PHILIP'S

CW00336572

NAVIGATOR Britain

NAVIGATOR

Contents

www.philips-maps.co.uk

First published in 1994 by Philip's,
a division of Octopus Publishing Group Ltd
www.octopusbooks.co.uk
Endeavour House, 189 Shaftesbury Avenue,
London WC2H 8JY
An Hachette UK Company
www.hachette.co.uk

Tenth edition 2012
First impression 2012

ISBN 978-1-84907-232-8

Cartography by Philip's

Copyright © 2012 Philip's

Ordnance Survey®

This product includes mapping data licensed from Ordnance Survey®, with the permission of the Controller of Her Majesty's Stationery Office. © Crown copyright 2012. All rights reserved. Licence number 100011710

No part of this publication may be reproduced, stored in a retrieval system or transmitted in any form or by any means, electronic, mechanical, photocopying, recording or otherwise, without the permission of the Publishers and the copyright owner.

While every reasonable effort has been made to ensure that the information compiled in this atlas is accurate, complete and up-to-date at the time of publication, some of this information is subject to change and the Publisher cannot guarantee its correctness or completeness.

The information in this atlas is provided without any representation or warranty, express or implied and the Publisher cannot be held liable for any loss or damage due to any use or reliance on the information in this atlas, nor for any errors, omissions or subsequent changes in such information.

The representation in this atlas of any road, drive or track is no evidence of the existence of a right of way.

Data for the speed cameras provided by **PocketGPSWorld.com Ltd**.

Information for National Parks, Areas of Outstanding Natural Beauty, National Trails and Country Parks in Wales supplied by the Countryside Council for Wales.

Information for National Parks, Areas of Outstanding Natural Beauty, National Trails and Country Parks in England supplied by Natural England. Data for Regional Parks, Long Distance Footpaths and Country Parks in Scotland provided by Scottish Natural Heritage.

Information for Forest Parks supplied by the Forestry Commission

Information for the RSPB reserves provided by the RSPB

Gaelic name forms used in the Western Isles provided by Comhairle nan Eilean.

Data for the National Nature Reserves in England provided by Natural England. Data for the National Nature Reserves in Wales provided by Countryside Council for Wales. Darparwyd data'n ymwneud â Gwarchodfeydd Natur Cenedlaethol Cymru gan Gyngor Cefn Gwlad Cymru.

Information on the location of National Nature Reserves in Scotland was provided by Scottish Natural Heritage.

Data for National Scenic Areas in Scotland provided by the Scottish Executive Office. Crown copyright material is reproduced with the permission of the Controller of HMSO and the Queen's Printer for Scotland. Licence number C02W0003960.

Printed in China

Road map symbols

M25 **Motorway**

16 17 **Motorway junctions** – full access, restricted access

Toll motorway

Pease Pottage Services **Motorway service area**

Motorway under construction

Primary route – dual, single carriageway, services
– under construction, narrow

Cardiff **Primary destination**

25 26 **Numbered junctions** – full, restricted access

A road – dual, single carriageway
– under construction, narrow

B road – dual, single carriageway
– under construction, narrow

Minor road – dual, single carriageway
Drive or track

Roundabout, multi-level junction

2 **Distance in miles**

Tunnel

Toll **Toll, steep gradient** – points downhill

40 **Speed camera** – single, multiple

CLEVELAND WAY **National trail** – England and Wales
GREAT GLEN WAY **Long distance footpath** – Scotland

YATTON ROPLEY **Railway with station, level crossing, tunnel**
Preserved railway with level crossing, station, tunnel
Tramway

National boundary
County or unitary authority boundary

Car ferry, catamaran
Passenger ferry, catamaran
CALAIS 1:30 **Ferry destination, journey time** – hours: minutes
Hovercraft
V P **Internal ferry** – car, passenger

Principal airport, other airport or airfield

MENDIP HILLS **Area of outstanding natural beauty, National Forest** – England and Wales, **Forest park**, **National park**, **National scenic area** – Scotland, **Regional park**
Woodland

Beach – sand, shingle

KENNET AND AVON CANAL **Navigable river or canal**
6 **Lock, flight of locks, canal bridge number**

965 **Viewpoint, spot height** – in metres
Linear antiquity
P&R **Park and ride**
29 **Adjoining page number**

SY 70 80 **Ordnance Survey National Grid reference** – see page 402

Road map scale 1: 100 000 or 1.58 miles to 1 inch

0 1 2 3 miles
0 1 2 3 4 5 km

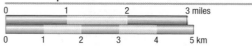

Road map scale (Isle of Man and parts of Scotland)

1: 200 000 or 3.15 miles to 1 inch

0 1 2 3 4 5 6 miles
0 1 2 3 4 5 6 7 8 9 10 km

Tourist information

BYLAND ABBEY **Abbey or priory**
WOODHENGE **Ancient monument**
SEALIFE CENTRE **Aquarium or dolphinarium**
CITY MUSEUM AND ART GALLERY **Art collection or museum**
TATE ST IVES **Art gallery**
1644 **Battle site and date**
ABBOTSBURY SWANNERY **Bird sanctuary or aviary**
Camping site
Caravan site
BAMBURGH CASTLE **Castle**
YORK MINSTER **Cathedral**
SANDHAM MEMORIAL CHAPEL **Church of interest**
Country park
SEVEN SISTERS – England and Wales
LOCHORE MEADOWS – Scotland
ROYAL BATH & WEST SHOWGROUND **County show ground**
MONK PARK FARM **Farm park**
HILLIER GARDENS AND ARBORETUM **Garden, arboretum**
ST ANDREWS **Golf course** – 18-hole
TYNTESFIELD **Historic house**
SS GREAT BRITAIN **Historic ship**
HATFIELD HOUSE **House and garden**
MUSEUM OF DARTMOOR LIFE **Local museum**
HOLTON HEATH **National nature reserve**
Marina
NAT MARITIME MUSEUM **Maritime or military museum**
SILVERSTONE **Motor racing circuit**
CUMBERLAND PENCIL MUSEUM **Museum**
Picnic area
WEST SOMERSET RAILWAY **Preserved railway**
THIRSK **Racecourse**
LEAHILL TURRET **Roman antiquity**
BOYTON MARSHES **RSPB reserve**
THRIGBY HALL **Safari park**
FREEPORT BRAINTREE **Shopping village**
MILLENNIUM STADIUM **Sports venue**
ALTON TOWERS **Theme park**
Tourist information centre
– open all year
– open seasonally
NATIONAL RAILWAY MUSEUM **Transport collection**
LEVANT MINE **World heritage site**
HELMSLEY **Youth hostel**
MARWELL **Zoo**
SUTTON BANK VISITOR CENTRE
GLENFIDDICH DISTILLERY **Other place of interest**

Approach map symbols

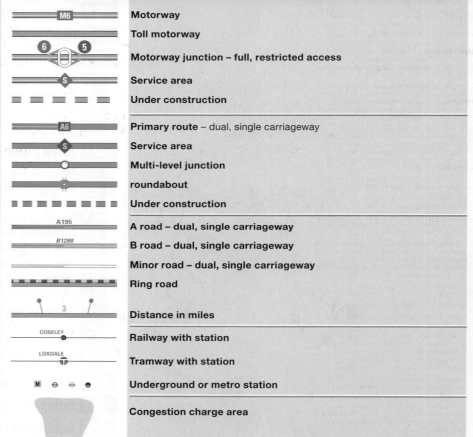

M6 **Motorway**

Toll motorway

6 5 **Motorway junction – full, restricted access**

Service area

Under construction

A6 **Primary route** – dual, single carriageway

Service area

Multi-level junction

roundabout

Under construction

A195 **A road – dual, single carriageway**

B1288 **B road – dual, single carriageway**

Minor road – dual, single carriageway

Ring road

3 **Distance in miles**

COSELEY **Railway with station**

LOXDALE **Tramway with station**

M **Underground or metro station**

Congestion charge area

Speed Cameras

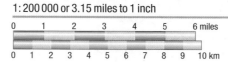

Fixed camera locations are shown using the 40 symbol. In congested areas the 40 symbol is used to show that there are two or more cameras on the road indicated.

Due to the restrictions of scale the camera locations are only approximate and cannot indicate the operating direction of the camera. Mobile camera sites, and cameras located on roads not included on the mapping are not shown. Where two or more cameras are shown on the same road, drivers are warned that this may indicate that a SPEC system is in operation. These cameras use the time taken to drive between the two camera positions to calculate the speed of the vehicle. At the time of going to press, some local authorities were considering decommissioning their speed cameras.

Sandwiches on the move

The Philip's team peels back the cellophane wrapper and reveals more than you probably want to see

By Stephen Mesquita, Philip's Correspondent on the Road

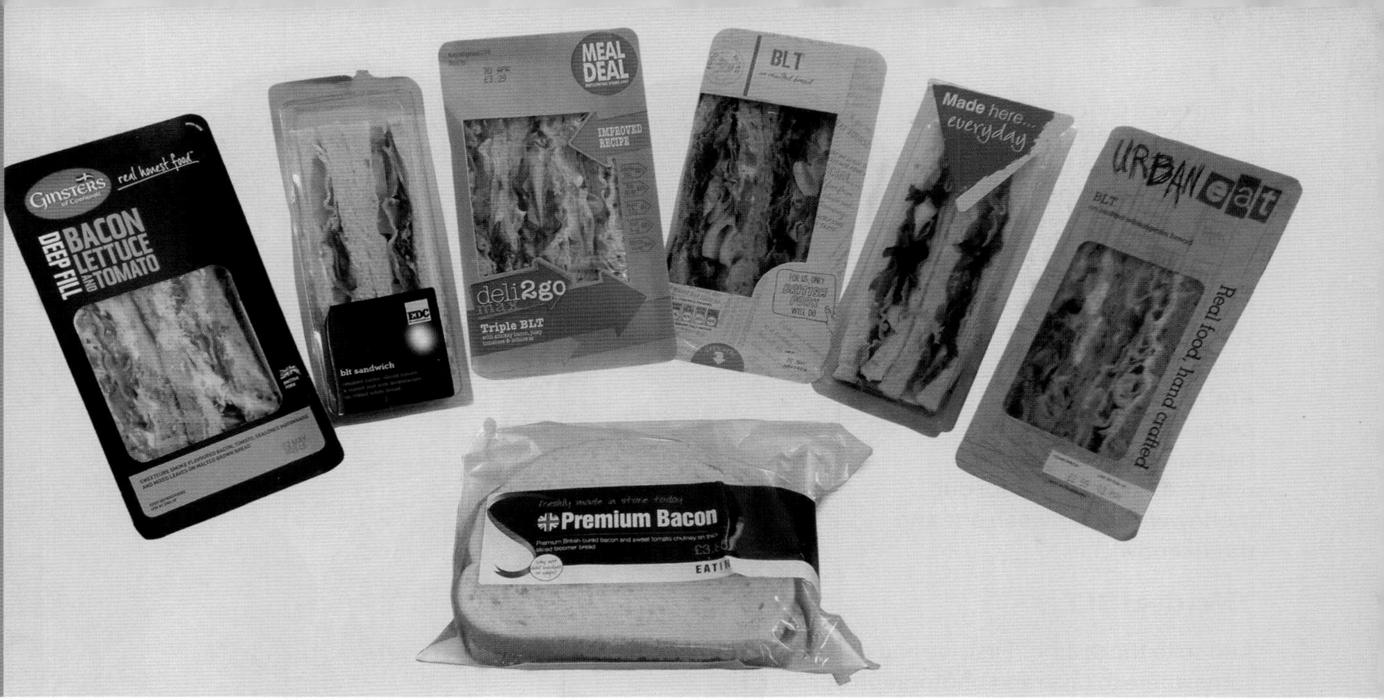

Grabbing a sandwich – the ultimate impulse purchase

We've probably all done it. You're on a car journey. You stop off at a petrol station or motorway service area. It's been a long time since your last meal. You haven't got time to stop for a proper meal. So you grab a sandwich.

Notice the word 'grab'. You don't stop, think, carefully inspect the wares, read the nutritional information on the packaging (if supplied – we'll return to that theme later) and take a rational decision. It's what the retail experts call an impulse purchase.

And we can say at the outset – it's probably not going to be one of your better impulse purchases.

So it was, on a fine spring day, that the Philip's sandwich tasting team met at Milton Keynes for a morning of recreational sandwich tasting. Milton Keynes had been hand-picked from a cast of thousands because it had petrol stations from four petrol companies and motorway service areas run by the three main operators all quickly and easily accessible.

This was the plan: we would 'grab a sandwich' at each, throw them in the back of the car and retreat to a suitable location to celebrate the gastronomic delights of our purchases.

Seven BLTs in quick succession – a challenge

One other word of explanation. Motorway service areas offer a more diverse shopping and eating experience than they used to. There is usually a newsagent, a coffee shop as well as a restaurant, all offering sandwiches. In this survey, we picked the sandwiches from the restaurant.

To make the survey as fair as possible, we chose sandwiches with the same filling – or its nearest equivalent – at each stop. And there wasn't really a choice when it came to choosing which sandwich. It had to be a BLT.

It was a daunting challenge. I enjoy a BLT as much as the next man. When the pangs of hunger strike, BLT offers a seductive mix of the fresh and healthy (the tomato and lettuce) with something a bit naughty and tasty (the bacon). But seven BLTs in quick succession – now that's what I call devotion to duty.

Touring the hotspots of Milton Keynes

It's a terrible confession for an atlas publisher to make, but if you ever have to visit seven petrol stations and service areas to buy seven BLTs in quick succession, sat nav is just the job. There are lots of things that an atlas can do that a sat nav can't – but putting in 'nearest petrol station' and getting the name up on the screen isn't one of them.

So off we went to spend £24.05 on seven BLTs. The first thing to say is that, with one exception, the seven people who served us were pleasant and helpful. We were offered trade ups to meal deals, we had smiles and thank you's. We asked for and got seven receipts without it causing a problem, the sun was shining and all was right in the world.

Price – not always an indication of quality or value

But that was as far as the pleasant experience went. First there was the price. We fast discovered that you don't always get what you pay for. Our BLTs varied in price from £2.99 to £3.99. If you happen to buy a BLT every day for lunch and don't want to spend an extra £365 a year, our advice would be to search out the best deal –

	Price	Sell-by date on 30 April	Number of sandwiches	Description on package	Tester's comments	Nutritional info	Marks out of 10
Texaco	£2.99	2 May	2	*'Deep Fill. Sweetcure Smoke Flavoured Bacon, Tomato, Seasoned Mayonnaise and Mixed Leaves on Malted Brown Bread'*	Bread soggy yet tasted stale; main taste was mayo; bacon chewy	34 ingredients • 439 calories fat 18.1gm • salt 2.42gm	**5**
Total	£2.99	2 May	2	*'BLT on malted wheatgrain bread. Real food, hand crafted'*	Soggy; too much mayo; bacon tasted cheap	45 ingredients • 460 calories fat 27.4gm • salt 1.50gm	**5.5**
Road Chef	£3.99	1 May	2	*'BLT Sandwich made here everyday'*	Bitter lettuce with grey edges; white bread; very unpleasant taste	None	**2**
BP	£3.25	1 May	2	*'BLT on malted bread. For us only British Pork will do'*	Decent sandwich – bacon quite tasty; mayo nice; bread a bit soggy; lettuce perhaps past its best but all in all edible	Approximately 40 ingredients 465 calories fat 20.8gm • salt 2.53gm	**6**
Moto	£3.69	1 May	2	*'BLT sandwich: smoked bacon, sliced tomato and mixed leaf with mayonnaise on sliced white bread'*	White bread; tasteless old lettuce; bacon unpleasant	None	**2**
Shell	£3.29	30 Apr	3	*'Improved recipe: Triple BLT with smokey bacon, juicy tomatoes and lettuce dip'*	Three sandwiches plus trade up to £3.99 lunch but salty; tomatoes and lettuce looked past their best; bacon unappetising	49 ingredients • 791 calories fat 48.2gm • salt 5.1gm	**4**
Welcome Break	£3.85	1 May	1	*Premium British cured bacon and sweet tomato chutney on thick sliced bloomer bread*	Disgusting – two bits of stale round white bread with a bit of tasteless bacon and ketchup	None	**1**

▶ **Top row**, left to right
Road Chef • Texaco • Moto • BP

▶ **Bottom row**, left to right
Shell • Total • Welcome Break

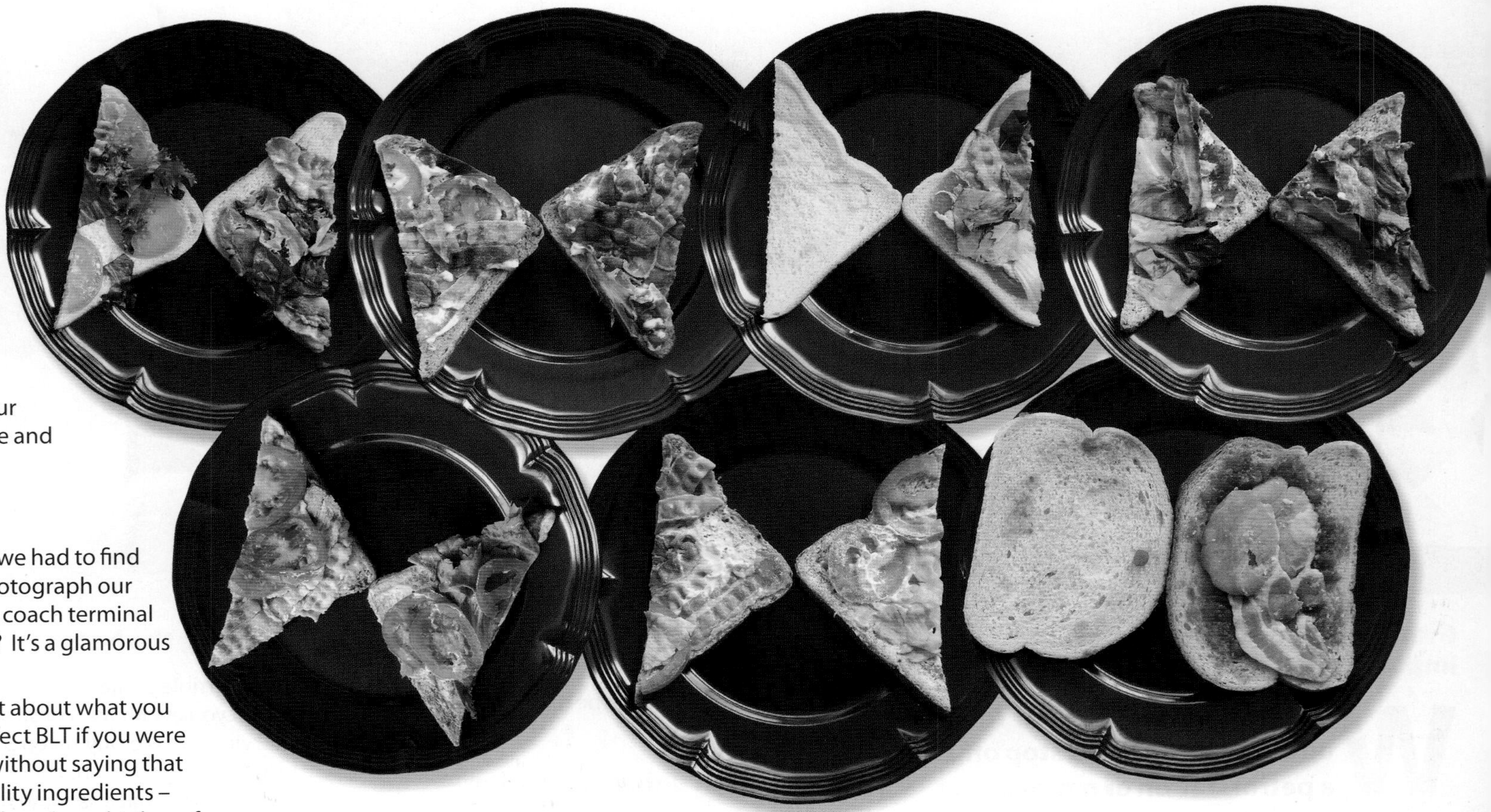

and, not surprisingly, these come from petrol stations rather than motorway service areas. And it's not just about price, it's about value. Our best sandwich was not the most expensive – and, for our money, we got between one and three sandwiches.

The ideal BLT

And so to the tasting. First, we had to find somewhere to taste and photograph our BLTs. Where better than the coach terminal off the M1 at Milton Keynes? It's a glamorous life, this sandwich tasting.

On the way, we had thought about what you would expect from the perfect BLT if you were making it at home. It goes without saying that you'd want fresh, good-quality ingredients – especially the bacon. Even if you bought these from a shop, it should be possible to source a tasty, ripe tomato, a piece of lettuce and one rasher of decent bacon for around 60p – offering a reasonable mark up on a £3.99 sandwich.

But it's only fair to admit that the home-made sandwich has one huge advantage that the packaged sandwich can never offer. It can be eaten immediately. Our packaged sandwiches mostly had a sell-by date of 48 to 72 hours after the start of the day we bought them. By this time neither the bread nor what goes inside it will be at its best.

Never open up a packaged sandwich

And now, the votes. Tasting these seven BLTs in quick succession could never be described as a pleasant experience. It was made less pleasant by having to open up the sandwiches and examine the contents. When you come face to face with the ingredients, the whole business of sandwich eating becomes rather less than appetising.

The results of our survey are presented here in word and pictures – and we will let them speak for themselves.

Finally, a health warning

Map making is our area of expertise at Philip's, not nutrition. But we thought it would be informative to offer you at least the headlines from the back of the boxes. Four out of the seven sandwiches came with a full list of ingredients.

The pack with three sandwiches contained nearly 40% of a woman's guideline intake of calories, nearly 70% of the guideline intake of fat and almost the entire daily guideline for salt. Even the two-sandwich packs had nearly a quarter of a woman's daily calories, over a third of fat and up to 40% for salt.

It is perhaps revealing that the three sandwiches which came without the contents list were the three made from white bread.

A telling moment

The team were quite hungry by the time they came to do the tasting. We took only one bite from each BLT. There was only one sandwich which we came back to at the end and took another bite from because the taste was enjoyable. Next time I think I'm going to stick to egg mayo.

Service areas on motorways and primary routes

Symbols

- Accommodation
- Baby change
- Barber shop
- Bureau de change
- Cash machine
- Footbridge
- Fuel
- Meeting room
- Free parking
- Showers
- Toilets
- Disabled toilets
- RADAR key scheme
- Truckstop
- Truck wash
- Free WiFi
- Work space
- Address
- Telephone number
- e-mail address
- website
- Details of shops and catering outlets that are normally open 24 hours are listed at the end of each entry. Other listed outlets may not be open 24 hours.

England

A1 Grantham South — Moto

A1 at Colsterworth • Northbound and southbound **155 E8** SK93822366
Costa *Esso* *Travelodge* 2hrs
A1 Colsterworth, Grantham NG33 5JR 01476 861006

A1 Grantham North — Moto

A1, 3 miles North of Grantham • Northbound and southbound **155 B7** SK88863988
Burger King • Costa • Eat In • EDC • WH Smith *BP* *Travelodge* 2hrs
Gonerby Moor, Grantham NG32 2AB 01476 563451

A1 Scotch Corner — Moto

A1, 6 miles North of Catterick • Northbound and southbound **224 D4** NZ21670542
Burger King • Costa • M&S Simply Food • WH Smith *Esso* *Travelodge* 2hrs
Middleton Tyas Lane, Scotch Corner, Richmond DL10 6PQ
01325 377719

A14 Cambridge — Extra

A14, 4 miles from northern end of M11 • Northbound and southbound **123 D7** TL35856537
KFC • Le Petit Four • M&S Simply Food • McDonald's • WH Smith *Shell* *Days Inn* 2 hrs
Boxworth, Cambridge CB3 8WU
Forecourt outlets open 24 hrs

A38 Saltash — Moto

A38 Carkeel Roundabout • Eastbound and westbound **7 C8** SX41186015
Costa *BP* *Travelodge* 2hrs
Carkeel Roundabout, Saltash PL12 6LF 07827978664

A50 Derby South – westbound — Welcome Break

A50 Junctions 1-2 • Westbound **153 C8** SK42463021
Burger King • Eat In • WH Smith *Shell* *Days Inn*
Shardlow, Derby DE72 2WW
01332 794194 derby.enquiry@welcomebreak.co.uk
www.welcomebreak.co.uk
WH Smith and forecourt outlet open 24 hrs

A50 Derby South – eastbound — Welcome Break

A50 Junctions 1-2 • Eastbound **153 C8** SK42673024
Burger King • Coffee Nation • Eat In • WH Smith *Shell, LPG available*
Shardlow, Derby DE72 2WW
01332 794194 derby.enquiry@welcomebreak.co.uk
www.welcomebreak.co.uk
WH Smith and forecourt outlet open 24 hrs

A1(M) Baldock — Extra MSA

A1(M) J10 • Northbound and southbound **104 D4** TL23443661
KFC Le Petit Four • M&S Simply Food • McDonald's • Starbucks *Shell* *Days Inn* 2hrs
A1(M), Junction 10, Baldock, Hertfordshire SG7 5TR
www.extraservices.co.uk
Forecourt shop, McDonald's and Starbucks open 24 hrs

A1(M) Peterborough — Extra MSA

A1(M) J17 • Northbound and southbound **138 E2** TL13939395
Costa • KFC • Le Petit Four • M&S Simply Food • McDonald's • WH Smith *Shell, LPG* *Days Inn* 2 hrs
Great North Road, Haddon, Peterborough PE7 8UQ
www.extraservices.co.uk
Forecourt shop open 24 hrs

A1(M) Blyth — Moto

A1(M) Junction 34 • Northbound and southbound **187 D10** SK62568827
Burger King • Costa • EDC • M&S Simply Food • WH Smith *Esso* *Travelodge*
Hill Top Roundabout, Blyth S81 8HG 01909 591841
www.moto-way.co.uk

A1(M) Wetherby — Moto

A1(M): J46 • Northbound and southbound **206 C4** SE41525025
Burger King • Costa • M&S Simply Food • Upper Crust • West Cornish Pasty • WH Smith *BP* *Days Inn* 2 hrs
Kirk Deighton, North Yorkshire LS22 5GT 01937 545080
www.moto-way.co.uk
Forecourt outlets open 24 hrs

A1(M) Durham — RoadChef

A1(M) J61 • Northbound and southbound **234 D2** NZ30843718
The Burger Company • Costa • Restbite! • WH Smith *Total* *Days Inn* 2 hrs
Tursdale Road, Bowburn, County Durham DH6 5NP 0191 377 9222
www.roadchef.com
Fast food outlet and forecourt shop open 24 hrs

A1(M) Washington — Moto

A1(M) just north of J64 • Northbound and southbound **243 F7** NZ28375506
Burger King • Costa • EDC • WH Smith *BP* *Travelodge* 2 hrs
Portobello, Birtley, County Durham DH3 2SJ 0191 410 3436 www.moto-way.co.uk
WH Smith and forecourt outlets open 24 hrs.

M1 London Gateway — Welcome Break

M1 between J2 and J4 • Northbound and southbound **85 G11** TQ20269369
Burger King • Eat In • Starbucks • Waitrose • WH Smith *Shell, LPG available* *Days Hotel* 2 hrs
M1 J2/4, Mill Hill, London NW7 3HB
0208 906 0611 lgw.enquiry@welcomebreak.co.uk
www.welcomebreak.co.uk
WH Smith open 24 hrs

M1 Toddington — Moto
M1, 1 mile south of J12 • Northbound and southbound **103 F10** TL03092878
Burger King • Costa • EDC • Krispy Kreme • M&S Simply Food • Starbucks • West Cornish Pasty (northbound) • WH Smith
BP, LPG available *Travelodge* P 2 hrs
Toddington, Bedfordshire LU5 6HR 01525 878400
www.moto-way.co.uk
Forecourt outlets open 24 hrs

M1 Newport Pagnell — Welcome Break
M1, north of J14 • Northbound and southbound **103 C7** SP85834351
Eat In • KFC • Starbucks • Waitrose • WH Smith *Shell* *Days Inn* P 2 hrs
M1 Motorway, J14/15, Newport Pagnell, Buckinghamshire MK16 8DS 01908 217722 newport.enquiry@welcomebreak.co.uk
www.welcomebreak.co.uk
WH Smith and forecourt shop open 24 hrs.

M1 Northampton — RoadChef
M1 J15A • Northbound and southbound **120 F4** SP72285732
The Burger Company (northbound) • Costa • Hot Food Co (southbound) • McDonald's (southbound) • Restbite! (northbound) • WH Smith
BP, LPG available P 2 hrs
M1 Junction 15A, Northampton, Northamptonshire NN4 9QY 01604 831888
www.roadchef.com
WH Smith, forecourt shop and (southbound) McDonald's open 24 hrs

M1 Watford Gap — RoadChef
M1 between J16 and J17 • Northbound and southbound **119 D11** SP59956802
Northbound: *Costa • Cotton Traders • Hot Food Co • McDonald's • WH Smith* **Southbound:** *The Burger Company • Costa • Restbite! • WH Smith* *Shell* *Days Inn (southbound)* P 2 hrs
M1 Motorway, Northamptonshire NN6 7UZ 01327 879001
www.roadchef.com

M1 Leicester Forest East — Welcome Break
M1 between J21 and J21A • Northbound and southbound **135 C10** SK53860267
Waitrose • WH Smith • Burger King • Eat In • KFC • Starbucks *BP, LPG available* *Days Inn* P 2 hrs
Leicester Forest East, M1, Leicester, Leicestershire LE3 3GB 0116 238 6801
lfe.enquiry@welcomebreak.co.uk
www.welcomebreak.co.uk
Eat In and WH Smith open 24 hrs

M1 Leicester — Eurogarages
M1 just off J22 • Northbound and southbound **153 G9** SK47651111
Burger King • Coffee Nation *BP, LPG available*
Littleshaw Lane, Markfield LE67 9PP 01530 244706
www.eurogarages.com

M1 Donington Park — Moto
M1 J23A • Northbound and southbound **153 E9** SK46712513
Burger King • Costa • EDC • M&S Simply Food • WH Smith *BP* *Travelodge* P 2 hrs
Castle Donington, Derby, East Midlands DE74 2TN 01509 672220
www.moto-way.co.uk
Forecourt shop and WH Smith open 24 hrs

M1 Trowell — Moto
M1 between J25 and J26 • Northbound and southbound **171 G7** SK49354073
Burger King • Costa • EDC • M&S Simply Food • WH Smith *BP* P 2 hrs
Ilkeston, Trowell, Nottinghamshire NG9 3PL 01159 320291
www.moto-way.co.uk
WH Smith and forecourt outlets are open 24 hrs.

M1 Tibshelf – northbound — RoadChef
M1, 2 miles north of J28 • **170 C6** SK44856031
The Burger Company • Costa • Restbite! • WH Smith *Shell* *Days Inn* P 2 hrs
Newton Wood Lane, Newton, Alfreton DE55 5TZ 01773 876600
www.roadchef.com WH Smith and forecourt shop open 24 hrs

M1 Tibshelf – southbound — RoadChef
M1, 2 miles north of J28 • **170 C6** SK44856031
Costa • McDonald's • Restbite! • WH Smith *Shell* *Days Inn* P 2 hrs
Newton Wood Lane, Newton, Alfreton DE55 5TZ 01773 876600
www.roadchef.com
WH Smith, forecourt shop and McDonald's open 24 hrs

M1 Woodall — Welcome Break
M1, 2.5 miles north of J30 • Northbound and southbound **187 E7** SK47928006
WH Smith • Burger King • Eat In • KFC • Starbucks *Shell, LPG available* *Days Inn* P 2 hrs
M1 Motorway, Sheffield, South Yorkshire S26 7XR 0114 248 7992
woodall.enquiry@welcomebreak.co.uk www.welcomebreak.co.uk
Eat In, WH Smith and forecourt outlets open 24 hrs.

M1 Woolley Edge — Moto
M1, just north of J38 • Northbound and southbound **197 E10** SE29841400
Burger King • Costa • EDC • M&S Simply Food • WH Smith *BP* *Travelodge* P 2 hrs
West Bretton, Wakefield, West Yorkshire WF4 4LQ 01924 830371
www.moto-way.co.uk
WH Smith and forecourt outlets open 24 hrs

M2 Medway — Moto
M2 between J4 and J5 • Eastbound and westbound **69 G10** TQ81756344
Burger King • Costa • WH Smith *BP, LPG available* *Travelodge* P 2 hrs
M2, Rainham, Gillingham, Kent ME8 8PQ 01634 236900
www.moto-way.co.uk
WH Smith and forecourt shop open 24 hrs

M3 Fleet — Welcome Break
M3 between J4A/J5 • Eastbound and westbound **49 B9** SU79885583
Waitrose • WH Smith • Burger King • Eat In • KFC • Starbucks *Shell, LPG available (southbound only)* *Days Inn* P 2 hrs
Fleet, Hampshire GU51 1AA 01252 788 500
fleet.enquiry@welcomebreak.co.uk
www.welcomebreak.co.uk
Eat In and WH Smith open 24 hrs

M3 Winchester — Moto
M3, 4 miles north of J9 • Northbound and southbound **48 F4** SU52303550
Burger King • Costa • EDC • Hot Food Co • Krispy Kreme • WH Smith *BP* *Days Inn* P 2 hrs
Shroner Wood, Winchester, Hampshire SO21 1PP 01962 791140
www.moto-way.co.uk
Forecourt outlets open 24 hrs

M4 Heston — Moto
M4 1 mile east of J3 • Eastbound and westbound **66 D6** TQ11777778
Burger King • Costa • EDC (westbound) • Krispy Kreme • WH Smith *BP, LPG (westbound)* *Travelodge* P 2 hrs
Phoenix Way, Heston, Hounslow, London TW5 9NB 0208 590 2101
www.moto-way.co.uk
WH Smith open 24 hrs

M4 Reading – eastbound — Moto
M4 Junctions 11-12 • Eastbound **65 E7** SU67177012
Burger King • Costa • EDC • Krispy Kreme • M&S Simply Food • West Cornish Pasty • WH Smith *BP, LPG available* *Travelodge* P 2 hrs
Burghfield, Reading RG30 3UQ 01189 566966
www.moto-way.co.uk
WH Smith and forecourt outlets open 24 hrs

M4 Reading – westbound — Moto
M4 Junctions 11-12 • Westbound **65 F7** SU67046985
Burger King • Costa • EDC • Krispy Kreme • M&S Simply Food • Upper Crust • West Cornish Pasty • WH Smith *BP, LPG available* *Travelodge* P 2 hrs
Burghfield, Reading RG30 3UQ 01189 566966
www.moto-way.co.uk
WH Smith and forecourt outlets open 24 hrs

M4 Chieveley — Moto
M4 J13 • Eastbound and westbound **64 E3** SU48157268
Burger King • Costa • EDC • Krispy Kreme • M&S Simply Food • West Cornish Pasty • WH Smith *BP, LPG available* *Travelodge* P 2 hrs
Oxford Road, Hermitage, Thatcham, Berkshire, RG18 9XX 01635 248024 www.moto-way.co.uk WH Smith open 24 hrs

M4 Membury — Welcome Break
M4, 4 miles west of J14 • Eastbound and westbound **63 D10** SU30847601
Waitrose • WH Smith • Burger King • Eat In • KFC • Starbucks *BP, LPG available (eastbound)* *Days Inn* P 2 hrs
Woodlands Road, Membury, near Lambourn, Berkshire RG17 7TZ 01488 674360 membury.enquiry@welcomebreak.co.uk
www.welcomebreak.co.uk
Eat In, WH Smith and forecourt shop open 24 hrs

M4 Leigh Delamere — Moto
M4 just west of J17 • Eastbound and westbound **61 D11** ST89077899
Burger King • Costa • EDC • Krispy Kreme • M&S Simply Food • West Cornish Pasty • WH Smith *BP, LPG available* *Travelodge* P 2 hrs
Chippenham, Wiltshire SN14 6LB 01666 837691 (eastbound); 01666 842015 (westbound)
www.moto.co.uk
WH Smith and shop and coffee shops in the forecourt are open 24 hrs

M5 Frankley — Moto
M5 J3 • Northbound and southbound **133 G9** SO98938120
Burger King • Costa • EDC • M&S Simply Food • WH Smith *Esso* *Travelodge (southbound only)* P 2 hrs
Illey Lane, Birmingham, West Midlands B32 4AR 0121 550 3131
www.moto-way.co.uk
Coffee Nation and WH Smith open 24 hrs

M5 Strensham – southbound — RoadChef
M5 southbound, just before J8 • Southbound only **99 D8** SO90413993
Costa • Cotton Traders • Hot Food Co • McDonald's • Soho Coffee Company • WH Smith *BP, LPG available* P 2 hrs
M5 Motorway, Lower Strensham, Worcestershire WR8 9LJ 01684 290577
www.roadchef.com
McDonald's and forecourt outlet open 24 hrs

M5 Strensham – northbound — RoadChef
M5, 1 mile north of J8 • Northbound only **99 C7** SO89344072
Costa • Cotton Traders • Hot Food Co • McDonald's • Pizza Hut Express • Subway • Starbucks • WH Smith *Texaco, LPG available* *Days Inn* P 2 hrs
M5 Motorway, Lower Strensham, Worcestershire WR8 9LJ 01684 293004
www.roadchef.com
McDonald's and forecourt outlets open 24 hrs

M5 Michaelwood — Welcome Break
M5, just north of J14 • Northbound and southbound **80 F2** ST70409541
WH Smith • Burger King • Eat In • KFC • Starbucks *BP, Ecotricity charge point* *Days Inn* P 2 hrs
Lower Wick, Dursley, Gloucestershire GL11 6DD 01454 260631 michaelwood.enquiry@welcomebreak.co.uk
www.welcomebreak.co.uk
WH Smith and forecourt shop open 24 hrs

M5 Gordano — Welcome Break
M5 J19 • Northbound and southbound **60 D4** ST50977563
Burger King • Eat In • KFC • Starbucks • Waitrose • WH Smith *Shell, LPG available* *Days Inn* P 2 hrs
Portbury, Bristol BS20 7XG 01275 373624 gordano.enquiry@welcomebreak.co.uk
www.welcomebreak.co.uk
WH Smith open 24 hrs

M5 Sedgemoor Southbound — RoadChef
M5, 7 miles south of J21 **43 C11** ST35815259
The Burger Company • Costa • Restbite! • WH Smith *Total* *Days Inn* P 2 hrs
M5 Southbound Rooksbridge, Axbridge, Somerset BS24 0JL 01934 750888
www.roadchef.com
Forecourt shop open 24 hrs

M5 Sedgemoor Northbound — Welcome Break
M5, 3 miles north of J22 **43 C11** ST35815259
Burger King • Eat In • KFC • Starbucks • Waitrose • WH Smith *Shell, Ecotricity charge point* *Days Inn* P 2 hrs
M5 Motorway Northbound, Bridgwater, Somerset BS24 0JL 01934 750730
sedgemoor.enquiry@welcomebreak.co.uk
www.welcomebreak.co.uk
WH Smith and shop on forecourt are open 24 hrs.

M5 Bridgwater — Moto
M5, J24 • Northbound and southbound **43 G10** ST30403441
Burger King • Costa • EDC • West Cornish Pasty • WH Smith *BP* *Travelodge* P 2 hrs
Huntsworth Business Park, Bridgwater, Somerset TA6 6TS 01278 456800
www.moto-way.co.uk
WH Smith and forecourt shop open 24 hrs

M5 Taunton Deane — RoadChef
M5 between J25 and J26 • Northbound and southbound **28 C2** ST19592035
The Burger Company • Costa • Restbite! • WH Smith *Shell* *Days Inn* P 2 hrs
Trull, Taunton, Somerset TA3 7PF 01823 271111
www.roadchef.com
Forecourt outlets are open 24 hrs

A38/M5 Tiverton — Moto
M5 Junction 27 • Northbound and southbound **27 E8** ST04901386
Costa • Burger King *Shell, LPG available* *Travelodge* P 2 hrs. No HGVs
Tiverton EX16 7HD 01884 829423
www.moto-way.co.uk

M5 Cullompton — Extra MSA
M5, J28 • Northbound and southbound **27 F8** ST02660798
Costa • McDonald's • WH Smith *Shell* P 2 hrs
Old Station Yard, Station Road, Cullompton, Devon EX15 1NS 01522 523737
www.extraservices.co.uk
WH Smith and forecourt shop open 24 hrs

M5 Exeter — Moto
M5 J30 • Northbound and southbound **14 C5** SX96779180
Burger King • Costa • Harry Ramsden • M&S Simply Food • West Cornish Pasty • WH Smith *BP* *Travelodge* P 2 hrs
Sandygate, Exeter, Devon EX2 7HF 01392 436266
www.moto-way.co.uk
WH Smith open 24 hrs

M6 Corley — Welcome Break
M6, 2.5 miles west of J3 • Eastbound and westbound **134 F6** SP30898604
Burger King • Eat In • KFC • Starbucks • Waitrose • WH Smith *Shell, LPG available* *Days Inn* P 2 hrs
Highfield Lane, Corley, Staffordshire CV7 8NR 01676 540111 corleyenquiry@welcomebreak.co.uk
www.welcomebreak.co.uk
WH Smith open 24 hrs

M6 Norton Canes — Road Chef
M6 Toll between JT6 and JT7 • Eastbound and westbound **133 B10** SK02290745
The Burger Company • Costa • Restbite! • WH Smith *BP, LPG available* *Days Inn* P 2 hrs
Betty's Lane, Norton Canes, Cannock, Staffordshire WS11 9UX 01543 272540
www.roadchef.co.uk
WH Smith and forecourt shop open 24 hrs

M6 Hilton Park — Moto
M6 J10A and J11 • Northbound and southbound **133 C9** SJ96200500
Burger King • Costa • EDC • M&S Simply Food • WH Smith *BP* *Travelodge* P 2 hrs
Essington, Wolverhampton, Staffordshire WV11 2AT 01922 412237
www.moto-way.co.uk
Coffee shops in forecourt and WH Smith are open 24 hrs

M6 Stafford – northbound — Moto
M6, 3 miles north of J14 • Northbound only **151 C7** SJ88613186
Burger King • Costa • EDC • Krispy Kreme • M&S Simply Food • WH Smith *BP, LPG available* *Travelodge* P 2 hrs
Stone, Staffordshire ST15 0EU 01785 811188
www.moto-way.co.uk
Forecourt outlets open 24 hrs

M6 Stafford – southbound — RoadChef
M6, 7.5 miles south of J15 • Southbound only **151 C7** SJ89243065
The Burger Company • Costa • Restbite! • WH Smith *Esso, LPG available* *Days Inn* P 2 hrs
M6 Southbound, Stone, Staffordshire ST15 0EU 01785 826300
www.roadchef.com

M6 Keele — Welcome Break
M6, 6 miles north of J15 • Northbound and southbound **168 G4** SJ80624406
Burger King • Eat In • KFC • Starbucks • Waitrose • WH Smith *Shell, LPG available (southbound)* P 2 hrs
Three Mile Lane, Keele, Newcastle under Lyme, Staffordshire ST5 5HG 01782 634230 keele.enquiry@welcomebreak.co.uk
www.welcomebreak.co.uk
Eat In and WH Smith open 24 hrs

M6 Sandbach — RoadChef
M6, just south of J17 • Northbound and southbound **168 C3** SK02290745
Northbound: *Costa • Restbite! • WH Smith* **Southbound:** *Costa • Hot Food Co • McDonald's • WH Smith* *Esso* P 2 hrs
M6 Northbound, Sandbach, Cheshire CW11 2FZ 01270 767134
www.roadchef.co.uk
Forecourt outlets and (southbound) McDonald's open 24 hrs

M6 Knutsford — Moto
M6, between J18 and J19 • Northbound and southbound **184 F2** SJ73267826
Burger King • Costa • EDC • Krispy Kreme • M&S Simply Food • West Cornish Pasty (southbound) • WH Smith *BP, LPG available* *Travelodge* P 2 hrs
Northwich Road, Knutsford, Cheshire WA16 0TL 01565 634167 www.moto-way.co.uk
Forecourt shop open 24 hrs

M6 Charnock Richard — Welcome Break
M6, 2.5 miles north of J27 • Northbound and southbound **194 E4** SD54411521
Burger King • Eat In • KFC • Starbucks • WH Smith *Shell* *Days Inn* P 2 hrs
Mill Lane, Chorley, Lancashire PR7 5LR 01257 791746
charnock.enquiry@welcomebreak.co.uk
www.welcomebreak.co.uk
Eat In and WH Smith open 24 hrs.

M6 Lancaster (Forton) Moto

M6 south of J33 • Northbound and southbound 202 C6 SD50145198

Burger King • Costa • Eat In • M&S Simply Food • West Cornish Pasty (northbound) • WH Smith BP, LPG available Travelodge 2 hrs

White Carr Lane, Bay Horse, Lancaster, Lancashire LA2 9DU

01524 791775

www.moto-way.co.uk

WH Smith and forecourt shop are open 24 hrs

M6 Burton-in-Kendal Moto

M6 between J35 and J36 • Northbound only 211 D10 SD52207617

Burger King • Costa • EDC • WH Smith BP Travelodge 2 hrs

Burton West, Carnforth, Lancashire LA6 1JF 01524 781234

www.moto-way.co.uk

M6 Killington Lake RoadChef

M6 just south of J37 • Southbound only 221 G11 SD58779111

The Burger Company • Costa • Restbite! • WH Smith BP Days Inn 2 hrs

M6 Southbound, near Kendal, Cumbria LA8 0NW 01539 620739

www.roadchef.com

WH Smith and forecourt shop open 24 hrs

M6 Tebay – northbound Westmorland

M6, just north of J38 • Northbound only 222 D2 NY60510626

Butcher's counter • cafe and coffee shop • farm shop • forecourt shop • takeaway snack bar Total, LPG available Westmorland Hotel Yes

M6, Old Tebay, Cumbria CA10 3ZA

01539 624511

www.westmorland.com

Petrol forecourt shop and takeaway open 24 hours

M6 Tebay – southbound Westmorland

M6, 4.5 miles south of J39 • Southbound only 222 D2 NY60790650

Butcher's counter • cafe and coffee shop • farm shop • forecourt shop • takeaway snack bar Total, LPG available Yes M6, Old Tebay, Cumbria CA10 3SB 01539 624511

www.westmorland.com

Petrol forecourt shop and takeaway open 24 hours

M6 Southwaite Moto

M6 Junctions 41-42 • Northbound and southbound 230 B4 NY44164523

Burger King • Costa • EDC • M&S Simply Food • West Cornish Pasty (southbound) • WH Smith BP Travelodge 2 hrs

Broadfield Road, Carlisle CA4 0NT

01697 473476

www.moto-way.co.uk

WH Smith and outlets on the forecourts are open 24 hours

M11 Birchanger Green Welcome Break

M11 at J8/J8a • Northbound and southbound 105 G10 TL51202149

Burger King • Eat In • KFC • Starbucks • Waitrose • WH Smith Shell, LPG available Days Hotel 2 hrs

Old Dunmow Road, Bishop's Stortford, Hertfordshire CM23 5QZ

01279 653388

www.welcomebreak.co.uk

WH Smith open 24 hrs

M18 Doncaster North Moto

M18 J5, at the western end of the M180 • Northbound and southbound 199 E7 SE66791104

Burger King • Costa • EDC • WH Smith BP, LPG available Travelodge 2 hrs Hatfield, Doncaster, South Yorkshire DN8 5GS

02920 891141

www.moto-way.co.uk

WH Smith open 24 hrs

M20 Maidstone RoadChef

M20 J8 53 C10 TQ82455523

Costa • McDonald's • Restbite! • WH Smith Esso Days Inn 2 hrs

M20 J8, Hollingbourne, Maidstone, Kent ME17 1SS

01622 631100

www.roadchef.com

McDonald's, WH Smith and forecourt outlets open 24 hrs

M20 Stop24 (Folkestone) Stop 24

M20 J11 54 F6 TR13283729

Coffee Stop • Haldane Express • Julian Graves • Just Spuds • KFC • Starbucks • WH Smith • Wimpy Shell, LPG available 2 hrs

Junction 11 M20, Stanford Intersection, Stanford, Kent CT21 4BL

01303 760273

info@stop24.co.uk

www.stop24.co.uk

Forecourt outlets open 24 hrs.

M23 Pease Pottage Moto

M23 J11 • Northbound and southbound 51 G9 TQ26183310

Burger King • Costa • EDC • Krispy Kreme • M&S Simply Food • West Cornish Pasty • WH Smith BP, LPG available 2 hrs Brighton Road, Pease Pottage, Crawley, West Sussex RH11 9AE 01293 562852

www.moto-way.co.uk

WH Smith and forecourt outlets open 24 hrs

M25 Clacket Lane RoadChef

M25 between J5 and J6 • Eastbound and westbound 52 C2 TQ42335457

Costa • Hot Food Co • McDonald's • WH Smith Total Days Inn 2hrs

M25 Westbound, Westerham, Kent TN16 2ER 01959 565577

www.roadchef.com

McDonald's open 24 hrs

M25 Cobham Extra MSA

M25 J9-10 • Clockwise and anti-clockwise TQ11345768

Eat In • KFC • M&S Simply Food • McDonald's • Starbucks • WH Smith Shell, LPG available Days Inn 2 hrs *www.extraservices.co.uk*

Forecourt outlets open 24 hrs

M25 South Mimms Welcome Break

M25 J23 and A1(M) J1 • Clockwise and anti-clockwise 86 E2 TL23000023

Burger King • Eat In • KFC • Starbucks • Waitrose • WH Smith BP, Ecotricity *charge point* Days Inn 2 hrs

Bignells Corner, Potters Bar, Hertfordshire EN6 3QQ

01707 621001 mimms.enquiry @welcomebreak.co.uk

www.welcomebreak.co.uk

Eat In, WH Smith and forecourt outlets open 24 hrs

M25 Thurrock Moto

M25, signposted from J30/J31 • Clockwise and anti-clockwise 68 C5 TQ57837947

Burger King • Costa • EDC • Krispy Kreme • M&S Simply Food • WH Smith Esso Travelodge 2 hrs

Arterial Road, West Thurrock, Grays, Essex RM16 3BG

01708 865487

www.moto-way.co.uk

WH Smith and forecourt outlet open 24 hrs

M27 Rownhams RoadChef

M27, between J3 and J4 • Eastbound and westbound 32 D5 SU38791769

The Burger Company (westbound) • Costa • Restbite! • WH Smith Esso Days Inn (westbound) 2 hrs

M27 Southbound, Southampton, Hampshire SO16 8AP

02380 734480

www.roadchef.com

The outlets in the forecourts are open 24 hrs

M40 Beaconsfield Extra MSA

M40 J2 • Eastbound and westbound 66 B3 SU95098897

KFC • Le Petit Four • M&S Simply Food • McDonald's • Presto • Starbucks • WH Smith Shell, LPG available *Etap Hotel* 2 hrs

A355 Windsor Drive, Beaconsfield, Buckinghamshire HP9 2SE

www.extraservices.co.uk

McDonald's and forecourt outlet open 24 hrs

M40 Oxford Welcome Break

M40 J8A • Eastbound and westbound 83 E10 SP62440479

Burger King • Eat In • KFC • Starbucks • Waitrose • WH Smith BP *Days Inn* 2 hrs M40 Junction 8A, Waterstock, Oxfordshire OX33 1JN

01865 877000 oxford.enquiry@ welcomebreak.co.uk

www.welcomebreak.co.uk

McDonald's and Starbucks open 24 hours

M40 Cherwell Valley Moto

M40 J10 • Northbound and southbound 101 F10 SP55162822

Burger King • Costa • EDC • Krispy Kreme • M&S Simply Food • West Cornish Pasty • WH Smith Esso Travelodge 2 hrs Northampton Road, Ardley, Bicester, Oxfordshire OX27 7RD 01869 346060

www.moto-way.co.uk

WH Smith open 24 hrs

M40 Warwick South Welcome Break

M40 between J12 and J13 • Southbound 118 F6 SP34075801

Burger King • Eat In • KFC • Starbucks • Waitrose • WH Smith

BP, LPG available Days Inn 2 hrs Banbury Road, Ashorne, Warwick CV35 0AA 01926 651681

warwicksouth.enquiry @welcomebreak.co.uk

www.welcomebreak.co.uk

Eat In, WH Smith and forecourt outlets open 24 hrs.

M40 Warwick North Welcome Break

M40 between J12 and J13 • Northbound 118 F6 SP33885770

Burger King • Eat In • KFC • Starbucks • Waitrose • WH Smith

BP, LPG available Days Inn 2 hrs Banbury Road, Ashorne, Warwick CV35 0AA 01926 650681

warwicknorth.enquiry @welcomebreak.co.uk

www.welcomebreak.co.uk

Eat In and WH Smith open 24 hrs

M42 Hopwood Park Welcome Break

M42 Junction 2 • Eastbound and westbound 117 C10 SP03637389

Burger King • Eat In • KFC • Starbucks • Waitrose • WH Smith Shell, LPG available 2 hrs Redditch Road, Alvechurch B48 7AU 0121 4474000

hopwood.enquiry @welcomebreak.co.uk

www.welcomebreak.co.uk

M42 Tamworth Moto

M42, just north of J10 • Northbound and southbound 134 C4 SK24440112

Burger King • Costa • EDC • M&S Simply Food • WH Smith Esso Travelodge 2 hrs Green Lane, Tamworth, Staffordshire B77 5PS

01827 260120

www.moto-way.co.uk

WH Smith and forecourt outlets are open 24 hrs.

M48 Severn View Moto

M48 J1 • Eastbound and westbound 60 B5 ST57118959

Burger King • Costa • Krispy Kreme • WH Smith BP Travelodge 2 hrs

Aust, South Gloucestershire BS35 4BH 01454 623851

www.moto-way.co.uk

Forecourt outlets open 24 hrs

M54 Telford Welcome Break

M54 J4 • Eastbound and westbound 132 B4 SJ73050890

Burger King • Eat In • Starbucks • WH Smith Shell, LPG available Days Inn 2 hrs Priorslee Road, Shifnal, Telford, Shropshire TF11 8TG 01952 238400

telford.enquiry @welcomebreak.co.uk

www.welcomebreak.co.uk

WH Smith and shop on forecourt open 24 hrs.

M56 Chester RoadChef

M56 J14 • Eastbound and westbound 183 G7 SJ46537491

Costa • Cotton Traders • Hot Food Co • McDonald's • WH Smith Shell Days Inn 2 hrs

Elton, Chester, Cheshire CH2 4QZ

01928 728500

www.roadchef.com

Costa and McDonald's open 24 hrs

M61 Rivington – northbound Euro Garages

M61 between J6 and J8 • Northbound and southbound 194 E6 SD62111168

Burger King • Spar • Starbucks • Subway BP 2 hrs M61, Horwich, Bolton, Lancashire BL6 5UZ

01254 56070

enquiries@eurogarages.com

www.eurogarages.com

Forecourt outlets open 24 hrs

M61 Rivington – southbound Euro Garages

M61 between J8 and J6 • Northbound and southbound 194 E6 SD62111168

Burger King • Spar • Starbucks • Subway BP Rivington Lodge 2 hrs

M61, Horwich, Bolton, Lancashire BL6 5UZ 01254 56070

enquiries@eurogarages.com

www.eurogarages.com

Forecourt outlets open 24 hrs

M62 Burtonwood Welcome Break

M62 J8 • Eastbound and westbound 183 C9 SJ57749129

KFC • Starbucks • WH Smith Shell 2 hrs M62 Great Sankey, Warrington, Cheshire WA5 3AX

01925 651656

burtonwood.enquiry @welcomebreak.co.uk

www.welcomebreak.co.uk

WH Smith open 24 hrs.

M62 Birch – eastbound Moto

M62 1.5 miles east of J18 • Eastbound and westbound 195 F10 SD84700797

Burger King • Costa • EDC • Krispy Kreme • M&S Simply Food • WH Smith BP Travelodge 2 hrs

Heywood, Lancashire OL10 2HQ

0161 643 0911

www.moto-way.co.uk

WH Smith is open 24 hrs.

M62 Birch – westbound Moto

M62 1.5 miles east of J18 • Eastbound and westbound 195 F10 SD84700797

Burger King • Costa • EDC • Krispy Kreme • M&S Simply Food • WH Smith BP Travelodge 2 hrs

Heywood, Lancashire OL10 2HQ

0161 643 0911

www.moto-way.co.uk

WH Smith is open 24 hrs.

M62 Hartshead Moor Welcome Break

M62, between J25 and J26 • Eastbound and westbound 197 C7 SE16892413

Burger King • Eat In • KFC • Starbucks • WH Smith Shell Days Inn 2 hrs

Clifton, Brighouse, West Yorkshire HD6 4JX 01274 876584

hartshead.enquiry @welcomebreak.co.uk

www.welcomebreak.co.uk

Eat In and WH Smith open 24 hrs

M62 Ferrybridge Moto

M62 Junction 33. Also A1(M) J40 (northbound) or J41 (southbound) • Northbound and southbound 198 C3 SE48512262

Burger King • Costa • EDC • M&S Simply Food • WH Smith BP Travelodge 2 hrs Ferrybridge, Knottingly, West Yorkshire WF11 0AF

01977 672767

www.moto-way.co.uk

Coffee Nation and WH Smith open 24 hrs

M65 Blackburn with Darwen Extra MSA

M65 J4. • Eastbound and westbound 195 C7 SD68592414

Co-op • Le Petit Four • McDonald's Shell, LPG Travelodge 2 hrs

Darwen Motorway Services Area, Darwen, Lancashire BB3 0AT

www.extraservices.co.uk

Forecourt shop is open 24 hrs.

Scotland

A1 Edinburgh Moto

A1 City Bypass, Old Craighall junction • Northbound and southbound 280 G6 NT33777084

Costa Esso Travelodge

A1 City Bypass, Old Craighall Junction, Musselburgh EH21 8RE

01316 653507

M9 Stirling Moto

M9 J9 • Northbound and southbound 278 D6 NS80438870

Burger King • Costa • EDC • WH Smith BP Travelodge 2 hrs

Pirnhall, Stirling FK7 8EU

01786 813614

www.moto-way.co.uk

WH Smith is open 24 hrs.

M74 Bothwell RoadChef

M74, south of J4 • southbound only 268 D4 NS70855980

Costa • Restbite! • WH Smith BP 2hrs M74 Southbound, Bothwell, Lanarkshire G71 8BG

01698 854123

www.roadchef.com

Forecourt shop is open 24 hrs.

M74 Hamilton RoadChef

M74, 1 mile north of J6 • northbound only 268 D4 NS72525672

Costa • Restbite! • WH Smith BP Days Inn 2hrs M74 Northbound, Hamilton, South Lanarkshire ML3 6JW

01698 282176

www.roadchef.com

Forecourt shop is open 24hrs

M74 Happendon Cairn Lodge

M74 between J11 and J12 on B7078 • Northbound and southbound 259 C8 NS85243364

Coffee shop • restaurant • retail shop Shell 2hrs Cairn Lodge, Douglas, Lanark, South Lanarkshire ML11 0RJ 01555 851880

Forecourt shop open 24 hrs

A74(M) Abington Welcome Break

A74(M) J13 • Northbound and southbound 259 D10 NS93022505

Burger King • Eat In • Starbucks • WH Smith Shell, LPG available Days Inn 2 hrs Abington, Biggar, South Lanarkshire ML12 6RG

01864 502637

abington.enquiry @welcomebreak.co.uk

www.welcomebreak.co.uk

Eat In open 24 hrs. Tourist information office

A74(M) Annandale Water Road Chef

A74(M) J16 • Northbound and southbound 248 E4 NY10389261

The Burger Company • Costa • Restbite! • WH Smith BP Days Inn 2hrs

Johnstone Bridge, near Lockerbie, Dumfries and Galloway DG11 1HD

01576 470870

www.roadchef.com

Restbite and forecourt shop are open 24 hrs.

A74(M) Gretna Green Welcome Break

A74(M), just north of J22 • Northbound and southbound 239 D8 NY30746872

Burger King • Eat In • KFC • Starbucks • WH Smith BP, LPG available Days Inn 2 hrs

M74A Trunk Road, Gretna Green, Dumfries and Galloway DG16 5HQ

01461 337567

gretna.enquiry @welcomebreak.co.uk

www.welcomebreak.co.uk

Eat In open 24 hrs

M80 Old Inns

M80 • Eastbound and Westbound
278 F5 NS77187671
Shell Select • Old Inns Cafe • Silk Cottage Cantonese buffet and take-away *Shell* Castlecary Road, Cumbernauld G68 0BJ
0843 2590190 (filling station)
www.shell.co.uk • www.oldinnscafe.com

M90 Kinross Moto

M90 J6 • Northbound and southbound 286 G5 NO10800282
Burger King • Costa • EDC • WH Smith *Esso* *Travelodge* 2 hrs
M90, Kinross, Perth and Kinross KY13 7NQ 01577 863123
www.moto-way.co.uk
WH Smith and forecourt shop open 24 hrs

Wales

M4 Magor RoadChef

M4 J23A • Eastbound and westbound 60 B2 ST42068796
Costa • McDonald's • Restbite! • WH Smith *Esso* *Days Inn*
2 hours M4 Magor, Caldicot, Monmouthshire NP26 3YL
01633 881515
info@firstmotorway.co.uk
www.roadchef.com
McDonald's open 24 hrs

M4 Cardiff Gate Welcome Break

M4 J30 • Eastbound and westbound 59 C8 ST21658283
Burger King • Starbucks • Waitrose • WH Smith *Total, LPG available*
2 hrs Cardiff Gate Business Park, Cardiff, South Glamorgan CF23 8RA
01758 822102 cardiff.enquiry @welcomebreak.co.uk
www.welcomebreak.co.uk
Forecourt shop open 24 hrs

M4 Cardiff West Moto

M4, off J33 • Eastbound and westbound 58 D5 ST09417967
Burger King • Costa • Krispy Kreme • WH Smith *Esso* *Travelodge*
2 hrs Pontyclun, Mid Glamorgan CF72 8SA
02920 891141
www.moto-way.co.uk
WH Smith is open 24 hrs.

M4 Sarn Park Welcome Break

M4 J36 • Eastbound and westbound 58 C2 SS90688290
Burger King • Cafe Primo • WH Smith *Shell* *Days Inn* 2 hrs
M4 Motorway, Junction 36, Sarn Park, Bridgend CF32 9RW
01656 655332 sarn.enquiry @welcomebreak.co.uk
www.welcomebreak.co.uk
WH Smith and forecourt shop open 24 hrs.

M4 Swansea Moto

M4 at J47 • Eastbound and westbound 75 F10 SS62159969
Burger King • Costa • WH Smith *BP* *Travelodge* 2 hrs
Penllergaer, Swansea, West Glamorgan SA4 1GT
01792 896222
www.moto-way.co.uk
Forecourt outlets open 24 hrs.

M4 Pont Abraham RoadChef

M4 J49 • Eastbound and westbound 75 D9 SN57470743
Costa • Restbite! • WH Smith *Texaco*
2 hours Llanedi, Pontarddulais, Swansea SA4 0FU 01792 884 663
www.roadchef.com
Forecourt outlets open 24 hrs

Service areas on motorways and primary routes

Primary route service area
Motorway service area
Kinross
M9
M90
Stirling
Old Inns
M8
Edinburgh
Bothwell
Hamilton
M74
Happendon
Abington
A74(M)
Annandale Water
Gretna Green
Washington
Southwaite
Durham
A1(M)
M6
Tebay
Scotch Corner
Killington Lake
Burton-in-Kendal
A1(M)
Lancaster
Wetherby
M6
M55
M65
Hartshead Moor
Darwen
Ferrybridge
Charnock Richard
M62
M62
Doncaster North
Birch
Rivington
Woolley Edge
M1
M180
Burtonwood
Blyth
Knutsford
Woodall
M56
Chester
Sandbach
Tibshelf
M1
Keele
Trowell
Grantham North
Stafford
Derby South
M6
Grantham South
Donington Park
Telford
Leicester
Norton Canes
M54
Leicester Forest East
Hilton Park
Tamworth
Peterborough
Corley
M1
A1(M)
Frankley
M6
Watford Gap
Cambridge
Hopwood Park
Northampton
Warwick
M5
Strensham
Newport Pagnell
M40
M1
Baldock
M11
M50
Cherwell Valley
Toddington
A1(M)
Birchanger Green
M5
Pont Abraham
Oxford
Swansea
South Mimms
M25
M25
Michaelwood
M4
Cardiff Gate
Magor
Beaconsfield
London Gateway
Sarn Park
Severn View
M4
Heston
Thurrock
Membury
M4
Cardiff West
Leigh Delamere
Reading
Gordano
Chieveley
Medway
M5
Cobham
M3
Fleet
M2
Sedgemoor
M25
Clacket Lane
Maidstone
M20
Stop 24
Winchester
M23
Bridgwater
Pease Pottage
Taunton Deane
Rownhams
Tiverton
M5
M27
M27
Cullompton
Exeter
Saltash

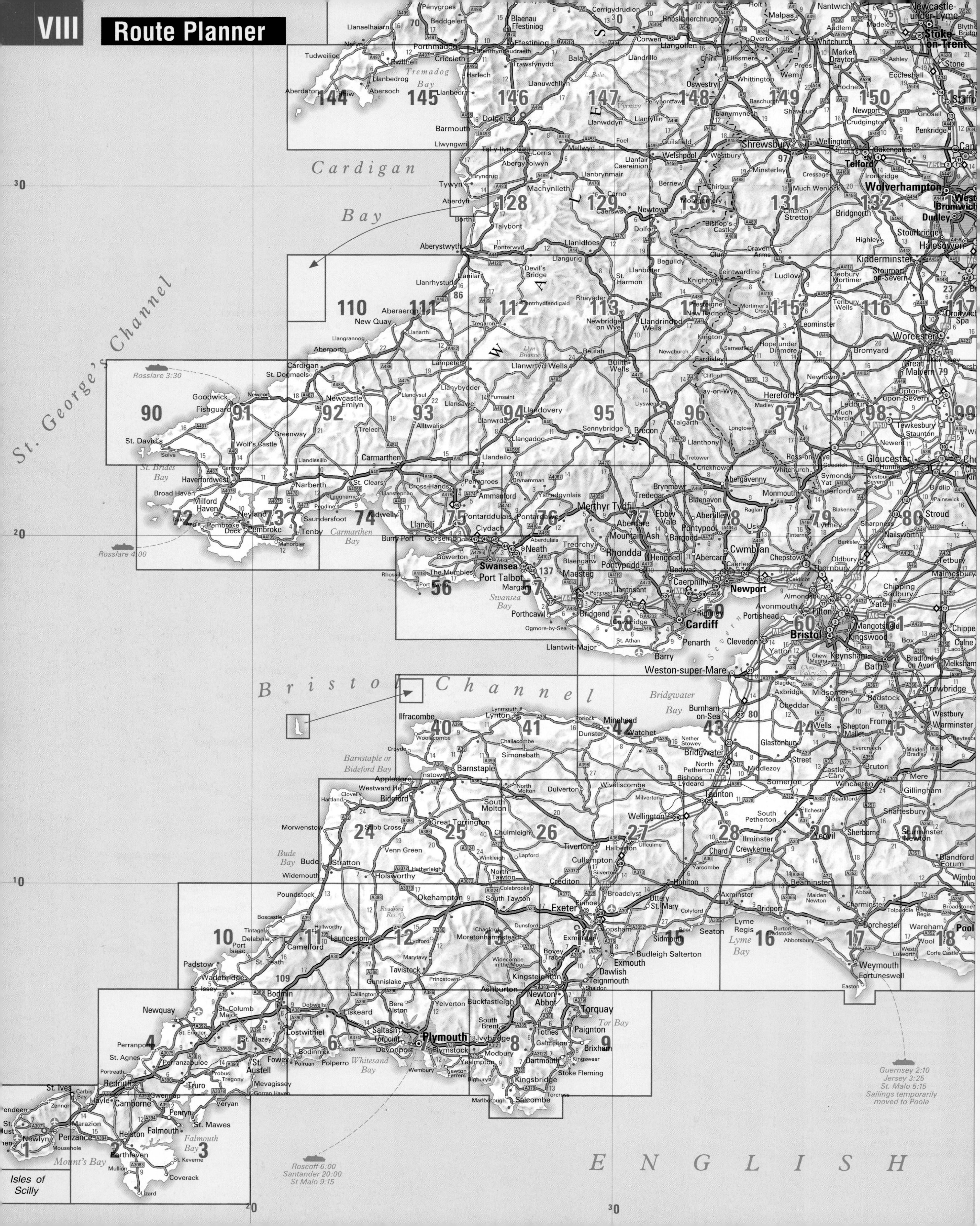
Cardigan
Bay
St. George's Channel
Bristol
Channel
Bridgwater Bay
Barnstaple or Bideford Bay
Carmarthen Bay
Swansea Bay
Tremadog Bay
Bude Bay
Lyme Bay
Tor Bay
Whitesand Bay
Falmouth Bay
Mount's Bay
St. Brides Bay
ENGLISH
Isles of Scilly
Rosslare 3:30
Rosslare 4:00
Roscoff 6:00
Santander 20:00
St Malo 9:15
Guernsey 2:10
Jersey 3:25
St. Malo 5:15
Sailings temporarily moved to Poole
Aberystwyth
Swansea
Cardiff
Newport
Bristol
Exeter
Plymouth
Torquay
Bath
Taunton
Shrewsbury
Hereford
Gloucester
Worcester
Wolverhampton
Telford
Stoke-on-Trent
Carmarthen
Merthyr Tydfil
Weston-super-Mare
Weymouth
Dorchester
Yeovil
Barnstaple
Truro
Penzance
Newquay
St. Austell
Falmouth
Bideford
Ilfracombe
Minehead
Brecon
Llandrindod Wells
Newtown
Dolgellau
Porthmadog
Haverfordwest
Pembroke
Fishguard
St. David's
Cardigan
New Quay
Llanelli
Neath
Port Talbot
Bridgend
Rhondda
Pontypridd
Caerphilly
Cwmbran
Chepstow
Monmouth
Abergavenny
Ross-on-Wye
Ledbury
Leominster
Ludlow
Kidderminster
Bridgnorth
Dudley
Welshpool
Oswestry
Wrexham
Bala
Machynlleth
Tywyn
Barmouth
Pwllheli
Cricieth
Blaenau Ffestiniog
Tiverton
Crediton
Okehampton
Tavistock
Launceston
Bodmin
Camborne
Redruth
Helston
Hayle
St. Ives
Padstow
Wadebridge
Liskeard
Totnes
Paignton
Brixham
Dartmouth
Kingsbridge
Salcombe
Exmouth
Sidmouth
Honiton
Chard
Crewkerne
Bridport
Lyme Regis
Wells
Glastonbury
Bridgwater
Frome
Shepton Mallet
Trowbridge
144
145
146
147
148
149
150
128
129
130
131
132
110
111
112
113
114
115
116
117
90
91
92
93
94
95
96
97
98
72
73
74
75
76
77
78
79
80
56
57
58
59
60
61
40
41
42
43
44
45
24
25
26
27
28
29
30
10
11
12
13
14
15
16
17
18
1
2
3
4
5
6
8
9
109
137

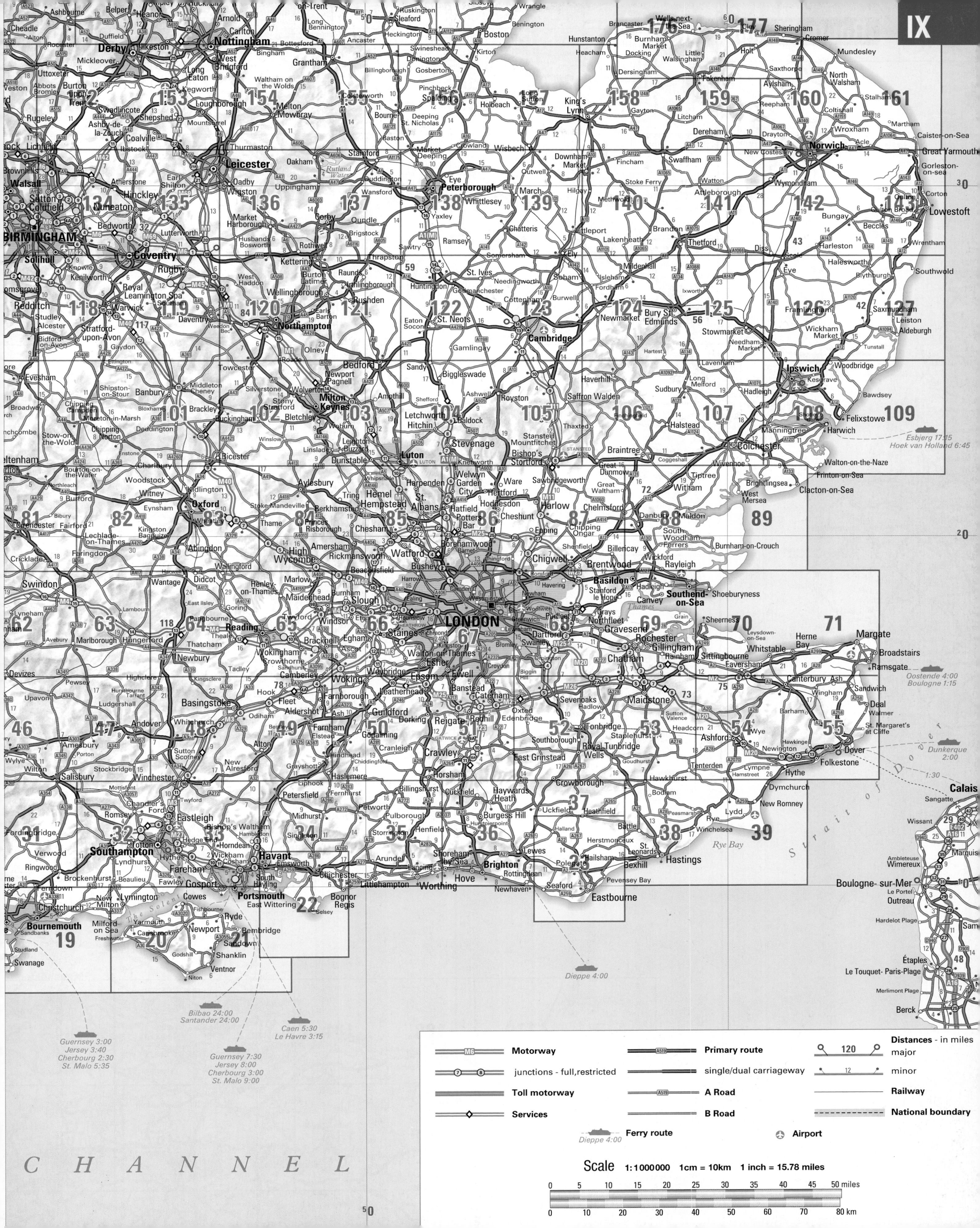
LONDON
CHANNEL
Strait of Dover
Motorway
junctions - full, restricted
Toll motorway
Services
Primary route
single/dual carriageway
A Road
B Road
Distances - in miles
major
minor
Railway
National boundary
Ferry route
Dieppe 4:00
Airport
Scale 1:1000000 1cm = 10km 1 inch = 15.78 miles
0 5 10 15 20 25 30 35 40 45 50 miles
0 10 20 30 40 50 60 70 80 km
Guernsey 3:00
Jersey 3:40
Cherbourg 2:30
St. Malo 5:35
Bilbao 24:00
Santander 24:00
Guernsey 7:30
Jersey 8:00
Cherbourg 3:00
St. Malo 9:00
Caen 5:30
Le Havre 3:15
Dieppe 4:00
Esbjerg 17:15
Hoek van Holland 6:45
Oostende 4:00
Boulogne 1:15
Dunkerque 2:00
1:30

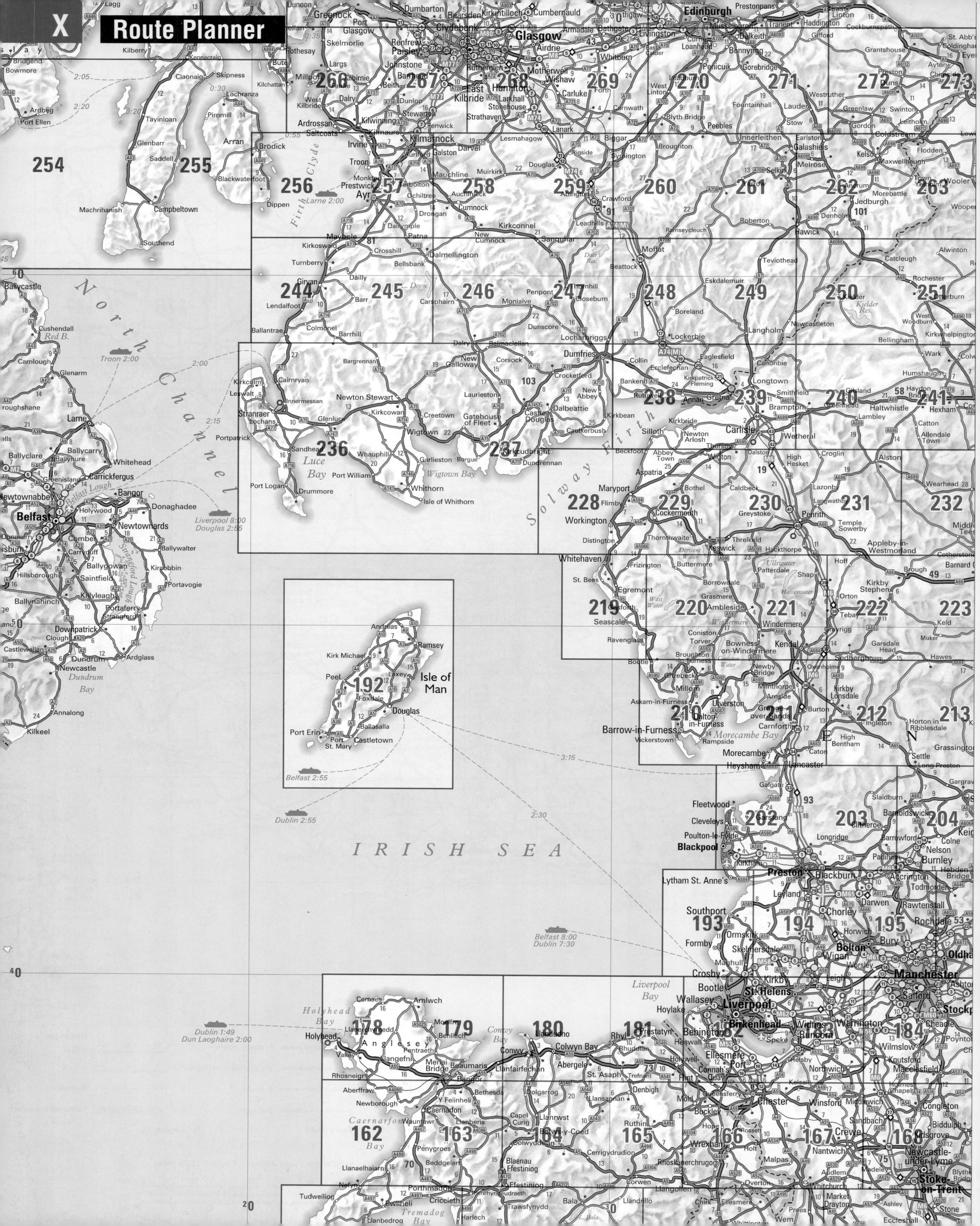
North Channel
IRISH SEA
Solway Firth
Firth of Clyde
Isle of Man
Anglesey
Luce Bay
Wigtown Bay
Morecambe Bay
Liverpool Bay
Conwy Bay
Holyhead Bay
Caernarfon Bay
Tremadog Bay
Dundrum Bay
Edinburgh
Glasgow
Belfast
Carlisle
Lancaster
Blackpool
Preston
Liverpool
Manchester
Stockport
Birkenhead
Chester
Stoke-on-Trent
Douglas
Ayr
Kilmarnock
Dumfries
Stranraer
Larne
Bangor
Holyhead
Troon 2:00
Larne 2:00
Liverpool 8:00
Douglas 2:55
Belfast 2:55
Dublin 2:55
Belfast 8:00
Dublin 7:30
Dublin 1:49
Dun Laoghaire 2:00
254
255
256
257
258
259
260
261
262
263
266
267
268
269
270
271
272
273
244
245
246
247
248
249
250
251
236
237
238
239
240
241
228
229
230
231
232
219
220
221
222
223
210
211
212
213
192
202
203
204
193
194
195
178
179
180
181
182
183
184
162
163
164
165
166
167
168

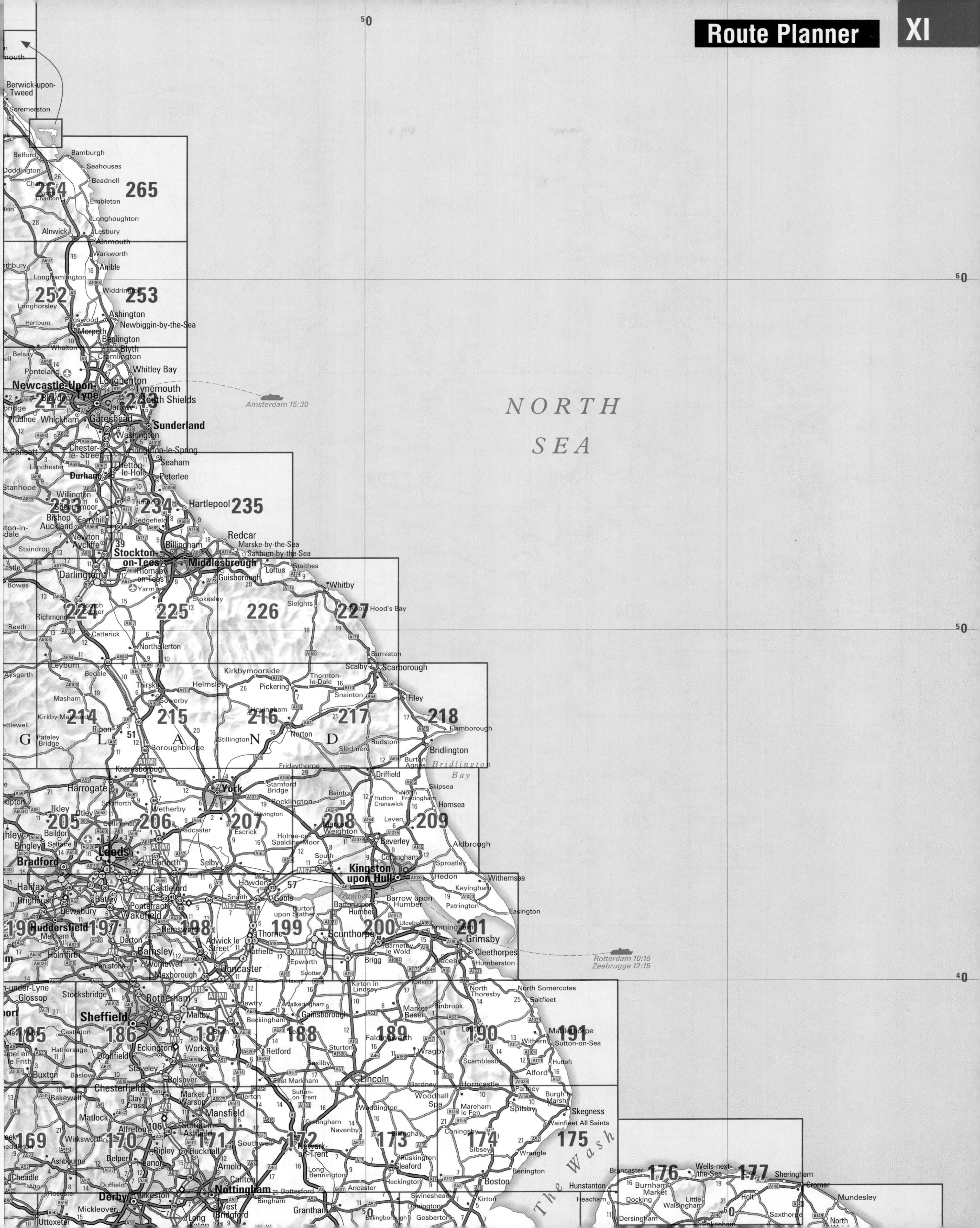
NORTH
SEA
Amsterdam 15:30
Rotterdam 10:15
Zeebrugge 12:15
Berwick-upon-Tweed
Scremerston
Belford
Bamburgh
Seahouses
Beadnell
Embleton
Longhoughton
Alnwick
Lesbury
Alnmouth
Warkworth
Amble
Longframlington
Widdrington
Longhorsley
Ashington
Newbiggin-by-the-Sea
Morpeth
Bedlington
Blyth
Cramlington
Whitley Bay
Ponteland
Longbenton
Newcastle-upon-Tyne
Tynemouth
South Shields
Jarrow
Prudhoe
Whickham
Gateshead
Sunderland
Washington
Consett
Chester-le-Street
Houghton-le-Spring
Seaham
Lanchester
Durham
Hetton-le-Hole
Peterlee
Stanhope
Willington
Spennymoor
Hartlepool
Bishop Auckland
Ferryhill
Sedgefield
Newton Aycliffe
Redcar
Marske-by-the-Sea
Saltburn-by-the-Sea
Staindrop
Stockton-on-Tees
Billingham
Middlesbrough
Loftus
Staithes
Darlington
Thornaby-on-Tees
Guisborough
Whitby
Yarm
Stokesley
Sleights
Robin Hood's Bay
Richmond
Reeth
Catterick
Northallerton
Burniston
Leyburn
Scalby
Scarborough
Aysgarth
Bedale
Kirkbymoorside
Thornton-le-Dale
Helmsley
Pickering
Snainton
Filey
Thirsk
Sowerby
Masham
Kirkby Malzeard
Ripon
Norton
Flamborough
Rudston
Bridlington
Pateley Bridge
Boroughbridge
Stillington
Sledmere
Burton Agnes
Bridlington Bay
Knaresborough
Fridaythorpe
Driffield
Harrogate
York
Stamford Bridge
Bainton
Skipsea
Spofforth
Wetherby
Pocklington
Hutton Cranswick
North Frodingham
Hornsea
Ilkley
Otley
Elvington
Market Weighton
Leven
Bingley
Baildon
Tadcaster
Escrick
Holme-on-Spalding-Moor
Beverley
Aldbrough
Leeds
Cottingham
Bradford
Garforth
Selby
South Cave
Sproatley
Kingston upon Hull
Hedon
Withernsea
Halifax
Castleford
Howden
Keyingham
Brighouse
Batley
Pontefract
Snaith
Goole
Barton-upon-Humber
Barrow upon Humber
Patrington
Dewsbury
Wakefield
Easington
Huddersfield
Hemsworth
Thorne
Scunthorpe
Immingham
Grimsby
Meltham
Darton
Adwick le Street
Barnsley
Hatfield
Barnetby le Wold
Cleethorpes
Holmfirth
Penistone
Wombwell
Epworth
Brigg
Laceby
Humberston
Doncaster
Mexborough
Kirton in Lindsey
Caistor
North Somercotes
North Thoresby
Saltfleet
Glossop
Stocksbridge
Rotherham
Bawtry
Walkeringham
Market Rasen
Binbrook
Sheffield
Maltby
Beckingham
Gainsborough
Louth
Mablethorpe
Castleton
Blyth
Faldingworth
Withern
Sutton-on-Sea
Hathersage
Eckington
Worksop
Retford
Sturton
Wragby
Chapel en le Frith
Dronfield
Staveley
Clowne
Saxilby
Scamblesby
Huttoft
Buxton
Baslow
Bolsover
East Markham
Lincoln
Alford
Bakewell
Chesterfield
Market Warsop
Ollerton
Sutton-on-Trent
Bardney
Horncastle
Partney
Burgh le Marsh
Clay Cross
Woodhall Spa
Matlock
Mansfield
Waddington
Mareham le Fen
Spilsby
Skegness
Alfreton
Sutton-in-Ashfield
Collingham
Navenby
Coningsby
Wainfleet All Saints
Wirksworth
Hucknall
Southwell
Newark-on-Trent
Billinghay
Sibsey
Wrangle
Belper
Heanor
Ripley
Ruskington
The Wash
Ashbourne
Arnold
Long Bennington
Sleaford
Benington
Cheadle
Carlton
Heckington
Boston
Hunstanton
Brancaster
Wells-next-the-Sea
Sheringham
Cromer
Burnham Market
Rocester
Derby
Ilkeston
Nottingham
Bottesford
Ancaster
Swineshead
Kirton
Heacham
Docking
Little Walsingham
Holt
Mundesley
Mickleover
West Bridgford
Bingham
Grantham
Donington
Gosberton
Dersingham
Fakenham
Saxthorpe
North Walsham
Uttoxeter
Long Eaton
Billingborough
ENGLAND
264
265
252
253
242
243
233
234
235
224
225
226
227
214
215
216
217
218
205
206
207
208
209
196
197
198
199
200
201
185
186
187
188
189
190
191
169
170
171
172
173
174
175
176
177
50
60
40

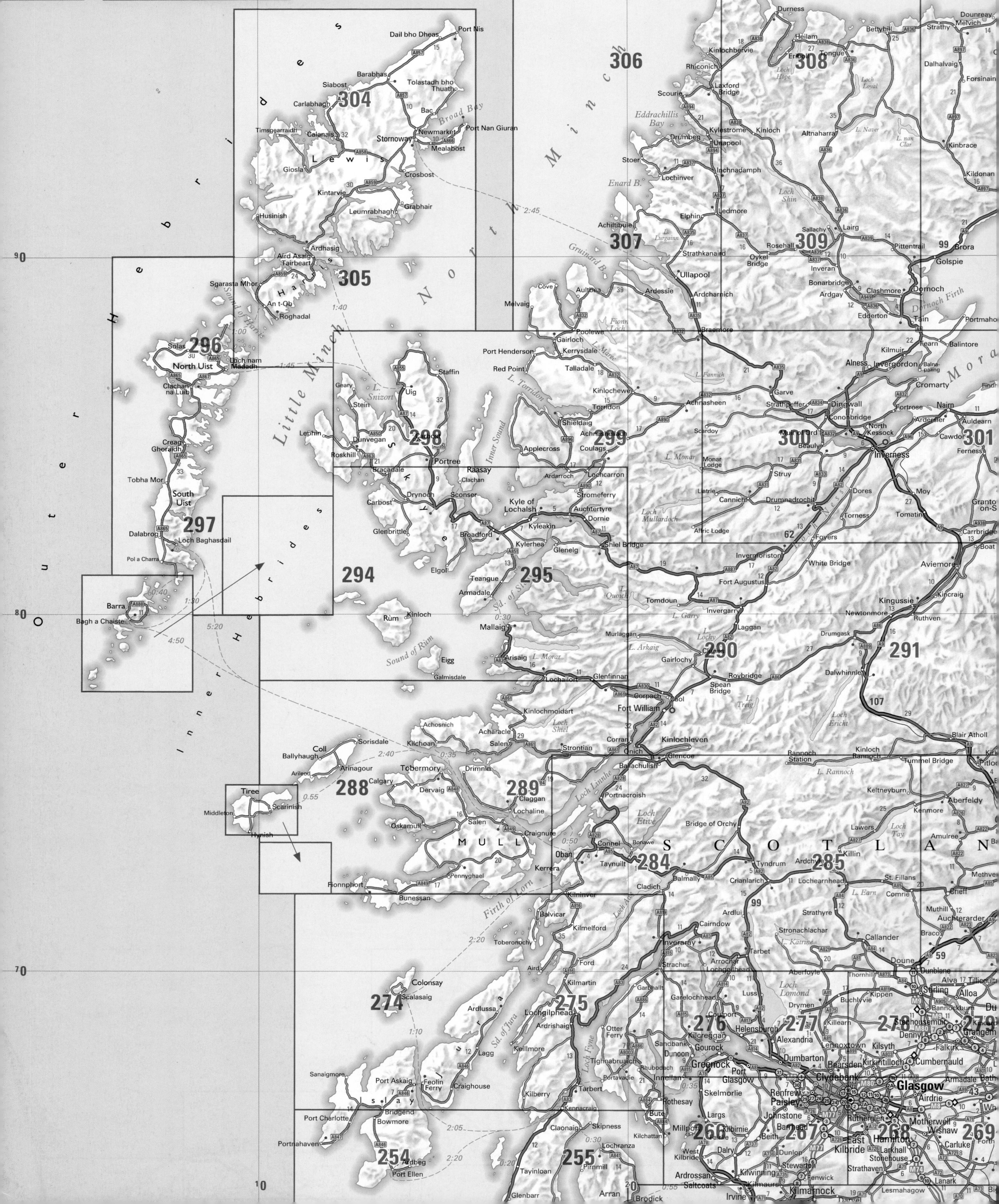

Outer Hebrides
Inner Hebrides
North Minch
Little Minch
Sound of Harris
Sound of Rum
Firth of Lorn
SCOTLAND
Lewis
Harris
North Uist
South Uist
Barra
Skye
Raasay
Rum
Eigg
Coll
Tiree
Mull
Colonsay
Jura
Islay
Port Nis
Dail bho Dheas
Barabhas
Siabost
Carlabhagh
Tolastadh bho Thuath
Bac
Broad Bay
Port Nan Giuran
Timsgearraidh
Calanais
Stornoway
Newmarket
Mealabost
Giosla
Crosbost
Kintarvie
Leumrabhagh
Grabhair
Husinish
Ardhasig
Aird Asaig
Tairbeart
Sgarasta Mhor
An t-Ob
Roghadal
Solas
Loch nam Madadh
Clachan na Luib
Creag Ghoraidh
Tobha Mor
Dalabrog
Loch Baghasdail
Pol a Charra
Bagh a Chaisteil
Durness
Kinlochbervie
Rhiconich
Laxford Bridge
Scourie
Eddrachillis Bay
Kylestrome
Drumbeg
Unapool
Kinloch
Stoer
Lochinver
Inchnadamph
Enard B.
Elphin
Ledmore
Achiltibuie
Strathkanaird
Ullapool
Gruinard B.
Ardessie
Ardcharnich
Cove
Aultbea
Melvaig
Poolewe
Gairloch
Kerrysdale
Port Henderson
Red Point
Talladale
Kinlochewe
Torridon
L. Torridon
Shieldaig
Achnasheen
Achnashellach
Applecross
Coulags
Lochcarron
Ardarroch
Stromeferry
Kyle of Lochalsh
Auchtertyre
Dornie
Kyleakin
Kylerhea
Glenelg
Shiel Bridge
Staffin
Uig
Geary
Stein
Lephin
Dunvegan
Portree
Roskhill
Bracadale
Carbost
Drynoch
Sconser
Clachan
Glenbrittle
Broadford
Elgol
Teangue
Armadale
Mallaig
Kinloch
Arisaig
Galmisdale
Lochailort
Glenfinnan
Corpach
Caol
Fort William
Kinlochmoidart
Acharacle
Salen
Strontian
Corran
Onich
Kinlochleven
Ballachulish
Glencoe
Achosnich
Kilchoan
Sorisdale
Ballyhaugh
Arinagour
Arileod
Tobermory
Calgary
Dervaig
Drimnin
Claggan
Lochaline
Middleton
Scarinish
Hynish
Oskamull
Salen
Craignure
Oban
Kerrera
Connel
Bonawe
Taynuilt
Pennyghael
Fionnphort
Bunessan
Kilninver
Balvicar
Kilmelford
Toberonochy
Ford
Aird
Kilmartin
Lochgilphead
Ardrishaig
Kilmore
Ardlussa
Lagg
Scalasaig
Sanaigmore
Port Askaig
Feolin Ferry
Craighouse
Bridgend
Bowmore
Port Charlotte
Portnahaven
Ardbeg
Port Ellen
Kilberry
Tarbert
Tayinloan
Claonaig
Skipness
Lochranza
Pirnmill
Glenbarr
Arran
Brodick
Kennacraig
Otter Ferry
Tighnabruaich
Portavadie
Rhubodach
Bute
Kilchattan
Millport
Rothesay
Innellan
Dunoon
Sandbank
Kilgreggan
Strachur
Inveraray
Cairndow
Arrochar
Lochgoilhead
Tarbet
Luss
Loch Lomond
Helensburgh
Gourock
Greenock
Port Glasgow
Skelmorlie
Largs
West Kilbride
Dalry
Ardrossan
Saltcoats
Irvine
Kilwinning
Kilmaurs
Kilmarnock
Stewarton
Beith
Dunlop
Barrhead
Paisley
Renfrew
Johnstone
Clydebank
Dumbarton
Alexandria
Glasgow
Rutherglen
East Kilbride
Hamilton
Motherwell
Wishaw
Airdrie
Bearsden
Kirkintilloch
Cumbernauld
Kilsyth
Lennoxtown
Denny
Falkirk
Grangemouth
Stirling
Bannockburn
Alloa
Dunblane
Doune
Callander
Aberfoyle
Drymen
Buchlyvie
Kippen
Thornhill
Killearn
Strathyre
Stronachlachar
L. Katrine
Balquhidder
Lochearnhead
Crianlarich
Tyndrum
Ardlui
Dalmally
Cladich
Bridge of Orchy
Killin
Comrie
Crieff
St. Fillans
Muthill
Auchterarder
Braco
Kenmore
Amulree
Aberfeldy
Keltneyburn
Tummel Bridge
Kinloch Rannoch
Rannoch Station
L. Rannoch
Blair Atholl
Dalwhinnie
L. Ericht
Drumgask
Newtonmore
Kingussie
Kincraig
Ruthven
Aviemore
Carrbridge
Boat of Garten
Tomatin
Moy
Grantown-on-Spey
Roybridge
Spean Bridge
Gairlochy
Clunes
L. Lochy
L. Treig
L. Arkaig
Murlaggan
Invergarry
Laggan
Fort Augustus
Tomdoun
L. Quoich
L. Garry
Invermoriston
White Bridge
Foyers
Torness
Dores
Drumnadrochit
Cannich
Struy
Affric Lodge
Loch Mullardoch
Monar Lodge
L. Monar
Scardoy
Muir of Ord
Beauly
Inverness
North Kessock
Dingwall
Conon Bridge
Strathpeffer
Garve
Braemore
L. Fannich
Alness
Invergordon
Cromarty
Fortrose
Ardersier
Nairn
Auldearn
Cawdor
Ferness
Kilmuir
Fearn
Balintore
Tain
Edderton
Dornoch
Dornoch Firth
Clashmore
Bonarbridge
Ardgay
Inveran
Oykel Bridge
Rosehall
Lairg
Sallachy
Pittentrail
Brora
Golspie
Loch Shin
Altnaharra
L. Naver
L. nan Clar
Kinbrace
Kildonan
Forsinain
Dalhalvaig
Strathy
Bettyhill
Melvich
Dounreay
Tongue
Heilam
Eriboll
Loch Hope
Loch Loyal
Ardersier
Moray Firth

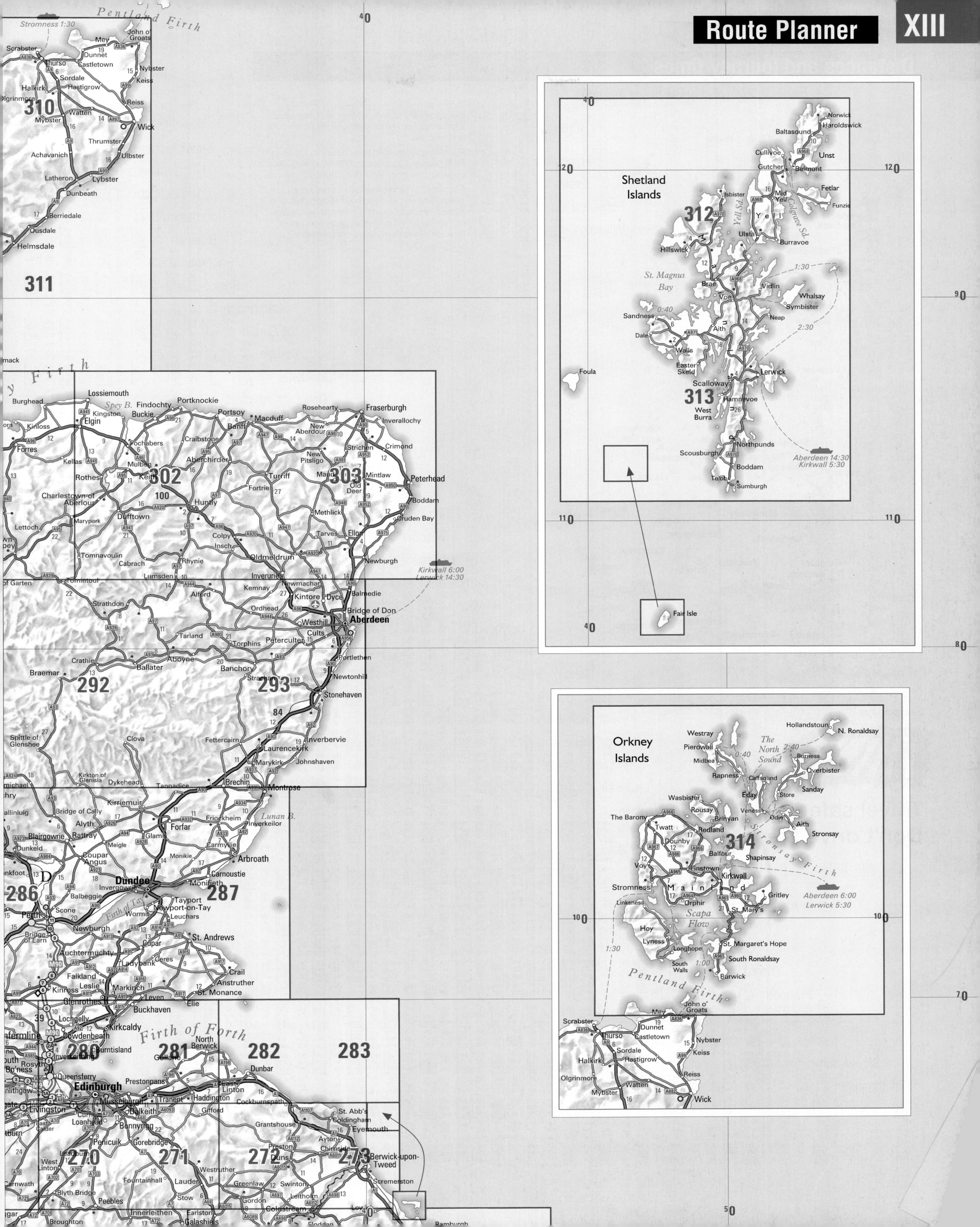
Pentland Firth
Stromness 1:30
Scrabster
Thurso
Mey
Dunnet
John o' Groats
Castletown
Nybster
Keiss
Sordale
Halkirk
Hastigrow
Reiss
310
Mybster
Watten
Wick
Thrumster
Achavanich
Ulbster
Latheron
Lybster
Dunbeath
Berriedale
Ousdale
Helmsdale
311
Shetland Islands
312
Norwick
Haroldswick
Baltasound
Unst
Cullivoe
Gutcher
Belmont
Fetlar
Funzie
Isbister
Mid Yell
Yell
Yell Sd.
Colgrave Sd.
Ulsta
Burravoe
Hillswick
St. Magnus Bay
Brae
Voe
Vidlin
Whalsay
Symbister
Sandness
Neap
Dale
Aith
Walls
Easter Skeld
Foula
Lerwick
Scalloway
313
Hamnavoe
West Burra
Northpunds
Scousburgh
Boddam
Toab
Sumburgh
Aberdeen 14:30
Kirkwall 5:30
Fair Isle
Orkney Islands
Hollandstoun
N. Ronaldsay
Westray
Pierowall
Midbea
The North Sound
Burness
Overbister
Sanday
Rapness
Calfsound
Eday
Store
Wasbister
Rousay
Veness
Odin
Aith
Stronsay
The Barony
Twatt
Brinyan
Redland
Dounby
314
Balfour
Shapinsay
Stronsay Firth
Voy
Finstown
Kirkwall
Stromness
Mainland
Gritley
Linksness
Orphir
St. Mary's
Aberdeen 6:00
Lerwick 5:30
Scapa Flow
Hoy
Lyness
Longhope
St. Margaret's Hope
South Walls
South Ronaldsay
Burwick
Pentland Firth
Lossiemouth
Burghead
Findochty
Portknockie
Spey B.
Kingston
Buckie
Portsoy
Macduff
Rosehearty
Fraserburgh
Inverallochy
Kinloss
Elgin
Banff
New Aberdour
Forres
Fochabers
Crimond
Cornhill
Strichen
Mulben
Aberchirder
New Pitsligo
Kellas
Rothes
Keith
302
Turriff
Maud
303
Mintlaw
Peterhead
Old Deer
Charlestown of Aberlour
100
Huntly
Fortrie
Boddam
Dufftown
Methlick
Cruden Bay
Marypark
Lettoch
Colpy
Tarves
Ellon
Insch
Tomnavoulin
Cabrach
Rhynie
Oldmeldrum
Newburgh
Kirkwall 6:00
Lerwick 14:30
Lumsden
Inverurie
Tomintoul
Kemnay
Newmachar
Alford
Kintore
Dyce
Balmedie
Strathdon
Ordhead
Westhill
Bridge of Don
Aberdeen
Tarland
Cults
Peterculter
Torphins
Crathie
Aboyne
Banchory
Portlethen
Braemar
Ballater
Newtonhill
292
Strachan
293
Stonehaven
84
Spittal of Glenshee
Clova
Fettercairn
Inverbervie
Laurencekirk
Marykirk
Johnshaven
Kirkton of Glenisla
Dykehead
Tannadice
Brechin
Montrose
Kirriemuir
Bridge of Cally
Friockheim
Lunan B.
Alyth
Inverkeilor
Blairgowrie
Rattray
Forfar
Glamis
Meigle
Carmyllie
Dunkeld
Coupar Angus
Monikie
Arbroath
Carnoustie
Dundee
Invergowrie
Monifieth
286
287
Balbeggie
Tayport
Newport-on-Tay
Firth of Tay
Scone
Perth
Wormit
Leuchars
Newburgh
St. Andrews
Bridge of Earn
Cupar
Auchtermuchty
Ceres
Crail
Ladybank
Falkland
Anstruther
Leslie
Markinch
St. Monance
Kinross
Glenrothes
Leven
Elie
Buckhaven
Lochgelly
Cowdenbeath
Kirkcaldy
Firth of Forth
Dunfermline
280
Burntisland
281
North Berwick
282
283
Inverkeithing
Gullane
Rosyth
Dunbar
Bo'ness
Queensferry
Prestonpans
East Linton
Linlithgow
Edinburgh
Tranent
Haddington
Musselburgh
Cockburnspath
Livingston
Dalkeith
Gifford
St. Abb's
Coldingham
Loanhead
Bonnyrigg
Eyemouth
East Calder
Grantshouse
Penicuik
Gorebridge
Ayton
Chirnside
270
271
272
Duns
273
Berwick-upon-Tweed
Preston
West Linton
Westruther
Fountainhall
Lauder
Scremerston
Carnwath
Greenlaw
Swinton
Blyth Bridge
Stow
Leitholm
Peebles
Gordon
Coldstream
Earlston
Innerleithen
Broughton
Galashiels
Bamburgh

Distances and journey times

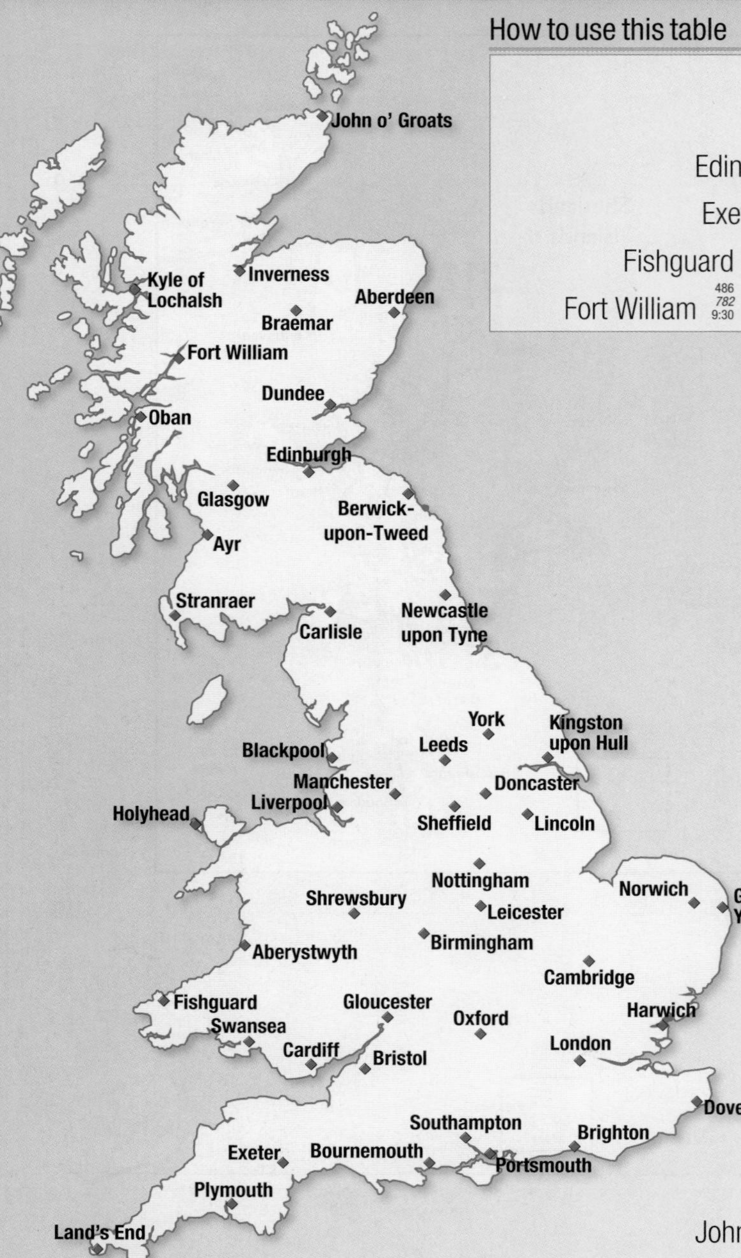

How to use this table

Dover						390 / 4:30
Dundee					523 / 842 / 9:10	275 / 443 / 5:00
Edinburgh				56 / 90 / 1:30	462 / 744 / 8:10	219 / 352 / 4:00
Exeter			450 / 724 / 8:00	518 / 834 / 9:10	248 / 399 / 4:40	251 / 404 / 4:30
Fishguard		230 / 370 / 4:30	399 / 642 / 7:30	460 / 740 / 8:30	331 / 533 / 6:20	247 / 398 / 4:50
Fort William	486 / 782 / 9:30	560 / 901 / 10:20	144 / 232 / 3:30	127 / 204 / 3:10	596 / 959 / 11:00	357 / 575 / 7:00

Distances are shown in miles and, in italics, kilometres with estimated journey times in hours and minutes.

For example, the distance between Dover and Fishguard is 331 miles or 533 kilometres with an estimated journey time of 6 hours, 20 minutes.

Estimated driving times are based on an average speed of 60mph on Motorways and 40mph on other roads. Drivers should allow extra time when driving at peak periods or through areas likely to be congested.

	Swansea	Stranraer	Southampton	Shrewsbury	Sheffield	Portsmouth	Plymouth	Oxford	Oban	Nottingham	Norwich	Newcastle upon Tyne	Manchester	Liverpool	Lincoln	Leicester	Leeds	Land's End	Kyle of Lochalsh	Kingston upon Hull	John o' Groats	Inverness	Holyhead	Harwich	Great Yarmouth	Gloucester	Glasgow	Fort William	Fishguard	Exeter	Edinburgh	Dundee	Dover	Doncaster	Carlisle	Cardiff	Cambridge	Bristol	Brighton	Braemar	Bournemouth	Blackpool	Birmingham	Berwick-upon-Tweed	Ayr	Aberystwyth	Aberdeen	London
London																																																
Aberdeen																																															517 / 832 / 11:20
Aberystwyth																																														445 / 716 / 8:40	211 / 340 / 4:40
Ayr																																													317 / 510 / 6:10	183 / 295 / 4:20	394 / 634 / 7:20
Berwick-upon-Tweed																																												134 / 216 / 3:00	311 / 501 / 6:20	182 / 293 / 4:40	352 / 567 / 7:30
Birmingham																																											274 / 441 / 5:30	289 / 465 / 5:30	114 / 183 / 2:50	420 / 676 / 8:30	117 / 188 / 2:50
Blackpool																																										123 / 198 / 2:40	181 / 291 / 3:50	180 / 290 / 3:30	153 / 246 / 3:20	308 / 496 / 6:20	226 / 364 / 4:30
Bournemouth																																									270 / 435 / 5:00	147 / 237 / 3:10	412 / 663 / 7:50	436 / 702 / 8:00	207 / 333 / 4:30	564 / 908 / 10:20	107 / 172 / 2:40
Braemar																																								524 / 843 / 9:30	281 / 452 / 5:20	385 / 620 / 7:10	148 / 238 / 3:20	143 / 230 / 3:00	405 / 652 / 7:50	59 / 95 / 1:30	482 / 776 / 10:30
Brighton																																							534 / 859 / 9:40	92 / 148 / 2:10	286 / 460 / 5:20	163 / 262 / 3:20	409 / 658 / 7:40	446 / 718 / 8:00	253 / 407 / 5:10	573 / 922 / 10:30	52 / 84 / 1:50
Bristol																																						147 / 237 / 4:10	477 / 768 / 8:40	82 / 132 / 2:30	204 / 328 / 3:50	81 / 130 / 2:00	362 / 583 / 6:50	370 / 595 / 6:40	125 / 201 / 3:00	493 / 793 / 9:10	122 / 196 / 2:50
Cambridge																																					169 / 272 / 3:10	116 / 187 / 2:20	438 / 705 / 7:50	154 / 248 / 3:00	208 / 335 / 3:50	100 / 161 / 2:10	306 / 493 / 5:40	357 / 575 / 6:20	214 / 344 / 4:20	471 / 758 / 10:00	54 / 87 / 1:30
Cardiff																																				190 / 306 / 3:30	45 / 72 / 1:20	182 / 293 / 3:40	483 / 778 / 8:40	117 / 188 / 3:00	209 / 336 / 4:00	103 / 166 / 2:20	368 / 592 / 7:00	382 / 615 / 7:00	105 / 169 / 2:40	505 / 813 / 9:20	157 / 253 / 3:20
Carlisle																																			289 / 465 / 5:20	264 / 425 / 4:40	277 / 446 / 5:00	370 / 596 / 6:40	196 / 316 / 3:50	343 / 552 / 6:20	87 / 140 / 1:50	196 / 315 / 3:50	87 / 140 / 2:10	93 / 150 / 2:00	224 / 360 / 4:30	221 / 356 / 4:30	301 / 484 / 5:40
Doncaster																																		142 / 229 / 3:00	209 / 336 / 4:00	116 / 187 / 2:10	175 / 282 / 3:20	236 / 380 / 4:30	310 / 499 / 5:40	235 / 378 / 4:20	94 / 151 / 1:50	94 / 151 / 2:00	184 / 296 / 3:50	235 / 378 / 4:20	176 / 283 / 3:40	344 / 554 / 6:50	171 / 275 / 3:30
Dover																																	242 / 390 / 4:30	389 / 626 / 7:00	238 / 383 / 4:30	125 / 201 / 2:30	202 / 325 / 3:50	82 / 132 / 2:20	553 / 890 / 9:50	174 / 280 / 4:30	312 / 502 / 5:40	194 / 312 / 3:50	424 / 683 / 7:50	478 / 769 / 8:30	297 / 478 / 5:50	588 / 947 / 10:40	71 / 114 / 2:00
Dundee																																523 / 842 / 9:10	275 / 443 / 5:00	152 / 245 / 3:00	441 / 710 / 8:00	406 / 654 / 7:10	430 / 692 / 7:40	517 / 832 / 9:10	52 / 84 / 1:20	495 / 797 / 8:50	239 / 385 / 4:30	349 / 562 / 6:20	113 / 182 / 2:40	117 / 188 / 2:30	376 / 605 / 7:10	67 / 108 / 1:50	448 / 721 / 8:40
Edinburgh																															56 / 90 / 1:30	462 / 744 / 8:10	219 / 352 / 4:00	96 / 154 / 2:00	385 / 620 / 7:00	345 / 555 / 6:10	373 / 600 / 6:50	456 / 734 / 8:20	91 / 146 / 2:10	439 / 707 / 8:00	183 / 295 / 3:30	292 / 470 / 5:30	57 / 92 / 1:40	73 / 117 / 1:50	320 / 515 / 6:20	125 / 201 / 3:10	390 / 628 / 7:20
Exeter																														450 / 724 / 8:00	518 / 834 / 9:10	248 / 399 / 4:40	251 / 404 / 4:30	353 / 568 / 6:20	121 / 195 / 2:30	249 / 401 / 4:30	76 / 122 / 1:40	184 / 296 / 5:00	550 / 885 / 9:40	82 / 132 / 2:20	282 / 454 / 5:10	157 / 253 / 3:10	428 / 689 / 7:50	446 / 718 / 7:50	201 / 323 / 4:10	569 / 916 / 10:20	181 / 291 / 3:40
Fishguard																													230 / 370 / 4:30	399 / 642 / 7:30	460 / 740 / 8:30	331 / 533 / 6:20	247 / 398 / 4:50	297 / 478 / 5:40	112 / 180 / 2:40	270 / 435 / 5:10	154 / 248 / 3:20	291 / 468 / 5:40	493 / 794 / 9:10	222 / 357 / 4:40	209 / 336 / 4:10	170 / 274 / 3:40	371 / 597 / 7:20	373 / 600 / 7:00	56 / 90 / 1:30	504 / 811 / 10:10	260 / 418 / 5:20
Fort William																												486 / 782 / 9:30	560 / 901 / 10:20	144 / 232 / 3:30	127 / 204 / 3:10	596 / 959 / 11:00	357 / 575 / 7:00	206 / 332 / 4:30	485 / 781 / 9:10	479 / 771 / 9:00	486 / 782 / 9:10	575 / 926 / 10:50	125 / 201 / 3:10	539 / 867 / 10:10	296 / 476 / 6:00	392 / 631 / 7:40	190 / 306 / 4:40	133 / 214 / 3:20	430 / 692 / 8:40	149 / 240 / 3:50	510 / 821 / 9:50
Glasgow																											101 / 163 / 2:50	376 / 605 / 7:10	449 / 723 / 8:00	44 / 71 / 1:20	83 / 134 / 2:00	488 / 786 / 8:40	249 / 401 / 4:40	96 / 154 / 2:10	385 / 620 / 7:00	372 / 599 / 6:40	373 / 600 / 6:50	468 / 753 / 8:30	110 / 177 / 2:30	439 / 707 / 8:00	183 / 295 / 3:40	292 / 470 / 5:30	101 / 163 / 2:40	33 / 53 / 1:10	320 / 515 / 6:20	145 / 233 / 3:30	397 / 639 / 7:30
Gloucester																										346 / 557 / 6:10	454 / 731 / 8:30	153 / 246 / 3:10	111 / 179 / 2:10	349 / 562 / 6:10	410 / 660 / 7:10	191 / 307 / 3:30	150 / 241 / 2:50	247 / 398 / 4:20	56 / 90 / 1:20	123 / 198 / 2:20	35 / 56 / 1:00	159 / 256 / 3:10	443 / 713 / 8:00	99 / 159 / 2:40	174 / 280 / 3:10	56 / 90 / 1:20	318 / 512 / 6:00	330 / 531 / 5:50	102 / 164 / 2:30	468 / 753 / 8:30	109 / 175 / 2:30
Great Yarmouth																									225 / 362 / 4:40	419 / 674 / 8:00	527 / 848 / 10:20	366 / 589 / 7:20	335 / 539 / 6:30	386 / 621 / 7:30	484 / 779 / 9:00	185 / 298 / 4:00	167 / 269 / 3:40	320 / 515 / 6:20	284 / 457 / 5:50	82 / 132 / 2:10	275 / 443 / 5:40	180 / 290 / 4:10	477 / 768 / 9:10	240 / 386 / 5:00	252 / 406 / 5:10	180 / 290 / 4:10	345 / 555 / 7:00	402 / 647 / 7:40	294 / 473 / 6:20	517 / 832 / 10:50	128 / 206 / 3:40
Harwich																								82 / 132 / 2:10	196 / 316 / 4:00	432 / 695 / 8:10	543 / 874 / 10:30	337 / 542 / 6:40	279 / 449 / 5:20	413 / 665 / 7:40	469 / 755 / 8:40	125 / 201 / 2:50	194 / 312 / 4:00	336 / 541 / 6:20	246 / 396 / 5:00	67 / 108 / 1:50	217 / 349 / 4:30	128 / 206 / 3:00	504 / 811 / 9:20	187 / 301 / 4:00	275 / 443 / 5:20	167 / 269 / 3:40	372 / 599 / 7:20	425 / 684 / 8:00	281 / 452 / 5:50	535 / 861 / 11:20	76 / 122 / 2:20
Holyhead																							349 / 562 / 7:10	334 / 538 / 7:00	191 / 307 / 4:00	330 / 531 / 6:40	438 / 705 / 8:50	167 / 269 / 4:00	282 / 454 / 5:40	333 / 536 / 6:40	394 / 634 / 7:30	360 / 580 / 7:00	181 / 291 / 3:50	231 / 372 / 4:50	216 / 348 / 5:40	270 / 435 / 5:20	206 / 332 / 4:30	334 / 538 / 6:40	426 / 686 / 8:20	288 / 463 / 5:50	141 / 227 / 3:20	148 / 238 / 3:30	311 / 501 / 6:30	305 / 491 / 6:10	111 / 179 / 2:50	439 / 707 / 8:40	269 / 433 / 5:40
Inverness																						474 / 763 / 9:40	569 / 916 / 11:00	553 / 890 / 11:00	504 / 811 / 9:30	166 / 267 / 4:00	66 / 106 / 1:40	542 / 872 / 10:30	618 / 995 / 11:30	158 / 254 / 3:50	132 / 212 / 3:20	622 / 1001 / 11:30	383 / 617 / 7:30	262 / 422 / 5:30	549 / 884 / 10:20	505 / 813 / 9:30	539 / 867 / 10:10	617 / 993 / 11:30	75 / 121 / 2:00	597 / 961 / 11:20	348 / 560 / 7:00	458 / 737 / 9:00	215 / 346 / 5:10	199 / 320 / 4:30	486 / 782 / 9:40	105 / 169 / 2:50	550 / 885 / 10:40
John o' Groats																					129 / 208 / 3:20	603 / 970 / 12:40	693 / 1116 / 14:00	677 / 1090 / 14:00	628 / 1011 / 12:30	295 / 475 / 7:10	195 / 314 / 5:00	671 / 1080 / 13:40	744 / 1197 / 14:30	285 / 459 / 7:00	259 / 417 / 6:30	746 / 1201 / 14:40	507 / 816 / 10:30	391 / 629 / 8:40	680 / 1094 / 13:30	630 / 1014 / 12:30	668 / 1075 / 13:20	741 / 1193 / 14:40	202 / 325 / 5:00	724 / 1165 / 14:20	478 / 769 / 10:00	574 / 924 / 11:50	342 / 550 / 8:10	328 / 528 / 7:40	601 / 967 / 12:40	232 / 373 / 5:50	663 / 1067 / 13:30
Kingston upon Hull																				518 / 834 / 10:50	394 / 634 / 7:50	231 / 372 / 4:50	196 / 316 / 4:10	207 / 333 / 5:20	169 / 272 / 3:10	254 / 409 / 4:50	369 / 594 / 7:20	280 / 451 / 5:30	309 / 497 / 5:40	234 / 377 / 4:30	295 / 475 / 5:30	256 / 412 / 4:50	47 / 76 / 1:10	158 / 254 / 3:00	244 / 393 / 4:40	139 / 224 / 3:10	233 / 375 / 4:20	245 / 394 / 4:40	327 / 526 / 6:10	264 / 425 / 5:00	127 / 204 / 2:30	134 / 216 / 2:50	185 / 298 / 3:50	251 / 404 / 4:40	223 / 359 / 4:40	364 / 586 / 7:20	184 / 296 / 3:50
Kyle of Lochalsh																			445 / 716 / 9:00	189 / 304 / 4:40	84 / 135 / 2:10	514 / 827 / 10:40	611 / 983 / 12:10	602 / 969 / 12:10	528 / 850 / 10:20	179 / 288 / 4:40	79 / 127 / 2:00	567 / 913 / 11:20	628 / 1011 / 12:00	216 / 348 / 5:20	186 / 299 / 4:40	671 / 1080 / 12:50	432 / 695 / 8:40	275 / 443 / 6:10	564 / 908 / 11:10	555 / 893 / 10:50	552 / 888 / 10:50	651 / 1048 / 12:40	159 / 256 / 4:00	618 / 995 / 12:10	372 / 599 / 7:50	471 / 758 / 9:40	263 / 423 / 6:20	212 / 341 / 5:10	499 / 803 / 10:20	189 / 304 / 4:50	586 / 943 / 11:40
Land's End																		763 / 1228 / 15:10	421 / 678 / 8:20	868 / 1397 / 17:20	741 / 1193 / 14:20	405 / 652 / 8:30	390 / 628 / 8:00	446 / 718 / 9:10	235 / 378 / 5:00	573 / 922 / 10:50	686 / 1104 / 13:20	353 / 568 / 7:20	123 / 198 / 3:20	574 / 924 / 10:50	642 / 1033 / 12:00	381 / 613 / 7:40	374 / 602 / 7:20	477 / 768 / 9:10	245 / 394 / 5:20	374 / 602 / 7:20	200 / 322 / 4:40	308 / 496 / 7:50	665 / 1070 / 12:30	205 / 330 / 5:20	405 / 652 / 8:00	281 / 452 / 6:00	552 / 888 / 10:40	570 / 917 / 10:50	313 / 504 / 6:50	692 / 1114 / 13:10	297 / 478 / 6:30
Leeds																	405 / 652 / 8:00	394 / 634 / 8:20	55 / 89 / 1:30	487 / 784 / 10:20	360 / 579 / 7:10	176 / 283 / 4:00	223 / 359 / 4:30	196 / 315 / 4:20	174 / 280 / 3:20	215 / 346 / 4:10	329 / 530 / 6:40	237 / 381 / 4:40	270 / 435 / 5:00	202 / 325 / 4:00	258 / 415 / 4:50	260 / 418 / 4:50	29 / 47 / 0:50	119 / 192 / 2:30	232 / 373 / 4:20	145 / 233 / 2:50	194 / 312 / 3:50	260 / 419 / 5:00	293 / 472 / 5:30	255 / 410 / 4:50	72 / 116 / 1:40	113 / 182 / 2:30	156 / 251 / 3:20	212 / 341 / 4:00	169 / 272 / 3:40	327 / 526 / 6:50	189 / 304 / 3:50
Leicester																95 / 153 / 2:00	320 / 515 / 6:30	500 / 805 / 9:50	102 / 164 / 2:10	588 / 947 / 11:50	461 / 742 / 8:50	190 / 306 / 4:00	147 / 237 / 3:10	140 / 225 / 3:20	85 / 137 / 1:40	314 / 505 / 5:40	422 / 679 / 8:00	209 / 336 / 4:10	196 / 315 / 3:40	296 / 476 / 5:20	349 / 562 / 6:20	185 / 298 / 3:30	74 / 119 / 1:30	206 / 332 / 3:50	154 / 248 / 3:00	68 / 109 / 1:20	120 / 193 / 2:30	166 / 267 / 3:20	389 / 626 / 7:00	158 / 254 / 3:10	140 / 225 / 2:40	39 / 63 / 1:10	252 / 406 / 5:00	299 / 481 / 5:20	153 / 246 / 3:20	414 / 666 / 7:40	97 / 156 / 2:20
Lincoln															51 / 82 / 1:20	68 / 109 / 1:50	371 / 597 / 7:30	476 / 766 / 9:40	44 / 71 / 1:20	554 / 892 / 11:30	427 / 687 / 8:30	216 / 348 / 4:40	155 / 249 / 3:30	128 / 206 / 3:20	159 / 256 / 3:10	291 / 468 / 5:30	399 / 642 / 7:50	272 / 438 / 5:30	247 / 398 / 4:40	258 / 415 / 5:00	314 / 505 / 5:50	202 / 325 / 4:00	39 / 63 / 1:10	191 / 307 / 3:40	208 / 335 / 4:10	85 / 137 / 2:20	183 / 295 / 3:40	197 / 317 / 4:00	357 / 575 / 6:40	209 / 336 / 4:10	128 / 206 / 2:40	90 / 145 / 2:10	224 / 360 / 4:40	274 / 441 / 5:10	199 / 320 / 4:20	383 / 616 / 7:20	131 / 211 / 3:10
Liverpool														129 / 208 / 2:50	130 / 209 / 2:40	75 / 121 / 1:50	361 / 581 / 7:20	407 / 655 / 8:30	130 / 209 / 2:40	511 / 822 / 10:40	382 / 615 / 7:40	102 / 164 / 2:40	265 / 427 / 5:20	240 / 386 / 5:00	140 / 225 / 2:40	216 / 348 / 4:10	329 / 530 / 6:40	160 / 257 / 3:30	237 / 381 / 4:30	216 / 348 / 4:10	286 / 460 / 5:20	299 / 481 / 5:30	86 / 138 / 1:50	120 / 193 / 2:30	169 / 272 / 3:20	194 / 312 / 3:40	161 / 259 / 3:10	272 / 438 / 5:10	318 / 512 / 6:00	234 / 377 / 4:30	49 / 79 / 1:20	93 / 150 / 2:10	219 / 352 / 4:30	213 / 343 / 4:10	104 / 167 / 2:40	341 / 549 / 6:40	202 / 325 / 4:10
Manchester													35 / 56 / 1:10	84 / 135 / 2:00	92 / 148 / 2:00	40 / 64 / 1:10	361 / 581 / 7:20	406 / 654 / 8:30	95 / 153 / 2:10	500 / 805 / 10:30	373 / 600 / 7:30	124 / 200 / 3:00	228 / 367 / 4:40	212 / 341 / 4:30	126 / 203 / 2:30	215 / 346 / 4:10	329 / 530 / 6:40	197 / 317 / 4:00	236 / 380 / 4:20	215 / 346 / 4:10	285 / 459 / 5:20	276 / 444 / 5:10	61 / 98 / 1:30	119 / 192 / 2:30	183 / 295 / 3:40	165 / 266 / 3:10	161 / 259 / 3:10	257 / 414 / 4:50	318 / 512 / 6:00	227 / 365 / 4:20	48 / 77 / 1:20	80 / 129 / 2:00	196 / 315 / 4:00	212 / 341 / 4:00	129 / 208 / 3:00	340 / 547 / 6:30	185 / 298 / 3:50
Newcastle upon Tyne												132 / 212 / 2:50	168 / 270 / 3:20	159 / 256 / 3:20	187 / 301 / 3:40	92 / 148 / 2:10	498 / 802 / 9:40	318 / 512 / 7:00	132 / 212 / 2:50	395 / 636 / 8:50	268 / 431 / 5:40	272 / 438 / 5:40	308 / 496 / 6:00	281 / 452 / 5:40	266 / 428 / 4:50	148 / 238 / 3:10	253 / 407 / 5:20	329 / 529 / 6:20	364 / 586 / 6:30	110 / 177 / 2:20	166 / 267 / 3:20	358 / 576 / 6:30	114 / 183 / 2:20	57 / 92 / 1:50	325 / 523 / 6:00	241 / 388 / 4:20	299 / 481 / 5:30	352 / 567 / 6:30	201 / 323 / 4:00	347 / 558 / 6:30	129 / 208 / 2:40	207 / 333 / 4:10	64 / 103 / 1:50	149 / 240 / 3:00	257 / 414 / 5:20	235 / 378 / 4:50	286 / 460 / 5:40
Norwich											264 / 425 / 5:20	185 / 298 / 4:30	220 / 354 / 4:40	105 / 169 / 2:50	119 / 192 / 3:20	176 / 283 / 3:50	421 / 678 / 8:40	582 / 937 / 11:50	149 / 240 / 4:00	654 / 1053 / 13:30	529 / 852 / 10:30	311 / 501 / 6:40	73 / 117 / 2:00	20 / 32 / 0:40	204 / 328 / 4:10	385 / 620 / 9:00	504 / 811 / 10:00	343 / 552 / 7:00	308 / 496 / 6:00	366 / 589 / 7:00	422 / 679 / 8:00	174 / 280 / 3:50	147 / 237 / 3:20	289 / 465 / 5:40	262 / 422 / 5:20	62 / 100 / 1:50	252 / 406 / 5:10	175 / 282 / 4:00	457 / 735 / 8:40	214 / 344 / 4:40	232 / 373 / 4:50	166 / 267 / 3:50	328 / 528 / 6:40	382 / 615 / 7:20	276 / 444 / 6:00	496 / 798 / 9:40	114 / 183 / 3:30
Nottingham										130 / 209 / 3:40	157 / 253 / 3:10	73 / 118 / 1:40	98 / 158 / 2:10	35 / 56 / 1:10	25 / 40 / 0:50	70 / 113 / 1:40	345 / 555 / 7:00	479 / 771 / 9:40	90 / 145 / 2:00	557 / 896 / 11:30	430 / 692 / 8:20	185 / 298 / 4:00	150 / 241 / 3:20	153 / 246 / 3:30	110 / 177 / 2:10	293 / 472 / 5:30	401 / 646 / 7:50	220 / 354 / 4:30	221 / 356 / 4:10	262 / 422 / 4:50	328 / 528 / 6:00	205 / 330 / 3:50	43 / 69 / 1:10	194 / 312 / 3:40	172 / 277 / 3:20	83 / 134 / 1:40	145 / 233 / 3:00	193 / 311 / 3:50	353 / 568 / 6:30	183 / 295 / 3:40	111 / 179 / 2:20	50 / 80 / 1:20	221 / 356 / 4:30	274 / 441 / 5:10	164 / 264 / 3:40	393 / 633 / 7:30	122 / 196 / 2:40
Oban									390 / 628 / 7:30	492 / 792 / 9:40	233 / 375 / 4:50	307 / 494 / 6:00	308 / 496 / 6:10	387 / 623 / 7:30	419 / 674 / 7:50	307 / 494 / 6:00	665 / 1070 / 12:50	128 / 206 / 3:10	346 / 557 / 6:40	244 / 393 / 6:10	117 / 188 / 3:00	427 / 687 / 8:30	524 / 843 / 10:00	515 / 829 / 10:00	441 / 710 / 8:10	92 / 148 / 2:30	49 / 79 / 1:20	481 / 774 / 9:10	549 / 884 / 10:00	123 / 198 / 3:00	117 / 188 / 2:50	585 / 942 / 10:40	346 / 557 / 6:40	188 / 303 / 4:00	477 / 768 / 9:00	468 / 753 / 8:40	465 / 748 / 8:40	565 / 910 / 10:30	141 / 227 / 3:30	530 / 853 / 9:50	285 / 459 / 5:40	384 / 618 / 7:30	180 / 290 / 4:20	94 / 151 / 2:20	412 / 663 / 8:10	178 / 286 / 4:20	499 / 803 / 9:30
Oxford								462 / 744 / 8:30	109 / 175 / 2:10	145 / 233 / 3:50	260 / 418 / 4:50	144 / 232 / 2:50	172 / 277 / 3:20	137 / 221 / 2:50	73 / 117 / 1:30	168 / 270 / 3:10	274 / 441 / 5:40	550 / 885 / 10:40	192 / 309 / 3:40	656 / 1056 / 13:00	532 / 856 / 10:00	238 / 383 / 4:50	145 / 233 / 3:10	200 / 322 / 4:20	52 / 84 / 1:30	356 / 573 / 6:30	472 / 760 / 9:00	205 / 330 / 4:10	156 / 251 / 3:00	372 / 599 / 6:40	433 / 697 / 7:40	141 / 227 / 2:50	145 / 233 / 2:40	260 / 418 / 4:40	108 / 174 / 2:20	83 / 134 / 1:40	74 / 119 / 1:40	108 / 174 / 2:20	465 / 749 / 8:20	90 / 145 / 2:00	187 / 301 / 3:30	64 / 103 / 1:30	324 / 521 / 6:10	353 / 568 / 6:20	154 / 248 / 3:20	483 / 777 / 8:50	57 / 92 / 1:40
Plymouth								199 / 320 / 4:00	587 / 945 / 11:00	267 / 430 / 5:10	343 / 552 / 7:00	410 / 660 / 7:40	283 / 455 / 5:30	283 / 455 / 5:30	293 / 472 / 5:50	242 / 389 / 4:40	316 / 509 / 6:00	89 / 143 / 2:20	674 / 1085 / 13:10	355 / 571 / 6:40	790 / 1271 / 15:40	664 / 1069 / 12:30	328 / 528 / 6:40	309 / 497 / 6:10	365 / 588 / 7:20	157 / 253 / 3:20	495 / 797 / 9:10	595 / 958 / 11:20	264 / 425 / 5:30	46 / 74 / 1:30	496 / 798 / 9:00	552 / 888 / 10:00	300 / 483 / 5:50	297 / 478 / 5:40	399 / 642 / 7:20	167 / 269 / 3:40	293 / 472 / 5:30	122 / 196 / 2:50	224 / 361 / 6:00	587 / 945 / 10:40	128 / 206 / 3:30	328 / 528 / 6:10	203 / 327 / 4:20	474 / 763 / 9:00	492 / 792 / 9:00	237 / 382 / 5:10	615 / 990 / 11:20	218 / 351 / 4:40
Portsmouth							176 / 283 / 4:50	77 / 124 / 1:40	545 / 877 / 10:00	191 / 307 / 3:40	207 / 333 / 4:20	337 / 542 / 6:10	236 / 380 / 4:30	254 / 409 / 4:50	201 / 323 / 4:00	162 / 261 / 3:10	257 / 414 / 4:50	259 / 417 / 5:40	633 / 1019 / 12:10	269 / 433 / 5:00	737 / 1186 / 14:30	613 / 987 / 11:30	311 / 501 / 6:10	166 / 267 / 3:40	221 / 356 / 4:40	119 / 192 / 3:00	448 / 721 / 8:10	555 / 893 / 10:20	251 / 404 / 5:00	135 / 217 / 2:40	453 / 729 / 8:10	514 / 827 / 9:00	130 / 209 / 2:50	234 / 377 / 4:20	348 / 560 / 6:10	142 / 229 / 3:00	144 / 232 / 2:50	97 / 156 / 2:10	48 / 77 / 1:40	547 / 881 / 9:50	52 / 84 / 1:30	264 / 425 / 4:50	141 / 227 / 3:00	401 / 645 / 7:30	430 / 692 / 7:40	222 / 357 / 4:40	560 / 901 / 10:10	70 / 113 / 2:00
Sheffield						230 / 370 / 4:20	283 / 455 / 5:30	135 / 217 / 2:40	339 / 546 / 6:30	37 / 60 / 1:00	146 / 235 / 3:20	125 / 201 / 2:40	38 / 61 / 1:00	72 / 116 / 1:40	46 / 74 / 1:20	62 / 100 / 1:20	33 / 53 / 1:00	361 / 581 / 7:10	427 / 687 / 8:40	65 / 105 / 1:30	520 / 837 / 10:50	393 / 632 / 7:40	168 / 270 / 3:40	187 / 301 / 3:50	166 / 267 / 3:40	126 / 203 / 2:20	248 / 399 / 4:40	348 / 560 / 6:50	215 / 346 / 4:20	237 / 381 / 4:20	235 / 378 / 4:20	291 / 468 / 5:20	245 / 394 / 4:30	18 / 29 / 0:40	152 / 245 / 3:00	194 / 312 / 3:40	120 / 193 / 2:20	161 / 259 / 3:10	226 / 364 / 4:20	320 / 515 / 6:00	216 / 348 / 4:10	86 / 138 / 1:50	76 / 122 / 1:50	190 / 306 / 4:00	245 / 394 / 4:30	159 / 256 / 3:30	360 / 579 / 6:50	159 / 256 / 3:20
Shrewsbury					82 / 132 / 2:10	207 / 333 / 3:50	225 / 362 / 4:40	106 / 171 / 2:10	364 / 586 / 7:00	93 / 150 / 2:00	205 / 330 / 4:20	201 / 323 / 3:50	69 / 111 / 1:40	58 / 93 / 1:50	133 / 214 / 2:50	84 / 135 / 1:40	109 / 175 / 2:20	303 / 488 / 6:10	451 / 726 / 9:00	169 / 272 / 3:10	567 / 912 / 11:30	438 / 705 / 8:20	113 / 182 / 2:50	240 / 386 / 4:40	225 / 362 / 4:40	77 / 124 / 1:30	272 / 438 / 5:00	382 / 615 / 7:20	145 / 233 / 3:10	179 / 288 / 3:20	274 / 441 / 5:00	330 / 531 / 6:00	251 / 404 / 4:30	109 / 175 / 2:10	176 / 283 / 3:20	111 / 179 / 2:20	159 / 256 / 3:00	103 / 166 / 2:50	226 / 364 / 4:20	371 / 597 / 6:50	185 / 298 / 3:40	98 / 158 / 2:00	45 / 72 / 1:20	265 / 426 / 5:10	269 / 433 / 5:00	77 / 124 / 2:10	399 / 642 / 7:30	160 / 258 / 3:20
Southampton				185 / 298 / 4:10	199 / 320 / 3:40	21 / 34 / 0:50	151 / 243 / 4:10	64 / 103 / 1:30	530 / 853 / 9:40	176 / 283 / 3:20	206 / 332 / 4:20	324 / 521 / 5:50	221 / 356 / 4:10	239 / 385 / 4:30	204 / 328 / 4:00	137 / 220 / 2:40	232 / 373 / 4:20	228 / 367 / 5:00	618 / 995 / 12:00	256 / 412 / 4:40	723 / 1164 / 14:10	598 / 963 / 11:10	293 / 472 / 5:50	164 / 264 / 3:30	220 / 354 / 4:40	105 / 169 / 2:40	433 / 697 / 7:40	541 / 871 / 10:00	233 / 375 / 4:40	105 / 169 / 3:00	438 / 705 / 7:50	500 / 805 / 8:50	143 / 230 / 2:50	209 / 336 / 3:50	324 / 521 / 5:50	121 / 195 / 2:30	148 / 238 / 2:50	76 / 122 / 2:20	61 / 98 / 1:50	532 / 856 / 9:30	31 / 50 / 1:00	251 / 404 / 4:40	128 / 206 / 2:40	388 / 624 / 7:10	417 / 671 / 7:30	201 / 323 / 4:10	547 / 880 / 10:00	77 / 124 / 2:00
Stranraer			445 / 716 / 8:20	277 / 446 / 5:30	263 / 423 / 5:20	461 / 742 / 8:40	500 / 805 / 9:40	379 / 610 / 7:10	148 / 238 / 3:40	290 / 467 / 5:50	403 / 649 / 8:10	158 / 254 / 3:40	220 / 354 / 4:40	221 / 356 / 4:40	298 / 480 / 6:00	330 / 531 / 6:20	220 / 354 / 4:40	585 / 942 / 11:30	263 / 423 / 6:30	259 / 417 / 5:20	379 / 610 / 9:00	262 / 422 / 6:00	338 / 544 / 7:00	410 / 660 / 8:10	426 / 686 / 8:40	343 / 552 / 6:30	84 / 135 / 2:30	195 / 314 / 4:50	392 / 631 / 7:50	454 / 731 / 8:30	124 / 200 / 3:00	167 / 269 / 3:40	496 / 798 / 9:10	257 / 414 / 5:10	101 / 163 / 2:40	390 / 628 / 7:30	379 / 610 / 7:10	378 / 608 / 7:20	475 / 765 / 9:00	194 / 312 / 4:20	444 / 715 / 8:30	188 / 303 / 4:00	297 / 478 / 6:00	170 / 274 / 4:10	51 / 82 / 1:20	325 / 523 / 6:50	228 / 367 / 5:10	402 / 647 / 7:50
Swansea		417 / 671 / 7:50	161 / 259 / 3:00	118 / 190 / 2:20	217 / 349 / 4:00	182 / 293 / 3:30	206 / 332 / 4:10	141 / 227 / 2:40	506 / 815 / 9:20	192 / 309 / 3:40	301 / 485 / 6:00	347 / 559 / 6:20	187 / 301 / 3:30	195 / 314 / 3:40	233 / 375 / 4:30	177 / 285 / 3:20	248 / 399 / 4:40	285 / 459 / 6:00	594 / 956 / 11:30	264 / 425 / 4:50	696 / 1120 / 13:40	572 / 921 / 10:40	184 / 296 / 4:50	267 / 430 / 5:10	329 / 530 / 6:30	89 / 143 / 1:50	409 / 658 / 7:20	496 / 798 / 9:20	67 / 108 / 1:50	161 / 259 / 3:00	412 / 663 / 7:20	473 / 761 / 8:20	274 / 441 / 5:00	232 / 373 / 4:10	309 / 497 / 5:30	41 / 66 / 1:10	227 / 365 / 4:10	85 / 137 / 1:50	222 / 357 / 4:20	505 / 813 / 9:00	167 / 269 / 3:20	216 / 348 / 4:00	119 / 192 / 2:30	383 / 616 / 7:10	379 / 610 / 6:50	73 / 117 / 2:00	507 / 816 / 9:20	194 / 312 / 4:00
York	272 / 438 / 5:10	222 / 357 / 4:40	258 / 415 / 5:10	133 / 214 / 2:40	52 / 84 / 1:20	278 / 448 / 5:10	333 / 536 / 6:20	181 / 291 / 3:20	309 / 497 / 6:00	77 / 124 / 1:40	181 / 291 / 4:20	84 / 135 / 2:20	64 / 103 / 1:30	99 / 159 / 2:10	75 / 121 / 1:50	108 / 174 / 2:10	24 / 39 / 0:50	411 / 661 / 8:00	407 / 655 / 8:20	37 / 60 / 1:10	479 / 771 / 10:10	352 / 566 / 7:00	204 / 328 / 4:20	228 / 367 / 4:40	201 / 323 / 4:20	189 / 304 / 3:30	217 / 349 / 4:10	330 / 531 / 6:30	261 / 420 / 5:10	287 / 462 / 5:10	194 / 312 / 3:40	250 / 402 / 4:40	282 / 454 / 5:10	34 / 55 / 1:00	121 / 195 / 2:30	244 / 393 / 4:40	165 / 266 / 3:10	222 / 357 / 4:10	275 / 443 / 5:10	285 / 459 / 5:20	269 / 433 / 5:00	96 / 154 / 2:00	130 / 209 / 2:40	148 / 238 / 3:10	214 / 344 / 4:00	195 / 314 / 4:10	319 / 513 / 6:10	207 / 333 / 4:10

Supporting THINK!

Travel safe – Don't drive tired

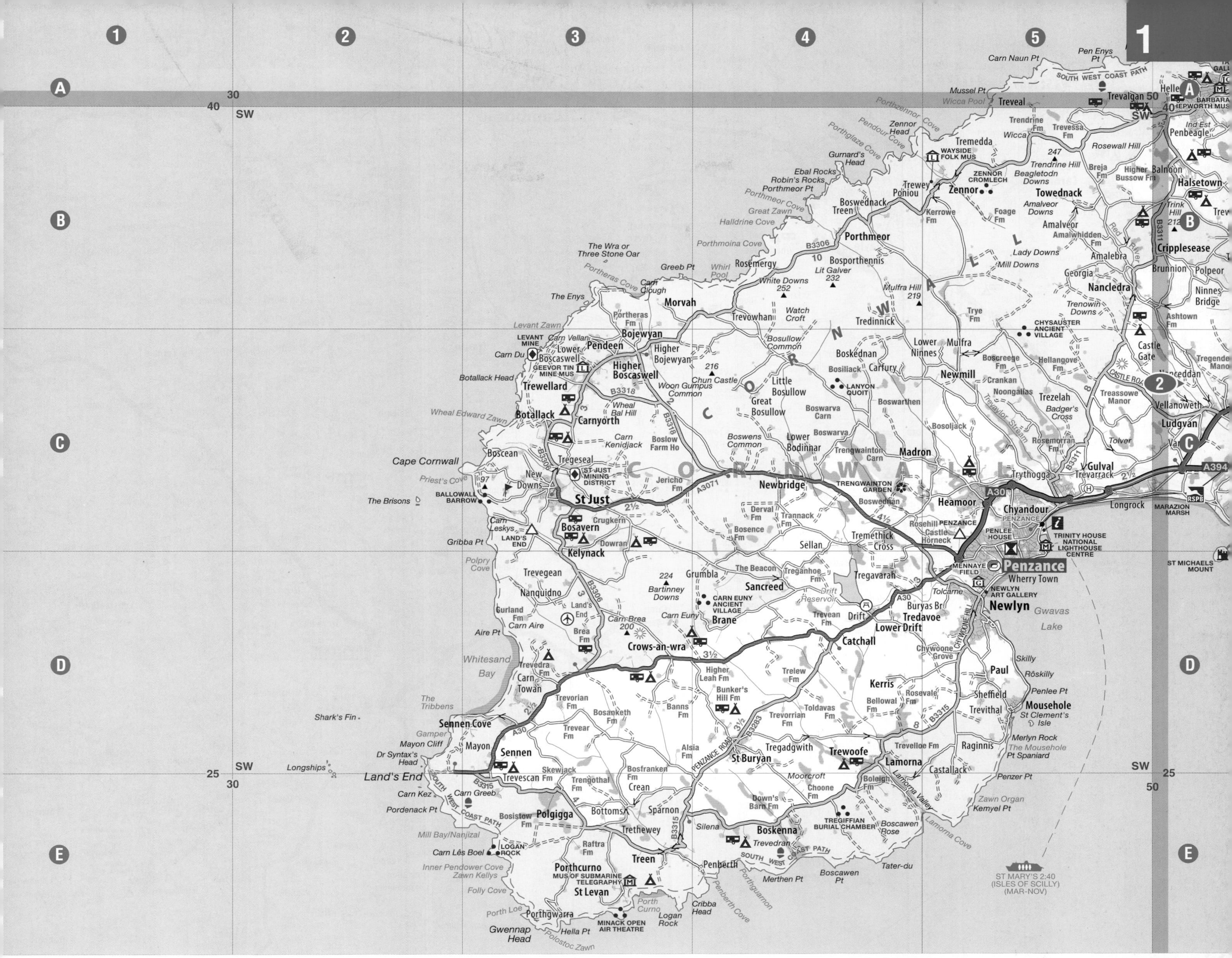

A
B
C
D
E
1
2
3
4
5
30
40
SW
25
50
Carn Naun Pt
Pen Enys Pt
SOUTH WEST COAST PATH
Mussel Pt
Wicca Pool
Treveal
Trevalgan
Porthzennor Cove
Pendour Cove
Zennor Head
Porthglaze Cove
Gurnard's Head
Tremedda
Wicca
Trendrine Fm
Trevessa Fm
Trendrine Hill
247
WAYSIDE FOLK MUS
ZENNOR CROMLECH
Zennor
Beagletodn Downs
Towednack
Rosewall Hill
Breja Fm
Higher Bussow Fm
Balnoon
Halsetown
Penbeagle
Ind Est
Ebal Rocks
Robin's Rocks
Porthmeor Pt
Porthmeor Cove
Great Zawn
Halldrine Cove
Trewey
Poniou
Bosewednack
Treen
Kerrowe Fm
Foage Fm
Amalveor Downs
Amalveor
Amalwhidden Fm
Trink Hill
Trevi
Porthmeor
B3306
Porthmoina Cove
Bosporthennis
10
Lady Downs
Mill Downs
Amalebra
Cripplesease
The Wra or Three Stone Oar
Greeb Pt
Whirl Pool
Rosemergy
White Downs
252
Lit Galver
232
Mulfra Hill
219
Georgia
Nancledra
Brunnion
Polpeor
Ninnes Bridge
Portheras Cove
Carn Clough
Morvah
The Enys
Portheras Fm
Trevowhan
Watch Croft
Tredinnick
Trye Fm
Trenowin Downs
Ashtown Fm
CHYSAUSTER ANCIENT VILLAGE
Levant Zawn
LEVANT MINE
Carn Vellan
Bojewyan
Lower Boscaswell
Pendeen
Higher Bojewyan
Bosullow Common
Lower Ninnes
Mulfra
Carn Du
GEEVOR TIN MINE MUS
Higher Boscaswell
216
Chun Castle
Boskednan
Bosiliack
Carfury
Boscreege Fm
Hellangove Fm
Castle Gate
Botallack Head
Trewellard
Woon Gumpus Common
Little Bosullow
LANYON QUOIT
Newmill
Crankan
CASTLE ROAD
Nanceddan
Tregender Manor
Wheal Edward Zawn
Botallack
B3318
Wheal Bal Hill
Great Bosullow
Noongallas
Trezelah
Badger's Cross
Treassowe Manor
Vellanoweth
Carnyorth
Boswarva Carn
Bosworthen
Ludgvan
Carn Kenidjack
Boslow Farm Ho
Boswens Common
Lower Bodinnar
Boswarva
Bosoljack
Trevaylor Stream
Rosemorran Fm
Tolver
Cape Cornwall
Boscean
Tregeseal
Trengwainton Carn
Madron
Gulval
Trevarrack
Priest's Cove
97
New Downs
ST JUST MINING DISTRICT
Jericho Fm
A3071
Trythogga
A394
BALLOWALL BARROW
The Brisons
St Just
Newbridge
TRENGWAINTON GARDEN
Boswedhan
A30
Heamoor
Chyandour
Longrock
MARAZION MARSH
RSPB
Carn Lesky
LAND'S END
Bosavern
Crugkern
Dorval Fm
Trannack Fm
Rosehill
Castle Horneck
PENZANCE HOUSE
PENLEE HOUSE
TRINITY HOUSE NATIONAL LIGHTHOUSE CENTRE
Gribba Pt
Kelynack
Dowran
Bosence Fm
Sellan
Tremethick Cross
ST MICHAEL'S MOUNT
Polpry Cove
224
The Beacon
Treganhoe Fm
Tregavarah
MENNAYE FIELD
Penzance
Wherry Town
Trevegean
Bartinney Downs
Grumbla
Sancreed
Drift Reservoir
Tolcarne
NEWLYN ART GALLERY
Nanquidno
Land's End
CARN EUNY ANCIENT VILLAGE
Burtyas Br
Newlyn
Gwavas Lake
Gurland Fm
Carn Aire
Carn Brea
200
Carn Euny
Brane
Trevean Fm
Drift
Tredavoe
Lower Drift
Aire Pt
Brea Fm
Crows-an-wra
Catchall
Chywoone Grove
Skilly
Whitesand Bay
Trevedra Fm
Carn Towan
Higher Leah Fm
Trelew Fm
Kerris
Paul
Rôskilly
The Tribbens
Trevorian Fm
Bosanketh Fm
Bunker's Hill Fm
Rosevale Fm
Sheffield
Penlee Pt
Mousehole
St Clement's Isle
Shark's Fin
Sennen Cove
Banns Fm
Trevorrian Fm
Toldavas Fm
Bellowal Fm
Trevithal
Gamper
Mayon Cliff
Dr Syntax's Head
Mayon
Trevear Fm
B3315
B3283
Merlyn Rock
Longships
Sennen
Alsia Fm
PENZANCE ROAD
St Buryan
Tregadgwith
Trewoofe
Trevelloe Fm
Raginnis
The Mousehole
Pt Spaniard
Land's End
Trevescan
Skewjack Fm
Trengothal Fm
Bosfranken Fm
Moorcroft
Lamorna
Castallack
Penzer Pt
Carn Kez
Carn Greeb
Crean
Choone Fm
Boleigh Fm
Lamorna Valley
Zawn Organ
Kemyel Pt
Pordenack Pt
Bosistow Fm
Polgigga
Bottoms
Sparnon
Down's Barn Fm
Mill Bay/Nanjizal
Trethewey
Silena
Boskenna
TREGIFFIAN BURIAL CHAMBER
Boscawen Rose
Lamorna Cove
Carn Lês Boel
LOGAN ROCK
Raftra Fm
Treen
Trevedran
Tater-du
Inner Pendower Cove
Zawn Kellys
Porthcurno
MUS OF SUBMARINE TELEGRAPHY
Penberth
Merthen Pt
Boscawen Pt
ST MARY'S 2:40 (ISLES OF SCILLY) (MAR-NOV)
Folly Cove
St Levan
Porth Curno
Logan Rock
Cribba Head
Penberth Cove
Porthguarnon
Porth Loe
Porthgwarra
MINACK OPEN AIR THEATRE
Gwennap Head
Hella Pt
Polostoc Zawn
CORNWALL

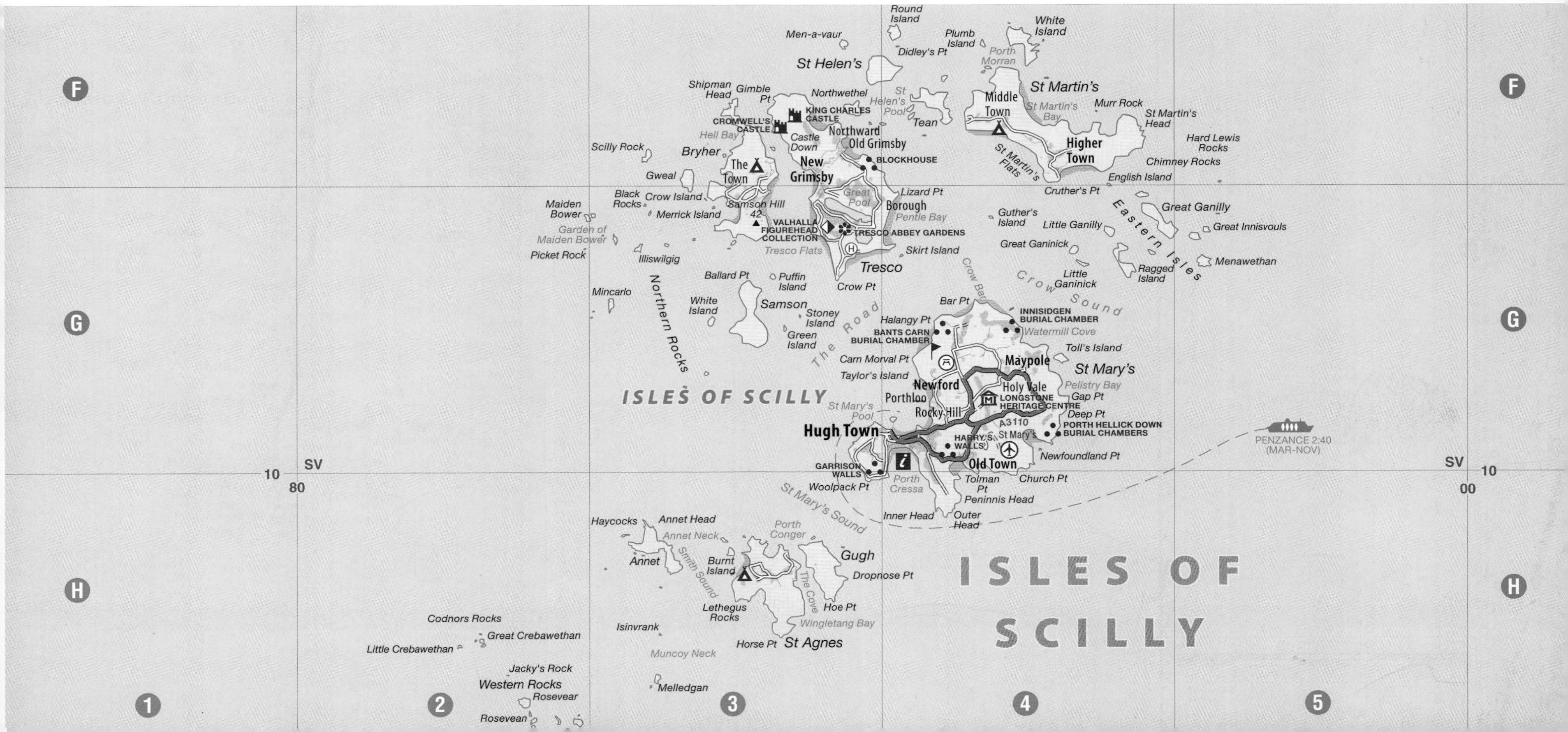

F
G
H
1
2
3
4
5
SV
10
80
00
Round Island
White Island
Men-a-vaur
Plumb Island
Didley's Pt
Porth Morran
St Helen's
St Martin's
Shipman Head
Gimble Pt
Northwethel
St Helen's Pool
Middle Town
St Martin's Bay
Murr Rock
St Martin's Head
KING CHARLES CASTLE
CROMWELL'S CASTLE
Tean
Hell Bay
Castle Down
Northward
Old Grimsby
Higher Town
Hard Lewis Rocks
Scilly Rock
Bryher
The Town
New Grimsby
BLOCKHOUSE
St Martin's Flats
Chimney Rocks
Gweal
English Island
Black Rocks
Crow Island
Great Pool
Lizard Pt
Cruther's Pt
Maiden Bower
Samson Hill
42
Borough
Great Ganilly
Merrick Island
Pentle Bay
Guther's Island
Little Ganilly
Great Innisvouls
Garden of Maiden Bower
VALHALLA FIGUREHEAD COLLECTION
TRESCO ABBEY GARDENS
Eastern Isles
Picket Rock
Great Ganinick
Illiswilgig
Tresco Flats
Skirt Island
Menawethan
Ballard Pt
Puffin Island
Tresco
Ragged Island
Mincarlo
Crow Bar
Little Ganinick
White Island
Crow Pt
Crow Sound
Northern Rocks
Samson
Bar Pt
INNISIDGEN BURIAL CHAMBER
Stoney Island
Halangy Pt
Green Island
BANTS CARN BURIAL CHAMBER
Watermill Cove
The Road
Toll's Island
Carn Morval Pt
Maypole
St Mary's
Taylor's Island
Holy Vale
Pelistry Bay
ISLES OF SCILLY
Newford
LONGSTONE HERITAGE CENTRE
Gap Pt
St Mary's Pool
Porthloo
Rocky Hill
Deep Pt
A3110
Hugh Town
HARRY'S WALLS
St Mary's
PORTH HELLICK DOWN BURIAL CHAMBERS
PENZANCE 2:40 (MAR-NOV)
GARRISON WALLS
Old Town
Newfoundland Pt
Woolpack Pt
Porth Cressa
Tolman Pt
Church Pt
Peninnis Head
St Mary's Sound
Inner Head
Outer Head
Haycocks
Annet Head
Porth Conger
Annet Neck
Gugh
Annet
Burnt Island
Smith Sound
Dropnose Pt
ISLES OF SCILLY
The Cove
Lethegus Rocks
Hoe Pt
Codnors Rocks
Wingletang Bay
Great Crebawethan
Isinvrank
Little Crebawethan
Horse Pt
St Agnes
Muncoy Neck
Jacky's Rock
Western Rocks
Melledgan
Rosevear
Rosevean

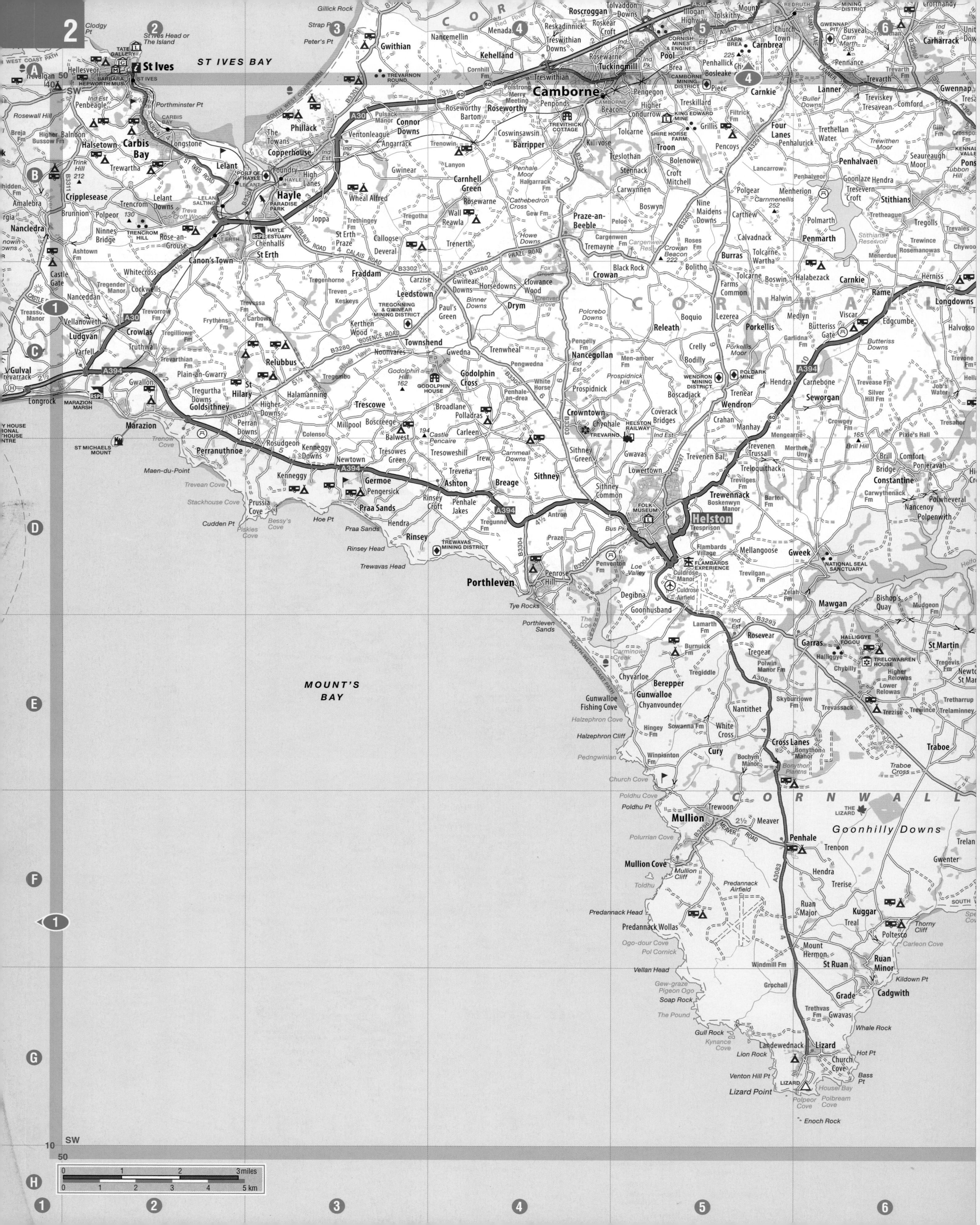
ST IVES BAY
MOUNT'S BAY
St Ives
Carbis Bay
Halsetown
Lelant
Hayle
Phillack
Copperhouse
Gwithian
Camborne
Tuckingmill
Pool
Carnbrea
Redruth
Roscroggan
Kehelland
Nancemellin
Connor Downs
Roseworthy
Barripper
Troon
Carharrack
Lanner
Four Lanes
Penhalvaen
Stithians
Praze-an-Beeble
Crowan
Leedstown
Fraddam
St Erth
Canon's Town
Nancledra
Cripplesease
Crowlas
Ludgvan
Gulval
Longrock
Marazion
St Michaels Mount
Perranuthnoe
Goldsithney
St Hilary
Relubbus
Townshend
Godolphin Cross
Trescowe
Germoe
Praa Sands
Ashton
Breage
Rinsey
Sithney
Porthleven
Nancegollan
Crowntown
Wendron
Porkellis
Releath
Carnkie
Rame
Helston
Gweek
Mawgan
Garras
St Martin
Constantine
Gunwalloe
Berepper
Cury
Cross Lanes
Mullion
Mullion Cove
Penhale
Goonhilly Downs
Predannack Wollas
Kuggar
Ruan Minor
Cadgwith
Grade
St Ruan
Landewednack
Lizard
Lizard Point
Church Cove
Traboe
A30
A394
A3083
B3280
B3302
B3303
B3304
B3297
B3293
B3296
C O R N W A L L
SW
10
50

Heads
Wheal Baddon
Fernsplatt
Coombe
Helston Water
Quenchwell
Playing Place
Old Kea
St Michael Penkevil
Ruan River
Caerhays
Hick's Mill
Greenwith Common
Chygwyne
Cowlands
Coombe
Higher Trelease
Veryan Green
Tretheake Manor
West Portholland
East Portholland
Treveor
Bosw
Cusgarne
Frogpool
Carnon Downs
Killiganoon
Penelewey
Treworga
Treburthes
Portholland
May's Rock
Porthluney Cove
Greeb Pt
Penare
Dodman Pt
Penveor Pt
Perranwell
Perranwell Station
Devoran
Goon Piper
Trevilla
Trelissick
TRELISSICK GARDEN
Borlase Wood
B3289
Philleigh
Ruan High Lanes
Trewartha
Hartriza Pt
Shag Rock
VERYAN BAY
High Pt
Lizard Pool
Perranarworthal
DEVORAN MINING DISTRICT
Chycoose
Penpol
Point
Feock
Treworthal
Treworlas
Crugsillick Manor
Lower Mill
Melinsey
Veryan
Tregamenna Manor Fm
Portloe
Manare Pt
Perran Wharf
Devichoys Wood
Carclew
Restronguet Creek
Restronguet Passage
Harcourt
Tregairewoon Fm
Carne
Pennare Fm
Gerrans Bay
Rosen Cliff
Commerrans Fm
Curgurrell
Pibyah Rock
Shannick Pt
Kiberick Cove
Lemoria Rock
Gull Rock
Nare Head
Angarrick
Trewithian
Burnthouse
Treluswell
Weir Pt
CARRICK ROADS
Messack Fm
Rosevine
Laity Moor
Roskrow
A39
Mylor Bridge
Mylor Creek
Messack Pt
Tretthewell
St Just Pool
St Just in Roseland
Gerrans
Portscatho
Trelever
Trelew
Penarrow Pt
Mylor Churchtown
A394
Carveth
Penryn
Bissom
St Gluvias
Ind Est
P&R
Mabe Burnthouse
Tregew
Flushing
Antron Fm
College Res
Trefusis Pt
St Mawes
Percuil
Greeb Pt
Argal Manor
ST MAWES CASTLE
Castle Pt
St Mawes Harbour
Porth Fm
Towan Beach
Mongleath
Falmouth
NAT MARITIME MUS CORNWALL
FALMOUTH DOCKS
Porthmellin Head
Argal Res
Budock Water
PENMERE
Bus Pk
PENDENNIS CASTLE
St Anthony
Bohortha
Killigerran Head
Porthbear Beach
Lamanva
Treverva
Trewen Fm
Boslowick
FALMOUTH TOWN
Gyllyngvase Beach
Swan Pool
Pendennis Pt
St Anthony Head
Place Barton
Zone Pt
Penjerrick
Penrose Fm
Pennance Pt
Carlidnack
Bareppa
Maenporth
High Cliff
Treworval Fm
Drift Fm
Boskensoe Fm
Mawnan Smith
FALMOUTH BAY
Bream Cove
Porth Navas
GLENDURGAN GARDENS
Trerose
Mawnan
Rosemullion Head
Helford Passage
TREBAH GDNS
Durgan
SOUTH WEST COAST PATH
Toll Pt
Treath
St Anthony-in-Meneage
Helford
Gillan Harbour
Flushing
Manaccan
Nare Pt
Polnare Cove
Gillan
Carne
Nare Head
Nare Cove
Roskorwell
Beacon 112
Porthallow
Porthkerris Pt
Tregidden
Tregarne
Polpidnick Fm
Porthoustock
Trelease Mill
Trelease
Laddenvean
Rosenithon
Ind Est
St Keverne
Godrevy Cove
Carn-du Rocks
Grugwith
Roskilly's Open Fm
Roskilly
Crousa Common
B3294
Zoar
Lowland Pt
North Corner
Polcoverack Fm
Penhallick
Coverack
COVERACK
Ponsongath
Perprean Cove
Treleaver Cliff
Ebber Rocks
Black Head
A
B
C
D
E
F
G
H
SW 40
00
SW 10
00
7
8
9
10
11

2
3
4
5
6
A
B
C
D
E
F
G
H
60
70
SW
10
Trescore Islands
Porth Mear
High Cove
Park Head
Diggory's Island
Queen Bess Rock
BEDRUTHEN STEPS
Pendarves Island
Carnewas Island
Trerathick Pt
High Cove
Trenance Pt
Berryl's Pt
Beacon Cove
Griffin's Pt
Stem Pt
Watergate Bay
Watergate or Tregurrian Beach
Horse Rock
Zacry's Islands
Flory Island
Trevelgue Head
Whipsiderry
Porth
Towan Head
Gazzle
Newquay Bay
Newquay
BLUE REEF AQUARIUM
Fistral Beach
Fistral Bay
St Columb Minor
Pentire Point East
NEWQUAY ZOO
Trenance
Gusti Veor
Trencreek
Chapel
Pentire Point West
Porth Joke
Crantock Beach
Pentire
Kelsey Head
Treninnick
Lane
Holywell Bay
West Pentire
Crantock
The Gannel
Trevemper
Trevithick Manor
Trevilley Court Fm
Trethiggy Fm
Holywell Beach
The Kelseys
Cubert Common
Trevowah
Gwills
River Gannel
Kestle Mill
Carter's or Gull Rocks
HOLYWELL BAY FUN PARK
Penhale Pt
Holywell
Carines
Tresean
Carevick
Trevail
Trerew Fm
Trewerry Mill
TRERICE
Hoblyn's Cove
Ellenglaze
Trenissick
Ligger Pt
Cubert
Trescowthick
Trewolla
Trevoll
Treoffal
BENNY HALT
Benny Mill
Ligger or Perran Bay
Neeham
LAPPA VALLEY STEAM RAILWAY
Perran Beach
ST PIRAN'S CHURCH (REMS)
Mount
Treworthen Fm
Rejerrah
Cargoll Ho
St Newlyn East
PERRAN CROSS
Stampas Fm
EAST WHEAL ROSE
Cotty's Pt
Hendra Fm
Hendra Croft
Treludderow Manor
Penhallow Moor
Trevilson
NEWLYN DOWNS HALT
Rose
PERRAN ROUND
Scotland Fm
Fiddlers Green
Droskyn Pt
Reen Sands
Reen Manor
Lower Rose
Shepherds Fm
PERRANPORTH
Perranporth
Rosehill
Carnebo Fm
Newlyn Downs
Cligga Head
Goonhavern
Ind Est
Bawden Rocks or Man & His Man
Hanover Cove
Bolingey
Reen Cross
Sixty Acres Fm
Perranporth
Perrancoombe
Cocks
Penwartha Coombe
Carnkief
Ennis Fm
Green Island
Trevellas Porth
Anchor
Perranwell
Killigrew Fm
Cross Coombe
Perranzabuloe
Wheal Frances
Zelah Hill
Newdowns Head
Crams
Penwartha Lambourne
Deer Park Wood
SOUTH WEST COAST PATH
Trevellas
Blowinghouse
Zelah
Trefronick Fm
St Agnes Head
Carn Gowla
New Downs
Wheal Kitty
Ventongimps
Chyverton Ho
Tolgroggan Fm
CORNWALL
Higher Bal
St Agnes
Barkla Shop
Peterville
Penhallow
Boswellick
Truthan
Tubby's Head
Mithian
CORNISH CYDER FARM
St Allen
Trispen
ST AGNES BEACON
Goonown
Gollawater
Callestick
Marazanvose
Chapel Porth
Goonvrea
ST AGNES MINING DISTRICT
Goonbell
Mithian Downs
Higher Callestick Fm
Tresawsen
Nanteague Fm
Pennare
Treworgan
PENWINNICK ROAD
Penwartha Ho
Coldharbour
Allet
Porth Towan
Towan Cross
Mingoose
Pendale
St Clement Woods
Banns
Silverwell
Mount Hawke
Gover Fm
Roscarnick Fm
Shortlanesend
Porthtowan
Tregavethan Manor
Roseworthy
Higher Carvinack
Calerick
Idless
Gullyn Rock
Penhallow Fm
Polwhele
Sheep Rock
Factory Fm
Manor Parsley
Two Burrows
Truro
Trevaskis
Little Croft West
Treheveras
Killagorden
Treworder
Blackwater
Three Burrows
Menagissey
Skinner's Bottom
Featherbeds
Buckshead
Tregurra
PORTREATH HARBOUR
Laity Moor
Boscolla
Nancemere
Croft West
Penstraze
Mawla
Kenwyn
Gull Rock
Horse Rock
Forge
Portreath
Cambrose
Stencoose
Carnhot
Jolly's Bottom
Green Bottom
P&R
New Mill
ROYAL CORNWALL MUSEUM
Samphire Island
Basset's Cove
Boscawen Fm
Treliske
Parc Erissey
Wheal Rose
Wheal Busy
Saveock
Gloweth
Threemilestone
Nance
Bridge
TOLGUS MILL
Radnor
WHEAL PEEVOR MINE
Chacewater
GWENNAP MINING DISTRICT
Tomperrow
Kerley Downs
Newbridge
Highertown
Truro
Illogan
Sparnon Gate
Gilbert's Coombe
Scorrier
Salem
Fishing Cove
Navax Pt
North Cliffs
TEHIDY
Killifreth Fm
Creegbrawse
Cusveorth Coombe
Carrine Common
Penweathers
St Clement
Hell's Mouth
Deadman's Cove
Old Merrose Fm
Paynter's Lane End
West Tolgus
North Country
Highway
Treskerby
Cox Hill
Todpool
Hugus
Baldhu
Goodern Manor Fm
Malpas
Oak Wood
Redruth
Treleigh
Mount Ambrose
Vogue
St Day
Goon Gumpas
Kea
Calenick
Coombe
Park Bottom
Plain-an-Gwarry
Hale Mills
Twelve Heads
Porth Kea
Roscroggan
Tolvaddon Downs
Tolgus Mount
REDRUTH MINING DISTRICT
Crofthandy
Sparnock Fm
Wheal Baddon
Carlyon Fm
Old Kea
Red River
Menadarva
Reskadinnick
Roskear Croft
Illogan Highway
Tolskithy
Gwithian
Nancemellin
Treswithian Downs
CORNISH MINES & ENGINES
Church Town
Carnbrea
SANDY LANE
GWENNAP PIT
Busveal
Carn Marth
Trevethan
United Downs
Fernsplatt
Coombe
Bissoe
Quenchwell
Playing Place
Kehelland
Rosewarne
Tuckingmill
Pool
CARN BREA
Ind Est
Carharrack
Helston Water
Chygwyne
Coombe
Higher Trelease Fm
Cornhill Fm
Brea
Penhallick
Bosleake
Church Coombe
Pennance
Sunny Corner
Hick's Mill
Carnon Downs
Cowlands
TREVARNON ROUND
Treswithian
CAMBORNE MINING DISTRICT
Trevarth
Cusgarne
Greenwith Common
Killiganoon
Penelewey
Polstrong
Merry Meeting
Camborne
Piece
Carnkie
Lanner
Gwennap
Frogpool
Tregye
Come-to-Good
Treskillard
Buller Downs
Treviskey
Tresamble
PERRANWELL
Perranwell Station
Trelissick
Pulsack Manor
Manor Downs
High Condurrow
KING EDWARD MINE
Filtrick Fm
Tresavean
Comford
Perranwell
Devoran
Goon Piper
TRELISSICK GARDEN
Angarrack
Trenowin
SHIRE HORSE FARM
Grillis
Four Lanes
Trethellan Water
Gilly Fm
Perranarworthal
Penpol
Trevilla
Killivose
Troon
Pencoys
Penhalurick
Crosspost Fm
KENNALL VALE
DEVORAN MINING DISTRICT
Chycoose
Point
Feock
Treslothan
Bolenowe
Penhalvaen
Seaureaugh
Perran Wharf
Carclew
Restronguet Creek
0 1 2 3 miles
0 1 2 3 4 5 km

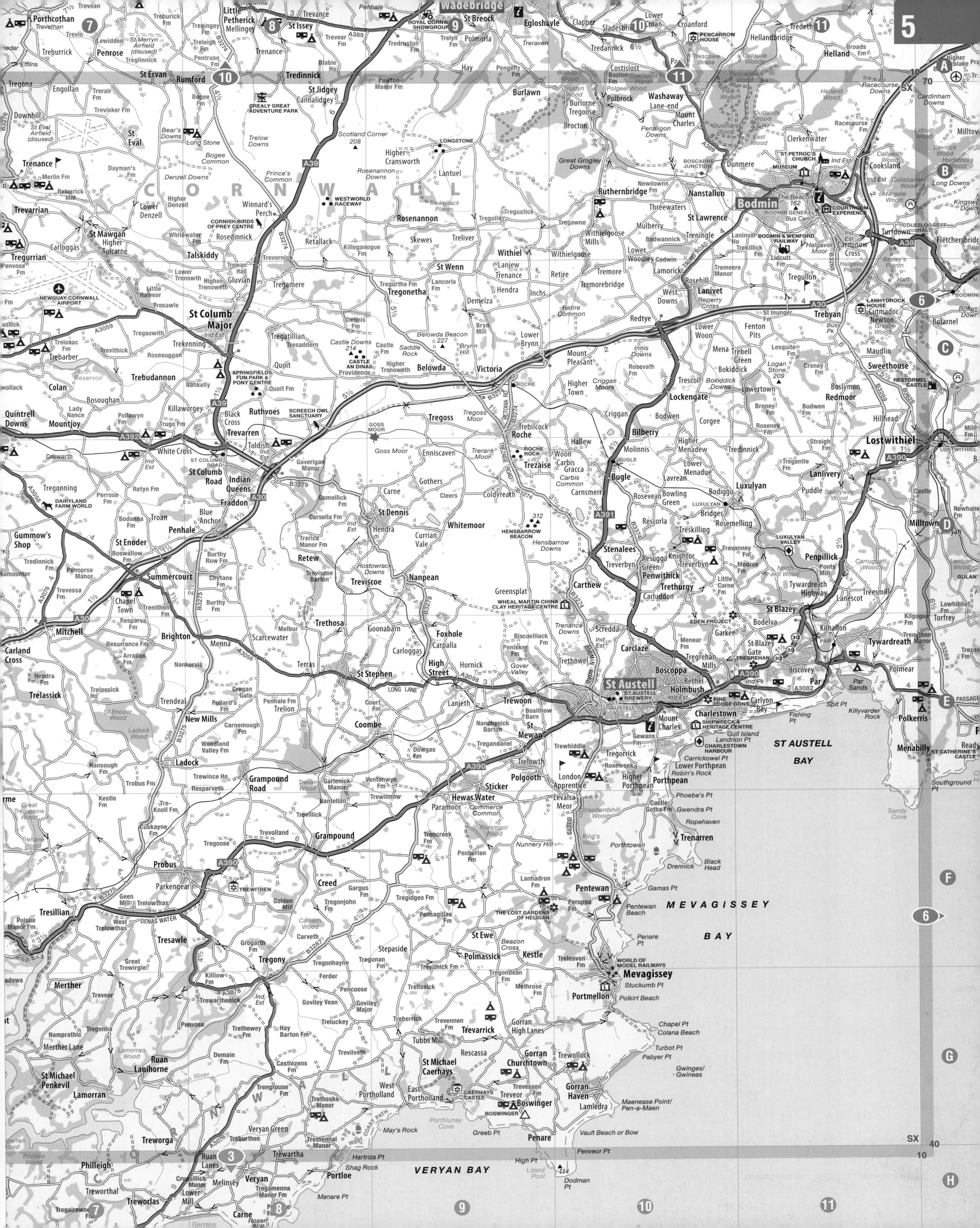
Wadebridge
Porthcothan
Trevethan
Little Petherick
Mellingey
St Issey
Trevance
Penhale
ROYAL CORNWALL SHOWGROUND
St Breock
Polmorla
Egloshayle
Clapper
Sladesbridge
Lower Croan
Croanford
PENCARROW HOUSE
Tredethy
Hellandbridge
Helland
Trevio
Lewidden
St Merryn Airfield (disused)
Penrose
Treburrick
Treglinnick
Trenance
Tredannick
Costislost
Hay
Pengelly Fm
St Ervan
Rumford
Tredinnick
St Jidgey
Cannalidgey
Pawton Manor Fm
Burlawn
Polbrock
Washaway
Lane-end
Mount Charles
Tregona
Engollan
Bogee Fm
CREALY GREAT ADVENTURE PARK
Downhill
St Eval Airfield (disused)
St Eval
Bear's Downs
Long Stone
Bogee Common
Trelow Downs
Scotland Corner 208
LONGSTONE
Higher Cransworth
Lantuel
Burlorne Tregoose
Brocton
Penaligon Downs
Clerkenwater
Cardinham Downs
Trenance
Merlin Fm
Dayman's Fm
Denzell Downs
Prince's Common
Rosenannon Downs
Great Grogley Downs
BOSCARNE JUNCTION
Dunmere
ST PETROC'S CHURCH
MUSEUM
Cooksland
CORNWALL
Winnard's Perch
WESTWORLD RACEWAY
Rutherbridge
Nanstallon
Bodmin
The Beacon 162
BODMIN GENERAL Bus Cen
COURTROOM EXPERIENCE
Long Downs
Trevarrian
Lower Denzell
Higher Denzell
CORNISH BIRDS OF PREY CENTRE
Rosedinnick
Rosenannon
Tregolls
Tregustick
Tregawne
Threewaters
St Lawrence
Turfdown
Fletchersbridge
St Mawgan
Higher Tolcarne
Carloggas
Talskiddy
Whitewater Fm
Retallack
Killeganogue Fm
Skewes
Treliver
Withielgoose Mills
Mulberry
Bodwannick
Treningle
BODMIN & WENFORD RAILWAY
Halgavor Moor
Carminow Cross
Tregurrian
Trevornick
St Wenn
Withiel
Withielgoose
Lower Woodley
Cadwin
Lamorick
Tremeere Manor
Tregullon
Trewan Hall
Lower Trenowth
Higher Trenowth
Gluvian
Tregamere
Tregurtha Fm
Tregonetha
Lancorla Fm
Lanjew
Trenance
Hendra
Retire
Tremore
Tremorebridge
Rosehill
Lanivet
Reperry Cross
NEWQUAY CORNWALL AIRPORT
Little Halveor
Tresawle
St Columb Major
Ind Est
Demelza
Inchs
Retire Common
West Downs
Redtye
St Ingunger
Trebyan
LANHYDROCK HOUSE
Cutmadoc
Newton
Treisaac Fm
Trebarber
Tregaswith
Trekenning
Tregatillian
Tresaddern
Dennis Fm
Castle Downs 214
CASTLE AN DINAS
Providence
Castle Fm
Saddle Rock
Higher Trenoweth
Belowda Beacon 227
Brynn Hill
Bryn Mill
Lower Brynn
Innis Downs
Lower Woon
Fenton Pits
Maudlin
Sweethouse
RESTORMEL CASTLE
Trevithick
Rosesugan
Quoit
Belowda
Victoria
Mount Pleasant
Mena
Trebell Green
Bokiddick
Lesquite Fm
Logan Stone 209
Creney Fm
Colan
Trebudannon
SPRINGFIELDS FUN PARK & PONY CENTRE
Nankelly
Quoit Fm
ROCHE
Higher Town
Criggan Moors
Rosevath Fm
Trescoll
Lockengate
Bokiddick Downs
Lowertown
Boslymon
Redmoor
Quintrell Downs
Mountjoy
Bosoughan
Lady Nance
Pollawyn Fm
Killaworgey
Trugo Fm
Black Cross
Ruthvoes
SCREECH OWL SANCTUARY
Tregoss
Tregoss Moor
Trebilcock
Roche
Criggan
Bodwen
Corgee
Bilberry
Breney
Roseney Fm
Hillhead
Lostwithiel
White Cross
Trevarren
Toldish
ST COLUMB ROAD
GOSS MOOR
Goss Moor
Enniscaven
Trerank Moor
ROCHE ROCK
Trezaise
Woon
Carbis
Gracca
Carbis Common
Hallew
Molinnis
Higher Menadew
Lower Menadue
Tredinnick
Streigh Fm
Tregantle Fm
Lanlivery
Coswarth
St Columb Road
Indian Queens
Gaverigan Manor
BUGLE
Bugle
Lavrean
Luxulyan
Tregonning
Retyn Fm
Carne
Gothers
Cleers
Coldvreath
Carnsmerry
Rosevean
Bowling Green
Bodiggo
Puddle
Sandyway Wood
DAIRYLAND FARM WORLD
Perrose Fm
Fraddon
Domellick Fm
Carsella Fm
St Dennis
Hendra
Whitemoor
312
HENSBARROW BEACON
Hensbarrow Downs
Rescorla
LUXULYAN
Bridges
Rosemelling
Gummow's Shop
Bodanna Fm
Troan
Blue Anchor
Penhale
St Enoder
Trerice Manor Fm
Retew
Currian Vale
Stenalees
Treskilling
Treverbyn
Resugga Green
Knightor
Treverbyn
Trevanney Fm
Medros Fm
LUXULYAN VALLEY
Penpillick
Ponts Mill
Milltown
Tredinnick Fm
Pencorse Manor
Boswallow Fm
Burthy Row Fm
Chytane Fm
Summercourt
Treviscoe Barton
Rostowrack Downs
Treviscoe
Nanpean
Penwithick
Trethurgy
Little Carne Fm
North Hill Wood
Tywardreath Highway
Carruggatt Wood
Lanescot
Treesmill
Trevessa Fm
Chapel Town
Trenithon Fm
Burthy Fm
Greensplat
WHEAL MARTIN CHINA CLAY HERITAGE CENTRE
Carthew
Carluddon
St Blazey
Bodelva
EDEN PROJECT
Garker
Kilhallon
Mitchell
Resparva Fm
Brighton
Trethosa
Melbur
Goonabarn
Foxhole
Carpalla
Biscovillack Fm
Trenance Downs
Scredda
Menear Fm
St Blazey Gate
TREGREHAN
PAR
Tywardreath
Carland Cross
Resurrance Fm
Menna
Scarcewater
Carloggas
Penisker Fm
Trethowel
Carclaze
Boscoppa
Tregrehan Mills
Biscovey
Polmear
Trenython Manor
Arrallas Fm
Nankervis
Terras
St Stephen
High Street
Hornick
Gover Valley
Bethel
Holmbush
Ind Est
St Austell
ST AUSTELL BREWERY
Par
Par Sands
Hendra Fm
Trelassick Fm
Trelassick
LONG LANE
Lanjeth
Trewoon
Bosithow Barn
PINE LODGE GDNS
Carlyon Bay
Spit Pt
Killyvarder Rock
Polkerris
Fishing Pt
St Enoder Wood
Trendeal
Grogan Gate
Pollard's Fm
Penhale Fm
Trelion
Court Fm
Coombe
Naphysick Barton
Tregandanel
St Mewan
Mount Charles
Gewans Fm
Charlestown
SHIPWRECK & HERITAGE CENTRE
Gull Island
Landrion Pt
CHARLESTOWN HARBOUR
ST AUSTELL BAY
Menabilly
ST CATHERINE'S CASTLE
Ladock Wood
New Mills
Carnemough Fm
Woodland Valley Fm
Dowgas Fm
Trewhiddle Fm
Tregorrick
Roseweek
Carrickowel Pt
Lower Porthpean
Robin's Rock
Nansough Fm
Ladock
Trewince Ho
Resparveth
Trobus Fm
Grampound Road
Trevan Wood
Garlenick Manor
Ventonwyn Fm
Trewinnow
Trelowth
Polgooth
London Apprentice
Higher Porthpean
Porthpean
Southground Pt
Great Tregassow Wood
Kestle Fm
Tre-Knoll Fm
Nantellan
Trevillick
Hewas Water
Sticker
Paramoor
Commerce Common
Levalsa Meor
Shepherdshill Wood
Castle Gotha Fm
Phoebe's Pt
Gwendra Pt
Ropehaven
Sandy Cove
Trehane Wood
Cuskayne Fm
Tregoose
Trevolland
Grampound
Trencreek Fm
Paramoor Wood
Penberlan Fm
Nunnery Hill
King's Wood
Porthtowan
Trenarren
Black Head
Drennick
Probus
TREWITHEN
Parkengear
Creed
Gargus Fm
Tregonjohn Fm
Golden Mill
Tregidgeo Fm
Lanhadron Fm
Pentewan
Peruppa Fm
Gamas Pt
Pentewan Beach
MEVAGISSEY BAY
Tresillian
Polsue Manor Fm
Green Mill
Trelowthas
West Trelowthas
DENAS WATER
Carveth Wood
Carveth
Pensagillas Fm
THE LOST GARDENS OF HELIGAN
Tresawle
Grogarth Fm
Great Trewirgie
Tregony
Stepaside
Tregonan Fm
St Ewe
Beacon Cross
Polmassick
Kestle
Treleaven Fm
Penare Pt
WORLD OF MODEL RAILWAYS
Mevagissey
Stuckumb Pt
Portmellon
Polkirt Beach
Merther
Killiow Fm
Trewarthenick
Tregonhayne
Ferder
Trevithick Fm
Tregondean Fm
Trelissick
Pencoose
Methrose Fm
Treveor
Goviley Vean
Goviley Major
Treluckey
Treberrick
Trevennen Fm
Trevarrick
Gorran High Lanes
Chapel Pt
Colana Beach
Nanprathic
Tregenna
Penvose
Trethewey Fm
Hay Barton Fm
Merther Lane
Lamorran Wood
Tubbs Mill
Rescassa
Gorran Churchtown
Trewollock
Turbot Pt
Pabyer Pt
Ruan Lanihorne
Ruan River
Demain Fm
Castlezens Fm
Treviveth
St Michael Caerhays
Gwinges/ Gwineas
St Michael Penkevil
Lamorran
Trengrouse Fm
West Portholland
East Portholland
CAERHAYS CASTLE
Treveor
Trevesson
Gorran Haven
Lamledra
Maenease Point/ Pen-a-Maen
Tretheake Manor
BOSWINGER
Boswinger
Veryan Green
Porthluney Cove
May's Rock
Vault Beach or Bow
Treworga
Tretheake
Trewartha
Greeb Pt
Penare
Trethennal Manor
SOUTH WEST COAST PATH
Penveor Pt
Philleigh
Ruan Lanes
Hartriza Pt
High Pt
Shag Rock
Lizard Pool
114
Dodman Pt
VERYAN BAY
Crugsillick Manor
Veryan
Portloe
Treworthal
Melinsey
Lower Mill
Tregamenna Manor Fm
Manare Pt
Tregairewoon
Treworlas
Carne
Rosen
A30
A39
A389
A38
A390
A391
A392
A3058
A3059
A3076
A3078
A3082
B3274
B3275
B3276
B3279
B3268
B3269
B3287
B3273
B3271
VICTORIA RD
TRURO ROAD
BODMIN ROAD
TREZAISE ROAD
SX
70
40
10
A
B
C
D
E
F
G
H
7
8
9
10
11
6

6
Cardinham Moor
Colliford Lake
Bunning's Park
Lord's Park Fm
Westerlake Fm
Sparretts Fm
THE HURLERS STONE CIRCLES
Minions
CARADON MINING DISTRICT
Caradon Hill 369
Gonamena
Upton Cross
Dunslea
Caradon Town
Downgate
Browda
Trewoodle
Golberdon
Tokenbury Manor
Millpool
Maidenwell
St Bellarmin's Tor
Letter Moor
Redhill Downs
Draynes Common
Siblyback Lake
Trekeivesteps
Commonmoor
Darite
Pensilva
Trevigro
Racecourse Downs
Cardinham Downs
Cardinham
Warleggan
Pantersbridge
Mutton's Downs
Wortha
Northwood
Carpuan
Draynes
GOLITHA FALLS
KING DONIERT'S INSCRIBED STONE
Treworrick
St Cleer
TRETHEVY QUOIT
Tremar
Crow's Nest
Tremarcoombe
Middlehill
Charaton Cross
Woolston
Frogwell
Trenant
Tremaddock
St Neot
Goonzion Downs
CARNGLAZE SLATE CAVERNS
Treverbyn
Old Cardinham Castle
Mount
Welltown
Trenay
Tredinnick
Ley
Ashford Br
Twelvewoods
Doublebois
Lampretten Ho
Treleathick
Trethinnick
East Tuelmenna
Old Park
Wayland
Gang
St Ive
Merryhue
Parkfield
St Ive Cross
Cookland
Long Downs
Kingswood Downs
Pinsla Park
Tawna Downs
Holtroad Downs
Turtdown
Fletchersbridge
Drawbridge
Dobwalls
Moorswater
Loe Mills
Liskeard
Trembraze
Addington
Pengover Green
Hendrabridge
Merrymeet
Quethiock
Hammett
BODMIN PARKWAY
LANHYDROCK HOUSE
Cutmadoc
Newton
Bofarnel
West Taphouse
Middle Taphouse
East Taphouse
Gelly Fm
St Pinnock
Trevelmond
Treburgie
Boduel
Camellion
LISKEARD
COOMBE
Lodge Hill
Roseland
Trewint
Trehunist
Menheniot
Doddycross
Blunt
Sweethouse
RESTORMEL CASTLE
Trewindle
Braddock
Connon
Penfrane Manor
Trussel Br
West Trevillies
Lower Clicker
MENHENIOT
Coldrenick
Trehurst
Tilland
Tideford Cross
Hillhead
Sandylake
Roselyon
Brooks
Woodlay Fm
Herodsfoot
St Keyne
MUSIC MACHINES
Horningtops
Great Trethew
Cutmere
Tideford
Lostwithiel
LOSTWITHIEL
Bridgend
Beacon Hill
Coombe Fm
Trebarret
Polmartin Fm
Bury Down
Black Down
Trewidland
Bylane End
Fursdon
Pensipple
Catchfrench Manor
Bethany
Budge's Shop
Couch's Mill
Netherton
Botallick
Abovetown
Landare Fm
Churchbridge
Polvean Cross
Duloe
Westnorth
Tregarlandbridge
Tregarland
Widegates
Shortacross
Trerulefoot
Hessenford
Milltown
Lantyan
St Winnow
Lerryn
Winnick
Bocaddon
LANREATH FOLK & FARM MUSEUM
Lanreath
Trefanny Hill
Tregarrick Mill
Tredinnick
Highercliff
SANDPLACE
Sandplace
Morval
Bin Down
Trelowia
Polbathic
GOLANT
Penquite
Golant
Tywardreath
Torfrey
St Veep
Trevollard
Muchlarnick
Snowden's Bridge
Milcombe
No Man's Land
Great Tree
St Martin
MONKEY SANCTUARY
Narkurs
Seaton
Downderry
Polmear
Penpoll
Lanteglos Highway
Trenewan
Pelynt
Barcelona
Trelawne Manor
Watergate
LOOE
Shutta
East Looe
Plaidy
Millendreath
Bodigga Cliff
Colmer Rocks
Polkerris
Mixtow
Bodinnick
Whitecross
Pont
West Watergate
West Looe
Hannafore
Looe
LOOE MUSEUM
Looe Bay
Tencreek
Portlooe
Porthallow
Talland
Talland Bay
Fowey
Readymoney
Menabilly
ST CATHERINE'S CASTLE
Polruan
Churchtown
Lansallos
Crumplehorn
Carey Park
Brent
HERITAGE MUSEUM
Polperro
Chapel Cliff
Hard Hd 132
Shag Rock
Lantivet Bay
West Coombe
Pencarrow Head
Lantic Bay
Blackbottle Rock
Washing Rocks
Coombe Hawne
Southground Pt
Sandy Cove
Portnadler Bay
St George's or Looe Island
WHITSAND
SOUTH WEST COAST PATH
C O R N W A L L
A38
A390
A387
A374
B3359
B3360
B3254
B3252
B3251
B3253
B3247
B3269
B3415
PASSAGE LANE
POLPERRO ROAD
SX
70
40
10
11
12
A
B
C
D
E
F
G
H
1
2
3
4
5
6
0 1 2 3 miles
0 1 2 3 4 5 km

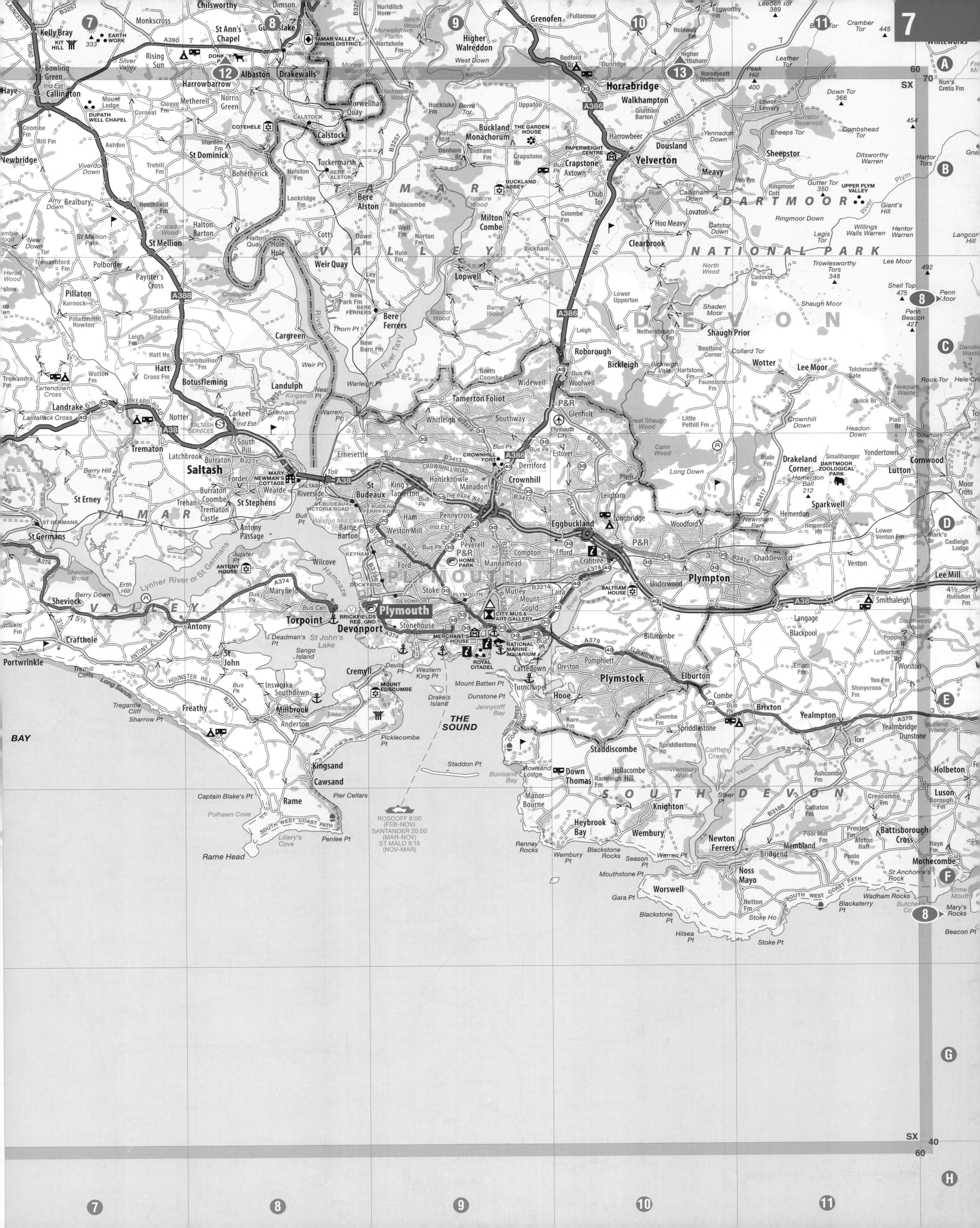
Kelly Bray
Chilsworthy
Monkscross
St Ann's Chapel
Gunnislake
Dimson
TAMAR VALLEY MINING DISTRICT
Hurdlitch Horn
Higher Walreddon
West Down
Grenofen
Fullamoor
Eggworthy Fm
Leeden Tor 389
Cramber Tor
445
Whiteworks
Bowling Green
Callington
Haye
Rising Sun
Albaston
Drakewalls
Harrowbarrow
Metherell
Norris Green
Morwellham Quay
Horrabridge
Walkhampton
Peek Hill 400
Down Tor 366
Nun's Cross Fm
DUPATH WELL CHAPEL
COTEHELE
Calstock
Buckland Monachorum
THE GARDEN HOUSE
Yelverton
Dousland
Sheeps Tor
Combshead Tor
Newbridge
St Dominick
Tuckermarsh
Bere Alston
BUCKLAND ABBEY
Crapstone
PAPERWEIGHT CENTRE
Sheepstor
Meavy
Ditsworthy Warren
Hartor Tors
T A M A R
V A L L E Y
Bealbury
Heathfield Fm
Halton Barton
Milton Combe
Chub Tor
Hoo Meavy
Gutter Tor 350
UPPER PLYM VALLEY
D A R T M O O R
Ringmoor Down
Giant's Hill
St Mellion
St Mellion Park
Cotts
Weir Quay
Hole's Hole
Clearbrook
N A T I O N A L   P A R K
Polborder
Paynter's Cross
Pillaton
Lopwell
Trowlesworthy Tors 348
Shell Top 475
Penn Beacon 427
Penn Moor
Langcombe Hill
Bere Ferrers
River Tamar
River Tavy
Cargreen
Leigh
Roborough
Bickleigh
Shaugh Prior
D E V O N
Shaugh Moor
Wotter
Lee Moor
Hatt
Botusfleming
Landulph
Widewell
Woolwell
Tamerton Foliot
Landrake
Notter
Carkeel
SALTASH SERVICES
Whitleigh
Southway
Glenholt
Plymouth City
Trematon
South Pill
Saltash
Burraton
Latchbrook
MARY NEWMAN'S COTTAGE
Forder
Ernesettle
CROWNHILL FORT
Derriford
Estover
Crownhill
Bude Fm
Drakeland Corner
DARTMOOR ZOOLOGICAL PARK
Hemerdon Ball 212
Sparkwell
Lutton
Cornwood
St Erney
St Stephens
Trehan
Wearde
Riverside
St Budeaux
King's Tamerton
Honicknowle
Manadon
Leigham
Longbridge
Eggbuckland
Woodford
Hemerdon
Newnham Park
Moor Cross
St Germans
Antony Passage
Barne Barton
Ham
Weston Mill
Pennycross
Peverell
Compton
Efford
Crabtree
Chaddlewood
Venton
Lee Mill
ANTONY HOUSE
Wilcove
KEYHAM
Ford
PLYMOUTH
Mannamead
Mutley
Mount Gould
Laira
SALTRAM HOUSE
Underwood
Plympton
Smithaleigh
Sheviock
Lynher River or St Germans
Maryfield
Torpoint
Devonport
Stoke
Plymouth
Stonehouse
CITY MUS & ART GALLERY
Langage
Blackpool
Crafthole
Antony
Deadman's Pt
St John's Lake
St John
MERCHANT'S HOUSE
NATIONAL MARINE AQUARIUM
ROYAL CITADEL
Billacombe
Oreston
Pomphlett
Cattedown
Plymstock
Elburton
Portwrinkle
Cremyll
Devils Pt
Western King Pt
MOUNT EDGCUMBE
Mount Batten Pt
Turnchapel
Hooe
Dunstone Pt
Combe
Brixton
Yealmpton
Yealmbridge
Dunstone
Worston
Freathy
Insworke
Southdown
Millbrook
Anderton
Drake's Island
THE SOUND
Jennycliff Bay
Staddiscombe
Spriddlestone
Torr
BAY
Tregantle Cliff
Sharrow Pt
Picklecombe Pt
Kingsand
Cawsand
Staddon Pt
Bovisand Lodge
Down Thomas
Hollacombe
Raneleigh Hill
Holbeton
Luson
Captain Blake's Pt
Rame
Pier Cellars
Manor Bourne
S O U T H   D E V O N
Knighton
Polhawn Cove
ROSCOFF 6:00 (FEB-NOV)
SANTANDER 20:00 (MAR-NOV)
ST MALO 9:15 (NOV-MAR)
Heybrook Bay
Wembury
Newton Ferrers
Membland
Battisborough Cross
Lillery's Cove
Penlee Pt
Rame Head
Renney Rocks
Wembury Pt
Blackstone Rocks
Warren Pt
Bridgend
Mothecombe
Mouthstone Pt
Noss Mayo
St Anchorite's Rock
Worswell
Gara Pt
Netton Fm
Wadham Rocks
Blackaterry Pt
Mary's Rocks
Blackstone Pt
Stoke Ho
Hilsea Pt
Stoke Pt
Beacon Pt
SOUTH WEST COAST PATH
A
B
C
D
E
F
G
H
7
8
9
10
11
12
13
SX
60
70
40

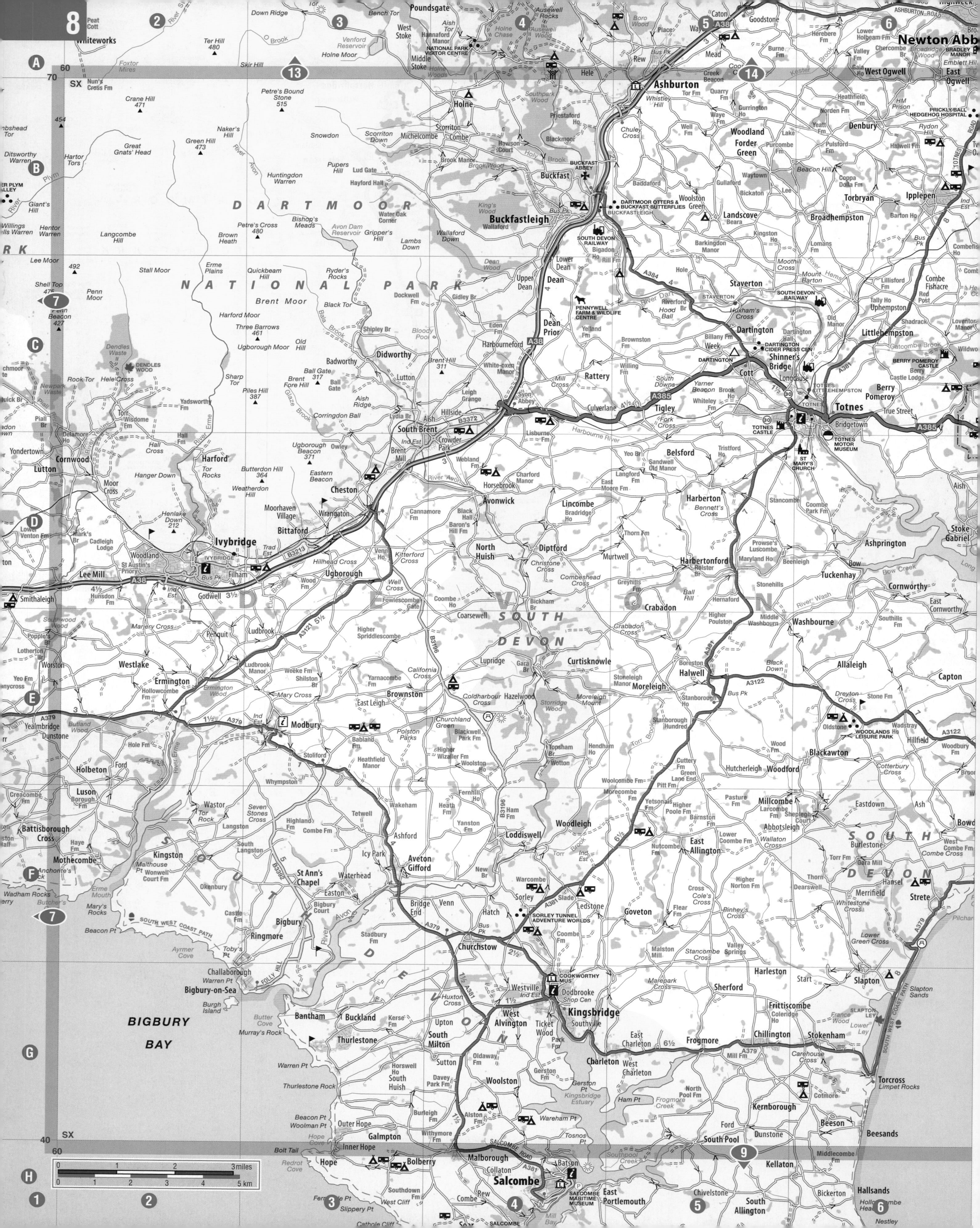
DARTMOOR
NATIONAL PARK
SOUTH DEVON
BIGBURY BAY
Ashburton
Buckfast
Buckfastleigh
Buckfast Abbey
Dartmoor Otters & Buckfast Butterflies
South Devon Railway
Pennywell Farm & Wildlife Centre
Dartington
Dartington Cider Press Cen
Shinner's Bridge
Totnes
Totnes Castle
Totnes Motor Museum
Bridgetown
Berry Pomeroy
Berry Pomeroy Castle
Newton Abbot
Denbury
Ipplepen
Torbryan
Broadhempston
Staverton
Landscove
Woodland
Forder Green
Littlehempston
Holne
Poundsgate
Hele
Scorriton
Michelcombe
Dean Prior
Dean
Rattery
Tigley
Harbourneford
Didworthy
South Brent
Avonwick
North Huish
Diptford
Lincombe
Harberton
Harbertonford
Ashprington
Tuckenhay
Cornworthy
Stoke Gabriel
Ivybridge
Bittaford
Ugborough
Cornwood
Lutton
Lee Mill
Smithaleigh
Ermington
Modbury
Westlake
Brownston
Crabadon
Curtisknowle
Moreleigh
Halwell
Allaleigh
Capton
Blackawton
Woodleigh
Loddiswell
Aveton Gifford
Kingston
Bigbury
Bigbury-on-Sea
Ringmore
Holbeton
Mothecombe
Battisborough Cross
Churchstow
Kingsbridge
Dodbrooke
Cookworthy Mus
West Alvington
Thurlestone
Bantham
Buckland
South Milton
Malborough
Salcombe
Salcombe Maritime Museum
East Portlemouth
Galmpton
Hope
Bolberry
Sherford
Frogmore
Chillington
Stokenham
Slapton
Strete
Torcross
Beesands
Kellaton
Chivelstone
South Allington
Hallsands
Woodlands Leisure Park
Sorley Tunnel Adventure Worlds
South West Coast Path
Burgh Island
Start
Slapton Sands
Ermington Wood
A38
A385
A384
A381
A379
A3121
A3122
B3372
B3213
B3196
B3392
SX
0 1 2 3 miles
0 1 2 3 4 5 km

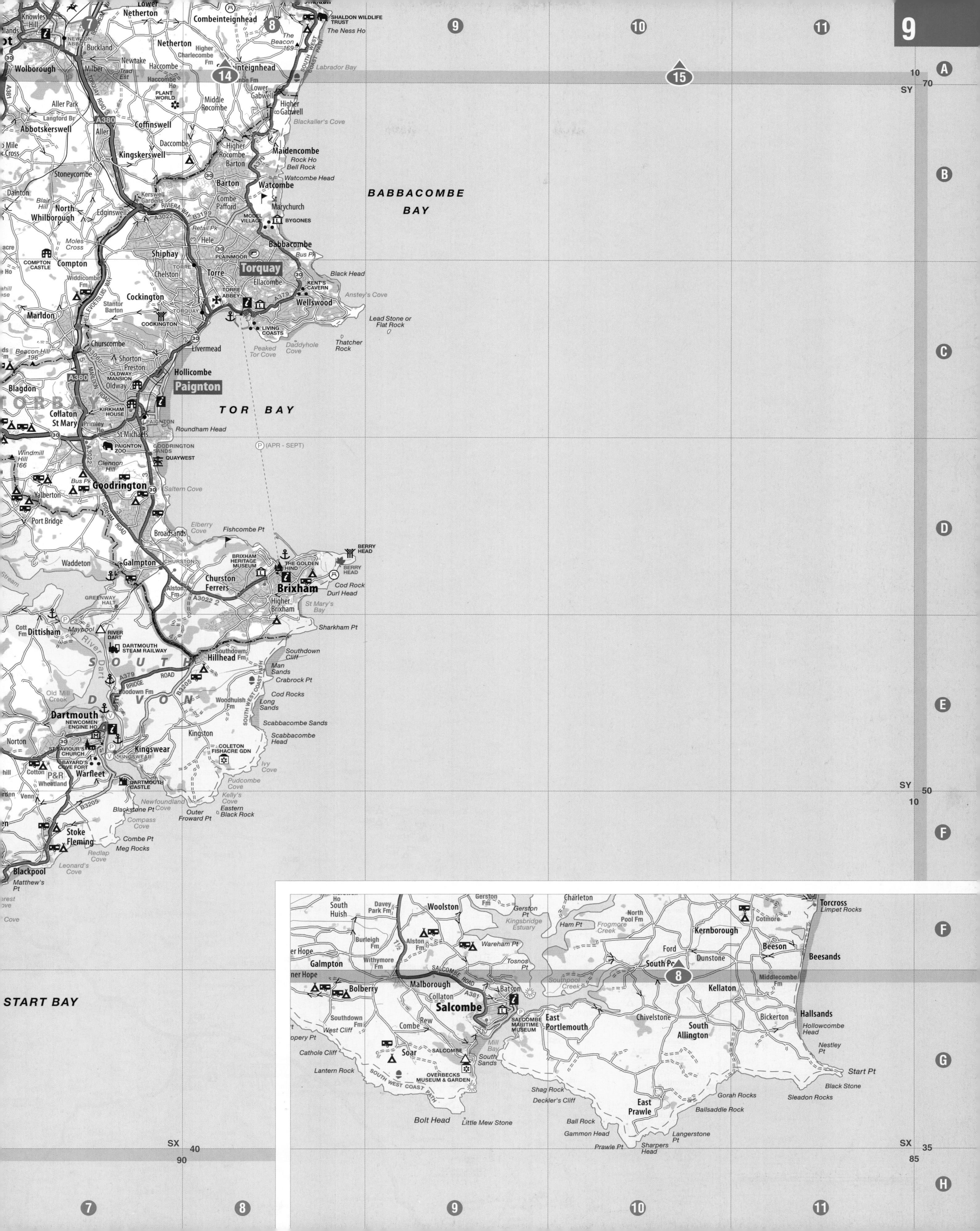

Netherton
Combeinteignhead
Shaldon Wildlife Trust
The Ness Ho
The Beacon 169
Labrador Bay
Newton Abbot
Buckland
Wolborough
Milber
Newtake
Haccombe
Higher Charlecombe Fm
Plant World
Lower Gabwell
Higher Gabwell
Blackaller's Cove
Aller Park
Langford Br
Abbotskerswell
Aller
Coffinswell
Middle Rocombe
Daccombe
Higher Rocombe Barton
Maidencombe
Rock Ho
Bell Rock
Watcombe Head
Kingskerswell
Stoneycombe
Dainton
Barton
Watcombe
Combe Pafford
St Marychurch
Babbacombe Bay
Blair Hill
North Whilborough
Kerswell Gardens
Riviera Way
Edginswell
Model Village
Bygones
Retail Pk
Hele
Moles Cross
Plainmoor
Babbacombe
Bus Pk
Compton Castle
Compton
Shiphay
Torquay
Black Head
Chelston
Torre
Ellacombe
Kent's Cavern
Widdicombe Fm
Torre Abbey
Wellswood
Anstey's Cove
Cockington
Stantor Barton
Lead Stone or Flat Rock
Marldon
Cockington
Living Coasts
Peaked Tor Cove
Daddyhole Cove
Thatcher Rock
Churscombe
Livermead
Beacon Hill 196
Shorton
Preston
Oldway Mansion
Oldway
Hollicombe
Paignton
Blagdon
Torbay
Kirkham House
Tor Bay
Collaton St Mary
Primley Ho
St Michaels
Roundham Head
Paignton Zoo
Goodrington Sands
Quaywest
(Apr - Sept)
Windmill Hill 166
Clennon Hill
Goodrington
Yalberton
Saltern Cove
Port Bridge
Brixham Road
Elberry Cove
Fishcombe Pt
Broadsands
Berry Head
Waddeton
Galmpton
Churston
Brixham Heritage Museum
The Golden Hind
Churston Ferrers
Brixham
Cod Rock
Durl Head
Greenway Halt
Alston Fm
Higher Brixham
St Mary's Bay
Cott Fm
Dittisham
Maypool
River Dart
Dartmouth Steam Railway
Sharkham Pt
South Devon
Southdown Fm
Hillhead
Southdown Cliff
Man Sands
Crabrock Pt
Bridge Road
Hoodown Fm
Old Mill Creek
Cod Rocks
Woodhuish Fm
Long Sands
Dartmouth
Newcomen Engine Ho
South West Coast Path
Scabbacombe Sands
Scabbacombe Head
Kingston
Norton
St Saviour's Church
Kingswear
Coleton Fishacre Gdn
Bayard's Cove Fort
Cotton
P&R
Warfleet
Ivy Cove
Wheatland
Dartmouth Castle
Pudcombe Cove
Venn
Kelly's Cove
Newfoundland Cove
Eastern Black Rock
Blackstone Pt
Outer Froward Pt
Compass Cove
Stoke Fleming
Combe Pt
Meg Rocks
Redlap Cove
Leonard's Cove
Blackpool
Matthew's Pt
Start Bay
South Huish
Davey Park Fm
Woolston
Gerston Fm
Charleton
Torcross
Limpet Rocks
Gerston Pt
Kingsbridge Estuary
Ham Pt
Frogmore Creek
North Pool Fm
Cotmore
Burleigh Fm
Alston Fm
Wareham Pt
Kernborough
Galmpton
Withymore Fm
Tosnos Pt
Ford
Dunstone
Beeson
Beesands
South Pool
Salcombe Road
Southpool Creek
Middlecombe Fm
Bolberry
Malborough
Batson
Kellaton
Collaton
Salcombe
Salcombe Maritime Museum
East Portlemouth
Chivelstone
Bickerton
Hallsands
Hollowcombe Head
Southdown Fm
Rew
South Allington
West Cliff
Combe
Nestley Pt
Cathole Cliff
Soar
Salcombe
Mill Bay
South Sands
Start Pt
Lantern Rock
Overbecks Museum & Garden
Black Stone
Shag Rock
Gorah Rocks
Sleadon Rocks
Deckler's Cliff
East Prawle
Ballsaddle Rock
Bolt Head
Little Mew Stone
Ball Rock
Gammon Head
Langerstone Pt
Prawle Pt
Sharpers Head
SY 70
SY 50
SX 40 90
SX 35 85

SW
The Island
Tintagel Head
Dunderhole Pt
TINTAGEL
Penhallic Pt
Gull Rock
Port William
Dennis Pt
Trebarwith Strand
Backways Cove
Start Pt
Trerubies Cove
Tregardock Cliff
Jacket's Pt
Crookmoyle Rock
Delabole Pt
Dannonchapel
Port Isaac Bay
Barrett's Zawn
Ranie Pt
SOUTH WEST COAST PATH
Tresungers Pt
Lobber Pt
Varley Head
Pine Haven
Kellan Head
Scarnor Pt
Doyden Pt
Port Quin Bay
The Mouls
Rumps Pt
Newland
Com Head
Pentire Pt
Pentire Fm
Carnweather Pt
Trevan Pt
Reedy Cliff
Port Quin
Port Isaac
Port Gaverne
Trewetha
Treore Fm
B3267
Scarrabine Fm
LONG CROSS VICTORIAN GDNS
Trelights
Pendoggett
Pentireglaze Haven
Hayle Bay
New Polzeath
Trenant
Porteath
Carruan
Plain Street
Padstow Bay
Gulland Rock
Polzeath
Shilla Mill
St Endellion
Poltreworgey
Pepper Hole
Stepper Pt
The Narrows
Butter Hole
Trebetherick
Gunvenna
Pennytinney
Lanow Fm
Trelill
Gunver Head
Daymer Bay
Trewiston Fm
Trevanger
Treglyn Down
Tregellist
Harbour Cove
Pityme
St Minver
Trevose Head
Merope Rocks
Round Hole
Stinking Cove
Dinas Head
Mother Ivey's or Polventon Bay
Quies
Porthmissen Bridge
Crugmeer
Tregirls Fm
Gun Pt
Tredrizzick
Trevine
Trewethern
Treguite
Greater Brighter Fm
St Kew
Trevone Bay
Round Hole
Trevone
PRIDEAUX PLACE
Splatt
Penmayne
Treglyn Fm
Rooke Fm
Chapel Amble
Carclaze Fm
Harlyn Bay
Toll
Trethillick
Rock
Trefresa Fm
Blakes Keiro
B3314
Hendra
St Kew Highway
Trevisquite Manor
Trethevan Fm
Harlyn
Treator
PADSTOW MUSEUM
Town Bar
Porthilly Cove
Stoptide
Porthilly
Penpont Fm
Booby's Bay
Constantine Bay
B3276
Padstow
Gutt Bridge
Lower Amble
Trewornan
Amble River
Tregorden
Kelly
Rocksea Fm
Dinham's Br
Treyarnon Pt
Windmill
Ind Est
Dinas
NATIONAL LOBSTER HATCHERY
Trevelver
Cant Cove
River Camel
Trethias Island
Warren Cove
Pepper Cove
Fox Cove
TREYARNON BAY
Towan
Treyarnon
Trewithen Fm
St Merryn
Trenavel Fm
A389
Dennis Hill
Oldtown
Oldtown Cove
Tregonce
Tregunna
Burniere
Bodieve
Ball
A39
Sea Mills
Trevorrick
Trevilgus Fm
Bodellick
Trevanson
Perlees Fm
Edmonton
Three Holes Cross
Minnows Islands
Will's Rock
Porthcothan Bay
Trehemborne
Carnevas
Shop
Trevorrick
Highlanes
CORNWALL
Burgois
Dunveth
Ind Est
Trenant
St Mabyn
Trethick Fm
Trescore Islands
Trevean
Treburick Fm
Tregonna
Whitecross
Wadebridge
Hingham Mill
Trevilder
Porth Mear
Porthcothan
Trevethan
Little Petherick
Mellingey
Trevance
Penhale
ROYAL CORNWALL SHOWGROUND
St Breock
Egloshayle
Clapper
Lower Croan
Sladesbridge
Croanford
High Cove
Trevemedar
Trevio
Lewidden
St Merryn Airfield (disused)
Treingey Fm
St Issey
Trevear Fm
A389
Polmorla
Treraven
Tredannick
PENCARROW HOUSE
Park Head
Treburrick
Penrose
Treleigh Fm
B3274
Trenance
Tredruston Fm
Trelyll Fm
Diggory's Island
Efflins
Treglinnick
Petrusse Fm
Blable Ho
Hay
Pengelly Fm
Costislost Fm
Bozion Fm
Polgeel Wood
Park
Trescowe Brake
Tregona
St Ervan
Rumford
Tredinnick
St Jidgey
Pawton Manor Fm
Bishop's Wood
Hustyn Wood
Queen Bess Rock
BEDRUTHEN STEPS
Trerair Fm
Cannalidgey
Burlawn
Polbrock
Washaway
Lane-end
Trevisker Fm
Bogee Fm
CREALY GREAT ADVENTURE PARK
Burlorne Tregoose
Mount Charles
St Eval Airfield (disused)
St Eval
Bear's Downs
Long Stone
Trelow Downs
Scotland Corner
208
Brocton
Penaligon Downs
High Cove
Trenance Pt
Trenance
Bogee Common
Higher Cransworth
Great Grogley
0 1 2 3 miles
0 1 2 3 4 5 km

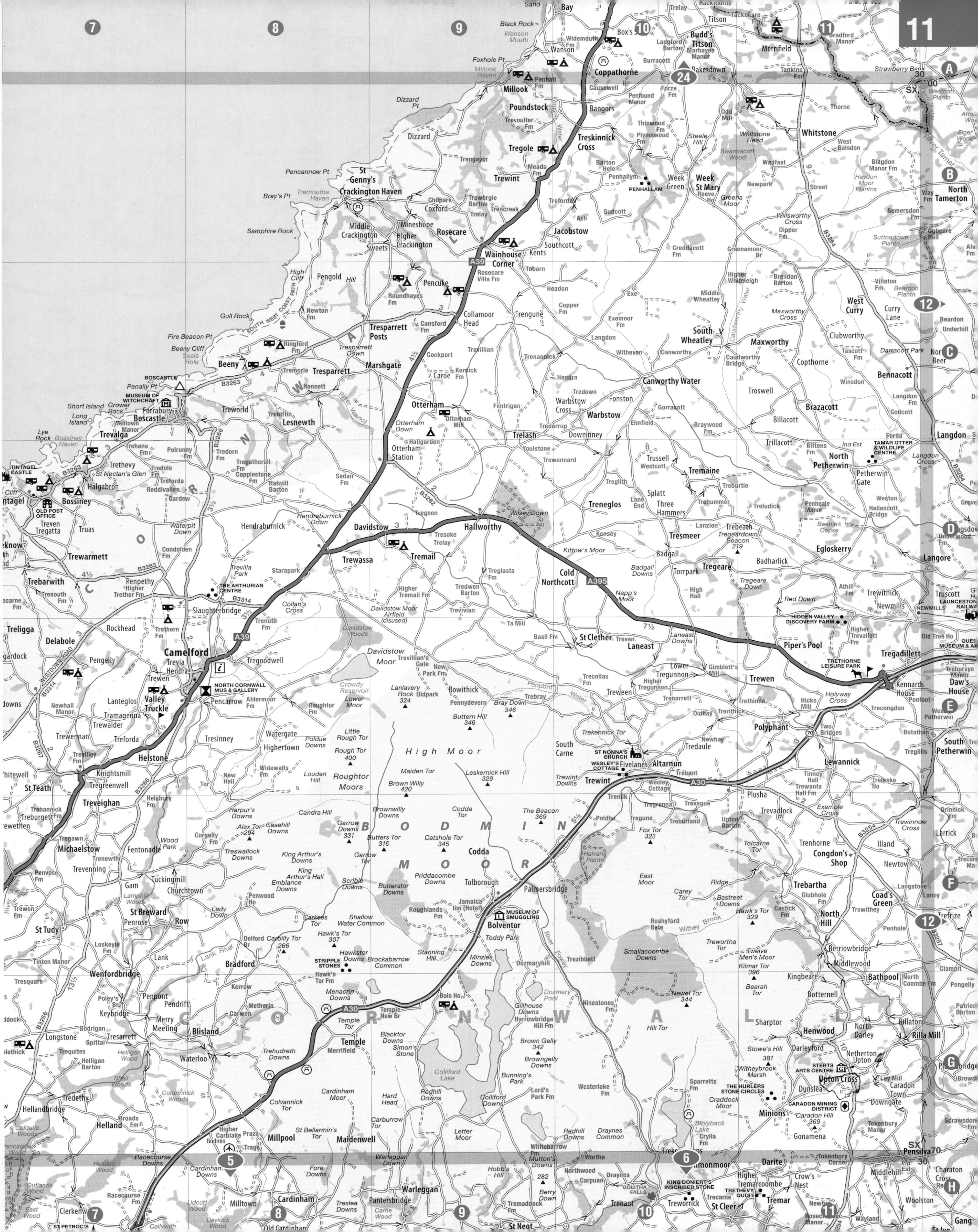
7
8
9
10
11
12
5
6
24
A
B
C
D
E
F
G
H
Black Rock
Wanson Mouth
Foxhole Pt
Millook Haven
Millook
Poundstock
Dizzard Pt
Dizzard
Trevoulter Fm
Tregole
Trewint
Treskinnick Cross
Coppathorne
Bangors
Box's
Budd's Titson
Marhayes Manor
Bakesdown
Titson
Merrifield
Bradford Manor
Strawberry Bank
Whitstone
Whitstone Head
Swannacott Wood
Week Green
Week St Mary
Penhallam
Jacobstow
Southcott
Kents
Wainhouse Corner
Pencannow Pt
Bray's Pt
Tremoutha Haven
St Genny's
Crackington Haven
Middle Crackington
Higher Crackington
Mineshope
Rosecare
Sweets
Samphire Rock
High Cliff
Pengold
Pencuke
Roundhayes Fm
Newton Fm
Gull Rock
Fire Beacon Pt
Beeny Cliff
Beeny
Ringford Fm
Tresparrett Posts
Tresparrett
Marshgate
Collamoor Head
Cansford Fm
Trengune
Trevillian
SOUTH WEST COAST PATH
Penally Pt
BOSCASTLE
MUSEUM OF WITCHCRAFT
Forrabury
Boscastle
Short Island
Long Island
Grower Rock
Welltown Manor
Treworld
Lesnewth
Otterham
Otterham Down
Otterham Mill
Otterham Station
Hallgarden
Lye Rock
Bossiney Haven
Trevalga
Trehane Fm
Polrunny Fm
Tredorn Fm
Tregatherall Fm
Copplestone Fm
Halwill Barton
Sedan Fm
TINTAGEL CASTLE
Tintagel
OLD POST OFFICE
St Nectan's Glen
Halgabron
Bossiney
Trethevy
Trefreda Fm
Reddivallen Fm
Cardew
Treven
Tregatta
Truas
Waterpit Down
Hendraburnick
Hendraburnick Down
Davidstow
Trewassa
Tremail
Tregeen
Hallworthy
Wilsey Down
Trelash
Warbstow
Warbstow Cross
Canworthy Water
Fonston
Tredown
Hendra
Trenannick
Elmfield
Downinney
Trewonnard
Youlstone
Gorracott
Braywood Fm
Billacott
Brazacott
Trillacott
Bittens Fm
Ind Est
TAMAR OTTER WILDLIFE CENTRE
North Petherwin
Petherwin Gate
Langdon
Trussell
Westcott
Tremaine
Splatt
Three Hammers
Treneglos
Lane End
Treburtle
Trehummer
Treludick
Penheale Manor
Hellescott Bridge
Weston
Trebeath
Tregardown Beacon 219
Lanzion
Beepark Copse
Tresmeer
Badgall
Badgall Downs
Torrpark
Tregeare
Badharlick
Egloskerry
Langore
Kittow's Moor
Cold Northcott
Napp's Moor
Kensey
Maxworthy
South Wheatley
Middle Wheatley
Higher Whiteleigh
Canworthy
Caudworthy Bridge
Copthorne
Troswell
Clubworthy
Tascott Fm
West Curry
Curry Lane
Maxworthy Cross
Bennacott
Winsdon
Langdon Fm
Godcott
North Tamerton
Street
Newpark
Greena Moor
Creddacott Fm
Greenamoor Br
Dipper Fm
Willsworthy Cross
Brendon Barton
Headon
Copper Fm
Exemoor Fm
Langdon
Witheven
Camelford
Trevia
Hendra
Tregoodwell
Slaughterbridge
THE ARTHURIAN CENTRE
Trevilla Park
Starapark
Penpethy
Higher Trether Fm
Collan's Cross
Trenuth Fm
Trethern Fm
Rockhead
Delabole
Treligga
Trebarwith
Trenouth Fm
Trewarmett
Condolden Fm
Pengelly
Trewen
Valley Truckle
NORTH CORNWALL MUS & GALLERY
Pencarrow
Aldermoor Fm
Lanteglos
Tramagenna
Trewalder
Treforda
Trewennan
Helstone
Knightsmill
Tregreenwell
St Teath
Treveighan
Michaelstow
Trenewth
Trevenning
Fentonadle
Tuckingmill
Churchtown
Davidstow Moor
Davidstow Moor Airfield (disused)
Davidstow Woods
Higher Tremail Fm
Tredwen Barton
Trevivian
Treglasta Fm
River Inny
Ta Mill
Basil Fm
St Clether
Laneast
Laneast Downs
Piper's Pool
Lower Tregunnon
Higher Tregunnon
Trewen
Treween
Trecollas Fm
Trebray
Penpont Water
Trenarrett
Trethinna
Hicks Mill
Oldhay
Trerithick
Polyphant
Two Bridges
Holyway Cross
Kennards House
Tregadillett
TRETHORNE LEISURE PARK
HIDDEN VALLEY DISCOVERY FARM
Higher Trevallett Fm
Red Down
Athill Fm
Trewithick
Newmills
Truscott
LAUNCESTON RAILWAY
Old Tree Ho
Daw's House
Trecongdon
Penfoot
Botathan
South Petherwin
Trekennick Tor
South Carne
ST NONNA'S CHURCH
WESLEY'S COTTAGE
Fivelanes
Altarnun
Trewint
Tredaule
Lewannick
Plusha
Trevadlock
Example Cross
Trenhorne
Congdon's Shop
Illand
Newtown
Trebartha
Glubhole Fm
North Hill
Coad's Green
Trewithey
Castick Fm
Berriowbridge
Middlewood
Bathpool
Kingbeare
Botternell
Sharptor
Henwood
Darleyford
North Darley
Rilla Mill
Netherton
Upton
Upton Cross
STERTS ARTS CENTRE
Dunslea
Caradon Town
CARADON MINING DISTRICT
Caradon Hill 369
Minions
THE HURLERS STONE CIRCLES
Gonamena
Pensilva
Darite
Tremarcoombe
Crow's Nest
Tremar
TRETHEVY QUOIT
KING DONIERT'S INSCRIBED STONE
Trecarne
St Cleer
Tremorrick
Trenant
GOLITHA FALLS
Draynes
Draynes Common
Little Rough Tor
Rough Tor 400
Roughtor Moors
High Moor
Maiden Tor
Brown Willy 420
Leskernick Hill 329
Buttern Hill 346
Bray Down 346
Lanlavery Rock 324
Bowithick
Oldpark
Pennydevern
Crowdy Reservoir
Lower Moor
Roughtor Fm
Watergate
Highertown
Poldue Downs
Louden Hill
Tresinney
Candra Hill
Harpur's Downs
Alex Tor 294
Casehill Downs
Garrow Downs 331
Butters Tor 316
Brownwilly Downs
Codda Tor
Catshole Tor 345
Codda
The Beacon 369
BODMIN MOOR
Fox Tor 323
Halvana Plantn
East Moor
Carey Tor
Bastreet Downs
Hawk's Tor 329
Rushyford Gate
Withey Brook
Tolborough
Palmersbridge
Jamaica Inn (Hotel)
MUSEUM OF SMUGGLING
Bolventor
Toddy Park
Roughlands Fm
Butterstor Downs
Priddacombe Downs
King Arthur's Downs
King Arthur's Hall
Emblance Downs
Scribble Downs
Carkees Tor
Shallow Water Common
Hawk's Tor 307
Carbilly Tor 266
STRIPPLE STONES
Hawkstor Downs
Brockabarrow Common
Stanning Hill
Minzies Downs
Dozmary Hill
Dozmary Pool
Trezibbett
Smallacoombe Downs
Treworrtha Tor
Twelve Men's Moor
Kilmar Tor 396
Bearah Tor
Newel Tor 344
Hill Tor
Stowe's Hill 381
Witheybrook Marsh
Sparretts Fm
Craddock Moor
Siblyback Lake
Crylla Fm
Ninestones Fm
Gillhouse Downs
Harrowbridge Hill Fm
Brown Gelly 342
Browngelly Downs
Bunning's Park
Lord's Park Fm
Westerlake Fm
Colliford Lake
Colliford Downs
Redhill Downs
Hard Head
Blacktor Downs
Simon's Stone
Temple Tor
Temple
Temple New Br
Menacrin Downs
Bois Ho
Cardinham Moor
Carburrow Tor
Letter Moor
St Bellarmin's Tor
Maidenwell
Millpool
Colvannick Tor
Trehudreth Downs
Merrifield
Mutton's Downs
Whitebarrow Fm
Hobb's Hill
Redhill Downs
Wortha
Northwood
Carpuan
Berry Down
Tremaddock
Warleggan Down
Warleggan
Pantersbridge
Carne Wood
Treslea Downs
Fore Downs
Cardinham Downs
Cardinham
Milltown
Old Cardinham
St Neot
Lidcutt Wood
Devlock Wood
Callywith
Racecourse Downs
Racecourse Wood
Helland Wood
Clerkenw
Outlands Wood
East Wood
ST PETROC'S
Higher Carblake
Praze
Trago
Bodmin
Helland
Broads Fm
Hellandbridge
Tredethy
Colquite Woods
Pencarrow Wood
Coldrinnick Woods
Shell Woods
Helligan Barton
Helligan Wood
Waterloo
Spittal
Bodrigan
Tresarrett
Trequites
Longstone
Blisland
Carwen
Merry Meeting
Pendrift
Penpont
Keybridge
Poley's Br
Kerrow
Metherin
Bradford
Lank River
Delford Br
Lank
Loskeyle Fm
Wenfordbridge
Tinten Manor
Tresquare
St Tudy
Penrose
Row
St Breward
Lady Down
Penwood Ho
Lamphill Downs
Gam
Corgelly Fm
Treswallock Downs
Wood Park
Penvose Fm
Trewen Fm
Newhall Manor
New Hall
Helsbury Fm
Widewalls Fm
Trehannick Fm
Treburgett
Trewethen
Tregawn
Westdown Road
A39
A395
A30
B3263
B3266
B3314
B3262
B3267
B3254
B3257
SX
River Tamar
River Ottery
River Valency
Caudworthy Water
River Lynher
River Fowey
Sedan Fm
Tinten Manor
Chilpark
Coxford
Trewornan Barton
Trelay
Trencreek
Trenguyor
Meads Fm
Treforda
Ash
Sudcott
Barton Hele
Penhallym
Thinwood Fm
Plymswood Fm
Steele Hill
Odd Mill
Furze Fm
Penfound Manor
Causewell
Burracott
Langford Barton
Tackbeare
Tankins Fm
Thorne
Westcott Plantn
West Balsdon
Wadfast
Blagdon Manor Fm
Haydon Moor Plantns
Semersdon Fm
Suttondown Plantn
Villaton Fm
Beardon Plantn
Beardon
Underhill
Darracott Park
Langdon Cross
Forda
Boswind
Tregorrick Down
Trenilk
Poldhu
Tregune
Trevague
Treburland
Upton Barton
Trebant
Wesley Cottage
Tolcarne Tor
Ridge
Trewinnow Cross
Larrick
Langstone
Trefrize
Penhole
Clampit
Middlehill
Woolston
Tokenbury Corner
Tokenbury Manor
Downgate
Ley Mill
North Coombe Fm
Billaton

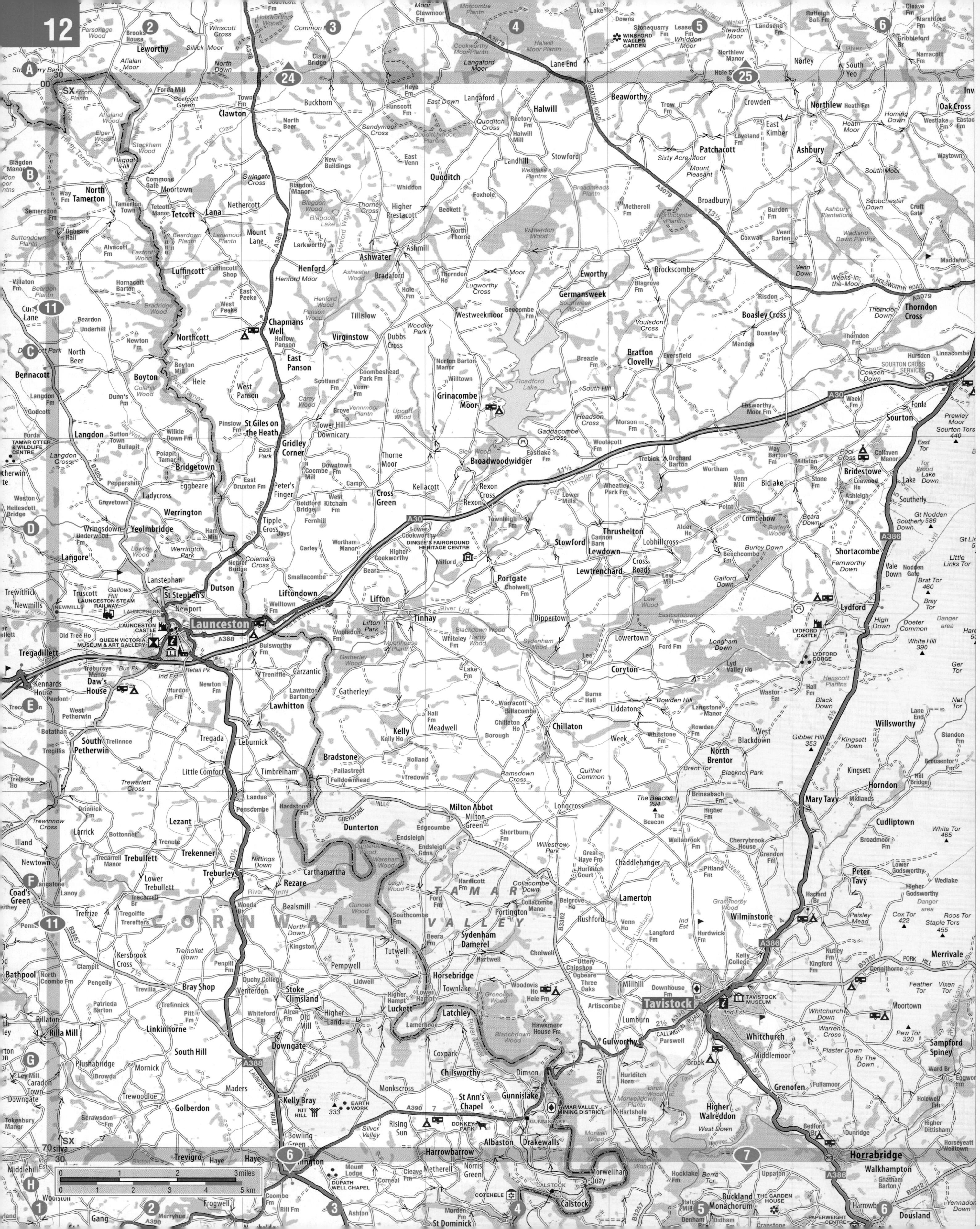
Leworthy
Clawton
Halwill
Beaworthy
Northlew
Oak Cross
Ashbury
Patchacott
Quoditch
Ashwater
Henford
North Tamerton
Tetcott
Lana
Luffincott
Chapmans Well
Virginstow
Northcott
Boyton
East Panson
West Panson
Germansweek
Eworthy
Boasley Cross
Bratton Clovelly
Thorndon Cross
Grinacombe Moor
Roadford Lake
St Giles on the Heath
Gridley Corner
Broadwoodwidger
Sourton
Bridestowe
Bennacott
Langdon
Bridgetown
Werrington
Yeolmbridge
Langore
Cross Green
Rexon
Thrushelton
Stowford
Lewdown
Lewtrenchard
Portgate
Shortacombe
Lydford
Lydford Castle
Lydford Gorge
Dutson
Liftondown
Lifton
Tinhay
Launceston
Launceston Castle
Launceston Steam Railway
Queen Victoria Museum & Art Gallery
St Stephen's
Newport
Tregadillett
Kennards House
Daw's House
Dingle's Fairground Heritage Centre
Dippertown
Coryton
Lawhitton
Kelly
Chillaton
Liddaton
North Brentor
Willsworthy
Mary Tavy
Horndon
South Petherwin
Bradstone
Milton Abbot
Dunterton
Lezant
Trebullett
Trekenner
Treburley
Rezare
Tamar Valley
Cornwall
Lamerton
Peter Tavy
Cudliptown
Wilminstone
Sydenham Damerel
Horsebridge
Stoke Climsland
Luckett
Latchley
Tavistock
Tavistock Museum
Whitchurch
Sampford Spiney
Merrivale
Gulworthy
Bray Shop
Linkinhorne
Rilla Mill
South Hill
Downgate
Kelly Bray
Kit Hill
Golberdon
Chilsworthy
Gunnislake
St Ann's Chapel
Tamar Valley Mining District
Harrowbarrow
Albaston
Drakewalls
Calstock
Cotehele
Morwellham Quay
Higher Walreddon
Grenofen
Horrabridge
Walkhampton
Buckland Monachorum
The Garden House
Dousland
Dupath Well Chapel
St Dominick
Bathpool
Coad's Green
Rising Sun
Metherell
A30
A388
A3079
A386
A390
B3362
B3257
B3254
B3357
B3212
SX
3 miles
5 km

Exbourne
Sampford Courtenay
North Tawton
Sampford Chapple
Trecott
A3072
Nymet Ho
Nicholls Nymett Cross
Hampson
Coplestone Ho
Knowle
Coleford
Appledore Fm
Walson Barton
South Coombe
Penstone
Hollacombe Cross
Colebrooke
Chapple Moor
Broadnymett Moor
Nymet Tracey
Langabeare Barton
Stockbeare Fm
Langabeer Moor
Teachmore Fm
South Dornaford
Dornaford Park
Newland Mill
Culm Cross
de Bathe Fm
Halse Fm
Falcadon Fm
Cocktree Moor
Newcott
Hilldown
Preston Moor
Lamerton Cross
A386
Common Moor
Beacon Cross
Rowden
North Wood Moor
Itton
Itton Moor
South Hill Fm
West Begbeer
Brownsland
Ham Fm
Brocks Cross
Yeoford
Neopardy
Berrydown Plantn
Sampford Courtenay
Belstone Corner
Black Moor
Halford Manor
Bowbeer
Grange Place
Hillerton
North Down
Folly Gate
Padson
Hill Barton
Wood Fm
Appledore Fm
Incott Fm
Brightley
Abberford Woods
Elmead
Chichacott
Webber Hill Fm
Dartmoor Railway
Trehill Fm
Wyke Moor Cross
Taw Green
Two Post Cross
Heath
Heath Cross
Spreyton
Dragdown Hill
Spreyton Wood
North Beer Fm
Wood Fm
Road Fm
Coltsfoot Fm
Ford Fm
Great Leigh Fm
Woodland Head
Blackdown Fm
Narraton
Pudson Fm
Ind Est
Church Hill Cross
Rat Combe
Ball Hill Fm
Woodgreen Fm
Shortridge
Hittisleigh Barton
Crayford
Westwood
Croft
Caddiford Fm
Hook Fm
Collihill
Coombe Valley
Higher Berry
Hilltown
Okehampton
Mus of Dartmoor Life
Corscombe Down
Spitlar Cross
Hollycombe Moor
Nethercott
Hittisleigh
Medland Manor
Tillerton
Fowley Cross
Manor Ho
Okehampton Castle
Tor Down
Coombe Head
Greenhill Fm
Sticklepath
Moon's Cross
South Tawton
Oxenham Manor
Brendis Cross
South Beer Fm
Fuidge Manor
Hittisleigh Mill
Wolfgar Fm
Lewdon Fm
Crosse Fm
Down Fm
Town Barton
Skaigh
East Hill 349
Cleave Ho
Belstone
Finch Foundry
South Zeal
Skaigh Warren
Hollycombe Ho
A30
Hill Fm
Forder Fm
Thorne Cross
Honeyford Fm
Cheriton Bishop
Venbridge Ho
Withycombe Fm
Estrayer Park
Okehampton Camp
Moorgate Fm
Scarey Tor
Culleever Steps 478
Ramsley
West Wyke
Fire Stone Cross
Fairhaven Fm
Whiddon Down
Grendon Fm
Manor Fm
Hole Fm
Melhuish Barton
Middletown
Meldon
Meldon Quarry
436
East Week
Gooseford
Redlake Fm
Puddicombe Ho
Veet Mill Fm
Cheriton Cross
Crockernwell
Haylake
Brook
South Down
Meldon Reservoir
Longstone Hill
Black Down
Rowtor
West Mill Tor
East Okement Fm
Higher Tor
Cosdon Hill
Clannaborough Fm
Well Fm
Ford Ho
Drewsteignton
Coombe Hall
Lower Eggbeer Fm
Corridge Fm
393
Homerton Hill
Okehampton Common
Yes Tor 619
New Bridge
East Mill Tor
Throwleigh
Shilstone Tor
Throwleigh Common
Rashleigh Fm
Spinsters Rock
France Hill
Stone Fm
Cross Fm
Castle Drogo
Rectory Wood
Drewston Wood
Prestonbury Castle
Upperton Fm
Westacombe Fm
Bigport Fm
Moor Fm
Branscombe's Loaf
Black Tor
High Willhays 621
Danger area
Oke Tor
Metheral Hill
Little Hound Tor
Kennon Hill 478
Moortown
Ensworthy
Wonson
Thorne Fm
Way Fm
Sandypark
Whiddon Wood
Hanicombe Wood
Hore Wood
Butterdon Wood
Wooston Castle
Hitchcombe Wood
Butts
Zeal Fm
Black-a-Tor Copse
Slipper Stones
Dinger Tor
Steeperton Tor
Hound Tor
Rippator or Rival Tor
Buttern Hill 413
Aysh
Thule
Murchington
Rushford Wood
Cranbrook Castle
Pinmoor Fm
River Teign
Dunsford
Bridford Wood
Logan Rock
Kitty Tor 585
Woodcock Hill
Lints Tor
Wild Tor
Gidleigh Common
Scorhill Tor
Gidleigh
Holystreet Manor
Rushford Mill Fm
Ind Pk
Chagford
Easton
Uppacott Fm
Bowden Fm
Smallridge Fm
Cod Wood
Steps Br
Okement Hill
Walla Brook
Gidleigh Tor
Leigh Br
Chagford Ho
Great Weeke
Howton Fm
Coombe Court
Ducksmoor Cottage
Leign Fm
Heltor Rock
Bleak Ho
Green Tor
Amicombe Hill
Hangingstone Hill 604
Watern Tor
Hew Down
Kestor
Teigncombe
Waye Barton
Thorn Fm
Meldon Hall
Middlecott
Meacombe Fm
Sloncombe
Moretonhampstead
Doccombe
Furzelands
Cossick Fm
Chat Tor 541
Gt Kneeset 568
Ockerton Court
Kestor Rock 436
Hole Fm
Meldon Hill 390
Weddicott
DEVON
Walla Brook Head
Stonetor Hill
Shovel Down
Frenchbeer
Higher Stiniel
Batworthy
Bughead Cross
Budleigh Fm
Pepperdon Fm
Blackingstone Rock
Laployd Plantn
Whitehorse Hill 601
Black Ridge
DARTMOOR
Quintin's Man 552
Black Hill 584
Collihole Fm
Fernworthy Reservoir
Shapley
Jurston
Miniature Pony Centre
Bovey Castle
Narramore Fm
Wray Barton
Kennick Reservoir
Lit.Kneeset 516
Hurston
Lettaford
North Bovey
Bowden Fm
Gratnar Fm
Canna Park
Lewdons Fm
Higher Elsford Fm
Tottiford Reservoir
Trenchford Reservoir
Watern Oke
Fur Tor 572
Sittaford Tor 537
Fernworthy Forest
Moor Gate
River Bovey
Aller
Clapper Br
Cut Hill 604
The Meads
NATIONAL
Chagford Common
Shapley Common
Coombe Down
Easdon Tor 439
Hunter's Tor
North West Passage
Winney's Down
White Ridge 504
Assycombe Hill
Lower Hookner
Langstone
Lustleigh Cleave
Caseley Court
Bullaton Fm
Beadon Fm
Standon Hill
Walkham Head
Dartmoor Forest
Stannon Tor 462
Water Hill 489
Hookney Tor
King Tor
Heathercombe
Vogwell Fm
Torhill Fm
Wingstone Fm
Manaton
Lustleigh
Wreyland
Slade Cross
Warren House Inn
Headland Warren
Grimspound (Earthwork)
Heatree Fm
Cripdon Down
Hayne Down
Water
Houndtor Wood
Lynch Tor 517
Broad Down
Merripit Hill 449
Hameldown Tor 529
Becky Falls Woodland Park
PARK
Rough Tor 546
Hartland Tor
Soussons Down
Soussons Fm
Natsworthy Manor
Hamel Down
Beckaford
Pullabrook Fm
Maiden Hill
Devil's Tor
Postbridge Information Centre
Postbridge
Runnage Fm
Hameldown Beacon 517
Hound Tor
Reddaford Water
Bovey Tracey Heritage Centre
Langstone Moor
Cocks Hill 501
Higher White Tor 525
Penlee Fm
Pizwell Fm
Smallacombe Rocks
East Dartmoor Woods & Heaths
Yarner Wood
Lower Down
Southbrook
Lydford Tor
Crow Tor
Arch Tor
Clapper Bridge
Grendon Fm
Blackaton Down
Chinkwell Tor 458
Greator Rocks
Haytor Down
Petertavy Great Common
Wistman's Wood
Beardown Tors 512
Dury Fm
Cator Common
Wooder Manor
Bonehill Down
Haytor Rocks 454
Ullacombe Fm
Whisselwell Fm
Five Wyches Fm
Black Dunghill 492
Bellever
Blackaton Manor
Hatchwell Fm
Bonehill
Haytor
Haytor Vale
Green Lane
House of Marbles
Gt Mis Tor 539
Powdermill
Cator Court
Widecombe in the Moor
B3387
Logan Stone
Lewthorn Cross
Haytor Information Centre
Brimley
Ilsington
Little Mis Tor
Littaford Tors
Bellever Tor 443
Riddon Ridge
Lower Cator
Dartmoor Expedition Centre
Top Tor
Hemsworthy Gate
Merrivale Prehistoric Settlement
Crockern Tor
Smith Hill
Laughter Tor
Dartmoor National Park
Wind Tor
Blackslade Down
473
Rippon Tor
Liverton
Rundlestone
Beardown Fm
Parson's Cottage
Babeny
Bagtor Ho
Two Bridges
Huccaby Tor
Corndon Tor 431
Corndon Ford Fm
Cold East Cross
Rora Ho
Blackpool
Yellowmeade Fm
HM Prison
400
King's Tor
North Hessary Tor 517
Princetown
Dunnabridge Fm
Moorlands Fm
Brimpts Fm
Yar Tor
Dartmeet
Ponsworthy
Buckland in the Moor
Welstor
Coombe Fm
Sigford
High Moorland Visitor Centre
Devil's Bridge
Sherberton
Sherberton Common
Sharp Tor
Lower Town
Spitchwick Manor
Buckland Beacon
Halshanger
Goodstone Woods
Yeo Fm
Lee Fm
Telegraph Hill
Ingra Tor
Leeden Tor 389
South Hessary Tor
Royal Hill 407
Hexworthy
Combestone Tor
Bel Tor 354
Auswell Cross
Whiddon Fm
Bickington
Down Ridge
Bench Tor
Poundsgate
Auswell Rocks
Boro Wood
Caton
Goodstone
Black Tor
Cramber Tor
445
Peat Cott
Whiteworks
River Swincombe
Ter Hill 480
West Stoke
Aish Tor
Hannaford Manor
National Park Visitor Centre
Holne Chase
Auswell Wood
Place
Waye
A38
Herebere Fm
Leather Tor
Peek Hill 400
Venford Reservoir
Holne Moor
Middle Stoke
Holne Woods
Rew
Bus Pk
Burne Fm
Mead
Coombe Cross
Foxtor Mires
Skir Hill
Hele
Creek Beacon
Ashburton
Down Tor 366
Crane Hill 471
Petre's Bound Stone 515
Holne
Southpark Wood
Tor Fm
Quarry Fm
Whistley Hill
Heath
Lower Lowery
Burrator Reservoir
454
Priestaford
Gurrington Fm
Waye Fm
Lake
Sheeps Tor
Combshead Tor
Naker's Hill
Snowdon
Scorriton Down
Scorriton
Michelcombe
Combe
Blackmoor
Chuley Cross
Well Fm
Woodland
Purcombe Fm
Forder Green
Pulsford Fm
Sheepstor
Ditsworthy
Great Gnats' Head
Green Hill 473
SX
80
70

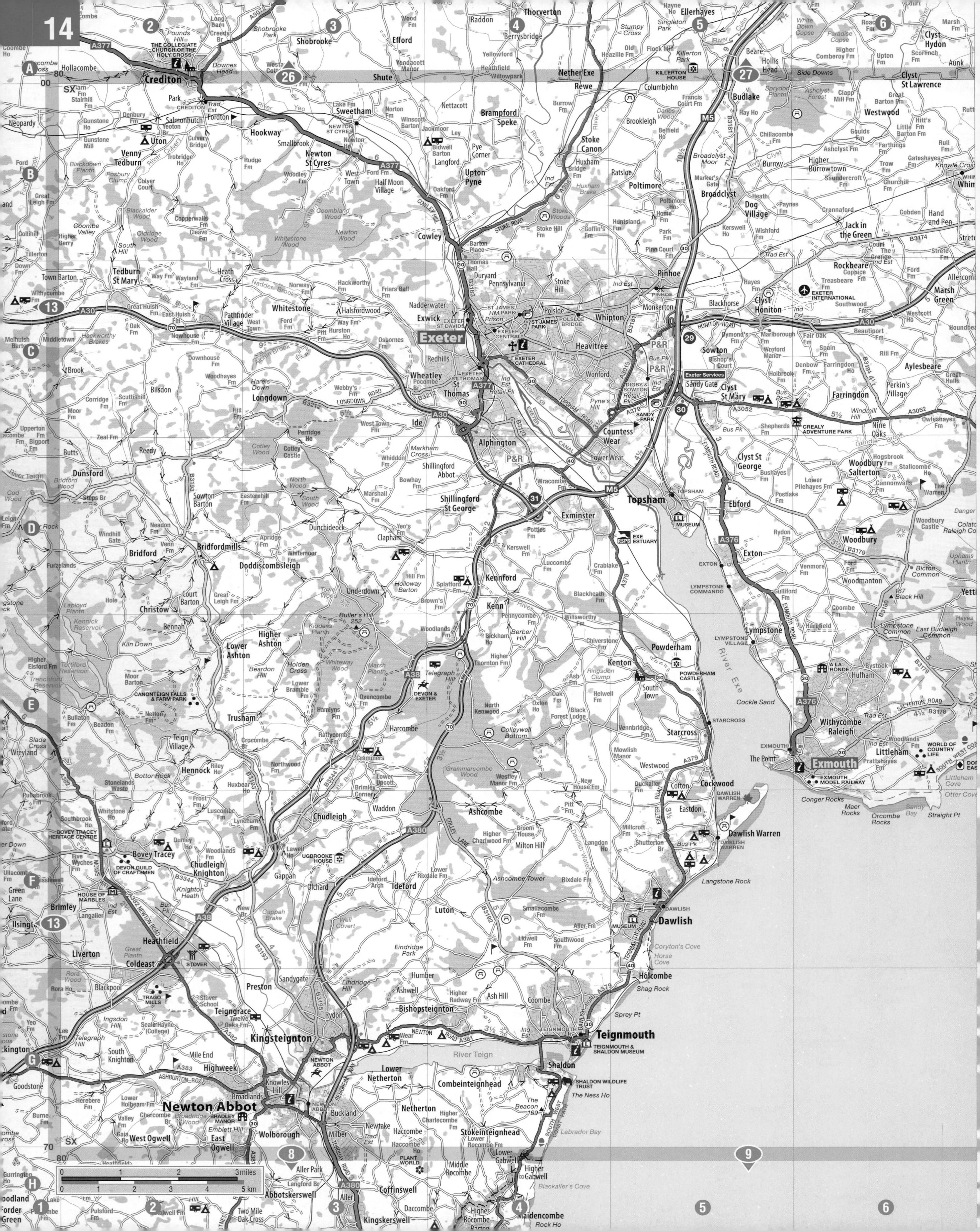
Crediton
THE COLLEGIATE CHURCH OF THE HOLY CROSS
Shobrooke
Efford
Raddon
Thorverton
Berrysbridge
Ellerhayes
Killerton House
Nether Exe
Rewe
Columbjohn
Shute
Sweetham
Hookway
Newton St Cyres
Brampford Speke
Stoke Canon
Upton Pyne
Cowley
Poltimore
Broadclyst
Budlake
Westwood
Clyst St Lawrence
Clyst Hydon
Jack in the Green
Rockbeare
Exeter International
Clyst Honiton
Marsh Green
Pinhoe
Monkerton
Whipton
Polsloe
Heavitree
Exeter
Exeter Cathedral
Exeter Services
Sowton
Sandy Gate
Clyst St Mary
Farringdon
Aylesbeare
Crealy Adventure Park
Exwick
Whitestone
Halsfordwood
Pathfinder Village
Tedburn St Mary
Uton
Venny Tedburn
Dunsford
Bridford
Bridfordmills
Doddiscombsleigh
Christow
Kennick Reservoir
Lower Ashton
Higher Ashton
Canonteign Falls & Farm Park
Trusham
Hennock
Wheatley
St Thomas
Longdown
Ide
Alphington
Countess Wear
Topsham
Shillingford Abbot
Shillingford St George
Exminster
Exe Estuary
Kennford
Kenn
Clyst St George
Woodbury Salterton
Ebford
Woodbury
Exton
Lympstone Commando
Lympstone
Powderham
Powderham Castle
Kenton
Starcross
Cockwood
Dawlish Warren
River Exe
Cockle Sand
A La Ronde
Withycombe Raleigh
Exmouth
Littleham
World of Country Life
Exmouth Model Railway
Devon & Exeter
Harcombe
Chudleigh
Ugbrooke House
Ashcombe
Dawlish
Bovey Tracey
Bovey Tracey Heritage Centre
Devon Guild of Craftsmen
Chudleigh Knighton
House of Marbles
Brimley
Heathfield
Liverton
Stover
Trago Mills
Teigngrace
Preston
Ideford
Luton
Bishopsteignton
Holcombe
Teignmouth
Teignmouth & Shaldon Museum
Kingsteignton
Newton Abbot
Highweek
Shaldon
Shaldon Wildlife Trust
Combeinteignhead
Netherton
Stokeinteignhead
Wolborough
West Ogwell
East Ogwell
Abbotskerswell
Coffinswell
Maidencombe
River Teign
M5
A30
A38
A380
A377
A379
A376
A3052
A381
A383
0 1 2 3 miles
0 1 2 3 4 5 km

Payhembury
Awliscombe
Raleigh
ALL HALLOWS MUSEUM
Northcote
Ham
Hawley Bottom
Mount Pleasant
Smallridge
Colestocks
Buckerell
Honiton
Littletown
Cleave
Wilmington
Offwell
Dalwood
Axminster
Weycroft
Millway Rise
Talaton
Feniton
Fenny Bridges
Gittisham
Widworthy
Lea
BURROW FARM
Shute
SHUTE BARTON
Kilmington
Millbrook
Alfington
Fairmile
Ottery St Mary
Church Green
Farway
Northleigh
Tricombe
Whitford
Musbury
Wyke Green
Trill
West Hill
Wiggaton
Southleigh
Colyton
Colyford
Holyford
Combpyne
Rousdon
Holcombe
Tipton St John
Venn Ottery
Metcombe
Sidbury
Harcombe
Harpford
Bowd
Sidford
Seaton
Axmouth
SEATON TRAMWAY
Beer
BEER QUARRY CAVES
Vicarage
Branscombe
Weston
Salcombe Regis
Sidmouth
Newton Poppleford
Hawkerland
Colaton Raleigh
BICTON PARK
OTTERTON MILL
Otterton
North Star
East Budleigh
Knowle
Budleigh Salterton
FAIRLYNCH ARTS CENTRE & MUSEUM
DORSET & EAST DEVON COAST
SEATON BAY
AXMOUTH TO LYME REGIS UNDERCLIFFS
Culverhole Pt
Dowlands Cliffs and Landslips
Beer Head
Ladram Bay
Chiselbury Bay
Brandy Head
SOUTH WEST COAST PATH
A30
A35
A3052
A375
A358
B3174
EAST DEVON
SY
A
B
C
D
E
F
G
H
7
8
9
10
11
16
27
28

Axminster
Smallridge
Weycroft
Millway Rise
Millbrook
Sector
Wadbrook
Tudhay
Castle
Brimley
Hawkchurch
Tillworth
Holditch
Marshwood
Lambert's Castle
Blackpool Corner
Birdsmoorgate
Marshalsea
Bettiscombe
Pilsdon
Pilsdon Pen
Blackney
Stoke Abbott
Stoke Water
Beaminster
Beaminster Museum
Shortmoor
Netherbury
Mapperton
Hooke
Melplash
North Poorton
South Poorton
Loscombe
Powerstock
Nettlecombe
West Milton
Loders
Uploders
Bradpole
Bridport
Bridport Museum
Allington
Symondsbury
Dottery
Salwayash
Kingsland
Broad Oak
DORSET
Whitchurch Canonicorum
Ryall
Morcombelake
Wootton Fitzpaine
Monkton Wyld
Penn
Harcombe Bottom
Uplyme
Holcombe
Combpyne
Rousdon
Lyme Regis
Dinosaurland
Aquarium
Charmouth
Charmouth Heritage Coast Centre
Chideock
Seatown
Golden Cap 191
Eype
Lower Eype
Eype's Mouth
West Bay
Watton
Bothenhampton
Walditch
Shipton Gorge
Burton Bradstock
Southover
Chilcombe
Askerswell
Swyre
Puncknowle
West Bexington
Litton Cheney
Burton Cliff
East Cliff
West Cliff
Ridge Cliff
St Gabriel's Mouth
Seven Rock Pt
Pinhay Bay
Humble Pt
Axmouth to Lyme Regis Undercliffs
Dorset & East Devon Coast
South West Coast Path
A35
A3052
B3165
B3157
B3162
A3066
L Y M E
B A Y
SY
0 1 2 3 miles
0 1 2 3 4 5 km
A B C D E F G H
1 2 3 4 5 6
15
28
29

Rampisham
Quintin
Higher Wraxall
Wraxall
Lower Wraxall
Sandhills
Higher Chalmington
Chalmington
Cattistock
Up Sydling
Cerne Abbas
Cerne Abbas Giant
Abbey
Plush
Bramblecombe
Higher Kingcombe
Lower Kingcombe
Chilfrome
Toller Porcorum
Tollerford
Maiden Newton
Toller Fratrum
Wynford Eagle
Cruxton
Frampton
Sydling St Nicholas
Godmanstone
Forston
Nether Cerne
Piddletrenthide
White Lackington
Piddlehinton
Cheselbourne
Dewlish
Milborne St Andrew
West Compton
Compton Valence
Grimstone
Muckleford
Stratton
Bradford Peverell
Charlton Down
Charminster
Wolfeton House
Puddletown
Athelhampton
Burleston
Tolpuddle
Martyrs Museum
Affpuddle
Northbrook
Higher Bockhampton
Hardy's Cottage & Garden
Stinsford
Kingston Maurward
Lower Bockhampton
Tincleton
Woodsford
Pallington
Kingston Russell
Winterbourne Abbas
Nine Stones
Winterbourne Steepleton
Litton Cheney
Long Bredy
Littlebredy
Poundbury
Military Mus
Tutankhamun Mus
Old Crown Court
County Mus
Dinosaur Museum
Dorchester
Maumbury Rings
Max Gate
Maiden Castle
West Stafford
Moreton
Crossways
Redbridge
Mill House Cider Museum
Martinstown or Winterbourne St Martin
Kingston Russell Stone Circle
Valley of Stones
Hardy Monument
Winterborne Monkton
Winterborne Herringston
Winterborne Came
Whitcombe
West Knighton
Broadmayne
Warmwell
Owermoigne
Tadnoll
Portesham
Abbotsbury
Abbey (Rems)
Abbotsbury Sub-Tropical Gardens
St Catherine's Chapel
Abbotsbury Children's Farm
Abbotsbury Swannery
Coryates
Upwey
Elwell
Broadwey
Bincombe
White Horse
Sutton Poyntz
Preston
Littlemoor
Osmington
Osmington Mills
Poxwell
Upton
Winfrith Newburgh
Chaldon Herring or East Chaldon
Chaldon Down
Holworth
Rodden
Langton Herring
Nottington
Redlands
Overcombe
Radipole
Melcombe Regis
Lodmoor
Sea Life Park
Weymouth Bay
Chickerell
Fleet
East Fleet
Putton
Southill
Charlestown
Bennetts Water Gardens
Westham
Weymouth
Deep Sea Adventure
Nothe Fort
Brewers Quay & Timewalk
Lanehouse
Rodwell
Southlands
Wyke Regis
Dorset & East Devon Coast
Chesil Beach
Portland Harbour
Guernsey 2:10
Jersey 3:25
St Malo 5:15
(Sailings temporarily moved to Poole)
Portland Castle
Nat. Sailing Academy
Castletown
Fortuneswell
Chiswell
Portland
Grove
Easton
Weston
Southwell
Bill of Portland
A35
A37
A354
A352
A353
B3157
B3159
B3143
SY
80
00
70

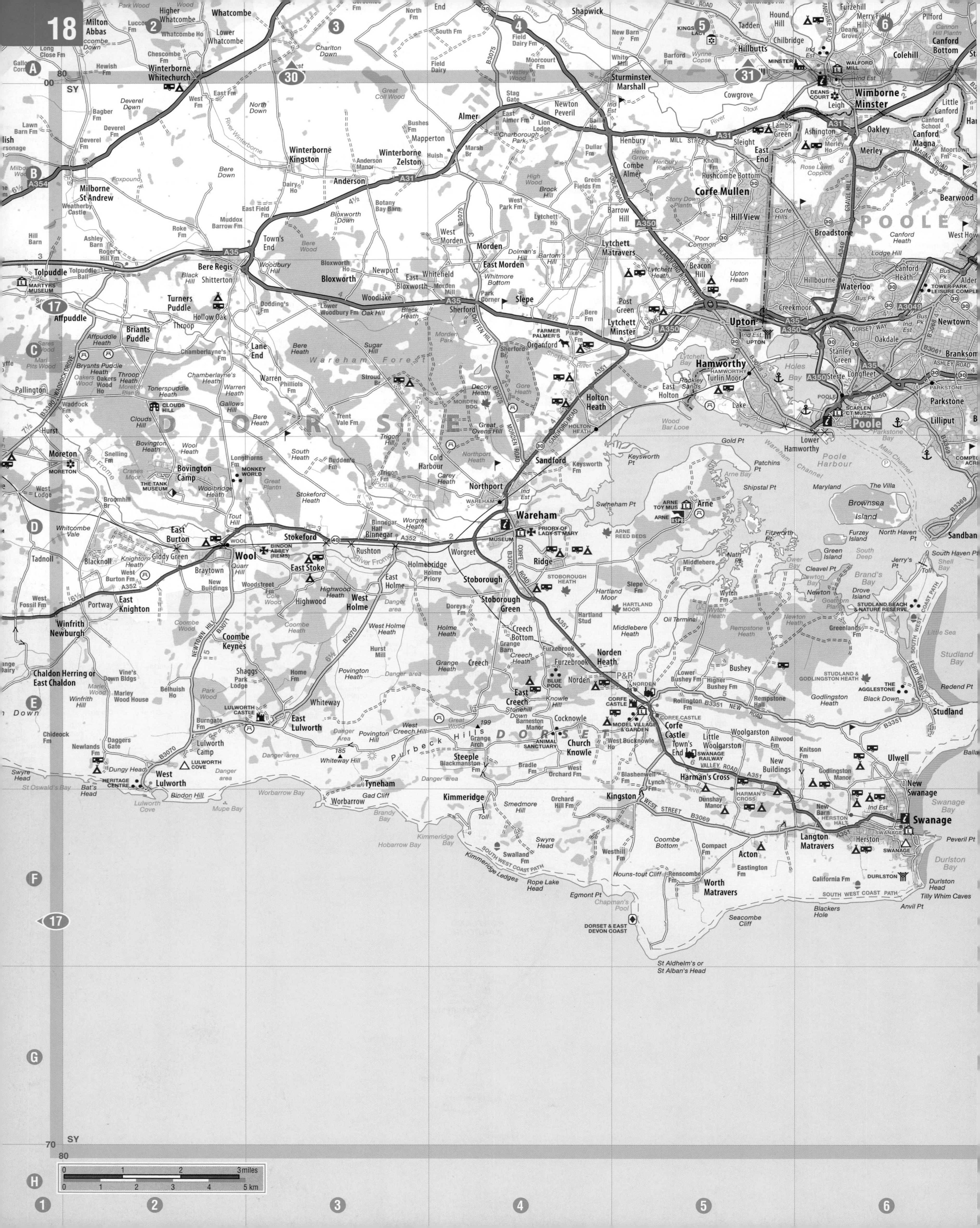
Milton Abbas
Higher Whatcombe
Whatcombe
Lower Whatcombe
Shapwick
Winterborne Whitechurch
Sturminster Marshall
Wimborne Minster
Canford Bottom
Colehill
Hillbutts
Tadden
Chilbridge
Hound Hill
Almer
Newton Peveril
Winterborne Kingston
Winterborne Zelston
Mapperton
Anderson
Henbury
Combe Almer
Corfe Mullen
Hill View
Sleight
East End
Ashington
Oakley
Merley
Canford Magna
Milborne St Andrew
POOLE
Broadstone
Bearwood
Lytchett Matravers
Morden
East Morden
Tolpuddle
Bere Regis
Shitterton
Bloxworth
Turners Puddle
Slepe
Lytchett Minster
Upton
Affpuddle
Briants Puddle
Lane End
Organford
Hamworthy
Turlin Moor
Creekmoor
Waterloo
Newtown
Oakdale
Branksome
Stanley Green
Longfleet
Parkstone
Lilliput
Poole
Lower Hamworthy
Holton Heath
Holes Bay
Poole Harbour
Brownsea Island
Sandbanks
Moreton
Bovington Camp
Sandford
Northport
Wareham
Arne
East Burton
Wool
Stokeford
East Stoke
Ridge
Stoborough
Stoborough Green
West Holme
East Holme
East Knighton
Winfrith Newburgh
Coombe Keynes
Chaldon Herring or East Chaldon
East Lulworth
East Creech
Norden
Corfe Castle
Church Knowle
Steeple
Tyneham
Kimmeridge
Kingston
Harman's Cross
Worth Matravers
Langton Matravers
Swanage
Studland
Ulwell
New Swanage
West Lulworth
Lulworth Camp
Worbarrow
D O R S E T
Studland Bay
Swanage Bay
Durlston Bay
St Aldhelm's or St Alban's Head
SY
00
70
80
0 1 2 3 miles
0 1 2 3 4 5 km

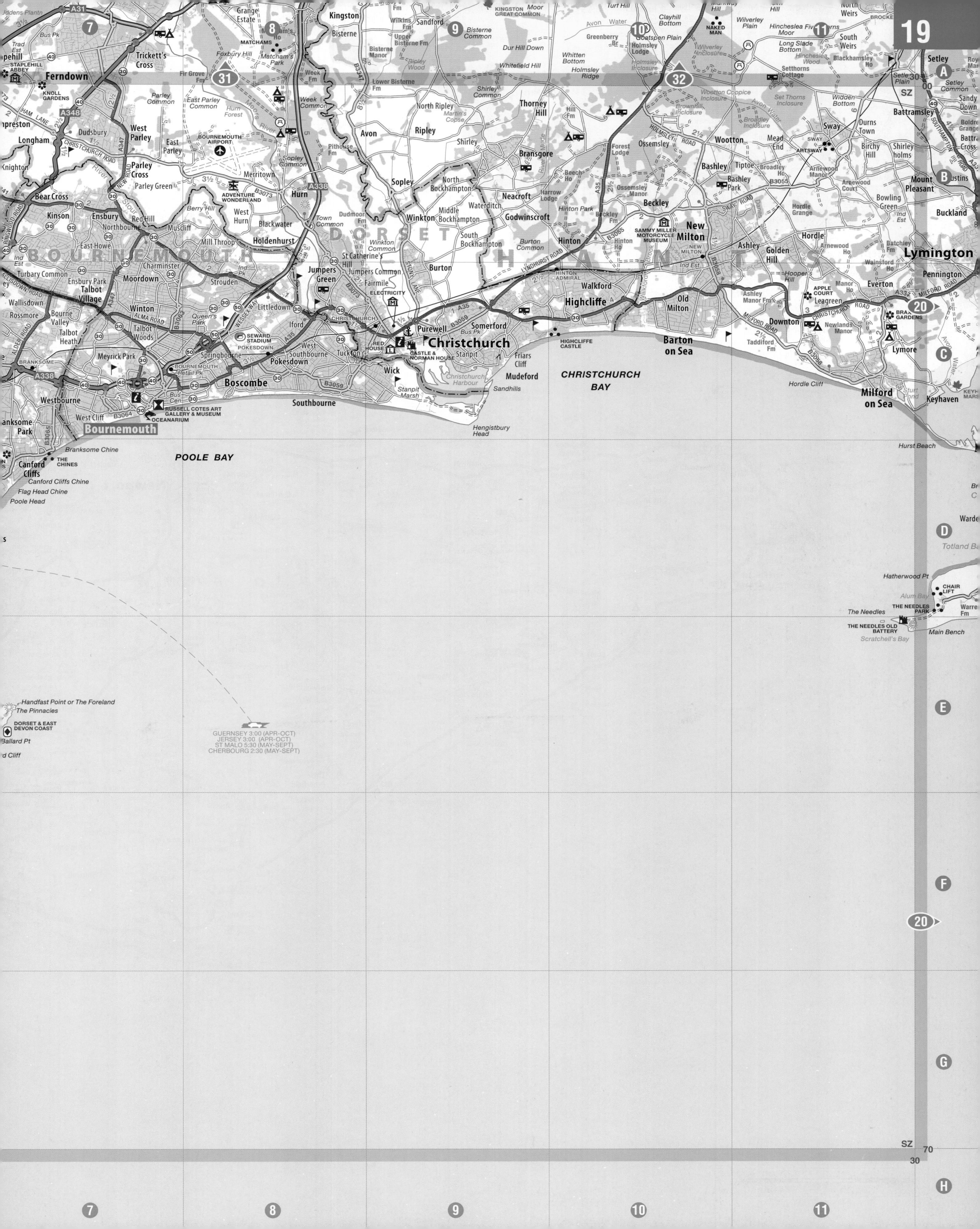
Ferndown
West Parley
Parley Cross
Bournemouth Airport
Kinson
Ensbury
Moordown
Winton
Talbot Village
Westbourne
Bournemouth
Boscombe
Southbourne
Pokesdown
Iford
Jumpers Green
Hurn
Christchurch
Mudeford
Highcliffe
Barton on Sea
New Milton
Milford on Sea
Lymington
Sway
Bransgore
Sopley
Ripley
Avon
Burton
Purewell
Somerford
Wick
Hengistbury Head
Christchurch Bay
Poole Bay
Canford Cliffs
Poole Head
The Needles
The Needles Old Battery
Alum Bay
Keyhaven
Hurst Beach
Handfast Point or The Foreland
The Pinnacles
Ballard Pt
GUERNSEY 3:00 (APR-OCT)
JERSEY 3:00 (APR-OCT)
ST MALO 5:30 (MAY-SEPT)
CHERBOURG 2:30 (MAY-SEPT)
DORSET
HANTS
BOURNEMOUTH

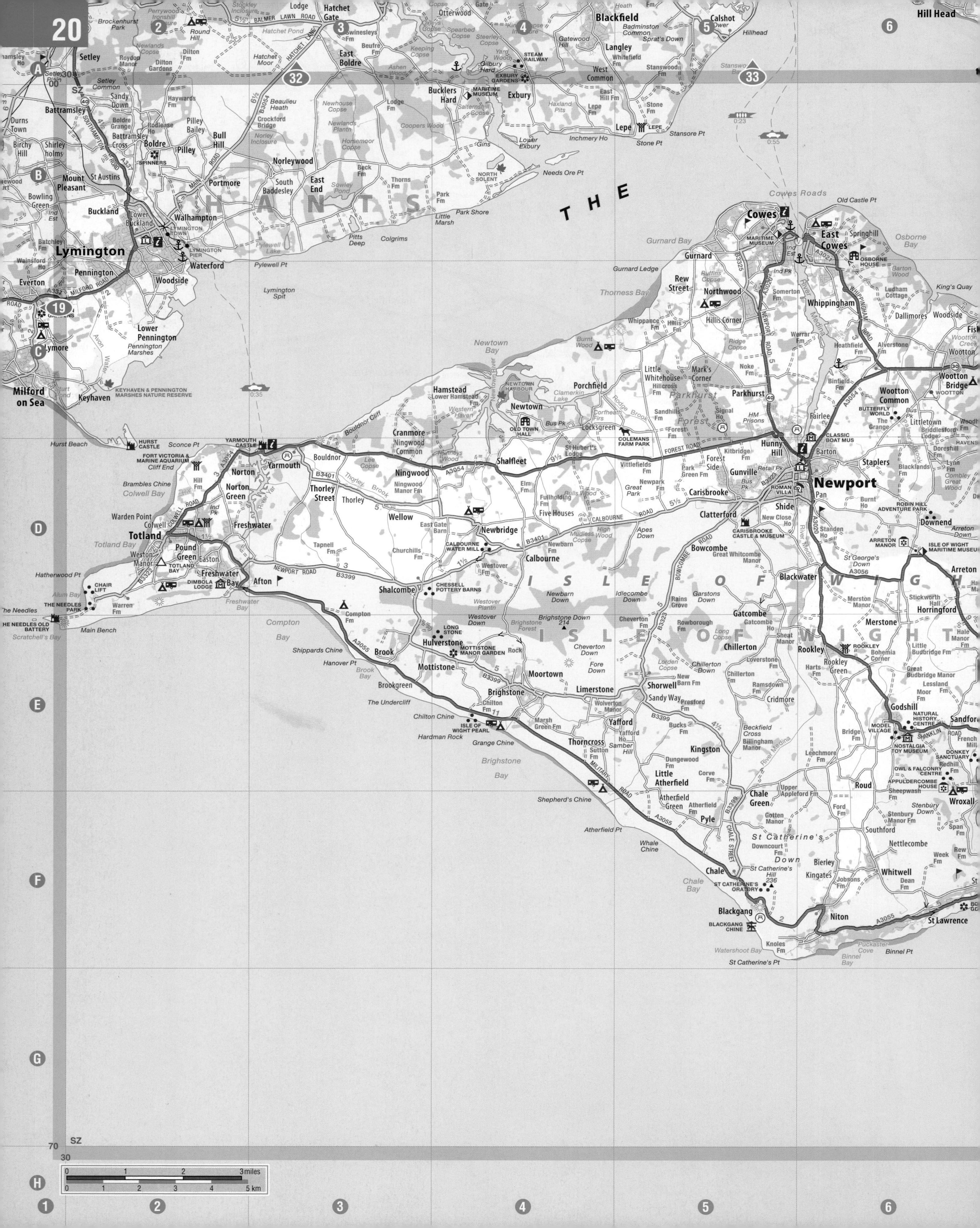

Hill Head
Brockenhurst Park
Round Hill
Hatchet Gate
Blackfield
Calshot
Badminton Common
Langley
Setley
East Boldre
Hatchet Moor
STEAM RAILWAY
Gilbury Hard
West Common
Bucklers Hard
MARITIME MUSEUM
Exbury
EXBURY GARDENS
Battramsley
Durns Town
Birchy Hill
Shirley holms
Boldre
SPINNERS
Pilley
Pilley Bailey
Bull Hill
Norleywood
Lepe
Stone Pt
Stansore Pt
Inchmery Ho
Lower Exbury
NORTH SOLENT
Needs Ore Pt
Mount Pleasant
St Austins
Portmore
South Baddesley
East End
Bowling Green
Buckland
Lower Buckland
Walhampton
HANTS
THE
Park Shore
Little Marsh
Pitts Deep
Colgrims
Lymington
LYMINGTON TOWN
LYMINGTON PIER
Pennington
Waterford
Woodside
Pylewell Pt
Lymington Spit
Everton
Lower Pennington
Pennington Marshes
Lymore
Milford on Sea
Keyhaven
KEYHAVEN & PENNINGTON MARSHES NATURE RESERVE
Hurst Beach
HURST CASTLE
Sconce Pt
YARMOUTH CASTLE
Yarmouth
FORT VICTORIA & MARINE AQUARIUM
Cliff End
Brambles Chine
Colwell Bay
Norton
Norton Green
Warden Point
Colwell
Totland
Totland Bay
Freshwater
Pound Green
Weston Manor
Easton
Freshwater Bay
DIMBOLA LODGE
TOTLAND BAY
Hatherwood Pt
Alum Bay
CHAIR LIFT
THE NEEDLES PARK
The Needles
THE NEEDLES OLD BATTERY
Scratchell's Bay
Main Bench
Warren Fm
Afton
Compton Bay
Compton Fm
Shippards Chine
Hanover Pt
Brook
Brook Bay
Brookgreen
The Undercliff
Chilton Chine
ISLE OF WIGHT PEARL
Hardman Rock
Grange Chine
Brighstone Bay
Shepherd's Chine
Atherfield Pt
Whale Chine
Chale Bay
Chale
Blackgang
BLACKGANG CHINE
ST CATHERINE'S ORATORY
St Catherine's Hill
St Catherine's Down
Watershoot Bay
Knoles Fm
St Catherine's Pt
Puckaster Cove
Binnel Bay
Binnel Pt
Niton
St Lawrence
Whitwell
Kingates
Bierley
Nettlecombe
Southford
Ventnor
Wroxall
APPULDURCOMBE HOUSE
OWL & FALCONRY CENTRE
DONKEY SANCTUARY
Roud
Godshill
NATURAL HISTORY CENTRE
MODEL VILLAGE
NOSTALGIA TOY MUSEUM
Sandford
Chale Green
Pyle
Atherfield Green
Little Atherfield
Kingston
Billingham Manor
Beckfield Cross
Thorncross
Yafford
Shorwell
Sandy Way
Limerstone
Brighstone
Moortown
Mottistone
MOTTISTONE MANOR GARDEN
Hulverstone
LONG STONE
Rock
Brighstone Down
Brighstone Forest
Westover Down
Shalcombe
CHESSELL POTTERY BARNS
Calbourne
CALBOURNE WATER MILL
Newbridge
Wellow
Thorley
Thorley Street
Bouldnor
Bouldnor Cliff
Cranmore
Ningwood Common
Ningwood
Shalfleet
Hamstead
Lower Hamstead
Newtown Bay
NEWTOWN HARBOUR
Newtown
OLD TOWN HALL
Porchfield
Locksgreen
COLEMANS FARM PARK
Five Houses
Fullholding
Vittlefields Fm
Great Park
Carisbrooke
CARISBROOKE CASTLE & MUSEUM
Clatterford
Bowcombe
Gunville
Forest Side
Parkhurst Forest
Parkhurst
HM Prisons
Hunny Hill
Newport
ROMAN VILLA
Shide
Pan
Barton
CLASSIC BOAT MUS
Fairlee
Staplers
Downend
ROBIN HILL ADVENTURE PARK
ARRETON MANOR
ISLE OF WIGHT MARITIME MUSEUM
Arreton
Horringford
Merstone
Blackwater
Gatcombe
Chillerton
Rookley
Rookley Green
ISLE OF WIGHT
Idlecombe Down
Garstons Down
Rowborough
Cheverton
Apes Down
Cowes
MARITIME MUSEUM
East Cowes
OSBORNE HOUSE
Osborne Bay
Old Castle Pt
Cowes Roads
Gurnard
Gurnard Bay
Gurnard Ledge
Thorness Bay
Rew Street
Northwood
Hillis Corner
Whippingham
Woodside
Wootton
Wootton Bridge
Wootton Common
BUTTERFLY WORLD
Littletown
Briddlesford Lodge
Havenstreet
King's Quay
Little Whitehouse
Mark's Corner
Sandhills Fm
A3054
A3055
A3020
A3056
B3401
B3399
B3323
B3325
0:35
0:23
0:55
32
33
19
SZ
30
70
00
0 1 2 3 miles
0 1 2 3 4 5 km
A B C D E F G H
1 2 3 4 5 6

Lee-on-the-Solent
Rowner
Elson
Hardway
Brockhurst
Ann's Hill
Privett
Gosport
Brownstone Pt
Stokes Bay
Alverstoke
Clayhall
Immigration Removal Centre
Fort Monckton
Gilkicker Pt
THE 1642 LIVING HISTORY MUSEUM
EXPLOSION
Burrow Island
MARY ROSE
HMS VICTORY
ROYAL NAVY SUBMARINE MUSEUM
Newtown
GUNWHARF QUAYS
Portsea
Old Portsmouth
CLARENCE PIER
D DAY MUSEUM
BLUE REEF AQUARIUM
SOUTHSEA CASTLE
Southsea
NATURAL HISTORY MUSEUM
Somers Town
Portsmouth
Landport
Kingston
DICKENS' BIRTHPLACE
FRATTON PARK
Fratton
Baffins
Portsea Island
Milton
Eastney
ROYAL MARINES MUSEUM
West Winner
East Winner
HARBOUR
Langstone Channel
Fleet
Manor Ho
Hayling Island
Gable Head
Westfield
West Town
South Hayling
Mengham
Selsmore
Hayling Bay
Eastoke
EAST HAYLING LIGHT RLY
Eastoke Pt
Black Pt
Emsworth Channel
Longmere Pt
PILSEY ISLAND
Pilsey Sand
Pilsey Island
Chichester Channel
East Head
West Wittering
Acre Street
Somerley
Lippering Fm
Oldhouse Fm
Stubcroft Fm
Holmes Fm
East Wittering
Bracklesham
Bracklesham Bay
SOLENT
SPITHEAD
Horse Sand Fort
No Mans Land Fort
St Helen's Fort
RYDE PIER HEAD
RYDE ESPLANADE
QUARR ABBEY
Pelhamfield
Ryde
Appley
St John's Park
Puckpool Pt
Binstead
Quarr Hill
Kite Hill
Puck Ho
Weeks
RYDE ST JOHNS ROAD
Oakfield
Elmfield
SEAVIEW WILDLIFE ENCOUNTER
Seagrove Bay
Seaview
Swanmore
Haylands
BRICKFIELDS HORSE COUNTRY
ROSEMARY VINEYARD
SMALLBROOK JUNCTION
Pondwell
Bullen Ho
The Priory
Priory Bay
Nettlestone
Upton
Havenstreet
Bartlett's Green Fm
WALTZING WATERS
Park Fm
Rowlands Wood
Whitefield Wood
Ashey
Whitefield Fm
BEAPER SHUTE
ISLE OF WIGHT STEAM RAILWAY
Guildford Fm
Hardingshute Fm
ASHEY
West Ashey
Rowlands Fm
St Helens
Bembridge Harbour
Bembridge Pt
BRADING MARSHES
Ethel Pt
Bembridge
Steyne Cross
Lane End
Foreland
Foreland Fields
Marsh Ho
BRADING THE EXPERIENCE
BEMBRIDGE WINDMILL
Ashey Down
Nunwell Fm
NUNWELL HO
Brading
Bembridge
The Run
Hillway
Long Ledge
Brading Down
BRADING
VINEYARD
Yarbridge
SANDOWN ROAD
Whitecliff Bay
Bembridge Down
Morton
MORTON MANOR
ROMAN VILLA
Alverstone
Adgestone
BEMBRIDGE FORT
Culver Down
Culver Cliff
Newchurch
Hill Fm
Yaverland
ISLE OF WIGHT ZOO
Ind Est
Queen's Bower
SANDOWN
Isle Of Wight (Sandown)
DINOSAUR ISLE
AMAZON WORLD
Winford
Sandown
Branstone
NEWPORT ROAD
Merrie Gardens
Lake
SANDOWN BAY
Apse Heath
Ind Est
Bus Cen
Landguard Manor
Bobberstone Fm
Whiteley Bank
Upper Hyde
SHANKLIN
Shanklin
Winstone Fm
Yard Fm
SHANKLIN CHINE
Horse Ledge
Shanklin Down
235
CHURCH ROAD
Luccombe Village
Luccombe Bay
Wroxall Manor Fm
Dunnose
Lowtherville
Upper Bonchurch
Bonchurch
Ventnor
Horseshoe Bay
Ventnor Bay
COASTAL VISITOR CENTRE
0:10
0:40
0:22
CAEN 5:30
LE HAVRE 3:15
ST MALO 9:00
GUERNSEY 7:30
JERSEY 8:00
SANTANDER 24:00 (MAR-NOV)
BILBAO 24:00
CAEN 3:45 (APR-SEPT)
CHERBOURG 3:00 (APR-NOV)
33
34
22
SZ
80
70
7
8
9
10
11
A
B
C
D
E
F
G
H

Havant
Leigh Park
Stockheath
Bedhampton
Rowlands Castle
Emsworth
Warblington
Langstone
Southbourne
Westbourne
Hermitage
Lumley
Hambrook
Nutbourne
Prinsted
Woodmancote
Funtington
Walderton
Stoughton
East Ashling
West Ashling
Woodend
West Stoke
Mid Lavant
East Lavant
Summersdale
Westerton
Strettington
Westhampnett
Boxgrove
Halnaker
Tangmere
Oving
Aldingbourne
Westergate
Chichester
Whyke
Portfield
Fishbourne
Broadbridge
Bosham
Apuldram
Stockbridge
Donnington
Hunston
North Mundham
South Mundham
Merston
Runcton
North Bersted
South Bersted
Rose Green
Aldwick
Bognor Regis
Nyetimber
Pagham
Sidlesham
Highleigh
Street End
Birdham
Somerley
Earnley
Bracklesham
East Wittering
West Wittering
Acre Street
Shipton Green
West Itchenor
West Thorney
Thorney Island
Chidham
CHICHESTER HARBOUR
LANGSTONE HARBOUR
North Hayling
Northney
Stoke
Fleet
Hayling Island
West Town
South Hayling
Mengham
Eastoke
Selsmore
Hayling Bay
Bracklesham Bay
Norton
Church Norton
East Beach
Selsey
Selsey Bill
Pagham Harbour
WEST SUSSEX
Goodwood
Goodwood Aerodrome & Motor Racing Circuit
CAEN 5:30
LE HAVRE 3:15
ST MALO 9:00
CAEN 3:45 (APR-SEPT)
CHERBOURG 3:00 (APR-NOV)
BILBAO 24:00
0 1 2 3 miles
0 1 2 3 4 5 km

Uckfield
Ridgewood
Little Horsted
Halland
East Hoathly
Framfield
Blackboys
Heathfield
Old Heathfield
Cade Street
Punnett's Town
Three Cups Corner
Broad Oak
Brightling
Dallington
Netherfield
Darwell Hole
Penhurst
Waldron
Horam
Maynard's Green
Warbleton
Rushlake Green
Foxhunt Green
Burlow
Chiddingly
Whitesmith
Laughton
Shortgate
Golden Cross
Gun Hill
Hellingly
Lower Horsebridge
Upper Horsebridge
Hailsham
Magham Down
Herstmonceux
Cowbeech
Foul Mile
Bodle Street Green
Windmill Hill
Boreham Street
Ninfield
Hooe
Hooe Common
Wartling
Little Common
Ponts Green
Ashburnham Forge
Glyndebourne
Ripe
Chalvington
Lower Dicker
Upper Dicker
Arlington
Selmeston
West Firle
Alciston
Berwick
Polegate
Wilmington
Folkington
Willingdon
Hampden Park
Langney
Pevensey
Westham
Pevensey Bay
Norman's Bay
Stone Cross
Alfriston
Litlington
Jevington
Friston
East Dean
Westdean
Seaford
Bishopstone
East Blatchington
Sutton
Eastbourne
Old Town
Upperton
Roselands
St Anthony's Hill
Meads
Holywell
Birling Gap
Beachy Head
EAST SUSSEX
Pevensey Levels
PEVENSEY BAY
A22
A27
A259
A267
A271
A2290
B2104

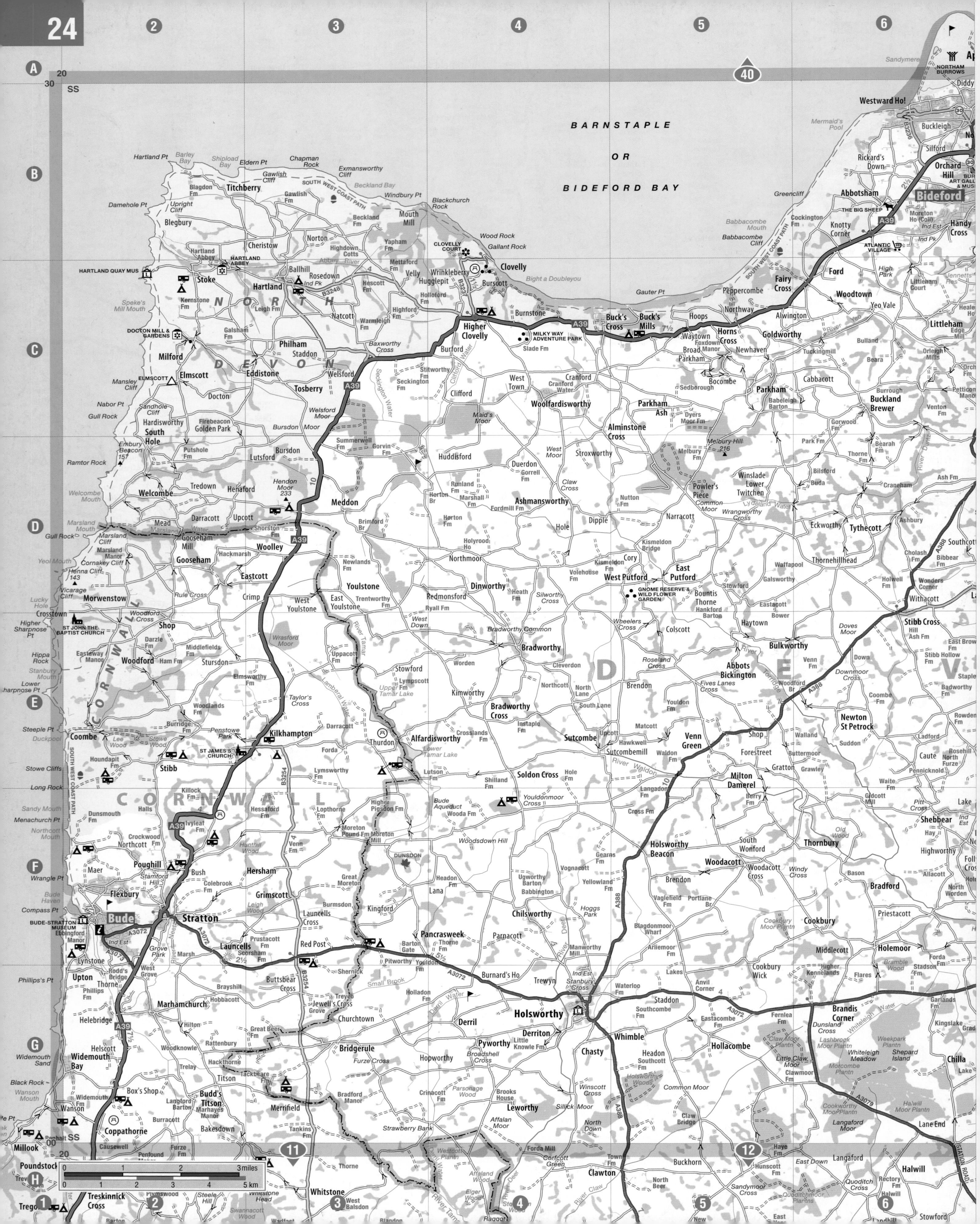
BARNSTAPLE
OR
BIDEFORD BAY
NORTH
DEVON
CORNWALL
D
E
V
Hartland Pt
Barley Bay
Shipload Bay
Eldern Pt
Chapman Rock
Gawlish Cliff
Exmansworthy Cliff
Beckland Bay
Windbury Pt
Blackchurch Rock
Wood Rock
Gallant Rock
CLOVELLY COURT
Clovelly
Bight a Doubleyou
Gauter Pt
SOUTH WEST COAST PATH
Titchberry
Blagdon Fm
Damehole Pt
Upright Cliff
Blegbury
Gawlish Fm
Beckland Fm
Mouth Mill
Norton
Cheristow
Hartland Abbey
HARTLAND ABBEY
HARTLAND QUAY MUS
Stoke
Hartland
Ballhill
Rosedown
Ind Pk
Yapham Fm
Highdown Cotts
Abbey River
Mettaford Fm
Velly
Wrinkleberry
Hugglepit
Burscott
Hescott Fm
Holloford Fm
Kernstone Fm
Speke's Mill Mouth
Leigh Fm
Natcott
Warmleigh Fm
Highford Fm
Burnstone
Higher Clovelly
MILKY WAY ADVENTURE PARK
Slade Fm
Buck's Cross
Buck's Mills
DOCTON MILL & GARDENS
Galsham Fm
Philham
Staddon
Baxworthy Cross
Burford
Milford
Elmscott
ELMSCOTT
Mansley Cliff
Eddistone
Welsford
Tosberry
Docton
Stitworthy Fm
Seckington Fm
Seckington Water
Clifford Water
Clifford
West Town
Cranford
Cranford Water
Woolfardisworthy
Nabor Pt
Gull Rock
Sandhole Cliff
Hardisworthy
South Hole
Firebeacon
Golden Park
Welsford Moor
Bursdon
Bursdon Moor
Maid's Moor
Embury Beacon 157
Putshole Fm
Lutsford
Summerwell Fm
Gorvin Fm
Huddisford
Ramtor Rock
Welcombe Mouth
Welcombe
Tredown
Henaford
Hendon Moor 233
Meddon
Horton Br
Rumland Fm
Marshall Fm
Fordmill Fm
Duerdon
Gorrell Fm
West Moor
Claw Cross
Stroxworthy
Ashmansworthy
Nutton Fm
Marsland Mouth
Mead
Darracott
Upcott
Shorston Fm
Marsland Water
Gull Rock
Marsland Cliff
Gooseham Mill
Woolley
Brimford Br
Horton Fm
Dipple
Hole
Holyrood Ho
Northmoor
Yeol Mouth
Marsland Manor
Cornakey Cliff
Henna Cliff 143
Hackmarsh
Gooseham
Eastcott
Newlands Fm
Youlstone
Dinworthy
Heath Fm
Silworthy Cross
Volehouse Fm
Kismeldon Fm
Cory
West Putford
Vicarage Cliff
Morwenstow
Rule Cross
Crimp
West Youlstone
East Youlstone
Trentworthy Fm
Redmonsford
Ryall Fm
Lucky Hole
Crosstown
ST JOHN THE BAPTIST CHURCH
Higher Sharpnose Pt
Woodford Cross
Shop
Wrasford Moor
West Down
Bradworthy Common
Bradworthy
Hippa Rock
Eastaway Manor
Darzle Fm
Ham Fm
Middlefields Fm
Stursdon
Woodford
Stanbury Mouth
Uppacott Fm
River Tamar
Stowford
Worden
Lympscott Fm
Upper Tamar Lake
Kimworthy
Cleverdon
Lower Sharpnose Pt
Elmsworthy Fm
Taylor's Cross
Lamberal Water
Woodlands Fm
Steeple Pt
Duckpool
Coombe
Lee Wood
Stowe Wood
Burridge Fm
Penstowe Park
ST JAMES'S CHURCH
Kilkhampton
Darracott
Thurdon
Alfardisworthy
Crosslands Fm
Bradworthy Cross
Instaple Fm
Stowe Cliffs
Houndapit Fm
Stibb
Forda
Lymsworthy Fm
Lower Tamar Lake
Lutson Fm
Shilland Fm
Soldon Cross
Hole Fm
Long Rock
Killock Fm
Halls
Hessaford Fm
Lopthorne Fm
Higher Pigsdon Fm
Bude Aqueduct
Wooda Fm
Youldenmoor Cross
Sandy Mouth
Menachurch Pt
Dunsmouth Fm
Ivyleaf Fm
Northcott Mouth
Crockwood Fm
Northcott
Moreton Pound Fm
Moreton Mill
Venn Fm
Huntbill Wood
Woodsdown Hill
DUNSDON
Maer
Poughill
Bush
Hersham
Great Moreton
Headon Fm
Wrangle Pt
Stamford Hill
Bude Haven
Colebrook Fm
Flexbury
Grimscott
Lana
Compass Pt
BUDE-STRATTON MUSEUM
Bude
Stratton
Leigh Wood
Burmsdon Fm
Launcells Cross
Kingford
Ebbingford Manor
A3072
Ind Est
Grove Park
Prustacott Fm
Launcells
Red Post
Barton Gate
Pancrasweek
Thorne Fm
Lynstone
Marsh
Scorsham Fm
Pitworthy
Youldon Fm
Burnard's Ho
Phillips's Pt
Upton
Rodd's Bridge
Thorne
West Grove
Phillips Fm
Brayshill
Buttsbear Cross
Shernick
Small Brook
Holladon Fm
Derril Water
Marhamchurch
Hobbacott
Jewell's Cross
Treyeo Grove
Churchtown
Helebridge
Hilton
Great Beer
Derril
Holsworthy
Helscott Fm
Rattenbury
Widemouth Sand
Widemouth Bay
Woodknowle
Bridgerule
Furze Cross
Hopworthy
Pyworthy
Broadshell Cross
Little Knowle Fm
Derriton
Black Rock
Hackthorne
Trelay
Titson
Tackbeare Fm
Wanson Mouth
Widemouth
Box's Shop
Langford Barton
Budd's Titson
Marhayes Manor
Bradford Manor
Merrifield
Crinacott Fm
Parsonage Wood
Brooks House
Leworthy
Wanson
Burracott
Strawberry Bank
Affalan Moor
Millook
Penhalt
Coppathorne
Bakesdown
Tankins Fm
Causewell
Penfound Manor
Furze Fm
Westcott Plantn
Affaland Wood
Elger Wood
River Tamar
River Deer
Poundstock
Trevi
Thorne
Whitstone
Whitstone Head
West Balsdon
Tregole
Treskinnick Cross
Plymswood
Steele Hill
Swannacott Wood
Barton
Watfoot
Blagdon
Raggot
Dinworthy
Buckleigh
Westward Ho!
Mermaid's Pool
NORTHAM BURROWS
Sandymere
Silford
Orchard Hill
Rickard's Down
Greencliff
Abbotsham
THE BIG SHEEP
Bideford
Cockington Fm
Babbacombe Mouth
Babbacombe Cliff
Knotty Corner
Moreton Ho (Coll)
Ind Est
Handy Cross
ATLANTIC VILLAGE
Ind Pk
Ford
High Park
Littleham Court
Fairy Cross
Peppercombe
Woodtown
Northway
Hoops
Waytown
Horns Cross
Alwington
Yeo Vale
Littleham
Goldworthy
Broad Parkham
Foxdown Manor
Newhaven
Tuckingmill
Bulland
Beara
Orleigh Mills
Sedborough
Bocombe
Cabbacott
Parkham
Parkham Ash
Dyers Moor Fm
Alminstone Cross
Babeleigh Barton
Buckland Brewer
Burrough Fm
Venton Fm
Gorwood Fm
Melbury Hill 216
Melbury Fm
Park Fm
Bearah Fm
Thorne Fm
Bilsford
Buda
Winslade
Lower Twitchen
Powler's Piece
Common Moor
Lydeland Water
Craneham
Ash Fm
Wrangworthy Cross
Narracott
Eckworthy
Tythecott
Ashbury
Kismeldon Bridge
Waffapool
Galsworthy
Thornehillhead
Cholash Fm
Bibbear Fm
East Putford
GNOME RESERVE & WILD FLOWER GARDEN
Stowford
Bountis Thorne
Hankford Barton
Eastacott
Holwell Fm
Wonders Corner
Withacott
Wheelers Cross
Colscott
Bower
Haytown
Doves Moor
Stibb Cross
Hill
Ash Fm
Bulkworthy
Stibb Hollow Fm
Roseland Cross
Abbots Bickington
Venn Fm
Down
Downmoor Cross
Brendon
Fives Lanes Cross
Woodford Fm
Badworthy Fm
Northcott
North Lane
South Lane
Youldon Fm
Coombe Fm
Newton St Petrock
Sutcombe
Upcott
Matcott
Hawkwell
Sutcombemill
Venn Green
Shop
Walland
Ladford
Forestreet
Buttermoor
Sutdon
Cauto
North Furze
River Waldon
Waldon Fm
Gratton
Grawley
Penniccknold
Milton Damerel
Langadon Fm
Cross Fm
Berry Fm
Waite Fm
Gidcott Mill
Pitt Cross
Shebbear
Holsworthy Beacon
South Wonford
Old Wood
Thornbury
Highworthy
Gearns Fm
Vognacott
Woodacott
Woodacott Cross
Windy Cross
Bason
Allacott
Ugworthy Barton
Babbington
Yellowland Fm
Brendon
Bradford
North Worden
Chilsworthy
Hoggs Park
Vaglefield Fm
Portlane Br
Priestacott
Cookbury Moor Plantn
Cookbury
Parnacott
Blagdonmoor Wharf
Manworthy Mill
Ind Est
Stanbury Cross
Arlemoor Fm
Middlecott
Holemoor
Forda Fm
Trewyn
Lakes
Cookbury Wick
Higher Kennelands
Bramble Wood
Flares
Stadson Fm
Waterloo Fm
Anvil Corner
Staddon
Southcombe Fm
Eastacombe Fm
Fernlea Fm
Brandis Corner
Garlands Fm
Whimble
Chasty
Headon
Southcott Fm
Hollacombe
Dunsland Cross
Claw Moor Plantn
Lashbrook Moor Plantn
Whiteleigh Water
Weekpark Plantn
Kingslake
Whiteleigh Meadow
Shepard Island
Little Claw Moor
Clawmoor Fm
Chilla
Winscott Cross
Holsworthy Woods
Common Moor
Silick Moor
Claw Bridge
Morcombe Plantn
Cookworthy Moor Plantn
Halwill Moor Plantn
Langaford Moor
Lane End
North Down
Forda Mill
Corfcott Green
Town Fm
Clawton
Buckhorn
Haye Fm
Hunscott Fm
East Down
Langaford
Halwill
North Beer
River Claw
Sandymoor Cross
Quoditch Cross
Rectory Fm
Quoditchmoor Plantns
Landhill
Stowford
New
East
STATION ROAD
A39
A388
A3072
A3079
A386
B3248
B3237
B3254
B3236
SS
20
30
40
11
12
0 1 2 3 miles
0 1 2 3 4 5 km
A B C D E F G H
1 2 3 4 5 6

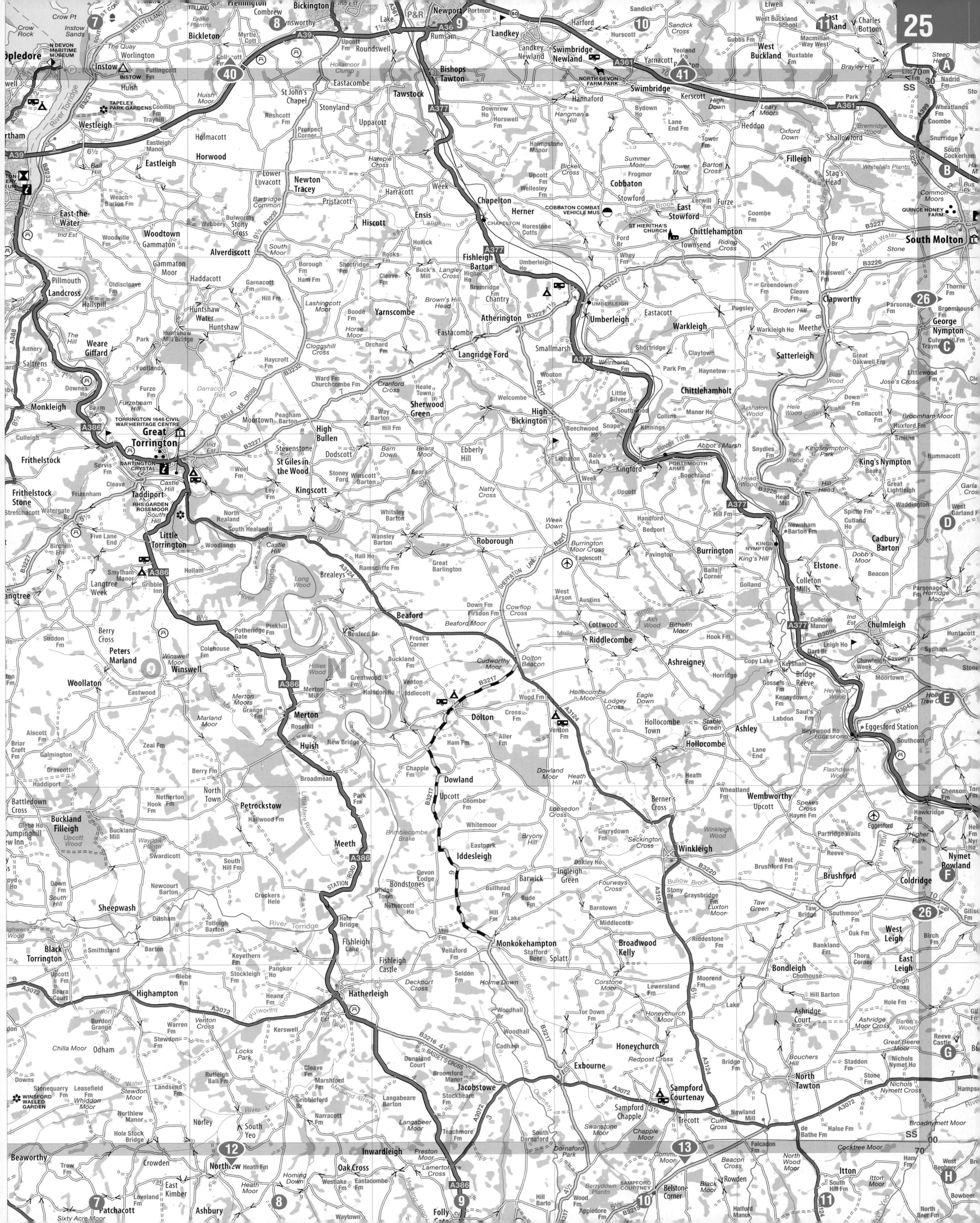

Appledore
Instow
Bickleton
Bickington
Newport
Landkey
Swimbridge Newland
Swimbridge
Harford
West Buckland
Westleigh
Horwood
Eastleigh
Bishops Tawton
Tawstock
Newton Tracey
Cobbaton
Filleigh
East-the-Water
Woodtown
Alverdiscott
Hiscott
Ensis
Chapelton
Herner
East Stowford
Chittlehampton
South Molton
Landcross
Fishleigh Barton
Umberleigh
Atherington
Yarnscombe
Warkleigh
Clapworthy
George Nympton
Weare Giffard
Langridge Ford
Satterleigh
Chittlehamholt
Monkleigh
Sherwood Green
High Bickington
High Bullen
Great Torrington
Frithelstock
St Giles in the Wood
Kingscott
Kingford
King's Nympton
Frithelstock Stone
Taddiport
Little Torrington
Roborough
Burrington
Cadbury Barton
Elstone
Langtree Week
Beaford
Cottwood
Riddlecombe
Chulmleigh
Peters Marland
Winswell
Woollaton
Ashreigney
Merton
Dolton
Ashley
Hollocombe
Huish
Dowland
Eggesford Station
Petrockstow
Buckland Filleigh
Wembworthy
Meeth
Iddesleigh
Winkleigh
Nymet Rowland
Brushford
Coldridge
Sheepwash
Black Torrington
Monkokehampton
Broadwood Kelly
West Leigh
East Leigh
Bondleigh
Highampton
Hatherleigh
Honeychurch
Exbourne
Jacobstowe
Sampford Courtenay
North Tawton
Inwardleigh
Oak Cross
Northlew
Beaworthy
Patchacott
Ashbury
Itton
A39
A361
A377
A386
A3124
A3072
B3227
B3217
B3220
A
B
C
D
E
F
G
H

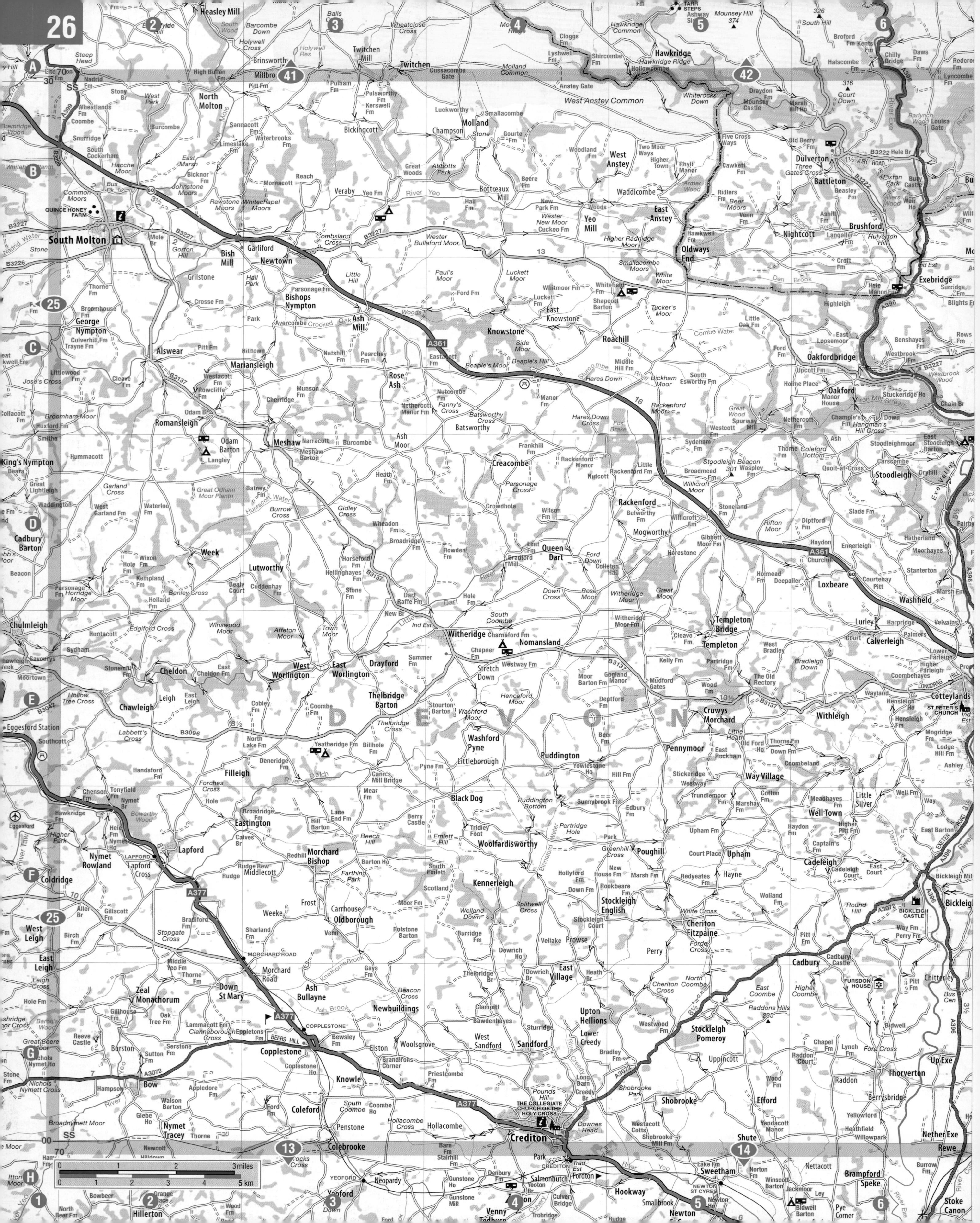
Heasley Mill
Tarr Steps
Mounsey Hill 374
Hawkridge Common
Hawkridge
Twitchen Mill
Twitchen
Molland Common
West Anstey Common
North Molton
Molland
Champson
Bickingcott
Dulverton
Battleton
Brushford
Nightcott
Exebridge
West Anstey
East Anstey
Yeo Mill
Oldways End
Waddicombe
South Molton
Quince Honey Farm
Bish Mill
Garliford
Newtown
Bishops Nympton
Ash Mill
George Nympton
Alswear
Mariansleigh
Knowstone
East Knowstone
Roachill
Rose Ash
Oakfordbridge
Oakford
Romansleigh
Meshaw
Ash Moor
Batsworthy
Creacombe
Rackenford
Stoodleigh
King's Nympton
Chulmleigh
Cadbury Barton
Week
Lutworthy
Queen Dart
Loxbeare
Washfield
Witheridge
Nomansland
Templeton Bridge
Templeton
Calverleigh
Cheldon
Chawleigh
West Worlington
East Worlington
Drayford
Thelbridge Barton
DEVON
Cruwys Morchard
Withleigh
Cotteylands
Eggesford Station
Washford Pyne
Puddington
Pennymoor
Filleigh
Way Village
Black Dog
Eastington
Lapford
Nymet Rowland
Morchard Bishop
Woolfardisworthy
Poughill
Upham
Cadeleigh
Coldridge
Kennerleigh
Stockleigh English
West Leigh
Oldborough
Cheriton Fitzpaine
Bickleigh
East Leigh
Morchard Road
Cadbury
Zeal Monachorum
Down St Mary
Ash Bullayne
Newbuildings
East Village
Upton Hellions
Copplestone
Bow
Knowle
Sandford
Stockleigh Pomeroy
Thorverton
Coleford
Nymet Tracey
Crediton
Shobrooke
Efford
Colebrooke
Shute
Nether Exe
Rewe
Sweetham
Brampford Speke
Hookway
Yeoford
Hillerton
Newton St Cyres
Stoke Canon
A361
A377
A396
A3072
B3227
B3137
3 miles
5 km

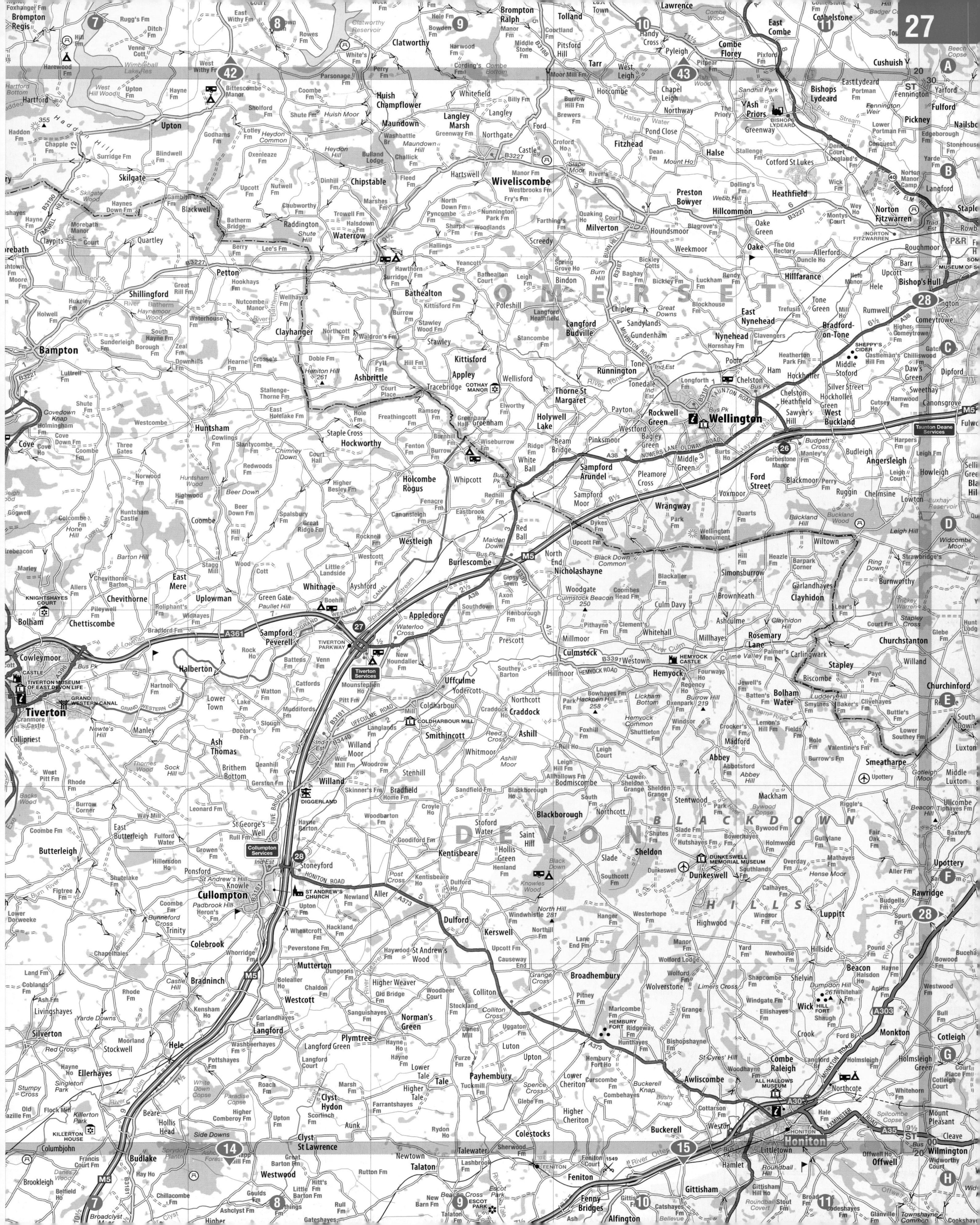
SOMERSET
DEVON
BLACKDOWN
HILLS
Brompton Regis
Clatworthy
Brompton Ralph
Tolland
Lawrence
East Combe
Cothelstone
Handy Cross
Pyleigh
Combe Florey
Cushuish
Bishops Lydeard
Ash Priors
West Leigh
Tarr
Pitsford Hill
Huish Champflower
Maundown
Langley Marsh
Langley
Northgate
Whitefield
Upton
Hartford
Skilgate
Chipstable
Wiveliscombe
Fitzhead
Halse
Pond Close
Cotford St Lukes
Pickney
Heathfield
Preston Bowyer
Hillcommon
Norton Fitzwarren
Milverton
Oake
Waterrow
Raddington
Petton
Shillingford
Bathealton
Hillfarance
Bishop's Hull
Clayhanger
Langford Budville
East Nynehead
Nynehead
Bradford-on-Tone
Bampton
Ashbrittle
Kittisford
Appley
Runnington
Thorne St Margaret
Holywell Lake
Rockwell Green
Wellington
West Buckland
Huntsham
Hockworthy
Greenham
Sampford Arundel
Wrangway
Ford Street
Angersleigh
Cove
Holcombe Rogus
Whipcott
Westleigh
Burlescombe
Nicholashayne
Wellington Monument
East Mere
Uplowman
Chevithorne
Whitnage
Appledore
Clayhidon
Bolham
Chettiscombe
Sampford Peverell
Culmstock
Hemyock
Churchstanton
Stapley
Cowleymoor
Halberton
Tiverton
Uffculme
Craddock
Ashill
Smithincott
Bolham Water
Churchinford
Ash Thomas
Manley
Willand
Abbey
Smeatharpe
Butterleigh
Kentisbeare
Blackborough
Sheldon
Dunkeswell
Upottery
Cullompton
Dulford
Kerswell
Luppitt
Rawridge
Colebrook
Bradninch
Mutterton
Westcott
Broadhembury
Wolverstone
Beacon
Wick
Silverton
Hele
Langford
Plymtree
Norman's Green
Monkton
Cotleigh
Ellerhayes
Payhembury
Awliscombe
Combe Raleigh
Tale
Clyst Hydon
Colestocks
Buckerell
Honiton
Wilmington
Offwell
Clyst St Lawrence
Talaton
Feniton
Gittisham
Budlake
Westwood
Fenny Bridges
Alfington
Columbjohn
M5
A38
A361
A373
A30
A35
A303
B3227
B3187
B3391
B3181
B3440
B3190
B3221
B3339
Taunton Deane Services
Tiverton Services
Cullompton Services
TIVERTON PARKWAY
KNIGHTSHAYES COURT
COTHAY MANOR
HEMYOCK CASTLE
COLDHARBOUR MILL
DIGGERLAND
ST ANDREW'S CHURCH
DUNKESWELL MEMORIAL MUSEUM
ALL HALLOWS MUSEUM
HEMBURY FORT
KILLERTON HOUSE
ESCOT PARK
SHEPPY'S CIDER
GRAND WESTERN CANAL
TIVERTON MUSEUM OF EAST DEVON LIFE
A
B
C
D
E
F
G
H
7
8
9
10
11
14
15
26
27
28
42
43

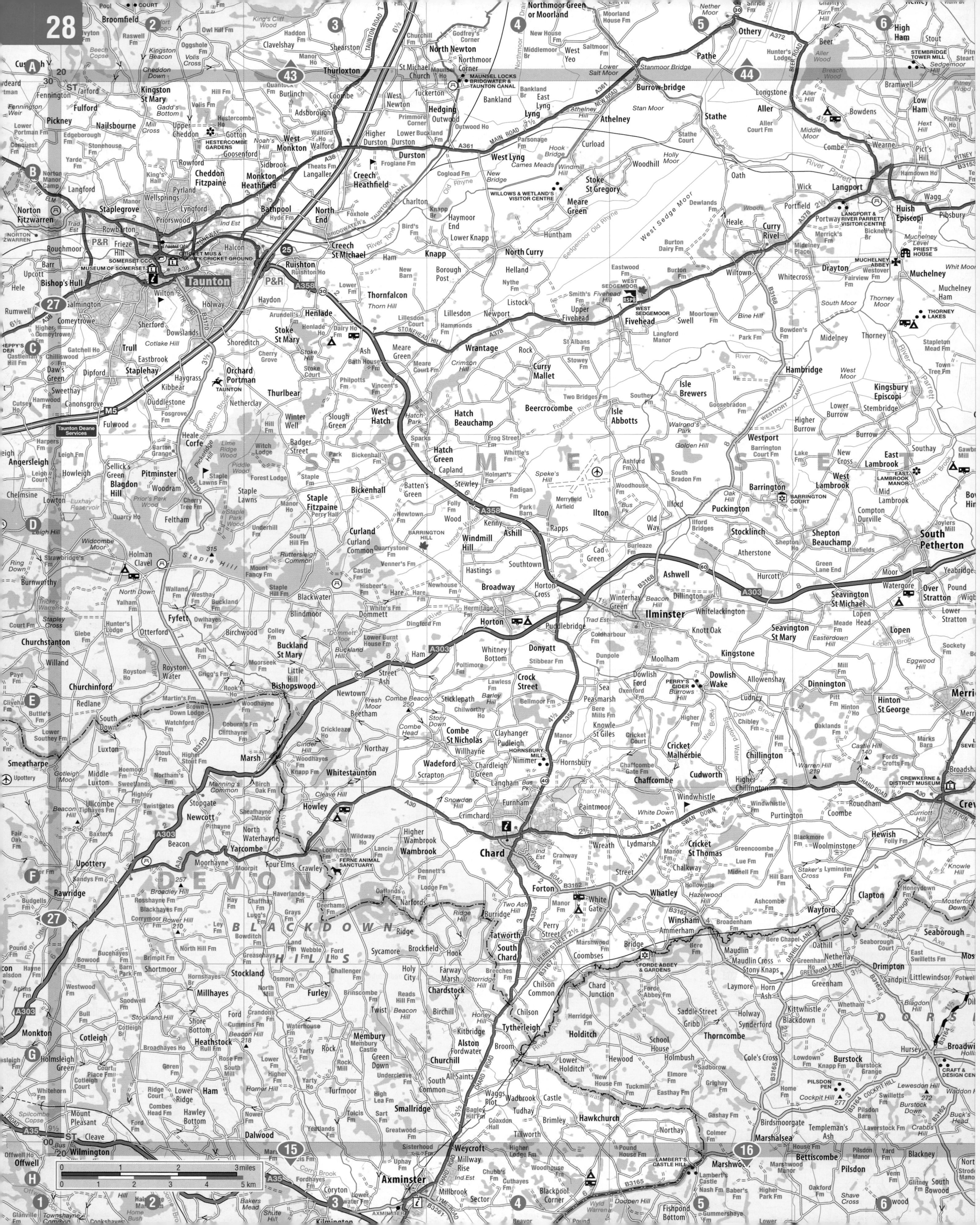

Taunton
Bishop's Hull
Norton Fitzwarren
Staplegrove
Kingston St Mary
Cheddon Fitzpaine
Monkton Heathfield
Bathpool
Creech St Michael
Creech Heathfield
North Newton
Thurloxton
St Michael Church
North Petherton
Durston
West Monkton
Hedging
Lyng
East Lyng
West Lyng
Athelney
Burrow-bridge
Othery
Pathe
Stathe
Aller
Langport
Huish Episcopi
Curry Rivel
Stoke St Gregory
Meare Green
North Curry
Knapp
Ruishton
Henlade
Thornfalcon
Stoke St Mary
Orchard Portman
Staplehay
Trull
Sherford
Wilton
Holway
Dowslands
Shoreditch
Thurlbear
West Hatch
Hatch Beauchamp
Hatch Green
Capland
Curry Mallet
Wrantage
Beercrocombe
Isle Brewers
Isle Abbotts
Fivehead
Upper Fivehead
Swell
Drayton
Muchelney
Kingsbury Episcopi
East Lambrook
West Lambrook
Barrington
Puckington
Westport
Hambridge
Ilton
Ashill
Kenny
Windmill Hill
Broadway
Horton
Ilminster
Dillington
Ashwell
Whitelackington
Donyatt
Puddlebridge
Shepton Beauchamp
South Petherton
Seavington St Michael
Seavington St Mary
Lopen
Over Stratton
Dinnington
Hinton St George
Kingstone
Dowlish Wake
Cricket Malherbie
Chillington
Cudworth
Chaffcombe
Knowle St Giles
Crock Street
Buckland St Mary
Bishopswood
Street Ash
Combe St Nicholas
Wadeford
Chard
Crimchard
Furnham
Whitestaunton
Howley
Wambrook
Cricket St Thomas
Winsham
Whatley
Forton
Tatworth
South Chard
Chardstock
Wayford
Clapton
Seaborough
Drimpton
Broadwindsor
Burstock
Pilsdon
Marshwood
Hawkchurch
Thorncombe
Holditch
Axminster
Membury
Stockland
Dalwood
Upottery
Yarcombe
Churchinford
Churchstanton
Pitminster
Blagdon Hill
Angersleigh
Staple Fitzpaine
Bickenhall
Curland
Smeatharpe
Rawridge
Monkton
Cotleigh
Wilmington
Offwell
Crewkerne
SOMERSET
DEVON
DORSET
BLACKDOWN HILLS
M5
A303
A358
A30
A38
A361
A372
A378
A35
0 1 2 3 miles
0 1 2 3 4 5 km

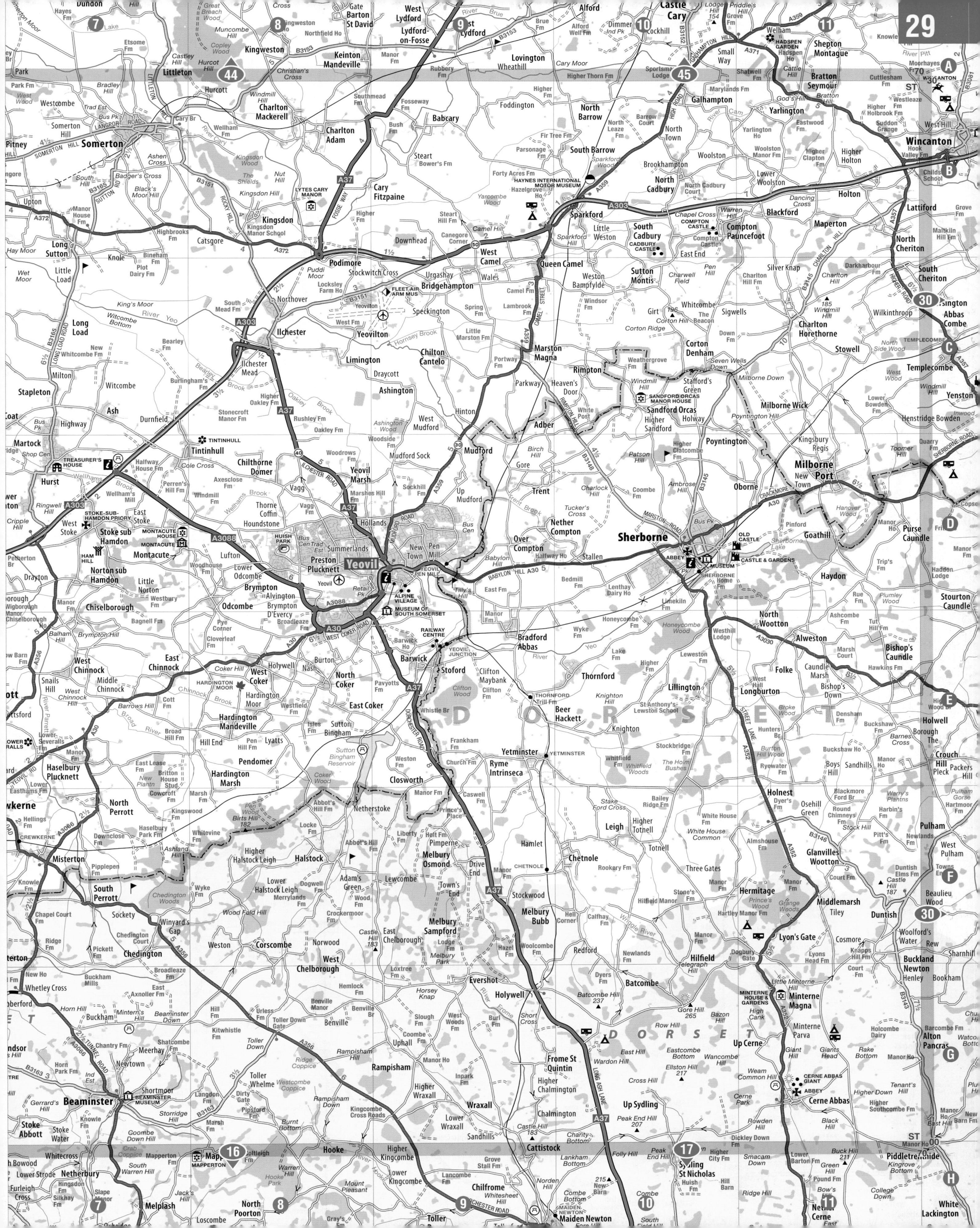
Somerton
Littleton
Kingweston
Keinton Mandeville
Lydford-on-Fosse
Castle Cary
Alford
Shepton Montague
Bratton Seymour
Wincanton
Charlton Mackerell
Charlton Adam
Babcary
North Barrow
South Barrow
Galhampton
Yarlington
Kingsdon
Cary Fitzpaine
Sparkford
North Cadbury
South Cadbury
Compton Pauncefoot
Blackford
Holton
Maperton
North Cheriton
South Cheriton
Long Sutton
Podimore
West Camel
Queen Camel
Bridgehampton
Yeovilton
Ilchester
Limington
Marston Magna
Rimpton
Corton Denham
Charlton Horethorne
Stowell
Templecombe
Ashington
Sandford Orcas
Milborne Wick
Milborne Port
Martock
Tintinhull
Chilthorne Domer
Yeovil Marsh
Mudford
Adber
Trent
Poyntington
Oborne
Stoke sub Hamdon
Montacute
Norton sub Hamdon
Preston Plucknett
Yeovil
Brympton
Odcombe
Nether Compton
Over Compton
Sherborne
Goathill
Purse Caundle
Haydon
Stourton Caundle
West Chinnock
East Chinnock
West Coker
North Coker
East Coker
Barwick
Stoford
Bradford Abbas
Thornford
Lillington
Longburton
Folke
Alweston
North Wootton
Bishop's Caundle
Hardington Mandeville
Haselbury Plucknett
Pendomer
Closworth
Yetminster
Ryme Intrinseca
Beer Hackett
Holwell
Crewkerne
Misterton
North Perrott
South Perrott
Halstock
Melbury Osmond
Leigh
Chetnole
Holnest
Glanvilles Wootton
Hermitage
Pulham
Chedington
Corscombe
Melbury Sampford
Melbury Bubb
Hilfield
Batcombe
Minterne Magna
Buckland Newton
Evershot
Holywell
Frome St Quintin
Up Cerne
Cerne Abbas
Alton Pancras
Beaminster
Rampisham
Wraxall
Up Sydling
Cattistock
Hooke
Netherbury
Sydling St Nicholas
Chilfrome
Maiden Newton
Piddletrenthide
Toller
DORSET

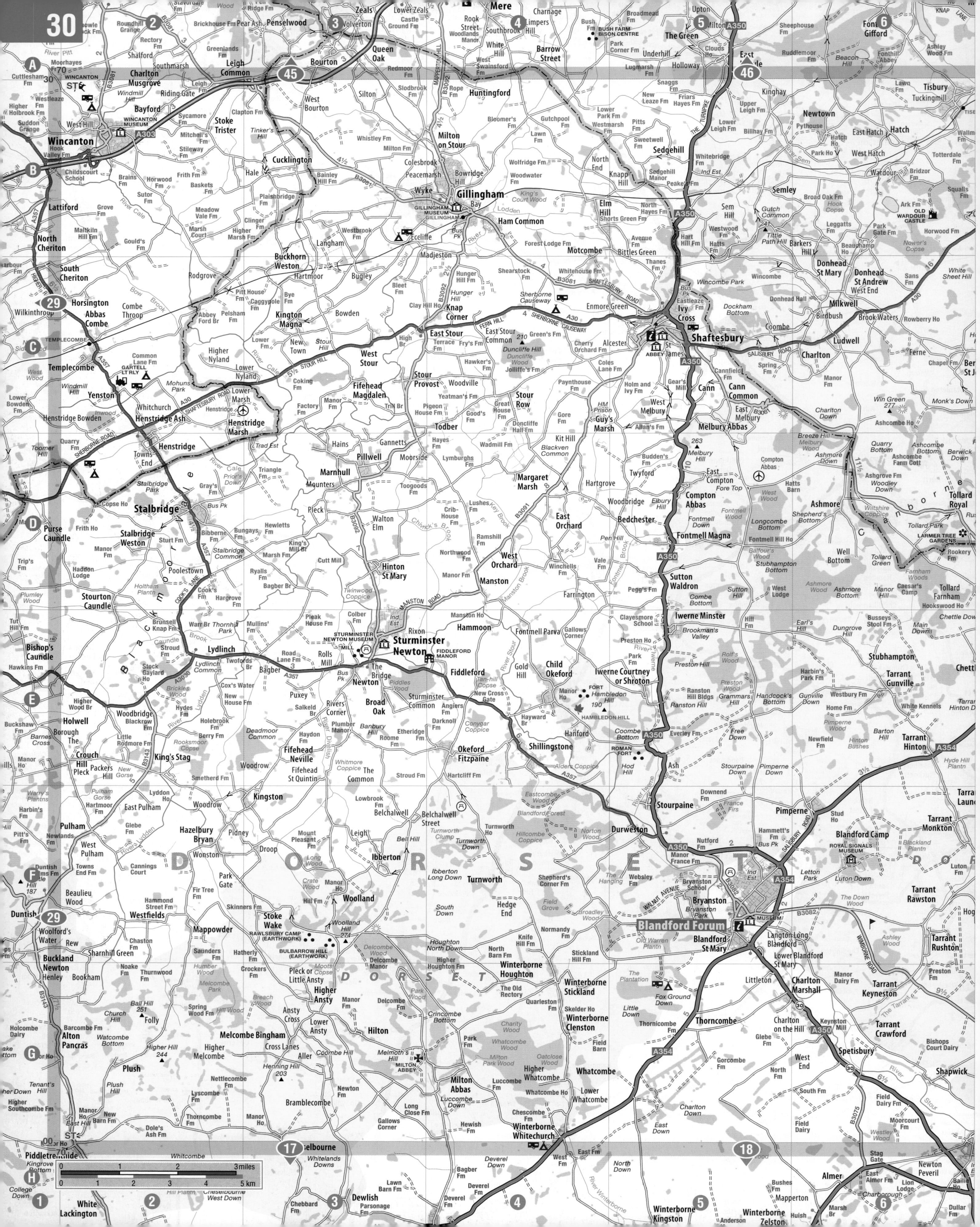
Zeals
Mere
Penselwood
Wolverton
Queen Oak
Bourton
West Bourton
Charlton Musgrove
Leigh Common
Bayford
Stoke Trister
Wincanton
WINCANTON MUSEUM
Cucklington
Milton on Stour
Gillingham
GILLINGHAM MUSEUM
Huntingford
Barrow Street
The Green
Holloway
Upton
Font Gifford
Tisbury
Tuckingmill
Newtown
Sedgehill
Semley
Hatch
East Hatch
West Hatch
Wardour
OLD WARDOUR CASTLE
Donhead St Mary
Donhead St Andrew
Milkwell
Birdbush
Ludwell
Charlton
Shaftesbury
ABBEY
St James
Cann
Cann Common
Melbury Abbas
Compton Abbas
Ashmore
Tollard Royal
LARMER TREE GARDENS
Fontmell Magna
Sutton Waldron
Iwerne Minster
Iwerne Courtney or Shroton
Stubhampton
Tarrant Gunville
Tarrant Hinton
Pimperne
Tarrant Monkton
Blandford Camp
ROYAL SIGNALS MUSEUM
Tarrant Rawston
Tarrant Rushton
Blandford Forum
Blandford St Mary
Langton Long Blandford
Lower Blandford St Mary
Charlton Marshall
Tarrant Keyneston
Tarrant Crawford
Spetisbury
Shapwick
Bryanston
Durweston
Stourpaine
Shillingstone
Hanford
Child Okeford
FORT HAMBLEDON HILL
HAMBLEDON HILL
Okeford Fitzpaine
Fiddleford
FIDDLEFORD MANOR
Sturminster Newton
STURMINSTER NEWTON MUSEUM
Hinton St Mary
Manston
West Orchard
East Orchard
Margaret Marsh
Todber
Stour Provost
East Stour
West Stour
Kington Magna
Buckhorn Weston
Motcombe
Enmore Green
Ham Common
Madjeston
Templecombe
GARTELL LT RLY
Henstridge
Henstridge Ash
Henstridge Marsh
Horsington
Abbas Combe
North Cheriton
South Cheriton
Lattiford
Stalbridge
Stalbridge Weston
Purse Caundle
Stourton Caundle
Bishop's Caundle
Lydlinch
Marnhull
Pillwell
Holwell
King's Stag
Fifehead Neville
Hazelbury Bryan
Kingston
Mappowder
Stoke Wake
RAWLSBURY CAMP (EARTHWORK)
BULBARROW HILL (EARTHWORK)
Woolland
Ibberton
Belchalwell
Turnworth
Winterborne Houghton
Winterborne Stickland
Winterborne Clenston
Whatcombe
Milton Abbas
MILTON ABBEY
Hilton
Higher Ansty
Melcombe Bingham
Buckland Newton
Alton Pancras
Plush
Winterborne Whitechurch
Winterborne Kingston
Winterborne Zelston
Almer
Dewlish
Thorncombe
D O R S E T
Cranborne Chase
A303
A30
A350
A357
A3030
A354
B3081
B3092
B3091
B3143
B3082
0 1 2 3 miles
0 1 2 3 4 5 km

Portash
Teffont Evias
Dinton
Baverstock
Barford St Martin
Ditchampton
Wilton
Fugglestone St Peter
Stratford Sub Castle
New Sarum
Quidhampton
Bemerton
Netherhampton
Laverstock
Salisbury
Milford
Chicksgrove
Compton Chamberlayne
Burcombe
Bulbridge
Harnham
West Harnham
East Harnham
Britford
Upper Chicksgrove
Fovant
Sutton Mandeville
Swallowcliffe
Ansty
Broad Chalke
Bishopstone
Stratford Tony
Coombe Bissett
Homington
Odstock
Nunton
Bodenham
Alderbury
Whaddon
West Grimstead
Fifield Bavant
Mount Sorrel
Stoke Farthing
Croucheston
West End
Ebbesbourne Wake
Alvediston
Bowerchalke
Woodminton
Charlton-All-Saints
Downton
WILTSHIRE
CRANBOURNE CHASE AND
WEST WILTSHIRE DOWNS
HAMPSHIRE
DORSET
Martin Drove End
Cobley
Martin
East Martin
Tidpit
Woodyates
New Town
Deanland
Pentridge
Woodcutts
Sixpenny Handley
Dean
Farnham
Wick
Morgan's Vale
Redlynch
Woodfalls
Lover
North Charford
Hale
Whitsbury
Rockbourne
Upper Street
Breamore
Woodgreen
Outwick
Flood Street
Damerham
North End
South End
Sandleheath
Fordingbridge
Ashford
Godshill
Burgate
Lower Burgate
Boveridge
Cranborne
Monkton Up Wimborne
Cashmoor
Gussage St Andrew
Lower Daggons
Alderholt
Cripplestyle
Daggons
Charing Cross
Bickton
Stuckton
Frogham
Hyde
Hungerford
North Gorley
South Gorley
Ibsley
Mockbeggar
Linwood
Gussage St Michael
Gussage All Saints
Wimborne St Giles
Edmondsham
Long Crichel
Knowlton
Sutton Holms
Romford
Verwood
Whitmore
Woodlands
Dewlands Common
Woodlands Common
Moor Crichel
Manswood
Witchampton
Chalbury
Horton
Chalbury Common
Wigbeth
Hinton Martell
Gaunt's Common
Holt Wood
Mannington
Three Legged Cross
Ebblake
Blashford
Ringwood
Poulner
Linford
Picket Post
Ashley Heath
Ashley
St Ives
St Leonards
Moortown
Crow
Burley Street
Burley
Holt
Stanbridge
Clapgate
Hinton Parva
Broom Hill
Holt Heath
West Moors
Ameysford
Pilford
Colehill
Stapehill
Canford Bottom
Ferndown
Trickett's Cross
Kingston
Bisterne
Wimborne Minster
Leigh
Hillbutts
Pamphill
Sturminster Marshall
Little Canford
Hampreston
Longham
Oakley
Merley
West Parley
East Parley
Dudsbury
Avon
Ripley
Sopley
Thorney Hill
Bransgore
BOURNEMOUTH AIRPORT
A30
A354
A338
A36
A31
A348
B3078
B3081
B3072
B3073
B3347
B3080
SU
7
8
9
10
11
46
47
32
18
19
A
B
C
D
E
F
G
H

Pitton
West Winterslow
Sparsholt
Somborne
King's Somborne
Ashley
Horsebridge
Bossington
Broughton Hill
Pitton Lodge
47
48
SU
Farley
West Tytherley
Stony Batter
East Tytherley
The Green
Farley Mount
Compton Manor
Compton Brook
Lower Brook
Furzedown
Ashley Down
Mount Down
Crabwood Farm Ho
East Grimstead
Frenchmoor
Lockerley Hall
Spearywell
Oakley Fm
Mottisfont Abbey
Mottisfont
Dunbridge
Hatt Hill
West Dean
East Dean
Lockerley
Clarendon Ho
Alderbury
Whaddon
West Grimstead
Butt's Green
Critchell's Green
Deanhill Barn
Pepperbox Hill
Kimbridge
Stonymarsh
Michelmersh
Braishfield
Pucknall
Hursley
Standon
Upper Slackstead
Lower Slackstead
Hall Place
Timsbury
Awbridge
Carter's Clay
Newtown
Kent's Oak
Upper Ratley
Lower Ratley
Whiteparish
Newton
Cowesfield Green
Brickworth Ho
Witherington Down
Hillier Gardens
Jermyns Ho
Abbotswood
Belbins
Ampfield
Knapp
Ratlake
Ladwell
Hocombe
Gosport
Broadgate
Hiltingbury
Cranbury Park
31
Barford Down Fm
Templeman Fm
Morgan's Vale
Redlynch
Lover
Woodfalls
North Charford
Hale
Bohemia
Newhouse
Earldoms Lodge
Langley Wood
Hamptworth Lodge
Hamptworth
Plaitford Green
Plaitford
Landford
Landford Manor
Landfordwood
Sherfield English
Wellow Wood
Woodington
East Wellow
West Wellow
Embley Park
Romsey
Romsey Abbey
Broadlands
Cupernham
Halterworth
Whitenap
Woodley
Crampmoor
North Baddesley
Flexford
Chandler's Ford
Valley Park
Fryern Hill
Eastleigh
Ashfield
Toothill
Rownhams Services
Chilworth
Chilworth Old Village
Rownhams
North Stoneham
Nomansland
Lyburn Ho
Pound Bottom
Hope Cottage
Canada
Canada Common
Wigley
Paultons Park
Ower
Ridge
Lee
Upton
Nursling
Bassett
Bassett Green
Swaythling
Lordswood
Coxford
Shirley Warren
Hampton Park
Highfield
Bitterne Park
Portswood
St Denys
Bramshaw
Furzley
Half Moon Common
Hillstreet
Stonyford
Newbridge
Copythorne
Cadnam
Winsor
Calmore
Testwood
Totton
Netley Marsh
Rushington
Eling
Redbridge
Millbrook
Maybush
Wimpson
Shirley
Upper Shirley
Freemantle
Southampton
Northam
Itchen
Woolston
Ocean Village
Town Quay
Fritham
Brook
Brook Hill
Wittensford
Bartley
Bartley Manor
Great Fletchwood
Ashurst Bridge
Woodlands
Foxhills
Hounsdown
Ashurst
Pooksgreen
Marchwood
Longdown Farm
Deerleap
Linwood
Broomy Lodge
Stoney Cross
Minstead
London Minstead
Newtown
Upper Canterton
Rufus Stone
Furzey Gardens
Acres Down Ho
Manor Park
Pikeshill
Emery Down
New Forest Centre
Lyndhurst
Goose Green
Clayhill
Custards
Bank
Fox Hill
Ashurst Lodge
New Forest Otter, Owl & Wildlife Park
Staplewood
Hythe
Dibden
Applemore
Langdown
Dibden Purlieu
Frostlane
Buttsash
The New Forest
National Park
Picket Post
Burley Lodge
Burley Street
Burley Lawn
Burley
Bisterne Close
Burley Beacon
Knightwood Oak
New Forest Reptiliary Centre
Denny Lodge
Park Hill
Black Down
Beaulieu Heath
Hardley
Holbury
Hill Top
Beaulieu
Hatchet Gate
Furzey Lodge
National Motor Museum
Beaulieu Abbey & Palace Ho
Otterwood
Rhinefield Ho
Brockenhurst
Balmerlawn
Brockenhurst Park
Ladycross Lodge
Round Hill
New Forest & Hants Showground
Great Huntley Bank
Naked Man
North Weirs
South Weirs
Setley
Roydon Manor
Dilton Gardens
East Boldre
Bucklers Hard
Maritime Museum
Exbury
Exbury Gardens
West Common
Sway
Durns Town
Battramsley
Boldre
Pilley
Pilley Bailey
Bull Hill
Wootton
Bransgore
Bashley
Tiptoe
Norleywood
19
20
0 1 2 3 miles
0 1 2 3 4 5 km

Winchester
Winnall
St Giles's Hill
Harestock
Weeke
Hyde
Chilcomb
Easton
Avington
Ovington
New Alresford
Bishop's Sutton
Ropley
Ropley Dean
Charlwood
Monkwood
Tichborne
Cheriton
New Cheriton
North End
Bramdean
West Tisted
Hinton Ampner
Beauworth
Kilmeston
Brockwood
Privett
Froxfield Green
Langrish
Ramsdean
West Meon
East End
Warnford
Exton
East Meon
Coombe
Corhampton
Meonstoke
Brockbridge
Droxford
Soberton
Chidden
Clanfield
Hambledon
Catherington
Horndean
Lovedean
Cowplain
Waterlooville
Havant
Purbrook
Bedhampton
Langstone
Drayton
Cosham
Farlington
Hilsea
Portsmouth
Southsea
Milton
Fratton
Eastney
Gosport
Alverstoke
Lee-on-the-Solent
Hill Head
Stubbington
Fareham
Portchester
Wallington
Wickham
Shedfield
Shirrell Heath
Waltham Chase
Bishop's Waltham
Upham
Lower Upham
Owslebury
Twyford
Shawford
Otterbourne
Colden Common
Fisher's Pond
Fair Oak
Bishopstoke
Horton Heath
West End
Hedge End
Botley
Curdridge
Burridge
Swanwick
Park Gate
Sarisbury
Locks Heath
Warsash
Titchfield
Bursledon
Hound
Netley
Hamble-le-Rice
Fawley
Calshot
Southwick
Boarhunt
North Boarhunt
Hundred Acres
Denmead
Anthill Common
Newtown
Hoe Gate
SOUTH DOWNS NATIONAL PARK
PORTSMOUTH
PORTSMOUTH HARBOUR
LANGSTONE HARBOUR
SOUTHAMPTON WATER
Hayling
M3
M27
M275
A3(M)
A31
A32
A272
A27
A334
B2177
B3035

Liphook
Petersfield
Midhurst
Havant
Emsworth
Southbourne
Chichester
Bognor Regis
WEST SUSSEX
SOUTH DOWNS NATIONAL PARK
CHICHESTER HARBOUR
LANGSTONE HARBOUR
Liss
West Liss
East Liss
Liss Forest
Longmoor Camp
Greatham
Empshott
Hawkley
Colemore
Langrish
Stroud
Steep
Sheet
Rogate
Rake
Hill Brow
Trotton
Iping
Stedham
Chithurst
Woolbeding
Easebourne
Fernhurst
Linchmere
Milland
Borden
Buriton
Nursted
South Harting
East Harting
Elsted
Treyford
Didling
Bepton
Cocking
Heyshott
Graffham
Selham
Lodsworth
Lickfold
Henley
Lurgashall
Upwaltham
Singleton
Charlton
West Dean
Chilgrove
East Dean
Compton
Up Marden
West Marden
East Marden
North Marden
Stoughton
Walderton
Forestside
Finchdean
Rowlands Castle
Horndean
Clanfield
Chalton
Catherington
Blendworth
Cowplain
Lovedean
Westbourne
Woodmancote
Funtington
West Stoke
East Ashling
West Ashling
Mid Lavant
East Lavant
Hermitage
Nutbourne
Bosham
Fishbourne
Apuldram
Donnington
Hunston
North Mundham
South Mundham
Runcton
Merston
Colworth
Shripney
North Bersted
South Bersted
Tangmere
Boxgrove
Westhampnett
Oving
Aldingbourne
Westergate
Woodgate
Halnaker
Eartham
West Thorney
West Itchenor
Birdham
Sidlesham
Nyetimber
Aldwick
West Wittering
Hayling Island
North Hayling
Northney
Langstone
Bedhampton
Warblington
Leigh Park
Stockheath
Hayling Bay
0 1 2 3 miles
0 1 2 3 4 5 km

Horsham
Billingshurst
Petworth
Pulborough
Storrington
Steyning
Henfield
Arundel
Littlehampton
Worthing
Lancing
Rustington
Angmering
Ferring
Goring-by-Sea
Durrington
Salvington
High Salvington
Findon
Washington
Ashington
West Chiltington
Fittleworth
Amberley
Houghton
Slindon
Fontwell
Walberton
Barnham
Yapton
Middleton-on-Sea
Felpham
Climping
Ford
Lyminster
Wick
Toddington
East Preston
Kingston Gorse
Hangleton
Clapham
Patching
Sompting
Shoreham
Bramber
Upper Beeding
Botolphs
Coombes
Cowfold
West Grinstead
Partridge Green
Shipley
Coolham
Southwater
Itchingfield
Slinfold
Broadbridge Heath
Rudgwick
Loxwood
Plaistow
Ifold
Kirdford
Wisborough Green
Tillington
Duncton
Sutton
Bignor
Bury
Madehurst
Burpham
Wepham
Crossbush
Poling
Hammerpot
Coldwaltham
Hardham
Wiggonholt
Greatham
Rackham
Cootham
Sullington
Thakeham
Warminghurst
Abingworth
Spear Hill
Dial Post
Ashurst
Wiston
Nepcote
Cissbury Ring
Chanctonbury Ring
South Downs Way
River Arun
A24
A27
A272
A283
A29
A280
A259
TQ
7
8
9
10
11
A
B
C
D
E
F
G
H

Horsham
Balcombe
Handcross
Ardingly
Highbrook
Chelwood Gate
Ashfold Crossways
Mannings Heath
Staplefield
Slaugham
Lower Beeding
Monk's Gate
Nuthurst
Warninglid
Crabtree
Cuckfield
Lindfield
Haywards Heath
Horsted Keynes
Danehill
Nutley
Maplehurst
Bolney
Ansty
Cowfold
Crosspost
Scayne's Hill
Fletching
Newick
North Chailey
Chailey
Wivelsfield
Wivelsfield Green
Burgess Hill
Hickstead
Twineham
Wineham
Shermanbury
Partridge Green
Sayers Common
Hurstpierpoint
Keymer
Hassocks
Ditchling
Plumpton Green
Plumpton
Chiltington
East Chiltington
Streat
South Street
Barcombe
Barcombe Cross
Cooksbridge
Hamsey
Offham
Henfield
West End
Small Dole
Upper Beeding
Bramber
Woodmancote
Albourne
Clayton
Pyecombe
Poynings
Fulking
Edburton
Saddlescombe
Westmeston
Lewes
South Malling
Wallands Park
Kingston near Lewes
Falmer
Stanmer
Patcham
Hollingbury
Coldean
Withdean
Westdene
Preston
Moulsecoomb
Bevendean
Woodingdean
BRIGHTON AND HOVE
Mile Oak
Portslade
Southwick
Shoreham-by-Sea
Kingston by Sea
Hove
Brighton
Kemp Town
Rottingdean
Ovingdean
Saltdean
Peacehaven
Telscombe
Telscombe Cliffs
Piddinghoe
Newhaven
Iford
Rodmell
Southease
Beddingham
Tarring Neville
South Lancing
Botolphs
Old Shoreham
Brighton Marina
SOUTH DOWNS WAY
A23
A27
A272
A275
A26
A259
A281
A283
A2300
A273
51
52
35
TQ
20
00
0 1 2 3 miles
0 1 2 3 4 5 km

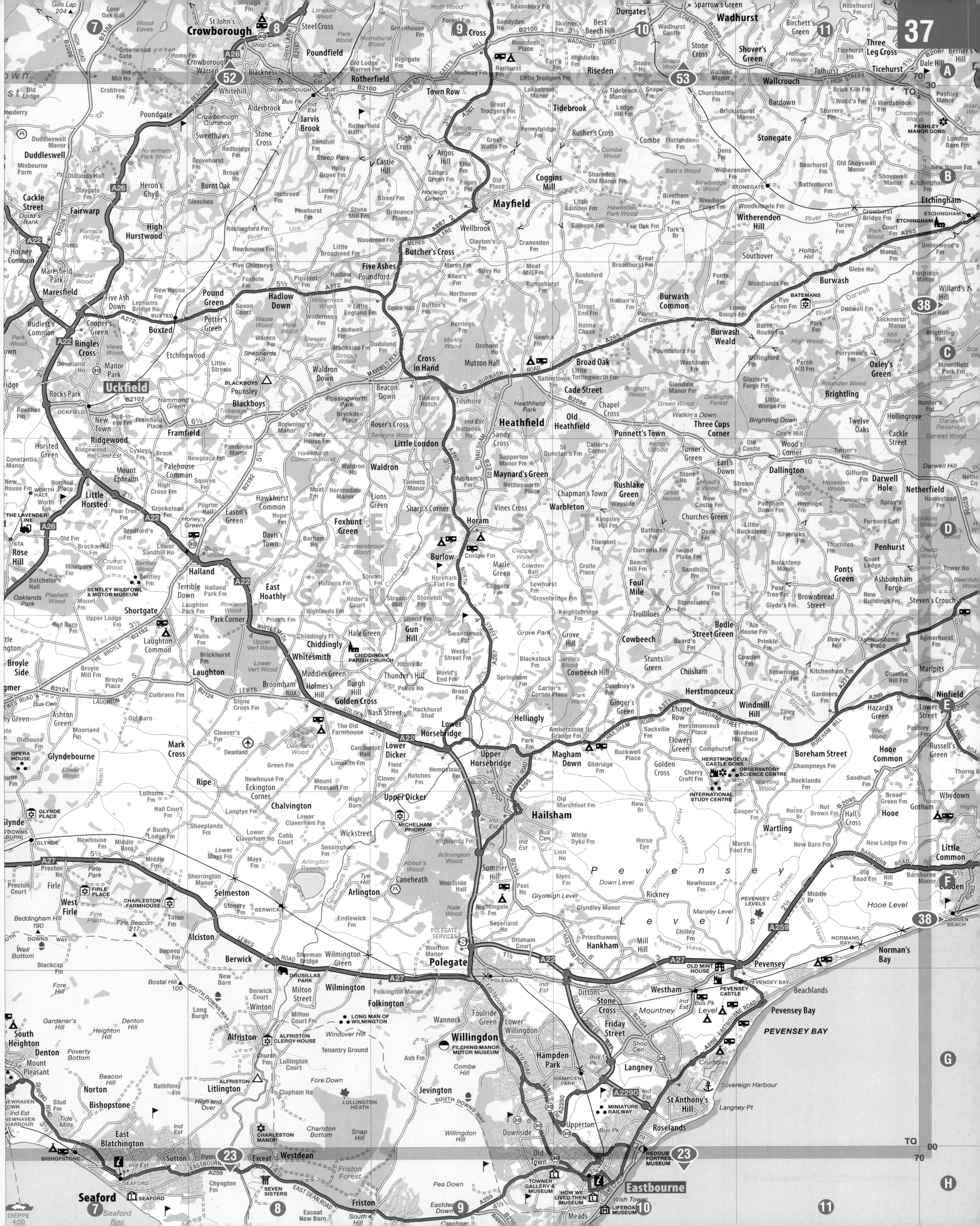
Crowborough
Rotherfield
Wadhurst
Ticehurst
Wallcrouch
Town Row
Mayfield
Stonegate
Etchingham
Burwash
Burwash Weald
Burwash Common
Five Ashes
Hadlow Down
Buxted
Maresfield
Uckfield
Framfield
Blackboys
Cross in Hand
Heathfield
Broad Oak
Punnett's Town
Three Cups Corner
Brightling
Dallington
Netherfield
Horam
Waldron
Little London
Halland
East Hoathly
Chiddingly
Gun Hill
Laughton
Herstmonceux
Windmill Hill
Ninfield
Hailsham
Hellingly
Magham Down
Hooe
Wartling
Pevensey
Norman's Bay
Pevensey Bay
Westham
Stone Cross
Polegate
Willingdon
Hampden Park
Langney
Eastbourne
Jevington
Friston
Westdean
Exceat
Alfriston
Litlington
Wilmington
Berwick
Selmeston
Alciston
Ripe
Chalvington
Glyndebourne
Glynde
Firle
West Firle
Seaford
East Blatchington
Bishopstone
Norton
South Heighton
Denton
Sutton
Pevensey Levels
EAST SUSSEX
PEVENSEY BAY
38
52
53
23
TQ

Hawkhurst
Flimwell
Gill's Green
Iden Green
Dingleden
Rolvenden
Rolvenden Layne
C M BOOTH COLLECTION OF HISTORIC VEHICLES
Small Hythe
SMALLHYTHE PLACE
Reading Street
Four Throws
The Moor
Horns Corner
Swiftsden
Sandhurst
Linkhill
Lamberden
Newenden
Peening Quarter
Isle of Oxney
Wittersham
The Stocks
Stone
KENT & EAST SUSSEX RAILWAY
Hurst Green
Etchingham
Burgh Hill
PASHLEY MANOR GDNS
Sandhurst Cross
Bodiam
BODIAM CASTLE
Northiam
GREAT DIXTER
BRICKWALL HOUSE
Rother Levels
River Rother
Four Oaks
Beckley
Clayhill
Ewhurst Green
Salehurst
Northbridge Street
Robertsbridge
ROTHER VALLEY RLY CENTRE
Peasmarsh
Iden
Houghton Green
Playden
Rye Foreign
Rye
East Guldeford
Horns Cross
Staplecross
Mill Corner
John's Cross
Cripp's Corner
Swaile's Green
Chitcombe
Broad Oak
Beckley Furnace
Broadland Row
Udimore
Mountfield
Vinehall Street
EAST SUSSEX
Sedlescombe
Sedlescombe Street
Brede
Cackle Street
Cock Marling
Rye Harbour
Camber Castle
TREASURY OF MECHANICAL MUSIC
YPRES TOWER
HERITAGE CENTRE & TOWN MODEL
Netherfield
Darwell Hole
Canada
Whatlington
Penhurst
Battle
BATTLE ABBEY
1066
Kent Street
Westfield
Brede Level
Winchelsea
WINCHELSEA COURT MUSEUM
Icklesham
Guestling Thorn
Winchelsea Beach
Pett Level
Telham
Starr's Green
Ninfield
Catsfield
Crowhurst
Three Oaks
Pett
Guestling Green
Baldslow
Hollington
St Helen's
Ore
Fairlight
Fairlight Cove
Cliff End
Silverhill
Bohemia
Blacklands
West Hill
ST CLEMENTS CAVE
SHIPWRECK HERITAGE CENTRE
UNDERWATER WORLD
Hastings
Old Town
St Leonards
West Marina
Bulverhythe
Glyne Gap
Pebsham
Sidley
Little Common
Cooden
Bexhill
DELAWARR PAVILION
Hooe
Hooe Common
Hooe Level
Norman's Bay
Lunsford's Cross
Henley's Down
A21
A28
A259
A268
A229
A271
A2100
37
53
54
0 1 2 3 miles
0 1 2 3 4 5 km

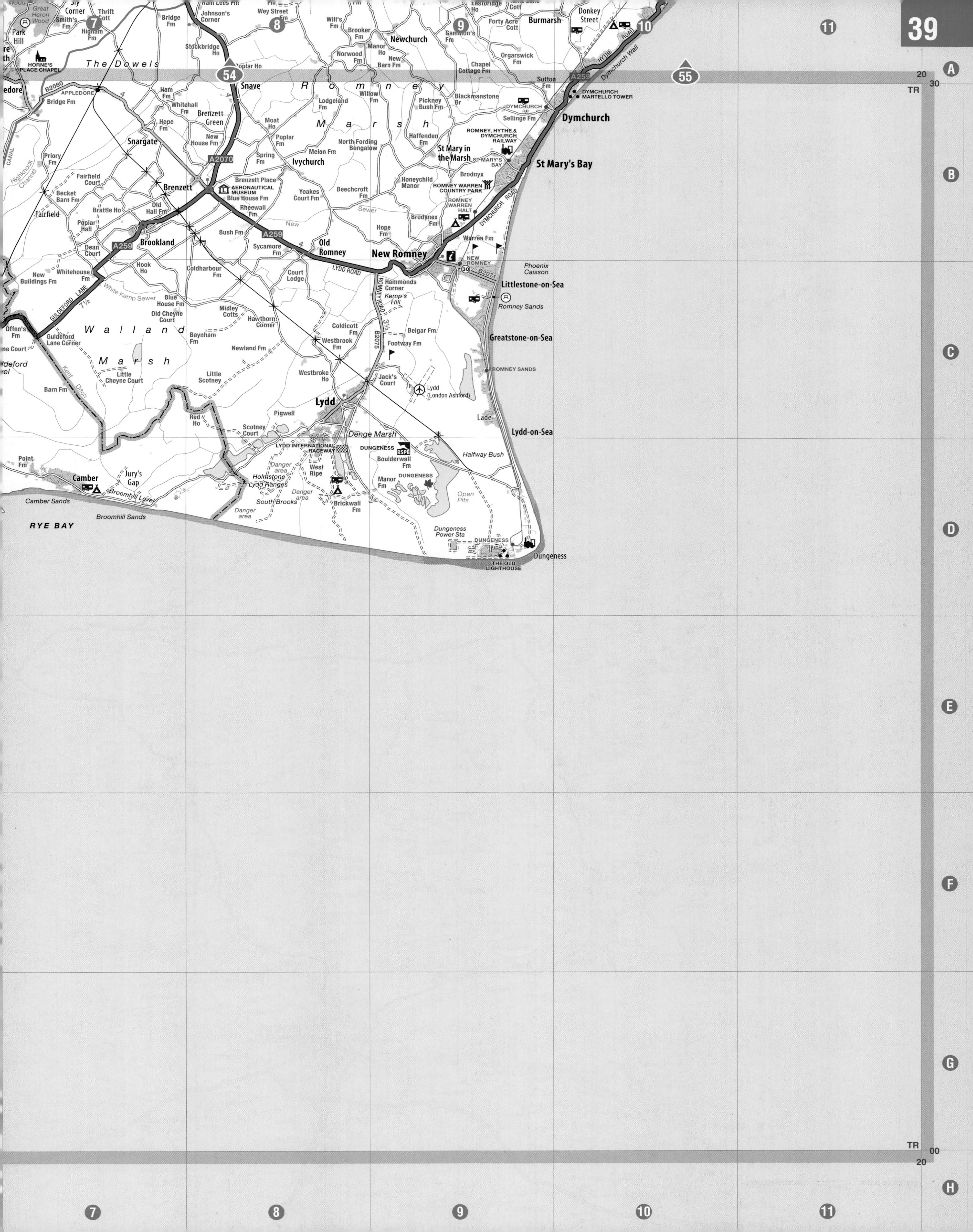
Park Hill
HORNE'S PLACE CHAPEL
Smith's Fm
Thrift Cott
Higham Fm
The Dowels
Bridge Fm
Johnson's Corner
Wey Street Fm
Stockbridge Ho
Poplar Ho
54
55
Will's Fm
Brooker Fm
Norwood Fm
Manor Ho
New Barn Fm
Newchurch
Gammon's Fm
Forty Acre Cott
Burmarsh
Donkey Street
Orgarswick Fm
Chapel Cottage Fm
HYTHE ROAD
Dymchurch Wall
A259
Sutton Fm
DYMCHURCH MARTELLO TOWER
Dymchurch
APPLEDORE
B2080
Bridge Fm
Ham Fm
Snave
Romney
Marsh
Willow Fm
Lodgeland Fm
Pickney Bush Fm
Blackmanstone Br
DYMCHURCH
Sellinge Fm
Whitehall Fm
Brenzett Green
Hope Fm
Moat Ho
New House Fm
Snargate
Poplar Fm
North Fording Bungalow
Haffenden Fm
ROMNEY, HYTHE & DYMCHURCH RAILWAY
St Mary in the Marsh
ST MARY'S BAY
St Mary's Bay
Priory Fm
CANAL
Highknock Channel
Spring Fm
Melon Fm
Ivychurch
A2070
Brodnyx
Honeychild Manor
ROMNEY WARREN COUNTRY PARK
Fairfield Court
Becket Barn Fm
Brenzett
Brenzett Place
AERONAUTICAL MUSEUM
Blue House Fm
Yoakes Court Fm
Beechcroft Fm
Fairfield
Brattle Ho
Old Hall Fm
Rheewall Fm
Sewer
New
ROMNEY WARREN HALT
Brodynex Fm
DYMCHURCH ROAD
Poplar Hall
Bush Fm
Hope Fm
Warren Fm
Dean Court
A259
Brookland
Sycamore Fm
Old Romney
New Romney
NEW ROMNEY
B2071
Phoenix Caisson
Whitehouse Fm
New Buildings Fm
Hook Ho
Coldharbour Fm
Court Lodge
LYDD ROAD
Hammonds Corner
Kemp's Hill
Littlestone-on-Sea
Romney Sands
GULDEFORD LANE
White Kemp Sewer
Blue House Fm
Old Cheyne Court
Midley Cotts
Hawthorn Corner
ROMNEY ROAD
Coldicott Fm
Belgar Fm
Offen's Fm
Walland
Marsh
Guldeford Lane Corner
Baynham Fm
Westbrook Fm
B2075
Footway Fm
Greatstone-on-Sea
Newland Fm
ROMNEY SANDS
Kent Ditch
Little Cheyne Court
Little Scotney
Westbroke Ho
Jack's Court
Lydd (London Ashford)
Barn Fm
Lydd
Pigwell
Red Ho
Lade
Scotney Court
Denge Marsh
Lydd-on-Sea
LYDD INTERNATIONAL RACEWAY
DUNGENESS
RSPB
Boulderwall Fm
Halfway Bush
Point Fm
Camber
Jury's Gap
Danger area
Holmstone
Lydd Ranges
West Ripe
Manor Fm
DUNGENESS
Broomhill Level
South Brooks
Brickwall Fm
Open Pits
Camber Sands
Broomhill Sands
RYE BAY
Danger area
Dungeness Power Sta
DUNGENESS
Dungeness
THE OLD LIGHTHOUSE
TR
20
30
00
A
B
C
D
E
F
G
H
7
8
9
10
11

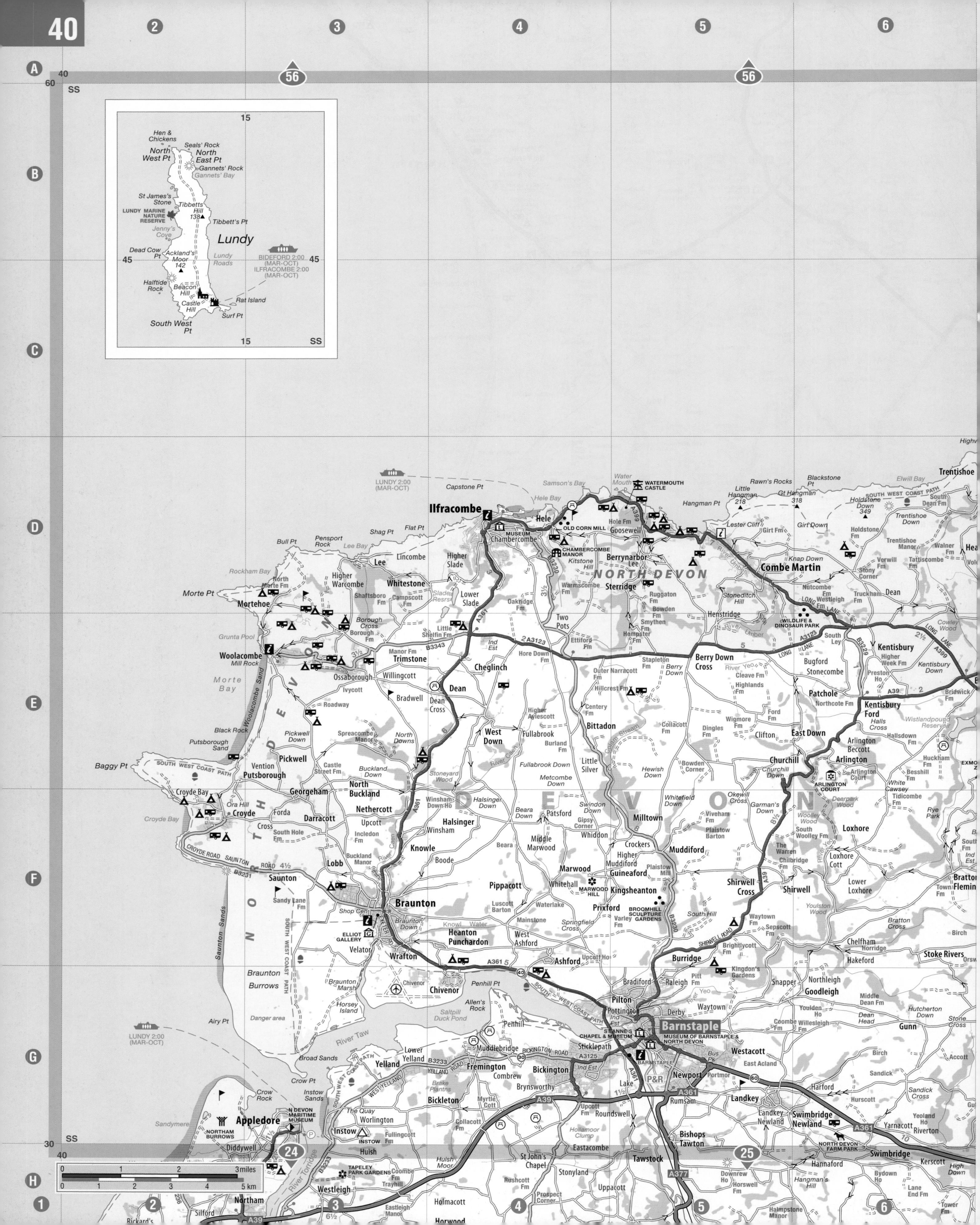

Lundy
North West Pt
North East Pt
Hen & Chickens
Seals' Rock
Gannets' Rock
Gannets' Bay
St James's Stone
Tibbetts Hill 138
Tibbett's Pt
LUNDY MARINE NATURE RESERVE
Jenny's Cove
Dead Cow Pt
Ackland's Moor 142
Lundy Roads
BIDEFORD 2:00 (MAR-OCT)
ILFRACOMBE 2:00 (MAR-OCT)
Halftide Rock
Beacon Hill
Castle Hill
Rat Island
Surf Pt
South West Pt
LUNDY 2:00 (MAR-OCT)
Capstone Pt
Ilfracombe
Hele
Samson's Bay
Water Mouth
WATERMOUTH CASTLE
OLD CORN MILL
Hole Fm
Goosewell
Chambercombe
CHAMBERCOMBE MANOR
Berrynarbor
Kitstone Hill
Little Hangman 218
Rawn's Rocks
Gt Hangman 318
Blackstone Pt
Hangman Pt
Lester Cliff
Combe Martin
Elwill Bay
Trentishoe
Holdstone Down 349
Trentishoe Down
Shag Pt
Flat Pt
Bull Pt
Pensport Rock
Lee Bay
Lee
Lincombe
Higher Slade
Lower Slade
Whitestone
Higher Warcombe
Rockham Bay
North Morte Fm
Morte Pt
Mortehoe
Shaftsboro Fm
Campscott Fm
Oakridge Fm
Warmscombe Fm
NORTH DEVON
Sterridge
Ruggaton Fm
Bowden Fm
Smythen Fm
Hempster Fm
Two Pots
Ettiford Fm
Stoneditch Hill
Henstridge
WILDLIFE & DINOSAUR PARK
LONG LANE
Kentisbury
Grunta Pool
Borough Cross
Borough Fm
Little Shelfin Fm
Woolacombe
Mill Rock
Manor Fm
Trimstone
Ind Est
Hore Down Fm
Berry Down Cross
Stapleton Fm
Berry Down
Outer Narracott
South Ley
Higher Week Fm
Kentisbury Down
Preston Ho
Bugford
Stonecombe
Morte Bay
Woolacombe Sand
Ossaborough
Willingcott
Ivycott
Bradwell
Dean Cross
Dean
Cheglinch
Hillcrest Fm
Cleave Fm
Highlands Fm
Patchole
Northcote Fm
Kentisbury Ford
Halls Cross
Bridwick
Roadway
Higher Aylescott
Centery Fm
Bittadon
Collacott Fm
Wigmore Fm
Ford Fm
Dingles Fm
Clifton
East Down
Wistlandpound Reservoir
Hallsdown Fm
Black Rock
Putsborough Sand
Pickwell Down
Spreacombe Manor
North Downs
West Down
Fullabrook
Burland Fm
Fullabrook Down
Little Silver
Hewish Down
Bowden Corner
Churchill
Churchill Down
Arlington Beccott
Arlington
Arlington Court
ARLINGTON COURT
Huckham Fm
Besshill Fm
White Cawsey
Baggy Pt
SOUTH WEST COAST PATH
Vention
Putsborough
Pickwell
Castle Street Fm
Buckland Down
Stoneyard Wood
Metcombe Down
Croyde Bay
Georgeham
North Buckland
Nethercott
Upcott
Ora Hill
Croyde
Forda
Darracott
Cross
South Hole Fm
Incledon Fm
Buckland Manor
Winsham Down Ho
Halsinger Down
Halsinger
Winsham
Beara Down
Patsford
Swindon Down
Gipsy Corner
Whiddon
Milltown
Whitefield Down
Okewill Cross
Viveham Fm
Plaistow Barton
Garman's Down
Deerpark Wood
Tidicombe Fm
Rye Park
Loxhore
Woolley Wood
South Woolley Fm
DEVON
CROYDE ROAD
SAUNTON ROAD
Lobb
Saunton
Knowle
Boode
Beara
Middle Marwood
Crockers
Higher Muddiford
Muddiford
The Warren
Chilbridge Fm
Loxhore Cott
Lower Loxhore
Marwood
Guineaford
Plaistow Mill
Shirwell Cross
Shirwell
Sandy Lane Fm
Braunton
Pippacott
Whitehall
MARWOOD HILL
Kingsheanton
BROOMHILL SCULPTURE GARDENS
Prixford
Varley Fm
Luscott Barton
Waterlake
Shop Cen
ELLIOT GALLERY
Braunton Down
Knowl Water
Mainstone
Springfield Cross
South Hill
Waytown Fm
Sepscott Fm
Youlston Wood
Bratton Cross
Town Fm
Saunton Sands
Heanton Punchardon
West Ashford
Brightlycott Fm
Chelfham
Horridge
Stoke Rivers
Birch
Velator
Wrafton
Ashford
Upcott Ho
Burridge
Kingdon's Gardens
Hakeford
Braunton Burrows
SOUTH WEST COAST PATH
Braunton Marsh
Chivenor
Penhill Pt
Bradiford
Raleigh
Pitt Fm
Snapper
Northleigh
Goodleigh
Horsey Island
Allen's Rock
Saltpill Duck Pond
Pilton
Pottington
Derby
Waytown
Middle Dean Fm
Dean Head
Hutcherton Down
Airy Pt
Danger area
River Taw
Penhill
ST ANNE'S CHAPEL & MUSEUM
Barnstaple
MUSEUM OF BARNSTAPLE & NORTH DEVON
Youlden Ho
Coombe Fm
Willesleigh Fm
Gunn
Stone Cross
Broad Sands
Lower Yelland
Muddlebridge
BICKINGTON ROAD
Sticklepath
Westacott
Birch
Accott
Yelland
Fremington
Combrew
Bickington
Ind Est
P&R
Newport
Portmor
Bus Pk
East Acland
Sandick
Crow Pt
Crow Rock
Instow Sands
WEST YELLAND
Brake Plantns
Brynsworthy
Lake
Harford
Sandick Cross
Bickleton
Myrtle Cott
Landkey
Hurscott
N DEVON MARITIME MUSEUM
Appledore
The Quay
Worlington
Collacott Fm
Upcott Fm
Roundswell
Rumsam
Landkey Newland
Swimbridge Newland
Yarnacott
Yeoland Ho
Riverton
Sandymere
NORTHAM BURROWS
Instow
INSTOW
Fullingcott Fm
Hollamoor Clump
Bishops Tawton
NORTH DEVON FARM PARK
Swimbridge
Kerscott
Diddywell
Huish
St John's Chapel
Eastacombe
Tawstock
Hannaford
Hangman's Hill
Bydown Ho
High Down
TAPELEY PARK GARDENS
Coombe Fm
Trayhill
Huish Moor
Stonyland
Downrew Ho
Horswell Fm
Lane End Fm
River Torridge
Westleigh
Rushcott Fm
Prospect Corner
Uppacott
Northam
Holmacott
Eastleigh Manor
Halmpstone Manor
Tower Fm
Silford
Rickard's
Horwood
A39
A361
A3123
B3343
B3231
B3233
A3125
A377
A399
B3230
B3229
B3232
56
24
25
SS
0 1 2 3 miles
0 1 2 3 4 5 km

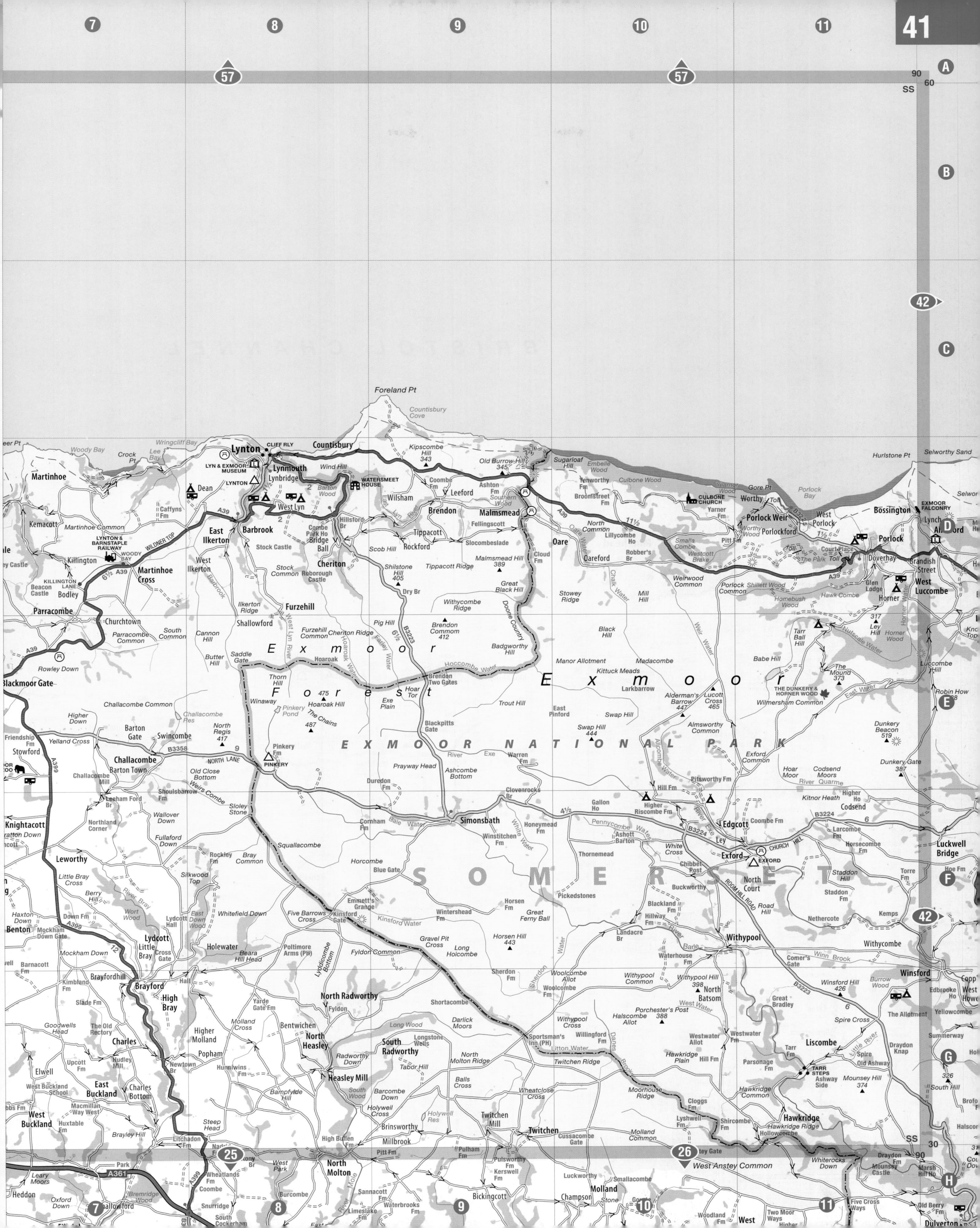
7
8
9
10
11
57
57
42
42
25
26
A
B
C
D
E
F
G
H
90
SS
60
30
BRISTOL CHANNEL
Foreland Pt
Countisbury Cove
Wringcliff Bay
Woody Bay
Crock Pt
Lee Bay
Lynton
CLIFF RLY
Countisbury
LYN & EXMOOR MUSEUM
LYNTON
Lynmouth
Lynbridge
Wind Hill
WATERSMEET HOUSE
Kipscombe Hill 343
Old Burrow Hill 345
Sugarloaf Hill
Embelle Wood
Culbone Wood
Yenworthy Fm
Broomstreet Fm
Gore Pt
Porlock Bay
Hurlstone Pt
Selworthy Sand
Martinhoe
Dean
Barton Wood
West Lyn
Coombe Fm
Leeford
Ashton Fm
Southern Wood
Wilsham
Brendon
Malmsmead
CULBONE CHURCH
Yarner Fm
Worthy
Porlock Weir
West Porlock
Porlockford
Bossington
EXMOOR FALCONRY
Lynch
Allerford
Kemacott
Martinhoe Common
Caffyns Fm
A39
WILDNER TOP
East Ilkerton
Barbrook
Hillsford Br
Combe Park Ho
Bridge Ball
Tippacott
Rockford
Fellingscott
Slocombeslade
North Common
Lillycombe Ho
Oare
Oareford
Robber's Br
Smalla Combe
Westcott Brake
Pitt Fm
Worthy Wood
Porlock
Court Place
Doverhay
Toll
The Park
Brandish Street
LYNTON & BARNSTAPLE RAILWAY
WOODY BAY
Killington
Martinhoe Cross
West Ilkerton
Stock Castle
Scob Hill
Cheriton
Stock Common
Roborough Castle
Shilstone Hill 405
Tippacott Ridge
Malmsmead Hill 389
Cloud Fm
Weirwood Common
Porlock Common
Shillett Wood
Glen Lodge
West Luccombe
Horner
KILLINGTON LANE
Beacon Castle
Bodley
Barbrook
Ilkerton Ridge
Furzehill
Dry Br
Great Black Hill
Stowey Ridge
Chalk Water
Mill Hill
Homebush Wood
Hawk Combe
Parracombe
Churchtown
Shallowford
Withycombe Ridge
Brendon Common 412
Parracombe Common
South Common
Cannon Hill
West Lyn River
Furzehill Common
Cheriton Ridge
Pig Hill
B3223
Doone Country
Black Hill
Weir Water
Tarr Ball Hill
Ley Hill 317
Horner Wood
Nutscale Water
Rowley Down
Butter Hill
Saddle Gate
Exmoor Forest
Hoaroak
Hoaroak Water
Farley Water
Badgworthy Hill
Hoccombe Water
Manor Allotment
Kittuck Meads
Madacombe
Babe Hill
The Mound 373
Luccombe Hill
Blackmoor Gate
Thorn Hill
Brendon Two Gates
Exmoor
Larkbarrow
Alderman's Barrow 447
Lucott Cross 465
THE DUNKERY & HORNER WOOD
Wilmersham Common
East Water
Robin How 428
Challacombe Common
Winaway
Hoaroak Hill 475
Exe Plain
Hoar Tor
Trout Hill
East Pinford
Swap Hill
Higher Down
Challacombe Res
Pinkery Pond
The Chains 487
North Regis 417
Blackpitts Gate
Swap Hill 444
Almsworthy Common
Dunkery Beacon 519
Friendship Fm
Yelland Cross
Barton Gate
Swincombe
EXMOOR NATIONAL PARK
Stowford
B3358
NORTH LANE
Pinkery Fm
PINKERY
River Exe
Warren Fm
Allcombe Water
Exford Common
Dunkery Gate 387
Challacombe
Barton Town
Prayway Head
Ashcombe Bottom
Hoar Moor
Codsend Moors
River Quarme
Challacombe Mill
Old Close Bottom
Weirs Combe
Duredon Fm
Pitsworthy Fm
Hill Fm
Higher Ho
Kitnor Heath
Codsend
Lecham Ford Br
Shoulsbarrow Fm
Sloley Stone
Clovenrocks Br
Gallon Ho
Higher Riscombe Fm
Knightacott
Northland Corner
Wallover Down
Cornham Fm
Barle Water
Simonsbath
Honeymead Fm
Pennycombe Water
Edgcott
Coombe Fm
B3224
Larcombe Fm
Luckwell Bridge
Fullaford Down
Winstitchen Fm
White Water
Ashott Barton
Ley
Horsecombe Fm
Leworthy
Squallacombe
Rockley Fm
Bray Common
Thornemead
White Cross
Exford
CHURCH HILL
EXFORD
Chibbet Post
Little Bray Cross
Horcombe
Blue Gate
SOMERSET
Silkwood Top
North Court
ROOM HILL ROAD
Staddon Hill
Torre Fm
Hoe Fm
Berry Hill
River Bray
Buckworthy
Pickedstones
Staddon Fm
Haxton Down
Wort Wood
East Down Wood
Emmett's Grange
Horsen Fm
Road Hill
Down Fm
Lydcott Hall
Whitefield Down
Five Barrows Cross
Kinsford Gate
Wintershead Fm
Great Ferny Ball
Blackland Fm
Hillway Fm
Nethercote
Kemps
Benton
Mockham Down Gate
A399
Kinsford Water
Landacre Br
River Barle
Withypool
Lydcott
Gravel Pit Cross
Long Holcombe
Horsen Hill 443
Withycombe
Mockham Down
Little Bray
Cross Gate
Holewater
Beara Hill Head
Poltimore Arms (PH)
Lydiacombe Bottom
Fyldon Common
Waterhouse Fm
Comer's Gate
Winn Brook
Barnacott Fm
Brayfordhill
Sherdon Fm
Sherdon Water
Woolcombe Allot
Woolcombe Fm
Withypool Common
Withypool Hill 398
North Batsom
Winsford Hill 426
Burrow Wood
Winsford
Edbrooke Ho
Kimbland Fm
Brayford
Hall
High Bray
Yarde Gate Fm
North Radworthy
Shortacombe
Great Bradley
West Water
The Allotment
Yellowcombe
Slade Fm
Fyldon
Darlick Moors
Withypool Cross
Halscombe Allot
Porchester's Post 388
Spire Cross
Goodwells Head
The Old Rectory
Higher Molland
Molland Cross
Bentwichen
Long Wood
Sportsman's Inn (PH)
Willingford Fm
Danes Brook
Westwater Allot
Westwater Fm
Summerway
Charles
North Heasley
South Radworthy
Longstone Wells
Litton Water
Liscombe
Draydon Knap
Popham
Little River
Elwell
Upcott Fm
Nudley Mill
Newtown Br
Hunniwins Fm
Radworthy Down
Tabor Hill
North Molton Ridge
Twitchen Ridge
Hawkridge Plain
Hill Fm
Tarr Fm
Parsonage Fm
TARR STEPS
Old Ashway
Ashway Side
Mounsey Hill 374
West Buckland School
East Buckland
Charles Bottom
Heasley Mill
Bampfylde Hill
Balls Cross
Wheatclose Cross
Moorhouse Ridge
Hawkridge Common
Macmillan Way West
South Wood
Barcombe Down
Holywell Cross
Holywell Res
Twitchen Mill
Cloggs Fm
South Hill
West Buckland
Huxtable Fm
Steep Head
Brinsworthy
Twitchen
Lyshwell Fm
Shircombe Fm
Hawkridge
Hawkridge Ridge
Hollowcombe
Brayley Hill
Eltchadon Fm
High Bullen Fm
Millbrook
Pulham Fm
Cussacombe Gate
Molland Common
Ley Gate
Park
Pitt Fm
North Molton
Putsworthy Fm
Kerswell Fm
West Anstey Common
Whiterocks Down
Draydon Fm
Mounsey Castle
Marsh Hall Ho
Leary Moors
A361
West Park
Wheatlands Fm
Coombe
Smallacombe
Luckworthy
Heddon
Bremridge Wood
Burcombe
Sannacott Fm
River Mole
Bickingcott
Molland
Champson
Stone
Five Cross Ways
Oxford Down
Chalowford
Snurridge
Limeslake Fm
Waterbrooks Fm
Woodland Fm
West
Two Moor Ways
Old Berry Fm
Dulverton
South Cockerham
A39

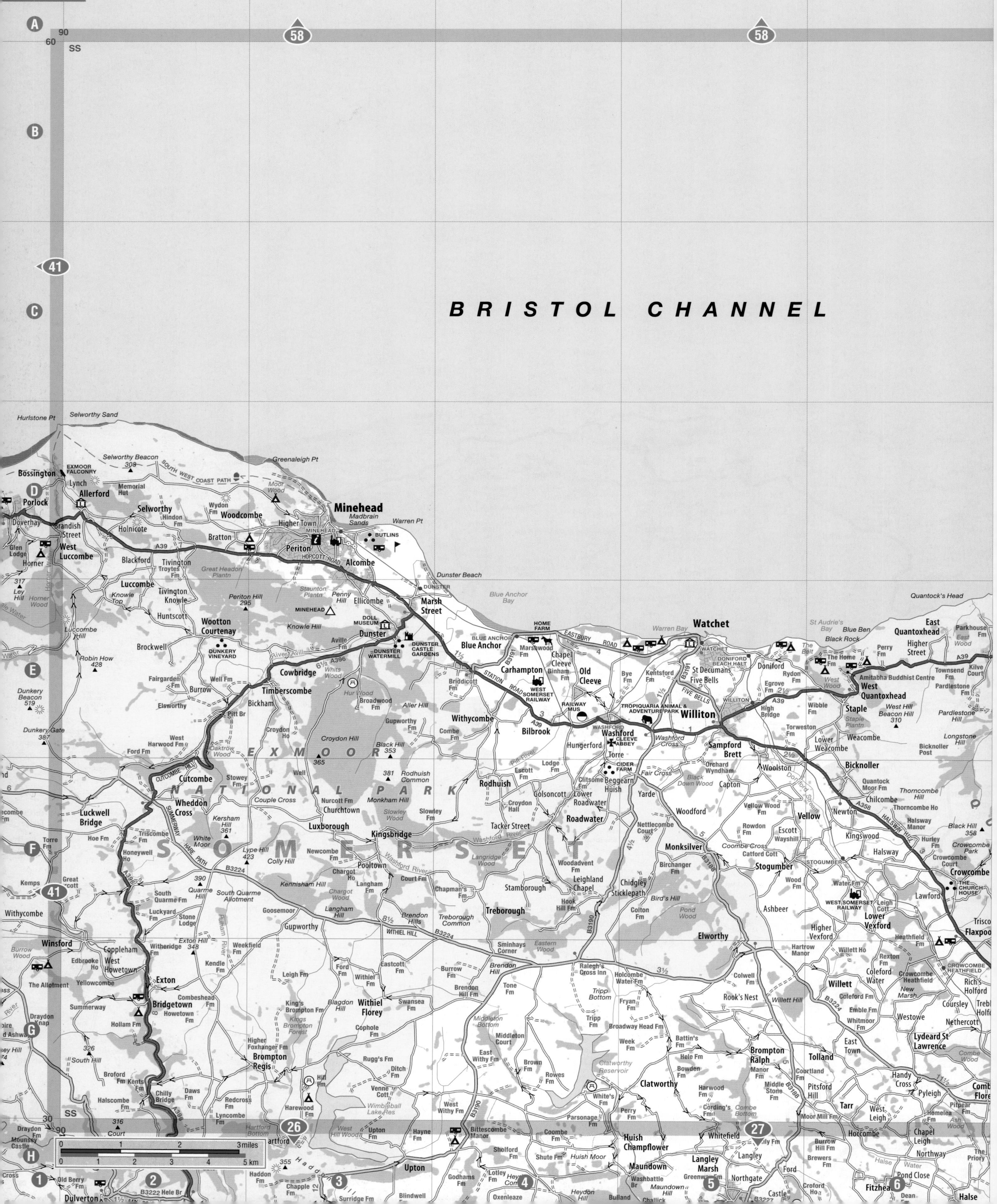
BRISTOL CHANNEL
EXMOOR NATIONAL PARK
SOMERSET
58
41
26
27
Hurlstone Pt
Selworthy Sand
Selworthy Beacon 308
SOUTH WEST COAST PATH
Greenaleigh Pt
Bossington
EXMOOR FALCONRY
Lynch
Memorial Hut
Porlock
Allerford
Selworthy
Wydon Fm
Moor Wood
Woodcombe
Minehead
Madbrain Sands
Warren Pt
Higher Town
BUTLINS
Doverhay
Brandish Street
Hindon Fm
Holnicote
Bratton
West Luccombe
Glen Lodge
Horner
Blackford
Tivington
Troytes Fm
Periton
HOPCOTT ROAD
Alcombe
A39
Great Headon Plantn
Luccombe
Knowle Top
Tivington Knowle
Horner Wood
Ley Hill
317
Staunton Plantn
Penny Hill
Ellicombe
DUNSTER
Dunster Beach
Marsh Street
Periton Hill 295
MINEHEAD
Huntscott
Wootton Courtenay
Knowle Hill
DOLL MUSEUM
Dunster
Luccombe Hill
Brockwell
DUNKERY VINEYARD
Avill Fm
DUNSTER WATERMILL
DUNSTER CASTLE GARDENS
Robin How 428
Cowbridge
Whits Wood
Dunkery Beacon 519
Fairgarden Fm
Well Fm
Burrow
Timberscombe
Hur Wood
Broadwood Fm
Elsworthy
Bickham
Pitt Br
Aller Hill
Croydon Ho
Gupworthy Fm
Dunkery Gate 387
Croydon Hill
West Harwood Fm
Ford Fm
Oaktrow Wood
Black Hill 353
365
381
Rodhuish Common
Cutcombe
Stowey Fm
Well
Wheddon Cross
Couple Cross
Nurcott Fm
Churchtown
Monkham Hill
Slowley Wood
Slowley Fm
Luckwell Bridge
Kersham Hill 361
Luxborough
Kingsbridge
Torre Fm
Hoe Fm
Triscombe
White Moor
Honeywell Ho
Lype Hill 423
Colly Hill
Newcombe Fm
Pooltown
Washford River
HARE PATH
SUMMERWAY
B3224
Chargot Ho
Langham Fm
Court Fm
Kennisham Hill
Chargot Wood
Kemps
Great Scott
390 Quarme Hill
South Quarme Allotment
South Quarme Fm
Goosemoor
Langham Hill
Brendon Hills
Treborough Common
Withycombe
Luckyard Fm
Stone Lodge
Gupworthy
WITHIEL HILL
Winsford
Exton Hill 348
Weekfield Fm
Coppleham
Witheridge Fm
Burrow Wood
Edbrooke Ho
West Howetown
Kendle Fm
Leigh Fm
Ford Fm
Withiel Fm
Eastcott Fm
The Allotment
Yellowcombe
Exton
Summerway
Bridgetown
Combeshead Fm
Hollam Fm
Hayne Fm
Hele Br
King's Brompton Fm
Blagdon Hill
Withiel Florey
Swansea Fm
Kings Brompton Forest
Draydon Knap
326
South Hill
Higher Foxhanger Fm
Brompton Regis
Cophole Fm
Broford Fm
Kents Fm
Rugg's Fm
Ditch Fm
Halscombe Fm
Chilly Bridge
Daws Fm
Redcross Fm
Venne Cott
Wimbleball Lake Res
Harewood Fm
Lyncombe Fm
316 Court
Draydon Fm
Mounsey Castle
Hartford Bottom
Hartford
West Hill Wood
Upton Fm
Haddon
355
Upton
Haddon Fm
Chapple Fm
Old Berry Fm
Dulverton
B3222
Surridge Fm
Blindwell
Blue Anchor Bay
HOME FARM
BLUE ANCHOR
Blue Anchor
Marshwood Fm
Chapel Cleeve
Binham Fm
Old Cleeve
EASTBURY ROAD
Warren Bay
Watchet
WATCHET
DONIFORD BEACH HALT
St Decumans
Five Bells
FIVE BELLS
Doniford
Bye Fm
Kentsford Fm
Carhampton
STATION ROAD
WEST SOMERSET RAILWAY
Briddicott Fm
RAILWAY MUS
TROPIQUARIA ANIMAL & ADVENTURE PARK
Williton
WILLITON
High Bridge
Withycombe
Bilbrook
WASHFORD
Washford
CLEEVE ABBEY
Combe Fm
Hungerford
Washford Cross
Sampford Brett
Torre
CIDER FARM
Lodge Fm
Escott Fm
Pill River
Rodhuish
Clitsome Fm
Beggearn Huish
Fair Cross
Orchard Wyndham
Black Down Wood
Golsoncott
Lower Roadwater
Capton
Yarde
Croydon Hall
Roadwater
Woodford
Tacker Street
Nettlecombe Court
Langridge Wood
Monksilver
Woodadvent Fm
Leighland Chapel
Birchanger Fm
Chidgley
Sticklepath
Stamborough
Hook Hill Fm
Bird's Hill
Treborough
Colton Fm
Pond Wood
B3190
B3188
Sminhays Corner
Eastern Wood
Elworthy
Brendon Hill
Raleigh's Cross Inn
Holcombe Water Fm
Burrow Fm
Brendon Hill Fm
Tone Fm
Tripp Bottom
Fryan Fm
Middleton Bottom
Tripp Fm
Broadway Head Fm
Middleton Court
East Withy Fm
Week Fm
Battin's Fm
Brown Fm
Hele Fm
Rowes Fm
Clatworthy Reservoir
Bowden Fm
Clatworthy
White's Fm
Harwood Fm
West Withy Fm
Perry Fm
Cording's Fm
Combe Bottom
Parsonage Fm
Bittescombe Manor
Coombe Fm
Huish Champflower
Whitefield
Sholford Fm
Shute Fm
Huish Moor
Langley Marsh
Langley
Maundown
Lotley Fm
Heydon Hill
Godhams Fm
Washbattle Br
Maundown Hill
Oxenleaze
Bulland
Challick
Northgate
Ford
Castle
B3227
Quantock's Head
St Audrie's Bay
Blue Ben
Black Rock
East Quantoxhead
Parkhouse Fm
East Wood
Perry Fm
Higher Street
The Belt
The Home Fm
Rydon Fm
Egrove Fm
Amitabha Buddhist Centre
Townsend Fm
Kilve Court
West Wood
West Quantoxhead
Pardlestone Fm
Wibble Fm
Staple
Staple Plantn
West Hill Beacon Hill 310
Pardlestone Hill
Torweston Fm
Lower Weacombe
Weacombe
Longstone Hill
Bicknoller Post
Woolston
Bicknoller
Quantock Moor Fm
Chilcombe
Thorncombe Hill
Doniford Stream
Newton
Thorncombe Ho
Yellow Wood Fm
Vellow
HALSWAY HILL
Halsway Manor
Black Hill 358
Rowdon Fm
Escott Fm
Wayshill
Kingswood
Hurley Fm
Coombe Cross
Catford Cott
Halsway
Crowcombe Park
Crowcombe Court
STOGUMBER
Stogumber
Crowcombe
THE CHURCH HOUSE
Wood Fm
Water Fm
WEST SOMERSET RAILWAY
Leigh Cott
Lawford
Ashbeer
Lower Vexford
Higher Vexford
Hartrow Manor
Heathfield Fm
Flaxpool
Willett Ho
Rexton Fm
CROWCOMBE HEATHFIELD
Coleford Water
Crowcombe Heathfield
Willett
Colwell Fm
Rich's Holford
New Marsh
Rook's Nest
Willett Hill
Coleford Fm
Coursley
Emble Fm
Whitmoor Fm
Westowe
Nethercott
Lydeard St Lawrence
East Town
Brompton Ralph
Manor Fm
Tolland
Combe Wood
Courtland Fm
Middle Stone Fm
Handy Cross
Pitsford Hill
Pyleigh
Tarr
West Leigh
Pitpear Fm
Homelea Fm
Ash Wood
Moor Mill Fm
Hoccombe
Chapel Leigh
Burrow Hill Fm
Northway
Brewers Fm
Halse Water
Pond Close
Croford Ho
Fitzhead
Halse
Dean
B3191
B3224
A358
A39
A396
B3190
A3
SS
90
60
30
3 miles
5 km

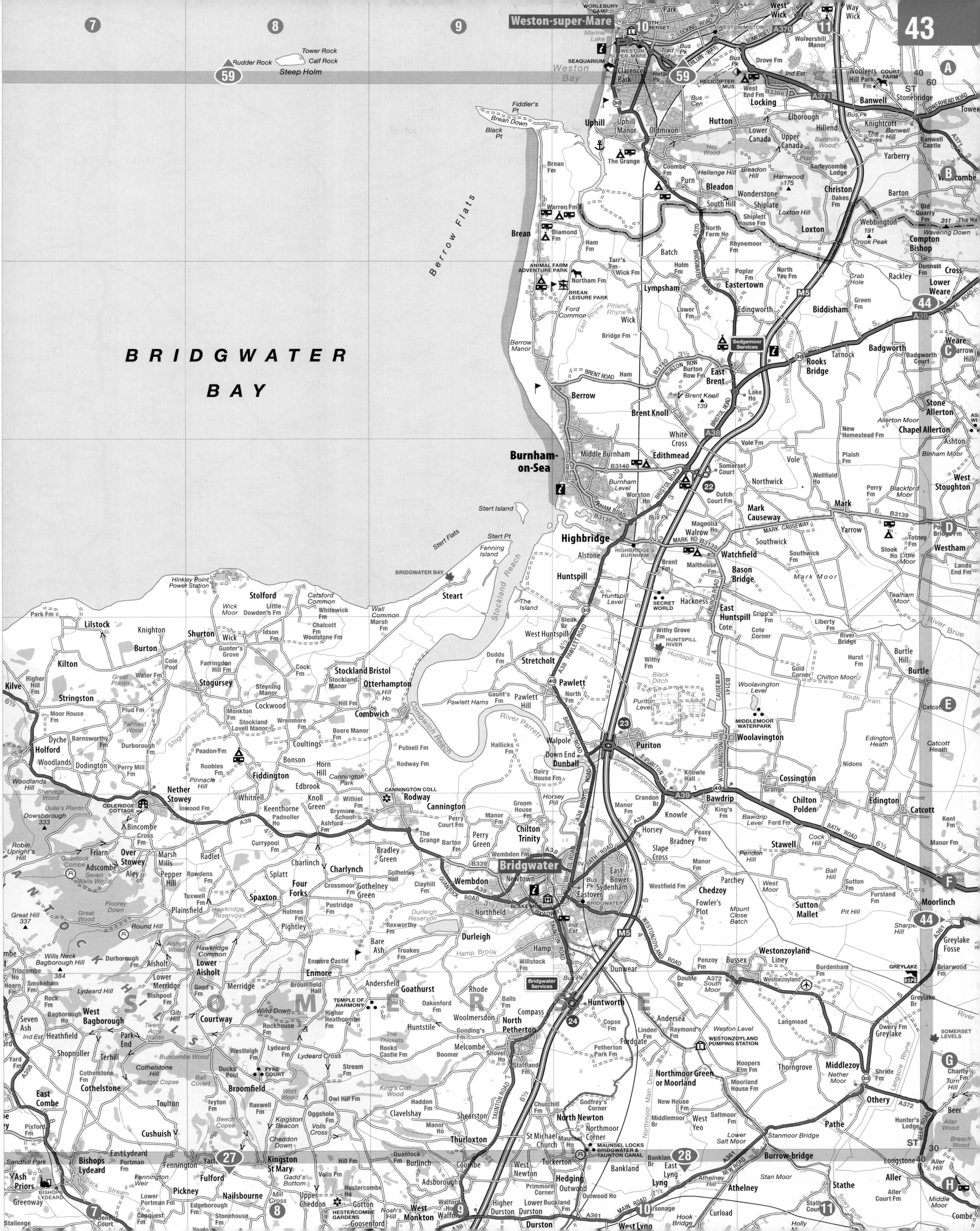

Weston-super-Mare
BRIDGWATER
BAY
Steep Holm
Rudder Rock
Tower Rock
Calf Rock
Weston Bay
Brean Down
Berrow Flats
Brean
Berrow
Burnham-on-Sea
Highbridge
Stert Island
Stert Flats
Fenning Island
Steart
Hinkley Point Power Station
Stolford
Lilstock
Kilton
Kilve
Stogursey
Stringston
Holford
Nether Stowey
Cannington
Combwich
Otterhampton
Pawlett
Puriton
Bridgwater
Wembdon
Durleigh
North Petherton
Huntworth
North Newton
Thurloxton
Bishops Lydeard
Kingston St Mary
Cothelstone
Broomfield
Spaxton
Enmore
Goathurst
Chedzoy
Westonzoyland
Middlezoy
Othery
Burrow-bridge
Athelney
Lyng
Bawdrip
Cossington
Woolavington
Chilton Polden
Edington
Catcott
Stawell
Sutton Mallet
Moorlinch
Burtle
Mark
Mark Causeway
Watchfield
East Huntspill
Huntspill
Bason Bridge
East Brent
Brent Knoll
Rooks Bridge
Biddisham
Badgworth
Lympsham
Eastertown
Edingworth
Loxton
Christon
Compton Bishop
Bleadon
Uphill
Locking
Hutton
Banwell
Uphill Manor
Oldmixon
West Huntspill
Dunball
Chilton Trinity
Bradney
Horsey
Westham
West Stoughton
Stone Allerton
Chapel Allerton
Lower Weare
Middle Burnham
Edithmead
Alstone
QUANTOCK HILLS
SOMERSET
Sedgemoor Services
Bridgwater Services
M5
A38
A39
A370
A371
A372
A361
B3139
B3140
B3141
59
27
28
44

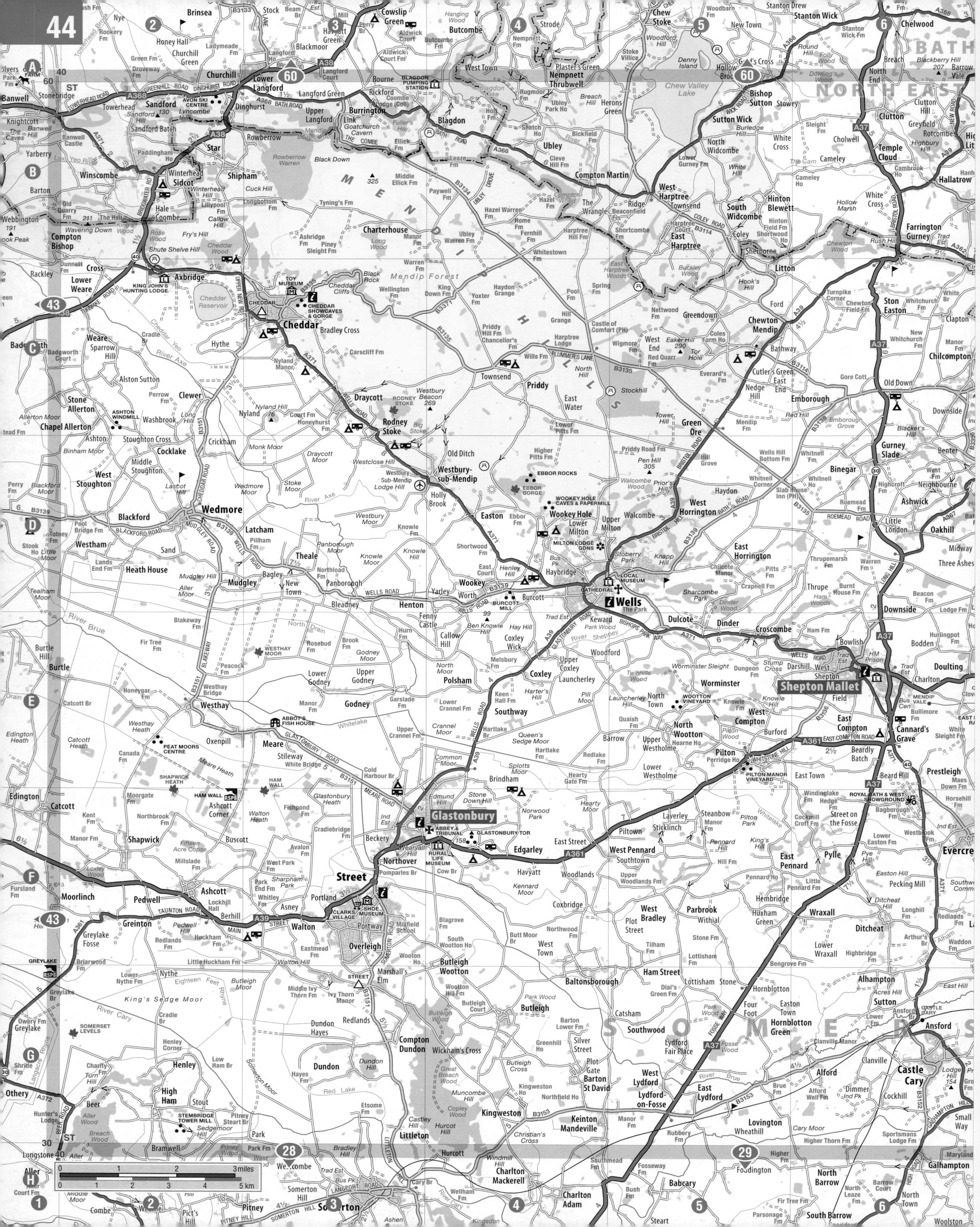

Brinsea
Stock
Cowslip Green
Butcombe
Strode
Chew Stoke
New Town
Stanton Drew
Stanton Wick
Chelwood
BATH
NORTH EAST
Honey Hall
Churchill Green
Blackmoor
Churchill
Lower Langford
Langford Green
Bourne
Rickford
BLAGDON PUMPING STATION
West Town
Nempnett Thrubwell
Chew Valley Lake
Bishop Sutton
Stowey
Breach
Clutton
Banwell
Stonebridge
Sandford
AVON SKI CENTRE
Dinghurst
Upper Langford
Burrington
Blagdon
Ubley
Sutton Wick
Temple Cloud
Star
Rowberrow
Shipham
Winscombe
Sidcot
Winterhead
Compton Martin
West Harptree
South Widcombe
Hinton Blewett
Farrington Gurney
Hallatrow
Webbington
Compton Bishop
Charterhouse
East Harptree
Litton
MENDIP HILLS
Axbridge
KING JOHN'S HUNTING LODGE
Cheddar Reservoir
CHEDDAR SHOWCAVES & GORGE
TOY MUSEUM
Cheddar
Bradley Cross
Mendip Forest
Lower Weare
Rackley
Cross
Weare
Hythe
Priddy
Townsend
Chewton Mendip
Green Ore
Ston Easton
Chilcompton
Emborough
Stone Allerton
Clewer
Draycott
Rodney Stoke
Westbury-sub-Mendip
EBBOR ROCKS
EBBOR GORGE
WOOKEY HOLE CAVES & PAPERMILL
Wookey Hole
Chapel Allerton
ASHTON WINDMILL
Cocklake
Wedmore
Blackford
Latcham
Theale
Easton
Wells
Dulcote
Dinder
Croscombe
Shepton Mallet
Doulting
Oakhill
Gurney Slade
Binegar
Ashwick
West Horrington
East Horrington
Westham
Heath House
Mudgley
Bagley
Panborough
Wookey
Henton
Yarley
Worth
Burcott
BURCOTT MILL
Coxley
Polsham
Southway
Worminster
North Wootton
WOOTTON VINEYARD
Pilton
PILTON MANOR VINEYARD
Burtle
Westhay
Godney
Meare
ABBOT'S FISH HOUSE
PEAT MOORS CENTRE
SHAPWICK HEATH
HAM WALL
Ashcott Corner
Edington
Catcott
Shapwick
Glastonbury
ABBEY & TRIBUNAL
GLASTONBURY TOR
RURAL LIFE MUSEUM
Edgarley
West Pennard
East Pennard
Pylle
Evercreech
East Compton
Cannard's Grave
Prestleigh
ROYAL BATH & WEST SHOWGROUND
Ashcott
Pedwell
Moorlinch
Greinton
Street
CLARKS VILLAGE
SHOE MUSEUM
Walton
Overleigh
Butleigh Wootton
Baltonsborough
West Bradley
Wraxall
Ditcheat
GREYLAKE RSPB
King's Sedge Moor
SOMERSET LEVELS
Henley
High Ham
STEMBRIDGE TOWER MILL
Butleigh
Compton Dundon
Dundon
Kingweston
Barton St David
Keinton Mandeville
West Lydford
East Lydford
Lydford-on-Fosse
Lovington
Alford
Castle Cary
Ansford
Charlton Mackerell
Charlton Adam
Babcary
North Barrow
South Barrow
Galhampton
Somerton
Pitney
Langport
Othery
Littleton
SOMERSET

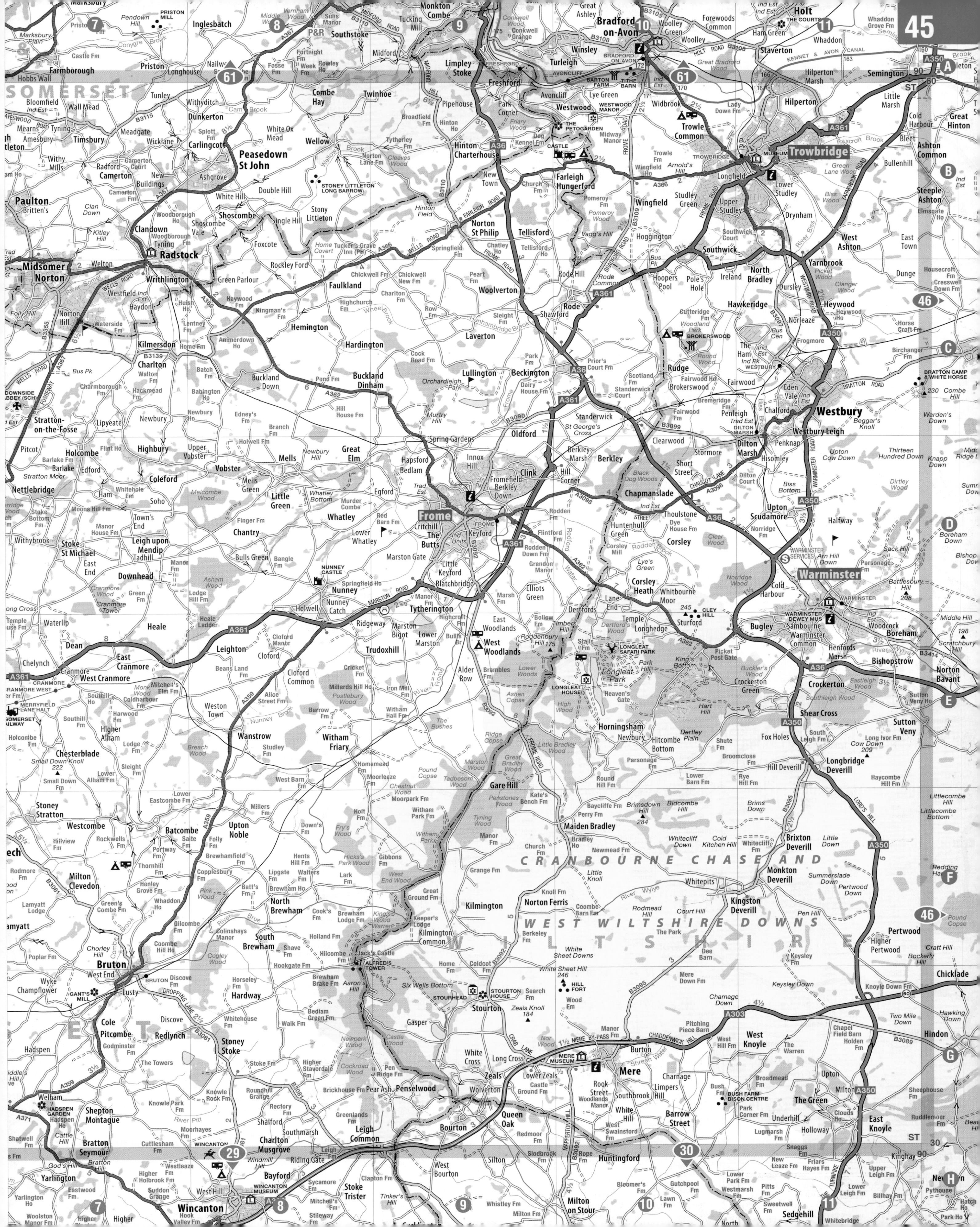
SOMERSET
WILTSHIRE
CRANBOURNE CHASE AND
WEST WILTSHIRE DOWNS
Bradford on-Avon
Trowbridge
Frome
Westbury
Warminster
Radstock
Midsomer Norton
Wincanton
Bruton
Mere
Holt
Freshford
Limpley Stoke
Monkton Combe
Southstoke
Midford
Priston
Inglesbatch
Farmborough
Paulton
Timsbury
Peasedown St John
Camerton
Dunkerton
Wellow
Combe Hay
Hinton Charterhouse
Farleigh Hungerford
Westwood
Winsley
Turleigh
Staverton
Semington
Hilperton
Wingfield
Southwick
North Bradley
Rode
Beckington
Lullington
Woolverton
Laverton
Buckland Dinham
Hemington
Hardington
Faulkland
Writhlington
Kilmersdon
Holcombe
Coleford
Vobster
Mells
Great Elm
Whatley
Chantry
Nunney
Tytherington
Berkley
Chapmanslade
Corsley
Dilton Marsh
Upton Scudamore
Leighton
East Cranmore
Trudoxhill
Witham Friary
West Woodlands
Longleat Park
Horningsham
Crockerton
Bishopstrow
Sutton Veny
Longbridge Deverill
Maiden Bradley
Kilmington
Stourton
Zeals
Kingston Deverill
Monkton Deverill
Brixton Deverill
North Brewham
South Brewham
Batcombe
Upton Noble
Penselwood
Bourton
Shepton Montague
Charlton Musgrove
Stoney Stoke
Redlynch
Pitcombe
Yarlington
Chicklade
Hindon
East Knoyle
West Knoyle
Sedgehill
Milton on Stour
Kinghay
Pertwood
Norton Bavant
Boreham
Heytesbury
Edington
Steeple Ashton
Bratton Camp & White Horse
Longleat Safari Park
Stourhead
Alfred's Tower
Hill Fort
Kennet & Avon Canal
A36
A361
A350
A362
A303
A359
A366
A371
B3092
B3095
B3109
61
29
30
46

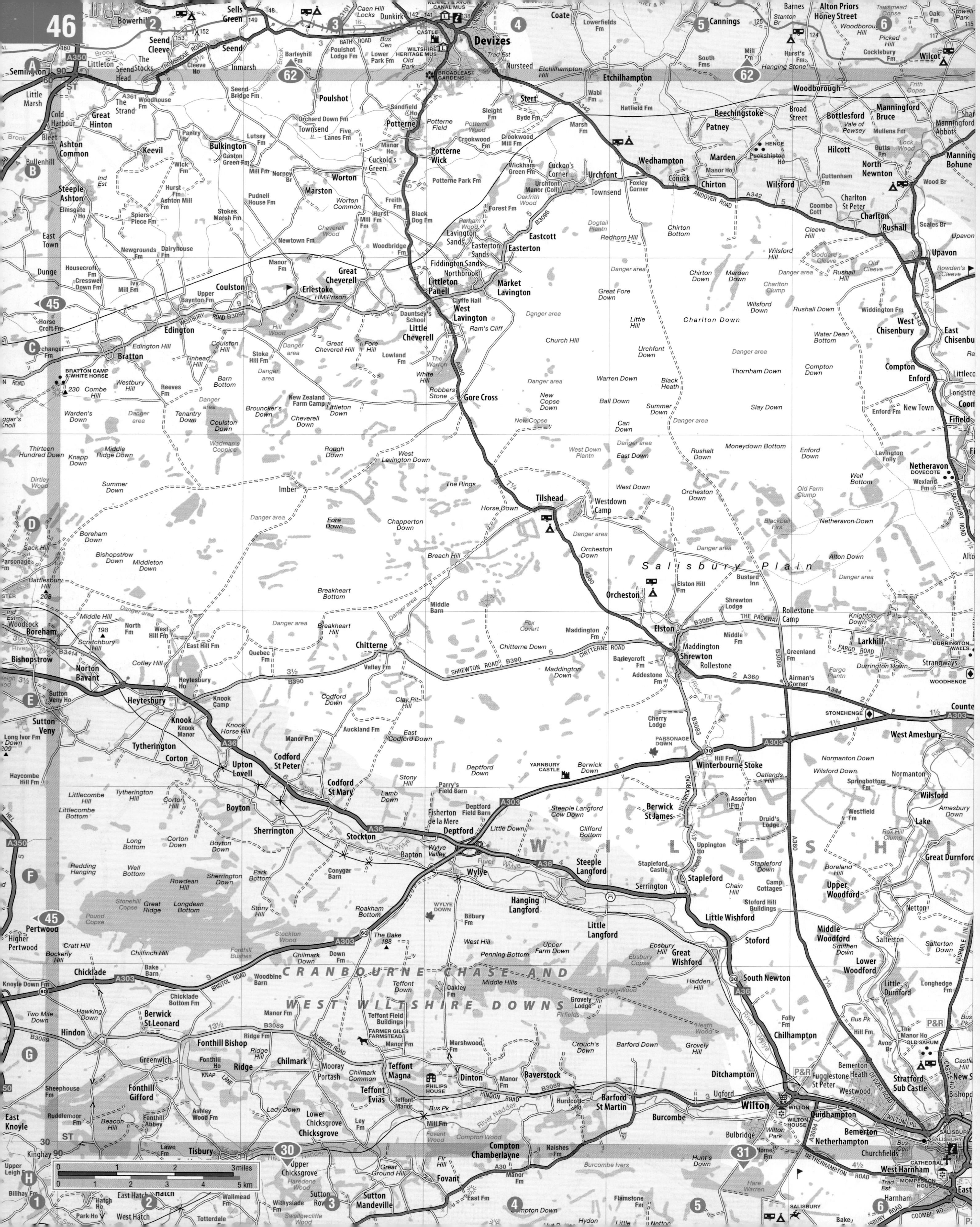
Devizes
Bowerhill
Sells Green
Seend Cleeve
Seend
Seend Head
The Stocks
Littleton
Semington
Little Marsh
Inmarsh
Poulshot
Caen Hill Locks
Dunkirk
Kennet & Avon Canal Mus
Castle
Wiltshire Heritage Mus
Broadleas Gardens
Nursteed
Etchilhampton Hill
Etchilhampton
Coate
Lowerfields Fm
Cannings
Barnes
Alton Priors
Honey Street
Woodborough
Wilcot
Stert
Sleight Fm
Byde Fm
Marsh Fm
Wabi Fm
Hatfield Fm
Beechingstoke
Patney
Broad Street
Bottlesford
Vale of Pewsey
Manningford Bruce
Manningford Abbots
Mullens Fm
Potterne
Potterne Field
Potterne Wood
Crookwood Fm
Crookwood Mill Fm
Potterne Wick
Potterne Park Fm
Wedhampton
Henge
Puckshipton Ho
Marden
Manor Ho
Conock
Chirton
Hilcott
North Newnton
Wilsford
Charlton St Peter
Charlton
Rushall
Upavon
Urchfont
Urchfont Manor (Coll)
Townsend
Foxley Corner
Wickham Green Fm
Cuckoo's Corner
Oakfrith Wood
Forest Fm
Cheverell Wood
Lavington Sands
Easterton Sands
Eastcott
Easterton
Redhorn Hill
Dogtail Plantn
Chirton Bottom
Cleeve Hill
Wilsford Hill
Worton
Worton Common
Marston
Cuckold's Green
Keevil
Bulkington
Gaston Green Fm
Great Hinton
The Strand
Cold Harbour
Bleet
Ashton Common
Bulkinghill
Steeple Ashton
Elmsgate Ho
Hurst Fm
Ashton Mill Fm
Spiers Piece Fm
Stokes Marsh Fm
Pudnell House Fm
East Town
Newgrounds Fm
Dairyhouse Fm
Dunge
Housecroft Fm
Cresswell Down Fm
Ivy Mill Fm
Coulston
Upper Baynton Fm
Erlestoke
HM Prison
Great Cheverell
Fiddington Sands
Northbrook
Littleton Panell
Market Lavington
Clyffe Hall
West Lavington
Dauntsey's School
Little Cheverell
Ram's Cliff
Edington
Edington Hill
Bratton
Bratton Camp & White Horse
Combe Hill
Westbury Hill
Reeves Fm
Barn Bottom
Coulston Hill
Tinhead Hill
Stoke Hill Fm
Great Cheverell Hill
Fore Hill
Lowland Fm
The Warren
White Hill
Robbers Stone
Gore Cross
New Zealand Farm Camp
Littleton Down
Cheverell Down
Brouncker's Down
Tenantry Down
Coulston Down
Wadman's Coppice
Warden's Down
Thirteen Hundred Down
Knapp Down
Middle Ridge Down
Rough Down
West Lavington Down
Summer Down
Imber
The Rings
Tilshead
Horse Down
Westdown Camp
West Down
West Down Plantn
East Down
Danger area
Church Hill
Urchfont Down
Warren Down
Black Heath
Ball Down
New Copse Down
Summer Down
Can Down
Rushalt Down
Moneydown Bottom
Enford Down
Great Fore Down
Little Hill
Charlton Down
Chirton Down
Marden Down
Charlton Clump
Wilsford Down
Rushall Down
Widdington Fm
West Chisenbury
East Chisenbury
Water Dean Bottom
Thornham Down
Compton Down
Compton
Enford
Slay Down
Enford Fm
New Town
Fifield
Lavington Folly
Netheravon
Dovecote
Wexland Fm
Well Bottom
Old Farm Clump
Netheravon Down
Blackball Firs
Orcheston Down
Fore Down
Chapperton Down
Boreham Down
Bishopstrow Down
Middleton Down
Breach Hill
Salisbury Plain
Alton Down
Bustard Inn
Elston Hill Fm
Orcheston
Breakheart Bottom
Middle Barn
Shrewton Lodge
Rollestone Camp
The Packway
Knighton Down
Larkhill
Durrington Walls
Fargo Road
Fox Covert
Maddington Fm
Elston
Maddington
Shrewton
Rollestone
Middle Fm
Greenland Fm
Durrington Down
Fargo Plantn
Strangways
Woodhenge
Battlesbury Hill
Middle Hill
Woodcock
Boreham
Scratchbury Hill
North Fm
West Hill Fm
East Hill Fm
Breakheart Hill
Quebec Fm
Chitterne
Chitterne Down
Chitterne Road
Shrewton Road
Valley Fm
Barleycroft Fm
Addestone Fm
Maddington Down
Airman's Corner
Bishopstrow
Norton Bavant
Cotley Hill
Heytesbury
Heytesbury Ho
Knook Camp
Sutton Veny
Sutton Veny Ho
Knook
Knook Manor
Knook Horse Hill
Codford Down
Clay Pit Hill
Auckland Fm
East Codford Down
Cherry Lodge
Stonehenge
Parsonage Down
Countess
West Amesbury
Normanton Down
Wilsford Down
Normanton
Springbottom Fm
Oatlands Hill
Tytherington
Corton
Upton Lovell
Codford St Peter
Manor Fm
Codford St Mary
Stony Hill
Deptford Down
Yarnbury Castle
Berwick Down
Hill Fm
Winterbourne Stoke
Asserton Fm
Druid's Lodge
Berwick St James
Lamb Down
Parry's Field Barn
Fisherton de la Mere
Deptford Field Barn
Deptford
Little Down
Steeple Langford Cow Down
Clifford Bottom
Westfield Fm
Wilsford
Amesbury Down
Lake
Great Durnford
Littlecombe Hill
Littlecombe Bottom
Tytherington Hill
Corton Hill
Boyton
Sherrington
Stockton
Bapton
Wylye Valley
Wylye
River Wylye
Steeple Langford
Stapleford Castle
Uppington Ho
Stapleford Down
Camp Cottages
Boreland Hill
Upper Woodford
Long Bottom
Corton Down
Boyton Down
Redding Hanging
Well Bottom
Sherrington Down
Park Bottom
Conygar Barn
Rowdean Hill
Serrington
Stapleford
Chain Hill
Stoford Hill Buildings
Stonehill Copse
Great Ridge
Longdean Bottom
Pound Copse
Stony Hill
Roakham Bottom
Wylye Down
Bilbury Fm
Hanging Langford
Little Langford
Little Wishford
Netton
Stockton Wood
The Bake
West Hill
Upper Farm Down
Penning Bottom
Ebsbury Hill
Ebsbury Copse
Great Wishford
Stoford
Middle Woodford
Salterton
Smithen Down
Salterton Down
Lower Woodford
Pertwood
Higher Pertwood
Cratt Hill
Bockerly Hill
Chilfinch Hill
Fonthill Bushes
Chilmark Down
Down Fm
Chicklade
Bake Barn
Woodbine Barn
Teffont Down
Oakley Fm
Middle Hills
Cranbourne Chase and West Wiltshire Downs
Grovely Wood
Grovely Lodge
Firfields
Hadden Hill
South Newton
Little Durnford
Longhedge Fm
Knoyle Down Fm
Two Mile Down
Hawking Down
Chicklade Bottom Fm
Berwick St Leonard
Manor Fm
Teffont Field Buildings
Farmer Giles Farmstead
Heath Wood
Folly Fm
Chilhampton
Bus Pk
Hill Fm
The Manor Ho
Old Sarum
Avon Br
Hindon
Fonthill Bishop
Ridge Fm
Ridge Hill
Salisbury Road
Marshwood Fm
Crouch's Down
Barford Down
Grovely Hill
Greenwich
Fonthill Ho
Knap Lane
Ridge
Chilmark
Mooray
Portash
Chilmark Common
Teffont Magna
Dinton
Philips House
Manor Fm
Baverstock
Ditchampton
Bemerton Heath
Fugglestone St Peter
Stratford sub Castle
Castle Rd
New Sarum
Bishopdown
Sheephouse Fm
Fonthill Gifford
Teffont Evias
Teffont Manor
Hindon Road
Hurdcott Ho
Barford St Martin
Ugford
Wilton
Wilton House
Westwood
Quidhampton
East Knoyle
Ruddlemoor Fm
Beacon Hill
Ashley Wood Fm
Fonthill Abbey
Lady Down
Lower Chicksgrove
Chicksgrove
Ley Fm
Bus Pk
Mill Fm
Fovant Wood
River Nadder
Burcombe
Wilton Park
Bulbridge
Bemerton
Netherhampton
Salisbury
Compton Wood
Compton Chamberlayne
Naishes Fm
Burcombe Ivers
Hunt's Down
Home Fm
Netherhampton Road
Churchfields
Bus Cen
Cathedral
Kinghay
Lawn Fm
Tisbury
Upper Chicksgrove
Hardene Wood
Great Ground Hill
Fir Hill
Fovant
Manor Fm
West Harnham
Trad Est
Mompesson House
East Harnham
Upper Leigh
Billhay Fm
East Hatch
Hatch
Park Ho
West Hatch
Wallmead Fm
Totterdale
Withyslade Fm
Sutton Row
Swallowcliffe Wood
Sutton Mandeville
East Fm
Compton Down
Hydon
Flamstone Fm
Hare Warren
Salisbury
Coombe Rd
0 1 2 3 miles
0 1 2 3 4 5 km
45
62
30
31

Pewsey
Southcott
Burbage
Eastcourt
Milton Lilbourne
Easton Royal
West Grafton
East Grafton
Marten
Wilton
Buttermere
Combe
Oxenwood
Tidcombe
Fosbury
Henley
Linkenholt
Faccombe
Ashmansworth
Netherton
Vernham Street
Vernham Dean
Upton
Aughton
Brunton
Collingbourne Kingston
Lower Everleigh
Everleigh
East Everleigh
Sunton
Cadley
Collingbourne Ducis
Mount Cowdown
Upper Chute
Lower Chute
Chute Standen
Chute Cadley
Tangley
Ibthorpe
Hurstbourne Tarrant
Stoke
NORTH WESSEX DOWNS
Ludgershall
Faberstown
Redenham
Hatherden
Wildhern
Little London
North Tidworth
Tidworth
South Tidworth
Perham Down
Great Shoddesden
Little Shoddesden
Appleshaw
Clanville
Penton Mewsey
Penton Grafton
Enham Alamein
Knights Enham
Smannell
Charlton
Picket Piece
Kimpton
Fyfield
Weyhill
Thruxton
Andover
Andover Down
Picket Twenty
Figheldean
Ablington
Milston
Brigmerston
Shipton Bellinger
Durrington
Bulford
Bulford Camp
Amesbury
Ratfyn
Cholderton
Quarley
Grateley
Amport
Monxton
Abbotts Ann
Anna Valley
Upper Clatford
Goodworth Clatford
Red Rice
Little Ann
Newton Tony
Palestine
Allington
Boscombe
Idmiston
Porton
Gomeldon
Over Wallop
Middle Wallop
Nether Wallop
Clatford Oakcuts
Fullerton
Leckford
Longstock
Chilbolton
Wherwell
Newton Stacey
Stockbridge
Winterbourne Dauntsey
Winterbourne Gunner
Winterbourne Earls
Lopcombe Corner
East Winterslow
Middle Winterslow
West Winterslow
The Common
Firsdown
Pitton
Broughton
Houghton
Little Somborne
Up Somborne
King's Somborne
Ashley
Bossington
Horsebridge
Laverstock
Salisbury
Milford
Farley
West Tytherley
East Tytherley
The Green
Compton
Compton Brook
HAMPSHIRE
A303
A338
A343
A342
A30
A3057
63
48
31
32

Highclere
Highclere Castle
Whitway
Old Burghclere
Sydmonton
Burghclere
Kingsclere
Wolverton
Ramsdell
Tadley
Baughurst
Pamber Green
Pamber End
Little London
Monk Sherborne
Sherborne St John
The Vyne
Faccombe
Ashmansworth
Crux Easton
Woodcott
Litchfield
Dunley
Binley
Hurstbourne Tarrant
Hannington
Upper Wootton
Ibworth
North Oakley
Wootton St Lawrence
Worting
Winklebury
Oakridge
South View
Basingstoke
Kempshott
Brighton Hill
Cliddesden
Hatch Warren
Kings Furlong
Eastrop
South Ham
Buckskin
Newfound
Church Oakley
Oakley
East Oakley
Clarken Green
Deane
Ashe
Overton
Quidhampton
Laverstoke
Freefolk
Whitchurch
Tufton
Southington
Foxdown
Cole Henley
St Mary Bourne
Stoke
Swampton
Egbury
Wadwick
Hurstbourne Priors
Longparish
Middleton
Forton
Bransbury
Andover Down
Picket Piece
Wherwell
Barton Stacey
Bullington
Newton Stacey
Chilbolton
Upper Bullington
Egypt
Sutton Scotney
Wonston
Hunton
Stoke Charity
Micheldever
Weston Colley
West Stratton
East Stratton
Northbrook
Steventon
North Waltham
Dummer
Popham
Woodmancott
Nutley
Axford
Farleigh Wallop
Ellisfield
Broadmere
Preston Candover
Bradley
Chilton Candover
Brown Candover
Lower Wield
Upper Wield
Hattingley
Northington
Swarraton
Abbotstone
Old Alresford
New Alresford
Bishop's Sutton
Ropley Dean
Gundleton
Bighton
Tichborne
Ovington
Itchen Stoke
Itchen Abbas
Avington
Easton
Martyr Worthy
Abbots Worthy
Kings Worthy
Headbourne Worthy
Littleton
Harestock
Weeke
Hyde
Winchester
Winnall
St Giles's Hill
Chilcomb
Stanmore
Sleepers Hill
Fulflood
Up Somborne
Sparsholt
Crawley
South Wonston
Kirton
Dean
Ham Green
Cheriton
Bramdean
NORTH WESSEX DOWNS
HAMPSHI
Basingstoke Road
Andover Road
Winchester Road
Kingsclere Road
Worting Road
Stockbridge Road
Alresford Road
Petersfield Road
Jacklyns Lane
South Downs Way
Mid Hants Railway (Watercress Line)
Winchester Services
Popham Services
Sutton Scotney Services
A34
A30
A303
A339
A33
A31
M3
B3400
B3048
B3046
B3047
B3049
B3051
B3404
A343
A3010
64
47
32
33
SU
0 1 2 3 miles
0 1 2 3 4 5 km

Camberley
Sandhurst
Yateley
Blackwater
Frimley
Hawley
Hook
Fleet
Farnborough
Church Crookham
Aldershot
Ash
Ash Vale
Odiham
North Warnborough
Farnham
Wrecclesham
Tongham
Crondall
Bentley
Alton
Chawton
Holybourne
Four Marks
Selborne
Kingsley
Bordon
Headley
Grayshott
Hindhead
Haslemere
Liphook
Liss
Frensham
Tilford
Elstead
Churt
Greatham
Whitehill
Old Basing
Chineham
Hartley Wintney
Winchfield
Long Sutton
South Warnborough
Herriard
Lasham
Medstead
Ropley
East Tisted
Newton Valence
Empshott
Hawkley
Liss Forest
Longmoor Camp
Kingsley Green
Fernhurst
SURREY
Fleet Services
M3
A31
A3
A30
A325
A287
A339
A32
A331
65
50
33
34
7
8
9
10
11
A
B
C
D
E
F
G
H

Lightwater
Bagshot Heath
Chobham
West End
Brook Place
Castle Green
Emmetts Mill
Mimbridge
Scotchers Fm
Horsell Common
Sheerwater
West Byfleet
Byfleet
Cobham
Fairmile
Oxshott Heath
Donkey Town
Greyspot Hill
Cuckoo Hill
Westend Common
Heatherside
Frimley Ridge
Lucas Green
Bisley
Whitfield Court
Horsell
Horsell Birch
Cheapside
Woking
Ridgway
Pyrford
Pyrford Common
Pyrford Green
Pyrford Village
Wisley
RHS Garden Wisley
Elm Corner
Downside
Stoke D'Abernon
Little Heath
Pains Hill
Painshill Park
Cobham Bus Mus
Foxwarren Park
Manor Ho
Bolder Mere
Cobham Court
Hatchford Park
Cobham Lodge
Frimley
Frimley Green
Deepcut
Farnborough Green
Colony Gate
Pirbright Common
Bisley Camp (National Shooting Centre)
Sheets Heath
Miles Green
Knaphill
St John's
Brookwood
Pirbright Camp
Mount Hermon
Hook Heath
Maybury
Kingfield
Old Woking
Roundbridge Fm
Park Fm
Papercourt Fm
Ripley
Bridge End
Church End
Ockham
Ockham Mill
Upton Fm
May's Green
Cobham Services
Bookham Lodge
Sheepbell Fm
Great Bookham Common
Little Bookham Common
Leatherhead
Mytchett
Mytchett Place
Basingstoke Canal Centre
Pirbright
Pirbright Lodge
Brookwood Cemetery
Dawney's Hill
West Hill
Mayford
Prey Heath
Smart's Heath
Westfield
Cartbridge
Lower Westfield Fm
Send
Send Marsh
Burntcommon
Boughton Hall
Hungry Hill
Ryde Fm
Blackmoor
Effingham Junction
Norwood Fm
Fetcham
Hinterland Ho
Little Bookham
Tunnel Hill
Stanford Common
Rails Fm
Hangman's Hill
Pirbright Common
Danger Area
Fox Corner
Worplesdon
Jordans Hill
Woodcorner Fm
Havering Fm
Whitmoor Ho
Sutton Green
Ladygrove Fm
Send Grove
Sendhurst Grange
Tythebarns Fm
Sussex Fm
Jury Fm
Holride Fm
HM Prison
East Horsley
Horsley Towers
Effingham
Great Bookham
Ash Vale
North Camp
Longhill Bottom
Bastion Hill
Cobbett Hill
Littlefield Common
Whitmoor Common
Cox's Fm
Nuthill Fm
Dedswell Manor Fm
Cotts Wood
Clandon
Gason Wood
West Horsley
Goldstone Fm
Phoenice Fm
Ricochet Hill
Fox Hills
Henley Park
Whipley Manor
Littlefield Manor
Pitch Place
Fairlands
Jacobs Well
Slyfield
Bellfields
Burpham
West Clandon
Norcote Wood
East Clandon
Hatchlands Park
Polesden Lacey
Tanners Hatch
Ash
Normandy
Willey Green
Wyke
East Wyke Fm
Westwood Place
Russellplace Fm
Wood Street Village
Wood Street
Rydeshill
Woodbridge Hill
Stoughton
Park Barn
Abbotswood
Bushy Hill
Merrow
Temple Court
Clandon Park
Clandon Downs
Blake's Lane Fm
Hook Wood
Mountain Wood
Hillside Fm
Effingham Forest
Dunley Hill Fm
Pigden Cott
Ranmore Common
Ash Green
Flexford
Wanborough Youth Ho
Onslow Village
Guildford
Guildford Park
Guildford House Gallery
Newland's Corner
Netherlands
Combe Bottom
Hollister Fm
Woodcote Lodge
Netley Heath
White Downs
Landbarn Fm
Stockman's Coomb Fm
Westcott
Tongham
White Lane Fm
Wanborough
Wanborough Manor
Hog's Back
Pewley Down
Merrow Downs
Tyting Fm
Albury Downs
Sherbourne Fm
Colekitchen Fm
Hackhurst Fm
Gomshall
Netley Ho
Shere
Albury
Puttenham
Puttenham Heath
Compton
Littleton
Loseley Park
Loseley House
Orange Grove
Artington
Shalford Mill
Chilworth Manor
Chilworth
Postford Ho
Albury Park
Burrows Cross
Abinger Hammer
Wotton
Logmore Fm
Binton Fm
Suffield Fm
Eastbury Manor
Lone Barn
Field Place
Broadford
Shalford
Shalford Common
Blackheath
Wonersh Common
Albury Heath
Brook
Cotterell Ho
Ponds Fm
Fulvens Ho
Raikes Fm
Goddards House & Garden
Culverswell Fm
Rodsall Manor
Cutt Mill Ho
Shackleford
Hurtmore
Binscombe
Farncombe
Peasmarsh
Gosden Ho
Chinthurst Hill
Wonersh
Farley Green
Dilton Fm
Sutton
Sutton Abinger
Abinger Common
Friday Street
Broadmoor
Holmbury St Mary
Peaslake
Shackleford Heath
Norney
Peper Harow
Eashing
Upper Eashing
Catteshall
Godalming
Bramley
Snowdenham Ho
Birtley Green
Norley Common
Shamley Green
Mayor House Fm
Surrey Hills
Charleshill
Elstead
Pot Common
Crownpits
Holloway Hill
Busbridge
Lordshill Common
Franklin's Fm
Winterfold Wood
Duke of Kent School
Holmbury Hill
Leith Hill
Coldharbour
Milford
Royal Common
Bagmoor Common
Mousehill
Rodborough Hill
Ockford Ridge
Tuesley
Thorncombe Street
Grafham
Stroud Common
Pitch Hill
Winterfold Ho
Ewhurst Place
Cornhill Manor
Forest Green
Hankley Common
Ockley Common
Thursley Common
Cramhurst
Witley Common
Wheelerstreet
Enton Green
Hydestile
Winkworth Arboretum
Juniper Valley
Scotsland Fm
Selhurst Common
Palmers Cross
Brooklands Fm
Rowly
Smithwood Common
St Joseph's School
Ewhurst
North Breache Manor
Lyefield Ho
Jayes Park
Thursley
Witley
Culmer
Hydon's Ball
Marepond Fm
Hascombe
Upper Ho
Hascombe Hill
Tilsey Fm
Rydinghurst
Bookhurst
Lower Breache Fm
Mayes Green
Parkland Farmhouse
Ewhurst Green
Cranleigh
Hyde Fm
Pitch Place
Bowlhead Green
Wormley
Sandhills
Brook
Hambledon
Oakhurst Cottage
Burgate Ho
Loxhill
Painshill Fm
Uttworth Manor
Knowle Park
New Park
Walliswood
Paynes Green
Peartree Green
Dunsfold Green
High Billinghurst Fm
Snoxhall Fm
Longhurst Hill
Oakwoodhill
Hindhead
Hindhead Common
Devil's Punch Bowl
Gibbet Hill
Combe Common
Dunsfold
Dunsfold Aerodrome (disused)
Laker's Green
Bookers Lee
Newhouse Fm
Vachery Pond
Baynard's Park
Ellen's Green
Ruckmans
Coombe Head
South Park Fm
Stroud
Grayswood
Chiddingfold
Highstreet Green
Dunsfold Common
Alfold Crossways
Ivelle Fm
Maybanks Manor
Honeywood Ho
Charmans Fm
Critchmere
Haslemere
High Prestwick
Grayswood Common
Clammer Hill
Bethwins Fm
Hazel Bridge
Follies
Sidney Wood
Upper Ifold
Sachel Court
Springbok Fm
Alfold
Pallinghurst Fm
Cox Green
Hermongers
Rowhook
Bury St Austen's
Rudgwick
Ramster Garden
Ramsnest Common
Furnace Place
Gostrode Fm
Robins Fm
Durfold Hall Fm
Sydney Fm
Alfold Bars
Monckton Hook
Hornshill Fm
Tisman's Common
Bucks Green
Warnham
Shepherd's Hill
Anstead Brook
Lythe Hill
Dickhurst
Stillands Fm
Shillinglee
Home Fm
Old Songhurst Fm
Strood Green
Red Court
Boxalland
Gaston's Fm
Deer Tower
Winkins Wood Fm
Hog Wood
Oakhurst Fm
Loxwood
Howick Fm
Park Street
Rapkyns
Broadbridge Heath
Marley Hill
Valewood Ho
Black Down
Roundhurst
Gospel Green
Fisherstreet
Newhouse Fm
Haymans Fm
Eastland Fm
Lyon's Fm
Plaistow Place
Plaistow
Ifold
Headfoldswood Fm
Brewhurst
Drungewick Manor
Rudgwick Grange
Gibbons Mill
Slinfold
Slinfold Lodge
Holmbush Manor
Wellcross Grange
Kingsley Green
Marley Heights
Aldworth Ho
Roundhurst Common
Greenland Fm
Park Mill Fm
Charleshurst Fm
The Haven
Hope Fm
Bignor Fm
Stane Street
Slinford Manor
Itchingfield
Fulfords Fm
Christ's Hospital
Weston's Fm
Fernhurst
Hatch Fm Hill
Cotchet Fm
Upper Diddlesfold
Dale's Fm
Upper Frithfold Fm
Lakers Lodge
Hurst Farm Ho
Northchapel
Freehold Fm
Roundwyck Ho
Scratchings Fm
Mackerel's Common
Burchett's Fm
Roundstreet Common
Great Wood
Menzies Wood Fm
Five Oaks
Shiprods Fm
Wedges Fm
Lower House Fm
Hillgrove
Navant Hill
Gof's Fm
Highnoons Fm
Hills Green Fm
Ebernoe
Dounhurst Fm
Fountain's
Loves
Great
School
Two Mile Ash
Surrey
Scale: 0 1 2 3 miles; 0 1 2 3 4 5 km

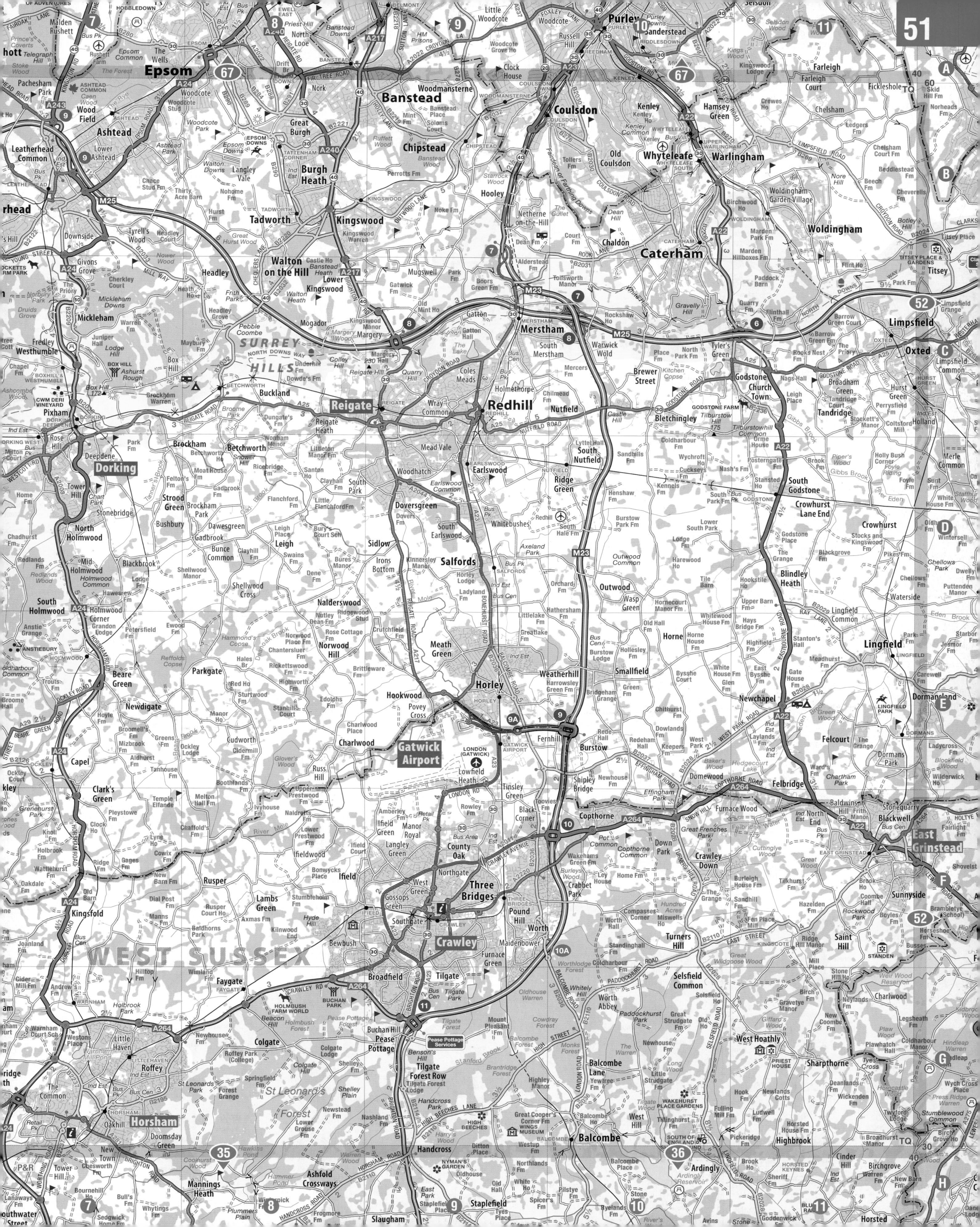
Epsom
Ashtead
Banstead
Chipstead
Coulsdon
Purley
Kenley
Whyteleafe
Warlingham
Woldingham
Caterham
Old Coulsdon
Burgh Heath
Tadworth
Kingswood
Walton on the Hill
Headley
Mickleham
Leatherhead
Merstham
Reigate
Redhill
Nutfield
Bletchingley
Godstone
Oxted
Limpsfield
Tandridge
Dorking
Pixham
Brockham
Betchworth
Buckland
Earlswood
Salfords
Horley
Smallfield
Lingfield
Dormansland
Felbridge
East Grinstead
Gatwick Airport
Crawley
Three Bridges
Pound Hill
Copthorne
Crawley Down
Turners Hill
West Hoathly
Sharpthorne
Horsham
Roffey
Colgate
Faygate
Rusper
Ifield
Charlwood
Newdigate
Capel
Kingsfold
Beare Green
North Holmwood
South Holmwood
Balcombe
Handcross
Ardingly
Pease Pottage
Tilgate
Worth
Turners Hill
Mannings Heath
Staplefield
Highbrook
SURREY HILLS
WEST SUSSEX
M25
M23
A22
A23
A24
A25
A264
A217
67
52
35
36

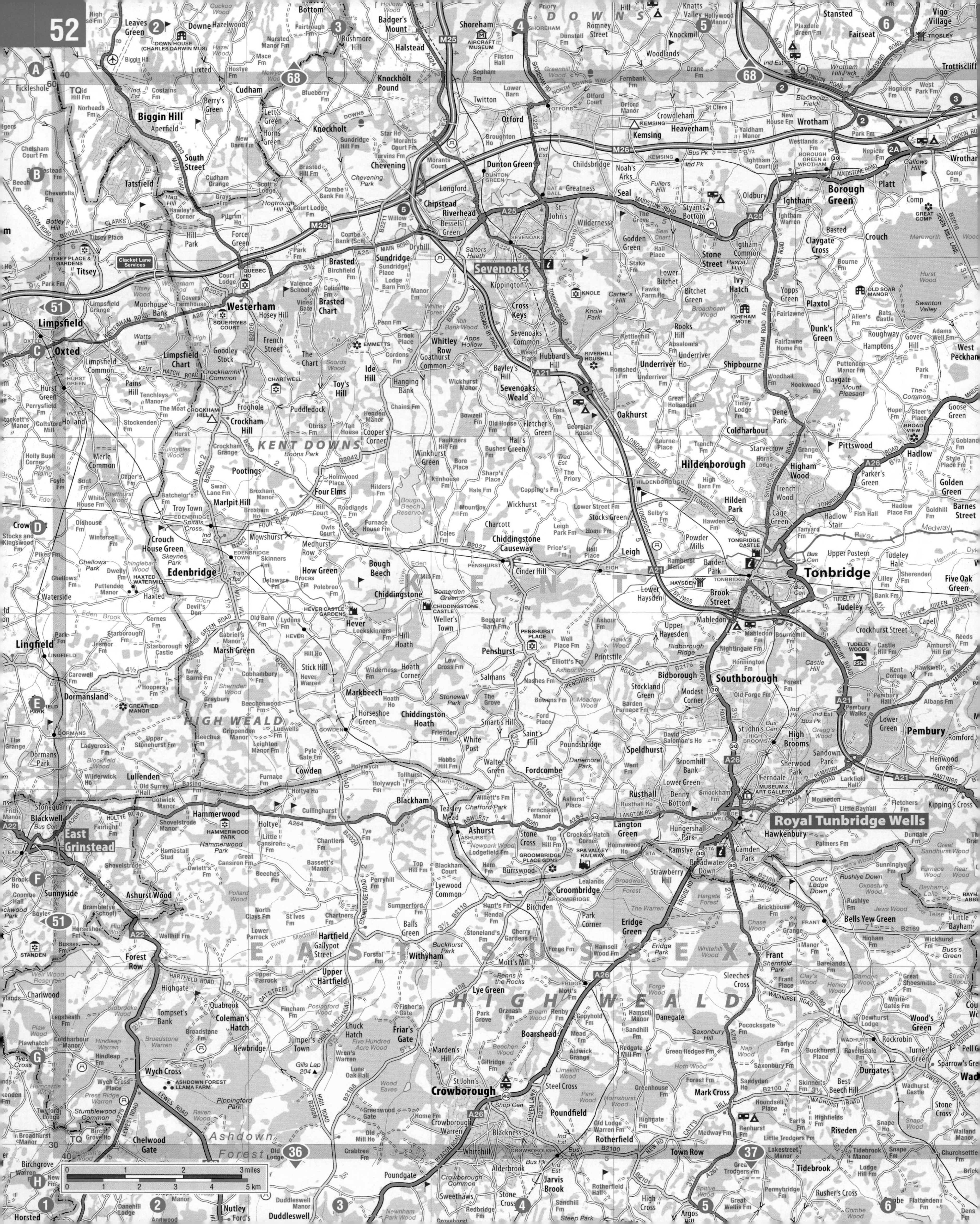
Biggin Hill
Westerham
Limpsfield
Oxted
Sevenoaks
Otford
Kemsing
Wrotham
Borough Green
Seal
Riverhead
Chipstead
Knockholt
Halstead
Shoreham
Sundridge
Brasted
Ightham
Hildenborough
Tonbridge
Hadlow
Edenbridge
Penshurst
Chiddingstone
Hever
Leigh
Southborough
Pembury
Royal Tunbridge Wells
Lingfield
Dormansland
East Grinstead
Forest Row
Hartfield
Groombridge
Crowborough
Rotherfield
Frant
Wadhurst
Ashdown Forest
KENT DOWNS
HIGH WEALD
KENT
EAST SUSSEX
0 1 2 3 miles
0 1 2 3 4 5 km

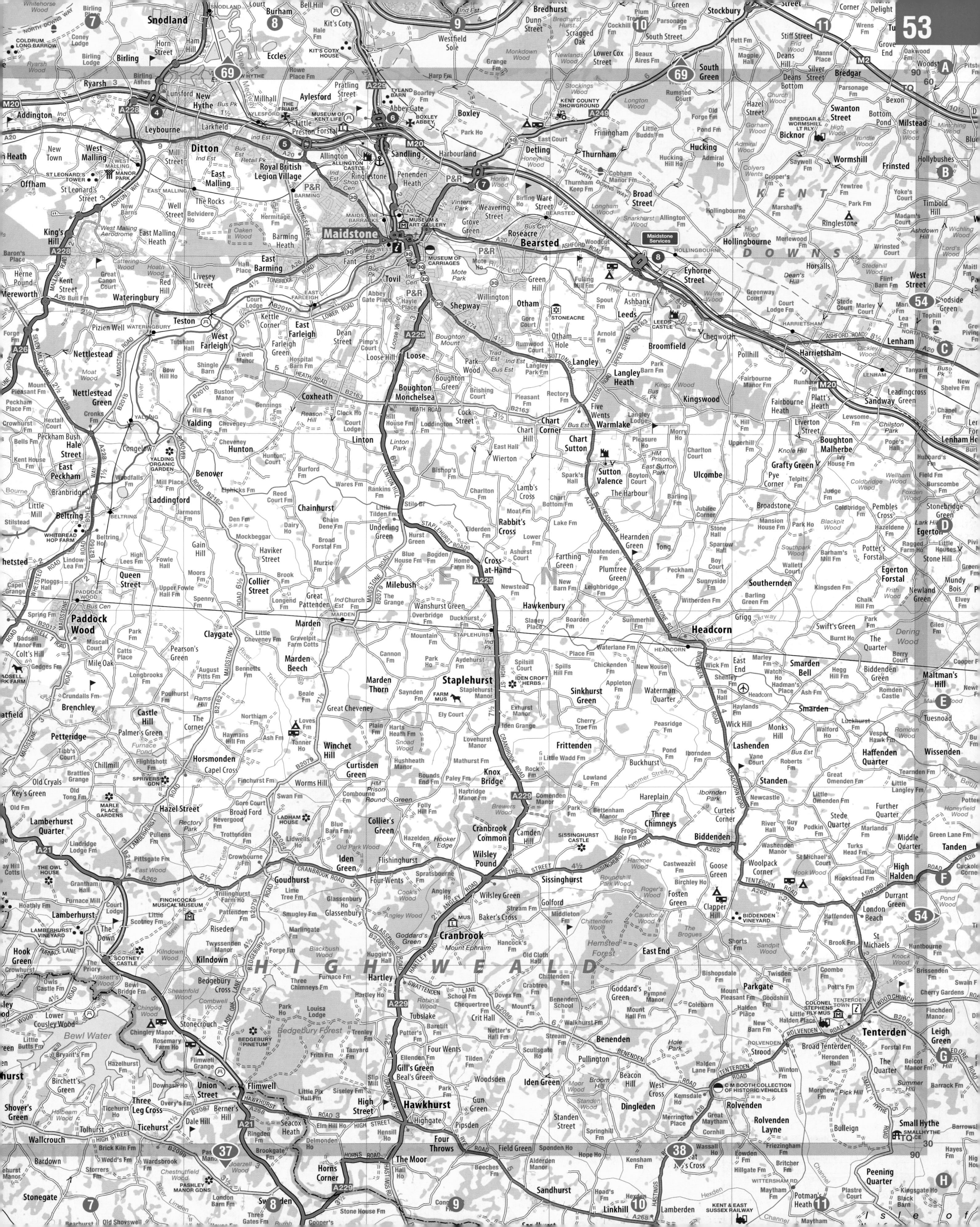
Snodland
Burham
Birling
Eccles
Aylesford
Leybourne
Ditton
Larkfield
New Hythe
Addington
West Malling
East Malling
Royal British Legion Village
Allington
Sandling
Boxley
Detling
Thurnham
Hucking
Bredgar
Bicknor
Wormshill
Frinsted
Maidstone
Bearsted
Tovil
Fant
East Barming
Barming Heath
Wateringbury
Teston
West Farleigh
East Farleigh
Otham
Leeds
Hollingbourne
Harrietsham
Lenham
Loose
Coxheath
Boughton Monchelsea
Langley
Langley Heath
Kingswood
Broomfield
Nettlestead
Nettlestead Green
Yalding
Hunton
Linton
Chart Sutton
Sutton Valence
Ulcombe
Grafty Green
Boughton Malherbe
Laddingford
Benover
Beltring
Collier Street
Marden
Staplehurst
Headcorn
Smarden
Paddock Wood
Brenchley
Horsmonden
Lamberhurst
Goudhurst
Cranbrook
Sissinghurst
Biddenden
Frittenden
High Halden
Tenterden
Hawkhurst
Flimwell
Ticehurst
Benenden
Rolvenden
Sandhurst
Bewl Water
Bedgebury Forest
K E N T
D O W N S
H I G H   W E A L D
M20
M2
A20
A21
A26
A228
A229
A274
A262
A28
A268
69
37
38
54

Faversham
Ospringe
Preston
Lynsted
Rodmersham
Newnham
Doddington
Eastling
North Downs
Sheldwich
Throwley
Selling
Boughton Street
Dunkirk
Harbledown
Rough Common
Blean
Chartham
Thanington
Chilham
Shottenden
Badlesmere
Leaveland
Molash
Challock
Godmersham
Kent Downs
King's Wood
Lenham
Charing
Charing Heath
Lenham Heath
Westwell
Eastwell Park
Boughton Aluph
Boughton Lees
Wye
Crundale
Waltham
Petham
Pluckley
Pluckley Thorne
Egerton
Little Chart
Hothfield
Kennington
Ashford
Willesborough
Kingsnorth
Great Chart
Bethersden
Shadoxhurst
Stubbs Cross
Mersham
Smeeth
Brabourne
Hastingleigh
Elmsted
Stowting
Postling
Sellindge
Aldington
Bonnington
Bilsington
Orlestone
Hamstreet
Ruckinge
Woodchurch
High Halden
Tenterden
Appledore
Snave
Newchurch
Burmarsh
Dymchurch
Lympne
West Hythe
Newingreen
Westenhanger
Romney Marsh
Isle of Oxney
M20
M2
A2
A28
A20
A2070
Stop 24 Folkestone Services

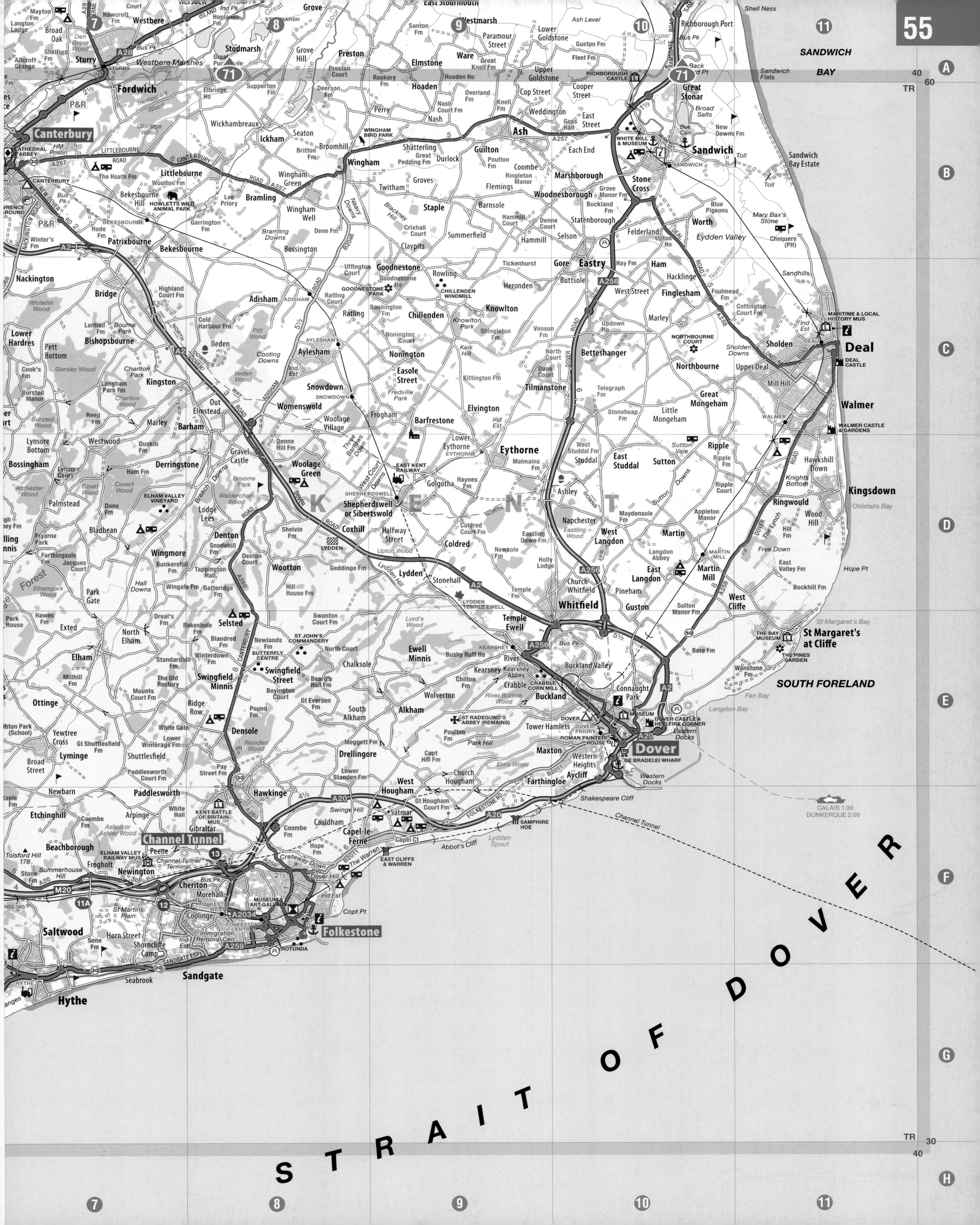
SANDWICH BAY
Shell Ness
Sandwich Flats
TR
40
60
Westbere
Sturry
Fordwich
Canterbury
Stodmarsh
Westbere Marshes
Grove
Preston
Westmarsh
Elmstone
Hoaden
Wickhambreaux
Ickham
Wingham
Littlebourne
Bekesbourne
Patrixbourne
Bridge
Nackington
Bishopsbourne
Kingston
Barham
Adisham
Aylesham
Nonington
Goodnestone
Chillenden
Knowlton
Ash
Sandwich
Richborough Port
Great Stonar
Worth
Eastry
Ham
Finglesham
Betteshanger
Northbourne
Deal
Sholden
Walmer
Great Mongeham
Ripple
Kingsdown
Ringwould
Martin Mill
St Margaret's at Cliffe
SOUTH FORELAND
Tilmanstone
Eythorne
Elvington
Barfrestone
Womenswold
Woolage Green
Shepherdswell or Sibertswold
Coxhill
Coldred
Lydden
Whitfield
Temple Ewell
Guston
East Langdon
West Langdon
Dover
River
Kearsney
Buckland
Maxton
Aycliff
Farthingloe
West Hougham
Capel-le-Ferne
Hawkinge
Densole
Swingfield Minnis
Elham
Lyminge
Etchinghill
Newington
Cheriton
Folkestone
Sandgate
Saltwood
Hythe
Channel Tunnel
Shakespeare Cliff
Channel Tunnel
CALAIS 1:30
DUNKERQUE 2:00
KENT
STRAIT OF DOVER
TR
30
40
7
8
9
10
11
A
B
C
D
E
F
G
H

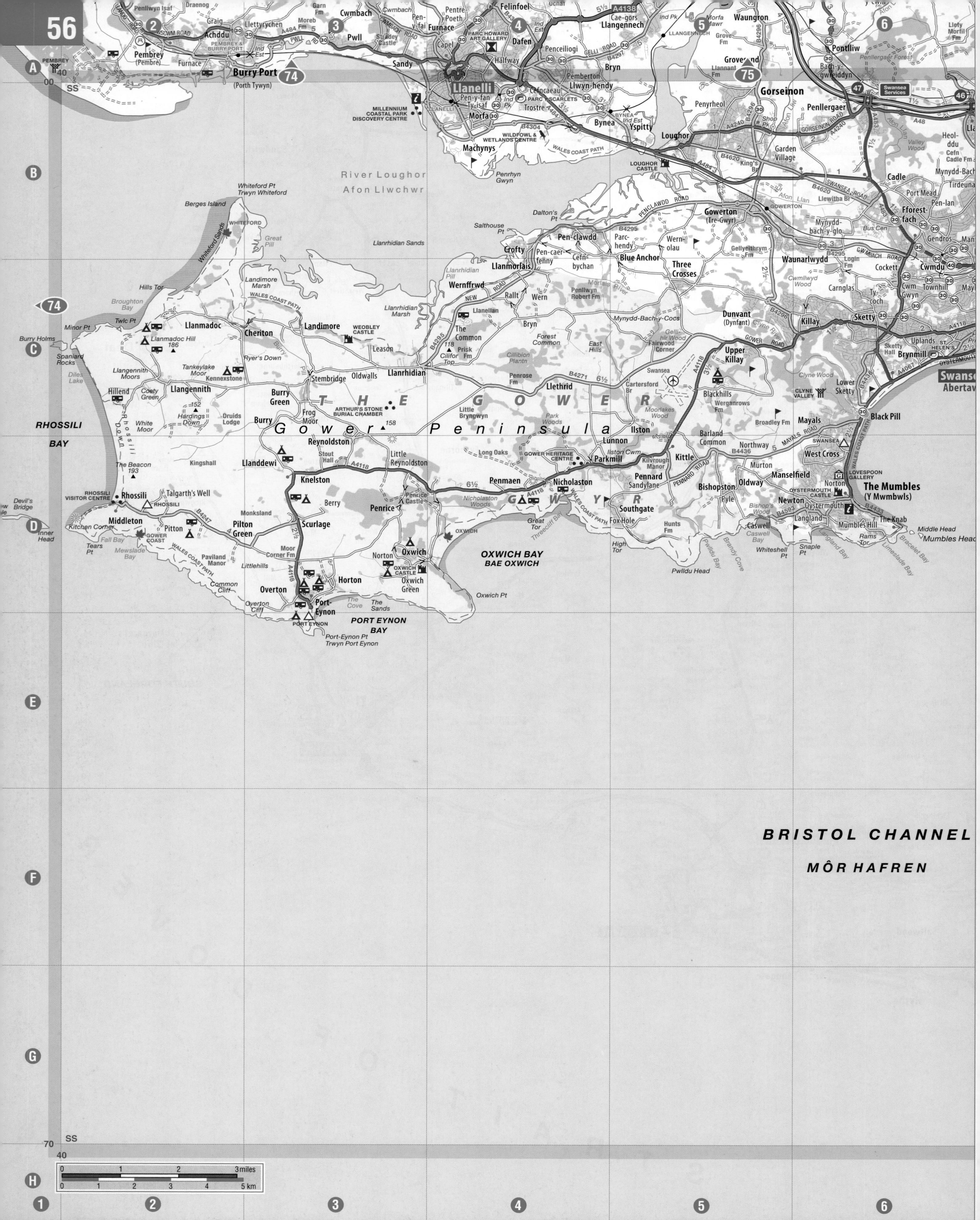
Pembrey
(Pembre)
Burry Port
(Porth Tywyn)
Llanelli
Felinfoel
Dafen
Llangennech
Pwll
Cwmbach
Furnace
Sandy
Morfa
Machynys
Bynea
Yspitty
Loughor
Gorseinon
Penllergaer
Pontlliw
Waungron
Gowerton
(Tre-Gwyr)
Dunvant
(Dynfant)
Killay
Upper Killay
Sketty
Cwmdu
Cockett
Fforest-fach
Cadle
Brynmill
Mayals
West Cross
Blackhills
Swansea
Abertawe
Waunarlwydd
Three Crosses
Blue Anchor
Pen-clawdd
Crofty
Llanmorlais
Wernffrwd
River Loughor
Afon Llwchwr
Llanrhidian Sands
Whiteford Pt
Trwyn Whiteford
Berges Island
Whiteford Sands
Llanmadoc
Cheriton
Landimore
Llanrhidian
Oldwalls
Stembridge
Burry Green
Llangennith
Hillend
Rhossili
RHOSSILI BAY
Middleton
Pitton
Pilton Green
Scurlage
Knelston
Llanddewi
Reynoldston
Penrice
Oxwich
OXWICH BAY
BAE OXWICH
Horton
Overton
Port-Eynon
PORT EYNON BAY
Port-Eynon Pt
Trwyn Port Eynon
Oxwich Pt
Penmaen
Nicholaston
Parkmill
Ilston
Lunnon
Llethrid
Southgate
Pennard
Bishopston
Kittle
Oldway
Murton
Manselfield
Newton
Langland
Mumbles Hill
The Mumbles
(Y Mwmbwls)
Mumbles Head
Pwlldu Head
THE GOWER
Gower Peninsula
Worms Head
Rhossili Down
BRISTOL CHANNEL
MÔR HAFREN
0 1 2 3 miles
0 1 2 3 4 5 km
A B C D E F G H
1 2 3 4 5 6

Clydach
Ynystawe
Pant-lasau
Morriston
(Treforys)
Heol-las
Birchgrove
Llansamlet
Landore
Skewen
Neath Abbey
Neath
Castell-Nedd
Cadoxton-Juxta-Neath
Aberdulais
Cilfrew
Bryn-coch
Rhydding
Tonna (Tonnau)
Clyne
Melincourt
Glyncorrwg
Abercregan
Cymer
Croeserw
Blaen-gwynfi
Aber-gwynfi
Duffryn
Tonmawr
AFAN ARGOED
FOREST PARK
Cimla
Briton Ferry
(Llansawel)
Baglan
Pontrhydyfen
Pwll-y-glaw
Cwmafan
Brynbryddan
Llandarcy
Port Tennant
St Thomas
Foxhole
Pentre-chwyth
SWANSEA BAY
BAE ABERTAWE
Aberavon
Sandfields
Port Talbot
Taibach
Goybre
Margam
Groes
Brombil
Maesteg
Llwydarth
Garth
Cwmfelin
Nantyffyllon
Spelter
Caerau
Dyffryn
Blaengarw
Pontycymer
BRIDGEND
(PEN-Y-BONT
AR OGWR)
Llangynwyd
Coytrahen
Brynmenyn
Tondu
Bryncethin
Aberkenfig
Sarn
Kenfig Hill
Cefn Cribbwr
Cefn Cross
Pyle (Y Pîl)
Mawdlam
Kenfig
North Cornelly
South Cornelly
Laleston
Pen-y-fai
Newcastle
Nottage
Porthcawl
Hutchwns
Newton
Merthyr Mawr
Ogmore
Ogmore-by-Sea
St Brides Major
Southerndown
Castle-upon-Alun
SWANSEA BAY
Margam Sands
Kenfig Sands
WALES COAST PATH
7
8
9
10
11

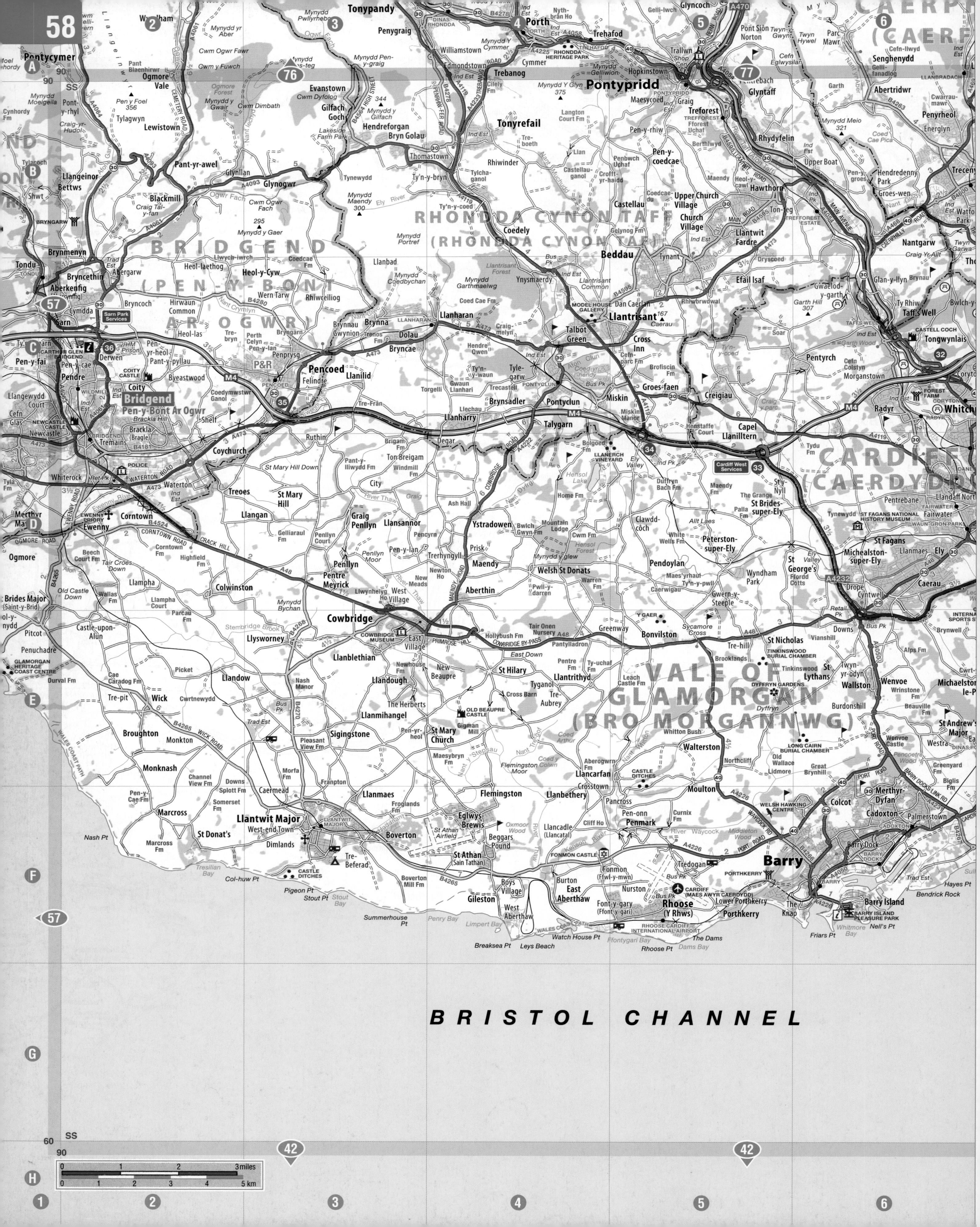

BRISTOL CHANNEL
BRIDGEND
(PEN-Y-BONT AR OGWR)
RHONDDA CYNON TAFF
(RHONDDA CYNON TAF)
VALE OF GLAMORGAN
(BRO MORGANNWG)
CARDIFF
CAERDYDD
Pontypridd
Tonypandy
Porth
Trehafod
Pontycymer
Ogmore Vale
Tonyrefail
Beddau
Llantrisant
Talbot Green
Pontyclun
Llanharan
Pencoed
Bridgend
Pen-y-Bont Ar Ogwr
Cowbridge
Llantwit Major
Barry
Rhoose
(Y Rhws)
Penarth
Barry Island
Radyr
Tongwynlais
Taff's Well
Creigiau
Pentyrch
St Fagans
Michaelston-super-Ely
Wenvoe
Dinas Powys
Cadoxton
Merthyr-Dyfan
Colcot
Bonvilston
St Nicholas
Peterston-super-Ely
Pendoylan
Welsh St Donats
Aberthin
Ystradowen
St Hilary
Llantrithyd
Llancarfan
Penmark
St Athan
(Sain Tathan)
Boverton
Llanmaes
Flemington
Eglwys-Brewis
St Donat's
Marcross
Monknash
Wick
Broughton
Llandow
Llysworney
Colwinston
Llangan
Treoes
Coychurch
Corntown
Ewenny
Ogmore
St Brides Major
Pentre Meyrick
Penllyn
Llansannor
Llanblethian
Llandough
St Mary Church
Sigingstone
Llanmihangel
Aberkenfig
Bryncethin
Sarn
Coity
Pendre
Brackla
Tremains
Heol-y-Cyw
Blackmill
Glynogwr
Llangeinor
Gilfach Goch
Evanstown
Penygraig
Trebanog
Cymmer
Williamstown
Treforest
Rhydyfelin
Hawthorn
Upper Church Village
Church Village
Llantwit Fardre
Efail Isaf
Groes-faen
Capel Llanilltern
Miskin
Talygarn
Llanharry
Brynsadler
Cross Inn
Nantgarw
Glyntaff
Abertridwr
Senghenydd
Pentrebane
Fairwater
Ely
Caerau
Drope
Culverhouse Cross
Tre-hill
Twyn-yr-odyn
Wallston
Lower Porthkerry
Porthkerry
Fonmon
East Aberthaw
West Aberthaw
Gileston
Boys Village
CARDIFF (MAES AWYR CAERDYDD)
M4
A48
A4226
A4232
A473
A4119
A470
57
76
77
42
BRIDGEND
Sarn Park Services
Cardiff West Services
Nash Pt
Col-huw Pt
Summerhouse Pt
Breaksea Pt
Leys Beach
Watch House Pt
Rhoose Pt
Friars Pt
Nell's Pt
Hayes Pt
Bendrick Rock
SS
60
90
0 1 2 3 miles
0 1 2 3 4 5 km
A B C D E F G H
1 2 3 4 5 6

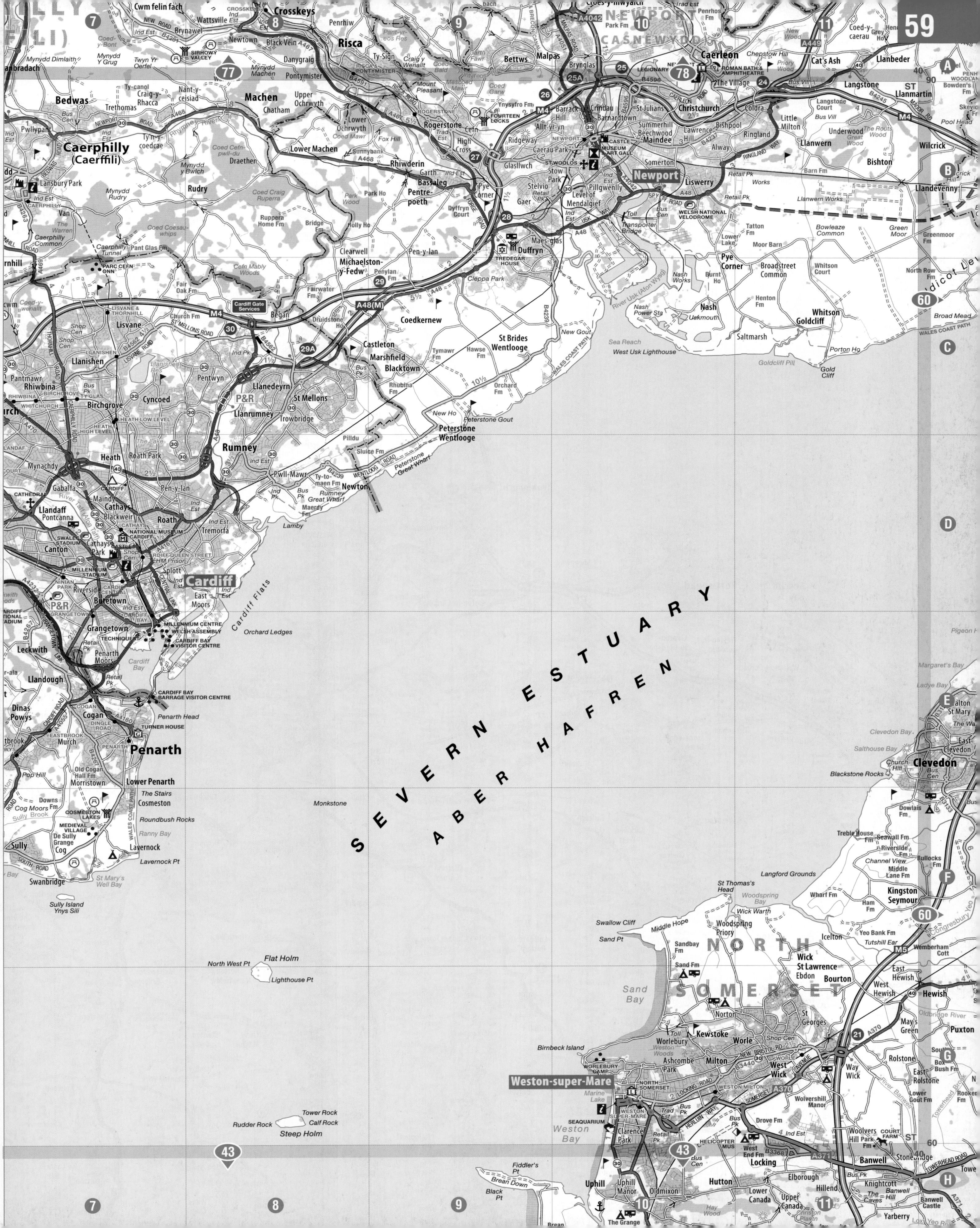
SEVERN ESTUARY
ABER HAFREN
Caerphilly
(Caerffili)
Newport
NEWPORT
CASNEWYDD
Cardiff
Weston-super-Mare
NORTH
SOMERSET
Crosskeys
Risca
Bettws
Malpas
Caerleon
Cat's Ash
Llanbeder
Bedwas
Machen
Rogerstone
Bassaleg
Rhiwderin
Lower Machen
Rudry
Duffryn
Maindee
Christchurch
Lliswerry
Langstone
Llanmartin
Wilcrick
Bishton
Llanwern
Llandevenny
Nash
Goldcliff
Whitson
Saltmarsh
Pye Corner
Coedkernew
Castleton
Marshfield
St Brides Wentlooge
Peterstone Wentlooge
Lisvane
Llanishen
Rhiwbina
Cyncoed
Pentwyn
Llanedeyrn
St Mellons
Llanrumney
Trowbridge
Rumney
Heath
Roath
Cathays
Canton
Llandaff
Butetown
Grangetown
Splott
Tremorfa
Leckwith
Llandough
Cogan
Penarth
Lower Penarth
Cosmeston
Lavernock
Sully
Swanbridge
Sully Island
Ynys Sili
Dinas Powys
Monkstone
Orchard Ledges
Cardiff Flats
Flat Holm
Steep Holm
Sand Bay
Weston Bay
Kewstoke
Worle
Milton
West Wick
Uphill
Hutton
Locking
Banwell
Clevedon
Kingston Seymour
Wick St Lawrence
Hewish
Puxton
Yatton
Bourton
Icelton
Woodspring Priory
Middle Hope
Sand Pt
Birnbeck Island
Brean Down
Langford Grounds
M4
M5
A48(M)
60
43
77
78

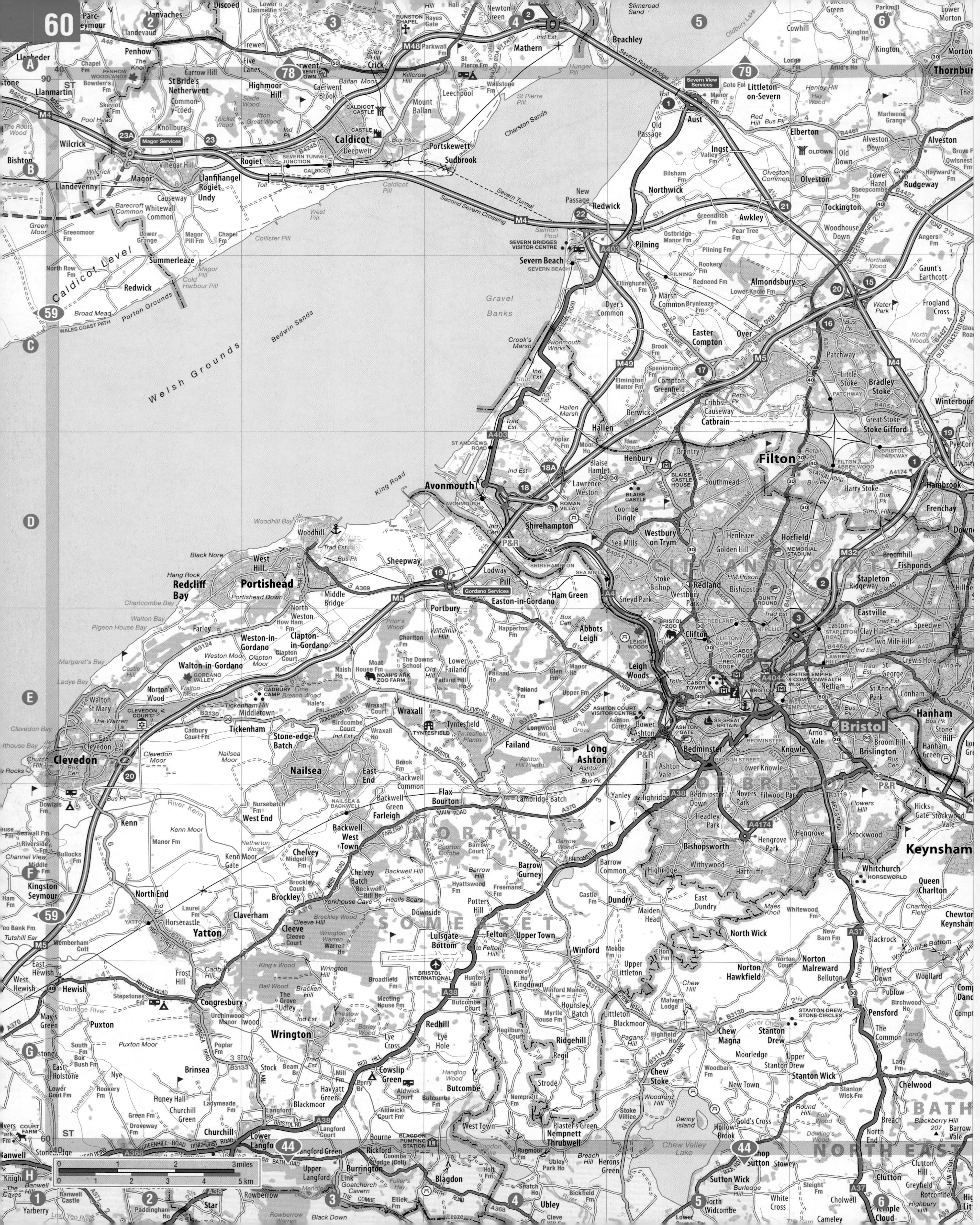
Parc-Seymour
Llanvaches
Penhow
Llanmartin
Magor
Magor Services
Rogiet
Caldicot
Portskewett
Sudbrook
Mathern
Beachley
Aust
Severn View Services
Littleton-on-Severn
Thornbury
Elberton
Olveston
Alveston
Rudgeway
Tockington
Almondsbury
Pilning
Redwick
Severn Beach
Severn Bridges Visitor Centre
Caldicot Level
Welsh Grounds
Bedwin Sands
Gravel Banks
Second Severn Crossing
Severn Road Bridge
Easter Compton
Patchway
Bradley Stoke
Stoke Gifford
Winterbourne
Hallen
Henbury
Filton
Avonmouth
Shirehampton
Frenchay
Hambrook
Fishponds
Westbury on Trym
Horfield
Redland
Clifton
Eastville
Stapleton
Kingswood
Hanham
Bristol
Bedminster
Brislington
Knowle
Keynsham
Whitchurch
Queen Charlton
Portishead
Redcliff Bay
Pill
Easton-in-Gordano
Portbury
Abbots Leigh
Leigh Woods
Long Ashton
Failand
Wraxall
Tyntesfield
Clapton-in-Gordano
Weston-in-Gordano
Walton-in-Gordano
Clevedon
Tickenham
Nailsea
Backwell
Flax Bourton
Barrow Gurney
Bishopsworth
Dundry
Winford
Felton
Bristol International
Kenn
Yatton
Claverham
Cleeve
Congresbury
Wrington
Redhill
Butcombe
Blagdon
Chew Magna
Chew Stoke
Stanton Drew
Pensford
Norton Malreward
North Wick
Puxton
Brinsea
Churchill
Langford
Burrington
Ubley
Chew Valley Lake
Bishop Sutton
Clutton
Temple Cloud
Chelwood
City and County of Bristol
North Somerset
Bath and North East Somerset
0 1 2 3 miles
0 1 2 3 4 5 km

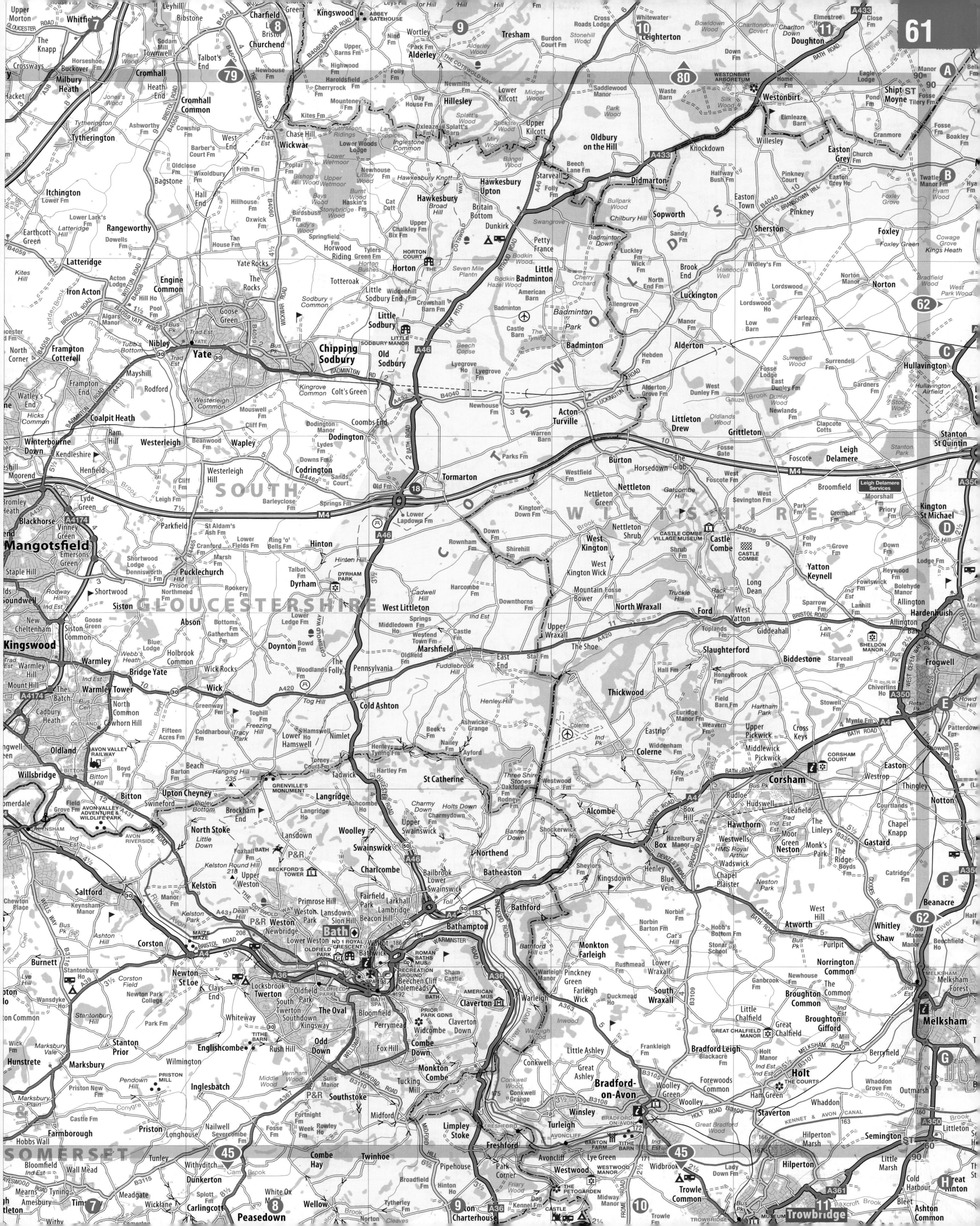
GLOUCESTERSHIRE
SOUTH
WILTSHIRE
COTSWOLDS
SOMERSET
Chipping Sodbury
Yate
Mangotsfield
Kingswood
Bath
Corsham
Melksham
Bradford-on-Avon
Trowbridge
Leighterton
Doughton
Westonbirt
Tresham
Alderley
Wickwar
Charfield
Kingswood
Cromhall
Tytherington
Hillesley
Hawkesbury
Hawkesbury Upton
Oldbury on the Hill
Didmarton
Sherston
Sopworth
Luckington
Badminton
Little Badminton
Acton Turville
Alderton
Hullavington
Norton
Foxley
Stanton St Quintin
Grittleton
Littleton Drew
Leigh Delamere
Burton
Nettleton
Kington St Michael
Yatton Keynell
Castle Combe
West Kington
North Wraxall
Ford
Biddestone
Slaughterford
Colerne
Marshfield
Tormarton
Dodington
Codrington
Westerleigh
Pucklechurch
Dyrham
Hinton
Cold Ashton
West Littleton
Wick
Warmley
Bitton
Saltford
Kelston
Corston
Newton St Loe
Keynsham
Marksbury
Priston
Englishcombe
Dunkerton
Peasedown
Combe Hay
Southstoke
Midford
Limpley Stoke
Freshford
Monkton Combe
Combe Down
Batheaston
Bathford
Box
Monkton Farleigh
South Wraxall
Atworth
Holt
Winsley
Westwood
Hilperton
Semington
Gastard
Frogwell
Chippenham
M4
A46
A4
A420
A433
A350
A36
A431
A432
A4174
B4040
B4039
Leigh Delamere Services
Dyrham Park
Castle Combe Village Museum
Corsham Court
Sheldon Manor
Great Chalfield Manor
Claverton American Mus
Roman Baths Mus
Westonbirt Arboretum
Prior Park Gdns
Avon Valley Adventure & Wildlife Park
Avon Valley Railway
Beckford's Tower
Grenville's Monument
Badminton Park
79
80
45
62

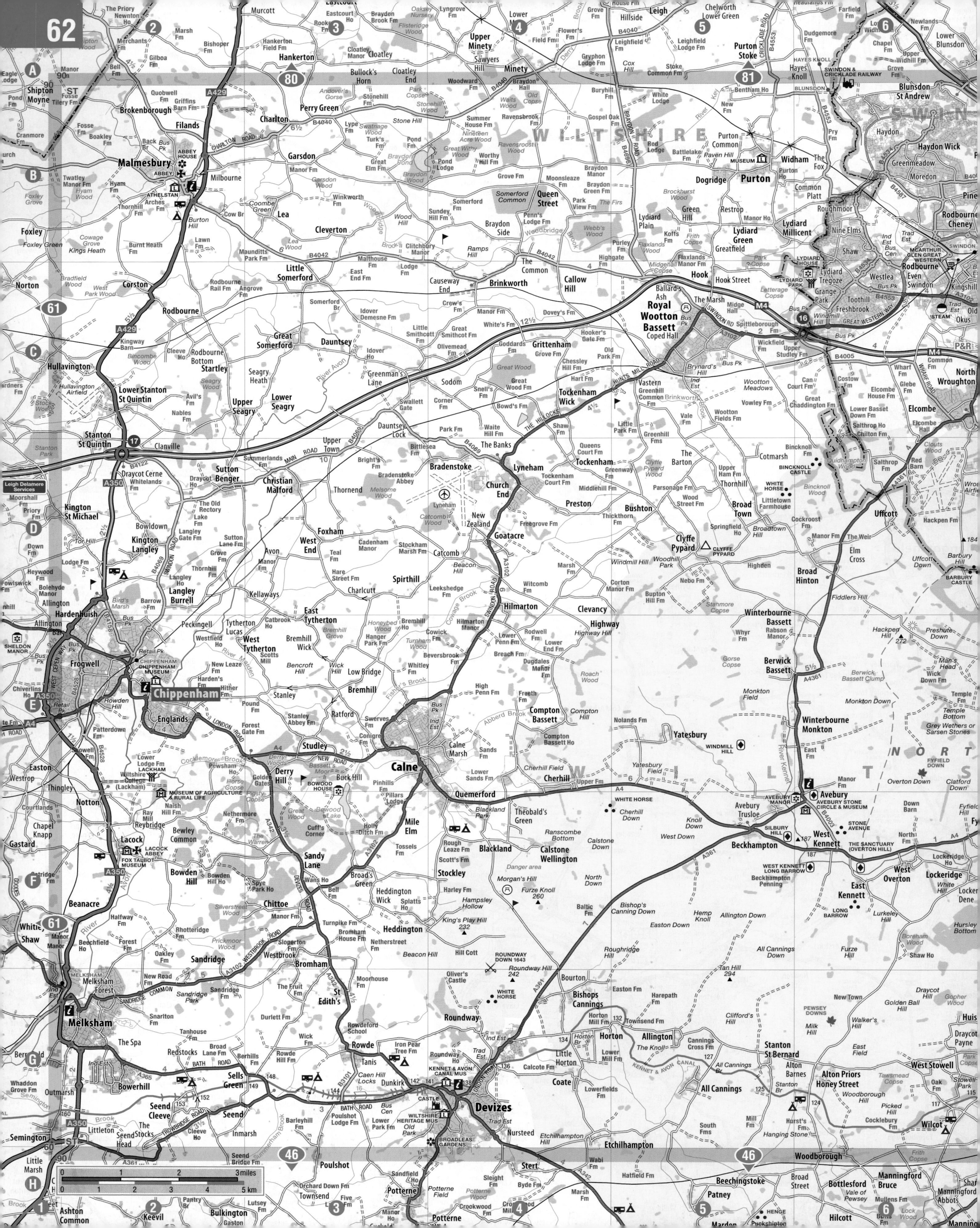
WILTSHIRE
Malmesbury
Chippenham
Calne
Melksham
Devizes
Royal Wootton Bassett
Lyneham
Purton
Avebury
Corsham
Lacock
Hullavington
Sutton Benger
Christian Malford
Brinkworth
Hankerton
Minety
Charlton
Garsdon
Lea
Cleverton
Little Somerford
Great Somerford
Dauntsey
Seagry
Stanton St Quintin
Kington St Michael
Kington Langley
Langley Burrell
Hardenhuish
Frogwell
Englands
Derry Hill
Studley
Bremhill
Hilmarton
Goatacre
Compton Bassett
Cherhill
Quemerford
Yatesbury
Winterbourne Bassett
Winterbourne Monkton
Broad Hinton
Broad Town
Clyffe Pypard
Bushton
Tockenham
Tockenham Wick
Grittenham
Hook
Lydiard Millicent
Lydiard Tregoze
Swindon
Haydon Wick
Blunsdon St Andrew
Wroughton
Elcombe
Uffcott
Beckhampton
West Kennett
East Kennett
West Overton
Lockeridge
Bishops Cannings
Horton
Allington
All Cannings
Stanton St Bernard
Alton Barnes
Alton Priors
Honey Street
Woodborough
Etchilhampton
Rowde
Poulshot
Potterne
Seend
Seend Cleeve
Bowerhill
Semington
Bromham
Sandy Lane
Heddington
Stockley
Calstone Wellington
Blackland
Roundway
Bowden Hill
Notton
Reybridge
Sandridge
Beanacre
Whitley
Shaw
Bulkington
Keevil
Ashton Common
Patney
Beechingstoke
Manningford Bruce
Wilcot
Oare
Pewsey
M4
A4
A350
A342
A3102
A361
A429
A4361
B4040
B4042
B4069
16
17
61
80
81
46
0 1 2 3 miles
0 1 2 3 4 5 km

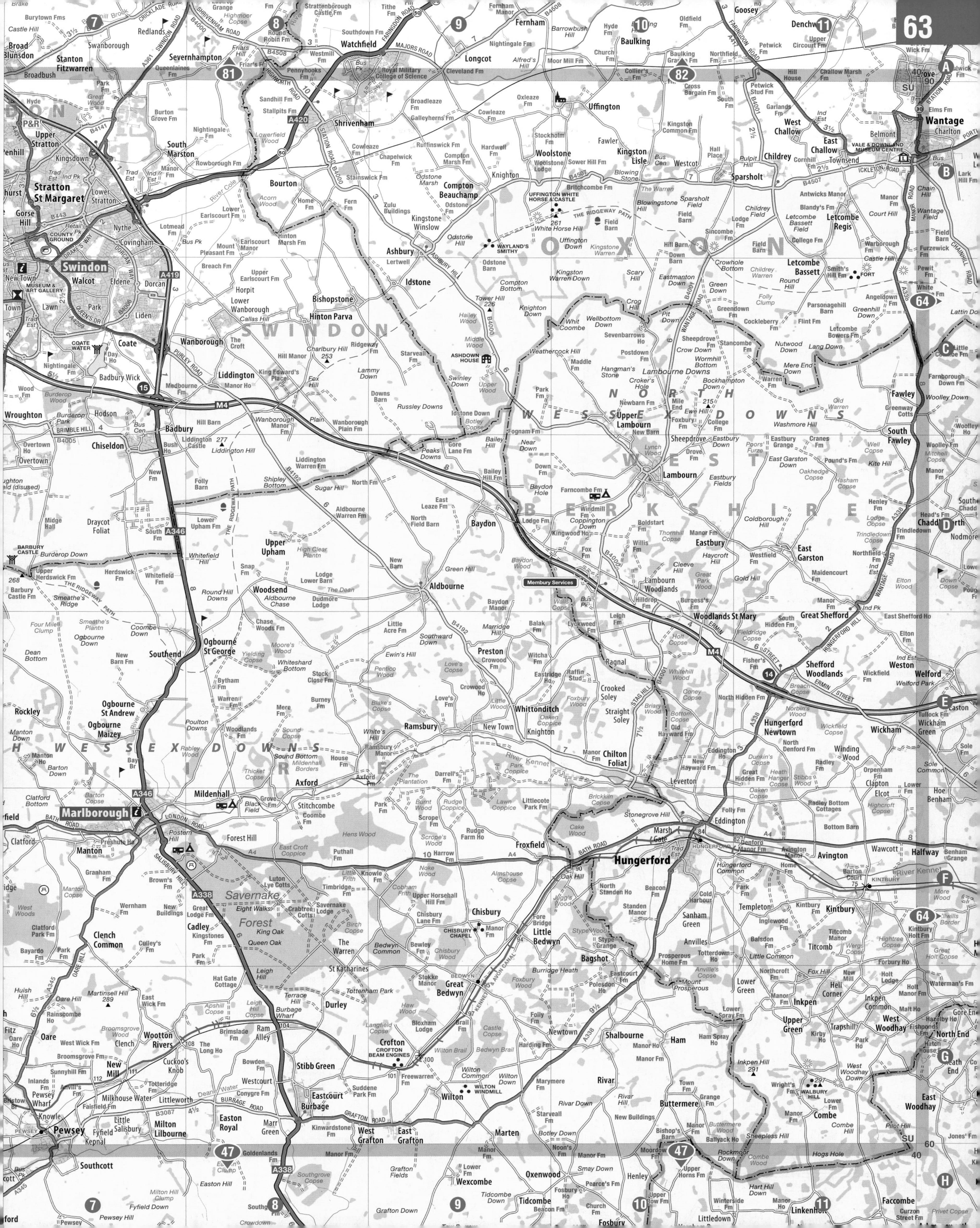

Swindon
Stratton St Margaret
Upper Stratton
Walcot
Wroughton
Chiseldon
Badbury
Liddington
Wanborough
Bishopstone
Hinton Parva
Ashbury
Idstone
Shrivenham
Watchfield
Bourton
South Marston
Longcot
Fernham
Baulking
Uffington
Woolstone
Compton Beauchamp
Kingston Lisle
Childrey
Sparsholt
West Challow
East Challow
Wantage
Letcombe Regis
Letcombe Bassett
Lambourn
Upper Lambourn
Eastbury
East Garston
Baydon
Aldbourne
Woodsend
Upper Upham
Ogbourne St George
Ogbourne St Andrew
Ogbourne Maizey
Marlborough
Mildenhall
Axford
Ramsbury
Whittonditch
Chilton Foliat
Hungerford
Froxfield
Great Shefford
Shefford Woodlands
Woodlands St Mary
Welford
Wickham
Kintbury
Inkpen
West Woodhay
East Woodhay
Combe
Buttermere
Shalbourne
Ham
Great Bedwyn
Little Bedwyn
Burbage
Pewsey
Easton Royal
Milton Lilbourne
Wootton Rivers
Clench Common
Savernake Forest
Wilton
Crofton
Marten
Oxenwood
Wexcombe
Grafton
Tidcombe
Fosbury
Faccombe
Linkenholt
NORTH WESSEX DOWNS
SWINDON
OXON
WEST BERKSHIRE
WILTSHIRE
WESSEX DOWNS
M4
A346
A338
A4
A419
Membury Services
THE RIDGEWAY PATH

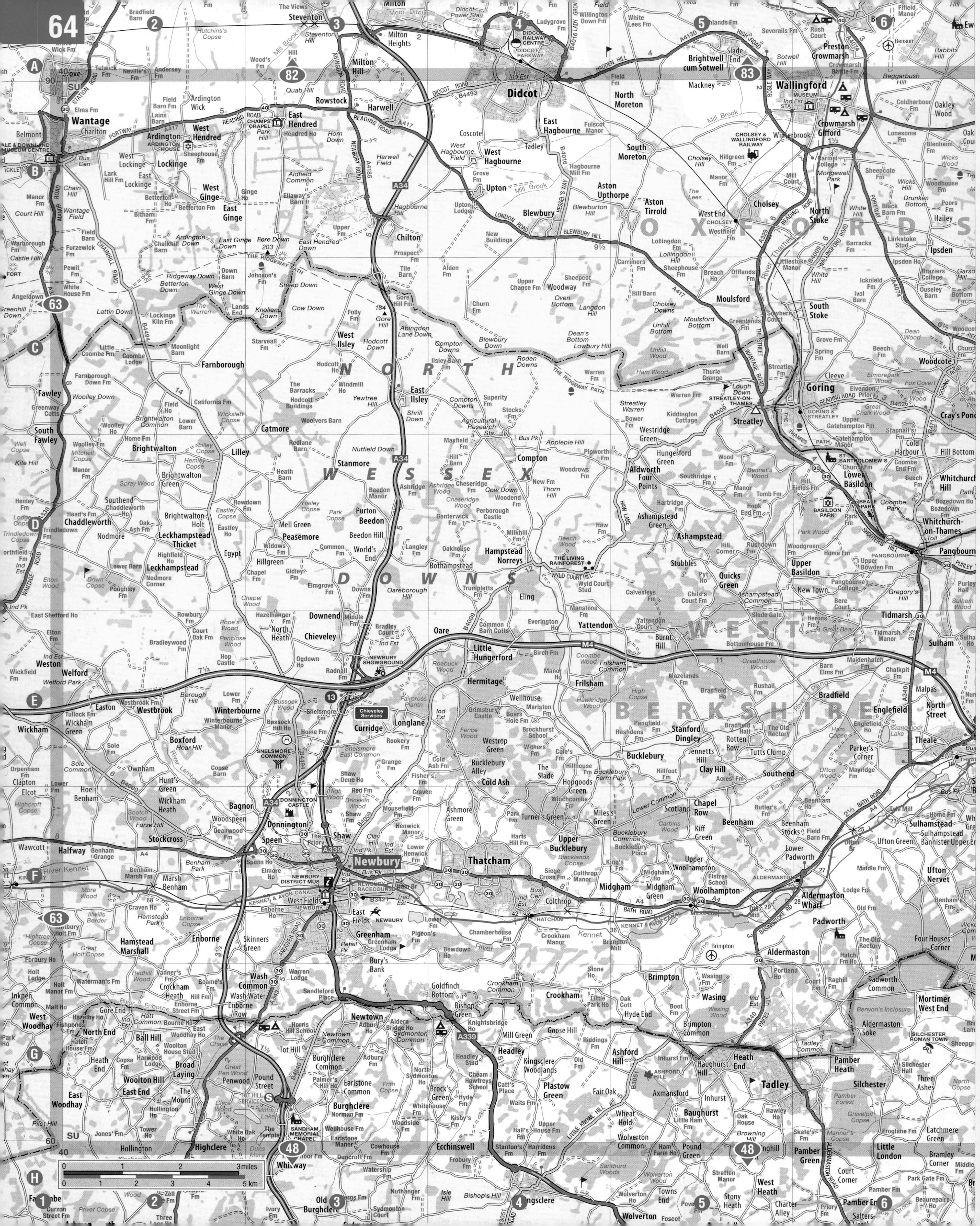

Wantage
Didcot
Wallingford
Goring
Streatley
Newbury
Thatcham
Tadley
Pangbourne
Lower Basildon
Whitchurch-on-Thames
Theale
Kingsclere
Highclere
Hungerford
O X F O R D S
N O R T H
W E S S E X
D O W N S
W E S T
B E R K S H I R E
Chieveley Services
Cholsey
Moulsford
South Stoke
Blewbury
Chilton
East Ilsley
West Ilsley
Compton
Hampstead Norreys
Yattendon
Hermitage
Curridge
Donnington
Speen
Greenham
Aldermaston
Woolhampton
Midgham
Bucklebury
Burghclere
Ecchinswell
Leckhampstead
Chaddleworth
Brightwalton
Farnborough
Fawley
Lambourn
Boxford
Winterbourne
Peasemore
Beedon
Chieveley
Cold Ash
Upper Bucklebury
Brimpton
Crookham
Headley
Baughurst
Pamber Heath
Silchester
Mortimer West End
Sulhamstead
Ufton Nervet
Padworth
Tidmarsh
Sulham
Bradfield
Englefield
Upper Basildon
Ashampstead
Aldworth
Crowmarsh Gifford
Brightwell cum Sotwell
Harwell
Milton
Steventon
Rowstock
East Hendred
Ardington
Lockinge
East Hagbourne
West Hagbourne
Upton
Aston Tirrold
Aston Upthorpe
North Moreton
South Moreton
Woodcote
Ipsden
Enborne
Hamstead Marshall
Inkpen Common
West Woodhay
East Woodhay
Ball Hill
Woolton Hill
Little London
Pamber Green
Wolverton
A34
A4
M4
A339
A417
A329
A340
82
83
63
48
A B C D E F G H
1 2 3 4 5 6
0 1 2 3 miles
0 1 2 3 4 5 km

Henley-on-Thames
Marlow
Maidenhead
Reading
Caversham
Tilehurst
Woodley
Earley
Twyford
Wokingham
Bracknell
Crowthorne
Sandhurst
Camberley
Yateley
Bagshot
Binfield
Whitley
Shinfield
Arborfield
Swallowfield
Finchampstead
Eversley
Hazeley
Frimley
Cookham
Bourne End
Taplow
Bray
Holyport
Hurley
Hambleden
Medmenham
Remenham
Wargrave
Sonning
Charvil
Nettlebed
Stoke Row
Checkendon
Mapledurham
Purley on Thames
Sonning Common
Harpsden
Shiplake
Burghfield
Stratfield Mortimer
Stratfield Saye
Heckfield
Riseley
Spencers Wood
Three Mile Cross
Pangbourne
Flackwell Heath
Loudwater
Little Marlow
Fingest
Turville
Stonor
Pishill
Fawley
Frieth
Lane End
Wooburn Green
Winkfield
Warfield
Easthampstead
College Town
Owlsmoor
Little Sandhurst
Hawley
Blackwater
York Town
BUCKS
WINDSOR & MAIDENHEAD
WOKINGHAM
BRACKNELL FOREST
READING
CHILTERNS
M4
M40
A4
A329(M)
A404
A4130
A33
A321
A30
River Thames

Beaconsfield
Loudwater
Knotty Green
Seer Green
Jordans
Chalfont St Peter
Harefield
Northwood
Ruislip
Harrow
Flackwell Heath
Gerrards Cross
Denham
Uxbridge
Ickenham
Eastcote
Northolt
Bourne End
Cookham
Burnham
Farnham Common
Stoke Poges
Iver Heath
Hillingdon
Yeading
Greenford
Taplow
Slough
Iver
Yiewsley
Hayes
Southall
Maidenhead
Langley
West Drayton
Bray
Eton
Datchet
Colnbrook
Harmondsworth
Heston
Windsor
Heathrow Airport
Hounslow
Old Windsor
Wraysbury
Stanwell
Feltham
Twickenham
Winkfield
Egham
Staines-upon-Thames
Ashford
Hanworth
Englefield Green
Laleham
Sunbury-on-Thames
Hampton
Ascot
Sunninghill
Virginia Water
Thorpe
Shepperton
Walton-on-Thames
Chertsey
Addlestone
Weybridge
Esher
Bagshot
Windlesham
Chobham
Woodham
Byfleet
Lightwater
West Byfleet
Cobham
Woking
Pyrford
Wisley
Oxshott
Stoke D'Abernon
M4
M25
M40
M3
A4
A30
A308
A316
1 2 3 miles
1 2 3 4 5 km

Stanmore
Finchley
Woodford
Wealdstone
Hendon
Tottenham
Wood Green
Hornsey
Walthamstow
Kenton
Kingsbury
Golders Green
Highgate
Wanstead
Leyton
Harrow on the Hill
Wembley
Hampstead
Stoke Newington
Islington
Sudbury
Willesden
Cricklewood
Camden
Hackney
Stratford
Alperton
Perivale
Kilburn
Shoreditch
Bethnal Green
West Ham
Harlesden
Paddington
Finsbury
Holborn
City
Poplar
Ealing
Acton
Shepherd's Bush
Notting Hill
Bayswater
Mayfair
Soho
Westminster
Southwark
Bermondsey
Blackwall Tunnel
Hammersmith
Kensington
Chiswick
Chelsea
Lambeth
Greenwich
Deptford
Kew Br
Brentford
Battersea
Fulham
Camberwell
Peckham
Isleworth
Richmond
Mortlake
Putney
Wandsworth
Clapham
Brixton
Lewisham
Roehampton
Balham
Dulwich
Catford
LONDON
Teddington
Wimbledon
Streatham
Sydenham
Kingston upon Thames
New Malden
Merton
Mitcham
Norwood
Penge
Beckenham
Bromley
Surbiton
Morden
Croydon
Sutton
Carshalton
Chessington
Ewell
Cheam
Wallington
Purley
Epsom
Banstead
Coulsdon
Ashtead
Chipstead
Whyteleafe
Warlingham

Woodford
Leytonstone
Wanstead
Stratford
West Ham
East Ham
Forest Gate
Ilford
Barking
Dagenham
Becontree
Goodmayes
Seven Kings
Romford
Gidea Park
Harold Hill
Harold Wood
Hornchurch
Upminster
Rainham
South Hornchurch
Cranham
Great Warley
Little Warley
West Horndon
North Ockendon
South Ockendon
Aveley
Purfleet
Grays
Little Thurrock
Thurrock Services
THURROCK
LONDON
Beckton
Canning Town
Blackwall Tunnel
Woolwich Ferry
Woolwich
North Woolwich
Silvertown
Greenwich
Charlton
Plumstead
Abbey Wood
Belvedere
Erith
Thamesmead
Welling
Bexleyheath
Bexley
Crayford
Dartford
Dartford Crossing
Greenhithe
Stone
Swanscombe
Northfleet
Blackheath
Kidbrooke
Eltham
Lee
Sidcup
Chislehurst
Mottingham
Bromley
Bickley
Orpington
St Paul's Cray
St Mary Cray
Petts Wood
Swanley
Hextable
Wilmington
Sutton at Hone
South Darenth
Farningham
Eynsford
Hartley
Longfield
New Ash Green
West Kingsdown
Halstead
Knockholt
Otford
Kemsing
Wrotham
Shoreham
KENT
KENT DOWNS
Hayes
Keston
Farnborough
Chelsfield
Green Street Green
Downe
Leaves Green
Cudham
Vigo Village
Culverstone Green
Trottiscliffe
Crockenhill
Hawley
Bean
Betsham
Southfleet
Istead Rise
M25
M20
M26
A2
A13
A12
A20
A127

E S S E X
Rayleigh
Hockley
Hawkwell
Rochford
Basildon
Laindon
Langdon Hills
Pitsea
Vange
North Benfleet
Thundersley
South Benfleet
Hadleigh
Leigh-on-Sea
Southend-on-Sea
Westcliff-on-Sea
Prittlewell
Southchurch
Eastwood
Canvey Island
Stanford-le-Hope
Corringham
Fobbing
Coryton
Mucking
Thames Haven
River Thames
Blythe Sands
West Tilbury
East Tilbury
Linford
Cliffe
Cooling
High Halstow
St Mary Hoo
Allhallows-on-Sea
Allhallows
Isle of Grain
Grain
Lower Stoke
Stoke
Hoo St Werburgh
M E D W A Y
River Medway
Higham
Cliffe Woods
Chattenden
Strood
Rochester
Chatham
Gillingham
Rainham
Walderslade
Wayfield
Luton
Hempstead
Wigmore
Medway Services
Cuxton
Halling
Snodland
Wouldham
Burham
Aylesford
Boxley
Detling
Leybourne
Ditton
Kemsley
Milton Regis
Sittingbourne
Queenborough
Newington
Upchurch
Hartlip
Stockbury
Borden
Bredgar
K E N T
D O W N S
Shorne
Cobham
Luddesdown
Birling
Ryarsh
Sole Street
Gravesend Reach
Medway
Tunstall
Highsted

Paglesham Eastend
Horseshoe Corner
Rugwood Fm
Eastwick Head
Great Burwood Fm
Island
Rugwood Head
Barling Marsh
Roper's Fm
Barling Hall Fm
Potton Island
Asplins Head
TQ
Bolts Fm
Fleet Head
New England Island
The Broomway
Butler's Fm
Barling
High Ho
Stonebridge
Little Wakering Wick
Rushley Island
Havengore Island
Shelford Head
Smither's Fm
Shopland Hall
Little Wakering
Oxenham Fm
Sharpness Head
Maplin Sands
Clay Street Fm
Oldbury Fm
Havengore Head
Haven Pt
HIGH STREET
Great Wakering
Ind Est
Samuel's Corner
Wakering Stairs
Trad Pk
Bournes Green
Southchurch
North Shoebury
Black Grounds
A13
A1159
B1015
THORPE BAY
Pig's Bay
KURSAAL
Thorpe Bay
Cambridge Town
SHOEBURYNESS
B1016
EASTERN ESPLANADE
THORPE ESPLANADE
SEA LIFE CENTRE
Shoeburyness
PIER RLY
Southend Pier
Shoebury Ness
West Knock
East Knock
THAMES ESTUARY
Roas Bank
Grain Spit
Grain
Garrison Pt
Jacob's Bank
Cheyney Rock
Blue Town
Trad Est
SHEERNESS ON-SEA
Sheerness
A249
Mile Town
Marine Town
Minster Marshes
Scrapsgate
The Lappel
West Minster
A250
Halfway Houses
Queenborough Spit
ABBEY
East End
Minster
Trouts
Warden Pt
Deadmans Island
QUEENBOROUGH
B2008
QUEENBOROUGH ROAD
MINSTER ROAD
Scocles Fm
Queenborough
Neats Court
LOWER ROAD
A2500
Norwood Manor
Barnland Fm
Warden
Eastchurch
Rushenden
Neatscourt Marshes
Parsonage Fm
New Hook Fm
Old Hook Fm
Groves Fm
HM Prison
LEYSDOWN ROAD
Bay View
B2231
Leysdown-on-Sea
Old Rides Fm
Minster Marshes
Southlees Marshes
FERRY ROAD
SHEPPEY WAY
Isle of Sheppey
Capel Hill Fm
COASTAL PARK
Muswell Manor
Stray Marshes
Ferry Marshes
The Dray
Windmill Creek
Leysdown Marshes
Ind Est
SWALE
ELMLEY
Elmley Island
Eastchurch Marshes
Capel Fleet
Ridham Dock
Iwade
ELMLEY MARSHES
RSPB
Kings Hill Fm
Elmley Marshes
Spitend Marshes
Harty
Marshes
Shell Ness
Coldharbour Marshes
Dutchman's Island
Elliots Fm
THE SWALE
Isle of Harty
Sharfleet Creek
The Swale
Peg Fleet
Mocketts
The Lilies
Spitend Pt
Sayes Court
Pheasant Fm
69
KEMSLEY DOWN
Kemsley
SITTINGBOURNE & KEMSLEY LIGHT RLY
Fowley Island
Conyer Creek
South Deep
Howt Green
Tonge Corner
Blacketts
The Ferry Inn
Horse Sands
Milton Creek
Milton Regis
Trad Est
MILTON REGIS HALT
Chalkwell
Binny Cotts
Teynham Level
Conyer
South Oaze
Cleve Marshes
Murston
Retail Pk
Teynham Street
Teynham Court
Nagden Marshes
Uplees
Poplar Hall
Court Lodge
Graveney Marshes
SITTINGBOURNE
Snipeshill
Bax
Luddenham Court
Barrow Green
Sittingbourne
Bapchild
TEYNHAM
Teynham
Deerton Street
Oare
Nash's Fm
Ham Marshes
Ham Fm
Nagden
Broom Street
Graveney Hill
Radfield
Haywood
Little Dully
The Old Farm Ho
Four Oaks
Rodmersham
Cellarhill
SHEPHERD NEAME BREWERY
The Brents
Faversham
Sandbanks
Graveney
Culmers
Dully Ho
Beacon Hill
Davington
FLEUR DE LIS HERITAGE CENTRE
FAVERSHAM
Goodnestone
Tunstall
Highsted
Rodmersham Green
Batteries Fm
Nouds Fm
Lewson Street
LONDON ROAD
Norton Ash
Ospringe
Judd's Hill
Ind Est
Ewell Fm
Langdon Court
Upper Rodmersham
Lynsted
Loyterton
MAISON DIEU
Perry Court
Preston
Woodstock
Pitstock Fm
Newbury
Lynsted Park
Kingsdown
Putt Wood
Nash Ct
FARMING WORLD
Brenley Corner
Penfield Ho
Whitehill
Copton
M2
Bexon
Hanslett's Ho
Plumford
Sole Street Ho
Brenley Ho
Churchman's Fm
Painter's Forstal
Selgrove
Sharsted Court
Champion Court
College Wood
Scocks Farm Ho
Littles Fm
Owens Court
Crouch
Bluetown
Hollybushes
Newnham
North
South Street
A251
DODDINGTON
Fairbrook Fm
Hernhill
Staplestreet
Dargate
Blean Wood
Acorn Cott
MOUNT EPHRAIM
Boughton Street
Courte Fm
Dunkirk
BOUGHTON BYPASS
Hickmans Green
Forester's Lodge Fm
Fishpond Wood
Church Wood
RSPB BLEAN WOODS
Rough Common
Upper Harbledown
Homestall Wood
Hall Place
Harbledown
CANTERBURY WEST
WEST GATE
TANKERTON BAY
Long Rock
Whitstable
Swalecliffe
Tankerton
Lower Island
WHITSTABLE BAY
B2205
A2990
CHESTFIELD & SWALECLIFFE
Chestfield
Bus Pk
WHITSTABLE
Seasalter
The Oaze
Duncan Down
South Street
Bogshole Fm
A299
Radfall
Graveney Marshes
Seasalter Level
Clapham Hill
Fox's Cross
Burgess Fm
Clowes Wood
Monkshill Fm
Yorkletts
Waterham
Highstreet
Pean Hill
Clowes Fm
THANET WAY
Dargate Common
Denstroude
Red Lion Ho
Well Court
Frog Hall
Fostall
Honey Hill
Amery Court
Honey Wood
Tyler Hill
Holly Hill
North Bishopden Wood
BLEAN WOODS
Blean
Hothe Court Fm
A290
Pucknall Fm
Parsonage Fm
Whitehill
Staplestreet
Wingham
Dargate
Ind Est
3 miles
5 km
88
89
54

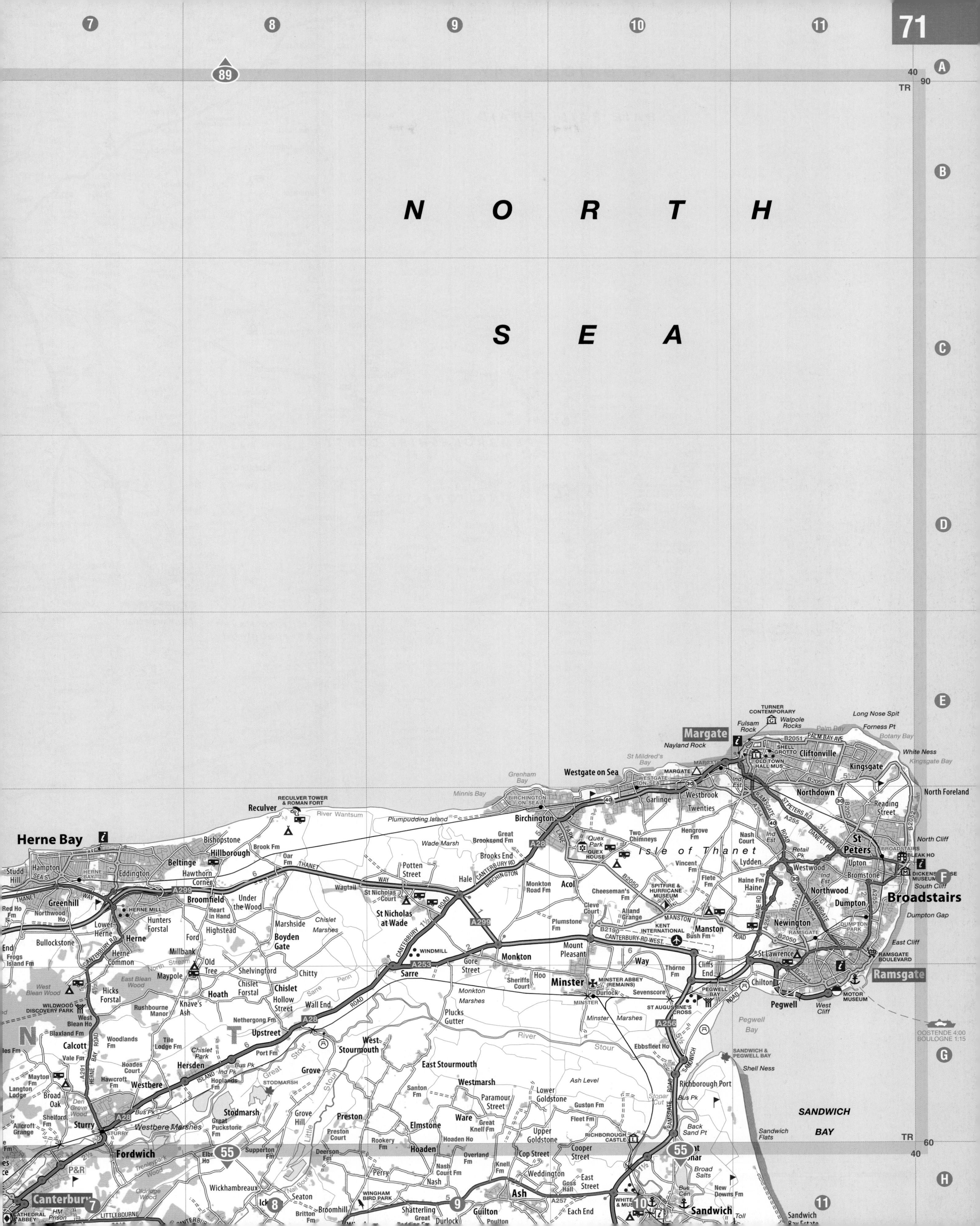

NORTH SEA
Margate
Westgate on Sea
Birchington
Reculver
Herne Bay
Hampton
Herne
Broomfield
Hillborough
Beltinge
Bishopstone
Eddington
Greenhill
Studd Hill
Hawthorn Corner
Under the Wood
Heart in Hand
Highstead
Marshside
Chislet Marshes
Boyden Gate
Hunters Forstal
Lower Herne
Herne Common
Bullockstone
Ford
Millbank
Old Tree
Maypole
Shelvingford
Chitty
Chislet Forstal
Chislet
Hollow Street
Hoath
Knave's Ash
Rushbourne Manor
Hicks Forstal
Wildwood Discovery Park
West Blean Ho
Blaxland Fm
Calcott
Vale Fm
Woodlands Fm
Tile Lodge Fm
Chislet Park
Hersden
Hoades Court
Hawcroft Fm
Westbere
Mayton Fm
Langton Lodge
Broad Oak
Den Grove Wood
Shelford Fm
Allcroft Grange
Sturry
Fordwich
Canterbury
Westbere Marshes
Stodmarsh
Great Puckstone Fm
Upstreet
Nethergong Fm
Wall End
Port Fm
Sarre
Grove
Grove Hill
Preston
Preston Court
Wickhambreaux
Seaton
Elbridge Ho
Supperton Fm
Deerson Fm
Rookery Fm
Hoaden
Hoaden Ho
Perry
Nash
Nash Court Fm
Ash
Overland Fm
Knell Fm
Guilton
Weddington
Cop Street
Goss Hall
East Street
Cooper Street
Each End
Sandwich
New Downs Fm
Broad Salts
Richborough Castle
Richborough Port
Back Sand Pt
Sandwich Bay
Sandwich Flats
Fleet Fm
Guston Fm
Ash Level
Lower Goldstone
Upper Goldstone
Elmstone
Ware
Great Knell Fm
Westmarsh
Paramour Street
Santon Fm
East Stourmouth
West Stourmouth
Plucks Gutter
Monkton Marshes
Gore Street
Monkton
Sheriffs Court
Hoo
Minster
Minster Abbey (Remains)
Durlock
Sevenscore
Minster Marshes
St Augustine's Cross
Ebbsfleet Ho
Pegwell Bay
Pegwell
Chilton
Cliffs End
Thorne Fm
Way
Mount Pleasant
Manston
Kent International
Alland Grange
Cleve Court
Plumstone Fm
Cheeseman's Fm
Spitfire & Hurricane Museum
Acol
Monkton Road Fm
Vincent Fm
Flete Fm
Isle of Thanet
Quex Park
Quex House
Two Chimneys
Hengrove Fm
Nash Court
Lydden
Haine
Haine Fm
Garlinge
Westbrook
Twenties
Great Brooksend Fm
Brooks End
Hale
Potten Street
Wade Marsh
St Nicholas Court
St Nicholas at Wade
Wagtail
Windmill
Plumpudding Island
River Wantsum
Reculver Tower & Roman Fort
Brook Fm
Oar Fm
Minnis Bay
Grenham Bay
St Mildred's Bay
Nayland Rock
Fulsam Rock
Turner Contemporary
Walpole Rocks
Shell Grotto
Old Town Hall Mus
Cliftonville
Palm Bay
Kingsgate
Kingsgate Bay
Long Nose Spit
Foreness Pt
Botany Bay
White Ness
North Foreland
Northdown
Reading Street
St Peters
North Cliff
Bleak Ho
Broadstairs
Dickens House Museum
Westwood
Bromstone
Upton
Northwood
Dumpton
Dumpton Gap
Newington
St Lawrence
East Cliff
Ramsgate
Ramsgate Boulevard
Motor Museum
West Cliff
Oostende 4:00
Boulogne 1:15
Shell Ness
Sandwich & Pegwell Bay
Stour
River

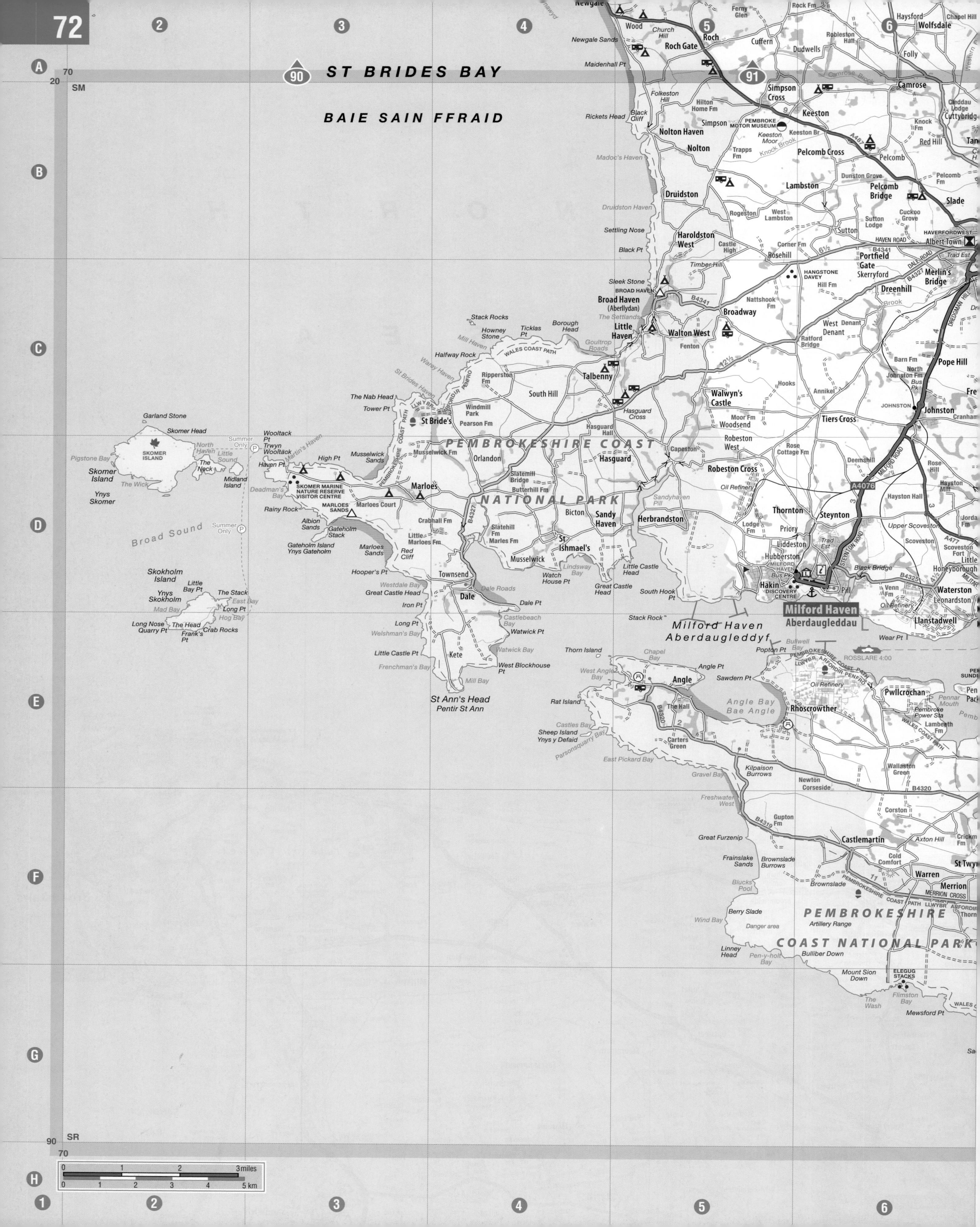
ST BRIDES BAY
BAIE SAIN FFRAID
90
91
SM
SR
70
20
90
Newgale
Newgale Sands
Wood
Church Hill
Roch Gate
Roch
Ferny Glen
Rock Fm
Cuffern
Dudwells
Robleston Hall
Haysford
Wolfsdale
Chapel Hill
Folly
Camrose Brook
Camrose
Maidenhall Pt
Folkeston Hill
Hilton Home Fm
Simpson Cross
Keeston
Simpson
PEMBROKE MOTOR MUSEUM
Keeston Moor
Keeston Br
Knock Brook
Rickets Head
Black Cliff
Nolton Haven
Nolton
Trapps Fm
Pelcomb Cross
Pelcomb
Cleddau Lodge
Cuttybridg
Knock Fm
Red Hill
Madoc's Haven
Druidston
Lambston
Dunston Grove
Pelcomb Bridge
Pelcomb Fm
Slade
Druidston Haven
Rogeston
West Lambston
Sutton Lodge
Cuckoo Grove
Settling Nose
Haroldston West
Sutton
HAVEN ROAD
HAVERFORDWEST
Albert Town
Black Pt
Castle High
Corner Fm
Rosehill
Portfield Gate
Skerryford
Merlin's Bridge
Trad Est
Timber Hill
HANGSTONE DAVEY
Hill Fm
Dreenhill
Sleek Stone
BROAD HAVEN
Broad Haven
(Aberllydan)
The Settlands
B4341
B4327
Nattshook Fm
Broadway
Little Haven
Walton West
Fenton
West Denant
Denant
Ratford Bridge
Merlin's Brook
Stack Rocks
Howney Stone
Ticklas Pt
Borough Head
Goultrop Roads
Mill Haven
WALES COAST PATH
Halfway Rock
Warey Haven
Talbenny
Barn Fm
North Johnston Fm
Pope Hill
St Brides Haven
Ripperston Fm
South Hill
Walwyn's Castle
Hooks
Annikel
Bus Pk
JOHNSTON
Johnston
The Nab Head
Tower Pt
Windmill Park
Pearson Fm
Hasguard Cross
Moor Fm
Woodsend
Tiers Cross
Garland Stone
Skomer Head
St Bride's
Hasguard Hall
PEMBROKESHIRE COAST
Wooltack Pt
Trwyn Wooltack
Summer Only
North Haven
Little Sound
Pigstone Bay
SKOMER ISLAND
Skomer Island
Ynys Skomer
The Neck
Midland Island
The Wick
Martin's Haven
High Pt
Musselwick Sands
Musselwick Fm
Orlandon
Hasguard
Capeston
Robeston West
Rose Cottage Fm
Deemshill
Rose Hill
Haven Pt
SKOMER MARINE NATURE RESERVE VISITOR CENTRE
Deadman's Bay
Marloes
Slatemill Bridge
Butterhill Fm
Robeston Cross
Oil Refinery
A4076
MILFORD ROAD
Hayston Mill
Hayston Hall
MARLOES SANDS
Marloes Court
Rainy Rock
NATIONAL PARK
Sandyhaven Pill
Thornton
Albion Sands
Gateholm Stack
Crabhall Fm
Slatehill Fm
Marles Fm
Bicton
Sandy Haven
Herbrandston
Steynton
Upper Scoveston
Broad Sound
Lodge Fm
Priory
Scoveston
Scoveston Fort
Gateholm Island
Ynys Gateholm
Little Marloes Fm
St Ishmael's
Liddeston
Trad Est
STEYNTON ROAD
A477
Marloes Sands
Red Cliff
Musselwick
Lindsway Bay
Hubberston
Skokholm Island
Ynys Skokholm
Little Bay Pt
The Stack
Hooper's Pt
Townsend
Watch House Pt
Little Castle Head
MILFORD HAVEN
Black Bridge
Honeyborough
Westdale Bay
Great Castle Head
Dale Roads
Great Castle Head
South Hook Pt
Hakin
DISCOVERY CENTRE
Bus Pk
Pill
Venn Fm
B4325
Waterston
Leonardston
Oil Refinery
Llanstadwell
East Bay
Mad Bay
Hog Bay
Long Pt
Iron Pt
Dale
Dale Pt
Long Nose Quarry Pt
The Head
Frank's Pt
Crab Rocks
Long Pt
Castlebeach Bay
Watwick Pt
Stack Rock
Milford Haven
Aberdaugleddyf
Aberdaugleddau
Welshman's Bay
Watwick Bay
Thorn Island
Chapel Bay
Popton Pt
Bullwell Bay
ROSSLARE 4:00
Wear Pt
Little Castle Pt
Kete
West Blockhouse Pt
West Angle Bay
Angle Pt
Sawdern Pt
PEMBROKESHIRE COAST PATH
LLWYBR ARFORDIR PENFRO
Frenchman's Bay
Mill Bay
Angle
Oil Refinery
Pwllcrochan
Pennar Mouth
St Ann's Head
Pentir St Ann
Rat Island
B4320
The Hall
Angle Bay
Bae Angle
Rhoscrowther
Pembroke Power Sta
Lambeeth Fm
Castles Bay
Sheep Island
Ynys y Defaid
Parsonsquarry Bay
Carters Green
East Pickard Bay
Kilpaison Burrows
Wallaston Green
Gravel Bay
Newton
Corseside
Freshwater West
B4319
Gupton Fm
Corston
Great Furzenip
Castlemartin
Axton Hill
Crickm Fm
Frainslake Sands
Brownslade Burrows
Cold Comfort
Warren
St Twy
Blucks Pool
Brownslade
Merrion
MERRION CROSS
Berry Slade
PEMBROKESHIRE
Artillery Range
Danger area
Wind Bay
COAST NATIONAL PARK
Linney Head
Pen-y-holt Bay
Bulliber Down
Mount Sion Down
ELEGUG STACKS
The Wash
Flimston Bay
Mewsford Pt
WALES C
0
1
2
3 miles
0
1
2
3
4
5 km
A
B
C
D
E
F
G
H
1
2
3
4
5
6

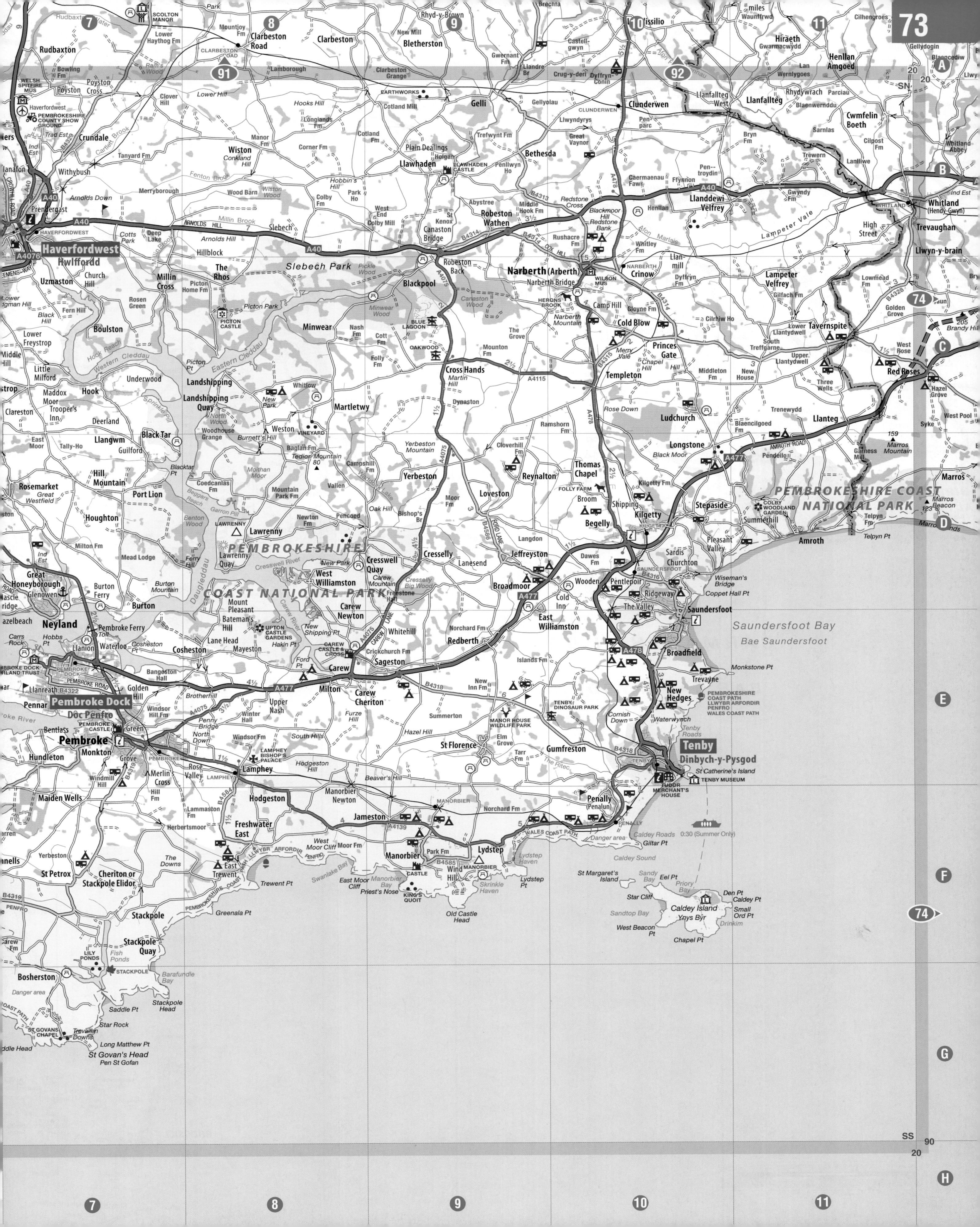
Rudbaxton
Clarbeston Road
Clarbeston
Bletherston
Rhyd-y-Brown
Scolton Manor
Mountjoy Fm
Lower Haythog Fm
Rudbaxton Water
Bowling Fm
Welsh Spitfire Mus
Poyston
Poyston Cross
Haverfordwest
Pembrokeshire County Show Ground
Crundale
Wiston
Conkland Hill
Withybush
Tanyard Fm
Prendergast
Arnolds Down
Merryborough
Wood Barn
Hobbin's Hill
Colby Fm
Plain Dealings
Llawhaden
Llawhaden Castle
Bethesda
Gelli
Clunderwen
Great Vaynor
Crug-y-deri
Dyffryn-Conin
Castell-gwyn
Llandre Br
Gwernant Fm
Earthworks
Cotland Mill
Hooks Hill
Longlands Fm
Lamborough
Clarbeston Grange
Lower Hill
Clover Hill
Manor Fm
Corner Fm
Cotland Fm
Trefwynt Fm
Llwyndyrys
Gellyolau
Pen-parc
Bryn Fm
Llanfallteg West
Llanfallteg
Henllan Amgoed
Hiraeth
Gwarmacwydd
Lan
Wernlygoes
Rhydywrach
Parciau
Blaenwernddu
Cwmfelin Boeth
Sarnias
Cilpost Fm
Whitland Abbey
Trewern
Lanlliwe
Caermaenau Fawr
Ffynnon
Pen-troydin
Llanddewi Velfrey
Gwyndy Fm
Whitland (Hendy-Gwyn)
Trevaughan
Llwyn-y-brain
High Street
Lampeter Vale
Henllan
Blackmoor Hill
Redstone Bank
Redstone Cross
Robeston Wathen
Middle Hook Fm
Abystree
Kenox
Canaston Bridge
West End
Colby Mill
Millin Brook
Arnolds Hill
Slebech
Deep Lake
Cotts Park
Hillblock
Haverfordwest
Hwlffordd
Slebech Park
Pickle Wood
Robeston Back
Blackpool
Narberth (Arberth)
Narberth Bridge
Wilson Mus
Crinow
Rushacre Fm
Whitley Fm
Llan-mill
Dyffryn Fm
Lampeter Velfrey
Gilfach Fm
Lowmead Fm
Golden Grove
Uzmaston
Church Hill
Millin Cross
The Rhos
Picton Home Fm
Rosen Green
Picton Park
Picton Castle
Black Hill
Fern Hill
Boulston
Minwear
Minwear Wood
Blue Lagoon
Oakwood
Nash Fm
Cott Fm
Folly Fm
Canaston Wood
Herons Brook
Narberth Mountain
Camp Hill
Gloyne Fm
Cold Blow
Cilrhiw Ho
Lower Llantydwell
Tavernspite
South Treffgarne
Upper Llantydwell
Red Roses
West Rose
Three Wells
Hazel Grove
Brandy Hill
The Grove
Mounton Fm
Cross Hands
Martin Hill
Princes Gate
Chapel Hill
Merry Vale
Templeton
Middleton Fm
New House
Lower Freystrop
Middle Hill
Little Milford
Hook Reach
Western Cleddau
Eastern Cleddau
Picton Pt
Underwood
Landshipping
Landshipping Quay
Maddox Moor
Hook
Trooper's Inn
Clareston
Deerland
New Park
Whitlow
Martletwy
Dynaston
Rose Down
Ludchurch
Trenewydd
Llanteg
Syke
West Pool
North Wood
Woodhouse Grange
Burnett's Hill
Weston
Vineyard
Ramshorn Fm
Blaencilgoed Fm
Longstone
Black Moor
Amroth Road
Pendeilo
Marros Mountain
Garness Mill
Llangwm
Black Tar
Guilford
East Moor
Tally-Ho
Baglan Fm
Tedion Mountain
Yerbeston Mountain
Cloverhill Fm
Reynalton
Thomas Chapel
Folly Farm
Kilgetty Fm
Marros
Hill Mountain
Blacktar Pt
Coedcanlas Fm
Mothan Moor
Upton Fm
Campshill Fm
Vallen
Yerbeston
Loveston
Moor Fm
Rosemarket
Great Westfield
Port Lion
Beggars Reach
Garron Pill
Mountain Park Fm
Oak Hill
Bishop's Br
Broom
Begelly
Shipping
Kilgetty
Stepaside
Colby Woodland Garden
Summerhill
Pembrokeshire Coast National Park
Marros Beacon
Telpyn Fm
Telpyn Pt
Amroth
Houghton
Benton Wood
Lawrenny
Newton Fm
Pencoed
Ford Lane
Langdon
Pleasant Valley
Milton Fm
Ind Est
Mead Lodge
Ferry Hill
Lawrenny Quay
Cresswell River
Pembrokeshire
Cresswell Quay
Cresselly
Lanesend
Jeffreyston
Dawes Fm
Sardis
Churchton
Saundersfoot
Wiseman's Bridge
Coppet Hall Pt
Great Honeyborough
Glenowen
Burton Ferry
Burton Mountain
Daugleddau
New Park
West Williamston
Carew Mountain
Cresselly Big Wood
Freestone Hall
Broadmoor
Wooden
Pentlepoir
Ridgeway
Coast National Park
Burton
Mount Pleasant
Bateman's Hill
Carew River
Carew Newton
Cold Inn
The Valley
Neyland
Hobbs Pt
Pembroke Ferry
Toll
Llanion
Waterloo
Cosheston
Upton Castle Gardens
Hakin Pt
New Shipping Pt
Whitehill
Norchard Fm
East Williamston
Saundersfoot Bay
Bae Saundersfoot
Lane Head
Mayeston
Carew Castle & Cross
Crickchurch Fm
Redberth
Broadfield
Pembroke Dock
Pembroke Road
Bangeston Hall
Ford Pt
Carew
Sageston
Islands Fm
Monkstone Pt
Llanreath
Golden Hill
Brotherhill
Upper Nash
Milton
Carew Cheriton
New Inn Fm
Trevayne
New Hedges
Pembrokeshire Coast Path
Llwybr Arfordir Penfro
Wales Coast Path
Pennar
Doc Penfro
Windsor Hill Fm
Winter Hall
Furze Hill
Summerton
Tenby Dinosaur Park
Manor House Wildlife Park
Cornish Down
Waterwynch
Bentlass
Pembroke Castle
Green
Penny Bridge
North Down
Windsor Fm
South Hills
Hazel Hill
St Florence
Elm Grove
Gumfreston
Tenby Roads
Tenby
Dinbych-y-Pysgod
Pembroke
Monkton
Grove
Hundleton
Lamphey Bishop's Palace
Lamphey
Rose Valley
Hodgeston Hill
Tarr Fm
The Ritec
St Catherine's Island
Tenby Museum
Tudor Merchant's House
Windmill Hill
Merlin's Cross
Beaver's Hill
Manorbier Newton
Maiden Wells
Hill Fm
Hodgeston
Norchard Fm
Penally (Penalun)
Lammaston Fm
Herbertsmoor
Freshwater East
Jameston
Manorbier
Wales Coast Path
Danger area
Caldey Roads
Giltar Pt
0:30 (Summer Only)
Yerbeston
West Moor Cliff
Moor Fm
Lydstep
Lydstep Haven
Caldey Sound
East Trewent
Park Fm
Wind Hill
St Petrox
Cheriton or Stackpole Elidor
The Downs
Trewent Pt
Swanlake Bay
Manorbier Bay
East Moor Cliff
Priest's Nose
King's Quoit
Castle
Skrinkle Haven
Lydstep Pt
St Margaret's Island
Sandy Bay
Eel Pt
Priory Bay
Star Cliff
Caldey Island
Ynys Byr
Den Pt
Caldey Pt
Small Ord Pt
Sandtop Bay
West Beacon Pt
Chapel Pt
Drinkim
Stackpole
Greenala Pt
Old Castle Head
Stackpole Quay
Lily Ponds
Fish Ponds
Stackpole
Barafundle Bay
Bosherston
Danger area
Stackpole Head
Saddle Pt
Star Rock
St Govans Chapel
Trevallen Downs
Long Matthew Pt
St Govan's Head
Pen St Gofan
A40
A4076
A477
A478
A4075
A4115
A4139
B4313
B4314
B4315
B4316
B4318
B4319
B4320
B4322
B4328
B4584
B4585
B4586
91
92
74
SN
SS
20
90
A
B
C
D
E
F
G
H
7
8
9
10
11

CARMARTHEN BAY
BAE CAERFYRDDIN
CARMARTHENSHIRE
(SIR GAERFYRDDIN)
Carmarthen
Caerfyrddin
St Clears
Sanclêr
Whitland
(Hendy-Gwyn)
Trevaughan
Llwyn-y-brain
Pwll-trap
Backe
Llanddowror
Red Roses
Marros
Pendine
(Pentywyn)
Laugharne
(Talacharn)
Broadway
Llansadurnen
Llandawke
Halfpenny
Furze
Brook
Plashett
Llanmiloe
Meidrim
Llangynin
Bancyfelin
Llangynog
Llansteffan
Llanybri
Ferryside
(Glan-y-Fferi)
Llansaint
Broadlay
Kidwelly
(Cydweli)
Pembrey
(Pembre)
Pinged
Llandyfaelog
Mynyddygarreg
Croesyceiliog
Idole
Bancycapel
Llangain
Morfa
Bach
Llanllwch
Johnstown
Llangunnor
Abergwili
Tanerdy
Merthyr
Sarnau
Llanmadoc
Llangennith
Rhossili
RHOSSILI
BAY
Pendine Sands
Laugharne Sands
Laugharne Burrows
Cefn Sidan Sands
Pembrey
Forest
River Taf Afon Taf
River Towy Afon Tywi
Gwendraeth
Whiteford Sands
Berges Island
Burry Holms
Hills Tor
Broughton Bay
Ginst Pt
Tywyn Pt
Salmon Point Scar
Wharley Pt
Dolwen Pt
Gilman Pt
Ragwen Pt
Telpyn Pt
Marros Sands
LAUGHARNE CASTLE
DYLAN THOMAS BOATHOUSE
LLANSTEFFAN CASTLE
KIDWELLY CASTLE
MUSEUM OF SPEED
WEST WALES CENTRE FOR THE CRAFTS
UNITED COUNTIES SHOWGROUND
WALES COAST PATH
A40
A477
A4066
A484
A48
B4312
B4314
B4328
B4299
B4298
B4308
B4317
B4309
B4306
73
92
93
56
SN
SS
0 1 2 3 miles
0 1 2 3 4 5 km
A
B
C
D
E
F
G
H
1
2
3
4
5
6

Llandeilo
Nantgaredig
Pont-ar-gothi
Llanegwad
Felindre
Dryslwyn
Dryslwyn Castle
Llanarthne
Golden Grove
Cilsan
Ffairfach
Maerdy
Capel Dewi
White Mill
Nantycaws
The National Botanic Garden of Wales
Paxton's Tower
Carreg Cennen Castle & Farm Centre
Trapp
Black Mountain
Llanddarog
Porthyrhyd
Penrhiwgoch
Maesybont
Temple Bar
Carmel
Milo
Pentre-Gwenlais
Llandyfan
Dre-fach
Llandybie
Cwmisfael
Llangendeirne
Foel-gastell
Castell-y-rhingyll
Cefneithin
Cwm-y-glo
Cross Hands
Gorslas
Drefach
Crwbin
Morfa
Saron
Ammanford (Rhydaman)
Betws
Glanaman
Garnant
Brynamman
Pontamman
Tumble (Y Tymbl)
Pontyberem
Bancffosfelen
Pentre
Capel Hendre
Penybanc
Tycroes
Pantyffynnon
Cwmgwili
Greynor
Four Roads
Pont-Henri
Pontyates (Pont-iets)
Llannon
Llwyn-Têg
Garnswllt
Cynheidre
Carway
Sylen
Horeb
Llanedi
Sardis
Five Roads
Trimsaran
SWANSEA (ABERTAWE)
Pontarddulais
Hendy
Fforest
Cwm-Dulais
Felindre
Rhyd-y-gwin
Rhyd-y-pandy
Craig-cefn-parc
Pontardawe
Trebanos
Clydach
Swiss Valley
Felinfoel
Allt
Llangennech
Waungron
Pontlliw
Pwll
Furnace
Dafen
Llanelli
Bryn
Llwyn-hendy
Gorseinon
Penllergaer
Llangyfelach
Morriston (Treforys)
Ynystawe
Bynea
Yspitty
Loughor
Machynys
Gowerton (Tre-Gwyr)
Fforest-fach
Cadle
Landore
Llansamlet
Birchgrove
River Loughor
Afon Llwchwr
Llanrhidian Sands
Pen-clawdd
Crofty
Llanmorlais
Blue Anchor
Three Crosses
Waunarlwydd
Cockett
Cwmdu
Manselton
Port Tennant
Dunvant (Dynfant)
Killay
Sketty
Uplands
Brynmill
Swansea Abertawe
Upper Killay
Wernffrwd
Landimore
Cheriton
Llanrhidian
Oldwalls
Burry Green
Llethrid
Blackhills
THE GOWER
Gower Peninsula
Reynoldston
Llanddewi
Knelston
Parkmill
Penmaen
Nicholaston
Pennard
Ilston
Kittle
Northway
Bishopston
Murton
Manselfield
West Cross
Black Pill
Mayals
Oldway
Newton
The Mumbles (Y Mwmbwls)
SWANSEA BAY
BAE ABERTAWE
Penrice
Southgate
Pontarddulais
A48
A483
A476
A4138
A4118
M4

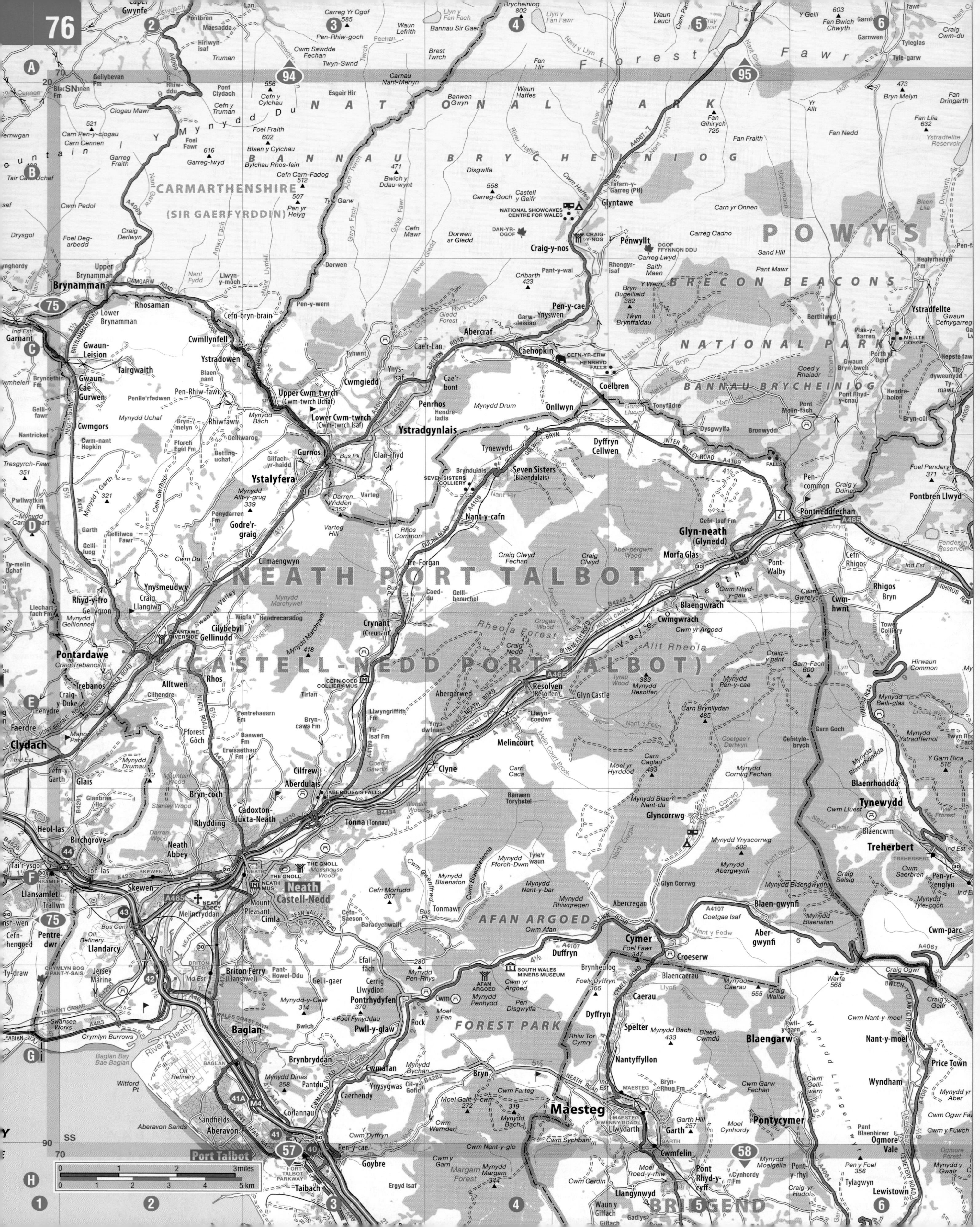
CARMARTHENSHIRE
(SIR GAERFYRDDIN)
BANNAU BRYCHEINIOG
NATIONAL PARK
Fforest Fawr
POWYS
BRECON BEACONS
NATIONAL PARK
BANNAU BRYCHEINIOG
NEATH PORT TALBOT
(CASTELL-NEDD PORT TALBOT)
AFAN ARGOED
FOREST PARK
BRIDGEND
Y Mynydd Du
Black Mountain
Brynamman
Upper Brynamman
Lower Brynamman
Rhosaman
Garnant
Gwaun-Leision
Tairgwaith
Gwaun-Cae-Gurwen
Cwmgors
Cwmllynfell
Ystradowen
Upper Cwm-twrch (Cwm-twrch Uchaf)
Lower Cwm-twrch (Cwm-twrch Isaf)
Cwmgiedd
Ystradgynlais
Abercraf
Caehopkin
Coelbren
Onllwyn
Penrhos
Gurnos
Glan-rhyd
Ystalyfera
Godre'r-graig
Seven Sisters (Blaendulais)
Dyffryn Cellwen
Nant-y-cafn
Glyn-neath (Glynedd)
Morfa Glas
Pontneddfechan
Blaengwrach
Cwmgwrach
Resolven (Resolfen)
Glyn Castle
Melincourt
Clyne
Crynant (Creunant)
Cilybebyll
Gellinudd
Pontardawe
Trebanos
Alltwen
Rhos
Ynysmeudwy
Rhyd-y-fro
Clydach
Glais
Bryn-coch
Cilfrew
Aberdulais
Cadoxton-Juxta-Neath
Rhydding
Tonna (Tonnau)
Neath Abbey
Skewen
Neath
Castell-Nedd
Cimla
Melincryddan
Llandarcy
Briton Ferry (Llansawel)
Baglan
Port Talbot
Aberavon
Sandfields
Taibach
Cwmafan
Pontrhydyfen
Pwll-y-glaw
Cymer
Croeserw
Duffryn
Glyncorrwg
Abercregan
Blaen-gwynfi
Abergwynfi
Caerau
Dyffryn
Spelter
Nantyffyllon
Maesteg
Llwydarth
Garth
Cwmfelin
Llangynwyd
Blaengarw
Pontycymer
Ogmore Vale
Nant-y-moel
Price Town
Wyndham
Lewistown
Treherbert
Tynewydd
Blaenrhondda
Cwm-parc
Hirwaun Common
Rhigos
Cwm-hwnt
Ystradfellte
Glyntawe
Craig-y-nos
Penwyllt
Pen-y-cae
Ynyswen
NATIONAL SHOWCAVES CENTRE FOR WALES
DAN-YR-OGOF
CEFN COED COLLIERY MUS
SOUTH WALES MINERS MUSEUM
ABERDULAIS FALLS
THE GNOLL
NEATH ABBEY
HENRHYD FALLS
SEVEN SISTERS COLLIERY
Rheola Forest
Vale of Neath
Swansea Bay
Bae Baglan
Aberavon Sands
Crymlyn Burrows
0 1 2 3 miles
0 1 2 3 4 5 km

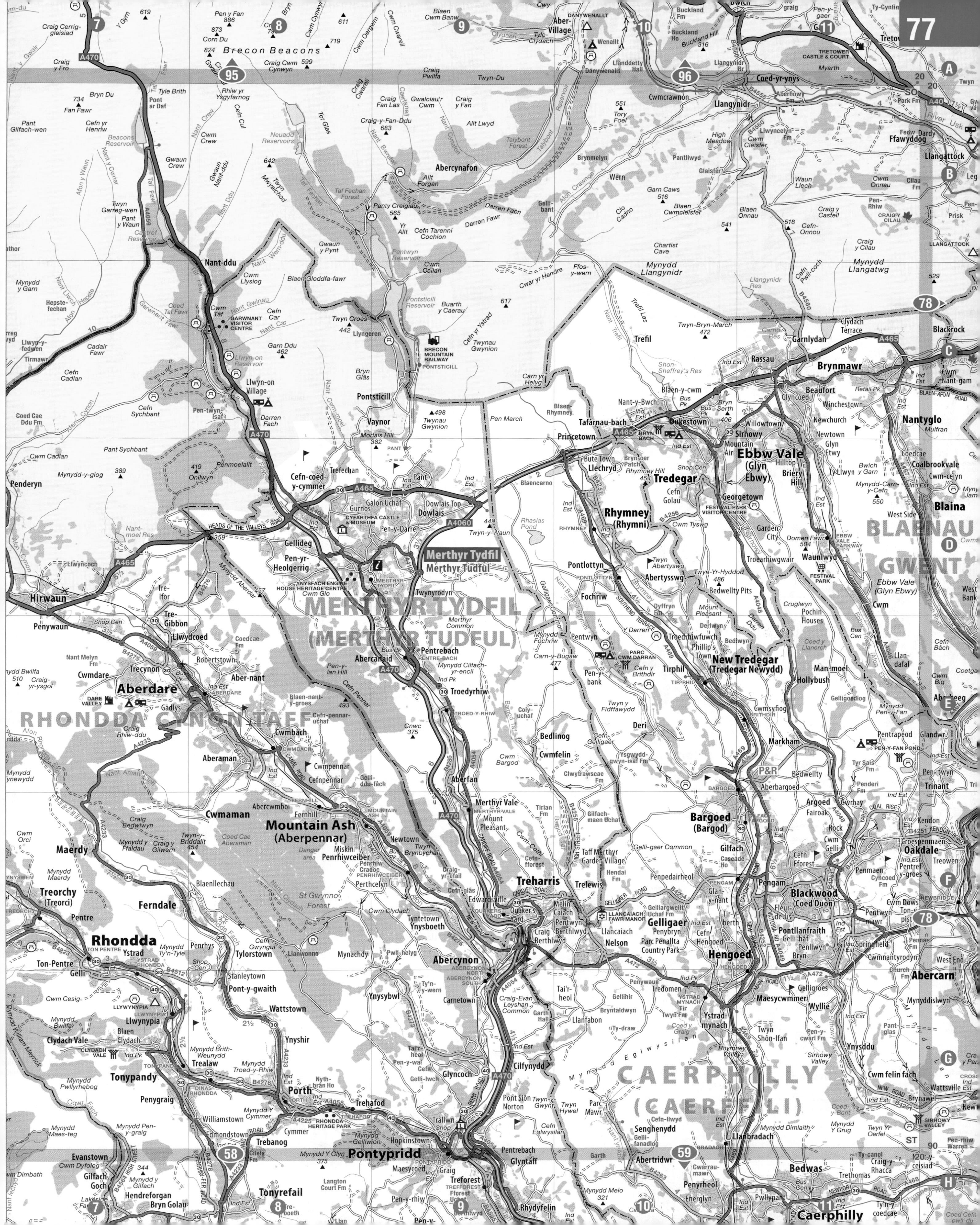
Brecon Beacons
Pen y Fan 886
Corn Du 873
Craig Cwm Cynwyn 599
95
96
9
10
11
8
7
Tretower Castle & Court
Llangynidr
Coed-yr-ynys
Cwmcrawnon
Llanddetty Hall
Buckland Hill
Dan-yr-ogof
Tyle Brith
Pont ar Daf
Fan Fawr 734
Bryn Du
Pant Gilfach-wen
Cefn yr Henriw
Craig Fan Las
Gwalciau'r Cwm
Craig y Fan
Allt Lwyd
Craig-y-Fan-Ddu 683
Neuadd Reservoirs
Talybont Forest
Talybont Reservoir
Tor Glas
Beacons Reservoir
Gwaun Crew
Abercynafon
Allt Forgan
Taf Fechan Forest
Twyn Mwyalchod
Twyn Garreg-wen
Pant y Waun
Cantref Reservoir
Panty Creigiau 565
Yr Allt
Cefn Tarenni Cochion
Darren Fach
Darren Fawr
Gelli-bant
Clo Cadno
Garn Caws 516
Blaen Cwmcleisfer
Brynmelyn
Wern
Pantllwyd
Glaisfer
High Meadow
Cwm Cleisfer
Llwyncelyn Fm
Waun Llech
Cwm Onnau
Blaen Onnau
Pen-Rhiw
Craig y Castell
Cefn Onnau
Craig y Cilau
Craig y Cilau
Mynydd Llangatwg
Mynydd Llangynidr
Chartist Cave
Cefn Pwll-coch
Llangynidr Res
Ffawyddog
Llangattock
Park Fm
River Usk
Prisk
Gwaun y Pynt
Pentwyn Reservoir
Cwm Callan
Nant-ddu
Cwm Llysiog
Blaen Gloddfa-fawr
Pontsticill Reservoir
Buarth y Caerau
Cwar yr Hendre
Ffos-y-wern
Mynydd y Garn
Hepste-fechan
Coed Taf Fawr
Cwm Tâf
Garwnant Visitor Centre
Cefn Car
Garn Ddu 462
Twyn Croes 442
Llyngeren
Brecon Mountain Railway
Pontsticill
Cefn yr Ystrad
Twynau Gwynion
Trefil
Twyn-Bryn-March 472
Shon-Sheffrey's Res
Garnlydan
Clydach Terrace
Blackrock
Rassau
Brynmawr
Cadair Fawr
Cefn Cadlan
Llwyn-y-fedwen
Tirmawr
Llwyn-on Reservoir
Llwyn-on Village
Cefn Sychbant
Pen-twyn-isaf
Darren Fach
Coed Cae Ddu Fm
Pontsticill
Twynau Gwynion 498
Vaynor
Morlais Hill 382
Pen March
Blaen-Rhymney
Tafarnau-bach
Princetown
Nant-y-Bwch
Blaen-y-cwm
Bryn Bach
Dukestown
Bryn Serth 406
Sirhowy
Willowtown
Beaufort
Glyncoed
Winchestown
Nantyglo
Newchurch
Newtown
Mountain Air
Ebbw Vale (Glyn Ebwy)
Glyn Etwy
Hilltop
Briery Hill
Ty Llwyn
Bwich y Garn
Coedcae
Coalbrookvale
Cwm-celyn
Mynydd-Carn-y-Cefn 550
Blaina
Cwm Cadlan
Pant Sychbant
Mynydd-y-glog 389
Penderyn
Onllwyn 419
Penmoelallt
Cefn-coed-y-cymmer
Trefechan
Pant
Galon Uchaf
Gurnos
Dowlais Top
Dowlais
Cyfarthfa Castle & Museum
Pen-y-Darren
Twyn-y-Waun 449
Blaencarno
Bute Town
Llechryd
Bryn-oer Patch
Rhymney Hill 454
Tredegar
Cefn Golau
Georgetown
Festival Park Visitor Centre
Rhymney (Rhymni)
Rhaslas Pond
Garden City
Cwm Tyswg
Domen Fawr 504
Waunlwyd
Festival Park
Troedrhiwgwair
Blaenau Gwent
Ebbw Vale (Glyn Ebwy)
West Side
Heads of the Valleys Road
Nant-moel Res
Gellideg
Pen-yr-Heolgerrig
Merthyr Tydfil
Merthyr Tudful
Ynysfach Engine House Heritage Centre
Cwm Glo
Twynyrodyn
Pontlottyn
Twyn Abertysswg
Abertysswg
Twyn-Yr-Hyddod 486
Bedwellty Pits
Fochriw
Hirwaun
Llwyncoch
Tre-Ifor
Mynydd Aberdar 457
Penywaun
Tre-Gibbon
Llwydcoed
Merthyr Tydfil (Merthyr Tudful)
Merthyr Common
Mynydd Fochriw
Pentwyn
Dyffryn Fm
Y Darren
Troedrhiwfuwch
Phillip's Town
Cwm Darran
Mount Pleasant
Derlwyn
Bedwellty
Pochin Houses
Coed y Llanerch
Cwm
Nant Melyn Fm
Cwmdare
Trecynon
Robertstown
Aber-nant
Coedcae Fm
Pentrebach
Abercanaid
Pen-y-lan Hill
Mynydd Cilfach-yr-encil
Carn-y-Bugaw 477
Pen-y-bank
Cefn y Brithdir
New Tredegar (Tredegar Newydd)
Tirphil
Man-moel
Hollybush
Cefn Bâch
Llan-dafal
Aberdare
Dare Valley
Gadlys
Craig-yr-ysgol 510
Rhondda Cynon Taf
Blaen-nant-y-groes
Cefn-pennar-uchaf
Troedyrhiw
Coly-uchaf
Twyn y Fidffawydd
Cwmsyfiog
Brithdir
Gelligoediog
Mynydd Pen-y-Fan
Aberbeeg
Craig Rhiw-ddu
Cwmbach
Aberaman
Cwmpennar
Cefnpennar
Gelli-ddu-fach
Cnwc 375
Aberfan
Bedlinog
Cwmfelin
Cefn Gelligaer
Deri
Ysgwydd-gwyn-isaf Fm
Markham
Pentrapeod
Pen-y-Fan Pond
Glandwr
Cwm Bargod
Clwytrawscae Fm
Bedwellty
Aberbargoed
Pen-twyn
Trinant
Tyr Sais Fm
Penderi Fm
Mynydd Ynewydd
Nant Aman Fach
Cwmaman
Abercwmboi
Fernhill
Mountain Ash (Aberpennar)
Merthyr Vale
Mount Pleasant
Tirlan Fm
Gilfach-maen Uchaf
Bargoed (Bargod)
Argoed
Fairoak
Rock
Cwm Gelli
Gwrhay
Kendon
Croespenmaen
Oakdale
Treowen
Cwm Orci
Craig Bedwlwyn
Mynydd y Ffaldau
Craig y Gilwern
Twyn-y-Briddallt 454
Coed Cae Aberaman
Miskin
Newtown
Twyn Brynbychan
Penrhiwceiber
Cwm-Cothi
Cefn-fforest
Taff Merthyr Garden Village
Hendai Fm
Gelli-gaer Common
Gilfach
Cascade
Cefn Fforest
Penmaen
Pentref-y-groes
Cynycoed Fm
Maerdy
Mynydd Maerdy
Danger area
Penrhiw Cradoc
Perthcelyn
Craig-yr-efail
Cefn-glâs
Treharris
Trelewis
Penpedairheol
Glan-y-nant
Pengam
Blackwood (Coed Duon)
Fleur-de-lis
Cwm Dows
Ton-y-pistyll
Treorchy (Treorci)
Ferndale
Blaenllechau
St Gwynno Forest
Nant Clydach
Edwardsville
Quakers Yard
Melin Caiach
Pentwyn Berthlwyd
Llancaiach Fawr Manor
Gelligaer
Gelliargwellt Uchaf Fm
Penybryn
Cefn Hengoed
Tir-y-berth
Pontllanfraith
Gelli-haf
Penllwyn
Bryn
Springfield
Pentwyn-mawr
Pentre
Cwm Clydach
Tyntetown
Ynysboeth
Craig Berthlwyd
Llancaiach
Nelson
Parc Penallta Country Park
Hengoed
Penyr Fm
Cwmnantyrodyn
West End
Rhondda
Ton Pentre
Ystrad Rhondda
Mynydd Ty'n-Tyle
Penrhys
Cefn Gwyngul
Tylorstown
Llanwonno
Mynachdy
Pwll-helyg
Abercynon
Ton-Pentre
Gelli
Stanleytown
Pont-y-gwaith
Carnetown
Craig-Evan Leyshan Common
Tai'r-heol
Gellihir
Penywaun
Tredomen
Ystrad Mynach
Maesycwmmer
Gelligroes
Wyllie
Abercarn
Mynyddislwyn
Cwm Cesig
Llwynypia
Mynydd Bwllfa
Ty'n-y-wern
Ynysybwl
Garth Hall
Llanfabon
Bryntaldwyn
Ty-draw
Tyn Fm
Cwm-llwyd
Coed y Graig
Twyn Shôn-Ifan
Pen-y-cwarl Fm
Pant-glas
Ynysddu
Sirhowy Valley
Clydach Vale
Blaen Clydach
Wattstown
Ynyshir
Tai'r-heol
Pen-y-wal
Cefn
Gelli-lwch
Mynydd Eglwysilan
Cilfynydd
Caerphilly
Rhymney Valley
Mynydd Brith-weunydd
Trealaw
Mynydd Troed-y-Rhiw
Tonypandy
Dinas Rhondda
Nyth-bran Ho
Glyncoch
Cwm felin fach
Wattsville
Brynawel
Mynydd Pwllyrhebog
Penygraig
Porth
Rhondda Heritage Park
Trehafod
Pont Siôn Norton
Twyn-y-Gwynt
Twyn Hywel
Parc Mawr
Caerffili
Newbridge
Williamstown
Mynydd Y Cymmer
Cymmer
Trallwn
Cefn Eglwysilan
Senghenydd
Gelli-fanadlog
Mynydd Dimlaith
Coed-y-Bont
Mynydd y Grug
Twyn Yr Oerfel
Sirhowy Valley
Mynydd Maes-teg
Mynydd Pen-y-graig
Edmondstown
Trebanog
Mynydd Gellwion
Hopkinstown
Pentrebach
Glyntaff
Garth
Abertridwr
Cwrrau-mawr
Llanbradach
Ty-canol
Craig-y-Rhacca
Trethomas
Bedwas
Evanstown
Cwm Dyfolog
Mynydd Y Glyn 375
Pontypridd
Maesycoed
Graig
Trefforest
Penyrheol
Energlyn
Ty'n-y-coedcae
Cwm Dimbath
Gilfach Goch
Mynydd y Gilfach 344
Hendreforgan
Bryn Golau
Tonyrefail
Langton Court Fm
Trefforest Industrial Estate
Pen-y-rhiw
Rhydyfelin
Mynydd Meio 321
Pwllypant
Penrhiw Warren
58
59
78
A470
A465
A4059
A4060
A469
A472
A4054
A4233
A4058
B4275
B4276
B4256
B4257
B4254
B4255
B4251
B4252
B4273
B4278
B4512
B4560
A40
A467
A4046
A4048
A4049
A4223
A4225
A4054
B4263

BRECON BEACONS
NATIONAL PARK
BANNAU BRYCHEINIOG
MONMOUTHSHIRE
(SIR FYNWY)
BLAENAU GWENT
TORFAEN
(TOR-FAEN)
NEWPORT
CASNEWYDD
Abergavenny
Y Fenni
Cwmbran
Pontypool
Blaenavon
Crickhowell
(Crug Hywel)
Usk
Raglan
Caerleon
Risca
Crosskeys
Abertillery
Blaina
Nantyglo
Brynmawr
Abersychan
Griffithstown
Pontnewydd
Llanfoist
Gilwern
Govilon
Clydach
Llanelly
Llangattock
Llangenny
Glangrwyney
Cwrt-y-gollen
Llanbedr
Partrishow Hill
Table Mountain
Sugar Loaf
596
Blorenge Carn
561
Llanvihangel Crucorney
Pandy
Stanton
Bettws
Mardy
Llantilio Pertholey
Llanvetherine
White Castle
Llantilio Crossenny
Llanvapley
Llanddewi Rhydderch
Wernyrheolydd
Coed Morgan
Llanarth
Bryngwyn
Llanover
Llanvihangel Gobion
Goetre
Penperlleni
Little Mill
Monkswood
Llanfair Kilgheddin
Nant-y-derry
Kemeys Commander
Gwehelog
Llandenny
Llangwm
Llancayo
Glascoed
Llanbadoc
Llangeview
Llanllowell
Llantrisant
Llangybi
Tredunnock
Newbridge-on-Usk
Llandegveth
Coed-y-paen
Llanfrechfa
Ponthir
Llanhennock
Croes-y-mwyalch
Llantarnam
Oakfield
Henllys
Castell-y-bwch
Bettws
Malpas
Christchurch
Rogerstone
Caerau
Llanmartin
Penhow
Llanvaches
Llandevaud
Parc-Seymour
Cat's Ash
Llanbeder
St Bride's Netherwent
Wilcrick
Crumlin
Newbridge
Oakdale
Abercarn
Cwmcarn
Pontywaun
Lanfach
Trinant
Llanhilleth
Brynithel
Swffryd
Aberbeeg
Six Bells
Cwmtillery
East Bank
Varteg
Cwmavon
Garndiffaith
Talywain
Pentre-Piod
Cwm Ffrwd-oer
New Inn
Sebastopol
Upper Cwmbran
Tranch
Penygarn
Trevethin
Garn-yr-erw
Forge Side
Rifle Green
Rhyd-y-meirch
Pencroesoped
Mamhilad
Llanellen
Cross Ash
Norton
Onen
Raglan Castle
Tregare
Penrhôs
Kingcoed
Twyn-y-Sheriff
Gwernesney
Tal-y-coed
Upper Green
Wayne Green
Llangattock Lingoed
Llanfaenor
Llanvihangel Ystern-Llewern
Bryn-y-gwenin
Llanddewi Skirrid
Ponthir
Lower Machen
Machen
Ty-Sign
Pontymister
Newtown
Wattsville
Brynawel
Penrhiw
Danygraig
Black Vein
Nine Wells
Gray Hill
275
Pen-y-cae-mawr
0 1 2 3 miles
0 1 2 3 4 5 km
96
97
77
59
60
A40
A465
A4042
A449
A472
A48
M4
B4233
B4598
B4235
B4246
B4248

Monmouth
Trefynwy
Chepstow
Coleford
Cinderford
Lydney
Thornbury
Caldicot
FOREST OF DEAN
FOREST PARK
GLOUCESTERSHIRE
SOUTH
GLOUCESTERSHIRE
River Severn
River Wye
Goodrich
Walford
Welsh Bicknor
English Bicknor
Symonds Yat
Mitcheldean
Longhope
Drybrook
Ruardean
Newnham
Blakeney
Awre
Arlingham
Sharpness
Berkeley
Newport
Woodford
Tortworth
Falfield
Whitfield
Rockhampton
Oldbury-on-Severn
Littleton-on-Severn
Alveston
Aust
Beachley
Sedbury
Tidenham
Woolaston
Alvington
Aylburton
Parkend
Yorkley
Bream
Whitecroft
St Briavels
Clearwell
Newland
Redbrook
Staunton
Christchurch
Berry Hill
Tintern Parva
Llandogo
Trellech
Catbrook
Itton Common
Shirenewton
Mathern
Crick
Caerwent
Portskewett
Wonastow
Mitchel Troy
Dixton
Rockfield
Llangarron
Coughton
Pontshill
Lea
Cheltenham
Sheperdine Sands
Oldbury Sands
Lydney Sand
Saniger Sands
Severn Road Bridge
M48
M5
A40
A48
A466
A4136
97
98
60
61
80

Gloucester
Stroud
GLOUCESTERSHIRE
COTSWOLDS
River Severn
Twigworth
Longford
Maisemore
Innsworth
Parton
Churchdown
Lansdown
Up Hatherley
Leckhampton
Shurdington
Hucclecote
Brockworth
Bentham
Barnwood
Elmbridge
Longlevens
Kingsholm
Wotton
Barton
Tredworth
Saintbridge
Abbeydale
Coney Hill
Linden
Podsmead
Matson
Tuffley
Lower Tuffley
Quedgeley
Hardwicke
Whaddon
Brookthorpe
Upton St Leonard's
Cranham
Birdlip
Painswick
Sheepscombe
Miserden
The Camp
Bisley
Slad
Edge
Harescombe
Haresfield
Standish
Stonehouse
Randwick
Whiteshill
Pitchcombe
Rodborough
Bowbridge
Thrupp
Brimscombe
Chalford
Eastcombe
Oakridge
Minchinhampton
Amberley
Nailsworth
Horsley
Avening
Cherington
Rodmarton
Tetbury
Long Newton
Westonbirt
Leighterton
Kingscote
Nympsfield
Uley
Dursley
Cam
Stinchcombe
North Nibley
Wotton-under-Edge
Kingswood
Charfield
Alderley
Hillesley
Tresham
Frampton on Severn
Whitminster
Saul
Slimbridge
Cambridge
Arlingham
Newnham
Awre
Blaisdon
Longhope
Huntley
Taynton
Tibberton
Rudford
Highnam
Minsterworth
Elmore
Longney
Westbury-on-Severn
Elton
Flaxley
Berkeley Heath
Woodford
Stone
Tortworth
Cromhall
Frocester
Eastington
Leonard Stanley
King's Stanley
Woodchester
Michaelwood Services
M5
A38
A40
A46
A419
A417
A4135
A433
A429
79
98
99
61
62
0 1 2 3 miles
0 1 2 3 4 5 km

Cheltenham
Charlton Kings
Whittington
Salperton
Notgrove
Cold Aston
Bourton-on-the-Water
Andoversford
Dowdeswell
Shipton
Hazleton
Turkdean
Clapton-on-the-Hill
Great Rissington
Little Rissington
Compton Abdale
Hampnett
Farmington
Coberley
Withington
Cassey Compton
Northleach
Sherborne
Great Barrington
Yanworth
Eastington
Windrush
Colesbourne
Elkstone
Chedworth
Fossebridge
COTSWOLDS
GLOUCESTERSHIRE
Coln St Dennis
Aldsworth
Winstone
Rendcomb
Coln Rogers
Foss Cross
Woodmancote
Calmsden
Winson
Duntisbourne Abbots
Duntisbourne Leer
North Cerney
Ablington
Arlington
Bibury
Duntisbourne Rouse
Bagendon
Daglingworth
Barnsley
Coln St Aldwyns
Hatherop
Eastleach Turville
Eastleach Martin
Baunton
Quenington
Fyfield
Stratton
Cirencester
Ampney Crucis
Ampney St Mary
Southrop
Coates
Chesterton
Preston
Ampney St Peter
Poulton
Milton End
Fairford
Harnhill
Driffield
Meysey Hampton
Horcott
Siddington
Lechlade-on-Thames
Whelford
Inglesham
Ewen
Kemble
South Cerney
Down Ampney
Marston Meysey
Dunfield
Kempsford
Shorncote
Poole Keynes
Somerford Keynes
Cerney Wick
Latton
Castle Eaton
Hannington Wick
Upper Inglesham
Chelworth
Oaksey
Ashton Keynes
Cricklade
Hannington
Highworth
Crudwell
Eastcourt
Leigh
Chelworth Upper Green
Upper Minety
Hankerton
Cloatley
Minety
Purton Stoke
Broad Blunsdon
Stanton Fitzwarren
Sevenhampton
Perry Green
Charlton
Garsdon
SWINDON
WILTSHIRE
Haydon Wick
Upper Stratton
Penhill
South Marston
Purton Common

COTSWOLDS
OXFORDSHIRE
100
101
81
63
64
Burford
Witney
Carterton
Charlbury
Faringdon
Lechlade-on-Thames
Highworth
Wantage
Grove
Eynsham
Bampton
Woodstock
Kiddington
Glympton
Chadlington
Spelsbury
Taston
Westcote
Church Westcote
Idbury
Fifield
Milton under Wychwood
Shipton-under-Wychwood
Ascott-under-Wychwood
Lyneham
Chilson
Shorthampton
Walcot
Fawler
Finstock
Stonesfield
Combe
Ramsden
Leafield
Asthall Leigh
Fordwells
Swinbrook
Asthall
Minster Lovell
Crawley
Hailey
New Yatt
North Leigh
Long Hanborough
Church Hanborough
Freeland
Barnard Gate
Cogges
High Cogges
South Leigh
Ducklington
Curbridge
Brize Norton
Shilton
Alvescot
Kencot
Filkins
Broughton Poggs
Langford
Broadwell
Black Bourton
Clanfield
Little Faringdon
Kelmscott
Radcot
Aston
Cote
Brighthampton
Standlake
Hardwick
Stanton Harcourt
Sutton
Northmoor
Appleton
Shifford
Chimney
Duxford
Buckland
Carswell Marsh
Longworth
Hinton Waldrist
Kingston Bagpuize
Southmoor
Fyfield
Frilford
Garford
Charney Bassett
Lyford
West Hanney
East Hanney
Denchworth
Goosey
Stanford in the Vale
Shellingford
Hatford
Littleworth
Buscot
Coleshill
Great Coxwell
Little Coxwell
Fernham
Baulking
Uffington
Longcot
Watchfield
Shrivenham
Upper Inglesham
Inglesham
Southrop
Fyfield
Eastleach Martin
Eastleach Turville
Holwell
Westwell
Signet
Taynton
Great Barrington
Little Barrington
Windrush
Great Rissington
Little Rissington
Upper Rissington
Westhall Hill
Fulbrook
Upton
Severnhampton
Redlands
Woolstone
West Challow
Childrey
Charlton
West Hendred
Ardington Wick
A40
A361
A420
A4095
A415
A417
A44
A338
B4437
B4022
B4020
B4477
B4449
B4047
B4019
B4508
B4000
B4001
B4425
WYCHWOOD
BLENHEIM PALACE
OXFORDSHIRE MUSEUM
MINSTER LOVELL HALL & DOVECOTE
COTSWOLD WILDLIFE PARK
COGGES MANOR FARM MUSEUM
KELMSCOTT MANOR
BUSCOT PARK
GREAT COXWELL BARN
KINGSTON BAGPUIZE HOUSE
NORTH LEIGH ROMAN VILLA
CHIMNEY MEADOWS
VALE & DOWNLAND MUSEUM CENTRE
Royal Military College of Science
THAMES PATH
River Windrush
River Evenlode
River Ock
0 1 2 3 miles
0 1 2 3 4 5 km
SP
SU

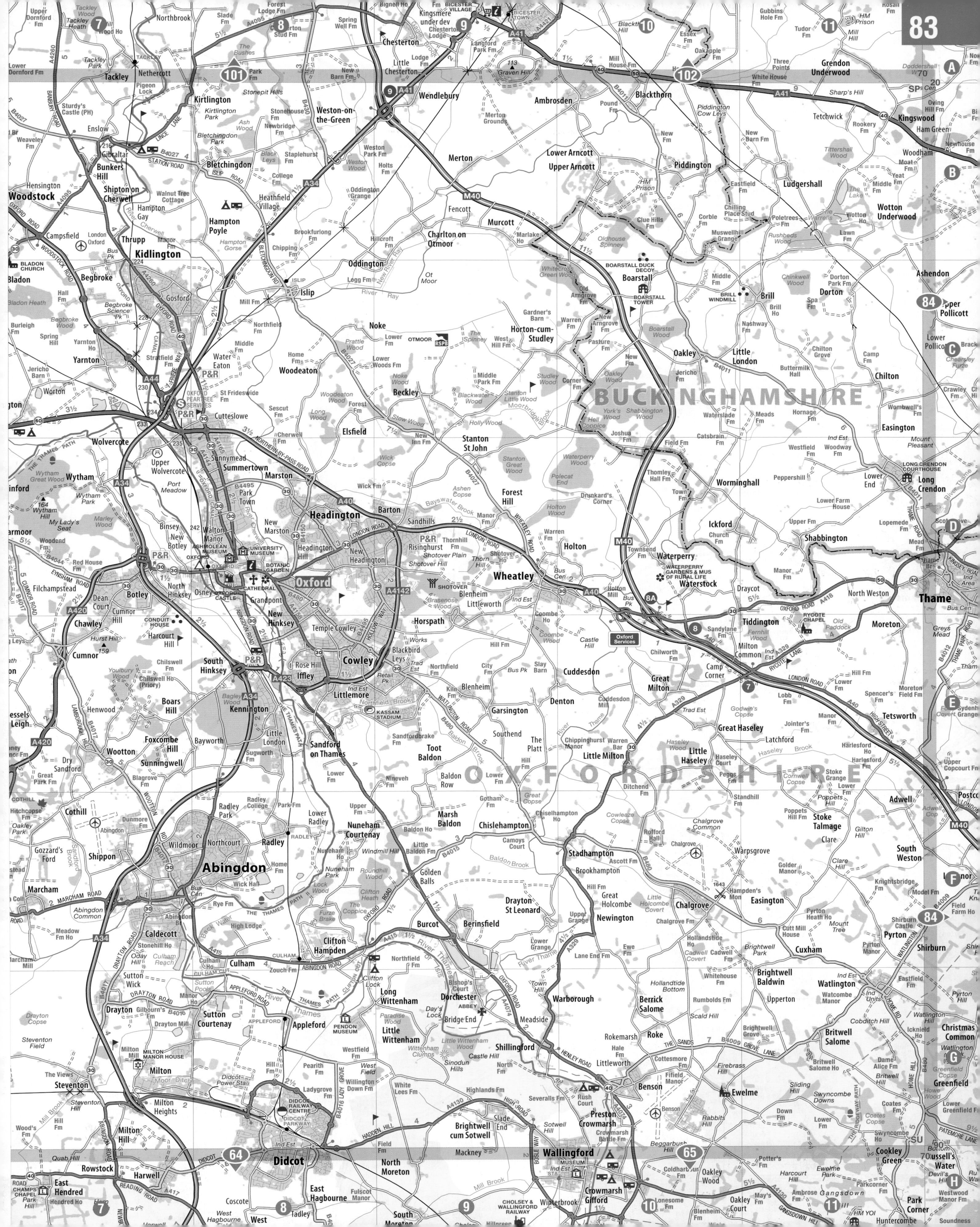

BUCKINGHAMSHIRE
OXFORDSHIRE
Oxford
Headington
Cowley
Kidlington
Woodstock
Abingdon
Didcot
Wallingford
Thame
Wheatley
Bicester
Chesterton
Weston-on-the-Green
Wendlebury
Ambrosden
Blackthorn
Kirtlington
Bletchingdon
Islip
Oddington
Charlton on Otmoor
Merton
Lower Arncott
Upper Arncott
Piddington
Ludgershall
Boarstall
Brill
Oakley
Horton-cum-Studley
Beckley
Elsfield
Marston
Barton
Stanton St John
Forest Hill
Holton
Waterperry
Waterstock
Tiddington
Long Crendon
Ickford
Shabbington
Worminghall
Great Milton
Little Milton
Great Haseley
Garsington
Cuddesdon
Horspath
Littlemore
Iffley
Kennington
Sandford on Thames
Toot Baldon
Marsh Baldon
Nuneham Courtenay
Radley
Chiselhampton
Stadhampton
Chalgrove
Drayton St Leonard
Berinsfield
Dorchester
Warborough
Shillingford
Benson
Ewelme
Watlington
Clifton Hampden
Culham
Sutton Courtenay
Appleford
Long Wittenham
Little Wittenham
Drayton
Milton
Steventon
Harwell
East Hendred
Botley
Cumnor
Wootton
Sunningwell
Kingston Bagpuize
Yarnton
Begbroke
Wolvercote
Wytham
Summertown
Tackley
Thrupp
Hampton Poyle
Wheatley
Tetsworth
Kingswood
Grendon Underwood
Wotton Underwood
Chilton
Easington
Dorton
Ashendon
Pyrton
Shirburn
Crowmarsh Gifford
North Moreton
South Moreton
East Hagbourne
Brightwell cum Sotwell
Preston Crowmarsh
Oxford Services
M40
A40
A34
A41
A4142
A329
A415
A4074
A418

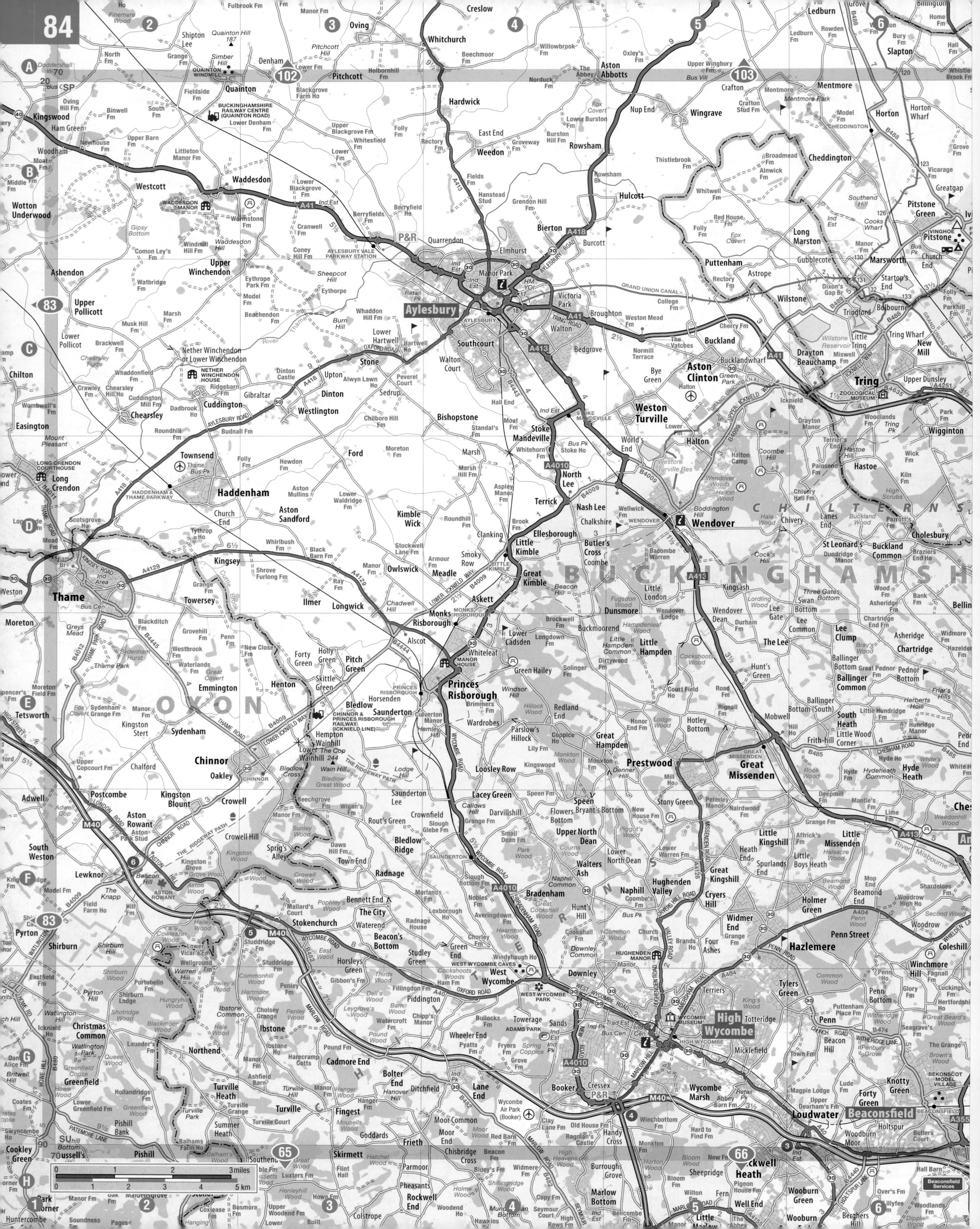

Creslow
Whitchurch
Oving
Quainton
Waddesdon
Westcott
Wotton Underwood
Kingswood
Ashendon
Upper Pollicott
Upper Winchendon
Nether Winchendon or Lower Winchendon
Chearsley
Cuddington
Long Crendon
Easington
Haddenham
Aston Sandford
Towersey
Thame
Kingsey
Moreton
Tetsworth
Sydenham
Chinnor
Oakley
Emmington
Henton
Kingston Blount
Aston Rowant
Postcombe
Adwell
South Weston
Lewknor
Pyrton
Shirburn
Christmas Common
Greenfield
Northend
Turville Heath
Turville
Fingest
Pishill
Ibstone
Stokenchurch
Radnage
Bledlow
Bledlow Ridge
Saunderton
Princes Risborough
Monks Risborough
Longwick
Ilmer
Owlswick
Meadle
Askett
Great Kimble
Little Kimble
Ellesborough
Terrick
Stoke Mandeville
Weston Turville
Aylesbury
Bierton
Hulcott
Weedon
Hardwick
Rowsham
Aston Abbotts
Wingrave
Mentmore
Cheddington
Marsworth
Long Marston
Puttenham
Wilstone
Buckland
Aston Clinton
Tring
Wigginton
Hastoe
Halton
Wendover
Cholesbury
Lee Clump
Chartridge
Dunsmore
Little Hampden
Great Hampden
Prestwood
Great Missenden
Little Missenden
Hyde Heath
Holmer Green
Hazlemere
Penn
Tylers Green
Loudwater
Beaconsfield
Wooburn Green
High Wycombe
West Wycombe
Downley
Hughenden Valley
Naphill
Walters Ash
Lacey Green
Loosley Row
Bradenham
Lane End
Frieth
Skirmett
Booker
Wycombe Marsh
Flackwell Heath
Marlow Bottom
Ivinghoe
Pitstone
Slapton
Ledburn
Horton
Buckingham
OXON
CHILTERNS
BUCKINGHAMSHIRE
A41
A413
A418
A4010
A4129
B4009
M40

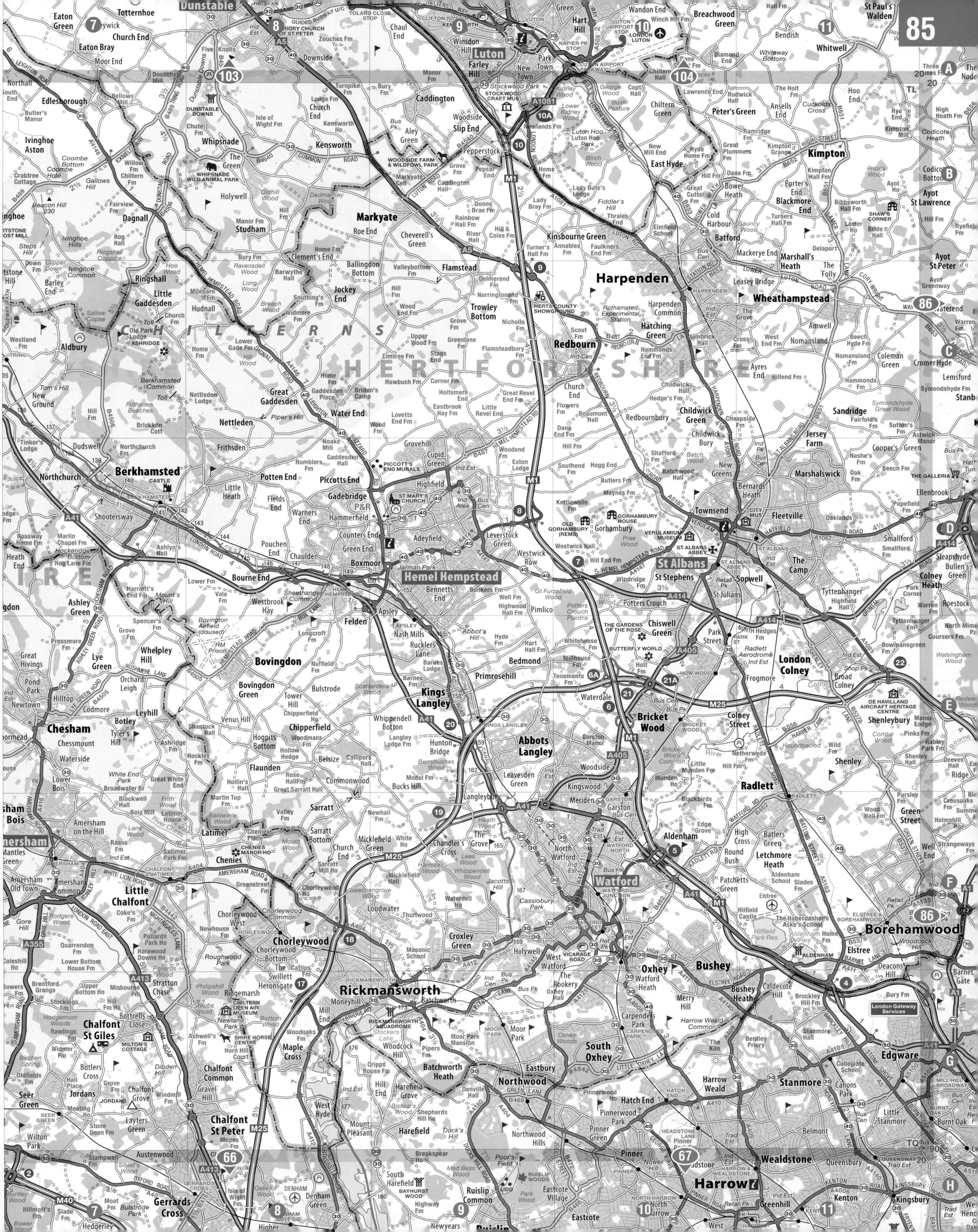
Dunstable
Luton
Harpenden
Wheathampstead
Kimpton
Markyate
Redbourn
Berkhamsted
Hemel Hempstead
St Albans
London Colney
Kings Langley
Abbots Langley
Bricket Wood
Radlett
Shenley
Chesham
Bovingdon
Watford
Bushey
Borehamwood
Elstree
Rickmansworth
Chorleywood
Little Chalfont
Chalfont St Giles
Chalfont St Peter
Gerrards Cross
Northwood
South Oxhey
Stanmore
Edgware
Harrow
Wealdstone
Pinner
Ruislip
Denham
Harefield
CHILTERNS
HERTFORDSHIRE

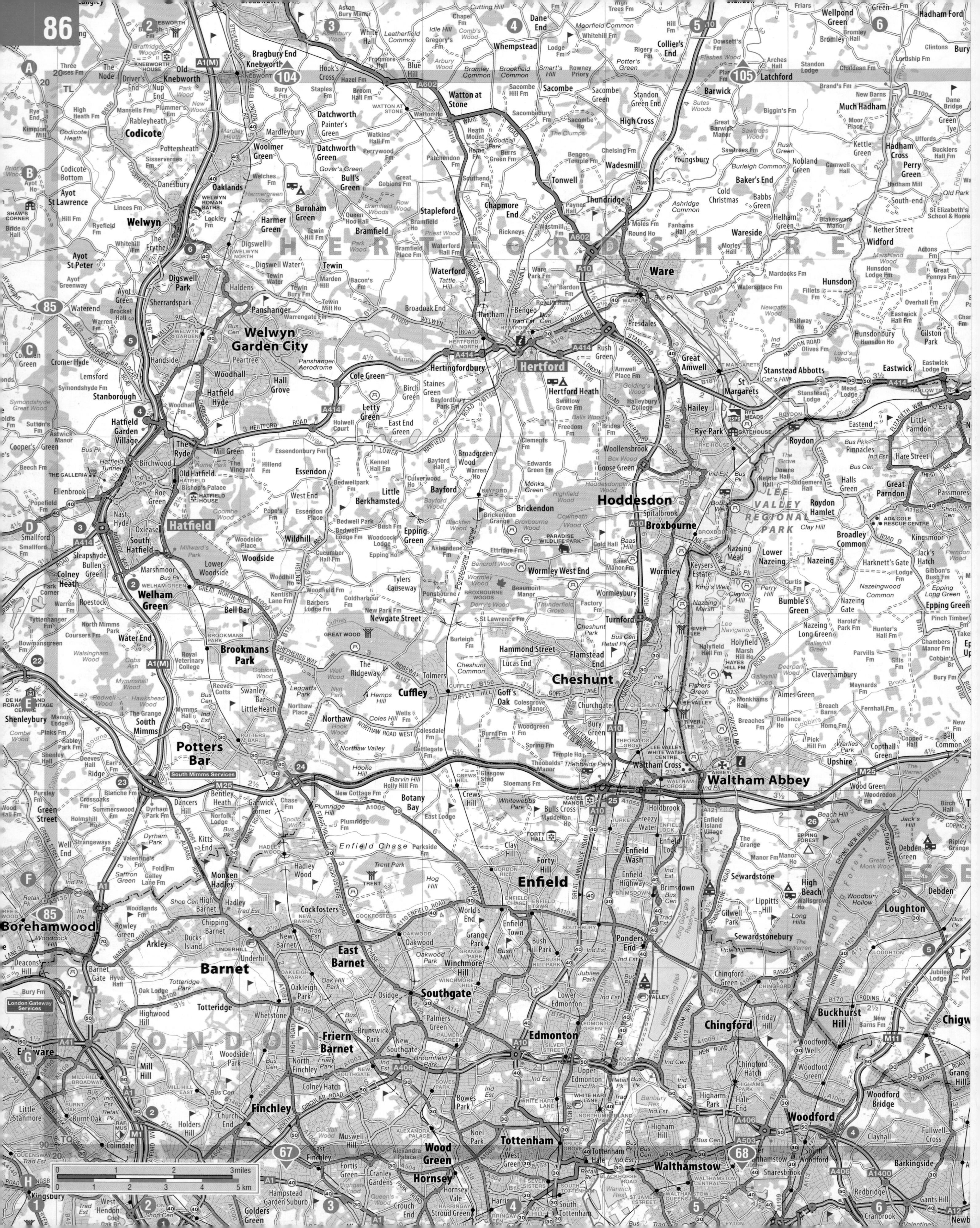
HERTFORDSHIRE
LONDON
Knebworth
Codicote
Welwyn
Welwyn Garden City
Hatfield
Potters Bar
Brookmans Park
Welham Green
Borehamwood
Barnet
East Barnet
Southgate
Finchley
Friern Barnet
Edmonton
Enfield
Tottenham
Wood Green
Hornsey
Walthamstow
Chingford
Woodford
Buckhurst Hill
Loughton
Waltham Abbey
Waltham Cross
Cheshunt
Cuffley
Broxbourne
Hoddesdon
Ware
Hertford
Hertingfordbury
Watton at Stone
Datchworth
Sacombe
High Cross
Wadesmill
Much Hadham
Hunsdon
Stanstead Abbotts
St Margarets
Roydon
Nazeing
Great Amwell
Essendon
Bayford
Brickendon
Wormley
Turnford
Goff's Oak
Northaw
South Mimms
Shenley
Arkley
Totteridge
Whetstone
Cockfosters
Hadley Wood
Enfield Chase
Epping Forest
Lee Valley Regional Park
Woolmer Green
Tewin
Stapleford
Letty Green
Cole Green
Welwyn Garden City
South Mimms Services
London Gateway Services
M25
A1(M)
A10
A414
A602
104
105
85
67
68
0 1 2 3 miles
0 1 2 3 4 5 km

Bishop's Stortford
Sawbridgeworth
Harlow
Epping
Great Dunmow
Chipping Ongar
Brentwood
Billericay
Romford
Ingatestone
Hatfield Heath
Sheering
High Wych
Thorley
Thorley Street
Spellbrook
Little Hallingbury
Great Hallingbury
Hatfield Broad Oak
Takeley
Takeley Street
Little Dunmow
Felsted
Barnston
High Easter
High Roding
Great Canfield
Pleshey
Great Waltham
Little Waltham
Broomfield
Chelmsford
Writtle
Widford
Moulsham
Galleywood
Margaretting
Stock
Mountnessing
Hutton
Shenfield
Pilgrims Hatch
Kelvedon Hatch
Navestock Heath
Navestock Side
Stapleford Abbotts
Stapleford Tawney
Theydon Bois
Theydon Mount
Abridge
Lambourne End
Chigwell Row
Hainault
Collier Row
Havering-atte-Bower
Harold Hill
Harold Wood
Gidea Park
Noak Hill
South Weald
Great Warley
Little Warley
West Horndon
Laindon
Great Burstead
Little Burstead
Crays Hill
Ramsden Heath
Downham
Fryerning
Blackmore
Doddinghurst
Stondon Massey
Norton Heath
High Ongar
Greensted
Toot Hill
North Weald Bassett
Bovinger
Moreton
Fyfield
Willingale
Shellow Bowells
Roxwell
Good Easter
Margaret Roding
Leaden Roding
Aythorpe Roding
White Roding
Abbess Roding
Beauchamp Roding
Matching
Matching Tye
Matching Green
High Laver
Little Laver
Magdalen Laver
Potter Street
Foster Street
Chignall Smealy
Chignall St James
Mashbury
Boyton Cross
ESSEX
M11
M25
A12
A414
A1060
A127
A120
A129
105
106
88
68
69

Great Notley
Black Notley
Cressing
Coggeshall Hamlet
Kelvedon
Feering
Tiptree
Witham
Terling
Fairstead
Faulkbourne
White Notley
Rivenhall
Great Leighs
Little Leighs
Hatfield Peverel
Boreham
Springfield
Chelmsford
Great Baddow
Danbury
Little Baddow
Woodham Walter
Maldon
Heybridge
Heybridge Basin
Langford
Wickham Bishops
Great Totham
Little Totham
Tolleshunt D'Arcy
Tolleshunt Major
Goldhanger
Osea Island
Mundon
Maylandsea
Mayland
Steeple
Latchingdon
Cold Norton
Purleigh
Stow Maries
Woodham Ferrers
Woodham Mortimer
East Hanningfield
West Hanningfield
South Hanningfield
Hanningfield Reservoir
Bicknacre
Rettendon
South Woodham Ferrers
North Fambridge
South Fambridge
Althorne
Ostend
Creeksea
Canewdon
Hullbridge
Battlesbridge
Runwell
Wickford
Shotgate
Rawreth
Ramsden Heath
Downham
Ramsden Bellhouse
Crays Hill
Nevendon
North Benfleet
Rayleigh
Hockley
Hawkwell
Ashingdon
Rochford
Great Stambridge
Paglesham Eastend
Paglesham Churchend
Ballards Gore
Thundersley
Pitsea
Eastwood
Daws Heath
Galleywood
Widford
Moulsham
Writtle
Broomfield
Great Waltham
Little Waltham
Howe Street
Stock
Sandon
Runsell Green
E S S E X
LONDON SOUTHEND AIRPORT
HANNINGFIELD RESERVOIR
MALDON 991

Wivenhoe
Alresford
Great Bentley
Weeley
Weeley Heath
Thorpe-le-Soken
Rowhedge
Fingringhoe
Langenhoe
Abberton
Abberton Reservoir
Layer de la Haye
Peldon
Little Wigborough
Great Wigborough
Thorrington
Aingers Green
South Heath
Hollybush Hill
St Osyth Heath
Row Heath
Little Clacton
Great Holland
Cook's Green
Burrsville Park
Brightlingsea
Hurst Green
St Osyth
Point Clear
Great Clacton
Clacton-on-Sea
Holland-on-Sea
Rush Green
Jaywick
Seawick
Lee-over-Sands
St Osyth Beach
Colne Bar
Colne Pt
Mersea Island
East Mersea
West Mersea
Blue Row
River Colne
Brightlingsea Reach
Pyefleet Channel
Strood Channel
COPT HALL MARSHES NATURE RESERVE
CUDMORE GROVE
COLNE ESTUARY
OLD HALL MARSHES
BLACKWATER ESTUARY
Tollesbury
Tollesbury Wick Marshes
The Nass
River Blackwater
St Lawrence Bay
Ramsey Island
Bradwell Waterside
East End
Bradwell on Sea
ST PETER'S ON THE WALL
Bradwell Marshes
St Lawrence
Tillingham
Tillingham Marshes
DENGIE
Dengie Flat
Asheldham
Dengie
Southminster
North Wycke
Ray Sand
Montsale
Deal Hall
Burnham-on-Crouch
River Crouch
Foulness Sands
Foulness Pt
Wallasea Island
WALLASEA WETLANDS
Churchend
Courtsend
River Roach
Foulness Island
Potton Island
New England Island
Rushley Island
Havengore Island
Maplin Sands
IRISH SEA
TM
TR
A
B
C
D
E
F
G
H
7
8
9
10
11
107
108
70
71

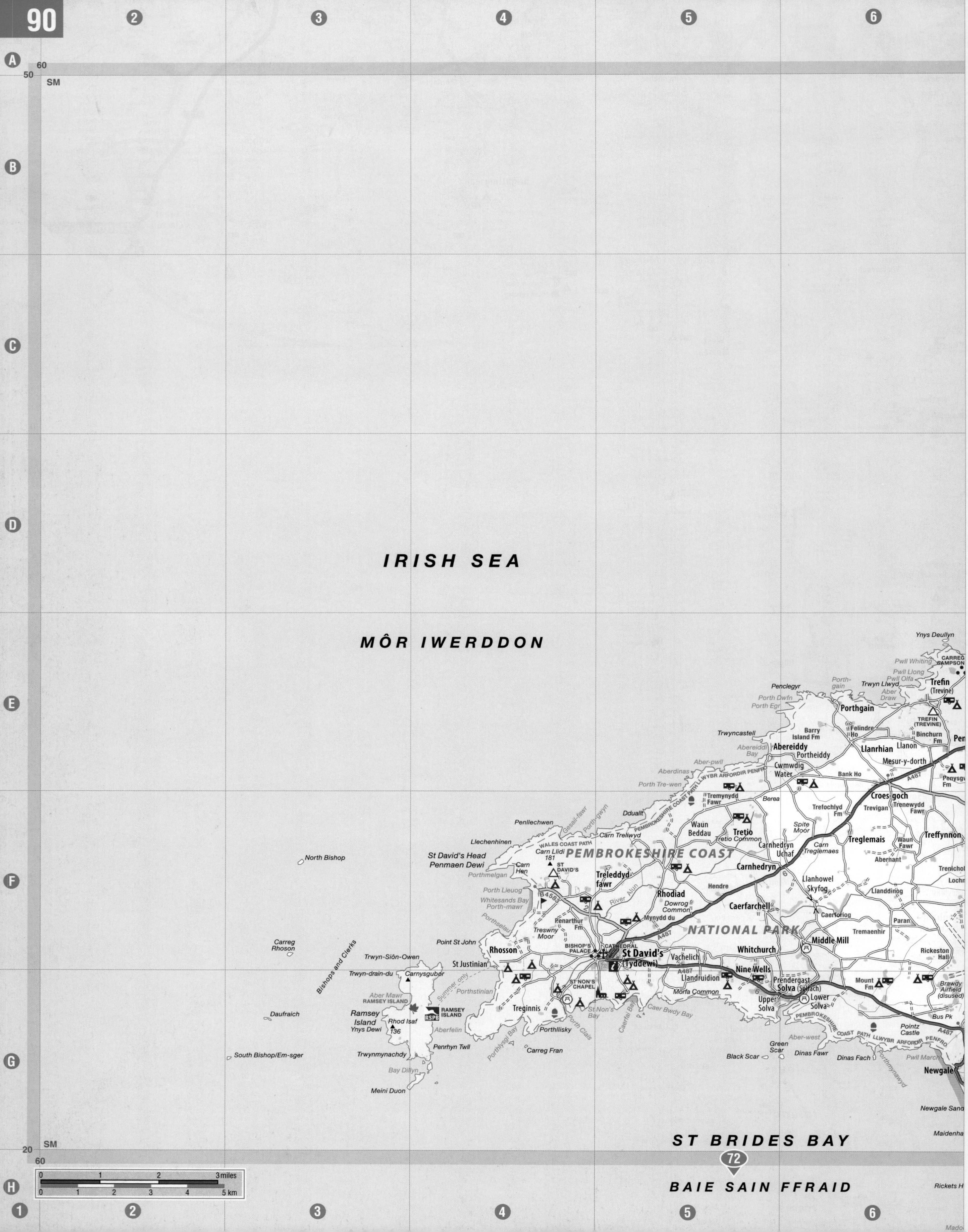
IRISH SEA
MÔR IWERDDON
ST BRIDES BAY
BAIE SAIN FFRAID
72
PEMBROKESHIRE COAST
NATIONAL PARK
St David's
(Tyddewi)
St David's Head
Penmaen Dewi
Ramsey Island
Ynys Dewi
RAMSEY ISLAND
RSPB
North Bishop
South Bishop/Em-sger
Carreg Rhoson
Daufraich
Bishops and Clerks
Meini Duon
Bay Dillyn
Trwynmynachdy
Penrhyn Twll
Aberfelin
Rhod Isaf
136
Carnysgubor
Aber Mawr
Trwyn-drain-du
Trwyn-Siôn-Owen
St Justinian
Point St John
Rhosson
Porthstinian
Treginnis
Porthlysgi Bay
Carreg Fran
Porthllisky
Porth Clais
St Non's Bay
ST NON'S CHAPEL
Caerfai Bay
Caer Bwdy Bay
Morfa Common
Llandruidion
Vachelich
Nine Wells
Whitchurch
Middle Mill
Solva (Solfach)
Prendergast
Upper Solva
Lower Solva
Green Scar
Black Scar
Dinas Fawr
Dinas Fach
Aber-west
PEMBROKESHIRE COAST PATH LLWYBR ARFORDIR PENFRO
Newgale
Newgale Sands
Maidenha
Rickets H
Pwll March
Pointz Castle
Bus Pk
Brawdy Airfield (disused)
Mount Fm
Rickeston Hall
Tremaenhir
Paran
Caerforiog
Llanhowel
Skyfog
Llanddinog
Caerfarchell
Hendre
Carnhedryn
Carnhedryn Uchaf
Rhodiad
Dowrog Common
Mynydd du
Treleddyd-fawr
Treswny Moor
Penarthur Fm
BISHOP'S PALACE
CATHEDRAL
Porthselau
Whitesands Bay
Porth-mawr
Porth Lleuog
Porthmelgan
Carn Hen
Carn Llidi
181
ST DAVID'S
WALES COAST PATH
Llechenhinen
Penllechwen
Gesail-fawr
Porth-gwyn
Carn Treliwyd
Dduallt
Waun Beddau
Tretio
Tretio Common
Tremynydd Fawr
Porth Tre-wen
Aberdinas
Aber-pwll
Cwmwdig Water
Berea
Spite Moor
Carn Treglemaes
Treglemais
Trefochlyd Fm
Waun Fawr
Abernant
Treffynnon
Trenichol
Lochn
Croes-goch
Trevigan
Trenewydd Fawr
Bank Ho
Mesur-y-dorth
Penysgw Fm
Llanrhian
Llanon
Abereiddy
Abereiddi Bay
Portheiddy
Barry Island Fm
Trwyncastell
Penclegyr
Porth Dwfn
Porth Egr
Porthgain
Porth-gain
Felindre Ho
Trwyn Llwyd
Aber Draw
Binchurn Fm
Trefin
(Trevine)
TREFIN (TREVINE)
Pwll Whiting
Pwll Llong
Pwll Olfa
CARREG SAMPSON
Ynys Deullyn
Pen
B4583
A487
Summer only
River Alun
SM
60
50
20
0 1 2 3 miles
0 1 2 3 4 5 km

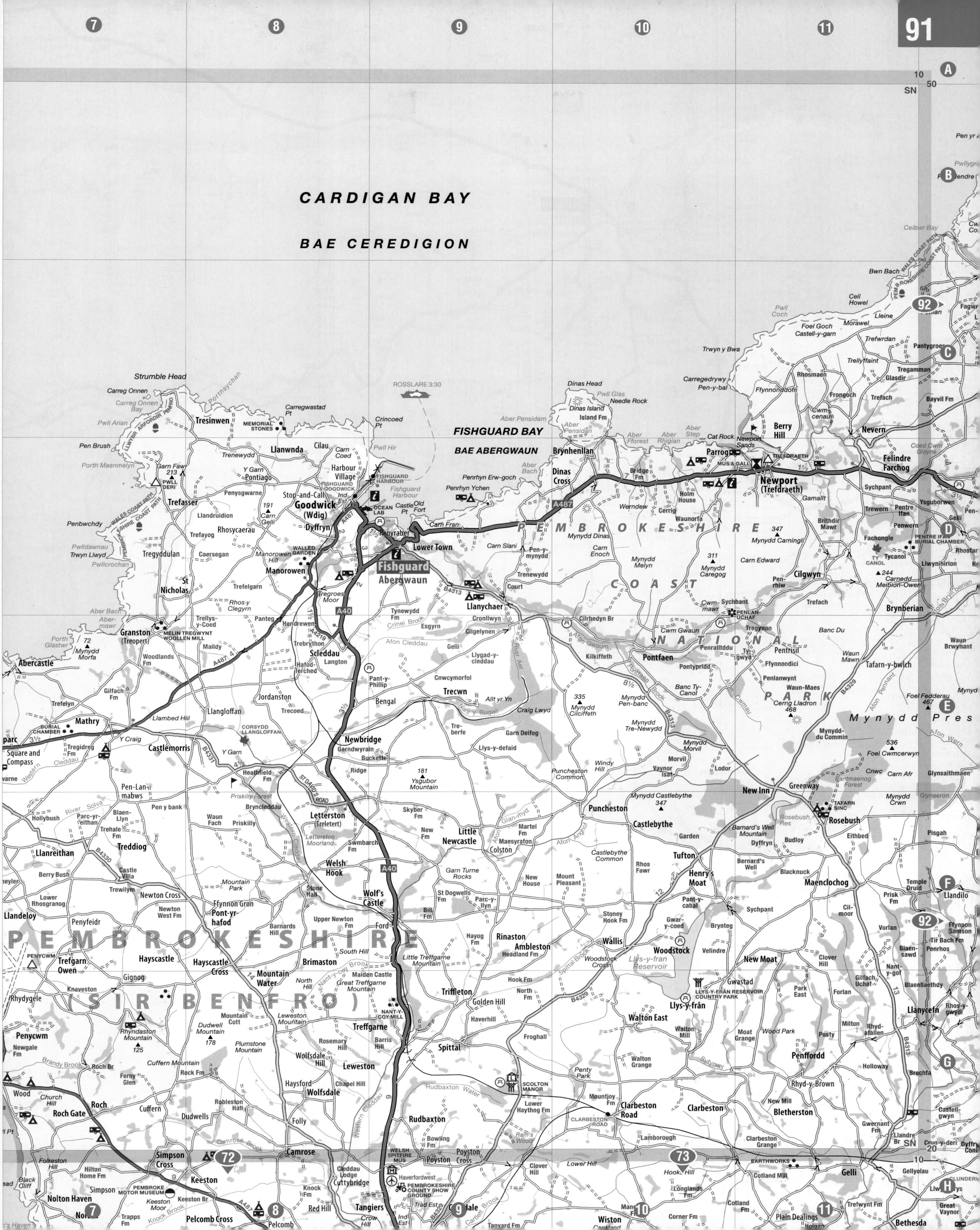
CARDIGAN BAY
BAE CEREDIGION
FISHGUARD BAY
BAE ABERGWAUN
PEMBROKESHIRE COAST NATIONAL PARK
PEMBROKESHIRE (SIR BENFRO)
Strumble Head
Carreg Onnen
Carreg Onnen Bay
Pwll Arian
Pen Brush
Porth Maenmelyn
Garn Fawr 213
Pwll Deri
Tresinwen
Memorial Stones
Carregwastad Pt
Llanwnda
Cilau
Carn Coed
Harbour Village
Fishguard Harbour
Crincoed Pt
Pwll Hir
ROSSLARE 3:30
Trenewydd
Y Garn Pontiago
Penysgwarne
Stop-and-Call
Goodwick (Wdig)
Ind Est
Ocean Lab
Castle Pt
Old Fort
Dyffryn
Carn Fran
Penyraber
Lower Town
Fishguard
Abergwaun
Trefasser
Llandruidion
191 Carn Gelli
Rhosycaerau
Trefayog
Penbwchdy
Pwlldawnau
Trwyn Llwyd
Pwllcrochan
Tregyddulan
Caersegan
Manorowen Hill
Walled Garden
Manorowen
St Nicholas
Trefelgarn
Rhos-y Clegyrn
Tregroes Moor
Aber Bach
Abermawr
Porth Glastwr
72 Mynydd Morfa
Granston (Treopert)
Melin Tregwynt Woollen Mill
Trellys-y-Coed
Panteg
Hendrewen
Maildy
Woodlands Fm
Abercastle
Trebrython
Scleddau
Langton
Hafod-Iferched
Gilfach Fm
Trefelyn
Jordanston
Trecoed
Pant-y-Phillip
Bengal
Llanbed Hill
Llangloffan
Mathry
Burial Chamber
Corsydd Llangloffan
Y Craig
Tregidreg Fm
Square and Compass
Castlemorris
Y Garn
Heathfield Fm
Priskilly Forest
St David's Road
Newbridge
Garndwyrain
Buckette
Ridge
181 Ysgubor Mountain
Pen-Lan-mabws
Pen y bank
River Solva
Hollybush
Blaen-Llyn
Parc-yr-eithan
Trehale Fm
Waun Fach
Priskilly
Bryncleddau
Letterston (Treletert)
Letterston Moorland
Skyber Fm
New Fm
Little Newcastle
Swmbarch Fm
Treddiog
Llanreithan
Berry Bush
Castle Villa
Trewilym
Newton Cross
Newton West Fm
Mountain Park
Lower Rhosgranog
Ffynnon Gron
Pont-yr-hafod
Llandeloy
Penyfeidr
Barnards Hill
Welsh Hook
Stone Hall
Upper Newton Fm
Wolf's Castle
Ford
Penycwm
Trefgarn Owen
Hayscastle
Hayscastle Cross
Gignog
Knaveston
Rhydygele
Mountain Water
North Hill
Brimaston
South Hill
Maiden Castle
Great Treffgarne Mountain
Little Treffgarne Mountain
Nant-y-Coy Mill
Leweston Mountain
Mountain Cott
Dudwell Mountain 178
Rhyndaston Mountain 125
Plumstone Mountain
Treffgarne
Rosemary Hill
Barris Hill
Wolfsdale Hill
Leweston
Newgale Fm
Brandy Brook
Roch Br
Cuffern Mountain
Rock Fm
Ferny Glen
Haysford
Chapel Hill
Wolfsdale
Wood
Church Hill
Roch Gate
Roch
Cuffern
Robleston Hall
Dudwells
Folly
Camrose Brook
Camrose
Simpson Cross
Folkeston Hill
Hilton Home Fm
Simpson
Keeston
Pembroke Motor Museum
Keeston Br
Keeston Moor
Knock Brook
Black Cliff
Nolton Haven
Pelcomb Cross
Pelcomb
Trapps Fm
Knock Fm
Red Hill
Cleddau Lodge
Cuttybridge
Welsh Spitfire Mus
Haverfordwest
Pembrokeshire County Show Ground
Tangiers
Crow Hill
Ind Est
Trad Est
Rudbaxton Water
Rudbaxton
Bowling Fm
Poyston
Poyston Cross
Western Cleddau
Crinoed Pt
Penrhyn Erw-goch
Penrhyn Ychen
Aber Bach
Carn Slani
Pen-y-mynydd
Trenewydd
Court
Llanychaer
Cronllwyn
Cilgelynen
Tynewydd Fm
Crinei Brook
Esgyrn
Afon Cleddau
Gelli
Llygad-y-cleddau
Cnwcymorfol
Trecwn
Allt yr Yn
Nant y Bugail
Craig Lwyd
Tre-berfe
Garn Deifog
Llys-y-defaid
Martel Fm
Maesyrafon
Colston
Afon Anghof
Glan-rhyd
Garn Turne Rocks
St Dogwells Fm
Parc-y-llyn
Bill Fm
Hayog Fm
Rinaston
Ambleston
Headland Fm
Hook Fm
North Fm
Triffleton
Golden Hill
Haverhill
Froghall
Scolton Manor
Penty Park
Mountjoy Fm
Lower Haythog Fm
Clarbeston Road
Lamborough
Ram's Wood
Clover Hill
Lower Hill
Dinas Head
Pwll Glas
Needle Rock
Dinas Island
Island Fm
Aber Pensidan
Aber Pensidam
Brynhenllan
Dinas Cross
Aber Fforest
Aber Rhigian
Aber Step
Cat Rock
Bridge Fm
Werndew
Cerrig
Holm House
Waunorfa
Mynydd Dinas
Carn Enoch
Mynydd Melyn
311 Mynydd Caregog
Cilrhedyn Br
Afon Gwaun
Kilkiffeth
Pontfaen
Cwm Gwaun
Penrallt-ddu
Pontypridd
Ty-gwyn
335 Mynydd Cilciffeth
Mynydd Pen-banc
Mynydd Tre-Newydd
Pontfaen Brook
Banc Ty-Canol
Puncheston Common
Windy Hill
Mynydd Morvil
Morvil
Vaynor Isaf
Lodor
Puncheston
Mynydd Castlebythe 347
Castlebythe
Castlebythe Common
Rhos Fawr
Tufton
Garden
Mount Pleasant
New House
Henry's Moat
Pant-y-cabal
Stoney Hook Fm
Wallis
Gwar-y-coed
Woodstock
Woodstock Cross
Spittal Brook
Llys-y-fran Reservoir
Llys-y-Fran Reservoir Country Park
Llys-y-frân
Walton East
Walton Mill
Walton Grange
Clarbeston
Hook's Hill
Longlands Fm
Cotland Fm
Corner Fm
Wiston
Tanyard Fm
Trwyn y Bwa
Carregedrywy
Pen-y-bal
Parrog
Mus & Gall
Newport Sands
Berry Hill
Trefdraeth
Newport (Trefdraeth)
Ffynnonddofn
Rhosmaen
Frongoch
Cwm-cenau
347 Mynydd Carningli
Carn Edward
Brithdir Mawr
Gamallt
Pen-rhiw
Cwm-mawr
Sychbant
Penlan-Uchaf
Tregynon
Banc Du
Pentrisil
Ffynnondici
Penlanwynt
Waun-Maes
Cerrig Lladron 468
Waun Mawn
Tafarn-y-bwlch
Mynydd-du Commin
Greenway
New Inn
Rosebush Res
Tafarn Sinc
Rosebush
Barnard's Well Mountain
Dyffryn
Budloy
Bernard's Well
Blacknuck
Maenclochog
Sychpant
Brynteg
Velindre
New Moat
Gwastad
Park East
Moat Grange
Wood Park
Penffordd
Posty
Milton
Rhyd-afallen
Rhyd-y-Brown
Holloway
New Mill
Bletherston
Clarbeston Grange
Gwernant Fm
Llandre Br
Earthworks
Cotland Mill
Gelli
Plain Dealings
Trefwynt Fm
Holgan
Ceibwr Bay
Bwn Bach
Pembrokeshire Coast Path
Cell Howel
Pwll Coch
Lleine
Morawel
Foel Goch
Castell-y-garn
Trefwrdan
Trellyffaint
Pantygroes
Tregamman
Glasdir
Trefach
Bayvil Fm
Nevern
Coed Cwm Gloyne
Felindre Farchog
Sychpant
Trewern
Pentre Ifan
Penwern
Ysgubor-wen
Gelli
Fachongle
Pentre Ifan Burial Chamber
Ty Canol
Tycanol
Rhostar
Llwynihirion
244 Carnedd Meibion-Owen
Cilgwyn
Trefach
Brynberian
Afon Brynberian
Waun Brwynant
Foel Fedderau 467
Mynydd Preseli
Afon Wern
536 Foel Cwmcerwyn
Cnwc
Carn Afr
Pantmaenog Forest
Glynsaithmaen
Mynydd Crwn
Glynaeron
Pisgah
Eithbed
Temple Druid
Prisk Fm
Llandilo
Cil-moor
Vorlan
Ffynnon Samson
Tir Bach Fm
Penrhos
Blaen-sawd
Clover Hill
Nant-y-got
Gilfach Uchaf
Forlan
Blaenllaethdy
Llanycefn
Rhos-y-gwydi
Brechfa
Castell-gwyn
Crug-y-deri
Dyffryn Conin
Gellyolau
Clunderwen
Llwyn-yrys
Great Vaynor
Bethesda
Pen yr Allt
Pwllygranant
Pantyrendre
Cwm
Fagwr
Penwern
Pen-y-bryn
Afon Pennant
Llanddewi Velfrey
A40
A487
B4313
B4329
B4330
B4331
SN
10
20
50
92
72
73
A B C D E F G H
7 8 9 10 11

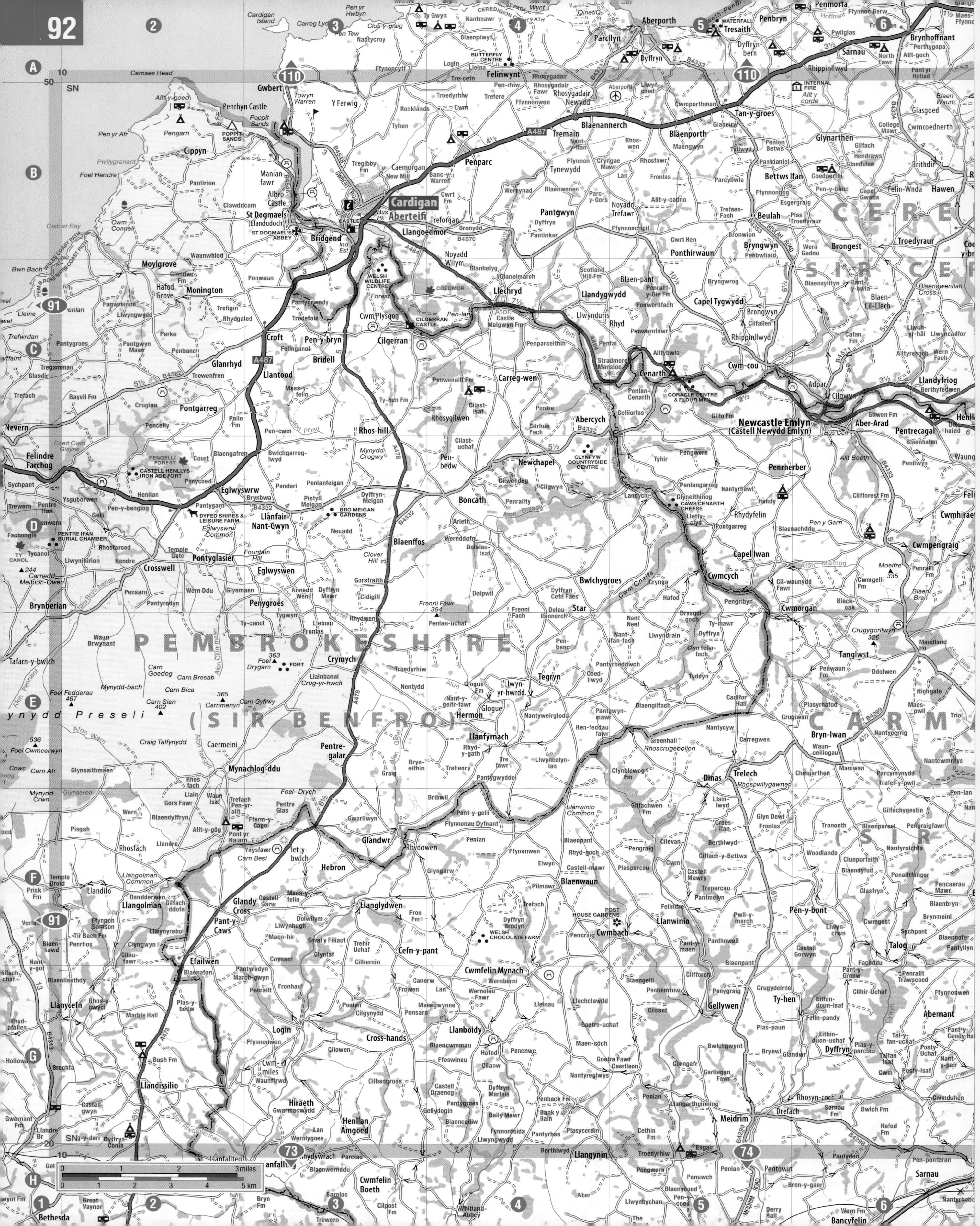
PEMBROKESHIRE
(SIR BENFRO)
CERE
(SIR CER
CARM
(SIR
Cardigan
Aberteifi
Newcastle Emlyn
(Castell Newydd Emlyn)
Aberporth
Cemaes Head
Cardigan Island
Gwbert
St Dogmaels
(Llandudoch)
Bridgend
Llangoedmor
Penparc
Tremain
Blaenannerch
Blaenporth
Tan-y-groes
Glynarthen
Penbryn
Tresaith
Parcllyn
Sarnau
Felinwynt
Beulah
Brongest
Troedyraur
Bettws Ifan
Hawen
Brithdir
Ponthirwaun
Bryngwyn
Capel Tygwydd
Brongwyn
Llechryd
Llandygwydd
Cilgerran
Cwm Plysgog
Pen-y-bryn
Bridell
Croft
Llantood
Glanrhyd
Moylgrove
Monington
Pontgarreg
Nevern
Felindre Farchog
Eglwyswrw
Llanfair Nant-Gwyn
Pontyglasier
Crosswell
Eglwyswen
Penygroes
Brynberian
Rhos-hill
Carreg-wen
Rhosygilwen
Abercych
Newchapel
Boncath
Blaenffos
Bwlchygroes
Star
Cenarth
Cwm-cou
Adpar
Cilgwyn
Llandyfriog
Aber-Arad
Pentrecagal
Penrherber
Capel Iwan
Cwmcych
Cwmorgan
Cwmpengraig
Tanglwst
Tegryn
Crymych
Hermon
Glogue
Llanfyrnach
Pentre-galar
Mynachlog-ddu
Bryn-Iwan
Trelech
Dinas
Glandwr
Rhydowen
Hebron
Blaenwaun
Llanglydwen
Glandy Cross
Pant-y-Caws
Efailwen
Llangolman
Llandilo
Cefn-y-pant
Cwmbach
Llanwinio
Pen-y-bont
Talog
Cwmfelin Mynach
Llanboidy
Login
Cross-hands
Llanycefn
Llandissilio
Gellywen
Ty-hen
Abernant
Dyffryn
Hiraeth
Henllan Amgoed
Meidrim
Llangynin
Cwmfelin Boeth
Sarnau
Bancyfelin
Whitland Abbey
Bethesda
Preseli
Foel Drygarn
Foel Cwmcerwyn
Frenni Fawr
394
Carn Sian
Foel Feddau
WELSH WILDLIFE CENTRE
CILGERRAN CASTLE
CASTELL HENLLYS IRON AGE FORT
PENTRE IFAN BURIAL CHAMBER
CORACLE CENTRE & FLOUR MILL
CAWS CENARTH CHEESE
CLYNFYW COUNTRYSIDE CENTRE
BRO MEIGAN GARDENS
DYFED SHIRES & LEISURE FARM
WELSH CHOCOLATE FARM
POST HOUSE GARDENS
BUTTERFLY CENTRE
INTERNAL FIRE
A487
A478
A484
B4332
B4333
B4570
B4582
B4299
B4298
B4313
B4571
B4334
110
91
73
74
0 1 2 3 miles
0 1 2 3 4 5 km
SN
A
B
C
D
E
F
G
H
1
2
3
4
5
6

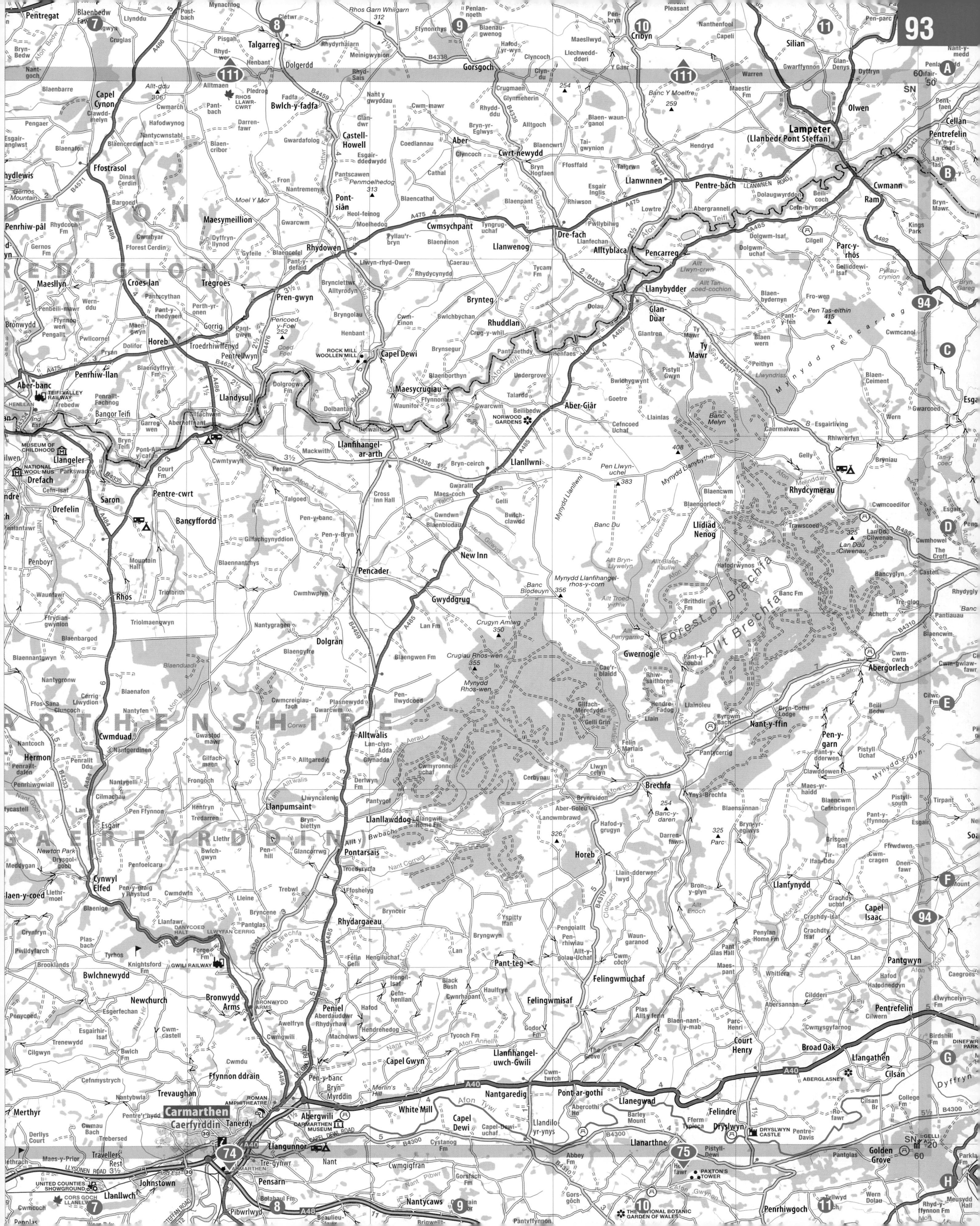
Pentregat
Talgarreg
Cribyn
Silian
Gorsgoch
Capel Cynon
Bwlch-y-fadfa
Lampeter
(Llanbedr Pont Steffan)
Olwen
Cellan
Pentrefelin
Ffostrasol
Castell-Howell
Aber
Cwrt-newydd
Llanwnnen
Pentre-bâch
Cwmann
Ram
Pont-siân
Maesymeillion
Cwmsychpant
Dre-fach
Penrhiw-pâl
Rhydowen
Llanwenog
Alltyblaca
Pencarreg
Parc-y-rhôs
Maesllyn
Croes-lan
Tregroes
Pren-gwyn
Brynteg
Llanybydder
Glan-Duar
Rhuddlan
Horeb
Ty Mawr
Capel Dewi
Penrhiw-llan
Aber-banc
Maesycrugiau
Llandysul
Aber-Giâr
Llangeler
Drefach
Saron
Pentre-cwrt
Llanfihangel-ar-arth
Llanllwni
Rhydcymerau
Drefelin
Bancyffordd
Llidiad Nenog
New Inn
Pencader
Gwyddgrug
Rhos
Dolgran
Forest of Brechfa
Allt Brechfa
Gwernogle
Abergorlech
Nant-y-ffin
Alltwalis
Cwmduad
Hermon
Pen-y-garn
Brechfa
Llanpumsaint
Llanllawddog
Pontarsais
Horeb
Cynwyl Elfed
Llanfynydd
Rhydargaeau
Capel Isaac
Pant-teg
Felingwmuchaf
Bwlchnewydd
Newchurch
Bronwydd Arms
Peniel
Felingwmisaf
Pentrefelin
Court Henry
Broad Oak
Llangathen
Capel Gwyn
Llanfihangel-uwch-Gwili
Ffynnon ddrain
Trevaughan
Nantgaredig
Pont-ar-gothi
Cilsan
Carmarthen
Caerfyrddin
Abergwili
White Mill
Capel Dewi
Llanegwad
Felindre
Dryslwyn
Tanerdy
Llangunnor
Llanarthne
Golden Grove
Johnstown
Llanllwch
Pensarn
Nantycaws
Penrhiwgoch
CARMARTHENSHIRE
(SIR GAERFYRDDIN)
CEREDIGION
A40
A48
A475
A482
A484
A485
A486
B4459
B4336
B4338
B4310
B4300

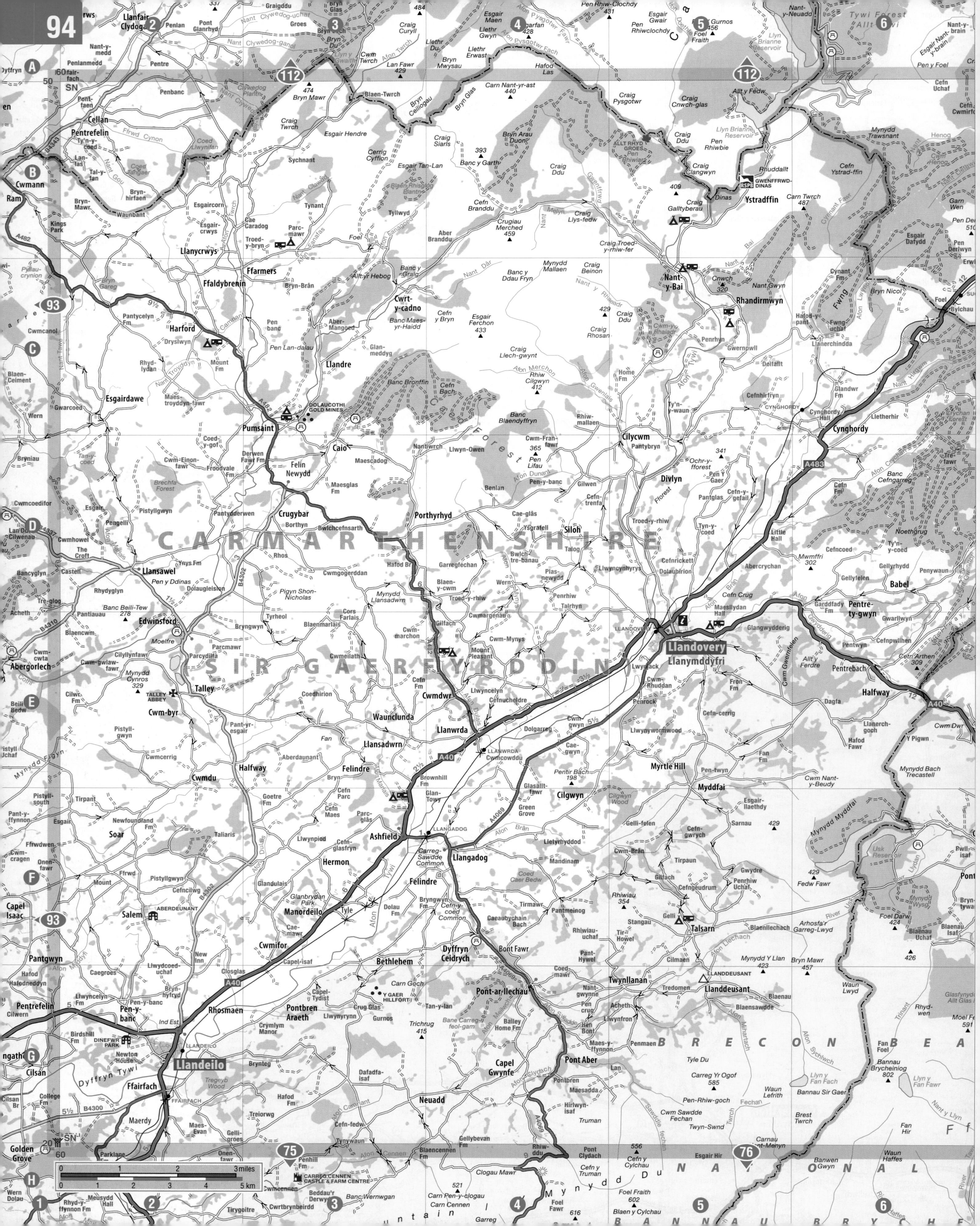
CARMARTHENSHIRE
SIR GAERFYRDDIN
BRECON BEACONS NATIONAL PARK
BANNAU BRYCHEINIOG
Tywi Forest
Llanfair Clydogau
Cellan
Pentrefelin
Cwmann
Llanycrwys
Ffarmers
Ffaldybrenin
Harford
Pumsaint
DOLAUCOTHI GOLD MINES
Caio
Crugybar
Esgairdawe
Llansawel
Edwinsford
Abergorlech
Talley
TALLEY ABBEY
Cwm-byr
Halfway
Cwmdu
Soar
Salem
ABERDEUNANT
Manordeilo
Cwmifor
Rhosmaen
Llandeilo
DINEFWR PARK
Ffairfach
Bethlehem
Y GAER HILLFORT
Pont-ar-llechau
Capel Gwynfe
Pont Aber
Llangadog
Ashfield
Llanwrda
Llansadwrn
Porthyrhyd
Cwrt-y-cadno
Llandre
Cilycwm
Siloh
Llandovery
Llanymddyfri
Myddfai
Cilgwyn
Myrtle Hill
Rhandirmwyn
Nant-y-Bai
Ystradffin
GWENFFRWD-DINAS
Llyn Brianne Reservoir
Cynghordy
Babel
Pentre-ty-gwyn
Halfway
Talsarn
Llanddeusant
Twynllanan
Usk Reservoir
Llyn y Fan Fach
Bannau Sir Gaer
Fan Foel
Bannau Brycheiniog 802
CARREG CENNEN CASTLE & FARM CENTRE
Mynydd Du
A40
A482
A483
A4069
B4302
B4300
B4337
B4310
A485
112
93
75
76
0 1 2 3 miles
0 1 2 3 4 5 km

Builth Wells
Llanfair-ym-Muallt
Llanelwedd
Cilmery
Beulah
Garth
Llanfechan
Llanwrtyd Wells
(Llanwrtud)
Llangammarch Wells
Cefn-gorwydd
Tirabad
Mynydd Eppynt
Sennybridge Training Area
Pentre Dolau-Honddu
Upper Chapel
Merthyr Cynog
Blaendyryn
Lower Chapel
Llandeilo'r Fan
Llanfihangel Nant Bran
Pont-faen
Pwllgloyw
Garthbrengy
Sarnau
Llandefaelog Fach
Battle
Llanddew
Llaneglwys
Crickadarn
Erwood
Gwenddwr
Aberedw
Alltmawr
Llanddewi'r Cwm
Maesmynis
Llandeilo Graban
Llandefalle
Talachddu
Felinfach
Pentre bach
Llywel
Trecastle
Pentre'r-felin
Trallong
Aberbran
Aberyscir
Sennybridge
(Pontsenni)
Defynnog
Penpont
Brecon
Aberhonddu
Llanfaes
Llanspyddid
Llechfaen
Groesffordd
Llanywern
Talyllyn
Tai'r-Bull
Libanus
Llanfrynach
Pencelli
Scethrog
Cross Oak
Talybont-on-Usk
Aber-Village
Crai
Felin-Crai
Heol Senni
Brecon Beacons
Forest Fawr
POWYS
A40
A470
A483
B4520
B4519
A4215
A4067
113
96
76
77

Newchurch
Michaelchurch on Arrow
Lower Welson
Eardisley
Rhulen
Bryngwyn
Dol-y-cannau
Crowther's Pool
Brilley
Little Merthyr
Millhalf
Whitney-on-Wye
Winforton
Willersley
Letton
Llanbadarn-y-Garreg
Rhos-goch
Rhydspence
Llanbedr
Painscastle
Clifford
Clifford Castle
Priory Wood
Merbach
Llandeilo Graban
Bronydd
Hardwicke
Bredwardine
Clyro
Hay-on-Wye
(Y Gelli Gandryll)
Hay on Wye Castle
The Bage
Erwood
Crickadarn
Llanstephan
Llowes
Cusop
Dorstone
Rhydness
Cwmbach
Llanigon
Snodhill
Boughrood
Glasbury
Heol-y-gaer
Llyswen
Pipton
Three Cocks
Tregoyd
Llanrosser
Hinton
H E R E F
Velindre
Felindre
Craswall
Urishay Common
Llandefalle
Bronllys
Bronllys Castle
Llanelieu
Upper Maes-coed
Michaelchurch Escley
Talgarth
Llanfilo
Felinfach
Tredustan
Trefecca
Tredomen
Capel-y-ffin
Newton
P O W Y S
Llanveynoe
Llandefaelog tre'r-graig
Pengenffordd
Brecon Beacons National Park
Llanywern
Llanfihangel Tal-y-llyn
Llangors
Llanthony
Longtown
Clodock
Talyllyn
Llanhamlach
Bannau Brycheiniog
The Black Mountains
Y Mynyddoedd Duon
Llangasty Talyllyn
Scethrog
Cathedine
Pencelli
Walterstone
Oldcastle
Cwmrhos
Cross Oak
Llansantffraed
Cwmdu
Cwmyoy
Talybont-on-Usk
Bwlch
Tre-wyn
Aber-Village
Gaer
Tretower
Tretower Castle & Court
Partrishow
Stanton
Pandy
Coed-yr-ynys
Llanbedr
Forest Coal Pit
Llanfihangel-Crucorney
Cwmcrawnon
Crickhowell
(Crug Hywel)
Bettws
Crossways
Ffawyddog
Llangattock
Llangenny
A438
A470
A479
A4078
A4079
A40
B4350
B4594
B4348
B4352
B4351
A4111
A4112
A465
B4560
B4558
95
114
77
78
0 1 2 3 miles
0 1 2 3 4 5 km

Weobley
Sarnesfield
Weobley Marsh
Bush Bank
King's Pyon
Westhope
Dinmore
Bodenham
Saffron's Cross
Bodenham Moor
Maund Bryan
Cowarne
Newchurch
Ledgemoor
Wistaston
Canon Pyon
Highway
Litmarsh
The Vauld
Ullingswick
Stoke Hill
Bleak Acre
Calver Hill
Norton Canon
Wormsley
Urdimarsh
Walker's Green
Moreton Jeffries
Felton
Burley Gate
Moorhampton
Yazor
Yarsop
Wellington
Marden
Preston Wynne
Ocle Pychard
Cowarn
Staunton on Wye
Mansel Lacy
Tillington Common
Tillington
Burghill
Moreton on Lugg
Sutton St Nicholas
Newtown
Mansell Gamage
Brinsop
Pipe and Lyde
Westhide
Monnington on Wye
Bishopstone
Credenhill
Shelwick
Withington
Moccas
Byford
Kenchester
Stretton Sugwas
Holmer
Yarkhill
Preston on Wye
Bridge Sollers
Swainshill
King's Acre
Shucknall
Holywell
Ploughfield
Lulham
Canon Bridge
Hagley
Lugwardine
Blakemere
Weston Beggard
Bartestree
Tarrington
Tyberton
Upper Breinton
Breinton Common
Tupsley
Dormington
Ruckhall
Breinton
Priors Frome
Madley
Eaton Bishop
Hampton Park
Hereford
Cublington
Shenmore
Lower Bullingham
Hampton Bishop
Checkley
Clehonger
Grafton
Mordiford
Vowchurch
Turnastone
Brampton
Allensmore
Portway
Dinedor
Woolhope
Kingstone
Thruxton
Winnal
Twyford Common
Holme Lacy
Fownhope
St Margaret's
Cockyard
Kerry's Gate
Callow
Dewshall Court
Kivernoll
Sollers Hope
Bacton
Didley
King's Thorn
Little Birch
Little Dewchurch
Bolstone
Falcon
Abbey Dore
St Devereux
Much Dewchurch
Much Birch
Ballingham
Carey
Brockhampton
Wormbridge
Kilpeck
Wormelow Tump
How Caple
Fawley Chapel
Ewyas Harold
Howton
Hoarwithy
King's Caple
Penalt
Orcop Hill
Llandinabo
Foy
Hole-in-the-Wall
Pontrilas
Red Rail
Sellack
Rowlestone
Bagwy Llydiart
Llanwarne
Harewood End
Monmouth Cap
Llangua
Kentchurch
Garway Hill
Orcop
Pencoyd
Michaelchurch
Upper Grove Common
Brampton Abbotts
Grosmont
White Rocks
St Weonards
Tretire
St Owens Cross
Peterstow
Bridstow
Ross-on-Wye
Garway
Three Ashes
Glewstone
Tudorville
Broad Oak
Llangarron
Pencraig
Coughton
Skenfrith
Llancloudy
Walford
Cross Ash
Norton
Crosswaty
Marstow
Goodrich
Kerne Bridge
Bont
Upper Green
Llanrothal
Llangrove
Wayne Green
Welsh Newton
Welsh Bicknor
115
78
79
98
HEREFORDSHIRE
WYE VALLEY

HEREFORDSHIRE
GLOUCES
MALVERN HILLS
Great Malvern
Malvern Link
West Malvern
Little Malvern
Malvern Wells
Ledbury
Newent
Ross-on-Wye
Mitcheldean
Longhope
Stoke Lacy
Bishops Frome
Much Cowarne
Stretton Grandison
Tarrington
Trumpet
Much Marcle
Dymock
Kempley
Upleadon
Hartpury
Maisemore
Highnam
Huntley
Staunton
Eldersfield
Bromsberrow Heath
Redmarley D'Abitot
Eastnor
Colwall
Coddington
Bosbury
Cradley
Storridge
Woolhope
Fownhope
Brampton Abbotts
Weston under Penyard
Aston Ingham
Clifford's Mesne
Glasshouse Hill
Tibberton
Rudford
Ashleworth
Tirley
Corse
Sandhurst
Twigworth
Longford
Welland
Castlemorton
Birtsmorton
Longdon
Hanley Swan
Hanley Castle
Upton Bishop
Linton
Gorsley
Kilcot
Pendock
Hollybush
Wellington Heath
Fromes Hill
Munsley
Putley
Aylton
Pixley
Little Marcle
Preston
Donnington
Ryton
Kent's Green
Taynton
Bulley
Birdwood
Churcham
Lea
Coughton
Tudorville
Rudhall
Crow Hill
Phocle Green
Hope Mansell
M50
A449
A417
A438
A4103
A40
116
97
79
80
3 miles
5 km
GLOUCESTER

WORCESTERSHIRE
COTSWOLDS
Evesham
Tewkesbury
Cheltenham
Pershore
Upton upon Severn
Broadway
Winchcombe
Bishop's Cleeve
Charlton Kings
Ashchurch
Bredon
Beckford
Kemerton
Overbury
Conderton
Eckington
Defford
Birlingham
Great Comberton
Little Comberton
Elmley Castle
Bricklehampton
Netherton
Fladbury
Cropthorne
Charlton
Hampton
Bengeworth
Fairfield
Badsey
Aldington
Bretforton
Offenham
Harvington
Norton
Lenchwick
Chadbury
Wickhamford
Murcot
Childswickham
Willersey
Hinton on the Green
Sedgeberrow
Aston Somerville
Dumbleton
Wormington
Ashton under Hill
Kersoe
Great Washbourne
Little Washbourne
Alderton
Teddington
Toddington
Stanway
Stanton
Laverton
Buckland
Snowshill
Didbrook
Hailes
Greet
Gretton
Gotherington
Woodmancote
Cleeve Hill
Prestbury
Southam
Charlton Abbots
Sevenhampton
Brockhampton
Whittington
Dowdeswell
Andoversford
Shipton
Temple Guiting
Guiting Power
Kineton
Ford
Cutsdean
Farmcote
Hawling
Notgrove
Salperton
Aylworth
Barton
Twyning
Ripple
Kinnersley
Kempsey
Hatfield
Stoulton
Pinvin
Throckmorton
Bishampton
Peopleton
Tewkesbury Abbey
Deerhurst
Apperley
Leigh
Coombe Hill
Boddington
Uckington
Elmstone Hardwicke
Swindon
Staverton
Churchdown
Parton
Innsworth
Shurdington
Leckhampton
Badgeworth
Up Hatherley
Golden Valley
M5
M50
A46
A44
A38
A40
A435
A436
Strensham Services North
Strensham Services South
117
100
80
81

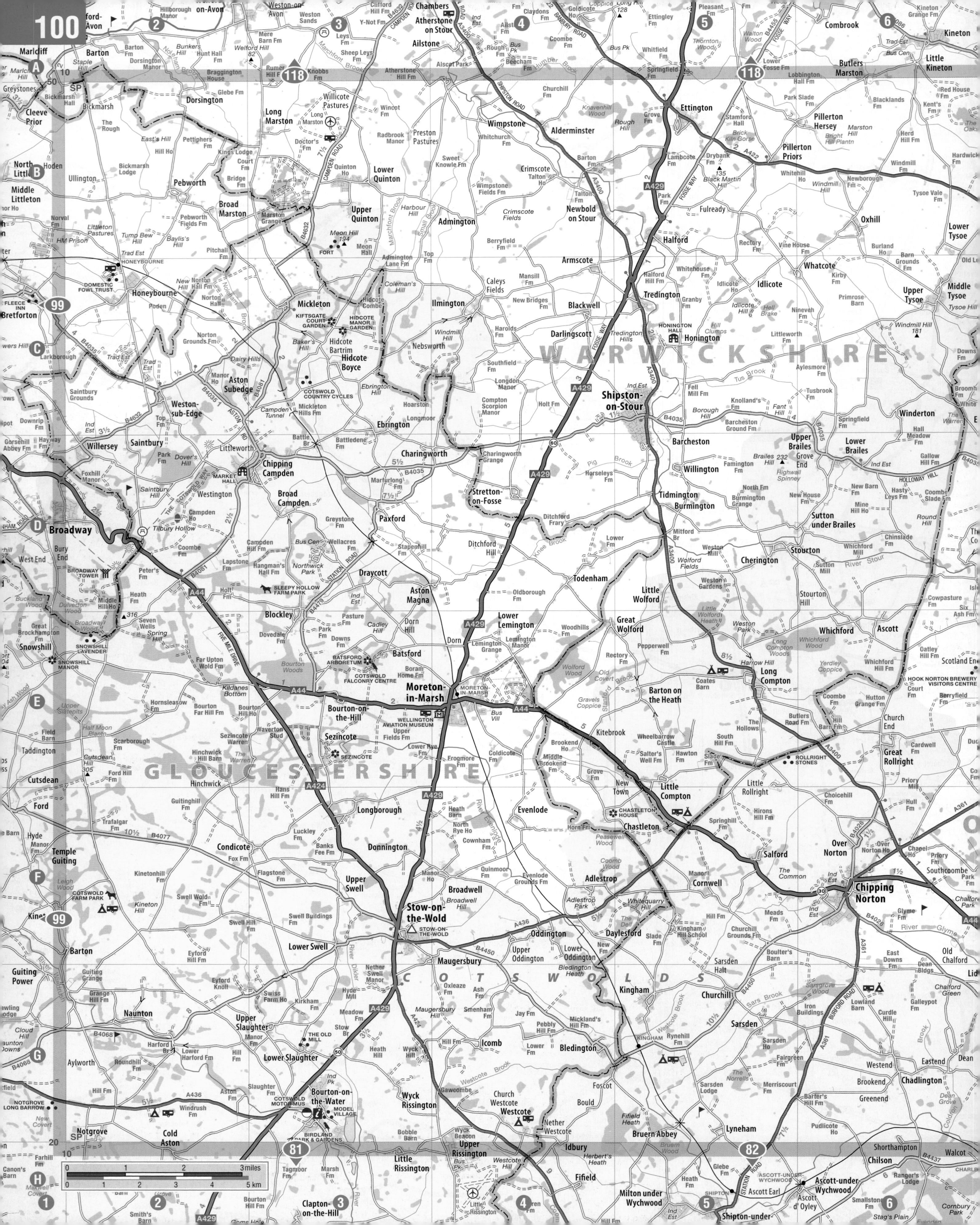
WARWICKSHIRE
GLOUCESTERSHIRE
COTSWOLDS
Marlcliff
Barton
Dorsington
Long Marston
Wimpstone
Alderminster
Ettington
Combrook
Kineton
Butlers Marston
Little Kineton
Cleeve Prior
Pillerton Hersey
Pillerton Priors
North Littleton
Middle Littleton
Pebworth
Broad Marston
Lower Quinton
Upper Quinton
Admington
Newbold on Stour
Halford
Fulready
Oxhill
Lower Tysoe
Whatcote
Honeybourne
Mickleton
Ilmington
Armscote
Blackwell
Tredington
Idlicote
Upper Tysoe
Middle Tysoe
Bretforton
Hidcote Bartrim
Hidcote Boyce
Nebsworth
Darlingscott
Honington
Aston Subedge
Weston-sub-Edge
Ebrington
Shipston-on-Stour
Willersey
Saintbury
Chipping Campden
Charingworth
Barcheston
Willington
Upper Brailes
Lower Brailes
Winderton
Broad Campden
Westington
Stretton-on-Fosse
Tidmington
Burmington
Sutton under Brailes
Broadway
Paxford
Ditchford Hill
Cherington
Stourton
Draycott
Aston Magna
Todenham
Little Wolford
Blockley
Lower Lemington
Great Wolford
Whichford
Ascott
Snowshill
Batsford
Long Compton
Moreton-in-Marsh
Barton on the Heath
Bourton-on-the-Hill
Sezincote
Kitebrook
Church End
Great Rollright
Cutsdean
Little Rollright
Longborough
Evenlode
Little Compton
Chastleton
Ford
Temple Guiting
Condicote
Donnington
Salford
Over Norton
Upper Swell
Broadwell
Adlestrop
Cornwell
Chipping Norton
Stow-on-the-Wold
Oddington
Daylesford
Lower Swell
Upper Oddington
Lower Oddington
Maugersbury
Old Chalford
Guiting Power
Kingham
Churchill
Naunton
Upper Slaughter
Icomb
Bledington
Sarsden
Lower Slaughter
Aylworth
Westend
Eastend
Chadlington
Wyck Rissington
Bourton-on-the-Water
Church Westcote
Westcote
Foscot
Bould
Notgrove
Cold Aston
Nether Westcote
Bruern Abbey
Lyneham
Upper Rissington
Idbury
Little Rissington
Fifield
Shorthampton
Chilson
Ascott-under-Wychwood
Clapton-on-the-Hill
Milton under Wychwood
Ascott Earl
Shipton-under-
A44
A429
A424
A3400
A422
A436
B4035
B4450
A361
118
99
81
82

Temple Herdewyke
Burton Dassett
Compton
Boddington
West Farm
Canons Ashby House
Canons Ashby
Eydon
Avon Dassett
Farnborough
Farnborough Hall
Granary Museum of Bygones
Claydon
Aston le Walls
Edgehill 1642
Radway
Arlescote
Warmington
Mollington
Chipping Warden
Edgcote
Culworth
Moreton Pinkney
Plumpton
Weedon Lois
Weston
Ratley
Edgehill
Upton House
Shotteswell
Cropredy
Wardington
Upper Wardington
Williamscott
Great Bourton
Little Bourton
Sulgrave
Sulgrave Manor
Thorpe Mandeville
Hornton
Horley
Hanwell
Chacombe
Helmdon
Shenington
Alkerton
Brook Cottage
Wroxton
Drayton
Balscote
Banbury
Neithrop
Ruscote
Hardwick
Grimsbury
Nethercote
Middleton Cheney
Overthorpe
Warkworth
Marston St Lawrence
Thenford
Greatworth
Falcutt
Halse
Radstone
Shutford
North Newington
Easington
Calthorpe
NORTHANTS
Great Purston
Farthinghoe
Whitfield
Sibford Gower
Swalcliffe Barn
Tadmarton
Broughton
Broughton Castle
Bodicote
Upper Astrop
King's Sutton
Astrop
Newbottle
Charlton
Brackley
Hinton-in-the-Hedges
Turweston
Sibford Ferris
Swalcliffe
Lower Tadmarton
Bloxham
Twyford
East End
Adderbury
West Adderbury
East Adderbury
Milton
Milcombe
Wigginton Heath
Evenley
Mixbury
Walton Grounds
Aynho
Croughton
Hook Norton
Wigginton
South Newington
Barford St John
Barford St Michael
Deddington
Deddington Castle
Clifton
Souldern
Swerford
Hempton
Nether Worton
Cottisford
Great Tew
Over Worton
The Green
North Aston
Somerton
Fritwell
Baynard's Green
Hardwick
Hethe
Fringford
OXFORDSHIRE
Little Tew
Heythrop
Ledwell
Duns Tew
Fewcott
Ardley
Cherwell Valley Services
Stoke Lyne
Sandford St Martin
Middle Aston
Upper Heyford
Westcott Barton
Middle Barton
Steeple Aston
Whistlow
Bucknell
Caversfield
Stratton Audley
Church Enstone
Gagingwell
Hopcroft's Holt
Steeple Barton
Barton Abbey
Rousham
Rousham Park House & Garden
Lower Heyford
Caulcott
Enstone
Neat Enstone
Cleveley
Radford
Fulwell
Radfordbridge
Kiddington
Over Kiddington
Middleton Stoney
Woodfield
Highfield
Bicester
Bicester Village
Kingsmere under dev
Taston
Spelsbury
Glympton
Ditchley Park
Tackley
Northbrook
Chesterton
Little Chesterton
Charlbury
Wootton
Woodleys
Kirtlington
Weston-on-the-Green
Wendlebury
Ambrosden
Old Woodstock
Enslow
Gibraltar
Merton
Lower Arncott
M40
A423
A361
A422
A43
A41
A44
A4260
B4100
B4030
B4031
B4525
119
102
82
83

NORTHAMPTONSHIRE
BUCKINGHAMSHIRE
Towcester
Buckingham
Winslow
Bicester
Stony Stratford
Wolverton
Brackley
Tiffield
Caldecote
Duncote
Blakesley
Greens Norton
Woodend
Bradden
Weedon Lois
Weston
Slapton
Abthorpe
Wappenham
Silverstone
Whittlebury
Syresham
Crowfield
Biddlesden
Whitfield
Turweston
Shalstone
Westbury
Evenley
Mixbury
Finmere
Tingewick
Water Stratford
Radclive
Dadford
Akeley
Lillingstone Lovell
Lillingstone Dayrell
Maids Moreton
Chackmore
Foscote
Leckhampstead
Thornton
Deanshanger
Wicken
Passenham
Calverton
Upper Weald
Beachampton
Nash
Whaddon
Thornborough
Singleborough
Great Horwood
Little Horwood
Padbury
Adstock
Addington
Gawcott
Lenborough
Barton Hartshorn
Chetwode
Newton Purcell
Preston Bissett
Hillesden
Steeple Claydon
Middle Claydon
East Claydon
Botolph Claydon
Granborough
Twyford
Poundon
Charndon
Calvert
Edgcott
Marsh Gibbon
Launton
Stratton Audley
Fringford
Hethe
North Marston
Oving
Whitchurch
Creslow
Cublington
Dunton
Hoggeston
Swanbourne
Mursley
Drayton Parslow
Pitchcott
Quainton
Grendon Underwood
Kingswood
Blackthorn
Ambrosden
Shutlanger
Stoke Bruerne
Ashton
Roade
Alderton
Grafton Regis
Paulerspury
Pury End
Potterspury
Yardley Gobion
Cosgrove
Hanslope
Castlethorpe
Haversham
Long Street
Tathall End
Gayhurst
Stoke Goldington
Ravenstone
Eakley Lanes
Old Wolverton
New Bradwell
Bradwell
Loughton
Shenley Church End
Shenley Brook End
Tattenhoe
SILVERSTONE
STOWE SCHOOL & GDNS
NEW INN STOWE VISITOR CENTRE
BUCKINGHAM THICK COPSE
CANAL MUSEUM
STOKE PARK PAVILIONS
CLAYDON HOUSE
WINSLOW HALL
CHANTRY CHAPEL
BUCKINGHAMSHIRE RAILWAY CENTRE (QUAINTON ROAD)
QUAINTON WINDMILL
NATIONAL HOCKEY STADIUM
A5 A43 A413 A421 A422 A508 A4421 A41 M1 B4525 B4033 B4032 B4011
WATLING STREET
GRAND UNION CANAL
120
101
83
84
0 1 2 3 miles
0 1 2 3 4 5 km

Olney
Weston Underwood
Clifton Reynes
Brayfield
Newton Blossomville
Bromham
Biddenham
Bedford
Great Denham
Queen's Park
Goldington
Putnoe
Brickhill
Emberton
Petsoe End
Stagsden
Box End
Kempston
Cardington
Fenlake
Cople
Harrowden
Elstow
Shortstown
Tyringham
Filgrave
Hardmead
Astwood
Sherington
Chicheley
Lathbury
Little Crawley
North Crawley
Newport Pagnell
Wootton
Keeley Green
Kempston Hardwick
Cotton End
Herring's Green
Littleworth
Wilstead
Bourne End
Upper Shelton
Wootton Broadmead
Stewartby
Cranfield
Broad Green
Lower Shelton
Caulcott
Marston Moretaine
Houghton Conquest
Haynes
Moulsoe
Great Linford
Giffard Park
Pineham
Tongwell
Willen
Downhead Park
Salford
Hulcote
Brogborough
Lidlington
Millbrook
Ampthill
Maulden
Clophill
Milton Keynes
Woolstone
Milton Keynes Village
Broughton
Kingston
Woughton on the Green
Eaglestone
Oldbrook
Wavendon
Walton
Walnut Tree
Browns Wood
Woburn Sands
Aspley Guise
Aspley Heath
Husborne Crawley
Ridgmont
Steppingley
Flitton
Wardhedges
Silsoe
Denel End
Flitwick
Greenfield
Pulloxhill
Bletchley
Fenny Stratford
Far Bletchley
Bow Brickhill
Woburn
Birchmoor Green
Eversholt
Tingrith
Westoning
Harlington
Sharpenhoe
Barton-le-Clay
Hexton
Little Brickhill
Great Brickhill
Stoke Hammond
Potsgrove
Milton Bryan
Battlesden
Toddington
Streatley
Upper Sundon
Lower Sundon
Soulbury
Stewkley
Leighton Buzzard
Linslade
Heath and Reach
Hockliffe
Tebworth
Wingfield
Chalgrave
Chalton
Sundon Park
Limbury
Eggington
Stanbridge
Tilsworth
Houghton Regis
Leagrave
Biscot
Stopsley
Luton
Dunstable
Billington
Wing
Ledburn
Eaton Bray
Totternhoe
Caddington
Slip End
Edlesborough
Whipsnade
Kensworth
Wingrave
Cheddington
Horton
Ivinghoe Aston
Pepperstock
CHILTERNS
CENTRAL BEDFORDSHIRE
LUTON
M1
A5
A6
A421
A428
A509
A4146
A505
A600
A507

CENTRAL BEDFORDSHIRE
CHILTERNS
LUTON
Sandy
Girtford
Blunham
Willington
Moggerhanger
Cople
Cardington
Beeston
Potton
Everton
Cockayne Hatley
Hatley St George
Arrington
New Wimpole
Croydon
Wendy
Whaddon
Tadlow
Wrestlingworth
Eyeworth
Sutton
Biggleswade
Upper Caldecote
Lower Caldecote
Northill
Ickwell Green
Old Warden
Southill
Broom
Stanford
Langford
Haynes
Shefford
Clifton
Henlow
Arlesey
Stotfold
Campton
Clophill
Meppershall
Upper Stondon
Lower Stondon
Upper Gravenhurst
Lower Gravenhurst
Shillington
Higham Gobion
Barton-le-Clay
Hexton
Pegsdon
Pirton
Holwell
Ickleford
Hitchin
Letchworth
Baldock
Radwell
Norton
Willian
Walsworth
Great Wymondley
Little Wymondley
Graveley
Stevenage
Shephall
Broadwater
Aston
Benington
Walkern
Weston
Clothall
Wallington
Sandon
Rushden
Cottered
Ardeley
Ashwell
Hinxworth
Edworth
Dunton
Guilden Morden
Steeple Morden
Abington Pigotts
Bassingbourn
Litlington
Therfield
Kelshall
Bygrave
Newnham
Caldecote
Astwick
Langley
Whitwell
St Paul's Walden
Preston
Gosmore
St Ippollytts
Knebworth
Old Knebworth
Codicote
Kimpton
Datchworth
Watton at Stone
Woolmer Green
Stopsley
Lilley
Offley
Great Offley
Little Offley
Cockernhoe Green
Tea Green
Breachwood Green
Whempstead
Dane End
Sacombe
Baldock Services

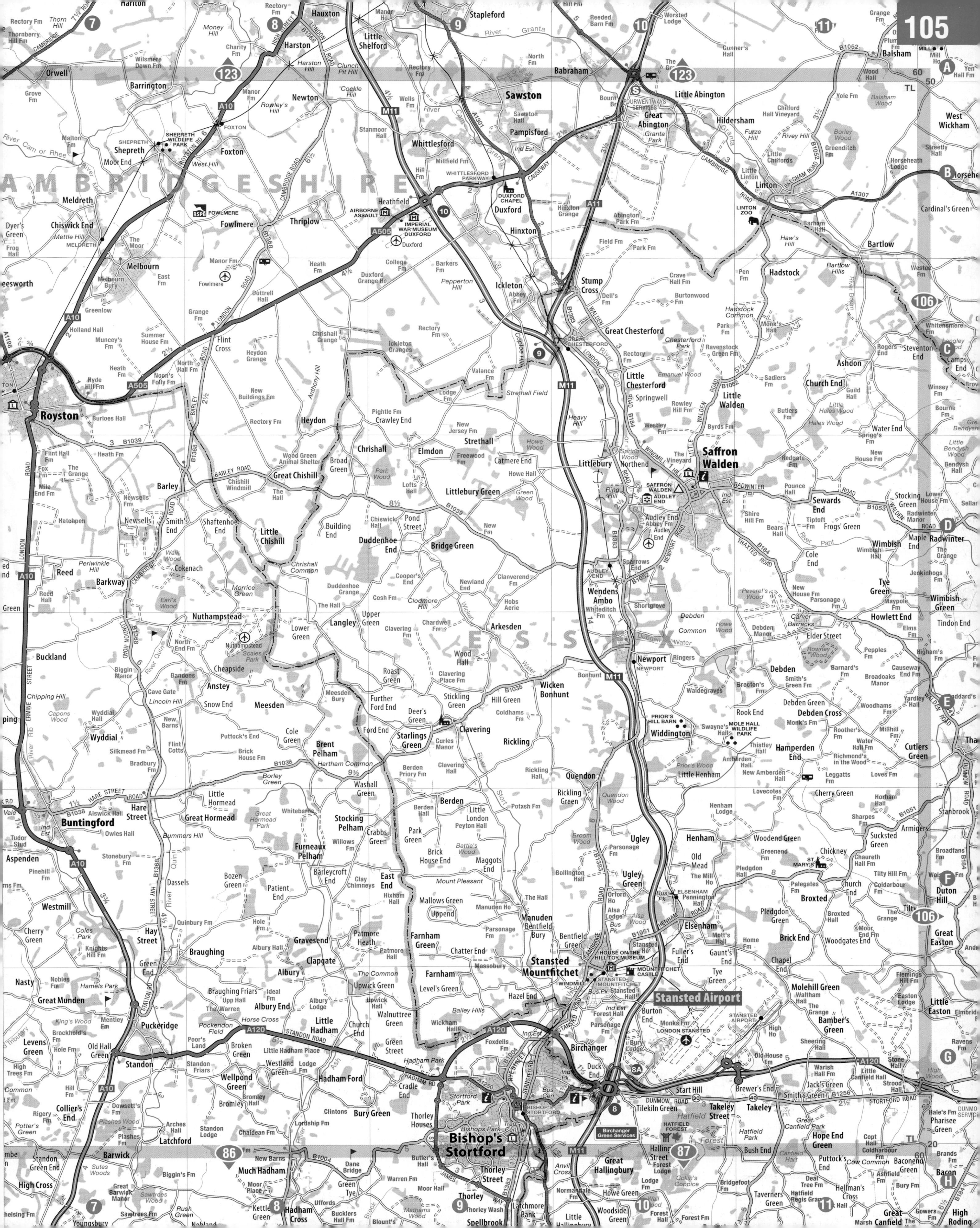
CAMBRIDGESHIRE
ESSEX
Harston
Hauxton
Little Shelford
Stapleford
Orwell
Barrington
Newton
Sawston
Babraham
Little Abington
Great Abington
Balsham
Hildersham
West Wickham
Shepreth
Foxton
Whittlesford
Pampisford
Linton
Meldreth
Fowlmere
Thriplow
Heathfield
Duxford
Hinxton
Melbourn
Ickleton
Stump Cross
Hadstock
Bartlow
Great Chesterford
Little Chesterford
Springwell
Ashdon
Royston
Heydon
Crawley End
Strethall
Elmdon
Chrishall
Great Chishill
Little Chishill
Littlebury
Littlebury Green
Saffron Walden
Little Walden
Barley
Reed
Barkway
Duddenhoe End
Bridge Green
Wendens Ambo
Audley End
Nuthampstead
Langley
Arkesden
Newport
Debden
Wimbish
Buckland
Anstey
Meesden
Wicken Bonhunt
Clavering
Rickling
Widdington
Wyddial
Brent Pelham
Starlings Green
Quendon
Hamperden End
Buntingford
Great Hormead
Stocking Pelham
Furneaux Pelham
Berden
Ugley
Henham
Aspenden
Westmill
Braughing
Gravesend
Clapgate
Albury
Farnham
Manuden
Stansted Mountfitchet
Stansted Airport
Elsenham
Broxted
Puckeridge
Great Munden
Standon
Little Hadham
Hadham Ford
Birchanger
Takeley
Bishop's Stortford
Much Hadham
Thorley
Great Hallingbury
Barwick
Latchford
High Cross
M11
A10
A11
A120
A505
A1307
B1038
B1039
B1368

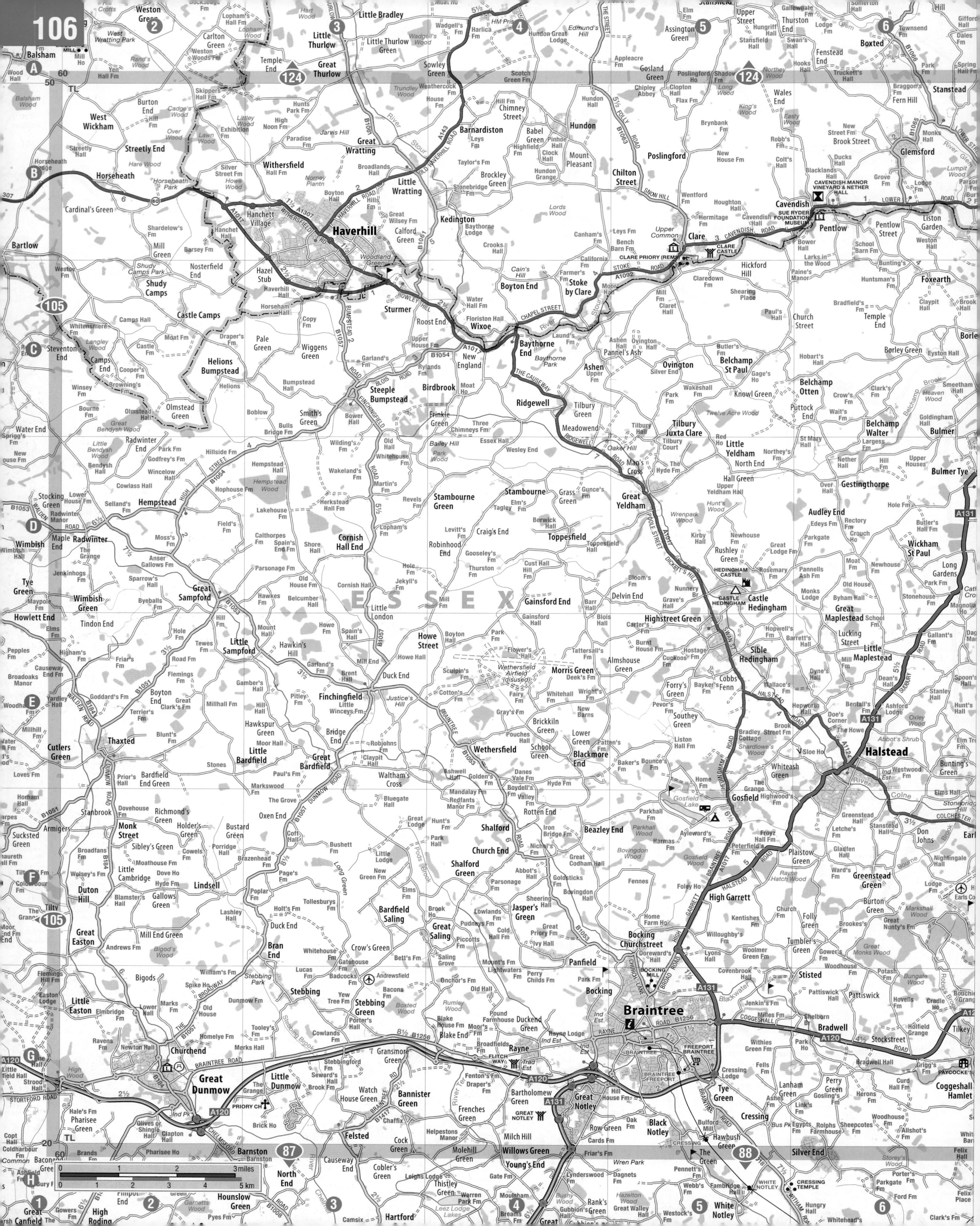
ESSEX
Haverhill
Braintree
Halstead
Great Dunmow
Balsham
Horseheath
West Wickham
Withersfield
Great Wratting
Little Wratting
Kedington
Barnardiston
Hundon
Poslingford
Chilton Street
Cavendish
Clare
Pentlow
Glemsford
Stoke by Clare
Boyton End
Sturmer
Wixoe
Baythorne End
Ashen
Ovington
Belchamp St Paul
Belchamp Otten
Belchamp Walter
Foxearth
Bulmer
Bulmer Tye
Castle Camps
Shudy Camps
Helions Bumpstead
Steeple Bumpstead
Birdbrook
Ridgewell
Tilbury Juxta Clare
Little Yeldham
Great Yeldham
Gestingthorpe
Hempstead
Radwinter
Wimbish
Great Sampford
Little Sampford
Stambourne
Stambourne Green
Toppesfield
Cornish Hall End
Gainsford End
Castle Hedingham
Sible Hedingham
Great Maplestead
Little Maplestead
Wickham St Paul
Highstreet Green
Finchingfield
Thaxted
Great Bardfield
Little Bardfield
Wethersfield
Gosfield
Shalford
High Garrett
Bocking Churchstreet
Bocking
Stisted
Panfield
Great Saling
Bardfield Saling
Stebbing
Lindsell
Great Easton
Little Easton
Monk Street
Duton Hill
Felsted
Rayne
Great Notley
Black Notley
Cressing
Bradwell
Coggeshall Hamlet
Silver End
White Notley
Little Dunmow
Bannister Green
Barnston
High Roding
Great Canfield
CAVENDISH MANOR VINEYARD & NETHER HALL
SUE RYDER FOUNDATION MUSEUM
CLARE PRIORY (REMS)
CLARE CASTLE
HEDINGHAM CASTLE
PRIORY CH
PAYCOCKE'S
CRESSING TEMPLE
FREEPORT BRAINTREE
Wethersfield Airfield (disused)
A120
A131
A1017
A1307
A1092
B1054
B1057
B1053
0 1 2 3 miles
0 1 2 3 4 5 km
124
105
87
88

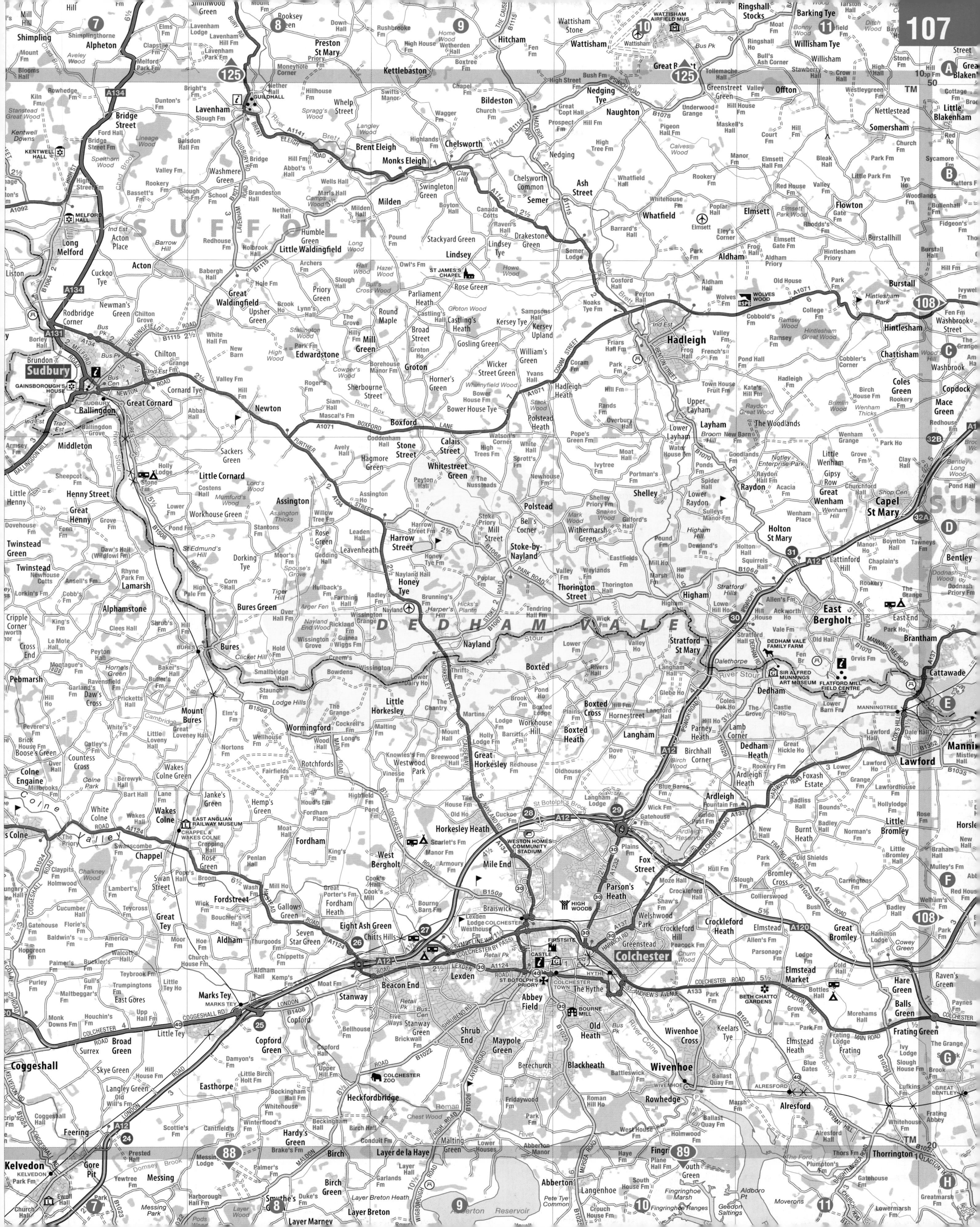
SUFFOLK
DEDHAM VALE
Sudbury
Lavenham
Long Melford
Hadleigh
Colchester
Wivenhoe
Coggeshall
Kelvedon
Lawford
Manningtree
Cattawade
East Bergholt
Dedham
Stratford St Mary
Nayland
Bures
Boxford
Kersey
Hitcham
Bildeston
Chelsworth
Monks Eleigh
Brent Eleigh
Lindsey
Polstead
Stoke-by-Nayland
Boxted
Langham
Great Horkesley
West Bergholt
Stanway
Lexden
Abbey Field
Old Heath
Rowhedge
Alresford
Elmstead Market
Great Bromley
Little Bromley
Ardleigh
Capel St Mary
Holton St Mary
Higham
Raydon
Layham
Shelley
Aldham
Elmsett
Whatfield
Nedging Tye
Naughton
Wattisham
Offton
Somersham
Hintlesham
Chattisham
Burstall
Washbrook
Bentley
Brantham
Acton
Chilton
Great Cornard
Ballingdon
Middleton
Henny Street
Twinstead
Lamarsh
Alphamstone
Pebmarsh
Colne Engaine
White Colne
Wakes Colne
Chappel
Fordham
Aldham
Marks Tey
Copford
Great Tey
Feering
Messing
Birch
Layer de la Haye
Abberton
Langenhoe
Thorrington
Frating Green
Great Bentley
Abberton Reservoir
COLCHESTER ZOO
A12
A120
A134
A131
A1071
A1141
A137
A133
B1508
125
108
88
89

Upper Street
Great Blakenham
Little Blakenham
Barham
Henley
Claydon
Akenham
Witnesham
Grundisburgh
Burgh
Hasketon
Melton
Bromeswell
Rendlesham Forest
Woodbridge Airfield (disused)
Nettlestead
Somersham
Westerfield
Tuddenham St Martin
Tuddenham
Culpho
Playford
Boot Street
Great Bealings
Little Bealings
Woodbridge
Kingston
Martlesham
Sutton Hoo
Sutton Common
Whitton
Bramford
Westbourne
Christchurch Mansion
Ipswich
California
Rushmere St Andrew
Rushmere Street
Kesgrave
Martlesham Heath
Waldringfield Heath
Waldringfield
Methersgate
Sutton
Shottisham
Burstall
Sproughton
Hintlesham
Washbrook
Chantry
Maidenhall
Stoke
Rose Hill
Racecourse
Greenwich
Priory Heath
Gainsborough
Warren Heath
Brightwell
Newbourne
Bucklesham
Hemley
Ramsholt
Alderton
Bawdsey
Copdock
Belstead
Wherstead
Nacton
Levington
Kirton
Falkenham
Trimley St Martin
Trimley St Mary
Felixstowe Ferry
Walton
Old Felixstowe
Felixstowe
Manning's Amusement Park
Landguard Fort
Felixstowe Museum
Landguard Pt
The Port of Felixstowe
Capel St Mary
SUFFOLK
Tattingstone
Tattingstone White Horse
Freston
Woolverstone
Pin Mill
Chelmondiston
River Orwell
Bentley
Holbrook
Lower Holbrook
Harkstead
Erwarton
Shotley
Shotley Gate
Trimley Marshes Nature Reserve
SUFFOLK COAST AND HEATHS
Brantham
Stutton
Cattawade
River Stour
Mistley
Manningtree
Lawford
Wrabness
Stour Estuary
Parkeston
Harwich
Dovercourt
Upper Dovercourt
Ramsey
Little Oakley
Bradfield
Bradfield Heath
Mistley Heath
Little Bromley
Horsleycross Street
Wix
Great Oakley
Esbjerg 17:15
Hoek van Holland 6:45
Crabknowe Spit
Pennyhole Bay
Pye Sand
Horsley Cross
Tendring Heath
Stones Green
Tendring Green
Little Bentley
Tendring
Beaumont
Hamford Water
Skipper's Island
Horsey Island
The Naze
Maritime Museum
Hare Green
Balls Green
Frating Green
Great Bentley
Weeley
Weeley Heath
Thorpe Green
Thorpe-le-Soken
Kirby-le-Soken
Kirby Cross
Walton-on-the-Naze
Frinton-on-Sea
Great Holland
Aingers Green
Thorrington
Little Clacton
St Osyth Heath
Holland Haven
0 1 2 3 miles
0 1 2 3 4 5 km

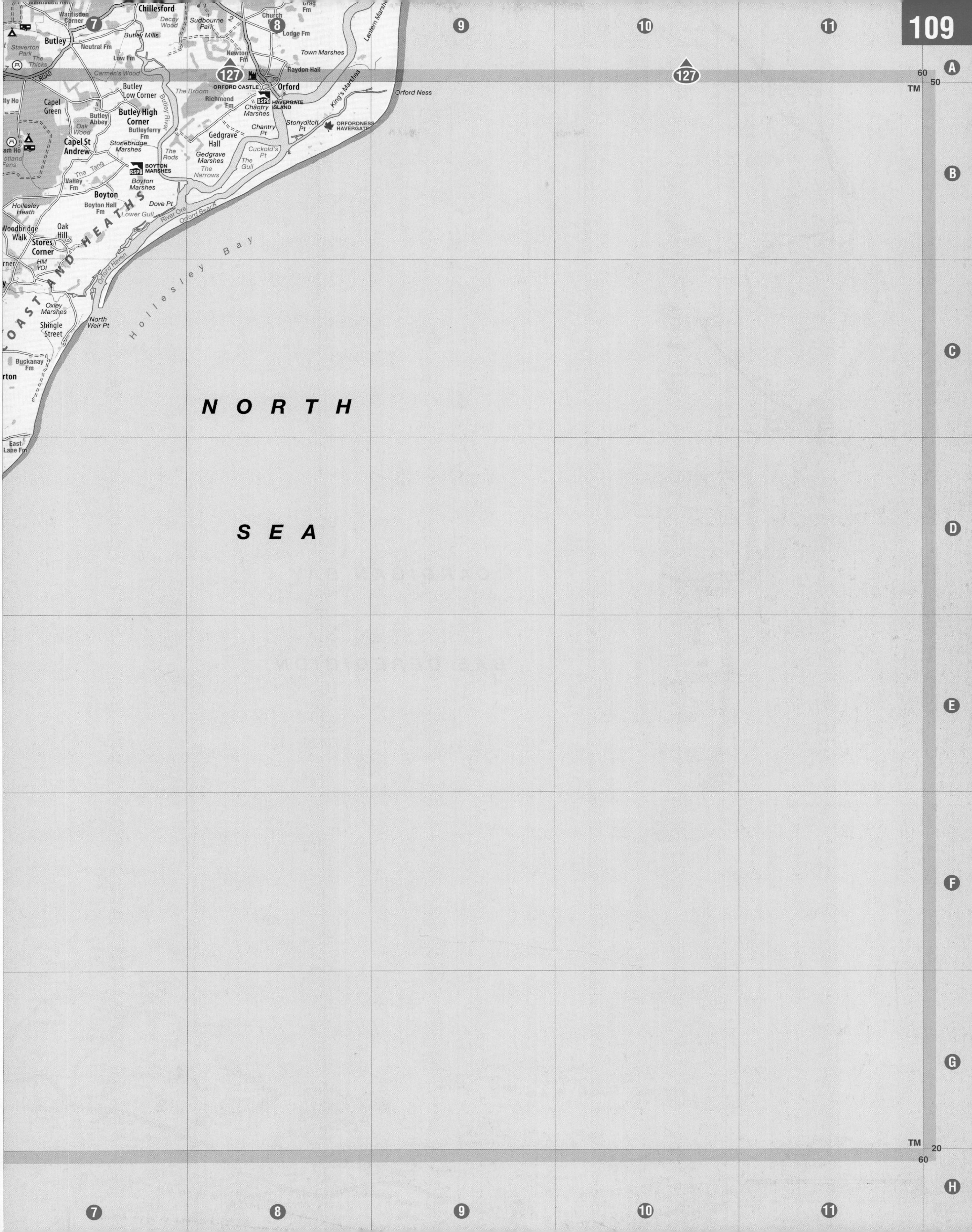

Chillesford
Wantisden Corner
Decoy Wood
Sudbourne Park
Church
Crag Fm
Lantern Marshes
Butley
Butley Mills
Lodge Fm
Staverton Park
The Thicks
Neutral Fm
Low Fm
Newton Fm
Town Marshes
Carmen's Wood
Raydon Hall
ROAD
127
ORFORD CASTLE
Orford
Butley Low Corner
The Broom
Orford Ness
Capel Green
Richmond Fm
HAVERGATE ISLAND
Chantry Marshes
King's Marshes
Butley High Corner
Butley Abbey
Butley River
Butleyferry Fm
Oak Wood
Capel St Andrew
Stonebridge Marshes
Gedgrave Hall
Chantry Pt
Stonyditch Pt
ORFORDNESS-HAVERGATE
Cuckold's Pt
Gedgrave Marshes
The Gull
The Rods
The Tang
BOYTON MARSHES
The Narrows
Valley Fm
Boyton Marshes
Boyton
Hollesley Heath
Boyton Hall Fm
Dove Pt
Lower Gull
River Ore
Orford Beach
Woodbridge Walk
Oak Hill
Stores Corner
HM YOI
COAST AND HEATHS
Orford Haven
Hollesley Bay
Oxley Marshes
North Weir Pt
Shingle Street
Buckanay Fm
East Lane Fm
NORTH SEA
TM
50
60
20
7
8
9
10
11
A
B
C
D
E
F
G
H

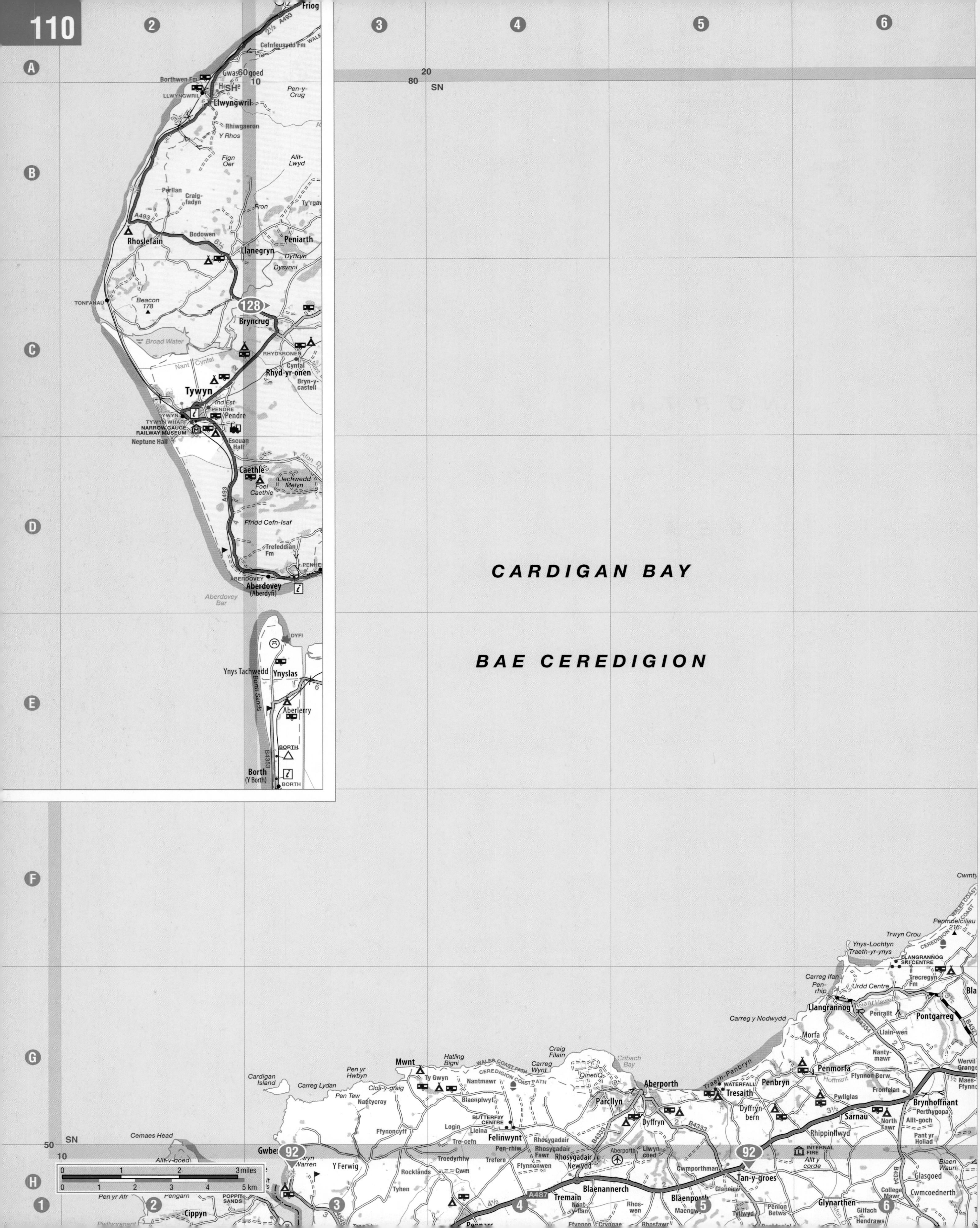

CARDIGAN BAY
BAE CEREDIGION
Friog
Cefnfeusydd Fm
Borthwen Fm
Gwastadgoed
Llwyngwril
Pen-y-Crug
Rhiwgaeron
Y Rhos
Fign Oer
Allt-Lwyd
Perllan
Craig-fadyn
Fron
Ty'rgaw
A493
Rhoslefain
Bodowen
Llanegryn
Peniarth
Dyffryn
Dysynni
TONFANAU
Beacon 178
128
Bryncrug
Broad Water
RHYDYRONEN
Nant Cynfal
Cynfal
Rhyd-yr-onen
Bryn-y-castell
Tywyn
Ind Est
PENDRE
Pendre
TYWYN
TYWYN WHARF
NARROW GAUGE RAILWAY MUSEUM
Neptune Hall
Escuan Hall
Caethle
Foel Caethle
Llechwedd Melyn
Ffridd Cefn-Isaf
Trefeddian Fm
ABERDOVEY
Aberdovey (Aberdyfi)
Aberdovey Bar
DYFI
Ynys Tachwedd
Ynyslas
Borth Sands
Aberleri
BORTH
B4353
Borth (Y Borth)
20
80
SN
50
SN
10
Cwmtydu
Penmoelciliau 216
Trwyn Crou
Ynys-Lochtyn
Traeth-yr-ynys
LLANGRANNOG SKI CENTRE
Trecregyn Fm
Carreg Ifan
Pen-rhip
Urdd Centre
Llangrannog
Pontgarreg
Carreg y Nodwydd
Penrallt
Llain-wen
Morfa
Nanty-mawr
Penmorfa
Hoffnant
Ffynnon Berw
Fronfelen
Wervil Grange
Maes-Ffynnon
Brynhoffnant
Perthygopa
Allt-goch
Pwliglas
Sarnau
North Fawr
Rhippinllwyd
Pant yr Holiad
INTERNAL FIRE
Allt y corde
Blaen Waun
Glasgoed
Cwmcoednerth
College Mawr
Gilfach
Hendraws
Glynarthen
Craig Filain
Cribach Bay
Traeth-Penbryn
WATERFALL
Tresaith
Penbryn
Dyffryn-bern
Aberporth
Parcllyn
Dyffryn
B4333
Mwnt
Hatling Bigni
WALES COAST PATH
CEREDIGION COAST PATH
Carreg Wynt
Ty Gwyn
Nantmawr
Blaenplwyf
Pen yr Hwbyn
Cardigan Island
Carreg Lydan
Pen Tew
Clos-y-graig
Nantycroy
Ffynoncyff
BUTTERFLY CENTRE
Login
Lleina
Felinwynt
Tre-cefn
Pen-rhiw
Rhosygadair
Rhosygadair Fawr
Rhosygadair Newydd
Trefere
Aberporth
Llwyn-coed
Troedyrhiw
Ffynnonwen
Cwm
Rocklands
Tyhen
Cwmporthman
Tan-y-groes
Glanrhyd
A487
Tremain
Blaenannerch
Nant-y-llan
Rhos-wen
Blaenporth
Maengwyn
Tyllwyd
Penlon Betws
Cemaes Head
Allt-y-goed
Gwbert
92
Y Ferwig
Warren
Pengarn
Pen yr Afr
POPPIT SANDS
Cippyn
0 1 2 3 miles
0 1 2 3 4 5 km

7
8
9
10
11
128
112
93
A
B
C
D
E
F
G
H
Aberystwyth
Trefechan
Penparcau
Southgate
Rhydyfelin
Llanfarian
Chancery (Rhydgaled)
Blaenplwyf
WALES COAST PATH
CEREDIGION COASTAL PATH
Llanddeiniol
Llangwyryfon
Llanrhystud
Ty-Newydd
Rhyd-Rosser
Rhydfudr
Trefenter
Llansantffraed
Llanon (Llan-non)
FANTASY FARM PARK
Trawsnant
Nebo
Rhos Haminiog
Cross Inn
Aberarth
Aberaeron
Bethania
Penuwch
Pennant
Monachty
Crynfryn
Cilcennin
Bwlch-Llan
New Quay (Ceinewydd)
New Quay Head
Birds Rock
Traethy Coubal
Cei-bach
Gilfachrheda
Llanarth
Llwyncelyn
Oakford
Henfynyw
Ffos-y-ffin
LLANERCHAERON
Ciliau Aeron
Newbridge
Capel Betws Lleucu
Trefilan
Tal-sarn
Gartheli
Llwyn-y-groes
Llundain-fach
Abermeurig
Ystrad Aeron
Felinfach
Felindre
Temple Bar
Dihewyd
Mydroilyn
CEREDIGION
(SIR CEREDIGION)
Maen-y-groes
Cross Inn
Nanternis
Caerwedros
Llwyndafydd
Synod Inn
Ffynnon-oer
Llangybi
Betws Bledrws
Silian
Cribyn
Talgarreg
Gorsgoch
Plwmp
Pentregat
Capel Cynon
Bwlch-y-fadfa
Castell-Howell
Cwrt-newydd
Lampeter (Llanbedr Pont Steffan)
Olwen
A487
A482
A485
A486
B4337
B4342
B4577
B4576
B4338
B4459

CEREDIGION
SIR CEREDIGION
Cambrian Mountains
Aberystwyth
Llanbadarn Fawr
Capel Dewi
Old Goginan
Goginan
Dollwen
Cwmbrwyno
Ponterwyd
Dyffryn Castell
Capel Bangor
Glanrafon
Penparcau
Southgate
Moriah
Rhydyfelin
Capel Seion
Pant-y-crûg
Aberffrwd
Nantyronen Station
Vale of Rheidol Light Railway
Rheidol Hydro Electric Station
Magic of Life Butterfly House
Llywernog Silver-Lead Mine
Ysbyty Cynfyn
Ystumtuen
Devil's Bridge (Pontarfynach)
Llanfarian
New Cross
Pisgah
Mynydd Bach
Trisant
Llanfihangel-y-Creuddyn
Cnwch-coch
Pentre-llyn
Llanilar
Abermagwr
New Row
Pont-rhyd-y-groes
Hafod Estate
Cwm Ystwyth
Cwmystwyth
Blaenycwm
Rhos-y-garth
Crosswood (Trawsgoed)
Llanafan
Wenallt
Ysbyty Ystwyth
Llangwyryfon
Lledrod
Tynygraig
Tanyrhydiau
Ffair-Rhos
Ystradmeurig
Pontrhydfendigaid
Strata Florida
Strata Florida Abbey
Trefenter
Bronnant
Rhydyfudr
Mynydd Bach
Bontnewydd
Swyddffynnon
Blaenpennal
Tyncelyn
Cors Caron
Ty'n-yr-eithin
Penuwch
Llangeitho
Tregaron
Rhiannon Welsh Gold Centre
Capel Betws Lleucu
Commins Capel Betws
Llanio
Olmarch
Cockshead
Llanddewi-Brefi
Pentre-rhew
Llangybi
Betws Bledrws
Llanfair Clydogau
Cwm Berwyn Plantation
Twyi Forest
Tywi Forest Allt Tywi
Soar-y-Mynydd
Llyn Brianne Reservoir
Claerwen
Claerwen Reservoir
Llyn Teifi
Llyn Egnant
Llyn Fyrddon Fawr
Abergwesyn
Devil's Staircase
Allt Rhyd y Groes
A44 A4120 A485 A487 B4340 B4343 B4574 B4575 B4576 B4577 B4578 B4342
128 111 94
3 miles
5 km

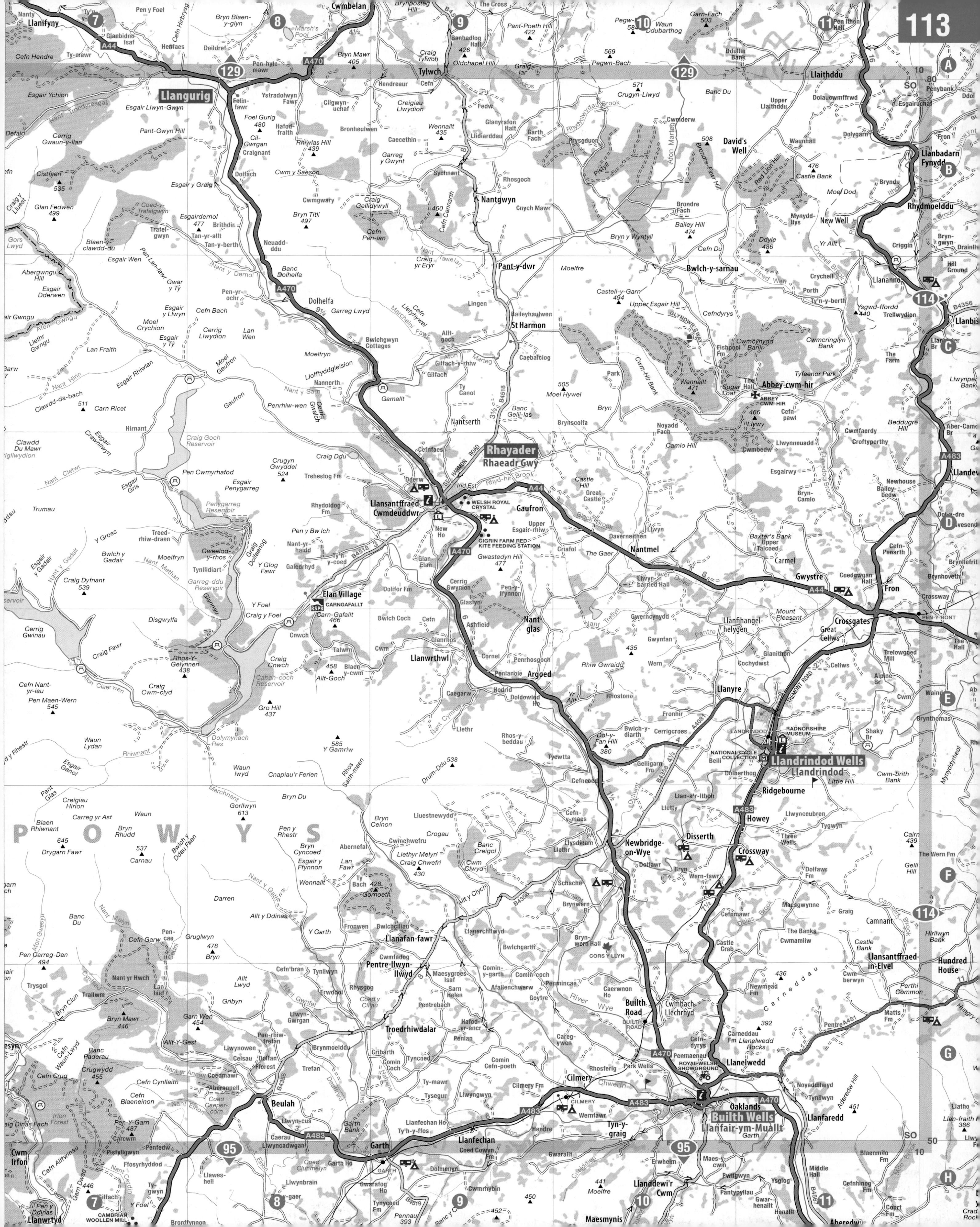

Llanifyny
Cwmbelan
Pen y Foel
Bryn Blaen-y-glyn
Marsh's Pool
Brynposteg Hill
The Cross
Pant-Poeth Hill 422
Pegwn 584
Waun Ddubarthog
Garn-Fach 503
Pen Ithon Hall
Glanbidno Isaf
Hirfaes
Deildref
Bryn Mawr 405
Banhadlog Hall
Oldchapel Hill
Craig Tylwch
Craig Iar
Pegwn-Bach 569
Dduallt Bank
Llaithddu
Cefn Hendre
Ty-mawr
Pen-hyle-mawr
A44
A470
129
Tylwch
Hendreaur
Cefn
Esgair Ychion
Llangurig
Ystradolwyn Fawr
Cilgwyn-uchaf
Creigiau Llwydion
Fedw
Crugyn-Llwyd 571
Banc Du
Upper Llaithddu
Dolaucwmffrwd
Penybank
Esgairuchaf
Felin-fawr
Esgair Llwyn-Gwyn
Foel Gurig 480
Hafod-fraith
Bronheulwen
Wennallt 435
Glanyrafon Halt
Llidiarddau
Garth Fach
Prysgduon
Cwmderw
Brondre-fawr Hill
David's Well
Waunhall
Dolygarn
Fron
Llanbadarn Fynydd
Pant-Gwyn Hill
Cerrig Gwaun-y-llan
Cil-Gwrgan
Craignant
Rhiwlas Hill 439
Caecethin
Garreg y Gwynt
Pistyll
508
Red Lion Hill
476
Castle Bank
Cistfaen 535
Dolfach
Esgair y Graig
Cwm y Saeson
Sychnant
Rhosgoch
Nantgwyn
Cnych Mawr
Moel Dod
Bryndu
Rhydmoelddu
Glan Fedwen 499
Coed-y-Trafelgwyn
Esgairdernol 477
Tan-yr-allt
Tan-y-berth
Brithdir
Cwmgwary
Craig Gellidywyll
Bryn Titli 497
Cefn Pen-lan
Cefn Cenarth
460
Brondre Fach
Bailey Hill 474
Mynydd-llys
New Well
Dyle 486
Criggin
Bryn-gwyn
Gors Lwyd
Blaen-y-clawdd-du
Trafel-gwyn
Neuadd-ddu
Yr Allt
Esgair Wen
Pen Lan-fawr Hill
Craig yr Eryr
Nant Tawelan
Pant-y-dwr
Moelfre
Bryn y Wyntyll
Cefn Du
Bwlch-y-sarnau
Crychell
Llanannoʼ
Hill Ground
Abergwngu Hill
Esgair Dderwen
Gwar y Tŷ
Pen-yr-ochr
Banc Dolhelfa
Dolhelfa
Garreg Lwyd
Cefn Lletyhywel
Lingen
Castell-y-Garn 494
Upper Esgair Hill
Porth
Ty'n-y-berth
Ysgwd-ffordd 440
Trellwydion
114
B4356
Esgair Gwngu
Cerrig Llwydion
Esgair y Llwyn
Cefn Bach
Moel Crychion
Esgair y Tŷ
Lan Wen
Baileyhaulwen
St Harmon
Glyndŵr's Way
Cefndyrys
Cwmcynydd Bank
Cwmcringlyn Bank
Lan Fraith
Bwlchgwyn Cottages
Allt-goch
Moelfryn
Gilfach-y-rhiw
Gilfach
Caebalciog
Fishpool Fm
Wennallt 471
The Farm
Esgair Rhiwlan
Moel Geufron
Lloftyddgleision
Nannerth
Nant y Sarn
Ty Canol
505
Moel Hywel
Park
Cwm-Hir Bank
Sugar Loaf
The Hall
Abbey-cwm-hir
Tyfaenor Park
Clawdd-da-bach 511
Carn Ricet
Penrhiw-wen
Cerrig Gwalch
Gamallt
B4518
Banc Gelli-las
Bryn
Abbey Cwm-Hir
Llywy 466
Cefn-pawl
Hirnant
Geufron
Craig Goch Reservoir
Nantserth
Brynscolfa
Noyadd Fach
Camlo Hill
Cwmfaerdy
Beddugre Hill
Croftyperthy
Clawdd Du Mawr
Esgair Crawnllwyn
Craig Ddu
Cefnfaes
Rhayader
Rhaeadr Gwy
Llwynneuadd
Cwmbedw
Esgairwy
Crugyn Gwyddel 524
Treheslog Fm
St Harmon Road
Rhyd-hir Brook
Castle Hill
Great Castle
Newhouse
Bailey-bedw
Llandev
Pen Cwmyrhafod
Esgair Gris
Esgair Penygarreg
Dderw
Ind Est
Gaufron
Welsh Royal Crystal
Bryn-Camlo
Trumau
Penygarreg Reservoir
Rhydoldog Fm
Llansantffraed Cwmdeuddwr
New Ho
Upper Esgair-rhiw
Gigrin Farm Red Kite Feeding Station
Daverneithen
Llwyn
Baxter's Bank
Upper Talcoed
Dolau-dre
Y Groes
Troed-rhiw-draen
Pen y Bw lch
Nant-yr-haidd
B4518
Gwastedyn Hill 477
Criafol
The Gaer
Nantmel
Carmel
Cefn-Penarth
Bwlch y Gadair
Gwaelod-y-rhos
Craig Dolfaenog
Ty'n-y-coed
Glan-Elan
Esgair y Gadair
Moelfryn
Tynlliidiart
Y Glog Fawr
Galedrhyd
Garreg-ddu Reservoir
Llwyn-barried Hall
River Dulas
Gwystre
Coedgwgan Hall
Brynllefrit
Craig Dyfnant 539
Glannau
Elan Village
Carngafallt
Dolifor Fm
Cerrig Gwynion
Pen-y-ffynnon
Fron
Brynhoveth
Y Foel
Carn-Gafallt 466
Bwlch Coch
Glaslyn
Nant-glas
Gwerncynydd
Llanfihangel-helygen
Mount Pleasant
Crossgates
Crossway
Pen-y-Bont
Disgwylfa
Craig y Foel
RSPB
Ashfield
Nant Treflyn
Pentre Brook
Great Cellws
The Hall
Cerrig Gwinau
Craig Fawr
Cnwch
Glanrhos
Cwm
435
Gwynfan
Glanithon
Trelowgoed Mill
Rhos-Y-Gelynnen 438
Craig Cnwch
Talwrn
Llanwrthwl
Cornel
Penrhosgoch
Rhiw Gwraidd
Wern
Cochydwst
Cellws
Alpine Br
Cefn Nant-yr-iau
Aton Claerwen
Craig Cwm-clyd
458
Allt-Goch
Blaen-y-cwm
Penlanole
Argoed
Llanyre
Caban-coch Reservoir
Hodrid
Doldowlod Ho
Yr Allt
Rhostono
Tremont Road
Cwm
Pen Maen-Wern 545
Gro Hill 437
Caegarw
Nant Cymrun
Fronhir
Waun Lydan
Dolymynach Res
Llethr
Rhos-y-beddau
Bwlch-y-diarth
Cerrigcroes
A4081
Llandrindod
Radnorshire Museum
Shaky Br
Brynthomas
Esgair Ganol
Rhiwnant
585
Y Gamriw
Dol-y-Fan Hill 380
Gelligarn Fm
National Cycle Collection
Beili
Llandrindod Wells
Waun Iwyd
Rhos Saith-maen
Drum-Ddu 538
Tycwtta
Cefncoed
B4358
Dolberthog
Cwm-brith Bank
Mynyddyrheol
Pant Glas
Creigiau Hirion
Marchnant
Capniau'r Ferlen
Bryn Du
Ridgebourne
Little Hill
Carreg yr Ast
Waun
Gorllwyn 613
Bryn Ceinon
Lluestnewydd
Estyn Brook
Llan-a'r-Ithon
Lletty
A483
Howey
Llwynceubren
Tygwyn
Blaen Rhiwnant
Bryn Rhudd
Pen y Rhestr
Abernefal
Crogau
Cefn-y-maes
Llysdinam
Disserth
Newbridge-on-Wye
P O W Y S
645
Drygarn Fawr
537
Carnau
Bwlch y Ddau Faen
Bryn Cyncoed
Esgair y Ffynnon
Cwmchwefru
Llethyr Melyn
Craig Chwefri 430
Banc Creigol
Cwm Clwyd
Llethr
Dolfawr
Crossway
Three Wells
Cairn 439
The Wern Fm
Gelli Hill
Lan Fawr
Wennallt
Ty Bach
428
Gornoeth
Schache
Bryn
Wern-fawr
Dolfawr Fm
Darren
Nant y Gaith
Allt y Clych
B4358
Brynwern Br
Cefnmawr
Maesgwynne
Graig
Camnant
114
Banc Du
Nant Melyn
Allt y Ddinas
Y Garth
Fronwen
Bwlchcilau
Llanafan-fawr
Llanerchllwyd
Bryn-wern Hall
Cors y Llyn
Castle Crab
The Banks
Cwmamliw
Hirllwyn Bank
Cefn Garw
Pen-cae
Gruglwyn
478
Bryn
Cwmfadog
Pentre-Llwyn-llwyd
Bwlchgarth
Castle Bank
Llansantffraed-in-Elvel
Hundred House
Pen Carreg-Dan 494
Cefn'bran
Tynllwyn
Comin-y-garth
Afallenchwerw
Comin-coch
Penmincae
Caerwnon Ho
436
Cwm-berwyn
Newmead Fm
Carneddau
Perthi Common
Trysgol
Nant yr Hwch
Lan Isaf
Allt Lwyd
Rhysgog
Maesygroes Isaf
Sarn Helen
Goytre
River Wye
Builth Road
Cwmbach Llechrhyd
Trallwm
Bryn Ciun
Gribyn
Erwddol
Coed y Cilliau
Pentrebach
Matts Fm
Pentre
A481
Bryn Mawr 446
Garn Wen 454
Llwyn-Gwrgan
Troedrhiwdalar
Hafod-yr-ancr
Penlan
Careg-ywen
392
Carneddau Fm
Llanelwedd Rocks
Cefn Waun-Lwyd
Allt-Y-Gest
Pen-rhiw-trefan
Brynmoelddu
Cefn-dyrys
Banc Paderau
Llwynowen
Celsau
Dolfan Fforest
Cribarth
Comin Coch
Tyncoed
Comin Cefn-poeth
A470
Penmaenau
Royal Welsh Showground
Llanelwedd
Crugwydd 455
Nant yr Aneill
Coedmawr
Trefan
Rhosferig
Park Wells
Aberedw Hill
Noyaddllwyd
Tynllwyn
Cefn Crug
Cefn Cynllaith
Aberannell
Ty-mawr
Cilmery Fm
Cilmery
Chwefri
Cefn Blaeneinon
Coed Caeper-corn
Nant Einon
B4358
Tysegur
Llwyngwgyn
Oaklands
Builth Wells
Llanfair-ym-Muallt
Llanfaredd
451
Llatho
Irfon Forest
Pen-Y-Garn 487
Beulah
Llwyn-cus
Garth Bank
Llanfechan Ho
Ty'h-y-ffos
A483
Wernfawr
Hendre
Tyn-y-graig
Garth
Llan-fraith 386
Dinas Fach
Carcwm
Penfedw
Caerau
Llwyncadwgan
Llanfechan
Coed Cowyn Fm
95
Cwm Irfon
Pistyllgwyn
Ffosyrhyddod
Coed Clunmelyn
Garth Ho
Dolmenyn
Gwaralt
Erwhelm
Maes-y-cwm
Blaenmilo Fm
Middle Hall
Cefn Alltwinau
Llawes-heli
Llwynbrain
Cwmrhybin
441
Moelfre
Pwllgwyn
Pantypyllau
Ysglog
Cefnhirog Fm
Garn Dwad
446
Gilfach
Ty-gwyn
Gwarafog Ho
Llanddewi'r Cwm
Garw-henallt
B4567
Y Foel
Tynycoed Fm
B4519
450
452
Henallt
Court Fm
Pen y Dinas
Llanwrtyd
Cambrian Woollen Mill
Bronffynnon
Pennau 393
Banc y Garth
Maesmynis
Aberedw
SO
10
80
50
A B C D E F G H

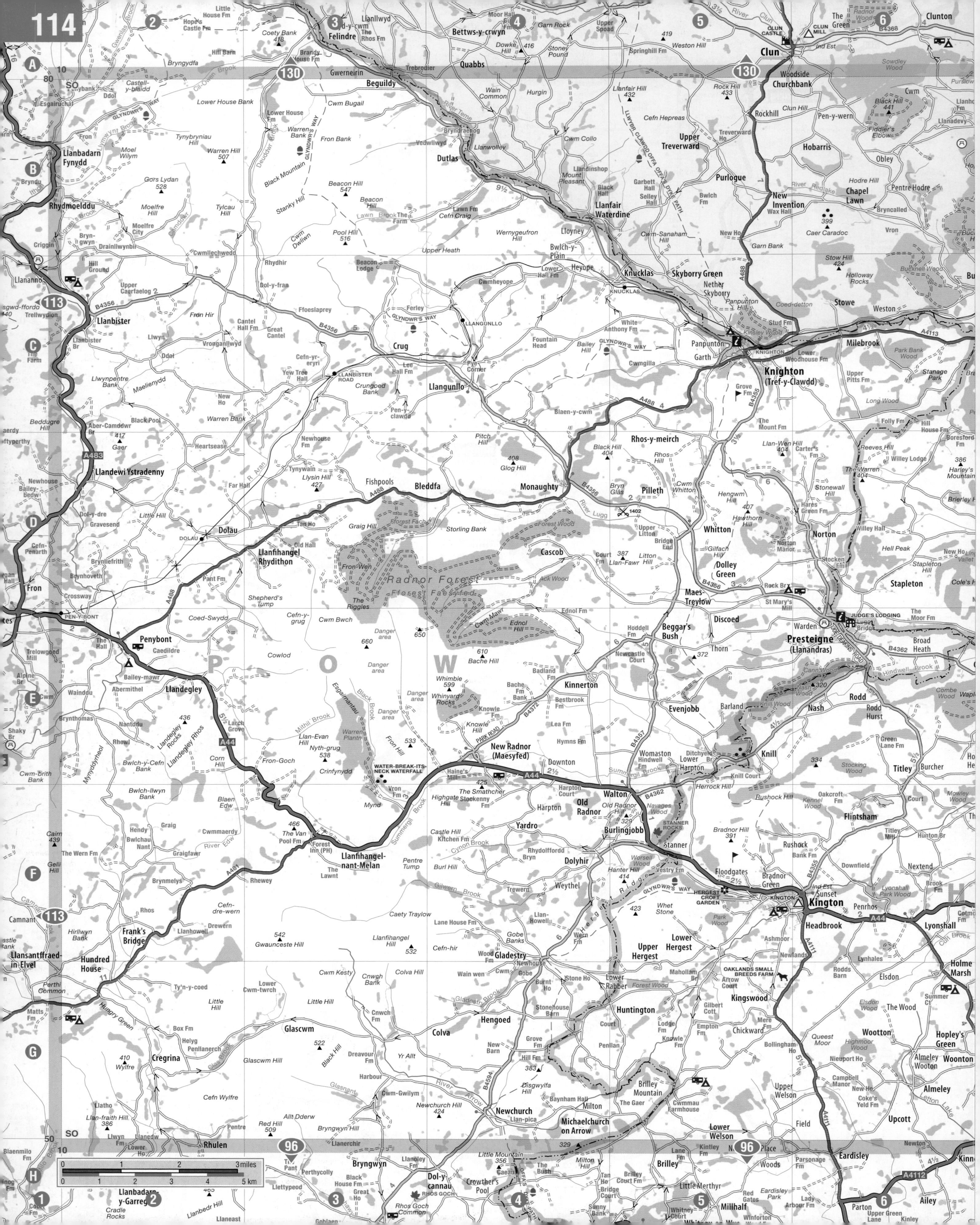

Felindre
Betws-y-crwyn
Clun
Clunton
Beguildy
Quabbs
Churchbank
Dutlas
Llanbadarn Fynydd
Upper Treverward
Hobarris
Purlogue
New Invention
Chapel Lawn
Llanfair Waterdine
Rhydmoelddu
Knucklas
Skyborry Green
Llanbister
Crug
Llangunllo
Knighton (Tref-y-Clawdd)
Milebrook
Panpunton
Garth
Llandewi Ystradenny
Rhos-y-meirch
Pilleth
Bleddfa
Monaughty
Dolau
Whitton
Norton
Llanfihangel Rhydithon
Cascob
Dolley Green
Stapleton
Radnor Forest
Fforest Faesyfed
Maes-Treylow
Discoed
Penybont
Beggar's Bush
Presteigne (Llanandras)
Kinnerton
Llandegley
Evenjobb
Rodd
Nash
P O W Y S
New Radnor (Maesyfed)
Knill
Titley
Walton
Old Radnor
Yardro
Burlingjobb
Llanfihangel-nant-Melan
Flintsham
Dolyhir
Kington
Frank's Bridge
Headbrook
Lyonshall
Upper Hergest
Lower Hergest
Hundred House
Llansantffraed-in-Elvel
Gladestry
Kingswood
Huntington
Hengoed
Glascwm
Colva
Cregrina
Newchurch
Michaelchurch on Arrow
Almeley
Rhulen
Bryngwyn
Brilley
Lower Welson
Eardisley
Dol-y-cannau
Llanbadarn-y-Garreg
Millhalf
Ailey
130
113
96
0 1 2 3 miles
0 1 2 3 4 5 km

SHROPSHIRE HILLS
HEREFORDSHIRE
Aston on Clun
Little Brampton
Purslow
Clunbury
Twitchen
Hopton Castle
Abcott
Clungunford
Three Ashes
Hoptonheath
Bedstone
Marlow
Broome
Craven Arms
Stokesay Castle
Stokesay
Aldon
Brandhill
The Wernlas Collection
Shelderton
Whittytree
Duxmoor
Onibury
Wootton
Norton
Culmington
Bache
Burley
Vernolds Common
Walton
Stanton Lacy
Bromfield
Bromfield Woodhouses
Old Field
Oakly Park
Lower Hayton
Upper Hayton
Hayton's Bent
Hoptongate
Titterhill
Milborough
Cleedownton
Hopton Cangeford
Cleeton St Mary
Bitterley
Middleton
Henley
Stoneylane
Angelbank
Dhustone
Cornbrook
Rockgreen
Snitton
Farden
Cleehill
Hints
Knowbury
Ludlow
Ludlow Museum
Ludlow Castle
Ludford
Priors Halton
Lady Halton
Bringewood Forge
Downton Castle
Downton on the Rock
Downton Gorge
Leintwardine
Kinton
Whitton
Todding
Lower Todding
Bucknell
Coxall
Buckton
Walford
Brampton Bryan
River Teme
Burrington
Aston
Pipe Aston
Overton
Mary Knoll
High Vinnalls
Steventon
Caynham
Whitton
Knowlegate
Hope Bagot
Nash
Adforton
Letton
Elton
Leinthall Starkes
Wigmore
Birtley
Newton
Richards Castle
Batchcott
Ashford Bowdler
Ashford Carbonell
Middleton
Greete
Boraston
Burford
Little Hereford
Woofferton
Gosford
Brimfield
Tenbury Wells
Burford House & Meadow Gallery
Ongar Street
Leinthall Earls
Yatton
Croft Ambrey Fort
Ashley Moor
Comberton
Orleton
Wyson
Lingen
Limebrook
Lower Lye
Upper Lye
Aymestrey
Croft Castle
Croft
Cock Gate
Bircher
Yarpole
Lucton
Stony Cross
Berrington
Callows Grave
St Michaels
Kinsham
Byton
Combe Moor
Mortimer's Cross
Mortimer's Cross Water Mill & Battle Centre
Byton Hand
Middleton on the Hill
Ashton
Eye
Berrington Hall
The Hundred
Leysters Pole
Leysters
Moreton
Shobdon
Ledicot
Lugg Green
Kingsland
Luston
Eyton
The Broad
Kimbolton
Stockton
Whyle
Grafton
Woonton
Staunton on Arrow
Cobnash
Shirl Heath
Cholstrey
Leominster
Barons Cross
Eaton
Lawton
Pembridge
Eardisland
Arrow Green
Stagbatch
Ebnall
Monkland
Monkland Cheese Dairy
Ryelands
Pudleston
Hatfield
Brockmanton
Steen's Bridge
Docklow
Grendon Green
Marston
Burton Court
Upper Hardwick
Lower Hardwick
Lower Burton
Sollers Dilwyn
Bearwood
Dunkertons Cider
Luntley
Ivington
Ivington Green
Brierley
Wharton
Stoke Prior
Humber
Risbury
Marston Stannett
Bredenbury
Broxwood
Haven
Dilwyn
Aulden
Marlbrook
Hegdon Hill
Newton
Upper Hill
Birley
Knapton Green
Hope under Dinmore
Hampton Court
Bowley
Pencombe
Weobley
Weobley Marsh
Sarnesfield
Bush Bank
King's Pyon
Ledgemoor
Westhope
Dinmore Manor
Queenswood
Bodenham
Bodenham Moor
Maund Bryan
Little Cowarne
Ullingswick
Canon Pyon
Wellington
Kingsfield
Vauld
Urdimarsh
Marden
Felton
Moreton Jeffries
Norton
Calver Hill
Wormsley
A49
A44
A4110
A4112
A456
A417
A4113
B4361
B4362
B4360
B4529
131
116
97

SHROPSHIRE
Wyre Forest
MALVERN HILLS
Cleedownton
Farlow
Oreton
Kinlet
Silvington
Catherton
Cleeton St Mary
Hopton Wafers
Doddington
Cleobury Mortimer
Neen Savage
Buttonoak
Upper Arley
Shatterford
Kingsford
Blakeshall
Wolverley
Franche
Kidderminster
Bewdley
Wribbenhall
Far Forest
Fingerpost
Callow Hill
Ribbesford
Bliss Gate
Pound Bank
Bayton
Milson
Coreley
Cleehill
Hints
Knowle
Nash
Neen Sollars
Mamble
Clows Top
Rock
Stourport-on-Severn
Areley Kings
Hartlebury
Boraston
Newnham Bridge
Burford
Tenbury Wells
Lindridge
Eardiston
Frith Common
Pensax
Stockton on Teme
Abberley
Dunley
Astley
Astley Cross
Lincomb
Crossway Green
Upper Rochford
Hanley William
Stanford on Teme
Orleton
Great Witley
Noutard's Green
Shrawley
Stanford Bridge
Broad Heath
Hanley Child
Little Witley
Ombersley
Holt Heath
Holt Fleet
Kyre Park
Stoke Bliss
Sweet Green
Upper Sapey
Sapey Common
Shelsley Walsh
Shelsley Beauchamp
Clifton upon Teme
Harpley
High Lane
Collington
Thornbury
Tedstone Wafer
Tedstone Delamere
Edvin Loach
Edwyn Ralph
Martley
Wichenford
Sinton Green
Grimley
Berrow Green
Horsham
Hallow
Grendon Green
Bredenbury
Bromyard
Bromyard Downs
Whitbourne
Knightwick
Lulsley
Broadwas
Worcester
St John's
Alfrick
Leigh
Bransford
Powick
Linley Green
Suckley
Stanford Bishop
Munderfield Row
Acton Beauchamp
Longley Green
Acton Green
Leigh Sinton
Malvern
Storridge
Bishops Frome
Evesbatch
Ridgeway
Pencombe
Little Cowarne
Hegdon Hill
Hatfield
Ullingswick
Jeffries
Newland
Stanbrook
Callow End
A456
A443
A4117
A44
A449
A4103
A442
B4202
B4203
B4204
B4214
132
115
98
0 1 2 3 miles
0 1 2 3 4 5 km

WORCESTERSHIRE
Hagley
West Hagley
Clent
Romsley
Frankley
Northfield
King's Norton
Bournville
Longbridge
Rubery
Rednal
Cofton Hackett
Hopwood
Alvechurch
Blakedown
Belbroughton
Bell End
Wildmoor
Fairfield
Catshill
Marlbrook
Lickey
Lickey End
Blackwell
Barnt Green
Harvington
Stone
Mustow Green
Shenstone
Chaddesley Corbett
Bluntington
Dodford
Sidemoor
Bromsgrove
Aston Fields
Charford
Finstall
Tutnall
Tardebigge
Redditch
Batchley
Enfield
Riverside
Smallwood
Southcrest
Lodge Park
Ipsley
Matchborough
Winyates Green
Headless Cross
Crabbs Cross
Hunt End
Studley
Hollywood
Drakes Cross
Wythall
Portway
Beoley
Holt End
Gorcott Hill
Mappleborough Green
Morton Bagot
Elmley Lovett
Cutnall Green
Rushock
Elmbridge
Stoke Prior
Stoke Heath
Upton Warren
Wychbold
Hampton Lovett
Doverdale
Droitwich Spa
Witton
Salwarpe
Hadzor
Hanbury
Woolmere Green
Bradley Green
Feckenham
Astwood Bank
Sambourne
Coughton
Alcester
Arrow
Inkberrow
Dormston
Stock Green
Himbleton
Huddington
Grafton Flyford
Tibberton
Oddingley
Martin Hussingtree
Fernhill Heath
Hindlip
Warndon
Kington
Flyford Flavell
Abberton
North Piddle
Upton Snodsbury
Broughton Hackett
Churchill
Spetchley
Whittington
White Ladies Aston
Naunton Beauchamp
Bishampton
Peopleton
Egdon
Throckmorton
Pinvin
Drake's Broughton
Kempsey
Norton
Littleworth
Hatfield
Rous Lench
Ab Lench
Church Lench
Atch Lench
Abbots Morton
Iron Cross
Dunnington
Salford Priors
Abbots Salford
Harvington
Bidford-on-Avon
Marlcliff
Cleeve Prior
Wixford
Broom
Exhall

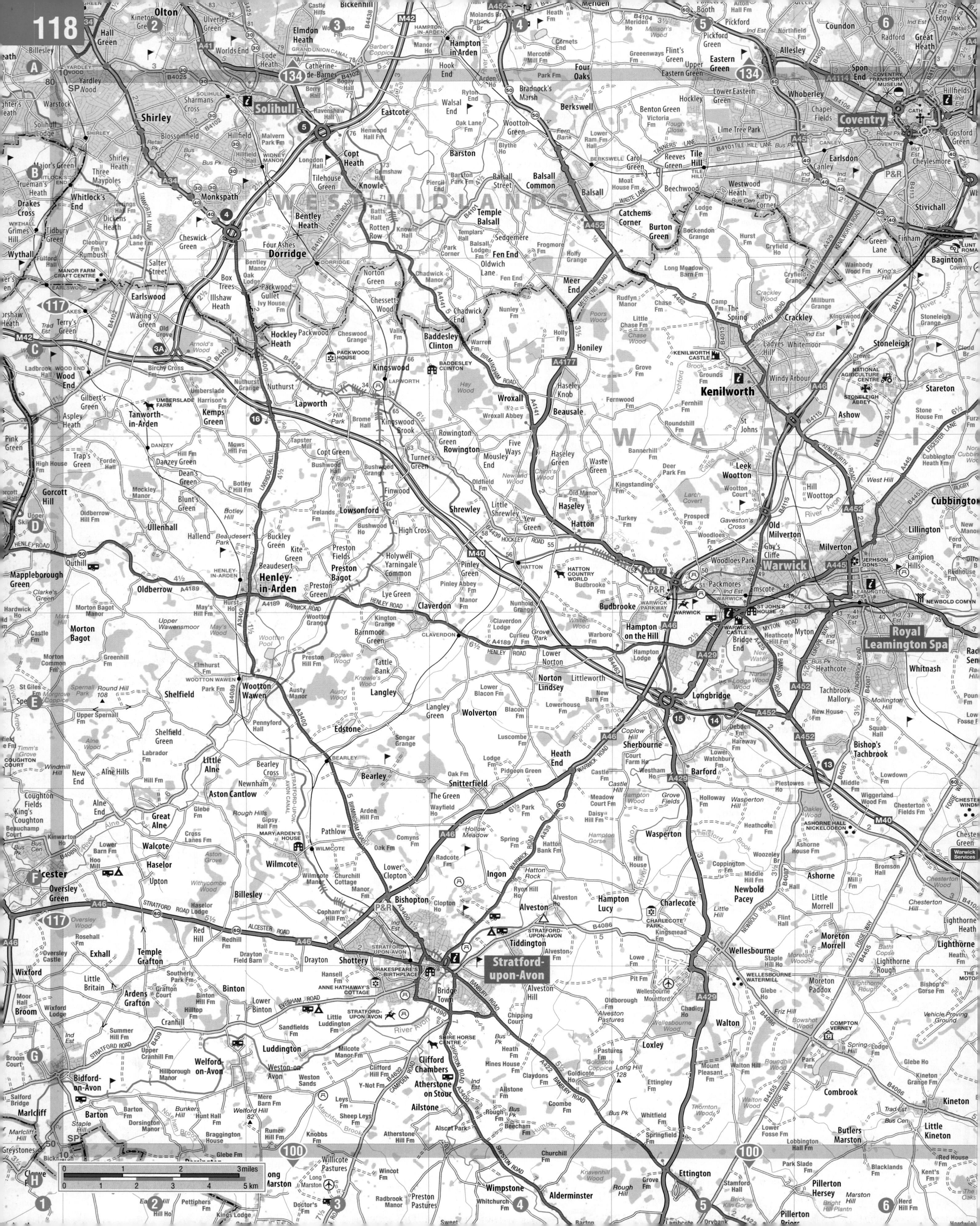
Olton
Hall Green
Elmdon Heath
Hampton in Arden
Meriden
Pickford Green
Coundon
Radford
Great Heath
Edgwick
Allesley
Solihull
Shirley
Catherine-de-Barnes
Eastcote
Berkswell
Four Oaks
Eastern Green
Coventry
Whoberley
Chapel Fields
Earlsdon
Canley
Cheylesmore
Tile Hill
Westwood Heath
Stivichall
Finham
Baginton
Monkspath
Whitlock's End
Tidbury Green
Wythall
Knowle
Copt Heath
Barston
Balsall Common
Balsall
Temple Balsall
Catchems Corner
Burton Green
WEST MIDLANDS
Bentley Heath
Dorridge
Cheswick Green
Earlswood
Hockley Heath
Packwood
Baddesley Clinton
Meer End
Honiley
Kenilworth
Crackley
Stoneleigh
Stareton
Ashow
Kingswood
Lapworth
Tanworth-in-Arden
Wroxall
Beausale
Haseley Knob
WARWICKSHIRE
Rowington
Shrewley
Lowsonford
Haseley
Hatton
Leek Wootton
Old Milverton
Cubbington
Lillington
Milverton
Warwick
Royal Leamington Spa
Henley-in-Arden
Preston Bagot
Claverdon
Budbrooke
Hampton on the Hill
Myton
Whitnash
Wootton Wawen
Langley
Norton Lindsey
Longbridge
Bishop's Tachbrook
Shelfield
Edstone
Wolverton
Sherbourne
Barford
Bearley
Snitterfield
Aston Cantlow
Great Alne
Wilmcote
Wasperton
Ingon
Alveston
Charlecote
Hampton Lucy
Newbold Pacey
Ashorne
Alcester
Oversley Green
Bishopton
Tiddington
Wellesbourne
Moreton Morrell
Lighthorne
Stratford-upon-Avon
Shottery
Binton
Temple Grafton
Exhall
Wixford
Broom
Luddington
Welford-on-Avon
Bidford-on-Avon
Clifford Chambers
Atherstone on Stour
Loxley
Walton
Combrook
Kineton
Marlcliff
Barton
Ailstone
Little Kineton
Butlers Marston
Long Marston
Wimpstone
Alderminster
Ettington
Pillerton Hersey
M40
M42
A46
A452
A429
A3400
1 2 3 miles
1 2 3 4 5 km

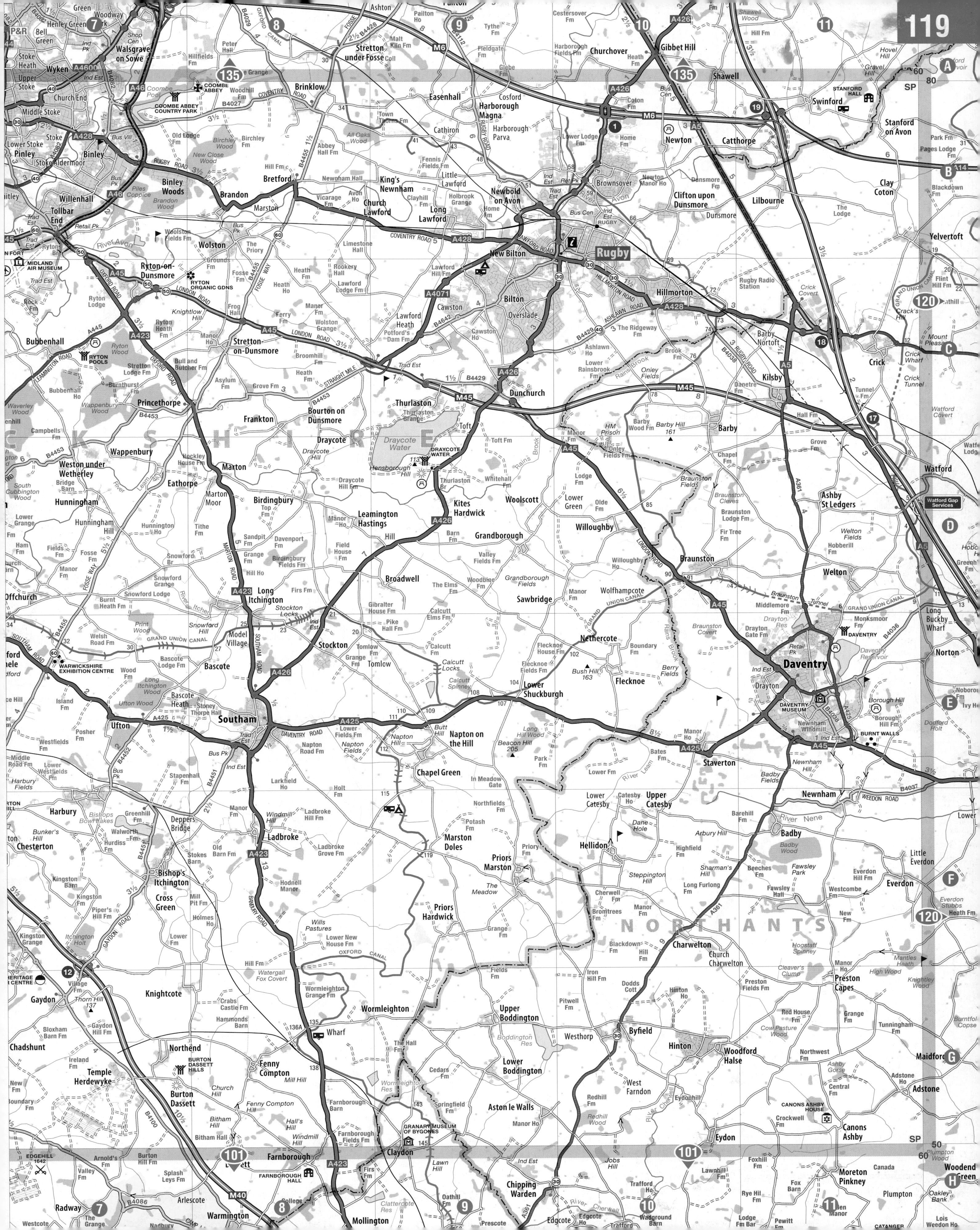
Walsgrave on Sowe
Wyken
Stoke Heath
Upper Stoke
Church End
Middle Stoke
Lower Stoke
Pinley
Binley
Binley Woods
Willenhall
Tollbar End
Stoke Aldermoor
Coombe Abbey
Coombe Abbey Country Park
Brinklow
Stretton under Fosse
Ashton
Easenhall
Harborough Magna
Harborough Parva
Cathiron
Churchover
Gibbet Hill
Shawell
Swinford
Stanford Hall
Stanford on Avon
Newton
Catthorpe
Clifton upon Dunsmore
Dunsmore
Lilbourne
Clay Coton
Yelvertoft
Brownsover
Newbold on Avon
Little Lawford
King's Newnham
Church Lawford
Long Lawford
Bretford
Brandon
Marston
Wolston
Ryton-on-Dunsmore
Ryton Organic Gdns
Midland Air Museum
Rugby
New Bilton
Bilton
Cawston
Overslade
Hillmorton
Rugby Radio Station
Barby Nortoft
Crick
Kilsby
Barby
Stretton-on-Dunsmore
Bubbenhall
Ryton Pools
Princethorpe
Frankton
Bourton on Dunsmore
Thurlaston
Dunchurch
Toft
Draycote
Draycote Water
Wappenbury
Weston under Wetherley
Hunningham
Eathorpe
Marton
Birdingbury
Leamington Hastings
Kites Hardwick
Woolscott
Grandborough
Willoughby
Lower Green
Braunston
Ashby St Ledgers
Watford
Watford Gap Services
Welton
Long Itchington
Broadwell
Sawbridge
Wolfhampcote
Offchurch
Stockton
Nethercote
Flecknoe
Lower Shuckburgh
Daventry
Daventry Museum
Drayton
Norton
Long Buckby Wharf
Bascote
Southam
Ufton
Napton on the Hill
Chapel Green
Staverton
Newnham
Badby
Warwickshire Exhibition Centre
Harbury
Deppers Bridge
Ladbroke
Marston Doles
Priors Marston
Priors Hardwick
Upper Catesby
Lower Catesby
Hellidon
Little Everdon
Everdon
Chesterton
Bishop's Itchington
Cross Green
Charwelton
Church Charwelton
Preston Capes
Gaydon
Knightcote
Wormleighton
Upper Boddington
Lower Boddington
Westhorp
Byfield
Hinton
Woodford Halse
Maidford
Chadshunt
Temple Herdewyke
Northend
Burton Dassett Hills
Fenny Compton
Burton Dassett
Aston le Walls
West Farndon
Eydon
Adstone
Canons Ashby House
Canons Ashby
Farnborough
Farnborough Hall
Claydon
Granary Museum of Bygones
Chipping Warden
Moreton Pinkney
Woodend Green
Radway
Arlescote
Warmington
Mollington
Edgcote
Edgehill 1642
NORTHANTS
M6
M45
M40
A45
A423
A426
A425
A428
A5
A361

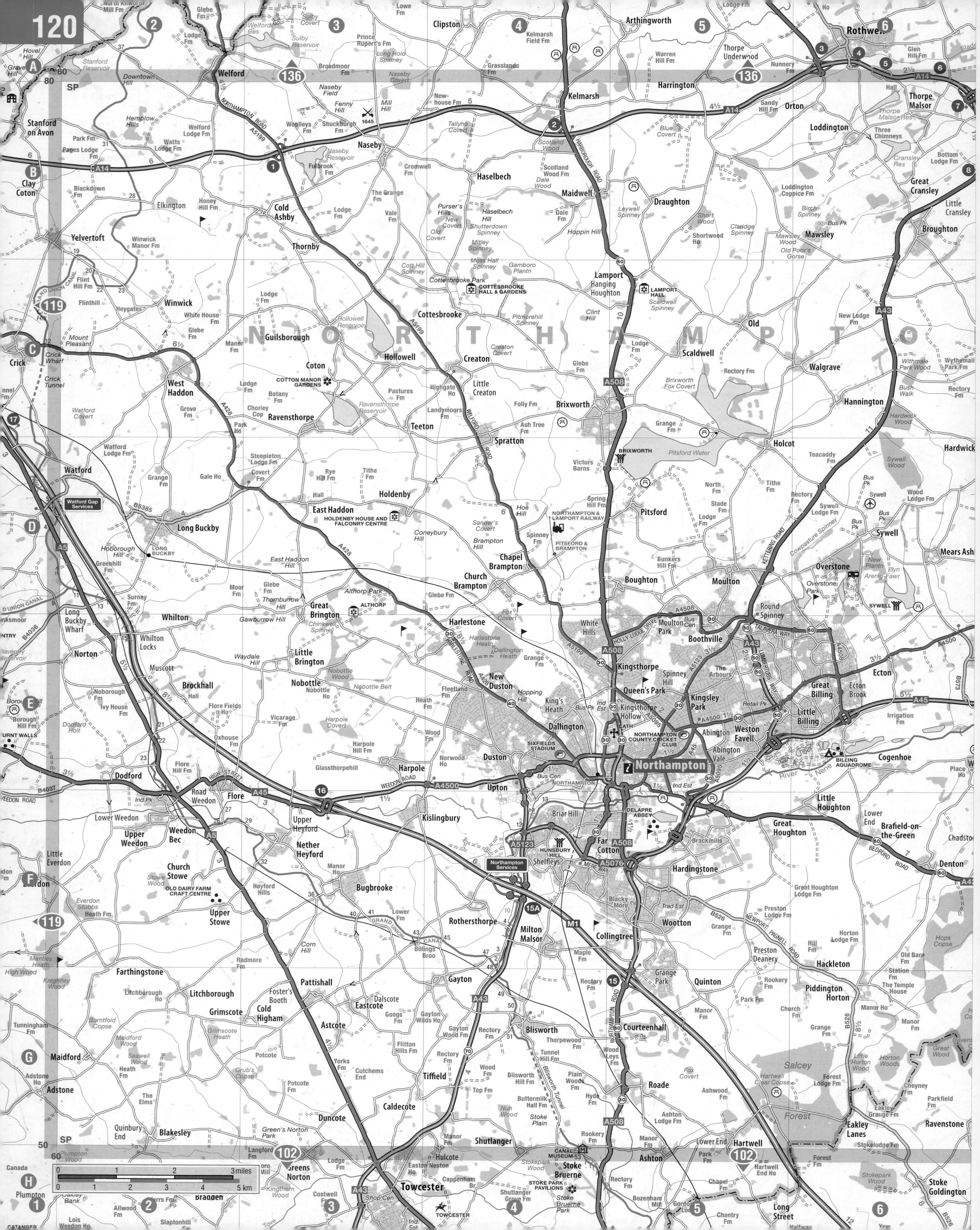

Welford
Sulby Reservoir
Clipston
Kelmarsh Field Fm
Arthingworth
Rothwell
Stanford on Avon
Naseby
Kelmarsh
Harrington
Thorpe Underwood
Thorpe Malsor
Orton
Loddington
Clay Coton
Elkington
Cold Ashby
Haselbech
Maidwell
Draughton
Great Cransley
Little Cransley
Broughton
Mawsley
Yelvertoft
Thornby
Lamport
Hanging Houghton
Winwick
Guilsborough
Cottesbrooke
Hollowell
Creaton
Old
Scaldwell
Walgrave
Crick
West Haddon
Coton
Little Creaton
Brixworth
Hannington
Ravensthorpe
Teeton
Spratton
Holcot
Hardwick
Watford
Watford Gap Services
Holdenby
East Haddon
Pitsford
Pitsford Water
Long Buckby
Chapel Brampton
Church Brampton
Boughton
Moulton
Overstone
Sywell
Mears Ashby
Whilton
Great Brington
Althorp
Harlestone
Moulton Park
Boothville
Norton
Little Brington
Kingsthorpe
Spinney Hill
Ecton
Brockhall
Nobottle
New Duston
Queen's Park
Kingsley Park
Great Billing
Little Billing
Dallington
Weston Favell
Abington
Duston
Northampton
Cogenhoe
Dodford
Flore
Harpole
Upton
Little Houghton
Weedon Bec
Upper Weedon
Lower Weedon
Kislingbury
Briar Hill
Upper Heyford
Nether Heyford
Great Houghton
Brafield-on-the-Green
Far Cotton
Hardingstone
Denton
Church Stowe
Upper Stowe
Bugbrooke
Northampton Services
Shelfleys
Wootton
Rothersthorpe
Milton Malsor
Collingtree
Farthingstone
Litchborough
Gayton
Grange Park
Quinton
Preston Deanery
Hackleton
Pattishall
Cold Higham
Eastcote
Piddington
Horton
Grimscote
Astcote
Blisworth
Courteenhall
Maidford
Tiffield
Roade
Salcey Forest
Adstone
Caldecote
Duncote
Blakesley
Shutlanger
Eakley Lanes
Ravenstone
Hulcote
Ashton
Hartwell
Greens Norton
Towcester
Stoke Bruerne
Stoke Goldington
Plumpton
Long Street
Gayton
M1
A5
A14
A43
A45
A428
A508
A5199
A4500
A5123
A5076
SP
3 miles
5 km

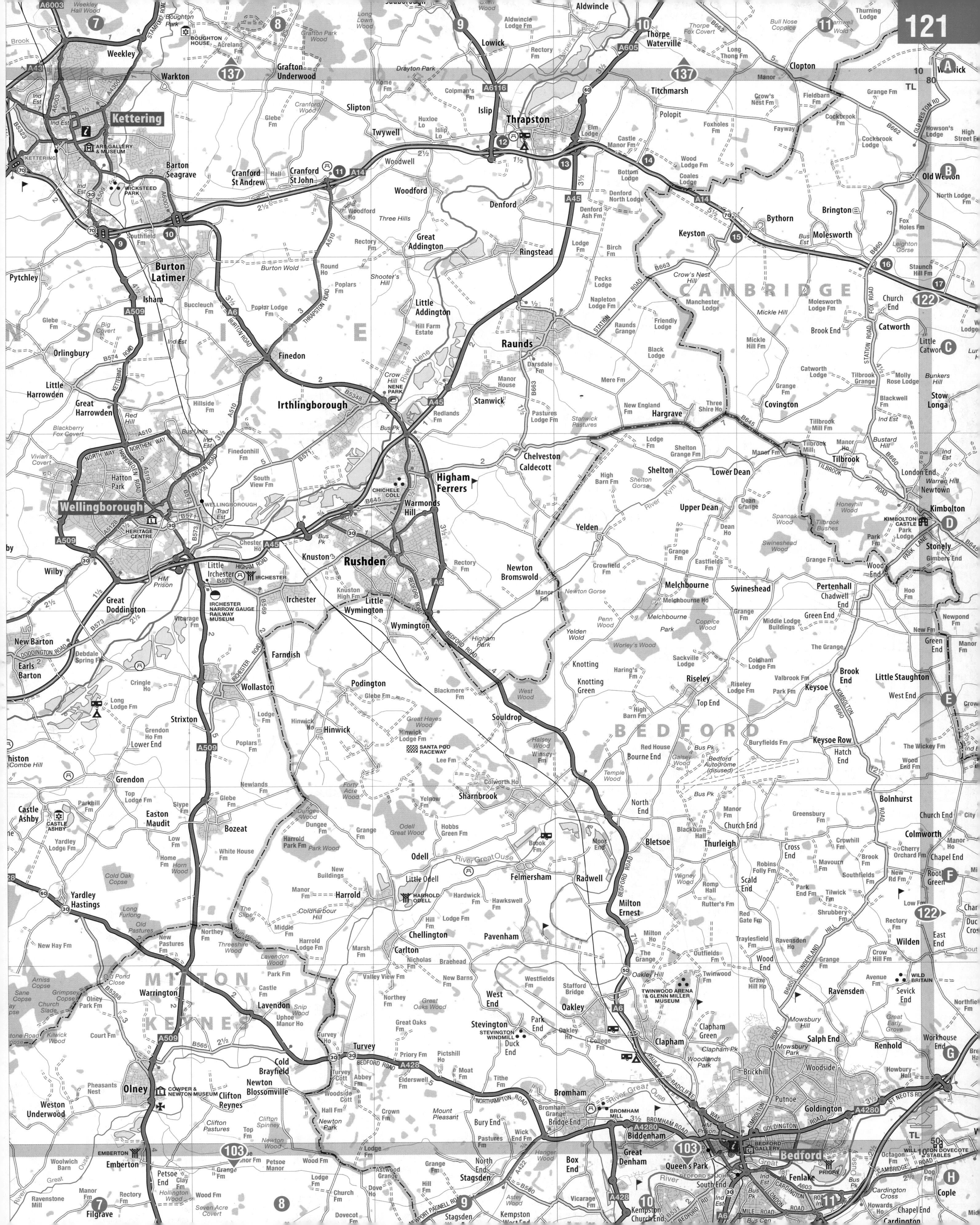
Kettering
Weekley
Warkton
Grafton Underwood
Lowick
Aldwincle
Thorpe Waterville
Clopton
Titchmarsh
Islip
Thrapston
Slipton
Twywell
Barton Seagrave
Cranford St Andrew
Cranford St John
Woodford
Denford
Keyston
Bythorn
Brington
Molesworth
Burton Latimer
Isham
Great Addington
Ringstead
Little Addington
Raunds
Pytchley
Orlingbury
Finedon
Irthlingborough
Little Harrowden
Great Harrowden
Stanwick
Hargrave
Covington
Catworth
Wellingborough
Higham Ferrers
Chelveston
Caldecott
Shelton
Lower Dean
Tilbrook
Kimbolton
Upper Dean
Rushden
Yelden
Stonely
Wilby
Great Doddington
Irchester
Little Wymington
Wymington
Newton Bromswold
Melchbourne
Swineshead
Pertenhall
Farndish
Knotting
Riseley
Keysoe
Little Staughton
Podington
Souldrop
Wollaston
Strixton
Hinwick
Sharnbrook
Grendon
Bozeat
Easton Maudit
Castle Ashby
Odell
Bletsoe
Thurleigh
Bolnhurst
Colmworth
Yardley Hastings
Harrold
Felmersham
Radwell
Milton Ernest
Chellington
Carlton
Pavenham
Wilden
Warrington
Lavendon
West End
Oakley
Ravensden
Stevington
Clapham
Salph End
Renhold
Turvey
Cold Brayfield
Olney
Newton Blossomville
Clifton Reynes
Bromham
Goldington
Biddenham
Bedford
Emberton
Great Denham
Queen's Park
Kempston
Stagsden
Filgrave
CAMBRIDGE
BEDFORD
MILTON KEYNES
A14
A45
A6
A509
A428
A4280
137
122
103

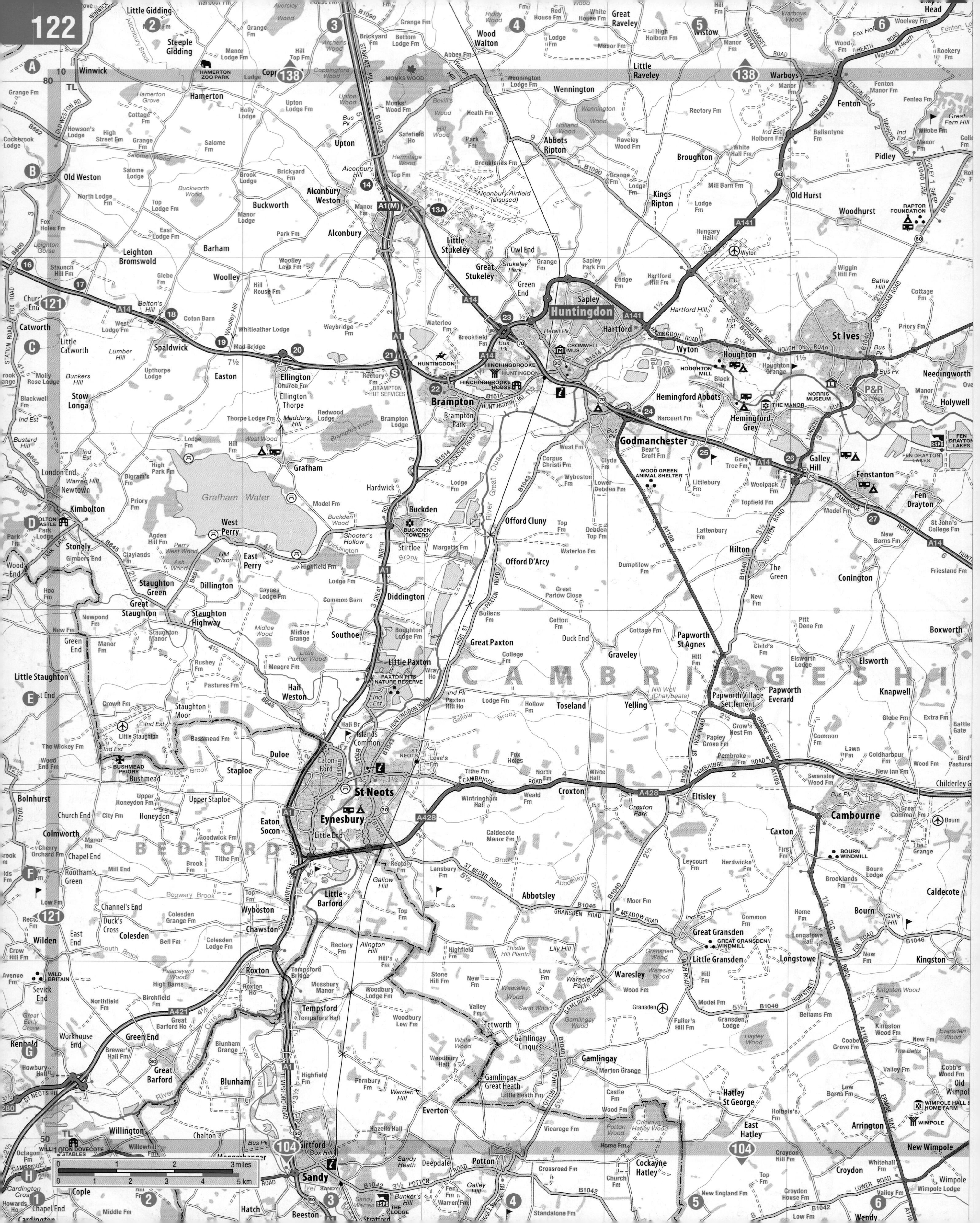
Little Gidding
Steeple Gidding
Winwick
HAMERTON ZOO PARK
Hamerton
Coppingford Wood
MONKS WOOD
Wood Walton
Great Raveley
Little Raveley
Wistow
Warboys
Wennington
Fenton
Old Weston
Upton
Alconbury Weston
Alconbury
Abbots Ripton
Broughton
Pidley
Buckworth
Alconbury Airfield (disused)
Kings Ripton
Old Hurst
Woodhurst
RAPTOR FOUNDATION
Leighton Bromswold
Barham
Little Stukeley
Great Stukeley
Owl End
Woolley
Catworth
Little Catworth
Spaldwick
Easton
Ellington
Ellington Thorpe
Stow Longa
Huntingdon
Sapley
Hartford
Wyton
Houghton
St Ives
HINCHINGBROOKE HOUSE
CROMWELL MUS
BRAMPTON HUT SERVICES
Brampton
Brampton Park
Hemingford Abbots
Hemingford Grey
NORRIS MUSEUM
THE MANOR
Needingworth
Holywell
Godmanchester
WOOD GREEN ANIMAL SHELTER
Galley Hill
Fenstanton
Fen Drayton
FEN DRAYTON LAKES
Kimbolton
Grafham
Grafham Water
West Perry
East Perry
Buckden
BUCKDEN TOWERS
Offord Cluny
Offord D'Arcy
Hilton
Conington
Stonely
Staughton Green
Dillington
Great Staughton
Staughton Highway
Diddington
Southoe
Great Paxton
Graveley
Papworth St Agnes
Boxworth
Elsworth
CAMBRIDGESHIRE
Little Paxton
PAXTON PITS NATURE RESERVE
Hail Weston
Toseland
Yelling
Papworth Village Settlement
Papworth Everard
Knapwell
Little Staughton
Duloe
BUSHMEAD PRIORY
Bushmead
Staploe
Eaton Ford
St Neots
Eynesbury
Eaton Socon
Croxton
Eltisley
Cambourne
Caxton
Bolnhurst
Colmworth
BEDFORD
Little End
Abbotsley
Little Barford
Wyboston
Chawston
Colesden
Wilden
Great Gransden
GREAT GRANSDEN WINDMILL
Little Gransden
Longstowe
Bourn
BOURN WINDMILL
Caldecote
Kingston
WILD BRITAIN
Roxton
Tempsford
Waresley
Tetworth
Gamlingay Cinques
Gamlingay
Great Barford
Blunham
Everton
Hatley St George
East Hatley
Arrington
WIMPOLE HALL & HOME FARM
WIMPOLE
Willington
Sandy
Potton
Cockayne Hatley
Croydon
New Wimpole
Wimpole
Cople
Beeston
A1(M)
A1
A14
A141
A428
A421
A1198
A603
B1040
B1043
B1046
B1090
0 1 2 3 miles
0 1 2 3 4 5 km

Mill Fm
Old Halves Fm
Mepal
North Fm
Toll Fm
Witcham Hythe
Wardy Hill
Coveney
Hale Fen
Wilbey Hill Fm
Frogs Abbey
West Fen Fm
Queen Adelaide
Oliver Cromwell's House
Swasedale Fm
Coronation Fm
Holwoods House Fm
Broadpiece Fm
Gault
Chatteris
Clare Fm
White Gate Fm
Witcham
Burnt Hill
Common Fm
Beald Fm
Coldmoor Fm
Ely
Cathedral & Mus
Wades Fm
Slyer's Fm
Warner's Fm
Sutton West Fen
Swarm Haugh Closes
Middle Fen
Thorney Hill
Shrubland Ho
North Fen Fm
The Meadow
Ind Est
Bus Pk
Somersham
Turkington Hill
Tubb's Fm
The Gullet
Sutton
The Beesons
Wentworth
Witchford
Paradise Fm
Causeway Fm
Red House Fm
Holwood Fm
Colne Fen
Colne Fen Fm
Chain Causeway
Old Bedford River
Haddenham Road
Stuntney
Nornea Fm
Hale Fields
Somersham Park
Salmon's Fm
South Fen
Grunty Fen Drain
St John's Fm
Castle Fm
Sutton Fen
Ring Fm
Haddenham End Field
Grunty Fen Fm
Valley Bottom or The Pools
Braham Fm
Harlock's Fm
Broad Hill
Hill Row Doles
Galls Fm
Causeway Fm
North Hill
Chambers Fm
Grangers Fm
Half Acre Fm
Barcham Fm
Crow Hall Fm
Great Hale Fm
Little Thetford
Saxon Fm
Longfield Fm
Colne
Willow Hall Fm
Haddenham Pastures
White Cross Hill
White Cross Field
Quarterway Ho
Barway
Blockmoor Fen
North Field
Northfield Windmill
Barnfield Fm
Bluntisham
Hermitage Fm
Haddenham
Chapel Hill
Hainey Fm
West Hill
Soham Cotes
Earith
The Hermitage
Wilburton
Windmill
Stretham
Old Fordey Ho
Padney
Padneyhill Fm
Sedge Fen
Shade Common
Qua Fen Common
Cracknell Fm
Adventurers' Fen
Linden End Field
Heavenly Valley Fm
Mitchell's Fm
Red Hill Fm
Starlock Hay Fen Common
Gravel Fm
Soham Mere
Soham
East Fen Common
Priors Field Fm
Ouse Fen
Potash Fm
Trinity College Fm
Bridge Fm
Aldreth
Bedlam Fm
Ash Tree Fm
High Fen Fm
Flat Bridge Fm
River Great Ouse
Brownshill Staunch
Woodhall Fm
Queen Holme
Ewell Fen
Grange Fm
Elford Closes
Dimmock's Cote Road
Angle Fm
Milking Hills Corner
Australia Fm
Thorn Hall
Down Field Windmill
Down Field
Bare Hill
Tredon Fm
Glebe Fm
Smithey Fen Fm
Fair View Fm
Chear Fen Fm
Chittering Fm
Spinney Abbey
Field Fm
Block Fm
Church End
Lingwood Fm
Setchel Fen
Chear Fen
Willow Grange Fm
Lark Hall Fm
Tibbitts Fm
Norris Fm
School Fm
Westside Fm
Willingham
Over
Mare Fen
Wicken
Wicken Fen
Wicken Corn Windmill
Upware
Westmere Fm
Chittering
Joist Fen
Joist Fm
Ness Fm
Swavesey
Church End
Cold Harbour Fm
Belsars Field
The Irams
Fenleigh Fm
Mitchell Hill Fm
Chestnut Fm
Denny Lodge
Varsity Mink Fm
Wicken Lode
Ducketts Fm
Priory Fm
Hundred Acre Fm
Hill Fm
Great North Fen
Lodge Fm
River Bank
Adventurers' Fen
Goosehall Fm
Crowhall Fm
The Busway Guided Bus
Two Bit Fm
Top Moor
Soldiers' Hill
Heron Fm
Bus Pk
New Fm
Green End Cow Pastures
Farmland Mus & Denny Abbey
New Fm
Longstanton
Cottenham
Rampton
Brookfield Fm
Brook Field
North Fen
North Fen Fm
Research Pk
Waterbeach Airfield (disused)
Lode Fm
Highfen Fm
Commissioners Fm
Swaffen Prior Fen
Lord's Ground Fm
Burwell Fen
Burwell
Boxworth End
Highfield Fm
Thorpes Fm
Trinity College Fm
Further or Farm Field
Goose Hall
Overbrook Fm
Lower Hinge Fm
Lythel's Fm
Reach
Northmore Fm
Bus Park
Cottenham Pastures
Highbridge Fm
Slades Fm
Ind Est
Landing Strip
Westwick Field
Lambs' Cross
Bar Fm
Rectory Fm
Landbeach
Denny End
Waterbeach
Hatley's Fm
Northfields Fm
Bottisham Fen
Hill Fm
Cambridge
Clare College Fm
Westwick
Oakington
Beck Fm
Oldfield Fm
Adventurers' Ground Fm
Swaffham Prior
Lower Portland Fm
Ditch Fm
Gravel Pit Fm
Manor House Fm
Yarmouth Fm
The Grange
New Close Fm
Phypers Fm
Oakington
Mill Lane Fm
Abbey Fm
Punch Fm
Queens Fm
Red Tile Fm
Clayhithe
Bulls Fm
Lolworth
Slate Hall Fm
Manor Fm
Bedlam Fm
Swaffham Prior Ho
Warbraham Mains Fm
Bar Hill
Craft's Hill
Histon
Poplar Fm
Stanton Fm
Eye Hall Fm
Cow Br
The Abbey
The Grange
Sterling Fm
Impington
Mere Way Fm
New Close Fm
Milton
Commercial End
Lode
Cadenham Fm
Vicarage Fm
Histon & Impington
Girton
Grange Fm
Catch Hall
Horningsea
Lode Mill
Anglesey Abbey
Long Meadow
Swaffham Bulbeck
Childerley Hall
Rectory Fm
Longwood
Dry Drayton
Beck Brook Fm
Kings Hedges
Science Park
Ind Est
Milton
Baits Bite Lock
Snout Corner
Allicky Fm
Bottisham Hall
Northfield
Hall Fm
Park End
New England Stud Fm
Newmarket
National Stud
Egerton Stud
New Fm
Arbury
Poplar Hall
Quy Water
Bottisham
Scotland Fm
Madingley
Wrangling Corner
Fen Ditton
Stow cum Quy
Honey Hill
Chalk Fm
Lordship Stud
American Forces Cemetery
Park Fm
Chesterton
Trad Est
Newmarket Road
Dunsley Corner
Spring Hall
Four Mile Stable Fm
Lower Hare Park Fm
Hardwick
High Cross
St Neots Rd
Coton
Kettle's Yard
Museum of Technology
Abbey Stad
Black Ho
Little Wilbraham
Hare Park
Highfields
Common Fm
King's College Chapel
Coldham's Common
Cambridge
Fulbourn Fen
Frog End
Hawk Mill Fm
Bungalow Fm
Lower Hill House Fm
Fitzwilliam Museum
Romsey Town
Teversham
Wilbraham Temple
Great Wilbraham
Six Mile Bottom
Coventry Fm
Hungry Hill
Westley Bottom
Hardwick Wood
Wood Fm
Jaggard's Fm
Danger area
Laundry Fm
Newnham
University Botanic Garden
Cambridge
Fernleigh Fm
Queens Fm
Herring's Ho
Wood Barn Fm
Asplins Fm
Highfield Fm
Haggis Fm
Cherry Hinton
Home Fm
The Hall
Green End
River Fm
Barton Road
Toft
Bennel Fm
Barton
Fulbourn
Lower Farm Barn
Comberton
Grantchester
Trumpington Hall
Clay Fm
Heath Fm
Church Fm
Fox's Bridge Fm
Long Road
Westbourn Fm
Limepit Hill
Mill Hill
Great Wilbraham Hall Fm
Lark Hall Heath Fm
Westfield Fm
Barton
Trumpington
Bishop's Fm
Mutlow Hill
Claypit Hill
Anstey Hall
Wimpole Road
Rectory Fm
Lark Hall
Cantelupe Fm
Nine Wells
Gog Magog Hills
Wandlebury
Spike Hall
Manor Fm
Great Eversden
Spring Hall Fm
Byron's Pool
Lower Valley Fm
New Fm
Shardelowes Fm
West Wratting Valley Fm
Wadlow Fm
Little Eversden
Brook Fm
White Hill
Heath Fm
Copley Hill
Lodge Fm
Valley Fm
Heath Fm
Weston Colville
Clarke's Hill
Middlefield
Meggs Hill
Dungate Fm
Green End Fm
Hall Fm
Frog End
Haslingfield
Great Shelford
Stone Hill
Magog Fm
Copley Hill Fm
Dotterell Hall
Harlton
Rectory Fm
Shelford
West Wratting
Rectory Fm
Thorn Hill
Hauxton
Manor Ho
Stapleford
Worsted Lodge
Reeded Barn Fm
Rectory Fm
Grange Fm
Oxcroft Fm
Thornberry Hill Fm
Money Hill
Harston
Little Shelford
River Granta
Plumian Fm
Smock Mill
Balsham
Charity Fm
Gunner's Hall
Wilsmere Down Fm
Harston Hill
Clunch Pit Hill
Rectory Fm
North Fm
Babraham
The Grange
Mill Ho
Wood Hall
Yen Hall Fm
Orwell
Barrington
Sawston
Abington
Grove Fm
Manor Fm
Newton
Cockle Hill
Wells Fm
Sawston Hall
Fourwentways Services
Great Abington
Yole Fm
Balsham Wood
Rowley's Hill
Foxton
Hildersham
Chilford Hall Vineyard
West Wickham
Stanmoor Hall
Bourn Br
Furze Hill
Malton Fm
Shepreth
Shepreth Wildlife Park
Whittlesford
Pampisford
Granta Park
Rivey Hill
Borley Wood
Greendith Fm
Streetly Hall
Foxton
Ind Est

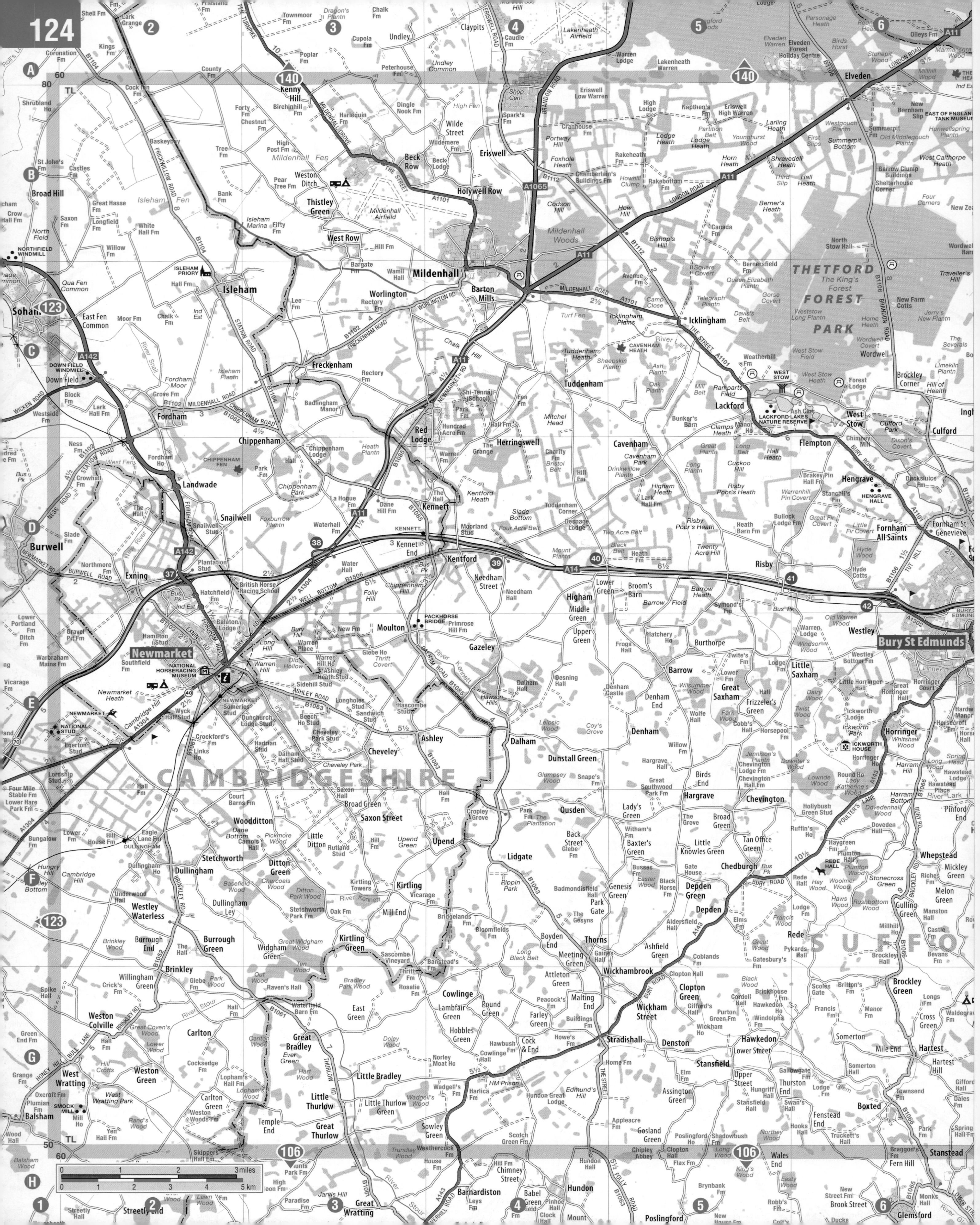

Mildenhall
Newmarket
Bury St Edmunds
Isleham
Soham
Burwell
Fordham
Chippenham
Landwade
Snailwell
Exning
Freckenham
Worlington
Barton Mills
Beck Row
Holywell Row
Eriswell
West Row
Thistley Green
Icklingham
Tuddenham
Herringswell
Red Lodge
Kennett
Kentford
Moulton
Gazeley
Higham
Cavenham
Lackford
Flempton
West Stow
Culford
Hengrave
Fornham All Saints
Risby
Westley
Little Saxham
Great Saxham
Barrow
Denham
Dalham
Ashley
Cheveley
Dunstall Green
Ousden
Hargrave
Chevington
Lidgate
Kirtling
Woodditton
Saxon Street
Stetchworth
Dullingham
Westley Waterless
Burrough Green
Brinkley
Carlton
Weston Colville
West Wratting
Balsham
Great Bradley
Little Bradley
Little Thurlow
Great Thurlow
Cowlinge
Wickhambrook
Stradishall
Denston
Stansfield
Hawkedon
Chedburgh
Depden
Rede
Whepstead
Horringer
Hartest
Boxted
Stanstead
Glemsford
Brockley Green
Barnardiston
Hundon
Poslingford
Great Wratting
Thetford Forest Park
Elveden
Wordwell
Mildenhall Woods
Cambridgeshire

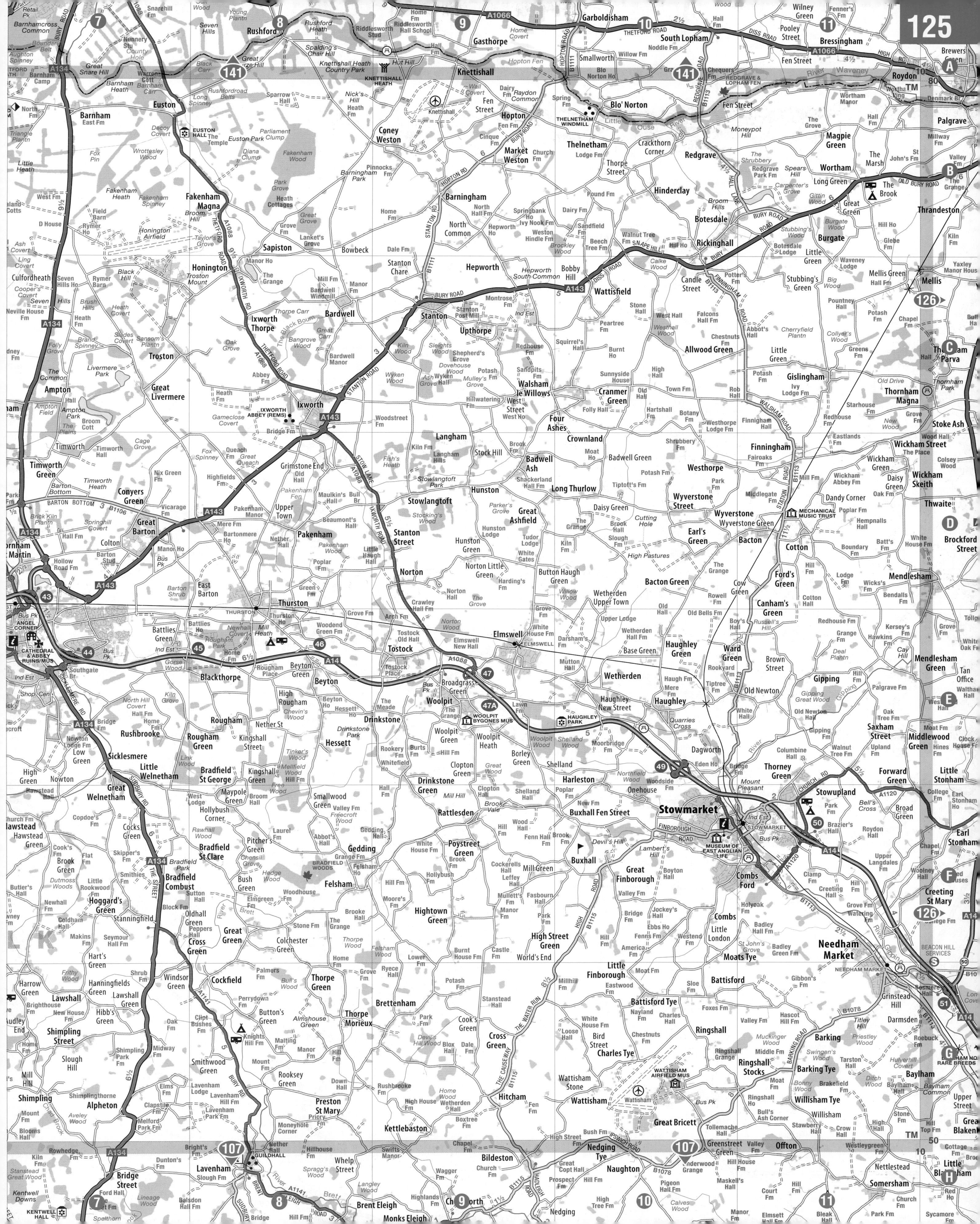

Rushford
Knettishall
Garboldisham
South Lopham
Bressingham
Roydon
Barnham
Euston
Coney Weston
Hopton
Blo' Norton
Thelnetham
Redgrave
Palgrave
Market Weston
Fakenham Magna
Barningham
Botesdale
Rickinghall
Wortham
Sapiston
Honington
Hepworth
Wattisfield
Burgate
Mellis
Thrandeston
Bardwell
Stanton
Ixworth Thorpe
Troston
Ampton
Great Livermere
Ixworth
Walsham le Willows
Cranmer Green
Gislingham
Thornham Magna
Allwood Green
Langham
Badwell Ash
Four Ashes
Finningham
Westhorpe
Wickham Skeith
Timworth Green
Conyers Green
Great Barton
Pakenham
Stowlangtoft
Great Ashfield
Long Thurlow
Wyverstone Street
Wyverstone
Bacton
Cotton
Brockford Street
Norton
Thurston
Elmswell
Bacton Green
Mendlesham
Tostock
Beyton
Haughley Green
Haughley
Wetherden
Blackthorpe
Rougham
Woolpit
Drinkstone
Hessett
Rushbrooke
Sicklesmere
Bradfield St George
Harleston
Stowmarket
Stowupland
Great Welnetham
Rattlesden
Buxhall
Gedding
Bradfield St Clare
Felsham
Great Finborough
Combs Ford
Combs
Needham Market
Bradfield Combust
Hightown Green
High Street Green
Great Green
Cockfield
Thorpe Green
Brettenham
Thorpe Morieux
Little Finborough
Battisford
Ringshall
Barking
Lawshall
Shimpling Street
Cross Green
Hitcham
Wattisham
Bildeston
Nedging Tye
Naughton
Great Bricett
Offton
Preston St Mary
Kettlebaston
Alpheton
Shimpling
Lavenham
Bridge Street
Brent Eleigh
Monks Eleigh
Somersham
A134
A143
A14
A1088
A1066
A1120
A1141
B1113
B1115
B1078
B1111
B1106
141
107
126

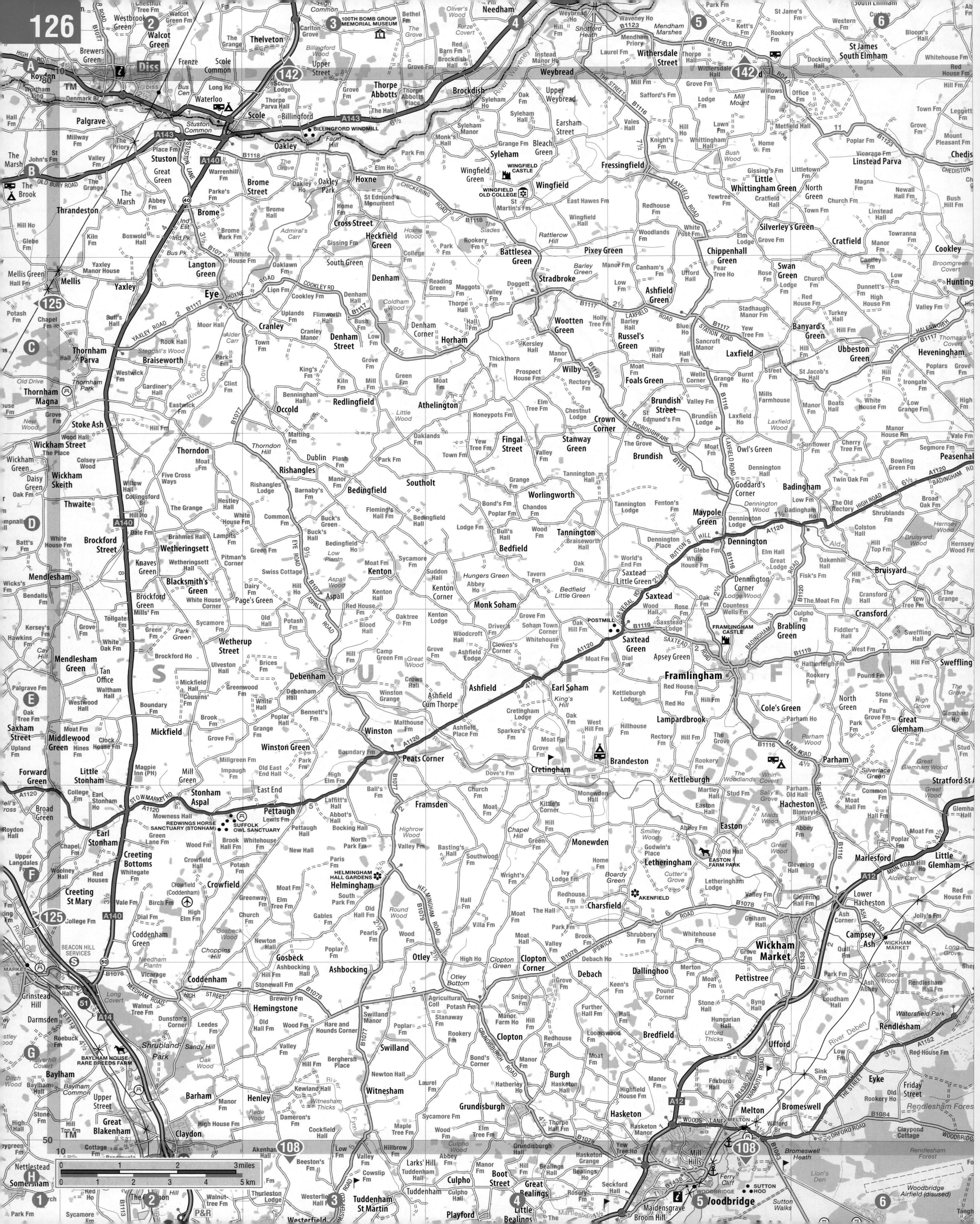
Diss
Roydon
Palgrave
Scole
Waterloo
Thelveton
Walcot Green
Brewers Green
Frenze
Scole Common
Stuston Common
Billingford
BILLINGFORD WINDMILL
Thorpe Abbotts
100TH BOMB GROUP MEMORIAL MUSEUM
Upper Street
Brockdish
Needham
Weybread
Upper Weybread
Withersdale Street
Mendham Marshes
St James South Elmham
Oakley
Stuston
Syleham
Hoxne
Fressingfield
WINGFIELD CASTLE
Wingfield Green
WINGFIELD OLD COLLEGE
Wingfield
Linstead Parva
Little Whittingham Green
Thrandeston
Brome Street
Brome
Cross Street
Heckfield Green
Battlesea Green
Pixey Green
Silverley's Green
Cratfield
Cookley
Mellis Green
Mellis
Yaxley
Langton Green
Eye
Denham
Stradbroke
Chippenhall Green
Swan Green
Ashfield Green
Huntingfield
Thornham Parva
Braiseworth
Cranley
Denham Street
Horham
Wootten Green
Russel's Green
Laxfield
Banyard's Green
Ubbeston Green
Heveningham
Thornham Magna
Occold
Redlingfield
Athelington
Wilby
Foals Green
Brundish Street
Stoke Ash
Wickham Street
Thorndon
Fingal Street
Stanway Green
Crown Corner
Brundish
Owl's Green
Peasenhall
Wickham Skeith
Rishangles
Dublin
Bedingfield
Southolt
Worlingworth
Badingham
Thwaite
Maypole Green
Brockford Street
Wetheringsett
Tannington
Bedfield
Dennington
Bruisyard
Mendlesham
Blacksmith's Green
Kenton
Aspall
Monk Soham
Saxtead Little Green
Saxtead
Cransford
Brabling Green
Wetherup Street
Saxtead Green
Apsey Green
FRAMLINGHAM CASTLE
Sweffling
Mendlesham Green
Debenham
Ashfield
Earl Soham
Framlingham
Cole's Green
North Green
Great Glemham
Mickfield
Winston
Winston Green
Lampardbrook
Middlewood Green
Peats Corner
Cretingham
Brandeston
Parham
Kettleburgh
Stratford St Andrew
Forward Green
Little Stonham
Stonham Aspal
Pettaugh
Framsden
Hacheston
REDWINGS HORSE SANCTUARY (STONHAM)
SUFFOLK OWL SANCTUARY
Earl Stonham
Creeting Bottoms
Easton
Monewden
Marlesford
Little Glemham
EASTON FARM PARK
Letheringham
HELMINGHAM HALL GARDENS
Helmingham
Crowfield
Creeting St Mary
AKENFIELD
Charsfield
Lower Hacheston
Campsey Ash
Coddenham Green
Wickham Market
Gosbeck
Ashbocking
Otley
Clopton Green
Clopton Corner
BEACON HILL SERVICES
Coddenham
Debach
Dallinghoo
Pettistree
Hemingstone
Rendlesham
BAYLHAM HOUSE RARE BREEDS FARM
Shrubland Park
Swilland
Clopton
Bredfield
Ufford
Baylham
Barham
Henley
Witnesham
Burgh
Eyke
Upper Street
Great Blakenham
Grundisburgh
Hasketon
Melton
Bromeswell
Friday Street
Rendlesham Forest
Claydon
Woodbridge Airfield (disused)
Nettlestead
Somersham
Culpho
Boot Street
Great Bealings
Little Bealings
Tuddenham
Tuddenham St Martin
Playford
Westerfield
Woodbridge
Mill Hills
SUTTON HOO
Sutton Walks
A140
A143
A1120
A12
A14
B1077
B1078
B1079
B1116
B1117
B1118
B1119
B1123
3 miles
5 km

Halesworth
Southwold
Southwold Museum
Walberswick
Blythburgh
Wangford
Reydon
Wenhaston
Holton
Spexhall
Wissett
Uggeshall
Westhall
Brampton
Stoven
Frostenden
Covehithe
South Cove
Cove Bottom
Blyford
Blackheath
Thorington
Bramfield
Walpole
Sibton
Sibton Green
Yoxford
Darsham
Westleton
Dunwich
Dunwich Underwater Exploration Museum
Dunwich Forest
Dunwich Heath
Minsmere
Middleton
Theberton
Eastbridge
Kelsale
Carlton
Saxmundham
Leiston
Leiston Abbey
Long Shop Museum
Sizewell
Knodishall
Aldringham
Thorpeness
Benhall Green
Sternfield
Friston
Farnham
Snape
Snape Maltings
Aldeburgh
Iken
Tunstall
Tunstall Forest
High Street
Sudbourne
Chillesford
Butley
Orford
Havergate Island
Orford Ness
Orfordness Havergate
Suffolk Coast and Heaths
Aldeburgh Bay
Hen Reedbeds Nature Reserve
Suffolk Coast
The Red House
North Warren
Blaxhall
A12
A144
A145
A1094
A1095
B1122
B1125
B1119
B1121
B1069
B1078
B1084
B1387
B1126
B1127
143
109
TM

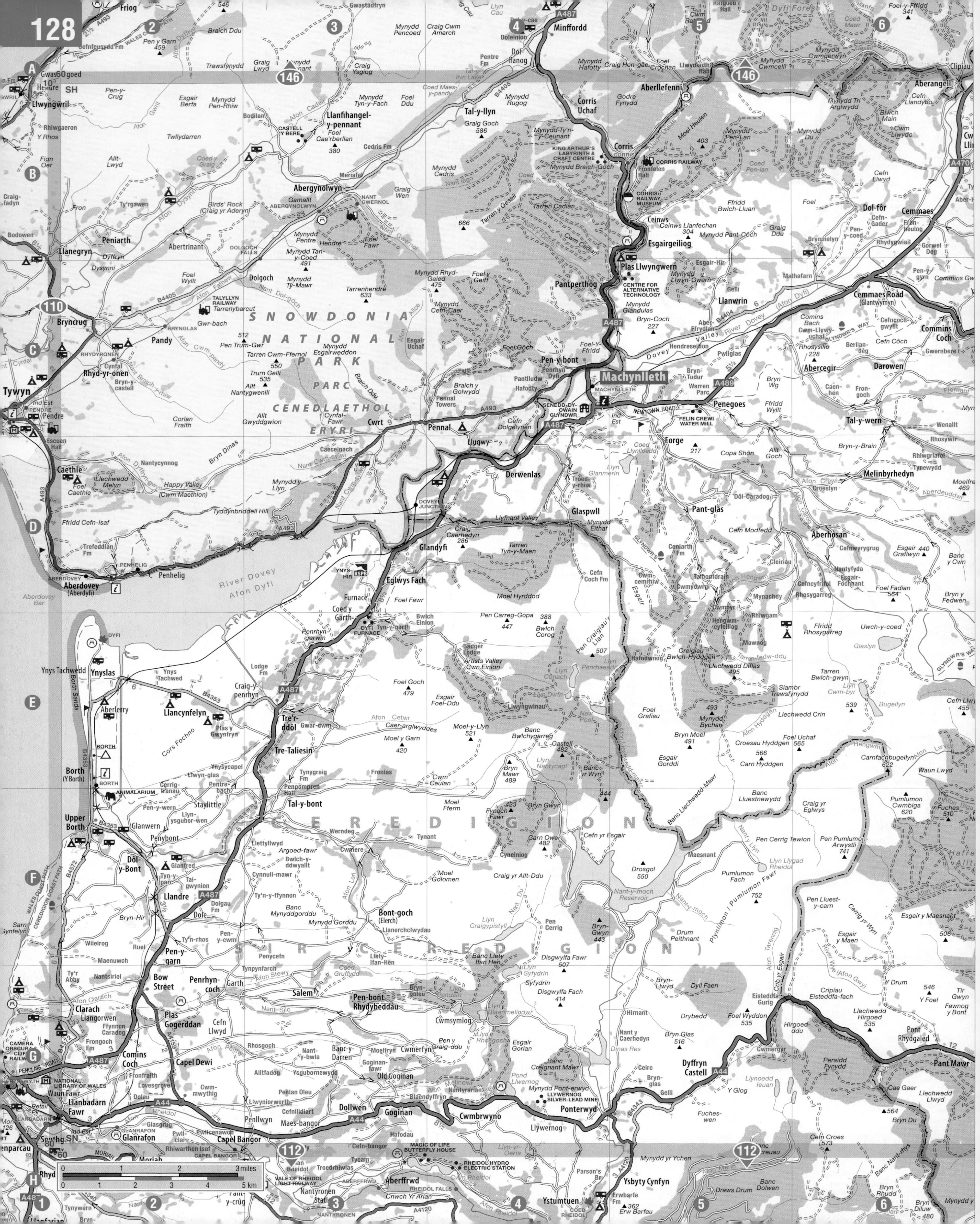
Friog
Minffordd
Corris Uchaf
Aberllefenni
Aberangell
Llwyngwril
Tal-y-llyn
Llanfihangel-y-pennant
Castell y Bere
Corris
King Arthur's Labyrinth & Craft Centre
Corris Railway
Corris Railway Museum
Abergynolwyn
Nant Gwernol
Peniarth
Llanegryn
Abertrinant
Dolgoch
Talyllyn Railway
Esgairgeiliog
Plas Llwyngwern
Centre for Alternative Technology
Pantperthog
Llanwrin
Cemmaes
Dol-fôr
Cemmaes Road (Glantwymyn)
Commins Coch
Bryncrug
Pandy
Snowdonia National Park
Parc Cenedlaethol Eryri
Rhyd-yr-onen
Tywyn
Pendre
Pen-y-bont
Machynlleth
Senedd-dy-Owain Glyndwr
Felin Crewi Water Mill
Penegoes
Abercegir
Darowen
Tal-y-wern
Pennal
Cwrt
Forge
Derwenlas
Melinbyrhedyn
Caethle
Happy Valley (Cwm Maethlon)
Dovey Junction
Glaspwll
Pant-glas
Aberhosan
Glandyfi
Eglwys Fach
Aberdovey (Aberdyfi)
Penhelig
River Dovey
Afon Dyfi
Aberdovey Bar
Furnace
Dyfi Furnace
Ynys-hir RSPB
Moel Hyrddod
Ynyslas
Ynys Tachwedd
Borth Sands
Llancynfelyn
Tre'r-ddôl
Tre-Taliesin
Cors Fochno
Borth (Y Borth)
Animalarium
Tal-y-bont
Upper Borth
Ceredigion
Dôl-y-Bont
Llandre
Bont-goch (Elerch)
Pen-y-garn
Bow Street
Penrhyn-coch
Salem
Pen-bont Rhydybeddau
Clarach
Llangorwen
Plas Gogerddan
Comins Coch
Capel Dewi
National Library of Wales
Waun Fawr
Llanbadarn Fawr
Penglais Road
Glanrafon
Capel Bangor
Dollwen
Goginan
Cwmbrwyno
Ponterwyd
Llywernog Silver-Lead Mine
Nant-y-moch Reservoir
Pumlumon Fach
Pen Pumlumon-Arwystli 741
Plynlimon / Pumlumon Fawr 752
Dyffryn Castell
Eisteddfa Gurig
Pant Mawr
Ysbyty Cynfyn
Ystumtuen
Aberffrwd
Magic of Life Butterfly House
Rheidol Hydro Electric Station
Vale of Rheidol Light Railway
Rheidol Falls
Nantyronen Station
Devil's Bridge
Sir Ceredigion
Glyndŵr's Way
Wales Coast Path
Ceredigion Coast Path
Dyfi Forest
0 1 2 3 miles
0 1 2 3 4 5 km

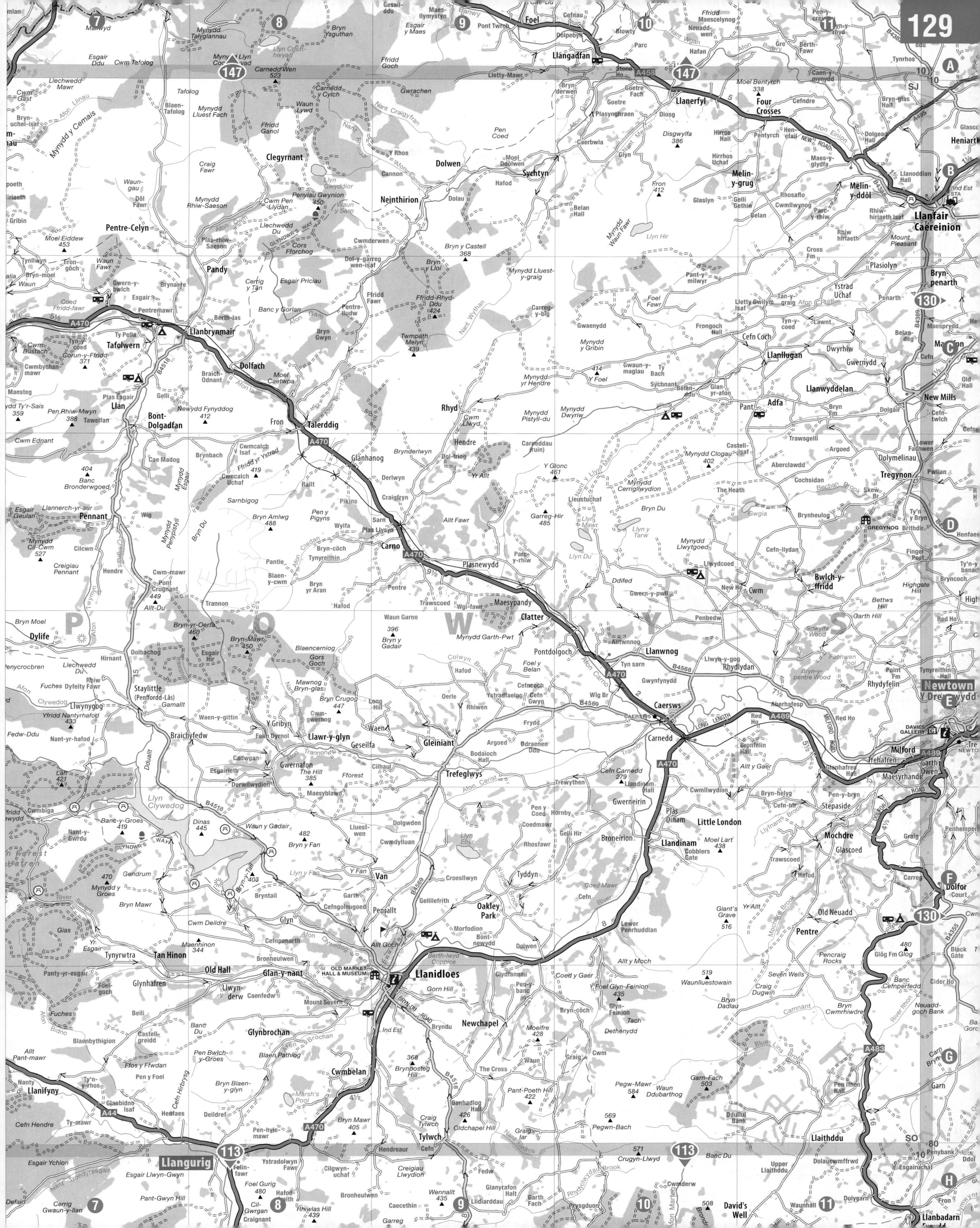

147
113
130
A470
A458
A489
A483
A44
B4518
B4568
B4569
B4390
B4389
B4355
POWYS
Newtown
Y Drenewydd
Llanidloes
OLD MARKET HALL & MUSEUM
Llangurig
Llanfair Caereinion
Caersws
Carno
Talerddig
Llanbrynmair
Llangadfan
Llanerfyl
Foel
Four Crosses
Melin-y-ddôl
Melin-y-grug
Llanllugan
Llanwyddelan
Adfa
Tregynon
GREGYNOG
Bwlch-y-ffridd
New Mills
Milford
Garth Owen
Maesyrhandir
Stepaside
Mochdre
Dolfor
Llandinam
Little London
Trefeglwys
Gleiniant
Llawr-y-glyn
Staylittle (Penffordd-Lâs)
Dylife
Llwynygog
Pennant
Bont-Dolgadfan
Llan
Tafolwern
Dolfach
Pandy
Pentre-Celyn
Clegyrnant
Dolwen
Sychtyn
Neinthirion
Rhyd
Hendre
Clatter
Maesypandy
Pontdolgoch
Llanwnog
Rhydlydan
Rhydyfelin
Carnedd
Van
Penrallt
Oakley Park
Newchapel
Glan-y-nant
Old Hall
Tan Hinon
Tynyrwtra
Llanifyny
Cwmbelan
Tylwch
Glynbrochan
Llaithddu
Pentre
Old Neuadd
DAVIES GALLERY
Llyn Clywedog
Mynydd Talyglannau
Carnedd Wen 523
Penylan Gwynion 450
Moel Eiddew 453
Corun-y-Ffridd 371
Newydd Fynyddog 412
Pen Rhiw-Mwyn 388
Twmpath Melyn 439
Ffridd-Rhyd-Ddu 424
Bryn Amlwg 488
Mynydd Cil-Cwm 527
Bryn-yr-Oerfa 460
Bryn-Mawr 450
Garreg-Hir 485
Y Glonc 461
Mynydd Clogau 402
Disgwylfa 386
Fron 412
Moel Bentyrch 338
Cefn Carnedd 279
Moel Lart 438
Giant's Grave 516
Pegwn-Mawr 584
Pegwn-Bach
Garn-Fach 503
Crugyn-Llwyd 571
Foel Glyn-Feinion 435
Moelfre 428
Pant-Poeth Hill 422
Bryn Mawr 405
Banhadlog Hall 426
Brynposteg Hill 368
Dinas 445
Banc-y-Groes 419
Mynydd y Groes 470
Bryn y Fan 482
GLYNDŴR'S WAY
Mynydd Garth-Pwt
Waun Garno 396
Bryn y Gadair
Maenhinon 344
Wennallt 435
Rhiwlas Hill 439
Foel Gurig 480
David's Well 508
Waunlluestowain 519
Banc Du
River Severn
Afon Clywedog
Afon Trannon
Afon Cerist
Afon Carno
Afon Iaen
Afon Gam
Afon Banwy
Afon Rhiw
Bechan Brook
Mochdre Brook
Blue Lins Brook
River Ithon
Llyn Hir
Llyn Ebyr
Llyn y Tarw
Llyn Du
Marsh's Pool
Fachwen Pool
Cwm Tafolog
Mynydd y Cemais
Esgair Ychion
Ty'n-y-rhos
Glanbidno Isaf
Cefn Hendre
Hendreaur
Ystradolwyn Fawr
Cilgwyn-uchaf
Fedw
Glanyrafon Halt
Garth Fm
Prysgduon
Lower Penrhuddlan
Coed Mawr
Broneirion
Plas Dinam
Cobblers Gate
Gwernerin
Bronfelin Hall
Aberhafesp
Red Ho
Trehafren
Glanhafren Hall
Penhempen
SJ
SO

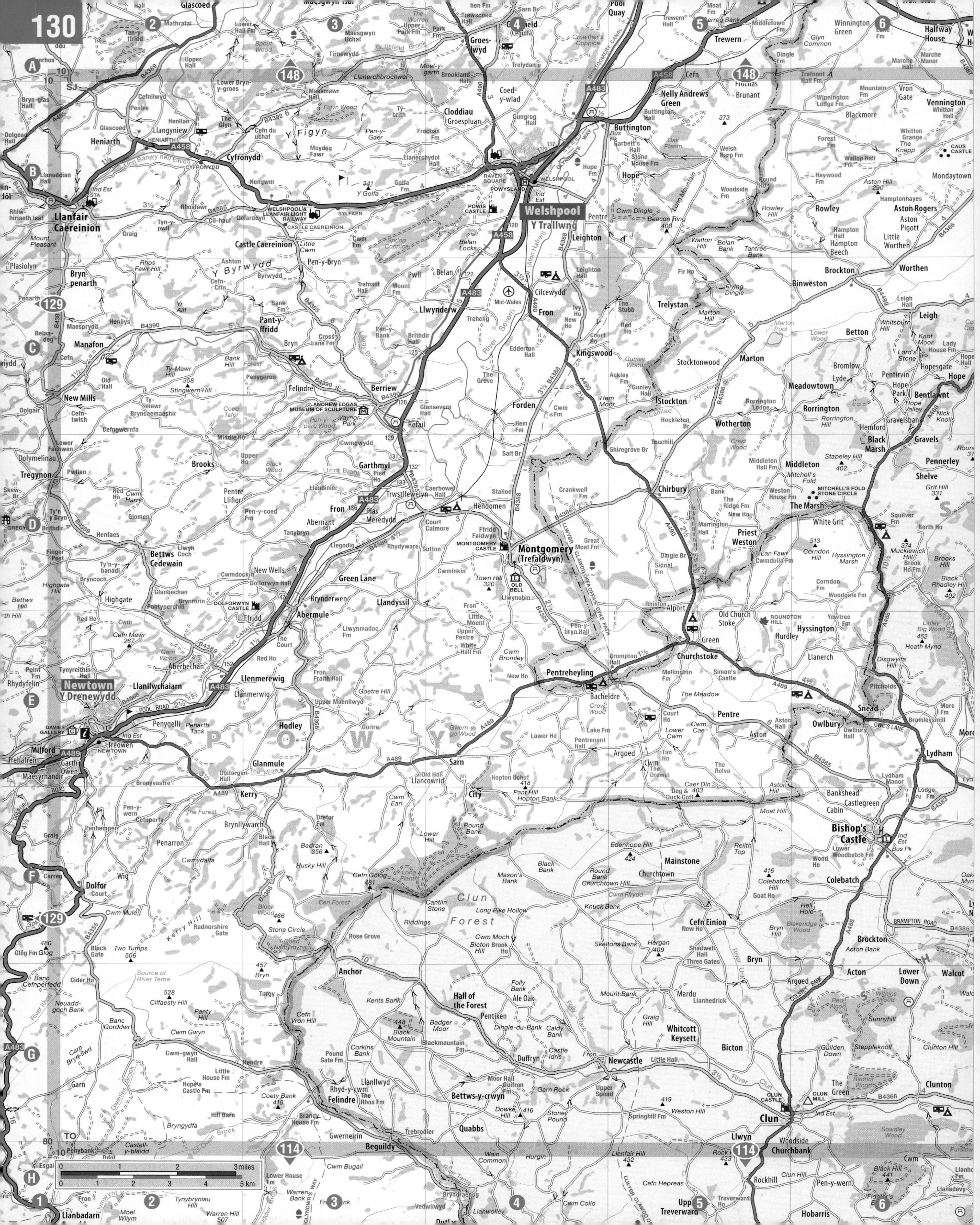

Welshpool
Y Trallwng
Llanfair Caereinion
Newtown
Y Drenewydd
Montgomery
(Trefaldwyn)
Bishop's Castle
Clun
Chirbury
Churchstoke
Kerry
Abermule
Berriew
Forden
Buttington
Leighton
Kingswood
Marton
Worthen
Brockton
Heniarth
Cyfronydd
Castle Caereinion
Manafon
New Mills
Tregynon
Bettws Cedewain
Garthmyl
Llandyssil
Sarn
Dolfor
Milford
Pentreheyling
Lydham
Snead
Mainstone
Newcastle
Bettws-y-crwyn
Felindre
Anchor
Beguildy
Colebatch
Clunton
Whitcott Keysett
Hyssington
Priest Weston
Middleton
The Marsh
Clun Forest
Kerry Hill
Long Mountain
Y Figyn
Y Byrwydd
P O W Y S
Mid-Wales
River Severn
Camlad
River Clun
River Teme
Montgomery Canal
Shropshire Union Canal
Glyndŵr's Way
Offa's Dyke Path
Powis Castle
Montgomery Castle
Dolforwyn Castle
Clun Castle
Andrew Logan Museum of Sculpture
Mitchell's Fold Stone Circle
A458
A483
A490
A489
A488
B4385
B4386
B4388
148
129
114
3 miles
5 km

Rowton
Cardeston
Hortonlane
Porthill
Kingsland
Belle Vue
Preston
Frogmore
Charlton
Meole Brace
Emstrey
Norton
Aston
Westbury
Yockleton
Cruckton
Cruckmeole
Hanwood
Redhill
Bayston Hill
Weeping Cross
Atcham
Uppington
Stoney Stretton
Edge
Lea
Hinwood
Farley
Hinton
Shorthill
Arscott
Annscroft
Great Lyth
Lythbank
Old Coppice
Little Lyth
Wroxeter
Donnington
Rushton
Westley
Asterley
Pontesbury
Pontesford
Malehurst
Pleasley
Longden
Exfords Green
Chatford
Condover
Berrington
Cantlop
Cross Houses
Longwood
Eaton Constantine
Dryton
Leighton
Minsterley
Oaks
Stapleton
Great Ryton
Little Ryton
Wheathall
Pitchford
Golding
Cound
Cressage
Ploxgreen
Habberley
Wrentnall
Church Pulverbatch
Pulverbatch
Dorrington
Acton Pigott
Acton Burnell
Snailbeach
Crowsnest
Westcott
Frodesley
Longnor
Harley
Stiperstones
Picklescott
Smethcott
Walkmills
Leebotwood
Ruckley
Kenley
Woolstaston
Betchcott
Church Preen
Hughley
Stretton Westwood
The Bog
Ratlinghope
Hollyhurst
Comley
Presthope
Bridges
All Stretton
Enchmarsh
Plaish
Cardington
Gretton
Willstone
Easthopewood
Bourton
Medlicott
Church Stretton
Longville in the Dale
Eastbope
Patton
Norbury
Wentnor
Hope Bowdler
Wall Bank
Wall under Heywood
Rushbury
Brockton
Weston
Little Stretton
Minton
Soudley
Ragdon
Chelmick
Ticklerton
Shipton
Stanton Long
Asterton
Marshbrook
Acton Scott
Hatton
Eaton
Broadstone
Holdgate
Myndtown
Whittingslow
Harton
Middlehope
Little London
Ditton Priors
Lea
Eaton
Choulton
Plowden
Woolston
Alcaston
Westhope
Munslow
Aston Munslow
Tugford
Abdon
Horderley
Wistanstow
Upper Affcot
Strefford
Diddlebury
Corfton
Boulden
Peaton
Upper Heath
Edgton
Cheny Longville
Lower Dinchope
Clee St Margaret
Newington
Halford
Hopesay
Sibdon Carwood
Seifton
Culmington
Great Sutton
Stoke St Milborough
Kempton
Aston on Clun
Craven Arms
Norton
Little Brampton
Stokesay
Broome
Hayton's Bent
Purslow
Clunbury
Vernolds Common
Cleedownton
Hopton Cangeford
Twitchen
Brandhill
Onibury
Stanton Lacy
Clungunford
Abcott
Shelderton
Wootton
Cleeton St Mary
Hopton Castle
SHROPSHIRE
SHROPSHIRE HILLS
The Long Mynd
Wenlock Edge
Corve Dale
A5
A49
A458
A488
B4368
B4371
B4370
B4365
132
149
115

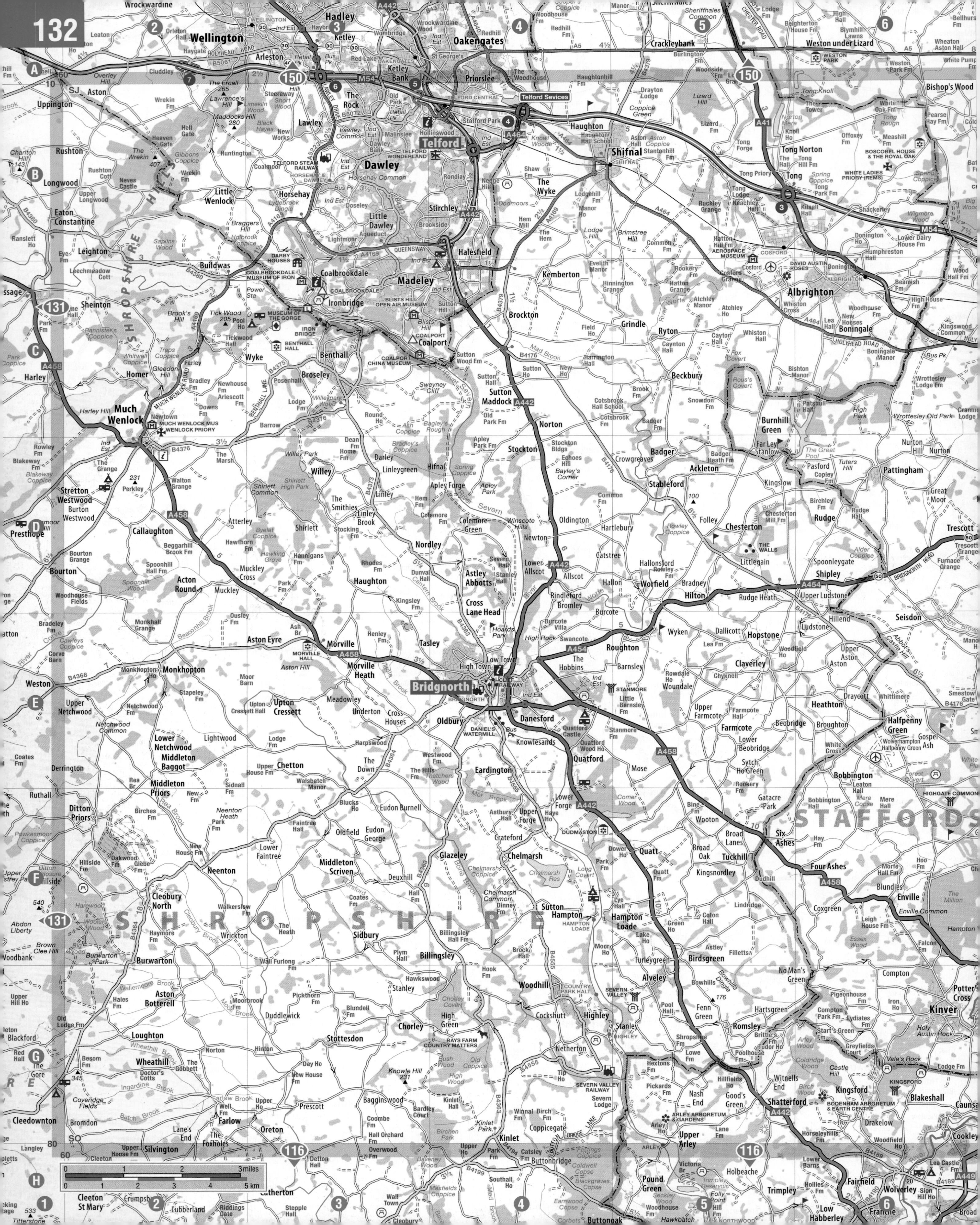
Wellington
Hadley
Ketley
Oakengates
Telford
Dawley
Shifnal
Weston under Lizard
Tong
Albrighton
Little Wenlock
Horsehay
Coalbrookdale
Ironbridge
Madeley
Buildwas
Much Wenlock
Broseley
Benthall
Coalport
Kemberton
Brockton
Grindle
Ryton
Beckbury
Boningale
Sutton Maddock
Norton
Stockton
Badger
Ackleton
Stableford
Chesterton
Pattingham
Rudge
Shipley
Trescott
Worfield
Hilton
Roughton
Seisdon
Bridgnorth
Morville
Aston Eyre
Monkhopton
Upton Cressett
Oldbury
Danesford
Quatford
Eardington
Claverley
Heathton
Bobbington
Six Ashes
Four Ashes
Enville
Kinver
Quatt
Chelmarsh
Glazeley
Middleton Scriven
Neenton
Cleobury North
Sidbury
Billingsley
Highley
Alveley
Romsley
Kingsford
Blakeshall
Woodhill
Chorley
Stottesdon
Kinlet
Upper Arley
Shatterford
Wolverley
Burwarton
Aston Botterell
Loughton
Wheathill
Farlow
Oreton
Cleedownton
Silvington
Cleeton St Mary
Ditton Priors
Middleton Priors
Callaughton
Acton Round
Muckley Cross
Stretton Westwood
Presthope
Harley
Homer
Sheinton
Leighton
Eaton Constantine
Uppington
Aston
Rushton
Longwood
Shirlett
Willey
Nordley
Astley Abbotts
Haughton
Tasley
Cross Lane Head
SHROPSHIRE
STAFFORDS
M54
A442
A458
A454
A5
131
150
116
A
B
C
D
E
F
G
H
1
2
3
4
5
6
0 1 2 3 miles
0 1 2 3 4 5 km

Cannock
Heath Hayes
Burntwood
Chasetown
Brewood
Cheslyn Hay
Great Wyrley
Brownhills
Codsall
Wolverhampton
Wednesfield
Willenhall
Walsall
Aldridge
Streetly
Bilston
Darlaston
Wednesbury
Great Barr
Kingstanding
Sedgley
Coseley
Tipton
West Bromwich
Handsworth
Wombourne
Dudley
Oldbury
Smethwick
Birmingham
Kingswinford
Brierley Hill
Rowley Regis
Wordsley
Stourbridge
Halesowen
Harborne
Edgbaston
Selly Oak
Bournville
Northfield
King's Norton
King's Heath
Moseley
Aston
Erdington
The Black Country
WEST
MIDLANDS
Hilton Park Services
Norton Canes Services
Frankley Services

Lichfield
Streethay
Huddlesford
Elford
Edingale
Harlaston
Haunton
Clifton Campville
Chilcote
Measham
Appleby Magna
Appleby Parva
Leomansley
Whittington
Hademore
Wigginton
Thorpe Constantine
No Man's Heath
Newton Regis
Seckington
Austrey
Norton-Juxta-Twycross
Twycross
Wall
Hopwas
Leyfields
Tamworth
Shuttington
Alvecote
Amington
Shenstone
Weeford
Hints
Bonehill
Fazeley
Glascote
Polesworth
Warton
Orton-on-the-Hill
Little Orton
Little Hay
Footherley
Watford Gap
Drayton Bassett
Dosthill
Wilnecote
Birchmoor
Dordon
St Helena
Grendon
Sheepy Magna
Sheepy Parva
Little Aston
Streetly
Four Oaks
Roughley
Hill
Middleton
Grendon Common
Baddesley Ensor
Atherstone
Witherley
Mancetter
Sutton Coldfield
Kingsbury
Wood End
Hurley
Baxterley
Bentley
Ridge Lane
Oldbury
Hartshill
Boldmere
New Oscott
Wylde Green
Walmley
Wishaw
Over Green
Lea Marston
Bodymoor Heath
Marston
Whiteacre Heath
Nether Whitacre
Church End
Ansley
Galley Common
Chapel End
Stockingford
Erdington
Pype Hayes
Minworth
Curdworth
Water Orton
Shustoke
Furnace End
Over Whitacre
Old Arley
New Arley
Astley
Castle Bromwich
Coleshill
Tyburn
Gravelly Hill
Nechells
Washwood Heath
Saltley
Kitt's Green
Tile Cross
Chelmsley Wood
Maxstoke
Fillongley
Corley Ash
Corley
Bedworth Heath
Birmingham
Yardley
Sheldon
Marston Green
Kinwalsey
Chapel Green
Corley Moor
Ash Green
Keresley
Sparkbrook
Sparkhill
Moseley
Acock's Green
Elmdon
Middle Bickenhill
Little Packington
Butler's End
Hollyberry End
Hawkes End
Olton
Bickenhill
Stonebridge
Meriden
Pinkett's Booth
Coundon
Hall Green
Springfield
Elmdon Heath
Hampton in Arden
Four Oaks
Allesley
Eastern Green
Catherine-de-Barnes
Hook End
Berkswell
Eastcote
Whoberley
Coventry
Solihull
Shirley
Copt Heath
Barston
Tile Hill
Earlsdon
STAFFS
WARWICKSHIRE
WEST MIDLANDS
LE
M6 TOLL
M42
M6
A5
A38
A51
A446
A452
A45
Tamworth Services
Corley Services
0 1 2 3 miles
0 1 2 3 4 5 km

THE NATIONAL FOREST
LEICESTERSHIRE
Ibstock
Ellistown
Heather
Swepstone
Stanton under Bardon
Markfield
Newtown Linford
Anstey
Thurcaston
Cropston
Birstall
Wanlip
Newton Burgoland
Battram
Bagworth
Thornton
Field Head
Groby
Odstone
Nailstone
Shackerstone
Barton in the Beans
Barlestone
Congerstone
Carlton
Bilstone
Ratby
Glenfield
Leicester
Botcheston
Newtown Unthank
Kirby Muxloe
Leicester Forest East
Market Bosworth
Newbold Verdon
Desford
Wellsborough
Cadeby
Peckleton
Braunstone Town
Shenton
Sutton Cheney
Kirkby Mallory
Aylestone
Knighton
Upton
Stapleton
Thurlaston
Enderby
Glen Parva
South Wigston
Dadlington
Earl Shilton
Normanton Turville
Narborough
Huncote
Whetstone
Blaby
Stoke Golding
Barwell
Elmesthorpe
Potters Marston
Littlethorpe
Cosby
Countesthorpe
Higham on the Hill
Croft
Stoney Stanton
Sutton in the Elms
Hinckley
Weddington
Nuneaton
Burbage
Aston Flamville
Sapcote
Primethorpe
Broughton Astley
Willoughby Waterleys
Peatling Magna
Sketchley
Sharnford
Attleborough
Whitestone
Burton Hastings
Smockington
Frolesworth
Leire
Dunton Bassett
Ashby Magna
Bruntingthorpe
Peatling Parva
Wigston Parva
Claybrooke Magna
Claybrooke Parva
Copston Magna
Wolvey Heath
Ashby Parva
Gilmorton
Griff
Bramcote
Shelford
Wolvey
Wibtoft
Ullesthorpe
Bedworth
Weston in Arden
Ryton
Bulkington
Cloudesley Bush
Bitteswell
Kimcote
Walton
Exhall
Hollyhurst
Lutterworth
Hawkesbury
Barnacle
Shilton
Hopsford
Withybrook
Monks Kirby
Willey
Little Walton
Cross in Hand
Misterton
Walcote
Ansty
Pailton
Street Ashton
Cotesbach
South Kilworth
Foleshill
Walsgrave on Sowe
Stretton under Fosse
Churchover
Gibbet Hill
Shawell
Wyken
Brinklow
Easenhall
Harborough Magna
Swinford
Stanford on Avon
Binley
Cathiron
Newton
Catthorpe
M1
M69
M6
A5
A47
A46
A426
A4303
B4114
153
136
119
7
8
9
10
11

Syston
Barsby
Ashby Folville
Thorpe Satchville
Burrough on the Hill
Somerby
Cold Overton
Langham
Barkby
Twyford
South Croxton
Barleythorpe
Birstall
Thurmaston
John O'Gaunt
Newbold
Knossington
Oakham
Beeby
Marefield
Owston
Hungarton
Lowesby
Braunston-in-Rutland
Keyham
Cold Newton
Tilton on the Hill
Halstead
New Humberstone
Humberstone
Scraptoft
Belgrave
Leicester
Crown Hills
North Evington
Bushby
Evington
Thurnby
Houghton on the Hill
Billesdon
Skeffington
Loddington
Ridlington
Stoneygate
Stoughton
Knighton
Oadby
Frisby
Gaulby
Tugby
Belton in Rutland
East Norton
Allexton
Wardley
Little Stretton
King's Norton
Illston on the Hill
Rolleston
Wigston
Goadby
Noseley
Great Glen
South Wigston
Newton Harcourt
Burton Overy
Carlton Curlieu
Stockerston
The Woodlands
Shangton
Hallaton
Horninghold
Glooston
Kilby Bridge
LEICESTERSHIRE
Wistow
Kilby
Stonton Wyville
Cranoe
Blaston
Kibworth Harcourt
Tur Langton
Bulwick
Fleckney
Slawston
Peatling Magna
Smeeton Westerby
Kibworth Beauchamp
Church Langton
Medbourne
Arnesby
Saddington
East Langton
Thorpe Langton
Welham
Weston by Welland
Drayton
Shearsby
Bruntingthorpe
Gumley
Foxton
Sutton Bassett
Ashley
Peatling Parva
Mowsley
Middleton
Laughton
Great Bowden
East Carlton
Wilbarston
Dingley
Stoke Albany
Walton
Lubenham
Little Bowden
Brampton Ash
Market Harborough
Carlton Purlieus
Theddingworth
Marston Trussell
Pipewell
East Farndon
Braybrooke
Husbands Bosworth
Great Oxendon
Rushton
North Kilworth
Sibbertoft
Desborough
South Kilworth
Clipston
Arthingworth
Rothwell
Welford
Thorpe Underwood
Harrington
Kelmarsh
Thorpe Malsor
Orton
Naseby
Loddington
A6
A47
A427
A508
A14
A4304
A5199
A607
A6030
A563
A606
B6047
B664
154
135
120
NOR
miles
km

Exton
Burley
Oakham
Oakham Castle
Rutland County Museum
Vale of Catmose
Barnsdale
Whitwell
Empingham
Rutland Water
Upper Hambleton
Egleton
Normanton
Edith Weston
Manton
Lyndon
Wing
Preston
North Luffenham
South Luffenham
Pilton
Ayston
Glaston
Morcott
Barrowden
Tixover
Uppingham
Bisbrooke
Seaton
Lyddington
Thorpe by Water
Harringworth
Caldecott
Gretton
Rockingham
Corby
Great Oakley
Little Oakley
Stanion
Brigstock
Geddington
Newton
Weekley
Warkton
Kettering
Grafton Underwood
Sudborough
Lowick
Slipton
Twywell
Islip
Thrapston
Titchmarsh
Tickencote
Great Casterton
Little Casterton
Ryhall
Belmesthorpe
Stamford
Tinwell
Ketton
Aldgate
Geeston
Easton on the Hill
Wothorpe
Collyweston
Duddington
Wakerley
Laxton
Blatherwycke
Bulwick
Deene
Deenethorpe
King's Cliffe
Apethorpe
Woodnewton
Nassington
Yarwell
Wansford
Stibbington
Sutton
Sibson
Water Newton
Elton
Fotheringhay
Southwick
Glapthorn
Cotterstock
Tansor
Warmington
Eaglethorpe
Oundle
Ashton
Polebrook
Lutton
Hemington
Barnwell
Barnwell St Andrew
Barnwell All Saints
Pilton
Wadenhoe
Achurch
Aldwincle
Thorpe Waterville
Wigsthorpe
Thurning
Luddington in the Brook
Clopton
Winwick
Upper Benefield
Lower Benefield
Great Weldon
Little Weldon
Stoke Doyle
Wittering
Thornhaugh
Southorpe
Barnack
Ufford
Bainton
Pilsgate
Uffington
Tallington
West Deeping
Barholm
Greatford
Upton
Burghley House
Rockingham Motor Speedway
A1
A47
A43
A6003
A606
A6121
A427
A6116
A605
A6086
NORTHAMPTONSHIRE

Market Deeping
Deeping St James
Towngate
Crowland
Northborough
Deeping Gate
West Deeping
Tallington
Maxey
Etton
Peakirk
Glinton
Helpston
Bainton
Ashton
Ufford
Upton
Newborough
PETERBOROUGH
Thorney
Thorney Toll
Eye
Eye Green
Werrington
Gunthorpe
Walton
Paston
Marholm
New England
Dogsthorpe
Bretton
Ravensthorpe
Millfield
Eastfield
Newark
Westwood
Longthorpe
Fengate
Peterborough
Woodston
Castor
Ailsworth
Sutton
Stibbington
Water Newton
Orton Wistow
Alwalton
Chesterton
Orton Waterville
Orton Longueville
Orton Malborne
Orton Brimbles
Orton Goldhay
Orton Southgate
Old Fletton
Stanground
Farcet
Hampton Hargate
Elton
Over End
Haddon
Morborne
Yaxley
Norman Cross
Folksworth
Stilton
Washingley
Caldecote
Denton
Holme
Conington
Glatton
Sawtry
Hemington
Luddington in the Brook
Great Gidding
Little Gidding
Steeple Gidding
Winwick
Coppingford
Hamerton
Whittlesey
Coates
Eastrea
Turves
Eldernell
Inham's End
Pondersbridge
Ramsey Mereside
Ramsey St Mary's
Ramsey Heights
Ramsey Forty Foot
Ramsey
Benwick
Bury
Upwood
Great Raveley
Little Raveley
Wood Walton
Church End
Wistow
Warboys
Wennington
Fenton
Chapel Head
Abbots Ripton
Bedford Level
North Level
CAMBRIDGESHIRE
Stone Bridge Corner
North Side
Peterborough Services
FLAG FEN BRONZE AGE EXCAVATIONS
NENE VALLEY RAILWAY
FERRY MEADOWS
SACREWELL FARM & COUNTRY CENTRE
EAST OF ENGLAND SHOWGROUND
CROWN LAKES
PETERBOROUGH MUSEUM
HAMERTON ZOO PARK
MONKS WOOD
RURAL MUSEUM
RAMSEY ABBEY GATEHOUSE
WOODWALTON FEN
HOLME FEN
UPWOOD MEADOWS
Peterborough (Conington)
Peterborough (Sibson)
Upwood Airfield (disused)
0 1 2 3 miles
0 1 2 3 4 5 km

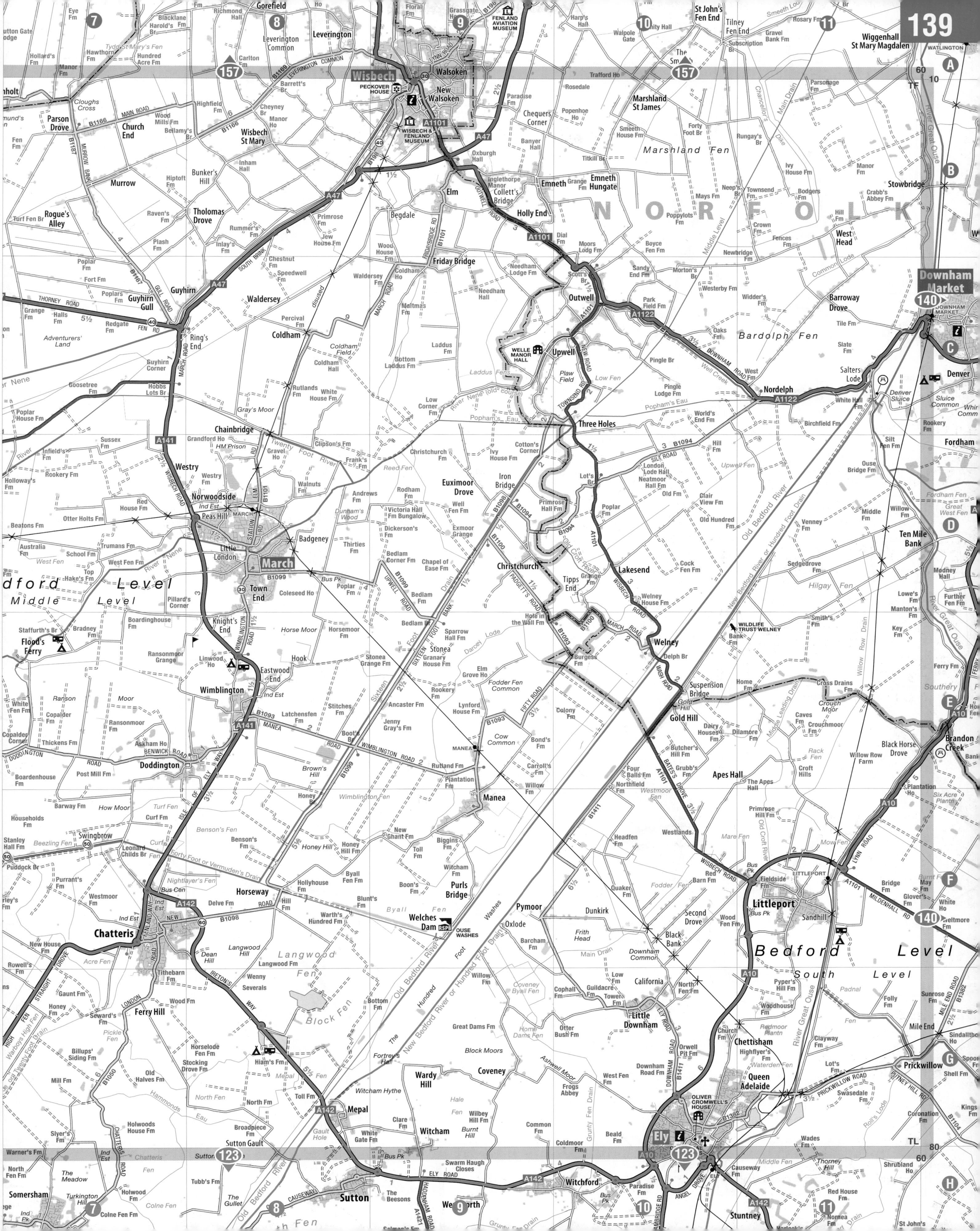
Gorefield
Leverington
Wisbech
Walsoken
New Walsoken
PECKOVER HOUSE
WISBECH & FENLAND MUSEUM
FENLAND AVIATION MUSEUM
St John's Fen End
Tilney Fen End
Wiggenhall St Mary Magdalen
Walpole Gate
Marshland St James
Marshland Fen
Parson Drove
Church End
Wisbech St Mary
Murrow
Tholomas Drove
Rogue's Alley
Guyhirn
Guyhirn Gull
Elm
Emneth
Emneth Hungate
Holly End
Friday Bridge
Outwell
Upwell
WELLE MANOR HALL
Stowbridge
N O R F O L K
West Head
Downham Market
Barroway Drove
Bardolph Fen
Nordelph
Salters Lode
Denver
Denver Sluice
Ring's End
Coldham
Waldersey
Chainbridge
Three Holes
Westry
Norwoodside
Peas Hill
March
Little London
Town End
Badgeney
Euximoor Drove
Iron Bridge
Christchurch
Tipps End
Lakesend
Welney
WILDLIFE TRUST WELNEY
Fordham
Ten Mile Bank
Hilgay Fen
Bedford Level
Middle Level
Flood's Ferry
Knight's End
Wimblington
Eastwood End
Stonea
Hook
Doddington
Manea
Gold Hill
Suspension Bridge
Apes Hall
Brandon Creek
Black Horse Drove
Littleport
Sandhill
Swingbrow
Chatteris
Horseway
Welches Dam
OUSE WASHES
Pymoor
Oxlode
Purls Bridge
Black Bank
Second Drove
Bedford Level
South Level
California
Little Downham
Ferry Hill
Langwood Fen
Block Fen
Coveney
Wardy Hill
Mepal
Witcham
Chettisham
Queen Adelaide
Prickwillow
Mile End
OLIVER CROMWELL'S HOUSE
Ely
Sutton Gault
Sutton
Somersham
Witchford
Wentworth
Stuntney
Old Bedford River
New Bedford River or Hundred Foot Drain
River Great Ouse
Sixteen Foot Drain
Forty Foot or Vermuden's Drain
A47
A141
A142
A1101
A1122
A10
B1098
B1099
B1093
B1100
B1094
B1411
B1382
B1104
B1050
B1166
B1167
B1169
B1187
157
140
123

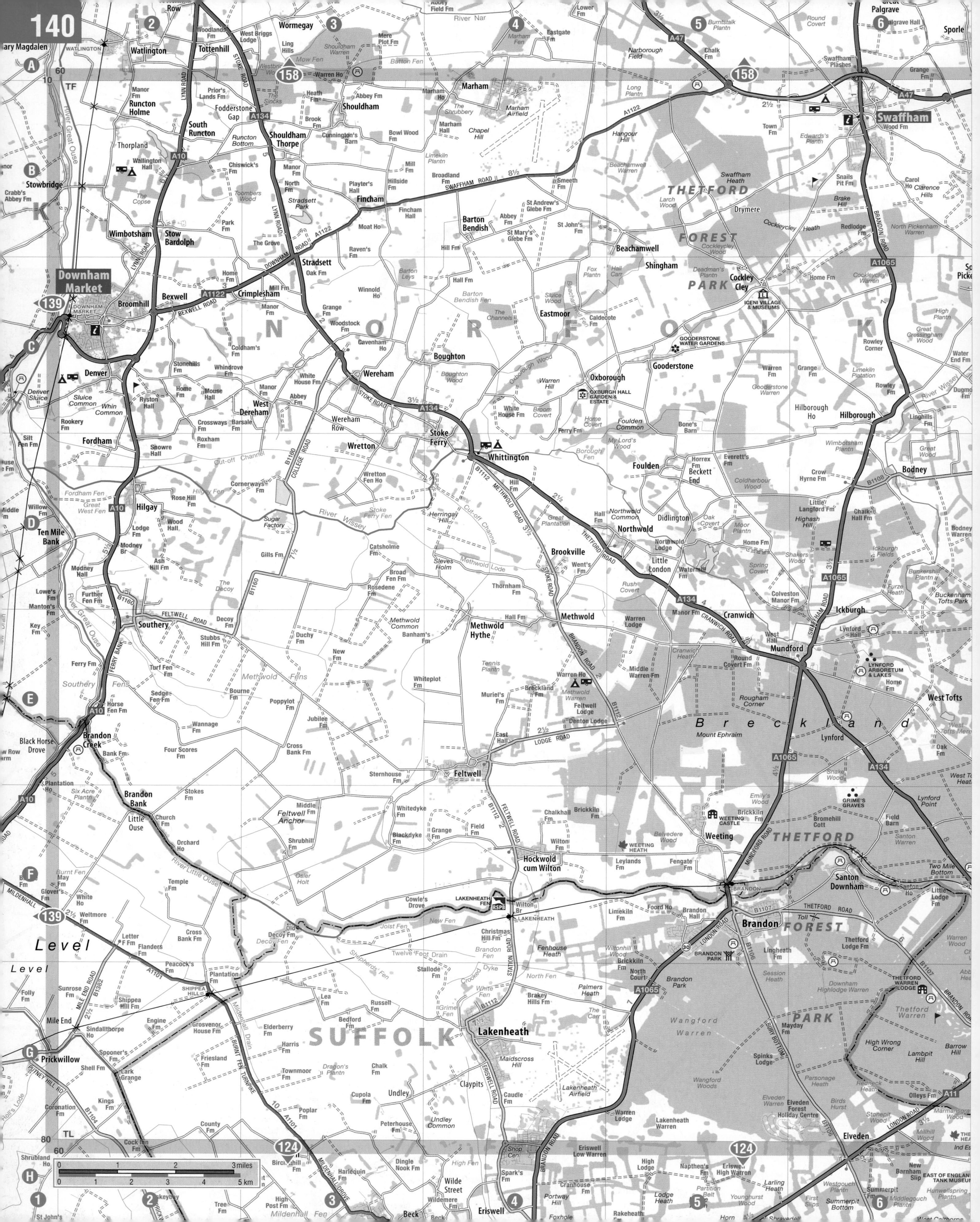

Downham Market
Swaffham
Watlington
Tottenhill
Wormegay
Marham
Runcton Holme
South Runcton
Shouldham
Shouldham Thorpe
Stowbridge
Wimbotsham
Stow Bardolph
Fincham
Barton Bendish
Stradsett
Crimplesham
Bexwell
Broomhill
Beachamwell
Shingham
Cockley Cley
Eastmoor
Boughton
Wereham
Denver
West Dereham
Fordham
Oxborough
Gooderstone
Hilborough
Stoke Ferry
Whittington
Wretton
Foulden
Bodney
Hilgay
Ten Mile Bank
Northwold
Brookville
Little London
Methwold
Methwold Hythe
Cranwich
Ickburgh
Mundford
Southery
West Tofts
Lynford
Feltwell
Brandon Creek
Brandon Bank
Little Ouse
Weeting
Hockwold cum Wilton
Santon Downham
Brandon
Lakenheath
Undley
Claypits
Elveden
Eriswell
Mile End
Prickwillow
Shippea Hill
THETFORD FOREST PARK
NORFOLK
SUFFOLK
Breckland
A10
A134
A1122
A1065
A47
A1101
A11
B1160
B1112
B1106
B1107
158
139
124
0 1 2 3 miles
0 1 2 3 4 5 km

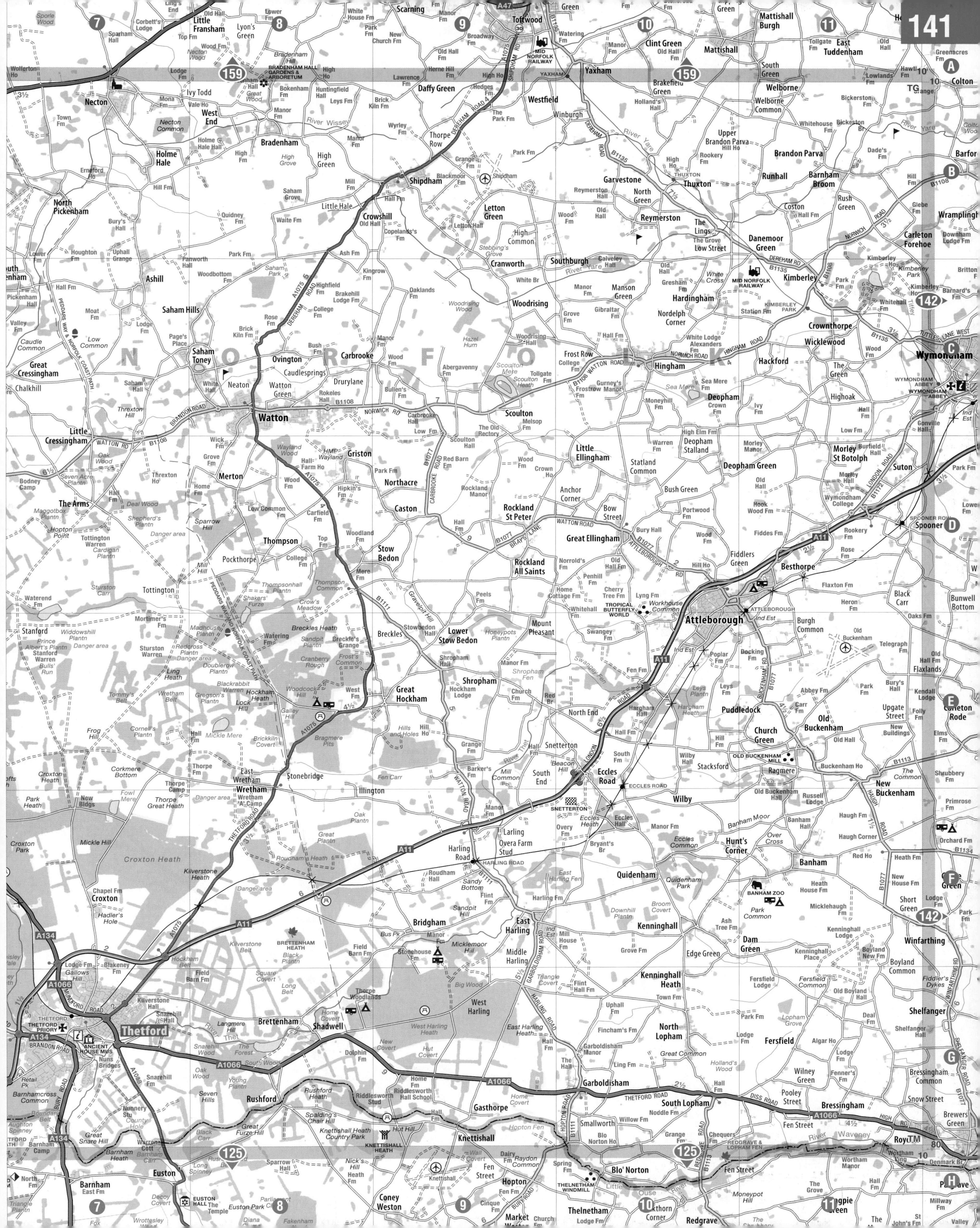
Necton
Little Fransham
Bradenham
Holme Hale
North Pickenham
Ashill
Saham Hills
Saham Toney
Ovington
Carbrooke
Watton
Little Cressingham
Great Cressingham
Merton
Griston
Thompson
Tottington
Stanford
Shipdham
Yaxham
Mattishall
East Tuddenham
Westfield
Garvestone
Thuxton
Reymerston
Letton Green
Cranworth
Southburgh
Woodrising
Hardingham
Kimberley
Hingham
Deopham
Wymondham
Scoulton
Little Ellingham
Great Ellingham
Rockland St Peter
Rockland All Saints
Caston
Stow Bedon
Breckles
Attleborough
Besthorpe
Great Hockham
Shropham
Snetterton
Eccles Road
Wilby
Old Buckenham
New Buckenham
Banham
Quidenham
Kenninghall
East Harling
Bridgham
Brettenham
Thetford
Croxton
Barnham
Euston
Rushford
Shadwell
Garboldisham
South Lopham
North Lopham
Fersfield
Bressingham
Winfarthing
Shelfanger
Knettishall
Hopton
Blo' Norton
Thelnetham
Coney Weston
Gasthorpe
NORFOLK

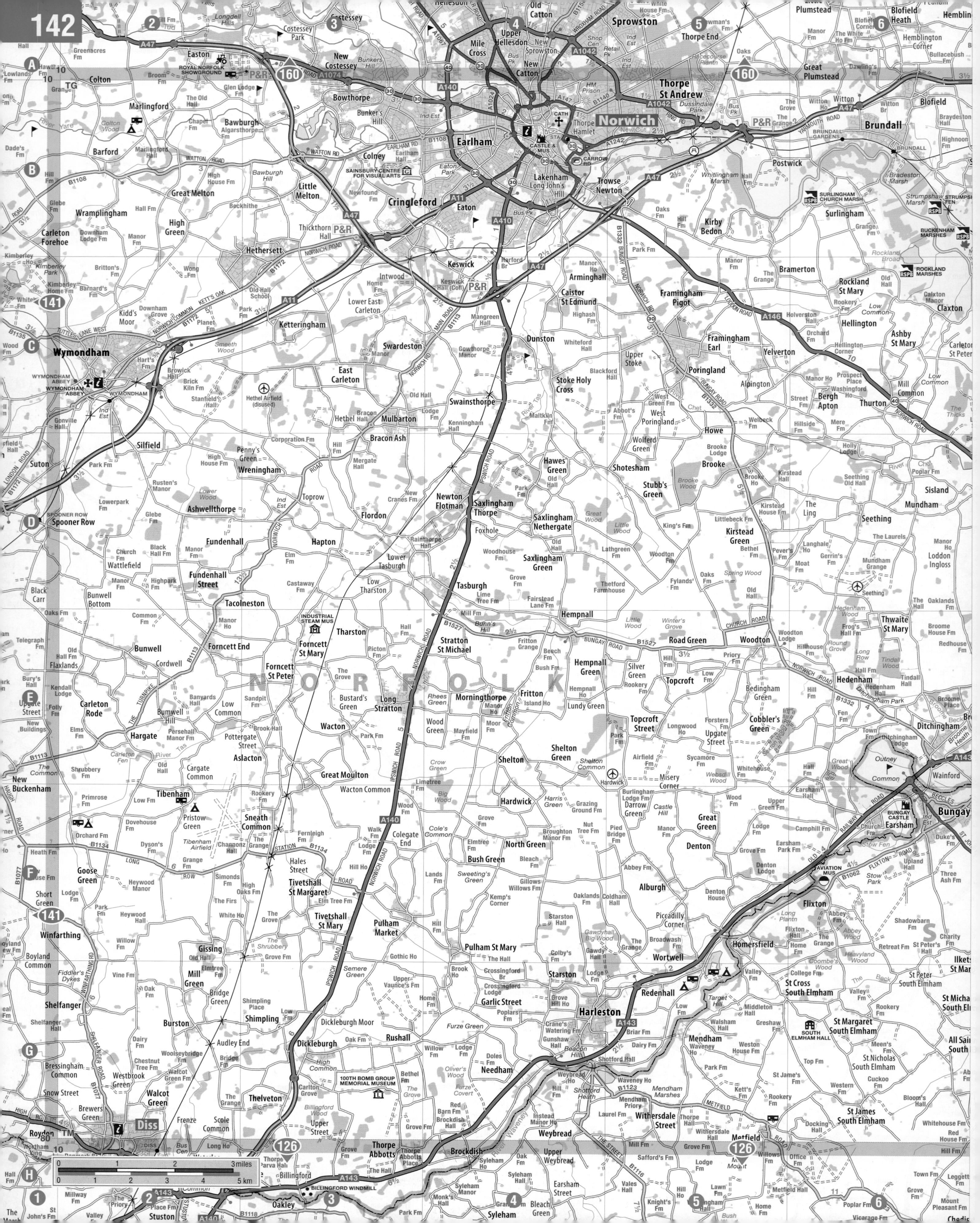
Norwich
Sprowston
Thorpe End
Old Catton
Upper Hellesdon
Mile Cross
New Sprowston
New Catton
Costessey
Costessey Park
New Costessey
Easton
ROYAL NORFOLK SHOWGROUND
Colton
Marlingford
Bawburgh
Bowthorpe
Bunker's Hill
Earlham
Colney
SAINSBURY CENTRE FOR VISUAL ARTS
Thorpe St Andrew
Thorpe Hamlet
Great Plumstead
Blofield
Blofield Heath
Hemblington
Brundall
Postwick
Barford
Great Melton
Little Melton
Cringleford
Eaton
Lakenham
Trowse Newton
Wramplingham
Carleton Forehoe
Hethersett
Thickthorn Hall
Keswick
Kirby Bedon
Surlingham
Bramerton
Rockland St Mary
Claxton
Arminghall
Caistor St Edmund
Framingham Pigot
Framingham Earl
Intwood
Lower East Carleton
Ketteringham
Kidd's Moor
Wymondham
Swardeston
Dunston
Upper Stoke
Stoke Holy Cross
Poringland
Hellington
Ashby St Mary
Yelverton
Alpington
Bergh Apton
Thurton
Mill Common
East Carleton
Hethel Airfield (disused)
Swainsthorpe
Mulbarton
Bracon Ash
West Poringland
Howe
Silfield
Suton
Wreningham
Shotesham
Brooke
Stubb's Green
Sisland
Mundham
Seething
Ashwellthorpe
Toprow
Flordon
Newton Flotman
Saxlingham Thorpe
Saxlingham Nethergate
Kirstead Green
Spooner Row
Fundenhall
Hapton
Wattlefield
Lower Tasburgh
Saxlingham Green
Loddon Ingloss
Fundenhall Street
Low Tharston
Tasburgh
Tacolneston
Bunwell Bottom
INDUSTRIAL STEAM MUS
Tharston
Hempnall
Thwaite St Mary
Bunwell
Forncett End
Forncett St Mary
Stratton St Michael
Road Green
Woodton
Forncett St Peter
NORFOLK
Hempnall Green
Topcroft
Hedenham
Carleton Rode
Long Stratton
Morningthorpe
Fritton
Lundy Green
Hargate
Wacton
Topcroft Street
Cobbler's Green
Ditchingham
New Buckenham
Aslacton
Great Moulton
Shelton
Shelton Green
Wainford
Bungay
Tibenham
Wacton Common
Hardwick
Sneath Common
Colegate End
Great Green
Earsham
Goose Green
Hales Street
Tivetshall St Margaret
North Green
Bush Green
Denton
Alburgh
Flixton
Winfarthing
Tivetshall St Mary
Pulham Market
Pulham St Mary
Homersfield
Gissing
Mill Green
Wortwell
Shelfanger
Garlic Street
Starston
Redenhall
St Cross South Elmham
Burston
Shimpling
Dickleburgh Moor
Rushall
Harleston
St Margaret South Elmham
Audley End
Dickleburgh
Mendham
Bressingham Common
Westbrook Green
100TH BOMB GROUP MEMORIAL MUSEUM
Needham
St Nicholas South Elmham
Snow Street
Walcot Green
Thelveton
Brewers Green
Diss
Frenze
Scole Common
Withersdale Street
St James South Elmham
Roydon
Upper Street
Weybread
Thorpe Abbotts
Brockdish
Upper Weybread
Metfield
Billingford
BILLINGFORD WINDMILL
Oakley
Syleham
Stuston
Earsham Street
0 1 2 3 miles
0 1 2 3 4 5 km

Caister-on-Sea
Caister Pt
West Caister
West End
Runham
Stokesby
Acle
North Burlingham
Burlingham Green
Fishley
Damgate
Lingwood
Lingwood Lodge
Beighton
South Burlingham
Moulton St Mary
Tunstall
THE
BROADS
Strumpshaw
Halvergate
Cucumber Corner
Freethorpe
Buckenham
Hassingham
Southwood
Wickhampton
Cantley
Limpenhoe
Limpenhoe Hill
Reedham
PETTITS ANIMAL ADVENTURE PARK
Langley Street
Hardley Street
Nogdam End
Chedgrave
Loddon
Hales
Heckingham
Thurlton
Lower Thurlton
Norton Subcourse
Thorpe
Thurlton Links
Haddiscoe
Three Cocked Hat
Raveningham
RAVENINGHAM GARDENS
Hales Green
HALES HALL BARN & GARDENS
Maypole Green
Brundish
Toft Monks
Kirby Cane
Stockton
Bull's Green
Waterheath
Wheatacre
Waterloo
Aldeby
Burgh St Peter
Ellingham
Kirby Row
Geldeston
Gillingham
Dockeney
Dunburgh
Beccles
BECCLES DISTRICT MUSEUM
Mettingham
Shipmeadow
Barsham
Worlingham
North Cove
Barnby
Ringsfield
Ringsfield Corner
Ilketshall St Andrew
Great Common
Weston
Ellough
Hulver Street
Mutford
Rushmere
Redisham
Shadingfield
Sotterley
Willingham
Ilketshall St Lawrence
Stone Street
Cox Common
Brampton
Mill Common
Stoven
Westhall
Frostenden
Wrentham
Uggeshall
Clay Common
Cove Bottom
South Cove
Covehithe
Spexhall
Wissett
Rumburgh
Broadway
Holton
Upper Holton
Wangford
Reydon
Reydon Smear
Halesworth
Henham Park
Great Yarmouth
Runham Vauxhall
Newtown
ELIZABETHAN HOUSE, NELSON & TOLHOUSE MUSEUMS
SEA LIFE CENTRE
PLEASURE BEACH
Southtown
Cobholm Island
Breydon Water
Burgh Castle
Bradwell
BERNEY ARMS WINDMILL
BERNEY MARSHES & BREYDON WATER
Gorleston-on-Sea
Belton
Browston Green
REDWINGS HORSE SANCTUARY (CALDECOTT)
Fritton
FRITTON LAKE COUNTRY WORLD
ST OLAVE'S PRIORY
St Olaves
Herringfleet
SOMERLEYTON HALL
Somerleyton
The Dell
Lound
Hopton on Sea
Blundeston
Corton
PLEASUREWOOD HILLS LEISURE PARK
Gunton
Oulton
Oulton Broad
Normanston
LOWESTOFT & EAST SUFFOLK MARITIME MUS
Lowestoft
CARLTON MARSHES NATURE RESERVE
Kirkley
Pakefield
Carlton Colville
TRANSPORT MUS
Gisleham
Kessingland
Kessingland Beach
AFRICA ALIVE
Henstead
Benacre
Benacre Ness
River Waveney
SUFFOLK

Trwyn Porth Dinllaen
Carreg Ddu
Pistyll
Moel Ty-Gwyn
Porth Dinllaen
Borth Wen
Penrhyn Nefyn
Morfa Nefyn
Porth Nefyn
Wern
Tir Bach
LLEYN HISTORICAL MARITIME MUSEUM
Mynydd Nefyn
Tyddyn Uchaf
Bodeilias
Aber Geirch
162
Nefyn
Edern
Garn Boduan 280
Hendre Penprys
Penrhyn Cwmistir
Cwmistir
Groesffordd
Plasyngheidio
Tan-y-graig
B4417
A497
B4412
B4354
Glanrhyd
Moelypenmaen
Porth Towyn
Rhos-y-llan
Porth Ysglaig
Tref-erwyn
Maesgglan
Glan-y-gors
Hendre
Boduan
Porth Ysgaden
Towyn
Cefn Leisiog
Nyffryn
Y Ddôl
CORS GEIRCH
Meillionen
Coed Bodfel
BODVEL ADVENTURE
Tudweiliog
Mochras
Traian
Porth Gwylan
Penrallt
Tan-llan
Brynodol
Madryn Castle
Mathan Isaf
Cefn Mine
Penllech Bach
Gwyndy
Pwllgoed
Rhos-ddû
Dinas
Moel Caerau
Gallt y Beren
Penrhyn Melyn
Ty-mawr
Cefntreuddyn
Cefnamwlch
Afon Soch
371
Carn Fadryn
CARN FADRUN (FORT)
Garn Bach
B4415
Tan-y-bryn
Porth Colmon
Ffridd-goch
Ffridd-wen
Penybryn
Tyn Llidiart
Nyfyr
Tyn Simdda
Garnfadryn
Rhyd-y-clafdy
Traeth Penllech
Berthaur
Penllech
Bryn Celyn Hall
Polish Home
Penrhos
Porth Wen Bâch
Porth Colmon
Bryn Geinach
Mynydd Cefnamwlch 182
Cefn Llanfair
Porth Ty-mawr
Pen-y-graig
Morfa
Tregwm
Bryn-mawr
Llaniestyn
Penbodlas
Wern Fawr
Tyddyncaled
Afon Rhyd-hir
WALES COAST PATH
Tynewydd
Carneddol
Llangwnnadl
Porth Widlin
Cellar Fm
Inkermann Br
Rhedyn
Foel Bach
Penarwel
Carreg y
Porth Ferin
Sarn Meyllteyrn
Trefaes
Foel Fawr
Henllys
A499
Penrhyn Mawr
Pen-y-bryn
B4413
Tyn-y-coed
Maen Mellt
Ty-mawr
Dinas
Bronphilip Fm
Mynytho Common
Llanbedrog
Plas Glyn-y-weddw
Porth Iago
Lleiniau
Pant
Bryncroes
Trygarn
Nanhoron
Mynydd Tirycwmwd 132
Trwyn Glas
Ty-hen
G W Y N E D D
Brynhunog Fawr
Llety'r Wym
Pen-y-groeslon
Coch-y-moel
Botwnnog
Capel Newydd
Mynytho
Trwyn Llanbed
Porth Oer
Porth y Wrâch
Tocia
Faerdre
Gelliwig
Bryn Llewelyn
Coed-y-fron
Tan-y-mynydd
Methlem
Rhydlios
Hirwaun
NEOLITHIC AXE FACTORY
Tyddyn Corn Fm
Llandegwning
Yalsarn
Barach
Nant
Bodwi
Rhandir
Dinas Bâch
Mynydd Carreg
Cruga Bach
304
Mynydd Rhiw
Tyn-y-parc
Saithbont
Tyddyn Gwyn
Dinas Fawr
Rhoshirwaun
Felin Uchaf
Meillionydd
Neigwl Ganol
Fach Fm
The Warren
Capel Carmel
Llawrdref Bellaf
Llangian
St Tudwal's Road
Porthorion
Carreg
L L E Y N
Glangors
PLAS-YN-RHIW
Ty Mawr
Glan Soch
Penbennar
Bryn-mawr
Mynydd Ystum
Afon Daron
Ty Cerrig
Abersoch
Angorfa St Tudwal
Braich Anelog
Hendre
Penycaerau
Rhiw
Trefollwyn
Morfa Gors
Anelog
Ty Croes Mawr
Mynydd Graig
Punt Gwynedd
Towyn
Porth Llanllawen
Llanllawen
Aberdaron
Llanfaelrhys
MYNYDD-Y-CRAIG HEADLAND
PORTH NEIGWL OR HELL'S MOUTH
Llanengan
Sarn Bach
Porth Tocyn
Penrhyn Du
Porth Bach
Maen Du
Braich y Noddfa
Uwchmynydd
Bryn Fm
Tai-morfa
Ty Newydd Fm
St Tudwal's Island East
Mynydd Mawr 160
Braich y Pwll
Porth Simdde
Aberdaron Bay
Porth Cadlan
Porth Ysgo
Bwlchtocyn
Marchroes
Gwyddel
Trwyn y Penrhyn
Ogof Lwyd
Trwyn Talfarach
Cim
Corn Fm
Nant y Fm
Trwyn Maen Melyn
Bodermid
Porth Cloch
Ebolion
Pant Fm
Trwyn y Gwyddel
Trwyn y Fulfran
Nant-y-big
St Tudwal's Island West
MYNUDD CILAN
Porth Felen
Ynys Gwylan-fawr
Porth y Pistyll
Porth Ceiriad
Pistyll Cim
Trwyn yr Wylfa
Parwyd
Hen Borth
Ynys Gwylan-bâch
Trwyn Carreg-y-tir
Trwyn y Ffosle
Mynydd Gilan
Pared-mawr
Pen y Cil
Cilan Uchaf
Trwyn Llech-y-doll
Maen Bugail
Bardsey Sound
Swnt Enlli
Trwyn Cilan
Bae y Rhigol
Trwyn y Gorlech
Bae'r Nant
ST MARY'S ABBEY (RUINS)
OLD CROSSES
Maen Iau
Plas-bach
Bardsey Island
Ynys Enlli
Carreg yr Honwy
YNYS ENLLI
Porth Solfach
Cafn Enlli
Ystwffwl Glas
Henllwyn
Ogof Lladron
Ogof Diban
SH
10
40
0 1 2 3 miles
0 1 2 3 4 5 km
A B C D E F G H
1 2 3 4 5 6

Penrhyn Llyn
Llwyndyrys
Pencaenewydd
Llangybi
Rhoslan
Penmorfa
Tremadog
Penrhyndeudraeth
Minffordd
Porthmadog
Borth-y-Gest
Morfa Bychan
Pentrefelin
Criccieth
CRICCIETH CASTLE
Llanystumdwy
LLOYD GEORGE MUSEUM
Chwilog
Llanarmon
Afon Wen
Abererch
Rhos-fawr
Y Ffôr
Efailnewydd
Denio
Penrallt
Pwllheli
South Beach
West End
Marian-y-mor
Traeth Crugan
HAFAN Y MOR
Penrhyn
Pen-ychain
Black Rock Sand
WALES COAST PATH
Portmeirion
Talsarnau
Traeth Bach
Harlech Pt
MORFA HARLECH
Morfa Harlech
Ynys
Glan-y-wern
Glyn-y-warch
TREMADOG BAY
BAE TREMADOG
Harlech
HARLECH CASTLE
Llanfair
SLATE CAVERNS
Llandanwg
Pen-sarn
Pentre Gwynfryn
Llanbedr
SHELL ISLAND
Morfa Dyffryn
MORFA DYFFRYN
Coed Ystumgwern
Llanenddwyn
Dyffryn Ardudwy
DYFFRYN BURIAL CHAMBER
Llanddwywe
Cors-y-Gedol
Tal-y-bont
Plas-canol
Llanaber
Barmouth (Abermaw)
RNLI LIFEBOAT MUSEUM
FAIRBOURNE RAILWAY
BARMOUTH BAY
BAE BERMO
Fairbourne
Gwastadgoed
Hendre
Llwyngwril
A497
A499
A487
A496
A493
163
146
7
8
9
10
11

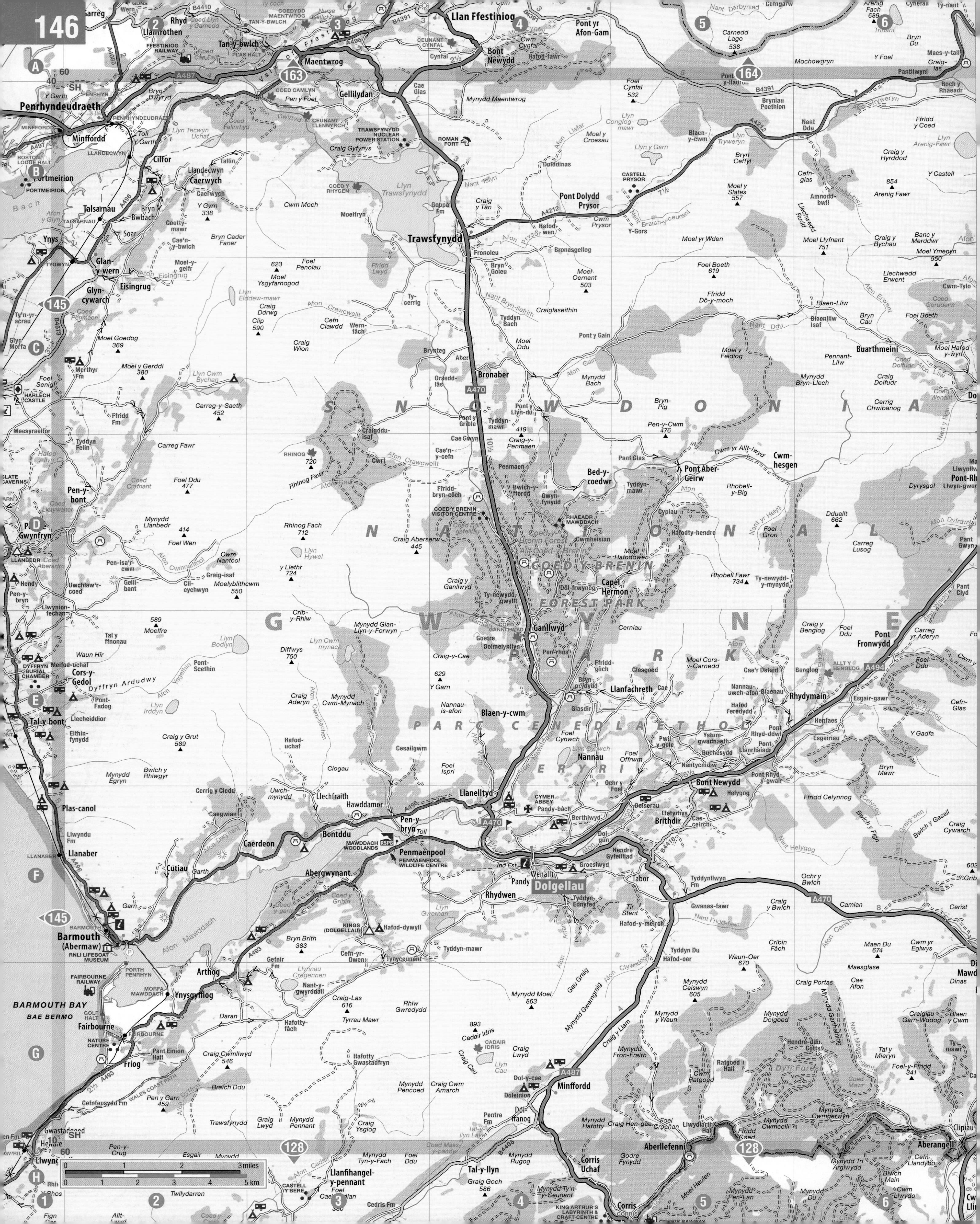
Llan Ffestiniog
Maentwrog
Tan-y-bwlch
Llanfrothen
Rhyd
Pont yr Afon-Gam
Bont Newydd
Cynfal
Penrhyndeudraeth
Minffordd
Gellilydan
Cae Glas
Mynydd Maentwrog
Foel Cynfal 532
Carnedd Lago 538
Arenig Fach 689
Pont y-llaflon
Mochowgryn
Y Foel
Bryn Du
Maes-y-tail
Graig-las
Pantllwyni
Boch y Rhaeadr
Bryniau Poethion
Nant Ddu
Ffridd y Coed
Llyn Arenig-Fawr
Craig y Hyrddod
Y Castell
854 Arenig Fawr
Portmeirion
Cilfor
Llandecwyn
Caerwych
Talsarnau
Soar
Bryn Bwbach
Y Gyrn 338
Llyn Trawsfynydd
TRAWSFYNYDD NUCLEAR POWER STATION
Craig Gyfynys
COED Y RHYGEN
Cwm Moch
Moelfryn
ROMAN FORT
Moel y Croesau
Dolddinas
Llyn Conglog-mawr
Llyn y Garn
CASTELL PRYSOR
Pont Dolydd Prysor
Cwm Prysor
Y-Gors
Blaen-y-cwm
Bryn Ceffyl
Cefn-glas
Amnodd-bwll
Moel y Slates 557
Trawsfynydd
Craig y Tân
Gopa Fm
Fronoleu
Bronasgellog
Hafod-wen
Moel yr Wden
Moel Llyfnant 751
Craig y Bychau
Banc y Merddwr
Moel Ymenyn 550
Ynys
Glan-y-wern
Glyn-cywarch
Eisingrug
Moel-y-geifr
Bryn Cader Faner
623
Foel Penolau
Moel Ysgyfarnogod
Ffridd Lwyd
Bryn Goleu
Moel Oernant 503
Foel Boeth 619
Ffridd Dô-y-moch
Llechwedd Erwent
Cwm-Tylo
Coed Gorddcrw
Foel Boeth
Llyn Eiddew-mawr
Craig Ddrwg
Clip 590
Cefn Clawdd
Wern-fâch
Ty-cerrig
Tyddyn Bach
Craiglaseithin
Blaen-Lliw
Blaenlliw Isaf
Bryn Cau
Buarthmeini
Moel Hafod-y-wŷn
Moel Goedog 369
Craig Wion
Moel y Gerddi 380
Llyn Cwm Bychan
Brynteg
Aber
Bronaber
Orsedd-lâs
Moel Ddu
Pont y Gain
Mynydd Bach
Moel y Feidiog
Pennant-Lliw
Mynydd Bryn-Llech
Craig Dolfudr
Craig Chwibanog
Harlech Castle
Foel Senigl
Merthyr Fm
Carreg-y-Saeth 452
Ffridd Fm
Tyddyn Felin
Maesyraelfor
Carreg Fawr
S N O W D O N I A
Craigddu-isaf
Pont y Grible
Tyddyn-mawr
Pont y Llyn-du
419
Craig-y-Penmaen
Cae Gwyn
Cae'n-y-cefn
Bryn-Pig
Pen-y-Cwm 476
Pant Glas
Cwm yr Allt-lwyd
Pont Aber-Geirw
Cwm-hesgen
Rhinog 720
Rhinog Fawr
Cwrt
Penmaen
Ffridd-bryn-côch
Bwlch-y-ffordd
Gwyn-fynydd
Bed-y-coedwr
Tyddyn-mawr
Rhobell-y-Big
Pen-y-bont
Coed Crafnant
Foel Ddu 477
COED Y BRENIN VISITOR CENTRE
RHAEADR MAWDDACH
Cyplau
Hafodty-hendre
Dduallt 662
Dyrysgol
Pont-Rhyd-Llwyn-gwern
Gwynfryn
Llanbedr
Mynydd Llanbedr
414
Foel Wen
Rhinog Fach 712
N A T I O N A L
Craig Aberserw 445
Cwmheisian
Moel Hafodowen
COED Y BRENIN FOREST PARK
Foel Gron
Carreg Lusog
Pant Gwyn
Hendy
Pen-y-bryn
Pen-isa'r-cwm
Cwm Nantcol
Llyn Hywel
y Llethr 724
Craig y Ganllwyd
Dôl-frwynog
Capel Hermon
Rhobell Fawr 734
Ty-newydd-y-mynydd
Pant Clyd
Uwchlaw'r-coed
Gelli-bant
Graig-isaf
Cil-cychwyn
Moelyblithcwm 550
Ty-newydd-gwyllt
Llwynion-fechan
589 Moelfre
Tal y ffnonau
Crib-y-Rhiw
G W Y N E D D
Mynydd Glan-Llyn-y-Forwyn
Ganllwyd
Cerniau
Craig y Benglog
Foel Ddu
Pont Fronwydd
Carreg yr Aderyn
Llyn Bodlyn
Llyn Cwm-mynach
Diffwys 750
Goetre
Dolmelynllyn
Pen-rhos
P A R K
Ffridd-gôch
Glasgoed
Moel Corsy-y-Garnedd
Caer Defaid
Benglog
ALLT Y BENGLOG
Waun Hîr
Meifod-uchaf
Cors-y-Gedol
Pont-Scethin
DYFFRYN BURIAL CHAMBER
Dyffryn Ardudwy
Craig-y-Cae
629 Y Garn
Bryn-prydydd
Llanfachreth
Cae
Hendre
Rhydymain
Esgair-gawr
Cefn-Glas
Craig Aderyn
Mynydd Cwm-Mynach
Pont-Fadog
Llecheiddior
Tal-y-bont
Llyn Irddyn
Nannau-is-afon
Blaen-y-cwm
Nannau-uchaf-afon
Blaenau
Hafod Feredydd
Glasdir
P A R C   C E N E D L A E T H O L
Eithin-fynydd
Craig y Grut 589
Hafod-uchaf
Cesailgwm
Foel Cynwch
Llyn Cynwch
Pwll-y-gele
Ystum-gwadnaeth
Pont Rhyd-ddwl
Henfaes
Esgeiriau
Y Gadfa
Foel Ispri
Nannau
Foel Offrwm
E R Y R I
Buchesydd
Llanrhaiadr
Nantycnidiw
Mynydd Egryn
Bwlch y Rhiwgyr
Clogau
Ochr y Foel
Bont Newydd
Helygog
Pont Rhyd-y-gwair
Bryn Mawr
Plas-canol
Cerrig y Cledd
Uwch-mynydd
Llechfraith
Hawddamor
Llanelltyd
CYMER ABBEY
Pandy-bâch
Dolserau
Lletyrhys
Brithdir
Cae-ceirch
Ffridd Celynnog
Bwlch y Gesail
Craig Cywarch
Caegwian
Bontddu
Pen-y-bryn
Berthlwyd
Bwlch y Fign
Llwyndu Fm
Llanaber
Caerdeon
MAWDDACH WOODLANDS
Penmaenpool
PENMAENPOOL WILDLIFE CENTRE
Dol-gûn
Hendre Gyfeilliad
Cutiau
Garth
Abergwynant
Ind Est
Wenallt
Groeslwyd
Pandy
Dolgellau
Tabor
Tyddynllwyn Fm
Ochr y Bwlch
Coed y Gribin
Rhydwen
Tyddyn-Ednyfed
Tir Stent
Gwanas-fawr
Craig y Bwlch
Camlan
Cerist
Garn
Barmouth (Abermaw)
RNLI LIFEBOAT MUSEUM
KINGS (DOLGELLAU)
Hafod-dywyll
Llyn Gwernan
Hafod-y-meirch
Nant Fridd-fawr
Bryn Brith 383
Cefn-yr-Owen
Tynyceunant
Tyddyn-mawr
Tyddyn Du
Hafod-oer
Cribin Fâch
Maen Du 674
Cwm yr Eglwys
Waun-Oer 670
Maesglase
PORTH PENRHYN
FAIRBOURNE RAILWAY
Arthog
Gefnir Fm
Llynnau Cregennen
Nant-y-gwyrddail
Gau Graig
Mynydd Ceiswyn 605
Craig Portas
Cae Afon
Dinas
BARMOUTH BAY
BAE BERMO
MORFA MAWDDACH
Ynysgyffiog
Craig-Las 616
Rhiw Gwredydd
Mynydd Moel 863
Mynydd Gwerngraig
Mynydd y Waun
Mynydd Dolgoed
Creigiau Garn-Wddog
Blaen y Cwm
Fairbourne
GOLF HALT
NATURE CENTRE
Daran
Hafotty-fâch
Tyrrau Mawr
893 Cadair Idris
Craig y Llam
Mynydd Fron-Fraith
Hendre-ddu Cotts
Ty-mawr
Friog
Pant Einion Hall
Craig Cwmllwyd 546
Hafotty Gwastadfryn
Craig Cau
CADAIR IDRIS
Llyn Cau
Craig Lwyd
Ratgoed Hall
Cwm Ratgoed
Tal y Mieryn
Foel-y-Ffridd 341
Braich Ddu
Cefnfeusydd Fm
WALES COAST PATH
Pen y Garn 459
Mynydd Pencoed
Craig Cwm Amarch
Dol-y-cae
Doleinion
Minffordd
Dyfi Forest
Coed Mawr
Gwastadgoed
Trawsfynydd
Graig Lwyd
Mynydd Pennant
Craig Ysgiog
Pentre Fm
Dol-ffanog
Mynydd Hafotty
Craig Hen-gae
Foel Crochan
Llwydiarth Hall
Ffridd Coed
Mynydd Cwmcelli
Mynydd Cwmgerwyn
Clipiau
Aberangell
Llwyngwril
Pen-y-Crug
Esgair
Mynydd
Coed Maes-y-pandy
Mynydd Tyn-y-Fach
Foel Ddu
Tal-y-llyn
Mynydd Rugog
Corris Uchaf
Godre Fynydd
Aberllefenni
Mynydd Tri Arglwydd
Cefn Llandybo
Blwch Main
Llanfihangel-y-pennant
CASTELL Y BERE
Graig Goch 586
Mynydd-Ty'n-y-Ceunant
Moel Heulen
Mynydd Pen-Lan
Mynydd Du
Cwm Llwydo
Twllydarren
Cedris Fm
Corris
KING ARTHUR'S LABYRINTH & CRAFT CENTRE
CORRIS RAILWAY
Fign
A487
A496
A470
A4212
A494
A493
B4391
B4410
B4573
B4416
B4405
A497
163
164
145
128
0 1 2 3 miles
0 1 2 3 4 5 km

DENBIGHSHIRE
(SIR DDYNBYCH)
P O W Y S
Bala
Y Bala
Llyn Celyn
Ciltalgarth
Frongoch
Llidiardau
Rhyd-uchaf
Glan-yr-afon
Wenallt
Bethel
Sarnau
Cefn-ddwysarn
Llandderfel
Rhiwlas
Llanfor
Palé
Cynwyd
Llandrillo
Pennant
Rhos-y-gwaliau
Llanycil
Parc
Llangower
Llanuwchllyn
Llyn Tegid or Bala Lake
BALA LAKE RAILWAY
Aber-Hirnant
Penllyn Forest
Cadair Berwyn 827
Cadair Bronwen 784
Moel Sych 827
Tan-y-pistyll
PISTYLL RHAEADR
Llangynog
Pentre
Pencraig
Pennant Melangell
Penybontfawr
Penygarnedd
Alltforgan
Y BERWYN
Aran Benllyn 885
Aran Fawddwy
Talardd
Ty-nant
Aber-Rhiwlech
Pont y Pennant
Llanymawddwy
Cywarch
Bryn Sion
Aber Cowarch
Cwm-Cewydd
Minllyn
MEIRION MILL
Mallwyd
Hirnant
Ty-uchaf
Llanwddyn
LAKE VYRNWY
RSPB
Abertridwr
Ddôl-Cownwy
Blaen-y-cwm
Llanfihangel-yng-Ngwynfa
Pont-Llogel
GLYNDWR'S WAY
Dolanog
Pontrobert
Tycrwyn
Wern
Foel
Llangadfan
Llanerfyl
Four Crosses
Heniarth
Dyfnant Forest
A494
A4212
A458
A495
B4391
B4393
B4396
B4395
B4401
B4402
B4403
B4382
B4390
164
165
148
129

Llangollen
Cefn-mawr
Pontcysyllte Aqueduct
Froncysyllte
Chirk (Y Waun)
Chirk Castle
Glyn-Ceiriog
Pontfadog
Llwynmawr
Bronygarth
Chirk Bank
Preesgweene
Weston Rhyn
Halton
Whittington
Whittington Castle
St Martin's
Gobowen
Hengoed
Selattyn
Craignant
Llechrydau
WREXHAM
(WRECSAM)
POWYS
SHROPSHIRE
Berwyn
Pandy
Tregeiriog
Llanarmon Dyffryn Ceiriog
Tyn-y-fedwen
Tyn-y-ffridd
Rhiwlas
Llangadwaladr
Llawnt
Rhydycroesau
Oswestry
Middleton
Morda
Tyn-y-coed
Trefonen
Pant-glas
Felin Newydd
Llansilin
Moelfre
Tai-bach
Llanarmon Mynydd-mawr
Llanrhaeadr-ym-Mochnant
Cefn Coch
Penybontfawr
Penygarnedd
Rhos-y-brithdir
Llangedwyn
Pen-y-bont
Llanerch Emrys
Porth-y-waen
Nantmawr
Treflach
Maesbury
Maesbury Marsh
West Felton
Morton
Llynclys
Llanyblodwel
Bwlchyddar
Abernaint
Llanfyllin
Llanfechain
Llansantffraid-ym-Mechain
Llanymynech
Pant
Maesbrook
Kinnerley
Knockin
Osbaston
Crickheath
Woolston
Llandysilio
Four Crosses
Llandrinio
Crosslanes
Melverley Green
Melverley
Deuddwr
Tycrwyn
Bwlch-y-cibau
Waen Fach
Trefnanney
Sarnau
Arddleen
Main
Pentrebeirdd
Geuffordd
Wern
Criggion
Coedway
Crewgreen
Middletown
Wollaston
Halfway House
Trewern
Pool Quay
Guilsfield (Cegidfa)
Groes-lwyd
Meifod
Maesgwyn-Isaf
Glascoed
Pontrobert
Cloddiau
Buttington
Nelly Andrews Green
Vennington
Heniarth
Cyfronydd
Oswestry Hill Fort
Old Oswestry
Offa's Dyke Path
Montgomery Canal
Shropshire Union Canal (Llangollen Branch)
Cambrian Heritage Railway
River Dee
Afon Tanat
Afon Cain
River Vyrnwy (Afon Efyrnwy)
A5
A483
A495
A490
A458
B4580
B4396
B4391
B4393
B4392
B4500
B4579
B5069
B5009
165
166
147
130
SJ
A
B
C
D
E
F
G
H
1
2
3
4
5
6
0 1 2 3 miles
0 1 2 3 4 5 km

Whitchurch
Overton (Owrtyn)
Ellesmere
Wem
Prees
Shawbury
Baschurch
Shrewsbury
Bayston Hill
Nesscliffe
Whixall
Tilstock
Hodnet
Hadnall
Harlescott
Battlefield
Upton Magna
Atcham
Westbury
Ightfield
Sandford
Cockshutt
Myddle
Loppington
Dudleston Heath
Welsh Frankton
Bettisfield
Penley
Hanmer
Bronington
Alkington
Prees Heath
Prees Higher Heath
Marchamley
Moreton Corbet
Stanton upon Hine Heath
High Hatton
Edgebolton
Muckleton
Rowton
High Ercall
Walton
Roden
Rodington
Withington
Walcot
Charlton
Uppington
Emstrey
Meole Brace
Porthill
Kingsland
Copthorne
Montford
Ford
Cardeston
Yockleton
Hanwood
Alberbury
Kinton
Kynaston
Ruyton-XI-Towns
Shotatton
Hordley
Tetchill
Lee
Colemere
Lyneal
Welshampton
Northwood
Newtown
Edstaston
Quina Brook
Waterloo
Noneley
Tilley
Aston
Burlton
Petton
Bagley
Weston Lullingfields
Stanwardine in the Fields
Marton
Walford
Merrington
Preston Gubbals
Albrighton
Leaton
Grafton
Yeaton
Little Ness
Great Ness
Felton Butler
Ensdon
Shrawardine
Bicton
Shelton
Nox
Cruckton
Pulley
Lea
Hinton
Edge
Farley
Stoney Stretton
Cruckmeole
Preston
Norton
Donnington
Wroxeter
Rushton
Aston
Cross
FENN'S WHIXALL & BETTISFIELD MOSSES
SHROPSHIRE UNION CANAL
MONTGOMERY CANAL
HAWKSTONE HISTORIC PARK & FOLLIES
HODNET HALL GARDENS
MORETON CORBET CASTLE
HAUGHMOND ABBEY
ATTINGHAM PARK
WROXETER ROMAN CITY (VIROCONIUM)
SHREWSBURY CASTLE
PRO STAR STADIUM
A41
A49
A53
A5
A458
A488
A528
A495
A525
A539
A442
B5476
B5063
B5062
B5061
B4397
B4380
B4386
B5065
B5067
166
167
150
131

SHROPSHIRE
TELFORD AND WREKIN
Market Drayton
Newport
Wellington
Hadley
Donnington
Oakengates
Telford
Eccleshall
Gnosall
Shifnal
Loggerheads
Ashley
Mucklestone
Hodnet
Ternhill
Hinstock
Cheswardine
Adderley
Norton in Hales
Whitmore
Maer
Blackbrook
Knighton
Woodseaves
Sambrook
Edgmond
Lilleshall
Weston under Lizard
Wrockwardine
Waters Upton
High Ercall
Sutton
Forton
Norbury
Standon
Croxton
Ellerton
Tibberton
Childs Ercall
Stoke on Tern
Muxton
Sheriffhales
Priorslee
M54
A41
A53
A442
A518
A519
A5
A51
167
168
149
132

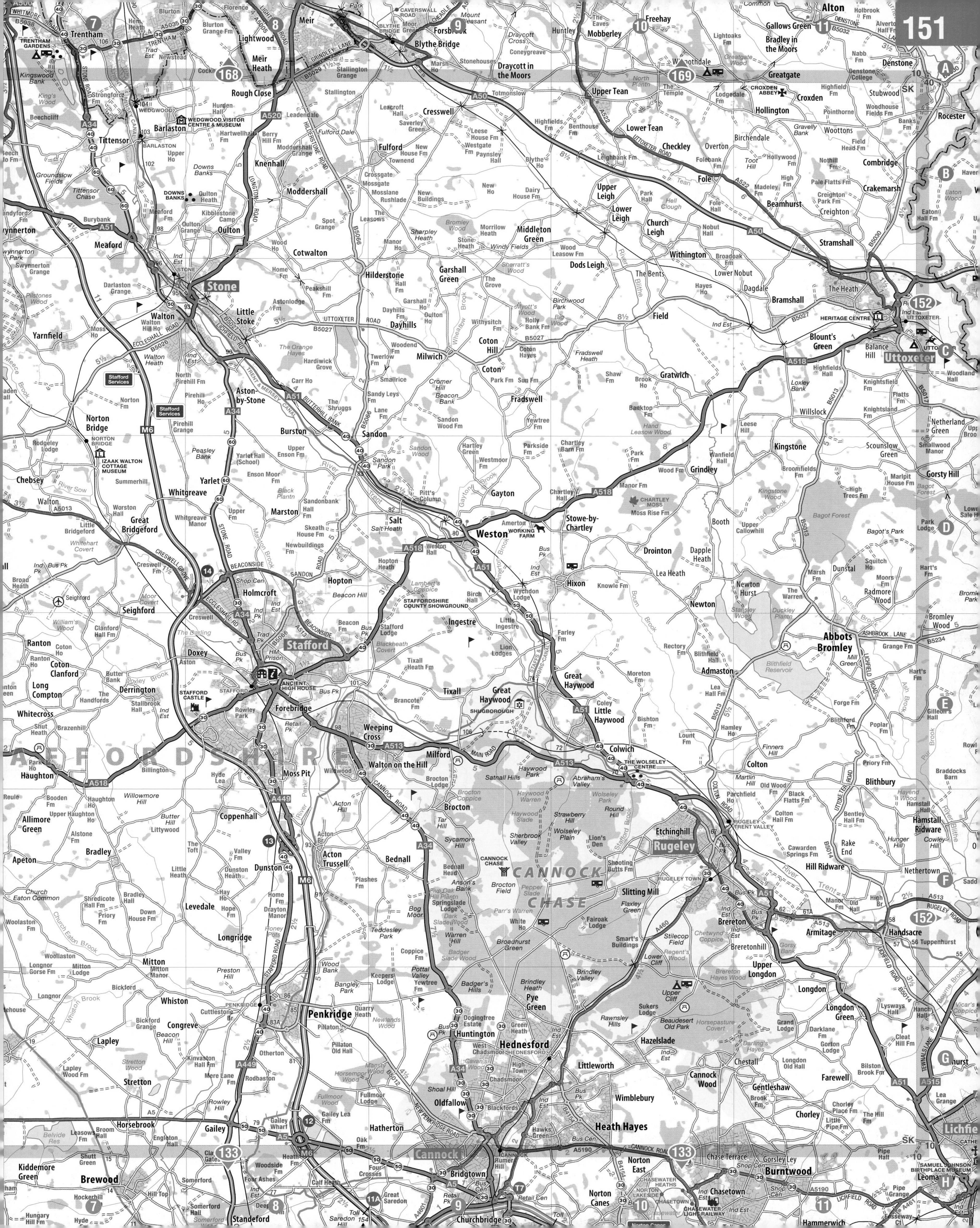
Trentham
Meir
Forsbrook
Blythe Bridge
Alton
Freehay
Mobberley
Lightwood
Meir Heath
Rough Close
Draycott in the Moors
Upper Tean
Lower Tean
Greatgate
Croxden
Hollington
Denstone
Rocester
Barlaston
Tittensor
Knenhall
Moddershall
Fulford
Checkley
Cresswell
Oulton
Meaford
Cotwalton
Hilderstone
Garshall Green
Middleton Green
Dods Leigh
Withington
Church Leigh
Upper Leigh
Lower Leigh
Stramshall
Bramshall
The Heath
Uttoxeter
Stone
Walton
Little Stoke
Yarnfield
Dayhills
Milwich
Coton Hill
Coton
Field
Gratwich
Blount's Green
Aston-by-Stone
Burston
Sandon
Fradswell
Norton Bridge
Chebsey
Yarlet
Whitgreave
Marston
Salt
Weston
Stowe-by-Chartley
Grindley
Kingstone
Great Bridgeford
Holmcroft
Hopton
Drointon
Hixon
Newton
Dunstal
Abbots Bromley
Seighford
Ranton
Coton Clanford
Doxey
Stafford
Ingestre
Great Haywood
Little Haywood
Admaston
Derrington
Forebridge
Tixall
Weeping Cross
Colwich
Milford
Walton on the Hill
Moss Pit
Haughton
Coppenhall
Brocton
Etchinghill
Rugeley
Blithbury
Hamstall Ridware
Hill Ridware
Bradley
Acton Trussell
Bednall
Dunston
Cannock Chase
Slitting Mill
Brereton
Armitage
Handsacre
Levedale
Longridge
Mitton
Upper Longdon
Longdon
Longdon Green
Whiston
Congreve
Penkridge
Pye Green
Huntington
Hednesford
Hazelslade
Lapley
Stretton
Littleworth
Cannock Wood
Gentleshaw
Farewell
Chorley
Oldfallow
Wimblebury
Heath Hayes
Gailey
Hatherton
Cannock
Horsebrook
Brewood
Kiddemore Green
Bridgtown
Norton East
Norton Canes
Burntwood
Chasetown
Chase Terrace
Churchbridge
Standeford
Great Saredon
STAFFORDSHIRE
CANNOCK CHASE

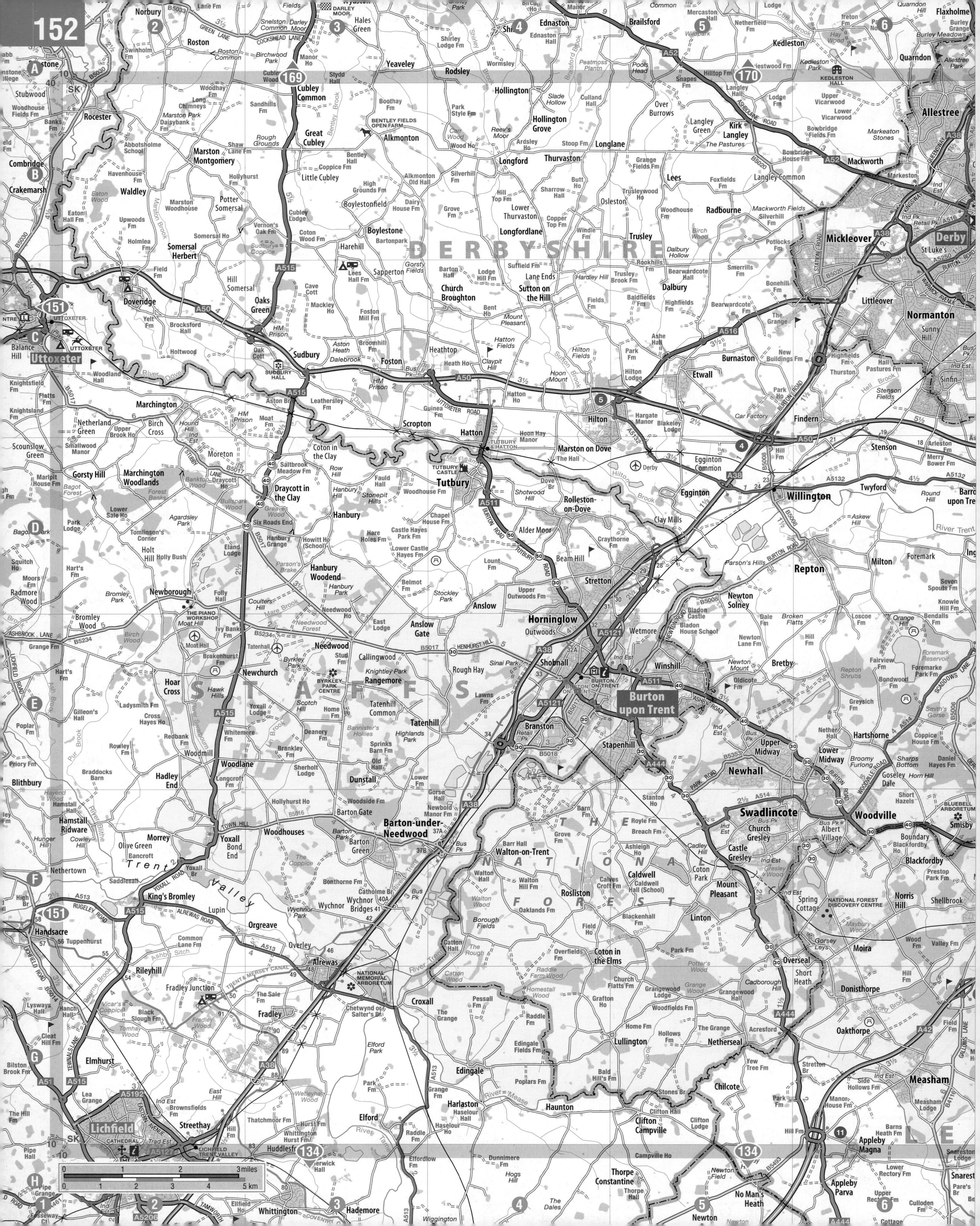
DERBYSHIRE
STAFFS
THE NATIONAL FOREST
Trent Valley
Norbury
Roston
Snelston Common
Darley Moor
Hales Green
Yeaveley
Shirley
Ednaston
Brailsford
Mercaston Hall
Kedleston
Flaxholme
Quarndon
Rocester
Stubwood
Cubley Common
Great Cubley
Alkmonton
Rodsley
Hollington
Hollington Grove
Longford
Thurvaston
Longlane
Kirk Langley
Langley Green
Allestree
Mackworth
Markeaton Stones
Combridge
Crakemarsh
Marston Montgomery
Waldley
Potter Somersal
Somersal Herbert
Little Cubley
Boylestonefield
Boylestone
Harehill
Sapperton
Church Broughton
Longfordlane
Lees
Langley Common
Radbourne
Osleston
Trusley
Mickleover
Derby
Littleover
Normanton
Sunny Hill
Doveridge
Uttoxeter
Balance Hill
Hill Somersal
Oaks Green
Sutton on the Hill
Lane Ends
Dalbury
Sudbury
Sudbury Hall
Foston
Heathtop
Etwall
Burnaston
Hilton
Hilton Lodge
Marchington
Scropton
Hatton
Tutbury
Tutbury Castle
Marston on Dove
Egginton
Egginton Common
Findern
Stenson
Willington
Twyford
Barrow upon Trent
Moreton
Marchington Woodlands
Gorsty Hill
Draycott in the Clay
Coton in the Clay
Rolleston-on-Dove
Hanbury
Six Roads End
Alder Moor
Clay Mills
Repton
Milton
Foremark
Beam Hill
Stretton
Hanbury Woodend
Anslow
Horninglow
Outwoods
Newton Solney
Newborough
Bromley Wood
Needwood
Anslow Gate
Callingwood
Rangemore
Shobnall
Winshill
Bretby
Burton upon Trent
Hoar Cross
Newchurch
Tatenhill
Tatenhill Common
Branston
Stapenhill
Upper Midway
Hartshorne
Lower Midway
Woodlane
Dunstall
Newhall
Swadlincote
Woodville
Blithbury
Hadley End
Hamstall Ridware
Barton-under-Needwood
Barton Gate
Barton Green
Walton-on-Trent
Church Gresley
Castle Gresley
Albert Village
Smisby
Morrey
Olive Green
Yoxall
Woodhouses
Rosliston
Caldwell
Mount Pleasant
Coton Park
Blackfordby
Nethertown
King's Bromley
Lupin
Wychnor
Wychnor Bridges
Linton
Spring Cottage
National Forest Discovery Centre
Norris Hill
Shellbrook
Handsacre
Orgreave
Overley
Coton in the Elms
Moira
Overseal
Short Heath
Rileyhill
Alrewas
National Memorial Arboretum
Fradley Junction
Fradley
Croxall
Donisthorpe
Oakthorpe
Lullington
Netherseal
Acresford
Elmhurst
Edingale
Chilcote
Measham
Lichfield
Streethay
Elford
Harlaston
Haunton
Clifton Campville
Appleby Magna
Huddlesford
Thorpe Constantine
No Man's Heath
Appleby Parva
Whittington
Hademore
Newton
A50
A515
A38
A52
A516
A511
A5121
A444
A513
A51
A5192
A5127
A514
A42
151
169
170
134
0 1 2 3 miles
0 1 2 3 4 5 km

NOTTINGHAM
Nottingham
NOTTINGHAMSHIRE
DERBY CITY
LEICESTERSHIRE
THE NATIONAL FOREST
Charnwood Forest
West Bridgford
Beeston
Stapleford
Long Eaton
Sandiacre
Risley
Chaddesden
Spondon
Borrowash
Ockbrook
Breadsall
Little Eaton
Morley
Dale Abbey
Kirk Hallam
West Hallam
Trowell
Wollaton
Lenton
Bramcote
Chilwell
Toton
Attenborough
Clifton
Ruddington
Edwalton
Tollerton
Plumtree
Keyworth
Bradmore
Gotham
Barton in Fabis
Thrumpton
Sawley
Draycott
Breaston
Elvaston
Ambaston
Alvaston
Osmaston
Allenton
Chellaston
Shardlow
Aston-on-Trent
Weston-on-Trent
Swarkestone
Stanton by Bridge
Cavendish Bridge
Castle Donington
Hemington
Lockington
Kegworth
Ratcliffe on Soar
Kingston on Soar
West Leake
East Leake
Costock
Wysall
Bunny
Rempstone
Wymeswold
Hoton
Prestwold
Cotes
Burton on the Wolds
Normanton on Soar
Stanford on Soar
Zouch
Hathern
Long Whatton
Diseworth
Isley Walton
Melbourne
King's Newton
Wilson
Breedon on the Hill
Tonge
Ticknall
Calke
Worthington
Belton
Osgathorpe
Shepshed
Thorpe Acre
Dishley
Loughborough
Shelthorpe
Nanpantan
Woodthorpe
Quorn or Quorndon
Barrow upon Soar
Walton on the Wolds
Sileby
Mountsorrel
Rothley
Cossington
Woodhouse
Woodhouse Eaves
Swithland
Thurcaston
Cropston
Anstey
Birstall
Newtown Linford
Markfield
Field Head
Copt Oak
Whitwick
Coalville
Greenhill
Bardon
Hugglescote
Ellistown
Ibstock
Stanton under Bardon
Swannington
Coleorton
Thringstone
Griffydam
Newbold
Lount
Ashby-de-la-Zouch
Packington
Ravenstone
Normanton le Heath
Heather
Swepstone
Newton Burgoland
Battram
Bagworth
Thornton
Odstone
Donington Park
East Midlands
Donington Park Services
Trowell Services
Leicester Services
M1
A52
A50
A6
A453
A42
A511
A512
A46
A60
170
171
135
154

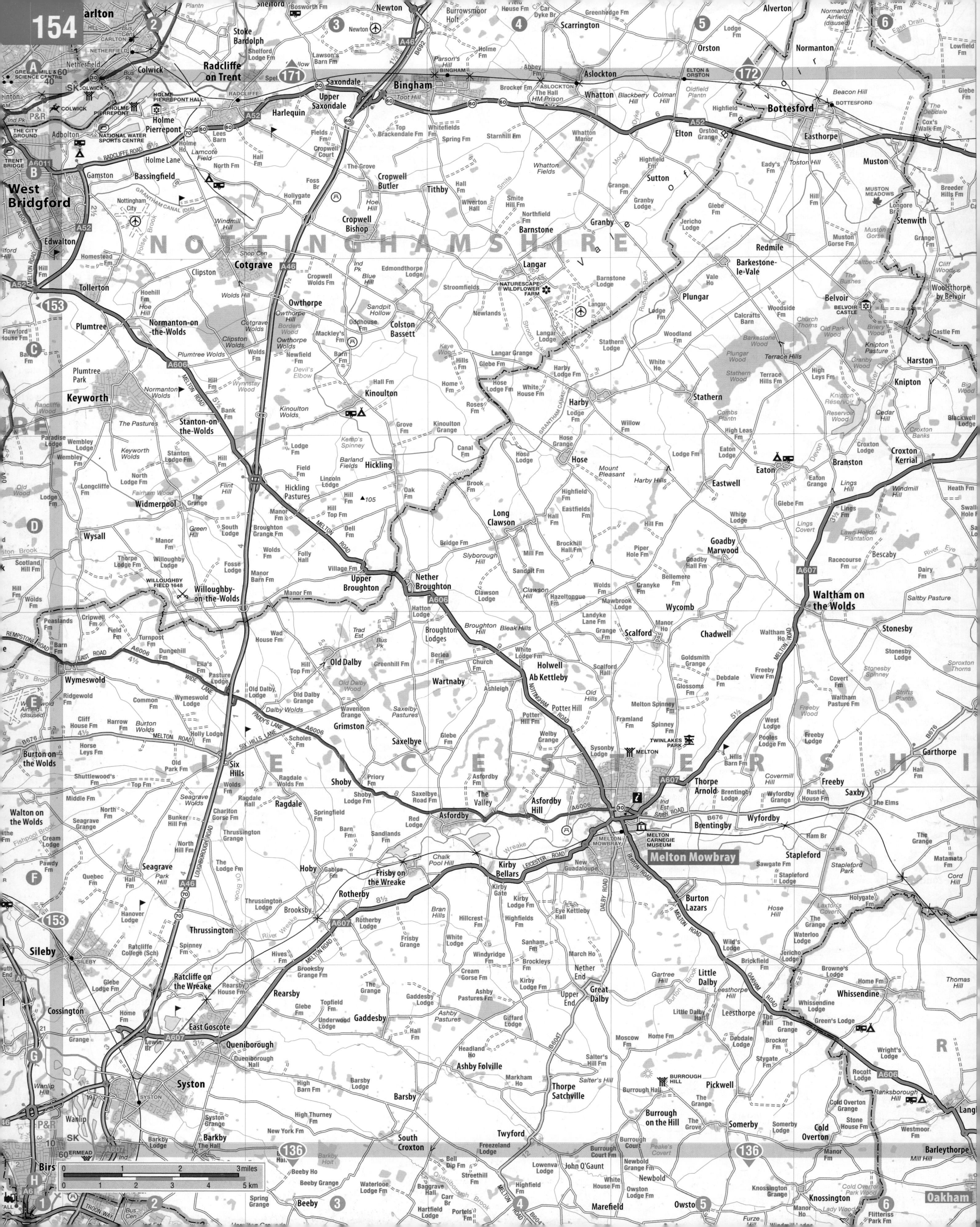
NOTTINGHAMSHIRE
LEICESTERSHIRE
Vale of Belvoir
West Bridgford
Radcliffe on Trent
Bingham
Bottesford
Cotgrave
Keyworth
Melton Mowbray
Syston
Sileby
Asfordby
Long Clawson
Harby
Waltham on the Wolds
Upper Broughton
Nether Broughton
Hickling
Kinoulton
Colston Bassett
Cropwell Bishop
Cropwell Butler
Tithby
Barnstone
Langar
Granby
Sutton
Elton
Whatton
Aslockton
Orston
Alverton
Normanton
Scarrington
Saxondale
Upper Saxondale
Harlequin
Holme Pierrepont
Gamston
Bassingfield
Edwalton
Tollerton
Plumtree
Normanton-on-the-Wolds
Stanton-on-the-Wolds
Widmerpool
Wysall
Willoughby-on-the-Wolds
Owthorpe
Redmile
Barkestone-le-Vale
Plungar
Belvoir
Knipton
Harston
Branston
Croxton Kerrial
Eaton
Eastwell
Stathern
Hose
Goadby Marwood
Wycomb
Chadwell
Scalford
Stonesby
Holwell
Ab Kettleby
Wartnaby
Old Dalby
Grimston
Saxelbye
Shoby
Ragdale
Six Hills
Wymeswold
Burton on the Wolds
Walton on the Wolds
Seagrave
Hoby
Rotherby
Frisby on the Wreake
Kirby Bellars
Brooksby
Thrussington
Ratcliffe on the Wreake
Rearsby
East Goscote
Queniborough
Cossington
Barsby
Gaddesby
Ashby Folville
Thorpe Satchville
Great Dalby
Little Dalby
Burton Lazars
Thorpe Arnold
Brentingby
Wyfordby
Stapleford
Freeby
Saxby
Garthorpe
Whissendine
Pickwell
Leesthorpe
Somerby
Burrough on the Hill
Cold Overton
Knossington
Owston
Marefield
Twyford
South Croxton
Barkby
Beeby
Barleythorpe
Oakham
Muston
Easthorpe
Stenwith
Woolsthorpe by Belvoir
NATURESCAPE WILDFLOWER FARM
BELVOIR CASTLE
TWINLAKES PARK
MELTON CARNEGIE MUSEUM
NATIONAL WATER SPORTS CENTRE
HOLME PIERREPONT HALL
BURROUGH HILL
WILLOUGHBY FIELD 1648
A46
A52
A606
A607
A6006
B676
A6
153
171
172
136
0 1 2 3 miles
0 1 2 3 4 5 km

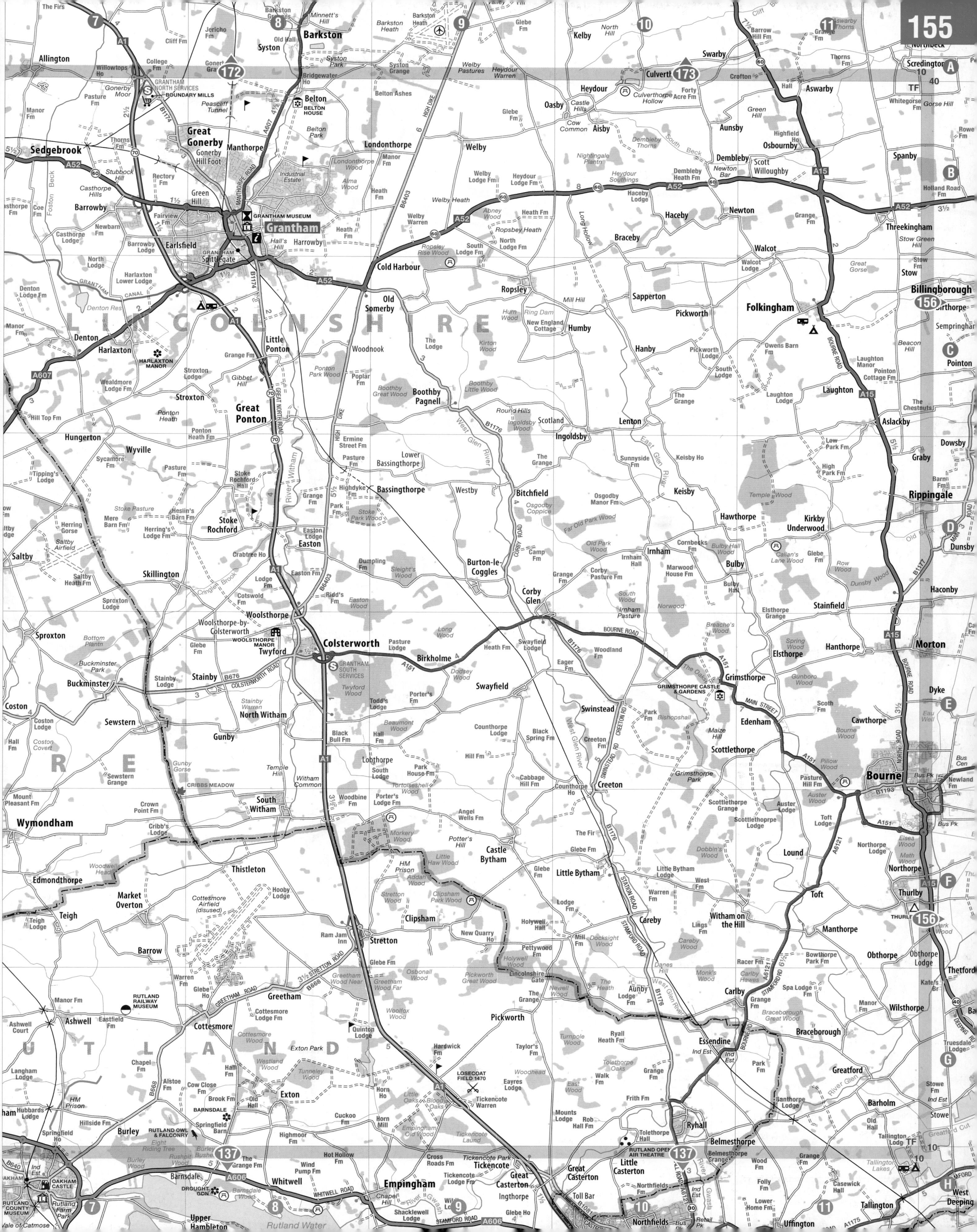
LINCOLNSHIRE
RUTLAND
Allington
Sedgebrook
Barrowby
Great Gonerby
Manthorpe
Grantham
Spittlegate
Earlsfield
Barkston
Syston
Belton
Belton House
Londonthorpe
Harrowby
Welby
Kelby
Oasby
Heydour
Aisby
Culverthorpe
Swarby
Aswarby
Aunsby
Osbournby
Dembleby
Scott Willoughby
Spanby
Threekingham
Haceby
Newton
Braceby
Walcot
Sapperton
Pickworth
Folkingham
Billingborough
Birthorpe
Sempringham
Pointon
Laughton
Aslackby
Dowsby
Graby
Rippingale
Dunsby
Haconby
Stainfield
Morton
Hanthorpe
Elsthorpe
Dyke
Cawthorpe
Bourne
Cold Harbour
Old Somerby
Ropsley
Humby
Hanby
Lenton
Ingoldsby
Keisby
Hawthorpe
Kirkby Underwood
Irnham
Bulby
Boothby Pagnell
Scotland
Bassingthorpe
Westby
Bitchfield
Burton-le-Coggles
Corby Glen
Swayfield
Grimsthorpe
Edenham
Scottlethorpe
Swinstead
Creeton
Denton
Harlaxton
Harlaxton Manor
Little Ponton
Great Ponton
Stroxton
Hungerton
Wyville
Stoke Rochford
Saltby
Skillington
Easton
Woolsthorpe
Woolsthorpe-by-Colsterworth
Colsterworth
Twyford
Birkholme
Sproxton
Buckminster
Stainby
Coston
Sewstern
Gunby
North Witham
South Witham
Wymondham
Edmondthorpe
Thistleton
Market Overton
Teigh
Barrow
Clipsham
Stretton
Greetham
Cottesmore
Ashwell
Exton
Burley
Whitwell
Empingham
Tickencote
Great Casterton
Little Casterton
Ryhall
Belmesthorpe
Essendine
Carlby
Careby
Little Bytham
Castle Bytham
Pickworth
Witham on the Hill
Toft
Lound
Manthorpe
Obthorpe
Thurlby
Northorpe
Wilsthorpe
Braceborough
Greatford
Barholm
Stowe
Tallington
West Deeping
Uffington
Northfields
Oakham
Upper Hambleton
Rutland Water
Thetford
Bourne Road
Great North Road
High Dike
Stamford Road
Colsterworth Road
Greetham Road
Stretton Road
Whitwell Road
Main Street
Station Road
Creeton Rd
Swinstead Rd
Corby Road
North Road
Grantham Canal
River Witham
West Glen River
East Glen River
Grantham Museum
Grimsthorpe Castle & Gardens
Rutland Railway Museum
Rutland Open Air Theatre
Losecoat Field 1470
Rutland County Museum
Oakham Castle
Grantham North Services
Grantham South Services
Boundary Mills
Cribbs Meadow
Barnsdale
Rutland Owl & Falconry
Drought Gdn
A1
A52
A151
A15
A607
A606
A6121
B1174
B1176
B6403
B676
B668
B1193
B1177
172
173
156
137
7
8
9
10
11
A
B
C
D
E
F
G
H
TF

173
174
155
138
LINCOLNSHIRE
TF
Helpringham
Scredington
Swaton
Spanby
Threekingham
Horbling
Billingborough
Birthorpe
Sempringham
Pointon
Millthorpe
Aslackby
Dowsby
Rippingale
Dunsby
Haconby
Morton
Dyke
Bourne
Northorpe
Thurlby
Obthorpe
Wilsthorpe
Baston
Langtoft
Barholm
Stowe
Towngate
Market Deeping
Deeping St James
Deeping St Nicholas
Hop Pole
Tongue End
Twenty
Guthram Gowt
Pode Hole
Pinchbeck
Pinchbeck West
Pinchbeck Bars
Northgate
Spalding
Little London
Clay Lake
Fulney
Low Fulney
Weston
Weston Hills
Moulton
Moulton Chapel
Moulton Eaugate
Moulton Seas End
Whaplode
Whaplode St Catherine
Whaplode Drove
Holbeach Drove
Shepeau Stow
Gedney Hill
Cowbit
Peak Hill
Brotherhouse Bar
Crowland
Dowsdale
Surfleet
Surfleet Seas End
Crossgate
Risegate
Gosberton
Gosberton Clough
Gosberton Cheal
Quadring
Quadring Eaudike
Westhorpe
Donington
Northorpe
Bicker
Swineshead
Drayton
Wigtoft
Sutterton
Algarkirk
Fosdyke
Kirton
Kirton Holme
Frampton
Frampton West End
Wyberton
Sandholme
Skeldyke
Seadyke
Bucklegate
Halesgate
Saracen's Head
Holbeach Clough
Austendike
Fenhouses
North End
Hubbert's Bridge
Asperton
Fishmere End
Burtoft
Sutterton Dowdyke
Belnie
Wargate
Wykeham
Loosegate
Stock's Hill
Thetford
Frognall
Stowgate
Maxey
Northborough
Castle End
Deeping
Tallington
Nene
Throckenholt
Spalding Tropical Forest
Springfields Gardens
Baytree Owl Centre
Ayscoughfee Hall
Gordon Boswell Romany Museum
Museum of Entertainment
Moulton Mill
A15
A16
A17
A52
A151
A152
A1175
B1397
B1177
B1166
B1165
B1357
River Welland
River Glen
South Forty Foot Drain
South Holland Main Drain
0 1 2 3 miles
0 1 2 3 4 5 km

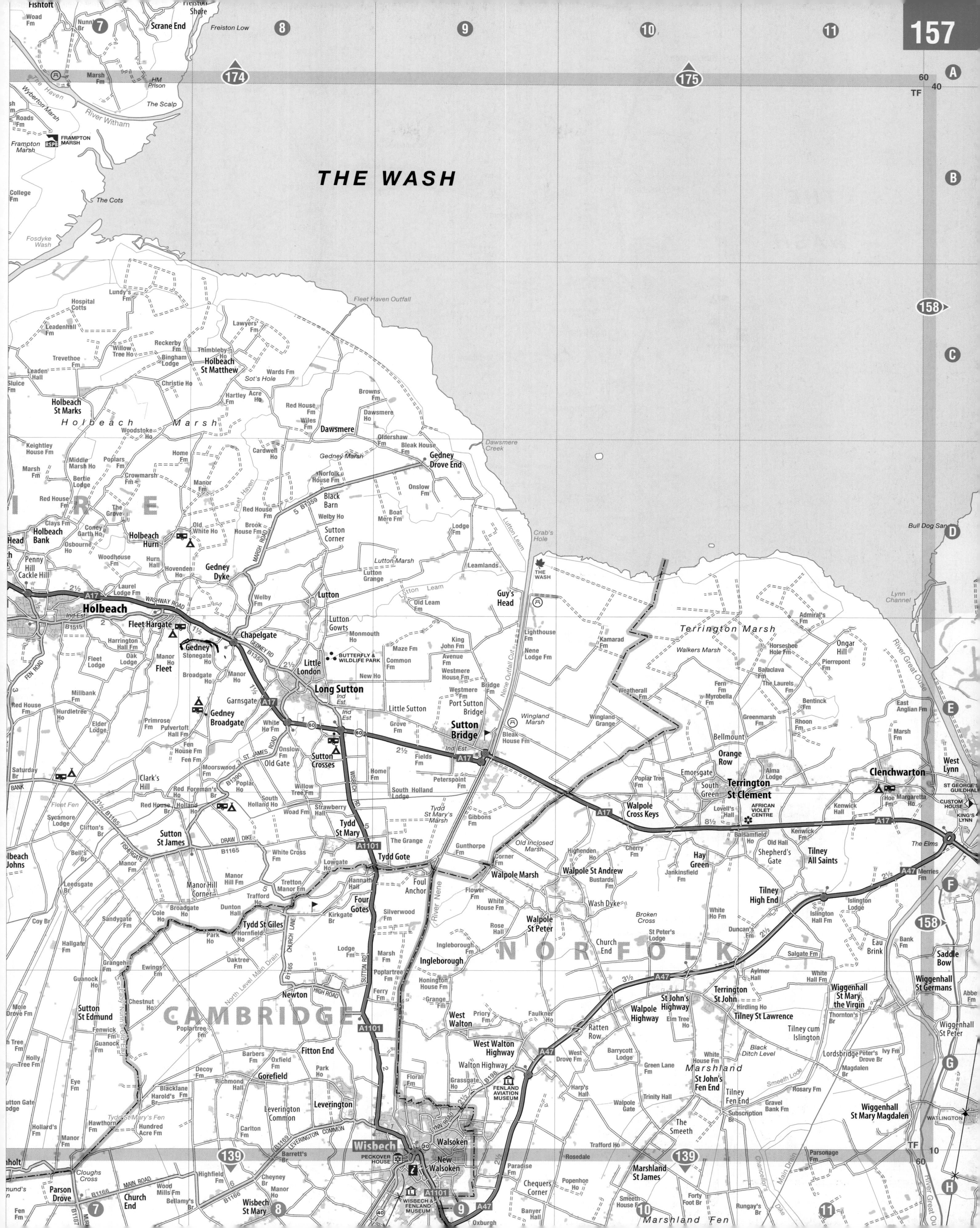
THE WASH
Fishtoft
Freiston Shore
Scrane End
Freiston Low
Marsh Fm
HM Prison
The Scalp
The Haven
Wyberton Marsh
River Witham
Frampton Marsh
FRAMPTON MARSH
RSPB
College Fm
The Cots
Fosdyke Wash
Fleet Haven Outfall
Lundy's Fm
Hospital Cotts
Leadenhall Fm
Lawyers' Fm
Reckerby Fm
Thimbleby Ho
Willow Tree Ho
Bingham Lodge
Holbeach St Matthew
Trevethoe Fm
Leaden Hall
Sot's Hole
Wards Fm
Christie Ho
Hartley Fm
Acre Ho
Browns Fm
Red House Fm
Wiles Fm
Dawsmere Ho
Dawsmere
Holbeach St Marks
Holbeach Marsh
Woodstoke Ho
Keightley House Fm
Home Fm
Cardwell Ho
Oldershaw Fm
Bleak House Fm
Dawsmere Creek
Gedney Marsh
Gedney Drove End
Middle Marsh Ho
Poplars Fm
Crowmarsh Fm
Marsh Fm
Bertie Lodge
Norfolk House Fm
Onslow Fm
Manor Fm
Fleet Haven
Red House Fm
The Grove
Red House Fm
Black Barn
Welby Ho
Boat Mere Fm
Clays Fm
Coney Garth Ho
Holbeach Bank
Old White Ho
Brook House Fm
Marsh Road
Sutton Corner
Lodge Fm
Lutton Leam
Crab's Hole
Bull Dog Sand
Holbeach Hurn
Osbourne Ho
Woodhouse Fm
Hurn Hall
Lutton Marsh
Gedney Dyke
Hovenden Ho
Lutton Grange
Leamlands
THE WASH
Penny Hill
Cackle Hill
Laurel Lodge Fm
Welby Fm
Lutton
Old Leam Fm
Guy's Head
Lynn Channel
Holbeach
Ind Est
Washway Road
Fleet Hargate
Chapelgate
Lutton Gowts
Monmouth Ho
Lighthouse Fm
Kamarad Fm
Terrington Marsh
Admiral's Fm
Harrington Hall Fm
Gedney
Stonegate Ho
Gedney Rd
Butterfly & Wildlife Park
Maze Fm
King John Fm
Nene Lodge Fm
Walkers Marsh
Horseshoe Hole Fm
Ongar Hill
Pierrepont Fm
Fleet Lodge
Oak Lodge
Manor Ho
Fleet
Little London
Common Fm
Avenue Fm
Westmere House Fm
Balaclava Fm
River Great Ouse
Fen Road
Broadgate Ho
Manor Ho
New Ho
Long Sutton
Bridge Fm
Nene Outfall Cut
Fern Fm
Myrobella Fm
The Laurels Fm
Millbank Fm
Garnsgate
Westmere Fm
Weatherall Fm
Bentinck Fm
East Anglian Fm
Red House Fm
Hurdletree Ho
Primrose Fm
Gedney Broadgate
Little Sutton
Port Sutton Bridge
Wingland Marsh
Wingland Grange
Greenmarsh Fm
Rhoon Fm
Elder Lodge
Pulvertoft Hall Fm
White Ho Fm
Grove Fm
Sutton Bridge
Bleak House Fm
Marsh Fm
Bellmount
Orange Row
Fen House Fm
Onslow Fm
St James Road
Fields Fm
Saturday Br
Clark's Hill
Moorswood Fm
Old Gate
Sutton Crosses
Home Fm
Peterspoint Fm
Emorsgate
Alma Lodge
West Lynn
Clenchwarton
Poplar Tree Fm
South Green
Terrington St Clement
Fleet Fen
Red Foreman's Br
Poplar Ho
Willow Tree Fm
Wisbech Rd
South Holland Lodge
Walpole Cross Keys
African Violet Centre
Lovell's Hall
Kenwick Hall
Hoe Fm
Margaretta Ho
St George's Guildhall
Custom House
King's Lynn
Sycamore Lodge
Red House Ho
Holland Ho
South Holland Ho
Strawberry Hall
Tydd St Mary's Marsh
Gibbons Fm
Balsamfield Ho
Kenwick Fm
The Elms
Clifton's Br
Sutton St James
Draw Dike
Woad Fm
Tydd St Mary
The Grange
Old Inclosed Marsh
Old Hall
Bell's Br
Fishergate
B1165
White Cross Fm
Gunthorpe Fm
Highdenden Ho
Cherry Fm
Hay Green
Shepherd's Gate
Tilney All Saints
Merries Fm
Holbeach St Johns
Manor Fm
Lowgate Ho
Tydd Gote
Corner Fm
Walpole Marsh
Walpole St Andrew
Bustards Fm
Jankinsfield Fm
Leedsgate Fm
Manor Hill Fm
Manor Hill Corner
Tretton Manor Fm
Hannath Hall
Foul Anchor
River Nene
Flower Fm
Wash Dyke
Tilney High End
Islington Lodge
Trafford Ho
Four Gotes
White House Fm
Broken Cross
White Ho Fm
Islington Hall Fm
Coy Br
Broadgate Ho
Dunton Hall
Cole Ho
Sandygate Fm
Tydd St Giles
Hornfield Ho
Kirkgate Br
Silverwood Fm
Rose Hall
Walpole St Peter
Duncan's Fm
Park Ho
Church Lane
Lodge Fm
Ingleborough Fm
Church End
St Peter's Lodge
Eau Brink
Bank Fm
Hallgate Fm
Grangehill Fm
Ewings Fm
Oaktree Fm
North Level Main Drain
Marsh Fm
Ingleborough
Salgate Fm
Saddle Bow
Poplartree Fm
Aylmer Hall
White Hall Fm
Wiggenhall St Germans
Guanock Ho
Sutton Rd
Honington House Fm
Terrington St John
Abbey Fm
Mole Drove Fm
Chestnut Ho
Lady Nunn's Old Eau
B1165
Newton
High Road
Ferry Fm
Grange Fm
St John's Highway
Walpole Highway
Wiggenhall St Mary the Virgin
Sutton St Edmund
CAMBRIDGESHIRE
NORFOLK
West Walton
Priory Fm
Faulkner Ho
Elm Tree Ho
Hirdling Ho
Tilney St Lawrence
Thornton's Br
Wiggenhall St Peter
Poplartree Fm
Fenwick Fm
A1101
Ratten Row
Tilney cum Islington
Guanock Fm
West Walton Highway
Barrycott Lodge
Black Ditch Level
Lordsbridge
Peter's Drove Br
Ivy Fm
Holly Tree Fm
Fitton End
West Drove Fm
White House Fm
Magdalen Br
Barbers Fm
Oxfield Ho
Walton Highway
Green Lane Fm
Marshland
Decoy Fm
Park Ho
Gorefield
Grassgate Ho
Fenland Aviation Museum
Harp's Hall
St John's Fen End
Smeeth Lode
Rosary Fm
Eye Fm
Blacklane Fm
Richmond Hall
Floral Fm
Trinity Hall
Tilney Fen End
Harold's Br
Walpole Gate
Gravel Bank Fm
Wiggenhall St Mary Magdalen
Leverington Common
Leverington
The Smeeth
Subscription Br
Tydd St Mary's Fen
Hawthorn Fm
Hundred Acre Fm
Holland's Fm
Carlton Fm
Lynn Road
Watlington
Manor Fm
Leverington Common
Trafford Ho
Walsoken
Wisbech
Peckover House
Barrett's Br
Rosedale
Parsonage Fm
Cloughs Cross
Highfield Fm
Cheyney Ho
New Walsoken
Paradise Fm
Marshland St James
Main Road
Wood Mills Fm
Manor Ho
Chequers Corner
Popenhoe Ho
Chancellor's Drain
Main Drain
Parson Drove
Church End
Bellamy's Br
Wisbech St Mary
Wisbech & Fenland Museum
Smeeth House Fm
Forty Foot Br
Rungay's Br
River Great Ouse
Fen Fm
Banyer Hall
Oxburgh
Marshland Fen
Dike
A17
A47
A1101
B1359
B1515
B1390
B1165
B1166
B1169
B1187
B198
174
175
158
139
TF

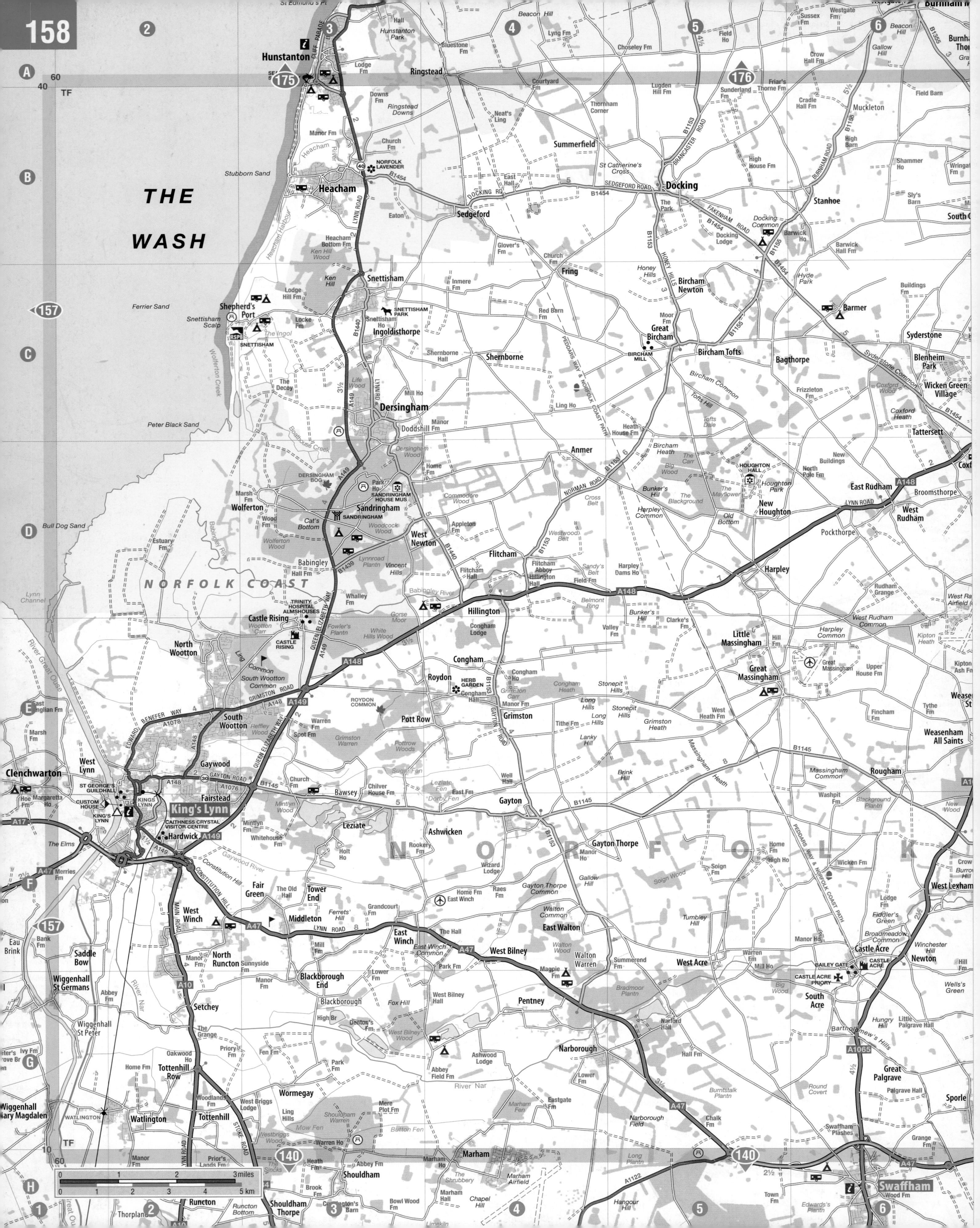
THE
WASH
NORFOLK COAST
NORFOLK
Hunstanton
Heacham
Snettisham
Shepherd's Port
Ingoldisthorpe
Dersingham
Wolferton
Sandringham
West Newton
Babingley
Castle Rising
North Wootton
South Wootton
Gaywood
King's Lynn
Fairstead
Hardwick
West Lynn
Clenchwarton
Ringstead
Sedgeford
Docking
Summerfield
Stanhoe
Fring
Bircham Newton
Great Bircham
Bircham Tofts
Bagthorpe
Barmer
Syderstone
Blenheim Park
Wicken Green Village
Tattersett
Shernborne
Anmer
Flitcham
Hillington
Congham
Roydon
Pott Row
Grimston
Gayton
Bawsey
Leziate
Ashwicken
Gayton Thorpe
Harpley
Little Massingham
Great Massingham
New Houghton
East Rudham
West Rudham
Rougham
Weasenham All Saints
West Lexham
Castle Acre
Newton
South Acre
West Acre
East Walton
West Bilney
Pentney
Narborough
Great Palgrave
Sporle
Swaffham
Marham
Shouldham
Shouldham Thorpe
Runcton
Wormegay
Tottenhill
Tottenhill Row
Watlington
Wiggenhall St Mary Magdalen
Wiggenhall St Peter
Wiggenhall St Germans
Saddle Bow
Setchey
North Runcton
West Winch
Middleton
Blackborough End
East Winch
Fair Green
Tower End
Stubborn Sand
Ferrier Sand
Peter Black Sand
Bull Dog Sand
Snettisham Scalp
Lynn Channel
River Great Ouse
River Nar
Gaywood River
Babingley River
Peddars Way & Norfolk Coast Path
A149
A148
A47
A10
A1065
A1122
B1145
B1153
B1154
B1155
B1454
B1440
B1439
175
176
157
140
0 1 2 3 miles
0 1 2 3 4 5 km

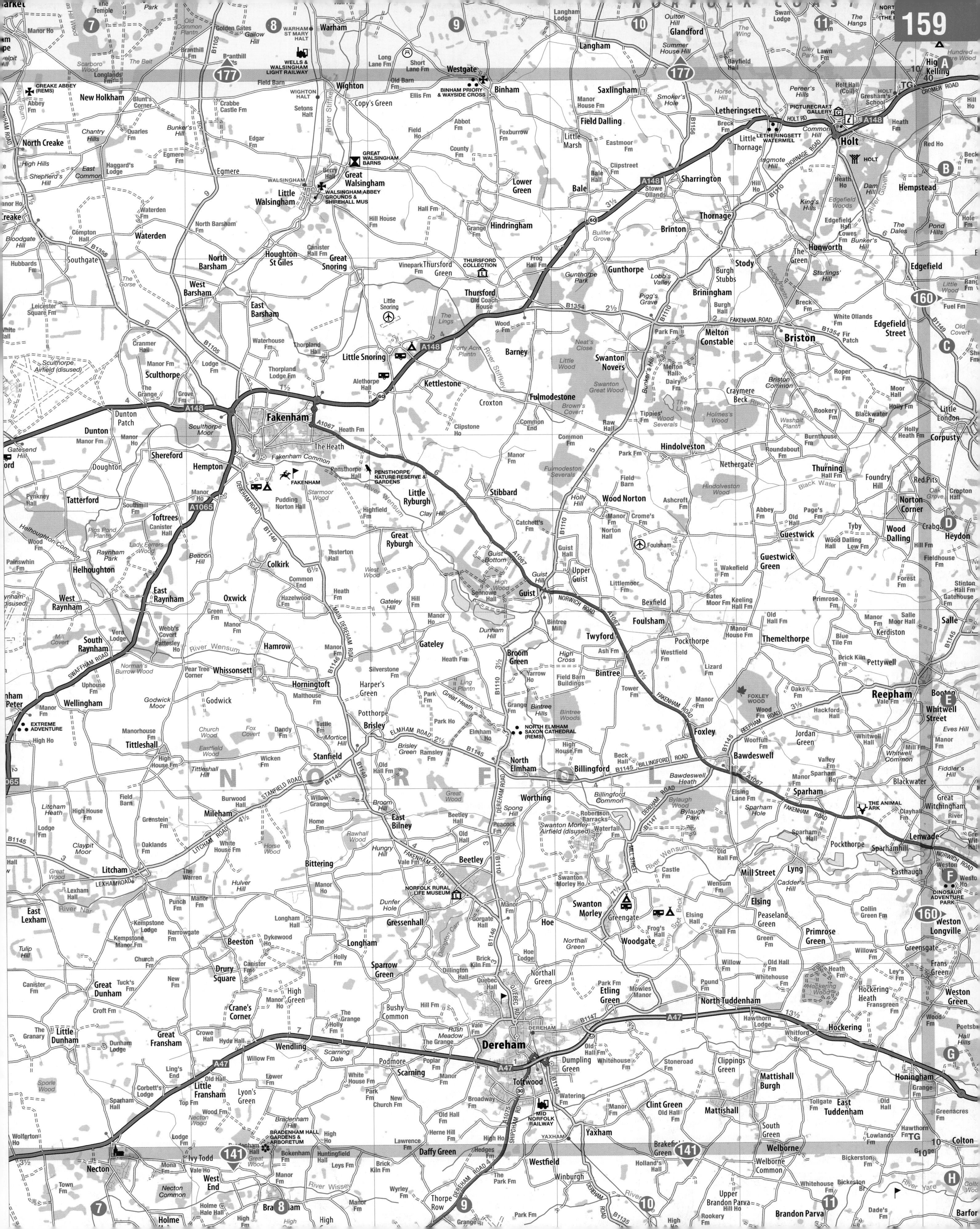
NORFOLK COAST
N O R F O L K
Warham
Wighton
Binham
Westgate
Langham
Glandford
Saxlingham
Letheringsett
Holt
Field Dalling
Sharrington
Bale
Lower Green
Hindringham
Thornage
Brinton
Hunworth
Stody
Edgefield
Hempstead
Gunthorpe
Briningham
Thursford
Melton Constable
Briston
Edgefield Street
Barney
Swanton Novers
Fulmodestone
Kettlestone
Little Snoring
Great Snoring
Houghton St Giles
Great Walsingham
Little Walsingham
New Holkham
North Creake
Waterden
North Barsham
West Barsham
East Barsham
Sculthorpe
Fakenham
Dunton
Shereford
Hempton
Tatterford
Toftrees
Little Ryburgh
Great Ryburgh
Stibbard
Wood Norton
Hindolveston
Thurning
Guestwick
Wood Dalling
Heydon
Corpusty
Helhoughton
West Raynham
East Raynham
South Raynham
Colkirk
Oxwick
Guist
Twyford
Foulsham
Bintree
Themelthorpe
Salle
Reepham
Whitwell Street
Hamrow
Whissonsett
Horningtoft
Gateley
Broom Green
Wellingham
Tittleshall
Brisley
Stanfield
North Elmham
Billingford
Foxley
Bawdeswell
Sparham
Lenwade
Mileham
Worthing
East Bilney
Beetley
Bittering
Litcham
East Lexham
Gressenhall
Swanton Morley
Hoe
Elsing
Lyng
Mill Street
Woodgate
Primrose Green
Weston Longville
Beeston
Longham
Drury Square
Great Dunham
Little Dunham
Crane's Corner
Sparrow Green
High Green
Great Fransham
Wendling
Scarning
Dereham
Toftwood
Dumpling Green
Etling Green
North Tuddenham
Hockering
Honingham
Mattishall
Mattishall Burgh
East Tuddenham
Little Fransham
Necton
Yaxham
Clint Green
Welborne
Daffy Green
Westfield
Holme
Thorpe Row
Brandon Parva
A148
A1067
A1065
A47
B1145
B1110
177
160
141

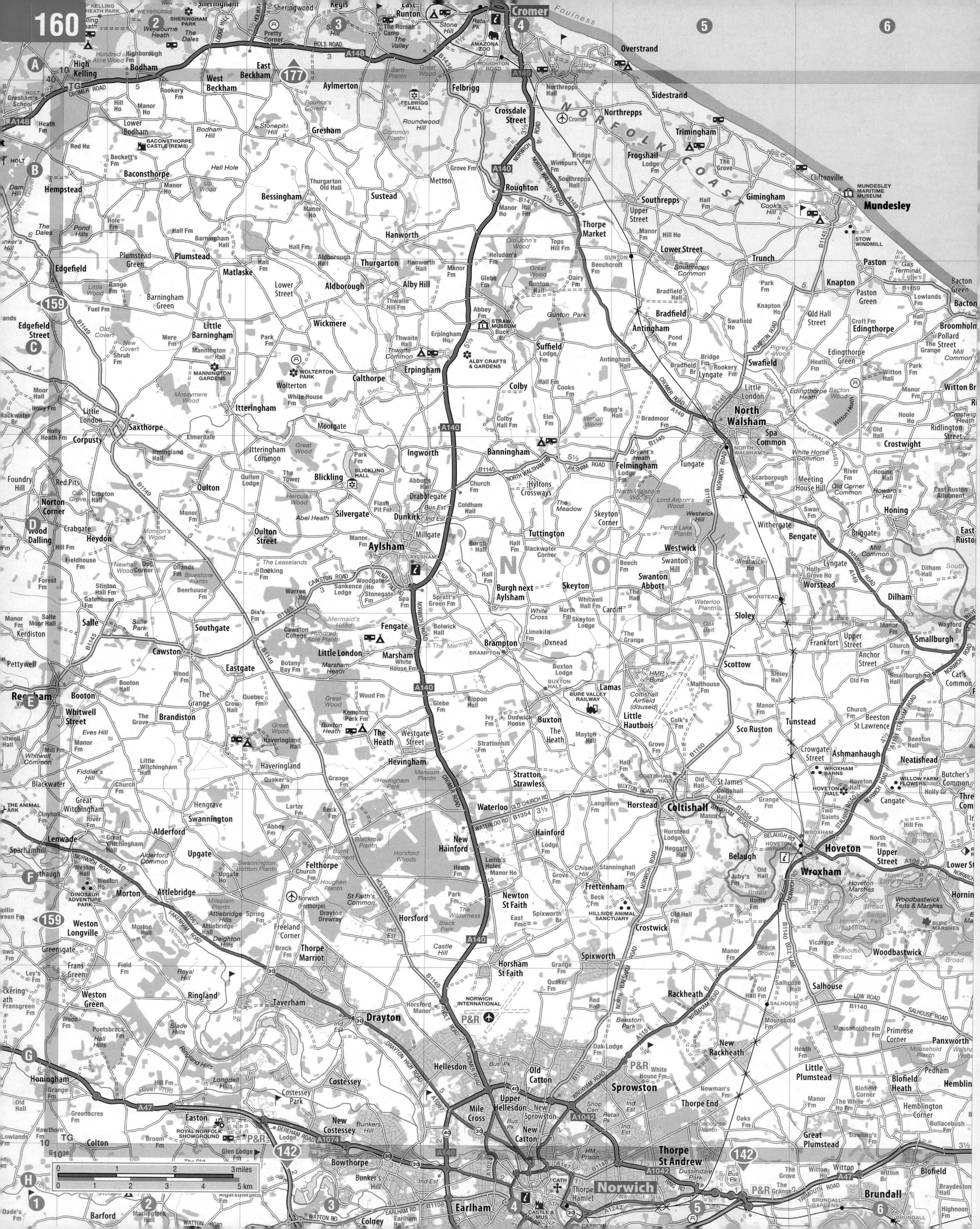
Cromer
Overstrand
Sidestrand
Northrepps
Trimingham
Mundesley
NORFOLK COAST
Felbrigg
Aylmerton
East Beckham
West Beckham
Bodham
High Kelling
Holt
Hempstead
Baconsthorpe
Gresham
Bessingham
Sustead
Metton
Roughton
Southrepps
Thorpe Market
Lower Street
Trunch
Knapton
Paston
Bacton
Edgefield
Plumstead
Matlaske
Aldborough
Thurgarton
Hanworth
Alby Hill
Wickmere
Little Barningham
Barningham Green
Itteringham
Wolterton
Calthorpe
Erpingham
Colby
Suffield
Antingham
Bradfield
Swafield
Edingthorpe
North Walsham
Saxthorpe
Corpusty
Blickling
Ingworth
Banningham
Felmingham
Oulton
Heydon
Aylsham
Burgh next Aylsham
Skeyton
Tuttington
Westwick
Swanton Abbott
Worstead
Dilham
Smallburgh
Honing
Sloley
Scottow
Cawston
Salle
Southgate
Eastgate
Marsham
Brampton
Oxnead
Lamas
Buxton
Little Hautbois
Tunstead
Sco Ruston
Ashmanhaugh
Neatishead
Booton
Whitwell Street
Brandiston
Haveringland
Hevingham
Stratton Strawless
Horstead
Coltishall
Belaugh
Hoveton
Wroxham
Great Witchingham
Swannington
Alderford
Lenwade
Morton
Attlebridge
Felthorpe
Horsford
Newton St Faith
Frettenham
Crostwick
Spixworth
Horsham St Faith
Rackheath
Salhouse
Woodbastwick
Weston Longville
Ringland
Taverham
Drayton
Hellesdon
Old Catton
Sprowston
Thorpe End
Costessey
Easton
Honingham
New Costessey
Bowthorpe
Thorpe St Andrew
Norwich
Earlham
Colney
Barford
Blofield
Brundall
Great Plumstead
Little Plumstead
Norwich International
A140
A148
A149
A1067
A47
A1042

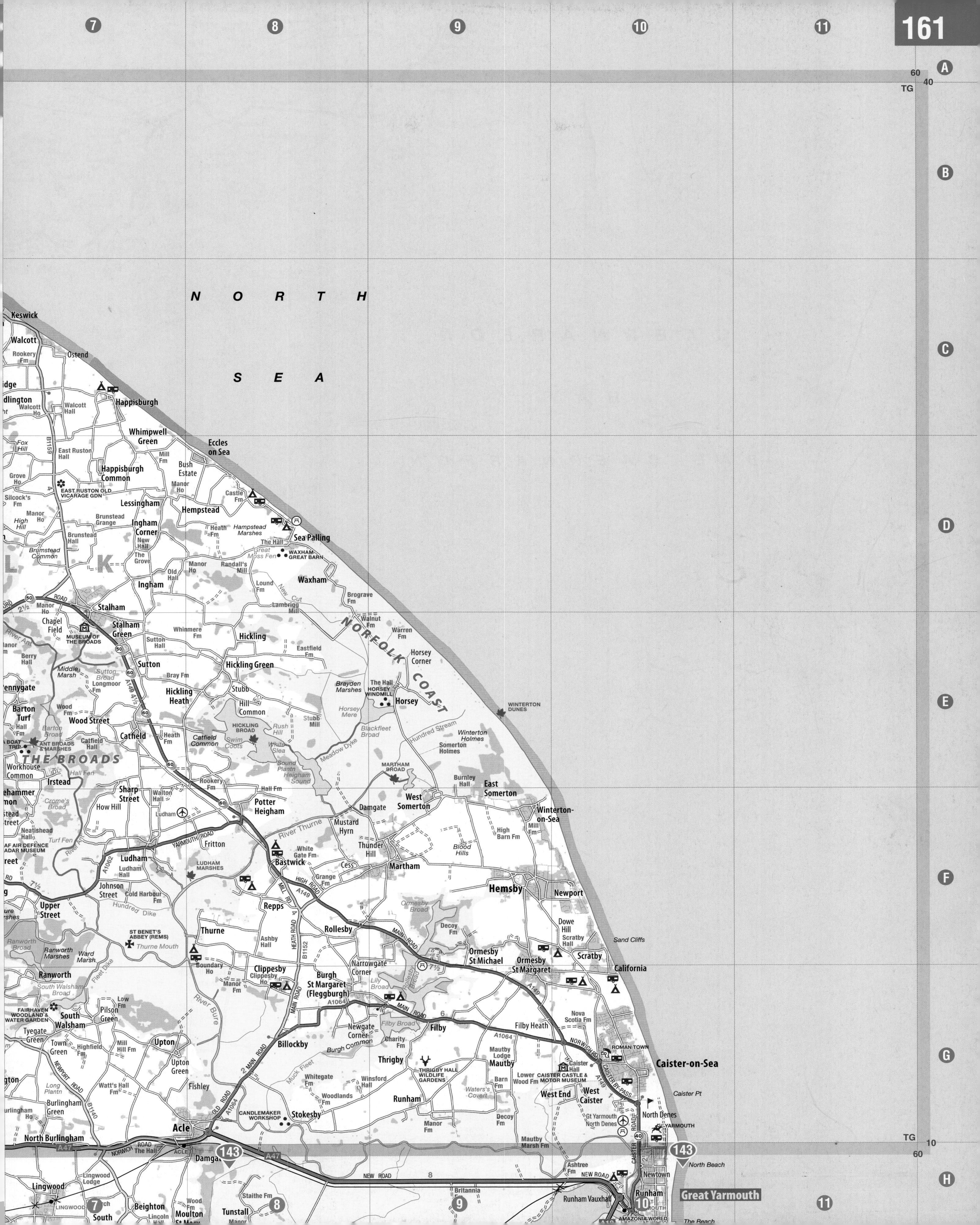
N O R T H
S E A
NORFOLK COAST
THE BROADS
Keswick
Walcott
Ostend
Happisburgh
Whimpwell Green
Eccles on Sea
Bush Estate
Happisburgh Common
EAST RUSTON OLD VICARAGE GDN
Lessingham
Hempstead
Castle Fm
Sea Palling
Hampstead Marshes
WAXHAM GREAT BARN
Ingham Corner
Brunstead Grange
Brunstead Hall
Brumstead Common
Ingham
Waxham
Lambrigg Mill
Brograve Fm
Stalham
Stalham Green
MUSEUM OF THE BROADS
Chapel Field
Sutton
Hickling
Hickling Green
Hickling Heath
Eastfield Fm
Horsey Corner
Warren Fm
Brayden Marshes
HORSEY WINDMILL
Horsey
Horsey Mere
WINTERTON DUNES
Hundred Stream
Winterton Holmes
Somerton Holmes
Wood Street
Catfield
Catfield Common
HICKLING BROAD
Meadow Dyke
Heigham Sound
ANT BROADS & MARSHES
Barton Turf
Irstead
Workhouse Common
MARTHAM BROAD
Burnley Hall
East Somerton
West Somerton
Winterton-on-Sea
Sharp Street
How Hill
Potter Heigham
Damgate
Mustard Hyrn
Ludham
Fritton
River Thurne
Thunder Hill
Martham
Blood Hills
Bastwick
LUDHAM MARSHES
Ludham Hall
Johnson Street
Cold Harbour Fm
Repps
Hemsby
Newport
Upper Street
Hundred Dike
Thurne
ST BENET'S ABBEY (REMS)
Thurne Mouth
Ashby Hall
Rollesby
Decoy Fm
Dowe Hill
Scratby Hall
Sand Cliffs
Ormesby St Michael
Ormesby St Margaret
Scratby
California
Ranworth Marshes
Ranworth
Ward Marsh
Boundary Ho
Clippesby
Narrowgate Corner
Burgh St Margaret (Fleggburgh)
Rollesby Broad
Lily Broad
South Walsham Broad
FAIRHAVEN WOODLAND & WATER GARDEN
South Walsham
Pilson Green
River Bure
Filby Broad
Filby
Filby Heath
Nova Scotia Fm
Tyegate Green
Town Green
Upton
Upton Green
Billockby
Newgate Corner
Burgh Common
Charity Fm
Thrigby
THRIGBY HALL WILDLIFE GARDENS
Mautby
ROMAN TOWN
Caister Hall
CAISTER CASTLE & MOTOR MUSEUM
Caister-on-Sea
Fishley
Whitegate Fm
Winsford Hall
Woodlands Fm
Runham
Waters's Covert
Lower Wood Fm
West End
West Caister
Caister Pt
Burlingham Green
CANDLEMAKER WORKSHOP
Stokesby
Acle
Decoy Fm
Manor Fm
Gt Yarmouth North Denes
North Denes
North Burlingham
Damgate
Mautby Marsh Fm
North Beach
Lingwood
Lingwood Lodge
Britannia
Ashtree Fm
Newtown
Beighton
Moulton St Mary
Tunstall
Staithe Fm
Runham Vauxhall
Runham
Great Yarmouth
AMAZONIA WORLD
The Beach
South
A149
A1062
A1064
A47
B1159
B1152
B1140
143
TG

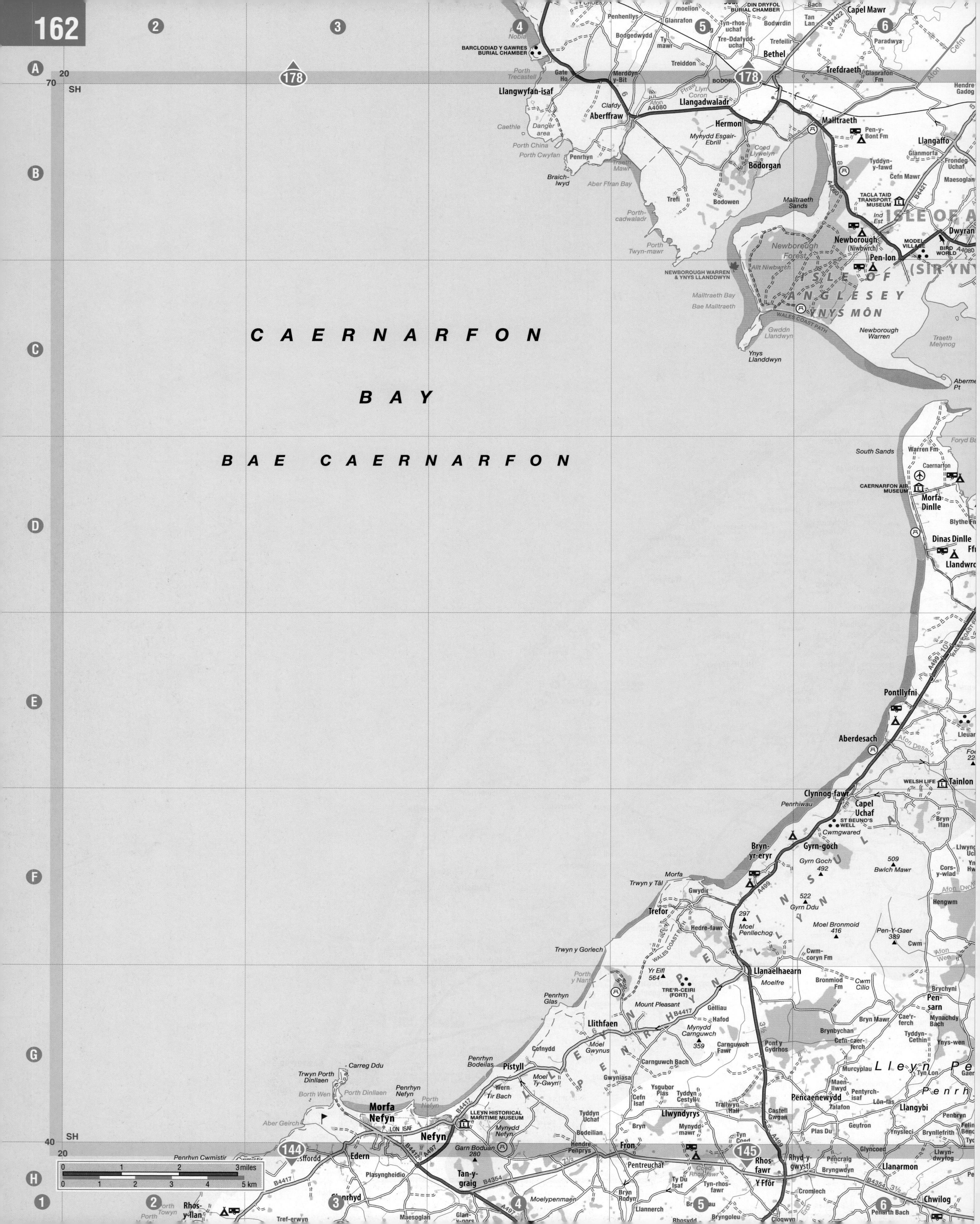
CAERNARFON
BAY
BAE CAERNARFON
ISLE OF ANGLESEY
YNYS MÔN
Lleyn Peninsula
PENRHYN LLŶN
BARCLODIAD Y GAWRES BURIAL CHAMBER
DIN DRYFOL BURIAL CHAMBER
Penhenllys
Glanrafon
Tyn-rhos-uchaf
Bodwrdin
Tan Lan
Capel Mawr
Bodgedwydd
Ty mawr
Tre-Ddafydd-uchaf
Trefeilir
Paradwys
Bethel
Treiddon
Trefdraeth
Glanrafon Fm
Hendre Gadog
Porth Trecastell
Gate Ho
Merddyn-y-Bit
Bodorgan
Llangwyfan-isaf
Llyn Coron
Clafdy
Afon Ffraw
Llangadwaladr
Aberffraw
Hermon
Malltraeth
Pen-y-Bont Fm
Llangaffo
Caethle
Danger area
Mynydd Esgair-Ebrill
Coed Llywelyn
Glanmorfa
Tyddyn-y-fawd
Frondeg Uchaf
Porth China
Porth Cwyfan
Penrhyn
Traeth Mawr
Bodorgan
Cefn Mawr
Maesoglan
Braich-lwyd
Aber Ffraw Bay
Trefi
Bodowen
Malltraeth Sands
TACLA TAID TRANSPORT MUSEUM
Ind Est
Porth-cadwaladr
Porth Twyn-mawr
Newborough Forest
Newborough (Niwbwrch)
MODEL VILLAGE
BIRD WORLD
Dwyran
Pen-lon
Allt Niwbwrch
NEWBOROUGH WARREN & YNYS LLANDDWYN
Malltraeth Bay
Bae Malltraeth
WALES COAST PATH
Gwddn Llandwyn
Ynys Llanddwyn
Newborough Warren
Traeth Melynog
Abermenai Pt
Foryd Bay
South Sands
Warren Fm
Caernarfon
CAERNARFON AIR MUSEUM
Morfa Dinlle
Blythe Fm
Dinas Dinlle
Llandwrog
Pontllyfni
Aberdesach
Afon Desach
WELSH LIFE
Tainlon
Clynnog-fawr
Penrhiwau
Capel Uchaf
ST BEUNO'S WELL
Cwmgwared
Bryn Hafn
Bryn-yr-eryr
Gyrn-goch
Gyrn Goch 492
509 Bwlch Mawr
Corsy-wlad
Morfa
Trwyn y Tâl
Gwydir
522 Gyrn Ddu
Hengwm
Trefor
297 Moel Penllechog
Hedre-fawr
Moel Bronmoid 416
Pen-Y-Gaer 389
Cwm
Trwyn y Gorlech
Cwm-coryn Fm
Afon Wen
Porth y Nant
Yr Eifl 564
TRE'R-CEIRI (FORT)
Llanaelhaearn
Moelfre
Bronmiod Fm
Cwm Cilio
Brychyni
Pen-sarn
Penrhyn Glas
Mount Pleasant
Gelliau
Hafod
Mynachdy Bach
Llithfaen
Mynydd Carnguwch 359
Bryn Mawr
Cae'r-ferch
Brynbychan
Tyddyn-Cethin
Ynys-wen
Moel Gwynus
Carnguwch Fawr
Pont y Gydrhos
Cefn-caer-ferch
Gefnydd
Carnguwch Bach
Penrhyn Bodeilas
Pistyll
Murcyplau
Tyn Lon
Trwyn Porth Dinllaen
Carreg Ddu
Moel Ty-Gwyn
Gwyniasa
Maen-llwyd
Pentyrch-isaf
Borth Wen
Porth Dinllaen
Penrhyn Nefyn
Wern
Tir Bach
Ysgubor Plas
Tyddyn Cestyll
Pencaenewydd
Talafon
Lôn-las
Llangybi
Porth Nefyn
Morfa Nefyn
LLEYN HISTORICAL MARITIME MUSEUM
Cefn Isaf
Trallwyn Hall
Castell Gwgan
Aber Geirch
Lôn Isaf
Tyddyn Uchaf
Llwyndyrys
Bryn
Geufron
Ynysleci
Penbryn
Brynllefrith
Nefyn
Mynydd Nefyn
Bodeilian
Mynydd-mawr
Plas Du
Tyn Coed
Garn Boduan 280
Hendre Penprys
Fron
Glyncoed
Llwyn-dwyfog
Penrhyn Cwmistir
Edern
Pentreuchaf
Rhos-fawr
Rhyd-y-gwystl
Pencraig
Bryngwdyn
Llanarmon
Plasyngheidio
Tan-y-graig
Ty Du Isaf
Coed Rhos-fawr
Tyn-rhos-fawr
Y Ffôr
Cromlech
Chwilog
Glanrhyd
Bryn Rodyn
Llannerch
Moelypenmaen
Porth Towyn
Rhos-y-llan
Tref-erwyn
Maesoglan
Glan-y-gors
Bryngoleu
Penarth Bach
Clogwyn
A4080
A499
A497
B4417
B4412
B4354
B4422
B4421
178
144
145
SH
0 1 2 3 miles
0 1 2 3 4 5 km

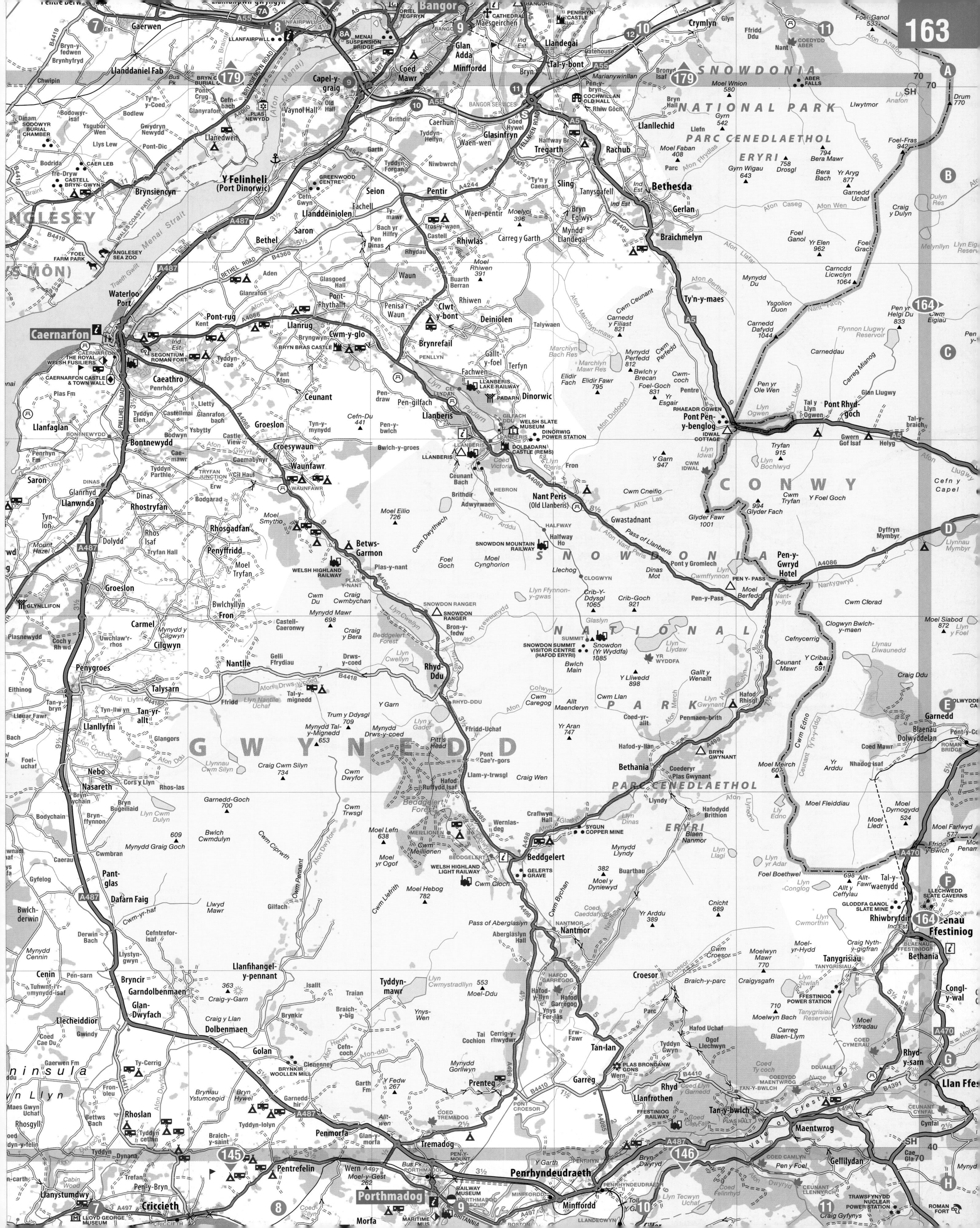
Bangor
Gaerwen
Llanfairpwll
Menai Suspension Bridge
Maesgeirchen
Penrhyn Castle
Llandegai
Tal-y-bont
Crymlyn
Glan Adda
Minffordd
Coed Mawr
Capel-y-graig
Llanddaniel Fab
Snowdonia
National Park
Parc Cenedlaethol
Eryri
Aber Falls
Moel Wnion 580
Drum 770
Foel-Fras 942
Bera Mawr 794
Drosgl 758
Yr Aryg 877
Garnedd Uchaf
Llanllechid
Rachub
Tregarth
Glasinfryn
Caerhun
Waen-wen
Vaynol Hall
Plas Newydd
Llanedwen
Brynsiencyn
Y Felinheli (Port Dinorwic)
Seion
Pentir
Sling
Bethesda
Gerlan
Braichmelyn
Anglesey
(Ynys Môn)
Menai Strait
Anglesey Sea Zoo
Llanddeiniolen
Saron
Bethel
Rhiwlas
Carreg y Garth
Moel Rhiwen 391
Waun
Waterloo Port
Caernarfon
Caernarfon Castle & Town Wall
Segontium Roman Fort
Pont-rug
Llanrug
Cwm-y-glo
Bryn Bras Castle
Clwt-y-bont
Deiniolen
Brynrefail
Caeathro
Ceunant
Llanberis
Llyn Padarn
Welsh Slate Museum
Dinorwig Power Station
Dolbadarn Castle (rems)
Dinorwic
Elidir Fawr 795
Foel-Goch 831
Yr Esgair
Carnedd y Filiast 821
Mynydd Perfedd 812
Carnedd Dafydd 1044
Pen yr Helgi Du 833
Carneddau
Carnedd Llewelyn 1064
Yr Elen 962
Foel Grach
Pen yr Ole Wen
Rhaeadr Ogwen
Pont Pen-y-benglog
Idwal Cottage
Tal y Llyn Ogwen
Pont Rhyd-goch
Glan Llugwy
Helyg
Tryfan 915
Y Garn 947
Glyder Fawr 1001
Glyder Fach 994
Conwy
Llanfaglan
Groeslon
Bontnewydd
Croesywaun
Waunfawr
Nant Peris (Old Llanberis)
Gwastadnant
Pass of Llanberis
Saron
Llanwnda
Dinas
Rhostryfan
Rhosgadfan
Moel Eilio 726
Betws-Garmon
Snowdon Mountain Railway
Halfway Ho
Pen-y-Gwryd Hotel
Pen-y-Pass
Moel Berfedd
Crib-Goch 921
Crib-Y-Ddysgl 1065
Snowdon (Yr Wyddfa) 1085
Snowdon Summit Visitor Centre (Hafod Eryri)
Snowdon Ranger
Llyn Cwellyn
Mynydd Mawr 698
Welsh Highland Railway
Groeslon
Carmel
Cilgwyn
Fron
Penygroes
Nantlle
Talysarn
Rhyd-Ddu
Y Lliwedd 898
Yr Aran 747
Gallt y Wenallt
Hafod Rhisgl
Penmaen-brith
Bryn Gwynant
Gwynedd
Trum y Ddysgl 709
Mynydd Tal-y-Mignedd 653
Craig Cwm Silyn 734
Llanllyfni
Nebo
Nasareth
Garnedd-Goch 700
Beddgelert Forest
Beddgelert
Sygun Copper Mine
Moel Hebog 782
Moel Lefn 638
Bethania
Craflwyn Hall
Yr Arddu 389
Cnicht 689
Nantmor
Pass of Aberglaslyn
Aberglaslyn Hall
Moel Siabod 872
Blaenau Ffestiniog
Dolwyddelan
Garnedd
Moel Meirch 607
Tanygrisiau
Ffestiniog Power Station
Moelwyn Mawr 770
Moelwyn Bach 710
Croesor
Llechwedd Slate Caverns
Gloddfa Ganol Slate Mine
Rhiwbryfdir
Pant-glas
Dafarn Faig
Bryncir
Garndolbenmaen
Glan-Dwyfach
Dolbenmaen
Llanfihangel-y-pennant
Tyddyn-mawr
Moel-Ddu 553
Golan
Brynkir Woollen Mill
Prenteg
Tan-lan
Garreg
Plas Brondanw Gdns
Llanfrothen
Rhyd
Tan-y-bwlch
Maentwrog
Ffestiniog Railway
Vale of Ffestiniog
Gellilydan
Trawsfynydd Nuclear Power Station
Rhoslan
Penmorfa
Tremadog
Pentrefelin
Criccieth
Llanystumdwy
Lloyd George Museum
Porthmadog
Penrhyndeudraeth
Minffordd
Morfa
Llan Ffestiniog
Rhyd-y-sarn
Congl-y-wal
Llyn Tecwyn Uchaf
Craig Gyfynys

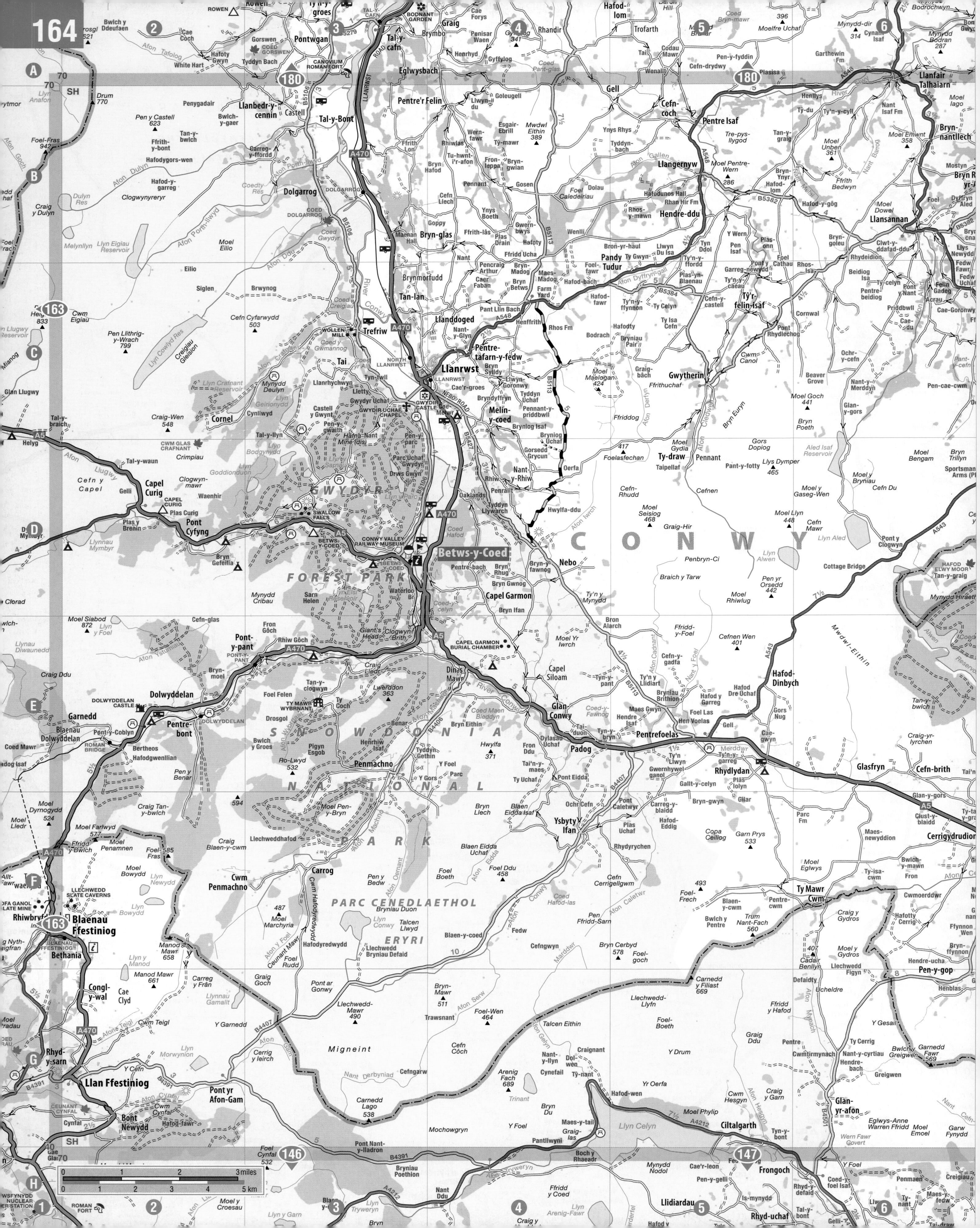
Rowen
Tyn-y-groes
Bodnant Garden
Graig
Cae Forys
Hafod-lom
Trofarth
Moelfre Uchaf
Mynydd-dir
Bodrochwyn
Bwlch y Ddeufaen
Pontwgan
Tal-y-cafn
Brymbo
Rhandir
Canovium Roman Fort
Eglwysbach
Pen-y-fyddin
Cefn-drydwy
Garthewin Fm
Llanfair Talhaiarn
Drum 770
Llanbedr-y-cennin
Castell
Tal-y-Bont
Pentre'r Felin
Gell
Cefn-coch
Pentre Isaf
Pen y Castell 623
Foel-Fras 942
Dolgarrog
Coed Dolgarrog
Llangernyw
Moel Pentre-Wern 286
Bryn-nantllech
Llansannan
Afon Dulyn
Hafodunos Hall
Hendre-ddu
Craig y Dulyn
Melynllyn
Llyn Eigiau Reservoir
Moel Eilio
Maenan Hall
Bryn-glas
Pandy Tudur
Eilio
Siglen
Brynwog
Brynmorfudd
Tan-lan
Llanddoged
Farm Yard
Cefn-y-castell
Ty'r-felin-isaf
Cwm Eigiau
Cefn Cyfarwydd 503
Trefriw
Pen Llithrig-y-Wrach 799
Pentre-tafarn-y-fedw
Llanrwst
Gwytherin
Tai
Cornel
Gwydyr Castle
Melin-y-coed
Moel Maelogan 424
Craig-Wen 548
Helyg
Capel Curig
Gwydyr
Swallow Falls
Pont Cyfyng
Betws-y-Coed
Conwy Valley Railway Museum
Forest Park
Capel Garmon
Nebo
Conwy
Moel Seisiog 468
Moel Llyn 448
Llyn Alwen
Pen yr Orsedd 442
Moel Siabod 872
Pont-y-pant
Capel Garmon Burial Chamber
Dinas Mawr
Dolwyddelan
Dolwyddelan Castle
Pentre-bont
Garnedd
Blaenau Dolwyddelan
Roman Bridge
Snowdonia National Park
Penmachno
Padog
Pentrefoelas
Glan Conwy
Capel Siloam
Hafod-Dinbych
Rhydlydan
Glasfryn
Cefn-brith
Ysbyty Ifan
Cerrigydrudion
Moel Dyrnogydd 524
Moel Farlwyd 577
Llechwedd Slate Caverns
Cwm Penmachno
Carrog
Parc Cenedlaethol Eryri
Blaenau Ffestiniog
Bethania
Manod Mawr 661
Congl-y-wal
Ty Mawr Cwm
Pen-y-gop
Carnedd y Filiast 669
Llyn Conwy
Migneint
Rhyd-y-sarn
Llan Ffestiniog
Pont yr Afon-Gam
Bont Newydd
Arenig Fach 689
Carnedd Lago 538
Llyn Celyn
Ciltalgarth
Glan-yr-afon
Frongoch
Llidiardau
Rhyd-uchaf
0 1 2 3 miles
0 1 2 3 4 5 km

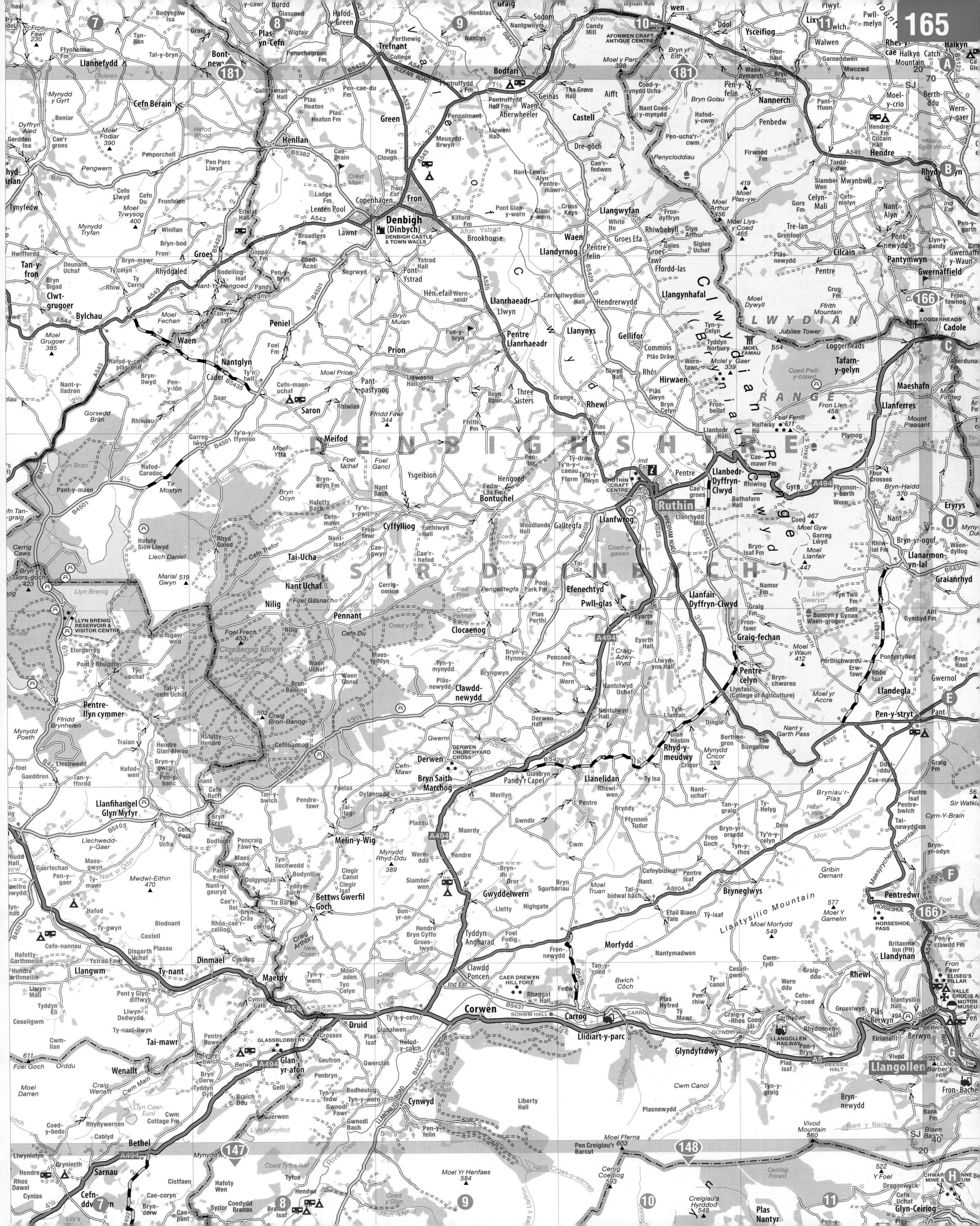
DENBIGHSHIRE
(SIR DDINBYCH)
CLWYDIAN RANGE
(Bryniau Clwyd)
Vale of Clwyd
Denbigh (Dinbych)
DENBIGH CASTLE & TOWN WALLS
Ruthin
RUTHIN CRAFT CENTRE
Corwen
Llangollen
Bodfari
Trefnant
Henllan
Llannefydd
Cefn Berain
Bylchau
Waen
Nantglyn
Saron
Peniel
Prion
Llanrhaeadr
Pentre Llanrhaeadr
Llanynys
Rhewl
Llangynhafal
Llandyrnog
Llangwyfan
Gellifor
Hirwaen
Llanbedr-Dyffryn-Clwyd
Llanfair-Dyffryn-Clwyd
Llanfwrog
Efenechtyd
Pwll-glas
Clocaenog
Clocaenog Forest
Cyffylliog
Bontuchel
Nant Uchaf
Pennant
Derwen
Bryn Saith Marchog
Melin-y-Wig
Betws Gwerfil Goch
Gwyddelwern
Llanelidan
Rhyd-y-meudwy
Graig-fechan
Pentre-celyn
Llandegla
Pen-y-stryt
Bryneglwys
Llantysilio Mountain
Carrog
Llidiart-y-parc
Glyndyfrdwy
Cynwyd
Druid
Maerdy
Dinmael
Ty-nant
Llangwm
Llanfihangel Glyn Myfyr
LLYN BRENIG RESERVOIR & VISITOR CENTRE
Llyn Brenig
Moel Famau
Jubilee Tower
Llanferres
Maeshafn
Llanarmon-yn-Ial
Graianrhyd
Eryrys
Cilcain
Nannerch
Caerwys
Halkyn
Hendre
Cadole
Gwernaffield
Pantymwyn
Loggerheads
HORSESHOE PASS
VALLE CRUCIS ABBEY
ELISEG'S PILLAR
LLANGOLLEN RAILWAY
Berwyn
Bethel
Sarnau
Glan-yr-afon
Tai-mawr
Wenallt
Moel Fferna 603
Vivod Mountain 560
AFONWEN CRAFT ANTIQUE CENTRE
CAER DREWYN HILL FORT
DERWEN CHURCHYARD CROSS
Llysfasi (College of Agriculture)
181
147
148
166

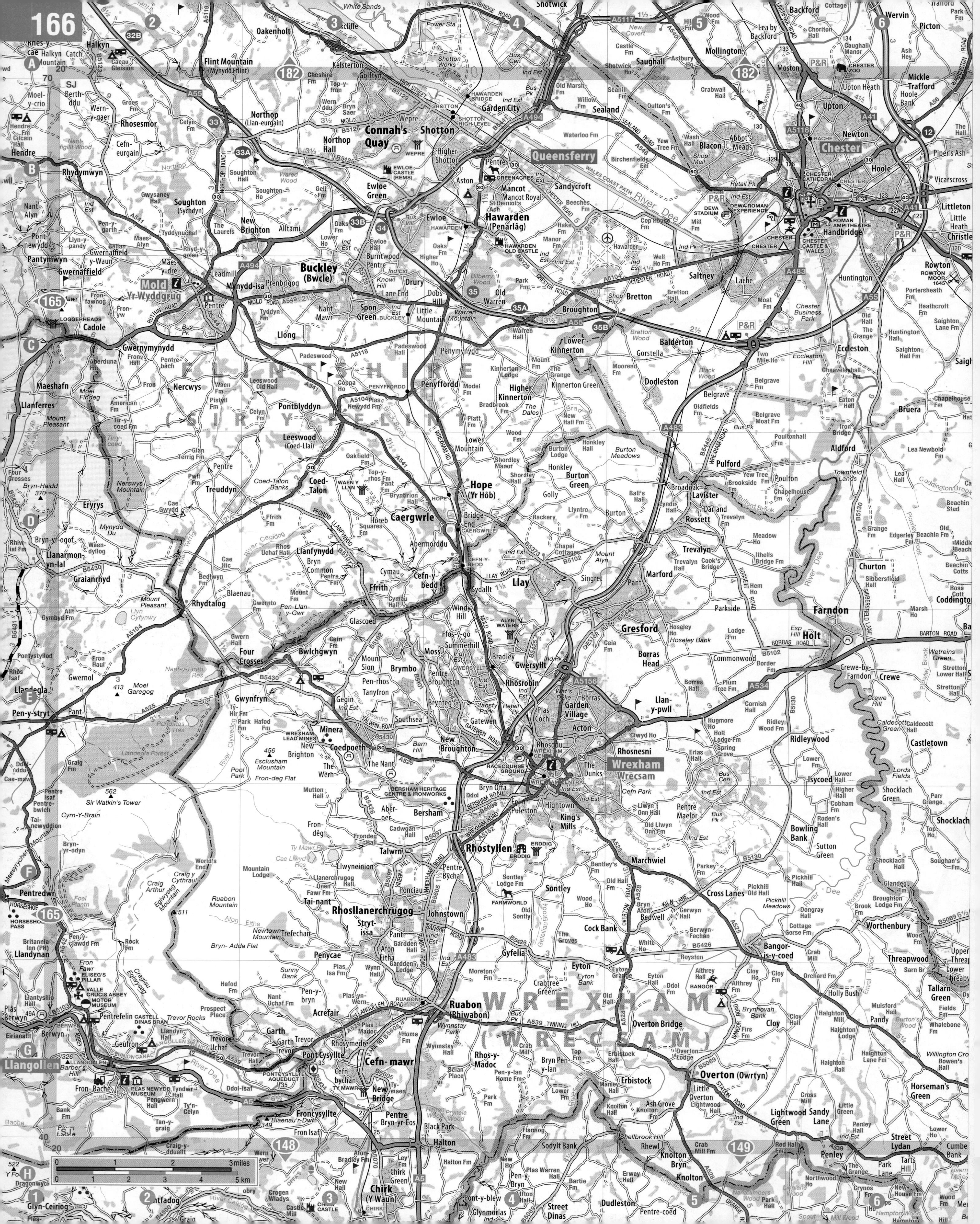
Chester
Queensferry
Wrexham
Wrecsam
Mold
Yr Wyddgrug
Llangollen
FLINTSHIRE
(SIR Y FFLINT)
WREXHAM
(WRECSAM)
Connah's Quay
Shotton
Hawarden
(Penarlâg)
Buckley
(Bwcle)
Northop
(Llan-eurgain)
Flint Mountain
(Mynydd Fflint)
Halkyn
Oakenholt
Saltney
Broughton
Bretton
Sealand
Saughall
Mollington
Backford
Upton
Hoole
Handbridge
Eccleston
Pulford
Rossett
Gresford
Llay
Hope
(Yr Hôb)
Caergwrle
Penyffordd
Leeswood
(Coed-Llai)
Pontblyddyn
Treuddyn
Coed-Talon
Ffrith
Cefn-y-bedd
Brymbo
Coedpoeth
Minera
Gwersyllt
Rhosrobin
Acton
Rhosnesni
Marford
Holt
Farndon
Churton
Aldford
Rhostyllen
Bersham
Marchwiel
Sontley
Rhosllanerchrugog
Johnstown
Penycae
Ruabon
(Rhiwabon)
Cefn-mawr
Pont Cysyllte
New Bridge
Chirk
(Y Waun)
Overton (Owrtyn)
Bangor-is-y-coed
Erbistock
Eyton
Gyfelia
Worthenbury
Threapwood
Llanarmon-yn-Ial
Graianrhyd
Rhydtalog
Four Crosses
Bwlchgwyn
Llandegla
Pen-y-stryt
Gwernymynydd
Cadole
Llanferres
Maeshafn
Nercwys
Mynydd-isa
Ewloe
Garden City
Sandycroft
Mancot
Aston
Llanfynydd
Pentrebach
Froncysyllte
Trevor
Garth
Acrefair
Halton
Penley
Dudleston
Glyn-Ceiriog
A55
A483
A41
A494
A541
A5104
A525
A534
A539
A528
A5
A5156
A5117
A5116
A548
A549
0
1
2
3 miles
0
1
2
3
4
5 km
SJ

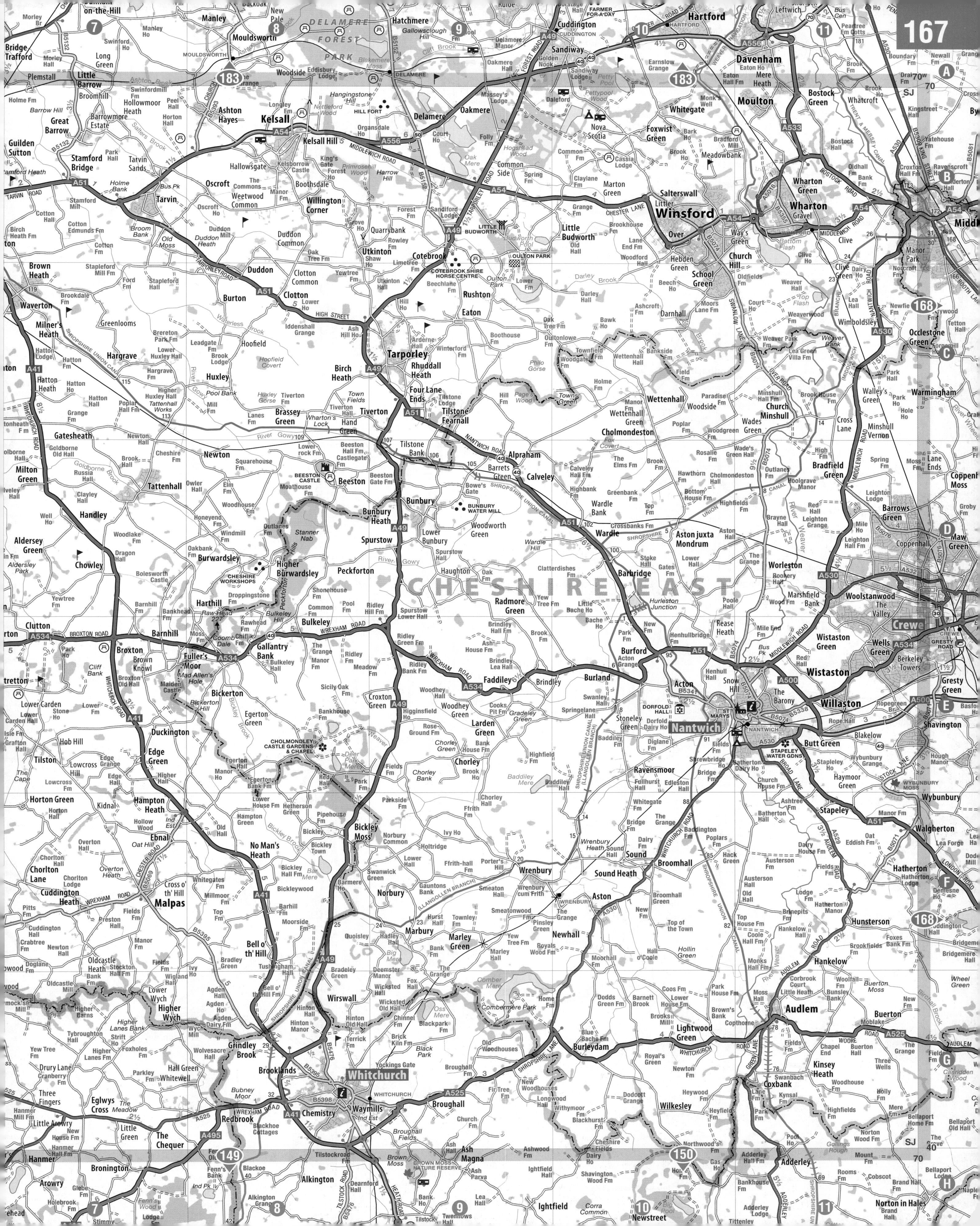
DELAMERE FOREST PARK
CHESHIRE EAST
Hartford
Davenham
Moulton
Winsford
Over
Cuddington
Sandiway
Kelsall
Tarvin
Tarporley
Cotebrook
Little Budworth
Oulton Park
Wharton
Church Minshull
Crewe
Nantwich
Willaston
Wistaston
Audlem
Wrenbury
Malpas
Whitchurch
Broxton
Bunbury
Beeston
Calveley
Barbridge
Wardle
Cholmondeston
Wettenhall
Peckforton
Burwardsley
Bickerton
Tattenhall
Waverton
Duddon
Clotton
Utkinton
Marbury
Hanmer
Adderley
Ightfield
Wybunbury
Hatherton
Hankelow
Shavington
Woolstanwood
Coppenhall
Stapeley
Baddiley
Burland
Acton
Aston
Newhall
Norbury
Chorley
Hampton Heath
Cuddington Heath
No Man's Heath
Bell o' th' Hill
Grindley Brook
Higher Wych
Redbrook
Bronington
Coxbank
Buerton
Kinsey Heath
Lightwood Green
Burleydam
Combermere Park
Cholmondeley Castle Gardens & Chapel
Beeston Castle
Shropshire Union Canal
Hurleston Junction
Stapeley Water Gdns

CHESHIRE EAST
STOKE-ON-TRENT
Middlewich
Holmes Chapel
Sandbach
Elworth
Congleton
Biddulph
Kidsgrove
Alsager
Crewe
Haslington
Tunstall
Burslem
Hanley
Newcastle-under-Lyme
Stoke-on-Trent
Fenton
Longton
Madeley
Audley
Goostrey
Byley
Cranage
Swettenham
Marton
Gawsworth
Bosley
Buglawton
Astbury
Mow Cop
Talke
Chesterton
Silverdale
Keele
Trentham
Meir
Barlaston
Whitmore
Betley
Wybunbury
Woore
Knighton
Rushton Spencer
Endon
Baddeley Green
Werrington
Sandbach Services
Keele Services
M6
A34
A50
A500
A53
A54
A534
A520
A51
A525
184
167
150
151
3 miles
5 km

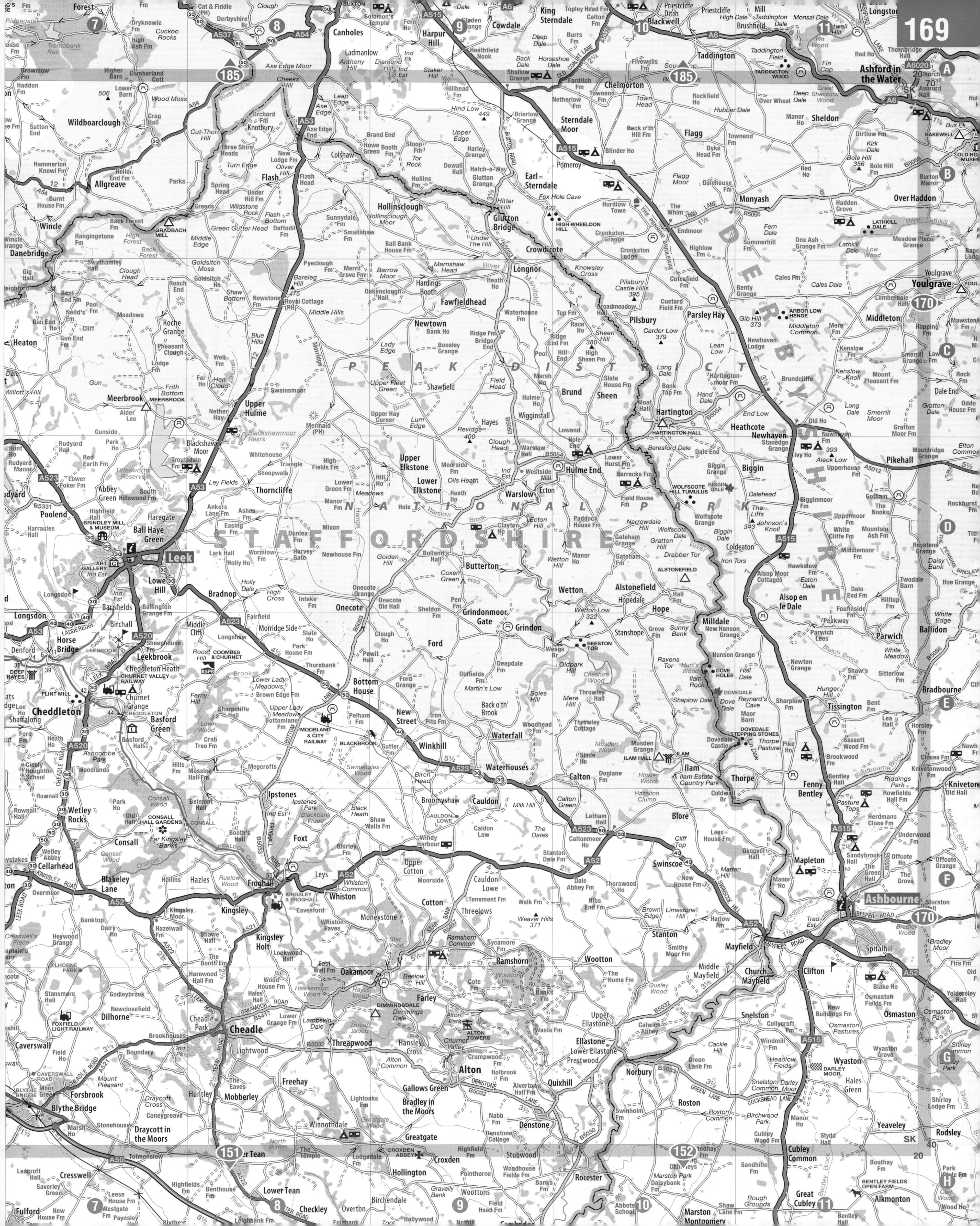

STAFFORDSHIRE
PEAK DISTRICT NATIONAL PARK
DERBYSHIRE
Leek
Ashbourne
Cheadle
Buxton
Ashford in the Water
Taddington
Chelmorton
Flagg
Sheldon
Over Haddon
Monyash
Youlgrave
Middleton
Hartington
Longnor
Hollinsclough
Flash
Wincle
Danebridge
Wildboarclough
Allgreave
Meerbrook
Upper Hulme
Warslow
Hulme End
Butterton
Wetton
Alstonefield
Ilam
Thorpe
Tissington
Parwich
Biggin
Onecote
Grindon
Waterhouses
Cauldon
Ipstones
Froghall
Kingsley
Oakamoor
Alton
Denstone
Rocester
Mayfield
Clifton
Norbury
Cheddleton
Blythe Bridge
Cubley Common
Great Cubley

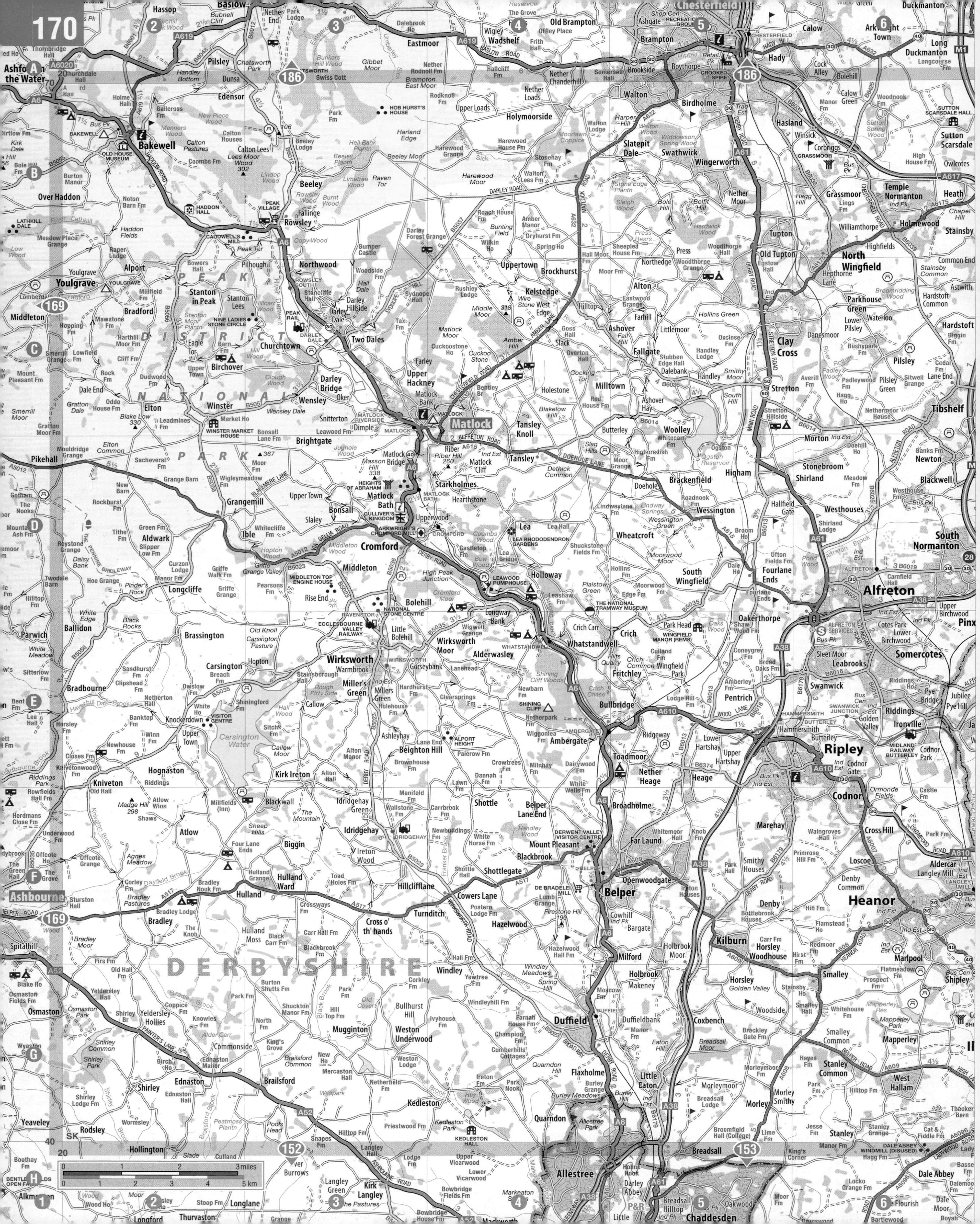
Hassop
Baslow
Eastmoor
Wigley
Wadshelf
Old Brampton
Chesterfield
Ashgate
Brampton
Calow
Arkwright Town
Duckmanton
Long Duckmanton
Ashford in the Water
Pilsley
Dunsa
Edensor
Bakewell
Nether Chanderhill
Brookside
Boythorpe
Walton
Birdholme
Hady
Cock Alley
Hasland
Sutton Scarsdale
Holymoorside
Slatepit Dale
Swathwick
Wingerworth
Corbriggs
Grassmoor
Temple Normanton
Heath
Over Haddon
Beeley
Rowsley
Northwood
Uppertown
Brockhurst
Kelstedge
Press
Nether Moor
Tupton
Old Tupton
North Wingfield
Williamthorpe
Holmewood
Stainsby
Alport
Youlgrave
Stanton in Peak
Middleton
Bradford
Darley Dale
Two Dales
Churchtown
Birchover
Ashover
Alton
Fallgate
Littlemoor
Clay Cross
Danesmoor
Pilsley
Hardstoft
Elton
Winster
Darley Bridge
Wensley
Upper Hackney
Matlock Bank
Matlock
Holestone
Milltown
Stretton
Tibshelf
Snitterton
Brightgate
Tansley Knoll
Tansley
Woolley
Morton
Pikehall
Matlock Bridge
Starkholmes
Riber
Higham
Shirland
Newton
Blackwell
Grangemill
Bonsall
Matlock Bath
Brackenfield
Wessington
Westhouses
Aldwark
Ible
Cromford
Lea
Wheatcroft
South Normanton
Middleton
Holloway
South Wingfield
Fourlane Ends
Alfreton
Longcliffe
Bolehill
Oakerthorpe
Ballidon
Parwich
Brassington
Wirksworth
Crich
Whatstandwell
Somercotes
Leabrooks
Carsington
Alderwasley
Fritchley
Bradbourne
Swanwick
Riddings
Ironville
Pentrich
Bullbridge
Ripley
Knockerdown
Ambergate
Kniveton
Hognaston
Kirk Ireton
Toadmoor
Nether Heage
Heage
Codnor
Atlow
Idridgehay
Shottle
Belper Lane End
Biggin
Mount Pleasant
Blackbrook
Shottlegate
Hulland Ward
Hulland
Belper
Heanor
Bradley
Turnditch
Cross o' th' hands
Hazelwood
Kilburn
Horsley Woodhouse
Marlpool
Ashbourne
DERBYSHIRE
Windley
Milford
Makeney
Smalley
Horsley
Shipley
Osmaston
Mugginton
Weston Underwood
Duffield
Coxbench
Mapperley
Stanley Common
West Hallam
Shirley
Ednaston
Brailsford
Flaxholme
Little Eaton
Morley
Yeaveley
Rodsley
Kedleston
Quarndon
Stanley
Hollington
Allestree
Breadsall
Dale Abbey
Longford
Thurvaston
Longlane
Kirk Langley
Chaddesden
186
169
152
153
0 1 2 3 miles
0 1 2 3 4 5 km

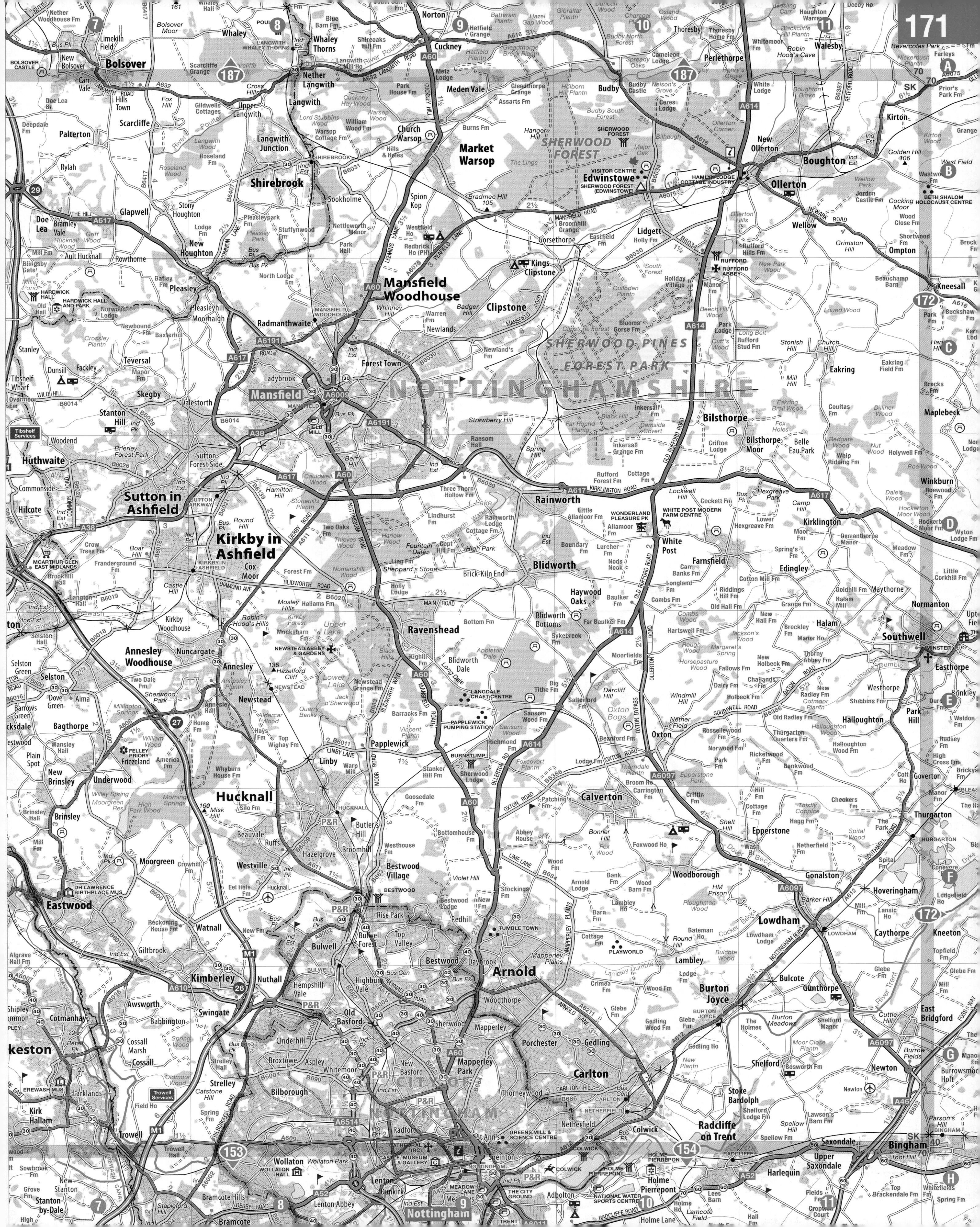
Bolsover
Whaley Thorns
Nether Langwith
Cuckney
Norton
Thoresby
Perlethorpe
Walesby
Budby
Meden Vale
Market Warsop
Church Warsop
Shirebrook
Langwith Junction
Scarcliffe
Palterton
Glapwell
Pleasley
Mansfield Woodhouse
Edwinstowe
SHERWOOD FOREST
New Ollerton
Ollerton
Boughton
Wellow
Ompton
Kneesall
Clipstone
Kings Clipstone
Lidgett
Rufford Abbey
Mansfield
Forest Town
Ladybrook
Teversal
Skegby
Dalestorth
Stanton Hill
Huthwaite
Sutton in Ashfield
Kirkby in Ashfield
SHERWOOD PINES FOREST PARK
NOTTINGHAMSHIRE
Rainworth
Bilsthorpe
Eakring
Kirklington
Farnsfield
Edingley
Blidworth
White Post
Ravenshead
Annesley Woodhouse
Annesley
Newstead
Papplewick
Linby
Hucknall
Southwell
Halam
Halloughton
Oxton
Calverton
Epperstone
Thurgarton
Woodborough
Lowdham
Caythorpe
Gonalston
Hoveringham
Lambley
Burton Joyce
Gunthorpe
East Bridgford
Shelford
Newton
Radcliffe on Trent
Bingham
Saxondale
Arnold
Mapperley
Gedling
Carlton
Netherfield
Colwick
Bestwood
Bulwell
Nuthall
Kimberley
Watnall
Eastwood
Brinsley
Underwood
Selston
Jacksdale
Ilkeston
Cossall
Trowell
Strelley
Bilborough
Wollaton
Lenton
Basford
Sherwood
Nottingham
Holme Pierrepont
West Bridgford
Adbolton
Stapleford
Bramcote
Kirk Hallam
Stanton-by-Dale
187
172
153
154

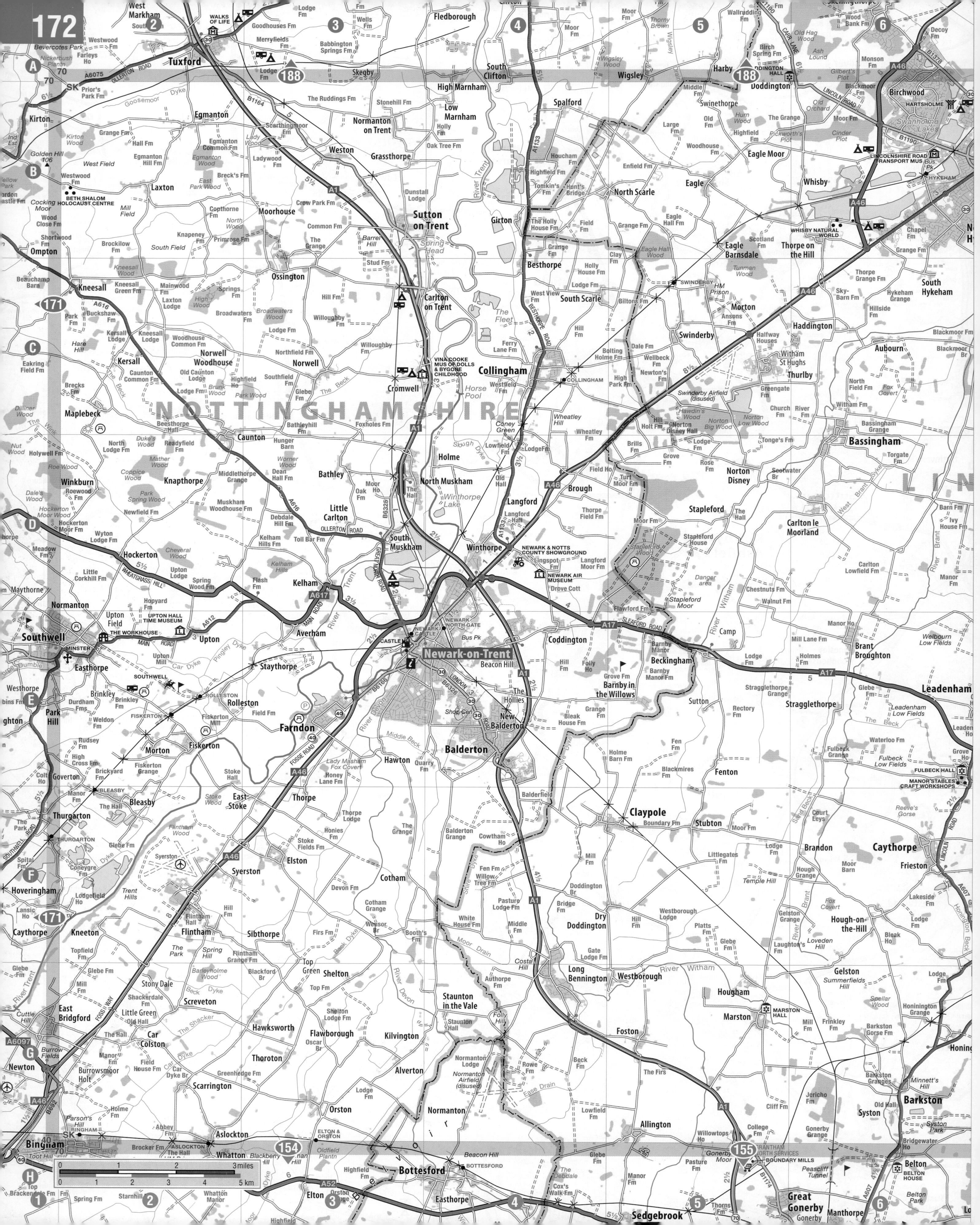
West Markham
Walks of Life
Goodhouses Fm
Wells Fm
Fledborough
Moor Fm
Thorny Brown
Wallrudding Fm
Wood Bank Fm
Decoy Fm
Beverotes Park
Westwood Fm
Farleys Ho
Tuxford
Merryfields Fm
Babbington Springs Fm
Moor Fm
Old Hag Wood
Birch Spring Fm
Ash Lound
Monson Fm
Skegby
Lodge Fm
188
South Clifton
Wigsley Wood
Wigsley
Harby
Doddington Hall
Doddington
Gilbert's Plot
A6075
Ollerton Road
Prior's Park Fm
High Marnham
Low Marnham
Middle Fm
Swinethorpe
Blackmoor Fm
Birchwood
Hartsholme
Lincoln Road
Kirton
Goosemoor
Egmanton
Scarthingmoor Fm
The Ruddings Fm
Stonehill Fm
Normanton on Trent
Holly Fm
Spalford
Large Fm
Old Fm
Hurn Wood
The Grange
Old Orchard
Cinder Plot
Moor Fm
Swanholme Lakes
Grange Fm
Kirton Wood
Half Fm
Egmanton Common Fm
Lady Wood
Weston
Grassthorpe
Oak Tree Fm
Houcham Fm
Highfield Fm
Pickworth's Plot
Woodhouse Fm
Eagle Moor
Lincolnshire Road Transport Mus
Golden Hill
West Field
Egmanton Hill Fm
Egmanton Wood
Ladywood Fm
Highfield Fm
Enfield Fm
Westwood Fm
Beth Shalom Holocaust Centre
Laxton
Breck's Fm
East Park Wood
Dunstall Lodge
Tomkin's Fm
Hunt's Bridge
North Scarle
Eagle
Whisby
Hykeham
Cocking Moor
Mill Field
Copthorne Fm
Moorhouse
Crow Park Fm
Sutton on Trent
Girton
The Holly House Fm
Field Fm
Grange Fm
Eagle Hall Fm
Whisby Natural World
Chapel Fm
Wood Close Fm
North Wood
Common Fm
Shortwood Fm
Knapeney Fm
Primrose Fm
The Grange
Barrel Hill
Spring Head
Ompton
Brockilow Fm
South Field
Stud Fm
Grange Fm
Besthorpe
Clay Fm
Eagle Hall Wood
Scotland Fm
Eagle Barnsdale
Thorpe on the Hill
Grange Fm
Holly House Fm
Lodge Fm
Tunman Wood
Swinderby
HM Prison
Kneesall Wood
Beauchamp Barn
Kneesall
Kneesall Green Fm
Mainwood Fm
Laxton Lodge
Springs Fm
High Wood
Ossington
Carlton on Trent
Thorpe Grange Fm
South Hykeham
West View Fm
South Scarle
Biltons Fm
Morton
Sky-Barn Fm
Hykeham Grange
171
Park Fm
Buckshaw Fm
Broadwaters Fm
Broadwaters Wood
Hill Fm
Willoughby Fm
The Fleet
Besthorpe Road
Ansons Fm
Haddington
Hillside Fm
Kersall Lodge
Kneesall Lodge
Lodge Fm
Ferry Lane Fm
Hill Fm
Swinderby
Halfway Houses
Blackmoor Fm
Hare Hill
Woodhouse Common Fm
Norwell Woodhouse
Northfield Fm
Willoughby Fm
Norwell
Dale Fm
Bolting Holme Fm
Wellbeck Fm
Newton's Fm
Witham St Hughs
Aubourn
Eakring Field Fm
Kersall
Caunton Common Fm
Old Caunton Lodge
Highfield Ho
Southfield Fm
Vina Cooke Mus of Dolls & Bygone Childhood
Collingham
Thurlby
North Field Fm
Fox Covert
Brecks Fm
Lodge Fm
Brunk Wood
Park Wood
Glebe Fm
The Beck
Cromwell
Westfield Fm
Horse Pool
High Park Fm
Swinderby Airfield (disused)
Greengate Fm
Witham Fm
Maplebeck
NOTTINGHAMSHIRE
Bathleyhill Fm
Foxholes Fm
Coney Green
Wheatley Hill
Hawdin's Wood
Norton Big Wood
Norton Disney Hall
Norton Low Wood
Church Fm
River Fm
Bassingham Houses
Beesthorpe Hall
Caunton
Hunger Barn
Slough Dyke
Lowfield Fm
Lodge Fm
Holt Fm
Tonge's Fm
Bassingham
North Lodge Fm
Duke's Wood
Readyfield Fm
Holme
Wheatley Ho
Brills Fm
Lodge Fm
Torgate Fm
Holywell Fm
Worner Wood
Old Hall
Field Ho
Grove Fm
Rose Fm
Norton Disney
Sootwater Br
Roe Wood
Mather Wood
Dean Hall Fm
Bathley
Moor Ho
North Muskham
Turf Moor Fm
Brough
Coppice Wood
Middlethorpe Grange
Knapthorpe
The Hall
Winthorpe Lake
Winkburn
Roewood Fm
Park Spring Wood
Muskham Woodhouse Fm
Oak Fm
Little Carlton
Langford
Thorpe Field Fm
Stapleford
The Hall
Barn Fm
Hockerton Moor Wood
Newfield Fm
Debdale Hill Fm
Langford Hall
Moor Fm
Carlton le Moorland
Ivy House Fm
Hockerton Moor Fm
Wyton Lodge Fm
Ollerton Road
South Muskham
Winthorpe
Stapleford House
Stapleford Wood
Meadow Fm
Hockerton
Cheveral Wood
Kelham Hills Fm
Toll Bar Fm
Great North Road
Newark & Notts County Showground
Lingspot Fm
Langford Moor Fm
Carlton Lowfield Fm
Little Corkhill Fm
Wheatgrass Hill
Upton Lodge
Spring Wood Fm
Flash Fm
Kelham Hills
Newark Air Museum
Danger area
Maythorne
Kelham
A617
Drove Cott
Stapleford Moor
Chestnuts Fm
Manor Fm
Hopyard Fm
Walnut Fm
Normanton
Upton Field
Upton Hall Time Museum
Main Road
Newark North Gate
Flawford Fm
Sleaford Road
Manor Ho
Southwell
The Workhouse
A612
Averham
Newark Castle
Coddington
Camp
Mill Lane Fm
Brant Broughton
Welbourn Low Fields
Minster
Main Road
Upton
Castle
Bus Pk
Newark-on-Trent
Barnby Manor
Beckingham
Lodge Fm
Holmes Fm
Upton Mill
Car Dyke
Pingley Dyke
Beacon Hill
Hill Fm
Folly Ho
A17
Easthorpe
Staythorpe
London Road
Grove Fm
Barnby Manor Fm
Westhorpe
Southwell
Rolleston
The Hollies
Barnby in the Willows
Stragglethorpe Grange
Glebe Fm
Leadenham
Brinkley
Durham Fms
Brinkley Ho
Rolleston
Field Fm
Farndon
Shop Cen
New Balderton
Bleak House Fm
Grange Fm
Sutton
Rectory Fm
Stragglethorpe
Leadenham Low Fields
Park Hill
Weldon Fm
Fiskerton
Fiskerton Mill
River Devon
Middle Beck
Balderton
The Beck
Rudsey Fm
Morton
Fiskerton
Fosse Road
Lady Masham Fox Cover
Hawton
Quarry Fm
Holme Barn Fm
Fen Fm
Waterloo Fm
Fulbeck Low Fields
Fulbeck Grange
Grove Ho
High Gross Fm
Brickyard Fm
Fiskerton Grange
Stoke Hall
Honey Lane Fm
Blackmires Fm
Fenton
Fulbeck Hall
Manor Stables Craft Workshops
Goverton
Bleasby
Balderfield
Manor Ho
Bleasby
East Stoke
Stoke Wood
Thorpe
Claypole
Boundary Fm
Stubton
Court Leys
Reeve's Gorse
The Hall
Thurgarton
Thorpe Lodge
The Park
The Grange
Balderton Grange
Cowtham Ho
Moor Fm
Caythorpe
Thurgarton
Flintham Wood
Honies Fm
Stoke Fields Fm
Lodge Fm
Brandon
Southwell Road
Glebe Fm
Littlegates Fm
Moor Barn
Frieston
Syerston
Elston
Spital Fm
Coneygre Fm
Syerston
Cotham
Fen Fm
Willow Tree Fm
Mill Fm
Hough Grange
Temple Hill
Hoveringham
Trent Hills
Devon Fm
Doddington Br
Lakeside Fm
Lodgefield Ho
Hill Fm
Cotham Grange
Pasture Lodge Fm
Bridge Fm
Dry Doddington
Hill Fm
Westborough Lodge
Fox Covert
Gelston Grange
Hough-on-the-Hill
Lansic Ho
171
Flintham Hall
Caythorpe
Kneeton
Flintham
Sibthorpe
Firs Fm
Wensor Br
Booth's Fm
White House Fm
Middle Fm
Platts Fm
Glebe Fm
Laughton's Fm
Loveden Hill
Bleak Ho
Lodge Fm
Topfield Ho
The Park
Spring Hill
Flintham Grange Fm
Moor Drain
Costa Hill
Gate Lodge Fm
Glebe Fm
Glebe Fm
Barleyholme Wood
Blackford Br
Top Green
Shelton
Long Bennington
Westborough
River Witham
Gelston
Summerfields Hill
Lodge Fm
Mill Fm
Stony Dale
Beck Dyke
Top Fm
Authorpe Fm
Hougham
Spellar Wood
Honington Grange
River Trent
Shackerdale Fm
Screveton
Shelton Lodge Fm
River Devon
Staunton in the Vale
Marston Hall
Marston
East Bridgford
Little Green
Old Hall
The Shacker
Hawksworth
Flawborough
Folly Hill
Foston
Mill Fm
Frinkley Fm
Barkston Gorse Fm
Honington
Cuttle Hill
Fosse Way
Car Colston
Oscar Br
Kilvington
Staunton Hall
A6097
The Hall
Burrow Fields
Manor Fm
Car Dyke
Thoroton
Normanton Lodge
Rowe Fm
Beck Fm
Newton
Field House Fm
Car Colston
Car Dyke Br
Greenhedge Fm
Alverton
Normanton Airfield (disused)
The Firs
Minnett's Hill
Burrowsmoor Holt
Scarrington
Ease Drain
Barkston Granges
Barkston
Holme Fm
Lodge Fm
Jericho Fm
Old Hall
Syston
A46
Orston
Normanton
Lowfield Fm
Cliff Fm
Syston Park
Parson's Hill
Abbey Fm
Allington
College Fm
Gonerby Grange
Bingham
Brocker Fm
Aslockton
Aslockton
Elton & Orston
154
Willowtops Fm
Bridgewater Ho
Toot Hill
Whatton
Blackberry Hill
Oldfield Plantn
Beacon Hill
Grantham North Services
155
Boundary Mills
Belton
Belton House
Highfield Fm
Bottesford
Bottesford
The Debdale
Glebe Fm
Manor Fm
Gonerby Moor
Pasture Fm
Peascliff Tunnel
Belton Park
Bracken Fm
Spring Fm
Starnhill
Whatton Manor
Elton
Orston
A52
Easthorpe
Cox's Walk Fm
Sedgebrook
Great Gonerby
Gonerby
Manthorpe
Thorns Fm
A607
0 1 2 3 miles
0 1 2 3 4 5 km

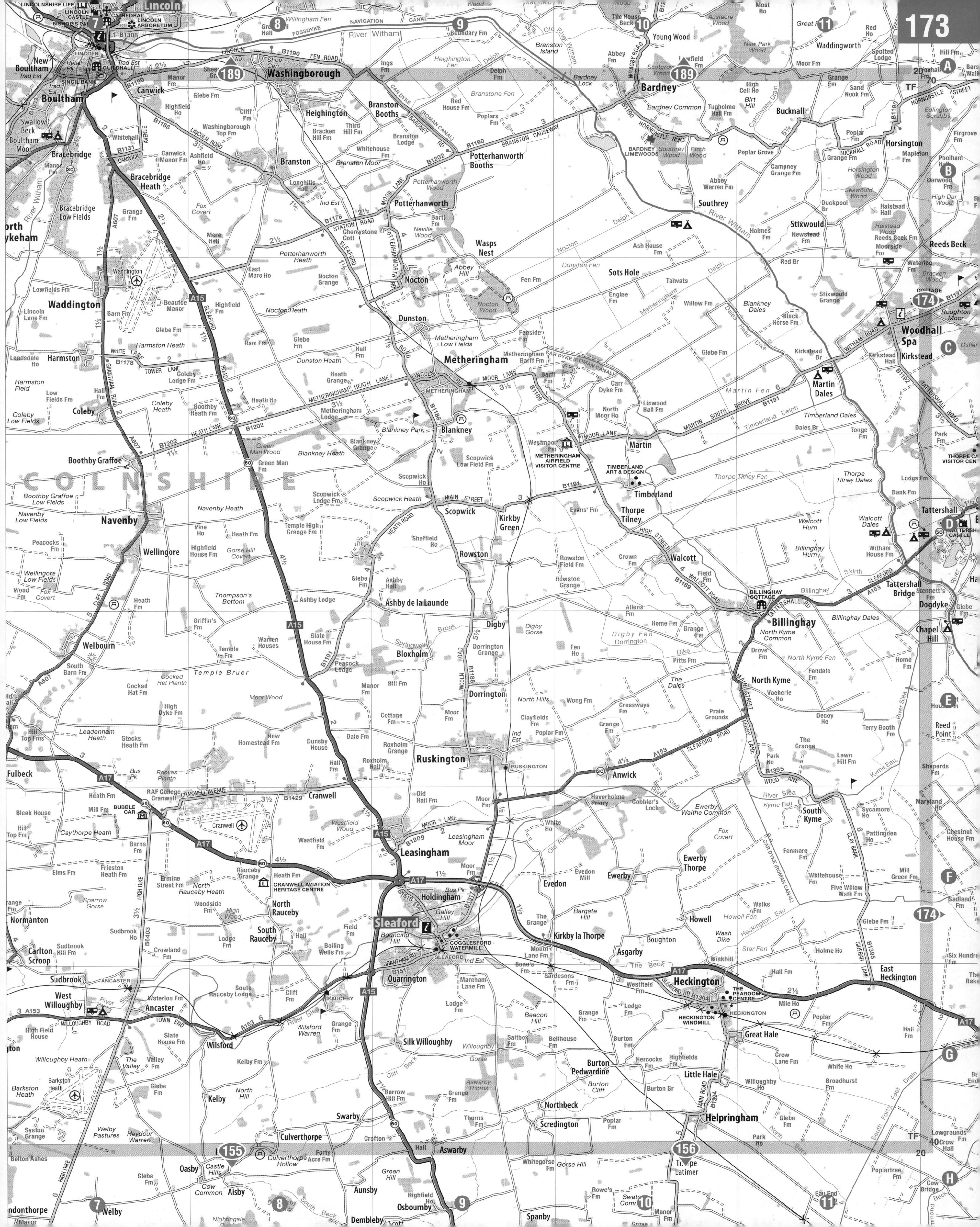

Lincoln
Lincolnshire Life
Lincoln Castle
Cathedral
Lincoln Arboretum
Bishop's Palace
New Boultham
Boultham
Trad Est
Sincil Bank
Guildhall
Canwick
Washingborough
Heighington
Branston Booths
Branston
Bracebridge
Bracebridge Heath
Bracebridge Low Fields
Swallow Beck
Boultham Moor
North Hykeham
Fossdyke Navigation
Willingham Fen
River Witham
Boundary Fm
Ings Fm
Heighington Fen
Branston Delph
Branstone Fen
Branston Island
Bardney Lock
Tile House Beck
Young Wood
Abbey Hill
Bardney
Bardney Common
Tupholme Hall Fm
Bucknall
Horsington
Bardney Limewoods
Southrey Wood
Birch Wood
Poplar Grove
Campney Grange Fm
Abbey Warren Fm
Southrey
Potterhanworth Booths
Potterhanworth
Potterhanworth Wood
Cherrystone Cott
Neville Wood
Barff Fm
Wasps Nest
Potterhanworth Heath
Nocton
Abbey Hill
Nocton Wood
Nocton Heath
Nocton Grange
Fen Fm
Sots Hole
Ash House Fm
Dunston Fen
Dunston
Dunston Heath
Metheringham
Metheringham Low Fields
Metheringham Barff Fm
Metheringham Heath Lane
Metheringham Lodge
Blankney
Blankney Park
Blankney Heath
Blankney Grange
Metheringham Airfield Visitor Centre
Westmoor Fm
Martin
Martin Dales
Martin Fen
Timberland Dales
Timberland
Timberland Art & Design
Thorpe Tilney
Thorpe Tilney Fen
Thorpe Tilney Dales
Stixwould
Reeds Beck
Woodhall Spa
Kirkstead
Roughton Moor
Tattershall
Tattershall Castle
Tattershall Bridge
Dogdyke
Chapel Hill
Walcott
Billinghay
Billinghay Cottage
Billinghay Dales
North Kyme
North Kyme Common
North Kyme Fen
Waddington
Harmston
Coleby
Boothby Graffoe
Navenby
Navenby Heath
Wellingore
Welbourn
Lincolnshire
Scopwick
Scopwick Heath
Kirkby Green
Rowston
Ashby de la Launde
Digby
Digby Fen
Dorrington
Bloxholm
Temple Bruer
Cocked Hat Plantn
Leadenham Heath
Fulbeck
Cranwell
RAF College Cranwell
Ruskington
Anwick
Leasingham
Leasingham Moor
Holdingham
Sleaford
Cogglesford Watermill
Cranwell Aviation Heritage Centre
North Rauceby
South Rauceby
Quarrington
Evedon
Ewerby
Ewerby Thorpe
Howell
Asgarby
Kirkby la Thorpe
Heckington
Heckington Windmill
The Pearoom Centre
East Heckington
Great Hale
Little Hale
Helpringham
South Kyme
Normanton
Carlton Scroop
Sudbrook
West Willoughby
Ancaster
Wilsford
Silk Willoughby
Kelby
Burton Pedwardine
Northbeck
Scredington
Swarby
Culverthorpe
Aswarby
Aunsby
Oasby
Aisby
Welby
Osbournby
Dembleby
Spanby
Threekingham
Barkston Heath
Syston Grange
Belton Ashes
A15
A17
A153
A607
B1188
B1189
B1190
B1191
B1202
B1394
B1395
TF

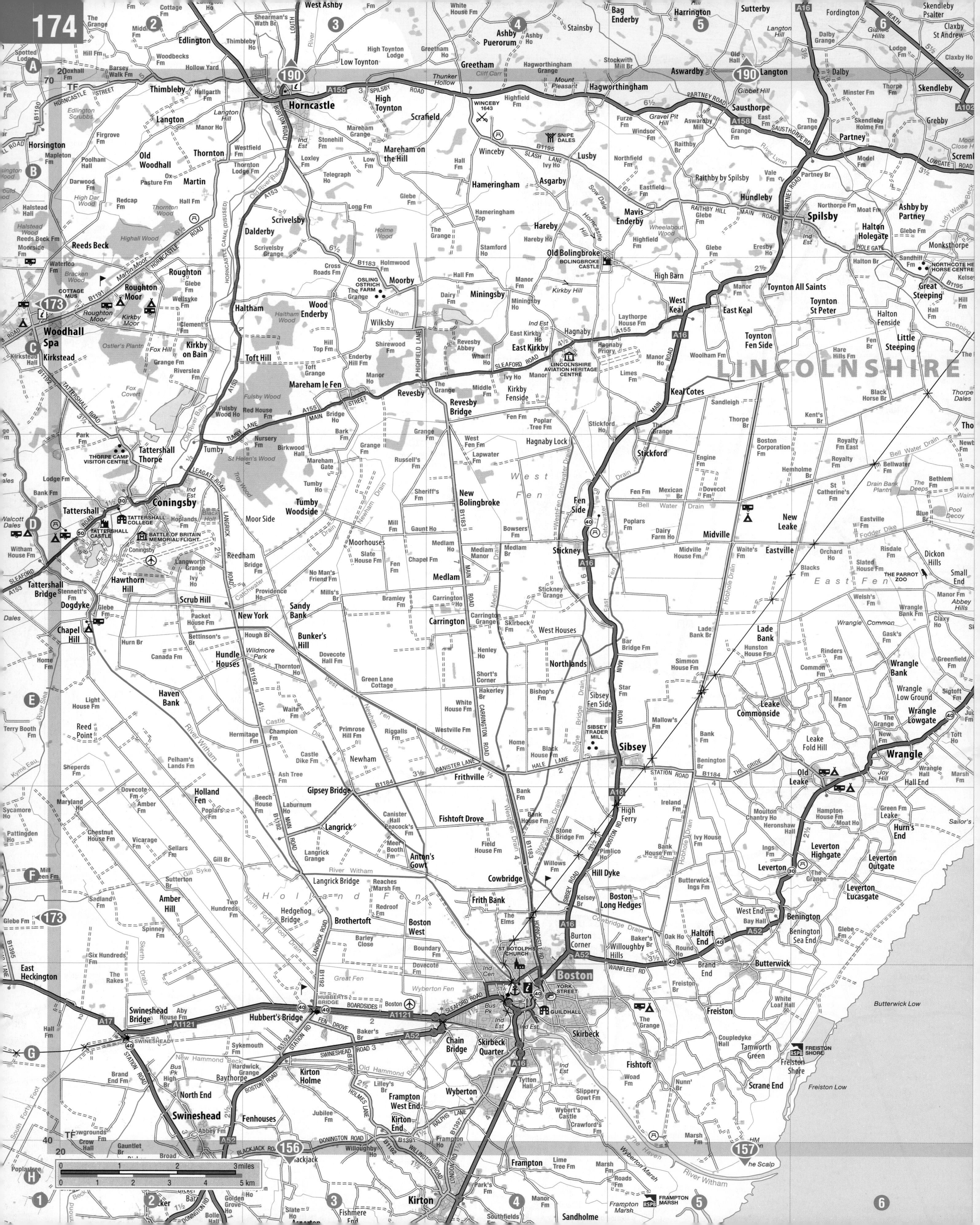
LINCOLNSHIRE
Horncastle
West Ashby
Edlington
Thimbleby
Langton
High Toynton
Scrafield
Greetham
Ashby Puerorum
Bag Enderby
Harrington
Sutterby
Fordington
Skendleby Psalter
Claxby St Andrew
Aswardby
Langton
Dalby
Hagworthingham
Sausthorpe
Skendleby
Grebby
Partney
Scremby
Horsington
Old Woodhall
Thornton
Martin
Mareham on the Hill
Winceby
Lusby
Asgarby
Hameringham
Raithby by Spilsby
Hundleby
Spilsby
Mavis Enderby
Hareby
Old Bolingbroke
Ashby by Partney
Halton Holegate
Monksthorpe
Scrivelsby
Dalderby
Reeds Beck
Roughton
Roughton Moor
Moorby
Miningsby
West Keal
East Keal
Toynton All Saints
Toynton St Peter
Great Steeping
Little Steeping
Woodhall Spa
Kirkstead
Kirkby on Bain
Haltham
Wood Enderby
Wilksby
Hagnaby
East Kirkby
Toft Hill
Mareham le Fen
Revesby
Revesby Bridge
Keal Cotes
Tattershall Thorpe
Tumby
Tumby Woodside
Stickford
Hagnaby Lock
Tattershall
Coningsby
New Bolingbroke
Fen Side
Moor Side
Midville
New Leake
Eastville
Stickney
Medlam
Carrington
Hawthorn Hill
Tattershall Bridge
Dogdyke
Scrub Hill
New York
Sandy Bank
Bunker's Hill
Chapel Hill
West Houses
Northlands
Lade Bank
Hundle Houses
Haven Bank
Wrangle Bank
Leake Commonside
Wrangle Lowgate
Wrangle
Sibsey
Frithville
Gipsey Bridge
Holland Fen
Old Leake
High Ferry
Fishtoft Drove
Langrick
Anton's Gowt
Hill Dyke
Leverton Highgate
Leverton Outgate
Leverton
Leverton Lucasgate
Amber Hill
Cowbridge
Frith Bank
Boston Long Hedges
Brothertoft
Boston West
Haltoft End
Benington
Butterwick
East Heckington
Swineshead Bridge
Hubbert's Bridge
Boston
Skirbeck
Freiston
Chain Bridge
Skirbeck Quarter
Fishtoft
Tamworth Green
Scrane End
Freiston Shore
Kirton Holme
Bicker
North End
Swineshead
Fenhouses
Wyberton
Frampton West End
Kirton End
Frampton
Kirton
Sandholme
A16
A17
A52
A153
A155
A158
A1121
B1183
B1184
B1192
Butterwick Low
Freiston Low
The Haven
River Witham
Scale 0 1 2 3 miles
0 1 2 3 4 5 km

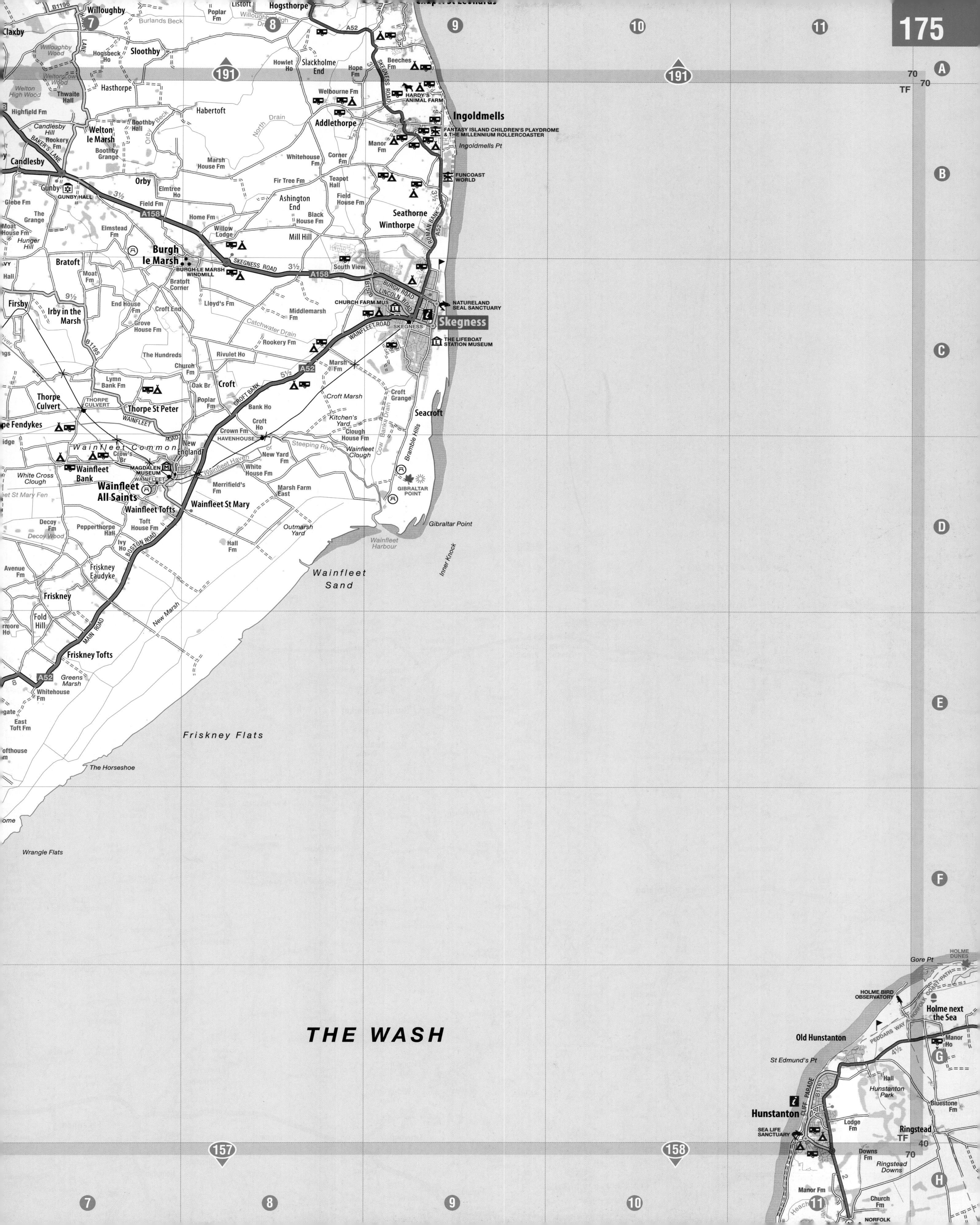
Willoughby
Claxby
Sloothby
Hogsthorpe
Burlands Beck
Poplar Fm
Slackholme End
Howlet Ho
Hope Fm
Beeches Fm
Hasthorpe
Thwaite Hall
Welton High Wood
Highfield Fm
Habertoft
Welbourne Fm
HARDY'S ANIMAL FARM
Ingoldmells
FANTASY ISLAND CHILDREN'S PLAYDROME & THE MILLENNIUM ROLLERCOASTER
Ingoldmells Pt
Addlethorpe
Manor Fm
Welton le Marsh
Boothby Grange
Candlesby
Marsh House Fm
Whitehouse Fm
Corner Fm
FUNCOAST WORLD
Orby
Gunby
GUNBY HALL
Elmtree Ho
Fir Tree Fm
Teapot Hall
Field House Fm
Ashington End
Field Fm
A158
Glebe Fm
Home Fm
Black House Fm
Seathorne
Winthorpe
Willow Lodge
Mill Hill
Elmstead Fm
Burgh le Marsh
BURGH LE MARSH WINDMILL
SKEGNESS ROAD
South View
Bratoft
Moat Fm
Bratoft Corner
Lloyd's Fm
NATURELAND SEAL SANCTUARY
Skegness
CHURCH FARM MUS
THE LIFEBOAT STATION MUSEUM
Firsby
Irby in the Marsh
End House Fm
Croft End
Middlemarsh Fm
Catchwater Drain
Grove House Fm
Rookery Fm
WAINFLEET ROAD
The Hundreds
Rivulet Ho
Marsh Fm
Church Fm
Lymn Bank Fm
Oak Br
Croft
A52
Croft Marsh
Croft Grange
Thorpe Culvert
Thorpe St Peter
Poplar Fm
CROFT BANK
Bank Ho
Seacroft
Kitchen's Yard
Croft Ho
Crown Fm
HAVENHOUSE
Clough House Fm
Bramble Hills
Wainfleet Common
New England
Steeping River
Wainfleet Clough
New Yard Fm
Wainfleet Bank
MAGDALEN MUSEUM
White House Fm
White Cross Clough
Wainfleet All Saints
Merrifield's Fm
Marsh Farm East
GIBRALTAR POINT
Wainfleet Tofts
Wainfleet St Mary
Gibraltar Point
Decoy Fm
Pepperthorpe Hall
Toft House Fm
Outmarsh Yard
Wainfleet Harbour
Ivy Ho
BOSTON ROAD
Hall Fm
Inner Knock
Avenue Fm
Friskney Eaudyke
Wainfleet Sand
Friskney
New Marsh
Fold Hill
MAIN ROAD
Friskney Tofts
Greens Marsh
Whitehouse Fm
East Toft Fm
Friskney Flats
The Horseshoe
Wrangle Flats
THE WASH
Gore Pt
HOLME DUNES
HOLME BIRD OBSERVATORY
Holme next the Sea
Old Hunstanton
PEDDARS WAY
Manor Ho
St Edmund's Pt
Hall
Hunstanton Park
CLIFF PARADE
Hunstanton
Bluestone Fm
SEA LIFE SANCTUARY
Lodge Fm
Ringstead
Downs Fm
Ringstead Downs
Manor Fm
Church Fm
NORFOLK
191
157
158
TF
70
40
A
B
C
D
E
F
G
H
7
8
9
10
11

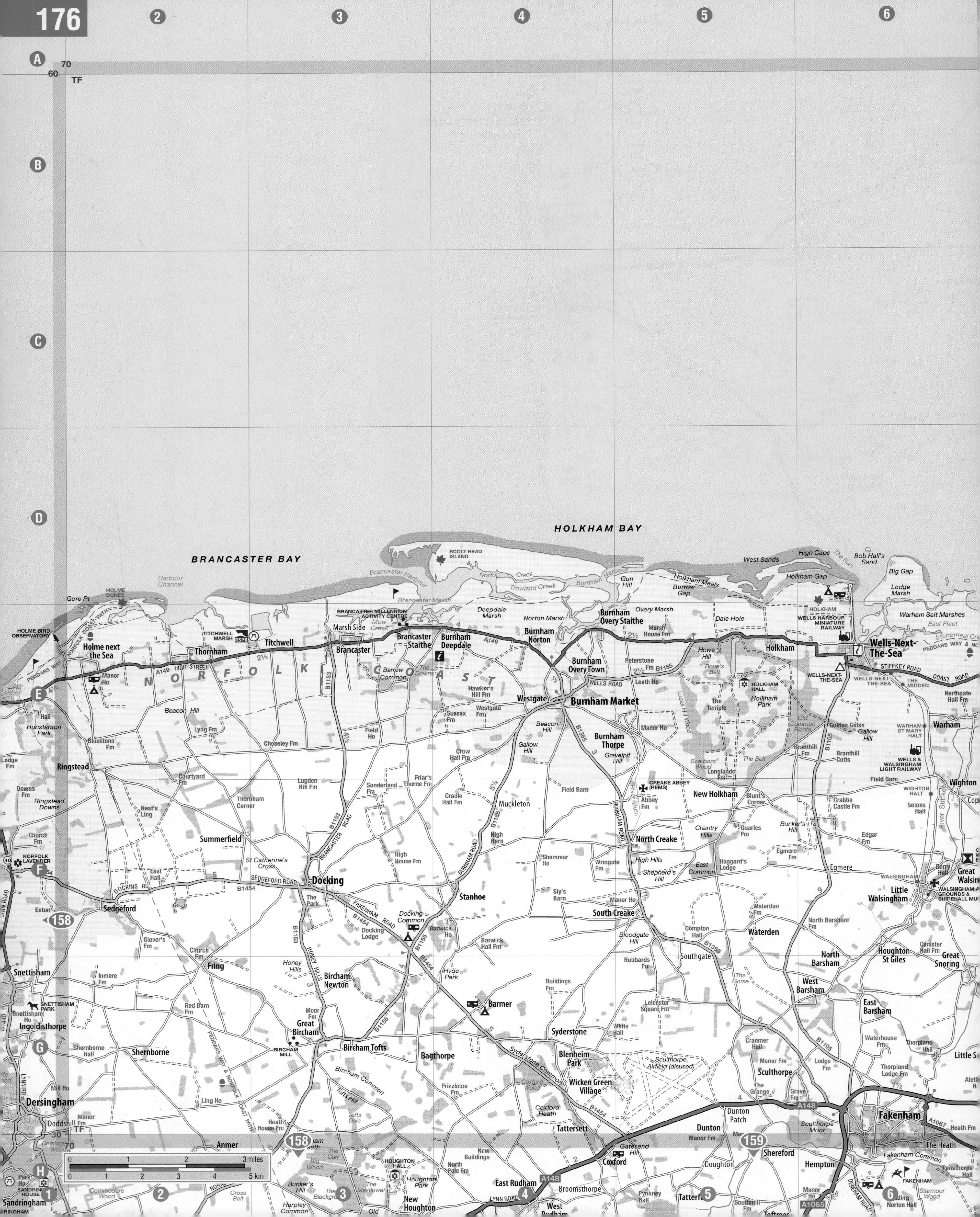
HOLKHAM BAY
BRANCASTER BAY
SCOLT HEAD ISLAND
Brancaster Harbour
Harbour Channel
Gore Pt
HOLME DUNES
HOLME BIRD OBSERVATORY
Holme next the Sea
TITCHWELL MARSH
RSPB
Titchwell
Thornham
N O R F O L K C O A S T
Brancaster
Marsh Side
BRANCASTER MILLENNIUM ACTIVITY CENTRE
Brancaster Staithe
Burnham Deepdale
Deepdale Marsh
Norton Creek
Trowland Creek
Burnham Harbour
Gun Hill
Norton Marsh
Burnham Norton
Burnham Overy Staithe
Overy Marsh
Burnham Overy Town
Westgate
Burnham Market
Burnham Thorpe
Holkham Meals
Burrow Gap
West Sands
High Cape
The Run
Bob Hall's Sand
Holkham Gap
Big Gap
Lodge Marsh
Warham Salt Marshes
East Fleet
HOLKHAM
WELLS HARBOUR MINIATURE RAILWAY
Wells-Next-The-Sea
Holkham
HOLKHAM HALL
Holkham Park
Dale Hole
Peterstone Fm
Leath Ho
Manor Ho
The Temple
Golden Gates
Warham
WARHAM ST MARY HALT
WELLS & WALSINGHAM LIGHT RAILWAY
Wighton
Ringstead
Hunstanton Park
Bluestone Fm
Lyng Fm
Beacon Hill
Choseley Fm
Courtyard Fm
Thornham Corner
Neat's Ling
Ringstead Downs
Summerfield
St Catherine's Cross
Lugden Hill Fm
Sunderland Fm
Friar's Thorne Fm
Cradle Hall Fm
Crow Hall Fm
Muckleton
High Barn
Field Barn
CREAKE ABBEY (REMS)
New Holkham
Abbey Fm
North Creake
Chantry Hills
Quarles Fm
Bunker's Hill
Egmere
Crabbe Castle Fm
Setons Halt
Edgar Fm
NORFOLK LAVENDER
Church Fm
Sedgeford
Docking
DOCKING RD
SEDGEFORD ROAD
East Hall
Eaton
Stanhoe
Docking Common
Docking Lodge
High House Fm
Shammer Ho
Wringate Fm
High Hills
Shepherd's Hill
East Common
Haggard's Lodge
Sly's Barn
South Creake
Waterden Fm
Waterden
Compton Hall
Bloodgate Hill
Southgate
Barwick Ho
Barwick Hall Fm
Little Walsingham
Great Walsingham
WALSINGHAM GROUNDS & SHIREHALL MUSEUM
North Barsham
Houghton St Giles
Great Snoring
Glover's Fm
Church Fm
Fring
Snettisham
Inmere Fm
Honey Hills
Bircham Newton
Hyde Park
Hubbards Fm
Buildings Fm
West Barsham
East Barsham
SNETTISHAM PARK
Ingoldisthorpe
Red Barn Fm
Great Bircham
Moor Fm
Barmer
Leicester Square Fm
Syderstone
White Hall
Shernborne Hall
Shernborne
BIRCHAM MILL
Bircham Tofts
Bagthorpe
Blenheim Park
Sculthorpe Airfield (disused)
Cranmer Hall
Manor Fm
Sculthorpe
Waterhouse Fm
Thorpland Hall
Little Snoring
Bircham Common
Tofts Hill
Frizzleton Fm
Coxford Wood
Wicken Green Village
Lodge Fm
Thorpland Lodge Fm
Dersingham
Mill Ho
Ling Ho
Manor
Doddshill Fm
Heath House Fm
Tofts Dale
Coxford Heath
Tattersett
Dunton
Dunton Patch
Fakenham
Sculthorpe Moor
Heath Fm
Anmer
New Buildings
Gatesend Hill
Coxford
Manor Fm
Shereford
The Heath
Fakenham Common
HOUGHTON HALL
Houghton Park
North Pole Fm
East Rudham
Doughton
Hempton
Pensthorpe Hall
FAKENHAM
Sandringham
Commodore Wood
Bunker's Hill
Harpley Common
The Mayflower
New Houghton
West Rudham
Broomsthorpe
Pynkney Hall
Tatterford
Southmill Fm
Norton Hall
Starmoor Wood
PEDDARS WAY & NORFOLK COAST PATH
A149
A148
A1065
A1067
B1153
B1155
B1454
B1355
B1105
B1355
BRANCASTER ROAD
BURNHAM ROAD
FAKENHAM ROAD
WELLS ROAD
STIFFKEY ROAD
LYNN ROAD
Syderstone Common
TF
158
159
0 1 2 3 miles
0 1 2 3 4 5 km

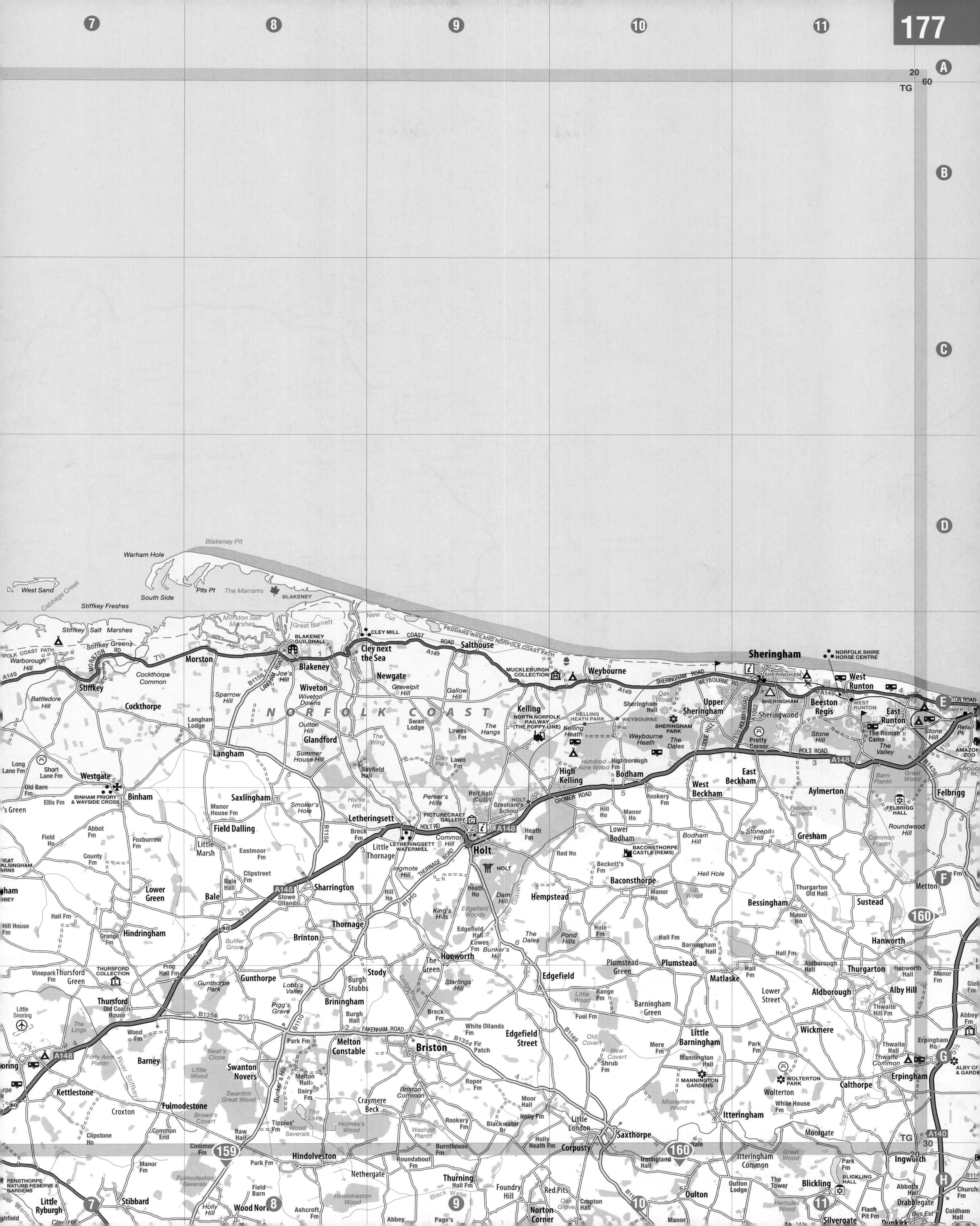
7
8
9
10
11
A
B
C
D
E
F
G
H
TG
20
60
30
Blakeney Pit
Warham Hole
West Sand
Cabbage Creek
Stiffkey Freshes
South Side
Pits Pt
The Marrams
BLAKENEY
Morston Salt Marshes
Great Barnett
New Cut
CLEY MILL
Stiffkey Salt Marshes
Stiffkey Greens
Agar Creek
BLAKENEY GUILDHALL
NORFOLK COAST PATH
MORSTON RD
COAST ROAD
PEDDARS WAY AND NORFOLK COAST PATH
Warborough Hill
A149
Morston
Blakeney
Cley next the Sea
Salthouse
Stiffkey
Cockthorpe Common
Newgate
Gravelpit Hill
Gallow Hill
MUCKLEBURGH COLLECTION
Weybourne
Sheringham
NORFOLK SHIRE HORSE CENTRE
SHERINGHAM
West Runton
Battledore Hill
Cockthorpe
Sparrow Hill
Joe's Hill
LANGHAM ROAD
B1156
Wiveton
Wiveton Downs
N O R F O L K   C O A S T
Kelling
NORTH NORFOLK RAILWAY (THE POPPY LINE)
KELLING HEATH PARK
WEYBOURNE
Sheringham Hall
Oak Wood
Upper Sheringham
SHERINGHAM PARK
SHERINGHAM ROAD
WEYBOURNE RD
Sheringwood
Beeston Regis
WEST RUNTON
East Runton
CROMER
Langham Lodge
Oulton Hill
Glandford
Swan Lodge
Lowes Fm
The Hangs
Kelling Heath
Weybourne Heath
The Dales
LODGE HILL
HOLWAY ROAD
A1082
Pretty Corner
Stone Hill
The Roman Camp
The Valley
Stone Hill
Retail Pk
AMAZONA ZOO
Long Lane Fm
Short Lane Fm
Langham
Summer House Hill
The Wing
Cley Park
Lawn Fm
Hundred Acre Wood
Highborough Fm
HOLT ROAD
A148
B1436
Westgate
Old Barn Fm
Ellis Fm
BINHAM PRIORY & WAYSIDE CROSS
Binham
Saxlingham
Bayfield Hall
High Kelling
Bodham
West Beckham
East Beckham
Aylmerton
Barn Plantn
Great Wood
Felbrigg
FELBRIGG HALL
Manor House Fm
Smoker's Hole
Horse Hill
Pereer's Hills
Holt Hall (Coll)
HOLT
Gresham's School
CROMER ROAD
Hill Ho
Manor Ho
Rookery Fm
Rounce's Coverts
Roundwood Hill
Abbot Fm
Field Dalling
Letheringsett
PICTURECRAFT GALLERY
HOLT RD
Heath Fm
Lower Bodham
Bodham Hill
Stonepit Hill
Gresham
Common Plantn
Field Ho
Foxburrow Fm
Little Marsh
Eastmoor Fm
Breck Fm
Little Thornage
LETHERINGSETT WATERMILL
Common Hill
Holt
Red Ho
BACONSTHORPE CASTLE (REMS)
County Fm
GREAT WALSINGHAM BARNS
Ingmote Hill
THORNAGE ROAD
Beckett's Fm
Hell Hole
Clipstreet Fm
Bale Hall
Lower Green
Bale
A148
Sharrington
Stowe Ollands
Hill Ho
B1110
Heath Ho
Dam Hill
River Glaven
Hempstead
Baconsthorpe
Manor Ho
Up Wood
Thurgarton Old Hall
Bessingham
Sustead
Metton
Hall Fm
Hill House Fm
Grange Fm
Hindringham
King's Hills
Edgefield Woods
Manor Ho
Thornage
Bullfer Grove
Brinton
Edgefield Hall
Lowes Fm
Bunker's Hill
The Dales
Pond Hills
Hole Fm
Hall Fm
Barningham Hall
Hanworth
160
Frog Hall Fm
Vinepark Fm
Thursford Green
THURSFORD COLLECTION
Gunthorpe Park
Gunthorpe
Lobb's Valley
Stody
The Green
Hunworth
Starlings' Hill
Edgefield
Plumstead Green
Plumstead
Matlaske
Hall Fm
Aldborough Hall
Thurgarton
Hanworth Hall
Manor Fm
Burgh Stubbs
Briningham
Little Woo
Range Fm
Barningham Green
Lower Street
Aldborough
Alby Hill
Thursford
Old Coach House
Little Snoring
The Lings
B1354
Pigg's Grave
Burgh Hall
Breck Fm
Fuel Fm
Thwaite Hill Fm
Abbey Fm
Wood Fm
FAKENHAM ROAD
White Ollands Fm
Edgefield Street
Little Barningham
Wickmere
A148
Forty Acre Plantn
Neat's Close
Park Fm
Melton Constable
Briston
B1354
Fir Patch
B1149
Old Covert
New Covert
Mere Fm
Mannington Hall
Park Fm
Thwaite Hall
Thwaite Common
Erpingham Ho
ALBY CRAFTS & GARDENS
Barney
Little Wood
Swanton Novers
Melton Hall
Dairy Fm
Briston Common
Roper Fm
Shrub Fm
MANNINGTON GARDENS
WOLTERTON PARK
Wolterton
Erpingham
Kettlestone
River Stiffkey
Swanton Great Wood
Bunker's Hill
The Lake
Craymere Beck
Moor Hall
Mossymere Wood
Calthorpe
Scarrow Beck
White House Fm
Croxton
Fulmodestone
Brown's Covert
Tipples' Fm
Wood Severals
Holmes's Wood
Washpit Plantn
Rookery Fm
Blackwater Br
Holly Fm
Little London
Saxthorpe
Itteringham
Moorgate
Common End
Clipstone Ho
Raw Hall
Common Fm
159
Burnthouse Fm
Holly Heath Fm
Corpusty
Hale
A140
Park Fm
Hindolveston
Roundabout Fm
Irmingland Hall
Itteringham Common
Great Wood
Ingworth
PENSTHORPE NATURE RESERVE & GARDENS
Manor Fm
Fulmodeston Severals
Field Barn
Nethergate
Thurning
Hall Fm
Foundry Hill
Red Pits
Oulton Lodge
The Tower
Blickling
BLICKLING HALL
Abbot's Hall
Church Fm
Little Ryburgh
Stibbard
Holly Hill
Wood Norton
Ashcroft Fm
Hindolveston Wood
Black Water
Oak Grove
Cropton Hall
Oulton
Hercules Wood
Flash Pit Fm
Drabblegate
Coldham Hall
Norton Corner
Silvergate
Abbey
Page's
Manor

The Skerries
Harry Furlough's Rocks
Wylfa Head
Wylfa Power Sta
WYLFA POWER STATION & OBSERVATION TOWER
Cemlyn Bay
Porth-y-pistyll
Porth Llanlleiana
Hell's Mouth/Porth Cynfor
Porth Wen
WALES COAST PATH
Porthllechog (Bull Bay)
Bull Bay/Porth Llechog
Llanbadrig
Cemaes
Tregele
Burwen
BULL BAY ROAD
Amlw
Carmel Head
Pen Carmel
Hen Borth
Porth y Dyfn
Caerdegog Uchaf
Ty Wian
Llanfairynghornwy
Porth y Bribys
Mynydd y Garn
Pen-yr-orsedd
Cefn-coch
Bwlch
Llanfechell
Nant-y-frân
Rhyd-y-groes
Criw
Carrog
Tai-hen
Brynddu
Dymchwa
Rhosbeirio
Hafodllin
Ysgellog
Werthyr
Bryn Llwyd
Pentrefelin
Ind Est
Penrhyd Lastra
Llyn Llaethdy
Tyddyn Dai
Parys Fm
Parys Mountain
Bodewryd
Bodelwyn
Clegyrog Blas
Tyddyn-Prys
Pentreheulyn
Gwredog
Craig y Gwynt
Llanrhyddlad
Llyn Llygeirian
Mynydd Mechell
Llanfflewyn
Carreglefn
Rhosgoch
Four Crosses
Trysglwyn
Church Bay
Porth Swtan
Rhydwyn
Bodwyn
Gamog
Salbri Fm
Llyn Hafodol
Rhosybol
Taldrwst Mawr
Yr-ynys
Pen Padrig
Glasgraig Fawr
Gorslwyd Fawr
Penbol
Penygraigwen
LON LAS
Porth Trwyn
Bryn Maethlu
Mynydd-blewog
Penbol Uchaf
Penrhyn
HOLYHEAD BAY
BAE CAERGYBI
Llanfaethlu
Llanbabo
Tyn-y-pwll
Pwllcoch Uchaf
Gaer Fm
Gaerwen
Clwch Dernog
Brwynog
Fferam-uchaf
Glan-y-gors
Llyn Alaw
Gwredog
DUN LAOGHAIRE 2:00 (Mar-Sept)
DUBLIN 1:49
DUBLIN 3:15
Porth Tywyn-mawr
Bodfardden-ddu
LLYNNON WINDMILL
Llanddeusant
Granalaw
LLYN ALAW VISITOR CENTRE
Ceidio
Llandyfrydog
Llwydiarth Fawr
Gronant
Bodfardden-wen
Llynon Hall
Elim
Pandy
Meinir
Chwaen-gôch
Llanerchymedd
Llwydiarth Esgob Fm
Llanfwrog
ISLE OF ANGLESEY (SIR YNYS MÔN)
ISLE OF ANGLESEY YNYS MÔN
Gogarth Bay
Porth Namarch
BREAKWATER
Soldiers' Pt
HOLYHEAD MARITIME MUSEUM
Salt Island
Holyhead
Caergybi
CAER Y TWR (FORT)
Holyhead Mountain
Mountain
Porth-y-felin
Llaingoch
Goferydd
HOLYHEAD MTN HUT CIRCLES
Pont Hwfa
HOLYHEAD ROMAN FORT
Twr
Stryd
Môrawelon
Nimrod Rocks
SOUTH STACK CLIFFS
Pen-las Rock
Kingsland
Retail Pk
Aluminium Smelting Works
Penrhos
Beddmanarch Bay
PENRHOS FEILW STANDING STONES
TY MAWR STANDING STONE
Penrhosfeilw
TREFIGNATH BURIAL CHAMBER
Porth Ruffydd
Porth Dafarch
Porth-y-post
Isallt Bach
Trearddur
Trearddur Bay
Porth Penrhyn-mawr
Llanfachraeth
Stryd y Facsen
Llantrisant
TREGWEHELYDD STANDING STONE
Chwaen Bach
Parc Newydd
Bachau
Cwyrt
Llanfigael
Pen-llyn
Rhiw Goch
Chwaen-wen
Carmel
Mynydd Mwyn Mawr
Ty-Hen Newydd
Tyn-y-Fawr
Bryn-Gwyddon
Ysgoldy
Tyns Bach
Llanynghenedl
Shop Fm
Rallt Fm
Llanllibio Groes
Llyn Llywenan
PRESADDFED BURIAL CHAMBER
Bodsuran
Clwch
Llechcynfarwy
Mynydd-Mwyn
Tryfil
Neuadd
Cae Mawr
Newlands Park
Valley (Y Fali)
Fadog
B5109
Bodedern
Trefor
B5112
Glan Gors
Cleifiog Isaf
Ty'n-y-graig
Bodowyr
Tre-Angharad
Ffynnon-y-mab
Clegir-Gwynion
Penyrorsedd
Gwyndy
Bryntwrog
Glyn Derw
Penrhyn-oer
Llangwyllog
Hafod
Foel
Glan-yr-afon
Eirianallt
Ty Mawr
Holy Island
Ynys Gybi
Porth Diana
Raven's Pt
Porth-y-garan
Glan-traeth
Four Mile Bridge
Ysbylldir
Rhosydd
Gwyddfor
Tai Uchaf
Ty Hên
Parc
Y Werthyr
Rhydydefaid
Afon Caradog
Bodfeillion
Llynfaes
Tyddyn Siencyn
Dolmeinir
Caergeiliog
HOLYHEAD ROAD
Penrhiw
Pandy Treban
Llanfihangel yn Nhowyn
Llyn Dinam
Cymunod
Cae Hywel
Bryngwran
Clegir Mawr
Bryn Ala
Bwlch-y-fen-bentir
Bodewran
Llanfairyneubwll
VALLEY WETLANDS
Llyn Penrhyn
Plâs Llechylched
Fach
Bodwrog
Cors Bodwrog
Llyn Hendref
Bodffordd
Cefni Reservoir
Gwaenfynydd
Llyn Traffwll
Engedi
Caer-glaw
Gwalchmai
Mona
Heneglwys
Ind Pk
Ty-moel
Pen-yr-allt
Rhoscolyn
Tai-croesion
Capel-gwyn
Gwalchmai Uchaf
Trehwfa Fawr
Druid Fm
Rhoscolyn Head
Cefnysgwydd Bach
Tan Rallt
Ty Mawr
Cefn Caer For
Hendre
Silver Bay
Borthwen
Valley
Bodfeddan
Ddrydwy
Cemaes
Cefn Du
Pen y Graig
Dothan
TY-NEWYDD BURIAL CHAMBER
Llain Wen Fm
Rhostrehwfa
Ynys Feirig
RHOSNEIGR
Llanfaelog
Fferam
Tal-y-llyn
Grugor-bach
Cerrigceinwen
Tyddyn Sadler
Llangristiolus
Rhosneigr
Llyn Maelog
Bryn Du
Pencarnisiog
Llyn Padrig
Treruffydd
Cerrig-myna
Cwyrtai
Tyn-rhos
Fferam Rhosydd
Cerrig Engan
Tyn Dryfol
Bodrwyn
Prysiorwerth
Taldrwst
HENBLAS
TY CROES
Rhosbadrig
Penhenllys
Glanrafon
Tai-moelion
Soar
DIN DRYFOL BURIAL CHAMBER
Plas Bach
Capel Mawr
Tan Lan
Bodgedwydd
Tyn-rhos-uchaf
Graig
Bodwrdin
Trefeilir
Tre-Ddafydd-uchaf
Paradwys
Porth Nobla
BARCLODIAD Y GAWRES BURIAL CHAMBER
Ty mawr
Bethel
Treiddon
Trefdraeth
Porth Trecastell
Gate Ho
Merddyn-y-Bit
BODORGAN
Glanrafon Fm
Afon Cefni
Llangwyfan-isaf
Clafdy
Llyn Coron
Llangadwaladr
Hendre Gadog
Aberffraw
Hermon
Malltraeth
Pen-y-Bont
Caethle
Danger area
China
Porth Cwyfan
Mynydd Esgair-ffrill
Coed Llywelyn
Llangaffo
Glanmorfa
Penrhyn
Tyddyn
Frondeg
SH
20
00
70
162
0 1 2 3 miles
0 1 2 3 4 5 km
A B C D E F G H
1 2 3 4 5 6

7
8
9
10
11
A
B
C
D
E
F
G
H
SH
70
00
180
Amlwch Port
Porthyrychen
Porth Eilian
Llaneilian
Fresh Water Bay
Pengorffwysfa
Cerrig-mân
Porthygwichiaid
Porth Helygen
Porth yr Aber
Ynys Dulas
Garreg Allan
Penysarn
Nebo
Gadfa
Dulas
Gwlybycoed
ISLE OF ANGLESEY
YNYS MÔN
Traeth yr Ora
Llaneuddog
City Dulas
Tyddyn Isaf
Lligwy Bay
Derz-Fawr
Brynrefail
Moelfre
MOELFRE SEAWATCH CENTRE
Y Swnt
Capel Parc
Rhôs Lligwy
DIN LLIGWY
LLIGWY BURIAL CHAMBER
Tal-y-bontan
Ty-mawr
Mynydd Bodafon
Plas Bodafon
Llanallgo
Caerhosliggwy
Parciau
Marianglas
Maenaddwyn
Penciau
Plas Llanfihangel
Frigan
Borth-wen
Tynygongl
Brynteg
Benllech
Dinas
Capel Coch
Cefn-du Mawr
Nant Isaf
Benllech Sand
Nant-uchaf
CORS ERDDREINIOG
Ynys Isaf
Nant Newydd
Bettws
CORS GOCH
Red Wharf Bay
Red Wharf Bay Traeth-coch
Llanbedrgoch
Tyn Coed
Erddreiniog
Prysan
Maen Eryr
Glan Gors
Hendre
Gwenfro Isaf
Tan-y-graig
STANDING STONE
Llanddyfnan
Gwenfro Uchaf
Pentraeth
Pencefn
Bonc Fadog
Carrog Uchaf
STONE SCIENCE
Rhosmeirch
Trefollwyn
Tyn Beudy
CORS BODEILIO
Hendre Fm
Clegyrdy-bach
Talwrn
ORIEL YNYS MON
The Dingle
Pencraig
Clegyrdy-mawr
Gylched
Ty-coch
Dyffryn
Rhoscefnhir
Taihirion
Trefor
Pen-y-garnedd
Hendrefor
Plas Penmynydd
Ind Est
Ind Pk
Llangefni
Ceint
Hirdre-faig
Penmynydd
Cefn-poeth
Nant
Tyddyn
Y Dolydd
Twll-y-clawdd
Castell
Ty'n Buarth
Tyddyn Mawr
Rhyd-yr-arian
Bwlch-gwyn
Cefn Du Isaf
Tyn Cae
PILI PALAS
Menai Bridge (Porthaethwy)
Pentre Berw
Llanfairpwll-gwyngyll
LLANFAIRPWLL
Gaerwen
MENAI SUSPENSION BRIDGE
ORIEL TEGFRYN
Bangor
Bryn-y-fedwen
Brynhyfryd
Llanddaniel Fab
BRYN CELLI DDU BURIAL CHAMBER
Capel-y-graig
Chwipin
Bus Pk
Pont Crug
Ty'n-y-Coed
Glanyrafon
PLAS NEWYDD
Vaynol Hall
Old Hall
Bodowyr-isaf
Bodlew
Dinam
SODOWYR BURIAL CHAMBER
Ysgubor Wen
Gwydryn Newydd
Llanedwen
Lew
Pont-Dic
Bodrida
CAER LEB
Wern Fm
WALES COAST PATH
Pentraeth Forest
Llanddona
Ffordd Deg
Rhôs
Carwad
Rhos Newydd
Pen-y-bryn
Bryn Cogail
Hafotty Covert
Llyn Bodgylched
Bodgylched
Llansadwrn
Coed Cefn
Cefn
Hen Bentref Llandegfan
Llandegfan
Beaumaris
BEAUMARIS CASTLE
GAOL & COURTHOUSE
ALLT GOCH FAWR
Gallows Point
Trwyn y Penrhyn
Fedw Fawr
Mariandyrys
Penhwnllys
Glan-yr-afon
Bryn Ddol
Cefn
Llangoed
Bryn Celyn
Caim
PENMON PRIORY
Penmon
Outer Road
Lavan Sands
Llanfaes
Fryars Road
Puffin Island or Priestholm Ynys Seiriol
CONWY BAY
BAE CONWY
Garth
Upper Bangor
Hirael
CATHEDRAL
BANGOR
Maesgeirchen
PENRHYN CASTLE
Glan Adda
Minffordd
Coed Mawr
Ind Est
Bryn
Llandegai
Tal-y-bont
Marianwinllan
Pen-y-bryn
COCHWILLAN OLD HALL
Rhiw Goch
BANGOR SERVICES
Caerhun
Brithdir
Tyddyn-Hefryn
Glasinfryn
Pen-wen
Halfway Br
Tregarth
Rachub
Garth
Tyddyn
Niwbwrch
Abergwyngregyn
Crymlyn
Glyn
Ffridd Ddu
Nant
COEDYDD ABER
Bronydd Isaf
ABER FALLS
Llanllechid
Llefn
Gyrn 542
Moel Wnion 580
Moel Faban 408
SNOWDONIA
NATIONAL PARK
PARC CENEDLAETHOL ERYRI
Bera Mawr
Gyrn Wigau
Drosgl 758
Penmaenan
Garizim
LLANFAIRFECHAN
Llanfairfechan
Nant-y-felin
Nant-y-pandy
Garreg Fawr 356
Gorddinog
Cammarnaint
Foel-Ganol 533
Afon Anafon
Pen Bryn-du
Drosgl 621
Bwlch y Ddeufaen
Moel 435
Llwytmor
Drum 770
Foel-Fras 942
Afon Goch
A55
A5
A5025
B5110
B5109
B5108
B5420
A545
A4087
163

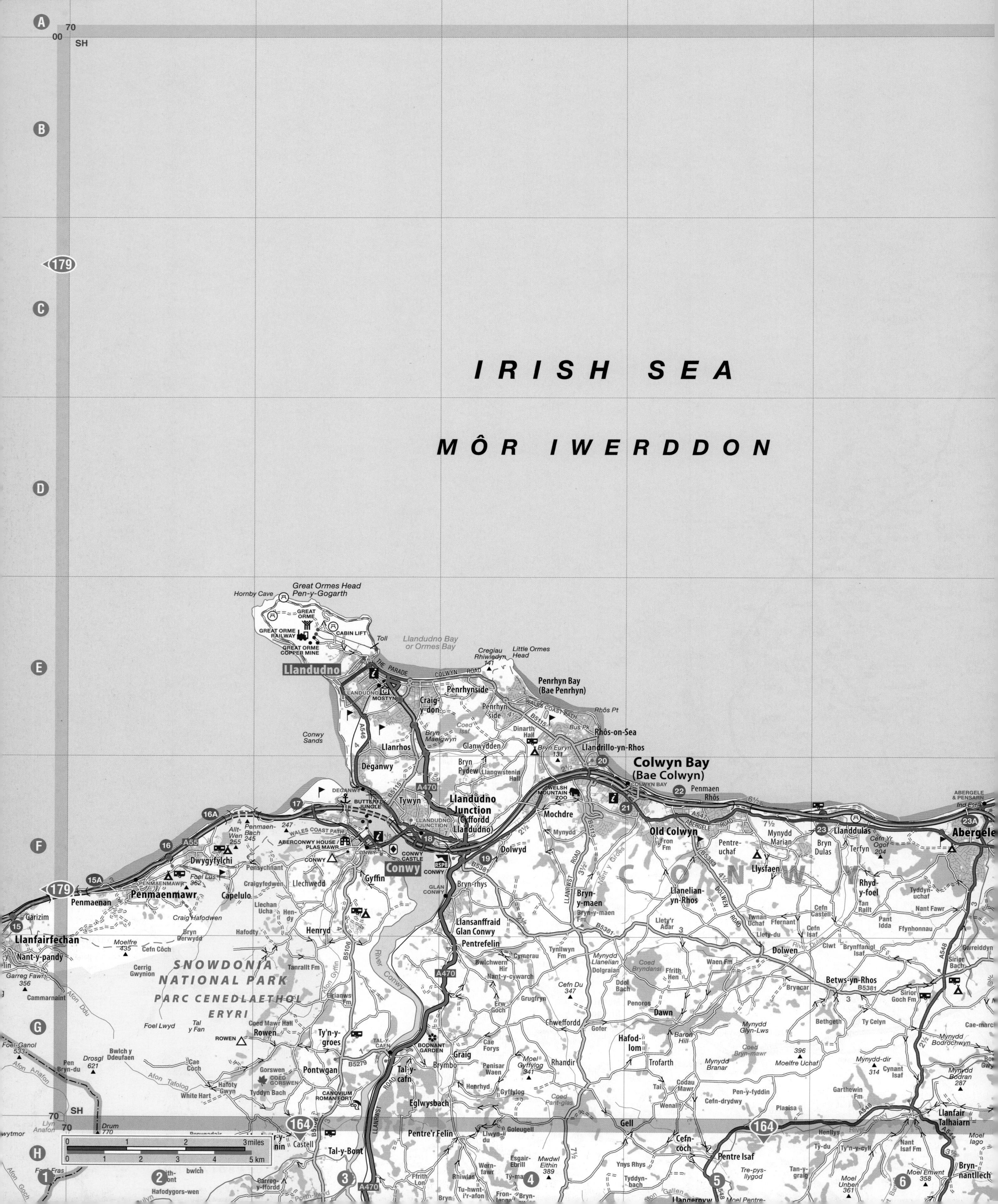

IRISH SEA
MÔR IWERDDON
Great Ormes Head
Pen-y-Gogarth
Hornby Cave
GREAT ORME
GREAT ORME RAILWAY
GREAT ORME COPPER MINE
CABIN LIFT
Toll
Llandudno Bay or Ormes Bay
Llandudno
THE PARADE
COLWYN ROAD
Cregiau Rhiwledyn 141
Little Ormes Head
Penrhyn Bay (Bae Penrhyn)
Penrhynside
Craig-y-don
Penrhyn side
Rhôs Pt
Rhôs-on-Sea
Llandrillo-yn-Rhos
Dinarth Hall
Bryn Euryn 131
Conwy Sands
Llanrhos
Glanwydden
Deganwy
Bryn Pydew
Llangwstenin Hall
Colwyn Bay (Bae Colwyn)
Penmaen Rhôs
Llandudno Junction (Cyffordd Llandudno)
Tywyn
WELSH MOUNTAIN ZOO
Mochdre
Old Colwyn
Llanddulas
Abergele
Mynydd Marian
Bryn Dulas
Terfyn
Cefn Yr Ogof 204
Pentre-uchaf
Llysfaen
Rhyd-y-foel
Dolwyd
Conwy
CONWY CASTLE
ABERCONWY HOUSE / PLAS MAWR
WALES COAST PATH
BUTTERFLY JUNGLE
Gyffin
Llechwedd
Bryn-rhys
Llansanffraid Glan Conwy
Pentrefelin
Bryn-y-maen
Llanelian-yn-Rhos
Dolwen
Betws-yn-Rhos
Penmaenmawr
Penmaenan
Dwygyfylchi
Capelulo
Foel Lus 362
Llanfairfechan
Garizim
Nant-y-pandy
SNOWDONIA NATIONAL PARK
PARC CENEDLAETHOL ERYRI
Henryd
Rowen
Ty'n-y-groes
Pontwgan
Tal-y-cafn
BODNANT GARDEN
Graig
Eglwysbach
Pentre'r Felin
Tal-y-Bont
Castell
Dawn
Hafod-lom
Trofarth
Gell
Cefn-coch
Pentre Isaf
Llanfair Talhaiarn
Bryn-nantllech
River Conwy
CONWY

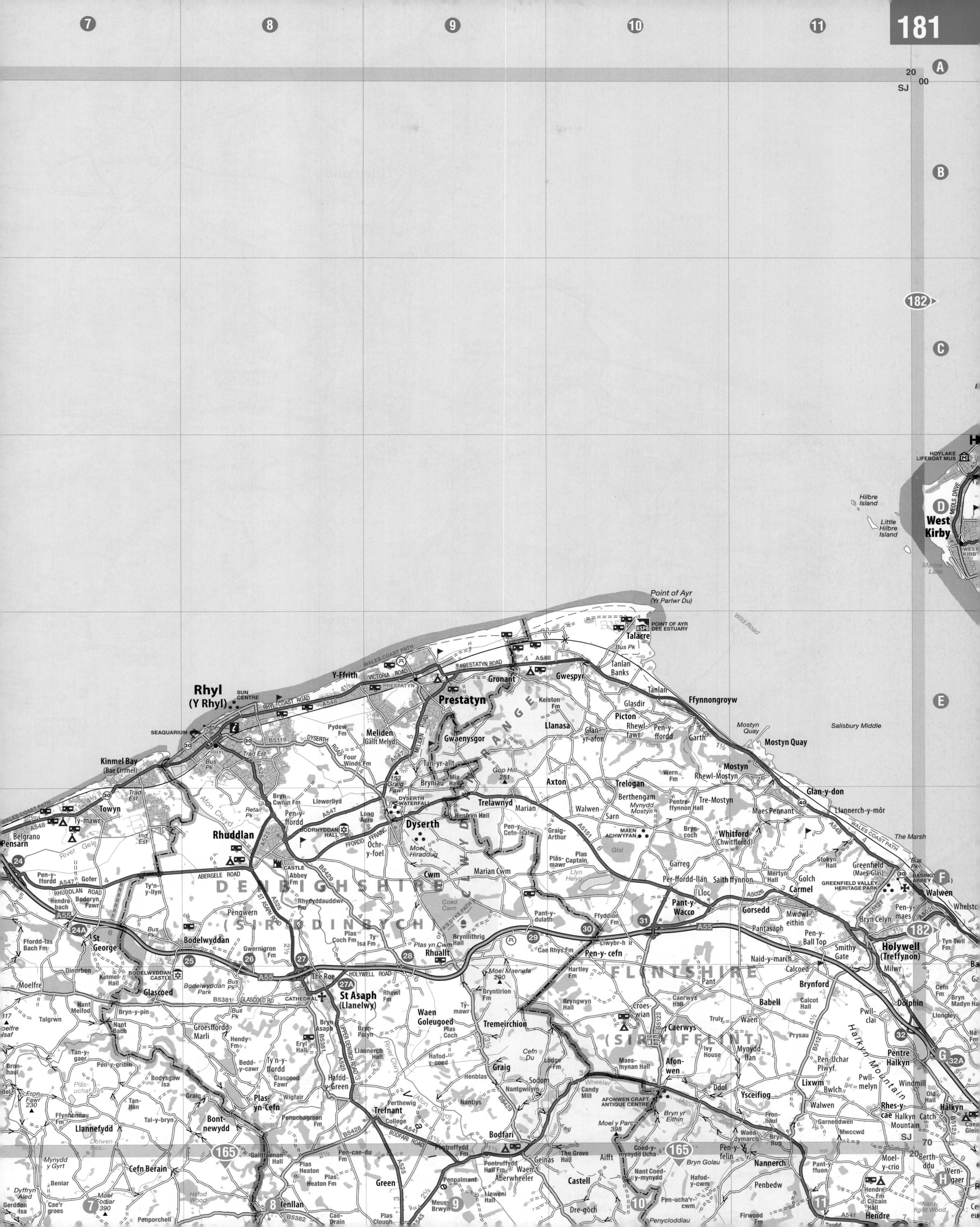
Point of Ayr
(Yr Parlwr Du)
POINT OF AYR DEE ESTUARY
Talacre
Hilbre Island
Little Hilbre Island
HOYLAKE LIFEBOAT MUS
West Kirby
Marine Lake
Rhyl
(Y Rhyl)
SUN CENTRE
SEAQUARIUM
Y-Ffrith
WALES COAST PATH
PRESTATYN ROAD
Prestatyn
Gronant
Gwespyr
Tanlan Banks
Tanlan
Ffynnongroyw
Mostyn Quay
Salisbury Middle
Kinmel Bay
(Bae Cinmel)
Towyn
Ty-mawr
Belgrano
Pensarn
Rhuddlan
Meliden
(Gallt Melyd)
Gwaenysgor
Gop Hill
251
Llanasa
Picton
Glasdir
Axton
Trelogan
Mostyn
Rhewl-Mostyn
Glan-y-don
Llannerch-y-môr
The Marsh
Dyserth
DYSERTH WATERFALL
BODRHYDDAN HALL
Trelawnyd
Marian
Walwen
Sarn
MAEN ACHWYFAN
Whitford
(Chwitffordd)
Maes Pennant
Greenfield
(Maes-Glas)
GREENFIELD VALLEY HERITAGE PARK
BASINGWERK ABBEY
Walwen
Carmel
Golch
Garreg
Per-ffordd-llân
Saith ffynnon
Lloc
Pant-y-Wacco
Gorsedd
Marian Cwm
Cwm
DENBIGHSHIRE
(SIR DDINBYCH)
FLINTSHIRE
(SIR Y FFLINT)
CLWYDIAN RANGE
St George
Bodelwyddan
BODELWYDDAN CASTLE
Kinmel Hall
Glascoed
Moelfre
Rhuallt
Pen-y-cefn
Holywell
(Treffynon)
Milwr
Brynford
Babell
Calcoed
Smithy Gate
The Roe
St Asaph
(Llanelwy)
CATHEDRAL
Waen Goleugoed
Tremeirchion
Moel Maenefa
290
Caerwys
Afon-wen
Dolphin
Pentre Halkyn
Halkyn Mountain
Halkyn
Lixwm
Ysceifiog
Graig
Sodom
AFONWEN CRAFT ANTIQUE CENTRE
Moel y Parc
398
Bont-newydd
Llannefydd
Trefnant
Bodfari
Cefn Berain
Nannerch
Penbedw
Rhes-y-cae
Windmill
Green
Tenllan
Aifft
Castell
Hendre
Moel Fodiar
390
A548
A55
A525
A547
A5151
A5026
A541
B5429
B5381
B5428
B5122
182
165
SJ
20
00
70
A
B
C
D
E
F
G
H
7
8
9
10
11

LIVERPOOL BAY
Crosby Channel
Crosby
Little Crosby
Thornton
Sefton
Netherton
Maghull
Melling
Kirkby
Blundellsands
Brighton le Sands
Great Crosby
Waterloo
Litherland
Seaforth
Bootle
Aintree
Fazakerley
Orrell
Walton
Norris Green
Knowsley
Croxteth
BELFAST 8:00
DOUGLAS 4:15 (WINTER ONLY)
DUBLIN 7:30
DOUGLAS 2:30 (MARCH-NOV)
New Brighton
Wallasey
Egremont
Liscard
Leasowe
Moreton
Poulton
Bidston
Hoylake
Meols
Dove Point
East Hoyle Bank
Hilbre Island
West Kirby
Upton
Greasby
Saughall Massie
Birkenhead
Claughton
Seacombe
Kirkdale
Anfield
Everton
Liverpool
Vauxhall
Kensington
Edge Hill
Wavertree
Toxteth
Dingle
Aigburth
Garston
Childwall
Roby
Huyton
Woolton
Gateacre
Allerton
Hunt's Cross
Liverpool Airport
River Mersey
MERSEYSIDE
Tranmere
Rock Ferry
New Ferry
Prenton
Oxton
Noctorum
Woodchurch
Arrowe Hill
Frankby
Grange
Caldy
Irby
Thurstaston
Landican
Thingwall
Pensby
Barnston
Heswall
Gayton
Storeton
Higher Bebington
Bebington
Port Sunlight
Bromborough
Eastham
Brimstage
Thornton Hough
Raby
Parkgate
Neston
Little Neston
Ness
Willaston
Hooton
Little Sutton
Overpool
Ellesmere Port
Stanlow
Whitby
Great Sutton
Ledsham
Capenhurst
Puddington
Burton
Shotwick
Saughall
Mollington
Backford
Chester
Upton
Hoole
CHESHIRE WEST & CHESTER
Dawpool Bank
Flint (Y Fflint)
Holywell (Treffynon)
Bagillt
Greenfield
Mount Pleasant
Oakenholt
Flint Mountain
Halkyn
Connah's Quay
Shotton
Queensferry
Sealand
Garden City
M53
M57
M62
A41
A540
A550
193
181
166
0 1 2 3 miles
0 1 2 3 4 5 km

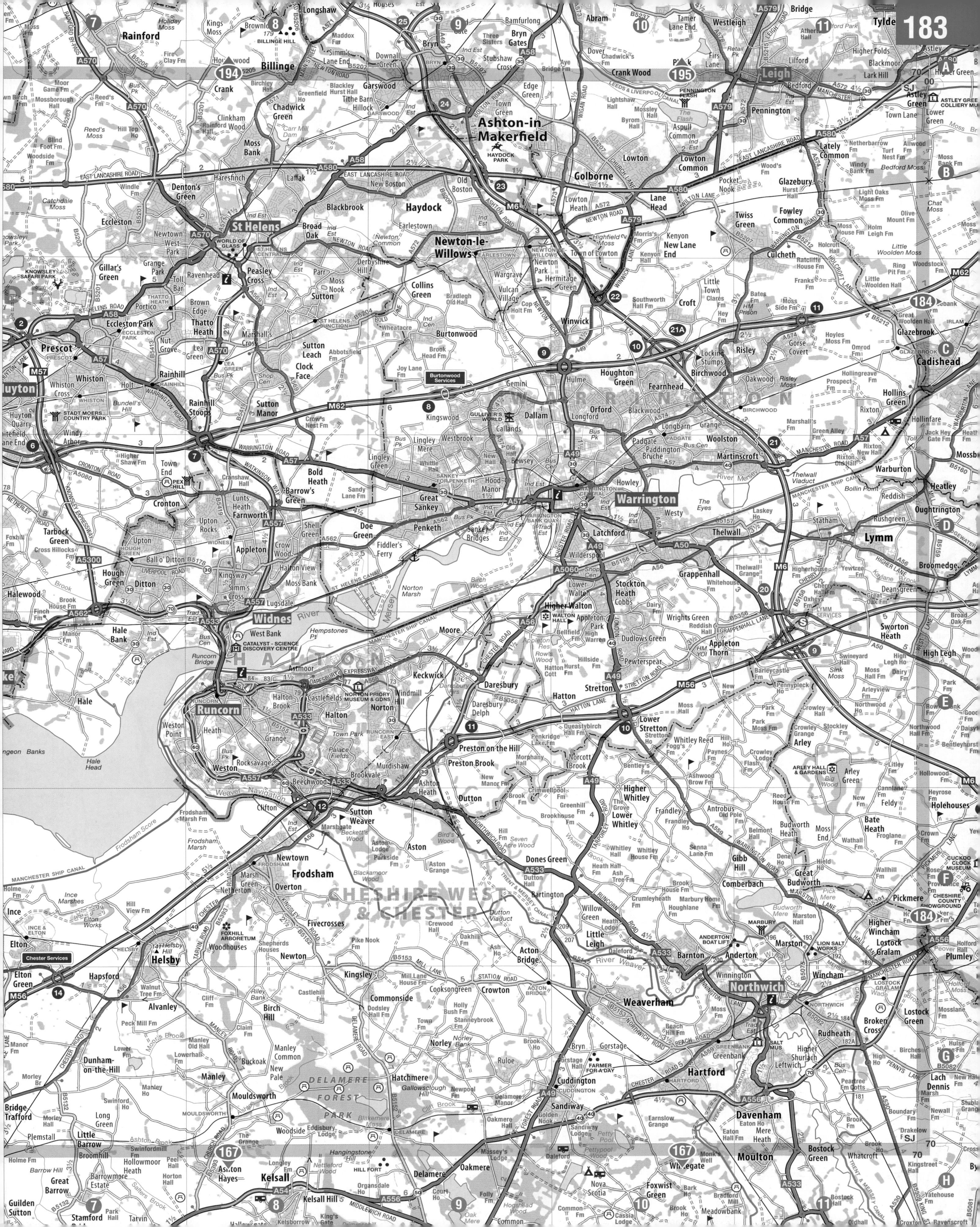
Rainford
Billinge
Longshaw
Bryn Gates
Abram
Westleigh
Tyldesley
Crank
Garswood
Ashton-in Makerfield
Golborne
Leigh
Pennington
Lowton
Lowton Common
Lane Head
Glazebury
Astley
Haydock
St Helens
Eccleston
Newton-le-Willows
Culcheth
Prescot
Whiston
Huyton
Rainhill
Sutton
Burtonwood
Winwick
Croft
Risley
Birchwood
Glazebrook
Cadishead
Fearnhead
Orford
Hulme
Houghton Green
Dallam
Warrington
Great Sankey
Penketh
Woolston
Martinscroft
Hollins Green
Rixton
Warburton
Heatley
Lymm
Thelwall
Statham
Latchford
Grappenhall
Appleton Thorn
Stockton Heath
Higher Walton
Farnworth
Cronton
Widnes
Ditton
Halewood
Hale
Hale Bank
Moore
Daresbury
Halton
Runcorn
Norton
Keckwick
Hatton
Stretton
Lower Stretton
Arley
High Legh
Preston on the Hill
Preston Brook
Dutton
Aston
Frodsham
Helsby
Elton
Alvanley
Kingsley
Crowton
Acton Bridge
Weaverham
Barnton
Anderton
Marston
Northwich
Hartford
Davenham
Moulton
Cuddington
Sandiway
Delamere
Kelsall
Tarvin
Manley
Mouldsworth
Norley
Little Leigh
Comberbach
Great Budworth
Pickmere
Lach Dennis
Rudheath
Lostock Gralam
Wincham
CHESHIRE WEST & CHESTER
DELAMERE FOREST PARK
HALTON
WARRINGTON
M6
M62
M56
M57
A57
A49
A56
A580
A533
A556

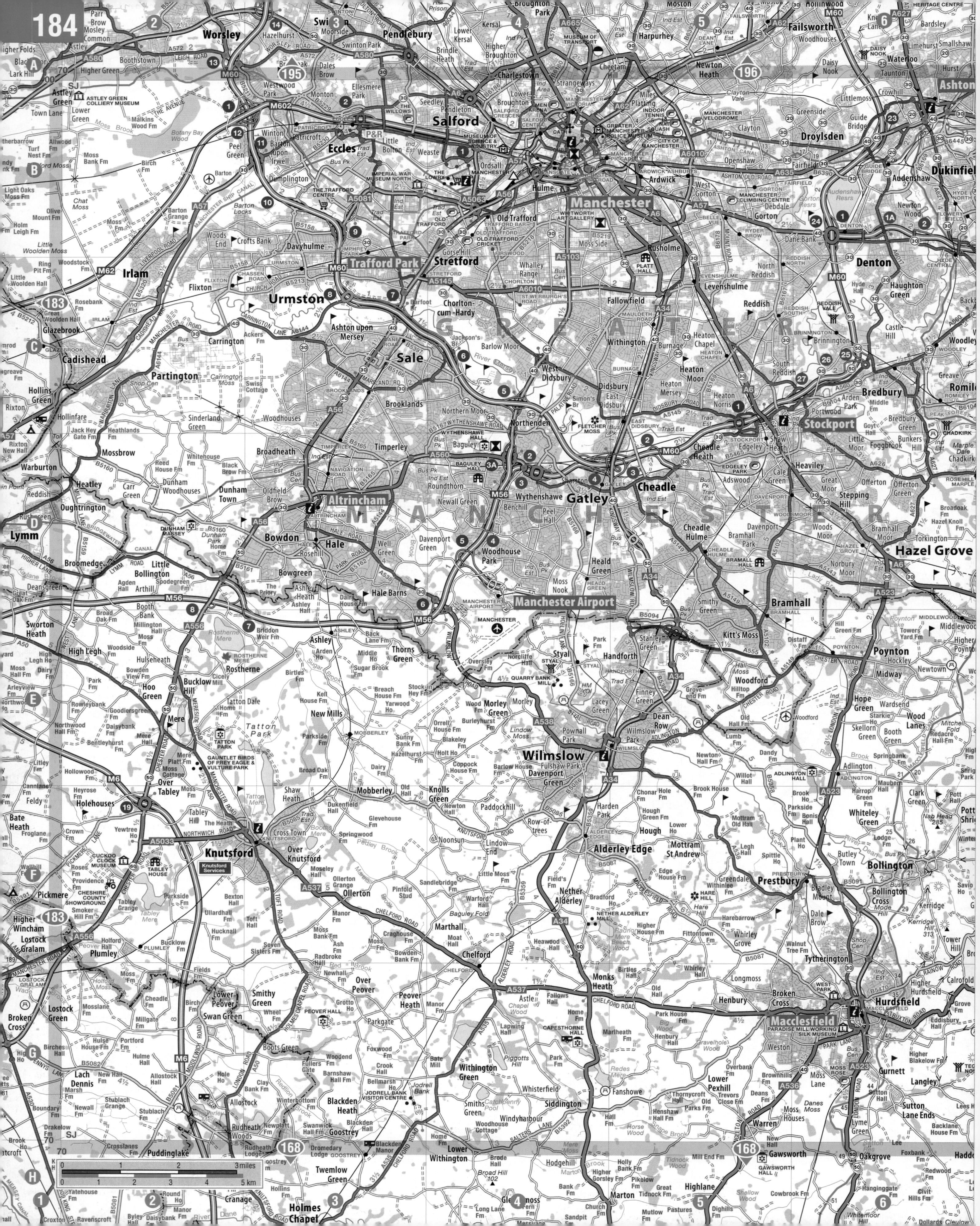
Worsley
Swinton
Pendlebury
Salford
Eccles
Manchester
Failsworth
Droylsden
Ashton
Dukinfield
Denton
Trafford Park
Stretford
Irlam
Flixton
Urmston
Cadishead
Partington
Sale
Carrington
Chorlton-cum-Hardy
Withington
Didsbury
Northenden
Stockport
Bredbury
Cheadle
Gatley
Altrincham
Bowdon
Hale
Lymm
Hazel Grove
Bramhall
Manchester Airport
Poynton
Wilmslow
Knutsford
Alderley Edge
Prestbury
Bollington
Macclesfield
Hurdsfield
Mobberley
Chelford
Goostrey
Holmes Chapel
Twemlow Green
Siddington
Marton
Gawsworth
Oakgrove
G R E A T E R
M A N C H E S T E R
0 1 2 3 miles
0 1 2 3 4 5 km

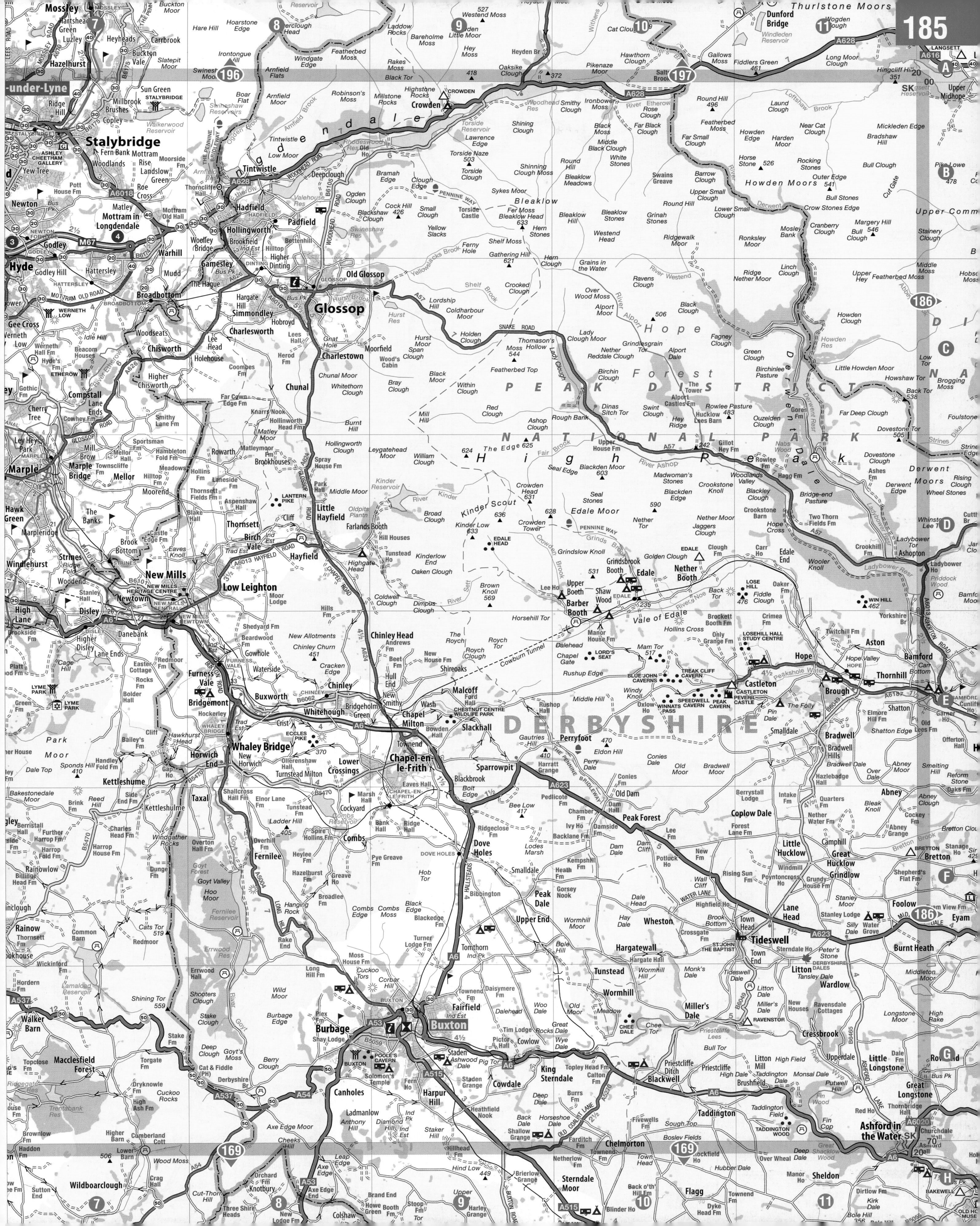

Mossley
Stalybridge
Hyde
Marple
Newton
Godley
Mottram in Longdendale
Hollingworth
Hadfield
Padfield
Tintwistle
Glossop
Old Glossop
Simmondley
Charlesworth
Chisworth
Broadbottom
Compstall
Mellor
Marple Bridge
New Mills
Newtown
Disley
High Lane
Low Leighton
Birch Vale
Hayfield
Little Hayfield
Chunal
Charlestown
Furness Vale
Bridgemont
Whaley Bridge
Horwich End
Chinley
Chapel-en-le-Frith
Chapel Milton
Buxworth
Combs
Dove Holes
Peak Dale
Buxton
Fairfield
Burbage
Harpur Hill
King Sterndale
Chelmorton
Taddington
Tideswell
Litton
Wardlow
Great Longstone
Ashford in the Water
Bradwell
Hope
Castleton
Edale
Aston
Bamford
Thornhill
Brough
Peak Forest
Wormhill
Miller's Dale
Crowden
Dunford Bridge
Langsett
Macclesfield Forest
Wildboarclough
Rainow
Kettleshulme
Taxal
Longdendale
Bleaklow
Kinder Scout
Edale Moor
Howden Moors
Derwent Moors
PEAK DISTRICT NATIONAL PARK
High Peak
Hope Forest
Vale of Edale
DERBYSHIRE
Ladybower Reservoir
Derwent Reservoir
Howden Reservoir
Kinder Reservoir
Errwood Reservoir
Fernilee Reservoir
Woodhead Reservoir
Torside Reservoir
Rhodeswood Reservoir
Valehouse Reservoir
Bottoms Reservoir
Snake Road
Pennine Way
The Pennine Bridleway
Cowburn Tunnel
A628
A57
A6
A623
A624
A515
A537
A54
A53
M67
196
197
186
169

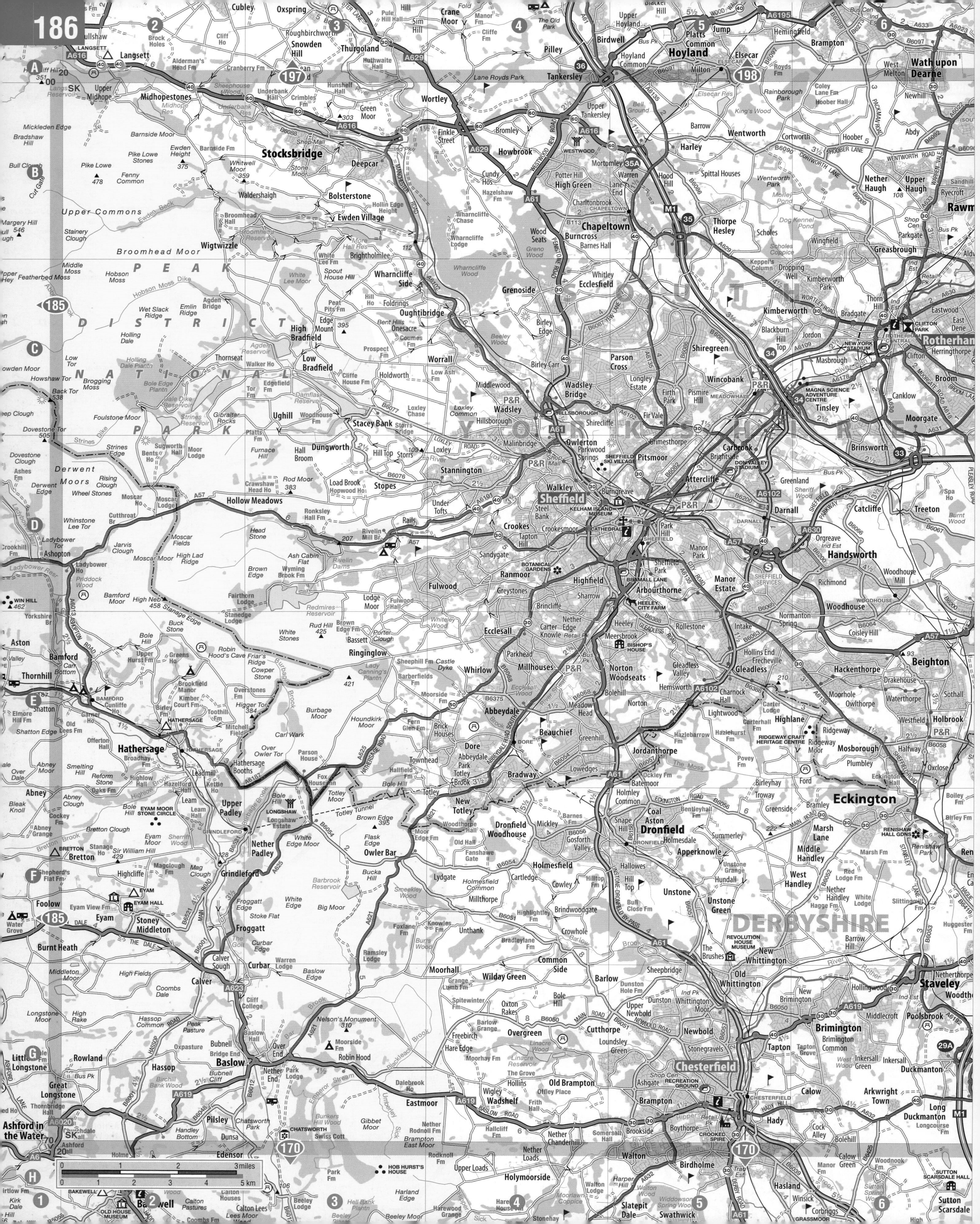

Langsett
Midhopestones
Stocksbridge
Deepcar
Bolsterstone
Ewden Village
Wigtwizzle
Broomhead Moor
Upper Commons
Oxspring
Thurgoland
Wortley
Tankersley
Birdwell
Hoyland
Elsecar
Jump
Brampton
Wath upon Dearne
Chapeltown
High Green
Ecclesfield
Grenoside
Wharncliffe Side
Oughtibridge
Worrall
High Bradfield
Low Bradfield
Dungworth
Stannington
Hollow Meadows
Wadsley Bridge
Hillsborough
Sheffield
Crookes
Fulwood
Ranmoor
Ecclesall
Rotherham
Kimberworth
Tinsley
Brinsworth
Catcliffe
Treeton
Darnall
Handsworth
Woodhouse
Beighton
Mosborough
Halfway
Eckington
Dronfield
Coal Aston
Unstone
Totley
Dore
Bradway
Abbeydale
Beauchief
Norton
Gleadless
Bamford
Thornhill
Hathersage
Grindleford
Eyam
Stoney Middleton
Froggatt
Curbar
Calver
Baslow
Hassop
Great Longstone
Ashford in the Water
Pilsley
Edensor
Bakewell
Holymoorside
Old Brampton
Brampton
Chesterfield
Newbold
Old Whittington
New Whittington
Staveley
Brimington
Calow
Hasland
Birdholme
Walton
Duckmanton
Long Duckmanton
Arkwright Town
Barlow
Sutton Scarsdale
Peak District National Park
South Yorkshire
Derbyshire
185
197
198
170
miles
km

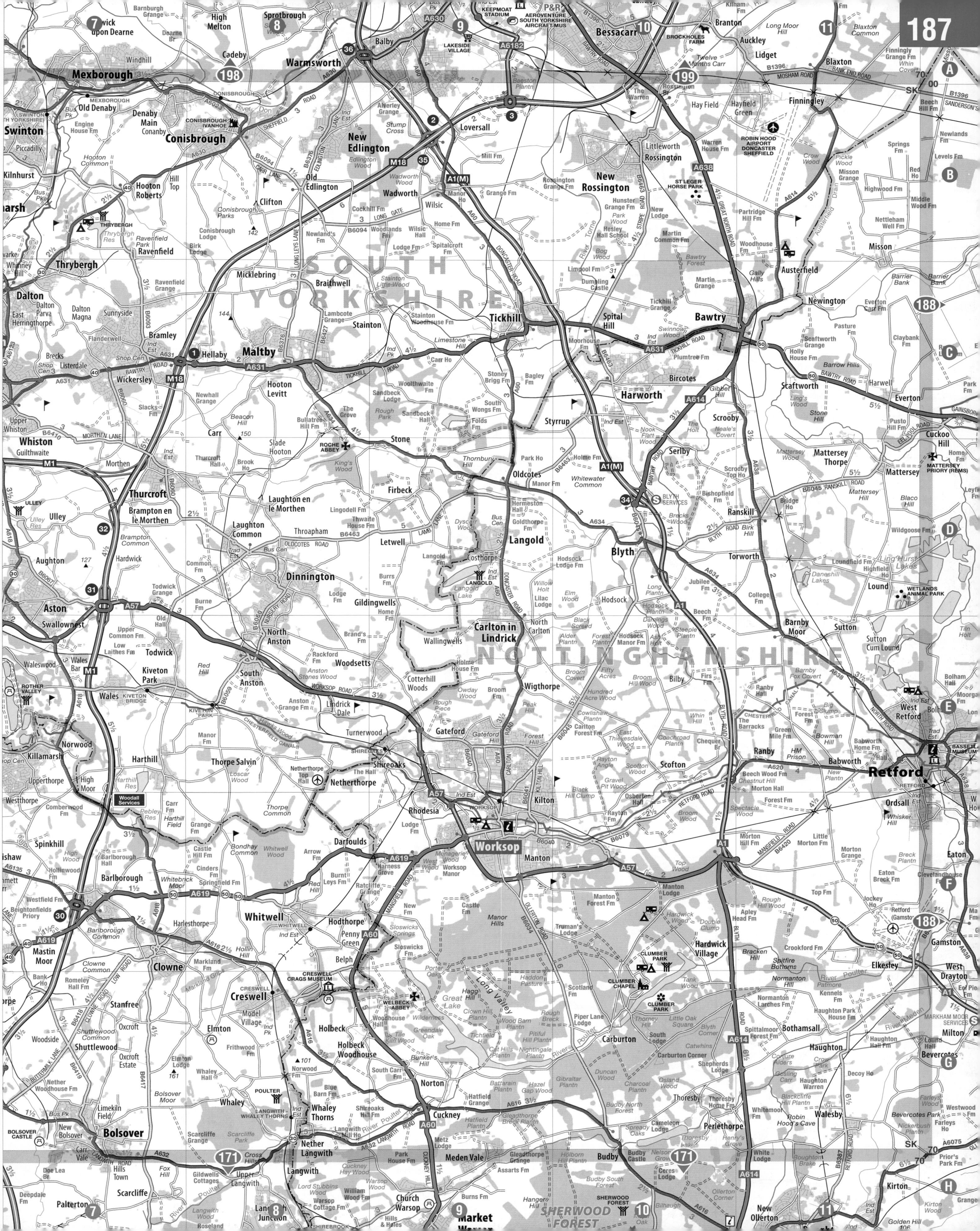
Mexborough
Old Denaby
Denaby Main
Conanby
Conisbrough
Swinton
Cadeby
Sprotbrough
High Melton
Warmsworth
Balby
Bessacarr
Branton
Auckley
Lidget
Blaxton
Finningley
Hayfield Green
Hay Field
ROBIN HOOD AIRPORT DONCASTER SHEFFIELD
Loversall
New Edlington
Old Edlington
Hooton Roberts
Clifton
Wadworth
Wilsic
New Rossington
Littleworth Rossington
Thrybergh
Ravenfield
Dalton
Micklebring
Braithwell
SOUTH YORKSHIRE
Stainton
Tickhill
Spital Hill
Bawtry
Austerfield
Misson
Newington
Maltby
Hellaby
Bramley
Wickersley
Hooton Levitt
Harworth
Bircotes
Styrrup
Scrooby
Serlby
Scaftworth
Everton
Whiston
Stone
Oldcotes
Firbeck
Thurcroft
Brampton en le Morthen
Laughton en le Morthen
Laughton Common
Letwell
Langold
Blyth
Ranskill
Torworth
Mattersey
Mattersey Thorpe
Ulley
Aughton
Aston
Dinnington
Gildingwells
Carlton in Lindrick
North Carlton
Hodsock
Barnby Moor
Sutton
Sutton Cum Lound
Lound
Swallownest
North Anston
South Anston
Todwick
Kiveton Park
Woodsetts
Wallingwells
NOTTINGHAMSHIRE
Wigthorpe
Bilby
Wales
Norwood
Killamarsh
Harthill
Thorpe Salvin
Shireoaks
Netherthorpe
Gateford
Rhodesia
Worksop
Kilton
Manton
Scofton
Ranby
Babworth
Retford
West Retford
Ordsall
Eaton
Spinkhill
Barlborough
Whitwell
Hodthorpe
Darfoulds
Clowne
Creswell
Belph
Elkesley
Gamston
West Drayton
Hardwick Village
Carburton
Bothamsall
Haughton
Milton
Bevercotes
Stanfree
Shuttlewood
Elmton
Holbeck
Holbeck Woodhouse
Norton
Cuckney
Whaley
Whaley Thorns
Bolsover
Nether Langwith
Langwith
Meden Vale
Budby
Perlethorpe
Walesby
Kirton
New Ollerton
Palterton
Scarcliffe
Upper Langwith
Market Warsop
Church Warsop
SHERWOOD FOREST
M1
M18
A1(M)
A1
A57
A60
A614
A619
A631
A634
A638
198
199
188
171

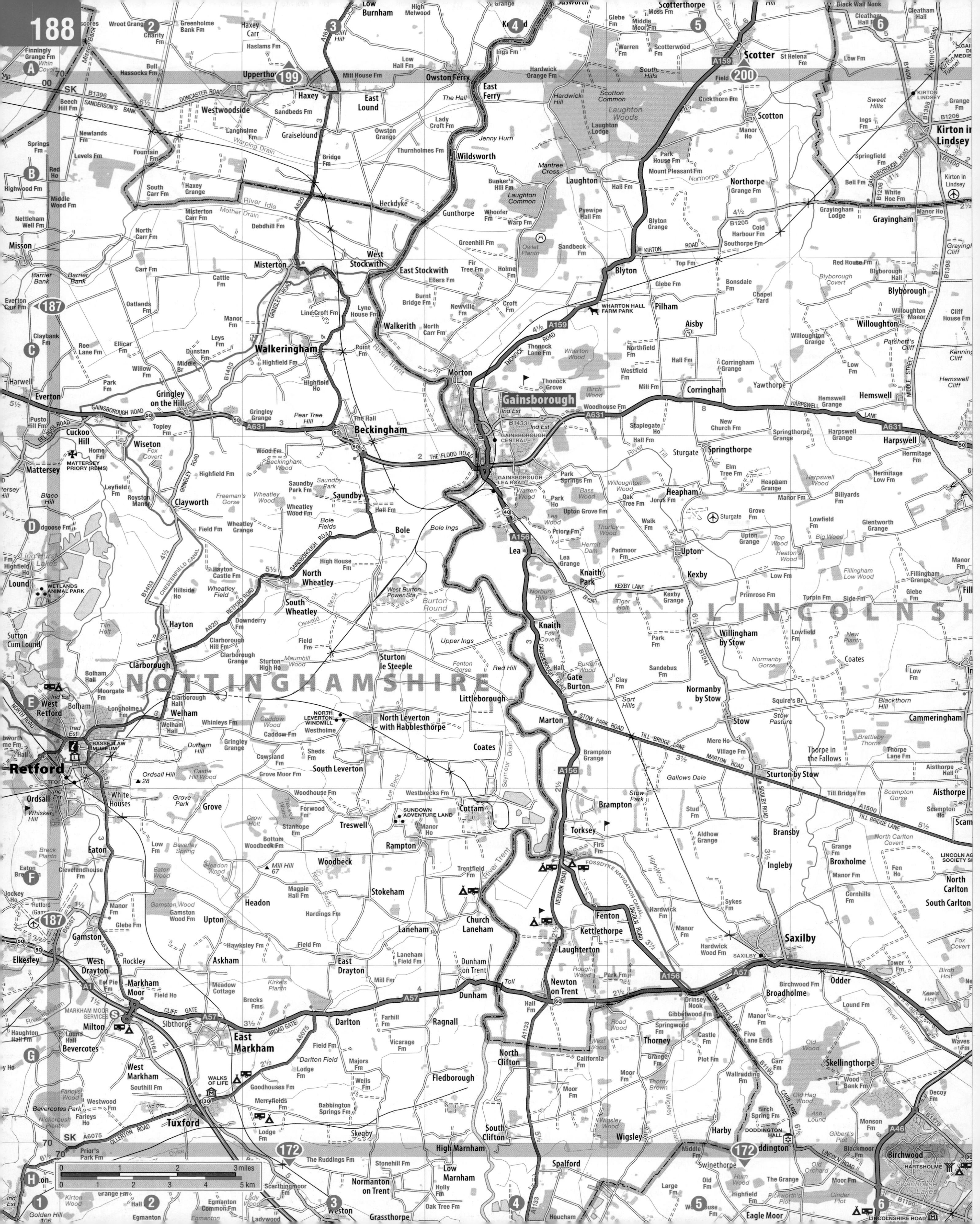
NOTTINGHAMSHIRE
LINCOLNSHIRE
Gainsborough
Retford
Scotter
Kirton in Lindsey
Haxey
Westwoodside
Owston Ferry
East Ferry
East Lound
Graiselound
Wildsworth
Laughton
Scotton
Northorpe
Grayingham
Misson
Misterton
West Stockwith
East Stockwith
Blyton
Pilham
Aisby
Blyborough
Willoughton
Walkeringham
Walkerith
Morton
Corringham
Hemswell
Harpswell
Everton
Gringley on the Hill
Beckingham
Cuckoo Hill
Wiseton
Mattersey
Clayworth
Saundby
Bole
Lea
Heapham
Springthorpe
Sturgate
Upton
Kexby
Knaith Park
North Wheatley
South Wheatley
Hayton
Knaith
Willingham by Stow
Clarborough
Sturton le Steeple
Gate Burton
Normanby by Stow
Coates
West Retford
Bolham
Welham
North Leverton with Habblesthorpe
Littleborough
Marton
Stow
Cammeringham
Sturton by Stow
Aisthorpe
South Leverton
Thorpe in the Fallows
Ordsall
Grove
Treswell
Cottam
Brampton
Torksey
Eaton
Rampton
Woodbeck
Bransby
Ingleby
Broxholme
Stokeham
Headon
Church Laneham
Laneham
Fenton
Kettlethorpe
Saxilby
North Carlton
South Carlton
Gamston
Upton
Askham
Laughterton
Elkesley
West Drayton
East Drayton
Dunham on Trent
Newton on Trent
Markham Moor
Dunham
Odder
Broadholme
Milton
Sibthorpe
Darlton
Ragnall
East Markham
Bevercotes
Thorney
West Markham
North Clifton
Skellingthorpe
Fledborough
Tuxford
Skegby
South Clifton
Wigsley
Harby
Birchwood
High Marnham
Low Marnham
Spalford
Normanton on Trent
Swinethorpe
Weston
Grassthorpe
Eagle Moor
Doddington
A159
A631
A156
A620
A161
A57
A1
A638
A1133
A1500
A6075
A46
B1396
B1403
B1241
B1205
B1398
B1400
B1164
B1190
LINCOLNSHIRE ROAD
187
199
200
172
0 1 2 3 miles
0 1 2 3 4 5 km

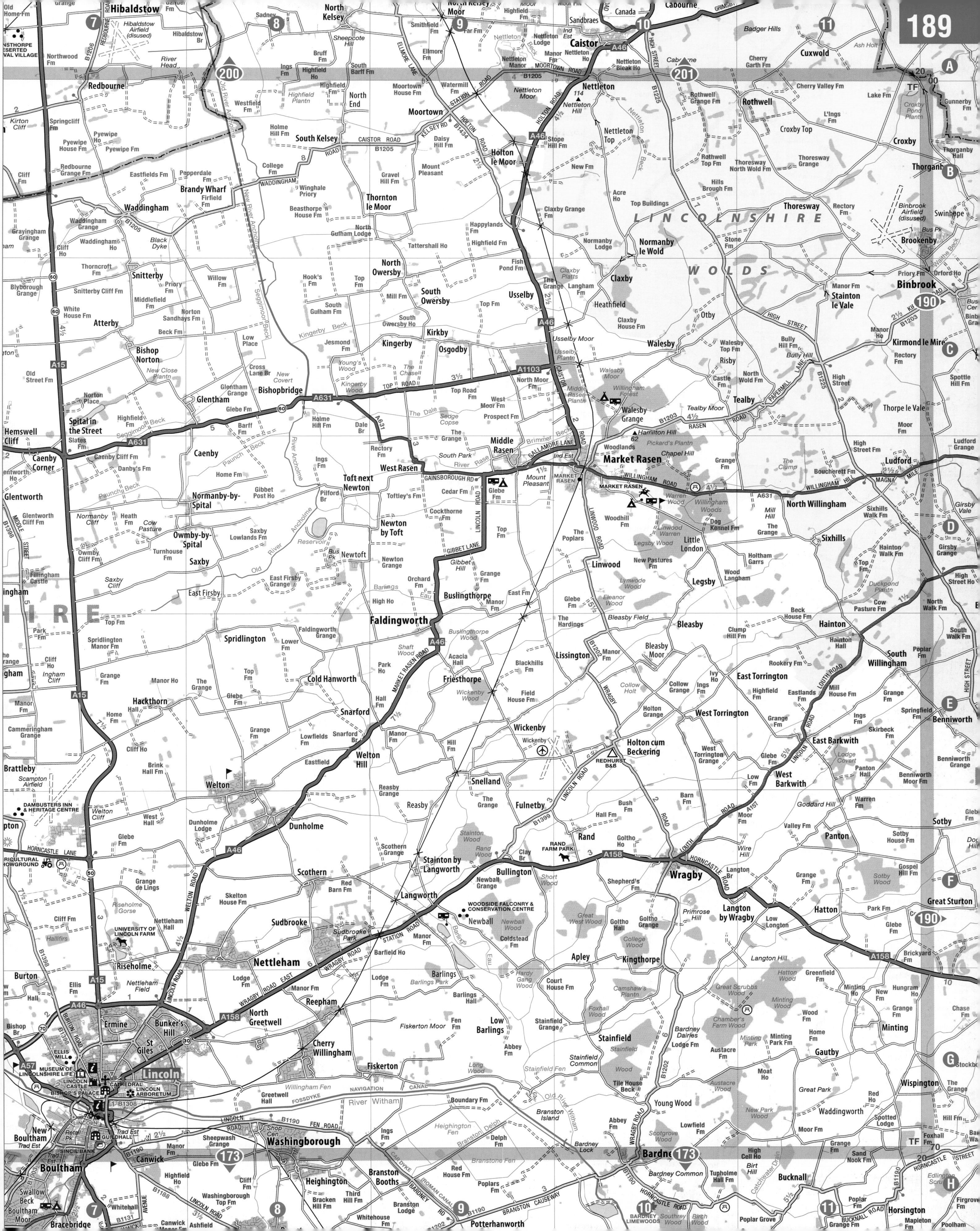
Hibaldstow
North Kelsey
North Kelsey Moor
Caistor
Cabourne
Canada
Sandbraes
Cuxwold
Redbourne
Nettleton
Moortown
South Kelsey
Holton le Moor
Rothwell
Croxby Top
Croxby
Thorganby
Waddingham
Brandy Wharf
Thornton le Moor
Thoresway
LINCOLNSHIRE
WOLDS
Normanby le Wold
Binbrook
Brookenby
Swinhope
Snitterby
North Owersby
South Owersby
Usselby
Claxby
Stainton le Vale
Atterby
Kirkby
Kingerby
Osgodby
Walesby
Kirmond le Mire
Bishop Norton
Glentham
Bishopbridge
Tealby
Hemswell Cliff
Spital in the Street
Caenby
Caenby Corner
Middle Rasen
West Rasen
Toft next Newton
Market Rasen
Ludford
North Willingham
Glentworth
Normanby-by-Spital
Owmby-by-Spital
Newton by Toft
Newtoft
Saxby
Sixhills
Little London
Linwood
Legsby
Buslingthorpe
Faldingworth
Spridlington
Lissington
Bleasby
Hainton
South Willingham
Cold Hanworth
Friesthorpe
East Torrington
Hackthorn
Snarford
West Torrington
Wickenby
Benniworth
Holton cum Beckering
East Barkwith
Welton Hill
Snelland
West Barkwith
Brattleby
Welton
Fulnetby
Reasby
Dunholme
Rand
Sotby
Panton
Stainton by Langworth
Bullington
Wragby
Scothern
Langworth
Langton by Wragby
Hatton
Great Sturton
Sudbrooke
Newball
Nettleham
Apley
Kingthorpe
Riseholme
Burton
Barlings
Reepham
Minting
Ermine
Bunker's Hill
North Greetwell
Low Barlings
Stainfield
St Giles
Cherry Willingham
Gautby
Fiskerton
Wispington
Lincoln
Young Wood
Waddingworth
Washingborough
Canwick
Boultham
Heighington
Branston Booths
Bardney
Bucknall
Potterhanworth
Bracebridge
Horsington
A15
A46
A631
A1103
A158
A157
B1205
B1225
B1203
B1202
B1399
B1190
B1398
200
201
173
190

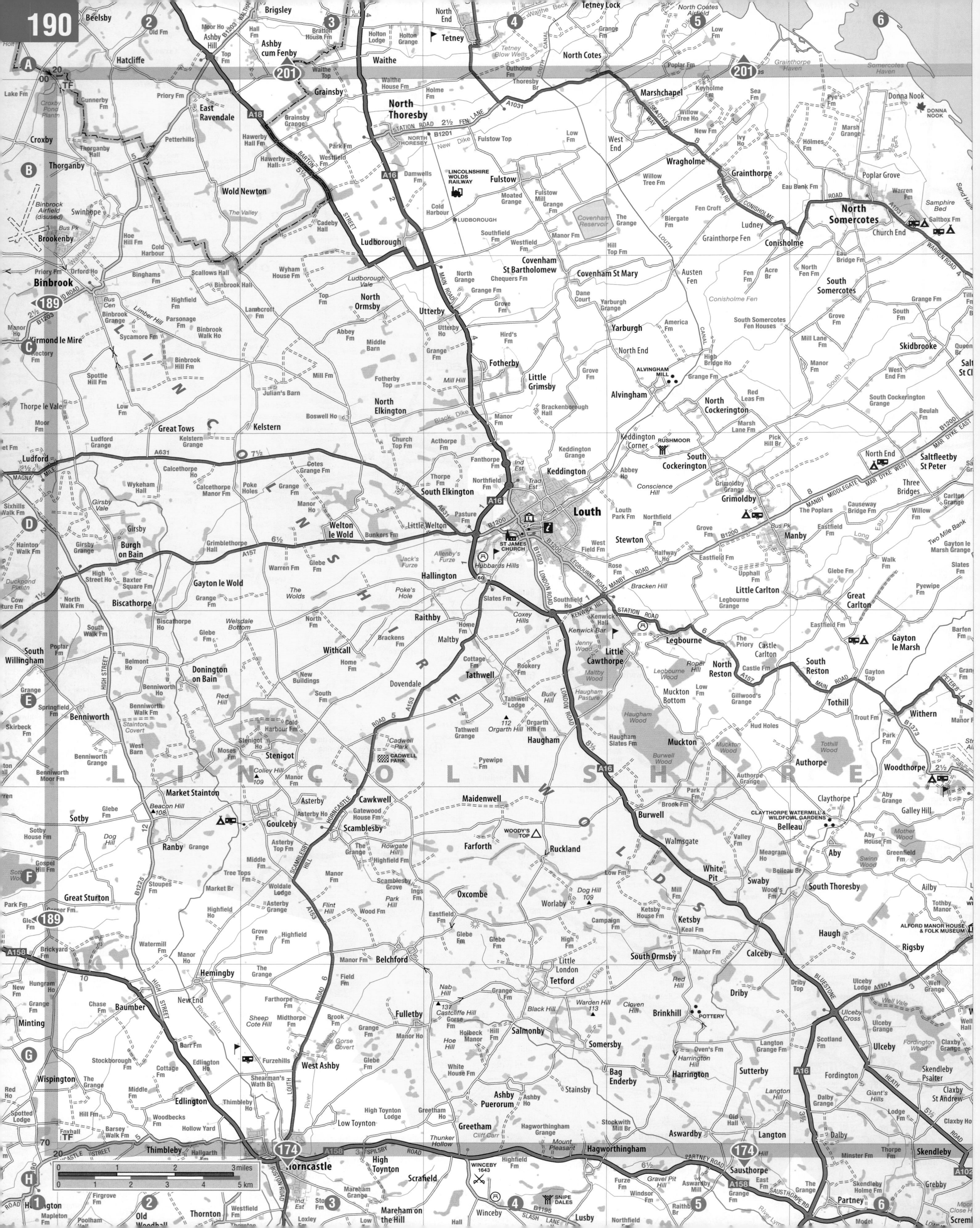
Beelsby
Brigsley
Tetney Lock
North Coates
Ashby Hill
Ashby cum Fenby
Holton Lodge
Holton Grange
Tetney
North End
Waithe
Hatcliffe
North Cotes
201
Grainsby
Marshchapel
North Thoresby
East Ravendale
Croxby
Thorganby
Wold Newton
Fulstow
Wragholme
Grainthorpe
Poplar Grove
North Somercotes
Donna Nook
Binbrook Airfield (disused)
Brookenby
Swinhope
Binbrook
189
Kirmond le Mire
Ludborough
Covenham Reservoir
Covenham St Bartholomew
Covenham St Mary
Conisholme
Ludney
South Somercotes
Utterby
North Ormsby
Yarburgh
Fotherby
Little Grimsby
Alvingham
North Cockerington
Skidbrooke
Thorpe le Vale
Great Tows
Kelstern
North Elkington
South Elkington
Ludford
Keddington
Louth
South Cockerington
Grimoldby
Saltfleetby St Peter
Manby
Stewton
Welton le Wold
Burgh on Bain
Girsby
Gayton le Wold
Hallington
Biscathorpe
Raithby
Maltby
Little Carlton
Great Carlton
Legbourne
Little Cawthorpe
Withcall
South Willingham
Donington on Bain
Tathwell
North Reston
South Reston
Gayton le Marsh
Tothill
Withern
Benniworth
Haugham
Muckton
Stenigot
Cadwell Park
Authorpe
Woodthorpe
LINCOLNSHIRE
Market Stainton
Cawkwell
Maidenwell
Burwell
Claythorpe
Belleau
Sotby
Goulceby
Asterby
Scamblesby
Farforth
Ruckland
Ranby
Walmsgate
Aby
Galley Hill
White Pit
Swaby
South Thoresby
Great Sturton
Oxcombe
Worlaby
Ketsby
Haugh
Rigsby
Belchford
Calceby
South Ormsby
Little London
Tetford
Hemingby
Baumber
Driby
Minting
Fulletby
Brinkhill
Salmonby
Ulceby Cross
Ulceby
Somersby
Wispington
West Ashby
Bag Enderby
Harrington
Sutterby
Fordington
Edlington
Ashby Puerorum
Stainsby
Skendleby Psalter
Claxby St Andrew
Low Toynton
Greetham
Aswardby
Langton
Dalby
Thimbleby
174
Hagworthingham
Skendleby
Horncastle
High Toynton
Scrafield
Winceby 1643
Sausthorpe
Grebby
Partney
Thornton
Winceby
Lusby
Mareham on the Hill
Old Woodhall
A16
A18
A157
A631
A153
A158
A1031
A104
B1200
B1373
0 1 2 3 miles
0 1 2 3 4 5 km

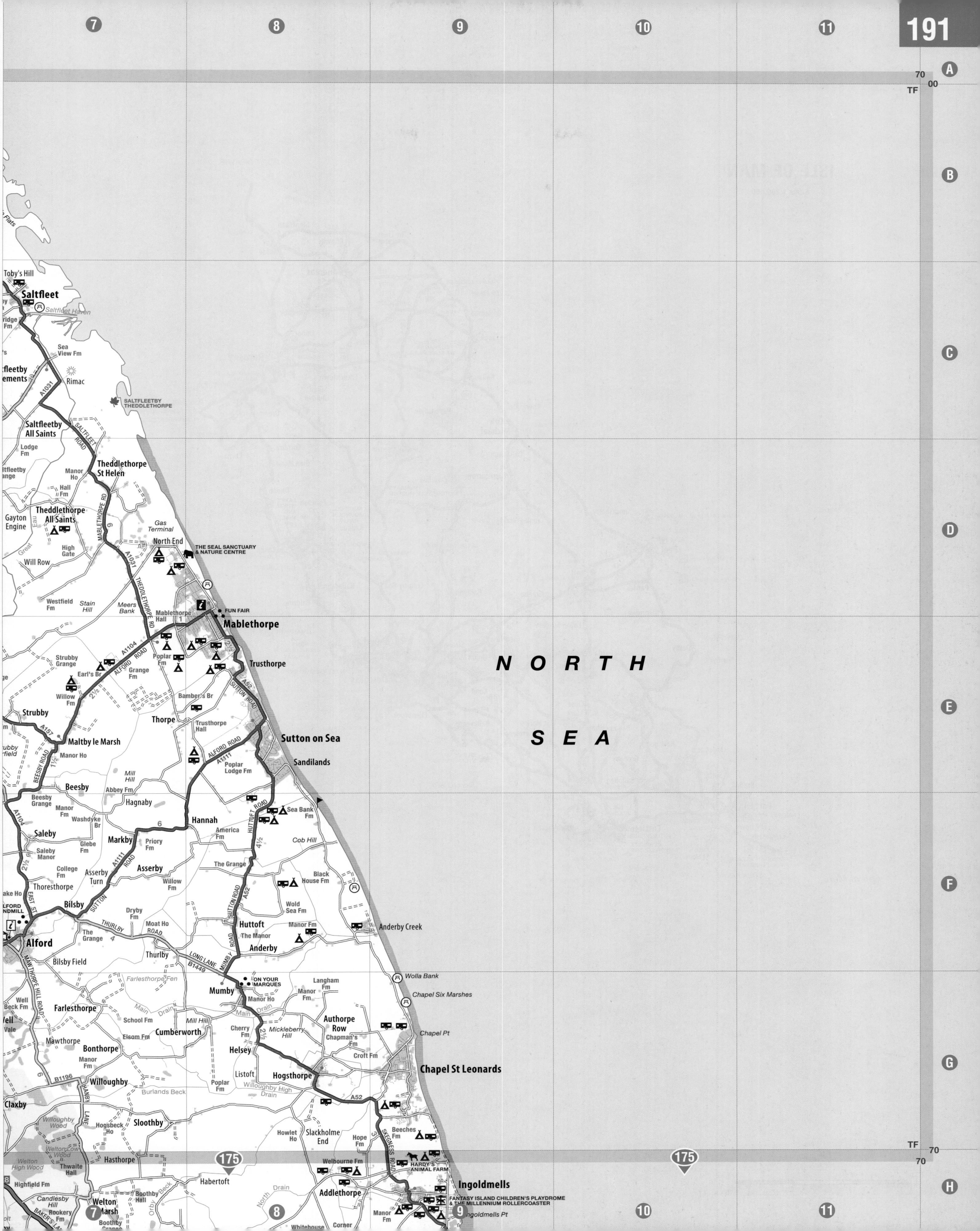
7
8
9
10
11
A
B
C
D
E
F
G
H
TF
70
00
NORTH
SEA
Toby's Hill
Saltfleet
Saltfleet Haven
Sea View Fm
Rimac
A1031
SALTFLEETBY THEDDLETHORPE
Saltfleetby All Saints
SALTFLEET ROAD
Lodge Fm
Manor Ho
Theddlethorpe St Helen
Hall Fm
Theddlethorpe All Saints
Gayton Engine
MABLETHORPE RD
Gas Terminal
North End
THE SEAL SANCTUARY & NATURE CENTRE
High Gate
Will Row
Westfield Fm
Stain Hill
Meers Bank
THEDDLETHORPE RD
FUN FAIR
Mablethorpe Hall
Mablethorpe
A1104
Strubby Grange
Earl's Br
ALFORD ROAD
Poplar Fm
Grange Fm
Trusthorpe
A52
SUTTON ROAD
Willow Fm
Bamber's Br
Strubby
A157
Thorpe
Trusthorpe Hall
Sutton on Sea
Maltby le Marsh
ALFORD ROAD
A1111
Manor Ho
Sandilands
BEESBY ROAD
Poplar Lodge Fm
Mill Hill
Beesby
Abbey Fm
Beesby Grange
Hagnaby
Manor Fm
HUTTOFT ROAD
Sea Bank Fm
Washdyke Br
Hannah
A1104
America Fm
Saleby
Markby
Priory Fm
Cob Hill
Glebe Fm
Saleby Manor
ROAD
Asserby
The Grange
College Fm
Asserby Turn
Black House Fm
Thoresthorpe
Willow Fm
EAST ST
SUTTON ROAD
A52
Bilsby
SUTTON
Dryby Fm
Wold Sea Fm
THURLBY
Moat Ho
Huttoft
Manor Fm
Anderby Creek
ROAD
The Manor
Alford
The Grange
MUMBY ROAD
Anderby
Thurlby
LONG LANE
Bilsby Field
B1449
Wolla Bank
Farlesthorpe Fen
ON YOUR MARQUES
Langham Fm
Mumby
Manor Fm
Chapel Six Marshes
Well Beck Fm
MAWTHORPE HILL ROAD
Farlesthorpe
Main Drain
Manor Ho
School Fm
Mill Hill
Authorpe Row
Mickleberry Hill
Cumberworth
Chapel Pt
Elsom Fm
Cherry Fm
Chapman's Fm
Mawthorpe
Bonthorpe
Helsey
Croft Fm
Manor Fm
Chapel St Leonards
Listoft
Hogsthorpe
B1196
Willoughby
Willoughby High Drain
Poplar Fm
A52
Burlands Beck
Claxby
MAMBY LANE
Willoughby Wood
Hogsbeck Ho
Sloothby
Howlet Ho
Slackholme End
Beeches Fm
Hope Fm
SKEGNESS ROAD
Welton Low Wood
Hasthorpe
175
Welbourne Fm
HARDY'S ANIMAL FARM
Welton High Wood
Thwaite Hall
Highfield Fm
Habertoft
Ingoldmells
Drain
Addlethorpe
Candlesby Hill
Boothby Hall
FANTASY ISLAND CHILDREN'S PLAYDROME & THE MILLENNIUM ROLLERCOASTER
Welton le Marsh
Rookery Fm
Manor Fm
Ingoldmells Pt
BAKER'S LANE
Boothby Grange
Whitehouse
Corner

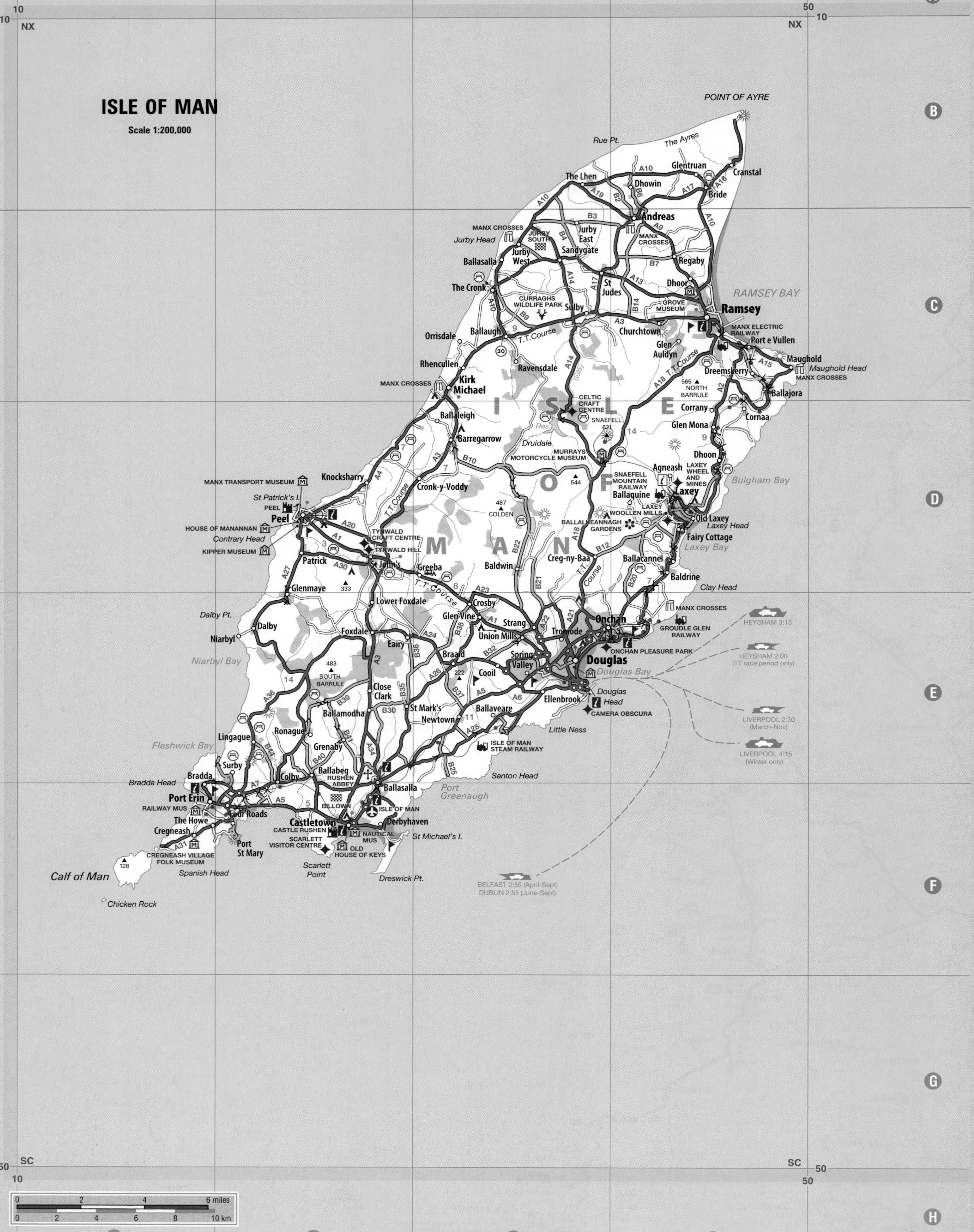
ISLE OF MAN
Scale 1:200,000
NX
SC
POINT OF AYRE
The Ayres
Rue Pt.
Glentruan
Cranstal
The Lhen
Dhowin
Bride
Andreas
MANX CROSSES
Jurby Head
JURBY SOUTH
Jurby East
Jurby West
Sandygate
Ballasalla
Regaby
The Cronk
St Judes
Dhoor
CURRAGHS WILDLIFE PARK
Sulby
GROVE MUSEUM
RAMSEY BAY
Ramsey
MANX ELECTRIC RAILWAY
Port e Vullen
Orrisdale
Ballaugh
Churchtown
Glen Auldyn
Maughold
Maughold Head
Rhencullen
Ravensdale
T.T. Course
Dreemskerry
Kirk Michael
NORTH BARRULE
Ballajora
CELTIC CRAFT CENTRE
Corrany
Cornaa
Ballaleigh
SNAEFELL
Glen Mona
Barregarrow
Druidale
MURRAYS MOTORCYCLE MUSEUM
Dhoon
Knocksharry
Agneash
LAXEY WHEEL AND MINES
Bulgham Bay
MANX TRANSPORT MUSEUM
SNAEFELL MOUNTAIN RAILWAY
Cronk-y-Voddy
Ballaquine
Laxey
St Patrick's I.
PEEL
COLDEN
LAXEY WOOLLEN MILLS
Peel
Old Laxey
HOUSE OF MANANNAN
BALLALHEANNAGH GARDENS
Laxey Head
Contrary Head
TYNWALD CRAFT CENTRE
Fairy Cottage
KIPPER MUSEUM
TYNWALD HILL
Laxey Bay
Patrick
St John's
Creg-ny-Baa
Ballacannel
Greeba
Baldwin
Baldrine
Glenmaye
Clay Head
Lower Foxdale
Crosby
MANX CROSSES
Dalby Pt.
Glen Vine
HEYSHAM 3:15
Dalby
Strang
Onchan
GROUDLE GLEN RAILWAY
Niarbyl
Foxdale
Union Mills
Tromode
Eairy
ONCHAN PLEASURE PARK
HEYSHAM 2:00 (TT race period only)
Braaid
Spring Valley
Douglas
Niarbyl Bay
SOUTH BARRULE
Cooil
Douglas Bay
Close Clark
Douglas Head
Ellenbrook
Ballamodha
St Mark's
Ballaveare
CAMERA OBSCURA
Newtown
LIVERPOOL 2:30 (March-Nov)
Lingague
Ronague
Little Ness
Fleshwick Bay
Grenaby
ISLE OF MAN STEAM RAILWAY
LIVERPOOL 4:15 (Winter only)
Surby
Ballabeg
RUSHEN ABBEY
Santon Head
Bradda
Colby
Bradda Head
Ballasalla
Port Greenaugh
Port Erin
BILLOWN
RAILWAY MUS
Four Roads
ISLE OF MAN
The Howe
Castletown
Derbyhaven
Cregneash
CASTLE RUSHEN
NAUTICAL MUS
St Michael's I.
Port St Mary
SCARLETT VISITOR CENTRE
OLD HOUSE OF KEYS
CREGNEASH VILLAGE FOLK MUSEUM
Spanish Head
Scarlett Point
Dreswick Pt.
Calf of Man
BELFAST 2:55 (April-Sept)
DUBLIN 2:55 (June-Sept)
Chicken Rock
0 2 4 6 miles
0 2 4 6 8 10 km

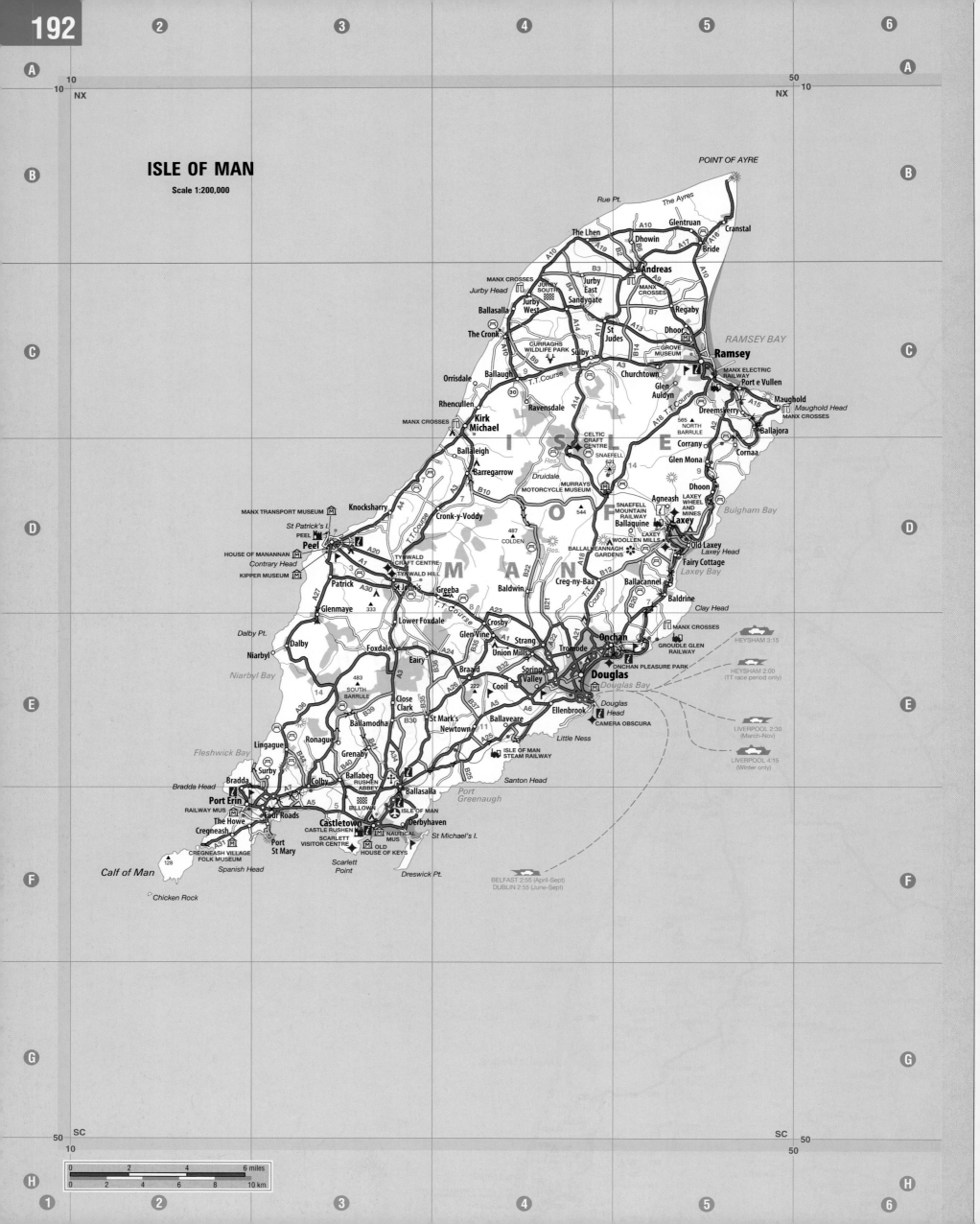

7
8
9
A
B
C
D
E
F
G
H
SD
Crusader Bank
North Hollow
TOY & TEDDY BEAR MUS
St Annes
Salter's Bank
Lytham St Anne's
Fairhaven
Ansdell
Hey Houses
Lytham
LYTHAM HALL
LYTHAM WINDMILL MUSEUM
Church Scar
Fairhaven Lake
BLACKPOOL INTERNATIONAL
Great Marton Moss
Peel
Higher Ballam
Lower Ballam
Moss Side
Westby
Moss Hall Fm
Birks Fm
Eastham Hall
Saltcotes
Bryning Hall Fm
Little Carr Side Fm
Kellamergh
Warton
Warton Bank
New House Fm
River Ribble
Hesketh Sands
Banks Sands
George's Brow
Banks Marsh
RIBBLE MARSHES
Long Bank
Great Bank
Foulnaze
Marshside Sands
Crossens Marsh
Horse Bank
Angry Brow
Southport Sands
MARSHSIDE
Goose Dub Fm
Fiddler's Ferry
Banks
Crossens
Hollywood Fm
Holmes Moss
Old Hollow Fm
Taylor's Fm
Far Banks
Marshside
ECO VISITOR CENTRE
BOTANIC GARDENS MUSEUM
Meol's Hall
Churchtown
SOUTHPORT MODEL RAILWAY VILLAGE
Southport
High Park
Blowick
Birkdale Sands
Birkdale
Brown Edge
Pool Hey
Hillside
Birkdale Hills
Ainsdale
Ainsdale-on-Sea
Ainsdale Sands
Ainsdale Hills
Woodvale
AINSDALE SAND DUNES
White Otter Fm
Halsall Moss
LANCS
Shirdley Hill
Scarisbrick
Carr Cross
Snape Green
Bescar
Drummersdale
Smithy Lane Ends
Pinfold
Hurlston Green
Hurlston
Primrose Hill
Halsall
Barton
Haskayne
Ormskirk
Formby Hills
Mad Wharf
Freshfield
Formby
Formby Pt
Little Altcar
Great Altcar
Downholland Moss
Downholland Cross
Clieves Hills
Aughton Park
Aughton
Town Green
Lydiate
The Withins
CABIN HILL
Taylor's Bank
North End
Hightown
Lady Green
Carr Houses
Ince Blundell
Formby Bank
Crosby Channel
Little Crosby
Thornton
Netherton
Sefton
Lunt
Maghull
Homer Green
Moss Side
Melling
Melling Mount
Waddicar
Blundellsands
Brighton le Sands
Great Crosby
Buckley Hill
Aintree
Westvale
Crosby
Waterloo
181
182
194
202

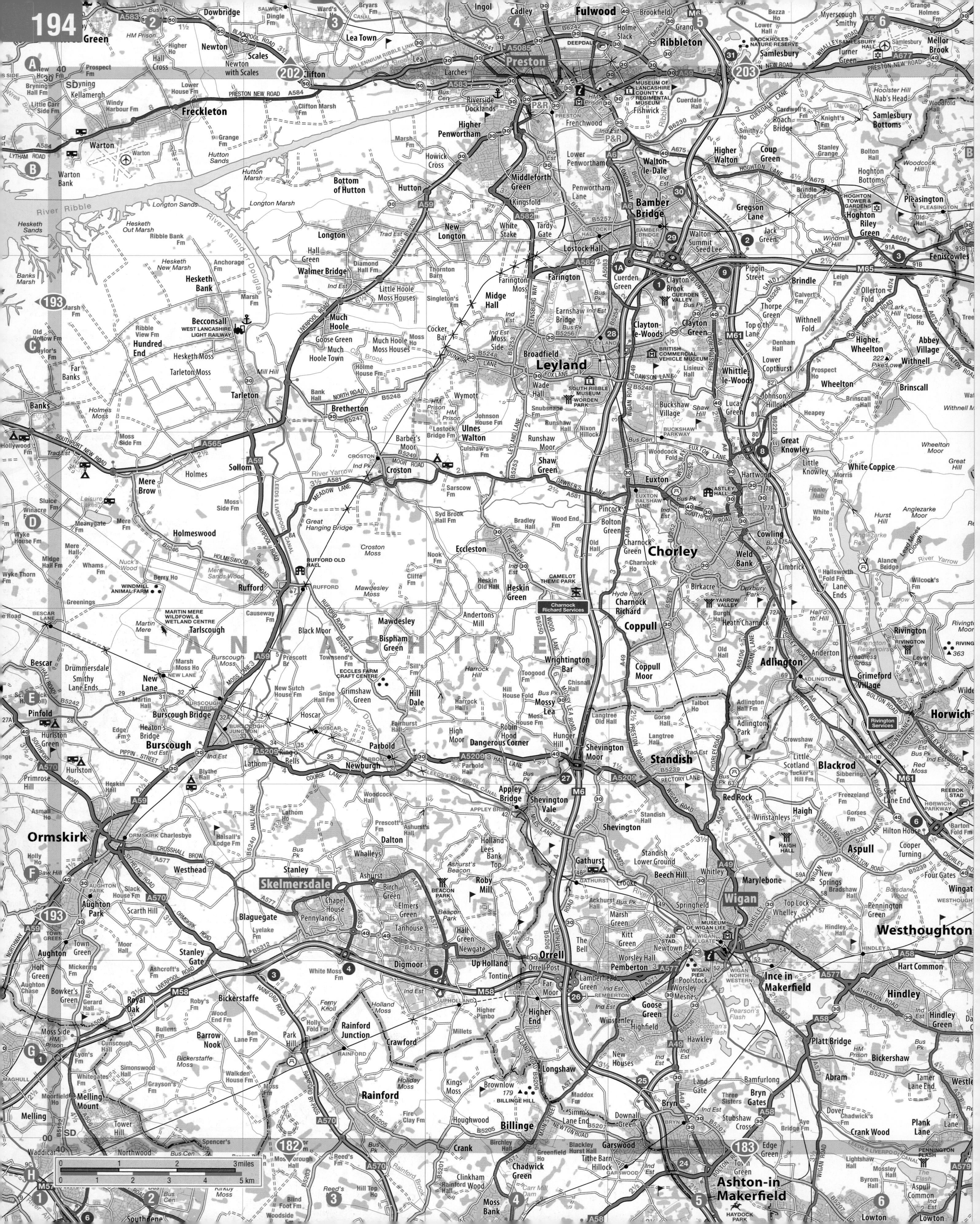
Preston
Fulwood
Ribbleton
Ingol
Cadley
Dowbridge
Newton
Scales
Clifton
Lea Town
Lea
Larches
Samlesbury
Mellor Brook
Freckleton
Warton
Kellamergh
Higher Penwortham
Riverside Docklands
Frenchwood
Fishwick
Walton-le-Dale
Higher Walton
Coup Green
Bamber Bridge
Middleforth Green
Kingsfold
Hutton
Longton
Lostock Hall
Farington
Walmer Bridge
Much Hoole
Tarleton
Hesketh Bank
Becconsall
Leyland
Broadfield
Clayton-le-Woods
Clayton Green
Cuerden Green
Whittle-le-Woods
Wheelton
Brinscall
Withnell
Feniscowles
Hoghton
Bretherton
Croston
Ulnes Walton
Euxton
Buckshaw Village
Chorley
Eccleston
Heskin Green
Mawdesley
Rufford
Holmeswood
Sollom
Mere Brow
Banks
Tarlscough
Bescar
Burscough
Burscough Bridge
Coppull
Charnock Richard
Adlington
Horwich
Standish
Shevington
Appley Bridge
Parbold
Newburgh
Lathom
Ormskirk
Aughton
Skelmersdale
Dalton
Upholland
Orrell
Wigan
Westhoughton
Hindley
Ince in Makerfield
Aspull
Blackrod
Pemberton
Billinge
Rainford
Garswood
Ashton-in Makerfield
Bryn
Abram
Platt Bridge
Crank
Melling
LANCASHIRE
River Ribble
River Yarrow
River Douglas
M6
M61
M65
M58
A59
A6
A49
A58
A5209
A570
A581
A565
202
203
193
182
183
0 1 2 3 miles
0 1 2 3 4 5 km

LANCASHIRE
BLACKBURN WITH DARWEN
GREATER MANCHESTER
Forest of Rossendale
Blackburn
Great Harwood
Clayton-le-Moors
Rishton
Accrington
Church
Oswaldtwistle
Haslingden
Rawtenstall
Bacup
Darwen
Edgworth
Ramsbottom
Whitworth
Rochdale
Bolton
Bury
Heywood
Tottington
Radcliffe
Farnworth
Whitefield
Prestwich
Middleton
Royton
Atherton
Tyldesley
Walkden
Worsley
Swinton
Pendlebury
Salford
Eccles
Leigh
Little Lever
Kearsley
Failsworth
Droylsden
Chadderton
Shawforth
Haslingden
Helmshore
Stubbins
Edenfield
Summerseat
Belmont
Horwich
203
204
196
183
184

204
205
195
184
185
Hebden Bridge
Heptonstall
Mytholmroyd
Todmorden
Walsden
Littleborough
Rochdale
Milnrow
Royton
Shaw
Chadderton
Oldham
Failsworth
Hollinwood
Lees
Mossley
Stalybridge
Uppermill
Greenfield
Delph
Diggle
Dobcross
Marsden
Slaithwaite
Meltham
Halifax
Illingworth
Sowerby Bridge
Elland
Brighouse
Ripponden
Rishworth
Holmfirth
Crowden
Droylsden
Whitworth
Denshaw
Bleak Hey Nook
Saddleworth Moor
Wessenden Moor
Langfield Common
GREATER MANCHESTER
PEAK DISTRICT NATIONAL PARK
M62
M60
A62
A58
A646
A672
A640
A635
A629
A6033
Ashton-under-Lyne
0 1 2 3 miles
0 1 2 3 4 5 km

Bradford
Cleckheaton
Batley
Heckmondwike
Liversedge
Dewsbury
Mirfield
Morley
Middleton
Rothwell
Wakefield
Ossett
Horbury
Normanton
Crigglestone
Darton
Royston
Barnsley
Dodworth
Worsbrough
Hoyland
Wombwell
Cudworth
Penistone
Denby Dale
Skelmanthorpe
Clayton West
Stocksbridge
Thurlstone Moors
YORKSHIRE
SOUTH YORKSHIRE

Micklefield
Kippax
Ledston
Ledston Luck
Great Preston
Ledsham
Fairburn
South Milford
Lumby
Monk Fryston
Hillam
Burton Salmon
Hambleton
Thorpe Willoughby
Brayton
Gateforth
Burn
Birkin
West Haddlesey
Chapel Haddlesey
Camblesforth
Temple Hirst
Hirst Courtney
Carlton
Allerton Bywater
Mickletown
Methley
Castleford
New Fryston
Wheldale
Water Fryston
Brotherton
Byram
Sutton
Beal
Kellington
Kellingley
Ferrybridge
Knottingley
Eggborough
Hensall
Gowdall
Whitwood
Normanton
North Featherstone
Pontefract
Ackton
Featherstone
Snydale
Purston Jaglin
Chequerfield
Darrington
Cridling Stubbs
High Eggborough
Whitley
Great Heck
Pollington
Balne
West Cowick
NORTH
YORKSHIRE
Sharlston
West Hardwick
High Ackworth
East Hardwick
Wentbridge
Stapleton
Womersley
Little Smeaton
Walden Stubbs
Sykehouse
Eskholme
Topham
Wragby
Low Ackworth
Ackworth Moor Top
Thorpe Audlin
Kirk Smeaton
Fenwick
Fitzwilliam
Ryhill
Kinsley
Badsworth
Norton
Campsall
Askern
Moss
Havercroft
Hemsworth
Upton
Wrangbrook
Instoneville
South Hiendley
North Elmsall
Skelbrooke
Sutton
Haywood
Braithwaite
SOUTH
YORKSHIRE
Shafton
Brierley
Moorthorpe
South Elmsall
South Kirkby
Hampole
Burghwallis
Owston
Skellow
Carcroft
Kirk Bramwith
Thorpe in Balne
Cudworth
Grimethorpe
Barnby Dun
Adwick le Street
Woodlands
Toll Bar
Almholme
Clayton
Hooton Pagnell
Brodsworth
Kirk Sandall
Great Houghton
Little Houghton
Thurnscoe
Marr
Sunnyfields
Bentley
Armthorpe
Darfield
Goldthorpe
Hickleton
Scawsby
Cusworth
Wheatley
Intake
Doncaster
Bolton upon Dearne
Barnburgh
Harlington
Hyde Park
Newton
Hexthorpe
Cantley
Wombwell
Brampton
Adwick upon Dearne
High Melton
Sprotbrough
Bessacarr
Balby
Warmsworth
Cadeby
Wath upon Dearne
Mexborough
Old Denaby
Denaby Main
Conisbrough
Swinton
Loversall
New Edlington
Wentworth
Rossington
0 1 2 3 miles
0 1 2 3 4 5 km

EAST RIDING OF YORKSHIRE
NORTH LINCOLNSHIRE
Lane Fm
Wressle Grange
Wressle
Castle Fm
Woodhouse Fm
Woodhall
Goule Hall Fm
Newhay
White Ho Fm
Hemingbrough
HULL ROAD
Hagthorpe Hall
207
A63
Leys Fm
Spaldington Grange
Brindleys Plantn
Wood Fm
Brind
Rowland Hall
Wynn Cottage Fm
North Howden
Caville Hall Fm
HOWDEN
Portington
Manor Fm
Portington Grange
Grange
Greaves End
Common Wood
Metham Grange
Hive
Sandholme
Cow Bridge
Hill Fm
Sandholme Lodge
Stoney Carr Fm
Newport
Cave Wood Grange
Jarratt Hills
Saltmarsh Grange
Everthorpe
Newholme
Barmby Marsh
Newsholme Parks
Parks Fm
Park Fm
Thorpe Hall
Cavil
Skelton Common
Mill Fm
Eastrington
Newland
EASTRINGTON
Gilberdyke
Scalby
208
New Village Ho
Walling Fen
Skelton Grange
Codd Hall
Thorpe Grange
New Village Grange
Staddlethorpe
GILBERDYKE
Higham Grange
White House Fm
Mole Lodge
Barmby on the Marsh
River Derwent
Barnhill Hall
Old Hall
B1230
Belby Hall
Saltmarshe Grange
Bennetland
Trad Est
Marr Grange
Broomfleet Ho
BROOMFLEET
Long Drax
Asselby
Knedlington
Howden
HOWDEN MINSTER
M62
West Linton Fm
East Lynton Fm
Balkholme
Greenoak
Bellasize
Bellasize Grange
Woodfield Ho
Oxmardyke Grange
Thornton Ho
Marr Ho
Northfield Ho
Crabley Fm
Drax Power Station
Boothferry
BOOTHFERRY ROAD
River Ouse
Kilpin Pike
Kilpin
Nine Acre Plantn
Northside Fm
Low Metham Grange
Warwick Ho
Sober Hill
Staddlethorpe Grange
North Hall
Broomfleet
Drax
Asselby Island
Groves Fm
Little Airmyn
River Aire
Airmyn
Brock Holes
Hook
Skelton
SALTMARSHE
Laxton
Newland
Goole
Brickhill Fm
The Grange
Carlton Towers
RAWCLIFFE ROAD
Airmyn Grange
Sutton Lodge Fm
Pasture Fm
Dowlands Plantn
Saltmarshe
Metham Hall
Hall Fm
Yokefleet
Blacktoft
Faxfleet
Whitton Channel
Blacktoft Channel
Whitton
200
Willwick Hill Plantn
Carlton Marsh
Rawcliffe
Hazel Bank Fm
Mill Fm
RAWCLIFFE
Potter Grange
GOOLE
THE YORKSHIRE WATERWAYS MUSEUM
Old Goole
Whitgift Ness
River Ouse
Reedness
Little Reedness
Whitgift
Ousefleet
BLACKTOFT SANDS
Trent Falls
Flatts Fm
Bishopthor
JULIAN'S BOWER (TURF MAZE)
Alkborough
East Cowick
Rawcliffe Bridge
AIRE & CALDER NAVIGATION
Dobella Fm
Decoy Fm
Swinefleet
A161
Rabbit Hill Fm
South Fm
A1041
M62
Moorfields Fm
Field Ho
Goole Grange
New Brakes Fm
KINGS CAUSEWAY
Adlingfleet
Garthorpe Grange
Walcot
The Elms
West Halton
Southdale Fm
Island Fm
Elms Fm
Commons Fm
College Fm
Readingate Fm
Mawgre Fm
Highfields Fm
Park Grounds Fm
Pasture Fm
Greenland Fm
Greenland Fm
Top Ho
Hookmoor Fm
Bankside Fm
Bracken Hill
Adlingfleet Drain
Nessfield Ho
Garthorpe
Coleby Wood
Halton Drain
Coleby
Poplars Fm
M18
Greenland
Priory Fm
Rawcliffe Moors
Sand House Fm
Haldenby Grange
Haldenby Hall Fm
Fockerby
River Trent
Burton Stather
Burton upon Stather
B1430
BURTON ROAD
Barkers Holt
Thealby
Old Cliff Fm
Pincheon Green
Goole Moors
Moors Fm
Moor Ends
Red House Fm
Luddington
Swinefleet Warping Drain
Burton Wood
FARM MUS
Normanby
NORMANBY HALL
Bagmoor Fm
Eastoft
Rainsbutt Fm
Easingwold Ho
Haldenby Ness
High Bridge
B1392
Pauper's Drain
NORTHFIELD LANE
NORMANBY ROAD
Sheffield's Hill
Moorends
Thorne Waste or Moors
Will Pitts
Crowle Waste or Moors
HUMBERHEAD PEATLANDS
Eastoft Grange
Cottage Fm
Carr Ho
Flixborough
River Don
Hangsman Hill
Merriville Fm
Fishlake
Thorne North
Dairy Fm
Ind Est
Sand Moors or South Moors
Crowle Common
Crowle Hill
Leam Fm
Poplar Fm
Boskeydyke Fm
Pasture Fm
Amcotts
Flixborough Stather
Dragonby
Foxhills Park
Conesby
Crosby Warren
WINTERTON ROAD
Canal Side
Thorne
THORNE SOUTH
Maud's Br
Medge Hall
Old River Don
Crowle
Crowle Park
Crowle Grange
North Moor Fm
Warping Drain
Grange Fm
Ind Pk
THORNE & KEADBY CANAL
Wike Well End
Buildings Fm
STAINFORTH & KEADBY CANAL
Windsor
SEVEN LAKES COUNTRY PARK
Tetley
Ealand
Ealand Grange
Keadby
Gunness
Crosby
Frodingham
Sandhill Fm
Dirtness Levels
Godnow Br
Grove Ho
Boating Dike
Red Ho
Sand Hall Fm
Keadby Grange
DONCASTER ROAD
Retail Pk
SCUNTHORPE
Scunthorpe
GLANFORD PARK
Brumby Hall
Brumby
Doncaster North Services
Hatfield Water Park
Brierholme Carr
HM Prison
Hatfield Chase
Bank House Fm
Hains Fm
Poplars Fm
Hirst Priory
CROWLE
Pilfrey Br
Althorpe
ALTHORPE
Burringham
Brumby Grove
Hatfield
Dunscroft
Severals Fm
Slay Pits
Elder House
Plains House Fm
Dirtness Br
M180
Common Fm
North Moor
Derrythorpe
M181
Carisbrooke Manor
QUEENSWAY
Bus Pk
Brier Hills Fm
Hatfield Woodhouse
The Lings
Stone Hill
Moor Fm
Low Levels
Goodcop Fm
Sandtoft
Woodcarr Fm
THE TROLLEYBUS MUSEUM AT SANDTOFT
River Torne
Woodhouse
Belwood Fm
Old Fm
North Grange Fm
Ashby
Lings Fm
West End
Lindholme Grange
West Carr
Westgate
Bracon
Grey Green
Belton
Beltoft
Yaddlethorpe
Bus Pk
Bottesford
Holme Hall
Aspen Fm
Woodhouse Grange
West Hale Fm
Stockholes Turbary
Isle of Axholme
West Butterwick
Butterwick Common
Snake Plantn
Red Ho
Lindholme Hall
West Carr Houses
Church Town
Woods Fm
East Butterwick
North Field Fm
Slate Ho
M18
Holme Ho
Holme Wood
HM Prison
Hatfield Moors
Roe Carr
Samuel Closes Fm
Scawcett Fm
North Idle Drain
South Engine Drain
Ellers Cottage
Lawns Fm
Glebe Fm
Lowhill Fm
Gate Wood Fm
Great Gate Wood
Boston Park
Ellerholme Fm
Tunnel Pits
Ninevah Fm
Sandhill Fm
Poplar Grove Fm
Ings Fm
West Grange
Sand House Fm
Briggate Fm
Messingham
Gate Fm
Carrside
OLD RECTORY
South Field Drain
Kelfield Catchwater
North Ewster
Cockwood Fm
Torne Br
Woodside
Candy Fm
Wroot
Holmes Fm
Aucklands Fm
Epworth Turbary
Epworth
Melwood Grange
Black Bank Fm
Carcar Fm
KIRTON ROAD
Scallow Grove
Landmoor Fm
Long Plantn
Field House Fm
Harvester Fm
River Torne
Acomb Fm
Low Burnham
High Melwood
Susworth
Kelfield Grange
Scotterthorpe
Moss Fm
Beggar Hill
Long Moor Fm
Blaxton Common
Ninescores Fm
Wroot Grange
Greenholme Bank Fm
Haxey Carr
Cliff Hill
Kelfield
Glebe Fm
Middle Moor Fm
Auckley
Missen Bank
Charity Fm
Haslams Fm
Warren Fm
Scotterwood Fm
Scotter
St Helena Fm
Lidget
B1396
MOSHAM ROAD
BANK END ROAD
Blaxton
Finningly Grange Fm
Whin Covert
Bull Hassocks Fm
Upperthorpe
Low Hall Fm
Mill House Fm
Owston Ferry
Ings Fm
Hardwick Grange Fm
South Hills
Field Ho
Finningley
Beech Hill Fm
187
SANDERSON'S BANK
DONCASTER ROAD
Haxey
East Lound
East Ferry
The Hall
188
Hardwick
Scotton Common
Laughton Woods
Cockthorn Fm
Scotton
Westwoodside
Sandbeds Fm
Lady Croft Fm
Laughton Lodge
ROBIN HOOD AIRPORT DONCASTER SHEFFIELD
Newlands Fm
Springs Fm
Levels Fm
Fountain
Langholme Fm
Graiseloud
Warping Drain
Owston Grange
Thornholmes Fm
Jenny Hu
Wildsworth
Manor Ho
Park House Fm
Bridge
SE
90
00
A
B
C
D
E
F
G
H
7
8
9
10
11

South Cave
Riplingham
Eppleworth
Inglemire
Newland
Sutton Ings
Stoneferry
Summergangs
KINGSTON UPON HULL
Sculcoates
Marfleet
West End
Willerby
Kirk Ella
West Ella
Anlaby
East Ella
Anlaby Park
Ellerker
Brantingham
Elloughton
Swanland
Brough
Welton
Melton
North Ferriby
Hessle
Northfield
Gipsyville
Kingston upon Hull
Victoria Dock Village
THE DEEP
WILBERFORCE HOUSE
St Andrews Quay
King George Dock
Humber Bridge
River Humber
Whitton
Whitton Ness
Redcliff Channel
Read's Island
Barton Waterside
Barton-upon Humber
Barrow upon Humber
Barrow Haven
New Holland
Goxhill
Goxhill Haven
Skitter Ness
East Halton
Winteringham
West Halton
South Ferriby
Horkstow
Winterton
Thealby
Roxby
Coleby
Saxby All Saints
Kingsforth
Thornton Curtis
THORNTON ABBEY
NORTH LINCOLNSHIRE
Burnham
Wootton
North Killingholme
Ulceby
Ulceby Skitter
Habrough
Bonby
Worlaby
Appleby
Dragonby
Elsham
ELSHAM HALL
Croxton
Kirmington
Melton Ross
New Barnetby
Barnetby le Wold
HUMBERSIDE INTERNATIONAL
Little Limber
Great Limber
Frodingham
Scunthorpe
Brumby
Santon
Broughton
Wressle
Wrawby
Brigg
Ashby
Bottesford
Holme
Scawby
Sturton
Bigby
Somerby
Searby
Owmby
Grasby
Clixby
LINCOLNSHIRE
Messingham
Manton
Howsham
Cadney
Hibaldstow
North Kelsey
North Kelsey Moor
Caistor
Cabourne
Nettleton
Scotter
Redbourne
Moortown
South Kelsey
Holton
Kirton in Lindsey
GAINSTHORPE DESERTED MEDIEVAL VILLAGE
M180
A15
A18
A1077
A180
A63
0 1 2 3 miles
0 1 2 3 4 5 km

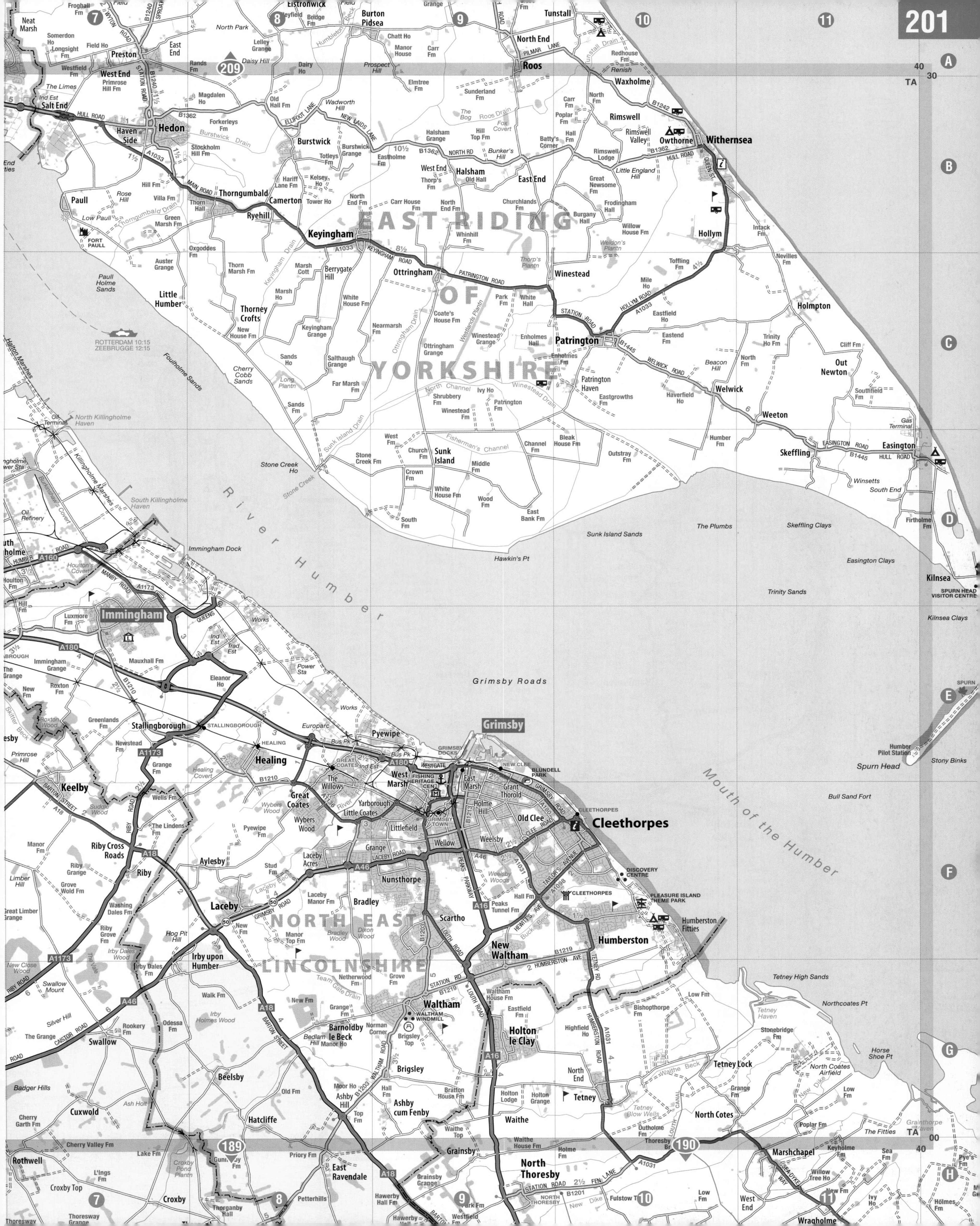

EAST RIDING OF YORKSHIRE
NORTH EAST LINCOLNSHIRE
River Humber
Mouth of the Humber
Grimsby Roads
Hedon
Salt End
Haven Side
Preston
West End
Thorngumbald
Paull
Fort Paull
Ryehill
Camerton
Keyingham
Burstwick
Ottringham
Halsham
Roos
Tunstall
North End
Waxholme
Rimswell
Owthorne
Withernsea
Hollym
Winestead
Patrington
Patrington Haven
Sunk Island
Welwick
Weeton
Skeffling
Easington
Holmpton
Out Newton
Kilnsea
Spurn Head
Spurn Head Visitor Centre
Humber Pilot Station
Stony Binks
Bull Sand Fort
Sunk Island Sands
Trinity Sands
Easington Clays
Kilnsea Clays
Skeffling Clays
The Plumbs
Hawkin's Pt
Stone Creek Ho
Little Humber
Thorney Crofts
Paull Holme Sands
Foulholme Sands
Rotterdam 10:15
Zeebrugge 12:15
Immingham
Immingham Dock
Stallingborough
Healing
Grimsby
Pyewipe
Great Coates
West Marsh
East Marsh
Grant Thorold
Cleethorpes
Old Clee
Weelsby
Nunsthorpe
Scartho
Bradley
Laceby
Laceby Acres
Aylesby
Riby
Riby Cross Roads
Keelby
Irby upon Humber
New Waltham
Humberston
Humberston Fitties
Waltham
Holton le Clay
Barnoldby le Beck
Brigsley
Ashby cum Fenby
Tetney
Tetney Lock
North Cotes
Marshchapel
Grainsby
North Thoresby
East Ravendale
Hatcliffe
Beelsby
Cuxwold
Swallow
Croxby
Rothwell
Wragholme
Tetney High Sands
Northcoates Pt
Horse Shoe Pt
Pleasure Island Theme Park
Discovery Centre
Fishing Heritage Centre
Waltham Windmill
A1033
A180
A160
A1173
A18
A16
A46
A1031
B1362
B1445
209
189
190
TA

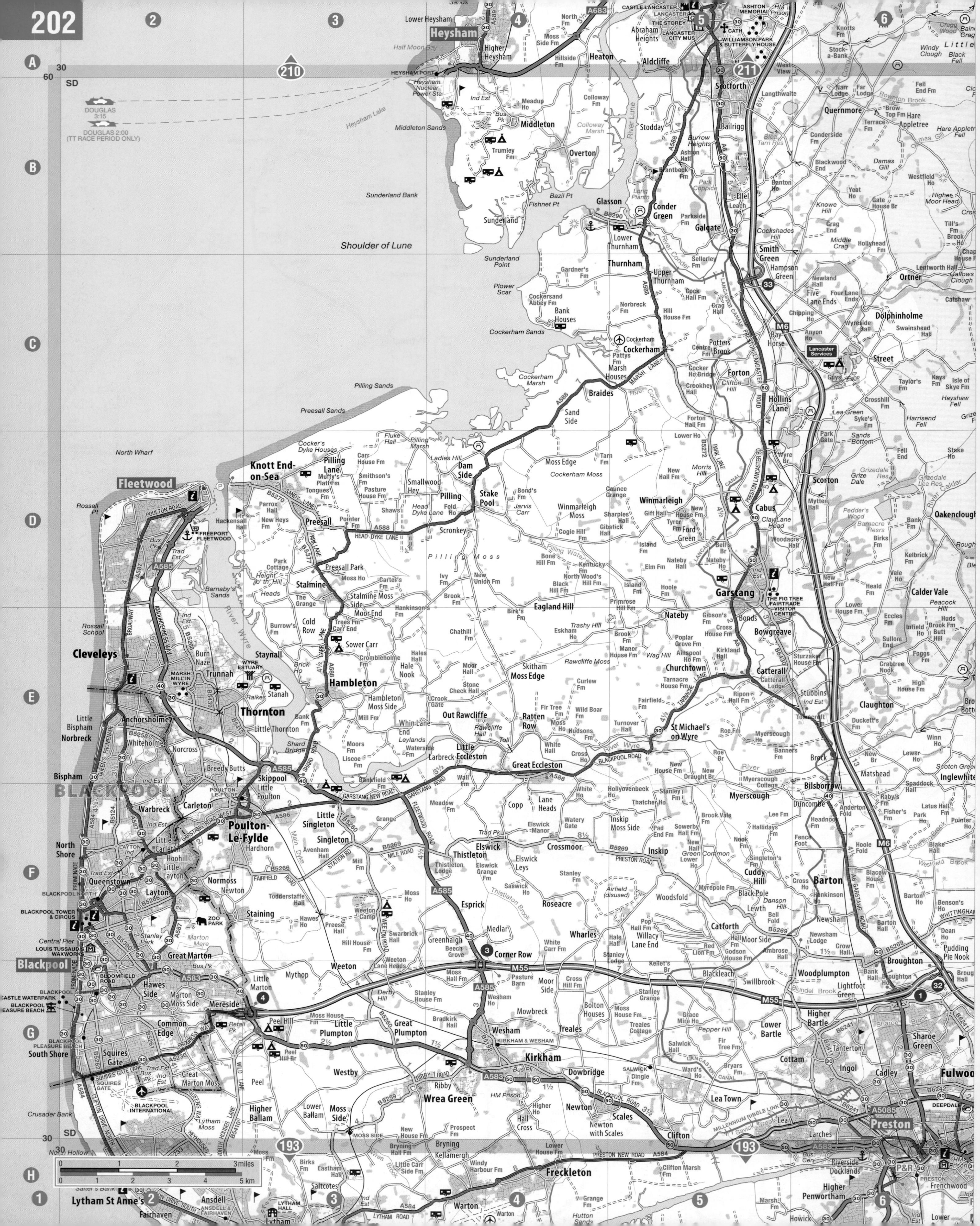
Heysham
Lancaster
Heaton
Aldcliffe
Scotforth
Quernmore
Middleton
Overton
Bailrigg
Glasson
Conder Green
Galgate
Sunderland
Shoulder of Lune
Thurnham
Smith Green
Ortner
Cockerham
Dolphinholme
Forton
Street
Pilling Sands
Preesall Sands
Braides
Hollins Lane
North Wharf
Knott End-on-Sea
Pilling
Stake Pool
Winmarleigh
Scorton
Fleetwood
Preesall
Pilling Moss
Garstang
Calder Vale
Stalmine
Eagland Hill
Nateby
Bowgreave
Cleveleys
Hambleton
Churchtown
Catterall
Thornton
Out Rawcliffe
Claughton
St Michael's on Wyre
Norbreck
Little Eccleston
Great Eccleston
Bispham
BLACKPOOL
Skippool
Myerscough
Bilsborrow
Inglewhite
Poulton-Le-Fylde
Carleton
Little Singleton
Singleton
Elswick
Thistleton
Crossmoor
Inskip
North Shore
Queenstown
Layton
Cuddy Hill
Barton
Staining
Esprick
Roseacre
Woodsfold
Catforth
Blackpool
Great Marton
Weeton
Medlar
Wharles
Corner Row
Woodplumpton
Broughton
Little Marton
Mythop
Hawes Side
Mereside
M55
Higher Bartle
Wesham
Treales
Great Plumpton
Little Plumpton
Squires Gate
South Shore
Kirkham
Cottam
Ingol
Fulwood
Westby
Ribby
Wrea Green
Dowbridge
Lea Town
Preston
Peel
Newton
Higher Ballam
Moss Side
Clifton
Freckleton
Warton
Lytham St Anne's
Ansdell
Fairhaven
Higher Penwortham
Frenchwood
210
211
193
M6
A6
A585
A583
A584
A588
A586

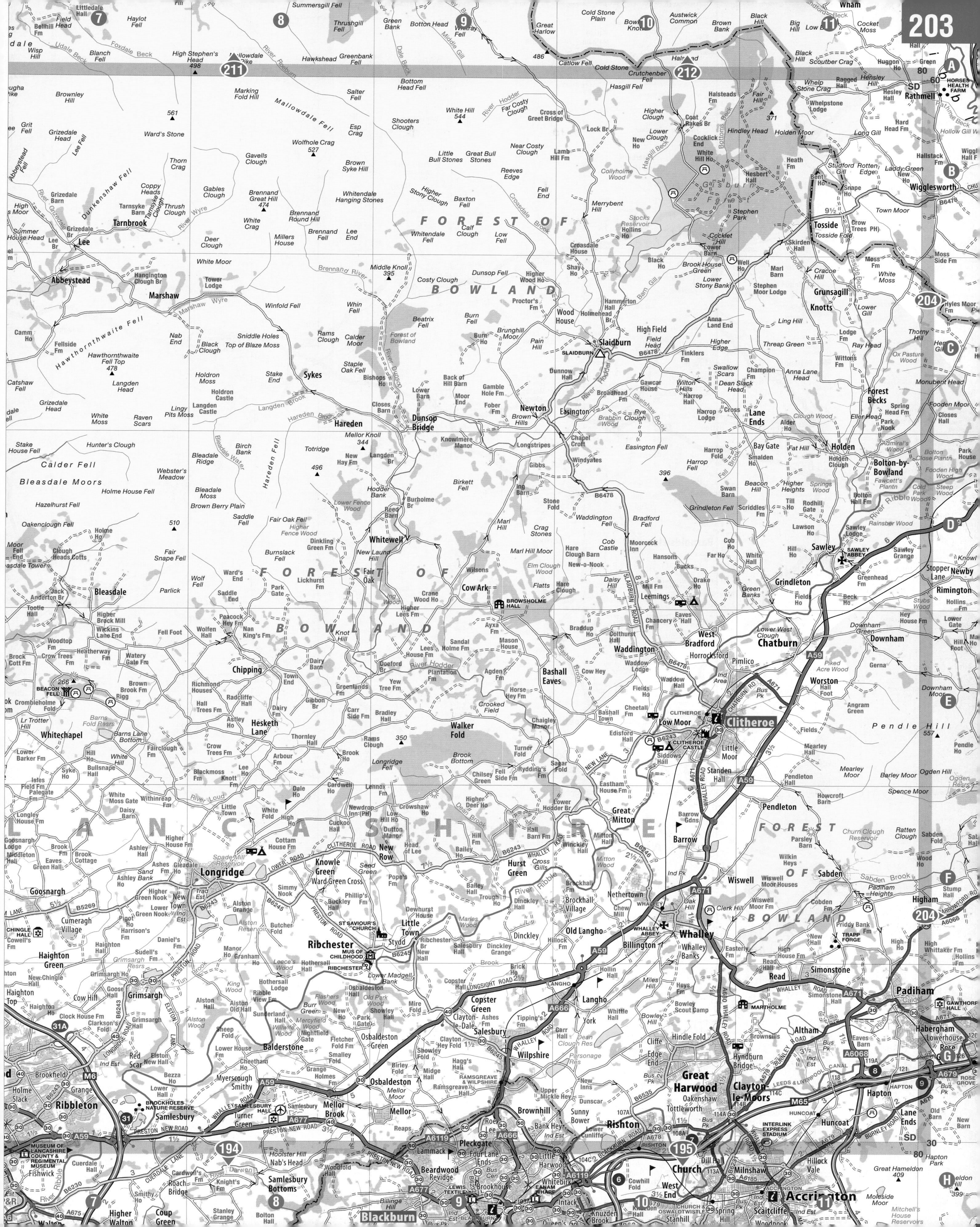
FOREST OF BOWLAND
FOREST OF BOWLAND
LANCASHIRE
FOREST OF BOWLAND
Abbeystead
Marshaw
Tarnbrook
Lee
Dunsop Bridge
Hareden
Newton
Slaidburn
Easington
Bolton-by-Bowland
Holden
Sawley
Grindleton
Rathmell
Wigglesworth
Tosside
Grunsagill
Knotts
Forest Becks
Whitewell
Chipping
Bleasdale
Whitechapel
Hesketh Lane
Longridge
Goosnargh
Ribchester
Great Mitton
Waddington
West Bradford
Chatburn
Clitheroe
Downham
Rimington
Worston
Barrow
Whalley
Wiswell
Sabden
Pendleton
Higham
Padiham
Read
Simonstone
Altham
Great Harwood
Clayton-le-Moors
Rishton
Church
Accrington
Blackburn
Langho
Billington
Wilpshire
Salesbury
Mellor
Osbaldeston
Samlesbury
Ribbleton
Grimsargh
Haighton Green
Balderstone
Mellor Brook
Calder Fell
Bleasdale Moors
Pendle Hill
Longridge Fell
Walker Fold
Cow Ark
Browsholme Hall
Stonyhurst
Hapton
Huncoat
Pleckgate
Sawley Abbey
Whalley Abbey
Clitheroe Castle
Beacon Fell
211
212
204
194
195
A59
A671
A666
A6119
A677
A678
A679
A680
M6
M65
B6478
B6243
B6245
B6246
SD 60 80
SD 30 80

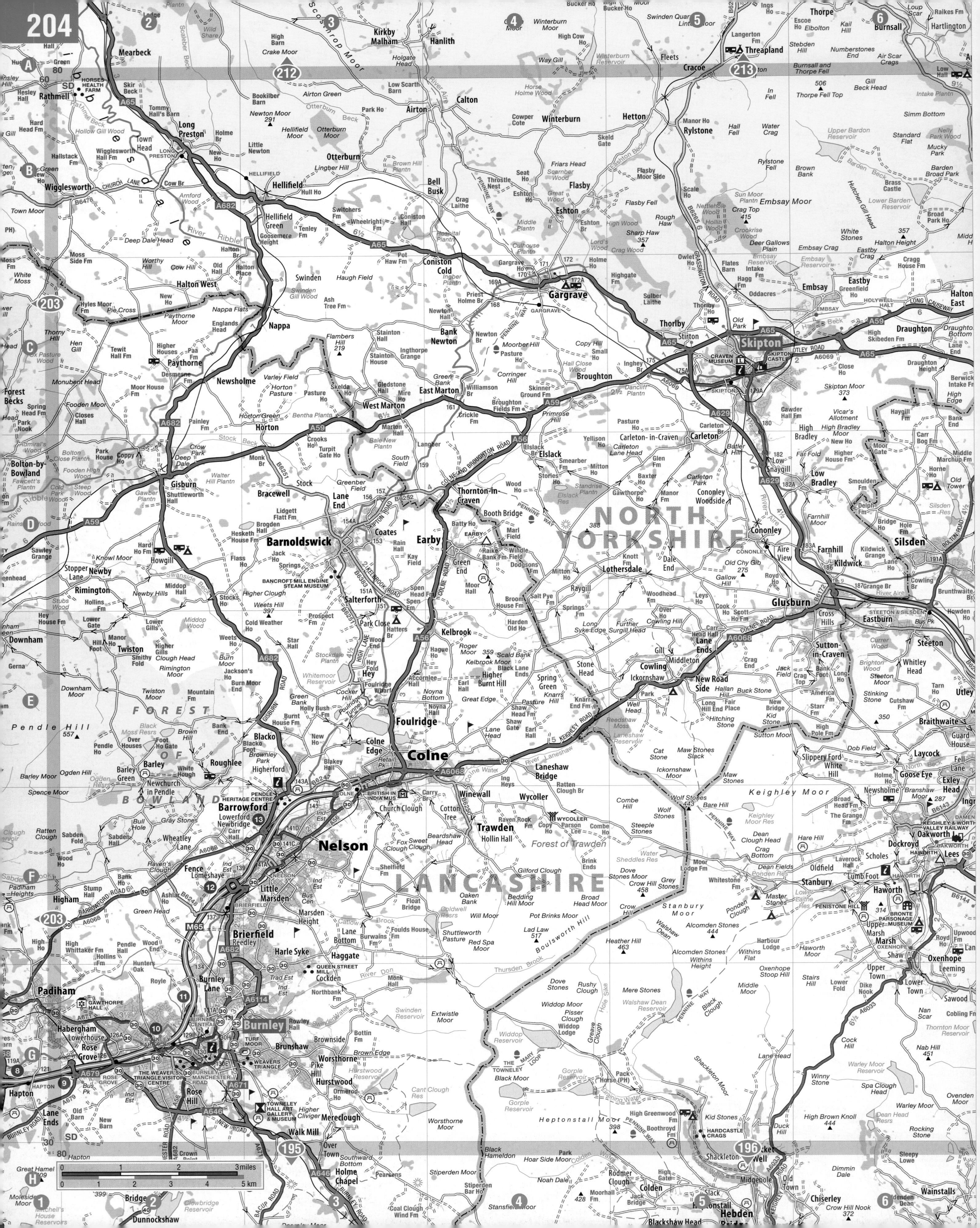
212
213
203
195
196
NORTH YORKSHIRE
LANCASHIRE
FOREST OF BOWLAND
Pendle Hill
Forest of Trawden
Keighley Moor
Embsay Moor
Ribblesdale
Mearbeck
Rathmell
Wigglesworth
Long Preston
Hellifield
Otterburn
Airton
Calton
Kirkby Malham
Hanlith
Winterburn
Hetton
Cracoe
Threapland
Burnsall
Thorpe
Rylstone
Flasby
Eshton
Gargrave
Bell Busk
Coniston Cold
Thorlby
Skipton
Embsay
Eastby
Halton East
Draughton
Nappa
Paythorne
Newsholme
Horton
West Marton
East Marton
Broughton
Elslack
Carleton
Carleton-in-Craven
Halton West
Gisburn
Bolton-by-Bowland
Bracewell
Barnoldswick
Coates
Earby
Thornton-in-Craven
Lothersdale
Cononley
Farnhill
Kildwick
Silsden
Glusburn
Cross Hills
Eastburn
Steeton
Sutton-in-Craven
Cowling
Ickornshaw
Middleton
Salterforth
Kelbrook
Foulridge
Colne
Laneshaw Bridge
Trawden
Winewall
Wycoller
Nelson
Barrowford
Blacko
Roughlee
Barley
Newchurch in Pendle
Fence
Brierfield
Burnley
Padiham
Higham
Twiston
Rimington
Downham
Howgill
Newby
Haworth
Oakworth
Oxenhope
Stanbury
Laycock
Goose Eye
Utley
Braithwaite
Worsthorne
Hurstwood
Cliviger
Holme Chapel
Hebden Bridge
Heptonstall Moor
Colden
Midgehole
Chiserley
Wainstalls
Lane Ends
Hapton
Rose Grove
Habergham
Brunshaw
Mereclough
Walk Mill
Widdop Reservoir
Boulsworth Hill
A65
A59
A682
A56
A6068
A629
M65
A646
A671
A679
A6114
A6033
B6252
B6251
B6383
B6265
B6172
3 miles
5 km

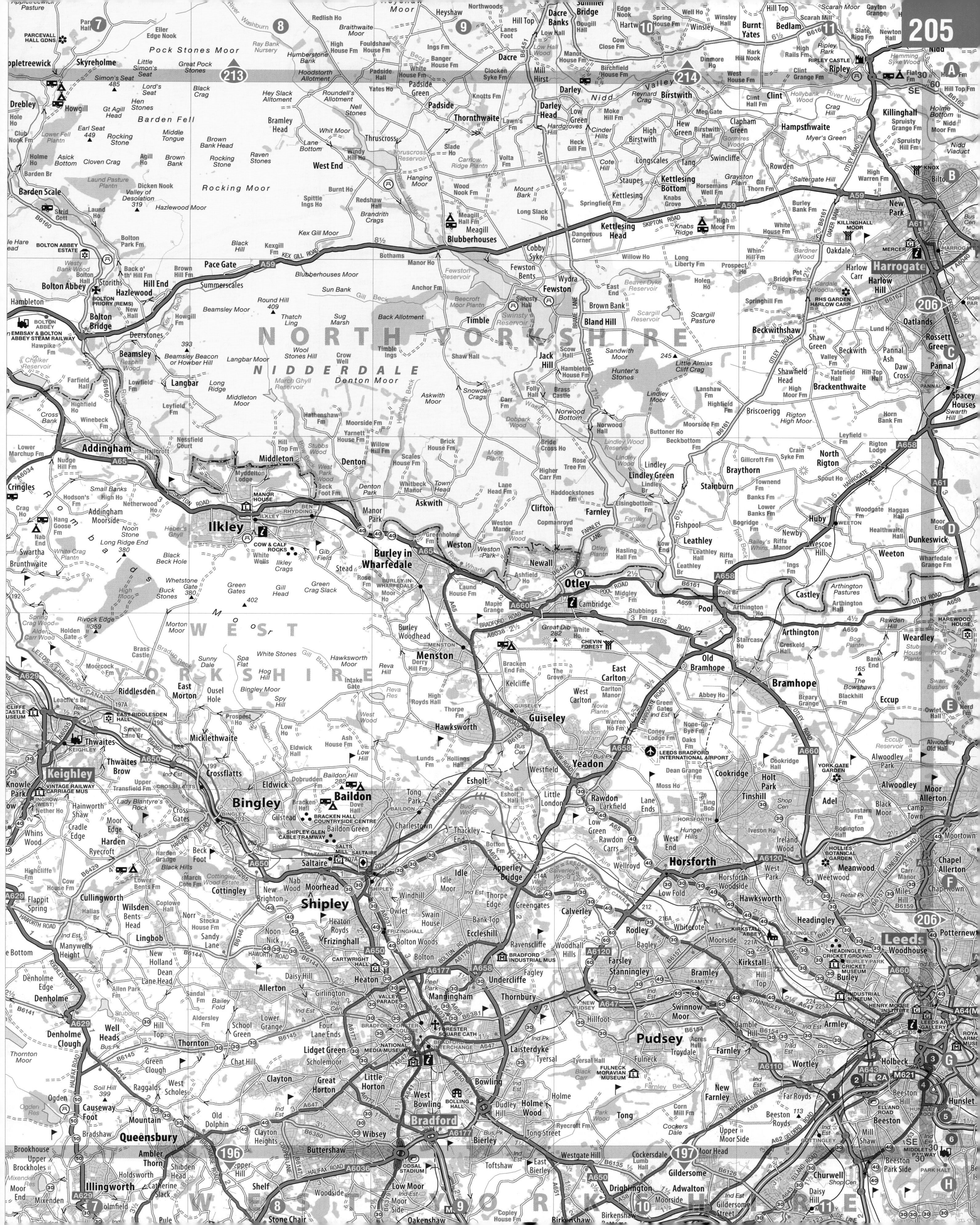
NORTH YORKSHIRE
NIDDERDALE
WEST YORKSHIRE
Harrogate
Leeds
Bradford
Keighley
Ilkley
Otley
Bingley
Shipley
Baildon
Guiseley
Yeadon
Horsforth
Pudsey
Menston
Burley in Wharfedale
Addingham
Bolton Abbey
Pannal
Killinghall
Ripley
Queensbury
Denholme
Illingworth
Bramhope
Pool
Adel
Headingley
Armley
Beeston
Holbeck
Kirkstall
Stanningley
Farsley
Calverley
Rodley
Bramley
Saltaire
Cottingley
Thornton
Clayton
Allerton
Heaton
Manningham
Eccleshill
Idle
Thornbury
Crossflatts
Riddlesden
Thwaites
Harden
Wilsden
Cullingworth
Blubberhouses
Fewston
Timble
Darley
Birstwith
Hampsthwaite
Beckwithshaw
Huby
Weeton
Castley
Arthington
Leathley
Stainburn
Lindley Green
Farnley
Clifton
Askwith
Denton
Middleton
Langbar
Beamsley
Hazlewood
Pace Gate
Dacre
Summerbridge
Skyreholme
Appletreewick
Drebley
Barden Fell
Rocking Moor
Denton Moor
Leeds Bradford International Airport
Harewood House
Chapel Allerton
Moortown
Alwoodley
Meanwood
Cookridge
Tinshill
Holt Park
Drighlington
Gildersome
Birkenshaw
Churwell
Wibsey
Buttershaw
Bierley
Tong
Holme Wood
Laisterdyke
Dudley Hill
Bowling
A59
A65
A660
A658
A61
A629
A650
A647
A6120
M621
213
214
206
196
197

Harrogate
Knaresborough
Wetherby
Leeds
Tadcaster
Garforth
Sherburn in Elmet
Collingham
Boston Spa
Bramham
Thorp Arch
Spofforth
North Deighton
Kirk Deighton
Little Ribston
Walshford
Hunsingore
Cowthorpe
Tockwith
Marston Moor
Long Marston
Hutton Wandesley
Rufforth
Askham Richard
Bilbrough
Bilton in Ainsty
Healaugh
Wighill
Catterton
Newton Kyme
Toulston
Stutton
Towton
Saxton
Barkston
Church Fenton
Little Fenton
Biggin
Ulleskelf
Kirkby Wharfe
Bolton Percy
Colton
South Milford
Lumby
Monk Fryston
Hillam
Fairburn
Ledsham
Ledston
Kippax
Great Preston
Little Preston
Swillington
Rothwell
Oulton
Methley
Micklefield
New Micklefield
Aberford
Parlington
Barwick in Elmet
Scholes
Thorner
Shadwell
Scarcroft
Bardsey
East Keswick
Harewood
Wike
Weardley
Alwoodley
Moor Allerton
Chapel Allerton
Roundhay
Moortown
Potternewton
Harehills
Sheepscar
Halton
Colton
Whitkirk
Manston
Cross Gates
Seacroft
Wellington Hill
Osmondthorpe
Hunslet
Beeston
Stourton
Woodhouse
Sicklinghall
Linton
Kearby Town End
Netherby
Dunkeswick
Weeton
Follifoot
Pannal
Spacey Houses
Oatlands
Rossett Green
Harlow Hill
High Harrogate
Starbeck
Forest Lane Head
Calcutt
Goldsborough
Flaxby
Coneythorpe
Scriven
Scotton
Farnham
Ferrensby
Arkendale
Brearton
Nidd
Killinghall
Bilton
New Park
Allerton Mauleverer
Hopperton
Great Ouseburn
Little Ouseburn
Whixley
Green Hammerton
Kirk Hammerton
Cattal
Thorpe Underwood
Linton-on-Ouse
Newton on Ouse
Nun Monkton
Moor Monkton
Beningbrough
Hessay
Poppleton
YORKSHIRE
WEST
A1(M)
A59
A61
A64
A63
A58
A659
A661
A168
M1
M621
A64(M)
0 1 2 3 miles
0 1 2 3 4 5 km

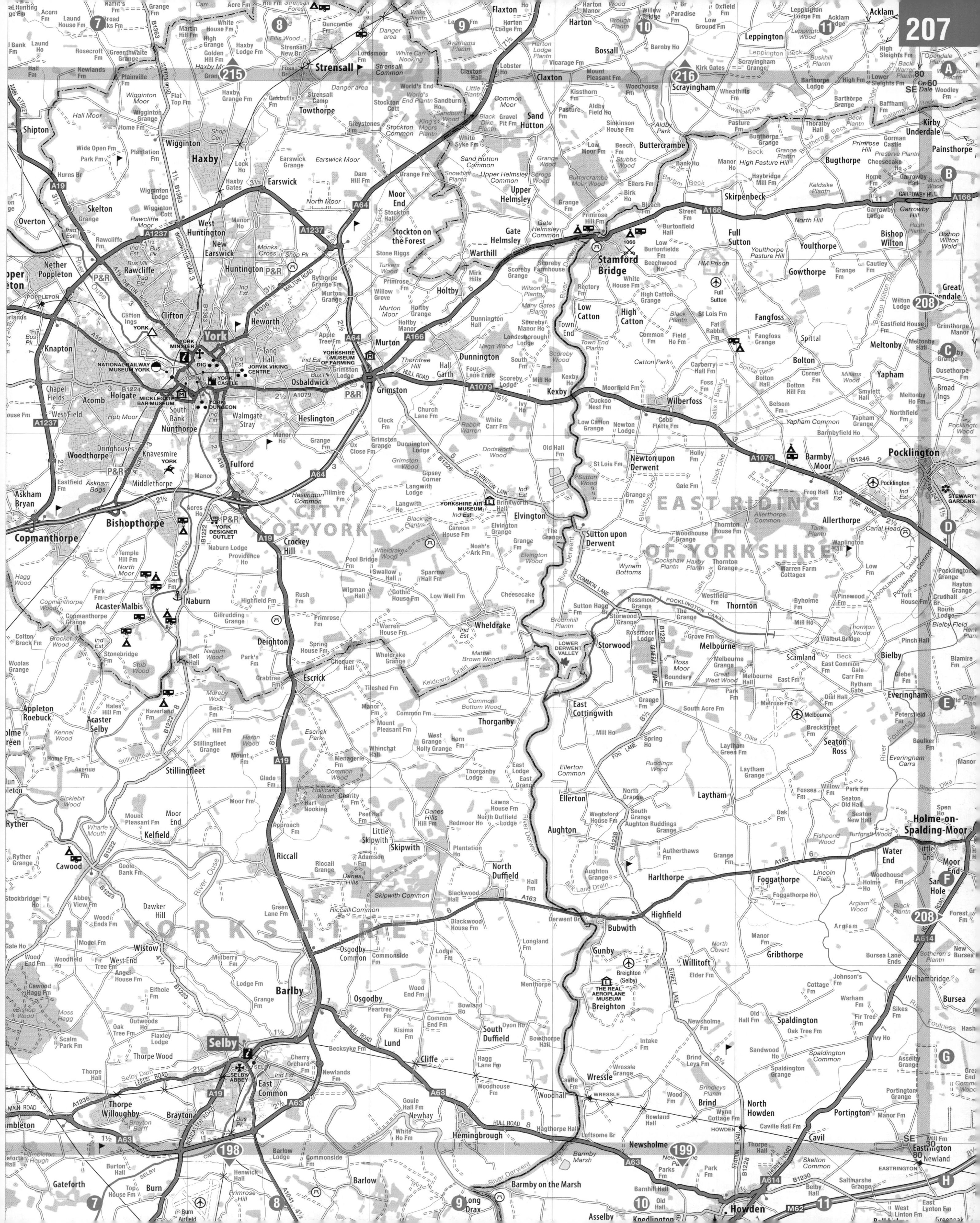

York
Strensall
Haxby
Wigginton
Earswick
Heworth
Huntington
New Earswick
Clifton
Rawcliffe
Skelton
Shipton
Nether Poppleton
Knapton
Acomb
Holgate
Dringhouses
Woodthorpe
Askham Bryan
Copmanthorpe
Bishopthorpe
Middlethorpe
Fulford
Heslington
Osbaldwick
Murton
Dunnington
Grimston
Kexby
Stamford Bridge
Gate Helmsley
Upper Helmsley
Warthill
Holtby
Sand Hutton
Claxton
Flaxton
Harton
Bossall
Buttercrambe
Scrayingham
Leppington
Acklam
Kirby Underdale
Painsthorpe
Bugthorpe
Skirpenbeck
Full Sutton
Youlthorpe
Bishop Wilton
Great Givendale
Gowthorpe
Fangfoss
Spittal
Meltonby
Bolton
Yapham
Wilberfoss
Low Catton
High Catton
Newton upon Derwent
Barmby Moor
Pocklington
Allerthorpe
Elvington
Sutton upon Derwent
Thornton
Melbourne
Storwood
Wheldrake
Deighton
Escrick
Crockey Hill
Naburn
Acaster Malbis
Acaster Selby
Appleton Roebuck
Stillingfleet
Kelfield
Riccall
Skipwith
North Duffield
Thorganby
East Cottingwith
Ellerton
Aughton
Laytham
Seaton Ross
Everingham
Bielby
Holme-on-Spalding-Moor
Harlthorpe
Foggathorpe
Highfield
Bubwith
Gunby
Willitoft
Gribthorpe
Breighton
Spaldington
Wressle
Brind
North Howden
Howden
Portington
Cavil
Eastrington
Newsholme
Hemingbrough
Barmby on the Marsh
Cliffe
Lund
South Duffield
Osgodby
Barlby
Selby
Brayton
Thorpe Willoughby
Wistow
Cawood
Gateforth
Burn
Barlow
Long Drax
Asselby
CITY OF YORK
EAST RIDING OF YORKSHIRE
NORTH YORKSHIRE
YORK MINSTER
NATIONAL RAILWAY MUSEUM YORK
JORVIK VIKING CENTRE
YORK CASTLE
YORK DUNGEON
MICKLEGATE BAR MUSEUM
YORKSHIRE MUSEUM OF FARMING
YORKSHIRE AIR MUSEUM
YORK DESIGNER OUTLET
LOWER DERWENT VALLEY
THE REAL AEROPLANE MUSEUM
SELBY ABBEY
STEWART'S GARDENS
A19
A64
A166
A1079
A1237
A163
A63
A614
A1041
M62
B1363
B1228
B1222
B1223
B1224
B1246
B1230
River Ouse
River Derwent
Pocklington Canal
215
216
208
198
199
7
8
9
10
11
A
B
C
D
E
F
G
H

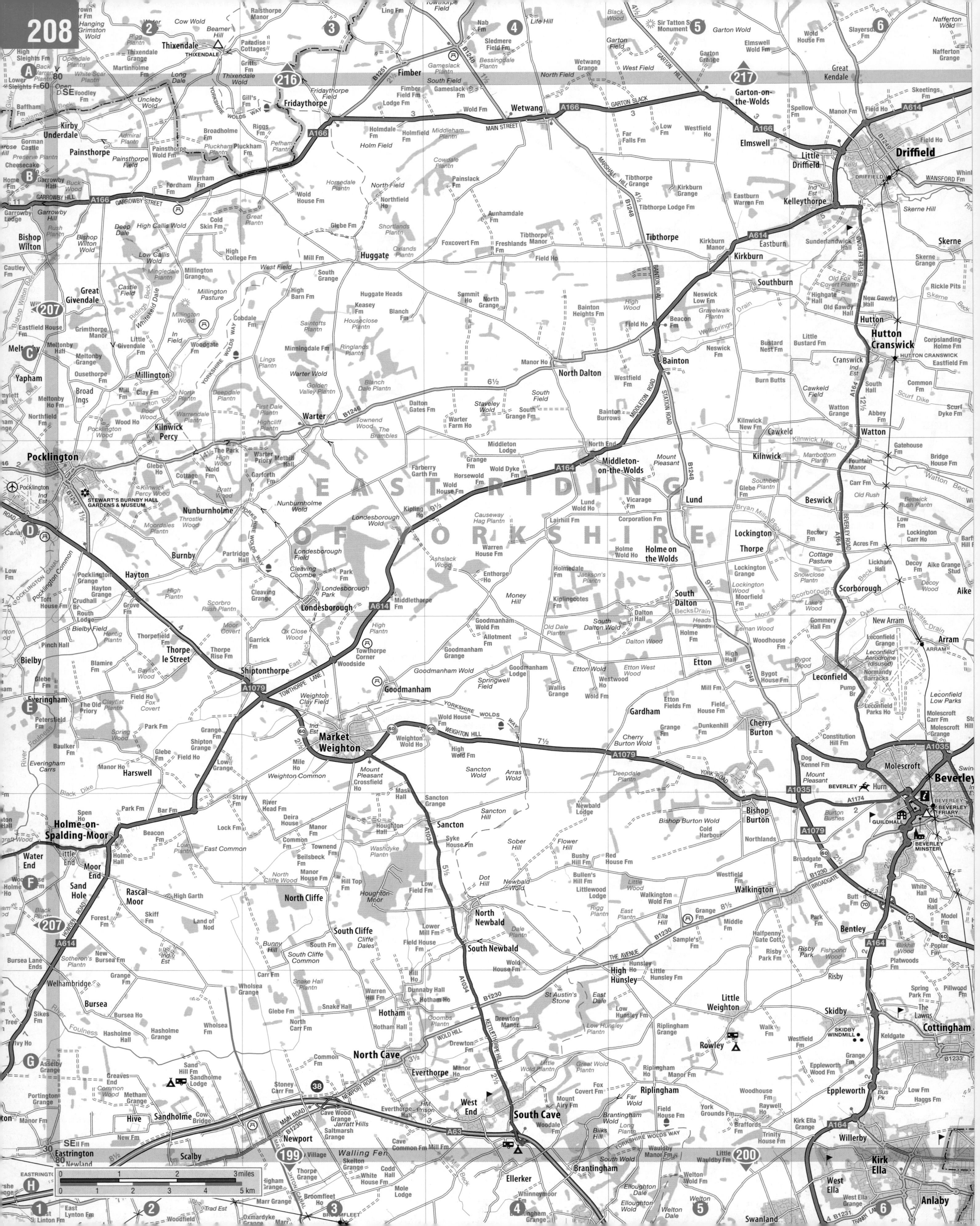
EAST RIDING OF YORKSHIRE
Thixendale
Fimber
Wetwang
Fridaythorpe
Garton-on-the-Wolds
Driffield
Little Driffield
Elmswell
Kelleythorpe
Kirby Underdale
Painsthorpe
Bishop Wilton
Great Givendale
Huggate
Tibthorpe
Kirkburn
Southburn
Bainton
North Dalton
Hutton Cranswick
Hutton
Millington
Yapham
Warter
Kilnwick Percy
Pocklington
Middleton-on-the-Wolds
Kilnwick
Watton
Lund
Beswick
Nunburnholme
Burnby
Hayton
Londesborough
Lockington
Thorpe
Holme on the Wolds
Scorborough
South Dalton
Thorpe le Street
Shiptonthorpe
Bielby
Everingham
Goodmanham
Etton
Leconfield
Arram
Gardham
Cherry Burton
Market Weighton
Harswell
Molescroft
Beverley
Holme-on-Spalding-Moor
Sancton
Bishop Burton
Walkington
Moor End
Sand Hole
Rascal Moor
North Cliffe
North Newbald
South Newbald
South Cliffe
Bentley
High Hunsley
Little Weighton
Skidby
Cottingham
Hotham
North Cave
Everthorpe
Rowley
Riplingham
West End
South Cave
Eppleworth
Willerby
Kirk Ella
West Ella
Anlaby
Hive
Sandholme
Newport
Eastrington
Scalby
Ellerker
Brantingham
Swanland
Welton
YORKSHIRE WOLDS WAY
A166
A614
A164
A1079
A1035
A1034
A63
B1248
B1246
B1230
216
217
207
199
200
0 1 2 3 miles
0 1 2 3 4 5 km

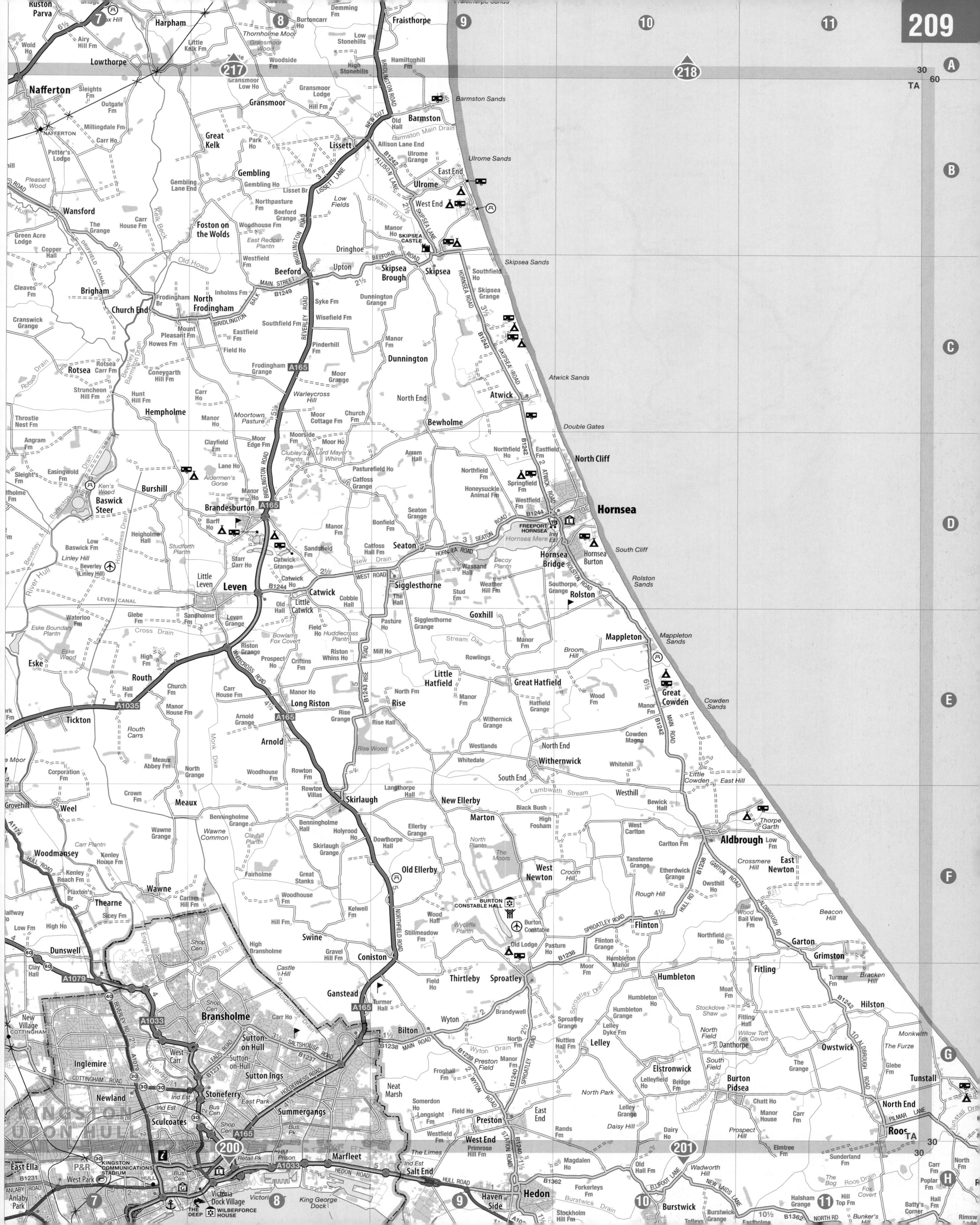
Ruston Parva
Harpham
Burtoncarr Ho
Demming Fm
Fraisthorpe
Wold Ho
Airy Hill Fm
Little Kelk Fm
Thornholme Moor
Gransmoor Wood
Low Stonehills
Lowthorpe
Woodside Fm
High Stonehills
Hamiltonhill Fm
217
218
Nafferton
Sleights Fm
Gransmoor Low Ho
Gransmoor Lodge
Outgate Fm
Gransmoor
Hill Fm
Barmston Sands
Millingdale Fm
Old Hall
Barmston
Nafferton
Carr Ho
Great Kelk
Park Ho
Barmston Main Drain
Potter's Lodge
Lissett
Allison Lane End
Ulrome Grange
Ulrome Sands
Pleasant Wood
Gembling
Gembling Lane End
Gembling Ho
Lisset Br
East End
Ulrome
Wansford
Northpasture Fm
Low Fields
West End
Beeford Grange
Carr House Fm
The Grange
Foston on the Wolds
Woodhouse Fm
Manor Ho
Skipsea Castle
Green Acre Lodge
East Redcarr Plantn
Copper Hall
Dringhoe
Old Howe
Westfield Fm
Upton
Skipsea Brough
Skipsea
Beeford
Skipsea Sands
Southfield Ho
Cleaves Fm
Brigham
Inholms Fm
Skipsea Grange
Frodingham Br
North Frodingham
Syke Fm
Dunnington Grange
Church End
Wisefield Fm
Cranswick Grange
Mount Pleasant Fm
Southfield Fm
Eastfield Fm
Howes Fm
Pinderhill Fm
Manor Fm
Field Ho
Dunnington
Rotsea Carr Fm
Rotsea
Frodingham Grange
Coneygarth Hill Fm
Moor Grange
Atwick Sands
Struncheon Hill Fm
Warleycross Hill
Atwick
Hunt Hill Fm
Carr Ho
North End
Hempholme
Moortown Pasture
Throstle Nest Fm
Manor Ho
Moor Cottage Fm
Church Fm
Bewholme
Double Gates
Moorside Fm
Moor Ho
Angram Fm
Clayfield Fm
Moor Edge Fm
Clubley's Plantn
Lord Mayor's Whins
Arram Hall
Northfield Ho
Eastfield Fm
North Cliff
Lane Ho
Pasturefield Ho
Sleight's Fm
Easingwold Fm
Aldermen's Gorse
Northfield Fm
Springfield Fm
Ken's Wood
Burshill
Catfoss Grange
Honeysuckle Animal Fm
Manor Ho
Westfield Fm
Hornsea
Baswick Steer
Brandesburton
Seaton Grange
Barff Ho
Bonfield Fm
Freeport Hornsea
Heigholme Hall
Manor Fm
Hornsea Mere
Low Baswick Fm
Studforth Plantn
Sandsfield Fm
Catfoss Hall Fm
Seaton
Hornsea Burton
South Cliff
Linley Hill
Starr Carr Ho
Catwick Grange
Hornsea Bridge
Beverley (Linley Hill)
Wassand Hall
Decoy Plantn
Rolston Sands
Little Leven
Catwick Ho
Weather Hill Fm
Southorpe Grange
Rolston
Leven
Catwick
Sigglesthorne
Leven Canal
Old Hall
Little Catwick
Cobble Hall
The Hall
Stud Fm
Waterloo Fm
Glebe Fm
Sandholme Fm
Leven Grange
Goxhill
Eske Boundary Plantn
Cross Drain
Sigglesthorne Grange
Pasture Ho
Bowlams Fox Covert
Field Ho
Huddlecross Plantn
Mappleton Sands
Mappleton
Riston Grange
Manor Fm
Eske Wood
Eske
Stream Dike
Broom Hill
Prospect Ho
Riston Whins Ho
Mill Ho
Rowlings
High Fm
Criftins Fm
Little Hatfield
Great Hatfield
Routh
Great Cowden
Hall Fm
Church Fm
Carr House Fm
Manor Ho
North Fm
Manor Fm
Wood Fm
Cowden Sands
Long Riston
Rise
Hatfield Grange
Manor Fm
Tickton
Manor House Fm
Rise Grange
Arnold Grange
Rise Hall
Withernwick Grange
Cowden Magna
Routh Carrs
Arnold
Rise Wood
Westlands
North End
Whitedale
Withernwick
Whitehill
Meaux Abbey Fm
Corporation Fm
North Grange
Woodhouse Fm
Rowton Fm
South End
Little Cowden
East Hill
Crown Fm
Rowton Villas
Langthorpe Hall
Lambwath Stream
Westhill
Grovehill
Weel
Meaux
Skirlaugh
New Ellerby
Black Bush
Bewick Hall
Marton
High Fosham
Thorpe Garth
Benninghome Grange
Benninghome Hall
Holyrood Ho
Ellerby Grange
West Carlton
Aldbrough
Low Fm
Wawne Grange
Wawne Common
Clayhill Plantn
Carr Plantn
Skirlaugh Grange
Dowthorpe Hall
North Plantn
Carlton Fm
Woodmansey
Kenley House Fm
The Moors
Tansterne Grange
Crossmere Hill
East Newton
Kenley Reach Fm
Fairholme
Great Stanks
Old Ellerby
West Newton
Croom Hill
Etherdwick Grange
Owsthill Ho
Plaxton's Br
Wawne
Woodhouse Fm
Burton Constable Hall
Rough Hill
Thearne
Carlam Hill Fm
Bail Wood
Bail View Fm
Beacon Hill
Sicey Fm
Kelwell Fm
Wood Hall
Wycliffe Plantn
Burton Constable
Flinton
Halfway Ho
Hill Fm
Swine
Stillmeadow Fm
Northfield Ho
Garton
Low Fm
High Ho
Engine Drain
Shop Cen
Pasture Ho
Flinton Grange
Dunswell
High Bransholme
Gravel Hill Fm
Coniston
Old Lodge
Humbleton Manor
Grimston
Wawne Drain
Clay Hill
Moor Fm
Fitling
A1079
Castle Hill
Field Ho
Thirtleby
Sproatley
Humbleton
Turmar Fm
Bracken Hill
Moat Fm
Ganstead
Turmer Hall
Sproatley Drain
Humbleton Ho
Stockdove Shaw
Hilston
New Village
Cottingham
Bransholme
Carr Ho
Brandywell
Humbleton Grange
Fitling Hall
Monkwith
Wyton
Sproatley Grange
Lelley Dyke Fm
North Field
Willow Toft Fox Covert
The Furze
Bilton
Sutton on Hull
Holderness Drain
North Hall
Nuttles Hall Fm
Lelley
Danthorpe
Owstwick
Inglemire
West Carr
Sutton-on-Hull
Wyton Drain
Preston Field
Manor Fm
South Field
The Grange
Glebe Fm
Sutton Ings
Froghall Fm
Elstronwick
Burton Pidsea
Tunstall
Newland
Cottingham Road
Stoneferry
Neat Marsh
Lelleyfield Ho
Bridge Fm
Ind Est
East Park
North Park
Chatt Ho
North End
Kingston upon Hull
Bus Cen
Summergangs
Somerdon Ho
Field Ho
East End
Humbleton Beck
Manor House
Carr Fm
Longsight Fm
Lelley Grange
Roos Lane
Sculcoates
Shop Cen
Bus Pk
Preston
Rands Fm
Daisy Hill
Prospect Hill
Roos
Westfield Fm
West End
Dairy Ho
200
201
Primrose Hill Fm
Elmtree Fm
Kingston Communications Stadium
Retail Pk
HM Prison
Marfleet
The Limes
Magdalen Ho
Old Hall Fm
Wadworth Hill
Sunderland Fm
North Fm
East Ella
P&R
Hull
Salt End
Carr Fm
West Park
Hedon Road
The Bog
Roos Drain
Poplar Fm
Anlaby Park
Victoria Dock Village
Victoria
King George Dock
Haven Side
Hedon
Forkerleys Fm
Fox Covert
The Deep
Wilberforce House
Burstwick Drain
Burstwick
Halsham Grange
Hill Top Fm
Hall Fm
Batty's Corner
Stockholm Hill Fm
Totleys Fm
Burstwick Grange
Fastholme
Bunker's Hill
Rimsw
A165
A1035
A1033
A1079
B1242
B1249
B1244
B1243
B1238
B1239
B1240
B1237
B1231
B1362
Bridlington Road
Beverley Road
Hornsea Road
Skipsea Road
Atwick Road
Main Road
Whitecross Road
Northfield Road
Sproatley Road
Wyton Road
Station Road
Hull Road
Garton Road
Aldbrough Road
Holderness Road
Saltshouse Road
Leads Road
Beverley Rd
Pilmar Lane
Ellifoot Lane
New Laids Lane
North Rd
TA
30
60

Corney
Swallowhurst
Hycemoor
Bootle
Kiskin
Annaside
Black Combe
Whitbeck
Whicham
Silecroft
Kirksanton
Millom
MILLOM FOLK MUSEUM
DUDDON ESTUARY
Haverigg
HM Prison
Haverigg Point
Hodbarrow Point
HODBARROW
Steel Green
Borwick Rails
The Green
Hallthwaites
The Hill
Duddon Bridge
Broughton in Furness
Broughton Mills
Foxfield
Grizebeck
Kirkby-in-Furness
Sand Side
Soutergate
Beck Side
Duddon Sands
Duddon Channel
Askam in Furness
Ireleth
Dunnerholme
Sandscale Haws
Lowsy Point
Scarth Channel
North Walney
Walney Meetings
Earnse Pt
North Scale
Vickerstown
Barrow Island
Barrow-in-Furness
Hawcoat
Ormsgill
Newbarns
Hindpool
Salthouse
Yarlside
Roose
Furness Abbey
Dalton-in-Furness
DALTON CASTLE
SOUTH LAKES WILD ANIMAL PARK
Lindal in Furness
Ulverston
LAUREL & HARDY MUS
Swarthmoor
SWARTHMOOR HALL
Pennington
Great Urswick
Little Urswick
Stainton with Adgarley
Gleaston
GLEASTON WATERMILL
Dendron
Leece
Newbiggin
Aldingham
Baycliff
Scales
Bardsea
CONISHEAD PRIORY
Rampside
Roosebeck
Roosecote
Roa Island
Piel Island
PIEL CASTLE
Foulney Island
Sheep Island
Biggar
Biggar Sands
South End
Scar End Point
Haws Point
South East Point
Piel Bar
Isle of Walney
Walney Channel
Rampside Sands
Roosebeck Sands
Ulverston Sands
Ulverston Channel
Lancaster Sound
South Channel
Gawthwaite
Lowick Green
Lowick Bridge
Blawith
Water Yeat
Spark Bridge
Penny Bridge
Greenodd
Broughton Beck
Mansriggs
Arrad Foot
Newland
Haverthwaite
Rusland
Furness Fells
High Nibthwaite
Colton
Bouth
Force Mills
A590
A595
A5092
A5093
A5087
A5084
B5281
220
202
DOUGLAS 3:15
DOUGLAS 2:00 (TT RACE PERIOD ONLY)
0 1 2 3 miles
0 1 2 3 4 5 km
SD

Killington Lake Services (Southbound Only)
Burton-in-Kendal Services (Northbound Only)
LAKE DISTRICT NATIONAL PARK
ARNSIDE AND SILVERDALE
MORECAMBE BAY
LANCS
Kendal
Abbot Hall Art Gallery & Museum
K Village Heritage Centre
Ludderburn
Crosthwaite
Underbarrow
Gregg Hall
Bowland Bridge
Brigsteer
Natland
Oxenholme
New Hutton
Millholme
Killington
Cartmel Fell
The Howe
Sizergh Castle
Barrows Green
Middleshaw
Old Hutton
Finsthwaite
Lakeside
Aquarium of the Lakes
Staveley-in-Cartmel
Newby Bridge
Cotes
Levens
Sedgwick
Halfpenny
Sampool Bridge
Causeway End
Levens Hall
Crosscrake
Summerlands
Stainton
Gatebeck
Endmoor
Hincaster
Backbarrow
Witherslack
Mill Side
Town End
Leasgill
Heversham
Woodhouse
Deepthwaite
Crooklands
Milton
Millness
Ayside
High Newton
Low Newton
Milnthorpe
Old Town
Mansergh
Field Broughton
Meathop
Lindale
Lupton
Farleton
Sandside
Storth
Beetham
Holme
Kearstwick
Cartmel
Cartmel Priory Gatehouse
Grange-over-Sands
Arnside
Hazelslack
Slack Head
Hale
Clawthorpe
Hutton Roof
Holker
Allithwaite
Kents Bank
Cark
Flookburgh
Far Arnside
Burton-in-Kendal
Whittington
Nether Burrow
Yealand Redmayne
Silverdale
Yealand Conyers
Ravenstown
Lakeland Riding Centre
Newton
Tunstall
Priest Hutton
Borwick
Warton
Capernwray
Arkholme
Wrayton
Melling
Carnforth
Millhead
Over Kellet
Gressingham
Tatham
Hornby
Bolton-le-Sands
Nether Kellet
Aughton
Farleton
Wray
Bolton Town End
Claughton
Hest Bank
Slyne
Halton
Caton Green
Caton
Brookhouse
Caton Moor
Morecambe
Bare
Torrisholme
West End
Sandylands
White Lund
Skerton
Lancaster
Ashton Memorial
Williamson Park & Butterfly House
Salter
Crossgill
Littledale
Heysham
Lower Heysham
Higher Heysham
Heaton
Aldcliffe
Scotforth
Quernmore
Middleton
Overton
Bailrigg
Stodday
Heysham Port
Heysham Nuclear Power Sta
Kent Channel
Keer Channel
Salt Marsh
Jenny Brown's Point
Humphrey Head
Humphrey Head Point
M6
A590
A591
A6
A65
A683
A601 (M)
A589
A588
221
212
202
203

Killington Lake Services (Southbound Only)
Sedbergh
Millthrop
Killington
Beckside
Middleton
Barbon
Casterton
Kirkby Lonsdale
Old Town
Mansergh
Kearstwick
Whittington
Nether Burrow
Tunstall
Cantsfield
Wrayton
Melling
Wennington
Tatham
Wray
Salter
FOREST OF BOWLAND
Goodber Common
Tatham Fells
Lowgill
Burton in Lonsdale
Low Bentham
High Bentham
Ingleton
Westhouse
Masongill
Ireby
Leck
Cowan Bridge
Clapham
Newby
Austwick
Lawkland
Eldroth
Keasden
Mewith Head
Burn Moor
Giggleswick
Settle
Langcliffe
Stainforth
Little Stainforth
Feizor
Wharfe
Helwith Bridge
Horton in Ribblesdale
Brackenbottom
Ribblehead
Chapel-le-Dale
Ingleborough Hill
Whernside
Dent
Cowgill
Gawthrop
Deepdale
Garsdale
Rise Hill
Widdale Fell
Dodd Fell
Horton Moor
Mearbeck
Rathmell
Long Preston
CUMBRIA
YORKSHIRE DALES NATIONAL PARK
A65
A683
A687
B6480
B6255
B6479
222
211
203
204
0 1 2 3 miles
0 1 2 3 4 5 km

Shaw
Hardraw Force Waterfall
Hardraw
Sedbusk
Sedbusk High Pasture
Cote Pasture
Litherskew
Simonstone
Leas Ho
Helm
Low Mill Outdoor Centre
Newbiggin Pasture
Newbiggin
Askrigg
Nappa Scar
Swinehaw Bottom
Blue Scar
Bolton Parks
Castle Bolton
Redmire Pasture
Redmire Scar
Elm Ho
Preston-under-Scar
Gillfield Wood
Bellerby Camp
Cote Pasture
Redmire
Wood End
Leyburn
Flosh Hill
Dales Countryside Museum
Brown Moor
Wensleydale
Ingleby Lodge
Yorebridge
Askrigg Bottoms
Nappa Hall
Woodhall
Ivy Scar
New Pasture
Hawes
River Ure
Bainbridge
Worton
Carperby
Sunny Bank
Haremire Ho
White Rose Candles
West Wood
Bolton Hall
Howe Hills
Wensleydale Creamery
Bainbridge Ings
High Hall
Cubeck
Warren Ho
Manor Ho
Hollins Ho
Swinithwaite
Wanlass Park
Alma Fm
Wensley
Gayle
Burtersett
Burtersett Bottoms
Raygill Ho
Bainbridge Low Pasture
Gill Edge
Scar Top
Bear Park
Aysgarth Falls
West Witton
Gale Bank
Gaudy Ho
Burtersett High Pasture
515
Yorburgh
Semerdale Hall
Bainbridge High Pasture
Holly Ho
Addlebrough
476
Devil's Stone
Thornton Rust
High Gill
Seata Fm
Aysgarth
Nossill Scars
Scot Gate
Holl Gate
Parki Gate
Mount Park Fm
Middleham Moor
Park Fm
Sleddale Pasture
Wether Fell
Countersett
Low Force
Thornton Rust Moor
Aysgarth Moor
Riggs Ho
Castle Dykes
Gill Beck
Spigot Lodge
Cappelbank Plantn
Drumaldrace
614
Wood End Lodge
Low Blean
High Blean
Carpley Green
Haw Beck
Thoralby
Flanders Hall
Dove Scar
Penhill Fm
West Witton Moor
Cotescue Park
Abbey (Rems)
Knight Close or Bella
Carr End Fm
Semer Water
Blean West Pasture
Water Ling Pasture
Stake Fell
495
Black Pasture
Haw Head
Bishopdale Valley
West Burton
Black Scar
546
Penhill
Middleham High Moor
Agglethorpe
Tupgill Park
Countersett Bardale
Marsett
Stalling Busk
Blean High Pasture
Skellicks Beck
Newbiggin
Long Ing Wood
Height of Hazely
Melmerby Moor
Gildersbeck Fm
Low Wood
Coverham
Close Ing
Bardale Beck
West Duerley Pasture
Fairy Haw
Heck Brow
Barker
Street Head Bank
Forelands Rigg
Cat Gill
Melmerby
Caldbergh
Raydale Grange
Thoralby Common
Bardale Head
Raydale Ho
Busk Moss
High Scar
East Lane Ho
Burton Pasture
Harland Hill
535
Howden Lodge
Carlton
East Scrafton
Billinside Moor
Raydale
Dale Foot
Newbiggin Pasture
Carlton Moor
Widdiman Pasture
New Ho
New Gill
Wasset Fell
Cowstone Gill Ho
Walden Beck
Mount Pleasant
High Field
Any Binks Moss
Ribba Hall
Gammersgill Moor
Gammersgill
Quarry Lodge
West Scrafton
Woldside
Cragdale Water
Cragdale Moor
High Wood
Bishopdale Edge
Mile Stone Hill
Walden
Fleensop
Coverdale
Grainings
West Fell
Stake Moss
Naughtberry Hill
573
Hill Top Fm
East Scrafton Moor
Swineside Moor
Nethergill
Bridge End Fm
Well Ho
Cocklee Fell
High Pasture
Cray Moss
Kidstones
Bishopdale Lane
Fleemis Gill
Fleensop Moor
Hindlethwaite Hall
Lead Up
Barnley Moss
Oughtershaw
Cush Rigg
Kidstones Fell
Kidstones Gill
Rountengil
Walden Head
Denman's Hill
482
Horsehouse
West Scrafton Moor
Colsterdale Moor
Arundel Grange
Beckermonds Scar
Beckermonds
Yockenthwaite Moor
High Pasture
Kidstones Bank
Bishopdale Head
Kentucky Ho
Hindlethwaite Moor
Little Haw
486
Middle Pasture
Chapel Moor
584
Brown Haw
Woodale Moor
Braidley
Deepdale
Walden Moor
Great Haw
544
Steel House Gill
West Moor
River Wharfe
Yockenthwaite
Deepdale Head
Woodale
Arkleside Moor
Carle Fell
River Cover
Cow Pasture
Buckden Pike
702
Masham Moor
Strans Wood
Rais Wood
Todd's Wood
Cray
Out Moor
Grove End
Raven Scar
Coverhead Fm
Woo Gill
Thorny Grane Gill
Eller Carr Moss
Hagg Beck
Hubberholme
Cow Side
Dead Mans Hill
North Moor
Gipsey Ho
Cosh Beck
Horse Head
Grange Fm
Rakes Wood
Little Whernside
604
Brown Ridge
Ber Gill
Great Pasture
Horse Head Moor
Mooring Head
Kirk Gill Moor
Starbotton Fell
North Moor
Scar House Reservoir
Carle Side
High Woodale
Low Woodale
River Nidd
Summerstone Lodge
Throstle Hill
Buckden
High Pasture
Bracken Ridge
Foxup
Halton Gill
Foxup Beck
Birks Wood
Buckden Wood Lane
Knuckle Bone Pasture
Great Hunters Stone
Nidderdale
Moss Top
Birks Fell
Eshber Wood
Cam Gill Beck
Starbotton Out Moor
Tor Mere Top
617
Angram Reservoir
Woodale Scar
New Houses
Thwaite Ho
Lofthouse Moor
High Bergh
Potts Moor
Crystal Beck
Out Moor
Nidd Head
River Nidd
Angram Low Pasture
Rain Stang
453
In Moor
How Gill Ho
Limley Fm
Hesleden Bergh
Firth Fell
Firth Wood
Cam Head
Armathwaite Gill
Northside Head
Thrope Fm
North
607
Starbotton
Slater Barn
Kay Head Allotment
Intake Fm
Intake Gill
Thrope Plantn
Nether Hesleden
Hesleden Beck
Ackerley Moor
Haw Fell
Fosse Wood
West Scale Park
East Scale Lodge
Lodge Moor
Stone Beck
High Riggs
Well Ho
Ling Hall
Middlesmoor
Pen-y-ghent Fell
Pen-y-ghent Gill
Litton
Capple Stones
Moor End Fell
Great Whernside
704
Whernside Pasture
Aygill Pike
How Stean Beck
Halfway Ho
Lofthouse
Pen-y-ghent Ho
Littondale
Skirfare
Bracken Gill
Old Cote High Moor
Wibbertons Fields
Cam Pasture
Hay Tonge
Hag Dike
Nidd Heads
Stean
Cow Close Fell
Old Cote Low Moor
Moor End
Riggs Moor
Stott Crags
Moor Ho
Out Sleets
Scoska Moor
Scoska Wood
Kettlewell
Stock Ridge
472
Blayshaw Crags
West House Fm
Darnbrook Fell
Old Cote Little Moor
Byre Bank Wood
Bown Scar Wood
Yorkshire
Brootes Barn
Arncliffe
Hawkswick Wood
Langcliffe
Straight Stean Beck
Grinstone Hill Ho
West Moor
Darnbrook Beck
Field Ho Barn
Hawkswick Moor
434
Scargill Ho
Backstean Gill
Sandy Gate
Blayshaw Gill
Raygill House Plantn
Pennine Way
Darnbrook Ho
Blue Scar
Great Stangate
Meugher
575
Stean Moor
465
Brown Hill
Raygill Ho
Fountains Fell
Hawkswick
Tennant Gill
Thoragill Beck Ho
Nab End
Cowside Beck
Yew Cogar Scar
Knipe Scar
Mile Ho
Conistone Moor
Cowside
Low Cote Moor
Mossdale Scar
Out Fell
Far Fell
Dew Bottoms
High Cote Moor
Ragstaff Hill
Black Edge
Father Bed Moss
Raygill House Wig Stones
Swine Beck Knotts
Parson's Pulpit
538
Skirfare Br
Raygill House Moor
Flat Moss
Rough Close
Westside Ho
Knowe Fell
Stanggill Barn
Back Pasture
Low Far Moor
Pinder Stile
Gill Ho
Bycliff Hill
Ashford Gill Head
Goutwaite Moor
Heathfield Moor
Middle Ho
Flock Rake
Kilnsey Crag
Sleet Moor
Middle Barn
Flout Hill
434
Water Houses
Procter High Mark
Kilnsey
Nook
Burrows Pasture
Brown Hill Plain
Malham Tarn
Conistone
Downs Pasture
Blea Beck
Ashfold Side Beck
Capon Hall
Kilnsey Park
Outgang Hill
Gate Up Gill
Spiggot Hill
Great Close Scar
Green Haw Hill
Chapel Ho
Bare Ho
416
Wig Stones Allotments
High Stony Bank
Mastiles Gate
Holgates Kilnsey Moor
River Wharfe
Wharfedale
Malham Tarn
Thompson Hole Ridge
Hebden Moor
Loss Gill Bank
Near Hardcastle
Street Gate
High Long Ridge
Malham Moor
Grass Wood
Bastow Wood
Gill Allotment
Trunla Allotment
Cross Gill Moor
The Settle Loop
Low Stony Bank
Kealcup Hill
Netherside Hall School
Appletreewick Moor
Back Scar
Ewe Moor
Bordley
Spring House
High Garnshaw Ho
Backstone Edge
Grimwith Reservoir
Jack Hole Flat
North Side Moss
Lily Green
Great Scar
Malham Cove
Gordale Scar
Lee Gate
New Ho
Bark Plantn
Firth Hill Plantn
Wood Nook
Skirethorns
Grassington
Upper Wharfedale Mus
Scar Top Ho
Hartlington Pasture
Grimwith Fell
Craven Moor
Rye Loaf Hill
547
Pikedaw Hill
Field Barns
Shorkley Hill
Malham
New House Farm Malham
Bordley Hall
Bordley Beck
Lower Height
Grysedale Ho
Bow Br
Scar Side Ho
Garnshaw Ho
Edge Ho
Nussey House Fm
Keld Houses
Kirkby Fell
Park Ho
Threshfield
Visitor Centre
River Dibb
Dibbles Br
Fancarl Ho
Stump Cross Caverns
Scosthrop High Moor
Longlands Barn
Malham
Aire Head
Hanlith Moor
Lane Head
Threshfield Moor
Lainger Ho
Linton
Lythe Ho
B6265
B6160
Hebden
Holes Beck Ho
Langerton Hill
Fancarl Crag
Black Hill
High Crag
Scosthrop Moor
Kirkby Beck
Brown Hill
Hetton Common
Low Bucker Ho
High Bucker Ho
Boss Moor
Ings Ho
Ranelands Fm
Loup Scar
278
Appletreewick Pasture
Raikes Fm
Parcevall Hall
High Barn
Crake Moor
Kirkby Malham
Hanlith
Calton Moor
Winterburn Moor
Swinden Quarry
Linton Moor
Thorpe
Escoe Ho
Elbolton
Kail Hill
Burnsall
Hartlington
Parcevall Hall Gdns
Eller Edge Nook
Holgate Head
High Cow Ho
Langerton Fm
Threapland
Stebden Hill
Numberstones End
Air Scar Crags
Pock Stones Moor
Way Gill
Winterburn Reservoir
Fleets
Cracoe
Skelterton Hill
Burnsall and Thorpe Fell
Appletreewick
Skyreholme
Little Simon's Seat
Great Pock Stones
Bookilber Barn
Low Scarth Barn
Airton Green
River Aire
Horse Holme Wood
506
Thorpe Fell Top
Gill Beck Head
Low Hall
Simon's Seat
485
Lord's Seat
Black Hill
Newton Moor
291
Otterburn Beck
Park Ho
Airton
Calton
In Fell
Lake Plantn
Drebley
Howgill
Gt Agill Head
Hen Stones
Hellifield Moor
Otterburn
Cowper Cote
Winterburn
Hetton
Manor Ho
Rylstone
Hall Fell
Water Crag
Simm Bottom
Hole Ho
Barden Fell
Middle Tongue
Earl Seat
449
Little Newton
Otterburn
Skeld Gate
Upper Barden Reservoir
Standard Flat
Nelly Park Wood
Mucky Path
Club Nook Fm
Lower Fell Plantn
Rocking Stone
Brown Bank Head
Holme
Asick
Agill
Brown
Rocking
A684
B6160
B6265
Yorkshire Dales National Park
7
8
9
10
11
223
214
204
205
A
B
C
D
E
F
G
H
SE
90
60

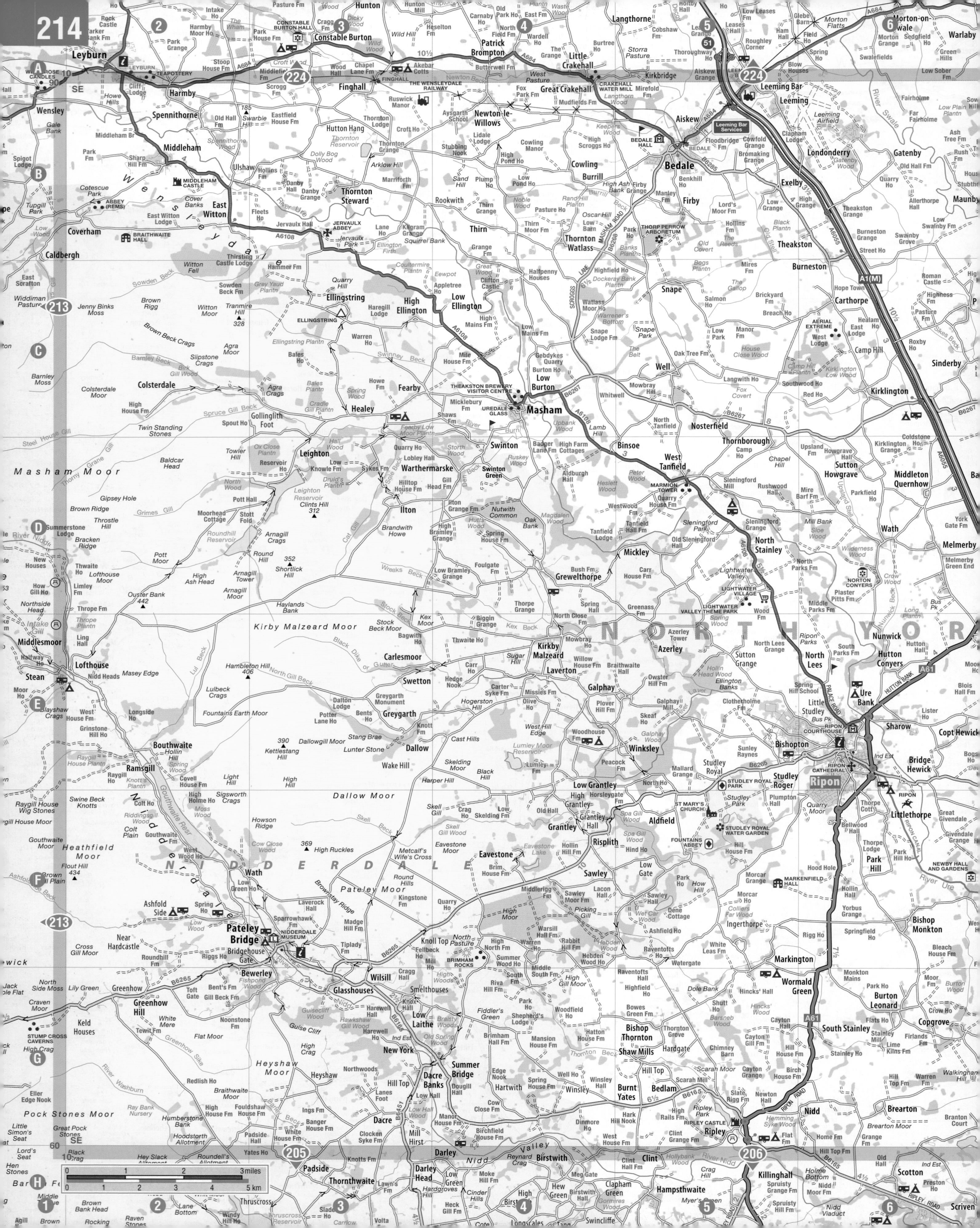
Leyburn
Harmby
Wensley
Spennithorne
Middleham
Constable Burton
Finghall
Patrick Brompton
Hunton
Langthorne
Little Crakehall
Great Crakehall
Newton-le-Willows
Leeming Bar
Leeming
Aiskew
Bedale
Morton-on-Swale
Warlaby
Londonderry
Gatenby
Exelby
Firby
Burrill
Cowling
Thornton Steward
Rookwith
Thirn
Thornton Watlass
East Witton
Coverham
Caldbergh
Jervaulx Abbey
Ellingstring
High Ellington
Low Ellington
Snape
Theakston
Burneston
Carthorpe
Masham
Fearby
Healey
Colsterdale
Leighton
Swinton
Warthermarske
Ilton
Well
Nosterfield
Thornborough
West Tanfield
Binsoe
Kirklington
Sinderby
Middleton Quernhow
Sutton Howgrave
Wath
Melmerby
North Stainley
Mickley
Grewelthorpe
Kirkby Malzeard
Laverton
Galphay
Azerley
Carlesmoor
Swetton
Greygarth
Dallow
Winksley
Nunwick
Hutton Conyers
North Lees
Ure Bank
Sharow
Copt Hewick
Bishopton
Ripon
Bridge Hewick
Littlethorpe
Studley Roger
Studley Royal
Low Grantley
High Grantley
Grantley
Risplith
Aldfield
Eavestone
Sawley
Markington
Wormald Green
Bishop Monkton
Burton Leonard
South Stainley
Copgrove
Nidd
Brearton
Ripley
Killinghall
Scotton
Scriven
Hampsthwaite
Birstwith
Clint
Darley
Darley Head
Dacre
Dacre Banks
Summer Bridge
New York
Low Laithe
Glasshouses
Wilsill
Bewerley
Pateley Bridge
Wath
Ramsgill
Bouthwaite
Lofthouse
Middlesmoor
Stean
Greenhow
Greenhow Hill
Keld Houses
Ashfold Side
Heyshaw
Thornthwaite
Padside
Bishop Thornton
Shaw Mills
Burnt Yates
Bedlam
Masham Moor
Kirby Malzeard Moor
Dallow Moor
Pateley Moor
Heathfield Moor
Heyshaw Moor
Pock Stones Moor
NIDDERDALE
NORTH YORKSHIRE
A684
A6108
A1(M)
A61
B6265
B6267
B6285
B6165
B6451
B6160
224
213
205
206
0 1 2 3 miles
0 1 2 3 4 5 km

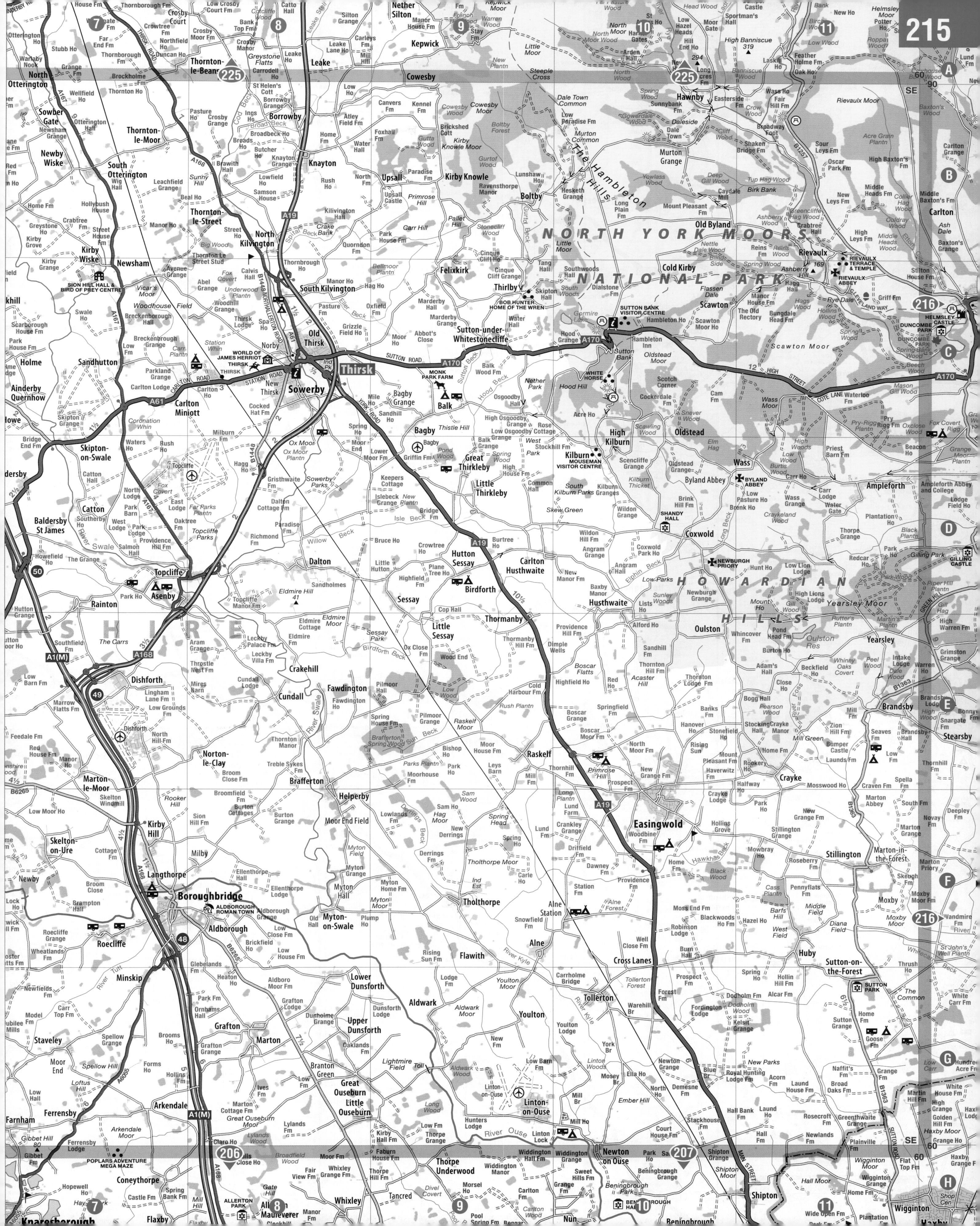
NORTH YORK MOORS
NATIONAL PARK
HOWARDIAN
HILLS
The Hambleton Hills
Thirsk
Sowerby
Old Thirsk
Thornton-le-Beans
Thornton-le-Moor
Thornton-le-Street
North Kilvington
South Kilvington
Borrowby
Knayton
Leake
Cowesby
Kepwick
Nether Silton
Upsall
Kirby Knowle
Boltby
Felixkirk
Thirlby
Sutton-under-Whitestonecliffe
Sutton Bank
Hawnby
Murton Grange
Old Byland
Cold Kirby
Rievaulx
Scawton
Carlton
Helmsley Castle
Duncombe Park
High Kilburn
Kilburn
Oldstead
Wass
Byland Abbey
Ampleforth
Coxwold
Newburgh Priory
Gilling Castle
Yearsley
Oulston
Husthwaite
Carlton Husthwaite
Hutton Sessay
Sessay
Little Sessay
Thormanby
Birdforth
Bagby
Balk
Great Thirkleby
Little Thirkleby
Dalton
Topcliffe
Asenby
Rainton
Dishforth
Cundall
Crakehill
Fawdington
Norton-le-Clay
Brafferton
Helperby
Marton-le-Moor
Kirby Hill
Skelton-on-Ure
Langthorpe
Boroughbridge
Aldborough
Roecliffe
Minskip
Myton-on-Swale
Tholthorpe
Flawith
Alne
Alne Station
Raskelf
Easingwold
Crayke
Brandsby
Stearsby
Stillington
Marton-in-the-Forest
Moxby
Huby
Sutton-on-the-Forest
Cross Lanes
Tollerton
Youlton
Aldwark
Linton-on-Ouse
Newton on Ouse
Lower Dunsforth
Upper Dunsforth
Great Ouseburn
Little Ouseburn
Branton Green
Grafton
Marton
Staveley
Arkendale
Ferrensby
Farnham
Coneythorpe
Thorpe Underwood
Whixley
Tancred
Shipton
Wigginton
Sandhutton
Carlton Miniott
Skipton-on-Swale
Catton
Baldersby St James
Newby Wiske
South Otterington
North Otterington
Sowber Gate
Kirby Wiske
Newsham
Holme
Ainderby Quernhow
Knaresborough
Helmsley
A19
A170
A168
A61
A1(M)
A167
B1448
B1363
B6265
B1257
River Swale
River Ouse
River Kyle
World of James Herriot
Sion Hill Hall & Bird of Prey Centre
Aldborough Roman Town
Poplars Adventure Mega Maze
Sutton Bank Visitor Centre
Mouseman Visitor Centre
Shandy Hall
Rievaulx Terrace & Temple
Rievaulx Abbey
Byland Abbey
Monk Park Farm
Bob Hunter Home of the Wren
White Horse
Sutton Park
Allerton Park
225
216
206
207
A B C D E F G H
7 8 9 10 11

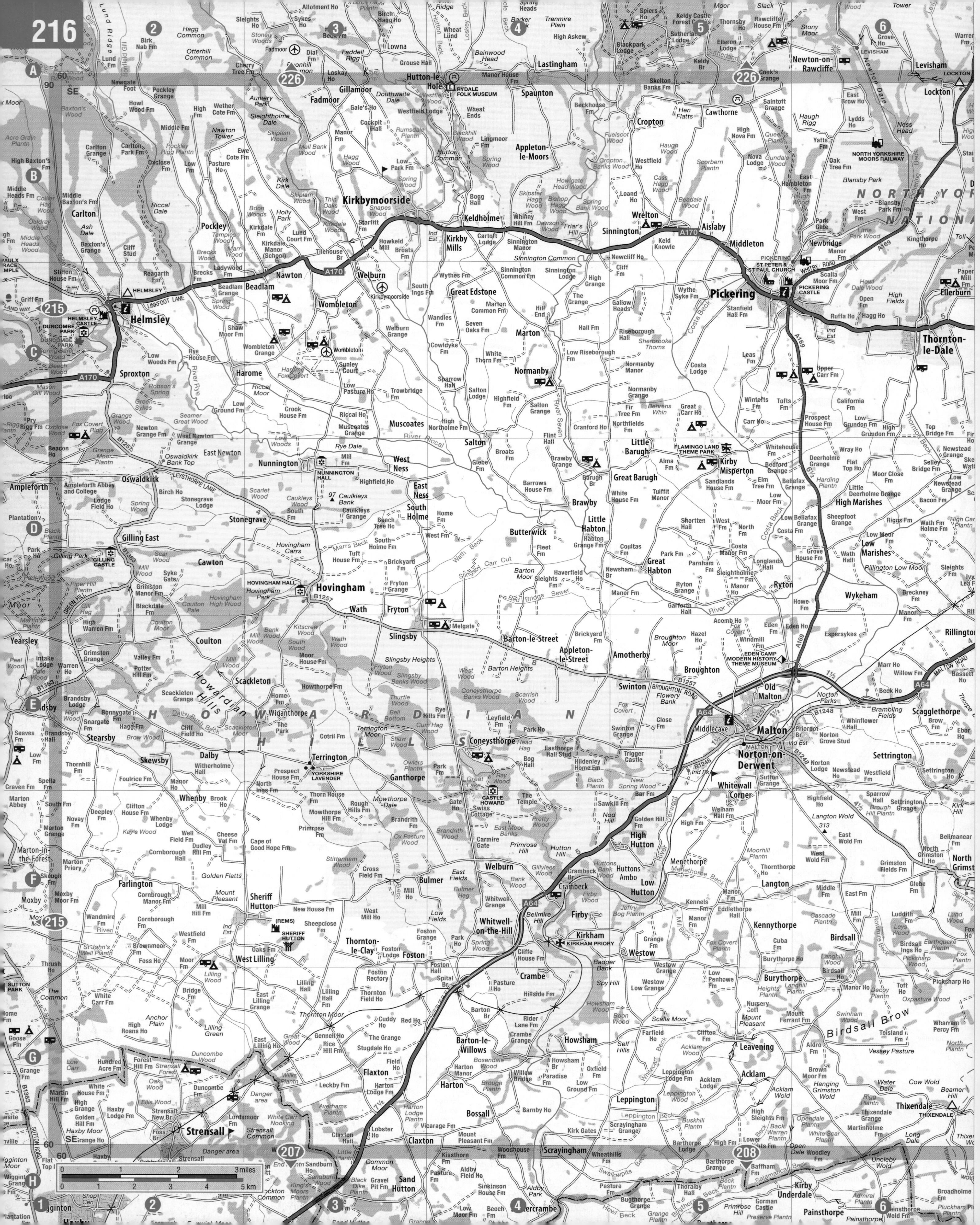
Helmsley
Kirkbymoorside
Pickering
Malton
Norton-on-Derwent
Old Malton
Hovingham
Slingsby
Terrington
Sheriff Hutton
Strensall
Flaxton
Bossall
Leppington
Acklam
Leavening
Langton
Birdsall
Settrington
Thornton-le-Dale
Lastingham
Spaunton
Cropton
Appleton-le-Moors
Sinnington
Wrelton
Aislaby
Middleton
Nawton
Beadlam
Wombleton
Welburn
Harome
Sproxton
Oswaldkirk
Ampleforth
Gilling East
Stonegrave
Nunnington
Salton
Normanby
Marton
Great Edstone
Little Barugh
Great Barugh
Kirby Misperton
Brawby
Little Habton
Great Habton
Ryton
Butterwick
Amotherby
Broughton
Swinton
Appleton-le-Street
Barton-le-Street
Coneysthorpe
Castle Howard
Whitwell-on-the-Hill
Kirkham
Westow
Crambe
Foston
Thornton-le-Clay
West Lilling
Bulmer
Welburn
Howsham
Barton-le-Willows
Harton
Claxton
Sand Hutton
Scrayingham
Kirby Underdale
Thixendale
Scagglethorpe
Rillington
Wykeham
High Marishes
Low Marishes
Coulton
Scackleton
Dalby
Skewsby
Whenby
Stearsby
Farlington
Yearsley
Cawton
Wath
Fryton
Huttons Ambo
High Hutton
Low Hutton
Menethorpe
Kennythorpe
Burythorpe
Whitewall Corner
Firby
Ganthorpe
Howardian Hills
North York Moors National Park
A170
A169
A64
B1257
B1363
B1248
Hutton-le-Hole
Rydale Folk Museum
Flamingo Land Theme Park
Eden Camp Modern History Theme Museum
Kirkham Priory
Helmsley Castle
Duncombe Park
Pickering Castle
Nunnington Hall
Hovingham Hall
Gilling Castle
Yorkshire Lavender
North Yorkshire Moors Railway
Birdsall Brow
Newton-on-Rawcliffe
Levisham
Lockton
Ellerburn
0 1 2 3 miles
0 1 2 3 4 5 km

NORTH YORK MOORS FOREST PARK
NORTH YORKSHIRE
EAST RIDING OF YORKSHIRE
The Wolds
Scarborough
Scalby
Newby
Scalby Ness Rocks
SEA LIFE CENTRE
Peasholm Park
Castle Cliff
SCARBOROUGH CASTLE
ROTUNDA MUSEUM
TOY MUS
Old & East Harbours
South Bay
South Sands
Black Rocks
White Nab
Cornelian Bay
Frank Cliff
Osgodby Pt
Cayton Cliff
Cayton Bay
Tenants' Cliff
Yons Nab
Lebberston Cliff
Gristhorpe Cliff
Cunstone Nab
The Wyke
Filey
Newbiggin
Barrowcliff
Throxenby
Falsgrave
McCAIN STADIUM
Falsgrave Moor Fm
Osgodby
Eastfield
Crossgates
Seamer
Irton
East Ayton
West Ayton
THE HONEY FARM
Cayton
LITTLE HOPPERS ADVENTURE WORLD
PLAYDALE FARM PARK
Lebberston
Gristhorpe
Muston
Hunmanby
Royal Oak
Reighton
Flixton
Folkton
Staxton
Willerby
Ganton
Potter Brompton
Sherburn
East Heslerton
West Heslerton
East Knapton
West Knapton
Scampton
SCAMPSTON HALL
WOLDS WAY LAVENDER
Yedingham
Wykeham
Hutton Buscel
Ruston
Brompton
Brompton-by-Sawdon
WORDSWORTH GALLERY
Snainton
Ebberston
EBBERSTON HALL
Allerston
Wilton
Sawdon
Hackness
Suffield
Everley
Langdale End
Broxa
Wrench Green
FORGE VALLEY WOODLANDS
Wykeham Forest
Dalby Forest
Thorpe Bassett
Wintringham
Place Newton
Settrington Beacon 651
Foxholes
Fordon
Wold Newton
Burton Fleming
Thwing
Octon
Octon Cross Roads
Langtoft
Butterwick
Weaverthorpe
Helperthorpe
East Lutton
West Lutton
Kirby Grindalythe
Duggleby
Wharram le Street
Wharram Percy
WHARRAM PERCY CHURCH & DESERTED MEDIEVAL VILLAGE
Sledmere
SLEDMERE HOUSE
Cottam
Kilham
Rudston
Thornholme
BURTON AGNES HALL
BURTON AGNES MANOR HOUSE
Burton Agnes
Harpham
Lowthorpe
Ruston Parva
Nafferton
Driffield
Little Driffield
Elmswell
Garton-on-the-Wolds
Wetwang
Fimber
Fridaythorpe
Towthorpe
Sir Tatton Sykes' Monument
Great Kendale
Great Kelk
Little Kelk
A170
A171
A165
A64
A1039
A166
A614
B1253
B1248
B1249
B1251
B1252
B1258
B1261
B1415
B1427
SCARBOROUGH ROAD
DRIFFIELD ROAD
SPITAL ROAD
HIGH STREET
MAIN STREET
GARTON SLACK
YORKSHIRE WOLDS WAY
CLEVELAND WAY
227
218
208
209
7
8
9
10
11
A
B
C
D
E
F
G
H
TA

NORTH SEA
FILEY BAY
BRIDLINGTON BAY
EAST RIDING OF YORKSHIRE
Yons Nab
Lebberston Cliff
217
Cunstone Nab
The Wyke
Gristhorpe Cliff
Cliff Fm
Club Pt
WOLDS WAY
Newbiggin
North Cliff
Gristhorpe
Filey Field
Filey Brigg
Brigg End
Filey Sands
Carr Ho
Filey
Beacon Hill
A1039
A165
MUSTON ROAD
Muston
Muston Grange
Muston Sands
Lowfield Fm
Royal Oak
Hunmanby Sands
Pilmoor Fm
Primrose Valley
Foxhill Fm
MOOR ROAD
Airy Hill Fm
Hunmanby Moor
Hunmanby Gap
Ind Est
HUNMANBY
Hill Fm
Rosedale Fm
Moor Fm
Reighton Sands
Graffitoe Fm
Moor Ho
Reighton Gap
Barf Fm
Moor Fm
Speeton Sands
Howe Fm
Vicarage Fm
HUNMANBY ROAD
Reighton
Speeton Hills
Speeton Cliffs
Dale Fm
Speeton
Buckton Cliffs
Reighton Field
Speeton Grange
Speeton Moor
SPEETON GATE
Buckton Hall
BEMPTON CLIFFS
RSPB
Bempton Cliffs
Scale Nab
Standard Hill
Wandale Fm
Cat Nab
Bempton Grange
Gull Nook
Hill Fm
Bartindale Fm
Speeton
Field Greenlands Fm
Buckton
Dykes Plantn
Thornwick Bay
Wasters Plantn
High Huntow Fm
Bempton
DANE'S DYKE
North Cliff
Burton Fleming
Grindale Field
North Dale
B1229
FLAMBOROUGH ROAD
North Landing
BEMPTON
Cradle Head
Maidensgrave Fm
Newsham Field
Butterwicks Fm
BEMPTON LANE
North Moor
Stottle Bank Nook
Grindale
East Leys Fm
High Barn
B1255
NORTH MARINE ROAD
Flatmere Plantn
Selwicks Bay
Flamborough Head
Finley Hill
Fox Covert Plantn
SCARBOROUGH ROAD
North Mount
Lynhams
The Crofts
LIGHTHOUSE ROAD
B1259
FLAMBOROUGH HEAD LIGHTHOUSE
Charlestone Fm
Field Ho
FLAMBOROUGH ROAD
Old Fall Plantn
High Stacks
Flamborough
Beacon Fm
Highcliffe Manor
Danes Dyke Fm
Beacon Hill
North Wood
High Easton Fm
Ind Est
MARTON GATE
Sewerby
SEWERBY HALL & GARDEN
South Landing
Springdale Fm
Binsdale Fm
East Crags Wood
Boynton
Eastfield Fm
MARTON ROAD
Sewerby Rocks
BONDSVILLE MODEL VILLAGE
B1253
PRIORY
Rudston
Thorpe Hall
West Lawn Wood
Fish Ponds Wood
Wandale Fm
BAYLE MUS
Old Town
North Sands
Carr Plantn
BRIDLINGTON
Bridlington
Sands Wood
Temple Fm
Carnaby Temple
High Wood
West Hill
The Spa
OLD PENNY MEMORIES
South Side Mount
Hallowkilm Wood
Ind Est
Wold Gate
Tufthill Fm
Bessingby
Hilderthorpe
Carnaby
KINGSGATE
P&R
Haisthorpe Field
Thornholme Field
Haisthorpe
A614
Wilsthorpe
South Sands
Burton Agnes Field
Thornholme
PARK ROSE BIRD OF PREY CENTRE
Ind Est
Carnaby Moor
BURTON AGNES HALL
Brackendale Fm
BURTON AGNES MANOR HOUSE
Harpham Grange
Burton Agnes
Oak Wood Fm
Auburn Fm
Hords Covert
Burton Agnes Stud Fm
A165
Fraisthorpe Sands
Harpham
Burtoncarr Ho
Demming Fm
Fraisthorpe
Thornholme Moor
Gransmoor Wood
Little Kelk Fm
Low Stonehills
Turtle Hill Fm
Woodside Fm
Hamiltonhill Fm
High Stonehills
BRIDLINGTON ROAD
Gransmoor Low Ho
Gransmoor Lodge
209
Barmston Sands
Barmston
Barmston Main Drain
Great Kelk
Park Ho
Lissett
Allison Lane End
Ulrome Grange
Ulrome Sands
TA
0 1 2 3 miles
0 1 2 3 4 5 km

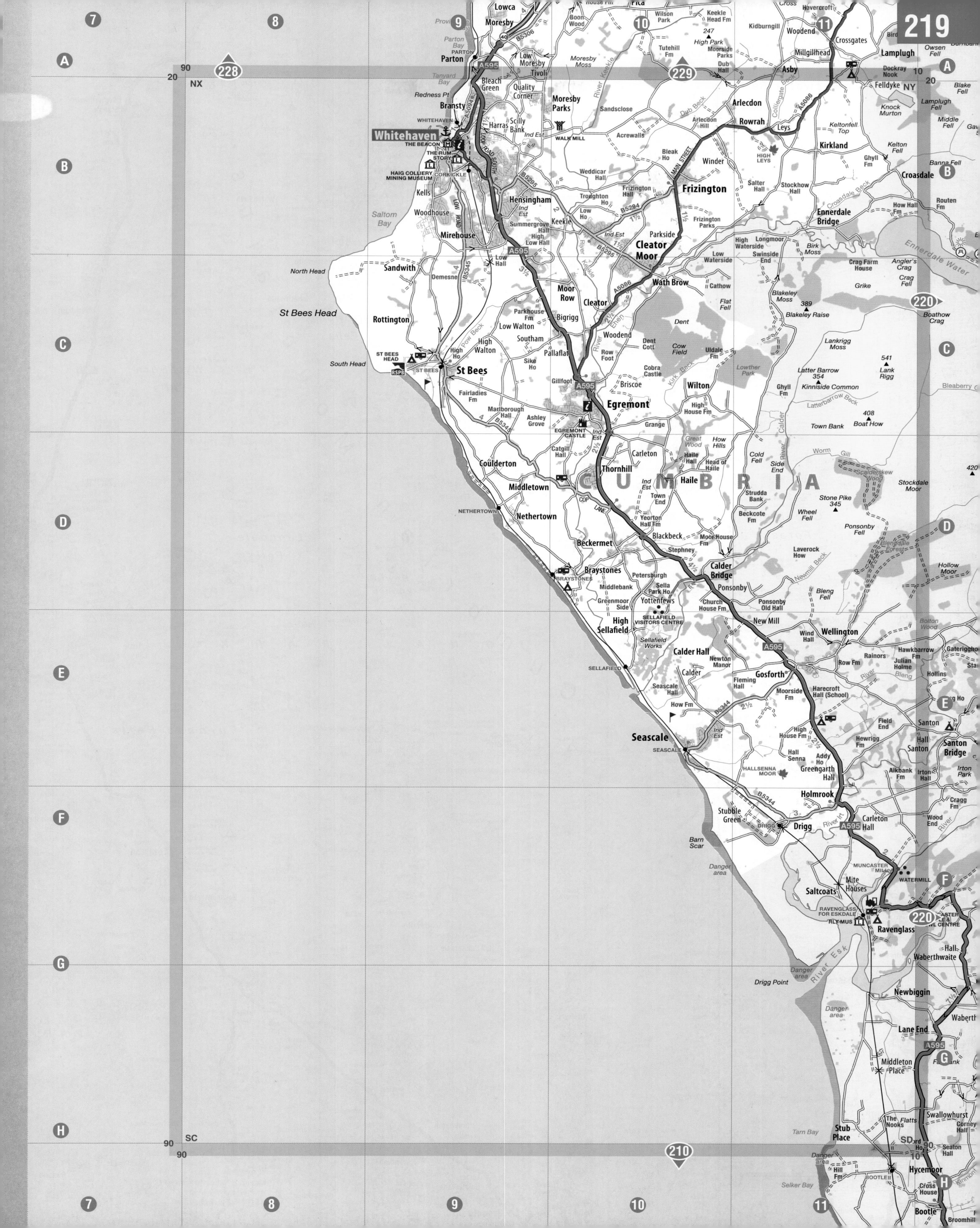

Lowca
Moresby
Parton
Bleach Green
Low Moresby
Tivoli
Quality Corner
Moresby Parks
Moresby Moss
Bransty
Redness Pt
Tanyard Bay
Parton Bay
WHITEHAVEN
Whitehaven
THE BEACON
THE RUM STORY
HAIG COLLIERY MINING MUSEUM
CORKICKLE
Harras
Scilly Bank
Ind Est
WALK MILL
Kells
Woodhouse
Mirehouse
Saltom Bay
Hensingham
Summergrove Hall
High Low Hall
Low Hall
Keekle
Troughton Ho
Low Ho
Weddicar Hall
Frizington Hall
Frizington
Frizington Parks
Sandsclose
Acrewalls
Bleak Ho
Winder
Salter Hall
Arlecdon
Arlecdon Hill
Rowrah
Leys
HIGH LEYS
Kirkland
Keltonfell Top
Kelton Fell
Knock Murton
Lamplugh
Lamplugh Fell
Felldyke
Dockray Nook
Owsen Fell
Blake Fell
Middle Fell
Banna Fell
Ghyll Fm
Croasdale
Stockhow Hall
Ennerdale Bridge
How Hall Fm
Routen Fm
Ennerdale Water
Asby
Millgillhead
Crossgates
Woodend
Kidburngill
Wilson Park
Keekle Head Fm
Tutehill Fm
High Park
Moorside Parks
Dub Hall
Havercroft
Boon Wood
Cleator Moor
Parkside
Ind Est
Cleator
Wath Brow
Cathow
Moor Row
Bigrigg
Woodend
Dent Cott
Row Foot
Cobra Castle
Briscoe
Gillfoot
Egremont
Grange
Wilton
High House Fm
Dent
Cow Field
Uldale Fm
Flat Fell
Lowther Park
High Waterside
Low Waterside
Longmoor
Swinside End
Blakeley Moss
389
Blakeley Raise
Birk Moss
Crag Farm House
Angler's Crag
Crag Fell
Grike
Boathow Crag
Lankrigg Moss
541
Lank Rigg
Latter Barrow
354
Kinniside Common
Latterbarrow Beck
Ghyll Fm
Bleaberry
408
Boat How
Town Bank
Worm Gill
Cold Fell
Side End
Scalderskew Wood
Stockdale Moor
420
Stone Pike
345
Wheel Fell
Ponsonby Fell
North Head
Sandwith
Demesne
St Bees Head
Rottington
South Head
ST BEES HEAD
RSPB
ST BEES
St Bees
High Ho
High Walton
Parkhouse Fm
Low Walton
Southam
Sike Ho
Pallaflat
Fairladies Fm
Marlborough Hall
Ashley Grove
EGREMONT CASTLE
Catgill Hall
Carleton
Great Wood
How Hills
Haile Hall
Head of Haile
Haile
Thornhill
Ind Est
Town End
Coulderton
Middletown
CUMBRIA
NETHERTOWN
Nethertown
Yeorton Hall Fm
COP LANE
Strudda Bank
Beckcote Fm
Blackbeck
Moor House Fm
Stephney
Beckermet
Braystones
BRAYSTONES
Calder Bridge
Ponsonby
Petersburgh
Sella Park Ho
Middlebank
Greenmoor Side
Yottenfews
SELLAFIELD VISITORS CENTRE
High Sellafield
Sellafield Works
Church House Fm
Ponsonby Old Hall
Laverock How
Newmill Beck
Bleng Fell
Hollow Moor
New Mill
Wind Hall
Wellington
Bolton Wood
Calder Hall
Newton Manor
Calder
Row Fm
Rainors
Hawkbarrow Fm
Julian Holme
Gateriggho
Hollins
River Bleng
SELLAFIELD
Seascale Hall
Fleming Hall
Gosforth
Harecroft Hall (School)
Moorside Fm
How Fm
Ind Est
Seascale
SEASCALE
High House Fm
Field End
Hewrigg Fm
Santon
Hall Santon
Santon Bridge
Hall Senna
Addy Ho
Greengarth Hall
HALLSENNA MOOR
Aikbank Fm
Irton Hall
Irton Park
Cragg Fm
Holmrook
Stubble Green
DRIGG
Drigg
River Irt
Carleton Hall
Wood End
Barn Scar
Danger area
MUNCASTER MILL
WATERMILL
Mite Houses
Saltcoats
RAVENGLASS FOR ESKDALE
RLY MUS
Ravenglass
Hall
Waberthwaite
Danger area
River Esk
Drigg Point
Newbiggin
Danger area
Lane End
Middleton Place
Stub Place
The Nooks
Flatts
Swallowhurst
Corney Hall
Seaton Hall
Ford Ho
Tarn Bay
Danger area
Hill Fm
BOOTLE
Hycemoor
Selker Bay
Cross House
Bootle
Broomhill
A595
A5094
A5086
B5306
B5295
B5294
B5345
B5344
228
229
220
210
NX
NY
SC
SD
A
B
C
D
E
F
G
H
7
8
9
10
11
20
90

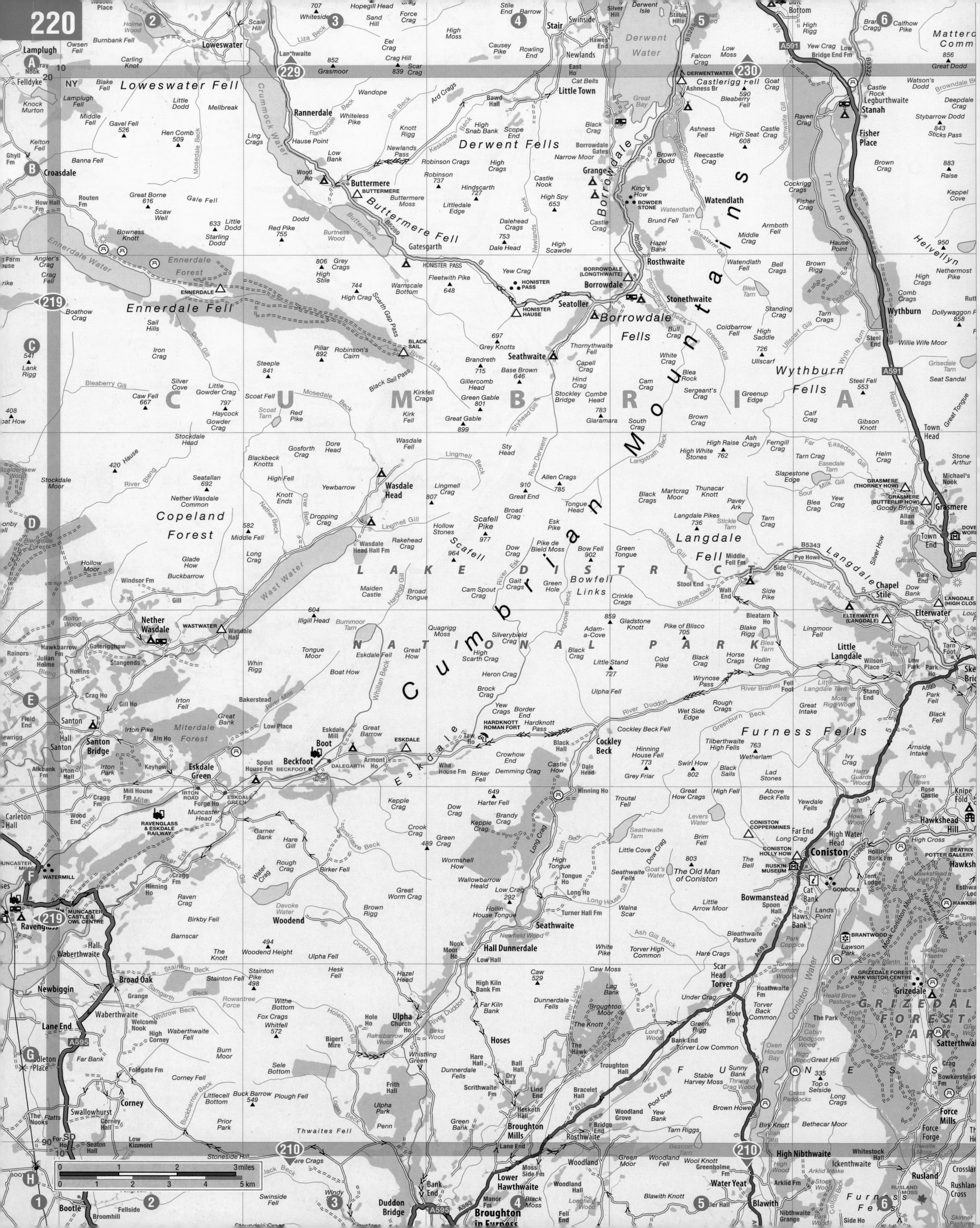
Lamplugh
Loweswater
Loweswater Fell
Crummock Water
Lanthwaite
Grasmoor
Rannerdale
Hause Point
Whiteless Pike
Derwent Fells
Derwent Water
Derwentwater
Stair
Swinside
Newlands
Little Town
Castlerigg Fell
Stanah
Fisher Place
Thirlmere
Helvellyn
Croasdale
Gale Fell
Great Borne
Red Pike
Buttermere
Buttermere Fell
Gatesgarth
Honister Pass
Grange
Bowder Stone
Borrowdale
Watendlath
Rosthwaite
Stonethwaite
Seatoller
Ennerdale Water
Ennerdale Forest
Ennerdale Fell
Ennerdale
Black Sail
Pillar
Great Gable
Seathwaite
Borrowdale Fells
Wythburn
Wythburn Fells
Cumbria
Cumbrian Mountains
Grasmere
Wasdale Head
Scafell Pike
Scafell
Great End
Glaramara
Langdale Fell
Langdale Pikes
Chapel Stile
Elterwater
Copeland Forest
Lake District National Park
West Water
Nether Wasdale
Wastwater
Bowfell
Crinkle Crags
Pike of Blisco
Little Langdale
Hardknott Pass
Hardknott Roman Fort
Wrynose Pass
Cockley Beck
Furness Fells
Santon Bridge
Miterdale Forest
Eskdale Green
Eskdale
Boot
Beckfoot
Dalegarth
Muncaster Castle & Owl Centre
Ravenglass
Ravenglass & Eskdale Railway
Coniston
The Old Man of Coniston
Coniston Water
Hawkshead
Grizedale Forest Park
Grizedale
Torver
Seathwaite
Hall Dunnerdale
Ulpha
Woodend
Broad Oak
Waberthwaite
Newbiggin
Lane End
Corney
Swallowhurst
Broughton Mills
Broughton in Furness
Lower Hawthwaite
Duddon Bridge
Bootle
Water Yeat
Blawith
Rusland
Satterthwaite
Force Mills
High Nibthwaite
A591
A593
A595
B5289
B5343
219
229
230
210
0 1 2 3 miles
0 1 2 3 4 5 km

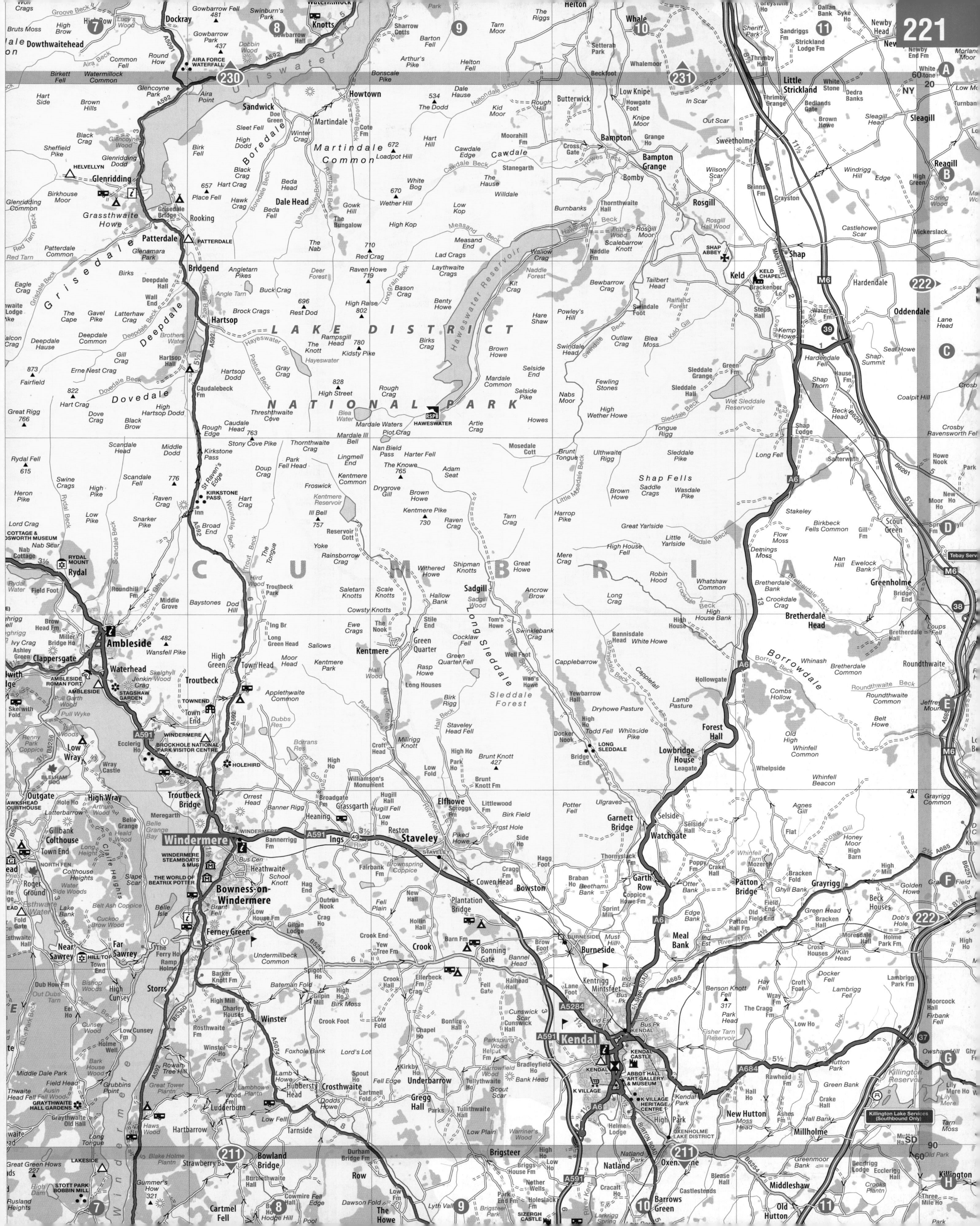
LAKE DISTRICT NATIONAL PARK
CUMBRIA
Ullswater
Haweswater Reservoir
Windermere
Shap Fells
Martindale Common
Boredale
Grisedale
Deepdale
Dovedale
Borrowdale
Long Sleddale
Sleddale Forest
Glenridding
Patterdale
Hartsop
Dockray
Howtown
Sandwick
Bampton
Bampton Grange
Shap
Keld
Rosgill
Little Strickland
Sleagill
Reagill
Oddendale
Greenholme
Ambleside
Rydal
Troutbeck
Windermere
Bowness-on-Windermere
Ings
Staveley
Kentmere
Sadgill
Burneside
Kendal
Crook
Crosthwaite
Underbarrow
Natland
Oxenholme
Grayrigg
Patton Bridge
Selside
Watchgate
Garnett Bridge
Forest Hall
Lowbridge House
Meal Bank
New Hutton
Millholme
Middleshaw
Hawkshead
Near Sawrey
Far Sawrey
Storrs
Winster
Ludderburn
Bowland Bridge
Cartmel Fell
Brigsteer
Barrows Green
Old Hutton
Killington
Tebay Services
Killington Lake Services (Southbound Only)
HAWESWATER
SHAP ABBEY
KIRKSTONE PASS
BROCKHOLE NATIONAL PARK VISITOR CENTRE
HOLEHIRD
WINDERMERE STEAMBOATS & MUSEUM
THE WORLD OF BEATRIX POTTER
STAGSHAW GARDEN
AMBLESIDE ROMAN FORT
RYDAL MOUNT
AIRA FORCE WATERFALL
KENDAL CASTLE
ABBOT HALL ART GALLERY & MUSEUM
K VILLAGE HERITAGE CENTRE
OXENHOLME LAKE DISTRICT
STOTT PARK BOBBIN MILL
LAKESIDE
GRAYTHWAITE HALL GARDENS
HILL TOP
SIZERGH CASTLE
M6
A6
A591
A592
A684
A685
B6261
230
231
222
211
7
8
9
10
11

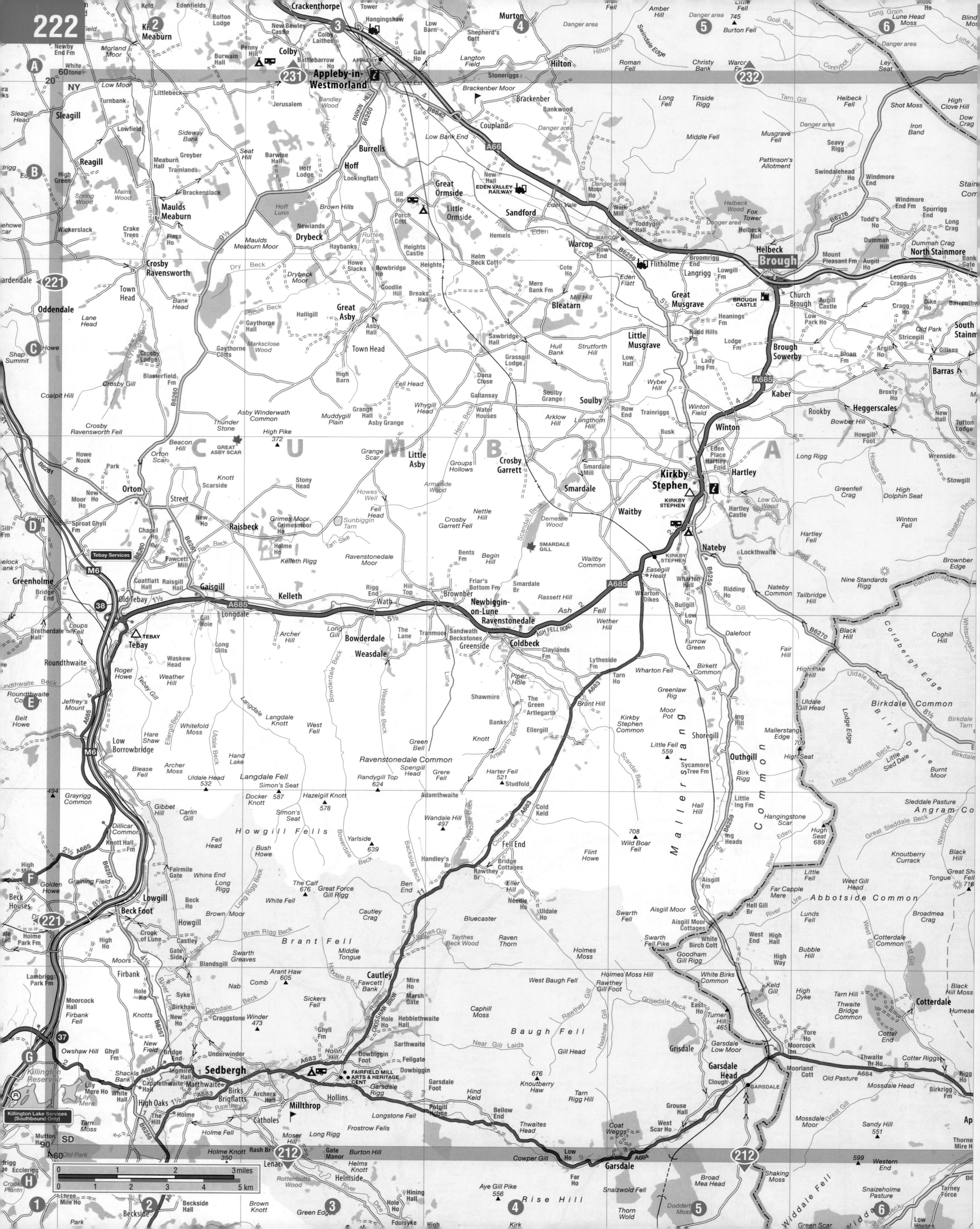
Crackenthorpe
Murton
Meaburn
Colby
Appleby-in-Westmorland
Hilton
Battlebarrow
Brackenber Moor
Brackenber
Coupland
Sleagill
Reagill
Burrells
Hoff
Great Ormside
Little Ormside
Sandford
EDEN VALLEY RAILWAY
Maulds Meaburn
Maulds Meaburn Moor
Drybeck
Warcop
Helbeck
North Stainmore
Brough
Church Brough
BROUGH CASTLE
Flitholme
Crosby Ravensworth
Oddendale
Great Asby
Bleatarn
Great Musgrave
Little Musgrave
Brough Sowerby
Barras
Kaber
Soulby
Winton
Heggerscales
Asby Winderwath Common
High Pike 372
GREAT ASBY SCAR
C U M B R I A
Little Asby
Crosby Garrett
Smardale
Kirkby Stephen
Hartley
Orton
Raisbeck
Waitby
Nateby
SMARDALE GILL
Tebay Services
M6
Greenholme
Gaisgill
Kelleth
Old Tebay
Newbiggin-on-Lune
Ravenstonedale
Tebay
A685
Coldbeck
Bowderdale
Weasdale
ASH FELL ROAD
Ravenstonedale Common
Langdale Fell
Howgill Fells
Mallerstang
Outhgill
Birkdale Common
Abbotside Common
Brant Fell
Cautley
Baugh Fell
Grisdale
Garsdale Head
Cotterdale
Lowgill
Beck Foot
Howgill
Sedbergh
Millthrop
Garsdale
FAIRFIELD MILL ARTS & HERITAGE CENT
Killington Reservoir
Killington Lake Services (Southbound Only)
Rise Hill
A684
A683
B6259
B6260
231
232
221
212
NY
SD
0 1 2 3 miles
0 1 2 3 4 5 km

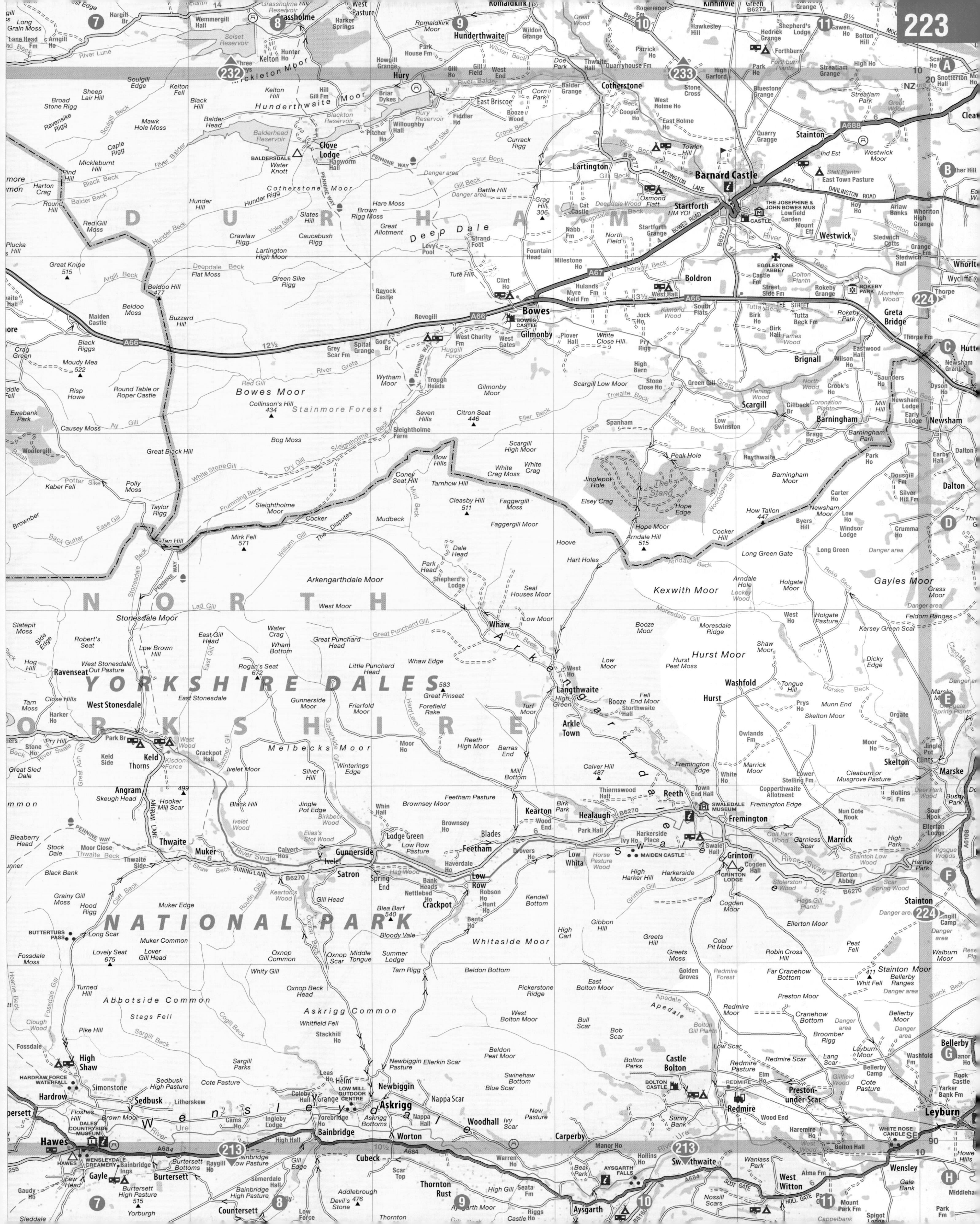

DURHAM
NORTH
YORKSHIRE
YORKSHIRE DALES
NATIONAL PARK
Barnard Castle
Startforth
Bowes
Gilmonby
Lartington
Cotherstone
Boldron
Greta Bridge
Brignall
Scargill
Barningham
Newsham
Dalton
Stainton
Westwick
Hunderthwaite
Grassholme
Romaldkirk
Hury
Clove Lodge
Baldersdale
Bowes Moor
Stainmore Forest
Deep Dale
Arkengarthdale Moor
Whaw
Langthwaite
Arkle Town
Reeth
Fremington
Healaugh
Grinton
Marrick
Marske
Skelton
Hurst
Washfold
Kexwith Moor
Hurst Moor
Gayles Moor
Keld
Thorns
Angram
Thwaite
Muker
Gunnerside
Ivelet
Satron
Feetham
Kearton
Low Row
Crackpot
Melbecks Moor
Whitaside Moor
West Stonesdale
Ravenseat
Stonesdale Moor
Abbotside Common
Askrigg Common
High Shaw
Hardrow
Simonstone
Sedbusk
Hawes
Gayle
Burtersett
Askrigg
Bainbridge
Worton
Newbiggin
Woodhall
Carperby
Castle Bolton
Redmire
Preston-under-Scar
Leyburn
Wensley
West Witton
Swinithwaite
Aysgarth
Countersett
Thornton Rust
Wensleydale
Arkengarthdale
Swaledale
Tan Hill
A66
A67
A684
A688
B6270
B6277
PENNINE WAY

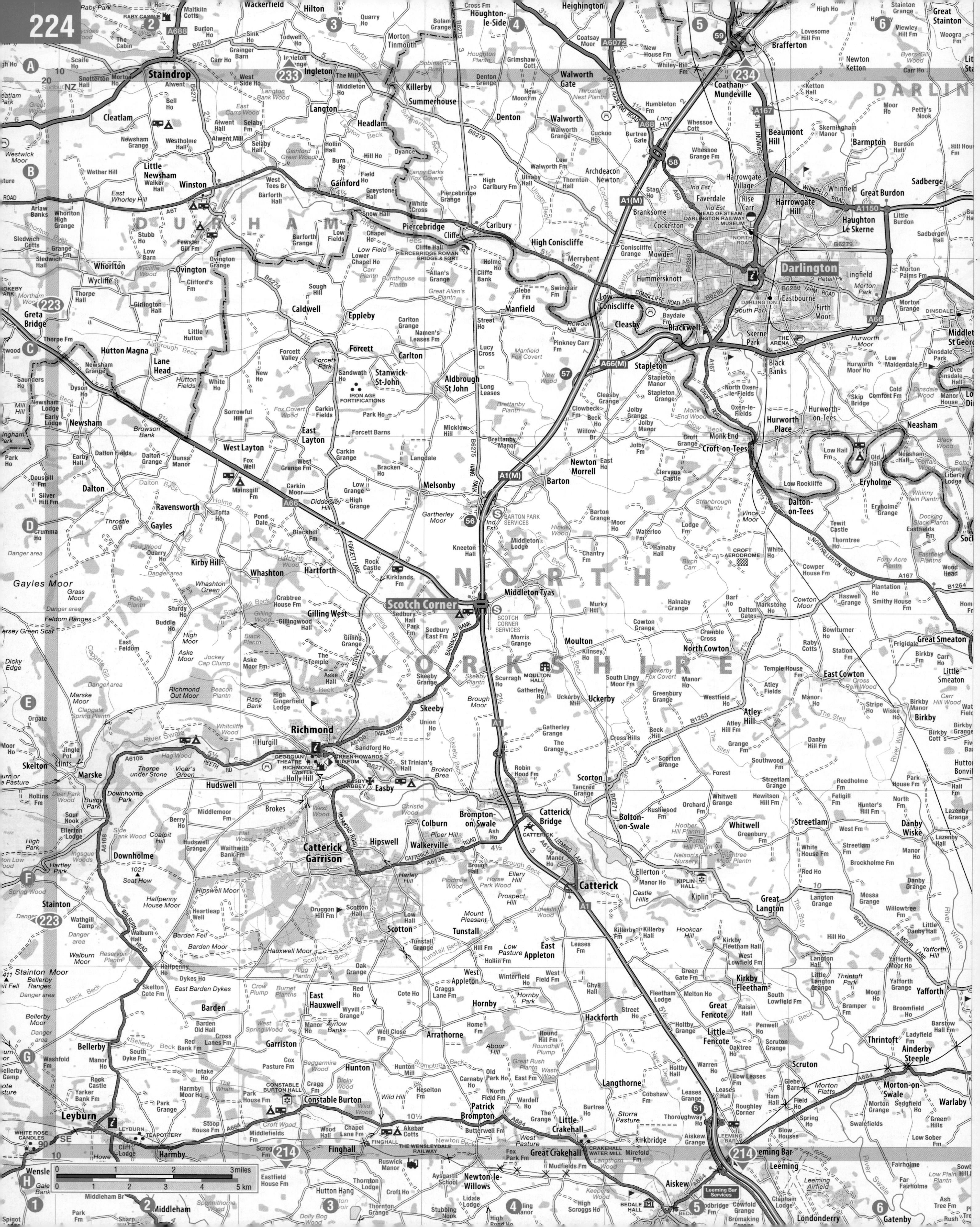
Raby Park
Staindrop
Wackerfield
Hilton
Houghton-le-Side
Heighington
Ingleton
Killerby
Summerhouse
Denton
Walworth
Walworth Gate
Coatham Mundeville
Brafferton
DARLIN
Cleatlam
Langton
Headlam
Beaumont Hill
Barmpton
Little Newsham
Winston
Gainford
Archdeacon Newton
Harrowgate Village
Harrowgate Hill
Whinfield
Great Burdon
Sadberge
D U R H A M
Piercebridge
Carlbury
High Coniscliffe
Merrybent
Faverdale
Branksome
Cockerton
Mowden
Hummersknott
Darlington
Haughton Le Skerne
Lingfield
Eastbourne
Firth Moor
Whorlton
Ovington
Wycliffe
Greta Bridge
Caldwell
Eppleby
Manfield
Low Coniscliffe
Cleasby
Blackwell
Skerne Park
Hutton Magna
Lane Head
Forcett
Carlton
Stanwick-St-John
Aldbrough St John
Stapleton
Black Banks
Hurworth Place
Hurworth-on-Tees
Neasham
Newsham
East Layton
West Layton
Melsonby
Barton
Newton Morrell
Croft-on-Tees
Eryholme
Dalton-on-Tees
Dalton
Ravensworth
Gayles
Kirby Hill
Whashton
Hartforth
N O R T H
Middleton Tyas
Scotch Corner
Gayles Moor
Gilling West
Moulton
North Cowton
Great Smeaton
Y O R K S H I R E
East Cowton
Skeeby
Uckerby
Atley Hill
Birkby
Richmond
Marske
Skelton
Hudswell
Easby
Scorton
Brompton-on-Swale
Catterick Bridge
Bolton-on-Swale
Whitwell
Streetlam
Danby Wiske
Colburn
Hipswell
Walkerville
Catterick Garrison
Downholme
Catterick
Kiplin
Great Langton
Stainton
Scotton
Tunstall
East Appleton
Barden
East Hauxwell
West Appleton
Hornby
Kirkby Fleetham
Great Fencote
Yafforth
Hackforth
Little Fencote
Garriston
Arrathorne
Bellerby
Thrintoft
Ainderby Steeple
Hunton
Langthorne
Scruton
Morton-on-Swale
Constable Burton
Patrick Brompton
Little Crakehall
Warlaby
Leyburn
Harmby
Finghall
Great Crakehall
Leeming Bar
Leeming
Newton-le-Willows
Aiskew
Wensley
Middleham
Hutton Hang
Londonderry
Gatenby
1
2
3
4
5
6
A
B
C
D
E
F
G
H
0
1
2
3 miles
0
1
2
3
4
5 km

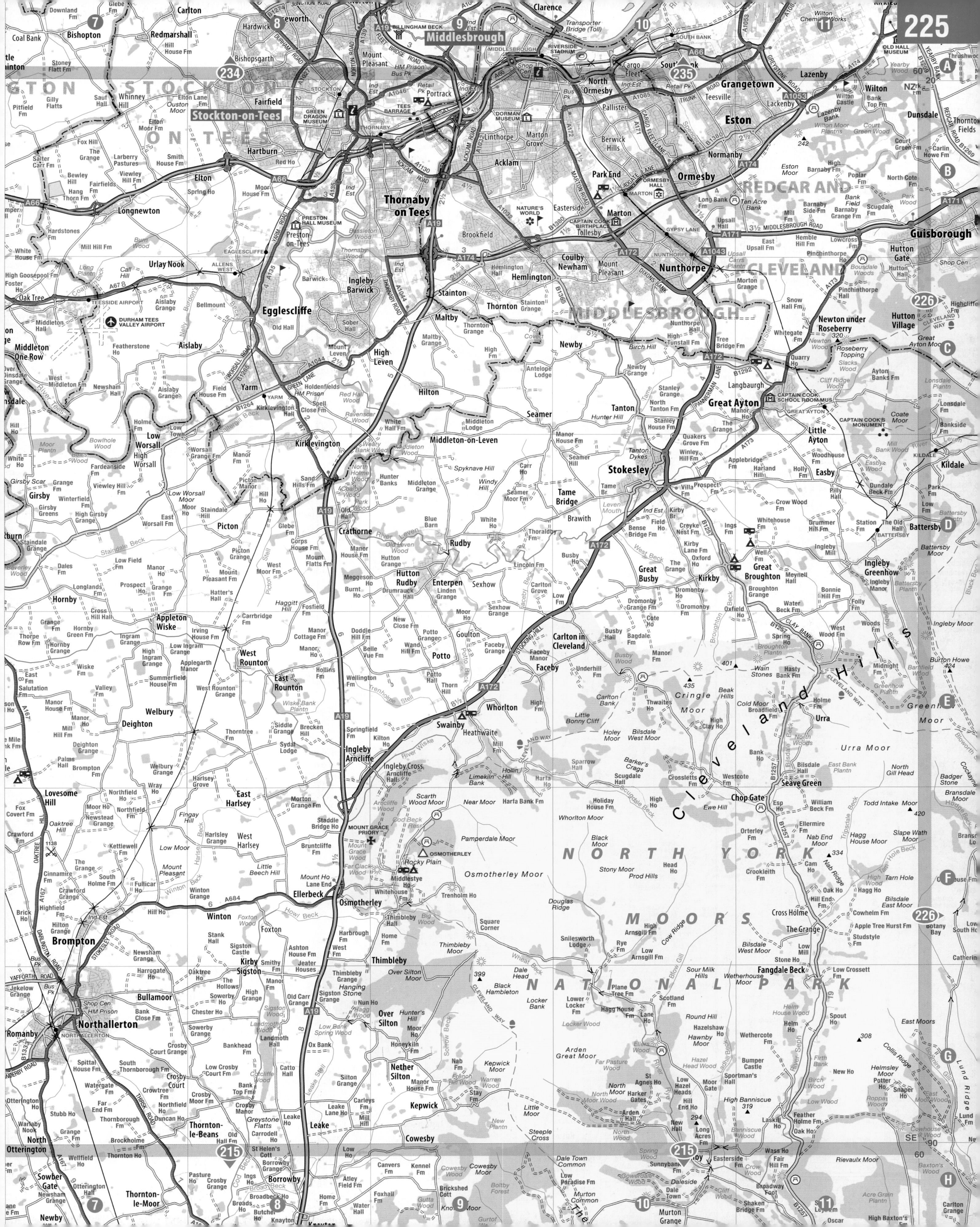
Middlesbrough
Stockton-on-Tees
STOCKTON ON TEES
Thornaby on Tees
Billingham Beck
Transporter Bridge (Toll)
Riverside Stadium
Clarence
Hardwick
Bishopsgarth
Bishopton
Redmarshall
Carlton
Coal Bank
Fairfield
Hartburn
Elton
Longnewton
Preston Hall Museum
Preston-on-Tees
Eaglescliffe
Urlay Nook
Teesside Airport
Durham Tees Valley Airport
Egglescliffe
Aislaby
Middleton One Row
Yarm
Kirklevington
Low Worsall
High Worsall
Girsby
Picton
Hornby
Appleton Wiske
West Rounton
East Rounton
Welbury
Deighton
Lovesome Hill
East Harlsey
West Harlsey
Brompton
Northallerton
Romanby
Bullamoor
Thornton-le-Beans
North Otterington
Thornton-le-Moor
Newby
Ingleby Barwick
Stainton
Maltby
Thornton
Hemlington
Coulby Newham
Acklam
Linthorpe
Marton
Nunthorpe
Ormesby
Eston
Normanby
Grangetown
South Bank
North Ormesby
Lazenby
Wilton
Dunsdale
Guisborough
Hutton Gate
REDCAR AND CLEVELAND
MIDDLESBROUGH
Newton under Roseberry
Roseberry Topping
Hutton Village
High Leven
Hilton
Middleton-on-Leven
Crathorne
Rudby
Hutton Rudby
Enterpen
Sexhow
Seamer
Newby
Tanton
Stokesley
Great Ayton
Little Ayton
Langbaurgh
Kildale
Easby
Battersby
Tame Bridge
Great Busby
Kirkby
Great Broughton
Ingleby Greenhow
Carlton in Cleveland
Faceby
Potto
Goulton
Whorlton
Swainby
Ingleby Arncliffe
Cleveland Hills
Cringle Moor
Urra Moor
Chop Gate
Seave Green
Mount Grace Priory
Osmotherley
Osmotherley Moor
Ellerbeck
Winton
NORTH YORK MOORS NATIONAL PARK
Kirby Sigston
Thimbleby
Over Silton
Nether Silton
Kepwick
Leake
Cowesby
Borrowby
Black Hambleton
Fangdale Beck
Bilsdale
Hawnby
Arden Great Moor
Rievaulx Moor
Cleveland Way
A19
A172
A173
A174
A171
A66
A67
A167
A684
B1257
234
235
215
226

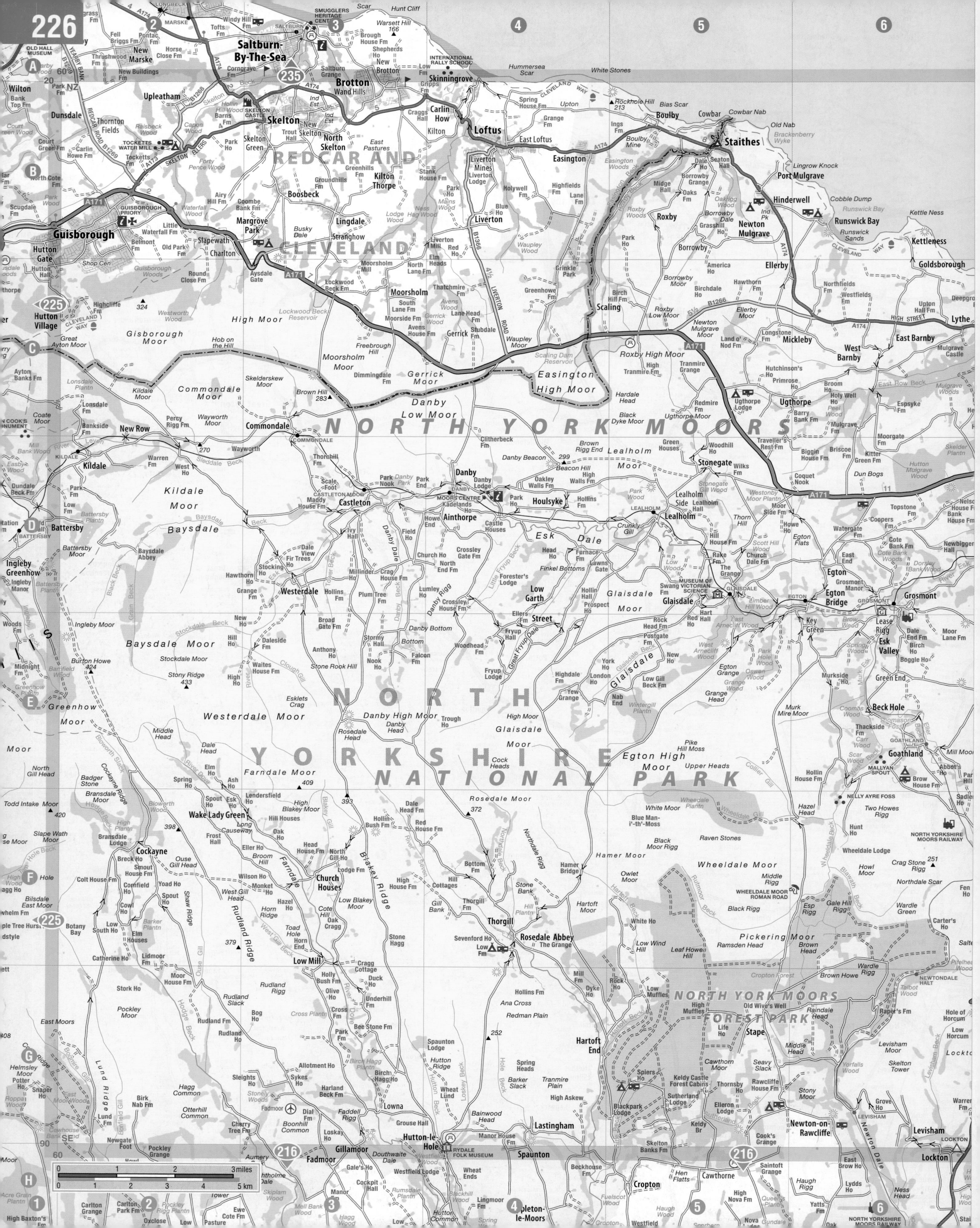
Saltburn-By-The-Sea
New Marske
Brotton
Skinningrove
Carlin How
Loftus
Staithes
Port Mulgrave
Hinderwell
Runswick Bay
Kettleness
Goldsborough
Lythe
East Barnby
Mickleby
Ellerby
Newton Mulgrave
Roxby
Easington
Skelton
Upleatham
Guisborough
Margrove Park
Lingdale
Boosbeck
Kilton Thorpe
Liverton
Moorsholm
Gerrick
Scaling
REDCAR AND CLEVELAND
NORTH YORK MOORS
NORTH YORKSHIRE NATIONAL PARK
Commondale
Kildale
Castleton
Danby
Ainthorpe
Houlsyke
Lealholm
Stonegate
Glaisdale
Egton
Egton Bridge
Grosmont
Esk Valley
Goathland
Beck Hole
Westerdale
Battersby
Ingleby Greenhow
Baysdale
Low Garth
Street
Church Houses
Cockayne
Wake Lady Green
Low Mill
Thorgill
Rosedale Abbey
Hartoft End
Stape
Lastingham
Hutton-le-Hole
Lowna
Gillamoor
Fadmoor
Spaunton
Cropton
Cawthorne
Newton-on-Rawcliffe
Levisham
Lockton
Hutton Village
Gisborough Moor
Commondale Moor
Kildale Moor
Danby High Moor
Glaisdale Moor
Egton High Moor
Westerdale Moor
Baysdale Moor
Farndale Moor
Rosedale Moor
Wheeldale Moor
Pickering Moor
Hamer Moor
NORTH YORK MOORS FOREST PARK
Easington High Moor
Roxby High Moor
Danby Low Moor
Rudland Ridge
Blakey Ridge
Farndale
Esk Dale
Glaisdale
A171
A174
B1366
B1266
B1268
B1269
A173
235
225
216
RYEDALE FOLK MUSEUM
NORTH YORKSHIRE MOORS RAILWAY
MUSEUM OF VICTORIAN SCIENCE
MOORS CENTRE
0 1 2 3 miles
0 1 2 3 4 5 km

7
8
9
10
11
A
B
C
D
E
F
G
H
OV
TA
Loop Wyke
Deepgrove Wyke
Sandsend Ness
Sandsend Wyke
Sandsend
Upgang Beach
Whitby
East Row
West Cliff
West Pier
East Pier
WHITBY ABBEY
The Scar
SALTWICK NAB
Saltwick Bay
Dunsley
Straggleton Fm
High Stakesby
WHITBY
CAPTAIN COOK MEMORIAL MUS
Black Nab
Newholm
A171
GUISBOROUGH ROAD
Airy Hill
Ind Est
Manor House Fm
Hawthorndale Fm
Selly Hill
Ruswarp
RUSWARP
Stripes Fm
Aislaby
Maw Wyke Hole
Briggswath
SLEIGHTS
Topping Riggs Wood
Stainsacre
Sneaton
Dale Fm
Low Hawsker
High Hawsker
White Stone Hole
Esk Hall
Tinkler Hall
Red Barn Wood
Rigg Mill Wood
Asp Ho
Bottom Ho
CLEVELAND WAY
Homerell Hole
Sleights
Ugglebarnby
Mortar Hall Fm
Castle Chamber
North Cheek or Ness Pt
Laund Ho
Dean Hall
Sneatonthorpe
Moor Fm
Hempsyke Hall
Knaggy House Fm
Rigg Hall
Raw
BLUE BANK
Robin Hood's Bay
ROBIN HOOD'S BAY ROAD
Haxby Plantn
White Moor Hill
Skerry Hall
Fylingthorpe
Hillside Fm
Moor House Fm
Littlebeck
Belt Plantns
Graystone Hills
Park Gate
Robin Hood's Bay
Black Brow
Intake Fm
Little Beck Wood
Soulsgrave Fm
Low Moor
Latter Gate Hills
BOGGLE HOLE
Newton Ho
Leas Head Fm
FALLING FOSS
Oak Wood
Ramsdale Beck
Demesne Fm
Foss Plantn
Whinstone Ridge
St Ives Fm
Swallow Head Fm
Old Peak or South Cheek
Foulsike Fm
Brock Hall Fm
Stoupe Brow
Shooting House Rigg
Hogarth Hall
Howdale Fm
Brow Moor
Blea Wyke Pt
Low Moor
Oxbank Wood
Biller Howe
Ravenscar
Sneaton High Moor
Foster Howes Rigg
Flyingdales Moor
Cook Ho
Pike Hill
Biller Howe
Turf Rigg
Stony Marl Moor
Dobbiner Head
Flask Inn
Wragby Wood
Rudda Fm
Bell Hill Fm
Louven Howe Side
Green Swang
Stony Leas 299
Jugger Howe Moor
Prospect House Fm
Beast Cliff
Staintondale Moor
Low Moor
High Moor
Tofta Fm
White Hall Fm
Little Eller Beck
Burn Howe Rigg
Burn Howe Moor
Staintondale
Plane Tree Fm
STAINTONDALE SHIRE HORSE FARM
Eller Beck Br
Lilla Rigg
Bloody Beck
Falcon Inn
Crowdon
Castlebeck Wood
Lownorth Moor
Providence Heath
Redhouse Fm
Brown Hill
Scar Wood
Harwood Dale Forest
Wyke Lodge
Hayburn Wyke
Stony Rigg 245
Riverhead Fm
Standingstones Rigg
Hayburn Beck Fm
Worm Sike Rigg
Woof Howe Grain
Chapel Fm
Moor Cottage Fm
Linglands Fm
Rodger Trod
Grey Stones
Barley Carr Tongue
Keasbeck Hill Fm
Cloughton Newlands
Langdale Forest
Cloughton Plantns
Allerston High Moor
High Langdale End
Hardwick Fm
Harwood Dale
Ellis Close Fm
WHITE WAY
Cloughton Wyke
Nab Fm
Cober Hill
NORTH YORK MOORS
Langdale Rigg End
Thirley Cote Fm
Hundale Pt
Hazelhead Moor
Warsman Head
Breckenhurst
Ripley's Fm
Cloughton
Cloughton Fields Fm
Thorn Hill Head
Barns Cliff
Kirkless Fm
Long Nab
Blakey Topping
FOREST PARK
Surgate Brow Fm
Burniston
Crook Ness
Whisper Dales
Silpho Brow Fm
Low Moor Fm
Newgate Foot
High Dales
Beacon Fm
Cromer Pt
Highdales Fm
Sailors Grave
Low Moor
Thompson's Rigg
Red Ho
School Fm
Black Beck
Birch Hall Cott
COASTAL ROAD
Four Lanes Ends
Grime Moor
North Side Ho
Springwood Cott
Silpho
Ind Est
Low Dales
Binkleys Fm
Keeper's Old Ho
Deepdale Fm
Howdale Hill
Foulsyke Fm
High House Fm
Bickley Gate Fm
Broxa
Hilda Wood
Scalby Ness Rocks
Stain Dale
Langdale End
West Head Coll
Low Fm
Northfield Fm
BURNISTON ROAD
SCALBY ROAD
Pasture Fm
Deep Dale
Redbrow Plantn
Suffield
Hackness
Scalby
SCARBOROUGH
SEA LIFE CENTRE
Green Dale
Peathead Rigg
Backleys Fm
Troutsdale Low Hall
South Moor Fm
Suffield Quarry
Swanbeck Fm
Newby
Thwaite Head
Ebberston Common Fm
Rock House Fm
Wood Ho
Suffield Heights
Intake Wood
Keld Runnels Fm
Sea Cut
Barrowcliff
Castle Cliff
SCARBOROUGH CASTLE
Swair Dale
Jingleby Ho
Mount Misery
Everley Bank Wood
Raincliffe Fm
Throxenby
Ind Est
Scarborough
High Dalby Ho
High Rigg Fm
Seive Dale
Troutsdale Moor
Brompton Moor Ho
Wrench Green
Cockrah Foot
Everley
ROTUNDA MUSEUM
Old & East Harbours
Dalby Forest
Wykeham Forest
Hawthorn Wood
TOY MUS
Row Brow Fm
South Bay
Snever Dale
Broad Head Fm
Manor Ho
Cockrah Wood
Thorn Park Fm
Raincliffe Woods
Rowbrow Wood
Hern
Row
217

EAST
STEWARTRY
COAST
Auchencairn
Auchencairn Bay
Drungans
Auchencairn Ho
Moyl
White Port
Almorness Pt
Hestan Island
Balcary Bay
Balcary Pt
Airds Cott
Airds
Airds Pt
Cairn Hill
Nether Hazelfield
Rascarrel
Rascarrel Bay
Castle Muir Pt
Barlocco Bay
NX
237
238
219
Bank End
SENHOUSE ROMAN MUSEUM
LAKE DISTRICT COAST AQUARIUM
MARITIME MUS
Maryport
THE WAVE CENTRE
Ind Est
MARYPORT
Netherton
Ewanrigg
Risehow Fm
Risehow
Fothergill
Woodside
FLIMBY
Flimby
Standingstone
MAIN ROAD
St Helens
Camerton Grange
A596
Stud Fm
Siddick
Seaton
Camerton
Camerton Hall
Ribton Hall
Bus Pk
North Side
Hawk Hill
Salmon Hall
Barepot
Stainburn Hall Fm
Great Clifton
Clifton Hall
WORKINGTON
WORKINGTON HALL
Stainburn
Workington
A66
Close End
HELENA THOMPSON MILL MUSEUM
Moorclose
Schoose
Quarry Hill
Mossbay
Westfield
Moss Bay
East Town End Fm
Winscales
A595
Salterbeck
Harrington
HARRINGTON
High Harrington
Gale Ho
Lucy Close Fm
Wythemoor Ho
Lillyhall Industrial Estate
Distington Works
Grayson Green
West Ghyll End Fm
Wythemoor Head
Branthwaite Row Fm
Harrington Parks
Kelmore Hill Fm
Park Ho
Distington
Gilgarran
Cunning Pt
Barngill Ho
Common End
B5306
High House Fm
Pica
Lowca
Boon Wood
Wilson Park
Keekle Head Fm
Providence Bay
Moresby
247
High Park
Parton Bay
PARTON
Parton
Low Moresby
Tivoli
Moresby Moss
Tutehill Fm
Moorside Parks
Dub Hall
Tanyard Bay
Redness Pt
Bransty
Moresby Parks
Sandsclose
Dub Beck
Arlecdon Hill
WHITEHAVEN
Whitehaven
THE BEACON
THE RUM
Harras
Scilly Bank
Ind Est
WALK MILL
Acrewalls
Bleak
River Keekle
Lostrigg Beck
0 1 2 3 miles
0 1 2 3 4 5 km

Blitterlees
Abbey Town
Kelsick
Wigton
Waverbridge
Beckfoot
Newtown
Mawbray
Holme St Cuthbert
Dubmill Pt
Salta
Edderside
Allonby
Allonby Bay
Aspatria
Westnewton
Hayton
Prospect
Oughterside
Crosby Villa
Crosscanonby
Crosby
Gilcrux
Bullgill
Dearham
Tallentire
Dovenby
Bridekirk
Papcastle
Cockermouth
Brigham
Great Broughton
Little Broughton
Greysouthen
Eaglesfield
Deanscales
Dean
Mockerkin
Lamplugh
Loweswater
Loweswater Fell
Low Lorton
High Lorton
Lorton Vale
Embleton
Wythop Mill
Bassenthwaite
Bassenthwaite Lake
Whinlatter Forest Park
Thornthwaite
Braithwaite
Portinscale
Keswick
Derwent Water
Castlerigg
Applethwaite
Millbeck
Skiddaw
Skiddaw Forest
Lake District National Park
Derwent Fells
Rannerdale
Crummock Water
Bothel
Torpenhow
Ireby
Uldale
Sandale
Boltongate
Mealsgate
Fletchertown
Bolton Low Houses
Waverton
Red Dial
Westward
Sunderland
Bewaldeth
Blindcrake
Isel
Plumbland
Threapland
Parsonby
Cumbria
Solway Coast
A596
A595
A591
A66
A5086
B5300
B5301
B5302
B5299
B5292
B5289
238
239
230
219
220
NY

Baldwinholme
Thursby
Dalston
Durdar
Brisco
Cotehill
Hornsby
Carlatton Mill
Cumwhitton
West Curthwaite
East Curthwaite
Cardew
Cardewlees
Buckabank
Unthank
Sprunston
Wreay
Foulbridge
Holmwrangle
Brackenthwaite
Rosley
Raughton Head
Gaitsgill
Aiketgate
Armathwaite
Ainstable
Welton
Stockdalewath
Southwaite
Southwaite Services
High Hesket
Low Hesket
Ruckcroft
Old Town
Ivegill
Low Braithwaite
Sebergham
Churchtown
Middlesceugh
I n g l e w o o d
F o r e s t
Calthwaite
Thomas Close
Hutton End
Plumpton Foot
Townhead
Caldbeck
Hesket Newmarket
Whelpo
Upton
Sowerby Row
Millhouse
Plumpton
Brockleymoor
New Rent
Hutton-in-the-Forest
Unthank
Skelton
Lamonby
Ellonby
High Row
Caldbeck Fells
C U M B R I A
Plumpton Head
Hutton Roof
Mosedale
Johnby
Little Blencow
Great Blencow
Laithes
Catterlen
Greystoke Forest
Newton Reigny
Fair Hill
Penrith
LAKE DISTRICT
NATIONAL PARK
Skiddaw Forest
Mungrisdale
Berrier
Greystoke
Newbiggin
Carleton
Eamont Bridge
Whitbarrow Village
Motherby
Penruddock
Stainton
Sockbridge
Scales
Troutbeck
Hutton
Dacre
Tirril
Clifton
Threlkeld
Soulby
Pooley Bridge
Waterfoot
Matterdale End
Longthwaite
Wreay
Askham
Lowther
Hackthorpe
Watermillock
Helton
Whale
Dockray
Knotts
Matterdale Common
Dowthwaitehead
Ullswater
Howtown
Sandwick
Martindale
Martindale Common
Bampton
Butterwick
Low Knipe
Bampton Grange
Blencathra
Great Calva
Skiddaw House
Castlerigg Stone Circle
Aira Force Waterfall
Dalemain
Rheged
Lakeland Bird of Prey Centre
Lowther Castle
Mayburgh Henge
Brougham Castle
Countess Pillar
Penrith Castle
High Head Sculpture Valley
Beckstones
Tarn Moss
A596
A595
A591
A592
A5091
A66
A6
M6
B5299
B5305
B5288
B5320
B5322
B6413
B6412
B6262
42
41
40
0 1 2 3 miles
0 1 2 3 4 5 km

Turnberry Ho
Cumrew Fell
Geltsdale Middle
Three Pikes 585
Hartchyside
Bertram Hill
Far Ho
Knarsdale Common
Shawhead
Dewley Fell
Dewley Field
Willyshaw Rigg
Ouston Fell
NINEBANKS
Spartywell
Farneyside
Greenley
Brownley Hill 533
Cumrew
New Water
Butt Hill
240
Lintley
Far Town
Ayle Common
241
Long Cross
White Hill
Mohope Head
Broadlee
Kevelin Moor
NY
Bove Wood
Newbiggin
Newbiggin Fell
Blotting Raise 591
Croglin Fell
The Combs
Green Hill
Thornhope Fell
Kirkhaugh
Ayle
Castle Nook
Whitley Castle
Kirkside Wood
Clarghyll Hall
White Ho
Newshield Moss
Hard Rigg
Mohope Moor
Halley Moor
The Nook
Limestone Brae
Broad Mea
High Shield
Lawyer's Cross
Farlam Currick
South Tynedale Railway
Broad Meadows
New Ho
The Meres
Black Cleugh
Sumburgh Ho
Fieldhead
Grey Nag 656
Thornhope Burn
Black Hill
Wanwood Hill
Blagill
Hesleywell Moor
Wellhope Burn
Middle Rigg
Hazelgill
Croglin
Scarrowmanwick
Scarrowmanwick Fell
637
Thack Moor 609
Gossipgate Gallery
Alston
Raise
Foreshield
East Cocklake
Smallburns Moor
Carrshield
Caber Fm
Croglin High Hall
Davygill
Watch Hill
Tom Smith's Stone
Woldgill Burn
Black Ho
Whitewell Fm
Nent
Nenthall
Galligill
Browngill
The Dodd
614
Carrshield Moor
Middle Moor
Renwick Fell
Woldgill Moss
Park Fell
Bayle Hill Fm
Middle Fell
Whimsey Hill
Greenends
Coalcleugh
Lowhall Building
Long Moor
Scale Houses
The Dod
Watcher's Hill
Horse Edge
Hill Ho
Bayles
Nettle Hall
Wellgill
Black Hill
Killhope Law
Bank Wood
Whin Fell
Crindledyke Fm
Dyrah
Green Rigg
Long Tongue
664 Black Fell
Gilderdale Forest
Brownside Moss
Ghyll Ho
Rise
Middle Fell
Coalcleugh Moor
Lincowell
Scales Moor
Skelling Moor
Haresceugh Fell
Leadgate
575
Nenthead
Slate Hill
232
Killhope Cross
Renwick
Haresceugh
Hartside Cotts
Rotherhope Tower
Meadow Flatt
Rice Head
Alston Moor
Old Mill
Nenthead Mines Heritage Centre
Shaw Side
Westgarth Hill
How Moor
Ravenbridge Mill
Benty Hill
Hartside Height
Meathaw Hill 486
Blackburn Bank
Dryburn
Cropshall
Nunnery Hill
High Bankhill
Scales
Huddlesceugh Hall
Busk
High Skyles
Flinty Fell 614
Low Mill
Viol Moor
Gamblesby Fell
Loaning Head
Garrigill
Cawood Hill
Rotherhope Fell
Nag's Head
Knoutberry Hill
Kirkoswald
Park Head
Twotop Hill
Fiend's Fell 634
Unthank
Hazel Rigg
Crossgill
Pasture Houses
Ash Gill
Mount Pleasant
Eden Br
The Mains
Old Parks
Viol Moor
Long Crags
Black Burn
Staneshaw Rigg
Long Grain
Lamb's Head 648
Lazonby
Gamblesby
Glassonbybeck
Little Knapside Hill 657
Smittergill Burn
Hound Hill 596
Alston Moor
Lee Hos
West Ashgill
High Ashgill
709
Dead Stones
White Edge
Eden Lacy
Glassonby
Hause in the Scar
685 Knapside Hill
Melmerby Fell
Smittergill Head
Paper Hill
Pasture Ho
Hole Ho
Windy Brow
Sally Grain
Lacy's Caves
Maughanby Fm
Melmerby Mire
Todhills
Melmerby High Scar
Rigg End
Ousby Fell
Pikeman Hill
Hill Ho
Tynehead
Yad Moss
Burnhope Seat 746
Tarn Ho
Long Meg & Her Daughters
Marian Lodge
Great Salkeld
Melmerby
Stony Rigg
Bullman Hills
Pennine Way
Long Man Hill
Robberby Fm
Colstons Fm
Gale Hall
Cuns Fell
Green Fell 740
Raehow End
Lambgreen Hills
Round Hill 686
Tyne Head
Slack's Rigg
Scaud Hill
Little Salkeld
Nunwick Hall
Hunsonby
Ousby Moor
Jardine's Fm
Muska Hill
Brown Hill
NORTH
Skirwith Fell
Fallow Hill
Calvert End
Crossgill Head
Tynehead Fell
Yad Moss
Harwood Common
Ashgill Head
Thack Moor
Bellbeaver Rigg 620
Winskill
Crewgarth
Ousby
Rayson Hall
Row
Cross Fell 893
High Cap
Kirkdale
Tees Head
River Tees
Frog Hall
Langwathby
Townhead
Beck Mill
Kirkland Fell
Little Dun Fell
Hard Hill 678
Metalband Hill
Viewing Hill
Greencomb Sike
Herdship Fell
Edenhall
High Barn
Langwathby Moor
Skirwith High Moor
Bank Hall
Kirkland
Middle Tongue
Great Dun Fell 848
Milburn Forest
Moor House Upper Teesdale
Moor Ho
Dodgen Pot
Home Fm
Appleside Hill
Whamthorn Plantn
Skirwith Abbey
Skirwith
Hanging Walls of Mark Anthony
Grumply Hill
Crowdundle Beck
Iron Howe
Green Castle
Moss Burn
Rough Sike
Green Burn
Backside Fell
West Common
Touting Hill
Dolphenby
Moorlands Plantn
Primrose Bank
Blencarn
High Slack
PENNINES
Red Carle
Knock Fell
Force Burn
Cow Green Reservoir
Udford
Moorside
Cross How
Lounthwaite
Knock Ore Gill
Lodgegill Sike
Highbarn Cott
River Eamont
Hornby Hall
Culgaith
Underwood
Loscars
Burney Hill
Green Fell
Woodside
Howgill Castle
Milburn
Meldon Hill 767
Dufton Fell
A66
Whinfell Ho
Mill Rigg Fm
Newbiggin
Kirk Ho
Moorlands Head
Gullom Holme
Slakes Fm
Milburn Grange
Close Ho
Knock Pike
Swindale Beck
High Scald Fell
Cauldron Snout Waterfall
Haversheaf Hall
Sawmill Cotts
Whinfell Forest
Ash Hill
Oglebird Plantn
Acorn Bank Garden
Temple Sowerby
Houtsay Park
Halefield Fm
Low Abbey
Knock Moor
Knock
Brownber Hill
Grain Beck
Oasis Lakeland Forest Village
Leacet Hill
Salter Wood
Skygarth Fm
Lowmoor Row
Hale Grange
Kirkby Thore
Stamp Hill Fm
Knock Cross
Dufton Pike
Bluethwaite Hill
Great Rundale Beck
Backstone Edge
Narrowgate Beacon
High Cup Nick
Rasp Hill
Maize Beck
Cliburn Moss
Brown Howe
Melkinthorpe
Town Head
Town End
Town Head
Marton Moor
Coatsike Fm
Pusgill Ho
Bow Hall
503 Peeping Hill
High Cup Gill
Danger area
Swarth Beck
Fisher Sike
Shaw Ho
Ousen Stand
Bridge End
Sleastonhow
Marton Ho
Birks Head
Dufton
Mickle Fell
Wood Ho
Cliburn
Long Marton
Park Ho
Murton Fell
Melkinthorpe Wood
Leith Bank
Crossrigg Hall
Winter Ho
Edenbank Fm
Eden Grove
Redlands Bank
Trout Beck
Broom
Town Head
Middle Tongue
Street Ho
Glenton Vale
Town Wood
Stanley Bank Plantn
Bolton
Brampton
Croft Ends
Dufton Wood
Scalehowe Wood
Harbour Flatt
594 Murton Pike
Keekham Beck Head
Great Strickland
Morland
Town Head
Roger Head
Crackenthorpe
Brampton Tower
Brackenthwaite
Hilton Fell
Philip Reed M
Greystone Ho
Dallan Bank
Syke Ho
Keld
Edenfields
Bolton Lodge
Hangingshaw
Low Barn
Murton
Mell Fell
Amber Hill
Little Fell 745
Burton Fell
Danger area
Sheriff Park
Sandriggs Fm
Strickland Lodge Fm
Newby Head
Newby
High Field
King's Meaburn
New Bewley Castle
Colby Laithes
Shepherd's Gott
Swindale Edge
Goal Sike
Thrimby Hall
Newby End Fm
Morland Moor
Penny Hill
Colby
Burwain Hall
Battlebarrow Ho
Appleby
Gale Ho
Langton Field
Hilton Beck
Roman Fell
Christy Bank
Warcop Fell
Connypot Beck
Little Strickland
White Stone
White Stone
Appleby-in-Westmorland
Stoneriggs
Hilton
221
222
Thrimby Grange
Dedra Banks
Littlebeck
Jerusalem
Bandley Wood
Parkin Hill
Brackenber Moor
Brackenber
Bankwood
Long Fell
Tinside Rigg
Helbeck Fell
Bedlands Gate
Brown Howe
Sleagill Head
Sleagill
Lowfield
Sideway Bank
Coupland
Danger area
Middle Fell
Musgrave Fell
Low Bank End
Seavy Rigg
Seat Hill
Barwise Hall
Burrells
Greyber
Meaburn
Reagill
Pattinson's

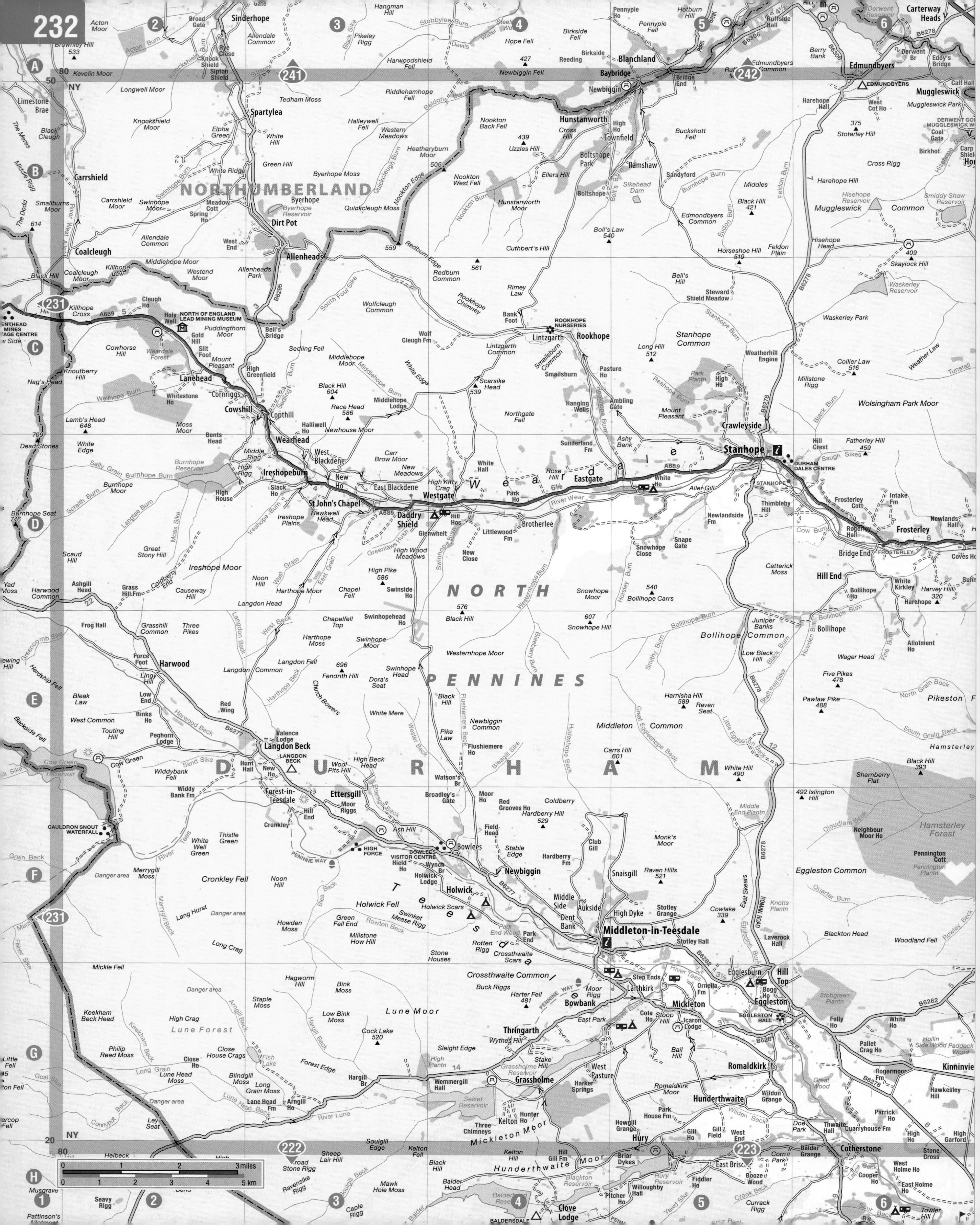
NORTHUMBERLAND
NORTH
PENNINES
DURHAM
Weardale
Teesdale
Sinderhope
Spartylea
Carrshield
Coalcleugh
Allenheads
Dirt Pot
Blanchland
Baybridge
Newbiggin
Hunstanworth
Townfield
Ramshaw
Edmundbyers
Muggleswick
Rookhope
Lintzgarth
Lanehead
Cowshill
Copthill
Wearhead
Ireshopeburn
St John's Chapel
Daddry Shield
Westgate
Eastgate
Stanhope
Crawleyside
Frosterley
Hill End
Harwood
Langdon Beck
Forest-in-Teesdale
Ettersgill
Bowlees
Newbiggin
Holwick
Middleton-in-Teesdale
Laithkirk
Mickleton
Eggleston
Hill Top
Thringarth
Bowbank
Grassholme
Romaldkirk
Hunderthwaite
Kelton
Hury
Cotherstone
Kinninvie
Clove Lodge
NORTH OF ENGLAND LEAD MINING MUSEUM
ROOKHOPE NURSERIES
DURHAM DALES CENTRE
BOWLEES VISITOR CENTRE
HIGH FORCE
CAULDRON SNOUT WATERFALL
EGGLESTON HALL
Cow Green Reservoir
Selset Reservoir
Grassholme Reservoir
Hury Reservoir
Blackton Reservoir
Balderhead Reservoir
Burnhope Reservoir
Derwent Reservoir
Waskerley Reservoir
Smiddy Shaw Reservoir
River Wear
River Tees
River Lune
A689
B6277
B6278
B6282
B6295
B6306
PENNINE WAY
Lune Moor
Lune Forest
Middleton Common
Bollihope Common
Stanhope Common
Eggleston Common
Hamsterley Forest
Wolsingham Park Moor
Ireshope Moor
Cronkley Fell
Mickle Fell
Crossthwaite Common
Mickleton Moor
Hunderthwaite Moor
Burnhope Seat 746
Black Hill 604
Fendrith Hill 696
Carrs Hill 601
Snowhope Hill 607
241
242
222
223
231
NY
50
20
80
0 1 2 3 miles
0 1 2 3 4 5 km

Consett
Leadgate
Annfield Plain
Chester-le-Street
Allensford
Iveston
Maiden Law
Edmondsley
Waldridge
Castleside
Knitsley
Delves
Burnhope
Holmside
Great Lumley
Lanchester
Sacriston
Kimblesworth
Plawsworth
Nettlesworth
Witton Gilbert
Waskerley
East Butsfield
Langley Park
Framwellgate Moor
Pity Me
Satley
Cornsay
Cornsay Colliery
Quebec
Esh
Bearpark
Ushaw Moor
Durham
Gilesgate
Esh Winning
Waterhouses
New Brancepeth
Brandon
Shincliffe
High Stoop
Tow Law
Sunniside
Wolsingham
Thornley
Billy Row
Crook
Willington
Brancepeth
Bowburn
Sunderland Bridge
Croxdale
Tudhoe
Spennymoor
Ferryhill
Howden-le-Wear
Witton-le-Wear
Bedburn
Hamsterley
Redford
Toronto
Escomb
Coundon
Bishop Auckland
Shildon
Newton Aycliffe
Chilton
Rushyford
West Auckland
Evenwood
Cockfield
Copley
Woodland
Butterknowle
Staindrop
Heighington
Redworth
Aycliffe
Killerby
Summerhouse
Walworth
Denton
Headlam
Cleatlam
Wackerfield
Hilton
Bolam
Royal Oak
Coatham Mundeville
DURHAM

Houghton-Le-Spring
Seaham
Hetton-le-Hole
Murton
Seaton
Northlea
West Lea
Deneside
Parkside
Dawdon
Dalton-le-Dale
Cold Hesleden
Easington
Easington Colliery
Peterlee
Horden
Blackhall Colliery
Shotton Colliery
Shotton
Wheatley Hill
Wingate
Thornley
Haswell
Haswell Plough
Ludworth
Sherburn
Sherburn Hill
Carrville
Belmont
Gilesgate
Pittington
Littletown
Shadforth
Shincliffe
High Shincliffe
Bowburn
Cassop
Old Cassop
Quarrington Hill
Kelloe
Coxhoe
Cornforth
West Cornforth
Ferryhill
Ferryhill Station
Chilton Lane
Chilton
Mainsforth
Bishop Middleham
Trimdon
Trimdon Colliery
Trimdon Grange
Fishburn
Sedgefield
Bradbury
Mordon
Butterwick
Embleton
Castle Eden
Hesleden
High Hesleden
Monk Hesleden
Crimdon Park
Station Town
Hutton Henry
Sheraton
Hart
Hart Station
West View
Elwick
Dalton Piercy
West Park
Rift House
Hartlepool
Seaton Carew
Owton Manor
Brierton
Greatham
Graythorp
Newton Bewley
Wolviston
Billingham
Cowpen Bewley
Haverton Hill
Port Clarence
Wynyard Village
Thorpe Larches
Grindon
Foxton
Stillington
Old Stillington
Whitton
Thorpe Thewles
Carlton
Redmarshall
Bishopton
Great Stainton
Little Stainton
Brafferton
Newton Ketton
Aycliffe
Preston-le-Skerne
Elstob
Norton
Roseworth
Hardwick
Bishopsgarth
Fairfield
Mount Pleasant
Portrack
Stockton-on-Tees
Middlesbrough
North Ormesby
South Bank
Cargo Fleet
Teesville
Pallister
Marton Grove
Berwick Hills
Linthorpe
Hartburn
Whinney Hill
Great Lumley
Fence Houses
Colliery Row
Leamside
West Rainton
East Rainton
Low Moorsley
High Moorsley
Easington Lane
South Hetton
Elemore Vale
Hetton Downs
Great Eppleton
Sunniside
Newbottle
Burdon
Featherbed Rocks
Nose's Pt
Chourdon Pt
Shippersea Bay
Horden Pt
Fox Holes
North Sands
Parton Rocks
The Headland
Middleton
Hartlepool Bay
Seaton Sands
Seal Sands
Tees Mouth
TYNE AND WEAR
DURHAM
HARTLEPOOL
DARLINGTON
STOCKTON ON TEES
243
233
224
225
0 1 2 3 miles
0 1 2 3 4 5 km

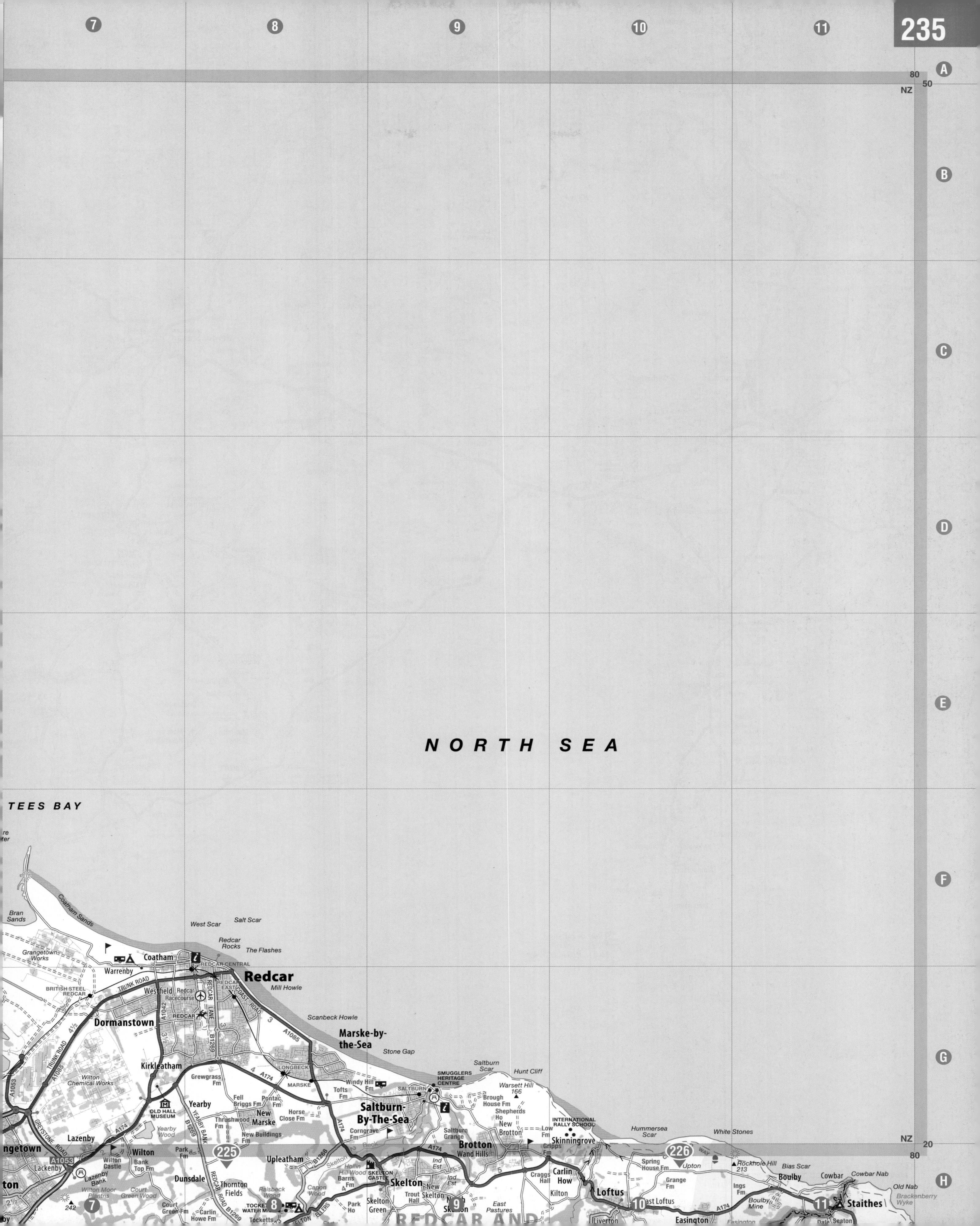

7
8
9
10
11
A
B
C
D
E
F
G
H
80
50
NZ
20
NORTH SEA
TEES BAY
Coatham Sands
Bran Sands
West Scar
Salt Scar
Redcar Rocks
The Flashes
Grangetown Works
Coatham
Warrenby
REDCAR CENTRAL
Redcar
Mill Howle
TRUNK ROAD
BRITISH STEEL REDCAR
Westfield
Redcar Racecourse
REDCAR EAST
COAST ROAD
REDCAR LANE
REDCAR
A1042
B1269
A1085
Dormanstown
Scanbeck Howle
Marske-by-the-Sea
Stone Gap
LONGBECK
Kirkleatham
Wilton Chemical Works
Grewgrass Fm
A174
MARSKE
Windy Hill Fm
SALTBURN
Saltburn Scar
Hunt Cliff
SMUGGLERS HERITAGE CENTRE
Warsett Hill 166
Brough House Fm
Shepherds Ho
New Brotton
Tofts Fm
Saltburn-By-The-Sea
OLD HALL MUSEUM
Yearby
Fell Briggs Fm
Pontac Fm
New Marske
Horse Close Fm
Thrushwood Fm
New Buildings Fm
Corngrave Fm
Saltburn Grange
Brotton
Wand Hills
INTERNATIONAL RALLY SCHOOL
Low Fm
Skinningrove
Gripps Fm
Hummersea Scar
White Stones
A1053
GREYSTONE ROAD
Lazenby
Yearby Wood
YEARBY BANK
ngetown
Wilton
Wilton Castle
Bank Top Fm
Park Fm
225
Upleatham
B1268
Skelton
Hollin Hill Wood
Barns Fm
SKELTON CASTLE
Ind Est
Spring House Fm
226
Upton
Rockhole Hill 213
Bias Scar
Boulby
Cowbar
Cowbar Nab
Lackenby
Lazenby Bank
Dunsdale
Thornton Fields
Raisbeck Wood
Capon Wood
Skelton
New Skelton
Craggs Hall
Carlin How
Kilton
Loftus
Grange Fm
Ings Fm
Old Nab
Brackenberry Wyke
ton
242
Wilton Moor Plantns
Court Green Wood
Court Green Fm
Carlin Howe Fm
REDCAR ROAD B1269
TOCKETTS WATER MILL
Tocketts
Park Ho
Skelton Green
Trout Hall
North Skelton
East Pastures
East Loftus
Boulby Mine
Staithes
REDCAR AND
Liverton
Easington
Dale
Seaton
A174

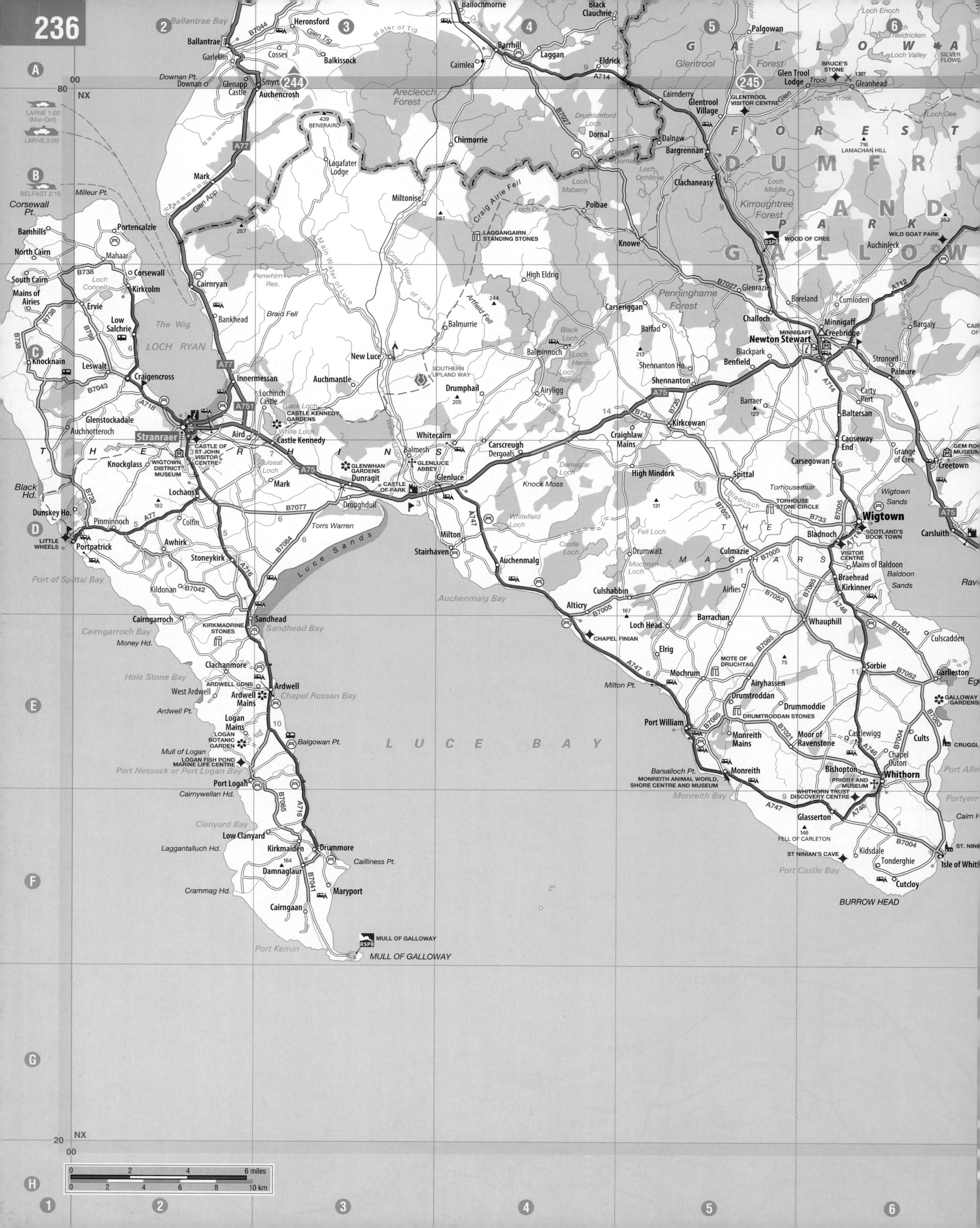
Ballantrae Bay
Ballantrae
Garleffin
Heronsford
Glen Tig
Cosses
Balkissock
Water of Tig
Ballochmorrie
Black Clauchrie
Barrhill
Cairnlea
Laggan
Eldrick
A714
Palgowan
Water of Minnoch
Loch Enoch
Loch Neldricken
Loch Valley
SILVER FLOWE
G A L L O W A Y
F O R E S T
D U M F R I E S
P A R K
G A L L O W A Y
Glentrool Forest
Downan Pt.
Downan
Glenapp Castle
Smyrt
Auchencrosh
244
245
Arecleoch Forest
Cairnderry
Glentrool Village
GLENTROOL VISITOR CENTRE
Glen Trool Lodge
Trool
Loch Trool
BRUCE'S STONE
1307
Gleanhead
Loch Dee
LARNE 1:00 (Mar-Oct)
LARNE 2:00
NX
80
00
439 BENERAIRD
Drumlamford Loch
B7027
Dornal
Dalnaw
Bargrennan
716 LAMACHAN HILL
Chirmorrie
Lagafater Lodge
Loch Dornal
Loch Ochiltree
Clachaneasy
A77
Mark
BELFAST 2:15
Milleur Pt.
Corsewall Pt.
Glen App
Miltonise
Loch Maberry
Loch Middle
Kirroughtree Forest
Polbae
Loch Derry
Craig Airie Fell
287
257
LAGGANGAIRN STANDING STONES
Knowe
WOOD OF CREE
RSPB
WILD GOAT PARK
353
Auchinleck
Portencalzie
Barnhills
North Cairn
Mahaar
Corsewall
South Cairn
Mains of Airies
B738
Loch Connell
Kirkcolm
Ervie
Cairnryan
Bankhead
Penwhirn Res.
Main Water of Luce
Cross Water of Luce
High Eldrig
A714
B7027
Glenrazie
Boreland
Cumloden
A712
Palnure Burn
Penkiln Burn
Penninghame Forest
Carseriggan
Challoch
Minnigaff
Creebridge
Bargaly
Newton Stewart
MINNIGAFF
Blackpark
Benfield
Low Salchrie
B798
The Wig
LOCH RYAN
Braid Fell
Arrfield Fell
244
Balmurrie
Black Loch
Barfad
213
Shennanton Ho.
Stronord
Palnure
Knocknain
Leswalt
Craigencross
New Luce
SOUTHERN UPLAND WAY
Balminnoch
Loch Heron
Loch Ronald
Shennanton
Innermessan
Auchmantle
Drumphail
205
Airyligg
Tarf Water
A75
B735
Barraer
123
Carty Port
Baltersan
Cree
B7043
Lochinch Castle
Black Loch
CASTLE KENNEDY GARDENS
White Loch
A718
A751
Glenstockadale
Auchnotteroch
Stranraer
CASTLE OF ST JOHN VISITOR CENTRE
Aird
Castle Kennedy
Whitecairn
Balmesh
Carscreugh
Dergoals
B733
Craighlaw Mains
Kirkcowan
Causeway End
Grange of Cree
GEM ROCK MUSEUM
Creetown
T H E R H I N S
Knockglass
WIGTOWN DISTRICT MUSEUM
Soulseat Loch
GLENWHAN GARDENS
GLENLUCE ABBEY
Glenluce
Dernaglar Loch
Knock Moss
High Mindork
Spittal
Carsegowan
Torhousemuir
Wigtown Sands
Black Hd.
Lochans
Mark
Dunragit
CASTLE OF PARK
Bladnoch
TORHOUSE STONE CIRCLE
B733
B7005
Wigtown
A75
182
Droughduil
B7077
Whitefield Loch
131
B7052
Dunskey Ho.
Pinminnoch
Colfin
Torrs Warren
A747
Fell Loch
T H E M A C H A R S
SCOTLAND'S BOOK TOWN
Carsluith
LITTLE WHEELS
Portpatrick
Awhirk
Stoneykirk
B7084
Luce Sands
Milton
Stairhaven
Castle Loch
Drumwalt
Mochrum Loch
Culmazie
B7005
VISITOR CENTRE
Mains of Baldoon
Baldoon Sands
A714
Port of Spittal Bay
Kildonan
B7042
A716
Auchenmalg
Culshabbin
Airlies
B7052
B7085
Braehead
Kirkinner
Auchenmalg Bay
Alticry
B7005
197
Barrachan
Whauphill
A746
B7004
Culscadden
Cairngarroch
Sandhead
KIRKMADRINE STONES
Sandhead Bay
Cairngarroch Bay
Money Hd.
Loch Head
CHAPEL FINIAN
Elrig
Hole Stone Bay
Clachanmore
ARDWELL GDNS
Ardwell
Ardwell Mains
Chapel Rossan Bay
West Ardwell
Ardwell Pt.
MOTE OF DRUCHTAG
75
Mochrum
Airyhassen
Sorbie
B7052
Garlieston
Milton Pt.
Drumtroddan
Drummoddie
DRUMTRODDAN STONES
GALLOWAY GARDENS
Logan Mains
LOGAN BOTANIC GARDEN
Balgowan Pt.
L U C E B A Y
Port William
Monreith Mains
B7021
Moor of Ravenstone
Castlewigg
B7063
Cults
CRUGGLETON
Mull of Logan
LOGAN FISH POND MARINE LIFE CENTRE
Port Nessock or Port Logan Bay
Port Logan
Cairnywellan Hd.
B7065
Barsalloch Pt.
MONREITH ANIMAL WORLD, SHORE CENTRE AND MUSEUM
Monreith
Monreith Bay
Bishopton
Chapel Outon
Whithorn
PRIORY AND MUSEUM
WHITHORN TRUST DISCOVERY CENTRE
Port Allen
Portyerrock
Clanyard Bay
Low Clanyard
Laggantalluch Hd.
Kirkmaiden
Drummore
164
Damnaglaur
B7041
Cailliness Pt.
Glasserton
146 FELL OF CARLETON
ST NINIAN'S CAVE
Kidsdale
Tonderghie
B7004
Isle of Whithorn
Port Castle Bay
Crammag Hd.
Maryport
Cairngaan
Cutcloy
BURROW HEAD
MULL OF GALLOWAY
Port Kemin
RSPB
20
NX
00
0 2 4 6 miles
0 2 4 6 8 10 km
A
B
C
D
E
F
G
H
1
2
3
4
5
6

St John's Town of Dalry
New Galloway
Castle Douglas
Dalbeattie
Kirkcudbright
Gatehouse of Fleet
Dumfries
Maxwelltown
Lincluden
Locharbriggs
Kirkton
Tinwald
Torthorwald
Collin
New Abbey
Kirkconnell
Glencaple
Bankend
Shearington
Bowhouse
Overton
Drumburn
Carsethorn
Kirkbean
Southerness
Southerness Pt.
Mainsriddle
Caulkerbush
Prestonmill
Sandyhills
Colvend
Rockcliffe
Kippford or Scaur
Palnackie
Barnbarroch
Auchencairn
Rascarrel
Orroland
Dundrennan
Netherlaw
Balmae
Townhead
Mutehill
Bombie
Kirkcarswell
Borgue
Knockbrex
Kirkandrews
Chapelton Row
Borness
Ross
Sandgreen
Carrick
Barharrow
Rainton
Girthon
Twynholm
Tongland
Ringford
Valleyfield
Bridge of Dee
Rhonehouse or Kelton Hill
Gelston
Airieland
Whinnieliggate
Auchenleck
Culnaightrie
Laurieston
Crossmichael
Parton
Mossdale
Balmaclellan
Kenmure
Glenlee
Garroch
Drumbuie
Earlstoun
Millquarter
Duchrae
Bogue
Corriedoo
Blackcraig
Knocklearn
Gibbshill
Corsock
Merkland
Glenlair
Crofts
Brooklands
Crocketford or Ninemile Bar
Milton
Springholm
Kirkpatrick Durham
Haugh of Urr
Hardgate
Kirkgunzeon
Beeswing
Lochfoot
Brae
Cargenbridge
Congeith
Barhill
Clarebrand
Townhead of Greenlaw
Old Bridge of Urr
Drumpark
Irongray
Newbridge
Terregles Banks
Glenkiln
Margreig
Glen
Shawhead
Holywood
Newtonairds
Sundaywell
Milton
Throughgate
Duncow
Amisfield
Gallaberry
Heathhall
Islesteps
Mabie
Kingholm Quay
Kelton
Horseholm
Anwoth
Lagganmullan
Barholm
Pulcree
Fleuchlang
Glengap
Glen
Mark
Culcronchie
Dromore
Craignell
Craigencallie Ho.
Mid Garrary
Ironmacannie
Craig
Drumrash
Redcroft
Glenlochar
Leaths
Maryport
Flimby
Siddick
Seaton
North Side
Workington
Stainburn
Mossbay
Westfield
Harrington
High Harrington
Winscales
Distington
Lowca
Pica
Moresby
Parton
Bransty
Whitehaven
Frizington
Hensingham
Mirehouse
Cleator Moor
WIGTOWN BAY
SOLWAY FIRTH
NITH ESTUARY
EAST STEWARTRY COAST
FLEET VALLEY
Clatteringshaws Forest
Bennan Forest
Fleet Forest
Laurieston Forest
Glengap Forest
Dalbeattie Forest
Mabie Forest
Corriedoo Forest
Mersehead Sands
Rascarrel Bay
Auchencairn Bay
Hestan I.
Balcary Pt.
Abbey Hd.
Port Mary
Little Ross
Kirkcudbright Bay
Islands of Fleet
Ringdoo Pt.
Fleet Bay
Borness Pt.
Castlehill Pt.
Rough I.
Saltom Bay
THREAVE CASTLE
THREAVE GARDENS
KELTON MAINS OPEN FARM
KEN-DEE MARSHES
STEWARTRY MUSEUM
BROUGHTON HOUSE AND GARDEN
GALLOWAY HYDRO VISITOR CENTRE
DUNDRENNAN ABBEY
CARDONESS CASTLE
MILL ON THE FLEET
CAIRNHOLY CAIRNS
CLATTERINGSHAWS FOREST WILDLIFE CENTRE
RAIDERS ROAD FOREST DRIVE
BLOWPLAIN OPEN FARM
CAIRNSMORE OF FLEET
DRUMCOLTRAN TOWER
OLD BUITTLE TOWER
ORCHARDTON TOWER
MOTE OF MARK
ROUGH ISLAND
RSPB MERSEHEAD
JOHN PAUL JONES COTTAGE MUSEUM
ARBIGLAND GARDENS
NATIONAL MUS OF COSTUME
SWEETHEART ABBEY
NEW ABBEY CORN MILL
WILDFOWL AND WETLAND CENTRE
CAERLAVEROCK CASTLE
DUMFRIES MUSEUM & CAMERA OBSCURA
BURNS HOUSE
ROBERT BURNS CENTRE
OLD BRIDGE HOUSE MUS
LINCLUDEN COLLEGE
DUMFRIES AND GALLOWAY AVIATION MUS
ELLISLAND FARM
MARYPORT MARITIME MUSEUM
HELENA THOMPSON MUS
THE RUM STORY
HAIG COLLIERY MINING MUSEUM
WALK MILL
246
247
238
228
219

Shaw's Hill
Long Plantn
Priesthead
Kirk Loch
Castle Loch
LOCHMABEN CASTLE
Castle Mains
Ladyward
Millhill
Lockerbie
LOCKERBIE
Mounthoolie
Rosebank
B7068
Scroggs
Bankshill
Northburn
Grange Fell
Birrens Hill
Tinwald Parks
Tinwald Ho
Hempland Hill
Rye Muir
Blackrig
Parkfoot
Whitelaird
Priestdykes
A709
South Tummuir Plantn
Millantae
The Linns
Tundergarth Mains
Powhaffet
Risp Hill
Carruthers
Crossbank
Branetrigg
Hightae Mill Loch
Heck
Mossgrove
Well Springs Plantn
Blackford
Westwood
248
Ind Est
NY
Heathhall
A701
Glenclair Hill
Woodlands
Ind Est
Downs Bank
West Roucan
The Broom
Corsegreen
Parkend
Greenhill
Skairfield
Millriggs
Muirfield
Courstein
Torbeckhill Res
Howat's Hill
Beacon Hill
Hartwood Hill
Tinlaw
Hallmuir
Pilmuir Common
BURNSWARK HILL FORT
Burnswark
Stockbridge
Darlawhill
Gilmartin
Ind Est
AVIATION MUS
Torthorwald
Hightae
Mossburn
The Grove
Lochar Moss
A709
Whiteside Hill
Carthat Hill
RAMMERSCALES
Smallholm
Woodlands
Birkshaw Forest
Shawhead Plantn
B723
A74(M)
Castlemilk
Gimmenbie
Haregills
Relief
Dougiashall
Grainhall
Purdomstone Res
Craighouse
Dockenflat
Stoneybeck
Dirrops
Greystone
Barton's House
Gasstown
A75
A780
Dourievale
Mid Dargavel
Nether Dargavel
Isle of Man
Georgetown
Collin
West Mains
Hazelshaw Hill
Holmains Moor
Range Castle
217
Linn Mill
Glenholm
Kettleholm
Cowdens
Axletreewell
Whitehill
Orchard
Langdyke
Paulsland
Middlebie
Blackwoodridge
Yesket
B7076
Middleshaw
Almagill
Rockhall Mains
Greenlea
Woodside
Elizafield
Mouswald Banks
Newton
Kirkwood
Dormont
Hunter's Gate
Nether Collinhirst
Ecclefechan
Cleuchbrae Mill
Johnstone Hall
BIRRENS FORT
Ashyards Gate
Burnfoot Hall
The Braes
Eaglesfield
Craigs Fm
Racks
Drummuir
B724
Brocklehirst
Cleughbrae
Hallidayhill
Dalton
Kirkwood Mains
Dalton Green
Sorrysike Moor
Shawbrae Moor Plantn
THOMAS CARLYLE'S BIRTHPLACE
Donkins
Allerbeck
Burnhead
Cairn of Craigs
237
Craigs Moss
Mouswald Grange
Townhead Fm
West Denbie Fm
Meikle Dyke
Isle of Dalton
Waterside Ho
B725
Hoddom Mill
Buckie Cott
Hoddomcross
Whins
Kirtlebridge
Barnkin of Craigs
Ironhirst
Mouswald
A75
West Raffles
East Raffles
Denbie Mains
Murraythwaite
Edge
Hoddom Mains
Woodcock Air
Quarry Park
Breconbeds
Bush of Craigs
Mabie Forest
Ironhirst Moss
Mount Kedar
Langdyke
Carrutherstown
Searigg Cott
Mains
Phyllis Park
Greycraig
Dumbretton
Robgill Tower
Kelton Ho
Keltonbank
Kelton
Horseholm
Holmhead Moss
Fostermeadowfoot
Gillbrae
Stenries
Oakbank
Nether Stenries
B7020
Wintersheugh Plantn
Millside Plantn
Brydekirk Mains
Brydekirk
Allalea
East Bretton
Robgill Mains
Johnstonlee
Beltedstane
Creca
Boreland
GLENCAPLE ROAD
Ballieknowe
Black Grain
Stragglingwath Plantn
Denbieyett
Windyknowe
Kirkblane Fm
Longbridge Muir
Longbridgemuir
Long Plantn
Plans
Upper Mains
Kelhead Moss Plantn
Winterseugh
Park
Mount Annan
Power Sta
Creca Hall
Black Grain Plantn
Comlongon Mains
Mains Cotts
Newfield Plantn
Outerford
Limekilns
B722
Glencaple
Byers Fm
Bankend
Clarencefield
Cocklicks
Charlesfield
Spittalriddinghill
Gullielands Burn
Highmains Hill
Bankend Hill
RUTHWELL CROSS
Newfield
Holly Bush Wood
Beetylands Park
Preston Hall
Stapleton Grange
Highmains Fm
Dockridding Wood
Comlongon Wood
Burnside
B6357
Tulliesfield
SHORE ROAD
Southfield
Cockpool Plantn
B725
Brow Well
Ruthwell
Mackwhinny Park
Justenlees
Newbie Mill
Woodhead
Woodhall
Lochar Water
DUNCAN SAVINGS BANK MUSEUM
Greenhill Plantn
Hitchill
B721
Topping Hall
Hardrigg Lodge
Airds Pt
Shearington
NITH
Croftheads Cotts
Annan
STAPLETON RD
Scar Pt
Airds
Mains
Blackshaw
Priestside
Priestside Flow
Cummertrees
Ind Est
ANNAN
Watchhill
Lowther
Eastriggs
SHORE ROAD
Bowhouse
ESTUARY
Eastpark
Saltcot Hills
Powfoot
Welldale
Dornock
CAERLAVEROCK CASTLE
WILDFOWL & WETLAND CENTRE
Nethertown
Newbie
Shawhill
Merse
CAERLAVEROCK
River Annan
Overton
Blackshaw Bank
Newbie Mains
Barnkirk Pt
Burnfoot
Bowness-on-Solway
Drum Bay
Herd Hill
Biglands Ho
Bowness Hall
VALLUM (COURSE OF)
Port Carlisle
CAMPFIELD MARSH
RSPB
Cardurnock Flats
Glasson Moss
Carse Bay
Herd Hill
Bowness Common
Carsethorn
Low Flow
SOLWAY FIRTH
Hogus Pt
Cardurnock
Anthorn
Millrigg Fm
Borron Pt
Longcroft
Whitrigg
ARBIGLAND GARDENS
JOHN PAUL JONES COTTAGE MUSEUM
Whitrigg
Grune Pt
Channel of River Wampool
Angerton
237
Skinburness
Skinburness Marsh
Channel of River Waver
Kirkbride
Starry Hill
Newton Marsh
Newton Arlosh
Longlands Head
Powhill
Shaw Ho
Kirkbride
Wampool
Shaw Hill
Watch Hill
Border
Silloth
Ind Est
Calvo
Salt Coates
Low Eskrigg
Meadow Lodge
Seaville
Sleightholme
Grassings
Ind Est
Causewayhead
B5307
SOUTH SOLWAY MOSSES
Lawrenceholme
Greenrow
Orchard Ho
Moss Side
Blackdyke
Raby Grange
Wedholme Ho
B5301
Blitterlees
Parkhead
High Ho
Raby
Wedholme Hill
Corbet Houses
Flagstaff
B5300
Heather Bank
Wolsty Hall
Dryholme
Kingside Hill
River Waver
Middle Houses
B5302
Oulton Ho
Pelutho Grange
COLDMIRE ROAD
Abbey Town
Kelsick
Oulton
Colmire Sough
Wolsty
The Hill Ho
NY
Highlaws
Lessonhall
Dundraw
228
229
Beckfoot
Kelsickhouse Fm
Moor Row
Aikhead
Station Hill
Pelutho
Foulsyke Fm
Southerfield Hall
Wheyrigg Fm
Dian Ho Fm
Waverbridge
West Ho
THORNHILL MOSS & MEADOW
Waverbridge Mill
Grayson Ho
Western Bank
East Fm
Newtown
Lowsay Fm
Aldoth
B5302
River Wiza
Hill Ho
Beck Fm
Weary Hall
Crooklands
Blencogo
Glebelands
Tarns
Southerfield Ho
Low Houses
0 1 2 3 miles
0 1 2 3 4 5 km
A
B
C
D
E
F
G
H
1
2
3
4
5
6

Crowdieknowe Hill
Bigholms Burn
Bloch Fm
Burian Hill
Tinnisburn Forest
Hardenside
Upper Millsteads
Green Knowe
Greena Hill
Stonegarthside Hall
Longcleughside
Gowd Muir
Collin Hags 255
249
Kerr Height
Tarrasfoot Hill
Mumbie Cottages
The Hill
Albierig
Irvine Ho
Bushfield
Kirtleton
Crosslands
West Linnbridgeford
Leaheads Hill
Viewy Knowe
Hagg Hill
Greenburn
Outer Woodhead
Orchard
Under Millsteads
Liddel Lodge
Old Hall
Nook
Crookburn Hill
Baileyhead
Kerr
Claygate
Byreburnside
Harelaw Pike
Barrascrofts
Harelaw Mill
Craigs
Allfornought Hill
Outer Hill
March Cottage
Enthorn
GILNOCKIE TOWER
Harelawhill
Arthur Seat
Hollows
Tomshielburn
Barnglies
Tarcoon
Loophill
Archerbeck
Kingfield Ho
Lads Lodge
High Muir
Allfornought
Solwaybank
Wattaman
Chapelhills
Newbie
Airnlee
Rowanburn
Liddel Park
KIELDER FOREST PARK
Chamot Hill
Bartle's Hill
Sheala Hill
High Stenries
Mossknowe
Greenrigg
Esk Bank
Catlowdy
Chapel Hill
Warwicksland
Crossings
Outerland
Kennedy's Corner
Craigshaws
Bell's Flow
Bogrie
Bogra
Evertown
Canonbie
Beyond the Moss
Sleetbeck
CONNEL CHYARD
The Forest
Springkell
Branteth
Parkhead
Milltown
Netherton
Dykehead
Beyond-the-Wood
Riggcroft
Rae Burn
Wakey Hill
Nether Hill
Kinkry Hill
Bellstown
Cadgillside
Hillhead Fm
Cadgill Wood
Scotland Gate
Woodhouselees Plantn
Riddings Fm
Hilltop
Redgate Head
Trough Head
Roadhead
Burnfoot
Crawn Knowe
Woodhouselees
Riddingshill
Barns
High Plains
Scuggate
Scugg Fm
Shawstown
Roan Fm
Moat
Livingstone Ho
Bruntons Hill
Raeburn
Hope's Ho
Westfield Ho
High Parkfoot
Gillshaw Wood
Logan Mains
Cadgillfoot
Cubbyhill
SCOTS DYKE
Todhillwood
Netherhirst
Haggbeck
Friar Hill
240
Gillshaw Flow
Chapelknowe
Englishtown
Scotsdike
The Green
Lynebrook
Kays Bank
Southwoodhead
Stubby Knowe
Campers' Corner
Carwinley
Todhillrigg Fm
Park Ho
Park Rigg
Skyehead
Low Luckens
MERKLAND CROSS
Faudingcleuch
Dunskellyrig
Frankstown Fm
Corries Mill
Easton
Gibstown
Raeburn Flow
Hayfield
Nether Woodhouse
Netherby
Oakshaw Hill
Jenkinstown
Shankhill
Harper Hill
Raeburnfoot
Batenbush
Laws Hall
New Pallyards
Lynedale
Stapleton
Milligansbush
Raeburn
Silverhill Wood
Cloughfoot Wood
Whiteclosergg
Newton
Bruce's Cave
Williamsfield
Aitchisons Bank
Stealandsburn
Patties Hill
Kirkpatrick-Fleming
Valley
Slackbraes Wood
Low Plains
Hollee
Broats
Mossknowe
Gap Wood
DLO Smalmstown
Sandbed
Dry Beck
Wellknowe Rigg
Brackenhill Rigg
High Dubwath
Barracks
White Close
A74(M)
OLD BLACKSMITHS SHOP CENTRE
Solway Moss
Jackson Rigg
Bolton Fell
Calvertsholm
Gretna Green Services
SOLWAY MOSS 1542
Smalmstown
Longtown
Ind Est
Drakeknowe Plantn
Prior Rigg
Boltonfellend
Riggheads
Springfield
Nutberry Moss
Gretna Green
GRETNA GREEN
Stonehouse
Mill Hill
Fauld Mill
Brisco Hill
Prior House
Mossedge
Todholes
White Moss
Black Snib
Kirklinton Hall
Appleby Ho
Henry's Hill
High Hills
Cocklet Hill Fm
Leaps
Gretna
GRETNA GATEWAY
DLO Longtown
Francismoor Wood
Kirklinton
Hethersgill
Irvington
Rigg
Old Graitney
River Esk
Hopesike Woods
Bush-on-Lyne Fm
Lonning Park
Prior Rigg
Broomhill Moss
Walton Moss
WALTON MOSS
Green
Muirhouse
Burnfoot
Hornickhill
East Cliff
Hetherside
Kirklinton Park
Westhills Moss
Cliff Ho
Willow Hill
Skitby
Smithfield
Breaks Moss
Browhouses
Redkirk Pt
Sarkfoot Pt
Mossband Hall
Sandysike
Alstonby Hall
Willow Bank
Brown Dyke
Hill Ho
West Knowe
Metal Bridge
Justicetown
Mossband Hall Marsh
Westlinton
Alstonby Grange
Standingstone Rigg
Brown Rigg
Highberries
Blackhouse Plantns
Young's Close
Torduff Pt
Channel of River Esk
Moor Ho
Hespin Wood
Ross Castle
Scaleby Moss
The Nooks
Brightenflat
Hall Flatt
Seat Hill Fm
Morrell Hill
Heads Wood
Kylesyke Hill
HADRIAN'S WALL PATH
Rockliffe Marsh
Far Gulf
Halltown
Wether Hill
Todhills Rest Area
Todhills
Rockcliffe Moss
Dyke Nook
Scalebyhill
Fordsyke
Bullersike
The Beck Fm
Newtown
Near Gulf
Rockcliffe Cross
CASTLETOWN HOUSE
Moorcock Plantn
Barclose
Scaleby
Woodhead
Pateshill
Laversdale
Burghmarsh Pt
Blackford
Wide open Dykes
Longpark
Scaleby Castle
CUMBRIA
Old Sandsfield
New Sandsfield
Casson Dyke Fm
Rockcliffe
Green Acres
Dykeside
Brunstock Beck
Irthington
Red Hills
Old Church Fm
Bankend
Harker
Hougton Ho
High Knells
Walldub
Walby
Wall Head
White Moss
Carlisle Airport
Beanlands Park
Middle Fm
Burgh Marsh
Cargoilhill
Ind Est
Harker Grange
Knells Ho
HADRIAN'S WALL (COURSE OF)
VALLUM (COURSE OF)
STANEGATE (COURSE OF)
Ruleholme Br
Drumburgh
Watch Hill
North End
Burgh by Sands
Bus Pk
Brunstock
Watch Hill
Crosby-on-Eden
Watch Cross
Park Barns
Easton
Boustead Hill
Beaumont
St Ann's Well
Cargo
Kingstown
Houghton
Low Crosby
Gelt Fm
Drumburgh Moss
DRUMBURGH MOSS
Longburgh
Hill Fm
West End
Monkhill Lough
Monkhill
Grinsdale
Kingmoor Ho
Tarraby
Park Broom
Warwick Holme
Bank Head
Edmond Castle
Kirkandrews on Eden
Knowefield
Linstock
Holme Ends
The Hall
Newby East
Fingland Moss
Fingland Rigg
Farhill
Hosket Hill
Etterby
Belah
Edentown
Moor Ho
Whiteclosegate
Holme Gate
Little Corby
Western Ridge
Stanwix
River Eden
Corby Hill
Toppin Castle
Fingland
Thurstonfield
Moorhouse
Stainton
Willow Holme
Rickerby
Warwick on Eden
Warwick Bridge
FINGLANDRIGG WOODS
Longrigg
Kirkbampton
CUMBERLAND BIRD OF PREY CENTRE
Thurstonfield Lough
Cobble Hall
Ind Est
CARLISLE CASTLE
TULLIE HOUSE MUSEUM & ART GALLERY
BRUNTON PARK
Aglionby
Moorhouse Hall
Corry Hill
Allenwood
Stockdale Hall
Fenton
Ploughlands
Oughterby
Woodlands
Prior Rigg
Belle Vue
CARLISLE
Carlisle
Botcherby
Scotby Ho
Warwick Moor Wood
Burnrigg
Low Wood
Fenton Lane Head
Windmill Ho
Little Bampton
Flat
TOWN WALLS
Newtown
Denton Holme
Wetheral Plain
Heads Nook
Broadwath
Westfield Ho
Lanshaw Ho
Bampton Beck
Quarry Gill
Park Ho
Bank Ho
Orton Moss
Little Orton
Suttle Ho
Morton
Longsowerby
Scotby
Wetheral
Gleneairn Mill
Moss Knowe
Faugh
Great Orton
Red Ho
Currock
Garlands
Orchard Ho
Great Corby
CORBY CASTLE
Aikton Ho
Fisher Gill
Newby West
Upperby
Harraby
Scotby Shield
Birk Hill
Aikton
Roblaw Hall
Fallow Field
Orton Park Fm
Newby Cross
Gladsmuir
Wetheral Pasture
Morley Hill
Whitehead
Gamelsby
Wiggonby
Cummersdale
Blackwell
Carleton
Gillhead
High Wood
Cumwhinton
Cote Ho
Shield Head
Clint Head Fm
Cumwhitton
Down Hall
Thornby
Woodhouses
Orton Rigg
Lingyclose Head
High Woodbank
Wampool
Wiggon Rigg
Baldwinholme
Orton Grange Fm
Sowerby Wood
CARLISLE
Scugger Ho
Brisco
Brisco Hill
Wrayside
Greyrigg Ho
Hardcake Hall
High Whinnow
Nealhouse
Cardewlees
Flosh
Blackhall Wood
Eden Banks
Moorthwaite Moss
Moorhouse
Moorhouse Hall
Parton
Moorend
Wood Fm
Springfield Fm
Low Cotehill
Dockrayrigg Ho
Low Whinnow
Bankend
DALSTON
Durdar
Oakland Ho
Burthwaite Hill
Newbiggin Hall
Knott Hill
Dockray Hall
Micklethwaite
Crofton
Thursby
Flanders
Hilltouse Nook
Durdar Ho
Carleton Ho
Cotehill
Dalston
Ratten Row
Pow Bank
Stone Raise
Burthwaite
Wragmire Ho
Warathwaite Head
Standingstone
Spittal
Bridge Ho
West End
229
Evening Hill
Cardew Hall
Nooklane Foot
Green Head
230
Wragmire Moss
Stoney Wath Fm
Greenwood Ho
West Woodside
West Curthwaite
Cardew Lodge
Cardew
Wreay
Wragmire Head
High Stand Plantn
Kirkland
Hazel Head
Moorthwaite Lough
Cumdivock
Chalkfoot
Buckabank
Bridge End
Unthank
Wreay Hall
Wigton
Ghyll Head Fm
Jacob's Gill
East Curthwaite
Broomfield
Nook
Hawksdale Hall
Spurnston
Bankdale Fm
Foulbridge
Petteril Crook's Mill
Lowthian Gill
Ivy Cottage
Low Ho
Drybeck

Kershope Forest
Bewcastle Fell
KIELDER FOREST PARK
Sighty Crag 518
Horse Head
Black Knowe 492
Rushy Knowe
Black Cleugh
Allerybank
Cuddy's Hill
Blacklyne Ho
Kettle Hall
Whitelyne Common
Long Bar
Long Crags
Hopehouse
Greenmeath Sike
Black Knors 248
Smuggy's Pike
Black Stantling
Stubbins Hill
Bailey Head
Black Knors
Baileyhead
Crookburn Hill
Slaty Crag
Long Crag 456
The Shanks
Kielder Mires
Claver Hill
The Flatt
Watch Rigg
Greyfell Common
Tarn Beck
Lowe Bush
Paddaburn
Muckle Samuel's Crags
Little Dodd Hill
High Capon Edge
Arthur Seat
Bailey Mill
Blackpool Gate
Holmehead
Nook
Crew Crag
Whiteside End
Gaylock Hill
Irthing Head
Blind Sike
Whitehill
Green
Sheala Hill
Crew Moor
Cammock Rigg
Felecia Crags
Round Hill 310
Battle Hill
Crossings
Oakshaw Ford
Bankhead
White Brae
Breakshaw Hill
Churnsike Lodge
Great Tongue Rigg
Round Top 325
Shank End
Wark Forest
Sleetbeck
Shawhead
Brownhill
Grey Hill
Bullcleugh Gate
Blackrigg Foot
Dry Sike
Wreay Hill
Butterburn Flow
Long Rigg
West Cleugh
Rawney
Park Head
Danger area
Spy Rigg
NORTHUMBERLAND
Nether Hill
Heather Ho
Peel o'Hill
Borderrigg
Leafy Rigg
Hen Hill
Gowany Knowe
Great Watch Hill
Haining
Blue Hemmel
Kinkry Hill
Roughsike
Ann's Hill
Bewcastle
356
Barron's Pike
Roadhead
Nobelstown
Scotstown
Kirkbeckstown
Shopford
Gilbert's Hill
Greymare Hill
Blackshaws Sike
Butterburn
Lampert
NATIONAL PARK
Roan Fm
Kilnstown
Kirk Beck
Whipper Slack
Gowk Bank
Black Fell
Westfield Ho
High Parkfoot
Bushley Bank
Jock's Hill
Butterburn Hill
Cheeseburn Hill
Grindon Green
Lynecrook
Birk Bush
Cocklett Rigg
Luke's Ho
Collin Bank
Side Fell
Hen Hill
Rough Sike
Deer Hill
Selbystown
Kays Bank
Bellbank
Green Knowe
Low King Hill
Spadeadam Forest
Jerrycalf Rigg
Berry Hill
Great Buckster
Caud Beck
Tip Hill
Gavelock Hill
The Show
Low Park
The Beacon 310
Standingstone Rigg
Harper Hill
Allergarth
Show Burn
Askerton Park
Gillalees Beacon
White Rigg
Green Rigg
Hopealone
Stapleton
Crowrigg Sike
Kingturn Rigg
Rashbush Rigg
Wileysike Ho
Bell's Braes
Robinrock Flothers
Hugh's Hill
Patties Hill
Low Park
Mollen Wood
Spadeadam Fm
Dumbliar Rigg
Middle Shield Rigg
Peat Rigg
White Rigg
Burn Divot
Parkgate Cotts
Ash Moss
Trout Beck
Forster's Hill
Rushey Hill
White Close
High Green Hill
Rinnion Hills
Long Moss
River Irthing
Black Rigg
Wall Shield
Highstead Ash
Jamie's Hill Sike
Thirlwall Common (North Side)
Whiteside
Bolton Fell
Bonfellend
Kirkcambeck
Gallowberry
Palmer Hill
Waterhead Common
Popping Stone
Watch Hill
Moss Peteral
Benkshill
Swallow Crags
Benks Hills
Ventners Hall
Edges Green
Cowburn Rigg
CUMBRIA
Tweedy Hill
Wardrew Fm
Seed Rigg
Cocklet Hill Fm
Leaps Rigg
Barns
Lees Hill
West Hall
Kingbridge Ford Br
Gilsland Spa
War Carr
Hangingshields Rigg
Chesters Pike
Cleughfoot
Sook Hill
Well Ho
Hill Ho
Khorren Beck
B6318
Cairny Croft
Barron House
Hadrian's Wall
Hadrian's Wall (course of)
Cawfields Milecastle
Pennine Way
Vallum (course of)
Broomhill Moss
Walton Moss
Spout Bank
Swaites
Craigsyke Ford
Park Nook
Miller Hill
Willowford Bridge Abutment
Midgeholme Moss
Gilsland
Burnt Walls
Low Old Shields
Walltown
Cockmount Hill
Hainings
Walton Woodhead
Allieshaw Rigg
Leahill Turret
Birdoswald (Camboglanna) Roman Fort
Birdoswald
Harrow's Scar Milecastle
Poltross Burn Milecastle
Gap
Greenhead
Haltwhistle Common
Milestone Ho
Stanegate (course of)
Breaks Moss
White Hill
Hill Head
Craig Hill
High Ho
Denton Mains
Throp
Wardoughan
Fell End
Lees Hall
Blackhouse Plantns
Low Rigg
Walton
Garthside
Hare Hill
Banks
Bank's East Turret
Upper Denton
Mains Rigg
Gapshield
The College Fm
Edge Hill
Hollin Crags
Common Ho
Morrell Hill
Low Wall
Howgill
Nook
Banks Ho
Lanercost
Trywell Lodge
A69
Thirlwall Common (South Side)
Todholes
Blenkinsopp Common
Blenkinsopp Hall
Haltwhistle
Town Foot
Low House Fm
Melkridge
Heads Wood
Kylesyke Hill
Lanercost Priory
Burtholme
Kellwood
St Mary's Vale
Low Broom Hill
Denton Hall
Lodges
Low Row
Hill Head
Hole Ho
Haltwhistle Ind Est
B6322
Plenmeller
A6071
The Beck Fm
River Irthing
Naworth Castle
Naworth Park
Birch Craig
Black Rigg
Wain Rigg
Cross Bank
Bellister Castle
Sandyford Rigg
Unthank Hall
East Unthank
Newtown
Cotehill Fm
Quarrybeck Ho
Denton Foot
Denton Fell
Featherstone Common
Wydon Eals
Broomhouse
Irthington
Kirby Moor
Low Houses
Cleugh Head
Glencune Burn
Hartleyburn Common (North Side)
Warren Ho
Broomhouse Common
Howden Burn
Blackcleugh Rigg
Red Hills
Brampton
Old Church Fm
Scarrow Hill
Miltonrigg Wood
Greentarn Rigg
Whamoss Rigg
Cross Rigg
Peat Gate
Bridge End
River South Tyne
Park Village
Bridle Green
Plenmeller Common
Beanlands Park
Ind Est
Middle Fm
A689
Aaron's Town
Milton Hall
Milton Hill
Back Dike
Greenside Rigg
Cocklit Hill
Kellah Burn
Rowfoot
Ramshaw Fell
Cairn End
Rulesholme
B6413
Milton
Kirkhouse
Moss Hill
Follysyke Cotts
Byers Hall
Hartley Burn
Park Barns
Wood's Hill
Low Geltbridge
Talkin Tarn
Hallbankgate
Tarnhouse Rigg
Tindale
Haining Burn
Haining Ho
Hill Ho
Lambley Fm
Wood Houses
Coanwood
Hargill Ho
Todhillwood
Peat Hill
Gelt Ho
Gelt Woods
Farlam
Boon Hill
Highfell
Clesketts
Geltsdale
Bishop Hill
Midgeholme
Clover Hill
Lambley
Burn Ho
Garbutt Hill
Wolf Hills
Edmond Castle
Tindale Tarn
Bruthwaite Forest
Tindale Fells
Halton Lea Gate
Pennine Road
Hag Wood
Stonehouse
Western Ridge
Forest Head
Byers Fell
Lambley Common
Quarry Ho
Laws Fell
Hayton
Talkin
Whinney Fell
458
Byers Pike
Haltonlea Fell
Hartleyburn Common (South Side)
Tows Bank
Coanwood Common
Corby Hill
Street Ho
Chapel Ho
Turkey Hall
Brown Fell
Whitwham
Redscar Burn
Warwick Bridge
How
Cote Hill
Hill Ho
Greenwell
Talkin Head Fm
Talkin Fell 381
Kelky Fell
Butt of Blackburn
Glendue Burn
NORTHUMBERLAND
Wallace's Crags
Ashholme Common
Brown Rigg
Allenwood
Stockdale Hall
Fenton
Ring Gate
Castle Carrock
Garth Head
River Gelt
Simmerson Hill
Cold Fell 621
Blackburn Head
Eals
Dun Hill
Parkhead Fell
Heads Nook
Fenton Lane Head
Whin Hill
Hayton Moss
How Gill
Larchet Hill
Knowe Head
Eals Fell
Blaeberry Hill
Glencairn Mill
Faugh
Tarn Lodge
Oaktree Hall
Knotts Wood
Tarnmonath Fell
Glendue Fell
Side Ho
Snope Burn
Moss Knowe
Park Ho
Long Dyke
Castle Carrock Fell
Knarsdale Hall
The Bog
Snope Common
Pike Rigg
Mainsrigg Fell
Nixon Head
Geltsdale Ho
Binney Bank
King's Forest of Geltsdale
Great Blacklaw Hill 595
Faugh Cleugh
Thinhope Burn
Knarsdale
Whitfield Moor
Longdyke Fm
PENNINE
Town Green
Williamston Common
Low Bradshaw Hill
Whitfield Law
Morley Hill
Whitehead Hill
Black Dub
Albyfield
482
Black Hill
Knarsdale Forest
Aules Hill
Slaggyford
Morleyhill Fell
Cumwhitton
Cardunneth Pike
Middle Top
West Dun Hill
Barhaugh Common
Dewley Fell
Carlatton Mill
Turnberry Ho
Bertram Hill
Shawhead
Moorthwaite Moss
Cumrew Fell
Geltsdale Middle
Three Pikes 585
Hartchyside
Far Ho
Dewley Field
Willyshaw Rigg
497
Eden Banks
Chapel Well
New Water
Knarsdale Common
Lintley
Ayle Common
Cumrew
Butt Hill
Gelt Burn
Long Cross
Hornsby
Far Town
Far Hornsby
Gateshaw Mill
Newbiggin Fell
Blotting Raise 591
Thornhope Fell
Kirkhaugh
Ayle
Fishgarth Wood
Green Hill
Newbiggin
Croglin Fell
Castle Nook
Kirkside Wood
Clarghyll Hall
High Stand Plantn
The Combs
Broad Mea
High Shield
Whitley Castle
South Tynedale Railway
White Ho
Newshield Moss
Hard Rigg
Low Hill
Lawson Hill
Cairnhead
Sumburgh
Croglin
Grey Nag 656
Black Hill
Drybeck
Fieldhead
Farlam
A686
A688
A689
A69
B6318
B6413
250
239
230
231
NY
80
50
0 1 2 3 miles
0 1 2 3 4 5 km

Redesmouth
Shitlington Common
Ealinghamrigg Common
Ealingham Rigg
Countesspark Wood
Green Rigg
Cowstand Hill
Birney Hill
Sweethope Crags
Great Bavington
Watson's Walls
Dun's Pike
Cairnglastenhope
Pundershaw
Shitlington Crags
Shitlington Hall
Stone Ho
Anton Hill
Lee Hall Fm
Lee Hall
Lowshield Green
Tone Hall
Carrycoats Hall
Waterfalls
White Ho
Quarry Ho
Newonstead Fm
Bavington Hill Head
Greatlaw
Merry Shiels
Esp Hill
Bridge Ho
Esp Mill
High Carry Ho
Low Carry Ho
Pitland Hills
Rushey Law
Colt Crag Reservoir
Thockrington
Little Bavington
Bavington Hall
Thockrington Crags
Moss Barns
Brier Hill
Camstone Rigg
Watergate Moor
Blackaburn
Manor Fm
Warksfield Head
South Fm
Rubbingstob Hill
Short Knowes
Bavington Mount
White Ho
Birtley
Cowstand Burn
Colt Crag
Trinket
Leadgate
Crossridge
Longstrother
Gold Island
Rouchester Fm
Gunnerton Fell
Folly Moss
Kirkheaton Wind Farm
Birk Hill 230
Horneystead
The Ash
Pasture Ho
Threpwood Hill
Dinley Hill
Little Swinburne
Hallington High Fm
Harelaw
White Hill
Windy Edge
The Barnes
Woodley Shield
Wark
Comogan Fm
Parkhouse Fm
Barrasford Park
Hallington Reservoirs
Fell Ho
Whygate
Stonehaugh
Low Moralee
High Moralee
Warks Haugh
Pit Ho
Mallowburn Cottages
Blackhill Fm
Hallington
Moatlaw
Coldcotes
Sadbury Hill
Bleaklaw
Park End
Steward's Ho
Great Swinburne
Whiteside Law
Hallington New Ho
Crookbank
Broadpool Common
Standard Hill
Lyndhurst
Green's Fell
Swinburne Castle
Liddell Hall
Coldcotes Hill
Willowbog
Short Moor
Gunnerton
Colwell
Middleburn
Coalcleugh
NORTHUMBERLAND
Black Rigg
Burnmouth Cotts
Shepherdshield
Allgood Fm
Fell Lane Fm
Haggle Rigg
Black Law
Burn Ho
Nunwick Mill
Wood Hall Fm
Well Ho
High Well Ho
Ryal
Long Edge
Simonburn
Ellwood Ho
Barrasford
Barrasford Green
Bingfield East Quarter
Townshield Bank
Hopeshield Burn
Hall Barns
Fairshaw Fm
Middle Fm
New Bingfield
Bingfield Eastside
Bell Crags
Edge Ho
Beaumont Ho
Byreshaw Hill
Simonburn Common
Greenhaugh
Uppertown
Wester Hall
Haughton Castle
Bellcrag Flow
Stoopprigg
Sharpley
Haughton Pasture
Chollerton
Bingfield
Haughton Common
Banno Crags
Cockplay
Low Errington
Tudridge Fell
Long Rigg
Long Crag
Haughton Mains
Errington Red Ho
Tudridge
Shellbraes
Crow Crags
Well Rigg
Teppermoor
Rye Hill
Lincoln Hill
Humshaugh
Keepwick Fm
Halleypike Lough
Hemmel Rigg
Black Carts Turret
Carrawburgh Temple of Mithras
Chollerford
Walwick
Cocklaw
Sweet Rigg
Stonefolds
Queen's Crags
Hadrian's Wall (course of)
Vallum (course of)
Hadrian's Wall Path
Walwick Fell
Beukley
Rose's Bower
The Whiggs
Great Whittington
Sewingshields Wall Turrets & Milecastle
Old Repeater Station
Brown Moor
Torney's Fell
Chesters Museum
Chesters (Cilurnum) Roman Fort
Low Brunton
Brunton Bank
Grottington Fm
Errington Hill Head
Greenlee Lough
Broomlee Lough
Middle Ho
Lane Ho
Brunton Turret
Planetrees Roman Wall
Little Whittington
Bonnyrigg Hall
Hotbank Crags
Housesteads (Vercovicium) Roman Fort
Howden Hill
Cowey Sike
Settlingstones
Frankham Fell
Wall
Hill Head
Halton Red House
Crag Lough
Hadrian's Wall
Grindon Mill Hills
Grindon Hill
Stonecroft Ho
Newbrough Lodge
Frankham
Fourstones
Written Crag
Codlaw Hill
Wall Fen Fm
Port Gate
Winshields Milecastle
Grindon Lough
East Wood
Stagshaw Bank
Carr Houses
Steel Rigg
Bradley Hall
Grandy's Knowe
Newbrough
Nether Warden
Halton
Once Brewed
Muckle Moss
Honeycrook Burn
Hindshield
Fell Cott
Wharmley
High Warden
Warden
Fern Hill Fm
Stagshaw High Ho
Black Hill
Holly Hall
Long Stone
Thorngrafton Common
Whinnetley Moss
Haydon Fell
High Ho
Allerwash Hall
Woodshield Fm
Greenshaw Plain
Broom Park
Carr Hill
Salmonswell Fm
Stagshaw
Chantry Fm
Aydon Castle
Chesterholm (Vindolanda) Roman Fort & Museum
East Mill Hills
Bridge End
Acomb
The Riding
Beaufront Hill Head
Shawwell Ho
Aydon
Thorngrafton
Westley Bank
Glendue
Bush Fm
Ind Est
Oakwood
Sandhoe
Beaufront Castle
Hampstead
Westend Town
Birkshaw
Whitechapel Hill Prior Ho
Chesterwood
Anick
Anick Grange
Brown Rigg
Henshaw
Tow House
Bardon Mill
Lipwood Hall
Haydon Bridge
Wood Hall
Hackford Fm
High Wood
Tyne Green
Bridge End
Corstopitum Roman Station
Thornbrough
Redburn
Crow Hall
Lipwood Well
Hill Ho
Lowe's Fell
Low Gate
Hexham
Hexham Abbey
Wide Haugh
Corbridge
High Barns
High Barn
Beltingham
Ridley
Ellfoot Ho
Elrington
Bagraw Fm
Moot Hall
Delegate Hall
Border History Mus
Dilston Park
Dilston
Howden Dene
Haughstrother Wood
Wool Ho
Burn Ho
Allen Banks
West Land Ends
Threepwood
Breckon Hill
Cock Wood
Swallowship Hill
High Town
West Fell
Grey Court
Prospect Hill
Vauce Wood
Blackhall Plantns
Benson's Fell
Oakerland
Sunnyside
Riding Mill
Farrow Shields
Ridley Common
Plankey Mill
Yellow Rigg
Blackhill Fm
Plover Hill 227
Black Ho
Linnels
Temperley Grange
Beauclerc
Hag Bank
Harlow Field
Langley
The Paise
Peterel Field
Red Ho
Hole Ho
Lamb Shield
Kingswood Common
Kingswood Rigg
Staward Manor
Nilston Rigg
Stublick Hill
Stublick Moor
Greenridge
Loadman
Diptonmill
Channel Well
Dipton Wood
Broomhaugh
Red Hemmels
High Plains
Beacon Hill 337
Fell Ho
Haining Hall
Crag Head
Catton Beacon 337
Emertley Hill
Rebel Hill
Greenrigg Moor
Edge Ho
Dotland Park
Todburn Steel
Broomley Pit Ho
Fellhouse Fell
Spitalshield Moor
Lord's Lot
Ordley
Lee
Linnel Wood
Hirst Hill 185
Marley Cote Walls
Eastwood Ho
Dingbell Hill
Whitfield
Highfield Fm
White Ho
Bulman's Rigg
Cook's Ho
Low Lane Ho
Barker Ho
Juniper
Black Hall
Dye House
Finechambers Mill
Shield Hall
Low Ho
Peel Flatt
Bearsbridge
Old Town
Gaterley Hill
Moss Well
Reeds Rigg
Hamburn Hall
Dalton
Whitley Mill
Steel
Slaley
Burnt Ho
Healey Mill
Emley
Hindley Hill
Catton
Lea Hall
Stone Hall
Lough Hill
Raven Currick Rigg
Eshells Moor
Springwell Ho
Whitley Chapel
Mire Ho
Dukesfield
Ridley Hills
Strothers Dale
Hill Top
Holly Hall
Park Head
Whitfield Hall
Keenley
Chapel Ho
Pia Troon
Thornley Gate
Moorhouse Gate
Allendale Town
Whapweasel Burn
Salmon Field
Rawgreen
Leadpipe Hill
White Ho
Fell Cotts
Quarry Ho
Monk Cott
High Oustley
Broadwood Halls
Crawberry Hill
Burntridge Moor
Burnt Ridge
Rowley Head
Stotsfold Hall
Steel Hall
Fell Plantn
Spring Ho
Trygill
Colpitts Grange
Parmentley Hall
Wentworth Place
Finney Hill
Glen Hill
Stotsfold Fm
Rennys Barn
Gate Ho
Wager Ho
Scotch Halls
Herds Law
Rowley Burn
357
Slaley Forest
Espershields Fm
Morley Hill
Round Hill
Park Gill
Mount Pleasant
Nettle Hill
King's Law
White Hall
Acton Fell
White Ho
Parmentley Cott
Hexhamshire Common
Broadwell Ho
Park Ho
Embley Fell
315
Pithouse Fell
Ninebanks
Middle Edge
Haggburn Gate
Studdon Park
Green Hill
Lilswood Grange
Grouse Ho
War Law
Burntshield Haugh
Blanchland Moor
Derwent Reservoir
Ouston
Park
Green Dike
Garrets Hill
Newfold Ho
Loaning Ho
Burntshieldhaugh Fell
Cowbyers Fell
413
Dean Rigg
Round Hill
Herd's Ho
Dryburn Moor
Sinderhope Gate
Ladle Well
Hangman Hill
Pow Hill
Ruffside Hall
Whitewalls Burn
Hawkuplee
Black Hill
Broad Gate
Sinderhope
Pennypie Ho
Hotburn Hill
Ouston Fell
Spartywell
Farneyside
Acton Moor
Allendale Common
Stobbylee Burn
Steelcrags Wood
Pennypie Fell
Birkside Fell
Greenleycleugh
Brownley Hill 533
Pikeley Rigg
Hope Fell
Rye Close
Harwoodshield Fell
Birkside
Reeding
Blanchland
Berry Bank
Edmundbyers Common
White Hill
Mohope Head
Park Ho
Knock Shield
Broadlee
Kevelin Moor
Sipton Shield
427
Newbiggin Fell
Baybridge
Ruffside Moor
Mohope Moor
The Nook
Limestone Brae
Longwell Moor
Tedham Moss
Riddlehamhope Fell
Newbiggin
Harehope Hall
Halley Moor
Broad Meadows
546
New Ho
The Meres
Black Cleugh
Knockshield Moor
Spartylea
Elpha Green
Halleywell Fell
Western Meadows
Nookton Back Fell
Hunstanworth
High Ho
Cross Hill
Townfield
Buckshott Fell
Heatheryburn Moor
Uzzles Hill
White Hill
Hesleywell
Boltshope
Stote
River North Tyne
River South Tyne
River Tyne
River Allen
River East Allen
River West Allen
Dere Street
Front Street
Cross Bank
Pennine Way
A68
A69
A686
A695
A6079
B6318
B6319
B6320
B6342
B6304
B6305
B6295
B6303
B6306
B6307
B6321
B6531
B6530
251
231
232
242
7
8
9
10
11
A
B
C
D
E
F
G
H
00
80
50
NY

NORTHUMBERLAND
DURHAM
Capheaton
Belsay
Ogle
Shilvington
Saltwick
Stannington
Bedlington
Kirkheaton
Black Heddon
West Newham
Higham Dykes
Berwick Hill
Brenkley
Seaton Burn
Hallington
Ingoe
Ryal
Heugh
Milbourne
Ponteland
Prestwick
Dinnington
Brunswick Village
Hazlerigg
Fenwick
Matfen
Stamfordham
Dalton
Great Whittington
Ouston
Eachwick
Medburn
Darras Hall
High Callerton
Black Callerton
Woolsington
Kenton Bankfoot
Gosforth
Harlow Hill
Halton
Aydon
Heddon-on-the-Wall
Throckley
Newburn
North Walbottle
Westerhope
Kenton
Fenham
Newton Hall
Horsley
Wylam
Clara Vale
Ryton
Newton
Ovingham
Ovington
West Wylam
Prudhoe
Blaydon
Riding Mill
Stocksfield
Mickley Square
Branch End
Greenside
Winlaton
Whickham
Dunston
Broomhaugh
Broomley
New Ridley
High Mickley
Coalburns
Barlow
Hedley on the Hill
Leadgate
High Spen
Rowlands Gill
Sunniside
Healey
Whittonstall
Chopwell
Blackhall Mill
Highfield
Lintzford
Leazes
Byermoor
Marley Hill
Lamesley
Hamsterley
Burnopfield
Hobson
Tanfield
Newlands
Ebchester
High Westwood
Kiln Pit Hill
Medomsley
Dipton
Tantobie
Shotley Bridge
Leadgate
Stanley
Beamish
Consett
Annfield Plain
Carterway Heads
Edmundbyers
Muggleswick
Templetown
Iveston
Allensford
Castleside
Knitsley
Delves
Maiden Law
Burnhope
Craghead
Edmondsley
Waldridge
A696
A69
A68
A695
A694
A692
A693
A691
A1
A167
A184
B6318
B6309
B6321
B6545
NEWCASTLE INTERNATIONAL AIRPORT
BELSAY HALL CASTLE & GARDENS
KIRKLEY HALL
HADRIAN'S WALL (COURSE OF)
VALLUM (COURSE OF)
GEORGE STEPHENSON'S BIRTHPLACE
GIBSIDE CHAPEL & AVENUE
DERWENT WALK
BEAMISH OPEN AIR MUSEUM
TANFIELD RAILWAY
DERWENTCOTE STEEL FURNACE
AYDON CASTLE
CHERRYBURN
GREAT NORTH MUSEUM
METROCENTRE
Derwent Reservoir
252
241
232
233
NZ
0 1 2 3 miles
0 1 2 3 4 5 km

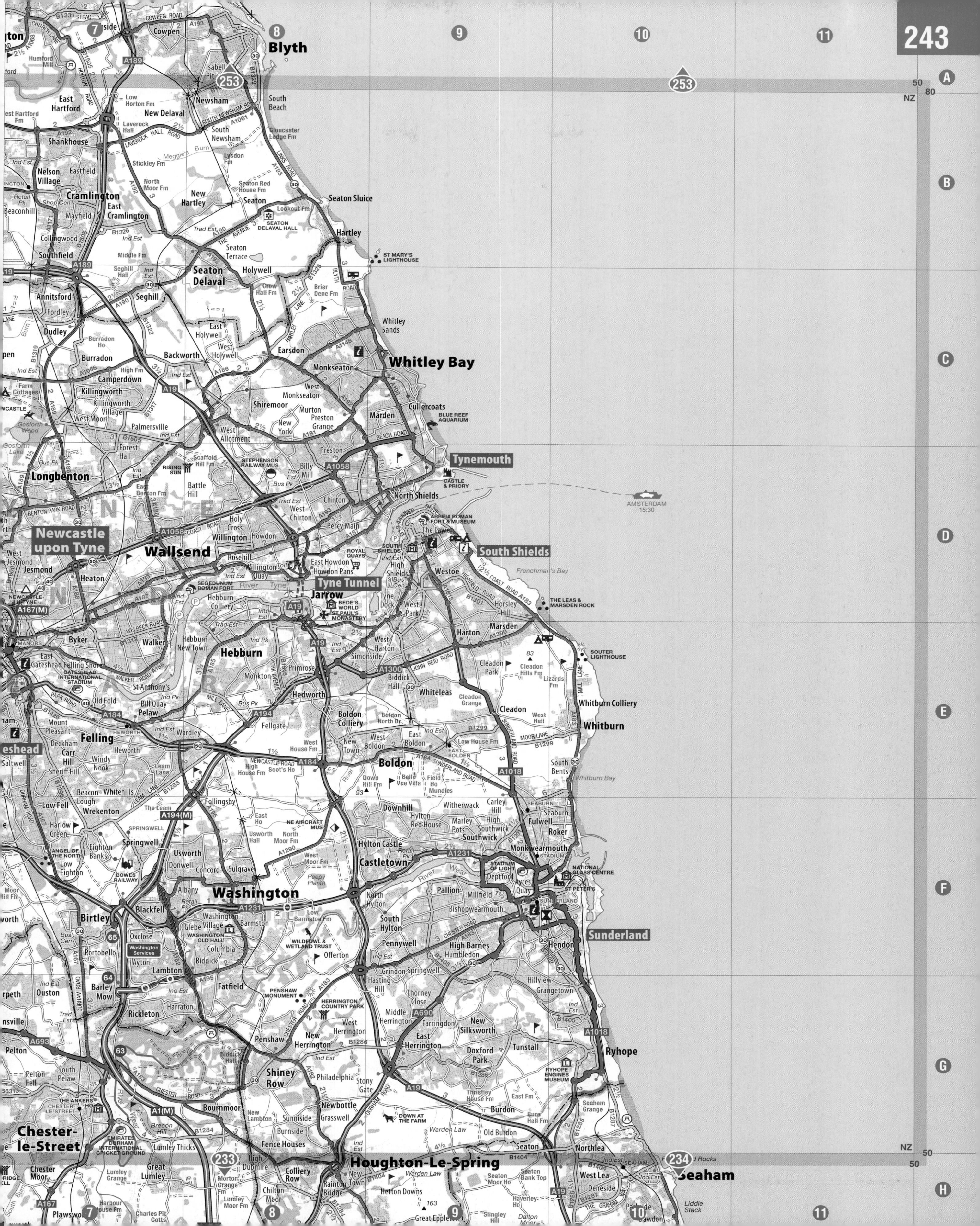
Blyth
Cowpen
Isabella Pit
South Beach
Newsham
New Delaval
East Hartford
Low Horton Fm
Laverock Hall
South Newsham
Gloucester Lodge Fm
Shankhouse
Stickley Fm
Lysdon Fm
Meggie's Burn
Nelson Village
Eastfield
Cramlington
East Cramlington
North Moor Fm
New Hartley
Seaton Red House Fm
Seaton
Seaton Sluice
Lookout Fm
Seaton Delaval Hall
Mayfield
Beaconhill
Collingwood
Southfield
Middle Fm
Seaton Terrace
Hartley
St Mary's Lighthouse
Seaton Delaval
Holywell
Seghill Hall
Crow Hall Fm
Brier Dene Fm
Annitsford
Seghill
Fordley
Dudley
Whitley Sands
East Holywell
West Holywell
Burradon Ho
Burradon
Backworth
Earsdon
Whitley Bay
Monkseaton
Camperdown
Killingworth
Killingworth Village
West Moor
High Fm
West Monkseaton
Shiremoor
Murton
Preston Grange
New York
Marden
Cullercoats
Blue Reef Aquarium
Gosforth Wood
Palmersville
West Allotment
Forest Hall
Preston
Tynemouth
Scaffold Hill Fm
Rising Sun
Stephenson Railway Mus
Billy Mill
Castle & Priory
Longbenton
Battle Hill
East Benton Fm
North Shields
Amsterdam 15:30
Chirton
West Chirton
Percy Main
Arbeia Roman Fort & Museum
The Lawe
Holy Cross
Willington
Howdon
Newcastle upon Tyne
Wallsend
South Shields
Frenchman's Bay
Jesmond
West Jesmond
Rosehill
Willington Quay
Royal Quays
East Howdon
Howdon Pans
Heaton
Segedunum Roman Fort
River Tyne
Tyne Tunnel
High Shields
Westoe
Jarrow
Hebburn Colliery
Bede's World
St Paul's Monastery
Tyne Dock
West Park
Horsley Hill
The Leas & Marsden Rock
Harton
Marsden
Byker
Walker
Hebburn New Town
Hebburn
West Harton
Simonside
Souter Lighthouse
Gateshead
Felling Shore
Gateshead International Stadium
Monkton
Primrose
Biddick Hall
Cleadon Park
Cleadon Hills Fm
Lizards Fm
St Anthony's
Old Fold
Hedworth
Whiteleas
Cleadon Grange
Bill Quay
Pelaw
Cleadon
Whitburn Colliery
Mount Pleasant
Wardley
Fellgate
Boldon Colliery
Boldon North Br
West Hall
Whitburn
Felling
Heworth
Deckham
Carr Hill
Windy Nook
Leam Lane
Sheriff Hill
West House Fm
High House Fm
Scot's Ho
West Boldon
East Boldon
Low House Fm
New Town
Boldon
South Bents
Whitburn Bay
Saltwell
Down Hill Fm
Belle Vue Villa
Field Ho
Mundles
Beacon Lough
Whitehills
Wrekenton
Low Fell
Follingsby
The Leam
Downhill
Witherwack
Carley Hill
Seaburn
Fulwell
Hylton Red House
Marley Pots
High Southwick
Southwick
Roker
Harlow Green
Springwell
East Ho
Usworth Hall
North Moor Fm
NE Aircraft Mus
Hylton Castle
Castletown
Monkwearmouth
Angel of the North
Eighton Banks
Low Eighton
Bowes Railway
Usworth
Donwell
Concord
Sulgrave
West Moor Fm
Peepy Plantn
Stadium of Light
Deptford
Ayres Quay
National Glass Centre
St Peter's
River Wear
Pallion
Millfield
Bishopwearmouth
Albany
Washington
North Hylton
Sunderland
Birtley
Blackfell
Washington Village
Barmston
Low Barmston Fm
South Hylton
Glebe
Washington Old Hall
Oxclose
Columbia
Wildfowl & Wetland Trust
Pennywell
High Barnes
Humbledon
Hendon
Portobello
Washington Services
Offerton
Grindon
Springwell
Ayton
Biddick
Lambton
Hasting Hill
Hillview
Grangetown
Barley Mow
Ouston
Fatfield
Penshaw Monument
Herrington Country Park
Thorney Close
Harraton
Rickleton
Middle Herrington
Farringdon
New Silksworth
Penshaw
New Herrington
West Herrington
East Herrington
Doxford Park
Tunstall
Ryhope
Pelton
South Pelton
Pelton Fell
Biddick Hall
Shiney Row
Philadelphia
Stony Gate
Ryhope Engines Museum
Chester Road
Thristley House Fm
East Fm
Burdon
Seaham Grange
The Ankers House
Chester-le-Street
Bournmoor
New Lambton
Sunniside
Newbottle
Grasswell
Down at the Farm
Burn Hall Fm
Brecon Hill
Emirates Durham International Cricket Ground
Burnside
Warden Law
Old Burdon
Lumley Thicks
Fence Houses
Seaton
Northlea
Houghton-Le-Spring
Seaham
Chester Moor
Lumley Grange
Great Lumley
High Dubmire
Colliery Row
Warden Law
Seaton Moor Ho
Seaton Bank Top
West Lea
Deneside
Murton Grange
Chilton Moor
Rainton Bridge
New Town
Hetton Downs
Haverley Ho
Liddle Stack
Harbour House Fm
Plawsworth
Charles Pit Cotts
Lumley Moor Fm
Great Eppleton
Slingley Hill
Dalton Moor
Dawdon
Parkside

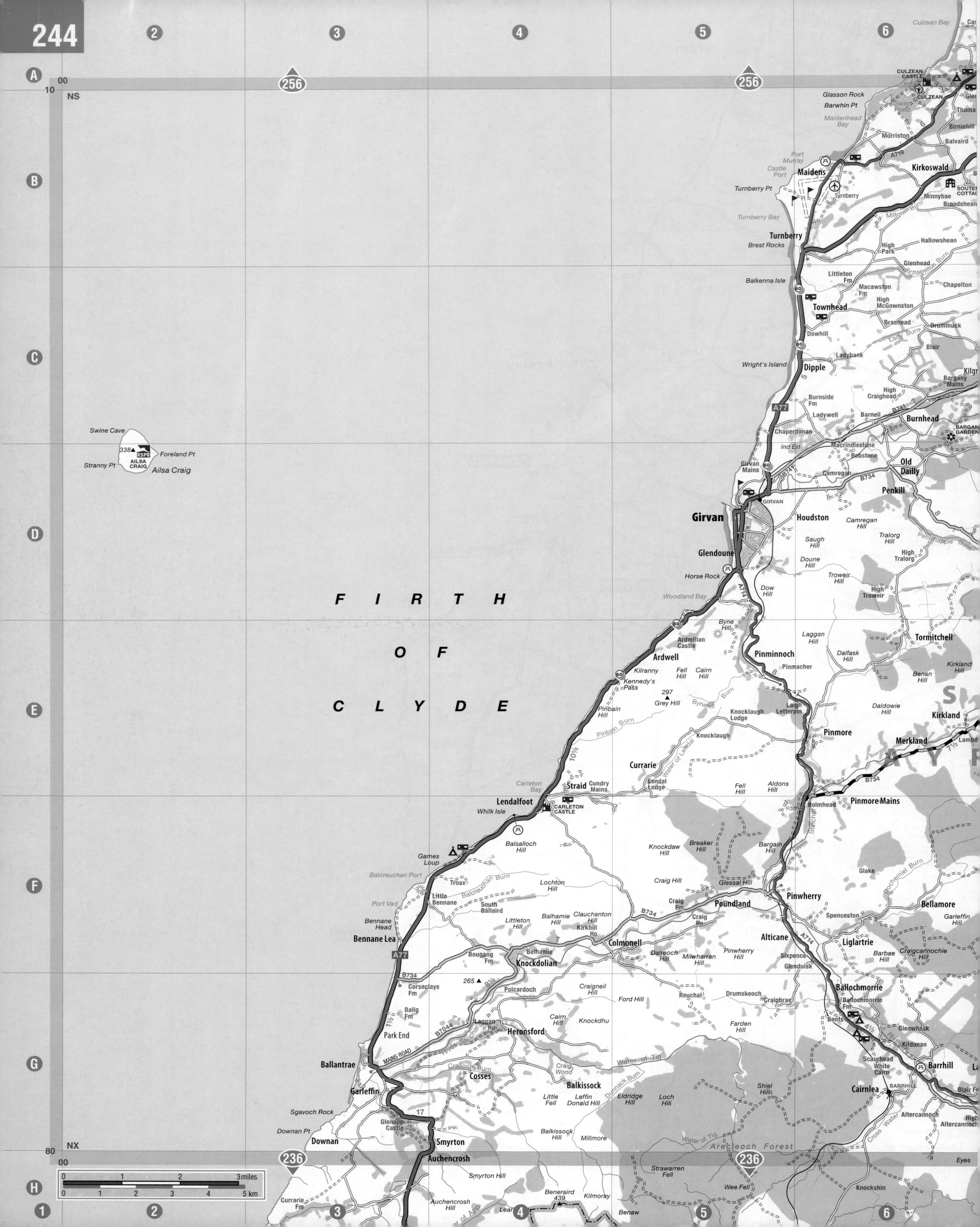
FIRTH OF CLYDE
256
236
NS
NX
Culzean Bay
CULZEAN CASTLE
CULZEAN
Glasson Rock
Barwhin Pt
Swan Pond
Maidenhead Bay
Morriston
Thomas
Birniehill
Balvaird
A719
Port Murray
Castle Port
Maidens
Kirkoswald
Turnberry Pt
Turnberry
Minnybae
Broadshean
Turnberry Bay
Milton Burn
Turnberry
Brest Rocks
Hallowshean
High Park
Glenhead
Chapelton Burn
Balkenna Isle
Littleton Fm
Macawston Fm
Chapelton
Townhead
High McGownston
Braehead
Drummuck
Dowhill
Lady Burn
Blair
Ladybank
Wright's Island
Dipple
Bargany Mains
Burnside Fm
High Craighead
Ladywell
Barneil
B741
Burnhead
A77
Chaperdonan
Ind Est
Macrindlestone
Robstone
Old Dailly
Girvan Mains
Camregan
B734
Penkill
GIRVAN
Girvan
Houdston
Camregan Hill
Saugh Hill
Tralorg Hill
Penwhapple Burn
Glendoune
High Tralorg
Doune Hill
Horse Rock
Troweir Hill
High Troweir
Dow Hill
Woodland Bay
A714
Byne Hill
Laggan Hill
Tormitchell
Ardmillan Castle
Ardwell
Pinminnoch
Dalfask Hill
Pinmacher
Kirkland Hill
Kilranny
Fell Hill
Cairn Hill
Benan Hill
Kennedy's Pass
297
Grey Hill
Byne Hill Burn
Laigh Letterpin
Daldowie Hill
Kirkland
Pinbain Hill
Knocklaugh Lodge
Pinbain Burn
Knocklaugh
Pinmore
Merkland
Water of Lendal
Currarie
B734
Carleton Bay
Straid
Cundry Mains
Lendal Lodge
Fell Hill
Aldons Hill
Lendalfoot
CARLETON CASTLE
Holmhead
Pinmore Mains
Whilk Isle
Balsalloch Hill
Knockdaw Hill
Breaker Hill
Bargain Hill
Games Loup
River Stinchar
Balcreuchan Port
Troax
Balcreuchan Burn
Lochton Hill
Craig Hill
Glessal Hill
Glake
Docherniel Burn
Little Bennane
Craig Fm
Poundland
Pinwherry
Port Vad
South Ballaird
Bellamore
Bennane Head
Littleton Hill
Balhamie Hill
Clauchanton Hill
Kirkhill Ho
Craig Ho
Spencestown
Garleffin Hill
Bennane Lea
Colmonell
Alticane
Liglartrie
Bougang Fm
Belhamie
Knockdolian
Dalreoch Hill
Milwharran Hill
Pinwherry Hill
Sixpence
Glenduisk
Barbae Hill
Craigcannochie Hill
Corseclays Fm
265
Polcardoch
Craigneil Hill
Ford Hill
Reuchal
Drumskeoch
Craigbrae
Ballochmorrie
Ballochmorrie Fm
Balig Fm
Cairn Hill
Knockdhu
Bents
Park End
B7044
Laggan Ho
Heronsford
Farden Hill
Glenwhask
Kildonan
MAINS ROAD
River Stinchar
Scaurhead
White Cairn
Barrhill
Ballantrae
Craig Wood
Water of Tig
Crailoch Burn
Cosses
Dunnack Burn
Balkissock
Shiel Hill
Cairnlea
BARRHILL
Garleffin
Little Fell
Leffin Donald Hill
Eldridge Hill
Loch Hill
Sgavoch Rock
Altercannoch
Glenapp Castle
Cross Water
Downan Pt
Balkissock Hill
Millmore
Water of Tig
Downan
Smyrton
Arecleoch Forest
Auchencrosh
Eyes
Strawarren Fell
Smyrton Hill
Wee Fell
Knockshin
Currarie Fm
Beneraird 439
Kilmoray
Auchencrosh Hill
Benaw
Swine Cave
338
RSPB
AILSA CRAIG
Foreland Pt
Stranny Pt
Ailsa Craig
0 1 2 3 miles
0 1 2 3 4 5 km
A B C D E F G H
1 2 3 4 5 6
00 10 80

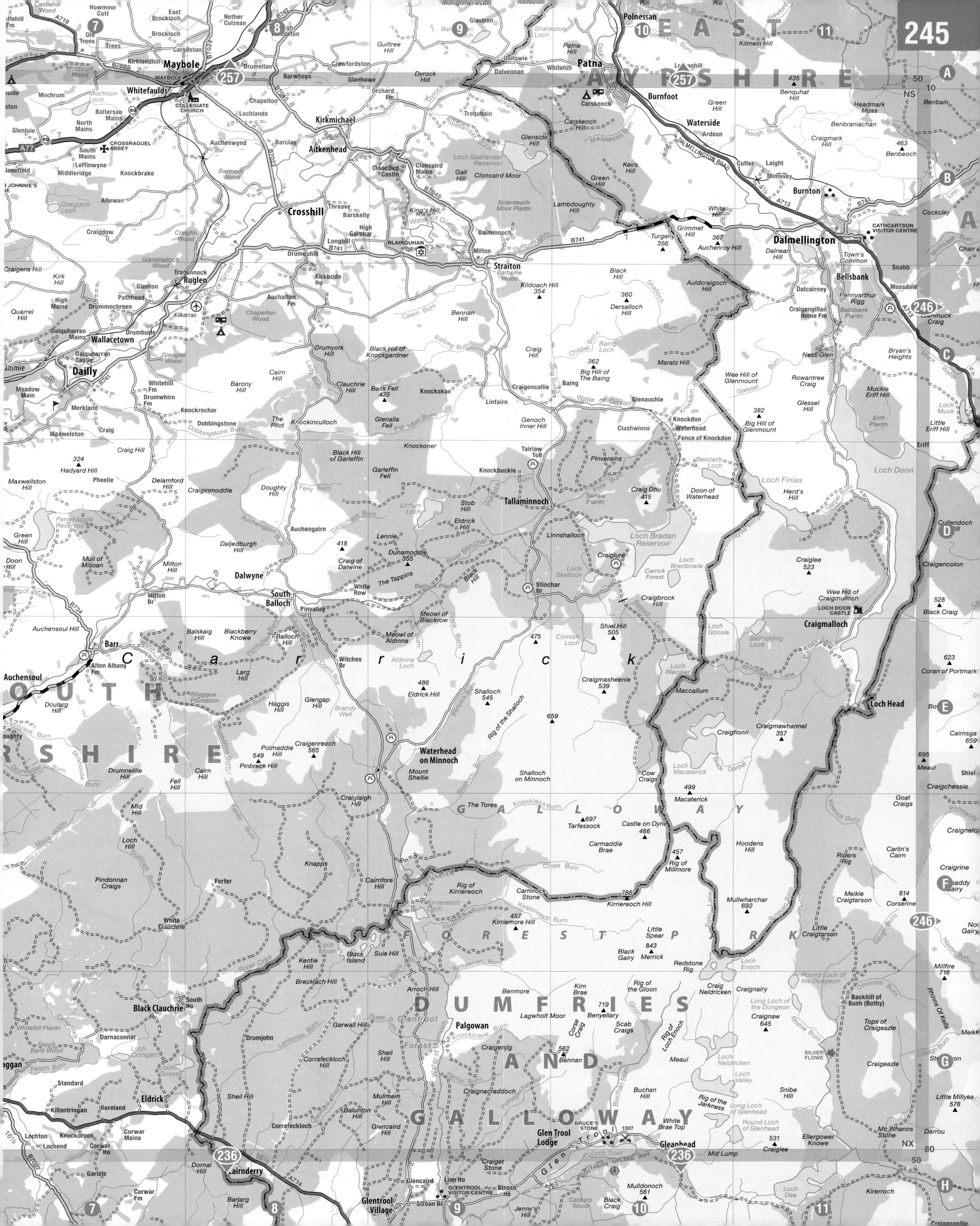
EAST AYRSHIRE
SOUTH AYRSHIRE
Carrick
GALLOWAY
FOREST PARK
DUMFRIES AND GALLOWAY
Maybole
Whitefaulds
Collegiate Church
Crossraguel Abbey
Kirkmichael
Aitkenhead
Crosshill
Blairquhan
Straiton
Patna
Burnfoot
Waterside
Dalmellington Road
Burnton
Cathcartson Visitor Centre
Dalmellington
Bellsbank
Kildoach Hill 354
Dersalloch Hill 360
Big Hill of The Baing 362
Glenauchie
Water of Girvan
Knockdon Waterhead
Fence of Knockdon
Big Hill of Glenmount 382
Loch Finlas
Loch Doon
Craig Dhu 415
Tallaminnoch
Loch Bradan Reservoir
Craiglure
Stinchar Br
Craigbrock Hill
Loch Doon Castle
Craigmalloch
Craiglee 523
Wee Hill of Craigmulloch
Loch Head
Shiel Hill 505
Craigmasheenie 539
Maccallum
Craigfionn
Craigmawhannel 357
Loch Macaterick
Macaterick 499
Tarfessock 697
Castle on Oyne 466
Rig of Millmore 457
Kirriereoch Hill 786
Mullwharchar 692
Little Craigtarson
Corserine 814
Merrick 843
Black Gairy
Kirriemore Hill 457
Redstone Rig
Loch Enoch
Craig Neldricken
Round Loch of the Dungeon
Backhill of Bush (Bothy)
Long Loch of the Dungeon
Craignaw 645
Benyellary 719
Lagwholt Moor
Palgowan
Bennan 562
Rig of Loch Enoch
Silver Flowe
Buchan Hill
Snibe Hill
Glen Trool Lodge
Bruce's Stone
Gleanhead
Loch Trool
Southern Upland Way
Mid Lump
Craiglee 531
Mulldonoch 561
Glentrool Village
Glentrool Visitor Centre
Stroan Br
Cairnderry
Black Clauchrie
Eldrick
Waterhead on Minnoch
Mount Shellie
Shalloch on Minnoch
Shalloch 545
Eldrick Hill 486
Polmaddie Hill
Cairn Hill
Pinbreck Hill 549
Craigenreoch 565
Barr
Alton Albany Fm
Auchensoul
Pinvalley
South Balloch
Dalwyne
Dunamoddie 355
Craig of Dalwine 418
The Tappins
Black Hill of Garleffin
Garleffin Fell
Back Fell 425
Knockskae
Glenalla Fell
Dailly
Wallacetown
Drummochreen
Kilkerran
Ruglen
Tradunnock
Drumochill
Hadyard Hill 324
Maxwelston
Merkland
Penwhapple Reservoir
Mull of Miljoan
Turgeny 356
Auchenroy Hill 367
Benquhat Hill 435
Benbeoch 463
Mulldonoch 561
Corserine 814
Millfire 716
Little Millyea 578
Coran of Portmark 623
Black Craig 528
Rhinns Of Kells
NS
NX
A77
A713
B741
B7023
B7045
B734
A714
257
236
246
A
B
C
D
E
F
G
H
7
8
9
10
11

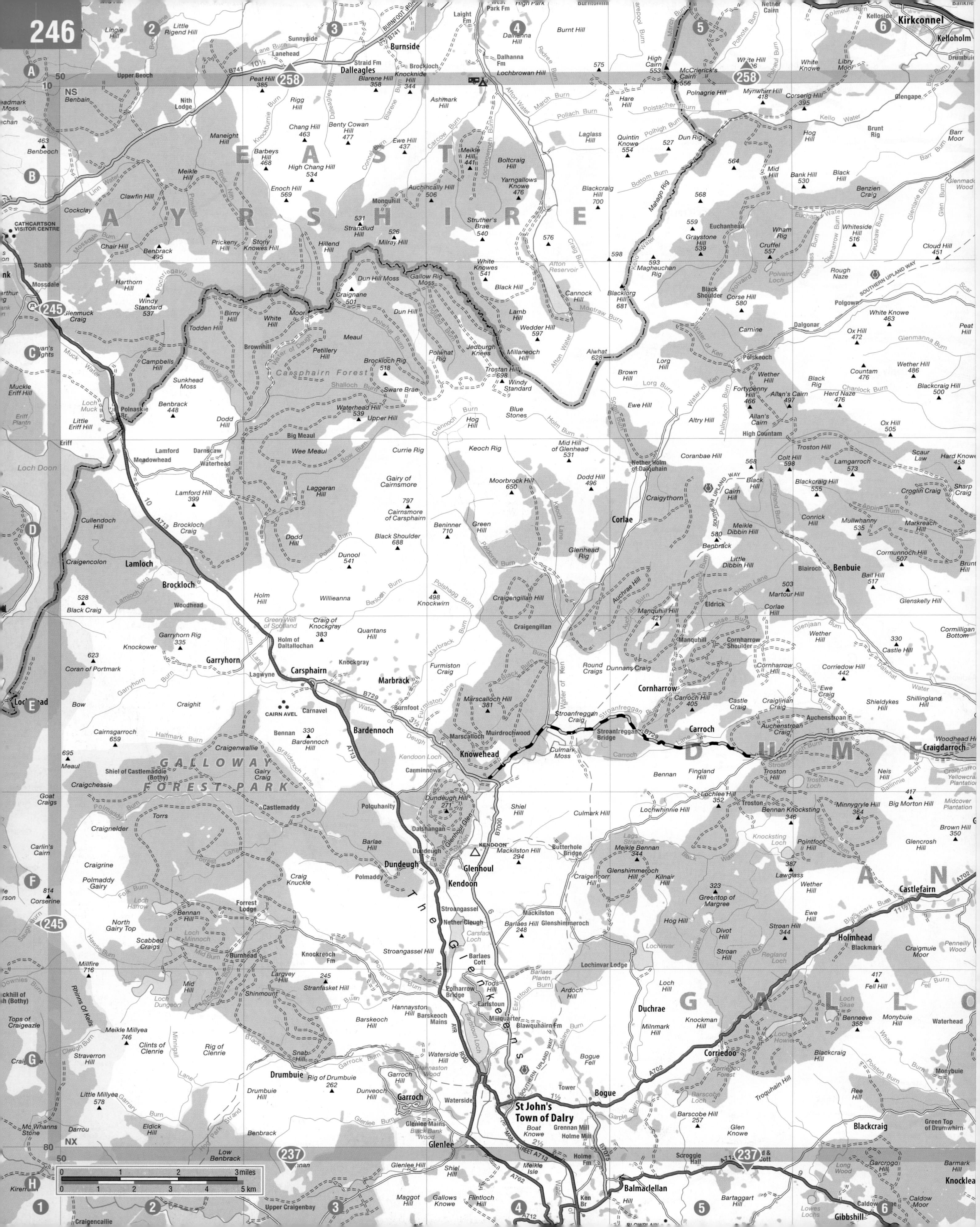

EAST AYRSHIRE
DUMFRIES
GALLOWAY
GALLOWAY FOREST PARK
Carsphairn Forest
The Glenkens
SOUTHERN UPLAND WAY
CATHCARTSON VISITOR CENTRE
CAIRN AVEL
KENDOON
Kirkconnel
Kelloholm
Burnside
Dalleagles
Sunnyside
Lanehead
Upper Beech
Peat Hill 385
Blarene Hill 358
Knocknide Hill 344
Lochbrowan Hill
Burnt Hill
Dalhanna Hill
High Cairn 553
McCrierick's Cairn 556
Polnagrie Hill
White Hill 536
Mynwhirr Hill 418
Corserig Hill 395
Glengape
Kello Water
Benbain
Nith Lodge
Rigg Hill
Chang Hill 463
Benty Cowan Hill 477
Ewe Hill 437
Ashmark Hill
Afton Water
Hare Hill
Laglass Hill
Quintin Knowe 554
Dun Rig
Hog Hill
Brunt Rig
Barr Moor
Benbeoch 463
Maneight Hill
Barbeys Hill 468
High Chang Hill 534
Meikle Hill 441
Boltcraig Hill
Meikle Hill
Enoch Hill 569
Auchincally Hill 506
Yarngallows Knowe 476
Blackcraig Hill 700
Manago Rig
Mid Hill
Bank Hill 530
Black Hill
Benzien Craig
Clawfin Hill
Cockclay
Monquhill
Strandlud Hill 531
Milray Hill 526
Struther's Brae 540
Euchanhead
Graystone Hill 539
Wham Rig
Cruffel 557
Whiteside Hill 516
Cloud Hill 451
Chair Hill
Benbrack 495
Prickeny Hill
Stony Knowes Hill
Hillend Hill
Afton Reservoir
Magheuchan Rig
Rough Naze
Harthorn Hill
Windy Standard 537
Dun Hill Moss
Gallow Rig Moss
Craignane 501
White Knowes 541
Black Hill
Cannock Hill
Blacklorg Hill 681
Black Shoulder
Corse Hill 580
Polgown
Glenmuck Craig
Birny Hill
White Hill
Moor
Dun Hill
Lamb Hill
Wedder Hill 597
Carnine
Dalgonar
White Knowe 463
Ox Hill 472
Todden Hill
Brownhill
Meaul
Petillery Hill
Campbells Hill
Brockloch Rig 518
Polwhat Rig
Jedburgh Knees
Millaneoch Hill
Alwhat 628
Lorg Hill
Polskeoch
Countam 476
Wether Hill 486
Sunkhead Moss
Trostan Hill 698
Windy Standard
Brown Hill
Black Rig
Herd Naze 476
Blackcraig Hill 500
Muckle Eriff Hill
Polnaskie Br
Benbrack 448
Sware Brae
Waterhead Hill 539
Upper Hill
Hog Hill
Blue Stones
Ewe Hill
Fortypenny Hill 466
Allan's Cairn 497
Allan's Cairn
High Countam
Little Eriff Hill
Dodd Hill
Big Meaul
Altry Hill
Ox Hill 505
Eriff
Lamford
Darnscaw
Meadowhead
Waterhead
Wee Meaul
Currie Rig
Keoch Rig
Mid Hill of Glenhead 531
Coranbae Hill
Troston Hill
Scaur Law
Hard Knowe 458
Loch Doon
Nether Holm of Dalquhain
Colt Hill 598
Lamgarroch 573
Gairy of Cairnsmore
Moorbrock Hill 650
Dodd Hill 496
Black Hill
Blackcraig Hill 555
Croglin Craig
Sharp Craig
Lamford Hill 399
Laggeran Hill
797
Cairnsmore of Carsphairn
Craigythorn
Cairn Hill
Corlae
Cullendoch Hill
Brockloch Craig
Green Hill
Meikle Dibbin Hill
Conrick Hill
Mullwhanny 535
Markreach Hill
Beninner 710
Black Shoulder 688
Dodd Hill
Benbrack 580
Glenhead Rig
Craigencolon
Lamloch
Dunool 541
Little Dibbin Hill
Cormunnoch Hill 507
Brockloch
Blairoch
Benbuie
Bail Hill 517
Woodhead
Holm Hill
Willieanna
Knockwirn 498
Craigengillan Hill
Martour Hill 503
Glenskelly Hill
Black Craig 528
Auchrae Hill
Eldrick
Corlae Hill
Manquhill Hill 421
Green Well of Scotland
Craig of Knockgray 383
Quantans Hill
Craigengillan
Wether Hill
Cormilligan Bottom
Garryhorn Rig 335
Holm of Daltallochan
Castle Hill 330
Knockower
Manquhill
Cornharrow Shoulder
623
Coran of Portmark
Garryhorn
Carsphairn
Knockgray
Furmiston Craig
Round Craigs
Dunnans Craig
Corriedow Hill 442
Cornharrow Hill
Lagwyne
Marbrack
Cornharrow
Ewe Craig
Bow
Craighit
Carnavel
Burnfoot
Marscalloch Hill 381
Carroch Hill 405
Castle Craig
Craiglinan Craig
Shieldykes Hill
Shillingland Hill
Stroanfreggan Craig
Auchenstroan
Cairnsgarroch 659
Bennan 330
Bardennoch Hill
Bardennoch
Muirdrochwood
Stroanfreggan Bridge
Carroch
Auchenstroan Craig
Woodhead Hill
Craigdarroch
Marscalloch
Culmark Moss
Craigenwallie
Kendoon Loch
Knowehead
Meaul 695
Gairy Craig
Shiel of Castlemaddie (Bothy)
Carminnows
Bennan
Fingland Hill
Troston Hill
Neis Hill
Yellowcraig Plantation
Craigchessie
Lochlee Hill 352
Troston
Big Morton Hill 417
Goat Craigs
Castlemaddy
Polquhanity
Dundeugh Hill 271
Shiel Hill
Culmark Hill
Lochwhinnie Hill
Bennan Knocksting 346
Minnygryle Hill 364
Midcover Plantation
Torrs
Craignelder
Dalshangan
Carlin's Cairn
Barlae Hill
Dundeugh
Mackilston Hill 294
Butterhole Bridge
Meikle Bennan 344
Knocksting Loch
Pointfoot Hill
Glencrosh Hill
Brown Hill 350
Craigrine
Polmaddy Gairy
Craig Knuckle
Polmaddy
Glenhoul
Kendoon
Craigencorr Hill
Glenshimmeroch Hill
Kilnair Hill
Lawglass 387
Castlefairn
Corserine 814
Forrest Lodge
Loch Harrow
Greentop of Margree 323
Wether Hill
Stroangassel
Nether Cleugh
Mackilston
Glenshimmeroch
Ewe Hill
North Gairy Top
Bennan Hill
Loch Minnoch
Carsfad Loch
Barlaes Hill 248
Hog Hill
Divot Hill
Stroan Hill 344
Holmhead
Blackmark
Craigmuie Moor
Penneilly Wood
Scabbed Craigs
Burnhead
Knockreoch Fm
Stroangassel Hill
Barlaes Cott
Lochinvar Lodge
Lochinvar
Stroan Hill
Regland Loch
Millfire 716
Largvey Hill
Stranfasket Hill 245
Barlaes Plantn
Tods Hill
Polharrow Bridge
Earlstoun
Ardoch Hill
Loch Hill
Fell Hill 417
Mid Hill
Loch Dungeon
Shinmount
Hannayston Hill
Barskeoch Mains
Barskeoch Hill
Millquarter
Blawquhairn Fm
Duchrae
Milnmark Hill
Knockman Hill
Loch Skae
Benneeve 358
Monybuie Hill
Waterhead
Rhinns Of Kells
Tops of Craigeazle
Meikle Millyea 746
Clints of Clenrie
Rig of Clenrie
Earlstoun Loch
Loch Howie
Straverron Hill
Snab Hill
Waterside Hill
Hannaston Wood
Bogue Fell
Corriedoo
Corriedoo Forest
Blackcraig Hill
Monybuie
Drumbuie
Rig of Drumbuie 262
Garroch Hill
Tower
Bogue
Troquhain Hill
Little Millyea 578
Drumbuie Hill
Dunveoch Hill
Garroch
Waterside
St John's Town of Dalry
Barscobe Loch
Rae Hill
Barscobe Hill 257
Mc Whanns Stone
Darrou
Eldrick Hill
Glenlee Mains
Black Bank Wood
Boat Knowe
Grennan Mill
Holme Mill
Glen Knowe
Blackcraig
Green Top of Drumwhirn
Benbrack
Glenlee
Low Benbrack
Glenlee Hill
Shiel Hill
Holme Fm
Scroggie Hill
Garcrogo Hill
Barmark Hill
Knocklea
Meikle Isle
Balmaclellan
Long Wood
Maggot Hill
Gallows Knowe
Flintloch Hill
Upper Craigenbay
Ken Br
Bartaggart Hill
Lowes Lochs
Gibbshill
Caldow Moor
Craigencallie
NS
NX
258
245
237
B741
B729
B7000
B7075
A713
A702
A762
A712
0 1 2 3 miles
0 1 2 3 4 5 km

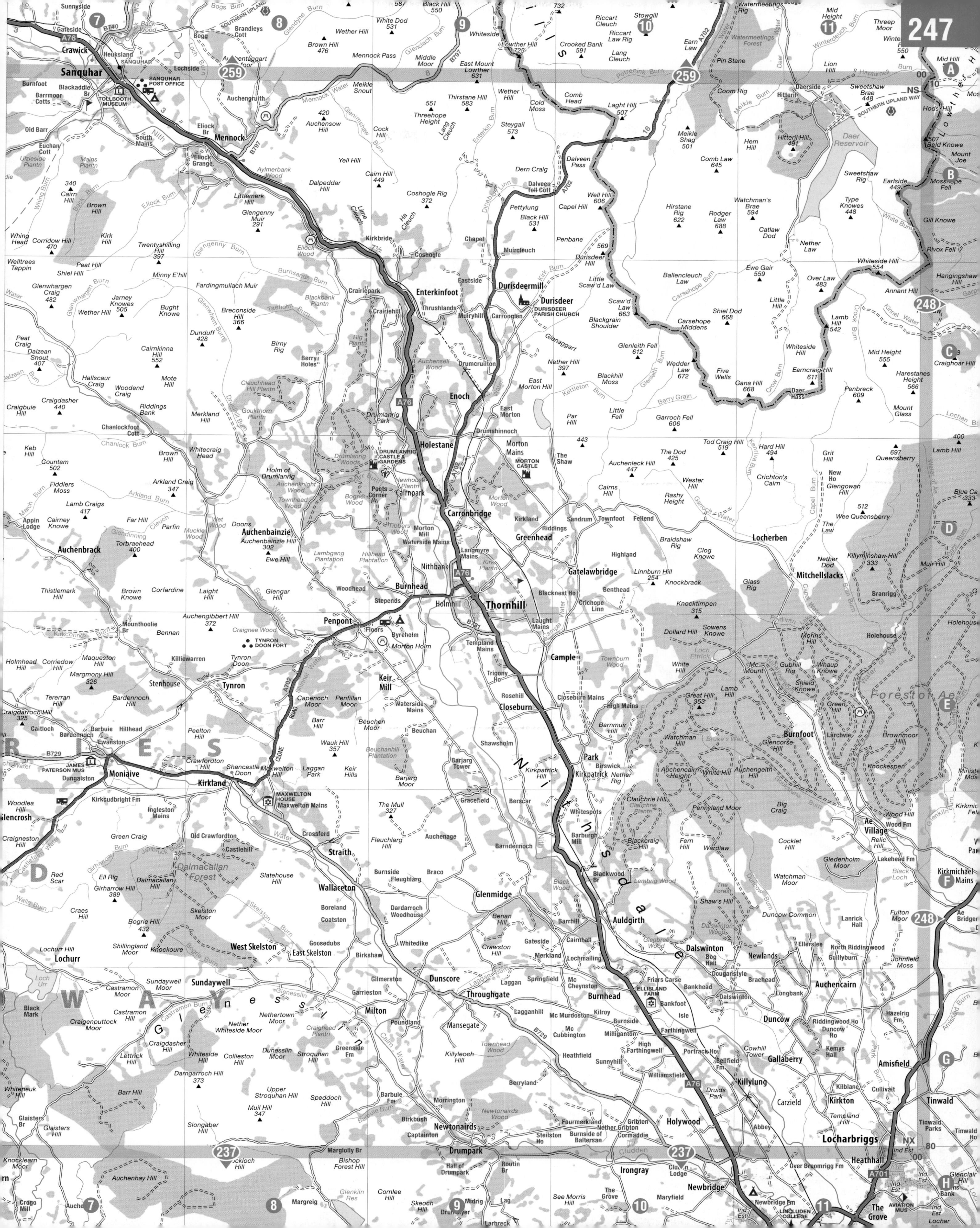
Sanquhar
Crawick
Heuksland
Gateside
Sunnyside
Bogg
Brandleys Cott
Lochside
Auchentaggart Moor
Burnfoot
Blackaddie Br
Barrmoor Cotts
SANQUHAR POST OFFICE
TOLLBOOTH MUSEUM
Auchengruith
Meikle Snout
Mennock Pass
Middle Moor
White Dod 531
Wether Hill
Brown Hill 476
Black Hill 550
Whiteside
East Mount Lowther 631
Lowther Hill 725
Riccart Cleuch
Riccart Law Rig
Stowgill
Crooked Bank 591
Lang Cleuch
Earn Law
Pin Stane
Watermeetings Forest
Mid Height
Threep Moor
Mid Hill
Old Barr
Euchan Cott
Ulzieside Plantn
South Mains
Mennock
Eliock Br
Eliock Grange
420 Auchensow Hill
Cock Hill
551 Threehope Height
Thirstane Hill 583
Lang Cleuch
Wether Hill
Cold Moss
Steygail 573
Comb Head
Laght Hill 507
Coom Rig
Daerside
Hitterin
Sweetshaw Brae 448
SOUTHERN UPLAND WAY
Hods Hill
Meikle Shag 501
Hem Hill
Hitteril Hill 491
Daer Reservoir
Beld Knowe
Mount Joe
Mains Plantn
Yell Hill
Cairn Hill 449
Dern Craig
Dalveen Pass
Dalveen Toll Cott
Comb Law 645
Sweetshaw Rig
Earlside 449
Mossnope Fell
340 Cairn Hill
Brown Hill
Aylmerbank Wood
Dalpeddar Hill
Littlemerk Hill
Glengenny Muir 291
Coshogle Rig 372
Pettylung
Black Hill 531
Well Hill 606
Capel Hill
Hirstane Rig 622
Rodger Law 688
Watchman's Brae 594
Catlaw Dod
Type Knowes 448
Gill Knowe
Whing Head
Corridow Hill 470
Kirk Hill
Twentyshilling Hill 397
Eliock Wood
Kirkbride
Chapel
Muircleuch
Penbane
Durisdeer Hill
Nether Law
Rivox Fell
Welltrees Tappin
Peat Hill
Shiel Hill
Minny E'hill
Coshogle
Ewe Gair 559
Whiteside Hill 554
Glenwhargen Craig 482
Jarney Knowes 505
Wether Hill
Bught Knowe
Fardingmullach Muir
Crairiepark
Crairiehill
Blackbank Plantn
Enterkinfoot
Thrushlands
Eastside
Muiryhill
Durisdeermill
Carronglen
Durisdeer
DURISDEER PARISH CHURCH
Little Scaw'd Law
Scaw'd Law 663
Blackgrain Shoulder
Ballencleuch Law
Carsehope Middens
Shiel Dod 668
Little Hill
Over Law 483
Hangingshaw Hill
Annant Hill
Lamb Hill 542
Breconside Hill 366
Dunduff 428
Peat Craig
Dalzean Snout 407
Cairnkinna Hill 552
Mote Hill
Birny Rig
Berry Holes
Auchensell Wood
Drumcruilton
Glenaggart
Glenleith Fell 612
Wedder Law 672
Five Wells
Whiteside Hill
Earncraig Hill 611
Mid Height 555
Craighoar Hill
Harestanes Height 566
Hallscaur Craig
Woodend Craig
Craigdasher 440
Craigbuie Hill
Riddings Bank
Cleuchhead Hill Plantn
Goukthorn Plantn
Merkland Hill
Enoch
East Morton Hill
Nether Hill 397
Blackhill Moss
Gana Hill 668
Daer Hass
Penbreck 609
Mount Glass
Chanlockfoot Cott
Drumlanrig Park
East Morton
Par Hill
Little Fell
Garroch Fell 606
Keb Hill
Countam 502
Brown Hill
Whitecraig Head
Holestane
Drumshinnoch
Morton Mains
MORTON CASTLE
The Shaw
443
Auchenleck Hill 447
The Dod 425
Tod Craig Hill 519
Hard Hill 494
Grit Hill
697 Queensberry
Lamb Hill
Fiddlers Moss
Arkland Craig 347
Holm of Drumlanrig
DRUMLANRIG CASTLE & GARDENS
Drumlanrig Woods
Auchenknight Wood
Townhead Wood
Poets Corner
Cairnpark
Newhouse Plantn
Cairns Hill
Wester Hill
Rashy Height
Crichton's Cairn
New Ho
Glengowan Hill
Blue Cairn 333
Lamb Craigs 417
Appin Lodge
Cairney Knowe
Far Hill
Parfin
Muckle Wood
Doons
Auchenbainzie
Auchenbainzie Hill 302
Bogrie Wood
Tibbers Wood
Morton Mill
Carronbridge
Morton Wood
Kirkland
Riddings
Sandrum
Townfoot
Fellend
Braidshaw Rig
Clog Knowe
512 Wee Queensberry
The Law
Locherben
Auchenbrack
Torbraehead 400
Ewe Hill
Lambgang Plantation
Hillhead Plantation
Waterside Mains
Langmyre Mains
Greenhead
Gatelawbridge
Highland
Linnburn Hill 254
Knockbrack
Glass Rig
Nether Dod
Mitchellslacks
Killyminshaw Hill 333
Muir Hill
Branrigg
Thistlemark Hill
Brown Knowe
Corfardine
Laight Hill
Glengar Hill
Woodhead
Nithbank
Burnhead
Stepends
Holmhill
Thornhill
Blacknest Ho
Crichope Linn
Benthead
Knocktimpen 315
Auchengibbert Hill 372
Mounthoolie Br
Bennan
Craignee Wood
TYNRON DOON FORT
Penpont
Floors
Byreholm
Morton Holm
Laught Mains
Templand Mains
Dollard Hill
Sowens Knowe
Loch Ettrick
Morins Hill
Holehouse
Holmhead Hill
Corriedow Hill
Maqueston Hill
Killiewarren
Tynron Doon
Cample
Townburn Wood
White Hill
Mc Mount
Gubhill Rig
Whaup Knowe
Margmony Hill 326
Stenhouse
Tynron
Keir Mill
Trigony Ho
Shiel Knowe
Forest of Ae
Tererran Hill
Bardennoch Hill
Capenoch Moor
Penfillan Moor
Waterside Mains
Rosehill
Closeburn Mains
Great Hill 353
Lamb Hill
Green Hill
Craigdarroch Hill 325
Caitloch
Closeburn
High Mains
Barr Hill
Beuchen Moor
Beuchan
Barnmuir Hill
Watchman Hill
Bruce's Well
Glencorse Hill
Burnfoot
Larchvie
Brownmoor Hill
Barbuie
Hillhead
Bardennoch
Ewanston
Peelton Hill
Wauk Hill 357
Beuchanhill Plantation
Shawsholm
Park
B729
JAMES PATERSON MUS
Dungalston
Moniaive
Crawfordton Hill
Shancastle Doon
Maxwelton Hill
Laggan Park
Keir Hills
Barjarg Tower
Barjarg Moor
Kirkpatrick Hill
Kirkpatrick
Birswick
Nether Rig
Auchencairn Height
White Hill
Auchengeith Hill
Knockespen
Kirkland
MAXWELTON HOUSE
Maxwelton Mains
Kirkcudbright Fm
Ingleston Mains
Woodlea Hill
Glencrosh
The Mull 327
Gracefield
Berscar
Whitespots
Clauchrie Hill
Clauchrie Plantn
Pennyland Moor
Big Craig
Ae Village
Wood Hill
Wood Fm
Craigneston Hill
Green Craig
Old Crawfordton
Castlehill
Crossford
Fleuchlarg Hill
Auchenage
Barburgh Mill
Blackcraig Hill
Fern Hill
Wardlaw
Cocklet Hill
Relic Hill
Lakehead Fm
Red Scar
Ell Rig
Dalmacallan Forest
Dalmacallan Hill
Girharrow Hill 389
Slatehouse Hill
Straith
Burnside
Fleughlarg
Braco
Barndennoch
Blackwood Br
Lambrig Wood
The Forest
Watchman Moor
Gledenholm Moor
Black Loch
Kirkmichael Mains
Craes Hill
Skelston Moor
Wallaceton
Boreland
Coatston
Dardarroch Woodhouse
Glenmidge
Black Wood
Shaw's Hill
Duncow Common
Lanrick Hall
Fulton Moor
Bogrie Hill 432
Shillingland Moor
Knockoure
West Skelston
Goosedubs
East Skelston
Whitedike
Benan Hill
Barrhill
Auldgirth
Dalswinton Wood
Gateside
Merkland
Crawston Hill
Cairnhall
Lochmailling
Glenbrae Wood
Dalswinton
Bog Hall
Douganstyle
Newlands
Ellerslee
North Riddingwood
Guillyburn
Johnfield Moss
Lochurr Hill
Lochurr
Birkshaw
Loch Urr
Castramon Moor
Sundaywell Moor
Sundaywell
Gilmerston
Garrieston
Dunscore
Laggan
Springfield
Mc Cheynston
Burnhead
Friars Carse
ELLISLAND FARM
Bankfoot
Bankhead
Braehead
Auchencairn
Longbank
Black Mark
Castramon Hill
Craigenputtock Moor
Nethertown Moor
Milton
Poundland
Throughgate
Lagganhill
Mc Murdoston
Kilroy
Burnside
Milliganton
Isle
Duncow
Riddingwood Ho
Duncow Ho
Hazelrig Fm
Craighead Plantn
Nether Whiteside Moor
Mansegate
Mc Cubbington
High Farthingwell
Farthingwell
Craigdasher Hill
Lettrick Hill
Whiteside Hill
Collieston Hill
Dunesslin Moor
Stroquhan Hill
Greenside Fm
Killyleoch Hill
Townhead Wood
Heathfield
Sunnyhill
Portrack Ho
Bellfield Fm
Cowhill Tower
Gallaberry
Kemys Hall
Amisfield
Darngarroch Hill 373
Barr Hill
Berryland
Williamsfield
Killylung
Kilblane
Cullivait
Whiteneuk Hill
Upper Stroquhan Hill
Speddoch Hill
Barbuie Fm
Morrington
Druids Park
Carzield
Kirkton
Tinwald
Glaisters Br
Muil Hill 347
Slongaber Hill
Newtonairds Wood
Birkbush
Newtonairds
Captainton
Fourmerkland
Nether Gribton
Gribton
Cormaddie
Holywood
Abbey
Templand Hill
Tinwald Parks
Glaisters Hill
Knocklearn Moor
Auchenhay Hill
Margolly Br
Bishop Forest Hill
Drumpark
Steilston Ho
Burnside of Baltersan
Cluden
Locharbriggs
Heathhall
Over Broomrigg Fm
Hall of Drumpark
Routin Br
Irongray
Cluden Lodge
Newbridge
Glenkiln Res
Cornlee Hill
Skeoch Hill
Midrig
See Morris Hill
The Grove
Maryfield
Newbridge Fm
LINCLUDEN COLLEGE
The Grove
AVIATION MUS
Ind Est
Glenclair
Bank
Locha
Crogo Mill
Margreig
Lag
Larbreck
A76
A702
B797
B740
B729
B731
A701
259
248
237
NS
NX
00
80
7
8
9
10
11
A
B
C
D
E
F
G
H
D R I E S
W A Y
G l e n e s s l i n
N i t h s d a l e

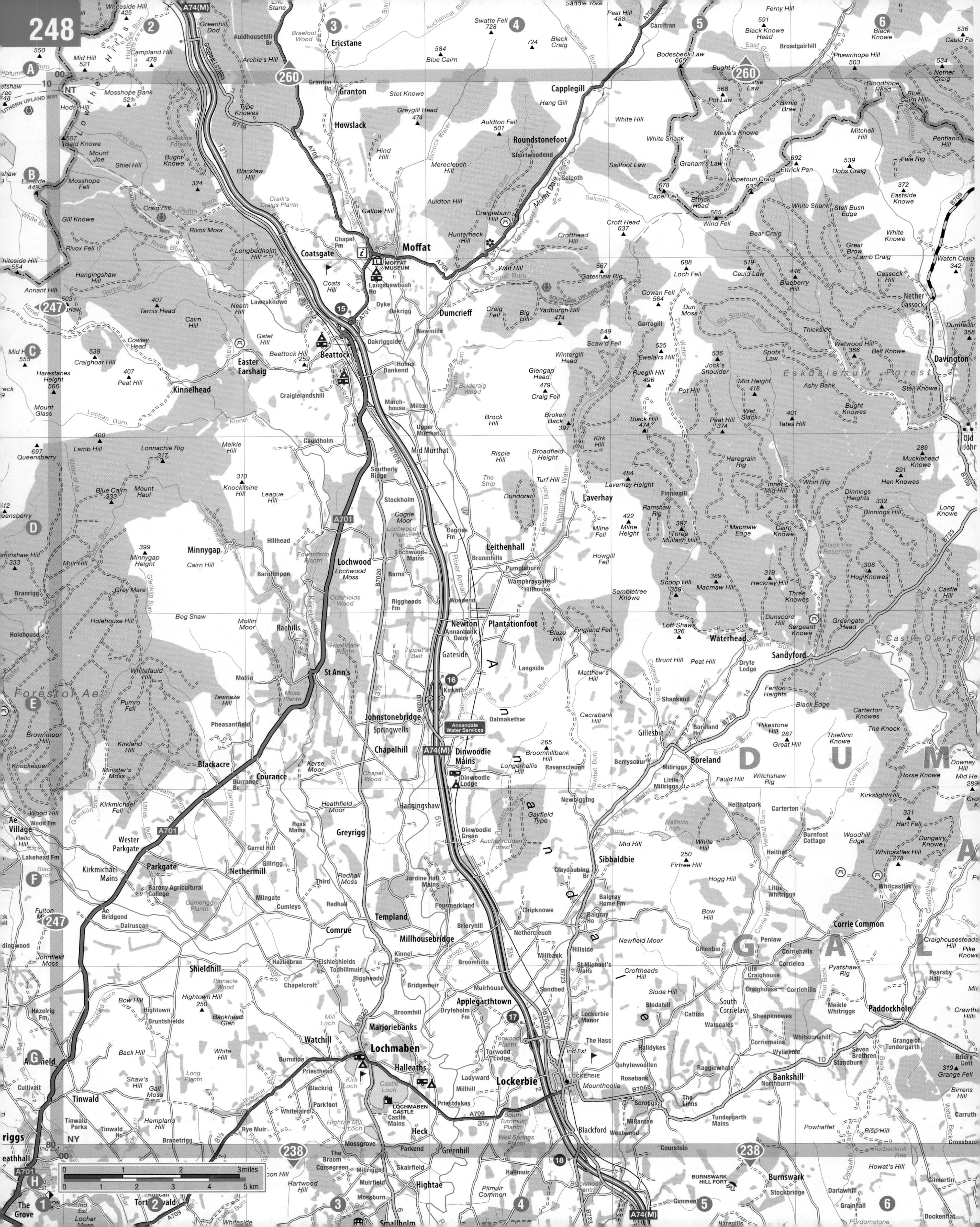

A74(M)
Whiteside Hill 425
Greenhill Dod
Auldhousehill Br
Archie's Hill
Braefoot Wood
Ericstane
Swatte Fell 728
584 Blue Cairn
724
Black Craig
Peat Hill 488
Carrifran
Ferny Hill
591 Black Knowe Head
Broadgairhill
Black Knowe
536 Cauld Fa
550
Mid Hill 521
Campland Hill 478
260
Bodesbeck Law 665
Bught Hill
Phawhope Hill 503
534 Nether Craig
NT
Mosshope Bank 521
Granton Ho
Granton
Stot Knowe
Capplegill
568 Pot Law
Bushie Law
Bloodhope Head
Blue Cairn Hill
Hods Hill
Type Knowes
Howslack
Greygill Head 474
Hang Gill
White Hill
Birnie Brae
SOUTHERN UPLAND WAY
B719
Auldton Fell 501
Roundstonefoot
Shortwoodend
White Shank
Maiden's Knowe
Mitchell Hill
507 Beld Knowe
Mount Joe
Shiel Hill
Bught Knowe
Greskine Forest
Hind Hill
Merecleuch Hill
Sailfoot Law
Graham's Law
692 Ettrick Pen
539 Dobs Craig
Ewe Rig
Pentland Hill
Earlside 449
Mosshope Fell
324
Blacklaw Hill
A701
Selcoth
678 Capel Fell
Hopetoun Craig 632
372 Eastside Knowe
B709
Craig Hill
Cloffin Burn
Craik's Craigs Plantn
Gallow Hill
Auldton Hill
Moffat Dale
Craigieburn Hill
Ettrick Head
665 Wind Fell
White Shank
Stell Bush Edge
Gill Knowe
Rivox Moor
Croft Head 637
Bear Craig
White Knowe
Rivox Fell
Longbedholm Hill
Chapel Fm
Coatsgate
Moffat
MOFFAT MUSEUM
Hunterheck Hill
A708
Crofthead Hill
Great Brow
Lamb Craig
Whiteside Hill 554
Hangingshaw Hill
Coats Hill
Langshawbush Ho
Wait Hill
567 Gateshaw Rig
688 Loch Fell
519 Cauld Law
446 Blaeberry Hill
Cassock Hill
Watch Craig 342
Annant Hill
503 Earlaw
247
407 Tarnis Head
Neath Hill
Laweskknowe
Dyke
Oakrigg
Dumcrieff
Craig Fell
Big Hill
Yadburgh Hill 474
Cowan Fell 564
Dun Moss
Nether Cassock
Cairn Hill
Gatet Hill
Newmills
Garrogill
Big Strushel Burn
Thickside
Dumfedling 358
Cowley Head
Mid Hill 555
538 Craighoar Hill
Beattock Hill 259
Beattock
Oakriggside
549 Scaw'd Fell
525 Ewelairs Hill
536 Jock's Shoulder
Spots Law
Wetwood Hill 366
Belt Knowe
Davington
Easter Earshaig
Holms Bankend
Wintergill Head
Ruegill Hill 496
Glengap Head 479
Craig Fell
Eskdalemuir Forest
Harestanes Height 566
407 Peat Hill
Kinnelhead
Craigielandshill
Beldcraig Wood
Pot Hill
Mid Height 418
Ashy Bank
Stell Knowe
Mount Glass
March-house
Milton
Broken Back 397
Brock Hill
Black Hill 474
Wet Slack
Bught Knowes
Peat Hill 374
401 Tates Hill
Upper Murthat
Mid Murthat
697 Queensberry
Lamb Hill
400
Lonnachie Rig 317
Meikle Hill
Cauldholm
Rispie Hill
Broadfield Height
Kirk Hill
Haregrain Rig
289 Mucklehead Knowe
291 Hen Knowes
Southerly Ridge
310 Knockilsine Hill
The Strip
Turf Hill
484 Laverhay Height
Inner Mid Hill
Whirl Rig
Blue Cairn 333
Mount Haul
League Hill
Stockholm
Dundoran
Laverhay
Finniegill
Dinnings Heights
332 Dinnings Hill
Long Knowe
Cogrie Moor
Lochwood Plantn
Cogries Fm
422 Milne Height
Milne Fell
Ramshaw Rig
397 Three Mullach Hill
Macmaw Edge
Cairn Knowe
B723
399 Minnygap Height
Minnygap
Cairn Hill
Hillhead
Edwardsrig Plantn
Lochwood
Lochwood Moss
Lochwood Mains
Leithenhall
Broomhills
Howgill Fell
Black Esk Reservoir
Muir Hill
Barntimpen
B7020
Barns
River Annan
Pumplaburn
Wamphraygate
Hillhouse
389 Macmaw Hill
Scoop Hill 359
319 Heckney Hill
308 Hog Knowes
Castle Hill
Branrigg
Grey Mare
Oldshields Wood
Riggheads Fm
Woodend
Sembletree Knowe
Three Knowes
Bog Shaw
Mollin Moor
Holehouse Hill
Raehills
Newton
Annanbank Dairy
Plantationfoot
Dunscore Hill
Greengate Head
Holehouse
Hazelbank Plantn
Tippet's Belt
Gateside
Blaze Hill
Fingland Fell
Loft Shaws 326
Waterhead
Sergeant Knowe
Castle O'er Forest
Sandyford
Brunt Hill
Peat Hill
Dryfe Lodge
Mollin
St Ann's
Langside
Whitefauld Hill
Matthew's Hill
Kirkhill
16
Forest of Ae
Tawnaze Hill
Moss Plantn
Pumro Fell
Dalmakethar
Shankend
Fenton Heights
Black Edge
Johnstonebridge
Springwells
Annandale Water Services
Carterton Knowes
Cacrabank Hill
Gillesbie
Boreland Ho
Pikestone Hill 287
The Knock
Pheasantfield
Brownmoor Hill
265 Broomhillbank Hill
Great Hill
Thieflinn Knowe
Kirkland Hill
Chapelhill
Blackacre
Dinwoodie Mains
Berryscaur
Boreland
Millriggs
D
U
M
Downey Hill
Knockespen
Minister's Moss
Kerse Moor
Longerhallis Hill
Ravenscleugh
Little Millriggs
Fauld Hill
Witchshaw Rig
Horse Knowe
Mid He 289
Courance
Chapel Wood
Dinwoodie Lodge
Burrance
Newbigging
Kirkslight Hill
Wood Hill
Ae Village
Wood Fm
Kirkmichael Fell
Heathfield Moor
Hangingshaw
Heithatpark
Carterton
Hallhills Loch
331 Hart Fell
Relic Hill
Wester Parkgate
Garrel Hill
Ross Mains
Gayfield Type
Dinwoodie Green
Auchenroddan Forest
Mid Hill
White Hill
Burnfoot Cottage
Woodhill Edge
Dungairy Knowe
Lakehead Fm
Parkgate
Kirkmichael Mains
Gillrigg
Greyrigg
Nethermill
Jardine Hall Mains
Redhall Moss
Sibbaldbie
Claydaubing Br
250 Firtree Hill
Heithat
Whitcastles Hill 278
Barony Agricultural College
Gamerigg Plantn
Third
Hogg Hill
Whitcastles
Little Whitriggs
Ae Bridgend
Milngate
Cumleys
Redhall
Fourmerkland
Balgray Home Fm
Balgray Ho
Fulton
Templand
Chipknowe
Bow Hill
Dalruscan
Comrue
Brieryhill
Corrie Common
Nethercleuch
Newfield Moor
Penlaw
Craighousesteads Hill
Pike Knowe
Millhousebridge
Hillside
Gillenbie
Corriehalls
G
A
L
Johnfield Moss
Hazliebrae
Elshieshields
Kinnel Br
Broomhills
Millbank
St Michael's Walls
Crofthead Hill
Corrielea
Pyatshaws Rig
Pearsby Hall
Shieldhill
Todhillmuir
Chapelcroft
Riggheads
Bridgemuir
Muirhouse
Sandbed
Old Craighouse
Craighouse
Corriehills
Pinnacle Wood
Hightown Hill 250
Applegarthtown
Sloda Hill
Slodahill
South Corrielaw
Meikle Whitriggs
Paddockhole
Bow Hill
Hightown
Bruntshields
Bankhead Glen
Broomhill
Dryfeholm Fm
17
Lockerbie Manor
Catlins
Sheepknowes
Crawthat Hill
Hazelrig Fm
Mill Loch
Marjoriebanks
Watscales
Whitestonehill
Grange of Tundergarth
White Hill
Watchill
Lochmaben
Torwood Plantn
The Hass
Corriemains
Wyliehole
Seven Brethren
Standburn
Back Hill
Ashfield
Burnside
Halleaths
Torwood Lodge
Ind Est
Halldykes
Quhytewoollen
Raggiewhate
Bankshill
319 Grange Fell
Berry Cott
Priesthead
Kirk Loch
Castle Loch
Ladyward
Lockerbie
Rosebank
Northburn
Shaw's Hill
Gall Moss
Long Plantn
Blackrig
Millhill
Mounthoolie
B7068
Birrens Hill
Cullivait
Tinwald
Whitelaird
Parkfoot
LOCHMABEN CASTLE
Priestdykes
Scroggs
The Linns
Carruth
Tinwald Parks
Tinwald Ho
Hempland Hill
Hightae Mill Loch
Castle Mains
A709
South Turnmuir Plantn
Millantae
Tundergarth Mains
Powhaffet
Branetrigg
Rye Muir
Heck
Blackford
Westwood
Risp Hill
riggs
NY
Mossgrove
Well Springs Plantn
Parkend
Greenhill
Courstein
238
Crossbank
eathhall
The Broom
Corsegreen
Millriggs
Skairfield
18
Torbeckhill Res
Howat's Hill
Hallmuir
Burnswark
BURNSWARK HILL FORT
Stockbridge
Gilmartin
Hartwood Hill
Muirfield
Hightae
Pilmuir Common
Darlawhill
The Grove
Ind Est
Lochar Moss
Mossburn
Gimmen
Grainhall
Dockenflat
Whiteside
Smallholm
Harepills
Purdomstone
0 1 2 3 miles
0 1 2 3 4 5 km

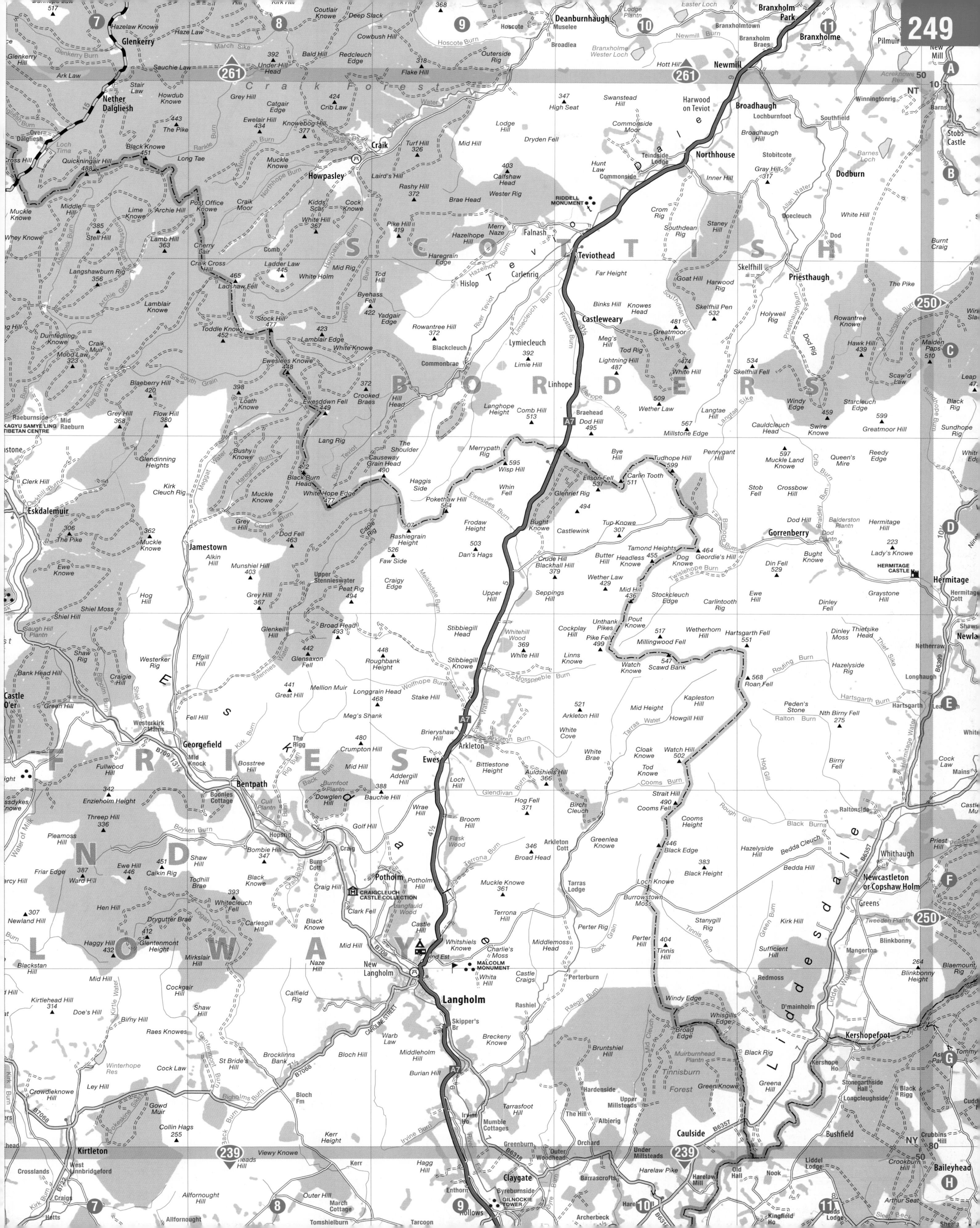

Glenkerry
Nether Dalgliesh
Craik Forest
Craik
Howpasley
Deanburnhaugh
Branxholm Park
Branxholme
Newmill
Harwood on Teviot
Broadhaugh
Northhouse
Teviothead
Riddell Monument
Falnash
Carlenrig
Hislop
Castleweary
Lymiecleuch
Linhope
Skelfhill
Priesthaugh
Dodburn
Stobs Castle
SCOTTISH BORDERS
Eskdalemuir
Jamestown
Upper Stennieswater
Arkleton
Ewes
Georgefield
Bentpath
Westerkirk Mains
Boonies Cottage
Potholm
Craigcleuch Castle Collection
Langholm
New Langholm
Malcolm Monument
Tarras Lodge
Gorrenberry
Hermitage
Hermitage Castle
Newcastleton or Copshaw Holm
Greens
Whithaugh
Kershopefoot
Liddesdale
Kagyu Samye Ling Tibetan Centre
DUMFRIES AND GALLOWAY
Eskdale
Ewesdale
Kirtleton
Claygate
Gilnockie Tower
Hollows
Caulside
Harelaw Mill
Baileyhead
Tinnisburn Forest
A7
B709
B7068
B6357
B6318
B6399
261
250
239

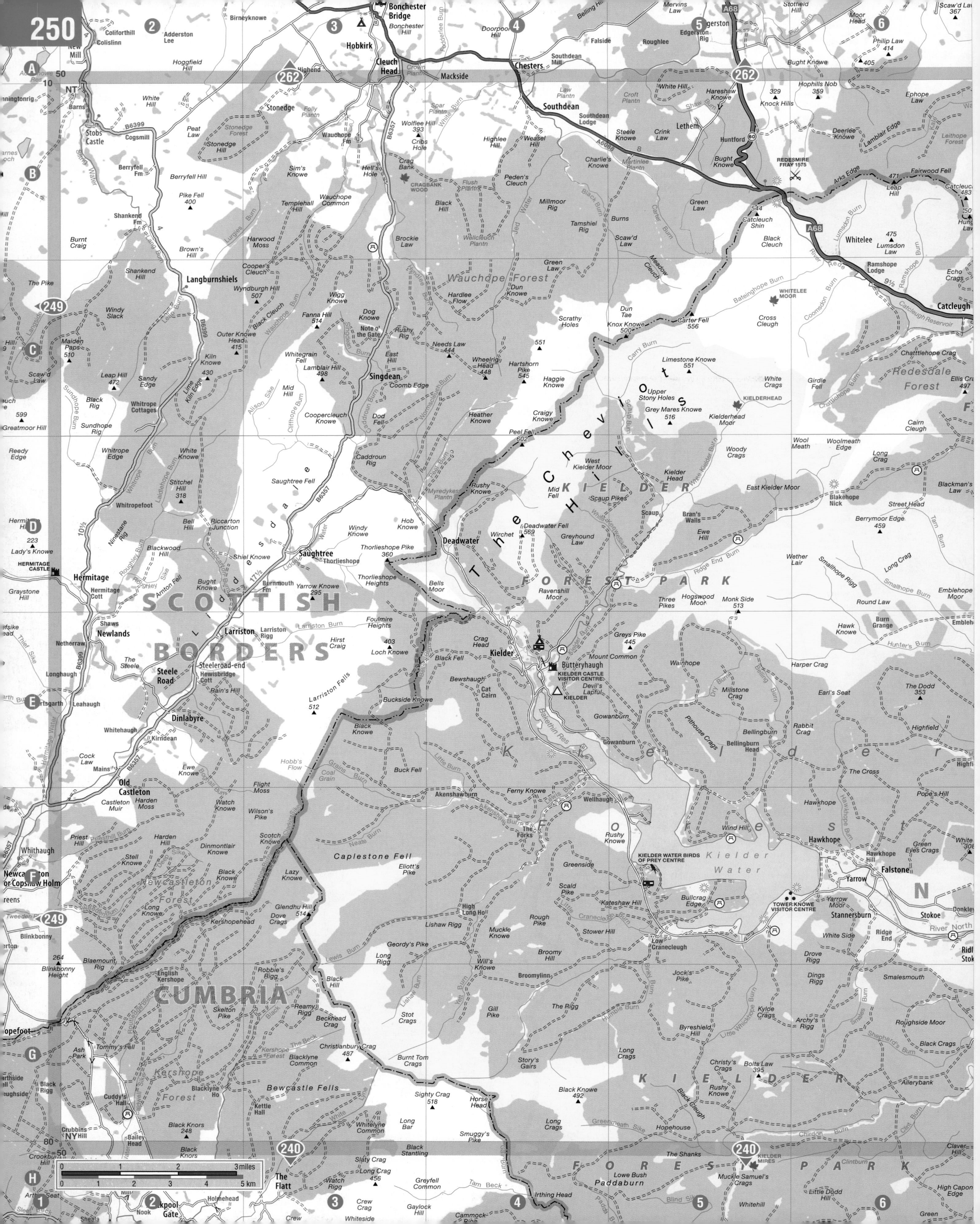
Bonchester Bridge
Bonchester Hill
Hobkirk
Cleuch Head
Mackside
Chesters
Southdean
Southdean Lodge
Colliforthill
Colislinn
Birneyknowe
Adderston Lee
Hoggfield Hill
New Mill
Highend
Doorpool Hill
Falside
Roughlee
Mervins Law
Edgerston Rig
Bught Knowe
Philip Law 414
Moor Head
Scaw'd Law 367
Stotfield Hill
Stonedge
Folly Plantn
White Hill
Stobs Castle
Cogsmill
Peat Law
Stonedge Forest
Stonedge Hill
Wauchope Fm
Wolflee Hill 393
Cribs Hole
Spar Plantn
Highlee Hill
Weasel Hill
Steele Knowe
Crink Law
Lethem
Huntford
Bught Knowe
Hareshaw Knowe
White Hill
329 Knock Hills
Hophills Nob 359
Ephope Law
Deerlee Knowe
Lamblair Edge
Leithope Forest
Berryfell Fm
Berryfell Hill
Sim's Knowe
Hell's Hole
Crag Bank
CRAGBANK WOOD
Flush Plantn
Peden's Cleuch
Charlie's Knowe
Martinlee Plantn
REDESMIRE FRAY 1575
Arks Edge
471 Leap Hill
Fairwood Fell
Catcleugh 483
Pike Fell 400
Templehall Hill
Wauchope Common
Black Hill
Millmoor Rig
Burns
Green Law
544 Catcleuch Shin
Shankend Fm
Burnt Craig
Harwood Moss
Brown's Hill
Brockie Law
Wellcleuch Plantn
Tamshiel Rig
Scaw'd Law
Black Cleuch
Whitelee
475 Lumsdon Law
Ramshope Lodge
Echo Crags
Shankend Hill
Langburnshiels
Cooper's Cleuch
Wyndburgh Hill 507
Wauchope Forest
Hardlee Flow
Dun Knowe
Green Law
Meadow Cleuch
Bateinghope Burn
WHITELEE MOOR
Catcleugh
Catcleugh Reservoir
The Pike
Windy Slack
Wigg Knowe
Dog Knowe
Black Cleuch
Fanna Hill 514
Note o' the Gate
Rushy Rig
Scrathy Holes
Dun Tae
Knox Knowe 500
Carter Fell 556
Cross Cleugh
Maiden Paps 510
Outer Knowe Head 415
Kiln Knowe
Whitegrain Fell
Lamblair Hill 498
East Hill
Needs Law 444
Wheelrig Head 448
551
Hartshorn Pike 545
Limestone Knowe 551
Chattlehope Crag
Scaw'd Law
Leap Hill 472
Sandy Edge
Lime Kiln Edge
430
Singdean
Coomb Edge
Haggie Knowe
White Crags
Girdle Fell
Redesdale Forest
Ellis Crag 497
Black Rig
Whitrope Cottages
Mid Hill
Coopercleuch Knowe
Dod Fell
Heather Knowe
Craigy Knowe
Upper Stony Holes
Grey Mares Knowe 516
KIELDERHEAD
Kielderhead Moor
599
Greatmoor Hill
Sundhope Rig
Peel Fell 602
Cairn Cleugh
Reedy Edge
Whitrope Edge
White Knowe
Caddroun Rig
West Kielder Moor
Woody Crags
Wool Meath
Woolmeath Edge
Long Crag
Kielder Head
Stitchel Hill 318
Saughtree Fell
Myredykes Plantn
Rushy Knowe
Mid Fell
KIELDER
East Kielder Moor
Blackman's Law
Blakehope Nick
Street Head
Whitropefoot
Scaup Pikes
Scaup
Bran's Walls
Berrymoor Edge 459
Hermitage Hill
223
Lady's Knowe
Ninestane Rig
Bell Hill
Riccarton Junction
Windy Knowe
Hob Knowe
Deadwater
Wirchet
Deadwater Fell 569
Greyhound Law
Ewe Hill
The Cheviots
Liddesdale
HERMITAGE CASTLE
Hermitage
Blackwood Hill
Shiel Knowe
Saughtree
Thorlieshope
Thorlieshope Pike 360
Wether Lair
Smallhope Rigg
Long Crag
Graystone Hill
Hermitage Cott
Arnton Fell
Bugh Knowe
Burnmouth Fm
Yarrow Knowe 295
Thorlieshope Heights
Bells Moor
Ravenshill Moor
FOREST PARK
Three Pikes
Hogswood Moor
Monk Side 513
Round Law
Emblehope Moor
SCOTTISH BORDERS
Shaws
Newlands
Larriston
Larriston Rigg
Larriston Burn
Foulmire Heights
Hirst Craig
403 Loch Knowe
Crag Head
Black Fell
Kielder
Greys Pike 445
Mount Common
Butteryhaugh
Hawk Knowe
Burn Grange
Netherraw
The Steele
Steele Road
Steeleroad-end
Hewisbridge Cott
Rain's Hill
Longhaugh
Bewshaugh
Cat Cairn
KIELDER CASTLE VISITOR CENTRE
Devil's Lapful
KIELDER
Wainhope
Harper Crag
Earl's Seat
The Dodd 353
Leahaugh
Larriston Fells 512
Buckside Knowe
Millstone Crag
Gowanburn
Dinlabyre
Whitehaugh
Kirndean
Black Knowe
Bellingburn
Bellingburn Head
Rabbit Crag
Highfield
Pithouse Crags
Cock Law
Mains
Ewe Knowe
Hobb's Flow
Coal Grain
Buck Fell
Bakethin Res
The Cross
Old Castleton
Castleton Muir
Harden Moss
Flight Moss
Watch Knowe
Wilson's Pike
Akenshawburn
Ferny Knowe
Wellhaugh
Hawkhope
Pope's Hill
Priest Hill
Harden Hill
Dinmontlair Knowe
Scotch Knowe
The Forks
Rushy Knowe
Wind Hill
Hawkhope
Whithaugh
Stell Knowe
Caplestone Fell
KIELDER WATER BIRDS OF PREY CENTRE
Kielder Water
Hawkhope Hill
Green Eyes Crags
Falstone
Newcastleton or Copshaw Holm
Newcastleton Forest
Black Knowe
Lazy Knowe
Elliott's Pike
Greenside
Scald Pike
Bullcrag Edge
TOWER KNOWE VISITOR CENTRE
Yarrow
Yarrow Moor
Stannersburn
Stokoe
Long Knowe
Kershopehead
Glendhu Hill 514
Dove Crags
High Long Ho
Kateshaw Hill
Rough Pike
Stower Hill
Lishaw Rigg
Muckle Knowe
Low Cranecleugh
White Side
Ridge End
Blinkbonny
Geordy's Pike
Long Rigg
Broomy Hill
Drove Rigg
264
Blinkbonny Height
Blaemount Rig
Will's Knowe
Broomylinn
Jock's Pike
Dings Rigg
Smalesmouth
English Kershope
Robbie's Rigg
CUMBRIA
Black Hill
Skelton Pike
Reamy Rigg
Beckhead Crag
Stot Crags
Gill Pike
The Rigg
Kyloe Crags
Archy's Rigg
Roughside Moor
Byreshield Hill
Black Crags
Ash Park
Tommy's Fell
Christianbury Crag 487
Burnt Tom Crags
Kershope Forest
Blacklyne Common
Story's Gairs
Long Crags
Christy's Crags
Bolts Law 395
Black Rigg
Cuddy's Hall
Blacklyne Ho
Bewcastle Fells
Kettle Hall
Sighty Crag 518
Horse Head
Black Knowe 492
Rushy Knowe
Allerybank
Crubbins Hill
Black Knors 248
Bailey Head
Whitelyne Common
Long Bar
Smuggy's Pike
Long Crags
Hopehouse
Crookburn Hill
Black Knors
Black Stantling
The Shanks
KIELDER MIRES
Claver Hill
The Flatt
Slaty Crag
Long Crag 456
Watch Rigg
Greyfell Common
Tarn Beck
Lowe Bush
Paddaburn
Muckle Samuel's Crags
Little Dodd Hill
High Capon Edge
Irthing Head
Whitehill
Green
Arthur's Seat
Nook
Holmehead
Crew Crag
Crew
Gaylock Hill
Cammock
Whiteside
Sheala
Blackpool Gate
0 1 2 3 miles
0 1 2 3 4 5 km

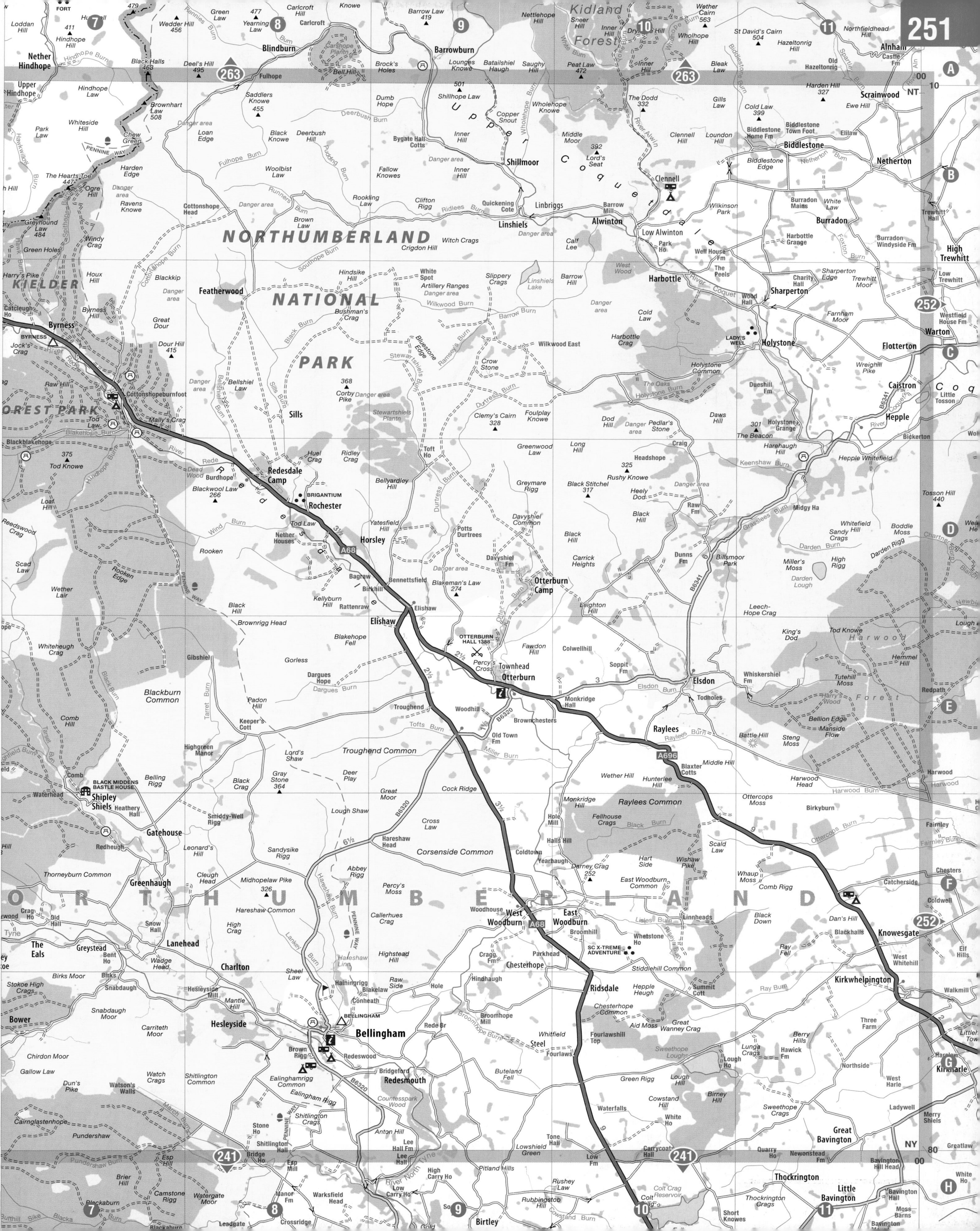

Kidland Forest
NORTHUMBERLAND NATIONAL PARK
Upper Coquetdale
KIELDER
OREST PARK
NORTHUMBERLAND
Harwood Forest
Nether Hindhope
Upper Hindhope
Hindhope Hill
Hindhope Law
Whiteside Hill
Park Law
Chew Green
PENNINE WAY
Loddan Hill
FORT
Wedder Hill 456
Green Law
Yearning Law 477
Carlcroft Hill
Carlcroft
Blindburn
Knowe
Barrow Law 419
Barrowburn
Nettlehope Hill
Sneer Hill
Inner Hill
Dryhope Hill
Wether Cairn 563
Wholhope Hill
St David's Cairn 504
Northfieldhead Hill
Hazeltonrig Hill
Alnham
Alnham Castle Fm
Old Hazeltonrig
Black Halls 463
Deel's Hill 495
Fulhope
Brock's Holes
Lounges Knowe
Batailshiel Haugh
Saughy Hill
Peat Law 472
Inner Hill
Bleak Law
Harden Hill 327
Scrainwood
Ewe Hill
Brownhart Law 508
Saddlers Knowe 455
Dumb Hope
Shillhope Law 501
Copper Snout
Wholehope Knowe
The Dodd 332
Gills Law
Cold Law 399
Biddlestone Home Fm
Biddlestone Town Foot
Biddlestone
Biddlestone Edge
Netherton
Loan Edge
Black Knowe
Deerbush Hill
Bygate Hall Cotts
Inner Hill
Middle Moor
Lord's Seat 392
Clennell Hill
Loundon Hill
Clennell
Harden Edge
The Hearts Toe 447
Ogre Hill
Woolbist Law
Fallow Knowes
Inner Hill
Shillmoor
Linbriggs
Burradon Mains
White Law
Burradon
Trewhitt Hall
Ravens Knowe
Cottonshope Head
Rookling Law
Clifton Rigg
Quickening Cote
Linshiels
Barrow Mill
Alwinton
Low Alwinton
Wilkinson Park
Greyhound Law 484
Windy Crag
Green Holes
Brown Law
Witch Crags
Crigdon Hill
Calf Lee
Park Ho
Well House Fm
Harbottle Grange
Burradon Windyside Fm
High Trewhitt
Low Trewhitt
Harry's Pike
Houx Hill
Featherwood
Blackkip
Hindsike Hill
White Spot
Artillery Ranges
Slippery Crags
Linshiels Lake
Barrow Hill
West Wood
Harbottle
The Peels
Charity Hall
Sharperton Edge
Trewhitt Moor
Sharperton
Wood Hall
Catcleugh Ho
Byrness Hill
Byrness
BYRNESS
Jock's Crag
Great Dour
Bushman's Crag
Wilkwood Burn
Bluestone Edge
Cold Law
Harbottle Crag
LADY'S WELL
Holystone
Farnham Moor
Westfield House Fm
Warton
Flotterton
Dour Hill 415
Wilkwood East
Crow Stone
Holystone Common
Wreighill Pike
Caistron
Little Tosson
Raw Hill
Cottonshopeburnfoot
Bellshiel Law
Corby Pike 368
Sills
Stewartshiels Plantn
The Oaks
Dueshill Fm
Tod Law
Mally's Crag
Blakehope Burn
Clemy's Cairn 328
Foulplay Knowe
Dod Hill
Pedlar's Stone
Daws Hill
Holystone Grange
Hepple
The Beacon 301
Bickerton
Blackblakehope
Tod Knowe 375
Huel Crag
Ridley Crag
Toft Ho
Greenwood Law
Long Hill
Headshope
Rushy Knowe 325
Harehaugh Hill
Hepple Whitefield
Redesdale Camp
Burdhope
Dead Wood
Blackwool Law 266
BRIGANTIUM
Rochester
Bellyardley Hill
Greymare Rigg
Black Stitchel 317
Heely Dod
Craig
Tosson Hill 440
Loaf Hill
Tod Law
Nether Houses
Yatesfield Hill
Potts Durtrees
Davyshiel Common
Black Hill
Raw Fm
Midgy Ha
Whitefield Hill
Sandy Crags
Boddle Moss
Reedswood Crag
Rooken
Horsley
Black Hill
Carrick Heights
Dunns Fm
Billsmoor Park
Miller's Moss
High Rigg
Darden Rigg
Scad Law
Rooken Edge
Bagraw
Birkhill
Bennettsfield
Davyshiel Fm
Otterburn Camp
Darden Lough
Wether Lair
Kellyburn Hill
Rattenraw
Blakeman's Law 274
Elishaw
Leighton Hill
Leech-Hope Crag
Black Hill
Brownrigg Head
OTTERBURN HALL 1388
King's Dod
Tod Knowe
Whiteheugh Crag
Blakehope Fell
Fawdon Hill
Colwellhill
Hemmel Hill
Gibshiel
Gorless
Percy's Cross
Townhead
Otterburn
Soppit Fm
Elsdon
Whiskershiel Fm
Tutehill Moss
Blackburn Common
Dargues Hope
Monkridge Hall
Todholes
Harry's Wood
Redpath
Padon Hill
Troughend
Woodhill
Brownchesters
Raylees
Bellion Edge
Manside Flow
Comb Hill
Keeper's Cott
Old Town Fm
Battle Hill
Steng Moss
Lord's Shaw
Troughend Common
Highgreen Manor
Middle Hill
Blaxter Cotts
Harwood Head
Harwood
Comb
BLACK MIDDENS BASTLE HOUSE
Belling Rigg
Black Crag
Gray Stone 364
Deer Play
Cock Ridge
Wether Hill
Hunterlee Hill
Shipley Shiels
Waterhead
Heathery Hall
Great Moor
Monkridge Hill
Raylees Common
Ottercops Moss
Birkyburn
Smiddy-Well Rigg
Lough Shaw
Cross Law
Fellhouse Crags
Hole Mill
Fairnley
Gatehouse
Hareshaw Head
Halls Hill
Scald Law
Redheugh
Leonard's Hill
Sandysike Rigg
Corsenside Common
Coldtown
Yearbaugh
Hart Side
Wishaw Pike
Thorneyburn Common
Cleugh Head
Midhopelaw Pike 326
Abbey Rigg
Percy's Moss
Darney Crag 252
East Woodburn Common
Whaup Moss
Comb Rigg
Chesters
Catcherside
Greenhaugh
Hareshaw Common
Callerhues Crag
Woodhouse
West Woodburn
East Woodburn
Linnheads
Black Down
Coldwell
Crag Ho
Old Hall
Snow Hall
High Crag
Broomhill
Dan's Hill
Blackhalls
Knowesgate
The Eals
Greystead
Bent Ho
Lanehead
Wadge Head
Highstead Hill
Cragg Fm
Parkhead
Whetstone Ho
SC X-TREME ADVENTURE
Ray Fell
West Whitehill
Elf Hills
Birks Moor
Birks
Charlton
Sheel Law
Chesterhope
Stiddlehill Common
Stokoe High Crags
Snabdaugh
Hesleyside Mill
Hainingrigg
Blakelaw
Raw Side
Hole
Hindhaugh
Ridsdale
Hepple Heugh
Summit Cott
Kirkwhelpington
Walkmill
Bower
Snabdaugh Moor
Mantle Hill
Conheath
Chesterhope Common
BELLINGHAM
Broomhope Mill
Aid Moss
Great Wanney Crag
Three Farm
Carriteth Moor
Hesleyside
Bellingham
Rede Br
Whitfield Hill
Fourlawshill Top
Steel
Fourlaws
Berry Hills
Hawick Fm
Chirdon Moor
Brown Rigg
Redeswood
Sweethope Loughs
Lough Ho
Lunga Crags
Northside
Kirkharle
Gallow Law
Watch Crags
Shitlington Common
Bridgeford
Redesmouth
Buteland Fell
Green Rigg
Lough Hill
West Harle
Duns Pike
Watson's Walls
Ealinghamrigg Common
Ealingham Rigg
Countesspark Wood
Birney Hill
Cowstand Hill
Waterfalls
White Ho
Sweethope Crags
Ladywell
Merry Shields
Cairnglastenhope
Pundershaw
Stone Ho
Shitlington Crags
Anton Hill
Great Bavington
Shitlington Hall
Lee Hall Fm
Lee Hall
Tone Hall
Lowshield Green
Low Fm
Carrycoats Hall
Quarry Ho
Newonstead Fm
Greatlaw
Esp Hill
Bridge Ho
Esp Mill
Brier Hill
High Carry Ho
Pitland Hills
Bavington Hall Head
White Ho
Camstone Rigg
Watergate Moor
Manor Fm
Warksfield Head
Low Carry Ho
Rushey Law
Colt Crag Reservoir
Thockrington
Little Bavington
Thockrington Crags
Rubbingstob Hill
Bavington Hall
Blackaburn
Leadgate
Crossridge
Birtley
Short Knowes
Moss Barns
A68
A696
B6320
B6341
252
263
241
7
8
9
10
11
A
B
C
D
E
F
G
H
NT
NY
00
10
80

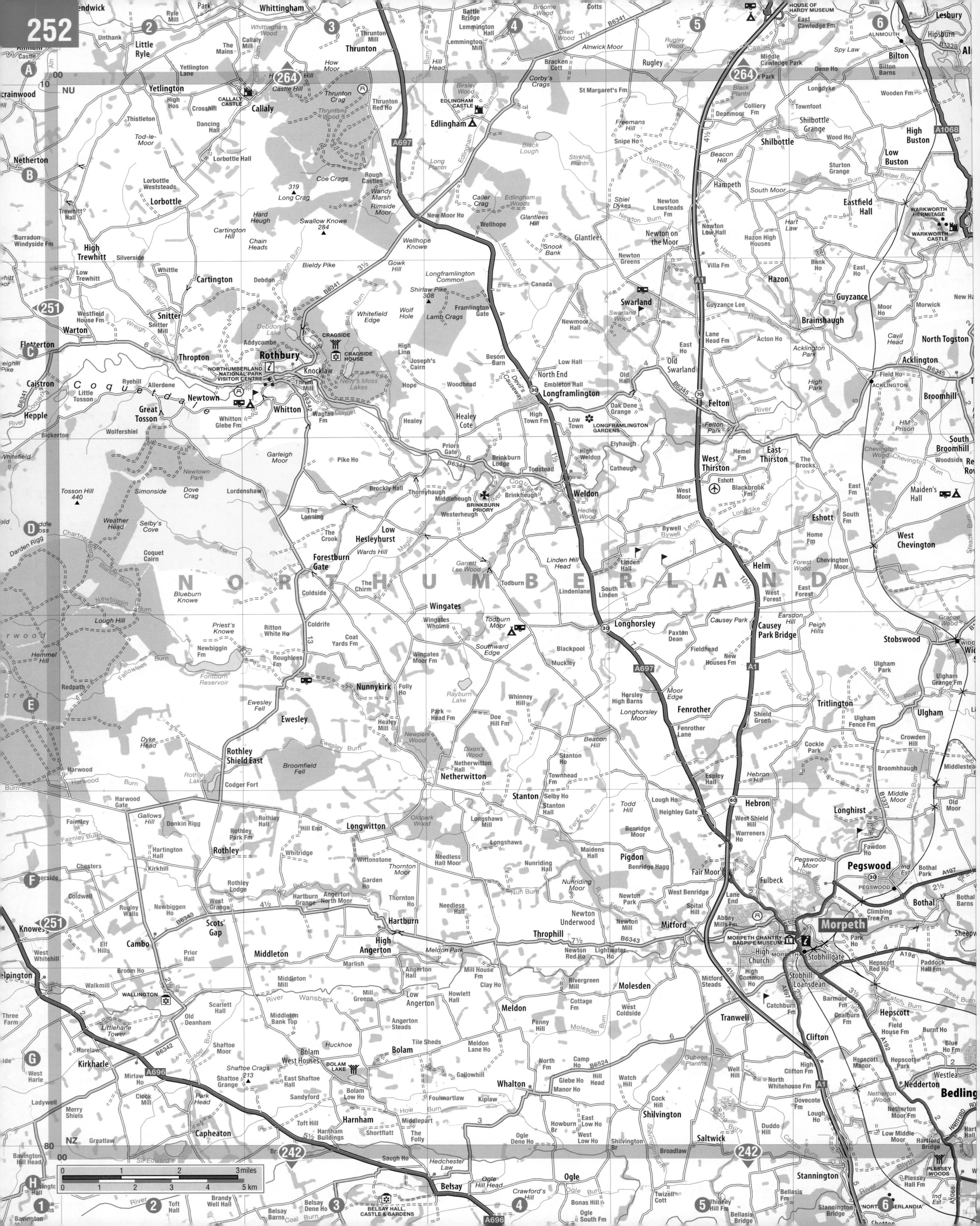
NORTHUMBERLAND
Rothbury
Morpeth
Longframlington
Longhorsley
Felton
Swarland
Old Swarland
Weldon
Thropton
Snitter
Cartington
Callaly
Yetlington
Whittingham
Thrunton
Edlingham
Lorbottle
Netherton
Whitton
Newtown
Great Tosson
Hepple
Caistron
Coquetdale
Cragside
Northumberland National Park Visitor Centre
Brinkburn Priory
Longframlington Gardens
Hesleyhurst
Forestburn Gate
Wingates
Nunnykirk
Ewesley
Rothley
Rothley Shield East
Netherwitton
Stanton
Longwitton
Hartburn
Middleton
Cambo
Wallington
Kirkharle
Capheaton
Bolam
Meldon
Whalton
Harnham
Belsay
Belsay Hall, Castle & Gardens
Ogle
Mitford
Pigdon
Hebron
Fenrother
Causey Park Bridge
Tritlington
Ulgham
Longhirst
Pegswood
Bothal
Hepscott
Clifton
Tranwell
Molesden
Shilvington
Saltwick
Stannington
Nedderton
Morpeth Chantry Bagpipe Museum
High Church
Stobhillgate
Stobhill
Loansdean
Throphill
Thirston
West Thirston
East Thirston
Eshott
Helm
West Chevington
Chevington Moor
Maiden's Hall
Acklington
Broomhill
North Togston
Guyzance
Brainshaugh
Hazon
Shilbottle
Bilton
Lesbury
Hipsburn
Alnmouth
Warkworth Hermitage
Warkworth Castle
Newton on the Moor
Rugley
Glantlees
Eastfield Hall
High Buston
Low Buston
A1
A697
A696
A1068
A192
A196
A197
B6341
B6342
B6343
B6344
B6345
B6524
B1337
264
251
242
Tosson Hill 440
Shirlaw Pike 308
Long Crag 319
Swallow Knowe 284
Shaftoe Crags 213
Fontburn Reservoir
NU
NZ
0 1 2 3 miles
0 1 2 3 4 5 km

NORTH SEA
Marden Rocks
Alnmouth Bay
Birling
Warkworth
Warkworth Harbour
Pan Pt
Wellhaugh Pt
Coquet Island
Gloster Hill
Amble
Moorhouse Fm
High Hauxley
Togston Hall
Radcliffe
Low Hauxley
Togston Barns
Togston East Fm
A1068
Danger area
Ladyburn Lake
Hadston
DRURIDGE BAY
Druridge Bay
Whitefield Ho
Chibburn Fm
High Chibburn
Widdrington
Hemscott Hill
Widdrington Station
Highthorn
Cresswell
Warkworthlane Cott
Hagg House
North Linton Fm
Ellington
Linton
Cresswell Home Fm
Lynemouth
East Moor Fm
Potland Fm
Potland Burn
Works
QUEEN ELIZABETH II
A189
Woodhorn
WOODHORN COLLIERY MUS
WOODHORN CHURCH MUS
Bus Cen
Woodbridge
Ashington
Newbiggin-by-the-Sea
Newbiggin Bay
Hirst
North Seaton
Ind Est
WANSBECK
North Seaton Colliery
Stakeford
West Sleekburn
STAKEFORD LANE
Guide Post
Scotland Gate
Bomarsund
Bus Cen
Cambois
Choppington
East Sleekburn
Bedlington Station
Mount Pleasant Fm
North Blyth
COWPEN ROAD
A193
Bebside
Cowpen
Blyth
Humford Mill
A189
Isabella Pit
B1329
South Beach
Low Horton Fm
East Hartford
New Delaval
West Hartford Fm
Laverock Hall
South Newsham
Gloucester Lodge Fm
Shankhouse
LAVEROCK HALL ROAD
Meggie's Burn
Lysdon Fm
Stickley Fm
Ind Est
265
243
NU
NZ

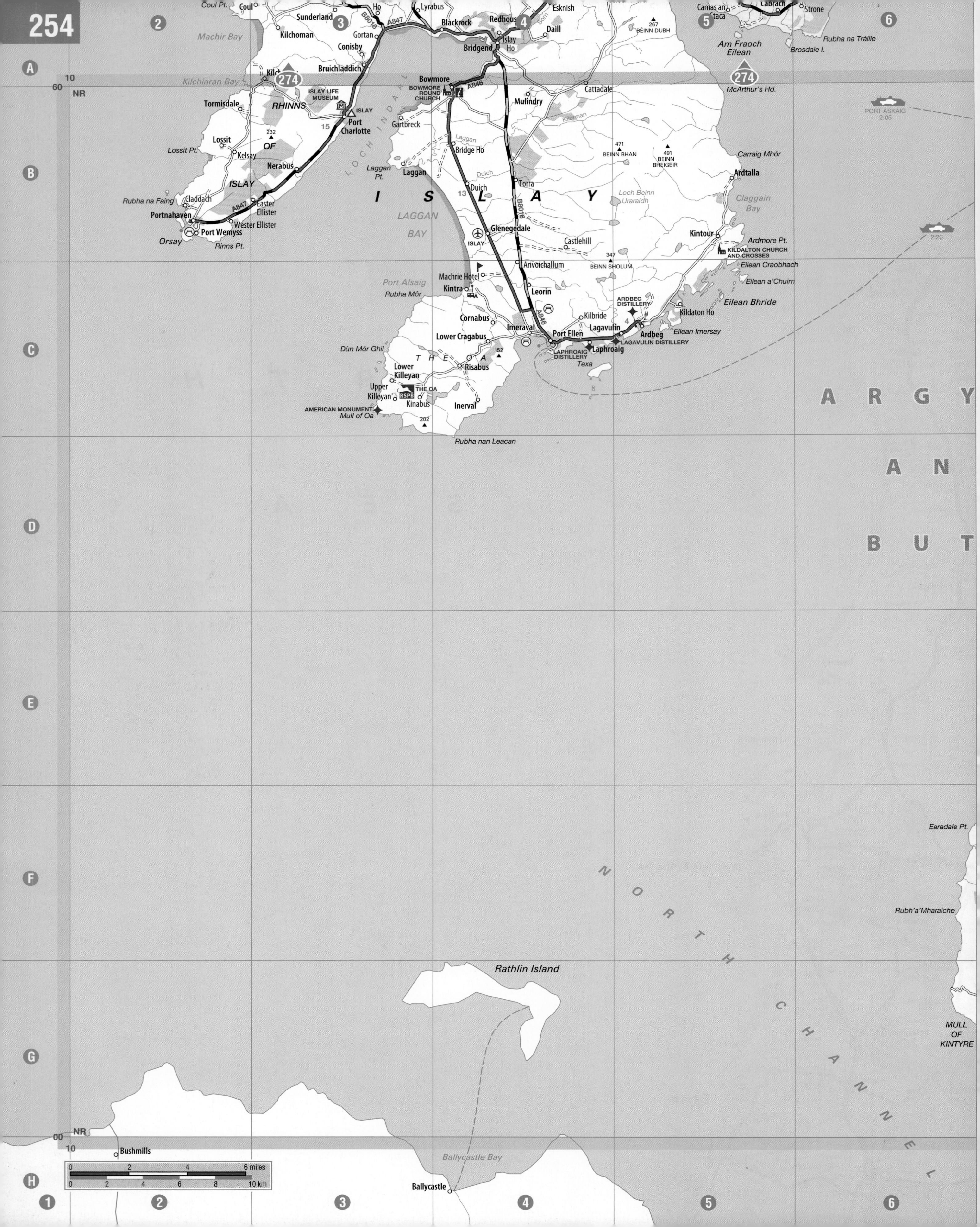
Coul Pt.
Coul
Sunderland
Kilchoman
Machir Bay
Gortan
Conisby
Bruichladdich
Kilchiaran Bay
Lyrabus
Blackrock
Redhouse
Esknish
Daill
Islay Ho
Bridgend
267
BEINN DUBH
Camas an Staca
Cabrach
Strone
Rubha na Tràille
Brosdale I.
Am Fraoch Eilean
McArthur's Hd.
PORT ASKAIG
2:05
Bowmore
BOWMORE ROUND CHURCH
ISLAY LIFE MUSEUM
ISLAY
Port Charlotte
RHINNS
OF
ISLAY
Tormisdale
Lossit
Lossit Pt.
Kelsay
232
Nerabus
Claddach
Rubha na Faing
Portnahaven
Port Wemyss
Orsay
Rinns Pt.
Easter Ellister
Wester Ellister
A847
B8018
A846
B8016
LOCH INDAAL
Gartbreck
Bridge Ho
Laggan
Laggan Pt.
Duich
Torra
Mulindry
Cattadale
Kilennan
471
BEINN BHAN
491
BEINN BHEIGEIR
Carraig Mhór
Ardtalla
Loch Beinn Uraraidh
Claggain Bay
I S L A Y
LAGGAN BAY
Glenegedale
ISLAY
Castlehill
347
BEINN SHOLUM
Kintour
Ardmore Pt.
2:20
KILDALTON CHURCH AND CROSSES
Eilean Craobhach
Eilean a'Chuirn
Arivoichallum
Machrie Hotel
Port Alsaig
Rubha Môr
Kintra
Leorin
ARDBEG DISTILLERY
Kildaton Ho
Eilean Bhride
Cornabus
Kilbride
Imeraval
Port Ellen
Lagavulin
Ardbeg
Eilean Imersay
Lower Cragabus
LAPHROAIG DISTILLERY
Laphroaig
LAGAVULIN DISTILLERY
Texa
Dùn Mór Ghil
THE OA
152
Risabus
Lower Killeyan
Upper Killeyan
RSPB
THE OA
Kinabus
Inerval
AMERICAN MONUMENT
Mull of Oa
202
Rubha nan Leacan
ARGYLL AND BUTE
NORTH CHANNEL
Earadale Pt.
Rubh'a'Mharaiche
MULL OF KINTYRE
Rathlin Island
Bushmills
Ballycastle Bay
Ballycastle
NR
10
60
00
0 2 4 6 miles
0 2 4 6 8 10 km
A
B
C
D
E
F
G
H
1
2
3
4
5
6
274

Kilberry
SCULPTURED STONES
Carse Ho.
Dunmore
Tarbert
Torinturk
Rhu
West Loch Tarbert
Kennacraig
Redhouse
Kilchamaig
Whitehouse
422 CNOC A'BHAILESHIOS
Ardlamont Pt.
Rubha Leathan
Loch Stornoway
275
Ardpatrick
Ardpatrick Ho.
Gartnagrenach
Glenreasdell Mains
Skipness
SKIPNESS CASTLE
Skipness Pt.
Skipness Bay
Claonaig
Claonaig Bay
Ardpatrick Pt.
Portachoillan
Eilean Traighe
Ronachan Pt.
Ronachan Ho.
Clachan
269 CRUACH NAM FIADH
Loch Ciaran
Eilean Garbh
West Tarbert Bay
East Tarbert Bay
Tarbert
Ardailly
Gigha Island
Ardminish
Ardminish Bay
Ardlamey
ACHAMORE GARDENS
Gigalum I.
Cara Island
SOUND OF GIGHA
Balochroy
Crossaig Glen
Loch Garasdale
Crossaig
248 CRUACH MHIC GOUGAN
Cour Bay
Cour
Rhunahaorine
Gortinanane
241 BEINN BHREAC
Tayinloan
322 CNOC NAN CRAOBH
Braids
Killean
Beacharr
CRUACH MHIC-AN T-SAOIR 364
Auchenbreck
Carradale Water
Grogport
Brackley
354 CRUACH NAN GABHAR
Clachaig Water
Achaglass
Muasdale
Rhonadale
Carradale
Port Righ
Glenacardoch Pt.
Belloch
Amod
426 BEINN BHREAC
Glenbarr
CLAN MACALISTER CENTRE
Barr Water
Bridgend
Waterfoot
Torrisdale-Square
Torrisdale Castle
Carradale Pt.
Carradale Bay
454 BEINN AN TUIRC
Killegruer
Cleongart
Bellochantuy Bay
Saddell Glen
Saddell
SADDELL ABBEY
341 A'CHRUACH
Saddell Ho
Saddell Bay
Bellochantuy
Killocraw
Corrylach
Lussa Loch
397 SGREADAN HILL
Ugadale
Tangy Loch
Tangy
Skeroblingarry
Glenlussa Ho
Kilkeddan
Glenlussa Water
Black Bay
Westport
Kilchenzie
Peninver
Ardnacross Bay
West Darlochan
CAMPBELTOWN
Kilmichael
Low Smerby
Machrihanish Bay
Machrihanish
Trodigal
Drumore
CAMPBELTOWN HERITAGE CENTRE
Campbeltown
Campbeltown Loch
Island Davaar
DAVAAR ISLAND CAVE PAINTING
Moy
Drumlemble
Stewarton
Kilkerran
Kildalloig
Ballygroggan
High Tirfergus
Knocknaha
352 BEINN GHUILEAN
Achinhoan Hd.
385 THE SLATE
Lochorodale
Woodbank
446 CNOC MOY
Largiebaan
Feochaig
Johnston's Pt.
Glen Breackerie
277 CNOC ODHAR
Conie Glen
Knockstapplemore
Keprigan
Strone
North Carrine
Strone Glen
Polliwilline
Polliwilline Bay
Macharioch
Mill Park
Southend
Carskiey
Cove Pt.
Brunerican Bay
Port Mean
Rubha Chlachan
Sheep I.
123
Sanda Island
KINTYRE
KILBRANNAN SOUND
SOUND OF BUTE
Inchmarnock
Rothesay
Ardroscadale
Straad
Woodend Ho
Loch Fad
Northpark
Midpark
Scalpsie
Loch Quien
Scoulag
MOUNT STUART HOUSE AND GARDEN
Piperhall
Ardscalpsie Pt.
Scalpsie Bay
Stravanan Bay
Kingarth
Kilchattan Bay
157
ST BLANE'S CHAPEL
Garroch Hd.
ISLE OF BUTE
Cock of Arran
LOCHRANZA CASTLE
Lochranza
Loch Ranza
Millstone Pt.
LOCHRANZA
Catacol
Catacol Bay
ISLE OF ARRAN DISTILLERY
444
Fairhaven
570 MEALL NAN DAMH
Thundergay
573
Sannox
Sannox Bay
Pirnmill
Loch Tanna
859
Glen Sannox
798 CIR MHÒR
Whitefarland
721 BEINN BHARRAIN
BEINN TARSUINN 825
874 GOAT FELL
Corrie
Imachar
Balliekine
Merkland
BRODICK
Glen Iorsa
Glen Rosa
Glenrosa
BRODICK CASTLE
ARRAN AROMATICS VISITOR CENTRE
Dougarie
228
Auchencar
ISLE OF ARRAN HERITAGE MUSEUM
Brodick Bay
Brodick
Strathwhillan
North Corriegills
South Corriegills
Auchagallon
Machrie Water
Machrie
Glenloig
A'CHRUACH 512
Glen Cloy
Machrie Bay
Clauchlands Pt.
Tormore
MACHRIE MOOR STANDING STONES
503
KING'S CAVE
BALMICHAEL VISITOR CENTRE
Balmichael
Blairbeg
Margnaheglish
Lamlash
Lamlash Bay
Holy Island
Cordon
314
Torbeg
Drumadoon Pt.
Shiskine
Birchburn
North Feorline
Blackwaterfoot
Drumadoon Bay
Kilpatrick
KILPATRICK DUN
458 TIGHVEIN
Kingscross Pt.
Auchencairn
Kingscross
Knockenkelly
Whiting Bay
North Kiscadale
South Kiscadale
Glenree
Sliddery Water
Corriecravie Moor
Corriecravie
Brown Hd.
CARN BAN
Clachaig
Auchareoch
Kilmory Water
GLENASHDALE FALLS
Largymore
Largymeanoch
Largybeg
Dippin
Dippin Head
Sliddery
Lagg
Shannochie
Levencorroch
Kilmory
Bennan
TORRYLINN CAIRN
Bennan Hd.
Kildonan
Sound of Pladda
Pladda
NORTH AYRSHIRE
ISLE OF ARRAN
ARDROSSAN 0:55
0:30
0:20
266
256
244
338
Ailsa Craig
NS
A83
B842
B8001
B843
A841
B880
A844
B878
B881

FIRTH OF CLYDE
Isle of Arran
NORTH AYRSHIRE
Port nam Balach
Maol Donn 368
A841
NS
Glenshant Hill
Glen Rosa
Creag Rosa
Merkland
Merkland Wood
Merkland Pt
Wine Port
BRODICK
Cladach
Glenrosa
Torr Breac
BRODICK CASTLE
Old Quay
ARRAN AROMATICS VISITOR CENTRE
ARDROSSAN 0:55
Glen Shurig
B880
THE STRING
ISLE OF ARRAN HERITAGE MUSEUM
Brodick
Glen Cloy
Corriegills Pt
Strathwhillan
Glen Ormidale
Fairy Glen
North Corriegills
Sgiath Bhàn
Dun Dubh
South Corriegills
Clauchland Hills
Clauchlands Fm
Clauchlands Pt
Hamilton Isle
Kerr's Port
Cnoc Dubh
Meall Buidhe
Clauchlands
Margnaheglish
Blairbeg
Benlister Glen
Benlister Burn
Lamlash
Mullach Beag
Holy Island
The Ross 311
Monamore Br
Cordon
White Pt
314 Mullach Mor
Monamore Glen
Gortonallister
Pillar Rock Pt
The Knowe Fm
Kingscross Pt
Kingscross
Cnoc Dubh
Urie Loch
Auchencairn
Knockenkelly
Sandbraes
Glas Choirein
Borrach
Allt Garbh
North Kiscadale
Whiting Bay
Cnoc Donn
Cnoc an Fheidh
Cnoc Mòr
South Kiscadale
GLENASHDALE FALLS
Glenashdale Burn
Largymore
Auchareoch
Kilmory Water
Largymeanoch
Cnoc Craobhach
Cnoc na Garbad
Cnoc na Comhairle
Largybeg
Largybeg Pt
Port na Gaillin
Dippin Head
Torr a' Chaisteil
Margenaish Fm
Levencorroch Hill
Dippin
Southbank
East Bennan
Levencorroch
Auchenhew
Drumla
Porta Leacach
West Bennan
Port a'Ghillie Ghlais
Porta Buidhe
Port Dearg
Kildonan
STRUEY ROCKS
Bennan Head
Sound of Pladda
Pladda
BRODICK 0:55
Ardrossan
ARDROSSAN HARBOUR
ARDROSSAN TOWN
ARDROSSAN SOUTH BEACH
South Bay
NORTH AYRSHIRE MUSEUM
Saltcoats
Outer Nebbock
Broad Craig
Culzean Bay
CULZEAN CASTLE
CULZEAN
Glasson Rock
Barwhin Pt
Maidenhead Bay
Swan Pond
Birniehill
Morriston
Balvaird
A719
255
266
244
0 1 2 3 miles
0 1 2 3 4 5 km

EAST AYRSHIRE
SOUTH AYRSHIRE
Irvine
Kilmarnock
Ayr
Troon
Prestwick
Monkton
Maybole
Patna
Galston
Mauchline
Tarbolton
Kilmaurs
Dreghorn
Dundonald
Symington
Riccarton
Hurlford
Crosshouse
Gatehead
Drybridge
Shewalton
Fullarton
Barassie
Muirhead
Loans
Bogend
Craigie
Hansel Village
Mossgiel
Failford
Crossroads
Annbank
Mossblown
St Quivox
Whitletts
Newton on Ayr
Wallacetown
Woodfield
Heathfield
Dalmilling
Holmston
Craigie
Masonhill
Belmont
Seafield
Doonfoot
Alloway
Kincaidston
Laigh Glengall
Coylton
Joppa
Hillhead
Drongan
Coalhall
Stair
Trabboch
Ochiltree
Sinclairston
Hayhill
Littlemill
Rankinston
Dalrymple
Hollybush
Culroy
Minishant
Fisherton
Whitefaulds
Kirkmichael
Waterside
Polnessan
Lady Isle
Irvine Bay
Bracken Bay
Lappock Rock
Barassie Sands
Stinking Rocks
Mill Rock
North Sands
Pan Rocks
South Bay
South Sands
Seal Rock
Little Craigs
Black Rocks
Meikle Craigs
Bell Rock
St Nicholas Rock
Blackburn Rocks
Longhill Pt
LARNE 2:00 (MARCH-OCT)
INTERNATIONAL AIRPORT
GLASGOW PRESTWICK
DUNDONALD CASTLE
SCOTTISH MARITIME MUSEUM
GLASGOW VENNEL MUSEUM
DEAN CASTLE
DICK INSTITUTE
BURNS HOUSE MUSEUM
BACHELOR'S CLUB
AYR GORGE WOODLANDS
HEADS OF AYR FARM PARK
ROBERT BURNS BIRTHPLACE MUS
TAM O'SHANTER EXPERIENCE & BURNS NATIONAL HERITAGE PARK
MACLAURIN GALLERY & ROZELLE HOUSE
COLLEGIATE CHURCH
CROSSRAGUEL ABBEY
ELECTRIC BRAE
Carsekeoch
A71
A76
A77
A78
A719
A70
A713
A759
B730
B742
B743
B744
B7034
B7024
266
267
258
245
50
NS
40
10
A
B
C
D
E
F
G
H
7
8
9
10
11

EAST AYRSHIRE
Mauchline
Galston
Newmilns
Darvel
Greenholm
Catrine
Sorn
Auchinleck
Cumnock
Netherthird
Craigens
Ochiltree
Logan
Lugar
Muirkirk
Smallburn
Kames
New Cumnock
Pathhead
Mansfield
Kirkconnel
Kelloholm
Kirkland
Drumclog
Caldermill
Gilmourton
Stobieside
Skares
Bankglen
Connel Park
Dalleagles
Burnside
Netherwood
Dalblair
Cronberry
Back Rogerton
Holmhead
Barshare
Sornhill
Auchmillan
Haugh
Kingencleugh Ho
Welton
Glenbuck
A76
A70
A71
A719
B743
B7037
B705
B713
B7036
B7083
B7046
B745
B741
B744
KILMARNOCK ROAD
BARONY ROAD
DARVEL ROAD
MUIRKIRK ROAD
SMALLBURN ROAD
SKARES ROAD
DUMFRIES ROAD
BURNFOOT ROAD
WINDY WIZEN
River Irvine
River Ayr
Lugar Water
Greenock Water
Glenmuir Water
Gass Water
Garpel Water
Crawick Water
Kello Water
Afton Water
River Nith
Glengavel Reservoir
Sorn Castle
Boswell Museum & Mausoleum
Baird Institute Museum
Kier Hardie Statue
Doon Valley Rare Breeds Centre
Burns House Museum
1648
Cairn Table 593
Wardlaw Hill 497
Middlefield Law 466
Priesthill Height 493
Starpet Rig 451
Bibblon Hill 431
Nutberry Hill 522
Spirebush Hill 469
Goodbush Hill 475
Auchengilloch 462
Dungavel Hill 457
Wedder Hill 434
Tulloch Hill 300
Distinkhorn 386
Loudoun Hill 316
Fingland Hill 462
Stony Hill 562
White Hill 480
Clocklowie Hill 442
Halfmerk Hill 453
Crook Brae 385
Black Hill 431
Benalt 382
Edge Hill 345
Cairnscadden Hill 314
Avisyard Hill 330
Carnivan Hill 324
High Mount 365
Niviston Hill 460
Corsencon Hill 475
Kirkland Hill 507
Todholes Hill 481
Blarene Hill 358
Knocknide Hill 344
Peat Hill 385
McCrierick's Cairn 556
High Cairn 553
White Hill 406
Corserig Hill 395
Chang Hill 463
Benty Cowan Hill 477
Ewe Hill 437
Quintin Knowe 554
Stannery Knowe 363
Little Cairn Table 517
NS
257
267
268
246
0 1 2 3 miles
0 1 2 3 4 5 km

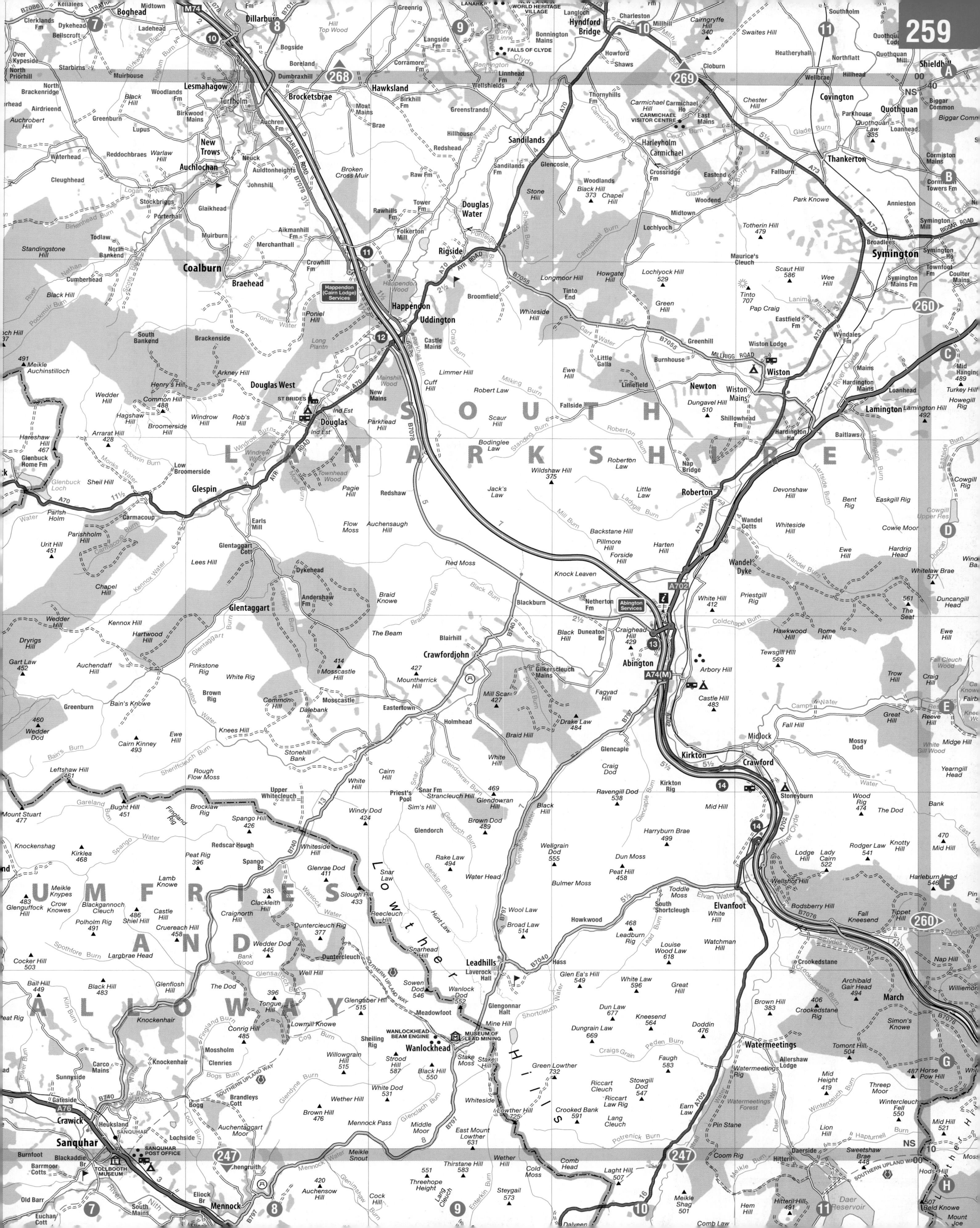
SOUTH LANARKSHIRE
DUMFRIES AND GALLOWAY
Lowther Hills
Boghead
Dillarburn
Hyndford Bridge
Lesmahagow
Turfholm
Brocketsbrae
Hawksland
New Trows
Auchlochan
Sandilands
Carmichael
Harleyholm
Covington
Quothquan
Thankerton
Douglas Water
Rigside
Coalburn
Braehead
Happendon
Uddington
Happendon (Cairn Lodge) Services
Symington
Wiston
Newton
Lamington
Douglas West
Douglas
Glespin
Roberton
Wandel Dyke
Glentaggart
Crawfordjohn
Abington
Abington Services
Kirkton
Crawford
Midlock
Elvanfoot
Leadhills
Wanlockhead
WANLOCKHEAD BEAM ENGINE
MUSEUM OF LEAD MINING
Watermeetings
March
Crawick
Sanquhar
SANQUHAR POST OFFICE
TOLLBOOTH MUSEUM
Mennock
FALLS OF CLYDE
NEW LANARK WORLD HERITAGE VILLAGE
CARMICHAEL VISITOR CENTRE
Tinto 707
Daer Reservoir
SOUTHERN UPLAND WAY
Green Lowther 732
Lowther Hill 725
M74
A70
A73
A702
A74(M)
A76
B7078
B7055
B7040
B740
B797
268
269
260
247

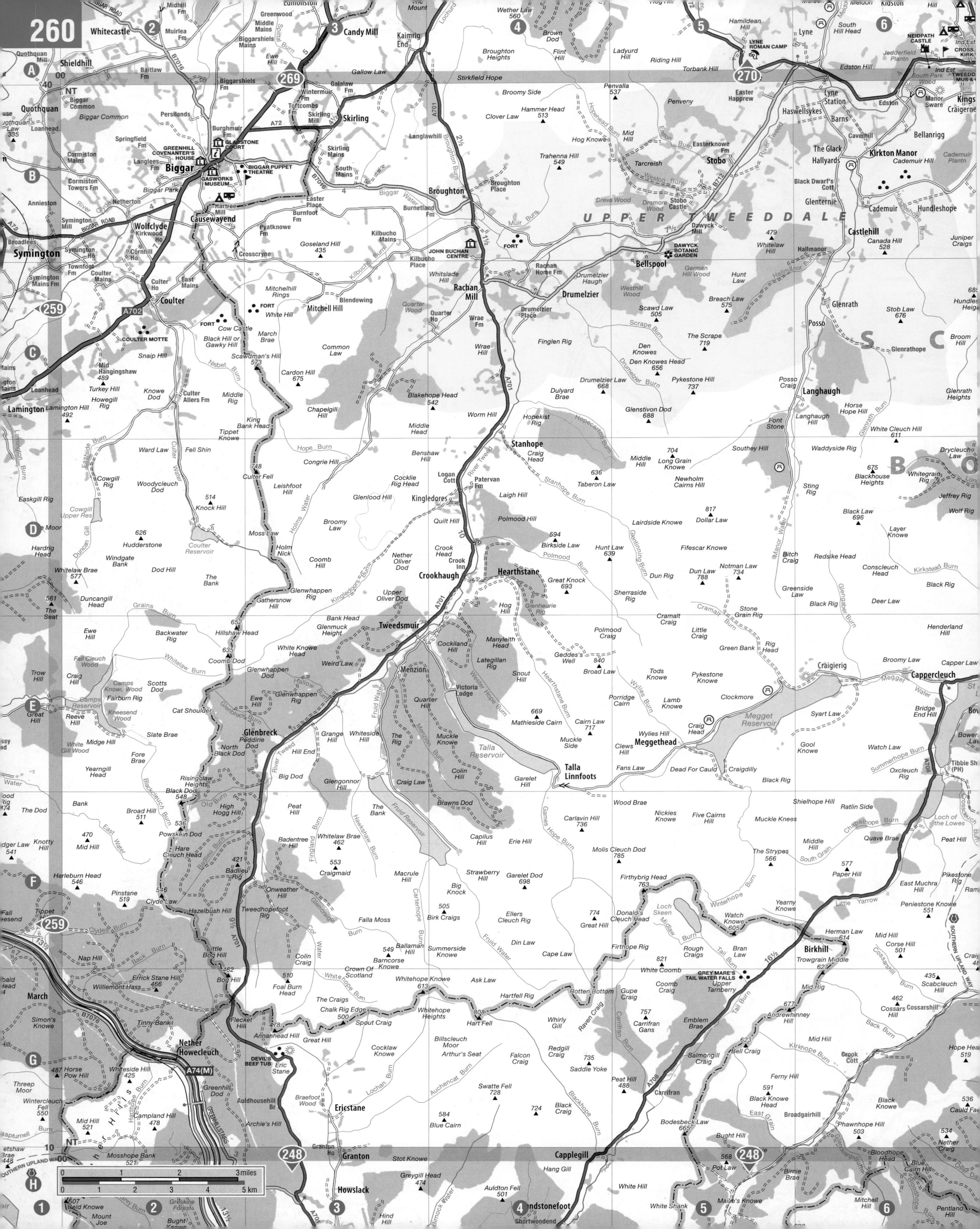
Whitecastle
Candy Mill
Kaimrig End
Wether Law 560
Brown Dod
Hamildean Hill
Lyne
Lyne Roman Camp
South Hill Head
Neidpath Castle
Quothquan
Shieldhill
Biggarshiels Mains
Broughton Heights
Flint Hill
Ladyurd Hill
Riding Hill
Torbanck Hill
Jedderfield Plantn
Edston Hill
Baitlaw Fm
Gallow Law
Stirkfield Hope
Biggarshiels Fm
Galalaw Fm
Penvalla 537
Easter Happrew
Lyne Station
Edston
Manor Sware
Kings
Craigerne
Biggar Common
Wintermuir Fm
Toftcombs Fm
Skirling Mill
Skirling
Broomy Side
Penveny
Haswellsykes
Barns
Persilands
Hammer Head 513
Clover Law
Caverhill
Bellanrigg
Quothquan Law 335
Loanhead
Springfield Fm
Burghmuir Fm
Gladstone Court
Greenhill Covenanter's House
Langlawhill
Hog Knowe
Mid Hill
Easterknowe Fm
The Glack
Hallyards
Kirkton Manor
Cadernuir Hill
Cadernuir Plantn
Cormiston Mains
Langlees Fm
Biggar
Gasworks Museum
Biggar Puppet Theatre
Skirling Mains
South Mains
Trahenna Hill 549
Tarcreish
Stobo
Black Dwarf's Cott
Cormiston Towers Fm
Biggar Park
Broughton
Broughton Place
Dreva Wood
Dramore Wood
Stobo Castle
Glenternie
Annieston
Netherton
Hartree Mill
Easter Place
Burnetland Fm
Cademuir
Hundleshope
Symington Mill
Wolfclyde
Kirkwood Ho
Causewayend
Burnfoot Fm
Pyatknowe Fm
Upper Tweeddale
Dawyck Mill
Castlehill
Juniper Craigs
Broadlees
Symington
Cornhill Ho
Crosscryne
Goseland Hill 435
Kilbucho Mains
Fort
John Buchan Centre
Dawyck Botanic Garden
Whitelaw Hill 479
Hallmanor
Canada Hill 528
Townfoot Fm
Coulter Mains
Kilbucho Place
Whitslade Hill
Rachan Home Fm
Bellspool
German Hill Wood
Hunt Law
Symington Mains Fm
Culter Ho
East Mains
Mitchelhill Rings
Rachan Mill
Drumelzier Haugh
Westhill Wood
Coulter
Blendewing
Mitchell Hill
Quarter Wood
Drumelzier
Breach Law 575
Glenrath
Hundleshope Heights
White Hill
Quarter Ho
Drumelzier Place
Scawd Law 505
Stob Law 676
Cow Castle
Coulter Motte
Wrae Fm
Posso
Glenrathope
Black Hill or Gawky Hill
March Brae
Finglen Rig
Den Knowes
The Scrape 719
Broom Hill
Common Law
Wrae Hill
Den Knowes Head 656
Snaip Hill
Scawdman's Hill 573
Mid Hangingshaw 489
Cardon Hill 675
Drumelzier Law 668
Pykestone Hill 737
Posso Craig
Langhaugh
Glenrath Heights
Turkey Hill
Loanhead
Howegill Rig
Knowe Dod
Culter Allers Fm
Middle Rig
Blakehope Head 542
Dulyard Brae
Horse Hope Hill
Lamington
Lamington Hill 492
Chapelgill Hill
Worm Hill
Glenstivon Dod 688
Font Stone
Langhaugh Hill
King Bank Head
Hopekist Rig
Middle Head
White Cleuch Hill 611
Tippet Knowe
Stanhope
Ward Law
Fell Shin
Hope Burn
Congrie Hill
Benshaw Hill
Craig Head
Long Grain Knowe 704
Middle Hill
Southey Hill
Waddyside Rig
Drycleuch Law
Culter Fell 748
Logan Cott
Patervan Fm
Taberon Law 636
Newholm Cairns Hill
Blackhouse Heights 675
Whitegrain Rig
Cowgill Rig
Woodycleuch Dod
Leishfoot Hill
Cocklie Rig Head
Sting Rig
Easkgill Rig
Cowgill Upper Res
Knock Hill 514
Glenlood Hill
Kingledores
Laigh Hill
Jeffrey Rig
Dollar Law 817
Black Law 696
Wolf Rig
Quilt Hill
Polmood Hill
Lairdside Knowe
Moor
Hudderstone 626
Moss Law
Broomy Law
Birkside Law 594
Hunt Law 639
Fifescar Knowe
Layer Knowe
Hardrig Head
Coulter Reservoir
Holm Nick
Crook Head
Crook Inn
Nether Oliver Dod
Windgate Bank
Dod Hill
Coomb Hill
Bitch Craig
Redsike Head
Whitelaw Brae 577
The Bank
Crookhaugh
Hearthstane
Dun Rig
Dun Law 788
Notman Law 734
Conscleuch Head
Great Knock 693
Black Rig
Glenwhappen Rig
Upper Oliver Dod
Sherraside Rig
Greenside Law
Duncangill Head
Gathersnow Hill
Hog Hill
Glenheurie Rig
Black Rig
Deer Law
The Seat 561
Stone Grain Rig
Bank Head
Cramalt Craig
Tweedsmuir
Glenmuck Height
Hillshaw Head 652
Polmood Craig
Little Craig
Henderland Hill
Ewe Hill
Backwater Rig
Manyleith Head
Rig Head
Green Bank
White Knowe Head
Cockiland Hill
Geddes's Well
Broad Law 840
Craigierig
Broomy Law
Capper Law
Cappercleuch
Trow Hill
Fall Cleuch Wood
Coomb Dod 635
Weird Law
Lateglllan Rig
Tods Knowe
Pykestone Knowe
Craig Hill
Glenwhappen Dod
Menzion
Snout Hill
Camps Knowe Wood
Scotts Dod
Camps Reservoir
Fairburn Rig
Victoria Lodge
Porridge Cairn
Clockmore
Ewe Hill
Glenwhappen Rig
Quarter Hill
Lamb Knowe
Syart Law
Bridge End Hill
Cat Shoulder
Megget Reservoir
Great Hill
Reeve Hill
Kneesend Wood
Mathieside Cairn 669
Cairn Law 717
Craig Head
Glenbreck
Peddirie Dod
Grange Hill
Whiteside Hill
The Rig
Muckle Knowe
Wylies Hill
Meggethead
Slate Brae
North Black Dod
Muckle Side
Clews Hill
Gool Knowe
Watch Law
White Gill Wood
Midge Hill
Fore Brae
Hill End
Talla Reservoir
Talla Linnfoots
Fans Law
Dead For Cauld
Craigdilly
Tibbie Shiels (PH)
Yearngill Head
Big Dod
Glengonnor Hill
Colin Hill
Garelet Hill
Black Rig
Oxcleuch Rig
Risingclaw Heights
Black Dod 548
Craig Law
Bank
High Hogg Hill
Peat Hill
The Bank
Brawns Dod
Wood Brae
Nickies Knowe
Five Cairns Hill
Muckle Knees
Shielhope Hill
Ratlin Side
Loch of the Lowes
The Dod
Broad Hill 511
Carlavin Hill 736
Powskein Dod 536
Mid Hill 470
Knotty Hill
Badentree Hill
Whitelaw Brae 462
Capilus Hill
Erie Hill
Middle Hill
Quave Brae
Peat Hill
Hare Cleuch Head
Molis Cleuch Dod 785
The Strypes 566
Badlieu Rig 421
Craigmaid 553
Macrule Hill
Strawberry Hill
Garelet Dod 698
Paper Hill 577
Harleburn Head 546
Firthybrig Head 763
Pikestone Rig
Onweather Hill
Big Knock
East Muchra Hill
Pinstane 519
Clyde Law 546
Hazelbush Hill
Tweedhopefoot Rig
Birk Craigs 505
Ellers Cleuch Rig
Great Hill 774
Donald's Cleuch Head
Loch Skeen
Yearny Knowe
Peniestone Knowe 551
Tippet
Falla Moss
Watch Knowe 605
Nap Hill
Little Bog Hill
Colin Craig
Barncorse Knowe 549
Ballaman Hill
Summerside Knowe
Din Law
Cape Law
Firthope Rig
Rough Craigs
Bran Law
Herman Law 614
Birkhill
Mid Hill
Corse Hill 501
Trowgrain Middle 627
Errick Stane Hill 466
Williemont Hass
Bog Hill 462
Crown Of Scotland
Foal Burn Head 510
White Coomb 821
Grey Mare's Tail Water Falls
Upper Tarnberry
Scabcleuch Hill 435
March
Whitehope Knowe 613
Ask Law
Coomb Craig
Gupe Craig
Rotten Bottom
Hartfell Rig
Mid Rig
Southern Upland Way
The Craigs
Chalk Rig Edge 500
Whitehope Heights
Hart Fell 808
Whirly Gill
Raven Craig
Carrifran Gans 757
Emblem Brae
Andrewhinney Hill 677
Cossars Hill 462
Cossarshill
Simon's Knowe
Tinny Bank
Flecket Hill
Annanhead Hill 478
Spout Craig
Great Hill
Billscleuch Moor
Arthur's Seat
Falcon Craig
Redgill Craig
Saddle Yoke 735
Bell Craig 623
Salmongill Craig
Mid Hill
Crook Cott
Hope Head 519
Nether Howecleuch
Devil's Beef Tub
Eric Stane
Cocklaw Knowe
Peat Hill 488
Carrifran
Ferny Hill
Horse Pow Hill 487
Whiteside Hill 425
Swatte Fell 728
Black Knowe Head 591
Threep Moor
Greenhill Dod
Auldhousehill Br
Braefoot Wood
Ericstane
Blue Cairn 584
724
Black Craig
Broadgairhill
Black Knowe
Cauld Face 536
Wintercleuch Fell 550
Campland Hill 478
Mid Hill 521
Archie's Hill
Bodesbeck Law 665
Phawnhope Hill 503
Bught Hill
Nether Craig 534
Granton Ho
Granton
Stot Knowe
Capplegill
Pot Law 568
Bloodhope Head
Mosshope Bank 521
Hang Gill
Birnie Brae
Blue Cairn Hill
Greygill Head 474
Howslack
Auldton Fell 501
White Hill
Mitchell Hill
Beld Knowe 507
Greskine Forest
Bught Knowe
Mount Joe
Hind Hill
Shortwoodend
White Shank
Mallie's Knowe
Pentland Hill
A701
A702
A72
A708
A74(M)
B7016
B712
B7076
259
269
270
248
0 1 2 3 miles
0 1 2 3 4 5 km

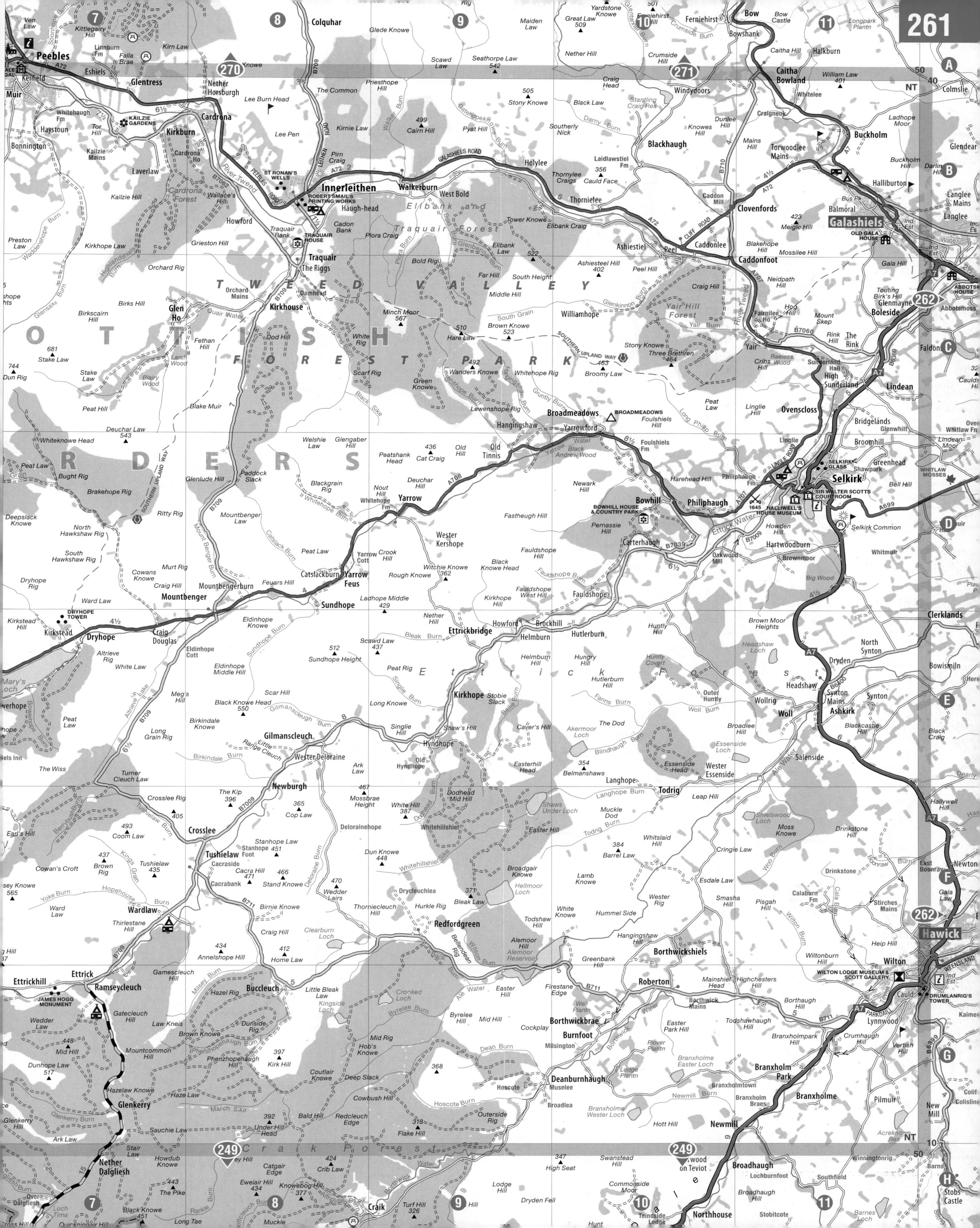
Peebles
Kerfield
Eshiels
Glentress
Muir
Kittlegairy Hill
Linnburn Fm
Falla Brae
Kirn Law
Colquhar
Glede Knowe
Maiden Law
Great Law 509
Yardstone Knowe
Fernichirst
Bow
Bow Castle
Bowshank
Longpark Plantn
Caitha Hill
Halkburn
270
271
Knowe
Scawd Law
Seathorpe Law 542
Nether Hill
Crumside Hill
Nether Horsburgh
Lee Burn Head
The Common
Priesthope Hill
Craig Head
Stantling Craig Res
Windydoors
Caitha Bowland
William Law 401
Whitelee
Colmslie
Cardrona
Whitehaugh Fm
KAILZIE GARDENS
Haystoun
Tor Hill
Kirkburn
Bonnington
Kailzie Mains
Cardrona Ho
Laverlaw
Kailzie Hill
Cardrona Forest
Wallace's Hill
Preston Law
Kirkhope Law
Howford
Grieston Hill
Orchard Rig
505 Stony Knowe
Black Law
Darny Burn
Southerly Nick
Pyat Hill
499 Cairn Hill
Kirnie Law
Lee Pen
Pirn Craig
Dunlee Hill
Knowes Hill
Blackhaugh
Mains Hill
Torwoodlee Mains
Craigneuk
Ladhope Moor
Buckholm
Glendear
Buckholm Hill
Darling Hill
Halliburton
Langlee Mains
Langlee
ST RONAN'S WELLS
Innerleithen
ROBERT SMAIL'S PRINTING WORKS
Haugh-head
Walkerburn
West Bold
Elibank and Traquair Forest
Holylee
Laidlawstiel Fm
Thornylee Craigs
356 Cauld Face
Thornielee
Caddon Mill
Clovenfords
Balmoral
Galashiels
OLD GALA HOUSE
423 Meigle Hill
Mossilee Hill
Blakehope Hill
Gala Hill
GALASHIELS ROAD
LEITHEN ROAD
PEEBLES ROAD
CLIFF ROAD
River Tweed
Traquair Bank
TRAQUAIR HOUSE
Traquair
The Riggs
Cadon Bank
Plora Craig
Bold Rig
Elibank Law
Tower Knowe
Elibank Craig
522
Ashiestiel
Peel
Caddonlee
Caddonfoot
Ashiestiel Hill 402
Peel Hill
Neidpath Hill
Touting Birk's Hill
Glenmayne
Boleside
ABBOTSFORD HOUSE
Abbotsmoss
262
TWEED VALLEY
SCOTTISH FOREST PARK
BORDERS
Orchard Mains
Kirkhouse
Damhead
Far Hill
South Height
Middle Hill
Williamhope
Craig Hill
Yair Hill Forest
Glenkinnon Burn
Glen Ho
Quair Water
Birks Hill
Birkscairn Hill
Minch Moor 567
South Grain
Brown Knowe 523
510 Hare Law
Dod Hill
White Rig
Fethan Hill
Larch Wood
Stony Knowe
Three Brethren 464
Fairnilee Ho
Hog Hill
Mount Skep
Rink Hill
The Rink
Yair
Faldonside
681 Stake Law
744 Dun Rig
Stake Law
Blairy Wood
Scarf Rig
492 Wanders Knowe
Whitehope Rig
SOUTHERN UPLAND WAY
463 Broomy Law
Cribs Hill
Raeless Wood
Sunderland Hall
High Sunderland
Lindean
Green Knowe
Lewenshope Rig
Peat Law
Linglie Hill
Ovensclose
Peat Hill
Blake Muir
Hangingshaw
Broadmeadows
BROADMEADOWS
Foulshiels Hill
Yarrowford
Bridgelands
Glenwhillt
Deuchar Law 543
Whiteknowe Head
Welshie Law
Glengaber Hill
436 Cat Craig
Peatshank Head
Old Hill
Old Tinnis
Black Andrew Wood
Foulshiels Fm
Broomhill
Lindean Moor
Greenhead
Shawpark
WHITLAW MOSSES
Peat Law
Bught Rig
Brakehope Rig
Glenlude Hill
Paddock Slack
Blackgrain Rig
Deuchar Hill
Nout Hill
Whitehope Fm
Yarrow
Newark Hill
Harehead Hill
Philiphaugh Fm
SELKIRK GLASS
Selkirk
SIR WALTER SCOTTS COURTROOM
HALLIWELL'S HOUSE MUSEUM
Bell Hill
Bowhill
Philiphaugh
1645
BOWHILL HOUSE & COUNTRY PARK
Fastheugh Hill
Selkirk Common
Ritty Rig
Deepslack Knowe
North Hawkshaw Rig
Mountbenger Law
Mount Benger Burn
Catslack Burn
Wester Kershope
Pernassie Hill
Carterhaugh
Ettrick Water
Howden Hill
Hartwoodburn
Brownmoor
Whitmuir
South Hawkshaw Rig
Murt Rig
Cowans Knowe
Craig Hill
Peat Law
Yarrow Cott
Crook Hill
Catslackburn
Yarrow Feus
Witchie Knowe 362
Rough Knowe
Black Knowe Head
Fauldshope Hill
Oakwood Mill
Big Wood
Dryhope Rig
Mountbengerburn
Mountbenger
Feuars Hill
Sundhope
Ladhope Middle 429
Fauldshope West Hill
Kirkhope Hill
Fauldshope
Ward Law
DRYHOPE TOWER
Kirkstead Hill
Kirkstead
Dryhope
Craig Douglas
Eldinhope Knowe
Nether Hill
Ettrickbridge
Howford
Brockhill
Helmburn
Hutlerburn
Huntly Hill
Brown Moor Heights
Clerklands
North Synton
Altrieve Rig
White Law
Eldinhope Cott
Eldinhope Middle Hill
512 Sundhope Height
Scawd Law 437
Peat Rig
Helmburn Hill
Hungry Hill
Huntly Covert
Headshaw Loch
Dryden
Bowismiln
Ettrick Forest
Hutlerburn Hill
Outer Huntly
Headshaw
Synton Mains
Synton
Ashkirk
Mary's Loch
Meg's Hill
Black Knowe Head 550
Scar Hill
Kirkhope
Stobie Slack
Long Knowe
Fanns Burn
Woll Burn
Wollrig
Woll
Peat Law
Long Grain Rig
Birkindale Knowe
Gilmanscleuch Burn
Singlie Hill
Shaw's Hill
Caver's Hill
Akermoor Loch
The Dod
Broadlee Hill
Blackcastle Hill
Black Craig
Gilmanscleuch
Little Range Cleuch
Hyndhope
Old Hyndhope
Essenside Loch
Essenside Head
Wester Essenside
Salenside
The Wiss
Birkindale Burn
Wester Deloraine
Ark Law
Easterhill Head
354 Belmanshaws
Langhope
Todrig
Leap Hill
Turner Cleuch Law
Newburgh
467 Mossbrae Height
Dodhead Mid Hill
Shaws Under Loch
Langhope Burn
Muckle Dod
Shielswood Loch
Hallywell Hill
Crosslee Rig
The Kip 396
365 Cop Law
White Hill 387
Whitehillshiel
Todrig Burn
Easter Hill
Moss Knowe
Drinkstone Hill
Earl's Hill
493 Coom Law
405
Crosslee
Deloraine hope
Whitslaid Hill
384 Barrel Law
Cringie Law
437 Brown Rig
Tushielaw 435
Tushielaw
Stanhope Law
Stanhope Foot 451
Dun Knowe 448
Drinkstone
East Boonraw
Newton
Cowan's Croft
Cacraside
Cacra Hill 471
466 Stand Knowe
470 Wedder Lairs
Broadgair Knowe
Lamb Knowe
Esdale Law
Smasha Hill
Pisgah Hill
Calaburn Fm
Gala Law
Yoke Burn
Cacrabank
Drycleuchlea
371 Bleak Law
Hellmoor Loch
Wester Rig
Stirches Mains
565
Ward Law
Wardlaw
Birnie Knowe
Thorniecleuch Hill
Hurkle Rig
White Knowe
Hummel Side
Thirlestane Hill
Craig Hill
Clearburn Loch
Redfordgreen
Todshaw Hill
Hangingshaw Hill
Hawick
434 Annelshope Hill
412 Home Law
Bellendean Rig
Alemoor Hill
Alemoor Reservoir
Borthwickshiels
Heip Hill
Wiltonburn Hill
Wilton
WILTON LODGE MUSEUM & SCOTT GALLERY
Greenbank Hill
Gamescleuch Hill
Ettrickhill
Ettrick
Ramseycleuch
Buccleuch
Little Bleak Law
Easter Hill
Firestane Edge
Roberton
Mainshiel Head
Highchesters Hill
WEENSLAND
JAMES HOGG MONUMENT
Hazel Rig
Kingside Loch
Crooked Loch
Ale Water
Well Plantn
Borthwick Mains
Borthaugh Hill
Cauld
DRUMLANRIG'S TOWER
Kaimend
Wedder Law
Gatecleuch Hill
Law Kneis
Dunside Rig
Byrelee Burn
Byrelee Hill
Mid Hill
Borthwickbrae
Burnfoot
Easter Park Hill
Todshawhaugh Hill
Lynnwood
Brown Knowe
Mid Rig
Cockplay
Branxholmpark Hill
Crumhaugh Hill
Vertish Hill
448 Mid Hill
Mountcommon Hill
Phenzhopehaugh Burn
Hob's Knowe
Dean Burn
Milsington
Plover Plantn
Branxholme Easter Loch
Dunhope Law 517
Phenzhopehaugh Hill
397 Kirk Hill
368
Deanburnhaugh
Lodge Plantn
Branxholm Park
Hazelaw Knowe
Haze Law
Coutlair Knowe
Deep Slack
Cowbush Hill
Hoscote
Muselee
Branxholmtown
Branxholme
Pilmuir
Glenkerry
March Sike
Hoscote Burn
Broadlea
Newmill Burn
Branxholm Braes
Glenkerry Burn
392 Under Hill Head
Bald Hill
Redcleuch Edge
318 Flake Hill
Outerside Rig
Branxholme Wester Loch
Hott Hill
Newmill
Glenkerry Hill
Sauchie Law
Ark Law
Stair Law
Craik Forest
Howdub Knowe
Catgair Edge
424 Crib Law
347 High Seat
Swanstead Hill
Acreknowe Res
New Mill
Colislinn
Winningtonrig
249
Nether Dalgliesh
443 The Pike
Ewelair Hill 434
Knowebog Hill 377
Lodge Hill
Commonside Moor
Broadhaugh
Lochburnfoot
Southfield
Barnes
Stobs Castle
Over Dalgliesh
Loch Tima
Black Knowe 451
Quickningair Hill
Long Tae
Muckle
Craik
Turf Hill 326
Dryden Fell
Teindside Lodge
Northhouse
Stobitcote
Barnes Loch
Hunt
A72
A7
A707
A708
A699
B709
B7062
B710
B7060
B7009
B7039
B711
B6400
B6359
NT
50
40
10
A
B
C
D
E
F
G
H
7
8
9
10
11

Colmslie
Colmslie
Bluecairn
Mains
Cocklee
Chapel on Leader
Birkenside
Legerwood Hill
West Morriston
Morriston
Fans
Fans Hill
Falsidehill
Hume
Hassington East Mains
Over Langshaw
Langshaw
Kedslie Hill
Kedslie
271
Huntshaw Hill
Earlston Mains
Earlston
Darlingfield
Mellerstain House
Whitehill Ho
272
Hareheugh Craigs
Hardiesmill Place
Lurgie Craigs
Sweethope Hill
Stichill Home Fm
Blue Houses
Hassington West Mains
Harpertoun
Stichill Eastfield
Kaimflat
Stichill
Caldronbrae
Mosshouses
Cairneymount
Leadervale Ho
Ladhope Moor
Chatto Craigs
Craigsford Mains
Sheep Covert
Blinkbonny
Parkend
Glendearg
Buckholm Hill
Darling's Hill
Easter Housebyres
White Hill
Cowdenknowes Mains
Shielfield Wood
Fans Loanend Covert
Rachelfield
Hundy Mundy
Girrick
Nenthorn
Newtonlees
Ednam Hill
Ednam
Halliburton
Sorrowlessfield Mains
Brotherstone Moor
Girnick
Eden Water
Nenthorn Ho
Old Nenthorn
Spotsmains
Newton Don
Langlee Mains
Langlee
Wester Housebyres
Easter Langlee
Ferny Hill
Faw Plantn
Packman's Burn
Redpath Hill
The Park
Brotherstone Hill
East Third
West Third
Smailholm
Courthill
Easter Muirdean
Kaimknowe
Berryhill
Hendersyde Fm
Edenbank
Galashiels
Gala House
Pavilion Fm
Gattonside Mains
Gattonside
Eildon
and
Redpath
Craighouse
Brotherstone
Smailholm Mains
Mien's Plantn
Bettyfield
Kelso
Queen's Ho
Hendersyde Park
Floors Home Fm
Floors Castle
Gala Hill
Lowood
Gattonside Ho
Priorwood Gardens
Melrose Abbey
Leaderfoot
Halidean Mill
Smailholm Tower
Whitrighill
Haymount
Touting Birk's Hill
Glen
Boleside
261
Abbotsford House
Darnick
Melrose
Dingleton
The Three Hills Roman Heritage Centre
Newstead
Main Street
Bemersyde
Bemersyde Moss
Butchercote
Fox Covert
Kelso Abbey
Border Union Showground
Springwood
Maxwellheugh
Wooden Ho
Abbotsmoss
Huntlyburn Ho
Leadfoot
Eildon
Monksford
Maidenhall
Sucklawridge
Wallacenick
Roxburgh Barns
Ind Est
Faldonside
Cauldshiels Loch
Rhymer's Glen
422
Eildon Hills
Newtown St Boswells
Dryburgh
Mertoun Br
Clintmains
Magdalene Hall
Dalcove Mains
Manorhill
Trows
Maisondieu
Spylaw
329
Cauldshiels Hill
Bowden Moor
Greenwells
Whiterigg
Dryburgh Abbey
Mertoun Gardens
Lessudden Bank
River Tweed
Rutherford Lodge
Heiton Mill
Lindean
Faughill Moor
Longlee foot
Whitelee
Fens
St Boswells
Benrig
Littledean
Ploughlands
Rutherford Mains
Roxburgh Newtown
Roxburgh Mill
Roxburgh
Heiton
Ladyrig
Faughill
Bowden
Riddletonhill
Maxton
Rutherford
Over Whitlaw Fm
Mainhill
Camieston
Charlesfield
Kelly Burn
Big Wood
Roxburgh Moor
Roxburgh Mains
Sunlaws Mill
River Teviot
Lindean Moor
Northfield
Morridgehall
Forest Lodge
Greenhead
Whitlaw Mosses
Kippilaw Mains
Old Prieston
Prieston
Thornielaw
Elliston
Eastfield
Kippilaw
Fox Covert
Steelmoor Plantn
Muirhouselaw
Upper Nisbet Moor
Duke's Strip
Graham's Law
Bowmont Forest
Grahamslaw Plantn
Bell Hill
Midlem
Whitmuir Hall
Clarilaw
Alerigg
Greenend
Longnewton
Longnewton Forest
Ancrum Moor 1545
Upper Nisbet
Kalemouth
Ormiston Mains
Teviot Water Gardens
Caverton Hillhead
Old Caverton
Midlem Mirloghall
Ale Water
Scottish
Shawburn
Cavers Carre
Lilliardsedge Park
Down Law
Peniel Heugh
237
Waterloo Monument
Blackrig Plantn
Ploughlands
Mosstower
Eckford
Eckfordmoss
Marlefield
Chesterknowes
Toftbarns
Alewater Ho
Chapel Fm
Bewlie Mains
Bewlie
Belses Mill Fm
Palacehill
Nisbet
Wooden Loch
Playknowe Plantn
Lilliesleaf
Belses
Pinnacle
Woodhead Fm
Howden
Woodside
Nisbetmill
Kirkmains
Crailing Tofts
Crailing
Clerklands
Riddell
Craggs
Old Belses
Rawflat
Ancrum
Shortacres
Crailing Ho
Wooden Hill
Rocky Covert
North Synton
West Middles
Bloomfield
Whitehouse
Copland
Harestanes Countryside Visitor Centre
Mounthooly
Netherraw
Greenhouse
Belses Muir
Ancrum Craig
Broom Covert
Ancrum West Mains
Bonjedward
Baittens
Littledeanlees
Blakeman's Crag
Castle Knowe
Cessford
Bowismiln
Newhouse
Firth
231
Troneyhill
Oxnam Water
Langdales
Hermiston
Harelaw
Catshawhill
Chesters Grange
Chesters
Bonjedward Ho
Mount Ulston
Bank Hill
230
Synton
Droveroad Plantn
Minto Kames
North Lodge
Grange Banks
Lanton Mill
Crailinghall
Lanton
Black Craig
Huntlaw
Barnhills Moor Plantn
Barnhills Fm
Lanton Moor
Ulston Moor
Marchcleuch
Newlands
Minto Hills
Lambslair Plantn
Crouchie Wood
Old Hall
Samieston
Mary Queen of Scots House
Cleuchhead
Newton
Wildcat Gate
Overwells Cott
Faw Laws
Hassendean Common
Gospel Hall Fm
Lanton Hill
Jedburgh
Jedburgh Abbey
Cappuck Br
Rennieston
Upper Samieston
Hassendean
Minto
Deanfoot
Menslaws
Spittal-on-Rule
Jedburgh Castle Jail Mus
Howden
Harden Mains
Shibden Hill
307
Whitton Loch
Hallywell Hill
Horsleyhill
Melgund Glen
Dunion Hill
Todlaw
Hunthill
Hardenpeel
Crook Knowes
Hassendean Burn
River Teviot
Jedburgh Road
Hassendean Bank
Bedrule Mill
Townfoot Hill
Clarilaw
Knowetownhead
Teviot Bank
Hundalee
Scraesburgh
Oxnam
Bloodylaws Hill
246
Cunzierton Fm
East Bonnraw
Newton
Appletreehall
Midshiels
Ashybank
Denholm
Bedrule
Black Law
Hag Plantn
Ferniehirst Castle
Glendouglas
Oxnamrow Hill
Denholm Dean
Spital Tower
Langlee
Gala Law
Cavers Mains
Watch Knowe
Swinnie
Kersheugh
Oxnam Sawmill
Swinside Hall
Harkers Hill
Stirches Mains
261
Burnhead
Bucklands
Burnfoot
Mill Court
Midgard
Denholmhill
Gilboa Wood
West Lees
Gilliestongues
Mossburnford
Borders
Hawick
Midgard
Effledge
Whitriggs
Fort
Rubers Law
424
Billerwell
Swinnie Plantn
Bairnkine
Mossburnford Bank
Newbigging
Heip Hill
Wilton
Weensland Road
Cauldmill
Cavers Knowes
Nether Tofts
Old Fodderlee
Easter Fodderlee
Willowford Burn
Jed Water
Dolphinston
Museum & Art Gallery
Cauld
Drumlanrig's Tower
Ind Est
Deanbrae
Ormiston
Hallrule
Wester Fodderlee
Woodhouse
Peg Law
Kaimend
Kirkton
Burnt Plantn
Faw Hill
Jedforest Deer & Farm Park
Mervinslaw
Camptown
Falla
North Riccalton
Lynnwood
Parkdaill
Vertish Hill
White Hill
Kirkton Hill
Weensmoor Fm
Hallrule Mill
Weens Ho
Abbotrule
Ruletownhead
Mervins Law
Lawsuit Law
Dod Hill
Stotfield Hill
Moor Head
Scaw'd Law
367
Bonchester Bridge
Bonchester Hill
Belling Hill
Edgerston
Edgerston Rig
Birneyknowe
Colifort hill
Adderston Lee
Colislinn
Pilmuir
Hobkirk
Doorpool Hill
Falside
Roughlee
Philip Law
414
405
New Mill
Hoggfield Hill
Highend
Cleuch Head
Crown Plantn
Mackside
Chesters
Southdean Mill
Bught Knowe
Acreknowe Res
White
250
Stonedge
Folly Plantn
Spar Plantn
Law Plantn
Southdean
Croft Plantn
White Hill
Haresha Knowe
329
Knock Hills
Hophills Nob
359
Ephope Law
Southdean Lodge
Shaw Burn
Lethem
Wolfelee Hill
393
Cribs Hole
Steele Knowe
Crink Law
Hundford
Deerlee Knowe
Lamblair Edge
Leithope Forest
Stobs Castle
Cogsmill
Stonedge Hill
Wauchope Fm
Highlee Hill
Weasel Hill
Redesmire
Charlie's Knowe
Martinlee
Bught Knowe
Southern Upland Way
A7
A68
A698
A699
A6091
A6088
A6089
B6397
B6404
B6356
B6398
B6400
B6358
B6357
B6359
B6405
B6453
B6361
B6360
B6374
B6350
B6352
B6436
B6401
B6364
B6356
St Street
Lauder Road
East End
NT
40
50
10
0 1 2 3 miles
0 1 2 3 4 5 km
A
B
C
D
E
F
G
H
1
2
3
4
5
6

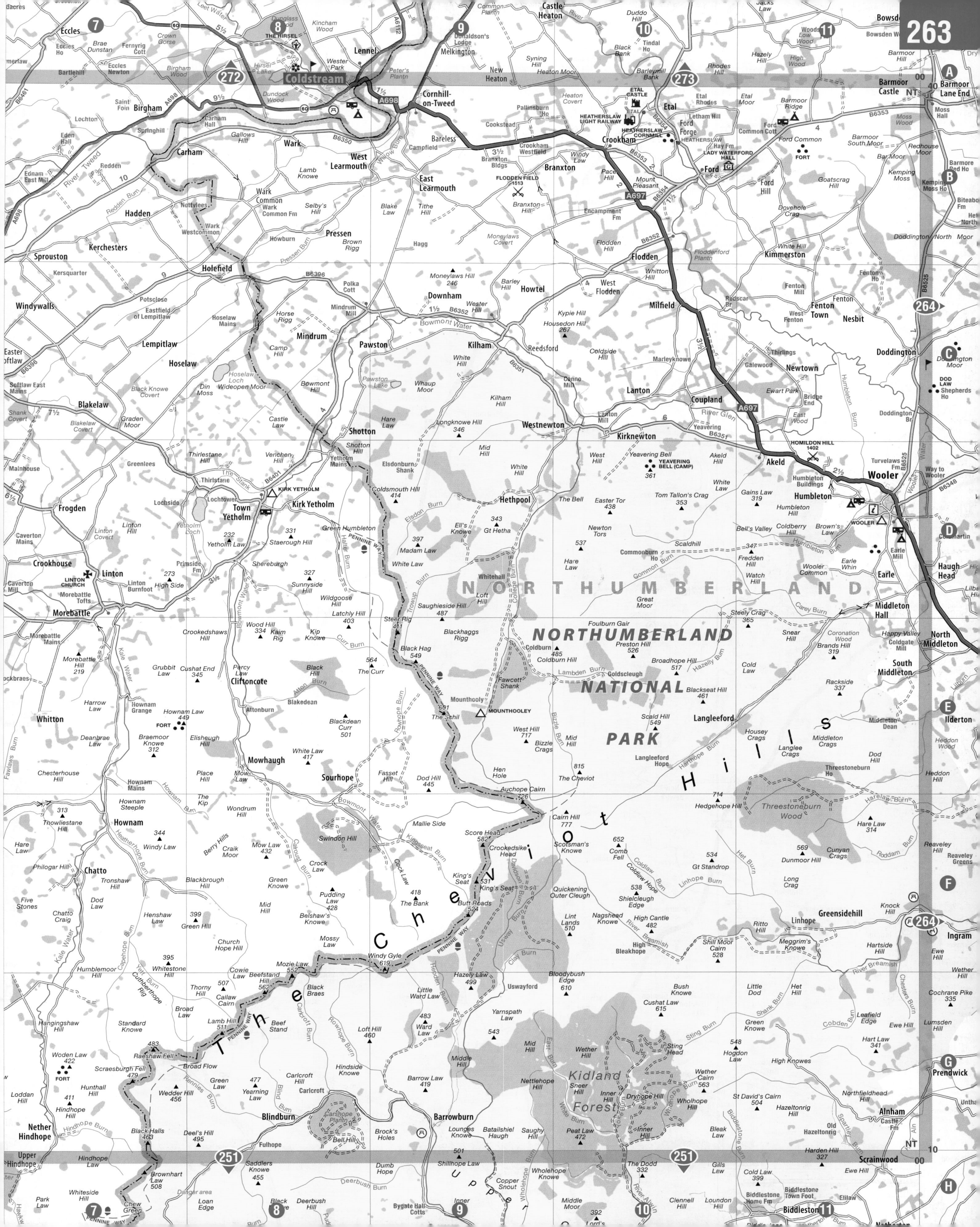
Eccles
Coldstream
THE HIRSEL
Lennel
Melkington
Castle Heaton
Duddo Hill
Tindal Ho
Bowsden
Barmoor Castle
Barmoor Lane End
Birgham
Cornhill-on-Tweed
Carham
Wark
West Learmouth
East Learmouth
Bareless
Campfield
Crookham
Etal
ETAL CASTLE
HEATHERSLAW LIGHT RAILWAY
HEATHERSLAW CORNMILL
Ford
Ford Forge
LADY WATERFORD HALL
Ford Common
FLODDEN FIELD 1513
Branxton
River Tweed
Hadden
Sprouston
Kerchesters
Pressen
Wark Common
Holefield
Windywalls
Lempitlaw
Hoselaw
Mindrum
Pawston
Downham
Kilham
Howtel
West Flodden
Flodden
Milfield
Kimmerston
Fenton Town
Nesbit
Doddington
Reedsford
Lanton
Coupland
Newtown
Westnewton
Kirknewton
Akeld
HOMILDON HILL 1402
Wooler
Humbleton
Earle
Haugh Head
Middleton Hall
North Middleton
South Middleton
Blakelaw
Shotton
Hethpool
YEAVERING BELL (CAMP)
Yeavering Bell
KIRK YETHOLM
Kirk Yetholm
Town Yetholm
Frogden
Crookhouse
Linton
LINTON CHURCH
Morebattle
Cliftoncote
Mowhaugh
Sourhope
Whitton
Hownam
Chatto
NORTHUMBERLAND
NORTHUMBERLAND NATIONAL PARK
The Cheviot
The Cheviot Hills
Auchope Cairn
Langleeford
Ilderton
Threestoneburn Wood
Cairn Hill
Windy Gyle
PENNINE WAY
Uswayford
Greensidehill
Ingram
Linhope
Kidland Forest
Barrowburn
Blindburn
Alnham
Prendwick
Scrainwood
Biddlestone
Nether Hindhope
Upper Hindhope
Chew Green
Upper Coquetdale
A697
A698
A6112
B6352
B6351
B6396
B6401
B6350
B6353
B6354
B6525
B6348
272
273
264
251

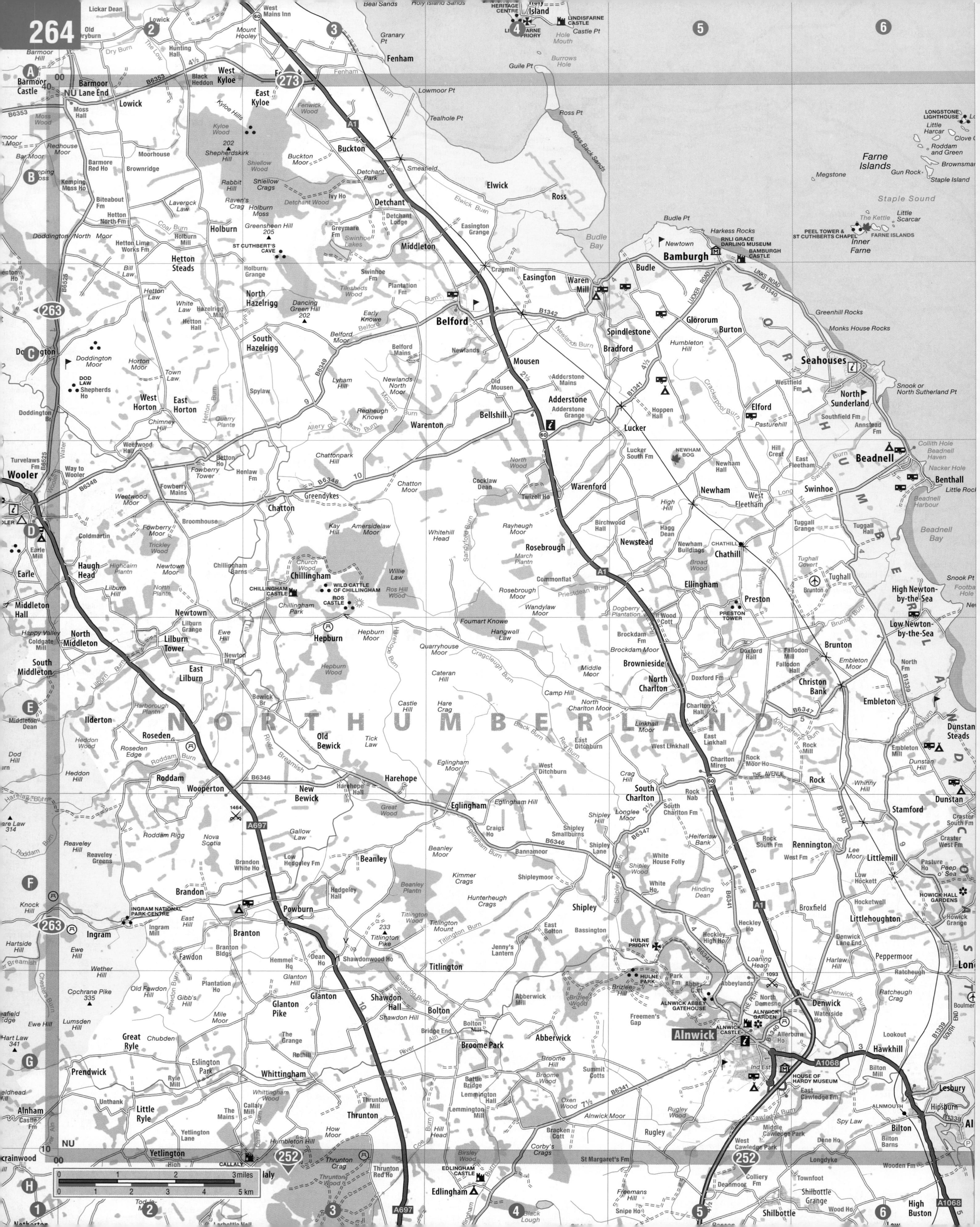

Lickar Dean
Lowick
West Mains Inn
Mount Hooley
Old Berryburn
Holy Island
LINDISFARNE CASTLE
Castle Pt
Hole Mouth
Burrows Hole
Guile Pt
Beal Sands
Holy Island Sands
Granary Pt
Fenham
Barmoor Hill
Barmoor Castle
Barmoor Lane End
NU
Dry Burn
Hunting Hall
West Kyloe
Black Heddon
East Kyloe
Fenwick Wood
Lowmoor Pt
Tealhole Pt
Ross Pt
Ross Back Sands
Moss Hall
Moss Wood
Kyloe Hills
Kyloe Wood
Shepherdskirk Hill
202
Redhouse Moor
Bar Moor
Moorhouse
Brownridge
Barmore Red Ho
Buckton
Buckton Moor
Smeafield
Shiellow Wood
Shiellow Crags
Rabbit Hill
Raven's Crag
Holburn Moss
Detchant Park
Detchant Wood
Ivy Ho
Detchant
Detchant Lodge
Elwick
Elwick Burn
Ross
Kemping Moss Ho
Biteabout Fm
Hetton North Fm
Laverock Law
Coal Burn
Doddington North Moor
Holburn Mill
Holburn
Greensheen Hill 205
Greymare Fm
Swinhoe Lakes
Easington Grange
Middleton
Hetton Lime Works Fm
ST CUTHBERT'S CAVE
Hetton Steads
Bill Law
Holburn Grange
Swinhoe Fm
Tileshelds Wood
Plantation Fm
Cragmill
Easington
Budle Bay
Budle Pt
Newtown
Harkess Rocks
RNLI GRACE DARLING MUSEUM
Bamburgh
BAMBURGH CASTLE
Budle
Waren Mill
LINKS ROAD
B1340
LUCKER ROAD
Farne Islands
LONGSTONE LIGHTHOUSE
Little Harcar
Clove
Roddam and Green
Brownsman
Megstone
Gun Rock
Staple Island
Staple Sound
The Kettle
Little Scarcar
PEEL TOWER & ST CUTHBERTS CHAPEL
FARNE ISLANDS
Inner Farne
Hetton Law
White Law
Hazelrigg Mill
Hetton Hall
North Hazelrigg
Dancing Green Hill 202
Early Knowe
Belford
B1342
Newlands Burn
Spindlestone
Glororum
Burton
Greenhill Rocks
Monks House Rocks
Doddington Moor
Horton Moor
Town Law
South Hazelrigg
Belford Moor
Belford Mains
Newlands
Mousen
Bradford
Humbleton Hill
Seahouses
DOD LAW
Shepherds Ho
West Horton
East Horton
Spylaw
B6349
Lyham Hill
Newlands North Moor
Old Mousen
Adderstone Mains
Adderstone
Adderstone Grange
B1341
Hoppen Hall
Crackerpool Burn
Westfield Fm
Elford
North Sunderland
Snook or North Sutherland Pt
Doddington Br
Chimney Hill
Hetton Burn
Quarry Plantn
Redheugh Knowe
Allery or Lyham Burn
Warenton
Bellshill
Lucker
Pasturehill
Southfield Fm
Annstead Fm
Weetwood Hall
Way to Wooler
Turvelaws Fm
Wooler
Hetton Ho
Fowberry Tower
Henlaw Fm
Chattonpark Hill
North Wood
Lucker South Fm
NEWHAM BOG
Hill Crest
East Fleetham
Collith Hole
Beadnell Haven
Beadnell
Nacker Hole
Benthall
Little Rock
B6348
Weetwood Moor
Fowberry Mains
Chatton Moor
Cocklaw Dean
Warenford
Newham Hall
Newham
West Fleetham
Swinhoe
Beadnell Harbour
Greendykes
Chatton
Twizell Ho
High Hill
Beadnell Bay
Broomhouse
Coldmartin
Fowberry Moor
Trickley Wood
Kay Hill
Amersidelaw Moor
Whitehill Head
Sandyford Burn
Rayheugh Moor
Birchwood Hall
Hagg Dean
Newstead
Newham Buildings
CHATHILL
Chathill
Tuggall Grange
Tuggall Hall
Earle Mill
Earle
Haugh Head
Highcairn Plantn
Newtown Moor
Chillingham Barns
Church Wood
Chillingham
Willie Law
Rosebrough
March Plantn
Broad Wood
Tughall Covert
Tughall
Snook Pt
Football Hole
WILD CATTLE OF CHILLINGHAM
CHILLINGHAM CASTLE
ROS CASTLE
Ros Hill Wood
Commonflat
Priestdean Burn
Rosebrough Moor
Ellingham
Brunton
High Newton-by-the-Sea
Middleton Hall
Lilburn Hill
North Plantn
Chillingham Park
Wandylaw Moor
Dogberry Plantation
Wood Cott
PRESTON TOWER
Preston
Low Newton-by-the-Sea
Happy Valley
Coldgate Mill
North Middleton
Newtown
Lilburn Grange
Lilburn Tower
Ewe Hill
Hepburn
Hepburn Moor
Foumart Knowe
Hangwell Law
Brockdam Fm
Brockdam Moor
Doxford Hall
Fallodon Mill
Fallodon Hall
Embleton Moor
Brunton
South Middleton
Newton Mill
Quarryhouse Moor
Cragcleugh Burn
Hepburn Wood
Middle Moor
Brownieside
North Charlton
Doxford Fm
Christon Bank
North Fm
East Lilburn
Lilburn Burn
Cateran Hill
Camp Hill
North Charlton Moor
Embleton
Ilderton
Middleton Dean
Harborough Plantn
Bewick Br
Castle Hill
Hare Crag
Charlton Hall
B6347
Kittycarter Burn
NORTHUMBERLAND
Roseden
Roseden Edge
Heddon Wood
Old Bewick
Tick Law
Black Burn
Red Burn
East Ditchburn
Linkhall Moor
West Linkhall
East Linkhall
Rock Mill
Embleton Mill
Dunstan Steads
Dod Hill
Heddon Hill
Roddam Burn
River Breamish
Eglingham Moor
West Ditchburn
Charlton Mires
Rock Moor Ho
THE AVENUE
Dunstan Hill
Roddam
Wooperton
B6346
New Bewick
Harehope
Harehope Hall
Crag Hill
South Charlton
Rock Nab
Rock
Whinny Hill
Dunstan
1464
A697
Great Wood
Eglingham
Eglingham Hill
Longlee Moor
South Charlton Fm
Stamford
Craster South Fm
Hare Law 314
Roddam Rigg
Nova Scotia
Gallow Law
Craigs Ho
Shipley Hill
Shipley Smallburns
Heiferlaw Bank
Rock South Fm
West Fm
Rennington
Craster West Fm
Reaveley Hill
Reaveley Greens
Low Hedgeley Fm
Brandon White Ho
Beanley
Beanley Moor
Eglingham Burn
Bannamoor
Shipley Lane
White House Folly
Shipley Wood
Lee Moor
Littlemill
Pasture Ho
Peep o' Sea
Kimmer Crags
Shipleymoor
White Ho
Hinding Dean
B6341
Low Hockett
Brandon
Hedgeley Hall
Beanley Plantn
Hunterheugh Crags
Shipley
A1
Broxfield
Hocketwell
HOWICK HALL GARDENS
Knock Hill
INGRAM NATIONAL PARK CENTRE
East Hill
Powburn
Tittington Wood
Tittington Mount
Tittington Burn
East Bolton
Bassington
Heckley Ho
Littlehoughton
Howick Grange
Ingram
Ingram Mill
Branton
233
Tittington Pike
Jenny's Lantern
HULNE PRIORY
Heckley High Ho
Denwick Lane End
Peppermoor
Hartside Hill
Ewe Hill
Fawdon
Branton Bldgs
Hemmel Ho
Dean Ho
Shawdonwood Ho
Titlington
Loaning Head
Harlaw Hill
Ratcheugh
Wether Hill
Old Fawdon Hill
Plantation Ho
Glanton Hill
Shawdon Burn
HULNE PARK
Park Fm
Abbey Cott
Abbeylands
1093
Cochrane Pike 335
Gibb's Hill
Glanton
Glanton Pike
Shawdon Hall
Abberwick Mill
Brizlee Hill
Brizlee Wood
ALNWICK ABBEY GATEHOUSE
North Demesne
ALNWICK GARDEN
Denwick
Denwick Burn
Ratcheugh Crag
Lumsden Hill
Ewe Hill
Mile Moor
Shawdon Hill
Bolton
Freemen's Gap
Waterside Ho
Boulmer
Hart Law 341
Great Ryle
Chubden
The Grange
Bridge End
Bolton Mill
Broome Park
Abberwick
ALNWICK CASTLE
Alnwick
Allerburn Ho
Lookout
Hawkhill
Rothill
River Aln
Broome Hill
Summit Cotts
Ind Est
A1068
Bilton Mill
Prendwick
Eslington Park
Ryle Mill
Whittingham
Battle Bridge
Lemmington Hall
Broome Wood
HOUSE OF HARDY MUSEUM
East Cawledge Fm
Lesbury
Unthank
Whittingham Wood
Thrunton Mill
Lemmington Mill
Oxen Wood
B6341
Alnwick Moor
Rugley Wood
ALNMOUTH
Hipsburn
Alnham
Little Ryle
The Mains
Callaly Mill
Thrunton
Hill Head
Bracken Cott
Rugley
Cawledge Burn
Middle Cawledge Park
Spy Law
Bilton
Bilton Barns
Alnham Castle Fm
Yetlington Lane
How Moor
Corby's Crags
West Cawledge Park
Dene Ho
Yetlington
CALLAJLY
Humbleton Hill
Thrunton Crag
Birsley Wood
St Margaret's Fm
Longdyke
Wooden Fm
Scrainwood
Callaly
Thrunton Wood
Thrunton Red Ho
EDLINGHAM CASTLE
Edlingham
Colliery Fm
Deanmoor
Townfoot
Shilbottle Grange
Freemans Hill
Snipe Ho
Black Lough
Shilbottle
Wood Ho
High Buxton
A1068
Todd Hill
Netherton
0 1 2 3 miles
0 1 2 3 4 5 km
263
273
252
A B C D E F G H
1 2 3 4 5 6

N O R T H
S E A
Embleton Bay
Castle Pt
DUNSTANBURGH CASTLE
Queen Margaret's Cove
Craster
Cullernose Pt
Howick
Rumbling Kern
Red Stead
Howick Haven
Sugar Sands
Low Stead
Howdiemont Sands
Red Ends
Boulmer
Boulmer Haven
Field Ho
Seaton Pt
Marden Rocks
Alnmouth Bay
NU
50
40
10
253
253
7
8
9
10
11
A
B
C
D
E
F
G
H

FIRTH OF CLYDE
INVERCLYDE
CLYDE-MUIRSHIEL REGIONAL PARK
NORTH AYRSHIRE
Island of Bute
Great Cumbrae Island
Little Cumbrae Island
Inverkip
Wemyss Bay
Skelmorlie
Upper Skelmorlie
Meigle
Largs
Fairlie
Millport
West Kilbride
Seamill
Ardrossan
Saltcoats
Stevenston
Kilwinning
Dalry
Kilbirnie
Beith
Lochwinnoch
Irvine
Innellan
Toward
Castle Toward
Craigmore
Montford
Ascog
Kerrycroy
Scoulag
Piperhall
Kingarth
Kilchattan Bay
Portencross
Hunterston Power Sta
Garvock
Shielhill
Routenburn
Glengarnock
Longbar
Drakemyre
Chapelhill
Auchenharvie
Dreghorn
Girdle Toll
BRODICK 0:55
276
275
255
256
257
NS
0 1 2 3 miles
0 1 2 3 4 5 km

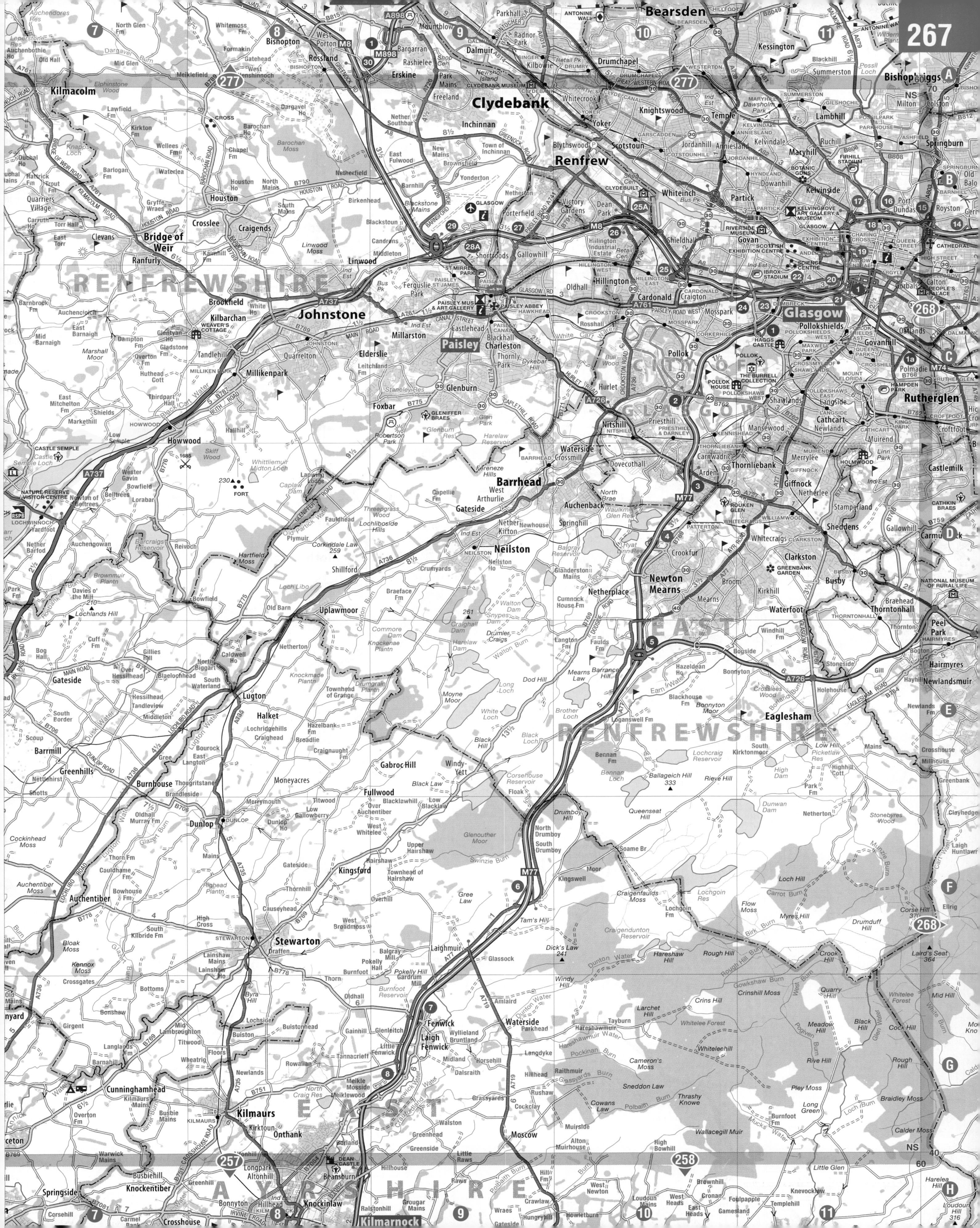
Bearsden
Clydebank
Renfrew
Paisley
Glasgow
Johnstone
Barrhead
Neilston
Newton Mearns
Kilmacolm
Bridge of Weir
Houston
Erskine
Bishopton
Dalmuir
Drumchapel
Kessington
Bishopbriggs
Scotstoun
Knightswood
Maryhill
Springburn
Partick
Govan
Kelvinside
Hillington
Cardonald
Linwood
Kilbarchan
Elderslie
Howwood
Lochwinnoch
Pollok
Pollokshields
Govanhill
Rutherglen
Cathcart
Thornliebank
Giffnock
Clarkston
Busby
Castlemilk
Eaglesham
Uplawmoor
Lugton
Dunlop
Stewarton
Fenwick
Kilmaurs
Kilmarnock
Knockentiber
Springside
Cunninghamhead
Auchentiber
Burnhouse
Barrmill
Gateside
Waterside
Moscow
RENFREWSHIRE
CITY OF GLASGOW
EAST RENFREWSHIRE
EAST AYRSHIRE
AYRSHIRE
A737
A761
A736
A726
A77
M77
M8
A735
A719
B778
B769
Glenouther Moor
Whitelee Forest
Loch Libo
Caplaw Dam
277
268
257
258
NS
40
60
70

NORTH
LANARKSHIRE
SOUTH
LANARKSHIRE
CITY OF GLASGOW
Cadder
Jellyhill
Lenzie
Auchinloch
Bishopbriggs
Lumloch
Springburn
Balornock
Stepps
Garnkirk
Muirhead
Chryston
Moodiesburn
Bridgend
Mollinburn
Marnock
Glenboig
Glenmavis
Riggend
Greengairs
Longriggend
Stand
Caldercruix
Airdrie
Plains
Coatbridge
Garthamlock
Easthouse
Riddrie
Carntyne
Shettleston
Baillieston
Bargeddie
Old Monkland
Calderbank
Chapelhall
Salsburgh
Rutherglen
Cambuslang
Uddingston
Bothwell
Viewpark
Bellshill
Mossend
Holytown
Newhouse
Newarthill
Motherwell
Wishaw
Cleland
Newmains
Blantyre
High Blantyre
Hamilton
East Kilbride
Carmunnock
Castlemilk
Thorntonhall
Larkhall
Stonehouse
Strathaven
Glassford
Quarter
Blackwood
Kirkmuirhill
Lesmahagow
Crossford
Gilmourton
Carnduff
Chapelton
Hareshaw
Auchenheath
Dalserf
Ashgill
Netherburn
268
278
267
258
259
0 1 2 3 miles
0 1 2 3 4 5 km

Uphall
Dechmont
Wester Dechmont
Uphall Station
Pumpherston
Livingston
East Calder
Mid Calder
Oakbank
Bathgate
Boghall
Armadale
Bathville
Blackridge
Westrigg
Whitburn
Blackburn
Harthill
Greenrigg
East Whitburn
Polbeth
West Calder
Addiewell
Stoneyburn
Loganlea
Bents
Longridge
Fauldhouse
Greenburn
Breich
Shotts
Stane
Dykehead
Allanton
Woolfords Cottages
Tarbrax
Wilsontown
Rootpark
Haywood
Auchengray
Forth
Climpy
Braehead
Carluke
Yieldshields
Roadmeetings
Kilncadzow
Carnwath
Carstairs
Carstairs Junction
Ravenstruther
Cleghorn
Lanark
New Lanark
Kirkfieldbank
Hyndford Bridge
Pettinain
Libberton
Newbigging
Walston
Dunsyre
Dolphinton
Elsrickle
Melbourne
Candy Mill
Whitecastle
Shieldhill
Quothquan
Covington
Thankerton
Sandilands
Skirling
Hawksland
Carmichael
M8
A70
A71
A721
A73
A702
A706
A743
279
270
259
260

EDINBURGH
MIDLOTHIAN
PENTLAND HILLS REGIONAL PARK
Pentland Hills
SCOTTISH BORDERS
TWEED VALLEY FOREST PARK
Moorfoot
Ratho Station
Ratho
Ratho Mains
Clifton Hall
Hermiston
Sighthill
Stenhouse
Saughton
Slateford
Longstone
Merchiston
Morningside
Craiglockhart
Kingsknowe
Wester Hailes
Baberton Mains
Juniper Green
Colinton
Bonaly
Dreghorn
Braid
Braid Hills
Liberton
Fairmilehead
Kaimes
Swanston
Oxgangs
Comiston
Gracemount
Gilmerton
Newington
Prestonfield
Craigmillar
Niddrie
The Inch
Moredun
Danderhall
Millerhill
Newcraighall
Stoneybank
Shawfair
Whitecraig
Dalkeith
Eskbank
Newbattle
Easthouses
Bonnyrigg and Lasswade
Lothianbridge
Newtongrange
Gorebridge
Arniston
Carrington
Temple
Loanhead
Straiton
Damhead Holdings
Bilston
Polton
Roslin
Rosewell
Auchendinny
Milton Bridge
Penicuik
Kirkhill
Howgate
Leadburn
Silverburn
Nine Mile Burn
Carlops
Wilkieston
Bonnington
Burnwynd
Currie
Balerno
Malleny Mills
Kirknewton
Glenbrook
Torphin
Edinburgh Canal Centre
Union Canal
Hillend Ski Centre
Allermuir Hill 493
Castlelaw Hill 488
Bell's Hill 406
Black Hill 501
Hare Hill 449
Carnethy Hill 573
Scald Law 579
West Kip 551
East Cairn Hill 561
West Cairn Hill 562
Harlaw Reservoir
Threipmuir Reservoir
Loganlea Reservoir
Glencorse Reservoir
North Esk Reservoir
Baddinsgill Reservoir
West Water Reservoir
Gladhouse Reservoir
Rosebery Reservoir
Edgelaw Reservoir
Portmore Loch
Mt Maw 535
King Seat 463
Muckle Knock 465
Mendick Hill 451
West Linton
Romannobridge
Halmyre Mains
Mountain Cross
Blyth Bridge
Kirkurd
Drochil
Dolphinton
Melbourne
Whim Farm
Cowdenburn
Waterheads
Eddleston
Milkieston
Peebles
Kerfield
Kings Muir
Eshiels
Cardrona
Kirkburn
Lyne
Lyne Station
Hallyne
Lyne Roman Camp
Neidpath Castle
Cross Kirk
Tweeddale Mus & Gal
Kailzie Gardens
Tweeddaleburn
Blackhope Scar 651
Dundreich 622
Cardon Law 588
Deepsyke Forest
Auchencorth Moss
Rosslyn Chapel
Castlelaw Fort
Arniston House
A70
A71
A72
A701
A702
A703
A720
A6094
B7059
M8
269
260
261
280
0 1 2 3 miles
0 1 2 3 4 5 km

Inveresk
Wallyford
Elphinstone
New Winton
New Town
Samuelston
Bolton
Garvald
Nunraw Abbey
Crossgatehall
Cousland
Ormiston
Pencaitland
East Saltoun
West Saltoun
Gifford
Carfrae
White Castle (Fort)
Danskine
Glenkinchie Distillery
Peastonbank
Gilchrist
Quarryford
Longyester
Chesterhill
Peaston
Pathhead
Mayfield
Dewartown
Long Newton
Fort
EAST LOTHIAN
Vogrie
Newlandrig
Humbie
Stobshiel
Crichton
Crichton Castle
Blegbie
Fala Dam
Fala
Lammer Law 527
Meikle Says Law 535
Tynehead
North Middleton
Blackcastle
Soutra Hill 368
Killpallet Heights
Crib Law 509
Seene's Law 513
Little Law 456
Middleton
Falahill
Gilston
Dun Law 393
Turf Law
Headshaw Hill
Hillhouse
Pulpit Law 450
Hogs Law 448
Longcroft Hillfort
Peat Law 414
Constable Hill 411
Addinston
Addinston Fort
Kirktonhill
Oxton
Heriot
Carcant
Hartside Hill 468
Clints Hill 465
Edgarhope Law 367
Dabshead Hill 383
Collie Law 381
Southern Upland Way
Blythe
Fountainhall
Allanshaugh
Torquhan
Symington
Inchkeith Hill 366
Lauder
Thirlestane Castle
Thirlestane
Cambridge
Whiteburn
Mitchelston
Cathpair
Watherston
Craigend
Killochyett
Stow
Woodheads
Boon
Boon Hill 326
Legerwood
Gately Rig 388
Deaf Heights 562
Scroof Hill 497
Windlestraw Law 659
Yardstone Knowe 513
Great Law 509
Ferniehirst Hill 501
Seathorpe Law 542
Torsonce Mains
Bow
Ferniehirst
Bowshank
Halkburn
Caitha Bowland
William Law 401
Colmslie
Langshaw
Over Langshaw
Chapel on Leader
Birkenside
West Morriston
Earlston
Blackhaugh
Buckholm
Cairn Hill 499
Glendearg
Galashiels Road
Lauder Road
A68
A7
B6368
B6362
B709
A697
261
262
272
281

EAST LOTHIAN
SCOTTISH BORDERS
Lammermuir
Merse
Cockburnspath
Cove
Oldhamstocks
Dunbar Common
White Castle (Fort)
Spartleton Edge
Monynut Edge
Ecclaw
Grantshouse
Old Cambus
Nether Monynut
Abbey St Bathans
Southern Upland Way
Whiteadder Reservoir
Cranshaws
Ellemford
Longformacus
Watch Water Reservoir
Twin Law 447
Dirrington Gt Law 398
Dirrington Lit Law 363
Eve Law 311
Edinshall Broch
Preston
Cumledge
Edrom
Norman Arch
Edrom Church
Blanerne
Lintlaw
Buxley
Manderston
Duns
Jim Clark Room
Crumstane Farm Park
Clockmill
Cheeklaw
Gavinton
Choicelee
Polwarth
Wedderlie
Westruther
Thornydykes
Halliburton
Greenlaw
Houndslow
Whiteburn
Cambridge
Legerwood
Green Knowe Tower
Gordon
Huntlywood
West Morriston
Fans
Middlethird
Easter Howlaws
Lambden
Hume
Falsidehill
Stichill
Eccles
Orange Lane
Leitholm
Sisterpath
Fogo
Fogorig
Bogend
Sinclair's Hill
Swinton
Swinton Kirk
Swintonmill
Charterhall
The Hirsel
Coldstream
Birgham
Carham
Lennel
Blackadder West
NT
282
271
262
263
0 1 2 3 miles
0 1 2 3 4 5 km

7
8
9
10
11
283
263
264
A
B
C
D
E
F
G
H
NU
Fast Castle Head
Wheat Stack
Telegraph Hill
FAST CASTLE
Oatlee Hill
St Abb's Head
ST ABB'S HEAD
Horsecastle Bay
Mire Loch
Lumsdaine
Lumsdaine Moor
Coldingham Loch
Cross Law
Moorside Plantn
Bell Hill
Starney Bay
Northfield
KITTIWAKE GALLERY
St Abbs
St Abb's Haven
Coldingham Bay
Yellow Craig
COLDINGHAM SANDS
Coldingham Moor
Buskinburn Ho
Long Latch
Huxton
SCHOOL ROAD
Temple Hall
PRIORY
Coldingham
Press Castle
Press Mains
Abbey Park
Three Burn Grange
Grange Plantn
Gallows Law
Callercove Pt
Hairy Ness
EYEMOUTH MUSEUM
Hallydown
A1107
Eyemouth
Ind Est
Ale Water
North Wood
Blackhill
Cairncross
Scout Pt
Horse Head
Fancove Head
Heugh Head
Howburn
MAIN STREET
Littledean Fm
Aytonwood Ho
Fox Covert
Reston
East Reston Mill
A1
Ayton Mains
Breeches Rock
Loanside
Auchencrow
AYTON CASTLE
Ayton
Burnmouth
Ross
Ross Pt
Berrybank
Peelwalls Ho
Cocklaw
Ayton Hill 199
Chester Hill
Bowie's Plantn
Prenderguest
Peelwalls Fm
Hilton Bay
Causeway Bank
Horn Burn
Millerton Hill
Greenfield Plantn
Lamberton Moor
Lamberton Beach
Meg's Dub
Oldcastles
Edington Covert
Westmains Moor
Foulden Hill
Hag Wood
North Crowlea Plantn
Witches' Knowe
Lamberton
Deans Hill
Lazybeds Plantn
Chirnside
B6355
Kilbann
Mordington Holdings
Marshall Meadows Bay
Foulden New Mains
FOULDEN TITHE BARN
Marshall Meadows
St John's Haven
Chirnsidebridge
A6105
Nether Mains
Mordington Ho
Clappers
West Edge Fm
Stuartslaw
West Foulden
Mains
Foulden Bastle
Foulden
Edrington Ho
Whiteadder Water
Bus Pk
Allanton
Hutton Hall Barns
Broadmeadows Ho
Clarabad Mill
Edrington Mains
DUNS ROAD
1333
Halidon Hill
Highfields
Sharper's Head
Hutton
Meadow House Mains
Baldersbury Hill
Berwick-upon-Tweed
BERWICK-UPON-TWEED
Bucket Rocks
Blackadder Mount
Broomdykes
Paxton North Mains
Spital Mains
New Mills
Grangeburn Mill Fm
BERWICK BOROUGH MUSEUM
Blackadder Bank
Hutton Mains
Paxton
Mill Fm
Tweedmouth
Sandstell Pt
Sunwick Fm
SHIELFIELD PARK
Spittal
Doons Law
Winfield
PAXTON HOUSE
River Tweed
East Ord
Bear's Head
Whitsome
Hilton
Fishwick
UNION SUSPENSION BRIDGE
Loanend
Ord Mains
ETAL ROAD
Prior Park
Redshin Cove
Jardinefield
Fishwick Mains
Horncliffe
Longridge Towers
Tweedmouthmoor
Whitsomehill
Horncliffe Mains
Borewell Fm
East Newton
Horndean
Green Hill
Norham East Mains
Ewe Hill
Murton
Scremerston
Saltpan Rocks
Fellow Hills
Horndean Burn
Norham West Mains
Velvet Hall
Thornton Park
Murton White Ho
Unthank Fm
Unthank Blue Ho
Old Town Covert
New Ladykirk
Thornton Cottage
Cheswick Black Rocks
Ladykirk
NORHAM CASTLE
Emerick Fm
Royalty Fm
Thornton Mains
Allerdean Mill
Scremerston Town Fm
Greenside Cotts
Norham
Morris Hall
Thornton
Scremerston Hill
Allerdeanmill Burn
Camphouses
Fox Covert
Shoreswood
Shoreswood Hall
Cheswick Sands
Shoresdean
West Allerdean
Cheswick Ho
Cheswick
Simprim Mains
East Newbiggin
Allerdean Greens
Cheswick Buildings
Ladykirk House
Battle Moor
Grievestead Moor
Allerdean Grange
Coal Burn
Windmill Hill
Goswick
Milne Graden East Mains
Groat Haugh
Ancroft Northmoor
Ancroft
Simprim
Wideopen Plantn
Grindon
Ancroft Mill
Goswick Sands
Holy Island (Lindisfarne)
Milne Graden West Mains
Tillmouth Fm
NORTHUMBERLAND
Ancroft Southmoor
Westmoor Plantn
Felkington
Haydon Dean
Berrington Law
Bridge Mill
Haggerston
Snook Pt
Berrington Ho
Berrington
Toft Hill
Mattilees Hill
Berrington Lough
New Haggerston
Brockmill Fm
Beal Pt
Tweedmill
Shellacres
Dean Burn
Bowsden Moor
Beal
LINDISFARNE
Twizel Mill
Brick Kiln Plantn
Fadden Hill
Duddo
Mattilees Cott
Jacks Law
Lickar Dean
West Mains Inn
Beal Sands
Holy Island Sands
Common Plantn
Castle Heaton
Duddo Hill
River Till
Bowsden
Lowick Mill
Old Dryburn
Bowsden West Fm
Mount Hooley
Donaldson's Lodge
Melkington
Tindal Ho
Black Bank
Woodside Fm
Low Wood
Dry Burn
Hunting Hall
Granary Pt
Hazely Hill
High Wood
Barmoor Hill
The Low
Fenham
Syning Hill
Heaton Moor
Barleymill Bank
Rhodes Hill
West Kyloe
Peter's Plantn
New Heaton
Barmoor Castle
Barmoor Lane End
Black Heddon
B6353
Fenwick
Cornhill-on-Tweed
Heaton Covert
ETAL CASTLE
Etal Rhodes
Etal Moor
Barmoor Ridge
East Kyloe
Lowmoor Pt
Pallinsburn Ho
HEATHERSLAW LIGHT RAILWAY
Etal
Letham Hill
Moss Hall
Lowick
Kyloe Hills
Fenwick Wood
Cookstead
HEATHERSLAW CORNMILL
Ford Forge
Common Cott
Ford
Moss Wood
Kyloe Wood
Teal
Bareless
Crookham
HEATHERSLAW
Ford Common
Barmoor South Moor
Campfield
Crookham Westfield
Branxton
Windy Law
Hay Fm
LADY WATERFORD HALL
FORT
Redhouse Moor
Bar Moor
Barmoor
Moorhouse
202 Shepherdskirk Hill
Buckton Moor
Buckton
A698
A6112
B6437
B6438
B6461
B6470
B6460
B6354
B6525
A1
Goswick Sands
Snook Pt
Holy Island (Lindisfarne)
Snipe Pt
Keel Head
Emmanuel Head
Beal Pt
LINDISFARNE
Beal Sands
Holy Island Sands
LINDISFARNE HERITAGE CENTRE
Holy Island
LINDISFARNE CASTLE
LINDISFARNE PRIORY
Castle Pt
Granary Pt
Hole Mouth
Fenham
Burrows Hole
Guile Pt
Lowmoor Pt
Tealhole Pt
Ross Pt
Ross Back Sands
Buckton

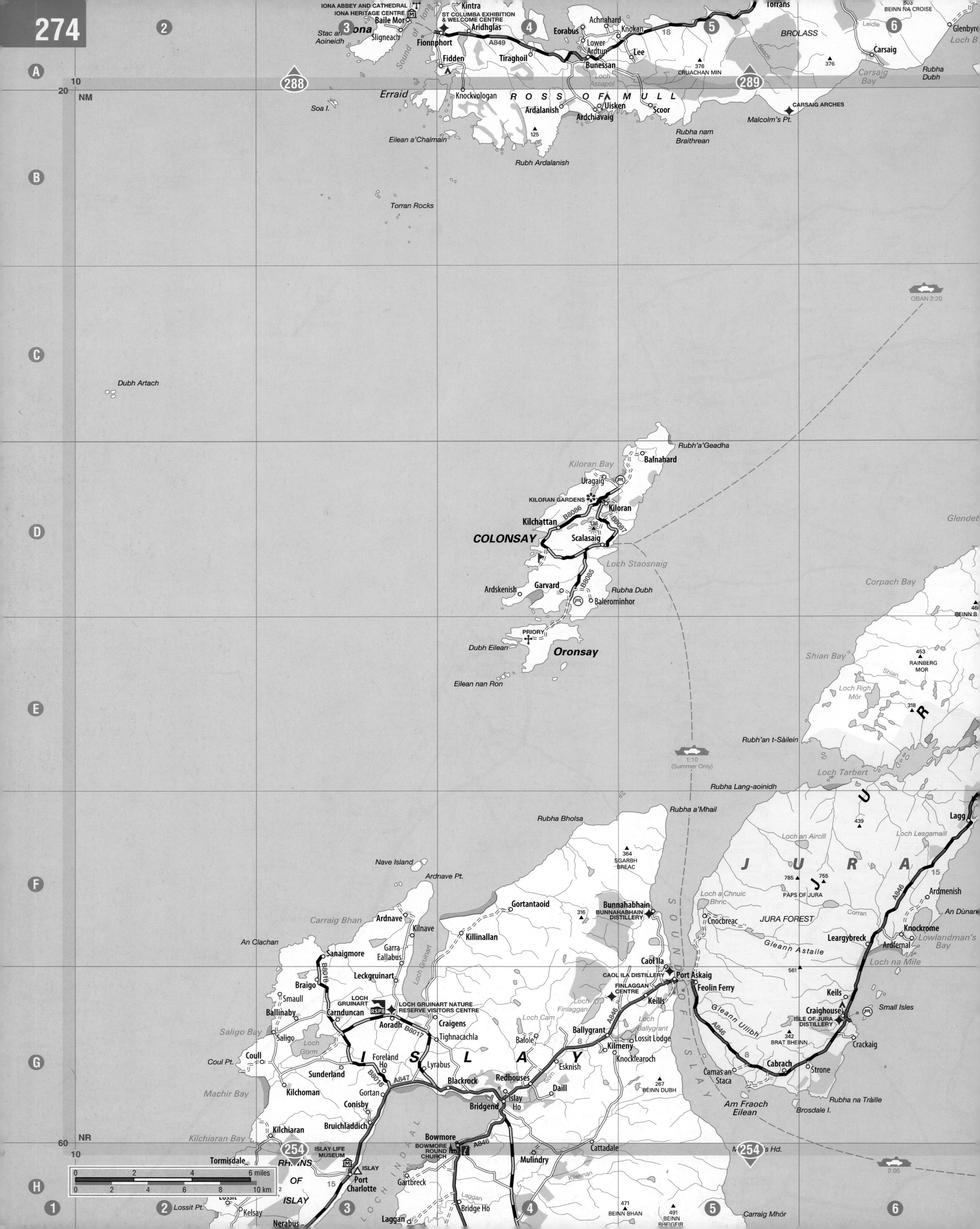
IONA ABBEY AND CATHEDRAL
IONA HERITAGE CENTRE
Baile Mor
Iona
Stac an Aoineidh
Sligneach
Sound of Iona
Kintra
ST COLUMBA EXHIBITION & WELCOME CENTRE
Aridhglas
Fionnphort
A849
Fidden
Tiraghoil
Eorabus
Achnahard
Knokan
Lower Ardtun
Bunessan
Lee
18
Torrans
376
CRUACHAN MIN
BROLASS
Beach
503
BEINN NA CROISE
Leidle
Glenbyre
Loch B
Carsaig
376
Carsaig Bay
Rubha Dubh
288
289
NM
10
20
Erraid
Knockvologan
ROSS OF MULL
Loch Assapol
Uisken
Ardalanish
Ardchiavaig
Scoor
Soa I.
Eilean a'Chalmain
125
Rubh Ardalanish
Rubha nam Braithrean
CARSAIG ARCHES
Malcolm's Pt.
Torran Rocks
OBAN 2:20
Dubh Artach
Rubh'a'Geadha
Kiloran Bay
Balnahard
Uragaig
KILORAN GARDENS
Kiloran
B8086
B8087
Kilchattan
136
COLONSAY
Scalasaig
Loch Staosnaig
Glendet
B8085
Ardskenish
Garvard
Rubha Dubh
Baleromindhor
Corpach Bay
PRIORY
Dubh Eilean
Oronsay
Eilean nan Ron
Shian Bay
453
RAINBERG MOR
Shian
Loch Righ Mòr
318
Rubh'an t-Sàilein
1:10 (Summer Only)
Loch Tarbert
Rubha Lang-aoinidh
Rubha a'Mhail
Rubha Bholsa
Lagg
439
Loch an Aircill
Loch Lesgamaill
364
SGARBH BREAC
JURA
Nave Island
Ardnave Pt.
785
755
PAPS OF JURA
15
Ardmenish
A846
Loch a Chnuic Bhric
An Dùnan
Gortantaoid
316
Bunnahabhain
BUNNAHABHAIN DISTILLERY
Cnocbreac
JURA FOREST
Corran
Carraig Bhan
Ardnave
Kilnave
Killinallan
Knockrome
Leargybreck
Lowlandman's Bay
An Clachan
Garra Eallabus
Gleann Astaile
Ardfernal
Sanaigmore
Loch Gruinart
Caol Ila
Loch na Mile
B8018
Leckgruinart
SOUND OF ISLAY
561
Braigo
CAOL ILA DISTILLERY
Port Askaig
Feolin Ferry
Smaull
LOCH GRUINART
RSPB
LOCH GRUINART NATURE RESERVE VISITORS CENTRE
FINLAGGAN CENTRE
Loch Finlaggan
Keills
Keils
Ballinaby
Carnduncan
Craigens
Loch Cam
Loch Ballygrant
Gleann Ullibh
Craighouse
Small Isles
Saligo Bay
Saligo
Aoradh
B8017
Tighnacachla
Balole
Ballygrant
A846
ISLE OF JURA DISTILLERY
342
BRAT BHEINN
Loch Gorm
Kilmeny
Lossit Lodge
Crackaig
Coull
Coul Pt.
Foreland Ho
ISLAY
Lyrabus
Knockfearoch
8
Cabrach
Strone
Sunderland
B8018
A847
Blackrock
Redhouses
Esknish
Camas an Staca
Machir Bay
Kilchoman
Gortan
Islay Ho
Daill
267
BEINN DUBH
Rubha na Tràille
Conisby
Bridgend
Am Fraoch Eilean
Brosdale I.
Bruichladdich
Kilchiaran
Bowmore
Kilchiaran Bay
NR
60
10
254
ISLAY LIFE MUSEUM
BOWMORE ROUND CHURCH
A846
Cattadale
Mull of Oa Hd.
LOCH INDAAL
Tormisdale
RHINNS OF ISLAY
Port Charlotte
Mulindry
Kilennan
2:05
0 2 4 6 miles
0 2 4 6 8 10 km
Gartbreck
Laggan
15
Lossit
Lossit Pt.
Kelsay
Nerabus
Bridge Ho
Laggan
471
BEINN BHAN
491
BEINN BHEIGEIR
Carraig Mhór
A B C D E F G H
1 2 3 4 5 6

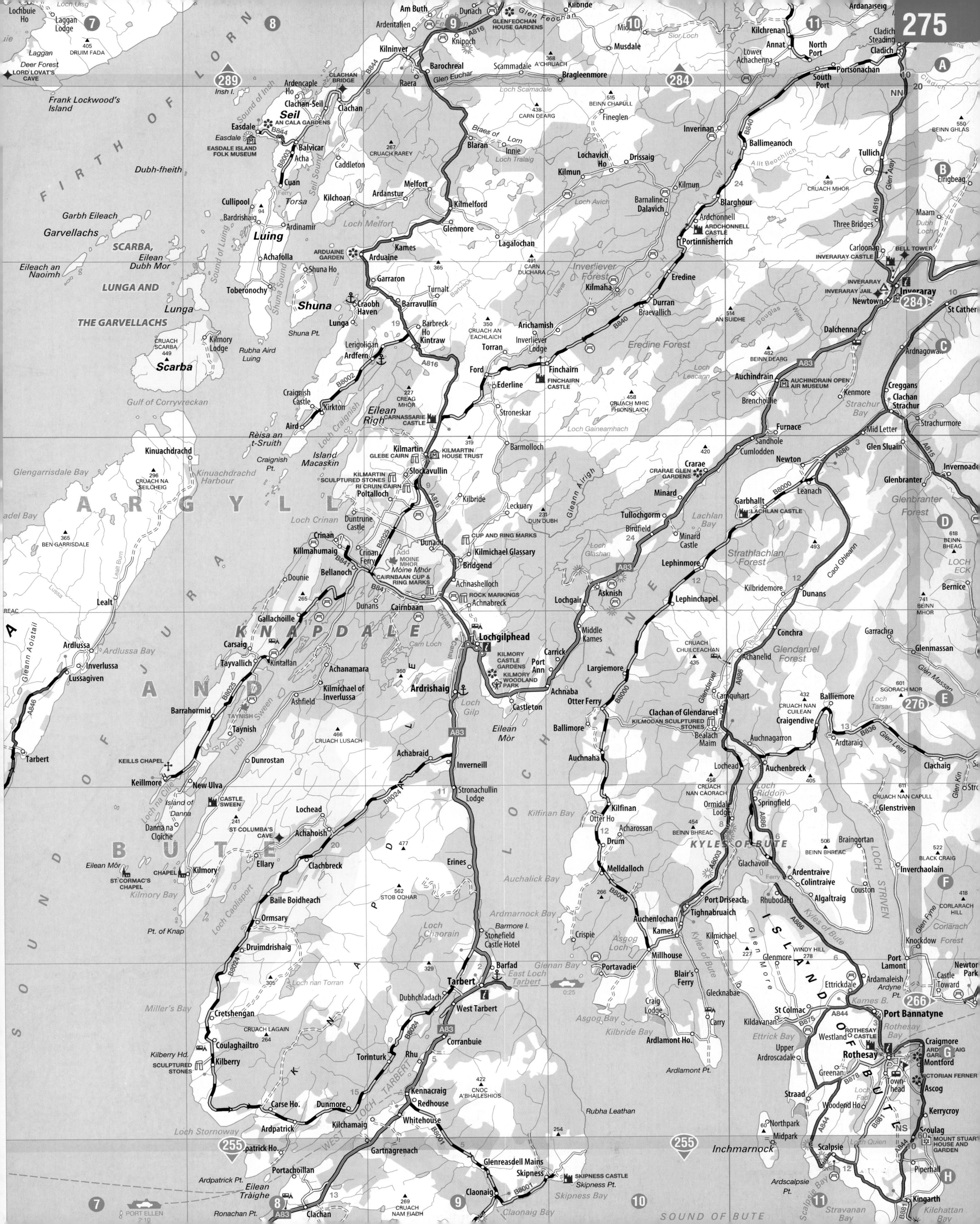

Lochbuie Ho
Loch Uisg
Laggan Lodge
405 DRUIM FADA
Laggan
Deer Forest
LORD LOVAT'S CAVE
Frank Lockwood's Island
FIRTH OF LORN
289
Insh I.
Am Buth
Dunach
Glen Feochan
GLENFEOCHAN HOUSE GARDENS
Kilbride
Ardanaiseig
Ardentallen
Knipoch
Kilninver
Barochreal
Raera
Glen Euchar
Scammadale
368 A'CHRUACH
Bragleenmore
Midpark
Musdale
Kilchrenan
Annat
North Port
Lower Achachenna
Cladich Steading
Cladich
Portsonachan
South Port
284
Ardencaple Ho
CLACHAN BRIDGE
Clachan-Seil
Seil
Clachan
Sound of Insh
Easdale
AN CALA GARDENS
EASDALE ISLAND FOLK MUSEUM
Balvicar
Acha
Cuan
Caddleton
267 CRUACH RAREY
Loch Scammadale
438 CARN DEARG
515 BEINN CHAPULL
Fineglen
Braes of Lorn
Blaran
Innie
Loch Tralaig
Inverinan
Ballimeanoch
Allt Beochlich
550 BEINN GHLAS
Tullich
Glen Aray
Elrigbeag
Dubh-fheith
Cullipool
Bardrishaig
Torsa
Seil Sound
Kilchoan
Ardanstur
Melfort
Kilmelford
Lochavich Ho
Drissaig
Kilmun
Loch Avich
Barnaline
Dalavich
Blarghour
24
589 CRUACH MHOR
Maam
Dubh Loch
Garbh Eileach
Garvellachs
Luing
Ardinamir
Loch Melfort
Glenmore
Lagalochan
Ardchonnell
ARDCHONNELL CASTLE
Portinnisherrich
Three Bridges
Carloonan
BELL TOWER
INVERARAY CASTLE
SCARBA, Eilean Dubh Mor
Sound of Luing
Achafolla
ARDUAINE GARDEN
Arduaine
Kames
365
491 CARN DUCHARA
Inverliever Forest
Eilean an Naoimh
LUNGA AND THE GARVELLACHS
Toberonochy
Shuna Ho
Shuna Sound
Garraron
Turnalt
Barbreck
Kilmaha
Eredine
INVERARAY
INVERARAY JAIL
Inveraray
Newtown
284
St Catherines
Lunga
Shuna
Craobh Haven
Barravullin
Durran
Braevallich
514 AN SUIDHE
Douglas Water
Shuna Pt.
Lunga
Barbreck Ho
Kintraw
350 CRUACH AN EACHLAICH
Arichamish
Inverliever Lodge
Torran
B840
Dalchenna
Ardnagowan
CRUACH SCARBA 449
Kilmory Lodge
Rubha Aird Luing
Scarba
Lerigoligan
Ardfern
A816
Ford
Ederline
Finchairn
FINCHAIRN CASTLE
Eredine Forest
482 BEINN DEARG
Loch Leacann
Auchindrain
AUCHINDRAIN OPEN AIR MUSEUM
Kenmore
Creggans
Clachan
Strachur
Gulf of Corryvreckan
Craignish Castle
Kirkton
227 CREAG MHOR
Eilean Righ
CARNASSARIE CASTLE
Stroneskar
458 CRUACH MHIC PHIONNLAICH
Brenchoillie
Strachur Bay
Strachurmore
Aird
Loch Craignish
Rèisa an t-Sruith
Loch Gaineamhach
Furnace
Mid Letter
Glen Sluain
Kinuachdrachd
Craignish Pt.
Island Macaskin
Kilmartin
GLEBE CAIRN
KILMARTIN HOUSE TRUST
319
Barmolloch
420
Sandhole
Cumlodden
Newton
A815
Invernoaden
Glengarrisdale Bay
296 CRUACH NA SEILCHEIG
Kinuachdrachd Harbour
KILMARTIN SCULPTURED STONES
RI CRUIN CAIRN
Slockavullin
Poltalloch
Crarae
CRARAE GLEN GARDENS
Minard
B8000
Leanach
Glenbranter
ARGYLL
Kilbride
Leckuary
231 DUN DUBH
Gleann Airigh
Garbhallt
LACHLAN CASTLE
Glenbranter Forest
Loch Crinan
Duntrune Castle
Tullochgorm
Lachlan Bay
Birdfield
Minard Castle
618 BEINN BHEAG
493
Loch Eck
365 BEN GARRISDALE
Crinan
Killmahumaig
Crinan Ferry
B8025
Dunadd
CUP AND RING MARKS
Kilmichael Glassary
Loch Glashan
A83
Strathlachlan Forest
Caol Ghleann
MOINE MHOR
Mòine Mhòr
CAIRNBAAN CUP & RING MARKS
Bridgend
Lephinmore
Bellanoch
B841
Dounie
Lealt
Lealt Burn
Achnashelloch
ROCK MARKINGS
Achnabreck
Lochgair
Asknish
Lephinchapel
Kilbridemore
Dunans
Bernice
741 BEINN MHOR
265
Dunans
Cairnbaan
Crinan Canal
Gallachoille
KNAPDALE
Lochgilphead
Middle Kames
Conchra
Garrachra
Ardlussa
Ardlussa Bay
Carsaig
Tayvallich
Kintallan
Cam Loch
KILMORY CASTLE GARDENS
KILMORY WOODLAND PARK
Port Ann
Carrick
Largiemore
CRUACH CHUILCEACHAN 435
Glendaruel Forest
Achanelid
Glenmassan
Glen Massan
Inverlussa
Lussagiven
Gleann Aoistail
Achanamara
Kilmichael of Inverlussa
360
Ardrishaig
Achnaba
Otter Ferry
Glendaruel
Camquhart
432 CRUACH NAN CUILEAN
Balliemore
601 SGORACH MOR
Loch Tarsan
276
A846
AND
Ashfield
Loch Gilp
Castleton
Clachan of Glendaruel
KILMODAN SCULPTURED STONES
Bealach Maim
Craigendive
Barrahormid
TAYNISH
Taynish
Loch Sween
466 CRUACH LUSACH
Eilean Mòr
Ballimore
Auchnagarron
Ardtaraig
B836
Glen Lean
Tarbert
KEILLS CHAPEL
Dunrostan
Achabraid
Inverneill
Auchnaha
Lochead
Auchenbreck
405
Clachaig
Glen Kin
Keillmore
Loch na Cille
New Ulva
CASTLE SWEEN
Island of Danna
B8024
Stronachullin Lodge
Kilfinan Bay
Kilfinan
Otter Ho
458 CRUACH NAN CAORACH
Ormidale Lodge
Loch Riddon
Springfield
611 CRUACH NAN CAPULL
Glenstriven
Lochead
Achahoish
Danna na Cloiche
241
ST COLUMBA'S CAVE
477
Acharossan
Drum
454 BEINN BHREAC
A886
KYLES OF BUTE
506 BEINN BHREAC
Braingortan
Loch Striven
BUTE
Eilean Mòr
ST CORMAC'S CHAPEL
CHAPEL
Kilmory
Ellary
Clachbreck
Erines
Melldalloch
Glachavoil
Ardentraive
Colintraive
522 BLACK CRAIG
Inverchaolain
Kilmory Bay
Loch Caolisport
Baile Boidheach
562 STOB ODHAR
Auchalick Bay
266
B8003
Port Driseach
Tighnabruaich
Rhubodach
Algaltraig
Couston
418 CORLARACH HILL
Pt. of Knap
Ormsary
Ardmarnock Bay
Loch Chaorain
Barmore I.
Stonefield Castle Hotel
Crispie
Auchenlochan
Kames
Kilmichael
Glen More
ISLAND OF BUTE
Glen Fyne
Corlarach
Knockdow
Forest
Druimdrishaig
Asgog Loch
Portavadie
Millhouse
Kyles of Bute
227
Glenmore
WINDY HILL 278
Port Lamont
Newton Park
305
Loch nan Torran
329
Barfad
Glenan Bay
East Loch Tarbert
0:25
Castle Toward
Miller's Bay
Tarbert
Dubhchladach
West Tarbert
Blair's Ferry
Gecknabae
Ettrickdale
Ardamaleish
Ardyne Pt.
266
Kames B.
Port Bannatyne
Cretshengan
CRUACH LAGAIN 264
Asgog Bay
Carry
St Colmac
Kildavanan
A844
B875
ROTHESAY CASTLE
Rothesay Bay
Corranbuie
Kilbride Bay
Ardlamont Ho.
Ettrick Bay
Westland
Rothesay
Craigmore
Montford
Coulaghailtro
Kilberry Hd.
SCULPTURED STONES
Kilberry
Torinturk
Rhu
422 CNOC A'BHAILESHIOS
Ardlamont Pt.
Upper Ardroscadale
Greenan
B878
Town head
VICTORIAN FERNERY
Ascog
Loch Fad
Straad
Carse Ho.
Dunmore
Kennacraig
Redhouse
Woodend Ho
Rubha Leathan
Kerrycroy
Ardpatrick
Kilchamaig
Whitehouse
Northpark
Midpark
Scoulag
Loch Stornoway
255
Ardpatrick Ho.
WEST LOCH TARBERT
B8001
Gartnagrenach
254
255
Inchmarnock
Loch Quien
MOUNT STUART HOUSE AND GARDEN
Scalpsie
Glenreasdell Mains
Portachoillan
Skipness
SKIPNESS CASTLE
Skipness Pt.
Ardscalpsie Pt.
Piperhall
Ardpatrick Pt.
Eilean Traighe
PORT ELLEN 2:10
Claonaig
269 CRUACH NAM FIADH
Skipness Bay
Kingarth
Ronachan Pt.
Clachan
Claonaig Bay
SOUND OF BUTE
Scalpsie Bay
Stravanan Bay
Kilchattan Bay
SOUND OF JURA

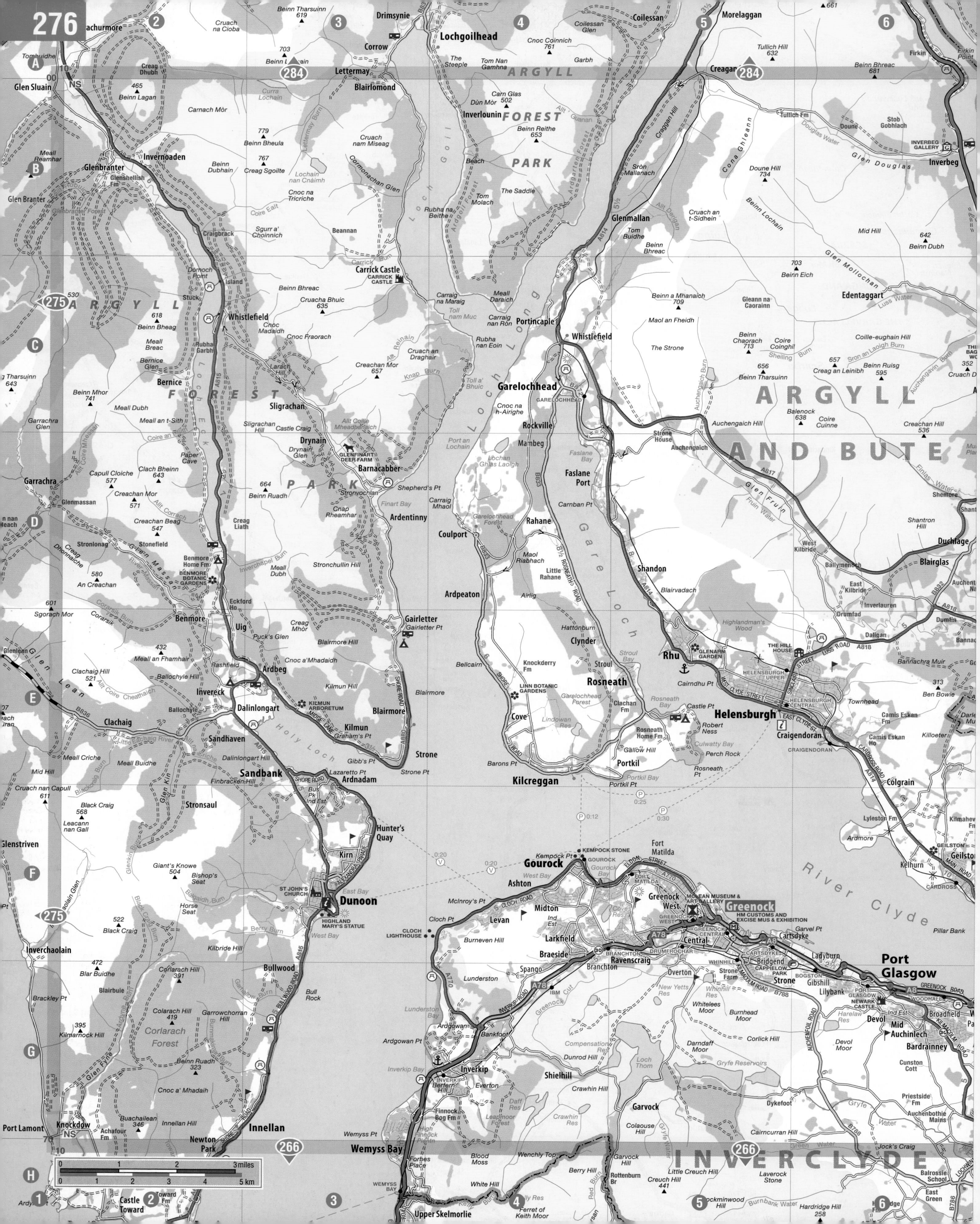
ARGYLL
FOREST
PARK
ARGYLL AND BUTE
INVERCLYDE
River Clyde
Lochgoilhead
Drimsynie
Corrow
Lettermay
Blairlomond
Coilessan
Morelaggan
Creagan
Glen Sluain
Glenbranter
Invernoaden
Glen Branter
Carrick Castle
Whistlefield
Portincaple
Garelochhead
Rockville
Mambeg
Faslane Port
Rahane
Shandon
Rhu
Helensburgh
Craigendoran
Colgrain
Kelhurn
Cardross
Inverbeg
Edentaggart
Duchlage
Blairglas
Glen Douglas
Glen Fruin
Loch Long
Loch Goil
Loch Eck
Gare Loch
Holy Loch
Sligrachan
Drynain
Barnacabber
Ardentinny
Coulport
Ardpeaton
Gairletter
Blairmore
Strone
Kilmun
Benmore
Uig
Ardbeg
Invereck
Dalinlongart
Sandhaven
Clachaig
Sandbank
Ardnadam
Stronsaul
Hunter's Quay
Kirn
Dunoon
Bullwood
Innellan
Newton Park
Knockdow
Port Lamont
Inverchaolain
Glenstriven
Garrachra
Glenmassan
Castle Toward
Kilcreggan
Rosneath
Clynder
Cove
Portkil
Gourock
Ashton
Midton
Levan
Larkfield
Braeside
Spango
Lunderston
Greenock
Greenock West
Central
Ravenscraig
Branchton
Port Glasgow
Gibshill
Bridgend
Strone
Ladyburn
Devol
Mid Auchinlech
Bardrainney
Inverkip
Wemyss Bay
Upper Skelmorlie
Garvock
Shielhill
Ardgowan
Bankfoot
Everton
Kempock Pt
Cloch Lighthouse
Highland Mary's Statue
Kilmun Arboretum
Benmore Botanic Gardens
Glenfinart Deer Farm
Linn Botanic Gardens
Glenarn Garden
The Hill House
McLean Museum & Art Gallery
HM Customs and Excise Mus & Exhibition
Inverbeg Gallery
275
284
266
0 1 2 3 miles
0 1 2 3 4 5 km

QUEEN ELIZABETH FOREST PARK
STIRLING
LOCH LOMOND AND THE TROSSACHS NATIONAL PARK
WEST DUNBARTONSHIRE
EAST DUNBARTONSHIRE
Loch Lomond
Loch Ard
Aberfoyle
David Marshall Lodge Visitor Centre
Scottish Wool Centre
Trossachs Discovery Centre
Milton
Kirkton
Balleich
Port of Menteith
Lake of Menteith
Inchmahome Priory
Malling
Arntamie
Nether Glenny
Portend
Stonefield
Windygate
Shannochill
Cobleland
Gartur
Dykehead
Gartmore
Barbadoes
Fir Hill
Dalmary
Borland Fm
Ward
Turner
Gartclach
Gartachoil
Buchlyvie
Arnprior
Kepdowrie
Garchell
Cretlevane
Badivow
Hoish
Douchlage
Ballochneck
Gowston
Thirds
Badenkep
Whiteleys
Knockingalloch
Balgair Muir
Glenfoot
Gaisland
Tombrake
Camoquhill
Balfron
Balfron Station
Harvieston
Dalfoil
Ballochearn
Ballikinrain
Boquhan
Clayland
Overton
Fintry
Dunmore
Dechrode
Gartness
Spittal
Killearn
Drumore
Heron's Court
Auchenibert
Kilmorie
Allanrowie
Earl's Seat 578
Garloch Hill 543
Dumgoyne
Craighat
Glengoyne Distillery
Stockiemuir
Blairquhosh
Strathblane Hills
Owsen Hill
Dumbreck 508
Fin Glen
Hog Hill
Hart
Knocknair
Netherton
Blanefield
Strathblane
Clachan of Campsie
Balcorrach
Craigend Fm
Craigend Muir
Dunglass
Mugdock
Mugdock Castle
Craigmaddie Muir
Blairskaith Muir
Blochairn
Blairskaith
Barraston
Langshot
Fluchter
Back o' Hill
Bardowie
Balmore
Buchley
Cadder
Jellyhill
Kessington
Summerston
Bishopbriggs
Springburn
Lambhill
Maryhill
Milngavie
Lillie Art Gallery
Bearsden
Roman Bath House
Antonine Wall
Hardgate
Faifley
Duntocher
Old Kilpatrick
Erskine Bridge
Mountblow
Parkhall
Radnor Park
Dalmuir
Drumchapel
Clydebank
Clydebank Museum
Whitecrook
Yoker
Knightswood
Temple
Scotstoun
Jordanhill
Anniesland
Kelvindale
Renfrew
Blythswood
Inchinnan
Town of Inchinnan
Freeland
Erskine
Park Mains
Rashielee
Bargarran
Bishopton
Rossland
West Porton
Formakin
Langbank
East Langbank
Finlaystone House & Gardens
Woodhall
Kilmacolm
Lawfield
Kirkton
Barochan
Dargavel
Mid Glen
Old Hall
Auchenbothie
Meiklefield
Bowling
Milton
Hill of Dun
Dumbarton
Dumbarton Castle
Strathclyde Stadium
Silverton
Dennystown
Brucehill
Kirktonhill
Castlehill
Ardoch
Cardross
Kipperoch
Renton
Bonhill
Alexandria
Jamestown
Balloch
Balloch Castle
Loch Lomond Shores
National Park Gateway Visitor Centre
Loch Lomond Outlet Centre
Mill of Haldane
Dumbain
Auchencarroch
Tullichewan
Arden
Luss
Rowardennan
Rowardennan Lodge
Milarrochy
Balmaha
Milton of Buchanan
Drymen
Buchanan Smithy
Buchanan Castle
The Rowan Gallery
Croftamie
Badshalloch
Gartocharn
Ross Priory
Gartochraggan
Tullycross
Duncryne 142
Caldarvan
Gallangad Muir
Cameron Muir
Stockie Muir
Auchineden Hill 357
Pappert Hill 257
Dumbarton Muir
Meikle White Hill 353
Doughnot Hill 374
Kilpatrick Hills
Cochno Hill
The Slacks
Maidens Paps
Edinbarnet
Whitehill Fm
Duntiglennan Fm
Inchmurrin
Inchcailloch
Inchfad
Inchcruin
Inchtavannach
Inchmoan
Inchconnachan
Inchlonaig
Creinch
Torrinch
Conic Hill 358
Beinn Bhreac 577
Beinne Uird 597
Beinn Bhan 569
Gualann 461
Tom Fithich
Sron Aonaich 577
Ben Lomond
Couligartan
Drum of Clashmore
Lime Hill
Corrie
Moor Park
Bad Ochainaich
Muir Park Reservoir
West Highland Way
Stirling Road
A81
A811
A809
A875
A82
A814
A898
M8
M898
B837
B835
B818
B834
B822
B821
B8050

Doune
Dunblane
Deanston
Thornhill
Flanders Moss
Blair Drummond
Bridge of Allan
Blairlogie
Menstrie
Kippen
Arnprior
Cauldhame
Gargunnock
Stirling
Raploch
Cambuskenneth
Cambusbarron
Torbrex
St Ninians
Bannockburn
Fallin
Gargunnock Hills
Touchadam Muir
STIRLING
Fintry Hills
Fintry
Plean
Cowie
Dunipace
Denny
Torwood
Carron Valley Reservoir
Carron Bridge
Kilsyth Hills
Campsie Fells
Meikle Bin
Lecket Hill
Lennoxtown
Clachan of Campsie
Milton of Campsie
Kilsyth
Queenzieburn
Banknock
Longcroft
Haggs
Castlecary
Bonnybridge
High Bonnybridge
Dullatur
Croy
Cumbernauld Village
Cumbernauld
Kirkintilloch
Lenzie
Torrance
Bishopbriggs
Cadder
Balloch
Condorrat
Westfield
Mollinsburn
Moodiesburn
Chryston
Muirhead
Glenboig
Riggend
Greengairs
Caldercruix
Longriggend
EAST DUNBARTONSHIRE
NORTH LANARKSHIRE
FALKIRK
Blair Drummond Moss
Blair Drummond Safari Park
Doune Castle
The National Wallace Monument
Culcreuch Castle
Colzium House
Antonine Wall
Forth & Clyde Canal
Stirling Services
Old Inns Services
M9
M80
M876
M73
A811
A84
A9
A91
A803
A80
A872
A873
A891
B818
B822
285
286
277
268
0 1 2 3 miles
0 1 2 3 4 5 km

Ben Buck
Grodwell Hill
Cairnmorris Hill
Whitewisp Hill
Commonedge Hill
Seamab Hill
Yetts o' Muckhart
Claysyke Fm
White Hill
North Kilduff
Craighorn 583
Craighorn
Bengengie Hill
Ben Cleuch 721
Ben Ever
Andrew Gannel Hill
Tarmangie Hill 645
Saddle Hill
Hillfoot Hill
Castleton Hill
Balruddie
Lendrick Muir School
Crook of Devon
Pool of Muckhart
South Kilduff
Drum
Wood of Coldrain
Colsnaur Hill 553
The Law 638
King's Seat Hill 648
Rumbling Bridge
Rumbling Bridge Gorge
Coldrain
Bank Hill
Gloom Hill
Castle Campbell
Law Hill
Cowden Fm
Muckhart Mill
Hilton of Aldie
Middleton of Aldie
Gateside
Craigton
Cockairney
Craig Leith 513
Wood Hill 525
Dollar Glen
Lawhill Ho
Gairney Ho
Myreton Hill
The Nebit
Elistoun Hill
Dollar
Keppoch Ho
Keith Hills
Threapmuir
Mill Glen
Ochil Hills Woodland Park
Silver Glen
Devonshaw Fm
Powmill
Cleish Mains
Cleish
Cleish Mill Fm
Tillicoultry
Kelly Br
Lower Mains
Vicar's Br
Westmuir
Blackhill Plantn
Balquharn
Mill Trail Visitor Centre
Alva
Dams
Boghall
Whitegates
Pow Fm
Hardiston
Fort
Cleish Castle
Sterling Mills
River Devon
Blairingone
Morelands Fm
Cleish Hills
Clackmannanshire
Dollarbeg
Cult Hill
Dowhill Muir
Marchglen
Devonside
Barnhill Fm
Wether Hill
Hill End
Outh Hill
Devon Village
Lawmuir Fm
Ditch
Collyland
Coalsnaughton
Meeks Park
Aberdona Mains
Solsgirth
Howfold Fm
Busses Fm
Tipperton Moss
Outh Muir
Craigencat Craigs
Tullibody
Lornshill
Branshill
Fairfield
Fishcross
Schaw Park
Aberdona Ho
Gartenkeir
Allaleckie
Newhall
Netty Burn
Lethans Muir
Black Rigg Moss
Roscobie Muir
Sauchie
Sheriffyards Ho
Forest Mill
West Saline
West Lethans Knock Hill 364
Knockhill
Inglewood
Keilarsbrae
Gartmorn Dam
Milton Fm
Grey Craig
Cambus
Jellyholm
Saline Shaw Fm
Langfaulds Fm
Balgonar
Roscobie Res
Recreation Park
Hillend
Black Devon
Gartknowie
Piperpool
359 Saline Hill
Din Moss
Roscobie Hills
Alloa
Alloa Tower
Hilton
The Forest
Fearns
Linn Mill
Dun Moss
Kitchen Green
Aikey Hill
Craig Ho
Saline
Steelend
Lynn Fm
Valley of Balmule
Clackmannan Tower
Clackmannan
Red Yetts
Gartfinnan Fm
Bluther Burn
Kinneddar Mains
The Temple
Myrie Hall
The Bents Fm
Dolly Fm
Craigduckie
Throsk
South Alloa
Brucefield
Slack
Bath Moor Plantn
Cattle Moss
Big Wood
Craigluscar Hill
Dunduff
Hillhead
Bowershall
Meadowend
Kennet
Gartarry
Brankstone Grange
Shepherdlands
Cowstrandburn
Lochhead
Dunmore Home Fm
Muirside of Kinneddar
Carnock Moor
Craigluscar Resrs
Townhill
Town Loch
Dunmore
Kilbagie
Inch of Ferryton
Peppermill Dam
West Grange
Blairhall
Blair Ho
Luscar Ho
Rosebank Mains
Dunmore Moss
Dunmore Park
The Pineapple
Craigton
Broomknowe
Windyhill Fm
Middle Grange
Carnock Ho
Gowkhall
Wellwood
Moor Loch
Hawkhill
Balgownie Mains
Comrie Burn
Comrie
Oakley
Carnock
Carnock Road
Milesmark
Parkneuk
Headwell
Kingseathill
Bellyeoman
Darnbogue
Castleton
North Doll
Tulliallan Castle (College)
Fife
East Grange
Carneil Hill
W Camps
E Camps
Back Muir
River Forth
Devilla Forest
Inzievar Wood
Dean Plantn
Airth
Clackmannanshire Bridge
Kincardine
Toll Rd
Lundin Fm
Andrew Carnegie Birthplace Mus
Retail Pk
East End Park
Garvock Hill
Bullions
South Doll
Culross Moor
Blairhall Mains
High Valleyfield
Duck Hill
Dunfermline Abbey
Dunfermline Mus
Abbot House
Airth Mains
South Approach Road
Kincardine Bridge
A985
Cairneyhill
Pitconochie
Pittencrieff Park
Brucefield
Powdrake
Powside
Pow Burn
Culross
Low Valleyfield
Newmills
Main Street
Crossford
Dunfermline
Aberdour Rd
Letham Moss
Bowtrees
Inch Fm
Blair Mains
Culross Palace
Low Torry
Torryburn
Mire End
Lyne Burn
Pitcorthie
Queensferry Road
Letham
Blairburn
Bankhead Fm
Gallowridge Hill
Lochymuir Plantn
Kersebrock
Drum of Kinnaird
Mains of Powfoulis
Longannet Pt
Longannet Power Sta
Preston Island
Torry Bay
Pitliver Ho
Bogend
M876
Hardilands
Crombie
St Margaret's Stone
Crombie Pt
Waulkmill
Craigs Plantn
Limekilns Road
Stonehouse Fm
Bellsdyke Road
Horse Craig
Ironmill Bay
Charlestown
Pattiesmuir
Admiralty Road
North Broomage
Bensfield
Orchardhead
Antonshill
Ochilview
King Street
Limekilns
Rosyth
Stenhousemuir
Carronshore
Skinflats
Bruce Haven
Castlandhill
Larbert
South Broomage
Carron
Main Street
Langlees
Glensburgh
Grangemouth
Oil Refinery
Bo'ness
Grangepans
Bainsford
Earl's Road
Bo'ness Road
Abbots Rd
Bo'ness Ind Est
Bridgeness
St Margaret's Hope
Bankside
Camelon
Grahamston
Firs Park
Middlefield
Inchyra Road
Wholeflats
Kinneil Kerse
Bo'ness & Kinneil Railway
Kinneil Ho
Carriden
Falkirk Wheel
Falkirk Stadium
Maidenpark
Kinneil
Grahamsdyke Road
Muirhouses
Blackness Bay
Blackness Castle
Forth Road Br
Tamfourhill
Falkirk
Laurieston
Inveravon
Antonine Wall (Course of)
Blackness
Bantaskin
Westburn Avenue
Beancross
Wholeflats Road
Birkhill Clay Mine
Woodhead Fm
Bo'mains Fm
Dyland Cotts
Union Canal
Callendar House
Old Polmont
Port Edgar
Greenbank
Callendar Park
Westquarter Dovecote
Clay Mine
Birkhill
Swordie Mains
Cauldcoats Holdings
Wester Shore Wood
Hopetoun House
Glen Village
Shop Cen
Hallglen
Westquarter
Redding
Avonbank
Grange
Grougfoot
Manners ton
House of the Binns
Abercorn
Seafield
Reddingmuirhead
Polmont
Linlithgow Loch
Midhope
Binns Mill
Queensferry
Falkirk
Glen Fm
Shieldhill Road
Brightons
Pardovan Ho
Old Philpstoun
Hopetoun Wood
Newton
Woodend
Auchengean
Middlerig
Wallacestone
Rumford
Whitecross
Linlithgow Bridge
Linlithgow Palace
Philpstoun
Fawnspark
Greenwells
Shieldhill
Maddiston
Linlithgow
Champfleurie Ho
Bridgend Fm
Dundas Mains
Wester Shieldhill Lands
California
Kendieshill
Manuel Ho
Parkley Place
Parkley Craigs
Kingscavil
Greencraig
Loan
Preston Ho
Haugh Burn
Humbie Ho
River Avon
Darnrig Moss
Gardrum Moss
Tarduf
Muiravonside
Bridgend
Threemiletown
Blackrig
Snabhead
Loch Ellrig
Standburn
Cocklerov 278
Waterstone
Winchburgh
Niddry Mains
Strathavon
Lochend
Grayrigg Fm
Coxhill Fm
Carribber Mill
Beecraigs
Longmuir Plantn
Ochiltree Mill
Binny Craig
Tar Hill
Faucheldean
Ross's Plantn
Dyke
Redbrae
Candie Ho
Lochcote Reservoir
Niddry Burn
Binny Ho
Ecclesmachan
Newliston
Slamannan
Hillhead
Loanrigg
North Bankhead
Newlees Fm
Brunton Fm
Torphichen Preceptory
North Mains
Broxburn
Ind Est
West Fm
Newbridge
Crossburn
Avonbridge
Strath House
Wallhouse
Gormyre
South Mains
Mains Burn
East Broadlaw
Kirkhill
Binniehill
Neucks Cotts
Middle Strath
Torphichen
Craigmailing
West Main Street
Uphall
Burnside
Westfield
Dykehead
Buiondale Fm
Linhouse Fm
Hilderston Fm
Couston Water
Cairnpapple Hill
Craig Binning
Brox Il Burn
Birdsmill
Salterhill Fm
Arnloss
Muckraw
Craigengall
Loch Ho
Barns
Ballencrief Mains
Bathgate Hills
Dechmont
Holehousemuir
Lochside Road
Easter Righead
Bridge Castle
Ballencrieff Toll
Byres
Wester Dechmont
Uphall
Roman Camp Cotts
Drumshoreland Muir
Clifton Hall
Clifton Mains
Burnhead
Drumcross
Uphall Station
Heights
Barbauchlaw Woodend Fm
Colinshiel
Belvedere
Glenmavis
Whitelaw
Knightsridge
Clapperton Ho
Pumpherston
West Clifton
Hillhead
Easter Whin
Wester Whin
Blawhorn Moss
Bennie Museum
Bathgate
Old Clapperton Hall
Almondell & Calderwood
Whiteside
Easteraigs Hill
Windyknowe
Boghall
Craigshill
Ladywell
Livingston North
Wilkieston
Blawhorn Moss
Armadale
Falside
Bathville
Livingston
286
280
269

Loch Leven
Loch Leven Castle
Kinross House Gardens
St Serf's Island
Scotlandwell
Auchmuirbridge
Leslie
Glenrothes
Markinch
Milton of Balgonie
Balcurvie
Windygates
Cameron Bridge
Coaltown of Balgonie
Kinglassie
Thornton
Gairney Bank
Vane Farm Nature Centre
Cleish
Cleish Castle
Ballingry
Lochore
Lochore Meadows
Fife Regional Park
Lochran
Kelty
Blairadam
Maryburgh
Keltybridge
Crosshill
Woodend
Auchterderran
Bowhill
Cardenden
Cluny
Dogton Stone
East Wemyss
Coaltown of Wemyss
West Wemyss
Boreland
Blair
Dysart
Glencraig
Lochgelly
Lumphinnans
Chapel
Dunnikier
Gallatown
Sinclairtown
Templehall
Smeaton
Hayfield
Pathhead
Kirkcaldy
Kirkcaldy Art Gallery & Mus
Ravenscraig Castle
Port Brae
Panhall
Kirkcaldy Sands
Link Sands
Linktown
Long Craig
Cowdenbeath
Lassodie
Kingseat
Bowershall
Hill of Beath
Cowdenend
Loch Gelly
Auchtertool
Boglily
Lambert's Mill
Kilrie Fm
West Balbairdie
Meadowfield
Balbie Fm
Orrock
Grange
Grange Cottages
Kinghorn
Linton Court
Hummel Rocks
Kinghorn Ness
Pettycur
Alexander III Monument
Townhill
Wellwood
Headwell
Kingseathill
Bellyeoman
Halbeath
Crossgates
Fordell
Donibristle
Balmule
Stenhouse Reservoir
Dunfermline
Garvock Hill
Bruce field
Pitcorthie
Duloch
Annfield
Rosyth
Pattiesmuir
Hillend
Dalgety Bay
Aberdour
Aberdour Castle & Gardens
Burntisland
Kirkton
Ross Pt
Common Rocks
Black Rocks
Inverkeithing
St Davids Harbour
Jamestown
West Ness
Inverkeithing Bay
Hawkcraig Pt
Port Haven
Barnhill Bay
Braefoot Bay
Mortimer's Deep
Car Craig
Swallow Craig
St Colm's Abbey
Inchcolm
Downing Pt
Inchkeith
Iron Craig
Long Craig
FIRTH OF FORTH
Cow & Calves
Inchmickery
North Queensferry
Deep Sea World
Forth Road Bridge
Forth Bridges Mus
Inch Garvie
Whitehouse Pt
Hound Pt
St Margaret's Hope
Hopetoun House
Port Edgar
Maid of the Forth Cruises
Queensferry
Queensferry Mus
Dalmeny
Dalmeny House
Cramond Island
Drum Sands
Snab Pt
Granton Pt
Granton Harbour
Newhaven
HMY Britannia
Leith
Black Rocks
Silverknowes
Lauriston Castle
Muirhouse
Granton
Pilton
Trinity
Cramond
Davidson's Mains
Drylaw
Royal Botanic Garden
Inverleith
Warriston
Pilrig
Broughton
Easter Road
Craigentinny
Edinburgh
Restalrig
Barnton
Cramond Bridge
Craigiehall
Clermiston
Blackhall
Craigleith
Lochend
Portobello
Joppa
Musselburgh
Kirkliston
Turnhouse
Edinburgh Airport
Royal Highland Showground
Newbridge
Ratho Station
Gogar
Corstorphine
Edinburgh Zoo
Ravelston
Murrayfield
Dean
New Town
Palace of Holyroodhouse
Abbeyhill
Old Town
St Giles Cathedral
National Mus of Scotland
Arthur's Seat
Meadowbank
Northfield
Duddingston
Bingham
Brunstane
Newhailes
Newcraighall
Stoneybank
Sighthill
Stenhouse
Saughton
Slateford
Gorgie
Merchiston
Newington
Prestonfield
Craigmillar
Craigmillar Castle
Niddrie
Ratho
Edinburgh Canal Centre
Union Canal
Suntrap
Longstone
Morningside
Craiglockhart
Royal Observatory
Blackford Hill
The Inch
Edmonstone
Shawfair
Whitecraig
Hermiston
Wester Hailes
Kingsknowe
Braid
Braid Hills
Liberton
Danderhall
Millerhill
Colinton
Oxgangs
Juniper Green
Bonaly
Swanston
Fairmilehead
Kaimes
Gracemount
Gilmerton
Burnwynd
Currie
Burnside
CITY OF EDINBURGH
FIFE
0 1 2 3 miles
0 1 2 3 4 5 km
279
286
270

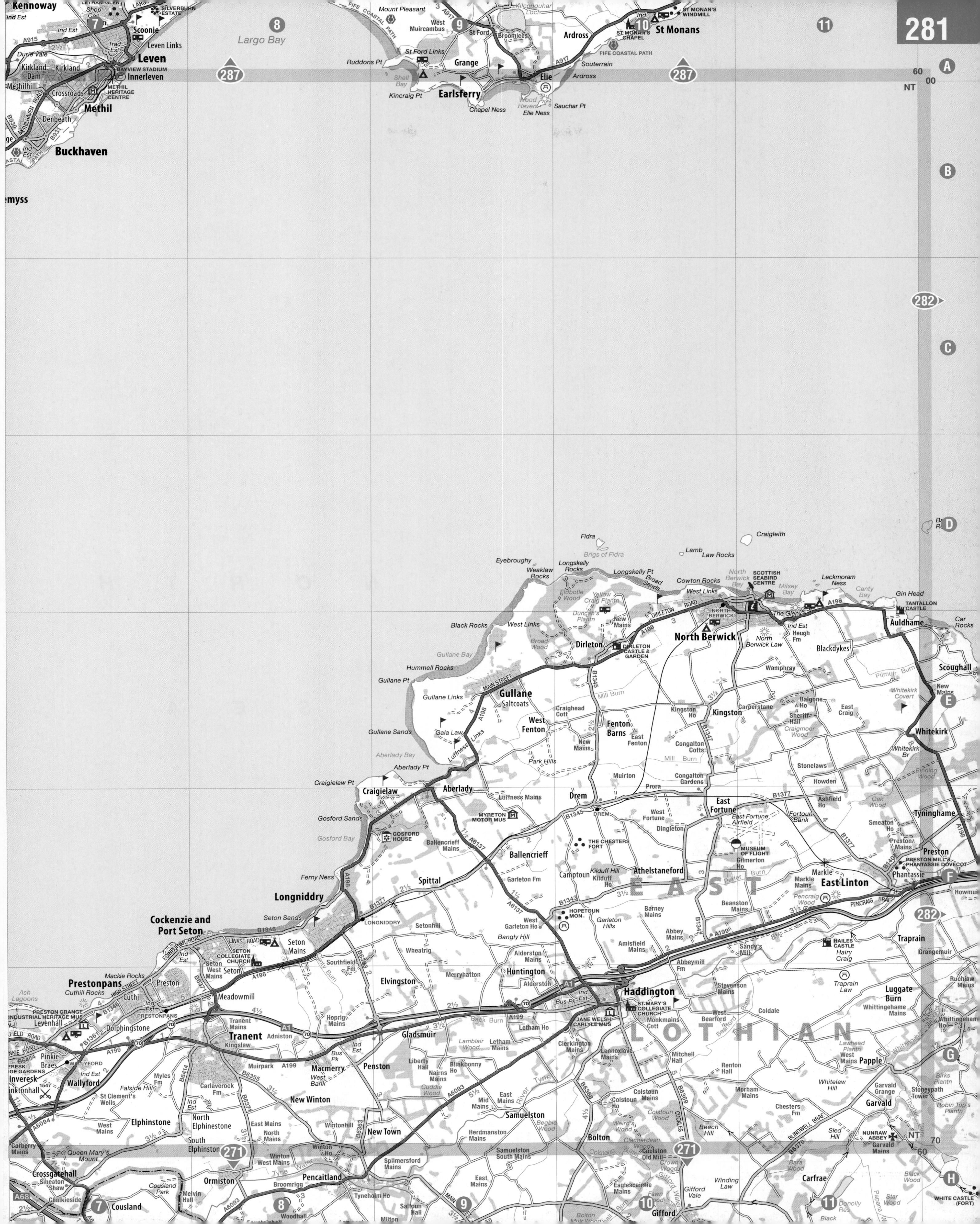
Kennoway
Ind Est
Scoonie
Leven Links
Leven
Durie Vale
Kirkland Dam
Kirkland
Innerleven
BAYVIEW STADIUM
Methilhill
Crossroads
METHIL HERITAGE CENTRE
Methil
Denbeath
Buckhaven
Largo Bay
Mount Pleasant
West Muircambus
St Ford
Broomlees
St Ford Links
Grange
Ruddons Pt
Shell Bay
Kincraig Pt
Earlsferry
Chapel Ness
Elie
Wood Haven
Elie Ness
Sauchar Pt
Ardross
Souterrain
St Monans
ST MONAN'S WINDMILL
ST MONAN'S CHAPEL
FIFE COASTAL PATH
A915
A917
287
NT
282
271
emyss
Fidra
Brigs of Fidra
Craigleith
Lamb
Law Rocks
Eyebroughy
Weaklaw Rocks
Longskelly Rocks
Longskelly Pt
Broad Sands
Cowton Rocks
North Berwick Bay
SCOTTISH SEABIRD CENTRE
Milsey Bay
Leckmoram Ness
Canty Bay
Gin Head
TANTALLON CASTLE
Car Rocks
Auldhame
West Links
Yellow Craig Plantn
Eldbotle Wood
Duncan's Plantn
New Mains
Black Rocks
Broad Wood
Dirleton
DIRLETON CASTLE & GARDEN
North Berwick
North Berwick Law
Ind Est
Heugh Fm
The Glen
Blackdykes
Scoughall
Gullane Bay
Hummell Rocks
Gullane Pt
Gullane Links
Gullane
Saltcoats
Gullane Sands
Gala Law
Luffness Links
Aberlady Bay
Aberlady Pt
Craigielaw Pt
Craigielaw
Aberlady
Craighead Cott
West Fenton
Fenton Barns
East Fenton
New Mains
Park Hills
Kingston Ho
Kingston
Congalton Cotts
Congalton Gardens
Muirton
Prora
Carperstane
Balgone Ho
Sheriff Hall
Craigmoor Wood
East Craig
Wamphray
Whitekirk
Whitekirk Covert
Whitekirk Br
New Mains
Stonelaws
Howden
Binning Wood
Drem
East Fortune
East Fortune Airfield
West Fortune
Dingleton
Fortune Bank
Ashfield Ho
Oak Wood
Tyninghame
Smeaton Ho
Preston Mains
Preston
PRESTON MILL & PHANTASSIE DOVECOT
Phantassie
Luffness Mains
MYRETON MOTOR MUS
Gosford Sands
Gosford Bay
GOSFORD HOUSE
Ballencrieff Mains
Ballencrieff
THE CHESTERS FORT
MUSEUM OF FLIGHT
Gilmerton Ho
Ferny Ness
Spittal
Longniddry
Garleton Fm
Kilduff Hill
Kilduff Ho
Camptoun
Athelstaneford
Markle
Markle Mains
East Linton
Pencraig Wood
Pencraig Brae
Howmuir
EAST
LOTHIAN
Seton Sands
Cockenzie and Port Seton
SETON COLLEGIATE CHURCH
Seton Mains
Setonhill
West Garleton Ho
Bangly Hill
HOPETOUN MON
Garleton Hills
Barney Mains
Beanston Mains
Abbey Mains
Amisfield Mains
Sandy's Mill
HAILES CASTLE
Hairy Craig
Traprain
Grangemuir
Mackie Rocks
Preston
Seton West Mains
Seton
Southfield Fm
Wheatrig
Alderston Mains
Huntington
Alderston
Elvingston
Merryhatton
Abbeymill Fm
Stevenson Mains
Traprain Law
Ruchlaw Mains
Luggate Burn
Whittingehame Mains
Prestonpans
Cuthill Rocks
Ash Lagoons
Cuthill
Meadowmill
PRESTON GRANGE INDUSTRIAL HERITAGE MUS
Levenhall
Dolphingstone
Tranent Mains
Tranent
Kingslaw
Adniston
Hopring Mains
Gladsmuir
Haddington
ST MARY'S COLLEGIATE CHURCH
JANE WELSH CARLYLE MUS
Monkmains Cott
West Bearford
Coldale
Letham Ho
Lamblair Wood
Letham Mains
Clerkington Mains
Lennoxlove Mains
Mitchell Hall
Renton Hall
Lawhead Plantn
West Mains
Papple
Pinkie Braes
Inveresk
Wallyford
Muirpark
Macmerry
West Bank
Penston
Liberty Hall
Nairns Mains
Blinkbonny Ho
Cuddie Wood
Myles Fm
Falside Hill
St Clement's Wells
Carlaverock Fm
New Winton
Mid Mains
East Mains
River Tyne
Colstoun Mains
Colstoun Ho
Colstoun Wood
Morham Mains
Chesters Fm
Whitelaw Hill
Garvald Grange
Garvald
Stoneypath Tower
Birks Plantn
Robin Tup's Plantn
West Mains
Elphinstone
North Elphinstone
South Elphinstone
East Mains
North Mains
Wintonhill
New Town
Samuelston
Begbie Wood
Herdmanston Mains
Bolton
Weirds Wood
Clacherdean Wood
Beech Hill
Sled Hill
NUNRAW ABBEY
Garvald Mains
Carberry Mains
Queen Mary's Mount
Crossgatehall
Sineaton Shaw
Chalkieside
Cousland Park
Cousland
Melvin Hall
Ormiston
Winton Ho
Winton West Mains
Tyne Water
Broomrigg
Pencaitland
Spilmersford Mains
Samuelston South Mains
East Mains
Colstoun Old Mill
Crowny Wood
Eaglescairnie Mains
Winding Law
Carfrae
Bara Wood
Black Wood
Star Wood
WHITE CASTLE (FORT)
Tyneholm Ho
Saltoun Hall
Gifford
Gifford Vale
Fawn Wood
Donolly Res
Woodhall
Milton
A1
A198
A199
A6137
A6093
B1345
B1347
B1377
B1343
B1348
B6363
B6355
B6368
B6369
B6370
Bus Pk
Ind Est
Kirkland
A

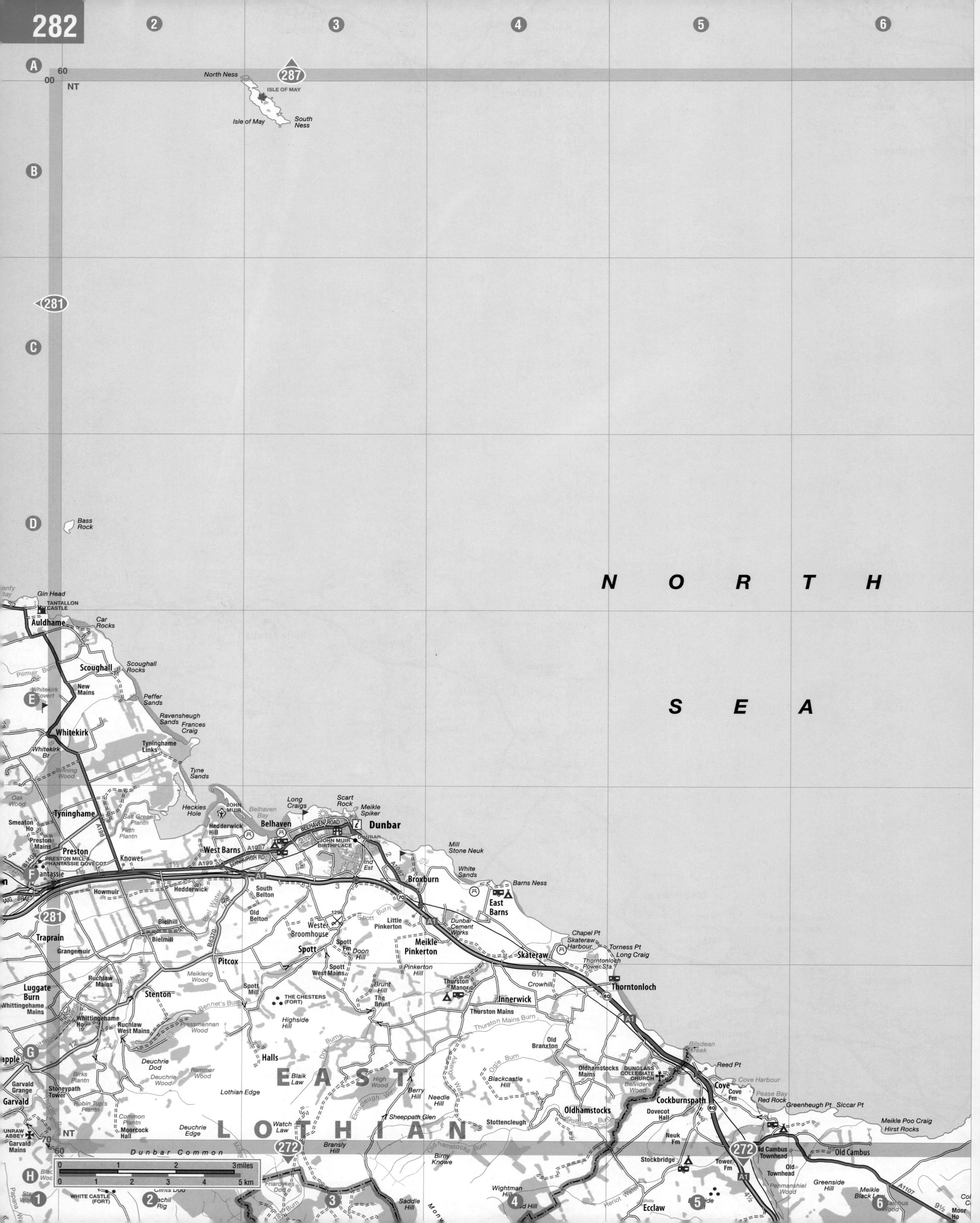

North Ness
287
ISLE OF MAY
Isle of May
South Ness
281
Bass Rock
N O R T H
S E A
Gin Head
TANTALLON CASTLE
Auldhame
Car Rocks
Scoughall
Scoughall Rocks
Pilmuir Burn
New Mains
Whitekirk Covert
Peffer Sands
Ravensheugh Sands
Frances Craig
Whitekirk
Whitekirk Br
Tyninghame Links
Binning Wood
Tyne Sands
Oak Wood
Tyninghame
Heckies Hole
JOHN MUIR
Belhaven Bay
Long Craigs
Scart Rock
Meikle Spiker
Smeaton Ho
Salt Greens Plantn
Firth Plantn
Hedderwick Hill
Belhaven
BELHAVEN ROAD
Dunbar
JOHN MUIR BIRTHPLACE
Preston Mains
Preston
West Barns
Mill Stone Neuk
PRESTON MILL
PHANTASSIE DOVECOT
Knowes
EDINBURGH RD
White Sands
Phantassie
Howmuir
Hedderwick
South Belton
Broxburn
Barns Ness
East Barns
Bielhill
Old Belton
Wester Broomhouse
Little Pinkerton
Dunbar Cement Works
Traprain
Bielmill
Spott
Spott Fm
Doon Hill
Meikle Pinkerton
Chapel Pt
Skateraw Harbour
Torness Pt
Long Craig
Grangemuir
Pitcox
Skateraw
Thorntonloch Power Sta
Pinkerton Hill
Ruchlaw Mains
Meiklerig Wood
Spott West Mains
Crowhill
Thorntonloch
Luggate Burn
Whittingehame Mains
Stenton
Spott Mill
THE CHESTERS (FORT)
Brunt Hill
The Brunt
Thurston Manor
Innerwick
Bennet's Burn
Thurston Mains
Whittingehame Ho
Ruchlaw West Mains
Pressmennan Wood
Highside Hill
Thurston Mains Burn
Old Branxton
Bilsdean Creek
Halls
Dry Burn
Ogle Burn
Reed Pt
Deuchrie Dod
Birks Plantn
Rammer Wood
Deuchrie Wood
E A S T
Blaik Law
High Wood
Blackcastle Hill
Oldhamstocks Mains
DUNGLASS COLLEGIATE CHURCH
Belvidere Wood
Cove Harbour
Coye
Cove Fm
Garvald Grange
Stoneypath Tower
Lothian Edge
Berry Hill
Pease Bay
Red Rock
Garvald
Robin Tup's Plantn
Needle Hill
Cockburnspath
Oldhamstocks
Greenheugh Pt
Siccar Pt
Common Plantn
Moorcock Hall
Deuchrie Edge
L O T H I A N
Watch Law
Sheeppath Glen
Stottencleugh
Dovecot Hall
Meikle Poo Craig
Hirst Rocks
Neuk Fm
NUNRAW ABBEY
Garvald Mains
Dunbar Common
272
Bransly Hill
Oldhamstocks Burn
Birny Knowe
Stockbridge
Tower Fm
Old Cambus Townhead
Old Cambus
Old Townhead
Penmanshiel Wood
Greenside Hill
Meikle Black Law
Friardykes Dod
WHITE CASTLE (FORT)
Saddle Hill
Wightman Hill
Heriot Water
Ecclaw
0 1 2 3 miles
0 1 2 3 4 5 km
NT
A1
A198
A199
A1087
B6370
A1107

7
8
9
10
11
A
B
C
D
E
F
G
H
10
00
NT
NT
70
10
Fast Castle Head
Wheat Stack
Telegraph Hill
FAST CASTLE
Oatlee Hill
Dowlaw Burn
Lumsdaine
Lumsdaine Moor
Coldingham Loch
Moorside
273
St Abb's Head
ST ABB'S HEAD
Horsecastle Bay
Mire Loch
Bell Hill

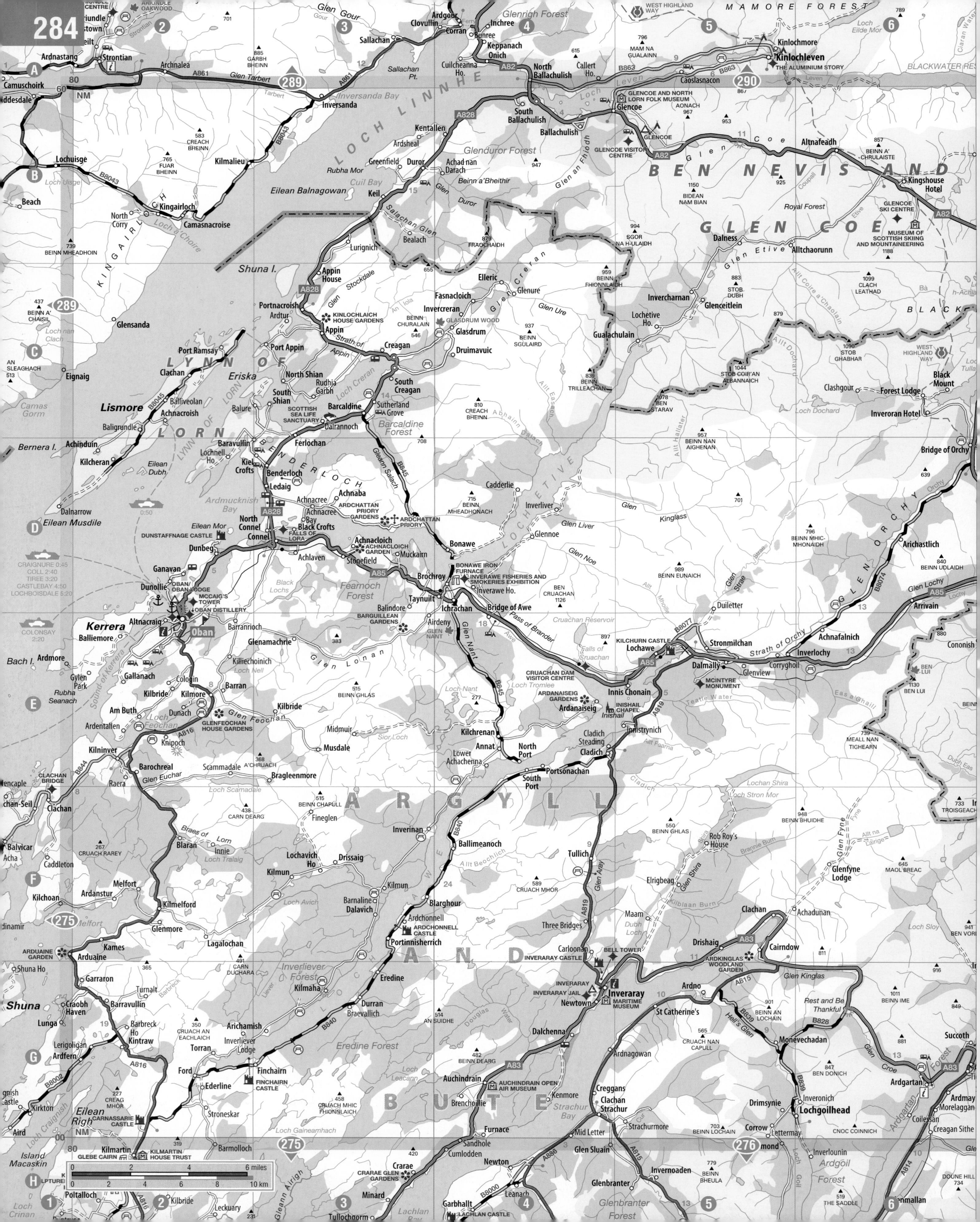

LOCH LINNHE
BEN NEVIS AND GLEN COE
ARGYLL AND BUTE
MAMORE FOREST
Ardgour
Clovullin
Corran
Inchree
Onich
Keppanach
Sallachan
Strontian
Ardnastang
Camuschoirk
Archnalea
Glen Tarbert
Inversanda
Inversanda Bay
North Ballachulish
South Ballachulish
Ballachulish
Callert Ho.
Kinlochmore
Kinlochleven
THE ALUMINIUM STORY
Caolasnacon
GLENCOE AND NORTH LORN FOLK MUSEUM
Glencoe
GLENCOE VISITOR CENTRE
Altnafeadh
Kingshouse Hotel
GLENCOE SKI CENTRE
MUSEUM OF SCOTTISH SKIING AND MOUNTAINEERING
Royal Forest
Dalness
Alltchaorunn
Glen Etive
Kentallen
Ardsheal
Greenfield
Duror
Achad nan Darach
Glenduror Forest
Rubha Mor
Cuil Bay
Eilean Balnagowan
Keil
Lochuisge
Kingairloch
North Corry
Camasnacroise
Beach
KINGAIRLOCH
Shuna I.
Lurignich
Bealach
Appin House
Portnacroish
Ardtur
KINLOCHLAICH HOUSE GARDENS
Appin
Port Appin
Creagan
Strath of Appin
Elleric
Glenure
Fasnacloich
Invercreran
GLASDRUM WOOD
Glasdrum
Druimavuic
Glen Ure
Glensanda
Port Ramsay
LYNN OF LORN
Clachan
Eriska
North Shian
South Shian
Rudhja Garbh
South Creagan
Loch Creran
Barcaldine
SCOTTISH SEA LIFE SANCTUARY
Dalrannoch
Sutherland Grove
Barcaldine Forest
Lismore
Balliveolan
Achnacroish
Baligrundle
Balure
Achinduin
Kilcheran
Bernera I.
Baravullin
Lochnell Ho
Kiel Crofts
Benderloch
Ferlochan
Ledaig
BENDERLOCH
Achnacree
Achnaba
ARDCHATTAN PRIORY GARDENS
ARDCHATTAN PRIORY
Ardmucknish Bay
Dalnarrow
Eilean Musdile
Eilean Mor
DUNSTAFFNAGE CASTLE
North Connel
Connel
FALLS OF LORA
Black Crofts
Dunbeg
Achlaven
Achnacloich
ACHNACLOICH GARDEN
Muckairn
Stonefield
Bonawe
BONAWE IRON FURNACE
INVERAWE FISHERIES AND SMOKERIES EXHIBITION
Brochroy
Taynuilt
Inverawe Ho.
Ganavan
Dunollie
OBAN/OBAN LODGE
MCCAIG'S TOWER
OBAN DISTILLERY
Oban
Altnacraig
Kerrera
Balliemore
Barranrioch
Glenamachrie
Glen Lonan
Balindore
BARGUILLEAN GARDENS
Airdeny
Ichrachan
Bridge of Awe
Pass of Brander
CRAIGNURE 0:45
COLL 2:40
TIREE 3:20
CASTLEBAY 4:50
LOCHBOISDALE 5:20
COLONSAY 2:20
Bach I.
Ardmore
Gylen Park
Gallanach
Rubha Seanach
Kilbride
Kilmore
Barran
Cologin
Dunach
Am Buth
Ardentallen
Glen Feochan
GLENFEOCHAN HOUSE GARDENS
Knipoch
Kilninver
Barochreal
Raera
Scammadale
Bragleenmore
Midmuir
Musdale
Kilchrenan
Annat
North Port
Lower Achachenna
Portsonachan
South Port
Cladich
Innis Chonain
Lochawe
KILCHURN CASTLE
CRUACHAN DAM VISITOR CENTRE
ARDANAISEIG GARDENS
Ardanaiseig
INISHAIL CHAPEL
Inistrynich
Dalmally
MCINTYRE MONUMENT
Glenview
Stronmilchan
Strath of Orchy
Corryghoil
Inverlochy
Achnafalnich
Arrivain
Duiletter
Glen Lochy
Arichastlich
GLEN ORCHY
Bridge of Orchy
Inveroran Hotel
Forest Lodge
Clashgour
Black Mount
Loch Dochard
Invercharnan
Glenceitlein
Lochetive Ho.
Gualachulain
Cadderlie
Inverliver
Glen Liver
Glennoe
Glen Noe
Glen Kinglass
LOCH ETIVE
Clachan Bridge
Clachan
Balvicar
Caddleton
Melfort
Kilchoan
Ardanstur
Kilmelford
Glenmore
Blaran
Braes of Lorn
Innie
Fineglen
Inverinan
Ballimeanoch
Lochavich Ho
Drissaig
Kilmun
Barnaline
Dalavich
Blarghour
Ardchonnell
ARDCHONNELL CASTLE
Portinnisherrich
Eredine
Kilmaha
Durran
Braevallich
Arichamish
Lagalochan
Kames
Arduaine
ARDUAINE GARDEN
Shuna Ho
Garraron
Turnalt
Barravullin
Craobh Haven
Shuna
Lunga
Barbreck Ho
Kintraw
Ardfern
Lerigoligan
Torran
Inverliever Lodge
Ford
Finchairn
FINCHAIRN CASTLE
Ederline
Stroneskar
Kirkton
Eilean Righ
CARNASSARIE CASTLE
Aird
Island Macaskin
Kilmartin
GLEBE CAIRN
KILMARTIN HOUSE TRUST
Barmolloch
Poltalloch
Kilbride
Leckuary
Tullochgorm
Minard
CRARAE GLEN GARDENS
Crarae
Furnace
Sandhole
Cumlodden
Newton
Auchindrain
AUCHINDRAIN OPEN AIR MUSEUM
Brenchoillie
Kenmore
Leacann
Garbhallt
Leanach
LACHLAN CASTLE
Dalchenna
Inveraray
INVERARAY JAIL
INVERARAY CASTLE
MARITIME MUSEUM
BELL TOWER
Newtown
Carloonan
Three Bridges
Tullich
Glen Aray
Maam
Dubh Loch
Elrigbeag
Glen Shira
Rob Roy's House
Glenfyne Lodge
Glen Fyne
Clachan
Achadunan
Drishaig
Cairndow
ARDKINGLAS WOODLAND GARDEN
Ardno
Glen Kinglas
St Catherine's
Hell's Glen
Rest and Be Thankful
Monevechadan
Arnagowan
Creggans
Clachan Strachur
Strachurmore
Strachur Bay
Mid Letter
Glen Sluain
Invernoaden
Glenbranter
Glenbranter Forest
Drimsynie
Inveronich
Lochgoilhead
Corrow
Lettermay
Inverlounin
Ardgoil Forest
Succoth
Ardgartan
Ardmay
Morelaggan
Coilessan
Creagan Sithe
Glen Croe
Eredine Forest
Inverliever Forest
Loch Avich
Loch Awe
Loch Fyne
Loch Scamadale
Loch Tralaig
Loch Nell
Loch Tromlee
Cruachan Reservoir
BEN CRUACHAN 1126
BEN LUI 1130
BIDEAN NAM BIAN 1150
BEN STARAV 1078
BEINN EUNAICH 989
BEINN IME 1011
BEINN BHUIDHE 948
BEINN LOCHAIN 703
CRUACH NAN CAPULL 565
Sior Loch
Loch Gaineamhach
WEST HIGHLAND WAY
BLACKWATER RES
289
290
275
276
0 2 4 6 miles
0 2 4 6 8 10 km

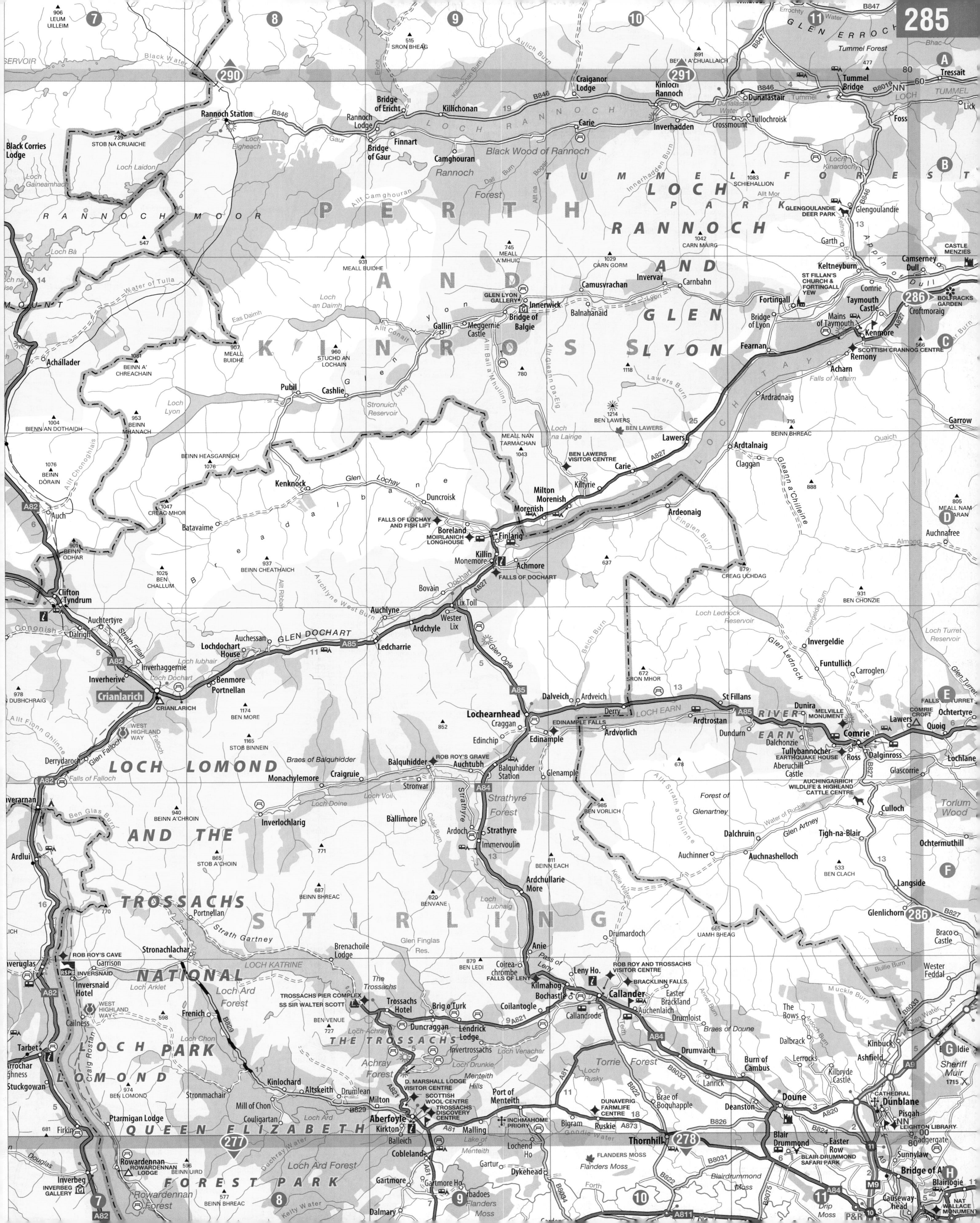
PERTH AND KINROSS
LOCH RANNOCH AND GLEN LYON
LOCH LOMOND AND THE TROSSACHS NATIONAL PARK
STIRLING
QUEEN ELIZABETH FOREST PARK
TUMMEL FOREST PARK
RANNOCH MOOR
BREADALBANE
290
291
286
277
278
Rannoch Station
Black Corries Lodge
Loch Laidon
STOB NA CRUAICHE
Bridge of Ericht
Killichonan
Craiganor Lodge
Kinloch Rannoch
Dunalastair
Tummel Bridge
Tressait
Rannoch Lodge
Bridge of Gaur
Finnart
Camghouran
Carie
Inverhadden
Crossmount
Tullochroisk
Foss
Black Wood of Rannoch
LOCH RANNOCH
SCHIEHALLION
GLENGOULANDIE DEER PARK
Glengoulandie
Garth
CASTLE MENZIES
Camserney
Dull
Keltneyburn
ST FILLAN'S CHURCH & FORTINGALL YEW
Fortingall
Comrie
Taymouth Castle
Kenmore
BOLFRACKS GARDEN
Croftmoraig
Bridge of Lyon
Mains of Taymouth
Fearnan
SCOTTISH CRANNOG CENTRE
Remony
Acharn
Falls of Acharn
Ardradnaig
CARN GORM
CARN MAIRG
Inverar
Carnbahn
Camusvrachan
GLEN LYON GALLERY
Innerwick
Bridge of Balgie
Balnahanaid
Gallin
Meggernie Castle
MEALL BUIDHE
STUCHD AN LOCHAIN
Pubil
Cashlie
Stronuich Reservoir
Loch Lyon
Achallader
BEINN A' CHREACHAIN
BEINN MHANACH
BIENN AN DOTHAIDH
BEINN DÒRAIN
BEINN HEASGARNICH
CREAG MHOR
Kenknock
Glen Lochay
Duncroisk
Batavaime
FALLS OF LOCHAY AND FISH LIFT
Boreland
MOIRLANICH LONGHOUSE
Finlarig
Killin
Monemore
Achmore
FALLS OF DOCHART
BEINN CHEATHAICH
BEN CHALLUM
BEINN ODHAR
Auch
MEALL NAN TARMACHAN
BEN LAWERS
BEN LAWERS VISITOR CENTRE
Lawers
Carie
Kiltyrie
Milton Morenish
Morenish
LOCH TAY
Ardtalnaig
Claggan
Ardeonaig
BEINN BHREAC
Garrow
Auchnafree
CREAG UCHDAG
BEN CHONZIE
Loch Lednock Reservoir
Loch Turret Reservoir
Clifton
Tyndrum
Auchtertyre
Dalrigh
Strath Fillan
Inverhaggernie
Inverherive
Crianlarich
Benmore
Portnellan
BEN MORE
STOB BINNEIN
Lochdochart House
Auchessan
GLEN DOCHART
Ledcharrie
Auchlyne
Ardchyle
Wester Lix
Lix Toll
Bovain
Glen Ogle
SRON MHOR
Dalveich
Ardveich
Lochearnhead
Craggan
Edinchip
Edinample
EDINAMPLE FALLS
Ardvorlich
LOCH EARN
St Fillans
Ardtrostan
Dundurn
Dunira
MELVILLE MONUMENT
COMRIE CROFT
Comrie
Dalchonzie
Tullybannocher
EARTHQUAKE HOUSE
Ross
Dalginross
Aberuchill Castle
AUCHINGARRICH WILDLIFE & HIGHLAND CATTLE CENTRE
Invergeldie
Funtullich
Carroglen
Lawers
Ochtertyre
Quoig
Lochlane
Glascorrie
Culloch
Torlum Wood
Ochtermuthill
Tigh-na-Blair
Dalchruin
Auchinner
Auchnashelloch
Forest of Glenartney
BEN VORLICH
BEN CLACH
Langside
Glenlichorn
Braco Castle
Wester Feddal
ROB ROY'S GRAVE
Balquhidder
Auchtubh
Balquhidder Station
Glenample
Braes of Balquhidder
Monachylemore
Craigruie
Stronvar
Loch Voil
Loch Doine
Inverlochlarig
BEINN A'CHROIN
Ballimore
Strathyre
Strathyre Forest
Ardoch
Immervoulin
STOB A'CHOIN
BEINN EACH
Ardchullarie More
BEINN BHREAC
BENVANE
Loch Lubnaig
Derrydaroch
Glen Falloch
Falls of Falloch
WEST HIGHLAND WAY
Inverarnan
Ardlui
Portnellan
Strath Gartney
Stronachlachar
Brenachoile Lodge
Glen Finglas Res.
Anie
Drumardoch
UAMH BHEAG
ROB ROY'S CAVE
Garrison
Inversnaid
Inversnaid Hotel
LOCH KATRINE
BEN LEDI
Coilrea-chrombe
FALLS OF LENY
Pass of Leny
Leny Ho.
ROB ROY AND TROSSACHS VISITOR CENTRE
BRACKLINN FALLS
Kilmahog
Bochastle
Callander
Easter Brackland
Auchenlaich
Drumloist
Braes of Doune
Callandrode
Coilantogle
Loch Arklet
Loch Ard Forest
Frenich
TROSSACHS PIER COMPLEX
SS SIR WALTER SCOTT
The Trossachs
Trossachs Hotel
Brig o'Turk
BEN VENUE
Duncraggan
Lendrick Lodge
Invertrossachs
Loch Venachar
Loch Achray
THE TROSSACHS
Loch Chon
Tarbet
Arrochar
Stuckgowan
Inveruglas
Cailness
Kinlochard
Altskeith
Drumlean
Achray Forest
D. MARSHALL LODGE VISITOR CENTRE
SCOTTISH WOOL CENTRE
TROSSACHS DISCOVERY CENTRE
Menteith Hills
Port of Menteith
Milton
Aberfoyle
Kirkton
Balleich
Cobleland
Stronmachair
Mill of Chon
Couligartan
Loch Ard
BEN LOMOND
Ptarmigan Lodge
Firkin
INCHMAHOME PRIORY
Malling
Lake of Menteith
Lochend Ho
Gartur
Dykehead
Gartmore
Gartmore Ho
Dalmary
Rowardennan
ROWARDENNAN LODGE
BEINN UIRD
BEINN BHREAC
Inverbeg
INVERBEG GALLERY
Rowardennan Forest
Torrie Forest
Loch Rusky
DUNAVERIG FARMLIFE CENTRE
Ruskie
Bigram
Thornhill
FLANDERS MOSS
Flanders Moss
Blairdrummond Moss
Brae of Boquhapple
Lanrick
Deanston
Doune
Drumvaich
Burn of Cambus
The Bows
Dalbrack
Lerrocks
Kilbryde Castle
Blair Drummond
BLAIR DRUMMOND SAFARI PARK
Easter Row
Kinbuck
Ashfield
Sheriff Muir
CATHEDRAL
Dunblane
Pisgah
LEIGHTON LIBRARY
Badgergate
Sunnylaw
Bridge of Allan
Blairlogie
Causewayhead
NAT WALLACE MONUMENT
Gleddie

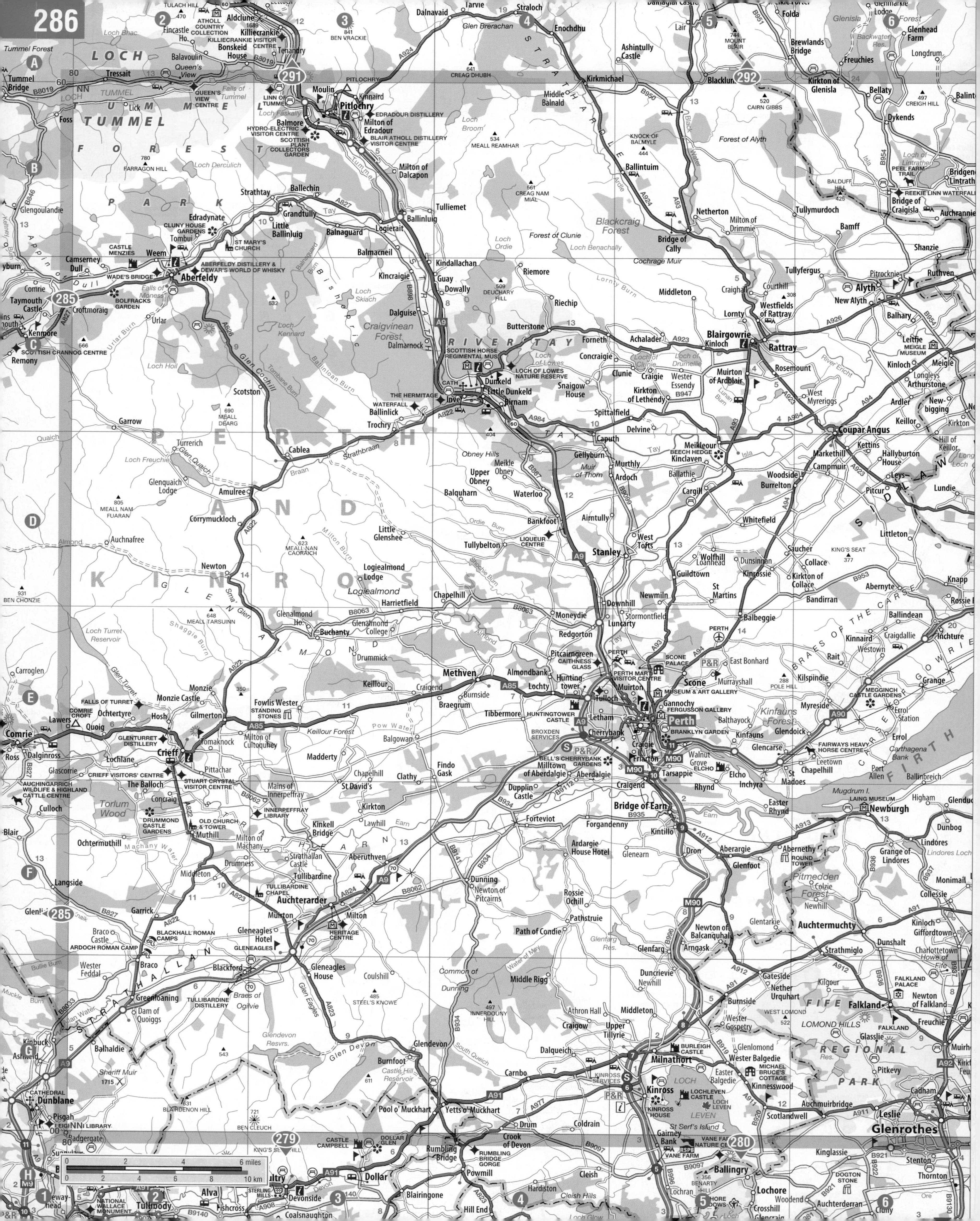
Tummel Forest
LOCH TUMMEL
TUMMEL FOREST PARK
Tummel Bridge
Tressait
Foss
Fincastle Ho.
Aldclune
Killiecrankie
Bonskeid House
Balavoulin
Queen's View
Pitlochry
Moulin
Kinnaird
Balmore
Milton of Edradour
Edradour Distillery
Blair Atholl Distillery Visitor Centre
Milton of Dalcapon
Dalnavaid
Tarvie
Straloch
Enochdhu
Glen Brerachan
Ashintully Castle
Kirkmichael
Middle Balnald
Strathardle
Ballintuim
Blacklunans
Lair
Mount Blair
Folda
Brewlands Bridge
Freuchies
Kirkton of Glenisla
Bellaty
Dykends
Forest of Alyth
Glenshee
Bridge of Craigisla
Reekie Linn Waterfall
Netherton
Milton of Drimmie
Tullymurdoch
Bamff
Bridge of Cally
Blackcraig Forest
Forest of Clunie
Loch Benachally
Cochrage Muir
Tullyfergus
Pitcrocknie
Alyth
New Alyth
Ruthven
Craighall
Courthill
Westfields of Rattray
Lornty
Middleton
Blairgowrie
Kinloch
Rattray
Rosemount
Balhary
Leitfie
Meigle Museum
Meigle
Longleys
Arthurstone
West Myreriggs
Ardler
Newbigging
Keillor
Kirkton
Coupar Angus
Kettins
Hill of Keillor
Hallyburton House
Markethill
Campmuir
Woodside
Burrelton
Leys
Pitcur
Lundie
Sidlaw
Strathtay
Ballechin
Grandtully
Little Ballinluig
Balnaguard
Logierait
Ballinluig
Tulliemet
Edradynate
Cluny House Gardens
Tombuie
St Mary's Church
Castle Menzies
Weem
Camserney
Dull
Aberfeldy
Aberfeldy Distillery & Dewar's World of Whisky
Wade's Bridge
Falls of Moness
Bolfracks Garden
Comrie
Taymouth Castle
Kenmore
Croftmoraig
Urlar
Remony
Scottish Crannog Centre
Glengoulandie
Appin of Dull
Balmacneil
Kincraigie
Kindallachan
Guay
Dowally
Dalguise
Loch Skiach
Craigvinean Forest
Loch Kennard
Dalmarnock
Riemore
Deuchary Hill
Riechip
Butterstone
Forneth
Achalader
Loch of Clunie
Loch of Drumellie
Concraigie
Clunie
Craigie
Wester Essendy
Muirton of Ardblair
Kirkton of Lethendy
Snaigow House
River Tay
Scottish Horse Regimental Museum
Loch of Lowes Nature Reserve
Dunkeld
Little Dunkeld
Birnam
Inver
The Hermitage
Ballinlick
Trochry
Spittalfield
Delvine
Caputh
Meikleour
Beech Hedge
Kinclaven
Ballathie
Cargill
Gellyburn
Murthly
Ardoch
Muir of Thorn
Obney Hills
Meikle Obney
Upper Obney
Balquharn
Waterloo
Bankfoot
Airntully
Liqueur Centre
Whitefield
Littleton
West Tofts
Stanley
Wolfhill
Loanhead
Dunsinnan
Saucher
Collace
King's Seat
Kinrossie
Kirkton of Collace
Abernyte
Knapp
Guildtown
St Martins
Bandirran
Rossie
Newmiln
Balbeggie
Ballindean
Craigdallie
Kinnaird
Westown
Inchture
Rait
Braes of the Carse
Kilspindie
Grange
Megginch Castle Gardens
Errol Station
Errol
Glendoick
Carse of Gowrie
Scotston
Glen Cochill
Loch Hoil
Garrow
Meall Dearg
Turrerich
Loch Freuchie
Glen Quaich
Cablea
Strathbraan
Glenquaich Lodge
Amulree
Meall nam Fuaran
Corrymuckloch
Auchnafree
Little Glenshee
Meall nan Caorach
Tullybelton
Newton
Glen Almond
Ben Chonzie
Meall Tarsuinn
Logiealmond Lodge
Logiealmond
Chapelhill
Harrietfield
Glenalmond Ho.
Glenalmond College
Buchanty
Moneydie
Downhill
Stormontfield
Luncarty
Redgorton
Pitcairngreen
Caithness Glass
Perth Mart Visitor Centre
Scone Palace
Scone
East Bonhard
Murrayshall
Pole Hill
Loch Turret Reservoir
Carroglen
Drummick
Keillour
Methven
Craigend
Almondbank
Huntingtower
Lochty
Burnside
Braegrum
Tibbermore
Huntingtower Castle
Muirton
Tulloch
Museum & Art Gallery
Gannochy
Fergusson Gallery
Letham
Perth
Kinfauns Forest
Balthayock
Myreside
Kinfauns
Branklyn Garden
Cherrybank
Broxden Services
Craigie
Friarton
Walnut Grove
Elcho
Glencarse
Fairways Heavy Horse Centre
Leetown
Chapelhill
St Madoes
Port Allen
Ballinbreich
Tarsappie
Inchyra
Rhynd
Craigend
Easter Rhynd
Firth of Tay
Mugdrum I.
Laing Museum
Newburgh
Higham
Monzie
Monzie Castle
Falls of Turret
Comrie Croft
Ochtertyre
Lawers
Quoig
Hosh
Gilmerton
Fowlis Wester
Standing Stones
Glenturret Distillery
Comrie
Ross
Dalginross
Crieff
Tomaknock
Milton of Cultoquhey
Keillour Forest
Pow Water
Balgowan
Madderty
Findo Gask
Clathy
Chapelhill
St David's
Lochlane
Glascorrie
Crieff Visitors' Centre
Stuart Crystal Visitor Centre
Pittachar
Auchingarrich Wildlife & Highland Cattle Centre
The Balloch
Concraig
Torlum Wood
Drummond Castle Gardens
Old Church & Tower
Muthill
Mains of Innerpeffray
Innerpeffray Library
Kirkton
Lawhill
Kinkell Bridge
Bell's Cherrybank Gardens
Milltown of Aberdalgie
Aberdalgie
Dupplin Castle
Forteviot
Forgandenny
Bridge of Earn
Kintillo
Culloch
Blair
Ochtermuthill
Machany Water
Milton of Machany
Strathearn
Strathallan Castle
Aberuthven
Tullibardine
Drumness
Ardargie House Hotel
Glenearn
Dron
Aberargie
Abernethy
Round Tower
Glenfoot
Grange of Lindores
Lindores
Dunbog
Langside
Middleton
Tullibardine Chapel
Auchterarder
Dunning
Newton of Pitcairns
Rossie Ochill
Pitmedden Forest
Colzie
Newhill
Monimail
Collessie
Glenleith
Garrick
Braco Castle
Ardoch Roman Camp
Blackhall Roman Camps
Gleneagles Hotel
Gleneagles
Milton
Heritage Centre
Pathstruie
Path of Condie
Glenfarg Res.
Glenfarg
Arngask
Newton of Balcanquhal
Glentarkie
Auchtermuchty
Dunshalt
Kinloch
Giffordtown
Strathmiglo
Charlottetown
Howe of Fife
Braco
Blackford
Wester Feddal
Gleneagles House
Coulshill
Glen Eagles
Common of Dunning
Middle Rigg
Duncrievie
Newhill
Gateside
Nether Urquhart
Kilgour
Falkland Palace
Newton of Falkland
Greenloaning
Tullibardine Distillery
Braes of Ogilvie
Dam of Quoiggs
Steel's Knowe
Innerdouny Hill
Athron Hall
Middleton
Burnside
West Lomond
Fife
Falkland
Lomond Hills
Freuchie
Kinbuck
Ashfield
Balhaldie
Glendevon Resvrs.
Glen Devon
Glendevon
Craigow
Upper Tillyrie
Wester Gospetry
Glenlomond
Wester Balgedie
Regional Park
Glasslie
Sheriff Muir
Burnfoot
Castle Hill Reservoir
South Queich
Dalqueich
Milnathort
Burleigh Castle
Easter Balgedie
Michael Bruce's Cottage
Kinnesswood
Pitkevy
Cathedral
Dunblane
Pisgah
Leighton Library
Blairdenon Hill
Ben Cleuch
Pool o' Muckhart
Yetts o' Muckhart
Carnbo
Kinross Services
Kinross
Loch Leven
Lochleven Castle
Kinross House
St Serf's Island
Drum
Coldrain
Scotlandwell
Auchmuirbridge
Cadham
Leslie
Glenrothes
Badgergate
King's Seat Hill
Castle Campbell
Dollar Glen
Rumbling Bridge
Rumbling Bridge Gorge
Crook of Devon
Gairney Bank
Vane Farm
Vane Farm Nature Centre
Ballingry
Kinglassie
Stenton
Thornton
Dollar
Devonside
Sterling Mills
Alva
Tullibody
National Wallace Monument
Fishcross
Coalsnaughton
Blairingone
Powmill
Cleish
Hardiston
Cleish Hills
Hill End
Benarty Hill
Lochore
Lochran
Woodend
Crosshill
Dogton Stone
Auchterderran
Cluny
0 2 4 6 miles
0 2 4 6 8 10 km

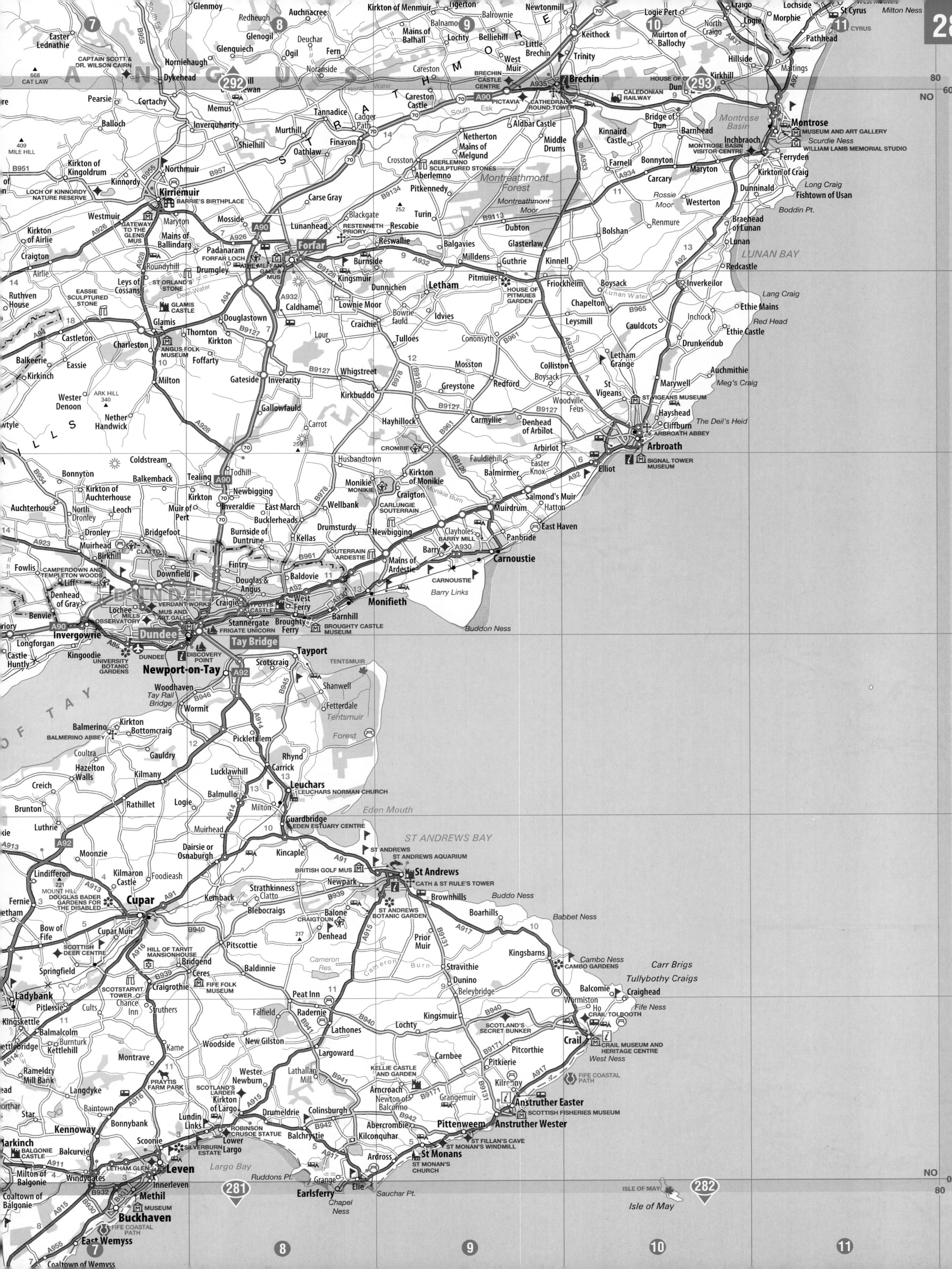

A
B
C
D
E
F
G
H
7
8
9
10
11
292
293
281
282
Glenmoy
Redheugh
Auchnacree
Kirkton of Menmuir
Tigerton
Balrownie
Newtonmill
Logie Pert
Lochside
Morphie
St Cyrus
Milton Ness
CYRUS
Easter Lednathie
Glenogil
Deuchar
Fern
Balnamoon
Mains of Balhall
Lochty
Belliehill
Little Brechin
Keithock
Muirton of Ballochy
North Craigo
Logie
Pathhead
CAPTAIN SCOTT & DR. WILSON CAIRN
Glenquiech
Ogil
West Muir
Trinity
Hillside
668 CAT LAW
Dykehead
Horniehaugh
Noranside
Careston
BRECHIN CASTLE CENTRE
Brechin
HOUSE OF DUN
Kirkhill
Maltings
Noran Water
Careston Castle
A90
A935
PICTAVIA
CATHEDRAL & ROUND TOWER
CALEDONIAN RAILWAY
Pearsie
Cortachy
Memus
Tannadice
Cadger Path
South Esk
Montrose Basin
Montrose
MUSEUM AND ART GALLERY
Scurdie Ness
WILLIAM LAMB MEMORIAL STUDIO
Balloch
Inverquharity
Murthill
Aldbar Castle
Bridge of Dun
Kinnaird Castle
Barnhead
Inchbraoch
MONTROSE BASIN VISITOR CENTRE
Ferryden
409 MILE HILL
Shielhill
Finavon
Oathlaw
Netherton
Mains of Melgund
Middle Drums
Farnell
Bonnyton
Maryton
Kirkton of Craig
Kirkton of Kingoldrum
Northmuir
B951
B955
B957
Crosston
ABERLEMNO SCULPTURED STONES
Aberlemno
Montreathmont Forest
A934
Carcary
Dunninald
Long Craig
Fishtown of Usan
LOCH OF KINNORDY NATURE RESERVE
Kinnordy
Kirriemuir
BARRIE'S BIRTHPLACE
Carse Gray
B9134
Pitkennedy
Rossie Moor
Westerton
Boddin Pt.
Westmuir
Maryton
Mosside
Blackgate
252
Turin
Montreathmont Moor
Renmure
Braehead of Lunan
Kirkton of Airlie
GATEWAY TO THE GLENS MUS
Mains of Ballindarg
A926
A90
Lunanhead
RESTENNETH PRIORY
Rescobie
B9113
Dubton
Bolshan
Lunan
Padanaram
Forfar
Reswallie
Balgavies
Glasterlaw
LUNAN BAY
Craigton
FORFAR LOCH
Burnside
Milldens
Guthrie
Kinnell
Redcastle
Airlie
Roundyhill
Drumgley
THE MEFFAN GALL & MUS
A932
Kingsmuir
Pitmuies
HOUSE OF PITMUIES GARDEN
Friockheim
Boysack
Inverkeilor
Leys of Cossans
ST ORLAND'S STONE
Dunnichen
Letham
Lunan Water
Lang Craig
Ruthven House
EASSIE SCULPTURED STONE
GLAMIS CASTLE
Dean Water
A94
Caldhame
Lowrie Moor
Bowriefauld
Idvies
Chapelton
B965
Ethie Mains
Inchock
Red Head
Glamis
Douglastown
Craichie
Leysmill
Cauldcots
Ethie Castle
Castleton
B9127
Lour
Tulloes
Cononsyth
B961
Drunkendub
Charleston
ANGUS FOLK MUSEUM
Thornton
Kirkton
Balkeerie
Eassie
Foffarty
Mosston
Colliston
Letham Grange
Auchmithie
Meg's Craig
Kirkinch
Milton
Gateside
Inverarity
Whigstreet
B978
Boysack
Greystone
Redford
St Vigeans
Marywell
Wester Denoon
ARK HILL 340
Kirkbuddo
ST VIGEANS MUSEUM
Nether Handwick
Gallowfauld
Carmyllie
Denhead of Arbilot
Woodville Feus
Hayshead
Cliffburn
The Deil's Heid
ARBROATH ABBEY
A928
Carrot
Hayhillock
Arbroath
259
CROMBIE
Arbirlot
SIGNAL TOWER MUSEUM
Coldstream
Husbandtown
Faulddiehill
Easter Knox
Elliot
Bonnyton
Balkemback
Tealing
Todhill
Kirkton of Monikie
Balmirmer
Kirkton of Auchterhouse
Newbigging
Monikie
MONIKIE
Craigton
Salmond's Muir
Auchterhouse
North Dronley
Leoch
Kirkton
Inveraldie
East March
Wellbank
CARLUNGIE SOUTERRAIN
Muirdrum
Hatton
Muir of Pert
Bucklerheads
Dronley
Bridgefoot
Burnside of Duntrune
Drumsturdy
Newbigging
Clayholes
BARRY MILL
East Haven
Panbride
Muirhead
Birkhill
CLATTO
Kellas
SOUTERRAIN ARDESTIE
Barry
A930
Carnoustie
Fowlis
CAMPERDOWN AND TEMPLETON WOODS
Fintry
B961
Mains of Ardestie
Liff
Downfield
Douglas & Angus
Baldovie
CARNOUSTIE
Barry Links
Denhead of Gray
DUNDEE
VERDANT WORKS
Craigie
West Ferry
Monifieth
Benvie
Lochee
MILLS OBSERVATORY
MUS AND ART GALL
Stannergate
Broughty Ferry
Barnhill
Invergowrie
Dundee
FRIGATE UNICORN
BROUGHTY CASTLE MUSEUM
Buddon Ness
Longforgan
Kingoodie
DUNDEE
Tay Bridge
Tayport
Castle Huntly
UNIVERSITY BOTANIC GARDENS
DISCOVERY POINT
Newport-on-Tay
Scotscraig
TENTSMUIR
Woodhaven
Tay Rail Bridge
Shanwell
Wormit
Fetterdale
Tentsmuir Forest
Balmerino
Kirkton
Bottomcraig
BALMERINO ABBEY
Pickletillem
Coultra
Gauldry
Rhynd
Hazelton Walls
Kilmany
Lucklawhill
Carrick
Creich
Leuchars
LEUCHARS NORMAN CHURCH
Brunton
Rathillet
Logie
Balmullo
Milton
Eden Mouth
Luthrie
Guardbridge
EDEN ESTUARY CENTRE
Muirhead
ST ANDREWS BAY
Dairsie or Osnaburgh
Moonzie
Kincaple
ST ANDREWS
ST ANDREWS AQUARIUM
Lindifferon
BRITISH GOLF MUS
St Andrews
221 MOUNT HILL
Kilmaron Castle
Foodieash
Newpark
CATH & ST RULE'S TOWER
Fernie
DOUGLAS BADER GARDENS FOR THE DISABLED
Cupar
Kemback
Strathkinness
Clatto
Brownhills
Buddo Ness
Blebocraigs
ST ANDREWS BOTANIC GARDEN
Boarhills
Babbet Ness
Bow of Fife
Cupar Muir
CRAIGTOUN
Balone
Denhead
217
Prior Muir
SCOTTISH DEER CENTRE
HILL OF TARVIT MANSIONHOUSE
Pitscottie
Kingsbarns
Cambo Ness
CAMBO GARDENS
Bridgend
Ceres
Cameron Res.
Stravithie
Carr Brigs
Springfield
Baldinnie
Dunino
Tullybothy Craigs
SCOTSTARVIT TOWER
FIFE FOLK MUSEUM
Craigrothie
Peat Inn
Beleybridge
Balcomie
Craighead
Ladybank
Chance Inn
Cults
Wormiston Ho
Fife Ness
Pitlessie
Struthers
Falfield
Radernie
Kingsmuir
SCOTLAND'S SECRET BUNKER
CRAIL TOLBOOTH
Kingskettle
Balmalcolm
Lathones
Lochty
Crail
Burnturk
Kettlebridge
Kettlehill
Kame
Woodside
New Gilston
Pitcorthie
CRAIL MUSEUM AND HERITAGE CENTRE
Montrave
Largoward
Carnbee
Pitkierie
West Ness
Rameldry Mill Bank
Wester Newburn
Lathallan Mill
KELLIE CASTLE AND GARDEN
FIFE COASTAL PATH
Kilrenny
PRAYTIS FARM PARK
SCOTLAND'S LARDER
Arncroach
Newton of Balcormo
Grangemuir
Anstruther Easter
Langdyke
Kirkton of Largo
Star
Baintown
Lundin Links
Drumeldrie
Colinsburgh
SCOTTISH FISHERIES MUSEUM
Kennoway
Bonnybank
Abercrombie
Pittenweem
Anstruther Wester
Markinch
BALGONIE CASTLE
Balcurvie
Scoonie
ROBINSON CRUSOE STATUE
Lower Largo
Balchrystie
Kilconquhar
ST FILLAN'S CAVE
ST MONAN'S WINDMILL
SILVERBURN ESTATE
Leven
LETHAM GLEN
Largo Bay
Ardross
St Monans
ST MONAN'S CHURCH
Milton of Balgonie
Windygates
Innerleven
Ruddons Pt.
Grange
Elie
ISLE OF MAY
Methil
Earlsferry
Sauchar Pt.
Coaltown of Balgonie
Chapel Ness
Isle of May
Buckhaven
MUSEUM
FIFE COASTAL PATH
East Wemyss
Coaltown of Wemyss
NO
80
60
00

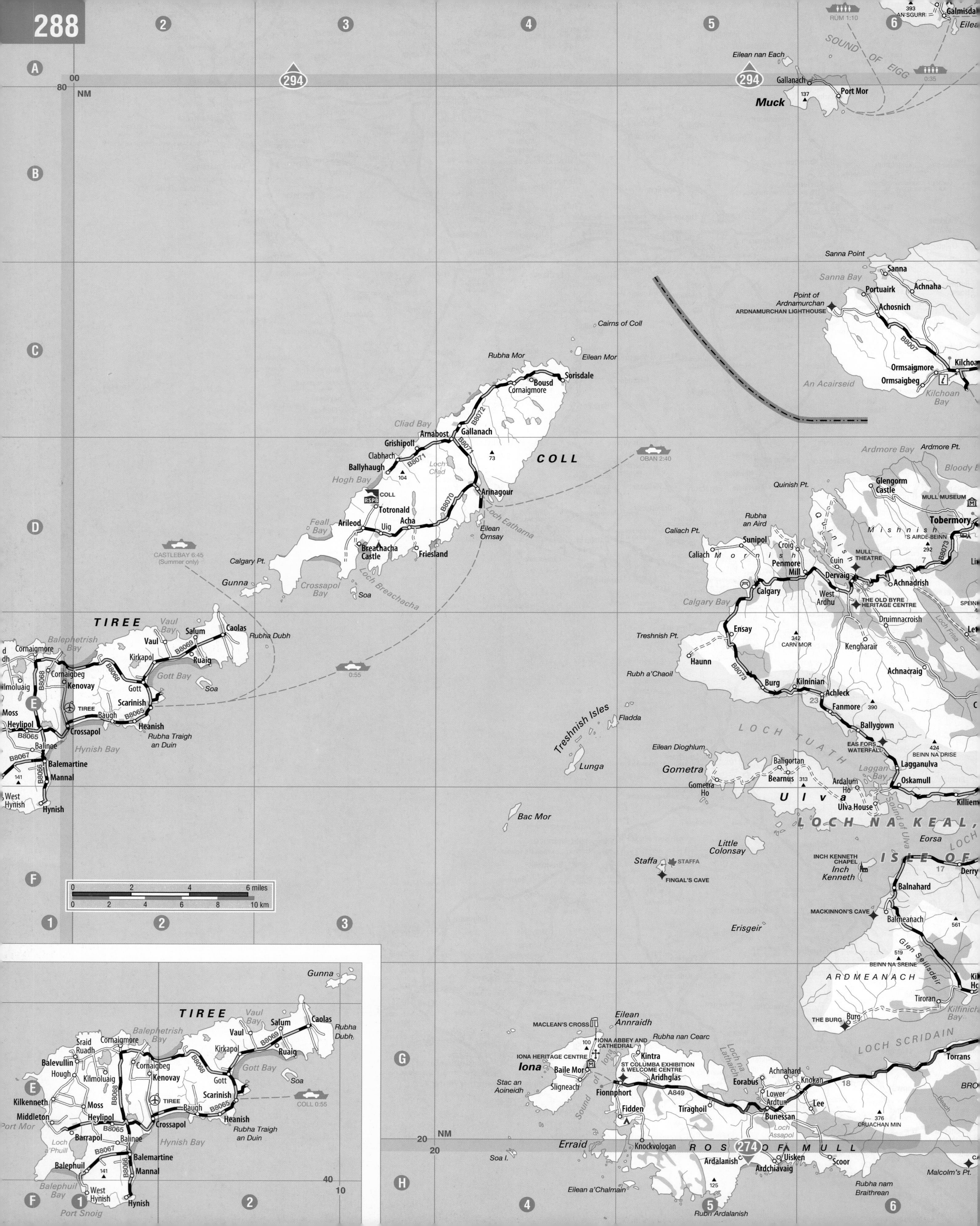

294
Eilean nan Each
Gallanach
Port Mor
Muck
137
RUM 1:10
393
AN SGURR
Galmisdale
SOUND OF EIGG
0:35
NM
Sanna Point
Sanna
Sanna Bay
Portuairk
Achnaha
Point of Ardnamurchan
ARDNAMURCHAN LIGHTHOUSE
Achosnich
B8007
Ormsaigmore
Ormsaigbeg
Kilchoan Bay
An Acairseid
Cairns of Coll
Eilean Mor
Rubha Mor
Sorisdale
Bousd
Cornaigmore
Cliad Bay
Arnabost
Gallanach
Grishipoll
Clabhach
Ballyhaugh
Loch Cliad
COLL
104
73
Hogh Bay
RSPB
Arinagour
OBAN 2:40
Totronald
Feall Bay
Arileod
Uig
Acha
Breachacha Castle
Friesland
Loch Eatharna
Eilean Ornsay
Calgary Pt.
Gunna
Crossapol Bay
Loch Breachacha
Soa
CASTLEBAY 6:45 (Summer only)
B8072
B8071
B8070
Ardmore Bay
Ardmore Pt.
Bloody Bay
Quinish Pt.
Glengorm Castle
MULL MUSEUM
Tobermory
Rubha an Aird
Mishnish
Caliach Pt.
Sunipol
Croig
Quinish
Caliach
Mornish
Penmore Mill
MULL THEATRE
Cuin
Dervaig
Achnadrish
292
B8073
Calgary
Calgary Bay
West Ardhu
THE OLD BYRE HERITAGE CENTRE
Druimnacroish
Treshnish Pt.
Ensay
342
CARN MOR
Kengharair
Haunn
Rubh a'Chaoil
Burg
Kilninian
Achleck
Achnacraig
Fanmore
390
Ballygown
LOCH TUATH
EAS FORS WATERFALL
424
BEINN NA DRISE
Lagganulva
Laggan Bay
Oskamull
Treshnish Isles
Fladda
Lunga
Eilean Dioghlum
Gometra
Gometra Ho
Baligortan
Bearnus
313
Ulva
Ardalum Ho
Ulva House
Sound of Ulva
Killiemor
LOCH NA KEAL
Eorsa
Bac Mor
Little Colonsay
Staffa
STAFFA
FINGAL'S CAVE
INCH KENNETH CHAPEL
Inch Kenneth
ISLE OF
Derry
Balnahard
MACKINNON'S CAVE
Balmeanach
561
Erisgeir
519
Glen Seilisdeir
BEINN NA SREINE
ARDMEANACH
Tiroran
THE BURG
Burg
Kilfinichen Bay
LOCH SCRIDAIN
Torrans
TIREE
Vaul Bay
Balephetrish Bay
Salum
Caolas
Vaul
Rubha Dubh
Cornaigmore
Kirkapol
B8069
Ruaig
Gott Bay
Cornaigbeg
B8068
Kenovay
Gott
Soa
Scarinish
TIREE
Baugh
B8065
Heanish
Rubha Traigh an Duin
Moss
Heylipol
Crossapol
Balinoe
Hynish Bay
B8067
Balemartine
141
B8066
Mannal
West Hynish
Hynish
0:55
0 2 4 6 miles
0 2 4 6 8 10 km
Gunna
Sraid Ruadh
Balevullin
Hough
Kilmoluaig
Kilkenneth
Middleton
Port Mor
Loch a'Phuill
Barrapol
Balephuil
Balephuil Bay
Port Snoig
COLL 0:55
MACLEAN'S CROSS
Eilean Annraidh
IONA ABBEY AND CATHEDRAL
Rubha nan Cearc
100
IONA HERITAGE CENTRE
Iona
Baile Mor
Kintra
ST COLUMBA EXHIBITION & WELCOME CENTRE
Aridhglas
Loch na Lathaich
Achnahard
Knokan
Stac an Aoineidh
Sligneach
Sound of Iona
Fionnphort
A849
Eorabus
Lower Ardtun
Lee
Fidden
Tiraghoil
Bunessan
376
CRUACHAN MIN
Loch Assapol
Erraid
Knockvologan
ROSS OF MULL
274
Ardalanish
Uisken
Ardchiavaig
Scoor
Soa I.
125
Eilean a'Chalmain
Rubh Ardalanish
Rubha nam Braithrean
Malcolm's Pt.

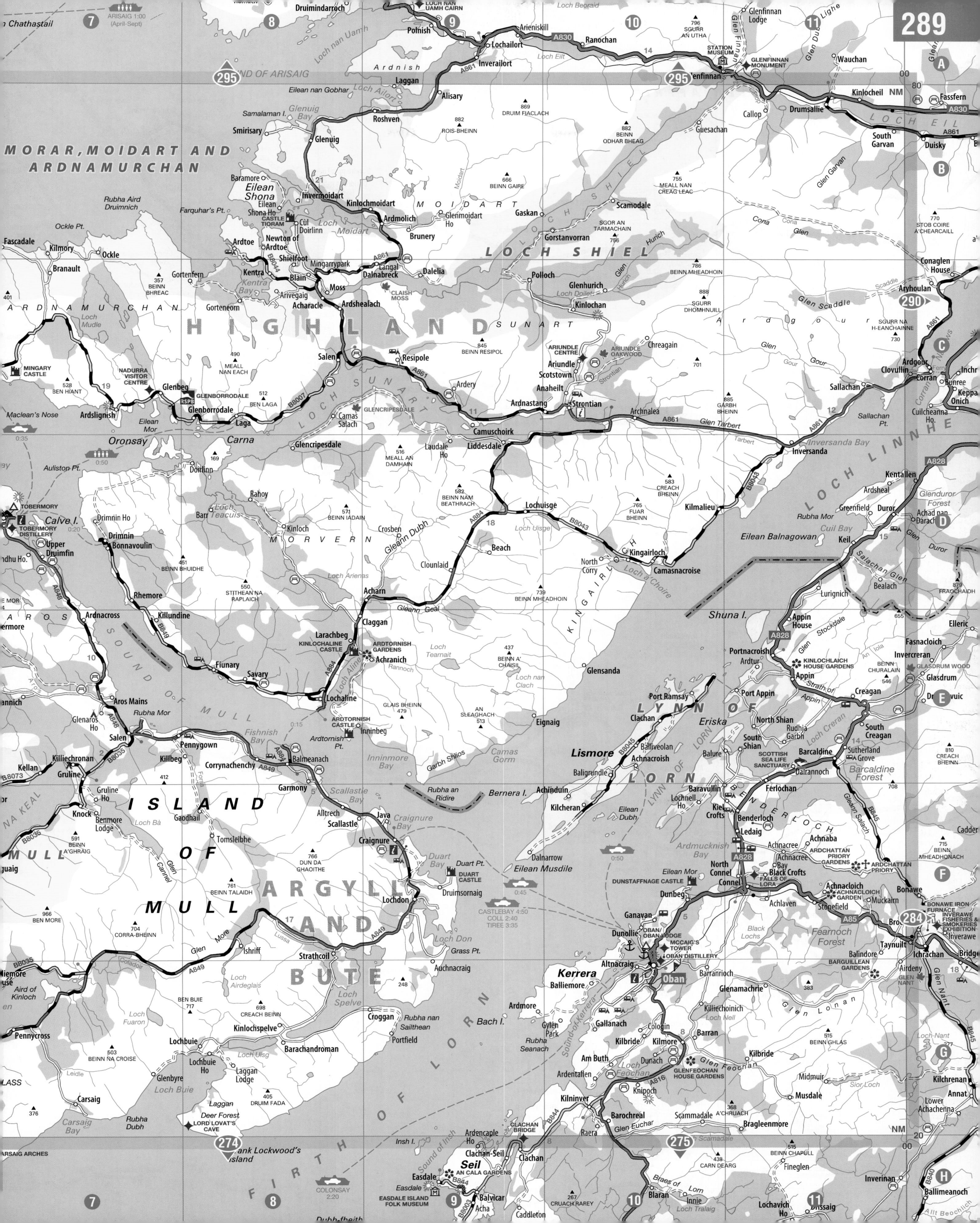

MORAR, MOIDART AND ARDNAMURCHAN
HIGHLAND
ISLAND OF MULL
ARGYLL AND BUTE
LOCH SHIEL
LOCH SUNART
MOIDART
SUNART
Ardgour
MORVERN
KINGAIRLOCH
LYNN OF LORN
LORN
BENDERLOCH
LOCH LINNHE
SOUND OF MULL
FIRTH OF LORN
LOCH EIL
SOUND OF ARISAIG
ARISAIG 1:00 (April-Sept)
Chathastail
Druimindarroch
LOCH NAN UAMH CAIRN
Polnish
Arieniskill
Lochailort
Inverailort
Ranochan
Loch Beoraid
Loch Eilt
Loch nan Uamh
Ardnish
Laggan
Alisary
Eilean nan Gobhar
Loch Ailort
Samalaman I.
Glenuig Bay
Roshven
Smirisary
Glenuig
796 SGURR AN UTHA
Glenfinnan Lodge
Glen Finnan
Glen Dubh Lighe
STATION MUSEUM
GLENFINNAN MONUMENT
Glenfinnan
Wauchan
Kinlocheil
Fassfern
Drumsallie
Callop
Guesachan
South Garvan
Duisky
869 DRUIM FIACLACH
882 ROIS-BHEINN
882 BEINN ODHAR BHEAG
666 BEINN GAIRE
755 MEALL NAN CREAG LEAC
Glen Garvan
770 STOB COIRE A'CHEARCAILL
Baramore
Eilean Shona
Eilean Shona Ho
CASTLE TIORAM
Invermoidart
Kinlochmoidart
Ardmolich
Glenmoidart Ho
Gaskan
Scamodale
Rubha Aird Druimnich
Farquhar's Pt.
Ockle Pt.
Cùl Doirlinn
Loch Moidart
Brunery
Gorstanvorran
SGOR AN TARMACHAIN 756
Cona Glen
Fascadale
Kilmory
Ockle
Branault
Ardtoe
Newton of Ardtoe
Shielfoot
Mingarrypark
Langal
Dalnabreck
Dalelia
Polloch
Glen Hurich
Glenhurich
Loch Doilet
786 BEINN MHEADHOIN
Conaglen House
Aryhoulan
Glen Scaddle
357 BEINN BHREAC
Gortenfern
Kentra
Kentra Bay
Blain
Arivegaig
Moss
CLAISH MOSS
Acharacle
Ardshealach
Gorteneorn
Kinlochan
888 SGURR DHOMHNUILL
SGURR NA H-EANCHAINNE 730
401
ARDNAMURCHAN
Loch Mudle
Salen
Resipole
845 BEINN RESIPOL
ARIUNDLE CENTRE
ARIUNDLE OAKWOOD
Ariundle
Chreagain
Glen Gour
701
Ardgour
Clovullin
Corran
Inchree
Bunree
Keppanach
Onich
MINGARY CASTLE
528 BEN HIANT
NADURRA VISITOR CENTRE
490 MEALL NAN EACH
Glenbeg
GLENBORRODALE
Glenborrodale
512 BEN LAGA
Ardery
Scotstown
Anaheilt
Ardnastang
Strontian
885 GARBH BHEINN
Sallachan
Cuilcheanna Ho.
Sallachan Pt.
Maclean's Nose
Ardslignish
Eilean Mor
Laga
Camas Salach
GLENCRIPESDALE
Camuschoirk
Archnalea
Glen Tarbert
Tarbert
Inversanda Bay
Inversanda
Oronsay
Carna
Glencripesdale
516 MEALL AN DAMHAIN
Laudale Ho
Liddesdale
169
Auliston Pt.
Doirlinn
Rahoy
Loch Teacuis
Barr
582 BEINN NAM BEATHRACH
583 CREACH BHEINN
Kentallen
Ardsheal
Glenduror Forest
Greenfield
Duror
Achadh nan Darach
TOBERMORY
TOBERMORY DISTILLERY
Calve I.
Drimnin Ho
Drimnin
Bonnavoulin
Upper Druimfin
Kinloch
571 BEINN IADAIN
Crosben
Gleann Dubh
Lochuisge
Loch Uisge
765 FUAR BHEINN
Kilmalieu
Rubha Mor
Cuil Bay
Eilean Balnagowan
Keil
Salachan Glen
Beach
North Corry
Kingairloch
Camasnacroise
Loch a' Choire
Cloundaid
Loch Arienas
451 BEINN BHUIDHE
550 STITHEAN NA RAPLAICH
739 BEINN MHEADHOIN
Bealach
879 FRAOCHAIDH
Lurignich
Acharn
Gleann Geal
Rhemore
Killundine
Ardnacross
Claggan
Shuna I.
Appin House
Glen Stockdale
655
Elleric
Larachbeg
KINLOCHALINE CASTLE
ARDTORNISH GARDENS
Achranich
Loch Teárnait
437 BEINN A' CHAISIL
Loch nan Clach
Glensanda
Portnacroish
Ardtur
Fasnacloich
Invercreran
KINLOCHLAICH HOUSE GARDENS
BEINN CHURALAIN 546
GLASDRUM WOOD
Glasdrum
Appin
Fiunary
Savary
Lochaline
Loch Aline
Rannoch
Port Ramsay
Port Appin
Strath of Appin
Creagan
Aros Mains
Rubha Mor
Glenaros Ho
GLAIS BHEINN 479
AN SLEAGHACH 513
Eignaig
Clachan
Eriska
North Shian
South Shian
Rudhja Garbh
Loch Creran
South Creagan
Sutherland Grove
Salen
Pennygown
ARDTORNISH CASTLE
Inninbeg
Ardtornish Pt.
Fishnish Bay
Lismore
Balliveolan
Achnacroish
Balure
SCOTTISH SEA LIFE SANCTUARY
Barcaldine
Dalrannoch
Barcaldine Forest
810 CREACH BHEINN
Kellan
Killiechronan
Gruline
Killbeg
Corrynachenchy
Balmeanach
Inninmore Bay
Garbh Shlios
Camas Gorm
Baligrundle
412
Forsa
Garmony
Scallastle Bay
Rubha an Ridire
Bernera I.
Achinduin
Kilcheran
Baravullin
Lochnell Ho
Kiel Crofts
Ferlochan
Gleann Salach
708
Gruline Ho
Knock
Benmore Lodge
Loch Bà
Gaodhail
Alltrech
Scallastle
Java
Craignure Bay
Eilean Dubh
Benderloch
Ledaig
Ardmucknish Bay
Achnacree
Achnaba
ARDCHATTAN PRIORY GARDENS
ARDCHATTAN PRIORY
715 BEINN MHEADHONACH
Cadder
591 BEINN A'GHRAIG
Tomsleibhe
Glen Cannel
Craignure
766 DUN DA GHAOITHE
Duart Bay
Duart Pt.
DUART CASTLE
Dalnarrow
Eilean Musdile
Eilean Mor
Achnacree Bay
North Connel
Black Crofts
FALLS OF LORA
DUNSTAFFNAGE CASTLE
Connel
Bonawe
966 BEN MORE
761 BEINN TALAIDH
Lochdon
Druimsornaig
0:45
CASTLEBAY 4:50 COLL 2:40 TIREE 3:35
Dunbeg
Achnacloich
ACHNACLOICH GARDEN
Muckairn
Stonefield
Achlaven
BONAWE IRON FURNACE
INVERAWE FISHERIES & SMOKERIES EXHIBITION
Inverawe
704 CORRA-BHEINN
Glen More
Lussa
Ishriff
Strathcoil
Loch Don
Grass Pt.
Ganavan
Dunollie
OBAN/OBAN LODGE
MCCAIG'S TOWER
OBAN DISTILLERY
Black Lochs
Fearnoch Forest
Taynuilt
Ichrachan
Bridge of Awe
Balindore
BARGUILLEAN GARDENS
Airdeny
GLEN NANT
Glen Nant
Auchnacraig
248
Altnacraig
Kerrera
Oban
Barranrioch
Balliemore
383
Aird of Kinloch
Loch Airdeglais
BEN BUIE 717
698 CREACH BEINN
Loch Spelve
Glenamachrie
Glen Lonan
Loch Fuaron
Kinlochspelve
Croggan
Rubha nan Sailthean
Bach I.
Ardmore
Gylen Park
Gallanach
Killiechoinich
Loch Nell
Pennycross
Lochbuie
Portfield
Rubha Seanach
Sound of Kerrera
Cologin
Barran
Kilbride
Kilmore
515 BEINN GHLAS
Loch Nant
503 BEINN NA CROISE
Barachandroman
Lochbuie Ho
Loch Uisg
Am Buth
Dunach
Glen Feochan
Kilbride
Glenbyre
Laggan Lodge
Loch Buie
Ardentallen
Loch Feochan
GLENFEOCHAN HOUSE GARDENS
Midmuir
Kilchrenan
Annat
Lower Achachenna
Leidle
Carsaig
405 DRUIM FADA
Kilninver
Knipoch
Musdale
376
Laggan Deer Forest
LORD LOVAT'S CAVE
Rubha Dubh
Carsaig Bay
Barochreal
Glen Euchar
Scammadale
368 A'CHRUACH
Bragleenmore
CARSAIG ARCHES
Frank Lockwood's Island
Insh I.
Ardencaple Ho
CLACHAN BRIDGE
Raera
515 BEINN CHAPULL
Sound of Insh
Clachan-Seil
Seil
AN CALA GARDENS
Clachan
438 CARN DEARG
Fineglen
Inverinan
Ballimeanoch
Easdale
Easdale
EASDALE ISLAND FOLK MUSEUM
Balvicar
Acha
267 CRUACH RAREY
Braes of Lorn
Innie
Loch Tralaig
Blarran
Lochavich Ho
Dussaig
COLONSAY 2:20
Caddleton
Dubh-fheith
Allt Beochlich
A830
A861
A828
A884
A849
A848
A85
A816
B8007
B8043
B8044
B8045
B849
B8035
B8073
B844
B8003
B845
B840
295
290
284
274
275
7
8
9
10
11
A
B
C
D
E
F
G
H
NM

GLEN AFFRIC
KINTAIL
Kintail Forest
Morvich
Glenlicht Ho.
1067 FIVE SISTERS
979 CISTE DHUBH
1032 BEINN FADA OR BEN ATTOW
1151 SGURR NAN CEATHREAMHNAN
Loch a'Bhealaich
Glen Gniomhaidh
Affric Lodge
Glen Affric
Glenaffric Forest
Athnamulloch
Loch Affric
539
Cougie
Guisachan Forest
PLODDA FALLS
Hilton Lodge
Loch a'Mheadhoin
MEALL A' CHRATHAICH 679
Loch ma Stac
Loch nan Eun
Loch a' Chràthaich
Loch na Beinne Bàine
Loch nam Breac Dearga
Balbeg
Grotaig
Foyers
Creaganeun Forest
Alltsigh
LOCH NESS
Levishie Forest
Levishie
Achnaconeran
Invermoriston
FALLS OF MORISTON
INVERNESS 1:20 (May-Dec)
Bhlàraidh
Portclair Forest
Portclair
Loch Knockie
Knockie Lodge
Knockcarrach
Glenbrein Lodge
Dundreggan Forest
680
Dundreggan Lodge
Dundreggan
Torgyle
Inverwick Forest
607 BURACH
GREAT GLEN WAY
Balnacarn
Dalchreichart
Tomchrasky
Ceannacroc Forest
Ceannacroc Lodge
888 AONACH SHASUINN
706 CARN A CHAOCHAIN
1120 A'CHRALAIG
1109 SGURR NAN CONBHAIREAN
1027
1719
GLEN SHIEL
Cluanie Inn
Cluanie Lodge
Lundie
LOCH CLUANIE
SGURR AN LOCHAIN 1004
918
Cluanie Forest
Bun Loyne
Bunloinn Forest
Beinneun Forest
788 MEALL DUBH
Inchnacardoch Hotel
Inchnacardoch Forest
Fort Augustus
CLANSMAN CENTRE
CANAL HERITAGE CENTRE
Auchteraw
Glendoe Lodge
Loch Tarff
Glendoebeg
555
Glen Brein
779 CARN EASGANN BANA
906 SGURR THIONAIL
295
Glen Quoich
Alltbeithe
1021 AONACH AIR CHRITH
1027 SGURR A'MHAORAICH
1035 GLEOURAICH
LOCH LOYNE
Loyne
Glenquoich Forest
540
LOCH QUOICH
Kingie
Aultnaslat
Inchlaggan
Tomdoun
Glen Garry
Garrygualach
Greenfield
Ardochy House
LOCH GARRY
Munerigie
Faichem
Invergarry
Mandally
Bridge of Oich
Caledonian Canal
Newtown
Aberchalder
CARN A'CHUILINN 816
Glendoe Forest
HIGH
Glen Tarff
Culachy Forest
919 GAIRICH
1003
Glen Kingie
556 GLAS BHEINN
Allt Choire a' Bhalachain
North Laggan
LOCH LOCHY
LAGGAN LOCKS
WELLS OF THE SEVEN HEADS
Laggan
901 BEN TEE
Glengarry Forest
Kilfinnan
884 CARN LEAC
Corrieyairack Forest
896 GAIRBEINN
815 CARN DEARG
Melgarve
656 MEALL BLAIR
Loch Blàir
880 SGURR MHURLAGAIN
858
804 GEAL CHARN
935 SRON A'CHOIRE GHAIRBH
Drummin
Murlaggan
Strathan
LOCH ARKAIG
Ardechvie
636
Letterfinlay
Annat
Brae Roy Lodge
Glen Roy
CARN LIATH 1006
Aberarder Forest
Gleann Camgharadh
727
Locheil Forest
Inver Mallie
Achnasaul
B8005
Clunes Forest
Clunes
Altrua
Glen Gloy
PARALLEL ROADS
Upper Glenfintaig
834 CARN DEARG
987 GAOR BHEINN
Glen Mallie
Achnacarry
Bunarkaig
Glenfintaig Ho.
684
GLEN ROY
1128 CREAG MEAGAIDH
CREAG MEAGAIDH
Aberarder
Achnanellan
796 BEINN BHAN
CLAN CAMERON MUSEUM
Gairlochy
Stronaba
654 COIRE CEIRSLE HILL
915
Glas Dhoire
1049 BEINN A' CHAORUINN
Moy Forest
Glen Loy
Gleann Suileag
Kilmonivaig
COMMANDO MEMORIAL
Bohuntine
Bohuntinville
Bohenie
Moy
Moy Lodge
LOCH LAGGAN
Wauchan
Druim Fada
Glen Loy Forest
Brackletter
Highbridge
Spean Bridge
Inverroy
Roybridge
Achluachrach
Murlaggan
Roughburn
Strone
Muirshearlich
Aonachan
Altour
Killiechonate
Bunroy
A86
Braes o' Lochaber
Tulloch
Achindaul
MONESSIE FALLS
GLEN SPEAN
Kinlocheil
Fassfern
Loch Eil
A830
TREASURES OF THE EARTH
B8004
TOR CASTLE
Leanachan
Leanachan Forest
LOCH EIL
South Garvan
Duisky
Blaich
A861
Corpach
Banavie
NEPTUNE'S STAIRCASE LOCKS
Torlundy
Creag Aoil
NEVIS RANGE SKI CENTRE
724 BEINN CHLIANAIG
Fersit
1087 BEINN A'CHLACHAIR
Caol
Camaghael
Lochyside
Achaphubuil
Camusnagaul
INVERLOCHY CASTLE
Inverlochy
BEN NEVIS DISTILLERY VISITOR CENTRE
Claggan
Trislaig
Fort William
Achintee
WEST HIGHLAND MUSEUM
GLEN NEVIS VISITOR CENTRE
GLEN NEVIS
Ach'an Todhair
Glen Nevis House
289
Stronchreggan
770 STOB COIRE A'CHEARCAILL
Goirtean a'Chladaich
Druimarbin
1344 BEN NEVIS
1234 AONACH BEAG
1094
1106
1177 STOB CHOIRE CLAURIGH
1115 STOB COIRE EASAIN
Bothy
Lairig Leacach
LOCH TREIG
1046 CHNO DEARG
Loch Ghuilbinn
1114 AONACH BEAG
1148 BEN ALDER
Conaglen House
Aryhoulan
Inverscaddle Bay
Coruanan Lodge
Blarmachfoldach
Achriabhach
Water of Nevis
BEN NEVIS AND MAMORE FOREST GLEN COE
Creaguaineach Lodge
Luibeilt
Amhainn Rath
937 BEINN NA LAP
Corrour Shooting Lodge
LOCH OSSIAN
Corrour Forest
Prince Charlie's Cave
Lundavra
Blar a'Chaorainn
1099 SGURR A' MHAIM
1130 BINNEIN MOR
630
Corrour
583
952 SGOR GAIBHRE
SGURR NA H-EANCHAINNE 730
616 BEINN NA GUCAIG
Loch Eilde Beag
Glenrigh Forest
WEST HIGHLAND WAY
789
Loch Eilde Mor
906 LEUM UILLEIM
Rannoch Forest
Ardgour
Clovullin
Corran
Corran Narrows
Inchree
Sallachan
Bunree
Keppanach
Onich
Kinlochmore
796 MAM NA GUALAINN
Kinlochleven
THE ALUMINIUM STORY
Sallachan Pt.
Cuilcheanna Ho.
North Ballachulish
Callert Ho.
615
B863
Caolasnacon
Leven
BLACKWATER RESERVOIR
Black Water
867
284
285
NORTH LORN MUSEUM
Glencoe
AONACH EAGACH 967
953
Rannoch Station
B846
0 2 4 6 miles
0 2 4 6 8 10 km
Kentallen
Ardsheal
Glenduror Forest
Greenfield
Duror
Achadh nan Darach
947
GLENCOE
GLENCOE VISITOR CENTRE
Glen a' Chaolais Fhiodh
Glen Coe
Altnafeadh
BEINN A' CHRULAISTE 857
Black Corries Lodge
STOB NA CRUAICHE 739
Loch Eigheach
A82
A87
A887
300
299
NH
NN

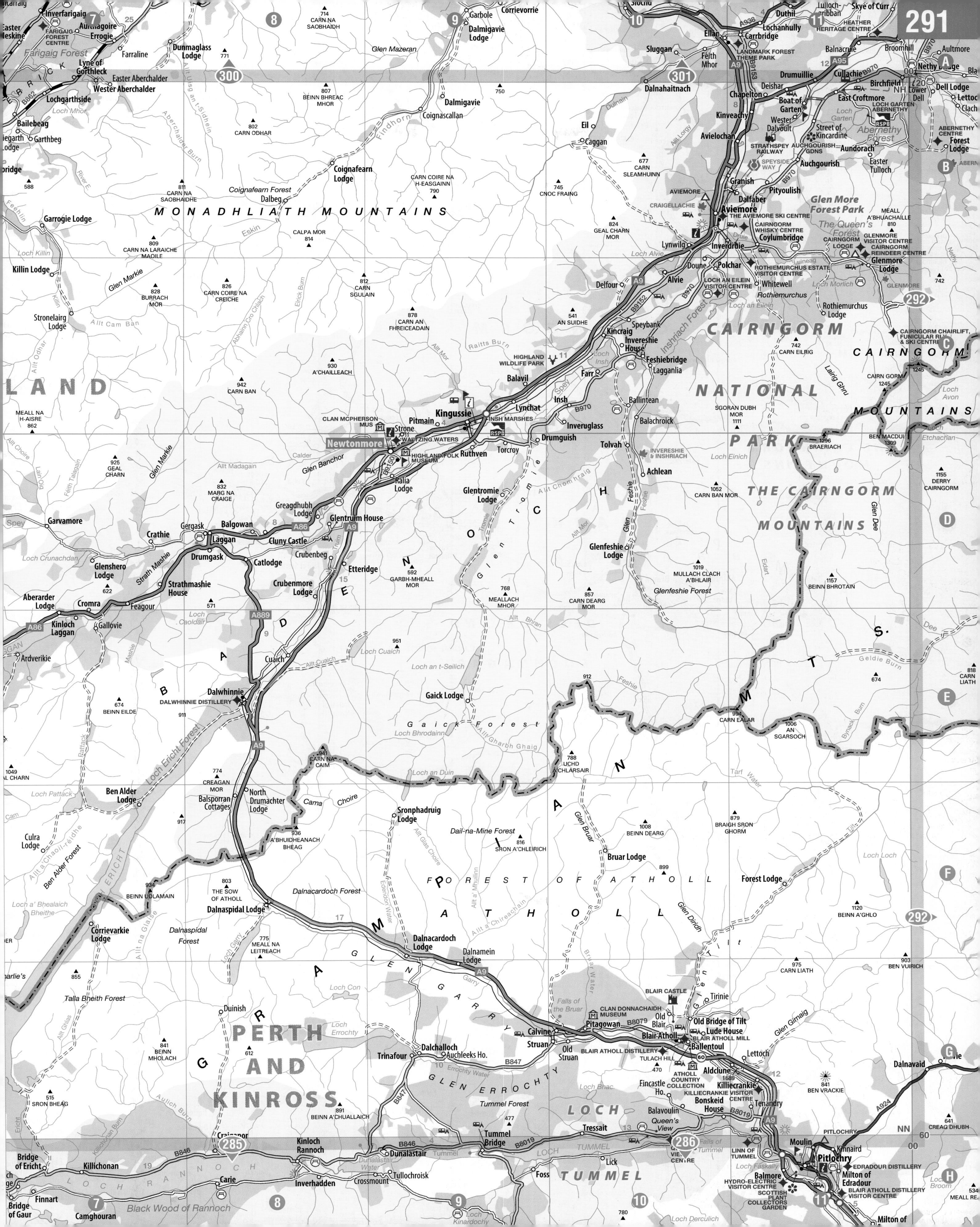

Inverfarigaig
Foyers
Aultnagoire
Errogie
Farigaig Forest
Farraline
Dunmaglass Lodge
Lyne of Gorthleck
Easter Aberchalder
Wester Aberchalder
Lochgarthside
Loch Mhor
Bailebeag
Garthbeg
Garbole
Corrievorrie
Dalmigavie Lodge
Glen Mazeran
Dalmigavie
Coignascallan
Findhorn
Coignafearn Lodge
Coignafearn Forest
Dalbeg
MONADHLIATH MOUNTAINS
Garrogie Lodge
Loch Killin
Killin Lodge
Glen Markie
Stronelairg Lodge
Carrbridge
Ellan
Sluggan
Feith Mhor
Dalnahaitnach
Lochanhully
Dulnain Bridge
Skye of Curr
Heather Heritage Centre
Landmark Forest Theme Park
Balnacruie
Broomhill
Aultmore
Nethy Bridge
Drumuillie
Cullachie
Deishar
Chapelton
Boat of Garten
Birchfield
Dell Lodge
Kinveachy
East Croftmore
Loch Garten
Abernethy
Wester Dalvoult
Street of Kincardine
Abernethy Forest
Avielochan
Strathspey Railway
Auchgourish Gdns
Aundorach
Forest Lodge
Auchgourish
Easter Tulloch
Eil
Caggan
Carn Sleamhuinn
Cnoc Fraing
Granish
Dalfaber
Pityoulish
Aviemore
Craigellachie
Glen More Forest Park
The Aviemore Ski Centre
Cairngorm Whisky Centre
Coylumbridge
The Queen's Forest
Glenmore Visitor Centre
Cairngorm Reindeer Centre
Glenmore Lodge
Lynwilg
Inverdruie
Loch Alvie
Doune
Polchar
Rothiemurchus Estate Visitor Centre
Alvie
Whitewell
Loch an Eilein Visitor Centre
Delfour
Rothiemurchus
Loch Morlich
Rothiemurchus Lodge
Cairngorm Chairlift, Funicular Railway & Ski Centre
Kincraig
Speyside
Invereshie House
Feshiebridge
Lagganlia
Inshriach Forest
CAIRNGORM
Carn Eilrig
CAIRNGORM MOUNTAINS
Highland Wildlife Park
Balavil
Farr
Insh
NATIONAL PARK
Lynchat
Kingussie
Pitmain
Clan McPherson Mus
Strone
Waltzing Waters
Newtonmore
Highland Folk Museum
Insh Marshes
Ruthven
Torcroy
Drumguish
Inveruglass
Ballintean
Balachroick
Tolvah
Achlean
Invereshie & Inshriach
Sgoran Dubh Mor
Braeriach
Ben Macdui
Derry Cairngorm
Carn Ban Mor
THE CAIRNGORM MOUNTAINS
Glen Dee
Glentromie Lodge
Glen Tromie
Glen Feshie
Glenfeshie Lodge
Mullach Clach a' Bhlair
Glenfeshie Forest
Beinn Bhrotain
Carn Dearg Mor
Meallach Mhor
Garbh-mheall Mor
Glen Banchor
Ralia Lodge
Geal Charn
Marg na Craige
Garvamore
Crathie
Gergask
Laggan
Balgowan
Greagdhubh Lodge
Glentruim House
Cluny Castle
Crubenbeg
Drumgask
Catlodge
Etteridge
Glenshero Lodge
Strath Mashie
Strathmashie House
Crubenmore Lodge
Aberarder Lodge
Cromra
Feagour
Kinloch Laggan
Gallovie
Loch Caoldair
Ardverikie
Cuaich
Loch Cuaich
Loch an t-Seilich
Gaick Lodge
Gaick Forest
Loch Bhrodainn
Dalwhinnie
Dalwhinnie Distillery
Beinn Eilde
Loch Ericht Forest
Carn na Caim
Loch an Duin
An Sgarsoch
Carn Ealar
Ben Alder Lodge
Loch Pattack
Balsporran Cottages
North Drumachter Lodge
Cama Choire
Sronphadruig Lodge
Dail-na-Mine Forest
Beinn Dearg
Bruar Lodge
Braigh Sron Ghorm
Culra Lodge
Ben Alder Forest
Loch a' Bhealaich Bheithe
Beinn Udlamain
The Sow of Atholl
Dalnaspidal Lodge
Dalnacardoch Forest
FOREST OF ATHOLL
Forest Lodge
Beinn a' Ghlo
Corrievarkie Lodge
Dalnaspidal Forest
Meall na Leitreach
Dalnacardoch Lodge
Dalnamein Lodge
Glen Garry
Carn Liath
Ben Vuirich
Loch Con
Talla Bheith Forest
Duinish
Falls of the Bruar
Clan Donnachaidh Museum
Blair Castle
Tirinie
Pitagowan
Old Blair
Old Bridge of Tilt
Lude House
Blair Atholl
Blair Atholl Mill
Calvine
Struan
Old Struan
Blair Atholl Distillery
Tulach Hill
Ballentoul
Lettoch
Glen Girnaig
Dalnavaird
PERTH AND KINROSS
Beinn Mholach
Loch Errochty
Dalchalloch
Auchleeks Ho.
Trinafour
Glen Errochty
Atholl Country Collection
Aldclune
Killiecrankie
Killiecrankie Visitor Centre
Fincastle Ho.
Bonskeid House
Tenandry
Ben Vrackie
Sron Bheag
Beinn a' Chuallaich
Tummel Forest
Balavoulin
Loch Tummel
Tressait
Queen's View
Craiganour
Kinloch Rannoch
Dunalastair
Tummel Bridge
Pitlochry
Moulin
Kinnaird
Creag Dhubh
Bridge of Ericht
Killichonan
Loch Rannoch
Carie
Dunalastair Water
Tullochroisk
Crossmount
Inverhadden
Lick
Foss
Linn of Tummel
Edradour Distillery
Milton of Edradour
Balmore
Hydro-Electric Visitor Centre
Scottish Plant Collectors Garden
Blair Atholl Distillery Visitor Centre
Finnart
Bridge of Gaur
Camghouran
Black Wood of Rannoch
Loch Kinardochy
Loch Derculich
Milton of

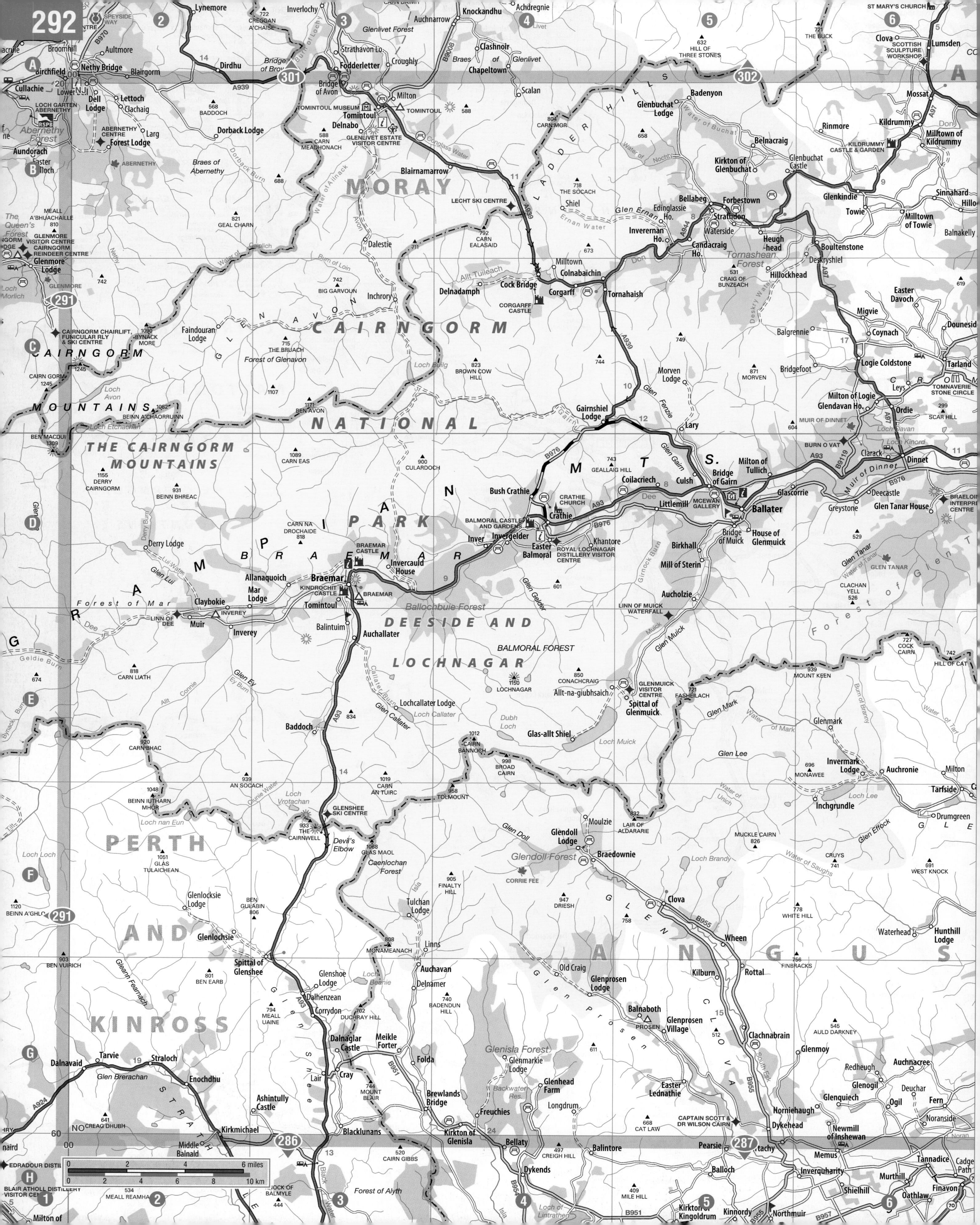

MORAY
CAIRNGORM
NATIONAL
PARK
CAIRNGORM MOUNTAINS
THE CAIRNGORM MOUNTAINS
GRAMPIAN MTS.
BRAEMAR
DEESIDE AND LOCHNAGAR
PERTH AND KINROSS
ANGUS
LADDER HILLS
GLEN CLOVA
STRATH
Lynemore
Inverlochy
Knockandhu
Achdregnie
ST MARY'S CHURCH
Broomhill
Aultmore
Nethy Bridge
Birchfield
Blairgorm
Dirdhu
Bridge of Brown
Strathavon Lo.
Fodderletter
Croughly
Braes of Glenlivet
Clashnoir
Chapeltown
Glenlivet Forest
Auchnarrow
Scalan
Bridge of Avon
Milton
Tomintoul
TOMINTOUL MUSEUM
Delnabo
GLENLIVET ESTATE VISITOR CENTRE
Cullachie
Lower Dell
Dell Lodge
Lettoch
Clachaig
LOCH GARTEN ABERNETHY
RSPB
Abernethy Forest
ABERNETHY CENTRE
Forest Lodge
Larg
Dorback Lodge
Aundorach
Easter Tulloch
Braes of Abernethy
Dorback Burn
568 BADDOCH
588 CARN MEADHONACH
588
Blairnamarrow
Conglass Water
Water of Ailnack
Avon
Dalestie
LECHT SKI CENTRE
792 CARN EALASAID
804 CARN MOR
718 THE SOCACH
Shiel
Glen Ernan
Ernan Water
Edinglassie Ho.
Inverernan Ho.
Badenyon
Glenbuchat Lodge
Water of Buchat
Belnacraig
Kirkton of Glenbuchat
Glenbuchat Castle
Bellabeg
Forbestown
Strathdon
Waterside
Candacraig Ho.
Heugh-head
Tornashean Forest
Boultenstone
Deskryshiel
Hillockhead
531 CRAIG OF BUNZEACH
632 HILL OF THREE STONES
721 THE BUCK
Clova
SCOTTISH SCULPTURE WORKSHOP
Lumsden
Mossat
Rinmore
Kildrummy
KILDRUMMY CASTLE & GARDEN
Milltown of Kildrummy
Glenkindie
Towie
Milltown of Towie
Sinnahard
Balnakelly
Easter Davoch
Migvie
Coynach
Balgrennie
Logie Coldstone
Tarland
Bridgefoot
Leys
TOMNAVERIE STONE CIRCLE
Milton of Logie
Glendavan Ho.
Ordie
299 SCAR HILL
MUIR OF DINNET
BURN O VAT
Clarack
Dinnet
Loch Kinord
Loch Davan
Muir of Dinnet
Deecastle
Glen Tanar House
BRAELOIN INTERPRETIVE CENTRE
Greystone
Glascorrie
Milton of Tullich
Bridge of Gairn
Cullsh
Ballater
MCEWAN GALLERY
House of Glenmuick
Bridge of Muick
Birkhall
Mill of Sterin
Aucholzie
LINN OF MUICK WATERFALL
Glen Muick
GLENMUICK VISITOR CENTRE
Spittal of Glenmuick
Allt-na-giubhsaich
Loch Muick
Glas-allt Shiel
850 CONACHCRAIG
1150 LOCHNAGAR
Dubh Loch
BALMORAL FOREST
Ballochbuie Forest
Glen Gelder
Girnock Burn
Khantore
ROYAL LOCHNAGAR DISTILLERY VISITOR CENTRE
Easter Balmoral
BALMORAL CASTLE AND GARDENS
Crathie
CRATHIE CHURCH
Bush Crathie
Inver
Invergelder
Coilacriech
Littlemill
743 GEALLAIG HILL
Glen Gairn
Gairnshiel Lodge
Lary
Glen Fenzie
Morven Lodge
871 MORVEN
749
744
604
Milltown
Colnabaichin
Cock Bridge
Corgarff
CORGARFF CASTLE
Tornahaish
Delnadamph
Allt Tuileach
673
Inchrory
742 BIG GARVOUN
Burn of Loin
Glen Avon
Faindouran Lodge
715 THE BRUACH
Forest of Glenavon
Loch Builg
823 BROWN COW HILL
1107
1171 BEN AVON
1090 BYNACK MORE
CAIRNGORM CHAIRLIFT, FUNICULAR RLY & SKI CENTRE
CAIRN GORM 1245
Loch Avon
BEINN A'CHAORRUINN
Loch Etchachan
BEN MACDUI 1309
1155 DERRY CAIRNGORM
931 BEINN BHREAC
1089 CARN EAS
900 CULARDOCH
CARN NA DROCHAIDE 818
Derry Lodge
Lui Water
Glen Lui
Allanaquoich
Mar Lodge
Braemar
BRAEMAR CASTLE
KINDROCHIT CASTLE
Invercauld House
Claybokie
Forest of Mar
LINN OF DEE
Muir
INVEREY
Inverey
Tomintoul
Balintuim
Auchallater
Dee
Geldie Burn
818 CARN LIATH
Glen Ey
Ey Burn
Allt Connie
Callater Burn
Lochcallater Lodge
Loch Callater
Glen Callater
Baddoch
834
920 CARN BHAC
939 AN SOCACH
1048 BEINN IUTHARN MHOR
Loch nan Eun
Baddoch Burn
Loch Vrotachan
1019 CARN AN TUIRC
958 TOLMOUNT
1012 CAIRN BANNOCH
998 BROAD CAIRN
GLENSHEE SKI CENTRE
933 THE CAIRNWELL
Devil's Elbow
1068 GLAS MAOL
Caenlochan Forest
1051 GLAS TULAICHEAN
Loch Loch
1120 BEINN A'GHLO
BEN GULABIN 806
Glenlocksie Lodge
Glenlochsie
Spittal of Glenshee
903 BEN VUIRICH
Gleann Fearnach
801 BEN EARB
794 MEALL UAINE
Glenshoe Lodge
Dalhenzean
Corrydon
702 DUCHRAY HILL
Glen Shee
Dalnaglar Castle
Lair
Cray
744 MOUNT BLAIR
Dalnavaid
Tarvie
Straloch
Glen Brerachan
Enochdhu
Ashintully Castle
641 CREAG DHUBH
Kirkmichael
Middle Bainald
Blacklunans
520 CAIRN GIBBS
EDRADOUR DISTILLERY
534 MEALL REAMHAR
BLAIR ATHOLL DISTILLERY VISITOR CENTRE
Milton of
Forest of Alyth
KNOCK OF BALMYLE 444
Black Water
905 FINALTY HILL
Tulchan Lodge
Isla
808 MONAMEANACH
Linns
Auchavan
Delnamer
740 BADENDUN HILL
Meikle Forter
Folda
Brewlands Bridge
Kirkton of Glenisla
Freuchies
Glenisla Forest
Glenmarkie Lodge
Glenhead Farm
Backwater Res.
Longdrum
Bellaty
497 CREIGH HILL
Balintore
Dykends
Loch of Lintrathen
Glendoll Lodge
Glen Doll
Glendoll Forest
CORRIE FEE
Braedownie
Moulzie
832 LAIR OF ALDARARIE
947 DRIESH
758
Clova
Old Craig
Glen Prosen
Glenprosen Lodge
Balnaboth
PROSEN
Glenprosen Village
611
512
Wheen
Kilburn
Rottal
Clachnabrain
South Esk
Easter Lednathie
CAPTAIN SCOTT & DR WILSON CAIRN
668 CAT LAW
Pearsie
Dykehead
Balloch
409 MILE HILL
Kirkton of Kingoldrum
Kinnordy
Northmuir
Loch Brandy
MUCKLE CAIRN 826
778 WHITE HILL
756 FINBRACKS
545 AULD DARKNEY
Glenmoy
Redheugh
Glenogil
Auchnacree
Glenquiech
Deuchar
Ogil
Fern
Noranside
Hornieheugh
Newmill of Inshewan
Memus
Inverquharity
Tannadice
Murthill
Shielhill
Finavon
Oathlaw
Cadger Path
Waterhead
Hunthill Lodge
691 WEST KNOCK
741 CRUYS
Water of Saughs
Glen Effock
Drumgreen
Inchgrundle
Loch Lee
Tarfside
Invermark Lodge
Auchronie
Milton
696 MONAWEE
Glenmark
Glen Lee
Water of Mark
Water of Unich
Burn of Branny
939 MOUNT KEEN
721 FASHEILACH
727 COCK CAIRN
742 HILL OF CAT
Forest of Glen Tanar
CLACHAN YELL 526
GLEN TANAR
Glen Tanar
529
619
Douneside
722 CREGGAN A'CHAISE
SPEYSIDE WAY
Glenmore Lodge
GLENMORE VISITOR CENTRE
CAIRNGORM REINDEER CENTRE
The Queen's Forest
MEALL A'BHUACHAILLE 810
821 GEAL CHARN
688
742
711
658
Loch Morlich
A939
A944
A97
A93
B976
B9119
B970
B9008
B955
B951
B954
A924
0 2 4 6 miles
0 2 4 6 8 10 km

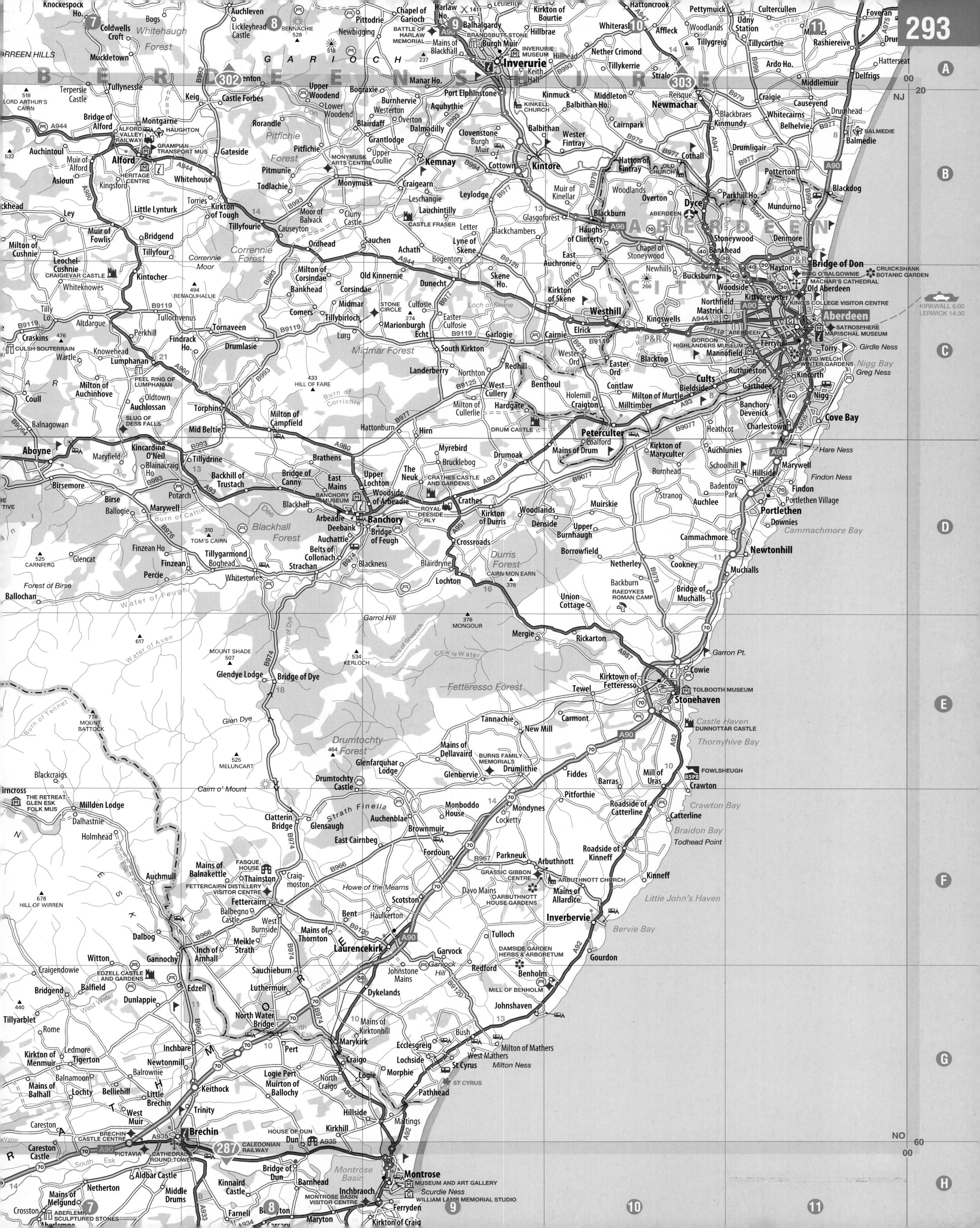

Knockespock Ho.
Coldwells Croft
Whitehaugh Forest
Auchleven
Lickleyhead Castle
BENNACHIE 528
Chapel of Garioch
Pittodrie
Newbigging
Harlaw Ho.
BATTLE OF HARLAW MEMORIAL
Balhalgardy
BRANDSBUTT STONE
Burgh Muir
Kirkton of Bourtie
Hillbrae
Hattoncrook
Whiterashes
Pettymuick
Woodlands
Tillygreig
Udny Station
Cultercullen
Tillycorthie
Foveran
Minnes
Rashierieve
Hatterseat
Delfrigs
Muckletown
G A R I O C H
B E R D E E N S H I R E
Inverurie
INVERURIE MUSEUM
Keith Hall
Mains of Blackhall
Manar Ho.
Nether Crimond
Tillykerrie
Stralochy
Ardo Ho.
Middlemuir
Terpersie Castle
Tullynessle
Keig
Castle Forbes
Upper Woodend
Bograxie
Lower Woodend
Port Elphinstone
Kinmuck
Middleton
Balbithan Ho.
Reisque
Newmachar
Craigie
Causeyend
Drumhead
LORD ARTHUR'S CAIRN
Bridge of Alford
Montgarrie
ALFORD VALLEY RAILWAY
HAUGHTON
GRAMPIAN TRANSPORT MUS
Alford
HERITAGE CENTRE
Burnhervie
Westerton
Overton
Aquhythie
Rorandle
Blairdaff
Dalmadilly
KINKELL CHURCH
Balbithan
Cloveston
Burgh Muir
Wester Fintray
Cairnpark
Blackbraes
Kinmundy
Whitecairns
Belhelvie
Balmedie
BALMEDIE
Pitfichie
Grantlodge
Auchintoul
Muir of Alford
Asloun
Kingsford
Gateside
Whitehouse
Pitfichie Forest
Pitmunie
Upper Coullie
MONYMUSK ARTS CENTRE
Kemnay
Cottown
Kintore
Hatton of Fintray
OLD CHURCH
Cothall
Drumligair
Potterton
Corby Loch
Blackdog
Todlachie
Monymusk
Craigearn
Leylodge
Muir of Kinellar
Woodlands
Overton
Dyce
Parkhill Ho.
Mundurno
Ley
Little Lynturk
Torries
Kirkton of Tough
Tillyfourie
Causeyton
Moor of Balvack
Cluny Castle
Leschangie
Lauchintilly
CASTLE FRASER
Letter
Glasgoforest
Blackburn
ABERDEEN
Stoneywood
Denmore
A B E R D E E N C I T Y
Muir of Fowlis
Bridgend
Tillyfour
Milton of Cushnie
Corrennie Forest
Corrennie Moor
Leochel-Cushnie
CRAIGIEVAR CASTLE
Ordhead
Sauchen
Achath
Lyne of Skene
Blackchambers
Haughs of Clinterty
Chapel of Stoneywood
Bankhead
East Auchronie
Newhills
Bucksburn
Hayton
Bridge of Don
CRUICKSHANK BOTANIC GARDEN
BRIG O' BALGOWNIE
ST MACHAR'S CATHEDRAL
Old Aberdeen
Woodside
Kittybrewster
KING'S COLLEGE VISITOR CENTRE
Kintocher
494 BENAQUHALLIE
Whiteknowes
Milton of Corsindae
Old Kinnernie
Bogentory
Dunecht
Skene Ho.
Kirkton of Skene
Northfield
Mastrick
Aberdeen
KIRKWALL 6:00
LERWICK 14:30
Corsindae
Bankhead
Midmar
STONE CIRCLE
Culfosie
Loch of Skene
Westhill
Kingswells
SATROSPHERE
MARISCHAL MUSEUM
Tilly Lo.
Tullochvenus
Comers
Tillybirloch
Marionburgh
Easter Culfosie
Echt
Garlogie
Cairnie
Elrick
GORDON HIGHLANDERS MUSEUM
Ferryhill
Torry
Girdle Ness
Altdargue
Craskins
Perkhill
Tornaveen
Lurg
South Kirkton
Wester Ord
Easter Ord
Blacktop
Mannofield
DAVID WELCH WINTER GARDENS
Nigg Bay
Greg Ness
CULSH SOUTERRAIN
Wartle
Knowehead
Lumphanan
Findrack Ho.
Drumlasie
Midmar Forest
Landerberry
Northton
Redhill
Kincorth
PEEL RING OF LUMPHANAN
433 HILL OF FARE
West Cullery
Benthoul
Contlaw
Cults
Bieldside
Ruthrieston
Garthdee
Nigg
Coull
Milton of Auchinhove
Oldtown
Auchlossan
Burn of Corrichie
Milton of Cullerlie
Hardgate
Holemill
Craigton
Milton of Murtle
Milltimber
Banchory-Devenick
Cove Bay
Balnagowan
SLUG OF DESS FALLS
Torphins
Mid Beltie
Milton of Campfield
Hattonburn
Hirn
DRUM CASTLE
Peterculter
Coalford
Heathcot
Charlestown
Aboyne
Maryfield
Kincardine O'Neil
Tillydrine
Blainacraig Ho
Brathens
Myrebird
Bricklebog
Drumoak
Mains of Drum
Kirkton of Maryculter
Auchlunies
Hare Ness
Birsemore
Backhill of Trustach
Bridge of Canny
East Mains
Upper Lochton
The Neuk
CRATHES CASTLE AND GARDENS
Burnhead
Schoolhill
Marywell
Hillside
Findon Ness
Findon
Potarch
BANCHORY MUSEUM
Woodside of Arbeadie
Badentoy Park
Stranog
Auchlee
Portlethen Village
Portlethen
Birse
Ballogie
Marywell
Blackhall
Arbeadie
Banchory
ROYAL DEESIDE RLY
Crathes
Kirkton of Durris
Woodlands
Denside
Muirskie
Downies
Burn of Cattie
Blackhall Forest
310 TOM'S CAIRN
Deebank
Auchattie
Bridge of Feugh
Crossroads
Upper Burnhaugh
Cammachmore
Cammachmore Bay
Finzean Ho
Tillygarmond
Boghead
Belts of Collonach
Durris Forest
Borrowfield
Newtonhill
525 CARNFERG
Glencat
Finzean
Percie
Whitestone
Strachan
Blackness
Blairdryne
CAIRN-MON EARN 378
Lochton
Netherley
Cookney
Muchalls
Forest of Birse
Ballochan
Water of Feugh
Backburn
RAEDYKES ROMAN CAMP
Bridge of Muchalls
Union Cottage
Garrol Hill
376 MONGOUR
Mergie
Rickarton
Garron Pt.
617
MOUNT SHADE 507
534 KERLOCH
Cowie Water
Cowie
Glendye Lodge
Bridge of Dye
Fetteresso Forest
Kirktown of Fetteresso
Tewel
TOLBOOTH MUSEUM
Stonehaven
Burn of Tennet
778 MOUNT BATTOCK
Glen Dye
Tannachie
New Mill
Carmont
Castle Haven
DUNNOTTAR CASTLE
Thornyhive Bay
Drumtochty Forest
464
525 MELUNCART
Mains of Dellavaird
BURNS FAMILY MEMORIALS
Glenbervie
Drumlithie
Fiddes
Barras
Mill of Uras
FOWLSHEUGH
RSPB
Crawton
Blackcraigs
Glenfarquhar Lodge
Drumtochty Castle
Cairn o' Mount
Pitforthie
THE RETREAT GLEN ESK FOLK MUS
Millden Lodge
Dalhastnie
Strath Finella
Monboddo House
Mondynes
Cocketty
Roadside of Catterline
Catterline
Crawton Bay
Holmhead
Clatterin Bridge
Glensaugh
Auchenblae
Brownmuir
Braidon Bay
Todhead Point
East Cairnbeg
Fordoun
Parkneuk
Arbuthnott
Roadside of Kinneff
Auchmull
Mains of Balnakettle
FASQUE HOUSE
Thainston
Craigmoston
GRASSIC GIBBON CENTRE
ARBUTHNOTT CHURCH
Kinneff
FETTERCAIRN DISTILLERY VISITOR CENTRE
Howe of the Mearns
Davo Mains
ARBUTHNOTT HOUSE GARDENS
Mains of Allardice
678 HILL OF WIRREN
Fettercairn
Balbegno Castle
Scotston
Little John's Haven
West Burnside
Bent
Haulkerton
Inverbervie
Dalbog
Mains of Thornton
Tulloch
Bervie Bay
Inch of Arnhall
Meikle Strath
Laurencekirk
Garvock
DAMSIDE GARDEN HERBS & ARBORETUM
Witton
Gannochy
Garvock Hill
Redford
Benholm
Gourdon
Craigendowie
EDZELL CASTLE AND GARDENS
Sauchieburn
Johnstone Mains
Bridgend
Balfield
Edzell
Luthermuir
Dykelands
MILL OF BENHOLM
Dunlappie
Johnshaven
440
Tillyarblet
North Water Bridge
Mains of Kirktonhill
Rome
Inchbare
Pert
Marykirk
Bush
Ecclesgreig
Milton of Mathers
West Mathers
Milton Ness
Kirkton of Menmuir
Ledmore
Tigerton
Newtonmill
Balrownie
Craigo
Logie Pert
Muirton of Ballochy
Lochside
St Cyrus
Balnamoon
Mains of Balhall
Lochty
Belliehill
Little Brechin
Keithock
North Craigo
Logie
Morphie
ST CYRUS
Pathhead
West Muir
Trinity
Hillside
Careston
Brechin
HOUSE OF DUN
Dun
Kirkhill
Maltings
BRECHIN CASTLE CENTRE
PICTAVIA
CATHEDRAL ROUND TOWER
CALEDONIAN RAILWAY
Careston Castle
Aldbar Castle
Bridge of Dun
Montrose Basin
Barnhead
Montrose
MUSEUM AND ART GALLERY
Scurdie Ness
Netherton
Mains of Melgund
Middle Drums
Kinnaird Castle
Inchbraoch
MONTROSE BASIN VISITOR CENTRE
WILLIAM LAMB MEMORIAL STUDIO
Crosston
ABERLEMNO SCULPTURED STONES
Farnell
Ferryden
Maryton
Kirkton of Craig
A B C D E F G H
NJ
NO
7 8 9 10 11
302
303
287

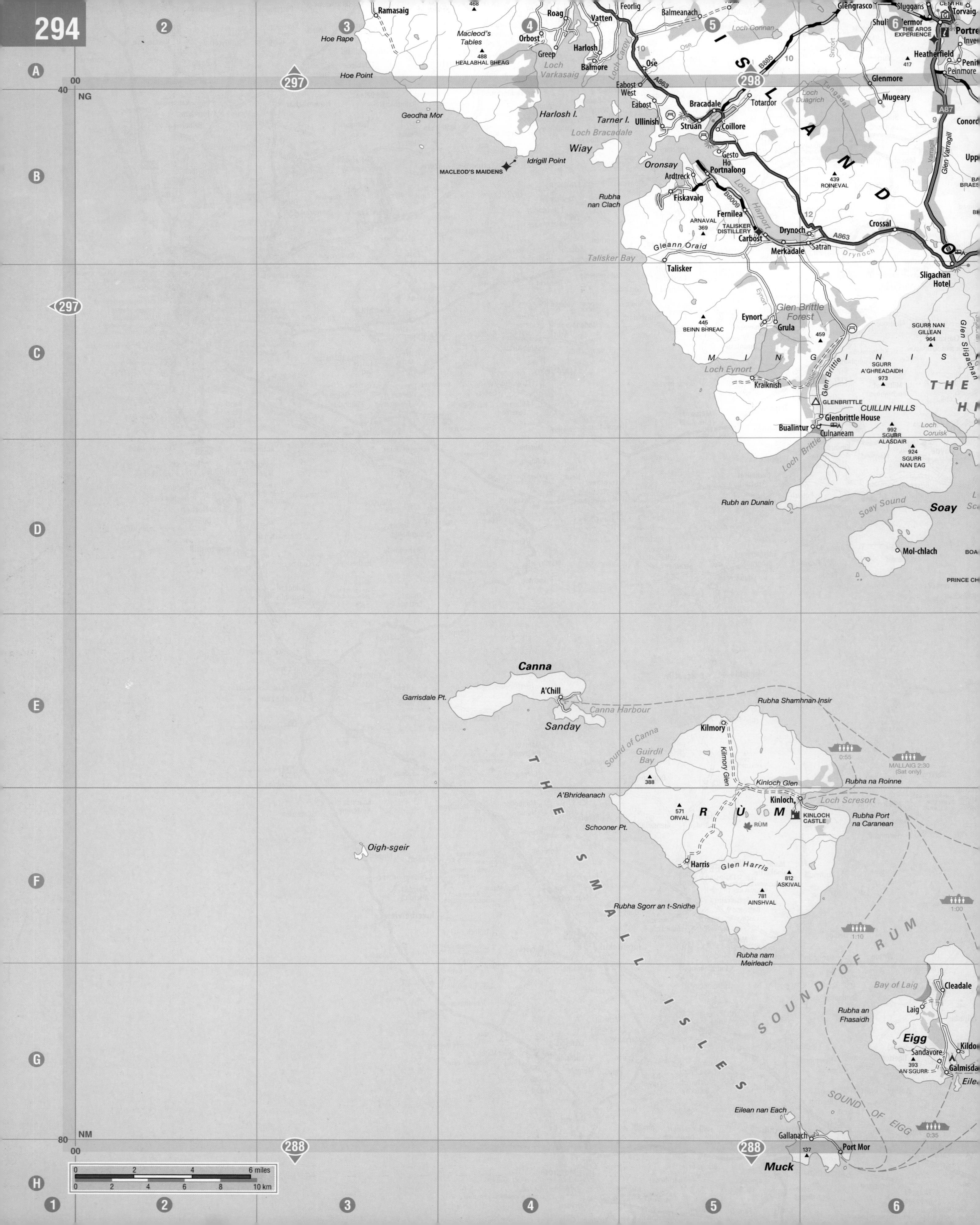
Ramasaig
Hoe Rape
Hoe Point
Macleod's Tables
488
HEALABHAL BHEAG
Roag
Orbost
Greep
Loch Varkasaig
Vatten
Harlosh
Balmore
Feorlig
Balmeanach
Loch Connan
Loch Caroy
Ose
Eabost West
Eabost
A863
B885
298
297
I S L A N D
Glengrasco
Sluggans
Torvaig
Portree
THE AROS EXPERIENCE
Heatherfield
Penifiler
Peinmore
417
Glenmore
Mugeary
Loch Duagrich
Tungadal
Totardor
Bracadale
Coillore
Struan
Ullinish
Tarner I.
Harlosh I.
Geodha Mor
Loch Bracadale
Wiay
Idrigill Point
MACLEOD'S MAIDENS
Oronsay
Gesto
Ho
Portnalong
Ardtreck
Fiskavaig
Rubha nan Clach
B8009
Loch Harport
Fernilea
ARNAVAL
369
TALISKER DISTILLERY
Carbost
Drynoch
Merkadale
Satran
A863
Crossal
439
ROINEVAL
A87
Conordan
Glen Varragill
Sligachan Hotel
Gleann Oraid
Talisker Bay
Talisker
Eynort
Glen Brittle Forest
Eynort
Grula
445
BEINN BHREAC
459
SGURR NAN GILLEAN
964
Glen Sligachan
M I N G I N I S
SGURR A' GHREADAIDH
973
THE
Loch Eynort
Kraiknish
Glen Brittle
GLENBRITTLE
Glenbrittle House
CUILLIN HILLS
Bualintur
Culnaneam
992
SGURR ALASDAIR
Loch Coruisk
924
SGURR NAN EAG
Loch Brittle
Rubh an Dunain
Soay Sound
Soay
Mol-chlach
PRINCE CH
Canna
A'Chill
Garrisdale Pt.
Canna Harbour
Sanday
Rubha Shamhnan Insir
Kilmory
Sound of Canna
Guirdil Bay
Kilmory Glen
0:55
MALLAIG 2:30 (Sat only)
388
Kinloch Glen
Rubha na Roinne
A'Bhrideanach
Kinloch
Loch Scresort
571
ORVAL
R Ù M
RÙM
KINLOCH CASTLE
Rubha Port na Caranean
Schooner Pt.
Oigh-sgeir
Harris
Glen Harris
812
ASKIVAL
781
AINSHVAL
Rubha Sgorr an t-Snidhe
1:00
1:10
Rubha nam Meirleach
SOUND OF RÙM
THE SMALL ISLES
Bay of Laig
Cleadale
Rubha an Fhasaidh
Laig
Eigg
Sandavore
393
AN SGURR
Galmisdale
SOUND OF EIGG
0:35
Eilean nan Each
Gallanach
Port Mor
137
Muck
288
NG
NM
40
80
00
A B C D E F G H
1 2 3 4 5 6
0 2 4 6 miles
0 2 4 6 8 10 km

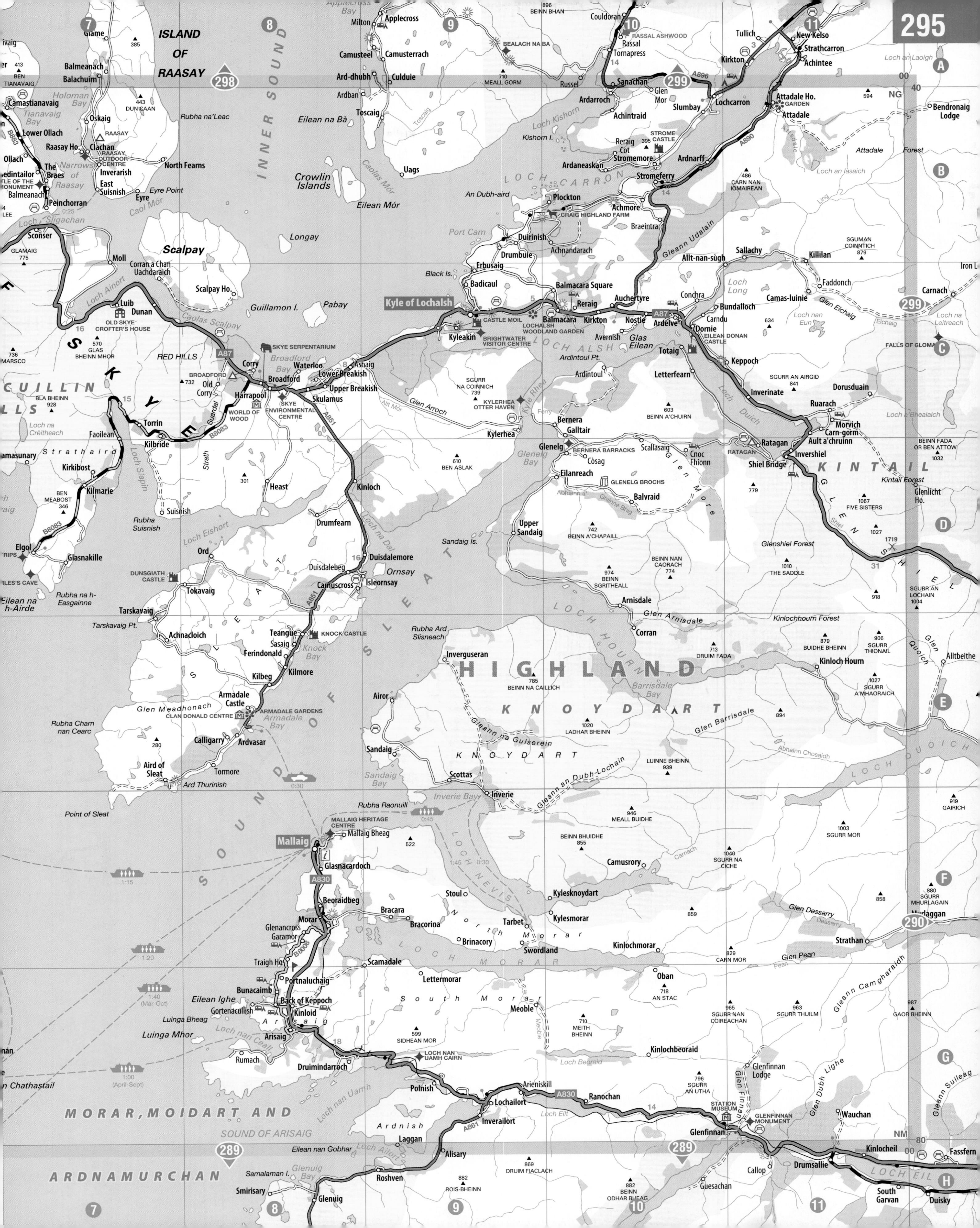

ISLAND OF RAASAY
INNER SOUND
Applecross
Milton
Camusteel
Camusterrach
Ard-dhubh
Culduie
Ardban
Toscaig
Eilean na Bà
Crowlin Islands
Eilean Mór
Uags
BEALACH NA BA
BEINN BHAN
Couldoran
RASSAL ASHWOOD
Rassal
Tornapress
MEALL GORM
Russel
Sanachan
Glen Mor
Ardarroch
Achintraid
Slumbay
Lochcarron
Kirkton
Tullich
New Kelso
Strathcarron
Achintee
Loch an Laoigh
Attadale Ho.
GARDEN
Attadale
Bendronaig Lodge
Attadale Forest
Loch Kishorn
Kishorn I.
Reraig Cot
STROME CASTLE
Stromemore
Ardaneaskan
Ardnarff
Stromeferry
CARN NAN IOMAIREAN
Loch an Iasaich
LOCH CARRON
Plockton
Achmore
CRAIG HIGHLAND FARM
Braeintra
An Dubh-aird
Port Cam
Duirinish
Drumbuie
Achnandarach
Gleann Udalain
Allt-nan-sùgh
Sallachy
Killilan
SGUMAN COINNTICH
Iron Lodge
Loch Long
Faddonch
Carnach
Conchra
Camas-luinie
Glen Elchaig
Bundalloch
Loch nan Eun
Loch na Leitreach
FALLS OF GLOMACH
Glame
Balmeanach
Balachuirn
BEN TIANAVAIG
Holoman Bay
DUN CAAN
Camastianavaig
Tianavaig Bay
Oskaig
Lower Ollach
RAASAY
Raasay Ho.
Clachan
RAASAY OUTDOOR CENTRE
Inverarish
North Fearns
Ollach
The Braes
Narrows of Raasay
East Suisnish
Eyre Point
Eyre
Peinchorran
Balmeanach
Caol Mór
Loch Sligachan
Sconser
Scalpay
Longay
GLAMAIG
Moll
Corran a Chan Uachdaraich
Scalpay Ho.
Loch Ainort
Luib
Dunan
OLD SKYE CROFTER'S HOUSE
GLAS BHEINN MHOR
MARSCO
Caolas Scalpay
Guillamon I.
Pabay
Black Is.
Erbusaig
Badicaul
Balmacara Square
Reraig
Auchertyre
Kyle of Lochalsh
CASTLE MOIL
LOCHALSH WOODLAND GARDEN
Balmacara
Kirkton
Nostie
Ardelve
Dornie
EILEAN DONAN CASTLE
Carndu
Kyleakin
BRIGHTWATER VISITOR CENTRE
LOCH ALSH
Avernish
Glas Eilean
Totaig
Keppoch
Ardintoul Pt.
Ardintoul
SKYE SERPENTARIUM
RED HILLS
Broadford Bay
Corry
Waterloo
Ashaig
Lower Breakish
Upper Breakish
BROADFORD
Broadford
Old Corry
Harrapool
Skulamus
SKYE ENVIRONMENTAL CENTRE
WORLD OF WOOD
CUILLIN HILLS
BLA BHEINN
SKYE
Torrin
Suardal
Loch na Crèitheach
Glen Arroch
SGURR NA COINNICH
KYLERHEA OTTER HAVEN
Kyle Rhea
Kylerhea
Bernera
Galltair
Letterfearn
Invermate
Loch Duich
SGURR AN AIRGID
Dorusduain
BEINN A'CHUIRN
Ruarach
Loch a'Bhealaich
Morvich
Carn-gorm
Ault a'chruinn
Inverhiel
Shiel Bridge
Ratagan
RATAGAN
BEINN FADA OR BEN ATTOW
KINTAIL
Kintail Forest
Glenlicht Ho.
Faoilean
Strathaird
Kilbride
Loch Slapin
Strath
Camasunary
Kirkibost
Kilmarie
BEN MEABOST
Heast
Suisnish
Rubha Suisnish
BEN ASLAK
Kinloch
Glenelg
Glenelg Bay
BERNERA BARRACKS
Còsag
Scallasaig
Cnoc Fhionn
Glen More
Eilanreach
GLENELG BROCHS
Balvraid
Abhainn a' Ghlinne Bhig
FIVE SISTERS
GLEN SHIEL
Elgol
Glasnakille
SPAR CAVE
Loch Eishort
Ord
Drumfearn
Loch na Dal
Upper Sandaig
BEINN A'CHAPAILL
Sandaig Is.
Glenshiel Forest
THE SADDLE
Duisdalemore
Duisdalebeg
Ornsay
DUNSGIATH CASTLE
Tokavaig
Camuscross
Isleornsay
BEINN NAN CAORACH
BEINN SGRITHEALL
Arnisdale
SGURR AN LOCHAIN
Rubha na h-Easgainne
Eilean na h-Airde
Tarskavaig
Tarskavaig Pt.
SLEAT
Achnacloich
Teangue
Sasaig
KNOCK CASTLE
Ferindonald
Knock Bay
Rubha Ard Slisneach
LOCH HOURN
Glen Arnisdale
Corran
Kinlochhourn Forest
BUIDHE BHEINN
SGURR THIONAIL
Glen Quoich
Alltbeithe
DRUIM FADA
Inverguseran
HIGHLAND
BEINN NA CAILLICH
Kinloch Hourn
SGURR A'MHAORAICH
Barrisdale Bay
Kilbeg
Kilmore
Armadale Castle
Glen Meadhonach
CLAN DONALD CENTRE
ARMADALE GARDENS
Armadale Bay
Airor
KNOYDART
Rubha Charn nan Cearc
Calligarry
Ardvasar
Gleann na Guiserein
LADHAR BHEINN
Glen Barrisdale
Sandaig
Sandaig Bay
LUINNE BHEINN
Abhainn Chosaidh
LOCH QUOICH
Aird of Sleat
Tormore
Ard Thurinish
Scottas
Gleann an Dubh-Lochain
Inverie
Inverie Bay
GAIRICH
Point of Sleat
SOUND OF SLEAT
Rubha Raonuill
MALLAIG HERITAGE CENTRE
Mallaig Bheag
Mallaig
MEALL BUIDHE
SGURR MOR
BEINN BHUIDHE
LOCH NEVIS
Camusrory
SGURR NA CICHE
Carnach
Glasnacardoch
Stoul
Kyleskoydart
Beoraidbeg
Bracara
Bracorina
North Morar
Tarbet
Kylesmorar
Glen Dessarry
SGURR MHURLAGAIN
Murlaggan
Morar
Glenancross
Garamor
Brinacory
Swordland
LOCH MORAR
Kinlochmorar
CARN MOR
Glen Pean
Strathan
Traigh Ho.
Scamadale
Oban
Portnaluchaig
Lettermorar
AN STAC
Gleann Camgharaidh
Bunacaimb
Eilean Ighe
Back of Keppoch
Gortenacullish
South Morar
Meoble
SGURR NAN COIREACHAN
SGURR THUILM
GAOR BHEINN
Kinloid
Luinga Bheag
Luinga Mhor
Arisaig
Loch nan Ceall
SIDHEAN MOR
MEITH BHEINN
Kinlochbeoraid
Rumach
Druimindarroch
LOCH NAN UAMH CAIRN
Loch Beoraid
Glenfinnan Lodge
Glen Dubh Lighe
Gleann Suileag
Polnish
Arieniskill
Ranochan
SGURR AN UTHA
Glen Finnan
Lochailort
Loch Eilt
STATION MUSEUM
GLENFINNAN MONUMENT
Wauchan
MORAR, MOIDART AND ARDNAMURCHAN
Loch nan Uamh
Inverailort
Ardnish
Glenfinnan
SOUND OF ARISAIG
Laggan
Alisary
Kinlocheil
Fassfern
Eilean nan Gobhar
Loch Ailort
DRUIM FIACLACH
Callop
Drumsallie
LOCH EIL
Samalaman I.
Glenuig Bay
Roshven
ROIS-BHEINN
BEINN ODHAR BHEAG
Guesachan
Smirisary
Glenuig
South Garvan
Duisky

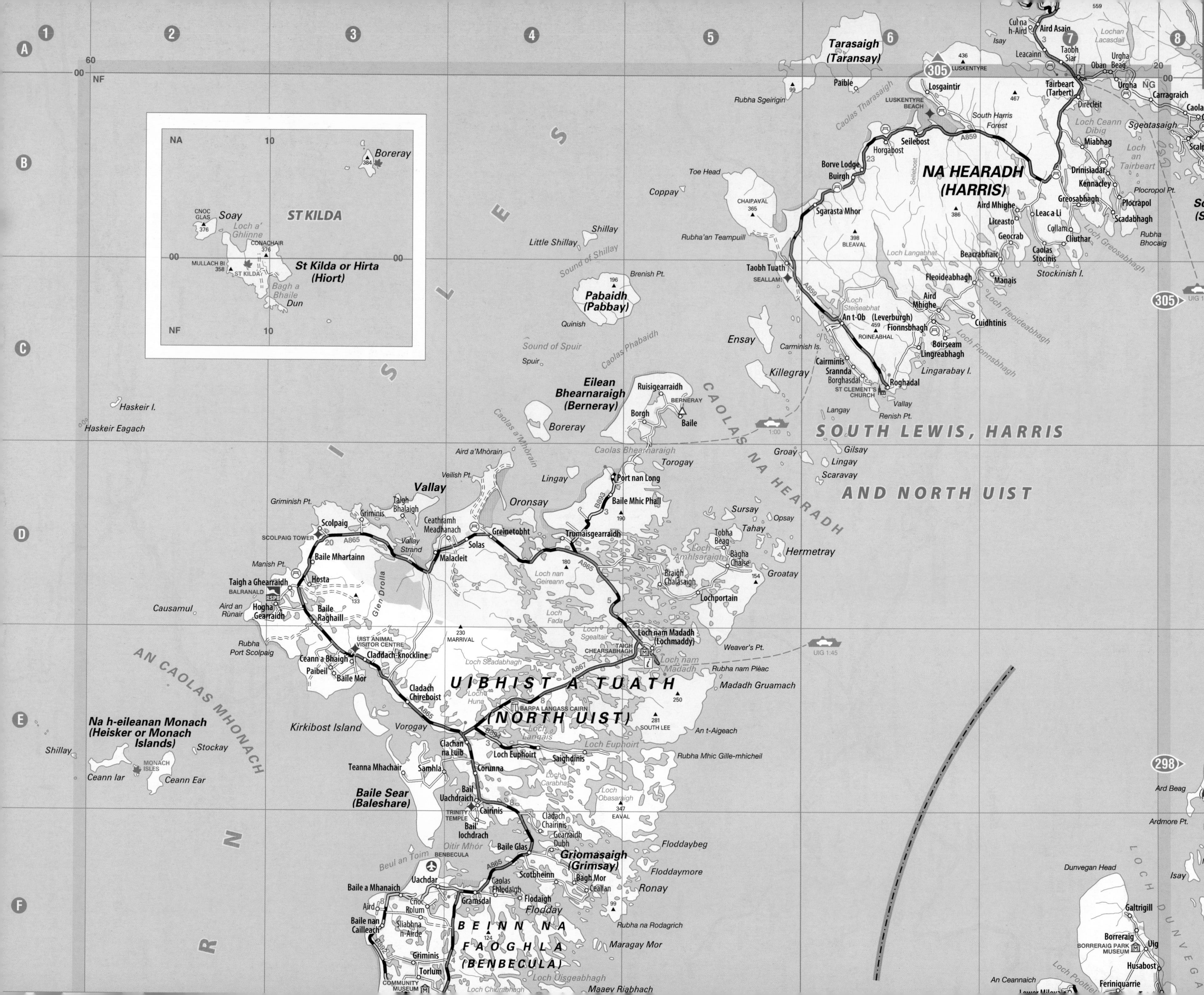
NA HEARADH (HARRIS)
SOUTH LEWIS, HARRIS AND NORTH UIST
UIBHIST A TUATH (NORTH UIST)
BEINN NA FAOGHLA (BENBECULA)
ST KILDA
St Kilda or Hirta (Hiort)
Soay
Boreray
Tarasaigh (Taransay)
Eilean Scalpaigh (Scalpay)
Pabaidh (Pabbay)
Eilean Bhearnaraigh (Berneray)
Baile Sear (Baleshare)
Griomasaigh (Grimsay)
Na h-eileanan Monach (Heisker or Monach Islands)
CAOLAS NA HEARADH
AN CAOLAS MHONACH
Tairbeart (Tarbert)
An t-Ob (Leverburgh)
Loch nam Madadh (Lochmaddy)
Vallay
Ensay
Killegray
Berneray
Oronsay
Kirkibost Island
Haskeir I.
Haskeir Eagach
Shillay
Little Shillay
Sound of Shillay
Sound of Spuir
Caolas Tharasaigh
Caolas Bhearnaraigh
LOCH DUNVEGA
305
298
UIG 1:40
UIG 1:45
1:00

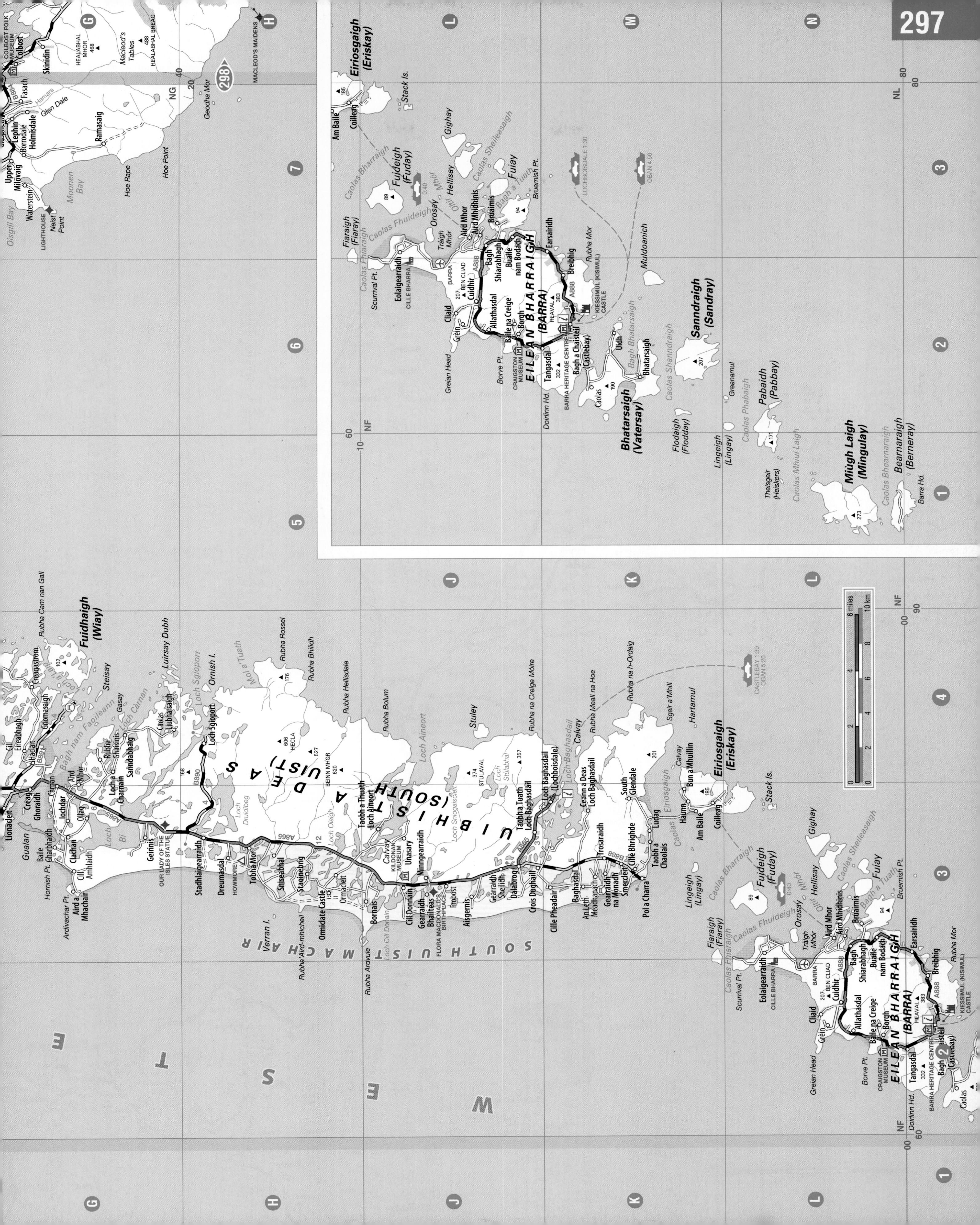

UIBHIST A DEAS (SOUTH UIST)
SOUTH UIST MACHAIR
W E S T
Fuidhaigh (Wiay)
Rubha Cam nan Gall
Creagastrom
Steisay
Gasay
Loch Carnan
Luirsay Dubh
Caolas Liubharsaigh
Loch Sgioport
Ornish I.
Mol a Tuath
Rubha Rossel
Rubha Bhilidh
Rubha Hellisdale
Rubha Bolum
HECLA 606
BEINN MHÒR 620
STULAVAL 374
Loch Aineort
Stuley
Rubha na Creige Mòire
Calvay
Rubha Meall na Hoe
Rubha na h-Ordaig
Sgeir a'Mhill
Hartamul
CASTLEBAY 1:30
OBAN 5:20
Eiriosgaigh (Eriskay)
Bun a' Mhuillin
Haunn
Am Baile
Coilleag
Stack Is.
Lionacleit
Creag Ghoraidh
Cill Eireabhagh
Iochdar
Gualan
Baile Gharbhaidh
Hornish Pt.
Cill Amhlaidh
Aird a' Mhachair
Ardivachar Pt.
Clachan
Loch Bì
Geirinis
OUR LADY OF THE ISLES STATUE
Stadhlaigearraidh
Dreumasdal
HOWMORE
Tobha Mòr
Snaoisbhal
Staoinebrig
Ormacleit
Ormiclate Castle
Bornais
Rubha Ardvule
Loch Cill Donnain
Cill Donnain
KILDONAN MUSEUM
Unasary
Gearraidh Bhailteas
FLORA MACDONALD'S BIRTHPLACE
Frobost
Aisgernis
Gearraidh Sheilidh
Dalabrog
Taobh a Tuath Loch Baghasdail
Loch Baghasdail (Lochboisdale)
Crois Dughaill
Cille Pheadair
Baghasdal
Ceann a Deas Loch Baghasdail
Trosaraidh
Gearraidh na Monadh
Smercleit
Cille Bhrighde
South Glendale
Pol a Charra
Taobh a Chaolais
Ludag
Verran I.
Rubha Aird-mhicheil
Loch Druidibeg
Loch Sgioport
Colbost
COLBOST FOLK MUSEUM
Skinidin
HEALABHAL MHOR 468
Macleod's Tables
HEALABHAL BHEAG 488
MACLEOD'S MAIDENS
Fasach
Hamara
Glen Dale
Lephin
Borrodale
Holmisdale
Ramasaig
Upper Milovaig
Waterstein
Neist Point
LIGHTHOUSE
Moonen Bay
Oisgill Bay
Hoe Rape
Hoe Point
Geodha Mor
298
EILEAN BHARRAIGH (BARRA)
Fiaraigh (Fiaray)
Fuideigh (Fuday)
Gighay
Hellisay
Fuiay
Orosay
Caolas Fhuideigh
Caolas Bharraigh
Caolas Sheileasaigh
Bagh a Tuath
Bruernish Pt.
Traigh Mhòr
Aird Mhor
Aird Mhidhinis
Bruairnis
Eolaigearraidh
CILLE BHARRA
Scurrival Pt.
BARRA
BEN CLIAD 207
Cuidhir
Bagh Shiarabhagh
Buaile nam Bodach
Earsairidh
Breibhig
Rubha Mor
Cliaid
Grèin
Greian Head
Allathasdal
Baile na Creige
Borgh
Borve Pt.
CRAIGSTON MUSEUM
HEAVAL 383
KIESSIMUL (KISIMUL) CASTLE
Tangasdal 332
Dorlinn Hd.
BARRA HERITAGE CENTRE
Bagh a Chaisteil (Castlebay)
LOCHBOISDALE 1:30
OBAN 4:50
Muldoanich
Sanndraigh (Sandray)
Caolas Shanndraigh
Uidh
Bagh Bhatarsaigh
Bhatarsaigh
Caolas
Bhatarsaigh (Vatersay)
Greanamul
Caolas Phabaigh
Pabaidh (Pabbay)
Flodaigh (Flodday)
Lingeigh (Lingay)
Theisgeir (Heiskers)
Caolas Mhiùl Laigh
Mìugh Laigh (Mingulay)
Caolas Bhearnaraigh
Bearnaraigh (Berneray)
Barra Hd.
NG
NF
NL

Fladda-chùain
305
307
Eilean Trodday
Rubha Hunish
Rubha na h-Aiseig
TARBERT 1:40
LOCHMADDY 1:45
Shulista
Balmacqueen
DUNTULM CASTLE
Duntulm
Kilmaluag
Connista
Lub Score
Eilean Flodigarry
Flodigarry
Hungladder
MUSEUM OF ISLAND LIFE
Peingown
Borneskètaig
Heribusta
MEALL NA SUIRAMACH 543
Staffin I.
Kilmuir
FLORA MACDONALD'S MEMORIAL
Digg
Staffin Bay
Kilvaxter
THE QUIRAING
Glashvin
Brogaig
Garafad
Balgown
Staffin
Stenscholl
TROTTERNISH
Kilt Rock
Clachan
KILT ROCK & MEALT FALLS
296
Waternish Point
Linicro
Totscore
466 BIOD BUIDHE
Kilbride Point
Scuddaborg
Elishader
Maligar
Loch Mealt
Valtos
Ascrib Islands
Idrigill
Uig
Marishader
Uig Bay
Conon
Rubha nam Brathairean
UIG
South Cuil
Balnaknock
611 BEINN EDRA
Garros
Breckrey
Culnaknock
BEN GEARY 284
Ru Chorachan
Lealt
Ard Beag
Geary
LEALT FALLS
TRUMPAN CHURCH
Trumpan
Knockbreck
Earlish
LOCH
Lower Tote
Gillen
Upper Tote
Lower Halistra
Upper Halistra
SNIZORT
Ardmore Pt.
A87
Peinlich
Peinaha
Hallin
Hinnisdal
607 CREAG A'LAIN
Island of Rona
125
Mingay
Lyndale Pt.
Isay
Greshornish Pt.
Lusta
Stein
Eilean Garbh
Kingsburgh
Loch Bay
719 THE STORR
Galtrigill
Lyndale Ho.
Callakille
Claigan
Greshornish
Kildonan
Romesdal
OLD MAN OF STORR
Borreraig
Eilean Tigh
Garbh Eilean
327 BEINN BHREAC
Treaslane
Bearreraig Bay
Uig
Flashader
Suladale
TROTTERNISH
Lonbain
PIPING MUSEUM
Husabost
The Aird
Keistle
Loch a' Sguirr
An Caol
Edinbane
Kensaleyre
Rhenetra
Holm I.
Bernisdale
Haultin
Eilean Fladday
Feriniquarrie
Annishader
Loch Leathan
254
DUNVEGAN CASTLE
Blackhill
Totaig
Glaspheìn
COLBOST FOLK MUSEUM
Tote
Torran
Lephin
Colbost
Borrodale
Fasach
Crepkill
Borve
Manish Pt.
Loch Arnish
Arnish
Holmisdale
Glen Bernisdale
Loch Fada
Skeabost
Carbost
PRINCE CHARLES'S CAVE
Skinidin
GIANT ANGUS MACASKILL MUSEUM
Dunvegan
CRUACHAN BEINN A'CHEARCAILL 266
Kilmuir
Lonmore
Uigshader
Drumuie
Achachork
392
BROCHEL CASTLE
Glen Dale
HEALABHAL MHOR 468
Rubha na h Airde Glaise
Brochel
Roskhill
Glen Vic Askil
Upper Feorlig
AN TUIREANN ARTS CENTRE
Ramasaig
Roag
Glengrasco
Torvaig
Balmeanach
Vatten
Sluggans
Shulishadermor
THE AROS EXPERIENCE
Portree
Loch Connan
ISLAND OF RAASAY
Macleod's Tables
Orbost
Glame
Inverallvaig
385
488 HEALABHAL BHEAG
Greep
Harlosh
Ose
Heatherfield
Penifiler
417
Ose
Loch Varkasaig
Balmore
413 BEN TIANAVAIG
Balmeanach
Peinmore
Balachuirn
Eabost West
Glenmore
Holoman Bay
Mugeary
443 DUN CAAN
Geodha Mor
Harlosh I.
Eabost
Loch Duagrich
Camastianavaig
Tarner I.
Totardor
Tianavaig Bay
Rubha na'Leac
Ullinish
Bracadale
Oskaig
Loch Bracadale
Struan
Coillore
Conordan
Eilean na Bà
Wiay
Lower Ollach
RAASAY
Raasay Ho.
Clachan
Idrigill Point
RAASAY OUTDOOR CENTRE
MACLEOD'S MAIDENS
Oronsay
Gesto Ho
Upper Ollach
The Braes
Narrows of Raasay
Inverarish
North Fearns
Ardtreck
Portnalong
439 ROINEVAL
Glen Varragill
Gedintailor
BATTLE OF THE BRAES MONUMENT
Crowlin Islands
Rubha nan Clach
Fiskavaig
East Suisnish
Eyre Point
Balmeanach
Eyre
297
Fernilea
444 BEN LEE
Peinchorran
Caol Mòr
ARNAVAL 369
TALISKER DISTILLERY
Loch Harport
Loch Sligachan
Crossal
Drynoch
Sconser
Longay
Carbost
Gleann Oraid
Merkadale
Satran
A863
Drynoch
GLAMAIG 775
Scalpay
Talisker Bay
Talisker
Sligachan Hotel
Moll
Corran a Chan Uachdaraich
Eynort
Loch Ainort
Scalpay Ho.
Glen Brittle Forest
Luib
Dunan
Pabay
445 BEINN BHREAC
Eynort
Grula
459
OLD SKYE CROFTER'S HOUSE
Caolas Scalpay
Guillamon I.
SGURR NAN GILLEAN 964
Glen Sligachan
SKYE
570 GLAS BHEINN MHOR
SKYE SERPENTARIUM
736 MARSCO
RED HILLS
Broadford Bay
Loch Eynort
MINGINISH
SGURR A'GHREADAIDH 973
Corry
Waterloo
Lower Breakish
Kraiknish
Glen Brittle
THE CUILLIN HILLS
BROADFORD
Broadford
732
Old Corry
Upper Breakish
BLA BHEINN 928
Harrapool
GLENBRITTLE
CUILLIN HILLS
WORLD OF WOOD
SKYE ENVIRONMENTAL CENTRE
Skulamus
Glenbrittle House
Loch na Crèitheach
Torrin
Bualintur
992 SGURR ALASDAIR
Loch Coruisk
Faoilean
Culnaneam
Strathaird
Kilbride
294
295
Loch Brittle
924 SGURR NAN EAG
Camasunary
Strath
Kirkibost
Loch Slapin
301
Heast
BEN MEABOST 346
Kilmarie
Rubh an Dunain
Soay Sound
Soay
Loch Scavaig
Suisnish
Drumfearn
0 2 4 6 miles
0 2 4 6 8 10 km

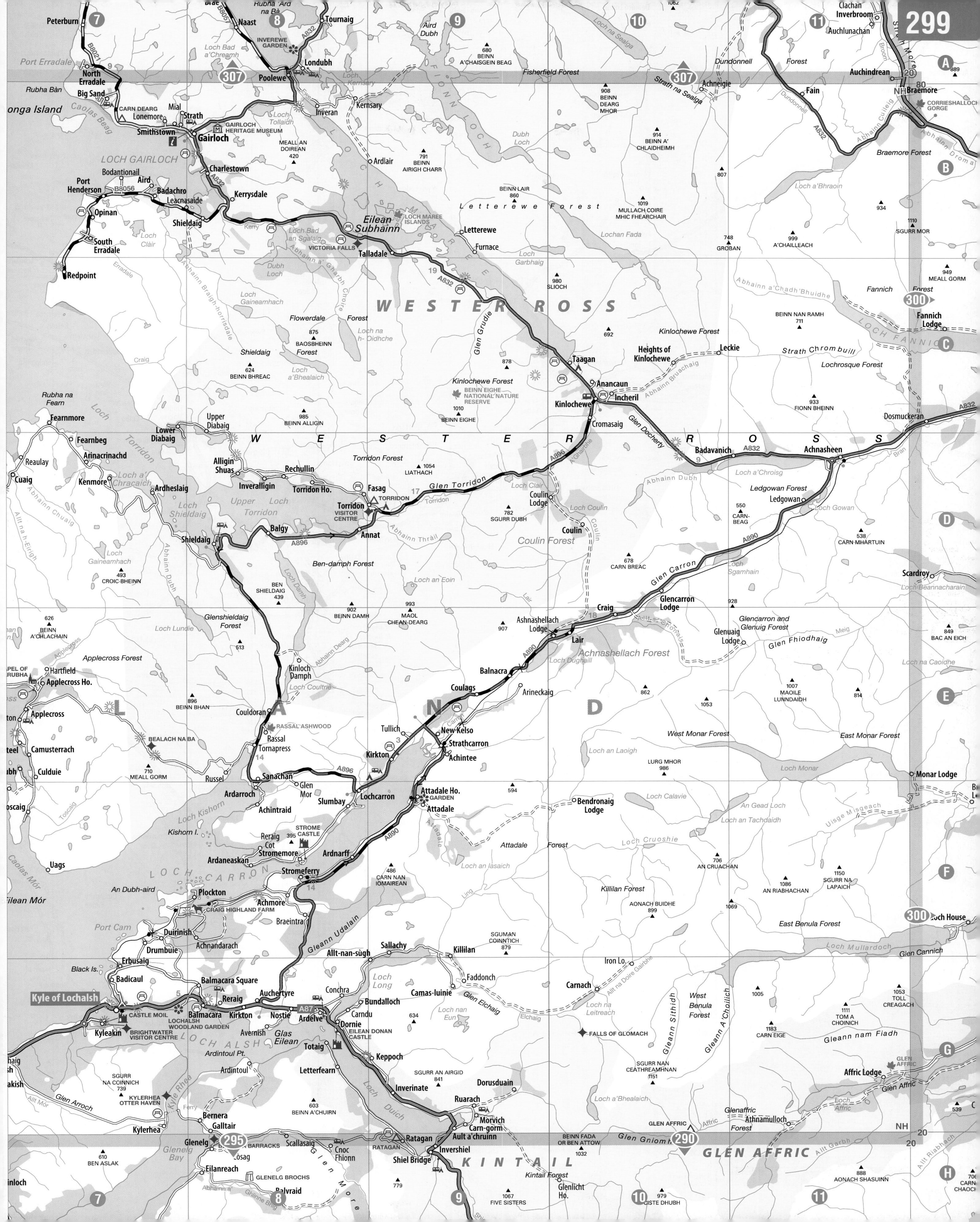
Peterburn
Naast
Tournaig
Aird Dubh
Loch Bad a'Chreamh
Inverewe Garden
Londubh
Poolewe
Port Erradale
North Erradale
Big Sand
Rubha Bàn
Longa Island
Caolas Beag
Carn Dearg
Lonemore
Mial
Strath
Smithstown
Gairloch
Gairloch Heritage Museum
Loch Gairloch
Charlestown
Bodantionail
Aird
Port Henderson
Badachro
Leacnasaide
Kerrysdale
Opinan
Shieldaig
South Erradale
Redpoint
Loch Tollaidh
Inveran
Kernsary
Ardlair
Meall an Doirean 420
791 Beinn Airigh Charr
680 Beinn a'Chaisgein Beag
Fisherfield Forest
908 Beinn Dearg Mhor
914 Beinn a' Chlaidheimh
Dubh Loch
Fionn Loch
Loch na Sealga
Dundonnell
Strath na Sealga
Achneigie
Forest
Fain
Clachan Inverbroom
Auchlunachan
Auchindrean
Braemore
Corrieshalloch Gorge
Braemore Forest
Strath More
Beinn Lair 860
Mullach Coire Mhic Fhearchair 1019
Letterewe Forest
Loch Maree Islands
Eilean Subhainn
Loch Maree
Letterewe
Furnace
Victoria Falls
Talladale
Loch Bad an Sgalaig
Dubh Loch
Lochan Fada
Loch Garbhaig
980 Slioch
748 Groban
999 A'Chailleach
1110 Sgurr Mor
Loch a'Bhraoin
807
934
949 Meall Gorm
Fannich Forest
Abhainn a'Chadh Bhuidhe
Wester Ross
Loch Gaineamhach
Flowerdale Forest
875 Baosbheinn
Loch na h-Oidhche
Glen Grudie
692
Kinlochewe Forest
Heights of Kinlochewe
Leckie
Beinn nan Ramh 711
Fannich Lodge
Loch Fannich
Strath Chrombuill
Lochrosque Forest
Shieldaig Forest
624 Beinn Bhreac
Loch a'Bhealaich
878
Taagan
Anancaun
Kinlochewe
Incheril
Beinn Eighe National Nature Reserve
1010 Beinn Eighe
933 Fionn Bheinn
Dosmuckeran
A832
Rubha na Fearn
Fearnmore
Fearnbeg
Reaulay
Cuaig
Arinacrinachd
Kenmore
Loch a' Chracaich
Loch Torridon
Upper Diabaig
Lower Diabaig
985 Beinn Alligin
Alligin Shuas
Inveralligin
Rechullin
Torridon Ho.
Fasag
Torridon
Torridon Visitor Centre
Torridon Forest
1054 Liathach
Glen Torridon
Loch Clair
Coulin Lodge
782 Sgurr Dubh
Cromasaig
Glen Docherty
Badavanich
Achnasheen
Loch a'Chroisg
Abhainn Dubh
Ledgowan Forest
Ledgowan
Loch Gowan
550 Carn-Beag
538 Carn Mhartuin
Ardheslaig
Loch Shieldaig
Upper Loch Torridon
Loch Coulin
Coulin
Coulin Forest
Shieldaig
Balgy
Annat
Abhainn Thrail
Ben-damph Forest
Loch Gaineamhach
493 Croic-Bheinn
Loch an Eoin
678 Carn Breac
Glen Carron
Loch Sgamhain
Scardroy
Loch Beannacharain
Ben Shieldaig 439
Loch Damh
902 Beinn Damh
993 Maol Chean-Dearg
Glencarron Lodge
928
Craig
Ashnashellach Lodge
Lair
907
Glencarron and Glenuaig Forest
Glenuaig Lodge
Glen Fhiodhaig
849 Bac an Eich
626 Beinn a'Chlachain
Loch Lundie
Glenshieldaig Forest
513
Applecross Forest
Hartfield
Applecross Ho.
Kinloch Damph
Loch Coultrie
Achnashellach Forest
Loch Dughaill
Balnacra
Coulags
Arineckaig
Loch na Caoidhe
896 Beinn Bhan
Applecross
Couldoran
Rassal Ashwood
Rassal
Tornapress
Tullich
New Kelso
Strathcarron
Achintee
862
1053
1007 Maoile Lunndaidh
814
West Monar Forest
East Monar Forest
Bealach na Ba
Camusterrach
Culduie
710 Meall Gorm
Russel
Sanachan
Kirkton
Loch an Laoigh
Lurg Mhor 986
Loch Monar
Monar Lodge
Ardarroch
Glen Mor
Slumbay
Lochcarron
Attadale Ho.
Garden
Attadale
594
Bendronaig Lodge
Loch Calavie
An Gead Loch
Loch an Tachdaidh
Uisge Misgeach
Toscaig
Loch Kishorn
Kishorn I.
Achintraid
Reraig
Cot
Strome Castle
395
Stromemore
Ardaneaskan
Ardnarff
Attadale Forest
Loch Cruoshie
706 An Cruachan
Uags
Caolas Mòr
Eilean Mór
Loch Carron
Stromeferry
486 Carn nan Iomairean
Loch an Iasaich
1150 Sgurr na Lapaich
1086 An Riabhachan
An Dubh-aird
Plockton
Craig Highland Farm
Achmore
Killilan Forest
Aonach Buidhe 899
1069
East Benula Forest
Loch House
Port Cam
Duirinish
Braeintra
Drumbuie
Achnandarach
Sguman Coinntich 879
Glen Cannich
Loch Mullardoch
Glean Udalain
Erbusaig
Black Is.
Badicaul
Sallachy
Allt-nan-sùgh
Killilan
Loch Long
Faddonch
Iron Lo.
Carnach
Balmacara Square
Kyle of Lochalsh
Reraig
Auchertyre
Conchra
Bundalloch
Camas-luinie
Glen Elchaig
West Benula Forest
Gleann Sithidh
Gleann A'Choilich
1005
1053 Toll Creagach
Castle Moil
Balmacara
Kirkton
Nostie
Ardelve
Carndu
Dornie
Eilean Donan Castle
Loch nan Eun
634
Loch na Leitreach
1111 Tom a Choinich
1183 Carn Eige
Gleann nam Fiadh
Lochalsh Woodland Garden
Kyleakin
Brightwater Visitor Centre
Loch Alsh
Avernish
Glas Eilean
Totaig
Falls of Glomach
Ardintoul Pt.
Ardintoul
Letterfearn
Keppoch
Glen Affric
Affric Lodge
Sgurr na Coinnich 739
Kylerhea Otter Haven
Kyle Rhea
Glen Arroch
Sgurr an Airgid 841
Invernate
Dorusduain
Sgurr nan Ceathreamhnan 1151
Loch a'Bhealaich
Loch Affric
539
603 Beinn a'Chuirn
Ruarach
Loch Duich
Bernera
Galltair
Kylerhea
Morvich
Carn-gorm
Glenaffric
Athnamulloch
Forest
888
NH
Glenelg
Barracks
Scallasaig
Cnoc Fhionn
Ratagan
Ault a'chruinn
Beinn Fada or Ben Attow 1032
Glen Gniomh
Glen Affric
Allt Garbh
Allt Riabhach
Glenelg Bay
Cosag
Eilanreach
Glenelg Brochs
Glen More
Shiel Bridge
Invershiel
Kintail
610 Ben Aslak
779
Kintail Forest
Glenlicht Ho.
1067 Five Sisters
979 Ciste Dhubh
888 Aonach Shasuinn
706 Carn Chaoich
Balvraid
Inverinate
Abhainn a'
Glenbeg
Inloch
Land
Wester Ross
307
300
290
295
7
8
9
10
11
A
B
C
D
E
F
G
H
NH
80
20
A832
A896
A890
A87
B8021
B8056
B8057

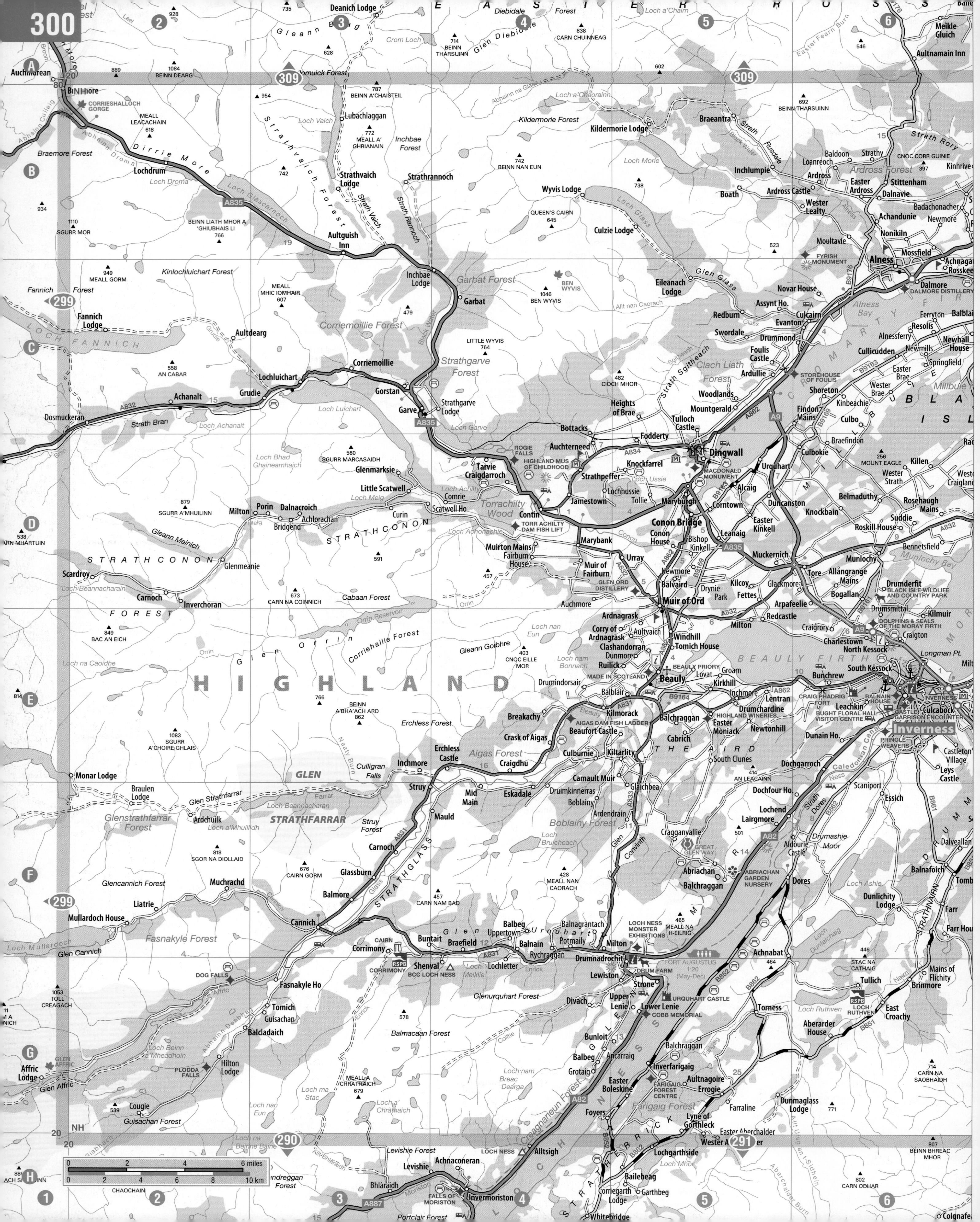

Deanich Lodge
EASTER ROSS
Diebidale Forest
Loch a'Chairn
928
735
Gleann Beag
Crom Loch
714 BEINN THARSUINN
Glen Diebidale
838 CARN CHUINNEAG
Meikle Gluich
546
Aultnamain Inn
Auchmdrean
889
1084 BEINN DEARG
309
Alladale
787 BEINN A'CHAISTEIL
602
Black Water
CORRIESHALLOCH GORGE
MEALL LEACACHAIN 618
954
Loch Vaich
Lubachlaggan
Loch a'Chaorainn
Kildermorie Forest
Kildermorie Lodge
Braeantra
692 BEINN THARSUINN
772 MEALL A' GHRIANAIN
Inchbae Forest
Strath Rusdale
Strath Rory
Braemore Forest
Dirrie More
Strathvaich Forest
742 BEINN NAN EUN
Loch Morie
Baldoon
Strathy
CNOC CORR GUINIE
Loanreoch
Ardross Forest
397
Kinhrive
Lochdrum
Loch Droma
742
Strathvaich Lodge
Strathrannoch
Inchlumpie
Ardross
Easter Ardross
Stittenham
Dalnavie
Wyvis Lodge
738
Boath
Ardross Castle
Wester Lealty
Badachonacher
934
A835
Loch Glascarnoch
Strath Vaich
Strath Rannoch
QUEEN'S CAIRN 645
Loch Glass
Achandunie
Newmore
1110 SGURR MOR
BEINN LIATH MHOR A 'GHIUBHAIS LI 766
Aultguish Inn
Culzie Lodge
Nonikiln
Moultavie
Mossfield
523
FYRISH MONUMENT
Alness
Achnagarron
Rosskeen
949 MEALL GORM
Kinlochluichart Forest
Inchbae Lodge
Garbat Forest
BEN WYVIS
1046 BEN WYVIS
Glen Glass
Eileanach Lodge
Novar House
Dalmore
DALMORE DISTILLERY
Fannich Forest
299
MEALL MHIC IOMHAIR 607
479
Garbat
Allt nan Caorach
Assynt Ho.
Alness Bay
Ferryton
Balblair
Fannich Lodge
LOCH FANNICH
Auldearg
Corriemoillie Forest
Redburn
Culcairn
Evanton
Resolis
Swordale
Drummond
Alnessferry
Newhall House
Cullicudden
Newmills
LITTLE WYVIS 764
Strathgarve Forest
Foulis Castle
Clach Liath Forest
Springfield
558 AN CABAR
Corriemoillie
Ardullie
STOREHOUSE OF FOULIS
Easter Brae
Lochluichart
Gorstan
482 CIOCH MHOR
Shoreton
Wester Brae
Millbuie
Achanalt
Grudie
Strath Sgitheach
Woodlands
Kinbeachie
Strathgarve Lodge
Heights of Brae
Mountgerald
Findon Mains
Culbo
BLACK ISLE
Dosmuckeran
A832
Strath Bran
Loch Luichart
Garve
Loch Achanalt
Loch Garve
Tulloch Castle
Braefindon
Bottacks
Fodderty
Auchterneed
ROGIE FALLS
Dingwall
Culbokie
256 MOUNT EAGLE
Killen
Loch Bhad Ghaineamhaich
580 SGURR MARCASAIDH
Tarvie
HIGHLAND MUS OF CHILDHOOD
Knockfarrel
Strathpeffer
MACDONALD MONUMENT
Urquhart
Wester Strath
Craiglan
Glenmarksie
Craigdarroch
Loch Ussie
Alcaig
Little Scatwell
Loch Achilty
Comrie
Torrachilty Wood
Lochussie
Tollie
Jamestown
Maryburgh
Corntown
Duncanston
Belmaduthy
Rosehaugh Mains
Loch Meig
879 SGURR A'MHUILINN
Milton
Porin
Dalnacroich
Achlorachan
Curin
Scatwell Ho
Contin
TORR ACHILTY DAM FISH LIFT
Conon Bridge
Conon House
Easter Kinkell
Knockbain
Suddie
Bridgend
STRATHCONON
Loch Achonachie
Leanaig
Roskill House
538 CARN MHARTUIN
Gleann Meinich
Marybank
Bishop Kinkell
A835
Bennetsfield
Muirton Mains
Fairburn House
Urray
Muckernich
Munlochy
Munlochy Bay
Glenmeanie
591
Muir of Fairburn
Newmore
Tore
Allangrange Mains
Scardroy
457
Balvaird
Drynie Park
Kilcoy
Glackmore
Drumderfit
Loch Beannacharain
GLEN ORD DISTILLERY
BLACK ISLE WILDLIFE AND COUNTRY PARK
Carnoch
Inverchoran
673 CARN NA COINNICH
Cabaan Forest
Fettes
Bogallan
Muir of Ord
Arpafeelie
Orrin
Auchmore
Drumsmittal
Kilmuir
FOREST
Orrin Reservoir
Ardnagrask
Redcastle
849 BAC AN EICH
Corriehallie Forest
Loch nan Eun
Corry of Ardnagrask
Aultvaich
Milton
DOLPHINS & SEALS OF THE MORAY FIRTH
Windhill
Craigrory
Craigton
Glen Orrin
Gleann Goibhre
Clashandorran
Tomich House
Charlestown
North Kessock
Longman Pt.
Loch na Caoidhe
403 CNOC EILLE MOR
Loch nam Bonnach
Dunmore
Ruilick
BEAULY PRIORY
BEAULY FIRTH
South Kessock
814
HIGHLAND
Drumindorsair
MADE IN SCOTLAND
Lovat
Groam
Bunchrew
Beauly
Kirkhill
766
Balblair
B9164
Inchmore
A862
CRAIG PHADRIG FORT
BALNAIN HOUSE
INVERNESS CASTLE
BEINN A'BHA'ACH ARD 862
Breakachy
Kilmorack
Balchraggan
Drumchardine
Lentran
Leachkin
GARRISON ENCOUNTER
Culcabock
Erchless Forest
AIGAS DAM FISH LADDER
HIGHLAND WINERIES
Easter Moniack
Newtonhill
BUGHT FLORAL HALL VISITOR CENTRE
Inverness
1083 SGURR A'CHOIRE GHLAIS
Crask of Aigas
Beaufort Castle
Cabrich
Dunain Ho.
PRINGLE WEAVERS
Erchless Castle
Aigas Forest
Culburnie
Kiltarlity
THE AIRD
South Clunes
Castleton Village
Leys Castle
Monar Lodge
Inchmore
Craigdhu
Culligran Falls
414 AN LEACAINN
Dochgarroch
GLEN
Neaty Burn
Caledonian Canal
Struy
Camault Muir
Braulen Lodge
Glen Strathfarrar
Mid Main
Eskadale
Druimkinnerras
Glaichbea
Dochfour Ho.
Scaniport
Loch Beannacharan
Boblainy
Essich
Glenstrathfarrar Forest
Ardchuilk
STRATHFARRAR
Struy Forest
Mauld
Ardendrain
Lochend
Loch a'Mhuillidh
Boblainy Forest
Lairgmore
Strath Dores
Loch Bruicheach
Cragganvallie
501
Drumashie Moor
Dalvealian
818 SGOR NA DIOLLAID
Carnoch
GREAT GLEN WAY
Aldourie Castle
676 CAIRN GORM
Glassburn
428 MEALL NAN CAORACH
Glen Convinth
Abriachan
ABRIACHAN GARDEN NURSERY
Balnafoich
Glencannich Forest
Muchrachd
STRATHGLASS
Balchraggan
Dores
Tomb
Loch Ashie
Dunlichity Lodge
Liatrie
Balmore
457 CARN NAM BAD
299
Mullardoch House
Cannich
Balbeg
Uppertown
Balnagrantach
LOCH NESS MONSTER EXHIBITIONS
465 MEALL NA H-EILRIG
Farr
Glen Urquhart
Potmaily
Farr House
Loch Mullardoch
Fasnakyle Forest
Buntait
Braefield
Balnain
Milton
Loch Duntelchaig
Glen Cannich
CAIRN
Corrimony
Rychraggan
Drumnadrochit
FORT AUGUSTUS 1:20 (May-Dec)
Achnabat
446 STAC NA CATHAIG
RSPB CORRIMONY
Shenval
BCC LOCH NESS
Loch Meiklie
Lochletter
Enrick
464
Mains of Flichity
DOG FALLS
Lewiston
DRUM FARM
Fasnakyle Ho
Strone
Tullich
Brinmore
1053 TOLL CREAGACH
Glenurquhart Forest
URQUHART CASTLE
Divach
Upper Lenie
Lower Lenie
Torness
COBB MEMORIAL
RSPB LOCH RUTHVEN
Loch Ruthven
East Croachy
Tomich
Guisachan
578
Aberarder House
Balcladaich
Balmacaan Forest
Bunloit
Loch Beinn a'Mheadhoin
Abhainn Deabhag
Balchraggan
GLEN AFFRIC
PLODDA FALLS
Hilton Lodge
Ancarraig
Balbeg
Inverfarigaig
714 CARN NA SAOBHAIDH
Affric Lodge
Glen Affric
Grotaig
Loch nam Breac Dearga
MEALL A CHRATHAICH 679
Easter Boleskine
FARIGAIG FOREST CENTRE
Aultnagoire
Errogie
Loch ma Stac
Creagnaneun Forest
Farigaig Forest
539
Cougie
Guisachan Forest
Loch nan Eun
Loch a'Chrathaich
Foyers
Farraline
Dunmaglass Lodge
771
Lyne of Gorthleck
NH
Loch na Beinne Baine
290
Easter Aberchalder
Wester Aberchalder
291
807 BEINN BHREAC MHOR
Levishie Forest
LOCH NESS
Alltsigh
STRATHERRICK
Lochgarthside
Achnaconeran
Levishie
Loch Mhor
886 ACH SLINN
Bhlaraidh
Bailebeag
802 CARN ODHAR
CHAOCHAIN
Dundreggan Forest
FALLS OF MORISTON
Corriegarth Lodge
Garthbeg
Invermoriston
Coignafe
A887
Portclair Forest
Whitebridge
0 2 4 6 miles
0 2 4 6 8 10 km

Tain
Morangie
GLENMORANGIE DISTILLERY
ALDIE WATERMILL
ST DUTHUS'S CHAPEL
TAIN THROUGH TIME VISITOR CENTRE
TAIN TOLBOOTH
TARBAT DISCOVERY CENTRE
Portmahomack
Bindal
Seafield
Rockfield
Balcherry
Inver
Balnagall
Arboll
Tarrel
Lochslin
Wester Arboll
Toulvaddie
Upper Bogrow
Quarryhill
Arthurville
Morangie Forest
Aldie
Hilton
Rhynie
Lower Pitkerrie
Geanies House
Kingscauseway
Loandhu
Fearn Station
East Lamington
Hartmount
Hill of Fearn
Fearn
FEARN ABBEY
Cadboll
Lamington
Newfield
Marybank
Logie Hill
Loans of Tullich
Hilton of Cadboll
Torran
Scotsburn
Pithmaduthy
Arabella
Balintore
Kildary
Broomton
SHANDWICK STONE
Shandwick
Tullich Muir
Milton
Ankerville
Tarbat Ho.
Chapelhill
NIGG BAY
Kilmuir
Pitcalnie
Port an Righ
Nigg Bay
Barbaraville
Nigg
Northfield
Sands of Nigg
Balintraid
Mount Canisp
King's Cave
Saltburn
Balnapaling
Balnabruaich
Castlecraig
Invergordon
Nigg Ferry
Cromarty
CROMARTY COURT HOUSE
Newhall Point
Cromarty Bay
Sutors of Cromarty
HUGH MILLER'S COTTAGE
UDALE BAY
Udale Bay
Newton
Shore Mill
Jemimaville
Davidston
Navity
Poyntzfield
Muirton
Glenurquhart
Upper Eathie
Craighead
MORAY FIRTH
Whitebog
Balmungie
Whiteness Head
GROAM HOUSE MUSEUM AND PICTISH CENTRE
Rosemarkie
Rosemarkie Bay
FORTROSE CATHEDRAL
Fortrose
Fort George
QUEEN'S OWN HIGHLANDERS MUS.
Kirkton
Baddock
Ardersier
Chanonry Pt.
HERITAGE EXHIBITION
Avoch
Avoch Bay
NAIRN FISHERTOWN MUSEUM
NAIRN LITERARY INSTITUTE MUSEUM
CULBIN SANDS
Nairn
Druim
Kingsteps
Tradespark
BOATH DOVECOTE
Auldearn
Moss-side
Househill
Gollanfield
Milton of Gollanfield
Muir of the Clans
Geddes House
Foynesfield
Lochside
Rosefield
Lakken Forest
Regoul
Fisherton
INVERNESS
CASTLE STUART
Castle Stuart
Alturlie Pt.
Clephanton
Cawdor
Piperhill
Culcharry
Tornagrain
Croy
KILRAVOCK CASTLE
CAWDOR CASTLE AND GARDENS
Mid Urchany
Littlemill
Achavelgin
Morayhill
Newton
Easter Galcantray
Achindown
Achavraat
Cantraywood
Balloch
Culloden Forest
Western Galcantray
Kirkton of Barevan
Culloden
Smithton
Newlands
Cantraydoune
Cantraybruich
Mains of Clunas
INVERNESS MUS AND ART GALLERY
CULLODEN BATTLEFIELD
CLAVA CAIRNS
Assich Forest
Balmore
Westhill
Castletown
Mains of Daltulich
House of Daviot
BEINN BHUIDHE MHOR
CARN SGUMAIN
Banchor
Dulsie
Milltown
Daviot
Craggie
Auchnahillin
BEINN BHREAC
CARN NAN TRI-TIGHEARNAN
Drynachan Lodge
Daless
Ballachrochin
Moy Burn
MEALL A'BHREACRAIBH
MEALL MOR
Moy Hall
Loch Moy
Moy
Strathdearn Forest
Ruthven
CARN NA H-EASGAINN
CARN AN T-SEAN-LIATHANAICH
Upper Inverbrough
Balvraid
Corrybrough
TOMATIN DISTILLERY
Tomatin
Raigbeg
CARN A'CHOIRE MHOIR
CARN GLAS-CHOIRE
Findhorn Bridge
BEINN BHREAC
Glen Kyllachy
Kyllachy House
Clune
Knockandoo
Corrievorrie
Garbole
Dalmigavie Lodge
Glen Mazeran
Slochd
STRATHDEARN
Dalmigavie
Coignascallan
Findhorn
Eil
Caggan
Culbin Forest
The Bar
Kincorth Ho.
Kintessack
Cloddymoss
Moy Ho.
Maviston
BRODIE CASTLE
Brodie
Dyke
Earlsmill
Darnaway Castle
Blackhills
Whitemire
Conicavel
Easter Milton
Wester Milton
Lethen Ho.
Clune
Darnaway Forest
LOGIE STEADING VISITOR CENTRE
Logie
Fornighty
Coulmony Ho.
Relugas
Redburn
Newlands of Fleenas Wood
ARDCLACH TOWER
Ardclach
Mount
Ferness
Glenferness House
Glenernie
Beachans
Shenvault
Dava
Aitnoch
HILL OF AITNOCH
Lochindorb
LOCHINDORB CASTLE
Lochindorb Lodge
CARN-RUIGH CHARRACH
Findhorn
Findhorn Bay
Forres
SUENO'S STONE
NELSON TOWER
FALCONER MUSEUM
Springfield
KINLOSS ABBEY
Kinloss
Grange Hall
Blervie Castle
Califer
DALLAS DHU DISTILLERY
Mundale
Rafford
Altyre Ho.
Moor of Granary
Damhead
Briach
Altyre Woods
Drumine Forest
Phorp
Newtyle Forest
MORAY
Loch Dallas
Burghead
BURGHEAD MUSEUM
BURGHEAD BAY
Hopeman
Cummingston
Roseisle
Roseisle Forest
College of Roseisle
Lower Hempriggs
Miltonhill
Coltfield
East Grange
Alves
Mains of Burgie
Monaughty Forest
PLUSCARDEN ABBEY
Barnhill
Stoneyfield
Dallas Forest
Hatton
Branchill
Dallas Lodge
Dallas
Craigroy
MILL BUIE
Ballachraggan
CARN KITTY
LARIG HILL
CARN NA LOINE
Upper Derraid
Auchnagallin
Wester Auchnagallin
Lettoch
Glaschoil
Lynmore
Delliefure
Cameroy
Cottartown
Upper Port
Dreggie
Glenbeg
Grantown-on-Spey
Anagach
Craggan
Speybridge
REVACK ESTATE
Congash
Cromdale
Auchroisk
Haughs of Cromdale
Dalriach
Mains of Dalvey
Advie
Achnahannet
BEINN MHOR
CLAN GRANT MAUSOLEUM & CHURCH
Dulnain Bridge
Tulloch-gribban
Skye of Curr
HEATHER HERITAGE CENTRE
Duthil
Lochanhully
Carrbridge
LANDMARK FOREST THEME PARK
Ellan
Sluggan
Feith Mhor
Balnacruie
Broomhill
CAIRNGORMS NATIONAL PARK
Aultmore
Nethy Bridge
Blairgorm
Dirdhu
Drumuillie
Cullachie
Birchfield
East Croftmore
LOCH GARTEN ABERNETHY
Loch Garten
Abernethy Forest
Deishar
Dalnahaitnach
Chapelton
Boat of Garten
Kinveachy
Wester Dalvoult
Street of Kincardine
Aundorach
Avielochan
STRATHSPEY RAILWAY
Lower Dell
Dell Lodge
Lettoch
Clachaig
BADDOCH
Larg
ABERNETHY CENTRE
Forest Lodge
Dorback Lodge
CREGGAN A'CHAISE
Lynemore
Inverlochy
HILLS OF CROMDALE
Bridge of Brown
Bridge of Avon
Strathavon Lo.
Fodderletter
Croughly
TOMINTOUL MUSEUM
Tomintoul
Delnabo
CARN MEADHONACH
GLENLIVET ESTATE VISITOR CENTRE
Milton
TOMINTOUL
Covesea
LOSSIEMOUTH FISHERIES & COMMUNITY MUSEUM
Covesea Skerries
Stotfield
Lossiemouth
Duffus
Gordonstoun
Westerfolds
Old Duffus
DUFFUS CASTLE
PALACE OF SPYNIE
Spynie
Bishopmill
Quarrywood
Rosebrae
Laverackloch
Newton
Ardgye
Elgin
OLD MILLS
MORAY MOTOR MUSEUM
New Elgin
Pittendreich
Cloves
Miltonduff
Mayne Ho.
Glassgreen
Muir of Miltonduff
Paddockhaugh
Auchtertyre
BIRNIE CHURCH
Foresterseat
Upper Bogside
Thornhill
Kellas
Glenlatterach
CARN UISH
Elchies Forest
CARN NA CAILLICHE
Archiestown
CARDHU DISTILLERY
Cardow
Upper Knockando
SPEYSIDE WAY
Knockando Ho.
Knockando
Carron
Marypark
GLENFARCLAS DISTILLERY
Bellehiglash
CRAGGANMORE DISTILLERY
Craggenmore
Bridge of Avon
Dalchirach
Haugh of Kilnmaichlie
Craggan
Drumin
Downan
GLENLIVET DISTILLERY
Glenlivet
Shenval
Auchbreck
Castleton
Ballcorach
Tomnavoulin
CARN DAIMH
Knockandhu
Auchnarrow
Glenlivet Forest
Clashnoir
Strath Avon
Stratha Avon
Conglass Water
Ruthven
Firth
A9
A96
A939
A940
A95
A938
B9007
B9006
B9090
B9091
B9092
B9101
B9165
B9166
B9175
B817
B9163
A832
B851
B9154
B9010
B9011
B9089
B9013
B9012
B9040
B9135
A941
B9102
B9138
B9008
B9009
B9136
B970
B9153
302
309
311
291
292
7
8
9
10
11
A
B
C
D
E
F
G
H
NJ

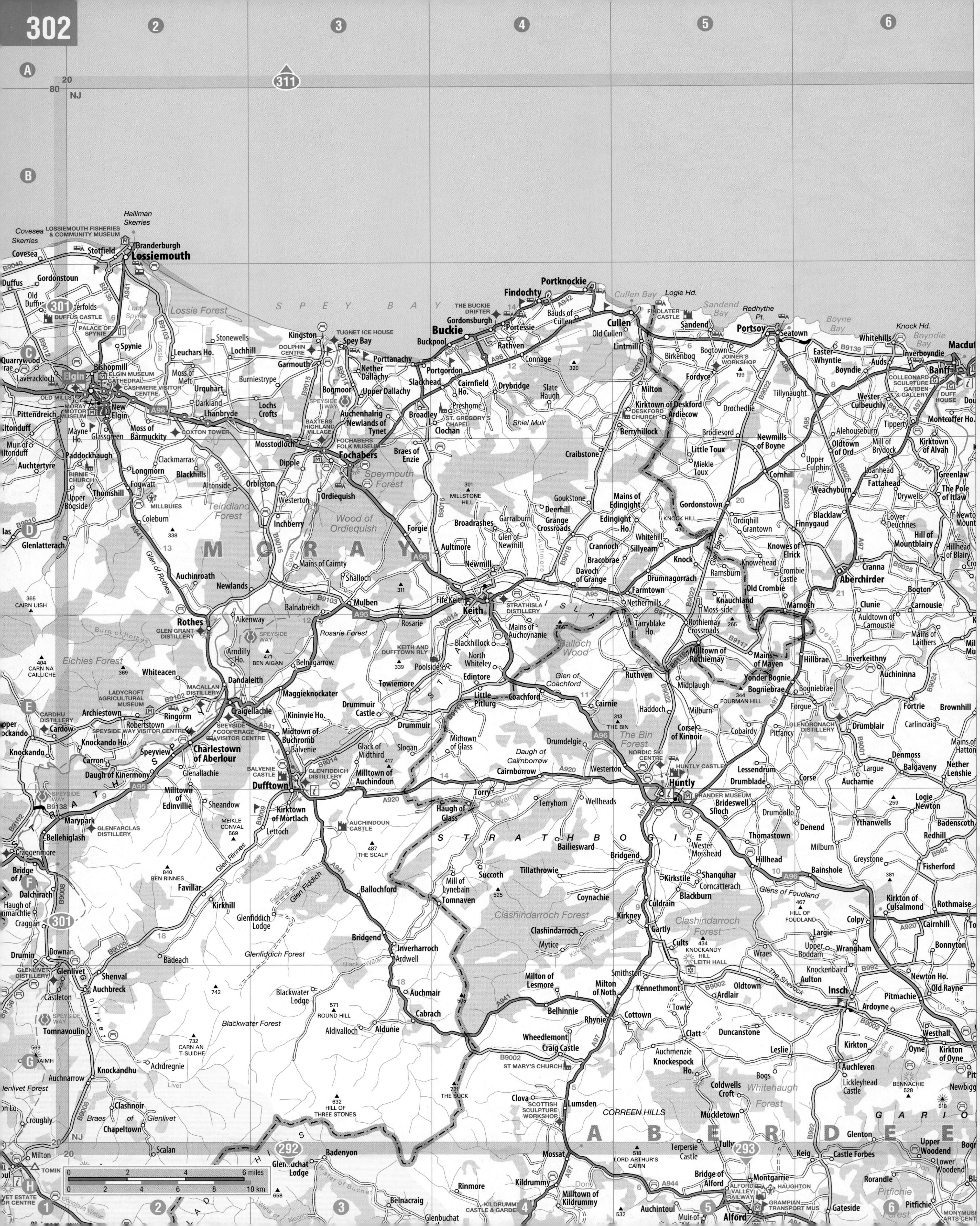

311
SPEY BAY
Lossiemouth
Branderburgh
Stotfield
Covesea
Covesea Skerries
Halliman Skerries
LOSSIEMOUTH FISHERIES & COMMUNITY MUSEUM
Duffus
Gordonstoun
DUFFUS CASTLE
PALACE OF SPYNIE
Spynie
Lossie Forest
Leuchars Ho.
Lochhill
Stonewells
Kingston
Garmouth
DOLPHIN CENTRE
TUGNET ICE HOUSE
Spey Bay
Portannachy
Nether Dallachy
Upper Dallachy
Bogmoor
Buckpool
Buckie
Gordonsburgh
THE BUCKIE DRIFTER
Findochty
Portknockie
Portessie
Rathven
Bauds of Cullen
Cullen
Cullen Bay
Logie Hd.
FINDLATER CASTLE
Sandend
Sandend Bay
Redhythe Pt.
Portsoy
Seatown
Boyne Bay
Knock Hd.
Boyndie Bay
Whitehills
Inverboyndie
Macduff
Banff
Elgin
ELGIN MUSEUM
ELGIN CATHEDRAL
CASHMERE VISITOR CENTRE
OLD MILLS
Bishopmill
New Elgin
Lhanbryde
Urquhart
Burniestrype
Darkland
Lochs Crofts
Mosstodloch
COXTON TOWER
Fochabers
FOCHABERS FOLK MUSEUM
Speymouth Forest
Slackhead
Portgordon
Cairnfield Ho.
Drybridge
Preshome
ST. GREGORY'S CHAPEL
Clochan
Broadley
Shiel Muir
Slate Haugh
Lintmill
Milton
Kirktown of Deskford
DESKFORD CHURCH
Ardiecow
Berryhillock
Fordyce
JOINER'S WORKSHOP
Birkenbog
Bogtown
Drochedlie
Brodiesord
Little Toux
Mickle Toux
Newmills of Boyne
Tillynaught
Wester Culbeuchly
Montcoffer Ho.
Tipperty
Alehouseburn
Kirktown of Alvah
Pittendreich
Mayne Ho.
Glassgreen
Moss of Barmuckity
Paddockhaugh
Auchtertyre
Longmorn
Fogwatt
Thornhill
BIRNIE CHURCH
Upper Bogside
MILLBUIES
Coleburn
Blackhills
Clackmarras
Altonside
Orbliston
Dipple
Westerton
Ordiequish
Wood of Ordiequish
Teindland Forest
Inchberry
Braes of Enzie
Forgie
Aultmore
Newmill
Broadrashes
Garralburn
Glen of Newmill
Deerhill
Grange Crossroads
Goukstone
Craibstone
Mains of Edingight
Edingight Ho.
Whitehill
Sillyearn
KNOCK HILL
Gordonstown
Ordiqhill
Grantown
Finnygaud
Blacklaw
Cornhill
Crannoch
Bracobrae
Davoch of Grange
Knock
Drumnagorrach
Farmtown
Nethermills
Knowehead
Ramsburn
Crombie Castle
Old Crombie
Aberchirder
Cranna
Knowes of Elrick
MORAY
Glenlatterach
Glen of Rothes
Auchinroath
Newlands
Mains of Cairnty
Shalloch
CAIRN UISH
Rothes
GLEN GRANT DISTILLERY
Aikenway
Balnabreich
Mulben
Fife Keith
Keith
STRATHISLA DISTILLERY
ISLA
Mains of Auchoynanie
Balloch Wood
Rosarie
Rosarie Forest
Burn of Rothes
Elchies Forest
CARN NA CAILLICHE
Arndilly Ho.
BEN AIGAN
Belnagarrow
KEITH AND DUFFTOWN RLY
Poolside
Blackhillock
North Whiteley
Edintore
Glen of Coachford
Coachford
Little Pitlurg
Ruthven
Tarryblake Ho.
Rothiemay Crossroads
Milltown of Rothiemay
Mains of Mayen
Yonder Bognie
Bogniebrae
FOURMAN HILL
Midplaugh
Haddoch
Milburn
Cairnie
THE BIN
The Bin Forest
Corse of Kinnoir
Cobairdy
Pitfancy
GLENDRONACH DISTILLERY
Forgue
Hillbrae
Inverkeithny
Auchininna
Fortrie
Brownhill
Drumblair
Whiteacen
Dandaleith
MACALLAN DISTILLERY
LADYCROFT AGRICULTURAL MUSEUM
Archiestown
CARDHU DISTILLERY
Cardow
Knockando
Knockando Ho.
Carron
Daugh of Kinermony
Speyview
Ringorm
Craigellachie
SPEYSIDE COOPERAGE VISITOR CENTRE
Charlestown of Aberlour
Glenallachie
Maggieknockater
Kininvie Ho.
Drummuir Castle
Drummuir
Towiemore
Midtown of Buchromb
Balvenie
Glack of Midthird
Slogan
Midtown of Glass
Drumdelgie
Daugh of Cairnborrow
Cairnborrow
Westerton
NORDIC SKI CENTRE
HUNTLY CASTLE
Huntly
BRANDER MUSEUM
Brideswell
Slioch
Lessendrum
Drumblade
Corse
Largue
Aucharnie
Denmoss
Balgaveny
Nether Lenshie
BALVENIE CASTLE
GLENFIDDICH DISTILLERY
Milltown of Auchindoun
Dufftown
Torry
Haugh of Glass
Terryhorn
Wellheads
Milltown of Edinvillie
Sheandow
Marypark
GLENFARCLAS DISTILLERY
Bellehiglash
Craggenmore
Kirktown of Mortlach
Lettoch
MEIKLE CONVAL
AUCHINDOUN CASTLE
THE SCALP
STRATHBOGIE
Bailiesward
Bridgend
Wester Mosshead
Drumdollo
Denend
Ythanwells
Thomastown
Hillhead
Bainshole
Milburn
Greystone
Redhill
Fisherford
Badenscoth
Logie Newton
BEN RINNES
Glen Rinnes
Favillar
Kirkhill
Glenfiddich Lodge
Glen Fiddich
Ballochford
Mill of Lynebain
Tomnaven
Succoth
Tillathrowie
Coynachie
Shanquhar
Corncatterach
Kirkstile
Blackburn
Culdrain
Glens of Foudland
HILL OF FOUDLAND
Kirkton of Culsalmond
Rothmaise
Colpy
Cairnhill
Clashindarroch Forest
Clashindarroch
Kirkney
Gartly
Mytice
Cults
KNOCKANDY HILL
LEITH HALL
Largie
Upper Boddam
Wrangham
Bonnyton
Wraes
Knockenbaird
Aulton
Newton Ho.
Old Rayne
Dalchirach
Haugh of Glenmaichlie
Craggan
Drumin
Downan
GLENLIVET DISTILLERY
Glenlivet
Shenval
Auchbreck
Castleton
Badeach
Glenfiddich Forest
Bridgend
Inverharroch
Ardwell
Blackwater Lodge
ROUND HILL
Auchmair
Cabrach
Aldivalloch
Aldunie
Blackwater Forest
Milton of Lesmore
Milton of Noth
Smithston
Kennethmont
Oldtown
Ardlair
Towie
The Shevock
Insch
Pitmachie
Ardoyne
Belhinnie
Rhynie
Cottown
Wheedlemont
Craig Castle
Clatt
Duncanstone
Auchmenzie
Knockespock Ho.
Leslie
Kirkton
Westhall
Oyne
Kirkton of Oyne
Auchleven
Lickleyhead Castle
BENNACHIE
Tomnavoulin
CARN AN T-SUIDHE
Knockandhu
Achdregnie
Auchnarrow
Glenlivet Forest
Clashnoir
Braes of Glenlivet
Chapeltown
Croughly
Scalan
HILL OF THREE STONES
THE BUCK
B9002
ST MARY'S CHURCH
Clova
SCOTTISH SCULPTURE WORKSHOP
Lumsden
CORREEN HILLS
Coldwells Croft
Bogs
Whitehaugh Forest
Muckletown
ABERDEEN
GARIOCH
Glenton
Newbigging
Milton
Glenbuchat Lodge
Badenyon
Mossat
Terpersie Castle
Tully
LORD ARTHUR'S CAIRN
Keig
Castle Forbes
Upper Woodend
Lower Woodend
Rinmore
Kildrummy
Milltown of Kildrummy
KILDRUMMY CASTLE & GARDEN
Bridge of Alford
Montgarrie
ALFORD VALLEY RAILWAY
HAUGHTON
GRAMPIAN TRANSPORT MUS
Rorandle
Pitfichie Forest
Pitfichie
Gateside
Alford
Auchintoul
Muir of
Belnacraig
Glenbuchat
Water of Buchat
Don
Deveron
Isla
Livet
301
292
293
0 2 4 6 miles
0 2 4 6 8 10 km
NJ
20
80
1 2 3 4 5 6
A B C D E F G H

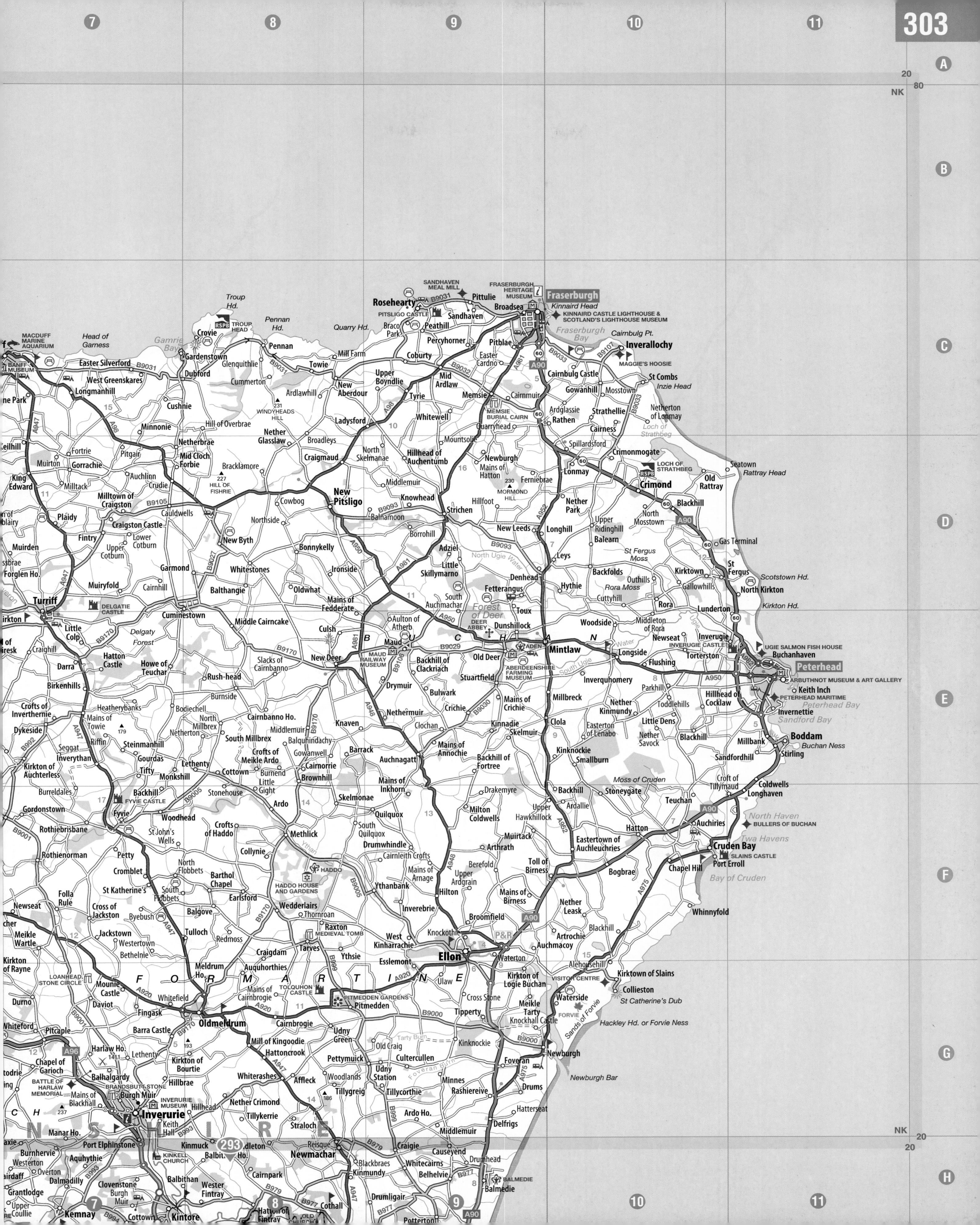

7
8
9
10
11
A
B
C
D
E
F
G
H
NK
20
80
Troup Hd.
Pennan Hd.
Quarry Hd.
SANDHAVEN MEAL MILL
Pittulie
FRASERBURGH HERITAGE MUSEUM
Fraserburgh
Kinnaird Head
KINNAIRD CASTLE LIGHTHOUSE & SCOTLAND'S LIGHTHOUSE MUSEUM
Rosehearty
PITSLIGO CASTLE
Sandhaven
Broadsea
Braco Park
Peathill
Fraserburgh Bay
Cairnbulg Pt.
Inverallochy
MAGGIE'S HOOSIE
MACDUFF MARINE AQUARIUM
Head of Garness
Gamrie Bay
Crovie
TROUP HEAD
Gardenstown
Pennan
Glenquithlie
Mill Farm
Towie
Coburty
Percyhorner
Pitblae
Easter Cardno
Cairnbulg Castle
St Combs
Inzie Head
BANFF MUSEUM
Easter Silverford
West Greenskares
Dubford
Cummerton
New Aberdour
Upper Boyndlie
Mid Ardlaw
Memsie
Cairnmuir
Gowanhill
Mosstown
Longmanhill
Cushnie
Ardlawhill
WINDYHEADS HILL
Tyrie
MEMSIE BURIAL CAIRN
Ardglassie
Rathen
Strathellie
Netherton of Lonmay
Minnonie
Hill of Overbrae
Nether Glasslaw
Ladysford
Whitewell
Quarryhead
Cairness
Loch of Strathbeg
Netherbrae
Broadleys
Mountsolie
Spillardsford
Crimonmogate
Fortrie
Pitgair
Mid Cloch Forbie
Craigmaud
North Skelmanae
Hillhead of Auchentumb
Newburgh
Mains of Hatton
Lonmay
LOCH OF STRATHBEG
Seatown
Rattray Head
Muirton
Gorrachie
Bracklamore
Ferniebrae
Crimond
Old Rattray
King Edward
Milltack
Auchlinn
Crudie
HILL OF FISHRIE
Middlemuir
MORMOND HILL
Milltown of Craigston
Cowbog
New Pitsligo
Knowhead
Hillfoot
Nether Park
Blackhill
Plaidy
Cauldwells
Northside
Balnamoon
Strichen
Upper Ridinghill
North Mosstown
Craigston Castle
Fintry
Lower Cotburn
Upper Cotburn
New Byth
Borrohill
New Leeds
Longhill
Balearn
Gas Terminal
Muirden
Bonnykelly
Adziel
North Ugie Water
Leys
St Fergus Moss
Forglen Ho.
Garmond
Whitestones
Ironside
Little Skillymarno
Backfolds
Kirktown
St Fergus
Scotstown Hd.
Muiryfold
Cairnhill
Balthangie
Oldwhat
Denhead
Hythie
Outhills
Gallowhills
Fetterangus
Rora Moss
North Kirkton
Turriff
DELGATIE CASTLE
Cuminestown
Mains of Fedderate
South Auchmachar
Cuttyhill
Rora
Kirkton Hd.
Toux
Forest of Deer
Lunderton
Middle Cairncake
Aulton of Atherb
Dunshillock
DEER ABBEY
Woodside
Middleton of Rora
Little Colp
Delgaty Forest
Culsh
Maud
Mintlaw
Newseat
Inverugie
INVERUGIE CASTLE
UGIE SALMON FISH HOUSE
Buchanhaven
Craighill
Hatton Castle
Slacks of Cairnbanno
New Deer
MAUD RAILWAY MUSEUM
Backhill of Clackriach
Old Deer
ABERDEENSHIRE FARMING MUSEUM
Longside
Flushing
Torterston
Peterhead
Darra
Howe of Teuchar
Rush-head
Stuartfield
South Ugie Water
Inverquhomery
ARBUTHNOT MUSEUM & ART GALLERY
Keith Inch
PETERHEAD MARITIME
Birkenhills
Burnside
Drymuir
Bulwark
Parkhill
Hillhead of Cocklaw
Peterhead Bay
Crofts of Inverthernie
Heatherybanks
Bodiechell
North Millbrex
Cairnbanno Ho.
Nethermuir
Crichie
Mains of Crichie
Millbreck
Nether Kinmundy
Toddlehills
Invernettie
Sandford Bay
Dykeside
Mains of Towie
Netherton
Middlemuir
Knaven
Clochan
Kinnadie
Clola
Easterton of Lenabo
Little Dens
Skelmuir
Nether Savock
Blackhill
Boddam
Buchan Ness
Seggat
Riffin
Steinmanhill
South Millbrex
Balquhindachy
Barrack
Mains of Annochie
Kinknockie
Smallburn
Millbank
Stirling
Inverythan
Gourdas
Crofts of Meikle Ardo
Gowanwell
Auchnagatt
Backhill of Fortree
Sandfordhill
Kirkton of Auchterless
Tifty
Lethenty
Cottown
Burnend
Cairnorrie
Brownhill
Moss of Cruden
Croft of Tillymaud
Monkshill
Little Gight
Mains of Inkhorn
Drakemyre
Backhill
Stoneygate
Coldwells
Longhaven
Burreldales
Backhill
FYVIE CASTLE
Stonehouse
Ardo
Skelmonae
Milton Coldwells
Upper Hawkhillock
Ardallie
Teuchan
Gordonstown
Fyvie
Woodhead
Quilquox
North Haven
BULLERS OF BUCHAN
Auchiries
Rothiebrisbane
St John's Wells
Crofts of Haddo
Methlick
South Quilquox
Muirtack
Eastertown of Auchleuchries
Hatton
Twa Havens
Collynie
Drumwhindle
Arthrath
Cruden Bay
SLAINS CASTLE
Port Erroll
Rothienorman
Petty
North Flobbets
Cairnleith Crofts
Berefeld
Toll of Birness
Bogbrae
Chapel Hill
Bay of Cruden
Cromblet
Barthol Chapel
HADDO
Mains of Arnage
Upper Ardgrain
St Katherine's
South Flobbets
HADDO HOUSE AND GARDENS
Ythanbank
Hilton
Mains of Birness
Folla Rule
Earlsford
Wedderlairs
Nether Leask
Whinnyfold
Newseat
Cross of Jackston
Byebush
Balgove
Thornroan
Inverebrie
Broomfield
Raxton
MEDIEVAL TOMB
Blackhill
Artrochie
Meikle Wartle
Jackstown
Tulloch
West Kinharrachie
Knockothie
Auchmacoy
Westertown
Bethelnie
Redmoss
Craigdam
Tarves
Ythsie
Ellon
Waterton
Kirkton of Rayne
LOANHEAD STONE CIRCLE
Meldrum Ho.
Auquhorthies
Esslemont
Alehousehill
Kirktown of Slains
Mounie Castle
F O R M A R T I N E
Ulaw
Kirkton of Logie Buchan
VISITOR CENTRE
Collieston
Durno
Daviot
Whitefield
Mains of Cairnbrogie
TOLQUHON CASTLE
PITMEDDEN GARDENS
Pitmedden
Cross Stone
Waterside
St Catherine's Dub
Fingask
Oldmeldrum
Tipperty
Meikle Tarty
FORVIE
Knockhall Castle
Sands of Forvie
Hackley Hd. or Forvie Ness
Whiteford
Pitcaple
Barra Castle
Cairnbrogie
Udny Green
Tarty Burn
Kinknockie
Newburgh
Harlaw Ho.
Lethenty
Mill of Kingoodie
Hattoncrook
Old Craig
Culterculien
Foveran
Chapel of Garioch
Kirkton of Bourtie
Pettymuick
Udny Station
Foveran Burn
Newburgh Bar
Balhalgardy
Hillbrae
Whiterashes
Affleck
Woodlands
Minnes
BATTLE OF HARLAW MEMORIAL
BRANDSBUTT STONE
Burgh Muir
Mains of Blackhall
INVERURIE MUSEUM
Hillhead
Nether Crimond
Tillygreig
Tillycorthie
Rashiereive
Drums
Tillykerrie
Ardo Ho.
Hatterseat
Inverurie
Keith Hall
Straloch
Middlemuir
Delgatie
Manar Ho.
Port Elphinstone
Kinmuck
Balbithan Ho.
Reisque
Craigie
Causeyend
Drumhead
Newmachar
Burnhervie
Aquhythie
KINKELL CHURCH
Blackbraes
Whitecairns
Westerton
Overton
Kinmundy
Belhelvie
Dalmadilly
Cairnpark
BALMEDIE
Balmedie
Clovenstone
Balbithan
Wester Fintray
Grantlodge
Burgh Muir
Drumligair
Cothall
Upper Coullie
Kemnay
Cottown
Kintore
Hatton of Fintray
OLD CHURCH
Potterton
C H
N S H I R E
A90
A98
A947
A950
A952
A981
A948
A975
A920
A96
A93
B9031
B9032
B9033
B9107
B9105
B9027
B9170
B9093
B9029
B9030
B9106
B9005
B9001
B9000
B999
B979
B977
B993
B994
B992
293
P&R
RSPB

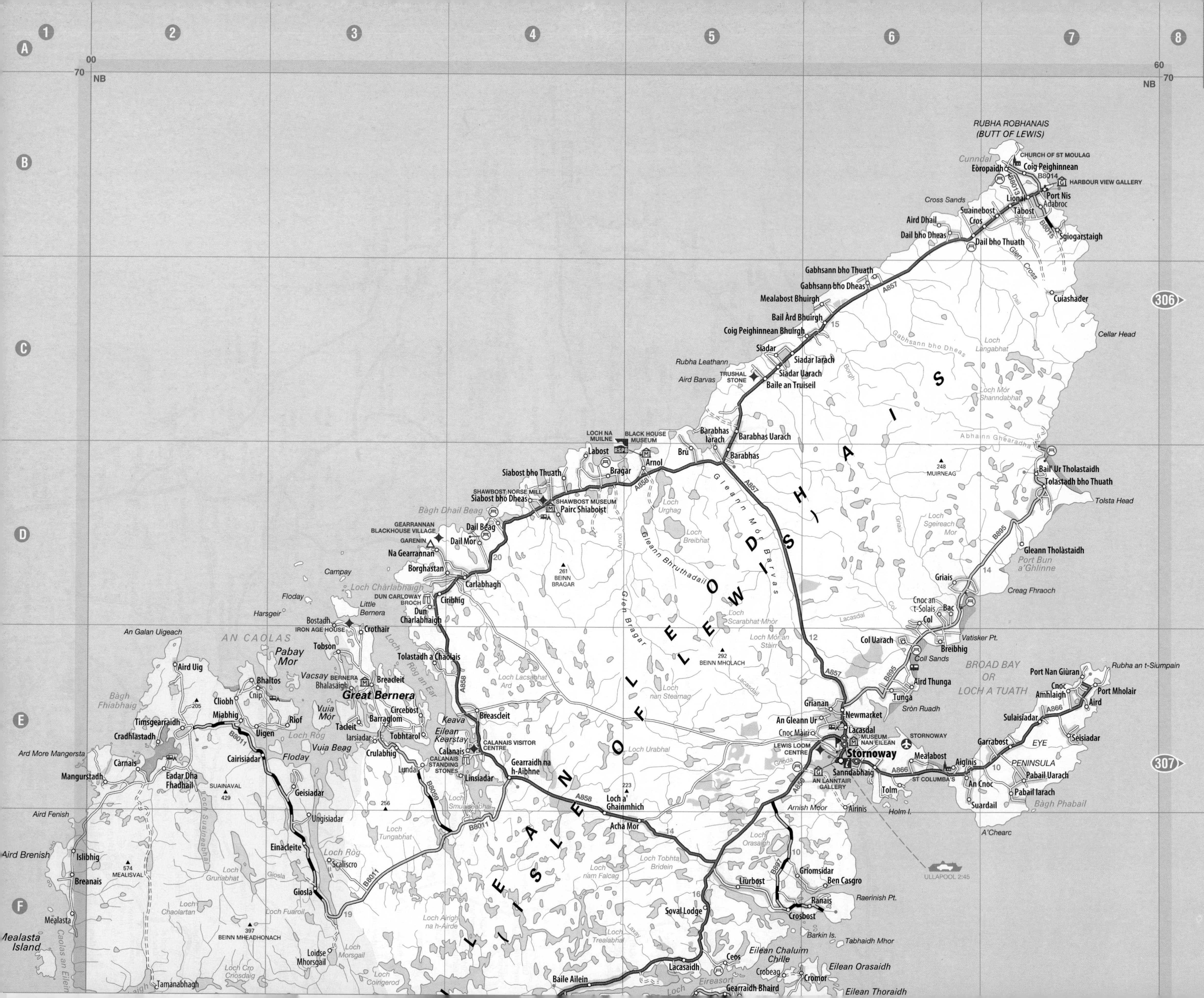
ISLE OF LEWIS (LEÒDHAS)
RUBHA ROBHANAIS
(BUTT OF LEWIS)
CHURCH OF ST MOULAG
Eòropaidh
Coig Peighinnean
HARBOUR VIEW GALLERY
Cunndal
Cross Sands
Lional
Port Nis
Adabroc
Suainebost
Cros
Tabost
Aird Dhail
Dail bho Dheas
Dail bho Thuath
Sgiogarstaigh
Glen Cross
Gabhsann bho Thuath
Gabhsann bho Dheas
Mealabost Bhuirgh
Bail Àrd Bhuirgh
Coig Peighinnean Bhuirgh
Cuiashader
Cellar Head
Siadar
Siadar Iarach
Siadar Uarach
Baile an Truiseil
Rubha Leathann
Aird Barvas
TRUSHAL STONE
Loch Langabhat
Loch Mòr Shanndabhat
Abhainn Ghearadha
Barabhas Iarach
Barabhas Uarach
Barabhas
LOCH NA MUILNE
BLACK HOUSE MUSEUM
Labost
Brù
Arnol
Bragar
248 MUIRNEAG
Bail' Ur Tholastaidh
Tolastadh bho Thuath
Tolsta Head
Siabost bho Thuath
SHAWBOST NORSE MILL
Siabost bho Dheas
SHAWBOST MUSEUM
Pairc Shiaboist
Bàgh Dhail Beag
GEARRANNAN BLACKHOUSE VILLAGE
GARENIN
Dail Beag
Dail Mòr
Na Gearrannan
Loch Urghag
Loch Breibhat
Gleann Bhruthadail
Gleann Mòr Barvas
Loch Sgeireach Mor
Gleann Tholàstaidh
Port Bun a'Ghlinne
261 BEINN BRAGAR
Borghastan
Carlabhagh
Campay
Loch Chàrlabhaigh
DUN CARLOWAY BROCH
Little Bernera
Floday
Ciribhig
Dun Charlabhaigh
Glen Bragar
Griais
Creag Fhraoch
Cnoc an t-Solais
Bac
Col
Harsgeir
Bostadh
IRON AGE HOUSE
Crothair
Loch Scarabhat Mhòr
An Galan Uigeach
AN CAOLAS
Pabay Mor
Tobson
Loch Mòr an Stàirr
Col Uarach
Vatisker Pt.
Breibhig
Coll Sands
Tolastadh a Chaolais
292 BEINN MHOLACH
Aird Uig
Bhaltos
Vacsay
BERNERA
Bhalasaigh
Breacleit
Great Bernera
Loch Lacsabhat Ard
Loch nan Stearnag
BROAD BAY OR LOCH A TUATH
Port Nan Giùran
Rubha an t-Siumpain
Aird Thunga
Cnoc
Amhlaigh
Port Mholair
Aird
Bàgh Fhiabhaig
Cliobh
Cnip
Vuia Mor
Circebost
Tunga
Sròn Ruadh
Grianan
Sulaisiadar
Timsgearraidh
Miabhig
Uigen
Riof
Tacleit
Barraglom
Keava
Breascleit
Newmarket
An Gleann Ur
Lacasdal
Cradhlastadh
Loch Ròg
Iarsiadar
Tobhtarol
Eilean Kearstay
CALANAIS VISITOR CENTRE
Cnoc Màiri
MUSEUM NAN EILEAN
STORNOWAY
Garrabost
EYE PENINSULA
Seisiadar
Ard More Mangersta
Càrnais
Cairisiadar
Floday
Vuia Beag
Crulabhig
Calanais
Loch Urabhal
LEWIS LOOM CENTRE
Stornoway
Mealabost
Aiginis
Mangurstadh
Eadar Dha Fhadhail
Lundal
CALANAIS STANDING STONES
Gearraidh na h-Aibhne
Sanndabhaig
AN LANNTAIR GALLERY
ST COLUMBA'S
10
Pabail Uarach
SUAINAVAL 429
Geisiadar
Linsiadar
223
Tolm
An Cnoc
Pabail Iarach
Aird Fenish
Loch Suaineabhal
256
Loch Smuaisbhal
Loch a' Ghainmhich
Arnish Moor
Airinis
Suardail
Bàgh Phabail
Ungisiadar
Loch Tungabhat
Acha Mor
Holm I.
A'Chearc
Aird Brenish
Islibhig
Einacleite
Loch Ròg
Scaliscro
Loch Orasaigh
Loch Tobhta Brìdein
574 MEALISVAL
Loch Grunabhat
Giosla
Loch nam Falcag
Liurbost
Griomsidar
Ben Casgro
ULLAPOOL 2:45
Breanais
Giosla
Raerinish Pt.
Ranais
Loch Chaolartan
Loch Fuaroil
Soval Lodge
Crosbost
Mealasta
Loch Airigh na h-Airde
Mealasta Island
Caolas an Eilein
397 BEINN MHEADHONACH
Barkin Is.
Tabhaidh Mhor
Loch Trealabhal
Laxay
Loidse Mhorsgail
Loch Morsgail
Eilean Chaluim Chille
Ceos
Eilean Orasaidh
Loch Cro Criosdaig
Loch Coirigerod
Lacasaidh
Crobeag
Cromor
Tamanabhagh
Baile Ailein
Eireasort
Gearraidh Bhaird
Eilean Thoraidh
A857
A858
A859
A866
B895
B897
B8011
B8013
B8014
B8015
B8059
306
307
NB
00
60
70

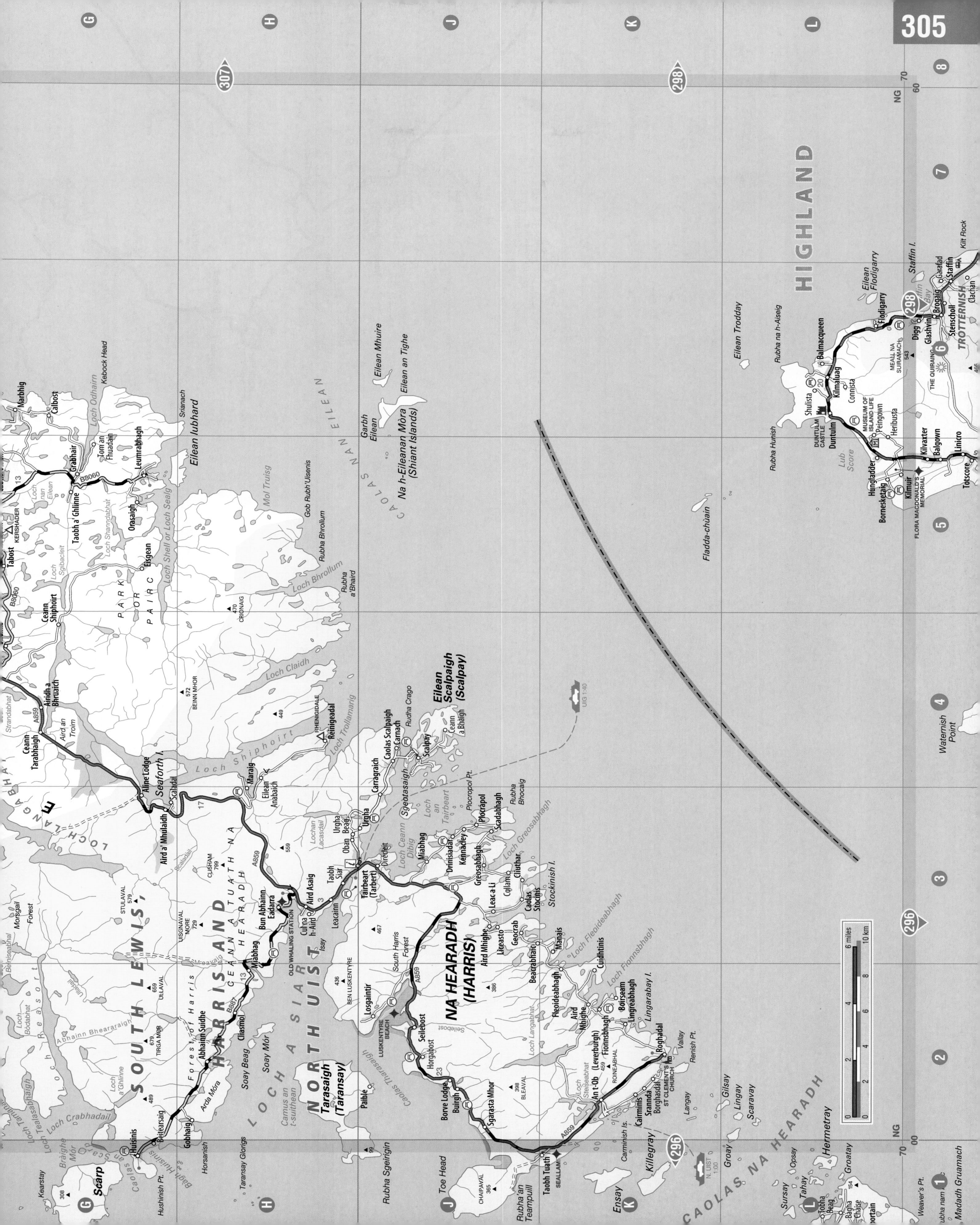
HIGHLAND
SOUTH LEWIS
HARRIS AND
NORTH UIST
NA HEARADH (HARRIS)
CEANN A TUATH NA HEARADH
PARK OR PAIRC
CAOLAS NAN EILEAN
LOCH A SIAR
CAOLAS NA HEARADH
Na h-Eileanan Mòra (Shiant Islands)
Eilean Scalpaigh (Scalpay)
Tarasaigh (Taransay)
Scarp
Tairbeart (Tarbert)
An t-Ob (Leverburgh)
Eilean Iubhard
Eilean Mhuire
Eilean an Tighe
Garbh Eilean
Eilean Trodday
Eilean Flodigarry
Fladda-chùain
Staffin I.
Kilt Rock
TROTTERNISH
Duntulm
DUNTULM CASTLE
MUSEUM OF ISLAND LIFE
FLORA MACDONALD'S MEMORIAL
THE QUIRAING
Waternish Point
Loch Shiphoirt
Loch Claidh
Loch Bhrollum
Seaforth I.
Aline Lodge
Loch Seaforth
Ceann Tarabhaigh
Ceann Shiphoirt
Leumrabhagh
Graibhair
Marbhig
Calbost
Kebock Head
Loch Odhairn
Loch Shell or Loch Sealg
Rubha Bhrollum
Gob Rubh'Uisenis
Reinigeadal
Loch Trollamarig
Caolas Scalpaigh
Urgha
Miabhag
Plocrapol
Scadabhagh
Loch Greosabhagh
Stockinish I.
Loch Fleoideabhagh
Loch Fionnsbhagh
Lingarabay I.
Roghadal
Renish Pt.
Killegray
Ensay
Gilsay
Lingay
Scaravay
Hermetray
Groay
Toe Head
Rubha an Teampuill
Taobh Tuath
Seallam!
Sgarasta Mhor
Borve Lodge
Horgabost
Seilebost
Luskentyre Beach
Losgaintir
Clasmol
Soay Mòr
Soay Beag
Abhainn Suidhe
Huisinis
Hushinish Pt.
Kearstay
Taransay Glorigs
Rubha Sgeirigin
Paible
Old Whaling Station
Bun Abhainn Eadarra
Aird Asaig
Leacainn
Uig 1:40
N. Uist 1:00
Eilean Lacasdale
A859
B887
B8060
307
298
296
NG
Forest of Harris
South Harris Forest
Clisham 799
Uisgnaval More 729
Stulaval 579
Beinn Mhor 572
Crionaig 470
Bleaval 398
Ben Luskentyre 436
Roineabhal 459
Chaipaval 365
Ullaval 659
Tirga Mor 679
6 miles
10 km

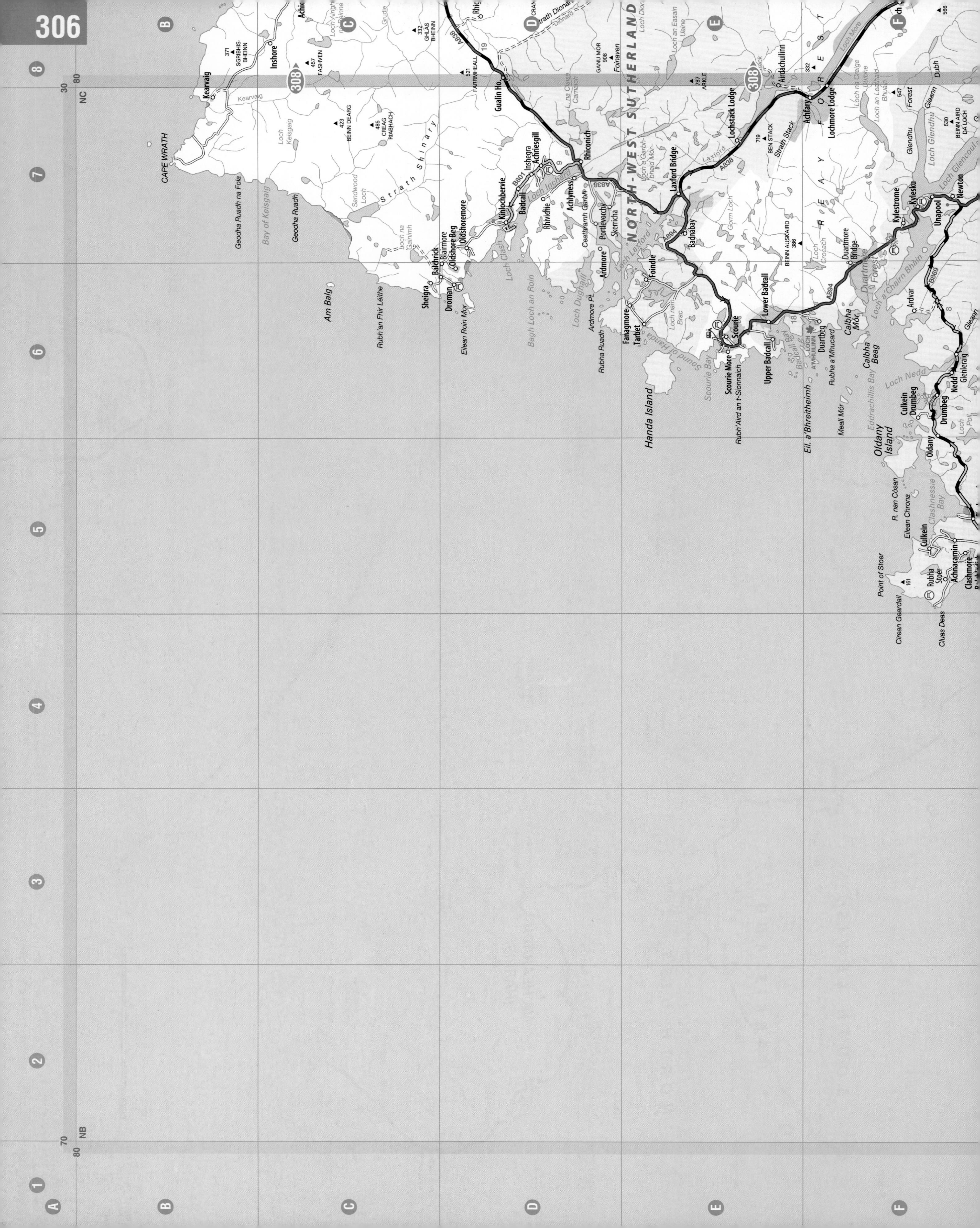
CAPE WRATH
Kearvaig
Inshore
SGRIBHIS-BHEINN
FASHVEN
BEINN DEARG
CREAG RIABHACH
GHLAS BHEINN
FARRMHEALL
Strath Shinary
Sandwood Loch
Loch Keisgaig
Bay of Keisgaig
Geodha Ruadh na Fola
Geodha Ruadh
Am Balg
Rubh'an Fhir Léithe
Sheigra
Balchrick
Blairmore
Oldshore Beg
Oldshoremore
Droman
Eilean Roin Mor
Kinlochbervie
Badcall
Inshegra
Achriesgill
Loch Inchard
Rhiconich
Gualin Ho.
Rhivichie
Achlyness
Portlevorchy
Skerricha
Ardmore
Ardmore Pt.
Loch Clash
Bagh Loch an Roin
Loch Dughaill
Rubha Ruadh
Strath Dionard
GANU MOR
Foinaven
ARKLE
NORTH-WEST SUTHERLAND
Laxford Bridge
Loch Laxford
Foindle
Fanagmore
Tarbet
Handa Island
Sound of Handa
Badnabay
Lochstack Lodge
BEN STACK
Strath Stack
Achfary
Lochmore Lodge
Airdachuilinn
REAY FOREST
Scourie
Scourie More
Scourie Bay
Rubh'Aird an t-Sionnaich
Lower Badcall
Upper Badcall
Badcall Bay
Eil. a'Bhreitheimh
Duartbeg
Duartmore Bridge
Duartmore Forest
BEINN AUSKAIRD
Loch Crocach
Rubha a'Mhucard
Calbha Mòr
Calbha Beag
Meall Mòr
Eddrachillis Bay
Kylestrome
Kylesku
Unapool
Newton
Loch Glencoul
Loch Glendhu
Glendhu Forest
BEINN AIRD DA LOCH
Ardvar
Loch a'Chairn Bhàin
Loch Nedd
Nedd
Glenleraig
Drumbeg
Culkein Drumbeg
Oldany
Oldany Island
R. nan Còsan
Eilean Chrona
Clashnessie Bay
Culkein
Achnacarnin
Clashmore
Rubha Stoer
Point of Stoer
Cirean Geardail
Cluas Deas
A838
A894
B801
B869
308
NC
NB

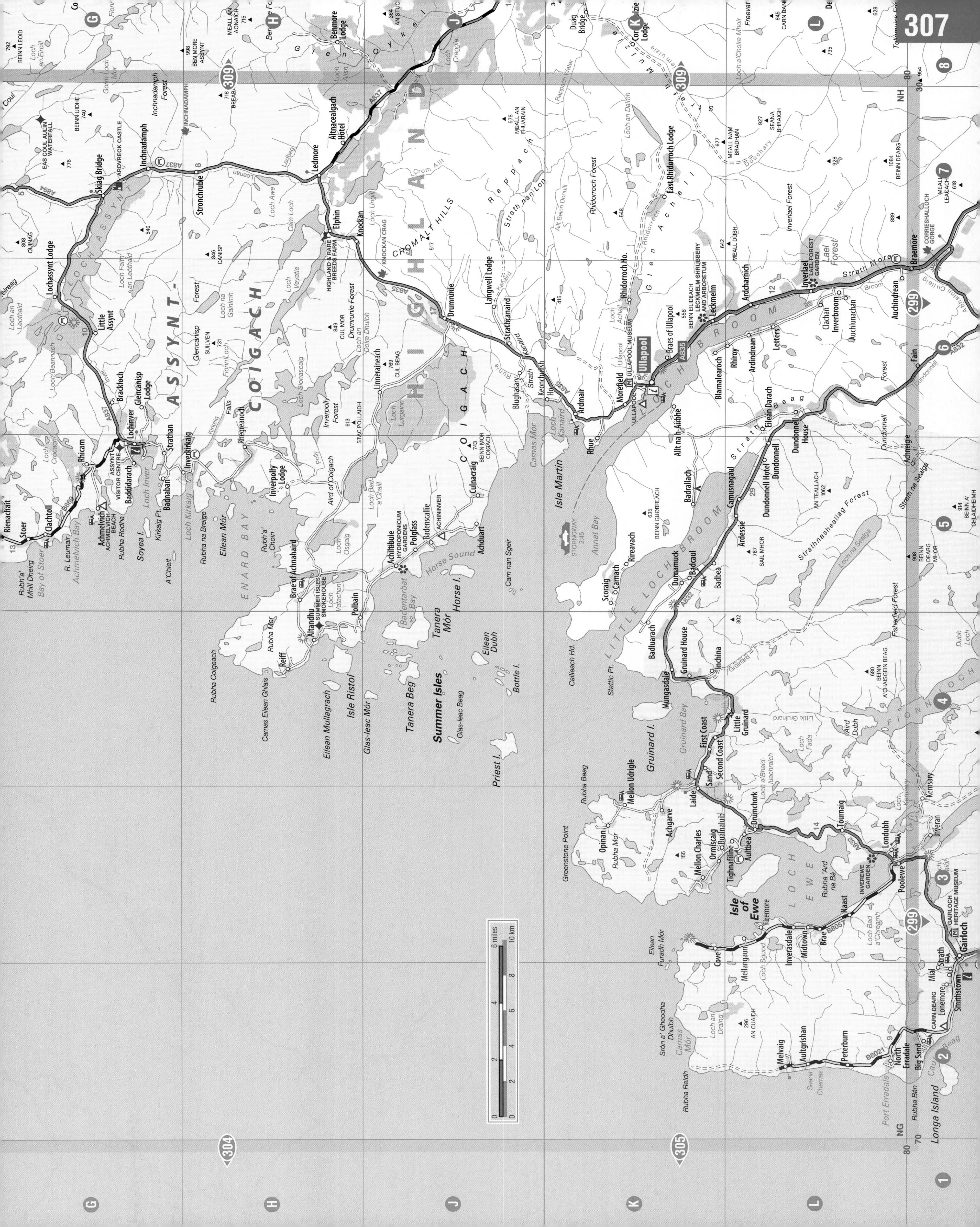

ASSYNT
COIGACH
HIGHLAND
Lochinver
Ullapool
Gairloch
Poolewe
Aultbea
Laide
Achiltibuie
Polbain
Altandhu
Reiff
Stoer
Clachtoll
Achmelvich
Inverkirkaig
Strathan
Badnaban
Baddidarach
Inverpolly Lodge
Culnacraig
Achduart
Polglass
Badenscallie
Elphin
Knockan
Ledmore
Inchnadamph
Skiag Bridge
Little Assynt
Drumrunie
Strathcanaird
Ardmair
Morefield
Rhue
Braes of Ullapool
Leckmelm
Ardcharnich
Inverlael
Braemore
Auchindrean
Inverbroom
Fain
Dundonnell
Camusnagaul
Badcaul
Scoraig
Badluarach
Mungasdale
Inchina
Little Gruinard
First Coast
Second Coast
Sand
Achgarve
Mellon Udrigle
Opinan
Drumchork
Tournaig
Londubh
Inverewe Garden
Naast
Brae
Inverasdale
Cove
Melvaig
Peterburn
North Erradale
Big Sand
Smithstown
Strath
Isle Martin
Tanera Mòr
Tanera Beg
Summer Isles
Isle Ristol
Priest I.
Gruinard I.
Isle of Ewe
Longa Island
Enard Bay
Little Loch Broom
Loch Broom
Loch Ewe
Gruinard Bay
Rubha Reidh
Greenstone Point
Ullapool Museum
Gairloch Heritage Museum
Highland & Rare Breeds Farm
Knockan Crag
Cromalt Hills
Ardvreck Castle
Eas Coul Aulin Waterfall
Stac Pollaidh
Cul Beag
Cul Mor
Suilven
Canisp
Ben More Assynt
An Teallach
Strathnasheallag Forest
Fisherfield Forest
Rhidorroch Forest
Inverlael Forest
Corrieshalloch Gorge
A835
A837
A832
A894
B869
B8021
6 miles
10 km
304
305
309
299

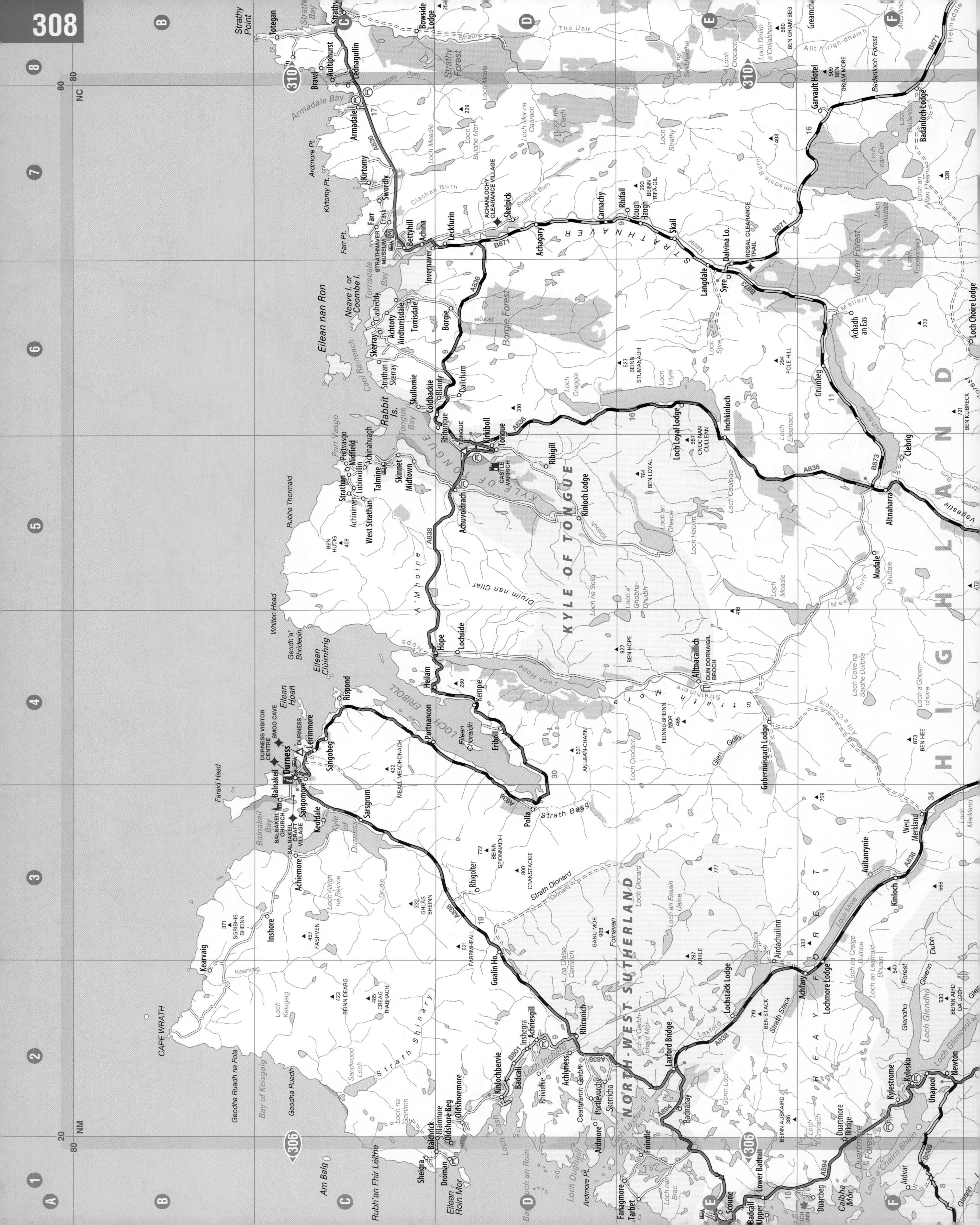
CAPE WRATH
Kearvaig
Inshore
Achiemore
Balnakeil Bay
BALNAKEIL CHURCH
BALNAKEIL CRAFT VILLAGE
Balnakeil
Faraid Head
Durness
DURNESS VISITOR CENTRE
SMOO CAVE
Sangomore
Keoldale
Kyle of Durness
Sarsgrum
Sangobeg
Leirinmore
Eilean Hoan
Rispond
Portnancon
LOCH ERIBOLL
Eilean Choraidh
Eriboll
Polla
Strath Beag
Heilam
Kempie
Hope
Lochside
Loch Hope
BEN HOPE
Alltnacaillich
DUN DORNAIGIL BROCH
Strathmore
Gobernuisgach Lodge
Glen Golly
Whiten Head
Eilean Clùimhrig
A'Mhoine
West Strathan
Achininver
Strathan
Talmine
Skinnet
Midtown
Melness
Achuvoldrach
KYLE OF TONGUE
CASTLE VARRICH
Tongue
Kirkiboll
Ribigill
Kinloch Lodge
BEN LOYAL
Rabbit Is.
Tongue Bay
Coldbackie
Skullomie
Dalcharn
Loch Loyal
Loch Loyal Lodge
Inchkinloch
Borgie
Borgie Forest
Torrisdale
Skerray
Eilean nan Ron
Neave I. or Coombe I.
Invernaver
STRATHNAVER MUSEUM
Bettyhill
Farr
Farr Pt.
Swordly
Kirtomy
Armadale
Armadale Bay
Lednagullin
Strathy Point
Strathy
Strathy Forest
Leckfurin
Skelpick
ACHANLOCHY CLEARANCE VILLAGE
Achagary
Carnachy
Rhifail
Skail
Syre
Langdale
Dalvina Lo.
ROSAL CLEARANCE TRAIL
STRATHNAVER
Naver Forest
Grumbeg
Achadh an Eas
Clebrig
Altnaharra
Mudale
Garvault Hotel
Badanloch Lodge
Badanloch Forest
HIGHLAND
NORTH-WEST SUTHERLAND
Foinaven
ARKLE
Gualin Ho.
Rhiconich
Achriesgill
Inshegra
Kinlochbervie
Oldshoremore
Blairmore
Balchrick
Sheigra
Strath Shinary
Sandwood Loch
Laxford Bridge
Lochstack Lodge
Achfary
Lochmore Lodge
Aultanrynie
Kinloch
West Merkland
REAY FOREST
Kylestrome
Kylesku
Unapool
Newton
Scourie
Badcall
Fanagmore
Tarbet
Foindle
Duartmore Bridge
Duartbeg
Loch Glencoul
Rhiconich
Achlyness
Badnabay
Ardmore
Skerricha
A836
A838
A894
B801
B871
B873
310
306
NC
NM
A B C D E F

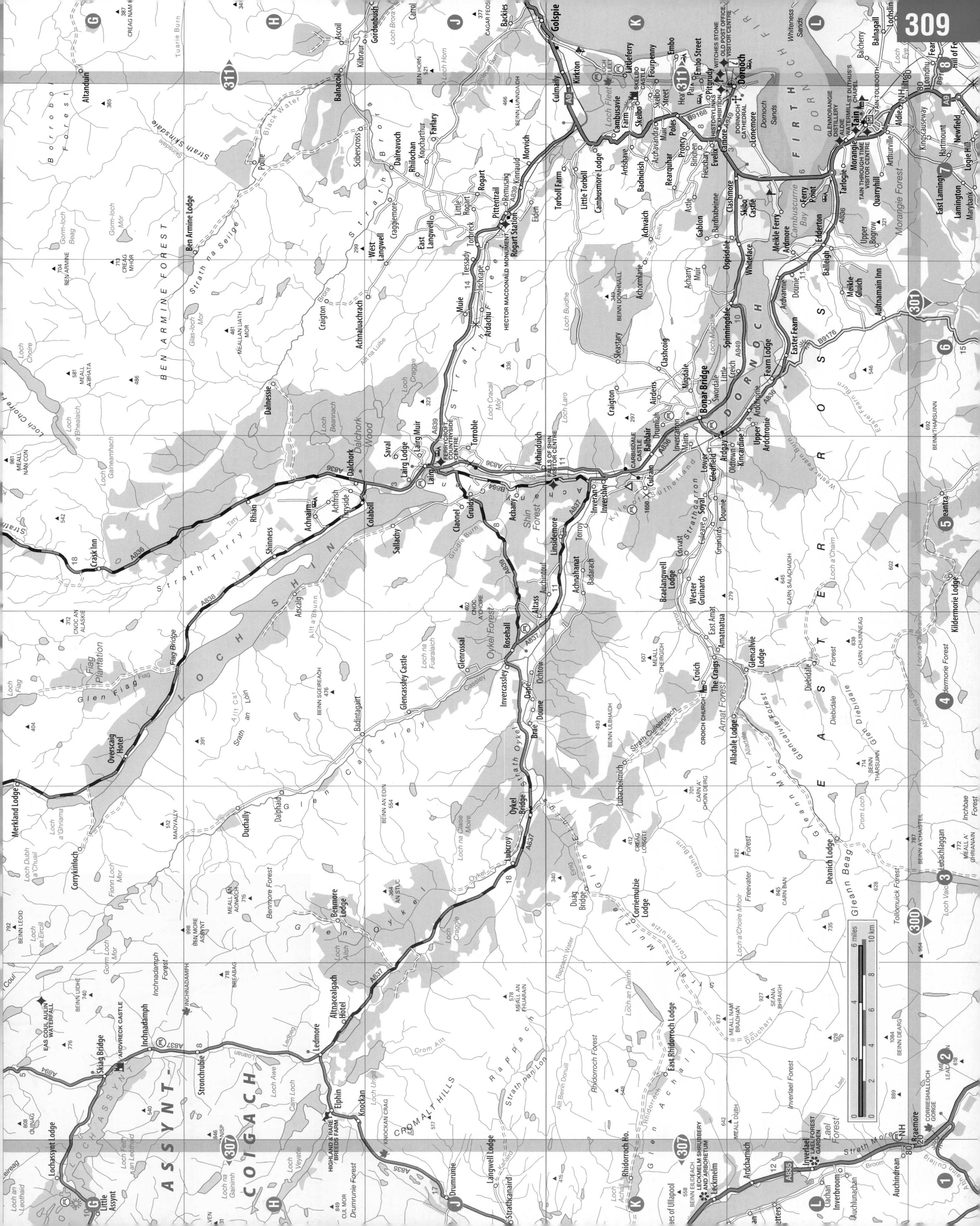

Golspie
Backies
Gordonbush
Loch Brora
Carrol
Ascoil
Kilbraur
Balnacoil
Altanduin
Borrobol Forest
Strath Skinsdale
Black Water
Ben Armine Lodge
BEN ARMINE FOREST
Strath na Seilge
Sciberscross
Dalreavoch
Rhilochan
Knocharthur
Farlary
Rogart
Little Rogart
Craggiemore
West Langwell
East Langwell
Torbreck
Pittentrail
Rogart Station
Remusaig
Kinnauld
Morvich
HECTOR MACDONALD MONUMENT
Eiden
Tressady
Inchcape
Muie
Ardachu
Achnaluachrach
Craigton
Dalnessie
Loch Craggie
Lairg Muir
Lairg Lodge
Saval
Lairg
Dalchork
Dalchork Wood
FERRYCROFT COUNTRYSIDE CENTRE
Torroble
Achinduich
FALLS OF SHIN VISITOR CENTRE
Crask Inn
Rhian
Shinness
Strath Tirry
Achnairn
Achfrish
Tirryside
Colaboll
Sallachy
LOCH SHIN
Claonel
Gruids
Achany
Shin Forest
Linsidemore
Torroy
Achnahanat
Badarach
Auchintoul
Altass
Aoscaig
Fiag Plantation
Glen Fiag
Fiag Bridge
Loch Fiag
Overscaig Hotel
Merkland Lodge
Glencassley Castle
Glenrossal
Rosehall
Oykel Forest
Invercassley
Badintagairt
Glen Cassley
Ochtow
Doune
Brae
Oape
Strath Oykel
Oykel Bridge
Lubcroy
Dalphaid
Duchally
Corrykinloch
Benmore Lodge
Benmore Forest
Glen Oykel
Loch Ailsh
Altnacealgach Hotel
Ledmore
Inchnadamph
Inchnadamph Forest
ARDVRECK CASTLE
Skiag Bridge
EAS COUL AULIN WATERFALL
Stronchrubie
Loch Assynt
Lochassynt Lodge
Little Assynt
ASSYNT-COIGACH
Elphin
Knockan
HIGHLAND & RARE BREEDS FARM
KNOCKAN CRAG
CROMALT HILLS
Drumrunie
Drumrunie Forest
Langwell Lodge
Strathcanaird
Strath nan Lon
Rappach Water
Rhidorroch Forest
Rhidorroch Ho.
East Rhidorroch Lodge
Glen Achall
LECKMELM SHRUBBERY AND ARBORETUM
Leckmelm
Ardcharnich
Inverlael
LAEL FOREST GARDEN
Lael Forest
Inverlael Forest
Strath More
Braemore
CORRIESHALLOCH GORGE
Inverbroom
Auchlunachan
Auchindrean
Clachan
Duag Bridge
Corriemulzie Lodge
Glen Einig
Lubachoinnich
Strath Cuileannach
CROICH CHURCH
Croich
The Craigs
Amat Forest
Amat Lodge
Alladale Lodge
Glencalvie Forest
Glencalvie Lodge
Gleann Mor
Deanich Lodge
Gleann Beag
Freevater Forest
Diebidale
Diebidale Forest
Kildermorie Lodge
East Amat
Amatnatua
Wester Gruinards
Braelangwell Lodge
Corvost
Culrain
Gruinards
Strathcarron
Invershin
Inveran
Kyle of Sutherland
CARBISDALE CASTLE
Balblair
Drumliah
Airdens
Invercarron Mains
Ardgay
Lower Gledfield
Oldtown
Kincardine
Upper Ardchronie
Ardchronie
Bonar Bridge
Swordale
Migdale
Loch Migdale
Spinningdale
Clashcoig
Creich
Fearn Lodge
Easter Fearn
Ospisdale
Whiteface
Gablon
Achvaich
Acharry Muir
Achormlarie
Sleastary
Loch Buidhe
Cambusmore Lodge
Little Torboll
Torboll Farm
Culmaily
Kirkton
Loch Fleet
LOCH FLEET
Littleferry
SKELBO CASTLE
Skelbo
Skelbo Street
Skelbo Muir
Cambusavie Farm
Fourpenny
Embo
Embo Street
WITCHES STONE
OLD POST OFFICE VISITOR CENTRE
Dornoch
DORNOCH CATHEDRAL
HISTORYLINKS EXHIBITION
Pitgrudy
Poles
Achavandra Muir
Ardshave
Badninish
Rearquhar
Proncy
Birichen
Evelix
Fleuchary
Astle
Bardnabeinne
Clashmore
Skibo Castle
Cuthill
Camore
Lonemore
Dornoch Sands
DORNOCH FIRTH
Cambuscurrie Bay
Ferry Point
Meikle Ferry
Ardmore
Edderton
Balleigh
Meikle Gluich
Ardvannie
Aultnamain Inn
Tarlogie
Morangie
TAIN THROUGH TIME VISITOR CENTRE
Tain
GLENMORANGIE DISTILLERY
TAIN TOLBOOTH
Aldie
Arthurville
Kingscauseway
Hartmount
Newfield
Logie Hill
Quarryhill
Upper Bogrow
Morangie Forest
East Lamington
Lamington
Marybank
Balnagall
Balcherry
Lochslin
Loandhu
Whiteness Sands
Lubachlaggan
Tollomuick Forest

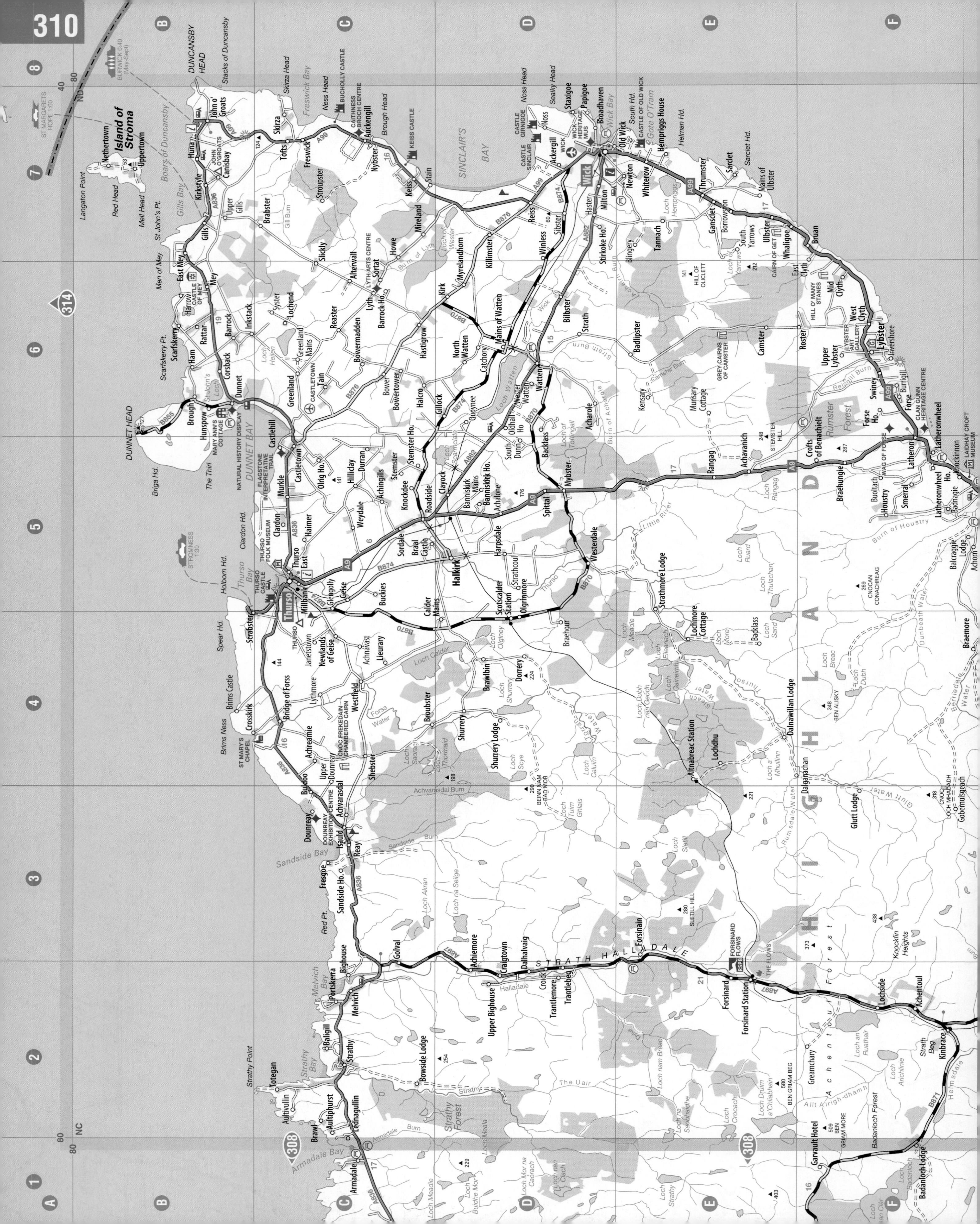
DUNCANSBY HEAD
Stacks of Duncansby
Island of Stroma
Nethertown
Uppertown
John o' Groats
Canisbay
Huna
Freswick
Skirza
Auckengill
Nybster
Keiss
Stain
SINCLAIR'S BAY
Wick
Wick Bay
Noss Head
Staxigoe
Papigoe
Broadhaven
Old Wick
CASTLE OF OLD WICK
Hempriggs House
Thrumster
Sarclet
Ulbster
Whaligoe
Bruan
East Clyth
Mid Clyth
West Clyth
Lybster
Forse
Latheron
Latheronwheel
Dunbeath Water
Braemore
DUNNET HEAD
Dunnet
Dunnet Bay
Brough
Castletown
Mey
CASTLE OF MEY
East Mey
Gills Bay
Thurso
Thurso Bay
Scrabster
Halkirk
Watten
Mains of Watten
Bilbster
Spittal
Mybster
Westerdale
Georgemas
Strathmore Lodge
Altnabreac Station
Dalnawillan Lodge
Glutt Lodge
Forsinard
Forsinard Station
FORSINARD FLOWS
STRATH HALLADALE
Kinbrace
Badanloch Lodge
Garvault Hotel
Melvich
Portskerra
Bighouse
Strathy
Strathy Point
Armadale
Armadale Bay
Reay
Dounreay
Sandside Bay
Crosskirk
Brims Ness
Bridge of Forss
Loch Calder
Loch Watten
H I G H L A N D
Achentoul Forest
Strathy Forest
Rumster Forest

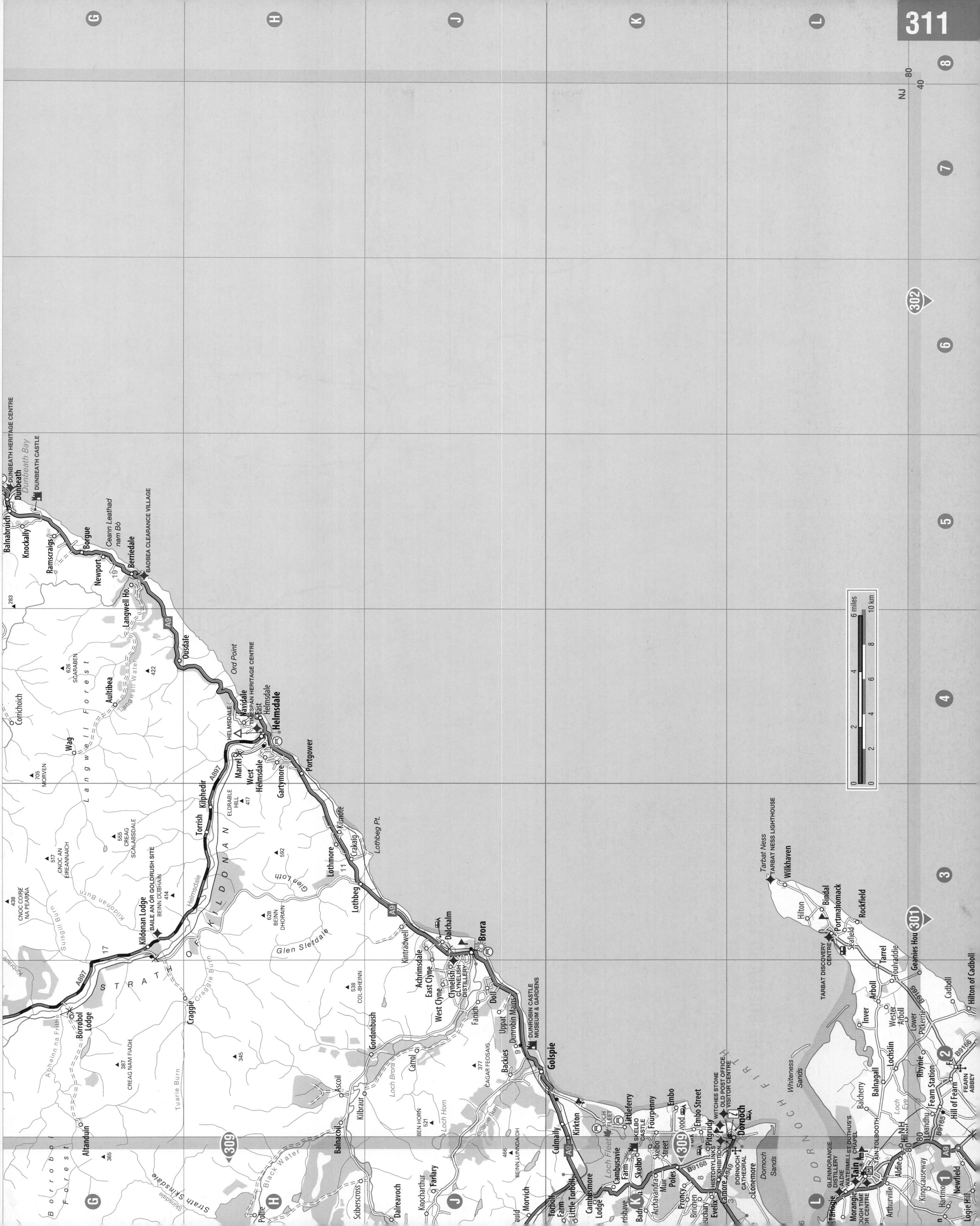

G
H
J
K
L
8
7
6
5
4
3
2
1
NJ
80
40
302
301
309
Dunbeath
DUNBEATH HERITAGE CENTRE
Dunbeath Bay
DUNBEATH CASTLE
Balnabruich
Knockally
Borgue
Ramscraigs
Ceann Leathad nam Bò
Newport
Berriedale
BADBEA CLEARANCE VILLAGE
Langwell Ho.
A9
Ousdale
Ord Point
Navidale
TIMESPAN HERITAGE CENTRE
East Helmsdale
Helmsdale
HELMSDALE
West Helmsdale
Marrel
Gartymore
Portgower
Corrichoich
Aultibea
Langwell Water
Langwell Forest
Wag
MORVEN
SCARABEN
CREAG SCALABSDALE
CNOC AN EIREANNAICH
CNOC COIRE NA FEARNA
Kilphedir
A897
Torrish
ELDRABLE HILL
Kildonan Lodge
BAILE AN OR GOLDRUSH SITE
BEINN DUBHAIN
Helmsdale
Kildonan Burn
Suisgill Burn
STRATH OF KILDONAN
Kilmote
Crakaig
Lothbeg Pt.
Lothmore
Lothbeg
Glen Loth
BEINN DHORAIN
Glen Sletdale
Craggie
Craggie Burn
Borrobol Lodge
Abhainn na Frithe
CREAG NAM FIADH
Tuarie Burn
Altanduin
Borrobol Forest
Strath Skinsdale
Skinsdale
Black Water
Balnacoil
Ascoil
Kilbraur
Gordonbush
Loch Brora
Carrol
BEN HORN
Loch Horn
Knocharthur
Farlary
Dalreavoch
Sciberscross
Pollie
Morvich
BEINN LUNNDAIDH
Backies
CAGAR FEOSAIG
Uppat
Dunrobin Mains
DUNROBIN CASTLE MUSEUM & GARDENS
Golspie
Fanich
Doll
West Clyne
East Clyne
Clynelish
CLYNELISH DISTILLERY
Achrimsdale
Kintradwell
Dalchalm
Brora
COL-BHEINN
Culmaily
Kirkton
Little Torboll
Torboll Farm
Cambusmore Lodge
Loch Fleet
LOCH FLEET
Littleferry
SKELBO CASTLE
Skelbo
Cambusavie Farm
Fourpenny
Skelbo Street
Embo
Embo Street
Poles
Pronsy
Pitgrudy
Dornoch
HISTORYLINKS EXHIBITION
WITCHES STONE
OLD POST OFFICE
VISITOR CENTRE
DORNOCH CATHEDRAL
Lonemore
Dornoch Sands
Evelix
Birichen
B9168
DORNOCH FIRTH
Whiteness Sands
Tarbat Ness
TARBAT NESS LIGHTHOUSE
Wilkhaven
Hilton
Bindal
Portmahomack
Rockfield
TARBAT DISCOVERY CENTRE
Seafield
Tarrel
Toulvaddie
Geanies House
Arboll
Inver
Wester Arboll
Lower Pitkerrie
Cadboll
Hilton of Cadboll
B9165
Lochslin
Balnagall
Balcherry
Rhynie
Fearn Station
Hill of Fearn
FEARN ABBEY
B9166
Loandhu
Tain
Aldie
Arthurville
Kingscauseway
Newfield
Logie Hill
GLENMORANGIE DISTILLERY
ALDIE WATERMILL
DUTHUS'S CHAPEL
TAIN TOLBOOTH
0 2 4 6 miles
0 2 4 6 8 10 km

THE SHETLAND ISLANDS

Scale 1:250,000

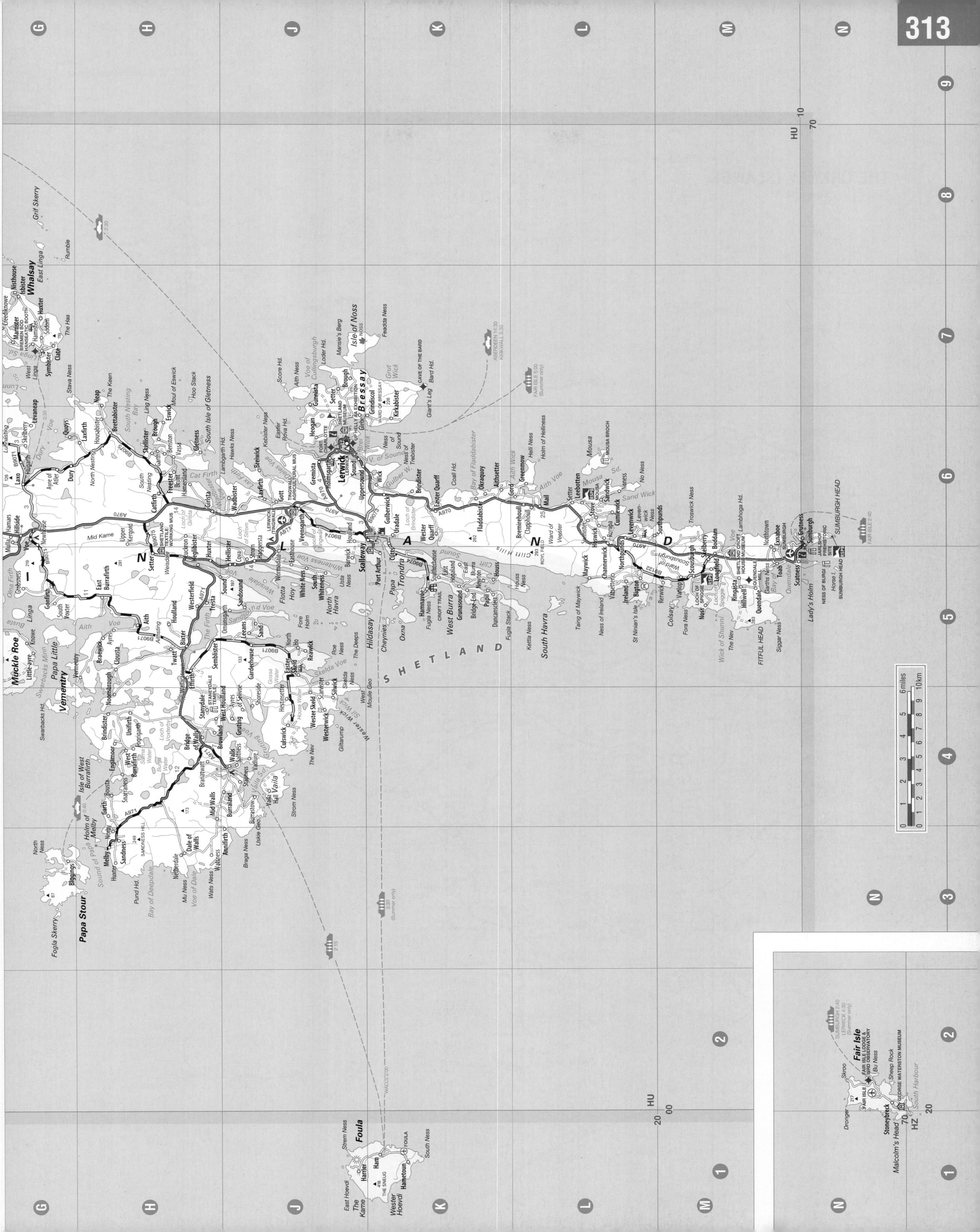
SHETLAND
Whalsay
Isle of Noss
Bressay
Lerwick
Scalloway
Trondra
West Burra
East Burra
South Havra
Mousa
Muckle Roe
Papa Little
Vementry
Papa Stour
Isle of West Burrafirth
Vaila
Foula
Fair Isle
Sumburgh
SUMBURGH HEAD
FITFUL HEAD
St Ninian's Isle
Hildasay
Oxna
Papa
Aith
Bixter
Walls
Sandness
Gott
Tingwall
Whiteness
Weisdale
Cunningsburgh
Sandwick
Levenwick
Bigton
Quendale
Scatness
Grutness
Voe
Laxo
Catfirth
Girlsta
Nesting
Skellister
Brettabister
Symbister
Hamister
Cliff Hills
Royl Field
Ward of Bressay
Mid Kame
Hametoun
Ham
Harrier
The Sneug
Stoneybreck
Malcolm's Head
Sheep Rock
Bu Ness
Skroo
George Waterston Museum
Fair Isle Lodge & Bird Observatory
Jarlshof Prehistoric Site
Mousa Broch
Shetland Museum
Fort Charlotte
Croft Trail
Stanydale Temple
Cave of the Bard
Shetland Croft House Museum
Aberdeen 14:30
Kirkwall 5:30
Fair Isle 5:00 (Summer only)
Sumburgh 2:40
Lerwick 4:30 (Summer only)
Fair Isle 2:40
Walls 2:00
3:30 (Summer only)
0 1 2 3 4 5 6 miles
0 1 2 3 4 5 6 7 8 9 10 km
HU
HZ
G H J K L M N
1 2 3 4 5 6 7 8 9

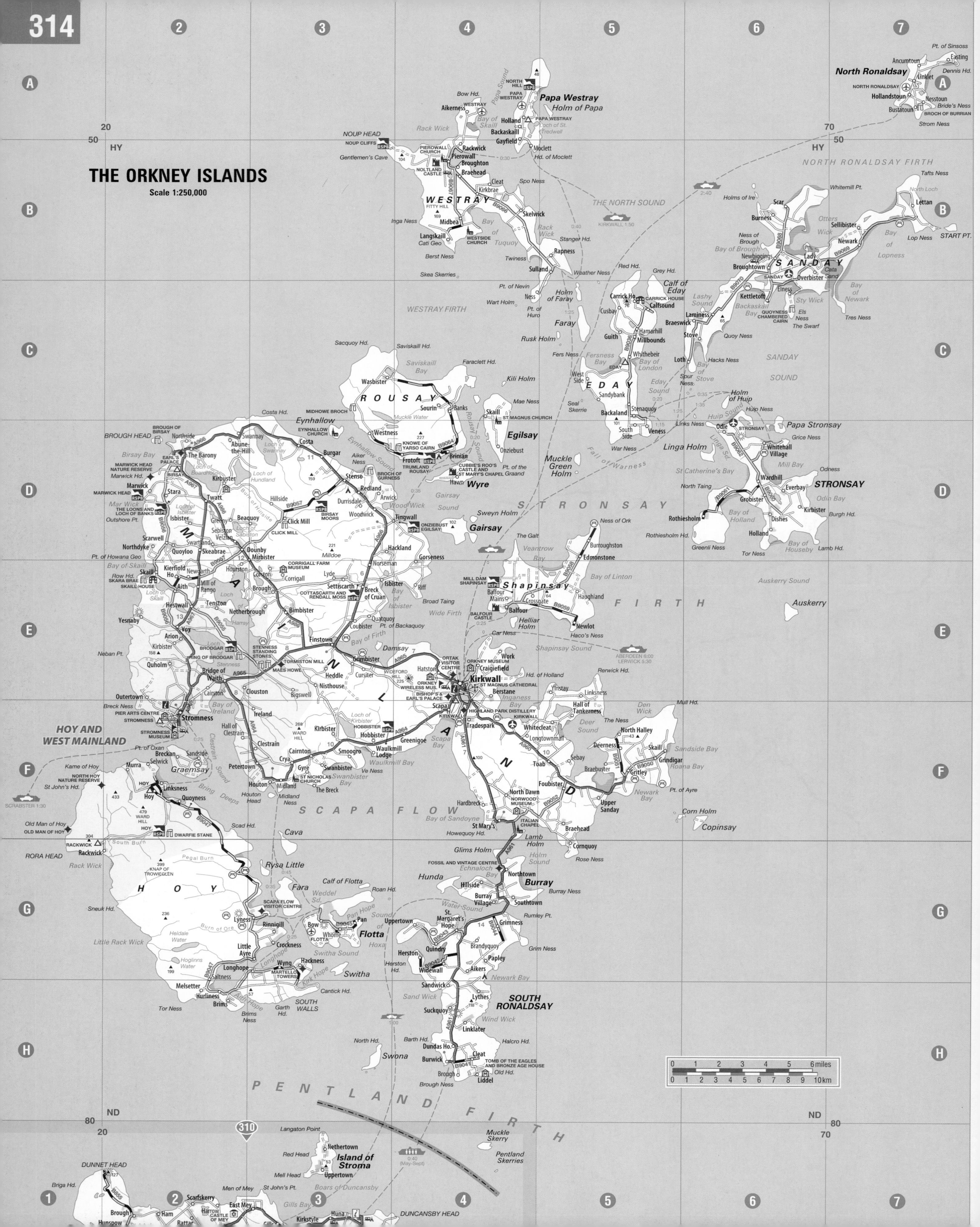
THE ORKNEY ISLANDS
Scale 1:250,000
HOY AND WEST MAINLAND
North Ronaldsay
Papa Westray
Holm of Papa
WESTRAY
Westray Firth
THE NORTH SOUND
NORTH RONALDSAY FIRTH
SANDAY
SANDAY SOUND
Calf of Eday
EDAY
Faray
ROUSAY
Eynhallow
Egilsay
Wyre
Gairsay
Muckle Green Holm
Papa Stronsay
STRONSAY
Linga Holm
Shapinsay
Auskerry
Auskerry Sound
STRONSAY FIRTH
Kirkwall
Stromness
MAINLAND
Finstown
Copinsay
SCAPA FLOW
Cava
Rysa Little
Fara
Flotta
Hunda
Burray
Switha
HOY
SOUTH RONALDSAY
SOUTH WALLS
Swona
Muckle Skerry
Pentland Skerries
PENTLAND FIRTH
Island of Stroma
DUNNET HEAD
DUNCANSBY HEAD
Noup Head
Pierowall
Rapness
Pt. of Sinsoss
Dennis Hd.
Start Pt.
Tafts Ness
Lop Ness
Tres Ness
Marwick Hd.
Brough Head
Yesnaby
Neban Pt.
Rora Head
Old Man of Hoy
Tor Ness
Brough Ness
Rose Ness
Mull Hd.
Scrabster 1:30
Aberdeen 6:00 Lerwick 5:30
0 1 2 3 4 5 6 miles
0 1 2 3 4 5 6 7 8 9 10 km

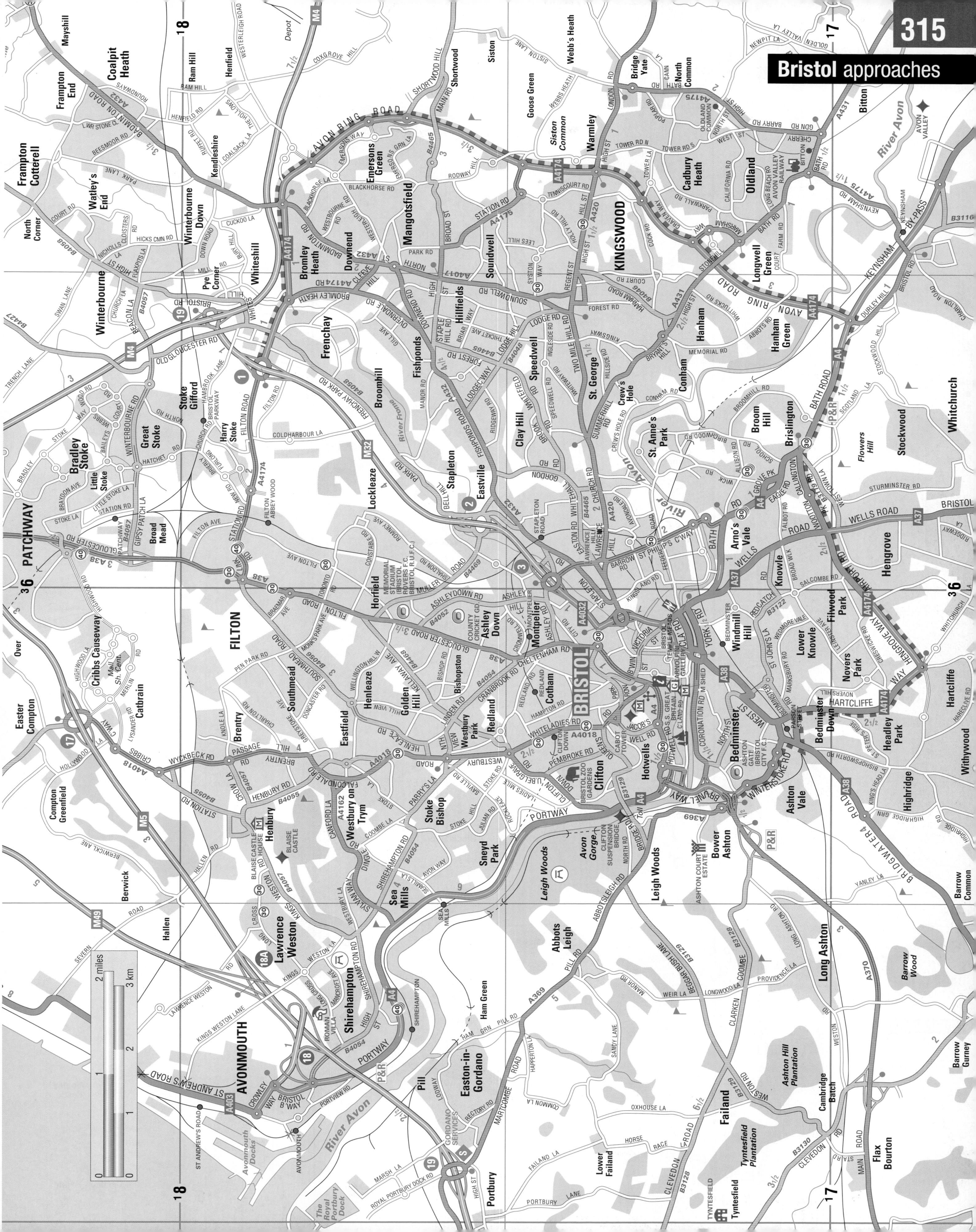
BRISTOL
AVONMOUTH
KINGSWOOD
FILTON
PATCHWAY
Frampton Cotterell
Frampton End
Coalpit Heath
Mayshill
Ram Hill
Henfield
Siston
Webb's Heath
Bridge Yate
North Common
Bitton
Goose Green
Siston Common
Warmley
Emersons Green
Mangotsfield
Kendleshire
Winterbourne Down
Watley's End
North Corner
Winterbourne
Whiteshill
Pye Corner
Bromley Heath
Downend
Soundwell
Oldland
Cadbury Heath
Longwell Green
Hanham
Hanham Green
Frenchay
Fishponds
Hillfields
Staple Hill
Speedwell
St. George
Crew's Hole
Conham
Broomhill
Stoke Gifford
Harry Stoke
Great Stoke
Bradley Stoke
Little Stoke
Broad Mead
Lockleaze
Stapleton
Eastville
Clay Hill
St. Anne's Park
Broom Hill
Brislington
Stockwood
Whitchurch
Flowers Hill
Arno's Vale
Knowle
Hengrove
Filwood Park
Horfield
Ashley Down
Montpelier
Windmill Hill
Lower Knowle
Novers Park
Hartcliffe
Cribbs Causeway
Over
Catbrain
Easter Compton
Southmead
Henleaze
Golden Hill
Bishopston
Redland
Cotham
Brentry
Eastfield
Westbury Park
Clifton
Hotwells
Bedminster
Bedminster Down
Headley Park
Withywood
Compton Greenfield
Henbury
Westbury on Trym
Stoke Bishop
Sneyd Park
Leigh Woods
Avon Gorge
Bower Ashton
Ashton Vale
Highridge
Berwick
Hallen
Lawrence Weston
Sea Mills
Abbots Leigh
Shirehampton
Ham Green
Long Ashton
Barrow Wood
Barrow Common
Pill
Easton-in-Gordano
Failand
Lower Failand
Tyntesfield
Tyntesfield Plantation
Ashton Hill Plantation
Cambridge Batch
Flax Bourton
Barrow Gurney
Portbury
Avonmouth Docks
The Royal Portbury Dock
River Avon
River Frome
Keynsham
AVON RING ROAD
M4
M5
M32
M49
A4
A38
A37
A4174
A432
A4018
A403
A369
A370
2 miles
3 km
18
17
36

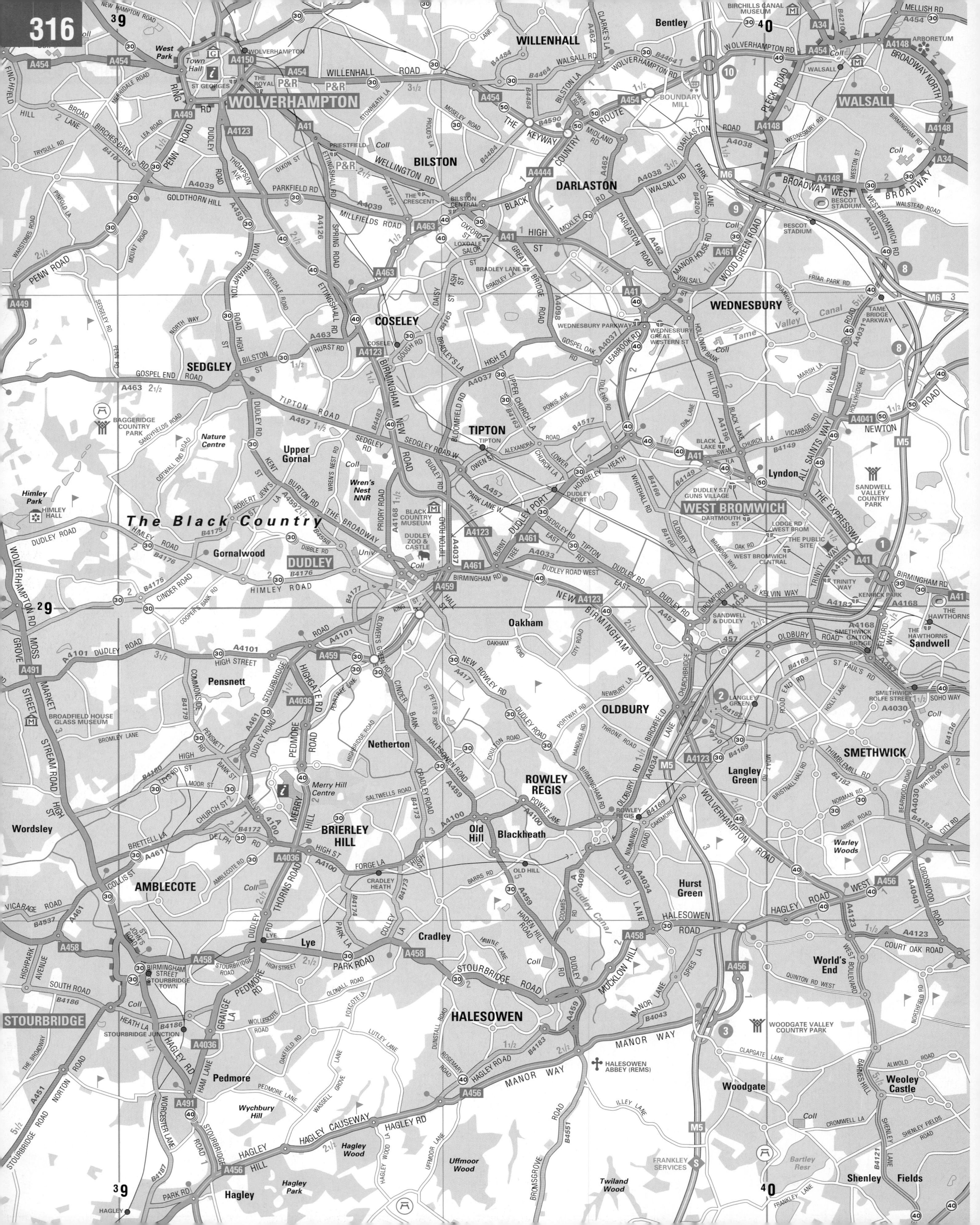

WOLVERHAMPTON
WILLENHALL
Bentley
WALSALL
BILSTON
DARLASTON
COSELEY
WEDNESBURY
SEDGLEY
TIPTON
Upper Gornal
Wren's Nest NNR
Black Country Museum
Dudley Zoo & Castle
Lyndon
WEST BROMWICH
NEWTON
Sandwell Valley Country Park
Himley Park
Himley Hall
The Black Country
Gornalwood
DUDLEY
Oakham
Sandwell
Pensnett
Broadfield House Glass Museum
OLDBURY
Netherton
SMETHWICK
Langley Green
ROWLEY REGIS
Merry Hill Centre
Wordsley
BRIERLEY HILL
Old Hill
Blackheath
Warley Woods
AMBLECOTE
Cradley Heath
Hurst Green
Lye
Cradley
World's End
STOURBRIDGE
HALESOWEN
Woodgate Valley Country Park
Halesowen Abbey (REMS)
Pedmore
Woodgate
Weoley Castle
Wychbury Hill
Hagley Wood
Uffmoor Wood
Frankley Services
Bartley Resr
Hagley
Hagley Park
Twiland Wood
Shenley
Fields
Baggeridge Country Park
Nature Centre
Dudley Canal
Tame Valley Canal

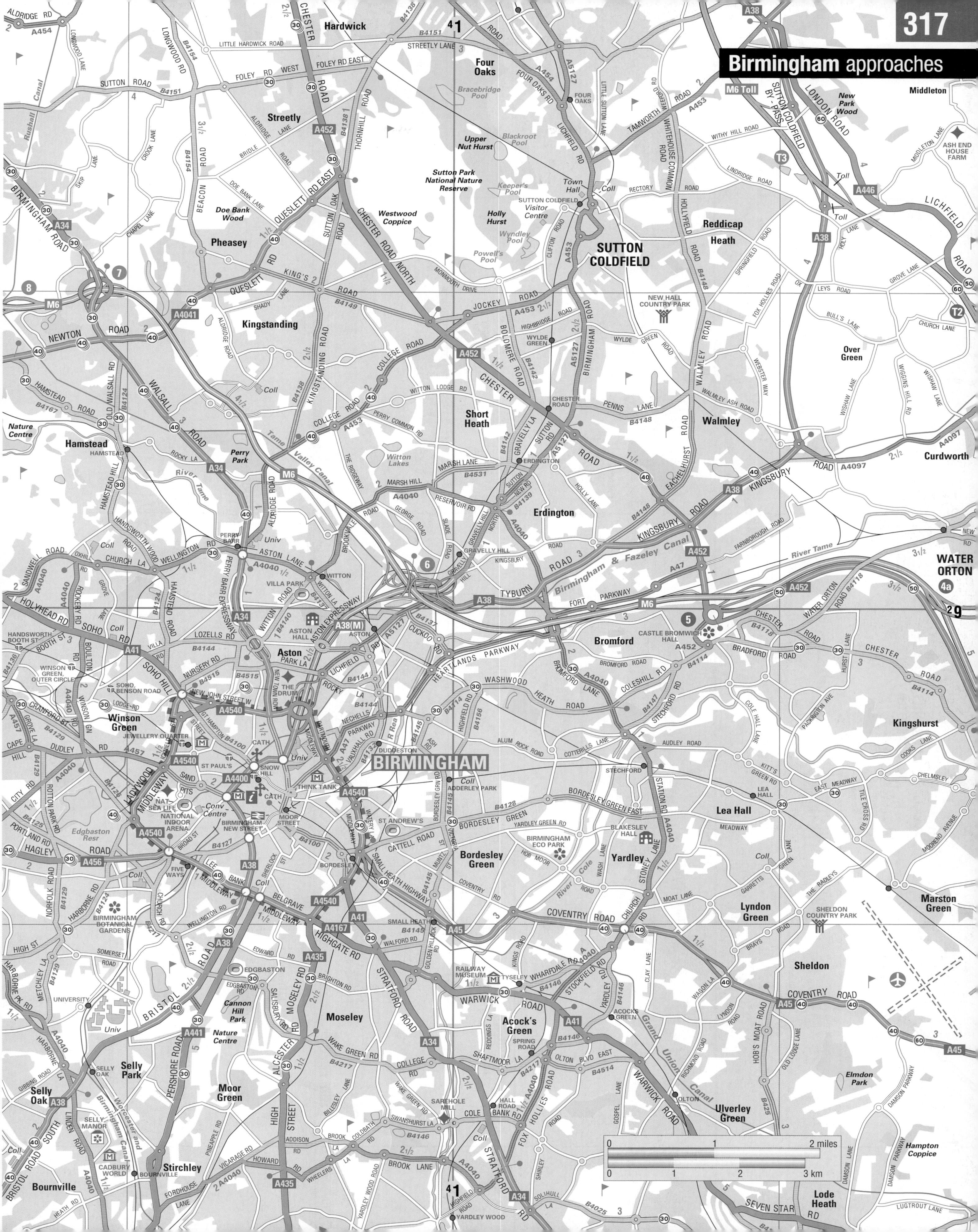
Hardwick
Four Oaks
Streetly
Upper Nut Hurst
Sutton Park National Nature Reserve
Westwood Coppice
Holly Hurst
Doe Bank Wood
Pheasey
SUTTON COLDFIELD
Reddicap Heath
Middleton
New Park Wood
ASH END HOUSE FARM
Kingstanding
NEW HALL COUNTRY PARK
Over Green
Short Heath
Walmley
Hamstead
Nature Centre
Perry Park
Witton Lakes
Erdington
Curdworth
WATER ORTON
VILLA PARK
ASTON HALL
Aston
Bromford
CASTLE BROMWICH HALL
Kingshurst
Winson Green
BIRMINGHAM
Lea Hall
Edgbaston Resr
BIRMINGHAM ECO PARK
BLAKESLEY HALL
Bordesley Green
Yardley
Lyndon Green
SHELDON COUNTRY PARK
Marston Green
BIRMINGHAM BOTANICAL GARDENS
Sheldon
RAILWAY MUSEUM
Moseley
Cannon Hill Park
Nature Centre
Acock's Green
Selly Park
Selly Oak
Moor Green
Elmdon Park
Ulverley Green
SAREHOLE MILL
CADBURY WORLD
Stirchley
Bournville
Hampton Coppice
Lode Heath
0 1 2 miles
0 1 2 3 km

Cardiff approaches

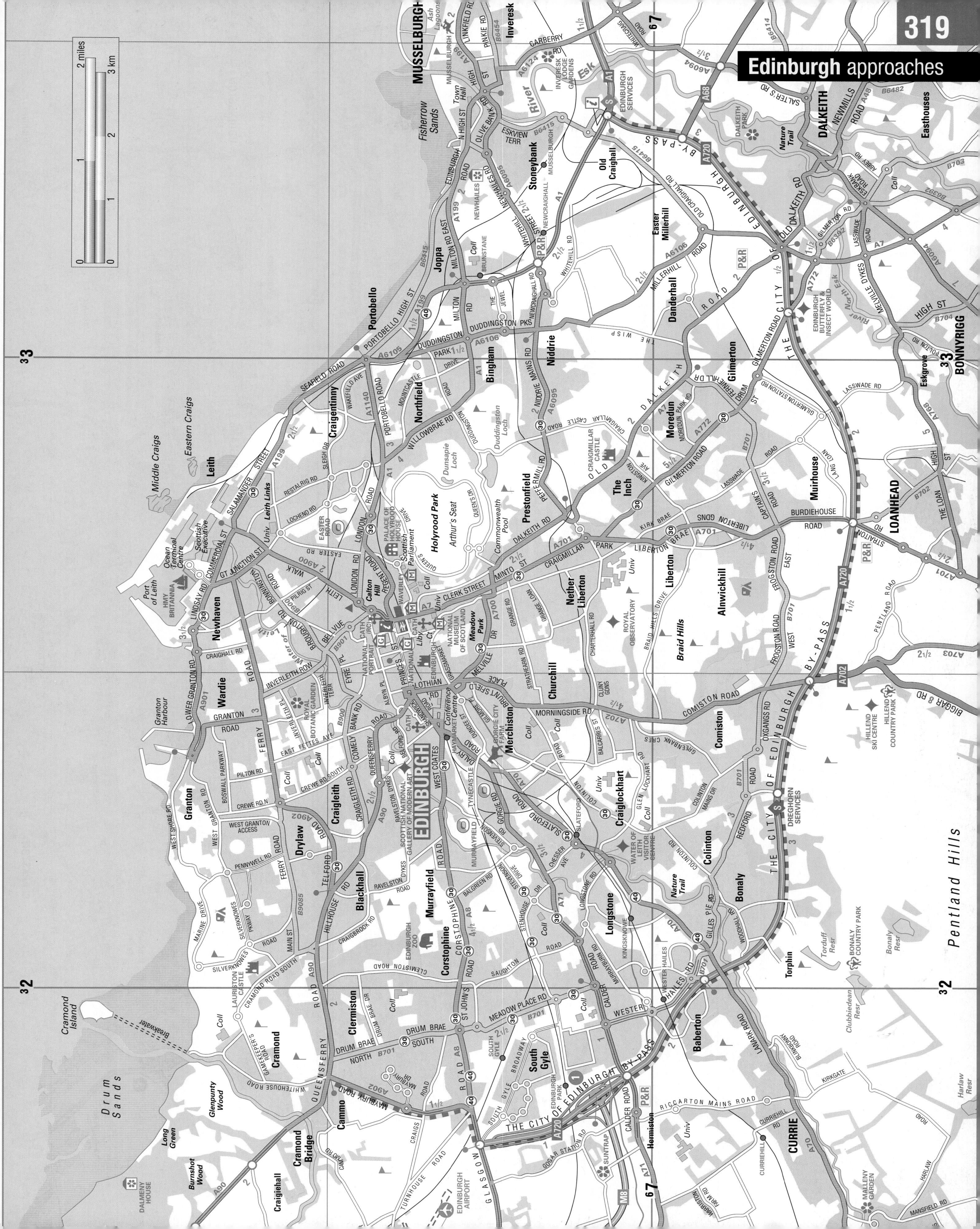
EDINBURGH
Leith
Newhaven
Granton
Wardie
Portobello
Joppa
Musselburgh
Inveresk
Dalkeith
Eskbank
Bonnyrigg
Loanhead
Easthouses
Newmills
Old Craighall
Stoneybank
Easter Millerhill
Danderhall
Niddrie
Bingham
Northfield
Craigentinny
Prestonfield
The Inch
Moredun
Gilmerton
Muirhouse
Alnwickhill
Liberton
Nether Liberton
Braid Hills
Churchill
Merchiston
Comiston
Craiglockhart
Colinton
Bonaly
Torphin
Longstone
Baberton
Currie
Hermiston
South Gyle
Corstorphine
Murrayfield
Blackhall
Craigleith
Drylaw
Cramond
Clermiston
Cammo
Cramond Bridge
Craigiehall
Cramond Island
Drum Sands
Fisherrow Sands
Middle Craigs
Eastern Craigs
Granton Harbour
Port of Leith
Holyrood Park
Arthur's Seat
Pentland Hills
Edinburgh Airport
Dalmeny House
Hillend Country Park
Bonaly Country Park
Edinburgh Zoo
Royal Botanic Garden
Royal Observatory
Palace of Holyroodhouse
Scottish Parliament
Calton Hill
Edinburgh Services
Dreghorn Services
The City of Edinburgh By-Pass
2 miles
3 km

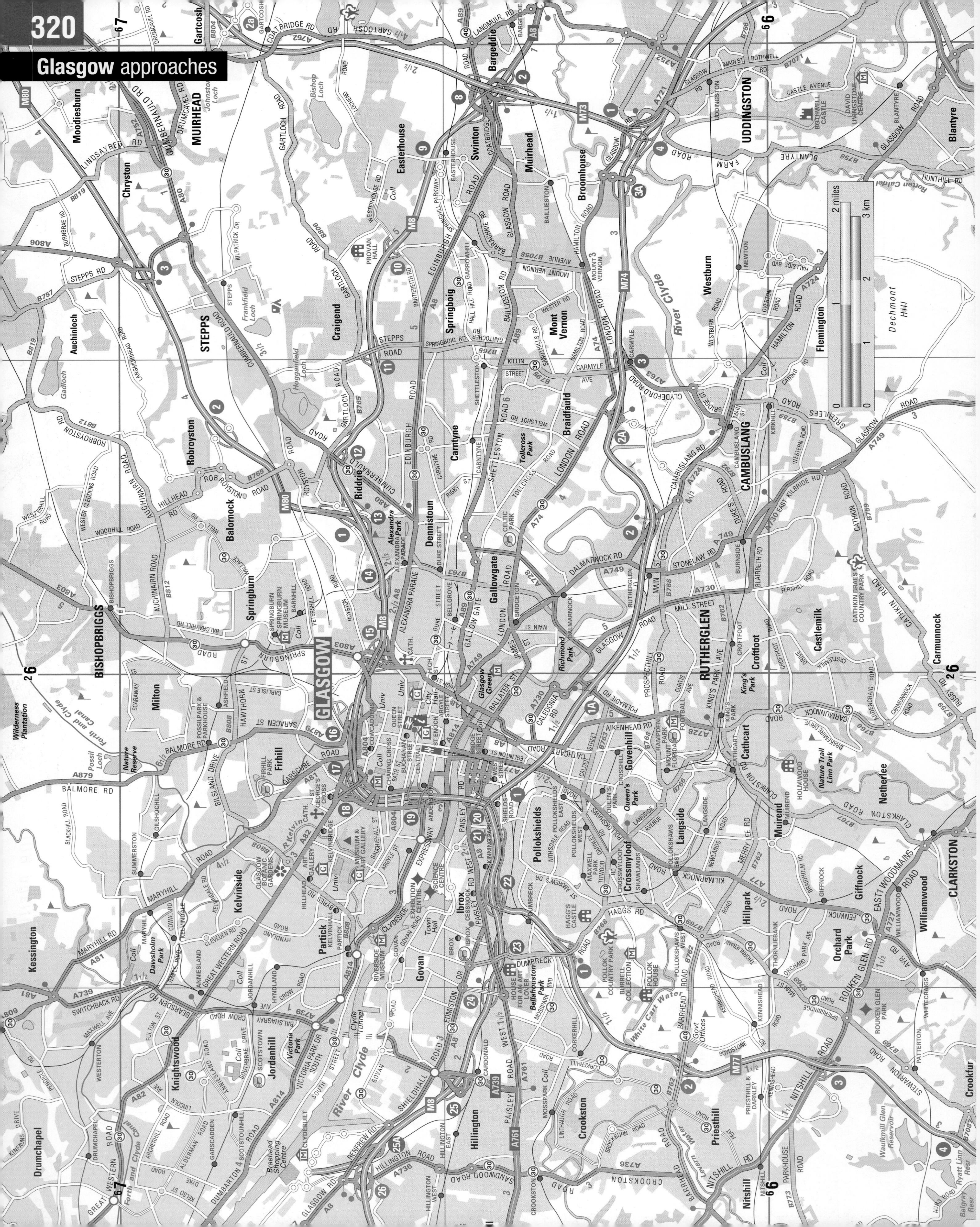
Gartcosh
Bargeddie
Moodiesburn
Muirhead
Chryston
Easterhouse
Swinton
Muirhead
Broomhouse
Uddingston
Bothwell Castle
David Livingstone Centre
Blantyre
Stepps
Auchinloch
Craigend
Springboig
Mont Vernon
Westburn
Flemington
Dechmont Hill
Robroyston
Carntyne
Braidfauld
Cambuslang
Riddrie
Balornock
Dennistoun
Tollcross Park
Celtic Park
Gallowgate
Springburn
Bishopbriggs
Rutherglen
Castlemilk
Carmunnock
Croftfoot
King's Park
Glasgow
Milton
Firhill
Govanhill
Cathcart
Netherlee
Pollokshields
Crossmyloof
Langside
Muirend
Kelvinside
Partick
Ibrox
Govan
Hillpark
Giffnock
Williamwood
Clarkston
Kessington
Dawsholm Park
Jordanhill
Knightswood
Victoria Park
Orchard Park
Rouken Glen Park
Pollok Country Park
Burrell Collection
Pollok House
Crookston
Hillington
Priesthill
Nitshill
Crookfur
Drumchapel
River Clyde
White Cart Water
Forth and Clyde Canal
M8
M73
M74
M77
M80

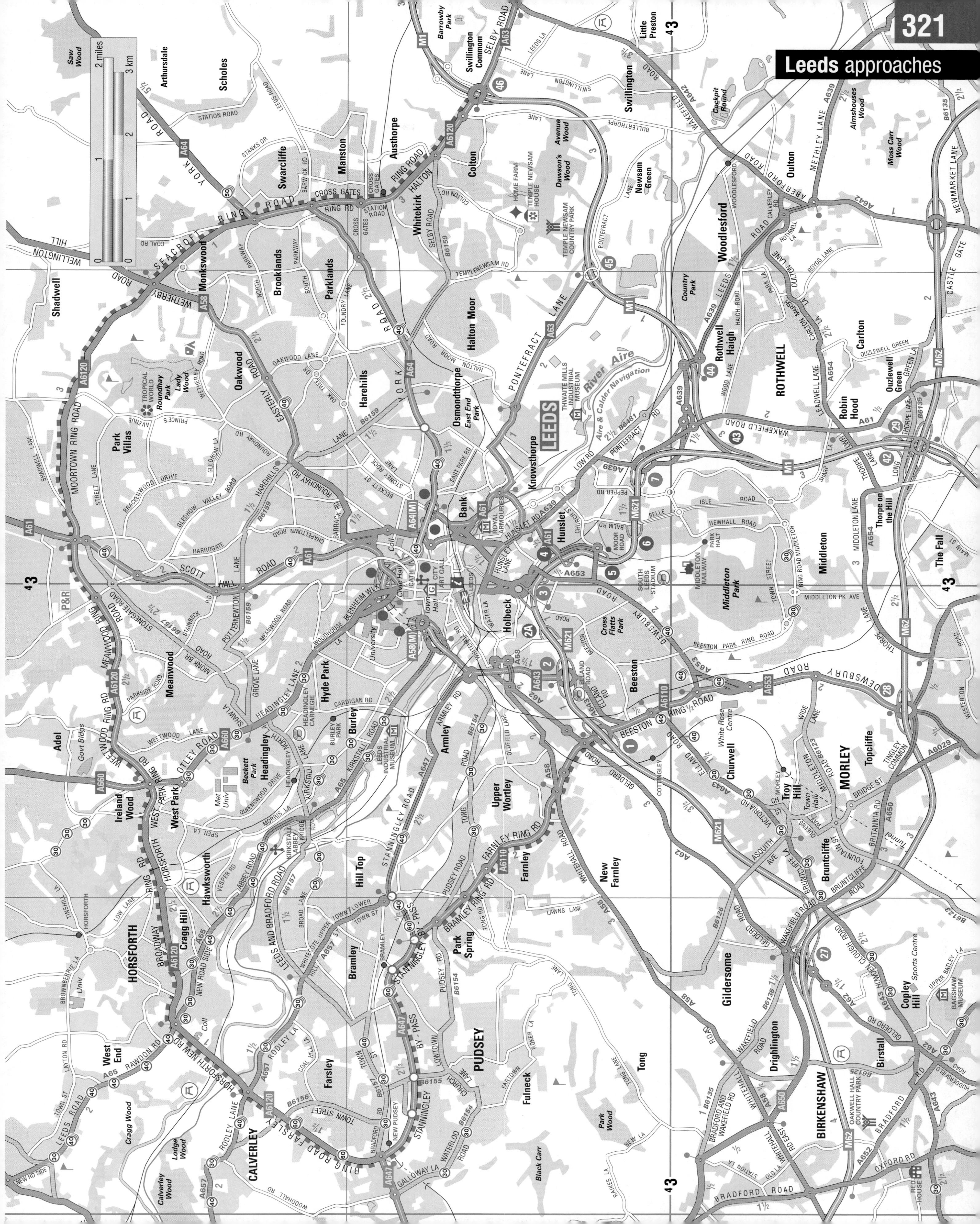
LEEDS
Saw Wood
Arthursdale
Scholes
Swarcliffe
Manston
Austhorpe
Colton
Whitekirk
Shadwell
Monkswood
Brooklands
Parklands
Halton Moor
Oakwood
Harehills
Osmondthorpe
Knowsthorpe
Park Villas
Roundhay Park
Lady Wood
Tropical World
Temple Newsam House
Temple Newsam Country Park
Home Farm
Dawson's Wood
Avenue Wood
Swillington
Swillington Common
Little Preston
Barrowby Park
Newsam Green
Woodlesford
Oulton
Almshouses Wood
Moss Carr Wood
Country Park
Rothwell Haigh
ROTHWELL
Carlton
Oulzewell Green
Robin Hood
Thorpe on the Hill
The Fall
Middleton
Middleton Park
Middleton Railway
South Leeds Stadium
Hunslet
Bank
Holbeck
Beeston
Cross Flatts Park
Thwaite Mills Industrial Museum
River Aire
Aire & Calder Navigation
Royal Armouries
University
City Art Gall
Civic Hall
Town Hall
Hyde Park
Burley
Burley Park
Headingley
Beckett Park
Met Univ
Meanwood
Adel
Govt Bldgs
Ireland Wood
West Park
Hawksworth
Kirkstall Abbey
Leeds Industrial Museum
Armley
Upper Wortley
Farnley
New Farnley
Hill Top
Bramley
Park Spring
PUDSEY
Fulneck
Tong
Park Wood
Black Carr
Farsley
CALVERLEY
Calverley Wood
Lodge Wood
Cragg Wood
West End
HORSFORTH
Cragg Hill
Gildersome
Drighlington
BIRKENSHAW
Birstall
Copley Hill
Bagshaw Museum
Oakwell Hall Country Park
Red House
MORLEY
Topcliffe
Tingley Common
Churwell
White Rose Centre
Troy Hill
Bruntcliffe
Sports Centre
Cockpit Round
P&R
RING ROAD
YORK ROAD
WETHERBY ROAD
SEACROFT RING ROAD
MOORTOWN RING ROAD
MEANWOOD RING ROAD
OTLEY ROAD
HORSFORTH RING RD
BRAMLEY RING RD
FARNLEY RING RD
STANNINGLEY BY-PASS
STANNINGLEY ROAD
DEWSBURY ROAD
WAKEFIELD ROAD
PONTEFRACT LANE
SELBY ROAD
BRADFORD ROAD
GELDERD ROAD
ELLAND ROAD
M1
M62
M621
A58(M)
A64(M)
A61
A63
A64
A65
A660
A6120
A639
A642
A650
A653
A654
A643
A647
A657
A6110
A62
A58
A652
A6029
43

Osidge
EAST BARNET
Whetstone
North Finchley
Colney Hatch
Muswell Hill
Fortis Green
Highgate Wood
Queen's Wood
Highgate
Dartmouth Park
Gospel Oak
Hampstead Heath
Parliament Hill
HAMPSTEAD
Belsize Park
Swiss Cottage
Primrose Hill
Regents Park
MARYLEBONE
FINCHLEY
East Finchley
Hampstead Garden Suburb
Golders Green
Temple Fortune
Golders Hill Park
Child's Hill
West Hampstead
Kilburn
Maida Vale
St John's Wood
Westbourne Park
Woodside Park
West Finchley
Church End
Totteridge
Underhill
BARNET
Arkley
Barnet Gate
Mill Hill
Mill Hill East
HENDON
Brent Cross
Cricklewood
Dollis Hill
Gladstone Park
WILLESDEN
Brondesbury
Brondesbury Park
Kensal Rise
Harlesden
Wormwood Scrubs Park
Old Oak Common
Neasden
West Hendon
Colindale
Grahame Park
Burnt Oak
EDGWARE
Edgware Bury
Elstree
Kingsbury
Wembley Park
Barn Hill
Queensbury
Little Stanmore
Canons Park
Stonebridge
Park Royal
West Acton
Alperton
WEMBLEY
North Wembley
Preston Road
KENTON
Sudbury
South Kenton
Northwick Park
Belmont
STANMORE
Stanmore Common
Wealdstone
Greenhill
HARROW
Harrow on the Hill
Perivale
EALING
Bushey Heath
BUSHEY
OXHEY
South Oxhey
Oxhey Woods
Harrow Weald
Headstone
Headstone Lane
Hatch End
North Harrow
West Harrow
Roxeth
South Harrow
Rayners Lane
PINNER
Eastcote
Eastcote Village
Ruislip Manor
South Ruislip
NORTHOLT
GREENFORD
Yeading

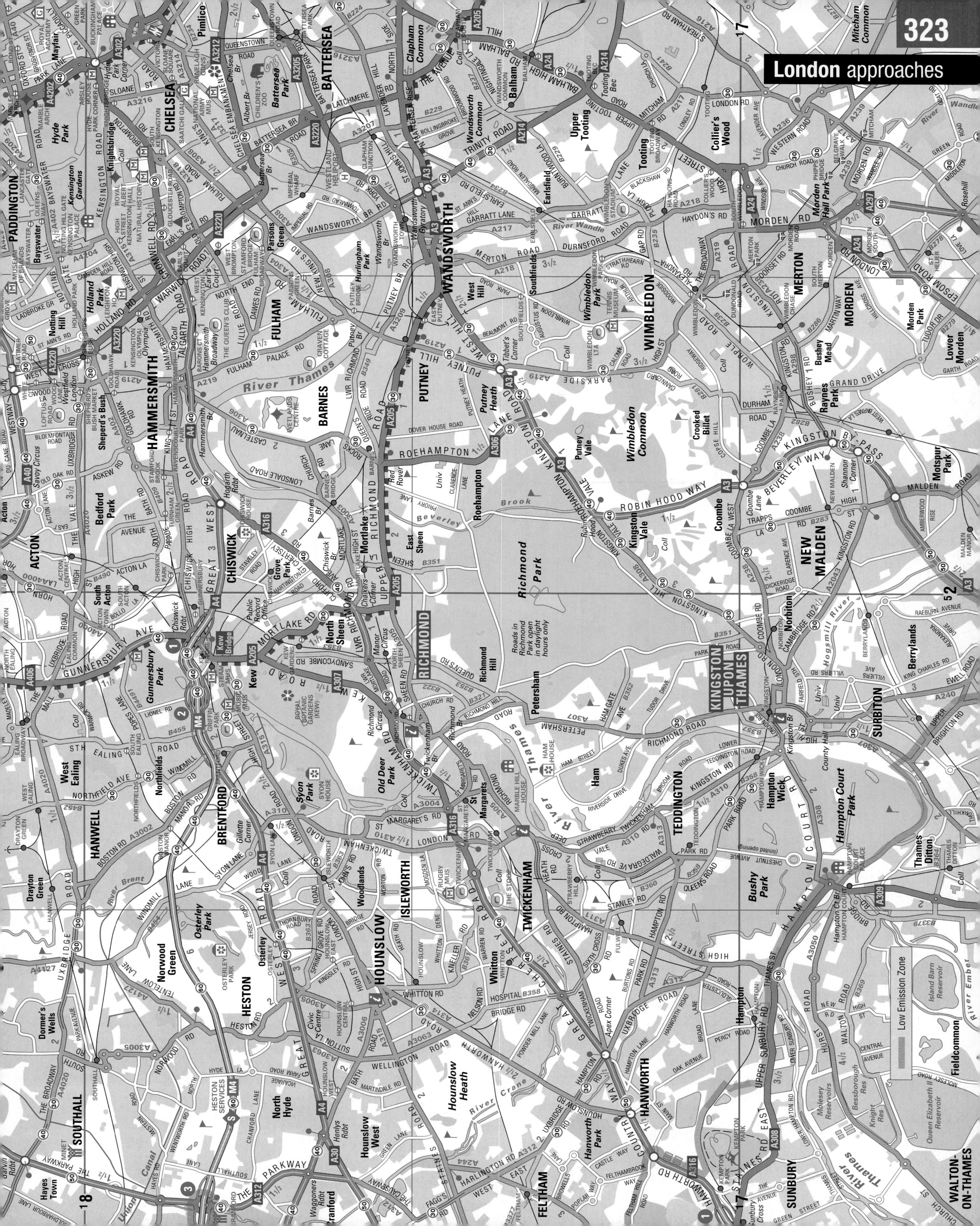
PADDINGTON
Mayfair
Pimlico
BATTERSEA
Battersea Park
CHELSEA
Hyde Park
Kensington Gardens
Knightsbridge
Bayswater
Notting Hill
Holland Park
Clapham Common
Balham
Upper Tooting
Tooting Bec
Tooting
Collier's Wood
Mitcham Common
Wandsworth Common
WANDSWORTH
Earlsfield
Parsons Green
Hurlingham Park
FULHAM
HAMMERSMITH
Shepherd's Bush
West Hill
Southfields
Wimbledon Park
WIMBLEDON
MERTON
MORDEN
Morden Park
Lower Morden
Morden Hall Park
Rosehill
River Thames
BARNES
PUTNEY
Putney Heath
Putney Vale
Wimbledon Common
Crooked Billet
Raynes Park
Motspur Park
ACTON
Bedford Park
CHISWICK
Roehampton
Mortlake
East Sheen
Kingston Vale
Coombe
NEW MALDEN
Richmond Park
Norbiton
Berrylands
South Acton
North Sheen
Kew
Gunnersbury Park
RICHMOND
Richmond Hill
Petersham
KINGSTON UPON THAMES
SURBITON
West Ealing
Northfields
BRENTFORD
Syon Park
Old Deer Park
St Margarets
Ham
TEDDINGTON
Hampton Wick
Hampton Court Park
Thames Ditton
HANWELL
Drayton Green
ISLEWORTH
Woodlands
TWICKENHAM
Bushy Park
Osterley Park
Osterley
Norwood Green
HESTON
HOUNSLOW
Whitton
Hampton
Dormer's Wells
Hounslow Heath
HANWORTH
Fieldcommon
SOUTHALL
North Hyde
Hounslow West
Hanworth Park
FELTHAM
SUNBURY
WALTON-ON-THAMES
Hayes Town
Cranford
Low Emission Zone

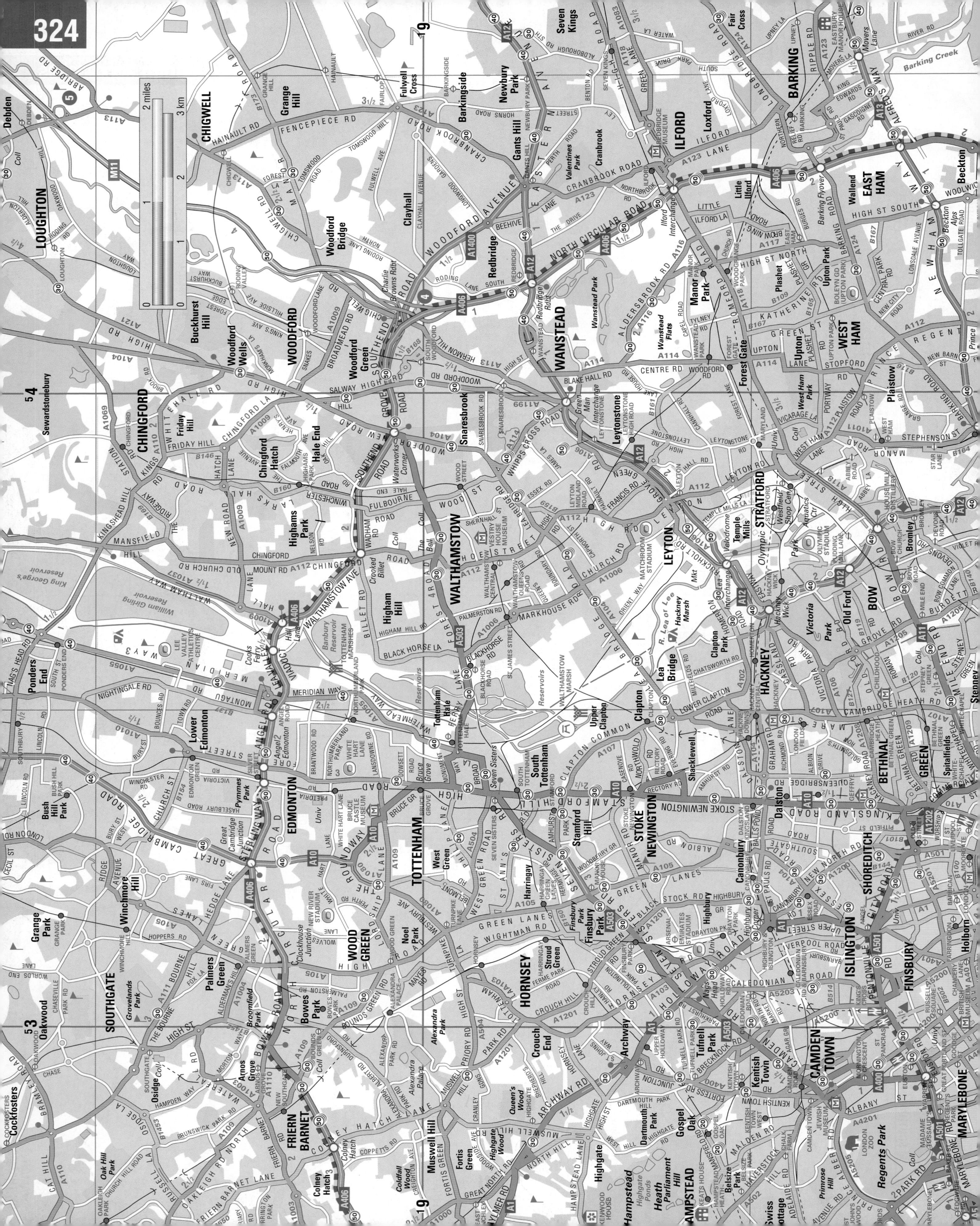

LOUGHTON
CHIGWELL
Grange Hill
Buckhurst Hill
WOODFORD
Woodford Wells
Woodford Green
Woodford Bridge
CHINGFORD
Chingford Hatch
Hale End
Highams Park
WALTHAMSTOW
Higham Hill
Snaresbrook
WANSTEAD
Redbridge
Gants Hill
Barkingside
Newbury Park
ILFORD
Loxford
BARKING
EAST HAM
WEST HAM
Plaistow
Forest Gate
Leytonstone
LEYTON
STRATFORD
Manor Park
Upton Park
Plashet
Beckton
Bromley
BOW
HACKNEY
Clapton Park
Lea Bridge
Upper Clapton
Clapton
Stoke Newington
Stamford Hill
South Tottenham
TOTTENHAM
Tottenham Hale
EDMONTON
Lower Edmonton
Ponders End
Bush Hill Park
Winchmore Hill
SOUTHGATE
Palmers Green
WOOD GREEN
Noel Park
HORNSEY
Crouch End
Finsbury Park
Highbury
Canonbury
ISLINGTON
Dalston
Shacklewell
SHOREDITCH
BETHNAL GREEN
FINSBURY
Holborn
CAMDEN TOWN
Kentish Town
Tufnell Park
Archway
Highgate
Muswell Hill
FRIERN BARNET
Colney Hatch
Arnos Grove
Bowes Park
Osidge
Oakwood
Cockfosters
Gospel Oak
Dartmouth Park
Belsize Park
Primrose Hill
Regents Park
MARYLEBONE
Hampstead Heath
Sewardstonebury
Seven Kings
Fair Cross
Fulwell Cross
Clayhall
Cranbrook
Little Ilford
Wallend
Victoria Park
Old Ford
Spitalfields
Stepney

River Thames
North Woolwich
Plumstead
Shooters Hill
East Wickham
Falconwood
Oxleas Wood
Avery Hill
New Eltham
Longlands
Chislehurst
Chislehurst Common
Petts Wood
Woolwich Ferry
WOOLWICH
Eltham Common
ELTHAM
Woolwich Common
Charlton
Thames Barrier
Silvertown
Custom House
Canning Town
LONDON CITY AIRPORT
Royal Albert Dock
King George V Dock
Royal Victoria Dock
Kidbrooke
Sun in the Sands Rbdt
Yorkshire Grey
Clifton's Rbdt
Mottingham
Grove Park
Elmstead Wood
Sundridge Park
Widmore
Bickley
Southborough
Bromley Common
BROMLEY
North Greenwich
Blackwall Tunnel
Blackwall
Blackheath Park
Lee
GREENWICH
Greenwich Park
BLACKHEATH
LEWISHAM
Hither Green
Downham
Plaistow
Shortlands
POPLAR
Canary Wharf
ISLE OF DOGS
Millwall
CATFORD
Catford Gyratory
Brockley
Ladywell
Bellingham
Bell Green
Beckenham Place Park
BECKENHAM
Eden Park
Limehouse
Rotherhithe
Surrey Quays
Rotherhithe Tunnel
New Cross
Forest Hill
PENGE
Elmers End
DEPTFORD
Nunhead
Honor Oak
Wapping
BERMONDSEY
Peckham
Peckham Rye Park
Dulwich
Anerley
Woodside
Aldgate
Tower Br
East Dulwich
CAMBERWELL
Dulwich Park
Elephant & Castle
Walworth
Camberwell Green
West Dulwich
South Norwood
Selhurst
Kennington
LAMBETH
BRIXTON
Brockwell Park
Tulse Hill
STREATHAM
Streatham Common
Norbury
Vauxhall
Vauxhall Cross
Houses of Parliament
Westminster
Lambeth
St James's Park
Green Park
Mayfair
Pimlico
CLAPHAM
Clapham Common
BATTERSEA
Battersea Park
Grange Mills
Tooting Bec Common
Furzedown
Streatham Vale
Mitcham Common
MITCHAM
CHELSEA
Hyde Park
Balham
Wandsworth Common
Upper Tooting
Tooting Bec
Collier's Wood
Thornton Heath

Great Crosby
CROSBY
Waterloo
Seaforth
Melling
Kirkby Park
AINTREE
LITHERLAND
Westvale
KIRKBY
Fazakerley
Croxteth
Knowsley
BOOTLE
Walton
West Derby
Stockbridge Village
New Brighton
WALLASEY
Anfield
Stanley Park
Newsham Park
HUYTON-WITH-ROBY
Roby
Broad Green
Wavertree Park
Edge Hill
Wavertree
Childwall
BIRKENHEAD
Birkenhead Park
LIVERPOOL
Toxteth
Sefton Park
Oxton
Tranmere
Dingle
Aigburth
Otterspool
Allerton
Woolton
Hunt's Cross
GARSTON
River Mersey
BEBINGTON
Port Sunlight
Spital
Brimstage
Bromborough
Eastham Ferry
SPEKE
LIVERPOOL JOHN LENNON AIRPORT
LIVERPOOL AIRPORT
Terminal Building
Ferries to Belfast, Douglas & Dublin
Kingsway
Queensway
Rail Tunnel
AINTREE RACE COURSE
CROXTETH COUNTRY PARK
RIMROSE VALLEY COUNTRY PARK
CALDERSTONES PARK
HALEWOOD COUNTRY PARK
EASTHAM COUNTRY PARK
LADY LEVER ART GALLERY
SUDLEY HOUSE
SPEKE HALL
MARITIME MUSEUM
TATE GALLERY
BEATLES STORY
MUS OF LIVERPOOL
M57
M62
M53
A5036
A580
A59
A5058
A561
A562
A41
0 1 2 miles
0 1 2 3 km

MANCHESTER
SALFORD
TRAFFORD PARK
STRETFORD
SALE
ECCLES
SWINTON
PENDLEBURY
PRESTWICH
WHITEFIELD
ALTRINCHAM
WYTHENSHAWE
GATLEY
CHEADLE HULME
REDDISH
Outwood
Ringley
Park Lane
Besses o' th' Barn
Simister
Rhodes
Higher Blackley
Alkrington Garden Village
Heaton Park
Charlestown
Newtown
Clifton Green
Kersal
Broughton Park
Crumpsall
Boggart Hole Clough
Moston
New Moston
Hollinwood
Harpurhey
Newton Heath
Miles Platting
Strangeways
Westwood Park
Ellesmere Park
Little Bolton
Seedley
Patricroft
Barton upon Irwell
Clayton
Openshaw
Ardwick
Gorton
Hulme
Salford Quays
Trafford Centre
Old Trafford
Moss Side
Rusholme
Ryder Brow
Levenshulme
Firswood
Whalley Range
Longford Park
North Reddish
Chorlton-cum-Hardy
Withington
Ashton upon Mersey
Barlow Moor
West Didsbury
Burnage
South Reddish
Woodhouses
Brooklands
Heaton Mersey
Heaton Norris
Northern Moor
Timperley
Roundthorn
Newall Green
Manchester Ship Canal
River Irwell
River Mersey
River Medlock
Bridgewater Canal
M60
M602
M62
M66
M56
A56
A57
A6
A34
A5103
A560
A62
A635
A6010
2 miles
3 km

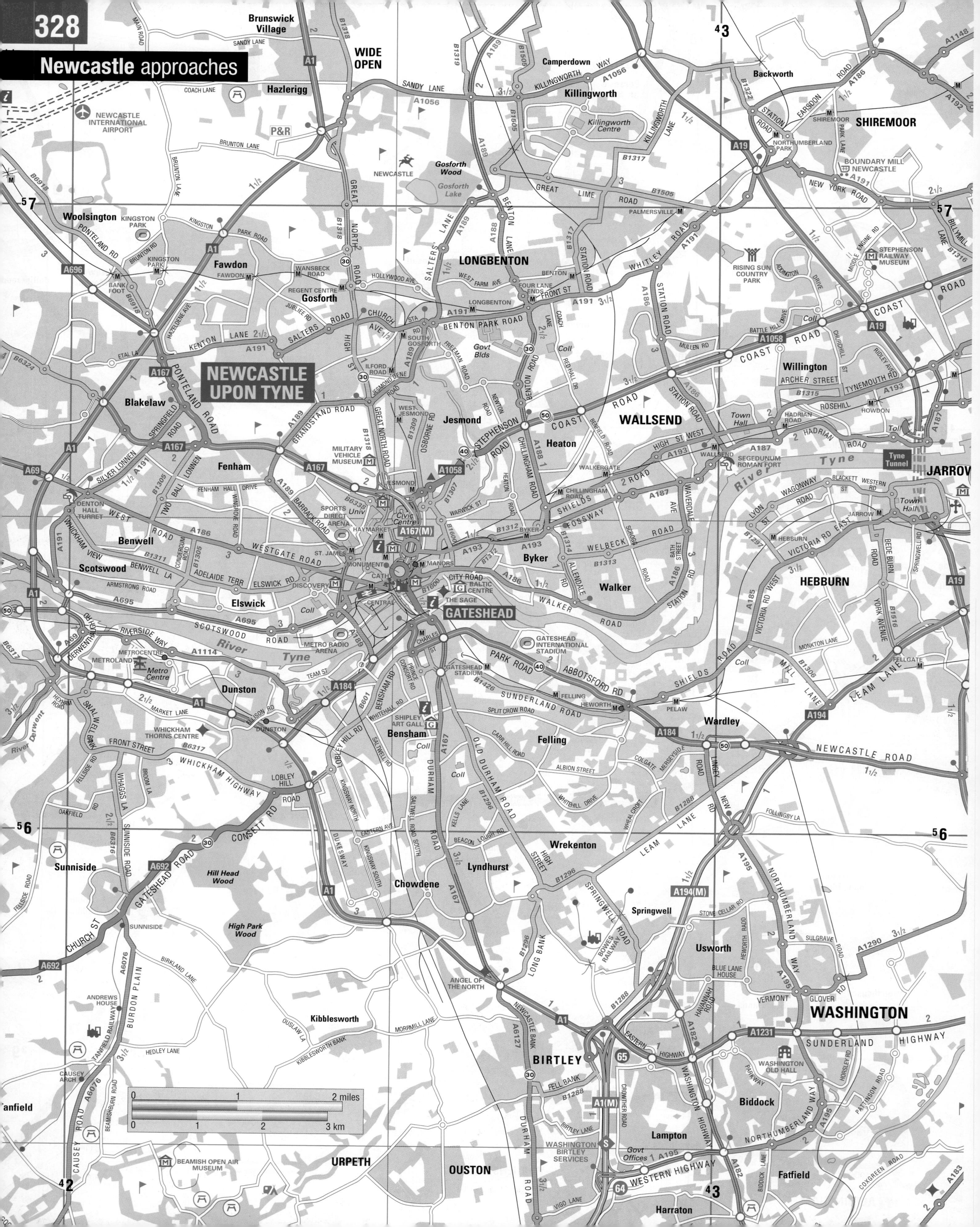
Brunswick Village
WIDE OPEN
Hazlerigg
Camperdown
Killingworth
Killingworth Centre
Backworth
SHIREMOOR
NEWCASTLE INTERNATIONAL AIRPORT
P&R
Gosforth Wood
Gosforth Lake
NEWCASTLE
Woolsington
KINGSTON PARK
Fawdon
Gosforth
LONGBENTON
RISING SUN COUNTRY PARK
STEPHENSON RAILWAY MUSEUM
BOUNDARY MILL NEWCASTLE
Govt Blds
Willington
NEWCASTLE UPON TYNE
Blakelaw
Jesmond
WALLSEND
Town Hall
Heaton
Fenham
MILITARY VEHICLE MUSEUM
SEGEDUNUM ROMAN FORT
Tyne Tunnel
JARROW
River Tyne
SPORTS DIRECT ARENA
Civic Centre
Benwell
Scotswood
Byker
Walker
HEBBURN
Elswick
DISCOVERY
CENTRAL
BALTIC CENTRE
THE SAGE
GATESHEAD
METRO RADIO ARENA
GATESHEAD INTERNATIONAL STADIUM
METROCENTRE
METROLAND
Metro Centre
Dunston
WHICKHAM THORNS CENTRE
SHIPLEY ART GALL
Bensham
Felling
Wardley
LOBLEY HILL
River Derwent
Sunniside
Hill Head Wood
Wrekenton
Lyndhurst
Chowdene
Springwell
BOWES RAILWAY
Usworth
High Park Wood
ANGEL OF THE NORTH
ANDREWS HOUSE
Kibblesworth
WASHINGTON
WASHINGTON OLD HALL
BIRTLEY
CAUSEY ARCH
Tanfield
Biddock
Lampton
WASHINGTON BIRTLEY SERVICES
Govt Offices
BEAMISH OPEN AIR MUSEUM
URPETH
OUSTON
Fatfield
Harraton
0 1 2 miles
0 1 2 3 km

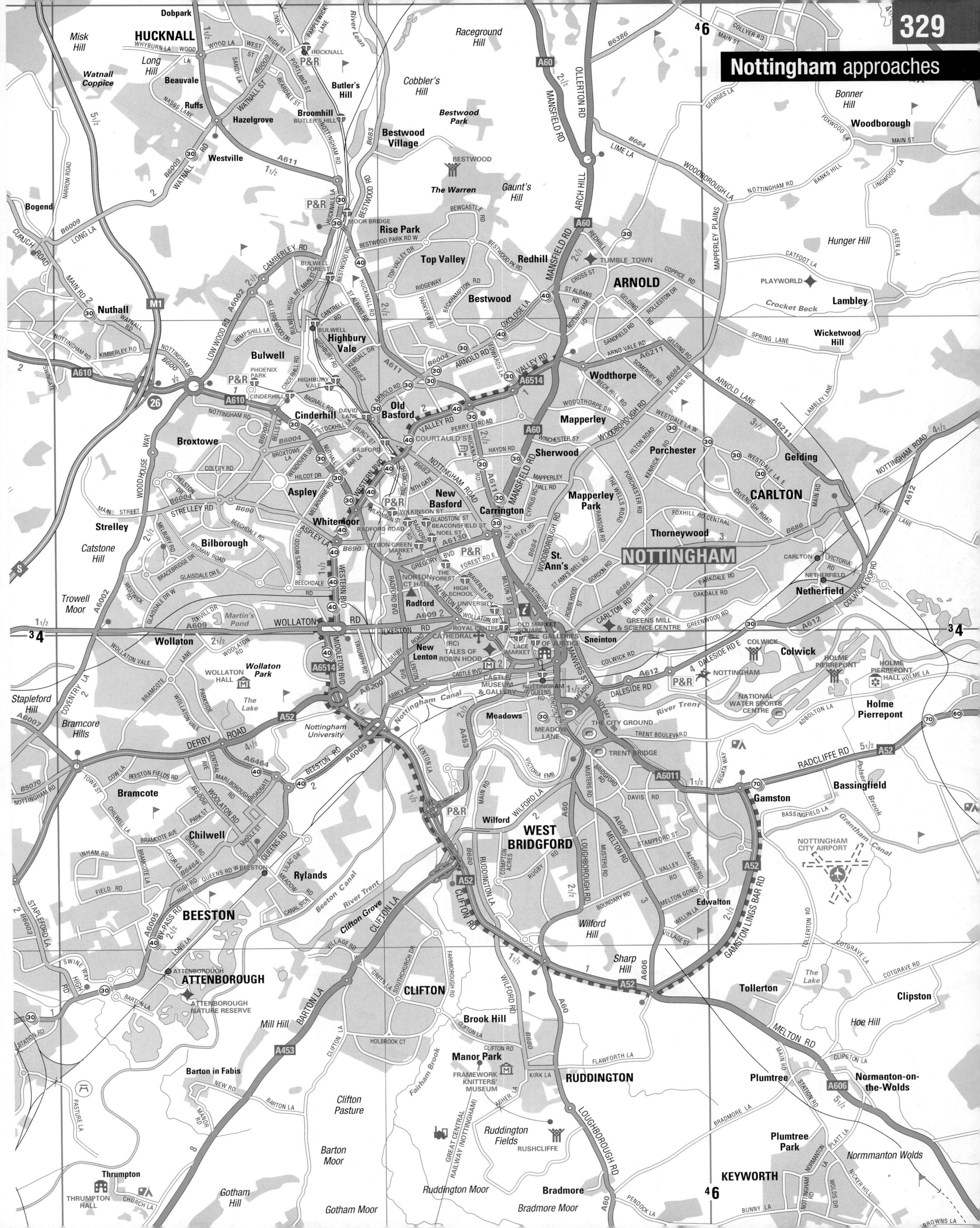
HUCKNALL
Dobpark
Misk Hill
Long Hill
Watnall Coppice
Beauvale
Ruffs
Hazelgrove
Westville
Butler's Hill
Broomhill
Raceground Hill
Cobbler's Hill
Bestwood Park
Bestwood Village
BESTWOOD
The Warren
Gaunt's Hill
Bogend
Nuthall
Rise Park
Top Valley
Redhill
Bestwood
ARNOLD
TUMBLE TOWN
Bulwell
Highbury Vale
Cinderhill
Old Basford
Broxtowe
Aspley
Whitemoor
Strelley
Bilborough
Catstone Hill
Trowell Moor
Wodthorpe
Mapperley
Sherwood
Mapperley Park
Porchester
Gelding
CARLTON
Thorneywood
NOTTINGHAM
St. Ann's
Netherfield
New Basford
Carrington
Radford
Wollaton
Martin's Pond
Wollaton Park
WOLLATON HALL
The Lake
New Lenton
TALES OF ROBIN HOOD
CASTLE MUSEUM & GALLERY
LACE MARKET
GALLERIES OF JUSTICE
Sneinton
GREENS MILL & SCIENCE CENTRE
Colwick
HOLME PIERREPONT HALL
Holme Pierrepont
NATIONAL WATER SPORTS CENTRE
Meadows
THE CITY GROUND
TRENT BRIDGE
River Trent
Nottingham Canal
Nottingham University
Stapleford Hill
Bramcore Hills
Bramcote
Chilwell
Rylands
BEESTON
Beeston Canal
ATTENBOROUGH
ATTENBOROUGH NATURE RESERVE
Wilford
WEST BRIDGFORD
Gamston
Bassingfield
NOTTINGHAM CITY AIRPORT
Grantham Canal
Edwalton
Wilford Hill
Sharp Hill
Clifton Grove
CLIFTON
Mill Hill
Brook Hill
Manor Park
FRAMEWORK KNITTERS' MUSEUM
RUDDINGTON
Tollerton
The Lake
Clipston
Hoe Hill
Plumtree
Normanton-on-the-Wolds
Barton in Fabis
Clifton Pasture
Barton Moor
Ruddington Fields
RUSHCLIFFE
Thrumpton
THRUMPTON HALL
Gotham Hill
Gotham Moor
Ruddington Moor
Bradmore
Bradmore Moor
Plumtree Park
KEYWORTH
Normmanton Wolds
Bonner Hill
Woodborough
Hunger Hill
PLAYWORLD
Lambley
Crocket Beck
Wicketwood Hill
M1
A60
A610
A611
A6514
A612
A52
A6005
A453
A606
A6011
A6211
A6002
A6200

ROTHERHAM
SHEFFIELD
ECCLESFIELD
GRENOSIDE
HILLSBOROUGH
Wickersley
Sunnyside
Listerdale
Dalton Magna
Dalton
Dalton Parva
Brecks
Whinney Hill
Herringthorpe
Moorgate
Eastwood
Clifton
Broom
Canklow
Masbrough
Greasbrough
Bradgate
Kimberworth Park
Kimberworth
Dropping Well
Blackburn
Tinsley
Jordan
Brinsworth
Whiston
Upper Whiston
Morthen
Ulley
Treeton
Guilthwaite
Aughton
Aston
Swallownest
Fence
Woodhouse Mill
Catcliffe
Handsworth
Orgreave
Woodhouse
Richmond
Beighton
Sothall
Holbrook
Westfield
Halfway
Waterthorpe
Drakehouse
Hackenthorpe
Moorhole
Owlthorpe
Plumbley
Birley
Highlane
Normanton Spring
Frecheville
Ridgeway
Ridgeway Moor
Ford
Hollins End
Intake
Gleadless
Lightwood
Wales
Woodall
Norwood
Killamarsh
Upperthorpe
Brampton en le Morthen
Greenland
Darnall
Attercliffe
Brightside
Carbrook
Wincobank
Concord Park
Pismire Hill
Shiregreen
Firth Park
Grimesthorpe
Pitsmoor
Fir Vale
Parson Cross
Longley Estate
Shirecliffe
Burngreave
Parkwood Springs
Owlerton
Wadsley Bridge
Birley Carr
Birley Edge
Beeley Wood
Oughtibridge
Wharncliffe Wood
Wadsley
Worrall
Loxley
Knowle Top
Malin Bridge
Walkley
Crookesmoor
Steel Bank
Crookes
Tapton Hill
Sandygate
Ranmoor
Greystones
Fulwood
Ecclesall
Brincliffe
Nether Edge
Sharrow
Heeley
Lowfield
Sheffield Park
Arbourthorne
Manor Park
Manor Estate
Newfield Green
Hemsworth
Backmoor
Gleadless Valley
Norton Woodseats
Norton
Jordanthorpe
Meersbrook
Carter Knowle
Millhouses
Whirlow
Abbeydale
Abbeydale Park
Beauchief
Meadow Head
Greenhill
Lowedges
Totley Rise
Totley Bents
Dore
Parkhead
Ecclesall Wood
Sheffield City Airport
Tinsley Park
Sheffield Services
Meadowhall
Rother Valley
Rother Valley Lake
Ulley Reservoir
River Rother
River Don
Sheffield to Keadby Canal
M1
M18
A57
A61
A6102
A630
A631
A618
A6135
A625
A621
A6109
A6178
A6123
A629
A6021
A6012
A6022
A6101
A57
B6060
B6200
B6053
B6058
B6059
B6066
B6067
B6085
B6082
B6086
B6087
B6076
B6077
B6388
B6057
B6158
B6068
B6069
B6070
B6071
B6074
B6089
B6410
B6533

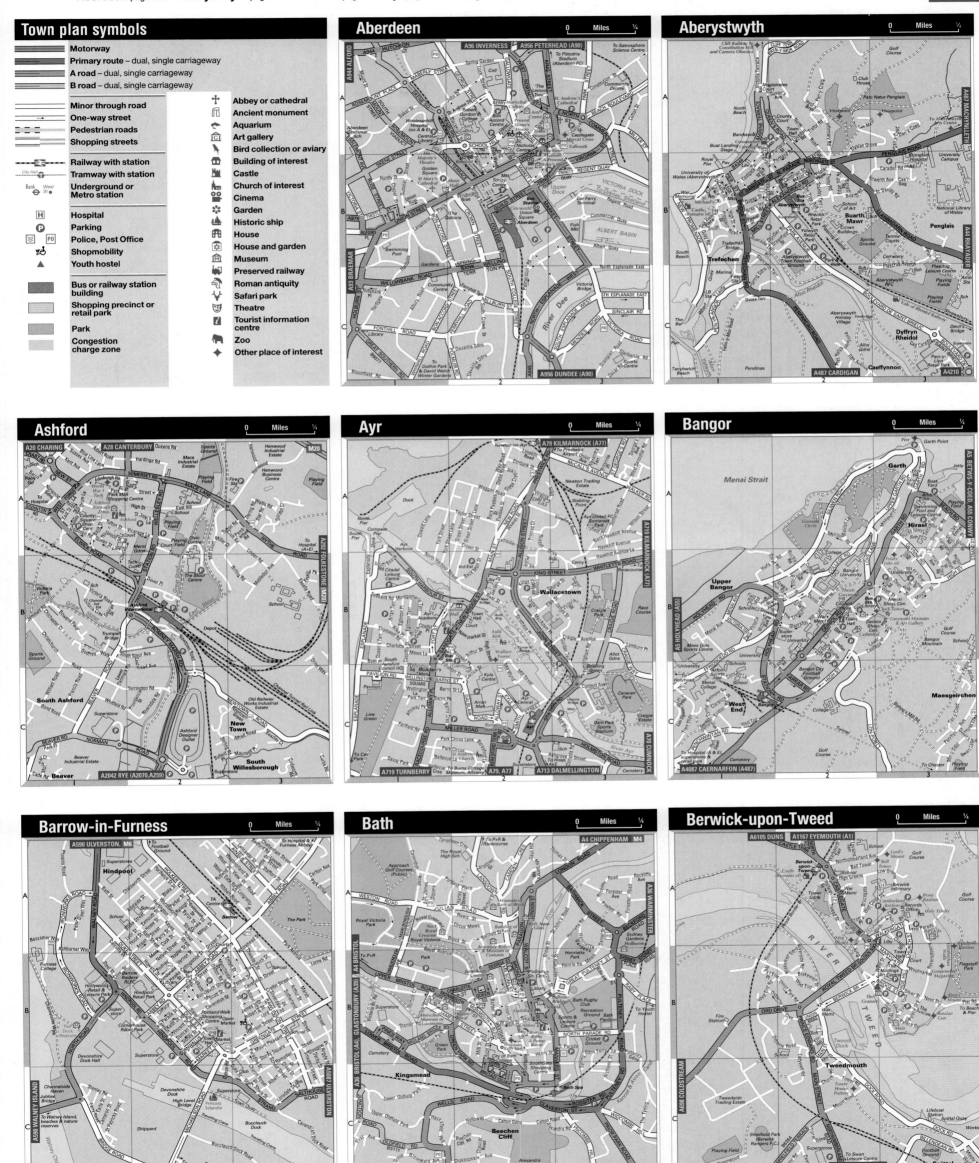

Town plan symbols

- Motorway
- Primary route – dual, single carriageway
- A road – dual, single carriageway
- B road – dual, single carriageway
- Minor through road
- One-way street
- Pedestrian roads
- Shopping streets
- Railway with station
- Tramway with station
- Underground or Metro station
- Hospital
- Parking
- Police, Post Office
- Shopmobility
- Youth hostel
- Bus or railway station building
- Shopping precinct or retail park
- Park
- Congestion charge zone
- Abbey or cathedral
- Ancient monument
- Aquarium
- Art gallery
- Bird collection or aviary
- Building of interest
- Castle
- Church of interest
- Cinema
- Garden
- Historic ship
- House
- House and garden
- Museum
- Preserved railway
- Roman antiquity
- Safari park
- Theatre
- Tourist information centre
- Zoo
- Other place of interest

Aberdeen

0 Miles ¼

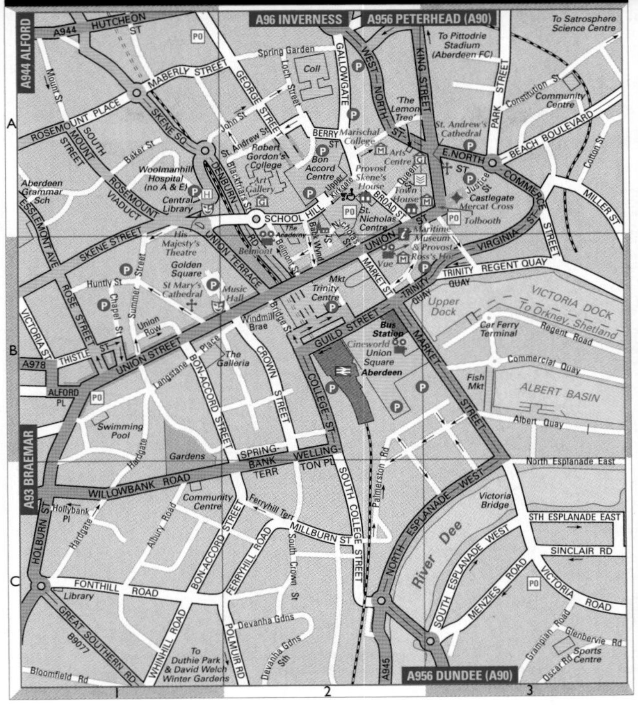

Aberystwyth

0 Miles ¼

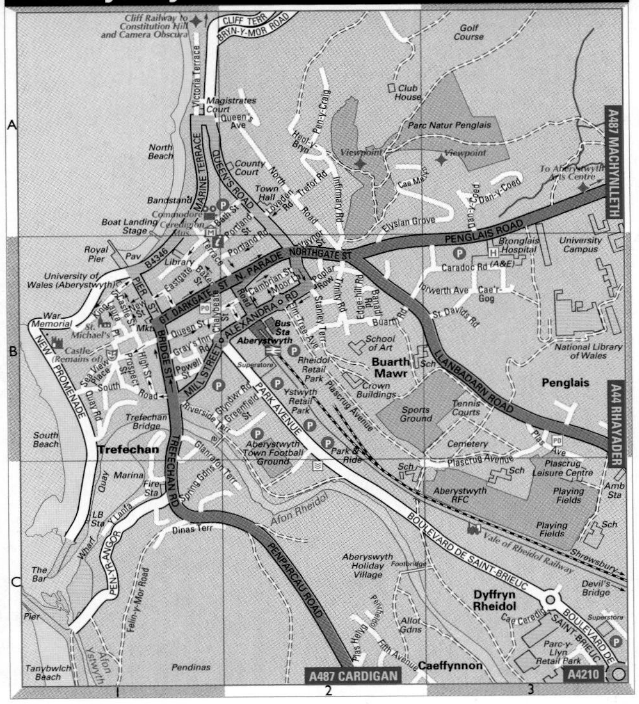

Ashford

0 Miles ¼

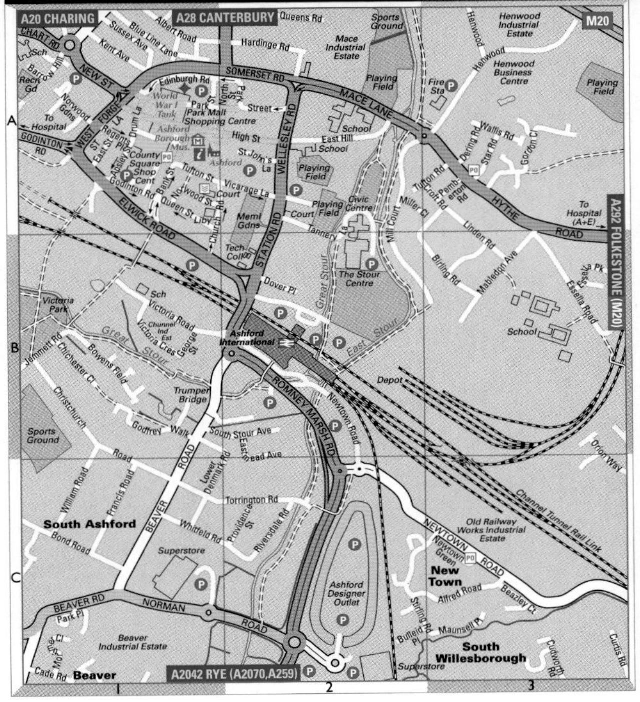

Ayr

0 Miles ¼

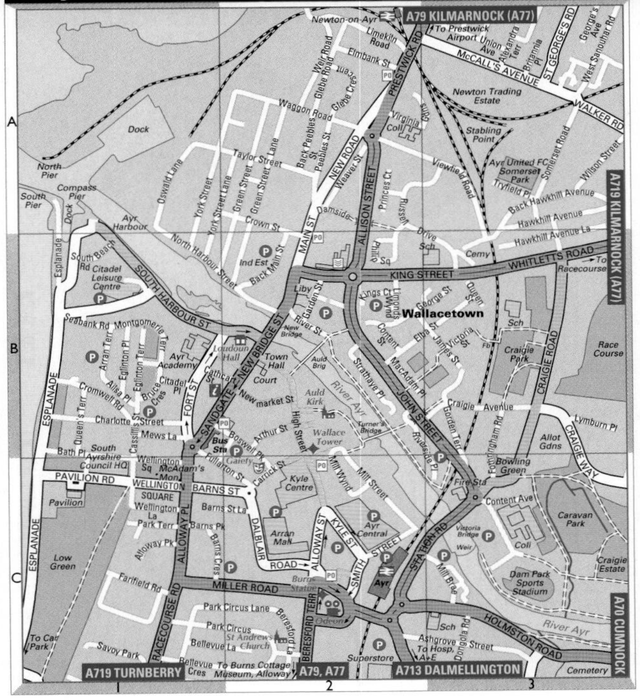

Bangor

0 Miles ¼

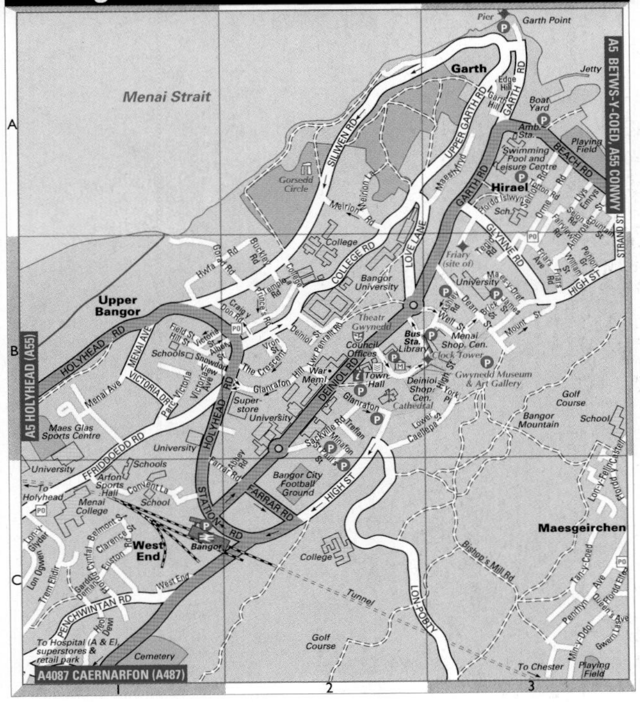

Barrow-in-Furness

0 Miles ¼

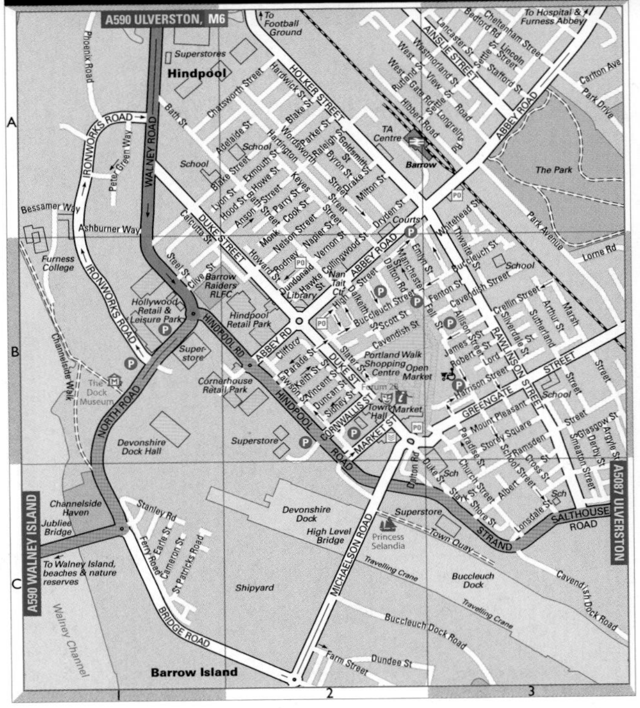

Bath

0 Miles ¼

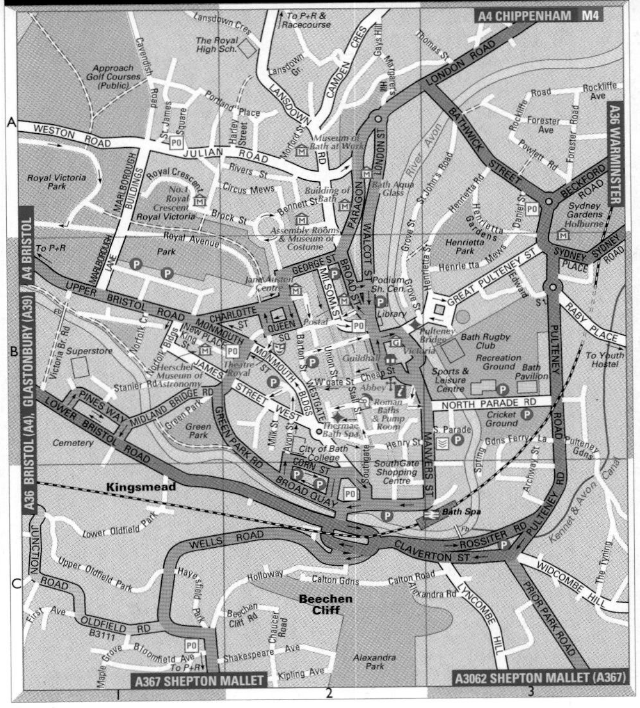

Berwick-upon-Tweed

0 Miles ¼

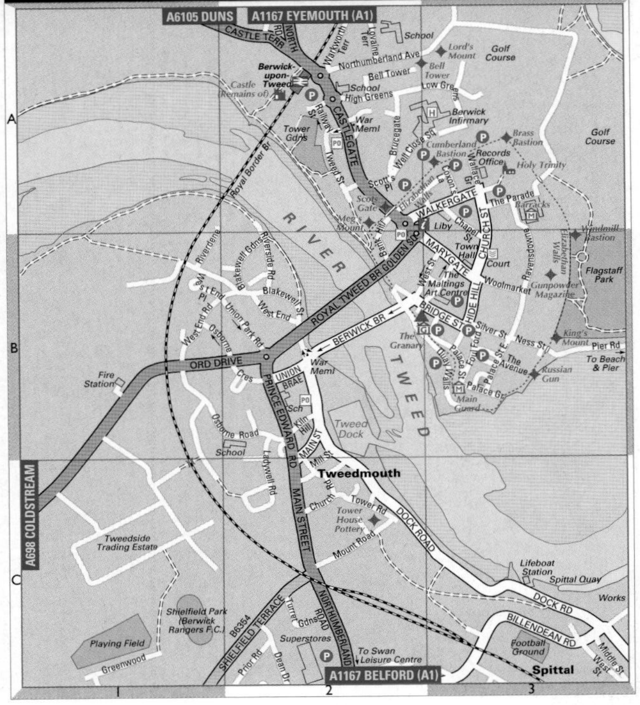

Birmingham

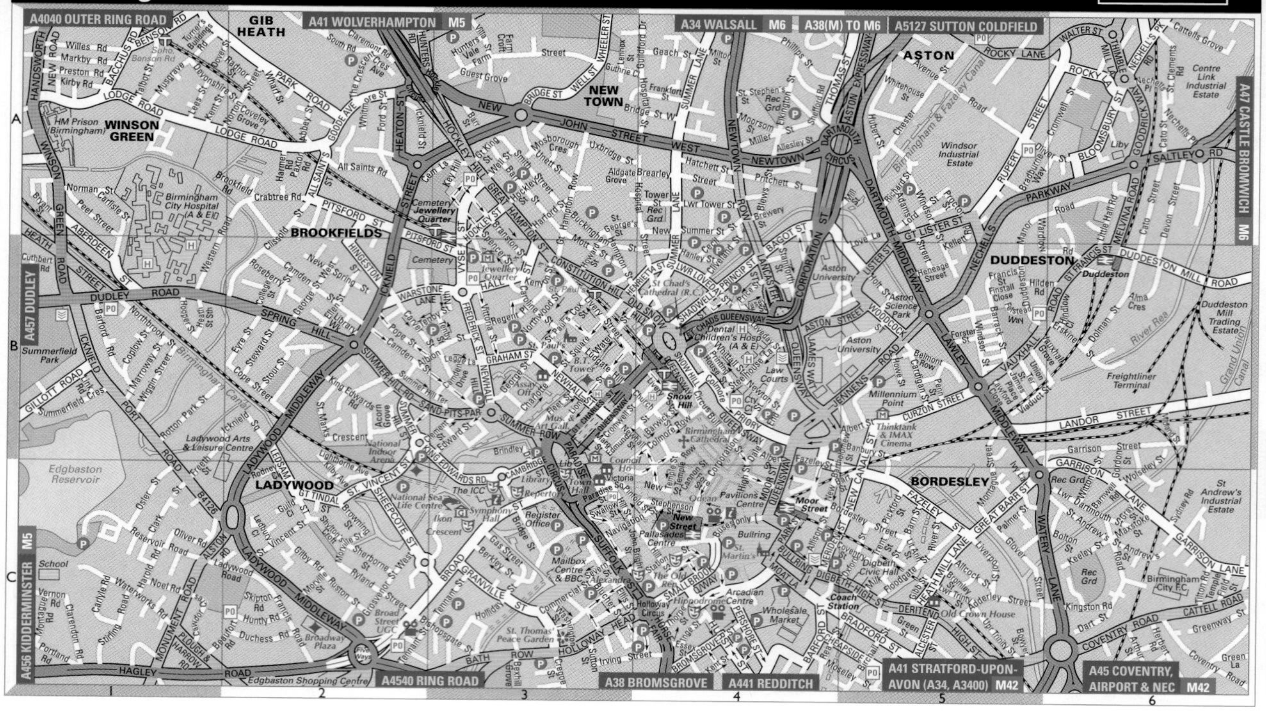

Blackpool

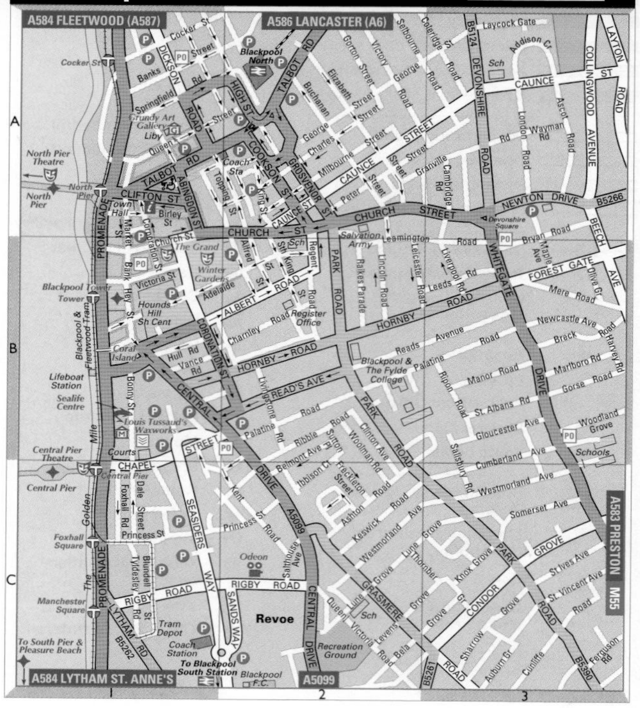

Bournemouth

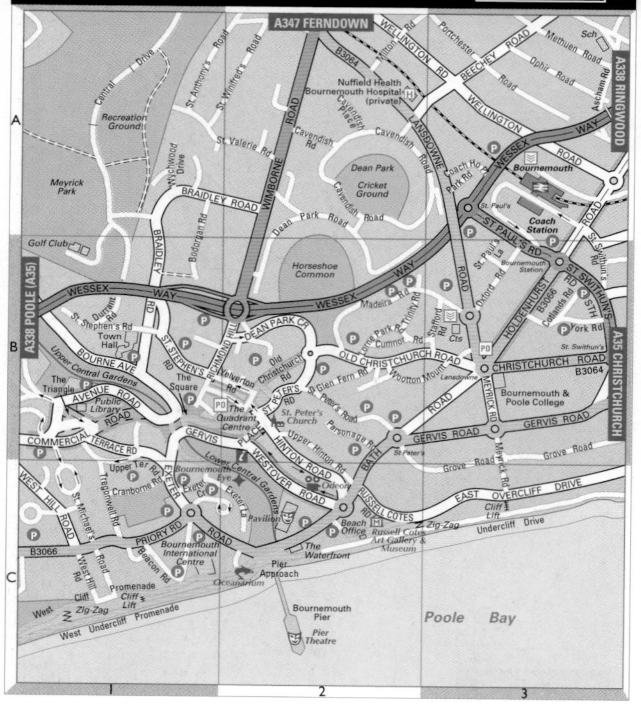

Bradford

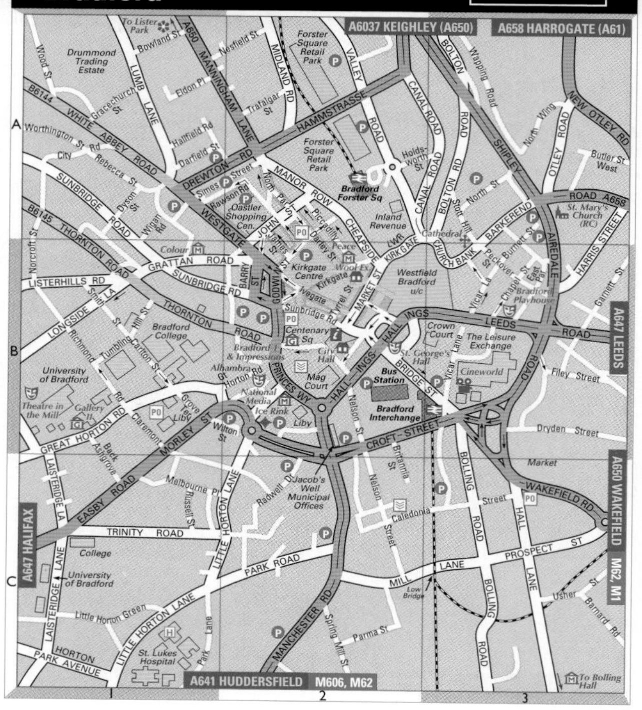

Brighton

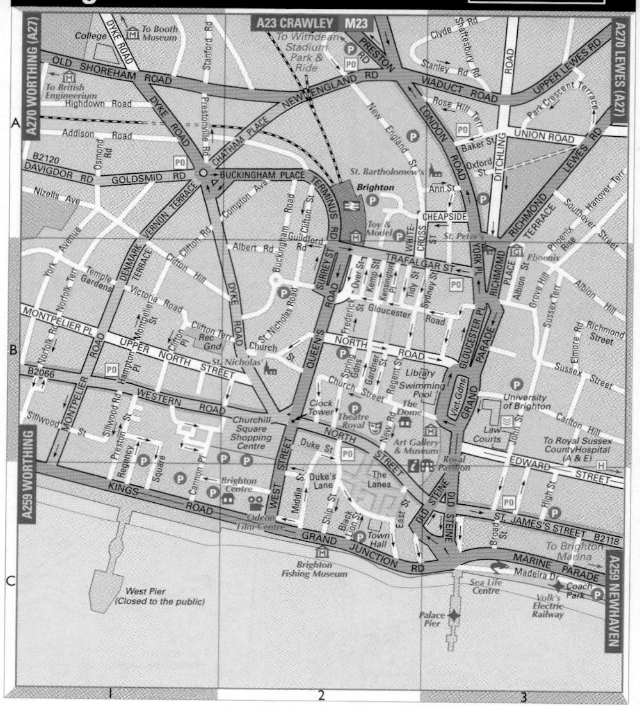

Bristol

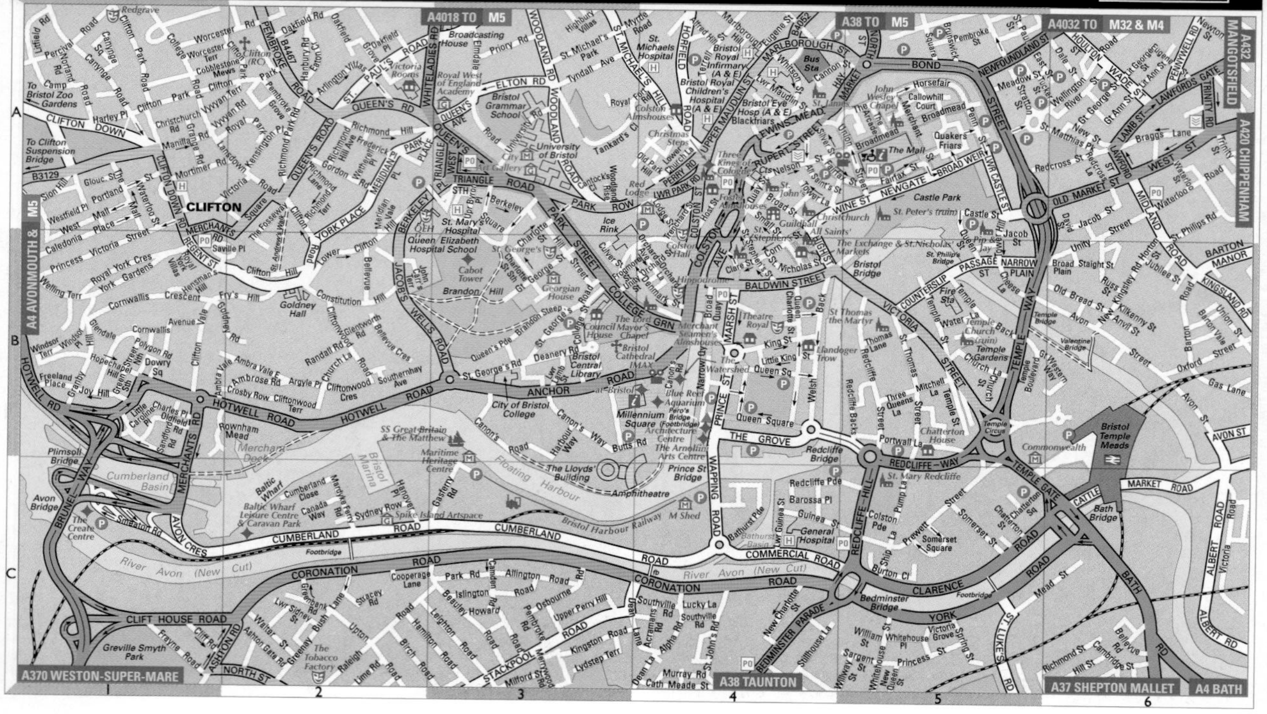

Bury St Edmunds

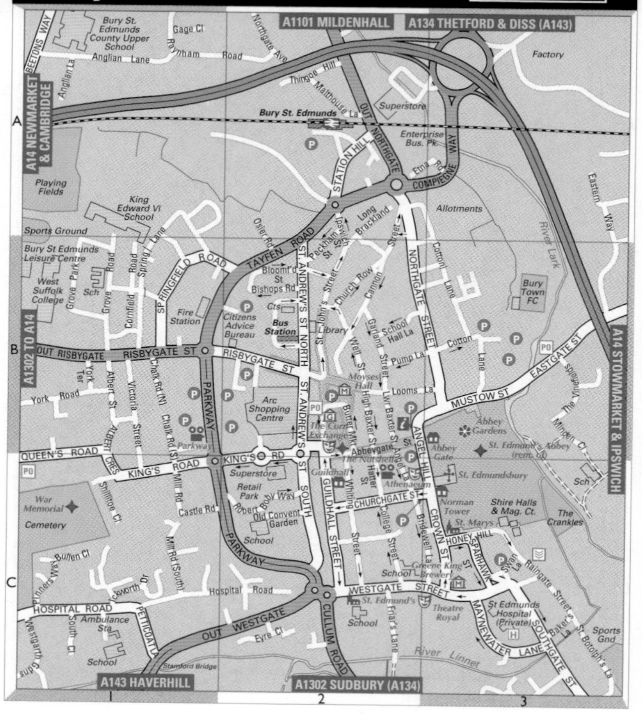

Cambridge

0 Miles ¼

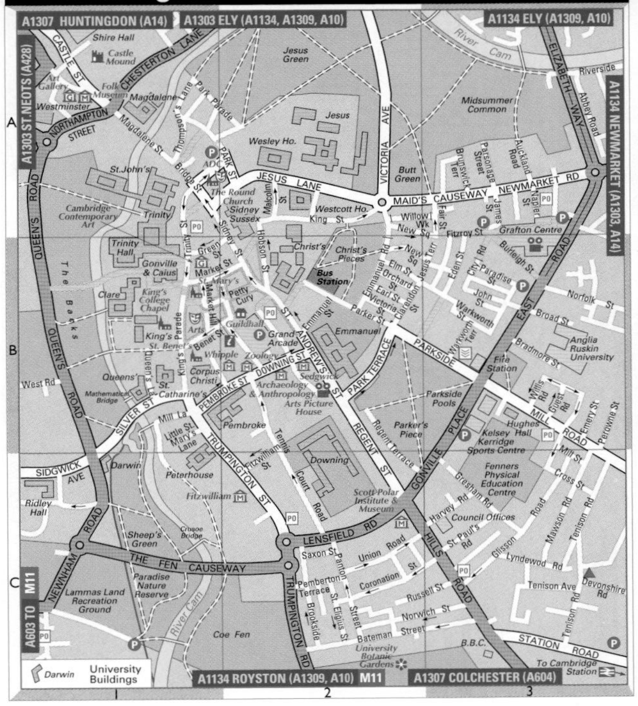

Canterbury

0 Miles ¼

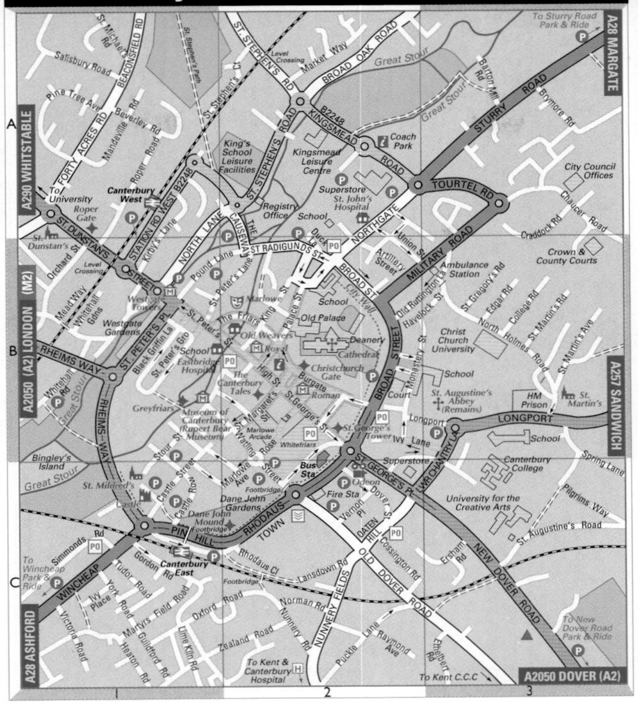

Cardiff / Caerdydd

0 Miles ¼

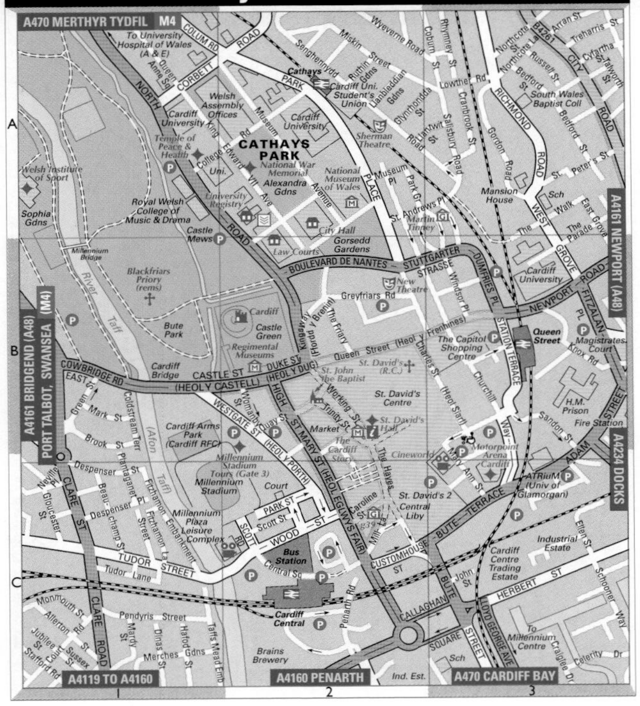

Carlisle

0 Miles ¼

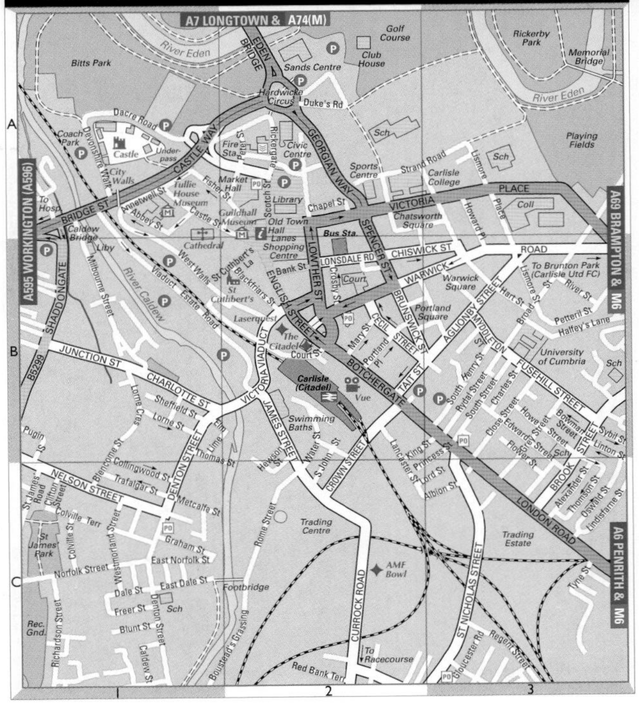

Chelmsford

0 Miles ¼

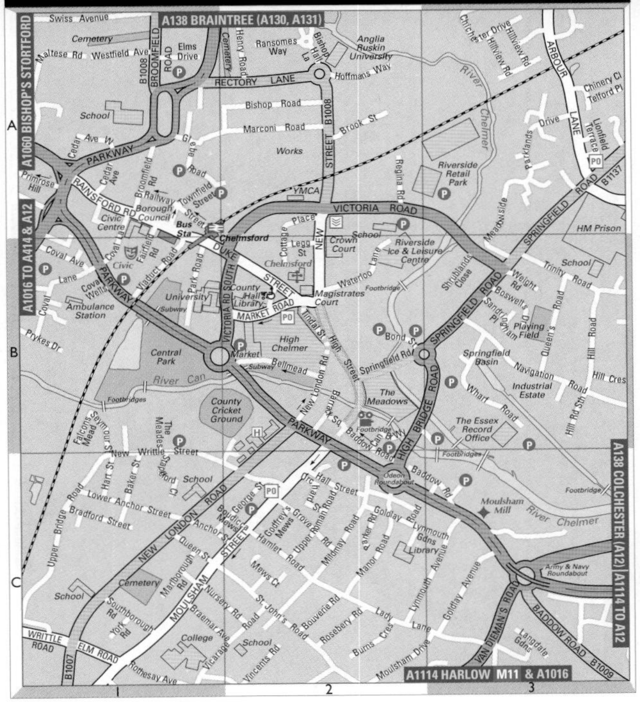

Cheltenham

0 Miles ¼

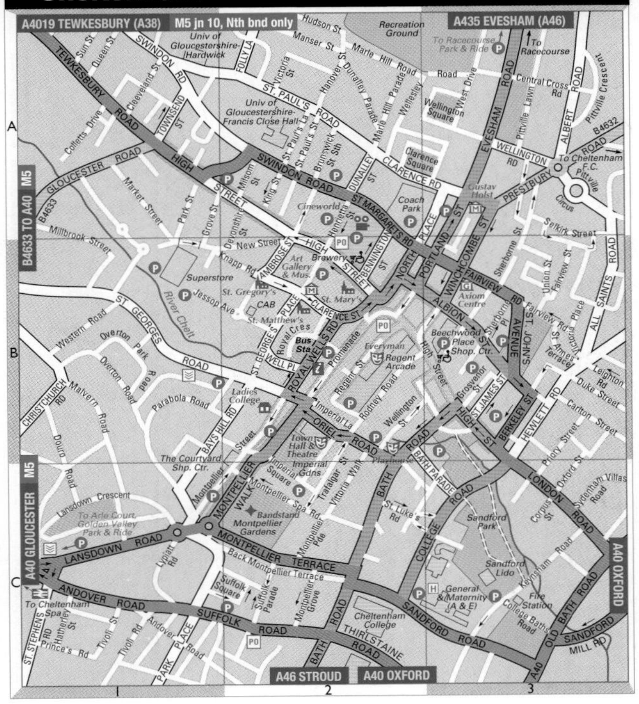

Chester

0 Miles ¼

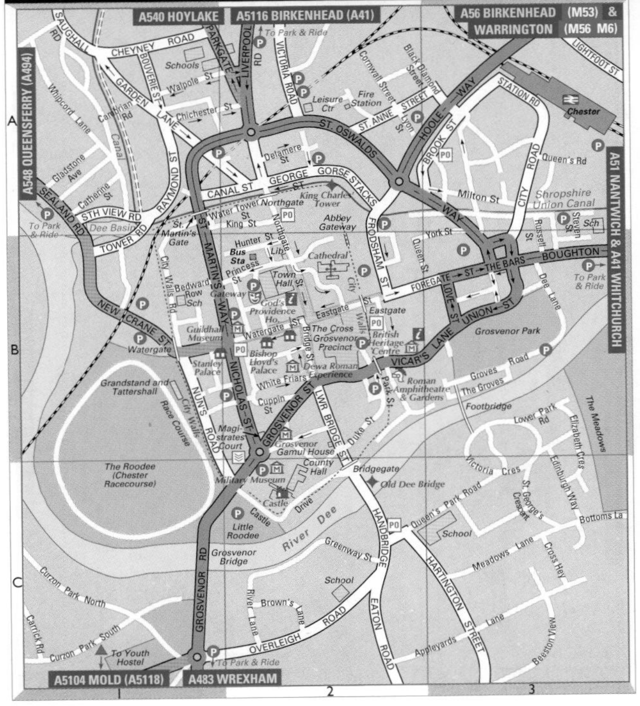

Chichester

0 Miles ¼

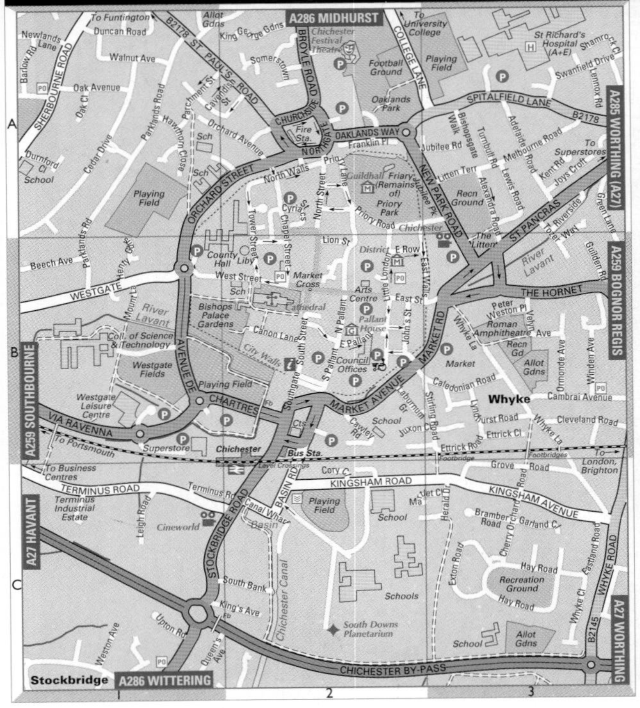

Colchester

0 Miles ¼

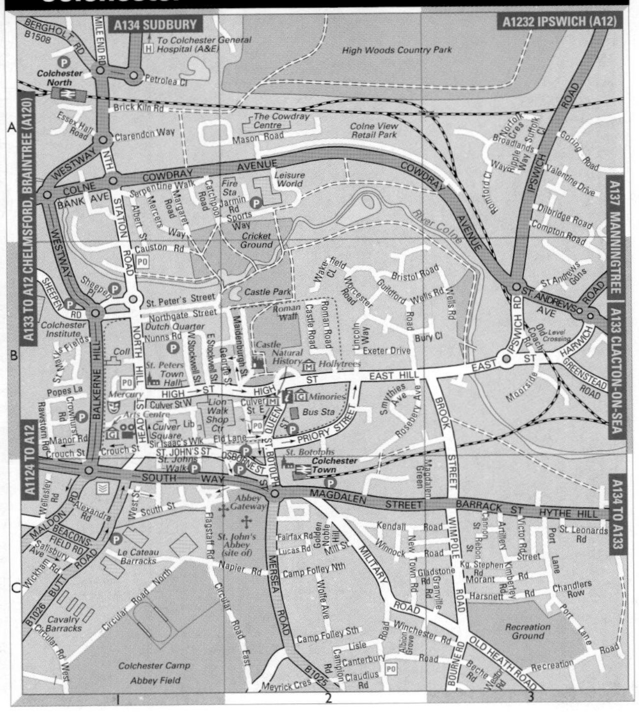

Coventry

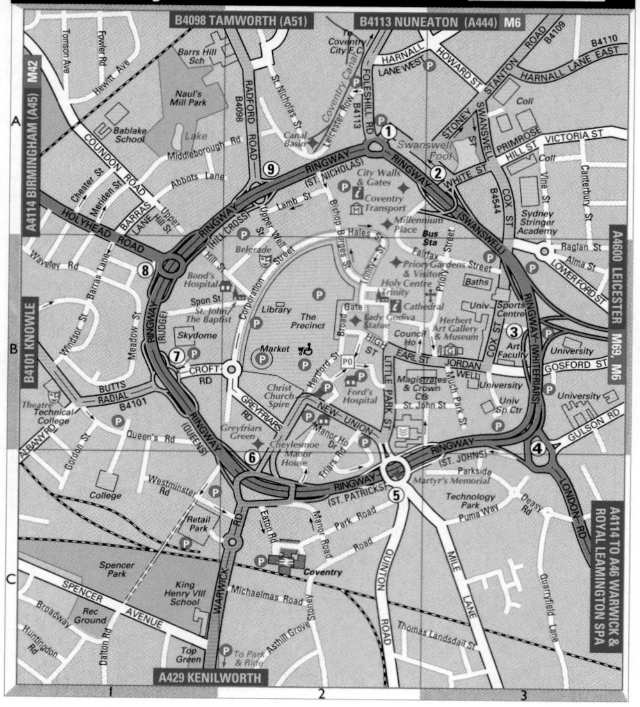

Derby

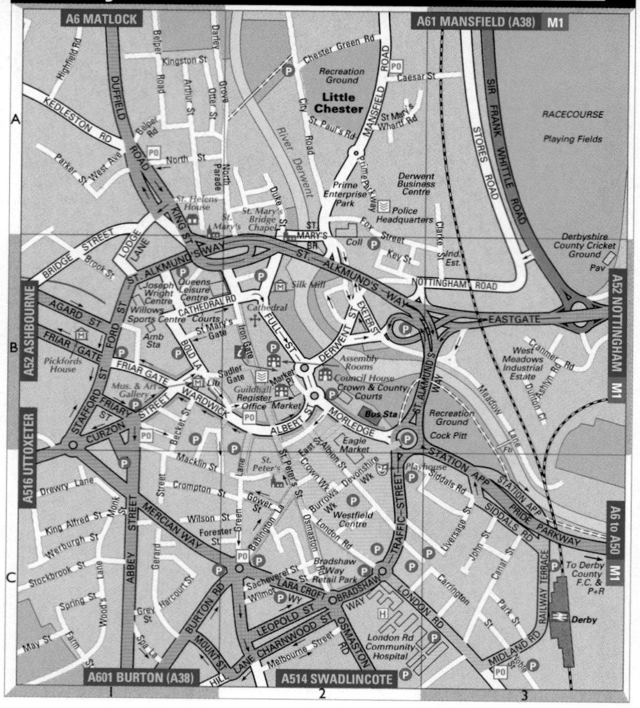

Dorchester

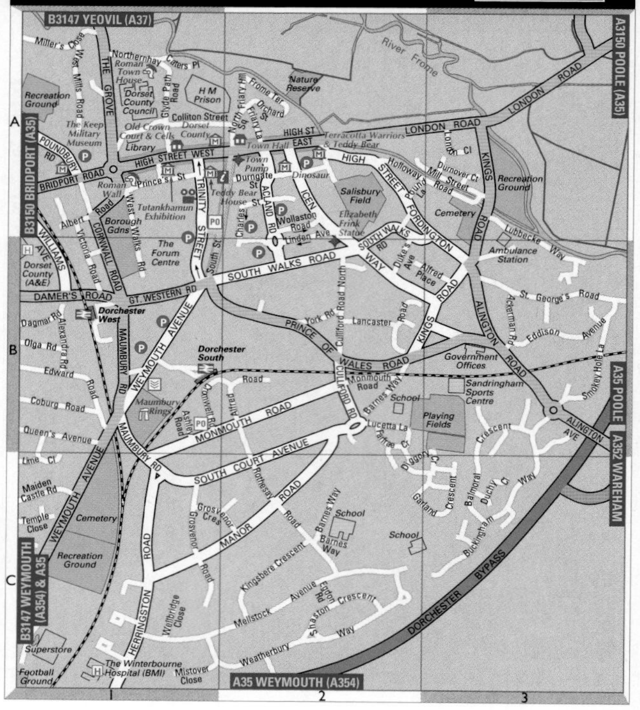

Dumfries

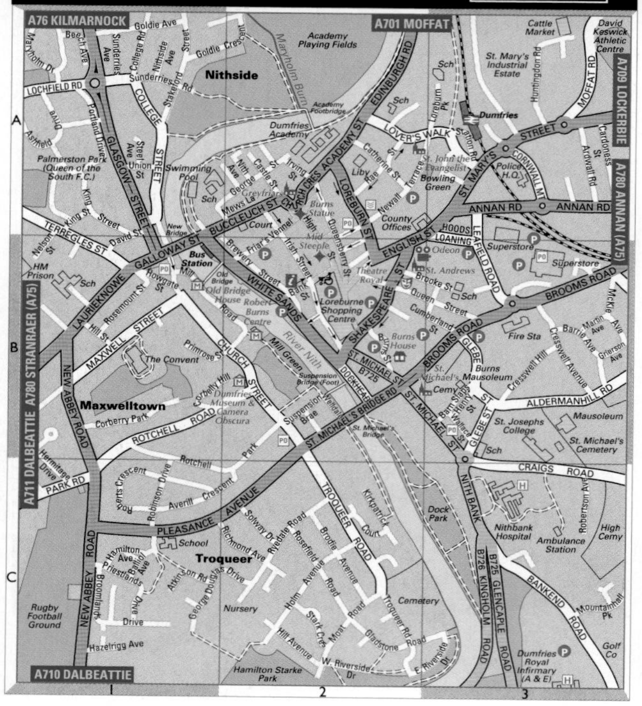

Dundee

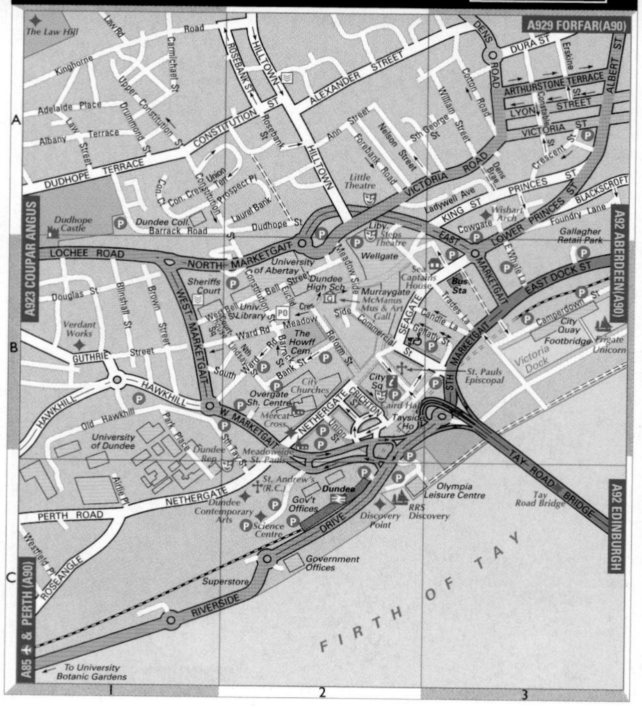

Durham

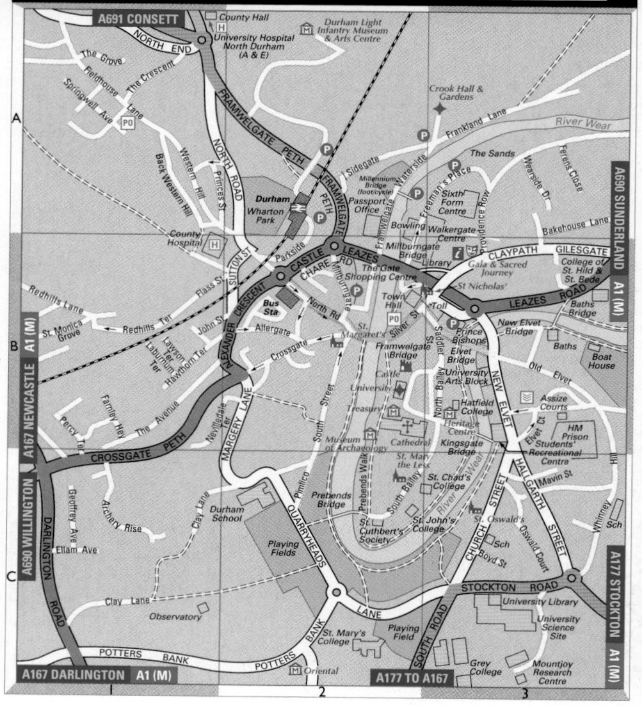

Edinburgh

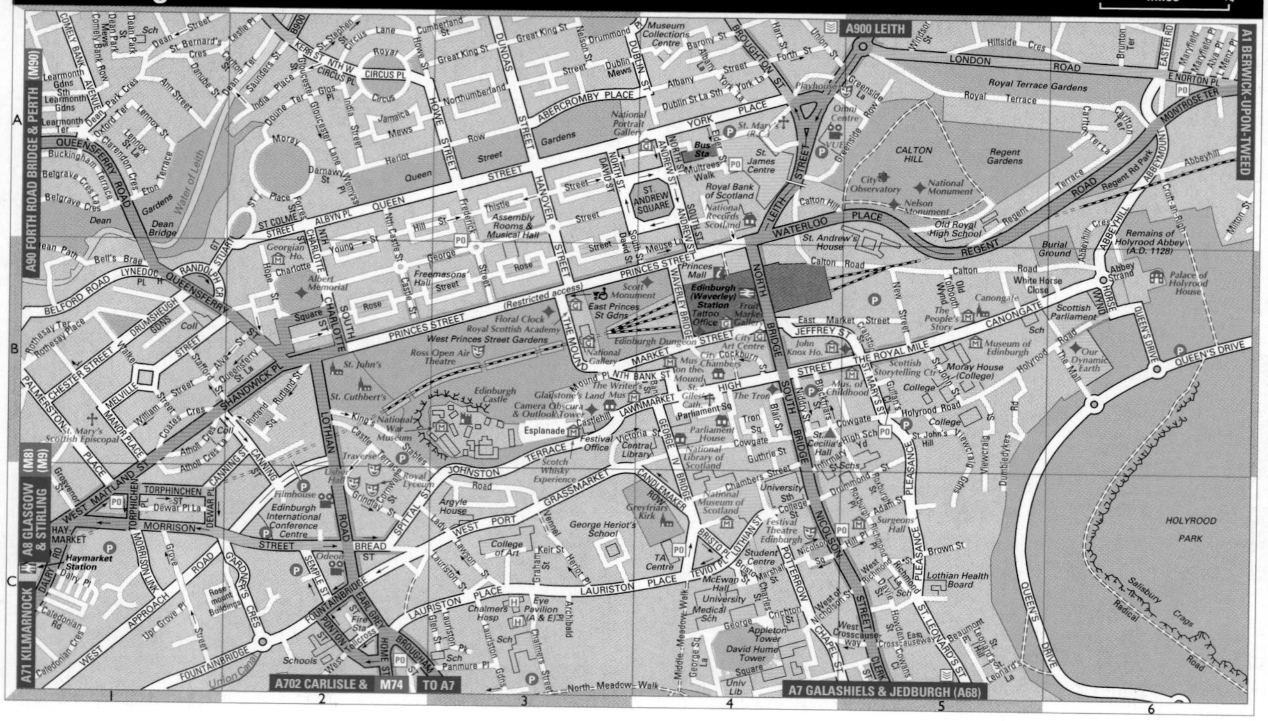

Exeter

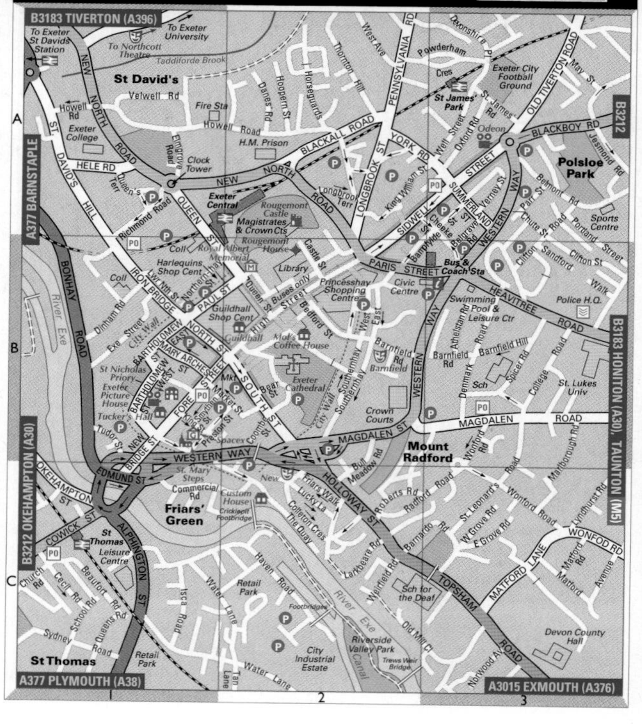

Fort William

0 Miles ¼

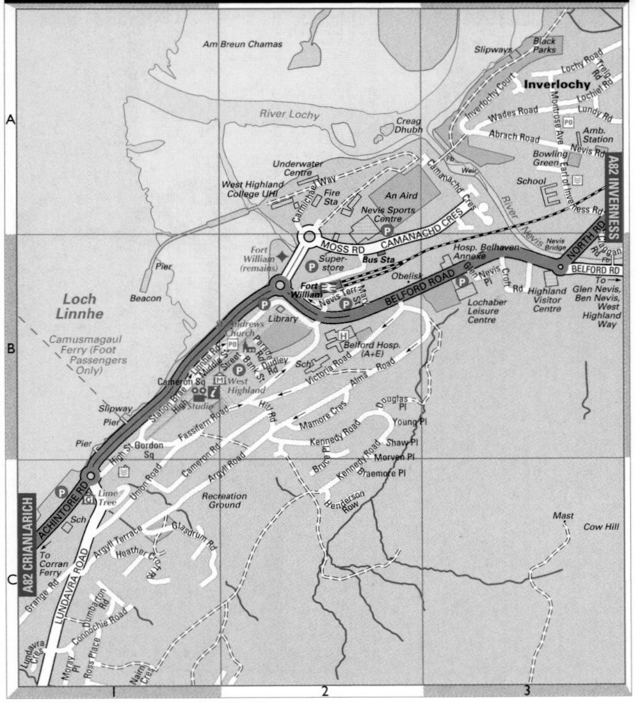

Glasgow

0 Miles ¼

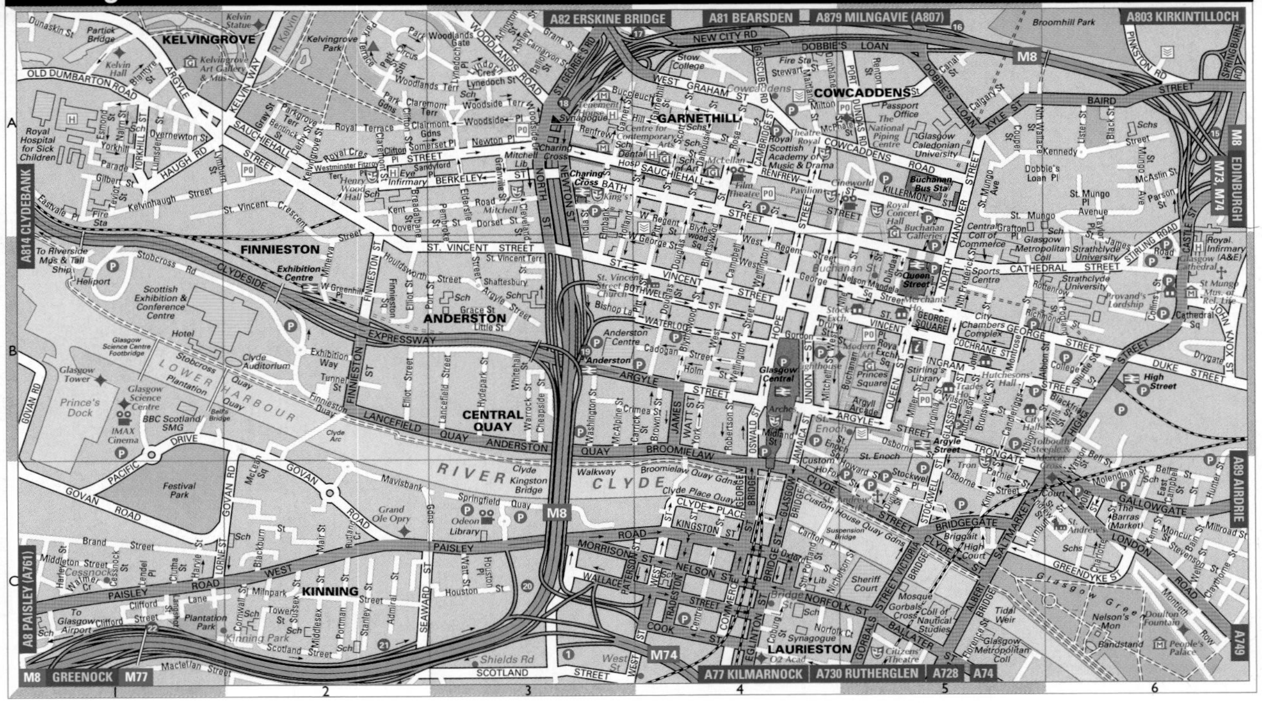

Gloucester

0 Miles ¼

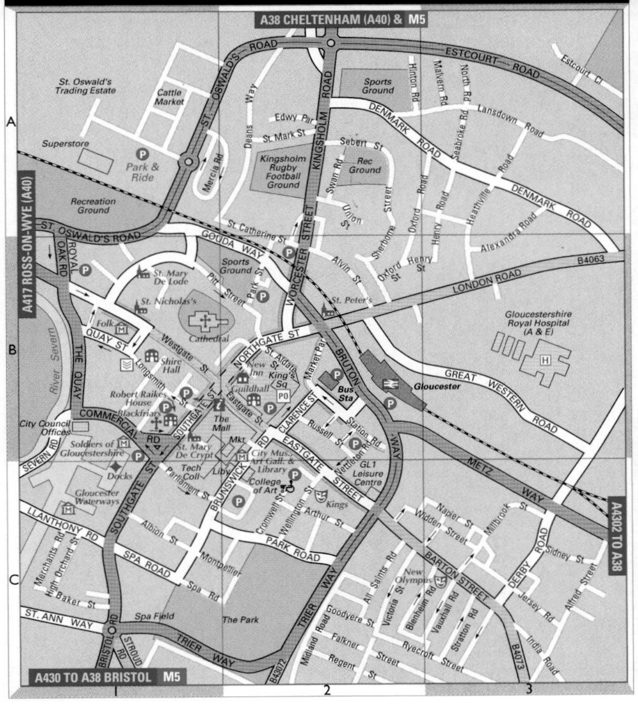

Grimsby

0 Miles ¼

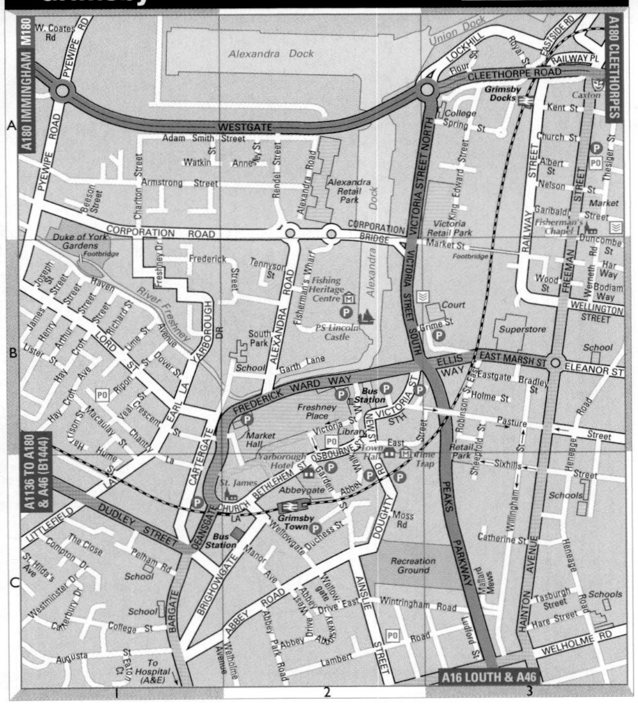

Hanley (Stoke-on-Trent)

0 Miles ¼

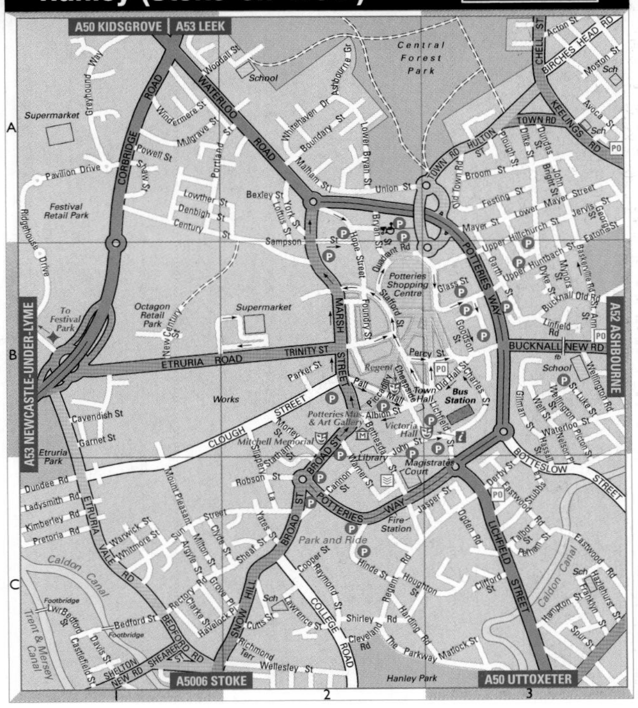

Harrogate

0 Miles ¼

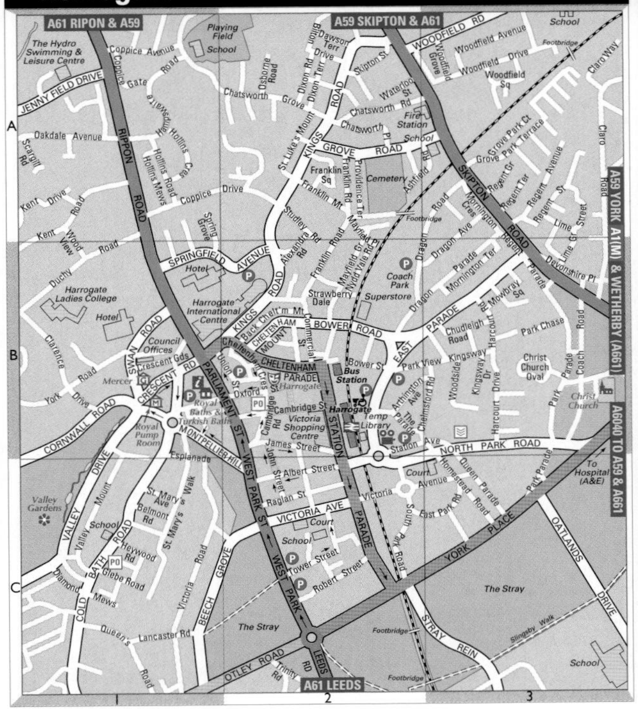

Holyhead / Caergybi

0 Miles ¼

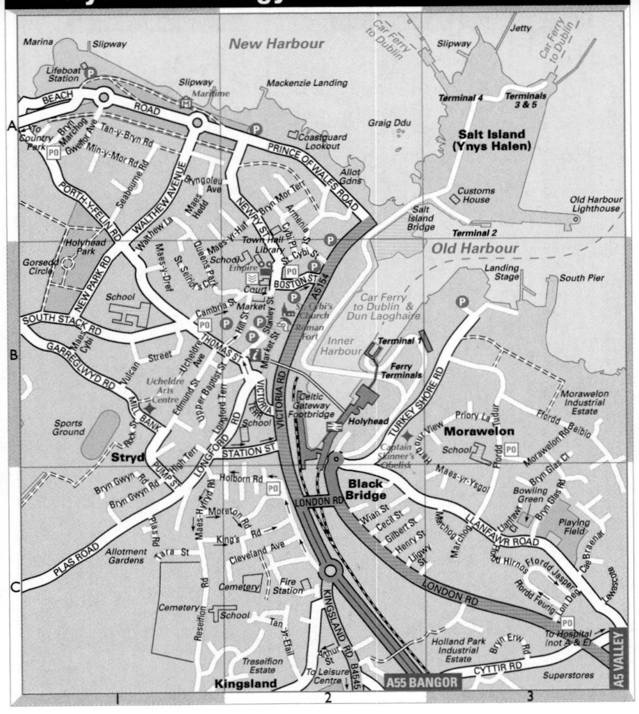

Hull

0 Miles ¼

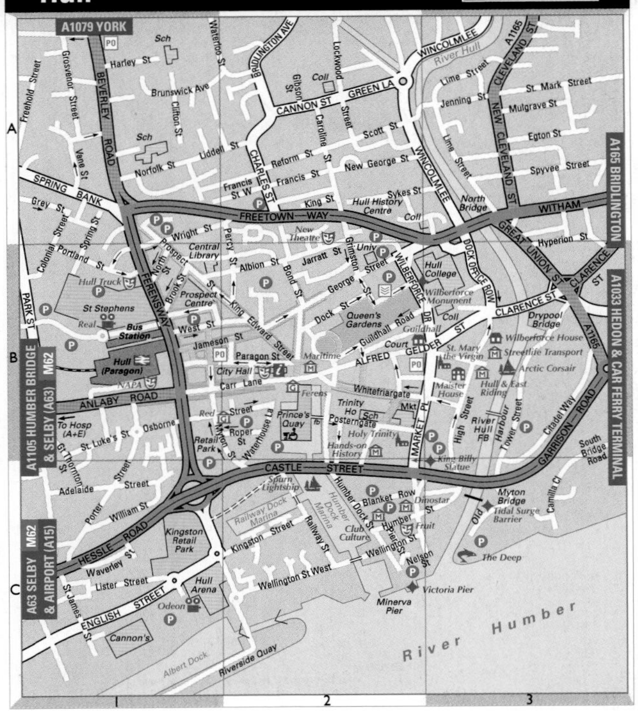

Inverness

0 Miles ¼

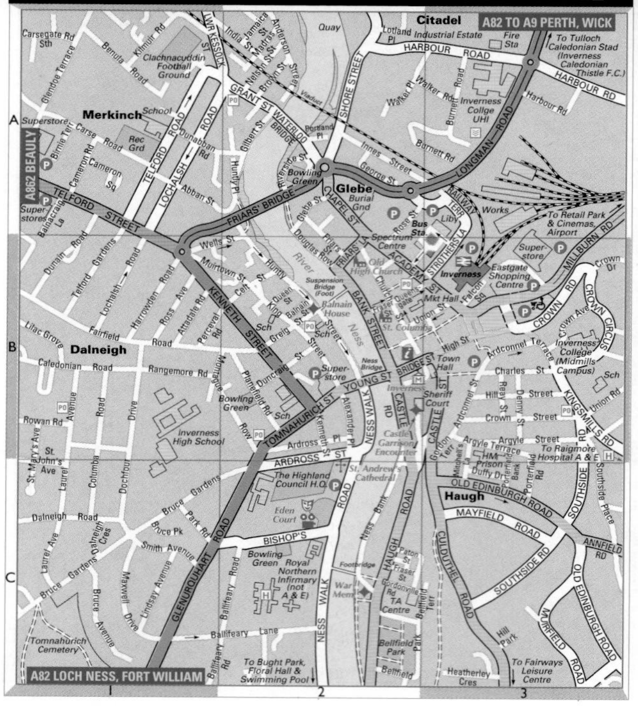

Ipswich

0 Miles ¼

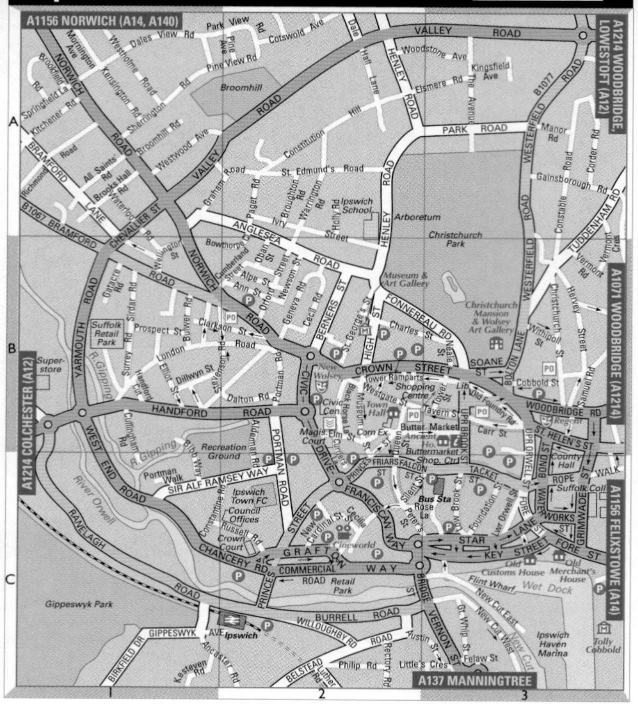

Kendal

0 Miles ¼

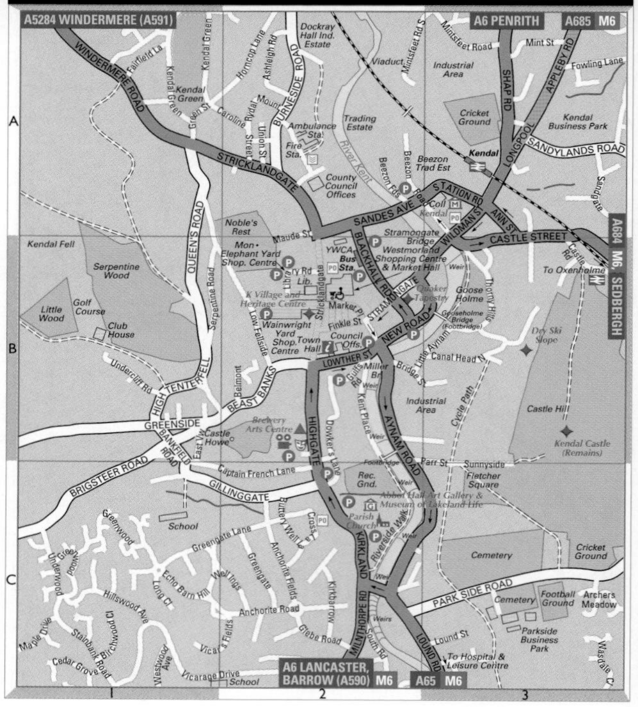

King's Lynn

0 Miles ¼

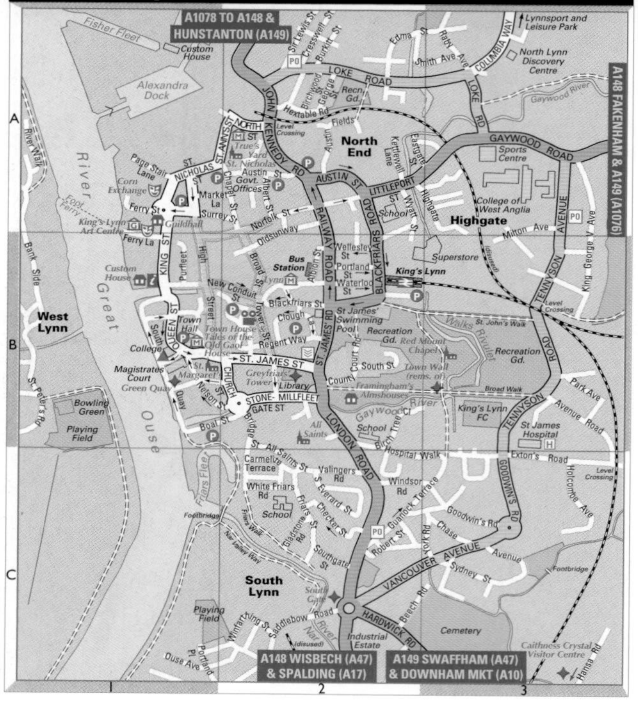

Leeds

0 Miles ¼

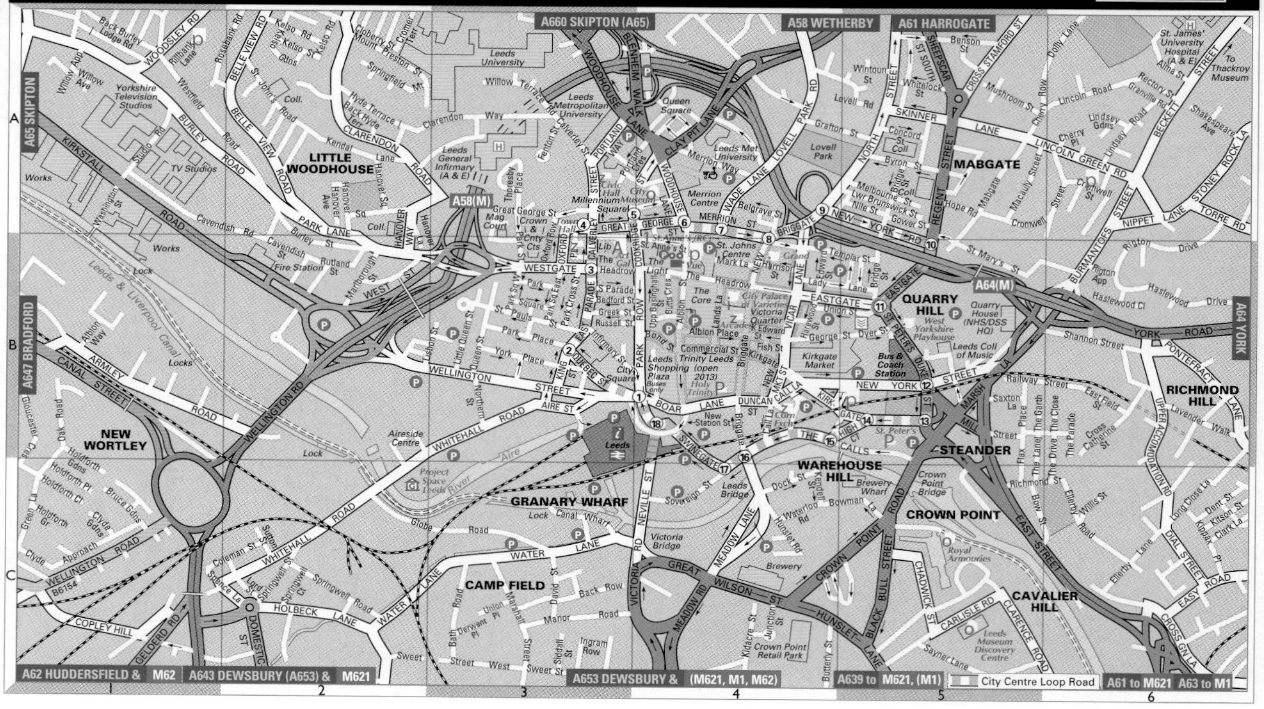

Lancaster

0 Miles ¼

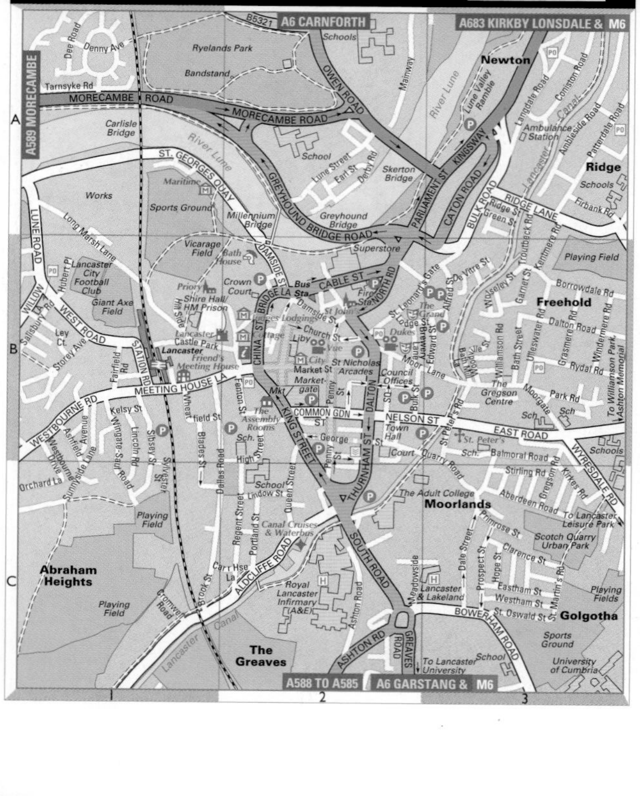

Leicester

0 Miles ¼

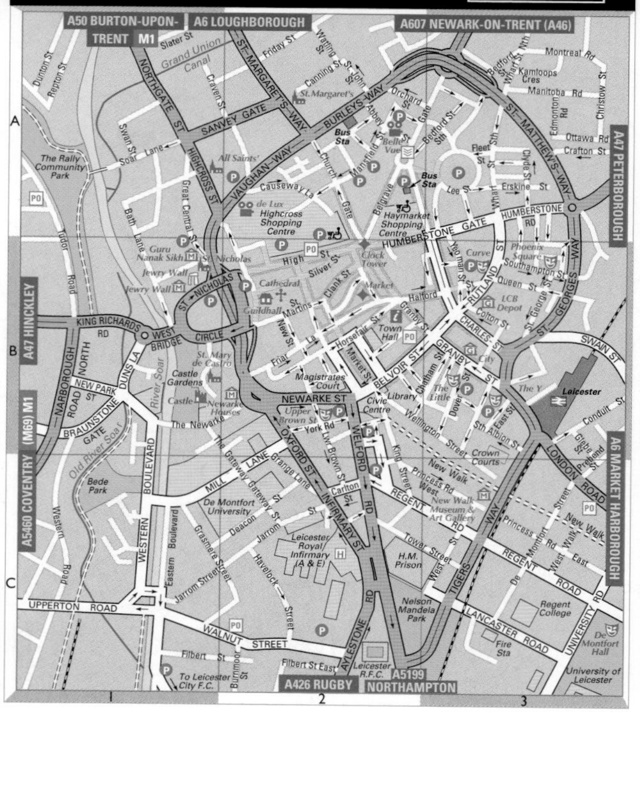

Lewes

0 Miles ¼

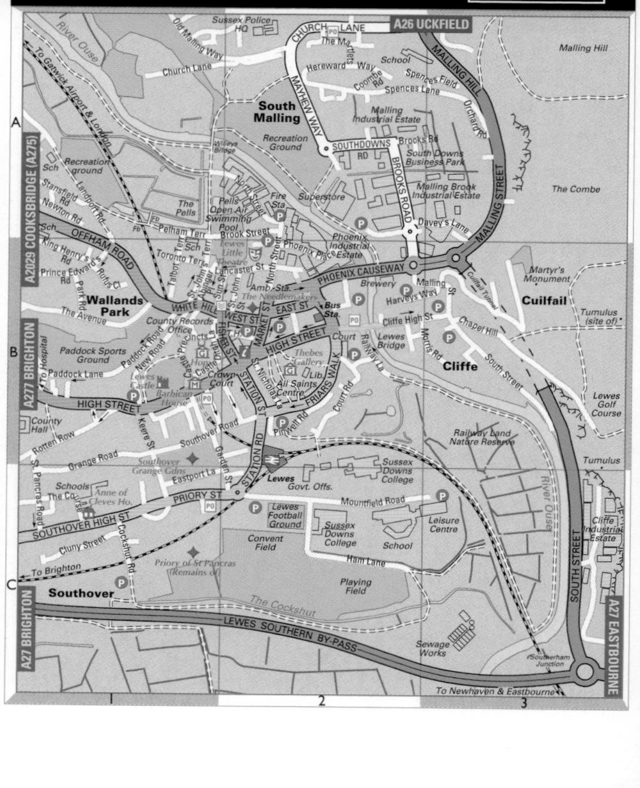

Lincoln

0 Miles ¼

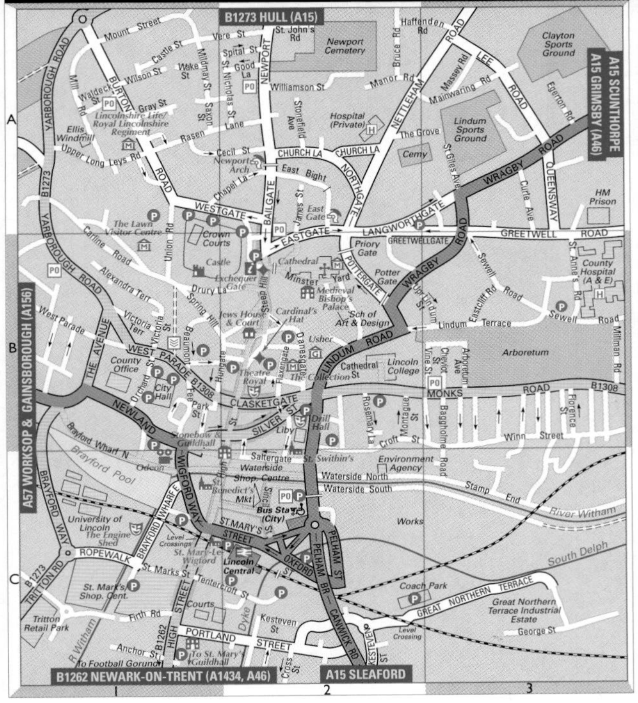

Liverpool

0 Miles ¼

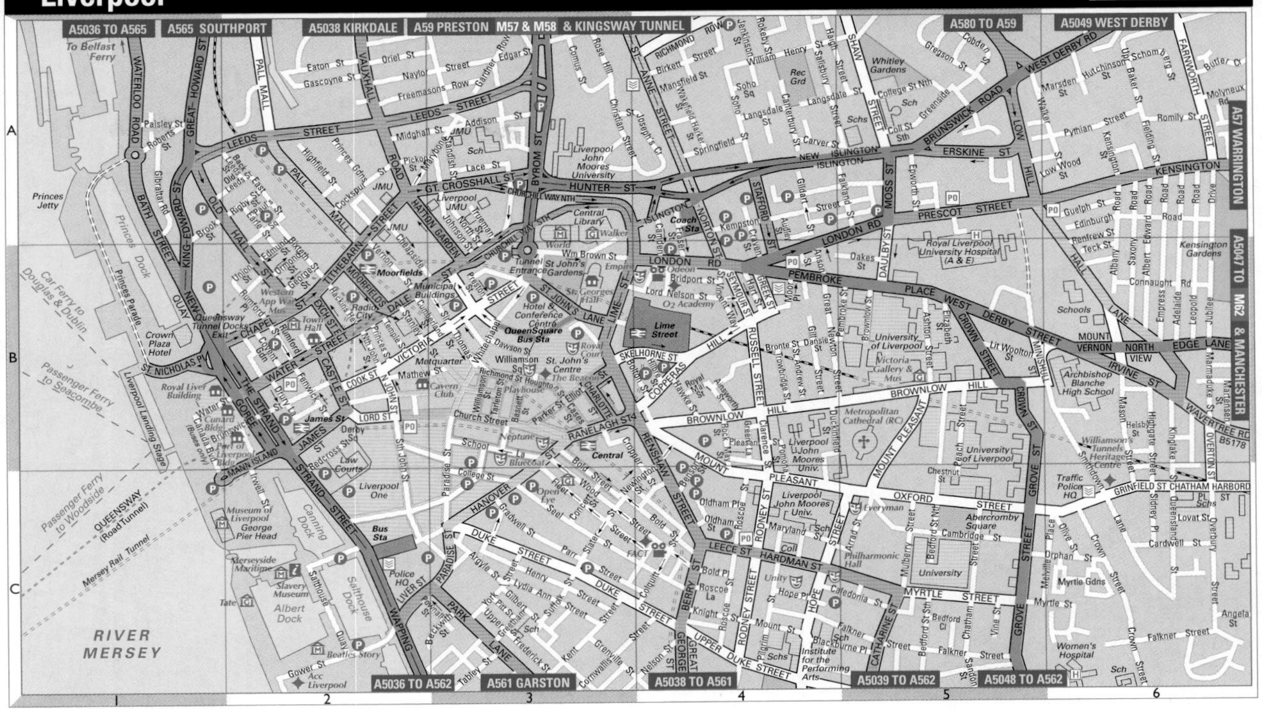

Llandudno

0 Miles ¼

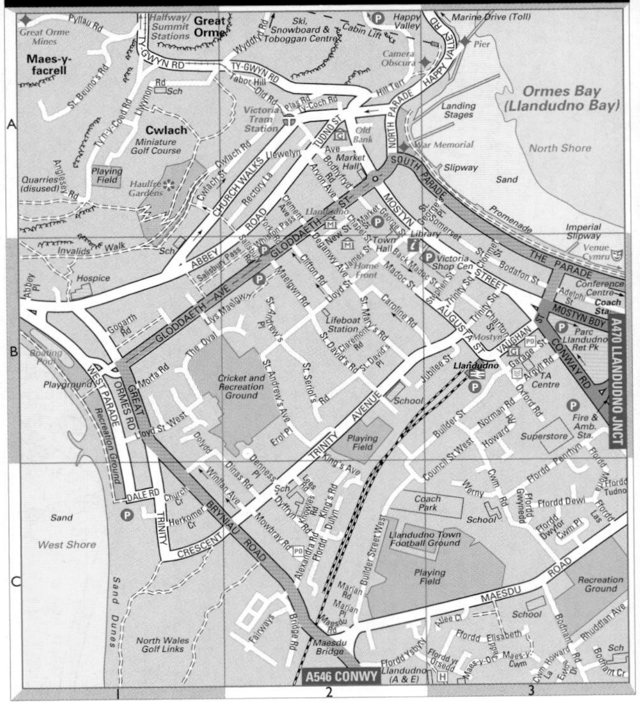

Llanelli

0 Miles ¼

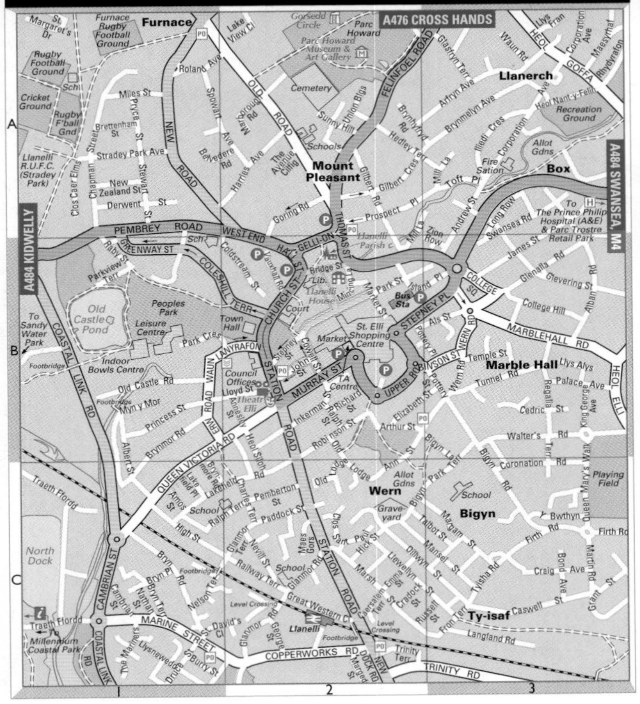

Luton

0 Miles ¼

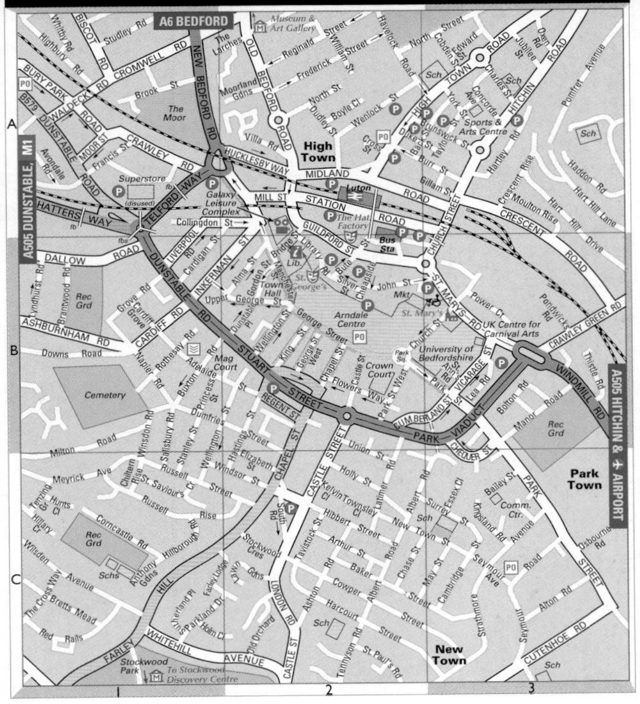

Macclesfield

0 Miles ¼

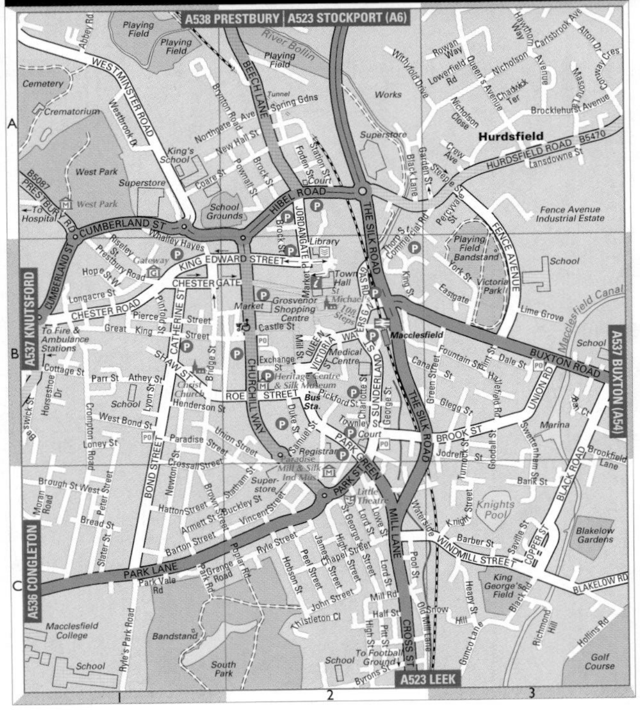

Manchester

0 Miles ¼

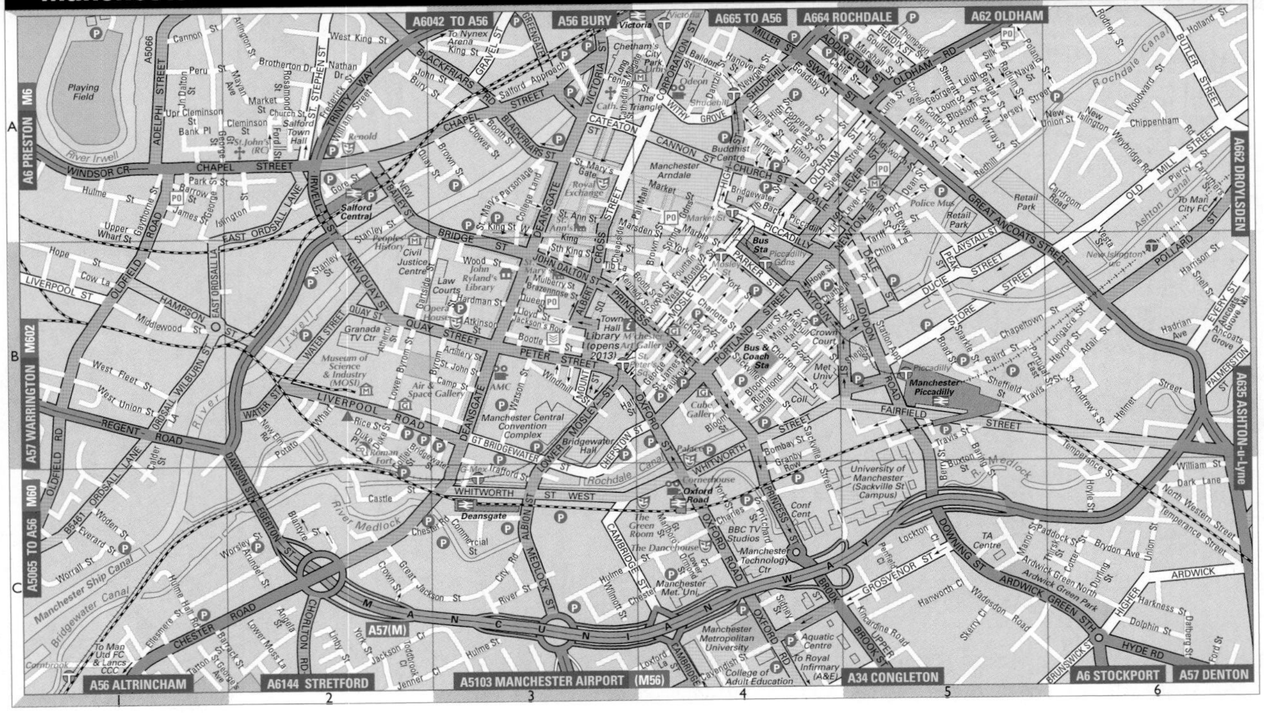

ST. JOHN'S WOOD
REGENT'S PARK
SOMERS TOWN
LISSON GREEN
PADDINGTON
BLOOMSBURY
FITZROVIA
SOHO
MAYFAIR
ST. JAMES'S
HYDE PARK
KENSINGTON GARDENS
GREEN PARK
ST. JAMES'S PARK
KNIGHTSBRIDGE
BROMPTON
WESTMINSTER
PIMLICO
THE SERPENTINE
Buckingham Palace
Euston
Victoria
Marylebone
St. Pancras International
Charing Cross
British Museum
Lord's Cricket Ground (M.C.C. & Middlesex C.C.C.)
Madame Tussaud's
Natural History Museum
Science Museum
Victoria & Albert Museum
Royal Albert Hall
Westminster Abbey
Tate Britain
Piccadilly Circus
Oxford Circus
Marble Arch
Hyde Park Corner
Trafalgar Square
National Gallery
Wellington Arch
Queen Victoria Memorial

HOXTON
FINSBURY
SHOREDITCH
CLERKENWELL
HOLBORN
THE CITY
SOUTHWARK
SOUTH BANK
BERMONDSEY
NEWINGTON
LAMBETH
RIVER THAMES
Liverpool Street
Cannon Street
London Bridge
Waterloo
Blackfriars
Farringdon
City Thameslink
Fenchurch Street
Elephant & Castle
Tower Gateway
The Tower of London
St Paul's Cathedral
Tate Modern
Imperial War Museum
Lincoln's Inn Fields
Bunhill Fields
The Barbican
Museum of London
London Eye
Tower Bridge
Blackfriars Bridge
Southwark Bridge
London Bridge
Waterloo Bridge
Westminster Bridge
The Millennium Bridge (Footbridge)
Miles
0
½
5
6
7
8
B
C
D
E
F

Maidstone

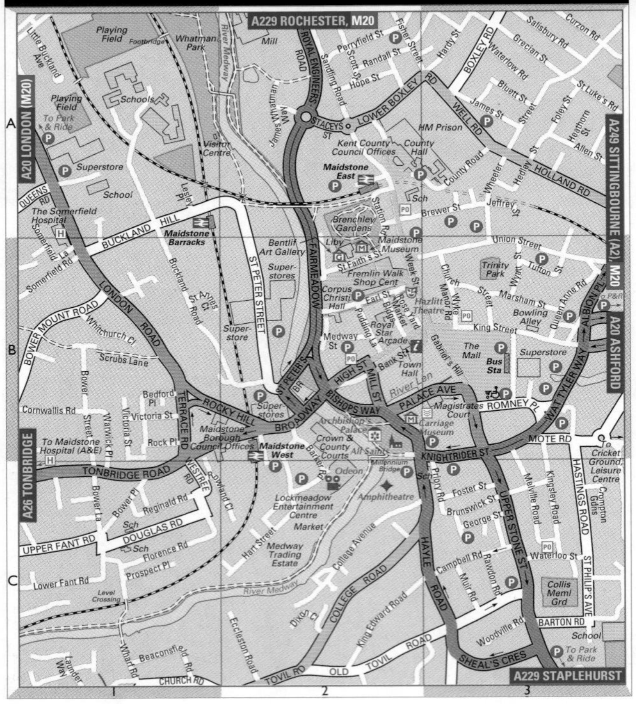

Merthyr Tydfil / Merthyr Tudful

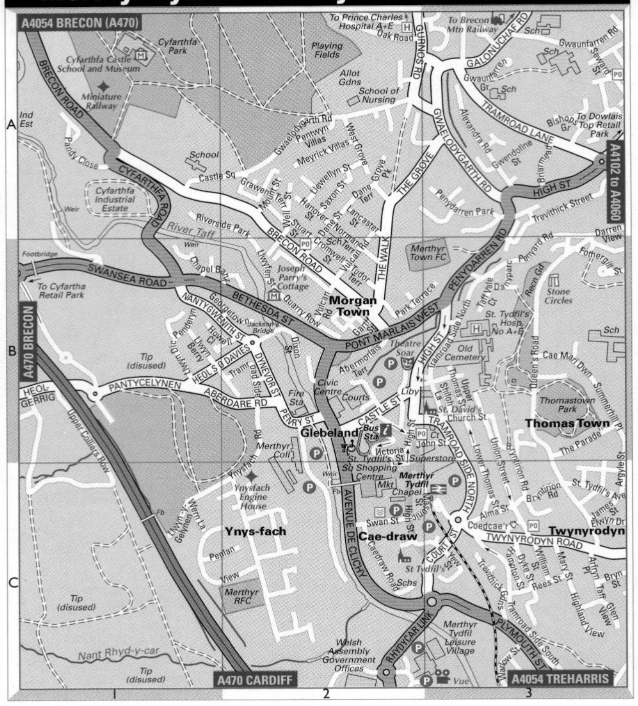

Middlesbrough

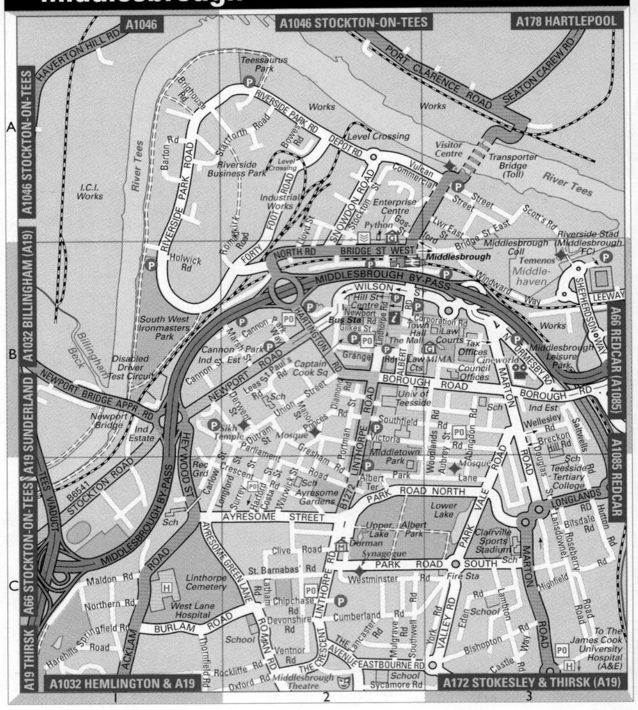

Milton Keynes

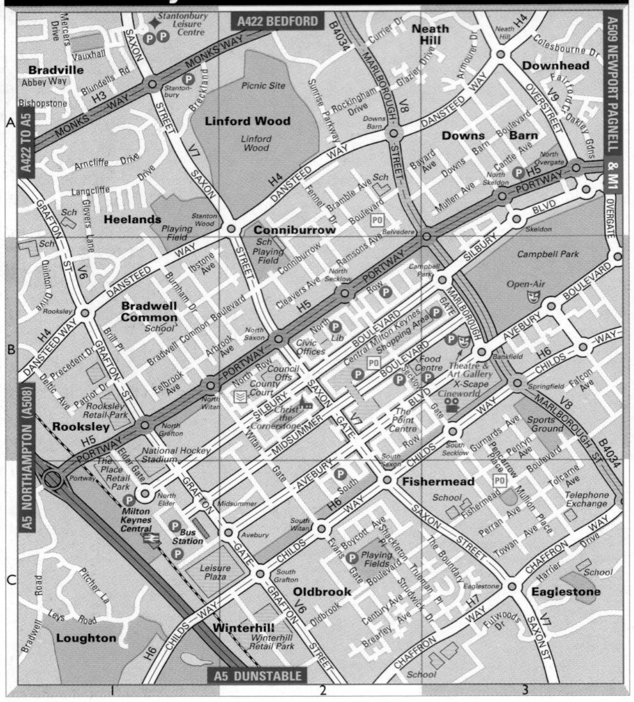

Newcastle upon Tyne

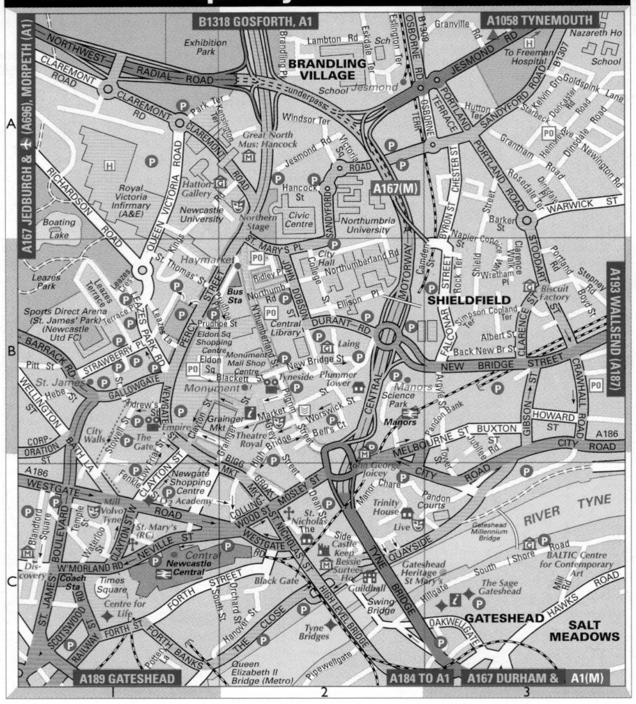

Newport / Casnewydd

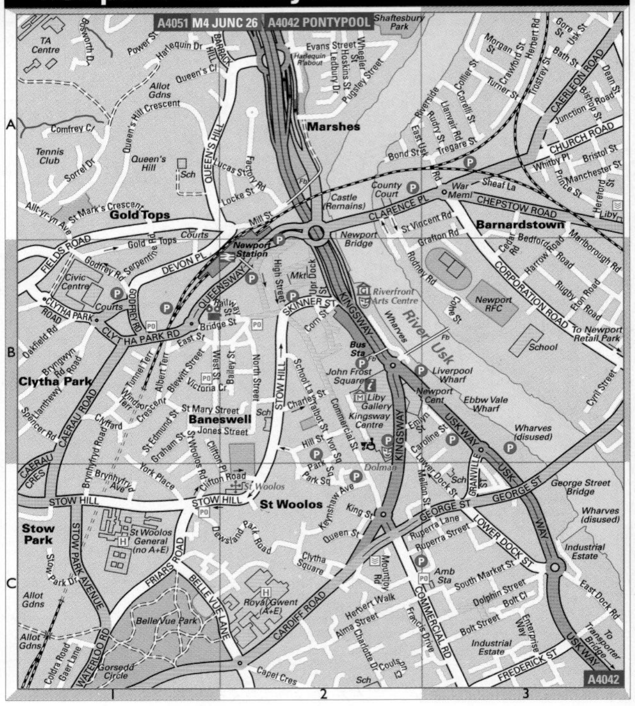

Newquay

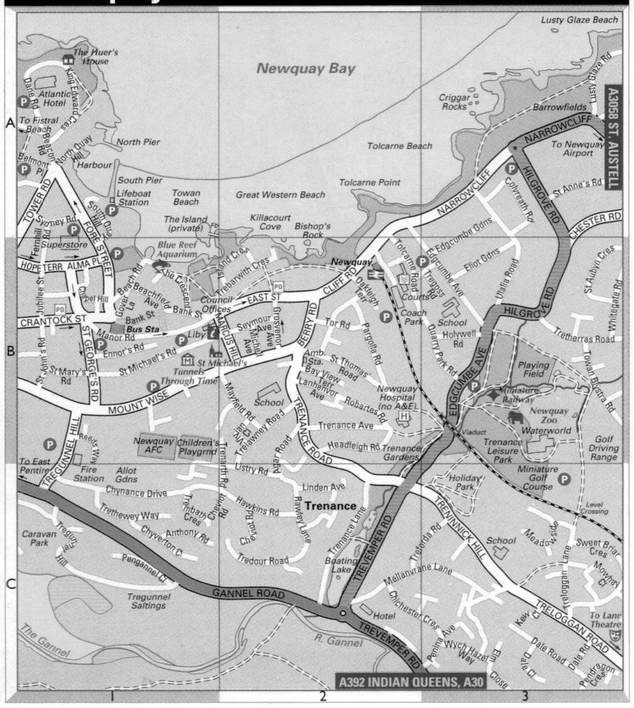

Newtown / Y Drenewydd

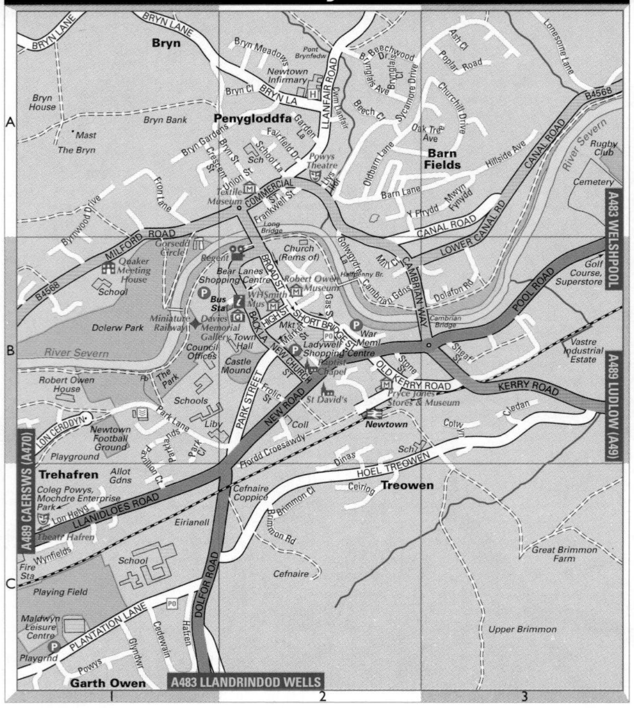

Northampton

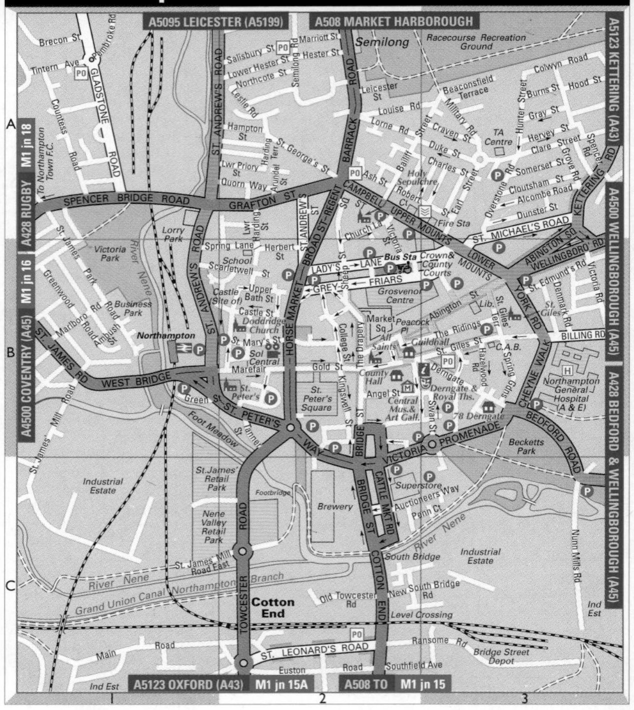

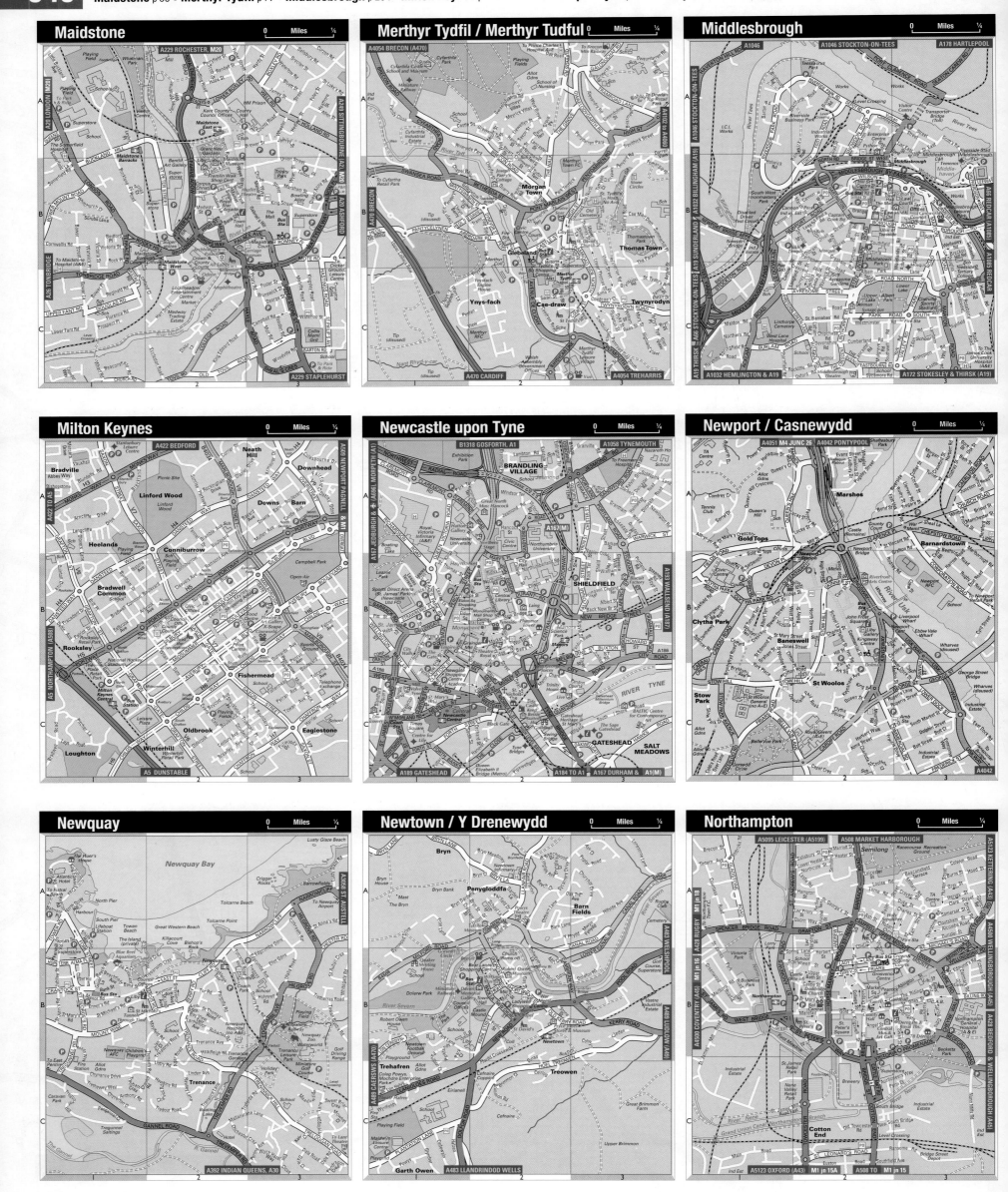

Norwich

0 Miles ¼

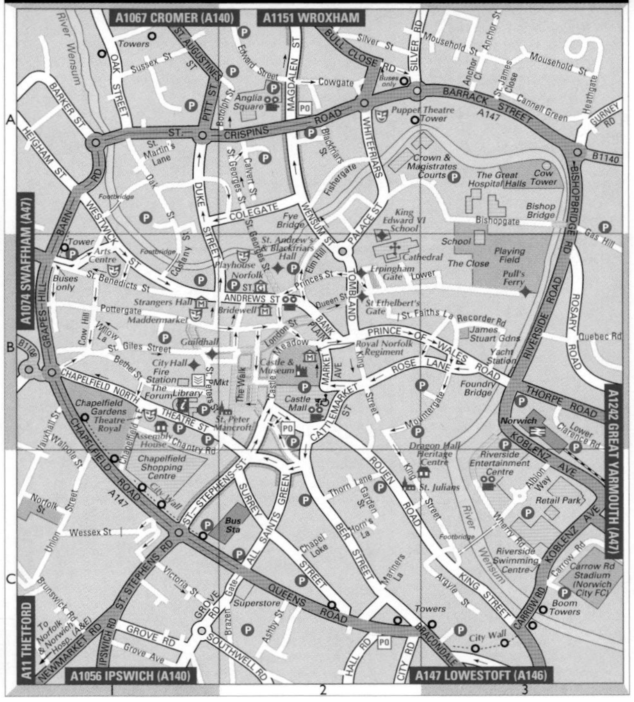

Nottingham

0 Miles ¼

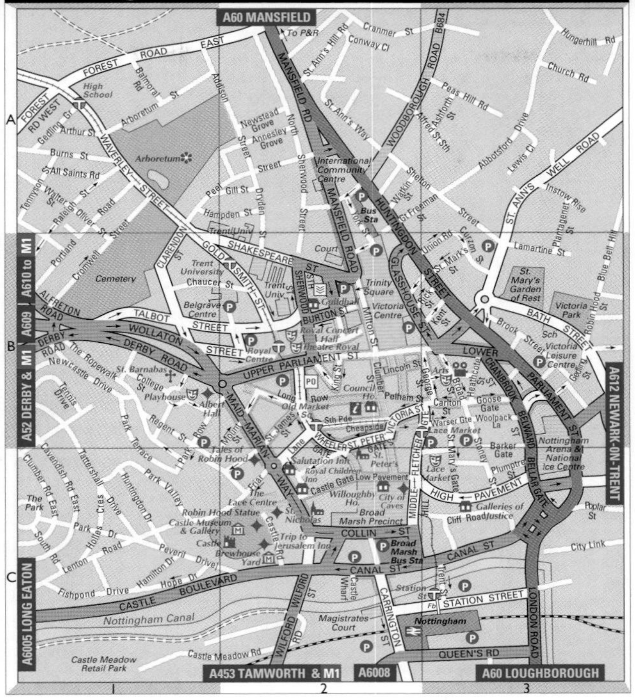

Oban

0 Miles ¼

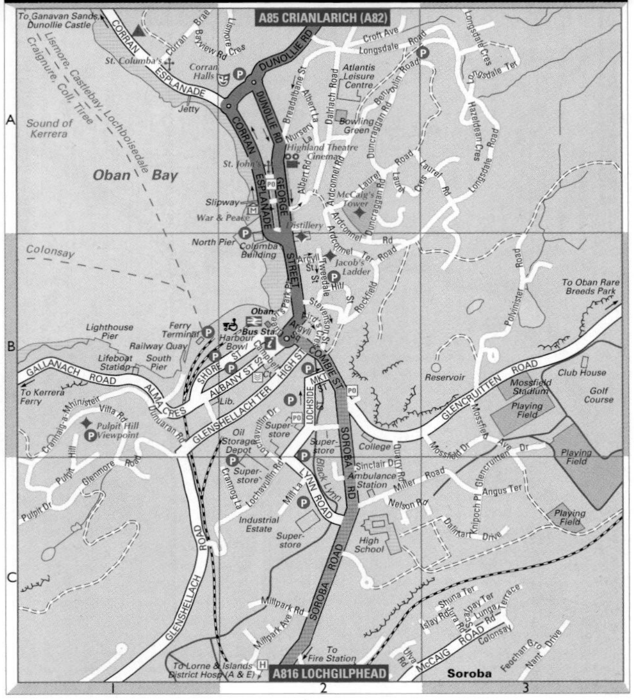

Oxford

0 Miles ¼

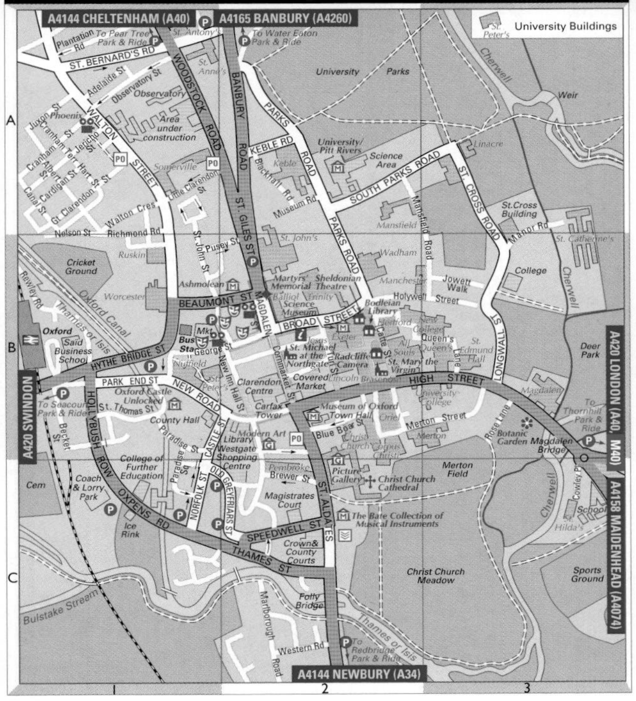

Perth

0 Miles ¼

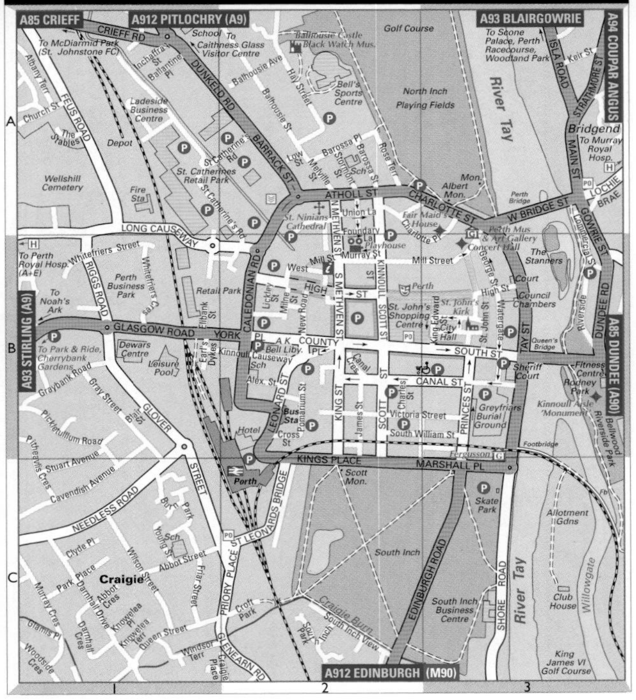

Peterborough

0 Miles ¼

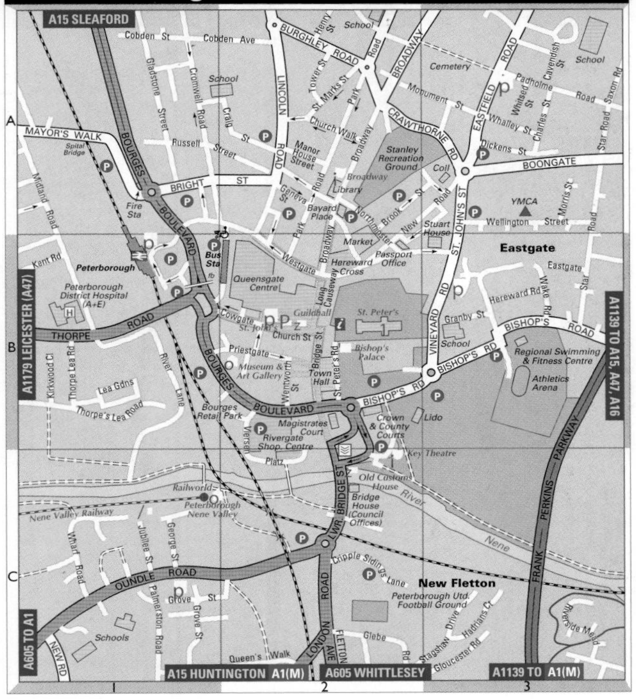

Plymouth

0 Miles ¼

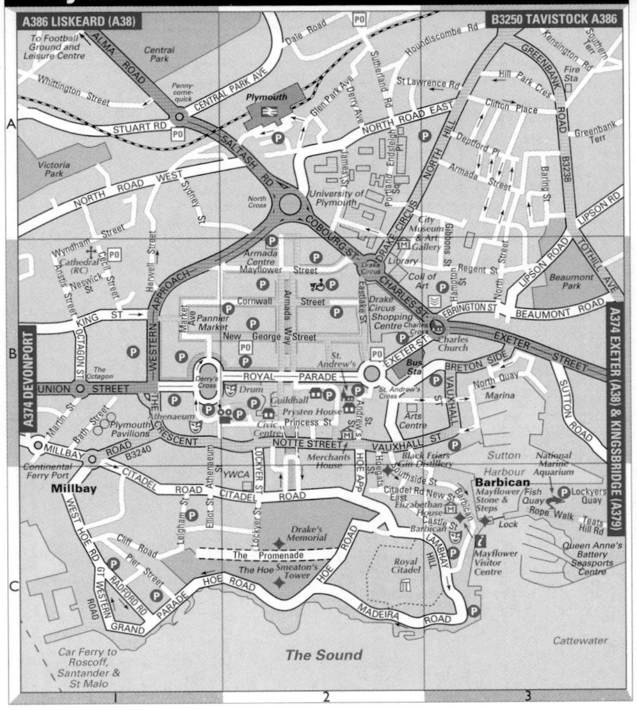

Poole

0 Miles ¼

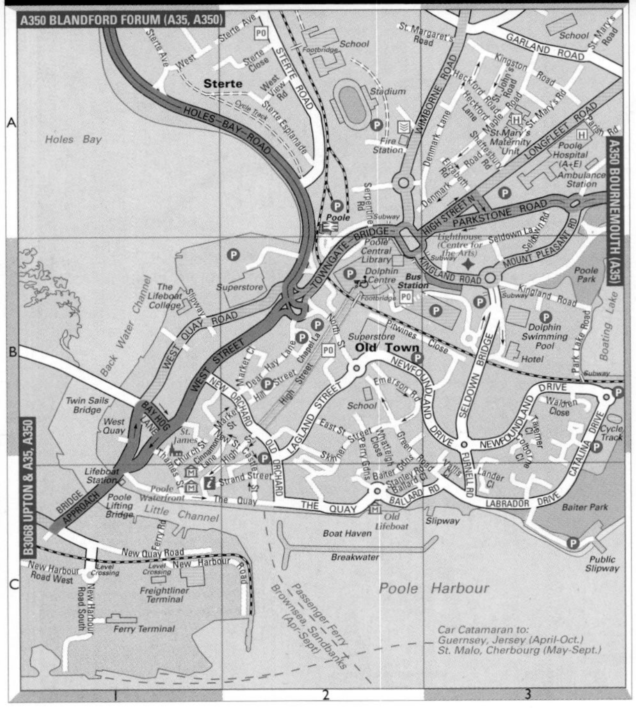

Portsmouth

0 Miles ¼

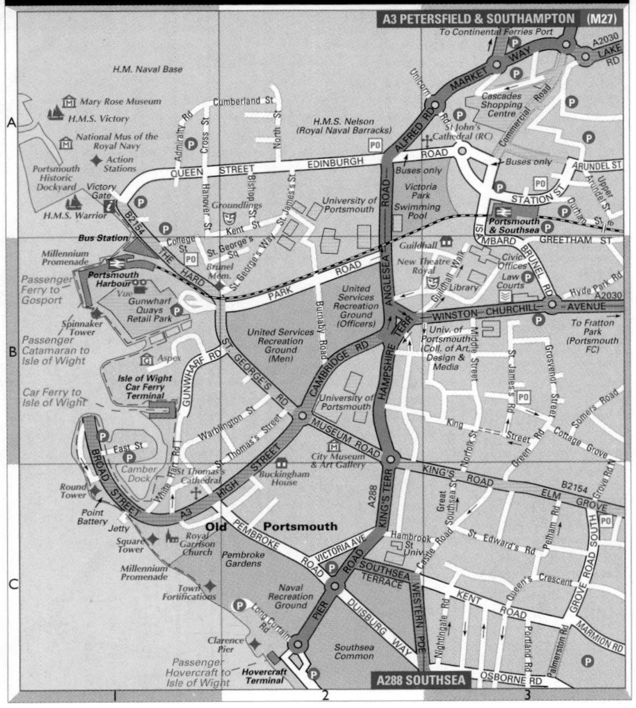

Preston

0 Miles ¼

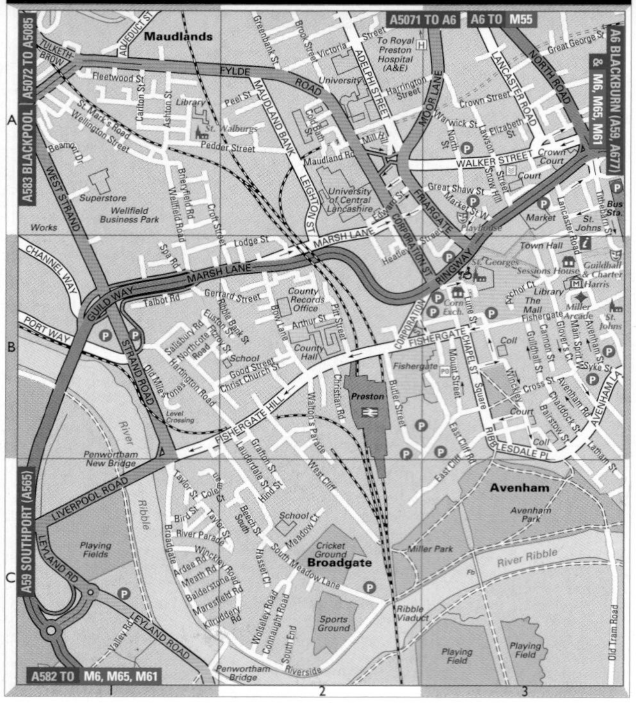

Reading

0 Miles ¼

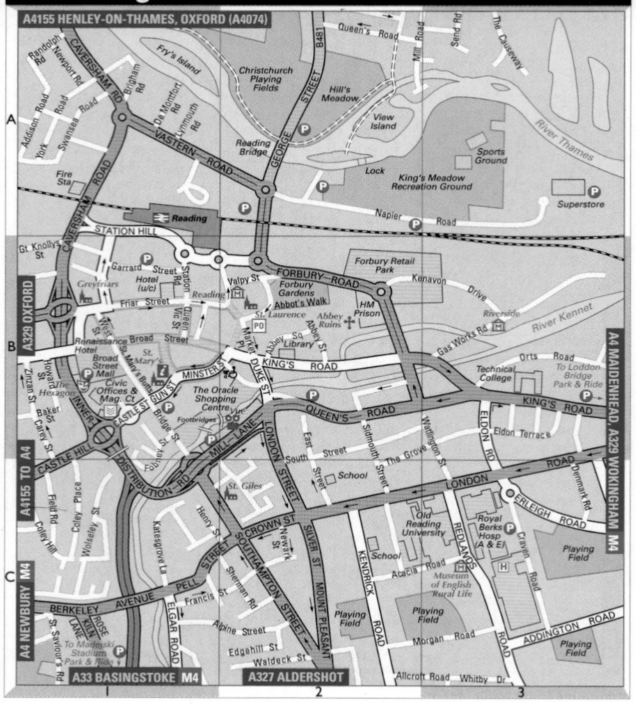

St Andrews

0 Miles ¼

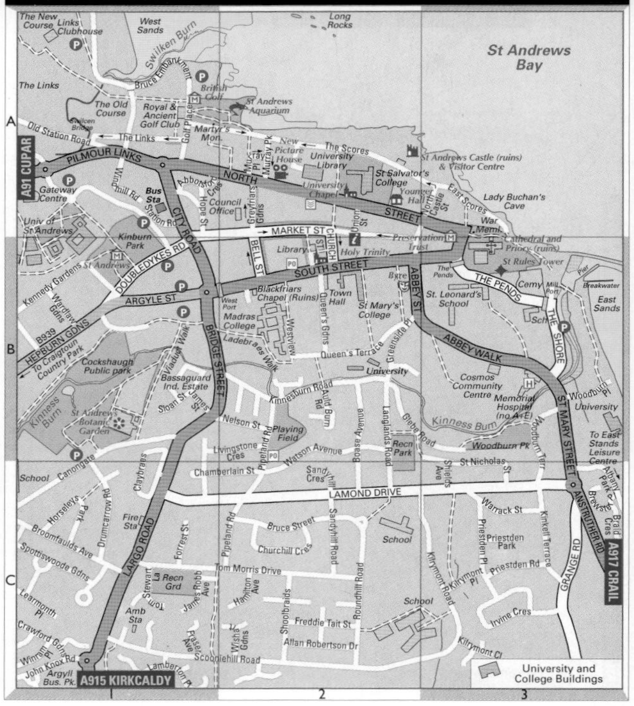

Salisbury

0 Miles ¼

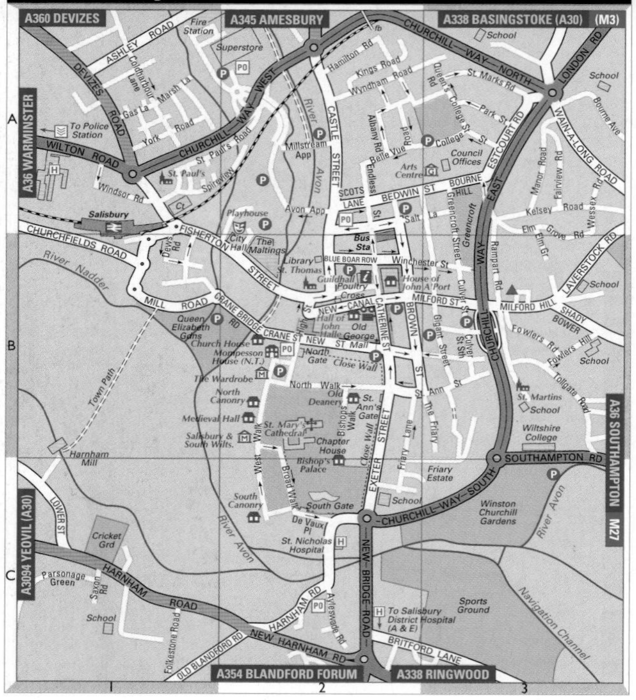

Scarborough

0 Miles ¼

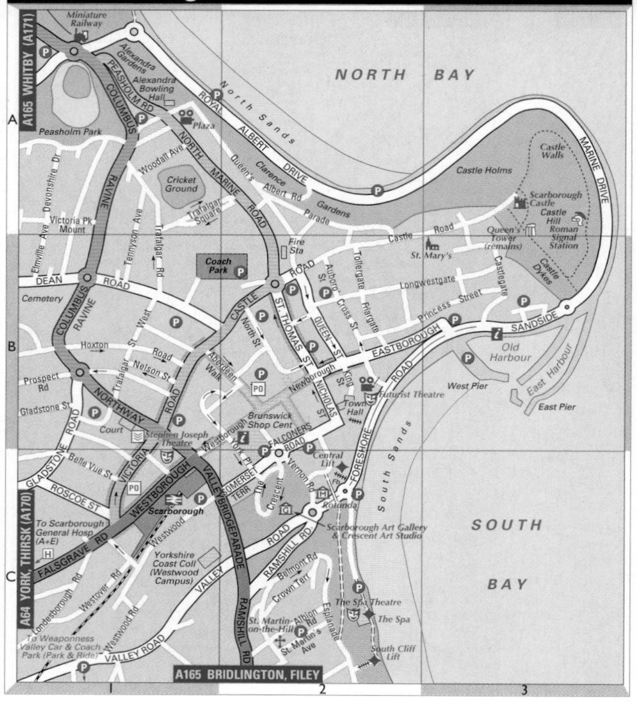

Shrewsbury

0 Miles ¼

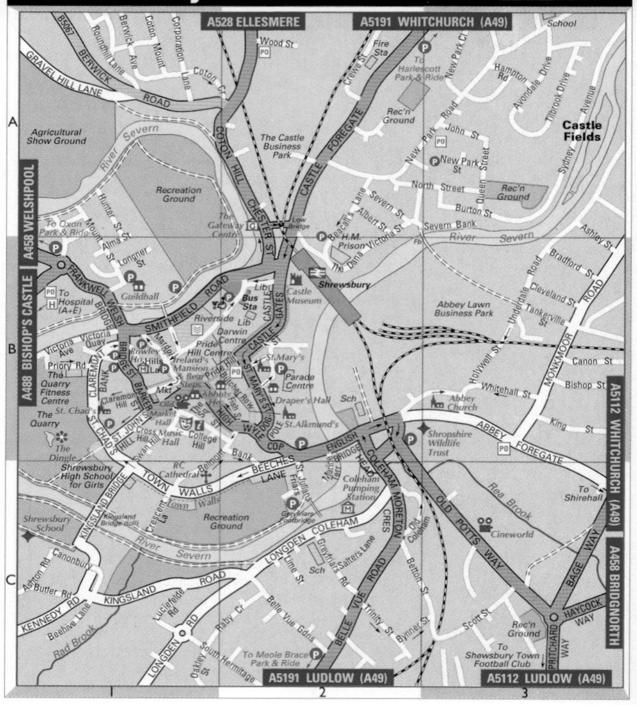

Sheffield

0 Miles ¼

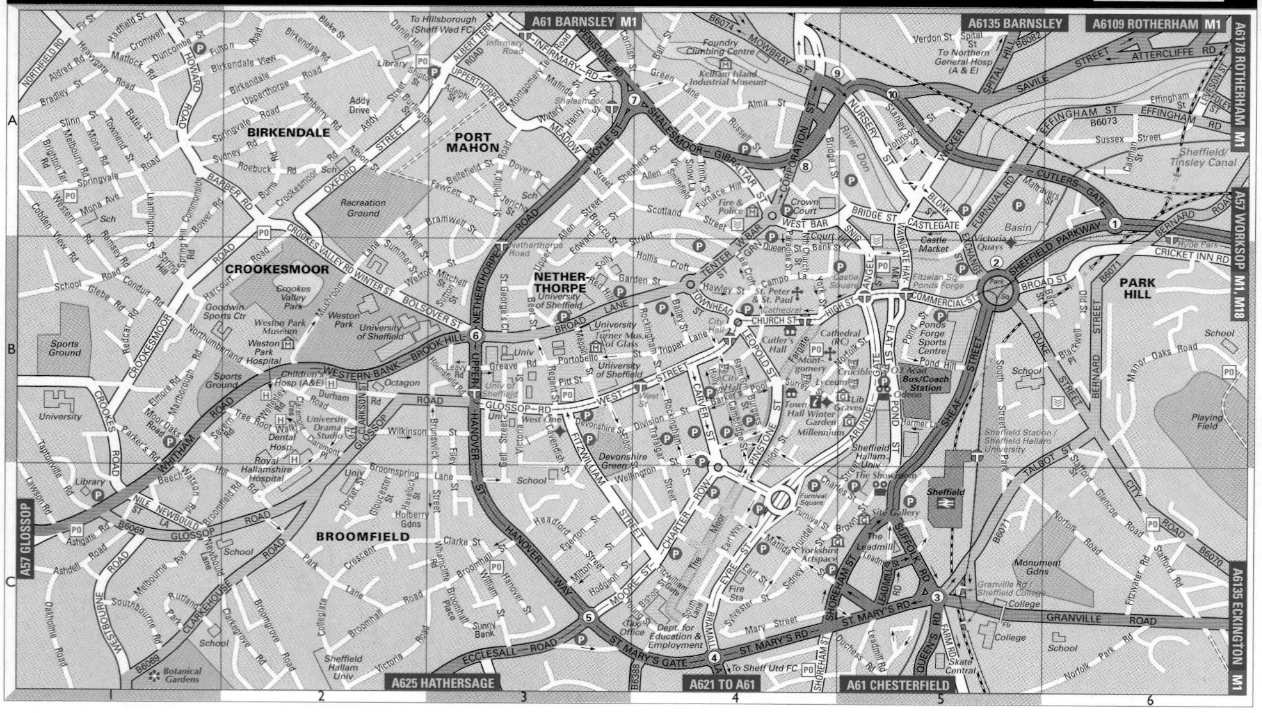

Southampton

0 Miles ¼

Southend-on-Sea

0 Miles ¼

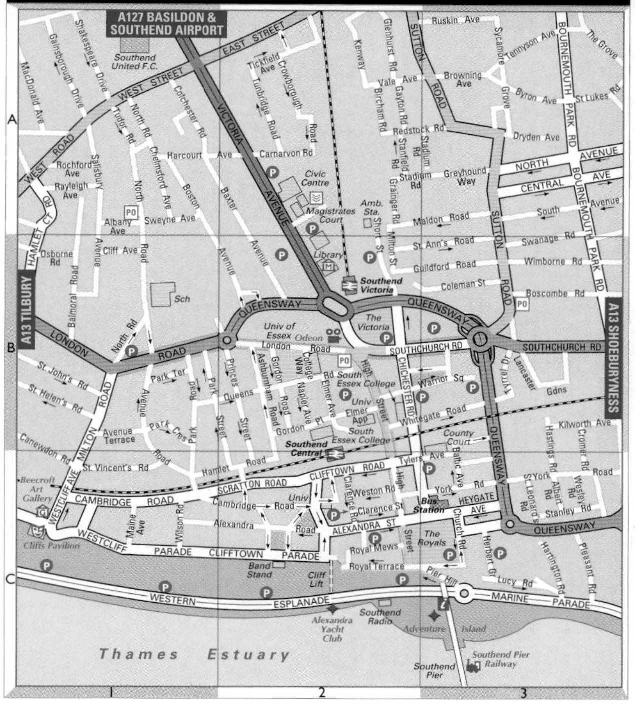

Stirling

0 Miles ¼

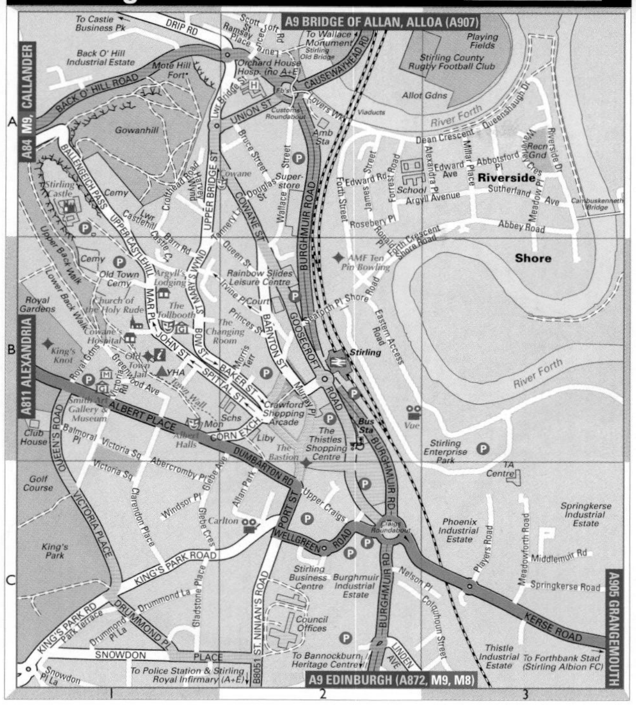

Stoke

0 Miles ¼

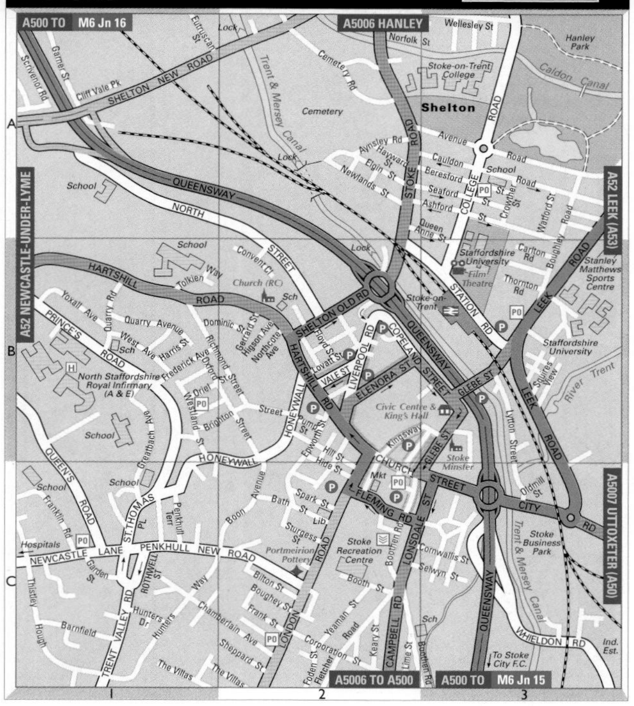

Stratford-upon-Avon

0 Miles ¼

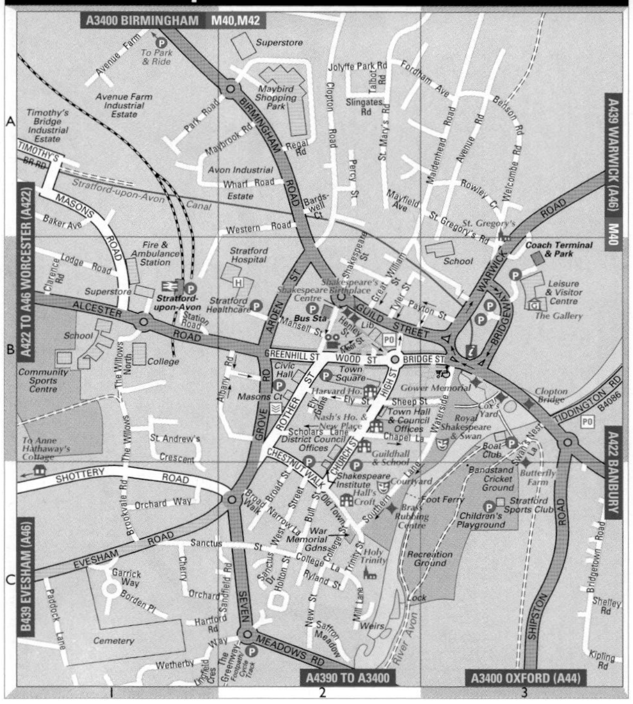

Sunderland

0 Miles ¼

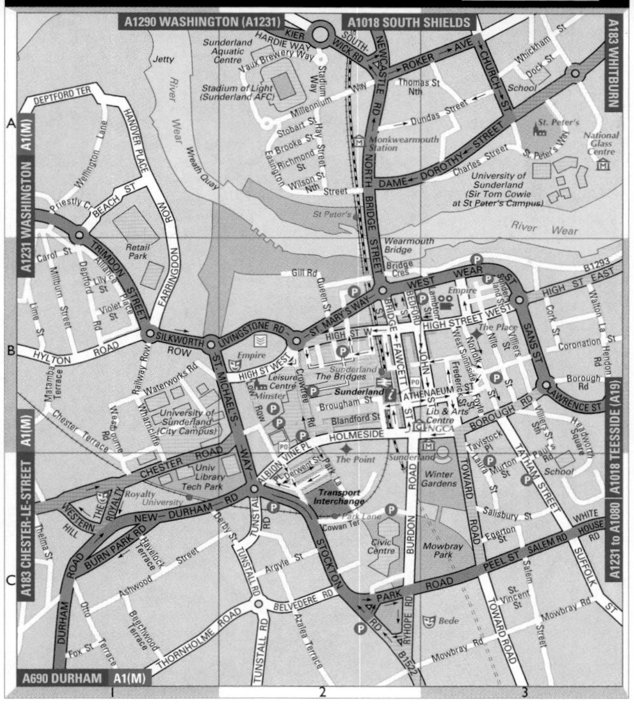

Swansea / Abertawe

0 Miles ¼

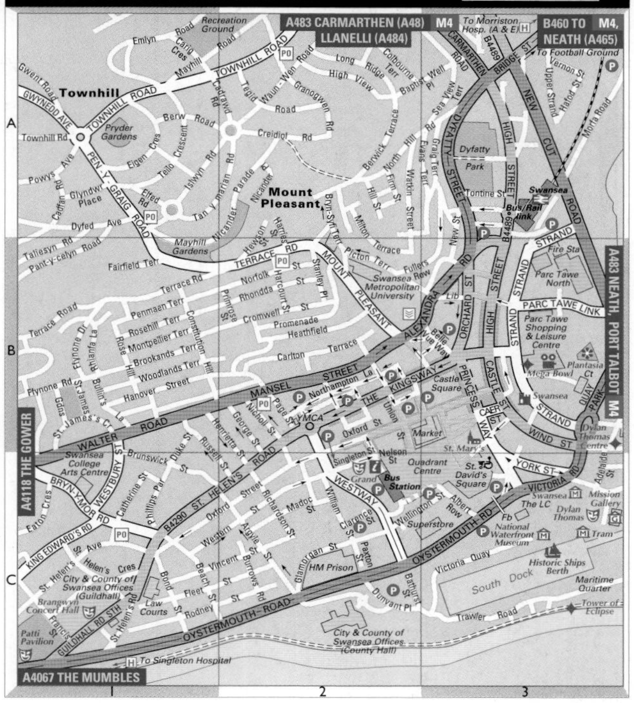

Swindon

0 Miles ¼

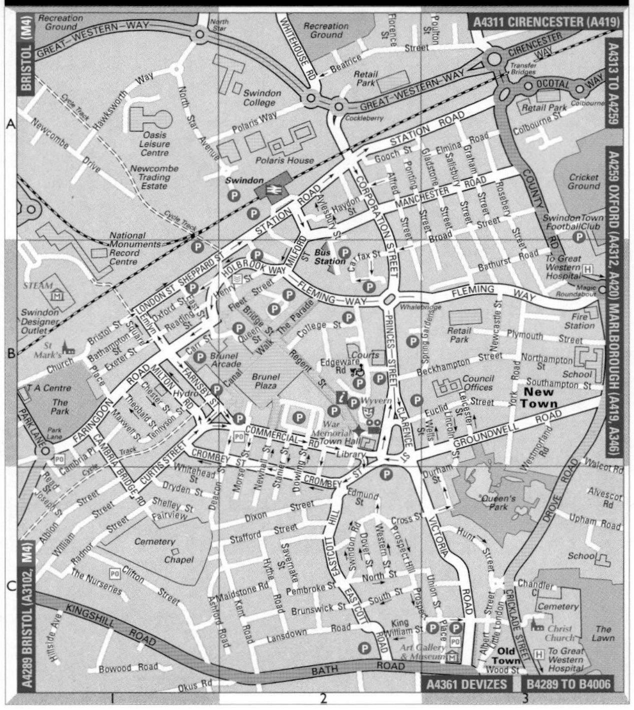

Taunton

0 Miles ¼

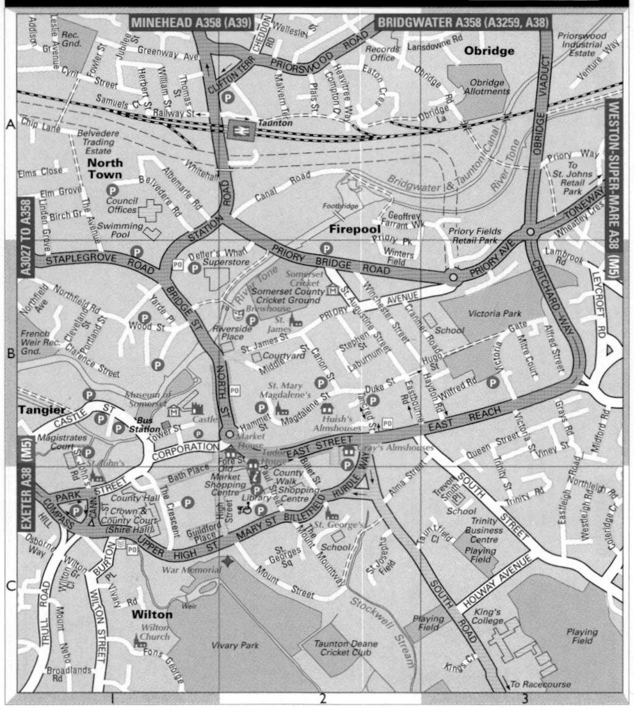

Telford

0 Miles ¼

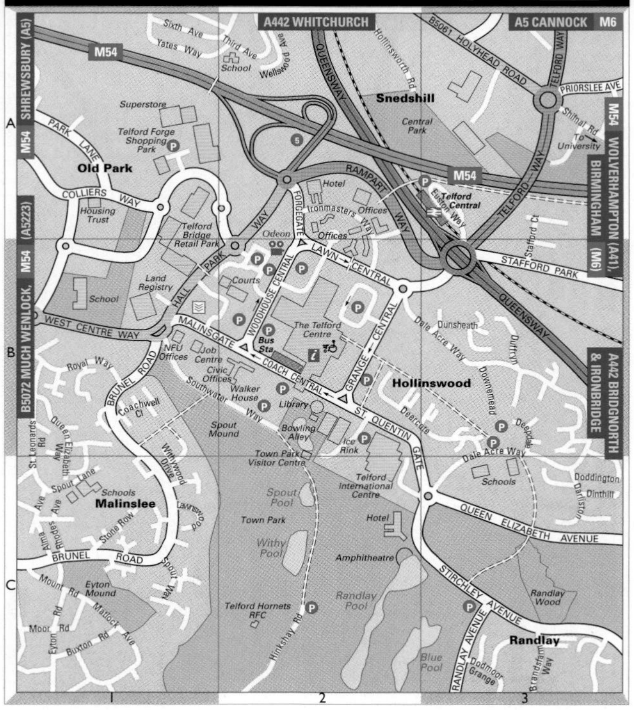

Torquay

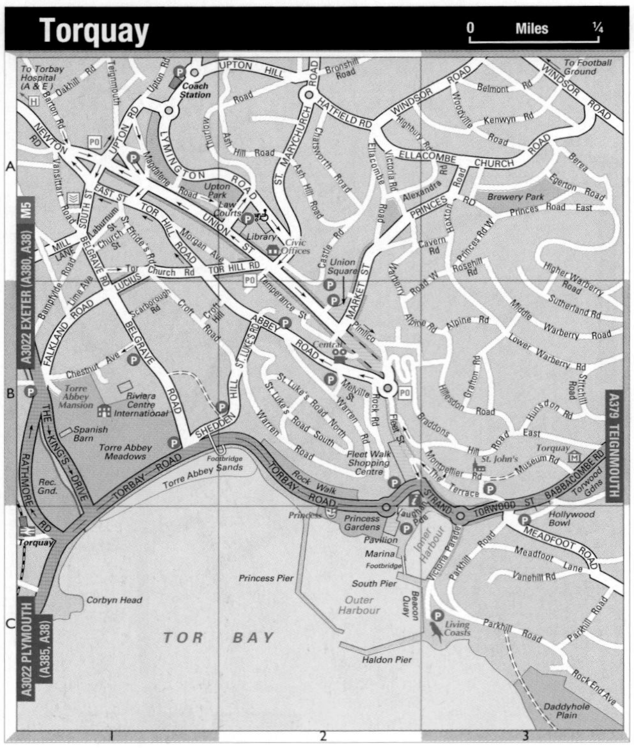

Truro

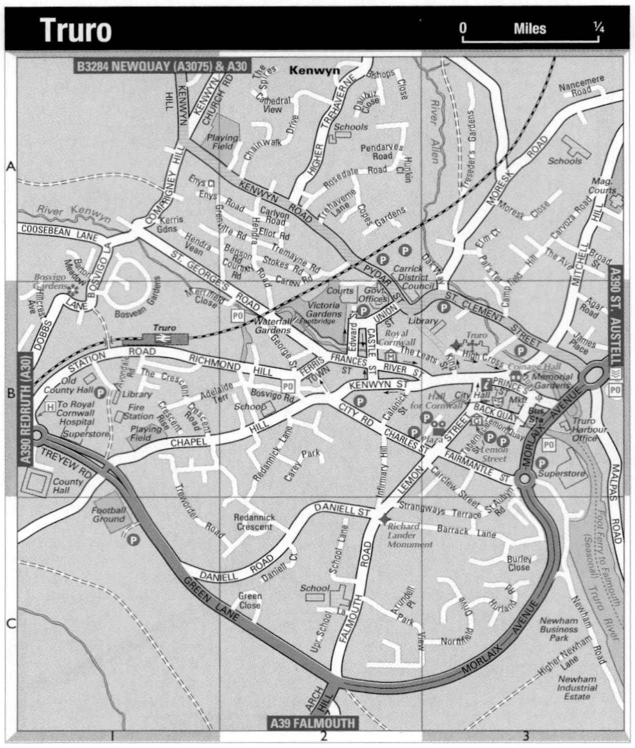

Wick

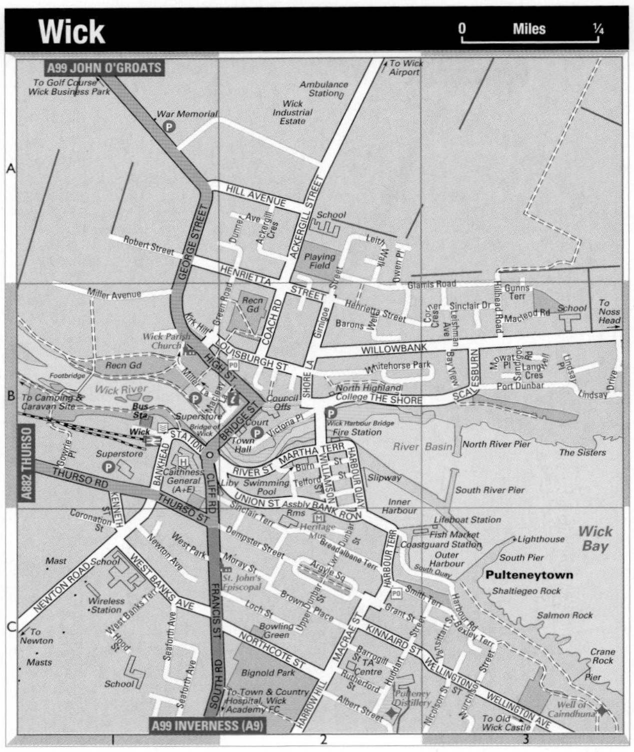

Winchester

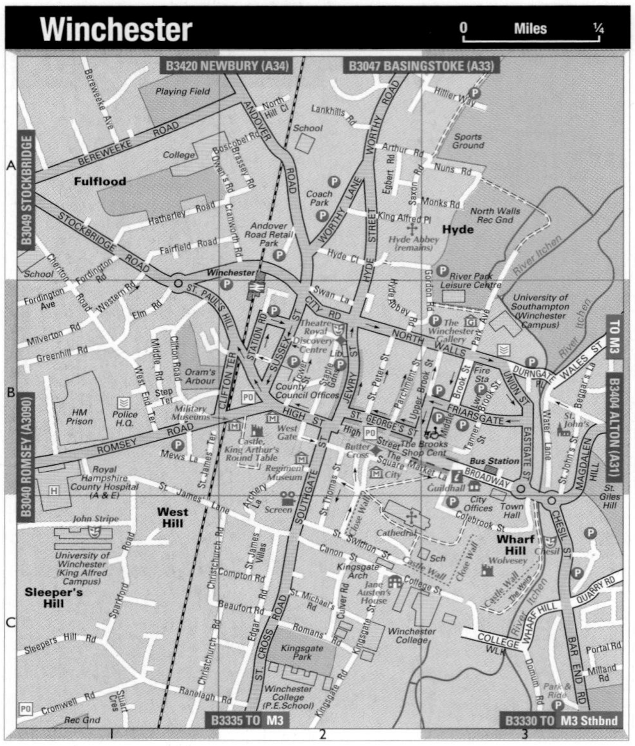

Windsor

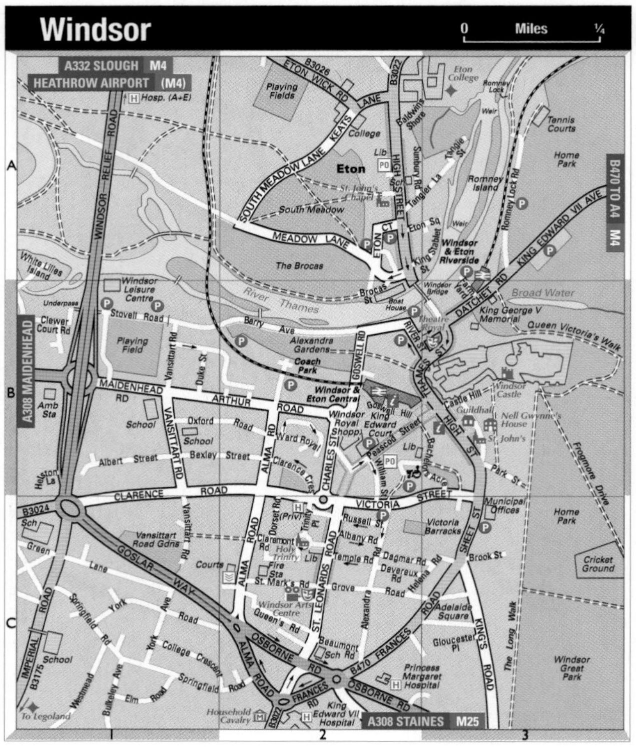

Wolverhampton

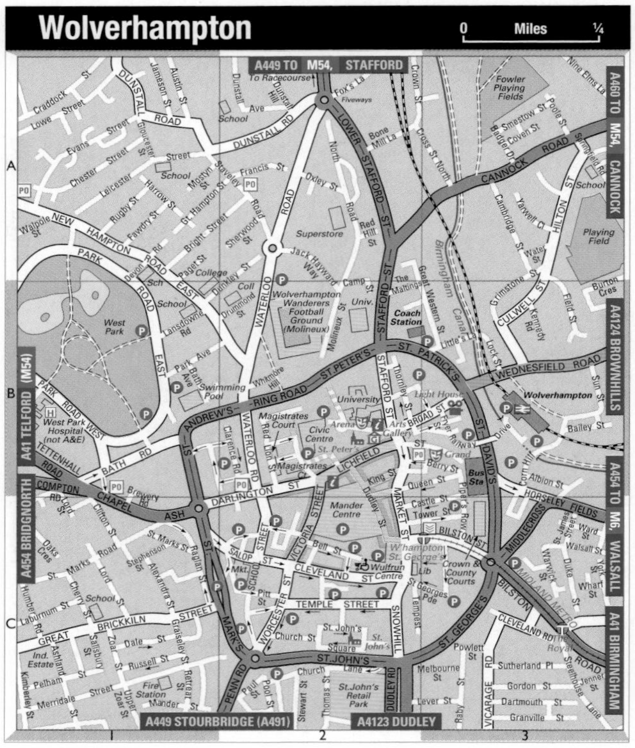

Worcester

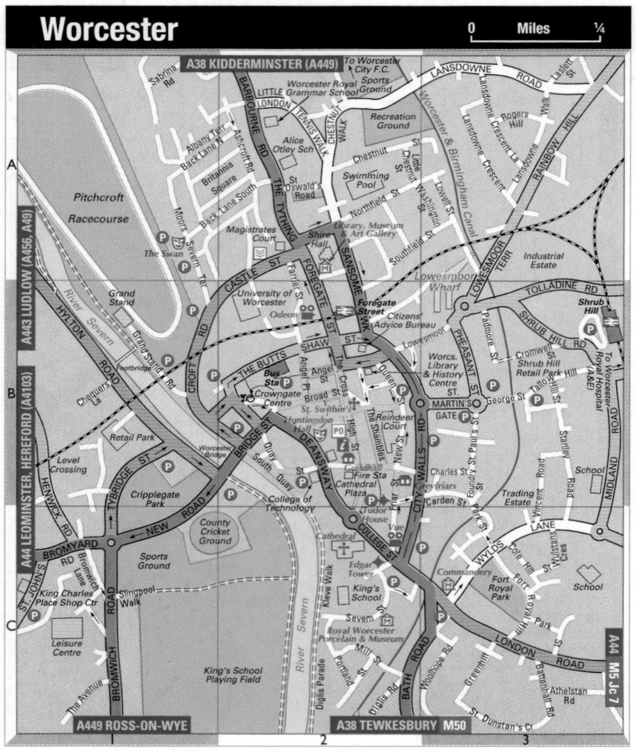

Wrexham / Wrecsam

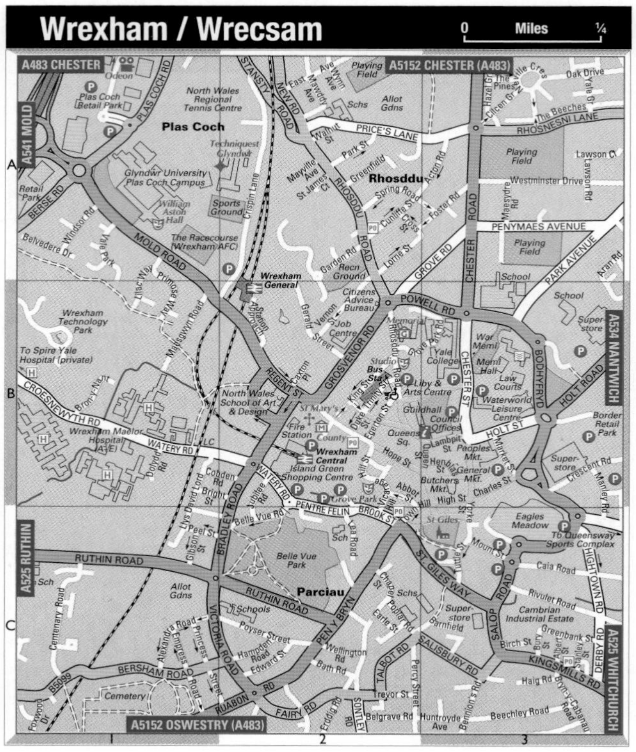

York

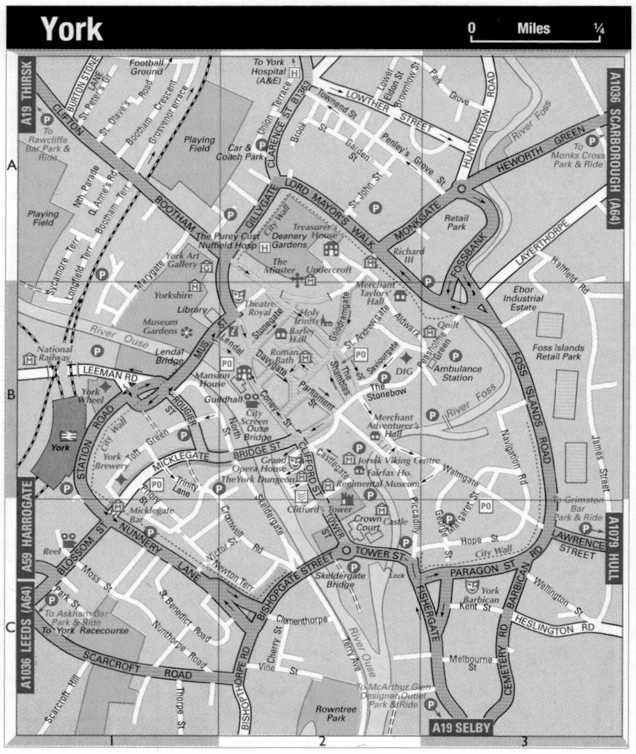

Town plan indexes

Blackpool 332

Bournemouth 332

Bradford 332

Brighton 332

Bristol 332

City Museum A3
City of Bristol College B3
Clare St B4
Clarence Rd C5
Cliff Rd C1
Clift House Rd C1
Clifton Cath (RC) ✝ A2
Clifton Down A1
Clifton Down Rd A1
Clifton Hill B2
Clifton Park A1/A2
Clifton Park Rd A1
Clifton Rd A2
Cliftonwood Cr B2
Cliftonwood Rd B2
Cliftonwood Terr B2
Clifton Vale B1
Cobblestone Mews A1
College Green B3
College Rd A1
College St B3
Colston Almshouses A4
Colston Ave B4
Colston Hall B4
Colston Parade C5
Colston St A4
Commercial Rd C4
Constitution Hill B2
Cooperage La C2
Corn St B4
Cornwallis Ave B1
Cornwallis Cr B1
Coronation Rd C2/C4
Council House B3
Counterslip B5
Courts A4
Create Ctr, The ✦ C1
Crosby Row B2
Culver St B3
Cumberland Basin C1
Cumberland Cl C2
Cumberland Rd C2/C3
Dale St A6
David St A6
Dean La C4
Deanery Rd B3
Denmark St B4
Dowry Sq B1
East St A5
Eaton Cr A2
Elmdale Rd A3
Elton Rd A3
Eugene St A4/A6
Exchange, The and St Nicholas' Mkts B4
Fairfax St A4
Fire Station B5
Floating Harbour C3
Foster Almshouses A4
Frayne Rd C1
Frederick Pl A2
Freeland Pl B1
Frogmore St B3
Fry's Hill B2
Gas La B6
Gasferry Rd C3
General Hospital C4
Georgian House B3
Glendale B1
Glentworth Rd B2
Gloucester St A1
Goldney Hall B2
Goldney Rd B1
Gordon Rd A2
Granby Hill B1
Grange Rd A1
Great Ann St A6
Great George St A6/B3
Great George Rd B3
Great Western Way B6
Green St North B1
Green St South B1
Greenay Bush La C2
Greenbank Rd C2
Greville Smyth Park C1
Guildhall A4
Guinea St C4
Hamilton Rd C3
Hanbury Rd A2
Hanover Pl C2
Harbour Way B3
Harley Pl A1
Haymarket A5
Hensman's Hill B1
High St B4
Highbury Villas A3
Hill St B3
Hill St C6
Hippodrome B4
Hopechapel Hill B1
Horfield Rd A4
Horton St B6
Host St A4
Hotwell Rd B1/B2
Houlton St A6
Howard Rd C3
Ice Rink B3
IMAX Cinema B4
Information Ctr B4
Islington Rd C3
Jacob St A5/A6
Jacob's Wells Rd B2
John Carr's Terr B2
John Wesley's Chapel A5
Joy Hill B1
Jubilee St B6
Kensington Pl A2
Kilkenny St B6
King St B4
Kingsland Rd B6
Kingston Rd C3
Lamb St A6
Lansdown Rd A2
Lawford St A6
Lawfords Gate A6
Leighton Rd C3
Lewins Mead A4
Lime Rd C2
Little Ann St A6
Little Caroline Pl B1
Little George St A6
Little King St B4
Litfield Rd A1
Llandoger Trow B4
Lloyds' Building, The C3
Lodge St A4
Lord Mayor's Chapel, The B4
Lower Castle St A5
Lower Church La A4
Lower Clifton Hill B2
Lower Guinea St C4
Lower Lamb St B3
Lower Maudlin St A4
Lower Park Rd A4
Lower Sidney St C2
Lucky La C4
Lydstep Terr C3
Mall (Galleries Shopping Ctr), The A5
Manilla Rd A1
Mardyke Ferry Rd C2
Maritime Heritage Ctr B3
Marlborough Hill A4
Marlborough St A4
Marsh St B4
Mead St C5
Meadow St A5
Merchant Dock B2
Merchant Seamen's Almshouses B4
Merchant St A5
Merchants Rd A1
Merchants Rd C1
Meridian Pl A2
Meridian Vale A2
Merrywood Rd C3
Midland Rd A6
Milford St C3
Millennium Sq B3
Mitchell La B5
Mortimer Rd A1
M Shed C4
Murray Rd C4
Myrtle Rd A3
Narrow Plain B5
Narrow Quay B4
Nelson St A4
New Charlotte St C4
New Kingsley Rd B6
New Queen St C5
New St A6
Newfoundland St A5
Newgate A5
Newton St A6
Norland Rd A1
North St C2
Oakfield Gr A2
Oakfield Pl A2
Oakfield Rd A2
Old Bread St B6
Old Market St A6
Old Park Hill A4
Oldfield Rd B1
Orchard Ave B4
Orchard La B4
Orchard St B4
Osbourne Rd C3
Oxford St B6
Park Pl A2
Park Rd C3
Park Row A3
Park St A3
Passage St B5
Pembroke Gr A2
Pembroke Rd A2
Pembroke Rd C3
Pembroke St A5
Penn St A5
Pennywell Rd A6
Percival Rd A1
Pero's Bridge B4
Perry Rd A4
Pip & Jay A5
Plimsoll Bridge B1
Police Sta A4/A6
Polygon Rd B1
Portland St A1
Portwall La B5
Post Office A1/A3/A4/A5/A6/B1/B4/C4/C5
Prewett St C5
Prince St B4
Prince St Bridge C4
Princess St C5
Princess Victoria St B1
Priory Rd A3
Pump La C5
QEH Theatre A2
Queen Charlotte St B4
Quakers Friars A5
Quay St A4
Queen Elizabeth Hospital School B2
Queen Sq B4
Queen St A5
Queen's Ave A3
Queen's Parade B3
Queen's Rd A2/A3
Raleigh Rd C2
Randall Rd B2
Redcliffe Backs B5
Redcliffe Bridge B4
Redcliffe Hill C5
Redcliffe Parade C4
Redcliffe St B5
Redcliffe Way B5
Redcross La A6
Redcross St A6
Redgrave Theatre A1
Red Lodge A4
Regent St B1
Richmond Hill A2
Richmond Hill Ave A2
Richmond La A2
Richmond Park Rd A2
Richmond St C6
Richmond Terr A2
River St A6
Rownham Mead B2
Royal Fort Rd A3
Royal Park A2
Royal West of England Academy A3
Royal York Cr B1
Royal York Villas B1
Rupert St A4
Russ St B6
St Andrew's Walk B2
St George's B3
St George's Rd B3
St James A4
St John's A4
St John's Rd C4
St Luke's Rd C5
St Mary Redcliffe C5
St Mary's Hospital A3
St Matthias Park A6
St Michael's Hill A3
St Michael's Hospl A4
St Michael's Park A3
St Nicholas St B4
St Paul St A5
St Paul's Rd A2
St Peter's (ruin) A5
St Philip's Bridge B5
St Philips Rd A6
St Stephen's B4
St Stephen's St B4
St Thomas St B5
St Thomas the Martyr B5
Sandford Rd B1
Sargent St C5
Saville Pl B1
Ship La C5
Silver St A4
Sion Hill A1
Small St A4
Smeaton Rd C1
Somerset Sq C5
Somerset St C5
Southernhay Ave B2
Southville Rd C4
Spike Island Artspace C2
Spring St C5
SS Great Britain and The Matthew B2
Stackpool Rd C3
Staight St B6
Stillhouse La C4
Stracey Rd C2
Stratton St A5
Sydney Row C2
Tankard's Cl A3
Temple Back B5
Temple Boulevard B5
Temple Bridge B5
Temple Church B5
Temple Circus B5
Temple Gate C5
Temple St B5
Temple Way B5
Terrell St A4
The Arcade A5
The Fosseway A2
The Grove B4
The Horsefair A5
The Mall A1
Theatre Royal B4
Thomas La B5
Three Kings of Cologne A4
Three Queens La B5
Tobacco Factory, The C2
Tower Hill B5
Tower La A4
Trenchard St A4
Triangle South A3
Triangle West A3
Trinity Rd A6
Trinity St A6
Tucker St A5
Tyndall Ave A3
Union St A5
Union St B6
Unity St A6
Unity St B3
University of Bristol A3
University Rd A3
Upper Maudlin St A4
Upper Perry Hill C3
Upper Byron Pl A3
Upton Rd C2
Valentine Bridge B6
Victoria Gr C5
Victoria Rd C6
Victoria Rooms A2
Victoria Sq A2
Victoria St B5
Vyvyan Rd A1
Vyvyan Terr A1
Wade St A6
Walter St C2
Wapping Rd C4
Water La B5
Waterloo Rd A6
Waterloo St A1
Waterloo St A6
Watershed, The ✦ B4
Welling Terr B1
Wellington Rd A6
Welsh Back B4
West Mall A1
West St A6
Westfield Pl A1
Wetherell Pl A2
Whitehouse Pl C5
Whitehouse St C5
Whiteladies Rd A2
Whitson St A4
William St C5
Willway St C5
Windsor Pl B1
Windsor Terr B1
Wine St A4
Woodland Rise A3
Woodland Rd A3
Worcester Rd A1
Worcester Terr A1
YHA ▲ B4
York Gdns B1
York Pl A2
York Rd C5

Bury St Edmunds 332

Abbey Gardens B3
Abbey Gate B3
Abbeygate St B2
Albert Cr B1
Albert St B1
Ambulance Sta C1
Angel Hill B2
Angel La B2
Anglian Lane A1
Arc Shopping Ctr B2
Athenaeum C2
Baker's La C3
Beetons Way A1
Bishops Rd B2
Bloomfield St B2
Bridewell La C2
Bullen Cl C1
Bury St Edmunds ≥ A2
Bury St Edmunds County Upper School A1
Bury St Edmunds L Ctr B1
Bury Town FC B3
Bus Station B2
Butter Mkt B2
Cannon St B2
Castle Rd C1
Cemetery C1
Chalk Rd (N) B1
Chalk Rd (S) B1
Church Row B2
Churchgate St C2
Citizens Advice Bureau B2
College St C2
Compiegne Way A3
Corn Exchange, The B2
Cornfield Rd B1
Cotton Lane B3
Courts B2
Covent Garden C2
Crown St C3
Cullum Rd C2
Eastern Way A3
Eastgate St B3
Enterprise Bsns Park A2
Etna Rd A2
Eyre Cl C2
Fire Station B1
Friar's Lane C2
Gage Cl A1
Garland St B2
Greene King Brewery C3
Grove Park B1
Grove Rd B1
Guildhall C2
Guildhall St C2
Hatter St C2
High Baxter St B2
Honey Hill C2
Hospital Rd C1/C2
Ickworth Dr C1
Information Ctr B2
Ipswich St A2
King Edward VI School A1
King's Rd C1/B2
Library B2
Long Brackland A2
Looms La B2
Lwr Baxter St B2
Malthouse La A2
Maynewater La C3
Mill Rd C1
Mill Rd (South) C1
Minden Close B3
Moyses Hall B2
Mustow St B3
Norman Tower C3
Northgate Ave A2
Northgate St B2
Nutshell, The B2
Osier Rd A2
Out Northgate A2
Out Risbygate B1
Out Westgate C2
Parkway B1/C2
Parkway B1
Peckham St B2
Petticoat La C1
Phoenix Day Hospl C1
Pinners Way C1
Police Station C3
Post Office B2/B3
Pump La B2
Queen's Rd B1
Raingate St C3
Raynham Rd A1
Retail Park C2
Risbygate St B1/B2
Robert Boby Way C2
St Andrew's St North B2
St Andrew's St South B2
St Botolph's La C3
St Edmunds Hospital (private) C3
St Edmund's C2
St Edmund's Abbey (Remains) ✦ B3
St Edmundsbury ✝ C3
St John's St B2
St Marys C3
School Hall La B2
Shillitoe Cl C1
Shire Halls & Magistrates Ct C3
South Cl C1
Southgate St C3
Sparhawk St C3
Spring Lane B1
Springfield Rd B1
Station Hill A2
Swan La C3
Tayfen Rd B2
The Vinefields B3
Theatre Royal C3
Thingoe Hill A2
Victoria St B1
War Memorial ✦ C1
Well St B2
West Suffolk College B1
Westgarth Gdns C1
Westgate St C2
Whiting St C2
York Rd B1
York Terr B1

Cambridge 333

Abbey Rd A3
ADC A2
Anglia Ruskin Univ B3
Archaeology & Anthropology B2
Art Gallery A1
Arts Picture House B2
Arts Theatre B1
Auckland Rd A3
Bateman St C2
BBC C3
Benet St B1
Bradmore St B3
Bridge St A1
Broad St B3
Brookside C2
Brunswick Terr A3
Burleigh St B3
Bus Station B2
Butt Green A2
Cambridge Contemporary Art Gallery B1
Castle Mound A1
Castle St A1
Chesterton La A1
Christ's (Coll) B2
Christ's Pieces B2
City Rd B3
Clare (Coll) B1
Clarendon St B2
Coe Fen C2
Coronation St C2
Corpus Christi (Coll) B1
Council Offices C3
Cross St C3
Crusoe Bridge C1
Darwin (Coll) C1
Devonshire Rd C3
Downing (Coll) C2
Downing St B2
Earl St B2
East Rd B3
Eden St B3
Elizabeth Way A3
Elm St B2
Emery St B3
Emmanuel (Coll) B2
Emmanuel Rd B2
Emmanuel St B2
Fair St A3
Fenners Physical Education Ctr C3
Fire Station B3
Fitzroy St A3
Fitzwilliam Mus C2
Fitzwilliam St C2
Folk Museum A1
Glisson Rd C3
Gonville & Caius (Coll) B1
Gonville Place C2
Grafton Ctr A3
Grand Arcade B2
Gresham Rd C3
Green St B1
Guest Rd B3
Guildhall B2
Harvey Rd C3
Hills Rd C3
Hobson St B2
Hughes Hall (Coll) B3
Information Ctr B2
James St A3
Jesus (Coll) A2
Jesus Green A2
Jesus La A2
Jesus Terr B3
John St B3
Kelsey Kerridge Sports Ctr B3
King St A2
King's (Coll) B1
King's Coll Chapel B1
King's Parade B1
Lammas Land Rec Gd C1
Lensfield Rd C2
Little St Mary's La B1
Lyndewod Rd C3
Magdalene (Coll) A1
Magdalene St A1
Maid's Causeway A3
Malcolm St A2
Market Hill B1
Market St B1
Mathematical Bridge B1
Mawson Rd C3
Midsummer Common A3
Mill La B1
Mill Rd B3
Mill St C3
Napier St A3
New Square A3
Newmarket Rd A3
Newnham Rd C1
Norfolk St B3
Northampton St A1
Norwich St C2
Orchard St B2
Panton St C2
Paradise Nature Reserve C1
Paradise St B3
Park Parade A1
Park St A2
Park Terr B2
Parker St B2
Parker's Piece B2
Parkside B3
Parkside Pools B3
Parsonage St A3
Pemberton Terr C2
Pembroke (Coll) B2
Pembroke St B1
Perowne St B3
Peterhouse (Coll) C1
Petty Cury B2
Police Station B3
Post Office A1/A3/B2/B3/C1/C2/C3
Queens' (Coll) B1
Queen's La B1
Queen's Rd B1
Regent St B2
Regent Terr B2
Ridley Hall (Coll) C1
Riverside A3
Round Church, The A1
Russell St C2
St Andrew's St B2
St Benet's B1
St Catharine's (Coll) B1
St Eligius St C2
St John's (Coll) A1
St Mary's B1
St Paul's Rd C3
Saxon St C2
Scott Polar Institute & Museum C2
Sedgwick Museum B2
Sheep's Green C1
Shire Hall A1
Sidgwick Ave C1
Sidney St A2
Sidney Sussex (Coll) A2
Silver St B1
Station Rd C3
Tenison Ave C3
Tenison Rd C3
Tennis Court Rd B2
The Backs B1
The Fen Causeway C1
Thompson's La A1
Trinity (Coll) A1
Trinity Hall (Coll) B1
Trinity St B1
Trumpington Rd C2
Trumpington St B1
Union Rd C2
University Botanic Gardens C2
Victoria Ave A2
Victoria St B2
Warkworth St B3
Warkworth Terr B3
Wesley House (Coll) A2
West Rd B1
Westcott House (Coll) A2
Westminster (Coll) A1
Whipple A2
Willis Rd B3
Willow Walk A2
Zoology B2

Canterbury 333

Artillery St B2
Barton Mill Rd A3
Beaconsfield Rd A1
Beverley Rd A1
Bingley's Island B1
Black Griffin La B1
Broad Oak Rd A2
Broad St B2
Brymore Rd A3
Burgate B2
Bus Station C2
Canterbury College C3
Canterbury East ≥ C1
Canterbury Tales, The ✦ B2
Canterbury West ≥ A1
Castle C1
Castle Row C1
Castle St C1
Cathedral ✝ B2
Chaucer Rd A3
Christ Church Univ B3
Christchurch Gate ✦ B2
City Council Offices A3
City Wall B2
Coach Park A2
College Rd B3
Cossington Rd C2
Court B2
Craddock Rd A3
Crown & County Courts B3
Dane John Gdns C2
Dane John Mound ✦ C1
Deanery B2
Dover St C2
Duck La B2
Eastbridge Hospl B1
Edgar Rd B3
Ersham Rd C3
Ethelbert Rd C3
Fire Station C2
Forty Acres Rd A1
Gordon Rd C1
Greyfriars ✦ B1
Guildford Rd C1
Havelock St B2
Heaton Rd C1
High St B2
HM Prison B3
Information Ctr A2/B2
Ivy La B2
Ivy Pl C1
King St B2
King's School B2/B3
King's School Leisure Facilities A2
Kingsmead Leisure Ctr A2
Kingsmead Rd A2
Kirby's La B1
Lansdown Rd C2
Lime Kiln Rd C1
Longport B3
Lower Chantry La C3
Mandeville Rd A1
Market Way A2
Marlowe Arcade B2
Marlowe Ave C2
Marlowe Theatre B2
Martyrs Field Rd C1
Mead Way B1
Military Rd B2
Monastery St B2
Mus of Canterbury (Rupert Bear Mus) B1
New Dover Rd C3
Norman Rd C2
North Holmes Rd B3
North La B1
Northgate A2
Nunnery Fields C2
Nunnery Rd C2
Oaten Hill C2
Odeon Cinema C2
Old Dover Rd C2
Old Palace B2
Old Ruttington La B2
Old Weavers B2
Orchard St B1
Oxford Rd C1
Palace St B2
Pilgrims Way C3
Pin Hill C1
Pine Tree Ave A1
Police Station C2
Post Office B2/C1/C2
Pound La B1
Puckle La C2
Raymond Ave C2
Registry Office A2
Rheims Way B1
Rhodaus Cl C2
Rhodaus Town C2
Roman Museum B2
Roper Gateway A1
Roper Rd A1
Rose La B2
Royal Museum B2
St Augustine's Abbey (remains) ✝ B3
St Augustine's Rd C3
St Dunstan's A1
St Dunstan's St A1
St George's Pl C2
St George's St B2
St George's Tower ✦ B2
St Gregory's Rd B3
St John's Hospital B2
St Margaret's St B2
St Martin's B3
St Martin's Ave B3
St Martin's Rd B3
St Michael's Rd A1
St Mildred's C1
St Peter's Gr B1
St Peter's La B2
St Peter's Pl B1
St Peter's St B1
St Radigunds St B2
St Stephen's Ct A1
St Stephen's Path A1
St Stephen's Rd A2
Salisbury Rd A1
Simmonds Rd C1
Spring La C3
Station Rd West B1
Stour St B1
Sturry Rd A3
The Causeway A2
The Friars B2
Tourtel Rd A3
Tudor Rd C1
Union St B2
University for the Creative Arts C3
Vernon Pl C2
Victoria Rd C1
Watling St B2
Westgate Gdns B1
Westgate Towers B1
Whitefriars B2
Whitehall Gdns B1
Whitehall Rd B1
Wincheap C1
York Rd C1
Zealand Rd C2

Cardiff *Caerdydd* 333

Adam St B3
Alexandra Gdns A2
Allerton St C1
Arran St A3
ATRiuM (Univ of Glamorgan) C3
Beauchamp St C1
Bedford St A3
Blackfriars Priory (rems) ✝ B1
Boulevard De Nantes B2
Brains Brewery C2
Brook St B1
Bus Station C2
Bute Park B1
Bute St C2
Bute Terr C3
Callaghan Sq C2/C3
Capitol Sh Ctr, The B3
Cardiff Arms Park (Cardiff RFC) B1
Cardiff Bridge B1
Cardiff Castle B2
Cardiff Central Sta ≥ C2
Cardiff Ctr Trading Est C3
Cardiff Univ A1/A2/B3
Cardiff University Student's Union A2
Caroline St C2
Castle Green B2
Castle Mews A1
Castle St (Heol y Castell) B1
Cathays Station ≥ A2
Celerity Drive C3
Central Library C2
Central Sq C2
Charles St (Heol Siarl) B3
Churchill Way B3
City Hall A2
City Rd A3
Clare Rd C1
Clare St C1
Coburn St A3
Coldstream Terr B1
College Rd A1
Colum Rd A1
Court C2
Court Rd C1
Craiglee Drive C3
Cranbrook St A3
Customhouse St C2
Cyfartha St A3
Despenser Place C1
Despenser St C1
Dinas St C1
Duke St (Heol y Dug) B2
Dumfries Place B3
East Grove A3
Ellen St C3
Fire Station B3
Fitzalan Place B3
Fitzhamon Emb C1
Fitzhamon La C1
g39 B2
Gloucester St C1
Glynrhondda St A2
Gordon Rd A3
Gorsedd Gdns B2
Green St B1
Greyfriars Rd B2
HM Prison B3
Hafod St C1
Herbert St C3
High St B2
Industrial Estate C3
John St C3
Jubilee St C1
King Edward VII Ave A1
Kingsway (Ffordd y Brenin) B2
Knox Rd B3
Law Courts B2
Llanbleddian Gdns A2
Llantwit St A2
Lloyd George Ave C3
Lower Cathedral Rd B1
Lowther Rd A3
Magistrates Court B3
Mansion House A3
Mardy St C1
Mark St B1
Market B2
Mary Ann St C3
Merches Gdns C1
Mill La C2
Millennium Bridge B1
Millennium Plaza Leisure Complex C1
Millennium Stadium C1
Millennium Stadium Tours (Gate 3) ✦ B2
Miskin St A2
Monmouth St C1
Motorpoint Arena Cardiff ✦ C3
Museum Ave A2
Museum Place A2
National Museum of Wales A2
National War Meml ✦ A2
Neville Place C1
New Theatre B2
Newport Rd B3
Northcote La A3
Northcote St A3
Park Grove A4
Park Place A2
Park St C2
Penarth Rd C2
Pendyris St C1
Plantaganet St C1
Quay St B2
Queen Anne Sq A1
Queen St (Heol y Frenhines) B2
Queen St Station ≥ B3
Regimental Museums B2
Rhymney St A3
Richmond Rd A3
Royal Welsh College of Music and Drama A1
Russell St A3
Ruthin Gdns A2
St Andrews Place A2
St David's ✝ B2
St David's 2 C2
St David's Ctr B2
St David's Hall ✦ B2
St John The Baptist B2
St Mary St (Heol Eglwys Fair) B2
St Peter's St A3
Salisbury Rd A3
Sandon St B3
Schooner Way C3
Scott Rd C2
Scott St C2
Senghennydd Rd A2
Sherman Theatre A2
Sophia Gardens A1
South Wales Baptist College A3
Stafford Rd C1
Station Terr B3
Stuttgarter Strasse B2
Sussex St C1
Taffs Mead Emb C1
Talworth St A3
Temple of Peace & Health ✦ A1
The Cardiff Story B2
The Friary B2
The Hayes B2
The Parade A3
The Walk A3
Treharris St A3
Trinity St B2
Tudor La C1
Tudor St C1
Welsh Assembly Offices A1
Welsh Inst of Sport ✦ A1
West Grove A3
Westgate St (Heol y Porth) B2
Windsor Place B3
Womanby St B2
Wood St C2
Working St B2
Wyeverne Rd A2

Carlisle 333

Abbey St A1
Aglionby St B3
Albion St C3
Alexander St C3
AMF Bowl ✦ C2
Annetwell St A1
Bank St B2
Bitts Park A1
Blackfriars St B2
Blencome St C1
Blunt St C1
Botchergate B2
Boustead's Grassing C2
Bowman St B3
Broad St B3
Bridge St A1
Brook St C3
Brunswick St B2
Bus Station B2
Caldew Bridge A1
Caldew St C1
Carlisle (Citadel) Station ≥ B2
Carlisle College A2
Castle A1
Castle St A1
Castle Way A1
Cathedral ✝ A1
Cecil St B2
Chapel St A2
Charles St B3
Charlotte St B1
Chatsworth Square A2
Chiswick St B2
Citadel, The ✦ B2
City Walls A1
Civic Ctr A2
Clifton St C1
Close St B3
Collingwood St C1
Colville St C1
Colville Terr C1
Court B2
Court St B2
Crosby St B2
Crown St C2
Currock Rd C2
Dacre Rd A1
Dale St C1
Denton St C1
Devonshire Walk A1
Duke's Rd A2
East Dale St C1
East Norfolk St C1
Eden Bridge A2
Edward St B3
Elm St B1
English St B2
Fire Station A2
Fisher St A1
Flower St B3
Freer St C1
Fusehill St B3
Georgian Way A2
Gloucester Rd C3
Golf Course A2
Graham St C1
Grey St B3
Guildhall Museum A2
Halfey's La B3
Hardwicke Circus A2
Hart St B3
Hewson St C2
Howard Pl A3
Howe St B3
Information Ctr A2
James St B2
Junction St B1
King St B2
Lancaster St B2
Lanes Shopping Ctr B2
Laserquest ✦ B2
Library A2/B1
Lime St B1
Lindisfarne St C3
Linton St B3
Lismore Pl A3
Lismore St B3
London Rd C3
Lonsdale Rd B2
Lord St C3
Lorne Cres B1
Lorne St B1
Lowther St B2
Market Hall A2
Mary St B2
Memorial Bridge A3
Metcalfe St C1
Milbourne St B1
Myddleton St B3

Dorset County Mus .A1
Duchy Close .C3
Duke's Ave. .B2
Durngate St .B2
Durnover Court .A3
Eddison Ave. .B3
Edward Rd .B1
Egdon Rd .C2
Elizabeth Frink Statue ✦ .B2
Farfrae Cres .B2
Forum Ctr, The .B1
Friary Hill .A2
Friary Lane .A2
Frome Terr .A2
Garland Cres .C3
Glyde Path Rd .A1
Government Offices .B3
Gt Western Rd .B1
Grosvenor Cres .C1
Grosvenor Rd .C1
HM Prison .A1
Herringston Rd .C1
High St East .A2
High St Fordington .A2
High Street West .A1
Holloway Rd .A2
Icen Way .A2
Keep Military Museum, The .A1
Kings Rd .A3/B3
Kingsbere Cres .C2
Lancaster Rd .B2
Library .A1
Lime Cl .C1
Linden Ave .B2
London Cl .A3
London Rd .A2/A3
Lubbecke Way .A3
Lucetta La .B2
Maiden Castle Rd .C1
Manor Rd .C2
Maumbury Rd .B1
Maumbury Rings .B1
Mellstock Ave .C2
Mill St .A3
Miller's Cl .A1
Mistover Cl .C1
Monmouth Rd .B1/B2
Nature Reserve .A2
North Sq .A2
Northernhay .A1
Old Crown Court & Cells .A1
Olga Rd .B1
Orchard St .A2
Police Station .B1
Post Office .A1/B1
Pound Lane .A2
Poundbury Rd .A1
Prince of Wales Rd .B2
Prince's St .A1
Queen's Ave .B1
Roman Town House .A1
Roman Wall .A1
Rothesay Rd .C2
St George's Rd .B3
Salisbury Field .A2
Sandringham Sports Ctr .B3
Shaston Cres .C2
Smokey Hole La .B3
South Court Ave .C1
South St .B1
South Walks Rd .B2
Superstore .C3
Teddy Bear House .A1
Temple Cl .C1
Terracotta Warriors & Teddy Bear Mus .A2
The Grove .A1
Town Hall .A2
Town Pump ✦ .A2
Trinity St .A1
Tutankhamun Ex .A1
Victoria Rd .B1
Weatherbury Way .C2
Wellbridge Cl .C1
West Mills Rd .A1
West Walks Rd .A1
Weymouth Ave .C1
Williams Ave .B1
Winterbourne (BMI) .C1
Wollaston Rd .A2
York Rd .B2

Dumfries 334

Academy St .A2
Aldermanhill Rd .B3
Ambulance Station .C3
Annan Rd .A3
Ardwall Rd .A3
Ashfield Dr .A1
Atkinson Rd .C1
Averill Cres .C1
Balliol Ave .C1
Bank St .B2
Bankend Rd .C3
Barn Slaps .B3
Barrie Ave .B3
Beech Ave .A1
Bowling Green .A3
Brewery St .B2
Brodie Ave .C2
Brooke St .B2
Broomlands Dr .C1
Brooms Rd .B3
Buccleuch St .A2
Burns House .B2
Burns Mausoleum .B3
Burns St .B2
Burns Statue ✦ .A2
Bus Station .B1
Cardoness St .A3
Castle St .A2
Catherine St .A2
Cattle Market .A3
Cemetery .B3
Cemetery .C2
Church Cres .A2
Church St .B2
College Rd .A1
College St .A1
Corbelly Hill .B1
Convent, The .B1
Corberry Park .B1
Cornwall Mt .A3
County Offices .A2
Court .A2
Craigs Rd .C3
Cresswell Ave .B3
Cresswell Hill .B3
Cumberland St .B3
David Keswick Athletic Ctr .A3
David St .B1
Dock Park .C3
Dockhead .B2
Dumfries .A3
Dumfries Academy .A2
Dumfries Museum & Camera Obscura .B2
Dumfries Royal Infirmary (A&E) .C3
East Riverside Dr .C3
Edinburgh Rd .A2
English St .B2
Fire Station .B3
Friar's Vennel .A2
Galloway St .B1
George Douglas Dr .C1
George St .A2
Gladstone Rd .C2
Glasgow St .A1
Glebe St .B3
Glencaple Rd .C3
Goldie Ave .A1
Goldie Cres .A1
Golf Course .C3
Greyfriars .A2
Grierson Ave .B3
HM Prison .B1
Hamilton Ave .C1
Hamilton Starke Park .C2
Hazelrigg Ave .C1
Henry St .B3
Hermitage Dr .C1
High Cemetery .C3
High St .A2
Hill Ave .C2
Hill St .B1
Holm Ave .C2
Hoods Loaning .A3
Howgate St .B1
Huntingdon Rd .A3
Information Ctr .B2
Irish St .B2
Irving St .A2
King St .A1
Kingholm Rd .C3
Kirkpatrick Ct .C2
Laurieknowe .B1
Leafield Rd .B3
Library .A2
Lochfield Rd .A1
Loreburn Pk .A3
Loreburn St .A2
Loreburne Sh Ctr .B2
Lover's Walk .A2
Martin Ave .B3
Maryholm Dr .A1
Mausoleum .B3
Maxwell St .B1
McKie Ave .B3
Mews La .A2
Mid Steeple ✦ .B2
Mill Green .B2
Mill Rd .B1
Moat Rd .C2
Moffat Rd .A3
Mountainhall Pk .C3
Nelson St .B1
New Abbey Rd .B1/C1
New Bridge .B1
Newall Terr .A2
Nith Ave .A2
Nith Bank .C3
Nithbank Hospital .C3
Nithside Ave .A1
Odeon .B2
Old Bridge .B1
Old Bridge House .B1
Palmerston Park (Queen of the South FC) .A1
Park Rd .C1
Pleasance Ave .C1
Police HQ .A3
Police Station .A2
Portland Dr .A1
Post Office .A2/B1/B2/B3/B3
Priestlands Dr .C1
Primrose St .B1
Queen St .B3
Queensberry St .A2
Rae St .A2
Richmond Ave .C2
Robert Burns Ctr .B2
Roberts Cres .C1
Robertson Ave .C3
Robinson Dr .C1
Rosefield Rd .C2
Rosemount St .B1
Rotchell Park .C1
Rotchell Rd .B1
Rugby Football Gd .C1
Ryedale Rd .C2
St Andrews .B2
St John the Evangelist .A2
St Josephs College .B3
St Mary's Ind Est .A3
St Mary's St .A3
St Michael St .B2
St Michael's .B2
St Michael's Bridge .B2
St Michael's Bridge Rd B2
St Michael's Cemetery B3
Shakespeare St .B2
Solway Dr .C2
Stakeford St .A1
Stark Cres .C2
Station Rd .A3
Steel Ave .A1
Sunderries Ave .A1
Sunderries Rd .A1
Suspension Brae .B2
Swimming Pool .A1
Terregles St .B1
Theatre Royal .B2
Troqueer Rd .C2
Union St .A1
Wallace St .B3
Welldale .B2
West Riverside Dr .C2
White Sands .B2

Dundee 334

Adelaide Pl .A1
Airlie Pl .C1
Albany Terr .A1
Albert St .A3
Alexander St .A2
Ann St .A2
Arthurstone Terr .A3
Bank St .B2
Barrack Rd .A1
Barrack St .B2
Bell St .B2
Blackscroft .A3
Blinshall St .B1
Brown St .B1
Bus Station .B3
Caird Hall .B2
Camperdown St .B3
Candle La .B3
Carmichael St .A1
City Churches .B2
City Quay .B3
City Sq .B2
Commercial St .B2
Constable St .A3
Constitution Ct .A1
Constitution Cres .A1
Constitution St .A1/B2
Cotton Rd .A3
Courthouse Sq .B1
Cowgate .A3
Crescent St .A3
Crichton St .B2
Dens Brae .A3
Dens Rd .A3
Discovery Point ✦ .C2
Douglas St .B1
Drummond St .A1
Dudhope Castle .A1
Dudhope St .A2
Dudhope Terr .A1
Dundee .C2
Dundee College .A1
Dundee Contemporary Arts ✦ .C2
Dundee High School .B2
Dundee Repertory .C2
Dura St .A3
East Dock St .B3
East Whale La .B3
East Marketgait .B3
Erskine St .A3
Euclid Cr .B2
Forebank Rd .A2
Foundry La .A3
Frigate Unicorn ✦ .B3
Gallagher Retail Park .B3
Gellatly St .B3
Government Offices .C2
Guthrie St .B1
Hawkhill .B1
Hilltown .A2
Howff Cemetery, The .B2
Information Ctr .B2
King St .A3
Kinghorne Rd .A1
Ladywell Ave .A3
Laurel Bank .A2
Law Hill, The ✦ .A1
Law Rd .A1
Law St .A1
Library .A2
Little Theatre .A2
Lochee Rd .B1
Lower Princes St .A3
Lyon St .A3
McManus Museum & Art Gallery .B2
Meadow Side .B2
Meadowside St Pauls .B2
Mercat Cross ✦ .B2
Murraygate .B2
Nelson St .A2
Nethergate .B2/C1
North Marketgait .B2
North Lindsay St .B2
Old Hawkhill .B1
Olympia Leisure Ctr .B3
Overgate Shopping Ctr B2
Park Pl .B1
Perth Rd .C1
Police Station .A2/B1
Post Office .B2
Princes St .A3
Prospect Pl .A2
Reform St .B2
Riverside Dr .C2
Roseangle .C1
Rosebank St .A2
RRS Discovery .C2
St Andrew's ✝ .C2
St Pauls Episcopal ✝ .B3
Science Ctr ✦ .C2
Seagate .B2
Sheriffs Court .B1
South George St .A2
South Marketgait .B3
South Tay St .B2
South Ward Rd .B2
Steps .A2
Tay Road Bridge ✦ .C3
Tayside House .B2
Trades La .B3
Union St .B2
Union Terr .A1
University Library .B2
University of Abertay .B2
University of Dundee .B1
Upper Constitution St .A1
Verdant Works ✦ .B1
Victoria Dock .B3
Victoria Rd .A2
Victoria St .A3
West Marketgait .B1/B2
Ward Rd .B1
Wellgate .B2
West Bell St .B1
Westfield Pl .C1
William St .A3
Wishart Arch ✦ .A3

Durham 334

Alexander Cr .B2
Allergate .B2
Archery Rise .C1
Assize Courts .B3
Back Western Hill .A1
Bakehouse La .A3
Baths .B3
Baths Bridge .B3
Boat House .B3
Bowling .A2
Boyd St .C3
Bus Station .B2
Castle .B2
Castle Chare .B2
Cathedral ✝ .B2
Church St .C3
Clay La .C1
Claypath .B3
College of St Hild & St Bede .B3
County Hall .A1
County Hospital .B1
Crook Hall & Gardens ✦ .A3
Crossgate .B2
Crossgate Peth .C1
Darlington Rd .C1
Durham .A2
Durham Light Infantry Mus & Arts Ctr .A2
Durham School .C2
Ellam Ave .C1
Elvet Bridge .B3
Elvet Court .B3
Farnley Hey .B1
Ferens Cl .A3
Fieldhouse La .A1
Flass St .B1
Framwelgate .A2
Framewelgate Bridge .B2
Framwelgate Peth .A2
Framwelgate Waterside .A2
Frankland La .A3
Freeman's Pl .A3
Gala & Sacred Journey .B3
Gate Sh Ctr, The .B2
Geoffrey Ave .C1
Gilesgate .B3
Grey College .C3
Hallgarth St .C3
Hatfield College .B3
Hawthorn Terr .B1
Heritage Ctr .B3
HM Prison .B3
Information Ctr .B3
John St .B1
Kingsgate Bridge .B3
Laburnum Terr .B1
Lawson Terr .B1
Leazes Rd .B2/B3
Library .B2
Margery La .B2
Mavin St .C3
Millburngate .B2
Millburngate Bridge .B2
Millennium Bridge (foot/cycle) .A2
Mountjoy Research Ctr .C3
Mus of Archaeology .B2
Nevilledale Terr .B1
New Elvet .B3
New Elvet Bridge .B3
North Bailey .B3
North End .A1
North Rd .A1/B2
Observatory .C1
Old Elvet .B3
Oriental Museum .C2
Oswald Court .C3
Parkside .B2
Passport Office .A2
Percy Terr .B1
Pimlico .C2
Police Station .B3
Post Office .A1/B2
Potters Bank .C1/C2
Prebends Bridge .C2
Prebends Walk .C2
Prince Bishops Sh Ctr .B3
Princes St .A1
Providence Row .A3
Quarryheads La .C2
Redhills La .B1
Redhills Terr .B1
Saddler St .B3
St Chad's College .C3
St Cuthbert's Society .C2
St John's College .C2
St Margaret's .B2
St Mary The Less .C2
St Mary's College .C2
St Monica Grove .B1
St Nicholas' .B3
St Oswald's .C3
Sidegate .A2
Silver St .B2
Add Sixth Form Ctr (Durham Gilesgate) .A3
South Bailey .C2
South Rd .C3
South St .B2
Springwell Ave .A1
Stockton Rd .C3
Students' Rec Ctr .B3
Sutton St .B2
The Avenue .B1
The Crescent .A1
The Grove .A1
The Sands .A3
Town Hall .B2
Treasury Museum .B2
University ✦ .B2
University Arts Block .B3
University Library .C3
Univ Science Site .C3
Walkergate Ctr .A3
Wearside Dr .A3
Western Hill .A1
Wharton Park .A2
Whinney Hill .C3

Edinburgh 334

Abbey Strand .B6
Abbeyhill .A6
Abbeyhill Cr .B6
Abbeymount .A6
Abercromby Pl .A3
Adam St .C5
Albany La .A4
Albany St .A4
Albert Memorial ✦ .B2
Albyn Pl .A2
Alva Pl .A6
Alva St .B1
Ann St .A1
Appleton Tower .C4
Archibald Pl .C3
Argyle House .C3
Assembly Rooms & Musical Hall .A3
Atholl Cr .B1
Atholl Crescent La .C1
Bank St .B4
Barony St .A4
Beaumont Pl .C5
Belford Rd .B1
Belgrave Cr .A1
Belgrave Crescent La .A1
Bell's Brae .B1
Blackfriars St .B4
Blair St .B4
Bread St .C2
Bristo Pl .C4
Bristo St .C4
Brougham St .C2
Broughton St .A4
Brown St .C5
Brunton Terr .A6
Buckingham Terr .A1
Burial Ground .A6
Bus Station .A4
Caledonian Cr .C1
Caledonian Rd .C1
Calton Hill .A4
Calton Hill .A5
Calton Rd .B4
Camera Obscura & Outlook Tower ✦ .B3
Candlemaker Row .C4
Canning St .B2
Canongate .B5
Canongate .B5
Carlton St .A1
Carlton Terr .A6
Carlton Terrace La .A6
Castle St .B2
Castle Terr .B2
Castlehill .B3
Central Library .B4
Chalmers Hospital .C3
Chalmers St .C3
Chambers St .C4
Chapel St .C4
Charles St .C4
Charlotte Sq .B2
Chester St .B1
Circus La .A2
Circus Pl .A2
City Art Ctr .B4
City Chambers .B4
City Observatory ✦ .A5
Clarendon Cr .A1
Clerk St .C5
Coates Cr .B1
Cockburn St .B4
College of Art .C3
Comely Bank Ave .A1
Comely Bank Row .A1
Cornwall St .C2
Cowans Cl .C5
Cowgate .B4
Cranston St .B5
Crichton St .C4
Croft-An-Righ .A6
Cumberland St .A2
Dalry Pl .C1
Dalry Rd .C1
Danube St .A1
Darnawy St .A2
David Hume Tower .C4
Davie St .C5
Dean Bridge .A1
Dean Gdns .A1
Dean Park Cr .A1
Dean Park Mews .A1
Dean Park St .A1
Dean Path .B1
Dean St .A1
Dean Terr .A1
Dewar Pl .C1
Dewar Place La .C1
Doune Terr .A2
Drummond Pl .A3
Drummond St .C5
Drumsheugh Gdns .B1
Dublin Mews .A3
Dublin St .A4
Dublin Street La South A4
Dumbiedykes Rd .B5
Dundas St .A3
Earl Grey St .C2
East Crosscauseway .C5
East Market St .B4
East Norton Pl .A6
East Princes St Gdns .B3
Easter Rd .A6
Edinburgh (Waverley) .B4
Edinburgh Castle .B3
Edinburgh Dungeon ✦ B4
Edinburgh International Conference Ctr .C2
Elder St .A4
Esplanade .B3
Eton Terr .A1
Eye Pavilion .C3
Festival Office .B3
Festival Theatre Edinburgh .C4
Filmhouse .C2
Fire Station .C2
Floral Clock ✦ .B3
Forres St .A2
Forth St .A4
Fountainbridge .C2
Frederick St .A3
Freemasons' Hall .B3
Fruit Market .B4
Gardner's Cr .C2
George Heriot's School .C3
George IV Bridge .B4
George Sq .C4
George Sq La .C4
George St .B3
Georgian House .B2
Gladstone's Land .B3
Glen St .C3
Gloucester La .A2
Gloucester Pl .A2
Gloucester St .A2
Graham St .C3
Grassmarket .C3
Great King St .A3
Great Stuart .B1
Greenside La .A5
Greenside Row .A5
Greyfriars Kirk .C4
Grindlay St .C2
Grosvenor St .C1
Grove St .C1
Gullan's Cl .B5
Guthrie St .B4
Hanover St .A3
Hart St .A4
Haymarket .C1
Haymarket Station .C1
Heriot Pl .C3
Heriot Row .A2
High School Yard .B5
High St .B4
Hill Pl .C5
Hill St .A2
Hillside Cr .A5
Holyrood Park .C6
Holyrood Rd .B5
Home St .C2
Hope St .B2
Horse Wynd .B6
Howden St .C5
Howe St .A2
India Pl .A2
India St .A2
Infirmary St .B4
Information Ctr .B4
Jamaica Mews .A2
Jeffrey St .B4
John Knox House .B4
Johnston Terr .C3
Keir St .C3
Kerr St .A2
King's Stables Rd .B2
Lady Lawson St .C3
Lauriston Gdns .C3
Lauriston Park .C3
Lauriston Pl .C3
Lauriston St .C3
Lawnmarket .B3
Learmonth Gdns .A1
Learmonth Terr .A1
Leith St .A4
Lennox St .A1
Lennox St La .A1
Leslie Pl .A2
London Rd .A5
Lothian Health Board .C5
Lothian Rd .B2
Lothian St .C4
Lower Menz Pl .A6
Lynedoch Pl .B1
Manor Pl .B1
Market St .B4
Marshall St .C4
Maryfield .A6
Maryfield Pl .A6
McEwan Hall .C4
Medical School .C4
Melville St .B1
Meuse La .B4
Middle Meadow Walk .C4
Milton St .A6
Montrose Terr .A6
Moray House (college) B5
Moray Place .A2
Morrison Link .C1
Morrison St .C1
Mound Pl .B3
Multrees Walk .A4
Mus Collections Ctr .A4
Mus of Childhood .B5
Mus of Edinburgh .B5
Mus on the Mound .B4
National Gallery .B3
National Library of Scotland .B4
National Monument ✦ A5
National Museum of Scotland .C4
National Portrait Gallery .B4
National Records Scotland .A4
Nelson Monument ✦ .A5
Nelson St .A3
New St .B5
Nicolson Sq .C4
Nicolson St .C4
Niddry St .B4
North Bridge .B4
North Meadow Walk .C3
North Bank St .B3
North Castle St .A2
North Charlotte St .A2
North St Andrew St .A4
North St David St .A3
North West Circus Pl .A2
Northumberland St .A3
Odeon .C2
Old Royal High School A5
Old Tolbooth Wynd .B5
Omni Ctr ✦ .A4
Our Dynamic Earth ✦ .B6
Oxford Terr .A1
Pal of Holyrood Ho .B6
Palmerston Pl .B1
Panmure Pl .C3
Parliament House .B4
Parliament Sq .B4
People's Story, The B5
Playhouse Theatre .A4
Pleasance .C5
Police Station .A4
Ponton St .C2
Post Office .A3/A4/B5/C1/C2/C4/C5
Potterrow .C4
Princes Mall .B4
Princes St .B3
Queen St .A2
Queen Street Gdns .A3
Queen's Dr .B6/C6
Queensferry Rd .A1
Queensferry St .B1
Queensferry Street La B2
Radical Rd .C6
Randolph Cr .B1
Regent Gdns .A5
Regent Rd .B5
Regent Rd Park .A6
Regent Terr .A5
Remains of Holyrood Abbey (AD 1128) .A6
Richmond La .C5
Richmond Pl .C5
Rose St .B2
Rosemount Bldgs .C1
Ross Open Air Theatre .B3
Rothesay Pl .B1
Rothesay Terr .B1
Roxburgh Pl .C5
Roxburgh St .C5
Royal Bank of Scotland .A4
Royal Circus .A2
Royal Lyceum .C2
Royal Scottish Acad B3
Royal Terr .A5
Royal Terrace Gdns .A5
Rutland Sq .B2
Rutland St .B2
St Andrew Sq .A3
St Andrew's House .A4
St Bernard's Cr .A1
St Cecilia's Hall .B4
St Colme St .A2
St Cuthbert's .B2
St Giles' ✝ .B4
St James Ctr .A4
St John St .B5
St John's .B2
St John's Hill .B5
St Leonard's Hill .C5
St Leonard's La .C5
St Leonard's St .C5
St Mary's (RC) ✝ .A4
St Mary's Scottish Episcopal ✝ .B1
St Mary's St .B5
St Stephen St .A2
Salisbury Crags .C6
Saunders St .A2
Scotch Whisky Experience ✦ .B3
Scott Monument ✦ .B4
Scottish Parliament .B6
Scottish Storytelling Ctr ✦ .B5
Semple St .C2
Shandwick Pl .B2
South Bridge .B4
South Charlotte St .B2
South College St .C4
South Learmonth Gdns .A1
South St Andrew St .A4
South St David St .A3
Spittal St .C2
Stafford St .B1
Student Ctr .C4
Surgeons' Hall .C5
TA Ctr .C4
Tattoo Office .B4
Teviot Pl .C4
The Mall .B6
The Mound .B3
The Royal Mile .B5
The Writer's Mus .B4
Thistle St .A3
Torphichen Pl .C1
Torphichen St .C1
Traverse Theatre .B2
Tron Sq .B4
Tron, The ✦ .B4
Union St .A4
University .C4
University Library .C4
Upper Grove Pl .C1
Usher Hall .C2
Vennel .C3
Victoria St .B3
Viewcraig Gdns .B5
Viewcraig St .B5
VUE .A4
Walker St .B1
Waterloo Pl .A4
Waverley Bridge .B4
Wemyss Pl .A2
West Approach Rd .C1
West Crosscauseway .C5
West Maitland St .C1
West of Nicholson St .C4
West Port .C3
West Princes St Gdns .B3
West Richmond St .C5
West Tollcross .C2
White Horse Cl .B5
William St .B1
Windsor St .A5
York La .A4
York Pl .A4
Young St .B2

Exeter 334

Alphington St .C1
Athelstan Rd .B3
Bampfylde St .B2
Barnardo Rd .C3
Barnfield Hill .B3
Barnfield Rd .B2/B3
Barnfield Theatre .B2
Bartholomew St East .B1
Bartholomew St West .B1
Bear St .B2
Beaufort Rd .C1
Bedford St .B2
Belgrave Rd .A3
Belmont Rd .A3
Blackall Rd .A2
Blackboy Rd .A3
Bonhay Rd .B1
Bull Meadow Rd .C2
Bus & Coach Sta .B3
Castle St .B2
Cecil Rd .C1
Cheeke St .A3
Church Rd .C1
Chute St .A3
City Industrial Estate .C2
City Wall .B1/B2
Civic Ctr .B2
Clifton Rd .B3
Clifton St .B3
Clock Tower .A1
College Rd .B3
Colleton Cr .C2
Commercial Rd .C1
Coombe St .B2
Cowick St .C1
Crown Courts .B2
Custom House .C2
Danes' Rd .A2
Denmark Rd .B3
Devon County Hall .C3
Devonshire Pl .A3
Dinham Rd .B1
East Grove Rd .C3
Edmund St .C1
Elmgrove Rd .A1
Exe St .B1
Exeter Cathedral ✝ .B2
Exeter Central Sta .A1
Exeter City Football Ground .A3
Exeter College .A1
Exeter Picture Ho .B1
Fire Station .A1
Fore St .B1
Friars Walk .C2
Guildhall .B2
Guildhall Shopping Ctr B2
Harlequins Sh Ctr .B1
Haven Rd .C2
Heavitree Rd .B3
Hele Rd .A1
High St .B2
HM Prison .A2
Holloway St .C2
Hoopern St .A2
Horseguards .A2
Howell Rd .A1
Information Ctr .B3
Iron Bridge .B1
Isca Rd .C1
Jesmond Rd .A3
King William St .A2
King St .B1
Larkbeare Rd .C2
Leisure Ctr .C1
Library .B2
Longbrook St .A2
Longbrook Terr .A2
Lower North St .B1
Lucky La .C2
Lyndhurst Rd .C3
Magdalen Rd .B3
Magdalen St .B2
Magistrates & Crown Courts .A2
Market .B2
Market St .B2
Marlborough Rd .C3
Mary Arches St .B1
Matford Ave .C3
Matford La .C3
Matford Rd .C3
May St .A3
Mol's Coffee House B2
New Theatre .C2
New Bridge St .B1
New North Rd .A1/A2
North St .B1
Northernhay St .B1
Norwood Ave .C3
Odeon .A3
Okehampton St .C1
Old Mill Cl .C2
Old Tiverton Rd .A3
Oxford Rd .A3
Paris St .B2
Parr St .A3
Paul St .B1
Pennsylvania Rd .A2
Police HQ .B3
Portland Street .A3
Post Office .A3/B1/B3/C1
Powderham Cr .A3
Preston St .B1
Princesshay Sh Ctr .B2
Queen St .A1
Queens Rd .C1
Queen's Terr .A1
Radford Rd .C2
Richmond Rd .A1
Roberts Rd .C2
Rougemont Castle .A2
Rougemont House ✦ .B2
Royal Albert Memorial Museum .B2
St David's Hill .A1
St James' Pk Sta .A3
St James' Rd .A3
St Leonard's Rd .C3
St Lukes University .B3
St Mary Steps .C1
St Nicholas Priory .B1
St Thomas Station .C1
Sandford Walk .B3
School for the Deaf .C2
School Rd .C1
Sidwell St .A2
Smythen St .B1
South St .B2
Southernhay East .B2
Southernhay West .B2
Spacex Gallery .B1
Spicer Rd .B3
Sports Ctr .A3
Summerland St .A3
Swimming Pool & L Ctr B3
Sydney Rd .C1
Tan La .C2
The Quay .C2
Thornton Hill .A2
Topsham Rd .C3
Tucker's Hall .B1
Tudor St .B1
Velwell Rd .A1
Verney St .A3
Water La .C1/C2
Weirfield Rd .C2
Well St .A3
West Ave .A2
West Grove Rd .C3
Western Way .A3/B1/B2
Wonford Rd .B3/C3
York Rd .A2

Fort William 335

Abrach Rd .A3
Achintore Rd .C1
Alma Rd .B2
Am Breun Chamas .A2
Ambulance Station .A3
An Aird .A2
Argyll Rd .C1
Argyll Terr .C1
Bank St .B2
Belford Hospital .B2
Belford Rd .B2/B3
Black Parks .A3
Braemore Pl .C2
Bruce Pl .C2
Bus Station .B2
Camanachd Cr .A3/B2
Cameron Rd .C1
Cameron Sq .B1
Carmichael Way .A2
Claggan Rd .B3
Connochie Rd .C1
Cow Hill .C3
Creag Dhubh .A2
Croft Rd .B3
Douglas Pl .B2
Dudley Rd .B2
Dumbarton Rd .C1
Earl of Inverness Rd .A3
Fassifern Rd .B1
Fire Station .A2
Fort William .B2
Fort William (Remains) ✦ .B2
Glasdrum Rd .C1
Glen Nevis Pl .B3
Gordon Sq .B1
Grange Rd .C1
Heather Croft Rd .C1
Henderson Row .C2
High St .B1
Highland Visitor Ctr .B3
Hill Rd .B2
Hospital Belhaven Annexe .B3
Information Ctr .A3
Inverlochy Ct .A3
Kennedy Rd .B2/C2
Library .B2
Lime Tree Gallery ✦ .C1
Linnhe Rd .B1
Lochaber Leisure Ctr .B3
Lochiel Rd .A3
Lochy Rd .A3
Lundavra Cres .C1
Lundavra Rd .C1
Lundy Rd .A3
Mamore Cr .B2
Mary St .B2
Middle St .B1
Montrose Ave .A3

Moray Pl C1
Morven Pl C2
Moss Rd B2
Nairn Cres C1
Nevis Bridge B3
Nevis Rd A3
Nevis Sports Ctr A2
Nevis Terr B2
North Rd B3
Obelisk B2
Parade Rd B2
Police Station A3/C1
Post Office A3/B2
Ross Pl C1
St Andrews B2
Shaw Pl B2
Station Brae B1
Studio B1
Treig Rd A3
Underwater Ctr A2
Union Rd C1
Victoria Rd B2
Wades Rd A3
West Highland B2
West Highland College UHI A2
Young Pl B2

Glasgow 335

Admiral St C2
Albert Bridge C5
Albion St B5
Anderston B3
Anderston Ctr B3
Anderston Quay B3
Arches B4
Argyle St A1/A2/B3/B4/B5
Argyle Street B5
Argyll Arcade B5
Arlington St A3
Arts Ctr B3
Ashley St A3
Bain St C6
Baird St A6
Baliol St A3
Ballater St C5
Barras, The (Market) C6
Bath St A3
BBC Scotland/SMG B1
Bell St C6
Bell's Bridge B1
Bentinck St A2
Berkeley St A3
Bishop La B3
Black St A6
Blackburn St C2
Blackfriars St B6
Blantyre St A1
Blythswood Sq A4
Blythswood St B4
Bothwell St B4
Brand St C1
Breadalbane St A2
Bridge St C4
Bridge St C4
Bridgegate C5
Briggait C5
Broomhill Park A6
Broomielaw B4
Broomielaw Quay Gdns B3
Brown St B4
Brunswick St B5
Buccleuch St A3
Buchanan Bus Station A5
Buchanan Galleries A5
Buchanan St B5
Buchanan St B5
Cadogan St B4
Caledonian University A5
Calgary St A5
Cambridge St A4
Canal St A5
Candleriggs B5
Carlton Pl C4
Carnarvon St A3
Carrick St B4
Castle St B6
Cathedral Sq B6
Cathedral St B5
Central College of Commerce B5
Ctr for Contemporary Arts A4
Centre St C4
Cessnock C1
Cessnock St C1
Charing Cross A3
Charlotte St C6
Cheapside St B3
Cineworld A5
Citizens' Theatre C5
City Chambers Complex B5
City Halls B5
Clairmont Gdns A2
Claremont St A2
Claremont Terr A2
Claythorne St C6
Cleveland St A3
Clifford La C1
Clifford St C1
Clifton Pl A2
Clifton St A2
Clutha St C1
Clyde Arc B2
Clyde Auditorium B2
Clyde Pl C4
Clyde Place Quay C4
Clyde St C5
Clyde Walkway C3
Clydeside Expressway B2
Coburg St C4
Cochrane St B5
College of Nautical Studies C5
College St B6
Collins St B6
Commerce St C4
Cook St C4
Cornwall St C2
Couper St A5
Cowcaddens A4
Cowcaddens Rd A4
Crimea St B3
Custom House C4
Custom Ho Quay Gdns C4
Dalhousie St A4
Dental Hospital A4
Derby St A2
Dobbie's Loan A4/A5
Dobbie's Loan Pl A5
Dorset St A3
Douglas St B4
Doulton Fountain C6
Dover St A2
Drury St B4
Drygate B6
Duke St B6
Dunaskin St A1
Dunblane St A4
Dundas St B5
Dunlop St C5
East Campbell St C6
Eastvale Pl A1
Eglinton St C4
Elderslie St A3
Elliot St B2
Elmbank St A3
Esmond St A1
Exhibition Ctr B2
Exhibition Way B2
Eye Infirmary A2
Festival Park C1
Film Theatre A4
Finnieston Quay B2
Finnieston Sq B2
Finnieston St B2
Fitzroy Pl A2
Florence St C5
Fox St C5
Gallowgate C6
Garnet St A3
Garnethill St A4
Garscube Rd A4
George Sq B5
George St B5
George V Bridge C4
Gilbert St A1
Glasgow Bridge C4
Glasgow Cathedral B6
Glasgow Central B4
Glasgow Green C6
Glasgow Metropolitan College B5/C5
Glasgow Tower B1
Glasgow Science Ctr B1
Glasgow Science Ctr Footbridge B1
Glassford St B5
Glebe St A6
Gorbals Cross C5
Gorbals St C5
Gordon St B4
Govan Rd B1/C1/C2
Grace St B3
Grand Ole Opry C2
Grafton Pl A5
Grant St A3
Granville St A3
Gray St A2
Greendyke St C6
Harley St C1
Harvie St C1
Haugh Rd A1
Heliport B1
Henry Wood Hall A2
High Court C5
High St B6
High Street B6
Hill St A3
Holland St A3
Holm St B4
Hope St A5
Houldsworth St B2
Houston Pl C3
Houston St C3
Howard St C5
Hunter St C6
Hutcheson St B5
Hutchesons Hall B5
Hydepark St B3
Imax Cinema B1
India St A3
Information Ctr B5
Ingram St B5
Jamaica St B4
James Watt St B4
John Knox St B6
John St B5
Kelvin Hall A1
Kelvin Statue A2
Kelvin Way A2
Kelvingrove Art Gallery & Museum A1
Kelvingrove Park A2
Kelvingrove St A2
Kelvinhaugh St A1
Kennedy St A6
Kent Rd A2
Killermont St A5
King St B5
King's C5
Kingston Bridge C3
Kingston St C4
Kinning Park C2
Kyle St A5
Lancefield Quay B2
Lancefield St B3
Langshot St C1
Lendel Pl C1
Lighthouse B4
Lister St A6
Little St B3
London Rd C6
Lorne St C1
Lower Harbour B1
Lumsden St A1
Lymburn St A1
Lyndoch Cr A3
Lynedoch Pl A3
Lynedoch St A3
Maclellan St C1
Mair St C2
Maitland St A4
Mavisbank Gdns C2
Mcalpine St B3
Mcaslin St A6
McLean Sq C2
McLellan Gallery A4
McPhater St A4
Merchants' House B5
Middlesex St C2
Middleton St C1
Midland St B4
Miller St B5
Millroad St C6
Milnpark St C2
Milton St A4
Minerva St B2
Mitchell Library A3
Mitchell St West B4
Mitchell Theatre A3
Modern Art Gallery B5
Moir St C6
Molendinar St C6
Moncur St C6
Montieth Row C6
Montrose St B5
Morrison St C3
Mosque C5
Nairn St A1
Nelson Mandela Sq B5
Nelson St C4
Nelson's Monument C6
New City Rd A4
Newton St A3
Newton Pl A3
Nicholson St C4
Nile St B5
Norfolk Court C4
Norfolk St C4
North Frederick St B5
North Hanover St B5
North Portland St B6
North St A3
North Wallace St A5
O2 Academy C4
Odeon C3
Old Dumbarton Rd A1
Osborne St B5/C5
Oswald St B4
Overnewton St A1
Oxford St C4
Pacific Dr B1
Paisley Rd C3
Paisley Rd West C1
Park Circus A2
Park Gdns A2
Park St South A2
Park Terr A2
Parkgrove Terr A2
Parnie St C5
Parson St A6
Partick Bridge A1
Passport Office A5
Pavilion Theatre A4
Pembroke St A3
People's Palace C6
Pinkston Rd A6
Piping Ctr, The National A5
Pitt St A4/B4
Plantation Park C1
Plantation Quay B1
Police Sta A4/A6/B5
Port Dundas Rd A5
Port St B2
Portman St C2
Prince's Dock B1
Princes Sq B5
Provand's Lordship B6
Queen St B5
Queen Street B5
Renfrew St A3/A4
Renton St A5
Richmond St B5
Robertson St B4
Rose St A4
Rottenrow B5
Royal Concert Hall A5
Royal Cr A2
Royal Exchange Sq B5
Royal Highland Fusiliers Museum A3
Royal Hospital For Sick Children A1
Royal Infirmary B6
Royal Scottish Academy of Music & Drama A4
Royal Terr A2
Rutland Cr C2
St Kent St C6
St Andrew's (RC) C5
St Andrew's C6
St Andrew's St C5
St Enoch B5
St Enoch Shopping Ctr B5
St Enoch Sq B4
St George's Rd A3
St James Rd B6
St Mungo Ave A5/A6
St Mungo Museum of Religious Life B6
St Mungo Pl A6
St Vincent Cr A2
St Vincent Pl B5
St Vincent St B3/B4
St Vincent Street Church B4
St Vincent Terr B3
Saltmarket C5
Sandyford Pl A3
Sauchiehall St A2/A4
School of Art A4
Scotland St C2
Scott St A4
Scottish Exhibition & Conference Ctr B1
Seaward St C2
Shaftesbury St B3
Sheriff Court C5
Shields Rd C3
Shuttle St B6
Somerset Pl A2
South Portland St C4
Springburn Rd A6
Springfield Quay C3
Stanley St C2
Stevenson St C6
Stewart St A4
Stirling Rd B6
Stirling's Library B5
Stobcross Quay B1
Stobcross Rd B1
Stock Exchange B5
Stockwell Pl C5
Stockwell St B5
Stow College A4
Strathclyde University B6
Sussex St C2
Synagogues A3/C4
Taylor Pl A6
Tenement House A3
Teviot St A1
Theatre Royal A4
Tolbooth Steeple & Mercat Cross C6
Tower St C2
Trades House B5
Tradeston St C4
Transport Museum A1
Tron C5
Trongate B5
Tunnel St B2
Turnbull St C5
Union St B4
Victoria Bridge C5
Virginia St B5
West Greenhill Pl B2
West Regent St A4
Wallace St C3
Walls St B6
Walmer Cr C1
Warrock St B3
Washington St B3
Waterloo St B4
Watson St B6
Watt St C3
Wellington St B4
West Campbell St B4
West George St B4
West Graham St A4
West Regent St B4
West St C4
West St C4
Westminster Terr A2
Whitehall St B3
Wilson St B5
Woodlands Gate A3
Woodlands Rd A3
Woodlands Terr A2
Woodside Cr A3
Woodside Pl A3
Woodside Terr A3
York St B4
Yorkhill Pde A1
Yorkhill St A1

Gloucester 335

Albion St C1
Alexandra Rd B3
Alfred St C3
All Saints Rd C2
Alvin St B2
Arthur St C2
Baker St C1
Barton St C2
Blackfriars B1
Blenheim Rd C2
Bristol Rd C1
Brunswick Rd C2
Bruton Way B2
Bus Station B2
Cattle Market A1
City Council Offices B1
City Mus, Art Gall & Library B2
Clarence St B2
College of Art C2
Commercial Rd B1
Cromwell St C2
Deans Way A2
Denmark Rd A3
Derby Rd C3
Docks C1
Eastgate St B2
Edwy Pde A2
Estcourt Cl A3
Estcourt Rd A3
Falkner St C2
Folk Museum B1
GL1 Leisure Ctr C2
Gloucester Cath B1
Gloucester Station B2
Gloucestershire Royal Hospital (A&E) B3
Gloucester Waterways C1
Goodyere St C2
Gouda Way A1
Great Western Rd B3
Guildhall B2
Heathville Rd A3
Henry Rd B3
Henry St B2
High Orchard St C1
Hinton Rd A2
India Rd C3
Information Ctr B1
Jersey Rd C3
King's C2
King's Sq B2
Kingsholm Rd A2
Kingsholm Rugby Football Ground A2
Lansdown Rd A3
Library C2
Llanthony Rd C1
London Rd B3
Longsmith St B1
Malvern Rd A3
Market Pde B2
Merchants Rd C1
Mercia Rd A1
Metz Way C3
Midland Rd C2
Millbrook St C3
Market B2
Montpellier C1
Napier St C3
Nettleton Rd C2
New Inn B2
New Olympus C3
North Rd A3
Northgate St B2
Oxford Rd A2
Oxford St B2
Pk & Ride Gloucester A1
Park Rd C2
Park St B2
Parliament St C1
Pitt St B1
Police Station B1
Post Office B2
Quay St B1
Recreation Gd A1/A2
Regent St C2
Robert Raikes Ho B1
Royal Oak Rd B1
Russell St B2
Ryecroft St C2
St Aldate St B2
St Ann Way C1
St Catherine St A2
St Mark St A2
St Mary De Crypt B1
St Mary De Lode B1
St Nicholas's B1
St Oswald's Rd A1
St Oswald's Trading Estate A1
St Peter's B2
Seabroke Rd A3
Sebert St A2
Severn Rd C1
Sherborne St B2
Shire Hall B1
Sidney St C3
Soldiers of Gloucestershire B1
Southgate St B1/C1
Spa Field C1
Spa Rd C1
Sports Ground A2/B2
Station Rd B2
Stratton Rd C3
Stroud Rd C1
Superstore A1
Swan Rd A2
Technical College C1
The Mall B1
The Park C2
The Quay B1
Trier Way C1/C2
Union St A2
Vauxhall Rd C3
Victoria St C2
Wellington St C2
Westgate St B1
Widden St C2
Worcester St B2

Grimsby 335

Abbey Drive East C2
Abbey Drive West C2
Abbey Park Rd C2
Abbey Rd C2
Abbey Walk C2
Abbeygate Sh Ctr C2
Abbotsway C2
Adam Smith St A1/A2
Ainslie St C2
Albert St A3
Alexandra Dock A2/B2
Alexandra Retail Park A2
Alexandra Rd A2/B2
Annesley St A2
Armstrong St A1
Arthur St B1
Augusta St C1
Bargate C1
Beeson St A1
Bethlehem St C2
Bodiam Way B3
Bradley St B3
Brighowgate C1/C2
Bus Station B2/C2
Canterbury Dr C1
Cartergate B1/C1
Catherine St C3
Caxton A3
Chantry La B1
Charlton St A1
Church La C2
Church St A3
Cleethorpe Rd A3
College C2
College St C1
Compton Dr C1
Corporation Bridge A2
Corporation Rd A1
Court B3
Crescent St B1
Deansgate C1
Doughty Rd C2
Dover St B1
Duchess St C2
Dudley St C1
Duke of York Gardens B1
Duncombe St B3
Earl La B1
East Marsh St B3
East St B2
Eastgate B3
Eastside Rd A3
Eaton Ct C1
Eleanor St B3
Ellis Way B3
Fisherman's Chapel A3
Fisherman's Wharf B2
Fishing Heritage Ctr B2
Flour Sq A3
Frederick St B1
Frederick Ward Way B2
Freeman St A3/B3
Freshney Dr B1
Freshney Pl B2
Garden St C2
Garibaldi St A3
Garth La B2
Grime St B3
Grimsby Docks Sta A3
Grimsby Town Sta C2
Hainton Ave C3
Har Way B3
Hare St C3
Harrison St B1
Haven Ave B1
Hay Croft Ave B1
Hay Croft St B1
Heneage Rd B3/C3
Henry St B1
Holme St B3
Hume St C1
James St B1
Joseph St B1
Kent St A3
King Edward St A3
Lambert Rd C2
Library B2
Lime St B1
Lister St B1
Littlefield La C1
Lockhill A3
Lord St B1
Ludford St C3
Macaulay St B1
Mallard Mews C3
Manor Ave C2
Market A3
Market Hall B2
Market St B3
Moss Rd C2
Nelson St A3
New St B2
Osbourne St B2
Pasture St B3
Peaks Parkway C3
Pelham Rd C1
Police Station A3
Post Office B1/B2/C2
PS Lincoln Castle B2
Pyewipe Rd A1
Railway Pl A3
Railway St A3
Recreation Ground C2
Rendel St A2
Retail Park B3
Richard St B1
Ripon St B1
Robinson St East B3
Royal St A3
St Hilda's Ave C1
St James C2
Sheepfold St B3/C3
Sixhills St C3
South Park B2
Spring St A3
Superstore B3
Tasburgh St C3
Tennyson St B2
The Close C1
Thesiger St A3
Time Trap C2
Town Hall B2
Veal St B1
Victoria Retail Park A3
Victoria St North A2
Victoria St South B2
Victoria St West B2
Watkin St A1
Welholme Ave C2
Welholme Rd C3
Wellington St B3
Wellowgate C2
Werneth Rd B3
West Coates Rd A1
Westgate A2
Westminster Dr C1
Willingham St C3
Wintringham Rd C2
Wood St B3
Yarborough Dr B1
Yarborough Hotel C2

Hanley 335

Acton St A3
Albion St B2
Argyle St C1
Ashbourne Gr A2
Avoca St A3
Baskerville Rd B3
Bedford Rd C1
Bedford St C1
Bethesda St B2
Bexley St A2
Birches Head Rd A3
Botteslow St C3
Boundary St A2
Broad St C2
Broom St A3
Bryan St A2
Bucknall New Rd B3
Bucknall Old Rd B3
Bus Station B3
Cannon St C2
Castlefield St C1
Cavendish St B1
Central Forest Pk A2
Charles St B3
Cheapside B2
Chell St A3
Clarke St C1
Cleveland Rd C2
Clifford St C3
Clough St B2
Clyde St C1
College Rd C2
Cooper St C2
Corbridge Rd A1
Cutts St C2
Davis St C1
Denbigh St A1
Derby St C3
Dilke St A3
Dundas St A3
Dundee Rd C1
Dyke St B3
Eastwood Rd C3
Eaton St A3
Etruria Park B1
Etruria Rd B1
Etruria Vale Rd C1
Festing St A3
Festival Retail Park A1
Fire Station C2
Foundry St B2
Franklyn St C3
Garnet St B1
Garth St B3
George St A3
Gilman St B3
Glass St B3
Goodson St B3
Greyhound Way A1
Grove Pl C1
Hampton St C3
Hanley Park C2
Harding Rd C2
Hassall St B3
Havelock Pl C1
Hazlehurst St C3
Hinde St C2
Hope St B2
Houghton St C2
Hulton St A3
Information Ctr B3
Jasper St C2
Jervis St A3
John Bright St A3
John St B2
Keelings Rd A3
Kimberley Rd C1
Ladysmith Rd C1
Lawrence St C2
Leek Rd C3
Library C2
Lichfield St C3
Linfield Rd B3
Loftus St A2
Lower Bedford St C1
Lower Bryan St A2
Lower Mayer St A3
Lowther St A1
Magistrates Court C2
Malham St A2
Marsh St B2
Matlock St C3
Mayer St A3
Milton St C1
Mitchell Memorial Theatre B2
Morley St B2
Moston St A3
Mount Pleasant C1
Mulgrave St A1
Mynors St B3
Nelson Pl B3
New Century St B1
Octagon Retail Park B1
Ogden Rd C3
Old Hall St B3
Old Town Rd A3
Pall Mall B2
Palmerston St C3
Park and Ride C2
Parker St B2
Pavilion Dr A1
Pelham St C3
Percy St B2
Piccadilly B2
Picton St B3
Plough St A3
Police Station C2
Portland St A1
Post Office A3/B3/C3
Potteries Museum & Art Gallery B2
Potteries Sh Ctr B2
Potteries Way C2
Powell St A1
Pretoria Rd C1
Quadrant Rd B2
Ranelagh St C2
Raymond St C2
Rectory Rd C1
Regent Rd C2
Regent Theatre B2
Richmond Terr C2
Ridgehouse Dr A1
Robson St C2
St Ann St B3
St Luke St B3
Sampson St B2
Shaw St A1
Sheaf St C2
Shearer St C1
Shelton New Rd C1
Shirley Rd C2
Slippery La B2
Snow Hill C2
Spur St C3
Stafford St B2
Statham St B2
Stubbs La C3
Sun St C1
Supermarket A1/B2
Talbot St C3
The Parkway C2
Town Hall B2
Town Rd A3
Trinity St B2
Union St A2
Upper Hillchurch St A3
Upper Huntbach St B3
Victoria Hall Theatre B3
Warner St C2
Warwick St C1
Waterloo Rd A1
Waterloo St B3
Well St B3
Wellesley St C2
Wellington Rd B3
Wellington St B3
Whitehaven Dr A2
Whitmore St C1
Windermere St A1
Woodall St A1
Yates St C2
York St A2

Harrogate 335

Albert St C2
Alexandra Rd B2
Arthington Ave B2
Ashfield Rd A2
Back Cheltenham Mount B2
Beech Grove C1
Belmont Rd C1
Bilton Dr A2
Bower Rd B2
Bower St B2
Bus Station B2
Cambridge Rd B2
Cambridge St B2
Cemetery A2
Chatsworth Pl A2
Chatsworth Grove A2
Chatsworth Rd A2
Chelmsford Rd B3
Cheltenham Cr B2
Cheltenham Mt B2
Cheltenham Pde B2
Christ Church B3
Christ Church Oval B3
Chudleigh Rd B3
Clarence Dr B1
Claro Rd A3
Claro Way A3
Coach Park B2
Coach Rd B3
Cold Bath Rd C1
Commercial St B2
Coppice Ave A1
Coppice Dr A1
Coppice Gate A1
Cornwall Rd B1
Council Offices B1
Court C3
Crescent Gdns B1
Crescent Rd B1
Dawson Terr A2
Devonshire Pl B3
Diamond Mews C1
Dixon Rd A2
Dixon Terr A2
Dragon Ave B3
Dragon Parade B2
Dragon Rd B2
Duchy Rd B1
East Parade B2
East Park Rd C3
Esplanade B1
Fire Station A2
Franklin Mount A2
Franklin Rd B2
Franklin Square A2
Glebe Rd C1
Grove Park Ct A3
Grove Park Terr A3
Grove Rd A2
Hampswaite Rd A1
Harcourt Dr B3
Harcourt Rd B3
Harrogate B2
Harrogate Int Ctr B1
Harrogate Ladies Coll B1
Harrogate Theatre B2
Heywood Rd C1
Hollins Cr A1
Hollins Mews A1
Hollins Rd A1
Homestead Rd C3
Hydro Leisure Ctr, The A1
Information Ctr B1
James St B2
Jenny Field Dr A1
John St B2
Kent Dr A1
Kent Rd A1
Kings Rd A2
Kingsway B3
Kingsway Dr B3
Lancaster Rd C1
Leeds Rd C2
Lime Grove B3
Lime St A3
Mayfield Grove B2
Mayfield Pl A2
Mercer B1
Montpellier Hill B1
Mornington Cr A3
Mornington Terr B3
Mowbray Sq B3
North Park Rd B3
Nydd Vale Rd B2
Oakdale Ave A1
Oatlands Dr C3
Odeon B2
Osborne Rd A2
Otley Rd C2
Oxford St B2
Park Chase B3
Park Parade B3
Park View B2
Parliament St B1
Police Station B3
Post Office B2/C1
Providence Terr A2
Queen Parade C3
Queen's Rd C1
Raglan St C2
Regent Ave A3
Regent Grove A3
Regent Parade A3
Regent St A3
Regent Terr A3
Rippon Rd A1
Robert St C2
Royal Baths & Turkish Baths B1
Royal Pump Room B1
St Luke's Mount A2
St Mary's Ave C1
St Mary's Walk C1
Scargill Rd A1
Skipton Rd A3
Skipton St A2
Slingsby Walk C3
South Park Rd C2
Spring Grove A1
Springfield Ave B1
Station Ave B2
Station Parade B2
Strawberry Dale B2
Stray Rein C3
Studley Rd A2
Superstore B2
Swan Rd B1
The Parade B2
The Stray C2/C3
Tower St C2
Trinity Rd C2
Union St B2
Valley Dr C1
Valley Gardens C1
Valley Mount C1
Victoria Ave C2
Victoria Rd C1
Victoria Shopping Ctr B2
Waterloo St A2
West Park C2
West Park St C2
Wood View A1
Woodfield Ave A3
Woodfield Dr A3
Woodfield Grove A3
Woodfield Rd A3
Woodfield Square A3
Woodside B3
York Pl C3
York Rd B1

Holyhead *Caergybi* 335

Armenia St A2
Arthur St C2
Beach Rd A1
Boston St B2
Bowling Green C3
Bryn Erw Rd C3
Bryn Glas Cl C3
Bryn Glas Rd C3
Bryn Gwyn Rd C1
Bryn Marchog A1
Bryn Mor Terr A2
Bryngoleu Ave A1
Cae Braenar C3
Cambria St B1
Captain Skinner's Obelisk B2
Cecil St C2
Celtic Gateway Footbridge B2
Cemetery C1/C2
Cleveland Ave C2
Coastguard Lookout A2
Court B2
Customs House A3
Cybi Pl A2
Cyttir Rd C3
Edmund St B1
Empire B2
Ferry Terminals B2
Ffordd Beibio B3
Ffordd Feurig C3
Ffordd Hirnos C3
Ffordd Jasper C3
Ffordd Tudur B3
Fire Station C2
Garreglwyd Rd B1
Gilbert St C2
Gorsedd Circle B1
Gwelfor Ave A1
Harbour View B3
Henry St C2
High Terr C1
Hill St B2
Holborn Rd C2
Holland Park Ind Est C3
Holyhead Park B1
Holyhead Station B2
Information Ctr B2
King's Rd C2
Kingsland Rd C2
Lewascote C3
Library B2
Lifeboat Station A1
Llanfawr Cl C3
Llanfawr Rd C3
Lligwy St C2
Lon Deg C3
London Rd C3
Longford Rd B1
Longford Terr B1
Maes Cybi B1
Maes Hedd A1
Maes-Hyfryd Rd C1
Maes-y-Dref B1
Maes-yr-Haf A2/B1
Maes-yr-Ysgol C3
Marchog C3
Marina A1
Maritime Museum A1
Market B2
Market St B2
Mill Bank B1
Min-y-Mor Rd A1
Morawelon Ind Est B3

Morawelon Rd B3
Moreton Rd C1
New Park Rd B1
Newry St A2
Old Harbour Lighthouse A3
Plas Rd C1
Police Station B2
Porth-y-Felin Rd A1
Post Office A1/B1/B2/B3/C2/C3
Prince of Wales Rd A2
Priory La B3
Pump St C1
Queens Park B1
Reseifion Rd C1
Rock St B1
Roman Fort B2
St Cybi St B2
St Cybi's Church B2
St Seiriol's Cl B1
Salt Island Bridge A2
Seabourne Rd A1
South Stack Rd B1
Sports Ground B1
Stanley St B2
Station St B2
Tan-y-Bryn Rd A1
Tan-yr-Efail C2
Tara St C1
Thomas St B1
Town Hall A2
Treseifion Estate C2
Turkey Shore Rd B2
Ucheldre Arts Ctr B1
Ucheldre Ave B1
Upper Baptist St B1
Victoria Rd B2
Victoria Terr B2
Vulcan St B1
Walthew Ave A1
Walthew La A1
Wian St C2

Hull 335

Adelaide St C1
Albert Dock C1
Albion St B2
Alfred Gelder St B2
Anlaby Rd B1
Arctic Corsair B3
Beverley Rd A1
Blanket Row C2
Bond St B2
Bridlington Ave A2
Brook St B1
Brunswick Ave A1
Bus Station B1
Camilla Cl C3
Cannon St A2
Cannon's C1
Caroline St A2
Carr La B2
Castle St C2
Central Library B1
Charles St A2
Citadel Way B3
City Hall B2
City Hall Theatre B2
Clarence St B3
Cleveland St A3
Clifton St A1
Club Culture C2
Colonial St B1
Court B2
Deep, The C3
Dock Office Row B3
Dock St B2
Dinostar C2
Drypool Bridge B3
Egton St A3
English St C1
Ferens Gallery B2
Ferensway B1
Francis St A2
Francis St West A2
Freehold St A1
Freetown Way A2
Fruit Theatre C2
Garrison Rd B3
George St B2
Gibson St A2
Great Thornton St B1
Great Union St A3
Green La A2
Grey St A1
Grimston St B2
Grosvenor St A1
Guildhall B2
Guildhall Rd B2
Hands-on History B2
Harley St A1
Hessle Rd C1
High St B3
Holy Trinity B2
Hull & East Riding Museum B3
Hull Arena C1
Hull College B3
Hull History Ctr A2
Hull (Paragon) Sta B1
Hull Truck Theatre B1
Humber Dock Marina C2
Humber Dock St C2
Humber St C2
Hyperion St A3
Information Ctr B2
Jameson St B1
Jarratt St B2
Jenning St A3
King Billy Statue C2
King Edward St B2
King St A2
Kingston Retail Park C1
Kingston St C2
Liddell St A1
Lime St A3
Lister St C1
Lockwood St A2
Maister House B3
Maritime Museum B2
Market B2
Market Place B2
Minerva Pier C2
Mulgrave St A3
Myton Bridge C3
Myton St B1
NAPA (Northern Acad of Performing Arts) B1
Nelson St C2
New Cleveland St A3
New George St A2
New Theatre A2
Norfolk St A1
North Bridge A3
North St B1
Odeon C1
Old Harbour C3
Osborne St B1
Paragon St B2
Park St B1
Percy St A2
Pier St C2
Police Station B2
Post Office A1/B1/B2
Porter St C1
Portland St B1
Posterngate B2
Prince's Quay B2
Prospect Ctr B1
Prospect St B1
Queen's Gdns B2
Railway Dock Marina C2
Railway St C2
Real B1
Red Gallery B1
Reform St A2
Retail Park B1
River Hull Footbridge B3
Riverside Quay C2
Roper St B2
St James St C1
St Luke's St B1
St Mark St A3
St Mary the Virgin B3
St Stephens Sh Ctr B1
Scott St A2
South Bridge Rd B3
Spring Bank A1
Spring St B1
Spurn Lightship C2
Spyvee St A3
Streetlife Transport Museum B3
Sykes St A2
Tidal Surge Barrier C3
Tower St B3
Trinity House B2
University B2
Vane St A1
Victoria Pier C2
Waterhouse La B2
Waterloo St A1
Waverley St C1
Wellington St C2
Wellington St West C2
West St B1
Whitefriargate B2
Wilberforce Dr B2
Wilberforce House B3
Wilberforce Monument B3
William St C1
Wincolmlee A3
Witham A3
Wright St A1

Inverness 336

Abban St A1
Academy St B2
Alexander Pl B2
Anderson St A2
Annfield Rd C3
Ardconnel St B3
Ardconnel Terr B3
Ardross Pl B2
Ardross St B2
Argyle St B3
Argyle Terr B3
Attadale Rd B1
Ballifeary La C2
Ballifeary Rd C1/C2
Balnacraig La A1
Balnain House B2
Balnain St B2
Bank St B2
Bellfield Park C2
Bellfield Terr C3
Benula Rd A1
Birnie Terr A1
Bishop's Rd C2
Bowling Green A2
Bowling Green B2
Bowling Green C2
Bridge St B2
Brown St A2
Bruce Ave C1
Bruce Gdns C1
Bruce Pk C1
Burial Ground A2
Burnett Rd A3
Bus Station B3
Caledonian Rd B1
Cameron Rd A1
Cameron Sq A1
Carse Rd A1
Carsegate Rd Sth A1
Castle Garrison Encounter B2
Castle Rd B2
Castle St B3
Celt St B2
Chapel St A2
Charles St B3
Church St B2
Clachnacuddin Football Ground A1
Columba Rd B1/C1
Crown Ave B3
Crown Circus B3
Crown Dr B3
Crown Rd B3
Crown St B3
Culduthel Rd C3
Dalneigh Cres C1
Dalneigh Rd C1
Denny St B3
Dochfour Dr B1/C1
Douglas Row B2
Duffy Dr C3
Dunabban Rd A1
Dunain Rd B1
Duncraig St B2
Eastgate Shopping Ctr B3
Eden Court C2
Fairfield Rd B1
Falcon Sq B3
Fire Station A3
Fraser St B2
Fraser St C2
Friars' Bridge A2
Friars' La B2
Friars' St A2
George St A2
Gilbert St A2
Glebe St A2
Glendoe Terr A1
Glenurquhart Rd C1
Gordon Terr B3
Gordonville Rd C2
Grant St A2
Greig St B2
HM Prison B3
Harbour Rd A3
Harrowden Rd B1
Haugh Rd C2
Heatherley Cres C3
High St B3
Highland Council HQ, The C2
Hill Park C3
Hill St B3
Huntly Pl A2
Huntly St B2
India St A2
Industrial Estate A3
Information Ctr B2
Innes St A2
Inverness B3
Inverness College (Midmills Campus) B3
Inverness College UHI A3
Inverness High School B1
Inverness Museum B2
Jamaica St A2
Kenneth St B2
Kilmuir Rd A1
King St B2
Kingsmills Rd B3
Laurel Ave B1/C1
Library A3
Lilac Gr B1
Lindsay Ave C1
Lochalsh Rd A1/B1
Longman Rd A3
Lotland Pl A2
Lower Kessock St A1
Madras St A2
Market Hall B3
Maxwell Dr C1
Mayfield Rd C3
Millburn Rd B3
Mitchell's La C3
Montague Row B2
Muirfield Rd C3
Muirtown St B1
Nelson St A2
Ness Bank C2
Ness Bridge B2
Ness Walk B2/C2
Old Edinburgh Rd C3
Old High Church B2
Park Rd C1
Paton St C2
Perceval Rd B1
Planefield Rd B2
Police Station A3
Porterfield Bank C3
Porterfield Rd C3
Portland Pl A2
Post Office A2/B1/B2/B3
Queen St B2
Queensgate B2
Railway Terr A3
Rangemore Rd B1
Reay St B3
Riverside St A2
Rose St A2
Ross Ave B1
Rowan Rd B1
Royal Northern Infirmary C2
St Andrew's Cath C2
St Columba B2
St John's Ave C1
St Mary's Ave C1
Sheriff Court B3
Shore St A2
Smith Ave C1
Southside Pl C3
Southside Rd C3
Spectrum Ctr B2
Strothers La B3
Superstore B2
TA Ctr C2
Telford Gdns B1
Telford Rd A1
Telford St A1
Tomnahurich Cemetery C1
Tomnahurich St B2
Town Hall B3
Union Rd B3
Union St B3
Walker Pl A2
Walker Rd A3
War Memorial C2
Waterloo Bridge A2
Wells St B1
Young St B2

Ipswich 336

Alderman Rd B2
All Saints' Rd A1
Alpe St B2
Ancaster Rd C1
Ancient House B3
Anglesea Rd B2
Ann St B2
Arboretum A2
Austin St C2
Belstead Rd C2
Berners St B2
Bibb Way B1
Birkfield Dr C1
Black Horse La B2
Bolton La B3
Bond St C3
Bowthorpe Cl B2
Bramford La A1
Bramford Rd A1
Bridge St C2
Brookfield Rd A1
Brooks Hall Rd A1
Broomhill A2
Broomhill Rd A1
Broughton Rd A2
Bulwer Rd B1
Burrell Rd C2
Butter Market B2
Butter Market Ctr B3
Carr St B3
Cecil Rd B2
Cecilia St C2
Chancery Rd C2
Charles St B2
Chevallier St A1
Christchurch Mansion & Wolsey Art Gallery B3
Christchurch Park A3
Christchurch St B3
Cineworld C2
Civic Ctr B2
Civic Dr B2
Clarkson St B1
Cobbold St B3
Commercial Rd C2
Constable Rd A3
Constantine Rd C1
Constitution Hill A2
Corder Rd A3
Corn Exchange B2
Cotswold Ave A2
Council Offices C2
County Hall B3
Crown Court C2
Crown St B2
Cullingham Rd B1
Cumberland St B2
Curriers La B2
Dale Hall La A2
Dales View Rd A1
Dalton Rd B2
Dillwyn St B1
Elliot St B1
Elm St B2
Elsmere Rd A3
Falcon St C2
Felaw St C3
Flint Wharf C3
Fonnereau Rd B2
Fore St C3
Foundation St C3
Franciscan Way C2
Friars St C2
Gainsborough Rd A3
Gatacre Rd B1
Geneva Rd B2
Gippeswyk Ave C1
Gippeswyk Park C1
Grafton Way C2
Graham Rd A1
Grimwade St C3
Great Whip St C3
Handford Cut B1
Handford Rd B1
Henley Rd A2
Hervey St B3
High St B2
Holly Rd A2
Information Ctr B3
Ipswich Haven Marina C3
Ipswich School A2
Ipswich Station C2
Ipswich Town FC (Portman Road) C2
Ivry St A2
Kensington Rd A1
Kesteven Rd C1
Key St C3
Kingsfield Ave A3
Kitchener Rd A1
Magistrates Court B2
Little's Cr C2
London Rd B1
Low Brook St C3
Lower Orwell St C3
Luther Rd C2
Manor Rd A3
Mornington Ave A1
Mus & Art Gallery B2
Museum St B2
Neale St B3
New Cardinal St C2
New Cut East C3
New Cut West C3
New Wolsey B2
Newson St B2
Norwich Rd A1/B1
Oban St B2
Old Customs House C3
Old Foundry Rd B3
Old Merchant's Ho C3
Orford St B2
Paget Rd A2
Park Rd A3
Park View Rd A2
Peter's St C2
Philip Rd C2
Pine Ave A2
Pine View Rd A2
Police Station B2
Portman Rd B2
Portman Walk C1
Post Office B2/B3
Princes St C2
Prospect St B1
Queen St B2
Ranelagh Rd C1
Recreation Ground B1
Rectory Rd C2
Regent Theatre B3
Retail Park C2
Richmond Rd A1
Rope Walk C3
Rose La C2
Russell Rd C2
St Edmund's Rd A2
St George's St B2
St Helen's St B3
Samuel Rd B3
Sherrington Rd A1
Silent St C2
Sir Alf Ramsey Way C1
Sirdar Rd B1
Soane St B3
Springfield La A1
Star La C3
Stevenson Rd B1
Suffolk College C3
Suffolk Retail Park B1
Superstore B1
Surrey Rd B1
Tacket St C3
Tavern St B3
The Avenue A3
Tolly Cobbold Mus C3
Tower Ramparts B2
Tower Ramparts Shopping Ctr B2
Tower St B3
Town Hall B2
Tuddenham Rd A3
Upper Brook St B3
Upper Orwell St B3
Valley Rd A2
Vermont Cr B3
Vermont Rd B3
Vernon St C3
Warrington Rd A2
Waterloo Rd A1
Waterworks St C3
Wellington St B1
West End Rd B1
Westerfield Rd A3
Westgate St B2
Westholme Rd A1
Westwood Ave A1
Willoughby Rd C2
Withipoll St B3
Woodbridge Rd B3
Woodstone Ave A3
Yarmouth Rd B1

Kendal 336

Abbot Hall Art Gallery & Museum of Lakeland Life C2
Ambulance Station A2
Anchorite Fields C2
Anchorite Rd C2
Ann St A3
Appleby Rd A3
Archers Meadow C3
Ashleigh Rd A2
Aynam Rd B2
Bankfield Rd B1
Beast Banks B2
Beezon Fields A2
Beezon Rd A2
Beezon Trad Est A3
Belmont B2
Birchwood Cl C1
Blackhall Rd B2
Brewery Arts Ctr B2
Bridge St B2
Brigsteer Rd C1
Burneside Rd A2
Bus Station B2
Buttery Well La C2
Canal Head North B3
Captain French La C2
Caroline St A2
Castle Hill B3
Castle Howe B2
Castle Rd B3
Castle St A3/B3
Cedar Gr C1
Council Offices B2
County Council Offices A2
Cricket Ground A3
Cricket Ground C3
Cross La C2
Dockray Hall Ind Est A2
Dowker's La B2
Dry Ski Slope B3
East View B1
Echo Barn Hill C1
Elephant Yard Sh Ctr B2
Fairfield La A1
Finkle St B2
Fire Station A2
Fletcher Square C3
Football Ground C3
Fowling La A3
Gillinggate C2
Glebe Rd C2
Golf Course B1
Goose Holme B3
Gooseholme Bridge B3
Green St A1
Greengate C2
Greengate La C1/C2
Greenside B1
Greenwood C1
Gulfs Rd B2
High Tenterfell B1
Highgate B2
Hillswood Ave C1
Horncop La A2
Information Ctr B2
K Village and Heritage Ctr B2
Kendal Business Park A3
Kendal Castle (Remains) B3
Kendal Fell B1
Kendal Green A1
Kendal A3
Kendal Station A3
Kent Pl B2
Kirkbarrow C2
Kirkland C2
Library B2
Library Rd B2
Little Aynam B3
Little Wood B1
Long Cl C1
Longpool A3
Lound Rd C3
Lound St C3
Low Fellside B2
Lowther St B2
Maple Dr C1
Market Pl B2
Maude St B2
Miller Bridge B2
Milnthorpe Rd C2
Mint St A3
Mintsfeet Rd A3
Mintsfeet Rd South A2
New Rd B2
Noble's Rest B2
Parish Church C2
Park Side Rd C3
Parkside Bsns Park C3
Parr St B3
Police Station A2
Post Office A3/B2/C2
Quaker Tapestry B2
Queen's Rd B1
Riverside Walk C2
Rydal Mount A2
Sandes Ave A2
Sandgate A3
Sandylands Rd A3
Serpentine Rd B1
Serpentine Wood B1
Shap Rd A3
South Rd C2
Stainbank Rd C1
Station Rd A3
Stramongate B2
Stramongate Bridge A2/B2
Stricklandgate A2/B2
Sunnyside C3
Thorny Hills B3
Town Hall B2
Undercliff Rd B1
Underwood C1
Union St A2
Vicar's Fields C2
Vicarage Dr C1/C2
Wainwright Yd Sh Ctr B2
Wasdale Cl C3
Well Ings C2
Westmorland Shopping Ctr & Market Hall B2
Westwood Ave C1
Wildman St A3
Windermere Rd A1
YHA B2
YWCA B2

King's Lynn 336

Albert St A2
Albion St B2
All Saints B2
All Saints St B2
Austin Fields A2
Austin St A2
Avenue Rd B3
Bank Side B1
Beech Rd C2
Birch Tree Cl B2
Birchwood St A2
Blackfriars Rd B2
Blackfriars St B2
Boal St B1
Bridge St B2
Broad St B2
Broad Walk B3
Burkitt St A2
Bus Station A2
Carmelite Terr C2
Chapel St A2
Chase Ave C3
Checker St C2
Church St B2
Clough La B2
Coburg St B2
College of West Anglia A3
Columbia Way A3
Corn Exchange A1
County Court Rd B2
Cresswell St A2
Custom House A1
Eastgate St A2
Edma St A2
Exton's Rd C3
Ferry La B1
Ferry St A1
Framingham's Almshouses B2
Friars St C2
Friars Walk C2
Gaywood Rd A3
George St A2
Gladstone Rd C2
Goodwin's Rd C3
Green Quay B1
Greyfriars' Tower B2
Guanock Terr C2
Guildhall A1
Hansa Rd C3
Hardwick Rd C2
Hextable Rd A2
High St B1
Holcombe Ave C3
Hospital Walk C2
Information Ctr B1
John Kennedy Rd A2
Kettlewell Lane A2
King George V Ave B3
King's Lynn Art Ctr A1
King's Lynn FC B3
King's Lynn Station B2
King St B1
Library B2
Littleport St A2
Loke Rd A2
London Rd B2
Lynn Museum B2
Majestic B2
Magistrates Court B1
Market La A1
Millfleet B2
Milton Ave A3
Nar Valley Walk C2
Nelson St B1
New Conduit St B2
Norfolk St A2
North Lynn Discovery Ctr A3
North St A2
Oldsunway B2
Ouse Ave C1
Page Stair Lane A1
Park Ave B3
Police Station B2
Portland Pl C1
Portland St B2
Post Office A3/C2
Purfleet B1
Queen St B1
Raby Ave A3
Railway Rd A2
Red Mount Chapel B3
Regent Way B2
River Walk A1
Robert St C2
Saddlebow Rd C2
St Ann's St A1
St James' Rd B2
St James' Swimming Pool B2
St James St B2
St John's Walk B3
St Margaret's B1
St Nicholas A2
St Nicholas St A1
St Peter's Rd B1
Sir Lewis St A2
Smith Ave A3
South Everard St C2
South Gate C2
South Quay B1
South St B2
Southgate St C2
Stonegate St B2
Surrey St A1
Sydney St C3
Tennyson Ave B3
Tennyson Rd B3
Tower St B2
Town Hall B1
Town Ho & Tales of The Old Gaol Ho B1
Town Wall (Remains) B3
True's Yard Mus A2
Valingers Rd C2
Vancouver Ave C2
Waterloo St B2
Wellesley St B2
White Friars Rd C2
Windsor Rd C2
Winfarthing St C2
Wyatt St A2
York Rd C3

Lancaster 336

Aberdeen Rd C3
Adult College, The C3
Aldcliffe Rd C2
Alfred St B3
Ambleside Rd A3
Ambulance Sta A3
Ashfield Ave B1
Ashton Rd C2
Assembly Rooms B2
Balmoral Rd B3
Bath House B2
Bath Mill La B3
Bath St B3
Blades St B1
Borrowdale Rd B3
Bowerham Rd C3
Brewery La B2
Bridge La B2
Brook St C1
Bulk Rd A3
Bulk St B2
Bus Station B2
Cable St B2
Canal Cruises & Waterbus C2
Carlisle Bridge A1
Carr House La C2
Castle B1
Castle Park B1
Caton Rd A3
China St B2
Church St B2
City Museum B2
Clarence St C3
Common Gdn St B2
Coniston Rd A3
Cottage Museum B2
Council Offices B2
Court B2
Cromwell Rd C1
Crown Court B1
Dale St C3
Dallas Rd B1/C1
Dalton Rd B3
Dalton Sq B2
Damside St B2
De Vitre St B3
Dee Rd A1
Denny Ave A1
Derby Rd A2
Dukes B2
Earl St A2
East Rd B3
Eastham St C3
Edward St B3
Fairfield Rd B1
Fenton St B2
Firbank Rd A3
Fire Station B2
Friend's Meeting Ho B1
Garnet St B3
George St B2
Giant Axe Field B1
Grand, The B2
Grasmere Rd B3
Greaves Rd C2
Green St A3
Gregson Ctr, The B3
Gregson Rd C3
Greyhound Bridge A2
Greyhound Bridge Rd A2
High St B2
Hill Side B1
Hope St C3
Hubert Pl B1
Information Ctr B2
Judges Lodgings B2
Kelsy St B1
Kentmere Rd B3
King St B2
Kingsway A3
Kirkes Rd C3
Lancaster & Lakeland C3
Lancaster City Football Club B1
Lancaster Station B1
Langdale Rd A3
Ley Ct B1
Library B2
Lincoln Rd B1
Lindow St C2
Lodge St B2
Long Marsh La B1
Lune Rd A1
Lune St A2
Lune Valley Ramble A3
Mainway A2
Maritime Museum A1
Market St B2
Marketgate Sh Ctr B2
Meadowside C2
Meeting House La B1
Millennium Bridge A2
Moor La B2
Moorgate B3
Morecambe Rd A1/A2
Nelson St B2
North Rd B2
Orchard La C1
Owen Rd A2
Park Rd B3
Parliament St A3
Patterdale Rd A3
Penny St B2
Police Station B2
Portland St C2
Post Office A3/B1/B2/B3/C3
Primrose St C3
Priory B1
Prospect St C3
Quarry Rd B3
Queen St C2
Regent St C2
Ridge La A3
Ridge St A3
Royal Lancaster Infirmary (A&E) C2
Rydal Rd B3
Ryelands Park A1
St Georges Quay A1
St John's B2
St Leonard's Gate B2
St Martin's Rd C3
St Nicholas Arcades Shopping Ctr B2
St Oswald St C3
St Peter's B3
St Peter's Rd B3
Salisbury Rd B1
Scotch Quarry Urban Park C3
Shire Hall/HM Prison B1
Sibsey St B1
Skerton Bridge A2
South Rd C2
Station Rd B1
Stirling Rd C3
Storey Ave B1
Sunnyside La C1
Sylvester St C1
Tarnsyke Rd A1
Thurnham St C2
Town Hall B2
Troutbeck Rd B3
Ulleswater Rd B3
University of Cumbria C3
Vicarage Field B1
Vue B2
West Rd B1
Westbourne Dr C1
Westbourne Rd B1
Westham St C3
Wheatfield St B1
Williamson Rd B3
Willow La B1
Windermere Rd B3
Wingate-Saul Rd B1
Wolseley St B3
Woodville St B3
Wyresdale Rd C3

Leeds 336

Aire St B3
Aireside Ctr B2
Albion Pl B4
Albion St B4
Albion Way B1
Alma St A6
Arcades B4
Armley Rd B1
Back Burley Lodge Rd A1
Back Hyde Terr A2
Back Row C3
Bath Rd C3
Beckett St A6
Bedford St B3
Belgrave St A4
Belle View Rd A2
Benson St A5
Black Bull St C5
Blenheim Walk A3
Boar La B4
Bond St B4
Bow St C5
Bowman La C4
Brewery C4
Bridge St A5/B5
Briggate B4
Bruce Gdns C1
Burley Rd A1
Burley St B1
Burmantofs St B6
Bus & Coach Station B5
Butterly St C4
Butts Cr B4
Brewery Wharf C5
Byron St A5
Call La B4
Calverley St A3/B3
Canal St B1
Canal Wharf C3
Carlisle Rd C5
Cavendish Rd A1
Cavendish St A2
Chadwick St C5
Cherry Pl A6
Cherry Row A5
City Museum A4
City Pal of Varieties B4
City Sq B3
Civic Hall A3
Clarence Road C5
Clarendon Rd A2
Clarendon Way A3
Clark La C6
Clay Pit La A4
Cloberry St A2
Clyde Approach C1
Clyde Gdns C1
Coleman St C2
Commercial St B4
Concord St A5
Cookridge St A4
Copley Hill C1
Corn Exchange B4
Cromer Terr A2
Cromwell St A5
Cross Catherine St B6
Cross Green La C6
Cross Stamford St A5
Crown & County Courts A3
Crown Point Bridge C5
Crown Point Retail Pk C4
Crown Point Rd C4
David St C3
Dent St C6
Derwent Pl C3
Dial St C6
Dock St C4
Dolly La A6
Domestic St C2
Duke St B5
Duncan St B4
Dyer St B5
East Field St B6
East Pde B3
East St C5
Eastgate B5
Easy Rd C6
Edward St B4
Ellerby La C6
Ellerby Rd C6
Fenton St A3
Fire Station B2
Fish St B4
Flax Pl B5
Gelderd Rd C1
George St B4
Globe Rd C2
Gloucester Cr B1
Gower St A5
Grafton St A4
Grand Theatre B4
Granville Rd A6
Great George St A3
Great Wilson St C4
Greek St B3
Green La C1
Hanover Ave A2
Hanover La A2
Hanover Sq A2
Hanover Way A2
Harewood St B4
Harrison St B4
Haslewood Cl B6
Haslewood Drive B6
High Court B5
Holbeck La C2
Holdforth Cl C1
Holdforth Gdns B1
Holdforth Gr C1
Holdforth Pl C1
Holy Trinity B4

Hope Rd A5
Hunslet La C4
Hunslet Rd C4
Hyde Terr A2
Infirmary St B3
Information Ctr B3
Ingram Row C3
Junction St C4
Kelso Gdns A2
Kelso Rd A2
Kelso St A2
Kendal La A2
Kendell St C4
Kidacre St C4
King Edward St B4
King St B3
Kippax Pl C6
Kirkgate B4
Kirkgate Market B4
Kirkstall Rd A1
Kitson St C6
Lady La B4
Lands La B4
Lavender Walk B6
Leeds Art Gallery B3
Leeds Bridge C4
Leeds Coll of Music B5
Leeds General Infirmary (A&E) A3
Leeds Metropolitan University A3/A4
Leeds Museum Discovery Ctr C5
Leeds Shopping Plaza B4
Leeds Station B3
Leeds University A3
Library B3
Lincoln Green Rd A6
Lincoln Rd A6
Lindsey Gdns A6
Lindsey Rd A6
Lisbon St B3
Little Queen St B3
Long Close La C6
Lord St C2
Lovell Park A4
Lovell Park Rd A4
Lovell Rd A5
Lower Brunswick St A5
Mabgate A5
Macauly St A5
Magistrates Court A3
Manor Rd C3
Mark La B4
Marlborough St B2
Marsh La B5
Marshall St C3
Meadow La C4
Meadow Rd C4
Melbourne St A5
Merrion Ctr A4
Merrion St A4
Merrion Way A4
Mill St B5
Millennium Sq A3
Mount Preston St A2
Mushroom St A5
Neville St C4
New Briggate A4/B4
New Market St B4
New Station St B4
New York Rd A5
New York St B5
Nile St A5
Nippet La A6
North St A4
Northern St B3
Oak Rd B1
Oxford Pl B3
Oxford Row A3
Park Cross St B3
Park La A2
Park Pl B3
Park Row B4
Park Sq B3
Park Sq East B3
Park Sq West B3
Park St B3
Police Station B5
Pontefract La B6
Portland Cr A3
Portland Way A3
Post Office B4/B5
Project Space Leeds C2
Quarry House (NHS/DSS Headquarters) B5
Quebec St B3
Queen St B3
Railway St B5
Rectory St A6
Regent St A5
Richmond St C5
Rigton Approach B6
Rigton Dr B6
Rillbank La A1
Rosebank Rd A1
Royal Armouries C5
Russell St B3
Rutland St B2
St Anne's Cath (RC) ✝ A4
St Anne's St B4
St James' Hospital A6
St Johns Ctr B4
St John's Rd A2
St Mary's St B5
St Pauls St B3
St Peter's B5
Saxton La B5
Sayner La C5
Shakespeare Ave A6
Shannon St B6
Sheepscar St South A5
Siddall St C3
Skinner La A5
South Pde B3
Sovereign St C4
Spence La C2
Springfield Mount A2
Springwell Ct C2
Springwell Rd C2
Springwell St C2
Stoney Rock La A6
Studio Rd A1
Sutton St C2
Sweet St C3
Sweet St West C3
Swinegate B4
Templar St B5
The Calls B5
The Close B6
The Core B4
The Drive B6
The Garth B5
The Headrow B3/B4
The Lane B5
The Light B4
The Parade B6
Thoresby Pl A3
Torre Rd A6
Town Hall A3
Union Pl C3
Union St B5
Upper Accomodation Rd B6
Upper Basinghall St B4
Vicar La B4
Victoria Bridge C4
Victoria Quarter B4
Victoria Rd C4
Vue B4
Wade La A4
Washington St A1
Water La C3
Waterloo Rd C4
Wellington Rd B2/C1
Wellington St B3
West St B2
West Yorkshire Playhouse B5
Westfield Rd A1
Westgate B3
Whitehall Rd B3/C2
Whitelock St A5
Willis St C6
Willow Approach A1
Willow Ave A1
Willow Terrace Rd A3
Wintoun St A5
Woodhouse La A3/A4
Woodsley Rd A1
York Pl B3
York Rd B6
Yorkshire TV Studios A1

Leicester 336

Abbey St A2
All Saints' A1
Aylestone Rd C2
Bath La A1
Bede Park C1
Bedford St A3
Bedford St South A3
Belgrave Gate A2
Belle Vue A2
Belvoir St B2
Braunstone Gate B1
Burleys Way A2
Burnmoor St C2
Bus Station A2
Canning St A2
Carlton St C2
Castle B1
Castle Gardens B1
Cathedral ✝ B2
Causeway La A2
Charles St B3
Chatham St B2
Christow St A3
Church Gate A2
City Gallery B3
Civic Ctr B2
Clank St B2
Clock Tower ✦ B2
Clyde St A3
Colton St B3
Conduit St B3
Crafton St A3
Craven St A1
Crown Courts B3
Curve B3
De Lux A2
De Montfort Hall C3
De Montfort St C3
De Montfort Univ C1
Deacon St C2
Dover St B3
Duns La B1
Dunton St A1
East St B3
Eastern Boulevard C1
Edmonton Rd A3
Erskine St A3
Filbert St C1
Filbert St East C2
Fire Station C3
Fleet St A3
Friar La B2
Friday St A2
Gateway St C2
Glebe St B3
Granby St B3
Grange La C2
Grasmere St C1
Great Central St A1
Guildhall B2
Guru Nanak Sikh Museum B1
Halford St B2
Havelock St C2
Haymarket Sh Ctr A2
High St A2
Highcross St A1
Highcross Sh Ctr A2
HM Prison C2
Horsefair St B2
Humberstone Gate B2
Humberstone Rd A3
Infirmary St C2
Information Ctr B2
Jarrom St C2
Jewry Wall B1
Kamloops Cr A3
King Richards Rd B1
King St B2
Lancaster Rd C3
LCB Depot B3
Lee St A3
Leicester RFC C2
Leicester Royal Infirmary (A&E) C2
Leicester Station B3
Library B2
Little Theatre, The B3
London Rd C3
Lower Brown St B2
Magistrates Court B2
Manitoba Rd A3
Mansfield St A2
Market ✦ B2
Market St B2
Mill La C2
Montreal Rd A3
Narborough Rd North B1
Nelson Mandela Park C2
New Park St B1
New St B2
New Walk C3
New Walk Museum & Art Gallery C3
Newarke Houses B2
Newarke St B2
Northgate St A1
Orchard St A2
Ottawa Rd A3
Oxford St C2
Upper Brown St B2
Phoenix Square B3
Police Station A3
Post Office A1/B2/C2/C3
Prebend St C3
Princess Rd East C3
Princess Rd West C3
Queen St B3
Regent College C3
Regent Rd C2/C3
Repton St A1
Rutland St B3
St George St B3
St Georges Way B3
St John St A2
St Margaret's A2
St Margaret's Way A2
St Martins B2
St Mary de Castro B1
St Matthew's Way A3
St Nicholas B1
St Nicholas Circle B1
Sanvey Gate A2
Silver St B2
Slater St A1
Soar La A1
South Albion St B3
Southampton St B3
Swain St B3
Swan St A1
The Gateway C2
The Newarke B1
The Rally Com Park A2
Tigers Way C3
Tower St C3
Town Hall B2
Tudor Rd B1
University of Leicester C3
University Rd C3
Upperton Rd C1
Vaughan Way A2
Walnut St C2
Watling St A2
Welford Rd B2
Wellington St B2
West Bridge B1
West St C3
West Walk C3
Western Boulevard C1
Western Rd C1
Wharf St North A3
Wharf St South A3
Y' Theatre, The B3
Yeoman St B3
York Rd B2

Lewes 336

Abinger Pl B1
All Saints Ctr B2
Ambulance Station B2
Anne of Cleves Ho C1
Barbican Ho Mus B1
Brewery B2
Brook St A2
Brooks Rd A2
Bus Station B2
Castle Ditch La B1
Castle Precincts B1
Chapel Hill B3
Church La A1/A2
Cliffe High St B2
Cliffe Industrial Estate C3
Cluny St C1
Cockshut Rd C1
Convent Field C2
Coombe Rd A2
County Hall B1
County Records Office B1
Court B2
Court Rd B2
Crown Court B2
Cuilfail Tunnel B3
Davey's La A3
East St B2
Eastport La C1
Fire Station A2
Fisher St B2
Friars Walk B2
Garden St B1
Government Offices C2
Grange Rd B1
Ham La C2
Harveys Way B2
Hereward Way A2
High St B1/B2
Hop Gallery B2
Information Ctr B2
Keere St B1
King Henry's Rd B1
Lancaster St B2
Landport Rd A1
Leisure Ctr C3
Lewes Bridge B2
Lewes Castle B1
Lewes Football Gd C2
Lewes Golf Course B3
Lewes Southern By-Pass C2
Lewes Station B2
Library B2
Malling Ind Est A2
Malling Brook Ind Est A3
Malling Hill A3
Malling St A3/B3
Market St B2
Martyr's Monument B3
Mayhew Way A2
Morris Rd B3
Mountfield Rd C2
New Rd B1
Newton Rd A1
North St A2/B2
Offham Rd B1
Old Malling Way A1
Orchard Rd A3
Paddock La B1
Paddock Rd B1
Paddock Sports Gd B1
Park Rd B1
Pelham Terr A1
Pells Open Air Swimming Pool A1
Phoenix Causeway B2
Phoenix Ind Est B2
Phoenix Pl B2
Pinwell Rd B2
Police Station B1
Post Office A2/B1/B2/C1
Prince Edward's Rd B1
Priory St C1
Priory of St Pancras (remains of) ✦ C1
Railway La B2
Railway Land Nature Reserve B3
Rotten Row B1
Rufus Cl B1
St Pancras Rd C1
St John St B2
St John's Terr B2
St Nicholas La B2
Sewage Works C3
South Downs Bsns Pk A3
South St B3/C3
Southdowns Rd A2
Southerham Junction C3
Southover Grange Gdns ✦ B1
Southover High St C1
Southover Rd B1
Spences Field A3
Spences La A2
Stansfield Rd A1
Station Rd B2
Station St B2
Sun St B1
Sussex Downs College C2
Sussex Police HQ A2
Talbot Terr B1
The Avenue B1
The Course C1
The Martlets A2
The Needlemakers ✦ B2
The Pells A1
Thebes Gallery B2
Toronto Terr B1
Town Hall B2
West St B2
White Hill B1
Willeys Bridge A1

Lincoln 337

Alexandra Terr B1
Anchor St C1
Arboretum B3
Arboretum Ave B3
Baggholme Rd B3
Bailgate A2
Beaumont Fee B1
Brayford Way C1
Brayford Wharf East C1
Brayford Wharf North B1
Bruce Rd A2
Burton Rd A1
Bus Station (City) C2
Canwick Rd C2
Cardinal's Hat ✦ B2
Carline Rd B1
Castle B1
Castle St A1
Cathedral ✝ B2
Cathedral St B2
Cecil St A2
Chapel La A2
Cheviot St B3
Church La A2
City Hall B1
Clasketgate B2
Clayton Sports Gd A3
Coach Park C2
Collection, The B2
County Hospl (A&E) B3
County Office B1
Courts C1
Croft St B2
Cross St C2
Crown Courts B1
Curle Ave A3
Danesgate B2
Drill Hall B2
Drury La B1
East Bight A2
East Gate A2
Eastcliff Rd B3
Eastgate B2
Egerton Rd A3
Ellis Windmill A1
Engine Shed, The C1
Environment Agency C2
Exchequer Gate ✦ B2
Firth Rd C1
Flaxengate B2
Florence St B3
George St C3
Good La A2
Gray St A1
Great Northern Terr C3
Great Northern Terrace Industrial Estate C3
Greetwell Rd B3
Greetwellgate B3
Haffenden Rd A2
High St B2/C1
HM Prison A3
Hospital (Private) A2
Hungate B2
James St A2
Jews House & Ct B2
Kesteven St C2
Langworthgate A2
Lawn Visitor Ctr, The B1
Lee Rd A3
Library B2
Lincoln College B2
Lincoln Central Sta C2
Lincolnshire Life/Royal Lincolnshire Regiment Museum A1
Lindum Rd B2
Lindum Sports Ground A3
Lindum Terr B3
Mainwaring Rd A3
Manor Rd A2
Market C2
Massey Rd A3
Medieval Bishop's Palace B2
Mildmay St A1
Mill Rd A1
Millman Rd B3
Minster Yard B2
Monks Rd B3
Montague St B2
Mount St A1
Nettleham Rd A2
Newland B1
Newport A2
Newport Arch A2
Newport Cemetery A2
Northgate A2
Odeon C1
Orchard St B1
Oxford St C2
Park St B1
Pelham Bridge C2
Pelham St C2
Police Station B1
Portland St C2
Post Office A1/A2/B1/B3/C2
Potter Gate B2
Priory Gate B2
Queensway A3
Rasen La A1
Ropewalk C1
Rosemary La B2
St Anne's Rd B3
St Benedict's C1
St Giles Ave A3
St John's Rd A2
St Marks St C1
St Mark's Sh Ctr C1
St Mary-Le-Wigford C1
St Mary's St C2
St Nicholas St A2
St Swithin's B2
Saltergate C1
Saxon St A1
Sch of Art & Design B2
Sewell Rd B3
Silver St B2
Sincil St C2
Spital St A2
Spring Hill B1
Stamp End C3
Steep Hill B2
Stonebow & Guildhall C2
Stonefield Ave A2
Tentercroft St C1
The Avenue B1
The Grove A3
Theatre Royal B2
Tritton Retail Park C1
Tritton Rd C1
Union Rd B1
University of Lincoln C1
Upper Lindum St B3
Upper Long Leys Rd A1
Usher B2
Vere St A2
Victoria St B1
Victoria Terr B1
Vine St B3
Wake St A1
Waldeck St A1
Waterside Sh Ctr C2
Waterside North C2
Waterside South C2
West Pde B1
Westgate A2
Wigford Way C1
Williamson St A2
Wilson St A1
Winn St B3
Wragby Rd A3
Yarborough Rd A1

Liverpool 337

Abercromby Sq C5
Acc Liverpool ✦ C2
Addison St A3
Adelaide Rd B6
Ainsworth St B4
Albany Rd B6
Albert Dock C2
Albert Edward Rd B6
Angela St C6
Anson St B4
Archbishop Blanche High School B6
Argyle St C3
Arrad St C4
Ashton St B5
Audley St A4
Back Leeds St A2
Basnett St B3
Bath St A1
Beatles Story C2
Beckwith St C3
Bedford Close C5
Bedford St North C5
Bedford St South C5
Benson St C4
Berry St C4
Birkett St A4
Bixteth St B2
Blackburne Place C4
Bluecoat B3
Bold Place C4
Bold St C4
Bolton St B3
Bridport St B4
Bronte St B4
Brook St A1
Brownlow Hill B4/B5
Brownlow St B5
Brunswick Rd A5
Brunswick St B1
Bus Station C2
Butler Cr A6
Byrom St A3
Caledonia St C4
Cambridge St C5
Camden St A4
Canada Blvd B1
Canning Dock C2
Canterbury St A4
Cardwell St C6
Carver St A4
Cases St B3
Castle St B2
Catherine St C5
Cavern Club B3
Central Library A3
Central Station B3
Chapel St B2
Charlotte St B3
Chatham Place C6
Chatham St C5
Cheapside B2
Chestnut St C5
Christian St A3
Church St B3
Churchill Way North A3
Churchill Way South B3
Clarence St B4
Coach Station A4
Cobden St A5
Cockspur St A2
College St C3
College St North A5
College St South A5
Colquitt St C4
Comus St A3
Concert St C3
Connaught Rd B6
Cook St B2
Copperas Hill B4
Cornwallis St C3
Covent Garden B2
Craven St A4
Cropper St B3
Crown St B5/C6
Cumberland St B2
Cunard Building B1
Dale St B2
Dansie St B4
Daulby St B5
Dawson St B3
Derby Sq B2
Drury La B2
Duckinfield St B4
Duke St C3
Earle St A2
East St A2
Eaton St A2
Edgar St A3
Edge La B6
Edinburgh Rd A6
Edmund St B2
Elizabeth St B5
Elliot St B3
Empire Theatre B4
Empress Rd B6
Epworth St A5
Erskine St A5
Everyman Theatre C5
Exchange St East B2
Fact Ctr, The ✦ C4
Falkland St A5
Falkner St C5/C6
Farnworth St A6
Fenwick St B2
Fielding St A6
Fleet St C3
Fraser St A4
Freemasons Row A2
Gardner Row A3
Gascoyne St A2
George Pier Head C1
George St B2
Gibraltar Road A1
Gilbert St C3
Gildart St A4
Gill St B4
Goree B2
Gower St C2
Gradwell St C3
Great Crosshall St A3
Great George St C4
Great Howard St A1
Great Newton St A4
Greek St B4
Green La B4
Greenside A5
Greetham St C3
Gregson St A5
Grenville St C3
Grinfield St C6
Grove St C5
Guelph St A6
Hackins Hey B2
Haigh St A4
Hall La B6
Hanover St B3
Harbord St C6
Hardman St C4
Harker St A4
Hart St B4
Hatton Garden A2
Hawke St B4
Helsby St B6
Henry St C3
HM Customs & Excise National Museum C2
Highfield St A2
Highgate St B6
Hilbre St B4
Hope Place C4
Hope St C4
Houghton St B3
Hunter St A3
Hutchinson St A6
Information Ctr C2
Institute For The Performing Arts C4
Irvine St B6
Irwell St B2
Islington A4
James St B2
James St Station B2
Jenkinson St A4
Johnson St A3
Jubilee Drive B6
Kempston St A4
Kensington A6
Kensington Gdns B6
Kensington St A6
Kent St C3
King Edward St A1
Kinglake St B6
Knight St C4
Lace St A3
Langsdale St A4
Law Courts C2
Leece St C4
Leeds St A2
Leopold Rd B6
Lime St B3
Lime St Station B4
Little Woolton St B5
Liver St C2
Liverpool John Moores University A3/B4/C4
Liverpool Landing Stage B1
Liverpool One C2
London Rd A4/B4
Lord Nelson St B4
Lord St B2
Lovat St C6
Low Hill A5
Low Wood St A6
Lydia Ann St C3
Mansfield St A4
Marmaduke St B6
Marsden St A6
Martensen St B6
Marybone A3
Maryland St C4
Mason St B6
Mathew St B2
May St B4
Melville Place C6
Merseyside Maritime Museum C2
Metquarter B3
Metropolitan Cathedral (RC) ✝ B5
Midghall St A2
Molyneux Rd A6
Moor Place B4
Moorfields B2
Moorfields Station B2
Moss St A5
Mount Pleasant B4/B5
Mount St C4
Mount Vernon B6
Mulberry St C5
Municipal Buildings B2
Mus of Liverpool C2
Myrtle Gdns C6
Myrtle St C5
Naylor St A2
Nelson St C4
Neptune Theatre B3
New Islington A4
New Quay B1
Newington St C3
North John St B2
North St A3
North View B6
Norton St A4
Oakes St B5
O2 Academy
Odeon B4
Old Hall St A1
Old Leeds St A2
Oldham Place C4
Oldham St C4
Olive St C5
Open Eye Gallery C3
Oriel St A2
Ormond St B2
Orphan St C6
Overbury St C6
Overton St B6
Oxford St C5
Paisley St A1
Pall Mall A2
Paradise St C3
Park La C3
Parker St B3
Parr St C3
Peach St B5
Pembroke Place B4
Pembroke St B5
Philharmonic Hall C5
Pickop St A2
Pilgrim St C4
Pitt St C3
Playhouse Theatre B3
Pleasant St B4
Police HQ C2
Police Station A4/B4
Pomona St B4
Port of Liverpool Building B2
Post Office A2/A4/A5/A6/B2/B3/B4/C4
Pownall St C2
Prescot St A5
Preston St B3
Princes Dock A1
Princes Gdns A2
Princes Jetty A1
Princes Pde B1
Princes St B2
Pythian St A6
Queen Sq Bus Station B3
Queensland St C6
Queensway Tunnel (Docks exit) B1
Queensway Tunnel (Entrance) B3
Radio City B2
Ranelagh St B3
Redcross St B2
Renfrew St B6
Renshaw St B4
Richmond Row A4
Richmond St B3
Rigby St A2
Roberts St A1
Rock St B4
Rodney St C4
Rokeby St A4
Romily St A6
Roscoe La C4
Roscoe St C4
Rose Hill A3
Royal Court Theatre B3
Royal Liver Building B1
Royal Liverpool Hospital (A&E) B5
Royal Mail St B4
Rumford Place B2
Rumford St B2
Russell St B4
St Andrew St B4
St Anne St A4
St Georges Hall B3
St John's Ctr B3
St John's Gdns B3
St John's La B3
St Joseph's Cr A4
St Minishull St B5
St Nicholas Place B1
St Paul's Sq A2
St Vincent Way B4
Salisbury St A4
Salthouse Dock C2
Salthouse Quay C2
Sandon St C5
Saxony Rd B6
Schomberg St A6
School La B2
Seel St C3
Seymour St B4
Shaw St A5
Sidney Place C6
Sir Thomas St B3
Skelhorne St B4
Slater St C3
Slavery Museum C2
Smithdown La B6
Soho Sq A4
Soho St A4
South John St B2
Springfield A4
Stafford St A4
Standish St A3
Stanley St B2
Strand St C2
Suffolk St C3
Tabley St C3
Tarleton St B3
Tate Gallery C2
Teck St B6
Temple St B2
The Beacon ✦ B3
The Strand B2
Tithebarn St B2
Town Hall B2
Traffic Police HQ C6
Trowbridge St B4
Trueman St A3
Union St B2
Unity Theatre C4
University C5
University of Liverpool B5
Upper Duke St C4
Upper Frederick St C3
Upper Baker St A6
Vauxhall Rd A2
Vernon St B2
Victoria Gallery & Museum B5
Victoria St B2
Vine St C5
Wakefield St A4
Walker Art Gallery A3
Walker St A6
Wapping C2
Water St B1/B2
Waterloo Rd A1
Wavertree Rd B6
West Derby Rd A6
West Derby St B5
Whitechapel B3
Western Approaches War Museum B2
Whitley Gdns A5
William Brown St B3
William Henry St A4
Williamson Sq B3
Williamson St B3
Williamson's Tunnels Heritage Ctr ✦ C6
Women's Hospital C6
Wood St B3
World Museum, Liverpool A3
York St C3

Llandudno 337

Abbey Pl B1
Abbey Rd B1
Adelphi St B3
Alexandra Rd C2
Anglesey Rd A1
Argyll Rd B3
Arvon Ave A2
Atlee Cl C3
Augusta St B3
Back Madoc St B2
Bodafon St B3
Bodhyfryd Rd A2
Bodnant Cr C3
Bodnant Rd C3
Bridge Rd C2
Bryniau Rd C1
Builder St B3
Builder St West C2
Cabin Lift A2
Camera Obscura ✦ A3
Caroline Rd B2
Chapel St A2
Charlton St B3
Church Cr C1
Church Walks A2
Claremont Rd B2
Clement Ave A2
Clifton Rd B2
Clonmel St B3
Coach Station B3
Conway Rd B3
Council St West C3
Cricket and Rec Gd B2
Cwlach Rd A2
Cwlach St A1
Cwm Howard La C3
Cwm Pl C3
Cwm Rd C3
Dale Rd C1
Deganwy Ave B2
Denness Pl C2
Dinas Rd C2
Dolydd B1
Erol Pl B2
Ewloe Dr C3
Fairways C2
Ffordd Dewi C3
Ffordd Dulyn C2
Ffordd Dwyfor C3
Ffordd Elisabeth C3
Ffordd Gwynedd C3
Ffordd Las C3
Ffordd Morfa C3
Ffordd Penrhyn C3
Ffordd Tudno C3
Ffordd yr Orsedd C3
Ffordd Ysbyty C2
Fire & Ambulance Sta B3
Garage St B3
George St A2
Gloddaeth Ave B1
Gloddaeth St B2
Gogarth Rd B1
Great Orme Mines ✦ A1
Great Ormes Rd B1
Happy Valley A2
Happy Valley Rd A3
Haulfre Gardens A1
Herkomer Cr C1
Hill Terr A2
Home Front Mus B2
Hospice B1
Howard Rd B3
Information Ctr B2
Invalids' Walk B1
James St B2
Jubilee St B3
King's Ave C2
King's Rd C2
Knowles Rd C2
Lees Rd C2
Library B2
Lifeboat Station B2
Llandudno A2
Llandudno (A&E) C2
Llandudno Station B3
Llandudno Town Football Ground C2
Llewelyn Ave A2
Lloyd St West B1
Lloyd St B2
Llwynon Rd A1
Llys Maelgwn B1
Madoc St B2
Maelgwn Rd B2
Maesdu Bridge C2
Maesdu Rd C2/C3
Maes-y-Cwm C3
Maes-y-Orsedd C3
Marian Pl C2
Marian Rd C2
Marine Drive (Toll) A3
Market Hall A2
Market St A2
Miniature Golf Course A1
Morfa Rd B1
Mostyn B3
Mostyn Broadway B3

Sherwood St D4
Shoe La C6
Shoreditch High St B8
Shoreditch High St ⊖ B8
Shorts Gdns C5
Shouldham St C2
Sidmouth St B5
Silk St C7
Sir John Soane's Museum 🏛 C5
Skinner St B6
Sloane Ave F2
Sloane Sq F2
Sloane Square ⊖ F3
Sloane St E2
Snow Hill C6
Soho Sq C4
Somerset House 🏛 D5
South Audley St D3
South Carriage Dr E2
South Eaton Pl F3
South Kensington ⊖ F1
South Molton St C3
South Parade F1
South Pl C7
South St D3
South Terr F2
South Wharf Rd C1
Southampton Row C5
Southampton St D5
Southwark ⊖ D6
Southwark Bridge D7
Southwark Bridge Rd D7
Southwark Cath ✝ D7
Southwark Park Rd F8
Southwark St D7
Spa Rd E8
Speakers' Corner D2
Spencer St B6
Spital Sq C8
Spring St C1
Stamford St D6
Stanhope St B4
Stanhope Terr D1
Stephenson Way B4
Stock Exchange C6
Stoney St D7
Strand C5
Strathearn Pl D2
Stratton St D3
Sumner St D6
Sussex Gdns C1
Sussex Pl C1
Sussex Sq D1
Sussex St F3
Sutton's Way B7
Swan St E7
Swanfield St B8
Swinton St B5
Sydney Pl F1
Sydney St F2
Tabard St E7
Tabernacle St B7
Tachbrook St F4
Tanner St E8
Tate Britain 🏛 F5
Tate Modern 🏛 D7
Tavistock Pl B5
Tavistock Sq B4
Tea & Coffee Mus 🏛 D7
Temple ⊖ D6
Temple Ave D6
Temple Pl D5
Terminus Pl E3
Thayer St C3
The Barbican Centre for Arts C7
The Cut E6
The Mall E4
Theobald's Rd C5
Thorney St F5
Threadneedle St C7
Throgmorton St C7
Thurloe Pl F1
Thurloe Sq F2
Tonbridge St B5
Tooley St D8
Torrington Pl B4
Tothill St E4
Tottenham Court Rd B4
Tottenham Ct Rd ⊖ C4
Tottenham St C4
Tower Bridge ✦ D8
Tower Bridge App D8
Tower Bridge Rd E8
Tower Hill D8
Tower Hill ⊖ D8
Tower of London, The D8
Toynbee St C8
Trafalgar Square D4
Trinity Sq D8
Trinity St E7
Trocadero Centre D4
Tudor St D6
Turin St B9
Turnmill St C6
Tyers St F5
Ufford St E6
Union St D6
Univ Coll Hospl H B4
University of London C4
Univ of Westminster C3
University St B4
Upper Belgrave St E3
Upper Berkeley St C2
Upper Brook St D3
Upper Grosvenor St D3
Upper Ground D6
Upper Montague St C2
Upper St Martin's La D5
Upper Thames St D7
Upper Wimpole St C3
Upper Woburn Pl B4
Vauxhall Bridge Rd F4
Vauxhall St F5
Vere St C3
Vernon Pl C5
Vestry St B7
Victoria ⇌⊖ E3
Victoria and Albert Mus 🏛 E1
Victoria Coach Station F3
Victoria Embankment D5
Victoria Pl Sh Ctr F3
Victoria St E4
Villiers St D5
Vincent Sq F4
Vinopolis City of Wine 🏛 D7
Virginia Rd B8
Wakley St B6
Walbrook C7
Walcot Sq F6
Wallace Collection 🏛 C3
Walnut Tree Walk F6
Walton St F2
Walworth Rd F7
Wardour St C4/D4
Warner St B6
Warren St ⊖ B4
Warren St B4
Warwick Sq F4
Warwick Way F3
Waterloo ⇌⊖ E6
Waterloo Bridge D5
Waterloo East ⇌ D6
Waterloo Rd E6
Watling St C7
Webber St E6
Welbeck St C3
Wellington Arch ✦ E3
Wellington Mus 🏛 E3
Wellington Rd B2
Wellington Row B9
Wells St C4
Wenlock St A7
Wentworth St C8
West Carriage Dr D2
West Smithfield C6
West Sq E6
Westbourne St D1
Westbourne Terr C1
Westminster ⊖ E5
Westminster Abbey ✝ E5
Westminster Bridge E5
Westminster Bridge Rd E6
Westminster Cathedral (RC) ✝ E4
Westminster City Hall E4
Westminster Hall 🏛 E5
Weston St E7
Weymouth St C3
Wharf Rd A7
Wharton St B5
Whitcomb St D4
White Cube 🏛 B8
White Lion Hill D6
White Lion St A6
Whitechapel Rd C9
Whitecross St B7
Whitefriars St C6
Whitehall D5
Whitehall Pl D5
Wigmore Hall C3
Wigmore St C3
William IV St D5
Willow Walk F8
Wilmington Sq B6
Wilson St C7
Wilton Cres E3
Wilton Rd F4
Wimpole St C3
Winchester St F3
Wincott St F6
Windmill Walk D6
Woburn Pl B5
Woburn Sq B4
Wood St C7
Woodbridge St B6
Wootton St D6
Wormwood St C8
Worship St B7
Wren St B5
Wynyatt St B6
York Rd E5
York St C2
York Terrace East B3
York Terrace West B3
York Way A5

Luton 337

Adelaide St B1
Albert Rd C2
Alma St B2
Alton Rd C3
Anthony Gdns C1
Arndale Ctr B2
Arthur St C2
Ashburnham Rd B1
Ashton Rd C2
Avondale Rd A1
Back St A2
Bailey St C3
Baker St C2
Biscot Rd A1
Bolton Rd B3
Boyle Cl A2
Brantwood Rd B1
Bretts Mead C1
Bridge St B2
Brook St A1
Brunswick St A3
Burr St A3
Bury Park Rd A1
Bus Station B2
Bute St B2
Buxton Rd B2
Cambridge St C3
Cardiff Grove B1
Cardiff Rd B1
Cardigan St A2
Castle St B2/C2
Chapel St C2
Charles St A3
Chase St C2
Cheapside B2
Chequer St C3
Chiltern Rise C1
Church St B2/B3
Cinema A2
Cobden St A3
Collingdon St A1
Community Ctr C3
Concorde Ave A3
Corncastle Rd C1
Cowper St C2
Crawley Green Rd B3
Crawley Rd A1
Crescent Rise A3
Crescent Rd A3
Cromwell Rd A1
Cross St A2
Crown Court B2
Cumberland St B2
Cutenhoe Rd C3
Dallow Rd B1
Downs Rd B1
Dudley St A2
Duke St A2
Dumfries St B1
Dunstable Place B2
Dunstable Rd A1/B1
Edward St A3
Elizabeth St C2
Essex Cl C3
Farley Hill C1
Farley Lodge C1
Flowers Way B2
Francis St A1
Frederick St A2
Galaxy L Complex A2
George St B2
George St West B2
Gillam St A2
Gordon St B2
Grove Rd B1
Guildford St A2
Haddon Rd A3
Harcourt St C2
Hart Hill Drive A3
Hart Hill Lane A3
Hartley Rd A3
Hastings St B2
Hat Factory, The ♥ B2
Hatters Way A1
Havelock Rd A2
Hibbert St C2
High Town Rd A3
Highbury Rd A1
Hightown Community Sports & Arts Ctr A3
Hillary Cres C1
Hillborough Rd C1
Hitchin Rd A3
Holly St C2
Holm C1
Hucklesby Way A2
Hunts Cl C1
Information Ctr ℹ B2
Inkerman St A2
John St B2
Jubilee St A3
Kelvin Cl C2
King St B2
Kingsland Rd C3
Latimer Rd C2
Lawn Gdns C2
Lea Rd B3
Library B2
Library Rd B2
Liverpool Rd B1
London Rd C2
Luton Station ⇌ A2
Lyndhurst Rd B1
Magistrates Court B2
Manchester St B2
Manor Rd B3
May St C3
Meyrick Ave C1
Midland Rd A2
Mill St A2
Milton Rd B1
Moor St A1
Moor, The A1
Moorland Gdns A2
Moulton Rise A3
Museum & Art Gallery 🏛🏛 A2
Napier Rd B1
New Bedford Rd A1
New Town St C2
North St A3
Old Bedford Rd A2
Old Orchard C2
Osbourne Rd C3
Oxen Rd A3
Park Sq B2
Park St B3/C3
Park St West B2
Park Viaduct B3
Parkland Drive C1
Police Station B1
Pomfret Ave A3
Pondwicks Rd B3
Post Office PO A1/A2/B2/C3
Power Court B3
Princess St B1
Red Rails C1
Regent St B2
Reginald St A2
Rothesay Rd B1
Russell Rise C1
Russell St C1
St Ann's Rd B3
St George's ♥ B2
St Mary's ⛪ B3
St Marys Rd B3
St Paul's Rd C2
St Saviour's Cres C1
Salisbury Rd B1
Seymour Ave C3
Seymour Rd C3
Silver St B2
South Rd C2
Stanley St B1
Station Rd A2
Stockwood Cres C2
Stockwood Park C1
Strathmore Ave C2
Stuart St B2
Studley Rd A1
Surrey St C3
Sutherland Place C1
Tavistock St C2
Taylor St A3
Telford Way A1
Tennyson Rd C2
Tenzing Grove C1
The Cross Way C1
The Larches A2
Thistle Rd B3
Town Hall B2
Townsley Cl C2
UK Ctr for Carnival Arts ✦ B3
Union St B2
Univ of Bedfordshire B3
Upper George St B2
Vicarage St B3
Villa Rd A2
Waldeck Rd A1
Wellington St B1/B2
Wenlock St A2
Whitby Rd A1
Whitehill Ave C1
William St A2
Wilsden Ave C1
Windmill Rd B3
Windsor St C2
Winsdon Rd B1
York St A3

Macclesfield 337

108 Steps B2
Abbey Rd A1
Alton Dr A3
Armett St C1
Athey St B1
Bank St C3
Barber St C3
Barton St C1
Beech La A2
Beswick St B1
Black La A2
Black Rd C3
Blakelow Gardens C3
Blakelow Rd C3
Bond St B1/C1
Bread St C1
Bridge St B1
Brock St A2
Brocklehurst Ave A3
Brook St B3
Brookfield La B3
Brough St West C1
Brown St C1
Brynton Rd A2
Buckley St C2
Bus Station B2
Buxton Rd B3
Byrons St C2
Canal St B3
Carlsbrook Ave A3
Castle St B2
Catherine St B1
Cemetery A1
Chadwick Terr A3
Chapel St C2
Charlotte St B2
Chester Rd B1
Chestergate B1
Christ Church ⛪ B1
Churchill Way B2
Coare St A1
Commercial Rd B2
Conway Cres A3
Copper St C3
Cottage St B1
Court A2
Court B2
Crematorium A1
Crew Ave A3
Crompton Rd B1/C1
Cross St C2
Crossall St C1
Cumberland St A1/B1
Dale St B3
Duke St B2
Eastgate B3
Exchange St B2
Fence Ave B3
Fence Ave Ind Est A3
Flint St B3
Foden St A2
Fountain St B3
Gateway Gallery ✦ B1
Garden St A3
Gas Rd B2
George St B2
Glegg St B3
Golf Course C3
Goodall St B3
Grange Rd C1
Great King St B1
Green St B3
Grosvenor Sh Ctr B2
Gunco La C3
Half St C2
Hallefield Rd B3
Hatton St C1
Hawthorn Way A3
Heapy St C3
Henderson St B1
Heritage Ctr & Silk Museum 🏛 B2
Hibel Rd A2
High St C2
Hobson St C2
Hollins Rd C3
Hope St West B1
Horseshoe Dr B1
Hurdsfield Rd A3
Information Ctr ℹ B2
James St C2
Jodrell St B3
John St C2
Jordangate A2
King Edward St B2
King George's Field C3
King St B2
King's School A1
Knight Pool C3
Knight St C3
Lansdowne St A3
Library B2
Lime Gr B3
Little Theatre ♥ C2
Loney St B1
Longacre St B1
Lord St C2
Lowe St C2
Lowerfield Rd A3
Lyon St B1
Macclesfield College C1
Macclesfield Sta ⇌ B2
Marina B3
Market B2
Market Pl B2
Masons La A3
Mill La C2
Mill Rd C2
Mill St B2
Moran Rd C1
New Hall St A2
Newton St C1
Nicholson Ave A3
Nicholson Cl A3
Northgate Ave A2
Old Mill La C2
Paradise Mill 🏛 C2
Paradise St B1
Park Green B2
Park La C1
Park Rd C1
Park St C2
Park Vale Rd C1
Parr St B1
Peel St C2
Percyvale St A3
Peter St C1
Pickford St B2
Pierce St B1
Pinfold St B1
Pitt St C2
Police Station B2
Pool St C2
Poplar Rd C2
Post Office PO B1/B2/B3
Pownall St A2
Prestbury Rd A1/B1
Queen Victoria St B2
Queen's Ave A3
Registrar B2
Richmond Hill C3
Riseley St B1
Roan Ct B3
Roe St B2
Rowan Way A3
Ryle St C2
Ryle's Park Rd C1
St George's St C2
St Michael's ⛪ B2
Samuel St B2
Saville St C3
Shaw St B1
Slater St C1
Snow Hill C3
South Park C1
Spring Gdns A2
Statham St C2
Station St A2
Steeple St A3
Sunderland St B2
Superstore A1/A2/C2
Swettenham St B3
The Silk Rd A2/B2
Thistleton Cl C2
Thorp St B2
Town Hall B2
Townley St B2
Turnock St C3
Union Rd B3
Union St B2
Victoria Park B3
Vincent St C2
Waters Green B2
Waterside C2
West Bond St B1
West Park A1
West Park Museum 🏛 A1
Westbrook Dr A1
Westminster Rd A1
Whalley Hayes B1
Windmill St C3
Withyfold Dr A2
York St B3

Maidstone 340

Albion Pl B3
All Saints ⛪ B2
Allen St A3
Amphitheatre ✦ C2
Archbishop's Pal B2
Bank St B2
Barker Rd C2
Barton Rd C3
Beaconsfield Rd C1
Bedford Pl B1
Bentlif Art Gallery 🏛 B2
Bishops Way B2
Bluett St A3
Bower La C1
Bower Mount Rd B1
Bower Pl C1
Bower St B1
Bowling Alley B3
Boxley Rd A3
Brenchley Gardens A2
Brewer St A3
Broadway B2
Brunswick St C3
Buckland Hill A1
Buckland Rd B1
Bus Station B3
Campbell Rd C3
Carriage Museum 🏛 B2
Church Rd C1
Church St B3
Cinema C2
College Ave C2
College Rd C2
Collis Memorial Gdn C3
Cornwallis Rd B1
Corpus Christi Hall B2
County Hall A2
County Rd A3
Crompton Gdns C3
Crown & County Courts B2
Curzon Rd A3
Dixon Cl C2
Douglas Rd C1
Earl St B2
Eccleston Rd C2
Fairmeadow B2
Fisher St A2
Florence Rd C1
Foley St A3
Foster St C3
Fremlin Walk Sh Ctr B2
Gabriel's Hill B3
George St C3
Grecian St A3
Hardy St A3
Hart St C2
Hastings Rd C3
Hayle Rd C3
Hazlitt Theatre ♥ B2
Heathorn St A3
Hedley St A3
High St B2
HM Prison A3
Holland Rd A3
Hope St A2
Information Ctr ℹ B2
James St A3
James Whatman Way A2
Jeffrey St A3
Kent County Council Offices A2
King Edward Rd C2
King St B3
Kingsley Rd C3
Knightrider St B3
Launder Way C1
Lesley Pl A1
Library B2
Little Buckland Ave A1
Lockmeadow Leisure Complex C2
London Rd B1
Lower Boxley Rd A2
Lower Fant Rd C1
Magistrates Court B3
Maidstone Barracks Station ⇌ A1
Maidstone Borough Council Offices B1
Maidstone East Sta ⇌ A2
Maidstone Museum 🏛 B2
Maidstone West Sta ⇌ B2
Market C2
Market Buildings B2
Marsham St B3
Medway St B2
Medway Trading Est C2
Melville Rd C3
Mill St B2
Millennium Bridge C2
Mote Rd B3
Muir Rd C3
Old Tovil Rd C2
Palace Ave B3
Perryfield St A2
Police Station B3
Post Office PO A2/B2/B3/C3
Priory Rd C3
Prospect Pl C1
Pudding La B2
Queen Anne Rd B3
Queens Rd A1
Randall St A2
Rawdon Rd C3
Reginald Rd C1
Rock Pl B1
Rocky Hill B1
Romney Pl B3
Rose Yard B2
Rowland Cl C1
Royal Engineers' Rd A2
Royal Star Arcade B2
St Annes Ct B1
St Faith's St B2
St Luke's Rd A3
St Peter's Br B2
St Peter St B2
St Philip's Ave C3
Salisbury Rd A3
Sandling Rd A2
Scott St A2
Scrubs La B1
Sheal's Cres C3
Somerfield La B1
Somerfield Rd B1
Staceys St A2
Station Rd A2
Superstore A1/B2/B3
Terrace Rd B1
The Mall B3
The Somerfield Hospital H A1
Tonbridge Rd C1
Tovil Rd C2
Town Hall B2
Trinity Park B3
Tufton St B3
Union St B3
Upper Fant Rd C1
Upper Stone St C3
Victoria St B1
Visitor Ctr A1
Warwick Pl B1
Wat Tyler Way B3
Waterloo St C3
Waterlow Rd A3
Week St B2
Well Rd A3
Westree Rd C1
Wharf Rd C1
Whatman Park A1
Wheeler St A3
Whitchurch Cl B1
Woodville Rd C3
Wyatt St B3
Wyke Manor Rd B3

Manchester 337

Adair St B6
Addington St A5
Adelphi St A1
Air & Space Gallery 🏛 B2
Albert Sq B3
Albion St C3
AMC Great Northern B3
Ancoats Gr B6
Ancoats Gr North B6
Angela St C2
Aquatic Ctr C4
Ardwick Green Park C5
Ardwick Green North C5
Ardwick Green South C5
Arlington St A2
Artillery St B3
Arundel St C2
Atherton St B2
Atkinson St B3
Aytoun St B4
Back Piccadilly A4
Baird St B5
Balloon St A4
Bank Pl A1
Baring St B5
Barrack St C1
Barrow St A1
BBC TV Studios C4
Bendix St A5
Bengal St A5
Berry St C5
Blackfriars Rd A3
Blackfriars St A3
Blantyre St C2
Bloom St B4
Blossom St A5
Boad St B5
Bombay St B4
Booth St A3
Booth St B4
Bootle St B3
Brazennose St B3
Brewer St A5
Bridge St A3
Bridgewater Hall B3
Bridgewater Pl A4
Bridgewater St B2
Brook St C4
Brotherton Dr A2
Brown St A3
Brown St B4
Brunswick St C6
Brydon Ave C6
Buddhist Ctr A4
Bury St A2
Bus & Coach Station B4
Bus Station B4
Butler St A6
Buxton St C5
Byrom St B3
Cable St A5
Calder St B1
Cambridge St C3/C4
Camp St B3
Canal St B4
Cannon St A1
Cannon St A4
Cardroom Rd A6
Carruthers St A6
Castle St C2
Cateaton St A3
Cathedral ✝ A3
Cathedral St A3
Cavendish St C4
Chapel St A1/A3
Chapeltown St B5
Charles St C4
Charlotte St B4
Chatham St B4
Cheapside A3
Chepstow St B3
Chester Rd C1/C2
Chester St C4
Chetham's (Dept Store) A3
China La B5
Chippenham Rd A6
Chorlton Rd C2
Chorlton St B4
Church St A2
Church St A4
City Park A4
City Rd C3
Civil Justice Ctr B2
Cleminson St A2
Clowes St A3
College Land A3
Coll of Adult Ed C4
Collier St B2
Commercial St C3
Conference Ctr C4
Cooper St B4
Copperas St A4
Cornbrook 🚊 C1
Cornell St A5
Cornerhouse C4
Corporation St A4
Cotter St C6
Cotton St A5
Cow La B1
Cross St B3
Crown Court B4
Crown St C2
Cube Gallery 🏛 B4
Dalberg St C6
Dale St A4/B5
Dancehouse, The ♥ C4
Dantzic St A4
Dark La C6
Dawson St C2
Dean St A5
Deansgate A3/B3
Deansgate Station ⇌ C3
Dolphin St C6
Downing St C5
Ducie St B5
Duke Pl B2
Duke St B2
Durling St C6
East Ordsall La A2/B1
Edge St A4
Egerton St C2
Ellesmere St C1
Everard St C1
Every St B6
Fairfield St B5
Faulkner St B4
Fennel St A3
Ford St A2
Ford St C6
Fountain St B4
Frederick St A2
Gartside St B2
Gaythorne St A1
George Leigh St A5
George St A1
George St B4
G-Mex 🚊 C3
Goadsby St A4
Gore St A2
Goulden St A5
Granada TV Ctr B2
Granby Row B4
Gravel St A3
Great Ancoats St A5
Great Bridgewater St B3
Great George St A1
Great Jackson St C2
Great Marlborough St C4
Greengate A3
Green Room, The ♥ C4
Grosvenor St C5
Gun St A5
Hadrian Ave B6
Hall St B3
Hampson St B1
Hanover St A4
Hanworth Cl C5
Hardman St B3
Harkness St C6
Harrison St B6
Hart St B4
Helmet St B6
Henry St A5
Heyrod St B6
High St A4
Higher Ardwick C6
Hilton St A4/A5
Holland St A6
Hood St A5
Hope St B1
Hope St B4
Houldsworth St A5
Hoyle St C6
Hulme Hall Rd C1
Hulme St A1
Hulme St C3
Hyde Rd C6
Information Ctr ℹ B3
Irwell St A2
Islington St A2
Jackson Cr C2
Jackson's Row B3
James St A1
Jenner Cl C2
Jersey St A5
John Dalton St A1
John Dalton St B3
John Ryland's Library 🏛 B3
John St A2
Kennedy St B3
Kincardine Rd C5
King St A3
King St West A3
Law Courts B3
Laystall St B5
Lever St A5
Library B3
Linby St C2
Little Lever St A4
Liverpool Rd B2
Liverpool St B1
Lloyd St B3
Lockton Cl C5
London Rd B5
Long Millgate A3
Longacre St B6
Loom St A5
Lower Byrom St B2
Lower Mosley St B3
Lower Moss La C2
Lower Ormond St C4
Loxford La C4
Luna St A5
Major St B4
Manchester Arndale A4
Manchester Art Gallery 🏛 B4
Manchester Central Convension Complex B3
Manchester Metropolitan University B4/C4
Manchester Piccadilly Station ⇌ B5
Manchester Technology Ctr C4
Mancunian Way C3
Manor St C5
Marble St A4
Market St A2
Market St A4
Market St 🚊 A4
Marsden St A3
Marshall St A5
Mayan Ave A2
Medlock St C3
Middlewood St B1
Miller St A4
Minshull St B4
Mosley St A4
Mosley St 🚊 B4
Mount St B3
Mulberry St B3
Murray St A5
Museum of Science & Industry (MOSI) 🏛 B2
Nathan Dr A2
Naval St A5
New Bailey St A2
New Elm Rd B2
New Islington A6
New Quay St B2
New Union St A6
Newgate St A4
Newton St A5
Nicholas St B4
North Western St C6
Oak St A4
Odeon A4
Old Mill St A6
Oldfield Rd A1/C1
Oldham Rd A5
Oldham St A4
Opera House ♥ B3
Ordsall La C1
Oxford Rd C4
Oxford Rd ⇌ C4
Oxford St B4
Paddock St C6
Palace Theatre ♥ B4
Pall Mall A3
Palmerston St B6
Park St A1
Parker St B4
Peak St B5
Penfield Cl C5
Peoples' History Museum 🏛 B2
Peru St A1
Peter St B3
Piccadilly A4
Piccadilly 🚊 B5
Piccadilly Gdns 🚊 B4
Piercy St A6
Poland St A5
Police Museum 🏛 A5
Police Station B3/B5
Pollard St B6
Port St A5
Portland St B4
Portugal St East B5
Post Office PO A1/A4/A5/B3
Potato Wharf B2
Princess St B3/C4
Pritchard St C4
Quay St A2
Quay St B2
Queen St B3
Radium St A5
Redhill St A5
Regent Rd B1
Renold Theatre ♥ A2
Retail Park A5
Rice St B2
Richmond St B4
River St C3
Roby St B5
Rodney St A6
Roman Fort B2
Rosamond St A2
Royal Exchange ♥ A3
Sackville St B4
St Andrew's St B6
St Ann St A3
St Ann's ⛪ A3
St George's Ave C1
St James St B4
St John St B3
St John's Cath (RC) ✝ A2
St Mary's ⛪ B3
St Mary's Gate A3
St Mary's Parsonage A3
St Peter's Sq 🚊 B3
St Stephen St A2
Salford Approach A3
Salford Central ⇌ A2
Sheffield St B5
Shepley St B5
Sherratt St A5
Shudehill A4
Shudehill 🚊 A4
Sidney St C4
Silk St A5
Silver St B4
Skerry Cl C5
Snell St B6
South King St B3
Sparkle St B5
Spear St A4
Spring Gdns A4
Stanley St A2/B2
Station Approach B5
Store St B5
Swan St A4
Tariff St B5
Tatton St C1
Temperance St B6/C6
The Triangle A4
Thirsk St C6
Thomas St A4
Thompson St A5
Tib La B3
Tib St A4
Town Hall (Manchester) B3
Town Hall (Salford) A2
Trafford St C3
Travis St B5
Trinity Way A2
Turner St A4
Union St C6

University of Manchester (Sackville Street Campus) C5
Upper Brook St C5
Upper Cleminson St A1
Upper Wharf St A1
Urbis Museum A4
Vesta St B6
Victoria A4
Victoria Station A4
Victoria St A3
Wadesdon Rd C5
Water St B2
Watson St B3
West Fleet St B1
West King St A2
West Mosley St B4
West Union St B1
Weybridge Rd A6
Whitworth St B4
Whitworth St West C3
Wilburn St B1
William St A2
William St C6
Wilmott St C3
Windmill St B3
Windsor Cr A1
Withy Gr A4
Woden St C1
Wood St B3
Woodward St A6
Worrall St C1
Worsley St C2
York St B4
York St C2
York St C4

Merthyr Tydfil
Merthyr Tudful 340

Aberdare Rd B2
Abermorlais Terr B2
Alexandra Rd A3
Alma St C3
Arfryn Pl C3
Argyle St C3
Avenue De Clichy C2
Bethesda St B2
Bishops Gr A3
Brecon Rd A1/B2
Briarmead A3
Bryn St C3
Bryntirion Rd B3/C3
Bus Station B2
Caedraw Rd C2
Cae Mari Dwn B3
Castle Sq A1
Castle St B2
Chapel C2
Chapel Bank B1
Church St B3
Civic Ctr B2
Coedcae'r Ct C3
Court B3
Courts B2
Court St C3
Cromwell St B2
Cyfarthfa Castle School and Museum A1
Cyfarthfa Ind Est A1
Cyfarthfa Park A1
Cyfarthfa Rd A1
Dane St A2
Dane Terr A2
Danyparc B3
Darren View A3
Dixon St B2
Dyke St C3
Dynevor St B2
Elwyn Dr C3
Fire Station B2
Fothergill St B3
Galonuchaf Rd A3
Garth St B2
Georgetown B2
Grawen Terr A2
Grove Pk A2
Gurnos Rd A2
Gwaelodygarth Rd A2/A3
Gwaunfarren Gr A3
Gwaunfarren Rd A3
Gwendoline St A3
Hampton St C3
Hanover St A2
Heol S O Davies B1
Heol-Gerrig B1
Highland View C3
High St A3/B2/B3/C2
Howell Cl B1
Information Ctr B2
Jackson's Bridge B2
James St C3
John St B3
Joseph Parry's Cott B2
Lancaster St A2
Library B2
Llewellyn St A2
Llwyfen St B2
Llwyn Berry B1
Llwyn Dic Penderyn B1
Llwyn-y-Gelynen C1
Lower Thomas St B3
Market C2
Mary St C3
Masonic St C2
Merthyr RFC C2
Merthyr College B2
Merthyr Town FC B3
Merthyr Tydfil Leisure Village C3
Merthyr Tydfil Sta C3
Meyrick Villas A2
Miniature Railway A1
Mount St A2
Nantygwenith St B1
Norman Terr B2
Oak Rd A2
Old Cemetery B3
Pandy Cl A1
Pantycelynen B1
Park Terr B2
Penlan View C2
Penry St B2
Pentwyn Villas A2
Penyard Rd B3
Penydarren Park A3
Penydarren Rd B3
Plymouth St C3
Police Station C2
Pont Marlais West B2
Post Office A3/B2/C3
Quarry Row B2
Queen's Rd B3
Rees St C3
Rhydycar Link C2
Riverside Park A1
St David's B3
St Tydfil's C2
St Tydfil's Ave C3
St Tydfil's Hospital (No A+E) B3
St Tydfil's Sq Sh Ctr C2
Saxon St A2
School of Nursing A2
Seward St A3
Shiloh La B3
Stone Circles B3
Stuart St A2
Summerhill Pl B3
Superstore B3
Swan St C2
Swansea Rd B1
Taff Glen View C3
Taff Vale Ct B3
Theatre Soar B2
The Grove A2
The Parade B3
The Walk B2
Thomastown Park B3
Tramroad La A3
Tramroad Side B2
Tramroad Side North B3
Tramroad Side South C3
Trevithick Gdns C3
Trevithick St A3
Tudor Terr B2
Twynyrodyn Rd C3
Union St B3
Upper Colliers Row B1
Upper Thomas St B3
Victoria St B2
Vue C3
Vulcan Rd B2
Warlow St C3
Well St A2
Welsh Assembly Government Offices C2
Wern La C1
West Gr A2
William St C3
Yew St C3
Ynysfach Engine Ho C2
Ynysfach Rd C2

Middlesbrough 340

Abingdon Rd C3
Acklam Rd C1
Albert Park C2
Albert Rd B2
Albert Terr C2
Aubrey St C3
Ayresome Gdns C2
Ayresome Green La C1
Ayresome St C2
Barton Rd A1
Bilsdale Rd C3
Bishopton Rd C3
Borough Rd B2/B3
Bowes Rd A2
Breckon Hill Rd B3
Bridge St East B3
Bridge St West B2
Brighouse Rd A1
Burlam Rd C1
Bus Station B2
Cannon Park B1
Cannon Park Way B2
Cannon St B1
Captain Cook Sq B2
Carlow St C1
Castle Way C3
Chipchase Rd C2
Cineworld B3
Clairville Sports Stadium C3
Cleveland Ctr B2
Clive Rd C2
Commercial St A2
Corporation Rd B2
Costa St C2
Council Offices B3
Crescent Rd C2
Cumberland Rd C2
Depot Rd A2
Derwent St B2
Devonshire Rd C2
Diamond Rd B2
Disabled Driver Test Circuit B1
Dorman Museum C2
Douglas St B3
Eastbourne Rd C2
Eden Rd C3
Enterprise Ctr A2
Forty Foot Rd A2
Gilkes St B2
Gosford St A2
Grange Rd B2
Gresham Rd B2
Harehills Rd C1
Harford St C2
Hartington Rd B2
Haverton Hill Rd A1
Hey Wood St B1
Highfield Rd C3
Hill St Ctr B2
Holwick Rd B1
Hutton Rd C3
ICI Works A1
Information Ctr B2
Lambton Rd C3
Lancaster Rd C2
Lansdowne Rd C3
Latham Rd C2
Law Courts B2/B3
Lees Rd B2
Leeway B3
Linthorpe Cemetery C1
Linthorpe Rd B2
Lloyd St B2
Longford St C2
Longlands Rd C3
Lower East St A3
Lower Lake C3
Maldon Rd C1
Manor St B2
Marsh St B2
Marton Rd B3
Middlehaven B3
Middlesbrough By-Pass B2/C1
Middlesbrough Coll B3
Middlesbrough L Park B3
Middlesbrough Sta B2
Middlesbrough Theatre C2
Middletown Park C2
MIMA B3
Mosque B2
Mosque C3
Mulgrave Rd C2
North Ormesby Rd B3
Newport Bridge B1
Newport Bridge Approach Rd B1
Newport Rd B2
North Rd B2
Northern Rd C1
Outram St B2
Oxford Rd C2
Park La C2
Park Rd North C2
Park Rd South C2
Park Vale Rd C3
Parliament Rd B1
Police Station A2
Port Clarence Rd A3
Portman St B2
Post Office B2/B3/C1/C2/C3
Princes Rd B2
Python A2
Riverside Bsns Park A2
Riverside Park Rd A1
Riverside Stadium (Middlesbrough FC) B3
Rockliffe Rd C2
Romaldkirk Rd B1
Roman Rd C2
Roseberry Rd C3
St Barnabas' Rd C2
St Paul's Rd B2
Saltwells Rd B3
Scott's Rd A3
Seaton Carew Rd A3
Shepherdson Way B3
Sikh Temple B2
Snowdon Rd A2
South West Ironmasters Park B1
Southfield Rd B2
Southwell Rd C2
Springfield Rd C1
Startforth Rd A2
Stockton Rd C1
Stockton St A2
Surrey St C2
Synagogue C2
Tax Offices B3
Tees Viaduct C1
Teessaurus Park A2
Teesside Tertiary Coll C3
Temenos B3
The Avenue C2
The Crescent C2
Thornfield Rd C1
Town Hall B2
Transporter Bridge (Toll) A3
Union St B2
University of Teesside B2
Upper Lake C2
Valley Rd C3
Ventnor Rd C2
Victoria Rd B2
Visitor Ctr A3
Vulcan St A2
Warwick St C2
Wellesley Rd B3
West Lane Hospital C1
Westminster Rd C2
Wilson St B2
Windward Way B3
Woodlands Rd B2
York Rd C3

Milton Keynes 340

Abbey Way A1
Arbrook Ave B1
Armourer Dr A3
Arncliffe Dr A1
Avebury C2
Avebury Blvd C2
Bankfield B3
Bayard Ave A2
Belvedere A2
Bishopstone A1
Blundells Rd A1
Boycott Ave C2
Bradwell Comm Blvd B1
Bradwell Rd C1
Bramble Ave A2
Brearley Ave C2
Breckland A1
Brill Place B1
Burnham Dr B1
Bus Station C1
Campbell Park B3
Castle Ave A3
Central Milton Keynes Shopping Area B2
Century Ave C2
Chaffron Way C3
Childs Way C1
Christ the Cornerstone B2
Cineworld B2
Civic Offices B2
Cleavers Ave B2
Colesbourne Dr A3
Conniburrow Blvd B2
County Court B2
Currier Dr A2
Dansteed Way A2/A3/B1
Deltic Ave B1
Downs Barn A2
Downs Barn Blvd A3
Eaglestone C3
Eelbrook Ave B1
Elder Gate B1
Evans Gate C2
Fairford Cr A3
Falcon Ave B3
Fennel Dr A2
Fishermead Blvd C3
Food Ctr B3
Fulwoods Dr C3
Glazier Dr A2
Glovers La A1
Grafton Gate C1
Grafton St A1/C2
Gurnards Ave B3
Harrier Dr C3
Ibstone Ave B1
Langcliffe Dr A1
Leisure Plaza C1
Leys Rd C1
Library B2
Linford Wood A2
Marlborough Gate B3
Marlborough St A2/B3
Mercers Dr A1
Midsummer C2
Midsummer Blvd B2
Milton Keynes Central C1
Monks Way A1
Mullen Ave A3
Mullion Pl C3
National Hockey Stadium B1
Neath Hill A3
North Elder C1
North Grafton B1
North Overgate A3
North Row B2
North Saxon B2
North Secklow B2
North Skeldon A3
North Witan B1
Oakley Gdns A3
Oldbrook Blvd C2
Open-Air Theatre B3
Overgate A3
Overstreet A3
Patriot Dr B1
Pencarrow Pl B3
Penryn Ave B3
Perran Ave C3
Pitcher La C1
Place Retail Park, The C1
Point Ctr, The B2
Police Station B2
Portway B2
Post Office A2/B2/C3
Precedent Dr B1
Quinton Dr B1
Ramsons Ave B2
Rockingham Dr A2
Rooksley B1
Rooksley Retail Park C1
Saxon Gate B2
Saxon St A1/C3
Secklow Gate B2
Shackleton Pl C2
Silbury Blvd B2
Skeldon A3
South Grafton C2
South Row C2
South Saxon C2
South Secklow B3
South Witan C2
Springfield B3
Stanton Wood A1
Stantonbury A1
Stantonbury L Ctr A1
Strudwick Dr C2
Sunrise Parkway A2
Telephone Exchange C3
The Boundary C3
Theatre & Art Gallery B3
Tolcarne Ave C3
Towan Ave C3
Trueman Pl C2
Vauxhall A1
Winterhill Retail Park C2
Witan Gate B2
X-Scape B3

Newcastle upon Tyne 340

Albert St B3
Argyle St B3
Back New Bridge St B3
BALTIC Ctr for Contemporary Art C3
Barker St A3
Barrack Rd B1
Bath La B1
Bell's Court B2
Bessie Surtees Ho C2
Bigg Market C2
Biscuit Factory B3
Black Gate C2
Blackett St B2
Blandford Sq C1
Boating Lake A1
Boyd St B3
Brandling Park A2
Bus Station B2
Buxton St B3
Byron St A3
Camden St B2
Castle Keep C2
Central C1
Central Library B2
Central Motorway B2
Chester St A3
City Hall B2
City Rd B3/C3
City Walls C1
Civic Ctr A2
Claremont Rd A1
Clarence St B3
Clarence Walk B3
Clayton St C1/B1
Clayton St West C1
Coach Station C1
College St B2
Collingwood St C2
Copland Terr B3
Coppice Way B3
Corporation St B1
Courts C3
Crawhall Rd B3
Dean St C2
Discovery C1
Dinsdale Pl A3
Dinsdale Rd A3
Doncaster Rd A3
Durant Rd B2
Eldon Sq B1
Eldon Sq Shopping Ctr B3
Ellison Pl B2
Empire B1
Eskdale Terr A2
Eslington Terr A2
Exhibition Park A1
Falconar St B3
Fenkle St C1
Forth Banks C1
Forth St C1
Gallowgate B1
Gateshead Heritage @ St Mary's C3
Gateshead Millennium Bridge C3
Gibson St B3
Goldspink La A3
Grainger Market B2
Grainger St B2
Grantham Rd A3
Granville Rd A3
Great North Mus:Hancock A2
Grey St B2
Groat Market C2
Guildhall C2
Hancock St A2
Hanover St C2
Hatton Gallery A1
Hawks Rd C3
Haymarket B2
Heber St B1
Helmsley Rd A3
High Bridge B2
High Level Bridge C2
Hillgate C3
Howard St B3
Hutton Terr A3
Information Ctr C3
Jesmond A2
Jesmond Rd A2/A3
John Dobson St B2
John George Joicey Museum C2
Jubilee Rd B3
Kelvin Gr A3
Kensington Terr A2
Laing Gallery B2
Lambton Rd A2
Leazes Cr B1
Leazes La B1
Leazes Park B1
Leazes Park Rd B1
Leazes Terr B1
Live C2
Low Friar St C1
Manor Chare C2
Manors B2
Manors Station B2
Market St B2
Melbourne St B2
Mill Rd C3
Mill Volvo Tyne C1
Monument B2
Monument Mall Sh Ctr B2
Morpeth St A2
Mosley St C2
Napier St A3
Nazareth House A3
New Bridge St B2/B3
Newcastle Central Station C1
Newcastle University A1
Newgate Shopping Ctr C1
Newgate St B1
Newington Rd A3
Northern Stage Theatre A2
Northumberland Rd B2
Northumberland St B2
Northumbria Univ A2
Northwest Radial Rd A1
O2 Academy C1
Oakwellgate C3
Orchard St C2
Osborne Rd A2
Osborne Terr A3
Pandon C3
Pandon Bank B3
Park Terr A1
Percy St B1
Pilgrim St B2
Pipewellgate C2
Pitt St B1
Plummer Tower A2
Police Station B1
Portland Rd A3/B3
Portland Terr A3
Post Office A3/B1/B2/B3
Pottery La C1
Prudhoe Pl B1
Prudhoe St B1
Quayside C2
Queen Elizabeth II Bridge C2
Queen Victoria Rd A1
Richardson Rd A1
Ridley Pl B2
Rock Terr B3
Rosedale Terr A3
Royal Victoria Infirmary A1
Sage Gateshead, The C3
St Andrew's St B1
St James B1
St James' Blvd C1
Sports Direct Arena (St James' Park) (Newcastle Utd FC) B1
St Mary's (RC) C1
St Mary's Place B2
St Nicholas C2
St Nicholas St C2
St Thomas' St B1
Sandyford Rd A2/A3
Science Park B2
Shield St B3
Shieldfield B3
Simpson Terr B3
South Shore Rd C3
South St C1
Starbeck Ave A3
Stepney Rd B3
Stoddart St B3
Stowell St B1
Strawberry Pl B1
Swing Bridge C2
Temple St C1
Terrace Pl B1
The Close C2
The Gate B1
The Side C2
Theatre Royal B2
Times Sq C1
Tower St B3
Trinity House C2
Tyne Bridge C2
Tyne Bridges C2
Tyneside B2
Victoria Sq A2
Warwick St A3
Waterloo St C1
Wellington St B1
Westgate Rd C1/C2
Windsor Terr A2
Worswick St B2
Wretham Pl B3

Newport
Casnewydd 340

Albert Terr B1
Allt-yr-Yn Ave A1
Alma St C2
Ambulance Station C3
Bailey St B2
Barrack Hill A2
Bath St A3
Bedford Rd B3
Belle Vue La C1
Belle Vue Park C1
Bishop St A3
Blewitt St B1
Bolt Cl C3
Bolt St C3
Bond St A2
Bosworth Dr A1
Bridge St B1
Bristol St A3
Bryngwyn Rd B1
Brynhyfryd Ave C1
Brynhyfryd Rd C1
Bus Station B2
Caerau Cres C1
Caerau Rd B1
Caerleon Rd A3
Capel Cres C2
Cardiff Rd C2
Caroline St B3
Castle (Remains) A2
Cedar Rd B3
Charles St B2
Charlotte Dr C2
Chepstow Rd A3
Church Rd A3
City Cinema B1
Civic Ctr B1
Clarence Pl A2
Clifton Pl B1
Clifton Rd C1
Clyffard Cres B1
Clytha Park Rd B1
Clytha Sq C2
Coldra Rd C1
Collier St A3
Colne St B3
Comfrey Cl A1
Commercial Rd C3
Commercial St B2
Corelli St A3
Corn St B2
Corporation Rd B3
Coulson Cl C2
County Court A2
Courts A1
Courts B1
Crawford St A3
Cyril St B3
Dean St A3
Devon Pl B1
Dewsland Park Rd C2
Dolman B2
Dolphin St C3
East Dock Rd C3
East St B1
East Usk Rd A3
Ebbw Vale Wharf B3
Emlyn St B2
Enterprise Way C3
Eton Rd B3
Evans St A2
Factory Rd A2
Fields Rd B1
Francis Dr C2
Frederick St C3
Friars Rd C1
Gaer La C1
George St C3
George Street Bridge C3
Godfrey Rd B1
Gold Tops B1
Gore St A3
Gorsedd Circle C1
Grafton Rd A3
Graham St B1
Granville St C3
Harlequin Dr A1
Harrow Rd B3
Herbert Rd A3
Herbert Walk C2
Hereford St A3
High St B2
Hill St B2
Hoskins St A2
Information Ctr B2
Ivor Sq B2
John Frost Sq B2
Jones St B1
Junction Rd A3
Keynshaw Ave C2
King St C2
Kingsway B2
Kingsway Ctr B2
Ledbury Dr A2
Library A3
Library, Museum & Art Gallery B2
Liverpool Wharf B3
Llanthewy Rd B1
Llanvair Rd A3
Locke St A2
Lower Dock St C3
Lucas St A2
Manchester St A3
Market B2
Marlborough Rd B3
Mellon St C3
Mill St A2
Morgan St A3
Mountjoy Rd C2
Newport Bridge A2
Newport Ctr B2
Newport RFC B3
Newport Station B2
North St B2
Oakfield Rd B1
Park Sq C2
Police Station A3/C2
Post Office B1/B2/C1/C3
Power St A1
Prince St A3
Pugsley St A2
Queen St C2
Queen's Cl A1
Queen's Hill A1
Queen's Hill Cres A1
Queensway B2
Railway St B2
Riverfront Arts Ctr B2
Riverside A3
Rodney Rd B2
Royal Gwent (A+E) C2
Rudry St A3
Rugby Rd B3
Ruperra La C3
Ruperra St C3
St Edmund St B1
St Mark's Cres A1
St Mary St B1
St Vincent Rd A3
St Woolos C2
St Woolos General (no A+E) C1
St Woolos Rd B1
School La B2
Serpentine Rd B1
Shaftesbury Park A2
Sheaf La A3
Skinner St B2
Sorrel Dr A1
South Market St C3
Spencer Rd B1
Stow Hill B2/C1/C2
Stow Park Ave C1
Stow Park Dr C1
TA Ctr A1
Talbot St B2
Tennis Club A1
Tregare St A3
Trostrey St A3
Tunnel Terr B1
Turner St A3
Upper Dock St B2
Usk St A3
Usk Way B3/C3
Victoria Cr B1
War Memorial A3
Waterloo Rd C1
West St B1
Wharves B2
Wheeler St A2
Whitby Pl A3
Windsor Terr B1
York Pl C1

Newquay 340

Agar Rd B2
Alma Pl B1
Ambulance Station B2
Anthony Rd C1
Atlantic Hotel A1
Bank St B1
Barrowfields A3
Bay View Terr B2
Beachfield Ave B1
Beach Rd B1
Beacon Rd A1
Belmont Pl A1
Berry Rd B2
Blue Reef Aquarium B1
Boating Lake C2
Bus Station B1
Chapel Hill B1
Chester Rd A3
Cheviot Rd C1/C2
Chichester Cres C2
Chynance Dr C1
Chyverton Cl C1
Cliff Rd B2
Coach Park B2
Colvreath Rd A3
Council Offices B1
Crantock St B1
Criggar Rocks A3
Dale Cl C3
Dale Rd C3
Dane Rd A1
East St B2
Edgcumbe Ave B3
Edgcumbe Gdns B3
Eliot Gdns B3
Elm Cl C3
Ennor's Rd B1
Fernhill Rd B1
Fire Station B1
Fore St B1
Gannel Rd C2
Golf Driving Range B3
Gover La B1
Great Western Beach A2
Grosvenor Ave B2
Harbour A1
Hawkins Rd C2
Headleigh Rd B2
Hilgrove Rd A3/B3
Holywell Rd B3
Hope Terr B1
Huer's House, The A1
Information Ctr B1
Island Cres B2
Jubilee St B1
Kew Cl C3
Killacourt Cove A2
King Edward Cres A1
Lanhenvor Ave B2
Library B1
Lifeboat Station A1
Linden Ave C2
Listry Rd C2
Lusty Glaze Beach A3
Lusty Glaze Rd A3
Manor Rd B1
Marcus Hill B2
Mayfield Rd B2
Meadowside C3
Mellanvrane La C2
Michell Ave B2
Miniature Golf Course C3
Miniature Railway B3
Mount Wise B1
Mowhay Cl C3
Narrowcliff A3
Newquay B2
Newquay Hospital (no A&E) B2
Newquay Town Football Ground B1
Newquay Zoo B3
North Pier A1
North Quay Hill A1
Oakleigh Terr B2
Pargolla Rd B2
Pendragon Cres C3
Pengannel Cl C1
Penina Ave C3
Police Sta & Courts B2
Post Office B1/B2
Quarry Park Rd B3
Rawley La C2
Reeds Way B1
Robartes Rd B2
St Anne's Rd A3
St Aubyn Cres B3
St George's Rd B1
St John's Rd B1
St Mary's Rd B1
St Michael's B1
St Michael's Rd B1
St Thomas' Rd B2
Seymour Ave B2
South Pier A1
South Quay Hill A1
Sweet Briar Cres C3
Sydney Rd A1
The Crescent B1
Tolcarne Beach A2
Tolcarne Point A2
Tolcarne Rd B2
Tor Rd B2
Towan Beach A1
Towan Blystra Rd B3
Tower Rd A1
Trebarwith Cres B2
Tredour Rd C2
Treforda Rd C3
Tregoss Rd B3
Tregunnel Hill B1/C1
Tregunnel Saltings C1
Trelawney Rd B2
Treloggan La C3
Treloggan Rd C3
Trembath Cres C1
Trenance Ave B2
Trenance Gardens B2
Trenance La C2
Trenance Leisure Park B3
Trenance Rd B2
Trenarth Rd B2
Treninnick Hill C3
Tretherras Rd B3
Trethewey Way C1
Trevemper Rd C2
Tunnels Through Time B1
Ulalia Rd B3
Vivian Cl B2
Waterworld B3
Whitegate Rd B3
Wych Hazel Way C3

Newtown
Y Drenewydd 340

Ash Cl C3
Back La B2
Baptist Chapel B2
Barn La A2
Bear Lanes Sh Ctr B2
Beech Cl A2
Beechwood Dr A2
Brimmon Cl C2
Brimmon Rd C2
Broad St B2
Bryn Bank A1
Bryn Cl A2
Bryn Gdns A1
Bryn House A1
Bryn La A1/A2
Bryn Meadows A2
Bryn St A2
Brynglais Ave A2
Brynglais Cl A2
Bus Station B2
Byrnwood Dr A1
Cambrian Bridge B3
Cambrian Gdns B2
Cambrian Way B2
Canal Rd A3
Castle Mound B2
Cedewain C1
Cefnaire C2
Cefnaire Coppice C2
Ceiriog C2
Cemetery A3
Church (Remains of) B2
Churchill Dr A3
Cledan B2
Colwyn B3
Commercial St A2
Council Offices B1
Crescent St A1
Cwm Llanfair A2
Davies Memorial Gallery B2
Dinas B2
Dolafon Rd B3
Dolerw Park B1
Dolfor Rd C1
Eirianell C1
Fairfield Dr A2
Ffordd Croesawdy B2
Fire Station C1
Frankwell St A2
Frolic St B2
Fron La A1
Garden La A2
Gas St B2
Glyndŵr C1
Golwgydre La B2
Gorsedd Circle B1
Great Brimmon Farm C3
Hafren C1
Halfpenny Bridge B2
High St B2
Hillside Ave A3
Hoel Treowen C2
Information Ctr B2
Kerry Rd B3
Ladywell Shopping Ctr B2
Library B1
Llanfair Rd A2
Llanidloes Rd C1
Llys Ifor A2
Lon Cerddyn B1
Lonesome La A3
Long Bridge A2
Lon Helyg C1
Lower Canal Rd B3
Maldwyn Leisure Ctr C1
Market B2
Market St B2
Milford Rd B1
Mill Cl B2
Miniature Railway B1
Mwyn Fynydd A3
New Church St B2
New Rd B2
Newtown Football Gd B1
Newtown Infirmary A2
Newtown Station B2
Oak Tree Ave A3
Old Kerry Rd B2
Oldbarn La A2
Park Cl B1
Parklands B1
Park La B1
Park St B2
Pavillion Ct C1
Plantation La C1
Police Station B1
Pont Brynfedw A2
Pool Rd B3
Poplar Rd A3
Post Office B2/C1
Powys C1
Powys Theatre A2
Pryce Jones Stores & Museum B2
Quaker Meeting Ho B1
Regent B2
Robert Owen House B1
Robert Owen Mus B2
Rugby Club A3
St David's B2
School La A2
Sheaf St B3
Short Bridge St B2

Stone St B2
Sycamore Dr A2
Textile Museum A2
The Bryn A1
The Park B1
Town Hall B2
Union St A2
Upper Brimmon C3
Vastre Industrial Est B3
War Memorial B2
WHSmith Museum B2
Wynfields C1
Y Ffrydd A3

Northampton 340

78 Derngate B3
Abington Sq B3
Abington St B3
Alcombe St A3
All Saints' B2
Ambush St B1
Angel St B2
Arundel St A2
Ash St A2
Auctioneers Way C2
Bailiff St A2
Barrack Rd A2
Beaconsfield Terr A3
Becketts Park C3
Bedford Rd B3
Billing Rd B3
Brecon St A1
Brewery C2
Bridge St C2
Bridge St Depot C3
Broad St B2
Burns St A3
Bus Station B2
Campbell St A2
Castle (Site of) B2
Castle St B2
Cattle Market Rd C2
Central Museum & Art Gallery B2
Charles St A3
Cheyne Walk B3
Church La A2
Clare St A3
Cloutsham St A3
College St B2
Colwyn Rd A3
Cotton End C2
Countess Rd A1
County Hall B2
Court A2
Craven St A3
Crown & County Courts B3
Denmark Rd B3
Derngate B3
Derngate & Royal Theatres B3
Doddridge Church B2
Duke St A3
Dunster St A3
Earl St A3
Euston Rd C2
Fire Station A3
Foot Meadow B2
Gladstone Rd A1
Gold St B2
Grafton St A2
Gray St A3
Green St B1
Greenwood Rd B1
Greyfriars B2
Grosvenor Ctr B2
Grove Rd A3
Guildhall B2
Hampton St A2
Harding Terr A2
Hazelwood Rd B3
Herbert St B2
Hervey St A3
Hester St A2
Holy Sepulchre A2
Hood St A3
Horse Market B2
Hunter St A3
Information Ctr B1
Kettering Rd A3
Kingswell St B2
Lady's La B2
Leicester St A2
Leslie Rd A2
Library B3
Lorne Rd A2
Lorry Park A1
Louise Rd A2
Lower Harding St A2
Lower Hester St A2
Lower Mounts B3
Lower Priory St A2
Main Rd C1
Marefair B2
Market Sq B2
Marlboro Rd B1
Marriott St A2
Military Rd A3
Nene Valley Retail Pk C1
New South Bridge Rd C2
Northampton General Hospital (A&E) B3
Northampton Sta B1
Northcote St A2
Nunn Mills Rd C3
Old Towcester Rd C2
Overstone Rd A3
Peacock Pl B2
Pembroke Rd A1
Penn Court C2
Police Station B3
Post Office A1/A2/B3/C2
Quorn Way A2
Ransome Rd C3
Regent Sq A2
Robert St A2
St Andrew's Rd B1
St Andrew's St A2
St Edmund's Rd B3
St George's St A2
St Giles B3
St Giles St B3
St Giles' Terr B3
St James' Mill Rd B1
St James' Mill Rd East C1
St James Park Rd B1
St James Retail Park C1
St James Rd B1
St Leonard's Rd C2
St Mary's St B2
St Michael's Rd A3
St Peter's B2
St Peter's Sq Sh Prec B2
St Peter's Way B2
Salisbury St A2
Scarletwell St B2
Semilong Rd A2
Sheep St B2
Sol Central (L Ctr) B2
Somerset St A3
South Bridge C2
Southfield Ave C2
Spencer Bridge Rd A1
Spencer Rd A3
Spring Gdns B3
Spring La B2
Swan St B3
TA Ctr A3
Tanner St B2
The Drapery B2
The Ridings B3
Tintern Ave A1
Towcester Rd C2
Upper Bath St B2
Upper Mounts A2
Victoria Park A1
Victoria Promenade B2
Victoria Rd B3
Victoria St A2
Wellingborough Rd B3
West Bridge B1
York Rd B3

Norwich 341

Albion Way C3
All Saints Green C2
Anchor Cl A3
Anchor St A3
Anglia Sq A2
Argyle St C3
Arts Ctr B1
Ashby St C2
Assembly House B1
Bank Plain B2
Barker St A1
Barn Rd A1
Barrack St A3
Ber St C2
Bethel St B1
Bishop Bridge A3
Bishopbridge Rd A3
Bishopgate A3
Blackfriars St A2
Botolph St A2
Bracondale C3
Brazen Gate C2
Bridewell B2
Brunswick Rd C1
Bull Close Rd A2
Bus Station C2
Calvert St A2
Cannell Green A3
Carrow Rd C3
Castle Mall B2
Castle Meadow B2
Castle & Museum B2
Cathedral B2
Cattlemarket St B2
Chantry Rd C1
Chapel Loke C2
Chapelfield East B1
Chapelfield Gdns B1
Chapelfield North B1
Chapelfield Rd B1
Chapelfield Sh Ctr C1
City Hall B1
City Rd C2
City Wall C1/C3
Colegate A2
Coslany St B1
Cow Hill B1
Cow Tower A3
Cowgate A2
Crown & Magistrates Courts A2
Dragon Hall Heritage Ctr C3
Duke St A1
Edward St A2
Elm Hill B2
Erpingham Gate B2
Fire Station B1
Fishergate A2
Foundry Bridge B3
Fye Bridge A2
Garden St C2
Gas Hill B3
Grapes Hill B1
Great Hospl Halls, The A3
Grove Ave C1
Grove Rd C1
Guildhall B1
Gurney Rd A3
Hall Rd C2
Heathgate A3
Heigham St A1
Horn's La C2
Information Ctr B1
Ipswich Rd C1
James Stuart Gdns B3
King Edward VI School B2
King St B2
King St C3
Koblenz Ave C3
Library B1
London St B2
Lower Clarence Rd B3
Lower Cl B3
Maddermarket B1
Magdalen St A2
Mariners La C2
Market B2
Market Ave B2
Mountergate B3
Mousehold St A3
Newmarket Rd C1
Norfolk Gallery B2
Norfolk St C1
Norwich City FC C3
Norwich Station B3
Oak St A1
Palace St A2
Pitt St A1
Playhouse B2
Post Office A2/B2/C2
Pottergate B1
Prince of Wales Rd B2
Princes St B2
Pull's Ferry B3
Puppet Theatre A2
Quebec Rd B3
Queen St B2
Queens Rd C2
Recorder Rd B3
Retail Park C3
Riverside Entertainment Ctr C3
Riverside Swimming Ctr C3
Riverside Rd B3
Rosary Rd B3
Rose La B2
Rouen Rd C2
Royal Norfolk Regiment Museum B2
St Andrew's & Blackfriars Hall B2
St Andrews St B2
St Augustines St A1
St Benedicts St B1
St Ethelbert's Gate B2
St Faiths La B3
St Georges St A2
St Giles St B1
St James Cl A3
St Julians C2
St Martin's La A1
St Peter Mancroft B2
St Peters St B1
St Stephens Rd C1
St Stephens St C1
Silver Rd A2
Silver St A2
Southwell Rd C2
Strangers Hall B1
Superstore C2
Surrey St C2
Sussex St A1
The Close B3
The Forum B1
The Walk B2
Theatre Royal B1
Theatre St B1
Thorn La C2
Thorpe Rd B3
Tombland B2
Union St C1
Vauxhall St B1
Victoria St C1
Walpole St B1
Wensum St A2
Wessex St C1
Westwick St A1
Wherry Rd C3
Whitefriars A2
Willow La B1
Yacht Station B3

Nottingham 341

Abbotsford Dr A3
Addison St A1
Albert Hall B1
Alfred St South A3
Alfreton Rd B1
All Saints Rd A1
Annesley Gr A2
Arboretum A1
Arboretum St A1
Arthur St A1
Arts Theatre B3
Ashforth St A3
Balmoral Rd A1
Barker Gate B3
Bath St B3
Belgrave Ctr B1
Bellar Gate B3
Belward St B3
Blue Bell Hill Rd B3
Brewhouse Yard C2
Broad Marsh Bus Sta C2
Broad Marsh Precinct C2
Broad St B3
Brook St B3
Burns St A1
Burton St B2
Bus Station A2
Canal St C2
Carlton St B3
Carrington St C2
Castle Blvd C1
Castle C2
Castle Gate C2
Castle Mdw Retail Pk C1
Castle Meadow Rd C1
Castle Museum & Gallery C2
Castle Rd C2
Castle Wharf C2
Cavendish Rd East C1
Cemetery B1
Chaucer St B1
Cheapside B2
Church Rd A3
City Link C3
City of Caves C2
Clarendon St B1
Cliff Rd C3
Clumber Rd East C1
Clumber St B2
College St B1
Collin St C2
Conway Cl A2
Council House B2
Court B2
Cranbrook St B3
Cranmer St A2
Cromwell St B1
Curzon St B3
Derby Rd B1
Dryden St A2
Fishpond Dr C1
Fletcher Gate B3
Forest Rd East A1
Forest Rd West A1
Friar La C2
Galleries of Justice C3
Gedling Gr A1
Gedling St B3
George St B3
Gill St A2
Glasshouse St B2
Goldsmith St B2
Goose Gate B3
Great Freeman St A2
Guildhall B2
Hamilton Dr C1
Hampden St A1
Heathcote St B3
High Pavement C3
High School A1
Holles Cr C1
Hope Dr C1
Hungerhill Rd A3
Huntingdon Dr C1
Huntingdon St A2
Information Ctr B2
Instow Rise A3
International Com Ctr A2
Kent St B3
King St B2
Lace Ctr, The C2
Lace Market B3
Lace Mkt Theatre C3
Lamartine St B3
Lenton Rd C1
Lewis Cl A3
Lincoln St B2
London Rd C3
Long Row B2
Low Pavement C2
Lower Parliament St B3
Magistrates Court C2
Maid Marian Way B2
Mansfield Rd A2/B2
Middle Hill C2
Milton St B2
Mount St B2
National Ice Ctr C3
Newcastle Dr B1
Newstead Gr A2
North Sherwood St A2
Nottingham Arena C3
Nottingham Station C3
Old Market Square B2
Oliver St A1
Park Dr C1
Park Row C1
Park Terr B1
Park Valley C1
Peas Hill Rd A3
Peel St A1
Pelham St B2
Peveril Dr C1
Plantagenet St A3
Playhouse Theatre B1
Plumptre St C3
Police Station B2
Poplar St C3
Portland Rd B1
Post Office B2
Queen's Rd C3
Raleigh St A1
Regent St B1
Rick St B3
Robin Hood Statue C2
Robin Hood St B3
Royal Ctr B2
Royal Children Inn C2
Royal Concert Hall B2
St Ann's Hill Rd A2
St Ann's Way A2
St Ann's Well Rd A3
St Barnabas B1
St James' St B2
St Mark's St B3
St Mary's Gdn of Rest B3
St Mary's Gate B3
St Nicholas C2
St Peter's C2
St Peter's Gate B2
Salutation Inn C2
Shakespeare St B2
Shelton St A2
South Pde B2
South Rd C1
South Sherwood St B2
Station St C3
Station Street C3
Stoney St B3
Talbot St B1
Tales of Robin Hood C2
Tattershall Dr C1
Tennis Dr B1
Tennyson St A1
The Park C1
The Ropewalk B1
Theatre Royal B2
Trent St C3
Trent University A2/B2
Trent University B2
Trinity Square Sh Ctr B2
Trip To Jerusalem Inn C2
Union Rd B3
Upper Parliament St B2
Victoria Ctr B2
Victoria Leisure Ctr B3
Victoria Park B3
Victoria St B2
Walter St A1
Warser Gate B3
Watkin St A2
Waverley St A1
Wheeler Gate B2
Wilford Rd C2
Wilford St C2
Willoughby House C2
Wollaton St B1
Woodborough Rd A2
Woolpack La B3
York St A2

Oban 341

Aird's Cres B2
Albany St B2
Albert La A2
Albert Rd A2
Alma Cres B1
Ambulance Station C2
Angus Terr C3
Ardconnel Rd A2
Ardconnel Terr B2
Argyll Sq B2
Argyll St B2
Atlantis Leisure Ctr A2
Bayview Rd A1
Benvoulin Rd A2
Bowling Green A2
Breadalbane St A2
Bus Station B2
Campbell St B2
College B2
Colonsay Terr C3
Columba Building B2
Combie St B2
Corran Brae A1
Corran Esplanade A1/A2
Corran Halls A2
Court B2
Crannaig-a-Mhinisteir B1
Crannog La C2
Croft Ave A2
Dalintart Dr C3
Dalriach Rd A2
Distillery B2
Drummore Rd C2
Duncraggan Rd A2
Dunollie Rd A2
Dunuaran Rd B1
Feochan Gr C3
Ferry Terminal B1
Gallanach Rd B1
George St A2
Glencruitten Dr C3
Glencruitten Rd B3
Glenmore Rd C1
Glenshellach Rd C1
Glenshellach Terr B2
Harbour Bowl B2
Hazeldean Cres A3
High St B2
Highland Theatre Cinema A2
Hill St B2
Industrial Estate C2
Information Ctr B2
Islay Rd C3
Jacob's Ladder B2
Jura Rd C3
Knipoch Pl C3
Laurel Cres A2
Laurel Rd A2/A3
Library B1
Lifeboat Station B1
Lighthouse Pier B1
Lismore Cres A2
Lochavullin Dr B2
Lochavullin Rd C2
Lochside St B2
Longsdale Cres A3
Longsdale Rd A2/A3
Longsdale Terr A3
Lunga Rd C3
Lynn Rd C2
Market St B2
McCaig Rd C3
McCaig's Tower A2
Mill La C2
Miller Rd C2
Millpark Ave C2
Millpark Rd C2
Mossfield Ave B3
Mossfield Dr B3
Mossfield Stadium B3
Nant Dr C3
Nelson Rd C2
North Pier B2
Nursery La A2
Oban B2
Police Station B2
Polvinister Rd B3
Post Office A2/B2
Pulpit Dr C1
Pulpit Hill C1
Pulpit Hill Viewpoint B1
Quarry Rd C2
Queen's Park Pl B2
Railway Quay B2
Rockfield Rd B2
St Columba's A1
St John's A2
Scalpay Terr C3
Shore St B1
Shuna Terr C3
Sinclair Dr C2
Soroba Rd B2/C2
South Pier B1
Stevenson St B2
Tweedale St B2
Ulva Rd C2
Villa Rd B1
War & Peace A2

Oxford 341

Adelaide St A1
Albert St A1
All Souls (Coll) B2
Ashmolean Mus B2
Balliol (Coll) B2
Banbury Rd A2
Bate Collection of Musical Instruments C2
Beaumont St B1
Becket St B1
Blackhall Rd A2
Blue Boar St B2
Bodleian Library B2
Botanic Garden B2
Brasenose (Coll) B2
Brewer St C2
Broad St B2
Burton-Taylor Theatre B2
Bus Station B1
Canal St A1
Cardigan St A1
Carfax Tower B2
Castle B1
Castle St B1
Catte St B2
Cemetery C1
Christ Church (Coll) B2
Christ Church Cath C2
Christ Church Mdw C2
Clarendon Ctr B2
Coach & Lorry Park C1
College B3
Coll of Further Ed C1
Cornmarket St B2
Corpus Christi (Coll) B2
County Hall B1
Covered Market B2
Cowley Pl C3
Cranham St A1
Cranham Terr A1
Cricket Ground B1
Crown & County Courts C2
Deer Park B3
Exeter (Coll) B3
Folly Bridge C2
George St B1
Great Clarendon St A1
Hart St A1
Hertford (Coll) B2
High St B3
Hollybush Row B1
Holywell St B2
Hythe Bridge St B1
Ice Rink C1
Information Ctr B2
Jericho St A1
Jesus (Coll) B2
Jowett Walk B3
Juxon St A1
Keble (Coll) A2
Keble Rd A2
Library B2
Linacre (Coll) A3
Lincoln (Coll) B2
Little Clarendon St A1
Longwall St B3
Magdalen (Coll) B3
Magdalen Bridge B2
Magdalen St B2
Magistrate's Court C2
Manchester (Coll) B2
Manor Rd B3
Mansfield (Coll) A2
Mansfield Rd A3
Market B1
Marlborough Rd C2
Martyrs' Memorial B2
Merton Field B3
Merton (Coll) B3
Merton St B2
Mus of Modern Art B2
Museum of Oxford B2
Museum Rd A2
New College (Coll) B3
New Inn Hall St B2
New Rd B1
New Theatre B2
Norfolk St C1
Nuffield (Coll) B1
Observatory A1
Observatory St A1
Odeon B1/B2
Old Fire Station B1
Old Greyfriars St C2
Oriel (Coll) B2
Oxford Station B1
Oxford Story, The B2
Oxford University Research Ctrs A1
Oxpens Rd C1
Paradise Sq C1
Paradise St B1
Park End St B1
Parks Rd A2/B2
Pembroke (Coll) C2
Phoenix A1
Picture Gallery C2
Plantation Rd A1
Playhouse B2
Police Station C2
Post Office A1/B2
Pusey St B1
Queen's La B3
Queen's (Coll) B3
Radcliffe Camera B2
Rewley Rd B1
Richmond Rd A1
Rose La B3
Ruskin (Coll) B1
Saïd Business School B1
St Aldates C2
St Anne's (Coll) A1
St Antony's (Coll) A1
St Bernard's Rd A1
St Catherine's (Coll) B3
St Cross Building A3
St Cross Rd A3
St Edmund Hall (Coll) B3
St Giles St A2
St Hilda's (Coll) C3
St John St B2
St John's (Coll) B2
St Mary the Virgin B2
St Michael at the Northgate B2
St Peter's (Coll) B1
St Thomas St B1
Science Area A2
Science Museum B2
Sheldonian Theatre B2
Somerville (Coll) A1
South Parks Rd A2
Speedwell St C2
Sports Ground C3
Thames St C2
Town Hall B2
Trinity (Coll) B2
Turl St B2
University Coll (Coll) B3
Univ Mus & Pitt Rivers Mus A2
University Parks A2
Wadham (Coll) B2
Walton Cr A1
Walton St A1
Western Rd C2
Westgate Sh Ctr B2
Woodstock Rd A1
Worcester (Coll) B1

Perth 341

A K Bell Library B2
Abbot Cres C1
Abbot St C1
Albany Terr A1
Albert Monument A3
Alexandra St B2
Atholl St A2
Balhousie Ave A2
Balhousie Castle Black Watch Museum A2
Balhousie St A2
Ballantine Pl A1
Barossa Pl A2
Barossa St A2
Barrack St A2
Bell's Sports Ctr A2
Bellwood B3
Blair St B1
Burn Park C1
Bus Station B2
Caledonian Rd B2
Canal Cres B2
Canal St B3
Cavendish Ave C1
Charles St B2
Charlotte Pl A2
Charlotte St A3
Church St A1
City Hall B3
Club House C3
Clyde Pl C1
Commercial St A3
Concert Hall B3
Council Chambers B3
County Pl B2
Court B3
Craigie Pl C2
Crieff Rd A1
Croft Park C2
Cross St B2
Darnhall Cres C1
Darnhall Dr C1
Dewars Ctr B1
Dundee Rd B3
Dunkeld Rd A1
Earl's Dykes B1
Edinburgh Rd C3
Elibank St B1
Fair Maid's House A3
Fergusson B3
Feus Rd A1
Fire Station A1
Fitness Ctr B3
Foundary La A2
Friar St C2
George St B3
Glamis Pl C1
Glasgow Rd B1
Glenearn Rd C2
Glover St B1/C1
Golf Course A2
Gowrie St A3
Gray St B1
Graybank Rd B1
Greyfriars Burial Grnd B3
Hay St A2
High St B2/B3
Hotel B2
Inchaffray St A1
Industrial/Retail Park B1
Information Ctr B2
Isla Rd A3
James St B2
Keir St A3
King Edward St B3
King James VI Golf Course C3
King St B2
Kings Pl C2
Kinnoull Causeway B2
Kinnoull Aisle 'Monument' B3
Kinnoull St B2
Knowelea Pl C1
Knowelea Terr C1
Ladeside Business Ctr A1
Leisure Pool B1
Leonard St B2
Lickley St B2
Lochie Brae A3
Long Causeway A1
Low St A2
Main St A3
Marshall Pl C3
Melville St A2
Mill St B3
Milne St B2
Murray Cres C1
Murray St B2
Needless Rd C1
New Rd B2
North Inch A3
North Methven St A2
Park Pl C1
Perth B2
Perth Bridge A3
Perth Business Park B1
Perth Museum & Art Gallery B3
Perth Station C2
Pickletullum Rd B1
Pitheavlis Cres C1
Playhouse B2
Police Station A2
Pomarium St B2
Post Office A3/B2/C2
Princes St B3
Priory Pl C2
Queen St C1
Queen's Bridge B3
Riggs Rd B1
Riverside B3
Riverside Park B3
Rodney Park B3
Rose Terr A2
St Catherines Ret Pk A1
St Catherine's Rd A1/A2
St John St B3
St John's Kirk B3
St John's Shopping Ctr B2
St Leonards Bridge C2
St Ninians Cathedral A2
Scott Monument C2
Scott St B2
Sheriff Court B3
Shore Rd C3
Skate Park C3
South Inch C2
South Inch Bsns Ctr C3
South Inch Park C2
South Inch View C2
South Methven St B2
South St B3
South William St B2
Stormont St A2
Strathmore St A3
Stuart Ave C1
Tay St B3
The Stables A1
The Stanners B3
Union La A2
Victoria St B2
Watergate B3
Wellshill Cemetery A1
West Bridge St A3
West Mill St B2
Whitefriers Cres B1
Whitefriers St B1
Wilson St C1
Windsor Terr C1
Woodside Cres C1
York Pl B2
Young St C1

Peterborough 341

Athletics Arena B3
Bishop's Palace B2
Bishop's Rd B2/B3
Boongate A3
Bourges Boulevard A1
Bourges Retail Pk B1/B2
Bridge House (Council Offices) C2
Bridge St B2
Bright St A1
Broadway A2
Broadway A2
Brook St A2
Burghley Rd A2
Bus Station B2
Cavendish St A3
Charles St A3
Church St B2
Church Walk A2
Cobden Ave A1
Cobden St A1
Cowgate B2
Craig St A2
Crawthorne Rd A2
Cripple Sidings La C2
Cromwell Rd A1
Dickens St A3
Eastfield Rd A3
Eastgate B3
Fire Station A1
Fletton Ave C2
Frank Perkins Parkway C3
Geneva St A2
George St C1
Gladstone St A1
Glebe Rd C2
Gloucester Rd C3
Granby St B3
Grove St C1
Guildhall B2
Hadrians Ct C3
Henry St A2
Hereward Cross (Sh) B2
Hereward Rd B3
Information Ctr B2
Jubilee St C1
Key Theatre C2
Kent Rd B1
Kirkwood Cl B1
Lea Gdns B1
Library A2
Lincoln Rd A2
London Rd C2
Long Causeway B2
Lower Bridge St C2
Magistrates Court B2
Manor House St A2
Mayor's Walk A1
Midland Rd A1
Monument St A2
Morris St A3
Mus & Art Gallery B2
Nene Valley Railway C1
New Rd A2
New Rd C1
Northminster A2
Old Customs House C2
Oundle Rd C1
Padholme Rd A3
Palmerston Rd C1
Park Rd A2
Passport Office B2
Peterborough District Hospital (A+E) B1
Peterborough Sta B1
Peterborough Nene Valley C1
Peterborough United FC C2
Police Station B2
Post Office A3/B1/B2/B3/C1
Priestgate B2
Queen's Walk C2
Queensgate Ctr B2
Railworld C1
Regional Swimming & Fitness Ctr B3
River La B1
Rivergate Sh Ctr B2
Riverside Mead C3
Russell St A1
St John's B2
St John's St A3
St Marks St A2
St Peter's B2
St Peter's Rd B2
Saxon Rd A3
Spital Bridge A1
Stagshaw Dr C3
Star Rd B3
Thorpe Lea Rd B1
Thorpe Rd B1
Thorpe's Lea Rd B1
Tower St A2
Town Hall B2
Viersen Platz B2
Vineyard Rd B3
Wake Rd B3
Wellington St A3
Wentworth St B2
Westgate B2
Whalley St A3
Wharf Rd C1
Whitsed St A3
YMCA A3

Plymouth 341

Alma Rd A1
Anstis St B1
Armada Ctr B2
Armada St A3
Armada Way B2
Arts Ctr B2
Athenaeum B1
Athenaeum St C1
Barbican C3
Barbican C3
Baring St A3
Bath St B1
Beaumont Park B3
Beaumont Rd B3
Black Friars Gin Distillery C2
Breton Side B3
Bus Station B2
Castle St C3
Cathedral (RC) B1
Cecil St B1
Central Park A1
Central Park Ave A2
Charles Church B3
Charles Cross B3
Charles St B2
City Museum & Art Gallery B2
Citadel Rd C2
Citadel Rd East C2
Civic Ctr B2
Cliff Rd C1
Clifton Pl A3
Cobourg St A2
College of Art B2
Continental Ferry Port B1
Cornwall St B2
Dale Rd A2
Deptford Pl A3
Derry Ave A2
Derry's Cross B1
Drake Circus B2
Drake Cir Sh Ctr B2
Drake's Memorial C2
Drum B2
Eastlake St B2
Ebrington St B3
Elizabethan House C3
Elliot St C1
Endsleigh Pl A2
Exeter St B3
Fire Station A3
Fish Quay C3
Gibbons St A3
Glen Park Ave A2
Grand Pde C1
Great Western Rd C1
Greenbank Rd A3
Greenbank Terr A3
Guildhall B2

Hampton St B3
Harwell St B1
Hill Park Cr A3
Hoe Approach B2
Hoe Rd C2
Hoegate St C2
Houndiscombe Rd A2
Information Ctr ℹ C3
James St A2
Kensington Rd A3
King St B1
Lambhay Hill C3
Leigham St C1
Library B2
Lipson Rd A3/B3
Lockyer St C2
Lockyers Quay C3
Madeira Rd C2
Marina B3
Market Ave B1
Martin St B1
Mayflower Stone & Steps ✦ C3
Mayflower St B2
Mayflower Visitor Ctr ✦ C3
Merchants House 🏛 B2
Millbay Rd B1
National Marine Aquarium 🐟 C3
Neswick St B1
New George St B2
New St C3
North Cross ⟳ A2
North Hill A3
North Quay B2
North Rd East A2
North Rd West A1
North St B3
Notte St B2
Octagon St B1
Pannier Market B1
Pennycomequick ⟳ A1
Pier St C1
Plymouth Pavilions B1
Plymouth Station ⇌ A2
Police Station ⊠ B3
Portland Sq A2
Post Office ✉ A1/B1/B2
Princess St B2
Prysten House ⛪ B2
Queen Anne's Battery Seasports Ctr C3
Radford Rd C1
Regent St B3
Rope Walk C3
Royal Citadel C2
Royal Pde B2
St Andrew's ⛪ B2
St Andrew's Cross ⟳ B2
St Andrew's St B2
St Lawrence Rd A2
Saltash Rd A2
Smeaton's Tower ✦ C2
Southern Terr A3
Southside St C2
Stuart Rd A1
Sutherland Rd A2
Sutton Rd B3
Sydney St A1
Teats Hill Rd C3
The Crescent B1
The Hoe C2
The Octagon ⟳ B1
The Promenade C2
Tothill Ave B3
Union St B1
Univ of Plymouth A2
Vauxhall St B2/3
Victoria Park A1
West Hoe Rd C1
Western Approach B1
Whittington St A1
Wyndham St B1
YMCA B2
YWCA C2

Poole 341

Ambulance Station A3
Baiater Gdns C2
Baiter Park C3
Ballard Cl C2
Ballard Rd C2
Bay Hog La B1
Bridge Approach C1
Bus Station B2
Castle St B2
Catalina Dr B3
Chapel La B2
Church St B1
Cinnamon La B1
Colborne Cl B3
Dear Hay La B2
Denmark La A3
Denmark Rd A3
East St B2
Elizabeth Rd A3
Emerson Rd B2
Ferry Rd C1
Ferry Terminal C1
Fire Station A2
Freightliner Terminal C1
Furnell Rd B3
Garland Rd A3
Green Rd B2
Heckford La A3
Heckford Rd A3
High St B2
High St North A3
Hill St B2
Holes Bay Rd A1
Hospital (A+E) H A3
Information Ctr ℹ C2
Kingland Rd B3
Kingston Rd A3
Labrador Dr C3
Lagland St B2
Lander Cl C3
Old Lifeboat 🏛 C2
Lighthouse – Poole Ctr for the Arts ✦ B3
Longfleet Rd A3
Maple Rd A3
Market Cl B2
Market St B2
Mount Pleasant Rd B3
New Harbour Rd C1
New Harbour Rd South C1
New Harbour Rd West C1
New Orchard B1
New Quay Rd C1
New St B2
Newfoundland Dr B2
North St B2
Old Orchard B2
Parish Rd A3
Park Lake Rd B3
Parkstone Rd A3
Perry Gdns B2
Pitwines Cl B2
Police Station ⊠ A2
Poole Central Library B2
Poole Lifting Bridge C1
Poole Park B2
Poole Station ⇌ A2
Poole Waterfront Museum 🏛 C1
Post Office ✉ A2/B2
St John's Rd A3
St Margaret's Rd A2
St Mary's Maternity Unit A3
St Mary's Rd A3
Seldown Bridge B3
Seldown La B3
Seldown Rd B3
Serpentine Rd A2
Shaftesbury Rd A3
Skinner St B2
Slipway B1
Stanley Rd C2
Sterte Ave A2
Sterte Ave West A1
Sterte Cl A2
Sterte Esplanade A2
Sterte Rd A2
Strand St C2
Swimming Pool B3
Taverner Cl B3
Thames St B1
The Lifeboat College B2
The Quay C2
Towngate Bridge B2
Vallis Cl C3
Waldren Cl B3
West Quay B1
West Quay Rd B1
West St B1
West View Rd A2
Whatleigh Cl B2
Wimborne Rd A3

Portsmouth 341

Action Stations ✦ C1
Admiralty Rd A1
Alfred Rd A2
Anglesea Rd B2
Arundel St B3
Aspex 🏛 B1
Bishop St A2
Broad St C1
Buckingham House ⛪ C2
Burnaby Rd B2
Bus Station B1
Camber Dock C1
Cambridge Rd B2
Car Ferry to Isle of Wight B1
Cascades Sh Ctr A3
Castle Rd C3
City Museum & Art Gallery 🏛 B2
Civic Offices B3
Clarence Pier C2
College St B1
Commercial Rd A3
Cottage Gr B3
Cross St A1
Cumberland St A2
Duisburg Way C2
Durham St A3
East St B1
Edinburgh Rd A2
Elm Gr C3
Great Southsea St C3
Green Rd B3
Greetham St B3
Grosvenor St B3
Groundlings 🎭 A2
Grove Rd North C3
Grove Rd South C3
Guildhall ⛪ B3
Guildhall Walk B3
Gunwharf Quays Retail Park B1
Gunwharf Rd B1
Hambrook St C2
Hampshire Terr B2
Hanover St A1
High St C2
HM Naval Base A1
HMS Nelson (Royal Naval Barracks) A2
HMS Victory ⛴ A1
HMS Warrior ⛴ A1
Hovercraft Terminal C2
Hyde Park Rd B3
Information Ctr ℹ A1/B3
Isambard Brunel Rd B3
Isle of Wight Car Ferry Terminal B1
Kent Rd C3
Kent St A2
King St B3
King's Rd C3
King's Terr C2
Lake Rd A3
Law Courts B3
Library B3
Long Curtain Rd C2
Market Way A3
Marmion Rd C3
Mary Rose Museum 🏛 A1
Middle St B3
Millennium Prom B1/C1
Museum Rd B2
National Museum of the Royal Navy 🏛 A1
Naval Recreation Gd C2
Nightingale Rd C3
Norfolk St B3
North St A2
Osborne Rd C3
Park Rd B2
Passenger Catamaran to Isle of Wight B1
Passenger Ferry to Gosport B1
Pelham Rd C3
Pembroke Gdns C2
Pier Rd C2
Point Battery C1
Police Station ⊠ B3
Portsmouth & Southsea ⇌ A3
Portsmouth Harbour ⇌ B1
Portsmouth Historic Dockyard 🏛 A1
Post Office ✉ A2/A3/B1/B3/C3
Queen St A1
Queen's Cr C3
Round Tower ✦ C1
Royal Garrison Church ⛪ C1
St Edward's Rd C3
St George's Rd B2
St George's Sq B1
St George's Way B2
St James's Rd B3
St James's St A2
St John's Cath (RC) ✝ A3
St Thomas's Cath ✝ C1
St Thomas's St B2
Somers Rd B3
Southsea Common C2
Southsea Terr C2
Spinnaker Tower ✦ B1
Square Tower ✦ C1
Station St A3
Swimming Pool A2
The Hard B1
Town Fortifications ✦ C1
Unicorn Rd A2
United Services Recreation Ground B2
University of Portsmouth A2/B2
University of Portsmouth – College of Art, Design & Media B3
Upper Arundel St A3
Victoria Ave C2
Victoria Park A2
Victory Gate A1
Vue 🎦 B1
Warblington St B1
Western Pde C2
White Hart Rd C1
Winston Churchill Ave B3

Preston 342

Adelphi St A2
Anchor Ct B3
Aqueduct St A1
Ardee Rd C1
Arthur St B2
Ashton St A1
Avenham La B3
Avenham Park C3
Avenham Rd B3
Avenham St B3
Bairstow St B3
Balderstone Rd C1
Beamont Dr A1
Beech St South C2
Bird St C1
Bow La B2
Brieryfield Rd A1
Broadgate C1
Brook St A2
Bus Station A3
Butler St B2
Cannon St B3
Carlton St A1
Chaddock St B3
Channel Way B1
Chapel St B3
Christ Church St B2
Christian Rd B2
Cold Bath St A2
Coleman Ct C1
Connaught Rd C2
Corn Exchange ⛪ B3
Corporation St A2/B2
County Hall B2
County Records Office B2
Court A3
Court B3
Cricket Ground C2
Croft St A1
Cross St B3
Crown Court A3
Crown St A3
East Cliff C3
East Cliff Rd B3
Edward St A2
Elizabeth St A3
Euston St B1
Fishergate B2/B3
Fishergate Hill B2
Fishergate Sh Ctr B2
Fitzroy St B1
Fleetwood St A1
Friargate A3
Fylde Rd A1/A2
Gerrard St B2
Glover's Ct B3
Good St B2
Grafton St B2
Great George St A3
Great Shaw St A3
Greenbank St A2
Guild Way B1
Guildhall & Charter 🎭 B3
Guildhall St B3
Harrington St A2
Harris Museum 🏛 B3
Hartington Rd B1
Hasset Cl C2
Heatley St B2
Hind St C2
Information Ctr ℹ B3
Kilruddery Rd C1
Lancaster Rd A3/B3
Latham St B3
Lauderdale St C2
Lawson St A3
Leighton St A2
Leyland Rd C1
Library A1
Library B3
Liverpool Rd C1
Lodge St B2
Lune St B3
Main Sprit West B3
Maresfield Rd C1
Market St West A3
Marsh La B1/B2
Maudland Bank A2
Maudland Rd A2
Meadow Ct C2
Meath Rd C1
Mill Hill A2
Miller Arcade ✦ B3
Miller Park C3
Moor La A3
Mount St B3
North Rd A3
North St A3
Northcote Rd B1
Old Milestones B1
Old Tram Rd C3
Pedder St A1/A2
Peel St A2
Penwortham Bridge C2
Penwortham New Bridge C1
Pitt St B2
Playhouse 🎭 A3
Police Station ⊠ A3
Port Way B1
Post Office ✉ B3
Preston Station ⇌ B2
Ribble Bank St B2
Ribble Viaduct C2
Ribblesdale Pl B3
Ringway B3
River Parade C1
Riverside C2
St Georges ⛪ B3
St Georges Sh Ctr B3
St Johns ⛪ B3
St Johns Shopping Centre A3
St Mark's Rd A1
St Walburges ⛪ A1
Salisbury Rd B1
Sessions House ⛪ B3
Snow Hill A3
South End C2
South Meadow La C2
Spa Rd B1
Sports Ground C2
Strand Rd B1
Syke St B3
Talbot Rd B1
Taylor St C1
Tithebarn St A3
Town Hall B3
Tulketh Brow A1
University of Central Lancashire A2
Valley Rd C1
Victoria St A2
Walker St A3
Walton's Parade B2
Warwick St A3
Wellfield Bsns Park A1
Wellfield Rd A1
Wellington St A1
West Cliff C2
West Strand A1
Winckley Rd C1
Winckley Square B3
Wolseley Rd C2

Reading 342

Abbey Ruins ✝ B2
Abbey Sq B2
Abbey St B2
Abbot's Walk B2
Acacia Rd C2
Addington Rd C3
Addison Rd A1
Allcroft Rd C3
Alpine St C2
Baker St B1
Berkeley Ave C1
Bridge St B2
Brigham Rd A1
Broad St B1
Broad Street Mall B1
Carey St B1
Castle Hill C1
Castle St B1
Caversham Rd A1
Christchurch Playing Fields A2
Civic Offices & Magistrate's Court B1
Coley Hill C1
Coley Pl C1
Craven Rd C3
Crown St C2
De Montfort Rd A1
Denmark Rd C3
Duke St B2
East St B2
Edgehill St C2
Eldon Rd B3
Eldon Terr B3
Elgar Rd C1
Erleigh Rd C3
Field Rd C1
Fire Station A1
Fobney St B1
Forbury Gdns B2
Forbury Retail Park B2
Forbury Rd B2
Francis St C1
Friar St B1
Garrard St B1
Gas Works Rd B3
George St A2
Great Knollys St B1
Greyfriars ⛪ B1
Gun St B1
Henry St C1
Hexagon Theatre, The 🎭 B1
Hill's Meadow A2
HM Prison B2
Howard St B1
Information Ctr ℹ B1
Inner Distribution Rd B1
Katesgrove La C1
Kenavon Dr B2
Kendrick Rd C2
King's Meadow Recreation Ground A2
King's Rd B2
Library B2
London Rd C3
London St B2
Lynmouth Rd A1
Market Pl B2
Mill La B2
Mill Rd A2
Minster St B1
Morgan Rd C3
Mount Pleasant C2
Museum of English Rural Life 🏛 C3
Napier Rd A2
Newark St C2
Newport Rd A1
Old Reading Univ C3
Oracle Sh Ctr, The B1
Orts Rd B3
Pell St C1
Queen Victoria St B1
Queen's Rd A2
Queen's Rd B2
Police Station ⊠ B1
Post Office ✉ B2
Randolph Rd A1
Reading Bridge A2
Reading Station ⇌ A1
Redlands Rd C3
Renaissance Hotel B1
Riverside Museum 🏛 B3
Rose Kiln La C1
Royal Berks Hospital (A & E) H C3
St Giles ⛪ C2
St Laurence ⛪ B2
St Mary's ⛪ B1
St Mary's Butts B1
St Saviour's Rd C1
Send Rd A3
Sherman Rd C2
Sidmouth St B2
Silver St C2
South St B2
Southampton St C2
Station Hill A1
Station Rd B1
Superstore A3
Swansea Rd A1
Technical College B3
The Causeway A3
The Grove B2
Valpy St B2
Vastern Rd A1
Vue 🎦 B2
Waldeck St C2
Watlington St B3
West St B1
Whitby Dr C3
Wolseley St C1
York Rd A1
Zinzan St B1

St Andrews 342

Abbey St B2
Abbey Walk B3
Abbotsford Cres A1
Albany Pk C3
Allan Robertson Dr C2
Ambulance Station C1
Anstruther Rd C3
Argyle St B1
Argyll Business Park C1
Auld Burn Rd B2
Bassaguard Ind Est B1
Bell St B2
Blackfriars Chapel (Ruins) B2
Boase Ave B2
Braid Cres C3
Brewster Pl C3
Bridge St B1
British Golf Mus 🏛 A1
Broomfaulds Ave C1
Bruce Embankment A1
Bruce St C2
Bus Station A1
Byre 🎭 B2
Canongate C1
Cathedral and Priory (Ruins) ✝ B3
Cemetery B3
Chamberlain St C1
Church St B2
Churchill Cres C2
City Rd A1
Claybraes C1
Cockshaugh Public Park B1
Cosmos Com Ctr B3
Council Office A2
Crawford Gdns C1
Doubledykes Rd B1
Drumcarrow Rd C1
East Sands B3
East Scores A3
Fire Station C1
Forrest St C1
Fraser Ave C1
Freddie Tait St C2
Gateway Ctr A1
Glebe Rd B2
Golf Pl A1
Grange Rd C3
Greenside Pl B2
Greyfriars Gdns A2
Hamilton Ave C2
Hepburn Gdns B1
Holy Trinity ⛪ B2
Horseleys Park C1
Information Ctr ℹ B2
Irvine Cres C3
James Robb Ave C1
James St B1
John Knox Rd C1
Kennedy Gdns B1
Kilrymont Cl C3
Kilrymont Pl C3
Kilrymont Rd C3
Kinburn Park B1
Kinkell Terr C3
Kinnesburn Rd B2
Ladebraes Walk B2
Lady Buchan's Cave A3
Lamberton Pl C1
Lamond Dr C2
Langlands Rd B2
Largo Rd C1
Learmonth Pl C1
Library B2
Links Clubhouse A1
Links, The A1
Livingstone Cres B2
Long Rocks A2
Madras College B2
Market St A2
Martyr's Monument A1
Memorial Hospital (No A+E) H B3
Murray Pk A2
Murray Pl A2
Nelson St B2
New Course, The A1
New Picture House 🎦 A2
North Castle St A3
North St A2
Old Course, The A1
Old Station Rd A1
Pends, The B3
Pilmour Links A1
Pipeland Rd B2/C2
Police Station ⊠ A2
Post Office ✉ B2
Preservation Trust 🏛 B3
Priestden Pk C3
Priestden Pl C3
Priestden Rd C3
Queen's Gdns B2
Queen's Terr B2
Roundhill Rd C2
Royal & Ancient Golf Club A1
St Andrews 🏛 B1
St Andrews Aquarium 🐟 A2
St Andrews Botanic Garden ✿ B1
St Andrews Castle (Ruins) & Visitor Ctr ♜ A2
St Leonard's School B3
St Mary St B3
St Mary's College B2
St Nicholas St C3
St Rules Tower ✦ B3
St Salvator's College A2
Sandyhill Cres C2
Sandyhill Rd C2
Scooniehill Rd C2
Shields Ave C3
Shoolbraids C2
Sloan St B1
South St B2
Spottiswoode Gdns C1
Station Rd A1
Swilcen Bridge A1
The Scores A2
The Shore B3
Tom Morris Dr C2
Tom Stewart La C1
Town Hall B2
Union St A2
University Chapel ⛪ A2
University Library A2
Univ of St Andrews A1
Viaduct Walk B1
War Memorial A3
Wardlaw Gdns B1
Warrack St C3
Watson Ave B2
West Port B2
West Sands A1
Westview B2
Windmill Rd A1
Winram Pl C1
Wishart Gdns C2
Woodburn Pk B3
Woodburn Pl B3
Woodburn Terr B3
Younger Hall ⛪ A2

Salisbury 342

Albany Rd A2
Arts Ctr 🏛 A3
Ashley Rd A1
Avon Approach A2
Ayleswade Rd C2
Bedwin St A2
Belle Vue A2
Bishop's Palace ⛪ C2
Bishops Walk B2
Blue Boar Row B2
Bourne Ave A3
Bourne Hill A3
Britford La C2
Broad Walk C2
Brown St B2
Bus Station B2
Castle St A2
Catherine St B2
Chapter House B2
Church House ⛪ B2
Churchfields Rd B1
Churchill Way East B3
Churchill Way North A3
Churchill Way South C2
Churchill Way West A1
City Hall B2
Close Wall B2
Coldharbour La A1
College St A3
Council Offices A3
Court A1
Crane Bridge Rd B2
Crane St B2
Cricket Ground C1
Culver St South B3
De Vaux Pl C2
Devizes Rd A1
Dews Rd B1
Elm Grove B3
Elm Grove Rd A3
Endless St A2
Estcourt Rd A3
Exeter St C2
Fairview Rd A3
Fire Station A1
Fisherton St A1
Folkestone Rd C1
Fowlers Hill B3
Fowlers Rd B3
Friary Estate C3
Friary La B2
Gas La A1
Gigant St B3
Greencroft B3
Greencroft St A3
Guildhall ⛪ B2
Hall of John Halle ⛪ B2
Hamilton Rd A2
Harnham Mill B1
Harnham Rd C1/C2
High St B2
Hospital H A1
Ho of John A'Port ⛪ B2
Information Ctr ℹ B2
Kelsey Rd A3
King's Rd A2
Laverstock Rd B3
Library B2
London Rd A3
Lower St C1
Maltings, The B2
Manor Rd A3
Marsh La A1
Medieval Hall ⛪ B2
Milford Hill B3
Milford St B3
Mill Rd B1
Millstream Approach A2
Mompesson House (NT) ⛪ B2
New Bridge Rd C2
New Canal B2
New Harnham Rd C2
New St B2
North Canonry ⛪ B2
North Gate B2
North Walk B2
Old George Hall B2
Old Blandford Rd C1
Old Deanery ⛪ B2
Park St A3
Parsonage Green C1
Playhouse Theatre 🎭 A2
Post Office ✉ A2/B2/C2
Poultry Cross B2
Queen Elizabeth Gdns B1
Queen's Rd A3
Rampart Rd B3
St Ann's Gate B2
St Ann St B2
St Marks Rd A3
St Martins ⛪ B3
St Mary's Cathedral ✝ B2
St Nicholas Hospital H C2
St Paul's ⛪ A1
St Paul's Rd A1
St Thomas ⛪ B2
Salisbury & South Wiltshire Museum 🏛 B2
Salisbury General Hospital (A&E) H C2
Salisbury Station ⇌ A1
Salt La A3
Saxon Rd C1
Scots La A2
Shady Bower B3
South Canonry ⛪ C2
South Gate C2
Southampton Rd B2
Spire View A1
Sports Ground C3
The Friary B3
Tollgate Rd B3
Town Path B1
Wain-a-Long Rd A3
Wardrobe, The 🏛 B2
Wessex Rd A3
West Walk C2
Wilton Rd A1
Wiltshire College B3
Winchester St B3
Windsor Rd A1
Winston Churchill Gdns C3
Wyndham Rd A2
YHA ▲ B3
York Rd A1

Scarborough 342

Aberdeen Walk B2
Albert Rd A2
Albion Rd C2
Alexandra Bowling Hall A1
Alexandra Gardens A1
Auborough St B2
Belle Vue St C1
Belmont Rd C2
Brunswick Sh Ctr B2
Castle Dykes B3
Castlegate B3
Castle Holms A3
Castle Hill A3
Castle Rd A2
Castle Walls A3
Cemetery B1
Central Lift ✦ C2
Clarence Gardens A2
Coach Park B1
Columbus Ravine A1
Court B1
Cricket Ground A1
Cross St B2
Crown Terr C2
Dean Rd B1
Devonshire Dr A1
East Harbour B3
East Pier B3
Eastborough B2
Elmville Ave B1
Esplanade C2
Falconers Rd B2
Falsgrave Rd C1
Fire Station B2
Foreshore Rd B2
Friargate B2
Futurist Theatre 🎭🎦 B2
Gladstone Rd B1
Gladstone St B1
Hoxton Rd B1
Information Ctr ℹ B2/B3
King St B2
Londesborough Rd C1
Longwestgate B3
Marine Dr A3
Miniature Railway 🚂 B1
Nelson St B1
Newborough B2
Nicolas St B2
North Marine Rd A1
North St B2
Northway B1
Old Harbour B3
Peasholm Park A1
Peasholm Rd A1
Plaza 🎦 A1
Police Station ⊠ B1
Post Office ✉ B2/C1
Princess St B3
Prospect Rd B1
Queen St B2
Queen's Parade A2
Queen's Tower (Remains) A3
Ramshill Rd C2
Roman Signal Sta A3
Roscoe St C1
Rotunda Museum 🏛 C2
Royal Albert Dr A2
St Martin-on-the-Hill ⛪ C2
St Martin's Ave C2
St Mary's ⛪ B3
St Thomas St B2
Sandside B3
Scarborough Art Gallery and Crescent Art Studio 🏛 C2
Scarborough Castle ♜ A3
Scarborough ⇌ C1
Somerset Terr C2
South Cliff Lift ✦ C2
Spa, The ✦ C2
Spa Theatre, The 🎭 C2
Stephen Joseph Theatre 🎭 B1
Tennyson Ave B1
The Crescent C2
Tollergate B2
Town Hall B2
Trafalgar Rd B1
Trafalgar Square A1
Trafalgar St West B1
Valley Bridge Parade C2
Valley Rd C1
Vernon Rd C2
Victoria Park Mount A1
Victoria Rd B1
West Pier B3
Westborough C1
Westover Rd C1
Westwood C1
Woodall Ave A1
York Pl B2
Yorkshire Coast College (Westwood Campus) C1

Sheffield 342

Addy Dr A2
Addy St A2
Adelphi St A3
Albert Terrace Rd A3
Albion St A2
Aldred Rd A1
Allen St A4
Alma St A4
Angel St B5
Arundel Gate B5
Arundel St C4
Ashberry Rd A2
Ashdell Rd C1
Ashgate Rd C1
Athletics Ctr B2
Attercliffe Rd A6
Bailey St B4
Ball St A4
Balm Green B4
Bank St B4
Barber Rd A2
Bard St B5
Barker's Pool B4
Bates St A1
Beech Hill Rd C1
Beet St B3
Bellefield St A3
Bernard Rd A6
Bernard St B6
Birkendale A2
Birkendale Rd A2
Birkendale View A1
Bishop St C4
Blackwell Pl B6
Blake St A2
Blonk St A5
Bolsover St B2
Botanical Gdns ✿ C1
Bower Rd A1
Bradley St A1
Bramall La C4
Bramwell St A3
Bridge St A4/A5
Brighton Terrace Rd A1
Broad La B3
Broad St B6
Brocco St A3
Brook Hill B3
Broomfield Rd C1
Broomgrove Rd C2
Broomhall Pl C3
Broomhall Rd C2
Broomhall St C3
Broomspring La C2
Brown St C5
Brunswick St B3
Burgess St B4
Burlington St A2
Burns Rd A2
Bus/Coach Station B5
Cadman St A6
Cambridge St B4
Campo La B4
Carver St B4
Castle Market B5
Castle Square 🚋 B5
Castlegate A5
Cathedral (RC) ✝ B4
Cathedral 🚋 B4
Cavendish St B3
Charles St C4
Charter Row C4
Children's Hospital (A&E) H B2
Church St B4
City Hall 🎭 B4
City Hall 🚋 B4
City Rd C6
Claremont Cr B2
Claremont Pl B2
Clarke St C3
Clarkegrove Rd C2
Clarkehouse Rd C1
Clarkson St B2
Cobden View Rd A1
Collegiate Cr C2
Commercial St B5
Commonside A1
Conduit Rd B1
Cornish St A3
Corporation St A4
Court B4
Cricket Inn Rd B6
Cromwell St A1
Crookes Rd B1
Crookes Valley Park B2
Crookes Valley Rd B2
Crookesmoor Rd A2
Crown Court A4
Crucible Theatre 🎭 B5
Cutlers Gate A6
Cutler's Hall ⛪ B4
Daniel Hill A2
Dental Hospital H B2
Dept for Education & Employment C4
Devonshire Green B3
Devonshire St B3
Division St B4
Dorset St C2
Dover St A3
Duchess Rd C5
Duke St B5
Duncombe St A1
Durham Rd B2
Earl St C4
Earl Way C4
Ecclesall Rd C3
Edward St B3
Effingham Rd A6
Effingham St A6
Egerton St C3
Eldon St B3
Elmore Rd B1
Exchange St B5
Eyre St C4
Fargate B4
Farm Rd C5
Fawcett St A3
Filey St B3
Fire & Police Mus 🏛 A4
Fire Station C4
Fir St A1
Fitzalan Sq/Ponds Forge 🚋 B5
Fitzwater Rd C6
Fitzwilliam Gate C4
Fitzwilliam St B3

Flat St B5
Foley St A6
Foundry Climbing Ctr A4
Fulton Rd A1
Furnace Hill A4
Furnival Rd A5
Furnival Sq C4
Furnival St C4
Garden St B3
Gell St B3
Gibraltar St A4
Glebe Rd B1
Glencoe Rd C6
Glossop Rd B2/B3/C1
Gloucester St C2
Granville Rd C6
Granville Rd/ Sheffield College C5
Graves Gallery B5
Greave Rd B3
Green La A4
Hadfield St A1
Hanover St C3
Hanover Way C3
Harcourt Rd B1
Harmer La B5
Havelock St C2
Hawley St B4
Haymarket B5
Headford St C3
Heavygate Rd A1
Henry St A3
High St B4
Hodgson St C3
Holberry Gdns C2
Hollis Croft B4
Holly St B4
Hounsfield Rd B3
Howard Rd A1
Hoyle St A3
Hyde Park A6
Infirmary Rd A3
Infirmary Rd A3
Information Ctr B4
Jericho St A3
Johnson St A5
Kelham Island Industrial Museum A4
Lawson Rd C1
Leadmill Rd C5
Leadmill St C5
Leadmill, The C5
Leamington St A1
Leavy Rd B3
Lee Croft B4
Leopold St B4
Leveson St A6
Library A2
Library B5
Library C1
Lyceum Theatre B5
Malinda St A3
Maltravers St A5
Manor Oaks Rd B6
Mappin St B3
Marlborough Rd B1
Mary St C4
Matilda St C4
Matlock Rd A1
Meadow St A3
Melbourn Rd A1
Melbourne Ave C1
Millennium Galleries B5
Milton St C3
Mitchell St B3
Mona Ave A1
Mona Rd A1
Montgomery Terr Rd A3
Montgomery Theatre B4
Monument Gdns C6
Moor Oaks Rd B1
Moore St C3
Mowbray St A4
Mushroom La B2
Netherthorpe Rd B3
Netherthorpe Rd B3
Newbould La C1
Nile St C1
Norfolk Park Rd C6
Norfolk Rd C6
Norfolk St B4
North Church St B4
Northfield Rd A1
Northumberland Rd B1
Nursery St A5
O2 Academy B5
Oakholme Rd C1
Octagon B2
Odeon B5
Old St B6
Oxford St A2
Paradise St B4
Park La C2
Park Sq B5
Parker's Rd B1
Pearson Building (Univ) C2
Penistone Rd A3
Pinstone St B4
Pitt St B3
Police Station A4/B5
Pond Hill B5
Pond St B5
Ponds Forge Sports Ctr B5
Portobello St B3
Post Office A1/A2/B3/B4/B5/B6/C1/C3/C4/C6
Powell St A2
Queen St B4
Queen's Rd C5
Ramsey Rd B1
Red Hill B3
Redcar Rd B1
Regent St B3
Rockingham St B4
Roebuck Rd A2
Royal Hallamshire Hospital C2
Russell St A4
Rutland Park C1
St George's Cl B3
St Mary's Gate C3
St Mary's Rd C4/C5
St Peter & St Paul Cathedral B4
St Philip's Rd A3
Savile St A5
School Rd B1
Scotland St A4
Severn Rd B1
Shalesmoor A4
Shalesmoor A3
Sheaf St B5
Sheffield Hallam Univ B5
Sheffield Ice Sports Ctr – Skate Central C5
Sheffield Parkway A6
Sheffield Station C5
Sheffield Sta/ Sheffield Hallam University B5
Sheffield University B2
Shepherd St A3
Shipton St A2
Shoreham St C4
Showroom, The C5
Shrewsbury Rd C5
Sidney St C4
Site Gallery C5
Slinn St A1
Smithfield A4
Snig Hill A5
Snow La A4
Solly St B3
Southbourne Rd C1
South La C4
South Street Park B5
Spital Hill A5
Spital St A5
Spring Hill B1
Spring Hill Rd B1
Springvale Rd A1
Stafford Rd C6
Stafford St B6
Stanley St A5
Suffolk Rd C5
Summer St B2
Sunny Bank C3
Surrey St B4
Sussex St A6
Sutton St B3
Sydney Rd A2
Sylvester St C4
Talbot St B5
Taptonville Rd B1
Tax Office C4
Tenter St B4
The Moor C4
Town Hall B4
Townend St A1
Townhead St B4
Trafalgar St B4
Tree Root Walk B2
Trinity St A4
Trippet La B4
Turner Mus of Glass B3
Union St B4
Univ Drama Studio B2
Univ of Sheffield B3
Upper Allen St A3
Upper Hanover St B3
Upperthorpe Rd A2/A3
Verdon St A5
Victoria Quays B5
Victoria Rd C2
Victoria St B3
Waingate B5
Watery St A3
Watson Rd C1
Wellesley Rd B2
Wellington St C3
West Bar A4
West Bar Green A4
West One B3
West St B3
West St B4
Westbourne Rd C1
Western Bank B2
Western Rd A1
Weston Park B2
Weston Park Hospl B2
Weston Park Mus B2
Weston St A2
Wharncliffe Rd C3
Whitham Rd B1
Wicker A5
Wilkinson St B2
William St C3
Winter Garden B4
Winter St B2
York St B4
Yorkshire Artspace C5
Young St C4

Shrewsbury 342

Abbey Church B3
Abbey Foregate B3
Abbey Lawn Bsns Park B3
Abbots House B2
Agricultural Show Gd A1
Albert St A2
Alma St B1
Ashley St A3
Ashton Rd C1
Avondale Dr A3
Bage Way C3
Barker St B1
Beacall's La A2
Beeches La C2
Beehive La C1
Belle Vue Gdns C2
Belle Vue Rd C2
Belmont Bank C1
Berwick Ave A1
Berwick Rd A1
Betton St C2
Bishop St B3
Bradford St B3
Bridge St B1
Bus Station B2
Butcher Row B2
Burton St A3
Butler Rd C1
Bynner St C2
Canon St B3
Canonbury C1
Castle Bsns Park, The A2
Castle Foregate A2
Castle Gates B2
Castle Museum B2
Castle St B2
Cathedral (RC) C1
Chester St A2
Cineworld C3
Claremont Bank B1
Claremont Hill B1
Cleveland St B3
Coleham Head B2
Coleham Pumping Station C2
College Hill B1
Corporation La A1
Coton Cres A1
Coton Hill A2
Coton Mount A1
Crescent La C1
Crewe St A2
Cross Hill B1
Darwin Ctr B2
Dingle, The B1
Dogpole B2
Draper's Hall B2
English Bridge B2
Fish St B2
Frankwell B1
Gateway Ctr, The A2
Gravel Hill La A1
Greyfriars Rd C2
Guildhall B1
Hampton Rd A3
Haycock Way C3
HM Prison B2
High St B1
Hills La B1
Holywell St B3
Hunter St A1
Information Ctr B1
Ireland's Mansion & Bear Steps B1
John St A3
Kennedy Rd C1
King St B3
Kingsland Bridge C1
Kingsland Bridge (toll) C1
Kingsland Rd C1
Library B2
Lime St C2
Longden Coleham C2
Longden Rd C1
Longner St B1
Luciefelde Rd C1
Mardol B1
Market B1
Marine Terr C2
Monkmoor Rd B3
Moreton Cr C2
Mount St A1
Music Hall B1
New Park Cl A3
New Park Rd A2
New Park St A3
North St A2
Oakley St C1
Old Coleham C2
Old Market Hall B1
Old Potts Way C3
Parade Ctr B2
Police Station B1
Post Office A2/B1/B2/B3
Pride Hill B1
Pride Hill Ctr B1
Priory Rd B1
Pritchard Way C3
Queen St A3
Raby Cr C2
Rad Brook C1
Rea Brook C3
Riverside B1
Roundhill La A1
Rowley's House B1
St Alkmund's B2
St Chad's B1
St Chad's Terr B1
St John's Hill B1
St Julians Friars C2
St Mary's B2
St Mary's St B2
Salters La C2
Scott St C3
Severn Bank A3
Severn St A2
Shrewsbury B2
Shrewsbury High School for Girls C1
Shrewsbury School C1
Shropshire Wildlife Trust B3
Smithfield Rd B1
South Hermitage C1
Swan Hill C1
Sydney Ave A3
Tankerville St B3
The Dana A2
The Quarry B1
The Square B1
Tilbrook Dr A3
Town Walls C1
Trinity St C2
Underdale Rd B3
Victoria Ave B1
Victoria Quay B1
Victoria St B2
Welsh Bridge B1
Whitehall St B3
Wood St A2
Wylie Cop B2

Southampton 342

Above Bar St A2
Albert Rd North B3
Albert Rd South C3
Anderson's Rd B3
Archaeology Mus (God's Ho Tower) C2
Argyle Rd A2
Arundel Tower B1
Bargate, The B2
Bargate Shopping Ctr B2
BBC Regional Ctr A1
Bedford Pl A1
Belvidere Rd A3
Bernard St C2
Blechynden Terr A1
Brazil Rd C3
Brinton's Rd A2
Britannia Rd A3
Briton St C2
Brunswick Pl A2
Bugle St C1
Canute Rd C3
Castle Way C2
Catchcold Tower B1
Central Bridge C3
Central Rd C2
Channel Way C3
Chapel Rd B3
Cineworld C3
City Art Gallery A1
City College B3
Civic Ctr A1
Civic Ctr Rd A1
Coach Station B1
Commercial Rd A1
Cumberland Pl A1
Cunard Rd C2
Derby Rd A3
Devonshire Rd A1
Dock Gate 4 C2
Dock Gate 8 B1
East Park A2
East Park Terr A2
East St B2
East St Shopping Ctr B2
Endle St B3
European Way C2
Fire Station A2
Floating Bridge Rd C3
Golden Gr A3
Graham Rd A2
Guildhall A1
Hanover Bldgs B2
Harbour Lights C3
Harbour Pde B1
Hartington Rd A3
Havelock Rd A1
Henstead Rd A1
Herbert Walker Ave B1
High St B2
Hoglands Park B2
Holy Rood (Rems), Merchant Navy Memorial B2
Houndwell Park B2
Houndwell Pl B2
Hythe Ferry C2
Information Ctr A1
Isle of Wight Ferry Terminal C1
James St B3
Java Rd C3
Kingsway A2
Leisure World B1
Library A1
Lime St B2
London Rd A2
Marine Pde B3
Maritime C1
Marsh La B2
Mayflower Meml C1
Mayflower Park C1
Mayflower Theatre, The A1
Medieval Merchant's House C1
Melbourne St B3
Millais A2
Morris Rd A1
National Oceanography Ctr C3
Neptune Way C3
New Rd A2
Nichols Rd A3
North Front A2
Northam Rd A3
Ocean Dock C2
Ocean Village Marina C3
Ocean Way C3
Odeon B1
Ogle Rd B1
Old Northam Rd A2
Orchard La B2
Oxford Ave A2
Oxford St C2
Palmerston Park A2
Palmerston Rd A2
Parsonage Rd A3
Peel St A3
Platform Rd C2
Police Station A1
Portland Terr B1
Post Office A2/A3/B2
Pound Tree Rd B2
Quays Swimming & Diving Complex, The B1
Queen's Park C2
Queen's Peace Fountain A2
Queen's Terr C2
Queen's Way B2
Radcliffe Rd A3
Rochester St A3
Royal Pier C1
Royal South Hants Hospital A2
St Andrew's Rd A2
St Mary St A2
St Mary's B3
St Mary's Leisure Ctr A2
St Mary's Pl B2
St Mary's Rd A2
St Mary's Stadium (Southampton FC) A3
St Michael's C1
Solent Sky C3
South Front B2
Southampton Central Station A1
Southampton Solent University A2
SS Shieldhall C2
Terminus Terr C2
The Mall, Marlands A1
The Polygon A1
Threefield La B2
Titanic Engineers' Memorial A2
Town Quay C1
Town Walls B2
Tudor House C1
Vincent's Walk B2
West Gate Hall C1
West Marlands Rd A1
West Park A1
West Park Rd A1
West Quay Rd B1
West Quay Retail Park B1
West Quay Sh Ctr B1
West Rd C2
Western Esplanade B1
Winton St A2

Southend-on-Sea 343

Adventure Island C3
Albany Ave A1
Albert Rd C3
Alexandra Rd C2
Alexandra St C2
Alexandra Yacht Club C2
Ashburnham Rd B2
Ave Rd B1
Avenue Terr B1
Balmoral Rd B1
Baltic Ave B3
Baxter Ave A2/B2
Beecroft Art Gallery C1
Bircham Rd A2
Boscombe Rd B3
Boston Ave A1/B2
Bournemouth Park Rd A3
Browning Ave A3
Bus Station C3
Byron Ave A3
Cambridge Rd C1/C2
Canewdon Rd B1
Carnarvon Rd A2
Central Ave A3
Chelmsford Ave A1
Chichester Rd B2
Church Rd C3
Civic Ctr A2
Clarence Rd C2
Clarence St C2
Cliff Ave B1
Cliffs Pavilion C1
Clifftown Parade C2
Clifftown Rd C2
Colchester Rd A1
College Way B2
Coleman St B3
County Court B3
Cromer Rd B3
Crowborough Rd A2
Dryden Ave A3
East St A2
Elmer App B2
Elmer Ave B2
Gainsborough Dr A1
Gayton Rd A2
Glenhurst Rd A2
Gordon Pl B2
Gordon Rd B2
Grainger Rd A2
Greyhound Way A3
Guildford Rd B3
Hamlet Ct Rd B1
Hamlet Rd C1
Harcourt Ave A1
Hartington Rd C3
Hastings Rd B3
Herbert Gr C3
Heygate Ave C3
High St B2/C2
Information Ctr C3
Kenway A2
Kilworth Ave B3
Lancaster Gdns B3
Library B2
London Rd B1
Lucy Rd C3
MacDonald Ave A1
Magistrates Court A2
Maldon Rd A2
Maine Ave C1
Marine Rd C1
Marine Parade C3
Milton Rd B1
Milton St B2
Napier Ave B2
North Ave A3
North Rd A1/B1
Odeon B2
Osborne Rd B1
Park Cres B1
Park Rd B1
Park St B1
Park Terr B1
Pier Hill C3
Pleasant Rd C3
Police Station A2
Post Office B2/B3
Princes St B2
Queens Rd B2
Queensway B2/B3/C3
Rayleigh Ave A1
Redstock Rd A2
Rochford Ave A1
Royal Mews C2
Royal Terr C2
Royals Sh Ctr, The C3
Ruskin Ave A3
St Ann's Rd B3
St Helen's Rd B1
St John's Rd B1
St Leonard's Rd C3
St Lukes Rd A3
St Vincent's Rd C1
Salisbury Ave A1/B1
Scratton Rd C2
Shakespeare Dr A1
Short St A2
South Ave A3
Southchurch Rd B3
South Essex College B2
Southend Central B2
Southend Pier Railway C3
Southend Radio C2
Southend United FC A1
Southend Victoria B2
Stadium Rd A2
Stanfield Rd A2
Stanley Rd C3
Sutton Rd A3/B3
Swanage Rd B3
Sweyne Ave A1
Sycamore Gr A3
Tennyson Ave A3
The Grove A3
Tickfield Ave A2
Tudor Rd A1
Tunbridge Rd A2
Tylers Ave B3
Tyrrel Dr B3
Univ of Essex B2/C2
Vale Ave A2
Victoria Ave A2
Victoria Sh Ctr, The B2
Warrior Sq B3
Wesley Rd C3
West Rd A1
West St A1
Westcliff Ave C1
Westcliff Parade C1
Western Esplanade C1
Weston Rd C2
Whitegate Rd B3
Wilson Rd C1
Wimborne Rd B3
York Rd C3

Stirling 343

Abbey Rd A3
Abbotsford Pl A3
Abercromby Pl C1
Albert Halls B1
Albert Pl B1
Alexandra Pl A3
Allan Park C2
Ambulance Station A2
AMF Ten Pin Bowling B2
Argyll Ave A3
Argyll's Lodging B1
Back O' Hill Ind Est A1
Back O' Hill Rd A1
Baker St B2
Ballengeich Pass A1
Balmoral Pl B1
Barn Rd B1
Barnton St B2
Bow St B1
Bruce St A2
Burghmuir Ind Est C2
Burghmuir Rd A2/B2/C2
Bus Station B2
Cambuskenneth Bridge A3
Carlton C2
Castle Ct B1
Causewayhead Rd A2
Cemetery A1
Church of the Holy Rude B1
Clarendon Pl C1
Club House B1
Colquhoun St C3
Corn Exchange B2
Council Offices C2
Court B2
Cowane A2
Cowane St A2
Cowane's Hospital B1
Crawford Sh Arc B2
Crofthead Rd A1
Dean Cres A3
Douglas St A2
Drip Rd A1
Drummond La C1
Drummond Pl C1
Drummond Pl La C1
Dumbarton Rd C2
Eastern Access Rd B2
Edward Ave A3
Edward Rd A2
Forrest Rd A2
Fort A1
Forth Cres B2
Forth St A2
Gladstone Pl C1
Glebe Ave C1
Glebe Cres C1
Golf Course C1
Goosecroft Rd B2
Gowanhill A1
Greenwood Ave B1
Harvey Wynd A1
Information Ctr B1
Irvine Pl B2
James St A2
John St B1
Kerse Rd C3
King's Knot B1
King's Park C1
King's Park Rd C1
Laurencecroft Rd A2
Leisure Pool B2
Library B2
Linden Ave C2
Lovers Wk A2
Lower Back Walk B1
Lower Bridge St A2
Lower Castlehill A1
Mar Pl B1
Meadow Pl A3
Meadowforth Rd C3
Middlemuir Rd C3
Millar Pl A3
Morris Terr B2
Mote Hill A1
Murray Pl B2
Nelson Pl C2
Old Town Cemetery B1
Old Town Jail B1
Orchard House Hospital (No A+E) A2
Park Terr C1
Phoenix Industrial Est C3
Players Rd C3
Port St C2
Princes St B2
Queen St B2
Queen's Rd B1
Queenshaugh Dr A3
Rainbow Slides B2
Ramsay Pl A2
Riverside Dr A3
Ronald Pl A1
Rosebery Pl A2
Royal Gardens B1
Royal Gdns B1
St Mary's Wynd B1
St Ninian's Rd C2
Scott St A2
Seaforth Pl B2
Shore Rd B2
Smith Art Gallery & Museum B1
Snowdon Pl C1
Snowdon Pl La C1
Spittal St B2
Springkerse Ind Est C3
Springkerse Rd C3
Stirling Business Ctr C2
Stirling Castle A1
Stirling County Rugby Football Club A3
Stirling Enterprise Pk B3
Stirling Old Bridge A2
Stirling Station B2
Superstore A2
Sutherland Ave A3
TA Ctr C3
Tannery La A2
The Bastion C2
The Changing Room B1
Thistle Industrial Est C3
Thistles Sh Ctr, The B2
Tollbooth, The B1
Town Wall B1
Union St A2
Upper Back Walk B1
Upper Bridge St A1
Upper Castlehill B1
Upper Craigs C2
Victoria Pl C1
Victoria Rd B1
Victoria Sq B1/C1
Vue B2
Wallace St A2
Waverley Cres A3
Wellgreen Rd C2
Windsor Pl C1
YHA B1

Stoke 343

Ashford St A3
Avenue Rd A3
Aynsley Rd A2
Barnfield C1
Bath St C2
Beresford St A3
Bilton St C2
Boon Ave C2
Booth St C2
Boothen Rd C2/C3
Boughey St C2
Boughey Rd C3
Brighton St B1
Campbell Rd C2
Carlton Rd B3
Cauldon Rd A3
Cemetery A2
Cemetery Rd A2
Chamberlain Ave C1
Church (RC) B2
Church St C2
City Rd C3
Civic Ctr & King's Hall B2
Cliff Vale Pk A1
College Rd A2
Convent Cl B2
Copeland St B2
Cornwallis St C2
Corporation St C2
Crowther St A3
Dominic St B1
Elenora St B2
Elgin St B2
Epworth St A3
Etruscan St A1
Film Theatre B3
Fleming Rd C2
Fletcher Rd C2
Floyd St B2
Foden St C2
Frank St C2
Franklin Rd C1
Frederick Ave B1
Garden St C1
Garner St A1
Gerrard St B2
Glebe St B3
Greatbach Ave B1
Hanley Park A3
Harris St B1
Hartshill Rd B1
Hayward St A2
Hide St B2
Higson Ave B2
Hill St B2
Honeywall B2
Hunters Dr C1
Hunters Way C1
Keary St C2
Kingsway B2
Leek Rd B3
Library C2
Lime St C2
Liverpool Rd B2
London Rd C2
Lonsdale St C2
Lovatt St B2
Lytton St B3
Market C2
Newcastle La C1
Newlands St A2
Norfolk St A2
North St A1/B2
North Staffordshire Royal Infirmary (A&E) B1
Northcote Ave B2
Oldmill St C3
Oriel St B1
Oxford St B1
Penkhull New Rd C1
Penkhull St C1
Police Station C2
Portmeirion Pottery C2
Post Office A3/B1/B3/C1/C2
Prince's Rd B1
Pump St B2
Quarry Ave C1
Quarry Rd C1
Queen Anne St A3
Queen's Rd C1
Queensway A1/B2/C3
Richmond St B1
Rothwell St C1
St Peter's B3
St Thomas Pl C1
Scrivenor Rd A1
Seaford St A3
Selwyn St C3
Shelton New Rd A1
Shelton Old Rd B2
Sheppard St C2
Spark St C2
Spencer Rd B3
Spode St C2
Squires View B3
Staffordshire Univ B3
Stanley Matthews Sports Ctr B3
Station Rd B3
Stoke Business Park C3
Stoke Recreation Ctr C2
Stoke Rd A2
Stoke-on-Trent Coll A3
Stoke-on-Trent Sta B3
Sturgess St C2
The Villas C1
Thistley Hough C1
Thornton Rd B3
Tolkien Way B1
Trent Valley Rd C1
Vale St B2
Watford St A3
Wellesley St A3
West Ave B1
Westland St B1
Yeaman St C2
Yoxall Ave B1

Stratford-upon-Avon 343

Albany Rd B1
Alcester Rd B1
Ambulance Station B1
Arden St B2
Avenue Farm A1
Ave Farm Ind Est A1
Avenue Rd A3
Avon Industrial Estate A2
Baker Ave A1
Bandstand C3
Benson Rd A3
Birmingham Rd A2
Boat Club B3
Borden Pl C1
Brass Rubbing Ctr C2
Bridge St B2
Bridgetown Rd C3
Bridgeway B3
Broad St C2
Broad Walk C2
Brookvale Rd C1
Bull St C2
Bus Station B2
Butterfly Farm C3
Cemetery C1
Chapel La B2
Cherry Orchard C1
Chestnut Walk B2
Children's Playground C3
Church St C2
Civic Hall B2
Clarence Rd B1
Clopton Bridge B3
Clopton Rd A2
Coach Terminal & Park B3
College B1
College La C2
College St C2
Community Sports Ctr B1
Council Offices (District) B2
Courtyard C2
Cox's Yard B3
Cricket Ground C3
Ely Gdns B2
Ely St B2
Evesham Rd C1
Fire Station B1
Foot Ferry C3
Fordham Ave A2
Gallery, The B3
Garrick Way C1
Gower Memorial B3
Great William St B2
Greenhill St B2
Grove Rd B2
Guild St B2
Guildhall & School B2
Hall's Croft C2
Hartford Rd C1
Harvard House B2
Henley St B2
High St B2
Holton St C2
Holy Trinity C2
Information Ctr B3
Jolyffe Park Rd A2
Kipling Rd C3
Leisure & Visitor Ctr B3
Library B2
Lodge Rd B1
Maidenhead Rd A3
Mansell St B2
Masons Court B2
Masons Rd A1
Maybird Shopping Pk A2
Maybrook Rd A1
Mayfield Ave A2
Meer St B2
Mill La C2
Moat House Hotel B3
Narrow La C2
Nash's Ho & New Pl B2
New St C2
Old Town C2
Orchard Way C1
Paddock La C1
Park Rd A1
Payton St B2
Percy St A2
Police Station B2
Post Office B2/B3
Recreation Ground C2
Regal Road A2
Rother St B2
Rowley Cr A3
Royal Shakespeare & Swan Theatres B3
Ryland St C2
Saffron Meadow C2
St Andrew's Cr B1
St Gregory's A3
St Gregory's Rd A3
St Mary's Rd A2
Sanctus Dr C2
Sanctus St C1
Sandfield Rd C2
Scholars La B2
Seven Meadows Rd C2
Shakespeare Ctr B2
Shakespeare Institute C2
Shakespeare St B2
Shakespeare's Birthplace B2
Sheep St B2
Shelley Rd C3
Shipston Rd C3
Shottery Rd C1
Slingates Rd A2
Southern La C2
Station Rd B1
Stratford Healthcare B2
Stratford Hospital B2
Stratford Sports Club B1
Stratford-upon-Avon Station B1
Swan's Nest La B3
Talbot Rd A2
The Greenway C2
The Willows B1
The Willows North B1
Tiddington Rd B3
Timothy's Bridge Industrial Estate A1
Timothy's Bridge Rd A1
Town Hall & Council Offices B2
Town Sq B2
Trinity St C2
Tyler St B2
War Memorial Gdns B3
Warwick Rd B3
Waterside B3
Welcombe Rd A3
West St C2
Western Rd A2
Wharf Rd A2
Wood St B2

Sunderland 343

Albion Pl C2
Alliance Pl B1
Argyle St C2
Ashwood St C1
Athenaeum St B2
Azalea Terr C2
Beach St A1
Bede Theatre C3
Bedford St B2
Beechwood Terr C1
Belvedere Rd C2
Blandford St B2
Borough Rd B3

Bridge Cr B2
Bridge St B2
Brooke St A2
Brougham St B2
Burdon Rd C2
Burn Park C1
Burn Park Rd C1
Burn Park Tech Park C1
Carol St B1
Charles St A3
Chester Rd C1
Chester Terr B1
Church St A3
Civic Ctr C2
Cork St B3
Coronation St B3
Cowan Terr C2
Crowtree Rd B2
Dame Dorothy St A2
Deptford Rd B1
Deptford Terr A1
Derby St C2
Derwent St C2
Dock St A3
Dundas St A2
Durham Rd C1
Easington St A2
Egerton St C3
Empire B2
Empire Theatre B2
Farringdon Row B1
Fawcett St B2
Fox St C1
Foyle St B3
Frederick St B3
Gill Rd B2
Hanover Pl A1
Havelock Terr C1
Hay St A2
Headworth Sq B3
Hendon Rd B3
High St East B3
High St West B2/B3
Holmeside B2
Hylton Rd B1
Information Ctr B2
John St B3
Kier Hardie Way A2
Lambton St B3
Laura St C3
Lawrence St B3
Leisure Ctr B2
Library & Arts Ctr B3
Lily St B1
Lime St B1
Livingstone Rd B2
Low Row B2
Matamba Terr B1
Millburn St B1
Millennium Way A2
Minster B2
Monkwearmouth Station Museum A2
Mowbray Park C3
Mowbray Rd C3
Murton St C3
National Glass Ctr A3
New Durham Rd C1
Newcastle Rd A2
Nile St B3
Norfolk St B3
North Bridge St A2
Northern Gallery for Contemporary Art B3
Otto Terr C1
Park La C2
Park Lane C2
Park Rd C2
Paul's Rd B3
Peel St C3
Police Station B2
Post Office B2
Priestly Cr A1
Queen St B2
Railway Row B1
Retail Park B1
Richmond St A2
Roker Ave A2
Royalty Theatre C1
Ryhope Rd C2
St Mary's Way B2
St Michael's Way B2
St Peter's A3
St Peter's A2
St Peter's Way A3
St Vincent St C3
Salem Rd C3
Salem St C3
Salisbury St C3
Sans St B3
Silkworth Row B1
Southwick Rd A2
Stadium of Light (Sunderland AFC) A2
Stadium Way A2
Stobart St A2
Stockton Rd C2
Suffolk St C3
Sunderland Aquatic Ctr C2
Sunderland B2
Sunderland Mus B3
Sunderland Station B2
Sunderland St B3
Tatham St C3
Tavistock Pl B3
The Bridges B2
The Place B3
The Royalty C1
Thelma St C1
Thomas St North A2
Thornholme Rd C1
Toward Rd C3
Transport Interchange C2
Trimdon St Way B1
Tunstall Rd C2
University C1
University Library C1
University of Sunderland (City Campus) B1
University of Sunderland (Sir Tom Cowle at St Peter's Campus) A3
Vaux Brewery Way A2
Villiers St B3
Villiers St South B3
Vine Pl C2
Violet St B1
Walton La B3
Waterworks Rd B1
Wearmouth Bridge B2
Wellington La A1
West Sunniside B3
West Wear St B3
Westbourne Rd B1
Western Hill C1
Wharncliffe B1
Whickham St A3
White House Rd C3
Wilson St North A2
Winter Gdns C3
Wreath Quay A1

Swansea *Abertawe* 343

Adelaide St C3
Albert Row C3
Alexandra Rd B3
Argyle St C1
Baptist Well Pl A2
Beach St C1
Belle Vue Way B3
Berw Rd A1
Berwick Terr A2
Bond St C1
Brangwyn Concert Hall C1
Bridge St A3
Brookands Terr B1
Brunswick St C1
Bryn-Syfi Terr A2
Bryn-y-Mor Rd C1
Bullins La B1
Burrows Rd C1
Bus/Rail link A3
Bus Station C2
Cadfan Rd A1
Cadrawd Rd A1
Caer St B3
Carig Cr A1
Carlton Terr B2
Carmarthen Rd A3
Castle Square B3
Castle St B3
Catherine St C1
City & County of Swansea Offices (County Hall) C2
City & County of Swansea Offices (Guildhall) C1
Clarence St C2
Colbourne Terr A2
Constitution Hill B1
Court B3
Creidiol Rd A2
Cromwell St B2
Duke St B1
Dunvant Pl C2
Dyfatty Park A3
Dyfatty St A3
Dyfed Ave A1
Dylan Thomas Ctr B3
Dylan Thomas Theatre C3
Eaton Cr C1
Eigen Cr A1
Elfed Rd A1
Emlyn Rd A1
Evans Terr A3
Fairfield Terr B1
Ffynone Dr B1
Ffynone Rd B1
Fire Station B3
Firm St A2
Fleet St C1
Francis St C1
Fullers Row B2
George St B2
Glamorgan St C2
Glyndŵr Pl A1
Graig Terr A3
Grand Theatre C2
Granogwen Rd A2
Guildhall Rd South C1
Gwent Rd A1
Gwynedd Ave A1
Hafod St A3
Hanover St B1
Harcourt St B2
Harries St A2
Heathfield B2
Henrietta St B1
Hewson St B2
High St A3/B3
High View A2
Hill St A2
Historic Ships Berth C3
HM Prison C2
Information Ctr C2
Islwyn Rd A1
King Edward's Rd C1
Law Courts C1
Library B3
Long Ridge A2
Madoc St C2
Mansel St B2
Maritime Quarter C3
Market B3
Mayhill Gdns B1
Mayhill Rd A1
Mega Bowl B3
Milton Terr A2
Mission Gallery C3
Montpellier Terr B1
Morfa Rd A3
Mount Pleasant B2
National Waterfront Museum C3
Nelson St C2
New Cut Rd A3
New St A3
Nicander Pde A2
Nicander Pl A2
Nicholl St B2
Norfolk St B2
North Hill Rd A2
Northampton La B2
Orchard St B3
Oxford St B2
Oystermouth Rd C1
Page St B2
Pant-y-Celyn Rd B1
Parc Tawe Link B3
Parc Tawe North B3
Parc Tawe Sh & L Ctr B3
Patti Pavilion C1
Paxton St C2
Penmaen Terr B1
Pen-y-Graig Rd A1
Phillips Pde C1
Picton Terr B2
Plantasia B3
Police Station B2
Post Office A1/A2/B2/C1
Powys Ave A1
Primrose St B2
Princess Way B3
Promenade B2
Pryder Gdns A1
Quadrant Ctr C2
Quay Park B3
Rhianfa La B1
Rhondda St B2
Richardson St C2
Rodney St C1
Rose Hill B1
Rosehill Terr B1
Russell St B1
St David's Sq C3
St Helen's Ave C1
St Helen's Cr C1
St Helen's Rd C1
St James Gdns B1
St James's Cr B1
St Mary's B3
Sea View Terr A3
Singleton St C2
South Dock C3
Stanley Pl B2
Strand B3
Swansea Castle B3
Swansea Coll Arts Ctr C1
Swansea Metropolitan University B2
Swansea Museum C3
Swansea Station A3
Taliesyn Rd B1
Tan y Marian Rd A1
Tegid Rd A2
Teilo Cr A1
Terrace Rd B1/B2
The Kingsway B2
The LC C3
Tontine St A3
Tower of Eclipse C3
Townhill Rd A1
Tram Museum C3
Trawler Rd C3
Union St B2
Upper Strand A3
Vernon St A3
Victoria Quay C3
Victoria Rd B3
Vincent St C1
Walter Rd B1
Watkin St A2
Waun-Wen Rd A2
Wellington St C2
Westbury St C1
Western St C1
Westway C2
William St C2
Wind St B3
Woodlands Terr B1
YMCA B2
York St C3

Swindon 343

Albert St C3
Albion St C1
Alfred St A2
Alvescot Rd C3
Art Gallery & Mus C3
Ashford Rd C1
Aylesbury St A2
Bath Rd C2
Bathampton St B1
Bathurst Rd B3
Beatrice St A2
Beckhampton St B3
Bowood Rd C1
Bristol St B1
Broad St A3
Brunel Arcade B2
Brunel Plaza B2
Brunswick St C2
Bus Station B2
Cambria Bridge Rd B1
Cambria Place B1
Canal Walk B2
Carfax St B2
Carr St B1
Cemetery C1/C3
Chandler Cl C3
Chapel C1
Chester St B1
Christ Church C3
Church Place B1
Cirencester Way A3
Clarence St B2
Clifton St C1
Cockleberry A2
Colbourne A3
Colbourne St A3
College St B2
Commercial Rd B2
Corporation St A2
Council Offices B3
County Rd A3
Courts B2
Cricket Ground A3
Cricklade Street C3
Crombey St B1/C2
Cross St C2
Curtis St B1
Deacon St C1
Designer Outlet (Great Western) B1
Dixon St C2
Dover St C2
Dowling St C2
Drove Rd C3
Dryden St C1
Durham St C3
East St B1
Eastcott Hill C2
Eastcott Rd C2
Edgeware Rd B2
Edmund St C2
Elmina Rd A3
Emlyn Square B1
Euclid St B3
Exeter St B1
Fairview C1
Faringdon Rd B1
Farnsby St B1
Fire Station B3
Fleet St B2
Fleming Way B2/B3
Florence St A2
Gladstone St A3
Gooch St A2
Graham St A3
Great Western Way A1/A2
Groundwell Rd B3
Hawksworth Way A1
Haydon St A2
Henry St B2
Hillside Ave C1
Holbrook Way B2
Hunt St C3
Hydro B1
Hythe Rd C2
Information Ctr B2
Joseph St C1
Kent Rd C2
King William St C2
Kingshill Rd C1
Lansdown Rd C2
Leicester St B3
Library B2
Lincoln St B3
Little London C3
London St B1
Magic Roundabout B3
Maidstone Rd C2
Manchester Rd A3
Maxwell St B1
Milford St B2
Milton Rd B1
Morse St C2
National Monuments Record Ctr B1
Newcastle St B3
Newcombe Drive A1
Newcombe Trading Estate A1
Newhall St C2
North St C2
North Star Ave A1
North Star A1
Northampton St B3
Oasis Leisure Ctr A1
Ocotal Way A3
Okus Rd C1
Old Town C3
Oxford St B1
Park Lane B1
Park Lane B1
Pembroke St C2
Plymouth St B3
Polaris House A2
Polaris Way A2
Police Station B2
Ponting St A2
Post Office B1/B2/C1/C3
Poulton St A3
Princes St B2
Prospect Hill C2
Prospect Place C2
Queen St B2
Queen's Park C3
Radnor St C1
Read St C1
Reading St B1
Regent St B2
Retail Park A2/A3/B3
Rosebery St A3
St Mark's B1
Salisbury St A3
Savernake St C2
Shelley St C1
Sheppard St B1
South St C2
Southampton St B3
Spring Gardens B3
Stafford Street C2
Stanier St C2
Station Road A2
STEAM B1
Swindon College A2
Swindon Rd C2
Swindon Station A2
Swindon Town Football Club A3
T A Ctr B1
Tennyson St B1
The Lawn C3
The Nurseries C1
The Parade B2
The Park B1
Theobald St B1
Town Hall B2
Transfer Bridges A3
Union St C2
Upham Rd C3
Victoria Rd C3
Walcot Rd B3
War Memorial B2
Wells St B3
Western St C2
Westmorland Rd B3
Whalebridge B2
Whitehead St C1
Whitehouse Rd A2
William St C1
Wood St C3
Wyvern Theatre & Arts Ctr B2
York Rd B3

Taunton 343

Addison Gr A1
Albemarle Rd A1
Alfred St B3
Alma St C2
Bath Pl C1
Belvedere Rd A1
Billet St B2
Billetfield C2
Birch Gr A1
Brewhouse Theatre B2
Bridge St B1
Bridgwater & Taunton Canal A2
Broadlands Rd C1
Burton Pl C1
Bus Station B1
Canal Rd A2
Cann St C1
Canon St B2
Castle B1
Castle St B1
Cheddon Rd A2
Chip Lane A1
Clarence St B1
Cleveland St B1
Clifton Terr A2
Coleridge Cres C3
Compass Hill C1
Compton Cl A2
Corporation St B1
Council Offices A1
County Walk Sh Ctr C2
Courtyard B2
Cranmer Rd B2
Critchard Way B3
Cyril St A1
Deller's Wharf B1
Duke St B2
East Reach B3
East St B3
Eastbourne Rd B2
Eastleigh Rd C3
Eaton Cres A2
Elm Gr A1
Elms Cl A1
Fons George C1
Fore St B2
Fowler St A1
French Weir Rec Grd B1
Geoffrey Farrant Wk A2
Gray's Almshouses B2
Grays Rd B3
Greenway Ave A1
Guildford Pl C1
Hammet St B2
Haydon Rd B3
Heavitree Way A2
Herbert St A2
High St C2
Holway Ave C3
Hugo St B3
Huish's Almshouses B2
Hurdle Way C2
Information Ctr C2
Jubilee St A1
King's College C3
Kings Cl C3
Laburnum St B2
Lambrook Rd B3
Lansdowne Rd A3
Leslie Ave A1
Leycroft Rd B3
Library C2
Linden Gr A1
Magdalene St B2
Magistrates Court B1
Malvern Terr A2
Market House B2
Mary St C2
Middle St B2
Midford Rd B3
Mitre Court B3
Mount Nebo C1
Mount St C2
Mountway C2
Mus of Somerset B1
North St B2
Northfield Ave B1
Northfield Rd B1
Northleigh Rd C3
Obridge Allotments A3
Obridge Lane A3
Obridge Rd A3
Obridge Viaduct A3
Old Mkt Shopping Ctr C2
Osborne Way C1
Park St C1
Paul St C2
Plais St A2
Playing Field C3
Police Station C1
Portland St B1
Post Office B1/B2/C1
Priorswood Ind Est A3
Priorswood Rd A2
Priory Ave B2
Priory Bridge Rd B2
Priory Fields Retail Pk A3
Priory Park A2
Priory Way A3
Queen St B3
Railway St A1
Records Office A2
Recreation Grd A1
Riverside Place B2
St Augustine St B2
St George's C2
St Georges Sq C2
St James B2
St James St B2
St John's C1
St John's Rd B1
St Josephs Field C2
St Mary Magdalene's B2
Samuels Ct A1
Shire Hall & Law Courts C1
Somerset County Cricket Ground B2
Somerset County Hall C1
Somerset Cricket B2
South Rd C3
South St C3
Staplegrove Rd B1
Station Rd A1
Stephen St B2
Swimming Pool A1
Tancred St B2
Tauntfield Cl C3
Taunton Dean Cricket Club C2
Taunton Station A2
The Avenue A1
The Crescent C1
The Mount C2
Thomas St A1
Toneway A3
Tower St B1
Trevor Smith Pl C3
Trinity Business Ctr C3
Trinity Rd C3
Trinity St B3
Trull Rd C1
Tudor House B2
Upper High St C1
Venture Way A3
Victoria Gate B3
Victoria Park B3
Victoria St B3
Viney St B3
Vivary Park C2
Vivary Rd C1
War Memorial C1
Wellesley St A2
Wheatley Cres A3
Whitehall A1
Wilfred Rd B3
William St A1
Wilton Church C1
Wilton Cl C1
Wilton Gr C1
Wilton St C1
Winchester St B2
Winters Field B2
Wood St B1
Yarde Pl B1

Telford 343

Alma Ave C1
Amphitheatre C2
Bowling Alley B2
Brandsfarm Way C3
Brunel Rd B1
Bus Station B2
Buxton Rd C1
Central Park A2
Civic Offices B2
Coach Central B2
Coachwell Cl B1
Colliers Way A1
Courts B2
Dale Acre Way B3
Darliston C3
Deepdale B3
Deercote B2
Dinthill C3
Doddington C3
Dodmoor Grange C3
Downemead B3
Duffryn B3
Dunsheath B3
Euston Way A3
Eyton Mound C1
Eyton Rd C1
Forgegate A2
Grange Central B2
Hall Park Way B1
Hinkshay Rd C2
Hollinsworth Rd A2
Holyhead Rd A3
Housing Trust A1
Ice Rink B2
Information Ctr B2
Ironmasters Way A2
Job Ctr B1
Land Registry B1
Lawn Central B2
Lawnswood C1
Library B2
Malinsgate B1
Matlock Ave C1
Moor Rd C1
Mount Rd C1
NFU Offices B1
Odeon B2
Park Lane A1
Police Station B1
Priorslee Ave A3
Queen Elizabeth Ave C3
Queen Elizabeth Way B1
Queensway A2/B3
Rampart Way A2
Randlay Ave C3
Randlay Wood C3
Rhodes Ave C1
Royal Way B1
St Leonards Rd B1
St Quentin Gate B2
Shifnal Rd A3
Sixth Ave A1
Southwater Way B1
Spout Lane C1
Spout Mound B1
Spout Way C1
Stafford Court B3
Stafford Park B3
Stirchley Ave C3
Stone Row C1
Telford Bridge Ret Pk A1
Telford Central Sta A3
Telford Ctr, The B2
Telford Forge Ret Pk A1
Telford Hornets RFC C2
Telford Int Ctr C2
Telford Way A3
Third Ave A2
Town Park C2
Town Park Visitor Ctr B2
Walker House B2
Wellswood Ave A2
West Ctr Way B1
Withywood Drive C1
Woodhouse Central B2
Yates Way A1

Torquay 344

Abbey Rd B2
Alexandra Rd A2
Alpine Rd B3
Ash Hill Rd A2
Babbacombe Rd B3
Bampfylde Rd B1
Barton Rd A1
Beacon Quay C2
Belgrave Rd A1/B1
Belmont Rd A3
Berea Rd A3
Braddons Hill Rd East B3
Brewery Park A3
Bronshill Rd A2
Castle Rd A2
Cavern Rd A3
Central B2
Chatsworth Rd A2
Chestnut Ave B1
Church St A1
Civic Offices A2
Coach Station A1
Corbyn Head C1
Croft Hill B1
Croft Rd B1
Daddyhole Plain C3
East St A1
Egerton Rd A3
Ellacombe Church Rd A3
Ellacombe Rd A2
Falkland Rd B1
Fleet St B2
Fleet Walk Sh Ctr B2
Grafton Rd B3
Haldon Pier C2
Hatfield Rd A2
Highbury Rd A2
Higher Warberry Rd A3
Hillesdon Rd B3
Hollywood Bowl C3
Hoxton Rd A3
Hunsdon Rd B3
Information Ctr B2
Inner Harbour C3
Kenwyn Rd A3
Laburnum St A1
Law Courts A2
Library A2
Lime Ave B1
Living Coasts C3
Lower Warberry Rd B3
Lucius St B1
Lymington Rd A1
Magdalene Rd A1
Marina C2
Market St B2
Meadfoot Lane C3
Meadfoot Rd C3
Melville St B2
Middle Warberry Rd B3
Mill Lane A1
Montpellier Rd B3
Morgan Ave A1
Museum Rd B3
Newton Rd A1
Oakhill Rd A1
Outer Harbour C2
Parkhill Rd C3
Pavilion C2
Pimlico B2
Police Station A1
Post Office A1/B2
Princes Rd A3
Princes Rd East A3
Princes Rd West A3
Princess Gdns C2
Princess Pier C2
Princess Theatre C2
Rathmore Rd B1
Recreation Grd B1
Riviera Ctr Int B1
Rock End Ave C3
Rock Rd B2
Rock Walk B2
Rosehill Rd A3
St Efride's Rd A1
St John's B3
St Luke's Rd B2
St Luke's Rd North B2
St Luke's Rd South B2
St Marychurch Rd A2
Scarborough Rd B1
Shedden Hill B2
South Pier C2
South St A1
Spanish Barn B1
Stitchill Rd B3
Strand B3
Sutherland Rd B3
Teignmouth Rd A1
Temperance St B2
The King's Drive B1
The Terrace B3
Thurlow Rd A1
Tor Bay B1
Tor Church Rd A1
Tor Hill Rd A1
Torbay Rd B2
Torquay Museum B3
Torquay Station C1
Torre Abbey Mansion B1
Torre Abbey Meadows B1
Torre Abbey Sands B1
Torwood Gdns B3
Torwood St C3
Union Square A2
Union St A1
Upton Hill A2
Upton Park A1
Upton Rd A1
Vanehill Rd C3
Vansittart Rd A1
Vaughan Parade C2
Victoria Parade C3
Victoria Rd A2
Warberry Rd West B2
Warren Rd B2
Windsor Rd A2/A3
Woodville Rd A3

Truro 344

Adelaide Ter B1
Agar Rd B3
Arch Hill C2
Arundell Pl C2
Avondale Rd B1
Back Quay B3
Barrack La C3
Barton Meadow A1
Benson Rd A2
Bishops Cl A2
Bosvean Gdns B1
Bosvigo Gardens B1
Bosvigo La A1
Bosvigo Rd B2
Broad St A3
Burley Cl C3
Bus Station B3
Calenick St B2
Campfield Hill B3
Carclew St B3
Carew Rd A2
Carey Park B2
Carlyon Rd A2
Carvoza Rd A3
Castle St B2
Cathedral View A2
Chainwalk Dr A2
Chapel Hill B1
Charles St B2
City Hall B3
City Rd B2
Coinage Hall B3
Comprigney Hill A1
Coosebean La A1
Copes Gdns A2
County Hall B1
Courtney Rd A2
Crescent Rd B1
Crescent Rise B1
Daniell Court C2
Daniell Rd C2
Daniell St C2
Daubuz Cl A2
Dobbs La B1
Edward St B2
Eliot Rd A2
Elm Court A3
Enys Cl A1
Enys Rd A1
Fairmantle St B3
Falmouth Rd C2
Ferris Town B2
Fire Station B1
Frances St B2
George St B2
Green Cl C2
Green La C1
Grenville Rd A2
Hall For Cornwall B3
Hendra Rd A2
Hendra Vean A1
High Cross B3
Higher Newham La C3
Higher Trehaverne A2
Hillcrest Ave B1
Hospital B2
Hunkin Cl A2
Hurland Rd C3
Infirmary Hill B2
James Pl B3
Kenwyn Church Rd A1
Kenwyn Hill A1
Kenwyn Rd A2
Kenwyn St B2
Kerris Gdns A1
King St B3
Lemon Quay B3
Lemon St Gallery B3
Library B1/B3
Malpas Rd B3
Market B3
Memorial Gdns B3
Merrifield Close B1
Mitchell Hill A3
Moresk Cl A3
Moresk Rd A3
Morlaix Ave C3
Nancemere Rd A3
Newham Bsns Park C3
Newham Industrial Est C3
Newham Rd C3
Northfield Dr C3
Oak Way A3
Old County Hall B1
Pal's Terr A3
Park View C2
Pendarves Rd A2
Plaza Cinema B3
Police Station B3
Post Office B2/B3
Prince's St B3
Pydar St A2
Quay St B3
Redannick Cres C2
Redannick La B2
Richard Lander Monument C2
Richmond Hill B1
River St B2
Rosedale Rd A2
Royal Cornwall Mus B2
St Aubyn Rd C3
St Clement St B3
St George's Rd A1
School La C2
Station Rd B1
Stokes Rd A2
Strangways Terr C3
Tabernacle St B3
The Avenue A3
The Crescent B1
The Leats B2
The Spires A2
Trehaverne La A2
Tremayne Rd A2
Treseder's Gdns A3
Treworder Rd B1
Treyew Rd B1
Truro Cathedral B3
Truro Harbour Office B3
Truro Station B3
Union St B2
Upper School La C2
Victoria Gdns B2
Waterfall Gdns B2

Wick 344

Ackergill Cres A2
Ackergill St A2
Albert St C2
Ambulance Station A2
Argyle Sq C2
Assembly Rooms C2
Bank Row C2
Bankhead B1
Barons Well B2
Barrogill St C2
Bay View B3
Bexley Terr C3
Bignold Park C2
Bowling Green C2
Breadalbane Terr C2
Bridge of Wick B1
Bridge St B2
Brown Pl C2
Burn St B2
Bus Station B1
Caithness General Hospital (A+E) B1
Cliff Rd B1
Coach Rd B2
Coastguard Station C3
Corner Cres B3
Coronation St C1
Council Offices B2
Court B2
Crane Rock C3
Dempster St C2
Dunnet Ave A2
Fire Station B2
Fish Market C3
Francis St C1
George St A1
Girnigoe St B2
Glamis Rd B2
Gowrie Pl B1
Grant St C2
Green Rd B2
Gunns Terr B3
Harbour Quay B2
Harbour Rd C3
Harbour Terr C2
Harrow Hill C2
Henrietta St A2/B2
Heritage Museum C2
High St B2
Hill Ave A2
Hillhead Rd B3
Hood St C1
Huddart St C2
Information Ctr B2
Kenneth St C1
Kinnaird St C2
Kirk Hill B1
Langwell Cres B3
Leishman Ave B3
Leith Walk A2
Library B2
Lifeboat Station C3
Lighthouse C3
Lindsay Dr B3
Lindsay Pl B3
Loch St C2
Louisburgh St B2
Lower Dunbar St C2
Macleay La B1
Macleod Rd B3
MacRae St C2
Martha Terr B2
Miller Ave B1
Miller La B1
Moray St C2
Mowat Pl B3
Murchison St C3
Newton Ave C1
Newton Rd C1
Nicolson St C3
North Highland Coll B2
North River Pier B3
Northcote St C2
Owen Pl A2
Police Station B1
Port Dunbar B3
Post Office B2/C2

Pulteney Distillery ✦ C2
River St B2
Robert St A1
Rutherford St C2
St John's Episcopal C2
Sandigoe Rd B3
Scalesburn B3
Seaforth Ave C1
Shore La B2
Sinclair Dr B3
Sinclair Terr C2
Smith Terr C3
South Pier C3
South Quay C3
South Rd C1
South River Pier B3
Station Rd B1
Swimming Pool B2
TA Ctr C2
Telford St B2
The Shore B2
Thurso Rd B1
Thurso St B1
Town Hall B2
Union St B2
Upper Dunbar St C2
Vansittart St C3
Victoria Pl B2
War Memorial A1
Well of Cairndhuna ✦ C3
Wellington Ave C3
Wellington St C3
West Banks Ave C1
West Banks Terr C1
West Park C1
Whitehorse Park B2
Wick Harbour Bridge B2
Wick Industrial Estate A2
Wick Parish Church B1
Wick Station B1
Williamson St B2
Willowbank B2

Winchester 344

Andover Rd A2
Andover Rd Retail Pk A2
Archery La C2
Arthur Rd A2
Bar End Rd C3
Beaufort Rd C2
Beggar's La B3
Bereweeke Ave A1
Bereweeke Rd A1
Boscobel Rd A2
Brassey Rd A2
Broadway B3
Brooks Sh Ctr, The B3
Bus Station B3
Butter Cross ✦ B2
Canon St C2
Castle Wall C2/C3
Castle, King Arthur's Round Table B2
Cathedral ✝ C2
Cheriton Rd A1
Chesil St C3
Chesil Theatre C3
Christchurch Rd C1
City Museum B2
City Offices C3
City Rd B2
Clifton Rd B1
Clifton Terr B2
Close Wall C2/C3
Coach Park A2
Colebrook St C3
College St C2
College Walk C3
Compton Rd C2
County Council Offices B2
Cranworth Rd A2
Cromwell Rd C1
Culver Rd C2
Domum Rd C3
Durngate Pl B3
Eastgate St B3
Edgar Rd C2
Egbert Rd A2
Elm Rd B1
Fairfield Rd A1
Fire Station B3
Fordington Ave B1
Fordington Rd A1
Friarsgate B3
Gordon Rd B3
Greenhill Rd B1
Guildhall B3
HM Prison B1
Hatherley Rd A1
High St B2
Hillier Way A3
Hyde Abbey (Remains) ✝ A2
Hyde Abbey Rd B2
Hyde Cl A2
Hyde St A2
Information Ctr B3
Jane Austen's Ho C2
Jewry St B2
John Stripe Theatre C1
King Alfred Pl A2
Kingsgate Arch C2
Kingsgate Park C2
Kingsgate Rd C2
Kingsgate St C2
Lankhills Rd A2
Library B2
Lower Brook St B3
Magdalen Hill B3
Market La B2
Mews La B1
Middle Brook St B3
Middle Rd B1
Military Museums B2
Milland Rd C3
Milverton Rd B1
Monks Rd A3
North Hill Cl A2
North Walls B2
North Walls Rec Gnd A3
Nuns Rd A3
Oram's Arbour B1
Owen's Rd A2
Parchment St B2
Park & Ride C3
Park Ave B3
Playing Field A1
Police HQ B1
Police Station B3
Portal Rd C3
Post Office B2/C1
Quarry Rd C3
Ranelagh Rd C1
Regiment Museum B2
River Park Leisure Ctr B3
Romans' Rd C2
Romsey Rd B1
Royal Hampshire County Hospital (A&E) B1
St Cross Rd C2
St George's St B2
St Giles Hill C3
St James' La B1
St James' Terr B1
St James Villas C2
St John's B3
St John's St B3
St Michael's Rd C2
St Paul's Hill B1
St Peter St B2
St Swithun St C2
St Thomas St C2
Saxon Rd A2
School of Art B3
Screen B2
Sleepers Hill Rd C1
Southgate St B2
Sparkford Rd C1
Staple Gdns B2
Station Rd B2
Step Terr B1
Stockbridge Rd A1
Stuart Cres C1
Sussex St B2
Swan Lane B2
Tanner St B3
The Square B2
The Weirs C3
The Winchester Gallery B3
Theatre Royal B2
Tower St B2
Town Hall C3
Union St B3
Univ of Winchester (King Alfred Campus) C1
Upper Brook St B2
Wales St B3
Water Lane B3
West End Terr B1
West Gate B2
Western Rd B1
Wharf Hill C3
Winchester College C2
Winchester Station A2
Wolvesey Castle C3
Worthy Lane A2
Worthy Rd A2

Windsor 344

Adelaide Sq C3
Albany Rd C2
Albert St B1
Alexandra Gdns B2
Alexandra Rd C2
Alma Rd B2
Ambulance Station B1
Arthur Rd B2
Bachelors Acre B3
Barry Ave B2
Beaumont Rd C2
Bexley St B1
Boat House B2
Brocas St B2
Brook St C3
Bulkeley Ave C1
Castle Hill B3
Charles St B2
Claremont Rd C2
Clarence Cr B2
Clarence Rd B1
Clewer Court Rd B1
Coach Park B2
College Cr C1
Courts C2
Cricket Ground C3
Dagmar Rd C2
Datchet Rd B3
Devereux Rd C2
Dorset Rd C2
Duke St B1
Elm Rd C1
Eton College ✦ A3
Eton Ct A2
Eton Sq A2
Eton Wick Rd A2
Fire Station C2
Farm Yard B3
Frances Rd C2
Frogmore Dr B3
Gloucester Pl C3
Goslar Way C1
Goswell Hill B2
Goswell Rd B2
Green La C1
Grove Rd C2
Guildhall B3
Helena Rd C2
Helston La B1
High St A2/B3
Holy Trinity C2
Hospital (Private) C2
Household Cavalry C2
Imperial Rd C1
Information Ctr B2/B3
Keats La A2
King Edward Ct B2
King Edward VII Ave A3
King Edward VII Hospital C2
King George V Meml B3
King's Rd C3
King Stable St A2
Library C2
Maidenhead Rd B1
Meadow La A2
Municipal Offices C3
Nell Gwynne's Ho B3
Osborne Rd C2
Oxford Rd B1
Park St B3
Peascod St B2
Police Station C2
Post Office A2
Princess Margaret Hospital C3
Queen Victoria's Walk B3
Queen's Rd C2
River St B2
Romney Island A3
Romney Lock A3
Romney Lock Rd A3
Russell St C2
St John's B3
St John's Chapel A2
St Leonards Rd C2
St Mark's Rd C2
Sheet St C3
South Meadow A2
South Meadow La A2
Springfield Rd C1
Stovell Rd B1
Sunbury Rd A3
Tangier La A2
Tangier St A3
Temple Rd C2
Thames St B3
The Brocas A2
The Home Park A3/C3
The Long Walk C3
Theatre Royal B3
Trinity Pl C2
Vansittart Rd B1/C1
Vansittart Rd Gdns C1
Victoria Barracks C2
Victoria St C2
Ward Royal B2
Westmead C1
White Lilies Island A1
William St B2
Windsor Arts Ctr C2
Windsor Castle B3
Windsor & Eton Central B2
Windsor & Eton Riverside A3
Windsor Bridge B3
Windsor Great Park C3
Windsor Leisure Ctr B1
Windsor Relief Rd A1
Windsor Royal Sh B2
York Ave C1
York Rd C1

Wolverhampton 344

Albion St B3
Alexandra St C1
Arena B2
Arts Gallery B2
Ashland St C1
Austin St A1
Badger Dr A3
Bailey St B3
Bath Ave B1
Bath Rd B1
Bell St C2
Berry St B3
Bilston Rd C3
Bilston St C3
Birmingham Canal A3
Bone Mill La A2
Brewery Rd B1
Bright St A1
Burton Cres B3
Bus Station B3
Cambridge St A3
Camp St B2
Cannock Rd A3
Castle St C2
Chapel Ash C1
Cherry St C1
Chester St A1
Church La C2
Church St C2
Civic Ctr B2
Clarence Rd B2
Cleveland St C2
Clifton St C1
Coach Station B2
Compton Rd B1
Corn Hill B3
Coven St A3
Craddock St A1
Cross St North A2
Crown & County Courts C3
Crown St A2
Culwell St B3
Dale St C1
Darlington St C1
Dartmouth St C3
Devon Rd A1
Drummond St B2
Dudley Rd C2
Dudley St B2
Duke St C3
Dunkley St B1
Dunstall Ave A2
Dunstall Hill A2
Dunstall Rd A1/A2
Evans St A1
Fawdry St A1
Field St B3
Fire Station C1
Fiveways A2
Fowler Playing Fields A3
Fox's La A2
Francis St A2
Fryer St B3
Gloucester St A1
Gordon St C3
Graiseley St C1
Grand B3
Granville St C3
Great Brickkiln St C1
Great Hampton St A1
Great Western St A2
Grimstone St B3
Harrow St A1
Hilton St A3
Horseley Fields C3
Humber Rd C1
Jack Hayward Way A2
Jameson St A1
Jenner St C3
Kennedy Rd B3
Kimberley St C1
King St B2
Laburnum St C1
Lansdowne Rd B1
Leicester St A1
Lever St C3
Library C3
Lichfield St B2
Light House B3
Little's La B3
Lock St B3
Lord St C1
Lowe St A1
Lower Stafford St A2
Magistrates Court B2
Mander Ctr C2
Mander St C1
Market St B2
Market C2
Melbourne St C3
Merridale St C1
Middlecross C3
Molineux St B2
Mostyn St A1
New Hampton Rd East A1
Nine Elms La A3
North Rd A2
Oaks Cres C1
Oxley St A2
Paget St A1
Park Ave B1
Park Road East A1
Park Road West B1
Paul St C2
Pelham St C1
Penn Rd C2
Piper's Row B3
Pitt St C2
Police Station C3
Pool St C2
Poole St A3
Post Office A1/A2/B2/B2
Powlett St C3
Queen St B2
Raby St C3
Raglan St C1
Railway Dr B3
Red Hill St A2
Red Lion St B2
Retreat St C1
Ring Rd B2
Rugby St A1
Russell St C1
St Andrew's B1
St David's B3
St George's C3
St George's Pde C2
St James St C3
St John's C2
St John's C2
St John's Retail Park C2
St John's Square C2
St Mark's C1
St Marks Rd C1
St Marks St C1
St Patrick's B2
St Peter's B2
St Peter's B2
Salisbury St C1
Salop St C2
School St C2
Sherwood St A2
Smestow St A3
Snowhill C2
Springfield Rd A3
Stafford St B2
Staveley Rd A1
Steelhouse La C3
Stephenson St C1
Stewart St C2
Sun St B3
Sutherland Pl C3
Tempest St C2
Temple St C2
Tettenhall Rd B1
The Maltings B2
The Royal (Metro) C3
Thomas St C2
Thornley St B2
Tower St C2
University B2
Upper Zoar St C1
Vicarage Rd C3
Victoria St C2
Walpole St A1
Walsall St C3
Ward St C3
Warwick St C3
Water St A3
Waterloo Rd B2
Wednesfield Rd B3
West Pk (not A&E) B1
West Park Swimming Pool B1
Wharf St C3
Whitmore Hill B2
Wolverhampton B3
Wolverhampton St George's (Metro) C2
Wolverhampton Wanderers Football Ground (Molineux) B2
Worcester St C2
Wulfrun Ctr C2
Yarwell Cl A3
York St C3
Zoar St C1

Worcester 344

Albany Terr A1
Alice Otley School A2
Angel Pl B2
Angel St B2
Ashcroft Rd A2
Athelstan Rd C3
Back Lane North A1
Back Lane South A1
Barbourne Rd A2
Bath Rd C2
Battenhall Rd C3
Bridge St B2
Britannia Sq A1
Broad St B2
Bromwich La C1
Bromwich Rd C1
Bromyard Rd C1
Bus Station B2
Carden St B3
Castle St A2
Cathedral ✝ C2
Cathedral Plaza B2
Charles St B3
Chequers La B1
Chestnut St A2
Chestnut Walk A2
Citizens' Advice Bureau B2
City Walls Rd B2
Cole Hill C3
College of Technology B2
College St C2
Commandery C3
County Cricket Gd C1
Cripplegate Park B1
Croft Rd B1
Cromwell St B3
Crowngate Ctr B2
Deansway B2
Diglis Pde C2
Diglis Rd C2
Edgar Tower ✦ C2
Farrier St A2
Fire Station B2
Foregate St B2
Foregate Street B2
Fort Royal Hill C3
Fort Royal Park C3
Foundry St B3
Friar St C2
George St B3
Grand Stand Rd B1
Greenhill C3
Greyfriars B2
Guildhall B2
Henwick Rd B1
High St B2
Hill St B3
Huntingdon Hall B2
Hylton Rd B1
Information Ctr B2
King Charles Place Shopping Centre C1
King's School C2
King's School Playing Field C2
Kleve Walk C2
Lansdowne Cr A3
Lansdowne Rd A3
Lansdowne Walk A3
Laslett St A3
Leisure Ctr A3
Library, Museum & Art Gallery A2
Little Chestnut St A2
Little London A2
London Rd C3
Lowell St A3
Lowesmoor B2
Lowesmoor Terr A3
Lowesmoor Wharf A3
Magistrates Court A2
Midland Rd B3
Mill St C2
Moors Severn Terr A1
New Rd C1
New St B2
Northfield St A2
Odeon B2
Padmore St B3
Park St C3
Pheasant St B3
Pitchcroft Racecourse A1
Police Station A2
Portland St C2
Post Office B2
Quay St B2
Queen St B2
Rainbow Hill A3
Recreation Ground A2
Reindeer Court B2
Rogers Hill A3
Sabrina Rd A1
St Dunstan's Cr C3
St John's C1
St Martin's Gate B3
St Oswald's Rd A2
St Paul's St B3
St Swithin's Church B2
St Wulstans Cr C3
Sansome Walk A2
Severn St C2
Shaw St B2
Shire Hall A2
Shrub Hill B3
Shrub Hill Retail Park B3
Shrub Hill Rd B3
Slingpool Walk C1
South Quay B2
Southfield St A2
Sports Ground A2/C1
Stanley Rd B3
Swan, The A1
Swimming Pool A2
Tallow Hill B3
Tennis Walk A2
The Avenue C1
The Butts B2
The Cross B2
The Shambles B2
The Tything A2
Tolladine Rd B3
Tudor House ✦ B2
Tybridge St B1
Univ of Worcester B2
Vincent Rd B3
Vue C2
Washington St A3
Woolhope Rd C3
Worcester Bridge B2
Worcester Library & History Ctr B3
Worcester Porcelain Museum C2
Worcester Royal Grammar School A2
Wylds La C3

Wrexham *Wrecsam* 344

Abbot St B2
Acton Rd A3
Albert St C3
Alexandra Rd C1
Aran Rd A3
Barnfield C3
Bath Rd C2
Beechley Rd C3
Belgrave Rd C2
Belle Vue Park C2
Belle Vue Rd C2
Belvedere Dr A1
Bennion's Rd C3
Berse Rd A1
Bersham Rd C1
Birch St C3
Bodhyfryd B3
Border Retail Park C3
Bradley Rd C2
Bright St B1
Bron-y-Nant B1
Brook St C2
Bryn-y-Cabanau Rd C3
Bury St C3
Bus Station B2
Butchers Market B3
Caia Rd C3
Cambrian Ind Est C3
Caxton Pl B2
Cemetery C1
Centenary Rd C1
Chapel St C2
Charles St B3
Chester Rd A3
Chester St B3
Cilcen Gr A3
Citizens Advice Bureau B2
Cobden Rd B1
Council Offices B3
County B2
Crescent Rd B3
Crispin La A2
Croesnewyth Rd B1
Cross St A2
Cunliffe St A2
Derby Rd C3
Dolydd Rd B1
Duke St B2
Eagles Meadow C3
Earle St C2
East Ave A2
Edward St C2
Egerton St B2
Empress Rd C1
Erddig Rd C2
Fairy Rd C2
Fire Station B2
Foster Rd A3
Foxwood Dr C1
Garden Rd A2
General Market B3
Gerald St B2
Gibson St C1
Glyndŵr University Plas Coch Campus A1
Greenbank St C3
Greenfield A2
Grosvenor Rd B2
Grove Park B2
Grove Park Rd B3
Grove Rd A3
Guildhall B2
Haig Rd C3
Hampden Rd C2
Hazel Gr A3
Henblas St B3
High St B3
Hightown Rd C3
Hill St B2
Holt Rd B3
Holt St B3
Hope St B2
Huntroyde Ave C3
Information Ctr B3
Island Gn Sh Ctr B2
Job Ctr B2
Jubilee Rd B2
King St B2
Kingsmills Rd C3
Lambpit St B3
Law Courts B3
Lawson Cl A3
Lawson Rd A3
Lea Rd C2
Library & Arts Ctr B2
Lilac Way B1
Llys David Lord B1
Lorne St A2
Maesgwyn Rd B1
Maesydre Rd A3
Manley Rd B3
Market St B3
Mawddy Ave A2
Mayville Ave A2
Memorial Gallery B2
Memorial Hall B3
Mold Rd A1
Mount St C3
Neville Cres A3
New Rd A2
North Wales Regional Tennis Ctr A1
North Wales School of Art & Design B2
Oak Dr A3
Park Ave A3
Park St A2
Peel St C1
Pentre Felin C2
Pen y Bryn C2
Penymaes Ave A3
Peoples Market B3
Percy St C2
Plas Coch Retail Park A1
Plas Coch Rd A1
Police Station B3
Poplar Rd C2
Post Office A2/B2/C2/C3
Powell Rd B3
Poyser St C2
Price's La A2
Primose Way B1
Princess St C1
Queen St B3
Queens Sq B2
Regent St B2
Rhosddu Rd A2/B2
Rhosnesni La A3
Rivulet Rd C3
Ruabon Rd C2
Ruthin Rd C1/C2
St Giles C3
St Giles Way C3
St James Ct A2
St Mary's ✝ B2
Salisbury Rd C3
Salop Rd C3
Sontley Rd C2
Spring Rd A2
Stanley St C3
Stansty Rd A2
Station Approach B2
Studio B2
Talbot Rd C2
Techniquest Glyndŵr ✦ A2
The Beeches A3
The Pines A3
Town Hill C2
Trevor St C2
Trinity St B2
Tuttle St C3
Vale Park A1
Vernon St B2
Vicarage Hill B2
Victoria Rd C2
Walnut St A2
War Memorial B3
Waterworld L Ctr ✦ B3
Watery Rd B1/B2
Wellington Rd C2
Westminster Dr A3
William Aston Hall A1
Windsor Rd A1
Wrexham AFC A1
Wrexham Central B2
Wrexham General B2
Wrexham Maelor Hospital (A+E) B1
Wrexham Technology Park B1
Wynn Ave A2
Yale College B3
Yale Gr A3
Yorke St C3

York 344

Aldwark B2
Ambulance Station B3
Barbican Rd C3
Barley Hall B2
Bishopgate St C2
Bishopthorpe Rd C2
Blossom St C1
Bootham A1
Bootham Cr A1
Bootham Terr A1
Bridge St B2
Brook St A2
Brownlow St A2
Burton Stone La A1
Castle Museum C2
Castlegate B2
Cemetery Rd C3
Cherry St C2
City Screen B2
City Wall A2/B1/C3
Clarence St A2
Clementhorpe C2
Clifford St B2
Clifford's Tower B2
Clifton A1
Coach park A2
Coney St B2
Cromwell Rd C2
Crown Court C2
Davygate B2
Deanery Gdns A2
DIG ✦ B2
Ebor Industrial Estate B3
Fairfax House C2
Fishergate C3
Foss Islands Retail Pk B3
Foss Islands Rd B3
Fossbank A3
Garden St A2
George St C3
Gillygate A2
Goodramgate B2
Grand Opera House B2
Grosvenor Terr A1
Guildhall B2
Hallfield Rd A3
Heslington Rd C3
Heworth Green A3
Holy Trinity B2
Hope St C3
Huntington Rd A3
Information Ctr B2
James St B3
Jorvik Viking Ctr B2
Kent St C3
Lawrence St C3
Layerthorpe A3
Leeman Rd B1
Lendal B2
Lendal Bridge B1
Library B1
Longfield Terr A1
Lord Mayor's Walk A2
Lower Eldon St A2
Lowther St A2
Mansion House B2
Margaret St C3
Marygate A1
Melbourne St C3
Merchant Adventurer's Hall B2
Merchant Taylors' Hall B2
Micklegate B1
Micklegate Bar C1
Minster, The ✝ A2
Monkgate A2
Moss St C1
Museum Gdns B1
Museum St B1
National Railway Museum B1
Navigation Rd B3
Newton Terr C2
North Pde A1
North St B2
Nunnery La C1
Nunthorpe Rd C1
Ouse Bridge B2
Paragon St C3
Park Gr A3
Park St C1
Parliament St B2
Peasholme Green B3
Penley's Grove St A2
Piccadilly B2
Police Station B2
Post Office B1/B2/C3
Priory St B1
Purey Cust Nuffield Hospital, The A2
Queen Anne's Rd A1
Quilt Museum B3
Reel C2
Regimental Mus B2
Richard III Museum A2
Roman Bath B2
Rowntree Park C2
St Andrewgate B2
St Benedict Rd C1
St John St A2
St Olave's Rd A1
St Peter's Gr A1
St Saviourgate B2
Scarcroft Hill C1
Scarcroft Rd C1
Skeldergate C2
Skeldergate Bridge C2
Station Rd B1
Stonegate B2
Sycamore Terr A1
Terry Ave C2
The Shambles B2
The Stonebow B2
Theatre Royal B2
Thorpe St C1
Toft Green B1
Tower St C2
Townend St A2
Treasurer's House A2
Trinity La B1
Undercroft Mus A2
Union Terr A2
Victor St C2
Vine St C2
Walmgate C3
Wellington St C3
York Art Gallery A1
York Barbican C3
York Brewery ✦ B1
York Dungeon, The B2
York Station B1

Abbreviations used in the index

Aberdeen	**Aberdeen City**
Aberds	**Aberdeenshire**
Ald	**Alderney**
Anglesey	**Isle of Anglesey**
Angus	**Angus**
Argyll	**Argyll and Bute**
Bath	**Bath and North East Somerset**
Bedford	**Bedford**
Bl Gwent	**Blaenau Gwent**
Blackburn	**Blackburn with Darwen**
Blackpool	**Blackpool**
Bmouth	**Bournemouth**
Borders	**Scottish Borders**
Brack	**Bracknell**
Bridgend	**Bridgend**
Brighton	**City of Brighton and Hove**
Bristol	**City and County of Bristol**
Bucks	**Buckinghamshire**
C Beds	**Central Bedfordshire**
Caerph	**Caerphilly**
Cambs	**Cambridgeshire**
Cardiff	**Cardiff**
Carms	**Carmarthenshire**
Ceredig	**Ceredigion**
Ches E	**Cheshire East**
Ches W	**Cheshire West and Chester**
Clack	**Clackmannanshire**
Conwy	**Conwy**
Corn	**Cornwall**
Cumb	**Cumbria**
Darl	**Darlington**
Denb	**Denbighshire**
Derby	**City of Derby**
Derbys	**Derbyshire**
Devon	**Devon**
Dorset	**Dorset**
Dumfries	**Dumfries and Galloway**
Dundee	**Dundee City**
Durham	**Durham**
E Ayrs	**East Ayrshire**
E Dunb	**East Dunbartonshire**
E Loth	**East Lothian**
E Renf	**East Renfrewshire**
E Sus	**East Sussex**
E Yorks	**East Riding of Yorkshire**
Edin	**City of Edinburgh**
Essex	**Essex**
Falk	**Falkirk**
Fife	**Fife**
Flint	**Flintshire**
Glasgow	**City of Glasgow**
Glos	**Gloucestershire**
Gtr Man	**Greater Manchester**
Guern	**Guernsey**
Gwyn	**Gwynedd**
Halton	**Halton**
Hants	**Hampshire**
Hereford	**Herefordshire**
Herts	**Hertfordshire**
Highld	**Highland**
Hrtlpl	**Hartlepool**
Hull	**Hull**
IoM	**Isle of Man**
IoW	**Isle of Wight**
Invclyd	**Inverclyde**
Jersey	**Jersey**
Kent	**Kent**
Lancs	**Lancashire**
Leicester	**City of Leicester**
Leics	**Leicestershire**
Lincs	**Lincolnshire**
London	**Greater London**
Luton	**Luton**
M Keynes	**Milton Keynes**
M Tydf	**Merthyr Tydfil**
Mbro	**Middlesbrough**
Medway	**Medway**
Mers	**Merseyside**
Midloth	**Midlothian**
Mon	**Monmouthshire**
Moray	**Moray**
N Ayrs	**North Ayrshire**
N Lincs	**North Lincolnshire**
N Lanark	**North Lanarkshire**
N Som	**North Somerset**
N Yorks	**North Yorkshire**
NE Lincs	**North East Lincolnshire**
Neath	**Neath Port Talbot**
Newport	**City and County of Newport**
Norf	**Norfolk**
Northants	**Northamptonshire**
Northumb	**Northumberland**
Nottingham	**City of Nottingham**
Notts	**Nottinghamshire**
Orkney	**Orkney**
Oxon	**Oxfordshire**
Pboro	**Peterborough**
Pembs	**Pembrokeshire**
Perth	**Perth and Kinross**
Plym	**Plymouth**
Poole	**Poole**
Powys	**Powys**
Ptsmth	**Portsmouth**
Reading	**Reading**
Redcar	**Redcar and Cleveland**
Renfs	**Renfrewshire**
Rhondda	**Rhondda Cynon Taff**
Rutland	**Rutland**
S Ayrs	**South Ayrshire**
S Glos	**South Gloucestershire**
S Lanark	**South Lanarkshire**
S Yorks	**South Yorkshire**
Scilly	**Scilly**
Shetland	**Shetland**
Shrops	**Shropshire**
Slough	**Slough**
Som	**Somerset**
Soton	**Southampton**
Staffs	**Staffordshire**
Southend	**Southend-on-Sea**
Stirling	**Stirling**
Stockton	**Stockton-on-Tees**
Stoke	**Stoke-on-Trent**
Suff	**Suffolk**
Sur	**Surrey**
Swansea	**Swansea**
Swindon	**Swindon**
T&W	**Tyne and Wear**
Telford	**Telford & Wrekin**
Thurrock	**Thurrock**
Torbay	**Torbay**
Torf	**Torfaen**
V Glam	**The Vale of Glamorgan**
W Berks	**West Berkshire**
W Dunb	**West Dunbartonshire**
W Isles	**Western Isles**
W Loth	**West Lothian**
W Mid	**West Midlands**
W Sus	**West Sussex**
W Yorks	**West Yorkshire**
Warks	**Warwickshire**
Warr	**Warrington**
Wilts	**Wiltshire**
Windsor	**Windsor and Maidenhead**
Wokingham	**Wokingham**
Worcs	**Worcestershire**
Wrex	**Wrexham**
York	**City of York**

Index to road maps of Britain

How to use the index

Example **Blatherwycke** Northants **137** D9

- grid square
- page number
- county or unitary authority

A

Aaron's Hill Sur 50 E3
Aaron's Town Cumb 240 E2
Ab Kettleby Leics 154 E4
Ab Lench Worcs 117 G10
Abbas Combe Som 30 C2
Abberley Worcs 116 D5
Abberton Essex 89 B8
Abberton Worcs 117 G9
Abberwick Northumb 264 G4
Abbess End Essex 87 C9
Abbess Roding Essex 87 C9
Abbey Devon 27 E10
Abbey-cwm-hir Powys 113 C11
Abbey Dore Hereford 97 E7
Abbey Field Essex 107 G9
Abbey Gate Kent 53 B9
Abbey Green Shrops 149 C10
Abbey Green Staffs 169 D7
Abbey Hey Gtr Man 184 B5
Abbey Hulton Stoke 168 F6
Abbey Mead Sur 66 F4
Abbey St Bathans Borders 272 C5
Abbey Town Cumb 238 G5
Abbey Village Lancs 194 C6
Abbey Wood London 68 D3
Abbeycwmhir Powys 113 C11
Abbeydale Glos 80 B5
Abbeydale S Yorks 186 E4
Abbeydale Park S Yorks 186 E4
Abbeyhill Edin 280 G5
Abbeystead Lancs 203 C7
Abbots Bickington Devon 24 E5
Abbots Bromley Staffs 151 E11
Abbots Langley Herts 85 E9
Abbots Leigh N Som 60 E4
Abbot's Meads W Ches 166 B5
Abbots Morton Worcs 117 F10
Abbots Ripton Cambs 122 B4
Abbots Salford Warks 117 G11
Abbots Worthy Hants 48 G3
Abbotsbury Dorset 17 D7
Abbotsford W Sus 36 C4
Abbotsham Devon 24 B6
Abbotskerswell Devon 9 B7
Abbotsleigh Devon 8 F6
Abbotsley Cambs 122 F4
Abbotstone Hants 48 G5
Abbotswood Hants 32 C5
Abbotswood Sur 50 C4
Abbotts Ann Hants 47 E10
Abcott Shrops 115 B7
Abdon Shrops 131 F11
Abdy S Yorks 186 B6
Aber Ceredig 93 B9
Aber-Arad Carms 92 D6
Aber-banc Ceredig 93 C7
Aber Cowarch Gwyn 147 F7
Aber-Giâr Carms 93 C10
Aber-gwynfi Neath 57 B11
Aber-Hirnant Gwyn 147 C9
Aber miwl = Abermule Powys 130 E3
Aber-nant Rhondda 77 E8
Aber-oer Wrex 166 F3
Aber-Rhiwlech Gwyn 147 E8
Aber-Village Powys 96 G2
Aberaeron Ceredig 111 E9
Aberaman Rhondda 77 E8
Aberangell Gwyn 146 G6
Aberarder Highld 290 E6
Aberarder House Highld 300 G6
Aberarder Lodge Highld 291 E7
Aberargie Perth 286 F5
Aberarth Ceredig 111 E9
Aberavon Neath 57 C8
Aberbargoed Caerph 77 E11
Aberbechan Powys 130 E2
Aberbeeg Bl Gwent 78 E2
Aberbran Powys 95 F9
Abercanaid M Tydf 77 E9
Abercarn Caerph 78 G2
Abercastle Pembs 91 E7
Abercegir Powys 128 C6
Aberchalder Highld 290 C5
Aberchirder Aberds 302 D6
Abercorn W Loth 279 F11
Abercraf Powys 76 C4
Abercregan Neath 57 B11
Abercrombie Fife 287 G9
Abercwmboi Rhondda 77 F8
Abercych Pembs 92 C4
Abercynafon Powys 77 B9
Abercynffig = Aberkenfig Bridgend 57 E11
Abercynon Rhondda 77 F9
Aberdâr = Aberdare Rhondda 77 E7
Aberdalgie Perth 286 E4
Aberdare = Aberdâr Rhondda 77 E7
Aberdaron Gwyn 144 D3
Aberdeen Aberdeen 293 C11
Aberdesach Gwyn 162 E6
Aberdour Fife 280 D3
Aberdovey = Aberdyfi Gwyn 128 D2
Aberdulais Neath 76 E3
Aberdyfi = Aberdovey Gwyn 128 D2
Aberedw Powys 95 B11
Abereiddy Pembs 90 E5
Abererch Gwyn 145 B7
Aberfan M Tydf 77 E9
Aberfeldy Perth 286 C2
Aberffraw Anglesey 162 B5
Aberffrwd Ceredig 112 B3
Aberffrwd Mon 78 D5
Aberford W Yorks 206 F4
Aberfoyle Stirl 285 G9
Abergarw Bridgend 58 C2
Abergarwed Neath 76 E4
Abergavenny Mon 78 C3
Abergele Conwy 180 F6
Abergorlech Carms 93 E11
Abergwaun = Fishguard Pembs 91 D9
Abergwesyn Powys 113 G7
Abergwili Carms 93 G8
Abergwynant Gwyn 146 F3
Abergwynfi Neath 57 B11
Abergwyngregyn Gwyn 179 G11
Abergynolwyn Gwyn 128 B3
Aberhosan Powys 128 D6
Aberkenfig = Abercynffig Bridgend 57 E11
Aberlady E Loth 281 E9
Aberlemno Angus 287 B9
Aberllerry Ceredig 128 E2
Aberllefenni Gwyn 128 B5
Aberllydan = Broad Haven Pembs 72 C5
Aberllynfi = Three Cocks Powys 96 D3
Abermagwr Ceredig 112 C3
Abermaw = Barmouth Gwyn 146 F2
Abermeurig Ceredig 111 F11
Abermorddu Flint 166 D4
Abermule = Aber-miwl Powys 130 E3
Abernaint Powys 148 E2
Abernant Carms 92 G6
Abernant Powys 130 D3
Abernethy Perth 286 F5
Abernyte Perth 286 D6
Aberogwr = Ogmore by Sea V Glam 57 F11
Aberpennar = Mountain Ash Rhondda 77 F8
Aberporth Ceredig 110 G5
Aberriw = Berriew Powys 130 C3
Abersoch Gwyn 144 D6
Abersychan Torf 78 E3
Abertawe = Swansea Swansea 56 C6
Aberteifi = Cardigan Ceredig 92 B3
Aberthin V Glam 58 D4
Abertillery Bl Gwent 78 E2
Abertridwr Caerph 58 B6
Abertridwr Powys 147 F10
Abertrinant Gwyn 128 B2
Abertysswg Caerph 77 D10
Aberuchill Castle Perth 285 E11
Aberuthven Perth 286 F3
Aberyscir Powys 95 F9
Aberystwyth Ceredig 111 A11
Abhainn Suidhe W Isles 305 H2
Abingdon Oxon 83 F7
Abinger Common Sur 50 D6
Abinger Hammer Sur 50 D5
Abington Northants 120 E5
Abington S Lnrk 259 E10
Abington Pigotts Cambs 104 C6
Abington Vale Northants 120 E5
Abingworth W Sus 35 D10
Ablington Glos 81 D10
Ablington Wilts 47 D7
Abney Derbys 185 F11
Aboyne Aberds 293 D7
Abraham Heights Lancs 211 G9
Abram Gtr Man 194 G6
Abriachan Highld 300 F5
Abridge Essex 87 F7
Abronhill N Lnrk 278 F5
Abshot Hants 33 F8
Abson S Glos 61 E8
Abthorpe Northants 102 B2
Abune-the-Hill Orkney 314 D2
Aby Lincs 190 F6
Acaster Malbis York 207 D7
Acaster Selby N Yorks 207 E7
Accrington Lancs 195 B9
Acha Argyll 275 B8
Acha Argyll 288 D3
Acha Mor W Isles 304 F5
Achabraid Argyll 275 E9
Achachork Highld 298 E4
Achad nan Darach Highld 284 B4
Achadh an Eas Highld 308 F6
Achadunan Argyll 284 F5
Achafolla Argyll 275 B8
Achagary Highld 308 D7
Achaglass Argyll 255 C8
Achahoish Argyll 275 F8
Achalader Perth 286 C5
Achallader Argyll 285 C7
Achalone Highld 310 D5
Ach'an Todhair Highld 290 F2
Achanalt Highld 300 C2
Achanamara Argyll 275 E8
Achandunie Highld 300 B6
Achanelid Argyll 275 E11
Achany Highld 309 J5
Achaphubuil Highld 290 F2
Acharacle Highld 289 C8
Acharn Highld 289 D9
Acharn Perth 285 C11
Acharole Highld 310 D6
Acharossan Argyll 275 F10
Acharry Muir Highld 309 K6
Achath Aberds 293 B9
Achavanich Highld 310 E5
Achavelgin Highld 301 D9
Achavraat Highld 301 E9
Achddu Carms 74 E6
Achdregnie Moray 302 G2
Achduart Highld 307 J5
Achentoul Highld 310 F2
Achfary Highld 306 F7
Achfrish Highld 309 H5
Achgarve Highld 307 K3
Achiemore Highld 308 C3
Achiemore Highld 310 D2
A'Chill Highld 294 E4
Achiltibuie Highld 307 J5
Achina Highld 308 C7
Achinahuagh Highld 308 C5
Achindaul Highld 290 E3
Achindown Highld 301 E8
Achinduich Highld 309 J5
Achinduin Argyll 289 F10
Achingills Highld 310 C5
Achininver Highld 308 C5
Achintee Highld 290 F3
Achintee Highld 299 E9
Achintraid Highld 295 B10
Achlaven Argyll 289 F11
Achlean Highld 291 D10
Achleck Argyll 288 E6
Achlorachan Highld 300 D3
Achluachrach Highld 290 E4
Achlyness Highld 306 D7
Achmelvich Highld 307 G5
Achmore Highld 295 B10
Achmore Stirl 285 D9
Achnaba Argyll 275 E10
Achnaba Argyll 289 F11
Achnabat Highld 300 F5
Achnabreck Argyll 275 D9
Achnacarnin Highld 306 F5
Achnacarry Highld 290 E3
Achnacloich Argyll 289 F11
Achnacloich Highld 295 E7
Achnaconeran Highld 290 B6
Achnacraig Argyll 288 E6
Achnacree Argyll 289 F11
Achnacree Bay Argyll 289 F11
Achnacroish Argyll 289 E10
Achnadrish Argyll 288 D6
Achnafalnich Argyll 284 E6
Achnagarron Highld 300 C6
Achnaha Highld 288 C6
Achnahanat Highld 309 K5
Achnahannet Highld 301 G9
Achnahard Argyll 288 G5
Achnairn Highld 309 H5
Achnaluachrach Highld 309 J6
Achnandarach Highld 295 B10
Achnanellan Highld 290 E2
Achnasaul Highld 290 E3
Achnasheen Highld 299 D11
Achnashelloch Argyll 275 D9
Achnavast Highld 310 C4
Achneigie Highld 299 B10
Achormlarie Highld 309 K6
Achorn Highld 310 F5
Achosnich Highld 288 C6
Achranich Highld 289 E9
Achreamie Highld 310 C4
Achriabhach Highld 290 G3
Achriesgill Highld 306 D7
Achrimsdale Highld 311 J3
Achtoty Highld 308 C6
Achurch Northants 137 G10
Achuvoldrach Highld 308 D5
Achvaich Highld 309 K7
Achvarasdal Highld 310 C3
Ackenthwaite Cumb 211 C10
Ackergill Highld 310 D7
Acklam M'bro 225 B9
Acklam N Yorks 216 G5
Ackleton Shrops 132 D5
Acklington Northumb 252 C6
Ackton W Yorks 198 C2
Ackworth Moor Top W Yorks 198 D2
Acle Norf 161 G8
Acock's Green W Mid 134 G2
Acol Kent 71 F10
Acomb Northumb 241 D10
Acomb York 207 C7
Acre Gtr Man 196 F2
Acre Lancs 195 C9
Acre Street W Sus 21 B11
Acrefair Wrex 166 G3
Acres Nook Staffs 168 E4
Acton Dorset 18 F5
Acton E Ches 167 E10
Acton London 67 C8
Acton Shrops 130 G6
Acton Staffs 168 G4
Acton Suff 107 C7
Acton Worcs 116 D6
Acton Wrex 166 E4
Acton Beauchamp Hereford 116 G3
Acton Bridge W Ches 183 F9
Acton Burnell Shrops 131 C10
Acton Green Hereford 116 G3
Acton Green London 67 D8
Acton Pigott Shrops 131 C10
Acton Place Suff 107 B7
Acton Reynald Shrops 149 E10
Acton Round Shrops 132 D2
Acton Scott Shrops 131 F9
Acton Trussell Staffs 151 F8
Acton Turville S Glos 61 C10
Adabroc W Isles 304 B7
Adambrae W Loth 269 A10
Adam's Green Dorset 29 F8
Adbaston Staffs 150 D5
Adber Dorset 29 C9
Adbolton Notts 154 B2
Adderbury Oxon 101 D9
Adderley Shrops 150 B3
Adderley Green Stoke 168 G6
Adderstone Northumb 264 C4
Addiewell W Loth 269 C9
Addingham W Yorks 205 D7
Addingham Moorside W Yorks 205 D7
Addington Bucks 102 F4
Addington Corn 6 B5
Addington Kent 53 B7
Addington London 67 G11
Addinston Borders 271 E10
Addiscombe London 67 F10
Addlestone Sur 66 G5
Addlestonemoor Sur 66 F4
Addlethorpe Lincs 175 B8
Adel W Yorks 205 F11
Adeney Telford 150 F4
Adeyfield Herts 85 D9
Adfa Powys 129 C11
Adforton Hereford 115 C8
Adgestone I o W 21 D7
Adisham Kent 55 C8
Adlestrop Glos 100 F4
Adlingfleet E Yorks 199 C10
Adlington E Ches 184 E6
Adlington Lancs 194 E6
Adlington Park Lancs 194 E5
Admaston Staffs 151 E10
Admaston Telford 150 G2
Admington Warks 100 B4
Adpar Ceredig 92 C6
Adsborough Som 28 B3
Adscombe Som 43 F7
Adstock Bucks 102 E4
Adstone Northants 119 G11
Adswood Gtr Man 184 D5
Adversane W Sus 35 C9
Advie Highld 301 F11
Adwalton W Yorks 197 B8
Adwell Oxon 83 F11
Adwick le Street S Yorks 198 F4
Adwick upon Dearne S Yorks 198 G3
Adziel Aberds 303 D9
Ae Dumfries 247 F11
Ae Village Dumfries 247 F11
Affetside Gtr Man 195 E9
Affleck Aberds 303 G8
Affpuddle Dorset 18 C2
Affric Lodge Highld 299 G11
Afon Eitha Wrex 166 F3
Afon-wen Flint 181 G10
Afon Wen Gwyn 145 B8
Afton I o W 20 D2
Agar Nook Leics 153 G9
Agbrigg W Yorks 197 D10
Aggborough Worcs 116 B6
Agglethorpe N Yorks 213 B11
Aglionby Cumb 239 F10
Agneash I o M 192 D5
Aifft Denb 165 B10
Aigburth Mers 182 D5
Aiginis W Isles 304 E6
Aike E Yorks 209 D7
Aikenway Moray 302 E2
Aikerness Orkney 314 A4
Aikers Orkney 314 G4
Aiketgate Cumb 230 B5
Aikton Cumb 239 G7
Ailby Lincs 190 F6
Ailey Hereford 96 B6
Ailstone Warks 118 G4
Ailsworth P'boro 138 D2
Aimes Green Essex 86 E5
Ainderby Quernhow N Yorks 215 C7
Ainderby Steeple N Yorks 224 G6
Aingers Green Essex 108 G2
Ainley Top W Yorks 196 D6
Ainsdale Mers 193 E10
Ainsdale-on-Sea Mers 193 E9
Ainstable Cumb 230 B6
Ainsworth Gtr Man 195 E9
Ainthorpe N Yorks 226 D4
Aintree Mers 182 B5
Aird Argyll 275 C8
Aird Dumfries 236 C2
Aird Highld 299 B7
Aird W Isles 296 F3
Aird W Isles 304 E7
Aird a Mhachair W Isles 297 G3
Aird a' Mhulaidh W Isles 305 G3
Aird Asaig W Isles 305 H3
Aird Dhail W Isles 304 B6
Aird Mhòr W Isles 297 G4
Aird Mhidhinis W Isles 297 L3
Aird Mhighe W Isles 296 C6
Aird Mhighe W Isles 305 J3
Aird Mhor W Isles 297 L3
Aird of Sleat Highld 295 E7
Aird Thunga W Isles 304 E6
Aird Uig W Isles 304 E2
Airdachuilinn Highld 306 E7
Airdens Highld 309 K6
Airdeny Argyll 289 G11
Airdrie N Lnrk 268 B5
Airds of Kells Dumfries 237 B8
Airdtorrisdale Highld 308 C6
Aire View N Yorks 204 D5
Airedale W Yorks 198 B3
Airidh a Bhruaich W Isles 305 G4
Airieland Dumfries 237 D9
Airinis W Isles 304 E6
Airlie Angus 287 B7
Airlies Dumfries 236 D5
Airmyn E Yorks 199 B8
Airntully Perth 286 D4
Airor Highld 295 E9
Airth Falk 279 D7
Airthrey Castle Stirl 278 B6
Airton N Yorks 204 B4
Airy Hill N Yorks 227 D7
Airyhassen Dumfries 236 E5
Airyligg Dumfries 236 C4
Aisby Lincs 155 B10
Aisby Lincs 188 C5
Aisgernis W Isles 297 J3
Aish Devon 8 C3
Aish Devon 8 D6
Aisholt Som 43 F7
Aiskew N Yorks 214 B5
Aislaby N Yorks 216 B5
Aislaby N Yorks 227 D7
Aislaby Stockton 225 C8
Aisthorpe Lincs 188 E6
Aith Orkney 314 E2
Aith Shetland 312 D8
Aith Shetland 313 H5
Aithnen Powys 148 E4
Aithsetter Shetland 313 K6
Aitkenhead S Ayrs 245 B8
Aitnoch Highld 301 F9
Akeld Northumb 263 D11
Akeley Bucks 102 D4
Akenham Suff 108 B2
Albany T & W 243 F7
Albaston Corn 12 G4
Alberbury Shrops 149 G7
Albert Town Pembs 72 B6
Albert Village Leics 152 F6
Albourne W Sus 36 D3
Albourne Green W Sus 36 D3
Albrighton Shrops 132 C6
Albrighton Shrops 149 F9
Albro Castle Ceredig 92 B3
Alburgh Norf 142 F5
Albury Herts 105 G8
Albury Sur 50 D5
Albury End Herts 105 G8
Albury Heath Sur 50 D5
Alby Hill Norf 160 C3
Albyfield Cumb 240 G2
Alcaig Highld 300 D5
Alcaston Shrops 131 F9
Alcester Dorset 30 C5
Alcester Warks 117 F11
Alcester Lane's End W Mid 133 G11
Alciston E Sus 23 D8
Alcombe Som 42 D3
Alcombe Wilts 61 F10
Alconbury Cambs 122 B3
Alconbury Weston Cambs 122 B3
Aldbar Castle Angus 287 B9
Aldborough N Yorks 215 F8
Aldborough Norf 160 C3
Aldborough Hatch London 68 B3
Aldbourne Wilts 63 D9
Aldbrough E Yorks 209 F10
Aldbrough St John N Yorks 224 C4
Aldbury Herts 85 C7
Aldcliffe Lancs 211 G9
Aldclune Perth 291 G11
Aldeburgh Suff 127 F9
Aldeby Norf 143 E8
Aldenham Herts 85 F10
Alder Forest Gtr Man 184 B3
Alder Moor Staffs 152 D4
Alder Row Som 45 E9
Alderbrook E Sus 37 B8
Alderbury Wilts 31 B11
Aldercar Derbys 170 F6
Alderford Norf 160 F2
Alderholt Dorset 31 E10
Alderley Glos 80 G3
Alderley Edge E Ches 184 F4
Alderman's Green W Mid 135 G7
Aldermaston W Berks 64 F5
Aldermaston Soke W Berks 64 G6
Aldermaston Wharf W Berks 64 F6
Alderminster Warks 100 B4
Aldermoor Soton 32 D5
Alderney Poole 18 C6
Alder's End Hereford 98 C2
Aldersbrook London 68 B2
Aldersey Green W Ches 167 D7
Aldershawe Staffs 134 B2
Aldershot Hants 49 C11
Alderton Glos 99 E10
Alderton Northants 102 B4
Alderton Shrops 149 E9
Alderton Suff 108 C6
Alderton Wilts 61 C10
Alderton Fields Glos 99 E10
Alderwasley Derbys 170 E4
Aldfield N Yorks 214 F5
Aldford W Ches 166 D6
Aldgate Rutland 137 C9
Aldham Essex 107 F8
Aldham Suff 107 B10
Aldie Highld 309 L7
Aldingbourne W Sus 22 B6
Aldingham Cumb 210 E5
Aldington Kent 54 F5
Aldington Worcs 99 C11
Aldington Frith Kent 54 F4
Aldivalloch Moray 302 G3
Aldochlay Argyll 277 C7
Aldon Shrops 115 B8
Aldoth Cumb 229 B8
Aldourie Castle Highld 300 F6
Aldreth Cambs 123 C8
Aldridge W Mid 133 C11
Aldringham Suff 127 E8
Aldrington Brighton 36 F3
Aldsworth Glos 81 C11
Aldunie Moray 302 G3
Aldwark Derbys 170 D2
Aldwark N Yorks 215 G9
Aldwarke S Yorks 186 C6
Aldwick W Sus 22 D6
Aldwincle Northants 137 G10
Aldworth W Berks 64 D5
Ale Oak Shrops 130 G4
Alehouseburn Aberds 302 C6
Alehousehill Aberds 303 G10
Alexandria W Dunb 277 F7
Aley Som 43 F7
Aley Green C Beds 85 B9
Alfardisworthy Devon 24 E3
Alfington Devon 15 B8
Alfold Sur 50 G4
Alfold Bars W Sus 50 G4
Alfold Crossways Sur 50 F4
Alford Aberds 293 B7
Alford Lincs 191 F7
Alford Som 44 G6
Alfred's Well Worcs 117 C8
Alfreton Derbys 170 D6
Alfrick Worcs 116 G4
Alfrick Pound Worcs 116 G4
Alfriston E Sus 23 E8
Algakirk Lincs 156 B5
Algaltraig Argyll 275 F11
Algarkirk Lincs 156 B5
Alhampton Som 44 G6
Aline Lodge W Isles 305 G3
Alisary Highld 289 B9
Alkborough N Lincs 199 C11
Alkerton Glos 80 D3
Alkerton Oxon 101 C7
Alkham Kent 55 E9
Alkington Shrops 149 B10
Alkmonton Derbys 152 B3
Alkrington Garden Village Gtr Man 195 G11
All Cannings Wilts 62 G5
All Saints Devon 28 G4
All Saints South Elmham Suff 142 G6
All Stretton Shrops 131 D9
Alladale Lodge Highld 309 L4
Allaleigh Devon 8 E6
Allanaquoich Aberds 292 D3
Allanbank Borders 271 F10
Allanbank N Lnrk 268 D6
Allangrange Mains Highld 300 D6
Allanshaugh Borders 271 F8
Allanshaws Borders 271 G9
Allanton Borders 273 E7
Allanton N Lnrk 269 D7
Allanton S Lnrk 268 E4
Allaston Glos 79 E10
Allathasdal W Isles 297 L2
Allbrook Hants 33 C7
Allen End Warks 134 D3
Allendale Town Northumb 241 F8
Allenheads Northumb 232 B3
Allens Green Herts 87 B7
Allensford Durham 242 G3
Allensmore Hereford 97 D9
Allenton Derby 153 C7
Allenwood Cumb 239 F11
Aller Devon 9 B7
Aller Devon 27 F9
Aller Dorset 30 G3
Aller Som 28 B6
Aller Park Devon 9 B7
Allerby Cumb 229 D7
Allerford Som 27 B11
Allerford Som 42 D2
Allerston N Yorks 217 C7
Allerthorpe E Yorks 207 D11
Allerton Mers 182 D6
Allerton W Yorks 205 G8
Allerton Bywater W Yorks 198 B2
Allerton Mauleverer N Yorks 206 B4
Allesley W Mid 134 G6
Allestree Derby 152 B6
Allet Corn 4 F5
Allexton Leics 136 C6
Allgreave E Ches 169 B7
Allhallows Medway 69 D10
Allhallows-on-Sea Medway 69 D10
Alligin Shuas Highld 299 D8
Allimore Green Staffs 151 F7
Allington Kent 53 B8
Allington Lincs 172 G5
Allington Wilts 47 F8
Allington Wilts 61 D11
Allington Wilts 62 G5
Allington Bar Wilts 61 E11
Allithwaite Cumb 211 D7
Alloa Clack 279 C7
Allonby Cumb 229 C7
Allostock W Ches 184 G2
Alloway S Ayrs 257 F8
Allowenshay Som 28 E5
Allscot Shrops 132 D4
Allscott Telford 150 G2
Allt Carms 75 E9
Allt-na-giubhsaich Aberds 292 E4
Allt na h-Airbhe Highld 307 K6
Allt-nan-sùgh Highld 295 C11
Allt-yr-yn Newport 59 B9
Alltami Flint 166 B3
Alltbeithe Highld 290 C2
Alltchaorunn Highld 284 B5
Alltforgan Powys 147 E9
Alltmawr Powys 95 B11
Alltnacaillich Highld 308 E4
Alltrech Argyll 289 F8
Alltsigh Highld 290 B6
Alltwalis Carms 93 E8
Alltwen Neath 76 E2
Alltyblaca Ceredig 93 B10
Allwood Green Suff 125 C10
Alma Notts 171 E7
Almagill Dumfries 238 B3
Almeley Hereford 114 G6

Almeley Wooton Hereford 114 G6
Almer Dorset 18 B4
Almholme S Yorks 198 F5
Almington Staffs 150 C4
Alminstone Cross Devon 24 C4
Almondbank Perth 286 E4
Almondbury W Yorks 197 D7
Almondsbury S Glos 60 C6
Almondvale W Loth 269 B11
Almshouse Green Essex 106 E5
Alne N Yorks 215 F9
Alne End Warks 118 F2
Alne Hills Warks 118 E2
Alne Station N Yorks 215 F10
Alness Highld 300 C6
Alnessferry Highld 300 C6
Alnham Northumb 263 G11
Alnmouth Northumb 264 G6
Alnwick Northumb 264 G5
Alperton London 67 C7
Alphamstone Essex 107 D7
Alpheton Suff 125 G7
Alphington Devon 14 C4
Alpington Norf 142 C5
Alport Derbys 170 C2
Alport Powys 130 D5
Alpraham E Ches 167 D9
Alresford Essex 107 G11
Alrewas Staffs 152 F3
Alsager E Ches 168 D3
Alsagers Bank Staffs 168 F4
Alscot Bucks 84 E4
Alsop en le Dale Derbys 169 D11
Alston Cumb 231 B10
Alston Devon 28 G4
Alston Sutton Som 44 C2
Alstone Glos 99 E9
Alstone Glos 99 G8
Alstone Som 43 D10
Alstonefield Staffs 169 D10
Alswear Devon 26 C2
Alt Gtr Man 196 G2
Alt Hill Gtr Man 196 G2
Altandhu Highld 307 H4
Altanduin Highld 311 G2
Altarnun Corn 11 E10
Altass Highld 309 J4
Altbough Hereford 97 E10
Altdargue Aberds 293 C7
Alterwall Highld 310 C6
Altham Lancs 203 G11
Althorne Essex 88 F6
Althorpe N Lincs 199 F10
Alticane S Ayrs 244 F6
Alticry Dumfries 236 D4
Altmore Windsor 65 D11
Altnabreac Station Highld 310 E4
Altnacealgach Hotel Highld 307 H7
Altnacraig Argyll 289 G10
Altnafeadh Highld 284 B6
Altnaharra Highld 308 F5
Altofts W Yorks 197 C11
Alton Derbys 170 C5
Alton Hants 49 F8
Alton Staffs 169 G9
Alton Wilts 47 D7
Alton Barnes Wilts 62 G6
Alton Pancras Dorset 30 G2
Alton Priors Wilts 62 G6
Altonhill E Ayrs 257 B10
Altonside Moray 302 D2
Altour Highld 290 E4
Altrincham Gtr Man 184 D3
Altrua Highld 290 E4
Altskeith Stirl 285 G8
Altyre Ho Moray 301 D10
Alum Rock W Mid 134 F2
Alva Clack 279 B7
Alvanley W Ches 183 G7
Alvaston Derby 153 C7
Alvechurch Worcs 117 C10
Alvecote Warks 134 C4
Alvediston Wilts 31 C7
Alveley Shrops 132 G5
Alverdiscott Devon 25 B8
Alverstoke Hants 21 B8
Alverstone I o W 21 D7
Alverthorpe W Yorks 197 C10
Alverton Notts 172 G3
Alves Moray 301 C11
Alvescot Oxon 82 E3
Alveston S Glos 60 B6
Alveston Warks 118 F4
Alveston Down S Glos 60 B6
Alveston Hill Warks 118 G4
Alvie Highld 291 C10
Alvingham Lincs 190 C5
Alvington Glos 79 E10
Alvington Som 29 D8
Alwalton Cambs 138 D2
Alway Newport 59 B10
Alweston Dorset 29 E11
Alwington Devon 24 C6
Alwinton Northumb 251 B10
Alwoodley W Yorks 205 E11
Alwoodley Gates W Yorks 206 E2
Alwoodley Park W Yorks 205 E11
Alyth Perth 286 C6
Am Baile W Isles 297 K3
Am Buth Argyll 289 G10
Amalebra Corn 1 B5
Amalveor Corn 1 B5
Amatnatua Highld 309 K4
Ambaston Derbys 153 C8
Amber Hill Lincs 174 F2
Ambergate Derbys 170 E4
Amberley Glos 80 E5
Amberley Hereford 97 B10
Amberley W Sus 35 E8
Amble Northumb 253 C7
Amblecote W Mid 133 F7
Ambler Thorn W Yorks 196 B5
Ambleside Cumb 221 E7
Ambleston Pembs 91 F10
Ambrosden Oxon 83 B10
Amcotts N Lincs 199 E11
Amen Corner Brack 65 F10
Amersham Bucks 85 F7
Amersham Common Bucks 85 F7
Amersham Old Town Bucks 85 F7
Amersham on the Hill Bucks 85 F7
Amerton Staffs 151 D9
Amesbury Bath 45 B7
Amesbury Wilts 47 E7
Ameysford Dorset 31 G9
Amington Staffs 134 C4
Amisfield Dumfries 247 G11
Amlwch Anglesey 178 C6
Amlwch Port Anglesey 179 C7
Ammanford = Rhydaman Carms 75 C10
Ammerham Som 28 F5
Amod Argyll 255 D8
Amotherby N Yorks 216 E4
Ampfield Hants 32 C6
Ampleforth N Yorks 215 D11
Ampney Crucis Glos 81 E9
Ampney St Mary Glos 81 E9
Ampney St Peter Glos 81 E9
Amport Hants 47 E9
Ampthill C Beds 103 D10
Ampton Suff 125 C7
Amroth Pembs 73 D11
Amulree Perth 286 D2
Amwell Herts 85 C11
An Caol Highld 298 D6
An Cnoc W Isles 304 E6
An Gleann Ur W Isles 304 E6
An Leth Meadhanach W Isles 297 K3
An t-Ob W Isles 296 C6
Anagach Highld 301 G10
Anaheilt Highld 289 C10
Anancaun Highld 299 C10
Ancarraig Highld 300 G4
Ancaster Lincs 173 G7
Anchor Shrops 130 G3
Anchor Corner Norf 141 D10
Anchor Street Norf 160 E6
Anchorage Park Ptsmth 33 G11
Anchorsholme Blkpool 202 E2
Ancoats Gtr Man 184 B5
Ancroft Northumb 273 F9
Ancroft Northmoor Northumb 273 F9
Ancrum Borders 262 E4
Ancton W Sus 35 G7
Ancumtoun Orkney 314 A7
Anderby Lincs 191 F8
Anderby Creek Lincs 191 F8
Andersea Som 43 G10
Andersfield Som 43 G8
Anderson Dorset 18 B3
Anderton Corn 7 E8
Anderton Lancs 194 E6
Anderton W Ches 183 F10
Andertons Mill Lancs 194 E4
Andover Hants 47 D11
Andover Down Hants 47 D11
Andoversford Glos 81 B8
Andreas I o M 192 C5
Andwell Hants 49 C7
Anelog Gwyn 144 D3
Anerley London 67 F10
Anfield Mers 182 C5
Angarrack Corn 2 B3
Angarrick Corn 3 B7
Angelbank Shrops 115 B11
Angersleigh Som 27 D11
Angerton Cumb 238 F6
Angle Pembs 72 E5
Angmering W Sus 35 G9
Angram N Yorks 206 D6
Angram N Yorks 223 F7
Anick Northumb 241 D11
Anie Stirl 285 F9
Ankerdine Hill Worcs 116 F4
Ankerville Highld 301 B8
Anlaby E Yorks 200 B4
Anlaby Park Hull 200 B5
Anmer Norf 158 D4
Anmore Hants 33 E11
Anna Valley Hants 47 E10
Annan Dumfries 238 D5
Annaside Cumb 210 B1
Annat Argyll 284 E4
Annat Highld 290 D5
Annat Highld 299 D8
Annbank S Ayrs 257 E10
Annesley Notts 171 E8
Annesley Woodhouse Notts 171 E7
Annfield Plain Durham 242 G5
Anniesland Glasgow 267 B10
Annifirth Shetland 313 J3
Annis Hill Suff 143 F7
Annishader Highld 298 D4
Annitsford T & W 243 C7
Ann's Hill Hants 33 G9
Annscroft Shrops 131 B9
Annwell Place Derbys 152 F6
Ansdell Lancs 193 B10
Ansells End Herts 85 B11
Ansford Som 44 G6
Ansley Warks 134 E5
Ansley Common Warks 134 E6
Anslow Staffs 152 D4
Anslow Gate Staffs 152 D3
Ansteadbrook Sur 50 G2
Anstey Herts 105 E8
Anstey Leics 135 B10
Anstruther Easter Fife 287 G9
Anstruther Wester Fife 287 G9
Ansty Hants 49 E8
Ansty W Sus 36 C3
Ansty Warks 135 G7
Ansty Wilts 31 B7
Ansty Coombe Wilts 31 B7
Ansty Cross Dorset 30 G3
Anthill Common Hants 33 E10
Anthony Corn 7 E7
Anthony's Cross Glos 98 G4
Anthorn Cumb 238 F5
Antingham Norf 160 C5
Anton's Gowt Lincs 174 F3
Antonshill Falk 279 E7
Antony Corn 7 E7
Antony Passage Corn 7 D8
Antrobus W Ches 183 F10
Anvil Green Kent 54 D6
Anvilles W Berks 63 F10
Anwick Lincs 173 E10
Anwoth Dumfries 237 D7
Aonachan Highld 290 E4
Aoradh Argyll 274 G3
Apedale Staffs 168 F4
Aperfield London 52 B2
Apes Dale Worcs 117 C9
Apes Hall Cambs 139 E11
Apethorpe Northants 137 D10
Apeton Staffs 151 F7
Apley Lincs 189 F10
Apley Forge Shrops 132 D4
Apperknowle Derbys 186 F5
Apperley Glos 99 F7
Apperley Bridge W Yorks 205 F9
Apperley Dene Northumb 242 F3
Appersett N Yorks 223 G7
Appin Argyll 289 E11
Appin House Argyll 289 E11
Appleby N Lincs 200 E3
Appleby-in-Westmorland Cumb 231 G9
Appleby Magna Leics 134 B6
Appleby Parva Leics 134 B6
Applecross Highld 299 E7
Applecross Ho Highld 299 E7
Appledore Devon 27 E9
Appledore Devon 40 G3
Appledore Kent 39 B7
Appledore Heath Kent 54 G3
Appleford Oxon 83 G8
Applegarthtown Dumfries 248 G4
Applehouse Hill Windsor 65 C10
Applemore Hants 32 F5
Appleshaw Hants 47 D10
Applethwaite Cumb 229 F11
Appleton Halton 183 D8
Appleton Oxon 82 E6
Appleton-le-Moors N Yorks 216 B4
Appleton-le-Street N Yorks 216 E4
Appleton Park Warr 183 E10
Appleton Roebuck N Yorks 207 E7
Appleton Thorn Warr 183 E10
Appleton Wiske N Yorks 225 E7
Appletreehall Borders 262 F2
Appletreewick N Yorks 213 G11
Appley I o W 21 C8
Appley Som 27 C9
Appley Bridge Lancs 194 F4
Apse Heath I o W 21 E7
Apsey Green Suff 126 E5
Apsley Herts 85 D9
Apsley End C Beds 104 E2
Apuldram W Sus 22 C4
Aqueduct Telford 132 B3
Aquhythie Aberds 293 B9
Arabella Highld 301 B8
Arbeadie Aberds 293 D8
Arberth = Narberth Pembs 73 C10
Arbirlot Angus 287 C10
Arboll Highld 311 L2
Arborfield Wokingham 65 F9
Arborfield Cross Wokingham 65 F9
Arborfield Garrison Wokingham 65 F9
Arbourthorne S Yorks 186 D5
Arbroath Angus 287 C10
Arbury Cambs 123 E8
Arbuthnott Aberds 293 F9
Archavandra Muir Highld 309 K7
Archdeacon Newton Darl 224 B5
Archenfield Hereford 96 C5
Archiestown Moray 302 E2
Archnalea Highld 289 C10
Arclid E Ches 168 C3
Arclid Green E Ches 168 C3
Ard-dhubh Highld 299 E7
Ardachu Highld 309 J6
Ardailly Argyll 255 B7
Ardalanish Argyll 274 B4
Ardallie Aberds 303 F10
Ardalum Ho Argyll 288 F6
Ardamaleish Argyll 275 G11
Ardanaiseig Argyll 284 E4
Ardaneaskan Highld 295 B10
Ardanstur Argyll 275 B9
Ardargie House Hotel Perth 286 F4
Ardarroch Highld 295 B10
Ardban Highld 295 B9
Ardbeg Argyll 254 C5
Ardbeg Argyll 276 E3
Ardcharnich Highld 307 L6
Ardchiavaig Argyll 274 B4
Ardchonnell Argyll 275 B10
Ardchronie Highld 309 L6
Ardchuilk Highld 300 F2
Ardchullarie More Stirl 285 F9
Ardchyle Stirl 285 E9
Ardclach Highld 301 E9
Arddleen Powys 148 F5
Ardechvie Highld 290 D3
Ardeley Herts 104 F6
Ardelve Highld 295 C10
Arden Argyll 277 E7
Arden E Renf 267 D10
Arden Park Gtr Man 184 C6
Ardencaple Ho Argyll 275 B8
Ardendrain Highld 300 F5
Ardens Grafton Warks 118 G2
Ardentallen Argyll 289 G10
Ardentinny Argyll 276 D3
Ardentraive Argyll 275 F11
Ardeonaig Stirl 285 D10
Ardersier Highld 301 D7
Ardery Highld 289 C9
Ardessie Highld 307 L5
Ardfern Argyll 275 C9
Ardfernal Argyll 274 F6
Ardgartan Argyll 284 G6
Ardgay Highld 309 K5
Ardglassie Aberds 303 C10
Ardgour Highld 290 G2
Ardgye Moray 301 C11
Ardheslaig Highld 299 D7
Ardiecow Moray 302 C5
Ardinamir Argyll 275 B8
Ardindrean Highld 307 L6
Ardingly W Sus 36 B4
Ardington Oxon 64 B2
Ardington Wick Oxon 64 B2
Ardintoul Highld 295 C10
Ardlair Aberds 302 G5
Ardlair Highld 299 B9
Ardlamey Argyll 255 C7
Ardlamont Ho Argyll 275 G10
Ardlawhill Aberds 303 C8
Ardleigh Essex 107 F11
Ardleigh Green London 68 B4
Ardleigh Heath Essex 107 E10
Ardler Perth 286 C6
Ardley Oxon 101 F10
Ardley End Essex 87 C8
Ardlui Argyll 285 F7
Ardlussa Argyll 275 E7
Ardmair Highld 307 K6
Ardmay Argyll 284 G6
Ardmenish Argyll 274 F6
Ardminish Argyll 255 C7
Ardmolich Highld 289 B9
Ardmore Argyll 289 G9
Ardmore Highld 306 D7
Ardmore Highld 309 L7
Ardnacross Argyll 289 E7
Ardnadam Argyll 276 E3
Ardnagowan Argyll 284 G4
Ardnagrask Highld 300 E5
Ardnarff Highld 295 B10
Ardnastang Highld 289 C10
Ardnave Argyll 274 F3
Ardneil N Ayrs 266 F3
Ardno Argyll 284 G5
Ardo Aberds 303 F8
Ardo Ho Aberds 303 G9
Ardoch Argyll 277 F7
Ardoch Perth 286 D4
Ardoch Stirl 285 F9
Ardochy House Highld 290 C4
Ardoyne Aberds 302 G6
Ardpatrick Argyll 275 G8
Ardpatrick Ho Argyll 255 B8
Ardpeaton Argyll 276 D4
Ardradnaig Perth 285 C11
Ardrishaig Argyll 275 E9
Ardross Fife 287 G9
Ardross Highld 300 B6
Ardross Castle Highld 300 B6
Ardrossan N Ayrs 266 G4
Ardshave Highld 309 K7
Ardsheal Highld 289 D11
Ardshealach Highld 289 C8
Ardskenish Argyll 274 D4
Ardsley S Yorks 197 F11
Ardslignish Highld 289 C7
Ardtalla Argyll 254 B5
Ardtalnaig Perth 285 D11
Ardtaraig Argyll 275 E11
Ardtoe Highld 289 B8
Ardtreck Highld 294 B5
Ardtrostan Perth 285 E10
Ardtur Argyll 289 E11
Arduaine Argyll 275 B8
Ardullie Highld 300 C5
Ardvannie Highld 309 L6
Ardvar Highld 306 F6
Ardvasar Highld 295 E8
Ardveich Stirl 285 E10
Ardverikie Highld 291 E7
Ardvorlich Perth 285 E10
Ardwell Dumfries 236 E3
Ardwell Moray 302 F3
Ardwell S Ayrs 244 E5
Ardwell Mains Dumfries 236 E3
Ardwick Gtr Man 184 B5
Areley Kings Worcs 116 C6
Arford Hants 49 F10
Argoed Caerph 77 F11
Argoed Powys 113 E9
Argoed Powys 130 E5
Argoed Shrops 130 G6
Argoed Shrops 148 E6
Argos Hill E Sus 37 B9
Arichamish Argyll 275 C10
Arichastlich Argyll 284 D6
Aridhglas Argyll 288 G5
Arienskill Highld 295 G9
Arileod Argyll 288 D3
Arinacrinachd Highld 299 D7
Arinagour Argyll 288 D4
Arineckaig Highld 299 E9
Arion Orkney 314 E2
Arisaig Highld 295 G8
Ariundle Highld 289 C10
Arivegaig Highld 289 C8
Arivoichallum Argyll 254 C4
Arkendale N Yorks 215 G7
Arkesden Essex 105 E9
Arkholme Lancs 211 E11
Arkle Town N Yorks 223 E10
Arkleby Cumb 229 D8
Arkleton Dumfries 249 E9
Arkley London 86 F2
Arksey S Yorks 198 F5
Arkwright Town Derbys 186 G6
Arle Glos 99 G8
Arlebrook Glos 80 D4
Arlecdon Cumb 219 B10
Arlescote Warks 101 B7
Arlesey C Beds 104 D3
Arleston Telford 150 G3
Arley E Ches 183 E11
Arley Green E Ches 183 E11
Arlingham Glos 80 C2
Arlington Devon 40 E6
Arlington E Sus 23 D8
Arlington Glos 81 D10
Arlington Beccott Devon 40 E6
Armadale Highld 308 C7
Armadale W Loth 269 B8
Armadale Castle Highld 295 E8
Armathwaite Cumb 230 B6
Armigers Essex 105 F11
Arminghall Norf 142 C5
Armitage Staffs 151 F11
Armitage Bridge W Yorks 196 E6
Armley W Yorks 205 G11
Armscote Warks 100 C4
Armsdale Staffs 150 C5
Armshead Staffs 168 F6
Armston Northants 137 F11
Armthorpe S Yorks 198 F6
Arnabost Argyll 288 D4
Arnaby Cumb 210 C3
Arncliffe N Yorks 213 E8
Arncroach Fife 287 G9
Arndilly Ho Moray 302 E2
Arne Dorset 18 D5
Arnesby Leics 136 E2
Arngask Perth 286 F5
Arnisdale Highld 295 D10
Arnish Highld 298 E5
Arniston Midloth 270 C6
Arnol W Isles 304 D5
Arnold E Yorks 209 E8
Arnold Notts 171 F9
Arno's Vale Bristol 60 E6
Arnprior Stirl 278 C2
Arnside Cumb 211 D9
Aros Mains Argyll 289 E7
Arowry Wrex 149 B9
Arpafeelie Highld 300 D6
Arpinge Kent 55 F7
Arrad Foot Cumb 210 C6
Arram E Yorks 208 E6
Arrathorne N Yorks 224 G4
Arreton I o W 20 D6
Arrington Cambs 122 G6
Arrivain Argyll 284 D6
Arrochar Argyll 284 G6
Arrow Warks 117 F11
Arrow Green Hereford 115 F8
Arrowe Hill Mers 182 D3
Arrowfield Top Worcs 117 C10
Arrunden W Yorks 196 F6
Arscaig Highld 309 H5
Arscott Shrops 131 B8
Arthill E Ches 184 D2
Arthington W Yorks 205 E11
Arthingworth Northants 136 G5
Arthog Gwyn 146 G2
Arthrath Aberds 303 F9
Arthursdale W Yorks 206 F3
Arthurstone Perth 286 C6
Arthurville Highld 309 L7
Artington Sur 50 D3
Artrochie Aberds 303 F10
Arundel W Sus 35 F8
Arwick Orkney 314 D3
Aryhoulan Highld 290 G2
Asby Cumb 229 G7
Ascog Argyll 266 C2
Ascoil Highld 311 H2
Ascot Windsor 66 F2
Ascott Warks 100 E6
Ascott d'Oyley Oxon 82 B4
Ascott Earl Oxon 82 B3
Ascott-under-Wychwood Oxon 82 B4
Asenby N Yorks 215 D7
Asfordby Leics 154 F4
Asfordby Hill Leics 154 F4
Asgarby Lincs 173 F10
Asgarby Lincs 174 B4
Ash Devon 8 F6
Ash Dorset 30 E5
Ash Kent 55 B9
Ash Kent 68 G5
Ash Som 28 C3
Ash Som 29 C7
Ash Sur 49 C11
Ash Bank Staffs 168 F6
Ash Bullayne Devon 26 G3
Ash Green Sur 50 D2
Ash Green Warks 134 F6
Ash Grove Wrex 166 G5
Ash Hill Devon 14 G4
Ash Magna Shrops 149 B11
Ash Mill Devon 26 C3
Ash Moor Devon 26 D3
Ash Parva Shrops 149 B11
Ash Priors Som 27 B11
Ash Street Suff 107 B10
Ash Thomas Devon 27 E8
Ash Vale Sur 49 C11
Ashaig Highld 295 C8
Ashampstead W Berks 64 D5
Ashampstead Green W Berks 64 D5
Ashansworth Hants 48 B2
Ashbank Kent 53 C10
Ashbeer Som 42 F5
Ashbocking Suff 126 G3
Ashbourne Derbys 169 F11
Ashbrittle Som 27 C9
Ashbrook Shrops 131 E9
Ashburnham Forge E Sus 23 B11
Ashburton Devon 8 B5
Ashbury Devon 12 B6
Ashbury Oxon 63 C9
Ashby N Lincs 200 F2
Ashby by Partney Lincs 174 B6
Ashby cum Fenby NE Lincs 201 G9
Ashby de la Launde Lincs 173 D9
Ashby-de-la-Zouch Leics 153 F7
Ashby Folville Leics 154 G4
Ashby Hill NE Lincs 201 G8
Ashby Magna Leics 135 E11
Ashby Parva Leics 135 F10
Ashby Puerorum Lincs 190 G4
Ashby St Ledgers Northants 119 D11
Ashby St Mary Norf 142 C6
Ashchurch Glos 99 E8
Ashcombe Devon 14 F4
Ashcombe Park N Som 59 G10
Ashcott Som 44 F2
Ashcott Corner Som 44 F2
Ashculme Devon 27 E10
Ashdon Essex 105 C11
Ashe Hants 48 D4
Asheldham Essex 89 E7
Ashen Essex 106 C4
Ashendon Bucks 84 C2
Asheridge Bucks 84 E6
Ashey I o W 21 D7
Ashfield Argyll 275 E8
Ashfield Carms 94 F3
Ashfield Hants 32 D5
Ashfield Hereford 97 G11
Ashfield Shrops 148 D6
Ashfield Stirl 285 G11
Ashfield Suff 126 E4
Ashfield Cum Thorpe Suff 126 E4
Ashfield Green Suff 124 F5
Ashfield Green Suff 126 C5
Ashfields Shrops 150 D4
Ashfold Crossways W Sus 36 B2
Ashfold Side N Yorks 214 F2
Ashford Devon 8 F3
Ashford Devon 40 F4
Ashford Hants 31 E10
Ashford Kent 54 E4
Ashford Sur 66 E5
Ashford Bowdler Shrops 115 C10
Ashford Carbonell Shrops 115 C10
Ashford Common Sur 66 E5
Ashford Hill Hants 64 G5
Ashford in the Water Derbys 185 G11
Ashgate Derbys 186 G5
Ashgill S Lnrk 268 F5
Ashgrove Bath 45 B8
Ashiestiel Borders 261 B10
Ashill Devon 27 E9
Ashill Norf 141 C7
Ashill Som 28 D4
Ashingdon Essex 88 G5
Ashington Northumb 253 F7
Ashington Poole 18 B6
Ashington Som 29 C9
Ashington W Sus 35 D10
Ashington End Lincs 175 B8
Ashintully Castle Perth 292 G3
Ashkirk Borders 261 E11
Ashlett Hants 33 G7
Ashleworth Glos 98 F6
Ashley Cambs 124 E3
Ashley Devon 25 E10
Ashley Dorset 31 G10
Ashley E Ches 184 E3
Ashley Glos 80 G6
Ashley Hants 19 B11
Ashley Hants 47 G11
Ashley Kent 55 D10
Ashley Northants 136 E5
Ashley Staffs 150 B5
Ashley Wilts 61 F10
Ashley Dale Staffs 150 B5
Ashley Down Bristol 60 D5
Ashley Green Bucks 85 D7
Ashley Heath Ches 184 D3
Ashley Heath Dorset 31 G10
Ashley Heath Staffs 150 B4
Ashley Moor Hereford 115 D9
Ashley Park Sur 66 F6
Ashleyhay Derbys 170 E3
Ashmanhaugh Norf 160 E6
Ashmansworth Hants 48 B2
Ashmansworthy Devon 24 D4
Ashmead Green Glos 80 F3
Ashmill Devon 12 B3
Ashmore Dorset 30 D6
Ashmore Green W Berks 64 F4
Ashmore Lake W Mid 133 D9
Ashmore Park W Mid 133 C9
Ashnashellach Lodge Highld 299 E10
Ashopton Derbys 185 D11
Ashorne Warks 118 F6
Ashover Derbys 170 C4
Ashover Hay Derbys 170 C5
Ashow Warks 118 C6
Ashperton Hereford 98 C2
Ashprington Devon 8 D6
Ashreigney Devon 25 E10
Ashridge Court Devon 25 G11
Ashtead Sur 51 B7
Ashton Corn 2 D4
Ashton Hants 33 D9
Ashton Hereford 115 E10
Ashton Invclyd 276 F4
Ashton Northants 102 B5
Ashton Northants 137 F11
Ashton P'boro 138 B2
Ashton Som 44 D2
Ashton Common Wilts 45 B11
Ashton Gate Bristol 60 E5
Ashton Green E Sus 23 C7
Ashton Hayes W Ches 167 B8
Ashton Heath Halton 183 F9
Ashton-in-Makerfield Gtr Man 183 B9
Ashton Keynes Wilts 81 G8
Ashton under Hill Worcs 99 D9
Ashton-under-Lyne Gtr Man 184 B6
Ashton upon Mersey Gtr Man 184 C3
Ashton Vale Bristol 60 E5
Ashurst Hants 32 E4
Ashurst Kent 52 F4
Ashurst Lancs 194 F3
Ashurst W Sus 35 D11
Ashurst Bridge Hants 32 E4
Ashurst Wood W Sus 52 F2
Ashvale Bl Gwent 77 C10
Ashwater Devon 12 B3
Ashwell Devon 14 G3
Ashwell Herts 104 D5
Ashwell Rutland 155 G7
Ashwell Som 28 D5
Ashwell End Herts 104 C5
Ashwellthorpe Norf 142 D2
Ashwick Som 44 D6
Ashwicken Norf 158 F4
Ashwood Staffs 133 F7
Ashybank Borders 262 F2
Askam in Furness Cumb 210 D4
Askern S Yorks 198 E5
Askerswell Dorset 16 C6
Askerton Hill Lincs 172 F4
Askett Bucks 84 D4
Askham Cumb 230 G6
Askham Notts 188 F3
Askham Bryan York 207 D7
Askham Richard York 206 D6
Asknish Argyll 275 D10
Askrigg N Yorks 223 G8
Askwith N Yorks 205 D9
Aslackby Lincs 155 C11
Aslacton Norf 142 E3
Aslockton Notts 154 B4
Asloun Aberds 293 B7
Asney Som 44 F3
Aspall Suff 126 D3
Aspatria Cumb 229 C8
Aspenden Herts 105 F7
Asperton Lincs 156 B5
Aspley Nottingham 171 G8
Aspley Staffs 150 C6
Aspley Guise C Beds 103 D8
Aspley Heath C Beds 103 D8
Aspley Heath Warks 117 C11
Aspull Gtr Man 194 F6
Aspull Common Gtr Man 183 B10
Assater Shetland 312 F4
Asselby E Yorks 199 B8
Asserby Lincs 191 F7
Asserby Turn Lincs 191 F7
Assington Suff 107 D8
Assington Green Suff 124 G5
Assynt Ho Highld 300 C5
Astbury E Ches 168 C4
Astcote Northants 120 G3
Asterby Lincs 190 F3
Asterley Shrops 131 B7
Asterton Shrops 131 E7
Asthall Oxon 82 C3
Asthall Leigh Oxon 82 C4
Astle E Ches 184 G4
Astle Highld 309 K7
Astley Gtr Man 195 G8
Astley Shrops 149 F10
Astley Warks 134 F6
Astley Worcs 116 D5
Astley Abbotts Shrops 132 D4
Astley Bridge Gtr Man 195 E8
Astley Cross Worcs 116 D6
Astley Green Gtr Man 184 B2
Astmoor Halton 183 E8
Aston Derbys 152 C3
Aston Derbys 185 E11
Aston E Ches 167 F10
Aston Flint 166 B4
Aston Hereford 115 C9
Aston Hereford 115 E9
Aston Herts 104 G5
Aston Oxon 82 E4
Aston Powys 130 E5
Aston S Yorks 187 D7
Aston Shrops 132 E6
Aston Shrops 149 D10
Aston Staffs 151 E7
Aston Staffs 168 G3
Aston Telford 132 B2
Aston W Ches 183 F9
Aston W Mid 133 F11
Aston Wokingham 65 C9
Aston Abbotts Bucks 102 G6
Aston Bank Worcs 116 C2
Aston Botterell Shrops 132 G2
Aston-by-Stone Staffs 151 C8
Aston Cantlow Warks 118 F2
Aston Clinton Bucks 84 C5
Aston Crews Hereford 98 G3
Aston Cross Glos 99 E8
Aston End Herts 104 G5
Aston Eyre Shrops 132 E3
Aston Fields Worcs 117 D9
Aston Flamville Leics 135 E9
Aston Ingham Hereford 98 G3
Aston juxta Mondrum E Ches 167 D11
Aston le Walls Northants 119 G9
Aston Magna Glos 100 D3
Aston Munslow Shrops 131 F10
Aston on Carrant Glos 99 E8
Aston on Clun Shrops 131 G7
Aston-on-Trent Derbys 153 D8
Aston Pigott Shrops 130 B6
Aston Rogers Shrops 130 B6
Aston Rowant Oxon 84 F2
Aston Sandford Bucks 84 D3
Aston Somerville Worcs 99 D10
Aston Square Shrops 148 D6
Aston Subedge Glos 100 C2
Aston Tirrold Oxon 64 B5
Aston Upthorpe Oxon 64 B5
Astrop Northants 101 D10
Astrope Herts 84 C5
Astwick C Beds 104 D4
Astwith Derbys 170 C6
Astwood M Keynes 103 B9
Astwood Worcs 117 D8
Astwood Worcs 117 F7
Astwood Bank Worcs 117 E10
Aswarby Lincs 173 G9
Aswardby Lincs 190 G5
Atch Lench Worcs 117 G10
Atcham Shrops 131 B10
Athelhampton Dorset 17 C11
Athelington Suff 126 C4
Athelney Som 28 B4
Athelstaneford E Loth 281 F10
Atherfield Green I o W 20 F5
Atherington Devon 25 C9
Atherington W Sus 35 G8
Athersley North S Yorks 197 F11
Athersley South S Yorks 197 F11
Atherstone Som 28 D5
Atherstone Warks 134 D6
Atherstone on Stour Warks 118 G4
Atherton Gtr Man 195 G7
Athnamulloch Highld 299 G11
Athron Hall Perth 286 G4
Atley Hill N Yorks 224 E5
Atlow Derbys 170 F2
Attadale Highld 295 B11
Attadale Ho Highld 295 B11
Attenborough Notts 153 B10
Atterbury M Keynes 103 D7
Atterby Lincs 189 C7
Attercliffe S Yorks 186 D5
Atterley Shrops 132 D2
Atterton Leics 135 D7
Attleborough Norf 141 D10
Attleborough Warks 135 E7
Attlebridge Norf 160 F2
Attleton Green Suff 124 G4
Atwick E Yorks 209 C9
Atworth Wilts 61 F11
Auberrow Hereford 97 B9
Aubourn Lincs 172 C6
Auch Argyll 285 D7
Auchagallon N Ayrs 255 D9
Auchallater Aberds 292 E3
Aucharnie Aberds 302 E6
Auchattie Aberds 293 D8
Auchavan Angus 292 G3
Auchbreck Moray 302 G2
Auchenback E Renf 267 D10
Auchenbainzie Dumfries 247 D8
Auchenblae Aberds 293 F9
Auchenbrack Dumfries 247 D7
Auchenbreck Argyll 255 C8
Auchenbreck Argyll 275 E11
Auchencairn Dumfries 237 D9
Auchencairn Dumfries 247 G11
Auchencairn N Ayrs 256 D2
Auchencairn Ho Dumfries 237 D10
Auchencar N Ayrs 255 D9
Auchencarroch W Dunb 277 E8
Auchencrosh S Ayrs 236 B3
Auchencrow Borders 273 C7
Auchendinny Midloth 270 C5
Auchengray S Lnrk 269 E9
Auchenhalrig Moray 302 C3
Auchenharvie N Ayrs 266 G5
Auchenheath S Lnrk 268 G6
Auchenhew N Ayrs 256 E2
Auchenlaich Stirl 285 G10
Auchenleck Dumfries 237 D9
Auchenlochan Argyll 275 F10
Auchenmalg Dumfries 236 D4
Auchenreoch E Dunb 278 F3
Auchensoul S Ayrs 245 E7
Auchentibber S Lnrk 268 E3
Auchentiber N Ayrs 267 F7
Auchertyre Highld 295 C10
Auchessan Stirl 285 E8
Auchgourish Highld 291 B11
Auchinairn E Dunb 268 B2
Auchindrain Argyll 284 G4
Auchindrean Highld 307 L6
Auchininna Aberds 302 E6
Auchinleck Dumfries 236 B6
Auchinleck E Ayrs 258 E3
Auchinloch N Lnrk 278 G3
Auchinner Perth 285 F10
Auchinraith S Lnrk 268 D3
Auchinroath Moray 302 D2
Auchinstarry N Lnrk 278 F4
Auchintoul Aberds 293 B7
Auchintoul Highld 309 K5
Auchiries Aberds 303 F10
Auchlee Aberds 293 D10
Auchleven Aberds 302 G6
Auchlinn Aberds 303 D7
Auchlochan S Lnrk 259 B8
Auchlossan Aberds 293 C7
Auchlunachan Highld 307 L6
Auchlunies Aberds 293 D10
Auchlyne Stirl 285 E9
Auchmacoy Aberds 303 F9
Auchmair Moray 302 G3
Auchmantle Dumfries 236 C3
Auchmenzie Aberds 302 G5
Auchmillan E Ayrs 258 D2
Auchmithie Angus 287 C10
Auchmore Highld 300 D4
Auchmuirbridge Fife 286 G6
Auchmull Angus 293 F7
Auchnacraig Argyll 289 G9
Auchnacree Angus 292 G6
Auchnafree Perth 286 D2
Auchnagallin Highld 301 F10
Auchnagarron Argyll 275 E11
Auchnagatt Aberds 303 E9
Auchnaha Argyll 275 E10
Auchnahillin Highld 301 F7
Auchnarrow Moray 302 G2
Auchnashelloch Perth 285 F11
Auchnotteroch Dumfries 236 C1
Aucholzie Aberds 292 D5
Auchrannie Angus 286 B6
Auchroisk Highld 301 G10
Auchronie Angus 292 E6
Auchterarder Perth 286 F3
Auchteraw Highld 290 C5
Auchterderran Fife 280 B4
Auchterhouse Angus 287 D7
Auchtermuchty Fife 286 F6
Auchterneed Highld 300 D4
Auchtertool Fife 280 C4
Auchtertyre Moray 301 D11
Auchtertyre Stirl 285 E7
Auchtubh Stirl 285 E9
Auckengill Highld 310 C7
Auckley S Yorks 199 G7
Audenshaw Gtr Man 184 B6
Audlem E Ches 167 G11
Audley Staffs 168 E3
Audley End Essex 105 D10
Audley End Essex 106 D6
Audley End Norf 142 G2
Audley End Suff 125 G7
Auds Aberds 302 C6
Aughertree Cumb 229 D11
Aughton E Yorks 207 F10
Aughton Lancs 193 F11
Aughton Lancs 211 F10
Aughton S Yorks 187 D7
Aughton Wilts 47 B8
Aughton Park Lancs 194 F2
Aukside Durham 232 F4
Auldearn Highld 301 D9
Aulden Hereford 115 G9
Auldgirth Dumfries 247 F10
Auldhame E Loth 281 E11
Auldhouse S Lnrk 268 E2
Auldtown of Carnoustie Aberds 302 E6
Ault a'chruinn Highld 295 C11
Ault Hucknall Derbys 171 B7
Aultanrynie Highld 308 F3
Aultbea Highld 307 L3
Aultdearg Highld 300 C2
Aultgrishan Highld 307 L2
Aultguish Inn Highld 300 B3
Aultibea Highld 311 G4
Aultiphurst Highld 310 C2
Aultivullin Highld 310 C2
Aultmore Highld 301 G10
Aultmore Moray 302 D4
Aultnagoire Highld 300 G5
Aultnamain Inn Highld 309 L6
Aultnaslat Highld 290 C3
Aulton Aberds 302 G6
Aulton of Atherb Aberds 303 E9
Aultvaich Highld 300 E5
Aunby Lincs 155 G10
Aundorach Highld 291 B11
Aunk Devon 27 G8
Aunsby Lincs 155 B10
Auquhorthies Aberds 303 G8
Aust S Glos 60 B5
Austen Fen Lincs 190 C5
Austendike Lincs 156 E5
Austenwood Bucks 66 B3
Austerfield S Yorks 187 C11
Austerlands Gtr Man 196 F3
Austhorpe W Yorks 206 G3
Austrey Warks 134 B5
Austwick N Yorks 212 F5
Authorpe Lincs 190 E6
Authorpe Row Lincs 191 G8
Avebury Wilts 62 F6
Avebury Trusloe Wilts 62 F5
Aveley Thurrock 68 C5
Avening Glos 80 F5
Avening Green S Glos 80 G2
Averham Notts 172 E3
Avernish Highld 295 C10
Avery Hill London 68 E2
Aveton Gifford Devon 8 F3
Avielochan Highld 291 B11
Aviemore Highld 291 B10
Avington Hants 48 G4
Avington W Berks 63 F11
Avoch Highld 301 D7
Avon Hants 19 B8
Avon Wilts 62 D3
Avon Dassett Warks 101 B8
Avonbridge Falk 279 G8
Avoncliff Wilts 45 B10
Avonmouth Bristol 60 D4
Avonwick Devon 8 D4
Awbridge Hants 32 C4
Awhirk Dumfries 236 D2
Awkley S Glos 60 B5
Awliscombe Devon 27 G10
Awre Glos 80 D2
Awsworth Notts 171 G7
Axbridge Som 44 C2
Axford Hants 48 E6
Axford Wilts 63 F8
Axmansford Hants 64 G5
Axminster Devon 15 B11
Axmouth Devon 15 C11
Axton Flint 181 E10
Axtown Devon 7 B10
Axwell Park T & W 242 E5
Aycliff Kent 55 E10
Aycliffe Durham 233 G11
Aydon Northumb 242 D2
Aykley Heads Durham 233 C11
Aylburton Glos 79 E10
Aylburton Common Glos 79 E10
Ayle Northumb 231 B10
Aylesbeare Devon 14 C6
Aylesbury Bucks 84 C4
Aylesby NE Lincs 201 F8
Aylesford Kent 53 B8
Aylesham Kent 55 C8
Aylestone Leicester 135 C11
Aylestone Hill Hereford 97 C10
Aylestone Park Leicester 135 C11
Aylmerton Norf 160 B3
Aylsham Norf 160 D3
Aylton Hereford 98 D3
Aylworth Glos 100 G2
Aymestrey Hereford 115 D8
Aynho Northants 101 E10
Ayot Green Herts 86 C2
Ayot St Lawrence Herts 85 B11
Ayot St Peter Herts 86 B2
Ayr S Ayrs 257 E8
Ayre of Atler Shetland 313 G6
Ayres Shetland 313 H5
Ayres End Herts 85 C11
Ayres of Selivoe Shetland 313 J4
Ayres Quay T & W 243 F9
Aysgarth N Yorks 213 B10
Ayshford Devon 27 D8
Ayside Cumb 211 C7
Ayston Rutland 137 C7
Aythorpe Roding Essex 87 B9
Ayton Borders 273 C8
Ayton T & W 243 F7
Ayton Castle Borders 273 C8
Aywick Shetland 312 E7
Azerley N Yorks 214 E5

B

Babbacombe Torbay 9 B8
Babbington Notts 171 G7
Babbinswood Shrops 148 C6
Babbs Green Herts 86 B5
Babcary Som 29 B9
Babel Carms 94 D6

Babel Green Suff 106 B4
Babell Flint 181 G11
Babeny Devon 13 F9
Babingley Norf 158 D3
Babraham Cambs 123 G10
Babworth Notts 187 E11
Bac W Isles 304 D6
Bach-y-gwreiddyn Swansea 75 E10
Bachau Anglesey 178 E6
Bache Shrops 131 G9
Bache Mill Shrops 131 F10
Bacheldre Powys 130 E4
Bachelor's Bump E Sus 38 E4
Back of Keppoch Highld 295 G8
Back o' th' Brook Staffs 169 E9
Back Muir Fife 279 D11
Back Rogerton E Ayrs 258 E3
Back Street Suff 124 F4
Backaland Orkney 314 C5
Backaskaill Orkney 314 A4
Backbarrow Cumb 211 C7
Backbower Gtr Man 185 C7
Backburn Aberds 293 D10
Backe Carms 74 B3
Backfolds Aberds 303 D10
Backford W Ches 182 G6
Backford Cross W Ches 182 G5
Backhill Aberds 303 F10
Backhill Aberds 303 F7
Backhill of Clackriach Aberds 303 E9
Backhill of Fortree Aberds 303 E9
Backhill of Trustach Aberds 293 D8
Backies Highld 311 J2
Backlass Highld 310 D6
Backlass Highld 310 E4
Backwell N Som 60 F3
Backwell Common N Som 60 F3
Backwell Green N Som 60 F3
Backworth T & W 243 C8
Bacon End Essex 87 B10
Baconend Green Essex 87 B10
Bacon's End W Mid 134 F3
Baconsthorpe Norf 160 B2
Bacton Hereford 97 E7
Bacton Norf 160 C6
Bacton Suff 125 D11
Bacton Green Norf 160 C6
Bacton Green Suff 125 D10
Bacup Lancs 195 C11
Badachonacher Highld 300 B6
Badachro Highld 299 B7
Badanloch Lodge Highld 308 F7
Badarach Highld 309 K5
Badavanich Highld 299 D11
Badbea Highld 307 K5
Badbury Swindon 63 C7
Badbury Wick Swindon 63 C7
Badby Northants 119 F11
Badcall Highld 306 D7
Badcaul Highld 307 K5
Baddeley Edge Stoke 168 E6
Baddeley Green Stoke 168 E6
Baddesley Clinton Warks 118 C4
Baddesley Ensor Warks 134 D5
Baddidarach Highld 307 G5
Baddoch Aberds 292 E3
Baddock Highld 301 D7
Baddow Park Essex 88 E2
Badeach Moray 302 F2
Badenscallie Highld 307 J5
Badenscoth Aberds 303 F7
Badentoy Park Aberds 293 D11
Badenyon Aberds 292 B5
Badgall Corn 11 D10
Badgeney Cambs 139 D8
Badger Shrops 132 D5
Badger Street Som 28 D3
Badgergate Stirl 278 B5
Badger's Hill Worcs 99 B10
Badger's Mount Kent 68 G3
Badgeworth Glos 80 B6
Badgworth Som 43 C11
Badharlick Corn 11 D11
Badicaul Highld 295 C9
Badingham Suff 126 D6
Badintagairt Highld 309 H4
Badlesmere Kent 54 C4
Badlipster Highld 310 E6
Badluarach Highld 307 K4
Badminton S Glos 61 C10
Badnaban Highld 307 G5
Badnabay Highld 306 E7
Badnagie Highld 310 F5
Badninish Highld 309 K7
Badrallach Highld 307 K5
Badsey Worcs 99 C11
Badshalloch W Dunb 277 D9
Badshot Lea Sur 49 D11
Badsworth W Yorks 198 E3
Badwell Ash Suff 125 D9
Badwell Green Suff 125 D10
Badworthy Devon 8 C3
Bae Cinmel = Kinmel Bay Conwy 181 E7
Bae Colwyn = Colwyn Bay Conwy 180 F4
Bae Penrhyn = Penrhyn Bay Conwy 180 E4
Baffins Ptsmth 33 G11
Bag Enderby Lincs 190 G5
Bagber Dorset 30 E3
Bagby N Yorks 215 C9
Bagby Grange N Yorks 215 C9
Bagendon Glos 81 D8
Bagginswood Shrops 132 G3
Baggrow Cumb 229 C9
Bàgha Chàise W Isles 296 D5
Bagh a Chaisteil W Isles 297 M2
Bagh Mor W Isles 296 F4
Bagh Shiarabhagh W Isles 297 L3
Bagham Kent 54 C5
Baghasdal W Isles 297 K3
Bagillt Flint 182 F2
Baginton Warks 118 C6
Baglan Neath 57 C8
Bagley Shrops 149 D8
Bagley Som 44 D3
Bagley W Yorks 205 F10
Bagley Green Som 27 D10
Bagley Marsh Shrops 149 D7
Bagmore Hants 49 E7
Bagnall Staffs 168 E6
Bagnor W Berks 64 F3
Bagpath Glos 80 E5
Bagpath Glos 80 G4
Bagshaw Derbys 185 E9
Bagshot Sur 66 G2
Bagshot Wilts 63 F10
Bagshot Heath Sur 66 G2
Bagslate Moor Gtr Man 195 E11
Bagstone S Glos 61 B7
Bagthorpe Norf 158 C5
Bagthorpe Notts 171 E7
Baguley Gtr Man 184 D4
Bagworth Leics 135 B8
Bagwy Llydiart Hereford 97 F8
Bagwyllydiart Hereford 97 F8
Bail Àrd Bhuirgh W Isles 304 C6
Bail' Iochdrach W Isles 296 F4
Bail Uachdraich W Isles 296 E4
Bail' Ur Tholastaidh W Isles 304 D7
Bailbrook Bath 61 F9
Baildon W Yorks 205 F9
Baildon Green W Yorks 205 F8
Baile W Isles 296 C5
Baile a Mhanaich W Isles 296 F3
Baile Ailein W Isles 304 F4
Baile an Truiseil W Isles 304 C5
Baile Boidheach Argyll 275 F8
Baile Gharbhaidh W Isles 297 G3
Baile Glas W Isles 296 F4
Baile Mhartainn W Isles 296 D3
Baile Mhic Phail W Isles 296 D4
Baile Mor Argyll 288 G4
Baile Mor W Isles 296 E3
Baile na Creige W Isles 297 L2
Baile nan Cailleach W Isles 296 F3
Baile Raghaill W Isles 296 D3
Bailebeag Highld 291 B7
Bailey Green Hants 33 B11
Baileyhead Cumb 240 B2
Bailiesward Aberds 302 F4
Bailiff Bridge W Yorks 196 C6
Baillieston Glasgow 268 C3
Bailrigg Lancs 202 B5
Bainbridge N Yorks 223 G8
Bainsford Falk 279 E7
Bainshole Aberds 302 F6
Bainton E Yorks 208 C5
Bainton Oxon 101 F11
Bainton P'boro 137 B11
Baintown Fife 287 G7
Bairnkine Borders 262 F5
Baker Street Thurrock 68 C6
Baker's Cross Kent 53 F9
Bakers End Herts 86 B5
Baker's Hill Glos 79 C9
Baker's Wood Bucks 66 B4
Bakesdown Corn 24 G2
Bakestone Moor Derbys 187 F8
Bakewell Derbys 170 B2
Bala = Y Bala Gwyn 147 B8
Balachroick Highld 291 C10
Balachuirn Highld 298 E5
Balance Hill Staffs 151 C11
Balavil Highld 291 C9
Balavoulin Perth 291 G10
Balbeg Highld 300 F4
Balbeg Highld 300 G4
Balbeggie Perth 286 E5
Balbegno Castle Aberds 293 F8
Balbithan Aberds 293 B9
Balbithan Ho Aberds 293 B10
Balblair Highld 300 E5
Balblair Highld 301 C7
Balblair Highld 309 K5
Balby S Yorks 198 G5
Balcherry Highld 311 L2
Balchladich Highld 306 F5
Balchraggan Highld 300 E5
Balchraggan Highld 300 F5
Balchraggan Highld 300 G5
Balchrick Highld 306 D6
Balchrystie Fife 287 G8
Balcladaich Highld 300 G2
Balcombe W Sus 51 G10
Balcombe Lane W Sus 51 G10
Balcomie Fife 287 F10
Balcraggie Lodge Highld 310 F5
Balcurvie Fife 287 G7
Baldersby N Yorks 215 D7
Baldersby St James N Yorks 215 D7
Balderstone Gtr Man 196 E2
Balderstone Lancs 203 G8
Balderton Notts 172 E4
Balderton W Ches 166 C5
Baldhu Corn 4 G5
Baldingstone Gtr Man 195 E10
Baldinnie Fife 287 F8
Baldock Herts 104 E4
Baldon Row Oxon 83 E9
Baldoon Highld 300 B6
Baldovie Dundee 287 D8
Baldrine I o M 192 D5
Baldslow E Sus 38 E3
Baldwin I o M 192 D4
Baldwinholme Cumb 239 G8
Baldwin's Gate Staffs 168 G3
Baldwins Hill W Sus 51 F11
Bale Norf 159 B10
Balearn Aberds 303 D10
Balemartine Argyll 288 E1
Balephuil Argyll 288 E1
Balerno Edin 270 B3
Balerominhor Argyll 274 D4
Balevullin Argyll 288 E1
Balfield Angus 293 G7
Balfour Orkney 314 E4
Balfour Mains Orkney 314 E4
Balfron Stirl 277 D10
Balfron Station Stirl 277 D10
Balgaveny Aberds 302 E6
Balgavies Angus 287 B9
Balgonar Fife 279 C10
Balgove Aberds 303 F8
Balgowan Highld 291 D8
Balgowan Perth 286 E3
Balgown Highld 298 C3
Balgrennie Aberds 292 C6
Balgrochan E Dunb 278 F2
Balgy Highld 299 D8
Balhaldie Stirl 286 G2
Balhalgardy Aberds 303 G7
Balham London 67 E9
Balhary Perth 286 C6
Baliasta Shetland 312 C8
Baligill Highld 310 C2
Baligortan Argyll 288 E5
Baligrundle Argyll 289 E10
Balindore Argyll 289 F11
Balinoe Argyll 288 E1
Balintore Angus 286 B6
Balintore Highld 301 B8
Balintraid Highld 301 B7
Balintuim Aberds 292 E3
Balk N Yorks 215 C9
Balk Field Notts 188 E2
Balkeerie Angus 287 C7
Balkemback Angus 287 D7
Balkholme E Yorks 199 B9
Balkissock S Ayrs 244 G4
Ball Shrops 148 D6
Ball Corn 10 G6
Ball Haye Green Staffs 169 D7
Ball Hill Hants 64 G2
Ball o'Ditton Halton 183 D7
Ballabeg I o M 192 E3
Ballacannel I o M 192 D5
Ballachraggan Moray 301 E11
Ballachrochin Highld 301 F8
Ballachulish Highld 284 B4
Balladen Lancs 195 C10
Ballajora I o M 192 C5
Ballaleigh I o M 192 D4
Ballamodha I o M 192 E3
Ballantrae S Ayrs 244 G3
Ballaquine I o M 192 D5
Ballard's Ash Wilts 62 C5
Ballards Gore Essex 88 G6
Ballard's Green Warks 134 E5
Ballasalla I o M 192 C4
Ballasalla I o M 192 E3
Ballater Aberds 292 D5
Ballathie Perth 286 D5
Ballaugh I o M 192 C4
Ballaveare I o M 192 E4
Ballcorach Moray 301 G11
Ballechin Perth 286 B3
Balleigh Highld 309 L7
Ballencrieff E Loth 281 F9
Ballencrieff Toll W Loth 279 G9
Ballentoul Perth 291 G10
Ballhill Devon 24 C3
Ballidon Derbys 170 E2
Balliekine N Ayrs 255 D9
Balliemore Argyll 275 E11
Balliemore Argyll 289 G10
Ballikinrain Stirl 277 D11
Ballimeanoch Argyll 284 F4
Ballimore Argyll 275 E10
Ballimore Stirl 285 F9
Ballinaby Argyll 274 G3
Ballinbreich Fife 286 E6
Ballindean Perth 286 E6
Ballingdon Suff 107 C7
Ballingdon Bottom Herts 85 C8
Ballinger Bottom Bucks 84 E6
Ballinger Bottom (South) Bucks 84 E6
Ballinger Common Bucks 84 E6
Ballingham Hereford 97 E11
Ballingham Hill Hereford 97 E11
Ballingry Fife 280 B3
Ballinlick Perth 286 C3
Ballinluig Perth 286 B3
Ballintean Highld 291 C10
Ballintuim Perth 286 B5
Balliveolan Argyll 289 E10
Balloch Angus 287 B7
Balloch Highld 301 E7
Balloch N Lnrk 278 G4
Balloch W Dunb 277 E7
Ballochan Aberds 293 D7
Ballochearn Stirl 277 D11
Ballochford Moray 302 F3
Ballochmorrie S Ayrs 244 G6
Ballogie Aberds 293 D7
Balls Cross W Sus 35 B7
Balls Green E Sus 52 F3
Balls Green Essex 107 G11
Ball's Green Glos 80 F5
Balls Green W Sus 35 C10
Balls Hill W Mid 133 E9
Ballygown Argyll 288 E6
Ballygrant Argyll 274 G4
Ballygroggan Argyll 255 F7
Ballyhaugh Argyll 288 D3
Balmacara Highld 295 C10
Balmacara Square Highld 295 C10
Balmaclellan Dumfries 237 B8
Balmacneil Perth 286 B3
Balmacqueen Highld 298 B4
Balmae Dumfries 237 E8
Balmaha Stirl 277 C8
Balmalcolm Fife 287 G7
Balmalloch N Lnrk 278 F4
Balmeanach Argyll 288 F6
Balmeanach Argyll 289 E8
Balmeanach Highld 295 B7
Balmeanach Highld 298 E3
Balmeanach Highld 298 E5
Balmedie Aberds 293 B11
Balmer Shrops 149 C8
Balmer Heath Shrops 149 C8
Balmerino Fife 287 E7
Balmerlawn Hants 32 G4
Balmesh Dumfries 236 D3
Balmichael N Ayrs 255 D10
Balminnoch Dumfries 236 C4
Balmirmer Angus 287 D9
Balmoral Borders 261 B11
Balmore E Dunb 278 G2
Balmore Highld 298 E2
Balmore Highld 300 F3
Balmore Highld 301 E8
Balmore Perth 286 B3
Balmule Fife 280 D4
Balmullo Fife 287 E8
Balmungie Highld 301 D7
Balmurrie Dumfries 236 C4
Balnaboth Angus 292 G5
Balnabreich Moray 302 D3
Balnabruaich Highld 301 C7
Balnabruich Highld 311 G5
Balnacarn Highld 290 B4
Balnacoil Highld 311 H2
Balnacra Highld 299 E9
Balnacruie Highld 301 G9
Balnafoich Highld 300 F6
Balnagall Highld 311 L2
Balnagowan Aberds 293 C7
Balnagrantach Highld 300 F4
Balnaguard Perth 286 B3
Balnahanaid Perth 285 C10
Balnahard Argyll 274 D5
Balnahard Argyll 288 F6
Balnain Highld 300 F4
Balnakeil Highld 308 C3
Balnakelly Aberds 293 B7
Balnaknock Highld 298 C4
Balnamoon Aberds 303 D9
Balnamoon Angus 293 G7
Balnapaling Highld 301 C7
Balne N Yorks 198 D5
Balnoon Corn 2 B2
Balochroy Argyll 255 B8
Balole Argyll 274 G4
Balone Fife 287 F8
Balornock Glasgow 268 B2
Balquharn Perth 286 D4
Balquhidder Stirl 285 E9
Balquhidder Station Stirl 285 E9
Balquhindachy Aberds 303 E8
Balrownie Angus 293 G7
Balsall W Mid 118 B4
Balsall Common W Mid 118 B4
Balsall Heath W Mid 133 G11
Balsall Street W Mid 118 B4
Balsam Cambs 123 G11
Balscote Oxon 101 C7
Balscott Oxon 101 C7
Balsham Cambs 123 G11
Balsporran Cottages Highld 291 F8
Balstonia Thurrock 69 C7
Baltasound Shetland 312 C8
Balterley Staffs 168 E3
Balterley Green Staffs 168 E3
Balterley Heath Staffs 168 E2
Baltersan Dumfries 236 C6
Balthangie Aberds 303 D8
Balthayock Perth 286 E5
Baltonsborough Som 44 G4
Balure Argyll 289 E11
Balvaird Highld 300 D5
Balvenie Moray 302 E3
Balvicar Argyll 275 B8
Balvraid Highld 295 D10
Balvraid Highld 301 F8
Balwest Corn 2 C3
Bamber Bridge Lancs 194 B5
Bamber's Green Essex 105 G11
Bamburgh Northumb 264 C5
Bamff Perth 286 B6
Bamford Derbys 186 E2
Bamford Gtr Man 195 E11
Bamfurlong Glos 99 G8
Bamfurlong Gtr Man 194 G5
Bampton Cumb 221 B10
Bampton Devon 27 C7
Bampton Oxon 82 E4
Bampton Grange Cumb 221 B10
Banavie Highld 290 F3
Banbury Oxon 101 C9
Banc-y-Darren Ceredig 128 G3
Bancffosfelen Carms 75 C7
Banchor Highld 301 E9
Banchory Aberds 293 D8
Banchory-Devenick Aberds 293 C11
Bancycapel Carms 74 B6
Bancyfelin Carms 74 B4
Bancyffordd Carms 93 D8
Bandirran Perth 286 D6
Bandonhill London 67 G9
Bandrake Head Cumb 210 B6
Banff Aberds 302 C6
Bangor Gwyn 179 G9
Bangor is y coed = Bangor on Dee Wrex 166 F5
Bangor on Dee = Bangor-is-y-coed Wrex 166 F5
Bangor Teifi Ceredig 93 C7
Bangors Corn 11 B10
Banham Norf 141 F11
Bank Hants 32 F3
Bank End Cumb 210 B3
Bank End Cumb 228 D6
Bank Fold Blkburn 195 C8
Bank Hey Blkburn 203 G9
Bank Houses Lancs 202 C4
Bank Lane Gtr Man 195 D9
Bank Newton N Yorks 204 C4
Bank Street Worcs 116 E2
Bank Top Gtr Man 195 E8
Bank Top Lancs 194 F4
Bank Top Stoke 168 E5
Bank Top T & W 242 D4
Bank Top W Yorks 196 C6
Bank Top W Yorks 205 F9
Bankend Dumfries 238 D2
Bankfoot Perth 286 D4
Bankglen E Ayrs 258 G4
Bankhead Aberdeen 293 B10
Bankhead Aberds 293 C8
Bankhead Dumfries 236 C2
Bankhead Falk 278 E6
Bankhead S Lnrk 269 G7
Bankland Som 28 B4
Banknock Falk 278 F5
Banks Cumb 240 E3
Banks Lancs 193 C11
Banks Orkney 314 C4
Bank's Green Worcs 117 D9
Bankshead Shrops 130 F6
Bankshill Dumfries 248 G5
Bankside Falk 279 E7
Banners Gate W Mid 133 D11
Banningham Norf 160 D4
Banniskirk Ho Highld 310 D5
Banniskirk Mains Highld 310 D5
Bannister Green Essex 106 G3
Bannockburn Stirl 278 C5
Banns Corn 4 F4
Banstead Sur 51 B8
Bantam Grove W Yorks 197 B9
Bantaskin Falk 279 F7
Bantham Devon 8 G3
Banton N Lnrk 278 F5
Banwell N Som 43 B11
Banyard's Green Suff 126 C5
Bapchild Kent 70 G2
Baptist End W Mid 133 F8
Bapton Wilts 46 F3
Bar End Hants 33 B7
Bar Hill Cambs 123 E7
Bar Hill Staffs 168 G3
Bar Moor T & W 242 E4
Barabhas W Isles 304 D5
Barabhas Iarach W Isles 304 D5
Barabhas Uarach W Isles 304 C5
Barachandroman Argyll 289 G8
Baramore Highld 289 B8
Barassie S Ayrs 257 C8
Baravullin Argyll 289 F10
Barbadoes Stirl 277 B11
Barbaraville Highld 301 B7
Barbauchlaw W Loth 269 B8
Barber Booth Derbys 185 E10
Barber Green Cumb 211 C7
Barber's Moor Lancs 194 D3
Barbican Plym 7 E9
Barbieston S Ayrs 257 F10
Barbon Cumb 212 C2
Barbourne Worcs 116 F6
Barbreck Ho Argyll 275 C9
Barbridge E Ches 167 D10
Barbrook Devon 41 D8
Barby Northants 119 C10
Barby Nortoft Northants 119 C11
Barcaldine Argyll 289 E11
Barcelona Corn 6 E4
Barcheston Warks 100 D5
Barclose Cumb 239 E10
Barcombe E Sus 36 E6
Barcombe Cross E Sus 36 D6
Barcroft W Yorks 204 F6
Barden N Yorks 224 G2
Barden Park Kent 52 D5
Barden Scale N Yorks 205 B7
Bardennoch Dumfries 246 E3
Bardfield End Green Essex 106 E2
Bardfield Saling Essex 106 F3
Bardister Shetland 312 F5
Bardnabeinne Highld 309 K7
Bardney Lincs 173 B10
Bardon Leics 153 G8
Bardon Mill Northumb 241 E7
Bardowie E Dunb 277 G11
Bardown E Sus 37 B11
Bardrainney Invclyd 276 G6
Bardrishaig Argyll 275 B8
Bardsea Cumb 210 E6
Bardsey W Yorks 206 E3
Bardsley Gtr Man 196 G2
Bardwell Suff 125 C8
Bare Lancs 211 G9
Bare Ash Som 43 F9
Bareless Northumb 263 B9
Barepot Cumb 228 F6
Bareppa Corn 3 D7
Barfad Argyll 275 G9
Barfad Dumfries 236 C5
Barford Norf 142 B2
Barford Sur 49 F11
Barford Warks 118 E5
Barford St John Oxon 101 E8
Barford St Martin Wilts 46 G5
Barford St Michael Oxon 101 E8
Barfrestone Kent 55 C9
Bargaly Dumfries 236 C6
Bargarran Renfs 277 G9
Bargate Derbys 170 F5
Bargeddie N Lnrk 268 C4
Bargod = Bargoed Caerph 77 F10
Bargoed Caerph 77 F10
Bargrennan Dumfries 236 B5
Barham Cambs 122 B2
Barham Kent 55 C8
Barham Suff 126 G2
Barharrow Dumfries 237 D8
Barhill Dumfries 237 C10
Barholm Dumfries 237 D7
Barholm Lincs 155 G11
Barkby Leics 136 B2
Barkby Thorpe Leics 136 B2
Barkers Green Shrops 149 D10
Barkers Hill Wilts 30 B6
Barkestone-le-Vale Leics 154 C5
Barkham Wokingham 65 F9
Barking London 68 C2
Barking Suff 125 G11
Barking Tye Suff 125 G11
Barkingside London 68 B2
Barkisland W Yorks 196 D5
Barkla Shop Corn 4 E4
Barkston Lincs 172 G6
Barkston N Yorks 206 F5
Barkston Ash N Yorks 206 F5
Barkway Herts 105 D7
Barlake Som 45 D7
Barlanark Glasgow 268 C3
Barland Powys 114 E5
Barland Common Swansea 56 D5
Barlaston Staffs 151 B7
Barlavington W Sus 35 D7
Barlborough Derbys 187 F7
Barlby N Yorks 207 G8
Barlestone Leics 135 B8
Barley Herts 105 D7
Barley Lancs 204 E2
Barley End Bucks 85 C7
Barley Green Lancs 204 E2
Barley Mow T & W 243 G7
Barleycroft End Herts 105 F8
Barleythorpe Rutland 136 B6
Barling Essex 70 B2
Barlings Lincs 189 G9
Barlow Derbys 186 G4
Barlow N Yorks 198 B6
Barlow T & W 242 E5
Barlow Moor Gtr Man 184 C4
Barmby Moor E Yorks 207 D11
Barmby on the Marsh E Yorks 199 B7
Barmer Norf 158 C6
Barming Heath Kent 53 B8
Barmolloch Argyll 275 D9
Barmoor Castle Northumb 263 B11
Barmoor Lane End Northumb 264 B2
Barmouth = Abermaw Gwyn 146 F2
Barmpton Darl 224 B6
Barmston E Yorks 209 B9
Barmston T & W 243 F8
Barmulloch Glasgow 268 B2
Barnaby Green Suff 127 B9
Barnacabber Argyll 276 D3
Barnack P'boro 137 B11
Barnacle Warks 135 G7
Barnaline Argyll 275 B10
Barnard Castle Durham 223 B11
Barnard Gate Oxon 82 C6
Barnardiston Suff 106 B4
Barnard's Green Worcs 98 B5
Barnardtown Newport 59 B10
Barnbarroch Dumfries 237 D10
Barnbow Carr W Yorks 206 F3
Barnburgh S Yorks 198 G3
Barnby Suff 143 F9
Barnby Dun S Yorks 198 F6
Barnby in the Willows Notts 172 E5
Barnby Moor Notts 187 E11
Barncluith S Lnrk 268 E4
Barndennoch Dumfries 247 F9
Barne Barton Plym 7 D8
Barnehurst London 68 D4
Barnes London 67 D8
Barnes Cray London 68 D4
Barnes Hall S Yorks 186 B4
Barnes Street Kent 52 D6
Barnet London 86 F2
Barnet Gate London 86 F2
Barnetby le Wold N Lincs 200 F5
Barnett Brook E Ches 167 G10
Barnettbrook Worcs 117 B7
Barney Norf 159 C9
Barnfield Kent 54 D2
Barnfields Hereford 97 C9
Barnfields Staffs 169 D7
Barnham Suff 125 B7
Barnham W Sus 35 G7
Barnham Broom Norf 141 B11
Barnhead Angus 287 B10
Barnhill Dundee 287 D8
Barnhill Moray 301 D11
Barnhill W Ches 167 E7
Barnhills Dumfries 236 B1
Barningham Durham 223 C11
Barningham Suff 125 B9
Barningham Green Norf 160 C2
Barnmoor Green Warks 118 E3
Barnoldby le Beck NE Lincs 201 G8
Barnoldswick Lancs 204 D3
Barnoldswick N Yorks 212 E3
Barns Borders 260 B6
Barns Green W Sus 35 B10
Barnsbury London 67 C10
Barnsdale Rutland 137 B8
Barnside W Yorks 197 F7
Barnsley Glos 81 D9
Barnsley S Yorks 197 F10
Barnsley Shrops 132 E5
Barnsole Kent 55 B9
Barnstaple Devon 40 G5
Barnston Essex 87 B10
Barnston Mers 182 E3
Barnstone Notts 154 B4
Barnt Green Worcs 117 C10
Barnton Edin 280 F3
Barnton W Ches 183 F10
Barnwell Cambs 123 F9
Barnwell Northants 137 G10
Barnwell All Saints Northants 137 G10
Barnwell St Andrew Northants 137 F10
Barnwood Glos 80 B5
Barochreal Argyll 289 G10
Barons Cross Hereford 115 F9
Barr Highld 289 D8
Barr S Ayrs 245 E7
Barr Som 27 C11
Barr Common W Mid 133 D11
Barra Castle Aberds 303 G7
Barrachan Dumfries 236 E5
Barrachnie Glasgow 268 C3
Barrack Aberds 303 E8
Barrack Hill Newport 59 B10
Barraer Dumfries 236 C5
Barraglom W Isles 304 E3
Barrahormid Argyll 275 E8
Barran Argyll 289 G10
Barranrioch Argyll 289 G10
Barrapol Argyll 288 E1
Barras Aberds 293 E10
Barras Cumb 222 C6
Barrasford Northumb 241 C10
Barravullin Argyll 275 C9
Barregarrow I o M 192 D4
Barrets Green E Ches 167 D9
Barrhead E Renf 267 D9
Barrhill S Ayrs 244 G6
Barrington Cambs 105 B7
Barrington Som 28 D5
Barripper Corn 2 B4
Barrmill N Ayrs 267 E7
Barrock Highld 310 B6
Barrock Ho Highld 310 C6
Barrow Glos 99 G7
Barrow Lancs 203 F10
Barrow Rutland 155 F7
Barrow S Yorks 186 B5
Barrow Shrops 132 C3
Barrow Som 44 E5
Barrow Suff 124 E5
Barrow Bridge Gtr Man 195 E7
Barrow Burn Northumb 263 G9
Barrow Common N Som 60 F4
Barrow Green Kent 70 G3
Barrow Gurney N Som 60 F4
Barrow Hann N Lincs 200 C5
Barrow Haven N Lincs 200 C5
Barrow Hill Derbys 186 F6
Barrow Hill Dorset 18 B5
Barrow-in-Furness Cumb 210 F4
Barrow Island Cumb 210 F3
Barrow Nook Lancs 194 G2
Barrow Street Wilts 45 G10
Barrow upon Humber N Lincs 200 C5
Barrow upon Soar Leics 153 F11
Barrow upon Trent Derbys 153 D7
Barrow Vale Bath 60 G6
Barrow Wake Glos 80 B6
Barroway Drove Norf 139 C11
Barrowburn Northumb 263 G9
Barrowby Lincs 155 B7
Barrowcliff N Yorks 217 B10
Barrowden Rutland 137 C8
Barrowford Lancs 204 F3
Barrowhill Kent 54 F6
Barrowmore Estate W Ches 167 B7
Barrows Green Cumb 211 B10
Barrows Green E Ches 167 D11
Barrow's Green Mers 183 D8
Barrows Green Notts 171 E7
Barry Angus 287 D9
Barry V Glam 58 F6
Barry Dock V Glam 58 F6
Barry Island V Glam 58 F6
Barsby Leics 154 G3
Barsham Suff 143 F7
Barshare E Ayrs 258 F3
Barstable Essex 69 B8
Barston W Mid 118 B4
Bartestree Hereford 97 C11
Barthol Chapel Aberds 303 F8
Bartholomew Green Essex 106 G4
Barthomley E Ches 168 E3
Bartington W Ches 183 F10
Bartley Hants 32 E4
Bartley Green W Mid 133 G10
Bartlow Cambs 105 B11
Barton Cambs 123 F8
Barton Glos 80 B4
Barton Glos 99 F11
Barton I o W 20 D6
Barton Lancs 193 F11
Barton Lancs 202 F6
Barton N Som 43 B11
Barton N Yorks 224 D4
Barton Oxon 83 D9
Barton Torbay 9 B8
Barton W Ches 166 E6
Barton Warks 118 G2
Barton Abbey Oxon 101 G9
Barton Bendish Norf 140 B4
Barton Court Hereford 98 C4
Barton End Glos 80 F4
Barton Gate Devon 41 E7
Barton Gate Staffs 152 F3
Barton Green Staffs 152 F3
Barton Hartshorn Bucks 102 E2
Barton Hill Bristol 60 E6
Barton Hill N Yorks 216 G4
Barton in Fabis Notts 153 C10
Barton in the Beans Leics 135 B7
Barton-le-Clay C Beds 103 E11
Barton-le-Street N Yorks 216 E4
Barton-le-Willows N Yorks 216 G4
Barton Mills Suff 124 C4
Barton on Sea Hants 19 C10
Barton on the Heath Warks 100 E5
Barton St David Som 44 G4
Barton Seagrave Northants 121 B7
Barton Stacey Hants 48 E2
Barton Town Devon 41 E7
Barton Turf Norf 161 E7
Barton Turn Staffs 152 F4
Barton-under-Needwood Staffs 152 F3
Barton-upon-Humber N Lincs 200 C4
Barton Upon Irwell Gtr Man 184 B3
Barton Waterside N Lincs 200 C4
Bartonsham Hereford 97 D10
Barugh S Yorks 197 F10
Barugh Green S Yorks 197 F10
Barway Cambs 123 B10
Barwell Leics 135 D8
Barwell London 67 G7
Barwick Devon 25 F9
Barwick Herts 86 B5
Barwick Som 29 E9
Barwick in Elmet W Yorks 206 F3
Baschurch Shrops 149 E8
Bascote Warks 119 E8
Bascote Heath Warks 119 E7
Base Green Suff 125 E10
Basford Shrops 131 F7
Basford Staffs 168 F5
Basford Green Staffs 169 E7
Bashall Eaves Lancs 203 E9
Bashley Hants 19 B10
Bashley Park Hants 19 B10
Basildon Essex 69 B8
Basingstoke Hants 48 C6
Baslow Derbys 186 G3
Bason Bridge Som 43 D10
Bassaleg Newport 59 B9
Bassenthwaite Cumb 229 E10
Bassett S Yorks 186 E3
Bassett Soton 32 D6
Bassett Green Soton 32 D6
Bassingbourn Cambs 104 C6
Bassingfield Notts 154 B2
Bassingham Lincs 172 C6
Bassingthorpe Lincs 155 D9
Bassus Green Herts 104 F6
Basta Shetland 312 D7
Basted Kent 52 B6
Baston Lincs 156 G2
Bastonford Worcs 116 G6
Bastwick Norf 161 F8
Baswich Staffs 151 E8
Baswick Steer E Yorks 209 D7
Batavaime Stirl 285 D8
Batch Som 43 B10
Batchcott Shrops 115 C9
Batchfields Hereford 98 B3
Batchley Worcs 117 D10
Batchworth Herts 85 G9
Batchworth Heath Herts 85 G9
Batcombe Dorset 29 G10
Batcombe Som 45 F7
Bate Heath E Ches 183 F11
Bateman's Green Worcs 117 B11
Bateman's Hill Pembs 73 E8
Batemoor S Yorks 186 E5
Batford Herts 85 B10
Bath Bath 61 F8
Bath Side Essex 108 E5
Bath Vale E Ches 168 C5
Bathampton Bath 61 F9
Bathealton Som 27 C9
Batheaston Bath 61 F9
Bathford Bath 61 F9
Bathgate W Loth 269 B9
Bathley Notts 172 D3
Bathpool Corn 11 G11
Bathpool Som 28 B3
Bathville W Loth 269 B8
Bathway Som 44 C5
Bathwick Bath 61 F9
Batlers Green Herts 85 F11
Batley W Yorks 197 C8
Batley Carr W Yorks 197 C8
Batsford Glos 100 E3
Batson Devon 9 G9
Batsworthy Devon 26 D4
Batten's Green Som 28 D3
Battenton Green Worcs 116 D6
Battersby N Yorks 225 D11
Battersea London 67 D9
Battisborough Cross Devon 7 F11
Battisford Suff 125 G11
Battisford Tye Suff 125 G10
Battle E Sus 38 D2
Battle Powys 95 E10
Battle Hill T & W 243 D8
Battledown Glos 99 G9
Battledown Cross Devon 25 F7
Battlefield Shrops 149 F10
Battlesbridge Essex 88 G3
Battlescombe Glos 80 D6
Battlesden C Beds 103 F9
Battlesea Green Suff 126 B4
Battleton Som 26 B6
Battlies Green Suff 125 E7
Battram Leics 135 B8
Battramsley Hants 20 B2
Battramsley Cross Hants 20 B2
Batt's Corner Hants 49 E10
Battyeford W Yorks 197 C7
Batworthy Devon 13 D10
Bauds of Cullen Moray 302 C4
Baugh Argyll 288 E2
Baughton Worcs 99 C7
Baughurst Hants 64 G5
Baulking Oxon 82 G4
Baumber Lincs 190 G2
Baunton Glos 81 E8
Baverstock Wilts 46 G4
Bawburgh Norf 142 B3
Bawdeswell Norf 159 E10
Bawdrip Som 43 F10
Bawdsey Suff 108 C6
Bawsey Norf 158 F3
Bawtry S Yorks 187 C11
Baxenden Lancs 195 B9
Baxterley Warks 134 D5
Baxter's Green Suff 124 F5
Bay Dorset 30 B4
Bay Highld 298 D2
Bay Gate Lancs 203 D11
Bay Horse Lancs 202 C5
Bay View Kent 70 E4
Baybridge Hants 33 C8
Baybridge Northumb 241 G11
Baycliff Cumb 210 E5
Baydon Wilts 63 D9
Bayford Herts 86 D4
Bayford Som 30 B2
Bayles Cumb 231 C10
Bayley's Hill Kent 52 C4
Baylham Suff 126 G2
Baylis Green Worcs 117 C11
Baynard's Green Oxon 101 F10
Baynhall Worcs 99 B7
Baysham Hereford 97 F11
Bayston Hill Shrops 131 B9
Bayswater London 67 C9
Baythorne End Essex 106 C4
Baythorpe Lincs 174 G2
Bayton Worcs 116 C3
Bayton Common Worcs 116 C4
Bayworth Oxon 83 E8
Beach Highld 289 D9
Beach S Glos 61 E8
Beach Hay Worcs 116 C4
Beachampton Bucks 102 D5
Beachamwell Norf 140 B5
Beachans Moray 301 E10
Beacharr Argyll 255 C7
Beachborough Kent 55 F7
Beachlands E Sus 23 E11
Beachley Glos 79 G9
Beacon Corn 2 B5
Beacon Devon 27 F11
Beacon Devon 28 F2
Beacon Down E Sus 37 C9
Beacon End Essex 107 G9
Beacon Hill Bath 61 F9
Beacon Hill Bucks 84 G6
Beacon Hill Cumb 210 E4
Beacon Hill Dorset 18 C5
Beacon Hill Essex 88 C5
Beacon Hill Kent 53 G10
Beacon Hill Notts 172 E4
Beacon Hill Suff 108 B4
Beacon Hill Sur 49 F11
Beacon Lough T & W 243 F7
Beaconhill Northumb 243 B7
Beacon's Bottom Bucks 84 F3
Beaconsfield Bucks 66 B2
Beaconside Staffs 151 E8
Beacrabhaic W Isles 305 J3
Beadlam N Yorks 216 C3
Beadlow C Beds 104 D2
Beadnell Northumb 264 D6
Beaford Devon 25 E9
Beal N Yorks 198 B4
Beal Northumb 273 G11
Bealach Highld 289 D11
Bealach Maim Argyll 275 E10
Bealbury Corn 7 B7
Beal's Green Kent 53 G9
Bealsmill Corn 12 F3
Beam Bridge Som 27 D10
Beam Hill Staffs 152 D4
Beambridge Shrops 131 F10
Beamhurst Staffs 151 B11
Beamhurst Lane Staffs 151 B11
Beaminster Dorset 29 G7
Beamish Durham 242 G6
Beamond End Bucks 84 F6
Beamsley N Yorks 205 C7
Bean Kent 68 E5
Beanacre Wilts 62 F2
Beancross Falk 279 F8
Beanhill M Keynes 103 D7
Beanley Northumb 264 F3
Beansburn E Ayrs 257 B10
Beanthwaite Cumb 210 C4
Beaquoy Orkney 314 D3
Bear Cross Bmouth 19 B7
Beard Hill Som 44 E6
Beardly Batch Som 44 E6
Beardwood Blkburn 195 B7
Beare Devon 27 G7
Beare Green Sur 51 E7
Bearley Warks 118 E3
Bearley Cross Warks 118 E3
Bearnus Argyll 288 E5
Bearpark Durham 233 C10
Bearsbridge Northumb 241 F7
Bearsden E Dunb 277 G10
Bearsted Kent 53 B9
Bearstone Shrops 150 B4
Bearwood Hereford 115 F7
Bearwood Poole 18 B6
Bearwood W Mid 133 F10
Beasley Staffs 168 F4
Beattock Dumfries 248 C3
Beauchamp Roding Essex 87 C9
Beauchief S Yorks 186 E4
Beauclerc Northumb 242 E2
Beaudesert Warks 118 D3
Beaufort Bl Gwent 77 C11
Beaufort Castle Highld 300 E5
Beaulieu Hants 32 G5
Beaulieu Wood Dorset 30 F2
Beauly Highld 300 E5
Beaumaris Anglesey 179 F10
Beaumont Cumb 239 F8
Beaumont Essex 108 G3
Beaumont Windsor 66 E3
Beaumont Hill Darl 224 B5
Beaumont Leys Leicester 135 B11
Beausale Warks 118 C4
Beauvale Notts 171 F8
Beauworth Hants 33 B9
Beavan's Hill Hereford 98 G3
Beaworthy Devon 12 B5
Beazley End Essex 106 F4
Bebington Mers 182 E4
Bebside Northumb 253 G7
Beccles Suff 143 E8
Becconsall Lancs 194 C2
Beck Bottom Cumb 210 C5
Beck Bottom W Yorks 197 C10
Beck Foot Cumb 222 F2
Beck Foot W Yorks 205 F8
Beck Head Cumb 211 C8
Beck Hole N Yorks 226 E6
Beck Houses Cumb 221 F11
Beck Row Suff 124 B3
Beck Side Cumb 210 C4
Beck Side Cumb 211 C7
Beckbury Shrops 132 C5
Beckces Cumb 230 F4
Beckenham London 67 F11
Beckermet Cumb 219 D10
Beckermonds N Yorks 213 C7
Beckery Som 44 F3
Beckett End Norf 140 D5
Beckfoot Cumb 220 E3
Beckfoot Cumb 229 B7
Beckford Worcs 99 D9
Beckhampton Wilts 62 F5
Beckingham Lincs 172 E5

Beckingham Notts 188 D3
Beckington Som 45 C10
Beckjay Shrops 115 B7
Beckley E Sus 38 C5
Beckley Hants 19 B10
Beckley Oxon 83 C9
Beckley Furnace E Sus 38 C4
Beckside Cumb 212 B2
Beckton London 68 C2
Beckwith N Yorks 205 C11
Beckwithshaw N Yorks 205 C11
Becontree London 68 B3
Bed-y-coedwr Gwyn 146 D4
Bedale N Yorks 214 B5
Bedburn Durham 233 E8
Bedchester Dorset 30 D5
Beddau Rhondda 58 B5
Beddgelert Gwyn 163 F9
Beddingham E Sus 36 F6
Beddington London 67 G10
Beddington Corner London 67 F9
Bedfield Suff 126 D4
Bedford Beds 121 G11
Bedford Gtr Man 183 B11
Bedford Park London 67 D8
Bedgebury Cross Kent 53 G8
Bedgrove Bucks 84 C4
Bedham W Sus 35 C8
Bedhampton Hants 22 B2
Bedingfield Suff 126 D3
Bedingham Green Norf 142 E5
Bedlam N Yorks 214 G5
Bedlam Som 45 D9
Bedlam Street W Sus 36 D3
Bedlar's Green Essex 105 G10
Bedlington Northumb 253 G7
Bedlington Station Northumb 253 G7
Bedlinog M Tydf 77 E9
Bedminster Bristol 60 E5
Bedminster Down Bristol 60 F5
Bedmond Herts 85 E9
Bednall Staffs 151 F9
Bednall Head Staffs 151 F9
Bedrule Borders 262 F4
Bedstone Shrops 115 B7
Bedwas Caerph 59 B7
Bedwell Herts 104 G4
Bedwell Wrex 166 F5
Bedwellty Caerph 77 E11
Bedwellty Pits Bl Gwent 77 D11
Bedwlwyn Wrex 148 B4
Bedworth Warks 135 F7
Bedworth Heath Warks 134 F6
Bedworth Woodlands Warks 134 F6
Beeby Leics 136 B3
Beech Hants 49 F7
Beech Staffs 151 B7
Beech Hill Gtr Man 194 F5
Beech Hill W Berks 65 G7
Beech Lanes W Mid 133 F10
Beechcliff Staffs 151 B7
Beechcliffe W Yorks 205 E7
Beechen Cliff Bath 61 G9
Beechingstoke Wilts 46 B5
Beechwood Halton 183 E8
Beechwood Newport 59 B10
Beechwood W Mid 118 B5
Beechwood W Yorks 206 F2
Beecroft C Beds 103 G10
Beedon W Berks 64 D3
Beedon Hill W Berks 64 D3
Beeford E Yorks 209 C8
Beeley Derbys 170 B3
Beelsby NE Lincs 201 G8
Beenham W Berks 64 F5
Beenham Stocks W Berks 64 F5
Beenham's Heath Windsor 65 D10
Beeny Corn 11 C8
Beer Devon 15 D10
Beer Som 44 G2
Beer Hackett Dorset 29 E9
Beercrocombe Som 28 C4
Beesands Devon 8 G6
Beesby Lincs 191 E7
Beeslack Midloth 270 C4
Beeson Devon 8 G6
Beeston C Beds 104 B3
Beeston Norf 159 F8
Beeston Notts 153 B10
Beeston W Ches 167 D8
Beeston W Yorks 205 G11
Beeston Hill W Yorks 205 G11
Beeston Park Side W Yorks 197 B9
Beeston Regis Norf 177 E11
Beeston Royds W Yorks 205 G11
Beeston St Lawrence Norf 160 E6
Beeswing Dumfries 237 C10
Beetham Cumb 211 D9
Beetham Som 28 E3
Beetley Norf 159 F9
Beffcote Staffs 150 F6
Began Cardiff 59 C8
Begbroke Oxon 83 C7
Begdale Cambs 139 B9
Begelly Pembs 73 D10
Beggar Hill Essex 87 E10
Beggarington Hill W Yorks 197 C9
Beggars Ash Hereford 98 D4
Beggar's Bush Powys 114 E5
Beggars Bush W Sus 35 F11
Beggars Pound V Glam 58 F4
Beggearn Huish Som 42 F4
Beguildy Powys 114 B3
Beighton Norf 143 B7
Beighton S Yorks 186 E6
Beighton Hill Derbys 170 E3
Beili-glas Mon 78 C4
Beitearsaig W Isles 305 G1
Beith N Ayrs 266 E6
Bekesbourne Kent 55 B7
Bekesbourne Hill Kent 55 B7
Belah Cumb 239 F9
Belan Powys 130 C4
Belaugh Norf 160 F5
Belbins Hants 32 C5
Belbroughton Worcs 117 B8
Belchalwell Dorset 30 F3
Belchalwell Street Dorset 30 F3
Belchamp Otten Essex 106 C6
Belchamp St Paul Essex 106 C5
Belchamp Walter Essex 106 C6
Belcher's Bar Leics 135 B8
Belchford Lincs 190 F3
Beleybridge Fife 287 F9
Belfield Gtr Man 196 E2
Belford Northumb 264 C4
Belgrano Conwy 181 F7
Belgrave Leicester 135 B11
Belgrave Staffs 134 C4
Belgrave W Ches 166 C5
Belgravia London 67 D9
Belhaven E Loth 282 F3
Belhelvie Aberds 293 B11
Belhinnie Aberds 302 G4
Bell Bar Herts 86 D3
Bell Busk N Yorks 204 B4
Bell Common Essex 86 E6
Bell End Worcs 117 B8
Bell Green London 67 E11
Bell Green W Mid 135 G7
Bell Heath Worcs 117 B9
Bell Hill Hants 34 C2
Bell o' th' Hill W Ches 167 F8
Bellabeg Aberds 292 B5
Bellamore S Ayrs 244 F6
Bellanoch Argyll 275 D8
Bellanrigg Borders 260 B6
Bellasize E Yorks 199 B10
Bellaty Angus 286 B6
Belle Eau Park Notts 171 D11
Belle Green S Yorks 197 F11
Belle Isle W Yorks 197 B10
Belle Vale Mers 182 D6
Belle Vale W Mid 133 G9
Belle Vue Cumb 229 E8
Belle Vue Cumb 239 F9
Belle Vue Gtr Man 184 B5
Belle Vue S Yorks 198 G5
Belle Vue Shrops 149 G9
Belle Vue W Yorks 197 D10
Belleau Lincs 190 F6
Bellehiglash Moray 301 F11
Bellerby N Yorks 224 G2
Bellever Devon 13 F9
Bellevue Worcs 117 C9
Bellfield E Ayrs 257 B10
Bellfields Sur 50 C3
Belliehill Angus 293 G7
Bellingdon Bucks 84 D6
Bellingham London 67 E11
Bellingham Northumb 251 G8
Bellmount Norf 157 E10
Belloch Argyll 255 D7
Bellochantuy Argyll 255 D7
Bell's Close T & W 242 E5
Bell's Corner Suff 107 D9
Bells Yew Green E Sus 52 F6
Bellsbank E Ayrs 245 C11
Bellshill N Lnrk 268 C4
Bellshill Northumb 264 C4
Bellside N Lnrk 268 D6
Bellsmyre W Dunb 277 F8
Bellspool Borders 260 B5
Bellsquarry W Loth 269 C10
Belluton Bath 60 G6
Bellyeoman Fife 280 D2
Belmaduthy Highld 300 D6
Belmesthorpe Rutland 155 G10
Belmont Blkburn 195 D7
Belmont Durham 234 C2
Belmont E Sus 38 E4
Belmont Harrow 67 G9
Belmont Oxon 63 B11
Belmont S Ayrs 257 E8
Belmont Shetland 312 C7
Belmont Sutton 85 G11
Belnacraig Aberds 292 B5
Belnagarrow Moray 302 E3
Belnie Lincs 156 C5
Belowda Corn 5 C9
Belper Derbys 170 F4
Belper Lane End Derbys 170 F4
Belph Derbys 187 F8
Belsay Northumb 242 B4
Belses Borders 262 D3
Belsford Devon 8 D5
Belsize Herts 85 E8
Belstead Suff 108 C2
Belston S Ayrs 257 E9
Belstone Devon 13 C8
Belstone Corner Devon 13 B8
Belthorn Blkburn 195 C8
Beltinge Kent 71 F7
Beltingham Northumb 241 E7
Beltoft N Lincs 199 F10
Belton Leics 153 E8
Belton Lincs 155 B8
Belton N Lincs 199 F9
Belton Norf 143 C9
Belton in Rutland Rutland 136 C6
Beltring Kent 53 D7
Belts of Collonach Aberds 293 D8
Belvedere London 68 D3
Belvedere W Loth 269 B9
Belvoir Leics 154 C6
Bembridge I o W 21 D8
Bemersyde Borders 262 C3
Bemerton Wilts 46 G6
Bemerton Heath Wilts 46 G6
Bempton E Yorks 218 E3
Ben Alder Lodge Highld 291 F7
Ben Armine Lodge Highld 309 H7
Ben Casgro W Isles 304 F6
Ben Rhydding W Yorks 205 D8
Benacre Suff 143 G10
Benbuie Dumfries 246 D6
Benchill Gtr Man 184 D4
Bencombe Glos 80 F3
Benderloch Argyll 289 F11
Bendish Herts 104 G3
Bendronaig Lodge Highld 299 F10
Benenden Kent 53 G10
Benfield Dumfries 236 C5
Benfieldside Durham 242 G3
Bengal Pembs 91 E9
Bengate Norf 160 D6
Bengeo Herts 86 C4
Bengeworth Worcs 99 C10
Bengrove Glos 99 E9
Benhall Glos 99 G8
Benhall Green Suff 127 E7
Benhall Street Suff 127 E7
Benhilton London 67 F9
Benholm Aberds 293 G10
Beningbrough N Yorks 206 B6
Benington Herts 104 G5
Benington Lincs 174 F5
Benington Sea End Lincs 174 F6
Benllech Anglesey 179 E8
Benmore Argyll 276 E2
Benmore Stirl 285 E8
Benmore Lodge Argyll 289 F7
Benmore Lodge Highld 309 H3
Bennacott Corn 11 C11
Bennah Devon 14 E2
Bennan N Ayrs 255 E10
Bennane Lea S Ayrs 244 F3
Bennetland E Yorks 199 B10
Bennetsfield Highld 300 D6
Bennett End Bucks 84 F3
Bennetts End Herts 85 D9
Benniworth Lincs 190 E2
Benover Kent 53 D8
Bensham T & W 242 E6
Benslie N Ayrs 266 G6
Benson Oxon 83 G10
Benston Shetland 313 H6
Bent Aberds 293 F8
Bent Gate Lancs 195 C9
Benter Som 44 D6
Bentfield Bury Essex 105 F9
Bentfield Green Essex 105 F10
Bentgate Gtr Man 196 E2
Benthall Northumb 264 D6
Benthall Shrops 132 C3
Bentham Glos 80 B6
Benthoul Aberdeen 293 C10
Bentilee Stoke 168 F6
Bentlass Pembs 73 E7
Bentlawnt Shrops 130 C6
Bentley E Yorks 208 F6
Bentley Essex 87 F9
Bentley Hants 49 E9
Bentley S Yorks 198 F5
Bentley Suff 108 D2
Bentley W Mid 133 D9
Bentley Warks 134 D5
Bentley Worcs 117 D9
Bentley Common Warks 134 D5
Bentley Heath Herts 86 F2
Bentley Heath W Mid 118 B3
Bentley Rise S Yorks 198 G5
Benton Devon 41 F7
Benton Green W Mid 118 B5
Bentpath Dumfries 249 E8
Bents W Loth 269 C9
Bents Head W Yorks 205 F7
Bentwichen Devon 41 G8
Bentworth Hants 49 E7
Benvie Dundee 287 D7
Benville Dorset 29 G8
Benwell T & W 242 E6
Benwick Cambs 138 E6
Beobridge Shrops 132 E5
Beoley Worcs 117 D11
Beoraidbeg Highld 295 F8
Bepton W Sus 34 D5
Berden Essex 105 F9
Bere Alston Devon 7 B8
Bere Ferrers Devon 7 C9
Bere Regis Dorset 18 C2
Berechurch Essex 107 G9
Berefold Aberds 303 F9
Berepper Corn 2 E5
Bergh Apton Norf 142 C6
Berghers Hill Bucks 66 B2
Berhill Som 44 F2
Berinsfield Oxon 83 F9
Berkeley Glos 79 F11
Berkeley Heath Glos 79 F11
Berkeley Road Glos 80 E2
Berkeley Towers E Ches 167 E11
Berkhamsted Herts 85 D7
Berkley Som 45 D10
Berkley Down Som 45 D9
Berkley Marsh Som 45 D10
Berkswell W Mid 118 B4
Bermondsey London 67 D10
Bermuda Warks 135 F7
Bernards Heath Herts 85 D11
Bernera Highld 295 C10
Berner's Cross Devon 25 F10
Berner's Hill E Sus 53 G8
Berners Roding Essex 87 D10
Bernice Argyll 276 C2
Bernisdale Highld 298 D4
Berrick Salome Oxon 83 G10
Berriedale Highld 311 G5
Berrier Cumb 230 F3
Berriew = Aberriw Powys 130 C3
Berrington Northumb 273 G10
Berrington Shrops 131 B10
Berrington Worcs 115 D11
Berrington Green Worcs 115 D11
Berriowbridge Corn 11 F11
Berrow Som 43 C10
Berrow Worcs 98 E5
Berrow Green Worcs 116 F4
Berry Swansea 56 D3
Berry Brow W Yorks 196 E6
Berry Cross Devon 25 E7
Berry Down Cross Devon 40 E5
Berry Hill Glos 79 C9
Berry Hill Pembs 91 C11
Berry Hill Stoke 168 F6
Berry Hill Worcs 117 E7
Berry Moor S Yorks 197 G9
Berry Pomeroy Devon 8 C6
Berryfield Wilts 61 G11
Berrygate Hill E Yorks 201 C8
Berryhillock Moray 302 C5
Berrylands London 67 F7
Berrynarbor Devon 40 D5
Berry's Green London 52 B2
Berrysbridge Devon 26 G6
Bersham Wrex 166 F4
Berstane Orkney 314 E4
Berth-ddu Flint 166 B2
Berthengam Flint 181 F10
Berwick E Sus 23 D8
Berwick Kent 54 F6
Berwick S Glos 60 C5
Berwick Bassett Wilts 62 E5
Berwick Hill Northumb 242 B5
Berwick Hills M'bro 225 B10
Berwick St James Wilts 46 F5
Berwick St John Wilts 30 C6
Berwick St Leonard Wilts 46 G2
Berwick-upon-Tweed Northumb 273 E9
Berwick Wharf Shrops 149 G10
Berwyn Denb 165 G11
Bescaby Leics 154 D6
Bescar Lancs 193 E11
Bescot W Mid 133 D10
Besford Shrops 149 E11
Besford Worcs 99 C8
Bessacarr S Yorks 198 G6
Bessels Green Kent 52 B4
Bessels Leigh Oxon 83 E7
Besses o' th' Barn Gtr Man 195 F10
Bessingby E Yorks 218 F3
Bessingham Norf 160 B3
Best Beech Hill E Sus 52 G6
Besthorpe Norf 141 D11
Besthorpe Notts 172 C4
Bestwood Nottingham 171 G9
Bestwood Village Notts 171 F9
Beswick E Yorks 208 D6
Beswick Gtr Man 184 B5
Betchcott Shrops 131 D8
Betchton Heath E Ches 168 C3
Betchworth Sur 51 D8
Bethania Ceredig 111 E11
Bethania Gwyn 163 E10
Bethania Gwyn 164 F2
Bethany Corn 6 D6
Bethel Anglesey 178 G5
Bethel Corn 5 E10
Bethel Gwyn 147 B9
Bethel Gwyn 163 B8
Bethelnie Aberds 303 F7
Bethersden Kent 54 E2
Bethesda Gwyn 163 B10
Bethesda Pembs 73 B9
Bethlehem Carms 94 F3
Bethnal Green London 67 C10
Betley Staffs 168 F3
Betley Common Staffs 168 F2
Betsham Kent 68 E6
Betteshanger Kent 55 C10
Bettiscombe Dorset 16 B3
Bettisfield Wrex 149 B9
Betton Shrops 130 C6
Betton Shrops 150 B3
Betton Strange Shrops 131 B10
Bettws Bridgend 58 B2
Bettws Mon 78 B3
Bettws Newport 78 G3
Bettws Cedewain Powys 130 D2
Bettws Gwerfil Goch Denb 165 F8
Bettws Ifan Ceredig 92 B6
Bettws Newydd Mon 78 D5
Bettws-y-crwyn Shrops 130 G4
Bettyhill Highld 308 C7
Betws Bridgend 57 D11
Betws Carms 75 C10
Betws Bledrws Ceredig 111 G11
Betws-Garmon Gwyn 163 D8
Betws Ifan Ceredig 92 B6
Betws-y-Coed Conwy 164 D4
Betws-yn-Rhos Conwy 180 G6
Beulah Ceredig 92 B5
Beulah Powys 113 G8
Bevendean Brighton 36 F4
Bevercotes Notts 187 G11
Bevere Worcs 116 F6
Beverley E Yorks 208 F6
Beverston Glos 80 G5
Bevington Glos 79 F11
Bewaldeth Cumb 229 E10
Bewbush W Sus 51 F8
Bewcastle Cumb 240 C3
Bewdley Worcs 116 B5
Bewerley N Yorks 214 G3
Bewholme E Yorks 209 C9
Bewley Common Wilts 62 F2
Bewlie Borders 262 D3
Bewlie Mains Borders 262 D3
Bewsey Warr 183 D9
Bexfield Norf 159 D10
Bexhill E Sus 38 F2
Bexley London 68 E3
Bexleyheath London 68 D3
Bexleyhill W Sus 34 B6
Bexon Kent 53 B11
Bexwell Norf 140 C2
Beyton Suff 125 E8
Beyton Green Suff 125 E8
Bhalasaigh W Isles 304 E3
Bhaltos W Isles 304 E2
Bhatarsaigh W Isles 297 M2
Bhlàraidh Highld 290 B5
Bibstone S Glos 79 G11
Bibury Glos 81 D10
Bicester Oxon 101 G11
Bickenhall Som 28 D3
Bickenhill W Mid 134 G3
Bicker Lincs 156 B4
Bicker Bar Lincs 156 B4
Bicker Gauntlet Lincs 156 B4
Bickershaw Gtr Man 194 G6
Bickerstaffe Lancs 194 G2
Bickerton Devon 9 G11
Bickerton E Ches 167 E8
Bickerton N Yorks 206 C5
Bickford Staffs 151 G7
Bickham Som 42 E3
Bickingcott Devon 26 B3
Bickington Devon 13 G11
Bickington Devon 40 G4
Bickleigh Devon 7 C10
Bickleigh Devon 26 F6
Bickleton Devon 40 G4
Bickley London 68 F2
Bickley W Ches 167 F8
Bickley Worcs 116 C2
Bickley Moss W Ches 167 F8
Bickley Town W Ches 167 F8
Bickleywood W Ches 167 F8
Bickmarsh Warks 100 B2
Bicknacre Essex 88 E3
Bicknoller Som 42 F6
Bicknor Kent 53 B11
Bickton Hants 31 E11
Bicton Hereford 115 E9
Bicton Pembs 72 D4
Bicton Shrops 130 G5
Bicton Shrops 149 F8
Bicton Heath Shrops 149 G9
Bidborough Kent 52 E5
Bidden Hants 49 D8
Biddenden Kent 53 F11
Biddenden Green Kent 53 E11
Biddenham Beds 103 B10
Biddestone Wilts 61 E11
Biddick T & W 243 F8
Biddick Hall T & W 243 E9
Biddisham Som 43 C11
Biddlesden Bucks 102 C2
Biddlestone Northumb 251 B11
Biddulph Staffs 168 D5
Biddulph Moor Staffs 168 D6
Bideford Devon 25 B7
Bideford-on-Avon Warks 118 G2
Bidlake Devon 12 D5
Bidston Mers 182 C3
Bidston Hill Mers 182 D3
Bidwell C Beds 103 G10
Bielby E Yorks 207 E11
Bieldside Aberdeen 293 C10
Bierley I o W 20 F6
Bierley W Yorks 205 G9
Bierton Bucks 84 B4
Big Mancot Flint 166 B4
Big Sand Highld 299 B7
Bigbury Devon 8 F3
Bigbury-on-Sea Devon 8 G3
Bigby Lincs 200 F5
Bigfrith Windsor 65 C11
Biggar Cumb 210 F3
Biggar S Lnrk 260 B2
Biggar Road N Lnrk 268 C5
Biggin Derbys 169 D11
Biggin Derbys 170 F3
Biggin N Yorks 206 F6
Biggin Thurrock 69 D7
Biggin Hill London 52 B2
Biggings Shetland 313 G3
Biggleswade C Beds 104 C3
Bighouse Highld 310 C2
Bighton Hants 48 G6
Biglands Cumb 239 G7
Bignall End Staffs 168 E4
Bignor W Sus 35 E7
Bigods Essex 106 G2
Bigram Stirl 285 G10
Bigrigg Cumb 219 C10
Bigswell Orkney 314 E3
Bigton Shetland 313 L5
Bilberry Corn 5 C10
Bilborough Nottingham 171 G8
Bilbrook Som 42 E4
Bilbrook Staffs 133 C7
Bilbrough N Yorks 206 D6
Bilbster Highld 310 D6
Bilby Notts 187 E10
Bildershaw Durham 233 G10
Bildeston Suff 107 B9
Bill Quay T & W 243 E7
Billacombe Plym 7 E10
Billacott Corn 11 C11
Billericay Essex 87 G11
Billesdon Leics 136 C4
Billesley W Mid 133 G11
Billesley Warks 118 F2
Billesley Common W Mid 133 G11
Billingborough Lincs 156 C2
Billinge Mers 194 G4
Billingford Norf 126 B3
Billingford Norf 159 E10
Billingham Stockton 234 G5
Billinghay Lincs 173 E11
Billingley S Yorks 198 G2
Billingshurst W Sus 35 B9
Billingsley Shrops 132 F4
Billington C Beds 103 G8
Billington Lancs 203 F10
Billington Staffs 151 E7
Billockby Norf 161 G8
Billy Mill T & W 243 D8
Billy Row Durham 233 D9
Bilmarsh Shrops 149 D9
Bilsborrow Lancs 202 F6
Bilsby Lincs 191 F7
Bilsby Field Lincs 191 F7
Bilsdon Devon 14 C2
Bilsham W Sus 35 G7
Bilsington Kent 54 G4
Bilson Green Glos 79 C11
Bilsthorpe Notts 171 C10
Bilsthorpe Moor Notts 171 D11
Bilston Midloth 270 C5
Bilston W Mid 133 D9
Bilstone Leics 135 B7
Bilting Kent 54 D5
Bilton E Yorks 209 G9
Bilton N Yorks 206 B2
Bilton Northumb 264 G6
Bilton Warks 119 C9
Bilton Haggs N Yorks 206 D5
Bilton in Ainsty N Yorks 206 D5
Bimbister Orkney 314 E3
Binbrook Lincs 190 C2
Binchester Blocks Durham 233 E10
Bincombe Dorset 17 E9
Bincombe Som 43 F7
Bindal Highld 311 L3
Bindon Som 27 C10
Binegar Som 44 D6
Bines Green W Sus 35 D11
Binfield Brack 65 E10
Binfield Heath Oxon 65 D8
Bingfield Northumb 241 C11
Bingham Edin 280 G6
Bingham Notts 154 B4
Bingley W Yorks 205 F8
Bings Heath Shrops 149 F10
Binham Norf 159 B9
Binley Hants 48 C2
Binley W Mid 119 B7
Binley Woods Warks 119 B7
Binnegar Dorset 18 D3
Binniehill Falk 279 G7
Binscombe Sur 50 D3
Binsey Oxon 83 D7
Binsoe N Yorks 214 D4
Binstead Hants 49 E9
Binstead I o W 21 C7
Binsted Hants 49 E9
Binsted W Sus 35 F7
Binton Warks 118 G2
Bintree Norf 159 E10
Binweston Shrops 130 C6
Birch Essex 88 B6
Birch Gtr Man 195 F11
Birch Acre Worcs 117 C11
Birch Berrow Worcs 116 E4
Birch Cross Staffs 152 C2
Birch Green Essex 88 B6
Birch Green Herts 86 C3
Birch Green Lancs 194 F3
Birch Green Worcs 99 B7
Birch Heath W Ches 167 C8
Birch Hill Brack 65 F11
Birch Hill W Ches 183 G8
Birch Vale Derbys 185 D8
Birch Wood Som 28 E2
Bircham Newton Norf 158 C5
Bircham Tofts Norf 158 C5
Birchan Coppice Worcs 116 C6
Birchanger Essex 105 G10
Birchburn N Ayrs 255 E10
Birchden E Sus 52 F4
Birchencliffe W Yorks 196 D6
Birchend Hereford 98 C3
Birchendale Staffs 151 B11
Bircher Hereford 115 D9
Birches Green W Mid 134 E2
Birches Head Stoke 168 F5
Birchett's Green E Sus 53 G7
Birchfield Highld 301 G9
Birchfield W Mid 133 E11
Birchgrove Cardiff 59 D7
Birchgrove E Sus 36 B6
Birchgrove Swansea 57 B8
Birchhall Corner Essex 107 E10
Birchill Devon 28 G4
Birchills W Mid 133 D10
Birchington Kent 71 F9
Birchley Heath Warks 134 E5
Birchmoor Warks 134 C5
Birchmoor Green C Beds 103 E8
Bircholt Forstal Kent 54 E5
Birchover Derbys 170 C2
Birchwood Herts 86 D2
Birchwood Lincs 172 B6
Birchwood Som 28 E2
Birchwood Warr 183 C10
Birchy Hill Hants 19 B11
Bircotes Notts 187 C10
Bird End W Mid 133 E10
Bird Street Suff 125 G10
Birdbrook Essex 106 C4
Birdbush Wilts 30 C6
Birdfield Argyll 275 D10
Birdforth N Yorks 215 D9
Birdham W Sus 22 D4
Birdholme Derbys 170 B5
Birdingbury Warks 119 D8
Birdlip Glos 80 C6
Birds Edge W Yorks 197 F8
Birds End Suff 124 E5
Birds Green Essex 87 D9
Birdsall N Yorks 216 F6
Birdsgreen Shrops 132 F5
Birdsmoorgate Dorset 28 G5
Birdston E Dunb 278 F3
Birdwell S Yorks 197 G10
Birdwood Glos 80 B2
Birgham Borders 263 B7
Birichen Highld 309 K7
Birkacre Lancs 194 D5
Birkby Cumb 229 D7
Birkby N Yorks 224 E6
Birkby W Yorks 196 D6
Birkdale Mers 193 D10
Birkenbog Aberds 302 C5
Birkenhead Mers 182 D4
Birkenhills Aberds 303 E7
Birkenshaw N Lnrk 268 C3
Birkenshaw S Lnrk 268 F5
Birkenshaw W Yorks 197 B8
Birkenshaw Bottoms W Yorks 197 B8
Birkenside Borders 271 G11
Birkett Mire Cumb 230 G2
Birkhall Aberds 292 D5
Birkhill Angus 287 D7
Birkhill Borders 260 F6
Birkhill Borders 271 G11
Birkholme Lincs 155 E9
Birkhouse W Yorks 197 C7
Birkin N Yorks 198 B4
Birks Cumb 222 G3
Birks W Yorks 197 B9
Birkshaw Northumb 241 D7
Birley Hereford 115 G9
Birley Carr S Yorks 186 C4
Birley Edge S Yorks 186 C4
Birleyhay Derbys 186 E5
Birling Kent 69 G7
Birling Northumb 252 B6
Birling Gap E Sus 23 F9
Birlingham Worcs 99 C8
Birmingham W Mid 133 F11
Birnam Perth 286 C4
Birniehill S Lnrk 268 E2
Birse Aberds 293 D7
Birsemore Aberds 293 D7
Birstall Leics 135 B11
Birstall W Yorks 197 B8
Birstall Smithies W Yorks 197 B8
Birstwith N Yorks 205 B10
Birthorpe Lincs 156 C2
Birtle Gtr Man 195 E10
Birtley Hereford 115 D7
Birtley Northumb 241 B9
Birtley Shrops 131 E9
Birtley T & W 243 F7
Birtley Green Sur 50 E4
Birts Street Worcs 98 D5
Birtsmorton Worcs 98 D6
Bisbrooke Rutland 137 D7
Biscathorpe Lincs 190 D2
Biscombe Som 27 E11
Biscot Luton 103 G11
Biscovey Corn 5 E11
Bish Mill Devon 26 B2
Bisham Windsor 65 C10
Bishampton Worcs 117 G9
Bishon Common Hereford 97 C8
Bishop Auckland Durham 233 F10
Bishop Burton E Yorks 208 F5
Bishop Kinkell Highld 300 D5
Bishop Middleham Durham 234 E2
Bishop Monkton N Yorks 214 F6
Bishop Norton Lincs 189 C7
Bishop Sutton Bath 44 B5
Bishop Thornton N Yorks 214 G5
Bishop Wilton E Yorks 207 B11
Bishopbridge Lincs 189 C8
Bishopbriggs E Dunb 278 G2
Bishopdown Wilts 47 G7
Bishopmill Moray 302 C2
Bishops Cannings Wilts 62 G4
Bishop's Castle Shrops 130 F6
Bishop's Caundle Dorset 29 E11
Bishop's Cleeve Glos 99 F9
Bishop's Down Dorset 29 E11
Bishops Frome Hereford 98 B3
Bishops Green Essex 87 B10
Bishop's Green W Berks 64 G4
Bishop's Hull Som 28 C2
Bishop's Itchington Warks 119 F7
Bishops Lydeard Som 27 B11
Bishop's Norton Glos 98 G6
Bishops Nympton Devon 26 C3
Bishop's Offley Staffs 150 D5
Bishop's Quay Corn 2 D6
Bishop's Stortford Herts 105 G9
Bishop's Sutton Hants 48 G6
Bishop's Tachbrook Warks 118 E6
Bishops Tawton Devon 40 G5
Bishop's Waltham Hants 33 D9
Bishop's Wood Staffs 132 B6
Bishopsbourne Kent 55 C7
Bishopsgarth Stockton 234 G4
Bishopsgate Sur 66 E3
Bishopsteignton Devon 14 G4
Bishopstoke Hants 33 D7
Bishopston Bristol 60 D5
Bishopston Swansea 56 D5
Bishopstone Bucks 84 C4
Bishopstone E Sus 23 E7
Bishopstone Hereford 97 C8
Bishopstone Kent 71 F8
Bishopstone Swindon 63 C8
Bishopstone Wilts 31 B9
Bishopstrow Wilts 45 E11
Bishopswood Som 28 E3
Bishopsworth Bristol 60 F5
Bishopthorpe York 207 D7
Bishopton Darl 234 G3
Bishopton Dumfries 236 E6
Bishopton N Yorks 214 E6
Bishopton Renfs 277 G8
Bishopton Warks 118 F3
Bishopwearmouth T & W 243 F9
Bishpool Newport 59 B10
Bishton Newport 59 B11
Bishton Staffs 151 E10
Bisley Glos 80 D6
Bisley Sur 50 B3
Bisley Camp Sur 50 B2
Bispham Blkpool 202 E2
Bispham Green Lancs 194 E3
Bissoe Corn 4 G5
Bissom Corn 3 C7
Bisterne Hants 31 G10
Bisterne Close Hants 32 G2
Bitchet Green Kent 52 C5
Bitchfield Lincs 155 D9
Bittadon Devon 40 E4
Bittaford Devon 8 D3
Bittering Norf 159 F8
Bitterley Shrops 115 B11
Bitterne Soton 33 E7
Bitterne Park Soton 32 E6
Bitterscote Staffs 134 C4
Bitteswell Leics 135 F10
Bittles Green Dorset 30 C5
Bitton S Glos 61 F7
Bix Oxon 65 B8
Bixter Shetland 313 H5
Blaby Leics 135 D11
Black Bank Cambs 139 F10
Black Bank Warks 135 F7
Black Banks Darl 224 C5
Black Barn Lincs 157 D8
Black Bourton Oxon 82 E3
Black Callerton T & W 242 D5
Black Carr Norf 141 D11
Black Clauchrie S Ayrs 245 G7
Black Corner W Sus 51 F9
Black Corries Lodge Highld 284 B6
Black Crofts Argyll 289 F11
Black Cross Corn 5 C8
Black Dam Hants 48 C6
Black Dog Devon 26 F4
Black Heddon Northumb 242 B3
Black Hill W Yorks 204 E6
Black Horse Drove Cambs 139 E11
Black Lake W Mid 133 E9
Black Lane Gtr Man 195 F9
Black Marsh Shrops 130 D6
Black Moor Lancs 194 E3
Black Moor W Yorks 205 F11
Black Mount Argyll 284 C6
Black Notley Essex 106 G5
Black Park Wrex 166 G4
Black Pill Swansea 56 C6
Black Pole Lancs 202 F5
Black Rock Brighton 36 G4
Black Rock Corn 2 C5
Black Street Suff 143 F10
Black Tar Pembs 73 D7
Black Torrington Devon 25 F7
Black Vein Caerph 78 G2
Blackacre Dumfries 248 E2
Blackadder West Borders 272 E6
Blackawton Devon 8 E6
Blackbeck Cumb 219 D10
Blackbird Leys Oxon 83 E9
Blackborough Devon 27 F9
Blackborough Norf 158 G3
Blackborough End Norf 158 G3
Blackboys E Sus 37 C8
Blackbraes Aberds 293 B10
Blackbrook Derbys 170 F4
Blackbrook Derbys 185 E9
Blackbrook Mers 183 B8
Blackbrook Staffs 150 B5
Blackbrook Sur 51 D7
Blackburn Aberds 293 B10
Blackburn Aberds 302 F5
Blackburn Blkburn 195 B7
Blackburn S Yorks 186 C5
Blackburn W Loth 269 B9
Blackcastle Midloth 271 D8
Blackchambers Aberds 293 B9
Blackcraig Dumfries 246 G6
Blackcraigs Angus 293 E7
Blackden Heath E Ches 184 G3
Blackditch Oxon 82 D6
Blackdog Aberds 293 B11
Blackdown Dorset 28 G5
Blackdown Hants 33 C8
Blackdown Warks 118 D6
Blackdyke Cumb 238 G4
Blackdykes E Loth 281 E11
Blacker Hill S Yorks 197 G11
Blacketts Kent 70 F2
Blackfell T & W 243 F7
Blackfen London 68 E3
Blackfield Hants 32 G6
Blackford Cumb 239 E9
Blackford Dumfries 248 G4
Blackford Perth 286 G2
Blackford Shrops 131 G11
Blackford Som 29 B11
Blackford Som 42 D2
Blackford Som 44 D2
Blackford Bridge Gtr Man 195 F10
Blackfordby Leics 152 F6
Blackfords Staffs 151 G9
Blackgang I o W 20 F5
Blackgate Angus 287 B8
Blackhall Aberds 293 D8
Blackhall Edin 280 G4
Blackhall Renfs 267 C9
Blackhall Colliery Durham 234 D5
Blackhall Mill T & W 242 F4
Blackhall Rocks Durham 234 D5
Blackham E Sus 52 F3
Blackhaugh Borders 261 B10
Blackheath Essex 107 G10
Blackheath London 67 D11
Blackheath Suff 127 C8
Blackheath Sur 50 D4
Blackheath W Mid 133 F9
Blackheath Park London 68 D2
Blackhill Aberds 303 D10
Blackhill Aberds 303 E10
Blackhill Aberds 303 F10
Blackhill Durham 242 G3
Blackhill Hants 32 D4
Blackhill Highld 298 D3
Blackhillock Moray 302 E4
Blackhills Highld 301 D9
Blackhills Moray 302 D2
Blackhills Swansea 56 D5
Blackhorse Devon 14 C5
Blackhorse S Glos 61 D7
Blackjack Lincs 156 B5
Blackland Wilts 62 F4
Blacklands E Sus 38 E4
Blacklands Hereford 98 C2
Blacklaw Aberds 302 D6
Blackleach Lancs 202 G5
Blackley Gtr Man 195 G11
Blackley W Yorks 196 D6
Blacklunans Perth 292 G3
Blackmarstone Hereford 97 D10
Blackmill Bridgend 58 B2
Blackminster Worcs 99 C11
Blackmoor Bath 60 G5
Blackmoor Gtr Man 195 G7
Blackmoor Hants 49 G9
Blackmoor N Som 60 G3
Blackmoor Som 27 D11
Blackmoor Gate Devon 41 E7
Blackmoorfoot W Yorks 196 E5
Blackmore Essex 87 E10
Blackmore Shrops 130 B6
Blackmore End Essex 106 E4
Blackmore End Herts 85 B11
Blackmore End Worcs 98 C6
Blackness Aberds 293 D8
Blackness E Sus 52 G4
Blackness Falk 279 F11
Blacknest Hants 49 E9
Blacknest Windsor 66 F3
Blacknoll Dorset 18 D2
Blacko Lancs 204 E3
Blackoe Shrops 149 B10
Blackpark Dumfries 236 C5
Blackpole Worcs 117 F7
Blackpool Blkpool 202 F2
Blackpool Devon 7 E11
Blackpool Devon 9 F7
Blackpool Devon 14 G2
Blackpool Pembs 73 C9
Blackpool Gate Cumb 240 B2
Blackridge W Loth 269 B7
Blackrock Argyll 274 G4
Blackrock Bath 60 F6
Blackrock Mon 78 C2
Blackrod Gtr Man 194 E6
Blackshaw Dumfries 238 D2
Blackshaw Head W Yorks 196 B3
Blackshaw Moor Staffs 169 D8
Blacksmith's Corner Suff 108 C2
Blacksmith's Green Suff 126 D2
Blacksnape Blkburn 195 C8
Blackstone W Sus 36 D2
Blackstone Worcs 116 C5
Blackthorn Oxon 83 B10
Blackthorpe Suff 125 E8
Blacktoft E Yorks 199 C10
Blacktop Aberdeen 293 C10
Blacktown Newport 59 C9
Blackwall Derbys 170 F3
Blackwall London 67 C11
Blackwall Tunnel London 67 C11
Blackwater Corn 4 F4
Blackwater Dorset 19 B8
Blackwater Hants 49 B11
Blackwater I o W 20 D6
Blackwater Norf 159 E11
Blackwater Som 28 D3
Blackwater Lodge Moray 302 G3
Blackwaterfoot N Ayrs 255 E9
Blackweir Cardiff 59 D7
Blackwell Cumb 239 G10
Blackwell Darl 224 C5
Blackwell Derbys 170 D6
Blackwell Derbys 185 G10
Blackwell Devon 27 B8
Blackwell W Sus 51 F11
Blackwell Warks 100 C4
Blackwell Worcs 117 C9
Blackwood Caerph 77 F11
Blackwood S Lnrk 268 G5
Blackwood Warr 183 C10
Blackwood Hill Staffs 168 D6
Blacon W Ches 166 B5
Bladbean Kent 55 D7
Blades N Yorks 223 F9
Bladnoch Dumfries 236 D6
Bladon Oxon 82 C6
Blaen-Cil-Llech Ceredig 92 B6
Blaen Clydach Rhondda 77 G7
Blaen-gwynfi Neath 57 B11
Blaen-pant Ceredig 92 C5
Blaen-waun Carms 92 F4
Blaen-waun Ceredig 111 G7
Blaen-y-coed Carms 92 F6
Blaen-y-Cwm Bl Gwent 77 C10
Blaen-y-cwm Denb 147 C10
Blaen-y-cwm Gwyn 146 E4
Blaen-y-cwm Powys 147 E11
Blaenannerch Ceredig 92 B4
Blaenau Carms 75 C10
Blaenau Flint 166 D2
Blaenau Dolwyddelan Conwy 164 E2
Blaenau Ffestiniog Gwyn 164 F2
Blaenau-Gwent Bl Gwent 78 E2
Blaenavon Torf 78 D3
Blaenbedw Fawr Ceredig 111 G7
Blaencaerau Bridgend 57 C11
Blaencelyn Ceredig 111 G7
Blaencwm Rhondda 76 F6
Blaendulais = Seven Sisters Neath 76 D4
Blaendyryn Powys 95 D8
Blaenffos Pembs 92 D3
Blaengarw Bridgend 76 G6
Blaengwrach Neath 76 D5
Blaengwynfi Neath 57 B11
Blaenllechau Rhondda 77 F8
Blaenpennal Ceredig 112 E2
Blaenplwyf Ceredig 111 B11
Blaenporth Ceredig 92 B5
Blaenrhondda Rhondda 76 E6
Blaenwaun Carms 92 F4
Blaenycwm Ceredig 112 B6
Blagdon N Som 44 B4
Blagdon Torbay 9 C7
Blagdon Hill Som 28 D2
Blagill Cumb 231 B10
Blaguegate Lancs 194 F3
Blaich Highld 290 F2
Blain Highld 289 C8
Blaina Bl Gwent 78 D2
Blainacraig Ho Aberds 293 D7
Blair Fife 280 C6
Blair Atholl Perth 291 G10
Blair Drummond Stirl 278 B4
Blairbeg N Ayrs 256 C2
Blairburn Fife 279 D9
Blairdaff Aberds 293 B8
Blairdryne Aberds 293 D9
Blairglas Argyll 276 D6
Blairgorm Highld 301 G10
Blairgowrie Perth 286 C5
Blairhall Fife 279 D10
Blairhill N Lnrk 268 B4
Blairingone Perth 279 B9
Blairland N Ayrs 266 F6
Blairlinn N Lnrk 278 G5
Blairlogie Stirl 278 B6
Blairlomond Argyll 276 B3
Blairmore Argyll 276 E3
Blairmore Highld 306 D6
Blairnamarrow Moray 292 B4
Blairquhosh Stirl 277 E10
Blair's Ferry Argyll 275 G10
Blairskaith E Dunb 277 F11
Blaisdon Glos 80 B2
Blaise Hamlet Bristol 60 D5
Blake End Essex 106 G4
Blakebrook Worcs 117 B7
Blakedown Worcs 117 B7
Blakelands M Keynes 103 C7
Blakelaw Borders 263 C7

Blakelaw T & W 242 D6
Blakeley Staffs 133 E7
Blakeley Lane Staffs 169 F7
Blakelow E Ches 167 E11
Blakemere Hereford 97 C7
Blakenall Heath W Mid 133 C10
Blakeney Glos 79 D11
Blakeney Norf 177 E8
Blakenhall E Ches 168 F2
Blakenhall W Mid 133 D8
Blakeshall Worcs 132 G6
Blakesley Northants 120 G2
Blanchland Northumb 241 G11
Bland Hill N Yorks 205 C10
Blandford Camp Dorset 30 F6
Blandford Forum Dorset 30 F5
Blandford St Mary Dorset 30 F5
Blandy Highld 308 D6
Blanefield Stirl 277 F11
Blanerne Borders 272 D6
Blank Bank Staffs 168 F4
Blankney Lincs 173 C9
Blantyre S Lnrk 268 D3
Blar a'Chaorainn Highld 290 G3
Blaran Argyll 275 B9
Blarghour Argyll 275 B10
Blarmachfoldach Highld 290 G2
Blarnalearoch Highld 307 K6
Blasford Hill Essex 88 C2
Blashford Hants 31 F11
Blaston Leics 136 D6
Blatchbridge Som 45 D9
Blatherwycke Northants 137 D9
Blawith Cumb 210 B5
Blaxhall Suff 127 F7
Blaxton S Yorks 199 G7
Blaydon T & W 242 E5
Blaydon Burn T & W 242 E5
Blaydon Haughs T & W 242 E5
Bleach Green Cumb 219 B9
Bleach Green Suff 126 B4
Bleadney Som 44 D3
Bleadon N Som 43 B10
Bleak Acre Hereford 98 B2
Bleak Hall M Keynes 103 D7
Bleak Hey Nook Gtr Man 196 F4
Bleak Hill Hants 31 E10
Blean Kent 70 G6
Bleasby Lincs 189 E10
Bleasby Notts 172 F2
Bleasby Moor Lincs 189 E10
Bleasdale Lancs 203 D7
Bleatarn Cumb 222 C4
Blebocraigs Fife 287 F8
Bleddfa Powys 114 D4
Bledington Glos 100 G4
Bledlow Bucks 84 E3
Bledlow Ridge Bucks 84 F3
Bleet Wilts 45 B11
Blegbie E Loth 271 C9
Blegbury Devon 24 B2
Blencarn Cumb 231 E8
Blencogo Cumb 229 B9
Blendworth Hants 34 E2
Blenheim Oxon 83 D9
Blenheim Oxon 83 E9
Blenheim Park Norf 158 C6
Blenkinsopp Hall Northumb 240 E5
Blennerhasset Cumb 229 C9
Blervie Castle Moray 301 D10
Bletchingdon Oxon 83 B8
Bletchingley Sur 51 C10
Bletchley M Keynes 103 E7
Bletchley Shrops 150 C2
Bletherston Pembs 91 G11
Bletsoe Beds 121 F10
Blewbury Oxon 64 B4
Bliby Kent 54 F4
Blickling Norf 160 D3
Blidworth Notts 171 D9
Blidworth Bottoms Notts 171 E9
Blidworth Dale Notts 171 E9
Blindburn Northumb 263 G8
Blindcrake Cumb 229 E8
Blindley Heath Sur 51 D11
Blindmoor Som 28 E3
Blingery Highld 310 E7
Blisland Corn 11 G8
Bliss Gate Worcs 116 C4
Blissford Hants 31 E11
Blisworth Northants 120 G4
Blithbury Staffs 151 E11
Blitterlees Cumb 238 G4
Blo' Norton Norf 125 B10
Blockley Glos 100 D3
Blofield Norf 142 B6
Blofield Heath Norf 160 G6
Bloodman's Corner Suff 143 D10
Bloomfield Bath 45 B7
Bloomfield Bath 61 G8
Bloomfield Borders 262 E3
Bloomfield W Mid 133 E9
Bloomsbury London 67 C10
Blore Staffs 150 C4
Blore Staffs 169 F10
Bloreheath Staffs 150 B4
Blossomfield W Mid 118 B2
Blount's Green Staffs 151 C11
Blowick Mers 193 D11
Blowinghouse Corn 4 E4
Bloxham Oxon 101 D8
Bloxholm Lincs 173 E9
Bloxwich W Mid 133 C9
Bloxworth Dorset 18 C3
Blubberhouses N Yorks 205 B9
Blue Anchor Corn 5 D8
Blue Anchor Som 42 E4
Blue Anchor Swansea 56 B4
Blue Bell Hill Kent 69 G8
Blue Hill Herts 104 G5
Blue Row Essex 89 C8
Blue Town Kent 70 D2
Blue Vein Wilts 61 F10
Bluebell Telford 149 G11
Bluecairn Borders 271 G10
Bluetown Kent 54 B2
Bluewater Kent 68 E5
Blughasary Highld 307 J6
Blundellsands Mers 182 B4
Blundeston Suff 143 D10
Blundies Staffs 132 F6
Blunham C Beds 122 G3
Blunsdon St Andrew Swindon 62 B6
Bluntington Worcs 117 C7
Bluntisham Cambs 123 C7
Blunts Corn 6 C6
Blunt's Green Warks 118 D2
Blurton Stoke 168 G5
Blyborough Lincs 188 C6
Blyford Suff 127 B8
Blymhill Staffs 150 G6
Blymhill Lawns Staffs 150 G6
Blyth Borders 270 F2
Blyth Northumb 253 G8
Blyth Notts 187 D10
Blyth Bridge Borders 270 F2
Blyth End Warks 134 E4
Blythburgh Suff 127 B9
Blythe Borders 271 F11
Blythe Bridge Staffs 169 G7
Blythe Marsh Staffs 169 G7
Blythswood Renfs 267 B10
Blyton Lincs 188 C5
Boarhills Fife 287 F9
Boarhunt Hants 33 F10
Boars Hill Oxon 83 E7
Boarsgreave Lancs 195 C10
Boarshead E Sus 52 G4
Boarstall Bucks 83 C10
Boasley Cross Devon 12 C5
Boat of Garten Highld 291 B11
Boath Highld 300 B5
Bobbing Kent 69 F11
Bobbington Staffs 132 E6
Bobbingworth Essex 87 D8
Bobby Hill Suff 125 C10
Boblainy Highld 300 F4
Bocaddon Corn 6 D3
Bochastle Stirl 285 G10
Bockhanger Kent 54 E4
Bocking Essex 106 G5
Bocking Churchstreet Essex 106 F5
Bocking's Elm Essex 89 B11
Bockleton Worcs 115 E11
Bockmer End Bucks 65 B10
Bocombe Devon 24 C5
Bodantionail Highld 299 B7
Boddam Aberds 303 E11
Boddam Shetland 313 M5
Bodden Som 44 E6
Boddington Glos 99 F7
Bodedern Anglesey 178 E4
Bodellick Corn 10 G5
Bodelva Corn 5 E11
Bodelwyddan Denb 181 F8
Bodenham Hereford 115 G10
Bodenham Wilts 31 B11
Bodenham Bank Hereford 98 E2
Bodenham Moor Hereford 115 G10
Bodermid Gwyn 144 D3
Bodewryd Anglesey 178 C5
Bodfari Denb 181 G9
Bodffordd Anglesey 178 F6
Bodham Norf 177 E10
Bodiam E Sus 38 B3
Bodicote Oxon 101 D9
Bodiechell Aberds 303 E7
Bodieve Corn 10 G5
Bodiggo Corn 5 D10
Bodilly Corn 2 C5
Bodinnick Corn 6 E2
Bodle Street Green E Sus 23 C11
Bodley Devon 41 D7
Bodmin Corn 5 B11
Bodmiscombe Devon 27 F10
Bodney Norf 140 D6
Bodorgan Anglesey 162 B5
Bodsham Kent 54 D6
Boduan Gwyn 144 B6
Boduel Corn 6 C4
Bodwen Corn 5 C10
Bodymoor Heath Warks 134 D4
Bofarnel Corn 6 C2
Bogallan Highld 300 D6
Bogbrae Aberds 303 F10
Bogend Borders 272 F5
Bogend Notts 171 F7
Bogend S Ayrs 257 C9
Bogentory Aberds 293 C9
Boghall Midloth 270 B4
Boghall W Loth 269 B9
Boghead Aberds 293 D8
Boghead S Lnrk 268 G5
Bogmoor Moray 302 C3
Bogniebrae Aberds 302 E5
Bogniebrae Aberds 302 E6
Bognor Regis W Sus 22 D6
Bograxie Aberds 293 B9
Bogs Aberds 302 G5
Bogs Bank Borders 270 E3
Bogside N Lnrk 268 E6
Bogthorn W Yorks 204 F6
Bogton Aberds 302 D6
Bogtown Aberds 302 C5
Bogue Dumfries 246 G4
Bohemia E Sus 38 E4
Bohemia Wilts 32 D2
Bohenie Highld 290 E4
Bohetherick Corn 7 B8
Bohortha Corn 3 C9
Bohuntine Highld 290 E4
Bohuntinville Highld 290 E4
Boirseam W Isles 296 C6
Bojewyan Corn 1 C3
Bokiddick Corn 5 C11
Bolahaul Fm Carms 74 B6
Bolam Durham 233 G9
Bolam Northumb 252 G3
Bolam West Houses Northumb 252 G3
Bolas Heath Telford 150 E3
Bolberry Devon 9 G8
Bold Heath Mers 183 D8
Boldmere W Mid 134 E2
Boldon T & W 243 E9
Boldon Colliery T & W 243 E8
Boldre Hants 20 B2
Boldron Durham 223 C10
Bole Notts 188 D3
Bole Hill Derbys 186 G4
Bolehall Staffs 134 C4
Bolehill Derbys 170 E3
Bolehill Derbys 186 G6
Bolehill S Yorks 186 E5
Bolenowe Corn 2 B5
Boleside Borders 261 C11
Boley Park Staffs 134 B2
Bolham Devon 27 E7
Bolham Notts 188 E2
Bolham Water Devon 27 E11
Bolholt Gtr Man 195 E9
Bolingey Corn 4 E5
Bolitho Corn 2 C5
Bollihope Durham 232 E6
Bollington E Ches 184 F6
Bollington Cross E Ches 184 F6
Bolney W Sus 36 C3
Bolnhurst Beds 121 F11
Bolnore W Sus 36 C4
Bolshan Angus 287 B10
Bolsover Derbys 187 G7
Bolsterstone S Yorks 186 B3
Bolstone Hereford 97 E11
Boltby N Yorks 215 B9
Bolter End Bucks 84 G3
Bolton Cumb 231 G8
Bolton E Loth 281 G10
Bolton E Yorks 207 C11
Bolton Gtr Man 195 F8
Bolton Northumb 264 G4
Bolton W Yorks 205 F9
Bolton Abbey N Yorks 205 C7
Bolton Bridge N Yorks 205 C7
Bolton-by-Bowland Lancs 203 D11
Bolton Green Lancs 194 D5
Bolton Houses Lancs 202 G4
Bolton-le-Sands Lancs 211 F9
Bolton Low Houses Cumb 229 C10
Bolton New Houses Cumb 229 C10
Bolton-on-Swale N Yorks 224 F5
Bolton Percy N Yorks 206 E6
Bolton Town End Lancs 211 F9
Bolton upon Dearne S Yorks 198 G3
Bolton Wood Lane Cumb 229 C11
Bolton Woods W Yorks 205 F9
Boltonfellend Cumb 239 D11
Boltongate Cumb 229 C10
Boltshope Park Durham 232 B4
Bolventor Corn 11 F9
Bomarsund Northumb 253 G7
Bombie Dumfries 237 D9
Bomby Cumb 221 B10
Bomere Heath Shrops 149 F9
Bon-y-maen Swansea 57 B7
Bonaly Edin 270 B4
Bonar Bridge Highld 309 K6
Bonawe Argyll 284 D4
Bonby N Lincs 200 D4
Boncath Pembs 92 D4
Bonchester Bridge Borders 262 G3
Bonchurch I o W 21 F7
Bond End Staffs 152 F2
Bondend Glos 80 B5
Bondleigh Devon 25 G11
Bondman Hays Leics 135 B9
Bonds Lancs 202 E5
Bondstones Devon 25 F9
Bonehill Devon 13 F10
Bonehill Staffs 134 C3
Bo'ness Falk 279 E9
Bonhill W Dunb 277 F7
Boningale Shrops 132 C6
Bonjedward Borders 262 E5
Bonkle N Lnrk 268 D6
Bonnavoulin Highld 289 D7
Bonning Gate Cumb 221 F9
Bonnington Borders 261 B7
Bonnington Edin 270 B2
Bonnington Kent 54 F5
Bonnybank Fife 287 G7
Bonnybridge Falk 278 E6
Bonnykelly Aberds 303 D8
Bonnyrigg and Lasswade Midloth 270 B6
Bonnyton Aberds 302 F6
Bonnyton Angus 287 B10
Bonnyton Angus 287 D7
Bonnyton E Ayrs 257 B10
Bonsall Derbys 170 D3
Bonskeid House Perth 291 G10
Bonson Som 43 E8
Bont Mon 78 B5
Bont-Dolgadfan Powys 129 C7
Bont Fawr Carms 94 F4
Bont goch = Elerch Ceredig 128 F3
Bont-newydd Conwy 181 G8
Bont Newydd Gwyn 146 E5
Bont Newydd Gwyn 164 G2
Bontddu Gwyn 146 F3
Bontuchel Denb 165 D9
Bonthorpe Lincs 191 G7
Bontnewydd Ceredig 112 D2
Bontnewydd Gwyn 163 D7
Bonvilston = Tresimwn V Glam 58 E5
Boode Devon 40 F4
Booker Bucks 84 G4
Bookham Dorset 30 G2
Booleybank Shrops 149 D11
Boon Borders 271 F11
Boon Hill Staffs 168 E4
Boorley Green Hants 33 E8
Boosbeck Redcar 226 B3
Boose's Green Essex 106 E6
Boot Cumb 220 E3
Boot Street Suff 108 B4
Booth Staffs 151 D10
Booth W Yorks 196 B4
Booth Bank E Ches 184 D2
Booth Bridge Lancs 204 D4
Booth Green E Ches 184 E6
Booth Wood W Yorks 196 D4
Boothby Graffoe Lincs 173 D7
Boothby Pagnell Lincs 155 C9
Boothen Stoke 168 G5
Boothferry E Yorks 199 B8
Boothgate Derbys 170 F5
Boothroyd W Yorks 197 C8
Boothsdale W Ches 167 B8
Boothstown Gtr Man 195 G8
Boothtown W Yorks 196 B5
Boothville Northants 120 E5
Bootle Cumb 210 B2
Bootle Mers 182 B4
Booton Norf 160 E2
Boots Green W Ches 184 G3
Booze N Yorks 223 E10
Boquhan Stirl 277 D10
Boquio Corn 2 C5
Boraston Shrops 116 D2
Boraston Dale Shrops 116 C2
Borden Kent 69 G11
Borden W Sus 34 C4
Border Cumb 238 G5
Bordesley W Mid 133 F11
Bordesley Green W Mid 134 F2
Bordlands Borders 270 F3
Bordley N Yorks 213 G8
Bordon Hants 49 F10
Bordon Camp Hants 49 F9
Boreham Essex 88 D3
Boreham Wilts 45 E11
Boreham Street E Sus 23 C11
Borehamwood Herts 85 F11
Boreland Dumfries 236 C5
Boreland Dumfries 248 E5
Boreland Fife 280 C6
Boreland Stirl 285 D9
Boreland of Southwick Dumfries 237 C11
Boreley Worcs 116 D6
Borestone Stirl 278 C5
Borgh W Isles 296 C5
Borgh W Isles 297 L2
Borghasdal W Isles 296 C6
Borghastan W Isles 304 D4
Borgie Highld 308 D6
Borgue Dumfries 237 E8
Borgue Highld 311 G5
Borley Essex 106 C6
Borley Green Essex 106 C6
Borley Green Suff 125 E9
Bornais W Isles 297 J3
Bornesketaig Highld 298 B3
Borness Dumfries 237 E8
Borough Scilly 1 G3
Borough Green Kent 52 B6
Borough Marsh Wokingham 65 D9
Borough Park Staffs 134 B4
Borough Post Som 28 C4
Boroughbridge N Yorks 215 F7
Borras Wrex 166 E4
Borras Head Wrex 166 E5
Borreraig Highld 296 F7
Borrobol Lodge Highld 311 G2
Borrodale Highld 297 G7
Borrohill Aberds 303 D9
Borrowash Derbys 153 C8
Borrowby N Yorks 215 B8
Borrowby N Yorks 226 B5
Borrowdale Cumb 220 C5
Borrowfield Aberds 293 D10
Borrowston Highld 310 E7
Borrowstoun Mains Falk 279 E9
Borstal Medway 69 F8
Borth = Y Borth Ceredig 128 E2
Borth-y-Gest Gwyn 145 B11
Borthwick Midloth 271 D7
Borthwickbrae Borders 261 G10
Borthwickshiels Borders 261 F10
Borve Highld 298 E4
Borve Lodge W Isles 305 J2
Borwick Lancs 211 E10
Borwick Rails Cumb 210 D3
Bosavern Corn 1 C3
Bosbury Hereford 98 C3
Boscadjack Corn 2 C5
Boscastle Corn 11 C8
Boscean Corn 1 C3
Boscombe Bmouth 19 C8
Boscombe Wilts 47 F8
Boscomoor Staffs 151 G8
Boscoppa Corn 5 E10
Boscreege Corn 2 C3
Bosham W Sus 22 C4
Bosham Hoe W Sus 22 C4
Bosherston Pembs 73 G7
Boskednan Corn 1 C4
Boskenna Corn 1 E4
Bosleake Corn 4 G3
Bosley E Ches 168 B6
Boslowick Corn 3 C7
Boslymon Corn 5 C11
Bosoughan Corn 5 C7
Bosporthennis Corn 1 B4
Bossall N Yorks 216 G4
Bossiney Corn 11 D7
Bossingham Kent 54 D6
Bossington Hants 47 G10
Bossington Kent 55 B8
Bossington Som 41 D11
Bostadh W Isles 304 D3
Bostock Green W Ches 167 B11
Boston Lincs 174 G4
Boston Long Hedges Lincs 174 F5
Boston Spa W Yorks 206 D4
Boston West Lincs 174 F3
Boswednack Corn 1 B4
Boswin Corn 2 C5
Boswinger Corn 5 G9
Boswyn Corn 2 B5
Botallack Corn 1 C3
Botany Bay London 86 F3
Botany Bay Mon 79 E8
Botcherby Cumb 239 F10
Botcheston Leics 135 B9
Botesdale Suff 125 B10
Bothal Northumb 252 F6
Bothampstead W Berks 64 D4
Bothamsall Notts 187 G11
Bothel Cumb 229 D9
Bothenhampton Dorset 16 C5
Bothwell S Lnrk 268 D4
Bothy Highld 290 F4
Botley Bucks 85 E7
Botley Hants 33 E8
Botley Oxon 83 D7
Botloe's Green Glos 98 F4
Botolph Claydon Bucks 102 G4
Botolphs W Sus 35 F11
Bottacks Highld 300 C4
Botternell Corn 11 G11
Bottesford Leics 154 B6
Bottesford N Lincs 199 F11
Bottisham Cambs 123 E10
Bottlesford Wilts 46 B6
Bottom Boat W Yorks 197 C11
Bottom House Staffs 169 E8
Bottom o' th' Moor Gtr Man 195 E7
Bottom of Hutton Lancs 194 B3
Bottom Pond Kent 53 B11
Bottomcraig Fife 287 E7
Bottomley W Yorks 196 D5
Bottoms Corn 1 E3
Botreaux Mill Devon 26 B4
Botrells Close Bucks 85 G7
Botts Green Warks 134 E4
Botusfleming Corn 7 C8
Botwnnog Gwyn 144 C5
Bough Beech Kent 52 D3
Boughrood Powys 96 D2
Boughrood Brest Powys 96 D2
Boughspring Glos 79 F9
Boughton Lincs 173 F10
Boughton Norf 140 C3
Boughton Northants 120 D5
Boughton Notts 171 B11
Boughton W Ches 166 B6
Boughton Aluph Kent 54 D4
Boughton Corner Kent 54 D4
Boughton Green Kent 53 C9
Boughton Heath W Ches 166 B6
Boughton Lees Kent 54 D4
Boughton Malherbe Kent 53 D11
Boughton Monchelsea Kent 53 C9
Boughton Street Kent 54 B5
Boulby Redcar 226 B5
Bould Oxon 100 G4
Boulden Shrops 131 F10
Boulder Clough W Yorks 196 C4
Bouldnor I o W 20 D3
Bouldon Shrops 131 F10
Boulmer Northumb 265 G7
Boulsdon Glos 98 G4
Boulston Pembs 73 C7
Boultenstone Aberds 292 B6
Boultham Lincs 173 B7
Boultham Moor Lincs 173 B7
Boulton Derbys 153 C7
Boulton Moor Derbys 153 C7
Boundary Leics 152 F6
Boundary Staffs 169 G7
Boundstone Sur 49 E10
Bountis Thorne Devon 24 D5
Bourn Cambs 122 F6
Bournbrook W Mid 133 G10
Bourne Lincs 155 E11
Bourne N Som 44 B3
Bourne End Beds 121 E10
Bourne End Bucks 65 B11
Bourne End C Beds 103 C9
Bourne End Herts 85 D8
Bourne Vale W Mid 133 D11
Bourne Valley Poole 19 C7
Bournemouth Bmouth 19 C7
Bournes Green Glos 80 E6
Bournes Green Sthend 70 B2
Bournes Green Worcs 117 C8
Bournheath Worcs 117 C9
Bournmoor Durham 243 G8
Bournside Glos 99 G8
Bournstream Glos 80 G2
Bournville W Mid 133 G10
Bourton Bucks 102 E4
Bourton Dorset 45 G9
Bourton N Som 59 G11
Bourton Oxon 63 B8
Bourton Shrops 131 D11
Bourton Wilts 62 G4
Bourton on Dunsmore Warks 119 C8
Bourton-on-the-Hill Glos 100 E3
Bourton-on-the-Water Glos 100 G3
Bourtreehill N Ayrs 257 B8
Bousd Argyll 288 C4
Bousta Shetland 313 H4
Boustead Hill Cumb 239 F7
Bouth Cumb 210 B6
Bouthwaite N Yorks 214 E2
Bouts Worcs 117 F10
Bovain Stirl 285 D9
Boveney Bucks 66 D2
Boveridge Dorset 31 E9
Boverton V Glam 58 F3
Bovey Tracey Devon 14 F2
Bovingdon Herts 85 E8
Bovingdon Green Bucks 65 B10
Bovingdon Green Herts 85 E8
Bovinger Essex 87 D8
Bovington Camp Dorset 18 D2
Bow Borders 271 G9
Bow Devon 8 D6
Bow Devon 26 G2
Bow Orkney 314 G3
Bow Oxon 82 G4
Bow Brickhill M Keynes 103 E8
Bow Broom S Yorks 187 B7
Bow Common London 67 C11
Bow of Fife Fife 287 F7
Bow Street Ceredig 128 G2
Bow Street Norf 141 D10
Bowbank Durham 232 G4
Bowbeck Suff 125 B8
Bowbridge Glos 80 E5
Bowbrook Shrops 149 G9
Bowburn Durham 234 D2
Bowcombe I o W 20 D5
Bowd Devon 15 C8
Bowden Borders 262 C3
Bowden Devon 8 F6
Bowden Dorset 30 C3
Bowden Hill Wilts 62 F2
Bowdens Som 28 B6
Bowderdale Cumb 222 E3
Bowdon Gtr Man 184 D3
Bower Highld 310 C6
Bower Northumb 251 G7
Bower Ashton Bristol 60 E5
Bower Heath Herts 85 B10
Bower Hinton Som 29 D7
Bower House Tye Suff 107 C9
Bowerchalke Wilts 31 C8
Bowerhill Wilts 62 G2
Bowermadden Highld 310 C6
Bowers Staffs 150 B6
Bowers Gifford Essex 69 B9
Bowershall Fife 279 C11
Bowertower Highld 310 C6
Bowes Durham 223 C9
Bowes Park London 86 G4
Bowgreave Lancs 202 E5
Bowgreen Gtr Man 184 D3
Bowhill Borders 261 D10
Bowhill Fife 280 B4
Bowhouse Dumfries 238 D2
Bowhousebog or Liquo N Lnrk 269 D7
Bowing Park Mers 182 D6
Bowismiln Borders 262 E2
Bowithick Corn 11 E9
Bowker's Green Lancs 194 G2
Bowland Bridge Cumb 211 B8
Bowldown Wilts 62 D2
Bowlee Gtr Man 195 F10
Bowlees Durham 232 F4
Bowler's Town E Sus 38 C6
Bowley Hereford 115 G10
Bowley Lane Hereford 98 C3
Bowley Town Hereford 115 G10
Bowlhead Green Sur 50 F2
Bowling W Dunb 277 G9
Bowling W Yorks 205 G9
Bowling Alley Hants 49 D9
Bowling Bank Wrex 166 F5
Bowling Green Corn 5 D10
Bowling Green Corn 12 G3
Bowling Green Glos 81 E8
Bowling Green Hants 19 B11
Bowling Green Shrops 150 D2
Bowling Green W Mid 133 F8
Bowling Green Worcs 116 G6
Bowlish Som 44 E6
Bowmans Kent 68 E4
Bowmanstead Cumb 220 F6
Bowmore Argyll 254 B4
Bowness-on-Solway Cumb 238 E6
Bowness-on-Windermere Cumb 221 F8
Bowridge Hill Dorset 30 B4
Bowrie-fauld Angus 287 C9
Bowsden Northumb 273 G9
Bowsey Hill Windsor 65 C10
Bowshank Borders 271 G9
Bowside Lodge Highld 310 C2
Bowston Cumb 221 F9
Bowthorpe Norf 142 B3
Bowyer's Common Hants 34 B3
Box Glos 80 E5
Box Wilts 61 F10
Box End Beds 103 B10
Box Hill Sur 51 C7
Box Hill Wilts 61 F10
Box Trees W Mid 118 C2
Boxbush Glos 80 C2
Boxbush Glos 98 G3
Boxford Suff 107 C9
Boxford W Berks 64 E2
Boxgrove W Sus 22 B6
Boxley Kent 53 B9
Boxmoor Herts 85 D9
Box's Shop Corn 24 G2
Boxted Essex 107 E9
Boxted Suff 124 G6
Boxted Cross Essex 107 E10
Boxted Heath Essex 107 E10
Boxwell Glos 80 G4
Boxworth Cambs 122 E6
Boxworth End Cambs 123 D7
Boyatt Wood Hants 32 C6
Boyden End Suff 124 F4
Boyden Gate Kent 71 F8
Boyland Common Norf 141 G11
Boylestone Derbys 152 B3
Boylestonfield Derbys 152 B3
Boyn Hill Windsor 65 C11
Boyndie Aberds 302 C6
Boynton E Yorks 218 F2
Boys Hill Dorset 29 E11
Boys Village V Glam 58 F4
Boysack Angus 287 C10
Boysack Angus 287 C9
Boythorpe Derbys 186 G5
Boyton Corn 12 C2
Boyton Suff 109 B7
Boyton Wilts 46 F3
Boyton Cross Essex 87 D10
Boyton End Essex 106 E2
Boyton End Suff 106 C4
Bozeat Northants 121 F8
Bozen Green Herts 105 F8
Brù W Isles 304 D5
Braaid I o M 192 E4
Braal Castle Highld 310 C5
Brabling Green Suff 126 E5
Brabourne Kent 54 E5
Brabourne Lees Kent 54 E5
Brabster Highld 310 C7
Bracadale Highld 294 B5
Bracara Highld 295 F9
Braceborough Lincs 155 G11
Bracebridge Lincs 173 B7
Bracebridge Heath Lincs 173 B7
Bracebridge Low Fields Lincs 173 B7
Braceby Lincs 155 B10
Bracewell Lancs 204 D3
Bracken Bank W Yorks 204 F6
Bracken Hill W Yorks 197 C7
Bracken Park W Yorks 206 E3
Brackenber Cumb 222 B4
Brackenbottom N Yorks 212 E6
Brackenfield Derbys 170 D5
Brackenhall W Yorks 197 D7
Brackenlands Cumb 229 B11
Brackenthwaite Cumb 229 B11
Brackenthwaite Cumb 229 G9
Brackenthwaite N Yorks 205 C11
Brackla = Bragle Bridgend 58 D2
Bracklamore Aberds 303 D8
Bracklesham W Sus 22 D4
Brackletter Highld 290 E3
Brackley Argyll 255 C8
Brackley Northants 101 D11
Brackloch Highld 307 G6
Bracknell Brack 65 F11
Braco Perth 286 G2
Braco Castle Perth 286 F2
Braco Park Aberds 303 C9
Bracobrae Moray 302 D5
Bracon N Lincs 199 F9
Bracon Ash Norf 142 D3
Bracorina Highld 295 F9
Bradaford Devon 12 C3
Bradbourne Derbys 170 E2
Bradbury Durham 234 F2
Bradda I o M 192 F2
Bradden Northants 102 B2
Braddock Corn 6 C3
Braddocks Hay Staffs 168 D5
Bradeley Stoke 168 E5
Bradeley Green E Ches 167 G8
Bradenham Bucks 84 F4
Bradenham Norf 141 B8
Bradenstoke Wilts 62 D4
Brades Village W Mid 133 E9
Bradfield Devon 27 F9
Bradfield Essex 108 E2
Bradfield Norf 160 C5
Bradfield W Berks 64 E6
Bradfield Combust Suff 125 F7
Bradfield Green E Ches 167 D11
Bradfield Heath Essex 108 F2
Bradfield St Clare Suff 125 F8
Bradfield St George Suff 125 E8
Bradford Corn 11 F8
Bradford Derbys 170 C2
Bradford Devon 24 F6
Bradford Gtr Man 184 B5
Bradford Northumb 264 C5
Bradford W Yorks 205 G9
Bradford Abbas Dorset 29 E9
Bradford Leigh Wilts 61 G10
Bradford-on-Avon Wilts 61 G10
Bradford-on-Tone Som 27 C11
Bradford Peverell Dorset 17 C9
Bradgate S Yorks 186 C6
Bradiford Devon 40 G5
Brading I o W 21 D8
Bradley Derbys 170 F2
Bradley Glos 80 G3
Bradley Hants 48 E6
Bradley NE Lincs 201 F8
Bradley Staffs 151 F7
Bradley W Mid 133 D8
Bradley W Yorks 197 C7
Bradley Wrex 166 E4
Bradley Cross Som 44 C3
Bradley Fold Gtr Man 195 F9
Bradley Green Glos 80 G2
Bradley Green Som 43 F9
Bradley Green W Ches 167 F8
Bradley Green Warks 134 C5
Bradley Green Worcs 117 E9
Bradley in the Moors Staffs 169 G9
Bradley Mills W Yorks 197 D7
Bradley Mount E Ches 184 F6
Bradley Stoke S Glos 60 C6
Bradlow Hereford 98 D4
Bradmore Notts 153 C11
Bradmore W Mid 133 D7
Bradney Shrops 132 D5
Bradney Som 43 F10
Bradninch Devon 27 G8
Bradnock's Marsh W Mid 118 B4
Bradnop Staffs 169 D8
Bradnor Green Hereford 114 F5
Bradpole Dorset 16 C5
Bradshaw Gtr Man 195 E8
Bradshaw Staffs 168 D6
Bradshaw W Yorks 196 E5
Bradshaw W Yorks 205 G7
Bradstone Devon 12 E3
Bradville M Keynes 102 C6
Bradwall Green E Ches 168 C3
Bradway S Yorks 186 E4
Bradwell Derbys 185 E11
Bradwell Devon 40 E3
Bradwell Essex 106 G6
Bradwell M Keynes 102 D6
Bradwell Norf 143 C10
Bradwell Staffs 168 F4
Bradwell Common M Keynes 102 D6
Bradwell Grove Oxon 82 D2
Bradwell Hills Derbys 185 E11
Bradwell on Sea Essex 89 D8
Bradwell Waterside Essex 89 D7
Bradworthy Devon 24 E4
Bradworthy Cross Devon 24 E4
Brae Dumfries 237 B10
Brae Highld 307 L3
Brae Highld 309 J4
Brae Shetland 312 G5
Brae of Achnahaird Highld 307 H5
Brae of Boquhapple Stirl 285 G10
Brae Roy Lodge Highld 290 D5
Braeantra Highld 300 B5
Braebuster Orkney 314 F5
Braedownie Angus 292 F4
Braeface Falk 278 E5
Braefield Highld 300 F4
Braefindon Highld 300 D6
Braegrum Perth 286 E4
Braehead Dumfries 236 D6
Braehead Orkney 314 B4
Braehead Orkney 314 F5
Braehead S Ayrs 257 E8
Braehead S Lnrk 259 C8
Braehead S Lnrk 267 D11
Braehead S Lnrk 269 E9
Braehead Stirl 278 C6
Braehead of Lunan Angus 287 B10
Braehoulland Shetland 312 F4
Braehour Highld 310 D4
Braehungie Highld 310 F5
Braeintra Highld 295 B10
Braelangwell Lodge Highld 309 K5
Braemar Aberds 292 D3
Braemore Highld 299 B11
Braemore Highld 310 F4
Braepark Edin 280 F3
Braes of Enzie Moray 302 D3
Braes of Ullapool Highld 307 K6
Braeside Invclyd 276 F4
Braeswick Orkney 314 C6
Braevallich Argyll 275 C10
Braewick Shetland 312 F4
Braewick Shetland 313 H5
Brafferton Darl 233 G11
Brafferton N Yorks 215 E8
Brafield-on-the-Green Northants 120 F6
Bragar W Isles 304 D4
Bragbury End Herts 104 G5
Bragenham Bucks 103 F8
Bragle = Brackla Bridgend 58 D2
Bragleenmore Argyll 289 G11
Braichmelyn Gwyn 163 B10
Braichyfedw Powys 129 E7
Braid Edin 280 G4
Braides Lancs 202 C4
Braidfauld Glasgow 268 C2
Braidley N Yorks 213 C10
Braids Argyll 255 C8
Braidwood S Lnrk 268 F6
Braigh Chalasaigh W Isles 296 D5
Braigo Argyll 274 G3
Brailsford Derbys 170 G3
Brailsford Green Derbys 170 G3
Braingortan Argyll 275 F11
Brain's Green Glos 79 D11
Brainshaugh Northumb 252 C6
Braintree Essex 106 G5
Braiseworth Suff 126 C2
Braishfield Hants 32 B5
Braiswick Essex 107 F9
Braithwaite Cumb 229 G10
Braithwaite S Yorks 198 E6
Braithwaite W Yorks 204 E6
Braithwell S Yorks 187 C8
Brakefield Green Norf 141 B10
Brakenhill W Yorks 198 D2
Bramber W Sus 35 E11
Bramblecombe Dorset 30 G3
Brambridge Hants 33 C7
Bramcote Notts 153 B10
Bramcote Warks 135 F8
Bramcote Hills Notts 153 B10
Bramcote Mains Warks 135 F8
Bramdean Hants 33 B10
Bramerton Norf 142 C5
Bramfield Herts 86 B3
Bramfield Suff 127 C7
Bramford Suff 108 B2
Bramford W Mid 133 E8
Bramhall Gtr Man 184 D5
Bramhall Moor Gtr Man 184 D6
Bramhall Park Gtr Man 184 D5
Bramham W Yorks 206 E4
Bramhope W Yorks 205 E11
Bramley Derbys 186 F6
Bramley Hants 48 B6
Bramley S Yorks 187 C7
Bramley Sur 50 D4
Bramley W Yorks 205 F10
Bramley Corner Hants 48 B6
Bramley Green Hants 49 B7
Bramley Head N Yorks 205 B8
Bramley Vale Derbys 171 B7
Bramling Kent 55 B8
Brampford Speke Devon 14 B4
Brampton Cambs 122 C4
Brampton Cumb 231 G9
Brampton Cumb 240 E2
Brampton Derbys 186 G5
Brampton Hereford 97 D8
Brampton Lincs 188 F4
Brampton Norf 160 E4
Brampton S Yorks 198 G2
Brampton Suff 143 G8
Brampton Abbotts Hereford 98 F2
Brampton Ash Northants 136 F5
Brampton Bryan Hereford 115 C7
Brampton en le Morthen S Yorks 187 D7
Brampton Park Cambs 122 C4
Brampton Street Suff 143 G8
Bramshall Staffs 151 C11
Bramshaw Hants 32 D3
Bramshill Hants 65 G8
Bramshott Hants 49 G10
Bramwell Som 28 B6
Bran End Essex 106 F3
Branatwatt Shetland 313 H4
Branault Highld 289 C7
Branbridges Kent 53 D7
Brancaster Norf 176 E3
Brancaster Staithe Norf 176 E3
Brancepeth Durham 233 D10
Branch End Northumb 242 E3
Branchill Moray 301 D10
Branchton Invclyd 276 F4
Brand End Lincs 174 F5
Brand Green Glos 98 F4
Brand Green Hereford 98 C5
Branderburgh Moray 302 B2
Brandesburton E Yorks 209 D8
Brandeston Suff 126 E4
Brandhill Shrops 115 B8
Brandis Corner Devon 24 G6
Brandish Street Som 42 D2
Brandiston Norf 160 E2
Brandlingill Cumb 229 F8
Brandon Durham 233 D10
Brandon Lincs 172 F6
Brandon Northumb 264 F2
Brandon Suff 140 F5
Brandon Warks 119 B8
Brandon Bank Cambs 140 F2
Brandon Creek Norf 140 E2
Brandon Parva Norf 141 B11
Brands Hill Windsor 66 D4
Brandsby N Yorks 215 E11
Brandwood Shrops 149 D9
Brandwood End W Mid 117 B11
Brandy Carr W Yorks 197 C10
Brandy Hole Essex 88 F4
Brandy Wharf Lincs 189 B8
Brandyquoy Orkney 314 G4
Brane Corn 1 D4
Branksome Darl 224 B5
Branksome Poole 18 C6
Branksome Park Poole 19 C7
Bransbury Hants 48 E2
Bransby Lincs 188 F5
Branscombe Devon 15 D9
Bransford Worcs 116 G5
Bransgore Hants 19 B9
Branshill Clack 279 C7
Bransholme Hull 209 G8
Branson's Cross Worcs 117 C11
Branston Leics 154 D6
Branston Lincs 173 B8
Branston Staffs 152 E4
Branston Booths Lincs 173 B9
Branstone I o W 21 E7
Bransty Cumb 219 B9
Brant Broughton Lincs 172 E6
Brantham Suff 108 E2
Branthwaite Cumb 229 D11
Branthwaite Cumb 229 G7
Branthwaite Edge Cumb 229 G7
Brantingham E Yorks 200 B2
Branton Northumb 264 F2
Branton S Yorks 198 G6
Branton Green N Yorks 215 G8
Branxholm Park Borders 261 G11
Branxholme Borders 261 G11
Branxton Northumb 263 B9
Brascote Leics 135 C8
Brassey Green W Ches 167 C8
Brassington Derbys 170 E2
Brasted Kent 52 C3
Brasted Chart Kent 52 C3
Brathens Aberds 293 D8
Bratoft Lincs 175 B7
Brattle Kent 54 G2
Brattleby Lincs 188 E6
Bratton Som 42 D2
Bratton Telford 150 G2
Bratton Wilts 46 C2
Bratton Clovelly Devon 12 C5
Bratton Fleming Devon 40 F6
Bratton Seymour Som 29 B11
Braughing Herts 105 F7
Braughing Friars Herts 105 G8
Braulen Lodge Highld 300 F2
Braunston Northants 119 D10
Braunston-in-Rutland Rutland 136 B6
Braunstone Leics 135 C11
Braunstone Town Leicester 135 C11
Braunton Devon 40 F3
Brawby N Yorks 216 D4
Brawith N Yorks 225 D10
Brawl Highld 310 C2
Brawlbin Highld 310 D4
Bray Windsor 66 D2
Bray Shop Corn 12 G2
Bray Wick Windsor 65 D11
Braybrooke Northants 136 G5
Braydon Side Wilts 62 B4
Brayford Devon 41 G7
Brayfordhill Devon 41 G7
Brays Grove Essex 87 D7
Braystones Cumb 219 D10
Brayswick Worcs 98 B6
Braythorn N Yorks 205 D10
Brayton N Yorks 207 G8
Braytown Dorset 18 D2
Braywoodside Windsor 65 D11
Brazacott Corn 11 C11
Brazenhill Staffs 151 E7
Brea Corn 4 G3
Breach Bath 60 G6
Breach Kent 69 F10
Breach W Sus 22 B3
Breachacha Castle Argyll 288 D3
Breachwood Green Herts 104 G2
Breacleit W Isles 304 E3
Bread Street Glos 80 D4
Breaden Heath Shrops 149 B8
Breadsall Derbys 153 B7
Breadsall Hilltop Derby 153 B7
Breadstone Glos 80 E2
Breage Corn 2 D4
Breakachy Highld 300 E4
Breakeys Devon 25 D8
Bream Glos 79 D10
Breamore Hants 31 D11
Brean Som 43 B9
Breanais W Isles 304 F1
Brearley W Yorks 196 B4
Brearton N Yorks 214 G6
Breascleit W Isles 304 E4
Breaston Derbys 153 C9
Brechfa Carms 93 E10
Brechin Angus 293 G7
Breck of Cruan Orkney 314 E3
Breckan Orkney 314 F2
Breckles Norf 141 E9
Breckrey Highld 298 C5
Brecks S Yorks 187 C7
Brecon Powys 95 F10
Bredbury Gtr Man 184 C6
Bredbury Green Gtr Man 184 C6
Brede E Sus 38 D4
Bredenbury Hereford 116 F2
Bredfield Suff 126 G5
Bredgar Kent 69 G11

Bredhurst Kent 69 G9
Bredicot Worcs 117 G8
Bredon Worcs 99 D8
Bredon's Hardwick Worcs 99 D8
Bredon's Norton Worcs 99 D8
Bredwardine Hereford 96 C6
Breedon on the Hill Leics 153 E8
Breeds Essex 87 C11
Breedy Butts Lancs 202 E2
Breibhig W Isles 297 M2
Breibhig W Isles 304 E6
Breich W Loth 269 C9
Breightmet Gtr Man 195 F8
Breighton E Yorks 207 G10
Breinton Hereford 97 D9
Breinton Common Hereford 97 C9
Breiwick Shetland 313 J6
Brelston Green Hereford 97 G11
Bremhill Wilts 62 E3
Bremhill Wick Wilts 62 E3
Bremirehoull Shetland 313 L6
Brenachoile Lodge Stirl 285 G8
Brenchley Kent 53 E7
Brenchoillie Argyll 284 G4
Brendon Devon 24 E5
Brendon Devon 24 F5
Brendon Devon 41 D9
Brenkley T & W 242 B6
Brent Corn 6 E4
Brent Eleigh Suff 107 B8
Brent Knoll Som 43 C10
Brent Mill Devon 8 D3
Brent Pelham Herts 105 E8
Brentford London 67 D7
Brentford End London 67 D7
Brentingby Leics 154 F5
Brentry Bristol 60 D5
Brentwood Essex 87 G9
Brenzett Kent 39 B8
Brenzett Green Kent 39 B8
Brereton Staffs 151 F11
Brereton Cross Staffs 151 F11
Brereton Green E Ches 168 C3
Brereton Heath E Ches 168 C4
Breretonhill Staffs 151 F11
Bressingham Norf 141 G11
Bressingham Common Norf 141 G11
Bretby Derbys 152 E5
Bretford Warks 119 B8
Bretforton Worcs 99 C11
Bretherdale Head Cumb 221 E11
Bretherton Lancs 194 C3
Brettabister Shetland 313 H6
Brettenham Norf 141 G8
Brettenham Suff 125 G9
Bretton Derbys 186 F2
Bretton Flint 166 C5
Bretton P'boro 138 C3
Brewer Street Sur 51 C10
Brewer's End Essex 105 G11
Brewers Green Norf 142 G2
Brewlands Bridge Angus 292 G3
Brewood Staffs 133 B7
Briach Moray 301 D10
Briants Puddle Dorset 18 C2
Briar Hill Northants 120 F4
Brick End Essex 105 F11
Brick Hill Sur 66 G3
Brick House End Essex 105 F9
Brick Houses S Yorks 186 E4
Brick-kiln End Notts 171 D9
Brickendon Herts 86 D4
Bricket Wood Herts 85 E10
Brickfields Worcs 117 F7
Brickhill Beds 121 G11
Brickhouses E Ches 168 C3
Brickkiln Green Essex 106 E4
Bricklehampton Worcs 99 C9
Bride I o M 192 B5
Bridekirk Cumb 229 E8
Bridell Pembs 92 C3
Bridestowe Devon 12 D6
Brideswell Aberds 302 F5
Bridford Devon 14 D2
Bridfordmills Devon 14 D2
Bridge Corn 2 D6
Bridge Corn 4 G3
Bridge Kent 55 C7
Bridge Som 28 F5
Bridge Ball Devon 41 D8
Bridge End Beds 121 G10
Bridge End Cumb 230 B3
Bridge End Devon 8 F3
Bridge End Durham 232 D6
Bridge End Essex 106 E3
Bridge End Flint 166 D4
Bridge End Hereford 98 B2
Bridge End Lincs 156 B2
Bridge End Northumb 241 D10
Bridge End Northumb 241 E10
Bridge End Oxon 83 G9
Bridge-End Shetland 313 K5
Bridge End Sur 50 B5
Bridge End Warks 118 E5
Bridge End Worcs 98 E6
Bridge Green Essex 105 D9
Bridge Green Norf 142 G2
Bridge Hewick N Yorks 214 E6
Bridge Ho Argyll 254 B4
Bridge of Alford Aberds 293 B7
Bridge of Allan Stirl 278 B5
Bridge of Avon Moray 301 F11
Bridge of Avon Moray 301 G11
Bridge of Awe Argyll 284 E4
Bridge of Balgie Perth 285 C9
Bridge of Cally Perth 286 B5
Bridge of Canny Aberds 293 D8
Bridge of Craigisla Angus 286 B6
Bridge of Dee Dumfries 237 D9
Bridge of Don Aberdeen 293 B11
Bridge of Dun Angus 287 B10
Bridge of Dye Aberds 293 E8
Bridge of Earn Perth 286 F5
Bridge of Ericht Perth 285 B9
Bridge of Feugh Aberds 293 D9
Bridge of Forss Highld 310 C4
Bridge of Gairn Aberds 292 D5
Bridge of Gaur Perth 285 B9
Bridge of Lyon Perth 285 C11
Bridge of Muchalls Aberds 293 D10
Bridge of Muick Aberds 292 D5
Bridge of Oich Highld 290 C5
Bridge of Orchy Argyll 284 D6
Bridge of Waith Orkney 314 E2
Bridge of Walls Shetland 313 H4
Bridge of Weir Renfs 267 B7
Bridge Reeve Devon 25 E11
Bridge Sollers Hereford 97 C8
Bridge Street Suff 107 B7
Bridge Town Warks 118 G4
Bridge Trafford W Ches 183 G7
Bridge Yate S Glos 61 E7
Bridgefoot Aberds 292 C6
Bridgefoot Angus 287 D7
Bridgefoot Cumb 229 F7
Bridgehampton Som 29 C9
Bridgehill Durham 242 G3
Bridgeholm Green Derbys 185 E8
Bridgehouse Gate N Yorks 214 F3
Bridgelands Borders 261 C11
Bridgemary Hants 33 G9
Bridgemere E Ches 168 F2
Bridgemont Derbys 185 E8
Bridgend Aberds 293 B7
Bridgend Aberds 302 F5
Bridgend Angus 293 G7
Bridgend Argyll 255 D8
Bridgend Argyll 274 G4
Bridgend Argyll 275 D9
Bridgend Corn 6 D2
Bridgend Cumb 221 C7
Bridgend Devon 7 F11
Bridgend Fife 287 F7
Bridgend Glos 80 E4
Bridgend Highld 300 D3
Bridgend Invclyd 276 F5
Bridgend Moray 302 F3
Bridgend N Lnrk 278 G3
Bridgend Pembs 92 B3
Bridgend W Loth 279 F10
Bridgend = Pen-y-Bont ar-ogwr Bridgend 58 C2
Bridgend of Lintrathen Angus 286 B6
Bridgeness Falk 279 E10
Bridgerule Devon 24 G3
Bridges Corn 5 D10
Bridges Shrops 131 D7
Bridgeton Glasgow 268 C2
Bridgetown Corn 12 D2
Bridgetown Devon 8 C6
Bridgetown Som 42 G2
Bridgetown Staffs 133 B9
Bridgham Norf 141 F9
Bridgnorth Shrops 132 E4
Bridgtown Staffs 133 B9
Bridgwater Som 43 F10
Bridlington E Yorks 218 F3
Bridport Dorset 16 C5
Bridstow Hereford 97 G11
Brierfield Lancs 204 F2
Brierholme Carr S Yorks 199 E7
Brierley Glos 79 B10
Brierley Hereford 115 F9
Brierley S Yorks 198 E2
Brierley Hill W Mid 133 F8
Brierton Hrtlpl 234 E5
Briery Cumb 229 G11
Briery Hill Bl Gwent 77 D11
Briestfield W Yorks 197 D8
Brig o'Turk Stirl 285 G9
Brigflatts Cumb 222 G2
Brigg N Lincs 200 F3
Brigg N Lincs 200 F4
Briggate Norf 160 D6
Briggswath N Yorks 227 D7
Brigham Cumb 229 E7
Brigham Cumb 229 G11
Brigham E Yorks 209 C7
Brighouse W Yorks 196 C6
Brighstone I o W 20 E4
Brightgate Derbys 170 D3
Brighthampton Oxon 82 E5
Brightholmlee S Yorks 186 B3
Brightley Devon 13 B7
Brightling E Sus 37 C11
Brightlingsea Essex 89 B9
Brighton Brighton 36 G4
Brighton Corn 5 E8
Brighton Hill Hants 48 D6
Brighton le Sands Mers 182 B4
Brightons Falk 279 F8
Brightside S Yorks 186 D5
Brightwalton W Berks 64 D2
Brightwalton Green W Berks 64 D2
Brightwalton Holt W Berks 64 D2
Brightwell Suff 108 C4
Brightwell Baldwin Oxon 83 F11
Brightwell cum Sotwell Oxon 83 G9
Brigmerston Wilts 47 D7
Brignall Durham 223 C11
Brigsley NE Lincs 201 G9
Brigsteer Cumb 211 B9
Brigstock Northants 137 F8
Brill Bucks 83 C11
Brill Corn 2 D6
Brilley Hereford 96 B5
Brilley Mountain Powys 114 G5
Brimaston Pembs 91 G8
Brimfield Hereford 115 D10
Brimington Derbys 186 G6
Brimington Common Derbys 186 G6
Brimley Devon 13 F11
Brimley Devon 28 G4
Brimps Hill Glos 79 B11
Brimpsfield Glos 80 C6
Brimpton W Berks 64 G5
Brimpton Common W Berks 64 G5
Brims Orkney 314 H2
Brims Castle Highld 310 B4
Brimscombe Glos 80 E5
Brimsdown London 86 F5
Brimstage Mers 182 E4
Brinacory Highld 295 F9
Brincliffe S Yorks 186 D4
Brind E Yorks 207 G10
Brindham Som 44 E4
Brindister Shetland 313 H4
Brindister Shetland 313 K6
Brindle Lancs 194 C6
Brindle Heath Gtr Man 195 G10
Brindley E Ches 167 E9
Brindley Ford Stoke 168 E5
Brindwoodgate Derbys 186 F4
Brineton Staffs 150 G6
Bringewood Forge Hereford 115 C9
Bringhurst Leics 136 E6
Bringsty Common Hereford 116 F4
Brington Cambs 121 B11
Brinian Orkney 314 D4
Briningham Norf 159 C10
Brinkhill Lincs 190 G5
Brinkley Cambs 124 G2
Brinkley Notts 172 E2
Brinkley Hill Hereford 97 E11
Brinklow M Keynes 103 D8
Brinklow Warks 119 B8
Brinkworth Wilts 62 C4
Brinmore Highld 300 G6
Brinnington Gtr Man 184 C6
Brinscall Lancs 194 C6
Brinsea N Som 60 G2
Brinsford Staffs 133 B8
Brinsley Notts 171 F7
Brinsop Hereford 97 C8
Brinsop Common Hereford 97 C8
Brinsworth S Yorks 186 D6
Brinsworthy Devon 41 G9
Brinton Norf 159 B10
Brisco Cumb 239 G10
Briscoe Cumb 219 C10
Briscoerigg N Yorks 205 C11
Brisley Norf 159 E8
Brislington Bristol 60 E6
Brissenden Green Kent 54 F2
Bristnall Fields W Mid 133 F9
Bristol Bristol 60 E5
Briston Norf 159 C11
Britain Bottom S Glos 61 B9
Britannia Lancs 195 C11
Britford Wilts 31 B11
Brithdir Caerph 77 E11
Brithdir Ceredig 92 B6
Brithdir Gwyn 146 F5
Brithem Bottom Devon 27 E8
British Torf 78 E3
Briton Ferry = Llansawel Neath 57 C8
Britten's Bath 45 B7
Britwell Slough 66 C3
Britwell Salome Oxon 83 G11
Brixham Torbay 9 D8
Brixton Devon 7 E11
Brixton London 67 D10
Brixton Deverill Wilts 45 F11
Brixworth Northants 120 C4
Brize Norton Oxon 82 D4
Broad Alley Worcs 117 D7
Broad Blunsdon Swindon 81 G11
Broad Campden Glos 100 D3
Broad Carr W Yorks 196 D5
Broad Chalke Wilts 31 B8
Broad Clough Lancs 195 C11
Broad Colney Herts 85 E11
Broad Common Worcs 117 D7
Broad Ford Kent 53 F8
Broad Green C Beds 103 C9
Broad Green Cambs 124 F3
Broad Green Essex 105 D8
Broad Green Essex 107 G7
Broad Green London 67 F10
Broad Green Mers 182 C6
Broad Green Suff 124 F5
Broad Green Suff 125 F11
Broad Green Worcs 116 F5
Broad Green Worcs 117 C9
Broad Haven = Aberllydan Pembs 72 C5
Broad Heath Powys 114 E6
Broad Heath Staffs 151 D7
Broad Heath Worcs 116 D3
Broad Hill Cambs 123 B11
Broad Hinton Wilts 62 D6
Broad Ings E Yorks 208 C2
Broad Lane Corn 4 G3
Broad Lanes Shrops 132 F5
Broad Laying Hants 64 G2
Broad Layings Hants 64 G2
Broad Marston Worcs 100 B2
Broad Meadow Staffs 168 F4
Broad Oak Carms 93 G11
Broad Oak Cumb 220 G2
Broad Oak Dorset 30 E3
Broad Oak E Sus 37 C10
Broad Oak E Sus 38 D4
Broad Oak Hants 49 C9
Broad Oak Hereford 97 G9
Broad Oak Kent 54 F4
Broad Oak Kent 71 G7
Broad Oak Mers 183 B8
Broad Oak Shrops 132 F5
Broad Parkham Devon 24 C5
Broad Street E Sus 38 D5
Broad Street Kent 53 B10
Broad Street Kent 54 E6
Broad Street Kent 55 E7
Broad Street Medway 69 E9
Broad Street Suff 107 C9
Broad Street Wilts 46 B6
Broad Street Green Essex 88 D5
Broad Tenterden Kent 53 G11
Broad Town Wilts 62 D5
Broadbottom Gtr Man 185 C7
Broadbridge W Sus 22 B4
Broadbridge Heath W Sus 50 G6
Broadbury Devon 12 B5
Broadbush Swindon 81 G11
Broadclyst Devon 14 B5
Broadfield Gtr Man 195 E10
Broadfield Invclyd 276 G6
Broadfield Lancs 194 C4
Broadfield Lancs 195 B8
Broadfield Pembs 73 E10
Broadfield W Sus 51 G9
Broadford Highld 295 C8
Broadford Sur 50 D3
Broadford Bridge W Sus 35 C9
Broadgate Hants 32 C6
Broadgrass Green Suff 125 E9
Broadgreen Wood Herts 86 D4
Broadhalgh Gtr Man 195 E11
Broadham Green Sur 51 C11
Broadhaugh Borders 249 B10
Broadhaven Highld 310 D7
Broadheath Gtr Man 184 D3
Broadhembury Devon 27 G10
Broadhempston Devon 8 B6
Broadholm Derbys 170 F4
Broadholme Derbys 170 F5
Broadholme Lincs 188 G5
Broadland Row E Sus 38 D4
Broadlands Devon 14 G3
Broadlane Corn 2 C4
Broadlay Carms 74 D5
Broadley Lancs 195 D11
Broadley Moray 302 C3
Broadley Common Essex 86 D6
Broadleys Aberds 303 C8
Broadmayne Dorset 17 D10
Broadmeadows Borders 261 C10
Broadmere Hants 48 D6
Broadmoor Pembs 73 D9
Broadmoor Sur 50 D6
Broadmoor Common Hereford 98 D2
Broadmore Green Worcs 116 G6
Broadoak Dorset 16 B4
Broadoak Glos 80 C2
Broadoak Hants 33 E8
Broadoak Shrops 149 F9
Broadoak Wrex 166 D5
Broadoak End Herts 86 C4
Broadoak Park Gtr Man 195 G9
Broadplat Oxon 65 C8
Broadrashes Moray 302 D4
Broadrock Glos 79 F8
Broad's Green Essex 87 C11
Broad's Green Wilts 62 F3
Broadsands Torbay 9 D7
Broadsea Aberds 303 C9
Broadshard Som 28 E6
Broadstairs Kent 71 F11
Broadstone Kent 53 D11
Broadstone Mon 79 E8
Broadstone Poole 18 B6
Broadstone Shrops 131 F10
Broadstreet Common Newport 59 C11
Broadwas Worcs 116 F5
Broadwater Herts 104 G4
Broadwater W Sus 35 G11
Broadwater Down Kent 52 F5
Broadwaters Worcs 116 B6
Broadwath Cumb 239 F11
Broadway Carms 74 D3
Broadway Carms 74 D5
Broadway Pembs 72 C5
Broadway Som 28 D4
Broadway Suff 127 B7
Broadway Worcs 99 D11
Broadway Lands Hereford 97 E11
Broadwell Glos 79 C9
Broadwell Glos 100 F4
Broadwell Oxon 82 E3
Broadwell Warks 119 D9
Broadwey Dorset 17 E9
Broadwindsor Dorset 28 G6
Broadwood Kelly Devon 25 F10
Broadwoodwidger Devon 12 D4
Brobury Hereford 96 C6
Brochel Highld 298 E5
Brochroy Argyll 284 D4
Brock Lancs 202 F6
Brock Hill Essex 88 F2
Brockamin Worcs 116 G5
Brockbridge Hants 33 D10
Brockdish Norf 126 B4
Brockencote Worcs 117 C7
Brockenhurst Hants 32 G4
Brocketsbrae S Lnrk 259 B8
Brockfield Devon 28 F4
Brockford Green Suff 126 D2
Brockford Street Suff 126 D2
Brockhall Northants 120 E2
Brockhall Village Lancs 203 F10
Brockham Sur 51 D7
Brockham End Bath 61 F8
Brockham Park Sur 51 D8
Brockhampton Glos 99 F8
Brockhampton Glos 99 G10
Brockhampton Hants 22 B2
Brockhampton Hereford 97 E11
Brockhampton Green Dorset 30 F2
Brockhill Borders 261 E9
Brockholes W Yorks 197 E7
Brockhollands Glos 79 D10
Brockhurst Derbys 170 C4
Brockhurst Hants 33 G10
Brockhurst Warks 135 G9
Brocklebank Cumb 230 C2
Brocklehirst Dumfries 238 C3
Brocklesby Lincs 200 E6
Brockley London 67 E11
Brockley N Som 60 F3
Brockley Corner Suff 124 C6
Brockley Green Suff 106 B4
Brockley Green Suff 124 G6
Brockleymoor Cumb 230 D5
Brockloch Dumfries 246 D2
Brockmanton Hereford 115 F10
Brockmoor W Mid 133 F8
Brock's Green Hants 64 G4
Brock's Watering Norf 142 E2
Brockscombe Devon 12 C5
Brockton Shrops 130 C6
Brockton Shrops 130 F6
Brockton Shrops 131 E11
Brockton Shrops 132 C4
Brockton Staffs 150 C6
Brockton Telford 150 F4
Brockweir Glos 79 E8
Brockwell Som 42 E2
Brockwood Hants 33 B10
Brockworth Glos 80 B5
Brocton Corn 5 B10
Brocton Staffs 151 F9
Brodick N Ayrs 256 B2
Brodie Moray 301 D9
Brodiesord Aberds 302 C5
Brodsworth S Yorks 198 F4
Brogaig Highld 298 C4
Brogborough C Beds 103 D9
Broke Hall Suff 108 C3
Broken Cross E Ches 184 G5
Broken Cross W Ches 183 G11
Broken Green Herts 105 G8
Brokenborough Wilts 62 B2
Brokerswood Wilts 45 C10
Brokes N Yorks 224 F3
Brombil Neath 57 D9
Bromborough Mers 182 E4
Bromborough Pool Mers 182 E4
Bromdon Shrops 132 G2
Brome Suff 126 B2
Brome Street Suff 126 B3
Bromesberrow Glos 98 E4
Bromesberrow Heath Glos 98 E4
Bromeswell Suff 126 G6
Bromfield Cumb 229 B9
Bromfield Shrops 115 B9
Bromford W Mid 134 E2
Bromham Beds 121 G10
Bromham Wilts 62 F3
Bromley Herts 105 G8
Bromley London 67 C11
Bromley S Yorks 186 B4
Bromley Shrops 132 D4
Bromley Shrops 149 D8
Bromley Tower Hamlets 68 F2
Bromley W Mid 133 F8
Bromley Common London 68 F2
Bromley Cross Essex 107 F11
Bromley Cross Gtr Man 195 E8
Bromley Green Kent 54 F3
Bromley Hall Staffs 150 C5
Bromley Heath S Glos 61 D7
Bromley Park London 67 F11
Bromley Wood Staffs 152 E2
Bromlow Shrops 130 C6
Brompton London 67 D9
Brompton Medway 69 F9
Brompton N Yorks 217 C8
Brompton N Yorks 225 F7
Brompton Shrops 131 B10
Brompton-by-Sawdon N Yorks 217 C8
Brompton-on-Swale N Yorks 224 F4
Brompton Ralph Som 42 G5
Brompton Regis Som 42 G3
Bromsash Hereford 98 G2
Bromsberrow Heath Glos 98 E4
Bromsgrove Worcs 117 C9
Bromstead Common Staffs 150 F6
Bromstead Heath Staffs 150 F6
Bromstone Kent 71 F11
Bromyard Hereford 116 G3
Bromyard Downs Hereford 116 F3
Bronaber Gwyn 146 C4
Broncroft Shrops 131 F10
Brondesbury London 67 C8
Brondesbury Park London 67 C8
Broneirion Powys 129 F10
Brongest Ceredig 92 B6
Brongwyn Ceredig 92 C5
Bronington Wrex 149 B9
Bronllys Powys 96 D2
Bronnant Ceredig 112 D2
Bronwydd Ceredig 93 C7
Bronwydd Arms Carms 93 G8
Bronydd Powys 96 B4
Bronygarth Shrops 148 B5
Brook Carms 74 D3
Brook Devon 12 G5
Brook Devon 14 C2
Brook Hants 32 B4
Brook Hants 32 E3
Brook I o W 20 E2
Brook Kent 54 E5
Brook Sur 50 D5
Brook Sur 50 F2
Brook Bottom Gtr Man 185 D7
Brook Bottom Gtr Man 196 G3
Brook Bottom Lancs 203 D8
Brook End Beds 121 E11
Brook End C Beds 104 B3
Brook End Cambs 121 C11
Brook End Herts 104 F6
Brook End M Keynes 103 C8
Brook End Wilts 61 C10
Brook End Worcs 99 B7
Brook Green London 67 D8
Brook Green Suff 125 F7
Brook Hill Hants 32 E3
Brook Hill Notts 153 C11
Brook Place Sur 66 G3
Brook Street Essex 87 G9
Brook Street Kent 52 D5
Brook Street Kent 54 G2
Brook Street Suff 106 B6
Brook Street W Sus 36 B4
Brook Waters Wilts 30 C6
Brooke Norf 142 D5
Brooke Rutland 136 B6
Brookenby Lincs 190 B2
Brookend Glos 79 E11
Brookend Glos 79 F9
Brookend Oxon 100 G6
Brookfield Derbys 185 B8
Brookfield Lancs 203 G7
Brookfield M'bro 225 B9
Brookfield Renfs 267 C8
Brookfoot W Yorks 196 C6
Brookgreen I o W 20 E3
Brookhampton Oxon 83 F10
Brookhampton Shrops 131 E11
Brookhampton Som 29 B10
Brookhouse Blkburn 195 B7
Brookhouse Denb 165 B9
Brookhouse E Ches 184 F6
Brookhouse Lancs 211 G10
Brookhouse S Yorks 187 D8
Brookhouse W Yorks 196 B5
Brookhouse Green E Ches 168 C4
Brookhouses Derbys 185 D8
Brookhouses Staffs 169 G7
Brookhurst Mers 182 E4
Brookland Kent 39 B7
Brooklands Dumfries 237 B10
Brooklands Gtr Man 184 C3
Brooklands Shrops 167 G8
Brooklands Sur 66 G5
Brooklands W Yorks 206 F2
Brookleigh Devon 14 B5
Brookmans Park Herts 86 E2
Brookpits W Sus 35 G8
Brookrow Shrops 116 C2
Brooks Corn 6 C3
Brooks Powys 130 D2
Brooks End Kent 71 F9
Brooks Green W Sus 35 C10
Brooksbottoms Gtr Man 195 D9
Brooksby Leics 154 F3
Brookside Brack 66 E2
Brookside Derbys 186 G5
Brookside Telford 132 B3
Brookthorpe Glos 80 C4
Brookvale Halton 183 E8
Brookville Norf 140 D4
Brookwood Sur 50 B2
Broom C Beds 104 C3
Broom Cumb 231 G9
Broom Devon 28 G4
Broom E Renf 267 D10
Broom Pembs 73 D10
Broom S Yorks 186 C5
Broom Warks 117 G11
Broom Green Norf 159 E9
Broom Hill Bristol 60 E6
Broom Hill Dorset 31 G8
Broom Hill Durham 242 G4
Broom Hill London 68 F3
Broom Hill Suff 108 B5
Broom Hill Worcs 117 B8
Broom Street Kent 70 G4
Broombank Worcs 116 C3
Broome Norf 143 E7
Broome Shrops 131 D10
Broome Shrops 131 G8
Broome Worcs 117 B8
Broome Park Northumb 264 G4
Broomedge Warr 184 D2
Broomer's Corner W Sus 35 C10
Broomershill W Sus 35 D9
Broomfield Aberds 303 F9
Broomfield Cumb 230 B2
Broomfield Essex 88 D2
Broomfield Kent 53 C10
Broomfield Kent 71 F7
Broomfield Som 43 G8
Broomfield Wilts 61 D11
Broomfields Shrops 149 F8
Broomfleet E Yorks 199 B11
Broomhall E Ches 167 F10
Broomhall Windsor 66 F3
Broomhall Green E Ches 167 F10
Broomham E Sus 23 C8
Broomhaugh Northumb 242 E2
Broomhill Borders 261 D11
Broomhill Bristol 60 D6
Broomhill Highld 301 G9
Broomhill Kent 55 B8
Broomhill Norf 140 C2
Broomhill Northumb 252 C6
Broomhill Notts 171 F8
Broomhill S Yorks 198 G2
Broomhill W Ches 167 B7
Broomhill Bank Kent 52 E5
Broomholm Norf 160 C6
Broomhouse Glasgow 268 C3
Broomlands N Ayrs 257 B8
Broomley Northumb 242 E2
Broompark Durham 233 C10
Broomridge Stirl 278 C6
Broom's Barn Suff 124 D5
Broom's Green Glos 98 E4
Broomsgrove E Sus 38 E4
Broomsthorpe Norf 158 D6
Broomton Highld 301 B8
Broomy Hill Hereford 97 D9
Broomy Lodge Hants 32 E2
Broomyshaw Staffs 169 F9
Brora Highld 311 J3
Broseley Shrops 132 C3
Brotherhouse Bar Lincs 156 G5
Brotheridge Green Worcs 98 C6
Brotherlee Durham 232 D4
Brotherstone Borders 262 B4
Brothertoft Lincs 174 F3
Brotherton N Yorks 198 B3
Brothybeck Cumb 230 C2
Brotton Redcar 226 B3
Broubster Highld 310 C4
Brough Cumb 222 C5
Brough Derbys 185 E11
Brough E Yorks 200 B2
Brough Highld 310 B6
Brough Notts 172 D4
Brough Orkney 314 H4
Brough Orkney 314 E3
Brough Shetland 312 C7
Brough Shetland 312 F6
Brough Shetland 312 F7
Brough Shetland 313 G7
Brough Shetland 313 H6
Brough Shetland 313 J7
Brough Lodge Shetland 312 D7
Brough Sowerby Cumb 222 C5
Broughall Shrops 167 G9
Broughton Borders 260 B4
Broughton Bucks 84 C4
Broughton Cambs 122 B5
Broughton Edin 280 F5
Broughton Flint 166 C4
Broughton Hants 47 G10
Broughton Lancs 202 F6
Broughton M Keynes 103 C7
Broughton N Lincs 200 F3
Broughton N Yorks 204 C4
Broughton N Yorks 216 E5
Broughton Northants 120 B6
Broughton Orkney 314 B4
Broughton Oxon 101 D8
Broughton Shrops 132 E6
Broughton Staffs 150 C5
Broughton V Glam 58 E2
Broughton Astley Leics 135 E10
Broughton Beck Cumb 210 C5
Broughton Common N Lincs 200 E3
Broughton Common Wilts 61 G11
Broughton Cross Cumb 229 E7
Broughton Gifford Wilts 61 G11
Broughton Green Worcs 117 E9
Broughton Hackett Worcs 117 G8
Broughton in Furness Cumb 210 B4
Broughton Lodges Leics 154 E4
Broughton Mills Cumb 220 G4
Broughton Moor Cumb 228 E6
Broughton Park Gtr Man 195 G10
Broughton Poggs Oxon 82 E2
Broughtown Orkney 314 B6
Broughty Ferry Dundee 287 D8
Brow Edge Cumb 211 C7
Browhouses Dumfries 239 D7
Browland Shetland 313 H4
Brown Bank N Yorks 205 C10
Brown Candover Hants 48 F5
Brown Edge Lancs 193 E11
Brown Edge Mers 183 C8
Brown Edge Staffs 168 E6
Brown Heath Hants 33 D8
Brown Heath W Ches 167 B7
Brown Knowl W Ches 167 E7
Brown Lees Staffs 168 D5
Brown Moor W Yorks 206 G3
Brown Street Suff 125 E11
Brownber Cumb 222 D4
Brownbread Street E Sus 23 B11
Brownedge E Ches 168 C3
Brownheath Devon 27 D10
Brownheath Shrops 149 D9
Brownheath Common Worcs 117 E7
Brownhill Aberds 302 E6
Brownhill Aberds 303 E8
Brownhill Blkburn 203 G9
Brownhill Shrops 149 E8
Brownhills Fife 287 F9
Brownhills Shrops 150 B3
Brownhills W Mid 133 B10
Brownieside Northumb 264 E5
Browninghill Green Hants 48 B5
Brownlow E Ches 168 C4
Brownlow Mers 194 G4
Brownlow Fold Gtr Man 195 E8
Brownlow Heath E Ches 168 C4
Brownmuir Aberds 293 F9
Brown's Bank E Ches 167 G10
Brown's End Glos 98 E4
Brown's Green W Mid 133 E10
Browns Wood M Keynes 103 D8
Brownshill Glos 80 E5
Brownshill Green W Mid 134 G6
Brownside Lancs 204 G3
Brownsover Warks 119 B10
Brownston Devon 8 E3
Browsburn N Lnrk 268 C5
Browston Green Norf 143 C9
Browtop Cumb 229 G7
Broxa N Yorks 227 G8
Broxbourne Herts 86 D5
Broxburn E Loth 282 F3
Broxburn W Loth 279 G11
Broxfield Northumb 264 F6
Broxholme Lincs 188 F6
Broxted Essex 105 F11
Broxton W Ches 167 E7
Broxtowe Nottingham 171 G8
Broxwood Hereford 115 G7
Broyle Side E Sus 23 C7
Bruairnis W Isles 297 L3
Bruan Highld 310 F7
Bruar Lodge Perth 291 F10
Brucefield Fife 280 D2
Brucehill W Dunb 277 F7
Bruche Warr 183 D10
Brucklebog Aberds 293 D9
Bruera W Ches 166 C6
Bruern Abbey Oxon 100 G5
Bruichladdich Argyll 274 G3
Bruisyard Suff 126 D6
Brumby N Lincs 199 F11
Brunant Powys 130 B5
Brund Staffs 169 C10
Brundall Norf 142 B6
Brundish Norf 143 D7
Brundish Suff 126 D5
Brundish Street Suff 126 C5
Brundon Suff 107 C7
Brunery Highld 289 B9
Brunnion Corn 2 B2
Brunshaw Lancs 204 G3
Brunstane Edin 280 G6
Brunstock Cumb 239 F10
Brunswick Gtr Man 184 B4
Brunswick Park London 86 G3
Brunswick Village T & W 242 C6
Brunt Hamersland Shetland 313 H6
Bruntcliffe W Yorks 197 B9
Brunthwaite W Yorks 205 D7
Bruntingthorpe Leics 136 F2
Brunton Fife 287 E7
Brunton Northumb 264 E6
Brunton Wilts 47 B8
Brushes Gtr Man 185 B7
Brushfield Derbys 185 G11
Brushford Devon 25 F11
Brushford Som 26 B6
Bruton Som 45 G7
Bryans Midloth 270 C6
Bryan's Green Worcs 117 D7
Bryanston Dorset 30 F5
Bryant's Bottom Bucks 84 F5
Brydekirk Dumfries 238 C5
Bryher Scilly 1 G3
Brymbo Conwy 180 G4
Brymbo Wrex 166 E3
Brympton Som 29 D8
Brympton D'Evercy Som 29 D8
Bryn Caerph 77 F11
Bryn Carms 75 E8
Bryn Gtr Man 194 G5
Bryn Gwyn 179 G9
Bryn Neath 57 C10
Bryn Powys 130 C3
Bryn Rhondda 76 D6
Bryn Shrops 130 F5
Bryn Swansea 56 C4
Bryn W Ches 183 G10
Bryn Bwbach Gwyn 146 B2
Bryn-coch Neath 57 B8
Bryn Celyn Anglesey 179 F10
Bryn Celyn Flint 181 F11
Bryn Common Flint 166 D3
Bryn Du Anglesey 178 G4
Bryn Dulas Conwy 180 F6
Bryn Eglwys Gwyn 163 B10
Bryn Gates Gtr Man 194 G5
Bryn-glas Conwy 164 B4
Bryn Golau Rhondda 58 B3
Bryn-henllan Pembs 91 D10
Bryn-Iwan Carms 92 E6
Bryn-mawr Gwyn 144 C4
Bryn Mawr Powys 148 F5
Bryn Myrddin Carms 93 G8
Bryn-nantllech Conwy 164 B6
Bryn-newydd Denb 165 G11
Bryn Offa Wrex 166 F4
Bryn Pen-y-lan Wrex 166 G4
Bryn-penarth Powys 130 C2
Bryn Pydew Conwy 180 F4
Bryn Rhyd-yr-Arian Conwy 165 B7
Bryn-rhys Conwy 180 F4
Bryn Saith Marchog Denb 165 E9
Bryn Sion Gwyn 147 F7
Bryn Tanat Powys 148 E4
Bryn-y-cochin Shrops 149 B7
Bryn-y-gwenin Mon 78 B4
Bryn-y-maen Conwy 180 F4
Bryn-yr-Eos Wrex 166 G3
Bryn-yr-eryr Gwyn 162 F5
Bryn-yr-ogof Denb 165 D11
Brynafan Ceredig 112 C4
Brynamman Carms 76 C2
Brynawel Caerph 77 G11
Brynberian Pembs 92 D2
Brynbryddan Neath 57 C9
Bryncae Rhondda 58 C3
Bryncethin Bridgend 58 C2
Brynbryddan Neath 57 C9
Bryncae Rhondda 58 C3
Bryncethin Bridgend 58 C2
Bryncir Gwyn 163 G7
Bryncoch Bridgend 58 C2
Bryncroes Gwyn 144 C4
Bryncrug Gwyn 128 C2
Brynderwen Powys 130 D3
Bryndu Carms 75 D8
Bryneglwys Denb 165 F10
Brynford Flint 181 G11
Brynglas Newport 59 B10
Brynglas Sta Gwyn 128 C2
Bryngwran Anglesey 178 F4
Bryngwyn Ceredig 92 B5
Bryngwyn Mon 78 D5
Bryngwyn Powys 96 B3
Brynhenllan Pembs 91 D10
Brynheulog Bridgend 57 C11
Brynhoffnant Ceredig 110 G6
Bryniau Denb 181 E9
Bryning Lancs 194 B2
Brynithel Bl Gwent 78 E2
Brynllywarch Powys 130 F3
Brynmawr Bl Gwent 77 C11
Brynmenyn Bridgend 58 B2
Brynmill Swansea 56 C6
Brynmorfudd Conwy 164 C4
Brynna Rhondda 58 C3
Brynnau Gwynion Rhondda 58 C3
Brynore Shrops 149 B7
Brynrefail Anglesey 179 D7
Brynrefail Gwyn 163 C9
Brynsadler Rhondda 58 C4
Brynsiencyn Anglesey 163 B7
Brynsworthy Devon 40 G4
Brynteg Anglesey 179 E7
Brynteg Ceredig 93 C9
Brynteg Wrex 166 E4
Bryntirion Bridgend 57 E11
Buaile nam Bodach W Isles 297 L3
Bualintur Highld 294 C6
Bualnaluib Highld 307 K3
Buarthmeini Gwyn 146 C6
Bubbenhall Warks 119 C7
Bubblewell Glos 80 E5
Bubnell Derbys 186 G2
Bubwith E Yorks 207 F10
Buccleuch Borders 261 G8
Buchan Hill W Sus 51 G9
Buchanhaven Aberds 303 E11
Buchanty Perth 286 E3
Buchley E Dunb 277 G11
Buchlyvie Stirl 277 C11
Buck Hill Wilts 62 E3
Buckabank Cumb 230 B3
Buckbury Worcs 98 E6
Buckden Cambs 122 D3
Buckden N Yorks 213 D8
Buckenham Norf 143 B7
Buckerell Devon 27 G10
Bucket Corner Hants 32 C6
Buckfast Devon 8 B4
Buckfastleigh Devon 8 B4
Buckham Dorset 29 G7
Buckhaven Fife 281 B7
Buckholm Borders 261 B11
Buckholt Mon 79 B8
Buckhorn Devon 12 B3
Buckhorn Weston Dorset 30 C3
Buckhurst Kent 53 E10
Buckhurst Hill Essex 86 G6
Buckie Moray 302 C4
Buckies Highld 310 C5
Buckingham Bucks 102 E3
Buckland Bucks 84 C5
Buckland Devon 8 G3
Buckland Devon 14 G3
Buckland Glos 99 D11
Buckland Hants 20 B2
Buckland Herts 105 E7
Buckland Kent 55 E10
Buckland Oxon 82 F4
Buckland Sur 51 C8
Buckland Brewer Devon 24 C6
Buckland Common Bucks 84 D6
Buckland Dinham Som 45 C9
Buckland Down Som 45 C8
Buckland End W Mid 134 F2
Buckland Filleigh Devon 25 F7
Buckland in the Moor Devon 13 G10
Buckland Marsh Oxon 82 F4
Buckland Monachorum Devon 7 B9
Buckland Newton Dorset 29 F11
Buckland Ripers Dorset 17 E8
Buckland St Mary Som 28 E3
Buckland Valley Kent 55 E10
Bucklands Borders 262 F2
Bucklandwharf Bucks 84 C5
Bucklebury W Berks 64 E5
Bucklebury Alley W Berks 64 E4
Bucklegate Lincs 156 B6
Buckleigh Devon 24 B6
Bucklerheads Angus 287 D8
Bucklers Hard Hants 20 B4
Bucklesham Suff 108 C4
Buckley = Bwcle Flint 166 C3
Buckley Green Warks 118 D3
Buckley Hill Mers 182 B4
Bucklow Hill E Ches 184 E2
Buckminster Leics 155 E7
Buckmoorend Bucks 84 E4
Bucknall Lincs 173 B11
Bucknall Stoke 168 F6
Bucknell Oxon 101 F11
Bucknell Shrops 115 C7
Buckoak W Ches 183 G8
Buckover S Glos 79 G11
Buckpool Moray 302 C4
Buckpool W Mid 133 F7
Buckridge Worcs 116 C4
Buck's Cross Devon 24 C4
Bucks Green W Sus 50 G5
Bucks Hill Herts 85 E9
Bucks Horn Oak Hants 49 E10
Buck's Mills Devon 24 C5
Bucksburn Aberdeen 293 C10
Buckshaw Village Lancs 194 C5
Buckskin Hants 48 C6
Buckton E Yorks 218 E3
Buckton Hereford 115 C7
Buckton Northumb 264 B3
Buckton Vale Gtr Man 196 G3
Buckworth Cambs 122 B2
Budbrooke Warks 118 D5
Budby Notts 171 B10
Buddgbrake Shetland 312 B8
Buddileigh Staffs 168 F3
Budd's Titson Corn 24 G2
Bude Corn 24 F2
Budge's Shop Corn 6 D6
Budlake Devon 14 B5
Budle Northumb 264 B5
Budleigh Som 27 D11
Budleigh Salterton Devon 15 E7
Budlett's Common E Sus 37 C7
Budock Water Corn 3 C7
Budworth Heath W Ches 183 F11
Buersil Head Gtr Man 196 E2
Buerton E Ches 167 G11
Buffler's Holt Bucks 102 D3
Bufton Leics 135 B8
Bugbrooke Northants 120 F3
Bugford Devon 40 E6
Bughtlin Edin 280 G3
Buglawton E Ches 168 C5
Bugle Corn 5 D10
Bugle Gate Worcs 116 D6
Bugley Dorset 30 C3
Bugley Wilts 45 E11
Bugthorpe E Yorks 207 B11
Building End Essex 105 D8
Buildwas Shrops 132 C2
Builth Road Powys 113 G10
Builth Wells Powys 113 G10
Buirgh W Isles 305 J2
Bulbourne Herts 84 C6
Bulbridge Wilts 46 G5
Bulby Lincs 155 D11
Bulcote Notts 171 G11
Buldoo Highld 310 C3
Bulford Wilts 47 E7
Bulford Camp Wilts 47 E7
Bulkeley E Ches 167 E8
Bulkeley Hall Shrops 168 G2
Bulkington Warks 135 F7
Bulkington Wilts 46 B2
Bulkworthy Devon 24 E5
Bull Bay = Porthllechog Anglesey 178 C6
Bull Hill Hants 20 B2
Bullamoor N Yorks 225 G7
Bullbridge Derbys 170 E5
Bullbrook Brack 65 F11
Bulleign Kent 53 G11
Bullenhill Wilts 45 B11
Bullen's Green Herts 86 D2
Bulley Glos 80 B3
Bullgill Cumb 229 D7
Bullhurst Hill Derbys 170 G3
Bullinghope Hereford 97 D10
Bullington Hants 48 E3
Bullington Lincs 189 F9

Bullo Glos 79 D11
Bullock's Horn Wilts 81 G7
Bullockstone Kent 71 F7
Bulls Cross London 86 F4
Bull's Green Herts 86 B3
Bull's Green Norf 143 E8
Bulls Green Som 45 D8
Bull's Hill Hereford 97 G11
Bullwood Argyll 276 G3
Bullyhole Bottom Mon 79 F7
Bulmer Essex 106 C6
Bulmer N Yorks 216 F3
Bulmer Tye Essex 106 D6
Bulphan Thurrock 68 B6
Bulstrode Herts 85 E8
Bulthy Shrops 148 G6
Bulverhythe E Sus 38 F3
Bulwark Aberds 303 E9
Bulwark Mon 79 G8
Bulwell Nottingham 171 F8
Bulwell Forest Nottingham 171 F8
Bulwick Leics 136 E3
Bulwick Northants 137 E9
Bumble's Green Essex 86 D6
Bumwell Hill Norf 142 E2
Bun Abhainn Eadarra W Isles 305 H3
Bun a'Mhuillin W Isles 297 K3
Bun Loyne Highld 290 C4
Bunacaimb Highld 295 G8
Bunarkaig Highld 290 E3
Bunbury E Ches 167 D9
Bunbury Heath E Ches 167 D9
Bunce Common Sur 51 D8
Bunchrew Highld 300 E6
Bundalloch Highld 295 C10
Buness Shetland 312 C8
Bunessan Argyll 288 G5
Bungay Suff 142 F6
Bunker's Hill Cambs 139 B8
Bunkers Hill Gtr Man 184 D6
Bunker's Hill Lincs 174 E3
Bunker's Hill Lincs 189 G7
Bunker's Hill Norf 142 B3
Bunkers Hill Oxon 83 B7
Bunker's Hill Suff 143 C10
Bunloit Highld 300 G5
Bunnahabhain Argyll 274 F5
Bunny Notts 153 D11
Bunny Hill Notts 153 D11
Bunree Highld 290 G2
Bunroy Highld 290 E4
Bunsley Bank E Ches 167 G11
Bunstead Hants 32 C6
Buntait Highld 300 F3
Buntingford Herts 105 F7
Bunting's Green Essex 106 E6
Bunwell Norf 142 E2
Bunwell Bottom Norf 142 D2
Buoltach Highld 310 F5
Burbage Derbys 185 G8
Burbage Leics 135 E8
Burbage Wilts 63 G8
Burcher Hereford 114 E6
Burchett's Green Windsor 65 C10
Burcombe Wilts 46 G5
Burcot Oxon 83 F9
Burcot Worcs 117 C9
Burcote Shrops 132 D4
Burcott Bucks 84 B4
Burcott Bucks 103 G7
Burcott Som 44 D4
Burdiehouse Edin 270 B5
Burdon T & W 243 G9
Burdonshill V Glam 58 E6
Burdrop Oxon 101 D7
Bures Suff 107 E8
Bures Green Suff 107 D8
Burford Devon 24 C4
Burford E Ches 167 E10
Burford Oxon 82 C3
Burford Shrops 115 D11
Burford Som 44 E5
Burg Argyll 288 E5
Burg Argyll 288 G6
Burgar Orkney 314 D3
Burgate Hants 31 D11
Burgate Suff 125 B11
Burgates Hants 34 B3
Burge End Herts 104 E2
Burgedin Powys 148 G4
Burgess Hill W Sus 36 D4
Burgh Suff 126 G4
Burgh by Sands Cumb 239 F8
Burgh Castle Norf 143 B9
Burgh Common Norf 141 E11
Burgh Heath Sur 51 B8
Burgh Hill E Sus 23 C8
Burgh Hill E Sus 38 B2
Burgh le Marsh Lincs 175 B8
Burgh Muir Aberds 293 B9
Burgh Muir Aberds 303 G7
Burgh next Aylsham Norf 160 D4
Burgh on Bain Lincs 190 D2
Burgh St Margaret = Fleggburgh Norf 161 G8
Burgh St Peter Norf 143 E9
Burgh Stubbs Norf 159 C10
Burghclere Hants 64 G3
Burghclere Common Hants 64 G3
Burghead Moray 301 C11
Burghfield W Berks 65 F7
Burghfield Common W Berks 64 F6
Burghfield Hill W Berks 65 F7
Burghill Hereford 97 C9
Burghwallis S Yorks 198 E4
Burgois Corn 10 G4
Burham Kent 69 G8
Burham Court Kent 69 G8
Buriton Hants 34 C2
Burland E Ches 167 E10
Burlawn Corn 10 G5
Burleigh Brack 65 E11
Burleigh Glos 80 E5
Burlescombe Devon 27 D9
Burleston Dorset 17 C11
Burlestone Devon 8 F6
Burley Hants 32 G2
Burley Rutland 155 G7
Burley Shrops 131 G9
Burley W Yorks 205 G11
Burley Beacon Hants 32 G2
Burley Gate Hereford 97 B11
Burley in Wharfedale W Yorks 205 D9
Burley Lawn Hants 32 G2
Burley Lodge Hants 32 F2
Burley Street Hants 32 G2
Burley Woodhead W Yorks 205 E9
Burleydam E Ches 167 G10
Burlinch Som 28 B3
Burlingham Green Norf 161 G7
Burlingjobb Powys 114 F5
Burlish Park Worcs 116 C6
Burlorne Tregoose Corn 5 B10
Burlow E Sus 23 B9
Burlton Shrops 149 D9
Burmantofts W Yorks 206 G2
Burmarsh Hereford 97 B10
Burmarsh Kent 54 G5
Burmington Warks 100 D5
Burn N Yorks 198 B5
Burn Bridge N Yorks 206 C2
Burn Naze Lancs 202 E2
Burn of Cambus Stirl 285 G11
Burnage Gtr Man 184 C5
Burnard's Ho Devon 24 G4
Burnaston Derbys 152 C5
Burnbank S Lnrk 268 D4
Burnby E Yorks 208 D2
Burncross S Yorks 186 B4
Burndell W Sus 35 G7
Burnden Gtr Man 195 F8
Burnedge Gtr Man 196 E2
Burnend Aberds 303 E8
Burneside Cumb 221 F10
Burness Orkney 314 B6
Burneston N Yorks 214 B6
Burnett Bath 61 F7
Burnfoot Borders 261 G10
Burnfoot Borders 262 F2
Burnfoot Dumfries 239 C7
Burnfoot Dumfries 247 E11
Burnfoot E Ayrs 245 B10
Burnfoot N Lnrk 268 B5
Burnfoot Perth 286 G3
Burngreave S Yorks 186 D5
Burnham Bucks 66 C2
Burnham N Lincs 200 D5
Burnham Deepdale Norf 176 E4
Burnham Green Herts 86 B3
Burnham Market Norf 176 E4
Burnham Norton Norf 176 E4
Burnham-on-Crouch Essex 88 F6
Burnham-on-Sea Som 43 D10
Burnham Overy Staithe Norf 176 E4
Burnham Overy Town Norf 176 E4
Burnham Thorpe Norf 176 E5
Burnhead Aberds 293 D10
Burnhead Borders 262 F2
Burnhead Dumfries 247 D9
Burnhead Dumfries 247 G10
Burnhead S Ayrs 244 C6
Burnhervie Aberds 293 B9
Burnhill Green Staffs 132 C5
Burnhope Durham 233 B9
Burnhouse N Ayrs 267 E7
Burnhouse Mains Borders 271 F8
Burniere Corn 10 G5
Burniestrype Moray 302 C3
Burniston N Yorks 227 G10
Burnlee W Yorks 196 F6
Burnley Lancs 204 G2
Burnley Lane Lancs 204 G2
Burnley Wood Lancs 204 G2
Burnmouth Borders 273 C9
Burnopfield Durham 242 F5
Burnrigg Cumb 239 F11
Burn's Green Herts 104 G6
Burnsall N Yorks 213 G10
Burnside Aberds 303 E8
Burnside Angus 287 B9
Burnside E Ayrs 258 G3
Burnside Fife 286 G5
Burnside Perth 286 E4
Burnside S Lnrk 268 C2
Burnside Shetland 312 F4
Burnside T & W 243 G8
Burnside W Loth 279 G11
Burnside of Duntrune Angus 287 D8
Burnstone Devon 24 C4
Burnswark Dumfries 238 B5
Burnt Ash Glos 80 E5
Burnt Heath Derbys 186 F2
Burnt Heath Essex 107 F11
Burnt Hill W Berks 64 E5
Burnt Houses Durham 233 G8
Burnt Mills Essex 88 G2
Burnt Oak E Sus 37 B8
Burnt Oak London 86 G2
Burnt Tree W Mid 133 E9
Burnt Yates N Yorks 214 G5
Burntcommon Sur 50 C4
Burntheath Derbys 152 C4
Burnthouse Corn 3 B7
Burntisland Fife 280 D4
Burnton E Ayrs 245 B11
Burnturk Fife 287 G7
Burntwood Staffs 133 B11
Burntwood Green Staffs 133 B11
Burntwood Pentre Flint 166 C3
Burnworthy Som 27 D11
Burnwynd Edin 270 B2
Burpham Sur 50 C4
Burpham W Sus 35 F8
Burradon Northumb 251 B11
Burradon T & W 243 C7
Burrafirth Shetland 312 B8
Burraland Shetland 312 F5
Burraland Shetland 313 J4
Burras Corn 2 C5
Burrastow Shetland 313 J4
Burraton Corn 7 D8
Burraton Coombe Corn 7 D8
Burravoe Shetland 312 F7
Burravoe Shetland 312 G5
Burray Village Orkney 314 G4
Burreldales Aberds 303 F7
Burrells Cumb 222 B3
Burrelton Perth 286 D6
Burridge Devon 28 F4
Burridge Devon 40 F5
Burridge Hants 33 E8
Burrigill Highld 310 F6
Burrill N Yorks 214 B4
Burringham N Lincs 199 F10
Burrington Devon 25 D10
Burrington Hereford 115 C8
Burrington N Som 44 B3
Burrough End Cambs 124 F2
Burrough Green Cambs 124 F2
Burrough on the Hill Leics 154 G5
Burroughs Grove Bucks 65 B11
Burroughston Orkney 314 D5
Burrow Devon 14 B5
Burrow Som 28 C6
Burrow Som 42 E2
Burrow-bridge Som 28 B5
Burrowbridge Som 43 G11
Burrowhill Sur 66 G3
Burrows Cross Sur 50 D5
Burrowsmoor Holt Notts 172 G2
Burrsville Park Essex 89 B11
Burrswood Kent 52 F4
Burry Swansea 56 C3
Burry Green Swansea 56 C3
Burry Port = Porth Tywyn Carms 74 E6
Burscott Devon 24 C4
Burscough Lancs 194 E2
Burscough Bridge Lancs 194 E2
Bursdon Devon 24 D3
Bursea E Yorks 208 G2
Burshill E Yorks 209 D7
Bursledon Hants 33 F7
Burslem Stoke 168 F5
Burstall Suff 107 C11
Burstallhill Suff 107 B11
Burstock Dorset 28 G6
Burston Devon 26 G2
Burston Norf 142 G2
Burston Staffs 151 C8
Burstow Sur 51 E10
Burstwick E Yorks 201 B8
Burtersett N Yorks 213 B7
Burtholme Cumb 240 E2
Burthorpe Suff 124 E5
Burthwaite Cumb 230 B4
Burtle Som 43 E11
Burtle Hill Som 43 E11
Burtoft Lincs 156 B5
Burton Dorset 17 C9
Burton Dorset 19 C9
Burton Lincs 189 G7
Burton Northumb 264 C5
Burton Pembs 73 D7
Burton Som 29 E8
Burton Som 43 E7
Burton V Glam 58 F4
Burton W Ches 167 C8
Burton W Ches 182 G4
Burton Wilts 45 G10
Burton Wilts 61 D10
Burton Wrex 166 D5
Burton Agnes E Yorks 218 G2
Burton Bradstock Dorset 16 D5
Burton Corner Lincs 174 F4
Burton Dassett Warks 119 G7
Burton End Cambs 106 B2
Burton End Essex 105 G10
Burton Ferry Pembs 73 D7
Burton Fleming E Yorks 217 E11
Burton Green Essex 106 F6
Burton Green W Mid 118 B5
Burton Green Wrex 166 D4
Burton Hastings Warks 135 E8
Burton-in-Kendal Cumb 211 D10
Burton in Lonsdale N Yorks 212 E3
Burton Joyce Notts 171 G10
Burton Latimer Northants 121 C8
Burton Lazars Leics 154 F5
Burton-le-Coggles Lincs 155 D9
Burton Leonard N Yorks 214 G6
Burton Manor Staffs 151 E8
Burton on the Wolds Leics 153 E11
Burton Overy Leics 136 D3
Burton Pedwardine Lincs 173 G10
Burton Pidsea E Yorks 209 G10
Burton Salmon N Yorks 198 B3
Burton Stather N Lincs 199 D11
Burton upon Stather N Lincs 199 D11
Burton upon Trent Staffs 152 E5
Burton Westwood Shrops 132 D2
Burtonwood Warr 183 C9
Burwardsley W Ches 167 D8
Burwarton Shrops 132 F2
Burwash E Sus 37 C11
Burwash Common E Sus 37 C10
Burwash Weald E Sus 37 C10
Burwell Cambs 123 D11
Burwell Lincs 190 F5
Burwen Anglesey 178 C6
Burwick Orkney 314 H4
Burwick Shetland 313 J5
Burwood Shrops 131 F9
Burwood Park Sur 66 G6
Bury Cambs 138 G5
Bury Gtr Man 195 E10
Bury Som 26 B6
Bury W Sus 35 E8
Bury End Beds 121 G9
Bury End C Beds 104 E2
Bury End Worcs 99 D11
Bury Green Herts 86 E4
Bury Green Herts 105 G8
Bury Hollow W Sus 35 E8
Bury Park Luton 103 G11
Bury St Edmunds Suff 125 E7
Buryas Br Corn 1 D4
Burybank Staffs 151 B7
Bury's Bank W Berks 64 F3
Burythorpe N Yorks 216 G5
Busbiehill N Ayrs 257 B9
Busbridge Sur 50 E3
Busby E Renf 267 D11
Buscot Oxon 82 F2
Buscott Som 44 F2
Bush Aberds 293 G9
Bush Corn 24 F2
Bush Bank Hereford 115 G9
Bush Crathie Aberds 292 D4
Bush End Essex 87 B9
Bush Estate Norf 161 D8
Bush Green Norf 141 D10
Bush Green Norf 142 F4
Bush Green Suff 125 F8
Bush Hill Park London 86 F4
Bushbury Sur 51 D7
Bushbury W Mid 133 C8
Bushby Leics 136 C3
Bushey Dorset 18 E5
Bushey Herts 85 G10
Bushey Ground Oxon 82 D4
Bushey Heath Herts 85 G11
Bushey Mead London 67 F8
Bushfield Cumb 249 G11
Bushley Worcs 99 E7
Bushley Green Worcs 99 E7
Bushmead Beds 122 E2
Bushmoor Shrops 131 F8
Bushton Wilts 62 D5
Bushy Common Norf 159 G9
Bushy Hill Sur 50 C4
Busk Cumb 231 C8
Busk Gtr Man 196 F2
Buslingthorpe Lincs 189 D9
Bussage Glos 80 E5
Bussex Som 43 F11
Busta Shetland 312 G5
Bustard Green Essex 106 F2
Bustard's Green Norf 142 E3
Bustatoun Orkney 314 A7
Busveal Corn 4 G4
Butcher's Common Norf 160 E6
Butcher's Cross E Sus 37 B9
Butcombe N Som 60 G4
Bute Town Caerph 77 D10
Butetown Cardiff 59 D7
Butlane Head Shrops 149 G8
Butleigh Som 44 G4
Butleigh Wootton Som 44 G4
Butler's Cross Bucks 84 D4
Butler's Cross Bucks 84 F6
Butlers End Warks 134 G4
Butler's Hill Notts 171 F8
Butlers Marston Warks 118 G6
Butlersbank Shrops 149 E11
Butley Suff 127 G7
Butley High Corner Suff 109 B7
Butley Low Corner Suff 109 B7
Butley Town E Ches 184 F6
Butlocks Heath Hants 33 F7
Butt Green E Ches 167 E11
Butt Lane Staffs 168 E4
Butt Yeats Lancs 211 F11
Butter Bank Staffs 151 E7
Butterburn Cumb 240 C5
Buttercrambe N Yorks 207 B10
Butteriss Gate Corn 2 C6
Butterknowle Durham 233 F8
Butterleigh Devon 27 F7
Butterley Derbys 170 C4
Butterley Derbys 170 E6
Buttermere Cumb 220 B3
Buttermere Wilts 63 G10
Butterrow Glos 80 E5
Butters Green Staffs 168 E4
Buttershaw W Yorks 196 B6
Butterstone Perth 286 C4
Butterton Staffs 168 G4
Butterton Staffs 169 D9
Butterwick Cumb 221 B10
Butterwick Durham 234 F3
Butterwick Lincs 174 G5
Butterwick N Yorks 216 D4
Butterwick N Yorks 217 E9
Butteryhaugh Northumb 250 E4
Buttington Powys 130 B5
Button Haugh Green Suff 125 D9
Buttonbridge Shrops 116 B4
Buttonoak Worcs 116 B5
Button's Green Suff 125 G8
Butts Devon 14 D2
Butt's Green Essex 88 E3
Butts Green Essex 105 E9
Butt's Green Hants 32 B4
Buttsash Hants 32 F6
Buttsbear Cross Corn 24 G3
Buttsbury Essex 87 F11
Buttsole Kent 55 C10
Buxhall Suff 125 F10
Buxhall Fen Street Suff 125 F10
Buxley Borders 272 E6
Buxted E Sus 37 C7
Buxton Derbys 185 G9
Buxton Norf 160 E4
Buxworth Derbys 185 E8
Bwcle = Buckley Flint 166 C3
Bwlch Flint 181 G11
Bwlch Powys 96 G2
Bwlch-derwin Gwyn 163 F7
Bwlch-Llan Ceredig 111 F11
Bwlch-newydd Carms 93 G7
Bwlch-y-cibau Powys 148 F3
Bwlch-y-cwm Cardiff 58 C6
Bwlch-y-fadfa Ceredig 93 B8
Bwlch-y-ffridd Powys 129 D11
Bwlch-y-Plain Powys 114 B4
Bwlch-y-sarnau Powys 113 C10
Bwlchgwyn Wrex 166 E3
Bwlchnewydd Carms 93 G7
Bwlchtocyn Gwyn 144 D6
Bwlchyddar Powys 148 E3
Bwlchygroes Pembs 92 D4
Bwlchyllyn Gwyn 163 D8
Bybrook Kent 54 E4
Bycross Hereford 97 C7
Bye Green Bucks 84 C5
Byeastwood Bridgend 58 C2
Byebush Aberds 303 F7
Byerhope Northumb 232 B3
Byermoor T & W 242 F5
Byers Green Durham 233 E10
Byfield Northants 119 G10
Byfleet Sur 66 G5
Byford Hereford 97 C7
Byford Common Hereford 97 C7
Bygrave Herts 104 D5
Byker T & W 243 E7
Byland Abbey N Yorks 215 D10
Bylchau Conwy 165 C7
Byley W Ches 168 B2
Bynea Carms 56 B4
Byram N Yorks 198 B3
Byrness Northumb 251 C7
Bythorn Cambs 121 B11
Byton Hereford 115 E7
Byton Hand Hereford 115 E7
Bywell Northumb 242 E2
Byworth W Sus 35 C7

C

Cabbacott Devon 24 C6
Cabbage Hill Brack 65 E11
Cabharstadh W Isles 304 F5
Cabin Shrops 130 F6
Cablea Perth 286 D3
Cabourne Lincs 200 G6
Cabrach Argyll 274 G5
Cabrach Moray 302 G3
Cabrich Highld 300 E5
Cabus Lancs 202 D5
Cackle Hill Lincs 157 D7
Cackle Street E Sus 23 B11
Cackle Street E Sus 37 B7
Cackle Street E Sus 38 D4
Cackleshaw W Yorks 204 F6
Cad Green Som 28 D4
Cadboll Highld 301 B8
Cadbury Devon 26 G6
Cadbury Barton Devon 25 D11
Cadbury Heath S Glos 61 E7
Cadder E Dunb 278 G2
Cadderlie Argyll 284 D4
Caddington C Beds 85 B9
Caddleton Argyll 275 B8
Caddonfoot Borders 261 C10
Caddonlee Borders 261 B10
Cade Street E Sus 37 C10
Cadeby Leics 135 C8
Cadeby S Yorks 198 G4
Cadeleigh Devon 26 F6
Cademuir Borders 260 B6
Cader Denb 165 C8
Cadger Path Angus 287 B8
Cadgwith Corn 2 G6
Cadham Fife 286 G6
Cadishead Gtr Man 184 C2
Cadle Swansea 56 B6
Cadley Lancs 202 G6
Cadley Wilts 47 C8
Cadley Wilts 63 F8
Cadmore End Bucks 84 G3
Cadnam Hants 32 E3
Cadney N Lincs 200 G4
Cadney Bank Wrex 149 C9
Cadole Flint 166 C2
Cadoxton V Glam 58 F6
Cadoxton-Juxta-Neath Neath 57 B9
Cadshaw Blkburn 195 D8
Cadwell Herts 104 E3
Cadzow S Lnrk 268 E4
Cae Clyd Gwyn 164 G2
Cae-gors Carms 75 E9
Caeathro Gwyn 163 C7
Caehopkin Powys 76 C4
Caemorgan Ceredig 92 B3
Caenby Lincs 189 D8
Caenby Corner Lincs 189 D7
Cae'r-bont Powys 76 C4
Cae'r-bryn Carms 75 C9
Caer-Estyn Wrex 166 D4
Caer-Farchell Pembs 90 F5
Cae'r-Lan Powys 76 C4
Caer Llan Mon 79 D7
Caerau Bridgend 57 C11
Caerau Cardiff 58 D6
Caerau Park Newport 59 B9
Caerdeon Gwyn 146 F2
Caerfarchell Pembs 90 F5
Caerffili = Caerphilly Caerph 59 B7
Caerfyrddin = Carmarthen Carms 93 G8
Caergeiliog Anglesey 178 F4
Caergwrle Flint 166 D4
Caergybi = Holyhead Anglesey 178 E2
Caerhendy Neath 57 C9
Caerhun Gwyn 163 B9
Caerleon Newport 78 G4
Caermead V Glam 58 F3
Caermeini Pembs 92 E2
Caernarfon Gwyn 163 C7
Caerphilly = Caerffili Caerph 59 B7
Caersws Powys 129 E10
Caerwedros Ceredig 111 F7
Caerwent Mon 79 G7
Caerwent Brook Mon 60 B3
Caerwych Gwyn 146 B2
Caerwys Flint 181 G10
Caethle Gwyn 128 D2
Cage Green Kent 52 D5
Caggan Highld 291 B10
Caggle Street Mon 78 B5
Cailness Stirl 285 G7
Caim Anglesey 179 E10
Cainscross Glos 80 D4
Caio Carms 94 D3
Cairinis W Isles 296 E4
Cairisiadar W Isles 304 E2
Cairminis W Isles 296 C6
Cairnbaan Argyll 275 D9
Cairnbanno Ho Aberds 303 E8
Cairnborrow Aberds 302 E4
Cairnbrogie Aberds 303 G8
Cairnbulg Castle Aberds 303 C10
Cairncross Angus 292 F6
Cairncross Borders 273 C7
Cairnderry Dumfries 236 B5
Cairndow Argyll 284 F5
Cairness Aberds 303 C10
Cairneyhill Fife 279 D10
Cairnfield Ho Moray 302 C4
Cairngaan Dumfries 236 F3
Cairngarroch Dumfries 236 E2
Cairnhill Aberds 302 F6
Cairnhill Aberds 303 D7
Cairnhill N Lnrk 268 C5
Cairnie Aberds 293 C10
Cairnie Aberds 302 E4
Cairnlea S Ayrs 244 G6
Cairnleith Crofts Aberds 303 F9
Cairnmuir Aberds 303 C9
Cairnorrie Aberds 303 E8
Cairnpark Aberds 293 B10
Cairnpark Dumfries 247 D9
Cairnryan Dumfries 236 C2
Cairnton Orkney 314 F3
Cairston Orkney 314 E2
Caister-on-Sea Norf 161 G10
Caistor Lincs 200 G6
Caistor St Edmund Norf 142 C4
Caistron Northumb 251 C11
Caitha Bowland Borders 271 G9
Cakebole Worcs 117 C7
Calais Street Suff 107 D9
Calanais W Isles 304 E4
Calbost W Isles 305 G6
Calbourne I o W 20 D4
Calceby Lincs 190 F5
Calcoed Flint 181 G11
Calcot Glos 81 C9
Calcot W Berks 65 E7
Calcot Row W Berks 65 E7
Calcott Kent 71 G7
Calcott Shrops 149 G8
Calcott's Green Glos 80 B3
Calcutt N Yorks 206 B2
Calcutt Wilts 81 G10
Caldback Shetland 312 C8
Caldbeck Cumb 230 D2
Caldbergh N Yorks 213 B11
Caldecote Cambs 122 F6
Caldecote Cambs 138 F2
Caldecote Herts 104 D4
Caldecote Northants 120 G3
Caldecote Warks 135 E7
Caldecote Hill Herts 85 G11
Caldecott Northants 121 D9
Caldecott Oxon 83 F7
Caldecott Rutland 137 E7
Caldecotte M Keynes 103 D7
Calder Cumb 219 E10
Calder Bridge Cumb 219 D10
Calder Grove W Yorks 197 D10
Calder Hall Cumb 219 E10
Calder Mains Highld 310 D4
Calder Vale Lancs 202 D6
Calderbank N Lnrk 268 C5
Calderbrook Gtr Man 196 D2
Caldercruix N Lnrk 268 B6
Caldermill S Lnrk 268 G3
Caldermoor Gtr Man 196 D2
Calderstones Mers 182 D6
Calderwood S Lnrk 268 D2
Caldhame Angus 287 C8
Caldicot = Cil-y-coed Mon 60 B3
Caldmore W Mid 133 D10
Caldwell Derbys 152 F5
Caldwell N Yorks 224 C3
Caldy Mers 182 D2
Cale Green Gtr Man 184 D5
Caledrhydiau Ceredig 111 G9
Calenick Corn 4 G6
Caleys Fields Worcs 100 C4
Calf Heath Staffs 133 B8
Calford Green Suff 106 B3
Calfsound Orkney 314 C5
Calgary Argyll 288 D5
Califer Moray 301 D10
California Cambs 139 G10
California Falk 279 F8
California Norf 161 G10
California Suff 108 C3
California W Mid 133 G10
Calke Derbys 153 E7
Callakille Highld 298 D6
Callaly Northumb 252 B3
Callander Stirl 285 G10
Callandrode Stirl 285 G10
Callands Warr 183 C9
Callaughton Shrops 132 D2
Callendar Park Falk 279 F7
Callert Ho Highld 290 G2
Callerton T & W 242 D5
Callerton Lane End T & W 242 D5
Callestick Corn 4 E5
Calligarry Highld 295 E8
Callington Corn 7 B7
Callingwood Staffs 152 E3
Calloose Corn 2 B3
Callop Highld 289 B11
Callow Derbys 170 E3
Callow Hereford 97 E9
Callow End Worcs 98 B6
Callow Hill Mon 79 B8
Callow Hill Som 44 E4
Callow Hill Wilts 62 C4
Callow Hill Worcs 116 C4
Callow Marsh Hereford 98 B3
Callows Grave Worcs 115 D11
Calmore Hants 32 E4
Calmsden Glos 81 D8
Calne Wilts 62 E4
Calne Marsh Wilts 62 E4
Calow Derbys 186 G6
Calow Green Derbys 170 B6
Calrofold E Ches 184 G6
Calshot Hants 33 G7
Calstock Corn 7 B8
Calstone Wellington Wilts 62 F4
Calthorpe Norf 160 C3
Calthorpe Oxon 101 D9
Calthwaite Cumb 230 C5
Calton Glasgow 268 C2
Calton N Yorks 204 B4
Calton Staffs 169 E10
Calton Lees Derbys 170 B3
Calvadnack Corn 2 B5
Calveley E Ches 167 D9
Calver Derbys 186 G2
Calver Hill Hereford 97 B7
Calver Sough Derbys 186 F2
Calverhall Shrops 150 B2
Calverleigh Devon 26 E6
Calverley W Yorks 205 F10
Calvert Bucks 102 G3
Calverton M Keynes 102 D5
Calverton Notts 171 F10
Calvine Perth 291 G10
Calvo Cumb 238 G4
Cam Glos 80 F3
Camaghael Highld 290 F3
Camas an Staca Argyll 274 G5
Camas-luinie Highld 295 C11
Camas Salach Highld 289 C8
Camasnacroise Highld 289 D10
Camastianavaig Highld 295 B7
Camasunary Highld 295 D7
Camault Muir Highld 300 E5
Camb Shetland 312 D7
Camber E Sus 39 D7
Camberley Sur 65 G11
Camberwell London 67 D10
Camblesforth N Yorks 199 B7
Cambo Northumb 252 F2
Cambois Northumb 253 G8
Camborne Corn 4 G3
Cambourne Cambs 122 F6
Cambridge Borders 271 F11
Cambridge Cambs 123 F9
Cambridge Glos 80 E3
Cambridge W Yorks 205 D10
Cambridge Batch N Som 60 F4
Cambridge Town Sthend 70 C2
Cambrose Corn 4 F3
Cambus Clack 279 C7
Cambusavie Farm Highld 309 K7
Cambusbarron Stirl 278 C5
Cambusdrenny Stirl 278 C5
Cambuskenneth Stirl 278 C6
Cambuslang S Lnrk 268 D2
Cambusmore Lodge Highld 309 K7
Cambusnethan N Lnrk 268 D6
Camden London 67 C9
Camden Hill Kent 53 F9
Camden Park Kent 52 F5
Camel Green Dorset 31 E10
Cameley Bath 44 B6
Camelford Corn 11 E8
Camelon Falk 279 E7
Camelsdale Sur 49 G11
Camer Kent 69 F7
Cameron Fife 280 B6
Cameron Bridge Fife 280 B6
Camerory Highld 301 F10
Camer's Green Worcs 98 D5
Camerton Bath 45 B7
Camerton Cumb 228 E6
Camerton E Yorks 201 B8
Camghouran Perth 285 B9
Cammachmore Aberds 293 D11
Cammeringham Lincs 188 E6
Camnant Powys 113 F11
Camoquhill Stirl 277 D10
Camore Highld 309 K7
Camp Lincs 172 E5
Camp Corner Oxon 83 E10
Camp Hill N Yorks 214 C6
Camp Hill Pembs 73 C10
Camp Hill W Yorks 196 D5
Camp Hill Warks 134 E6
Camp Town W Yorks 206 F2
Campbeltown Argyll 255 E8
Camperdown T & W 243 C7
Camphill Derbys 185 F11
Campion Hills Warks 118 D6
Campions Essex 87 C7
Cample Dumfries 247 E9
Campmuir Perth 286 D6
Camps End Cambs 106 C2
Camps Heath Suff 143 E10
Campsall S Yorks 198 E4
Campsea Ashe Suff 126 F6
Campsey Ash Suff 126 F6
Campsfield Oxon 83 B7
Campton C Beds 104 D2
Camptoun E Loth 281 F10
Camptown Borders 262 G5
Camquhart Argyll 275 E10
Camrose Pembs 91 G8
Camserney Perth 286 C2
Camster Highld 310 E6
Camuschoirk Highld 289 C9
Camuscross Highld 295 D8
Camusnagaul Highld 290 F2
Camusnagaul Highld 307 L5
Camusrory Highld 295 F10
Camusteel Highld 299 E7
Camusterrach Highld 299 E7
Camusvrachan Perth 285 C10
Canada Hants 32 D3
Canada Lincs 200 G6
Canadia E Sus 38 D2
Canal Foot Cumb 210 D6
Canal Side S Yorks 199 E7
Canbus Clack 279 C7
Candacraig Ho Aberds 292 B5
Candle Street Suff 125 C10
Candlesby Lincs 175 B7
Candy Mill S Lnrk 269 G11
Cane End Oxon 65 D7
Caneheath E Sus 23 D9
Canewdon Essex 88 G5
Canford Bottom Dorset 31 G8
Canford Cliffs Poole 19 D7
Canford Heath Poole 18 C6
Canford Magna Poole 18 B6
Cangate Norf 160 F6
Canham's Green Suff 125 D11
Canholes Derbys 185 G8
Canisbay Highld 310 B7
Canklow S Yorks 186 C6
Canley W Mid 118 B6
Cann Dorset 30 C5
Cann Common Dorset 30 C5
Cannalidgey Corn 5 B8
Cannard's Grave Som 44 E6
Cannich Highld 300 F3
Canning Town London 68 C2
Cannington Som 43 F9
Cannock Staffs 133 B9
Cannock Wood Staffs 151 G10
Cannon's Green Essex 87 D9
Cannop Glos 79 C10
Canon Bridge Hereford 97 C8
Canon Frome Hereford 98 C3
Canon Pyon Hereford 97 B9
Canonbie Dumfries 239 B9
Canonbury London 67 C10
Canons Ashby Northants 119 G11
Canons Park London 85 G11
Canon's Town Corn 2 B2
Canonsgrove Som 28 C2
Canterbury Kent 54 B6
Cantley Norf 143 C7
Cantley S Yorks 198 G6
Cantlop Shrops 131 B10
Canton Cardiff 59 D7
Cantraybruich Highld 301 E7
Cantraydoune Highld 301 E7
Cantraywood Highld 301 E7
Cantsfield Lancs 212 E2
Canvey Island Essex 69 C9
Canwick Lincs 173 B7
Canworthy Water Corn 11 C10
Caol Highld 290 F3
Caol Ila Argyll 274 F5
Caolas Argyll 288 E2
Caolas W Isles 297 M2
Caolas Fhlodaigh W Isles 296 F4
Caolas Liubharsaigh W Isles 297 G4
Caolas Scalpaigh W Isles 305 J4
Caolas Stocinis W Isles 305 J3
Caoslasnacon Highld 290 G3
Capel Carms 75 E8
Capel Kent 52 E6
Capel Sur 51 E7
Capel Bangor Ceredig 128 G3
Capel Betws Lleucu Ceredig 112 F2
Capel Carmel Gwyn 144 D3
Capel Coch Anglesey 179 E7
Capel Cross Kent 53 E8
Capel Curig Conwy 164 D2
Capel Cynon Ceredig 93 B7
Capel Dewi Carms 93 G9
Capel Dewi Ceredig 93 C9
Capel Dewi Ceredig 128 G2
Capel Garmon Conwy 164 D4
Capel Green Suff 109 B7
Capel-gwyn Anglesey 178 F4
Capel Gwyn Carms 93 G9
Capel Gwynfe Carms 94 G4
Capel Hendre Carms 75 C9
Capel Hermon Gwyn 146 D4
Capel Isaac Carms 93 F11
Capel Iwan Carms 92 D5
Capel-le-Ferne Kent 55 F8
Capel Llanilltern Cardiff 58 C5
Capel Mawr Anglesey 178 G6
Capel Newydd = Newchapel Pembs 92 D4
Capel Parc Anglesey 178 D6
Capel St Andrew Suff 109 B7
Capel St Mary Suff 107 D11
Capel Seion Carms 75 C8
Capel Seion Ceredig 112 B2
Capel Siloam Conwy 164 E4
Capel Tygwydd Ceredig 92 C5
Capel Uchaf Gwyn 162 F6
Capel-y-ffin Powys 96 E5
Capel-y-graig Gwyn 163 B8
Capelulo Conwy 180 F2
Capenhurst W Ches 182 G5
Capernwray Lancs 211 E10
Capheaton Northumb 252 G2
Capland Som 28 D4
Cappercleuch Borders 260 E6
Capplegill Dumfries 248 B4
Capstone Medway 69 F9
Captain Fold Gtr Man 195 E11
Capton Devon 8 E6
Capton Som 42 F5
Caputh Perth 286 D4
Car Colston Notts 172 G2
Caradon Town Corn 11 G11
Carbis Corn 5 D10
Carbis Bay Corn 2 B2
Carbost Highld 294 B5
Carbost Highld 298 E4
Carbrain N Lnrk 278 G5
Carbrook S Yorks 186 D5
Carbrooke Norf 141 C9
Carburton Notts 187 G10
Carcant Borders 271 E7
Carcary Angus 287 B10
Carclaze Corn 5 E10
Carclew Corn 3 B7
Carcroft S Yorks 198 E4
Cardenden Fife 280 C4
Cardeston Shrops 149 G7
Cardew Cumb 230 B2
Cardewlees Cumb 239 G8
Cardiff Cardiff 59 D7
Cardigan = Aberteifi Ceredig 92 B3
Cardinal's Green Cambs 106 B2
Cardington Beds 103 B11
Cardington Shrops 131 D10
Cardinham Corn 6 B2
Cardonald Glasgow 267 C10
Cardow Moray 301 E11
Cardrona Borders 261 B8
Cardross Argyll 276 F6
Cardurnock Cumb 238 F5
Care Village Leics 136 D4
Careby Lincs 155 F10
Careston Angus 293 G7
Careston Castle Angus 287 B9
Carew Pembs 73 E8
Carew Cheriton Pembs 73 E8
Carew Newton Pembs 73 E8
Carey Hereford 97 E11
Carey Park Corn 6 E4
Carfin N Lnrk 268 D5
Carfrae E Loth 271 B11
Carfury Corn 1 C4
Cargate Common Norf 142 E2
Cargenbridge Dumfries 237 B11
Cargill Perth 286 D5
Cargo Cumb 239 F9
Cargo Fleet M'bro 234 G6
Cargreen Corn 7 C8
Carham Northumb 263 B8
Carhampton Som 42 E4
Carharrack Corn 4 G4
Carie Perth 285 B10
Carie Perth 285 D10
Carines Corn 4 D5
Carisbrooke I o W 20 D5
Cark Cumb 211 D7
Carkeel Corn 7 C8
Carlabhagh W Isles 304 D4
Carland Cross Corn 5 E7
Carlbury N Yorks 224 B4
Carlby Lincs 155 G11
Carlecotes S Yorks 197 G7
Carleen Corn 2 C4
Carlenrig Borders 249 C9
Carlesmoor N Yorks 214 E3
Carleton Cumb 219 D10
Carleton Cumb 230 F6
Carleton Cumb 239 G10
Carleton Lancs 202 F2
Carleton N Yorks 204 D5
Carleton W Yorks 198 C3
Carleton Forehoe Norf 141 B11
Carleton Hall Cumb 219 F11
Carleton-in-Craven N Yorks 204 D5
Carleton Rode Norf 142 E2
Carleton St Peter Norf 142 C6
Carley Hill T & W 243 F9
Carlidnack Corn 3 D7
Carlin How Redcar 226 B4
Carlincraig Aberds 302 E6
Carlingcott Bath 45 B7
Carlinghow W Yorks 197 C8
Carlingwark Devon 27 E11
Carlisle Cumb 239 F10
Carloggas Corn 5 B7
Carloggas Corn 5 E9
Carloonan Argyll 284 F4
Carlops Borders 270 D3
Carlton Beds 121 F9
Carlton Cambs 124 G2
Carlton Leics 135 C7
Carlton N Yorks 198 C6
Carlton N Yorks 213 C11
Carlton N Yorks 216 B2
Carlton N Yorks 224 C3
Carlton Notts 171 G10
Carlton S Yorks 197 E11
Carlton Stockton 234 G3
Carlton Suff 127 E7
Carlton W Yorks 197 B10
Carlton Colville Suff 143 F10
Carlton Curlieu Leics 136 D3
Carlton Green Cambs 124 G2
Carlton Husthwaite N Yorks 215 D9
Carlton in Cleveland N Yorks 225 E10
Carlton in Lindrick Notts 187 E9
Carlton le Moorland Lincs 172 D6
Carlton Miniott N Yorks 215 C7
Carlton on Trent Notts 172 C3
Carlton Purlieus Northants 136 F6
Carlton Scroop Lincs 172 G6
Carluddon Corn 5 D10
Carluke S Lnrk 268 E6
Carlyon Bay Corn 5 E11
Carmarthen = Caerfyrddin Carms 93 G8
Carmel Anglesey 178 E5
Carmel Carms 75 B9
Carmel Flint 181 F11
Carmel Gwyn 163 E7
Carmel Powys 113 D11
Carmichael S Lnrk 259 B10
Carminow Cross Corn 5 B11
Carmont Aberds 293 E10
Carmunnock Glasgow 268 D2
Carmyle Glasgow 268 C2
Carmyllie Angus 287 C9
Carn Arthen Corn 2 B5
Carn Brea Village Corn 4 G3
Carn-gorm Highld 295 C11
Carn Towan Corn 1 D3
Carnaby E Yorks 218 F2
Carnach Highld 299 G10
Carnach Highld 307 K5
Carnach W Isles 305 J4
Carnachy Highld 308 D7
Càrnais W Isles 304 E2
Càrnan W Isles 297 G3
Carnbahn Perth 285 C10
Carnbee Fife 287 G9
Carnbo Perth 286 G4
Carnbrea Corn 4 G3
Carnbroe N Lnrk 268 C4
Carndu Highld 295 C10
Carnduff S Lnrk 268 F3
Carnduncan Argyll 274 G3
Carne Corn 3 B10
Carne Corn 3 E7
Carne Corn 5 D9
Carnebone Corn 2 C6
Carnedd Powys 129 E10
Carnetown Rhondda 77 G9
Carnforth Lancs 211 E10
Carnforth Lancs 211 E9
Carnglas Swansea 56 C6

Carnhedryn Pembs 90 F6
Carnhedryn Uchaf Pembs 90 F5
Carnhell Green Corn 2 B4
Carnhot Corn 4 F4
Carnkie Corn 2 B5
Carnkie Corn 2 C6
Carnkief Corn 4 E5
Carno Powys 129 D9
Carnoch Highld 300 D2
Carnoch Highld 300 F3
Carnock Fife 279 D10
Carnon Downs Corn 4 G5
Carnousie Aberds 302 D6
Carnoustie Angus 287 D9
Carnsmerry Corn 5 D10
Carntyne Glasgow 268 B2
Carnwadric E Renf 267 D10
Carnwath S Lnrk 269 F9
Carnyorth Corn 1 C3
Carol Corn 11 C9
Carol Green W Mid 118 B5
Carpalla Corn 5 E9
Carpenders Park Herts 85 G10
Carpenter's Hill Worcs 117 C11
Carperby N Yorks 213 B10
Carpley Green N Yorks 213 B8
Carr Gtr Man 195 D9
Carr S Yorks 187 C8
Carr Bank Cumb 211 D9
Carr Cross Lancs 193 E11
Carr Gate W Yorks 197 C10
Carr Green Gtr Man 184 D2
Carr Hill T & W 243 E7
Carr Houses Mers 193 G10
Carr Vale Derbys 171 B7
Carradale Argyll 255 D9
Carragraich W Isles 305 J3
Carrbridge Highld 301 G9
Carrbrook Gtr Man 196 G3
Carreg-wen Pembs 92 C4
Carreg y Garth Gwyn 163 B9
Carreglefn Anglesey 178 D5
Carrhouse Devon 26 F3
Carrick Argyll 275 E10
Carrick Dumfries 237 D7
Carrick Fife 287 E8
Carrick Castle Argyll 276 C3
Carrick Ho Orkney 314 C5
Carriden Falk 279 E10
Carrington Gtr Man 184 C2
Carrington Lincs 174 E4
Carrington Midloth 270 C6
Carrington Nottingham 171 G9
Carroch Dumfries 246 E5
Carrog Conwy 164 F3
Carrog Denb 165 G10
Carroglen Perth 285 E11
Carrol Highld 311 J2
Carron Falk 279 E7
Carron Moray 302 E2
Carron Bridge Stirl 278 E4
Carronbridge Dumfries 247 D9
Carronshore Falk 279 E7
Carrot Angus 287 C8
Carrow Hill Mon 78 G6
Carrway Head Staffs 134 D3
Carrshield Northumb 232 B2
Carrutherstown Dumfries 238 C4
Carrville Durham 234 C2
Carry Argyll 275 G10
Carsaig Argyll 275 E8
Carsaig Argyll 289 G7
Carscreugh Dumfries 236 D4
Carse Gray Angus 287 B8
Carse Ho Argyll 275 G8
Carsegowan Dumfries 236 D6
Carseriggan Dumfries 236 C5
Carsethorn Dumfries 237 D11
Carshalton London 67 G9
Carshalton Beeches London 67 G9
Carshalton on the Hill London 67 G9
Carsington Derbys 170 E3
Carskiey Argyll 255 G7
Carsluith Dumfries 236 D6
Carsphairn Dumfries 246 E3
Carstairs S Lnrk 269 F8
Carstairs Junction S Lnrk 269 F9
Carswell Marsh Oxon 82 F4
Cartbridge Sur 50 B4
Carter Knowle S Yorks 186 E4
Carterhaugh Borders 261 D10
Carter's Clay Hants 32 C4
Carter's Green Essex 87 C8
Carter's Hill Wokingham 65 F9
Carterspiece Glos 79 C9
Carterton Oxon 82 D3
Carterway Heads Northumb 242 G2
Carthamartha Corn 12 F3
Carthew Corn 2 B5
Carthew Corn 5 D10
Carthorpe N Yorks 214 C6
Cartington Northumb 252 C2
Cartland S Lnrk 269 F7
Cartledge Derbys 186 F4
Cartmel Cumb 211 D7
Cartmel Fell Cumb 211 B8
Cartsdyke Invclyd 276 F5
Cartworth W Yorks 196 F6
Carty Port Dumfries 236 C6
Carway Carms 75 D7
Carwinley Cumb 239 C10
Carwynnen Corn 2 B5
Cary Fitzpaine Som 29 B9
Carzantic Corn 12 E3
Carzield Dumfries 247 G11
Carzise Corn 2 C3
Cas Mael = Puncheston Pembs 91 F10
Cascob Powys 114 D4
Cashes Green Glos 80 D4
Cashlie Perth 285 C8
Cashmoor Dorset 31 E7
Cassey Compton Glos 81 C9
Cassington Oxon 83 C7
Cassop Durham 234 D2
Castallack Corn 1 D5
Castell Conwy 164 B3
Castell Denb 165 B10
Castell-Howell Ceredig 93 B8
Castell nedd = Neath Neath 57 B8
Castell Newydd Emlyn = Newcastle Emlyn Carms 92 C6
Castell-y-bwch Torf 78 G3
Castell-y-rhingyll Carms 75 C9
Castellau Rhondda 58 B5
Casterton Cumb 212 D2
Castle Devon 28 G4
Castle Som 27 B9
Castle Acre Norf 158 F6
Castle Ashby Northants 121 F7
Castle Bolton N Yorks 223 G10
Castle Bromwich W Mid 134 F2
Castle Bytham Lincs 155 F9
Castle Caereinion Powys 130 B3
Castle Camps Cambs 106 C2
Castle Carlton Lincs 190 E5
Castle Carrock Cumb 240 F2
Castle Cary Som 44 G6
Castle Combe Wilts 61 D10
Castle Donington Leics 153 D8
Castle Douglas Dumfries 237 C9
Castle Eaton Swindon 81 F10
Castle Eden Durham 234 D4
Castle End P'boro 138 B2
Castle Fields Shrops 149 G10
Castle Forbes Aberds 293 B8
Castle Frome Hereford 98 B3
Castle Gate Corn 1 C5
Castle Green London 68 C3
Castle Green S Yorks 197 G9
Castle Green Sur 66 G3
Castle Gresley Derbys 152 F5
Castle Heaton Northumb 273 G8
Castle Hedingham Essex 106 D5
Castle Hill E Sus 37 B9
Castle Hill Gtr Man 184 C6
Castle Hill Kent 53 E7
Castle Hill Suff 108 B3
Castle Hill Worcs 116 F5
Castle Huntly Perth 287 E7
Castle Kennedy Dumfries 236 D3
Castle O'er Dumfries 248 E6
Castle Rising Norf 158 E3
Castle Street W Yorks 196 C3
Castle Stuart Highld 301 E7
Castle Toward Argyll 266 B2
Castle Town W Sus 36 E2
Castle-upon-Alun V Glam 58 E2
Castle Vale W Mid 134 E2
Castlebythe Pembs 91 F10
Castlecary N Lnrk 278 F5
Castle Craig Borders 270 G2
Castlecraig Highld 301 C8
Castlecroft Staffs 133 D7
Castlefairn Dumfries 246 F6
Castlefields Halton 183 E8
Castleford W Yorks 198 B2
Castlegreen Shrops 130 F6
Castlehead Renfs 267 C9
Castlehill Argyll 254 B4
Castlehill Borders 260 B6
Castlehill Highld 310 C5
Castlehill S Ayrs 257 E9
Castlehill W Dunb 277 F7
Castlemaddy Dumfries 246 F3
Castlemartin Pembs 72 F6
Castlemilk Dumfries 238 B5
Castlemilk Glasgow 268 D2
Castlemorris Pembs 91 E8
Castlemorton Worcs 98 D5
Castlerigg Cumb 229 G11
Castleside Durham 233 B7
Castlethorpe M Keynes 102 C6
Castlethorpe N Lincs 200 F3
Castleton Angus 287 C7
Castleton Argyll 275 E9
Castleton Derbys 185 E11
Castleton Gtr Man 195 E11
Castleton Moray 301 G11
Castleton N Yorks 226 D3
Castleton Newport 59 C9
Castleton Village Highld 300 E6
Castletown Cumb 230 E6
Castletown Dorset 17 G9
Castletown Highld 301 E7
Castletown Highld 310 C5
Castletown I o M 192 F3
Castletown Staffs 151 E8
Castletown T & W 243 F9
Castletown W Ches 166 E6
Castletump Glos 98 F4
Castleweary Borders 249 C10
Castlewigg Dumfries 236 E6
Castley N Yorks 205 D11
Castling's Heath Suff 107 C9
Caston Norf 141 D9
Castor P'boro 138 D2
Caswell Swansea 56 D5
Cat Bank Cumb 220 F6
Cat Hill S Yorks 197 F8
Catacol N Ayrs 255 C10
Catbrain S Glos 60 C5
Catbrook Mon 79 E8
Catch Flint 182 G2
Catchall Corn 1 D4
Catchems Corner W Mid 118 B4
Catchems End Worcs 116 B5
Catchgate Durham 242 G5
Catchory Highld 310 D6
Catcleugh Northumb 250 C6
Catcliffe S Yorks 186 D6
Catcomb Wilts 62 D4
Catcott Som 43 F11
Caterham Sur 51 B10
Catfield Norf 161 E7
Catfirth Shetland 313 H6
Catford London 67 E11
Catforth Lancs 202 F5
Cathays Cardiff 59 D7
Cathays Park Cardiff 59 D7
Cathcart Glasgow 267 C11
Cathedine Powys 96 F2
Catherine-de-Barnes W Mid 134 G3
Catherine Slack W Yorks 196 B5
Catherington Hants 33 E11
Catherton Shrops 116 B3
Cathiron Warks 119 B9
Catholes Cumb 222 G3
Cathpair Borders 271 F9
Catisfield Hants 33 F8
Catley Lane Head Gtr Man 195 D11
Catley Southfield Hereford 98 C3
Catlodge Highld 291 D8
Catlowdy Cumb 239 B11
Catmere End Essex 105 D9
Catmore W Berks 64 C3
Caton Devon 13 G11
Caton Lancs 211 G10
Caton Green Lancs 211 F10
Catrine E Ayrs 258 D2
Cat's Ash Newport 78 G5
Cat's Common Norf 160 E6
Cats Edge Staffs 169 E7
Cat's Hill Cross Staffs 150 C6
Catsfield E Sus 38 E2
Catsfield Stream E Sus 38 E2
Catsgore Som 29 B8
Catsham Som 44 G5
Catshaw S Yorks 197 G8
Catshill W Mid 133 B11
Catshill Worcs 117 C9
Catslackburn Borders 261 D8
Catslip Oxon 65 B8
Catstree Shrops 132 D4
Cattadale Argyll 274 G4
Cattal N Yorks 206 C4
Cattawade Suff 108 E2
Cattedown Plym 7 E9
Catterall Lancs 202 E5
Catterick N Yorks 224 F4
Catterick Bridge N Yorks 224 F4
Catterick Garrison N Yorks 224 F3
Catterlen Cumb 230 E5
Catterline Aberds 293 F10
Catterton N Yorks 206 D6
Catteshall Sur 50 E3
Catthorpe Leics 119 B11
Cattistock Dorset 17 B7
Cattle End Northants 102 C3
Catton N Yorks 215 D7
Catton Northumb 241 F8
Catwick E Yorks 209 D8
Catworth Cambs 121 C11
Caudle Green Glos 80 C6
Caudlesprings Norf 141 C8
Caulcott C Beds 103 C9
Caulcott Oxon 101 G10
Cauld Borders 261 G11
Cauldcoats Holdings Falk 279 F10
Cauldcots Angus 287 C10
Cauldhame Stirl 278 C2
Cauldmill Borders 262 G2
Cauldon Staffs 169 F9
Cauldon Lowe Staffs 169 F9
Cauldwells Aberds 303 D7
Caulkerbush Dumfries 237 D11
Caulside Dumfries 249 G10
Caundle Marsh Dorset 29 E11
Caunsall Worcs 132 G6
Caunton Notts 172 D2
Causeway Hants 33 E11
Causeway Hants 34 C2
Causeway Mon 60 B2
Causeway End Cumb 210 C6
Causeway End Cumb 211 B9
Causeway End Dumfries 236 C6
Causeway End Essex 87 B11
Causeway End Wilts 62 C4
Causeway Foot W Yorks 197 E8
Causeway Foot W Yorks 205 G7
Causeway Green W Mid 133 F9
Causewayend S Lnrk 260 B2
Causewayhead Cumb 238 G4
Causewayhead Stirl 278 B6
Causewaywood Shrops 131 D10
Causey Durham 242 F6
Causey Park Bridge Northumb 252 E5
Causeyend Aberds 293 B11
Causeyton Aberds 293 B8
Caute Devon 24 E6
Cautley Cumb 222 G3
Cavendish Suff 106 B6
Cavendish Bridge Leics 153 D8
Cavenham Suff 124 D5
Cavers Carre Borders 262 D3
Caversfield Oxon 101 F11
Caversham Reading 65 E8
Caversham Heights Reading 65 D8
Caverswall Staffs 169 G7
Cavil E Yorks 207 G11
Cawdor Highld 301 D8
Cawkeld E Yorks 208 C5
Cawkwell Lincs 190 F3
Cawood N Yorks 207 F7
Cawsand Corn 7 E8
Cawston Norf 160 E2
Cawston Warks 119 C9
Cawthorne N Yorks 216 B5
Cawthorne S Yorks 197 F9
Cawthorpe Lincs 155 E11
Cawton N Yorks 216 D2
Caxton Cambs 122 F6
Caynham Shrops 115 C11
Caythorpe Lincs 172 F6
Caythorpe Notts 171 F11
Cayton N Yorks 217 C11
Ceallan W Isles 296 F4
Ceann a Bhàigh W Isles 305 J4
Ceann a Bhaigh W Isles 296 E3
Ceann a Deas Loch Baghasdail W Isles 297 K3
Ceann Shiphoirt W Isles 305 G4
Ceann Tarabhaigh W Isles 305 G4
Ceannacroc Lodge Highld 290 B4
Cearsiadair W Isles 304 F5
Ceathramh Meadhanach W Isles 296 D4
Cefn Newport 59 B9
Cefn Powys 148 G5
Cefn Berain Conwy 165 B7
Cefn-brith Conwy 164 E6
Cefn-bryn-brain Carms 76 C2
Cefn-bychan Swansea 56 B4
Cefn-bychan Wrex 166 G3
Cefn Canol Powys 148 C4
Cefn-coch Conwy 164 B5
Cefn Coch Powys 129 C10
Cefn Coch Powys 148 D2
Cefn-coed-y-cymmer M Tydf 77 D8
Cefn Cribbwr Bridgend 57 E11
Cefn Cross Bridgend 57 E11
Cefn-ddwysarn Gwyn 147 B9
Cefn Einion Shrops 130 F5
Cefn-eurgain Flint 166 B2
Cefn Fforest Caerph 77 F11
Cefn Glas Bridgend 57 E11
Cefn Golau Bl Gwent 77 D10
Cefn-gorwydd Powys 95 B8
Cefn Hengoed Caerph 77 F10
Cefn-hengoed Swansea 57 B7
Cefn Llwyd Ceredig 128 G2
Cefn-mawr Wrex 166 G3
Cefn Rhigos Rhondda 76 D6
Cefn-y-bedd Flint 166 D4
Cefn-y-Crib Torf 78 F2
Cefn-y-Garth Swansea 76 E2
Cefn-y-pant Carms 92 F3
Cefncaeau Carms 56 B4
Cefneithin Carms 75 C9
Cefnpennar Rhondda 77 E8
Cegidfa = Guilsfield Powys 148 G4
Cei-bach Ceredig 111 F8
Ceinewydd = New Quay Ceredig 111 F7
Ceint Anglesey 179 F7
Ceinws Powys 128 B5
Cellan Ceredig 94 B2
Cellarhead Staffs 169 F7
Cellarhill Kent 70 G3
Celyn-Mali Flint 165 B11
Cemaes Anglesey 178 C5
Cemmaes Powys 128 B6
Cemmaes Road = Glantwymyn Powys 128 C6
Cenarth Carms 92 C5
Cenin Gwyn 163 F7
Central Invclyd 276 F5
Central Milton Keynes M Keynes 102 D6
Ceos W Isles 304 F5
Ceres Fife 287 F8
Ceri = Kerry Powys 130 F2
Cerne Abbas Dorset 29 G11
Cerney Wick Glos 81 F9
Cerrig Llwydion Neath 57 C9
Cerrig-mân Anglesey 179 C7
Cerrigceinwen Anglesey 178 G6
Cerrigydrudion Conwy 165 F7
Cess Norf 161 F8
Cessford Borders 262 E6
Ceunant Gwyn 163 C8
Chaceley Glos 99 E7
Chaceley Hole Glos 98 E6
Chaceley Stock Glos 99 F7
Chacewater Corn 4 G4
Chackmore Bucks 102 D3
Chacombe Northants 101 C9
Chad Valley W Mid 133 F10
Chadbury Worcs 99 B10
Chadderton Gtr Man 196 F2
Chadderton Fold Gtr Man 195 F11
Chaddesden Derby 153 B7
Chaddesley Corbett Worcs 117 C7
Chaddlehanger Devon 12 F5
Chaddlewood Plym 7 D11
Chaddleworth W Berks 64 D2
Chadkirk Gtr Man 184 D6
Chadlington Oxon 100 G6
Chadshunt Warks 118 G6
Chadsmoor Staffs 151 G9
Chadstone Northants 121 F7
Chadwell Leics 154 E5
Chadwell Shrops 150 G5
Chadwell End Beds 121 D11
Chadwell Heath London 68 B3
Chadwell St Mary Thurrock 68 D6
Chadwick Worcs 116 D6
Chadwick End W Mid 118 C4
Chadwick Green Mers 183 B8
Chaffcombe Som 28 E5
Chafford Hundred Thurrock 68 D5
Chagford Devon 13 D10
Chailey E Sus 36 D5
Chain Bridge Lincs 174 G4
Chainbridge Cambs 139 C8
Chainhurst Kent 53 D8
Chalbury Dorset 31 F8
Chalbury Common Dorset 31 F8
Chaldon Sur 51 B10
Chaldon Herring or East Chaldon Dorset 17 E11
Chale I o W 20 F5
Chale Green I o W 20 F5
Chalfont Common Bucks 85 G8
Chalfont Grove Bucks 85 G7
Chalfont St Giles Bucks 85 G7
Chalfont St Peter Bucks 85 G8
Chalford Glos 80 E5
Chalford Oxon 84 E2
Chalford Wilts 45 C11
Chalford Hill Glos 80 E5
Chalgrave C Beds 103 F10
Chalgrove Oxon 83 F10
Chalk Kent 69 E7
Chalk End Essex 87 C10
Chalkfoot Cumb 230 B2
Chalkhill Norf 141 C7
Chalkhouse Green Oxon 65 D8
Chalkshire Bucks 84 D4
Chalksole Kent 55 E9
Chalkway Som 28 F5
Chalkwell Kent 69 G11
Chalkwell Sthend 69 B11
Challaborough Devon 8 G3
Challacombe Devon 41 E7
Challister Shetland 312 G7
Challoch Dumfries 236 C5
Challock Kent 54 C4
Chalmington Dorset 29 G9
Chalton C Beds 103 F10
Chalton Hants 34 D2
Chalvedon Essex 69 B8
Chalvey Slough 66 D3
Chalvington E Sus 23 D8
Chambercombe Devon 40 D4
Chamber's Green Kent 54 E2
Champson Devon 26 B4
Chance Inn Fife 287 F7
Chancery = Rhydgaled Ceredig 111 B11
Chance's Pitch Hereford 98 C4
Chandler's Cross Herts 85 F9
Chandler's Cross Worcs 98 D5
Chandler's Ford Hants 32 D6
Chandlers Green Hants 49 B8
Channel Tunnel Kent 55 F7
Channel's End Beds 122 F2
Channerwick Shetland 313 L6
Chantry Devon 25 C9
Chantry Som 45 D8
Chantry Suff 108 C2
Chapel Corn 4 C6
Chapel Cumb 229 E10
Chapel Fife 280 C5
Chapel Allerton Som 44 C2
Chapel Allerton W Yorks 206 F2
Chapel Amble Corn 10 F5
Chapel Brampton Northants 120 D4
Chapel Chorlton Staffs 150 B6
Chapel Cleeve Som 42 E4
Chapel Cross E Sus 37 C10
Chapel-en-le-Frith Derbys 185 E9
Chapel End Beds 103 B11
Chapel End Beds 122 F2
Chapel End C Beds 103 C11
Chapel End Cambs 138 G2
Chapel End E Ches 167 G11
Chapel End Essex 105 G11
Chapel End Northants 138 F2
Chapel End Warks 134 E6
Chapel Field Gtr Man 195 F9
Chapel Field Norf 161 E7
Chapel Fields W Mid 118 B6
Chapel Fields York 207 C7
Chapel Green Herts 104 D6
Chapel Green Warks 119 E9
Chapel Green Warks 134 F5
Chapel Haddlesey N Yorks 198 B5
Chapel Head Cambs 138 G6
Chapel Hill Aberds 303 F10
Chapel Hill Glos 79 E10
Chapel Hill Lincs 174 E2
Chapel Hill Mon 79 F8
Chapel Hill N Yorks 206 D2
Chapel House Lancs 194 F3
Chapel Knapp Wilts 61 F11
Chapel Lawn Shrops 114 B6
Chapel-le-Dale N Yorks 212 D4
Chapel Leigh Som 27 B10
Chapel Mains Borders 271 G11
Chapel Milton Derbys 185 E9
Chapel of Garioch Aberds 303 G7
Chapel of Stoneywood Aberdeen 293 B10
Chapel on Leader Borders 271 G11
Chapel Outon Dumfries 236 E6
Chapel Plaister Wilts 61 F10
Chapel Row E Sus 23 C10
Chapel Row Essex 88 E3
Chapel Row W Berks 64 F5
Chapel St Leonards Lincs 191 G9
Chapel Stile Cumb 220 D6
Chapel Town Corn 5 D7
Chapelgate Lincs 157 E8
Chapelhall N Lnrk 268 C5
Chapelhill Dumfries 248 E3
Chapelhill Highld 301 B8
Chapelhill N Ayrs 266 G4
Chapelhill Perth 286 D4
Chapelhill Perth 286 E3
Chapelhill Perth 286 E6
Chapelknowe Dumfries 239 C8
Chapels Blkburn 195 C7
Chapels Cumb 210 C4
Chapelthorpe W Yorks 197 D10
Chapelton Angus 287 C10
Chapelton Devon 25 B9
Chapelton Highld 291 B11
Chapelton S Lnrk 268 F3
Chapelton Row Dumfries 237 E8
Chapeltown Blkburn 195 D8
Chapeltown Moray 302 G2
Chapeltown S Yorks 186 B5
Chapeltown W Yorks 206 F2
Chapman's Hill Worcs 117 B9
Chapman's Town E Sus 23 B10
Chapmans Well Devon 12 C3
Chapmanslade Wilts 45 D10
Chapmore End Herts 86 B4
Chappel Essex 107 F7
Charaton Cross Corn 6 B6
Charcott Kent 52 D4
Chard Som 28 F4
Chard Junction Dorset 28 G4
Chardleigh Green Som 28 E4
Chardstock Devon 28 G4
Charfield S Glos 80 G2
Charfield Green S Glos 80 G2
Charfield Hill S Glos 80 G2
Charford Worcs 117 D9
Chargrove Glos 80 B6
Charing Kent 54 D3
Charing Cross Dorset 31 E10
Charing Heath Kent 54 D2
Charing Hill Kent 54 C3
Charingworth Glos 100 D4
Charlbury Oxon 82 B5
Charlcombe Bath 61 F8
Charlcutt Wilts 62 D3
Charlecote Warks 118 F5
Charlemont W Mid 133 E10
Charles Devon 41 G7
Charles Bottom Devon 41 G7
Charles Tye Suff 125 G10
Charlesfield Borders 262 D3
Charlesfield Dumfries 238 D5
Charleshill Sur 49 E11
Charleston Angus 287 C7
Charleston Renfs 267 C9
Charlestown Aberdeen 293 C11
Charlestown Corn 5 E10
Charlestown Derbys 185 C8
Charlestown Dorset 17 F9
Charlestown Fife 279 E11
Charlestown Gtr Man 195 G10
Charlestown Gtr Man 195 G11
Charlestown Highld 299 B8
Charlestown Highld 300 E6
Charlestown W Yorks 196 B3
Charlestown W Yorks 205 F9
Charlestown of Aberlour Moray 302 E2
Charlesworth Derbys 185 C8
Charleton Devon 8 G5
Charlinch Som 43 F8
Charlottetown Fife 286 F6
Charlton Hants 47 D11
Charlton Herts 104 F3
Charlton London 68 D2
Charlton Northants 101 D10
Charlton Northumb 251 F8
Charlton Oxon 64 B2
Charlton Redcar 226 B2
Charlton Som 28 B3
Charlton Som 44 E6
Charlton Som 45 C7
Charlton Sur 66 F5
Charlton Telford 149 G11
Charlton W Sus 34 E5
Charlton Wilts 30 C6
Charlton Wilts 46 B6
Charlton Wilts 62 B3
Charlton Worcs 99 B10
Charlton Worcs 116 C6
Charlton Abbots Glos 99 G10
Charlton Adam Som 29 B8
Charlton-All-Saints Wilts 31 C11
Charlton Down Dorset 17 C9
Charlton Horethorne Som 29 C11
Charlton Kings Glos 99 G9
Charlton Mackrell Som 29 B8
Charlton Marshall Dorset 30 G5
Charlton Musgrove Som 30 B2
Charlton on Otmoor Oxon 83 B9
Charlton on the Hill Dorset 30 G5
Charlton Park Glos 99 G9
Charlton St Peter Wilts 46 B6
Charltonbrook S Yorks 186 B4
Charlwood E Sus 51 G11
Charlwood Hants 49 G7
Charlwood Sur 51 E8
Charlynch Som 43 F8
Charminster Bmouth 19 C8
Charminster Dorset 17 C9
Charmouth Dorset 16 C3
Charnage Wilts 45 G10
Charndon Bucks 102 G3
Charnes Staffs 150 C5
Charney Bassett Oxon 82 G5
Charnock Green Lancs 194 D5
Charnock Hall S Yorks 186 E5
Charnock Richard Lancs 194 D5
Charsfield Suff 126 F5
Chart Corner Kent 53 C9
Chart Hill Kent 53 D9
Chart Sutton Kent 53 D10
Charter Alley Hants 48 B5
Charterhouse Som 44 B3
Chartershall Stirl 278 C6
Charterville Allotments Oxon 82 C4
Chartham Kent 54 C6
Chartham Hatch Kent 54 B6
Chartridge Bucks 84 E6
Charvil Wokingham 65 D9
Charwelton Northants 119 F10
Chase Cross London 87 G8
Chase End Street Worcs 98 D5
Chase Hill S Glos 61 B8
Chase Terrace Staffs 133 B10
Chasetown Staffs 133 B10
Chastleton Oxon 100 F4
Chasty Devon 24 G4
Chat Hill W Yorks 205 G8
Chatburn Lancs 203 E11
Chatcull Staffs 150 C5
Chatford Shrops 131 B9
Chatham Caerph 59 B8
Chatham Medway 69 F9
Chatham Green Essex 88 B2
Chathill Northumb 264 D5
Chatley Worcs 117 E7
Chattenden Medway 69 E9
Chatter End Essex 105 F9
Chatteris Cambs 139 F7
Chatterley Staffs 168 E4
Chattern Hill Sur 66 E5
Chatterton Lancs 195 D9
Chattisham Suff 107 C11
Chattle Hill Warks 134 E3
Chatto Borders 263 F7
Chatton Northumb 264 D3
Chaul End C Beds 103 G11
Chaulden Herts 85 D8
Chavel Shrops 149 G8
Chavenage Green Glos 80 F5
Chavey Down Brack 65 F11
Chawleigh Devon 26 E2
Chawley Oxon 83 E7
Chawson Worcs 117 E7
Chawston Beds 122 F3
Chawton Hants 49 F8
Chaxhill Glos 80 C2
Chazey Heath Oxon 65 D7
Cheadle Gtr Man 184 D5
Cheadle Staffs 169 G8
Cheadle Heath Gtr Man 184 D5
Cheadle Hulme Gtr Man 184 D5
Cheadle Park Staffs 169 G8
Cheam London 67 G8
Cheapside Herts 105 E8
Cheapside Sur 50 B4
Cheapside Windsor 66 F2
Chearsley Bucks 84 C2
Chebsey Staffs 151 D7
Checkendon Oxon 65 C7
Checkley E Ches 168 F2
Checkley Hereford 97 D11
Checkley Staffs 151 B11
Checkley Green E Ches 168 F2
Chedburgh Suff 124 F5
Cheddar Som 44 C3
Cheddington Bucks 84 B6
Cheddleton Staffs 169 E7
Cheddleton Heath Staffs 169 E7
Cheddon Fitzpaine Som 28 B2
Chedglow Wilts 80 G6
Chedgrave Norf 143 D7
Chedington Dorset 29 F7
Chediston Suff 127 B7
Chediston Green Suff 127 B7
Chedworth Glos 81 C9
Chedworth Laines Glos 81 C8
Chedzoy Som 43 F10
Cheeklaw Borders 272 E5
Cheeseman's Green Kent 54 F4
Cheetam Hill Gtr Man 195 G10
Cheglinch Devon 40 E4
Chegworth Kent 53 C10
Cheldon Devon 26 E2
Chelfham Devon 40 F6
Chelford E Ches 184 G4
Chell Heath Stoke 168 E5
Chellaston Derby 153 C7
Chells Herts 104 F5
Chelmarsh Shrops 132 F4
Chelmer Village Essex 88 D2
Chelmick Shrops 131 E9
Chelmondiston Suff 108 D4
Chelmorton Derbys 169 B10
Chelmsford Essex 88 D2
Chelmsine Som 27 D11
Chelmsley Wood W Mid 134 F3
Chelsea London 67 D9
Chelsfield London 68 G3
Chelsham Sur 51 B11
Chelston Som 27 C11
Chelston Torbay 9 C7
Chelston Heathfield Som 27 C11
Chelsworth Suff 107 B9
Chelsworth Common Suff 107 B9
Cheltenham Glos 99 G8
Chelveston Northants 121 D9
Chelvey N Som 60 F3
Chelvey Batch N Som 60 F3
Chelwood Bath 60 G6
Chelwood Common E Sus 36 B6
Chelwood Gate E Sus 36 B6
Chelworth Wilts 81 G7
Chelworth Lower Green Wilts 81 G9
Chelworth Upper Green Wilts 81 G9
Chelynch Som 45 E7
Chemistry Shrops 167 G8
Cheney Longville Shrops 131 G8
Chenhalls Corn 2 B3
Chenies Bucks 85 F8
Cheny Longville Shrops 131 G8
Chepstow Mon 79 G8
Chequerbent Gtr Man 195 F7
Chequerfield W Yorks 198 C3
Chequers Corner Norf 139 B9
Chequertree Kent 54 F4
Cherhill Wilts 62 E4
Cherington Glos 80 F6
Cherington Warks 100 D5
Cheristow Devon 24 B3
Cheriton Devon 41 D8
Cheriton Hants 33 B9
Cheriton Kent 55 F7
Cheriton Swansea 56 C3
Cheriton Bishop Devon 13 C11
Cheriton Cross Devon 13 C11
Cheriton Fitzpaine Devon 26 F5
Cheriton or Stackpole Elidor Pembs 73 F7
Cherrington Telford 150 E3
Cherry Burton E Yorks 208 E5
Cherry Green Essex 105 F11
Cherry Green Herts 105 F7
Cherry Hinton Cambs 123 F9
Cherry Orchard Shrops 149 G9
Cherry Orchard Worcs 117 G7
Cherry Tree Blkburn 195 B7
Cherry Tree Gtr Man 185 C7
Cherry Willingham Lincs 189 G8
Cherrybank Perth 286 E5
Cherrytree Hill Derby 153 B7
Chertsey Sur 66 F4
Chertsey Meads Sur 66 F5
Cheselbourne Dorset 17 B11
Chesham Bucks 85 E7
Chesham Gtr Man 195 E10
Chesham Bois Bucks 85 F7
Cheshunt Herts 86 E5
Chesley Kent 69 G11
Cheslyn Hay Staffs 133 B9
Chessetts Wood Warks 118 C3
Chessington London 67 G7
Chessmount Bucks 85 E7
Chestall Staffs 151 G11
Chester W Ches 166 B6
Chester-le-Street Durham 243 G7
Chester Moor Durham 233 B11
Chesterblade Som 45 E7
Chesterfield Derbys 186 G5
Chesterfield Staffs 134 B2
Chesterhill Midloth 271 B7
Chesterhope Northumb 251 F9
Chesterknowes Borders 262 D2
Chesters Borders 262 E4
Chesters Borders 262 G4
Chesterton Cambs 123 E9
Chesterton Cambs 138 D2
Chesterton Glos 81 E8
Chesterton Oxon 101 G11
Chesterton Shrops 132 D5
Chesterton Staffs 168 F4
Chesterton Warks 118 F6
Chesterton Green Warks 118 F6
Chesterwood Northumb 241 D8
Chestfield Kent 70 F6
Chestnut Hill Cumb 229 G11
Chestnut Street Kent 69 G11
Cheston Devon 8 D3
Cheswardine Shrops 150 D4
Cheswell Telford 150 F4
Cheswick Northumb 273 F10
Cheswick Buildings Northumb 273 F10
Cheswick Green W Mid 118 B2
Chetnole Dorset 29 F10
Chettiscombe Devon 27 E7
Chettisham Cambs 139 G10
Chettle Dorset 31 E7
Chetton Shrops 132 E3
Chetwode Bucks 102 F2
Chetwynd Aston Telford 150 F5
Cheveley Cambs 124 E3
Chevening Kent 52 B3
Cheverell's Green Herts 85 B9
Chevin End W Yorks 205 E9
Chevington Suff 124 F5
Chevithorne Devon 27 D7
Chew Magna Bath 60 G5
Chew Moor Gtr Man 195 F7
Chew Stoke Bath 60 G5
Chewton Keynsham Bath 61 F7
Chewton Mendip Som 44 C5
Cheylesmore W Mid 118 B6
Chichacott Devon 13 B8
Chicheley M Keynes 103 B8
Chichester W Sus 22 C5
Chickenley W Yorks 197 C9
Chickerell Dorset 17 E8
Chicklade Wilts 46 G2
Chickney Essex 105 F11
Chicksands C Beds 104 D2
Chicksgrove Wilts 46 G3
Chickward Hereford 114 G5
Chidden Hants 33 D11
Chiddingfold Sur 50 F3
Chiddingly E Sus 23 C8
Chiddingstone Kent 52 D3
Chiddingstone Causeway Kent 52 D4
Chiddingstone Hoath Kent 52 E3
Chideock Dorset 16 C4
Chidgley Som 42 F4
Chidham W Sus 22 C3
Chidswell W Yorks 197 C9
Chieveley W Berks 64 E3
Chignall St James Essex 87 D11
Chignall Smealy Essex 87 C11
Chigwell Essex 86 G6
Chigwell Row Essex 87 G7
Chilbolton Hants 47 F11
Chilbolton Down Hants 48 F2
Chilbridge Dorset 31 G7
Chilcomb Hants 33 B8
Chilcombe Dorset 16 C6
Chilcombe Som 42 F6
Chilcompton Som 44 C6
Chilcote Leics 152 G5
Child Okeford Dorset 30 E4
Childer Thornton W Ches 182 F5
Childerditch Essex 68 B6
Childerley Gate Cambs 123 F7
Childrey Oxon 63 B11
Child's Ercall Shrops 150 E3
Child's Hill London 67 B8
Childsbridge Kent 52 B5
Childswickham Worcs 99 D11
Childwall Mers 182 D6
Childwick Bury Herts 85 C10
Childwick Green Herts 85 C10
Chilfrome Dorset 17 B7
Chilgrove W Sus 34 E4
Chilham Kent 54 C5
Chilhampton Wilts 46 G5
Chilla Devon 24 G6
Chillaton Devon 12 E4
Chillenden Kent 55 C9
Chillerton I o W 20 E5
Chillesford Suff 127 G7
Chillingham Northumb 264 D3
Chillington Devon 8 G5
Chillington Som 28 E5
Chillmill Kent 53 E7
Chilmark Wilts 46 G3
Chilmington Green Kent 54 E3
Chilsham E Sus 23 C10
Chilson Oxon 82 B4
Chilson Som 28 G4
Chilson Common Som 28 G4
Chilsworthy Corn 12 G4
Chilsworthy Devon 24 F4
Chiltern Green Beds 85 B10
Chilthorne Domer Som 29 D8
Chiltington E Sus 36 D5
Chilton Bucks 83 C11
Chilton Durham 233 F11
Chilton Kent 71 G11
Chilton Oxon 64 B3
Chilton Suff 107 C7
Chilton Candover Hants 48 E5
Chilton Cantelo Som 29 C9
Chilton Foliat Wilts 63 E10
Chilton Lane Durham 234 E2
Chilton Moor T & W 234 B2
Chilton Polden Som 43 F11
Chilton Street Suff 106 B5
Chilton Trinity Som 43 F9
Chilvers Coton Warks 135 E7
Chilwell Notts 153 B10
Chilworth Hants 32 D6
Chilworth Sur 50 D4
Chilworth Old Village Hants 32 D6
Chimney Oxon 82 E5
Chimney-end Oxon 82 B4
Chimney Street Suff 106 B4
Chineham Hants 49 C7
Chingford London 86 G5
Chingford Green London 86 G5
Chingford Hatch London 86 G5
Chinley Derbys 185 E8
Chinley Head Derbys 185 E9
Chinnor Oxon 84 E3
Chipley Som 27 C10
Chipmans Platt Glos 80 D3
Chipnall Shrops 150 C4
Chippenhall Green Suff 126 B5
Chippenham Cambs 124 D3
Chippenham Wilts 62 E2
Chipperfield Herts 85 E8
Chipping Herts 105 E7
Chipping Lancs 203 E8
Chipping Barnet London 86 F2
Chipping Campden Glos 100 D3
Chipping Hill Essex 88 B4
Chipping Norton Oxon 100 F6
Chipping Ongar Essex 87 E8
Chipping Sodbury S Glos 61 C8
Chipping Warden Northants 101 B9
Chipstable Som 27 B8
Chipstead Kent 52 B3
Chipstead Sur 51 B9
Chirbury Shrops 130 D5
Chirk = Y Waun Wrex 148 B5
Chirk Bank Shrops 148 B5
Chirk Green Wrex 148 B5
Chirmorrie S Ayrs 236 B4
Chirnside Borders 273 D7
Chirnsidebridge Borders 273 D7
Chirton T & W 243 D8
Chirton Wilts 46 B5
Chisbridge Cross Bucks 65 B10
Chisbury Wilts 63 F9
Chiselborough Som 29 E7
Chiseldon Swindon 63 D7
Chiserley W Yorks 196 B4
Chislehampton Oxon 83 F9
Chislehurst London 68 E2
Chislehurst West London 68 E2
Chislet Kent 71 G8
Chislet Forstal Kent 71 G8
Chiswell Dorset 17 G9
Chiswell Green Herts 85 E10
Chiswick London 67 D8
Chiswick End Cambs 105 B7
Chisworth Derbys 185 C7
Chitcombe E Sus 38 C4
Chithurst W Sus 34 C4
Chittering Cambs 123 C9
Chitterley Devon 26 G6
Chitterne Wilts 46 E3
Chittlehamholt Devon 25 C11
Chittlehampton Devon 25 B10
Chittoe Wilts 62 F3
Chitts Hills Essex 107 F9
Chitty Kent 71 G8
Chivelstone Devon 9 G10
Chivenor Devon 40 G4
Chivery Bucks 84 D6
Chobham Sur 66 G3
Choicelee Borders 272 E4
Cholderton Wilts 47 E8
Cholesbury Bucks 84 D6
Chollerford Northumb 241 C10
Chollerton Northumb 241 C10
Cholmondeston E Ches 167 C10
Cholsey Oxon 64 B5
Cholstrey Hereford 115 F9
Cholwell Bath 44 B6
Chop Gate N Yorks 225 F11
Choppington Northumb 253 G7
Chopwell T & W 242 F4
Chorley E Ches 167 E9
Chorley Lancs 194 D5
Chorley Shrops 132 G3
Chorley Staffs 151 G11
Chorley Common W Sus 34 B4
Chorleywood Herts 85 F8
Chorleywood Bottom Herts 85 F8
Chorleywood West Herts 85 F8
Chorlton E Ches 168 E2
Chorlton-cum-Hardy Gtr Man 184 C4
Chorlton Lane W Ches 167 F7
Choulton Shrops 131 F7
Chowdene T & W 243 F7
Chowley W Ches 167 D7
Chownes Mead W Sus 36 C4
Chreagain Highld 289 C10
Chrishall Essex 105 D8
Christchurch Cambs 139 D9
Christchurch Dorset 19 C9
Christchurch Glos 79 C9
Christchurch Newport 59 B10
Christian Malford Wilts 62 D3
Christleton W Ches 166 B6
Christmas Common Oxon 84 G2
Christon N Som 43 B11
Christon Bank Northumb 264 E6
Christow Devon 14 D2
Chryston N Lnrk 278 G3
Chub Tor Devon 7 B10
Chuck Hatch E Sus 52 G3
Chudleigh Devon 14 F3
Chudleigh Knighton Devon 14 F2
Chulmleigh Devon 25 E11

Chunal Derbys 185 C8
Church Lancs 195 B8
Church Aston Telford 150 F4
Church Brampton Northants 120 D4
Church Brough Cumb 222 C5
Church Broughton Derbys 152 C4
Church Charwelton Northants 119 F10
Church Clough Lancs 204 F3
Church Common Hants 34 B2
Church Coombe Corn 4 G3
Church Cove Corn 2 G6
Church Crookham Hants 49 C10
Church Eaton Staffs 150 F6
Church End Barnet 86 G2
Church End Beds 122 F2
Church End Bucks 84 B6
Church End Bucks 84 D2
Church End Brent 67 C8
Church End C Beds 85 B8
Church End C Beds 103 E9
Church End C Beds 103 G9
Church End C Beds 104 D3
Church End C Beds 122 G3
Church End Cambs 121 C11
Church End Cambs 123 C7
Church End Cambs 123 D7
Church End Cambs 138 G4
Church End Cambs 139 B7
Church End E Yorks 209 C7
Church End Essex 88 B2
Church End Essex 105 C11
Church End Essex 105 F11
Church End Essex 106 F4
Church End Glos 80 D2
Church End Glos 99 D7
Church End Hants 49 B7
Church End Herts 85 C10
Church End Herts 85 F8
Church End Herts 104 E5
Church End Herts 105 G8
Church End Lincs 156 C4
Church End Lincs 190 B6
Church End Norf 157 F10
Church End Oxon 82 D5
Church End Oxon 100 E6
Church End Suff 108 D4
Church End Sur 50 B5
Church End W Mid 119 B7
Church End Warks 134 E4
Church End Warks 134 E5
Church End Wilts 62 D4
Church End Worcs 98 C6
Church Enstone Oxon 101 G7
Church Fenton N Yorks 206 F6
Church Green Devon 15 B9
Church Green Norf 141 E11
Church Gresley Derbys 152 F5
Church Hanborough Oxon 82 C6
Church Hill Pembs 73 C7
Church Hill Staffs 151 G10
Church Hill W Ches 167 C10
Church Hill W Mid 133 D9
Church Hill Worcs 117 D11
Church Hougham Kent 55 E9
Church Houses N Yorks 226 F3
Church Knowle Dorset 18 E4
Church Laneham Notts 188 F4
Church Langton Leics 136 E4
Church Lawford Warks 119 B8
Church Lawton E Ches 168 D4
Church Leigh Staffs 151 B10
Church Lench Worcs 117 G10
Church Mayfield Staffs 169 G11
Church Minshull E Ches 167 C11
Church Norton W Sus 22 D5
Church Oakley Hants 48 C5
Church Preen Shrops 131 D10
Church Pulverbatch Shrops 131 C8
Church Stowe Northants 120 F2
Church Street Essex 106 C5
Church Street Kent 69 E8
Church Stretton Shrops 131 E9
Church Town Corn 4 G3
Church Town Leics 153 F7
Church Town N Lincs 199 F9
Church Town Sur 51 C11
Church Village Rhondda 58 B5
Church Warsop Notts 171 B9
Church Westcote Glos 100 G4
Church Whitfield Kent 55 D10
Church Wilne Derbys 153 C8
Churcham Glos 80 B3
Churchbank Shrops 114 B6
Churchbridge Corn 6 D4
Churchbridge Staffs 133 B9
Churchdown Glos 80 B5
Churchend Essex 89 G8
Churchend Essex 106 G2
Churchend Glos 80 D3
Churchend Reading 65 E7
Churchend S Glos 80 G2
Churches Green E Sus 23 B10
Churchfield Hereford 98 B4
Churchfield W Mid 133 E10
Churchfields Wilts 31 B10
Churchgate Herts 86 E4
Churchgate Street Essex 87 C7
Churchill Devon 28 G4
Churchill Devon 40 E5
Churchill N Som 44 B2
Churchill Oxon 100 G5
Churchill Worcs 117 B7
Churchill Worcs 117 G8
Churchill Green N Som 60 G2
Churchinford Som 28 E2
Churchmoor Rough Shrops 131 F8
Churchover Warks 135 G10
Churchstanton Som 27 E11
Churchstoke Powys 130 E5
Churchstow Devon 8 F4
Churchtown Pembs 73 D10
Churchtown Corn 11 F7
Churchtown Cumb 230 C3
Churchtown Derbys 170 C3
Churchtown Devon 24 G3
Churchtown Devon 41 E7
Churchtown I o M 192 C5
Churchtown Lancs 202 E5
Churchtown Mers 193 D11
Churchtown Shrops 130 F5
Churchtown Som 42 F3
Churchwood W Sus 35 D8
Churnet Grange Staffs 169 E7
Churnsike Lodge Northumb 240 B5
Churscombe Torbay 9 C7
Churston Ferrers Torbay 9 D8
Churt Sur 49 F11
Churton W Ches 166 D6
Churwell W Yorks 197 B9
Chute Cadley Wilts 47 C10
Chute Standen Wilts 47 C10
Chwefforfdd Conwy 180 G4
Chwilog Gwyn 145 B8
Chwitffordd = Whitford Flint 181 F10
Chyandour Corn 1 C5
Chyanvounder Corn 2 E5
Chycoose Corn 3 B8
Chynhale Corn 2 C4
Chynoweth Corn 2 C2
Chyvarloe Corn 2 E5
Cicelyford Mon 79 E8
Cil y coed = Caldicot Mon 60 B3
Cilan Uchaf Gwyn 144 E5
Cilau Pembs 91 D8
Cilcain Flint 165 B11
Cilcennin Ceredig 111 E10
Cilcewydd Powys 130 C4
Cilfor Gwyn 146 B2
Cilfrew Neath 76 E3
Cilfynydd Rhondda 77 G9
Cilgerran Pembs 92 C3
Cilgwyn Carms 94 F4
Cilgwyn Ceredig 92 C6
Cilgwyn Gwyn 163 E7
Cilgwyn Pembs 91 D11
Ciliau Aeron Ceredig 111 F9
Cill Amhlaidh W Isles 297 G3
Cill Donnain W Isles 297 J3
Cill Eireabhagh W Isles 297 G4
Cille Bhrighde W Isles 297 K3
Cille Pheadair W Isles 297 K3
Cilmaengwyn Neath 76 D2
Cilmery Powys 113 G10
Cilsan Carms 93 G11
Ciltalgarth Gwyn 164 G5
Ciltwrch Powys 96 C3
Cilybebyll Neath 76 E2
Cilycwm Carms 94 D5
Cimla Neath 57 B9
Cinder Hill Gtr Man 195 F9
Cinder Hill Kent 52 D4
Cinder Hill W Mid 133 E8
Cinder Hill W Sus 36 B5
Cinderford Glos 79 C11
Cinderhill Derbys 170 F5
Cinderhill Nottingham 171 G8
Cinnamon Brow Warr 183 C10
Cippenham Slough 66 C2
Cippyn Pembs 92 B2
Circebost W Isles 304 E3
Cirencester Glos 81 E8
Ciribhig W Isles 304 D3
City London 67 C10
City Powys 130 F4
City V Glam 58 D3
City Dulas Anglesey 179 D7
Clabhach Argyll 288 D3
Clachaig Argyll 276 E2
Clachaig Highld 292 B2
Clachaig N Ayrs 255 E10
Clachan Argyll 255 B8
Clachan Argyll 275 B8
Clachan Argyll 284 F5
Clachan Argyll 289 E10
Clachan Highld 295 B7
Clachan Highld 298 C4
Clachan Highld 307 L6
Clachan W Isles 297 G3
Clachan na Luib W Isles 296 E4
Clachan of Campsie E Dunb 278 F2
Clachan of Glendaruel Argyll 275 E10
Clachan-Seil Argyll 275 B8
Clachan Strachur Argyll 284 G4
Clachaneasy Dumfries 236 B5
Clachanmore Dumfries 236 E2
Clachbreck Argyll 275 F8
Clachnabrain Angus 292 G5
Clachtoll Highld 307 G5
Clackmannan Clack 279 C8
Clackmarras Moray 302 D2
Clacton-on-Sea Essex 89 B11
Cladach N Ayrs 256 B2
Cladach Chairinis W Isles 296 F4
Cladach Chireboist W Isles 296 E3
Claddach Argyll 254 B2
Claddach-knockline W Isles 296 E3
Cladich Argyll 284 E4
Cladich Steading Argyll 284 E4
Cladswell Worcs 117 F10
Claggan Highld 289 E8
Claggan Highld 290 F3
Claggan Perth 285 D11
Claigan Highld 298 D2
Claines Worcs 117 F7
Clandown Bath 45 B7
Clanfield Hants 33 D11
Clanfield Oxon 82 E3
Clanking Bucks 84 D4
Clanville Hants 47 D10
Clanville Som 44 G6
Clanville Wilts 62 D2
Claonaig Argyll 255 B9
Claonel Highld 309 J5
Clap Hill Kent 54 F5
Clapgate Dorset 31 G8
Clapgate Herts 105 G8
Clapham Beds 121 G10
Clapham Devon 14 D3
Clapham London 67 D9
Clapham N Yorks 212 F4
Clapham W Sus 35 F9
Clapham Green Beds 121 G10
Clapham Green N Yorks 205 B10
Clapham Hill Kent 70 G6
Clapham Park London 67 E9
Clapper Corn 10 G6
Clapper Hill Kent 53 F10
Clappers Borders 273 D8
Clappersgate Cumb 221 E7
Clapphoull Shetland 313 L6
Clapton Som 28 F6
Clapton Som 44 C6
Clapton W Berks 63 E11
Clapton in Gordano N Som 60 E3
Clapton-on-the-Hill Glos 81 B11
Clapton Park London 67 B11
Clapworthy Devon 25 C11
Clara Vale T & W 242 E4
Clarach Ceredig 128 G2
Clarack Aberds 292 D6
Clarbeston Pembs 91 G10
Clarbeston Road Pembs 91 G10
Clarborough Notts 188 E2
Clardon Highld 310 C5
Clare Oxon 83 F11
Clare Suff 106 B5
Clarebrand Dumfries 237 C9
Claregate W Mid 133 C7
Claremont Park Sur 66 G6
Claremount W Yorks 196 B5
Clarence Park N Som 59 G10
Clarencefield Dumfries 238 D3
Clarendon Park Leicester 135 C11
Clareston Pembs 73 C7
Clarilaw Borders 262 D3
Clarilaw Borders 262 F2
Clark Green E Ches 184 F6
Clarken Green Hants 48 C5
Clark's Green Sur 51 F7
Clark's Hill Lincs 157 E7
Clarksfield Gtr Man 196 G2
Clarkston E Renf 267 D11
Clarkston N Lnrk 268 B5
Clase Swansea 57 B7
Clashandorran Highld 300 E5
Clashcoig Highld 309 K6
Clasheddy Highld 308 C6
Clashgour Argyll 284 C6
Clashindarroch Aberds 302 F4
Clashmore Highld 306 F5
Clashmore Highld 309 L7
Clashnessie Highld 306 F5
Clashnoir Moray 302 G2
Clate Shetland 313 G7
Clatford Wilts 63 F7
Clatford Oakcuts Hants 47 F10
Clathy Perth 286 F3
Clatt Aberds 302 G5
Clatter Powys 129 E9
Clatterford I o W 20 D5
Clatterford End Essex 87 C10
Clatterford End Essex 87 D9
Clatterford End Essex 87 E8
Clatterin Bridge Aberds 293 F8
Clatto Fife 287 F8
Clatworthy Som 42 G5
Claughlands N Ayrs 256 C2
Claughton Lancs 202 E6
Claughton Lancs 211 F11
Claughton Mers 182 D4
Clavelshay Som 43 G9
Claverdon Warks 118 E3
Claverham N Som 60 F2
Claverhambury Essex 86 E6
Clavering Essex 105 E9
Claverley Shrops 132 E5
Claverton Bath 61 G9
Claverton Down Bath 61 G9
Clawdd-côch V Glam 58 D5
Clawdd-newydd Denb 165 E9
Clawdd Poncen Denb 165 G9
Clawthorpe Cumb 211 D10
Clawton Devon 12 B3
Claxby Lincs 189 C10
Claxby Lincs 191 G7
Claxby St Andrew Lincs 191 G7
Claxton N Yorks 216 G3
Claxton Norf 142 C6
Clay Common Suff 143 G9
Clay Coton Northants 119 B11
Clay Cross Derbys 170 C5
Clay End Herts 104 F6
Clay Hill Bristol 60 E6
Clay Hill London 86 F4
Clay Hill W Berks 64 E5
Clay Lake Lincs 156 E5
Clay Mills Derbys 152 D5
Claybokie Aberds 292 D2
Claybrooke Magna Leics 135 F9
Claybrooke Parva Leics 135 F9
Claydon Glos 99 E8
Claydon Oxon 119 G9
Claydon Suff 126 G2
Claygate Dumfries 239 B9
Claygate Kent 52 C6
Claygate Kent 53 E8
Claygate Sur 67 G7
Claygate Cross Kent 52 B6
Clayhall Hants 21 B8
Clayhall London 86 G6
Clayhanger Devon 27 C8
Clayhanger Som 28 E4
Clayhanger W Mid 133 C10
Clayhidon Devon 27 D11
Clayhill E Sus 38 C4
Clayhill Hants 32 F4
Clayhithe Cambs 123 E10
Clayholes Angus 287 D9
Clayland Stirl 277 D11
Claylock Highld 310 D5
Claypit Hill Cambs 123 G7
Claypits Devon 27 B7
Claypits Glos 80 D3
Claypits Kent 55 B9
Claypits Suff 140 G4
Claypole Lincs 172 F5
Clays End Bath 61 G8
Claythorpe Lincs 190 F6
Clayton Gtr Man 184 B5
Clayton S Yorks 198 F3
Clayton Staffs 168 G5
Clayton W Sus 36 E3
Clayton W Yorks 205 G8
Clayton Brook Lancs 194 C5
Clayton Green Lancs 194 C5
Clayton Heights W Yorks 205 G8
Clayton-le-Dale Lancs 203 G9
Clayton-le-Moors Lancs 203 G10
Clayton-le-Woods Lancs 194 C5
Clayton West W Yorks 197 E9
Clayworth Notts 188 D2
Cleadale Highld 294 G6
Cleadon T & W 243 E9
Cleadon Park T & W 243 E9
Clearbrook Devon 7 B10
Clearwell Glos 79 D9
Clearwell Newport 59 B9
Clearwood Wilts 45 D10
Cleasby N Yorks 224 C5
Cleat Orkney 314 B4
Cleat Orkney 314 H4
Cleatlam Durham 224 B2
Cleator Cumb 219 C10
Cleator Moor Cumb 219 B10
Cleave Devon 28 G2
Clebrig Highld 308 F5
Cleckheaton W Yorks 197 B7
Cleddon Mon 79 E8
Clee St Margaret Shrops 131 G11
Cleedownton Shrops 131 G11
Cleehill Shrops 115 B11
Cleekhimin N Lnrk 268 D5
Cleemarsh Shrops 131 G11
Cleestanton Shrops 115 B11
Cleethorpes NE Lincs 201 F10
Cleeton St Mary Shrops 116 B2
Cleeve Glos 80 C2
Cleeve N Som 60 F3
Cleeve Oxon 64 C6
Cleeve Hill Glos 99 F9
Cleeve Prior Worcs 99 B11
Cleghorn S Lnrk 269 F8
Clegyrnant Powys 129 B8
Clehonger Hereford 97 D9
Cleirwy = Clyro Powys 96 C4
Cleish Perth 279 B11
Cleland N Lnrk 268 D5
Clement Street Kent 68 E4
Clement's End C Beds 85 B8
Clements End Glos 79 D9
Clench Wilts 63 G7
Clench Common Wilts 63 F7
Clencher's Mill Hereford 98 D4
Clenchwarton Norf 157 E11
Clennell Northumb 251 B10
Clent Worcs 117 B8
Cleobury Mortimer Shrops 116 B3
Cleobury North Shrops 132 F2
Cleongart Argyll 255 D7
Clephanton Highld 301 D8
Clerk Green W Yorks 197 C8
Clerkenwater Corn 5 B11
Clerkenwell London 67 C10
Clerklands Borders 262 E2
Clermiston Edin 280 G3
Clestrain Orkney 314 F3
Cleuch Head Borders 262 G3
Cleughbrae Dumfries 238 C3
Clevancy Wilts 62 D5
Clevans Renfs 267 B7
Clevedon N Som 60 E2
Cleveley Oxon 101 G7
Cleveleys Lancs 202 E2
Cleverton Wilts 62 B3
Clevis Bridgend 57 F10
Clewer Som 44 C2
Clewer Green Windsor 66 D2
Clewer New Town Windsor 66 D3
Clewer Village Windsor 66 D3
Cley next the Sea Norf 177 E8
Cliaid W Isles 297 L2
Cliasmol W Isles 305 H2
Cliburn Cumb 231 G7
Click Mill Orkney 314 D3
Cliddesden Hants 48 D6
Cliff Derbys 185 D8
Cliff Warks 134 D4
Cliff End E Sus 38 E5
Cliff End W Yorks 196 D6
Cliffburn Angus 287 C10
Cliffe Lancs 203 G10
Cliffe Medway 69 D8
Cliffe N Yorks 207 G9
Cliffe N Yorks 224 B4
Cliffe Woods Medway 69 E8
Clifford Devon 24 C4
Clifford Hereford 96 B4
Clifford W Yorks 206 E4
Clifford Chambers Warks 118 G3
Clifford's Mesne Glos 98 G4
Cliffs End Kent 71 G10
Clifftown Sthend 69 B11
Clifton Bristol 60 E5
Clifton C Beds 104 D3
Clifton Cumb 230 F6
Clifton Derbys 169 G11
Clifton Devon 40 E5
Clifton Gtr Man 195 G9
Clifton Lancs 202 G5
Clifton N Yorks 205 D9
Clifton Northumb 252 G6
Clifton Nottingham 153 C11
Clifton Oxon 101 E9
Clifton S Yorks 186 C6
Clifton S Yorks 187 B8
Clifton Stirl 285 D7
Clifton W Ches 183 F8
Clifton W Yorks 197 C7
Clifton Worcs 98 B6
Clifton York 207 C7
Clifton Campville Staffs 152 G5
Clifton Green Gtr Man 195 G9
Clifton Hampden Oxon 83 F8
Clifton Junction Gtr Man 195 G9
Clifton Manor C Beds 104 D3
Clifton Maybank Dorset 29 E9
Clifton Moor York 207 B7
Clifton Reynes M Keynes 121 G8
Clifton upon Dunsmore Warks 119 B10
Clifton upon Teme Worcs 116 E4
Cliftoncote Borders 263 E8
Cliftonville Kent 71 E11
Cliftonville N Lnrk 268 B4
Cliftonville Norf 160 B6
Climping W Sus 35 G8
Climpy S Lnrk 269 D8
Clink Som 45 D9
Clinkham Wood Mers 183 B8
Clint N Yorks 205 B11
Clint Green Norf 159 G10
Clintmains Borders 262 C4
Clints N Yorks 224 E2
Cliobh W Isles 304 E2
Clipiau Gwyn 146 G6
Clippesby Norf 161 G8
Clippings Green Norf 159 G10
Clipsham Rutland 155 F9
Clipston Northants 136 G4
Clipston Notts 154 C2
Clipstone C Beds 103 F8
Clipstone Notts 171 C9
Clitheroe Lancs 203 E10
Cliuthar W Isles 305 J3
Clive Shrops 149 E10
Clive W Ches 167 B11
Clive Green W Ches 167 C11
Clive Vale E Sus 38 E4
Clivocast Shetland 312 C8
Clixby Lincs 200 G6
Cloatley Wilts 81 G7
Cloatley End Wilts 81 G7
Clocaenog Denb 165 E9
Clochan Aberds 303 E9
Clochan Moray 302 C4
Clock Face Mers 183 C8
Clock House London 67 G9
Clock Mills Hereford 96 B5
Clockmill Borders 272 E5
Cloddiau Powys 130 B4
Cloddymoss Moray 301 D9
Clodock Hereford 96 F6
Cloford Som 45 E8
Cloford Common Som 45 E8
Cloigyn Carms 74 C6
Clola Aberds 303 E10
Clophill C Beds 103 D11
Clopton Northants 137 G11
Clopton Suff 126 G4
Clopton Corner Suff 126 G4
Clopton Green Suff 124 G5
Clopton Green Suff 125 E9
Close Clark I o M 192 E3
Close House Durham 233 F10
Closeburn Dumfries 247 E9
Closworth Som 29 E9
Clothall Herts 104 E5
Clothall Common Herts 104 E5
Clotton W Ches 167 C8
Clotton Common W Ches 167 C8
Cloud Side Staffs 168 C6
Cloudesley Bush Warks 135 F9
Clouds Hereford 97 D11
Clough Gtr Man 196 D2
Clough Gtr Man 196 F2
Clough W Yorks 196 E5
Clough Dene Durham 242 F5
Clough Foot W Yorks 196 C2
Clough Hall Staffs 168 E4
Clough Head W Yorks 196 C5
Cloughfold Lancs 195 C10
Cloughton N Yorks 227 G10
Cloughton Newlands N Yorks 227 F10
Clounlaid Highld 289 D9
Clousta Shetland 313 H5
Clouston Orkney 314 E2
Clova Aberds 302 G4
Clova Angus 292 F5
Clove Lodge Durham 223 B8
Clovelly Devon 24 C4
Clovenfords Borders 261 B10
Clovenstone Aberds 293 B9
Cloves Moray 301 C11
Clovullin Highld 290 G2
Clow Bridge Lancs 195 B10
Clowance Wood Corn 2 C4
Clowne Derbys 187 F7
Clows Top Worcs 116 C4
Cloy Wrex 166 G5
Cluanie Inn Highld 290 B2
Cluanie Lodge Highld 290 B2
Clubmoor Mers 182 C5
Clubworthy Corn 11 C11
Cluddley Telford 150 G2
Clun Shrops 130 G6
Clunbury Shrops 131 G7
Clunderwen Carms 73 B10
Clune Highld 301 D9
Clune Highld 301 G7
Clunes Highld 290 E4
Clungunford Shrops 115 B7
Clunie Aberds 302 D6
Clunie Perth 286 C5
Clunton Shrops 130 G6
Cluny Fife 280 B4
Cluny Castle Aberds 293 B8
Cluny Castle Highld 291 D8
Clutton Bath 44 B6
Clutton W Ches 167 E7
Clutton Hill Bath 44 B6
Clwt-grugoer Conwy 165 C7
Clwt-y-bont Gwyn 163 C9
Clwydyfagwyr M Tydf 77 D8
Clydach Mon 78 C2
Clydach Swansea 75 E11
Clydach Terrace Powys 77 C11
Clydach Vale Rhondda 77 G7
Clydebank W Dunb 277 G9
Clyffe Pypard Wilts 62 D5
Clynder Argyll 276 E4
Clyne Neath 76 E4
Clynelish Highld 311 J2
Clynnog-fawr Gwyn 162 F6
Clyro = Cleirwy Powys 96 C4
Clyst Honiton Devon 14 C5
Clyst Hydon Devon 27 G8
Clyst St George Devon 14 D5
Clyst St Lawrence Devon 27 G8
Clyst St Mary Devon 14 C5
Cnip W Isles 304 E2
Cnoc Amhlaigh W Isles 304 E7
Cnoc an t-Solais W Isles 304 D6
Cnoc Fhionn Highld 295 D10
Cnoc Màiri W Isles 304 E6
Cnoc Rolum W Isles 296 F3
Cnocbreac Argyll 274 F5
Cnwch-coch Ceredig 112 B3
Coachford Aberds 302 E4
Coad's Green Corn 11 F11
Coal Aston Derbys 186 F5
Coal Bank Darl 234 G3
Coal Pool W Mid 133 C10
Coalbrookdale Telford 132 C3
Coalbrookvale Bl Gwent 77 D11
Coalburn S Lnrk 259 C8
Coalburns T & W 242 E4
Coalcleugh Northumb 232 B2
Coaley Glos 80 E3
Coaley Peak Glos 80 E3
Coalford Aberds 293 D10
Coalhall E Ayrs 257 F10
Coalhill Essex 88 F3
Coalmoor Telford 132 B3
Coalpit Field Warks 135 F7
Coalpit Heath S Glos 61 C7
Coalpit Hill Staffs 168 E4
Coalport Telford 132 C3
Coalsnaughton Clack 279 B8
Coaltown of Balgonie Fife 280 B5
Coaltown of Wemyss Fife 280 B6
Coalville Leics 153 G8
Coalway Glos 79 C9
Coanwood Northumb 240 F5
Coarsewell Devon 8 E4
Coat Som 29 C7
Coatbridge N Lnrk 268 C4
Coatdyke N Lnrk 268 B5
Coate Swindon 63 C7
Coate Wilts 62 G4
Coates Cambs 138 D6
Coates Glos 81 E7
Coates Lancs 204 D3
Coates Lincs 188 E6
Coates Midloth 270 C4
Coates Notts 188 E4
Coates W Sus 35 D7
Coatham Redcar 235 F7
Coatham Mundeville Darl 233 G11
Coatsgate Dumfries 248 B3
Cobairdy Aberds 302 E5
Cobbaton Devon 25 B10
Cobbler's Corner Worcs 116 F5
Cobbler's Green Norf 142 E5
Cobbler's Plain Mon 79 E7
Cobbs Warr 183 D10
Cobb's Cross Glos 98 E5
Cobbs Fenn Essex 106 E5
Cobby Syke N Yorks 205 B9
Coberley Glos 81 B7
Cobhall Common Hereford 97 D9
Cobham Kent 69 F7
Cobham Sur 66 G6
Cobleland Stirl 277 B10
Cobler's Green Essex 87 B11
Cobley Dorset 31 C8
Cobley Hill Worcs 117 C10
Cobnash Hereford 115 E9
Cobridge Stoke 168 F5
Cobscot Shrops 150 B3
Coburty Aberds 303 C9
Cock and End Suff 124 G4
Cock Alley Derbys 186 G6
Cock Bank Wrex 166 F5
Cock Bevington Warks 117 G11
Cock Bridge Aberds 292 C4
Cock Clarks Essex 88 E4
Cock Gate Hereford 115 D9
Cock Green Essex 87 B11
Cock Hill N Yorks 206 B6
Cock Marling E Sus 38 D5
Cock Street Kent 53 C9
Cock Street Suff 107 D9
Cockadilly Glos 80 E4
Cockayne N Yorks 226 F2
Cockburnspath Borders 282 G5
Cockden Lancs 204 G3
Cockenzie and Port Seton E Loth 281 F8
Cocker Bar Lancs 194 C4
Cockerham Lancs 202 C5
Cockermouth Cumb 229 E8
Cockernhoe Herts 104 G2
Cockernhoe Green Herts 104 G2
Cockersdale W Yorks 197 B8
Cockerton Darl 224 B5
Cockett Swansea 56 C6
Cocketty Aberds 293 F9
Cockfield Durham 233 G8
Cockfield Suff 125 G8
Cockfosters London 86 F3
Cockhill Som 44 G6
Cocking W Sus 34 D5
Cocking Causeway W Sus 34 D5
Cockington Torbay 9 C7
Cocklake Som 44 D2
Cocklaw Northumb 241 C10
Cockleford Glos 81 C7
Cockley Beck Cumb 220 E4
Cockley Cley Norf 140 C5
Cockley Hill W Yorks 197 D7
Cocknowle Dorset 18 E4
Cockpole Green Wokingham 65 C9
Cocks Corn 4 E5
Cocks Green Suff 125 F7
Cockshead Ceredig 112 F2
Cockshoot Hereford 97 D11
Cockshutford Shrops 131 F11
Cockshutt Shrops 132 G4
Cockshutt Shrops 149 D8
Cockthorpe Norf 177 E7
Cockwells Corn 2 C2
Cockwood Devon 14 E5
Cockwood Som 43 E8
Cockyard Derbys 185 F8
Cockyard Hereford 97 E8
Codda Corn 11 F9
Coddenham Suff 126 G2
Coddenham Green Suff 126 F2
Coddington Hereford 98 C4
Coddington Notts 172 E4
Coddington W Ches 167 D7
Codford St Mary Wilts 46 F3
Codford St Peter Wilts 46 F3
Codicote Herts 86 B2
Codicote Bottom Herts 86 B2
Codmore Bucks 85 E7
Codmore Hill W Sus 35 C9
Codnor Derbys 170 F6
Codnor Breach Derbys 170 F6
Codnor Gate Derbys 170 E6
Codnor Park Derbys 170 E6
Codrington S Glos 61 D8
Codsall Staffs 133 C7
Codsall Wood Staffs 132 B6
Codsend Som 41 F11
Coed Cwnwr Mon 78 F6
Coed Eva Torf 78 G3
Coed Llai = Leeswood Flint 166 D3
Coed Mawr Gwyn 179 G9
Coed Morgan Mon 78 C5
Coed-Talon Flint 166 D3
Coed-y-bryn Ceredig 93 C7
Coed-y-caerau Newport 78 G5
Coed-y-fedw Mon 78 D6
Coed y Garth Ceredig 128 E3
Coed y go Shrops 148 D5
Coed-y-paen Mon 78 F4
Coed-y-parc Gwyn 163 B10
Coed-y-wlad Powys 130 B4
Coed-yr-ynys Powys 96 G3
Coed Ystumgwern Gwyn 145 E11
Coedcae Bl Gwent 77 D11
Coedcae Torf 78 D3
Coedely Rhondda 58 B4
Coedkernew Newport 59 C9
Coedpoeth Wrex 166 E3
Coedway Powys 148 G6
Coelbren Powys 76 C4
Coffee Hall M Keynes 103 D7
Coffinswell Devon 9 B7
Cofton Devon 14 E5
Cofton Common W Mid 117 B10
Cofton Hackett Worcs 117 B10
Cog V Glam 59 F7
Cogan V Glam 59 E7
Cogenhoe Northants 120 E6
Cogges Oxon 82 D5
Coggeshall Essex 106 G6
Coggeshall Hamlet Essex 107 G7
Coggins Mill E Sus 37 B9
Coig Peighinnean W Isles 304 B7
Coig Peighinnean Bhuirgh W Isles 304 C6
Coignafearn Lodge Highld 291 B8
Coignascallan Highld 291 B9
Coilacriech Aberds 292 D5
Coilantogle Stirl 285 G9
Coilessan Argyll 284 G6
Coilleag W Isles 297 K3
Coillemore Highld 300 B6
Coillore Highld 294 B5
Coirea-chrombe Stirl 285 G9
Coisley Hill S Yorks 186 E6
Coity Bridgend 58 C2
Cokenach Herts 105 D7
Cokhay Green Derbys 152 D5
Col W Isles 304 D6
Col Uarach W Isles 304 E6
Colaboll Highld 309 H5
Colan Corn 5 C7
Colaton Raleigh Devon 15 D7
Colbost Highld 298 E2
Colburn N Yorks 224 F3
Colby Cumb 231 G9
Colby I o M 192 E3
Colby Norf 160 C4
Colchester Essex 107 F10
Colchester Green Suff 125 F8
Colcot V Glam 58 F6
Cold Ash W Berks 64 F4
Cold Ash Hill Hants 49 G10
Cold Ashby Northants 120 B3
Cold Ashton S Glos 61 E9
Cold Aston Glos 81 B10
Cold Blow Pembs 73 C10
Cold Brayfield M Keynes 121 G8
Cold Christmas Herts 86 B5
Cold Cotes N Yorks 212 E4
Cold Elm Glos 98 E6
Cold Hanworth Lincs 189 E8
Cold Harbour Dorset 18 D4
Cold Harbour Herts 85 B10
Cold Harbour Kent 69 G11
Cold Harbour Lincs 155 C9
Cold Harbour Oxon 64 D6
Cold Harbour Wilts 45 B11
Cold Harbour Wilts 45 D11
Cold Harbour Windsor 65 D10
Cold Hatton Telford 150 E2
Cold Hatton Heath Telford 150 E2
Cold Hesledon Durham 234 B4
Cold Hiendley W Yorks 197 E11
Cold Higham Northants 120 G3
Cold Inn Pembs 73 D10
Cold Kirby N Yorks 215 C10
Cold Moss Heath E Ches 168 C3
Cold Newton Leics 136 B4
Cold Northcott Corn 11 D10
Cold Norton Essex 88 E4
Cold Overton Leics 154 G6
Cold Row Lancs 202 E3
Cold Well Staffs 151 G11
Coldbackie Highld 308 D6
Coldbeck Cumb 222 E4
Coldblow London 68 E4
Coldbrook Powys 96 D3
Coldean Brighton 36 F4
Coldeast Devon 14 G2
Coldeaton Derbys 169 D10
Colden W Yorks 196 B3
Colden Common Hants 33 C7
Coldfair Green Suff 127 E8
Coldham Cambs 139 C8
Coldham Staffs 133 B7
Coldham's Common Cambs 123 F9
Coldharbour Corn 4 F5
Coldharbour Devon 27 E9
Coldharbour Dorset 17 E9
Coldharbour Glos 79 E9
Coldharbour Kent 52 C5
Coldharbour London 68 D4
Coldharbour Sur 50 E6
Coldingham Borders 273 B8
Coldmeece Staffs 151 C7
Coldoch Stirl 278 B3
Coldra Newport 59 B11
Coldrain Perth 286 G4
Coldred Kent 55 D9
Coldridge Devon 25 F11
Coldstream Angus 287 D7
Coldstream Borders 263 B8
Coldvreath Corn 5 D9
Coldwaltham W Sus 35 D8
Coldwells Aberds 303 E11
Coldwells Croft Aberds 302 G5
Cole Som 45 G7
Cole End Essex 105 D11
Cole End Warks 134 F3
Cole Green Herts 86 C3
Cole Green Herts 105 E8
Cole Henley Hants 48 C3
Cole Park London 67 E7
Colebatch Shrops 130 F6
Colebrook Devon 27 F8
Colebrooke Devon 13 B11
Coleburn Moray 302 D2
Coleby Lincs 173 C7
Coleby N Lincs 199 D11
Coleford Devon 26 G3
Coleford Glos 79 C9
Coleford Som 45 D7
Coleford Water Som 42 G6
Colegate End Norf 142 F3
Colehall W Mid 134 F2
Colehill Dorset 31 G8
Coleman Green Herts 85 C11
Coleman's Hatch E Sus 52 G3
Colemere Shrops 149 C8
Colemore Hants 49 G8
Colemore Green Shrops 132 D4
Coleorton Leics 153 F8
Coleorton Moor Leics 153 F8
Colerne Wilts 61 E10
Cole's Cross Dorset 28 G5
Coles Green Suff 107 C11
Cole's Green Suff 126 E5
Coles Green Worcs 116 G5
Coles Meads Sur 51 C9
Colesbourne Glos 81 C7
Colesbrook Dorset 30 B4
Colesden Beds 122 F2
Coleshill Bucks 85 F7
Coleshill Oxon 82 G2
Coleshill Warks 134 F4
Colestocks Devon 27 G9
Colethrop Glos 80 C4
Coley Bath 44 B5
Coley Reading 65 E8
Coley W Yorks 196 B6
Colfin Dumfries 236 D2
Colgate W Sus 51 G8
Colgrain Argyll 276 E6
Colham Green London 66 C5
Colindale London 67 B8
Colinsburgh Fife 287 G8
Colinton Edin 270 B4
Colintraive Argyll 275 F11
Colkirk Norf 159 D8
Collace Perth 286 D6
Collafield Glos 79 C11
Collafirth Shetland 312 G6
Collam W Isles 305 J3
Collamoor Head Corn 11 C9
Collaton Devon 9 G9
Collaton St Mary Torbay 9 D7
College Milton S Lnrk 268 D2
College of Roseisle Moray 301 C11
College Park London 67 C8
College Town Brack 65 G11
Collennan S Ayrs 257 C8
Collessie Fife 286 F6
Colleton Mills Devon 25 D11
Collett's Br Norf 139 B9
Collett's Green Worcs 116 G6
Collier Row London 87 G8
Collier Street Kent 53 D8
Collier's End Herts 105 G7
Collier's Green E Sus 38 C3
Collier's Green Kent 53 F9
Colliers Hatch Essex 87 E8
Collier's Wood London 67 E9
Colliery Row T & W 234 B2
Collieston Aberds 303 G10
Collin Dumfries 238 B2
Collingbourne Ducis Wilts 47 C8
Collingbourne Kingston Wilts 47 B8
Collingham Notts 172 C4
Collingham W Yorks 206 D3
Collington Hereford 116 E2
Collingtree Northants 120 F5
Collingwood Northumb 243 B7
Collins End Oxon 65 D7
Collins Green Warr 183 C9
Collins Green Worcs 116 F4
Colliprest Devon 27 E7
Colliston Angus 287 C10
Colliton Devon 27 G9
Collycroft Warks 135 F7
Collyhurst Gtr Man 195 G11
Collynie Aberds 303 F8
Collyweston Northants 137 C9
Colmonell S Ayrs 244 F4
Colmslie Borders 262 B2
Colmsliehill Borders 271 G10
Colmworth Beds 122 F2
Coln Rogers Glos 81 D9
Coln St Aldwyns Glos 81 D10
Coln St Dennis Glos 81 C9
Colnabaichin Aberds 292 C4
Colnbrook Slough 66 D4
Colne Cambs 123 B7
Colne Lancs 204 E3
Colne Bridge W Yorks 197 C7
Colne Edge Lancs 204 E3
Colne Engaine Essex 107 E7
Colnefields Cambs 123 B7
Colney Norf 142 B3
Colney Hatch London 86 G3
Colney Heath Herts 86 D2
Colney Street Herts 85 E11
Cologin Argyll 289 G10
Colpitts Grange Northumb 241 F11
Colpy Aberds 302 F6
Colquhar Borders 270 G6
Colscott Devon 24 E5
Colshaw Staffs 169 B8
Colsterdale N Yorks 214 C2
Colsterworth Lincs 155 E8
Colston E Dunb 268 B2
Colston Pembs 91 F9
Colston Bassett Notts 154 C3
Colt Hill Hants 49 C8
Colt Park Cumb 210 E5
Coltfield Moray 301 C11
Colthouse Cumb 221 F7
Colthrop W Berks 64 F4
Coltishall Norf 160 F5
Coltness N Lnrk 268 D6
Colton Cumb 210 B6
Colton N Yorks 206 E6
Colton Norf 142 B2
Colton Staffs 151 E11
Colton Suff 125 D7
Colton W Yorks 206 G3
Colton Hills Staffs 133 D8
Colt's Green S Glos 61 C8
Colt's Hill Kent 52 E6
Columbia T & W 243 F8
Columbjohn Devon 14 B5
Colva Powys 114 G4
Colvend Dumfries 237 D10
Colvister Shetland 312 D7
Colwall Hereford 98 C4
Colwall Green Hereford 98 C4
Colwall Stone Hereford 98 C5
Colwell I o W 20 D2
Colwell Northumb 241 B11
Colwich Staffs 151 E10
Colwick Notts 171 G10
Colwinston = Tregolwyn V Glam 58 D2
Colworth W Sus 22 C6
Colwyn Bay = Bae Colwyn Conwy 180 F4
Colychurch Bridgend 58 D2
Colyford Devon 15 C10
Colyton Devon 15 C10
Colzie Fife 286 F6
Combe Devon 7 E10
Combe Devon 8 B4
Combe Devon 9 G9
Combe E Sus 37 B10
Combe Hereford 114 E6
Combe Oxon 82 B6
Combe Som 28 B6
Combe W Berks 63 G11
Combe Almer Dorset 18 B5
Combe Common Sur 50 F3
Combe Down Bath 61 G9
Combe Fishacre Devon 8 C6
Combe Florey Som 43 G7
Combe Hay Bath 45 B8
Combe Martin Devon 40 D5
Combe Moor Hereford 115 E7
Combe Pafford Torbay 9 B8
Combe Raleigh Devon 27 G11
Combe St Nicholas Som 28 E4
Combe Throop Som 30 C2
Combebow Devon 12 D5
Combeinteignhead Devon 14 G4
Comberbach W Ches 183 F10
Comberford Staffs 134 B3
Comberton Cambs 123 F7
Comberton Hereford 115 D9
Combpyne Devon 15 C11
Combrew Devon 40 G4
Combridge Staffs 151 B11
Combrook Warks 118 G6
Combs Derbys 185 F8
Combs Suff 125 F10
Combs W Yorks 197 D8
Combs Ford Suff 125 F11
Combwich Som 43 E9
Come-to-Good Corn 4 G6
Comers Aberds 293 C8
Comeytrowe Som 28 C2
Comford Corn 2 B6
Comfort Corn 2 D6
Comhampton Worcs 116 D6
Comins Coch Ceredig 128 G2
Comiston Edin 270 B4
Comley Shrops 131 D9
Commercial End Cambs 123 E11
Commins Denb 165 C10
Commins Capel Betws Ceredig 112 F2
Commins Coch Powys 128 C6
Common Cefn-llwyn Mon 78 G4
Common Edge Blkpool 202 G2
Common End Cumb 228 G6
Common End Derbys 170 C6
Common Hill Hereford 97 E11
Common Moor Corn 6 B4
Common Platt Wilts 62 B6
Common Side Derbys 170 F6
Common Side Derbys 186 F4
Common Side W Ches 167 B9
Common-y-coed Mon 60 B2

Commondale N Yorks 226 C3
Commonmoor Corn 6 B4
Commonside Derbys 170 G2
Commonside Notts 171 D7
Commonside W Ches 183 G8
Commonwood Herts 85 E8
Commonwood Shrops 149 D9
Commonwood Wrex 166 E5
Comp Kent 52 B6
Compass Som 43 G9
Compstall Gtr Man 185 C7
Compton Derbys 169 F11
Compton Devon 9 C7
Compton Farnham 49 D11
Compton Hants 32 B4
Compton Hants 33 B7
Compton Plym 7 D9
Compton Staffs 132 G6
Compton Sur 50 D3
Compton W Berks 64 D4
Compton W Mid 133 D7
Compton W Sus 34 E3
Compton W Yorks 206 E3
Compton Wilts 46 C6
Compton Abbas Dorset 30 D5
Compton Abdale Glos 81 B9
Compton Bassett Wilts 62 E4
Compton Beauchamp Oxon 63 B9
Compton Bishop Som 43 B11
Compton Chamberlayne Wilts 31 B8
Compton Common Bath 60 G6
Compton Dando Bath 60 G6
Compton Dundon Som 44 G3
Compton Durville Som 28 D6
Compton End Hants 33 B7
Compton Green Glos 98 F4
Compton Greenfield S Glos 60 C5
Compton Martin Bath 44 B4
Compton Pauncefoot Som 29 B10
Compton Valence Dorset 17 C7
Comrie Fife 279 D10
Comrie Highld 300 D4
Comrie Perth 285 C11
Comrie Perth 285 E11
Comrue Dumfries 248 F3
Conaglen House Highld 290 G2
Conanby S Yorks 187 B7
Conchra Argyll 275 E11
Conchra Highld 295 C10
Concord T & W 243 F8
Concraig Perth 286 F2
Concraigie Perth 286 C5
Conder Green Lancs 202 B5
Conderton Worcs 99 D9
Condicote Glos 100 F3
Condorrat N Lnrk 278 G4
Condover Shrops 131 B9
Coney Hall London 67 G11
Coney Hill Glos 80 B5
Coney Weston Suff 125 B9
Coneyhurst W Sus 35 C10
Coneysthorpe N Yorks 216 E4
Coneythorpe N Yorks 206 B3
Conford Hants 49 G10
Congash Highld 301 G10
Congdon's Shop Corn 11 F11
Congeith Dumfries 237 C10
Congelow Kent 53 D7
Congerstone Leics 135 B7
Congham Norf 158 E4
Congl-y-wal Gwyn 164 G2
Congleton E Ches 168 C5
Congleton Edge E Ches 168 C5
Congresbury N Som 60 G2
Congreve Staffs 151 G8
Conham Bristol 60 E6
Conicavel Moray 301 D9
Coningsby Lincs 174 D2
Conington Cambs 122 D6
Conington Cambs 138 F3
Conisbrough S Yorks 187 B8
Conisby Argyll 274 G3
Conisholme Lincs 190 B6
Coniston Cumb 220 F6
Coniston E Yorks 209 F9
Coniston Cold N Yorks 204 B4
Conistone N Yorks 213 F9
Conkwell Wilts 61 G9
Connage Moray 302 C4
Connah's Quay Flint 166 B3
Connel Argyll 289 F11
Connel Park E Ayrs 258 G4
Conniburrow M Keynes 103 D7
Connista Highld 298 B4
Connon Corn 6 C3
Connor Downs Corn 2 B3
Conock Wilts 46 B5
Conon Bridge Highld 300 D5
Conon House Highld 300 D5
Cononish Stirl 285 E7
Cononley N Yorks 204 D5
Cononley Woodside N Yorks 204 D5
Cononsyth Angus 287 C9
Conordan Highld 295 B7
Conquermoor Heath Telford 150 F3
Consall Staffs 169 F7
Consett Durham 242 G4
Constable Burton N Yorks 224 G3
Constable Lee Lancs 195 C10
Constantine Corn 2 D6
Constantine Bay Corn 10 G3
Contin Highld 300 D4
Contlaw Aberdeen 293 C10
Conwy Conwy 180 F3
Conyer Kent 70 G3
Conyers Green Suff 125 D7
Cooden E Sus 38 F2
Cooil I o M 192 E4
Cookbury Devon 24 F6
Cookbury Wick Devon 24 E5
Cookham Windsor 65 B11
Cookham Dean Windsor 65 C11
Cookham Rise Windsor 65 C11
Cookhill Worcs 117 F11
Cookley Suff 126 B6
Cookley Worcs 132 G6
Cookley Green Oxon 83 G11
Cookney Aberds 293 D10
Cookridge W Yorks 205 E11
Cook's Green Essex 89 B12
Cook's Green Suff 125 G9
Cooksbridge E Sus 36 E6
Cooksey Corner Worcs 117 D8
Cooksey Green Worcs 117 D8
Cookshill Staffs 168 G6
Cooksland Corn 5 B11
Cooksmill Green Essex 87 D10
Coolsongreen W Ches 183 G8
Coolham W Sus 35 C10
Cooling Medway 69 D9
Cooling Street Medway 69 E8
Coolinge Kent 55 F8
Coomb Hill Kent 69 G7
Coombe Bucks 84 D4
Coombe Corn 4 G2
Coombe Corn 4 G5
Coombe Corn 4 G6
Coombe Corn 5 E9
Coombe Corn 6 C4
Coombe Corn 24 E2
Coombe Devon 14 G4
Coombe Devon 27 D8
Coombe Glos 80 G3
Coombe Hants 33 C11
Coombe Kent 55 B9
Coombe London 67 E8
Coombe Som 28 B3
Coombe Som 28 F6
Coombe Wilts 30 C5
Coombe Wilts 47 C7
Coombe Bissett Wilts 31 B10
Coombe Dingle Bristol 60 D5
Coombe Hill Glos 99 F7
Coombe Keynes Dorset 18 E2
Coombes W Sus 35 F11
Coombesdale Staffs 150 B6
Coombeswood W Mid 133 F9
Coombs End S Glos 61 C9
Coombses Som 28 F4
Cooper Street Kent 55 B10
Cooper Turning Gtr Man 194 F6
Cooper's Corner Kent 52 D3
Cooper's Green E Sus 37 C7
Cooper's Green Herts 85 D11
Cooper's Hill C Beds 103 D10
Cooper's Hill Sur 66 E3
Coopersale Common Essex 87 E7
Coopersale Street Essex 87 E7
Cootham W Sus 35 E9
Cop Street Kent 55 B9
Copcut Worcs 117 E7
Copdock Suff 108 C2
Coped Hall Wilts 62 C5
Copenhagen Denb 165 B8
Copford Essex 107 G8
Copford Green Essex 107 G8
Copgrove N Yorks 214 G6
Copister Shetland 312 F6
Cople Beds 104 B2
Copley Durham 233 F7
Copley Gtr Man 185 B7
Copley W Yorks 196 C5
Copley Hill W Yorks 197 B8
Coplow Dale Derbys 185 F11
Copmanthorpe York 207 D7
Copmere End Staffs 150 D6
Copnor Ptsmth 33 G11
Copp Lancs 202 F4
Coppathorne Corn 24 G2
Coppenhall E Ches 168 D2
Coppenhall Staffs 151 F8
Coppenhall Moss E Ches 168 D2
Copperhouse Corn 2 B3
Coppice Gtr Man 196 G2
Coppicegate Shrops 132 G4
Coppingford Cambs 138 G3
Coppins Corner Kent 54 D2
Coppleham Som 42 G2
Copplestone Devon 26 G3
Coppull Lancs 194 E5
Coppull Moor Lancs 194 E5
Copsale W Sus 35 C11
Copse Hill London 67 E8
Copster Green Lancs 203 G9
Copster Hill Gtr Man 196 G2
Copston Magna Warks 135 F9
Copt Green Warks 118 D3
Copt Heath W Mid 118 B3
Copt Hewick N Yorks 214 E6
Copt Oak Leics 153 G9
Copthall Green Essex 86 E6
Copthill Durham 232 C3
Copthorne Corn 11 C11
Copthorne E Ches 167 G11
Copthorne Shrops 149 G9
Copthorne Sur 51 F10
Coptiviney Shrops 149 B8
Copton Kent 54 B4
Copy's Green Norf 159 B8
Copythorne Hants 32 E4
Corbets Tey London 68 B5
Corbridge Northumb 241 E11
Corbriggs Derbys 170 B6
Corby Northants 137 F7
Corby Glen Lincs 155 E9
Corby Hill Cumb 239 F11
Cordon N Ayrs 256 C2
Cordwell Norf 142 E2
Coreley Shrops 116 C2
Cores End Bucks 66 B2
Corfe Som 28 D2
Corfe Castle Dorset 18 E5
Corfe Mullen Dorset 18 B5
Corfton Shrops 131 F9
Corfton Bache Shrops 131 F9
Corgarff Aberds 292 C4
Corgee Corn 5 C10
Corhampton Hants 33 C10
Corlae Dumfries 246 D5
Corlannau Neath 57 C9
Corley Warks 134 F6
Corley Ash Warks 134 F5
Corley Moor Warks 134 F5
Cornaa I o M 192 D5
Cornabus Argyll 254 C4
Cornaigbeg Argyll 288 E1
Cornaigmore Argyll 288 C4
Cornaigmore Argyll 288 E1
Cornard Tye Suff 107 C8
Cornbank Midloth 270 C4
Cornbrook Shrops 116 B2
Corncatterach Aberds 302 F5
Cornel Conwy 164 C2
Corner Row Lancs 202 F4
Cornett Hereford 97 B11
Corney Cumb 220 G2
Cornforth Durham 234 E2
Cornharrow Dumfries 246 E5
Cornhill Aberds 302 D5
Cornhill Powys 96 C2
Cornhill Stoke 168 E5
Cornhill-on-Tweed Northumb 263 B9
Cornholme W Yorks 196 B2
Cornish Hall End Essex 106 D3
Cornquoy Orkney 314 G5
Cornriggs Durham 232 C2
Cornsay Durham 233 C8
Cornsay Colliery Durham 233 C9
Cornton Stirl 278 B5
Corntown Highld 300 D5
Corntown V Glam 58 D2
Cornwell Oxon 100 F5
Cornwood Devon 8 D2
Cornworthy Devon 8 D6
Corpach Highld 290 F2
Corpusty Norf 160 C2
Corran Highld 290 G2
Corran Highld 295 E10
Corran a Chan Uachdaraich Highld 295 C7
Corranbuie Argyll 275 G9
Corrany I o M 192 D5
Corrichoich Highld 311 G4
Corrie N Ayrs 255 C11
Corrie Common Dumfries 248 F6
Corriecravie N Ayrs 255 E10
Corriecravie Moor N Ayrs 255 E10
Corriedoo Dumfries 246 G5
Corriegarth Lodge Highld 291 B7
Corriemoillie Highld 300 C3
Corriemulzie Lodge Highld 309 K3
Corrievarkie Lodge Perth 291 F7
Corrievorrie Highld 301 G7
Corrigall Orkney 314 E3
Corrimony Highld 300 F3
Corringham Lincs 188 C5
Corringham Thurrock 69 C8
Corris Gwyn 128 B5
Corris Uchaf Gwyn 128 B4
Corrour Highld 290 G5
Corrour Shooting Lodge Highld 290 G6
Corrow Argyll 284 G5
Corry Highld 295 C8
Corry of Ardnagrask Highld 300 E5
Corrybrough Highld 301 G8
Corrydon Perth 292 G3
Corryghoil Argyll 284 E5
Corrykinloch Highld 309 G3
Corrylach Argyll 255 D8
Corrymuckloch Perth 286 D2
Corrynachenchy Argyll 289 E8
Cors-y-Gedol Gwyn 145 E11
Corsback Highld 310 B6
Corscombe Dorset 29 F8
Corse Aberds 302 E6
Corse Glos 98 F5
Corse Lawn Worcs 98 E6
Corse of Kinnoir Aberds 302 E5
Corsewall Dumfries 236 C2
Corsham Wilts 61 E11
Corsindae Aberds 293 C8
Corsley Wilts 45 D10
Corsley Heath Wilts 45 D10
Corsock Dumfries 237 B9
Corston Bath 61 F7
Corston Orkney 314 E3
Corston Wilts 62 C2
Corstorphine Edin 280 G3
Cortachy Angus 287 B7
Corton Suff 143 D10
Corton Wilts 46 E2
Corton Denham Som 29 C10
Cortworth S Yorks 186 B6
Coruanan Lodge Highld 290 G2
Corunna W Isles 296 E4
Corvast Highld 309 K5
Corwen Denb 165 G9
Cory Devon 24 D5
Coryates Dorset 17 D8
Coryton Cardiff 58 C6
Coryton Devon 12 E5
Coryton Thurrock 69 C8
Còsag Highld 295 D10
Cosby Leics 135 E10
Coscote Oxon 64 B4
Coseley W Mid 133 E8
Cosford Warks 119 B9
Cosgrove Northants 102 C5
Cosham Ptsmth 33 F11
Cosheston Pembs 73 E8
Cosmeston V Glam 59 F7
Cosmore Dorset 29 F11
Cossall Notts 171 G7
Cossall Marsh Notts 171 G7
Cosses S Ayrs 244 G4
Cossington Leics 154 G2
Cossington Som 43 E11
Costa Orkney 314 D3
Costessey Norf 160 G3
Costessey Park Norf 160 G3
Costhorpe Notts 187 D9
Costislost Corn 10 G6
Costock Notts 153 D11
Coston Leics 154 E6
Coston Norf 141 B11
Coswinsawsin Corn 2 B4
Cote Oxon 82 E4
Cote Som 43 E10
Cote W Sus 35 F10
Cotebrook W Ches 167 B9
Cotehill Cumb 239 G11
Cotes Cumb 211 B9
Cotes Leics 153 E11
Cotes Staffs 150 C6
Cotes Heath Staffs 150 C6
Cotes Park Derbys 170 E6
Cotesbach Leics 135 G10
Cotford St Lukes Som 27 B11
Cotgrave Notts 154 B2
Cothall Aberds 293 B10
Cotham Bristol 60 E5
Cotham Notts 172 F3
Cothelstone Som 43 G7
Cotheridge Worcs 116 G5
Cotherstone Durham 223 B10
Cothill Oxon 83 F7
Cotland Mon 79 E8
Cotleigh Devon 28 G2
Cotmanhay Derbys 171 G7
Cotmarsh Wilts 62 D5
Cotmaton Devon 15 D8
Coton Cambs 123 F8
Coton Northants 120 C3
Coton Shrops 149 C10
Coton Staffs 134 B3
Coton Staffs 150 E6
Coton Staffs 151 C9
Coton Clanford Staffs 151 E7
Coton Hayes Staffs 151 C9
Coton Hill Shrops 149 G9
Coton Hill Staffs 151 C9
Coton in the Clay Staffs 152 D3
Coton in the Elms Derbys 152 F4
Coton Park Derbys 152 F5
Cotonwood Shrops 149 B10
Cotonwood Staffs 150 E6
Cotswold Community Wilts 81 F8
Cott Devon 8 C5
Cottam E Yorks 217 F9
Cottam Lancs 202 G6
Cottam Notts 188 F4
Cottartown Highld 301 F10
Cottenham Cambs 123 D8
Cottenham Park London 67 F8
Cotterdale N Yorks 222 G6
Cottered Herts 104 F6
Cotterhill Woods S Yorks 187 E9
Cotteridge W Mid 117 B10
Cotterstock Northants 137 E10
Cottesbrooke Northants 120 C4
Cottesmore Rutland 155 G8
Cotteylands Devon 26 E6
Cottingham E Yorks 208 G6
Cottingham Northants 136 E6
Cottingley W Yorks 205 F8
Cottisford Oxon 101 E11
Cotton Staffs 169 F9
Cotton Suff 125 D11
Cotton End Beds 103 B11
Cotton End Northants 120 F5
Cotton Stones W Yorks 196 C4
Cotton Tree Lancs 204 F4
Cottonworth Hants 47 F11
Cottown Aberds 293 B9
Cottown Aberds 302 G5
Cottown Aberds 303 E8
Cotts Devon 7 B8
Cottwood Devon 25 E10
Cotwall Telford 150 F2
Cotwalton Staffs 151 B8
Coubister Orkney 314 E3
Couch Green Hants 48 G4
Couch's Mill Corn 6 D2
Coughton Hereford 97 G11
Coughton Warks 117 E11
Coughton Fields Warks 117 F11
Cougie Highld 300 G2
Coulaghailtro Argyll 275 G8
Coulags Highld 299 E9
Coulby Newham M'bro 225 B10
Coulderton Cumb 219 D9
Couldoran Highld 299 E8
Couligartan Stirl 285 G8
Coulin Highld 299 D10
Coulin Lodge Highld 299 D10
Coull Aberds 293 C7
Coull Argyll 274 G3
Coulmony Ho Highld 301 E9
Coulport Argyll 276 D4
Coulsdon London 51 B9
Coulshill Perth 286 G3
Coulston Wilts 46 C3
Coulter S Lnrk 260 C2
Coultings Som 43 E8
Coulton N Yorks 216 E2
Coultra Fife 287 E7
Cound Shrops 131 C11
Coundlane Shrops 131 B11
Coundmoor Shrops 131 C11
Coundon Durham 233 F10
Coundon W Mid 134 G6
Coundon Grange Durham 233 F10
Coundongate Durham 233 F10
Counters End Herts 85 D8
Countersett N Yorks 213 B8
Countess Wilts 47 E7
Countess Cross Essex 107 E7
Countess Wear Devon 14 D4
Countesthorpe Leics 135 D11
Countisbury Devon 41 D8
County Oak W Sus 51 F9
Coup Green Lancs 194 B5
Coupar Angus Perth 286 C6
Coupland Cumb 222 B4
Coupland Northumb 263 C10
Cour Argyll 255 C9
Courance Dumfries 248 E3
Coursley Som 42 G6
Court-at-Street Kent 54 F5
Court Barton Devon 14 D2
Court Colman Bridgend 57 E11
Court Corner Hants 48 B6
Court Henry Carms 93 G11
Court House Green W Mid 135 G7
Courteenhall Northants 120 G5
Courthill Perth 286 C5
Courtsend Essex 89 G8
Courtway Som 43 G8
Cousland Midloth 271 B7
Cousley Wood E Sus 53 G7
Couston Argyll 275 F11
Cova Shetland 313 J5
Cove Argyll 276 E4
Cove Borders 282 G5
Cove Devon 27 D7
Cove Hants 49 B11
Cove Highld 307 K3
Cove Bay Aberdeen 293 C11
Cove Bottom Suff 127 B9
Covehithe Suff 143 G10
Coven Staffs 133 B8
Coven Heath Staffs 133 C8
Coven Lawn Staffs 133 B8
Covender Hereford 98 C2
Coveney Cambs 139 G9
Covenham St Bartholomew Lincs 190 C4
Covenham St Mary Lincs 190 C4
Coventry W Mid 118 B6
Coverack Corn 3 F7
Coverack Bridges Corn 2 C5
Coverham N Yorks 214 B2
Covesea Moray 301 B11
Covingham Swindon 63 B7
Covington Cambs 121 C11
Covington S Lnrk 259 B11
Cow Ark Lancs 203 D9
Cow Green Suff 125 D11
Cow Hill Lancs 203 G7
Cow Roast Herts 85 C7
Cowan Bridge Lancs 212 D2
Cowbar Redcar 226 B5
Cowbeech E Sus 23 C10
Cowbeech Hill E Sus 23 C10
Cowbit Lincs 156 F5
Cowbog Aberds 303 D8
Cowbridge Lincs 174 F4
Cowbridge Som 42 E3
Cowbridge = Y Bont-Faen V Glam 58 E3
Cowcliffe W Yorks 196 D6
Cowdale Derbys 185 G9
Cowden Kent 52 E3
Cowdenbeath Fife 280 C3
Cowdenburn Borders 270 E4
Cowen Head Cumb 221 F9
Cowers Lane Derbys 170 F4
Cowes I o W 20 B5
Cowesby N Yorks 215 B9
Cowesfield Green Wilts 32 C3
Cowfold W Sus 36 C2
Cowgill Cumb 212 B5
Cowgrove Dorset 18 B5
Cowhill Derbys 170 F5
Cowhill S Glos 79 G10
Cowhorn Hill S Glos 61 E7
Cowie Aberds 293 E10
Cowie Stirl 278 D6
Cowlands Corn 4 G6
Cowleaze Corner Oxon 82 E4
Cowley Derbys 186 F4
Cowley Devon 14 B4
Cowley Glos 81 C7
Cowley London 66 C5
Cowley Oxon 83 E8
Cowley Peachy London 66 C5
Cowleymoor Devon 27 E7
Cowling Lancs 194 D5
Cowling N Yorks 204 E5
Cowling N Yorks 214 B4
Cowlinge Suff 124 G4
Cowlow Derbys 185 G9
Cowmes W Yorks 197 D7
Cowpe Lancs 195 C10
Cowpen Northumb 253 G7
Cowpen Bewley Stockton 234 G5
Cowplain Hants 33 E11
Cowshill Durham 232 C3
Cowslip Green N Som 60 G3
Cowstrandburn Fife 279 C10
Cowthorpe N Yorks 206 C4
Cox Common Suff 143 G8
Cox Green Gtr Man 195 E8
Cox Green Sur 50 G5
Cox Green Windsor 65 D11
Cox Hill Corn 4 G4
Cox Moor Notts 171 D8
Coxall Hereford 115 C7
Coxbank E Ches 167 G11
Coxbench Derbys 170 G5
Coxbridge Som 44 F4
Coxford Corn 11 B9
Coxford Norf 158 D6
Coxford Soton 32 D5
Coxgreen Staffs 132 F6
Coxheath Kent 53 C8
Coxhill Kent 55 D8
Coxhoe Durham 234 D2
Coxley Som 44 E4
Coxley W Yorks 197 D9
Coxley Wick Som 44 E4
Coxlodge T & W 242 D6
Coxpark Corn 12 G4
Coxtie Green Essex 87 F9
Coxwold N Yorks 215 D10
Coychurch Bridgend 58 D2
Coylton S Ayrs 257 E10
Coylumbridge Highld 291 B11
Coynach Aberds 292 C6
Coynachie Aberds 302 F4
Coytrahen Bridgend 57 D11
CoytrahÛn Bridgend 57 D11
Crab Orchard Dorset 31 F9
Crabadon Devon 8 E5
Crabbet Park W Sus 51 F10
Crabble Kent 55 E9
Crabbs Cross Worcs 117 E10
Crabbs Green Herts 105 F9
Crabgate Norf 159 D11
Crabtree Plym 7 D10
Crabtree W Sus 36 B2
Crabtree Green Wrex 166 G4
Crackaig Argyll 274 G6
Crackenedge W Yorks 197 C8
Crackenthorpe Cumb 231 G9
Crackington Haven Corn 11 B8
Crackley Staffs 168 E4
Crackley Warks 118 C5
Crackleybank Shrops 150 G5
Crackpot N Yorks 223 F9
Crackthorn Corner Suff 125 B10
Cracoe N Yorks 213 G9
Cracow Moss E Ches 168 F2
Cracow Moss Staffs 168 F3
Craddock Devon 27 E9
Cradhlastadh W Isles 304 E2
Cradle Edge W Yorks 205 F7
Cradle End Herts 105 G9
Cradley Hereford 98 B4
Cradley W Mid 133 G8
Cradley Heath W Mid 133 F8
Cradoc Powys 95 E10
Crafthole Corn 7 E7
Crafton Bucks 84 B5
Crag Bank Lancs 211 E9
Crag Foot Lancs 211 E9
Cragg Hill W Yorks 205 F10
Cragg Vale W Yorks 196 C4
Craggan Highld 301 G10
Craggan Moray 301 F11
Craggan Stirl 285 E9
Cragganvallie Highld 300 F5
Craggenmore Moray 301 F11
Craggie Highld 301 F7
Craggie Highld 311 H2
Craggiemore Highld 309 J7
Craghead Durham 242 G6
Crahan Corn 2 C5
Crai Powys 95 G7
Craibstone Moray 302 D4
Craichie Angus 287 C9
Craig Dumfries 237 B8
Craig Dumfries 237 C8
Craig Highld 299 E10
Craig Berthlwyd M Tydf 77 F9
Craig Castle Aberds 302 G4
Craig-cefn-parc Swansea 75 E11
Craig Douglas Borders 261 E7
Craig Llangiwg Neath 76 D2
Craig-llwyn Shrops 148 D4
Craig Lodge Argyll 275 G10
Craig-moston Aberds 293 F8
Craig Penllyn V Glam 58 D3
Craig-y-don Conwy 180 E3
Craig-y-Duke Swansea 76 E2
Craig-y-nos Powys 76 B4
Craig-y-penrhyn Ceredig 128 E3
Craig-y-Rhacca Caerph 59 B7
Craiganour Lodge Perth 285 B10
Craigdallie Perth 286 E6
Craigdam Aberds 303 F8
Craigdarroch Dumfries 246 E6
Craigdarroch Highld 300 D4
Craigdhu Highld 300 E4
Craigearn Aberds 293 B9
Craigellachie Moray 302 E2
Craigencallie Ho Dumfries 237 B7
Craigencross Dumfries 236 C2
Craigend Borders 271 F9
Craigend Glasgow 268 B3
Craigend Perth 286 E3
Craigend Perth 286 E5
Craigend Stirl 278 D5
Craigendive Argyll 275 E11
Craigendoran Argyll 276 E6
Craigendowie Angus 293 G7
Craigends Renfs 267 B8
Craigens Argyll 274 G3
Craigens E Ayrs 258 F3
Craigentinny Edin 280 G5
Craigerne Borders 261 B7
Craighall Perth 286 C5
Craighat Stirl 277 E9
Craighead Fife 287 G10
Craighead Highld 301 C7
Craighill Aberds 303 E7
Craighlaw Mains Dumfries 236 C5
Craighouse Argyll 274 G6
Craigie Aberds 293 B11
Craigie Dundee 287 D8
Craigie Perth 286 C5
Craigie Perth 286 E5
Craigie S Ayrs 257 C10
Craigie S Ayrs 257 E8
Craigiefield Orkney 314 E4
Craigiehall Edin 280 F3
Craigielaw E Loth 281 F9
Craigierig Borders 260 E6
Craigleith Edin 280 G4
Craiglockhart Edin 280 G4
Craigmalloch E Ayrs 245 E11
Craigmaud Aberds 303 D8
Craigmill Stirl 278 B6
Craigmillar Edin 280 G5
Craigmore Argyll 266 B2
Craignant Shrops 148 B5
Craignell Dumfries 237 B7
Craigneuk N Lnrk 268 C5
Craigneuk N Lnrk 268 D5
Craignish Castle Argyll 275 C8
Craignure Argyll 289 F9
Craigo Angus 293 G8
Craigow Perth 286 G4
Craigrory Highld 300 E6
Craigrothie Fife 287 F7
Craigroy Moray 301 D11
Craigruie Stirl 285 E8
Craig's End Essex 106 D4
Craigsford Mains Borders 262 B3
Craigshall Dumfries 237 D10
Craigshill W Loth 269 B11
Craigside Durham 233 D8
Craigston Castle Aberds 303 D7
Craigton Aberdeen 293 C10
Craigton Angus 287 B7
Craigton Angus 287 D9
Craigton Glasgow 267 C10
Craigton Highld 300 E6
Craigton Highld 309 H6
Craigton Highld 309 K6
Craigtown Highld 310 D2
Craik Borders 249 B8
Crail Fife 287 G10
Crailing Borders 262 E5
Crailinghall Borders 262 E5
Crakaig Highld 311 H3
Crakehill N Yorks 215 E8
Crakemarsh Staffs 151 B11
Crambe N Yorks 216 G4
Crambeck N Yorks 216 F4
Cramhurst Sur 50 E2
Cramlington Northumb 243 B7
Cramond Edin 280 F3
Cramond Bridge Edin 280 F3
Crampmoor Hants 32 C5
Cranage E Ches 168 B3
Cranberry Staffs 150 B6
Cranborne Dorset 31 E9
Cranbourne Brack 66 E2
Cranbourne Hants 48 C6
Cranbrook Kent 53 F9
Cranbrook London 68 B2
Cranbrook Common Kent 53 F9
Crane Moor S Yorks 197 G10
Crane's Corner Norf 159 G8
Cranfield C Beds 103 C9
Cranford Devon 24 C4
Cranford London 66 D6
Cranford St Andrew Northants 121 B8
Cranford St John Northants 121 B8
Cranham Glos 80 C5
Cranham London 68 B5
Cranhill Glasgow 268 B2
Cranhill Warks 118 G2
Crank Mers 183 B8
Crank Wood Gtr Man 194 G6
Crankwood Gtr Man 194 G6
Cranleigh Sur 50 F5
Cranley Suff 126 C3
Cranley Gardens London 67 B9
Cranmer Green Suff 125 C10
Cranmore I o W 20 D3
Cranmore Som 45 E7
Cranna Aberds 302 D6
Crannich Argyll 289 E7
Crannoch Moray 302 D4
Cranoe Leics 136 D5
Cransford Suff 126 E6
Cranshaws Borders 272 C3
Cranstal I o M 192 B5
Cranswick E Yorks 208 C6
Crantock Corn 4 C5
Cranwell Lincs 173 F8
Cranwich Norf 140 E5
Cranworth Norf 141 C9
Craobh Haven Argyll 275 C8
Crapstone Devon 7 B10
Crarae Argyll 275 D10
Crask Highld 308 C7
Crask Inn Highld 309 G5
Crask of Aigas Highld 300 E4
Craskins Aberds 293 C7
Craster Northumb 265 F7
Craswall Hereford 96 D5
Crateford Shrops 132 F4
Crateford Staffs 133 B8
Cratfield Suff 126 B6
Crathes Aberds 293 D9
Crathie Aberds 292 D4
Crathie Highld 291 D7
Crathorne N Yorks 225 D8
Craven Arms Shrops 131 G8
Crawcrook T & W 242 E4
Crawford Lancs 194 G3
Crawford S Lnrk 259 E11
Crawforddyke S Lnrk 269 F7
Crawfordjohn S Lnrk 259 E9
Crawick Dumfries 259 G7
Crawley Devon 28 F3
Crawley Hants 48 G2
Crawley Oxon 82 C4
Crawley W Sus 51 F9
Crawley Down W Sus 51 F10
Crawley End Essex 105 C8
Crawley Hill Sur 65 G11
Crawleyside Durham 232 C5
Crawshaw W Yorks 197 E8
Crawshawbooth Lancs 195 B10
Crawton Aberds 293 F10
Cray N Yorks 213 D8
Cray Perth 292 G3
Crayford London 68 E4
Crayke N Yorks 215 E11
Craymere Beck Norf 159 C11
Crays Hill Essex 88 G2
Cray's Pond Oxon 64 C6
Crazies Hill Wokingham 65 C9
Creacombe Devon 26 D4
Creag Aoil Highld 290 F3
Creag Ghoraidh W Isles 297 G3
Creagan Argyll 289 E11
Creagan Sithe Argyll 284 G6
Creagastrom W Isles 297 G4
Creaguaineach Lodge Highld 290 G5
Creaksea Essex 88 F6
Creamore Bank Shrops 149 C10
Crean Corn 1 E3
Creaton Northants 120 C4
Creca Dumfries 238 C6
Credenhill Hereford 97 C9
Crediton Devon 26 G4
Creebridge Dumfries 236 C6
Creech Dorset 18 E4
Creech Bottom Dorset 18 E4
Creech Heathfield Som 28 B3
Creech St Michael Som 28 B3
Creed Corn 5 F8
Creediknowe Shetland 312 G7
Creegbrawse Corn 4 G4
Creekmoor Poole 18 C6
Creekmouth London 68 C3
Creeksea Essex 88 F6
Creeting Bottoms Suff 126 F2
Creeting St Mary Suff 125 F11
Creeton Lincs 155 E10
Creetown Dumfries 236 D6
Creg-ny-Baa I o M 192 D4
Creggans Argyll 284 G4
Cregneash I o M 192 F2
Cregrina Powys 114 G2
Creich Fife 287 E7
Creigau Mon 79 F7
Creighton Staffs 151 B11
Creigiau Cardiff 58 C5
Crelly Corn 2 C5
Cremyll Corn 7 E9
Crendell Dorset 31 E9
Crepkill Highld 298 E4
Creslow Bucks 102 G6
Cress Green Glos 80 E3
Cressage Shrops 131 C11
Cressbrook Derbys 185 G11
Cresselly Pembs 73 D9
Cressex Bucks 84 G4
Cressing Essex 106 G5
Cresswell Northumb 253 E7
Cresswell Staffs 151 B9
Cresswell Quay Pembs 73 D9
Creswell Derbys 187 G8
Creswell Staffs 151 D7
Creswell Staffs 151 D8
Creswell Green Staffs 151 G11
Cretingham Suff 126 E4
Cretshengan Argyll 275 G8
Creunant = Crynant Neath 76 E3
Crewe E Ches 168 D2
Crewe W Ches 166 E6
Crewe-by-Farndon W Ches 166 E6
Crewgarth Cumb 231 E8
Crewgreen Powys 148 F6
Crewkerne Som 28 F6
Crews Hill London 86 F4
Crew's Hole Bristol 60 E6
Crewton Derby 153 C7
Crianlarich Stirl 285 E7
Cribbs Causeway S Glos 60 C5
Cribden Side Lancs 195 C9
Cribyn Ceredig 111 G10
Criccieth Gwyn 145 B9
Crich Derbys 170 E5
Crich Carr Derbys 170 E4
Crichie Aberds 303 E9
Crichton Midloth 271 C7
Crick Mon 79 G7
Crick Northants 119 C11
Crickadarn Powys 95 C11
Cricket Hill Hants 65 G10
Cricket Malherbie Som 28 E5
Cricket St Thomas Som 28 F5
Crickham Som 44 D2
Crickheath Shrops 148 E5
Crickheath Wharf Shrops 148 E5
Crickhowell Powys 78 B2
Cricklade Wilts 81 G10
Cricklewood London 67 B8
Crickmery Shrops 150 D3
Crick's Green Hereford 116 G2
Criddlestyle Hants 31 E11
Cridling Stubbs N Yorks 198 C4
Cridmore I o W 20 E5
Crieff Perth 286 E2
Criggan Corn 5 C10
Criggion Powys 148 F5
Crigglestone W Yorks 197 D10
Crimble Gtr Man 195 E11
Crimchard Som 28 F4
Crimdon Park Durham 234 D5
Crimond Aberds 303 D10
Crimonmogate Aberds 303 D10
Crimp Corn 24 D3
Crimplesham Norf 140 C3
Crimscote Warks 100 B4
Crinan Argyll 275 D8
Crinan Ferry Argyll 275 D8
Crindau Newport 59 B10
Crindledyke N Lnrk 268 D6
Cringleford Norf 142 B3
Cringles W Yorks 204 D6
Cringletie Borders 270 G4
Crinow Pembs 73 C10
Cripple Corner Essex 107 E7
Cripplesease Corn 2 B2
Cripplestyle Dorset 31 E9
Cripp's Corner E Sus 38 C3
Crispie Argyll 275 F10
Crist Derbys 185 E8
Crit Hall Kent 53 G9
Critchell's Green Hants 32 B3
Critchill Som 45 D9
Critchmere Sur 49 G11
Crizeley Hereford 97 E8
Croanford Corn 10 G6
Croasdale Cumb 219 B11
Crobeag W Isles 304 F5
Crock Street Som 28 E4
Crockenhill Kent 68 F4
Crocker End Oxon 65 B8
Crockerhill Hants 33 F9
Crockerhill W Sus 22 B6
Crockernwell Devon 13 C11
Crockers Devon 40 F5
Crocker's Ash Hereford 79 B8
Crockerton Wilts 45 E11
Crockerton Green Wilts 45 E11
Crocketford or Ninemile Bar Dumfries 237 B10
Crockey Hill York 207 D8
Crockham Heath W Berks 64 G2
Crockham Hill Kent 52 C2
Crockhurst Street Kent 52 E6
Crockleford Heath Essex 107 F10
Crockleford Hill Essex 107 F10
Crockness Orkney 314 G3
Croes-goch Pembs 87 E11
Croes-Hywel Mon 78 C4
Croes-lan Ceredig 93 C7
Croes Llanfair Mon 78 D4
Croes-wian Flint 181 G10
Croes-y-mwyalch Torf 78 G4
Croes y pant Mon 78 E4
Croesau Bach Shrops 148 D4
Croeserw Neath 57 B11
Croesor Gwyn 163 G10
Croespenmaen Caerph 77 F11
Croesyceiliog Carms 74 B6
Croesyceiliog Torf 78 F4
Croesywaun Gwyn 163 D8
Croft Hereford 115 D9
Croft Leics 135 D10
Croft Lincs 175 C8
Croft Pembs 92 C3
Croft Warr 183 C10
Croft Mitchell Corn 2 B5
Croft of Tillymaud Aberds 303 F11
Croft-on-Tees N Yorks 224 D5
Croftamie Stirl 277 D9
Croftfoot S Lnrk 268 C2
Crofthandy Corn 4 G4
Croftlands Cumb 210 D5
Croftmalloch W Loth 269 C8
Croftmoraig Perth 285 C11
Crofton Cumb 239 G8
Crofton London 68 F2
Crofton W Yorks 197 D11
Crofton Wilts 63 G9
Crofts Dumfries 237 B9
Crofts Bank Gtr Man 184 B3
Crofts of Benachielt Highld 310 F5
Crofts of Haddo Aberds 303 F8
Crofts of Inverthernie Aberds 303 E7
Crofts of Meikle Ardo Aberds 303 E8
Crofty Swansea 56 B4
Croggan Argyll 289 G9
Croglin Cumb 231 B7
Croich Highld 309 K4
Croick Highld 310 D2
Croig Argyll 288 D5
Crois Dughaill W Isles 297 J3
Cromarty Highld 301 C7
Cromasaig Highld 299 C10
Crombie Fife 279 D10
Crombie Castle Aberds 302 D5
Cromblet Aberds 303 F7
Cromdale Highld 301 G10
Cromer Herts 104 F5
Cromer Norf 160 A4
Cromer-Hyde Herts 86 C2
Cromford Derbys 170 D3
Cromhall S Glos 79 G11
Cromhall Common S Glos 61 B7
Cromor W Isles 304 F6
Crompton Fold Gtr Man 196 F2
Cromra Highld 291 D7
Cromwell Notts 172 C3
Cromwell Bottom W Yorks 196 C6
Cronberry E Ayrs 258 E4
Crondall Hants 49 D9
Cronk-y-Voddy I o M 192 D4
Cronton Mers 183 D7
Crook Cumb 221 G9
Crook Devon 27 G11
Crook Durham 233 D9
Crook of Devon Perth 286 G4
Crookdake Cumb 229 C9
Crooke Gtr Man 194 F5
Crooked Billet London 67 E8
Crooked Soley Wilts 63 E10
Crooked Withies Dorset 31 F9
Crookedholm E Ayrs 257 B11
Crookes S Yorks 186 D4
Crookesmoor S Yorks 186 D4
Crookfur E Renf 267 D10
Crookgate Bank Durham 242 F5
Crookhall Durham 242 G4
Crookham Northumb 263 B10
Crookham W Berks 64 G4
Crookham Village Hants 49 C9
Crookhaugh Borders 260 D4
Crookhill T & W 242 E5
Crookhouse Borders 263 D7
Crooklands Cumb 211 C10
Crookston Glasgow 267 C10
Cropredy Oxon 101 B9
Cropston Leics 153 G11
Cropthorne Worcs 99 C9
Cropton N Yorks 216 B5
Cropwell Bishop Notts 154 B3
Cropwell Butler Notts 154 B3
Cros W Isles 304 B7
Crosben Highld 289 D9
Crosbost W Isles 304 F5
Crosby Cumb 229 D7
Crosby I o M 192 E4
Crosby Mers 182 B4
Crosby N Lincs 199 E11
Crosby Court N Yorks 225 G7
Crosby Garrett Cumb 222 D4
Crosby-on-Eden Cumb 239 F11
Crosby Ravensworth Cumb 222 C2
Crosby Villa Cumb 229 D7
Croscombe Som 44 E5
Crosemere Shrops 149 D8
Crosland Edge W Yorks 196 E6
Crosland Hill W Yorks 196 E6
Crosland Moor W Yorks 196 D6
Croslands Park Cumb 210 E4
Cross Devon 40 F3
Cross Devon 40 G6
Cross Shrops 149 B7
Cross Som 44 C2
Cross Ash Mon 78 B6
Cross-at-Hand Kent 53 D9
Cross Bank Worcs 116 C4
Cross Coombe Corn 4 E4
Cross End Beds 121 F11
Cross End Essex 107 E7
Cross End M Keynes 103 D8
Cross Gate W Sus 35 E8
Cross Gates W Yorks 206 G3
Cross Green Devon 12 D3
Cross Green Staffs 133 B8
Cross Green Suff 124 G6
Cross Green Suff 125 F7
Cross Green Suff 125 G9
Cross Green Telford 150 G2
Cross Green W Yorks 206 G2
Cross Green Warks 119 F7
Cross Hands Carms 75 C9
Cross-hands Carms 92 G3
Cross Hands Pembs 73 C9
Cross Heath Staffs 168 F4
Cross Hill Corn 10 G6
Cross Hill Derbys 170 F6
Cross Hill Glos 79 F9
Cross Hills N Yorks 204 E6
Cross Holme N Yorks 225 F11
Cross Houses Shrops 131 B10
Cross Houses Shrops 132 E3
Cross in Hand E Sus 37 C9
Cross in Hand Leics 135 G10
Cross Inn Carms 74 C3
Cross Inn Ceredig 111 E10
Cross Inn Ceredig 111 F7
Cross Inn Rhondda 58 C5
Cross Keys Kent 52 C4
Cross Keys Wilts 61 E11
Cross Lane E Ches 167 C11
Cross Lane Head Shrops 132 D4
Cross Lanes Corn 2 E5
Cross Lanes Dorset 30 G3
Cross Lanes N Yorks 215 F10
Cross Lanes Oxon 65 D7

Cross Lanes Wrex 166 F5
Cross Llyde Hereford 97 F8
Cross o' th' hands Derbys 170 F3
Cross o' th' Hill W Ches 167 F7
Cross Oak Powys 96 G2
Cross of Jackston Aberds 303 F7
Cross Roads Devon 12 D5
Cross Roads W Yorks 204 F6
Cross Stone Aberds 303 G9
Cross Street Suff 126 B3
Cross Town E Ches 184 F3
Crossaig Argyll 255 B9
Crossal Highld 294 B6
Crossapol Argyll 288 E1
Crossbrae Aberds 302 D6
Crossburn Falk 279 G7
Crossbush W Sus 35 F8
Crosscanonby Cumb 229 D7
Crosscrake Cumb 211 B10
Crossdale Street Norf 160 B4
Crossens Mers 193 D11
Crossflatts W Yorks 205 E8
Crossford Fife 279 D11
Crossford S Lnrk 268 F6
Crossgate Lincs 156 D4
Crossgate Orkney 314 E4
Crossgate Staffs 151 B8
Crossgatehall E Loth 271 B7
Crossgates Cumb 229 G7
Crossgates Fife 280 D2
Crossgates N Yorks 217 C10
Crossgates Powys 113 E11
Crossgill Cumb 231 C10
Crossgill Lancs 211 G11
Crossgreen Shrops 149 F9
Crosshands Carms 92 G3
Crosshill E Ayrs 257 E11
Crosshill Fife 280 B3
Crosshill S Ayrs 245 B8
Crosshouse E Ayrs 257 B9
Crossings Cumb 240 B2
Crosskeys Caerph 78 G2
Crosskirk Highld 310 B4
Crosslands Cumb 210 B6
Crosslanes Shrops 148 F6
Crosslee Borders 261 F8
Crosslee Renfs 267 B8
Crossley Hall W Yorks 205 G8
Crossmichael Dumfries 237 C9
Crossmill E Renf 267 D10
Crossmoor Lancs 202 F4
Crossmount Perth 285 B11
Crosspost W Sus 36 C3
Crossroads Aberds 293 D9
Crossroads E Ayrs 257 C11
Crossroads Fife 281 B7
Crosston Angus 287 B9
Crosstown Corn 24 D2
Crosstown V Glam 58 F4
Crosswater Sur 49 F11
Crossway Hereford 98 E2
Crossway Mon 78 B6
Crossway Powys 113 F11
Crossway Green Mon 79 G8
Crossway Green Worcs 116 D6
Crossways Dorset 17 D11
Crossways Kent 68 D5
Crossways Mon 96 G6
Crossways S Glos 79 G11
Crossways Sur 49 F11
Crosswell = Ffynnongroes Pembs 92 D2
Crosswood Ceredig 112 C3
Crosthwaite Cumb 221 G8
Croston Lancs 194 D3
Crostwick Norf 160 F5
Crostwight Norf 160 D6
Crothair W Isles 304 E3
Crouch Kent 52 B6
Crouch Kent 54 B5
Crouch End London 67 B9
Crouch Hill Dorset 30 E2
Crouch House Green Kent 52 D2
Crouchers W Sus 22 C4
Croucheston Wilts 31 B9
Croughly Moray 301 G11
Croughton Northants 101 E10
Crovie Aberds 303 C8
Crow Hants 31 G11
Crow Edge S Yorks 197 G7
Crow Green Essex 87 F9
Crow Hill Hereford 98 F2
Crow Nest W Yorks 205 F8
Crow Wood Halton 183 D8
Crowan Corn 2 C4
Crowborough E Sus 52 G4
Crowborough Staffs 168 D6
Crowborough Warren E Sus 52 G4
Crowcombe Som 42 F6
Crowcroft Worcs 116 G5
Crowden Derbys 185 B9
Crowden Devon 12 B5
Crowder Park Devon 8 D4
Crowdhill Hants 33 C7
Crowdicote Derbys 169 B10
Crowdleham Kent 52 B5
Crowdon N Yorks 227 F9
Crowell Oxon 84 F2
Crowell Hill Oxon 84 F3
Crowfield Northants 102 C2
Crowfield Suff 126 F2
Crowgate Street Norf 160 E6
Crowgreaves Shrops 132 D4
Crowhill Gtr Man 184 B6
Crowhill M Keynes 102 D6
Crowhole Derbys 186 F4
Crowhurst E Sus 38 E3
Crowhurst Sur 51 D11
Crowhurst Lane End Sur 51 D11
Crowland Lincs 156 G4
Crowlas Corn 2 C2
Crowle N Lincs 199 E9
Crowle Worcs 117 F8
Crowle Green Worcs 117 F8
Crowle Hill N Lincs 199 E9
Crowle Park N Lincs 199 E9
Crowmarsh Gifford Oxon 64 B6
Crown Corner Suff 126 C5
Crown East Worcs 116 G6
Crown Hills Leicester 136 C2
Crown Wood Brack 65 F11
Crownfield Bucks 84 F4
Crownhill Plym 7 D9
Crownland Suff 125 D10
Crownpits Sur 50 E3
Crownthorpe Norf 141 C11
Crowntown Corn 2 C4
Crows-an-wra Corn 1 D3
Crow's Green Essex 106 F3
Crow's Nest Corn 6 B5
Crowshill Norf 141 B8
Crowsley Oxon 65 D8
Crowsnest Shrops 131 C7
Crowther's Pool Powys 96 B4
Crowthorne Brack 65 G10
Crowton W Ches 183 G9
Croxall Staffs 152 G3
Croxby Lincs 189 B11
Croxby Top Lincs 189 B11
Croxdale Durham 233 D11
Croxden Staffs 151 B11
Croxley Green Herts 85 F9
Croxteth Mers 182 B6
Croxton Cambs 122 E4
Croxton N Lincs 200 E5
Croxton Norf 141 F7
Croxton Norf 159 C9
Croxton Staffs 150 C5
Croxton Green E Ches 167 E8
Croxton Kerrial Leics 154 D6
Croxtonbank Staffs 150 C5
Croy Highld 301 E7
Croy N Lnrk 278 F4
Croyde Devon 40 F2
Croyde Bay Devon 40 F2
Croydon Cambs 104 B6
Croydon London 67 F10
Crozen Hereford 97 B11
Crubenbeg Highld 291 D8
Crubenmore Lodge Highld 291 D8
Cruckmeole Shrops 131 B8
Cruckton Shrops 149 G8
Cruden Bay Aberds 303 F10
Crudgington Telford 150 F2
Crudie Aberds 303 D7
Crudwell Wilts 81 G7
Crug Powys 114 C3
Crugmeer Corn 10 F4
Crugybar Carms 94 D3
Cruise Hill Worcs 117 E10
Crulabhig W Isles 304 E3
Crumlin Caerph 78 F2
Crumplehorn Corn 6 E4
Crumpsall Gtr Man 195 G10
Crumpsbrook Shrops 116 B2
Crumpton Hill Worcs 98 B5
Crundale Kent 54 D5
Crundale Pembs 73 B7
Cruwys Morchard Devon 26 E5
Crux Easton Hants 48 B2
Cruxton Dorset 17 B8
Crwbin Carms 75 C7
Crya Orkney 314 F3
Cryers Hill Bucks 84 F5
Crymlyn Gwyn 179 G10
Crymych Pembs 92 E3
Crynant = Creunant Neath 76 E3
Crynfryn Ceredig 111 E11
Cuaich Highld 291 E8
Cuaig Highld 299 D7
Cuan Argyll 275 B8
Cubbington Warks 118 D6
Cubeck N Yorks 213 B9
Cubert Corn 4 D5
Cubitt Town London 67 D11
Cubley S Yorks 197 G8
Cubley Common Derbys 152 B3
Cublington Bucks 102 G6
Cublington Hereford 97 D8
Cuckfield W Sus 36 B4
Cucklington Som 30 B3
Cuckney Notts 187 G9
Cuckold's Green Suff 143 G9
Cuckold's Green Wilts 46 B3
Cuckoo Green Suff 143 D10
Cuckoo Hill Notts 188 C2
Cuckoo Tye Suff 107 C7
Cuckoo's Corner Hants 49 E8
Cuckoo's Corner Wilts 46 B4
Cuckoo's Knob Wilts 63 G7
Cuckron Shetland 313 H6
Cucumber Corner Norf 143 B7
Cuddesdon Oxon 83 E10
Cuddington Bucks 84 C2
Cuddington W Ches 183 G10
Cuddington Heath W Ches 167 F7
Cuddy Hill Lancs 202 F5
Cudham London 52 B2
Cudlipptown Devon 12 F6
Cudliptown Devon 12 F6
Cudworth S Yorks 197 F11
Cudworth Som 28 E5
Cudworth Sur 51 E8
Cudworth Common S Yorks 197 F11
Cuerden Green Lancs 194 C5
Cuerdley Cross Warr 183 D8
Cufaude Hants 48 B6
Cuffern Pembs 91 G7
Cuffley Herts 86 E4
Cuiashader W Isles 304 C7
Cuidhir W Isles 297 L2
Cuidhtinis W Isles 296 C6
Cuiken Midloth 270 C4
Cuilcheanna Ho Highld 290 G2
Cuin Argyll 288 D6
Cul na h-Aird W Isles 305 H3
Cul Doirlinn Highld 289 B8
Culbo Highld 300 C6
Culbokie Highld 300 D6
Culburnie Highld 300 E4
Culcabock Highld 300 E6
Culcairn Highld 300 C6
Culcharry Highld 301 D8
Culcheth Warr 183 B11
Culcronchie Dumfries 237 C7
Culdrain Aberds 302 F5
Culduie Highld 299 E7
Culeave Highld 309 K5
Culford Suff 124 D6
Culfordheath Suff 125 C7
Culfosie Aberds 293 C9
Culgaith Cumb 231 F8
Culham Oxon 83 F8
Culkein Highld 306 F5
Culkein Drumbeg Highld 306 F6
Culkerton Glos 80 F6
Cullachie Highld 301 G9
Cullen Moray 302 C5
Cullercoats T & W 243 C9
Cullicudden Highld 300 C6
Cullingworth W Yorks 205 F7
Cullipool Argyll 275 B8
Cullivoe Shetland 312 C7
Culloch Perth 285 F11
Culloden Highld 301 E7
Cullompton Devon 27 F8
Culm Davy Devon 27 D10
Culmaily Highld 311 K2
Culmazie Dumfries 236 D5
Culmer Sur 50 F2
Culmers Kent 70 G5
Culmington Shrops 131 G9
Culmore Stirl 278 B3
Culmstock Devon 27 E10
Culnacraig Highld 307 J5
Culnaightrie Dumfries 237 D9
Culnaknock Highld 298 C5
Culnaneam Highld 294 C6
Culpho Suff 108 B4
Culra Lodge Highld 291 F7
Culrain Highld 309 K5
Culross Fife 279 D9
Culroy S Ayrs 257 G8
Culscadden Dumfries 236 E6
Culsh Aberds 292 D5
Culsh Aberds 303 E8
Culshabbin Dumfries 236 D5
Culswick Shetland 313 J4
Cultercullen Aberds 303 G9
Cults Aberdeen 293 C10
Cults Aberds 302 F5
Cults Dumfries 236 E6
Cults Fife 287 G7
Culverlane Devon 8 C4
Culverstone Green Kent 68 G6
Culverthorpe Lincs 173 G8
Culworth Northants 101 B10
Culzie Lodge Highld 300 B5
Cumberlow Green Herts 104 E6
Cumbernauld N Lnrk 278 G5
Cumbernauld Village N Lnrk 278 F5
Cumber's Bank Wrex 149 B8
Cumberworth Lincs 191 G8
Cumdivock Cumb 230 B2
Cumeragh Village Lancs 203 F7
Cuminestown Aberds 303 D8
Cumledge Borders 272 D5
Cumlewick Shetland 313 L6
Cummersdale Cumb 239 G9
Cummerton Aberds 303 C8
Cummertrees Dumfries 238 D4
Cummingston Moray 301 C11
Cumnock E Ayrs 258 E3
Cumnor Oxon 83 E7
Cumnor Hill Oxon 83 D7
Cumrew Cumb 240 G2
Cumwhinton Cumb 239 G10
Cumwhitton Cumb 240 G2
Cundall N Yorks 215 E8
Cundy Cross S Yorks 197 F11
Cundy Hos S Yorks 186 B4
Cunninghamhead N Ayrs 267 G7
Cunnister Shetland 312 D7
Cupar Fife 287 F7
Cupar Muir Fife 287 F7
Cupernham Hants 32 C5
Cupid Green Herts 85 D9
Cupid's Hill Mon 97 F8
Curbar Derbys 186 G3
Curborough Staffs 152 G2
Curbridge Hants 33 E8
Curbridge Oxon 82 D4
Curdridge Hants 33 E8
Curdworth Warks 134 E3
Curgurrell Corn 3 B9
Curin Highld 300 D3
Curland Som 28 D3
Curland Common Som 28 D3
Curlew Green Suff 127 D7
Curling Tye Green Essex 88 D4
Curload Som 28 B4
Currarie S Ayrs 244 E5
Currian Vale Corn 5 D9
Curridge W Berks 64 E3
Currie Edin 270 B3
Currock Cumb 239 G10
Curry Lane Corn 11 C11
Curry Mallet Som 28 C4
Curry Rivel Som 28 B5
Cursiter Orkney 314 E3
Curteis' Corner Kent 53 F11
Curtisden Green Kent 53 E8
Curtisknowle Devon 8 E4
Curtismill Green Essex 87 F8
Cury Corn 2 E5
Cusbay Orkney 314 C5
Cusgarne Corn 4 G5
Cushnie Aberds 303 C7
Cushuish Som 43 G7
Cusop Hereford 96 C4
Custards Hants 32 F3
Custom House London 68 C2
Cusveorth Coombe Corn 4 G5
Cusworth S Yorks 198 G4
Cutcloy Dumfries 236 F6
Cutcombe Som 42 F2
Cutgate Gtr Man 195 E11
Cuthill E Loth 281 G7
Cutiau Gwyn 146 F2
Cutlers Green Essex 105 E11
Cutler's Green Som 44 C5
Cutmadoc Corn 5 C11
Cutmere Corn 6 C6
Cutnall Green Worcs 117 D7
Cutsdean Glos 99 E11
Cutsyke W Yorks 198 C2
Cutteslowe Oxon 83 C8
Cutthorpe Derbys 186 G4
Cuttiford's Door Som 28 E4
Cutts Shetland 313 K6
Cuttybridge Pembs 72 B6
Cuttyhill Aberds 303 D10
Cuxham Oxon 83 F11
Cuxton Medway 69 F8
Cuxwold Lincs 201 G7
Cwm Bl Gwent 77 D11
Cwm Denb 181 F9
Cwm Neath 57 C10
Cwm Powys 129 D11
Cwm Powys 130 E5
Cwm Shrops 114 B6
Cwm Swansea 57 B7
Cwm-byr Carms 94 E2
Cwm Capel Carms 75 E7
Cwm-celyn Bl Gwent 78 D2
Cwm-Cewydd Gwyn 147 G7
Cwm-cou Ceredig 92 C5
Cwm Dows Caerph 78 F2
Cwm-Dulais Swansea 75 E10
Cwm felin fach Caerph 77 G11
Cwm Ffrwd-oer Torf 78 E3
Cwm-Fields Torf 78 E3
Cwm Gelli Caerph 77 F11
Cwm Gwyn Swansea 56 C6
Cwm Head Shrops 131 F8
Cwm-hesgen Gwyn 146 D5
Cwm-hwnt Rhondda 76 D6
Cwm Irfon Powys 95 B7
Cwm-Llinau Powys 128 B6
Cwm-mawr Carms 75 C8
Cwm-miles Carms 92 G3
Cwm Nant-gam Bl Gwent 78 C2
Cwm-parc Rhondda 77 F7
Cwm Penmachno Conwy 164 F3
Cwm Plysgog Ceredig 92 C3
Cwm-twrch Isaf Powys 76 C3
Cwm-twrch Uchaf Powys 76 C3
Cwm-y-glo Carms 75 C9
Cwm-y-glo Gwyn 163 C8
Cwmafan Neath 57 C9
Cwmaman Rhondda 77 F8
Cwmann Carms 93 B11
Cwmavon Torf 78 D3
Cwmbâch Rhondda 77 E8
Cwmbach Carms 75 E7
Cwmbach Carms 92 F5
Cwmbach Powys 96 D3
Cwmbach Rhondda 77 E8
Cwmbach Llechrhyd Powys 113 G10
Cwmbelan Powys 129 G8
Cwmbran Torf 78 G3
Cwmbrwyno Ceredig 128 G4
Cwmcarn Caerph 78 G2
Cwmcarvan Mon 79 D7
Cwmcoednerth Ceredig 92 B6
Cwmcrawnon Powys 77 B10
Cwmcych Carms 92 D5
Cwmdare Rhondda 77 E7
Cwmdu Carms 94 E2
Cwmdu Powys 96 G3
Cwmdu Swansea 56 C6
Cwmduad Carms 93 E7
Cwmdwr Carms 94 E4
Cwmerfyn Ceredig 128 G3
Cwmfelin Bridgend 57 D11
Cwmfelin M Tydf 77 E9
Cwmfelin Boeth Carms 73 B11
Cwmfelin Mynach Carms 92 G4
Cwmffrwd Carms 74 B6
Cwmgiedd Powys 76 C3
Cwmgors Neath 76 C2
Cwmgwili Carms 75 C9
Cwmgwrach Neath 76 E5
Cwmhiraeth Carms 92 D6
Cwmifor Carms 94 F3
Cwmisfael Carms 75 B7
Cwmllynfell Neath 76 C2
Cwmnantyrodyn Caerph 77 F11
Cwmorgan Pembs 92 E5
Cwmparc Rhondda 77 F7
Cwmpengraig Carms 92 D6
Cwmpennar Rhondda 77 E8
Cwmrhos Powys 96 G3
Cwmrhydyceirw Swansea 57 B7
Cwmsychpant Ceredig 93 B9
Cwmsyfiog Caerph 77 E11
Cwmsymlog Ceredig 128 G4
Cwmtillery Bl Gwent 78 D2
Cwmwdig Water Pembs 90 E6
Cwmwysg Powys 95 F7
Cwmyniscoy Torf 78 F3
Cwmyoy Mon 96 G5
Cwmystwyth Ceredig 112 C5
Cwrt Gwyn 128 C3
Cwrt-newydd Ceredig 93 B9
Cwrt-y-cadno Carms 94 C3
Cwrt-y-gollen Powys 78 B2
Cydweli = Kidwelly Carms 74 D6
Cyffordd Llandudno = Llandudno Junction Conwy 180 F3
Cyffylliog Denb 165 D9
Cyfronydd Powys 130 B2
Cymau Flint 166 D3
Cymdda Bridgend 58 C2
Cymer Neath 57 B11
Cymmer Rhondda 77 G8
Cyncoed Cardiff 59 C7
Cynghordy Carms 94 C6
Cynheidre Carms 75 D7
Cynonville Neath 57 B10
Cyntwell Cardiff 58 D6
Cynwyd Denb 165 G9
Cynwyl Elfed Carms 93 F7
Cywarch Gwyn 147 F7

D

Daccombe Devon 9 B8
Dacre Cumb 230 F5
Dacre N Yorks 214 G3
Dacre Banks N Yorks 214 G3
Daddry Shield Durham 232 D3
Dadford Bucks 102 D3
Dadlington Leics 135 D8
Dafarn Faig Gwyn 163 F7
Dafen Carms 75 E8
Daffy Green Norf 141 B9
Dagdale Staffs 151 C11
Dagenham London 68 C3
Daggons Dorset 31 E10
Daglingworth Glos 81 D7
Dagnall Bucks 85 B7
Dagtail End Worcs 117 E10
Dagworth Suff 125 E10
Dail Beag W Isles 304 D4
Dail bho Dheas W Isles 304 B6
Dail bho Thuath W Isles 304 B6
Dail Mor W Isles 304 D4
Daill Argyll 274 G4
Dailly S Ayrs 245 C7
Dainton Devon 9 B7
Dairsie or Osnaburgh Fife 287 F8
Daisy Green Suff 125 D10
Daisy Green Suff 125 D11
Daisy Hill Gtr Man 195 G7
Daisy Hill W Yorks 197 B9
Daisy Hill W Yorks 205 G8
Daisy Nook Gtr Man 196 G2
Dalabrog W Isles 297 J3
Dalavich Argyll 275 B10
Dalbeattie Dumfries 237 C10
Dalbeg Highld 291 B8
Dalblair E Ayrs 258 F4
Dalbog Angus 293 F7
Dalbrack Stirl 285 G11
Dalbury Derbys 152 C5
Dalby I o M 192 E3
Dalby Lincs 190 G6
Dalby N Yorks 216 E2
Dalchalloch Perth 291 G9
Dalchalm Highld 311 J3
Dalchenna Argyll 284 G4
Dalchirach Moray 301 F11
Dalchonzie Perth 285 E11
Dalchork Highld 309 H5
Dalchreichart Highld 290 B4
Dalchruin Perth 285 F11
Dalderby Lincs 174 B2
Dale Cumb 230 C6
Dale Gtr Man 196 F3
Dale Pembs 72 D4
Dale Shetland 312 G6
Dale Abbey Derbys 153 B8
Dale Bottom Cumb 229 G11
Dale Brow E Ches 184 F6
Dale End Derbys 170 C2
Dale End N Yorks 204 D5
Dale Head Cumb 221 B8
Dale Hill E Sus 53 G7
Dale Hill E Sus 53 G8
Dale Moor Derbys 153 B8
Dale of Walls Shetland 313 H3
Dalebank Derbys 170 C5
Dalelia Highld 289 C9
Dales Brow Gtr Man 195 G9
Dales Green Staffs 168 D5
Daless Highld 301 F8
Dalestie Moray 292 B3
Dalestorth Notts 171 C8
Dalfaber Highld 291 B11
Dalfoil Stirl 277 D11
Dalganachan Highld 310 E4
Dalgarven N Ayrs 266 F5
Dalgety Bay Fife 280 E3
Dalginross Perth 285 E11
Dalguise Perth 286 C3
Dalhalvaig Highld 310 D2
Dalham Suff 124 E4
Dalhastnie Angus 293 F7
Dalhenzean Perth 292 G3
Dalinlongart Argyll 276 E2
Dalkeith Midloth 270 B6
Dallam Warr 183 C9
Dallas Moray 301 D11
Dallas Lodge Moray 301 D11
Dallcharn Highld 308 D6
Dalleagles E Ayrs 258 G3
Dallicott Shrops 132 E5
Dallimores I o W 20 C6
Dallinghoo Suff 126 G5
Dallington E Sus 23 B11
Dallington Northants 120 E4
Dallow N Yorks 214 E3
Dalmadilly Aberds 293 B9
Dalmally Argyll 284 E5
Dalmarnock Glasgow 268 C2
Dalmarnock Perth 286 C3
Dalmary Stirl 277 B10
Dalmellington E Ayrs 245 B11
Dalmeny Edin 280 F2
Dalmigavie Highld 291 B9
Dalmigavie Lodge Highld 301 G7
Dalmilling S Ayrs 257 E9
Dalmore Highld 300 C6
Dalmuir W Dunb 277 G9
Dalnabreck Highld 289 C8
Dalnacardoch Lodge Perth 291 F9
Dalnacroich Highld 300 D3
Dalnaglar Castle Perth 292 G3
Dalnahaitnach Highld 301 G8
Dalnamein Lodge Perth 291 G10
Dalnarrow Argyll 289 F9
Dalnaspidal Lodge Perth 291 F8
Dalnavaid Perth 292 G2
Dalnavie Highld 300 B6
Dalnaw Dumfries 236 B5
Dalnawillan Lodge Highld 310 E4
Dalness Highld 284 B5
Dalnessie Highld 309 H6
Dalphaid Highld 309 H3
Dalqueich Perth 286 G4
Dalrannoch Argyll 289 E11
Dalreavoch Highld 309 J7
Dalriach Highld 301 F10
Dalrigh Stirl 285 E7
Dalry Edin 280 G4
Dalry N Ayrs 266 F5
Dalrymple E Ayrs 257 G9
Dalscote Northants 120 G3
Dalserf S Lnrk 268 E6
Dalshannon N Lnrk 278 G4
Dalston Cumb 239 G9
Dalston London 67 C10
Dalswinton Dumfries 247 F10
Dalton Cumb 211 D10
Dalton Dumfries 238 C4
Dalton Lancs 194 F3
Dalton N Yorks 215 D8
Dalton N Yorks 224 D2
Dalton Northum 241 F10
Dalton Northum 242 C4
Dalton S Lnrk 268 D3
Dalton S Yorks 187 C7
Dalton W Yorks 197 D7
Dalton-in-Furness Cumb 210 E4
Dalton-le-Dale Durham 234 B4
Dalton Magna S Yorks 187 C7
Dalton-on-Tees N Yorks 224 D5
Dalton Parva S Yorks 187 C7
Dalton Piercy Hrtlpl 234 E5
Dalveallan Highld 300 F6
Dalveich Stirl 285 E10
Dalvina Lo Highld 308 E6
Dalwey Telford 132 B3
Dalwhinnie Highld 291 E8
Dalwood Devon 28 G3
Dalwyne S Ayrs 245 D8
Dam Green Norf 141 F11
Dam Head W Yorks 196 B6
Dam Mill Staffs 133 C7
Dam of Quoiggs Perth 286 G2
Dam Side Lancs 202 D4
Damask Green Herts 104 F5
Damems W Yorks 204 F6
Damerham Hants 31 D10
Damery Glos 80 G2
Damgate Norf 143 B8
Damgate Norf 161 F9
Damhead Moray 301 D10
Damhead Holdings Midloth 270 B5
Damnaglaur Dumfries 236 F3
Damside Borders 270 F3
Dan Caerlan Rhondda 58 C5
Danaway Kent 69 G11
Danbury Essex 88 E3
Danbury Common Essex 88 E3
Danby N Yorks 226 D4
Danby Wiske N Yorks 224 F6
Dancers Hill Herts 86 F2
Dancing Green Hereford 98 G2
Dandaleith Moray 302 E2
Danderhall Midloth 270 B6
Dandy Corner Suff 125 D11
Dane Bank Gtr Man 184 B6
Dane End Herts 104 G6
Dane in Shaw E Ches 168 C5
Dane Street Kent 54 C5
Danebank E Ches 185 E7
Danebridge E Ches 169 B7
Danegate E Sus 52 G5
Danehill E Sus 36 B6
Danemoor Green Norf 141 B11
Danes Moss E Ches 184 G6
Danesbury Herts 86 B2
Danesfield Bucks 65 C10
Danesford Shrops 132 E4
Daneshill Hants 49 C7
Danesmoor Derbys 170 C6
Daneway Glos 80 E6
Dangerous Corner Gtr Man 195 G7
Dangerous Corner Lancs 194 E4
Daniel's Water Kent 54 E3
Danna na Cloiche Argyll 275 F7
Dannonchapel Corn 10 E6
Danskine E Loth 271 B11
Danthorpe E Yorks 209 G10
Danygraig Caerph 78 G2
Danzey Green Warks 118 D2
Dapple Heath Staffs 151 D10
Darby End W Mid 133 F9
Darby Green Hants 65 G10
Darbys Green Worcs 116 F4
Darby's Hill W Mid 133 F9
Darcy Lever Gtr Man 195 F8
Dardy Powys 78 B2
Darenth Kent 68 E5
Daresbury Halton 183 E9
Daresbury Delph Halton 183 E9
Darfield S Yorks 198 G2
Darfoulds Notts 187 F9
Dargate Kent 70 G5
Dargate Common Kent 70 G5
Darite Corn 6 B5
Darkland Moray 302 C2
Darland Wrex 166 D5
Darlaston W Mid 133 D9
Darlaston Green W Mid 133 D9
Darley N Yorks 205 B10
Darley Shrops 132 D3
Darley Abbey Derby 153 B7
Darley Bridge Derbys 170 C3
Darley Dale Derbys 170 C3
Darley Green Warks 118 C3
Darley Head N Yorks 205 B9
Darley Hillside Derbys 170 C3
Darleyford Corn 11 G11
Darleyhall Herts 104 G2
Darlingscott Warks 100 C4
Darlington Darl 224 C5
Darliston Shrops 149 C11
Darlton Notts 188 G3
Darmsden Suff 125 G11
Darn Hill Gtr Man 195 E10
Darnall S Yorks 186 D5
Darnaway Castle Moray 301 D9
Darnford Staffs 134 B2
Darnhall W Ches 167 C10
Darnhall Mains Borders 270 F4
Darnick Borders 262 C2
Darowen Powys 128 C6
Darra Aberds 303 E7
Darracott Devon 24 D2
Darracott Devon 40 F3
Darras Hall Northum 242 C5
Darrington W Yorks 198 D3
Darrow Green Norf 142 F5
Darsham Suff 127 D8
Darshill Som 44 E6
Dartford Kent 68 E4
Dartford Crossing Kent 68 D5
Dartington Devon 8 C5
Dartmeet Devon 13 G9
Dartmouth Devon 9 E7
Dartmouth Park London 67 B9
Darton S Yorks 197 F10
Darvel E Ayrs 258 B3
Darvillshill Bucks 84 F4
Darwell Hole E Sus 23 B11
Darwen Blkburn 195 C7
Dassels Herts 105 F7
Datchet Windsor 66 D3
Datchet Common Windsor 66 D3
Datchworth Herts 86 B3
Datchworth Green Herts 86 B3
Daubhill Gtr Man 195 F8
Daugh of Kinermony Moray 302 E2
Dauntsey Wilts 62 C3
Dauntsey Lock Wilts 62 C3
Dava Moray 301 F10
Davenham W Ches 183 G11
Davenport E Ches 168 B4
Davenport Gtr Man 184 D5
Davenport Green E Ches 184 F4
Davenport Green Gtr Man 184 D4
Daventry Northants 119 E11
David Street Kent 68 G6
David's Well Powys 113 B11
Davidson's Mains Edin 280 F4
Davidston Highld 301 C7
Davidstow Corn 11 D9
Davington Dumfries 248 C6
Davington Kent 70 G4
Daviot Aberds 303 G7
Daviot Highld 301 F7
Davis's Town E Sus 23 B8
Davo Mains Aberds 293 F9
Davoch of Grange Moray 302 D4
Davyhulme Gtr Man 184 B3
Daw Cross N Yorks 205 C11
Daw End W Mid 133 C10
Dawdon Durham 234 B4
Dawesgreen Sur 51 D8
Dawker Hill N Yorks 207 F7
Dawley Telford 132 B3
Dawley Bank Telford 132 B3
Dawlish Devon 14 F5
Dawlish Warren Devon 14 F5
Dawn Conwy 180 G5
Daw's Cross Essex 107 E7
Daw's Green Som 27 C11
Daws Heath Essex 69 B10
Daw's House Corn 12 E2
Dawshill Worcs 116 G6
Dawsmere Lincs 157 C8
Day Green E Ches 168 D3
Dayhills Staffs 151 C9
Dayhouse Bank Worcs 117 B9
Daylesford Glos 100 F4
Daywall Shrops 148 C5
Ddol Flint 181 G10
Ddôl Cownwy Powys 147 F10
Ddrydwy Anglesey 178 G5
De Beauvoir Town London 67 C10
Deacons Hill Herts 85 F11
Deadman's Cross C Beds 104 C2
Deadman's Green Staffs 151 B10
Deadwater Hants 49 F10
Deadwater Northum 250 D4
Deaf Hill Durham 234 D3
Deal Kent 55 C11
Deal Hall Essex 89 F8
Dean Cumb 229 F7
Dean Devon 8 C4
Dean Devon 40 D6
Dean Devon 40 E4
Dean Devon 41 D8
Dean Dorset 31 D7
Dean Edin 280 G4
Dean Hants 33 D9
Dean Hants 48 G2
Dean Lancs 195 B11
Dean Oxon 100 G6
Dean Som 45 E7
Dean Bank Durham 233 E11
Dean Court Oxon 83 D7
Dean Cross Devon 40 E4
Dean Head S Yorks 197 G9
Dean Lane Head W Yorks 205 G7
Dean Park Renfs 267 B10
Dean Prior Devon 8 C4
Dean Row E Ches 184 E5
Dean Street Kent 53 C8
Deanburnhaugh Borders 261 G9
Deane Gtr Man 195 F7
Deane Hants 48 C4
Deanend Dorset 31 D7
Deanich Lodge Highld 309 L3
Deanland Dorset 31 D7
Deanlane End W Sus 34 E2
Deans W Loth 269 B10
Deans Bottom Kent 69 G11
Dean's Green Warks 118 D2
Deans Hill Kent 69 G11
Deanscales Cumb 229 F7
Deansgreen E Ches 183 D11
Deanshanger Northants 102 D5
Deanston Stirl 285 G11
Dearham Cumb 229 D7
Dearnley Gtr Man 196 D2
Debach Suff 126 G4
Debdale Gtr Man 184 B5
Debden Essex 86 F6
Debden Essex 105 E11
Debden Cross Essex 105 E11
Debden Green Essex 86 F6
Debden Green Essex 105 E11
Debenham Suff 126 E3
Deblin's Green Worcs 98 B6
Dechmont W Loth 279 G10
Deckham T & W 243 E7
Deddington Oxon 101 E9
Dedham Essex 107 E11
Dedham Heath Essex 107 E11
Dedridge W Loth 269 B11
Dedworth Windsor 66 D2
Deebank Aberds 293 D8
Deecastle Aberds 292 D6
Deene Northants 137 E8
Deenethorpe Northants 137 E9
Deepcar S Yorks 186 B3
Deepclough Derbys 185 B8
Deepcut Sur 50 B2
Deepdale C Beds 104 B4
Deepdale Cumb 212 C4
Deepdale N Yorks 213 D7
Deepdene Sur 51 D7
Deepfields W Mid 133 E8
Deeping Gate Lincs 138 B2
Deeping St James Lincs 138 B3
Deeping St Nicholas Lincs 156 F4
Deepthwaite Cumb 211 C10
Deepweir Mon 60 B3
Deerhill Moray 302 D4
Deerhurst Glos 99 F7
Deerhurst Walton Glos 99 F7
Deerland Pembs 73 C7
Deerness Orkney 314 F5
Deer's Green Essex 105 E9
Deerstones N Yorks 205 C7
Deerton Street Kent 70 G3
Defford Worcs 99 C8
Defynnog Powys 95 F8
Deganwy Conwy 180 F3
Degar V Glam 58 D4
Degibna Corn 2 D5
Deighton N Yorks 225 E7
Deighton W Yorks 197 D7
Deighton York 207 E8
Deiniolen Gwyn 163 C9
Deishar Highld 291 B11
Delabole Corn 11 E7
Delamere W Ches 167 B9
Delfour Highld 291 C10
Delfrigs Aberds 303 G9
Dell Lodge Highld 292 B2
Dell Quay W Sus 22 C4
Delliefure Highld 301 F10
Delly End Oxon 82 C5
Delnabo Moray 292 B3
Delnadamph Aberds 292 C4
Delnamer Angus 292 G3
Delph Gtr Man 196 F3
Delves Durham 233 B8
Delvin End Essex 106 D5
Delvine Perth 286 C5
Dembleby Lincs 155 B10
Demelza Corn 5 C9
Denaby Main S Yorks 187 B7
Denbeath Fife 281 B7
Denbigh Denb 165 B8
Denbury Devon 8 B6
Denby Derbys 170 F5
Denby Bottles Derbys 170 F5
Denby Common Derbys 170 F6
Denby Dale W Yorks 197 F8
Denchworth Oxon 82 G5
Dendron Cumb 210 E4
Dene Park Kent 52 C5
Denel End C Beds 103 D10
Denend Aberds 302 F6
Deneside Durham 234 B4
Denford Northants 121 B9
Denford Staffs 169 E7
Dengie Essex 89 E7
Denham Bucks 66 B4
Denham Bucks 102 G5
Denham Suff 124 E5
Denham Suff 126 C3
Denham Corner Suff 126 C3
Denham End Suff 124 E5
Denham Green Bucks 66 B4
Denham Street Suff 126 C3
Denhead Aberds 303 D9
Denhead Fife 287 F8
Denhead of Arbilot Angus 287 C9
Denhead of Gray Dundee 287 D7
Denholm Borders 262 F3
Denholme W Yorks 205 G7
Denholme Clough W Yorks 205 G7
Denholme Edge W Yorks 205 G7
Denholme Gate W Yorks 205 G7
Denholmhill Borders 262 F3
Denio Gwyn 145 B7
Denmead Hants 33 E11
Denmore Aberdeen 293 B11
Denmoss Aberds 302 E6
Dennington Suff 126 D5
Dennington Corner Suff 126 D5
Dennington Hall Suff 126 D5
Denny Falk 278 E6
Denny Bottom Kent 52 F5
Denny End Cambs 123 D9
Denny Lodge Hants 32 F4
Dennyloanhead Falk 278 E6
Dennystown W Dunb 277 F7
Denshaw Gtr Man 196 E3
Denside Aberds 293 D10
Densole Kent 55 E8
Denston Suff 124 G5
Denstone Staffs 169 G9
Denstroude Kent 70 G6
Dent Cumb 212 B4
Dent Bank Durham 232 F4
Denton Cambs 138 F2
Denton Darl 224 B4
Denton E Sus 23 E7
Denton Gtr Man 184 B6
Denton Kent 55 D8
Denton Kent 69 E7
Denton Lincs 155 C7
Denton N Yorks 205 D8
Denton Norf 142 F5
Denton Northants 120 F6
Denton Oxon 83 E9
Denton Burn T & W 242 D5
Denton Holme Cumb 239 G10
Denton's Green Mers 183 B7
Denver Norf 140 C2
Denvilles Hants 22 B2
Denwick Northum 264 G6
Deopham Norf 141 C11
Deopham Green Norf 141 D10
Deopham Stalland Norf 141 D10
Depden Suff 124 F5
Depden Green Suff 124 F5
Deppers Bridge Warks 119 F7
Deptford London 67 D11
Deptford T & W 243 F9
Deptford Wilts 46 F4
Derby Derbys 153 B7
Derby Devon 40 G5
Derbyhaven I o M 192 F3
Derbyshire Hill Mers 183 C8
Dereham Norf 159 G9
Dergoals Dumfries 236 D4
Deri Caerph 77 E10
Derriford Plym 7 D9
Derril Devon 24 G4
Derringstone Kent 55 D8
Derrington Shrops 132 E2
Derrington Staffs 151 E7
Derriton Devon 24 G4
Derry Stirl 285 E10
Derry Downs London 68 F3
Derry Fields Wilts 81 G8
Derry Hill Wilts 62 E3
Derry Lodge Aberds 292 D2
Derrydaroch Stirl 285 E7
Derryguaig Argyll 288 F6
Derrythorpe N Lincs 199 F10
Dersingham Norf 158 C3
Dertfords Wilts 45 D10
Dervaig Argyll 288 D6
Derwen Bridgend 58 C2
Derwen Denb 165 E9
Derwenlas Powys 128 D4
Desborough Northants 136 G6
Desford Leics 135 C9
Deskryshiel Aberds 292 B6
Detchant Northum 264 B3
Detling Kent 53 B9
Deuchar Angus 292 G6
Deuddwr Powys 148 F4
Deuxhill Shrops 132 F3
Devauden Mon 79 F7
Deveral Corn 2 B3
Devil's Bridge = Pontarfynach Ceredig 112 B4
Devitts Green Warks 134 E5
Devizes Wilts 62 G4
Devol Invclyd 276 G6
Devon Village Clack 279 B8
Devonport Plym 7 E9
Devonside Clack 279 B8
Devoran Corn 3 B7
Dewar Borders 270 F6
Dewartown Midloth 271 C7
Dewes Green Essex 105 E9
Dewlands Common Dorset 31 F9
Dewlish Dorset 17 B11
Dewsbury W Yorks 197 C8
Dewsbury Moor W Yorks 197 C8
Dewshall Court Hereford 97 E9
Dhoon I o M 192 D5
Dhoor I o M 192 C5
Dhowin I o M 192 B5
Dhustone Shrops 115 B11
Dial Green W Sus 34 B6
Dial Post W Sus 35 D11
Dibberford Dorset 29 G7
Dibden Hants 32 F6
Dibden Purlieu Hants 32 F6
Dickens Heath W Mid 118 B2
Dickleburgh Norf 142 G3
Dickleburgh Moor Norf 142 G3
Dickon Hills Lincs 174 D6
Didbrook Glos 99 E11
Didcot Oxon 64 B4
Diddington Cambs 122 D3
Diddlebury Shrops 131 F10
Diddywell Devon 25 B7
Didley Hereford 97 E9
Didling W Sus 34 D4
Didlington Norf 140 D5
Didmarton Glos 61 B10
Didsbury Gtr Man 184 C4
Didworthy Devon 8 C3
Diebidale Highld 309 L4
Digbeth W Mid 133 F11
Digby Lincs 173 E9
Digg Highld 298 C4
Diggle Gtr Man 196 F4
Diglis Worcs 116 G6
Digmoor Lancs 194 F3
Digswell Herts 86 B3
Digswell Park Herts 86 C2
Digswell Water Herts 86 C3
Dihewyd Ceredig 111 F9
Dilham Norf 160 D6
Dilhorne Staffs 169 G7
Dill Hall Lancs 195 B8
Dillarburn S Lnrk 268 G6
Dillington Cambs 122 D2
Dillington Som 28 D5
Dilston Northum 241 E11
Dilston Marsh Wilts 45 D11
Dilwyn Hereford 115 G8
Dimlands V Glam 58 F3
Dimmer Som 44 G6
Dimple Derbys 170 C3
Dimple Gtr Man 195 D8
Dimsdale Staffs 168 F4
Dimson Corn 12 G4
Dinas Carms 92 E5
Dinas Corn 10 G4
Dinas Gwyn 144 B5
Dinas Gwyn 163 D7
Dinas Cross Pembs 91 D10
Dinas Dinlle Gwyn 162 D6
Dinas-Mawddwy Gwyn 147 G7
Dinas Mawr Conwy 164 E4
Dinas Powys V Glam 59 E7
Dinbych y Pysgod = Tenby Pembs 73 E10
Dinckley Lancs 203 F9
Dinder Som 44 E5
Dinedor Hereford 97 D10
Dinedor Cross Hereford 97 D10
Dines Green Worcs 116 F6
Dingestow Mon 79 C7
Dinghurst N Som 44 B2
Dingle Mers 182 D5
Dingleden Kent 53 G10
Dingleton Borders 262 C2
Dingley Northants 136 F5
Dingwall Highld 300 D5
Dinlabyre Borders 250 E2
Dinmael Conwy 165 G8
Dinnet Aberds 292 D6
Dinnington S Yorks 187 D8
Dinnington Som 28 E6
Dinnington T & W 242 C6
Dinorwic Gwyn 163 C9
Dinton Bucks 84 C3
Dinton Wilts 46 G4
Dinwoodie Mains Dumfries 248 E4

Dinworthy Devon 24 D4
Dipford Som 28 C2
Dipley Hants 49 B8
Dippenhall Sur 49 D10
Dippertown Devon 12 E4
Dippin N Ayrs 256 E2
Dipple Devon 24 D4
Dipple Moray 302 D3
Dipple S Ayrs 244 C6
Diptford Devon 8 D4
Dipton Durham 242 G5
Diptonmill Northumb 241 E10
Dirdhu Highld 301 G10
Direcleit W Isles 305 J3
Dirleton E Loth 281 E10
Dirt Pot Northumb 232 B3
Discoed Powys 114 E5
Discove Som 45 G7
Diseworth Leics 153 E9
Dishes Orkney 314 D6
Dishforth N Yorks 215 E7
Dishley Leics 153 E10
Disley E Ches 185 E7
Diss Norf 126 B2
Disserth Powys 113 F10
Distington Cumb 228 G6
Ditchampton Wilts 46 G5
Ditcheat Som 44 F6
Ditchfield Bucks 84 G4
Ditchford Hill Worcs 100 D4
Ditchingham Norf 142 E6
Ditchling E Sus 36 D4
Ditherington Shrops 149 G10
Ditteridge Wilts 61 F10
Dittisham Devon 9 E7
Ditton Halton 183 D7
Ditton Kent 53 B8
Ditton Green Cambs 124 F3
Ditton Priors Shrops 132 F2
Dittons E Sus 23 E10
Divach Highld 300 G4
Divlyn Carms 94 D5
Dixton Glos 99 E9
Dixton Mon 79 C8
Dizzard Corn 11 B9
Dobcross Gtr Man 196 F3
Dobs Hill Flint 166 C4
Dobson's Bridge Shrops 149 C9
Dobwalls Corn 6 C4
Doc Penfro = Pembroke Dock Pembs 73 E7
Doccombe Devon 13 D11
Dochfour Ho Highld 300 F6
Dochgarroch Highld 300 E6
Dockeney Norf 143 E7
Dockenfield Sur 49 E10
Docker Lancs 211 E11
Docking Norf 158 B5
Docklow Hereford 115 F11
Dockray Cumb 230 G3
Dockroyd W Yorks 204 F6
Docton Devon 24 C2
Dodbrooke Devon 8 G4
Dodburn Borders 249 B11
Doddenham Worcs 116 F5
Doddinghurst Essex 87 F9
Doddington Cambs 139 E7
Doddington Kent 54 B2
Doddington Lincs 188 G6
Doddington Northumb 263 C11
Doddington Shrops 116 B2
Doddiscombsleigh Devon 14 D3
Doddshill Norf 158 C3
Doddycross Corn 6 C6
Dodford Northants 120 E2
Dodford Worcs 117 C8
Dodington S Glos 61 C9
Dodington Som 43 E7
Dodleston W Ches 166 C5
Dodmarsh Hereford 97 C11
Dods Leigh Staffs 151 C10
Dodscott Devon 25 D8
Dodworth S Yorks 197 F10
Dodworth Bottom S Yorks 197 G10
Dodworth Green S Yorks 197 F10
Doe Bank W Mid 134 D2
Doe Green Warr 183 D9
Doe Lea Derbys 171 B7
Doehole Derbys 170 D5
Doffcocker Gtr Man 195 E7
Dog & Gun Mers 182 B5
Dog Hill Gtr Man 196 F3
Dog Village Devon 14 B5
Dogdyke Lincs 174 D2
Dogingtree Estate Staffs 151 G9
Dogley Lane W Yorks 197 E7
Dogmersfield Hants 49 C9
Dogridge Wilts 62 B5
Dogsthorpe P'boro 138 C3
Doirlinn Highld 289 D8
Dol-fôr Powys 128 B6
Dôl-ffanog Gwyn 146 G4
Dôl-y-Bont Ceredig 128 F2
Dol-y-cannau Powys 96 B3
Dolanog Powys 147 G11
Dolau Powys 114 D2
Dolau Rhondda 58 C3
Dolbenmaen Gwyn 163 G8
Dole Ceredig 128 F2
Dolemeads Bath 61 G9
Doley Staffs 150 D4
Dolfach Powys 129 C8
Dolfor Powys 130 F2
Dolgarrog Conwy 164 B3
Dolgellau Gwyn 146 F4
Dolgerdd Ceredig 111 G8
Dolgoch Gwyn 128 C3
Dolgran Carms 93 E8
Dolhelfa Powys 113 C8
Dolhendre Gwyn 147 C7
Doll Highld 311 J2
Dollar Clack 279 B9
Dolley Green Powys 114 D5
Dollis Hill London 67 B8
Dollwen Ceredig 128 G3
Dolphin Flint 181 G11
Dolphingstone E Loth 281 G7
Dolphinholme Lancs 202 C6
Dolphinston Borders 262 F5
Dolphinton S Lnrk 270 F2
Dolton Devon 25 E9
Dolwen Conwy 180 G5
Dolwen Powys 129 B9
Dolwyd Conwy 180 F4
Dolwyddelan Conwy 164 E2
Dolydd Gwyn 163 D7
Dolyhir Powys 114 F4
Dolymelinau Powys 129 D11
Dolywern Wrex 148 B4
Domewood Sur 51 E10
Domgay Powys 148 F5
Dommett Som 28 E3
Don Johns Essex 106 F6
Doncaster S Yorks 198 G5
Doncaster Common S Yorks 198 G6
Dones Green W Ches 183 F10
Donhead St Andrew Wilts 30 C6
Donhead St Mary Wilts 30 C6
Donibristle Fife 280 D3
Doniford Som 42 E5
Donington Lincs 156 B4
Donington Shrops 132 C6
Donington Eaudike Lincs 156 B4
Donington le Heath Leics 153 G8
Donington on Bain Lincs 190 E2
Donington South Ing Lincs 156 C4
Donisthorpe Leics 152 G6
Donkey Street Kent 54 G6
Donkey Town Sur 66 G2
Donna Nook Lincs 190 B6
Donnington Glos 100 F3
Donnington Hereford 98 E4
Donnington Shrops 131 B11
Donnington Telford 150 G4
Donnington W Berks 64 F3
Donnington W Sus 22 C5
Donnington Wood Telford 150 G4
Donwell T & W 243 F7
Donyatt Som 28 E4
Doomsday Green W Sus 35 B11
Doonfoot S Ayrs 257 F8
Dora's Green Hants 49 D10
Dorback Lodge Highld 292 B2
Dorcan Swindon 63 C7
Dorchester Dorset 17 C9
Dorchester Oxon 83 G9
Dordale Worcs 117 C8
Dordon Warks 134 C5
Dore S Yorks 186 E4
Dores Highld 300 F5
Dorking Sur 51 D7
Dorking Tye Suff 107 D8
Dorley's Corner Suff 127 D7
Dormans Park Sur 51 E11
Dormansland Sur 52 E2
Dormanstown Redcar 235 G7
Dormer's Wells London 66 C6
Dormington Hereford 97 C11
Dormston Worcs 117 F9
Dorn Glos 100 E4
Dorn Hill Worcs 100 E3
Dornal S Ayrs 236 B4
Dorney Bucks 66 D2
Dorney Reach Bucks 66 D2
Dornie Highld 295 C10
Dornoch Highld 309 L7
Dornock Dumfries 238 D6
Dorrery Highld 310 D4
Dorridge W Mid 118 B3
Dorrington Lincs 173 E9
Dorrington Shrops 131 C9
Dorsington Warks 100 B2
Dorstone Hereford 96 C6
Dorton Bucks 83 C11
Dorusduain Highld 295 C11
Doseley Telford 132 B3
Dosmuckeran Highld 300 C2
Dosthill Staffs 134 C4
Dosthill Staffs 134 D4
Dothan Anglesey 178 G5
Dothill Telford 150 G2
Dottery Dorset 16 B5
Double Hill Bath 45 B8
Doublebois Corn 6 C3
Dougarie N Ayrs 255 D9
Doughton Glos 80 G5
Doughton Norf 159 D7
Douglas I o M 192 E4
Douglas S Lnrk 259 C8
Douglas & Angus Dundee 287 D8
Douglas Water S Lnrk 259 B9
Douglas West S Lnrk 259 C8
Douglastown Angus 287 C8
Doulting Som 44 E6
Dounby Orkney 314 D2
Doune Highld 291 C10
Doune Highld 309 J4
Doune Stirl 285 G11
Doune Park Aberds 303 C7
Douneside Aberds 292 C6
Dounie Argyll 275 D8
Dounie Highld 309 K5
Dounie Highld 309 L6
Dounreay Highld 310 C3
Doura N Ayrs 266 G6
Dousland Devon 7 B10
Dovaston Shrops 149 E7
Dove Green Notts 171 E7
Dove Holes Derbys 185 F9
Dove Point Mers 182 C2
Dovecot Mers 182 C6
Dovecothall Glasgow 267 D10
Dovenby Cumb 229 E7
Dovendale Lincs 190 E4
Dover Gtr Man 194 G6
Dover Kent 55 E10
Dovercourt Essex 108 E5
Doverdale Worcs 117 D7
Doverhay Som 41 D11
Doveridge Derbys 152 C2
Doversgreen Sur 51 D9
Dowally Perth 286 C4
Dowanhill Glasgow 267 B11
Dowbridge Lancs 202 G4
Dowdeswell Glos 81 B7
Dowe Hill Norf 161 F10
Dowlais M Tydf 77 D10
Dowlais Top M Tydf 77 D9
Dowland Devon 25 E9
Dowles Worcs 116 B5
Dowlesgreen Wokingham 65 F10
Dowlish Ford Som 28 E5
Dowlish Wake Som 28 E5
Down Ampney Glos 81 F10
Down End Som 43 E10
Down Field Cambs 124 C2
Down Hall Cumb 239 G7
Down Hatherley Glos 99 G7
Down Park W Sus 51 F10
Down St Mary Devon 26 G2
Down Street E Sus 36 C6
Down Thomas Devon 7 E10
Downall Green Gtr Man 194 G5
Downan Moray 301 F11
Downan S Ayrs 244 G3
Downcraig Ferry N Ayrs 266 E3
Downderry Corn 6 E6
Downe London 68 G2
Downend Glos 80 F4
Downend I o W 20 D6
Downend S Glos 60 D6
Downend W Berks 64 D3
Downfield Dundee 287 D7
Downgate Corn 11 G11
Downgate Corn 12 G3
Downham Essex 88 F2
Downham Lancs 203 E11
Downham London 67 E11
Downham Northumb 263 C9
Downham Market Norf 140 C2
Downhead Som 29 B9
Downhead Som 45 D7
Downhead Park M Keynes 103 C7
Downhill Corn 5 B7
Downhill Perth 286 D4
Downhill T & W 243 F9
Downholland Cross Lancs 193 F11
Downholme N Yorks 224 F2
Downicary Devon 12 C3
Downies Aberds 293 D11
Downinney Corn 11 C10
Downley Bucks 84 G4
Downs V Glam 58 E6
Downside C Beds 103 G10
Downside E Sus 23 E9
Downside N Som 60 F3
Downside Som 44 D6
Downside Sur 50 B6
Downside Sur 51 B7
Downton Hants 19 C11
Downton Powys 114 E4
Downton Shrops 149 G10
Downton Wilts 31 C11
Downton on the Rock Hereford 115 C8
Dowsby Lincs 156 D2
Dowsdale Lincs 156 G5
Dowslands Som 28 C2
Dowthwaitehead Cumb 230 G3
Doxey Staffs 151 E8
Doxford Park T & W 243 G9
Doynton S Glos 61 E8
Drabblegate Norf 160 D4
Draethen Newport 59 B8
Draffan S Lnrk 268 F5
Dragley Beck Cumb 210 D5
Dragonby N Lincs 200 E2
Dragons Green W Sus 35 C10
Drakehouse S Yorks 186 E6
Drakeland Corner Devon 7 D11
Drakelow Worcs 132 G6
Drakemyre Aberds 303 F9
Drakemyre N Ayrs 266 E5
Drake's Broughton Worcs 99 B8
Drakes Cross Worcs 117 B11
Drakestone Green Suff 107 B9
Drakewalls Corn 12 G4
Draughton N Yorks 204 C6
Draughton Northants 120 B5
Drawbridge Corn 6 B3
Drax N Yorks 199 B7
Draycot Oxon 83 D10
Draycot Cerne Wilts 62 D2
Draycot Fitz Payne Wilts 62 G6
Draycot Foliat Swindon 63 D7
Draycote Warks 119 C8
Draycott Derbys 153 C8
Draycott Glos 80 E2
Draycott Glos 100 D3
Draycott Shrops 132 E6
Draycott Som 29 C8
Draycott Som 44 C3
Draycott Worcs 99 B7
Draycott in the Clay Staffs 152 D3
Draycott in the Moors Staffs 169 G7
Drayford Devon 26 E3
Drayton Leics 136 E6
Drayton Lincs 156 B4
Drayton Norf 160 G3
Drayton Northants 119 E11
Drayton Oxon 83 G7
Drayton Oxon 101 C8
Drayton Ptsmth 33 F11
Drayton Som 28 C6
Drayton Som 29 D7
Drayton Warks 118 F3
Drayton Worcs 117 B8
Drayton Bassett Staffs 134 C3
Drayton Beauchamp Bucks 84 C6
Drayton Parslow Bucks 102 F6
Drayton St Leonard Oxon 83 F10
Dre-fach Carms 75 B11
Dre-fach Ceredig 93 B10
Dre-gôch Denb 165 B10
Drebley N Yorks 205 B7
Dreemskerry I o M 192 C5
Dreenhill Pembs 72 C6
Drefach Carms 75 C8
Drefach Carms 92 G5
Drefach Carms 93 D7
Drefelin Carms 93 D7
Dreggie Highld 301 G10
Dreghorn Edin 270 B4
Dreghorn N Ayrs 257 B9
Drellingore Kent 55 E8
Drem E Loth 281 F10
Dresden Stoke 168 G6
Dreumasdal W Isles 297 H3
Drewsteignton Devon 13 C10
Driby Lincs 190 G5
Driffield E Yorks 208 B6
Driffield Glos 81 F9
Drift Corn 1 D4
Drigg Cumb 219 F11
Drighlington W Yorks 197 B8
Drimnin Highld 289 D7
Drimnin Ho Highld 289 D7
Drimpton Dorset 28 F6
Drimsynie Argyll 284 G5
Dringhoe E Yorks 209 C9
Dringhouses York 207 D7
Drinisiadar W Isles 305 J3
Drinkstone Suff 125 E9
Drinkstone Green Suff 125 E9
Drishaig Argyll 284 F5
Drissaig Argyll 275 B10
Drive End Dorset 29 F9
Driver's End Herts 86 B2
Drochedlie Aberds 302 C5
Drochil Borders 270 G3
Drointon Staffs 151 D10
Droitwich Spa Worcs 117 E7
Droman Highld 306 D6
Dromore Dumfries 237 C7
Dron Perth 286 F5
Dronfield Derbys 186 F5
Dronfield Woodhouse Derbys 186 F4
Drongan E Ayrs 257 F10
Dronley Angus 287 D7
Droop Dorset 30 F3
Drope Cardiff 58 D6
Dropping Well S Yorks 186 C5
Droughduil Dumfries 236 D3
Droxford Hants 33 D10
Droylsden Gtr Man 184 B6
Drub W Yorks 197 B7
Druggers End Worcs 98 D5
Druid Denb 165 G8
Druidston Pembs 72 B5
Druim Highld 301 D9
Druimarbin Highld 290 F2
Druimavuic Argyll 284 C4
Druimdrishaig Argyll 275 F8
Druimindarroch Highld 295 G8
Druimkinnerras Highld 300 F4
Druimnacroish Argyll 288 E6
Druimsornaig Argyll 289 F9
Druimyeon More Argyll 255 B7
Drum Argyll 275 F10
Drum Edin 270 B6
Drum Perth 286 G4
Drumardoch Stirl 285 F10
Drumbeg Highld 306 F6
Drumblade Aberds 302 E5
Drumblair Aberds 302 E6
Drumbuie Dumfries 246 G3
Drumbuie Highld 295 B9
Drumburgh Cumb 239 F7
Drumburn Dumfries 237 C11
Drumchapel Glasgow 277 G10
Drumchardine Highld 300 E5
Drumchork Highld 307 L3
Drumclog S Lnrk 258 B4
Drumdelgie Aberds 302 E4
Drumderfit Highld 300 D6
Drumdollo Aberds 302 F6
Drumeldrie Fife 287 G8
Drumelzier Borders 260 C4
Drumfearn Highld 295 D8
Drumgask Highld 291 D8
Drumgelloch N Lnrk 268 B5
Drumgley Angus 287 B8
Drumgreen Angus 292 F6
Drumguish Highld 291 D9
Drumhead Aberds 293 B11
Drumin Moray 301 F11
Drumindorsair Highld 300 E4
Drumlasie Aberds 293 C8
Drumlean Stirl 285 G8
Drumlemble Argyll 255 F7
Drumliah Highld 309 K6
Drumligair Aberds 293 B11
Drumlithie Aberds 293 E9
Drumloist Stirl 285 G10
Drummersdale Lancs 193 E11
Drummick Perth 286 E3
Drummoddie Dumfries 236 E5
Drummond Highld 300 C6
Drummore Dumfries 236 F3
Drummuir Moray 302 E3
Drummuir Castle Moray 302 E3
Drumnadrochit Highld 300 G5
Drumnagorrach Moray 302 D5
Drumness Perth 286 F2
Drumoak Aberds 293 D9
Drumore Argyll 255 E8
Drumpark Dumfries 247 G9
Drumpellier N Lnrk 268 B4
Drumphail Dumfries 236 C4
Drumrash Dumfries 237 B8
Drumrunie Highld 307 J6
Drumry W Dunb 277 G10
Drums Aberds 303 G9
Drumsallie Highld 289 B11
Drumsmittal Highld 300 E6
Drumstinchall Dumfries 237 D10
Drumsturdy Angus 287 D8
Drumtochty Castle Aberds 293 F8
Drumtroddan Dumfries 236 E5
Drumuie Highld 298 E4
Drumuillie Highld 301 G9
Drumvaich Stirl 285 G10
Drumwalt Dumfries 236 D5
Drumwhindle Aberds 303 F9
Drunkendub Angus 287 C10
Drury Flint 166 C3
Drury Lane Wrex 167 G7
Drury Square Norf 159 F8
Drurylane Norf 141 C8
Dry Doddington Lincs 172 F4
Dry Drayton Cambs 123 E7
Dry Hill Hants 49 F7
Dry Sandford Oxon 83 E7
Dry Street Essex 69 B7
Drybeck Cumb 222 B3
Drybridge Moray 302 C4
Drybridge N Ayrs 257 B9
Drybrook Glos 79 B10
Dryburgh Borders 262 C3
Dryden Borders 261 E11
Dryhill Kent 52 B3
Dryhope Borders 261 E7
Drylaw Edin 280 F4
Drym Corn 2 C4
Drymen Stirl 277 D9
Drymere Norf 140 B5
Drymuir Aberds 303 E9
Drynachan Lodge Highld 301 F8
Drynain Argyll 276 D3
Drynham Wilts 45 B11
Drynie Park Highld 300 D5
Drynoch Highld 294 B6
Dryslwyn Carms 93 G11
Dryton Shrops 131 B11
Drywells Aberds 302 D6
Duag Bridge Highld 309 K3
Duartbeg Highld 306 F6
Duartmore Bridge Highld 306 F6
Dubbs Cross Devon 12 C3
Dubford Aberds 303 C8
Dubhchladach Argyll 275 G9
Dublin Suff 126 D3
Dubton Angus 287 B9
Dubwath Cumb 229 E9
Duchally Highld 309 H3
Duchlage Argyll 276 D6
Duchrae Dumfries 246 G5
Duck Corner Suff 109 C7
Duck End Beds 103 C11
Duck End Beds 121 G9
Duck End Bucks 102 F5
Duck End Cambs 122 E4
Duck End Essex 105 G10
Duck End Essex 106 E3
Duck End Essex 106 F3
Duckend Green Essex 106 G4
Duckhole S Glos 79 G10
Duckington W Ches 167 E7
Ducklington Oxon 82 D5
Duckmanton Derbys 186 G6
Duck's Cross Beds 122 F2
Ducks Island London 86 F2
Duckswich Worcs 98 D6
Dudbridge Glos 80 E4
Dudden Hill London 67 B8
Duddenhoe End Essex 105 D9
Duddingston Edin 280 G5
Duddington Northants 137 C9
Duddlestone Som 28 C2
Duddleswell E Sus 37 B7
Duddlewick Shrops 132 G3
Duddo Northumb 273 G8
Duddon W Ches 167 C8
Duddon Bridge Cumb 210 B3
Duddon Common W Ches 167 B8
Dudleston Shrops 148 B6
Dudleston Grove Shrops 149 B7
Dudleston Heath (Criftins) Shrops 149 B7
Dudley T & W 243 C7
Dudley W Mid 133 E8
Dudley Hill W Yorks 205 G9
Dudley Port W Mid 133 E9
Dudley Wood W Mid 133 F8
Dudley's Fields W Mid 133 C9
Dudlows Green Warr 183 E10
Dudsbury Dorset 19 B7
Dudswell Herts 85 D7
Dudwells Pembs 91 G8
Duerdon Devon 24 D4
Duffield Derbys 170 G4
Duffieldbank Derbys 170 G5
Duffryn Neath 57 B10
Duffryn Newport 59 B9
Duffryn Shrops 130 G4
Dufftown Moray 302 F3
Duffus Moray 301 C11
Dufton Cumb 231 F9
Duggleby N Yorks 217 F7
Duich Argyll 254 B4
Duiletter Argyll 284 D5
Duinish Perth 291 G8
Duirinish Highld 295 B9
Duisdalebeg Highld 295 D8
Duisdalemore Highld 295 D9
Duisky Highld 290 F2
Duke End Warks 134 F4
Dukesfield Northumb 241 F10
Dukestown Bl Gwent 77 C10
Dukinfield Gtr Man 184 B6
Dulas Anglesey 179 D7
Dulcote Som 44 E5
Dulford Devon 27 F9
Dull Perth 286 C2
Dullatur N Lnrk 278 F4
Dullingham Cambs 124 F2
Dullingham Ley Cambs 124 F2
Dulnain Bridge Highld 301 G9
Duloch Fife 280 D2
Duloe Beds 122 E3
Duloe Corn 6 D4
Dulsie Highld 301 E9
Dulverton Som 26 B6
Dulwich London 67 E10
Dulwich Village London 67 E10
Dumbarton W Dunb 277 F7
Dumbleton Glos 99 D10
Dumcrieff Dumfries 248 C4
Dumfries Dumfries 237 B11
Dumgoyne Stirl 277 E10
Dummer Hants 48 D5
Dumpford W Sus 34 C4
Dumpinghill Devon 24 F6
Dumpling Green Norf 159 G10
Dumplington Gtr Man 184 B3
Dumpton Kent 71 F11
Dun Angus 287 B10
Dun Charlabhaigh W Isles 304 D3
Dunach Argyll 289 G10
Dunadd Argyll 275 D9
Dunain Ho Highld 300 E6
Dunalastair Perth 285 B11
Dunan Highld 295 C7
Dunans Argyll 275 D11
Dunans Argyll 275 D9
Dunball Som 43 E10
Dunbar E Loth 282 F3
Dunbeath Highld 311 G5
Dunbeg Argyll 289 F10
Dunblane Stirl 285 G11
Dunbog Fife 286 F6
Dunbridge Hants 32 B4
Duncansclett Shetland 313 K5
Duncanston Highld 300 D5
Duncanstone Aberds 302 G5
Dunchideock Devon 14 D3
Dunchurch Warks 119 C9
Duncombe Lancs 202 F6
Duncote Northants 120 G3
Duncow Dumfries 247 G11
Duncraggan Stirl 285 G9
Duncrievie Perth 286 G5
Duncroisk Stirl 285 D9
Duncton W Sus 35 D7
Dundas Ho Orkney 314 H4
Dundee Dundee 287 D8
Dundeugh Dumfries 246 F3
Dundon Som 44 G3
Dundon Hayes Som 44 G3
Dundonald Fife 280 C4
Dundonald S Ayrs 257 C9
Dundonnell Highld 307 L5
Dundonnell Hotel Highld 307 L5
Dundonnell House Highld 307 L6
Dundraw Cumb 229 B10
Dundreggan Highld 290 B5
Dundreggan Lodge Highld 290 B5
Dundrennan Dumfries 237 E9
Dundridge Hants 33 D9
Dundry N Som 60 F5
Dundurn Perth 285 E11
Dundyvan N Lnrk 268 C4
Dunecht Aberds 293 C9
Dunfermline Fife 279 D11
Dunfield Glos 81 F10
Dunford Bridge S Yorks 197 G7
Dungate Kent 54 B2
Dunge Wilts 45 C11
Dungeness Kent 39 D9
Dungworth S Yorks 186 D3
Dunham Notts 188 G4
Dunham-on-the-Hill W Ches 183 G7
Dunham on Trent Notts 188 G4
Dunham Town Gtr Man 184 D2
Dunham Woodhouses Gtr Man 184 D2
Dunhampstead Worcs 117 E8
Dunhampton Worcs 116 D6
Dunholme Lincs 189 F8
Dunino Fife 287 F9
Dunipace Falk 278 E6
Dunira Perth 285 E11
Dunkeld Perth 286 C4
Dunkerton Bath 45 B8
Dunkeswell Devon 27 F10
Dunkeswick N Yorks 206 D2
Dunkirk Cambs 139 F10
Dunkirk Kent 54 B5
Dunkirk Norf 160 D4
Dunkirk Nottingham 153 B11
Dunkirk S Glos 61 B9
Dunkirk Staffs 168 E4
Dunkirk W Ches 182 G5
Dunkirk Wilts 62 G3
Dunk's Green Kent 52 C6
Dunlappie Angus 293 G7
Dunley Hants 48 C3
Dunley Worcs 116 D5
Dunlichity Lodge Highld 300 F6
Dunlop E Ayrs 267 F8
Dunmaglass Lodge Highld 300 G5
Dunmere Corn 5 B10
Dunmore Argyll 275 G8
Dunmore Falk 279 D7
Dunmore Highld 300 E5
Dunn Street Kent 54 D3
Dunn Street Kent 69 G9
Dunnerholme Cumb 210 D4
Dunnet Highld 310 B6
Dunnichen Angus 287 C9
Dunnikier Fife 280 C5
Dunninald Angus 287 B11
Dunning Perth 286 F4
Dunnington E Yorks 209 C9
Dunnington Warks 117 G11
Dunnington York 207 C9
Dunningwell Cumb 210 C3
Dunnockshaw Lancs 195 B10
Dunnose I o W 21 F7
Dunnsheath Shrops 149 F9
Dunollie Argyll 289 F10
Dunoon Argyll 276 F3
Dunragit Dumfries 236 D3
Dunrobin Mains Highld 311 J2
Dunrostan Argyll 275 E8
Duns Borders 272 E5
Duns Tew Oxon 101 F9
Dunsa Derbys 186 G2
Dunsby Lincs 156 D2
Dunscar Gtr Man 195 E8
Dunscore Dumfries 247 G9
Dunscroft S Yorks 199 F7
Dunsdale Redcar 226 B2
Dunsden Green Oxon 65 D8
Dunsfold Sur 50 F4
Dunsfold Common Sur 50 F4
Dunsfold Green Sur 50 F4
Dunsford Devon 14 D2
Dunsford Sur 50 F4
Dunshalt Fife 286 F6
Dunshillock Aberds 303 E9
Dunsill Notts 171 C7
Dunsinnan Perth 286 D5
Dunskey Ho Dumfries 236 D2
Dunslea Corn 11 G11
Dunsley N Yorks 227 C7
Dunsley Staffs 133 G7
Dunsmore Bucks 84 D5
Dunsmore Warks 119 B10
Dunsop Bridge Lancs 203 C9
Dunstable C Beds 103 G10
Dunstal Staffs 151 D11
Dunstall Staffs 152 E3
Dunstall Common Worcs 99 C7
Dunstall Green Suff 124 E4
Dunstall Hill W Mid 133 C8
Dunstan Northumb 265 F7
Dunstan Steads Northumb 264 E6
Dunster Som 42 E3
Dunston Derbys 186 G5
Dunston Lincs 173 C9
Dunston Norf 142 C4
Dunston Staffs 151 F8
Dunston T & W 242 E6
Dunston Heath Staffs 151 F8
Dunston Hill T & W 242 E6
Dunstone Devon 7 E11
Dunstone Devon 8 G5
Dunsville S Yorks 198 F6
Dunswell E Yorks 209 F7
Dunsyre S Lnrk 269 F11
Dunterton Devon 12 F3
Dunthrop Oxon 101 F7
Duntisbourne Abbots Glos 81 D7
Duntisbourne Leer Glos 81 D7
Duntisbourne Rouse Glos 81 D7
Duntish Dorset 29 F11
Duntocher W Dunb 277 G9
Dunton Bucks 102 G6
Dunton C Beds 104 C4
Dunton Norf 159 C7
Dunton Bassett Leics 135 E10
Dunton Green Kent 52 B4
Dunton Patch Norf 159 C7
Dunton Wayletts Essex 87 G11
Duntrune Castle Argyll 275 D8
Duntulm Highld 298 B4
Dunure S Ayrs 257 F7
Dunvant = Dynfant Swansea 56 C5
Dunvegan Highld 298 E2
Dunveth Corn 10 G5
Dunwear Som 43 F10
Dunwich Suff 127 C9
Dunwood Staffs 168 D6
Dupplin Castle Perth 286 F4
Durdar Cumb 239 G10
Durgan Corn 3 D7
Durgates E Sus 52 G6
Durham Durham 233 C11
Durisdeer Dumfries 247 C9
Durisdeermill Dumfries 247 C9
Durkar W Yorks 197 D10
Durleigh Som 43 F9
Durleighmarsh W Sus 34 C3
Durley Hants 33 D8
Durley Wilts 63 G8
Durley Street Hants 33 D8
Durlock Kent 55 B9
Durlow Common Hereford 98 D2
Durn Gtr Man 196 D2
Durnamuck Highld 307 K5
Durness Highld 308 C4
Durnfield Som 29 C7
Durno Aberds 303 G7
Durns Town Hants 19 B11
Duror Highld 289 D11
Durran Argyll 275 C10
Durran Highld 310 C5
Durrant Green Kent 53 F11
Durrants Hants 22 B2
Durrington W Sus 35 F10
Durrington Wilts 47 E7
Durrisdale Orkney 314 D3
Dursley Glos 80 F3
Dursley Wilts 45 C11
Dursley Cross Glos 98 G3
Durston Som 28 B3
Durweston Dorset 30 F5
Dury Shetland 313 G6
Duryard Devon 14 C4
Duston Northants 120 E4
Dutch Village Essex 69 C9
Duthil Highld 301 G9
Dutlas Powys 114 B4
Duton Hill Essex 106 F2
Dutson Corn 12 D2
Dutton Ches 183 F9
Duxford Cambs 105 B9
Duxford Oxon 82 F5
Duxmoor Shrops 115 B8
Dwygyfylchi Conwy 180 F2
Dwyran Anglesey 162 B6
Dwyrhiw Powys 129 C11
Dyce Aberdeen 293 B10
Dyche Som 43 E7
Dye House Northumb 241 F10
Dyer's Common S Glos 60 C5
Dyer's Green Cambs 105 B7
Dyffryn Bridgend 57 C11
Dyffryn Carms 92 G6
Dyffryn Ceredig 110 G5
Dyffryn Pembs 91 D8
Dyffryn Ardudwy Gwyn 145 E11
Dyffryn-bern Ceredig 110 G5
Dyffryn Castell Ceredig 128 G5
Dyffryn Ceidrych Carms 94 F4
Dyffryn Cellwen Neath 76 D5
Dyke Lincs 156 E2
Dyke Moray 301 D9
Dykehead Angus 292 G5
Dykehead N Lnrk 269 D7
Dykehead Stirl 277 B11
Dykelands Aberds 293 G9
Dykends Angus 286 B6
Dykeside Aberds 303 E7
Dykesmains N Ayrs 266 G5
Dylife Powys 129 E7
Dymchurch Kent 39 B9
Dymock Glos 98 E4
Dynfant = Dunvant Swansea 56 C5
Dyrham S Glos 61 D8
Dysart Fife 280 C6
Dyserth Denb 181 F9

E

Eabost Highld 294 B5
Eabost West Highld 298 E3
Each End Kent 55 B10
Eachway Worcs 117 B9
Eachwick Northumb 242 C4
Eadar Dha Fhadhail W Isles 304 E2
Eagland Hill Lancs 202 D4
Eagle Lincs 172 B5
Eagle Barnsdale Lincs 172 B5
Eagle Moor Lincs 172 B5
Eagle Tor Derbys 170 C2
Eaglescliffe Stockton 225 B8
Eaglesfield Cumb 229 F7
Eaglesfield Dumfries 238 C6
Eaglesham E Renf 267 E11
Eaglestone M Keynes 103 D7
Eaglethorpe Northants 137 E11
Eagley Gtr Man 195 E8
Eairy I o M 192 E3
Eakley Lanes M Keynes 120 G6
Eakring Notts 171 C11
Ealand N Lincs 199 E9
Ealing London 67 C7
Eals Northumb 240 F5
Eamont Bridge Cumb 230 F6
Earby Lancs 204 D3
Earcroft Blkburn 195 C7
Eardington Shrops 132 E4
Eardisland Hereford 115 F8
Eardisley Hereford 96 B6
Eardiston Shrops 149 D7
Eardiston Worcs 116 D3
Earith Cambs 123 C7
Earl Shilton Leics 135 D9
Earl Soham Suff 126 E4
Earl Sterndale Derbys 169 B9
Earl Stoneham Suff 126 F2
Earl Stonham Suff 126 F2
Earle Northumb 263 D11
Earlestown Mers 183 B9
Earley Wokingham 65 E9
Earlham Norf 142 B4
Earlish Highld 298 C3
Earls Barton Northants 121 E7
Earls Colne Essex 107 F7
Earl's Common Worcs 117 F9
Earl's Court London 67 D9
Earl's Croome Worcs 99 C7
Earl's Down E Sus 23 B10
Earl's Green Suff 125 D10
Earlsdon W Mid 118 B6
Earlsferry Fife 281 B9
Earlsfield Lincs 155 B8
Earlsfield London 67 E9
Earlsford Aberds 303 F8
Earlsheaton W Yorks 197 C9
Earlsmill Moray 301 D9
Earlston Borders 262 B3
Earlston E Ayrs 257 B10
Earlstone Common Hants 64 G3
Earlstoun Dumfries 246 G4
Earlswood Mon 79 F7
Earlswood Sur 51 D9
Earlswood Warks 118 C2
Earnley W Sus 22 D4
Earnock S Lnrk 268 E3
Earnshaw Bridge Lancs 194 C4
Earsairidh W Isles 297 M3
Earsdon T & W 243 C8
Earsham Norf 142 F6
Earsham Street Suff 126 B4
Earswick York 207 B8
Eartham W Sus 22 B6
Earthcott Green S Glos 61 B7
Easby N Yorks 224 E3
Easby N Yorks 225 D11
Easdale Argyll 275 B8
Easebourne W Sus 34 C5
Easenhall Warks 119 B9
Eashing Sur 50 E2
Easington Bucks 83 C11
Easington Durham 234 C4
Easington E Yorks 201 D11
Easington Lancs 203 C10
Easington Northumb 264 C4
Easington Oxon 83 F11
Easington Oxon 101 D9
Easington Redcar 226 B4
Easington Colliery Durham 234 C4
Easington Lane T & W 234 B3
Easingwold N Yorks 215 F10
Easole Street Kent 55 C9
Eason's Green E Sus 23 B8
Eassie Angus 287 C7
East Aberthaw V Glam 58 F4
East Acton London 67 C8
East Adderbury Oxon 101 D9
East Allington Devon 8 F5
East Amat Highld 309 K4
East Anstey Devon 26 B5
East Anton Hants 47 D11
East Appleton N Yorks 224 F4
East Ardsley W Yorks 197 B10
East Ashling W Sus 22 B4
East Aston Hants 48 D2
East Auchronie Aberds 293 C10
East Ayton N Yorks 217 B9
East Bank Bl Gwent 78 D2
East Barkwith Lincs 189 E11
East Barming Kent 53 C8
East Barnby N Yorks 226 C6
East Barnet London 86 F3
East Barns E Loth 282 F4
East Barsham Norf 159 C8
East Barton Suff 125 D8
East Beach W Sus 22 E5
East Beckham Norf 177 E11
East Bedfont London 66 E5
East Bergholt Suff 107 D11
East Bierley W Yorks 197 B7
East Bilney Norf 159 F9
East Blackdene Durham 232 D3
East Blatchington E Sus 23 E7
East Bloxworth Dorset 18 C3
East Boldon T & W 243 E9
East Boldre Hants 32 G5
East Bower Som 43 F10
East Bonhard Perth 286 E5
East Brent Som 43 C11
East Bridgford Notts 171 G11
East Briscoe Durham 223 B9
East Buckland Devon 41 G7
East Budleigh Devon 15 E7
East Burnham Bucks 66 C3
East Burrafirth Shetland 313 H5
East Burton Dorset 18 D2
East Butsfield Durham 233 B8
East Butterleigh Devon 27 F7
East Butterwick N Lincs 199 F10
East Cairnbeg Aberds 293 F9
East Calder W Loth 269 B11
East Carleton Norf 142 C3
East Carlton Northants 136 F6
East Carlton W Yorks 205 E10
East Chaldon or Chaldon Herring Dorset 17 E11
East Challow Oxon 63 B11
East Charleton Devon 8 G5
East Chelborough Dorset 29 F9
East Chiltington E Sus 36 D5
East Chinnock Som 29 E7
East Chisenbury Wilts 46 C6
East Cholderton Hants 47 D9
East Clandon Sur 50 C5
East Claydon Bucks 102 F4
East Clevedon N Som 60 E2
East Clyne Highld 311 J3
East Clyth Highld 310 F7
East Coker Som 29 E8
East Combe Som 43 G7
East Common N Yorks 207 G8
East Compton Dorset 30 D5
East Compton Som 44 E6
East Cornworthy Devon 8 D6
East Cottingwith E Yorks 207 E10
East Cowes I o W 20 B6
East Cowick E Yorks 199 C7
East Cowton N Yorks 224 E6
East Cramlington Northumb 243 B7
East Cranmore Som 45 E7
East Creech Dorset 18 E4
East Croachy Highld 300 G6
East Croftmore Highld 291 B11
East Curthwaite Cumb 230 B2
East Dean E Sus 23 F9
East Dean Glos 98 G3
East Dean Hants 32 B3
East Dean W Sus 34 E6
East Dene S Yorks 186 C6
East Denton T & W 242 D6
East Didsbury Gtr Man 184 C5
East Down Devon 40 E6
East Drayton Notts 188 F3
East Dulwich London 67 E10
East Dundry N Som 60 F5
East Ella Hull 200 B5
East End Beds 122 F2
East End Bucks 84 B4
East End C Beds 103 C9
East End Dorset 18 B5
East End E Yorks 201 B9
East End E Yorks 209 B9
East End E Yorks 209 G9
East End Essex 89 D8
East End Glos 81 E11
East End Hants 20 B3
East End Hants 33 C11
East End Hants 64 G2
East End Herts 105 F9
East End Kent 53 E11
East End Kent 53 F10
East End Kent 70 E3
East End M Keynes 103 C8
East End N Som 60 E3
East End Oxon 82 C5
East End Oxon 101 D7
East End Oxon 101 E8
East End S Glos 61 E9
East End Som 29 B10
East End Som 44 C5
East End Som 45 D7
East End Suff 108 E2
East End Suff 126 F3
East End Green Herts 86 C3
East Everleigh Wilts 47 C8
East Ewell Sur 67 G8
East Farleigh Kent 53 C8
East Farndon Northants 136 F4
East Fen Common Cambs 124 C2
East Ferry Lincs 188 B4
East Fields W Berks 64 F3
East Finchley London 67 B9
East Finglassie Fife 280 B5
East Firsby Lincs 189 D8
East Fleet Dorset 17 E8
East Fortune E Loth 281 F10
East Garforth W Yorks 206 G4
East Garston W Berks 63 D11
East Gateshead T & W 243 E7
East Ginge Oxon 64 B2
East Gores Essex 107 G7
East Goscote Leics 154 G2
East Grafton Wilts 63 G9
East Grange Moray 301 C10
East Green Hants 49 E9
East Green Suff 124 G3
East Green Suff 127 D8
East Grimstead Wilts 32 B2
East Grinstead W Sus 51 F11
East Guldeford E Sus 38 C6
East Haddon Northants 120 D3
East Hagbourne Oxon 64 B4
East Halton N Lincs 200 D6
East Ham London 68 C2
East Hampnett W Sus 22 B6
East Hanney Oxon 82 G6
East Hanningfield Essex 88 E3
East Hardwick W Yorks 198 D3
East Harling Norf 141 F9
East Harlsey N Yorks 225 F8
East Harnham Wilts 31 B10
East Harptree Bath 44 B5
East Hartford Northumb 243 B7
East Harting W Sus 34 D3
East Hatch Wilts 30 B6
East Hatley Cambs 122 G5
East Hauxwell N Yorks 224 G3
East Heckington Lincs 173 G11
East Haven Angus 287 D9
East Hedleyhope Durham 233 C9
East Helmsdale Highld 311 H4
East Hendred Oxon 64 B3
East Herringthorpe S Yorks 187 C7
East Herrington T & W 243 G9
East Heslerton N Yorks 217 D8
East Hewish N Som 59 G11
East Hill Kent 68 G5

East Hoathly E Sus 23 B8
East Hogaland Shetland 313 K5
East Holme Dorset 18 D3
East Holton Dorset 18 C5
East Holywell Northumb 243 C8
East Horndon Essex 68 B6
East Horrington Som 44 D5
East Horsley Sur 50 C5
East Horton Northumb 264 C2
East Howdon T & W 243 D8
East Howe Bmouth 19 B7
East Huntspill Som 43 E10
East Hyde C Beds 85 B10
East Ilkerton Devon 41 D8
East Ilsley W Berks 64 C3
East Keal Lincs 174 C5
East Kennett Wilts 62 F6
East Keswick W Yorks 206 E3
East Kilbride S Lnrk 268 E2
East Kimber Devon 12 B5
East Kingston W Sus 35 G9
East Kirkby Lincs 174 C4
East Knapton N Yorks 217 D7
East Knighton Dorset 18 D2
East Knowstone Devon 26 C4
East Knoyle Wilts 45 G11
East Kyloe Northumb 264 B3
East Kyo Durham 242 G5
East Lambrook Som 28 D6
East Lamington Highld 301 B7
East Langdon Kent 55 D10
East Langton Leics 136 E4
East Langwell Highld 309 J7
East Lavant W Sus 22 B5
East Lavington W Sus 34 D6
East Law Northumb 242 G3
East Layton N Yorks 224 D3
East Leake Notts 153 D11
East Learmouth Northumb 263 B9
East Leigh Devon 8 E3
East Leigh Devon 25 F11
East Lexham Norf 159 F7
East Lilburn Northumb 264 E2
East Linton E Loth 281 F11
East Liss Hants 34 B3
East Lockinge Oxon 64 B2
East Loftus Redcar 226 B4
East Looe Corn 6 E5
East Lound N Lincs 188 B3
East Lulworth Dorset 18 E3
East Lutton N Yorks 217 F8
East Lydeard Som 27 B11
East Lydford Som 44 G5
East Lyng Som 28 B4
East Mains Aberds 293 D8
East Mains Borders 271 F11
East Mains S Lnrk 268 E2
East Malling Kent 53 B8
East Malling Heath Kent 53 B7
East March Angus 287 D8
East Marden W Sus 34 E4
East Markham Notts 188 G2
East Marsh NE Lincs 201 E9
East Martin Hants 31 D9
East Marton N Yorks 204 C4
East Melbury Dorset 30 C5
East Meon Hants 33 C11
East Mere Devon 27 D7
East Mersea Essex 89 C9
East Mey Highld 310 B7
East Molesey Sur 67 F7
East Moor W Yorks 197 C10
East Moors Cardiff 59 D8
East Morden Dorset 18 B4
East Morton W Yorks 205 E7
East Moulsecoomb Brighton 36 F4
East Ness N Yorks 216 D3
East Newton E Yorks 209 F11
East Newton N Yorks 216 D2
East Norton Leics 136 C5
East Nynehead Som 27 C11
East Oakley Hants 48 C5
East Ogwell Devon 14 G2
East Orchard Dorset 30 D4
East Ord Northumb 273 E9
East Panson Devon 12 C3
East Parley Dorset 19 B8
East Peckham Kent 53 D7
East Pennard Som 44 F5
East Perry Cambs 122 D3
East Portholland Corn 5 G9
East Portlemouth Devon 9 G9
East Prawle Devon 9 G10
East Preston W Sus 35 G9
East Pulham Dorset 30 F2
East Putford Devon 24 D5
East Quantoxhead Som 42 E6
East Rainton T & W 234 B2
East Ravendale NE Lincs 190 B2
East Raynham Norf 159 D7
East Rhidorroch Lodge Highld 307 K7
East Rigton W Yorks 206 E3
East Rolstone N Som 59 G11
East Rounton N Yorks 225 E8
East Row N Yorks 227 C7
East Rudham Norf 158 D6
East Runton Norf 177 E11
East Ruston Norf 160 D6
East Saltoun E Loth 271 B9
East Sheen London 67 D8
East Skelston Dumfries 247 F8
East Sleekburn Northumb 253 G7
East Somerton Norf 161 F9
East Stanley Durham 242 G6
East Stockwith Lincs 188 C3
East Stoke Dorset 18 D3
East Stoke Notts 172 F3
East Stoke Som 29 D7
East Stour Dorset 30 C4
East Stour Common Dorset 30 C4
East Stourmouth Kent 71 G9
East Stowford Devon 25 B10
East Stratton Hants 48 F4
East Street Kent 55 B10
East Street Som 44 F4
East Studdal Kent 55 D10
East Suisnish Highld 295 B7
East Taphouse Corn 6 C3
East-the-Water Devon 25 B7
East Third Borders 262 B4
East Thirston Northumb 252 D5
East Tilbury Thurrock 69 D7
East Tisted Hants 49 G8
East Torrington Lincs 189 E10
East Town Som 42 G6
East Town Som 44 E6
East Town Wilts 45 B11
East Trewent Pembs 73 F8
East Tuddenham Norf 159 G11
East Tuelmenna Corn 6 B4
East Tytherley Hants 32 B3
East Tytherton Wilts 62 E3
East Village Devon 26 F4
East Village V Glam 58 E3
East Wall Shrops 131 E10
East Walton Norf 158 F4
East Water Som 44 C4
East Week Devon 13 C9
East Wellow Hants 32 C4
East Wemyss Fife 280 B6
East Whitburn W Loth 269 B9
East Wickham London 68 D3
East Williamston Pembs 73 E9
East Winch Norf 158 F3
East Winterslow Wilts 47 G8
East Wittering W Sus 21 B11
East Witton N Yorks 214 B2
East Woodburn Northumb 251 F10
East Woodhay Hants 64 G2
East Woodlands Som 45 E9
East Worldham Hants 49 F8
East Worlington Devon 26 E3
East Worthing W Sus 35 G11
East Wretham Norf 141 E8
East Youlstone Devon 24 D3
Eastacombe Devon 25 B8
Eastacombe Devon 25 C9
Eastacott Devon 25 C10
Eastbourne Darl 224 C6
Eastbourne E Sus 23 F10
Eastbridge Suff 127 D9
Eastbrook Som 28 C2
Eastbrook V Glam 59 E7
Eastburn E Yorks 208 B5
Eastburn W Yorks 204 E6
Eastburn Br W Yorks 204 E6
Eastbury London 85 G9
Eastbury W Berks 63 D10
Eastby N Yorks 204 C6
Eastchurch Kent 70 E3
Eastcombe Glos 80 E5
Eastcote London 66 B6
Eastcote Northants 120 G3
Eastcote W Mid 118 B3
Eastcote Village London 66 B6
Eastcott Corn 24 D3
Eastcott Wilts 46 B4
Eastcotts Beds 103 B11
Eastcourt Wilts 63 G8
Eastcourt Wilts 81 G7
Eastdon Devon 14 F5
Eastdown Devon 8 F6
Eastend Essex 86 C6
Eastend Oxon 100 G6
Easter Aberchalder Highld 291 B7
Easter Ardross Highld 300 B6
Easter Balgedie Perth 286 G5
Easter Balmoral Aberds 292 D4
Easter Boleskine Highld 300 G5
Easter Brackland Stirl 285 G10
Easter Brae Highld 300 C6
Easter Cardno Aberds 303 C9
Easter Compton S Glos 60 C5
Easter Cringate Stirl 278 D4
Easter Culfosie Aberds 293 C9
Easter Davoch Aberds 292 C6
Easter Earshaig Dumfries 248 C2
Easter Ellister Argyll 254 B3
Easter Fearn Highld 309 L6
Easter Galcantray Highld 301 E8
Easter Housebyres Borders 262 B2
Easter Howgate Midloth 270 C4
Easter Howlaws Borders 272 G4
Easter Kinkell Highld 300 D5
Easter Knox Angus 287 D9
Easter Langlee Borders 262 B2
Easter Lednathie Angus 292 G5
Easter Milton Highld 301 D9
Easter Moniack Highld 300 E5
Easter Ord Aberdeen 293 C10
Easter Quarff Shetland 313 K6
Easter Rhynd Perth 286 F5
Easter Row Stirl 278 B5
Easter Silverford Aberds 303 C7
Easter Skeld Shetland 313 J5
Easter Softlaw Borders 263 C7
Easter Tulloch Highld 291 B11
Easter Whyntie Aberds 302 C6
Eastergate W Sus 22 B6
Easterhouse Glasgow 268 B3
Eastern Green W Mid 134 G5
Easterside M'bro 225 B10
Easterton Wilts 46 C4
Easterton of Lenabo Aberds 303 E10
Easterton Sands Wilts 46 B4
Eastertown Som 43 C10
Eastertown of Auchleuchries Aberds 303 F10
Eastfield Borders 262 D2
Eastfield Bristol 60 D5
Eastfield N Lnrk 269 C7
Eastfield N Lnrk 278 G4
Eastfield N Yorks 217 C10
Eastfield Northumb 243 B7
Eastfield P'boro 138 D4
Eastfield S Lnrk 268 C2
Eastfield S Yorks 197 G9
Eastfield Hall Northumb 252 B6
Eastgate Durham 232 D5
Eastgate Norf 160 E2
Eastgate P'boro 138 D4
Easthall Herts 104 G3
Eastham Mers 182 E5
Eastham Worcs 116 D2
Eastham Ferry Mers 182 E5
Easthampstead Brack 65 F11
Easthampton Hereford 115 E8
Easthaugh Norf 159 F11
Eastheath Wokingham 65 F10
Easthope Shrops 131 D11
Easthopewood Shrops 131 D11
Easthorpe Essex 107 G8
Easthorpe Leics 154 B6
Easthorpe Notts 172 E2
Easthouse Shetland 313 J5
Easthouses Midloth 270 B6
Easting Orkney 314 A7
Eastington Devon 26 F2
Eastington Glos 80 D3
Eastington Glos 81 C10
Eastland Gate Hants 33 E11
Eastleach Martin Glos 82 D2
Eastleach Turville Glos 81 D11
Eastleigh Devon 25 B7
Eastleigh Hants 32 D6
Eastling Kent 54 B3
Eastmoor Derbys 186 G4
Eastmoor Norf 140 C4
Eastney Ptsmth 21 B9
Eastnor Hereford 98 D4
Eastoft N Lincs 199 D10
Eastoke Hants 21 B10
Easton Bristol 60 E6
Easton Cambs 122 C2
Easton Cumb 239 C10
Easton Cumb 239 F7
Easton Devon 8 F3
Easton Devon 13 D10
Easton Dorset 17 G9
Easton Hants 48 G4
Easton I o W 20 D2
Easton Lincs 155 D8
Easton Norf 160 G2
Easton Som 44 D4
Easton Suff 126 F5
Easton W Berks 64 E2
Easton Wilts 61 E11
Easton Grey Wilts 61 B11
Easton in Gordano N Som 60 D4
Easton Maudit Northants 121 F7
Easton on the Hill Northants 137 C10
Easton Royal Wilts 63 G8
Easton Town Som 44 G5
Easton Town Wilts 61 B11
Eastover Som 43 F10
Eastpark Dumfries 238 D2
Eastrea Cambs 138 D5
Eastriggs Dumfries 238 D6
Eastrington E Yorks 199 B9
Eastrip Wilts 61 E10
Eastrop Hants 48 C6
Eastry Kent 55 C10
Eastville Bristol 60 E6
Eastville Lincs 174 D6
Eastwell Leics 154 D5
Eastwell Park Kent 54 D4
Eastwick Herts 86 C6
Eastwick Shetland 312 F5
Eastwood Hereford 98 C2
Eastwood Notts 171 F7
Eastwood S Yorks 186 C6
Eastwood Sthend 69 B10
Eastwood W Yorks 196 B3
Eastwood End Cambs 139 E8
Eastwood Hall Notts 171 F7
Eathorpe Warks 119 D7
Eaton C Ches 168 B5
Eaton Hereford 115 F10
Eaton Leics 154 D5
Eaton Norf 142 B4
Eaton Notts 188 F2
Eaton Oxon 82 E6
Eaton Shrops 131 F10
Eaton Shrops 131 F7
Eaton W Ches 167 C9
Eaton Bishop Hereford 97 D8
Eaton Bray C Beds 103 G9
Eaton Constantine Shrops 131 B11
Eaton Ford Cambs 122 E3
Eaton Green C Beds 103 G9
Eaton Hastings Oxon 82 F3
Eaton Mascott Shrops 131 B10
Eaton on Tern Shrops 150 E3
Eaton Socon Cambs 122 F3
Eaton upon Tern Shrops 150 E3
Eau Brink Norf 157 F11
Eau Withington Hereford 97 C10
Eaves Green W Mid 134 G5
Eavestone N Yorks 214 F4
Ebberly Hill Devon 25 D9
Ebberston N Yorks 217 C7
Ebbesbourne Wake Wilts 31 C7
Ebblake Hants 31 F10
Ebbw Vale Bl Gwent 77 D11
Ebchester Durham 242 F4
Ebdon N Som 59 G11
Ebernoe W Sus 35 B7
Ebford Devon 14 D5
Ebley Glos 80 D4
Ebnal W Ches 167 F7
Ebnall Hereford 115 F9
Ebreywood Shrops 149 F10
Ebrington Glos 100 C3
Ecchinswell Hants 48 B4
Ecclaw Borders 272 B5
Eccle Riggs Cumb 210 B4
Ecclefechan Dumfries 238 C5
Eccles Borders 272 G5
Eccles Gtr Man 184 B3
Eccles Kent 69 G8
Eccles on Sea Norf 161 D8
Eccles Road Norf 141 E10
Ecclesall S Yorks 186 E4
Ecclesfield S Yorks 186 C5
Ecclesgreig Aberds 293 G9
Eccleshall Staffs 150 D6
Eccleshill W Yorks 205 F9
Ecclesmachan W Loth 279 G11
Eccleston Lancs 194 D4
Eccleston Mers 183 B7
Eccleston W Ches 166 C6
Eccleston Park Mers 183 C7
Eccliffe Dorset 30 B3
Eccup W Yorks 205 E11
Echt Aberds 293 C9
Eckford Borders 262 D6
Eckfordmoss Borders 262 D6
Eckington Derbys 186 F6
Eckington Worcs 99 C8
Eckington Corner E Sus 23 D8
Ecklands S Yorks 197 G8
Eckworthy Devon 24 D6
Ecton Northants 120 E6
Ecton Staffs 169 D9
Ecton Brook Northants 120 E6
Edale Derbys 185 D10
Edale End Derbys 185 D11
Edbrook Som 43 E8
Edburton W Sus 36 E2
Edderside Cumb 229 B7
Edderton Highld 309 L7
Eddington Kent 71 F7
Eddington W Berks 63 F10
Eddistone Devon 24 C3
Eddleston Borders 270 F4
Eddlewood S Lnrk 268 E4
Eden Mount Cumb 211 D8
Eden Park London 67 F11
Eden Vale Durham 234 D4
Eden Vale Wilts 45 C11
Edenbridge Kent 52 D2
Edenfield Lancs 195 D9
Edenhall Cumb 231 E7
Edenham Lincs 155 E11
Edensor Derbys 170 B2
Edentaggart Argyll 276 C6
Edenthorpe S Yorks 198 F6
Edentown Cumb 239 F9
Ederline Argyll 275 C9
Edern Gwyn 144 B5
Edford Som 45 D7
Edgarley Som 44 F4
Edgbaston W Mid 133 G11
Edgcote Northants 101 B10
Edgcott Bucks 102 G3
Edgcott Som 41 F10
Edgcumbe Corn 2 C6
Edge Glos 80 D4
Edge Shrops 131 B7
Edge End Glos 79 C9
Edge End Lancs 203 G10
Edge Fold Blkburn 195 D8
Edge Fold Gtr Man 195 F8
Edge Green Gtr Man 183 B9
Edge Green Norf 141 F10
Edge Green W Ches 167 E7
Edge Hill Mers 182 C5
Edge Hill Warks 134 D4
Edge Mount S Yorks 186 C3
Edgebolton Shrops 149 E11
Edgefield Norf 159 C11
Edgefield Street Norf 159 C11
Edgehill Warks 101 B7
Edgeley Gtr Man 184 D5
Edgerley Shrops 148 F6
Edgerston Borders 262 G5
Edgerton W Yorks 196 D6
Edgeside Lancs 195 C10
Edgeworth Glos 80 D6
Edginswell Devon 9 B7
Edgiock Worcs 117 E10
Edgmond Telford 150 F4
Edgmond Marsh Telford 150 E4
Edgton Shrops 131 F7
Edgware London 85 G11
Edgwick W Mid 134 G6
Edgworth Blkburn 195 D8
Edham Borders 262 B6
Edial Staffs 133 B11
Edinample Stirl 285 E9
Edinbane Highld 298 D3
Edinburgh Edin 280 G5
Edinchip Stirl 285 E9
Edingale Staffs 152 G4
Edingight Ho Moray 302 D5
Edinglassie Ho Aberds 292 B5
Edingley Notts 171 D11
Edingthorpe Norf 160 C6
Edingthorpe Green Norf 160 C6
Edington Som 43 E11
Edington Wilts 46 C2
Edingworth Som 43 C11
Edintore Moray 302 E4
Edistone Devon 24 C2
Edith Weston Rutland 137 B8
Edithmead Som 43 D10
Edlaston Derbys 169 G11
Edlesborough Bucks 85 B7
Edlingham Northumb 252 B4
Edlington Lincs 190 G2
Edmondsham Dorset 31 E9
Edmondsley Durham 233 B10
Edmondstown Rhondda 77 G8
Edmondthorpe Leics 155 F7
Edmonston S Lnrk 269 G11
Edmonstone Orkney 314 D5
Edmonton Corn 10 G5
Edmonton London 86 G4
Edmundbyers Durham 242 G2
Ednam Borders 262 B6
Ednaston Derbys 170 G2
Edney Common Essex 87 E11
Edradynate Perth 286 B2
Edrom Borders 272 D6
Edstaston Shrops 149 C10
Edstone Warks 118 E3
Edvin Loach Hereford 116 F3
Edwalton Notts 153 B11
Edwardstone Suff 107 C8
Edwardsville M Tydf 77 F9
Edwinsford Carms 94 E2
Edwinstowe Notts 171 B10
Edworth C Beds 104 C4
Edwyn Ralph Hereford 116 F2
Edzell Angus 293 G7
Efail-fôch Neath 57 B9
Efail Isaf Rhondda 58 C5
Efailnewydd Gwyn 145 B7
Efailwen Carms 92 F2
Efenechtyd Denb 165 D10
Effingham Sur 50 C6
Effirth Shetland 313 H5
Effledge Borders 262 F3
Efflinch Staffs 152 F3
Efford Devon 26 G5
Efford Plym 7 D10
Egbury Hants 48 C2
Egdon Worcs 117 G8
Egerton Gtr Man 195 E8
Egerton Kent 54 D2
Egerton Forstal Kent 53 D11
Egerton Green E Ches 167 E8
Egford Som 45 D9
Eggbeare Corn 12 D2
Eggborough N Yorks 198 C5
Eggbuckland Plym 7 D10
Eggesford Station Devon 25 E11
Eggington C Beds 103 F9
Egginton Derbys 152 D5
Egginton Common Derbys 152 D5
Egglesburn Durham 232 G5
Egglescliffe Stockton 225 C8
Eggleston Durham 232 G5
Egham Sur 66 E4
Egham Hythe Sur 66 E4
Egham Wick Sur 66 E3
Egleton Rutland 137 B7
Eglingham Northumb 264 F4
Egloshayle Corn 10 G5
Egloskerry Corn 11 D11
Eglwys-Brewis V Glam 58 F4
Eglwys Cross Wrex 167 G7
Eglwys Fach Ceredig 128 D3
Eglwysbach Conwy 180 G4
Eglwyswen Pembs 92 D3
Eglwyswrw Pembs 92 D2
Egmanton Notts 172 B2
Egmere Norf 159 B8
Egremont Cumb 219 C10
Egremont Mers 182 C4
Egton N Yorks 226 D6
Egton Bridge N Yorks 226 D6
Egypt Bucks 66 B3
Egypt Hants 48 E3
Egypt W Berks 64 D2
Egypt W Yorks 205 G7
Eiden Highld 309 J7
Eight Ash Green Essex 107 F8
Eighton Banks T & W 243 F7
Eign Hill Hereford 97 D10
Eignaig Highld 289 E9
Eil Highld 291 B10
Eilanreach Highld 295 D10
Eildon Borders 262 C3
Eilean Anabaich W Isles 305 H4
Eilean Darach Highld 307 L6
Eilean Shona Ho Highld 289 B8
Eileanach Lodge Highld 300 C5
Einacleite W Isles 304 F3
Einsiob = Evenjobb Powys 114 E5
Eisgean W Isles 305 G5
Eisingrug Gwyn 146 C2
Elan Village Powys 113 D8
Eland Green Northumb 242 C5
Elberton S Glos 60 B6
Elborough N Som 43 B11
Elbridge Shrops 149 E7
Elbridge W Sus 22 C6
Elburton Plym 7 E10
Elcho Perth 286 E5
Elcock's Brook Worcs 117 E10
Elcombe Glos 80 F3
Elcombe Swindon 62 C6
Elcot W Berks 63 F11
Eldene Swindon 63 C7
Elder Street Essex 105 E11
Eldernell Cambs 138 D6
Eldersfield Worcs 98 E6
Elderslie Renfs 267 C8
Eldon Durham 233 F10
Eldon Lane Durham 233 F10
Eldrick S Ayrs 245 G7
Eldroth N Yorks 212 F5
Eldwick W Yorks 205 E8
Elemore Vale T & W 234 B3
Elerch = Bont-goch Ceredig 128 F3
Elfhowe Cumb 221 F9
Elford Northumb 264 C5
Elford Staffs 152 G3
Elford Closes Cambs 123 C10
Elgin Moray 302 C2
Elgol Highld 295 D7
Elham Kent 55 E7
Eliburn W Loth 269 B10
Elie Fife 287 G8
Elim Anglesey 178 D5
Eling Hants 32 E5
Eling W Berks 64 D4
Elishader Highld 298 C5
Elishaw Northumb 251 D9
Elizafield Dumfries 238 C2
Elkesley Notts 187 F11
Elkington Northants 120 B2
Elkins Green Essex 87 E10
Elkstone Glos 81 C7
Ellacombe Torbay 9 C8
Ellan Highld 301 G8
Elland W Yorks 196 C6
Elland Lower Edge W Yorks 196 C6
Elland Upper Edge W Yorks 196 C6
Ellary Argyll 275 F8
Ellastone Staffs 169 G10
Ellel Lancs 202 B5
Ellemford Borders 272 C4
Ellenborough Cumb 228 D6
Ellenbrook Herts 86 D2
Ellenbrook I o M 192 E4
Ellenglaze Corn 4 D5
Ellenhall Staffs 150 D6
Ellen's Green Sur 50 F5
Ellerbeck N Yorks 225 F8
Ellerburn N Yorks 216 C6
Ellerby N Yorks 226 C5
Ellerdine Telford 150 E2
Ellerdine Heath Telford 150 E2
Ellerhayes Devon 27 G7
Elleric Argyll 284 C4
Ellerker E Yorks 200 B2
Ellerton E Yorks 207 F10
Ellerton N Yorks 224 F5
Ellerton Shrops 150 D4
Ellesborough Bucks 84 D4
Ellesmere Shrops 149 C8
Ellesmere Park Gtr Man 184 B3
Ellesmere Port W Ches 182 F6
Ellicombe Som 42 E3
Ellingham Hants 31 F10
Ellingham Norf 143 E7
Ellingham Northumb 264 D5
Ellingstring N Yorks 214 C3
Ellington Cambs 122 C3
Ellington Northumb 253 E7
Ellington Thorpe Cambs 122 C3
Elliot Angus 287 D10
Elliots Green Som 45 D9
Elliot's Town Caerph 77 E10
Ellisfield Hants 48 D6
Elliston Borders 262 D3
Ellistown Leics 153 G8
Ellon Aberds 303 F9
Ellonby Cumb 230 D4
Ellough Suff 143 F8
Elloughton E Yorks 200 B2
Ellwood Glos 79 D9
Elm Cambs 139 B9
Elm Corner Sur 50 B5
Elm Cross Wilts 62 D6
Elm Hill Dorset 30 B4
Elm Park London 68 B4
Elmbridge Glos 80 B5
Elmbridge Worcs 117 D8
Elmdon Essex 105 D9
Elmdon W Mid 134 G3
Elmdon Heath W Mid 134 G3
Elmer W Sus 35 G7
Elmers End London 67 F11
Elmers Green Lancs 194 F3
Elmers Marsh W Sus 34 B5
Elmesthorpe Leics 135 D9
Elmfield I o W 21 C8
Elmhurst Bucks 84 B4
Elmhurst Staffs 152 G2
Elmley Castle Worcs 99 C9
Elmley Lovett Worcs 117 D7
Elmore Glos 80 B3
Elmore Back Glos 80 B3
Elms Green Hereford 115 F10
Elms Green Worcs 116 D4
Elmscott Devon 24 C2
Elmsett Suff 107 B11
Elmslack Lancs 211 D9
Elmstead Essex 107 F11
Elmstead London 68 E2
Elmstead Heath Essex 107 G11
Elmstead Market Essex 107 G11
Elmsted Kent 54 E6
Elmsthorpe Leics 135 D9
Elmstone Kent 71 G9
Elmstone Hardwicke Glos 99 F8
Elmswell E Yorks 208 B5
Elmswell Suff 125 E9
Elmton Derbys 187 G8
Elness Orkney 314 C6
Elphin Highld 307 H7
Elphinstone E Loth 281 G7
Elrick Aberds 293 C10
Elrig Dumfries 236 E5
Elrigbeag Argyll 284 F5
Elrington Northumb 241 E9
Elscar S Yorks 197 G11
Elsdon Hereford 114 G6
Elsdon Northumb 251 E10
Elsecar S Yorks 197 G11
Elsenham Essex 105 F10
Elsenham Sta Essex 105 F10
Elsfield Oxon 83 C8
Elsham N Lincs 200 E4
Elsing Norf 159 F11
Elslack N Yorks 204 D4
Elson Hants 33 G10
Elson Shrops 149 B7
Elsrickle S Lnrk 269 G11
Elstead Sur 50 E2
Elsted W Sus 34 D4
Elsthorpe Lincs 155 E11
Elstob Durham 234 G2
Elston Devon 26 G3
Elston Notts 172 F3
Elston Wilts 46 E5
Elstone Devon 25 D11
Elstow Beds 103 B11
Elstree Herts 85 F11
Elstronwick E Yorks 209 G10
Elswick Lancs 202 F4
Elswick T & W 242 E6
Elswick Leys Lancs 202 F4
Elsworth Cambs 122 E6
Elterwater Cumb 220 E6
Eltham London 68 E2
Eltisley Cambs 122 F5
Elton Cambs 137 E11
Elton Derbys 170 C2
Elton Glos 80 C2
Elton Gtr Man 195 E9
Elton Hereford 115 C9
Elton Notts 154 B5
Elton Stockton 225 B8
Elton W Ches 183 F7
Elton Green W Ches 183 G7
Elton's Marsh Hereford 97 C9
Eltringham Northumb 242 E3
Elvanfoot S Lnrk 259 F11
Elvaston Derbys 153 C8
Elveden Suff 124 B6
Elvet Hill Durham 233 C11
Elvingston E Loth 281 G9
Elvington Kent 55 C9
Elvington York 207 D9
Elwell Devon 41 G7
Elwell Dorset 17 E9
Elwick Hrtlpl 234 E5
Elwick Northumb 264 B4
Elworth E Ches 168 C2
Elworthy Som 42 G5
Ely Cambs 139 G10
Ely Cardiff 58 D6
Emberton M Keynes 103 B7
Embleton Cumb 229 E9
Embleton Durham 234 F4
Embleton Northumb 264 E6
Embo Highld 311 K2
Embo Street Highld 311 K2
Emborough Som 44 C6
Embsay N Yorks 204 C6
Emerson Park London 68 B4
Emerson Valley M Keynes 102 E6
Emersons Green S Glos 61 D7
Emery Down Hants 32 F3
Emley W Yorks 197 E8
Emmbrook Wokingham 65 F9
Emmer Green Reading 65 D8
Emmett Carr Derbys 187 F7
Emmington Oxon 84 E2
Emneth Norf 139 B9
Emneth Hungate Norf 139 B10
Emorsgate Norf 157 E10
Empingham Rutland 137 B8
Empshott Hants 49 G9
Empshott Green Hants 49 G8
Emscote Warks 118 D5
Emstrey Shrops 149 G10
Emsworth Hants 22 B2
Enborne W Berks 64 F2
Enborne Row W Berks 64 G2
Enchmarsh Shrops 131 D10
Enderby Leics 135 D10
Endmoor Cumb 211 C10
Endon Staffs 168 E6
Endon Bank Staffs 168 E6
Energlyn Caerph 58 B6
Enfield London 86 F4
Enfield Worcs 117 D10
Enfield Highway London 86 F5
Enfield Lock London 86 F5
Enfield Town London 86 F4
Enfield Wash London 86 F5
Enford Wilts 46 C6
Engamoor Shetland 313 H4
Engedi Anglesey 178 F5
Engine Common S Glos 61 C7
Englefield W Berks 64 E6
Englefield Green Sur 66 E3
Englesea-brook E Ches 168 E3
English Bicknor Glos 79 B9
English Frankton Shrops 149 D9
Englishcombe Bath 61 G8
Engollan Corn 10 G3
Enham Alamein Hants 47 D11
Enis Devon 25 B9
Enisfirth Shetland 312 F5
Enmore Som 43 G8
Enmore Field Hereford 115 E9
Enmore Green Dorset 30 C5
Ennerdale Bridge Cumb 219 B11
Enniscaven Corn 5 D9
Enoch Dumfries 247 C9
Enochdhu Perth 292 G2
Ensay Argyll 288 E5
Ensbury Bmouth 19 B7
Ensbury Park Bmouth 19 C7
Ensdon Shrops 149 F8
Ensis Devon 25 B9
Enslow Oxon 83 B7
Enstone Oxon 101 G7
Enterkinfoot Dumfries 247 C9
Enterpen N Yorks 225 D9
Enton Green Sur 50 E3
Enville Staffs 132 F6
Eolaigearraidh W Isles 297 L3
Eorabus Argyll 288 G5
Eòropaidh W Isles 304 B7
Epney Glos 80 C3
Epperstone Notts 171 F11
Epping Essex 87 E7
Epping Green Essex 86 D6
Epping Green Herts 86 D3
Epping Upland Essex 86 E6
Eppleby N Yorks 224 C3
Eppleworth E Yorks 208 G6
Epsom Sur 67 G8
Epwell Oxon 101 C7
Epworth N Lincs 199 G9
Epworth Turbary N Lincs 199 G9
Erbistock Wrex 166 G5
Erbusaig Highld 295 C9
Erchless Castle Highld 300 E4
Erdington W Mid 134 E2
Eredine Argyll 275 C10
Eriboll Highld 308 D4
Ericstane Dumfries 260 G3
Eridge Green E Sus 52 F5
Erines Argyll 275 F9
Eriswell Suff 124 B4
Erith London 68 D4
Erlestoke Wilts 46 C3
Ermine Lincs 189 G7
Ermington Devon 8 E2
Ernesettle Plym 7 D8
Erpingham Norf 160 C3
Erriottwood Kent 54 B2
Errogie Highld 300 G5
Errol Perth 286 E6
Errol Station Perth 286 E6
Erskine Renfs 277 G9
Erskine Bridge Renfs 277 G9
Ervie Dumfries 236 C2
Erwarton Suff 108 E4
Erwood Powys 95 C11
Eryholme N Yorks 224 D6
Eryrys Denb 166 D2
Escomb Durham 233 E9
Escott Som 42 F5
Escrick N Yorks 207 E8
Esgairdawe Carms 94 C2
Esgairgeiliog Powys 128 B5
Esgyryn Conwy 180 F4
Esh Durham 233 C9
Esh Winning Durham 233 C9
Esher Sur 66 G6
Eshiels Borders 261 B7
Esholt W Yorks 205 E9
Eshott Northumb 252 D6
Eshton N Yorks 204 B4
Esk Valley N Yorks 226 E6
Eskadale Highld 300 F4
Eskbank Midloth 270 B6
Eskdale Green Cumb 220 E2
Eskdalemuir Dumfries 249 D7
Eske E Yorks 209 E7
Eskham Lincs 190 B5
Eskholme S Yorks 198 D6
Esknish Argyll 274 G4
Eslington Park Northumb 264 G2
Esperley Lane Ends Durham 233 G8
Esprick Lancs 202 F4
Essendine Rutland 155 G10
Essendon Herts 86 D3
Essich Highld 300 F6
Essington Staffs 133 C9
Esslemont Aberds 303 G9
Eston Redcar 225 B11
Estover Plym 7 D10
Eswick Shetland 313 H6
Etal Northumb 263 B10
Etchilhampton Wilts 62 G4
Etchingham E Sus 38 B2
Etchinghill Kent 55 F7
Etchinghill Staffs 151 F10
Etchingwood E Sus 37 C8
Etherley Dene Durham 233 F9
Ethie Castle Angus 287 C10
Ethie Mains Angus 287 C10
Etling Green Norf 159 G10
Etloe Glos 79 D11
Eton Windsor 66 D3
Eton Wick Windsor 66 D2
Etruria Stoke 168 F5
Etsell Shrops 131 C7
Etterby Cumb 239 F9
Etteridge Highld 291 D8
Ettersgill Durham 232 F3
Ettiley Heath E Ches 168 C2
Ettingshall W Mid 133 D8
Ettingshall Park W Mid 133 D8
Ettington Warks 100 B5
Etton E Yorks 208 E5
Etton P'boro 138 B2
Ettrick Borders 261 G7
Ettrickbridge Borders 261 E9
Ettrickdale Argyll 275 G11
Ettrickhill Borders 261 G7
Etwall Derbys 152 C5
Etwall Common Derbys 152 C5
Eudon Burnell Shrops 132 F3
Eudon George Shrops 132 F3
Euston Suff 125 B7
Euximoor Drove Cambs 139 D9
Euxton Lancs 194 D5
Evanstown Bridgend 58 B3
Evanton Highld 300 C6
Evedon Lincs 173 F9
Eve Hill W Mid 133 E8
Evelix Highld 309 K7
Even Pits Hereford 97 D11
Even Swindon Swindon 62 B6
Evendine Hereford 98 C5
Evenjobb = Einsiob Powys 114 E5
Evenley Northants 101 E11
Evenlode Glos 100 F4
Evenwood Durham 233 G9
Evenwood Gate Durham 233 G9
Everbay Orkney 314 D6
Evercreech Som 44 F6
Everdon Northants 119 F11
Everingham E Yorks 208 E2
Everland Shetland 312 D8
Everleigh Wilts 47 C8
Everley N Yorks 217 B9
Eversholt C Beds 103 E9
Evershot Dorset 29 G9
Eversley Essex 69 B8
Eversley Hants 65 G9
Eversley Centre Hants 65 G9
Eversley Cross Hants 65 G9
Everthorpe E Yorks 208 G4
Everton C Beds 122 G4
Everton Hants 19 C11
Everton Mers 182 C5
Everton Notts 187 C11
Evertown Dumfries 239 B9
Evesbatch Hereford 98 B3
Evesham Worcs 99 C10
Evington Kent 54 D6
Evington Leicester 136 C2
Ewanrigg Cumb 228 D6
Ewden Village S Yorks 186 B3
Ewell Sur 67 G8
Ewell Minnis Kent 55 E9
Ewelme Oxon 83 G10
Ewen Glos 81 F8
Ewenny V Glam 58 D2
Ewerby Lincs 173 F10
Ewerby Thorpe Lincs 173 F10
Ewes Dumfries 249 E9
Ewesley Northumb 252 E3
Ewhurst Sur 50 E5
Ewhurst Green E Sus 38 C3
Ewhurst Green Sur 50 F5
Ewloe Flint 166 B4
Ewloe Green Flint 166 B3
Ewood Blkburn 195 B7
Ewood Bridge Lancs 195 C9
Eworthy Devon 12 C5
Ewshot Hants 49 D10
Ewyas Harold Hereford 97 F7
Exbourne Devon 25 G10
Exbury Hants 20 B4
Exceat E Sus 23 F8
Exebridge Devon 26 C6
Exelby N Yorks 214 B5
Exeter Devon 14 C4
Exford Som 41 F11
Exfords Green Shrops 131 B9
Exhall Warks 118 F2
Exhall Warks 135 F7
Exlade Street Oxon 65 C7
Exley W Yorks 196 C5
Exley Head W Yorks 204 F6
Exminster Devon 14 D4
Exmouth Devon 14 E6
Exnaboe Shetland 313 M5
Exning Suff 124 D2
Exted Kent 55 E7
Exton Devon 14 D5
Exton Hants 33 C10
Exton Rutland 155 G8
Exton Som 42 G2
Exwick Devon 14 C4
Eyam Derbys 186 F2
Eydon Northants 119 G10
Eye Hereford 115 E9
Eye P'boro 138 C4
Eye Suff 126 C2
Eye Green P'boro 138 C4
Eyemouth Borders 273 C8
Eyeworth C Beds 104 B4
Eyhorne Street Kent 53 C10
Eyke Suff 126 G6
Eynesbury Cambs 122 F3
Eynort Highld 294 C5
Eynsford Kent 68 F4
Eynsham Oxon 82 D6
Eype Dorset 16 C5
Eyre Highld 295 B7
Eyre Highld 298 D4
Eyres Monsell Leicester 135 D11
Eythorne Kent 55 D9
Eyton Hereford 115 E9
Eyton Shrops 131 F7
Eyton Shrops 149 G7
Eyton Wrex 166 G4
Eyton on Severn Shrops 131 B11
Eyton upon the Weald Moors Telford 150 G3

F

Faberstown Wilts 47 C9
Faccombe Hants 47 B11
Faceby N Yorks 225 E9
Fachell Gwyn 163 B8
Fachwen Gwyn 163 C9
Facit Lancs 195 D11
Fackley Notts 171 C7
Faddiley E Ches 167 E9
Faddonch Highld 295 C11
Fadmoor N Yorks 216 B3
Faerdre Swansea 75 E11
Fagley W Yorks 205 G9
Fagwyr Swansea 75 E11
Faichem Highld 290 C4
Faifley W Dunb 277 G10
Failand N Som 60 E4
Failford S Ayrs 257 D11
Failsworth Gtr Man 195 G11
Fain Highld 299 B11
Faindouran Lodge Moray 292 C2
Fair Cross London 68 B3
Fair Green Norf 158 F3
Fair Hill Cumb 230 E6
Fair Moor Northumb 252 F5
Fair Oak Hants 33 D7
Fair Oak Hants 64 G5
Fair Oak Lancs 203 D8
Fair Oak Green Hants 65 G7
Fairbourne Gwyn 146 G2
Fairbourne Heath Kent 53 C11
Fairburn N Yorks 198 B3
Fairburn House Highld 300 D4
Fairfield Clack 279 C7
Fairfield Derbys 185 G9
Fairfield Gtr Man 184 B6
Fairfield Gtr Man 195 E10
Fairfield Kent 39 B7
Fairfield Mers 182 C5
Fairfield Stockton 225 B8
Fairfield Worcs 99 C10
Fairfield Worcs 117 B8
Fairfield Park Bath 61 F9
Fairfields Glos 98 E4
Fairford Glos 81 E11
Fairford Park Glos 81 E11
Fairhaven Lancs 193 B10
Fairhaven N Ayrs 255 C10
Fairhill S Lnrk 268 E4
Fairlands Sur 50 C3
Fairlee I o W 20 C6
Fairlie N Ayrs 266 D4
Fairlight E Sus 38 E5
Fairlight Cove E Sus 38 E5
Fairlop London 87 G7
Fairmile Devon 15 B7
Fairmile Dorset 19 C9
Fairmile Sur 66 G6
Fairmilehead Edin 270 B4
Fairoak Caerph 77 F11
Fairoak Staffs 150 C5
Fairseat Kent 68 G6
Fairstead Essex 88 B3
Fairstead Norf 158 F2
Fairview Glos 99 G9
Fairwarp E Sus 37 B7
Fairwater Cardiff 58 D6
Fairwater Torf 78 G3
Fairwood Wilts 45 C10
Fairy Cottage I o M 192 D5
Fairy Cross Devon 24 C6
Fakenham Norf 159 D8
Fakenham Magna Suff 125 B8
Fala Midloth 271 C8
Fala Dam Midloth 271 C8
Falahill Borders 271 D7
Falcon Hereford 98 E2
Falcon Lodge W Mid 134 D2
Falconwood London 68 D3
Falcutt Northants 101 C11
Faldingworth Lincs 189 E9
Faldonside Borders 262 C2
Falfield Fife 287 G8
Falfield S Glos 79 G11
Falkenham Suff 108 D5
Falkenham Sink Suff 108 D5
Falkirk Falk 279 F7
Falkland Fife 286 G6
Falla Borders 262 G6
Fallgate Derbys 170 C5
Fallin Stirl 278 C6
Fallinge Derbys 170 B3
Fallings Heath W Mid 133 D9
Fallowfield Gtr Man 184 C5
Fallside N Lnrk 268 C4
Falmer E Sus 36 F5
Falmouth Corn 3 C8
Falnash Borders 249 B9
Falsgrave N Yorks 217 B10
Falside W Loth 269 B9
Falsidehill Borders 272 G3
Falstone Northumb 250 F6
Fanagmore Highld 306 E6
Fancott C Beds 103 F10
Fangdale Beck N Yorks 225 G11
Fangfoss E Yorks 207 C11
Fanich Highld 311 J2
Fankerton Falk 278 E5
Fanmore Argyll 288 E6
Fanner's Green Essex 87 C11
Fannich Lodge Highld 300 C2
Fans Borders 272 G2
Fanshowe E Ches 184 G5
Fant Kent 53 B8
Faoilean Highld 295 C7
Far Arnside Cumb 211 D8
Far Bank S Yorks 198 E6
Far Banks Lancs 194 C2
Far Bletchley M Keynes 103 E7

Far Coton Leics 135 C7
Far Cotton Northants 120 F4
Far End Cumb 220 F6
Far Forest Worcs 116 C4
Far Green Glos 80 E3
Far Hoarcross Staffs 152 E2
Far Laund Derbys 170 F5
Far Ley Staffs 132 D5
Far Moor Gtr Man 194 G4
Far Oakridge Glos 80 E6
Far Royds W Yorks 205 G11
Far Sawrey Cumb 221 F7
Far Thrupp Glos 80 E5
Farcet Cambs 138 E4
Farden Shrops 115 B11
Fareham Hants 33 F9
Farewell Staffs 151 G11
Farforth Lincs 190 F4
Farhill Derbys 170 C5
Faringdon Oxon 82 F3
Farington Lancs 194 B4
Farington Moss Lancs 194 C4
Farlam Cumb 240 F3
Farlands Booth Derbys 185 D9
Farlary Highld 309 J7
Farleigh N Som 60 F3
Farleigh Sur 67 G11
Farleigh Court Sur 67 G11
Farleigh Green Kent 53 C8
Farleigh Hungerford Som 45 B10
Farleigh Wallop Hants 48 D6
Farleigh Wick Wilts 61 G10
Farlesthorpe Lincs 191 G7
Farleton Cumb 211 C10
Farleton Lancs 211 F11
Farley Bristol 60 E2
Farley Derbys 170 C3
Farley Shrops 131 B7
Farley Shrops 132 C2
Farley Staffs 169 G9
Farley Wilts 32 B2
Farley Green Suff 124 G4
Farley Green Sur 50 D5
Farley Hill Luton 103 G11
Farley Hill Wokingham 65 G8
Farleys End Glos 80 B3
Farlington N Yorks 216 F2
Farlington Ptsmth 33 F11
Farlow Shrops 132 G2
Farm Town Leics 153 F7
Farmborough Bath 61 G7
Farmbridge End Essex 87 C10
Farmcote Glos 99 F11
Farmcote Shrops 132 E5
Farmington Glos 81 B10
Farmoor Oxon 82 D6
Farms Common Corn 2 C5
Farmtown Moray 302 D5
Farnah Green Derbys 170 F4
Farnborough Hants 49 C11
Farnborough London 68 G2
Farnborough W Berks 64 C2
Farnborough Warks 101 B8
Farnborough Green Hants 49 B11
Farnborough Park Hants 49 B11
Farnborough Street Hants 49 B11
Farncombe Sur 50 E3
Farndish Beds 121 E8
Farndon Notts 172 E3
Farndon W Ches 166 E6
Farnell Angus 287 B10
Farnham Dorset 31 D7
Farnham Essex 105 G9
Farnham N Yorks 215 G7
Farnham Suff 127 E7
Farnham Sur 49 D10
Farnham Common Bucks 66 C3
Farnham Green Essex 105 F9
Farnham Park Bucks 66 C3
Farnham Royal Bucks 66 C3
Farnhill N Yorks 204 D6
Farningham Kent 68 F4
Farnley N Yorks 205 D10
Farnley W Yorks 205 G11
Farnley Bank W Yorks 197 E7
Farnley Tyas W Yorks 197 E7
Farnsfield Notts 171 D10
Farnworth Gtr Man 195 F8
Farnworth Halton 183 D8
Farr Highld 291 C10
Farr Highld 300 F6
Farr Highld 308 C7
Farr House Highld 300 F6
Farraline Highld 300 G5
Farringdon Devon 14 C6
Farringdon T & W 243 G9
Farrington Dorset 30 D4
Farrington Gurney Bath 44 B6
Farsley W Yorks 205 F10
Farsley Beck Bottom W Yorks 205 F10
Farther Howegreen Essex 88 E4
Farthing Corner Medway 69 G10
Farthing Green Kent 53 D10
Farthinghoe Northants 101 D10
Farthingloe Kent 55 E9
Farthingstone Northants 120 F2
Fartown W Yorks 196 D6
Farway Devon 15 B9
Farway Marsh Devon 28 G4
Fasach Highld 297 G7
Fasag Highld 299 D8
Fascadale Highld 289 B7
Faslane Port Argyll 276 D4
Fasnacloich Argyll 284 C4
Fasnakyle Ho Highld 300 G3
Fassfern Highld 290 F2
Fatfield T & W 243 G8
Fattahead Aberds 302 D6
Faucheldean W Loth 279 G11
Faugh Cumb 240 G2
Faughill Borders 262 C2
Fauld Staffs 152 D3
Fauldhouse W Loth 269 C8
Fauldiehill Angus 287 D9
Fauldshope Borders 261 D10
Faulkbourne Essex 88 B3
Faulkland Som 45 C8
Fauls Shrops 149 C11
Faverdale Darl 224 B5
Faversham Kent 70 G4
Favillar Moray 302 F2
Fawdington N Yorks 215 E8
Fawdon Northumb 264 F2
Fawdon T & W 242 D6
Fawfieldhead Staffs 169 C9
Fawkham Green Kent 68 F5
Fawler Oxon 63 B10
Fawler Oxon 82 B5
Fawley Bucks 65 B9
Fawley Hants 33 G7
Fawley W Berks 63 C11
Fawley Bottom Bucks 65 B8
Fawley Chapel Hereford 97 F11
Faxfleet E Yorks 199 C11
Faygate W Sus 51 G8
Fazakerley Mers 182 B5
Fazeley Staffs 134 C4
Feagour Highld 291 D7
Fearby N Yorks 214 C3
Fearn Highld 301 B8
Fearn Lodge Highld 309 L6
Fearn Station Highld 301 B8
Fearnan Perth 285 C11
Fearnbeg Highld 299 D7
Fearnhead Warr 183 C10
Fearnmore Highld 299 C7
Fearnville W Yorks 206 F2
Featherstone Staffs 133 B8
Featherstone W Yorks 198 C2
Featherwood Northumb 251 C8
Feckenham Worcs 117 E10
Fedw Fawr Anglesey 179 E10
Feering Essex 107 G7
Feetham N Yorks 223 F9
Fegg Hayes Stoke 168 E5
Fèith Mhor Highld 301 G8
Feizor N Yorks 212 F5
Felbridge Sur 51 F11
Felbrigg Norf 160 B4
Felcourt Sur 51 E11
Felden Herts 85 E8
Felderland Kent 55 B10
Feldy E Ches 183 F11
Felhampton Shrops 131 F8
Felin-Crai Powys 95 G7
Felin Newydd Carms 94 D3
Felin-newydd Powys 96 D2
Felin Newydd = New Mills Powys 129 C11
Felin Puleston Wrex 166 F4
Felin-Wnda Ceredig 92 B6
Felindre Carms 75 C7
Felindre Carms 93 D7
Felindre Carms 93 G11
Felindre Carms 94 E3
Felindre Carms 94 F4
Felindre Ceredig 111 F10
Felindre Powys 96 D3
Felindre Powys 96 G3
Felindre Powys 130 C3
Felindre Powys 130 G3
Felindre Rhondda 58 C4
Felindre Swansea 75 E10
Felindre Farchog Pembs 92 D2
Felinfach Ceredig 111 F10
Felinfach Powys 95 E11
Felinfoel Carms 75 E8
Felingwmisaf Carms 93 G10
Felingwmuchaf Carms 93 G10
Felinwynt Ceredig 110 G4
Felixkirk N Yorks 215 C9
Felixstowe Suff 108 E5
Felixstowe Ferry Suff 108 D6
Felkington Northumb 273 G8
Felkirk W Yorks 197 E11
Fell End Cumb 222 F4
Fell Lane W Yorks 204 E6
Fell Side Cumb 230 D2
Felldyke Cumb 219 B11
Fellgate T & W 243 E8
Felling T & W 243 E7
Felling Shore T & W 243 E7
Fellside T & W 242 E5
Felmersham Beds 121 F9
Felmingham Norf 160 D5
Felmore Essex 69 B8
Felpham W Sus 35 H7
Felsham Suff 125 F8
Felsted Essex 106 G3
Feltham London 66 E6
Feltham Som 28 D2
Felthamhill London 66 E5
Felthorpe Norf 160 F3
Felton Hereford 97 B11
Felton N Som 60 F4
Felton Northumb 252 C5
Felton Butler Shrops 149 F7
Feltwell Norf 140 E4
Fen Ditton Cambs 123 E9
Fen Drayton Cambs 122 D6
Fen End Lincs 156 E4
Fen End W Mid 118 B4
Fen Side Lincs 174 D4
Fen Street Norf 141 G11
Fen Street Suff 125 B11
Fen Street Suff 125 B9
Fenay Bridge W Yorks 197 D7
Fence Lancs 204 F2
Fence Houses T & W 243 G8
Fencott Oxon 83 B9
Fengate Norf 160 E3
Fengate P'boro 138 D4
Fenham Northumb 273 G11
Fenham T & W 242 D6
Fenhouses Lincs 174 G3
Feniscliffe Blkburn 195 B7
Feniscowles Blkburn 194 B6
Feniton Devon 15 B8
Fenlake Beds 103 B11
Fenn Green Shrops 132 G5
Fenn Street Medway 69 D9
Fennington Som 27 B11
Fenn's Bank Wrex 149 B10
Fenny Bentley Derbys 169 E11
Fenny Bridges Devon 15 B8
Fenny Castle Som 44 E4
Fenny Compton Warks 119 G8
Fenny Drayton Leics 134 D6
Fenny Stratford M Keynes 103 E7
Fenrother Northumb 252 E5
Fenstanton Cambs 122 D6
Fenstead End Suff 124 G6
Fenton Cambs 122 B6
Fenton Cumb 240 F2
Fenton Lincs 172 E5
Fenton Lincs 188 F4
Fenton Northumb 263 C11
Fenton Stoke 168 G5
Fenton Barns E Loth 281 E10
Fenton Low Stoke 168 F5
Fenton Pits Corn 5 C11
Fenton Town Northumb 263 C11
Fentonadle Corn 11 F7
Fenwick E Ayrs 267 G9
Fenwick Northumb 242 C3
Fenwick Northumb 273 G11
Fenwick S Yorks 198 D5
Feochaig Argyll 255 F8
Feock Corn 3 B8
Feolin Ferry Argyll 274 G5
Ferguslie Park Renfs 267 C9
Ferindonald Highld 295 E8
Feriniquarrie Highld 296 F7
Ferlochan Argyll 289 E11
Fern Angus 292 G6
Fern Bucks 65 B11
Fern Bank Gtr Man 185 B7
Fern Hill Suff 106 B6
Ferndale Kent 52 E5
Ferndale Rhondda 77 F7
Ferndown Dorset 31 G9
Ferne Wilts 30 C6
Ferness Highld 301 E9
Ferney Green Cumb 221 F8
Fernham Oxon 82 G3
Fernhill Gtr Man 195 E10
Fernhill Rhondda 77 F8
Fernhill W Sus 51 E10
Fernhill Gate Gtr Man 195 F7
Fernhill Heath Worcs 117 F7
Fernhurst W Sus 34 B5
Fernie Fife 287 F7
Ferniebrae Aberds 303 D9
Ferniegair S Lnrk 268 E4
Ferniehirst Borders 271 G8
Fernilea Highld 294 B5
Fernilee Derbys 185 F8
Fernsplatt Corn 4 G5
Ferrensby N Yorks 215 G7
Ferring W Sus 35 G9
Ferry Hill Cambs 139 G7
Ferry Point Highld 309 L7
Ferrybridge W Yorks 198 C3
Ferryden Angus 287 B11
Ferryhill Aberdeen 293 C11
Ferryhill Durham 233 E11
Ferryhill Station Durham 234 E2
Ferryside = Glan-y-Ffer Carms 74 C5
Ferryton Highld 300 C6
Fersfield Norf 141 G11
Fersit Highld 290 F5
Feshiebridge Highld 291 C10
Fetcham Sur 50 B6
Fetterangus Aberds 303 D9
Fettercairn Aberds 293 F8
Fetterdale Fife 287 E8
Fettes Highld 300 D5
Fewcott Oxon 101 F10
Fewston N Yorks 205 C9
Fewston Bents N Yorks 205 C9
Ffair-Rhos Ceredig 112 D4
Ffairfach Carms 94 G2
Ffaldybrenin Carms 94 C2
Ffarmers Carms 94 C3
Ffawyddog Powys 78 B2
Ffodun = Forden Powys 130 C4
Ffont y gari = Font y gary V Glam 58 F5
Ffordd-las Denb 165 C10
Ffordd-y-Gyfraith Bridgend 57 E11
Fforddlas Powys 96 D4
Fforest Carms 75 E9
Fforest-fach Swansea 56 B6
Fforest Gôch Neath 76 E2
Ffos-y-ffin Ceredig 111 E8
Ffos-y-go Wrex 166 E4
Ffostrasol Ceredig 93 B7
Ffridd Powys 130 D3
Ffrith Wrex 166 D3
Ffrwd Gwyn 163 D7
Ffwl y mwn = Fonmon V Glam 58 F4
Ffynnon Carms 74 B5
Ffynnon ddrain Carms 93 G8
Ffynnon Gron Pembs 91 F8
Ffynnon Gynydd Powys 96 C3
Ffynnon-oer Ceredig 111 G10
Ffynnongroes = Crosswell Pembs 92 D2
Ffynnongroyw Flint 181 E10
Fickleshole Sur 67 G11
Fidden Argyll 288 G5
Fiddes Aberds 293 E10
Fiddington Glos 99 E8
Fiddington Som 43 E8
Fiddington Sands Wilts 46 C4
Fiddleford Dorset 30 E4
Fiddler' Green Norf 141 D10
Fiddler's Ferry Mers 193 C11
Fiddler's Ferry Warr 183 D9
Fiddler's Green Glos 99 G8
Fiddler's Green Hereford 97 D11
Fiddlers Hamlet Essex 87 E7
Field Hereford 114 G6
Field Som 44 E6
Field Staffs 151 C10
Field Assarts Oxon 82 C4
Field Broughton Cumb 211 C7
Field Common Sur 66 F6
Field Dalling Norf 159 B10
Field Green Kent 38 B3
Field Head Leics 135 B9
Fields End Herts 85 D8
Field's Place Hereford 115 G8
Fife Keith Moray 302 D4
Fifehead Magdalen Dorset 30 C3
Fifehead Neville Dorset 30 E3
Fifehead St Quintin Dorset 30 E3
Fifield Oxon 82 B2
Fifield Wilts 46 C6
Fifield Windsor 66 D2
Fifield Bavant Wilts 31 B8
Figheldean Wilts 47 D7
Filands Wilts 62 B2
Filby Norf 161 G9
Filby Heath Norf 161 G9
Filchampstead Oxon 83 D7
Filey N Yorks 218 C2
Filgrave M Keynes 103 B7
Filham Devon 8 D2
Filkins Oxon 82 E2
Filleigh Devon 25 B11
Filleigh Devon 26 E2
Fillingham Lincs 188 D6
Fillongley Warks 134 F5
Filmore Hill Hants 33 B11
Filton S Glos 60 D6
Filwood Park Bristol 60 F5
Fimber E Yorks 217 G7
Finavon Angus 287 B8
Fincastle Ho Perth 291 G10
Finchairn Argyll 275 C10
Fincham Mers 182 C6
Fincham Norf 140 B3
Finchampstead Wokingham 65 G9
Finchdean Hants 34 E2
Finchingfield Essex 106 E3
Finchley London 86 G3
Findern Derbys 152 C6
Findhorn Moray 301 C10
Findhorn Bridge Highld 301 G8
Findo Gask Perth 286 E4
Findochty Moray 302 C4
Findon Aberds 293 D11
Findon W Sus 35 F10
Findon Mains Highld 300 C6
Findon Valley W Sus 35 F10
Findrack Ho Aberds 293 C8
Fine Street Hereford 96 D6
Finedon Northants 121 C8
Fineglen Argyll 275 B10
Fingal Street Suff 126 D4
Fingask Aberds 303 G7
Fingerpost Worcs 116 C4
Fingest Bucks 84 G3
Finghall N Yorks 214 B3
Fingland Cumb 239 F7
Fingland Dumfries 259 F7
Finglesham Kent 55 C10
Fingringhoe Essex 107 G10
Finham W Mid 118 B6
Finkle Street S Yorks 186 B4
Finlarig Stirl 285 D9
Finmere Oxon 102 E2
Finnart Perth 285 B9
Finney Green E Ches 184 E5
Finney Green Staffs 168 F3
Finningham Suff 125 D11
Finningley S Yorks 187 B11
Finnygaud Aberds 302 D5
Finsbury London 67 C10
Finsbury Park London 67 B10
Finstall Worcs 117 D9
Finsthwaite Cumb 211 B7
Finstock Oxon 82 B5
Finstown Orkney 314 E3
Fintry Aberds 303 D7
Fintry Dundee 287 D8
Fintry Stirl 278 D2
Finwood Warks 118 D3
Finzean Aberds 293 D8
Finzean Ho Aberds 293 D7
Fionnphort Argyll 288 G5
Fionnsbhagh W Isles 296 C6
Fir Toll Kent 54 E2
Fir Tree Durham 233 E8
Fir Vale S Yorks 186 C5
Firbank Cumb 222 G2
Firbeck S Yorks 187 D9
Firby N Yorks 214 B5
Firby N Yorks 216 F4
Firemore Highld 307 L3
Firgrove Gtr Man 196 E2
Firkin Argyll 285 G7
Firle E Sus 23 D7
Firs Lane Gtr Man 194 G6
First Coast Highld 307 K4
Firsby Lincs 175 C7
Firsdown Wilts 47 G8
Firswood Gtr Man 184 B4
Firth Borders 262 E2
Firth Moor Darl 224 C6
Firth Park S Yorks 186 C5
Firwood Fold Gtr Man 195 E8
Fishbourne I o W 21 C7
Fishbourne W Sus 22 C4
Fishburn Durham 234 E3
Fishcross Clack 279 B7
Fisher Place Cumb 220 B6
Fisherford Aberds 302 F6
Fishermead M Keynes 103 D7
Fisherrow E Loth 280 G6
Fishers Green Herts 104 F4
Fisher's Pond Hants 33 C7
Fishersgate Brighton 36 F3
Fisherstreet W Sus 50 G3
Fisherton Highld 301 D7
Fisherton S Ayrs 257 F7
Fisherton de la Mere Wilts 46 F4
Fisherwick Staffs 134 B3
Fishery Windsor 65 C11
Fishguard = Abergwaun Pembs 91 D9
Fishlake S Yorks 199 E7
Fishleigh Devon 25 F8
Fishleigh Barton Devon 25 C9
Fishleigh Castle Devon 25 F8
Fishley Norf 161 G8
Fishley W Mid 133 C10
Fishmere End Lincs 156 B5
Fishponds Bristol 60 D6
Fishpool Glos 98 F3
Fishpool Gtr Man 195 F10
Fishpool N Yorks 205 D10
Fishpools Powys 114 D3
Fishtoft Lincs 174 G5
Fishtoft Drove Lincs 174 F4
Fishtown of Usan Angus 287 B11
Fishwick Borders 273 E8
Fishwick Lancs 194 B5
Fiskavaig Highld 294 B5
Fiskerton Lincs 189 G8
Fiskerton Notts 172 E2
Fitling E Yorks 209 G11
Fittleton Wilts 46 D6
Fittleworth W Sus 35 D8
Fitton End Cambs 157 G8
Fitton Hill Gtr Man 196 G2
Fitz Shrops 149 F8
Fitzhead Som 27 B10
Fitzwilliam W Yorks 198 D2
Fiunary Highld 289 E8
Five Acres Glos 79 C9
Five Ash Down E Sus 37 C7
Five Ashes E Sus 37 C9
Five Bells Som 42 E5
Five Bridges Hereford 98 B3
Five Houses I o W 20 D4
Five Lane Ends Lancs 202 C6
Five Lanes Mon 78 G6
Five Oak Green Kent 52 D6
Five Oaks W Sus 35 B9
Five Roads Carms 75 D7
Five Ways Warks 118 D4
Five Wents Kent 53 C10
Fivecrosses W Ches 183 F8
Fivehead Som 28 C5
Fivelanes Corn 11 E10
Fixby W Yorks 196 C6
Flackley Ash E Sus 38 C5
Flack's Green Essex 88 B3
Flackwell Heath Bucks 65 B11
Fladbury Worcs 99 B9
Fladbury Cross Worcs 99 B9
Fladda Shetland 312 E5
Fladdabister Shetland 313 K6
Flagg Derbys 169 B10
Flaggoners Green Hereford 116 G2
Flamborough E Yorks 218 E4
Flamstead Herts 85 C9
Flamstead End Herts 86 E4
Flansham W Sus 35 G7
Flanshaw W Yorks 197 C10
Flappit Spring W Yorks 205 F7
Flasby N Yorks 204 B4
Flash Staffs 169 B8
Flashader Highld 298 D3
Flask Inn N Yorks 227 E8
Flathurst W Sus 35 C7
Flaunden Herts 85 E8
Flawborough Notts 172 G3
Flawith N Yorks 215 F9
Flax Bourton N Som 60 F4
Flax Moss Lancs 195 C9
Flaxby N Yorks 206 B3
Flaxholme Derbys 170 G4
Flaxlands Norf 142 E2
Flaxley Glos 79 B11
Flaxpool Som 42 F6
Flaxton N Yorks 216 G3
Fleckney Leics 136 E2
Flecknoe Warks 119 E10
Fledborough Notts 188 G4
Fleet Dorset 17 E8
Fleet Hants 22 C2
Fleet Hants 49 C10
Fleet Lincs 157 E7
Fleet Downs Kent 68 E5
Fleet Hargate Lincs 157 E7
Fleetend Hants 33 F8
Fleetlands Hants 33 G9
Fleets N Yorks 213 G9
Fleetville Herts 85 D11
Fleetwood Lancs 202 D2
Fleggburgh = Burgh St Margaret Norf 161 G8
Fleming Field Durham 234 C3
Flemings Kent 55 B9
Flemingston V Glam 58 E4
Flemington S Lnrk 268 D3
Flemington S Lnrk 268 G4
Flempton Suff 124 D6
Fleoideabhagh W Isles 296 C6
Fletcher's Green Kent 52 C4
Fletchersbridge Corn 6 B2
Fletchertown Cumb 229 C10
Fletching E Sus 36 C6
Fletching Common E Sus 36 C6
Fleuchary Highld 309 K7
Fleuchlang Dumfries 237 D8
Fleur-de-lis Caerph 77 F11
Flexbury Corn 24 F2
Flexford Hants 32 C6
Flexford Sur 50 D2
Flimby Cumb 228 E6
Flimwell E Sus 53 G8
Flint Flint 182 G2
Flint Cross Cambs 105 C8
Flint Hill Durham 242 G5
Flint Mountain = Mynydd Fflint Flint 182 G2
Flintham Notts 172 F2
Flinton E Yorks 209 F10
Flint's Green W Mid 134 G5
Flintsham Hereford 114 F6
Flishinghurst Kent 53 F9
Flitcham Norf 158 D4
Flitholme Cumb 222 B5
Flitton C Beds 103 D11
Flitwick C Beds 103 D10
Flixborough N Lincs 199 D11
Flixborough Stather N Lincs 199 E11
Flixton Gtr Man 184 C2
Flixton N Yorks 217 D10
Flixton Suff 142 F6
Flockton W Yorks 197 E8
Flockton Green W Yorks 197 D8
Flockton Moor W Yorks 197 E8
Flodaigh W Isles 296 F4
Flodden Northumb 263 B10
Flodigarry Highld 298 B4
Flood Street Hants 31 D10
Floodgates Hereford 114 F5
Flood's Ferry Cambs 139 E7
Flookburgh Cumb 211 D7
Flordon Norf 142 D3
Flore Northants 120 E2
Florence Stoke 168 G6
Flotterton Northumb 251 C11
Flowers Bottom Bucks 84 F4
Flowers Green E Sus 23 C10
Flowery Field Gtr Man 184 B6
Flowton Suff 107 B11
Fluchter E Dunb 277 G11
Flugarth Shetland 313 G6
Flush House W Yorks 196 F6
Flushdyke W Yorks 197 C9
Flushing Aberds 303 E10
Flushing Corn 3 C8
Flushing Corn 3 D7
Flyford Flavell Worcs 117 G9
Foals Green Suff 126 C5
Fobbing Thurrock 69 C8
Fochabers Moray 302 D3
Fochriw Caerph 77 D10
Fockerby N Lincs 199 D10
Fodderletter Moray 301 G11
Fodderstone Gap Norf 140 B3
Fodderty Highld 300 D5
Foddington Som 29 B9
Foel Powys 147 G9
Foel-gastell Carms 75 C8
Foffarty Angus 287 C8
Foggathorpe E Yorks 207 F11
Foggbrook Gtr Man 184 D6
Fogo Borders 272 F5
Fogorig Borders 272 F5
Fogrigarth Shetland 313 H4
Fogwatt Moray 302 D2
Foindle Highld 306 E6
Fold Head Lancs 195 D11
Fold Hill Lincs 175 E7
Folda Angus 292 G3
Foldrings S Yorks 186 C3
Fole Staffs 151 B10
Foleshill W Mid 135 G7
Foley Park Worcs 116 B5
Folke Dorset 29 E11
Folkestone Kent 55 F8
Folkingham Lincs 155 C11
Folkington E Sus 23 E9
Folksworth Cambs 138 F2
Folkton N Yorks 217 D11
Folla Rule Aberds 303 F7
Folley Shrops 132 D5
Follifoot N Yorks 206 C2
Follingsby T & W 243 E8
Folly Dorset 30 G2
Folly Pembs 91 G8
Folly Cross Devon 25 F7
Folly Gate Devon 13 B7
Folly Green Essex 106 F6
Fonmon = Ffwl-y-mwn V Glam 58 F4
Fonston Corn 11 C10
Font-y-gary = Ffont-y-gari V Glam 58 F5
Fonthill Bishop Wilts 46 G2
Fonthill Gifford Wilts 46 G2
Fontmell Magna Dorset 30 D5
Fontmell Parva Dorset 30 E4
Fontwell W Sus 35 F7
Foodieash Fife 287 F7
Foolow Derbys 185 F11
Footbridge Glos 99 F10
Footherley Staffs 134 C2
Footrid Worcs 116 C3
Foots Cray London 68 E3
Forbestown Aberds 292 B5
Force Forge Cumb 220 G6
Force Green Kent 52 B2
Force Mills Cumb 220 G6
Forcett N Yorks 224 C3
Ford Argyll 275 C9
Ford Bucks 84 D3
Ford Derbys 186 E6
Ford Devon 8 E2
Ford Devon 8 G5
Ford Devon 24 C6
Ford Devon 28 G2
Ford Glos 99 F11
Ford Hereford 115 F10
Ford Kent 71 F8
Ford Mers 182 B4
Ford Northumb 263 B10
Ford Pembs 91 F9
Ford Plym 7 D9
Ford Shrops 149 G8
Ford Som 27 B9
Ford Som 44 C5
Ford Staffs 169 E9
Ford W Sus 35 G7
Ford Wilts 47 G7
Ford Wilts 61 E10
Ford End Essex 87 B11
Ford End Essex 105 E9
Ford Forge Northumb 263 B10
Ford Green Lancs 202 D5
Ford Green Stoke 168 E5
Ford Heath Shrops 149 G8
Ford Hill Northumb 263 B11
Ford Street Som 27 D11
Forda Devon 12 C6
Forda Devon 40 F3
Fordbridge W Mid 134 F3
Fordcombe Kent 52 E4
Fordell Fife 280 D3
Forden = Ffodun Powys 130 C4
Forder Corn 7 D8
Forder Green Devon 8 B5
Fordgate Som 43 G10
Fordham Cambs 124 C2
Fordham Essex 107 F8
Fordham Norf 140 D2
Fordham Heath Essex 107 F8
Fordhouses W Mid 133 C8
Fordingbridge Hants 31 E10
Fordington Lincs 190 G6
Fordley T & W 243 C7
Fordon E Yorks 217 D10
Fordoun Aberds 293 F9
Ford's Green E Sus 36 B6
Ford's Green Suff 125 D11
Fordstreet Essex 107 F8
Fordton Devon 14 B2
Fordwater Devon 28 G4
Fordwells Oxon 82 C4
Fordwich Kent 55 B7
Fordyce Aberds 302 C5
Forebridge Staffs 151 E8
Foredale N Yorks 212 F6
Forehill S Ayrs 257 E8
Foreland Fields I o W 21 D9
Foreland Ho Argyll 274 G3
Foremark Derbys 152 D6
Forest Lodge Argyll 284 C6
Forest Lodge Highld 292 B2
Forest Lodge Perth 291 F11
Forest Becks Lancs 203 C11
Forest Coal Pit Mon 96 G5
Forest Gate Hants 33 E10
Forest Gate London 68 C2
Forest Green Glos 80 E4
Forest Green Sur 50 E6
Forest Hall Cumb 221 E10
Forest Hall T & W 243 D7
Forest Head Cumb 240 F3
Forest Hill London 67 E11
Forest Hill Oxon 83 D9
Forest Hill Wilts 63 F8
Forest Holme Lancs 195 B10
Forest-in-Teesdale Durham 232 F3
Forest Lane Head N Yorks 206 B2
Forest Mill Clack 279 C9
Forest Moor N Yorks 206 B2
Forest Row E Sus 52 G2
Forest Side I o W 20 D5
Forest Town Notts 171 C9
Forestburn Gate Northumb 252 D3
Forestdale London 67 G11
Foresterseat Moray 301 D11
Forestreet Devon 24 E5
Forestside W Sus 34 E3
Forewoods Common Wilts 61 G10
Forfar Angus 287 B8
Forgandenny Perth 286 F4
Forge Corn 4 F3
Forge Powys 128 D5
Forge Hammer Torf 78 F3
Forge Side Torf 78 D2
Forgewood N Lnrk 268 D4
Forgie Moray 302 D3
Forglen Ho Aberds 302 D6
Forgue Aberds 302 E6
Forhill Worcs 117 B11
Formby Mers 193 F10
Forncett End Norf 142 E2
Forncett St Mary Norf 142 E3
Forncett St Peter Norf 142 E3
Forneth Perth 286 C4
Fornham All Saints Suff 124 D6
Fornham St Genevieve Suff 124 D6
Fornham St Martin Suff 125 D7
Fornighty Highld 301 D9
Forrabury Corn 11 C7
Forres Moray 301 D10
Forrest Lodge Dumfries 246 F3
Forrestfield N Lnrk 269 B7
Forry's Green Essex 106 E5
Forsbrook Staffs 169 G7
Forse Highld 310 F6
Forse Ho Highld 310 F6
Forshaw Heath Warks 117 C11
Forsinain Highld 310 E3
Forsinard Highld 310 E2
Forsinard Station Highld 310 E2
Forstal Kent 53 B8
Forston Dorset 17 B9
Fort Augustus Highld 290 C5
Fort George Highld 301 D7
Fort Matilda Invclyd 276 F5
Fort William Highld 290 F3
Forteviot Perth 286 F4
Forth S Lnrk 269 E8
Forth Road Bridge Edin 280 F2
Forthampton Glos 99 E7
Forthay Glos 80 F2
Fortingall Perth 285 C11
Fortis Green London 67 B9
Forton Hants 33 G10
Forton Hants 48 E2
Forton Lancs 202 C5
Forton Shrops 149 F8
Forton Som 28 F4
Forton Staffs 150 E5
Forton Heath Shrops 149 F8
Fortrie Aberds 302 E6
Fortrie Aberds 303 D7
Fortrose Highld 301 D7
Fortuneswell Dorset 17 G9
Forty Green Bucks 84 E3
Forty Green Bucks 84 G6
Forty Hill London 86 F4
Forward Green Suff 125 F11
Forwood Glos 80 E5
Fosbury Wilts 47 B10
Foscot Oxon 100 G4
Foscote Bucks 102 D4
Foscote Northants 102 B3
Foscote Wilts 61 D11
Fosdyke Lincs 156 C6
Fosdyke Bridge Lincs 156 C6
Foss Perth 285 B11
Foss Cross Glos 81 D9
Fossebridge Glos 81 C9
Fostall Kent 70 G5
Fosten Green Kent 53 F10
Foster Street Essex 87 D7
Fosterhouses S Yorks 199 E7
Foster's Booth Northants 120 G3
Foster's Green Worcs 117 D9
Foston Derbys 152 C3
Foston Leics 136 D2
Foston Lincs 172 G5
Foston N Yorks 216 F3
Foston on the Wolds E Yorks 209 B8
Fotherby Lincs 190 C4
Fothergill Cumb 228 E6
Fotheringhay Northants 137 E11
Foubister Orkney 314 F5
Foul Anchor Cambs 157 F9
Foul End Warks 134 E4
Foul Mile E Sus 23 B10
Foulbridge Cumb 230 B4
Foulby W Yorks 197 D11
Foulden Borders 273 D8
Foulden Norf 140 D5
Foulford Hants 31 F11
Foulis Castle Highld 300 C5
Foulride Green E Sus 23 E9
Foulridge Lancs 204 E3
Foulsham Norf 159 E10
Foundry Corn 2 B3
Foundry Hill Norf 159 D11
Fountain Bridgend 57 E11
Fountainhall Borders 271 F8
Four Ashes Bucks 84 F5
Four Ashes Staffs 132 F6
Four Ashes Staffs 133 B8
Four Ashes Suff 125 C10
Four Ashes W Mid 118 B3
Four Crosses Powys 129 B11
Four Crosses Powys 148 F5
Four Crosses Staffs 133 B9
Four Crosses Wrex 166 E3
Four Elms Devon 28 F3
Four Elms Kent 52 D3
Four Foot Som 44 G5
Four Forks Som 43 F8
Four Gates Gtr Man 194 F6
Four Gotes Cambs 157 F9
Four Houses Corner W Berks 64 F6
Four Lane End S Yorks 197 G9
Four Lane Ends Blkburn 195 B7
Four Lane Ends Gtr Man 195 E9
Four Lane Ends W Ches 167 C9
Four Lane Ends W Yorks 205 G8
Four Lanes Corn 2 B5
Four Marks Hants 49 G7
Four Mile Bridge Anglesey 178 F3
Four Mile Elm Glos 80 C4
Four Oaks E Sus 38 C5
Four Oaks Glos 98 F3
Four Oaks Kent 70 G3
Four Oaks W Mid 134 D2
Four Oaks W Mid 134 G4
Four Oaks Park W Mid 134 D2
Four Points W Berks 64 D5
Four Pools Worcs 99 C10
Four Roads Carms 74 D6
Four Roads I o M 192 F3
Four Throws Kent 38 B3
Four Wantz Essex 87 C10
Four Wents Kent 53 F9
Fourlane Ends Derbys 170 D5
Fourlanes End E Ches 168 D4
Fourpenny Highld 311 K2
Fourstones Northumb 241 D9
Fovant Wilts 31 B8
Foveran Aberds 303 G9
Fowey Corn 6 E2
Fowler's Plot Som 43 F10
Fowley Common Warr 183 B11
Fowlis Angus 287 D7
Fowlis Wester Perth 286 E3
Fowlmere Cambs 105 B8
Fownhope Hereford 97 E11
Fox Corner C Beds 103 F8
Fox Corner Sur 50 C3
Fox Hatch Essex 87 F9
Fox Hill Bath 61 G9
Fox Hill Hereford 98 B3
Fox Hole Swansea 56 D5
Fox Holes Wilts 45 E11
Fox Lane Hants 49 B11
Fox Royd W Yorks 197 D8
Fox Street Essex 107 F10
Foxash Estate Essex 107 E11
Foxbar Renfs 267 C9
Foxbury London 68 E2
Foxcombe Hill Oxon 83 E7
Foxcote Glos 81 B8
Foxcote Som 45 B8
Foxdale I o M 192 E3
Foxdown Hants 48 C4
Foxearth Essex 106 C6
Foxendown Kent 69 F7
Foxfield Cumb 210 B4
Foxford W Mid 135 G7
Foxham Wilts 62 D3
Foxhills Hants 32 E4
Foxhole Corn 5 E9
Foxhole Norf 142 D4
Foxhole Swansea 57 C7
Foxholes N Yorks 217 E10
Foxhunt Green E Sus 23 B8
Foxley Hereford 97 B8
Foxley Norf 159 E10
Foxley Staffs 168 E3
Foxley Wilts 61 B11
Foxlydiate Worcs 117 D10
Foxt Staffs 169 F8
Foxton Cambs 105 B8
Foxton Durham 234 F3
Foxton Leics 136 E4
Foxton N Yorks 225 F8
Foxup N Yorks 213 D7
Foxwist Green W Ches 167 B10
Foxwood Shrops 116 B2
Foy Hereford 97 F11
Foyers Highld 300 G4
Foynesfield Highld 301 D8
Fraddam Corn 2 C3
Fraddon Corn 5 D8
Fradley Staffs 152 G3
Fradley Junction Staffs 152 G2
Fradswell Staffs 151 C9
Fraisthorpe E Yorks 218 G3
Framfield E Sus 37 C7
Framingham Earl Norf 142 C5
Framingham Pigot Norf 142 C5
Framlingham Suff 126 E5
Frampton Dorset 17 B8
Frampton Lincs 156 B6
Frampton Cotterell S Glos 61 C7
Frampton Court Glos 99 E10
Frampton End S Glos 61 C7
Frampton Mansell Glos 80 E6
Frampton on Severn Glos 80 D2
Frampton West End Lincs 174 G3
Framsden Suff 126 F3
Framwellgate Moor Durham 233 C11
France Lynch Glos 80 E6
Franche Worcs 116 B6
Frandley W Ches 183 F10
Frankby Mers 182 D2
Frankfort Norf 160 E6
Franklands Gate Hereford 97 B10
Frankley Worcs 133 G9
Frankley Green Worcs 133 G9
Frankley Hill Worcs 117 B9
Frank's Bridge Powys 114 F2
Frankton Warks 119 C8
Frankwell Shrops 149 G9
Frans Green Norf 160 G2
Frant E Sus 52 F5
Fraserburgh Aberds 303 C9
Frating Essex 107 G11
Frating Green Essex 107 G11
Fratton Ptsmth 21 B9
Freasley Warks 134 D4
Freathy Corn 7 E8
Frecheville S Yorks 186 E5
Freckenham Suff 124 C3
Freckleton Lancs 194 B2
Fredley Sur 51 C7
Free Town Gtr Man 195 E10
Freebirch Derbys 186 G4
Freeby Leics 154 E6
Freefolk Hants 48 D3
Freehay Staffs 169 G8
Freeland Oxon 82 C6
Freeland Renfs 267 B9
Freeland Corner Norf 160 F3
Freemantle Soton 32 E6
Freeport Village W Loth 269 C10
Freester Shetland 313 H6
Freethorpe Norf 143 B8
Freezy Water London 86 F5
Freiston Lincs 174 G5
Freiston Shore Lincs 174 G5
Fremington Devon 40 G4
Fremington N Yorks 223 F10
French Street Kent 52 C3
Frenchay S Glos 60 D6
Frenchbeer Devon 13 D9
Frenches Green Essex 106 G4
Frenchmoor Hants 32 B3
Frenchwood Lancs 194 B4
Frenich Stirl 285 G8
Frensham Sur 49 E10
Frenze Norf 142 G2
Fresgoe Highld 310 C3
Freshbrook Swindon 62 C6
Freshfield Mers 193 F9
Freshford Bath 61 G9
Freshwater I o W 20 D2
Freshwater Bay I o W 20 D2
Freshwater East Pembs 73 F8
Fressingfield Suff 126 B5
Freston Suff 108 D3
Freswick Highld 310 C7
Fretherne Glos 80 D2
Frettenham Norf 160 F4
Freuchie Fife 286 G6
Freuchies Angus 292 G4
Freystrop Pembs 73 C7
Friar Park W Mid 133 E10
Friarn Som 43 F7
Friars Cliff Dorset 19 C9
Friar's Gate E Sus 52 G3
Friar's Hill E Sus 38 E5
Friarton Perth 286 E5
Friday Bridge Cambs 139 C9
Friday Hill London 86 G5
Friday Street E Sus 23 E10
Friday Street Suff 126 G6
Friday Street Suff 127 E7
Friday Street Sur 50 D6
Fridaythorpe E Yorks 208 B3
Friendly W Yorks 196 C5
Friern Barnet London 86 G3
Friesland Argyll 288 D3
Friesthorpe Lincs 189 E9
Frieston Lincs 172 F6
Frieth Bucks 84 G3
Frieze Hill Som 28 B2
Friezeland Notts 171 E7
Frilford Oxon 82 F6
Frilford Heath Oxon 82 F6
Frilsham W Berks 64 E4
Frimley Sur 49 B11
Frimley Green Sur 49 B11
Frimley Ridge Sur 49 B11
Frindsbury Medway 69 E8
Fring Norf 158 C4
Fringford Oxon 102 F2
Friningham Kent 53 B10
Frinkle Green Essex 106 C4
Frinsted Kent 53 B11
Frinton-on-Sea Essex 108 G4
Friockheim Angus 287 C9
Friog Gwyn 146 G2
Frisby Leics 136 C4
Frisby on the Wreake Leics 154 F3
Friskney Lincs 175 D7
Friskney Eaudyke Lincs 175 D7
Friskney Tofts Lincs 175 E7
Friston E Sus 23 F8
Friston Suff 127 E8
Fritchley Derbys 170 E5
Frith Kent 54 B2
Frith Bank Lincs 174 F4
Frith Common Worcs 116 D3
Frith-hill Bucks 84 E6
Frith Hill Sur 50 E3
Fritham Hants 32 E2
Frithelstock Devon 25 D7
Frithelstock Stone Devon 25 D7
Frithend Hants 49 F10
Frithsden Herts 85 D8
Frithville Lincs 174 E4
Frittenden Kent 53 E10
Frittiscombe Devon 8 G6
Fritton Norf 142 E4
Fritton Norf 143 C9
Fritton Norf 161 F8
Fritwell Oxon 101 F10
Frizinghall W Yorks 205 F8
Frizington Cumb 219 B10
Frizzeler's Green Suff 124 E5
Frobost W Isles 297 J3
Frocester Glos 80 E3
Frochas Powys 148 G5
Frodesley Shrops 131 C10
Frodingham N Lincs 199 E11
Frodsham W Ches 183 F8
Frog End Cambs 123 F10
Frog End Cambs 123 G8
Frog Moor Swansea 56 C3
Frog Pool Worcs 116 E5
Frogden Borders 263 D7
Froggatt Derbys 186 F2

Froghall Staffs 169 F8
Frogham Hants 31 E11
Frogham Kent 55 C9
Froghole Kent 52 C2
Frogholt Kent 55 F7
Frogland Cross S Glos 60 C6
Frogmore Devon 8 G5
Frogmore Hants 33 C11
Frogmore Hants 49 B10
Frogmore Herts 85 E11
Frognal S Ayrs 257 D8
Frognall Lincs 156 G3
Frogpool Corn 4 G5
Frogs' Green Essex 105 D11
Frogshail Norf 160 B5
Frogwell Corn 6 B6
Frolesworth Leics 135 E10
Frome Som 45 D9
Frome St Quintin Dorset 29 G9
Fromebridge Glos 80 D3
Fromes Hill Hereford 98 B3
Fromington Hereford 97 B10
Fron Denb 165 B9
Fron Gwyn 145 B7
Fron Gwyn 163 D8
Fron Powys 113 D11
Fron Powys 129 C8
Fron Powys 130 C4
Fron Powys 130 D3
Fron Shrops 148 B5
Fron-Bache Denb 166 G2
Fron-dêg Wrex 166 F3
Fron Isaf Wrex 166 G3
Froncysyllte Wrex 166 G3
Frongoch Gwyn 147 B8
Frost Devon 26 F3
Frost Hill N Som 60 G2
Frost Row Norf 141 C10
Frostenden Suff 143 G9
Frostenden Corner Suff 143 G9
Frosterley Durham 232 D6
Frostlane Hants 32 F6
Frotoft Orkney 314 D4
Froxfield C Beds 103 E9
Froxfield Wilts 63 F9
Froxfield Green Hants 34 B2
Froyle Hants 49 E9
Fryern Hill Hants 32 C6
Fryerning Essex 87 E10
Fryerns Essex 69 B8
Fryton N Yorks 216 E3
Fugglestone St Peter Wilts 46 G6
Fulbeck Lincs 172 E6
Fulbeck Northumb 252 F5
Fulbourn Cambs 123 F10
Fulbrook Oxon 82 C3
Fulflood Hants 33 B7
Fulford Som 28 B2
Fulford Staffs 151 B9
Fulford York 207 D8
Fulham London 67 D8
Fulking W Sus 36 E2
Full Sutton E Yorks 207 B10
Fullabrook Devon 40 E4
Fullarton Glasgow 268 C2
Fullarton N Ayrs 257 B8
Fuller Street Essex 88 B2
Fuller's End Essex 105 F10
Fuller's Moor W Ches 167 E7
Fullerton Hants 47 F11
Fulletby Lincs 190 G3
Fullshaw S Yorks 197 G8
Fullwell Cross London 86 G6
Fullwood E Ayrs 267 E8
Fullwood Gtr Man 196 F2
Fulmer Bucks 66 B3
Fulmodestone Norf 159 C9
Fulneck W Yorks 205 G10
Fulnetby Lincs 189 F9
Fulney Lincs 156 E5
Fulready Warks 100 B5
Fulshaw Park E Ches 184 E4
Fulstone W Yorks 197 F7
Fulstow Lincs 190 B4
Fulthorpe Stockton 234 G4
Fulwell Oxon 101 G7
Fulwell T & W 243 F9
Fulwood Lancs 202 G6
Fulwood S Yorks 186 D4
Fulwood Som 28 C2
Fundenhall Norf 142 D3
Fundenhall Street Norf 142 D2
Funtington W Sus 22 B3
Funtley Hants 33 F9
Funtullich Perth 285 E11
Funzie Shetland 312 D8
Furley Devon 28 G3
Furnace Argyll 284 G4
Furnace Carms 74 E6
Furnace Carms 75 E7
Furnace Ceredig 128 D3
Furnace Highld 299 B9
Furnace End Warks 134 E4
Furnace Green W Sus 51 F9
Furnace Wood W Sus 51 F11
Furneaux Pelham Herts 105 F8
Furner's Green E Sus 36 B6
Furness Vale Derbys 185 E8
Furneux Pelham Herts 105 F8
Furnham Som 28 F4
Further Ford End Essex 105 E9
Further Quarter Kent 53 F11
Furtho Northants 102 C5
Furze Devon 25 B10
Furze Hill Hants 31 E11
Furze Platt Windsor 65 C11
Furzebrook Dorset 18 E4
Furzedown Hants 32 B5
Furzedown London 67 E9
Furzehill Devon 41 D8
Furzehill Dorset 31 G8
Furzeley Corner Hants 33 E11
Furzey Lodge Hants 32 G5
Furzley Hants 32 D3
Furzton M Keynes 102 D6
Fyfett Som 28 E2
Fyfield Essex 87 D9
Fyfield Glos 82 E2
Fyfield Hants 47 D9
Fyfield Oxon 82 F6
Fyfield Wilts 63 F7
Fyfield Wilts 63 G7
Fylingthorpe N Yorks 227 D8
Fyning W Sus 34 C4
Fyvie Aberds 303 F7

G

Gabalfa Cardiff 59 D7
Gabhsann bho Dheas W Isles 304 C6
Gabhsann bho Thuath W Isles 304 C6
Gable Head Hants 21 B10
Gablon Highld 309 K7
Gabroc Hill E Ayrs 267 E9
Gadbrook Sur 51 D8
Gaddesby Leics 154 G3
Gadebridge Herts 85 D8
Gadfa Anglesey 179 D7
Gadfield Elm Worcs 98 E5
Gadlas Shrops 149 B7
Gadlys Rhondda 77 E7
Gadshill Kent 69 E8
Gaer Newport 59 B9
Gaer Powys 96 G3
Gaer-fawr Mon 78 F6
Gaerllwyd Mon 78 F6
Gaerwen Anglesey 179 G7
Gagingwell Oxon 101 F8
Gaick Lodge Highld 291 E9
Gailey Staffs 151 G8
Gailey Wharf Staffs 151 G8
Gain Hill Kent 53 D8
Gainfield Oxon 82 F4
Gainford Durham 224 B3
Gainsborough Lincs 188 C4
Gainsborough Suff 108 C3
Gainsford End Essex 106 D4
Gairletter Argyll 276 E3
Gairloch Highld 299 B8
Gairlochy Highld 290 E3
Gairney Bank Perth 280 B2
Gairnshiel Lodge Aberds 292 C4
Gaisgill Cumb 222 D2
Gaitsgill Cumb 230 B3
Galadean Borders 271 G11
Galashiels Borders 261 B11
Galdlys Flint 182 G2
Gale Gtr Man 196 D2
Galgate Lancs 202 B5
Galhampton Som 29 B10
Gallaberry Dumfries 247 G11
Gallachoille Argyll 275 E8
Gallanach Argyll 288 C4
Gallanach Argyll 289 G10
Gallanach Highld 294 G6
Gallantry Bank E Ches 167 E8
Gallatown Fife 280 C5
Galley Common Warks 134 E6
Galley Hill Cambs 122 D6
Galley Hill Lincs 190 F6
Galleyend Essex 88 E2
Galleywood Essex 88 E2
Gallin Perth 285 C9
Gallovie Highld 291 E7
Gallowfauld Angus 287 C8
Gallowhill Glasgow 267 D11
Gallowhill Renfs 267 B9
Gallowhills Aberds 303 D10
Gallows Corner London 87 G8
Gallows Green Essex 106 F2
Gallows Green Essex 107 F8
Gallows Green Staffs 169 G9
Gallows Green Worcs 117 E8
Gallows Inn Derbys 171 G7
Gallowsgreen Torf 78 D3
Gallowstree Common Oxon 65 C7
Gallt Melyd = Meliden Denb 181 E9
Gallt-y-foel Gwyn 163 C9
Galltair Highld 295 C10
Galltegfa Denb 165 D10
Gallypot Street E Sus 52 F3
Galmington Som 28 C2
Galmisdale Highld 294 G6
Galmpton Devon 8 G3
Galmpton Torbay 9 D7
Galon Uchaf M Tydf 77 D9
Galphay N Yorks 214 E5
Galston E Ayrs 258 B2
Galtrigill Highld 296 F7
Gam Corn 11 F7
Gamble Hill W Yorks 205 G11
Gamble's Green Essex 88 C3
Gamblesby Cumb 231 D8
Gamelsby Cumb 239 G7
Gamesley Derbys 185 C8
Gamlingay Cambs 122 G4
Gamlingay Cinques Cambs 122 G4
Gamlingay Great Heath Cambs 122 G4
Gammaton Devon 25 B7
Gammaton Moor Devon 25 C7
Gammersgill N Yorks 213 C11
Gamston Notts 154 B2
Gamston Notts 188 F2
Ganarew Hereford 79 B8
Ganavan Argyll 289 F10
Ganders Green Glos 98 G4
Gang Corn 6 B6
Ganllwyd Gwyn 146 E4
Gannetts Dorset 30 D3
Gannochy Angus 293 F7
Gannochy Perth 286 E5
Gansclet Highld 310 E7
Ganstead E Yorks 209 G9
Ganthorpe N Yorks 216 E3
Ganton N Yorks 217 D9
Gants Hill London 68 B2
Ganwick Corner Herts 86 F3
Gaodhail Argyll 289 F8
Gappah Devon 14 F3
Garafad Highld 298 C4
Garamor Highld 295 F8
Garbat Highld 300 C4
Garbhallt Argyll 275 D11
Garboldisham Norf 141 G10
Garbole Highld 301 G7
Garden City Bl Gwent 77 D11
Garden City Flint 166 B4
Garden Village S Yorks 186 B3
Garden Village Swansea 56 B5
Garden Village W Yorks 206 G4
Garden Village Wrex 166 E4
Gardeners Green Wokingham 65 F10
Gardenstown Aberds 303 C7
Garderhouse Shetland 313 J5
Gardham E Yorks 208 E5
Gardie Shetland 312 D7
Gardin Shetland 312 G6
Gare Hill Som 45 E9
Garelochhead Argyll 276 C4
Garford Oxon 82 F6
Garforth W Yorks 206 G4
Gargrave N Yorks 204 C4
Gargunnock Stirl 278 C4
Garizim Conwy 179 F11
Garker Corn 5 E10
Garlandhayes Devon 27 E11
Garlands Cumb 239 G10
Garleffin S Ayrs 244 G3
Garlic Street Norf 142 G4
Garlieston Dumfries 236 E6
Garliford Devon 26 B3
Garlinge Kent 71 F10
Garlinge Green Kent 54 C6
Garlogie Aberds 293 C9
Garmelow Staffs 150 D5
Garmond Aberds 303 D8
Garmondsway Durham 234 E2
Garmony Argyll 289 E8
Garmouth Moray 302 C3
Garmston Shrops 132 B2
Garn Powys 130 G2
Garn-swllt Swansea 75 D10
Garn-yr-erw Torf 78 C2
Garnant Carms 75 C11
Garndiffaith Torf 78 E3
Garndolbenmaen Gwyn 163 G7
Garnedd Conwy 164 E2
Garnett Bridge Cumb 221 F10
Garnetts Essex 87 B10
Garnfadryn Gwyn 144 C5
Garnkirk N Lnrk 268 B3
Garnlydan Bl Gwent 77 C11
Garnsgate Lincs 157 E8
Garnswllt Swansea 75 D10
Garra Eallabus Argyll 274 F3
Garrabost W Isles 304 E7
Garracha Argyll 275 E11
Garralburn Moray 302 D4
Garraron Argyll 275 C9
Garras Corn 2 E6
Garreg Flint 181 F10
Garreg Gwyn 163 G10
Garrets Green W Mid 134 F2
Garrick Perth 286 F2
Garrigill Cumb 231 C10
Garrison Stirl 285 G7
Garriston N Yorks 224 G3
Garroch Dumfries 246 G3
Garrogie Lodge Highld 291 B7
Garros Highld 298 C4
Garrow Perth 286 C2
Garrowhill Glasgow 268 C3
Garrygualach Highld 290 C3
Garryhorn Dumfries 246 E2
Garsdale Cumb 212 B4
Garsdale Head Cumb 222 G5
Garsdon Wilts 62 B3
Garshall Green Staffs 151 C9
Garsington Oxon 83 E9
Garstang Lancs 202 D5
Garston Herts 85 F10
Garston Mers 182 E6
Garswood Mers 183 B9
Gartachoil Stirl 277 C10
Gartbreck Argyll 254 B3
Gartcosh N Lnrk 268 B3
Garth Bridgend 57 C11
Garth Ceredig 128 G2
Garth Flint 181 E10
Garth Gwyn 179 G9
Garth Newport 59 B9
Garth Newport 78 G4
Garth Perth 285 B11
Garth Powys 95 B9
Garth Powys 114 C5
Garth Shetland 313 H4
Garth Shetland 313 H6
Garth Wrex 166 G3
Garth Owen Powys 130 E2
Garth Row Cumb 221 F10
Garth Trevor Wrex 166 G3
Garthamlock Glasgow 268 B3
Garthbeg Highld 291 B7
Garthbrengy Powys 95 E10
Garthdee Aberdeen 293 C11
Gartheli Ceredig 111 F11
Garthmyl Powys 130 D3
Garthorpe Leics 154 E6
Garthorpe N Lincs 199 D11
Gartlea N Lnrk 268 C5
Gartloch Glasgow 268 B3
Gartly Aberds 302 F5
Gartmore Stirl 277 B10
Gartmore Ho Stirl 277 B10
Gartnagrenach Argyll 255 B8
Gartness N Lnrk 268 C5
Gartness Stirl 277 D10
Gartocharn W Dunb 277 D8
Garton E Yorks 209 F11
Garton-on-the-Wolds E Yorks 208 B5
Gartsherrie N Lnrk 268 B4
Gartur Stirl 277 B11
Gartymore Highld 311 H4
Garvald E Loth 281 G11
Garvamore Highld 291 D7
Garvard Argyll 274 D4
Garvault Hotel Highld 308 F7
Garve Highld 300 C3
Garvestone Norf 141 B10
Garvock Aberds 293 F9
Garvock Invclyd 276 G5
Garvock Hill Fife 280 D2
Garway Hereford 97 G9
Garway Hill Hereford 97 F8
Gaskan Highld 289 B9
Gasper Wilts 45 G9
Gastard Wilts 61 F11
Gasthorpe Norf 141 G9
Gaston Green Essex 87 B7
Gatacre Park Shrops 132 F5
Gatcombe I o W 20 D5
Gate Burton Lincs 188 E4
Gate Helmsley N Yorks 207 B9
Gateacre Mers 182 D6
Gatebeck Cumb 211 B10
Gateford Notts 187 E9
Gateford Common Notts 187 E9
Gateforth N Yorks 198 B5
Gatehead E Ayrs 257 B9
Gatehouse Northumb 251 F7
Gatehouse of Fleet Dumfries 237 D8
Gatelawbridge Dumfries 247 D10
Gateley Norf 159 E9
Gatenby N Yorks 214 B6
Gatesgarth Cumb 220 B3
Gateshead T & W 243 E7
Gatesheath W Ches 167 C7
Gateside Aberds 293 B8
Gateside Angus 287 C8
Gateside Dumfries 248 E4
Gateside E Renf 267 D9
Gateside Fife 286 G5
Gateside N Ayrs 267 E7
Gateside Shetland 312 F4
Gatewen Wrex 166 E4
Gatherley Devon 12 E3
Gathurst Gtr Man 194 F4
Gatlas Newport 78 G4
Gatley Gtr Man 184 D4
Gatley End Cambs 104 C5
Gatton Sur 51 C9
Gattonside Borders 262 B2
Gatwick Glos 80 C2
Gatwick Airport W Sus 51 E9
Gaufron Powys 113 D9
Gaulby Leics 136 C3
Gauldry Fife 287 E7
Gauntons Bank E Ches 167 F9
Gaunt's Common Dorset 31 F8
Gaunt's Earthcott S Glos 60 C6
Gaunt's End Essex 105 F10
Gautby Lincs 189 G11
Gavinton Borders 272 E5
Gawber S Yorks 197 F10
Gawcott Bucks 102 E3
Gawsworth E Ches 168 B5
Gawthorpe W Yorks 197 C9
Gawthorpe W Yorks 197 D7
Gawthrop Cumb 212 B3
Gawthwaite Cumb 210 C5
Gay Bowers Essex 88 E3
Gay Street W Sus 35 C9
Gaydon Warks 119 G7
Gayfield Orkney 314 A4
Gayhurst M Keynes 103 B7
Gayle N Yorks 213 B7
Gayles N Yorks 224 D2
Gayton Mers 182 E3
Gayton Norf 158 F4
Gayton Northants 120 G4
Gayton Staffs 151 D9
Gayton Engine Lincs 191 D7
Gayton le Marsh Lincs 190 E6
Gayton le Wold Lincs 190 D2
Gayton Thorpe Norf 158 F4
Gaywood Norf 158 E2
Gaza Shetland 312 F5
Gazeley Suff 124 E4
Geàrraidh Sheilidh W Isles 297 J3
Geanies House Highld 301 B8
Gearraidh Bhailteas W Isles 297 J3
Gearraidh Bhaird W Isles 304 F5
Gearraidh Dubh W Isles 296 F4
Gearraidh na h-Aibhne W Isles 304 E4
Gearraidh na Monadh W Isles 297 K3
Geary Highld 298 C2
Geat Wolford Warks 100 E4
Geddes House Highld 301 D8
Gedding Suff 125 F9
Geddington Northants 137 G7
Gedgrave Hall Suff 109 B8
Gedintailor Highld 295 B7
Gedling Notts 171 G10
Gedney Lincs 157 E8
Gedney Broadgate Lincs 157 E8
Gedney Drove End Lincs 157 D9
Gedney Dyke Lincs 157 D8
Gedney Hill Lincs 156 G6
Gee Cross Gtr Man 185 C7
Geeston Rutland 137 C9
Gegin Wrex 166 E3
Geilston Argyll 276 F6
Geinas Denb 165 B9
Geirinis W Isles 297 G3
Geise Highld 310 C5
Geisiadar W Isles 304 E3
Geldeston Norf 143 E7
Gell Conwy 164 B5
Gelli Pembs 73 B9
Gelli Rhondda 77 G7
Gelli-gaer Neath 57 C9
Gelli-hôf Caerph 77 F11
Gellideg M Tydf 77 D8
Gellifor Denb 165 C10
Gelligaer Caerph 77 F10
Gelligroes Caerph 77 G11
Gellilydan Gwyn 146 B3
Gellinud Neath 76 E2
Gellinudd Neath 76 E2
Gellyburn Perth 286 D4
Gellygron Neath 76 E2
Gellywen Carms 92 G5
Gelsmoor Leics 153 F8
Gelston Dumfries 237 D9
Gelston Lincs 172 G6
Gembling E Yorks 209 B8
Gemini Warr 183 C9
Gendros Swansea 56 B6
Genesis Green Suff 124 F4
Gentleshaw Staffs 151 G11
Geocrab W Isles 305 J3
George Green Bucks 66 C4
George Nympton Devon 26 C2
Georgefield Dumfries 249 E7
Georgeham Devon 40 F3
Georgetown Bl Gwent 77 D10
Georgia Corn 1 B5
Gergask Highld 291 D8
Gerlan Gwyn 163 B10
Germansweek Devon 12 C4
Germiston Glasgow 268 B2
Germoe Corn 2 D3
Gernon Bushes Essex 87 E7
Gerrans Corn 3 B9
Gerrard's Bromley Staffs 150 C5
Gerrards Cross Bucks 66 B4
Gerrick Redcar 226 C4
Geseilfa Powys 129 E8
Gestingthorpe Essex 106 D6
Gesto Ho Highld 294 B5
Geuffordd Powys 148 G4
Geufron Denb 166 G2
Gib Heath W Mid 133 F11
Gibb Hill W Ches 183 F10
Gibbet Hill W Mid 118 C6
Gibbet Hill Warks 135 G10
Gibbshill Dumfries 237 B9
Gibraltar Beds 103 B10
Gibraltar Bucks 84 C3
Gibraltar Kent 55 F8
Gibraltar Oxon 83 B7
Gibraltar Suff 108 B3
Gibshill Invclyd 276 G6
Gibsmere Notts 172 F2
Giddeahall Wilts 61 E11
Giddy Green Dorset 18 D2
Gidea Park London 68 B4
Gidleigh Devon 13 D9
Giffard Park M Keynes 103 C7
Giffnock E Renf 267 D11
Gifford E Loth 271 B10
Giffordland N Ayrs 266 F5
Giffordtown Fife 286 F6
Gigg Gtr Man 195 F10
Giggetty Staffs 133 E7
Giggleswick N Yorks 212 G6
Giggshill Sur 67 F7
Gignog Pembs 91 G7
Gilberdyke E Yorks 199 B10
Gilbert Street Hants 49 G7
Gilbert's Coombe Corn 4 G3
Gilbert's End Worcs 98 C6
Gilbert's Green Warks 118 C2
Gilbertstone W Mid 134 G2
Gilchriston E Loth 271 B9
Gilcrux Cumb 229 D8
Gildersome W Yorks 197 B8
Gildersome Street W Yorks 197 B8
Gildingwells S Yorks 187 D9
Gilesgate Durham 233 C11
Gilesgate Moor Durham 233 C11
Gileston V Glam 58 F4
Gilfach Caerph 77 F11
Gilfach Hereford 96 E6
Gilfach Goch Rhondda 58 B3
Gilfachrheda Ceredig 111 F8
Gilgarran Cumb 228 G6
Gill N Yorks 204 E5
Gillamoor N Yorks 216 B3
Gillan Corn 3 E7
Gillar's Green Mers 183 B7
Gillbank Cumb 221 F7
Gillbent Gtr Man 184 E5
Gillen Highld 298 D2
Gillesbie Dumfries 248 E5
Gilling East N Yorks 216 D2
Gilling West N Yorks 224 D3
Gillingham Dorset 30 B4
Gillingham Medway 69 F9
Gillingham Norf 143 E8
Gillmoss Mers 182 B6
Gillock Highld 310 D6
Gillow Heath Staffs 168 D5
Gills Highld 310 B7
Gill's Green Kent 53 G9
Gillway Staffs 134 C4
Gilmanscleuch Borders 261 E8
Gilmerton Edin 270 B5
Gilmerton Perth 286 E2
Gilmonby Durham 223 C9
Gilmorton Leics 135 F11
Gilmourton S Lnrk 268 G3
Gilnow Gtr Man 195 F8
Gilroyd S Yorks 197 G10
Gilsland Cumb 240 D4
Gilsland Spa Cumb 240 D4
Gilson Warks 134 E3
Gilstead W Yorks 205 F8
Gilston Borders 271 D8
Gilston Herts 86 C6
Gilston Park Herts 86 C6
Giltbrook Notts 171 F7
Gilver's Lane Worcs 98 C6
Gilwell Park Essex 86 F5
Gilwern Mon 78 C2
Gimingham Norf 160 B5
Ginclough E Ches 185 F7
Ginger's Green E Sus 23 C10
Giosla W Isles 304 F3
Gipping Suff 125 E11
Gipsey Bridge Lincs 174 F3
Gipsy Row Suff 107 D11
Gipsyville Hull 200 B5
Gipton W Yorks 206 F2
Gipton Wood W Yorks 206 F2
Girdle Toll N Ayrs 266 G6
Girlington W Yorks 205 G8
Girlsta Shetland 313 H6
Girsby Lincs 190 D2
Girsby N Yorks 225 D7
Girt Som 29 C10
Girtford C Beds 104 B3
Girtford C Beds 122 G3
Girthon Dumfries 237 D8
Girton Cambs 123 E8
Girton Notts 172 B4
Girvan S Ayrs 244 D5
Gisburn Lancs 204 D2
Gisleham Suff 143 F10
Gislingham Suff 125 C11
Gissing Norf 142 F2
Gittisham Devon 15 B8
Givons Grove Sur 51 C7
Glachavoil Argyll 275 F11
Glack of Midthird Moray 302 E3
Glackmore Highld 300 D6
Gladestry Powys 114 F4
Gladsmuir E Loth 281 G9
Glaichbea Highld 300 F5
Glais Swansea 76 E2
Glaisdale N Yorks 226 D5
Glame Highld 298 E5
Glamis Angus 287 C7
Glan Adda Gwyn 179 G9
Glan-Conwy Conwy 164 E4
Glan-Duar Carms 93 C10
Glan-Dwyfach Gwyn 163 G7
Glan Gors Anglesey 179 F7
Glan-rhyd Gwyn 163 D7
Glan-rhyd Powys 76 D3
Glan-traeth Anglesey 178 F3
Glan-y-don Flint 181 F11
Glan y Ffer = Ferryside Carms 74 C5
Glan-y-llyn Rhondda 58 C6
Glan-y-môr Carms 74 C4
Glan-y-nant Caerph 77 F10
Glan-y-nant Powys 129 G8
Glan-y-wern Gwyn 146 C2
Glan-yr-afon Anglesey 179 E10
Glan-yr-afon Flint 181 E10
Glan-yr-afon Gwyn 164 G6
Glan-yr-afon Gwyn 165 G8
Glan-yr-afon Shrops 148 E4
Glanaber Terrace Conwy 164 F3
Glanafon Pembs 73 B7
Glanaman Carms 75 C11
Glandford Norf 177 E8
Glandwr Caerph 78 E2
Glandwr Pembs 92 F3
Glandy Cross Carms 92 F2
Glandyfi Ceredig 128 D3
Glangrwyney Powys 78 B2
Glanhanog Powys 129 D8
Glanmule Powys 130 E3
Glanrafon Ceredig 128 G2
Glanrhyd Gwyn 144 B5
Glanrhyd Pembs 92 C2
Glantlees Northumb 252 B4
Glanton Northumb 264 G3
Glanton Pike Northumb 264 G3
Glantwymyn = Cemmaes Road Powys 128 C6
Glanvilles Wootton Dorset 29 F11
Glanwern Ceredig 128 F2
Glanwydden Conwy 180 E4
Glapthorn Northants 137 E10
Glapwell Derbys 171 B7
Glas-allt Shiel Aberds 292 E4
Glasbury Powys 96 D3
Glaschoil Highld 301 F10
Glascoed Denb 181 G7
Glascoed Mon 78 E4
Glascoed Powys 129 F11
Glascoed Powys 148 G2
Glascoed Wrex 166 E3
Glascorrie Aberds 292 D5
Glascorrie Perth 286 E2
Glascote Staffs 134 C4
Glascwm Powys 114 G3
Glasdir Flint 181 E10
Glasdrum Argyll 284 C4
Glasfryn Conwy 164 E6
Glasgoed Ceredig 92 B6
Glasgoforest Aberds 293 B10
Glasgow Glasgow 267 B11
Glashvin Highld 298 C4
Glasinfryn Gwyn 163 B9
Glasllwch Newport 59 B9
Glasnacardoch Highld 295 F8
Glasnakille Highld 295 D7
Glasphein Highld 297 G7
Glaspwll Powys 128 D4
Glass Houghton W Yorks 198 C2
Glassburn Highld 300 F3
Glassenbury Kent 53 F8
Glasserton Dumfries 236 F6
Glassford S Lnrk 268 F4
Glassgreen Moray 302 C2
Glasshouse Glos 98 G4
Glasshouse Hill Glos 98 G4
Glasshouses N Yorks 214 G3
Glasslie Fife 286 G6
Glasson Cumb 228 D6
Glasson Cumb 239 E7
Glasson Lancs 202 B4
Glassonby Cumb 231 D7
Glasterlaw Angus 287 B9
Glaston Rutland 137 C7
Glastonbury Som 44 F4
Glatton Cambs 138 F3
Glazebrook Warr 183 C11
Glazebury Warr 183 B11
Glazeley Shrops 132 F4
Gleadless S Yorks 186 E5
Gleadless Valley S Yorks 186 E5
Gleadmoss E Ches 168 B4
Gleadsmoss E Ches 168 B4
Gleanhead Dumfries 245 G10
Gleann Tholàstaidh W Isles 304 D7
Gleaston Cumb 210 E5
Glebe Hants 33 D9
Glebe Shetland 313 J6
Glebe T & W 243 F8
Glecknabae Argyll 275 G11
Gledhow W Yorks 206 F2
Gledrid Shrops 148 B5
Gleiniant Powys 129 E9
Glemsford Suff 106 B6
Glen Dumfries 237 B10
Glen Dumfries 237 D7
Glen Auldyn I o M 192 C5
Glen Bernisdale Highld 298 E4
Glen Ho Borders 261 C7
Glen Mona I o M 192 D5
Glen Mor Highld 295 B10
Glen Nevis House Highld 290 F3
Glen of Newmill Moray 302 D4
Glen Parva Leics 135 D11
Glen Sluain Argyll 275 D11
Glen Tanar House Aberds 292 D6
Glen Trool Lodge Dumfries 245 G10
Glen Vic Askil Highld 298 E3
Glen Village Falk 279 F7
Glen Vine I o M 192 E4
Glenallachie Moray 302 E2
Glenalmond College Perth 286 E3
Glenalmond Ho Perth 286 E3
Glenamachrie Argyll 289 G11
Glenample Stirl 285 E9
Glenancross Highld 295 F8
Glenapp Castle S Ayrs 244 G3
Glenaros Ho Argyll 289 E7
Glenbarr Argyll 255 D7
Glenbeg Highld 289 C7
Glenbeg Highld 301 G10
Glenbervie Aberds 293 E9
Glenboig N Lnrk 268 B4
Glenborrodale Highld 289 C8
Glenbranter Argyll 276 B2
Glenbreck Borders 260 E3
Glenbrein Lodge Highld 290 B6
Glenbrittle House Highld 294 C6
Glenbrook Edin 270 B2
Glenbuchat Castle Aberds 292 B5
Glenbuchat Lodge Aberds 292 B5
Glenbuck E Ayrs 259 D7
Glenburn Renfs 267 C9
Glenbyre Argyll 289 G7
Glencalvie Lodge Highld 309 L4
Glencanisp Lodge Highld 307 G6
Glencaple Dumfries 237 C11
Glencarron Lodge Highld 299 D10
Glencarse Perth 286 E5
Glencassley Castle Highld 309 J4
Glencat Aberds 293 D7
Glenceitlein Highld 284 C5
Glencoe Highld 284 B4
Glencraig Fife 280 B3
Glencripesdale Highld 289 D8
Glencrosh Dumfries 247 F7
Glendavan Ho Aberds 292 C6
Glendearg Borders 262 B2
Glendevon Perth 286 G3
Glendoe Lodge Highld 290 C6
Glendoebeg Highld 290 C6
Glendoick Perth 286 E6
Glendoll Lodge Angus 292 F4
Glendoune S Ayrs 244 D5
Glenduckie Fife 286 F6
Glendye Lodge Aberds 293 E8
Gleneagles Hotel Perth 286 F3
Gleneagles House Perth 286 G3
Glenearn Perth 286 F5
Glenegedale Argyll 254 B4
Glenelg Highld 295 D10
Glenernie Moray 301 E10
Glenfarg Perth 286 F5
Glenfarquhar Lodge Aberds 293 E9
Glenferness House Highld 301 E9
Glenfeshie Lodge Highld 291 D10
Glenfiddich Lodge Moray 302 F3
Glenfield Leics 135 B10
Glenfinnan Highld 295 G10
Glenfinnan Lodge Highld 295 G11
Glenfintaig Ho Highld 290 E4
Glenfoot Perth 286 F5
Glenfyne Lodge Argyll 284 F6
Glengap Dumfries 237 D8
Glengarnock N Ayrs 266 E6
Glengolly Highld 310 C5
Glengorm Castle Argyll 288 D6
Glengoulandie Perth 285 B11
Glengrasco Highld 298 E4
Glenhead Farm Angus 292 G4
Glenholt Plym 7 C10
Glenhoul Dumfries 246 F4
Glenhurich Highld 289 C10
Glenkerry Borders 261 G7
Glenkiln Dumfries 237 B10
Glenkindie Aberds 292 B6
Glenlair Dumfries 237 B9
Glenlatterach Moray 301 D11
Glenlee Dumfries 246 G4
Glenleigh Park E Sus 38 F2
Glenleraig Highld 306 F6
Glenlichorn Perth 285 F11
Glenlicht Ho Highld 290 B2
Glenlivet Moray 301 G11
Glenlochar Dumfries 237 C9
Glenlochsie Perth 292 F2
Glenlocksie Lodge Perth 292 F2
Glenloig N Ayrs 255 D10
Glenlomond Perth 286 G5
Glenluce Dumfries 236 D4
Glenlussa Ho Argyll 255 E8
Glenmallan Argyll 276 B5
Glenmark Angus 292 E6
Glenmarkie Lodge Angus 292 G4
Glenmarksie Highld 300 D3
Glenmavis N Lnrk 268 B4
Glenmavis W Loth 269 B9
Glenmaye I o M 192 E3
Glenmayne Borders 261 C11
Glenmeanie Highld 300 D2
Glenmidge Dumfries 247 F9
Glenmoidart Ho Highld 289 B9
Glenmore Argyll 275 B9
Glenmore Argyll 275 G11
Glenmore Highld 298 E4
Glenmore Lodge Highld 291 C11
Glenmoy Angus 292 G6
Glennoe Argyll 284 D4
Glenogil Angus 292 G6
Glenowen Pembs 73 D7
Glenprosen Lodge Angus 292 G4
Glenprosen Village Angus 292 G5
Glenquaich Lodge Perth 286 D2
Glenquiech Angus 292 G6
Glenquithlie Aberds 303 C8
Glenrath Borders 260 C6
Glenrazie Dumfries 236 C5
Glenreasdell Mains Argyll 255 B9
Glenree N Ayrs 255 E10
Glenridding Cumb 221 B7
Glenrosa N Ayrs 256 B2
Glenrossal Highld 309 J4
Glenrothes Fife 286 G6
Glensanda Highld 289 E10
Glensaugh Aberds 293 F8
Glensburgh Falk 279 E8
Glenshero Lodge Highld 291 D7
Glenshoie Lodge Perth 292 G3
Glenstockadale Dumfries 236 C2
Glenstriven Argyll 275 F11
Glentaggart S Lnrk 259 D8
Glentarkie Perth 286 F5
Glenternie Borders 260 B6
Glentham Lincs 189 C8
Glentirranmuir Stirl 278 C3
Glenton Aberds 302 G6
Glentress Borders 261 B7
Glentromie Lodge Highld 291 D9
Glentrool Village Dumfries 236 B5
Glentruan I o M 192 B5
Glentruim House Highld 291 D8
Glentworth Lincs 188 D6
Glenuaig Lodge Highld 299 E11
Glenuig Highld 289 B8
Glenure Argyll 284 C4
Glenurquhart Highld 301 C7
Glenview Argyll 284 E5
Glespin S Lnrk 259 D8
Gletness Shetland 313 H6
Glewstone Hereford 97 G11
Glinton P'boro 138 B3
Globe Town London 67 C11
Glodwick Gtr Man 196 G2
Glogue Pembs 92 E4
Glooston Leics 136 D4
Glororum Northumb 264 C5
Glossop Derbys 185 C8
Gloster Hill Northumb 253 C7
Gloucester Glos 80 B4
Gloup Shetland 312 C7
Gloweth Corn 4 G5
Glusburn N Yorks 204 E6
Glutt Lodge Highld 310 F3
Glutton Bridge Staffs 169 B9
Gluvian Corn 5 C8
Glympton Oxon 101 G8
Glyn Mon 79 F7
Glyn Powys 129 F8
Glyn Castle Neath 76 E4
Glyn-Ceiriog Wrex 148 B4
Glyn-cywarch Gwyn 146 C2
Glyn Etwy Bl Gwent 77 D11
Glyn-neath = Glynedd Neath 76 D5
Glynarthen Ceredig 92 B6
Glynbrochan Powys 129 G8
Glyncoch Rhondda 77 G9
Glyncoed Bl Gwent 77 C11
Glyncorrwg Neath 57 B11
Glynde E Sus 23 D7
Glyndebourne E Sus 23 C7
Glyndyfrdwy Denb 165 G10
Glyne Gap E Sus 38 F3
Glynedd = Glyn neath Neath 76 D5
Glynhafren Powys 129 G7
Glynllan Bridgend 58 B2
Glynmorlas Shrops 148 B6
Glynogwr Bridgend 58 B3
Glyntaff Rhondda 58 B5
Glyntawe Powys 76 B4
Gnosall Staffs 150 E6
Gnosall Heath Staffs 150 E6
Goadby Leics 136 D4
Goadby Marwood Leics 154 D5
Goat Lees Kent 54 D4
Goatacre Wilts 62 D4
Goatham Green E Sus 38 C4
Goathill Dorset 29 D11
Goathland N Yorks 226 E6
Goathurst Som 43 G9
Goathurst Common Kent 52 C3
Gobernuisgach Lodge Highld 308 E4
Gobernuisgeach Highld 310 F3
Gobhaig W Isles 305 H2
Gobley Hole Hants 48 D6
Gobowen Shrops 148 C6
Godalming Sur 50 E3
Goddards Bucks 84 G3
Goddard's Corner Suff 126 D5
Goddard's Green Kent 53 G10
Goddard's Green W Berks 65 F7
Goddards' Green W Sus 36 C3
Godden Green Kent 52 B5
Goddington London 68 F3
Godley Gtr Man 185 B7
Godley Hill Gtr Man 185 C7
Godleybrook Staffs 169 G7
Godleys Green E Sus 36 D5
Godmanchester Cambs 122 C4
Godmanstone Dorset 17 B9
Godmersham Kent 54 C5
Godney Som 44 E3
Godolphin Cross Corn 2 C4
Godre'r-graig Neath 76 D3
God's Blessing Green Dorset 31 G8
Godshill Hants 31 E11
Godshill I o W 20 E6
Godstone Sur 51 C10
Godswinscroft Hants 19 B9
Godwell Devon 8 D2
Godwick Norf 159 E8
Godwinscroft Hants 19 B9
Goetre Mon 78 D4
Goferydd Anglesey 178 E2
Goff's Oak Herts 86 E4
Gogar Edin 280 G3
Goginan Ceredig 128 G3
Goirtean a'Chladaich Highld 290 F2
Golan Gwyn 163 G8
Golant Corn 6 E2
Golberdon Corn 12 G2
Golborne Gtr Man 183 B10
Golcar W Yorks 196 D6
Golch Flint 181 F11
Gold Hill Dorset 30 E4
Gold Hill Norf 139 E10
Goldcliff Newport 59 C11
Golden Balls Oxon 83 F9
Golden Cross E Sus 23 C10
Golden Cross E Sus 23 C8
Golden Green Kent 52 D6
Golden Grove Carms 75 B9
Golden Hill Bristol 60 D5
Golden Hill Hants 19 B11
Golden Hill Pembs 73 E7
Golden Hill Pembs 91 G9
Golden Park Devon 24 C2
Golden Pot Hants 49 E8
Golden Valley Derbys 170 E6
Golden Valley Glos 99 G8
Golden Valley Hereford 98 B3
Goldenhill Stoke 168 E5
Golder Field Hereford 115 E11
Golders Green London 67 B9
Goldfinch Bottom W Berks 64 G4
Goldhanger Essex 88 D6
Golding Shrops 131 C10
Goldington Beds 121 G11
Gold's Cross Bath 60 G5
Golds Green W Mid 133 E9
Goldsborough N Yorks 206 B3
Goldsborough N Yorks 226 C6
Goldsithney Corn 2 C2
Goldstone Shrops 150 D4
Goldthorn Park W Mid 133 D8
Goldthorpe S Yorks 198 G3
Goldworthy Devon 24 C5
Golford Kent 53 F9
Golftyn Flint 182 G3
Golgotha Kent 55 D9
Gollanfield Highld 301 D8
Gollawater Corn 4 E5
Gollinglith Foot N Yorks 214 C3
Golly Wrex 166 D4
Golsoncott Som 42 F4
Golspie Highld 311 J2
Golval Highld 310 C2
Golynos Torf 78 E3
Gomeldon Wilts 47 F7
Gomersal W Yorks 197 B8
Gometra Ho Argyll 288 E5
Gomshall Sur 50 D5
Gonalston Notts 171 F11
Gonamena Corn 11 G11
Gonerby Hill Foot Lincs 155 B8
Gonfirth Shetland 313 G5
Good Easter Essex 87 C10
Gooderstone Norf 140 C5
Goodleigh Devon 40 G6
Goodley Stock Kent 52 C2
Goodmanham E Yorks 208 E3
Goodmayes London 68 B3
Goodnestone Kent 55 C9
Goodnestone Kent 70 G4
Goodrich Hereford 79 B9
Goodrington Torbay 9 D7
Good's Green Worcs 132 G5
Goodshaw Lancs 195 B10
Goodshaw Chapel Lancs 195 B10
Goodshaw Fold Lancs 195 B10
Goodstone Devon 13 G11
Goodwick = Wdig Pembs 91 D8
Goodworth Clatford Hants 47 E11
Goodyers End Warks 134 F6
Goodyhills Cumb 229 B8
Goom's Hill Worcs 117 G10
Goon Gumpas Corn 4 G4
Goon Piper Corn 3 B8
Goonabarn Corn 5 E9
Goonbell Corn 4 F4
Goonhavern Corn 4 E5
Goonhusband Corn 2 D5
Goonlaze Corn 2 B6
Goonown Corn 4 E4
Goonvrea Corn 4 F4
Goose Eye W Yorks 204 E6
Goose Green Cumb 211 C10
Goose Green Essex 108 F2
Goose Green Gtr Man 194 G5
Goose Green Hants 32 F4
Goose Green Herts 86 D5
Goose Green Kent 52 C6
Goose Green Kent 53 F10
Goose Green Lancs 194 C3
Goose Green Norf 142 F2
Goose Green S Glos 61 C8
Goose Green W Sus 34 C3
Goose Green W Sus 35 D10
Goose Hill Hants 64 G4
Goose Pool Hereford 97 D9
Gooseberry Green Essex 87 F11
Gooseford Devon 13 C9
Gooseham Mill Devon 24 D2
Goosehill W Yorks 197 C11
Goosehill Green Worcs 117 E8
Goosemoor Staffs 150 F6
Goosemoor Green Staffs 151 G11
Goosenford Som 28 B2
Goosewell Devon 40 D5
Goosey Oxon 82 G5
Goosnargh Lancs 203 F7
Goostrey E Ches 184 G3
Gorbals Glasgow 267 C11
Gorcott Hill Warks 117 D11
Gord Shetland 313 L6
Gorddinog Conwy 179 G11
Gordon Borders 272 G2
Gordonbush Highld 311 J2
Gordonsburgh Moray 302 C4
Gordonstoun Moray 301 C11
Gordonstown Aberds 302 D5
Gordonstown Aberds 303 F7
Gore Dorset 29 D9
Gore Kent 55 B10
Gore Cross Wilts 46 C4
Gore End Hants 64 G2
Gore Pit Essex 88 B5
Gore Street Kent 71 F9
Gorebridge Midloth 270 C6
Gorefield Cambs 157 G8
Gorehill W Sus 35 C7
Gorgie Edin 280 G4

Gorhambury Herts 85 D10
Goring Oxon 64 C6
Goring-by-Sea W Sus 35 G10
Goring Heath Oxon 65 D7
Gorleston-on-Sea Norf 143 C10
Gornalwood W Mid 133 E8
Gorrachie Aberds 303 D7
Gorran Churchtown Corn 5 G9
Gorran Haven Corn 5 G10
Gorran High Lanes Corn 5 G9
Gorrenberry Borders 249 D11
Gorrig Ceredig 93 C8
Gorse Covert Warr 183 C11
Gorse Hill Gtr Man 184 B4
Gorse Hill Swindon 63 B7
Gorsedd Flint 181 F11
Gorseinon Swansea 56 B5
Gorseness Orkney 314 E4
Gorsethorpe Notts 171 B9
Gorseybank Derbys 170 E3
Gorsgoch Ceredig 111 G9
Gorslas Carms 75 C9
Gorsley Glos 98 F3
Gorsley Common Hereford 98 F3
Gorsley Ley Staffs 133 B11
Gorst Hill Worcs 116 C4
Gorstage W Ches 183 G10
Gorstan Highld 300 C3
Gorstanvorran Highld 289 B10
Gorstella W Ches 166 C5
Gorsteyhill E Ches 168 E2
Gorsty Hill Staffs 151 D11
Gorstyhill Staffs 168 E2
Gortan Argyll 274 G3
Gortantaoid Argyll 274 F4
Gortenacullish Highld 295 G8
Gorteneorn Highld 289 C8
Gortenfern Highld 289 C8
Gortinanane Argyll 255 C8
Gorton Gtr Man 184 B5
Gortonallister N Ayrs 256 D2
Gosbeck Suff 126 F3
Gosberton Lincs 156 C4
Gosberton Cheal Lincs 156 D4
Gosberton Clough Lincs 156 D3
Goscote W Mid 133 C10
Goseley Dale Derbys 152 E6
Gosfield Essex 106 F5
Gosford Hereford 115 D10
Gosford Oxon 83 C7
Gosford Green W Mid 118 B6
Gosforth Cumb 219 E11
Gosforth T & W 242 D6
Gosforth Valley Derbys 186 F4
Gosland Green Suff 124 G5
Gosling Green Suff 107 C9
Gosmere Kent 54 B4
Gosmore Herts 104 F3
Gospel Ash Staffs 132 E6
Gospel End Village Staffs 133 E7
Gospel Green W Sus 50 G2
Gospel Oak London 67 B9
Gosport Hants 21 B8
Gosport Hants 32 C5
Gossabrough Shetland 312 E7
Gossard's Green C Beds 103 C9
Gossington Glos 80 E2
Gossops Green W Sus 51 F9
Goswick Northumb 273 F11
Gotham Dorset 31 E9
Gotham E Sus 38 F2
Gotham Notts 153 C10
Gothelney Green Som 43 F9
Gotherington Glos 99 F9
Gothers Corn 5 D9
Gott Argyll 288 E2
Gott Shetland 313 J6
Gotton Som 28 B2
Goudhurst Kent 53 F8
Goukstone Moray 302 D4
Goulceby Lincs 190 F3
Goulton N Yorks 225 E9
Gourdas Aberds 303 E7
Gourdon Aberds 293 F10
Gourock Invclyd 276 F4
Govan Glasgow 267 B11
Govanhill Glasgow 267 C11
Gover Hill Kent 52 C6
Goverton Notts 172 E2
Goveton Devon 8 F5
Govilon Mon 78 C3
Gowanhill Aberds 303 C10
Gowanwell Aberds 303 E8
Gowdall E Yorks 198 C6
Gowerton = Tre-Gwyr Swansea 56 B5
Gowhole Derbys 185 E8
Gowkhall Fife 279 D11
Gowkthrapple N Lnrk 268 E5
Gowthorpe E Yorks 207 C11
Goxhill E Yorks 209 E9
Goxhill N Lincs 200 C6
Goxhill Haven N Lincs 200 B6
Goybre Neath 57 D9
Goytre Neath 57 D9
Gozzard's Ford Oxon 83 F7
Grabhair W Isles 305 G5
Graby Lincs 155 D11
Gracca Corn 5 D10
Gracemount Edin 270 B5
Grade Corn 2 G6
Graffham W Sus 34 D6
Grafham Cambs 122 D3
Grafham Sur 50 E4
Grafton Hereford 97 D9
Grafton N Yorks 215 G8
Grafton Oxon 82 E3
Grafton Shrops 149 F8
Grafton Worcs 99 D9
Grafton Worcs 115 E11
Grafton Flyford Worcs 117 F9
Grafton Regis Northants 102 B5
Grafton Underwood Northants 137 G8
Grafty Green Kent 53 D11
Grahamston Falk 279 E7
Graianrhyd Denb 166 D2
Graig Carms 74 E6
Graig Conwy 180 G4
Graig Denb 181 G9
Graig Rhondda 58 B5
Graig Wrex 148 B4
Graig-Fawr Swansea 75 E10
Graig-fechan Denb 165 E10
Graig Felen Swansea 75 E11
Graig Penllyn V Glam 58 D3
Graig Trewyddfa Swansea 57 B7
Grain Medway 69 D11
Grains Bar Gtr Man 196 F3
Grainsby Lincs 190 B3
Grainthorpe Lincs 190 B5
Grainthorpe Fen Lincs 190 B5
Graiselound N Lincs 188 B3
Grampound Corn 5 F8
Grampound Road Corn 5 E8
Gramsdal W Isles 296 F4
Granborough Bucks 102 F5
Granby Notts 154 B5
Grandborough Warks 119 D9
Grandpont Oxon 83 D8
Grandtully Perth 286 B3
Grange Cumb 220 B5
Grange Dorset 31 G8
Grange E Ayrs 257 B10
Grange Fife 287 G8
Grange Halton 183 E8
Grange Lancs 203 G7
Grange Medway 69 F9
Grange Mers 182 D2
Grange N Yorks 223 G8
Grange NE Lincs 201 F9
Grange Perth 286 E6
Grange Warr 183 C10
Grange Crossroads Moray 302 D4
Grange Estate Dorset 31 G10
Grange Hall Moray 301 C10
Grange Hill Durham 233 F10
Grange Hill Essex 86 G6
Grange Moor W Yorks 197 D8
Grange of Cree Dumfries 236 D6
Grange of Lindores Fife 286 F6
Grange-over-Sands Cumb 211 D8
Grange Park London 86 F4
Grange Park Mers 183 C7
Grange Park Northants 120 F5
Grange Park Swindon 62 C6
Grange Villa Durham 242 G6
Grange Village Glos 79 C11
Grangemill Derbys 170 D2
Grangemouth Falk 279 E8
Grangemuir Fife 287 G9
Grangepans Falk 279 E10
Grangetown Cardiff 59 E7
Grangetown Redcar 235 G7
Grangetown T & W 243 G10
Granish Highld 291 B11
Gransmoor E Yorks 209 B8
Gransmore Green Essex 106 G3
Granston = Treopert Pembs 91 E7
Grant Thorold NE Lincs 201 F9
Grantchester Cambs 123 F8
Grantham Lincs 155 B8
Grantley N Yorks 214 F4
Grantley Hall N Yorks 214 F4
Grantlodge Aberds 293 B9
Granton Dumfries 248 B3
Granton Edin 280 F4
Grantown Aberds 302 D5
Grantown-on-Spey Highld 301 G10
Grantsfield Hereford 115 E10
Grantshouse Borders 272 B6
Graplin Dumfries 237 E8
Grappenhall Warr 183 D10
Grasby Lincs 200 G5
Grasmere Cumb 220 D6
Grass Green Essex 106 D4
Grasscroft Gtr Man 196 G3
Grassendale Mers 182 D5
Grassgarth Cumb 221 F8
Grassgarth Cumb 230 C2
Grassholme Durham 232 G4
Grassington N Yorks 213 G10
Grassmoor Derbys 170 B6
Grassthorpe Notts 172 B3
Grasswell T & W 243 G8
Grateley Hants 47 E9
Gratton Devon 24 E5
Gratwich Staffs 151 C10
Gravel W Ches 167 B11
Gravel Castle Kent 55 D8
Gravel Hill Bucks 85 G8
Gravel Hole Gtr Man 196 F2
Gravel Hole Shrops 149 B7
Graveley Cambs 122 E4
Graveley Herts 104 F4
Gravelhill Shrops 149 G9
Gravelly Hill W Mid 134 E2
Gravels Shrops 130 D6
Gravelsbank Shrops 130 C6
Graven Shetland 312 F6
Graveney Kent 70 G5
Gravenhunger Moss Shrops 168 G2
Gravesend Herts 105 F8
Gravesend Kent 68 E6
Grayingham Lincs 188 B6
Grayrigg Cumb 221 F11
Grays Thurrock 68 D6
Grayshott Hants 49 F11
Grayson Green Cumb 228 F5
Grayswood Sur 50 G2
Graythorp Hrtlpl 234 F6
Grazeley Wokingham 65 F7
Grazeley Green W Berks 65 F7
Greagdhubh Lodge Highld 291 D8
Greamchary Highld 310 F2
Greasbrough S Yorks 186 B6
Greasby Mers 182 D3
Greasley Notts 171 F7
Great Abington Cambs 105 B10
Great Addington Northants 121 B9
Great Alne Warks 118 F2
Great Altcar Lancs 193 F10
Great Amwell Herts 86 C5
Great Asby Cumb 222 C3
Great Ashfield Suff 125 D9
Great Ashley Wilts 61 G10
Great Ayton N Yorks 225 C11
Great Baddow Essex 88 E2
Great Bardfield Essex 106 E3
Great Barford Beds 122 G2
Great Barrington Glos 82 C2
Great Barrow W Ches 167 B7
Great Barton Suff 125 D7
Great Barugh N Yorks 216 D4
Great Bavington Northumb 251 G11
Great Bealings Suff 108 B4
Great Bedwyn Wilts 63 G9
Great Bentley Essex 108 G2
Great Berry Essex 69 B7
Great Billing Northants 120 E6
Great Bircham Norf 158 C5
Great Blakenham Suff 126 G2
Great Blencow Cumb 230 E5
Great Bolas Telford 150 E2
Great Bookham Sur 50 C6
Great Bosullow Corn 1 C4
Great Bourton Oxon 101 B9
Great Bowden Leics 136 F4
Great Bower Kent 54 C4
Great Bradley Suff 124 G3
Great Braxted Essex 88 C5
Great Bricett Suff 125 G10
Great Brickhill Bucks 103 E8
Great Bridge W Mid 133 E9
Great Bridgeford Staffs 151 D7
Great Brington Northants 120 D3
Great Bromley Essex 107 F11
Great Broughton Cumb 229 E7
Great Broughton N Yorks 225 D10
Great Buckland Kent 69 G7
Great Budworth W Ches 183 F11
Great Burdon Darl 224 B6
Great Burgh Sur 51 B8
Great Burstead Essex 87 G11
Great Busby N Yorks 225 D10
Great Canfield Essex 87 B9
Great Carlton Lincs 190 D6
Great Casterton Rutland 137 B10
Great Casterton Rutland 137 B9
Great Cellws Powys 113 E11
Great Chalfield Wilts 61 G11
Great Chart Kent 54 E3
Great Chatwell Staffs 150 G5
Great Chell Stoke 168 E5
Great Chesterford Essex 105 C10
Great Cheveney Kent 53 E8
Great Cheverell Wilts 46 C3
Great Chilton Durham 233 E11
Great Chishill Cambs 105 D8
Great Clacton Essex 89 B11
Great Claydons Essex 88 E3
Great Cliff W Yorks 197 D10
Great Clifton Cumb 228 F6
Great Coates NE Lincs 201 F8
Great Comberton Worcs 99 C9
Great Common Suff 143 F7
Great Common W Sus 35 B8
Great Corby Cumb 239 G11
Great Cornard Suff 107 C7
Great Cowden E Yorks 209 E10
Great Coxwell Oxon 82 G3
Great Crakehall N Yorks 224 G4
Great Cransley Northants 120 B6
Great Cressingham Norf 141 C7
Great Crosby Mers 182 B4
Great Crosthwaite Cumb 229 G11
Great Cubley Derbys 152 B3
Great Dalby Leics 154 G4
Great Denham Beds 103 B10
Great Doddington Northants 121 E7
Great Doward Hereford 79 B9
Great Dunham Norf 159 G7
Great Dunmow Essex 106 G2
Great Durnford Wilts 46 F6
Great Easton Essex 106 F2
Great Easton Leics 136 E6
Great Eccleston Lancs 202 E4
Great Edstone N Yorks 216 C4
Great Ellingham Norf 141 D10
Great Elm Som 45 D8
Great Eppleton T & W 234 B3
Great Eversden Cambs 123 G7
Great Fencote N Yorks 224 G5
Great Finborough Suff 125 F10
Great Fransham Norf 159 G7
Great Gaddesden Herts 85 C8
Great Gate Staffs 169 G9
Great Gidding Cambs 138 G2
Great Givendale E Yorks 208 C2
Great Glemham Suff 126 E6
Great Glen Leics 136 D3
Great Gonerby Lincs 155 B7
Great Gransden Cambs 122 F5
Great Green Cambs 104 C5
Great Green Norf 142 F5
Great Green Suff 125 B11
Great Green Suff 125 F8
Great Green Suff 126 B2
Great Habton N Yorks 216 D5
Great Hale Lincs 173 G10
Great Hallingbury Essex 87 B8
Great Hampden Bucks 84 E4
Great Harrowden Northants 121 C7
Great Harwood Lancs 203 G10
Great Haseley Oxon 83 E10
Great Hatfield E Yorks 209 E9
Great Haywood Staffs 151 E10
Great Haywood Staffs 151 E9
Great Heath W Mid 134 G6
Great Heck N Yorks 198 C5
Great Henny Essex 107 D7
Great Hinton Wilts 46 B2
Great Hivings Bucks 85 E7
Great Hockham Norf 141 E9
Great Holcombe Oxon 83 F10
Great Holland Essex 89 B12
Great Hollands Brack 65 F11
Great Holm M Keynes 102 D6
Great Honeyborough Pembs 73 D7
Great Horkesley Essex 107 E9
Great Hormead Herts 105 F7
Great Horton W Yorks 205 G8
Great Horwood Bucks 102 E5
Great Houghton Northants 120 F5
Great Houghton S Yorks 198 F2
Great Howarth Gtr Man 196 D2
Great Hucklow Derbys 185 F11
Great Job's Cross Kent 38 B4
Great Kelk E Yorks 209 B8
Great Kendale E Yorks 217 G10
Great Kimble Bucks 84 D4
Great Kingshill Bucks 84 F5
Great Langton N Yorks 224 F5
Great Lea Common Reading 65 F8
Great Leighs Essex 88 B2
Great Lever Gtr Man 195 F8
Great Limber Lincs 200 F6
Great Linford M Keynes 103 C7
Great Livermere Suff 125 C7
Great Longstone Derbys 186 G2
Great Lumley Durham 233 B11
Great Lyth Shrops 131 B9
Great Malgraves Thurrock 69 C7
Great Malvern Worcs 98 B5
Great Maplestead Essex 106 E6
Great Marton Blkpool 202 F2
Great Marton Moss Blkpool 202 G2
Great Massingham Norf 158 E5
Great Melton Norf 142 B2
Great Milton Oxon 83 E10
Great Missenden Bucks 84 E5
Great Mitton Lancs 203 F10
Great Mongeham Kent 55 C10
Great Moor Gtr Man 184 D6
Great Moor Staffs 132 D6
Great Moulton Norf 142 E3
Great Munden Herts 105 G7
Great Musgrave Cumb 222 C5
Great Ness Shrops 149 F7
Great Notley Essex 106 G4
Great Oak Mon 78 D5
Great Oakley Essex 108 F3
Great Oakley Northants 137 F7
Great Offley Herts 104 F2
Great Ormside Cumb 222 B4
Great Orton Cumb 239 G8
Great Ouseburn N Yorks 215 G8
Great Oxendon Northants 136 G4
Great Oxney Green Essex 87 D11
Great Palgrave Norf 158 G6
Great Parndon Essex 86 D6
Great Pattenden Kent 53 E8
Great Paxton Cambs 122 E4
Great Plumpton Lancs 202 G3
Great Plumstead Norf 160 G6
Great Ponton Lincs 155 C8
Great Preston W Yorks 198 B2
Great Purston Northants 101 D10
Great Raveley Cambs 138 G5
Great Rissington Glos 81 B11
Great Rollright Oxon 100 E6
Great Ryburgh Norf 159 D9
Great Ryle Northumb 264 G2
Great Ryton Shrops 131 C9
Great Saling Essex 106 F4
Great Salkeld Cumb 231 D7
Great Sampford Essex 106 D2
Great Sankey Warr 183 D9
Great Saredon Staffs 133 B9
Great Saxham Suff 124 E5
Great Shefford W Berks 63 E11
Great Shelford Cambs 123 G9
Great Shoddesden Hants 47 D9
Great Smeaton N Yorks 224 E6
Great Snoring Norf 159 C8
Great Somerford Wilts 62 C3
Great Stainton Darl 234 G2
Great Stambridge Essex 88 G5
Great Staughton Cambs 122 E2
Great Steeping Lincs 174 C6
Great Stoke S Glos 60 C6
Great Stonar Kent 55 B10
Great Stretton Leics 136 C3
Great Strickland Cumb 231 G7
Great Stukeley Cambs 122 C4
Great Sturton Lincs 190 F2
Great Sutton Shrops 131 G10
Great Sutton W Ches 182 F5
Great Swinburne Northumb 241 B10
Great Tew Oxon 101 F7
Great Tey Essex 107 F7
Great Thirkleby N Yorks 215 D9
Great Thurlow Suff 124 G3
Great Torrington Devon 25 D7
Great Tosson Northumb 252 C2
Great Totham Essex 88 C5
Great Tows Lincs 190 C2
Great Tree Corn 6 D5
Great Urswick Cumb 210 E5
Great Wakering Essex 70 B2
Great Waldingfield Suff 107 C8
Great Walsingham Norf 159 B8
Great Waltham Essex 87 C11
Great Warley Essex 87 G9
Great Washbourne Glos 99 E9
Great Weeke Devon 13 D10
Great Weldon Northants 137 F8
Great Welnetham Suff 125 F7
Great Wenham Suff 107 D11
Great Whittington Northumb 242 C2
Great Wigborough Essex 89 C7
Great Wilbraham Cambs 123 F10
Great Wilne Derbys 153 C8
Great Wishford Wilts 46 F5
Great Witchingham Norf 160 E2
Great Witcombe Glos 80 C6
Great Witley Worcs 116 D5
Great Wolford Warks 100 E4
Great Wratting Suff 106 B3
Great Wymondley Herts 104 F4
Great Wyrley Staffs 133 B9
Great Wytheford Shrops 149 F11
Great Yarmouth Norf 143 B10
Great Yeldham Essex 106 D5
Greater Doward Hereford 79 B9
Greatfield Wilts 62 B5
Greatford Lincs 155 G11
Greatgap Bucks 84 B6
Greatgate Staffs 169 G9
Greatham Hants 49 G9
Greatham Hrtlpl 234 F5
Greatham W Sus 35 D8
Greatmoor Bucks 102 G4
Greatness Kent 52 B4
Greatstone-on-Sea Kent 39 C9
Greatworth Northants 101 C11
Greave Gtr Man 184 C6
Greave Lancs 195 C11
Grebby Lincs 174 B6
Greeba I o M 192 D4
Green Denb 165 B9
Green Pembs 73 E7
Green Powys 130 E5
Green Bank Cumb 211 C7
Green Bottom Corn 4 F5
Green Bottom Glos 79 B11
Green Close N Yorks 212 F4
Green Clough W Yorks 205 G7
Green Crize Hereford 97 D10
Green Cross Sur 49 F11
Green Down Devon 28 G3
Green End Beds 103 B10
Green End Beds 121 E11
Green End Beds 122 E2
Green End Beds 122 G2
Green End Bucks 84 F4
Green End Bucks 103 E8
Green End C Beds 103 D11
Green End Cambs 122 C4
Green End Cambs 123 F7
Green End Herts 85 D8
Green End Herts 104 E5
Green End Herts 104 E6
Green End Herts 104 G6
Green End Herts 105 F7
Green End Lancs 204 D4
Green End N Yorks 226 E6
Green End Warks 134 F5
Green Gate Devon 27 D8
Green Hailey Bucks 84 E4
Green Hammerton N Yorks 206 B5
Green Haworth Lancs 195 B9
Green Head Cumb 230 B3
Green Heath Staffs 151 G9
Green Hill Kent 53 C9
Green Hill Lincs 155 B8
Green Hill W Yorks 206 F4
Green Hill Wilts 62 B5
Green Lane Devon 13 F11
Green Lane Hereford 98 B2
Green Lane Powys 130 D3
Green Lane Warks 117 E11
Green Lane Warks 118 B6
Green Moor S Yorks 186 B3
Green Ore Som 44 C5
Green Parlour Bath 45 C8
Green Quarter Cumb 221 E9
Green St Green London 68 G3
Green Side W Yorks 197 E7
Green Side W Yorks 205 G11
Green Street E Sus 38 E3
Green Street Essex 87 F10
Green Street Glos 80 B5
Green Street Glos 80 E3
Green Street Herts 85 F11
Green Street Herts 105 G9
Green Street W Sus 35 C10
Green Street Worcs 99 B7
Green Street Worcs 99 C7
Green Street Green Kent 68 E5
Green Street Green London 68 G3
Green Tye Herts 86 B6
Greenacres Gtr Man 196 F2
Greenan Argyll 275 G11
Greenbank Falk 279 F7
Greenbank Shetland 312 C7
Greenbank W Ches 183 G10
Greenburn W Loth 269 C8
Greencroft Durham 242 G5
Greendale E Ches 184 F5
Greendikes Northumb 264 D3
Greendown Som 44 C5
Greendykes Northumb 264 D3
Greenend N Lnrk 268 C4
Greenend Oxon 100 G6
Greenfaulds N Lnrk 278 G5
Greenfield C Beds 103 E11
Greenfield Glasgow 268 C2
Greenfield Gtr Man 196 G3
Greenfield Highld 289 D11
Greenfield Highld 290 C4
Greenfield Oxon 84 G2
Greenfield = Maes-Glas Flint 181 F11
Greenfoot N Lnrk 268 B4
Greenford London 66 C6
Greengairs N Lnrk 278 G5
Greengarth Hall Cumb 219 E11
Greengate Gtr Man 196 D2
Greengate Norf 159 F10
Greengates W Yorks 205 F9
Greengill Cumb 229 D8
Greenhalgh Lancs 202 F4
Greenhall S Lnrk 268 D3
Greenham Dorset 28 G6
Greenham Som 27 C9
Greenham W Berks 64 F3
Greenhaugh Northumb 251 F7
Greenhead Borders 261 D11
Greenhead Dumfries 247 D9
Greenhead N Lnrk 268 E6
Greenhead Northumb 240 D5
Greenhead Staffs 169 F7
Greenheys Gtr Man 195 G8
Greenhill Dumfries 238 B4
Greenhill Durham 234 B3
Greenhill Falk 278 F6
Greenhill Hereford 98 B4
Greenhill Kent 71 F7
Greenhill Leics 153 G8
Greenhill London 67 B7
Greenhill S Yorks 186 E4
Greenhill Worcs 99 B10
Greenhill Worcs 116 B6
Greenhill Bank Shrops 149 B7
Greenhillocks Derbys 170 F6
Greenhills N Ayrs 267 E7
Greenhills S Lnrk 268 E2
Greenhithe Kent 68 E5
Greenholm E Ayrs 258 B2
Greenholme Cumb 221 D11
Greenhouse Borders 262 E3
Greenhow N Yorks 214 G2
Greenhow Hill N Yorks 214 G2
Greenigoe Orkney 314 F4
Greenland Highld 310 C6
Greenland S Yorks 186 D5
Greenland Mains Highld 310 C6
Greenlands Bucks 65 B9
Greenlands Worcs 117 D11
Greenlaw Aberds 302 D6
Greenlaw Borders 272 F4
Greenlaw Mains Midloth 270 C4
Greenlea Dumfries 238 B2
Greenloaning Perth 286 G2
Greenlooms W Ches 167 C7
Greenman's Lane Wilts 62 C3
Greenmeadow Swindon 62 B6
Greenmeadow Torf 78 F3
Greenmount Gtr Man 195 E9
Greenmow Shetland 313 L6
Greenoak E Yorks 199 B10
Greenock Invclyd 276 F5
Greenock West Invclyd 276 F5
Greenodd Cumb 210 C6
Greenrigg W Loth 269 C8
Greenrow Cumb 238 G4
Greens Borders 249 F11
Greens Norton Northants 102 B3
Greensforge Staffs 133 F7
Greensgate Norf 160 F2
Greenside Cumb 222 E4
Greenside Derbys 186 F5
Greenside Gtr Man 184 B6
Greenside T & W 242 E4
Greenside W Yorks 197 D7
Greensidehill Northumb 263 F11
Greensplat Corn 5 D9
Greenstead Essex 107 F10
Greenstead Green Essex 106 F6
Greensted Essex 87 E8
Greensted Green Essex 87 E8
Greenstreet Green Suff 107 B10
Greenway Hereford 98 E4
Greenway Pembs 91 E11
Greenway Som 27 B11
Greenway V Glam 58 E5
Greenway Worcs 116 C4
Greenwell Cumb 240 F2
Greenwells Borders 262 C3
Greenwich London 67 D11
Greenwich Suff 108 C3
Greenwich Wilts 46 G2
Greenwith Common Corn 4 G5
Greenwoods Essex 87 F11
Greeny Orkney 314 D2
Greep Highld 298 E2
Greet Glos 99 E10
Greet Kent 55 B9
Greete Shrops 115 C11
Greetham Lincs 190 G4
Greetham Rutland 155 G8
Greetland W Yorks 196 C5
Greetland Wall Nook W Yorks 196 C5
Greetwell N Lincs 200 G2
Gregg Hall Cumb 221 G9
Gregson Lane Lancs 194 B5
Gregynog Powys 129 D11
Greinetobht W Isles 296 D4
Grèin W Isles 297 L2
Greinton Som 44 F2
Gremista Shetland 313 J6
Grenaby I o M 192 E3
Grendon Northants 121 E7
Grendon Warks 134 C5
Grendon Bishop Hereford 115 F11
Grendon Common Warks 134 D5
Grendon Green Hereford 115 F11
Grendon Underwood Bucks 102 G3
Grenofen Devon 12 G5
Grenoside S Yorks 186 C4
Greosabhagh W Isles 305 J3
Gresford Wrex 166 E5
Gresham Norf 160 B3
Greshornish Highld 298 D3
Gressenhall Norf 159 F9
Gressingham Lancs 211 F11
Gresty Green E Ches 168 E2
Greta Bridge Durham 223 C11
Gretna Dumfries 239 D8
Gretna Green Dumfries 239 D8
Gretton Glos 99 E10
Gretton Northants 137 E7
Gretton Shrops 131 D10
Gretton Fields Glos 99 E10
Grewelthorpe N Yorks 214 D4
Grey Green N Lincs 199 F9
Greyfield Bath 44 B6
Greygarth N Yorks 214 E3
Greylake Som 43 G11
Greylake Fosse Som 44 F2
Greynor Carms 75 D9
Greynor-isaf Carms 75 D9
Greyrigg Dumfries 248 F3
Greys Green Oxon 65 C8
Greysouthen Cumb 229 F7
Greystead Northumb 251 F7
Greystoke Cumb 230 E4
Greystoke Gill Cumb 230 F4
Greystone Aberds 292 D6
Greystone Aberds 302 F6
Greystone Angus 287 C9
Greystone Cumb 211 D10
Greystone Dumfries 237 B11
Greystonegill N Yorks 212 F3
Greystones S Yorks 186 D4
Greystones Warks 99 B11
Greytree Hereford 97 F11
Greywell Hants 49 C8
Griais W Isles 304 D6
Grianan W Isles 304 E6
Gribb Dorset 28 G5
Gribthorpe E Yorks 207 F11
Gridley Corner Devon 12 C3
Griff Warks 135 F7
Griffins Hill W Mid 133 G10
Griffithstown Torf 78 F3
Griffydam Leics 153 F8
Grigg Kent 53 E11
Griggs Green Hants 49 G10
Grillis Corn 2 B5
Grilstone Devon 26 C2
Grimbister Orkney 314 E3
Grimblethorpe Lincs 190 D2
Grimeford Village Lancs 194 E6
Grimes Hill Worcs 117 B11
Grimesthorpe S Yorks 186 C5
Grimethorpe S Yorks 198 F2
Griminis W Isles 296 D3
Griminis W Isles 296 F3
Grimister Shetland 312 D6
Grimley Worcs 116 E6
Grimness Orkney 314 G4
Grimoldby Lincs 190 D5
Grimpo Shrops 149 D7
Grimsargh Lancs 203 G7
Grimsbury Oxon 101 C9
Grimsby NE Lincs 201 E9
Grimscote Northants 120 G3
Grimscott Corn 24 F3
Grimshaw Blkburn 195 C8
Grimshaw Green Lancs 194 E3
Grimsthorpe Lincs 155 E10
Grimston E Yorks 209 F11
Grimston Leics 154 E3
Grimston Norf 158 E4
Grimston York 207 C8
Grimstone Dorset 17 C8
Grimstone End Suff 125 D8
Grinacombe Moor Devon 12 C4
Grindale E Yorks 218 E2
Grindigar Orkney 314 F5
Grindiscol Shetland 313 K6
Grindle Shrops 132 C5
Grindleford Derbys 186 F2
Grindleton Lancs 203 D11
Grindley Staffs 151 D10
Grindley Brook Shrops 167 G8
Grindlow Derbys 185 F11
Grindon Northumb 273 G8
Grindon Staffs 169 E9
Grindon Stockton 234 F3
Grindon T & W 243 G9
Grindonmoor Gate Staffs 169 E9
Grindsbrook Booth Derbys 185 D10
Gringley on the Hill Notts 188 C2
Grinsdale Cumb 239 F9
Grinshill Shrops 149 E10
Grinstead Hill Suff 125 G11
Grinton N Yorks 223 F10
Griomasaigh W Isles 297 G4
Griomsidar W Isles 304 F5
Grisdale Cumb 222 G5
Grishipoll Argyll 288 D3
Grisling Common E Sus 36 C6
Gristhorpe N Yorks 217 C11
Griston Norf 141 D8
Gritley Orkney 314 F5
Grittenham Wilts 62 C4
Grittlesend Hereford 98 B4
Grittleton Wilts 61 C11
Grizebeck Cumb 210 C4
Grizedale Cumb 220 G6
Groam Highld 300 E5
Grobister Orkney 314 D6
Grobsness Shetland 313 G5
Groby Leics 135 B10
Groes Conwy 165 C8
Groes Neath 57 D9
Groes Efa Denb 165 B10
Groes-faen Rhondda 58 C5
Groes-fawr Denb 165 B10
Groes-lwyd Mon 96 G6
Groes-lwyd Powys 148 G4
Groes-wen Caerph 58 B6
Groesffordd Gwyn 144 B5
Groesffordd Powys 95 F11
Groesffordd Marli Denb 181 G8
Groeslon Gwyn 163 C8
Groeslon Gwyn 163 D7
Groespluan Powys 130 B4
Grogport Argyll 255 C9
Gromford Suff 127 F7
Gronant Flint 181 E9
Gronwen Shrops 148 D5
Groombridge E Sus 52 F4
Grosmont Mon 97 G8
Grosmont N Yorks 226 D6
Gross Green Warks 119 F7
Grotaig Highld 300 G4
Groton Suff 107 C9
Grotton Gtr Man 196 G3
Grougfoot Falk 279 F10
Grove Bucks 103 G8
Grove Dorset 17 G10
Grove Hereford 98 C2
Grove Kent 71 G8
Grove Notts 188 F2
Grove Oxon 82 G6
Grove Pembs 73 E7
Grove End Kent 69 G11
Grove End Warks 100 D6
Grove End Warks 134 D3
Grove Green Kent 53 B9
Grove Hill E Sus 23 C10
Grove Hill Kent 71 G8
Grove Park London 67 D8
Grove Park London 68 E2
Grove Town W Yorks 198 C3
Grove Vale W Mid 133 E10
Grovehill E Yorks 208 F6
Grovehill Herts 85 D9
Groves Kent 55 B9
Grovesend Swansea 75 E9
Grub Street Staffs 150 D5
Grubb Street Kent 68 F5
Grudie Highld 300 C3
Gruids Highld 309 J5
Gruinard House Highld 307 K4
Gruinards Highld 309 K5
Grula Highld 294 C5
Gruline Argyll 289 E7
Gruline Ho Argyll 289 F7
Grumbeg Highld 308 F6
Grumbla Corn 1 D4
Grunasound Shetland 313 K5
Grundisburgh Suff 126 G4
Grunsagill Lancs 203 C11
Gruting Shetland 313 J4
Grutness Shetland 313 N6
Gryn Goch Gwyn 162 F6
Gualachulain Highld 284 C5
Gualin Ho Highld 308 D3
Guard House W Yorks 204 E6
Guardbridge Fife 287 F8
Guarlford Worcs 98 B6
Guay Perth 286 C4
Gubbion's Green Essex 88 B2
Gubblecote Herts 84 C6
Guesachan Highld 289 B10
Guestling Green E Sus 38 E5
Guestling Thorn E Sus 38 D4
Guestwick Norf 159 D11
Guestwick Green Norf 159 D11
Guide Blkburn 195 B8
Guide Bridge Gtr Man 184 B6
Guide Post Northumb 253 F7
Guilden Morden Cambs 104 C5
Guilden Sutton W Ches 166 B6
Guildford Sur 50 D3
Guildford Park Sur 50 D3
Guildiehaugh W Loth 269 B9
Guildtown Perth 286 D5
Guilford Pembs 73 D7
Guilsborough Northants 120 C3
Guilsfield = Cegidfa Powys 148 G4
Guilthwaite S Yorks 187 D7
Guilton Kent 55 B9
Guineaford Devon 40 F5
Guisachan Highld 300 G3
Guisborough Redcar 226 B2
Guiseley W Yorks 205 E9
Guist Norf 159 D9
Guith Orkney 314 C5
Guiting Power Glos 99 G11
Gulberwick Shetland 313 K6
Gullane E Loth 281 E9
Guller's End Worcs 99 D7
Gulling Green Suff 124 F6
Gullom Holme Cumb 231 F9
Gulval Corn 1 C5
Gulworthy Devon 12 G4
Gumfreston Pembs 73 E10
Gumley Leics 136 E3
Gummow's Shop Corn 5 D7
Gun Green Kent 53 G9
Gun Hill E Sus 23 C9
Gunby E Yorks 207 F10
Gunby Lincs 155 E8
Gunby Lincs 175 B7
Gundenham Som 27 C10
Gundleton Hants 48 G6
Gunn Devon 40 G6
Gunnersbury London 67 D7
Gunnerside N Yorks 223 F9
Gunnerton Northumb 241 C10
Gunness N Lincs 199 E10
Gunnislake Corn 12 G4
Gunnista Shetland 313 J7
Guns Village W Mid 133 E9
Gunstone Staffs 133 C7
Gunter's Bridge W Sus 35 B7
Gunthorpe Lincs 188 B4
Gunthorpe Norf 159 C10
Gunthorpe Notts 171 G11
Gunthorpe P'boro 138 C3
Gunthorpe Rutland 137 B7
Gunton Suff 143 D10
Gunville I o W 20 D5
Gunwalloe Corn 2 E5
Gunwalloe Fishing Cove Corn 2 E5
Gupworthy Som 42 F3
Gurnard I o W 20 B5
Gurnett E Ches 184 G6
Gurney Slade Som 44 D6
Gurnos M Tydf 77 D8
Gurnos Powys 76 D3
Gushmere Kent 54 B4
Gussage All Saints Dorset 31 E8
Gussage St Andrew Dorset 31 E7
Gussage St Michael Dorset 31 E7
Gustard Wood Herts 85 B11
Guston Kent 55 E10
Gutcher Shetland 312 D7
Guthram Gowt Lincs 156 E3
Guthrie Angus 287 B9
Guyhirn Cambs 139 C7
Guyhirn Gull Cambs 139 C7
Guy's Cliffe Warks 118 D5
Guy's Head Lincs 157 D9
Guy's Marsh Dorset 30 C4
Guyzance Northumb 252 C6
Gwaelod-y-garth Cardiff 58 C6
Gwaenysgor Flint 181 E9
Gwalchmai Anglesey 178 F5
Gwalchmai Uchaf Anglesey 178 F5
Gwallon Corn 2 C2
Gwastad Pembs 91 G10
Gwastadgoed Gwyn 145 G11
Gwastadnant Gwyn 163 D10
Gwaun-Cae-Gurwen Neath 76 C2
Gwaun-Leision Neath 76 C2
Gwavas Corn 2 D5
Gwavas Corn 2 E5
Gwbert Ceredig 92 B3
Gwedna Corn 2 C4
Gweek Corn 2 D6
Gwehelog Mon 78 E5
Gwenddwr Powys 95 C11
Gwennap Corn 2 B6
Gwenter Corn 2 F6
Gwern y brenin Shrops 148 D6
Gwern-y-Steeple V Glam 58 D5
Gwernaffield-y-Waun Flint 166 C2
Gwernafon Powys 129 E8
Gwerneirin Powys 129 F10
Gwerneirin Powys 130 G3
Gwernesney Mon 78 E6
Gwernogle Carms 93 E10
Gwernol Denb 166 E2
Gwernydd Powys 129 C11
Gwernymynydd Flint 166 C2
Gwersyllt Wrex 166 E4
Gwespyr Flint 181 E10
Gwills Corn 4 D6
Gwinear Corn 2 B3
Gwinear Downs Corn 2 C4
Gwithian Corn 2 A3
Gwredog Anglesey 178 D6
Gwrhay Caerph 77 F11
Gwyddelwern Denb 165 F9
Gwyddgrug Carms 93 D9
Gwynfryn Wrex 166 E3
Gwystre Powys 113 D11
Gwytherin Conwy 164 C5
Gyfelia Wrex 166 F4
Gyffin Conwy 180 F3
Gylen Park Argyll 289 G10
Gyre Orkney 314 F3
Gyrn Denb 165 D11
Gyrn-goch Gwyn 162 F6

H

Habberley Shrops 131 C7
Habberley Worcs 116 B6
Habergham Lancs 204 G2
Habertoft Lincs 175 B8
Habin W Sus 34 C4
Habrough NE Lincs 200 E6
Haccombe Devon 14 G3
Haceby Lincs 155 B10
Hacheston Suff 126 F6
Hack Green E Ches 167 F10
Hackbridge London 67 F9
Hackenthorpe S Yorks 186 E6
Hackford Norf 141 C11
Hackforth N Yorks 224 G4
Hackland Orkney 314 D3
Hackleton Northants 120 F6
Hacklinge Kent 55 C10
Hackman's Gate Worcs 117 B7
Hackness N Yorks 227 G9
Hackness Orkney 314 G3
Hackness Som 43 D10
Hackney London 67 C10
Hackney Wick London 67 C11
Hackthorn Lincs 189 E7
Hackthorn Wilts 47 D7
Hackthorpe Cumb 230 G6
Haclait W Isles 297 G4
Haconby Lincs 156 D2
Hacton London 68 B4
Haddacott Devon 25 C8
Hadden Borders 263 B7
Haddenham Bucks 84 D2
Haddenham Cambs 123 B9
Haddenham End Field Cambs 123 B9
Haddington E Loth 281 G10
Haddington Lincs 172 C6
Haddiscoe Norf 143 D8
Haddoch Aberds 302 E5
Haddon Cambs 138 E2
Haddon E Ches 169 B7
Hade Edge W Yorks 196 F6
Hademore Staffs 134 B3
Haden Cross W Mid 133 F9
Hadfield Derbys 185 B8
Hadham Cross Herts 86 B6
Hadham Ford Herts 105 G8
Hadleigh Essex 69 B10
Hadleigh Suff 107 C10
Hadleigh Heath Suff 107 C9
Hadley London 86 F2
Hadley Telford 150 G3
Hadley Worcs 117 E7
Hadley Castle Telford 150 G3
Hadley End Staffs 152 E2
Hadley Wood London 86 F3
Hadlow Kent 52 D6
Hadlow Down E Sus 37 C8
Hadlow Stair Kent 52 D6
Hadnall Shrops 149 F10
Hadspen Som 45 G7
Hadstock Essex 105 C11
Hadston Northumb 253 D7
Hady Derbys 186 G5
Hadzor Worcs 117 E8
Haffenden Quarter Kent 53 E11
Hafod Swansea 57 C7
Hafod-Dinbych Conwy 164 E5
Hafod Grove Pembs 92 C2
Hafod-Iom Conwy 180 G5
Hafod-y-Green Denb 181 G8
Hafodiwan Ceredig 111 G7
Hafodyrynys Bl Gwent 78 F2
Hag Fold Gtr Man 195 G7
Haggate Gtr Man 196 F2
Haggate Lancs 204 F3
Haggbeck Cumb 239 C11
Haggersta Shetland 313 J5
Haggerston London 67 C10
Haggerston Northumb 273 G10
Hagginton Hill Devon 40 D5
Haggrister Shetland 312 F5
Haggs Falk 278 F5
Haghill Glasgow 268 B2
Hagley Hereford 97 C11
Hagley Worcs 133 G8
Hagloe Glos 79 D11
Hagmore Green Suff 107 D9
Hagnaby Lincs 174 C4
Hagnaby Lincs 191 F7
Hagnaby Lock Lincs 174 D4
Hague Bar Derbys 185 D7
Hagworthingham Lincs 174 B4
Haigh Gtr Man 194 F6
Haigh S Yorks 197 E9
Haigh Moor W Yorks 197 C9
Haighton Green Lancs 203 G7
Haighton Top Lancs 203 G7
Hail Weston Cambs 122 E3
Haile Cumb 219 D10
Hailes Glos 99 E10
Hailey Herts 86 C5
Hailey Oxon 64 B6
Hailey Oxon 82 C5
Hailsham E Sus 23 D9
Hailstone Hill Wilts 81 G9
Haimer Highld 310 C5
Haimwood Powys 148 F6
Hainault London 87 G7
Haine Kent 71 F11
Hainford Norf 160 F4

Hains Dorset 30 D3
Hainton Lincs 189 E11
Hainworth W Yorks 205 F7
Hainworth Shaw W Yorks 205 F7
Hairmyres S Lnrk 268 E2
Haisthorpe E Yorks 218 G2
Hakeford Devon 40 F6
Hakin Pembs 72 D5
Halabezack Corn 2 C6
Halam Notts 171 E11
Halamanning Corn 2 C3
Halbeath Fife 280 D2
Halberton Devon 27 E8
Halcon Som 28 B2
Halcro Highld 310 C6
Haldens Herts 86 C2
Hale Cumb 211 D10
Hale Gtr Man 184 D3
Hale Halton 183 E7
Hale Hants 31 D11
Hale Kent 71 F9
Hale Medway 69 F9
Hale Som 30 B3
Hale Sur 49 D10
Hale Bank Halton 183 E7
Hale Barns Gtr Man 184 D3
Hale Coombe N Som 44 B2
Hale End London 86 G5
Hale Green E Sus 23 C9
Hale Mills Corn 4 G5
Hale Nook Lancs 202 E3
Hale Street Kent 53 D7
Halecommon W Sus 34 C4
Hales Norf 143 D7
Hales Staffs 150 C4
Hales Bank Hereford 116 G2
Hales Green Derbys 169 G11
Hales Green Norf 143 D7
Hales Park Worcs 116 B5
Hales Place Kent 54 B6
Hales Street Norf 142 F3
Hales Wood Hereford 98 E2
Halesfield Telford 132 C4
Halesgate Lincs 156 D6
Halesowen W Mid 133 G9
Halesworth Suff 127 B7
Halewood Mers 183 D7
Half Moon Village Devon 14 B3
Halford Shrops 131 G8
Halford Warks 100 B5
Halfpenny Cumb 211 B10
Halfpenny Furze Carms 74 C3
Halfpenny Green Staffs 132 E6
Halfway Carms 75 E8
Halfway Carms 94 E2
Halfway Carms 94 E6
Halfway S Yorks 186 E6
Halfway W Berks 64 F2
Halfway Wilts 45 D11
Halfway Bridge W Sus 34 C6
Halfway House Shrops 148 G6
Halfway Houses Gtr Man 195 F9
Halfway Houses Kent 70 E2
Halfway Street Kent 55 D9
Halgabron Corn 11 D7
Halifax W Yorks 196 B5
Halkburn Borders 271 G9
Halket E Ayrs 267 E8
Halkirk Highld 310 D5
Halkyn = Helygain Flint 182 G2
Halkyn Mountain Flint 182 G2
Hall Bower W Yorks 196 E6
Hall Broom S Yorks 186 D3
Hall Cross Lancs 202 G4
Hall Dunnerdale Cumb 220 F4
Hall End Beds 103 B10
Hall End C Beds 103 D11
Hall End Lincs 174 E6
Hall End S Glos 61 B8
Hall End Warks 134 C5
Hall Flat Worcs 117 C9
Hall Garth York 207 C9
Hall Green E Ches 168 D4
Hall Green Essex 106 D5
Hall Green Lancs 194 C3
Hall Green Lancs 194 F4
Hall Green W Mid 133 E10
Hall Green W Mid 134 G2
Hall Green W Mid 135 G7
Hall Green W Yorks 197 D10
Hall Green Wrex 167 G7
Hall Grove Herts 89 C8
Hall i' th' Wood Gtr Man 195 E8
Hall of Clestrain Orkney 314 F2
Hall of Tankerness Orkney 314 F5
Hall of the Forest Shrops 130 G4
Hall Santon Cumb 220 F2
Hall Waberthwaite Cumb 220 F2
Hallam Fields Derbys 153 B9
Halland E Sus 23 B8
Hallaton Leics 136 D5
Hallatrow Bath 44 B6
Hallbankgate Cumb 240 F3
Hallbeaths Dumfries 248 G3
Hallen S Glos 60 C5
Hallend Warks 118 D2
Hallew Corn 5 D10
Hallfield Gate Derbys 170 D5
Hallgarth Durham 234 C2
Hallglen Falk 279 F7
Halliburton Borders 261 B11
Halliburton Borders 272 F3
Hallin Highld 298 D2
Halling Medway 69 G8
Hallingbury Street Essex 87 B8
Hallington Lincs 190 D4
Hallington Northumb 241 B11
Halliwell Gtr Man 195 E8
Hallon Shrops 132 D5
Hallonsford Shrops 132 D5
Halloughton Notts 171 E11
Hallow Worcs 116 F6
Hallow Heath Worcs 116 F6
Hallowes Derbys 186 F5
Hallowsgate W Ches 167 B8
Hallrule Borders 262 G3
Halls E Loth 282 G3
Hall's Cross E Sus 23 D11
Halls Green Essex 86 D6
Hall's Green Herts 104 F5
Hall's Green Kent 52 D4
Hallsands Devon 9 G11
Hallsford Bridge Essex 87 E9
Hallspill Devon 25 C7
Hallthwaites Cumb 210 B3
Hallwood Green Glos 98 E3
Hallworthy Corn 11 D9
Hallyards Borders 260 B6
Hallyburton House Perth 286 D6
Hallyne Borders 270 G3
Halmer End Staffs 168 F3
Halmond's Frome Hereford 98 B3
Halmore Glos 79 E11
Halmyre Mains Borders 270 F3
Halnaker W Sus 22 B6
Halsall Lancs 193 E11
Halse Northants 101 C11
Halse Som 27 B10
Halsetown Corn 2 B2
Halsfordwood Devon 14 C3
Halsham E Yorks 201 B9
Halsinger Devon 40 F4
Halstead Essex 106 E6
Halstead Kent 68 G3
Halstead Leics 136 B4
Halstock Dorset 29 F8
Halsway Som 42 F6
Haltcliff Bridge Cumb 230 D3
Halterworth Hants 32 C5
Haltham Lincs 174 C2
Haltoft End Lincs 174 F5
Halton Bucks 84 C5
Halton Halton 183 E8
Halton Lancs 211 G10
Halton Northumb 241 D11
Halton W Yorks 206 G2
Halton Wrex 148 B6
Halton Barton Corn 7 B8
Halton Brook Halton 183 E8
Halton East N Yorks 204 C6
Halton Fenside Lincs 174 C6
Halton Gill N Yorks 213 D7
Halton Green Lancs 211 F10
Halton Holegate Lincs 174 B6
Halton Lea Gate Northumb 240 F5
Halton Moor W Yorks 206 G2
Halton Shields Northumb 242 D2
Halton View Halton 183 D8
Halton West N Yorks 204 C2
Haltwhistle Northumb 240 E6
Halvergate Norf 143 B8
Halvosso Corn 2 C6
Halwell Devon 8 E5
Halwill Devon 12 B4
Halwill Junction Devon 24 G6
Halwin Corn 2 C5
Ham Devon 28 G2
Ham Glos 79 F11
Ham Glos 99 G9
Ham Highld 310 B6
Ham Kent 55 C10
Ham London 67 E7
Ham Plym 7 D9
Ham Shetland 313 K1
Ham Som 27 C11
Ham Som 28 B3
Ham Som 28 E3
Ham Som 45 D7
Ham Wilts 63 G10
Ham Common Dorset 30 B4
Ham Green Bucks 83 B11
Ham Green Hants 48 G2
Ham Green Hereford 98 C4
Ham Green Kent 38 B5
Ham Green Kent 69 F10
Ham Green N Som 60 D4
Ham Green Wilts 61 G11
Ham Green Worcs 117 E10
Ham Hill Kent 69 G8
Ham Moor Sur 66 G5
Ham Street Som 44 G5
Hamar Shetland 312 F5
Hamarhill Orkney 314 C5
Hamars Shetland 313 G6
Hamble-le-Rice Hants 33 F7
Hambleden Bucks 65 B9
Hambledon Hants 33 E10
Hambledon Sur 50 F3
Hambleton Lancs 202 E3
Hambleton N Yorks 205 C7
Hambleton N Yorks 207 G7
Hambleton Moss Side Lancs 202 E3
Hambridge Som 28 C5
Hambrook S Glos 60 D6
Hambrook W Sus 22 B3
Hameringham Lincs 174 B4
Hamerton Cambs 122 B2
Hametoun Shetland 313 K1
Hamilton S Lnrk 268 D3
Hamister Shetland 313 G7
Hamlet Dorset 29 F9
Hammer W Sus 49 G11
Hammer Bottom Hants 49 G11
Hammerfield Herts 85 D8
Hammerpot W Sus 35 F9
Hammersmith Derbys 170 E5
Hammersmith London 67 D8
Hammerwich Staffs 133 B11
Hammerwood E Sus 52 F2
Hammill Kent 55 B9
Hammond Street Herts 86 E4
Hammoon Dorset 30 E4
Hamnavoe Shetland 312 E4
Hamnavoe Shetland 312 E6
Hamnavoe Shetland 312 F6
Hamnavoe Shetland 313 K5
Hamnish Clifford Hereford 115 F10
Hamp Som 43 F10
Hampden Park E Sus 23 E10
Hampen Glos 81 B9
Hamperden End Essex 105 E11
Hamperley Shrops 131 F8
Hampers Green W Sus 35 C7
Hampeth Northumb 252 B5
Hampnett Glos 81 B10
Hampole S Yorks 198 E4
Hampreston Dorset 19 B7
Hampsfield Cumb 211 C8
Hampson Green Lancs 202 C5
Hampstead London 67 B9
Hampstead Garden Suburb London 67 B9
Hampstead Norreys W Berks 64 D4
Hampsthwaite N Yorks 205 B11
Hampton Kent 71 F7
Hampton London 66 F6
Hampton Shrops 132 F4
Hampton Swindon 81 G11
Hampton Worcs 99 C10
Hampton Bank Shrops 149 C9
Hampton Beech Shrops 130 B6
Hampton Bishop Hereford 97 D11
Hampton Fields Glos 80 F5
Hampton Gay Oxon 83 B7
Hampton Green Glos 80 E5
Hampton Green W Ches 167 F8
Hampton Hargate P'boro 138 E3
Hampton Heath W Ches 167 F7
Hampton Hill London 66 E6
Hampton in Arden W Mid 134 G4
Hampton Loade Shrops 132 F5
Hampton Lovett Worcs 117 D7
Hampton Lucy Warks 118 F5
Hampton Magna Warks 118 D5
Hampton on the Hill Warks 118 E5
Hampton Park Hereford 97 D10
Hampton Park Soton 32 D6
Hampton Poyle Oxon 83 B8
Hampton Wick London 67 F7
Hamptons Kent 52 C6
Hamptworth Wilts 32 D2
Hamrow Norf 159 E8
Hamsey E Sus 36 E6
Hamsey Green London 51 B10
Hamshill Glos 80 E3
Hamstall Ridware Staffs 152 F2
Hamstead I o W 20 C4
Hamstead W Mid 133 E10
Hamstead Marshall W Berks 64 F2
Hamsterley Durham 233 E8
Hamsterley Durham 242 F4
Hamstreet Kent 54 G4
Hamworthy Poole 18 C5
Hanbury Staffs 152 D3
Hanbury Worcs 117 E9
Hanbury Woodend Staffs 152 D3
Hanby Lincs 155 C10
Hanchett Village Suff 106 B3
Hanchurch Staffs 168 G4
Hand Green W Ches 167 C8
Handbridge W Ches 166 B6
Handcross W Sus 36 B3
Handforth E Ches 184 E5
Handless Shrops 131 E7
Handley Derbys 170 C5
Handley W Ches 167 D7
Handley Green Essex 87 E11
Handsacre Staffs 151 F11
Handside Herts 86 C2
Handsworth S Yorks 186 D6
Handsworth W Mid 133 E10
Handsworth Wood W Mid 133 E11
Handy Cross Bucks 84 G5
Handy Cross Devon 24 B6
Handy Cross Som 42 G6
Hanford Dorset 30 E4
Hanford Stoke 168 G5
Hangersley Hants 31 F11
Hanging Bank Kent 52 C3
Hanging Heaton W Yorks 197 C9
Hanging Houghton Northants 120 C5
Hanging Langford Wilts 46 F4
Hangingshaw Borders 261 C9
Hangingshaw Dumfries 248 F4
Hangleton Brighton 36 F3
Hangleton W Sus 35 G9
Hangsman Hill S Yorks 199 E7
Hanham S Glos 60 E6
Hanham Green S Glos 60 E6
Hankelow E Ches 167 F11
Hankerton Wilts 81 G7
Hankham E Sus 23 D10
Hanley Stoke 168 F5
Hanley Castle Worcs 98 C6
Hanley Child Worcs 116 E3
Hanley Swan Worcs 98 C6
Hanley William Worcs 116 D3
Hanlith N Yorks 213 G8
Hanmer Wrex 149 B9
Hannaford Devon 25 B10
Hannafore Corn 6 E5
Hannah Lincs 191 F8
Hanningfields Green Suff 125 G7
Hannington Hants 48 B4
Hannington Northants 120 C6
Hannington Swindon 81 G11
Hannington Wick Swindon 81 F11
Hanscombe End C Beds 104 E2
Hansel Devon 8 F6
Hansel Village S Ayrs 257 C9
Hansley Cross Staffs 169 G9
Hanslope M Keynes 102 B6
Hanthorpe Lincs 155 E11
Hanwell London 67 C7
Hanwell Oxon 101 C8
Hanwood Shrops 131 B8
Hanwood Bank Shrops 149 G8
Hanworth Brack 65 F11
Hanworth London 66 E6
Hanworth Norf 160 B3
Happendon S Lnrk 259 C9
Happisburgh Norf 161 C7
Happisburgh Common Norf 161 D7
Hapsford Som 45 D9
Hapsford W Ches 183 G7
Hapton Lancs 203 G11
Hapton Norf 142 D3
Hararden = Penarlâg Flint 166 B4
Harberton Devon 8 D5
Harbertonford Devon 8 D5
Harbledown Kent 54 B6
Harborne W Mid 133 G10
Harborough Magna Warks 119 B9
Harborough Parva Warks 119 B9
Harbottle Northumb 251 C10
Harbour Heights E Sus 36 G6
Harbour Village Pembs 91 D8
Harbourland Kent 53 B9
Harbourneford Devon 8 C4
Harbours Hill Worcs 117 D9
Harbridge Hants 31 E10
Harbridge Green Hants 31 E10
Harburn W Loth 269 C10
Harbury Warks 119 F7
Harby Leics 154 C4
Harby Notts 188 G5
Harcombe Devon 14 E3
Harcombe Devon 15 C9
Harcourt Corn 3 B8
Harcourt Hill Oxon 83 E7
Hardbreck Orkney 314 F4
Hardeicke Glos 80 C4
Harden S Yorks 197 G7
Harden W Mid 133 C10
Harden W Yorks 205 F7
Harden Park E Ches 184 F4
Hardendale Cumb 221 C11
Hardenhuish Wilts 62 E2
Hardgate Aberds 293 C9
Hardgate Dumfries 237 C10
Hardgate N Yorks 214 G5
Hardgate W Dunb 277 G10
Hardham W Sus 35 D8
Hardhorn Lancs 202 F3
Hardingham Norf 141 C10
Hardings Booth Staffs 169 C9
Hardings Wood Staffs 168 E4
Hardingstone Northants 120 F5
Hardington Som 45 C8
Hardington Mandeville Som 29 E8
Hardington Marsh Som 29 F8
Hardington Moor Som 29 E8
Hardiston Perth 279 B11
Hardisworthy Devon 24 C2
Hardley Hants 32 G6
Hardley Street Norf 143 C7
Hardmead M Keynes 103 B8
Hardrow N Yorks 223 G7
Hardstoft Derbys 170 C6
Hardstoft Common Derbys 170 C6
Hardway Hants 33 G10
Hardway Som 45 G8
Hardwick Bucks 84 B4
Hardwick Cambs 122 D3
Hardwick Cambs 123 F7
Hardwick Norf 142 F4
Hardwick Norf 158 F2
Hardwick Northants 121 D7
Hardwick Oxon 82 D5
Hardwick Oxon 101 C8
Hardwick Oxon 101 F11
Hardwick S Yorks 187 D7
Hardwick Shrops 131 E7
Hardwick Stockton 234 G4
Hardwick W Mid 133 D11
Hardwick Green Worcs 98 E6
Hardwick Village Notts 187 F10
Hardwicke Glos 80 C3
Hardwicke Glos 99 F8
Hardwicke Hereford 96 C5
Hardy's Green Essex 107 G8
Hare Som 28 D3
Hare Appletree Lancs 202 B6
Hare Edge Derbys 186 G4
Hare Green Essex 107 G11
Hare Hatch Wokingham 65 D10
Hare Street Essex 86 D6
Hare Street Herts 104 F6
Hare Street Herts 105 F7
Hareby Lincs 174 B4
Harecroft W Yorks 205 F7
Hareden Lancs 203 C8
Harefield London 85 G9
Harefield Soton 33 E7
Harefield Grove London 85 G9
Haregate Staffs 169 D7
Harehill Derbys 152 B3
Harehills W Yorks 206 G2
Harehope Borders 270 G4
Harehope Northumb 264 E3
Harelaw Durham 242 G5
Hareleeshill S Lnrk 268 E5
Hareplain Kent 53 F10
Haresceugh Cumb 231 C8
Harescombe Glos 80 C4
Haresfield Glos 80 C4
Haresfield Swindon 82 G2
Haresfinch Mers 183 B8
Hareshaw N Lnrk 268 C6
Hareshaw Head Northumb 251 F9
Harestanes E Dunb 278 G3
Harestock Hants 48 G3
Harewood W Yorks 206 D2
Harewood End Hereford 97 F10
Harewood Hill W Yorks 204 F6
Harford Carms 94 C2
Harford Devon 8 D2
Harford Devon 40 G6
Hargate Norf 142 E2
Hargate Hill Derbys 185 C8
Hargatewall Derbys 185 F10
Hargrave Northants 121 C10
Hargrave Suff 124 F5
Hargrave W Ches 167 C7
Harker Cumb 239 E9
Harker Marsh Cumb 229 E7
Harkland Shetland 312 E6
Harknett's Gate Essex 86 D6
Harkstead Suff 108 E3
Harlaston Staffs 152 G4
Harlaw Ho Aberds 303 G7
Harlaxton Lincs 155 C7
Harle Syke Lancs 204 F3
Harlech Gwyn 145 C11
Harlequin Notts 154 B3
Harlescott Shrops 149 F10
Harlesden London 67 C8
Harlesthorpe Derbys 187 F7
Harleston Devon 8 F5
Harleston Norf 142 G4
Harleston Suff 125 E10
Harlestone Northants 120 E4
Harley S Yorks 186 B5
Harley Shrops 131 C11
Harleyholm S Lnrk 259 B10
Harleywood Glos 80 F4
Harling Road Norf 141 F9
Harlington C Beds 103 E10
Harlington London 66 D5
Harlington S Yorks 198 G3
Harlosh Highld 298 E2
Harlow Essex 86 C6
Harlow Carr N Yorks 205 C11
Harlow Green T & W 243 F7
Harlow Hill N Yorks 205 C11
Harlow Hill Northumb 242 D3
Harlthorpe E Yorks 207 F10
Harlton Cambs 123 G7
Harlyn Corn 10 F3
Harman's Corner Kent 69 G11
Harman's Cross Dorset 18 E5
Harmans Water Brack 65 F11
Harmby N Yorks 214 B2
Harmer Green Herts 86 B3
Harmer Hill Shrops 149 E9
Harmondsworth London 66 D5
Harmston Lincs 173 C7
Harnage Shrops 131 C11
Harnham Northumb 242 B3
Harnham Wilts 31 B10
Harnham Wilts 31 B11
Harnhill Glos 81 E9
Harold Hill London 87 G8
Harold Park London 87 G9
Harold Wood London 87 G8
Haroldston West Pembs 72 B5
Haroldswick Shetland 312 B8
Harome N Yorks 216 C2
Harpenden Herts 85 C10
Harpenden Common Herts 85 C10
Harper Green Gtr Man 195 F8
Harperley Durham 242 G5
Harper's Gate Staffs 169 D7
Harper's Green Norf 159 E8
Harpford Devon 15 C7
Harpham E Yorks 217 G11
Harpley Norf 158 D5
Harpley Worcs 116 E3
Harpole Northants 120 E3
Harpsdale Highld 310 D5
Harpsden Oxon 65 C9
Harpsden Bottom Oxon 65 C9
Harpswell Lincs 188 D6
Harpton Powys 114 F4
Harpur Hill Derbys 185 G9
Harpurhey Gtr Man 195 G11
Harraby Cumb 239 G10
Harracott Devon 25 B9
Harrapool Highld 295 C8
Harras Cumb 219 B9
Harraton T & W 243 G7
Harrier Shetland 313 J1
Harrietfield Perth 286 E3
Harrietsham Kent 53 C11
Harringay London 67 B10
Harrington Cumb 228 F5
Harrington Lincs 190 G5
Harrington Northants 136 G5
Harringworth Northants 137 D8
Harris Highld 294 F5
Harriseahead Staffs 168 D5
Harriston Cumb 229 C9
Harrogate N Yorks 206 C2
Harrold Beds 121 F8
Harrop Dale Gtr Man 196 F4
Harrow Highld 310 B6
Harrow London 67 B7
Harrow Green Suff 125 G7
Harrow Hill Glos 79 B10
Harrow on the Hill London 67 B7
Harrow Street Suff 107 D9
Harrow Weald London 85 G11
Harrowbarrow Corn 7 B7
Harrowbeer Devon 7 B10
Harrowby Lincs 155 B8
Harrowden Beds 103 B11
Harrowgate Hill Darl 224 B5
Harrowgate Village Darl 224 B5
Harry Stoke S Glos 60 D6
Harston Cambs 123 G8
Harston Leics 154 C6
Harswell E Yorks 208 E2
Hart Hrtlpl 234 E5
Hart Common Gtr Man 194 F6
Hart Hill Luton 104 G2
Hart Station Hrtlpl 234 D5
Hartbarrow Cumb 221 G8
Hartburn Northumb 252 F3
Hartburn Stockton 225 B8
Hartcliffe Bristol 60 F5
Hartest Suff 124 G6
Hartest Hill Suff 124 G6
Hartfield E Sus 52 F3
Hartfield Highld 299 E7
Hartford Cambs 122 C5
Hartford W Ches 183 G10
Hartford End Essex 87 B11
Hartfordbeach W Ches 183 G10
Hartfordbridge Hants 49 B9
Hartforth N Yorks 224 D3
Hartgrove Dorset 30 D4
Hartham Herts 86 C4
Harthill N Lnrk 269 C8
Harthill S Yorks 187 E7
Harthill W Ches 167 D8
Hartington Derbys 169 C10
Hartland Devon 24 C3
Hartle Worcs 117 B8
Hartlebury Shrops 132 D4
Hartlebury Worcs 116 C6
Hartlebury Common Worcs 116 C6
Hartlepool Hrtlpl 234 E6
Hartley Cumb 222 D5
Hartley Kent 53 G9
Hartley Kent 68 F6
Hartley Northumb 243 B8
Hartley Plym 7 D9
Hartley Green Kent 68 F6
Hartley Green Staffs 151 D9
Hartley Mauditt Hants 49 F8
Hartley Westpall Hants 49 B7
Hartley Wintney Hants 49 B9
Hartlington N Yorks 213 G10
Hartlip Kent 69 G10
Hartmoor Dorset 30 C3
Hartmount Highld 301 B7
Hartoft End N Yorks 226 G5
Harton N Yorks 216 G4
Harton Shrops 131 F9
Harton T & W 243 E9
Hartpury Glos 98 F5
Hart's Green Suff 125 F7
Hart's Hill W Mid 133 F8
Hartsgreen Shrops 132 G5
Hartshead W Yorks 197 C7
Hartshead Green Gtr Man 196 G3
Hartshead Moor Side W Yorks 197 C7
Hartshead Moor Top W Yorks 197 B7
Hartshead Pike Gtr Man 196 G3
Hartshill Stoke 168 F5
Hartshill Warks 134 E6
Hartshill Green Warks 134 E6
Hartshorne Derbys 152 E6
Hartsop Cumb 221 C8
Hartswell Som 27 B9
Hartwell Northants 120 G5
Hartwell Staffs 151 B8
Hartwith N Yorks 214 G4
Hartwood Lancs 194 D5
Hartwood N Lnrk 268 D6
Hartwoodburn Borders 261 D11
Harvel Kent 68 G6
Harvest Hill W Mid 134 G5
Harvieston Stirl 277 D11
Harvills Hawthorn W Mid 133 E9
Harvington Worcs 99 B11
Harvington Worcs 117 C7
Harvington Cross Worcs 99 B11
Harvington Hill Worcs 99 B10
Harwell Notts 187 C11
Harwell Oxon 64 B3
Harwich Essex 108 E5
Harwood Durham 232 E2
Harwood Gtr Man 195 E8
Harwood Dale N Yorks 227 F9
Harwood Lee Gtr Man 195 E8
Harwood on Teviot Borders 249 B10
Harworth Notts 187 C10
Hasbury W Mid 133 G9
Hascombe Sur 50 E3
Haselbech Northants 120 B4
Haselbury Plucknett Som 29 E7
Haseley Warks 118 D4
Haseley Green Warks 118 D4
Haseley Knob Warks 118 C4
Haselor Warks 118 F2
Hasfield Glos 98 F6
Hasguard Pembs 72 D5
Haskayne Lancs 193 F11
Hasketon Suff 126 G4
Hasland Derbys 170 B5
Haslemere Sur 50 G2
Haslingbourne W Sus 35 C7
Haslingden Lancs 195 C9
Haslingfield Cambs 123 G8
Haslington E Ches 168 D2
Hasluck's Green W Mid 118 B2
Hassall E Ches 168 D3
Hassall Green E Ches 168 D3
Hassell Street Kent 54 D5
Hassendean Borders 262 E2
Hassingham Norf 143 B7
Hassocks W Sus 36 D3
Hassop Derbys 186 G2
Haster Highld 310 D7
Hasthorpe Lincs 175 B7
Hastigrow Highld 310 C6
Hasting Hill T & W 243 G9
Hastingleigh Kent 54 E5
Hastings E Sus 38 F4
Hastings Som 28 D4
Hastingwood Essex 87 D7
Hastoe Herts 84 D6
Haston Shrops 149 E10
Haswell Durham 234 C3
Haswell Moor Durham 234 C3
Haswell Plough Durham 234 C3
Haswellsykes Borders 260 B6
Hatch C Beds 104 B3
Hatch Devon 8 F4
Hatch Hants 49 C7
Hatch Wilts 30 B6
Hatch Beauchamp Som 28 C4
Hatch Bottom Hants 33 E7
Hatch End Beds 121 E11
Hatch End London 85 G10
Hatch Farm Hill W Sus 34 B6
Hatch Green Som 28 D4
Hatch Warren Hants 48 D6
Hatchet Gate Hants 32 G5
Hatchet Green Hants 31 D11
Hatching Green Herts 85 C10
Hatchmere W Ches 183 G9
Hatcliffe NE Lincs 201 G8
Hateley Heath W Mid 133 E10
Hatfield Hereford 115 F11
Hatfield Herts 86 D2
Hatfield S Yorks 199 F7
Hatfield Worcs 117 G7
Hatfield Broad Oak Essex 87 B8
Hatfield Chase S Yorks 199 E8
Hatfield Garden Village Herts 86 D2
Hatfield Heath Essex 87 B8
Hatfield Hyde Herts 86 C2
Hatfield Peverel Essex 88 C3
Hatfield Woodhouse S Yorks 199 F7
Hatford Oxon 82 G4
Hatherden Hants 47 C10
Hatherleigh Devon 25 G8
Hatherley Glos 99 G8
Hathern Leics 153 E9
Hatherop Glos 81 D11
Hathersage Derbys 186 E2
Hathersage Booths Derbys 186 E2
Hathershaw Gtr Man 196 G2
Hatherton E Ches 167 F11
Hatherton Staffs 151 G9
Hatley St George Cambs 122 G5
Hatston Orkney 314 E4
Hatt Corn 7 C7
Hatt Hill Hants 32 B4
Hatterseat Aberds 303 G9
Hattersley Gtr Man 185 C7
Hattingley Hants 48 F6
Hatton Aberds 303 F10
Hatton Angus 287 D9
Hatton Derbys 152 D4
Hatton Lincs 189 F11
Hatton London 66 D5
Hatton Moray 301 D11
Hatton Shrops 131 E9
Hatton Warks 118 D4
Hatton Warr 183 E9
Hatton Castle Aberds 303 E7
Hatton Grange Shrops 132 C5
Hatton Heath W Ches 167 C7
Hatton Hill Sur 66 G2
Hatton of Fintray Aberds 293 B10
Hatton Park Northants 121 D7
Hattonburn Aberds 293 C9
Hattoncrook Aberds 303 G8
Hattonknowe Borders 270 F4
Haugh E Ayrs 257 D11
Haugh Gtr Man 196 E2
Haugh Lincs 190 F6
Haugh-head Borders 261 B8
Haugh Head Northumb 264 D2
Haugh of Glass Moray 302 F4
Haugh of Kilnmaichlie Moray 301 F11
Haugh of Urr Dumfries 237 C10
Haugham Lincs 190 E4
Haughland Orkney 314 E5
Haughley Suff 125 E10
Haughley Green Suff 125 E10
Haughley New Street Suff 125 E10
Haughs of Clinterty Aberdeen 293 B10
Haughton E Ches 167 D9
Haughton Notts 187 G11
Haughton Powys 148 F6
Haughton Shrops 132 B4
Haughton Shrops 132 D3
Haughton Shrops 149 D7
Haughton Shrops 149 F11
Haughton Staffs 151 E7
Haughton Castle Northumb 241 C10
Haughton Green Gtr Man 184 C6
Haughton Le Skerne Darl 224 B6
Haughurst Hill W Berks 64 G5
Haulkerton Aberds 293 F9
Haultwick Herts 104 G6
Haunn Argyll 288 E5
Haunn W Isles 297 K3
Haunton Staffs 152 G4
Hauxton Cambs 123 G8
Havannah E Ches 168 C5
Havant Hants 22 B2
Haven Hereford 97 B11
Haven Hereford 115 G8
Haven Bank Lincs 174 E2
Haven Side E Yorks 201 B7
Havenstreet I o W 21 C7
Havercroft W Yorks 197 E11
Haverfordwest = Hwlffordd Pembs 73 B7
Haverhill Suff 106 B3
Haverigg Cumb 210 D3
Havering-atte-Bower London 87 G8
Haveringland Norf 160 E3
Haversham M Keynes 102 C6
Haverthwaite Cumb 210 C6
Haverton Hill Stockton 234 G5
Haviker Street Kent 53 D8
Havyatt Som 44 F4
Havyatt Green N Som 60 G3
Hawarden = Penarlâg Flint 166 B4
Hawbridge Worcs 99 B8
Hawbush Green Essex 106 G5
Hawcoat Cumb 210 E4
Hawcross Glos 98 E5
Hawddamor Gwyn 146 F3
Hawen Ceredig 92 B6
Hawes N Yorks 213 B7
Hawes' Green Norf 142 D4
Hawes Side Blkpool 202 G2
Hawford Worcs 116 E6
Hawgreen Shrops 150 D2
Hawick Borders 262 F2
Hawk Green Gtr Man 185 D7
Hawk Hill Cumb 228 F6
Hawkchurch Devon 28 G4
Hawkcombe Som 41 D11
Hawkedon Suff 124 G5
Hawkenbury Kent 52 F5
Hawkenbury Kent 53 E10
Hawkeridge Wilts 45 C11
Hawkerland Devon 15 D7
Hawkersland Cross Hereford 97 B10
Hawkes End W Mid 134 G6
Hawkesbury S Glos 61 B9
Hawkesbury Warks 135 G7
Hawkesbury Upton S Glos 61 B9
Hawkesley W Mid 117 B10
Hawkhill Northumb 264 G6
Hawkhope Northumb 250 F6
Hawkhurst Kent 53 G9
Hawkhurst Common E Sus 23 B8
Hawkinge Kent 55 F8
Hawkin's Hill Essex 106 E3
Hawkley Gtr Man 194 G5
Hawkley Hants 34 B2
Hawkridge Som 41 G11
Hawks Green Staffs 151 G9
Hawks Hill Bucks 66 B2
Hawk's Hill Sur 51 B7
Hawks Stones W Yorks 196 B2
Hawksdale Cumb 230 B3
Hawkshaw Blkburn 195 D9
Hawkshead Cumb 221 F7
Hawkshead Hill Cumb 220 F6
Hawksland S Lnrk 259 B8
Hawkspur Green Essex 106 E3
Hawkswick N Yorks 213 E9
Hawksworth Notts 172 G3
Hawksworth W Yorks 205 E9
Hawksworth W Yorks 205 F11
Hawkwell Essex 88 G4
Hawley Hants 49 B11
Hawley Kent 68 E4
Hawley Bottom Devon 28 G2
Hawley Lane Hants 49 B11
Hawling Glos 99 G11
Hawn Orkney 314 D4
Hawnby N Yorks 215 B10
Hawne W Mid 133 G9
Haworth W Yorks 204 F6
Haws Bank Cumb 220 F6
Hawstead Suff 125 F7
Hawstead Green Suff 125 F7
Hawthorn Durham 234 B4
Hawthorn Hants 49 G7
Hawthorn Rhondda 58 B6
Hawthorn Wilts 61 F11
Hawthorn Corner Kent 71 F8
Hawthorn Hill Brack 65 E11
Hawthorn Hill Lincs 174 D2
Hawthorns Staffs 168 F4
Hawthorpe Lincs 155 D10
Hawton Notts 172 E3
Haxby York 207 B8
Haxey N Lincs 188 B3
Haxey N Lincs 199 G9
Haxey Carr N Lincs 199 G9
Haxted Sur 52 D2
Haxton Wilts 46 D6
Hay Corn 10 G5
Hay Field S Yorks 187 B10
Hay Green Essex 87 E10
Hay Green Herts 104 D6
Hay Green Norf 157 F10
Hay Mills W Mid 134 G2
Hay-on-Wye Powys 96 C4
Hay Street Herts 105 F7
Haybridge Shrops 116 C2
Haybridge Som 44 D4
Haybridge Telford 150 G3
Hayden Glos 99 G8
Haydock Mers 183 B9
Haydon Bath 45 C7
Haydon Dorset 29 D11
Haydon Som 28 C3
Haydon Som 44 D5
Haydon Swindon 62 B6
Haydon Bridge Northumb 241 E8
Haydon Wick Swindon 62 B6
Haye Corn 7 B7
Haye Fm Corn 6 B6
Hayes Bromley 68 F2
Hayes Hillingdon 66 C6
Hayes Staffs 169 C9
Hayes End London 66 C5
Hayes Knoll Wilts 81 G10
Hayes Town London 66 C6
Hayfield Derbys 185 D8
Hayfield Fife 280 C5
Hayfield Green S Yorks 187 B11
Haygate Telford 150 G2
Haygrass Som 28 C2
Hayhill E Ayrs 257 F11
Hayhillock Angus 287 C9
Haylands I o W 21 C7
Hayle Corn 2 B3
Hayley Green W Mid 133 G8
Haymoor End Som 28 B4
Haymoor Green E Ches 167 E11
Hayne Devon 26 F5
Haynes C Beds 103 C11
Haynes Church End C Beds 103 C11
Haynes West End C Beds 103 C11
Hayscastle Pembs 91 F7
Hayscastle Cross Pembs 91 G8
Haysford Pembs 91 G8
Hayshead Angus 287 C10
Hayston E Dunb 278 G2
Haystoun Borders 261 B7
Haythorne Dorset 31 F8
Hayton Aberdeen 293 C11
Hayton Cumb 229 C8
Hayton Cumb 240 F2
Hayton E Yorks 208 D2
Hayton Notts 188 E2
Hayton's Bent Shrops 131 G10
Haytor Vale Devon 13 F11
Haytown Devon 24 E5
Haywards Heath W Sus 36 C4
Haywood S Lnrk 269 E9
Haywood S Yorks 198 E5
Haywood Oaks Notts 171 D10
Hazard's Green E Sus 23 C11
Hazel End Essex 105 G9
Hazel Grove Gtr Man 184 D6
Hazel Street Kent 53 B11
Hazel Street Kent 53 F7
Hazel Stub Suff 106 C3
Hazelbank S Lnrk 268 F6
Hazelbeach Pembs 72 E6
Hazelbury Bryan Dorset 30 F2
Hazeleigh Essex 88 E4
Hazeley Hants 49 B8
Hazeley Bottom Hants 49 B9
Hazeley Heath Hants 49 B9
Hazeley Lea Hants 49 B8
Hazelgrove Notts 171 F8
Hazelhurst Gtr Man 195 D9
Hazelhurst Gtr Man 195 G9
Hazelhurst Gtr Man 196 G3
Hazelslack Cumb 211 D9
Hazelslade Staffs 151 G10
Hazelton Glos 81 B9
Hazelton Walls Fife 287 E7
Hazelwood Derbys 170 F4
Hazelwood Devon 8 E4
Hazelwood London 68 G2
Hazlehead S Yorks 197 G7
Hazlemere Bucks 84 F5
Hazler Shrops 131 E9
Hazlerigg T & W 242 C6
Hazles Staffs 169 F8
Hazlescross Staffs 169 F8
Hazleton Glos 81 B9
Hazlewood N Yorks 205 C7
Hazon Northumb 252 C5
Heacham Norf 158 B3
Head of Muir Falk 278 E6
Headbourne Worthy Hants 48 G3
Headbrook Hereford 114 F6
Headcorn Kent 53 E10
Headingley W Yorks 205 F11
Headington Oxon 83 D8
Headington Hill Oxon 83 D8
Headlam Durham 224 B3
Headless Cross Cumb 211 D7
Headless Cross Worcs 117 D10
Headley Hants 49 F10
Headley Hants 64 G4
Headley Sur 51 C8
Headley Down Hants 49 F10
Headley Heath Worcs 117 B11
Headley Park Bristol 60 F5
Headon Devon 24 G5
Headon Notts 188 F2
Heads S Lnrk 268 F4
Heads Nook Cumb 239 F11
Headshaw Borders 261 E11
Headstone London 66 B6
Headwell Fife 279 D11
Heady Hill Gtr Man 195 E10
Heage Derbys 170 E5
Healaugh N Yorks 206 D5
Healaugh N Yorks 223 F10
Heald Green Gtr Man 184 D4
Healds Green Gtr Man 195 F11
Heale Devon 40 D6
Heale Som 28 B5
Heale Som 28 D2
Heale Som 45 E7
Healey Gtr Man 195 D11
Healey N Yorks 214 C3
Healey Northumb 242 F2
Healey W Yorks 197 C8
Healey W Yorks 197 D9
Healey Cote Northumb 252 C4
Healey Hall Northumb 242 F2
Healeyfield Durham 233 B7
Healing NE Lincs 201 E8
Heamoor Corn 1 C5
Heaning Cumb 221 F8
Heanish Argyll 288 E2
Heanor Derbys 170 F6
Heanor Gate Derbys 170 F6
Heanton Punchardon Devon 40 F4
Heap Bridge Gtr Man 195 E10
Heapham Lincs 188 D5
Hearn Hants 49 F10
Hearnden Green Kent 53 D10
Hearthstane Borders 260 D4
Hearthstone Derbys 170 D4
Hearts Delight Kent 69 G11
Heasley Mill Devon 41 G8
Heast Highld 295 D8
Heath Cardiff 59 D7
Heath Derbys 170 B6
Heath Halton 183 E8
Heath and Reach C Beds 103 F8
Heath Charnock Lancs 194 E5
Heath Common W Sus 35 E10
Heath Common W Yorks 197 D11
Heath Cross Devon 13 B10
Heath Cross Devon 14 C2
Heath End Bucks 84 F5
Heath End Bucks 85 D7
Heath End Derbys 153 E7
Heath End Hants 64 G2
Heath End Hants 64 G5
Heath End S Glos 61 B7
Heath End Sur 49 D10
Heath End W Mid 133 C10
Heath End W Sus 35 D7
Heath End Warks 118 E4
Heath Green Hants 48 F6
Heath Green Worcs 117 C11
Heath Hayes Staffs 151 G10
Heath Hill Shrops 150 G5
Heath House Som 44 D2
Heath Lanes Telford 150 E2
Heath Park London 68 B4
Heath Side Kent 68 E4
Heath Town W Mid 133 D8
Heathcot Aberds 293 C10
Heathcote Derbys 169 C10
Heathcote Shrops 150 D3
Heathcote Warks 118 E6
Heather Leics 153 G7
Heather Row Hants 49 C8
Heathercombe Devon 13 E10
Heatherfield Highld 298 E4
Heatherside Sur 50 B2
Heatherwood Park Highld 311 K2
Heatherybanks Aberds 303 E7
Heathfield Cambs 105 B9
Heathfield Devon 14 F2
Heathfield E Sus 37 C9
Heathfield Glos 80 F2
Heathfield Hants 33 F9
Heathfield Lincs 189 C10
Heathfield N Yorks 214 F2
Heathfield S Ayrs 257 E9
Heathfield Som 27 B11
Heathfield Som 43 G7
Heathfield Village Oxon 83 B8
Heathhall Dumfries 237 B11
Heathlands Wokingham 65 F10
Heathrow Airport London 66 D5
Heathstock Devon 28 G2
Heathton Shrops 132 E6
Heathtop Derbys 152 C4
Heathwaite Cumb 221 F8
Heathwaite N Yorks 225 E9
Heatley Staffs 151 D11
Heatley Warr 184 D2
Heaton Gtr Man 195 F7
Heaton Lancs 211 G8
Heaton Staffs 169 C7
Heaton T & W 243 D7
Heaton W Yorks 205 G8
Heaton Chapel Gtr Man 184 C5

Heaton Mersey Gtr Man 184 C5
Heaton Moor Gtr Man 184 C5
Heaton Norris Gtr Man 184 C5
Heaton Royds W Yorks 205 F8
Heaton Shay W Yorks 205 F8
Heaton's Bridge Lancs 194 E2
Heaven's Door Som 29 C10
Heaverham Kent 52 B5
Heaviley Gtr Man 184 D6
Heavitree Devon 14 C4
Hebburn T & W 243 E8
Hebburn Colliery T & W 243 D8
Hebburn New Town T & W 243 E8
Hebden N Yorks 213 G10
Hebden Bridge W Yorks 196 B3
Hebden Green W Ches 167 B10
Hebing End Herts 104 G6
Hebron Anglesey 179 E7
Hebron Carms 92 F3
Hebron Northumb 252 F5
Heck Dumfries 248 G3
Heckdyke N Lincs 188 B3
Heckfield Hants 65 G8
Heckfield Green Suff 126 B3
Heckfordbridge Essex 107 G8
Heckingham Norf 143 D7
Heckington Lincs 173 G10
Heckmondwike W Yorks 197 C8
Heddington Wilts 62 F3
Heddington Wick Wilts 62 F3
Heddle Orkney 314 E3
Heddon Devon 25 B11
Heddon-on-the-Wall Northumb 242 D4
Hedenham Norf 142 E6
Hedge End Dorset 30 F4
Hedge End Hants 33 E7
Hedgehog Bridge Lincs 174 F3
Hedgerley Bucks 66 B3
Hedgerley Green Bucks 66 B3
Hedgerley Hill Bucks 66 B3
Hedging Som 28 B4
Hedley Hill Durham 233 C9
Hedley on the Hill Northumb 242 F3
Hednesford Staffs 151 G9
Hedon E Yorks 201 B7
Hedsor Bucks 66 B2
Hedworth T & W 243 E8
Heelands M Keynes 102 D6
Heeley S Yorks 186 E5
Hegdon Hill Hereford 115 G11
Heggerscales Cumb 222 C6
Heggle Lane Cumb 230 D3
Heglibister Shetland 313 H5
Heighington Darl 233 G11
Heighington Lincs 173 B8
Heighley Staffs 168 F3
Height End Lancs 195 C9
Heightington Worcs 116 C5
Heights Gtr Man 196 F3
Heights of Brae Highld 300 C5
Heights of Kinlochewe Highld 299 C10
Heilam Highld 308 C4
Heiton Borders 262 C6
Helbeck Cumb 222 B5
Hele Devon 12 C2
Hele Devon 13 G10
Hele Devon 27 G7
Hele Devon 40 D4
Hele Som 27 C11
Hele Torbay 9 B8
Helebridge Corn 24 G2
Helensburgh Argyll 276 E5
Helford Corn 3 D7
Helford Passage Corn 3 D7
Helham Green Herts 86 B5
Helhoughton Norf 159 D7
Helions Bumpstead Essex 106 C3
Hell Corner W Berks 63 G11
Hellaby S Yorks 187 C8
Helland Corn 11 G7
Helland Som 28 C4
Hellandbridge Corn 11 G7
Hellesdon Norf 160 G4
Hellesveor Corn 2 A2
Hellidon Northants 119 F10
Hellifield N Yorks 204 B3
Hellifield Green N Yorks 204 B3
Hellingly E Sus 23 C9
Hellington Norf 142 C6
Hellister Shetland 313 J5
Hellman's Cross Essex 87 B9
Helm N Yorks 223 G8
Helm Northumb 252 D5
Helmburn Borders 261 E9
Helmdon Northants 101 C11
Helme W Yorks 196 E5
Helmingham Suff 126 F3
Helmington Row Durham 233 D9
Helmsdale Highld 311 H4
Helmshore Lancs 195 C9
Helmside Cumb 212 B3
Helmsley N Yorks 216 C2
Helperby N Yorks 215 F8
Helperthorpe N Yorks 217 E9
Helpringham Lincs 173 G10
Helpston P'boro 138 B2
Helsby W Ches 183 F7
Helscott Corn 24 G2
Helsey Lincs 191 G8
Helston Corn 2 D5
Helston Water Corn 4 G5
Helstone Corn 11 E7
Helton Cumb 230 G6
Helwith Bridge N Yorks 212 F6
Helygain = Halkyn Flint 182 G2
Hem Heath Stoke 168 G5
Hemblington Norf 160 G6
Hemblington Corner Norf 160 G6
Hembridge Som 44 F5
Hemel Hempstead Herts 85 D9
Hemerdon Devon 7 D11
Hemford Shrops 130 C6
Hemingbrough N Yorks 207 G9
Hemingby Lincs 190 G2
Hemingfield S Yorks 197 G11
Hemingford Abbots Cambs 122 C5
Hemingford Grey Cambs 122 C5
Hemingstone Suff 126 G3
Hemington Leics 153 D9
Hemington Northants 137 F11
Hemington Som 45 C8
Hemley Suff 108 C5
Hemlington M'bro 225 C10
Hemp Green Suff 127 D7
Hempholme E Yorks 209 C7
Hempnall Norf 142 E4
Hempnall Green Norf 142 E4
Hempriggs House Highld 310 E7
Hemp's Green Essex 107 F8
Hempshill Vale Notts 171 G8
Hempstead Essex 106 D2
Hempstead Medway 69 G9
Hempstead Norf 160 B2
Hempstead Norf 161 D8
Hempsted Glos 80 B4
Hempton Norf 159 D8
Hempton Oxon 101 E8
Hempton Wainhill Oxon 84 E3
Hemsby Norf 161 F9
Hemsted Kent 54 E6
Hemswell Lincs 188 C6
Hemswell Cliff Lincs 188 D6
Hemsworth Dorset 31 F7
Hemsworth S Yorks 186 E5
Hemsworth W Yorks 198 E2
Hemyock Devon 27 E10
Hen Bentref Llandegfan Anglesey 179 G9
Hên-efail Denb 165 C9
Henaford Devon 24 D2
Henbrook Worcs 117 D8
Henbury Bristol 60 D5
Henbury Dorset 18 B5
Henbury E Ches 184 G5
Hendomen Powys 130 D4
Hendon London 67 B8
Hendon T & W 243 F10
Hendra Corn 2 B6
Hendra Corn 2 C5
Hendra Corn 2 D3
Hendra Corn 2 F6
Hendra Corn 5 C9
Hendra Corn 5 D9
Hendra Corn 11 E7
Hendra Croft Corn 4 D5
Hendrabridge Corn 6 B5
Hendraburnick Corn 11 D8
Hendre Flint 165 B11
Hendre Gwyn 110 B2
Hendre Powys 129 D9
Hendre-ddu Conwy 164 B5
Hendredenny Park Caerph 58 B6
Hendreforgan Rhondda 58 B3
Hendrerwydd Denb 165 C10
Hendrewen Swansea 75 D10
Hendy Carms 75 E9
Hendy-Gwyn Carms 74 B2
Hendy Gwyn = Whitland Carms 73 B11
Heneglwys Anglesey 178 F6
Henfield S Glos 61 D7
Henfield W Sus 36 D2
Henford Devon 12 C3
Henfords Marsh Wilts 45 E11
Henghurst Kent 54 F3
Hengoed Caerph 77 F10
Hengoed Denb 165 D9
Hengoed Powys 114 G4
Hengoed Shrops 148 C5
Hengrave Norf 160 F2
Hengrave Suff 124 D6
Hengrove Bristol 60 F6
Hengrove Park Bristol 60 F5
Henham Essex 105 F10
Heniarth Powys 130 B2
Henlade Som 28 C3
Henleaze Bristol 60 D5
Henley Dorset 29 G11
Henley Glos 80 B6
Henley Shrops 115 B10
Henley Shrops 131 F9
Henley Som 44 G2
Henley Suff 126 G3
Henley W Sus 34 B5
Henley Wilts 47 B10
Henley Wilts 61 F10
Henley Common W Sus 34 B5
Henley Green W Mid 135 G7
Henley-in-Arden Warks 118 D3
Henley-on-Thames Oxon 65 C9
Henley Street Kent 69 F7
Henley's Down E Sus 38 E2
Henllan Ceredig 93 C7
Henllan Denb 165 B8
Henllan Amgoed Carms 92 G3
Henlle Shrops 148 C6
Henllys Torf 78 G3
Henllys Vale Torf 78 G3
Henlow C Beds 104 D3
Hennock Devon 14 E2
Henny Street Essex 107 D7
Henryd Conwy 180 G3
Henry's Moat Pembs 91 F10
Hensall N Yorks 198 C5
Henshaw Northumb 241 E7
Henshaw W Yorks 205 E10
Hensingham Cumb 219 B9
Hensington Oxon 83 B7
Henstead Suff 143 F9
Hensting Hants 33 C7
Henstridge Devon 40 E5
Henstridge Som 30 D2
Henstridge Ash Som 30 C2
Henstridge Bowden Som 29 C11
Henstridge Marsh Som 30 C2
Henton Oxon 84 E3
Henton Som 44 D3
Henwood Corn 11 G11
Henwood Oxon 83 E7
Henwood Green Kent 52 E6
Heogan Shetland 313 J6
Heol-ddu Carms 75 E7
Heol-ddu Swansea 56 B6
Heol-laethog Bridgend 58 C2
Heol-las Bridgend 58 C2
Heol-las Swansea 57 B7
Heol Senni Powys 95 G8
Heol-y-gaer Powys 96 D3
Heol-y-mynydd V Glam 57 G11
Heolgerrig M Tydf 77 D8
Hepburn Northumb 264 E3
Hepple Northumb 251 C11
Hepscott Northumb 252 G6
Hepthorne Lane Derbys 170 C6
Heptonstall W Yorks 196 B3
Hepworth Suff 125 C9
Hepworth W Yorks 197 F7
Herbrandston Pembs 72 D5
Hereford Hereford 97 C10
Heribusta Highld 298 B4
Heriot Borders 271 E7
Hermiston Edin 280 G3
Hermit Hill S Yorks 197 G10
Hermit Hole W Yorks 205 F7
Hermitage Borders 250 D2
Hermitage Dorset 29 F10
Hermitage W Berks 64 E4
Hermitage W Sus 22 B3
Hermitage Green Mers 183 C10
Hermon Anglesey 162 B5
Hermon Carms 93 E7
Hermon Carms 94 F3
Hermon Pembs 92 E4
Herne Kent 71 F7
Herne Bay Kent 71 F7
Herne Common Kent 71 F7
Herne Hill London 67 E10
Herne Pound Kent 53 C7
Herner Devon 25 B9
Hernhill Kent 70 G5
Herniss Corn 2 C6
Herodsfoot Corn 6 C4
Heron Cross Stoke 168 G5
Heronden Kent 55 C9
Herongate Essex 87 G10
Heron's Ghyll E Sus 37 B7
Herons Green Bath 44 B5
Heronsford S Ayrs 244 G4
Heronsgate Herts 85 G8
Heronston Bridgend 58 D2
Herra Shetland 312 D8
Herriard Hants 49 D7
Herringfleet Suff 143 D9
Herring's Green Beds 103 C11
Herringswell Suff 124 C4
Herringthorpe S Yorks 186 C6
Hersden Kent 71 G8
Hersham Corn 24 F3
Hersham Sur 66 G6
Herstmonceux E Sus 23 C10
Herston Dorset 18 F6
Herston Orkney 314 G4
Hertford Herts 86 C4
Hertford Heath Herts 86 C4
Hertingfordbury Herts 86 C4
Hesket Newmarket Cumb 230 D2
Hesketh Bank Lancs 194 C2
Hesketh Lane Lancs 203 E8
Hesketh Moss Lancs 194 C2
Heskin Green Lancs 194 D4
Hesleden Durham 234 D4
Hesleyside Northumb 251 G8
Heslington York 207 C8
Hessay York 206 C6
Hessenford Corn 6 D6
Hessett Suff 125 E8
Hessle E Yorks 200 B4
Hessle W Yorks 198 D2
Hest Bank Lancs 211 F9
Hester's Way Glos 99 G8
Hestinsetter Shetland 313 J4
Heston London 66 D6
Hestwall Orkney 314 E2
Heswall Mers 182 E3
Hethe Oxon 101 F11
Hethel Norf 142 C3
Hethelpit Cross Glos 98 F5
Hethersett Norf 142 C3
Hethersgill Cumb 239 D11
Hetherside Cumb 239 D10
Hetherson Green W Ches 167 F8
Hethpool Northumb 263 D9
Hett Durham 233 D11
Hetton N Yorks 204 B5
Hetton Downs T & W 234 B3
Hetton-le-Hill T & W 234 B3
Hetton-le-Hole T & W 234 B3
Hetton Steads Northumb 264 B2
Heugh Northumb 242 C3
Heugh-head Aberds 292 B5
Heveningham Suff 126 C6
Hever Kent 52 E3
Heversham Cumb 211 C9
Hevingham Norf 160 E3
Hew Green N Yorks 205 B10
Hewas Water Corn 5 F9
Hewelsfield Glos 79 E9
Hewelsfield Common Glos 79 E8
Hewer Hill Cumb 230 D3
Hewish N Som 60 G2
Hewish Som 28 F6
Hewood Dorset 28 G5
Heworth T & W 243 E7
Heworth York 207 C8
Hexham Northumb 241 E10
Hextable Kent 68 E4
Hexthorpe S Yorks 198 G5
Hexton Herts 104 E2
Hexworthy Devon 13 G9
Hey Lancs 204 E3
Hey Green W Yorks 196 E4
Hey Houses Lancs 193 B10
Heybridge Essex 88 D5
Heybridge Essex 87 F10
Heybridge Basin Essex 88 D5
Heybrook Bay Devon 7 F10
Heydon Cambs 105 C8
Heydon Norf 160 D2
Heydour Lincs 155 B10
Heyheads Gtr Man 196 G3
Heylipol Argyll 288 E1
Heylor Shetland 312 E4
Heyope Powys 114 C4
Heyrod Gtr Man 185 B7
Heysham Lancs 211 G8
Heyshaw N Yorks 214 G3
Heyshott W Sus 34 D5
Heyshott Green W Sus 34 D5
Heyside Gtr Man 196 F2
Heytesbury Wilts 46 E2
Heythrop Oxon 101 F7
Heywood Gtr Man 195 E11
Heywood Wilts 45 C11
Hibaldstow N Lincs 200 G3
Hibb's Green Suff 125 G7
Hickford Hill Essex 106 C5
Hickleton S Yorks 198 F3
Hickling Norf 161 E8
Hickling Notts 154 D3
Hickling Green Norf 161 E8
Hickling Heath Norf 161 E8
Hickling Pastures Notts 154 D3
Hickmans Green Kent 54 B5
Hicks Forstal Kent 71 G7
Hicks Gate Bath 60 F6
Hick's Mill Corn 4 G5
Hickstead W Sus 36 C3
Hidcote Bartrim Glos 100 C3
Hidcote Boyce Glos 100 C3
Hifnal Shrops 132 D4
Higginshaw Gtr Man 196 F2
High Ackworth W Yorks 198 D2
High Angerton Northumb 252 F3
High Bankhill Cumb 231 C7
High Banton N Lnrk 278 E4
High Barn Lincs 174 C5
High Barnes T & W 243 F9
High Barnet London 86 F2
High Beach Essex 86 F6
High Bentham N Yorks 212 F3
High Bickington Devon 25 C10
High Biggins Cumb 212 D2
High Birkwith N Yorks 212 D5
High Birstwith N Yorks 205 B10
High Blantyre S Lnrk 268 D3
High Bonnybridge Falk 278 F6
High Bradfield S Yorks 186 C3
High Bradley N Yorks 204 D6
High Bray Devon 41 G7
High Brooms Kent 52 E5
High Brotheridge Glos 80 C5
High Bullen Devon 25 C8
High Buston Northumb 252 B6
High Callerton Northumb 242 C5
High Cark Cumb 211 C7
High Casterton Cumb 212 D2
High Catton E Yorks 207 C10
High Church Northumb 252 F5
High Cogges Oxon 82 D5
High Common Norf 141 B9
High Coniscliffe Darl 224 B4
High Crompton Gtr Man 196 F2
High Cross Cambs 123 F8
High Cross Corn 2 D6
High Cross E Sus 37 B9
High Cross Hants 34 B2
High Cross Herts 85 F10
High Cross Herts 86 B5
High Cross Newport 59 B9
High Cross W Sus 36 D2
High Cross Warks 118 D3
High Crosshill S Lnrk 268 C2
High Cunsey Cumb 221 G7
High Dubmire T & W 234 B2
High Dyke Durham 232 F5
High Easter Essex 87 C10
High Eggborough N Yorks 198 C5
High Eldrig Dumfries 236 C4
High Ellington N Yorks 214 C3
High Ercall Telford 149 F11
High Etherley Durham 233 F9
High Ferry Lincs 174 F5
High Field Lancs 203 C10
High Flatts W Yorks 197 F8
High Forge Durham 242 G6
High Friarside Durham 242 F5
High Gallowhill E Dunb 278 G2
High Garrett Essex 106 F5
High Grange Durham 233 E9
High Grantley N Yorks 214 F4
High Green Cumb 221 E8
High Green Norf 141 B8
High Green Norf 142 B2
High Green Norf 159 G8
High Green S Yorks 186 B4
High Green Shrops 132 G4
High Green Suff 125 E7
High Green W Yorks 197 E7
High Green Worcs 99 B7
High Halden Kent 53 F11
High Halstow Medway 69 D9
High Ham Som 44 G2
High Handenhold Durham 242 G6
High Harrington Cumb 228 F6
High Harrogate N Yorks 206 B2
High Haswell Durham 234 C3
High Hatton Shrops 150 E2
High Hauxley Northumb 253 C7
High Hawsker N Yorks 227 D8
High Heath Shrops 150 D3
High Heath W Mid 133 C10
High Hesket Cumb 230 C5
High Hesleden Durham 234 D5
High Hill Cumb 229 G11
High Houses Essex 87 C11
High Hoyland S Yorks 197 E9
High Hunsley E Yorks 208 F4
High Hurstwood E Sus 37 B7
High Hutton N Yorks 216 F5
High Ireby Cumb 229 D10
High Kelling Norf 177 E10
High Kilburn N Yorks 215 D10
High Lands Durham 233 F8
High Lane Gtr Man 185 D7
High Lane Worcs 116 E3
High Lanes Corn 2 B3
High Laver Essex 87 D8
High Legh E Ches 184 E2
High Leven Stockton 225 C8
High Littleton Bath 44 B6
High Longthwaite Cumb 229 B11
High Lorton Cumb 229 F9
High Marishes N Yorks 216 D6
High Marnham Notts 188 G4
High Melton S Yorks 198 G4
High Mickley Northumb 242 E3
High Mindork Dumfries 236 D5
High Moor Derbys 187 E7
High Moor Lancs 194 E4
High Moorsley T & W 234 B2
High Nash Glos 79 C9
High Newton Cumb 211 C8
High Newton-by-the-Sea Northumb 264 D6
High Nibthwaite Cumb 210 B5
High Oaks Cumb 222 G2
High Offley Staffs 150 D5
High Ongar Essex 87 E9
High Onn Staffs 150 F6
High Onn Wharf Staffs 150 F6
High Park Cumb 221 G10
High Park Mers 193 D11
High Risby N Lincs 200 E2
High Roding Essex 87 B10
High Rougham Suff 125 E8
High Row Cumb 230 D3
High Row Cumb 230 G3
High Salvington W Sus 35 F10
High Scales Cumb 229 B9
High Sellafield Cumb 219 E10
High Shaw N Yorks 223 G7
High Shields T & W 243 D9
High Shincliffe Durham 233 C11
High Side Cumb 229 E10
High Southwick T & W 243 F9
High Spen T & W 242 F4
High Stakesby N Yorks 227 C7
High Stoop Durham 233 C8
High Street Corn 5 E9
High Street Kent 53 G8
High Street Pembs 73 B11
High Street Suff 107 B7
High Street Suff 127 D8
High Street Suff 127 F8
High Street Suff 143 G7
High Street Green Suff 125 F10
High Sunderland Borders 261 C11
High Throston Hrtlpl 234 E5
High Tirfergus Argyll 255 F7
High Town Luton 103 G11
High Town Shrops 132 E4
High Town Staffs 151 G9
High Toynton Lincs 174 B3
High Trewhitt Northumb 252 B2
High Urpeth Durham 242 G6
High Valleyfield Fife 279 D10
High Walton Cumb 219 C9
High Warden Northumb 241 D10
High Water Head Cumb 220 F6
High Westwood Durham 242 F4
High Whinnow Cumb 239 G8
High Woolaston Glos 79 F9
High Worsall N Yorks 225 D7
High Wray Cumb 221 F7
High Wych Herts 87 C7
High Wycombe Bucks 84 G5
Higham Derbys 170 D5
Higham Fife 286 F6
Higham Kent 69 E8
Higham Lancs 204 F2
Higham S Yorks 197 F10
Higham Suff 107 D10
Higham Suff 124 E4
Higham Common S Yorks 197 F10
Higham Dykes Northumb 242 B4
Higham Ferrers Northants 121 D9
Higham Gobion C Beds 104 E2
Higham Hill London 86 G5
Higham on the Hill Leics 135 D7
Higham Wood Kent 52 D5
Highampton Devon 25 G7
Highams Park London 86 G5
Highbridge Cumb 230 C3
Highbridge Hants 33 C7
Highbridge Highld 290 E3
Highbridge Som 43 D10
Highbridge W Mid 133 C10
Highbrook W Sus 51 G11
Highburton W Yorks 197 E7
Highbury London 67 B10
Highbury Ptsmth 33 G11
Highbury Som 45 D7
Highbury Vale Nottingham 171 G8
Highclere Hants 64 G2
Highcliffe Derbys 186 F2
Highcliffe Dorset 19 C10
Higher Alham Som 45 E7
Higher Ansty Dorset 30 G3
Higher Ashton Devon 14 E3
Higher Audley Blkburn 195 B7
Higher Bal Corn 4 E4
Higher Ballam Lancs 202 G3
Higher Bartle Lancs 202 G6
Higher Bebington Mers 182 D4
Higher Berry End C Beds 103 E9
Higher Blackley Gtr Man 195 G10
Higher Boarshaw Gtr Man 195 F11
Higher Bockhampton Dorset 17 C10
Higher Bojewyan Corn 1 C3
Higher Boscaswell Corn 1 C3
Higher Brixham Torbay 9 D8
Higher Broughton Gtr Man 195 G10
Higher Burrow Som 28 C6
Higher Burwardsley W Ches 167 D8
Higher Chalmington Dorset 29 G9
Higher Cheriton Devon 27 G10
Higher Chillington Som 28 E5
Higher Chisworth Derbys 185 C7
Higher Clovelly Devon 24 C4
Higher Condurrow Corn 2 B5
Higher Crackington Corn 11 B9
Higher Cransworth Corn 5 B9
Higher Croft Blkburn 195 B7
Higher Denham Bucks 66 B4
Higher Dinting Derbys 185 C8
Higher Disley E Ches 185 E7
Higher Downs Corn 2 C3
Higher Durston Som 28 B3
Higher End Gtr Man 194 G4
Higher Folds Gtr Man 195 G7
Higher Gabwell Torbay 9 B8
Higher Green Gtr Man 195 G8
Higher Halstock Leigh Dorset 29 F8
Higher Heysham Lancs 211 G8
Higher Hogshead Lancs 195 C11
Higher Holton Som 29 B11
Higher Hurdsfield E Ches 184 G6
Higher Kingcombe Dorset 16 B6
Higher Kinnerton Flint 166 C4
Higher Land Corn 12 G3
Higher Marsh Som 30 C2
Higher Melcombe Dorset 30 G2
Higher Menadew Corn 5 D10
Higher Molland Devon 41 G8
Higher Muddiford Devon 40 F5
Higher Nyland Dorset 30 C2
Higher Penwortham Lancs 194 B4
Higher Pertwood Wilts 45 F11
Higher Porthpean Corn 5 E10
Higher Poynton E Ches 184 E6
Higher Prestacott Devon 12 B3
Higher Rads End C Beds 103 E9
Higher Ridge Shrops 149 C7
Higher Rocombe Barton Devon 9 B8
Higher Row Dorset 31 G8
Higher Runcorn Halton 183 E8
Higher Sandford Dorset 29 C10
Higher Shotton Flint 166 B4
Higher Shurlach W Ches 183 G11
Higher Slade Devon 40 D4
Higher Street Som 42 E6
Higher Tale Devon 27 G9
Higher Tolcarne Corn 5 B7
Higher Totnell Dorset 29 F10
Higher Town Corn 5 C10
Higher Town Scilly 1 F4
Higher Town Som 42 D3
Higher Tremarcoombe Corn 6 B5
Higher Vexford Som 42 F6
Higher Walreddon Devon 12 G5
Higher Walton Lancs 194 B5
Higher Walton Warr 183 D9
Higher Wambrook Som 28 F3
Higher Warcombe Devon 40 D3
Higher Weaver Devon 27 G9
Higher Whatcombe Dorset 30 G4
Higher Wheelton Lancs 194 C6
Higher Whitley W Ches 183 E10
Higher Wincham W Ches 183 F11
Higher Woodsford Dorset 17 D11
Higher Wraxall Dorset 29 G9
Higher Wych W Ches 167 G7
Highercliff Corn 6 D4
Higherford Lancs 204 E3
Highertown Corn 4 G6
Highertown Corn 11 E8
Highfield E Yorks 207 F10
Highfield Glos 79 E10
Highfield Gtr Man 194 G5
Highfield Gtr Man 195 F8
Highfield Herts 85 D9
Highfield N Ayrs 266 E6
Highfield Oxon 101 G11
Highfield S Yorks 186 D5
Highfield Soton 32 E6
Highfield T & W 242 F4
Highfields Cambs 123 F7
Highfields Derbys 170 B6
Highfields Essex 88 B5
Highfields Glos 80 F3
Highfields Leicester 136 C2
Highfields Northumb 273 E9
Highfields S Yorks 198 F4
Highfields Staffs 151 E8
Highgate E Sus 52 G2
Highgate Kent 53 G9
Highgate London 67 B9
Highgate Powys 130 D2
Highgate S Yorks 198 G3
Highgate W Mid 133 F11
Highlane Derbys 186 E6
Highlane E Ches 168 B5
Highlanes Corn 10 G4
Highlanes Staffs 150 C5
Highlaws Cumb 229 B8
Highleadon Glos 98 G5
Highleigh W Sus 22 D4
Highley Shrops 132 G4
Highmoor Cumb 229 B11
Highmoor Oxon 65 B8
Highmoor Cross Oxon 65 C8
Highmoor Hill Mon 60 B3
Highnam Glos 80 B3
Highnam Green Glos 98 G5
Highoak Norf 141 C11
Highridge Bristol 60 F5
Highroad Well Moor W Yorks 196 B5
Highstead Kent 71 F8
Highsted Kent 70 G2
Highstreet Kent 70 G5
Highstreet Green Essex 106 E5
Highstreet Green Sur 50 F3
Hightae Dumfries 238 B3
Highter's Heath W Mid 117 B11
Hightown E Ches 168 C5
Hightown Hants 31 G11
Hightown Mers 193 G10
Hightown Soton 33 E7
Hightown W Yorks 197 C7
Hightown Wrex 166 F4
Hightown Green Suff 125 F9
Hightown Heights W Yorks 197 C7
Highway Corn 4 G4
Highway Hereford 97 B9
Highway Som 29 C7
Highway Wilts 62 E4
Highway Windsor 65 C11
Highweek Devon 14 G2
Highwood Devon 27 F10
Highwood Dorset 18 D3
Highwood Essex 87 E10
Highwood Hants 31 F11
Highwood Worcs 116 D3
Highwood Hill London 86 G2
Highworth Swindon 82 G2
Highworthy Devon 24 F6
Hilborough Norf 140 C6
Hilborough Ho Norf 140 C6
Hilcot Glos 81 B7
Hilcot End Glos 81 E9
Hilcote Derbys 171 D7
Hilcott Wilts 46 B6
Hilden Park Kent 52 D5
Hildenborough Kent 52 D5
Hildersham Cambs 105 B10
Hildersley Hereford 98 G2
Hilderstone Staffs 151 C8
Hilderthorpe E Yorks 218 F3
Hilfield Dorset 29 F10
Hilgay Norf 140 D2
Hill S Glos 79 G10
Hill W Mid 134 D2
Hill Warks 119 D9
Hill Bottom Oxon 64 D6
Hill Brow W Sus 34 B3
Hill Chorlton Staffs 150 B5
Hill Common Norf 161 E8
Hill Common Som 27 B11
Hill Corner Som 45 D10
Hill Croome Worcs 99 C7
Hill Dale Lancs 194 E3
Hill Deverill Wilts 45 E11
Hill Dyke Lincs 174 F4
Hill End Durham 232 D6
Hill End Fife 279 B10
Hill End Glos 99 D8
Hill End London 85 G8
Hill End N Yorks 205 C7
Hill End Som 29 E8
Hill End Worcs 117 E8
Hill Furze Worcs 99 B9
Hill Gate Hereford 97 F9
Hill Green Essex 105 E9
Hill Green Kent 69 G10
Hill Head Hants 33 G8
Hill Head Northumb 241 D10
Hill Hoath Kent 52 E3
Hill Hook W Mid 134 C2
Hill Houses Shrops 116 B2
Hill Mountain Pembs 73 D7
Hill of Beath Fife 280 C3
Hill of Drip Stirl 278 B5
Hill of Fearn Highld 301 B8
Hill of Keillor Angus 286 C6
Hill of Mountblairy Aberds 302 D6
Hill of Overbrae Aberds 303 C8
Hill Park Hants 33 F9
Hill Park Kent 52 B2
Hill Ridware Staffs 151 F11
Hill Side Hants 34 B3
Hill Side S Yorks 197 G8
Hill Side W Yorks 197 D7
Hill Side Worcs 116 E5
Hill Somersal Derbys 152 C2
Hill Street Kent 54 D6
Hill Top Derbys 186 F5
Hill Top Durham 232 G5
Hill Top Durham 233 C10
Hill Top Durham 242 G5
Hill Top Gtr Man 195 G8
Hill Top Hants 32 G6
Hill Top N Yorks 214 G3
Hill Top N Yorks 214 G5
Hill Top Notts 171 F7
Hill Top S Yorks 186 C5
Hill Top S Yorks 186 D3
Hill Top S Yorks 187 B7
Hill Top S Yorks 197 F9
Hill Top Staffs 133 B7
Hill Top W Mid 133 E9
Hill Top W Sus 34 C5
Hill Top W Yorks 196 E5
Hill Top W Yorks 197 D10
Hill Top W Yorks 205 G11
Hill Top W Yorks 205 G7
Hill Top Warks 134 E5
Hill Top Warks 135 E7
Hill View Dorset 18 B5
Hill Wood W Mid 134 C2
Hill Wootton Warks 118 D6
Hillam N Yorks 198 B4
Hillbeck Cumb 222 B5
Hillblock Pembs 73 B8
Hillborough Kent 71 F8
Hillbourne Poole 18 C6
Hillbrae Aberds 302 E6
Hillbrae Aberds 303 G7
Hillbutts Dorset 31 G7
Hillcliffe Warr 183 D10
Hillclifflane Derbys 170 F3
Hillcommon Som 27 B11
Hillcross Derbys 152 C6
Hilldyke Lincs 174 F4
Hillend Fife 280 E2
Hillend N Lnrk 268 B6
Hillend N Som 43 B11
Hillend Shrops 132 E6
Hillend Swansea 56 C2
Hillend Green Glos 98 F4
Hillersland Glos 79 C9
Hillerton Devon 13 B10
Hillesden Bucks 102 F3
Hillesden Hamlet Bucks 102 E3
Hillesley Glos 61 B9
Hillfarance Som 27 C11
Hillfarrance Som 27 C11
Hillfield Devon 8 E6
Hillfield W Mid 118 B2
Hillfields S Glos 60 D6
Hillfields W Mid 118 B6
Hillfoot Aberds 303 D9
Hillfoot W Yorks 205 G10
Hillfoot End C Beds 104 E2
Hillgreen W Berks 64 D3
Hillgrove W Sus 34 B6
Hillhampton Hereford 97 B11
Hillhead Aberds 302 F5
Hillhead Aberds 303 G8
Hillhead Corn 5 C11
Hillhead Devon 9 E8
Hillhead E Ayrs 257 B10
Hillhead S Ayrs 257 F10
Hillhead of Auchentumb Aberds 303 D9
Hillhead of Blairy Aberds 302 D6
Hillhead of Cocklaw Aberds 303 E10
Hillhouse Borders 271 D10
Hilliard's Cross Staffs 152 G3
Hilliclay Highld 310 C5
Hillingdon London 66 C5
Hillingdon Heath London 66 C5
Hillington Glasgow 267 C10
Hillington Norf 158 D4
Hillis Corner I o W 20 C5
Hillmoor Devon 27 E10
Hillmorton Warks 119 C10
Hillock Vale Lancs 195 B9
Hillockhead Aberds 292 B6
Hillockhead Aberds 292 C5
Hillpool Worcs 117 B7
Hillpound Hants 33 D9
Hills Town Derbys 171 B7
Hillsborough S Yorks 186 C4
Hillside Aberds 293 D11
Hillside Angus 293 G9
Hillside Devon 8 C4
Hillside Devon 27 F11
Hillside Hants 49 C9
Hillside Mers 193 E10
Hillside Orkney 314 G4
Hillside Orkney 314 D3
Hillside Shetland 313 G6
Hillside Shrops 131 F11
Hillside Wilts 81 G9
Hillstreet Hants 32 D4
Hillswick Shetland 312 F4
Hilltop Bl Gwent 77 D11
Hilltop Bucks 85 E7
Hilltop Derbys 170 C4
Hillview T & W 243 G9
Hillway I o W 21 D8
Hillwell Shetland 313 M5
Hillyfields Hants 32 D5
Hilmarton Wilts 62 D4
Hilperton Wilts 45 B11
Hilperton Marsh Wilts 45 B11
Hilsea Ptsmth 33 G11
Hilston E Yorks 209 G11
Hiltingbury Hants 32 C6
Hilton Aberds 303 F9
Hilton Borders 273 E7
Hilton Cambs 122 D5
Hilton Cumb 231 G10
Hilton Derbys 152 C4
Hilton Dorset 30 G3
Hilton Durham 233 G9
Hilton Highld 309 L7
Hilton Highld 311 L3
Hilton Shrops 132 D5
Hilton Staffs 133 B11
Hilton Stockton 225 C9
Hilton House Gtr Man 194 F6
Hilton Lodge Highld 300 G2
Hilton of Cadboll Highld 301 B8
Hilton Park Gtr Man 195 G10
Himbleton Worcs 117 F8
Himley Staffs 133 E7
Hincaster Cumb 211 C10
Hinchley Wood Sur 67 F7
Hinchliffe Mill W Yorks 196 F6
Hinchwick Glos 100 E2
Hinckley Leics 135 E8
Hinderclay Suff 125 B10
Hinderton W Ches 182 F4
Hinderwell N Yorks 226 B5
Hindford Shrops 148 C6
Hindhead Sur 49 F11
Hindle Fold Lancs 203 G10
Hindley Gtr Man 194 G6
Hindley Northumb 242 F2
Hindley Green Gtr Man 194 G6
Hindlip Worcs 117 F7
Hindolveston Norf 159 D10
Hindon Wilts 46 G2
Hindpool Cumb 210 F3
Hindringham Norf 159 B9
Hindsford Gtr Man 195 G7
Hingham Norf 141 C10
Hinstock Shrops 150 D3
Hintlesham Suff 107 C11
Hinton Glos 79 E11
Hinton Hants 19 B10
Hinton Hereford 96 D6
Hinton Northants 119 G10
Hinton S Glos 61 D8
Hinton Shrops 131 B8
Hinton Som 29 C9
Hinton Ampner Hants 33 B9
Hinton Blewett Bath 44 B5
Hinton Charterhouse Bath 45 B9
Hinton Cross Worcs 99 C10
Hinton-in-the-Hedges Northants 101 D11
Hinton Martell Dorset 31 F8
Hinton on the Green Worcs 99 C10
Hinton Parva Dorset 31 G7
Hinton Parva Swindon 63 C8
Hinton St George Som 28 E6
Hinton St Mary Dorset 30 D3
Hinton Waldrist Oxon 82 F5
Hints Shrops 116 C2
Hints Staffs 134 C3
Hinwick Beds 121 E8
Hinxhill Kent 54 E5
Hinxton Cambs 105 B9
Hinxworth Herts 104 C4
Hipperholme W Yorks 196 B6
Hipplecote Worcs 116 F4
Hipsburn Northumb 264 G6
Hipswell N Yorks 224 F3
Hirael Gwyn 179 G9
Hiraeth Carms 92 G3
Hirn Aberds 293 C9
Hirnant Powys 147 E11
Hirst N Lnrk 269 C7
Hirst Northumb 253 F7
Hirst Courtney N Yorks 198 C6
Hirwaen Denb 165 C10
Hirwaun Rhondda 77 D7
Hirwaun Common Bridgend 58 C2
Hiscott Devon 25 B8
Hislop Borders 249 C9
Hisomley Wilts 45 D11
Histon Cambs 123 E8
Hitcham Suff 125 G9
Hitchill Dumfries 238 D4
Hitchin Herts 104 F3
Hitchin Hill Herts 104 F3
Hitcombe Bottom Wilts 45 E10
Hither Green London 67 E11
Hittisleigh Devon 13 C10
Hittisleigh Barton Devon 13 B10
Hive E Yorks 208 G2
Hixon Staffs 151 D10
Hoaden Kent 55 B9
Hoar Cross Staffs 152 E2
Hoarwithy Hereford 97 F10
Hoath Kent 71 G8
Hoath Corner Kent 52 E3
Hob Hill W Ches 167 E7
Hobarris Shrops 114 B6
Hobbister Orkney 314 F3
Hobble End Staffs 133 B10
Hobbles Green Suff 124 G4
Hobbs Cross Essex 87 C7
Hobbs Cross Essex 87 F7
Hobbs Wall Bath 61 G7
Hobkirk Borders 262 G3
Hobroyd Derbys 185 C8
Hobson Durham 242 F5
Hoby Leics 154 F3
Hoccombe Som 27 B10
Hockenden London 68 F3
Hockerill Herts 105 G9
Hockering Norf 159 G11
Hockering Heath Norf 159 G11
Hockerton Notts 172 D2
Hockholler Som 27 C11
Hockholler Green Som 27 C11
Hockley E Ches 184 E6
Hockley Essex 88 G4
Hockley Kent 54 B3
Hockley Staffs 134 C4
Hockley W Mid 118 B5
Hockley Heath W Mid 118 C3
Hockliffe C Beds 103 F9
Hockwold cum Wilton Norf 140 F4
Hockworthy Devon 27 D8
Hocombe Hants 32 C6
Hoddesdon Herts 86 D5
Hoddlesden Blkburn 195 C8
Hoddom Mains Dumfries 238 C5
Hoddomcross Dumfries 238 C5
Hoden Worcs 99 B11
Hodgefield Staffs 168 E6
Hodgehill E Ches 168 B4
Hodgehill W Mid 134 F2
Hodgeston Pembs 73 F8
Hodgley Powys 130 E3
Hodnet Shrops 150 D2
Hodnetheath Shrops 150 D2
Hodsock Notts 187 D10
Hodsoll Street Kent 68 G6
Hodson Swindon 63 C7
Hodthorpe Derbys 187 F8
Hoe Hants 33 D9
Hoe Norf 159 F9
Hoe Sur 50 D5
Hoe Benham W Berks 64 F2
Hoe Gate Hants 33 E10
Hoff Cumb 222 B3
Hoffleet Stow Lincs 156 B4
Hog Hatch Sur 49 D10
Hogaland Shetland 312 F5
Hogben's Hill Kent 54 B4
Hogganfield Glasgow 268 B2
Hoggard's Green Suff 125 F7
Hoggeston Bucks 102 G6
Hoggington Wilts 45 B10
Hoggrill's End Warks 134 E4
Hogha Gearraidh W Isles 296 D3
Hoghton Lancs 194 B6
Hoghton Bottoms Lancs 194 B6
Hogley Green W Yorks 196 F6
Hognaston Derbys 170 E2
Hogpits Bottom Herts 85 E8
Hogsthorpe Lincs 191 G8
Hogstock Dorset 31 F7
Holbeach Lincs 157 E7
Holbeach Bank Lincs 157 D7
Holbeach Clough Lincs 156 D6
Holbeach Drove Lincs 156 G6
Holbeach Hurn Lincs 157 D7
Holbeach St Johns Lincs 156 F6
Holbeach St Marks Lincs 157 C7
Holbeach St Matthew Lincs 157 C8
Holbeache Worcs 116 B5
Holbeck Notts 187 G8
Holbeck W Yorks 205 G11
Holbeck Woodhouse Notts 187 G8
Holberrow Green Worcs 117 F10
Holbeton Devon 8 E2
Holborn London 67 C10
Holborough Kent 69 G8
Holbrook Derbys 170 G5
Holbrook S Yorks 186 E6
Holbrook Suff 108 D3
Holbrook Common S Glos 61 E7
Holbrook Moor Derbys 170 F5
Holbrooks W Mid 134 G6
Holburn Northumb 264 B2
Holbury Hants 32 G6
Holcombe Devon 14 G5
Holcombe Gtr Man 195 D9
Holcombe Som 45 D7
Holcombe Brook Gtr Man 195 E9
Holcombe Rogus Devon 27 D9
Holcot Northants 120 D5
Holdbrook London 86 F5
Holden Lancs 203 D11
Holden Fold Gtr Man 196 F2
Holdenby Northants 120 D3
Holdenhurst Bmouth 19 B8
Holder's Green Essex 106 F2
Holders Hill London 86 G2
Holdfast Worcs 99 D7
Holdgate Shrops 131 F11
Holdingham Lincs 173 F9
Holditch Dorset 28 G4

Holdsworth W Yorks 196 B5
Holdworth S Yorks 186 C3
Hole Devon 24 D4
Hole W Yorks 204 F6
Hole Bottom W Yorks 196 C2
Hole-in-the-Wall Hereford 98 F2
Hole Street W Sus 35 E10
Holefield Borders 263 C8
Holehills N Lnrk 268 B5
Holehouse Derbys 185 C8
Holehouses E Ches 184 F2
Holemill Aberdeen 293 C10
Holemoor Devon 24 F6
Hole's Hole Devon 7 B8
Holestane Dumfries 247 D9
Holestone Derbys 170 C4
Holewater Devon 41 F8
Holford Som 43 E7
Holgate York 207 C7
Holker Cumb 211 D7
Holkham Norf 176 E5
Hollacombe Devon 24 G5
Hollacombe Devon 26 G4
Hollacombe Hill Devon 7 E10
Holland Orkney 314 D6
Holland Orkney 314 A4
Holland Sur 52 C2
Holland Fen Lincs 174 F2
Holland Lees Lancs 194 F4
Holland-on-Sea Essex 89 B12
Hollands Som 29 D9
Hollandstoun Orkney 314 A7
Hollee Dumfries 239 D7
Hollesley Suff 109 C7
Hollicombe Torbay 9 C7
Hollies Common Staffs 150 E6
Hollin Hall Lancs 204 F4
Hollin Park W Yorks 206 F2
Hollinfare Warr 183 C11
Hollingbourne Kent 53 B10
Hollingbury Brighton 36 F4
Hollingdean Brighton 36 F4
Hollingdon Bucks 103 F7
Hollingrove E Sus 37 C11
Hollingthorpe W Yorks 197 D10
Hollington Derbys 152 B4
Hollington E Sus 38 E3
Hollington Hants 48 B2
Hollington Staffs 151 B11
Hollington Cross Hants 48 B2
Hollington Grove Derbys 152 B4
Hollingwood Derbys 186 G6
Hollingworth Gtr Man 185 B8
Hollins Cumb 222 G3
Hollins Derbys 186 G4
Hollins Gtr Man 195 F10
Hollins Gtr Man 195 F11
Hollins Gtr Man 195 F8
Hollins Staffs 168 D6
Hollins Staffs 168 E4
Hollins Staffs 169 F7
Hollins End S Yorks 186 E5
Hollins Green Warr 183 C11
Hollins Lane Lancs 202 C5
Hollins Lane Shrops 149 B10
Hollinsclough Staffs 169 B9
Hollinsgreen E Ches 168 C2
Hollinswood Telford 132 B4
Hollinthorpe W Yorks 206 G3
Hollinwood Gtr Man 196 G2
Hollinwood Shrops 149 B10
Hollis Green Devon 27 F9
Hollis Head Devon 27 G7
Hollocombe Devon 25 E10
Hollocombe Town Devon 25 E10
Hollow Brook Bath 60 G5
Hollow Meadows S Yorks 186 D2
Hollow Oak Dorset 18 C2
Hollow Street Kent 71 G8
Holloway Derbys 170 D4
Holloway Wilts 45 G11
Holloway Windsor 65 C10
Holloway Hill Sur 50 E3
Hollowell Northants 120 C3
Hollowmoor Heath W Ches 167 B7
Hollows Dumfries 239 B9
Holly Bank W Mid 133 C11
Holly Brook Som 44 D4
Holly Bush Wrex 166 G6
Holly Cross Windsor 65 C10
Holly End Norf 139 B9
Holly Green Bucks 84 E3
Holly Green Worcs 99 C7
Holly Hill N Yorks 224 E3
Hollyberry End W Mid 134 G5
Hollybush Caerph 77 E11
Hollybush E Ayrs 257 G9
Hollybush Stoke 168 G5
Hollybush Torf 78 G3
Hollybush Worcs 98 D5
Hollybush Corner Bucks 66 B3
Hollybush Corner Suff 125 F8
Hollybush Hill Bucks 66 C3
Hollybush Hill Essex 89 B10
Hollybushes Kent 54 B2
Hollycroft Leics 135 E8
Hollyhurst Shrops 131 D9
Hollyhurst Warks 135 F7
Hollym E Yorks 201 B10
Hollywaste Shrops 116 B2
Hollywater Hants 49 G10
Hollywood Worcs 117 B11
Holmacott Devon 25 B8
Holman Clavel Som 28 D2
Holmbridge W Yorks 196 F6
Holmbury St Mary Sur 50 E6
Holmbush Corn 5 E10
Holmbush Dorset 28 G5
Holmcroft Staffs 151 D8
Holme C Beds 104 C3
Holme Cambs 138 F3
Holme Cumb 211 D10
Holme N Lincs 200 F2
Holme N Yorks 215 C7
Holme Notts 172 D4
Holme W Yorks 196 F6
Holme W Yorks 205 G9
Holme Chapel Lancs 195 B11
Holme Green C Beds 104 C3
Holme Green N Yorks 207 E7
Holme Green Wokingham 65 F10
Holme Hale Norf 141 B7
Holme Hill NE Lincs 201 F9
Holme Lacy Hereford 97 D11
Holme Lane Notts 154 B2
Holme Marsh Hereford 114 G6
Holme Mills Cumb 211 D10
Holme next the Sea Norf 176 E2
Holme-on-Spalding-Moor E Yorks 208 F2
Holme on the Wolds E Yorks 208 D5
Holme Pierrepont Notts 154 B2
Holme St Cuthbert Cumb 229 B8
Holme Slack Lancs 203 G7
Holme Wood W Yorks 205 G9
Holmebridge Dorset 18 D3
Holmer Hereford 97 C10
Holmer Green Bucks 84 F6
Holmes Lancs 194 D2
Holmes Chapel E Ches 168 B3
Holmesdale Derbys 186 F5
Holmesfield Derbys 186 F4
Holmes's Hill E Sus 23 C8
Holmeswood Lancs 194 D2
Holmethorpe Sur 51 C9
Holmewood Derbys 170 B6
Holmfield W Yorks 196 B5
Holmfirth W Yorks 196 F6
Holmhead Angus 293 F7
Holmhead Dumfries 246 F6
Holmhead E Ayrs 258 E3
Holmhill Dumfries 247 D9
Holmisdale Highld 297 G7
Holmley Common Derbys 186 F5
Holmpton E Yorks 201 C11
Holmrook Cumb 219 F11
Holmsgarth Shetland 313 J6
Holmside Durham 233 B10
Holmsleigh Green Devon 28 G2
Holmston S Ayrs 257 E9
Holmwood Corner Sur 51 E7
Holmwrangle Cumb 230 B6
Holne Devon 8 B4
Holnest Dorset 29 E11
Holnicote Som 42 D2
Holsworthy Devon 24 G4
Holsworthy Beacon Devon 24 F5
Holt Dorset 31 G8
Holt Hants 49 C8
Holt Mers 183 C7
Holt Norf 159 B11
Holt Wilts 61 G11
Holt Worcs 116 E6
Holt Wrex 166 E6
Holt End Hants 49 F7
Holt End Worcs 117 D11
Holt Fleet Worcs 116 E6
Holt Green Lancs 193 G11
Holt Head W Yorks 196 E5
Holt Heath Dorset 31 G9
Holt Heath Worcs 116 E6
Holt Hill Kent 53 B8
Holt Hill Staffs 152 D2
Holt Park W Yorks 205 E11
Holt Pound Hants 49 E10
Holt Wood Dorset 31 F8
Holtby York 207 C9
Holton Oxon 83 D10
Holton Som 29 B11
Holton Suff 127 B7
Holton cum Beckering Lincs 189 E10
Holton Heath Dorset 18 C4
Holton le Clay Lincs 201 G9
Holton le Moor Lincs 189 B9
Holton St Mary Suff 107 D11
Holts Gtr Man 196 G3
Holtspur Bucks 84 G6
Holtye E Sus 52 F3
Holway Dorset 28 G5
Holway Dorset 29 C10
Holway Flint 181 F11
Holway Som 28 C2
Holwell Dorset 30 E2
Holwell Herts 104 E3
Holwell Leics 154 E4
Holwell Oxon 82 D2
Holwell Som 45 D8
Holwellbury C Beds 104 E3
Holwick Durham 232 F4
Holworth Dorset 17 E11
Holy City Devon 28 G3
Holy Cross T & W 243 D8
Holy Cross Worcs 117 B8
Holy Island Northumb 273 B11
Holy Vale Scilly 1 G4
Holybourne Hants 49 E8
Holyfield Essex 86 E5
Holyhead = Caergybi Anglesey 178 E2
Holylee Borders 261 B9
Holymoorside Derbys 170 B4
Holyport Windsor 65 D11
Holystone Northumb 251 C11
Holytown N Lnrk 268 C5
Holywell C Beds 85 B8
Holywell Cambs 122 C6
Holywell Corn 4 D5
Holywell Dorset 29 G9
Holywell E Sus 23 F9
Holywell Glos 80 G3
Holywell Hereford 97 C7
Holywell Herts 85 F9
Holywell Northumb 243 C8
Holywell Som 29 E8
Holywell Warks 118 D3
Holywell = Treffynnon Flint 181 F11
Holywell Green W Yorks 196 D5
Holywell Lake Som 27 C10
Holywell Row Suff 124 B4
Holywood Dumfries 247 G10
Hom Green Hereford 97 G11
Homedowns Glos 99 E8
Homer Shrops 132 C2
Homer Green Mers 193 G10
Homersfield Suff 142 F5
Homerton London 67 B11
Homington Wilts 31 B10
Honey Hall N Som 60 G2
Honey Hill Kent 70 G6
Honey Street Wilts 62 G6
Honey Tye Suff 107 D9
Honeybourne Worcs 100 C2
Honeychurch Devon 25 G10
Honeydon Beds 122 F2
Honeyhill Wokingham 65 F10
Honeystreet Wilts 62 G6
Honeywick C Beds 103 G9
Honicknowle Plym 7 D9
Honiley Warks 118 C4
Honing Norf 160 D6
Honingham Norf 160 G2
Honington Lincs 172 G6
Honington Suff 125 C8
Honington Warks 100 C5
Honiton Devon 27 G11
Honkley Wrex 166 D4
Honley W Yorks 196 E6
Honley Moor W Yorks 196 E6
Honnington Telford 150 F4
Honor Oak London 67 E11
Honor Oak Park London 67 E11
Honresfeld Gtr Man 196 D2
Hoo Kent 71 G9
Hoo End Herts 85 B11
Hoo Green E Ches 184 E2
Hoo Hole W Yorks 196 B4
Hoo Meavy Devon 7 B10
Hoo St Werburgh Medway 69 E9
Hoober S Yorks 186 B6
Hoobrook Worcs 116 C6
Hood Green S Yorks 197 G10
Hood Hill S Yorks 186 B5
Hood Manor Warr 183 D9
Hooe E Sus 23 D11
Hooe Plym 7 E10
Hooe Common E Sus 23 C11
Hoofield W Ches 167 C8
Hoohill Blkpool 202 F2
Hook Cambs 139 E8
Hook Devon 28 F4
Hook E Yorks 199 B9
Hook Hants 33 F8
Hook Hants 49 C8
Hook London 67 G7
Hook Pembs 73 C7
Hook Wilts 62 C5
Hook-a-gate Shrops 131 B9
Hook Bank Worcs 98 C6
Hook End Essex 87 F9
Hook End Oxon 65 C7
Hook End W Mid 134 G4
Hook Green Kent 53 F7
Hook Green Kent 68 F6
Hook Heath Sur 50 B3
Hook Norton Oxon 101 E7
Hook Park Hants 33 G7
Hook Street Glos 79 F11
Hook Street Wilts 62 C5
Hooke Dorset 16 B6
Hooker Gate T & W 242 F4
Hookgate Staffs 150 B4
Hook's Cross Herts 104 G5
Hookway W Sus 34 D4
Hookway Devon 14 B3
Hookwood Sur 51 E9
Hoole W Ches 166 B6
Hoole Bank W Ches 166 B6
Hooley Sur 51 B9
Hooley Bridge Gtr Man 195 E11
Hooley Brow Gtr Man 195 E11
Hooley Hill Gtr Man 184 B6
Hoop Mon 79 D8
Hoopers Pool Wilts 45 C10
Hoops Devon 24 C5
Hooton W Ches 182 F5
Hooton Levitt S Yorks 187 C8
Hooton Pagnell S Yorks 198 F3
Hooton Roberts S Yorks 187 B7
Hop Pole Lincs 156 G3
Hopcroft's Holt Oxon 101 F9
Hope Derbys 185 E11
Hope Devon 9 G8
Hope Highld 308 D4
Hope Powys 130 B5
Hope Shrops 130 C6
Hope Staffs 169 D10
Hope = Yr Hôb Flint 166 D4
Hope Bagot Shrops 115 C11
Hope Bowdler Shrops 131 E9
Hope End Green Essex 105 G11
Hope Green E Ches 184 E6
Hope Mansell Hereford 79 B10
Hope Park Shrops 130 C6
Hope under Dinmore Hereford 115 G10
Hopebeck Cumb 229 G9
Hopedale Staffs 169 D10
Hopeman Moray 301 C11
Hope's Green Essex 69 B9
Hope's Rough Hereford 98 B2
Hopesay Shrops 131 G7
Hopesgate Shrops 130 C6
Hopetown W Yorks 197 C11
Hopgoods Green W Berks 64 F4
Hopkinstown Rhondda 77 G9
Hopley's Green Hereford 114 G6
Hopperton N Yorks 206 B4
Hopsford Warks 135 G8
Hopstone Shrops 132 E5
Hopton Derbys 170 E3
Hopton Shrops 149 D11
Hopton Shrops 149 E7
Hopton Staffs 151 D8
Hopton Suff 125 B9
Hopton Cangeford Shrops 131 G10
Hopton Castle Shrops 115 B7
Hopton Heath Staffs 151 D9
Hopton on Sea Norf 143 D10
Hopton Wafers Shrops 116 B2
Hoptonbank Shrops 116 B2
Hoptongate Shrops 131 G10
Hoptonheath Shrops 115 B7
Hopwas Staffs 134 B3
Hopwood Gtr Man 195 F11
Hopwood Worcs 117 B10
Hopworthy Devon 24 G4
Horam E Sus 23 B9
Horbling Lincs 156 B2
Horbury W Yorks 197 D9
Horbury Bridge W Yorks 197 D9
Horbury Junction W Yorks 197 D10
Horcott Glos 81 E11
Horden Durham 234 C4
Horderley Shrops 131 F8
Hordle Hants 19 B11
Hordley Shrops 149 C7
Horeb Carms 75 D7
Horeb Carms 93 F10
Horeb Ceredig 93 C7
Horeb Flint 166 D3
Horfield Bristol 60 D6
Horgabost W Isles 305 J2
Horham Suff 126 C4
Horkesley Heath Essex 107 F9
Horkstow N Lincs 200 D3
Horkstow Wolds N Lincs 200 D3
Horley Oxon 101 C8
Horley Sur 51 E9
Horn Ash Dorset 28 G5
Horn Hill Som 43 E8
Horn Street Kent 55 F7
Horn Street Kent 69 G7
Hornblotton Som 44 G5
Hornblotton Green Som 44 G5
Hornby Lancs 211 F11
Hornby N Yorks 224 G4
Hornby N Yorks 225 D7
Horncastle Lincs 174 B3
Horncastle Reading 65 E7
Hornchurch London 68 B4
Horncliffe Northumb 273 F8
Horndean Borders 273 F7
Horndean Hants 34 E2
Horndon Devon 12 F6
Horndon on the Hill Thurrock 69 C7
Horne Sur 51 E10
Horne Row Essex 88 E3
Horner Som 41 D11
Horner's Green Suff 107 C9
Hornestreet Essex 107 E10
Horney Common E Sus 37 B7
Hornick Corn 5 E9
Horniehaugh Angus 292 G6
Horning Norf 160 F6
Horninghold Leics 136 D6
Horninglow Staffs 152 D4
Horningsea Cambs 123 E9
Horningsham Wilts 45 E10
Horningtoft Norf 159 E8
Horningtops Corn 6 C5
Horns Corner Kent 38 B2
Horns Cross Devon 24 C5
Horns Cross E Sus 38 C4
Horns Green Kent 52 B3
Hornsbury Som 28 E4
Hornsby Cumb 240 G2
Hornsea E Yorks 209 D10
Hornsea Bridge E Yorks 209 D10
Hornsea Burton E Yorks 209 D10
Hornsey London 67 B10
Hornsey Vale London 67 B10
Hornton Oxon 101 B7
Horpit Swindon 63 C8
Horrabridge Devon 7 B10
Horringer Suff 124 E6
Horringford I o W 20 D6
Horrocks Fold Gtr Man 195 E8
Horrocksford Lancs 203 E10
Horsalls Kent 53 C11
Horse Bridge Staffs 169 E7
Horsebridge Devon 12 G4
Horsebridge Hants 47 G10
Horsebridge Shrops 131 B7
Horsebrook Devon 8 D4
Horsebrook Staffs 151 G7
Horsecastle N Som 60 F2
Horsedown Wilts 61 D10
Horsedowns Corn 2 C4
Horsehay Telford 132 B3
Horseheath Cambs 106 B2
Horseholm Dumfries 238 C2
Horsehouse N Yorks 213 C10
Horseley Heath W Mid 133 E9
Horsell Sur 50 B3
Horsell Birch Sur 50 B3
Horseman Side Essex 87 F8
Horseman's Green Wrex 166 G6
Horsemere Green W Sus 35 G7
Horsenden Bucks 84 E3
Horsepools Glos 80 C4
Horseway Cambs 139 F8
Horseway Head Hereford 114 E6
Horsey Norf 161 E9
Horsey Som 43 F10
Horsey Corner Norf 161 E9
Horsey Down Wilts 81 G9
Horsford Norf 160 F3
Horsforth W Yorks 205 F10
Horsforth Woodside W Yorks 205 F10
Horsham W Sus 51 G7
Horsham Worcs 116 F4
Horsham St Faith Norf 160 F4
Horshoe Green Kent 52 E3
Horsington Lincs 173 B11
Horsington Som 30 C2
Horsley Derbys 170 G5
Horsley Glos 80 F4
Horsley Northumb 242 D3
Horsley Northumb 251 D8
Horsley Cross Essex 108 F2
Horsley Hill T & W 243 D9
Horsley Woodhouse Derbys 170 G5
Horsleycross Street Essex 108 F2
Horsleyhill Borders 262 F2
Horsleyhope Durham 233 B7
Horsleys Green Bucks 84 F3
Horsmonden Kent 53 E7
Horspath Oxon 83 E9
Horstead Norf 160 F5
Horsted Green E Sus 23 B7
Horsted Keynes W Sus 36 B5
Horton Bucks 84 B6
Horton Dorset 31 F8
Horton Kent 54 B6
Horton Lancs 204 C3
Horton Northants 120 G6
Horton S Glos 61 C9
Horton Shrops 149 D9
Horton Som 28 E4
Horton Staffs 168 D6
Horton Swansea 56 D3
Horton Telford 150 G3
Horton Wilts 62 G5
Horton Windsor 66 D4
Horton Common Dorset 31 F9
Horton Cross Som 28 D4
Horton-cum-Studley Oxon 83 C9
Horton Green W Ches 167 F7
Horton Heath Dorset 31 F9
Horton Heath Hants 33 D7
Horton in Ribblesdale N Yorks 212 E6
Horton Kirby Kent 68 F5
Horton Wharf Bucks 84 B6
Hortonlane Shrops 149 G8
Hortonwood Telford 150 G3
Horwich Gtr Man 194 E6
Horwich End Derbys 185 E8
Horwood Devon 25 B8
Horwood Riding S Glos 61 B8
Hoscar Lancs 194 E3
Hose Leics 154 D4
Hoselaw Borders 263 C8
Hoses Cumb 220 G4
Hosey Hill Kent 52 C3
Hosh Perth 286 E2
Hosta W Isles 296 D3
Hoswick Shetland 313 L6
Hotham E Yorks 208 G3
Hothfield Kent 54 D3
Hotley Bottom Bucks 84 E5
Hoton Leics 153 E11
Hotwells Bristol 60 E5
Houbans Shetland 312 F5
Houbie Shetland 312 D8
Houdston S Ayrs 244 D5
Hough Argyll 288 E1
Hough E Ches 168 E2
Hough E Ches 184 F5
Hough Green Halton 183 D7
Hough-on-the-Hill Lincs 172 F6
Hough Side W Yorks 205 G10
Hougham Lincs 172 G5
Houghton Cambs 122 C5
Houghton Cumb 239 F10
Houghton Hants 47 G10
Houghton Northumb 242 D4
Houghton Pembs 73 D7
Houghton W Sus 35 E8
Houghton Bank Darl 233 G10
Houghton Conquest C Beds 103 C10
Houghton Green E Sus 38 C6
Houghton Green Warr 183 C10
Houghton-le-Side Darl 233 G10
Houghton-le-Spring T & W 234 B2
Houghton on the Hill Leics 136 C3
Houghton Regis C Beds 103 G10
Houghton St Giles Norf 159 B8
Houghwood Mers 194 G4
Houlland Shetland 312 B7
Houlland Shetland 312 F7
Houlland Shetland 313 H5
Houlland Shetland 313 J6
Houlsyke N Yorks 226 D4
Hound Hants 33 F7
Hound Green Hants 49 B8
Hound Hill Dorset 31 G7
Houndmills Hants 48 C6
Houndscroft Glos 80 E5
Houndslow Borders 272 F2
Houndsmoor Som 27 B10
Houndstone Som 29 D8
Houndwood Borders 272 C6
Hounsdown Hants 32 E5
Hounsley Batch N Som 60 G4
Hounslow London 66 D6
Hounslow Green Essex 87 B11
Hounslow West London 66 D6
Hourston Orkney 314 E2
Housabister Shetland 313 H6
Housay Shetland 312 F8
House of Daviot Highld 301 E7
House of Glenmuick Aberds 292 D5
Househill Highld 301 D8
Houses Hill W Yorks 197 D7
Housetter Shetland 312 E5
Housham Tye Essex 87 C8
Houss Shetland 313 K5
Houston Renfs 267 B8
Housty Highld 310 F5
Houton Orkney 314 F3
Hove Brighton 36 G3
Hove Edge W Yorks 196 C6
Hoveringham Notts 171 F11
Hoveton Norf 160 F6
Hovingham N Yorks 216 D3
How Cumb 240 F2
How Caple Hereford 98 E2
How End C Beds 103 C10
How Green Kent 52 D3
How Hill Norf 161 F7
How Wood Herts 85 E10
Howbeck Bank E Ches 167 F11
Howbrook S Yorks 186 B4
Howden Borders 262 E5
Howden E Yorks 199 B8
Howden W Loth 269 B11
Howden Clough W Yorks 197 B8
Howden-le-Wear Durham 233 E9
Howdon T & W 243 D8
Howdon Pans T & W 243 D8
Howe Highld 310 C7
Howe N Yorks 214 C6
Howe Norf 142 C5
Howe Bridge Gtr Man 195 G7
Howe Green Essex 88 E2
Howe Green Essex 87 B8
Howe Green Warks 134 F6
Howe of Teuchar Aberds 303 E7
Howe Street Essex 87 C11
Howe Street Essex 106 E3
Howegreen Essex 88 E4
Howell Lincs 173 F10
Howey Powys 113 F11
Howford Borders 261 B8
Howford Borders 261 E9
Howgate Cumb 228 G5
Howgate Midloth 270 D4
Howgill Cumb 222 F2
Howgill Lancs 204 D2
Howgill N Yorks 205 B7
Howick Mon 79 F8
Howick Northumb 265 F7
Howick Cross Lancs 194 B4
Howle Durham 233 F7
Howle Telford 150 E3
Howleigh Som 28 D2
Howlett End Essex 105 E11
Howley Glos 80 G2
Howley Som 28 F3
Howley Warr 183 D10
Hownam Borders 263 F7
Hownam Mains Borders 263 E7
Howpasley Borders 249 B8
Howsen Worcs 116 G5
Howsham N Lincs 200 G4
Howsham N Yorks 216 G4
Howslack Dumfries 248 B3
Howt Green Kent 69 F11
Howtel Northumb 263 C9
Howton Hereford 97 F8
Howtown Cumb 221 B8
Howwood Renfs 267 C7
Hoxne Suff 126 B3
Hoxton London 67 C10
Hoy Orkney 314 F2
Hoylake Mers 182 D2
Hoyland S Yorks 197 G11
Hoyland Common S Yorks 197 G11
Hoylandswaine S Yorks 197 G9
Hoyle W Sus 34 D6
Hoyle Mill S Yorks 197 F11
Hubbard's Hill Kent 52 C4
Hubberholme N Yorks 213 D8
Hubberston Pembs 72 D5
Hubbersty Head Cumb 221 G8
Hubberton Green W Yorks 196 C4
Hubbert's Bridge Lincs 174 G3
Huby N Yorks 205 D11
Huby N Yorks 215 F11
Hucclecote Glos 80 B5
Hucking Kent 53 B10
Hucknall Notts 171 F8
Hud Hey Lancs 195 C9
Huddersfield W Yorks 196 D6
Huddington Worcs 117 F8
Huddisford Devon 24 D4
Huddlesford Staffs 134 B3
Hudnall Herts 85 C8
Hudnalls Glos 79 E8
Hudswell N Yorks 224 E3
Hudswell Wilts 61 F11
Huggate E Yorks 208 B3
Hugglepit Devon 24 C4
Hugglescote Leics 153 G8
Hugh Mill Lancs 195 C10
Hugh Town Scilly 1 G4
Hughenden Valley Bucks 84 F5
Hughley Shrops 131 D11
Hugus Corn 4 G5
Huish Devon 25 B7
Huish Devon 25 E8
Huish Wilts 62 G6
Huish Champflower Som 27 B9
Huish Episcopi Som 28 B6
Huisinis W Isles 305 G1
Hulcote C Beds 103 D8
Hulcote Northants 102 B4
Hulcott Bucks 84 B5
Hull End Derbys 185 E9
Hulland Derbys 170 F2
Hulland Moss Derbys 170 F3
Hulland Ward Derbys 170 F3
Hullavington Wilts 61 C11
Hullbridge Essex 88 G4
Hulme Gtr Man 184 B4
Hulme Staffs 168 F6
Hulme Warr 183 C10
Hulme End Staffs 169 D10
Hulme Walfield E Ches 168 B4
Hulseheath E Ches 184 E2
Hulver Street Suff 143 F9
Hulverstone I o W 20 E3
Humber Devon 14 G3
Humber Hereford 115 F10
Humber Bridge N Lincs 200 C4
Humberston NE Lincs 201 F10
Humberston Fitties NE Lincs 201 F10
Humberstone Leicester 136 B2
Humbie E Loth 271 C9
Humble Green Suff 107 B8
Humbledon T & W 243 F9
Humbleton E Yorks 209 G10
Humbleton Northumb 263 D11
Humby Lincs 155 C10
Hume Borders 272 G4
Hummersknott Darl 224 C5
Humshaugh Northumb 241 C10
Huna Highld 310 B7
Huncoat Lancs 203 G11
Huncote Leics 135 D10
Hundalee Borders 262 F4
Hundall Derbys 186 F5
Hunderthwaite Durham 232 G5
Hunderton Hereford 97 D9
Hundle Houses Lincs 174 E3
Hundleby Lincs 174 B5
Hundleshope Borders 260 B6
Hundleton Pembs 73 E7
Hundon Suff 106 B4
Hundred Acres Hants 33 E9
Hundred End Lancs 194 C2
Hundred House Powys 114 G2
Hungarton Leics 136 B3
Hungate W Yorks 197 B11
Hunger Hill Gtr Man 195 F7
Hunger Hill Lancs 194 E4
Hungerford Hants 31 E11
Hungerford Shrops 131 F10
Hungerford Som 42 E4
Hungerford W Berks 63 F10
Hungerford Windsor 65 E10
Hungerford Green W Berks 64 D5
Hungerford Newtown W Berks 63 E11
Hungershall Park Kent 52 F5
Hungerstone Hereford 97 D8
Hungerton Lincs 155 D7
Hungladder Highld 298 B3
Hungreyhatton Shrops 150 D3
Hunmanby N Yorks 217 D11
Hunmanby Moor N Yorks 218 D2
Hunningham Warks 119 D7
Hunningham Hill Warks 119 D7
Hunnington Worcs 133 G9
Hunny Hill I o W 20 D5
Hunsdon Herts 86 C6
Hunsdonbury Herts 86 C6
Hunsingore N Yorks 206 C4
Hunslet W Yorks 206 G2
Hunslet Carr W Yorks 206 G2
Hunsonby Cumb 231 D7
Hunspow Highld 310 B6
Hunstanton Norf 175 G11
Hunstanworth Durham 232 B5
Hunsterson E Ches 167 F11
Hunston Suff 125 D9
Hunston W Sus 22 C5
Hunston Green Suff 125 D9
Hunstrete Bath 60 G6
Hunsworth W Yorks 197 B7
Hunt End Worcs 117 E10
Huntenhull Green Wilts 45 D10
Huntercombe End Oxon 65 B7
Hunters Forstal Kent 71 F7
Hunter's Quay Argyll 276 F3
Huntham Som 28 B4
Hunthill Lodge Angus 292 F6
Hunting-tower Perth 286 E4
Huntingdon Cambs 122 C4
Huntingfield Suff 126 C6
Huntingford Dorset 45 G10
Huntingford S Glos 80 G2
Huntington E Loth 281 F9
Huntington Hereford 97 C9
Huntington Hereford 114 G5
Huntington Staffs 151 G9
Huntington Telford 132 B3
Huntington W Ches 166 C6
Huntington York 207 B8
Huntley Glos 80 B2
Huntley Staffs 169 G8
Huntly Aberds 302 F5
Huntlywood Borders 272 G2
Hunton Hants 48 F3
Hunton Kent 53 D8
Hunton N Yorks 224 G3
Hunton Bridge Herts 85 E9
Hunt's Corner Norf 141 F11
Hunt's Cross Mers 182 D6
Hunt's Green Bucks 84 E5
Hunt's Green W Berks 64 E2
Hunts Green Warks 134 D3
Hunt's Hill Bucks 84 F4
Hunt's Lane Leics 135 C9
Huntscott Som 42 E2
Huntsham Devon 27 C8
Huntshaw Devon 25 C8
Huntshaw Water Devon 25 C8
Huntspill Som 43 D10
Huntstile Som 43 G9
Huntworth Som 43 G10
Hunwick Durham 233 E9
Hunworth Norf 159 B11
Hurcott Som 28 D5
Hurcott Som 29 B8
Hurcott Worcs 117 B7
Hurdcott Wilts 47 G7
Hurdley Powys 130 E5
Hurdsfield E Ches 184 G6
Hurgill N Yorks 224 E3
Hurlet Glasgow 267 C10
Hurley Warks 134 D4
Hurley Windsor 65 C10
Hurley Bottom Windsor 65 C10
Hurley Common Warks 134 D4
Hurlford E Ayrs 257 B11
Hurliness Orkney 314 H2
Hurlston Lancs 194 E2
Hurlston Green Lancs 193 E11
Hurn Dorset 19 B8
Hurn E Yorks 208 E6
Hurn's End Lincs 174 F6
Hursey Dorset 28 G6
Hursley Hants 32 B6
Hurst Cumb 230 C4
Hurst Dorset 17 C11
Hurst Gtr Man 196 G2
Hurst N Yorks 223 E10
Hurst Som 29 D7
Hurst Wokingham 65 E9
Hurst Green E Sus 38 B2
Hurst Green Essex 89 B9
Hurst Green Lancs 203 F9
Hurst Green Sur 51 C11
Hurst Green W Mid 133 F9
Hurst Hill W Mid 133 E8
Hurst Park Sur 66 F6
Hurst Wickham W Sus 36 D3
Hurstbourne Priors Hants 48 D2
Hurstbourne Tarrant Hants 47 C11
Hurstead Gtr Man 196 D2
Hurstley Hereford 97 B7
Hurstpierpoint W Sus 36 D3
Hurstwood Lancs 204 G3
Hurtmore Sur 50 D3
Hurworth-on-Tees Darl 224 C6
Hurworth Place Darl 224 D5
Hury Durham 223 B9
Husabost Highld 298 D2
Husbands Bosworth Leics 136 G2
Husbandtown Angus 287 D8
Husborne Crawley C Beds 103 D9
Husthwaite N Yorks 215 D10
Hut Green N Yorks 198 C5
Hutcherleigh Devon 8 E5
Hutchesontown Glasgow 267 C11
Hutchwns Bridgend 57 F10
Huthwaite Notts 171 D7
Hutlerburn Borders 261 E10
Huttock Top Lancs 195 C11
Huttoft Lincs 191 F8
Hutton Borders 273 E9
Hutton Cumb 230 F4
Hutton E Yorks 208 C6
Hutton Essex 87 F10
Hutton Lancs 194 B3
Hutton N Som 43 B11
Hutton Bonville N Yorks 224 E6
Hutton Buscel N Yorks 217 C9
Hutton Conyers N Yorks 214 E6
Hutton Cranswick E Yorks 208 C6
Hutton End Cumb 230 D4
Hutton Gate Redcar 225 B11
Hutton Hang N Yorks 214 B3
Hutton Henry Durham 234 D4
Hutton-le-Hole N Yorks 226 G4
Hutton Magna Durham 224 C2
Hutton Mount Essex 87 G10
Hutton Roof Cumb 211 D11
Hutton Roof Cumb 230 E3
Hutton Rudby N Yorks 225 D9
Hutton Sessay N Yorks 215 D9
Hutton Village Redcar 225 C11
Hutton Wandesley N Yorks 206 C6
Huttons Ambo N Yorks 216 F5
Huxham Devon 14 B4
Huxham Green Som 44 F5
Huxley W Ches 167 C8
Huxter Shetland 313 G7
Huxter Shetland 313 H3
Huxter Shetland 313 H5
Huxton Borders 273 B7
Huyton Mers 182 C6
Huyton Park Mers 182 C6
Huyton Quarry Mers 183 C7
Hwlffordd = Haverfordwest Pembs 73 B7
Hycemoor Cumb 210 B1
Hyde Glos 80 E5
Hyde Glos 99 F11
Hyde Gtr Man 184 B6
Hyde Hants 31 E11
Hyde Hants 48 G3
Hyde Hereford 115 F9
Hyde Chase Essex 88 E4
Hyde End W Berks 64 G5
Hyde Heath Bucks 84 E6
Hyde Lea Staffs 151 E8
Hyde Park S Yorks 198 G5
Hydestile Sur 50 E3
Hylton Castle T & W 243 F9
Hylton Red House T & W 243 F9
Hyltons Crossways Norf 160 D4
Hyndburn Bridge Lancs 203 G10
Hyndford Bridge S Lnrk 269 G8
Hyndhope Borders 261 E9
Hynish Argyll 288 F1
Hyssington Powys 130 E6
Hystfield Glos 79 F11
Hythe Hants 32 F6
Hythe Kent 55 G7
Hythe Som 44 C2
Hythe Sur 66 E4
Hythe End Windsor 66 E4
Hythie Aberds 303 D10
Hyton Cumb 210 B1

I

Iarsiadar W Isles 304 E3
Ibberton Dorset 30 F3
Ible Derbys 170 D2
Ibsley Hants 31 F11
Ibstock Leics 153 G8
Ibstone Bucks 84 G3
Ibthorpe Hants 47 C11
Ibworth Hants 48 C5
Icelton N Som 59 F11
Ichrachan Argyll 284 D4
Ickburgh Norf 140 E6
Ickenham London 66 B5
Ickenthwaite Cumb 210 B6
Ickford Bucks 83 D11
Ickham Kent 55 B8
Ickleford Herts 104 E3
Icklesham E Sus 38 D5
Ickleton Cambs 105 C9
Icklingham Suff 124 C5
Ickornshaw N Yorks 204 E5
Ickwell C Beds 104 B3
Ickwell Green C Beds 104 B3
Icomb Glos 100 G4
Icy Park Devon 8 G3
Idbury Oxon 82 B2
Iddesleigh Devon 25 F9
Ide Devon 14 C3
Ide Hill Kent 52 C3
Ideford Devon 14 F3
Iden E Sus 38 C6
Iden Green Kent 53 F8
Iden Green Kent 53 G10
Idle W Yorks 205 F9
Idle Moor W Yorks 205 F9
Idless Corn 4 F6
Idlicote Warks 100 C5
Idmiston Wilts 47 F7
Idole Carms 74 B6
Idridgehay Derbys 170 F3
Idridgehay Green Derbys 170 F3
Idrigill Highld 298 C3
Idstone Oxon 63 C9
Idvies Angus 287 C9
Iet-y-bwlch Carms 92 F3
Iffley Oxon 83 E8
Ifield W Sus 51 F8
Ifield Green W Sus 51 F9
Ifieldwood W Sus 51 F8
Ifold W Sus 50 G4
Iford Bmouth 19 C8
Iford E Sus 36 F6
Ifton Heath Shrops 148 B6
Ightfield Shrops 149 B11
Ightfield Heath Shrops 149 B11
Ightham Kent 52 B5
Igtham Common Kent 52 B5
Iken Suff 127 F8
Ilam Staffs 169 E10
Ilchester Som 29 C8
Ilchester Mead Som 29 C8
Ilderton Northumb 264 E2
Ileden Kent 55 C8
Ilford London 68 B2
Ilford Som 28 D5
Ilfracombe Devon 40 D4
Ilkeston Derbys 171 G7
Ilketshall St Andrew Suff 143 F7
Ilketshall St Lawrence Suff 143 G7
Ilketshall St Margaret Suff 142 F6
Ilkley W Yorks 205 D8
Illand Corn 11 F11
Illey W Mid 133 G9
Illidge Green E Ches 168 C3
Illington Norf 141 F8
Illingworth W Yorks 196 B5
Illogan Corn 4 G3
Illogan Highway Corn 4 G3
Illshaw Heath W Mid 118 C2
Illston on the Hill Leics 136 D4
Ilmer Bucks 84 D3
Ilmington Warks 100 C4
Ilminster Som 28 E5
Ilsington Devon 13 F11
Ilston Swansea 56 C5
Ilton N Yorks 214 D3
Ilton Som 28 D5
Imachar N Ayrs 255 C9
Imber Wilts 46 D3
Imeraval Argyll 254 C4
Immervoulin Stirl 285 F9
Immingham NE Lincs 201 E7
Impington Cambs 123 E8
Ince W Ches 183 F7
Ince Blundell Mers 193 G10
Ince in Makerfield Gtr Man 194 G5
Inch of Arnhall Aberds 293 F8
Inchbae Lodge Highld 300 C4
Inchbare Angus 293 G8
Inchberry Moray 302 D3
Inchbraoch Angus 287 B11
Inchbrook Glos 80 E4
Inchcape Highld 309 J6
Incheril Highld 299 C10
Inchgrundle Angus 292 F6
Inchina Highld 307 K4
Inchinnan Renfs 267 B9
Inchkinloch Highld 308 E5
Inchlaggan Highld 290 C3
Inchlumpie Highld 300 B5
Inchmore Highld 300 E3
Inchmore Highld 300 F5
Inchnacardoch Hotel Highld 290 B5
Inchnadamph Highld 307 G7
Inchock Angus 287 C10
Inchree Highld 290 G2
Inchrory Moray 292 C3
Inchs Corn 5 C9
Inchture Perth 286 E6
Inchyra Perth 286 E5
Indian Queens Corn 5 D8
Inerval Argyll 254 C4
Ingatestone Essex 87 F11
Ingbirchworth S Yorks 197 F8
Ingerthorpe N Yorks 214 F5
Ingestre Staffs 151 E9
Ingham Lincs 188 E6
Ingham Norf 161 D7
Ingham Suff 125 C7
Ingham Corner Norf 161 D7
Ingleborough Norf 157 F9
Ingleby Derbys 152 D6
Ingleby Lincs 188 F5
Ingleby Arncliffe N Yorks 225 E8
Ingleby Barwick Stockton 225 C9
Ingleby Cross N Yorks 225 E9
Ingleby Greenhow N Yorks 225 D11
Ingleigh Green Devon 25 F10
Inglemire Hull 209 G7
Inglesbatch Bath 61 G8
Inglesham Swindon 82 F2
Ingleton Durham 233 G9
Ingleton N Yorks 212 E3
Inglewhite Lancs 202 E6
Ingmanthorpe N Yorks 206 C4
Ingoe Northumb 242 C2
Ingol Lancs 202 G6
Ingoldisthorpe Norf 158 C3
Ingoldmells Lincs 175 B9
Ingoldsby Lincs 155 C10
Ingon Warks 118 F4
Ingram Northumb 264 F2
Ingrams Green W Sus 34 C4
Ingrave Essex 87 G10
Ingrow W Yorks 205 F7
Ings Cumb 221 F8
Ingst S Glos 60 B5
Ingthorpe Rutland 137 B9
Ingworth Norf 160 D3
Inham's End Cambs 138 D5
Inhurst Hants 64 G5
Inkberrow Worcs 117 F10
Inkerman Durham 233 D8
Inkersall Derbys 186 G6
Inkersall Green Derbys 186 G6
Inkford Worcs 117 C11
Inkpen W Berks 63 G11
Inkpen Common W Berks 63 G11
Inkstack Highld 310 B6
Inlands W Sus 22 B3
Inmarsh Wilts 62 G2
Inn Cumb 221 D8
Innellan Argyll 276 G3
Inner Hope Devon 9 G8
Innerleithen Borders 261 B8
Innerleven Fife 287 G7
Innermessan Dumfries 236 C2
Innerwick E Loth 282 G4
Innerwick Perth 285 C9
Innie Argyll 275 B9
Inninbeg Highld 289 E8
Innis Chonain Argyll 284 E5
Innistrynich Argyll 284 E5
Innox Hill Som 45 D9
Innsworth Glos 99 G7

Insch Aberds 302 G6
Insh Highld 291 C10
Inshegra Highld 306 D7
Inshore Highld 308 C3
Inskip Lancs 202 F5
Inskip Moss Side Lancs 202 F5
Instoneville S Yorks 198 E5
Instow Devon 40 G3
Insworke Corn 7 E8
Intack Blkburn 195 B8
Intake S Yorks 186 E5
Intake S Yorks 198 G5
Intake W Yorks 205 F10
Interfield Worcs 98 B5
Intwood Norf 142 C3
Inver Aberds 292 D4
Inver Highld 311 L2
Inver Perth 286 C4
Inver Mallie Highld 290 E3
Inverailort Highld 295 G9
Inveraldie Angus 287 D8
Inveralivaig Highld 298 E4
Inveralligin Highld 299 D8
Inverallochy Aberds 303 C10
Inveran Highld 299 B8
Inveran Highld 309 K5
Inveraray Argyll 284 G4
Inverarish Highld 295 B7
Inverarity Angus 287 C8
Inverarnan Stirl 285 F7
Inverasdale Highld 307 L3
Inverawe Ho Argyll 284 D4
Inverbeg Argyll 276 B6
Inverbervie Aberds 293 F10
Inverboyndie Aberds 302 C6
Inverbroom Highld 307 L6
Invercarron Mains Highld 309 K5
Invercassley Highld 309 J4
Invercauld House Aberds 292 D3
Inverchaolain Argyll 275 F11
Invercharnan Highld 284 C5
Inverchoran Highld 300 D2
Invercreran Argyll 284 C4
Inverdruie Highld 291 B11
Inverebrie Aberds 303 F9
Invereck Argyll 276 E2
Inverernan Ho Aberds 292 B5
Invereshie House Highld 291 C10
Inveresk E Loth 280 G6
Inverey Aberds 292 E2
Inverfarigaig Highld 300 G5
Invergarry Highld 290 C5
Invergelder Aberds 292 D4
Invergeldie Perth 285 E11
Invergordon Highld 301 C7
Invergowrie Perth 287 D7
Inverguseran Highld 295 E9
Inverhadden Perth 285 B10
Inverhaggernie Stirl 285 E7
Inverharroch Moray 302 F3
Inverherive Stirl 285 E7
Inverie Highld 295 F9
Inverinan Argyll 275 B10
Inverinate Highld 295 C11
Inverkeilor Angus 287 C10
Inverkeithing Fife 280 E2
Inverkeithny Aberds 302 E6
Inverkip Invclyd 276 G4
Inverkirkaig Highld 307 H5
Inverlael Highld 307 L6
Inverleith Edin 280 F4
Inverliever Lodge Argyll 275 C9
Inverliver Argyll 284 D4
Inverlochlarig Stirl 285 F8
Inverlochy Argyll 284 E5
Inverlochy Highld 290 F3
Inverlochy Moray 301 G11
Inverlounin Argyll 276 B4
Inverlussa Argyll 275 E7
Invermark Lodge Angus 292 E6
Invermoidart Highld 289 B8
Invermoriston Highld 290 B6
Invernaver Highld 308 C7
Inverneill Argyll 275 E9
Inverness Highld 300 E6
Invernettie Aberds 303 E11
Invernoaden Argyll 276 B2
Inveronich Argyll 284 G6
Inveroran Hotel Argyll 284 C6
Inverpolly Lodge Highld 307 H5
Inverquharity Angus 287 B8
Inverquhomery Aberds 303 E10
Inverroy Highld 290 E4
Inversanda Highld 289 D11
Invershiel Highld 295 D11
Invershin Highld 309 K5
Invershore Highld 310 F6
Inversnaid Hotel Stirl 285 G7
Invertrossachs Stirl 285 G9
Inverugie Aberds 303 E11
Inveruglas Argyll 285 G7
Inveruglass Highld 291 C10
Inverurie Aberds 303 G7
Invervar Perth 285 C10
Inverythan Aberds 303 E7
Inwardleigh Devon 13 B7
Inwood Shrops 131 D9
Inworth Essex 88 B5
Iochdar W Isles 297 G3
Iping W Sus 34 C5
Ipplepen Devon 8 B6
Ipsden Oxon 64 B6
Ipsley Worcs 117 D11
Ipstones Staffs 169 F8
Ipswich Suff 108 C3
Irby Mers 182 E3
Irby in the Marsh Lincs 175 C7
Irby upon Humber NE Lincs 201 G7
Irchester Northants 121 D8
Ireby Cumb 229 D10
Ireby Lancs 212 D3
Ireland C Beds 104 C2
Ireland Orkney 314 F3
Ireland Shetland 313 L5
Ireland Wilts 45 C10
Ireland Wood W Yorks 205 F11
Ireland's Cross Shrops 168 G2
Ireleth Cumb 210 D4
Ireshopeburn Durham 232 D3
Ireton Wood Derbys 170 F3
Irlam Gtr Man 184 C2
Irlams o' th' Height Gtr Man 195 G9
Irnham Lincs 155 D10
Iron Acton S Glos 61 C7
Iron Bridge Cambs 139 D9
Iron Cross Warks 117 G11
Iron Lo Highld 299 G10
Ironbridge Telford 132 C3
Irongray Dumfries 237 B11
Ironmacannie Dumfries 237 B8
Irons Bottom Sur 51 D9
Ironside Aberds 303 D8
Ironville Derbys 170 E6
Irstead Norf 161 E7
Irstead Street Norf 161 F7
Irthington Cumb 239 E11
Irthlingborough Northants 121 C8
Irton N Yorks 217 C10
Irvine N Ayrs 257 B8
Irwell Vale Lancs 195 C9
Isabella Pit Northumb 253 G8
Isallt Bach Anglesey 178 F3
Isauld Highld 310 C3
Isbister Orkney 314 E3
Isbister Orkney 314 D2
Isbister Shetland 312 D5
Isbister Shetland 313 G7
Isel Cumb 229 E9
Isfield E Sus 36 D6
Isham Northants 121 C7
Ishriff Argyll 289 F8
Isington Hants 49 E9
Island Carr N Lincs 200 F3
Islands Common Cambs 122 E3
Islay Ho Argyll 274 G4
Isle Abbotts Som 28 C5
Isle Brewers Som 28 C5
Isle of Axholme N Lincs 199 F9
Isle of Dogs London 67 D11
Isle of Man Dumfries 238 B2
Isle of Whithorn Dumfries 236 F6
Isleham Cambs 124 C2
Isleornsay Highld 295 D9
Islesburgh Shetland 312 G5
Islesteps Dumfries 237 B11
Isleworth London 67 D7
Isley Walton Leics 153 D8
Islibhig W Isles 304 F1
Islington London 67 C10
Islington Telford 150 E4
Islip Northants 121 B9
Islip Oxon 83 C8
Isombridge Telford 150 G2
Istead Rise Kent 68 F6
Isycoed Wrex 166 E6
Itchen Soton 32 E6
Itchen Abbas Hants 48 G4
Itchen Stoke Hants 48 G5
Itchingfield W Sus 35 B10
Itchington S Glos 61 B7
Itteringham Norf 160 C2
Itteringham Common Norf 160 D3
Itton Devon 13 B9
Itton Mon 79 F7
Itton Common Mon 79 F7
Ivegill Cumb 230 C4
Ivelet N Yorks 223 F8
Iver Bucks 66 C4
Iver Heath Bucks 66 C4
Iverley Staffs 133 G7
Iveston Durham 242 G4
Ivinghoe Bucks 84 B6
Ivinghoe Aston Bucks 85 B7
Ivington Hereford 115 F9
Ivington Green Hereford 115 F9
Ivy Chimneys Essex 86 E6
Ivy Cross Dorset 30 C5
Ivy Hatch Kent 52 C5
Ivy Todd Norf 141 B7
Ivybridge Devon 8 D2
Ivychurch Kent 39 B8
Iwade Kent 69 F11
Iwerne Courtney or Shroton Dorset 30 E5
Iwerne Minster Dorset 30 E5
Iwood N Som 60 G3
Ixworth Suff 125 C8
Ixworth Thorpe Suff 125 C8

J

Jack Green Lancs 194 B5
Jack Hayes Staffs 168 F6
Jack Hill N Yorks 205 C10
Jack in the Green Devon 14 B6
Jackfield Telford 132 C3
Jack's Green Essex 105 G11
Jack's Green Glos 80 D5
Jack's Hatch Essex 86 D6
Jacksdale Notts 170 E6
Jackson Bridge W Yorks 197 F7
Jackstown Aberds 303 F7
Jacobs Well Sur 50 C3
Jacobstow Corn 11 B9
Jacobstowe Devon 25 G9
Jagger Green W Yorks 196 D5
Jameston Pembs 73 F9
Jamestown Dumfries 249 D8
Jamestown Highld 300 D4
Jamestown W Dunb 277 E7
Jamphlars Fife 280 B4
Janetstown Highld 310 C4
Janke's Green Essex 107 F8
Jarrow T & W 243 D8
Jarvis Brook E Sus 37 B8
Jasper's Green Essex 106 F4
Java Argyll 289 F9
Jaw Hill W Yorks 197 C9
Jawcraig Falk 278 F6
Jaywick Essex 89 C11
Jealott's Hill Brack 65 E11
Jeaniefield Borders 271 G10
Jedburgh Borders 262 E5
Jedurgh Borders 262 F5
Jeffreyston Pembs 73 D9
Jellyhill E Dunb 278 G2
Jemimaville Highld 301 C7
Jennetts Hill W Berks 64 E5
Jennyfield N Yorks 205 B11
Jericho Gtr Man 195 E10
Jersey Farm Herts 85 D11
Jersey Marine Neath 57 C8
Jerviswood S Lnrk 269 F7
Jesmond T & W 243 D7
Jevington E Sus 23 E9
Jewell's Cross Corn 24 G3
Jingle Street Mon 79 C7
Jockey End Herts 85 C8
Jodrell Bank E Ches 184 G3
John O'Gaunt Leics 136 B4
John O'Gaunts W Yorks 197 B11
John o'Groats Highld 310 B7
Johnby Cumb 230 E4
John's Cross E Sus 38 C2
Johnshaven Aberds 293 G9
Johnson Fold Gtr Man 195 E7
Johnson Street Norf 161 F7
Johnson's Hillock Lancs 194 C5
Johnston Pembs 72 C6
Johnstone Renfs 267 C8
Johnstone Mains Aberds 293 F9
Johnstonebridge Dumfries 248 E3
Johnstown Carms 74 B6
Johnstown Wrex 166 F4
Jolly's Bottom Corn 4 F5
Joppa Corn 2 B3
Joppa Edin 280 G6
Joppa S Ayrs 257 F10
Jordan Green Norf 159 E11
Jordanhill Glasgow 267 B10
Jordans Bucks 85 G7
Jordanston Pembs 91 E8
Jordanthorpe S Yorks 186 E5
Jordon S Yorks 186 C6
Joyford Glos 79 C9
Joy's Green Glos 79 B10
Jubilee Gtr Man 196 E2
Jubilee Notts 170 E6
Jugbank Staffs 150 B5
Jump S Yorks 197 G11
Jumpers Common Dorset 19 C8
Jumpers Green Dorset 19 C8
Jumper's Town E Sus 52 G3
Junction N Yorks 204 D6
Juniper Northumb 241 F10
Juniper Green Edin 270 B3
Jurby East I o M 192 C4
Jurby West I o M 192 C4
Jurston Devon 13 E9
Jury's Gap E Sus 39 D7

K

Kaber Cumb 222 C5
Kaimend S Lnrk 269 F9
Kaimes Edin 270 B5
Kaimrig End Borders 269 G11
Kalemouth Borders 262 D6
Kame Fife 287 G7
Kames Argyll 275 B9
Kames Argyll 275 F10
Kames E Ayrs 258 D5
Kates Hill W Mid 133 E9
Kea Corn 4 G6
Keadby N Lincs 199 E10
Keal Cotes Lincs 174 C5
Kearby Town End N Yorks 206 D2
Kearnsey Kent 55 E9
Kearsley Gtr Man 195 F9
Kearstwick Cumb 212 C2
Kearton N Yorks 223 F9
Kearvaig Highld 306 B7
Keasden N Yorks 212 F4
Kebroyd W Yorks 196 C4
Keckwick Halton 183 E9
Keddington Lincs 190 D4
Keddington Corner Lincs 190 D5
Kedington Suff 106 B4
Kedleston Derbys 170 G4
Kedslie Borders 271 G11
Keekle Cumb 219 B10
Keelars Tye Essex 107 G11
Keelby Lincs 201 E7
Keele Staffs 168 F4
Keeley Green Beds 103 B10
Keelham W Yorks 205 G7
Keenley Northumb 241 F7
Keenthorne Som 43 F8
Keeres Green Essex 87 C9
Keeston Pembs 72 B6
Keevil Wilts 46 B2
Kegworth Leics 153 D9
Kehelland Corn 4 G2
Keig Aberds 293 B8
Keighley W Yorks 205 E7
Keil Highld 289 D11
Keilarsbrae Clack 279 C7
Keilhill Aberds 303 D7
Keillmore Argyll 275 E7
Keillor Perth 286 C6
Keillour Perth 286 E3
Keills Argyll 274 G5
Keils Argyll 274 G6
Keinton Mandeville Som 44 G4
Keir Mill Dumfries 247 E9
Keisby Lincs 155 D10
Keiss Highld 310 C7
Keistle Highld 298 D4
Keith Moray 302 D4
Keith Hall Aberds 303 G7
Keith Inch Aberds 303 E11
Keithock Angus 293 G8
Kelbrook Lancs 204 E4
Kelby Lincs 173 G8
Kelcliffe W Yorks 205 E9
Keld Cumb 221 C11
Keld N Yorks 223 E7
Keld Houses N Yorks 214 G2
Keldholme N Yorks 216 B4
Kelfield N Lincs 199 G10
Kelfield N Yorks 207 F7
Kelham Notts 172 D3
Kelhurn Argyll 276 F6
Kellacott Devon 12 D4
Kellamergh Lancs 194 B2
Kellan Argyll 289 E7
Kellas Angus 287 D8
Kellas Moray 301 D11
Kellaton Devon 9 G11
Kellaways Wilts 62 D3
Kelleth Cumb 222 D3
Kelleythorpe E Yorks 208 B5
Kelleythorpe E Yorks 208 B6
Kelling Norf 177 E9
Kellingley N Yorks 198 C4
Kellington N Yorks 198 C5
Kelloe Durham 234 D2
Kelloholm Dumfries 258 G6
Kells Cumb 219 B9
Kelly Corn 10 G6
Kelly Devon 12 E3
Kelly Bray Corn 12 G3
Kelmarsh Northants 120 B4
Kelmscott Oxon 82 F3
Kelsale Suff 127 D7
Kelsall W Ches 167 B8
Kelsall Hill W Ches 167 B8
Kelsay Argyll 254 B2
Kelshall Herts 104 D6
Kelsick Cumb 238 G5
Kelso Borders 262 C6
Kelstedge Derbys 170 C4
Kelstern Lincs 190 C3
Kelsterton Flint 182 G3
Kelston Bath 61 F8
Keltneyburn Perth 285 C11
Kelton Dumfries 237 B11
Kelton Durham 232 G4
Kelty Fife 280 C2
Keltybridge Fife 280 B2
Kelvedon Essex 88 B5
Kelvedon Hatch Essex 87 F9
Kelvin S Lnrk 268 E2
Kelvindale Glasgow 267 B11
Kelvinside Glasgow 267 B11
Kelynack Corn 1 D3
Kemacott Devon 41 D7
Kemback Fife 287 F8
Kemberton Shrops 132 C4
Kemble Glos 81 F7
Kemble Wick Glos 81 F7
Kemerton Worcs 99 D8
Kemeys Commander Mon 78 E4
Kemincham E Ches 168 B4
Kemnay Aberds 293 B9
Kemp Town Brighton 36 G4
Kempe's Corner Kent 54 D4
Kempie Highld 308 D4
Kempley Glos 98 F3
Kempley Green Glos 98 F3
Kemps Green Warks 118 C2
Kempsey Worcs 99 B7
Kempsford Glos 81 F11
Kempshott Hants 48 C6
Kempston Beds 103 B10
Kempston Church End Beds 103 B10
Kempston Hardwick Beds 103 C10
Kempston West End Beds 103 B9
Kempton Shrops 131 G7
Kemsing Kent 52 B4
Kemsley Kent 70 F2
Kemsley Street Kent 69 G10
Kenardington Kent 54 G3
Kenchester Hereford 97 C8
Kencot Oxon 82 E3
Kendal Cumb 221 G10
Kendal End Worcs 117 C10
Kendleshire S Glos 61 D7
Kendon Caerph 77 F11
Kendoon Dumfries 246 F4
Kendray S Yorks 197 F11
Kenfig Bridgend 57 E10
Kenfig Hill Bridgend 57 E10
Kengharair Argyll 288 E6
Kenilworth Warks 118 C5
Kenknock Stirl 285 D8
Kenley London 51 B10
Kenley Shrops 131 C11
Kenmore Argyll 284 G4
Kenmore Highld 299 D7
Kenmore Perth 285 C11
Kenmure Dumfries 237 B8
Kenn Devon 14 D4
Kenn N Som 60 F2
Kenn Moor Gate N Som 60 F2
Kennacley W Isles 305 J3
Kennacraig Argyll 275 G9
Kennards House Corn 11 E11
Kenneggy Corn 2 D3
Kenneggy Downs Corn 2 D3
Kennerleigh Devon 26 F4
Kennet Clack 279 C8
Kennet End Suff 124 D4
Kennethmont Aberds 302 G5
Kennett Cambs 124 D3
Kennford Devon 14 D4
Kenninghall Norf 141 F10
Kenninghall Heath Norf 141 G10
Kennington Kent 54 E4
Kennington London 67 D10
Kennington Oxon 83 E8
Kennoway Fife 287 G7
Kenny Som 28 D4
Kenny Hill Suff 124 B3
Kennythorpe N Yorks 216 F5
Kenovay Argyll 288 E1
Kensal Green London 67 C8
Kensal Rise London 67 C8
Kensal Town London 67 C8
Kensaleyre Highld 298 D4
Kensary Highld 310 E6
Kensington London 67 D9
Kensington Mers 182 C5
Kensworth C Beds 85 B8
Kent Street E Sus 38 D3
Kent Street Kent 53 C7
Kent Street W Sus 36 C2
Kentallen Highld 284 B4
Kentchurch Hereford 97 F8
Kentford Suff 124 D4
Kentisbeare Devon 27 F9
Kentisbury Devon 40 E6
Kentisbury Ford Devon 40 E6
Kentish Town London 67 C9
Kentmere Cumb 221 E9
Kenton Devon 14 E5
Kenton London 67 B7
Kenton Suff 126 D3
Kenton T & W 242 D6
Kenton Bankfoot T & W 242 D6
Kenton Bar T & W 242 D6
Kenton Corner Suff 126 D4
Kenton Green Glos 80 C3
Kentra Highld 289 C8
Kentrigg Cumb 221 G10
Kents Corn 11 B9
Kents Bank Cumb 211 D7
Kent's Green Glos 98 G4
Kents Hill M Keynes 103 D7
Kent's Oak Hants 32 C4
Kenwick Shrops 149 C8
Kenwick Park Shrops 149 D8
Kenwyn Corn 4 F6
Kenyon Warr 183 B10
Keoldale Highld 308 C3
Keonchulish Ho Highld 307 K6
Kepdowrie Stirl 277 C11
Kepnal Wilts 63 G7
Keppanach Highld 290 G2
Keppoch Highld 295 C11
Keprigan Argyll 255 F7
Kepwick N Yorks 225 G9
Kerchesters Borders 263 B7
Kerdiston Norf 159 E11
Keresforth Hill S Yorks 197 F10
Keresley W Mid 134 G6
Keresley Newlands Warks 134 G6
Kerfield Borders 270 G5
Kerley Downs Corn 4 G5
Kernborough Devon 8 G5
Kerne Bridge Hereford 79 B9
Kernsary Highld 299 B8
Kerridge E Ches 184 F6
Kerridge-end E Ches 184 F6
Kerris Corn 1 D4
Kerry = Ceri Powys 130 F2
Kerry Hill Staffs 168 F6
Kerrycroy Argyll 266 C2
Kerry's Gate Hereford 97 E7
Kerrysdale Highld 299 B8
Kersal Gtr Man 195 G10
Kersall Notts 172 C2
Kersbrook Devon 15 E7
Kerscott Devon 25 B10
Kersey Suff 107 C10
Kersey Tye Suff 107 C9
Kersey Upland Suff 107 C9
Kershopefoot Cumb 249 G11
Kersoe Worcs 99 C9
Kerswell Devon 27 F9
Kerswell Green Worcs 99 B7
Kerthen Wood Corn 2 C3
Kesgrave Suff 108 B4
Kessingland Suff 143 F10
Kessingland Beach Suff 143 F10
Kessington E Dunb 277 G11
Kestle Corn 5 F9
Kestle Mill Corn 5 D7
Keston London 68 G2
Keston Mark London 68 F2
Keswick Cumb 229 G11
Keswick Norf 142 C4
Keswick Norf 161 C7
Kete Pembs 72 E4
Ketford Glos 98 E4
Ketley Telford 150 G3
Ketley Bank Telford 150 G3
Ketsby Lincs 190 F5
Kettering Northants 121 B7
Ketteringham Norf 142 C3
Kettins Perth 286 D6
Kettle Corner Kent 53 C8
Kettle Green Herts 86 B6
Kettlebaston Suff 125 G9
Kettlebridge Fife 287 G7
Kettlebrook Staffs 134 C4
Kettleburgh Suff 126 E5
Kettlehill Fife 287 G7
Kettleholm Dumfries 238 B4
Kettleness N Yorks 226 B6
Kettleshulme E Ches 185 F7
Kettleshume E Ches 185 F7
Kettlesing N Yorks 205 B10
Kettlesing Bottom N Yorks 205 B10
Kettlesing Head N Yorks 205 B10
Kettlestone Norf 159 C9
Kettlethorpe Lincs 188 F4
Kettlethorpe W Yorks 197 D10
Kettletoft Orkney 314 C6
Kettlewell N Yorks 213 E9
Ketton Rutland 137 C9
Kevingtown London 68 F3
Kew London 67 D7
Kew Bridge London 67 D7
Keward Som 44 E4
Kewstoke N Som 59 G10
Kexbrough S Yorks 197 F9
Kexby Lincs 188 D5
Kexby York 207 C10
Key Green E Ches 168 C5
Key Green N Yorks 226 E6
Key Street Kent 69 G11
Keybridge Corn 11 G7
Keycol Kent 69 G11
Keyford Som 45 D9
Keyham Leics 136 B3
Keyhaven Hants 20 C2
Keyingham E Yorks 201 B8
Keymer W Sus 36 D4
Keynsham Bath 61 F7
Key's Green Kent 53 F7
Keysers Estate Essex 86 D5
Keysoe Beds 121 E11
Keysoe Row Beds 121 E11
Keyston Cambs 121 B10
Keyworth Notts 154 C2
Khantore Aberds 292 D4
Kibbear Som 28 C2
Kibblesworth T & W 242 F6
Kibworth Beauchamp Leics 136 E3
Kibworth Harcourt Leics 136 E3
Kidbrooke London 68 D2
Kidburngill Cumb 229 G7
Kiddal Lane End W Yorks 206 F4
Kiddemore Green Staffs 133 B7
Kidderminster Worcs 116 B6
Kiddington Oxon 101 G8
Kidd's Moor Norf 142 C2
Kidlington Oxon 83 C7
Kidmore End Oxon 65 D7
Kidnal W Ches 167 F7
Kidsdale Dumfries 236 F6
Kidsgrove Staffs 168 E4
Kidstones N Yorks 213 C9
Kidwelly = Cydweli Carms 74 D6
Kiel Crofts Argyll 289 F11
Kielder Northumb 250 E4
Kierfiold Ho Orkney 314 E2
Kiff Green W Berks 64 F5
Kilbagie Fife 279 D8
Kilbarchan Renfs 267 C8
Kilbeg Highld 295 E8
Kilberry Argyll 275 G8
Kilbirnie N Ayrs 266 E6
Kilbowie W Dunb 277 G10
Kilbraur Highld 311 H2
Kilbride Argyll 254 C4
Kilbride Argyll 275 D9
Kilbride Argyll 289 G10
Kilbride Argyll 289 G11
Kilbride Highld 295 C7
Kilbridemore Argyll 275 D11
Kilbryde Castle Stirl 285 G11
Kilburn Angus 292 G5
Kilburn Derbys 170 F5
Kilburn London 67 C9
Kilburn N Yorks 215 D10
Kilby Leics 136 D2
Kilby Bridge Leics 136 D2
Kilchamaig Argyll 275 G9
Kilchattan Argyll 274 D4
Kilchattan Bay Argyll 266 E2
Kilchenzie Argyll 255 E7
Kilcheran Argyll 289 F10
Kilchiaran Argyll 274 G3
Kilchoan Argyll 275 B8
Kilchoan Highld 288 C6
Kilchoman Argyll 274 G3
Kilchrenan Argyll 284 E4
Kilconquhar Fife 287 G8
Kilcot Glos 98 F3
Kilcoy Highld 300 D5
Kilcreggan Argyll 276 E4
Kildale N Yorks 226 D2
Kildallog Argyll 255 F8
Kildary Highld 301 B7
Kildaton Ho Argyll 254 C5
Kildavanan Argyll 275 G11
Kildermorie Lodge Highld 300 B5
Kildonan Dumfries 236 D2
Kildonan Highld 298 D3
Kildonan N Ayrs 256 E2
Kildonan Lodge Highld 311 G3
Kildonnan Highld 294 G6
Kildrum N Lnrk 278 F5
Kildrummy Aberds 292 B6
Kildwick N Yorks 204 D6
Kilfinan Argyll 275 F10
Kilfinnan Highld 290 D4
Kilgetty Pembs 73 D10
Kilgour Fife 286 G6
Kilgrammie S Ayrs 245 C7
Kilgwrrwg Common Mon 79 F7
Kilhallon Corn 5 E11
Kilham E Yorks 217 G11
Kilham Northumb 263 C9
Kilkeddan Argyll 255 E8
Kilkenneth Argyll 288 E1
Kilkenny Glos 81 B8
Kilkerran Argyll 255 F8
Kilkhampton Corn 24 E3
Killamarsh Derbys 187 E7
Killaworgey Corn 5 C8
Killay Swansea 56 C6
Killbeg Argyll 289 E8
Killean Argyll 255 C7
Killearn Stirl 277 D10
Killegruer Argyll 255 D7
Killen Highld 300 D6
Killerby Darl 224 B3
Killichonan Perth 285 B9
Killiechoinich Argyll 289 G10
Killiechonate Highld 290 E4
Killiechronan Argyll 289 E7
Killiecrankie Perth 291 G11
Killiemor Argyll 288 F6
Killiemore House Argyll 288 G6
Killilan Highld 295 B11
Killimster Highld 310 D7
Killin Stirl 285 D9
Killin Lodge Highld 291 C7
Killinallan Argyll 274 F4
Killingbeck W Yorks 206 G2
Killinghall N Yorks 205 B11
Killington Cumb 212 B2
Killington Devon 41 D7
Killingworth T & W 243 C7
Killingworth Moor T & W 243 C7
Killingworth Village T & W 243 C7
Killivose Corn 2 B4
Killmahumaig Argyll 275 D8
Killochyett Borders 271 F9
Killocraw Argyll 255 D7
Killundine Highld 289 E7
Killylung Dumfries 247 G11
Kilmacolm Invclyd 267 B7
Kilmaha Argyll 275 C10
Kilmahog Stirl 285 G10
Kilmalieu Highld 289 D10
Kilmaluag Highld 298 B4
Kilmany Fife 287 E7
Kilmarie Highld 295 D7
Kilmarnock E Ayrs 257 B10
Kilmaron Castle Fife 287 F7
Kilmartin Argyll 275 D9
Kilmaurs E Ayrs 267 G8
Kilmelford Argyll 275 B9
Kilmeny Argyll 274 G4
Kilmersdon Som 45 C7
Kilmeston Hants 33 B9
Kilmichael Argyll 255 E7
Kilmichael Argyll 275 F10
Kilmichael Glassary Argyll 275 D9
Kilmichael of Inverlussa Argyll 275 E8
Kilmington Devon 15 B11
Kilmington Wilts 45 F9
Kilmington Common Wilts 45 F9
Kilmoluaig Argyll 288 E1
Kilmonivaig Highld 290 E3
Kilmorack Highld 300 E4
Kilmore Argyll 289 G10
Kilmore Highld 295 E8
Kilmory Argyll 275 F8
Kilmory Highld 289 B7
Kilmory Highld 294 E5
Kilmory N Ayrs 255 E10
Kilmory Lodge Argyll 275 C8
Kilmote Highld 311 H3
Kilmuir Highld 298 B3
Kilmuir Highld 298 E2
Kilmuir Highld 300 E6
Kilmuir Highld 301 B7
Kilmun Argyll 275 B10
Kilmun Argyll 276 E3
Kiln Green Hereford 79 B10
Kiln Green Wokingham 65 D10
Kiln Pit Hill Northumb 242 G2
Kilnave Argyll 274 F3
Kilncadzow S Lnrk 269 F7
Kilndown Kent 53 G8
Kilnhill Cumb 229 E10
Kilnhurst S Yorks 187 B7
Kilninian Argyll 288 E5
Kilninver Argyll 289 G10
Kilnsea E Yorks 201 D12
Kilnsey N Yorks 213 G9
Kilnwick E Yorks 208 D5
Kilnwick Percy E Yorks 208 C2
Kiloran Argyll 274 D4
Kilpatrick N Ayrs 255 E10
Kilpeck Hereford 97 E8
Kilphedir Highld 311 H3
Kilpin E Yorks 199 B9
Kilpin Pike E Yorks 199 B9
Kilrenny Fife 287 G9
Kilsby Northants 119 C11
Kilspindie Perth 286 E6
Kilsyth N Lnrk 278 F4
Kilton Notts 187 F9
Kilton Redcar 226 B4
Kilton Som 43 E7
Kilton Thorpe Redcar 226 B3
Kilvaxter Highld 298 C3
Kilve Som 43 E7
Kilvington Notts 172 G3
Kilwinning N Ayrs 266 G6
Kimberley Norf 141 C11
Kimberley Notts 171 G8
Kimberworth S Yorks 186 C6
Kimberworth Park S Yorks 186 C6
Kimble Wick Bucks 84 D4
Kimblesworth Durham 233 B11
Kimbolton Cambs 121 D11
Kimbolton Hereford 115 E10
Kimbridge Hants 32 B4
Kimcote Leics 135 F11
Kimmeridge Dorset 18 F4
Kimmerston Northumb 263 B11
Kimpton Hants 47 D9
Kimpton Herts 85 B11
Kimworthy Devon 24 E4
Kinabus Argyll 254 C3
Kinbeachie Highld 300 C6
Kinbrace Highld 310 F2
Kinbuck Stirl 285 G11
Kincaidston S Ayrs 257 F9
Kincaple Fife 287 F8
Kincardine Fife 279 D8
Kincardine Highld 309 L6
Kincardine Bridge Falk 279 D8
Kincardine O'Neil Aberds 293 D7
Kinclaven Perth 286 D5
Kincorth Aberdeen 293 C11
Kincorth Ho Moray 301 C10
Kincraig Highld 291 C10
Kincraigie Perth 286 C3
Kindallachan Perth 286 C3
Kine Moor S Yorks 197 G9
Kineton Glos 99 F11
Kineton Warks 118 G6
Kineton Green W Mid 134 G2
Kinfauns Perth 286 E5
King Edward Aberds 303 D7
King Sterndale Derbys 185 G9
King Street Essex 87 E9
Kingairloch Highld 289 D10
Kingarth Argyll 255 B11
Kingates I o W 20 F6
Kingbeare Corn 11 G11
Kingcoed Mon 78 D6
Kingdown N Som 60 G4
Kingerby Lincs 189 C9
Kingfield Sur 50 B4
Kingford Devon 24 F3
Kingford Devon 25 D10
Kingham Oxon 100 G5
Kinghay Wilts 30 B5
Kingholm Quay Dumfries 237 B11
Kinghorn Fife 280 D5
Kingie Highld 290 C3
Kinglassie Fife 280 B4
Kingledores Borders 260 D4
Kingoodie Perth 287 E7
King's Acre Hereford 97 C9
King's Bromley Staffs 152 F2
King's Caple Hereford 97 F11
King's Cliffe Northants 137 D10
Kings Clipstone Notts 171 C10
King's Coughton Warks 117 F11
King's Dyke Cambs 138 D4
King's End Oxon 101 G11
King's End Worcs 116 G6
King's Furlong Hants 48 C6
King's Green Glos 98 E5
King's Green Worcs 116 E5
King's Heath Northants 120 E4
King's Heath W Mid 133 G11
Kings Hedges Cambs 123 E9
Kings Hill Glos 81 E8
King's Hill Kent 53 C7
King's Hill W Mid 133 D9
Kings Langley Herts 85 E9
King's Lynn Norf 158 E2
King's Meaburn Cumb 231 G8
King's Mills Derbys 153 D8
King's Mills Wrex 166 F4
Kings Moss Mers 194 G4
Kings Muir Borders 261 B7
King's Newnham Warks 119 B9
King's Newton Derbys 153 D7
King's Norton Leics 136 C3
King's Norton W Mid 117 B11
King's Nympton Devon 25 D11
King's Pyon Hereford 115 G8
Kings Ripton Cambs 122 B5
King's Somborne Hants 47 G11
King's Stag Dorset 30 E2
King's Stanley Glos 80 E4
King's Sutton Northants 101 D9
King's Tamerton Plym 7 D9
King's Thorn Hereford 97 E10
King's Walden Herts 104 G3
Kings Worthy Hants 48 G3
Kingsand Corn 7 E8
Kingsash Bucks 84 D5
Kingsbarns Fife 287 F9
Kingsbridge Devon 8 G4
Kingsbridge Som 42 F3
Kingsburgh Highld 298 D3
Kingsbury London 67 B8
Kingsbury Warks 134 D4
Kingsbury Episcopi Som 28 C6
Kingsbury Regis Som 29 D11
Kingscauseway Highld 301 B7
Kingscavil W Loth 279 F10
Kingsclere Hants 48 B4
Kingsclere Woodlands Hants 64 G4
Kingscote Glos 80 F4
Kingscott Devon 25 D8
Kingscourt Glos 80 E4
Kingscross N Ayrs 256 D2
Kingsditch Glos 99 G8
Kingsdon Som 29 B8
Kingsdown Kent 54 B2
Kingsdown Kent 55 D11
Kingsdown Swindon 63 B7
Kingsdown Wilts 61 F10
Kingseat Fife 280 C2
Kingseathill Fife 280 D2
Kingsett Devon 12 E6
Kingsey Bucks 84 D2
Kingsfield Hereford 97 B10
Kingsfold Lancs 194 B4
Kingsfold W Sus 51 F7
Kingsford Aberds 293 B7
Kingsford E Ayrs 267 F8
Kingsford Worcs 132 G6
Kingsforth N Lincs 200 D4
Kingsgate Kent 71 E11
Kingshall Green Suff 125 E8
Kingshall Street Suff 125 E8
Kingsheanton Devon 40 F5
Kingshill Glos 80 F3
Kingshill Swindon 62 C6
Kingsholm Glos 80 B4
Kingshouse Hotel Highld 284 B6
Kingshurst W Mid 134 F3
Kingside Hill Cumb 238 G5
Kingskerswell Devon 9 B7
Kingskettle Fife 287 G7
Kingsknowe Edin 280 G4
Kingsland Anglesey 178 E2
Kingsland Hereford 115 E8
Kingsland London 67 C10
Kingsland Shrops 149 G9
Kingsley Hants 49 F9
Kingsley Staffs 169 F8
Kingsley W Ches 183 G9
Kingsley Green W Sus 49 G11
Kingsley Holt Staffs 169 F8
Kingsley Moor Staffs 169 F7
Kingsley Park Northants 120 E5
Kingslow Shrops 132 D5
Kingsmead Hants 33 E9
Kingsmoor Essex 86 D6
Kingsmuir Angus 287 C8
Kingsmuir Fife 287 G9
Kingsnordley Shrops 132 F5
Kingsnorth Kent 54 F4
Kingstanding W Mid 133 E11
Kingsteignton Devon 14 G3
Kingsteps Highld 301 D9
Kingsthorpe Northants 120 E5
Kingsthorpe Hollow Northants 120 E5
Kingston Cambs 122 F6
Kingston Devon 8 F2
Kingston Devon 9 E8
Kingston Dorset 18 F5
Kingston Dorset 30 F3
Kingston E Loth 281 E10
Kingston Gtr Man 184 B6
Kingston Hants 31 G11
Kingston I o W 20 E5
Kingston Kent 55 C7
Kingston M Keynes 103 D8
Kingston Moray 302 C3
Kingston Ptsmth 33 G11
Kingston Suff 108 B5
Kingston Bagpuize Oxon 82 F6
Kingston Blount Oxon 84 F2
Kingston by Sea W Sus 36 G2
Kingston Deverill Wilts 45 F10
Kingston Gorse W Sus 35 G9
Kingston Lisle Oxon 63 B10
Kingston Maurward Dorset 17 C10
Kingston near Lewes E Sus 36 F5
Kingston on Soar Notts 153 D10
Kingston Park T & W 242 D6
Kingston Russell Dorset 17 C7
Kingston St Mary Som 28 B2
Kingston Seymour N Som 60 F2
Kingston Stert Oxon 84 E2
Kingston upon Hull Hull 200 B5
Kingston upon Thames London 67 F7
Kingston Vale London 67 E8
Kingstone Hereford 97 D8
Kingstone Hereford 98 G2
Kingstone S Yorks 197 F10
Kingstone Som 28 E5
Kingstone Staffs 151 D11
Kingstone Winslow Oxon 63 B9
Kingstown Cumb 239 F9
Kingsway Bath 61 G8
Kingsway Halton 183 D8
Kingswear Devon 9 E7
Kingswells Aberdeen 293 C10
Kingswinford W Mid 133 F7
Kingswood Bucks 83 B11
Kingswood Essex 69 B8
Kingswood Glos 80 G2
Kingswood Hereford 114 G5
Kingswood Herts 85 E10
Kingswood Kent 53 C10
Kingswood Powys 130 C4
Kingswood S Glos 60 E6
Kingswood Som 42 F6
Kingswood Sur 51 B8
Kingswood Warks 118 C3
Kingswood Warr 183 C9
Kingswood Brook Warks 118 C3
Kingswood Common Staffs 132 C6
Kingswood Common Worcs 116 D4
Kingthorpe Lincs 189 F10
Kington Hereford 114 F5
Kington S Glos 79 G10
Kington Worcs 117 F9
Kington Langley Wilts 62 D2
Kington Magna Dorset 30 C3
Kington St Michael Wilts 62 D2
Kingussie Highld 291 C9
Kingweston Som 44 G4
Kininvie Ho Moray 302 E3
Kinkell Bridge Perth 286 F3
Kinknockie Aberds 303 E10
Kinknockie Aberds 303 G9
Kinkry Hill Cumb 240 B2
Kinlet Shrops 132 G4
Kinloch Fife 286 F6
Kinloch Highld 289 D8
Kinloch Highld 294 F5
Kinloch Highld 295 D8
Kinloch Highld 308 F3
Kinloch Perth 286 C5
Kinloch Perth 286 C6
Kinloch Damph Highld 299 E8
Kinloch Hourn Highld 295 E11
Kinloch Laggan Highld 291 E7
Kinloch Lodge Highld 308 D5
Kinloch Rannoch Perth 285 B10
Kinlochan Highld 289 C10
Kinlochard Stirl 285 G8
Kinlochbeoraid Highld 295 G10
Kinlochbervie Highld 306 D7
Kinlocheil Highld 289 B11
Kinlochewe Highld 299 C10
Kinlochleven Highld 290 G3
Kinlochmoidart Highld 289 B9
Kinlochmorar Highld 295 F10
Kinlochmore Highld 290 G3
Kinlochspelve Argyll 289 G8
Kinloid Highld 295 G8
Kinloss Moray 301 C10
Kinmel Bay = Bae Cinmel Conwy 181 E7
Kinmuck Aberds 293 B10
Kinmundy Aberds 293 B10
Kinnadie Aberds 303 E9
Kinnaird Perth 286 B3
Kinnaird Perth 286 E6
Kinnaird Castle Angus 287 B10
Kinnauld Highld 309 J7
Kinneff Aberds 293 F10
Kinneil Falk 279 E9
Kinnelhead Dumfries 248 C2
Kinnell Angus 287 B10
Kinnerley Shrops 148 E6
Kinnersley Hereford 96 B6
Kinnersley Worcs 99 C7
Kinnerton Powys 114 E4
Kinnerton Green Flint 166 C4
Kinnesswood Perth 286 G5
Kinninvie Durham 233 G7
Kinnordy Angus 287 B7
Kinoulton Notts 154 C3
Kinross Perth 286 G5
Kinrossie Perth 286 D5
Kinsbourne Green Herts 85 B10
Kinsey Heath E Ches 167 G11
Kinsham Hereford 115 E7
Kinsham Worcs 99 D8
Kinsley W Yorks 198 E2
Kinson Bmouth 19 B7
Kintallan Argyll 275 E8
Kintbury W Berks 63 F11
Kintessack Moray 301 C9
Kintillo Perth 286 F5
Kintocher Aberds 293 C7
Kinton Hereford 115 C8
Kinton Shrops 149 F7
Kintore Aberds 293 B9
Kintour Argyll 254 B5
Kintra Argyll 254 C4
Kintra Argyll 288 G5
Kintradwell Highld 311 J3
Kintraw Argyll 275 C9
Kinuachdrach Argyll 275 D8
Kinveachy Highld 291 B11
Kinver Staffs 132 G6
Kinwalsey Warks 134 F5
Kip Hill Durham 242 G6
Kiplin N Yorks 224 F5
Kippax W Yorks 206 G4
Kippen Stirl 278 C3
Kippford or Scaur Dumfries 237 D10

Kippilaw Borders 262 D2
Kippilaw Mains Borders 262 D2
Kipping's Cross Kent 52 F6
Kippington Kent 52 C4
Kirbister Orkney 314 E2
Kirbister Orkney 314 D6
Kirbister Orkney 314 F3
Kirbuster Orkney 314 D2
Kirby Bedon Norf 142 B5
Kirby Bellars Leics 154 F4
Kirby Cane Norf 143 E7
Kirby Corner W Mid 118 B5
Kirby Cross Essex 108 G4
Kirby Fields Leics 135 C10
Kirby Green Norf 143 E7
Kirby Grindalythe N Yorks 217 F8
Kirby Hill N Yorks 215 F7
Kirby Hill N Yorks 224 D2
Kirby Knowle N Yorks 215 B9
Kirby-le-Soken Essex 108 G4
Kirby Misperton N Yorks 216 D5
Kirby Moor Cumb 240 E2
Kirby Muxloe Leics 135 C10
Kirby Row Norf 143 E7
Kirby Sigston N Yorks 225 G8
Kirby Underdale E Yorks 208 B2
Kirby Wiske N Yorks 215 C7
Kirdford W Sus 35 B8
Kirk Highld 310 D6
Kirk Bramwith S Yorks 198 E6
Kirk Deighton N Yorks 206 C3
Kirk Ella E Yorks 200 B4
Kirk Hallam Derbys 171 G7
Kirk Hammerton N Yorks 206 B5
Kirk Ireton Derbys 170 E3
Kirk Langley Derbys 152 B5
Kirk Merrington Durham 233 E11
Kirk Michael I o M 192 C4
Kirk of Shotts N Lnrk 268 C6
Kirk Sandall S Yorks 198 F6
Kirk Smeaton N Yorks 198 D4
Kirk Yetholm Borders 263 D8
Kirkabister Shetland 312 G6
Kirkabister Shetland 313 K6
Kirkandrews Dumfries 237 E8
Kirkandrews-on-Eden Cumb 239 F9
Kirkapol Argyll 288 E2
Kirkbampton Cumb 239 F8
Kirkbean Dumfries 237 D11
Kirkborough Cumb 229 D7
Kirkbrae Orkney 314 B4
Kirkbride Cumb 238 F6
Kirkbridge N Yorks 224 G5
Kirkbuddo Angus 287 C9
Kirkburn Borders 261 B7
Kirkburn E Yorks 208 B5
Kirkburton W Yorks 197 E7
Kirkby Lincs 189 C9
Kirkby Mers 182 B6
Kirkby N Yorks 225 D10
Kirkby Fenside Lincs 174 C4
Kirkby Fleetham N Yorks 224 G5
Kirkby Green Lincs 173 D9
Kirkby Hill N Yorks 215 F7
Kirkby in Ashfield Notts 171 D8
Kirkby-in-Furness Cumb 210 C4
Kirkby la Thorpe Lincs 173 F10
Kirkby Lonsdale Cumb 212 D2
Kirkby Malham N Yorks 213 G7
Kirkby Mallory Leics 135 C9
Kirkby Malzeard N Yorks 214 E4
Kirkby Mills N Yorks 216 B4
Kirkby on Bain Lincs 174 C2
Kirkby Overblow N Yorks 206 D2
Kirkby Stephen Cumb 222 D5
Kirkby Thore Cumb 231 F8
Kirkby Underwood Lincs 155 D11
Kirkby Wharfe N Yorks 206 E6
Kirkby Woodhouse Notts 171 E7
Kirkbymoorside N Yorks 216 B3
Kirkcaldy Fife 280 C5
Kirkcambeck Cumb 240 D2
Kirkcarswell Dumfries 237 E9
Kirkcolm Dumfries 236 C2
Kirkconnel Dumfries 258 G6
Kirkconnell Dumfries 237 C11
Kirkcowan Dumfries 236 C5
Kirkcudbright Dumfries 237 D8
Kirkdale Mers 182 C4
Kirkfieldbank S Lnrk 269 G7
Kirkforthar Feus Fife 286 G6
Kirkgunzeon Dumfries 237 C10
Kirkham Lancs 202 G4
Kirkham N Yorks 216 F4
Kirkhamgate W Yorks 197 C9
Kirkhams Gtr Man 195 F10
Kirkharle Northumb 252 G2
Kirkheaton Northumb 242 B2
Kirkheaton W Yorks 197 D7
Kirkhill Angus 293 G8
Kirkhill E Renf 267 D11
Kirkhill Highld 300 E5
Kirkhill Midloth 270 C4
Kirkhill Moray 302 F2
Kirkhill W Loth 279 G11
Kirkholt Gtr Man 195 E11
Kirkhope Borders 261 E9
Kirkhouse Borders 261 C8
Kirkhouse Cumb 240 F3
Kirkiboll Highld 308 D5
Kirkibost Highld 295 D7
Kirkinch Angus 287 C7
Kirkinner Dumfries 236 D6
Kirkintilloch E Dunb 278 G3
Kirkland Cumb 219 B11
Kirkland Cumb 229 B11
Kirkland Cumb 231 E8
Kirkland Dumfries 247 E8
Kirkland Dumfries 258 G6
Kirkland S Ayrs 244 E6
Kirkland Guards Cumb 229 C9
Kirkleatham Redcar 235 G7
Kirklees Gtr Man 195 E9
Kirklevington Stockton 225 D8
Kirkley Suff 143 E10
Kirklington N Yorks 214 C6
Kirklington Notts 171 D11
Kirklinton Cumb 239 D10
Kirkliston Edin 280 G2
Kirkmaiden Dumfries 236 F3
Kirkmichael Perth 286 B4
Kirkmichael S Ayrs 245 B8
Kirkmichael Mains Dumfries 248 F2
Kirkmuirhill S Lnrk 268 G5
Kirknewton Northumb 263 C10
Kirknewton W Loth 270 B2
Kirkney Aberds 302 F5
Kirkoswald Cumb 231 C7
Kirkoswald S Ayrs 244 B6
Kirkpatrick Dumfries 247 E10
Kirkpatrick Durham Dumfries 237 B9
Kirkpatrick-Fleming Dumfries 239 C7
Kirksanton Cumb 210 C2
Kirkshaw N Lnrk 268 C4
Kirkstall W Yorks 205 F11
Kirkstead Borders 261 E7
Kirkstead Lincs 173 C11
Kirkstile Aberds 302 F5
Kirkstyle Highld 310 B7
Kirkthorpe W Yorks 197 C11
Kirkton Aberds 302 E6
Kirkton Aberds 302 G6
Kirkton Angus 286 C6
Kirkton Angus 287 C8
Kirkton Angus 287 D8
Kirkton Argyll 275 C8
Kirkton Borders 262 G2
Kirkton Dumfries 247 G11
Kirkton Fife 280 D4
Kirkton Fife 287 E7
Kirkton Highld 295 C10
Kirkton Highld 299 E9
Kirkton Highld 301 D7
Kirkton Highld 309 K7
Kirkton Perth 286 F3
Kirkton S Lnrk 259 E10
Kirkton Stirl 285 G9
Kirkton W Loth 269 B10
Kirkton Manor Borders 260 B6
Kirkton of Airlie Angus 287 B7
Kirkton of Auchterhouse Angus 287 D7
Kirkton of Auchterless Aberds 303 E7
Kirkton of Barevan Highld 301 E8
Kirkton of Bourtie Aberds 303 G8
Kirkton of Collace Perth 286 D5
Kirkton of Craig Angus 287 B11
Kirkton of Culsalmond Aberds 302 F6
Kirkton of Durris Aberds 293 D9
Kirkton of Glenbuchat Aberds 292 B5
Kirkton of Glenisla Angus 292 G4
Kirkton of Kingoldrum Angus 287 B7
Kirkton of Largo Fife 287 G8
Kirkton of Lethendy Perth 286 C5
Kirkton of Logie Buchan Aberds 303 G9
Kirkton of Maryculter Aberds 293 D10
Kirkton of Menmuir Angus 293 G7
Kirkton of Monikie Angus 287 D9
Kirkton of Oyne Aberds 302 G6
Kirkton of Rayne Aberds 302 G6
Kirkton of Skene Aberds 293 C10
Kirkton of Tough Aberds 293 B8
Kirktonhill Borders 271 E9
Kirktonhill W Dunb 277 G7
Kirktown E Ayrs 267 G8
Kirktown Aberds 303 D10
Kirktown of Alvah Aberds 302 C6
Kirktown of Deskford Moray 302 C5
Kirktown of Fetteresso Aberds 293 E10
Kirktown of Mortlach Moray 302 F3
Kirktown of Slains Aberds 303 G10
Kirkurd Borders 270 G2
Kirkwall Orkney 314 E4
Kirkwhelpington Northumb 251 G11
Kirkwood Dumfries 238 B4
Kirkwood N Lnrk 268 C4
Kirmington N Lincs 200 E6
Kirmond le Mire Lincs 189 C11
Kirn Argyll 276 F3
Kirriemuir Angus 287 B7
Kirstead Green Norf 142 D5
Kirtlebridge Dumfries 238 C6
Kirtleton Dumfries 249 G7
Kirtling Cambs 124 F3
Kirtling Green Cambs 124 F3
Kirtlington Oxon 83 B7
Kirtomy Highld 308 C7
Kirton Lincs 156 B6
Kirton Notts 171 B11
Kirton Suff 108 D5
Kirton Campus W Loth 269 B10
Kirton End Lincs 174 G3
Kirton Holme Lincs 174 G3
Kirton in Lindsey N Lincs 188 B6
Kiskin Cumb 210 B1
Kislingbury Northants 120 F3
Kit Hill Dorset 30 D4
Kitbridge Devon 28 G4
Kitchenroyd W Yorks 197 F8
Kite Green Warks 118 D3
Kite Hill I o W 21 C7
Kitebrook Warks 100 E4
Kites Hardwick Warks 119 D9
Kitlye Glos 80 E5
Kit's Coty Kent 69 G8
Kitt Green Gtr Man 194 F5
Kittisford Som 27 C9
Kittle Swansea 56 D5
Kitts End Herts 86 F2
Kitt's Green W Mid 134 F3
Kitt's Moss Gtr Man 184 E5
Kittwhistle Dorset 28 G5
Kittybrewster Aberdeen 293 C11
Kitwell W Mid 133 G9
Kitwood Hants 49 G7
Kivernoll Hereford 97 E9
Kiveton Park S Yorks 187 E7
Knaith Lincs 188 E4
Knaith Park Lincs 188 D4
Knap Corner Dorset 30 C4
Knaphill Sur 50 B3
Knapp Hants 32 C6
Knapp Perth 286 D6
Knapp Som 28 B4
Knapp Wilts 31 B8
Knapp Hill Wilts 30 B5
Knapthorpe Notts 172 D2
Knaptoft Leics 136 F2
Knapton Norf 160 C6
Knapton York 207 C7
Knapton Green Hereford 115 G8
Knapwell Cambs 122 E6
Knaresborough N Yorks 206 B3
Knarsdale Northumb 240 G5
Knatts Valley Kent 68 G5
Knauchland Moray 302 D5
Knaven Aberds 303 E8
Knave's Ash Kent 71 G7
Knaves Green Suff 126 D2
Knavesmire York 207 D7
Knayton N Yorks 215 B8
Knebworth Herts 104 G5
Knedlington E Yorks 199 B8
Kneesall Notts 172 C2
Kneesworth Cambs 104 C6
Kneeton Notts 172 F2
Knelston Swansea 56 D3
Knenhall Staffs 151 B8
Knettishall Suff 141 G9
Knightacott Devon 41 F7
Knightcote Warks 119 G7
Knightcott N Som 43 B11
Knightley Staffs 150 D6
Knightley Dale Staffs 150 E6
Knighton Devon 7 F10
Knighton Dorset 29 E10
Knighton Leicester 135 C11
Knighton Oxon 63 B9
Knighton Poole 18 B6
Knighton Som 43 E7
Knighton Staffs 150 D4
Knighton Staffs 168 G2
Knighton Wilts 63 E9
Knighton Worcs 117 F10
Knighton = Tref-y-Clawdd Powys 114 C5
Knighton Fields Leicester 135 C11
Knighton on Teme Worcs 116 C2
Knightor Corn 5 D10
Knight's End Cambs 139 E8
Knights Enham Hants 47 D11
Knight's Hill London 67 E10
Knightsbridge Glos 99 F7
Knightsbridge London 67 D9
Knightsmill Corn 11 E7
Knightsridge W Loth 269 B10
Knightswood Glasgow 267 B10
Knightwick Worcs 116 F4
Knill Hereford 114 E5
Knipe Fold Cumb 220 F6
Knipoch Argyll 289 G10
Knipton Leics 154 C6
Knitsley Durham 233 B8
Kniveton Derbys 170 E2
Knocharthur Highld 309 J7
Knock Argyll 289 F7
Knock Cumb 231 F9
Knock Moray 302 D5
Knockally Highld 311 G5
Knockan Highld 307 H7
Knockandhu Moray 302 G2
Knockando Moray 301 E11
Knockando Ho Moray 302 E2
Knockandoo Highld 301 G7
Knockbain Highld 300 D6
Knockbreck Highld 298 C2
Knockbrex Dumfries 237 E7
Knockcarrach Highld 290 B6
Knockdee Highld 310 C5
Knockdolian S Ayrs 244 F4
Knockdow Argyll 276 G2
Knockdown Glos 61 B10
Knockenbaird Aberds 302 G6
Knockenkelly N Ayrs 256 D2
Knockentiber E Ayrs 257 B9
Knockerdown Derbys 170 E2
Knockespock Ho Aberds 302 G5
Knockfarrel Highld 300 D5
Knockglass Dumfries 236 D2
Knockhall Kent 68 E5
Knockhall Castle Aberds 303 G9
Knockholt Kent 52 B3
Knockholt Pound Kent 52 B3
Knockie Lodge Highld 290 B6
Knockin Shrops 148 E6
Knockin Heath Shrops 149 E7
Knockinlaw E Ayrs 257 B10
Knockinnon Highld 310 F5
Knocklaw Northumb 252 C3
Knocklearn Dumfries 237 B9
Knocklearoch Argyll 274 G4
Knockmill Kent 68 G5
Knocknaha Argyll 255 F7
Knocknain Dumfries 236 C1
Knockothie Aberds 303 F9
Knockrome Argyll 274 F6
Knocksharry I o M 192 D3
Knockstapplemore Argyll 255 F7
Knockvologan Argyll 274 B4
Knodishall Suff 127 E8
Knokan Argyll 288 G6
Knole Som 29 B7
Knoll Green Som 43 F8
Knoll Top N Yorks 214 F3
Knollbury Mon 60 B2
Knolls Green E Ches 184 F4
Knolton Wrex 149 B7
Knolton Bryn Wrex 149 B7
Knook Wilts 46 E2
Knossington Leics 136 B6
Knotbury Staffs 169 B8
Knott End-on-Sea Lancs 202 D3
Knott Lanes Gtr Man 196 G2
Knott Oak Som 28 E5
Knotting Beds 121 E10
Knotting Green Beds 121 E10
Knottingley W Yorks 198 C4
Knotts Cumb 230 G4
Knotts Lancs 203 C11
Knotty Ash Mers 182 C6
Knotty Corner Devon 24 B6
Knotty Green Bucks 84 G6
Knowbury Shrops 115 C11
Knowe Dumfries 236 B5
Knowe Shetland 313 G5
Knowefield Cumb 239 F10
Knowehead Aberds 293 C7
Knowehead Aberds 302 D5
Knowehead Dumfries 246 E4
Knowes E Loth 282 F2
Knowes of Elrick Aberds 302 D6
Knowesgate Northumb 251 F11
Knoweton N Lnrk 268 D5
Knowetop N Lnrk 268 D5
Knowhead Aberds 303 D9
Knowl Bank Staffs 168 F3
Knowl Green Essex 106 C5
Knowl Hill Windsor 65 D10
Knowl Wall Staffs 151 B7
Knowl Wood W Yorks 196 C2
Knowle Bristol 60 E6
Knowle Devon 15 E7
Knowle Devon 26 G3
Knowle Devon 27 F8
Knowle Devon 40 F3
Knowle Hants 33 F9
Knowle Shrops 115 C11
Knowle Som 43 F10
Knowle W Mid 118 B3
Knowle Wilts 63 G7
Knowle Fields Worcs 117 F10
Knowle Green Lancs 203 F8
Knowle Green Sur 66 E4
Knowle Grove W Mid 118 B3
Knowle Hill Sur 66 F3
Knowle Park W Yorks 205 E7
Knowle St Giles Som 28 E4
Knowlegate Shrops 115 C11
Knowles Hill Devon 14 G3
Knowlesands Shrops 132 E4
Knowlton Dorset 31 E8
Knowlton Kent 55 C9
Knowsley Mers 182 B6
Knowsthorpe W Yorks 206 G2
Knowstone Devon 26 C4
Knox Bridge Kent 53 E9
Knucklas Powys 114 C5
Knuston Northants 121 D8
Knutsford E Ches 184 F3
Knutton Staffs 168 F4
Knuzden Brook Lancs 195 B8
Knypersley Staffs 168 D5
Kraiknish Highld 294 C5
Krumlin W Yorks 196 D5
Kuggar Corn 2 F6
Kyle of Lochalsh Highld 295 C9
Kyleakin Highld 295 C9
Kylepark N Lnrk 268 C3
Kylerhea Highld 295 C9
Kylesknoydart Highld 295 F10
Kylesku Highld 306 F7
Kylesmorar Highld 295 F10
Kylestrome Highld 306 F7
Kyllachy House Highld 301 G7
Kymin Hereford 97 B11
Kymin Mon 79 C8
Kynaston Hereford 97 F10
Kynaston Shrops 149 E7
Kynnersley Telford 150 F3
Kyre Worcs 116 E2
Kyre Green Worcs 116 E2
Kyre Magna Worcs 116 E2
Kyre Park Worcs 116 E2
Kyrewood Worcs 116 D2

L

Labost W Isles 304 D4
Lacasaidh W Isles 304 F5
Lacasdal W Isles 304 E6
Laceby NE Lincs 201 F8
Laceby Acres NE Lincs 201 F8
Lacey Green Bucks 84 F4
Lacey Green E Ches 184 E4
Lach Dennis W Ches 184 G2
Lache W Ches 166 C5
Lackenby Redcar 225 B11
Lackford Suff 124 C5
Lacock Wilts 62 F2
Ladbroke Warks 119 F8
Laddenvean Corn 3 E7
Laddingford Kent 53 D7
Lade Kent 39 C9
Lade Bank Lincs 174 E5
Ladies Riggs N Yorks 214 F2
Ladmanlow Derbys 185 G8
Ladock Corn 5 E7
Ladwell Hants 32 C6
Lady Orkney 314 B6
Lady Green Mers 193 G10
Lady Hall Cumb 210 B3
Lady Halton Shrops 115 B9
Lady House Gtr Man 196 E2
Lady Park T & W 242 F6
Lady Wood W Yorks 206 F2
Ladybank Fife 287 F7
Ladybrook Notts 171 C8
Ladyburn Invclyd 276 F6
Ladycross Corn 12 D2
Ladyes Hill Warks 118 C5
Ladykirk Borders 273 F7
Ladyoak Shrops 131 C7
Ladyridge Hereford 97 E11
Lady's Green Suff 124 F5
Ladysford Aberds 303 C9
Ladywell London 67 E11
Ladywell Shrops 149 C9
Ladywell W Loth 269 B10
Ladywood Telford 132 C3
Ladywood W Mid 133 F11
Ladywood Worcs 117 E7
Laffak Mers 183 B8
Laga Highld 289 C8
Lagafater Lodge Dumfries 236 B3
Lagalochan Argyll 275 B9
Lagavulin Argyll 254 C5
Lagg Argyll 274 F6
Lagg N Ayrs 255 E10
Laggan Argyll 254 B3
Laggan Highld 289 B9
Laggan Highld 290 D4
Laggan Highld 291 D8
Laggan S Ayrs 245 G7
Laggan Lodge Argyll 289 G8
Lagganlia Highld 291 C10
Lagganmullan Dumfries 237 D7
Lagganulva Argyll 288 E6
Lagness W Sus 22 C5
Laide Highld 307 K3
Laig Highld 294 G6
Laigh Carnduff S Lnrk 268 F3
Laigh Fenwick E Ayrs 267 G9
Laigh Glengall S Ayrs 257 F8
Laighmuir E Ayrs 267 F9
Laighstonehall S Lnrk 268 E4
Laindon Essex 69 B7
Lair Highld 299 E10
Lair Perth 292 G3
Laira Plym 7 D10
Lairg Highld 309 J5
Lairg Lodge Highld 309 J5
Lairg Muir Highld 309 J5
Lairgmore Highld 300 F5
Laisterdyke W Yorks 205 G9
Laithes Cumb 230 E5
Laithkirk Durham 232 G5
Laity Moor Corn 4 F3
Lake Devon 12 D6
Lake Devon 24 F6
Lake Devon 40 G5
Lake I o W 21 E7
Lake Poole 18 C5
Lake Wilts 46 F6
Lake End Bucks 66 D2
Lakenham Norf 142 B4
Lakenheath Suff 140 G4
Laker's Green Sur 50 F4
Lakesend Norf 139 D10
Lakeside Cumb 211 B7
Lakeside Thurrock 68 D5
Lakeside Worcs 117 D11
Laleham Sur 66 F5
Laleston = Trelales Bridgend 57 F11
Lamanva Corn 3 C7
Lamarsh Essex 107 D7
Lamas Norf 160 E4
Lamb Corner Essex 107 E10
Lambden Borders 272 G4
Lamberden Kent 38 B4
Lamberhead Green Gtr Man 194 G4
Lamberhurst Kent 53 F7
Lamberhurst Quarter Kent 53 F7
Lamberton Borders 273 D9
Lambert's End W Mid 133 E9
Lambeth London 67 D10
Lambfair Green Suff 124 G4
Lambfoot Cumb 229 E9
Lambhill Glasgow 267 B11
Lambley Northumb 240 F5
Lambley Notts 171 F10
Lambourn W Berks 63 D10
Lambourn Woodlands W Berks 63 D10
Lambourne Corn 4 E5
Lambourne Essex 87 F7
Lambourne End Essex 87 G7
Lambridge Bath 61 F9
Lamb's Cross Kent 53 D9
Lambs' Green Dorset 18 B5
Lambs Green W Sus 51 F8
Lambston Pembs 72 B6
Lambton T & W 243 G7
Lamellion Corn 6 C4
Lamerton Devon 12 F5
Lamesley T & W 243 F7
Laminess Orkney 314 C6
Lamington Highld 301 B7
Lamington S Lnrk 259 C11
Lamlash N Ayrs 256 C2
Lamledra Corn 5 G10
Lamloch Dumfries 246 D2
Lammack Blkburn 195 B7
Lamonby Cumb 230 D4
Lamorick Corn 5 C10
Lamorna Corn 1 E4
Lamorran Corn 5 G7
Lampardbrook Suff 126 E5
Lampeter = Llanbedr Pont Steffan Ceredig 93 B11
Lampeter Velfrey Pembs 73 C11
Lamphey Pembs 73 E8
Lamplugh Cumb 229 G7
Lamport Northants 120 C5
Lampton London 66 D6
Lamyatt Som 45 F7
Lana Devon 12 B2
Lana Devon 24 F4
Lanark S Lnrk 269 G7
Lancaster Lancs 211 G9
Lanchester Durham 233 B9
Lancing W Sus 35 G11
Land Gate Gtr Man 194 G5
Landbeach Cambs 123 D9
Landcross Devon 25 C7
Landerberry Aberds 293 C9
Landewednack Corn 2 G6
Landford Wilts 32 D3
Landford Manor Wilts 32 C3
Landfordwood Wilts 32 C3
Landguard Manor I o W 21 E7
Landhill Devon 12 B4
Landican Mers 182 D3
Landimore Swansea 56 C3
Landkey Devon 40 G5
Landkey Newland Devon 40 G5
Landore Swansea 57 B7
Landport E Sus 36 E6
Landport Ptsmth 33 G10
Landrake Corn 7 C7
Landscove Devon 8 B5
Landshipping Pembs 73 C8
Landshipping Quay Pembs 73 C8
Landslow Green Gtr Man 185 B7
Landulph Corn 7 C8
Landwade Suff 124 D2
Landywood Staffs 133 B9
Lane Corn 4 C6
Lane Bottom Lancs 204 F3
Lane Bottom W Yorks 205 F7
Lane End Bucks 84 G4
Lane-end Corn 5 B10
Lane End Cumb 220 G2
Lane End Derbys 170 C6
Lane End Devon 24 G6
Lane End Dorset 18 C3
Lane End Flint 166 C3
Lane End Glos 79 B10
Lane End Hants 33 B11
Lane End Hants 33 B9
Lane End I o W 21 D9
Lane End Kent 68 E5
Lane End Lancs 204 D3
Lane End S Yorks 186 B5
Lane End Sur 49 E10
Lane End W Yorks 204 F6
Lane End Wilts 45 D10
Lane Ends Cumb 210 C6
Lane Ends Derbys 152 C4
Lane Ends E Ches 168 D2
Lane Ends E Ches 185 E7
Lane Ends Gtr Man 185 C7
Lane Ends Lancs 194 D6
Lane Ends Lancs 203 C11
Lane Ends Lancs 203 G11
Lane Ends N Yorks 204 E5
Lane Ends Stoke 168 E5
Lane Ends W Yorks 205 F10
Lane Green Staffs 133 C7
Lane Head Derbys 185 F11
Lane Head Durham 224 C2
Lane Head Gtr Man 183 B10
Lane Head Pembs 73 E8
Lane Head W Mid 133 C9
Lane Head W Yorks 197 F7
Lane Heads Lancs 202 F4
Lane Side Lancs 195 C9
Laneast Corn 11 E10
Laneham Notts 188 F4
Lanehead Durham 232 C2
Lanehead Northumb 251 F7
Lanehouse Dorset 17 F9
Lanercost Cumb 240 E3
Lanes End Bucks 84 D6
Lane's End Shrops 132 G2
Lanescot Corn 5 D11
Lanesend Pembs 73 D9
Lanesfield W Mid 133 D8
Laneshaw Bridge Lancs 204 E4
Laney Green Staffs 133 B9
Lanfach Caerph 78 F2
Langaford Devon 12 B4
Langage Devon 7 E11
Langal Highld 289 C9
Langaller Som 28 B3
Langar Notts 154 C4
Langbank Renfs 277 G7
Langbar N Yorks 205 C7
Langbaurgh N Yorks 225 C11
Langburnshiels Borders 250 C2
Langcliffe N Yorks 212 G6
Langdale Highld 308 E6
Langdale End N Yorks 227 G8
Langdon Corn 12 D2
Langdon Beck Durham 232 E3
Langdon Hills Essex 69 B7
Langdown Hants 32 F6
Langdyke Dumfries 238 C3
Langdyke Fife 287 G7
Langenhoe Essex 89 B8
Langford C Beds 104 C3
Langford Devon 14 B4
Langford Devon 27 G8
Langford Essex 88 D4
Langford Notts 172 D4
Langford Oxon 82 E2
Langford Som 28 B2
Langford Budville Som 27 C10
Langford Green Devon 27 G8
Langford Green N Som 44 B3
Langham Dorset 30 B3
Langham Essex 107 E10
Langham Norf 177 E8
Langham Rutland 154 G6
Langham Som 28 E4
Langham Suff 125 C9
Langhaugh Borders 260 C6
Langho Lancs 203 G10
Langholm Dumfries 249 G9
Langholme N Lincs 188 B3
Langhope Borders 261 E10
Langland Swansea 56 D6
Langlee Borders 262 B2
Langlee Mains Borders 262 B2
Langleeford Northumb 263 E10
Langlees Falk 279 E7
Langley Derbys 170 F6
Langley E Ches 184 G6
Langley Essex 105 D8
Langley Glos 99 F10
Langley Gtr Man 195 F11
Langley Hants 32 G6
Langley Herts 104 G4
Langley Kent 53 C10
Langley Northumb 241 E8
Langley Oxon 82 B4
Langley Slough 66 D4
Langley Som 27 B9
Langley W Mid 133 F9
Langley W Sus 34 B4
Langley Warks 118 E3
Langley Burrell Wilts 62 D2
Langley Common Derbys 152 B5
Langley Common Wokingham 65 F9
Langley Corner Bucks 66 C4
Langley Green Derbys 152 B5
Langley Green Essex 107 G7
Langley Green W Mid 133 F9
Langley Green W Sus 51 F9
Langley Green Warks 118 E3
Langley Heath Kent 53 C10
Langley Marsh Som 27 B9
Langley Mill Derbys 170 F6
Langley Moor Durham 233 C11
Langley Park Durham 233 C10
Langley Street Norf 143 C7
Langley Vale Sur 51 B8
Langleybury Herts 85 E9
Langloan N Lnrk 268 C4
Langney E Sus 23 E10
Langold Notts 187 D9
Langore Corn 12 D2
Langport Som 28 B6
Langrick Lincs 174 F3
Langrick Bridge Lincs 174 F3
Langridge Bath 61 F8
Langridge Ford Devon 25 C9
Langrigg Cumb 222 C5
Langrigg Cumb 229 B9
Langrish Hants 34 C2
Langsett S Yorks 197 G8
Langshaw Borders 262 B2
Langside Glasgow 267 C11
Langside Perth 285 F11
Langskaill Orkney 314 B4
Langstone Devon 13 E10
Langstone Hants 22 C2
Langstone Newport 78 G5
Langthorne N Yorks 224 G5
Langthorpe N Yorks 215 F7
Langthwaite N Yorks 223 E10
Langtoft E Yorks 217 F10
Langtoft Lincs 156 G2
Langton Durham 224 B3
Langton Lincs 174 B2
Langton Lincs 190 G5
Langton N Yorks 216 F5
Langton by Wragby Lincs 189 F11
Langton Green Kent 52 F4
Langton Green Suff 126 C2
Langton Herring Dorset 17 E8
Langton Long Blandford Dorset 30 F5
Langton Matravers Dorset 18 F6
Langtree Devon 25 D7
Langtree Week Devon 25 D7
Langwathby Cumb 231 E7
Langwell Ho Highld 311 G5
Langwell Lodge Highld 307 J6
Langwith Derbys 171 B8
Langwith Junction Derbys 171 B8
Langworth Lincs 189 F9
Lanham Green Essex 106 G5
Lanivet Corn 5 C10
Lanjeth Corn 5 E9
Lanjew Corn 5 C9
Lank Corn 11 F7
Lanlivery Corn 5 D11
Lanner Corn 2 B6
Lanreath Corn 6 D3
Lanrick Stirl 285 G10
Lansallos Corn 6 E3
Lansbury Park Caerph 59 B7
Lansdown Bath 61 F8
Lansdown Glos 99 G8
Lanstephan Corn 12 D2
Lanteglos Corn 11 E7
Lanteglos Highway Corn 6 E3
Lanton Borders 262 E4
Lanton Northumb 263 C10
Lantuel Corn 5 B9
Lantyan Corn 6 D2
Lapal W Mid 133 G9
Lapford Devon 26 F2
Lapford Cross Devon 26 F2
Laphroaig Argyll 254 C4
Lapley Staffs 151 G7
Lapworth Warks 118 C3
Larachbeg Highld 289 E8
Larbert Falk 279 E7
Larbreck Lancs 202 E4
Larches Lancs 202 G6
Larden Green E Ches 167 E9
Larg Highld 292 B2
Largie Aberds 302 F6
Largiebaan Argyll 255 F7
Largiemore Argyll 275 E10
Largoward Fife 287 G8
Largs N Ayrs 266 D4
Largue Aberds 302 E6
Largybeg N Ayrs 256 E3
Largymeanoch N Ayrs 256 E2
Largymore N Ayrs 256 E2
Lark Hill Gtr Man 195 G7
Larkfield Invclyd 276 F4
Larkfield Kent 53 B8
Larkfield W Yorks 205 F10
Larkhall Bath 61 F9
Larkhall S Lnrk 268 E5
Larkhill Wilts 46 E6
Larklands Derbys 171 G7
Larks' Hill Suff 108 B3
Larling Norf 141 F9
Larport Hereford 97 D11
Larrick Corn 12 F2
Larriston Borders 250 E2
Lartington Durham 223 B10
Lary Aberds 292 C5
Lasborough Glos 80 G4
Lasham Hants 49 E7
Lashenden Kent 53 E10
Lask Edge Staffs 168 D6
Lassington Glos 98 G5
Lassodie Fife 280 C2
Lastingham N Yorks 226 G4
Latcham Som 44 D2
Latchbrook Corn 7 D8
Latchford Herts 105 G7
Latchford Oxon 83 E11
Latchford Warr 183 D10
Latchingdon Essex 88 E5
Latchley Corn 12 G4
Latchmere Green Hants 64 G6
Latchmore Bank Essex 87 B7
Lately Common Warr 183 B11
Lathallan Mill Fife 287 G8
Lathbury M Keynes 103 B7
Latheron Highld 310 F5
Latheronwheel Highld 310 F5
Latheronwheel Ho Highld 310 F5
Lathom Lancs 194 E3
Lathones Fife 287 G8
Latimer Bucks 85 F8
Latteridge S Glos 61 C7
Lattiford Som 29 B11
Lattinford Hill Suff 107 D11
Latton Wilts 81 F9
Latton Bush Essex 87 D7
Lauchintilly Aberds 293 B9
Laudale Ho Highld 289 D9
Lauder Borders 271 F10
Lauder Barns Borders 271 F10
Laugharne = Talacharn Carms 74 C4
Laughern Hill Worcs 116 F5
Laughterton Lincs 188 F4
Laughton E Sus 23 C8
Laughton Leics 136 F3
Laughton Lincs 155 C11
Laughton Lincs 188 B4
Laughton Common E Sus 23 C7
Laughton Common S Yorks 187 D8
Laughton en le Morthen S Yorks 187 D8
Launcells Corn 24 F2
Launcells Cross Corn 24 F3
Launceston Corn 12 D2
Launcherley Som 44 E4
Laund Lancs 195 C10
Launton Oxon 102 G2
Laurencekirk Aberds 293 F9
Laurieston Dumfries 237 C8
Laurieston Falk 279 F8
Lavendon M Keynes 121 G8
Lavenham Suff 107 B8
Laverackloch Moray 301 C11
Laverhay Dumfries 248 D4
Laverlaw Borders 261 B7
Laverley Som 44 F5
Lavernock V Glam 59 F7
Laversdale Cumb 239 E11
Laverstock Wilts 47 G7
Laverstoke Hants 48 D3
Laverton Glos 99 D11
Laverton N Yorks 214 E4
Laverton Som 45 C9
Lavington Sands Wilts 46 B4
Lavister Wrex 166 D5
Lavrean Corn 5 D10
Law Hill S Lnrk 268 E6
Lawers Perth 285 D10
Lawers Perth 285 E11
Lawford Essex 107 E11
Lawford Som 42 F6
Lawford Heath Warks 119 C9
Lawhill Perth 286 F3
Lawhitton Corn 12 E3
Lawkland N Yorks 212 F5
Lawkland Green N Yorks 212 F5
Lawley Telford 132 B3
Lawn Swindon 63 C7
Lawnhead Staffs 150 E6
Lawns W Yorks 197 C10
Lawnswood W Yorks 205 F11
Lawnt Denb 165 B8
Lawrence Hill Newport 59 B10
Lawrence Weston Bristol 60 D4
Lawrenny Pembs 73 D8
Lawrenny Quay Pembs 73 D8
Lawshall Suff 125 G7
Lawshall Green Suff 125 G7
Lawton Hereford 115 F8
Lawton Shrops 131 G10
Lawton-gate E Ches 168 D4
Lawton Heath End E Ches 168 D3
Laxey I o M 192 D5
Laxfield Suff 126 C5
Laxfirth Shetland 313 H6
Laxfirth Shetland 313 J6
Laxford Bridge Highld 306 E7
Laxo Shetland 313 G6
Laxobigging Shetland 312 F6
Laxton E Yorks 199 B9
Laxton Northants 137 D8
Laxton Notts 172 B2
Laycock W Yorks 204 E6
Layer Breton Essex 88 B6
Layer de la Haye Essex 89 B7
Layer Marney Essex 88 B6
Layerthorpe York 207 C8
Layham Suff 107 C10
Laymore Dorset 28 G5
Layters Green Bucks 85 G7
Laytham E Yorks 207 F10
Layton Blkpool 202 F2
Lazenby Redcar 225 B11
Lazonby Cumb 230 D6
Le Skerne Haughton Darl 224 B6
Lea Derbys 170 D4
Lea Hereford 98 G3
Lea Lancs 202 G5
Lea Lincs 188 D4
Lea Shrops 131 B8
Lea Shrops 131 F7
Lea Wilts 62 B3
Lea Bridge London 67 B11
Lea by Backford W Ches 182 G5
Lea End Worcs 117 B10
Lea Forge E Ches 168 F2
Lea Green Mers 183 C8
Lea Hall W Mid 134 F2
Lea Heath Staffs 151 D10
Lea Line Hereford 98 G3
Lea Marston Warks 134 E4
Lea Town Lancs 202 G5
Lea Valley Herts 85 B11
Lea Yeat Cumb 212 B5
Leabrooks Derbys 170 E6
Leac a Li W Isles 305 J3
Leacainn W Isles 305 H3
Leachkin Highld 300 E6
Leacnasaide Highld 299 B7
Leadburn Midloth 270 D4
Leaden Roding Essex 87 C9
Leadendale Staffs 151 B8
Leadenham Lincs 173 E7
Leadgate Cumb 231 C10
Leadgate Durham 242 G4
Leadgate T & W 242 F4
Leadhills S Lnrk 259 G9
Leadingcross Green Kent 53 C11
Leadmill Derbys 186 E2
Leadmill Flint 166 C2
Leafield Oxon 82 B4
Leafield Wilts 61 F11
Leagrave Luton 103 G10
Leagreen Hants 19 C11
Leake Lincs 174 F6
Leake N Yorks 225 G8
Leake Commonside Lincs 174 E5
Leake Fold Hill Lincs 174 E6
Lealholm N Yorks 226 D5
Lealholm Side N Yorks 226 D5
Lealt Argyll 275 D7
Lealt Highld 298 C5
Leam Derbys 186 F2
Leamington Hastings Warks 119 D8
Leamoor Common Shrops 131 F8
Leamore W Mid 133 C9
Leamside Durham 234 B2
Leanach Argyll 275 D11
Leanachan Highld 290 F4
Leanaig Highld 300 D5
Leapgate Worcs 116 C6
Leargybreck Argyll 274 F6
Lease Rigg N Yorks 226 E6
Leasey Bridge Herts 85 C11
Leasgill Cumb 211 C9
Leasingham Lincs 173 F9
Leasingthorne Durham 233 F11
Leason Swansea 56 C3
Leasowe Mers 182 C3
Leatherhead Sur 51 B7
Leatherhead Common Sur 51 B7
Leathern Bottle Glos 80 E2
Leathley N Yorks 205 D10
Leaths Dumfries 237 C9
Leaton Shrops 149 F9
Leaton Telford 150 G2
Leaton Heath Shrops 149 F9
Leaveland Kent 54 C4
Leavenheath Suff 107 D9
Leavening N Yorks 216 G5
Leaves Green London 68 G2
Leavesden Green Herts 85 E9
Leazes Durham 242 F5
Lebberston N Yorks 217 C11
Leburnick Corn 12 E3
Lechlade-on-Thames Glos 82 F2
Leck Lancs 212 D2
Leckford Hants 47 F11
Leckfurin Highld 308 D7
Leckgruinart Argyll 274 G3
Leckhampstead Bucks 102 D4
Leckhampstead W Berks 64 D2
Leckhampstead Thicket W Berks 64 D2
Leckhampton Glos 80 B6
Leckie Highld 299 C10
Leckmelm Highld 307 K6
Leckuary Argyll 275 D9
Leckwith V Glam 59 E7
Leconfield E Yorks 208 E6
Ledaig Argyll 289 F11
Ledburn Bucks 103 G8
Ledbury Hereford 98 D4
Ledcharrie Stirl 285 E9
Leddington Glos 98 E3
Ledgemoor Hereford 115 G8
Ledgowan Highld 299 D11
Ledicot Hereford 115 E8
Ledmore Angus 293 G7
Ledmore Highld 307 H7
Lednagullin Highld 308 C7
Ledsham W Ches 182 G5
Ledsham W Yorks 198 B3
Ledston W Yorks 198 B2
Ledston Luck W Yorks 206 G4
Ledstone Devon 8 F4
Ledwell Oxon 101 F8
Lee Argyll 288 G6
Lee Devon 40 D3
Lee Devon 40 D5
Lee Hants 32 D5
Lee Lancs 203 B7
Lee London 67 E11
Lee Northumb 241 F10
Lee Shrops 149 C8
Lee Bank W Mid 133 F11
Lee Brockhurst Shrops 149 D10
Lee Chapel Essex 69 B7
Lee Clump Bucks 84 E6
Lee Common Bucks 84 E6
Lee Gate Bucks 84 D5
Lee Ground Hants 33 F8
Lee Head Derbys 185 C8
Lee Mill Devon 8 D2
Lee Moor Devon 7 C11
Lee Moor W Yorks 197 B10
Lee-on-the-Solent Hants 33 G9
Lee-over-Sands Essex 89 C10
Leeans Shetland 313 J5
Leebotten Shetland 313 L6
Leebotwood Shrops 131 D9
Leece Cumb 210 F4
Leechpool Mon 60 B4
Leeds Kent 53 C10
Leeds W Yorks 205 G11
Leedstown Corn 2 C4
Leeford Devon 41 D9
Leegomery Telford 150 G3
Leeholme Durham 233 E10
Leek Staffs 169 D7
Leek Wootton Warks 118 D5
Leekbrook Staffs 169 E7
Leeming N Yorks 214 B5
Leeming W Yorks 204 G6
Leeming Bar N Yorks 224 G5
Leemings Lancs 203 D10
Lees Derbys 152 B5
Lees Gtr Man 196 G3

Lees W Yorks 204 F6
Leesthorpe Leics 154 G5
Leeswood = Coed-Llai Flint 166 D3
Leetown Perth 286 E6
Leftwich W Ches 183 G11
Legar Powys 78 B2
Legbourne Lincs 190 E5
Legburthwaite Cumb 220 B6
Legerwood Borders 271 G11
Leggatt Hill W Sus 34 C6
Legsby Lincs 189 D10
Leicester Leicester 135 C11
Leicester Forest East Leics 135 C10
Leicester Grange Warks 135 E8
Leigh Devon 26 E2
Leigh Dorset 18 B6
Leigh Dorset 29 F10
Leigh Dorset 30 F3
Leigh Glos 99 F7
Leigh Gtr Man 195 G7
Leigh Kent 52 D4
Leigh Shrops 130 C6
Leigh Sur 51 D8
Leigh Wilts 81 G9
Leigh Worcs 116 G5
Leigh Beck Essex 69 C10
Leigh Common Som 30 B2
Leigh Delamere Wilts 61 D11
Leigh Green Kent 54 G2
Leigh-on-Sea Sthend 69 B10
Leigh Park Hants 22 B2
Leigh Sinton Worcs 116 G5
Leigh upon Mendip Som 45 D7
Leigh Woods N Som 60 E5
Leigham Plym 7 D10
Leighland Chapel Som 42 F4
Leighswood W Mid 133 C11
Leighterton Glos 80 G4
Leighton N Yorks 214 D3
Leighton Shrops 132 B2
Leighton Som 45 E8
Leighton = Tre'r llai Powys 130 B4
Leighton Bromswold Cambs 122 B2
Leighton Buzzard C Beds 103 F8
Leinthall Earls Hereford 115 D8
Leinthall Starkes Hereford 115 D8
Leintwardine Hereford 115 C8
Leire Leics 135 E10
Leirinmore Highld 308 C4
Leiston Suff 127 E8
Leitfie Perth 286 C6
Leith Edin 280 F5
Leithenhall Dumfries 248 D4
Leitholm Borders 272 G5
Lelant Corn 2 B2
Lelant Downs Corn 2 B2
Lelley E Yorks 209 G10
Lem Hill Worcs 116 C4
Lemington T & W 242 E5
Lemmington Hall Northumb 264 G4
Lempitlaw Borders 263 C7
Lemsford Herts 86 C2
Lenacre Cumb 212 B3
Lenborough Bucks 102 E3
Lenchwick Worcs 99 B10
Lendalfoot S Ayrs 244 F4
Lendrick Lodge Stirl 285 G9
Lenham Kent 53 C11
Lenham Forstal Kent 54 C2
Lenham Heath Kent 54 D2
Lennel Borders 273 G7
Lennoxtown E Dunb 278 F2
Lent Bucks 66 C2
Lent Rise Bucks 66 C2
Lenten Pool Denb 165 B8
Lenton Lincs 155 C10
Lenton Nottingham 153 B11
Lenton Abbey Nottingham 153 B10
Lentran Highld 300 E5
Lenwade Norf 159 F11
Leny Ho Stirl 285 G10
Lenzie E Dunb 278 G3
Lenziemill N Lnrk 278 G5
Leoch Angus 287 D7
Leochel-Cushnie Aberds 293 B7
Leominster Hereford 115 F9
Leomonsley Staffs 134 B2
Leonard Stanley Glos 80 E4
Leonardston Pembs 72 D6
Leorin Argyll 254 C4
Lepe Hants 20 B5
Lephin Highld 297 G7
Lephinchapel Argyll 275 D10
Lephinmore Argyll 275 D10
Leppington N Yorks 216 G5
Lepton W Yorks 197 D8
Lepton Edge W Yorks 197 D8
Lerigoligan Argyll 275 C9
Lerrocks Stirl 285 G11
Lerryn Corn 6 D2
Lerwick Shetland 313 J6
Lesbury Northumb 264 G6
Leschangie Aberds 293 B9
Leslie Aberds 302 G5
Leslie Fife 286 G6
Lesmahagow S Lnrk 259 B8
Lesnewth Corn 11 C8
Lessendrum Aberds 302 E5
Lessingham Norf 161 D7
Lessness Heath London 68 D3
Lessonhall Cumb 238 G6
Leswalt Dumfries 236 C2
Letchmore Heath Herts 85 F11
Letchworth Herts 104 E4
Letcombe Bassett Oxon 63 B11
Letcombe Regis Oxon 63 B11
Letham Angus 287 C9
Letham Falk 279 D7
Letham Fife 287 F7
Letham Perth 286 E4
Letham Grange Angus 287 C10
Lethem Borders 250 B5
Lethen Ho Highld 301 D9
Lethenty Aberds 303 E8
Lethenty Aberds 303 G7
Letheringham Suff 126 F5
Letheringsett Norf 159 B11
Lettaford Devon 13 E10
Lettan Orkney 314 B7
Letter Aberds 293 B9
Letterewe Highld 299 B9
Letterfearn Highld 295 C10
Letterfinlay Highld 290 D4
Lettermay Argyll 284 G5
Lettermorar Highld 295 G9
Lettermore Argyll 288 E6
Letters Highld 307 L6
Letterston = Treletert Pembs 91 F8
Lettoch Highld 292 B2
Lettoch Highld 301 F10
Lettoch Moray 302 F3
Lettoch Perth 291 G11
Letton Hereford 96 B6
Letton Hereford 115 C7
Letton Green Norf 141 B9
Lett's Green Kent 52 B3
Letty Brongu Bridgend 57 D11
Letty Green Herts 86 C3
Letwell S Yorks 187 D9
Leuchars Fife 287 E8
Leuchars Ho Moray 302 C2
Leumrabhagh W Isles 305 G5
Levalsa Meor Corn 5 F10
Levan Invclyd 276 F4
Levaneap Shetland 313 G6
Levedale Staffs 151 F7
Level of Mendalgief Newport 59 B10
Level's Green Essex 105 G9
Leven E Yorks 209 D8
Leven Fife 287 G7
Leven Seat W Loth 269 D8
Levencorroch N Ayrs 256 E2
Levenhall E Loth 281 G7
Levens Cumb 211 B9
Levens Green Herts 105 G7
Levenshulme Gtr Man 184 C5
Leventhorpe W Yorks 205 G8
Levenwick Shetland 313 L6
Lever-Edge Gtr Man 195 F8
Leverington Cambs 157 G8
Leverington Common Cambs 157 G8
Leverstock Green Herts 85 D9
Leverton Lincs 174 F6
Leverton W Berks 63 E10
Leverton Highgate Lincs 174 F6
Leverton Lucasgate Lincs 174 F6
Leverton Outgate Lincs 174 F6
Levington Suff 108 D4
Levisham N Yorks 226 G6
Levishie Highld 290 B6
Lew Oxon 82 D4
Lewannick Corn 11 E11
Lewcombe Dorset 29 F9
Lewdown Devon 12 D4
Lewes E Sus 36 E6
Leweston Pembs 91 G8
Lewisham London 67 D11
Lewiston Highld 300 G5
Lewistown Bridgend 58 B2
Lewknor Oxon 84 F2
Leworthy Devon 24 G4
Leworthy Devon 41 F7
Lewson Street Kent 70 G3
Lewth Lancs 202 F5
Lewthorn Cross Devon 13 F11
Lewtrenchard Devon 12 D5
Lexden Essex 107 G9
Ley Aberds 293 B7
Ley Corn 6 B3
Ley Som 41 F10
Ley Green Herts 104 G3
Ley Hey Park Gtr Man 185 D7
Ley Hill W Mid 134 D2
Leybourne Kent 53 B7
Leyburn N Yorks 224 G2
Leycett Staffs 168 F3
Leyfields Staffs 134 B4
Leyhill Bucks 85 E7
Leyhill S Glos 79 G11
Leyland Lancs 194 C4
Leylodge Aberds 293 B9
Leymoor W Yorks 196 D6
Leys Aberds 292 C6
Leys Aberds 303 D10
Leys Cumb 219 B11
Leys Perth 286 D6
Leys Staffs 169 F8
Leys Castle Highld 300 E6
Leys Hill Hereford 79 B9
Leys of Cossans Angus 287 C7
Leysdown-on-Sea Kent 70 E4
Leysmill Angus 287 C10
Leysters Hereford 115 E11
Leysters Pole Hereford 115 E11
Leyton London 67 B11
Leytonstone London 67 B11
Lezant Corn 12 F2
Lezerea Corn 2 C5
Leziate Norf 158 F3
Lhanbryde Moray 302 C2
Liatrie Highld 300 F2
Libanus Powys 95 F9
Libberton S Lnrk 269 G9
Libbery Worcs 117 F9
Liberton Edin 270 B5
Liceasto W Isles 305 J3
Lichfield Staffs 134 B2
Lick Perth 286 B2
Lickey Worcs 117 B9
Lickey End Worcs 117 C9
Lickfold W Sus 34 B6
Lickhill Worcs 116 C6
Lickleyhead Castle Aberds 302 G6
Liddaton Devon 12 E5
Liddel Orkney 314 H4
Liddesdale Highld 289 D9
Liddeston Pembs 72 D5
Liddington Swindon 63 C8
Liden Swindon 63 C7
Lidgate Suff 124 F4
Lidget S Yorks 199 G7
Lidget Green W Yorks 205 G8
Lidgett Notts 171 B10
Lidgett Park W Yorks 206 F2
Lidham Hill E Sus 38 D4
Lidlington C Beds 103 D9
Lidsey W Sus 22 C6
Lidsing Kent 69 G9
Lidstone Oxon 101 G7
Lieurary Highld 310 C4
Liff Angus 287 D7
Lifford W Mid 117 B11
Lifton Devon 12 D3
Liftondown Devon 12 D3
Light Oaks Staffs 168 E6
Lightcliffe W Yorks 196 B6
Lighteach Shrops 149 C10
Lightfoot Green Lancs 202 G6
Lighthorne Warks 118 F6
Lighthorne Heath Warks 119 F7
Lighthorne Rough Warks 118 F6
Lightmoor Telford 132 B3
Lightpill Glos 80 E4
Lightwater Sur 66 G2
Lightwood S Yorks 186 E5
Lightwood Shrops 132 E2
Lightwood Shrops 150 D3
Lightwood Staffs 169 G8
Lightwood Stoke 168 G6
Lightwood Green E Ches 167 G10
Lightwood Green Wrex 166 G5
Liglartrie S Ayrs 244 F6
Lilbourne Northants 119 B11
Lilburn Tower Northumb 264 E2
Lilford Gtr Man 195 G7
Lilleshall Telford 150 F4
Lilley Herts 104 F2
Lilley W Berks 64 D2
Lilliesleaf Borders 262 E2
Lillingstone Dayrell Bucks 102 D4
Lillingstone Lovell Bucks 102 C4
Lillington Dorset 29 E10
Lillington Warks 118 D6
Lilliput Poole 18 C6
Lilstock Som 43 E7
Lilybank Invclyd 276 G6
Lilyhurst Shrops 150 G4
Lilyvale Kent 54 F5
Limbrick Lancs 194 D6
Limbury Luton 103 G11
Lime Side Gtr Man 196 G2
Lime Street Worcs 98 E6
Lime Tree Park W Mid 118 B5
Limebrook Hereford 115 D7
Limefield Gtr Man 195 E10
Limehouse London 67 C11
Limehurst Gtr Man 196 G2
Limekiln Field Derbys 187 G7
Limekilnburn S Lnrk 268 E4
Limekilns Fife 279 E11
Limerigg Falk 279 G7
Limerstone I o W 20 E4
Limestone Brae Northumb 231 B11
Limington Som 29 C8
Limpenhoe Norf 143 C7
Limpenhoe Hill Norf 143 C8
Limpers Hill Wilts 45 G10
Limpley Stoke Wilts 61 G9
Limpsfield Sur 52 C2
Limpsfield Chart Sur 52 C2
Limpsfield Common Sur 52 C2
Linbriggs Northumb 251 B9
Linburn W Loth 270 B2
Linby Notts 171 E8
Linchmere W Sus 49 G11
Lincluden Dumfries 237 B11
Lincoln Lincs 189 G7
Lincomb Worcs 116 D6
Lincombe Devon 8 D4
Lincombe Devon 40 D3
Lindal in Furness Cumb 210 D5
Lindale Cumb 211 C8
Lindean Borders 261 C11
Linden Glos 80 B4
Lindfield W Sus 36 B4
Lindford Hants 49 F10
Lindifferon Fife 287 F7
Lindley N Yorks 205 D10
Lindley W Yorks 196 D6
Lindley Green N Yorks 205 D10
Lindores Fife 286 F6
Lindow End E Ches 184 F4
Lindrick Dale S Yorks 187 E8
Lindridge Worcs 116 D3
Lindsell Essex 106 F2
Lindsey Suff 107 C9
Lindsey Tye Suff 107 B9
Lindwell W Yorks 196 C5
Lineholt Worcs 116 D6
Lineholt Common Worcs 116 D6
Liney Som 43 F11
Linfitts Gtr Man 196 F3
Linford Hants 31 F11
Linford Thurrock 69 D7
Lingague I o M 192 E3
Lingards Wood W Yorks 196 E5
Lingbob W Yorks 205 F7
Lingdale Redcar 226 B3
Lingen Hereford 115 D7
Lingfield Darl 224 C6
Lingfield Sur 51 E11
Lingfield Common Sur 51 E11
Lingley Green Warr 183 D9
Lingley Mere Warr 183 D10
Lingreabhagh W Isles 296 C6
Lingwood Norf 143 B7
Linhope Borders 249 C10
Linhope Northumb 263 F11
Linicro Highld 298 C3
Link N Som 44 B3
Linkend Worcs 98 E6
Linkenholt Hants 47 B11
Linkhill Kent 38 B4
Linkinhorne Corn 12 G2
Linklater Orkney 314 H4
Linklet Orkney 314 A7
Linksness Orkney 314 E5
Linksness Orkney 314 F2
Linktown Fife 280 C5
Linley Shrops 131 E7
Linley Shrops 132 D3
Linley Brook Shrops 132 D3
Linley Green Hereford 116 G3
Linleygreen Shrops 132 D3
Linlithgow W Loth 279 F10
Linlithgow Bridge W Loth 279 F9
Linndhu Ho Argyll 289 D7
Linneraineach Highld 307 J6
Linns Angus 292 F3
Linnyshaw Gtr Man 195 G8
Linshiels Northumb 251 B9
Linsiadar W Isles 304 E4
Linsidemore Highld 309 K5
Linslade C Beds 103 F8
Linstead Parva Suff 126 B6
Linstock Cumb 239 F10
Linthorpe M'bro 225 B9
Linthurst Worcs 117 C9
Linthwaite W Yorks 196 E6
Lintlaw Borders 272 D6
Lintmill Moray 302 C5
Linton Borders 263 D7
Linton Cambs 105 B11
Linton Derbys 152 F5
Linton Hereford 98 F3
Linton Kent 53 D9
Linton N Yorks 213 G9
Linton Northumb 253 E7
Linton W Yorks 206 D3
Linton Heath Derbys 152 F5
Linton Hill Hereford 98 G3
Linton-on-Ouse N Yorks 215 G9
Lintridge Glos 98 E4
Lintz Durham 242 F5
Lintzford T & W 242 F4
Lintzgarth Durham 232 C4
Linwood Hants 31 F11
Linwood Lincs 189 D10
Linwood Renfs 267 C8
Lionacleit W Isles 297 G3
Lional W Isles 304 B7
Lions Green E Sus 37 D9
Liphook Hants 49 G10
Lipley Shrops 150 C4
Lippitts Hill Essex 86 F5
Liquo or Bowhousebog N Lnrk 269 D7
Liscard Mers 182 C4
Liscombe Som 41 G11
Liskeard Corn 6 C5
Liss Hants 34 B3
Liss Forest Hants 34 B3
Lissett E Yorks 209 B8
Lissington Lincs 189 E10
Lisson Grove London 67 C9
Listerdale S Yorks 187 C7
Listock Som 28 C4
Listoft Lincs 191 G8
Liston Essex 107 C7
Liston Garden Essex 106 B6
Lisvane Cardiff 59 C7
Liswerry Newport 59 B10
Litcham Norf 159 F7
Litchard Bridgend 58 C2
Litchborough Northants 120 G2
Litchfield Hants 48 C3
Litchurch Derbys 153 B7
Litherland Mers 182 B4
Litlington Cambs 104 C6
Litlington E Sus 23 E8
Litmarsh Hereford 97 B10
Little Abington Cambs 105 B10
Little Addington Northants 121 C9
Little Airmyn E Yorks 199 B8
Little Almshoe Herts 104 F3
Little Alne Warks 118 E2
Little Altcar Mers 193 F10
Little Ann Hants 47 E10
Little Arowry Wrex 167 G7
Little Asby Cumb 222 D3
Little Ashley Wilts 61 G10
Little Assynt Highld 307 G6
Little Aston Staffs 133 C11
Little Atherfield I o W 20 E5
Little Ayre Orkney 314 G3
Little-ayre Shetland 313 G5
Little Ayton N Yorks 225 C11
Little Baddow Essex 88 D3
Little Badminton S Glos 61 C10
Little Ballinluig Perth 286 B3
Little Bampton Cumb 239 F7
Little Bardfield Essex 106 E3
Little Barford Beds 122 F3
Little Barningham Norf 160 C2
Little Barrington Glos 82 C2
Little Barrow W Ches 183 G7
Little Barugh N Yorks 216 D5
Little Bavington Northumb 241 B11
Little Bayham E Sus 52 F6
Little Bealings Suff 108 B4
Little Beckford Glos 99 E9
Little Bedwyn Wilts 63 F9
Little Bentley Essex 108 F2
Little Berkhamsted Herts 86 D3
Little Billing Northants 120 E6
Little Billington C Beds 103 G8
Little Birch Hereford 97 E10
Little Bispham Blkpool 202 E2
Little Blakenham Suff 108 B2
Little Blencow Cumb 230 E5
Little Bloxwich W Mid 133 C10
Little Bognor W Sus 35 C8
Little Bolehill Derbys 170 E3
Little Bollington E Ches 184 D2
Little Bolton Gtr Man 184 B3
Little Bookham Sur 50 C6
Little Bosullow Corn 1 C4
Little Bourton Oxon 101 C9
Little Bowden Leics 136 F4
Little Boys Heath Bucks 84 F6
Little Bradley Suff 124 G3
Little Braithwaite Cumb 229 G10
Little Brampton Shrops 131 G7
Little Braxted Essex 88 C4
Little Bray Devon 41 F7
Little Brechin Angus 293 G7
Little Brickhill M Keynes 103 E8
Little Bridgeford Staffs 151 D7
Little Brington Northants 120 E3
Little Bristol S Glos 80 G2
Little Britain Warks 118 G2
Little Bromley Essex 107 F11
Little Bromwich W Mid 134 F2
Little Broughton Cumb 229 E7
Little Budworth W Ches 167 B9
Little Burstead Essex 87 G11
Little Bytham Lincs 155 F10
Little Cambridge Essex 106 F2
Little Canfield Essex 105 G11
Little Canford Poole 18 B6
Little Carleton Lancs 202 F2
Little Carlton Lincs 190 D5
Little Carlton Notts 172 D3
Little Casterton Rutland 137 B10
Little Catwick E Yorks 209 E8
Little Catworth Cambs 122 C2
Little Cawthorpe Lincs 190 E5
Little Chalfield Wilts 61 G11
Little Chalfont Bucks 85 F7
Little Chart Kent 54 D2
Little Chart Forstal Kent 54 D3
Little Chell Stoke 168 E5
Little Chester Derby 153 B7
Little Chesterford Essex 105 C10
Little Chesterton Oxon 101 G11
Little Cheverell Wilts 46 C3
Little Chishill Cambs 105 D8
Little Clacton Essex 89 B11
Little Clanfield Oxon 82 E3
Little Clegg Gtr Man 196 E2
Little Clifton Cumb 229 F7
Little Coates NE Lincs 201 F8
Little Colp Aberds 303 E7
Little Comberton Worcs 99 C9
Little Comfort Corn 12 E2
Little Common E Sus 38 F2
Little Common Lincs 156 D6
Little Common Shrops 115 B7
Little Common W Sus 34 C6
Little Compton Warks 100 E5
Little Corby Cumb 239 F11
Little Cornard Suff 107 D7
Little Cowarne Hereford 116 G2
Little Coxwell Oxon 82 G3
Little Crakehall N Yorks 224 G4
Little Cransley Northants 120 B6
Little Crawley M Keynes 103 B8
Little Creaton Northants 120 C4
Little Creich Highld 309 L6
Little Cressingham Norf 141 D7
Little Crosby Mers 193 G10
Little Cubley Derbys 152 B3
Little Dalby Leics 154 G5
Little Dawley Telford 132 B3
Little Dens Aberds 303 E10
Little Dewchurch Hereford 97 E10
Little Ditton Cambs 124 F3
Little Doward Hereford 79 B8
Little Downham Cambs 139 G10
Little Drayton Shrops 150 C3
Little Driffield E Yorks 208 B6
Little Drybrook Glos 79 D9
Little Dunham Norf 159 G7
Little Dunkeld Perth 286 C4
Little Dunmow Essex 106 G3
Little Durnford Wilts 46 G6
Little Eastbury Worcs 116 F6
Little Easton Essex 106 G2
Little Eaton Derbys 170 G5
Little Eccleston Lancs 202 E4
Little Ellingham Norf 141 D10
Little End Cambs 122 F3
Little End E Yorks 208 F2
Little End Essex 87 E8
Little Everdon Northants 119 F11
Little Eversden Cambs 123 G7
Little Faringdon Oxon 82 E2
Little Fencote N Yorks 224 G5
Little Fenton N Yorks 206 F6
Little Finborough Suff 125 G10
Little Fransham Norf 159 G8
Little Frith Kent 54 B2
Little Gaddesden Herts 85 C7
Little Gidding Cambs 138 G2
Little Gight Aberds 303 F8
Little Glemham Suff 126 F6
Little Glenshee Perth 286 D3
Little Gorsley Glos 98 F3
Little Gransden Cambs 122 F5
Little Green Cambs 104 B5
Little Green Notts 172 G2
Little Green Som 45 D8
Little Green Suff 125 C11
Little Green Wrex 167 G7
Little Grimsby Lincs 190 C4
Little Gringley Notts 188 E2
Little Gruinard Highld 307 L4
Little Habton N Yorks 216 D4
Little Hadham Herts 105 G8
Little Hale Lincs 173 G10
Little Hale Norf 141 B8
Little Hallam Derbys 171 G7
Little Hallingbury Essex 87 B7
Little Hampden Bucks 84 E5
Little Haresfield Glos 80 D4
Little Harrowden Northants 121 C7
Little Harwood Blkburn 195 B7
Little Haseley Oxon 83 E10
Little Hatfield E Yorks 209 E9
Little Hautbois Norf 160 E5
Little Haven Pembs 72 C5
Little Haven W Sus 51 G7
Little Hay Staffs 134 C2
Little Hayfield Derbys 185 D8
Little Haywood Staffs 151 E10
Little Heath E Ches 167 G11
Little Heath Herts 85 D8
Little Heath Herts 86 E3
Little Heath London 68 B3
Little Heath Staffs 151 F8
Little Heath Sur 66 G6
Little Heath W Berks 65 E7
Little Heath W Ches 166 B6
Little Heath W Mid 134 G6
Little Heck N Yorks 198 C5
Little Henham Essex 105 E10
Little Henny Essex 107 D7
Little Herbert's Glos 81 B7
Little Hereford Hereford 115 D11
Little Hill Hereford 97 F9
Little Hill Som 28 E3
Little Holbury Hants 32 G6
Little Honeyborough Pembs 73 D7
Little Hoole Moss Houses Lancs 194 C3
Little Horkesley Essex 107 E9
Little Hormead Herts 105 F8
Little Horsted E Sus 23 B7
Little Horton W Yorks 205 G9
Little Horton Wilts 62 G4
Little Horwood Bucks 102 E5
Little Houghton Northants 120 F6
Little Houghton S Yorks 198 G2
Little Hucklow Derbys 185 F11
Little Hulton Gtr Man 195 G8
Little Humber E Yorks 201 C8
Little Hungerford W Berks 64 E4
Little Ilford London 68 B2
Little Ingestre Staffs 151 E9
Little Inkberrow Worcs 117 F10
Little Irchester Northants 121 D8
Little Keyford Som 45 D9
Little Kimble Bucks 84 D4
Little Kineton Warks 118 G6
Little Kingshill Bucks 84 F5
Little Knowles Green Suff 124 F5
Little Langdale Cumb 220 E6
Little Langford Wilts 46 F4
Little Laver Essex 87 D8
Little Lawford Warks 119 B9
Little Layton Blkpool 202 F2
Little Leigh W Ches 183 F10
Little Leighs Essex 88 B2
Little Lepton W Yorks 197 E8
Little Leven E Yorks 209 D8
Little Lever Gtr Man 195 F9
Little Limber Lincs 200 E6
Little Linford M Keynes 102 C6
Little Load Som 29 C7
Little London Bucks 83 C10
Little London Bucks 84 D5
Little London Cambs 139 D8
Little London E Sus 23 B9
Little London Essex 105 F9
Little London Essex 106 D3
Little London Glos 80 B2
Little London Hants 47 D11
Little London Hants 48 B6
Little London Lincs 156 E4
Little London Lincs 157 E8
Little London Lincs 189 D10
Little London Lincs 190 F4
Little London Norf 139 D11
Little London Norf 160 C2
Little London Norf 160 C5
Little London Norf 160 E3
Little London Oxon 83 E8
Little London Powys 129 F10
Little London Shrops 131 F10
Little London Som 44 D6
Little London Suff 125 F10
Little London W Yorks 205 F10
Little London Worcs 116 C2
Little Longstone Derbys 185 G11
Little Lynturk Aberds 293 B7
Little Lyth Shrops 131 B9
Little Madeley Staffs 168 F3
Little Malvern Worcs 98 C5
Little Mancot Flint 166 B4
Little Maplestead Essex 106 D6
Little Marcle Hereford 98 D3
Little Marlow Bucks 65 B11
Little Marsden Lancs 204 F3
Little Marsh Bucks 102 G3
Little Marsh Norf 159 B10
Little Marsh Wilts 45 B11
Little Marton Blkpool 202 G2
Little Mascalls Essex 88 E2
Little Massingham Norf 158 E5
Little Melton Norf 142 B3
Little Merthyr Hereford 96 B5
Little Milford Pembs 73 C7
Little Mill Kent 53 D7
Little Mill Mon 78 E4
Little Milton Newport 59 B11
Little Milton Oxon 83 E10
Little Minster Oxon 82 C4
Little Missenden Bucks 84 F6
Little Mongeham Kent 55 C10
Little Moor Gtr Man 184 D6
Little Moor Lancs 203 E10
Little Moor End Lancs 195 B8
Little Morrell Warks 118 F6
Little Mountain Flint 166 C3
Little Musgrave Cumb 222 C5
Little Ness Shrops 149 F8
Little Neston W Ches 182 F3
Little Newcastle Pembs 91 F9
Little Newsham Durham 224 B2
Little Norlington E Sus 23 C7
Little Norton Som 29 D7
Little Oakley Essex 108 F4
Little Oakley Northants 137 F7
Little Odell Beds 121 F9
Little Offley Herts 104 F2
Little Onn Staffs 150 F6
Little Ormside Cumb 222 B4
Little Orton Cumb 239 F9
Little Orton Leics 134 B6
Little Ouse Norf 140 F2
Little Ouseburn N Yorks 215 G8
Little Overton Wrex 166 G5
Little Oxney Green Essex 87 D11
Little Packington Warks 134 G4
Little Parndon Essex 86 C6
Little Paxton Cambs 122 E3
Little Petherick Corn 10 G4
Little Pitlurg Moray 302 E4
Little Plumpton Lancs 202 G3
Little Plumstead Norf 160 G6
Little Ponton Lincs 155 C8
Little Posbrook Hants 33 G8
Little Poulton Lancs 202 F3
Little Preston Kent 53 B8
Little Preston W Yorks 206 G3
Little Raveley Cambs 122 B5
Little Reedness E Yorks 199 C10
Little Reynoldston Swansea 56 D3
Little Ribston N Yorks 206 C3
Little Rissington Glos 81 B11
Little Rogart Highld 309 J7
Little Rollright Oxon 100 E5
Little Ryburgh Norf 159 D9
Little Ryle Northumb 264 G2
Little Ryton Shrops 131 C9
Little Salisbury Wilts 63 G7
Little Salkeld Cumb 231 D7
Little Sampford Essex 106 E3
Little Sandhurst Brack 65 G10
Little Saredon Staffs 133 B8
Little Saxham Suff 124 E5
Little Scatwell Highld 300 D3
Little Scotland Gtr Man 194 E6
Little Sessay N Yorks 215 E9
Little Shelford Cambs 123 G9
Little Shoddesden Hants 47 D9
Little Shrewley Warks 118 D4
Little Shurdington Glos 80 B6
Little Silver Devon 26 F6
Little Silver Devon 40 E4
Little Singleton Lancs 202 F3
Little Skillymarno Aberds 303 D9
Little Skipwith N Yorks 207 F9
Little Smeaton N Yorks 198 D4
Little Smeaton N Yorks 224 E6
Little Snoring Norf 159 C9
Little Sodbury S Glos 61 C9
Little Sodbury End S Glos 61 C8
Little Somborne Hants 47 G11
Little Somerford Wilts 62 C3
Little Soudley Shrops 150 D4
Little Stainforth N Yorks 212 F6
Little Stainton Darl 234 G2
Little Stanmore London 85 G11
Little Stanney W Ches 182 G6
Little Staughton Beds 122 E2
Little Steeping Lincs 174 C6
Little Stoke S Glos 60 C6
Little Stoke Staffs 151 C8
Little Stonham Suff 126 E2
Little Stretton Leics 136 C3
Little Stretton Shrops 131 E8
Little Strickland Cumb 221 B11
Little Studley N Yorks 214 E6
Little Stukeley Cambs 122 B4
Little Sugnall Staffs 150 C6
Little Sutton Lincs 157 E9
Little Sutton Shrops 131 G10
Little Sutton W Ches 182 F5
Little Swinburne Northumb 241 B10
Little Tarrington Hereford 98 C2
Little Tew Oxon 101 F7
Little Tey Essex 107 G7
Little Thetford Cambs 123 B10
Little Thirkleby N Yorks 215 D9
Little Thornage Norf 159 B11
Little Thornton Lancs 202 E3
Little Thorpe Durham 234 C4
Little Thorpe W Yorks 197 C7
Little Thurlow Suff 124 G3
Little Thurlow Green Suff 124 G3
Little Thurrock Thurrock 68 D6
Little Torboll Highld 309 K7
Little Torrington Devon 25 D7
Little Totham Essex 88 C5
Little Toux Aberds 302 D5
Little Town Cumb 220 B4
Little Town Lancs 203 F9
Little Town Warr 183 C10
Little Tring Herts 84 C6
Little Twycross Leics 134 B6
Little Urswick Cumb 210 E5
Little Vantage W Loth 270 C2
Little Wakering Essex 70 B2
Little Walden Essex 105 C10
Little Waldingfield Suff 107 B8
Little Walsingham Norf 159 B8
Little Waltham Essex 88 C2
Little Walton Warks 135 G9
Little Warley Essex 87 G10
Little Warton Warks 134 C5
Little Washbourne Glos 99 E9
Little Weighton E Yorks 208 G5
Little Weldon Northants 137 F8
Little Welland Worcs 98 D6
Little Welnetham Suff 125 E7
Little Welton Lincs 190 D4
Little Wenham Suff 107 D11
Little Wenlock Telford 132 B2
Little Weston Som 29 B10
Little Whitehouse I o W 20 C5
Little Whittingham Green Suff 126 B5
Little Wigborough Essex 89 B7
Little Wilbraham Cambs 123 F10
Little Wisbeach Lincs 156 C2
Little Wishford Wilts 46 F5
Little Witcombe Glos 80 B6
Little Witley Worcs 116 E5
Little Wittenham Oxon 83 G9
Little Wolford Warks 100 D5
Little Wood Corner Bucks 84 E6
Little Woodcote London 67 G9
Little Woolgarston Dorset 18 E5
Little Worthen Shrops 130 B6
Little Wratting Suff 106 B3
Little Wymington Beds 121 D9
Little Wymondley Herts 104 F4
Little Wyrley Staffs 133 B10
Little Wytheford Shrops 149 F11
Little Yeldham Essex 106 D5
Littlebeck N Yorks 227 D7
Littleborough Gtr Man 196 D2
Littleborough Notts 188 E4
Littlebourne Kent 55 B8
Littlebredy Dorset 17 D7
Littlebury Essex 105 D10
Littlebury Green Essex 105 D9
Littlecote Bucks 102 G6
Littlecott Wilts 46 C6
Littledean Glos 79 C11
Littledean Hill Glos 79 C11
Littledown Bmouth 19 C8
Littledown Hants 47 B10
Littleferry Highld 311 K2
Littlefield NE Lincs 201 F9
Littlefield Common Sur 50 C3
Littlefield Green Windsor 65 D11
Littlegain Shrops 132 D5
Littleham Devon 14 E6
Littleham Devon 24 C6
Littlehampton W Sus 35 G8
Littlehempston Devon 8 C6
Littlehoughton Northumb 264 F6
Littlemill Aberds 292 D5
Littlemill E Ayrs 257 F11
Littlemill Highld 301 D9
Littlemill Northumb 264 F6
Littlemoor Derbys 170 C5
Littlemoor Dorset 17 E9
Littlemore Oxon 83 E8
Littlemoss Gtr Man 184 B6
Littleover Derby 152 C6
Littleport Cambs 139 F11
Littler W Ches 167 B10
Littlestead Green Oxon 65 D8
Littlestone-on-Sea Kent 39 C9
Littlethorpe Leics 135 D10
Littlethorpe N Yorks 214 F6
Littleton Bath 60 G5
Littleton Dorset 30 G5
Littleton Guildford 50 D3
Littleton Hants 48 G3
Littleton Perth 286 D6
Littleton Som 44 G3
Littleton Spelthorne 66 F5
Littleton W Ches 166 B6
Littleton Wilts 62 G2
Littleton Common Sur 66 E5
Littleton Drew Wilts 61 C10
Littleton-on-Severn S Glos 60 B5
Littleton Panell Wilts 46 C4
Littleton-upon-Severn S Glos 79 G9
Littletown Durham 234 C2
Littletown I o W 20 C6
Littletown W Yorks 197 C8
Littlewick Green Windsor 65 D10
Littlewindsor Dorset 28 G6
Littlewood Staffs 133 B9
Littlewood Green Warks 117 E11
Littleworth Beds 103 C11
Littleworth Glos 80 E4
Littleworth Glos 100 D2
Littleworth Oxon 82 F4
Littleworth Oxon 83 D9
Littleworth Oxon 83 E9
Littleworth S Yorks 187 B10
Littleworth Staffs 151 E8
Littleworth Staffs 151 G10
Littleworth W Sus 35 C11
Littleworth Warks 118 E4
Littleworth Wilts 63 F7
Littleworth Worcs 117 E9
Littleworth Worcs 117 G7
Littleworth Common Bucks 66 B2
Littleworth End Warks 134 D3
Littley Green Essex 87 B11
Litton Derbys 185 F11
Litton N Yorks 213 E8
Litton Som 44 C5
Litton Cheney Dorset 17 C7
Litton Mill Derbys 185 G11
Liurbost W Isles 304 F5
Livermead Torbay 9 C8
Liverpool Mers 182 C4
Liverpool Airport Mers 182 E6
Liversedge W Yorks 197 C8
Liverton Devon 14 F2
Liverton Redcar 226 B4
Liverton Mines Redcar 226 B4
Liverton Street Kent 53 C11
Livesey Street Kent 53 C8
Livingshayes Devon 27 G7
Livingston W Loth 269 B11
Livingston Village W Loth 269 B10
Lix Toll Stirl 285 D9
Lixwm Flint 181 G11
Lizard Corn 2 G6
Llaingoch Anglesey 178 E2
Llaithddu Powys 129 G11
Llampha V Glam 58 D2
Llan Powys 129 C7
Llan-dafal Bl Gwent 77 E11
Llan eurgain = Northop Flint 166 B2
Llan Ffestiniog Gwyn 164 G2
Llan-mill Pembs 73 C10
Llan-non = Llanon Ceredig 111 D10
Llan-y-pwll Wrex 166 E5
Llanaber Gwyn 146 F2
Llanaelhaearn Gwyn 162 G5
Llanafan Ceredig 112 C3
Llanafan-fawr Powys 113 F9
Llanallgo Anglesey 179 D7
Llananno Powys 113 C11
Llanarmon Gwyn 145 B8
Llanarmon Dyffryn Ceiriog Wrex 148 C3
Llanarmon Mynydd-mawr Powys 148 D2
Llanarmon-yn-Ial Denb 165 D11
Llanarth Ceredig 111 F8
Llanarth Mon 78 C5
Llanarthne Carms 93 G10
Llanasa Flint 181 E10
Llanbabo Anglesey 178 D5
Llanbad Rhondda 58 C3
Llanbadarn Fawr Ceredig 128 G2
Llanbadarn Fynydd Powys 114 B2
Llanbadarn-y-Garreg Powys 96 B2
Llanbadoc Mon 78 E5
Llanbadrig Anglesey 178 C5
Llanbeder Newport 78 G5
Llanbedr Gwyn 145 D11
Llanbedr Powys 96 B2
Llanbedr Powys 96 G4
Llanbedr-Dyffryn-Clwyd Denb 165 D10
Llanbedr Pont Steffan = Lampeter Ceredig 93 B11
Llanbedr-y-cennin Conwy 164 B3
Llanbedrgoch Anglesey 179 E8
Llanbedrog Gwyn 144 C6
Llanberis Gwyn 163 C9
Llanbethery V Glam 58 F4
Llanbister Powys 114 C2
Llanblethian = Llanfleiddan V Glam 58 E3
Llanboidy Carms 92 G4
Llanbradach Caerph 77 G10
Llanbrynmair Powys 129 C7
Llancadle = Llancatal V Glam 58 F4
Llancaiach Caerph 77 F10
Llancarfan V Glam 58 E5
Llancatal = Llancadle V Glam 58 F4
Llancayo Mon 78 E5
Llancloudy Hereford 97 G9
Llancowrid Powys 130 E3
Llancynfelyn Ceredig 128 E2
Llandaff Cardiff 59 D7
Llandaff North Cardiff 59 D7
Llandanwg Gwyn 145 D11
Llandarcy Neath 57 B8
Llandawke Carms 74 C3
Llanddaniel Fab Anglesey 179 G7
Llanddarog Carms 75 B8
Llanddeiniol Ceredig 111 C11
Llanddeiniolen Gwyn 163 B8
Llandderfel Gwyn 147 B9
Llanddeusant Anglesey 178 D4
Llanddeusant Carms 94 G5
Llanddew Powys 95 E11
Llanddewi Swansea 56 D3
Llanddewi-Brefi Ceredig 112 F3
Llanddewi Fach Mon 78 F4
Llanddewi Rhydderch Mon 78 C5
Llanddewi Skirrid Mon 78 B4
Llanddewi Velfrey Pembs 73 B10
Llanddewi Ystradenni Powys 114 D2
Llanddewi'r Cwm Powys 95 B10
Llanddoged Conwy 164 C4
Llanddona Anglesey 179 F9
Llanddowror Carms 74 C3
Llanddulas Conwy 180 F6
Llanddwywe Gwyn 145 E11
Llanddyfynan Anglesey 179 F8
Llandecwyn Gwyn 146 B2
Llandefaelog Powys 95 E10
Llandefaelog Fach Powys 95 E10
Llandefaelog-tre'r-graig Powys 96 F2
Llandefalle Powys 96 D2
Llandegai Gwyn 179 G9
Llandegfan Anglesey 179 G9
Llandegla Denb 165 E11
Llandegley Powys 114 E2
Llandegveth Mon 78 F4
Llandegwning Gwyn 144 C5
Llandeilo Carms 94 G2
Llandeilo Graban Powys 95 C11
Llandeilo'r Fan Powys 95 E7
Llandeloy Pembs 91 F7
Llandenny Mon 78 E6
Llandenny Walks Mon 78 E5
Llandevaud Newport 78 G6
Llandevenny Mon 60 B2
Llandewi Ystradenny Powys 114 D2
Llandilo Pembs 92 F2
Llandilo-yr-ynys Carms 93 G9
Llandinabo Hereford 97 F10
Llandinam Powys 129 F10
Llandissilio Pembs 92 G2
Llandogo Mon 79 E8
Llandough V Glam 58 E3
Llandough V Glam 59 E7
Llandovery = Llanymddyfri Carms 94 E5
Llandow = Llandw V Glam 58 E2
Llandre Carms 94 C3
Llandre Ceredig 128 F2
Llandrillo Denb 147 B10
Llandrillo-yn-Rhôs Conwy 180 E4
Llandrindod Wells Powys 113 E11
Llandrinio Powys 148 F5
Llandruidion Pembs 90 G5
Llandudno Conwy 180 E3
Llandudno Junction = Cyffordd Llandudno Conwy 180 F3
Llandudoch = St Dogmaels Pembs 92 B3
Llandw = Llandow V Glam 58 E2
Llandwrog Gwyn 163 D7
Llandybie Carms 75 B10
Llandyfaelog Carms 74 C6
Llandyfan Carms 75 B10
Llandyfriog Ceredig 92 C6
Llandyfrydog Anglesey 178 D6
Llandygwydd Ceredig 92 C4
Llandynan Denb 165 F11
Llandyrnog Denb 165 B10
Llandysilio Powys 148 F5
Llandyssil Powys 130 D3
Llandysul Ceredig 93 C8

Lower Menadue Corn 5 D10
Lower Merridge Som 43 G8
Lower Mickletown W Yorks 198 B2
Lower Middleton Cheney Northants 101 C10
Lower Midway Derbys 152 E6
Lower Mill Corn 3 B10
Lower Milovaig Highld 296 F7
Lower Milton Som 44 D4
Lower Moor Wilts 81 G8
Lower Moor Worcs 99 B9
Lower Morton S Glos 79 G10
Lower Mountain Flint 166 D4
Lower Nazeing Essex 86 D5
Lower Netchwood Shrops 132 E2
Lower Netherton Devon 14 G3
Lower New Inn Torf 78 F4
Lower Ninnes Corn 1 C5
Lower Nobut Staffs 151 C10
Lower North Dean Bucks 84 F5
Lower Norton Warks 118 E4
Lower Nyland Dorset 30 C2
Lower Ochrwyth Caerph 59 B8
Lower Odcombe Som 29 D8
Lower Oddington Glos 100 F4
Lower Ollach Highld 295 B7
Lower Padworth W Berks 64 F6
Lower Penarth V Glam 59 F7
Lower Penn Staffs 133 D7
Lower Pennington Hants 20 C2
Lower Penwortham Lancs 194 B4
Lower Peover W Ches 184 G2
Lower Pexhill E Ches 184 G5
Lower Pilsley Derbys 170 C6
Lower Pitkerrie Highld 311 L2
Lower Place Gtr Man 196 E2
Lower Place London 67 C8
Lower Pollicot Bucks 84 C2
Lower Porthkerry V Glam 58 F5
Lower Porthpean Corn 5 E10
Lower Quinton Warks 100 B3
Lower Rabber Hereford 114 G5
Lower Race Torf 78 E3
Lower Radley Oxon 83 F8
Lower Rainham Medway 69 F10
Lower Ratley Hants 32 C4
Lower Raydon Suff 107 D10
Lower Rea Glos 80 B4
Lower Ridge Devon 28 G2
Lower Ridge Shrops 148 C6
Lower Roadwater Som 42 F4
Lower Rochford Worcs 116 D2
Lower Rose Corn 4 E5
Lower Row Dorset 31 G8
Lower Sapey Worcs 116 E3
Lower Seagry Wilts 62 C3
Lower Sheering Essex 87 C7
Lower Shelton C Beds 103 C9
Lower Shiplake Oxon 65 D9
Lower Shuckburgh Warks 119 E9
Lower Skelty Swansea 56 C6
Lower Slackstead Hants 32 B5
Lower Slade Devon 40 D4
Lower Slaughter Glos 100 G3
Lower Solva Pembs 87 G11
Lower Soothill W Yorks 197 C9
Lower Soudley Glos 79 D11
Lower Southfield Hereford 98 C3
Lower Stanton St Quintin Wilts 62 C2
Lower Stoke Medway 69 D10
Lower Stoke W Mid 119 B7
Lower Stondon C Beds 104 D3
Lower Stone Glos 79 G11
Lower Stonnall Staffs 133 C11
Lower Stow Bedon Norf 141 E9
Lower Stratton Som 28 D6
Lower Stratton Swindon 63 B7
Lower Street E Sus 38 E2
Lower Street Norf 160 B5
Lower Street Norf 160 C3
Lower Street Norf 160 F6
Lower Street Suff 108 E3
Lower Street Suff 124 G5
Lower Strensham Worcs 99 C8
Lower Stretton Warr 183 E10
Lower Studley Wilts 45 B11
Lower Sundon C Beds 103 F10
Lower Swainswick Bath 61 F9
Lower Swanwick Hants 33 F7
Lower Swell Glos 100 F3
Lower Sydenham London 67 E11
Lower Tadmarton Oxon 101 D8
Lower Tale Devon 27 G9
Lower Tasburgh Norf 142 D3
Lower Tean Staffs 151 B10
Lower Thorpe Northants 101 B10
Lower Threapwood Wrex 166 G6
Lower Thurlton Norf 143 D8
Lower Thurnham Lancs 202 C5
Lower Thurvaston Derbys 152 B4
Lower Todding Hereford 115 B8
Lower Tote Highld 298 C5
Lower Town Devon 27 E8
Lower Town Hereford 98 C2
Lower Town Pembs 91 D9
Lower Town W Yorks 204 G6
Lower Town Worcs 117 F7
Lower Trebullett Corn 12 F2
Lower Tregunnon Corn 11 E10
Lower Treworrick Corn 6 B4
Lower Tuffley Glos 80 C4
Lower Turmer Hants 31 F10
Lower Twitchen Devon 24 D5
Lower Twydall Medway 69 F10
Lower Tysoe Warks 100 B6
Lower Upham Hants 33 D8
Lower Upnor Medway 69 E9
Lower Vexford Som 42 F6
Lower Wainhill Oxon 84 E3
Lower Walton Warr 183 D10
Lower Wanborough Swindon 63 C8
Lower Weacombe Som 42 E6
Lower Weald M Keynes 102 D5
Lower Wear Devon 14 D4
Lower Weare Som 44 C2
Lower Weedon Northants 120 F2
Lower Welson Hereford 114 G5
Lower Westholme Som 44 E5
Lower Westhouse N Yorks 212 E3
Lower Westmancote Worcs 99 D8
Lower Weston Bath 61 F8
Lower Whatcombe Dorset 30 G4
Lower Whatley Som 45 D8
Lower Whitley W Ches 183 F10
Lower Wick Glos 80 F2
Lower Wick Worcs 116 G6
Lower Wield Hants 48 E6
Lower Willingdon E Sus 23 E9
Lower Winchendon or Nether Winchendon Bucks 84 C2
Lower Withington E Ches 168 B4
Lower Wolverton Worcs 117 G8
Lower Woodend Aberds 293 B8
Lower Woodend Bucks 65 B10
Lower Woodford Wilts 46 G6
Lower Woodley Corn 5 B10
Lower Woodside Herts 86 D2
Lower Woolston Som 29 B11
Lower Woon Corn 5 C10
Lower Wraxall Dorset 29 G9
Lower Wraxall Som 44 F6
Lower Wraxall Wilts 61 G10
Lower Wych W Ches 167 G7
Lower Wyche Worcs 98 C5
Lower Wyke W Yorks 197 B7
Lower Yelland Devon 40 G3
Lower Zeals Wilts 45 G9
Lowerford Lancs 204 F3
Lowerhouse E Ches 184 F6
Lowerhouse Lancs 204 G2
Lowertown Corn 2 D5
Lowertown Corn 5 C11
Lowertown Devon 12 E5
Lowes Barn Durham 233 C11
Lowesby Leics 136 B4
Lowestoft Suff 143 E10
Loweswater Cumb 229 G8
Lowfield S Yorks 186 D5
Lowfield Heath W Sus 51 E9
Lowford Hants 33 E7
Lowgill Cumb 222 F2
Lowgill Lancs 212 G3
Lowick Cumb 210 B5
Lowick Northants 137 G9
Lowick Northumb 264 B2
Lowick Bridge Cumb 210 B5
Lowick Green Cumb 210 B5
Lowlands Torf 78 F3
Lowmoor Row Cumb 231 F8
Lowna N Yorks 226 G3
Lownie Moor Angus 287 C8
Lowood Borders 262 B2
Lowsonford Warks 118 D3
Lowther Cumb 230 G6
Lowthertown Dumfries 238 D6
Lowtherville I o W 21 F7
Lowthorpe E Yorks 217 G11
Lowton Gtr Man 183 B10
Lowton Som 27 D11
Lowton Common Gtr Man 183 B10
Lowton Heath Gtr Man 183 B10
Lowton St Mary's Gtr Man 183 B10
Loxbeare Devon 26 D6
Loxford London 68 B2
Loxhill Sur 50 F4
Loxhore Devon 40 F6
Loxhore Cott Devon 40 F6
Loxley S Yorks 186 D4
Loxley Warks 118 G5
Loxley Green Staffs 151 C11
Loxter Hereford 98 C4
Loxton N Som 43 B11
Loxwood W Sus 50 G4
Loyter's Green Essex 87 C8
Loyterton Kent 70 G3
Lozells W Mid 133 F11
Lubachlaggan Highld 300 B3
Lubachoinnich Highld 309 K4
Lubberland Shrops 116 B2
Lubcroy Highld 309 J3
Lubenham Leics 136 F4
Lubinvullin Highld 308 C5
Lucas End Herts 86 E4
Lucas Green Lancs 194 C5
Lucas Green Sur 50 B2
Luccombe Som 42 E2
Luccombe Village I o W 21 F7
Lucker Northumb 264 C5
Luckett Corn 12 G3
Lucking Street Essex 106 E6
Luckington Wilts 61 C10
Lucklawhill Fife 287 E8
Luckwell Bridge Som 42 F2
Lucton Hereford 115 E8
Ludag W Isles 297 K3
Ludborough Lincs 190 B3
Ludbrook Devon 8 E3
Ludchurch Pembs 73 C10
Luddenden W Yorks 196 B4
Luddenden Foot W Yorks 196 C4
Ludderburn Cumb 221 G8
Luddesdown Kent 69 F7
Luddington N Lincs 199 D10
Luddington Warks 118 G3
Luddington in the Brook Northants 138 G2
Lude House Perth 291 G10
Ludford Lincs 190 D2
Ludford Shrops 115 C10
Ludgershall Bucks 83 B11
Ludgershall Wilts 47 C9
Ludgvan Corn 2 C2
Ludham Norf 161 F7
Ludlow Shrops 115 C10
Ludney Lincs 190 B5
Ludney Som 28 E5
Ludstock Hereford 98 D3
Ludstone Shrops 132 E6
Ludwell Wilts 30 C6
Ludworth Durham 234 C3
Luffenhall Herts 104 F5
Luffincott Devon 12 C2
Lufton Som 29 D8
Lugar E Ayrs 258 E3
Lugate Borders 271 G8
Lugg Green Hereford 115 E9
Luggate Burn E Loth 282 G2
Luggiebank N Lnrk 278 G5
Lugsdale Halton 183 D8
Lugton E Ayrs 267 E8
Lugwardine Hereford 97 C11
Luib Highld 295 C7
Luibeilt Highld 290 G4
Lulham Hereford 97 C8
Lullenden Sur 52 E2
Lullington Derbys 152 G5
Lullington Som 45 C9
Lulsgate Bottom N Som 60 F4
Lulsley Worcs 116 F4
Lulworth Camp Dorset 18 E2
Lumb Lancs 195 C10
Lumb Lancs 195 D9
Lumb W Yorks 196 C4
Lumb W Yorks 197 E7
Lumb Foot W Yorks 204 F6
Lumburn Devon 12 G5
Lumbutts W Yorks 196 C3
Lumby N Yorks 206 G5
Lumley W Sus 22 B3
Lumley Thicks Durham 243 G8
Lumloch E Dunb 268 B2
Lumphanan Aberds 293 C7
Lumphinnans Fife 280 C3
Lumsdaine Borders 273 B7
Lumsden Aberds 302 G4
Lunan Angus 287 B10
Lunanhead Angus 287 B8
Luncarty Perth 286 E4
Lund E Yorks 208 D5
Lund N Yorks 207 G9
Lund Shetland 312 C7
Lundal W Isles 304 E3
Lundavra Highld 290 G2
Lunderton Aberds 303 E11
Lundie Angus 286 D6
Lundie Highld 290 B3
Lundin Links Fife 287 G8
Lundwood S Yorks 197 F11
Lundy Green Norf 142 E4
Lunga Argyll 275 C8
Lunna Shetland 312 G6
Lunning Shetland 312 G7
Lunnister Shetland 312 F5
Lunnon Swansea 56 D4
Lunsford Kent 53 B7
Lunsford's Cross E Sus 38 E2
Lunt Mers 193 G10
Luntley Hereford 115 F7
Lunts Heath Halton 183 D8
Lupin Staffs 152 F2
Luppitt Devon 27 F11
Lupridge Devon 8 E4
Lupset W Yorks 197 D10
Lupton Cumb 211 C11
Lurg Aberds 293 C8
Lurgashall W Sus 34 B6
Lurignich Argyll 289 D11
Lurley Devon 26 E6
Lusby Lincs 174 B4
Lushcott Shrops 131 D11
Luson Devon 8 F2
Luss Argyll 277 C7
Lussagiven Argyll 275 E7
Lusta Highld 298 D2
Lustleigh Devon 13 E11
Lustleigh Cleave Devon 13 E11
Luston Hereford 115 E9
Lusty Som 45 G7
Luthermuir Aberds 293 G8
Luthrie Fife 287 F7
Lutley W Mid 133 G8
Luton Devon 14 F4
Luton Devon 27 G9
Luton Luton 103 G11
Luton Medway 69 F9
Lutsford Devon 24 D3
Lutterworth Leics 135 G10
Lutton Devon 7 D11
Lutton Devon 8 C3
Lutton Lincs 157 D8
Lutton Northants 138 F2
Lutton Gowts Lincs 157 E8
Lutworthy Devon 26 D3
Luxborough Som 42 F3
Luxley Glos 98 G3
Luxted London 68 G2
Luxton Devon 28 E2
Luxulyan Corn 5 D11
Luzley Gtr Man 196 G3
Luzley Brook Gtr Man 196 F2
Lyatts Som 29 E8
Lybster Highld 310 F6
Lydbury North Shrops 131 F7
Lydcott Devon 41 F7
Lydd Kent 39 C8
Lydd on Sea Kent 39 C9
Lydden Kent 55 D9
Lydden Kent 71 F11
Lyddington Rutland 137 D7
Lyde Orkney 314 E3
Lyde Shrops 130 C6
Lyde Cross Hereford 97 C10
Lyde Green Hants 49 B8
Lyde Green S Glos 61 D7
Lydeard St Lawrence Som 42 G6
Lydford Devon 12 E6
Lydford Fair Place Som 44 G5
Lydford-on-Fosse Som 44 G5
Lydgate Derbys 186 F4
Lydgate Gtr Man 196 G3
Lydgate W Yorks 196 B2
Lydham Shrops 130 E6
Lydiard Green Wilts 62 B5
Lydiard Millicent Wilts 62 B5
Lydiard Plain Wilts 62 B5
Lydiard Tregoze Swindon 62 C6
Lydiate Mers 193 G11
Lydiate Ash Worcs 117 B9
Lydlinch Dorset 30 E2
Lydmarsh Som 28 F5
Lydney Glos 79 E10
Lydstep Pembs 73 F9
Lye W Mid 133 G8
Lye Cross N Som 60 G3
Lye Green Bucks 85 E7
Lye Green E Sus 52 G4
Lye Green Warks 118 D3
Lye Green Wilts 45 B10
Lye Head Worcs 116 C5
Lye Hole N Som 60 G4
Lyewood Common E Sus 52 F4
Lyford Oxon 82 G5
Lymbridge Green Kent 54 E6
Lyme Green E Ches 184 G6
Lyme Regis Dorset 16 C2
Lymiecleuch Borders 249 C9
Lyminge Kent 55 E7
Lymington Hants 20 B2
Lyminster W Sus 35 G8
Lymm Warr 183 D11
Lymore Hants 19 C11
Lympne Kent 54 F6
Lympsham Som 43 C10
Lympstone Devon 14 E5
Lynbridge Devon 41 D8
Lynch Hants 48 D4
Lynch Som 42 D2
Lynch Hill Hants 48 D3
Lynch Hill Slough 66 C2
Lynchat Highld 291 C9
Lynchgate Shrops 131 F7
Lyndale Ho Highld 298 D3
Lyndhurst Hants 32 F4
Lyndon Rutland 137 C8
Lyndon Green W Mid 134 F2
Lyne Borders 270 G4
Lyne Sur 66 F4
Lyne Down Hereford 98 E2
Lyne of Gorthleck Highld 300 G5
Lyne of Skene Aberds 293 B9
Lyne Station Borders 260 B6
Lyneal Shrops 149 C8
Lyneal Mill Shrops 149 C9
Lyneal Wood Shrops 149 C9
Lyneham Oxon 100 G5
Lyneham Wilts 62 D4
Lynemore Highld 301 G10
Lynemouth Northumb 253 E7
Lyness Orkney 314 G3
Lynford Norf 140 E6
Lyng Norf 159 F11
Lyng Som 28 B4
Lyngate Norf 160 C5
Lyngford Som 28 B2
Lynmore Highld 301 F10
Lynmouth Devon 41 D8
Lynn Staffs 133 C11
Lynn Telford 150 F5
Lynnwood Borders 261 G11
Lynsore Bottom Kent 55 D7
Lynsted Kent 70 G2
Lynstone Corn 24 F2
Lynton Devon 41 D8
Lynwilg Highld 291 B10
Lynworth Glos 99 G9
Lyons T & W 234 B3
Lyon's Gate Dorset 29 F11
Lyon's Green Norf 159 G8
Lyons Hall Essex 88 B2
Lyonshall Hereford 114 F6
Lypiatt Glos 80 D6
Lyrabus Argyll 274 G3
Lytchett Matravers Dorset 18 B4
Lytchett Minster Dorset 18 C5
Lyth Highld 310 C6
Lytham Lancs 193 B11
Lytham St Anne's Lancs 193 B10
Lythbank Shrops 131 B9
Lythe N Yorks 226 C6
Lythes Orkney 314 H4
Lythmore Highld 310 C4

M

Maam Argyll 284 F5
Mabe Burnthouse Corn 3 C7
Mabie Dumfries 237 B11
Mabledon Kent 52 E5
Mablethorpe Lincs 191 D8
Macclesfield E Ches 184 G6
Macclesfield Forest E Ches 185 G7
Macduff Aberds 303 C7
Mace Green Suff 108 C2
Machan S Lnrk 268 E5
Macharioch Argyll 255 G8
Machen Caerph 59 B8
Machrie N Ayrs 255 D9
Machrie Hotel Argyll 254 C4
Machrihanish Argyll 255 E7
Machroes Gwyn 144 D6
Machynlleth Powys 128 C4
Machynys Carms 56 B4
Mackerel's Common W Sus 35 B8
Mackerye End Herts 85 B11
Mackham Devon 27 F11
Mackney Oxon 64 B5
Mackside Borders 262 G4
Mackworth Derbys 152 B6
Macmerry E Loth 281 G8
Madderty Perth 286 E3
Maddington Wilts 46 E5
Maddiston Falk 279 F8
Maddox Moor Pembs 73 C7
Madehurst W Sus 35 E7
Madeley Staffs 168 G3
Madeley Telford 132 C3
Madeley Heath Staffs 168 F3
Madeley Heath Worcs 117 B9
Madeley Park Staffs 168 G3
Madeleywood Telford 132 C3
Maders Corn 12 G2
Madford Devon 27 E10
Madingley Cambs 123 E7
Madjeston Dorset 30 B4
Madley Hereford 97 D8
Madresfield Worcs 98 B6
Madron Corn 1 C5
Maen-y-groes Ceredig 111 F7
Maenaddwyn Anglesey 179 E7
Maenclochog Pembs 91 F11
Maendy V Glam 58 D4
Maenporth Corn 3 D7
Maentwrog Gwyn 163 G11
Maer Corn 24 F2
Maer Staffs 150 B5
Maerdy Carms 94 G2
Maerdy Conwy 165 G8
Maerdy Rhondda 77 F7
Maes-bangor Ceredig 128 G3
Maes-glas Newport 59 B9
Maes Glas = Greenfield Flint 181 F11
Maes llyn Ceredig 93 C7
Maes Pennant Flint 181 F11
Maes-Treylow Powys 114 D5
Maes-y-dre Flint 166 C2
Maesbrook Shrops 148 E5
Maesbury Shrops 148 D6
Maesbury Marsh Shrops 148 D6
Maesgeirchen Gwyn 179 G9
Maesgwyn-Isaf Powys 148 G3
Maeshafn Denb 166 C2
Maesllyn Ceredig 93 C7
Maesmynis Powys 95 B10
Maesteg Bridgend 57 C10
Maesybont Carms 75 B9
Maesycoed Rhondda 58 B5
Maesycrugiau Carms 93 C9
Maesycwmmer Caerph 77 G11
Maesygwartha Mon 78 C2
Maesymeillion Ceredig 93 B8
Maesypandy Powys 129 D9
Maesyrhandir Powys 129 E11
Magdalen Laver Essex 87 D8
Maggieknockater Moray 302 E3
Maggots End Essex 105 F9
Magham Down E Sus 23 C10
Maghull Mers 193 G11
Magor Mon 60 B2
Magpie Green Suff 125 B11
Mahaar Dumfries 236 B2
Maida Vale London 67 C9
Maiden Bradley Wilts 45 F10
Maiden Head N Som 60 F5
Maiden Law Durham 233 B9
Maiden Newton Dorset 17 B7
Maiden Wells Pembs 73 F7
Maidenbower W Sus 51 F9
Maidencombe Torbay 9 B8
Maidenhall Suff 108 C3
Maidenhead Windsor 65 C11
Maidenhead Court Windsor 66 C2
Maidenpark Falk 279 E9
Maidens S Ayrs 244 B6
Maiden's Green Brack 65 E11
Maiden's Hall Northumb 252 D6
Maidensgrave Suff 108 B5
Maidensgrove Oxon 65 B8
Maidenwell Corn 11 G8
Maidenwell Lincs 190 F4
Maidford Northants 120 G2
Maids Moreton Bucks 102 D4
Maidstone Kent 53 B9
Maidwell Northants 120 B4
Mail Shetland 313 L6
Mailand Shetland 312 C8
Mailingsland Borders 270 G4
Main Powys 148 F3
Maindee Newport 59 B10
Maindy Cardiff 59 D7
Mainholm S Ayrs 257 E9
Mains Cumb 229 G7
Mains of Airies Dumfries 236 C1
Mains of Allardice Aberds 293 F10
Mains of Annochie Aberds 303 E9
Mains of Ardestie Angus 287 D9
Mains of Arnage Aberds 303 F9
Mains of Auchoynanie Moray 302 E4
Mains of Baldoon Dumfries 236 D6
Mains of Balhall Angus 293 G7
Mains of Ballindarg Angus 287 B8
Mains of Balnakettle Aberds 293 F8
Mains of Birness Aberds 303 F9
Mains of Blackhall Aberds 303 G7
Mains of Burgie Moray 301 D10
Mains of Cairnbrogie Aberds 303 G8
Mains of Cairnty Moray 302 D3
Mains of Clunas Highld 301 E8
Mains of Crichie Aberds 303 E9
Mains of Daltulich Highld 301 E7
Mains of Dalvey Highld 301 F11
Mains of Dellavaird Aberds 293 E9
Mains of Drum Aberds 293 D10
Mains of Edingight Moray 302 D5
Mains of Fedderate Aberds 303 E8
Mains of Flichity Highld 300 G6
Mains of Hatton Aberds 303 D9
Mains of Hatton Aberds 303 E7
Mains of Inkhorn Aberds 303 F9
Mains of Innerpeffray Perth 286 F3
Mains of Kirktonhill Aberds 293 G8
Mains of Laithers Aberds 302 E6
Mains of Mayen Moray 302 E5
Mains of Melgund Angus 287 B9
Mains of Taymouth Perth 285 C11
Mains of Thornton Aberds 293 F8
Mains of Towie Aberds 303 E7
Mains of Ulbster Highld 310 E7
Mains of Watten Highld 310 D6
Mainsforth Durham 234 E2
Mainsriddle Dumfries 237 D11
Mainstone Shrops 130 F5
Maisemore Glos 98 G6
Maitland Park London 67 C9
Major's Green W Mid 118 B2
Makeney Derbys 170 G5
Malacleit W Isles 296 D3
Malborough Devon 9 G9
Malcoff Derbys 185 E9
Malden Rushett London 67 G7
Maldon Essex 88 D4
Malehurst Shrops 131 B7
Malham N Yorks 213 G8
Maligar Highld 298 C4
Malinbridge S Yorks 186 D4
Malinslee Telford 132 B3
Malkin's Bank E Ches 168 D3
Mallaig Highld 295 F8
Mallaig Bheag Highld 295 F8
Malleny Mills Edin 270 B3
Malling Stirl 285 G9
Mallows Green Essex 105 F9
Malltraeth Anglesey 162 B6
Mallwyd Gwyn 147 G7
Malmesbury Wilts 62 B2
Malmsmead Devon 41 D9
Malpas Corn 4 G6
Malpas Newport 78 G4
Malpas W Berks 64 E6
Malpas W Ches 167 F7
Malswick Glos 98 F4
Maltby Lincs 190 E4
Maltby S Yorks 187 C8
Maltby Stockton 225 C9
Maltby le Marsh Lincs 191 E7
Malting End Suff 124 G4
Malting Green Essex 107 G9
Maltings Angus 293 G9
Maltman's Hill Kent 54 E2
Malton N Yorks 216 E5
Malvern Common Worcs 98 C5
Malvern Link Worcs 98 B5
Malvern Wells Worcs 98 C5
Mambeg Argyll 276 D4
Mamble Worcs 116 C3
Mamhilad Mon 78 E4
Man-moel Caerph 77 E11
Manaccan Corn 3 E7
Manadon Plym 7 D9
Manafon Powys 130 C2
Manais W Isles 296 C7
Manar Ho Aberds 303 G7
Manaton Devon 13 E11
Manby Lincs 190 D5
Mancetter Warks 134 D6
Manchester Gtr Man 184 B4
Manchester Airport Gtr Man 184 D4
Mancot Flint 166 B4
Mancot Royal Flint 166 B4
Mandally Highld 290 C4
Manea Cambs 139 F9
Maney W Mid 134 D2
Manfield N Yorks 224 C4
Mangaster Shetland 312 F5
Mangotsfield S Glos 61 D7
Mangrove Green Herts 104 G2
Mangurstadh W Isles 304 E2
Manhay Corn 2 C5
Manian-fawr Pembs 92 B3
Mankinholes W Yorks 196 C3
Manley Devon 27 E7
Manley W Ches 183 G8
Manley Common W Ches 183 G8
Manmoel Caerph 77 E11
Mannal Argyll 288 E1
Mannamead Plym 7 D9
Mannerston W Loth 279 F10
Manningford Abbots Wilts 46 B6
Manningford Bohune Wilts 46 B6
Manningford Bruce Wilts 46 B6
Manningham W Yorks 205 G9
Mannings Heath W Sus 36 B2
Mannington Dorset 31 F9
Manningtree Essex 107 E11
Mannofield Aberdeen 293 C11
Manor London 68 B2
Manor Bourne Devon 7 F9
Manor Estate S Yorks 186 D5
Manor Hill Corner Lincs 157 F8
Manor House W Mid 135 G7
Manor Park Bucks 84 C4
Manor Park E Sus 37 C7
Manor Park London 68 B2
Manor Park Notts 153 C11
Manor Park S Yorks 186 D5
Manor Park Slough 66 C3
Manor Park W Ches 167 B11
Manor Park W Yorks 205 D9
Manor Parsley Corn 4 F4
Manor Royal W Sus 51 F9
Manorbier Pembs 73 F9
Manorbier Newton Pembs 73 F8
Manordeilo Carms 94 F3
Manorhill Borders 262 C5
Manorowen Pembs 91 D8
Man's Cross Essex 106 D5
Mansegate Dumfries 247 G9
Mansel Lacy Hereford 97 B8
Mansell Gamage Hereford 97 C7
Manselfield Swansea 56 D5
Manselton Swansea 57 B7
Mansergh Cumb 212 C2
Mansewood Glasgow 267 C11
Mansfield E Ayrs 258 G4
Mansfield Notts 171 C8
Mansfield Woodhouse Notts 171 C8
Manson Green Norf 141 C10
Mansriggs Cumb 210 C5
Manston Dorset 30 D4
Manston Kent 71 F10
Manston W Yorks 206 F3
Manswood Dorset 31 F7
Manthorpe Lincs 155 B8
Manthorpe Lincs 155 F11
Mantles Green Bucks 85 F7
Manton N Lincs 200 G2
Manton Notts 187 F9
Manton Rutland 137 C7
Manton Wilts 63 F7
Manton Warren N Lincs 200 F2
Manuden Essex 105 F9
Manwood Green Essex 87 C8
Manywells Height W Yorks 205 F7
Maperton Som 29 B11
Maple Cross Herts 85 G8
Maple End Essex 105 D11
Maplebeck Notts 172 C2
Mapledurham Oxon 65 D7
Mapledurwell Hants 49 C7
Maplehurst W Sus 35 C11
Maplescombe Kent 68 G5
Mapleton Derbys 169 F11
Mapperley Derbys 170 G6
Mapperley Nottingham 171 G9
Mapperley Park Nottingham 171 G9
Mapperton Dorset 16 B6
Mapperton Dorset 18 B4
Mappleborough Green Warks 117 D11
Mappleton E Yorks 209 E10
Mapplewell S Yorks 197 F10
Mappowder Dorset 30 F2
Mar Lodge Aberds 292 D2
Maraig W Isles 305 H3
Marazanvose Corn 4 E6
Marazion Corn 2 C2
Marbhig W Isles 305 G6
Marbrack Dumfries 246 E3
Marbury E Ches 167 F9
March Cambs 139 D8
March S Lnrk 259 G11
Marcham Oxon 83 F7
Marchamley Shrops 149 D11
Marchamley Wood Shrops 149 C11
Marchington Staffs 152 C2
Marchington Woodlands Staffs 152 D2
Marchroes Gwyn 144 D6
Marchwiel Wrex 166 F5
Marchwood Hants 32 E5
Marcross V Glam 58 F2
Marden Hereford 97 B10
Marden Kent 53 E8
Marden T & W 243 C9
Marden Wilts 46 B5
Marden Ash Essex 87 E9
Marden Beech Kent 53 E8
Marden Thorn Kent 53 E9
Marden's Hill E Sus 52 G3
Mardleybury Herts 86 B3
Mardu Shrops 130 G5
Mardy Mon 78 B4
Mardy Shrops 148 C5
Marefield Leics 136 B4
Mareham le Fen Lincs 174 C3
Mareham on the Hill Lincs 174 B3
Marehay Derbys 170 F5
Marehill W Sus 35 D9
Maresfield E Sus 37 C7
Maresfield Park E Sus 37 C7
Marfleet Hull 200 B6
Marford Wrex 166 D5
Margam Neath 57 D9
Margaret Marsh Dorset 30 D4
Margaret Roding Essex 87 C9
Margaretting Essex 87 E11
Margaretting Tye Essex 87 E11
Margate Kent 71 E11
Margery Sur 51 C9
Margnaheglish N Ayrs 256 C2
Margrie Dumfries 237 D8
Margrove Park Redcar 226 B3
Marham Norf 158 G4
Marhamchurch Corn 24 G2
Marholm P'boro 138 C2
Marian Flint 181 F9
Marian Cwm Denb 181 F9
Marian-glas Anglesey 179 E8
Marian y de = South Beach Gwyn 145 C7
Marian y mor = West End Gwyn 145 C7
Mariandyrys Anglesey 179 E10
Marianglas Anglesey 179 E8
Mariansleigh Devon 26 C2
Marine Town Kent 70 E2
Marionburgh Aberds 293 C9
Marishader Highld 298 C4
Marjoriebanks Dumfries 248 G3
Mark Dumfries 236 D3
Mark Dumfries 237 C7
Mark S Ayrs 236 B2
Mark Som 43 D11
Mark Causeway Som 43 D11
Mark Cross E Sus 23 C7
Mark Cross E Sus 52 G5
Mark Hall North Essex 87 C7
Mark Hall South Essex 87 C7
Markbeech Kent 52 E3
Markby Lincs 191 F7
Markeaton Derbys 152 B6
Market Bosworth Leics 135 C8
Market Deeping Lincs 138 B2
Market Drayton Shrops 150 C3
Market Harborough Leics 136 F4
Market Lavington Wilts 46 C4
Market Overton Rutland 155 F7
Market Rasen Lincs 189 D10
Market Stainton Lincs 190 F2
Market Warsop Notts 171 B9
Market Weighton E Yorks 208 E3
Market Weston Suff 125 B9
Markethill Perth 286 D6
Markfield Leics 153 G9
Markham Caerph 77 E11
Markham Moor Notts 188 G2
Markinch Fife 286 G6
Markington N Yorks 214 F5
Markland Hill Gtr Man 195 F7
Markle E Loth 281 F11
Marks Corner I o W 20 C5
Marks Gate London 87 G7
Marks Tey Essex 107 G8
Marksbury Bath 61 G7
Markyate Herts 85 B9
Marl Bank Worcs 98 C5
Marland Gtr Man 195 E11
Marlas Hereford 97 F8
Marlborough Wilts 63 F7
Marlbrook Hereford 115 G10
Marlbrook Worcs 117 C9
Marlcliff Warks 117 G11
Marldon Devon 9 C7
Marle Green E Sus 23 B9
Marle Hill Glos 99 G9
Marlesford Suff 126 F6
Marley Kent 55 C10
Marley Kent 55 C7
Marley Green E Ches 167 F9
Marley Heights W Sus 49 G11
Marley Hill T & W 242 F6
Marley Pots T & W 243 F9
Marlingford Norf 142 B2
Marloes Pembs 72 D3
Marlow Bucks 65 B10
Marlow Hereford 115 B8
Marlow Bottom Bucks 65 B11
Marlow Common Bucks 65 B10
Marlpit Hill Kent 52 D2
Marlpits E Sus 38 E2
Marlpool Derbys 170 F6
Marnhull Dorset 30 D3
Marnoch Aberds 302 D5
Marnock N Lnrk 268 B4
Marple Gtr Man 185 D7
Marple Bridge Gtr Man 185 D7
Marpleridge Gtr Man 185 D7
Marr S Yorks 198 F4
Marr Green Wilts 63 G8
Marrel Highld 311 H4
Marrick N Yorks 223 F11
Marrister Shetland 313 G7
Marros Carms 74 D2
Marsden T & W 243 E9
Marsden W Yorks 196 E4
Marsden Height Lancs 204 F3
Marsett N Yorks 213 B8
Marsh Bucks 84 D4
Marsh Devon 28 E3
Marsh W Yorks 196 D6
Marsh W Yorks 204 F6
Marsh Baldon Oxon 83 F9
Marsh Benham W Berks 64 F2
Marsh Common S Glos 60 C5
Marsh End Worcs 98 D6
Marsh Gate W Berks 63 F10
Marsh Gibbon Bucks 102 G2
Marsh Green Devon 14 C6
Marsh Green Gtr Man 194 F5
Marsh Green Kent 52 E2
Marsh Green Staffs 168 D5
Marsh Green Telford 150 G2
Marsh Green W Ches 183 F8
Marsh Houses Lancs 202 C5
Marsh Lane Derbys 186 F6
Marsh Lane Glos 79 D9
Marsh Mills Som 43 F7
Marsh Side Norf 176 E3
Marsh Street Som 42 E3
Marshall Meadows Northumb 273 D9
Marshall's Cross Mers 183 C8
Marshall's Elm Som 44 G3
Marshall's Heath Herts 85 B11
Marshalsea Dorset 28 G5
Marshalswick Herts 85 D11
Marsham Norf 160 E3
Marshaw Lancs 203 C7
Marshborough Kent 55 B10
Marshbrook Shrops 131 F8
Marshchapel Lincs 190 B5
Marshfield Newport 59 C9
Marshfield S Glos 61 E9
Marshfield Bank E Ches 167 D11
Marshgate Corn 11 C9
Marshland St James Norf 139 B10
Marshmoor Herts 86 D2
Marshside Kent 71 F8
Marshside Mers 193 D11
Marshwood Dorset 16 B3
Marske N Yorks 224 E2
Marske-by-the-Sea Redcar 235 G8
Marston Hereford 115 F7
Marston Lincs 172 G5
Marston Oxon 83 D8
Marston Staffs 150 G6
Marston Staffs 151 D8
Marston W Ches 183 F11
Marston Warks 119 B8
Marston Warks 134 E4
Marston Wilts 46 B3
Marston Bigot Som 45 E9
Marston Doles Warks 119 F9
Marston Gate Som 45 D9
Marston Green W Mid 134 F3
Marston Hill Glos 81 F10
Marston Jabbett Warks 135 F7
Marston Magna Som 29 C9
Marston Meysey Wilts 81 F10
Marston Montgomery Derbys 152 B2
Marston Moretaine C Beds 103 C9
Marston on Dove Derbys 152 D4
Marston St Lawrence Northants 101 C10
Marston Stannett Hereford 115 F11
Marston Trussell Northants 136 F3
Marstow Hereford 79 B9
Marsworth Bucks 84 C6
Marten Wilts 47 B9
Marthall E Ches 184 F4
Martham Norf 161 F9
Marthwaite Cumb 222 G2
Martin Hants 31 D9
Martin Kent 55 D10
Martin Lincs 173 D10
Martin Lincs 174 B2
Martin Dales Lincs 173 C11
Martin Drove End Hants 31 C9
Martin Hussingtree Worcs 117 E7
Martin Mill Kent 55 D10
Martin Moor Lincs 174 C2
Martinhoe Devon 41 D7
Martinhoe Cross Devon 41 D7
Martin's Moss E Ches 168 C4
Martinscroft Warr 183 D11
Martinstown Dorset 17 D8
Martinstown or Winterbourne St Martin Dorset 17 D8
Martlesham Suff 108 B4
Martlesham Heath Suff 108 B4
Martletwy Pembs 73 C8
Martley Worcs 116 E5
Martock Som 29 D7
Marton Cumb 210 D4
Marton E Ches 168 B5
Marton E Yorks 209 F9
Marton Lincs 188 E4
Marton M'bro 225 B10
Marton N Yorks 215 G8
Marton N Yorks 216 C4
Marton Shrops 130 C5
Marton Shrops 149 E8
Marton W Ches 167 B10
Marton Warks 119 D8
Marton Green W Ches 167 B10
Marton Grove M'bro 225 B9
Marton-in-the-Forest N Yorks 215 F11
Marton-le-Moor N Yorks 215 E7
Marton Moor Warks 119 D8
Marton Moss Side Blkpool 202 G2
Martyr Worthy Hants 48 G4
Martyr's Green Sur 50 B5
Marwick Orkney 314 D2
Marwood Devon 40 F4
Mary Tavy Devon 12 F6
Marybank Highld 300 D4
Marybank Highld 301 B7
Maryburgh Highld 300 D5
Maryfield Aberds 293 D7
Maryfield Corn 7 D8
Maryhill Glasgow 267 B11
Marykirk Aberds 293 G8
Maryland Mon 79 D8
Marylebone Gtr Man 194 F5
Marypark Moray 301 F11
Maryport Cumb 228 D6
Maryport Dumfries 236 F3
Maryton Angus 287 B10
Maryton Angus 287 B7
Marywell Aberds 293 D11
Marywell Aberds 293 D7
Marywell Angus 287 C10
Masbrough S Yorks 186 C6
Mascle Bridge Pembs 73 D7
Masham N Yorks 214 C4
Mashbury Essex 87 C11
Masongill N Yorks 212 D3
Masonhill S Ayrs 257 E9
Mastin Moor Derbys 187 F7
Mastrick Aberdeen 293 C10
Matchborough Worcs 117 D11
Matching Essex 87 C8
Matching Green Essex 87 C8
Matching Tye Essex 87 C8
Matfen Northumb 242 C2
Matfield Kent 53 E7
Mathern Mon 79 G8
Mathon Hereford 98 B4
Mathry Pembs 91 E7
Matlaske Norf 160 C3
Matley Gtr Man 185 B7
Matlock Derbys 170 C3
Matlock Bank Derbys 170 C3
Matlock Bath Derbys 170 D3
Matlock Bridge Derbys 170 D3
Matlock Cliff Derbys 170 D4
Matlock Dale Derbys 170 D3
Matshead Lancs 202 E6
Matson Glos 80 B4
Matterdale End Cumb 230 G3
Mattersey Notts 187 D11
Mattersey Thorpe Notts 187 D11
Matthewsgreen Wokingham 65 F10
Mattingley Hants 49 B8
Mattishall Norf 159 G11
Mattishall Burgh Norf 159 G11
Mauchline E Ayrs 257 D11
Maud Aberds 303 E9
Maudlin Corn 5 C11
Maudlin Dorset 28 F5
Maudlin W Sus 22 B5
Maudlin Cross Dorset 28 F5
Maugersbury Glos 100 F4
Maughold I o M 192 C5
Mauld Highld 300 F4
Maulden C Beds 103 D11
Maulds Meaburn Cumb 222 B2
Maunby N Yorks 215 B7
Maund Bryan Hereford 115 G11
Maundown Som 27 B9
Mauricewood Midloth 270 C4
Mautby Norf 161 G9
Mavesyn Ridware Staffs 151 F11
Mavis Enderby Lincs 174 B5
Maviston Highld 301 D9
Maw Green E Ches 168 D2
Mawbray Cumb 229 B7
Mawdesley Lancs 194 E3
Mawdlam Bridgend 57 E10
Mawgan Corn 2 D6
Mawgan Porth Corn 5 B7
Mawla Corn 4 F4
Mawnan Corn 3 D7
Mawnan Smith Corn 3 D7
Mawsley Northants 120 B6
Mawson Green S Yorks 198 D6
Mawthorpe Lincs 191 G7
Maxey P'boro 138 B2
Maxstoke Warks 134 F4

Maxted Street Kent 54 E6
Maxton Borders 262 C4
Maxton Kent 55 E10
Maxwellheugh Borders 262 C6
Maxwelltown Dumfries 237 B11
Maxworthy Corn 11 C11
May Bank Staffs 168 F5
May Hill Mon 79 C8
May Hill Village Glos 98 G4
Mayals Swansea 56 C6
Maybole S Ayrs 257 G8
Maybury Sur 50 B4
Maybush Soton 32 E5
Mayer's Green W Mid 133 E10
Mayes Green Sur 50 F6
Mayeston Pembs 73 E8
Mayfair London 67 C9
Mayfield E Sus 37 B9
Mayfield Midloth 271 C7
Mayfield Northumb 243 B7
Mayfield Staffs 169 F11
Mayfield W Loth 269 B8
Mayford Sur 50 B3
Mayhill Swansea 56 C6
Mayland Essex 88 E6
Maylandsea Essex 88 E6
Maynard's Green E Sus 23 B9
Mayne Ho Moray 302 C2
Mayon Corn 1 D3
Maypole Bromley 68 G3
Maypole Dartford 68 E4
Maypole Kent 71 G7
Maypole Mon 79 B7
Maypole Scilly 1 G4
Maypole Green Essex 107 G9
Maypole Green Norf 143 D8
Maypole Green Suff 125 F8
Maypole Green Suff 126 D5
May's Green N Som 59 G11
Mays Green Oxon 65 C8
May's Green Sur 50 B5
Mayshill S Glos 61 C7
Maythorn S Yorks 197 F7
Maythorne Notts 171 D11
Maywick Shetland 313 L5
Mead Devon 13 G11
Mead Devon 24 D2
Mead End Hants 19 B11
Mead End Hants 33 E11
Mead End Wilts 31 C8
Mead Vale Sur 51 D9
Meadgate Bath 45 B7
Meadle Bucks 84 D4
Meadow Green Hereford 116 F4
Meadow Hall S Yorks 186 C5
Meadow Head S Yorks 186 E4
Meadowbank Edin 280 G5
Meadowbank W Ches 167 B11
Meadowend Essex 106 C4
Meadowfield Durham 233 D10
Meadowfoot N Ayrs 266 F4
Meadowley Shrops 132 E3
Meadowmill E Loth 281 G8
Meadows Nottingham 153 B11
Meadowtown Shrops 130 C6
Meads E Sus 23 F10
Meadside Oxon 83 G9
Meadwell Devon 12 E4
Meaford Staffs 151 B7
Meagill N Yorks 205 B9
Meal Bank Cumb 221 F10
Meal Hill W Yorks 197 F7
Mealabost Bhuirgh W Isles 304 C6
Mealabost W Isles 304 E6
Mealasta W Isles 304 F1
Mealrigg Cumb 229 B8
Mealsgate Cumb 229 C10
Meanwood W Yorks 205 F11
Mearbeck N Yorks 212 G6
Meare Som 44 E3
Meare Green Som 28 B4
Meare Green Som 28 C3
Mearns Bath 45 B7
Mearns E Renf 267 D10
Mears Ashby Northants 120 D6
Measborough Dike S Yorks 197 F11
Measham Leics 152 G6
Meath Green Sur 51 E9
Meathop Cumb 211 C8
Meaux E Yorks 209 F7
Meaver Corn 2 F5
Meavy Devon 7 B10
Medbourne Leics 136 E5
Medbourne M Keynes 102 D6
Medburn Northumb 242 C4
Meddon Devon 24 D3
Meden Vale Notts 171 B9
Medhurst Row Kent 52 D3
Medlam Lincs 174 D4
Medlar Lancs 202 F4
Medlicott Shrops 131 E8
Medlyn Corn 2 C6
Medmenham Bucks 65 C10
Medomsley Durham 242 G4
Medstead Hants 49 F7
Meer Common Hereford 115 G7
Meer End W Mid 118 C4
Meerbrook Staffs 169 C7
Meerhay Dorset 29 G7
Meers Bridge Lincs 191 D7
Meersbrook S Yorks 186 E5
Meesden Herts 105 E8
Meeson Telford 150 E3
Meeson Heath Telford 150 E3
Meeth Devon 25 F8
Meethe Devon 25 C11
Meeting Green Suff 124 F4
Meeting House Hill Norf 160 D6
Meggernie Castle Perth 285 C9
Meggethead Borders 260 E4
Meidrim Carms 92 G5
Meifod Denb 165 D8
Meifod Powys 148 G3
Meigle N Ayrs 266 B3
Meigle Perth 286 C6
Meikle Earnock S Lnrk 268 E4
Meikle Ferry Highld 309 L7
Meikle Forter Angus 292 G3
Meikle Gluich Highld 309 L6
Meikle Obney Perth 286 D4
Meikle Pinkerton E Loth 282 F4
Meikle Strath Aberds 293 F8
Meikle Tarty Aberds 303 G9
Meikle Wartle Aberds 303 F7
Meikleour Perth 286 D5
Meinciau Carms 75 C7
Meir Stoke 168 G6
Meir Heath Staffs 168 G6
Melbourn Cambs 105 C7
Melbourne Derbys 153 D7
Melbourne E Yorks 207 E11
Melbourne S Lnrk 269 G11
Melbury Abbas Dorset 30 D5
Melbury Bubb Dorset 29 F9
Melbury Osmond Dorset 29 F9
Melbury Sampford Dorset 29 F9
Melby Shetland 313 H3
Melchbourne Beds 121 D10
Melcombe Som 43 G9
Melcombe Bingham Dorset 30 G3
Melcombe Regis Dorset 17 E9
Meldon Devon 13 C7
Meldon Northumb 252 G4
Meldreth Cambs 105 B7
Meldrum Ho Aberds 303 G8
Melfort Argyll 275 B9
Melgarve Highld 290 D6
Meliden = Gallt Melyd Denb 181 E9
Melin Caiach Caerph 77 F10
Melin-y-coed Conwy 164 C4
Melin-y-ddôl Powys 129 B11
Melin-y-grug Powys 129 B11
Melin-y-Wig Denb 165 F8
Melinbyrhedyn Powys 128 D6
Melincourt Neath 76 E4
Melincryddan Neath 57 B8
Melinsey Corn 3 B10
Melkington Northumb 273 G7
Melkinthorpe Cumb 231 F7
Melkridge Northumb 240 E6
Melksham Wilts 62 G2
Melksham Forest Wilts 62 G2
Mell Green W Berks 64 D3
Mellangaun Highld 307 L3
Mellangoose Corn 2 D5
Melldalloch Argyll 275 F10
Mellguards Cumb 230 B4
Melling Lancs 211 E11
Melling Mers 193 G11
Melling Mount Mers 194 G2
Mellingey Corn 10 G4
Mellis Suff 126 C2
Mellis Green Suff 125 C11
Mellon Charles Highld 307 K3
Mellon Udrigle Highld 307 K3
Mellor Gtr Man 185 D7
Mellor Lancs 203 G9
Mellor Brook Lancs 203 G8
Mells Som 45 D8
Mells Suff 127 B8
Mells Green Som 45 D8
Melmerby Cumb 231 D8
Melmerby N Yorks 213 B11
Melmerby N Yorks 214 D6
Melon Green Suff 124 F6
Melplash Dorset 16 B5
Melrose Borders 262 C2
Melsetter Orkney 314 H2
Melsonby N Yorks 224 D3
Meltham W Yorks 196 E6
Meltham Mills W Yorks 196 E6
Melton E Yorks 200 B3
Melton Suff 126 G5
Melton Constable Norf 159 C10
Melton Mowbray Leics 154 F5
Melton Ross N Lincs 200 E5
Meltonby E Yorks 207 C11
Melvaig Highld 307 L2
Melverley Shrops 148 F6
Melverley Green Shrops 148 F6
Melvich Highld 310 C2
Membland Devon 7 F11
Membury Devon 28 G3
Memsie Aberds 303 C9
Memus Angus 287 B8
Mena Corn 5 C10
Menabilly Corn 5 E11
Menadarva Corn 4 G2
Menagissey Corn 4 F4
Menai Bridge = Porthaethwy Anglesey 179 G9
Mendham Suff 142 G5
Mendlesham Suff 126 D2
Mendlesham Green Suff 125 E11
Menethorpe N Yorks 216 F5
Mengham Hants 21 B10
Menheniot Corn 6 C5
Menherion Corn 2 B6
Menithwood Worcs 116 D4
Menna Corn 5 E8
Mennock Dumfries 247 B8
Menston W Yorks 205 E9
Menstrie Clack 278 B6
Mentmore Bucks 84 B6
Menzion Borders 260 E3
Meoble Highld 295 G9
Meole Brace Shrops 149 G9
Meols Mers 182 C2
Meon Hants 33 G8
Meonstoke Hants 33 D10
Meopham Kent 68 F6
Meopham Green Kent 68 F6
Meopham Station Kent 68 F6
Mepal Cambs 139 G8
Meppershall C Beds 104 D2
Merbach Hereford 96 B6
Mercaton Derbys 170 G3
Merchant Fields W Yorks 197 B7
Merchiston Edin 280 G4
Mere Ches 184 E2
Mere Wilts 45 G10
Mere Brow Lancs 194 D2
Mere Green W Mid 134 D2
Mere Green Worcs 117 E9
Mere Heath W Ches 183 G11
Mereclough Lancs 204 G3
Merehead Wrex 149 B9
Meresborough Medway 69 G10
Mereside Blkpool 202 G2
Meretown Staffs 150 E5
Mereworth Kent 53 C7
Mergie Aberds 293 E9
Meriden Herts 85 F10
Meriden W Mid 134 G4
Merkadale Highld 294 B5
Merkland Dumfries 237 B9
Merkland N Ayrs 256 B2
Merkland S Ayrs 244 E6
Merkland Lodge Highld 309 G4
Merle Common Sur 52 D2
Merley Poole 18 B6
Merlin's Bridge Pembs 72 C6
Merlin's Cross Pembs 73 E7
Merridale W Mid 133 D7
Merridge Som 43 G8
Merrie Gardens I o W 21 E7
Merrifield Devon 8 F6
Merrifield Devon 24 G3
Merrington Shrops 149 E9
Merrion Pembs 72 F6
Merriott Dorset 16 B6
Merriott Som 28 E6
Merriottsford Som 28 E6
Merritown Dorset 19 B8
Merrivale Devon 12 F6
Merrivale Hereford 98 G2
Merrow Sur 50 C4
Merry Field Hill Dorset 31 G8
Merry Hill Herts 85 G10
Merry Hill W Mid 133 D7
Merry Lees Leics 135 B9
Merry Meeting Corn 11 G7
Merry Oak Soton 32 E6
Merrybent Darl 224 C4
Merryhill Green Wokingham 65 E9
Merrylee E Renf 267 D11
Merrymeet Corn 6 B5
Mersham Kent 54 F5
Merstham Sur 51 C9
Merston W Sus 22 C5
Merstone I o W 20 E6
Merther Corn 5 G7
Merther Lane Corn 5 G7
Merthyr Carms 93 G7
Merthyr Cynog Powys 95 D9
Merthyr-Dyfan V Glam 58 F6
Merthyr Mawr Bridgend 57 F11
Merthyr Tydfil M Tydf 77 D8
Merthyr Vale M Tydf 77 F9
Merton Devon 25 E8
Merton London 67 E9
Merton Norf 141 D8
Merton Oxon 83 B9
Merton Park London 67 F9
Mervinslaw Borders 262 G5
Meshaw Devon 26 D3
Messing Essex 88 B5
Messingham N Lincs 199 G11
Mesty Croft W Mid 133 E9
Mesur-y-dorth Pembs 87 E11
Metal Bridge Durham 233 E11
Metfield Suff 142 G5
Metherell Corn 7 B8
Metheringham Lincs 173 C9
Methersgate Suff 108 B5
Methil Fife 281 B7
Methilhill Fife 281 B7
Methlem Gwyn 144 C3
Methley W Yorks 197 B11
Methley Junction W Yorks 197 B11
Methley Lanes W Yorks 197 B11
Methlick Aberds 303 F8
Methven Perth 286 E4
Methwold Norf 140 E4
Methwold Hythe Norf 140 E4
Mettingham Suff 143 F7
Metton Norf 160 B3
Mevagissey Corn 5 G10
Mewith Head N Yorks 212 F4
Mexborough S Yorks 187 B7
Mey Highld 310 B6
Meyrick Park Bmouth 19 C7
Meysey Hampton Glos 81 F10
Miabhag W Isles 305 H2
Miabhag W Isles 305 J3
Miabhig W Isles 304 E2
Mial Highld 299 B7
Michaelchurch Hereford 97 F10
Michaelchurch Escley Hereford 96 E6
Michaelchurch on Arrow Powys 114 G4
Michaelston-le-Pit V Glam 59 E7
Michaelston-y-Fedw Newport 59 C8
Michaelstow Corn 11 F7
Michealston-super-Ely Cardiff 58 D6
Michelcombe Devon 8 B3
Micheldever Hants 48 F4
Michelmersh Hants 32 B4
Mickfield Suff 126 E2
Mickle Trafford W Ches 166 B6
Micklebring S Yorks 187 C8
Mickleby N Yorks 226 C6
Micklefield Bucks 84 G5
Micklefield W Yorks 206 G4
Micklefield Green Herts 85 F8
Mickleham Sur 51 C7
Micklehurst Gtr Man 196 G3
Mickleover Derby 152 C6
Micklethwaite Cumb 239 G7
Micklethwaite W Yorks 205 E8
Mickleton Durham 232 G5
Mickleton Glos 100 C3
Mickletown W Yorks 197 B11
Mickley Derbys 186 F4
Mickley N Yorks 214 D5
Mickley Shrops 150 C2
Mickley Green Suff 124 F6
Mickley Square Northumb 242 E3
Mid Ardlaw Aberds 303 C9
Mid Auchinleck Invclyd 276 G6
Mid Beltie Aberds 293 C8
Mid Calder W Loth 269 B11
Mid Cloch Forbie Aberds 303 D7
Mid Clyth Highld 310 F6
Mid Garrary Dumfries 237 B7
Mid Holmwood Sur 51 D7
Mid Lambrook Som 28 D6
Mid Lavant W Sus 22 B5
Mid Letter Argyll 284 G4
Mid Main Highld 300 F4
Mid Murthat Dumfries 248 D3
Mid Urchany Highld 301 E8
Mid Walls Shetland 313 H4
Mid Yell Shetland 312 D7
Midanbury Hants 33 E7
Midbea Orkney 314 B4
Middle Assendon Oxon 65 B8
Middle Aston Oxon 101 F9
Middle Balnald Perth 286 B4
Middle Barton Oxon 101 F8
Middle Bickenhill W Mid 134 G4
Middle Bockhampton Dorset 19 B9
Middle Bourne Sur 49 E10
Middle Bridge N Som 60 D3
Middle Burnham Som 43 D10
Middle Cairncake Aberds 303 E8
Middle Chinnock Som 29 E7
Middle Claydon Bucks 102 F4
Middle Cliff Staffs 169 E8
Middle Crackington Corn 11 B9
Middle Drums Angus 287 B9
Middle Duntisbourne Glos 81 D7
Middle Green Bucks 66 C4
Middle Green Som 27 D10
Middle Green Suff 124 D4
Middle Handley Derbys 186 F6
Middle Harling Norf 141 F9
Middle Herrington T & W 243 G9
Middle Hill Pembs 73 C7
Middle Hill Staffs 133 B9
Middle Kames Argyll 275 E10
Middle Littleton Worcs 99 B11
Middle Luxton Devon 28 E2
Middle Madeley Staffs 168 F3
Middle Maes-coed Hereford 96 E6
Middle Marwood Devon 40 F4
Middle Mayfield Staffs 169 G10
Middle Mill Pembs 87 F11
Middle Quarter Kent 53 F11
Middle Rainton T & W 234 B2
Middle Rasen Lincs 189 D9
Middle Rigg Perth 286 G4
Middle Rocombe Devon 9 B8
Middle Side Durham 232 F4
Middle Stoford Som 27 C11
Middle Stoke Devon 13 G9
Middle Stoke Medway 69 D10
Middle Stoke W Mid 119 B7
Middle Stoughton Som 44 D2
Middle Strath W Loth 279 G8
Middle Street Glos 80 E3
Middle Taphouse Corn 6 C3
Middle Town Scilly 1 F4
Middle Tysoe Warks 100 C6
Middle Wallop Hants 47 F9
Middle Weald M Keynes 102 D5
Middle Wick Glos 80 F2
Middle Winterslow Wilts 47 G8
Middle Woodford Wilts 46 F6
Middlebie Dumfries 238 B6
Middlecave N Yorks 216 E5
Middlecliffe S Yorks 198 F2
Middlecott Devon 13 D10
Middlecott Devon 24 F6
Middlecott Devon 26 F3
Middlecroft Derbys 186 G6
Middlefield Falk 279 E7
Middleforth Green Lancs 194 B4
Middleham N Yorks 214 B2
Middlehill Corn 6 B5
Middlehill Wilts 61 F10
Middlehope Shrops 131 F9
Middlemarsh Dorset 29 F11
Middlemoor Devon 12 G5
Middlemuir Aberds 303 D9
Middlemuir Aberds 303 E8
Middlemuir Aberds 303 G9
Middleport Stoke 168 F5
Middlerig Falk 279 F8
Middlesbrough M'bro 234 G5
Middlesceugh Cumb 230 C4
Middleshaw Cumb 211 B11
Middlesmoor N Yorks 213 E11
Middlestone Durham 233 E11
Middlestone Moor Durham 233 E10
Middlestown W Yorks 197 D9
Middlethird Borders 272 G3
Middlethorpe York 207 D7
Middleton Aberds 293 B10
Middleton Argyll 288 E1
Middleton Cumb 212 B2
Middleton Derbys 169 C11
Middleton Derbys 170 D3
Middleton Essex 107 D7
Middleton Gtr Man 195 F11
Middleton Hants 48 E2
Middleton Hereford 115 D10
Middleton Hrtlpl 234 E6
Middleton I o W 20 D2
Middleton Lancs 202 B4
Middleton Midloth 271 D7
Middleton N Yorks 204 E5
Middleton N Yorks 205 D8
Middleton N Yorks 216 B5
Middleton Norf 158 F3
Middleton Northants 136 F6
Middleton Northumb 252 F3
Middleton Northumb 264 B4
Middleton Perth 286 C5
Middleton Perth 286 F2
Middleton Perth 286 G5
Middleton Shrops 115 B10
Middleton Shrops 130 D5
Middleton Shrops 148 D6
Middleton Suff 127 D8
Middleton Swansea 56 D2
Middleton W Yorks 197 B10
Middleton Warks 134 D3
Middleton Baggot Shrops 132 E2
Middleton Cheney Northants 101 C9
Middleton Green Staffs 151 B9
Middleton Hall Northumb 263 D11
Middleton-in-Teesdale Durham 232 F4
Middleton Junction Gtr Man 195 G11
Middleton Moor Suff 127 D8
Middleton of Rora Aberds 303 E10
Middleton-on-Leven N Yorks 225 D9
Middleton-on-Sea W Sus 35 G7
Middleton on the Hill Hereford 115 E10
Middleton-on-the-Wolds E Yorks 208 D4
Middleton One Row Darl 225 C7
Middleton Place Cumb 219 G11
Middleton Priors Shrops 132 E2
Middleton Quernhow N Yorks 214 D6
Middleton St George Darl 224 C6
Middleton Scriven Shrops 132 F3
Middleton Stoney Oxon 101 G10
Middleton Tyas N Yorks 224 D4
Middletown Cumb 219 D9
Middletown N Som 60 E3
Middletown Powys 148 G6
Middletown Warks 117 E11
Middlewich E Ches 167 B11
Middlewick Wilts 61 E11
Middlewood Corn 11 F11
Middlewood E Ches 184 E6
Middlewood S Yorks 186 C4
Middlewood Green Suff 125 E11
Middleyard Glos 80 E4
Middlezoy Som 43 G11
Middridge Durham 233 F11
Midelney Som 28 C6
Midfield Highld 308 C5
Midford Bath 61 G9
Midgard Borders 262 F3
Midge Hall Lancs 194 C4
Midgehole W Yorks 196 B3
Midgeholme Cumb 240 F4
Midgham W Berks 64 F5
Midgham Green W Berks 64 F5
Midgley W Yorks 196 B4
Midgley W Yorks 197 E9
Midhopestones S Yorks 186 B2
Midhurst W Sus 34 C5
Midland Orkney 314 F3
Midlem Borders 262 D2
Midlock S Lnrk 259 E11
Midmar Aberds 293 C8
Midmuir Argyll 289 G11
Midpark Argyll 255 B11
Midplaugh Aberds 302 E5
Midsomer Norton Bath 45 C7
Midton Invclyd 276 F4
Midtown Highld 307 L3
Midtown Highld 308 C5
Midtown of Buchromb Moray 302 E3
Midtown of Glass Aberds 302 E4
Midville Lincs 174 D5
Midway E Ches 184 E6
Midway Som 45 D7
Miekle Toux Aberds 302 D5
Migdale Highld 309 K6
Migvie Aberds 292 C6
Milarrochy Stirl 277 C8
Milber Devon 14 G3
Milborne Port Som 29 D11
Milborne St Andrew Dorset 18 B2
Milborne Wick Som 29 C11
Milbourne Northumb 242 B4
Milbourne Wilts 62 B2
Milburn Aberds 302 E5
Milburn Aberds 302 F6
Milburn Cumb 231 F9
Milbury Heath S Glos 79 G11
Milby N Yorks 215 F8
Milch Hill Essex 106 G4
Milcombe Corn 6 D4
Milcombe Oxon 101 E8
Milden Suff 107 B9
Mildenhall Suff 124 C4
Mildenhall Wilts 63 F8
Mile Cross Norf 160 G4
Mile Elm Wilts 62 F3
Mile End Cambs 140 G2
Mile End Devon 14 G2
Mile End Essex 107 F9
Mile End Glos 79 C9
Mile End London 67 C11
Mile End Suff 124 G6
Mile Oak Brighton 36 F2
Mile Oak Kent 53 E7
Mile Oak Shrops 148 D6
Mile Oak Staffs 134 C3
Mile Town Kent 70 E2
Milebrook Powys 114 C6
Milebush Kent 53 D9
Mileham Norf 159 F8
Miles Green Staffs 168 F4
Miles Green Sur 50 B3
Miles Hill W Yorks 205 F11
Miles Platting Gtr Man 184 B5
Milesmark Fife 279 D11
Miles's Green W Berks 64 F4
Milfield Northumb 263 C10
Milford Derbys 170 F5
Milford Devon 24 C2
Milford Powys 129 E11
Milford Shrops 149 E8
Milford Staffs 151 E9
Milford Sur 50 E2
Milford Wilts 31 B11
Milford Haven Pembs 72 D6
Milford on Sea Hants 19 C11
Milkhouse Water Wilts 63 G7
Milkieston Borders 270 F4
Milkwall Glos 79 D9
Milkwell Wilts 30 C6
Mill Bank W Yorks 196 C4
Mill Brow Gtr Man 185 D7
Mill Common Norf 142 C6
Mill Common Suff 143 G8
Mill Corner E Sus 38 C4
Mill Dam N Yorks 212 F3
Mill End Bucks 65 C9
Mill End Cambs 124 F3
Mill End Glos 81 C10
Mill End Herts 85 G8
Mill End Herts 104 E6
Mill End Green Essex 106 F2
Mill Farm Aberds 303 C8
Mill Green Cambs 106 B2
Mill Green Essex 87 E10
Mill Green Hants 64 G4
Mill Green Herts 86 D2
Mill Green Norf 142 G2
Mill Green Shrops 150 D3
Mill Green Suff 107 C9
Mill Green Suff 125 F9
Mill Green Suff 126 E2
Mill Green W Mid 133 C11
Mill Hall Dumfries 237 E8
Mill Hill Blkburn 195 B7
Mill Hill E Sus 23 D10
Mill Hill Essex 88 G4
Mill Hill Glos 79 D10
Mill Hill Gtr Man 195 F8
Mill Hill Kent 55 C11
Mill Hill Lincs 175 B8
Mill Hill London 86 G2
Mill Hill Suff 125 G7
Mill Hills Suff 108 B5
Mill Hirst N Yorks 214 G3
Mill Lane Hants 49 C9
Mill Meads London 67 C11
Mill of Brydock Aberds 302 D6
Mill of Chon Stirl 285 G8
Mill of Haldane W Dunb 277 E8
Mill of Kingoodie Aberds 303 G8
Mill of Lynebain Aberds 302 F4
Mill of Muiresk Aberds 302 E6
Mill of Rango Orkney 314 E2
Mill of Sterin Aberds 292 D5
Mill of Uras Aberds 293 E10
Mill Park Argyll 255 G8
Mill Place N Lincs 200 F3
Mill Shaw W Yorks 205 G11
Mill Side Cumb 211 C8
Mill Street Kent 53 B7
Mill Street Norf 159 F11
Mill Street Suff 107 D9
Mill Throop Bmouth 19 B8
Milland W Sus 34 B4
Millarston Renfs 267 C9
Millbank Aberds 303 E11
Millbank Highld 310 C5
Millbank Kent 71 F8
Millbeck Cumb 229 F11
Millbounds Orkney 314 C5
Millbreck Aberds 303 E10
Millbridge Sur 49 E10
Millbrook C Beds 103 D10
Millbrook Corn 7 E8
Millbrook Devon 41 G9
Millbrook Gtr Man 185 B7
Millbrook Soton 32 E5
Millburn S Ayrs 257 D10
Millcombe Devon 8 F6
Millcorner E Sus 38 C4
Milldale Staffs 169 E10
Millden Lodge Angus 293 F7
Milldens Angus 287 B9
Millend Glos 80 D3
Millend Glos 80 F3
Millendreath Corn 6 E5
Millerhill Midloth 270 B6
Miller's Dale Derbys 185 G10
Miller's Green Derbys 170 E3
Miller's Green Essex 87 D9
Millersneuk E Dunb 278 G3
Millerston Glasgow 268 B2
Millfield P'boro 138 C3
Millfield T & W 243 F9
Millgate Lancs 195 D11
Millgate Norf 160 D3
Millgillhead Cumb 229 G7
Millhalf Hereford 96 B5
Millhall Kent 53 B8
Millhayes Devon 27 E10
Millhayes Devon 28 G2
Millhead Lancs 211 E9
Millheugh S Lnrk 268 E5
Millhill Devon 12 G5
Millholme Cumb 221 G11
Millhouse Argyll 275 F10
Millhouse Cumb 230 D3
Millhouse Green S Yorks 197 G8
Millhousebridge Dumfries 248 F4
Millhouses S Yorks 186 E4
Millhouses S Yorks 198 G2
Millikenpark Renfs 267 C8
Millin Cross Pembs 73 C7
Millington E Yorks 208 C2
Millington Green Derbys 170 F3
Millmeece Staffs 150 C6
Millmoor Devon 27 E10
Millness Cumb 211 C10
Millom Cumb 210 C3
Millook Corn 11 B9
Millow C Beds 104 C4
Millpool Corn 2 C3
Millpool Corn 11 G8
Millport N Ayrs 266 E3
Millquarter Dumfries 246 G4
Milltack Aberds 303 D7
Millthorpe Derbys 186 F4
Millthorpe Lincs 156 C2
Millthrop Cumb 222 G3
Milltimber Aberdeen 293 C10
Milltown Aberds 292 C4
Milltown Corn 6 B2
Milltown Corn 6 D2
Milltown Derbys 170 C5
Milltown Devon 40 F5
Milltown Highld 301 E9
Milltown of Aberdalgie Perth 286 E4
Milltown of Auchindoun Moray 302 E3
Milltown of Craigston Aberds 303 D7
Milltown of Edinvillie Moray 302 E2
Milltown of Kildrummy Aberds 292 B6
Milltown of Rothiemay Moray 302 E5
Milltown of Towie Aberds 292 B6
Millwall London 67 D11
Milnathort Perth 286 G5
Milner's Heath W Ches 167 C7
Milngavie E Dunb 277 G11
Milnquarter Falk 278 F6
Milnrow Gtr Man 196 E2
Milnsbridge W Yorks 196 D6
Milnshaw Lancs 195 B9
Milnthorpe Cumb 211 C9
Milnthorpe W Yorks 197 D10
Milnwood N Lnrk 268 D4
Milo Carms 75 B9
Milson Shrops 116 C2
Milstead Kent 54 B2
Milston Wilts 47 D7
Milthorpe Northants 101 B11
Milton Angus 287 C7
Milton Angus 292 E6
Milton Cambs 123 E9
Milton Cumb 211 C10
Milton Cumb 240 E3
Milton Derbys 152 D6
Milton Dumfries 236 D4
Milton Dumfries 237 B10
Milton Dumfries 247 G8
Milton Fife 287 E8
Milton Glasgow 267 B11
Milton Highld 299 E7
Milton Highld 300 D3
Milton Highld 300 E5
Milton Highld 300 F4
Milton Highld 301 B7
Milton Highld 301 E7
Milton Highld 310 D7
Milton Kent 69 E7
Milton Moray 292 B3
Milton Moray 302 C5
Milton N Som 59 G10
Milton Notts 188 G2
Milton Oxon 83 G7
Milton Oxon 101 E8
Milton Pembs 73 E8
Milton Perth 286 F3
Milton Powys 114 G4
Milton Ptsmth 21 B9
Milton S Yorks 197 G11
Milton Som 29 C7
Milton Stirl 285 G9
Milton Stoke 168 E6
Milton W Dunb 277 G8
Milton Wilts 45 G11
Milton Abbas Dorset 30 G4
Milton Bridge Midloth 270 C4
Milton Bryan C Beds 103 E9
Milton Clevedon Som 45 F7
Milton Coldwells Aberds 303 F9
Milton Combe Devon 7 B9
Milton Common Oxon 83 E11
Milton Coombe Devon 7 B9
Milton Damerel Devon 24 E5
Milton End Glos 80 C2
Milton End Glos 81 E10
Milton Ernest Beds 121 F10
Milton Green Devon 12 F4
Milton Green W Ches 167 D7
Milton Heights Oxon 83 G7
Milton Hill Devon 14 F4
Milton Hill Oxon 83 G7
Milton Keynes M Keynes 103 D7
Milton Keynes Village M Keynes 103 D7
Milton Lilbourne Wilts 63 G7
Milton Malsor Northants 120 F4
Milton Morenish Perth 285 D10
Milton of Auchinhove Aberds 293 C7
Milton of Balgonie Fife 287 G7
Milton of Buchanan Stirl 277 C8
Milton of Campfield Aberds 293 C8
Milton of Campsie E Dunb 278 F3
Milton of Corsindae Aberds 293 C8
Milton of Cullerlie Aberds 293 C9
Milton of Cultoquhey Perth 286 E2
Milton of Cushnie Aberds 293 B7
Milton of Dalcapon Perth 286 B3
Milton of Drimmie Perth 286 B5
Milton of Edradour Perth 286 B3
Milton of Gollanfield Highld 301 D7
Milton of Lesmore Aberds 302 G4
Milton of Logie Aberds 292 C6
Milton of Machany Perth 286 F3
Milton of Mathers Aberds 293 G9
Milton of Murtle Aberdeen 293 C10
Milton of Noth Aberds 302 G5
Milton of Tullich Aberds 292 D5
Milton on Stour Dorset 30 B3
Milton Regis Kent 70 F2
Milton Street E Sus 23 E8
Milton under Wychwood Oxon 82 B3
Miltonduff Moray 301 C11
Miltonhill Moray 301 C10
Miltonise Dumfries 236 B3
Milverton Som 27 B10
Milverton Warks 118 D6
Milwich Staffs 151 C9
Milwr Flint 181 G11
Mimbridge Sur 66 G3
Minard Argyll 275 D10
Minard Castle Argyll 275 D10
Minchington Dorset 31 E7
Minchinhampton Glos 80 E5
Mindrum Northumb 263 C8
Minehead Som 42 D3
Minera Wrex 166 E3
Mineshope Corn 11 B9
Minety Wilts 81 G8
Minffordd Gwyn 145 B11
Minffordd Gwyn 146 G4
Minffordd Gwyn 179 G9
Mingarrypark Highld 289 C8
Mingoose Corn 4 F4
Miningsby Lincs 174 C4
Minions Corn 11 G11
Minishant S Ayrs 257 G8
Minllyn Gwyn 147 G7
Minnes Aberds 303 G9
Minngearraidh W Isles 297 J3
Minnigaff Dumfries 236 C6
Minnonie Aberds 303 C7
Minnow End Essex 88 C2
Minnygap Dumfries 248 D2
Minshull Vernon E Ches 167 C11
Minskip N Yorks 215 G7
Minstead Hants 32 E3
Minsted W Sus 34 C5
Minster Kent 70 E3
Minster Kent 71 G10
Minster Lovell Oxon 82 C4
Minsterley Shrops 131 C7
Minsterworth Glos 80 B3
Minterne Magna Dorset 29 G11
Minterne Parva Dorset 29 G11
Minting Lincs 189 G11
Mintlaw Aberds 303 E10
Minto Borders 262 E3
Minto Kames Borders 262 E3
Minton Shrops 131 E8
Mintsfeet Cumb 221 G10
Minwear Pembs 73 C8
Minworth W Mid 134 E3
Mirbister Orkney 314 E2
Mirehouse Cumb 219 B9
Mireland Highld 310 C7
Mirfield W Yorks 197 D8
Miserden Glos 80 D6
Misery Corner Norf 142 F5
Miskin Rhondda 58 C4
Miskin Rhondda 77 F8
Misselfore Wilts 31 C8
Misson Notts 187 C11
Misterton Leics 135 G11
Misterton Notts 188 C3
Misterton Som 29 F7
Misterton Soss Notts 188 B3
Mistley Essex 108 E2
Mistley Heath Essex 108 E2
Mitcham London 67 F9
Mitchel Troy Mon 79 C7
Mitcheldean Glos 79 B11
Mitchell Corn 5 E7
Mitchell Hill Borders 260 C3
Mitchellslacks Dumfries 247 D11
Mitchelston Borders 271 F9
Mitcheltroy Common Mon 79 D7
Mite Houses Cumb 219 F11
Mitford Northumb 252 F5
Mithian Corn 4 E4
Mithian Downs Corn 4 F4
Mitton Staffs 151 F7
Mitton Worcs 99 E8
Mixbury Oxon 102 E2
Mixenden W Yorks 196 B5
Mixtow Corn 6 E2
Moat Cumb 239 C10
Moats Tye Suff 125 F10
Mobberley E Ches 184 F3
Mobberley Staffs 169 G8
Moblake E Ches 167 G11
Mobwell Bucks 84 E5
Moccas Hereford 97 C7
Mochdre Conwy 180 F4
Mochdre Powys 129 F11
Mochrum Dumfries 236 E5
Mockbeggar Hants 31 F11
Mockbeggar Kent 54 E6
Mockbeggar Medway 69 E8
Mockerkin Cumb 229 G7
Moclett Orkney 314 B4
Modbury Devon 8 E3
Moddershall Staffs 151 B8
Model Village Derbys 187 G8
Model Village Warks 119 E8
Modest Corner Kent 52 E5
Moel Tryfan Gwyn 163 D8
Moel-y-crio Flint 165 B11
Moelfre Anglesey 179 D8
Moelfre Conwy 181 G7
Moelfre Powys 148 D3
Moffat Dumfries 248 B3
Moffat Mills N Lnrk 268 C5
Mogador Sur 51 C8
Moggerhanger C Beds 104 B2
Mogworthy Devon 26 D5
Moira Leics 152 F6
Moity Powys 96 C3
Mol-chlach Highld 294 D6
Molash Kent 54 C4
Mold Flint 166 C2
Moldgreen W Yorks 197 D7
Molehill Green Essex 105 G11
Molehill Green Essex 106 G4
Molescroft E Yorks 208 E6
Molesden Northumb 252 G4
Molesworth Cambs 121 B11
Molinnis Corn 5 D10
Moll Highld 295 B7
Molland Devon 26 B4
Mollington Oxon 101 B8
Mollington W Ches 182 G5
Mollinsburn N Lnrk 278 G4
Monachty Ceredig 111 E10
Monachylemore Stirl 285 F8
Monar Lodge Highld 300 E2
Monaughty Powys 114 D4
Monboddo House Aberds 293 F9
Mondaytown Shrops 130 B6
Mondynes Aberds 293 F9
Monemore Stirl 285 D9
Monevechadan Argyll 284 G5
Monewden Suff 126 F4
Money Hill Leics 153 F7
Moneyacres E Ayrs 267 E8
Moneydie Perth 286 E4
Moneyhill Herts 85 G8
Moneyrow Green Windsor 65 D11
Moneystone Staffs 169 F9
Mongleath Corn 3 C7
Moniaive Dumfries 247 E7
Monifieth Angus 287 D8
Monikie Angus 287 D8
Monimail Fife 286 F6
Monington Pembs 92 C2
Monk Bretton S Yorks 197 F11
Monk End N Yorks 224 D5
Monk Fryston N Yorks 198 B4
Monk Hesleden Durham 234 D5
Monk Sherborne Hants 48 B6
Monk Soham Suff 126 D4
Monk Street Essex 106 F2
Monken Hadley London 86 F3
Monkerton Devon 14 C5
Monkhide Hereford 98 C2
Monkhill Cumb 239 F8
Monkhill W Yorks 198 C3
Monkhopton Shrops 132 E2
Monkland Hereford 115 F9
Monkleigh Devon 25 C7
Monkmoor Shrops 149 G10
Monknash V Glam 58 E2
Monkokehampton Devon 25 F9
Monks Eleigh Suff 107 B9
Monk's Gate W Sus 36 B2
Monks Heath E Ches 184 G4
Monks Hill Kent 53 E11
Monks Kirby Warks 135 G9
Monks Orchard London 67 F11
Monk's Park Wilts 61 F11
Monks Risborough Bucks 84 E4
Monkscross Corn 12 G3
Monkseaton T & W 243 C8
Monkshill Aberds 303 E7
Monksilver Som 42 F5
Monkspath W Mid 118 B2
Monksthorpe Lincs 174 B6
Monkston Park M Keynes 103 D7
Monkswood Midloth 270 C6
Monkswood Mon 78 E4
Monkswood W Yorks 206 F2
Monkton Devon 27 G11
Monkton Kent 71 G9
Monkton Pembs 73 E7
Monkton S Ayrs 257 D9
Monkton T & W 243 E8
Monkton V Glam 58 E2
Monkton Combe Bath 61 G9
Monkton Deverill Wilts 45 F11
Monkton Farleigh Wilts 61 F10
Monkton Heathfield Som 28 B3
Monkton Up Wimborne Dorset 31 E8
Monktonhall E Loth 280 G6
Monkwearmouth T & W 243 F9
Monkwood Hants 49 G7
Monkwood Green Worcs 116 E6
Monmarsh Hereford 97 B10
Monmore Green W Mid 133 D8
Monmouth = Trefynwy Mon 79 C8
Monmouth Cap Mon 97 F7
Monnington on Wye Hereford 97 C7
Monreith Dumfries 236 E5
Monreith Mains Dumfries 236 E5
Montacute Som 29 D7
Montcliffe Gtr Man 195 E7
Montcoffer Ho Aberds 302 C6
Montford Argyll 266 C2
Montford Shrops 149 G8
Montford Bridge Shrops 149 F8
Montgarrie Aberds 293 B7
Montgomery Powys 130 D4
Montgomery Lines Hants 49 C11
Monton Gtr Man 184 B3
Montpelier Bristol 60 E5
Montrave Fife 287 G7
Montrose Angus 287 B11
Montsale Essex 89 F8
Monwode Lea Warks 134 E5
Monxton Hants 47 E10
Monyash Derbys 169 B11
Monymusk Aberds 293 B8
Monzie Perth 286 E2
Monzie Castle Perth 286 E2
Moodiesburn N Lnrk 278 G3
Moolham Som 28 E5
Moon's Green Kent 38 B5
Moon's Moat Worcs 117 D11
Moonzie Fife 287 F7
Moor Som 28 D6
Moor Allerton W Yorks 205 F11
Moor Common Bucks 84 G4
Moor Crichel Dorset 31 F7
Moor Cross Devon 8 D2
Moor Edge W Yorks 205 F7
Moor End Bucks 84 G4
Moor End C Beds 103 G9
Moor End Cambs 105 B7
Moor End Durham 234 C2
Moor End E Yorks 208 F2
Moor End Glos 99 G9
Moor End Lancs 202 E3
Moor End N Yorks 207 F7
Moor End N Yorks 215 G7
Moor End S Yorks 197 G9
Moor End W Yorks 196 B5
Moor End W Yorks 206 D4
Moor End Worcs 117 F8
Moor End York 207 B9
Moor End Field N Yorks 215 F8
Moor Green Herts 104 F6
Moor Green Staffs 169 G7
Moor Green W Mid 133 G11
Moor Green Wilts 61 F11
Moor Hall W Mid 134 D2
Moor Head W Yorks 197 B8
Moor Head W Yorks 197 E8
Moor Monkton N Yorks 206 B6
Moor Monkton Moor N Yorks 206 B6

Moor of Balvack Aberds 293 B8
Moor of Granary Moray 301 D10
Moor of Ravenstone Dumfries 236 E5
Moor Park Cumb 229 D7
Moor Park Hereford 97 C9
Moor Park Herts 85 G9
Moor Park Sur 49 D11
Moor Row Cumb 219 C10
Moor Row Cumb 229 B10
Moor Side Lancs 202 F5
Moor Side Lancs 202 G4
Moor Side Lincs 174 D2
Moor Side W Yorks 197 B7
Moor Side W Yorks 204 F6
Moor Street Kent 69 F10
Moor Top W Yorks 197 C7
Mooradale Shetland 312 F6
Mooray Wilts 46 G3
Moorby Lincs 174 C3
Moorclose Cumb 228 F5
Moorclose Gtr Man 195 F11
Moorcot Hereford 115 F7
Moordown Bmouth 19 C7
Moore Halton 183 E9
Moorend Cumb 239 G8
Moorend Derbys 170 F2
Moorend Dumfries 239 C7
Moorend Glos 80 C5
Moorend Glos 80 E2
Moorend Gtr Man 185 D7
Moorend S Glos 61 D7
Moorend Cross Hereford 98 B4
Moorends S Yorks 199 D7
Moorfield Derbys 185 C8
Moorgate Norf 160 C3
Moorgate S Yorks 186 C6
Moorgreen Hants 33 D7
Moorgreen Notts 171 F7
Moorhaigh Notts 171 C8
Moorhall Derbys 186 G4
Moorhampton Hereford 97 B7
Moorhaven Village Devon 8 D3
Moorhayne Devon 28 F2
Moorhead W Yorks 205 F8
Moorhey Gtr Man 196 G2
Moorhole S Yorks 186 E6
Moorhouse Cumb 239 F8
Moorhouse Cumb 239 G7
Moorhouse Notts 172 B3
Moorhouse S Yorks 198 E3
Moorhouse Bank Sur 52 C2
Moorhouses Lincs 174 D3
Moorland or **Northmoor Green** Som 43 G10
Moorledge Bath 60 G5
Moorlinch Som 43 F11
Moorsholm Redcar 226 C3
Moorside Dorset 30 D3
Moorside Durham 233 B7
Moorside Gtr Man 195 G9
Moorside Gtr Man 196 F3
Moorside W Ches 182 F3
Moorside W Yorks 197 B8
Moorside W Yorks 205 F10
Moorstock Kent 54 F6
Moorswater Corn 6 C4
Moorthorpe W Yorks 198 E3
Moortown Devon 12 B2
Moortown Devon 12 G6
Moortown Devon 25 C8
Moortown Hants 31 G11
Moortown I o W 20 E4
Moortown Lincs 189 B9
Moortown Telford 150 F2
Moortown W Yorks 206 F2
Morangie Highld 309 L7
Morar Highld 295 F8
Moravian Settlement Derbys 153 B8
Môrawelon Anglesey 178 E3
Morayhill Highld 301 E7
Morborne Cambs 138 E2
Morchard Bishop Devon 26 F3
Morchard Road Devon 26 G3
Morcombelake Dorset 16 C4
Morcott Rutland 137 C8
Morda Shrops 148 D5
Morden Dorset 18 B4
Morden London 67 F9
Morden Green Cambs 104 C5
Morden Park London 67 F8
Mordiford Hereford 97 D11
Mordington Holdings Borders 273 D8
Mordon Durham 234 F2
More Shrops 130 E6
More Crichel Dorset 31 F7
Morebath Devon 27 C7
Morebattle Borders 263 E7
Morecambe Lancs 211 G8
Moredon Swindon 62 B6
Moredun Edin 270 B5
Morefield Highld 307 K6
Morehall Kent 55 F8
Morelaggan Argyll 284 G6
Moreleigh Devon 8 E5
Morenish Perth 285 D9
Moresby Cumb 228 G5
Moresby Parks Cumb 219 B9
Morestead Hants 33 B8
Moreton Dorset 18 D2
Moreton Essex 87 D8
Moreton Hereford 115 E10
Moreton Mers 182 C3
Moreton Oxon 82 E6
Moreton Oxon 83 E11
Moreton Staffs 150 F5
Moreton Staffs 152 D2
Moreton Corbet Shrops 149 E11
Moreton-in-Marsh Glos 100 E4
Moreton Jeffries Hereford 98 B2
Moreton Morrell Warks 118 F6
Moreton on Lugg Hereford 97 B10
Moreton Paddox Warks 118 G6
Moreton Pinkney Northants 101 B11
Moreton Say Shrops 150 C2
Moreton Valence Glos 80 D3
Moretonhampstead Devon 13 D11
Moretonwood Shrops 150 C2
Morfa Carms 56 B4
Morfa Carms 75 C9
Morfa Ceredig 110 G6
Morfa Gwyn 144 C3
Morfa Bach Carms 74 C5
Morfa Bychan Gwyn 145 B10
Morfa Dinlle Gwyn 162 D6
Morfa Glas Neath 76 D5
Morfa Nefyn Gwyn 162 G3
Morfydd Denb 165 F10
Morgan's Vale Wilts 31 C11
Morganstown Cardiff 58 C6
Moriah Ceredig 112 B2
Mork Glos 79 D9
Morland Cumb 231 G7
Morley Derbys 170 G5
Morley Durham 233 F8
Morley E Ches 184 E4
Morley W Yorks 197 B9
Morley Green E Ches 184 E4
Morley Park Derbys 170 F5
Morley St Botolph Norf 141 D11
Morley Smithy Derbys 170 G5
Morleymoor Derbys 170 G5
Mornick Corn 12 G2
Morningside Edin 280 G3
Morningside N Lnrk 268 D6
Morningthorpe Norf 142 E4
Morpeth Northumb 252 F6
Morphie Aberds 293 G9
Morrey Staffs 152 F2
Morridge Side Staffs 169 E8
Morrilow Heath Staffs 151 B9
Morris Green Essex 106 E4
Morriston = Treforys Swansea 57 B7
Morristown V Glam 59 E7
Morston Norf 177 E8
Mortehoe Devon 40 D3
Morthen S Yorks 187 D7
Mortimer W Berks 65 G7
Mortimer West End Hants 64 G6
Mortimer's Cross Hereford 115 E8
Mortlake London 67 D8
Mortomley S Yorks 186 B4
Morton Cumb 230 D4
Morton Cumb 239 G9
Morton Derbys 170 C6
Morton I o W 21 D8
Morton Lincs 155 E11
Morton Lincs 172 C5
Morton Lincs 188 C4
Morton Norf 160 F2
Morton Notts 172 E2
Morton S Glos 79 G10
Morton Shrops 148 E5
Morton Bagot Warks 118 E2
Morton Common Shrops 148 E5
Morton Mains Dumfries 247 D9
Morton Mill Shrops 149 E11
Morton-on-Swale N Yorks 224 G6
Morton Spirt Warks 117 G10
Morton Tinmouth Durham 233 G9
Morton Underhill Worcs 117 F10
Morvah Corn 1 B4
Morval Corn 6 D5
Morven Lodge Aberds 292 C5
Morvich Highld 295 C11
Morvich Highld 309 J7
Morville Shrops 132 E3
Morville Heath Shrops 132 E3
Morwellham Quay Devon 7 B8
Morwenstow Corn 24 E2
Mosborough S Yorks 186 E6
Moscow E Ayrs 267 G9
Mose Shrops 132 E5
Mosedale Cumb 230 E3
Moseley W Mid 133 D8
Moseley W Mid 133 G11
Moseley Worcs 116 F6
Moses Gate Gtr Man 195 F8
Mosley Common Gtr Man 195 G8
Moss Argyll 288 E1
Moss Highld 289 C8
Moss S Yorks 198 E5
Moss Wrex 166 E4
Moss Bank Halton 183 D8
Moss Bank Mers 183 B8
Moss Edge Lancs 202 D4
Moss Edge Lancs 202 E4
Moss End Brack 65 E11
Moss End E Ches 183 F11
Moss Houses E Ches 184 G5
Moss Lane E Ches 184 G6
Moss Nook Gtr Man 184 D4
Moss Nook Mers 183 C8
Moss of Barmuckity Moray 302 C2
Moss of Meft Moray 302 C2
Moss Pit Staffs 151 E8
Moss Side Cumb 238 G5
Moss Side Gtr Man 184 B4
Moss-side Highld 301 D8
Moss Side Lancs 193 G11
Moss Side Lancs 194 C4
Moss Side Lancs 202 G3
Moss Side Mers 182 B6
Moss-side Moray 302 D5
Mossat Aberds 292 B6
Mossbank Shetland 312 F6
Mossbay Cumb 228 F5
Mossblown S Ayrs 257 E10
Mossbrow Gtr Man 184 D2
Mossburnford Borders 262 F5
Mossdale Dumfries 237 B8
Mossedge Cumb 239 D11
Mossend N Lnrk 268 C4
Mosser Mains Cumb 229 F8
Mossfield Highld 300 B6
Mossgate Staffs 151 B8
Mossgiel E Ayrs 257 D11
Mosshouses Borders 262 B2
Mosside Angus 287 B8
Mossley E Ches 168 C5
Mossley Gtr Man 196 G3
Mossley Brow Gtr Man 196 G3
Mossley Hill Mers 182 D5
Mosspark Glasgow 267 C10
Mosstodloch Moray 302 D3
Mosston Angus 287 C9
Mosstown Aberds 303 C10
Mossy Lea Lancs 194 E4
Mosterton Dorset 29 F7
Moston E Ches 168 C2
Moston Gtr Man 195 G11
Moston Shrops 149 D11
Moston W Ches 182 G6
Moston Green E Ches 168 C2
Mostyn Flint 181 E11
Mostyn Quay Flint 181 E11
Motcombe Dorset 30 B5
Mothecombe Devon 8 F2
Motherby Cumb 230 F4
Motherwell N Lnrk 268 D5
Motspur Park London 67 F8
Mottingham London 68 E2
Mottisfont Hants 32 B4
Mottistone I o W 20 E4
Mottram in Longdendale Gtr Man 185 B7
Mottram Rise Gtr Man 185 B7
Mottram St Andrew E Ches 184 F5
Mott's Green Essex 87 B8
Mott's Mill E Sus 52 F4
Mouldsworth W Ches 183 G8
Moulin Perth 286 B3
Moulsecoomb Brighton 36 F4
Moulsford Oxon 64 C5
Moulsham Essex 88 D2
Moulsoe M Keynes 103 C8
Moultavie Highld 300 B6
Moulton Lincs 156 E6
Moulton N Yorks 224 E4
Moulton Northants 120 D5
Moulton Suff 124 E3
Moulton V Glam 58 E5
Moulton W Ches 167 B11
Moulton Chapel Lincs 156 F5
Moulton Eaugate Lincs 156 F6
Moulton Park Northants 120 E5
Moulton St Mary Norf 143 B7
Moulton Seas End Lincs 156 D6
Moulzie Angus 292 F4
Mounie Castle Aberds 303 G7
Mount Corn 4 D5
Mount Corn 6 B2
Mount Highld 301 E9
Mount W Yorks 196 D5
Mount Ambrose Corn 4 G4
Mount Ballan Mon 60 B3
Mount Batten Plym 7 E9
Mount Bovers Essex 88 G4
Mount Bures Essex 107 E8
Mount Canisp Highld 301 B7
Mount Charles Corn 5 B10
Mount Charles Corn 5 E10
Mount Cowdown Wilts 47 C9
Mount End Essex 87 E7
Mount Ephraim E Sus 23 B7
Mount Gould Plym 7 D9
Mount Hawke Corn 4 F4
Mount Hermon Corn 2 F6
Mount Hermon Sur 50 B4
Mount Hill S Glos 61 E7
Mount Lane Devon 12 B3
Mount Pleasant Bucks 102 E3
Mount Pleasant Corn 5 C10
Mount Pleasant Derbys 152 D6
Mount Pleasant Derbys 152 F5
Mount Pleasant Derbys 170 F4
Mount Pleasant Devon 27 G11
Mount Pleasant Durham 233 E11
Mount Pleasant E Ches 168 D4
Mount Pleasant E Sus 23 E7
Mount Pleasant E Sus 36 D6
Mount Pleasant Flint 182 G2
Mount Pleasant Hants 19 B11
Mount Pleasant Kent 71 F10
Mount Pleasant London 85 G8
Mount Pleasant M Tydf 77 F9
Mount Pleasant Neath 57 B9
Mount Pleasant Norf 141 E9
Mount Pleasant Pembs 73 D8
Mount Pleasant Shrops 149 G9
Mount Pleasant Stockton 234 G4
Mount Pleasant Stoke 168 G5
Mount Pleasant Suff 106 B4
Mount Pleasant T & W 243 E7
Mount Pleasant W Yorks 197 C8
Mount Pleasant Warks 135 F7
Mount Pleasant Worcs 99 D10
Mount Pleasant Worcs 117 E10
Mount Sion Wrex 166 E3
Mount Skippett Oxon 82 B5
Mount Sorrel Wilts 31 C8
Mount Tabor W Yorks 196 B5
Mount Vernon Glasgow 268 C3
Mount Wise Corn 7 E9
Mountain Anglesey 178 E2
Mountain W Yorks 205 G7
Mountain Air Bl Gwent 77 D11
Mountain Ash = Aberpennar Rhondda 77 F8
Mountain Bower Wilts 61 D10
Mountain Cross Borders 270 F2
Mountain Street Kent 54 C5
Mountain Water Pembs 91 G8
Mountbenger Borders 261 D8
Mountbengerburn Borders 261 D8
Mountblow W Dunb 277 G9
Mounters Dorset 30 D3
Mountfield E Sus 38 C2
Mountgerald Highld 300 C5
Mountjoy Corn 5 C7
Mountnessing Essex 87 F10
Mounton Mon 79 G8
Mountsolie Aberds 303 D9
Mountsorrel Leics 153 F11
Mousehill Sur 50 E2
Mousehole Corn 1 D5
Mousen Northumb 264 C4
Mousley End Warks 118 D4
Mouswald Dumfries 238 C3
Mouth Mill Devon 24 B3
Mow Cop E Ches 168 D5
Mowbreck Lancs 202 G4
Mowden Darl 224 B5
Mowden Essex 88 C3
Mowhaugh Borders 263 E8
Mowmacre Hill Leicester 135 B11
Mowshurst Kent 52 D3
Mowsley Leics 136 F2
Moxby N Yorks 215 F11
Moxley W Mid 133 D9
Moy Argyll 255 E8
Moy Highld 290 E6
Moy Highld 301 F7
Moy Hall Highld 301 F7
Moy Ho Moray 301 C10
Moy Lodge Highld 290 E6
Moyles Court Hants 31 F11
Moylgrove = Trewyddel Pembs 92 C2
Muasdale Argyll 255 C7
Much Birch Hereford 97 E10
Much Cowardne Hereford 98 B2
Much Cowarne Hereford 98 B2
Much Dewchurch Hereford 97 E9
Much Hadham Herts 86 B5
Much Hoole Lancs 194 C3
Much Hoole Moss Houses Lancs 194 C3
Much Hoole Town Lancs 194 C3
Much Marcle Hereford 98 E3
Much Wenlock Shrops 132 C2
Muchalls Aberds 293 D11
Muchelney Som 28 C6
Muchelney Ham Som 28 C6
Muchlarnick Corn 6 D4
Muchrachd Highld 300 F2
Muckairn Argyll 289 F11
Muckernich Highld 300 D5
Mucking Thurrock 69 C7
Muckle Breck Shetland 312 G7
Muckleford Dorset 17 C8
Mucklestone Staffs 150 B4
Muckleton Norf 158 B6
Muckleton Shrops 149 E11
Muckletown Aberds 302 G5
Muckley Shrops 132 D2
Muckley Corner Staffs 133 B11
Muckley Cross Shrops 132 D2
Muckton Lincs 190 E5
Muckton Bottom Lincs 190 E5
Mudale Highld 308 F5
Mudd Gtr Man 185 C7
Muddiford Devon 40 F5
Muddlebridge Devon 40 G4
Muddles Green E Sus 23 C8
Mudeford Dorset 19 C9
Mudford Som 29 D9
Mudford Sock Som 29 D9
Mudgley Som 44 D2
Mugdock Stirl 277 F11
Mugeary Highld 294 B6
Mugginton Derbys 170 G3
Muggintonlane End Derbys 170 G3
Muggleswick Durham 232 B6
Mugswell Sur 51 C9
Muie Highld 309 J6
Muir Aberds 292 E2
Muir of Alford Aberds 293 B7
Muir of Fairburn Highld 300 D4
Muir of Fowlis Aberds 293 B7
Muir of Kinellar Aberds 293 B10
Muir of Miltonduff Moray 301 D11
Muir of Ord Highld 300 D5
Muir of Pert Angus 287 D8
Muircleugh Borders 271 F10
Muirden Aberds 303 D7
Muirdrum Angus 287 D9
Muiredge Fife 281 B7
Muirend Glasgow 267 C11
Muirhead Angus 287 D7
Muirhead Fife 286 G6
Muirhead Fife 287 F8
Muirhead N Lnrk 268 B3
Muirhead S Ayrs 257 C8
Muirhouse Edin 280 F4
Muirhouse N Lnrk 268 D5
Muirhouselaw Borders 262 D4
Muirhouses Falk 279 E10
Muirkirk E Ayrs 258 D5
Muirmill Stirl 278 E4
Muirshearlich Highld 290 E3
Muirskie Aberds 293 D10
Muirtack Aberds 303 F9
Muirton Aberds 303 D7
Muirton Highld 301 C7
Muirton Perth 286 E5
Muirton Perth 286 F3
Muirton Mains Highld 300 D4
Muirton of Ardblair Perth 286 C5
Muirton of Ballochy Angus 293 G8
Muiryfold Aberds 303 D7
Muker N Yorks 223 F8
Mulbarton Norf 142 C3
Mulben Moray 302 D3
Mulberry Corn 5 B10
Mulfra Corn 1 C5
Mulindry Argyll 254 B4
Mulla Shetland 313 G6
Mullardoch House Highld 300 F2
Mullenspond Hants 47 D9
Mullion Corn 2 F5
Mullion Cove Corn 2 F5
Mumbles Hill Swansea 56 D6
Mumby Lincs 191 G8
Mumps Gtr Man 196 F2
Mundale Moray 301 D10
Munderfield Row Hereford 116 G2
Munderfield Stocks Hereford 116 G2
Mundesley Norf 160 B6
Mundford Norf 140 E6
Mundham Norf 142 D6
Mundon Essex 88 E5
Mundurno Aberdeen 293 B11
Mundy Bois Kent 54 D2
Munerigie Highld 290 C4
Muness Shetland 312 C8
Mungasdale Highld 307 K4
Mungrisdale Cumb 230 E3
Munlochy Highld 300 D6
Munsary Cottage Highld 310 E6
Munsley Hereford 98 C3
Munslow Shrops 131 F10
Munstone Hereford 97 C10
Murch V Glam 59 E7
Murchington Devon 13 D9
Murcot Worcs 99 C11
Murcott Oxon 83 B9
Murcott Wilts 81 G7
Murdieston Stirl 278 B3
Murdishaw Halton 183 E9
Murieston W Loth 269 C11
Murkle Highld 310 C5
Murlaggan Highld 290 D2
Murlaggan Highld 290 E5
Murra Orkney 314 F2
Murrayfield Edin 280 G4
Murrayshall Perth 286 E5
Murraythwaite Dumfries 238 C4
Murrell Green Hants 49 B8
Murrell's End Glos 98 E4
Murrell's End Glos 98 G5
Murrion Shetland 312 F4
Murrow Cambs 139 B7
Mursley Bucks 102 F6
Murston Kent 70 G2
Murthill Angus 287 B8
Murthly Perth 286 D4
Murton Cumb 231 G10
Murton Durham 234 B3
Murton Northumb 273 F9
Murton Swansea 56 D5
Murton T & W 243 C8
Murton York 207 C8
Murton Grange N Yorks 215 B10
Murtwell Devon 8 D5
Musbury Devon 15 C11
Muscliff Bmouth 19 B7
Muscoates N Yorks 216 C3
Muscott Northants 120 E2
Musdale Argyll 289 G11
Mushroom Green W Mid 133 F8
Musselburgh E Loth 280 G6
Musselwick Pembs 72 D4
Mustard Hyrn Norf 161 F8
Muston Leics 154 B6
Muston N Yorks 217 D11
Mustow Green Worcs 117 C7
Muswell Hill London 86 G3
Mutehill Dumfries 237 E8
Mutford Suff 143 F9
Muthill Perth 286 F2
Mutley Plym 7 D9
Mutterton Devon 27 G8
Mutton Hall E Sus 37 C9
Muxton Telford 150 G4
Mwdwl-eithin Flint 181 F11
Mwynbwll Flint 165 B11
Mybster Highld 310 D5
Myddfai Carms 94 F5
Myddle Shrops 149 E9
Myddlewood Shrops 149 E9
Myddyn-fych Carms 75 C10
Mydroilyn Ceredig 111 F9
Myerscough Lancs 202 F5
Myerscough Smithy Lancs 203 G8
Mylor Bridge Corn 3 B8
Mylor Churchtown Corn 3 B8
Mynachdy Cardiff 59 D7
Mynachdy Rhondda 77 F8
Mynachlog-ddu Pembs 92 E2
Mynd Shrops 115 C7
Myndd Llandegai Gwyn 163 B10
Myndtown Shrops 131 F7
Mynydd Bach Ceredig 112 B4
Mynydd-bach Mon 79 G7
Mynydd-Bach Swansea 57 B7
Mynydd-bach-y-glo Swansea 56 B6
Mynydd Bodafon Anglesey 179 D7
Mynydd Fflint = Flint Mountain Flint 182 G2
Mynydd Gilan Gwyn 144 D5
Mynydd-isa Flint 166 C3
Mynydd-llan Flint 181 G11
Mynydd Marian Conwy 180 F5
Mynydd Mechell Anglesey 178 D5
Mynyddislwyn Caerph 77 G11
Mynyddygarreg Carms 74 D6
Mynytho Gwyn 144 C6
Myrebird Aberds 293 D9
Myrelandhorn Highld 310 D6
Myreside Perth 286 E6
Myrtle Hill Carms 94 E5
Mytchett Sur 49 B11
Mytchett Place Sur 49 C11
Mytholm W Yorks 196 B3
Mytholmes W Yorks 204 F6
Mytholmroyd W Yorks 196 B4
Mythop Lancs 202 G3
Mytice Aberds 302 F4
Myton Warks 118 E6
Myton Hall N Yorks 215 F8
Myton-on-Swale N Yorks 215 F8
Mytton Shrops 149 F8

N

Na Gearrannan W Isles 304 D3
Naast Highld 307 L3
Nab Hill W Yorks 197 D7
Nab Wood W Yorks 205 F8
Nab's Head Lancs 194 B6
Naburn York 207 D7
Naccolt Kent 54 E4
Nackington Kent 55 C7
Nacton Suff 108 C4
Nadderwater Devon 14 C3
Nafferton E Yorks 209 B7
Nag's Head Glos 80 F5
Naid-y-march Flint 181 F11
Nailbridge Glos 79 B10
Nailsbourne Som 28 B2
Nailsea N Som 60 D3
Nailstone Leics 135 B8
Nailsworth Glos 80 F5
Nailwell Bath 61 G8
Nairn Highld 301 D8
Nalderswood Sur 51 D8
Nance Corn 4 G3
Nanceddan Corn 2 C2
Nancegollan Corn 2 C4
Nancemellin Corn 4 G2
Nancenoy Corn 2 D6
Nancledra Corn 1 B5
Nangreaves Lancs 195 D10
Nanhoron Gwyn 144 C5
Nanhyfer = Nevern Pembs 91 D11
Nannau Gwyn 146 E4
Nannerch Flint 165 B11
Nanpantan Leics 153 F10
Nanpean Corn 5 D9
Nanquidno Corn 1 D3
Nanstallon Corn 5 B10
Nant Carms 74 B6
Nant Denb 165 D11
Nant Alyn Flint 165 B11
Nant-ddu Powys 77 B8
Nant-glas Powys 113 E9
Nant Mawr Flint 166 C3
Nant Peris = Old Llanberis Gwyn 163 D10
Nant Uchaf Denb 165 D8
Nant-y-Bai Carms 94 C5
Nant-y-Bwch Bl Gwent 77 C10
Nant-y-cafn Neath 76 D4
Nant y Caws Shrops 148 D5
Nant-y-ceisiad Caerph 59 B8
Nant-y-derry Mon 78 D4
Nant-y-felin Conwy 179 G11
Nant-y-ffin Carms 93 E11
Nant-y-gollen Shrops 148 D4
Nant-y-moel Bridgend 76 G6
Nant-y-pandy Conwy 179 G11
Nant-y-Rhiw Conwy 164 D4
Nanternis Ceredig 111 F7
Nantgaredig Carms 93 G9
Nantgarw Rhondda 58 B6
Nantglyn Denb 165 C8
Nantgwyn Powys 113 B9
Nantithet Corn 2 E5
Nantlle Gwyn 163 E8
Nantmawr Shrops 148 E5
Nantmel Powys 113 D10
Nantmor Gwyn 163 F10
Nantwich E Ches 167 E11
Nantycaws Carms 75 B7
Nantyffyllon Bridgend 57 C11
Nantyglo Bl Gwent 77 C11
Nantyronen Station Ceredig 112 B3
Napchester Kent 55 D10
Naphill Bucks 84 F4
Napleton Worcs 99 B7
Napley Staffs 150 B4
Napley Heath Staffs 150 B4
Nappa N Yorks 204 C3
Nappa Scar N Yorks 223 G9
Napton on the Hill Warks 119 E9
Narberth = Arberth Pembs 73 C10
Narberth Bridge Pembs 73 C10
Narborough Leics 135 D10
Narborough Norf 158 G4
Narfords Som 28 F3
Narkurs Corn 6 D6
Narracott Devon 24 D5
Narrowgate Corner Norf 161 F8
Nasareth Gwyn 163 E7
Naseby Northants 120 B3
Nash Bucks 102 E5
Nash Hereford 114 E6
Nash Kent 55 B9
Nash London 68 G2
Nash Newport 59 C10
Nash Shrops 116 C2
Nash Som 29 E8
Nash End Worcs 132 G5
Nash Lee Bucks 84 D4
Nash Mills Herts 85 E9
Nash Street E Sus 23 C8
Nash Street Kent 68 F6
Nashend Glos 80 D5
Nashes Green Hants 49 D7
Nassington Northants 137 D11
Nast Hyde Herts 86 D2
Nastend Glos 80 D3
Nasty Herts 105 G7
Natcott Devon 24 C3
Nateby Cumb 222 D5
Nateby Lancs 202 E5
Nately Scures Hants 49 C8
Natland Cumb 211 B10
Natton Glos 99 E8
Naughton Suff 107 B10
Naunton Glos 100 G2
Naunton Worcs 99 D7
Naunton Beauchamp Worcs 117 G9
Navant Hill W Sus 34 B6
Navenby Lincs 173 D7
Navestock Heath Essex 87 F8
Navestock Side Essex 87 F9
Navidale Highld 311 H4
Navity Highld 301 C7
Nawton N Yorks 216 C3
Nayland Suff 107 E9
Nazeing Essex 86 D6
Nazeing Gate Essex 86 D6
Nazeing Long Green Essex 86 E6
Nazeing Mead Essex 86 D5
Neacroft Hants 19 B9
Nealhouse Cumb 239 G8
Neal's Green Warks 134 G6
Neames Forstal Kent 54 B5
Neap Shetland 313 H7
Near Hardcastle N Yorks 214 F2
Near Sawrey Cumb 221 F7
Nearton End Bucks 102 F6
Neasden London 67 B8
Neasham Darl 224 C6
Neat Enstone Oxon 101 G7
Neat Marsh E Yorks 209 G9
Neath = Castell-nedd Neath 57 B8
Neath Abbey Neath 57 B8
Neath Hill M Keynes 103 C7
Neatham Hants 49 E8
Neatishead Norf 160 E6
Neaton Norf 141 C8
Nebo Anglesey 179 C7
Nebo Ceredig 111 D10
Nebo Conwy 164 D4
Nebo Gwyn 163 E7
Nebsworth Warks 100 C3
Nechells W Mid 133 F11
Necton Norf 141 B7
Nedd Highld 306 F6
Nedderton Northumb 252 G6
Nedge Hill Som 44 C5
Nedge Hill Telford 132 B4
Nedging Suff 107 B9
Nedging Tye Suff 107 B10
Needham Norf 142 G4
Needham Green Essex 87 B9
Needham Market Suff 125 G11
Needham Street Suff 124 D4
Needingworth Cambs 122 C6
Needwood Staffs 152 E3
Neen Savage Shrops 116 B3
Neen Sollars Shrops 116 C3
Neenton Shrops 132 F2
Nefod Shrops 148 B6
Nefyn Gwyn 162 G4
Neighbourne Som 44 D6
Neight Hill Worcs 117 F8
Neilston E Renf 267 D9
Neinthirion Powys 129 B9
Neithrop Oxon 101 C8
Nelly Andrews Green Powys 130 B5
Nelson Caerph 77 F10
Nelson Lancs 204 F3
Nelson Village Northumb 243 B7
Nemphlar S Lnrk 269 G7
Nempnett Thrubwell N Som 60 G4
Nene Terrace Lincs 138 B5
Nenthall Cumb 231 B11
Nenthead Cumb 231 C11
Nenthorn Borders 262 B5
Neopardy Devon 13 B11
Nep Town W Sus 36 D2
Nepcote W Sus 35 F10
Nepgill Cumb 229 F7
Nerabus Argyll 254 B3
Nercwys Flint 166 C2
Nerston S Lnrk 268 D2
Nesbit Northumb 263 C11
Ness Orkney 314 C4
Ness W Ches 182 F4
Nesscliffe Shrops 149 F7
Nessholt W Ches 182 F4
Nesstoun Orkney 314 A7
Neston W Ches 182 F3
Neston Wilts 61 F11
Netchells Green W Mid 133 F11
Netham Bristol 60 E6
Nethanfoot S Lnrk 268 F6
Nether Alderley E Ches 184 F4
Nether Blainslie Borders 271 G10
Nether Booth Derbys 185 D10
Nether Broughton Leics 154 D3
Nether Burrow Lancs 212 D2
Nether Burrows Derbys 152 B5
Nether Cassock Dumfries 248 C6
Nether Cerne Dorset 17 B9
Nether Chanderhill Derbys 186 G4
Nether Compton Dorset 29 D9
Nether Crimond Aberds 303 G8
Nether Dalgliesh Borders 249 B7
Nether Dallachy Moray 302 C3
Nether Edge S Yorks 186 E4
Nether End Derbys 186 G3
Nether End Leics 154 G4
Nether End W Yorks 197 F8
Nether Exe Devon 26 G6
Nether Glasslaw Aberds 303 D8
Nether Hall Leicester 136 B2
Nether Handley Derbys 186 F6
Nether Handwick Angus 287 C7
Nether Haugh S Yorks 186 B6
Nether Headon Notts 188 F2
Nether Heage Derbys 170 E5
Nether Heyford Northants 120 F3
Nether Hindhope Borders 263 G7
Nether Horsburgh Borders 261 B8
Nether Howecleuch S Lnrk 260 G2
Nether Kellet Lancs 211 F10
Nether Kidston Borders 270 G4
Nether Kinmundy Aberds 303 E10
Nether Kirton E Renf 267 D9
Nether Langwith Notts 187 G8
Nether Leask Aberds 303 F10
Nether Lenshie Aberds 302 E6
Nether Loads Derbys 170 B4
Nether Monynut Borders 272 C4
Nether Moor Derbys 170 B5
Nether Padley Derbys 186 F3
Nether Park Aberds 303 D10
Nether Poppleton York 207 B7
Nether Row Cumb 230 D2
Nether Savock Aberds 303 E10
Nether Shiels Borders 271 F8
Nether Silton N Yorks 225 G9
Nether Skyborry Shrops 114 C5
Nether St Suff 125 E8
Nether Stowe Staffs 152 G2
Nether Stowey Som 43 F7
Nether Street Essex 87 C9
Nether Street Herts 86 B6
Nether Urquhart Fife 286 G5
Nether Wallop Hants 47 F10
Nether Warden Northumb 241 D10
Nether Wasdale Cumb 220 E2
Nether Welton Cumb 230 B3
Nether Westcote Glos 100 G4
Nether Whitacre Warks 134 E4
Nether Winchendon or **Lower Winchendon** Bucks 84 C2
Nether Worton Oxon 101 E8
Nether Yeadon W Yorks 205 E10
Netheravon Wilts 46 D6
Netherbrae Aberds 303 D7
Netherbrough Orkney 314 E3
Netherburn S Lnrk 268 F6
Netherbury Dorset 16 B5
Netherby Cumb 239 C9
Netherby N Yorks 206 D2
Netherclay Som 28 C3
Nethercote Oxon 101 C9
Nethercote Warks 119 E10
Nethercott Devon 12 B3
Nethercott Devon 40 F3
Nethercott Oxon 101 G9
Nethercott Som 42 G6
Netherdale Shetland 313 H3
Netherend Glos 79 E9
Netherfield E Sus 38 D2
Netherfield M Keynes 103 D7
Netherfield Notts 171 G10
Nethergate Norf 159 D11
Netherhampton Wilts 31 B10
Netherland Green Staffs 152 C2
Netherlaw Dumfries 237 E9
Netherlay Dorset 28 F6
Netherlee E Renf 267 D11
Netherley Aberds 293 D10
Netherley Mers 182 D6
Netherley W Yorks 196 E4
Nethermill Dumfries 248 F2
Nethermills Moray 302 D5
Nethermuir Aberds 303 E9
Netherne on-the-Hill Sur 51 B9
Netheroyd Hill W Yorks 196 D6
Netherplace E Renf 267 D10
Netherraw Borders 262 E3
Netherseal Derbys 152 G5
Netherstoke Dorset 29 F8
Netherthird E Ayrs 258 F3
Netherthong W Yorks 196 F6
Netherthorpe Derbys 186 G6
Netherthorpe S Yorks 187 E8
Netherton Aberds 303 E8
Netherton Angus 287 B9
Netherton Corn 11 G11
Netherton Cumb 228 D6
Netherton Devon 14 G3
Netherton Glos 81 E11
Netherton Hants 47 B11
Netherton Hereford 97 F10
Netherton Mers 193 G11
Netherton N Lnrk 268 E5
Netherton Northumb 251 B11
Netherton Oxon 82 F6
Netherton Perth 286 B5
Netherton Shrops 132 G4
Netherton Stirl 277 F11
Netherton W Ches 183 F8
Netherton W Mid 133 F8
Netherton W Yorks 196 E6
Netherton W Yorks 197 D9
Netherton Worcs 99 C9
Netherton of Lonmay Aberds 303 C10
Nethertown Cumb 219 D9
Nethertown Highld 310 B7
Nethertown Lancs 203 F10
Nethertown Staffs 152 F2
Netherwitton Northumb 252 E4
Netherwood E Ayrs 258 D5
Nethy Bridge Highld 301 G10
Netley Hants 33 F7
Netley Hill Soton 33 E7
Netley Marsh Hants 32 E4
Nettacott Devon 14 B4
Netteswell Essex 87 C7
Nettlebed Oxon 65 B8
Nettlebridge Som 44 D6
Nettlecombe Dorset 16 B6
Nettlecombe I o W 20 F6
Nettleden Herts 85 C8
Nettleham Lincs 189 F8
Nettlestead Kent 53 C7
Nettlestead Suff 107 B11
Nettlestead Green Kent 53 C7
Nettlestone I o W 21 C8
Nettlesworth Durham 233 B11
Nettleton Glos 80 C6
Nettleton Lincs 200 G6
Nettleton Wilts 61 D10
Nettleton Green Wilts 61 D10
Nettleton Hill W Yorks 196 D5
Nettleton Shrub Wilts 61 D10
Nettleton Top Lincs 189 B10
Netton Wilts 46 F6
Neuadd Carms 94 G3
Nevendon Essex 88 G2
Nevern = Nanhyfer Pembs 91 D11
Nevilles Cross Durham 233 C11
New Abbey Dumfries 237 C11
New Aberdour Aberds 303 C8
New Addington London 67 G11
New Alresford Hants 48 G5
New Alyth Perth 286 C6
New Arley Warks 134 F5
New Arram E Yorks 208 E6
New Ash Green Kent 68 F6
New Balderton Notts 172 E4
New Barn Kent 68 F6
New Barnet London 86 F3
New Barnetby N Lincs 200 E5
New Barton Northants 121 E7
New Basford Nottingham 171 G9
New Beaupre V Glam 58 E4
New Beckenham London 67 E11
New Bewick Northumb 264 E3
New-bigging Angus 286 C6
New Bilton Warks 119 B9
New Bolingbroke Lincs 174 D4
New Bolsover Derbys 187 G7
New Boston Mers 183 B9
New Botley Oxon 83 D7
New Boultham Lincs 189 G7
New Bradwell M Keynes 102 C6
New Brancepeth Durham 233 C10
New Bridge Wrex 166 G3
New Brighton Flint 166 B3
New Brighton Mers 182 C4
New Brighton W Sus 22 B3
New Brighton W Yorks 197 B9
New Brighton W Yorks 205 F8
New Brighton Wrex 166 E3
New Brimington Derbys 186 G6
New Brinsley Notts 171 E7
New Brotton Redcar 235 G9
New Broughton Wrex 166 E4
New Buckenham Norf 141 E11
New Buildings Bath 45 B7
New Buildings Dorset 18 F5
New Bury Gtr Man 195 F8
New Byth Aberds 303 D8
New Catton Norf 160 G4
New Charlton London 68 D2
New Cheltenham S Glos 61 E7
New Cheriton Hants 33 B9
New Clipstone Notts 171 C9
New Costessey Norf 160 G3
New Coundon Durham 233 E10
New Cowper Cumb 229 B8
New Crofton W Yorks 197 D11
New Cross Ceredig 112 B2
New Cross London 67 D11
New Cross Oxon 65 D9
New Cross Som 28 D6
New Cross Gate London 67 D11
New Cumnock E Ayrs 258 G4
New Deer Aberds 303 E8
New Delaval Northumb 243 B7
New Delph Gtr Man 196 F3
New Denham Bucks 66 C4
New Downs Corn 1 C3
New Downs Corn 4 E4
New Duston Northants 120 E4
New Earswick York 207 B8
New Eastwood Notts 171 F7
New Edlington S Yorks 187 B8
New Elgin Moray 302 C2
New Ellerby E Yorks 209 F9
New Eltham London 68 E2
New End Lincs 190 G2
New End Warks 118 E2
New End Worcs 117 F11
New England Essex 106 C4
New England Lincs 175 D8
New England P'boro 138 C3
New England Som 28 E4
New Farnley W Yorks 205 G10
New Ferry Mers 182 D4
New Fletton P'boro 138 D3
New Fryston W Yorks 198 B3
New Galloway Dumfries 237 B8
New Gilston Fife 287 G8
New Greens Herts 85 D10
New Grimsby Scilly 1 F3
New Ground Herts 85 C7
New Hainford Norf 160 F4
New Hall Hey Lancs 195 C10
New Hartley Northumb 243 B8
New Haw Sur 66 G5
New Headington Oxon 83 D9
New Heaton Northumb 273 G7
New Hedges Pembs 73 E10
New Herrington T & W 243 G8
New Hinksey Oxon 83 E8
New Ho Durham 232 D3
New Holkham Norf 159 B7
New Holland N Lincs 200 C5
New Holland W Yorks 205 F7
New Horwich Derbys 185 E8
New Houghton Derbys 171 B7
New Houghton Norf 158 D5
New House Kent 68 E6
New Houses Gtr Man 194 G5
New Houses N Yorks 212 E6
New Humberstone Leicester 136 B2
New Hunwick Durham 233 E9
New Hutton Cumb 221 G11
New Hythe Kent 53 B8
New Inn Carms 93 D9
New Inn Devon 24 F6
New Inn Mon 79 E7
New Inn Pembs 91 E11
New Inn Torf 78 F4
New Invention Shrops 114 B5
New Invention W Mid 133 C9
New Kelso Highld 299 E9
New Kingston Notts 153 D10
New Kyo Durham 242 G5
New Ladykirk Borders 273 F7
New Lanark S Lnrk 269 G7
New Lane Lancs 194 E2
New Lane End Warr 183 B10
New Langholm Dumfries 249 G9
New Leake Lincs 174 D6
New Leeds Aberds 303 D9
New Lodge S Yorks 197 F10
New Longton Lancs 194 B4
New Luce Dumfries 236 C3
New Malden London 67 F8
New Marske Redcar 235 G8
New Marston Oxon 83 D8
New Marton Shrops 148 C6
New Micklefield W Yorks 206 G4
New Mill Aberds 293 E9
New Mill Borders 262 G2
New Mill Corn 1 C5
New Mill Corn 4 G6
New Mill Cumb 219 E11
New Mill Herts 84 C6
New Mill W Yorks 197 F7
New Mill Wilts 63 G7
New Mills Borders 271 F10
New Mills Corn 5 E7
New Mills Derbys 185 D7
New Mills E Ches 184 E3
New Mills Glos 79 E10
New Mills Hereford 98 D4
New Mills = Felin Newydd Powys 129 C11
New Milton Hants 19 B10
New Mistley Essex 108 E2
New Moat Pembs 91 F11
New Moston Gtr Man 195 G11
New Ollerton Notts 171 B11
New Oscott W Mid 133 E11
New Pale W Ches 183 G8
New Park N Yorks 205 B11

New Parks Leicester 135 B11
New Passage S Glos 60 B4
New Pitsligo Aberds 303 D8
New Polzeath Corn 10 F4
New Quay = Ceinewydd Ceredig 111 F7
New Rackheath Norf 160 G5
New Radnor Powys 114 E4
New Rent Cumb 230 D5
New Ridley Northumb 242 F3
New Road Side N Yorks 204 E5
New Road Side W Yorks 197 B7
New Romney Kent 39 C9
New Rossington S Yorks 187 B10
New Row Ceredig 112 C4
New Row Lancs 203 F8
New Row N Yorks 226 C2
New Sarum Wilts 46 G6
New Sawley Derbys 153 C9
New Scarbro W Yorks 205 G10
New Sharlston W Yorks 197 C11
New Silksworth T & W 243 G9
New Skelton Redcar 226 B3
New Smithy Derbys 185 E9
New Southgate London 86 G3
New Springs Gtr Man 194 F6
New Sprowston Norf 160 G4
New Stanton Derbys 153 B9
New Stevenston N Lnrk 268 D5
New Street Kent 68 G6
New Street Staffs 169 E9
New Swanage Dorset 18 E6
New Swannington Leics 153 F8
New Thirsk N Yorks 215 C8
New Thundersley Essex 69 B9
New Totley S Yorks 186 F4
New Town Bath 45 B9
New Town Bath 60 G5
New Town Dartford 68 E4
New Town Dorset 30 C3
New Town Dorset 30 D6
New Town Dorset 31 D7
New Town Dorset 31 F7
New Town E Loth 281 G8
New Town E Sus 37 C7
New Town Edin 280 G4
New Town Edin 280 G5
New Town Glos 99 E10
New Town Lancs 203 F8
New Town Luton 103 G11
New Town Maidstone 53 B7
New Town Medway 69 G8
New Town Oxon 100 F5
New Town Reading 65 E8
New Town Shetland 312 E6
New Town Som 29 D11
New Town Som 29 D9
New Town Som 44 D3
New Town Soton 33 E7
New Town Swindon 63 C7
New Town T & W 234 B2
New Town T & W 243 E8
New Town W Berks 64 D6
New Town W Mid 133 B11
New Town W Mid 133 E9
New Town W Sus 35 B11
New Town W Yorks 198 C3
New Town Wilts 46 C6
New Town Wilts 63 E9
New Tredegar Caerph 77 E10
New Trows S Lnrk 259 B8
New Ulva Argyll 275 E8
New Village E Yorks 209 G7
New Village S Yorks 198 F5
New Walsoken Cambs 139 B9
New Waltham NE Lincs 201 G9
New Well Powys 113 B11
New Wells Powys 130 D3
New Whittington Derbys 186 F5
New Wimpole Cambs 104 B6
New Winton E Loth 281 G8
New Woodhouses Shrops 167 G9
New Works Telford 132 B3
New Wortley W Yorks 205 G11
New Yatt Oxon 82 C5
New York Lincs 174 D2
New York N Yorks 214 G3
New York T & W 243 C8
New Zealand Wilts 62 D4
Newall W Yorks 205 D10
Newall Green Gtr Man 184 D4
Newark Orkney 314 B7
Newark P'boro 138 C4
Newark-on-Trent Notts 172 E3
Newarthill N Lnrk 268 D5
Newball Lincs 189 F9
Newbarn Kent 55 F7
Newbarns Cumb 210 E4
Newbattle Midloth 270 B6
Newbie Dumfries 238 D5
Newbiggin Cumb 210 F5
Newbiggin Cumb 211 D11
Newbiggin Cumb 219 G11
Newbiggin Cumb 230 F5
Newbiggin Cumb 231 B7
Newbiggin Cumb 231 F8
Newbiggin Durham 232 B5
Newbiggin Durham 232 F4
Newbiggin Durham 233 B8
Newbiggin N Yorks 213 B9
Newbiggin N Yorks 223 G9
Newbiggin-by-the-Sea Northumb 253 F8
Newbiggin Hall Estate T & W 242 D6
Newbiggin-on-Lune Cumb 222 D4
Newbigging Aberds 303 G7
Newbigging Angus 287 D8
Newbigging Borders 262 F6
Newbigging Edin 280 F2
Newbigging S Lnrk 269 F10
Newbiggings Orkney 314 B6
Newbold Derbys 186 G5
Newbold Gtr Man 196 E2
Newbold Leics 136 B5
Newbold Leics 153 F8
Newbold Heath Leics 135 B8
Newbold on Avon Warks 119 B9
Newbold on Stour Warks 100 B4
Newbold Pacey Warks 118 F5
Newbold Verdon Leics 135 C8
Newbolds W Mid 133 C8
Newborough P'boro 138 B4
Newborough Staffs 152 D2
Newbottle Northants 101 D10
Newbottle T & W 243 G8
Newbourne Suff 108 C5
Newbridge Bath 61 F8
Newbridge Caerph 78 F2
Newbridge Ceredig 111 F10
Newbridge Corn 1 C4
Newbridge Corn 4 G5
Newbridge Corn 7 B7
Newbridge Dumfries 237 B11
Newbridge E Sus 52 G3
Newbridge Edin 280 G2
Newbridge Hants 32 D3
Newbridge I o W 20 D4
Newbridge Lancs 204 F3
Newbridge N Yorks 216 B6
Newbridge Oxon 82 E6
Newbridge Pembs 91 E8
Newbridge Shrops 148 D6
Newbridge W Mid 133 D7
Newbridge Wrex 166 G3
Newbridge Green Worcs 98 D6
Newbridge-on-Usk Mon 78 G5
Newbridge-on-Wye Powys 113 F10
Newbrough Northumb 241 D9
Newbuildings Devon 26 G3
Newburgh Aberds 303 D9
Newburgh Aberds 303 G9
Newburgh Borders 261 F8
Newburgh Fife 286 F6
Newburgh Lancs 194 E3
Newburn T & W 242 D5
Newbury Kent 54 B2
Newbury W Berks 64 F3
Newbury Wilts 45 E10
Newbury Park London 68 B2
Newby Cumb 231 G7
Newby Lancs 204 D2
Newby N Yorks 205 D11
Newby N Yorks 212 E4
Newby N Yorks 215 F7
Newby N Yorks 225 C10
Newby N Yorks 227 G10
Newby Bridge Cumb 211 B7
Newby Cote N Yorks 212 E4
Newby East Cumb 239 F11
Newby Head Cumb 231 G7
Newby West Cumb 239 G9
Newby Wiske N Yorks 215 B7
Newcastle Bridgend 58 D2
Newcastle Mon 78 B6
Newcastle Shrops 130 G4
Newcastle Emlyn = Castell Newydd Emlyn Carms 92 C6
Newcastle-under-Lyme Staffs 168 F4
Newcastle upon Tyne T & W 242 E6
Newcastleton or Copshaw Holm Borders 249 F11
Newchapel Powys 129 G9
Newchapel Staffs 168 E5
Newchapel Sur 51 E11
Newchapel = Capel Newydd Pembs 92 D4
Newchurch Bl Gwent 77 C11
Newchurch Carms 93 G7
Newchurch Hereford 115 G7
Newchurch I o W 21 D7
Newchurch Kent 54 G5
Newchurch Lancs 195 C10
Newchurch Mon 79 F7
Newchurch Powys 114 G4
Newchurch Staffs 152 E2
Newchurch in Pendle Lancs 204 F2
Newcott Devon 28 F2
Newcraighall Edin 280 G6
Newdigate Sur 51 E7
Newell Green Brack 65 E11
Newenden Kent 38 B4
Newent Glos 98 F4
Newerne Glos 79 E10
Newfield Durham 233 E10
Newfield Durham 242 G6
Newfield Highld 301 B7
Newfield Stoke 168 E6
Newford Scilly 1 G4
Newfound Hants 48 C5
Newgale Pembs 90 G6
Newgarth Orkney 314 E2
Newgate Lancs 194 F4
Newgate Norf 177 E9
Newgate Corner Norf 161 G8
Newgate Street Herts 86 D4
Newgrounds Hants 31 E11
Newhailes Edin 280 G6
Newhall Derbys 152 E5
Newhall E Ches 167 F10
Newhall Green Warks 134 F5
Newhall House Highld 300 C6
Newhall Point Highld 301 C7
Newham Lincs 174 E3
Newham Northumb 264 D5
Newhaven Derbys 169 C11
Newhaven Devon 24 C5
Newhaven E Sus 36 G6
Newhaven Edin 280 F5
Newhay N Yorks 207 G9
Newhey Gtr Man 196 E2
Newhill Fife 286 F6
Newhill Perth 286 G5
Newhill S Yorks 186 B6
Newhills Aberdeen 293 C10
Newholm N Yorks 227 C7
Newhouse Borders 262 E2
Newhouse N Lnrk 268 C5
Newhouse Shetland 313 G6
Newhouses Borders 271 G10
Newick E Sus 36 C6
Newingreen Kent 54 F6
Newington Edin 280 G5
Newington Kent 55 B7
Newington Kent 69 G11
Newington Kent 71 F11
Newington London 67 D10
Newington Notts 187 C11
Newington Oxon 83 F10
Newington Shrops 131 G8
Newington Bagpath Glos 80 G4
Newland Cumb 210 D6
Newland E Yorks 199 B10
Newland Glos 79 D9
Newland Hull 209 G7
Newland N Yorks 199 C7
Newland Oxon 82 C5
Newland Worcs 98 B5
Newland Bottom Cumb 210 C5
Newland Common Worcs 117 E8
Newland Green Kent 54 D2
Newlandrig Midloth 271 C7
Newlands Borders 250 E2
Newlands Borders 262 E2
Newlands Cumb 229 G10
Newlands Cumb 230 D2
Newlands Derbys 170 F6
Newlands Dumfries 247 F11
Newlands Glasgow 267 C11
Newlands Highld 301 E7
Newlands Moray 302 D3
Newlands Northumb 242 F3
Newlands Notts 171 C9
Newlands Staffs 151 E11
Newlands Corner Sur 50 D4
Newlands of Geise Highld 310 C4
Newlands of Tynet Moray 302 C3
Newlands Park Anglesey 178 E3
Newlandsmuir S Lnrk 268 E2
Newliston Edin 280 G2
Newliston Fife 280 C5
Newlot Orkney 314 E5
Newlyn Corn 1 D5
Newmachar Aberds 293 B10
Newmains N Lnrk 268 D6
Newman's End Essex 87 C8
Newman's Green Suff 107 C7
Newman's Place Hereford 96 B5
Newmarket Glos 80 F4
Newmarket Suff 124 E2
Newmarket W Isles 304 E6
Newmill Borders 261 G11
Newmill Corn 1 C5
Newmill Moray 302 D4
Newmill of Inshewan Angus 292 G6
Newmillerdam W Yorks 197 D10
Newmills Corn 11 D11
Newmills Fife 279 D10
Newmills Highld 300 C6
Newmills of Boyne Aberds 302 D5
Newmiln Perth 286 D5
Newmilns E Ayrs 258 B2
Newmore Highld 300 B6
Newmore Highld 300 D5
Newnes Shrops 149 C7
Newney Green Essex 87 D11
Newnham Cambs 123 F8
Newnham Glos 79 C11
Newnham Hants 49 C8
Newnham Herts 104 D4
Newnham Kent 54 B3
Newnham Northants 119 F11
Newnham Warks 118 E3
Newnham Bridge Worcs 116 D2
Newpark Fife 287 F8
Newpool Staffs 168 D5
Newport Corn 12 D2
Newport Devon 40 G5
Newport Dorset 18 C3
Newport E Yorks 208 G3
Newport Essex 105 E10
Newport Glos 79 F11
Newport Highld 311 G5
Newport I o W 20 D6
Newport Newport 59 B10
Newport Norf 161 F10
Newport Som 28 C4
Newport Telford 150 F4
Newport = Trefdraeth Pembs 91 D11
Newport-on-Tay Fife 287 E8
Newport Pagnell M Keynes 103 C7
Newpound Common W Sus 35 B9
Newquay Corn 4 C6
Newsam Green W Yorks 206 G3
Newsbank E Ches 168 B4
Newseat Aberds 303 E10
Newseat Aberds 303 F7
Newsells Herts 105 D7
Newsham Lancs 202 F6
Newsham N Yorks 215 C7
Newsham N Yorks 224 C2
Newsham Northumb 243 B8
Newsholme E Yorks 199 B8
Newsholme Lancs 204 C2
Newsholme W Yorks 204 F6
Newsome W Yorks 196 E6
Newstead Borders 262 C3
Newstead Northumb 264 D5
Newstead Notts 171 E8
Newstead Staffs 168 G5
Newstead W Yorks 197 E11
Newstreet Lane Shrops 150 B2
Newtake Devon 14 G3
Newthorpe N Yorks 206 G5
Newthorpe Notts 171 F7
Newthorpe Common Notts 171 F7
Newtoft Lincs 189 D8
Newton Argyll 275 D11
Newton Borders 262 E3
Newton Borders 262 F2
Newton Bridgend 57 F10
Newton C Beds 104 C4
Newton Cambs 105 B8
Newton Cambs 157 G8
Newton Cardiff 59 D8
Newton Corn 5 C11
Newton Cumb 210 E4
Newton Derbys 170 D6
Newton Dorset 30 E3
Newton Dumfries 239 C7
Newton Dumfries 248 E4
Newton Gtr Man 185 B7
Newton Hereford 96 C5
Newton Hereford 96 E6
Newton Hereford 115 D7
Newton Hereford 115 G10
Newton Highld 301 C7
Newton Highld 301 E7
Newton Highld 306 F7
Newton Highld 310 E7
Newton Lancs 202 F2
Newton Lancs 202 G4
Newton Lancs 203 C9
Newton Lancs 211 E11
Newton Lincs 155 B10
Newton Mers 182 D2
Newton Moray 301 C11
Newton Moray 302 C2
Newton Norf 158 F6
Newton Northants 137 G7
Newton Northumb 242 E2
Newton Notts 171 G11
Newton Perth 286 D2
Newton S Glos 79 G10
Newton S Lnrk 259 C10
Newton S Lnrk 268 C3
Newton S Yorks 198 G5
Newton Shetland 312 E5
Newton Shetland 313 K5
Newton Shrops 132 D4
Newton Shrops 149 C8
Newton Som 42 F6
Newton Staffs 151 D10
Newton Suff 107 C8
Newton Swansea 56 D6
Newton W Ches 166 B6
Newton W Ches 167 D8
Newton W Ches 183 F8
Newton W Loth 279 F11
Newton W Mid 133 E10
Newton Warks 119 B10
Newton Wilts 32 C2
Newton Abbot Devon 14 G3
Newton Arlosh Cumb 238 F5
Newton Aycliffe Durham 233 G11
Newton Bewley Hrtlpl 234 F5
Newton Blossomville M Keynes 121 G8
Newton Bromswold Northants 121 D9
Newton Burgoland Leics 135 B7
Newton by Toft Lincs 189 D9
Newton Cross Pembs 91 F7
Newton Ferrers Devon 7 F10
Newton Flotman Norf 142 D4
Newton Green Mon 79 G8
Newton Hall Durham 233 B11
Newton Hall Northumb 242 D2
Newton Harcourt Leics 136 D2
Newton Heath Gtr Man 195 G11
Newton Hill W Yorks 197 C10
Newton Ho Aberds 302 G6
Newton Hurst Staffs 151 D11
Newton Ketton Darl 234 G2
Newton Kyme N Yorks 206 E5
Newton-le-Willows Mers 183 B9
Newton-le-Willows N Yorks 214 B4
Newton Longville Bucks 102 E6
Newton Mearns E Renf 267 D10
Newton Morrell N Yorks 224 D4
Newton Morrell Oxon 102 F2
Newton Mulgrave N Yorks 226 B5
Newton of Ardtoe Highld 289 B8
Newton of Balcanqual Perth 286 F5
Newton of Balcormo Fife 287 G9
Newton of Falkland Fife 286 G6
Newton of Mountblairy Aberds 302 D6
Newton of Pitcairns Perth 286 F4
Newton on Ayr S Ayrs 257 E8
Newton on Ouse N Yorks 206 B6
Newton-on-Rawcliffe N Yorks 226 G6
Newton on the Hill Shrops 149 E9
Newton on the Moor Northumb 252 B5
Newton on Trent Lincs 188 G4
Newton Park Argyll 266 B2
Newton Park Mers 183 C9
Newton Peveril Dorset 18 B4
Newton Poppleford Devon 15 D7
Newton Purcell Oxon 102 E2
Newton Regis Warks 134 B5
Newton Reigny Cumb 230 E5
Newton Rigg Cumb 230 E5
Newton St Boswells Borders 262 C3
Newton St Cyres Devon 14 B3
Newton St Faith Norf 160 F4
Newton St Loe Bath 61 G8
Newton St Petrock Devon 24 E6
Newton Solney Derbys 152 D5
Newton Stacey Hants 48 E2
Newton Stewart Dumfries 236 C6
Newton Tony Wilts 47 E8
Newton Tracey Devon 25 B8
Newton under Roseberry Redcar 225 C11
Newton Underwood Northumb 252 F4
Newton upon Derwent E Yorks 207 D10
Newton Valence Hants 49 G8
Newton with Scales Lancs 202 G4
Newton Wood Gtr Man 184 B6
Newtonairds Dumfries 247 G9
Newtongrange Midloth 270 C6
Newtonhill Aberds 293 D11
Newtonhill Highld 300 E5
Newtonia E Ches 167 B11
Newtonmill Angus 293 G8
Newtonmore Highld 291 D9
Newtown Argyll 284 G4
Newtown Bl Gwent 77 C11
Newtown Bucks 85 E7
Newtown Caerph 78 G2
Newtown Cambs 121 D11
Newtown Corn 2 D3
Newtown Corn 11 F11
Newtown Cumb 229 B7
Newtown Cumb 239 F9
Newtown Cumb 240 E2
Newtown Derbys 185 E7
Newtown Devon 26 B3
Newtown Dorset 29 G7
Newtown E Ches 184 E6
Newtown Falk 279 E9
Newtown Glos 79 E11
Newtown Glos 80 D3
Newtown Glos 99 E8
Newtown Gtr Man 194 F5
Newtown Gtr Man 195 G9
Newtown Hants 21 B8
Newtown Hants 32 C4
Newtown Hants 32 E3
Newtown Hants 33 D8
Newtown Hants 33 E10
Newtown Hants 33 F7
Newtown Hants 49 F8
Newtown Hants 49 G10
Newtown Hants 64 G3
Newtown Hereford 97 E10
Newtown Hereford 98 C2
Newtown Highld 290 C5
Newtown I o W 20 C4
Newtown I o M 192 E4
Newtown Mers 183 B7
Newtown Norf 143 B10
Newtown Northumb 252 C2
Newtown Northumb 263 C11
Newtown Northumb 264 D2
Newtown Oxon 65 C9
Newtown Poole 18 C6
Newtown Powys 130 E2
Newtown Rhondda 77 F9
Newtown Shrops 132 C2
Newtown Shrops 149 C9
Newtown Shrops 149 E8
Newtown Som 28 E3
Newtown Som 43 F9
Newtown Staffs 133 C9
Newtown Staffs 168 C6
Newtown Staffs 169 C9
Newtown W Ches 183 F8
Newtown W Mid 133 F11
Newtown Wilts 30 B6
Newtown Wilts 63 G10
Newtown Worcs 116 F5
Newtown Worcs 117 E7
Newtown-in-St Martin Corn 2 E6
Newtown Linford Leics 135 B10
Newtown St Boswells Borders 262 C3
Newtown Unthank Leics 135 C9
Newtyle Angus 286 C6
Newyears Green London 66 B5
Nextend Hereford 114 F6
Neyland Pembs 73 D7
Niarbyl I o M 192 E3
Nib Heath Shrops 149 F8
Nibley Glos 79 D11
Nibley S Glos 61 C7
Nibley Green Glos 80 F2
Nibon Shetland 312 F5
Nicholashayne Devon 27 D10
Nicholaston Swansea 56 D4
Nidd N Yorks 214 G6
Niddrie Edin 280 G5
Nigg Aberdeen 293 C11
Nigg Highld 301 B8
Nigg Ferry Highld 301 C7
Nightcott Som 26 B5
Nilig Denb 165 D8
Nimble Nook Gtr Man 196 G2
Nimlet S Glos 61 E8
Nimmer Som 28 E4
Nine Ashes Essex 87 E9
Nine Elms London 67 D9
Nine Elms Swindon 62 B6
Nine Maidens Downs Corn 2 B5
Nine Mile Burn Midloth 270 D3
Nine Wells Pembs 90 G5
Ninebanks Northumb 241 G7
Nineveh Worcs 116 C3
Nineveh Worcs 116 E2
Ninewells Glos 79 C9
Ninfield E Sus 38 E2
Ningwood I o W 20 D3
Ningwood Common I o W 20 D3
Ninnes Bridge Corn 2 B2
Nisbet Borders 262 D5
Nisthouse Orkney 314 E3
Nisthouse Shetland 313 G7
Nithbank Dumfries 247 D9
Niton I o W 20 F6
Nitshill Glasgow 267 C10
No Man's Heath W Ches 167 F8
No Man's Heath Warks 134 B5
No Man's Land Corn 6 D5
No Man's Land Hants 33 B8
Noah's Arks Kent 52 B5
Noah's Green Worcs 117 E10
Noak Bridge Essex 87 G11
Noak Hill Essex 87 G11
Noak Hill London 87 G8
Nob End Gtr Man 195 F9
Nobland Green Herts 86 B5
Noblethorpe S Yorks 197 F9
Nobold Shrops 149 G9
Nobottle Northants 120 E3
Nob's Crook Hants 33 C7
Nocton Lincs 173 C9
Noctorum Mers 182 D3
Nodmore W Berks 64 D2
Noel Park London 86 G4
Nog Tow Lancs 202 G6
Nogdam End Norf 143 C7
Noke Oxon 83 C8
Noke Street Medway 69 E8
Nolton Pembs 72 B5
Nolton Haven Pembs 72 B5
Nomansland Devon 26 E4
Nomansland Herts 85 C11
Nomansland Wilts 32 D3
Noneley Shrops 149 D9
Noness Shetland 313 L6
Nonikiln Highld 300 B6
Nonington Kent 55 C9
Nook Cumb 211 C10
Noon Nick W Yorks 205 F8
Noonsbrough Shetland 313 H4
Noonsun E Ches 184 F4
Noonvares Corn 2 C3
Noranside Angus 292 G6
Norbiton London 67 F7
Norbreck Blkpool 202 E2
Norbridge Hereford 98 C4
Norbury Derbys 169 G10
Norbury E Ches 167 F9
Norbury London 67 F10
Norbury Shrops 131 E7
Norbury Staffs 150 E5
Norbury Common E Ches 167 F9
Norbury Junction Staffs 150 E5
Norbury Moor Gtr Man 184 D6
Norby N Yorks 215 C8
Norby Shetland 313 H3
Norchard Worcs 116 D6
Norcote Glos 81 E8
Norcott Brook W Ches 183 E10
Norcross Blkpool 202 E2
Nordelph Norf 139 C11
Nordelph Corner Norf 141 C10
Norden Dorset 18 E4
Norden Gtr Man 195 E11
Norden Heath Dorset 18 E4
Nordley Shrops 132 D3
Norham Northumb 273 F8
Norham West Mains Northumb 273 F8
Nork Sur 51 B8
Norland Town W Yorks 196 C5
Norleaze Wilts 45 C11
Norley Devon 25 G8
Norley W Ches 183 G9
Norley Common Sur 50 E4
Norleywood Hants 20 B3
Norlington E Sus 36 E6
Normacot Stoke 168 G6
Norman Cross Cambs 138 E3
Norman Hill Glos 80 F3
Normanby N Lincs 199 D11
Normanby N Yorks 216 C4
Normanby Redcar 225 B10
Normanby-by-Spital Lincs 189 D7
Normanby by Stow Lincs 188 E5
Normanby le Wold Lincs 189 B10
Normandy Sur 50 C2
Norman's Bay E Sus 23 D11
Norman's Green Devon 27 G9
Normanston Suff 143 E10
Normanton Derby 152 C6
Normanton Leics 172 G4
Normanton Lincs 172 F6
Normanton Notts 172 E2
Normanton Rutland 137 B8
Normanton W Yorks 197 C11
Normanton Wilts 46 E6
Normanton le Heath Leics 153 G7
Normanton on Soar Notts 153 E10
Normanton-on-the-Wolds Notts 154 C2
Normanton on Trent Notts 172 B3
Normanton Spring S Yorks 186 E6
Normanton Turville Leics 135 D9
Normoss Lancs 202 F2
Norney Sur 50 E2
Norr W Yorks 205 F7
Norrington Common Wilts 61 G11
Norris Green Corn 7 B8
Norris Green Mers 182 C5
Norris Hill Leics 152 F6
Norristhorpe W Yorks 197 C8
Norseman Orkney 314 E3
North Acton London 67 C8
North Anston S Yorks 187 E8
North Ascot Brack 66 F2
North Aston Oxon 101 F9
North Ayre Shetland 312 F6
North Baddesley Hants 32 D5
North Ballachulish Highld 290 G2
North Barrow Som 29 B10
North Barsham Norf 159 C8
North Batsom Som 41 G10
North Beer Corn 12 C2
North Benfleet Essex 69 B9
North Bersted W Sus 22 C6
North Berwick E Loth 281 D11
North Bitchburn Durham 233 E9
North Blyth Northumb 253 G8
North Boarhunt Hants 33 E10
North Bockhampton Dorset 19 B9
North Bovey Devon 13 E10
North Bradley Wilts 45 C11
North Brentor Devon 12 E5
North Brewham Som 45 F8
North Brook End Cambs 104 C5
North Broomage Falk 279 E7
North Buckland Devon 40 E3
North Burlingham Norf 161 G7
North Cadbury Som 29 B10
North Cairn Dumfries 236 B1
North Camp Hants 49 C11
North Carlton Lincs 188 F6
North Carlton Notts 187 E9
North Carrine Argyll 255 G7
North Cave E Yorks 208 G3
North Cerney Glos 81 D8
North Chailey E Sus 36 C5
North Charford Wilts 31 D11
North Charlton Northumb 264 E5
North Cheam London 67 F8
North Cheriton Som 29 B11
North Cliff E Yorks 209 D10
North Cliffe E Yorks 208 F3
North Clifton Notts 188 G4
North Close Durham 233 E11
North Cockerington Lincs 190 C5
North Coker Som 29 E8
North Collafirth Shetland 312 E5
North Common S Glos 61 E7
North Common Suff 125 B9
North Connel Argyll 289 F11
North Cornelly Bridgend 57 E10
North Corner Corn 3 F7
North Corner S Glos 61 C7
North Corriegills N Ayrs 256 C2
North Corry Highld 289 D10
North Cotes Lincs 201 G11
North Country Corn 4 G3
North Court Som 41 F11
North Cove Suff 143 F9
North Cowton N Yorks 224 E5
North Craigo Angus 293 G8
North Crawley M Keynes 103 C8
North Cray London 68 E3
North Creake Norf 159 B7
North Curry Som 28 B4
North Dalton E Yorks 208 C4
North Darley Corn 11 G11
North Dawn Orkney 314 F4
North Deighton N Yorks 206 C3
North Denes Norf 161 G10
North Dronley Angus 287 D7
North Drumachter Lodge Highld 291 F8
North Duffield N Yorks 207 F9
North Dykes Cumb 230 D6
North Eastling Kent 54 B3
North Elham Kent 55 E7
North Elkington Lincs 190 C3
North Elmham Norf 159 E9
North Elmsall W Yorks 198 E3
North Elmshall W Yorks 198 E3
North Elphinestone E Loth 281 G7
North End Bath 60 G6
North End Beds 103 B9
North End Beds 121 F10
North End Bexley 68 D4
North End Bucks 102 F4
North End Bucks 102 F6
North End Camden 67 B9
North End Cumb 239 F8
North End Devon 27 D10
North End Dorset 30 B4
North End Durham 233 C11
North End E Yorks 209 C9
North End E Yorks 209 E9
North End E Yorks 209 G11
North End Essex 87 B11
North End Essex 106 D5
North End Hants 31 D10
North End Hants 33 B9
North End Hants 64 G2
North End Leics 153 F11
North End Lincs 174 G2
North End Lincs 189 B8
North End Lincs 190 C5
North End Lincs 190 D6
North End Lincs 191 D7
North End Lincs 201 G10
North End N Lincs 200 C6
North End N Som 60 F2
North End Norf 141 E10
North End Northumb 252 C4
North End Ptsmth 33 G11
North End Som 28 B3
North End W Sus 35 F10
North End W Sus 35 G7
North End W Sus 51 F11
North End Wilts 81 G8
North Erradale Highld 307 L2
North Evington Leicester 136 C2
North Ewster N Lincs 199 G10
North Fambridge Essex 88 F5
North Fearns Highld 295 B7
North Featherstone W Yorks 198 C2
North Feltham London 66 E6
North Feorline N Ayrs 255 E10
North Ferriby E Yorks 200 B3
North Finchley London 86 G3
North Flobbets Aberds 303 F7
North Frodingham E Yorks 209 C8
North Gluss Shetland 312 F5
North Gorley Hants 31 E11
North Green Norf 141 B10
North Green Norf 142 F4
North Green Suff 126 B6
North Green Suff 126 E6
North Green Suff 127 D7
North Greetwell Lincs 189 G8
North Grimston N Yorks 216 F6
North Halley Orkney 314 F5
North Halling Medway 69 F8
North Harrow London 66 B6
North Hayling Hants 22 C2
North Hazelrigg Northumb 264 C3
North Heasley Devon 41 G8
North Heath W Berks 64 E3
North Heath W Sus 35 C9
North Hill Corn 11 F11
North Hillingdon London 66 C5
North Hinksey Oxon 83 D7
North Hinksey Village Oxon 83 D7
North Ho Shetland 313 J5
North Holmwood Sur 51 D7
North Houghton Hants 47 G10
North Howden E Yorks 207 G11
North Huish Devon 8 D4
North Hyde London 66 D6
North Hykeham Lincs 172 B6
North Hylton T & W 243 F8
North Kelsey Lincs 200 G4
North Kelsey Moor Lincs 200 G5
North Kensington London 67 C8
North Kessock Highld 300 E6
North Killingholme N Lincs 200 D6
North Kilvington N Yorks 215 B8
North Kilworth Leics 136 G2
North Kingston Hants 31 G11
North Kirkton Aberds 303 D11
North Kiscadale N Ayrs 256 D2
North Kyme Lincs 173 E11
North Laggan Highld 290 D4
North Lancing W Sus 35 F11
North Landing E Yorks 218 E4
North Lee Bucks 84 D4
North Lees N Yorks 214 E6
North Leigh Kent 54 D6
North Leigh Oxon 82 C5
North Leverton with Habblesthorpe Notts 188 E3
North Littleton Worcs 99 B11
North Looe Sur 67 G8
North Lopham Norf 141 G10
North Luffenham Rutland 137 C8
North Marden W Sus 34 D4
North Marston Bucks 102 G5
North Middleton Midloth 271 D7
North Middleton Northumb 264 E2
North Millbrex Aberds 303 E8
North Molton Devon 26 B2
North Moreton Oxon 64 B5
North Mosstown Aberds 303 D10
North Motherwell N Lnrk 268 D4
North Moulsecoomb Brighton 36 F4
North Mundham W Sus 22 C5
North Muskham Notts 172 D3
North Newbald E Yorks 208 F4
North Newington Oxon 101 D8
North Newnton Wilts 46 B6
North Newton Som 43 G9
North Nibley Glos 80 F2
North Oakley Hants 48 C4
North Ockendon London 68 C5
North Ormesby M'bro 234 G6
North Ormsby Lincs 190 C3
North Otterington N Yorks 215 B7
North Owersby Lincs 189 C9
North Perrott Som 29 F7
North Petherton Som 43 G9
North Petherwin Corn 11 D11
North Pickenham Norf 141 B7
North Piddle Worcs 117 G9
North Poorton Dorset 16 B6
North Port Argyll 284 E4
North Poulner Hants 31 F11
North Queensferry Fife 280 E2
North Radworthy Devon 41 G9
North Rauceby Lincs 173 F8
North Reddish Gtr Man 184 C5
North Reston Lincs 190 E5
North Rigton N Yorks 205 D11
North Ripley Hants 19 B9
North Rode E Ches 168 B5
North Roe Shetland 312 E5
North Row Cumb 229 E10
North Runcton Norf 158 F2
North Sandwick Shetland 312 D7
North Scale Cumb 210 F3
North Scarle Lincs 172 B5
North Seaton Northumb 253 F7
North Seaton Colliery Northumb 253 F7
North Sheen London 67 D7
North Shian Argyll 289 E11
North Shields T & W 243 D9
North Shoebury Sthend 70 B2
North Shore Blkpool 202 F2
North Side Cumb 228 F6
North Side P'boro 138 D5
North Skelmanae Aberds 303 D9
North Skelton Redcar 226 B3
North Somercotes Lincs 190 B6
North Stainley N Yorks 214 D5
North Stainmore Cumb 222 B6
North Stifford Thurrock 68 C6
North Stoke Bath 61 F8
North Stoke Oxon 64 B6
North Stoke W Sus 35 E8
North Stoneham Hants 32 D6
North Street Hants 31 D11
North Street Hants 48 G6
North Street Kent 54 B4
North Street Medway 69 E10
North Street W Berks 64 E6
North Sunderland Northumb 264 C6
North Synton Borders 261 E11
North Tamerton Corn 12 B2
North Tawton Devon 25 G11
North Thoresby Lincs 190 B3
North Tidworth Wilts 47 D8
North Togston Northumb 252 C6
North Town Devon 25 F8
North Town Hants 49 C11
North Town Som 29 B10
North Town Som 44 E5
North Town Windsor 65 C11
North Tuddenham Norf 159 G10
North Walbottle T & W 242 D5
North Walney Cumb 210 F3
North Walsham Norf 160 C5
North Waltham Hants 48 D5
North Warnborough Hants 49 C8
North Water Bridge Angus 293 G8
North Waterhayne Devon 28 F3
North Watford Herts 85 F10
North Watten Highld 310 D6
North Weald Bassett Essex 87 E7
North Weirs Hants 32 G3
North Wembley London 67 B7
North Weston N Som 60 D3
North Weston Oxon 83 D11
North Wheatley Notts 188 D3
North Whilborough Devon 9 B7
North Whiteley Moray 302 E4
North Wick Bath 60 F5
North Widcombe Bath 44 B5
North Willingham Lincs 189 D11
North Wingfield Derbys 170 B6
North Witham Lincs 155 E8
North Woolwich London 68 D2
North Wootton Dorset 29 E11
North Wootton Norf 158 E2
North Wootton Som 44 E5
North Wraxall Wilts 61 D10
North Wroughton Swindon 63 C7
Northacre Norf 141 D9
Northall Bucks 103 G9
Northall Green Norf 159 G9
Northallerton N Yorks 225 G7
Northam Devon 24 B6
Northam Soton 32 E6
Northampton Northants 120 E5
Northaw Herts 86 E3
Northay Devon 28 G5
Northay Som 28 E3
Northbeck Lincs 173 G9
Northborough P'boro 138 B3
Northbourne Bmouth 19 B7
Northbourne Kent 55 C10
Northbridge Street E Sus 38 C2
Northbrook Dorset 17 C11
Northbrook Hants 33 D9
Northbrook Hants 48 F4
Northbrook Oxon 101 G9
Northbrook Wilts 46 C4
Northchapel W Sus 35 B7
Northchurch Herts 85 D7
Northcote Devon 27 G11
Northcott Corn 24 F2
Northcott Devon 12 C2
Northcott Devon 27 E9
Northcott Devon 27 F10
Northcourt Oxon 83 F8
Northdown Kent 71 E11
Northdyke Orkney 314 D2
Northedge Derbys 170 B5
Northend Bath 61 F9
Northend Bucks 84 G2
Northend Essex 89 E7
Northend Essex 105 D10
Northend Warks 119 G7
Northenden Gtr Man 184 C4
Northern Moor Gtr Man 184 C4
Northfield Aberdeen 293 C11
Northfield Borders 262 D3
Northfield Borders 273 B8
Northfield E Yorks 200 B4
Northfield Edin 280 G5
Northfield Highld 301 B7
Northfield M Keynes 103 C7
Northfield Northants 137 E7
Northfield Som 43 F9
Northfield W Mid 117 B10
Northfields Hants 33 B7
Northfields Lincs 137 B10
Northfleet Kent 68 E6
Northfleet Green Kent 68 E6
Northgate Lincs 156 D3
Northgate Som 27 B9
Northgate W Sus 51 F9
Northiam E Sus 38 B4
Northill C Beds 104 B2
Northington Glos 80 D2
Northington Hants 48 F5
Northlands Lincs 174 E4
Northlea Durham 243 G10
Northleach Glos 81 C10
Northleigh Devon 15 B9
Northleigh Devon 40 G6
Northlew Devon 12 B6
Northmoor Devon 24 D4
Northmoor Oxon 82 E6
Northmoor Corner Som 43 G10
Northmoor Green or Moorland Som 43 G10
Northmuir Angus 287 B7
Northney Hants 22 C2
Northolt London 66 C6
Northop = Llan-eurgain Flint 166 B2
Northop Hall Flint 166 B3
Northorpe Lincs 155 F11
Northorpe Lincs 156 B4
Northorpe Lincs 188 B5
Northorpe W Yorks 197 C8
Northover Som 29 C8
Northover Som 44 F3
Northowram W Yorks 196 B6
Northpark Argyll 275 G11
Northport Dorset 18 D4
Northpunds Shetland 313 L6
Northrepps Norf 160 B4
Northside Aberds 303 D8
Northside Orkney 314 D2
Northton Aberds 293 C9
Northtown Orkney 314 G4
Northtown Shetland 313 M5
Northumberland Heath London 68 D4
Northville Torf 78 F3
Northway Devon 24 C5
Northway Glos 99 E8
Northway Som 27 B10
Northway Swansea 56 D5
Northwich W Ches 183 G11
Northwick S Glos 60 B5
Northwick Som 43 D11
Northwick Worcs 116 F6
Northwold Norf 140 D5
Northwood Derbys 170 C3
Northwood I o W 20 C5
Northwood Kent 71 F11
Northwood London 85 G9
Northwood Mers 182 B6
Northwood Shrops 149 C9
Northwood Staffs 168 F5
Northwood Stoke 168 F5
Northwood Green Glos 80 B2
Northwood Hills London 85 G9
Norton Devon 9 E7
Norton Devon 24 B3
Norton E Sus 23 E7
Norton Glos 99 G7
Norton Halton 183 E9
Norton Herts 104 E4
Norton I o W 20 D2

Norton Mon 78 B6
Norton N Som 59 G10
Norton Northants 120 E2
Norton Notts 187 G9
Norton Powys 114 D6
Norton S Yorks 186 E5
Norton S Yorks 198 D4
Norton Shrops 131 B11
Norton Shrops 131 G9
Norton Shrops 132 C4
Norton Stockton 234 G4
Norton Suff 125 D9
Norton Swansea 56 D3
Norton Swansea 56 D6
Norton W Mid 133 G7
Norton W Sus 22 B6
Norton W Sus 22 D5
Norton Wilts 61 C11
Norton Worcs 99 B10
Norton Worcs 117 G7
Norton Ash Kent 70 G3
Norton Bavant Wilts 46 E2
Norton Bridge Staffs 151 C7
Norton Canes Staffs 133 B10
Norton Canon Hereford 97 B7
Norton Corner Norf 159 D11
Norton Disney Lincs 172 D5
Norton East Staffs 133 B10
Norton Ferris Wilts 45 F9
Norton Fitzwarren Som 27 B11
Norton Green Herts 104 G4
Norton Green I o W 20 D2
Norton Green Staffs 168 E6
Norton Green W Mid 118 C3
Norton Hawkfield Bath 60 G5
Norton Heath Essex 87 E10
Norton in Hales Shrops 150 B4
Norton-in-the-Moors Stoke 168 E5
Norton-Juxta-Twycross Leics 134 B6
Norton-le-Clay N Yorks 215 E8
Norton Lindsey Warks 118 E4
Norton Little Green Suff 125 D9
Norton Malreward Bath 60 F6
Norton Mandeville Essex 87 E9
Norton-on-Derwent N Yorks 216 E5
Norton St Philip Som 45 B9
Norton sub Hamdon Som 29 D7
Norton Subcourse Norf 143 D8
Norton Woodseats S Yorks 186 E5
Norton's Wood N Som 60 E2
Norwell Notts 172 C3
Norwell Woodhouse Notts 172 C2
Norwich Norf 142 B4
Norwick Shetland 312 B8
Norwood Derbys 187 E7
Norwood Dorset 29 F8
Norwood End Essex 87 D9
Norwood Green London 66 D6
Norwood Green W Yorks 196 B6
Norwood Hill Sur 51 E8
Norwood New Town London 67 E10
Norwoodside Cambs 139 D8
Noseley Leics 136 D4
Noss Highld 310 D7
Noss Shetland 313 M5
Noss Mayo Devon 7 F11
Nosterfield N Yorks 214 C5
Nosterfield End Cambs 106 C2
Nostie Highld 295 C10
Notgrove Glos 100 G2
Nottage Bridgend 57 F10
Notter Corn 7 C7
Notting Hill London 67 C8
Nottingham Nottingham 153 B11
Nottington Dorset 17 E9
Notton W Yorks 197 E10
Notton Wilts 62 F2
Nounsley Essex 88 C3
Noutard's Green Worcs 116 D5
Nova Scotia W Ches 167 B10
Novar House Highld 300 C6
Novers Park Bristol 60 F5
Noverton Glos 99 G9
Nowton Suff 125 E7
Nox Shrops 149 G8
Noyadd Trefawr Ceredig 92 B5
Noyadd Wilym Ceredig 92 C4
Nuffield Oxon 65 B7
Nun Appleton N Yorks 207 F7
Nun Hills Lancs 195 C11
Nun Monkton N Yorks 206 B6
Nunburnholme E Yorks 208 D2
Nuncargate Notts 171 E8
Nunclose Cumb 230 B5
Nuneaton Warks 135 E7
Nuneham Courtenay Oxon 83 F9
Nuney Green Oxon 65 D7
Nunhead London 67 D11
Nunney Som 45 D8
Nunney Catch Som 45 E8
Nunnington N Yorks 216 D3
Nunnykirk Northumb 252 E3
Nunsthorpe NE Lincs 201 F9
Nunthorpe M'bro 225 C10
Nunthorpe York 207 C8
Nunton Wilts 31 B11
Nunwick N Yorks 214 E6
Nup End Bucks 84 B5
Nup End Herts 86 B2
Nupdown S Glos 79 F10
Nupend Glos 80 D3
Nupend Glos 80 F4
Nuper's Hatch Essex 87 G8
Nuppend Glos 79 E10
Nuptown Brack 65 E11
Nursling Hants 32 D5
Nursted Hants 34 C3
Nursteed Wilts 62 G4
Nurston V Glam 58 F5
Nurton Staffs 132 D6
Nurton Hill Staffs 132 D6
Nut Grove Mers 183 C7
Nutbourne W Sus 22 B3
Nutbourne W Sus 35 D9
Nutbourne Common W Sus 35 D9
Nutburn Hants 32 C5
Nutcombe Sur 49 G11
Nutfield Sur 51 C10
Nuthall Notts 171 G8
Nuthampstead Herts 105 E8
Nuthurst W Sus 35 B11
Nuthurst Warks 118 C3
Nutley E Sus 36 B3
Nutley Hants 48 E6
Nuttall Gtr Man 195 D9
Nutwell S Yorks 198 G6
Nybster Highld 310 C7
Nye N Som 60 G2
Nyetimber W Sus 22 D5
Nyewood W Sus 34 C4
Nyland Som 44 C3
Nymet Rowland Devon 26 F2
Nymet Tracey Devon 26 G2
Nympsfield Glos 80 E4
Nynehead Som 27 C10
Nythe Som 44 G2
Nythe Swindon 63 B7
Nyton W Sus 22 B6

O

Oad Street Kent 69 G11
Oadby Leics 136 C2
Oak Bank Gtr Man 195 F10
Oak Cross Devon 12 B6
Oak Hill Stoke 168 G5
Oak Hill Suff 109 B7
Oak Tree Darl 225 C7
Oakall Green Worcs 116 E6
Oakamoor Staffs 169 G9
Oakbank W Loth 269 B11
Oakdale Caerph 77 F11
Oakdale N Yorks 205 B11
Oakdale Poole 18 C6
Oake Som 27 B11
Oake Green Som 27 B11
Oaken Staffs 133 C7
Oakenclough Lancs 202 D6
Oakengates Telford 150 G4
Oakenholt Flint 182 G3
Oakenshaw Durham 233 D10
Oakenshaw Lancs 203 G10
Oakenshaw W Yorks 197 B7
Oakerthorpe Derbys 170 E5
Oakes W Yorks 196 D6
Oakfield Herts 104 F3
Oakfield I o W 21 C7
Oakfield Torf 78 G4
Oakford Ceredig 111 F9
Oakford Devon 26 C6
Oakfordbridge Devon 26 C6
Oakgrove E Ches 168 B6
Oakgrove M Keynes 103 D7
Oakham Rutland 137 B7
Oakham W Mid 133 F9
Oakhanger E Ches 168 E3
Oakhanger Hants 49 F9
Oakhill Som 44 D6
Oakhill W Sus 51 G7
Oakhurst Kent 52 C4
Oakington Cambs 123 E8
Oaklands Carms 74 B6
Oaklands Herts 86 B2
Oaklands Powys 113 G10
Oakle Street Glos 80 B3
Oakleigh Park London 86 G3
Oakley Beds 121 G10
Oakley Bucks 83 C10
Oakley Fife 279 D10
Oakley Glos 99 G9
Oakley Hants 48 C5
Oakley Oxon 84 E3
Oakley Poole 18 B6
Oakley Staffs 150 B4
Oakley Suff 126 B3
Oakley Court Oxon 64 B6
Oakley Green Windsor 66 D2
Oakley Park Powys 129 F9
Oakley Park Suff 126 B3
Oakley Wood Oxon 64 B6
Oakmere W Ches 167 B9
Oakridge Glos 80 E6
Oakridge Hants 48 C6
Oakridge Lynch Glos 80 E6
Oaks Shrops 131 C8
Oaks Green Derbys 152 C3
Oaks in Charnwood Leics 153 F9
Oaksey Wilts 81 G7
Oakshaw Ford Cumb 240 B2
Oakshott Hants 34 B2
Oakthorpe Leics 152 G6
Oakwell W Yorks 197 B8
Oakwood Derby 153 B7
Oakwood London 86 F3
Oakwood Northumb 241 D10
Oakwood W Yorks 206 F2
Oakwood Warr 183 C11
Oakwoodhill Sur 50 F6
Oakworth W Yorks 204 F6
Oape Highld 309 J4
Oare Kent 70 G4
Oare Som 41 D10
Oare W Berks 64 E4
Oare Wilts 63 G7
Oareford Som 41 D10
Oasby Lincs 155 B10
Oath Som 28 B5
Oathill Dorset 28 F6
Oathlaw Angus 287 B8
Oatlands Glasgow 267 C11
Oatlands N Yorks 205 C11
Oatlands Park Sur 66 G5
Oban Argyll 289 G10
Oban Highld 295 G10
Oban W Isles 305 H3
Obley Shrops 114 B6
Oborne Dorset 29 D11
Obthorpe Lincs 155 F11
Obthorpe Lodge Lincs 156 F2
Occlestone Green W Ches 167 C11
Occold Suff 126 C3
Ocean Village Soton 32 E6
Ochiltree E Ayrs 258 E2
Ochr-y-foel Denb 181 F9
Ochtermuthill Perth 286 F2
Ochtertyre Perth 286 E2
Ochtow Highld 309 J4
Ockbrook Derbys 153 B8
Ocker Hill W Mid 133 E9
Ockeridge Worcs 116 E5
Ockford Ridge Sur 50 E3
Ockham Sur 50 B5
Ockle Highld 289 B7
Ockley Sur 50 F6
Ocle Pychard Hereford 97 B11
Octon E Yorks 217 F10
Octon Cross Roads E Yorks 217 F10
Odam Barton Devon 26 D2
Odcombe Som 29 D8
Odd Down Bath 61 G8
Oddendale Cumb 221 C11
Odder Lincs 188 G6
Oddingley Worcs 117 F8
Oddington Glos 100 F4
Oddington Oxon 83 C9
Odell Beds 121 F9
Odham Devon 25 G7
Odie Orkney 314 D6
Odiham Hants 49 C8
Odsal W Yorks 197 B7
Odsey Cambs 104 D5
Odstock Wilts 31 B10
Odstone Leics 135 B7
Offchurch Warks 119 D7
Offenham Worcs 99 B11
Offenham Cross Worcs 99 B11
Offerton Gtr Man 184 D6
Offerton T & W 243 F8
Offerton Green Gtr Man 184 D6
Offham E Sus 36 E5
Offham Kent 53 B7
Offham W Sus 35 F8
Offleyhay Staffs 150 D5
Offleymarsh Staffs 150 D5
Offleyrock Staffs 150 D5
Offord Cluny Cambs 122 D4
Offord D'Arcy Cambs 122 D4
Offton Suff 107 B11
Offwell Devon 15 B9
Ogbourne Maizey Wilts 63 E7
Ogbourne St Andrew Wilts 63 E7
Ogbourne St George Wilts 63 E8
Ogden W Yorks 205 G7
Ogdens Hants 31 E11
Ogil Angus 292 G6
Ogle Northumb 242 B4
Ogmore V Glam 57 F11
Ogmore-by-Sea = Aberogwr V Glam 57 F11
Ogmore Vale Bridgend 76 G6
Okeford Fitzpaine Dorset 30 E4
Okehampton Devon 13 B7
Okehampton Camp Devon 13 C7
Oker Derbys 170 C3
Okewood Hill Sur 50 F6
Okle Green Glos 98 F5
Okraquoy Shetland 313 K6
Okus Swindon 62 C6
Olchard Devon 14 F3
Old Northants 120 C5
Old Aberdeen Aberdeen 293 C11
Old Alresford Hants 48 G5
Old Arley Warks 134 E5
Old Balornock Glasgow 268 B2
Old Basford Nottingham 171 G8
Old Basing Hants 49 C7
Old Belses Borders 262 E3
Old Bewick Northumb 264 E3
Old Bexley London 68 E3
Old Blair Perth 291 G10
Old Bolingbroke Lincs 174 B4
Old Boston Mers 183 B9
Old Bramhope W Yorks 205 E10
Old Brampton Derbys 186 G4
Old Bridge of Tilt Perth 291 G10
Old Bridge of Urr Dumfries 237 C9
Old Buckenham Norf 141 E11
Old Burdon T & W 243 G9
Old Burghclere Hants 48 B3
Old Byland N Yorks 215 B11
Old Cambus Borders 272 B6
Old Cardinham Castle Corn 6 B2
Old Carlisle Cumb 229 B11
Old Cassop Durham 234 D2
Old Castleton Borders 250 E2
Old Catton Norf 160 G4
Old Chalford Oxon 100 F6
Old Church Stoke Powys 130 E5
Old Clee NE Lincs 201 F9
Old Cleeve Som 42 E4
Old Colwyn Conwy 180 F5
Old Coppice Shrops 131 B9
Old Corry Highld 295 C8
Old Coulsdon London 51 B10
Old Country Hereford 98 C4
Old Craig Aberds 303 G9
Old Craig Angus 292 G4
Old Crombie Aberds 302 D5
Old Cryals Kent 53 E7
Old Cullen Moray 302 C5
Old Dailly S Ayrs 244 D6
Old Dalby Leics 154 E3
Old Dam Derbys 185 F10
Old Deer Aberds 303 E9
Old Denaby S Yorks 187 B7
Old Ditch Som 44 D4
Old Dolphin W Yorks 205 G8
Old Down S Glos 60 B6
Old Duffus Moray 301 C11
Old Edlington S Yorks 187 B8
Old Eldon Durham 233 F10
Old Ellerby E Yorks 209 F9
Old Fallings W Mid 133 C8
Old Farm Park M Keynes 103 D8
Old Felixstowe Suff 108 D6
Old Field Shrops 115 B9
Old Fletton P'boro 138 D3
Old Fold T & W 243 E7
Old Ford London 67 C11
Old Forge Hereford 79 B9
Old Furnace Torf 78 E3
Old Gate Lincs 157 E8
Old Glossop Derbys 185 C8
Old Goginan Ceredig 128 G3
Old Goole E Yorks 199 C8
Old Gore Hereford 98 F2
Old Graitney Dumfries 239 D8
Old Grimsby Scilly 1 F3
Old Hall Powys 129 G8
Old Hall Green Herts 105 G7
Old Hall Street Norf 160 C6
Old Harlow Essex 87 C7
Old Hatfield Herts 86 D2
Old Heath Essex 107 G10
Old Heathfield E Sus 37 C9
Old Hill W Mid 133 F9
Old Hills Worcs 98 B6
Old Hunstanton Norf 175 G11
Old Hurst Cambs 122 B5
Old Hutton Cumb 211 B11
Old Johnstone Dumfries 248 D6
Old Kea Corn 4 G6
Old Kilpatrick W Dunb 277 G9
Old Kinnernie Aberds 293 C9
Old Knebworth Herts 104 G4
Old Langho Lancs 203 F10
Old Laxey I o M 192 D5
Old Leake Lincs 174 E6
Old Leckie Stirl 278 C3
Old Lindley W Yorks 196 D5
Old Linslade C Beds 103 F8
Old Llanberis = Nant Peris Gwyn 163 D10
Old Malden London 67 F8
Old Malton N Yorks 216 E5
Old Marton Shrops 148 C6
Old Mead Essex 105 F10
Old Micklefield W Yorks 206 G4
Old Mill Corn 12 G3
Old Milton Hants 19 C10
Old Milverton Warks 118 D5
Old Monkland N Lnrk 268 C4
Old Nenthorn Borders 262 B5
Old Netley Hants 33 F7
Old Neuadd Powys 129 F11
Old Newton Suff 125 E11
Old Oak Common London 67 C8
Old Park Corn 6 B4
Old Park Telford 132 B3
Old Passage S Glos 60 B5
Old Perton Staffs 133 D7
Old Philpstoun W Loth 279 F11
Old Polmont Falk 279 F8
Old Portsmouth Ptsmth 21 B8
Old Quarrington Durham 234 D2
Old Radnor Powys 114 F5
Old Rattray Aberds 303 D10
Old Rayne Aberds 302 G6
Old Romney Kent 39 B8
Old Shirley Soton 32 E5
Old Shoreham W Sus 36 F2
Old Snydale W Yorks 198 C2
Old Sodbury S Glos 61 C9
Old Somerby Lincs 155 C9
Old Stillington Stockton 234 G3
Old Storridge Common Worcs 116 G4
Old Stratford Northants 102 C5
Old Struan Perth 291 G10
Old Swan Mers 182 C5
Old Swarland Northumb 252 C5
Old Swinford W Mid 133 G8
Old Tame Gtr Man 196 F3
Old Tebay Cumb 222 D2
Old Thirsk N Yorks 215 C8
Old Tinnis Borders 261 D9
Old Toll S Ayrs 257 E9
Old Town Cumb 211 C11
Old Town Cumb 230 C5
Old Town E Sus 23 F9
Old Town E Sus 38 F2
Old Town E Sus 38 F4
Old Town E Yorks 218 F3
Old Town Edin 280 G5
Old Town Herts 104 F4
Old Town Scilly 1 G4
Old Town Swindon 63 C7
Old Town W Yorks 196 B3
Old Trafford Gtr Man 184 B4
Old Tree Kent 71 G8
Old Tupton Derbys 170 B5
Old Warden C Beds 104 C2
Old Warren Flint 166 C4
Old Way Som 28 D5
Old Weston Cambs 121 B11
Old Wharf Hereford 98 D4
Old Whittington Derbys 186 G5
Old Wick Highld 310 D7
Old Wimpole Cambs 122 G6
Old Windsor Windsor 66 E3
Old Wingate Durham 234 D3
Old Wives Lees Kent 54 C5
Old Woking Sur 50 B4
Old Wolverton M Keynes 102 C6
Old Woodhall Lincs 174 B2
Old Woodhouses Shrops 167 G9
Old Woodstock Oxon 82 B6
Oldany Highld 306 F6
Oldberrow Warks 118 D2
Oldborough Devon 26 F3
Oldbrook M Keynes 103 D7
Oldbury Kent 52 B5
Oldbury Shrops 132 E4
Oldbury W Mid 133 F9
Oldbury Warks 134 E6
Oldbury Naite S Glos 79 G10
Oldbury-on-Severn S Glos 79 G10
Oldbury on the Hill Glos 61 B10
Oldcastle Mon 96 G6
Oldcastle Heath W Ches 167 F7
Oldcotes Notts 187 D9
Oldcroft Glos 79 D10
Oldend Glos 80 D3
Oldfallow Staffs 151 G9
Oldfield Cumb 229 F7
Oldfield Shrops 132 F3
Oldfield W Yorks 196 E6
Oldfield W Yorks 204 F6
Oldfield Worcs 116 E6
Oldfield Brow Gtr Man 184 D3
Oldfield Park Bath 61 G8
Oldford Som 45 C9
Oldfurnace Staffs 169 G8
Oldhall Renfs 267 C10
Oldhall Green Suff 125 F7
Oldhall Ho Highld 310 D6
Oldham Gtr Man 196 F2
Oldham Edge Gtr Man 196 F2
Oldhamstocks E Loth 282 G4
Oldhurst Cambs 122 B6
Oldington Shrops 132 D4
Oldland S Glos 61 E7
Oldland Common S Glos 61 E7
Oldmeldrum Aberds 303 G8
Oldmixon N Som 43 B10
Oldshore Beg Highld 306 D6
Oldshoremore Highld 306 D7
Oldstead N Yorks 215 C10
Oldtown Aberds 293 C7
Oldtown Aberds 302 G5
Oldtown Highld 309 L5
Oldtown of Ord Aberds 302 D6
Oldway Swansea 56 C3
Oldway Torbay 9 C7
Oldways End Devon 26 B5
Oldwhat Aberds 303 D8
Oldwich Lane W Mid 118 C4
Oldwood Worcs 115 D11
Olgrinmore Highld 310 D4
Olive Green Staffs 152 F2
Oliver's Battery Hants 33 B7
Ollaberry Shetland 312 E5
Ollag W Isles 297 G3
Ollerbrook Booth Derbys 185 D10
Ollerton E Ches 184 F3
Ollerton Notts 171 B11
Ollerton Shrops 150 D2
Ollerton Fold Lancs 194 C6
Ollerton Lane Shrops 150 D2
Olmarch Ceredig 112 F2
Olmstead Green Essex 106 C2
Olney M Keynes 121 G7
Olrig Ho Highld 310 C5
Olton W Mid 134 G2
Olveston S Glos 60 B6
Olwen Ceredig 93 B11
Ombersley Worcs 116 E6
Ompton Notts 171 B11
Omunsgarth Shetland 313 J5
Onchan I o M 192 E4
Onecote Staffs 169 D9
Onehouse Suff 125 F10
Onen Mon 78 C6
Onesacre S Yorks 186 C3
Ongar Hill Norf 157 E11
Ongar Street Hereford 115 D7
Onibury Shrops 115 B9
Onich Highld 290 G2
Onllwyn Neath 76 C4
Onneley Staffs 168 G3
Onslow Village Sur 50 D3
Onthank E Ayrs 267 G8
Onziebust Orkney 314 D4
Openshaw Gtr Man 184 B5
Openwoodgate Derbys 170 F5
Opinan Highld 299 B7
Opinan Highld 307 K3
Orange Lane Borders 272 G5
Orange Row Norf 157 E10
Orasaigh W Isles 305 G5
Orbiston N Lnrk 268 D4
Orbliston Moray 302 D3
Orbost Highld 298 E2
Orby Lincs 175 B7
Orchard Hill Devon 24 B6
Orchard Leigh Bucks 85 E7
Orchard Portman Som 28 C2
Orcheston Wilts 46 D5
Orcop Hereford 97 F9
Orcop Hill Hereford 97 F9
Ord Highld 295 D8
Ordale Shetland 312 C8
Ordhead Aberds 293 B8
Ordie Aberds 292 C6
Ordiequish Moray 302 D3
Ordiqhill Aberds 302 D5
Ordley Northumb 241 F10
Ordsall Gtr Man 184 B4
Ordsall Notts 187 E11
Ore E Sus 38 E4
Oreston Plym 7 E10
Oreton Shrops 132 G3
Orford Suff 109 B8
Orford Warr 183 C10
Organford Dorset 18 C4
Orgreave S Yorks 186 D6
Orgreave Staffs 152 F3
Oridge Street Glos 98 F5
Orlandon Pembs 72 D4
Orlestone Kent 54 G3
Orleton Hereford 115 D9
Orleton Worcs 116 D3
Orleton Common Hereford 115 D9
Orlingbury Northants 121 C7
Ormacleit W Isles 297 H3
Ormathwaite Cumb 229 F11
Ormesby Redcar 225 B10
Ormesby St Margaret Norf 161 G9
Ormesby St Michael Norf 161 G9
Ormiclate Castle W Isles 297 H3
Ormidale Lodge Argyll 275 F11
Ormiscaig Highld 307 K3
Ormiston Borders 262 G2
Ormiston E Loth 271 B8
Ormsaigbeg Highld 288 C6
Ormsaigmore Highld 288 C6
Ormsary Argyll 275 F8
Ormsgill Cumb 210 E3
Ormskirk Lancs 194 F2
Ornsby Hill Durham 233 B9
Orpington London 68 F3
Orrell Gtr Man 194 F4
Orrell Mers 182 B4
Orrell Post Gtr Man 194 G4
Orrisdale I o M 192 C4
Orrock Fife 280 D4
Orroland Dumfries 237 E9
Orsett Thurrock 68 C6
Orsett Heath Thurrock 68 D6
Orslow Staffs 150 F6
Orston Notts 172 G3
Orthwaite Cumb 229 E11
Ortner Lancs 202 C6
Orton Cumb 222 D2
Orton Northants 120 B6
Orton Staffs 133 D7
Orton Brimbles P'boro 138 D3
Orton Goldhay P'boro 138 D3
Orton Longueville P'boro 138 D3
Orton Malborne P'boro 138 D3
Orton-on-the-Hill Leics 134 C6
Orton Rigg Cumb 239 G8
Orton Southgate P'boro 138 E2
Orton Waterville P'boro 138 D3
Orton Wistow P'boro 138 D2
Orwell Cambs 123 G7
Osbaldeston Lancs 203 G8
Osbaldeston Green Lancs 203 G8
Osbaldwick York 207 C8
Osbaston Leics 135 C8
Osbaston Shrops 148 E6
Osbaston Telford 149 F11
Osbaston Hollow Leics 135 B8
Osbournby Lincs 155 B11
Oscroft W Ches 167 B8
Ose Highld 298 E3
Osea Island Essex 88 D6
Osehill Green Dorset 29 F11
Osgathorpe Leics 153 F8
Osgodby Lincs 189 C9
Osgodby N Yorks 207 G8
Osgodby N Yorks 217 C11
Osgodby Common N Yorks 207 F8
Osidge London 86 G3
Oskaig Highld 295 B7
Oskamull Argyll 288 E6
Osleston Derbys 152 B4
Osmaston Derby 153 C7
Osmaston Derbys 170 G2
Osmington Dorset 17 E10
Osmington Mills Dorset 17 E10
Osmondthorpe W Yorks 206 G2
Osmotherley N Yorks 225 F9
Osney Oxon 83 D8
Ospisdale Highld 309 L7
Ospringe Kent 70 G4
Ossaborough Devon 40 E3
Ossemsley Hants 19 B10
Osset Spa W Yorks 197 D9
Ossett W Yorks 197 C9
Ossett Street Side W Yorks 197 C9
Ossington Notts 172 C3
Ostend Essex 88 F6
Ostend Norf 161 C7
Osterley London 66 D6
Oswaldkirk N Yorks 216 D2
Oswaldtwistle Lancs 195 B8
Oswestry Shrops 148 D5
Otby Lincs 189 C10
Oteley Shrops 149 C8
Otford Kent 52 B4
Otham Kent 53 C9
Otham Hole Kent 53 C10
Otherton Staffs 151 G8
Othery Som 43 G11
Otley Suff 126 F4
Otley W Yorks 205 D10
Otter Ferry Argyll 275 E10
Otter Ho Argyll 275 F10
Otterbourne Hants 33 C7
Otterburn N Yorks 204 B3
Otterburn Northumb 251 E9
Otterburn Camp Northumb 251 D9
Otterden Place Kent 54 C2
Otterford Som 28 E2
Otterham Corn 11 C9
Otterham Quay Kent 69 F10
Otterham Station Corn 11 D9
Otterhampton Som 43 E8
Ottershaw Sur 66 G4
Otterspool Mers 182 D5
Otterswick Shetland 312 E7
Otterton Devon 15 D7
Otterwood Hants 32 G6
Ottery St Mary Devon 15 B8
Ottinge Kent 55 E7
Ottringham E Yorks 201 C9
Oughterby Cumb 239 F7
Oughtershaw N Yorks 213 C7
Oughterside Cumb 229 C8
Oughtibridge S Yorks 186 C4
Oughtrington Warr 183 D11
Oulston N Yorks 215 E10
Oulton Cumb 238 G6
Oulton Norf 160 D2
Oulton Staffs 150 E5
Oulton Staffs 151 B8
Oulton Suff 143 D10
Oulton W Yorks 197 B11
Oulton Broad Suff 143 E10
Oulton Grange Staffs 151 B8
Oulton Heath Staffs 151 B8
Oulton Street Norf 160 D3
Oultoncross Staffs 151 C8
Oundle Northants 137 F10
Ounsdale Staffs 133 E7
Ousby Cumb 231 E8
Ousdale Highld 311 G4
Ousden Suff 124 F4
Ousefleet E Yorks 199 C10
Ousel Hole W Yorks 205 E8
Ouston Durham 243 G7
Ouston Northumb 241 G7
Ouston Northumb 242 C3
Out Elmstead Kent 55 C8
Out Newton E Yorks 201 C11
Out Rawcliffe Lancs 202 E4
Outcast Cumb 210 D6
Outer Hope Devon 8 G3
Outertown Orkney 314 E2
Outgate Cumb 221 F7
Outhgill Cumb 222 E5
Outhill Warks 118 D2
Outhills Aberds 303 D10
Outlands Staffs 150 C5
Outlane W Yorks 196 D5
Outlane Moor W Yorks 196 D5
Outlet Village W Ches 182 G6
Outmarsh Wilts 61 G11
Outwell Norf 139 C10
Outwick Hants 31 D10
Outwood Gtr Man 195 F9
Outwood Som 28 B4
Outwood Sur 51 D10
Outwood W Yorks 197 C10
Outwoods Leics 153 F8
Outwoods Staffs 150 F5
Outwoods Staffs 152 E4
Outwoods Warks 134 G4
Ouzlewell Green W Yorks 197 B10
Ovenden W Yorks 196 B5
Ovenscloss Borders 261 C11
Over Cambs 123 C7
Over Glos 80 B4
Over S Glos 60 C5
Over W Ches 167 B10
Over Burrow Lancs 212 D2
Over Burrows Derbys 152 B5
Over Compton Dorset 29 D9
Over End Cambs 137 E11
Over End Derbys 186 G3
Over Green W Mid 134 E3
Over Haddon Derbys 170 B2
Over Hulton Gtr Man 195 F7
Over Kellet Lancs 211 E10
Over Kiddington Oxon 101 G8
Over Knutsford E Ches 184 F3
Over Langshaw Borders 271 G10
Over Monnow Mon 79 C8
Over Norton Oxon 100 F6
Over Peover E Ches 184 G3
Over Silton N Yorks 225 G9
Over Stowey Som 43 F7
Over Stratton Som 28 D6
Over Tabley E Ches 184 E2
Over Town Lancs 195 B11
Over Wallop Hants 47 F9
Over Whitacre Warks 134 E5
Over Worton Oxon 101 F8
Overa Farm Stud Norf 141 F9
Overbister Orkney 314 B6
Overbury Worcs 99 D9
Overcombe Dorset 17 E9
Overend W Mid 133 G9
Overgreen Derbys 186 G4
Overleigh Som 44 F3
Overley Staffs 152 F3
Overley Green Warks 117 F11
Overpool W Ches 182 F5
Overs Shrops 131 D7
Overscaig Hotel Highld 309 G4
Overseal Derbys 152 F5
Overslade Warks 119 C9
Oversland Kent 54 B5
Oversley Green Warks 117 F11
Overstone Northants 120 D6
Overstrand Norf 160 A4
Overthorpe Northants 101 C9
Overthorpe W Yorks 197 D8
Overton Aberdeen 293 B10
Overton Aberds 293 B9
Overton Dumfries 237 C11
Overton Glos 80 C2
Overton Hants 48 D4
Overton Involyd 276 G5
Overton Lancs 202 B4
Overton N Yorks 207 B7
Overton Shrops 115 C10
Overton Shrops 115 B10
Overton Staffs 151 B10
Overton Swansea 56 D3
Overton W Ches 183 F8
Overton W Yorks 197 D9
Overton = Owrtyn Wrex 166 G5
Overton Bridge Wrex 166 G5
Overtown Lancs 212 D2
Overtown N Lnrk 268 E6
Overtown Swindon 63 D7
Overtown W Yorks 197 D11
Oving Bucks 102 G5
Oving W Sus 22 C6
Ovingdean Brighton 36 G5
Ovingham Northumb 242 E3
Ovington Durham 224 C2
Ovington Essex 106 C5
Ovington Hants 48 G5
Ovington Norf 141 C8
Ovington Northumb 242 E3
Owen's Bank Staffs 152 D4
Ower Hants 32 D4
Owermoigne Dorset 17 D11
Owl End Cambs 122 B4
Owlbury Shrops 130 E6
Owlcotes Derbys 170 B6
Owler Bar Derbys 186 F3
Owlerton S Yorks 186 D4
Owlet W Yorks 205 F9
Owlpen Glos 80 F4
Owl's Green Suff 126 D5
Owlsmoor Brack 65 G11
Owlswick Bucks 84 D3
Owlthorpe S Yorks 186 E6
Owmby Lincs 200 G5
Owmby-by-Spital Lincs 189 D8
Ownham W Berks 64 E2
Owrtyn = Overton Wrex 166 G5
Owslebury Hants 33 C8
Owston Leics 136 B5
Owston S Yorks 198 E5
Owston Ferry N Lincs 199 G10
Owstwick E Yorks 209 G11
Owthorne E Yorks 201 B10
Owthorpe Notts 154 C3
Owton Manor Hrtlpl 234 F5
Oxborough Norf 140 C4
Oxclose S Yorks 186 E6
Oxclose T & W 243 F7
Oxcombe Lincs 190 F4
Oxcroft Derbys 187 G7
Oxcroft Estate Derbys 187 G7
Oxen End Essex 106 F3
Oxen Park Cumb 210 B6
Oxenhall Glos 98 F4
Oxenholme Cumb 211 B10
Oxenhope W Yorks 204 F6
Oxenpill Som 44 E2
Oxenton Glos 99 E9
Oxenwood Wilts 47 B10
Oxford Oxon 83 D8
Oxford Stoke 168 E5
Oxgang E Dunb 278 G3
Oxgangs Edin 270 B4
Oxhey Herts 85 F10
Oxhill Durham 242 G5
Oxhill Warks 100 B6
Oxlease Herts 86 D2
Oxley W Mid 133 C8
Oxley Green Essex 88 C6
Oxley's Green E Sus 37 C11
Oxlode Cambs 139 F9
Oxnam Borders 262 F5
Oxnead Norf 160 E4
Oxshott Sur 66 G6
Oxspring S Yorks 197 G9
Oxted Sur 51 C11
Oxton Borders 271 E9
Oxton Mers 182 D3
Oxton N Yorks 206 E6
Oxton Notts 171 E10
Oxton Rakes Derbys 186 G4
Oxwich Swansea 56 D3
Oxwich Green Swansea 56 D3
Oxwick Norf 159 D8
Oykel Bridge Highld 309 J3
Oyne Aberds 302 G6
Oystermouth Swansea 56 D6
Ozleworth Glos 80 G3

P

Pabail Iarach W Isles 304 E7
Pabail Uarach W Isles 304 E7
Pabo Conwy 180 F4
Pace Gate N Yorks 205 C8
Pachesham Park Sur 51 B7
Packers Hill Dorset 30 E2
Packington Leics 153 G7
Packmoor Staffs 168 E5
Packmores Warks 118 D5
Packwood W Mid 118 C3
Packwood Gullet W Mid 118 C3
Padanaram Angus 287 B8
Padbury Bucks 102 E4
Paddington London 67 C9
Paddington Warr 183 D10
Paddlesworth Kent 55 F7
Paddlesworth Kent 69 G7
Paddock Kent 54 C3
Paddock W Yorks 196 D6
Paddock Wood Kent 53 E7
Paddockhaugh Moray 302 D2
Paddockhill E Ches 184 F4
Paddockhole Dumfries 248 G6
Paddolgreen Shrops 149 C10
Padfield Derbys 185 B8
Padgate Warr 183 D10
Padham's Green Essex 87 F10
Padiham Lancs 203 G11
Padney Cambs 123 C10
Padog Conwy 164 E4
Padside N Yorks 205 B9
Padside Green N Yorks 205 B9
Padson Devon 13 B7
Padstow Corn 10 F4
Padworth W Berks 64 F6
Padworth Common Hants 64 G6
Paganhill Glos 80 D4
Page Bank Durham 233 D10
Page Moss Mers 182 C6
Page's Green Suff 126 D2
Pagham W Sus 22 D5
Paglesham Churchend Essex 88 G6
Paglesham Eastend Essex 88 G6
Paibeil W Isles 296 E3
Paible W Isles 305 J2
Paignton Torbay 9 C7
Pailton Warks 135 G9
Painleyhill Staffs 151 C10
Pains Hill Sur 52 C2
Painscastle Powys 96 B3
Painshawfield Northumb 242 E3
Painsthorpe E Yorks 208 B2
Painswick Glos 80 D5
Painter's Forstal Kent 54 B3
Painter's Green Herts 86 B3
Painters Green Wrex 167 G8
Painthorpe W Yorks 197 D10
Paintmoor Som 28 F4
Pairc Shiaboist W Isles 304 D4
Paisley Renfs 267 C9
Pakefield Suff 143 E10
Pakenham Suff 125 D8
Pale Gwyn 147 B9
Pale Green Essex 106 C3
Palehouse Common E Sus 23 B7
Palestine Hants 47 E9
Paley Street Windsor 65 D11
Palfrey W Mid 133 D10
Palgowan Dumfries 245 G9
Palgrave Suff 126 B2
Pallaflat Cumb 219 C9
Pallington Dorset 17 C11
Pallion T & W 243 F9
Pallister M'bro 225 B10
Palmarsh Kent 54 G6
Palmer Moor Derbys 152 C2
Palmers Cross Staffs 133 C7
Palmers Cross Sur 50 E4
Palmer's Flat Glos 79 D9
Palmer's Green Kent 53 E7
Palmers Green London 86 G4
Palmersbridge Corn 11 F9
Palmerstown V Glam 58 F
Palmersville T & W 243 C
Palmstead Kent 55 D
Palnackie Dumfries 237 D1
Palnure Dumfries 236 C
Palterton Derbys 171 B
Pamber End Hants 48 B
Pamber Green Hants 48 B
Pamber Heath Hants 64 G
Pamington Glos 99 E
Pamphill Dorset 31 G
Pampisford Cambs 105 B
Pan I o W 20 D
Pan Orkney 314 G
Panborough Som 44 D
Panbride Angus 287 D
Pancakehill Glos 81 C
Pancrasweek Devon 24 F
Pancross V Glam 58 F
Pandy Gwyn 128 C
Pandy Gwyn 146 F
Pandy Gwyn 147 D
Pandy Mon 96 G
Pandy Powys 129 C
Pandy Wrex 148 B
Pandy Wrex 166 G
Pandy Tudur Conwy 164 C
Pandy'r Capel Denb 165 E
Panfield Essex 106 F
Pangbourne W Berks 64 D
Panhall Fife 280 C
Panks Bridge Hereford 98 B
Pannal N Yorks 206 C
Pannal Ash N Yorks 205 C1
Pannel's Ash Essex 106 C
Panpunton Powys 114 C
Panshanger Herts 86 C
Pant Denb 166 E
Pant Flint 181 G1
Pant Gwyn 144 C
Pant M Tydf 77 D
Pant Powys 129 C1
Pant Shrops 148 E
Pant Wrex 166 D
Pant Wrex 166 F
Pant-glâs Powys 128 D
Pant-glas Gwyn 163 F
Pant-glas Shrops 148 C
Pant-lasau Swansea 57 E
Pant Mawr Powys 129 G
Pant-pastynog Denb 165 C
Pant-teg Carms 93 F
Pant-y-Caws Carms 92 F
Pant-y-crûg Ceredig 112 E
Pant-y-dwr Powys 113 B
Pant-y-dwr Powys 113 C
Pant-y-ffridd Powys 130 C
Pant-y-fyllau Bridgend 58 C
Pant-y-Wacco Flint 181 F
Pant-yr-awel Bridgend 58 B
Pantasaph Flint 181 F
Pantdu Neath 57 C
Panteg Ceredig 111 E
Panteg Torf 78 F
Pantersbridge Corn 6 B
Pantgwyn Carms 93 F1
Pantgwyn Ceredig 92 B
Pantmawr Cardiff 58 C
Panton Lincs 189 F1
Pantperthog Gwyn 128 C
Pantside Caerph 78 F
Pantyffynnon Carms 75 C
Pantygasseg Torf 78 F
Pantymwyn Flint 165 C1
Panxworth Norf 161 G
Papcastle Cumb 229 E
Papermill Bank Shrops 149 D
Papigoe Highld 310 D
Papil Shetland 313 K
Papley Northants 138 F
Papley Orkney 314 G
Papple E Loth 281 G
Papplewick Notts 171 E
Papworth Everard Cambs 122 E
Papworth St Agnes Cambs 122 E
Papworth Village Settlement Cambs 122 E
Par Corn 5 E
Paradise Glos 80 C
Paradise Green Hereford 97 B
Paramoor Corn 5 F
Paramour Street Kent 71 G
Parbold Lancs 194 E
Parbrook Som 44 F
Parbrook W Sus 35 B
Parc Gwyn 147 C
Parc Erissey Corn 4 G
Parc-hendy Swansea 56 B
Parc Mawr Caerph 77 G
Parc-Seymour Newport 78 G
Parc-y-rhôs Carms 93 B
Parchey Som 43 F
Parciau Anglesey 179 E
Parcllyn Ceredig 110 G
Pardown Hants 48 D
Pardshaw Cumb 229 G
Pardshaw Hall Cumb 229 F
Parham Suff 126 E
Park Corn 10 G
Park Devon 14 B
Park Dumfries 247 E
Park Som 44 G
Park Swindon 63 C
Park Barn Sur 50 C
Park Bottom Corn 4 G
Park Bridge Gtr Man 196 G
Park Broom Cumb 239 F
Park Close Lancs 204 E
Park Corner Bath 45 B
Park Corner E Sus 23 C
Park Corner E Sus 52 F
Park Corner Oxon 65 B
Park Corner Windsor 65 C
Park End Beds 121 G
Park End Cambs 123 E
Park End M'bro 225 B
Park End Northumb 241 B
Park End Som 43 G
Park End Staffs 168 E
Park End Worcs 116 C
Park Gate Dorset 30 F
Park Gate Hants 33 F
Park Gate Kent 55 D
Park Gate Suff 124 F
Park Gate W Yorks 197 E
Park Gate Worcs 117 C
Park Green Essex 105 F
Park Hall Shrops 148 C
Park Head Cumb 231 C
Park Head Derbys 170 E
Park Head W Yorks 197 F
Park Hill Glos 79 F
Park Hill Kent 54 G
Park Hill Mers 194 G
Park Hill N Yorks 214 F
Park Hill Notts 171 E
Park Hill S Yorks 186 D
Park Lane Staffs 133 B
Park Lane Wrex 149 B
Park Langley London 67 F

Park Mains Renfs 277 G9
Park Mill W Yorks 197 E9
Park Royal London 67 C7
Park Street Herts 85 E10
Park Street W Sus 50 G6
Park Town Luton 103 G11
Park Town Oxon 83 D8
Park Village Northumb 240 E5
Park Village W Mid 133 C8
Park Villas W Yorks 206 F2
Park Wood Kent 53 C9
Park Wood Medway 69 G10
Parkend Glos 79 D10
Parkend Glos 80 C3
Parkengear Corn 5 F8
Parker's Corner W Berks 64 E6
Parker's Green Herts 104 F6
Parker's Green Kent 52 D6
Parkeston Essex 108 E4
Parkfield Corn 6 B6
Parkfield S Glos 61 D7
Parkfield W Mid 133 D8
Parkfoot Falk 278 F6
Parkgate Cumb 229 B10
Parkgate Dumfries 248 F2
Parkgate E Ches 184 G3
Parkgate Essex 87 B11
Parkgate Kent 53 G11
Parkgate S Yorks 186 B6
Parkgate Sur 51 E8
Parkgate W Ches 182 F3
Parkhall W Dunb 277 G9
Parkham Devon 24 C5
Parkham Ash Devon 24 C5
Parkhead Cumb 230 C2
Parkhead Glasgow 268 C2
Parkhead S Yorks 186 E4
Parkhill Aberds 303 E10
Parkhill Invclyd 277 G7
Parkhill Ho Aberds 293 B10
Parkhouse Mon 79 E7
Parkhouse Green Derbys 170 C6
Parkhurst I o W 20 C5
Parklands W Yorks 206 F3
Parkmill Swansea 56 D4
Parkneuk Aberds 293 F9
Parkneuk Fife 279 D11
Parkside C Beds 103 G10
Parkside Cumb 219 B10
Parkside Durham 234 B4
Parkside N Lnrk 268 D6
Parkside Staffs 151 D8
Parkside Wrex 166 D5
Parkstone Poole 18 C6
Parkway Hereford 98 D4
Parkway Som 29 C9
Parkwood Springs S Yorks 186 D4
Parley Cross Dorset 19 B7
Parley Green Dorset 19 B7
Parliament Heath Suff 107 C9
Parlington W Yorks 206 F4
Parmoor Bucks 65 B9
Parnacott Devon 24 F4
Parney Heath Essex 107 E10
Parr Mers 183 C8
Parr Brow Gtr Man 195 G8
Parracombe Devon 41 E7
Parrog Pembs 91 D10
Parsley Hay Derbys 169 C10
Parslow's Hillock Bucks 84 E4
Parson Cross S Yorks 186 C5
Parson Drove Cambs 139 B7
Parsonage Green Essex 88 D2
Parsonby Cumb 229 D8
Parsons Green London 67 D9
Parson's Heath Essex 107 F10
Partick Glasgow 267 B11
Partington Gtr Man 184 C2
Partney Lincs 174 B6
Parton Cumb 228 G5
Parton Cumb 239 G7
Parton Dumfries 237 B8
Parton Glos 99 G7
Parton Hereford 96 B6
Partridge Green W Sus 35 D11
Partrishow Powys 96 G5
Parwich Derbys 169 E11
Pasford Staffs 132 D6
Passenham Northants 102 D5
Passfield Hants 49 G10
Passingford Bridge Essex 87 F8
Passmores Essex 86 D6
Paston Norf 160 C6
Paston P'boro 138 C3
Paston Green Norf 160 C6
Pasturefields Staffs 151 D9
Patchacott Devon 12 B5
Patcham Brighton 36 F4
Patchetts Green Herts 85 F10
Patching W Sus 35 F9
Patchole Devon 40 E6
Patchway S Glos 60 C6
Pategill Cumb 230 F6
Pateley Bridge N Yorks 214 F3
Paternoster Heath Essex 88 C6
Path Head T & W 242 E5
Path of Condie Perth 286 F4
Pathe Som 43 G11
Pather N Lnrk 268 E5
Pathfinder Village Devon 14 C2
Pathhead Aberds 293 G9
Pathhead E Ayrs 258 G4
Pathhead Fife 280 C5
Pathhead Midloth 271 C7
Pathlow Warks 118 F3
Pathstruie Perth 286 F4
Patient End Herts 105 F8
Patmore Heath Herts 105 F8
Patna E Ayrs 257 G10
Patney Wilts 46 B5
Patrick I o M 192 D3
Patrick Brompton N Yorks 224 G4
Patricroft Gtr Man 184 B3
Patrington E Yorks 201 C10
Patrington Haven E Yorks 201 C10
Patrixbourne Kent 55 B7
Patsford Devon 40 F4
Patterdale Cumb 221 B7
Pattiesmuir Fife 279 E11
Pattingham Staffs 132 D6
Pattishall Northants 120 G3
Pattiswick Essex 106 G6
Patton Shrops 131 E11
Patton Bridge Cumb 221 F11
Paul Corn 1 D5
Paulerspury Northants 102 B4
Paull E Yorks 201 B7
Paul's Green Corn 2 C4
Paulsgrove Ptsmth 33 F10
Paulton Bath 45 B7
Paulville W Loth 269 B9
Pave Lane Telford 150 F5
Pavenham Beds 121 F9
Pawlett Som 43 E10
Pawlett Hill Som 43 E9
Pawston Northumb 263 C9
Paxford Glos 100 D3
Paxton Borders 273 E8
Payden Street Kent 54 C2
Payhembury Devon 27 G9
Paynes Green Sur 50 F6
Paynter's Cross Corn 7 C7
Paynter's Lane End Corn 4 G3
Paythorne Lancs 204 C2
Payton Som 27 C10
Peacehaven E Sus 36 G6
Peacehaven Heights E Sus 36 G6
Peacemarsh Dorset 30 B4
Peak Dale Derbys 185 F9
Peak Forest Derbys 185 F10
Peak Hill Lincs 156 F5
Peakirk P'boro 138 B3
Pean Hill Kent 70 G6
Pear Ash Som 45 G9
Pear Tree Derby 153 C7
Pearsie Angus 287 B7
Pearson's Green Kent 53 E7
Peartree Herts 86 C2
Peartree Green Essex 87 F9
Peartree Green Hereford 97 E11
Peartree Green Soton 32 E6
Peartree Green Sur 50 F3
Peas Acre W Yorks 205 E8
Peas Hill Cambs 139 D8
Pease Pottage W Sus 51 G9
Peasedown St John Bath 45 B8
Peasehill Derbys 170 F6
Peaseland Green Norf 159 F11
Peasemore W Berks 64 D3
Peasenhall Suff 127 D7
Peaslake Sur 50 E5
Peasley Cross Mers 183 C8
Peasmarsh E Sus 38 C5
Peasmarsh Som 28 E4
Peasmarsh Sur 50 D3
Peaston E Loth 271 B8
Peastonbank E Loth 271 B8
Peat Inn Fife 287 G8
Peathill Aberds 303 C9
Peatling Magna Leics 135 E11
Peatling Parva Leics 135 F11
Peaton Shrops 131 G10
Peatonstrand Shrops 131 G10
Peats Corner Suff 126 E3
Pebmarsh Essex 107 E7
Pebsham E Sus 38 F3
Pebworth Worcs 100 B2
Pecket Well W Yorks 196 B3
Peckforton E Ches 167 D8
Peckham London 67 D10
Peckham Bush Kent 53 D7
Pecking Mill Som 44 F6
Peckingell Wilts 62 E2
Peckleton Leics 135 C9
Pedair-ffordd Powys 148 E2
Pedham Norf 160 G6
Pedlars End Essex 87 E8
Pedlar's Rest Shrops 131 G9
Pedlinge Kent 54 F6
Pedmore W Mid 133 G8
Pednor Bottom Bucks 84 E6
Pednormead End Bucks 85 E7
Pedwell Som 44 F2
Peebles Borders 270 G5
Peel Borders 261 B10
Peel I o M 192 D3
Peel Lancs 202 G3
Peel Common Hants 33 G9
Peel Green Gtr Man 184 B2
Peel Hall Gtr Man 184 D4
Peel Hill Lancs 202 G3
Peel Park S Lnrk 268 E2
Peene Kent 55 F7
Peening Quarter Kent 38 B5
Peggs Green Leics 153 F8
Pegsdon C Beds 104 E2
Pegswood Northumb 252 F6
Pegwell Kent 71 G11
Peinaha Highld 298 D4
Peinchorran Highld 295 B7
Peingown Highld 298 B4
Peinlich Highld 298 D4
Peinmore Highld 298 E4
Pelaw T & W 243 E7
Pelcomb Pembs 72 B6
Pelcomb Bridge Pembs 72 B6
Pelcomb Cross Pembs 72 B6
Peldon Essex 89 B7
Pelhamfield I o W 21 C7
Pell Green E Sus 52 G6
Pellon W Yorks 196 B5
Pelsall W Mid 133 C10
Pelsall Wood W Mid 133 C10
Pelton Durham 243 G7
Pelton Fell Durham 243 G7
Pelutho Cumb 229 B8
Pelynt Corn 6 D4
Pemberton Carms 75 E8
Pemberton Gtr Man 194 G5
Pembles Cross Kent 53 D11
Pembre = Pembrey Carms 74 E6
Pembrey = Pembre Carms 74 E6
Pembridge Hereford 115 F7
Pembroke Pembs 73 E7
Pembroke Dock = Doc Penfro Pembs 73 E7
Pembroke Ferry Pembs 73 E7
Pembury Kent 52 E6
Pempwell Corn 12 F3
Pen-allt Hereford 97 F11
Pen-bedw Pembs 92 D4
Pen-bont Rhydybeddau Ceredig 128 G3
Pen-caer-fenny Swansea 56 B4
Pen-clawdd Swansea 56 B4
Pen-common Powys 76 D6
Pen-gilfach Gwyn 163 C9
Pen-groes-oped Mon 78 D4
Pen-lan Swansea 56 B6
Pen-Lan-mabws Pembs 91 F7
Pen-llyn Anglesey 178 E4
Pen-lon Anglesey 162 B6
Pen Mill Som 29 D9
Pen-onn V Glam 58 F5
Pen-Rhiw-fawr Neath 76 C2
Pen-rhos Wrex 166 E3
Pen-sarn Gwyn 145 D11
Pen-sarn Gwyn 162 G6
Pen-twyn Caerph 78 E2
Pen-twyn Carms 75 C9
Pen-twyn Mon 79 D8
Pen-twyn Torf 78 E3
Pen-Uchar Plwyf Flint 181 G11
Pen-y-Ball Top Flint 181 F11
Pen-y-banc Carms 93 G8
Pen-y-banc Carms 94 G2
Pen-y-bank Caerph 77 E10
Pen-y-Bont Bl Gwent 78 D2
Pen-y-bont Carms 92 F6
Pen-y-bont Gwyn 128 C4
Pen-y-bont Gwyn 146 D2
Pen-y-bont Powys 148 E4
Pen y Bont ar ogwr = Bridgend Bridgend 58 C2
Pen-y-Bryn Gwyn 145 B9
Pen-y-bryn Gwyn 146 F3
Pen-y-bryn Pembs 92 C3
Pen-y-bryn Powys 130 C3
Pen-y-bryn Shrops 148 B6
Pen-y-bryn Wrex 166 G3
Pen-y-cae Bridgend 58 C2
Pen-y-cae Neath 57 D9
Pen-y-cae Powys 76 C4
Pen-y-cae-mawr Mon 78 F6
Pen-y-cefn Flint 181 F10
Pen-y-clawdd Mon 79 D7
Pen-y-coed Shrops 148 E5
Pen-y-coedcae Rhondda 58 B5
Pen-y-Darren M Tydf 77 D9
Pen-y-fai Bridgend 57 E11
Pen-y-fai Carms 75 E7
Pen-y-fan Carms 56 B4
Pen-y-fan Mon 79 D8
Pen-y-felin Flint 165 B11
Pen-y-ffordd Denb 181 F8
Pen-y-ffordd Flint 181 E10
Pen y Foel Shrops 148 E5
Pen-y-garn Carms 93 E11
Pen-y-garn Ceredig 128 F2
Pen-y-garnedd Anglesey 179 F8
Pen-y-gop Conwy 164 G6
Pen-y-graig Gwyn 144 C3
Pen-y-groes Carms 75 C9
Pen-y-groeslon Gwyn 144 C4
Pen-y-Gwryd Hotel Gwyn 163 D11
Pen-y-lan Cardiff 59 D7
Pen-y-lan Newport 59 B9
Pen-y-lan V Glam 58 D3
Pen-y-maes Flint 181 F11
Pen-y-Myndd Carms 75 E7
Pen-y-Park Hereford 96 C5
Pen-y-rhiw Rhondda 58 B5
Pen-y-stryt Denb 165 E11
Pen-y-wern Shrops 114 B6
Pen-yr-englyn Rhondda 76 F6
Pen-yr-heol Bridgend 58 C2
Pen-yr-heol Mon 78 C6
Pen-yr-Heolgerrig M Tydf 77 D8
Penallt Mon 79 C8
Penally = Penalun Pembs 73 F10
Penalt Hereford 97 F11
Penalun = Penally Pembs 73 F10
Penare Corn 5 G9
Penarlâg = Hawarden Flint 166 B4
Penarron Powys 130 F2
Penarth V Glam 59 E7
Penarth Moors Cardiff 59 E7
Penbeagle Corn 2 B2
Penberth Corn 1 E4
Penbidwal Mon 96 G6
Penbodlas Gwyn 144 C5
Penboyr Carms 93 D7
Penbryn Ceredig 110 G5
Pencader Carms 93 D8
Pencaenewydd Gwyn 162 G6
Pencaerau Neath 57 B8
Pencaitland E Loth 271 B8
Pencarnisiog Anglesey 178 G5
Pencarreg Carms 93 B10
Pencarrow Corn 11 E8
Penceiliogi Carms 75 E8
Pencelli Powys 95 F11
Pencoed Bridgend 58 C3
Pencombe Hereford 115 G11
Pencoyd Hereford 97 F10
Pencoys Corn 2 B5
Pencraig Anglesey 179 F7
Pencraig Hereford 97 G11
Pencraig Powys 147 D10
Pencroesoped Mon 78 D4
Pencuke Corn 11 C9
Pendas Fields W Yorks 206 F3
Pendeen Corn 1 C3
Pendeford W Mid 133 C7
Penderyn Rhondda 77 D7
Pendine = Pentywyn Carms 74 D2
Pendlebury Gtr Man 195 G9
Pendleton Gtr Man 184 B4
Pendleton Lancs 203 F11
Pendock Worcs 98 E5
Pendoggett Corn 10 F6
Pendomer Som 29 E8
Pendoylan V Glam 58 D5
Pendre Bridgend 58 C2
Pendre Gwyn 110 C2
Pendre Powys 95 F10
Pendrift Corn 11 G8
Penegoes Powys 128 C5
Penelewey Corn 4 G6
Penenden Heath Kent 53 B9
Penffordd Pembs 91 G11
Penffordd Lâs = Staylittle Powys 129 E7
Pengam Caerph 77 F11
Pengam Cardiff 59 D8
Penge London 67 E11
Pengegon Corn 2 B5
Pengelly Corn 11 E7
Pengenffordd Powys 96 E3
Pengersick Corn 2 D3
Pengold Corn 11 C8
Pengorffwysfa Anglesey 179 C7
Pengover Green Corn 6 B5
Pengwern Denb 181 F8
Penhale Corn 2 F5
Penhale Corn 5 D8
Penhale Corn 5 E8
Penhale Jakes Corn 2 D4
Penhallick Corn 3 F7
Penhallick Corn 4 G3
Penhallow Corn 4 E5
Penhalurick Corn 2 B6
Penhalvean Corn 2 B6
Penhelig Gwyn 128 D2
Penhill Devon 40 G4
Penhill Swindon 63 B7
Penhow Newport 78 G6
Penhurst E Sus 23 B11
Peniarth Gwyn 128 B2
Penicuik Midloth 270 C4
Peniel Carms 93 G8
Peniel Denb 165 C8
Penifiler Highld 298 E4
Peninver Argyll 255 E8
Penisa'r Waun Gwyn 163 C9
Penistone S Yorks 197 G8
Penjerrick Corn 3 C7
Penketh Warr 183 D9
Penkhull Stoke 168 G5
Penkill S Ayrs 244 D6
Penknap Wilts 45 D11
Penkridge Staffs 151 G8
Penleigh Wilts 45 C11
Penley Wrex 149 B8
Penllech Gwyn 144 C4
Penllergaer Swansea 56 B6
Penllwyn Caerph 77 F11
Penllwyn Ceredig 128 G3
Penllyn V Glam 58 D3
Penmachno Conwy 164 E3
Penmaen Caerph 77 F11
Penmaen Swansea 56 D4
Penmaen Rhôs Conwy 180 F5
Penmaenan Conwy 180 F2
Penmaenmawr Conwy 180 F2
Penmaenpool Gwyn 146 F3
Penmark V Glam 58 F5
Penmarth Corn 2 B6
Penmayne Corn 10 F4
Penmon Anglesey 179 E10
Penmore Mill Argyll 288 D6
Penmorfa Ceredig 110 G6
Penmorfa Gwyn 163 G8
Penmynydd Anglesey 179 G8
Penn Bucks 84 G6
Penn W Mid 133 D7
Penn Bottom Bucks 84 G6
Penn Street Bucks 84 F6
Pennal Gwyn 128 C4
Pennan Aberds 303 C8
Pennance Corn 4 G4
Pennant Ceredig 111 E10
Pennant Conwy 164 D5
Pennant Denb 147 C10
Pennant Denb 165 E8
Pennant Powys 129 D7
Pennant Melangell Powys 147 D10
Pennar Pembs 73 E7
Pennar Park Pembs 72 E6
Pennard Swansea 56 D5
Pennerley Shrops 131 D7
Pennington Cumb 210 D5
Pennington Gtr Man 183 B11
Pennington Hants 20 C2
Pennington Green Gtr Man 194 F6
Pennorth Powys 96 F2
Pennsylvania Devon 14 C4
Pennsylvania S Glos 61 E8
Penny Bridge Cumb 210 C6
Penny Green Derbys 187 F8
Penny Hill Lincs 157 D7
Penny Hill W Yorks 196 D5
Pennycross Argyll 289 G7
Pennycross Plym 7 D9
Pennygate Norf 160 E6
Pennygown Argyll 289 E7
Pennylands Lancs 194 F3
Pennymoor Devon 26 E5
Pennypot Kent 54 G6
Penny's Green Norf 142 D3
Pennytinney Corn 10 F6
Pennywell T & W 243 F9
Penparc Ceredig 92 B4
Penparc Pembs 91 E7
Penparcau Ceredig 111 B11
Penpedairheol Caerph 77 F10
Penpedairheol Mon 78 E4
Penpergym Mon 78 C4
Penperlleni Mon 78 E4
Penpethy Corn 11 D7
Penpillick Corn 5 D11
Penplas Carms 74 B5
Penpol Corn 3 B8
Penpoll Corn 6 E2
Penponds Corn 2 B4
Penpont Corn 11 G7
Penpont Dumfries 247 E8
Penpont Powys 95 F9
Penprysg Bridgend 58 C3
Penquit Devon 8 E2
Penrallt Gwyn 145 B7
Penrallt Powys 129 F9
Penrhôs Mon 78 C6
Penrherber Carms 92 D5
Penrhiw Caerph 78 G2
Penrhiw-llan Ceredig 93 C7
Penrhiw-pal Ceredig 92 B6
Penrhiwceiber Rhondda 77 F8
Penrhiwgarreg Bl Gwent 78 E2
Penrhiwtyn Neath 57 B8
Penrhos Anglesey 178 E3
Penrhos Gwyn 144 C6
Penrhos Hereford 114 F6
Penrhos Mon 78 C6
Penrhos Powys 76 C3
Penrhos-garnedd Gwyn 179 G9
Penrhosfeilw Anglesey 178 E2
Penrhyd Lastra Anglesey 178 C6
Penrhyn Bay = Bae-Penrhyn Conwy 180 E4
Penrhyn Castle Pembs 92 B2
Penrhyn-coch Ceredig 128 G2
Penrhyn side Conwy 180 E4
Penrhyndeudraeth Gwyn 146 B2
Penrhynside Conwy 180 E4
Penrhys Rhondda 77 F8
Penrice Swansea 56 D3
Penrith Cumb 230 E6
Penrose Corn 10 G3
Penrose Corn 11 F7
Penrose Hill Corn 2 D4
Penruddock Cumb 230 F4
Penryn Corn 3 C7
Pensarn Carms 74 B6
Pensarn Conwy 181 F7
Pensax Worcs 116 D4
Pensby Mers 182 E3
Penselwood Som 45 G9
Pensford Bath 60 G6
Pensham Worcs 99 C8
Penshaw T & W 243 G8
Penshurst Kent 52 E4
Pensilva Corn 6 B5
Pensnett W Mid 133 F8
Penston E Loth 281 G8
Penstone Devon 26 G3
Penstraze Corn 4 F5
Pentewan Corn 5 F10
Pentiken Shrops 130 G4
Pentir Gwyn 163 B9
Pentire Corn 4 C5
Pentirvin Shrops 130 C6
Pentlepoir Pembs 73 D10
Pentlow Essex 106 B6
Pentlow Street Essex 106 B6
Pentney Norf 158 G4
Penton Corner Hants 47 D10
Penton Grafton Hants 47 D10
Penton Mewsey Hants 47 D10
Pentonville London 67 C10
Pentowin Carms 74 B3
Pentraeth Anglesey 179 F8
Pentrapeod Caerph 77 E11
Pentre Carms 75 C8
Pentre Denb 165 D10
Pentre Flint 165 C11
Pentre Flint 166 B4
Pentre Flint 166 C2
Pentre Flint 166 D2
Pentre Powys 129 F11
Pentre Powys 130 B4
Pentre Powys 130 E5
Pentre Powys 147 D11
Pentre Powys 148 G3
Pentre Rhondda 77 F7
Pentre Shrops 148 D4
Pentre Shrops 149 F7
Pentre Wrex 148 B2
Pentre Wrex 166 G3
Pentre-bâch Ceredig 93 B11
Pentre-bach Powys 95 E8
Pentre Berw Anglesey 179 G7
Pentre-bont Conwy 164 E2
Pentre Broughton Wrex 166 E4
Pentre Bychan Wrex 166 F4
Pentre-cefn Shrops 148 D4
Pentre-celyn Denb 165 E11
Pentre-Celyn Powys 129 B7
Pentre-chwyth Swansea 57 B7
Pentre Cilgwyn Wrex 148 B4
Pentre-clawdd Shrops 148 C5
Pentre-coed Shrops 149 B7
Pentre-cwrt Carms 93 D7
Pentre Dolau-Honddu Powys 95 C9
Pentre-dwr Swansea 57 B7
Pentre-Ffwrndan Flint 182 G3
Pentre-galar Pembs 92 E3
Pentre-Gwenlais Carms 75 B10
Pentre Gwynfryn Gwyn 145 D11
Pentre Halkyn Flint 182 G2
Pentre Hodre Shrops 114 B6
Pentre Isaf Conwy 164 B5
Pentre Llanrhaeadr Denb 165 C9
Pentre Llifior Powys 130 D2
Pentre-llwyn-llwyd Powys 113 G9
Pentre-llyn Ceredig 112 C2
Pentre-llyn cymmer Conwy 165 E7
Pentre Maelor Wrex 166 F5
Pentre Meyrick V Glam 58 D3
Pentre-newydd Shrops 148 B5
Pentre-Piod Torf 78 E3
Pentre-Poeth Carms 75 E8
Pentre-poeth Newport 59 B9
Pentre-rhew Ceredig 112 G3
Pentre-tafarn-y-fedw Conwy 164 C4
Pentre-ty-gwyn Carms 94 D6
Pentre-uchaf Conwy 180 F5
Pentrebach Carms 94 E6
Pentrebach M Tydf 77 E9
Pentrebach Rhondda 58 B5
Pentrebach Swansea 75 D10
Pentrebane Cardiff 58 D6
Pentrebeirdd Powys 148 G3
Pentrecagal Carms 92 C6
Pentredwr Denb 165 F11
Pentref-y-groes Caerph 77 F11
Pentrefelin Anglesey 178 C6
Pentrefelin Carms 93 G11
Pentrefelin Ceredig 94 B2
Pentrefelin Conwy 180 G4
Pentrefelin Denb 166 G2
Pentrefelin Gwyn 145 B10
Pentrefoelas Conwy 164 E5
Pentregat Ceredig 111 G7
Pentreheyling Shrops 130 E4
Pentrellwyn Ceredig 93 C8
Pentre'r beirdd Powys 148 G3
Pentre'r Felin Conwy 164 B4
Pentre'r-felin Denb 165 B10
Pentre'r-felin Powys 95 E8
Pentreuchaf Gwyn 145 B7
Pentrich Derbys 170 E5
Pentridge Dorset 31 D8
Pentrisil Pembs 91 E11
Pentwyn Caerph 77 E10
Pentwyn Cardiff 59 C8
Pentwyn = Pendine Carms 74 D2
Pentwyn Berthlwyd Caerph 77 F10
Pentwyn-mawr Caerph 77 F11
Pentyrch Cardiff 58 C6
Penuchadre V Glam 57 G11
Penuwch Ceredig 111 E11
Penwartha Corn 4 E5
Penwartha Coombe Corn 4 E5
Penweathers Corn 4 G6
Penwithick Corn 5 D10
Penwood Hants 64 G2
Penwortham Lane Lancs 194 B4
Penwyllt Powys 76 B5
Penybanc Carms 75 C10
Penybedd Carms 74 E6
Penybont Ceredig 128 F2
Penybont Powys 114 E2
Penybontfawr Powys 147 E11
Penybryn Caerph 77 F10
Penycae Wrex 166 F3
Penycaerau Gwyn 144 D3
Penycwm Pembs 90 G6
Penydre Swansea 75 E11
Penyfeidr Pembs 91 F7
Penyffordd Flint 166 C4
Penyffridd Gwyn 163 D8
Penygarn Torf 78 E3
Penygarnedd Powys 148 E2
Penygelli Powys 130 E2
Penygraig Rhondda 77 G7
Penygraigwen Anglesey 178 D6
Penygroes Gwyn 163 E7
Penygroes Pembs 92 D3
Penymynydd Flint 166 C4
Penyraber Pembs 91 D9
Penyrheol Caerph 58 B6
Penyrheol Swansea 56 B5
Penyrheol Torf 78 F3
Penysarn Anglesey 179 C7
Penywaun Rhondda 77 E7
Penzance Corn 1 C5
Peopleton Worcs 117 G8
Peover Heath E Ches 184 G3
Peper Harow Sur 50 E2
Pepper Hill Som 43 F7
Pepper Hill W Yorks 196 B6
Peppercombe Devon 24 C5
Peppermoor Northumb 264 F6
Pepper's Green Essex 87 C10
Pepperstock C Beds 85 B9
Per-ffordd-llan Flint 181 F10
Perceton N Ayrs 267 G7
Percie Aberds 293 D7
Percuil Corn 3 C9
Percy Main T & W 243 D8
Percyhorner Aberds 303 C9
Perham Down Wilts 47 D9
Periton Som 42 D3
Perivale London 67 C7
Perkhill Aberds 293 C7
Perkinsville Durham 243 G7
Perlethorpe Notts 187 G11
Perran Downs Corn 2 C3
Perran Wharf Corn 3 B7
Perranarworthal Corn 3 B7
Perrancoombe Corn 4 E5
Perranporth Corn 4 E5
Perranuthnoe Corn 2 D2
Perranwell Corn 3 B7
Perranwell Corn 4 E5
Perranwell Station Corn 3 B7
Perranzabuloe Corn 4 E5
Perrott's Brook Glos 81 D8
Perry Devon 26 F5
Perry Kent 55 B9
Perry W Mid 133 E11
Perry Barr W Mid 133 E11
Perry Beeches W Mid 133 E11
Perry Common W Mid 133 E11
Perry Crofts Staffs 134 C4
Perry Green Essex 106 G6
Perry Green Herts 86 B6
Perry Green Som 43 F9
Perry Green Wilts 62 B3
Perry Street Kent 68 E6
Perry Street Som 28 F4
Perryfields Worcs 117 C8
Perryfoot Derbys 185 E10
Perrymead Bath 61 G9
Perrystone Hill Hereford 98 F2
Perrywood Kent 54 B4
Pershall Staffs 150 C6
Pershore Worcs 99 B8
Pert Angus 293 G8
Pertenhall Beds 121 D11
Perth Perth 286 E5
Perthcelyn Rhondda 77 F9
Perthy Shrops 149 C7
Perton Hereford 97 C11
Perton Staffs 133 D7
Pertwood Wilts 45 F11
Pested Kent 54 C4
Peter Tavy Devon 12 F6
Peterborough P'boro 138 D3
Peterburn Highld 307 L2
Peterchurch Hereford 96 D6
Peterculter Aberdeen 293 C10
Peterhead Aberds 303 E11
Peterlee Durham 234 C4
Peter's Finger Devon 12 D3
Peter's Green Herts 85 B10
Peters Marland Devon 25 E7
Petersburn N Lnrk 268 C5
Petersfield Hants 34 C2
Petersham London 67 E7
Peterston-super-Ely V Glam 58 D5
Peterstone Wentlooge Newport 59 C9
Peterstow Hereford 97 G11
Petertown Orkney 314 F3
Peterville Corn 4 E4
Petham Kent 54 C6
Petherwin Gate Corn 11 D11
Petrockstow Devon 25 F8
Petsoe End M Keynes 103 B7
Pett E Sus 38 E5
Pett Bottom Kent 54 E6
Pett Bottom Kent 55 C7
Pett Level E Sus 38 E5
Pettaugh Suff 126 F3
Petteridge Kent 53 E7
Pettinain S Lnrk 269 G9
Pettings Kent 68 G6
Pettistree Suff 126 G5
Petton Devon 27 C8
Petton Shrops 149 D8
Petts Wood London 68 F2
Petty Aberds 303 F7
Petty France S Glos 61 B9
Pettycur Fife 280 D5
Pettymuick Aberds 303 G9
Pettywell Norf 159 E11
Petworth W Sus 35 C7
Pevensey E Sus 23 E10
Pevensey Bay E Sus 23 E11
Peverell Plym 7 D9
Pewsey Wilts 63 G7
Pewsey Wharf Wilts 63 G7
Pewterspear Warr 183 E10
Phantassie E Loth 281 F11
Pharisee Green Essex 106 G2
Pheasants Bucks 65 B9
Pheasant's Hill Bucks 65 B9
Pheasey W Mid 133 D11
Pheonix Green Hants 49 B9
Phepson Worcs 117 F8
Philadelphia T & W 243 G8
Philham Devon 24 C3
Philiphaugh Borders 261 D10
Phillack Corn 2 B3
Philleigh Corn 3 B9
Phillip's Town Caerph 77 E10
Philpot End Essex 87 B10
Philpstoun W Loth 279 F10
Phocle Green Hereford 98 F2
Phoenix Green Hants 49 B9
Phoenix Row Durham 233 F9
Phorp Moray 301 D10
Pibsbury Som 28 B6
Pibwrlwyd Carms 74 B6
Pica Cumb 228 G6
Piccadilly S Yorks 187 B7
Piccadilly Warks 134 D4
Piccadilly Corner Norf 142 F5
Piccotts End Herts 85 D9
Pickburn S Yorks 198 F4
Picken End Worcs 98 C6
Pickering N Yorks 216 C5
Pickering Nook Durham 242 F5
Picket Hill Hants 31 F11
Picket Piece Hants 47 D11
Picket Post Hants 31 F11
Pickford W Mid 134 G5
Pickford Green W Mid 134 G5
Pickhill N Yorks 214 C6
Picklenash Glos 98 F4
Picklescott Shrops 131 D8
Pickletillem Fife 287 E8
Pickley Green Gtr Man 195 G7
Pickmere E Ches 183 F11
Pickney Som 27 B11
Pickstock Telford 150 E4
Pickup Bank Blkburn 195 C8
Pickwell Devon 40 E3
Pickwell Leics 154 G5
Pickwick Wilts 61 E11
Pickwood Scar W Yorks 196 C5
Pickworth Lincs 155 C10
Pickworth Rutland 155 G9
Picton Flint 181 E10
Picton N Yorks 225 D8
Picton W Ches 182 G6
Pict's Hill Som 28 B6
Piddinghoe E Sus 36 G6
Piddington Bucks 84 G4
Piddington Northants 120 G6
Piddington Oxon 83 B10
Piddlehinton Dorset 17 B10
Piddletrenthide Dorset 17 B10
Pidley Cambs 122 B6
Pidney Dorset 30 F2
Piece Corn 2 B5
Piercebridge Darl 224 B4
Piercing Hill Essex 86 F6
Pierowall Orkney 314 B4
Piff's Elm Glos 99 F8
Pig Oak Dorset 31 G8
Pigdon Northumb 252 F5
Pightley Som 43 F8
Pigstye Green Essex 87 D10
Pike End W Yorks 196 D4
Pike Hill Lancs 204 G3
Pike Law W Yorks 196 D4
Pikehall Derbys 169 D11
Pikeshill Hants 32 F3
Pikestye Hereford 97 B10
Pilford Dorset 31 G8
Pilgrims Hatch Essex 87 F9
Pilham Lincs 188 C5
Pilhough Derbys 170 C3
Pill N Som 60 D4
Pill Pembs 72 D6
Pillaton Corn 7 C7
Pillaton Staffs 151 G8
Pillerton Hersey Warks 100 B6
Pillerton Priors Warks 100 B5
Pilleth Powys 114 D5
Pilley Glos 81 B7
Pilley Hants 20 B2
Pilley S Yorks 197 G10
Pilley Bailey Hants 20 B2
Pillgwenlly Newport 59 B10
Pilling Lancs 202 D4
Pilling Lane Lancs 202 D3
Pillmouth Devon 25 C7
Pillowell Glos 79 D10
Pillows Green Glos 98 F5
Pillwell Dorset 30 D3
Pilmuir Borders 261 G11
Pilning S Glos 60 B5
Pilrig Edin 280 F5
Pilsbury Derbys 169 C10
Pilsdon Dorset 16 B4
Pilsgate P'boro 137 B11
Pilsley Derbys 170 C6
Pilsley Derbys 186 G2
Pilsley Green Derbys 170 C6
Pilson Green Norf 161 G7
Piltdown E Sus 36 C6
Pilton Devon 40 G5
Pilton Edin 280 F4
Pilton Northants 137 G10
Pilton Rutland 137 C8
Pilton Som 44 E5
Pilton Green Swansea 56 D2
Piltown Som 44 F5
Pimhole Gtr Man 195 E10
Pimlico Herts 85 D9
Pimlico Lancs 203 E10
Pimlico London 67 D9
Pimlico Northants 102 C2
Pimperne Dorset 29 F9
Pimperne Dorset 30 F6
Pin Green Herts 104 F4
Pin Mill Suff 108 D4
Pinchbeck Lincs 156 D4
Pinchbeck Bars Lincs 156 D3
Pinchbeck West Lincs 156 E4
Pincheon Green S Yorks 199 D7
Pinckney Green Wilts 61 G10
Pincock Lancs 194 D5
Pineham Kent 55 D10
Pineham M Keynes 103 C7
Pinehurst Swindon 63 B7
Pinfarthings Glos 80 E5
Pinfold Lancs 193 E11
Pinfold Hill S Yorks 197 G9
Pinfoldpond C Beds 103 E8
Pinford End Suff 124 F6
Pinged Carms 74 E6
Pingewood W Berks 65 F7
Pinhoe Devon 14 C5
Pink Green Worcs 117 D11
Pinkett's Booth W Mid 134 G5
Pinkie Braes E Loth 281 G7
Pinkney Wilts 61 B11
Pinkneys Green Windsor 65 C11
Pinksmoor Som 27 D10
Pinley W Mid 119 B7
Pinley Green Warks 118 D4
Pinminnoch Dumfries 236 D2
Pinminnoch S Ayrs 244 E5
Pinmore S Ayrs 244 E6
Pinmore Mains S Ayrs 244 E6
Pinnacles Essex 86 D6
Pinner London 66 B6
Pinner Green London 85 G10
Pinnerwood Park London 85 G10
Pin's Green Worcs 98 B6
Pinsley Green E Ches 167 F9
Pinstones Shrops 131 F9
Pinvin Worcs 99 B9
Pinwall Leics 134 C6
Pinwherry S Ayrs 244 F5
Pinxton Derbys 171 E7
Pipe and Lyde Hereford 97 C10
Pipe Aston Hereford 115 C9
Pipe Gate Shrops 168 G2
Pipe Ridware Staffs 151 F11
Pipehill Staffs 133 B11
Pipehouse Bath 45 B9
Piperhall Argyll 266 D2
Piperhill Highld 301 D8
Piper's Ash W Ches 166 B6
Piper's End Worcs 98 E6
Piper's Hill Worcs 117 D9
Piper's Pool Corn 11 E11
Pipewell Northants 136 F6
Pippacott Devon 40 F4
Pippin Street Lancs 194 C5
Pipps Hill Essex 69 B7
Pipsden Kent 53 G9
Pipton Powys 96 D3
Pirbright Sur 50 B2
Pirbright Camp Sur 50 B2
Pirnmill N Ayrs 255 C9
Pirton Herts 104 E2
Pirton Worcs 99 B7
Pisgah Ceredig 112 B3
Pisgah Stirl 285 G11
Pishill Oxon 65 B8
Pishill Bank Oxon 84 G2
Pismire Hill S Yorks 186 C5
Pistyll Gwyn 162 G4
Pit Mon 78 D5
Pitagowan Perth 291 G10
Pitblae Aberds 303 C9
Pitcairngreen Perth 286 E4
Pitcalnie Highld 301 B8
Pitcaple Aberds 303 G7
Pitch Green Bucks 84 E3
Pitch Place Sur 49 F11
Pitch Place Sur 50 C3
Pitchcombe Glos 80 D5
Pitchcott Bucks 102 G5
Pitcher's Green Suff 125 F8
Pitchford Shrops 131 C10
Pitcombe Som 45 G7
Pitcorthie Fife 280 D2
Pitcorthie Fife 287 G9
Pitcot Som 45 D7
Pitcot V Glam 57 G11
Pitcox E Loth 282 F2
Pitcur Perth 286 D6
Pitfancy Aberds 302 E5
Pitfichie Aberds 293 B8
Pitforthie Aberds 293 F10
Pitgair Aberds 303 D7
Pitgrudy Highld 309 K7
Pithmaduthy Highld 301 B7
Pitkennedy Angus 287 B9
Pitkevy Fife 286 G6
Pitkierie Fife 287 G9
Pitlessie Fife 287 G7
Pitlochry Perth 286 B3
Pitmachie Aberds 302 G6
Pitmain Highld 291 C9
Pitmedden Aberds 303 G8
Pitminster Som 28 D2
Pitmuies Angus 287 C9
Pitmunie Aberds 293 B8
Pitney Som 29 B7
Pitrocknie Perth 286 C6
Pitscottie Fife 287 F8
Pitsea Essex 69 B8
Pitses Gtr Man 196 G2
Pitsford Northants 120 D5
Pitsford Hill Som 42 G6
Pitsmoor S Yorks 186 D5
Pitstone Bucks 84 B6
Pitstone Green Bucks 84 B6
Pitstone Hill Bucks 85 C7
Pitt Hants 33 B7
Pitt Court Glos 80 F3
Pittachar Perth 286 E2
Pittendreich Moray 301 C11
Pittentrail Highld 309 J7
Pittenweem Fife 287 G9
Pitteuchar Fife 280 B5
Pittington Durham 234 C2
Pittodrie Aberds 302 G6
Pitton Swansea 56 D2
Pitton Wilts 47 G8
Pitts Hill Stoke 168 E5
Pittswood Kent 52 D6
Pittulie Aberds 303 C9
Pittville Glos 99 G9
Pity Me Durham 233 B11
Pityme Corn 10 F5
Pityoulish Highld 291 B11
Pixey Green Suff 126 B4
Pixham Sur 51 C7
Pixham Worcs 98 B6
Pixley Hereford 98 D3
Pixley Shrops 150 D3
Pizien Well Kent 53 C7
Place Newton N Yorks 217 E7
Plaidy Aberds 303 D7
Plaidy Corn 6 E5
Plain-an-Gwarry Corn 4 G3
Plain Dealings Pembs 73 B9
Plain Spot Notts 171 E7
Plain Street Corn 10 F5
Plains N Lnrk 268 B5
Plainsfield Som 43 F7
Plaish Shrops 131 D10
Plaistow Bromley 68 E2
Plaistow Newham 68 C2
Plaistow W Sus 50 G4
Plaistow Green Essex 106 F6
Plaitford Wilts 32 D3
Plaitford Green Hants 32 C3
Plank Lane Gtr Man 194 G6
Plans Dumfries 238 D3
Plantation Bridge Cumb 221 F9
Plantationfoot Dumfries 248 E4
Plardiwick Staffs 150 E6
Plas-canol Gwyn 145 F11
Plas Coch Wrex 166 E4
Plas Dinam Powys 129 F10
Plas Gogerddan Ceredig 128 G2
Plas Llwyngwern Powys 128 C5
Plas Meredydd Powys 130 D3
Plas Nantyr Wrex 148 B3
Plas-yn-Cefn Denb 181 G8
Plasau Shrops 149 E7
Plashet London 68 C2
Plashett Carms 74 D3
Plasiolyn Powys 129 C11
Plasnewydd Powys 129 D9
Plaster's Green Bath 60 G4
Plastow Green Hants 64 G4
Platt Kent 52 B6
Platt Bridge Gtr Man 194 G6
Platt Lane Shrops 149 B10
Platts Common S Yorks 197 G11
Platt's Heath Kent 53 C11
Plawsworth Durham 233 B11
Plaxtol Kent 52 C6
Play Hatch Oxon 65 D8
Playden E Sus 38 C6
Playford Suff 108 B4
Playing Place Corn 4 G6
Playley Green Glos 98 E5
Plealey Shrops 131 B8
Pleamore Cross Som 27 D10
Plean Stirl 278 D6
Pleasant Valley Pembs 73 D10
Pleasington Blkburn 194 B6
Pleasley Derbys 171 C8
Pleasleyhill Notts 171 C8
Pleck Dorset 30 D3
Pleck Dorset 30 E2
Pleck W Mid 133 D9
Pleck or Little Ansty Dorset 30 G3
Pleckgate Blkburn 203 G9
Pledgdon Green Essex 105 F11
Pledwick W Yorks 197 D10
Plemstall W Ches 183 G7
Plenmeller Northumb 240 E6
Pleshey Essex 87 C10
Plockton Highld 295 B10
Plocrapol W Isles 305 J3
Plot Gate Som 44 G4
Plot Street Som 44 F5
Plough Hill Warks 134 E6
Ploughfield Hereford 97 C7
Plowden Shrops 131 F7
Ploxgreen Shrops 131 C7
Pluckley Kent 54 D2
Pluckley Thorne Kent 54 E2
Plucks Gutter Kent 71 G9
Plumbland Cumb 229 D9
Plumbley S Yorks 186 E6
Plumford Kent 54 B4
Plumley E Ches 184 F2
Plump Hill Glos 79 B11
Plumpton Cumb 230 D5
Plumpton E Sus 36 E5
Plumpton Northants 101 B11
Plumpton End Northants 102 B4
Plumpton Foot Cumb 230 D5
Plumpton Green E Sus 36 D5
Plumpton Head Cumb 230 E6
Plumstead London 68 D3
Plumstead Norf 160 C2
Plumstead Common London 68 D3
Plumstead Green Norf 160 C2
Plumtree Notts 154 C2
Plumtree Green Kent 53 D10
Plumtree Park Notts 154 C2
Plungar Leics 154 C5
Plush Dorset 30 G2
Plusha Corn 11 E11
Plushabridge Corn 12 G2
Plusterwine Glos 79 F9
Plwmp Ceredig 111 G7
Plymouth Plym 7 E9

Plympton Plym 7 D10
Plymstock Plym 7 E10
Plymtree Devon 27 G9
Pobgreen Gtr Man 196 F4
Pochin Houses Caerph 77 E11
Pocket Nook Gtr Man 183 B10
Pockley N Yorks 216 B2
Pocklington E Yorks 208 D2
Pockthorpe Norf 141 D8
Pockthorpe Norf 158 D6
Pockthorpe Norf 159 E10
Pockthorpe Norf 159 F11
Pode Hole Lincs 156 E4
Podimore Som 29 C8
Podington Beds 121 E8
Podmoor Worcs 117 C7
Podmore Norf 159 G9
Podmore Staffs 150 B5
Podsmead Glos 80 B4
Poffley End Oxon 82 C5
Pogmoor S Yorks 197 F10
Point Corn 3 B8
Point Clear Essex 89 C9
Pointon Lincs 156 C2
Pokesdown Bmouth 19 C8
Pol a Charra W Isles 297 K3
Polbae Dumfries 236 B4
Polbain Highld 307 H4
Polbathic Corn 7 D7
Polbeth W Loth 269 C10
Polborder Corn 7 C7
Polbrock Corn 5 B10
Polchar Highld 291 C10
Pole Elm Worcs 98 B6
Pole Moor W Yorks 196 D5
Polebrook Northants 137 F11
Polegate E Sus 23 D9
Poles Highld 309 K7
Pole's Hole Wilts 45 C10
Polesden Lacey Sur 50 C6
Poleshill Som 27 C9
Polesworth Warks 134 C5
Polgear Corn 2 B5
Polgigga Corn 1 E3
Polglass Highld 307 J5
Polgooth Corn 5 E9
Poling W Sus 35 G8
Poling Corner W Sus 35 F8
Polkerris Corn 5 E11
Poll Hill Mers 182 E3
Polla Highld 308 D3
Polladras Corn 2 C4
Pollard Street Norf 160 C6
Pollhill Kent 53 C11
Pollie Highld 309 H7
Pollington E Yorks 198 D6
Polliwilline Argyll 255 G8
Polloch Highld 289 C9
Pollok Glasgow 267 C10
Pollokshields Glasgow 267 C11
Polmadie Glasgow 267 C11
Polmarth Corn 2 B6
Polmassick Corn 5 F9
Polmear Corn 5 E11
Polmont Falk 279 F8
Polmorla Corn 10 G5
Polnessan E Ayrs 257 G10
Polnish Highld 295 G9
Polopit Northants 121 B10
Polpenwith Corn 2 D6
Polpeor Corn 2 B2
Polperro Corn 6 E4
Polruan Corn 6 E2
Polsham Som 44 E4
Polsloe Devon 14 C4
Polstead Suff 107 D9
Polstead Heath Suff 107 C9
Poltalloch Argyll 275 D9
Poltesco Corn 2 F6
Poltimore Devon 14 B5
Polton Midloth 270 C5
Polwarth Borders 272 E4
Polwheveral Corn 2 D6
Polyphant Corn 11 E11
Polzeath Corn 10 F4
Pomeroy Derbys 169 B10
Pomphlett Plym 7 E10
Ponciau Wrex 166 F3
Pond Close Som 27 B10
Pond Park Bucks 85 E7
Pond Street Essex 105 D9
Ponde Powys 96 D2
Ponders End London 86 F5
Pondersbridge Cambs 138 E5
Pondtail Hants 49 C10
Pondwell I o W 21 C8
Poniou Corn 1 B4
Ponjeravah Corn 2 D6
Ponsanooth Corn 3 B7
Ponsford Devon 27 F8
Ponsonby Cumb 219 D11
Ponsongath Corn 3 F7
Ponsworthy Devon 13 G10
Pont Corn 6 E2
Pont Aber Carms 94 G4
Pont Aber-Geirw Gwyn 146 D5
Pont-ar-gothi Carms 93 G10
Pont ar Hydfer Powys 95 F7
Pont-ar-llechau Carms 94 G4
Pont Cyfyng Conwy 164 D2
Pont Cysyllte Wrex 166 G3
Pont Dolydd Prysor Gwyn 146 B4
Pont-faen Powys 95 E9
Pont-Faen Shrops 148 B5
Pont Fronwydd Gwyn 146 E6
Pont-gareg Pembs 92 C2
Pont-Henri Carms 75 D7
Pont Hwfa Anglesey 178 E2
Pont iets = Pontyates Carms 75 D7
Pont-Llogel Powys 147 F10
Pont-newydd Carms 74 D6
Pont-newydd Flint 165 B11
Pont Pen-y-benglog Gwyn 163 C10
Pont Rhyd-goch Conwy 163 C11
Pont-Rhyd-sarn Gwyn 147 D7
Pont Rhyd-y-berry Powys 95 D9
Pont Rhyd-y-cyff Bridgend 57 D11
Pont-rhyd-y-groes Ceredig 112 C4
Pont Rhydgaled Powys 128 G6
Pont-Rhythallt Gwyn 163 C8
Pont-rug Gwyn 163 C8
Pont Senni = Sennybridge Powys 95 F8
Pont Siôn Norton Rhondda 77 G9
Pont-siôn Ceredig 93 B8
Pont-Walby Neath 76 D5
Pont-y-blew Shrops 148 B6
Pont-y-gwaith Rhondda 77 G8
Pont-y-pant Conwy 164 E3
Pont y Pennant Gwyn 147 G8
Pont-y-rhyl Bridgend 58 B2
Pont-y-wal Powys 96 D2
Pont yr Afon-Gam Gwyn 164 G2
Pont-yr-hafod Pembs 91 F8
Pont-Ystrad Denb 165 C9
Pontamman Carms 75 C10
Pontantwn Carms 74 C6
Pontardawe Neath 76 E2
Pontarddulais Swansea 75 E9
Pontarfynach = Devils Bridge Ceredig 112 B4
Pontarsais Carms 93 F8
Pontblyddyn Flint 166 C3
Pontbren Araeth Carms 94 G3
Pontbren Llwyd Rhondda 76 D6
Pontcanna Cardiff 59 D7
Pontdolgoch Powys 129 E10
Pontefract W Yorks 198 C3
Ponteland Northumb 242 C5
Ponterwyd Ceredig 128 G4
Pontesbury Shrops 131 B7
Pontesbury Hill Shrops 131 B7
Pontesford Shrops 131 B8
Pontfadog Wrex 148 B4
Pontfaen Pembs 91 E10
Pontgarreg Ceredig 110 G6
Ponthen Shrops 148 F6
Ponthir Torf 78 G4
Ponthirwaun Ceredig 92 B5
Pontiago Pembs 91 D8
Pontithel Powys 96 D3
Pontllanfraith Caerph 77 F11
Pontlliw Swansea 75 E10
Pontllyfni Gwyn 162 E6
Pontlottyn Caerph 77 D10
Pontneddfechan Powys 76 D6
Pontnewydd Torf 78 F3
Pontnewynydd Torf 78 E3
Pontrhydfendigaid Ceredig 112 D4
Pontrhydyfen Neath 57 C9
Pontrhydyrun Torf 78 F3
Pontrilas Hereford 97 F7
Pontrobert Powys 148 G2
Ponts Green E Sus 23 B11
Pontshill Hereford 98 G2
Pontsticill M Tydf 77 C9
Pontwgan Conwy 180 G3
Pontyates = Pont-iets Carms 75 D7
Pontyberem Carms 75 C8
Pontyclun Rhondda 58 C4
Pontycymer Bridgend 76 G6
Pontyglasier Pembs 92 D2
Pontymister Caerph 78 G2
Pontymoel Torf 78 E3
Pontypool Torf 78 E3
Pontypridd Rhondda 58 B5
Pontywaun Caerph 78 G2
Pooksgreen Hants 32 E5
Pool Corn 4 G3
Pool W Yorks 205 D10
Pool Head Hereford 115 G11
Pool Hey Lancs 193 D11
Pool o' Muckhart Clack 286 G4
Pool Quay Powys 148 G5
Poolbrook Worcs 98 C5
Poole N Yorks 198 B3
Poole Poole 18 C6
Poole Som 27 C10
Poole Keynes Glos 81 F8
Poolend Staffs 169 D7
Poolestown Dorset 30 D2
Poolewe Highld 307 L3
Pooley Bridge Cumb 230 G5
Pooley Street Norf 141 G11
Poolfold Staffs 168 D5
Poolhead Shrops 149 C9
Poolhill Glos 98 F4
Poolmill Hereford 97 G11
Poolsbrook Derbys 186 G6
Poolside Moray 302 E4
Poolstock Gtr Man 194 G5
Pooltown Som 42 F3
Pootings Kent 52 D3
Pope Hill Pembs 72 C6
Pope's Hill Glos 79 C11
Popeswood Brack 65 F10
Popham Devon 41 G8
Popham Hants 48 E5
Poplar London 67 C11
Poplar Grove Lincs 190 B6
Poplars Herts 104 G5
Popley Hants 48 C6
Porchester Nottingham 171 G9
Porchfield I o W 20 C4
Porin Highld 300 D3
Poringland Norf 142 C5
Porkellis Corn 2 C5
Porlock Som 41 D11
Porlock Weir Som 41 D11
Porlockford Som 41 D11
Port Allen Perth 286 E6
Port Ann Argyll 275 E10
Port Appin Argyll 289 E11
Port Arthur Shetland 313 K5
Port Askaig Argyll 274 G5
Port Bannatyne Argyll 275 G11
Port Brae Fife 280 C5
Port Bridge Devon 9 D7
Port Carlisle Cumb 238 E6
Port Charlotte Argyll 254 B3
Port Clarence Stockton 234 G5
Port Dinorwic = Y Felinheli Gwyn 163 B8
Port Driseach Argyll 275 F10
Port Dundas Glasgow 267 B11
Port e Vullen I o M 192 C5
Port Edgar Edin 280 F2
Port Ellen Argyll 254 C4
Port Elphinstone Aberds 293 B9
Port Erin I o M 192 F2
Port Erroll Aberds 303 F10
Port-Eynon Swansea 56 D3
Port Gaverne Corn 10 E6
Port Glasgow Invclyd 276 G6
Port Henderson Highld 299 B7
Port Hill Oxon 65 B7
Port Isaac Corn 10 E5
Port Lamont Argyll 275 F11
Port Lion Pembs 73 D7
Port Logan Dumfries 236 E2
Port Mead Swansea 56 B6
Port Mholair W Isles 304 E7
Port Mor Highld 288 B6
Port Mulgrave N Yorks 226 B5
Port Nan Giùran W Isles 304 E7
Port nan Long W Isles 296 D4
Port Nis W Isles 304 B7
Port of Menteith Stirl 285 G9
Port Quin Corn 10 E5
Port Ramsay Argyll 289 E10
Port St Mary I o M 192 F3
Port Solent Ptsmth 33 F10
Port Sunlight Mers 182 E4
Port Sutton Bridge Lincs 157 E9
Port Talbot Neath 57 D9
Port Tennant Swansea 57 C7
Port Wemyss Argyll 254 B2
Port William Dumfries 236 E5
Portachoillan Argyll 255 B8
Portash Wilts 46 G3
Portavadie Argyll 275 G10
Portbury N Som 60 D4
Portchester Hants 33 F10
Portclair Highld 290 B6
Porteath Corn 10 F5
Portencalzie Dumfries 236 B2
Portencross N Ayrs 266 F3
Porterfield Renfs 267 B9
Porter's End Herts 85 B11
Portesham Dorset 17 D8
Portessie Moray 302 C4
Portfield Argyll 289 G9
Portfield Som 28 B6
Portfield W Sus 22 B5
Portfield Gate Pembs 72 B6
Portgate Devon 12 D4
Portgordon Moray 302 C3
Portgower Highld 311 H4
Porth Corn 4 C6
Porth Rhondda 77 G8
Porth Colmon Gwyn 144 C3
Porth Kea Corn 4 G6
Porth Navas Corn 3 D7
Porth Tywyn = Burry Port Carms 74 E6
Porth-y-felin Anglesey 178 E2
Porth-y-waen Shrops 148 E5
Porthallow Corn 3 E7
Porthallow Corn 6 E4
Porthcawl Bridgend 57 F10
Porthcothan Corn 10 G3
Porthcurno Corn 1 E3
Portheiddy Pembs 90 E6
Porthgain Pembs 90 E6
Porthgwarra Corn 1 E3
Porthhallow Corn 3 E7
Porthill Shrops 149 G9
Porthill Staffs 168 F5
Porthilly Corn 10 F4
Porthkerry V Glam 58 F5
Porthleven Corn 2 D4
Porthllechog = Bull Bay Anglesey 178 C6
Porthloo Scilly 1 G4
Porthmadog Gwyn 145 B11
Porthmeor Corn 1 B4
Porthoustock Corn 3 E8
Porthpean Corn 5 E10
Porthtowan Corn 4 F3
Porthyrhyd Carms 75 B8
Porthyrhyd Carms 94 D4
Portico Mers 183 C7
Portincaple Argyll 276 C4
Portington Devon 12 F4
Portington E Yorks 207 G11
Portinnisherrich Argyll 275 B10
Portinscale Cumb 229 G11
Portishead N Som 60 D3
Portkil Argyll 276 E5
Portknockie Moray 302 C4
Portland Som 44 F3
Portlethen Aberds 293 D11
Portlethen Village Aberds 293 D11
Portlevorchy Highld 306 D7
Portling Dumfries 237 D10
Portloe Corn 3 B10
Portlooe Corn 6 E4
Portmahomack Highld 311 L3
Portmeirion Gwyn 145 B11
Portmellon Corn 5 G10
Portmore Hants 20 B2
Portnacroish Argyll 289 E11
Portnahaven Argyll 254 B2
Portnalong Highld 294 B5
Portnaluchaig Highld 295 G8
Portnancon Highld 308 C4
Portnellan Stirl 285 E8
Portnellan Stirl 285 F8
Portobello Edin 280 G6
Portobello T & W 243 F7
Portobello W Mid 133 D9
Portobello W Yorks 197 D10
Porton Wilts 47 F7
Portpatrick Dumfries 236 D2
Portrack Stockton 225 B9
Portreath Corn 4 F3
Portree Highld 298 E4
Portscatho Corn 3 B9
Portsea Ptsmth 33 G10
Portsea Island Ptsmth 33 G11
Portskerra Highld 310 C2
Portskewett Mon 60 B4
Portslade Brighton 36 F3
Portslade-by-Sea Brighton 36 G3
Portslade Village Brighton 36 F3
Portsmouth Ptsmth 21 B9
Portsmouth W Yorks 196 B2
Portsonachan Argyll 284 E4
Portsoy Aberds 302 C5
Portswood Soton 32 E6
Porttanachy Moray 302 C3
Portuairk Highld 288 C6
Portvasgo Highld 308 C5
Portway Dorset 18 D2
Portway Glos 98 E5
Portway Hereford 97 B9
Portway Hereford 97 D9
Portway Som 28 B6
Portway Som 44 F3
Portway W Mid 133 F9
Portway Worcs 117 C11
Portwood Gtr Man 184 C6
Portwrinkle Corn 7 E7
Posenhall Shrops 132 C3
Poslingford Suff 106 B5
Posso Borders 260 C6
Post Green Dorset 18 C5
Post Mawr = Synod Inn Ceredig 111 G8
Postbridge Devon 13 F9
Postcombe Oxon 84 F2
Postling Kent 54 F6
Postlip Glos 99 F10
Postwick Norf 142 B5
Pot Common Sur 50 E2
Potarch Aberds 293 D8
Potash Suff 108 D2
Potbridge Hants 49 C8
Potholm Dumfries 249 F9
Potmaily Highld 300 F4
Potman's Heath Kent 38 B5
Potsgrove C Beds 103 F9
Pott Row Norf 158 E4
Pott Shrigley E Ches 184 F6
Potten End Herts 85 D8
Potten Street Kent 71 F9
Potter Brompton N Yorks 217 D9
Potter Heigham Norf 161 F8
Potter Hill Leics 154 E4
Potter Hill S Yorks 186 B4
Potter Somersal Derbys 152 B2
Potter Street Essex 87 D7
Pottergate Street Norf 142 E3
Potterhanworth Lincs 173 B9
Potterhanworth Booths Lincs 173 B9
Potterne Wilts 46 B3
Potterne Wick Wilts 46 B4
Potternewton W Yorks 206 F2
Potters Bar Herts 86 E3
Potters Brook Lancs 202 C5
Potters Corner Kent 54 E3
Potter's Cross Staffs 132 G6
Potters Crouch Herts 85 D10
Potter's Forstal Kent 53 D11
Potter's Green E Sus 37 C8
Potter's Green W Mid 135 G7
Potters Hill N Som 60 F4
Potters Marston Leics 135 D9
Pottersheath Herts 86 B2
Potterspury Northants 102 C5
Potterton Aberds 293 B11
Potterton W Yorks 206 F4
Pottery Field W Yorks 206 G2
Potthorpe Norf 159 E8
Pottington Devon 40 G5
Potto N Yorks 225 E9
Potton C Beds 104 B4
Pouchen End Herts 85 D8
Poughill Corn 24 F2
Poughill Devon 26 F5
Poulner Hants 31 F11
Poulshot Wilts 46 B3
Poulton Glos 81 E10
Poulton Mers 182 C4
Poulton Mers 182 E4
Poulton W Ches 166 D5
Poulton-le-Fylde Lancs 202 F2
Pound Som 28 D6
Pound Bank Worcs 98 B5
Pound Bank Worcs 116 C4
Pound Green E Sus 37 C8
Pound Green Hants 48 B5
Pound Green I o W 20 D2
Pound Green Suff 124 G4
Pound Green Worcs 116 B5
Pound Hill W Sus 51 F9
Pound Street Hants 64 G3
Poundbury Dorset 17 C9
Poundffald Swansea 56 C5
Poundfield E Sus 52 G4
Poundford E Sus 37 C9
Poundgate E Sus 37 B7
Poundgreen Wokingham 65 F7
Poundland S Ayrs 244 F5
Poundon Bucks 102 F2
Poundsbridge Kent 52 E4
Poundsgate Devon 13 G10
Poundstock Corn 11 B10
Pounsley E Sus 37 C8
Poverest London 68 F3
Povey Cross Sur 51 E9
Pow Green Hereford 98 C4
Powburn Northumb 264 F3
Powder Mills Kent 52 D5
Powderham Devon 14 E5
Powers Hall End Essex 88 B4
Powerstock Dorset 16 B6
Powfoot Dumfries 238 D4
Powhill Cumb 238 F6
Powick Worcs 116 G6
Powler's Piece Devon 24 D5
Powmill Perth 279 B10
Pownall Park E Ches 184 E4
Powntley Copse Hants 49 E8
Poxwell Dorset 17 E10
Poyle Slough 66 D4
Poynings W Sus 36 E3
Poyntington Dorset 29 D11
Poynton E Ches 184 E6
Poynton Telford 149 F11
Poynton Green Telford 149 F11
Poyntzfield Highld 301 C7
Poyston Pembs 73 B7
Poyston Cross Pembs 73 B7
Poystreet Green Suff 125 F9
Praa Sands Corn 2 D3
Pratling Street Kent 53 B8
Pratt's Bottom London 68 G3
Praze Corn 2 B3
Praze-an-Beeble Corn 2 B4
Predannack Wollas Corn 2 F5
Prees Shrops 149 C11
Prees Green Shrops 149 C11
Prees Heath Shrops 149 B11
Prees Higher Heath Shrops 149 B11
Prees Lower Heath Shrops 149 C11
Prees Wood Shrops 149 C11
Preesall Lancs 202 D3
Preesall Park Lancs 202 D3
Preesgweene Shrops 148 B5
Preeshenlle Shrops 148 C6
Pren-gwyn Ceredig 93 C8
Prenbrigog Flint 166 C3
Prendergast Pembs 73 B7
Prendergast Pembs 90 G6
Prendergust Borders 273 D8
Prendwick Northumb 264 G2
Prenteg Gwyn 163 G9
Prenton Mers 182 D4
Prescot Mers 183 C7
Prescott Devon 27 E9
Prescott Glos 99 F9
Prescott Shrops 132 G3
Prescott Shrops 149 E8
Presdales Herts 86 C5
Preshome Moray 302 C4
Press Derbys 170 B5
Pressen Northumb 263 B8
Prestatyn Denb 181 E9
Prestbury E Ches 184 F6
Prestbury Glos 99 G9
Presteigne Powys 114 E6
Presthope Shrops 131 D11
Prestleigh Som 44 E6
Prestolee Gtr Man 195 F9
Preston Borders 272 D5
Preston Brighton 36 F4
Preston Devon 14 G3
Preston Dorset 17 E10
Preston E Loth 281 F11
Preston E Loth 281 G7
Preston E Yorks 209 G9
Preston Glos 81 E8
Preston Glos 98 E3
Preston Herts 104 G3
Preston Kent 70 G4
Preston Kent 71 G8
Preston Lancs 194 B4
Preston London 67 B7
Preston Northumb 264 D5
Preston Rutland 137 C7
Preston Shrops 149 G10
Preston T & W 243 D8
Preston Torbay 9 C7
Preston Wilts 62 D4
Preston Wilts 63 E9
Preston Bagot Warks 118 D3
Preston Bissett Bucks 102 F3
Preston Bowyer Som 27 B10
Preston Brockhurst Shrops 149 E10
Preston Brook Halton 183 E9
Preston Candover Hants 48 E6
Preston Capes Northants 119 G11
Preston Crowmarsh Oxon 83 G10
Preston Deanery Northants 120 F5
Preston Fields Warks 118 D3
Preston Grange T & W 243 C8
Preston Green Warks 118 D3
Preston Gubbals Shrops 149 F9
Preston-le-Skerne Durham 234 G2
Preston Marsh Hereford 97 B11
Preston Montford Shrops 149 G8
Preston on Stour Warks 118 G4
Preston-on-Tees Stockton 225 B8
Preston on the Hill Halton 183 E9
Preston on Wye Hereford 97 C7
Preston Pastures Worcs 100 B3
Preston Plucknett Som 29 D8
Preston St Mary Suff 125 G8
Preston-under-Scar N Yorks 223 G11
Preston upon the Weald Moors Telford 150 F3
Preston Wynne Hereford 97 B11
Prestonfield Edin 280 G5
Prestonmill Dumfries 237 D11
Prestonpans E Loth 281 G7
Prestwich Gtr Man 195 G10
Prestwick Northumb 242 C5
Prestwick S Ayrs 257 D9
Prestwold Leics 153 E11
Prestwood Bucks 84 E5
Prestwood Staffs 133 F7
Prestwood Staffs 169 G10
Prey Heath Sur 50 B3
Price Town Bridgend 76 G6
Prickwillow Cambs 139 G11
Priddy Som 44 C4
Pride Park Derbys 153 B7
Priest Down Bath 60 G6
Priest Hutton Lancs 211 E10
Priest Weston Shrops 130 D5
Priestacott Devon 24 F6
Priestcliffe Derbys 185 G10
Priestcliffe Ditch Derbys 185 G10
Priestfield W Mid 133 D8
Priestfield Worcs 98 C6
Priesthaugh Borders 249 C11
Priesthill Glasgow 267 C10
Priesthorpe W Yorks 205 F10
Priestley Green W Yorks 196 B6
Prieston Borders 262 D2
Priestside Dumfries 238 D4
Priestthorpe W Yorks 205 F8
Priestwood Brack 65 F11
Priestwood Kent 69 G7
Priestwood Green Kent 69 G7
Primethorpe Leics 135 E10
Primrose T & W 243 E8
Primrose Corner Norf 160 G6
Primrose Green Norf 159 F11
Primrose Hill Bath 61 F8
Primrose Hill Lancs 193 F11
Primrose Hill London 67 C9
Primrose Hill W Mid 133 F8
Primrose Valley N Yorks 218 D2
Primrosehill Herts 85 E9
Primsland Worcs 117 E8
Prince Hill E Ches 168 G2
Prince Royd W Yorks 196 D6
Princes End W Mid 133 E9
Princes Gate Pembs 73 C10
Prince's Marsh Hants 34 B3
Princes Park Mers 182 D5
Princes Risborough Bucks 84 E4
Princethorpe Warks 119 C8
Princetown Caerph 77 C10
Princetown Devon 13 G7
Prinsted W Sus 22 B3
Printstile Kent 52 E5
Prion Denb 165 C9
Prior Muir Fife 287 F9
Prior Park Northumb 273 E9
Prior Rigg Cumb 239 D11
Priors Frome Hereford 97 D11
Priors Halton Shrops 115 B9
Priors Hardwick Warks 119 F9
Priors Marston Warks 119 F9
Prior's Norton Glos 99 G7
Priors Park Glos 99 E7
Priorslee Telford 150 G4
Priorswood Som 28 B2
Priory Pembs 72 D6
Priory Green Suff 107 C8
Priory Heath Suff 108 C3
Priory Wood Hereford 96 B5
Prisk V Glam 58 D4
Pristacott Devon 25 B8
Priston Bath 61 G7
Pristow Green Norf 142 F2
Prittlewell Sthend 69 B11
Privett Hants 21 B7
Privett Hants 33 B11
Prixford Devon 40 F4
Probus Corn 5 F7
Proncy Highld 309 K7
Prospect Cumb 229 C8
Prospect Village Staffs 151 G10
Prospidnick Corn 2 C4
Provanmill Glasgow 268 B2
Prowse Devon 26 F4
Prudhoe Northumb 242 E3
Prussia Cove Corn 2 D3
Ptarmigan Lodge Stirl 285 G7
Pubil Perth 285 C8
Publow Bath 60 G6
Puckeridge Herts 105 G7
Puckington Som 28 D5
Pucklechurch S Glos 61 D7
Pucknall Hants 32 B5
Puckrup Glos 99 D7
Puckshole Glos 80 D4
Puddaven Devon 8 C5
Pudding Pie Nook Lancs 202 F6
Puddinglake W Ches 168 B2
Puddington Devon 26 E4
Puddington W Ches 182 G4
Puddle Corn 5 D11
Puddlebridge Som 28 E4
Puddledock Kent 52 C3
Puddledock Kent 68 E4
Puddledock Norf 141 E11
Puddletown Dorset 17 C11
Pudleigh Som 28 E4
Pudleston Hereford 115 F11
Pudsey W Yorks 196 B2
Pudsey W Yorks 205 G10
Pulborough W Sus 35 D8
Pulcree Dumfries 237 D7
Pule Hill W Yorks 196 B5
Puleston Telford 150 E4
Pulford W Ches 166 D5
Pulham Dorset 30 F2
Pulham Market Norf 142 F3
Pulham St Mary Norf 142 F4
Pullens Green S Glos 79 G10
Pulley Shrops 131 B9
Pullington Kent 53 G10
Pulloxhill C Beds 103 E11
Pulverbatch Shrops 131 C8
Pumpherston W Loth 269 B11
Pumsaint Carms 94 C3
Puncheston = Cas -Mael Pembs 91 F10
Puncknowle Dorset 16 D6
Punnett's Town E Sus 37 C10
Purbrook Hants 33 F11
Purewell Dorset 19 C9
Purfleet Thurrock 68 D5
Puriton Som 43 E10
Purleigh Essex 88 E4
Purley London 67 G10
Purley on Thames W Berks 65 D7
Purlogue Shrops 114 B5
Purlpit Wilts 61 F11
Purls Bridge Cambs 139 F9
Purn N Som 43 B10
Purse Caundle Dorset 29 D11
Purslow Shrops 131 G7
Purston Jaglin W Yorks 198 D2
Purtington Som 28 F5
Purton Glos 79 E11
Purton W Berks 64 D3
Purton Wilts 62 B5
Purton Common Wilts 62 B5
Purton Stoke Wilts 81 G9
Purwell Herts 104 F4
Pury End Northants 102 B4
Pusey Oxon 82 F5
Putley Hereford 98 D2
Putley Common Hereford 98 D2
Putley Green Hereford 98 D3
Putloe Glos 80 D3
Putney London 67 D8
Putney Heath London 67 E8
Putney Vale London 67 E8
Putnoe Beds 121 G11
Putsborough Devon 40 E3
Putson Hereford 97 D10
Puttenham Herts 84 C5
Puttenham Sur 50 D2
Puttock End Essex 106 C6
Puttock's End Essex 87 B9
Putton Dorset 17 E9
Puxey Dorset 30 E3
Puxley Northants 102 C5
Puxton N Som 60 G2
Pwll Carms 75 E7
Pwll Powys 130 C3
Pwll-clai Flint 181 F11
Pwll-glas Denb 165 E10
Pwll-Mawr Cardiff 59 D8
Pwll-melyn Flint 181 G11
Pwll-trap Carms 74 B3
Pwll-y-glaw Neath 57 C9
Pwllcrochan Pembs 72 E6
Pwllgloyw Powys 95 E10
Pwllheli Gwyn 145 B7
Pwllmeyric Mon 79 G8
Pwllypant Caerph 59 B7
Pye Bridge Derbys 170 E6
Pye Corner Devon 14 B4
Pye Corner Kent 53 D11
Pye Corner Newport 59 B9
Pye Corner S Glos 60 D6
Pye Green Staffs 151 G9
Pye Hill Notts 170 E6
Pyecombe W Sus 36 E3
Pyewipe NE Lincs 201 E9
Pyle I o W 20 F5
Pyle Swansea 56 D5
Pyle = Y Pîl Bridgend 57 E10
Pyle Hill Sur 50 B3
Pylehill Hants 33 D7
Pyleigh Som 42 G6
Pylle Som 44 F6
Pymoor or Pymore Cambs 139 F9
Pype Hayes W Mid 134 E2
Pyrford Sur 50 B4
Pyrford Green Sur 50 B4
Pyrford Village Sur 50 B4
Pyrland Som 28 B2
Pyrton Oxon 83 F11
Pytchley Northants 121 C7
Pyworthy Devon 24 G4

Q

Quabbs Shrops 130 G4
Quabrook E Sus 52 G2
Quadring Lincs 156 C4
Quadring Eaudike Lincs 156 C4
Quags Corner W Sus 34 C5
Quainton Bucks 84 B2
Quaker's Yard M Tydf 77 F9
Quaking Houses Durham 242 G5
Quality Corner Cumb 219 B9
Quarhouse Glos 80 E5
Quarley Hants 47 E9
Quarmby W Yorks 196 D6
Quarndon Derbys 170 G4
Quarndon Common Derbys 170 G4
Quarr Hill I o W 21 C7
Quarrelton Renfs 267 C8
Quarrendon Bucks 84 B4
Quarriers Village Invclyd 267 B7
Quarrington Lincs 173 G9
Quarrington Hill Durham 234 D2
Quarry Bank W Mid 133 F8
Quarry Heath Staffs 151 G8
Quarry Hill Staffs 134 C4
Quarrybank W Ches 167 B8
Quarryford E Loth 271 B11
Quarryhead Aberds 303 C9
Quarryhill Highld 309 L7
Quarrywood Moray 301 C11
Quarter S Lnrk 268 E4
Quartley Devon 27 B7
Quatford Shrops 132 E4
Quatquoy Orkney 314 E3
Quatt Shrops 132 F5
Quebec Durham 233 C9
Quebec W Sus 34 C3
Quedgeley Glos 80 C4
Queen Adelaide Cambs 139 G11
Queen Camel Som 29 C9
Queen Charlton Bath 60 F6
Queen Dart Devon 26 D4
Queen Oak Dorset 45 G9
Queen Street Kent 53 D7
Queen Street Wilts 62 B4
Queenborough Kent 70 E2
Queenhill Worcs 99 D7
Queen's Bower I o W 21 E7
Queen's Corner W Sus 34 B5
Queen's Head Shrops 148 D6
Queen's Park Beds 103 B10
Queen's Park Blkburn 195 B7
Queen's Park Essex 87 F11
Queen's Park Northants 120 E5
Queen's Park W Ches 166 B6
Queensbury London 67 B7
Queensbury W Yorks 205 G8
Queensferry Edin 280 F2
Queensferry Flint 166 B4
Queenslie Glasgow 268 B3
Queenstown Blkpool 202 F2
Queensville Staffs 151 E8
Queenzieburn N Lnrk 278 F3
Quemerford Wilts 62 F4
Quendale Shetland 313 M5
Quendon Essex 105 E10
Queniborough Leics 154 G2
Quenington Glos 81 E10
Quernmore Lancs 202 B6
Queslett W Mid 133 E11
Quethiock Corn 6 C6
Quhamm Shetland 312 G6
Quholm Orkney 314 E2
Quick Gtr Man 196 G3
Quick Edge Gtr Man 196 G3
Quicks Green W Berks 64 D5
Quidenham Norf 141 F10
Quidhampton Hants 48 C4
Quidhampton Wilts 46 G6
Quilquox Aberds 303 F9
Quina Brook Shrops 149 C10
Quinbury End Northants 120 G2
Quindry Orkney 314 G4
Quinton Northants 120 G5
Quinton W Mid 133 G9
Quintrell Downs Corn 5 C7
Quixhill Staffs 169 G10
Quoditch Devon 12 B4
Quoig Perth 286 E2
Quoisley E Ches 167 F8
Quoit Corn 5 C8
Quorndon or Quorn Leics 153 F11
Quothquan S Lnrk 259 B11
Quoyloo Orkney 314 D2
Quoynee Highld 310 D6
Quoyness Orkney 314 F2
Quoys Shetland 312 B8
Quoys Shetland 313 G6

R

Raasay Ho Highld 295 B7
Rabbit's Cross Kent 53 D9
Rableyheath Herts 86 B2
Raby Cumb 238 G5
Raby Mers 182 F4
Racecourse Suff 108 C3
Racedown Hants 47 E9
Rachan Mill Borders 260 C4
Rachub Gwyn 163 B10
Rack End Oxon 82 E6
Rackenford Devon 26 D5
Rackham W Sus 35 E9
Rackheath Norf 160 G5
Rackley Som 43 C11
Racks Dumfries 238 C2
Rackwick Orkney 314 B4
Rackwick Orkney 314 G2
Radbourne Derbys 152 B5
Radcliffe Gtr Man 195 F9
Radcliffe Northumb 253 C7
Radcliffe on Trent Notts 154 B2
Radclive Bucks 102 E3
Radcot Oxon 82 F3
Raddery Highld 301 D7
Raddington Som 27 B8
Raddon Devon 26 G6
Radernie Fife 287 G8
Radfall Kent 70 G6
Radfield Kent 70 G2
Radford Bath 45 B7
Radford Nottingham 171 G9
Radford Oxon 101 G8
Radford W Mid 134 G6
Radford Worcs 117 F10
Radford Semele Warks 118 E6
Radfordbridge Oxon 101 G8
Radipole Dorset 17 E9
Radlet Som 43 F8
Radlett Herts 85 F11
Radley Oxon 83 F8
Radley Green Essex 87 D10
Radley Park Oxon 83 F8
Radlith Shrops 131 B8
Radmanthwaite Notts 171 C8
Radmoor Shrops 150 E2
Radmore Green E Ches 167 D9
Radmore Wood Staffs 151 D11
Radnage Bucks 84 F3
Radnor Corn 4 G4
Radnor Park W Dunb 277 G9
Radstock Bath 45 C7
Radstone Northants 101 C11
Radway Warks 101 B7
Radway Green E Ches 168 E3
Radwell Beds 121 F10
Radwell Herts 104 D4
Radwinter Essex 106 D2
Radwinter End Essex 106 D2
Radyr Cardiff 58 C6
Raehills Dumfries 248 E3
Raera Argyll 289 G10
Rafborough Hants 49 B11
Rafford Moray 301 D10
Raga Shetland 312 D6
Ragdale Leics 154 F3
Ragdon Shrops 131 E9
Raggalds W Yorks 205 G7
Ragged Appleshaw Hants 47 D10
Raginnis Corn 1 D5
Raglan Mon 78 D6
Ragmere Norf 141 E11
Ragnal Wilts 63 E10
Ragnall Notts 188 G4
Rahane Argyll 276 D4
Rahoy Highld 289 D8
Raigbeg Highld 301 G8
Rails S Yorks 186 D3
Rain Shore Gtr Man 195 D11
Rainbow Hill Worcs 117 F7
Rainford Mers 194 G3
Rainford Junction Mers 194 G3
Rainham London 68 C4
Rainham Medway 69 F10
Rainhill Mers 183 C7
Rainhill Stoops Mers 183 C8
Rainow E Ches 185 F7
Rainowlow E Ches 185 F7
Rainsough Gtr Man 195 G10
Rainton Dumfries 237 D8
Rainton N Yorks 215 D7
Rainton Bridge T & W 234 B2
Rainton Gate Durham 234 B2
Rainworth Notts 171 D9
Raisbeck Cumb 222 D2
Raise Cumb 231 B10
Rait Perth 286 E6
Raithby Lincs 190 E4
Raithby by Spilsby Lincs 174 B5
Rake W Sus 34 B4
Rake Common Hants 34 B3
Rake End Staffs 151 F11
Rake Head Lancs 195 C10
Rakes Dale Staffs 169 G9
Rakeway Staffs 169 G8
Rakewood Gtr Man 196 E2
Raleigh Devon 40 G5
Ralia Lodge Highld 291 D9
Rallt Swansea 56 C4
Ram Carms 93 B11
Ram Alley Wilts 63 G8
Ram Hill S Glos 61 D7
Ram Lane Kent 54 D3
Ramasaig Highld 297 G7
Rame Corn 2 C6
Rame Corn 7 F8
Rameldry Mill Bank Fife 287 G7
Ramnageo Shetland 312 C8
Rampisham Dorset 29 G9
Rampside Cumb 210 F4
Rampton Cambs 123 D8
Rampton Notts 188 F3
Ramsbottom Gtr Man 195 D9
Ramsburn Moray 302 D5
Ramsbury Wilts 63 E9
Ramscraigs Highld 311 G5
Ramsdean Hants 34 C2
Ramsdell Hants 48 B5
Ramsden London 68 F3
Ramsden Oxon 82 B5
Ramsden Worcs 99 B8
Ramsden Bellhouse Essex 88 G2
Ramsden Heath Essex 88 F2
Ramsden Wood W Yorks 196 C2
Ramsey Cambs 138 F5
Ramsey Essex 108 E4
Ramsey I o M 192 C5
Ramsey Forty Foot Cambs 138 F6
Ramsey Heights Cambs 138 F5
Ramsey Island Essex 89 D7
Ramsey Mereside Cambs 138 F5
Ramsey St Mary's Cambs 138 F5
Ramseycleuch Borders 261 G7
Ramsgate Kent 71 G11
Ramsgill N Yorks 214 E2
Ramshaw Durham 232 B5
Ramshaw Durham 233 F8
Ramsholt Suff 108 C6
Ramshorn Staffs 169 F9
Ramsley Devon 13 C8
Ramslye Kent 52 F5
Ramsnest Common Sur 50 G2
Ranais W Isles 304 F6
Ranby Lincs 190 F2
Ranby Notts 187 E11
Rand Lincs 189 F10
Randwick Glos 80 D4
Ranfurly Renfs 267 C7
Rangag Highld 310 E5
Rangemore Staffs 152 E3
Rangeworthy S Glos 61 B7
Rankinston E Ayrs 257 G11
Rank's Green Essex 88 B3
Ranmoor S Yorks 186 D4
Ranmore Common Sur 50 C6
Rannerdale Cumb 220 B3
Rannoch Lodge Perth 285 B9
Rannoch Station Perth 285 B8
Ranochan Highld 295 G10
Ranskill Notts 187 D11
Ranton Staffs 151 E7
Ranton Green Staffs 150 E6
Ranworth Norf 161 G7
Rapkyns W Sus 50 G6
Raploch Stirl 278 C5
Rapness Orkney 314 B5
Rapps Som 28 D4
Rascal Moor E Yorks 208 F2
Rascarrel Dumfries 237 E9
Rashielee Renfs 277 G9
Rashierieve Aberds 303 G9
Rashwood Worcs 117 D8
Raskelf N Yorks 215 E9
Rassal Highld 299 E8
Rassau Bl Gwent 77 C11
Rastrick W Yorks 196 C6
Ratagan Highld 295 D11
Ratby Leics 135 B10
Ratcliff London 67 C11
Ratcliffe Culey Leics 134 D6
Ratcliffe on Soar Leics 153 D9
Ratcliffe on the Wreake Leics 154 G2
Ratford Wilts 62 E3
Ratfyn Wilts 47 E7
Rathen Aberds 303 C10
Rathillet Fife 287 E7
Rathmell N Yorks 204 B2
Ratho Edin 280 G2
Ratho Station Edin 280 G2
Rathven Moray 302 C4
Ratlake Hants 32 C6
Ratley Warks 101 B7
Ratling Kent 55 C8
Ratlinghope Shrops 131 D8
Ratsloe Devon 14 B5
Rattar Highld 310 B6
Ratten Row Cumb 230 B3
Ratten Row Cumb 230 C3
Ratten Row Lancs 202 E4
Ratten Row Norf 157 G10
Rattery Devon 8 C4
Rattlesden Suff 125 F9
Rattray Perth 286 C5
Raughton Cumb 230 B3
Raughton Head Cumb 230 B3
Raunds Northants 121 C9
Ravelston Edin 280 G4
Ravenfield S Yorks 187 B7
Ravenglass Cumb 219 F11
Ravenhead Mers 183 C8
Ravenhills Green Worcs 116 G4
Raveningham Norf 143 D7
Raven's Green Essex 108 G2
Ravenscar N Yorks 227 E9
Ravenscliffe Stoke 168 E4
Ravenscliffe W Yorks 205 F9
Ravenscraig Invclyd 276 F5
Ravensdale I o M 192 C4
Ravensden Beds 121 G11
Ravenseat N Yorks 223 E7
Ravenshall Staffs 168 F3
Ravenshead Notts 171 E9
Ravensmoor E Ches 167 E10
Ravensthorpe Northants 120 C3
Ravensthorpe P'boro 138 C3
Ravensthorpe W Yorks 197 C8
Ravenstone Leics 153 G8
Ravenstone M Keynes 120 G6
Ravenstonedale Cumb 222 E4
Ravenstown Cumb 211 D7
Ravenstruther S Lnrk 269 F8
Ravenswood Village Settlement Wokingham 65 G10
Ravensworth N Yorks 224 D2
Raw N Yorks 227 D8
Raw Green S Yorks 197 F9

Rawcliffe E Yorks 199 C7
Rawcliffe York 207 C7
Rawcliffe Bridge E Yorks 199 C7
Rawdon W Yorks 205 F10
Rawdon Carrs W Yorks 205 F10
Rawfolds W Yorks 197 C7
Rawgreen Northumb 241 F10
Rawmarsh S Yorks 186 B6
Rawnsley Staffs 151 G10
Rawreth Essex 88 G3
Rawreth Shot Essex 88 G3
Rawridge Devon 28 F2
Rawson Green Derbys 170 F5
Rawtenstall Lancs 195 C10
Rawthorpe W Yorks 197 D7
Rawyards N Lnrk 268 B5
Raxton Aberds 303 F8
Raydon Suff 107 D11
Raygill N Yorks 204 D4
Raylees Northumb 251 E10
Rayleigh Essex 88 G4
Rayne Essex 106 G4
Rayners Lane London 66 B6
Raynes Park London 67 F8
Reabrook Shrops 131 C7
Reach Cambs 123 D11
Read Lancs 203 G11
Reader's Corner Essex 88 E2
Reading Reading 65 E8
Reading Street Kent 54 G2
Reading Street Kent 71 F11
Readings Glos 79 B10
Ready Token Glos 81 E10
Readymoney Corn 6 E2
Reagill Cumb 222 B2
Rearquhar Highld 309 K7
Rearsby Leics 154 G3
Reasby Lincs 189 F9
Rease Heath E Ches 167 E10
Reaster Highld 310 C6
Reaulay Highld 299 D7
Reawick Shetland 313 J5
Reawla Corn 2 B4
Reay Highld 310 C3
Rechullin Highld 299 D8
Reculver Kent 71 F8
Red Ball Devon 27 D9
Red Bridge Lancs 211 D9
Red Bull E Ches 168 D4
Red Bull Staffs 150 B4
Red Dial Cumb 229 B11
Red Hill Bmouth 19 B7
Red Hill Hants 34 E2
Red Hill Hereford 97 D10
Red Hill Kent 53 C7
Red Hill Leics 135 D10
Red Hill Pembs 72 B6
Red Hill W Yorks 198 B2
Red Hill Warks 118 F2
Red Hill Worcs 117 G7
Red House Common E Sus 36 C5
Red Lake Telford 150 G3
Red Lodge Suff 124 C3
Red Lumb Gtr Man 195 D10
Red Pits Norf 159 D11
Red Post Corn 24 F3
Red Rail Hereford 97 F10
Red Rice Hants 47 E10
Red Rock Gtr Man 194 F5
Red Roses Carms 74 C2
Red Row Northumb 253 D7
Red Scar Lancs 203 G7
Red Street Staffs 168 E4
Red Wharf Bay Anglesey 179 E8
Redberth Pembs 73 E9
Redbourn Herts 85 C10
Redbournbury Herts 85 C10
Redbourne N Lincs 189 B7
Redbourne N Lincs 200 G3
Redbridge Dorset 17 D11
Redbridge London 68 B2
Redbridge Soton 32 E5
Redbrook Mon 79 C8
Redbrook Wrex 167 G8
Redburn Highld 300 C5
Redburn Highld 301 E9
Redburn Northumb 241 E7
Redcar Redcar 235 G8
Redcastle Angus 287 B10
Redcastle Highld 300 E5
Redcliff Bay N Som 60 D2
Redcroft Dumfries 237 B9
Redcross Worcs 117 C7
Reddicap Heath W Mid 134 D2
Redding Falk 279 F8
Reddingmuirhead Falk 279 F8
Reddish Gtr Man 184 C5
Reddish Warr 183 D11
Redditch Worcs 117 D10
Rede Suff 124 F6
Redenhall Norf 142 G5
Redenham Hants 47 D10
Redesdale Camp Northumb 251 D8
Redesmouth Northumb 251 G9
Redford Aberds 293 F9
Redford Angus 287 C9
Redford Dorset 29 F10
Redford Durham 233 E7
Redford W Sus 34 B5
Redfordgreen Borders 261 F9
Redgorton Perth 286 E4
Redgrave Suff 125 B10
Redheugh Angus 292 G6
Redhill Aberds 293 C9
Redhill Aberds 302 F6
Redhill Herts 104 E6
Redhill N Som 60 G4
Redhill Notts 171 F9
Redhill Shrops 131 B9
Redhill Shrops 150 G4
Redhill Staffs 150 D6
Redhill Sur 51 C9
Redhill Telford 150 G4
Redhills Cumb 230 F6
Redhills Devon 14 C4
Redhouse Argyll 275 G9
Redhouses Argyll 274 G4
Redisham Suff 143 G8
Redland Bristol 60 D5
Redland Orkney 314 D3
Redland End Bucks 84 E4
Redlands Dorset 17 E9
Redlands Som 44 G3
Redlands Swindon 81 G11
Redlane Som 28 E2
Redlingfield Suff 126 C3
Redlynch Som 45 G8
Redlynch Wilts 32 C2
Redmain Cumb 229 E8
Redmarley D'Abitot Glos 98 E5
Redmarshall Stockton 234 G3
Redmile Leics 154 B5
Redmire N Yorks 223 G10
Redmonsford Devon 24 D4
Redmoor Corn 5 C11
Redmoss Aberds 293 C11
Rednal Shrops 149 D7
Rednal W Mid 117 B10
Redpath Borders 262 B3
Redpoint Highld 299 C7
Redruth Corn 4 G3
Redscarhead Borders 270 G4
Redstocks Wilts 62 G2
Redtye Corn 5 C10
Redvales Gtr Man 195 F10
Redwick Newport 60 C2
Redwick S Glos 60 B4
Redwith Shrops 148 E6
Redworth Darl 233 G10
Reed Herts 105 D7
Reed End Herts 104 D6
Reed Point Lincs 174 E2
Reedham Lincs 174 D2
Reedham Norf 143 C8
Reedley Lancs 204 F2
Reedness E Yorks 199 C9
Reeds Beck Lincs 174 B2
Reeds Holme Lancs 195 C10
Reedsford Northumb 263 C9
Reedy Devon 14 D2
Reen Manor Corn 4 E5
Reepham Lincs 189 G8
Reepham Norf 159 E11
Reeth N Yorks 223 F10
Reeves Green W Mid 118 B5
Refail Powys 130 C3
Regaby I o M 192 C5
Regil Bath 60 G4
Regoul Highld 301 D8
Reiff Highld 307 H4
Reigate Sur 51 C9
Reigate Heath Sur 51 C8
Reighton N Yorks 218 D2
Reighton Gap N Yorks 218 D2
Reinigeadal W Isles 305 H4
Reisque Aberds 293 B10
Reiss Highld 310 D7
Rejerrah Corn 4 D5
Releath Corn 2 C5
Relubbus Corn 2 C3
Relugas Moray 301 E9
Remenham Wokingham 65 C9
Remenham Hill Wokingham 65 C9
Remony Perth 285 C11
Rempstone Notts 153 E11
Remusaig Highld 309 J7
Rendcomb Glos 81 D8
Rendham Suff 126 E6
Rendlesham Suff 126 G6
Renfrew Renfs 267 B10
Renhold Beds 121 G11
Renishaw Derbys 186 F6
Renmure Angus 287 B10
Rennington Northumb 264 F6
Renshaw Wood Shrops 132 B6
Renton W Dunb 277 F7
Renwick Cumb 231 C7
Repps Norf 161 F8
Repton Derbys 152 D6
Reraig Highld 295 C10
Reraig Cot Highld 295 B10
Rerwick Shetland 313 M5
Rescassa Corn 5 G9
Rescobie Angus 287 B9
Rescorla Corn 5 D10
Resipole Highld 289 C9
Reskadinnick Corn 4 G2
Resolfen = Resolven Neath 76 E4
Resolis Highld 300 C6
Resolven = Resolfen Neath 76 E4
Restalrig Edin 280 G5
Reston Borders 273 C7
Reston Cumb 221 F9
Restronguet Passage Corn 3 B8
Restrop Wilts 62 B5
Resugga Green Corn 5 D10
Reswallie Angus 287 B9
Retallack Corn 5 B8
Retew Corn 5 D8
Retford Notts 188 E2
Retire Corn 5 C10
Rettendon Essex 88 F3
Rettendon Place Essex 88 F3
Revesby Lincs 174 C3
Revesby Bridge Lincs 174 C4
Revidge Blkburn 195 B7
Rew Devon 9 G9
Rew Devon 13 G11
Rew Dorset 29 F11
Rew Street I o W 20 C5
Rewe Devon 14 B4
Rexon Devon 12 D4
Rexon Cross Devon 12 D4
Reybridge Wilts 62 F2
Reydon Suff 127 B9
Reydon Smear Suff 127 B9
Reymerston Norf 141 B10
Reynalton Pembs 73 D9
Reynoldston Swansea 56 C3
Rezare Corn 12 F3
Rhadyr Mon 78 E5
Rhaeadr Gwy = Rhayader Powys 113 D9
Rhandir Conwy 180 G4
Rhandirmwyn Carms 94 C5
Rhayader = Rhaeadr Gwy Powys 113 D9
Rhedyn Gwyn 144 C5
Rhegreanoch Highld 307 H5
Rhemore Highld 289 D7
Rhencullen I o M 192 C4
Rhenetra Highld 298 D4
Rhes-y-cae Flint 181 G11
Rhewl Denb 165 C10
Rhewl Denb 165 F11
Rhewl Shrops 148 C6
Rhewl Wrex 149 B7
Rhewl-fawr Flint 181 E10
Rhewl-Mostyn Flint 181 E11
Rhian Highld 309 H5
Rhicarn Highld 307 G5
Rhiconich Highld 306 D7
Rhicullen Highld 300 B6
Rhidorroch Ho Highld 307 K6
Rhifail Highld 308 E7
Rhigolter Highld 308 D3
Rhigos Rhondda 76 D6
Rhilochan Highld 309 J7
Rhippinllwyd Ceredig 92 C5
Rhippinllwyd Ceredig 110 G6
Rhiroy Highld 307 L6
Rhitongue Highld 308 D6
Rhivichie Highld 306 D7
Rhiw Gwyn 144 D4
Rhiwabon = Ruabon Wrex 166 G4
Rhiwbebyll Denb 165 B10
Rhiwbina Cardiff 59 C7
Rhiwbryfdir Gwyn 163 F11
Rhiwceiliog Bridgend 58 C3
Rhiwderin Newport 59 B9
Rhiwen Gwyn 163 C9
Rhiwfawr Neath 76 C2
Rhiwinder Rhondda 58 B4
Rhiwlas Gwyn 147 B8
Rhiwlas Gwyn 163 B9
Rhiwlas Powys 148 C3
Rhode Som 43 G9
Rhode Common Kent 54 B5
Rhodes Gtr Man 195 F11
Rhodes Minnis Kent 55 E7
Rhodesia Notts 187 F9
Rhodiad Pembs 90 F5
Rhondda Rhondda 77 F7
Rhonadale Argyll 255 D8
Rhonehouse or Kelton Hill Dumfries 237 D9
Rhoose V Glam 58 F5
Rhos Carms 93 D7
Rhôs Neath 76 E2
Rhôs Denb 165 C10
Rhos Powys 148 F5
Rhôs Common Powys 148 F5
Rhos-ddû Gwyn 144 B5
Rhos-fawr Gwyn 145 B7
Rhos-goch Powys 96 B3
Rhos Haminiog Ceredig 111 E10
Rhos-hill Pembs 92 C3
Rhos Isaf Gwyn 163 D7
Rhôs Lligwy Anglesey 179 D7
Rhôs-on-Sea Conwy 180 E4
Rhos-y-brithdir Powys 148 E2
Rhos-y-garth Ceredig 112 C2
Rhos-y-gwaliau Gwyn 147 C8
Rhos-y-llan Gwyn 144 B4
Rhos-y-Madoc Wrex 166 G4
Rhos-y-meirch Powys 114 D5
Rhosaman Carms 76 C2
Rhosbeirio Anglesey 178 C5
Rhoscefnhir Anglesey 179 F8
Rhoscolyn Anglesey 178 F3
Rhoscrowther Pembs 72 E6
Rhosddu Wrex 166 E4
Rhosdylluan Gwyn 147 D7
Rhosesmor Flint 166 B2
Rhosfach Pembs 92 F2
Rhosgadfan Gwyn 163 D8
Rhosgoch Anglesey 178 D6
Rhosgoch Powys 96 B3
Rhosgyll Gwyn 163 G7
Rhoshirwaun Gwyn 144 D3
Rhoslan Gwyn 163 G7
Rhoslefain Gwyn 110 B2
Rhosllanerchrugog Wrex 166 F3
Rhosmaen Carms 94 G2
Rhosmeirch Anglesey 179 F7
Rhosneigr Anglesey 178 G4
Rhosnesni Wrex 166 E5
Rhosrobin Wrex 166 E4
Rhossili Swansea 56 D2
Rhosson Pembs 90 F4
Rhostrehwfa Anglesey 178 G6
Rhostryfan Gwyn 163 D7
Rhostyllen Wrex 166 F4
Rhoswiel Shrops 148 B5
Rhosybol Anglesey 178 D6
Rhosycaerau Pembs 91 D8
Rhosygadair Newydd Ceredig 92 B4
Rhosygadfa Shrops 148 C6
Rhosygilwen Pembs 92 C4
Rhosymedre Wrex 166 G3
Rhosyn-coch Carms 92 G5
Rhu Argyll 275 G9
Rhu Argyll 276 E5
Rhuallt Denb 181 F9
Rhubodach Argyll 275 F11
Rhuddall Heath W Ches 167 C9
Rhuddlan Ceredig 93 C9
Rhuddlan Denb 181 F8
Rhue Highld 307 K5
Rhulen Powys 96 B2
Rhunahaorine Argyll 255 C8
Rhyd Ceredig 92 C5
Rhyd Gwyn 163 G10
Rhyd Powys 129 C9
Rhyd-Ddu Gwyn 163 E9
Rhyd-Rosser Ceredig 111 D11
Rhyd-uchaf Gwyn 147 B8
Rhyd-y-Brown Pembs 91 G11
Rhyd-y-clafdy Gwyn 144 B6
Rhyd-y-cwm Shrops 130 G3
Rhyd-y-foel Conwy 180 F6
Rhyd-y-fro Neath 76 D2
Rhyd-y-gwin Swansea 75 E11
Rhyd-y-gwystl Gwyn 145 B8
Rhyd-y-meirch Mon 78 D4
Rhyd-y-meudwy Denb 165 E10
Rhyd-y-pandy Swansea 75 E11
Rhyd-y-sarn Gwyn 163 G11
Rhyd-yr-onen Gwyn 128 C2
Rhydaman = Ammanford Carms 75 C10
Rhydargaeau Carms 93 F8
Rhydcymerau Carms 93 D11
Rhydd Worcs 98 B6
Rhydd Green Worcs 98 B6
Rhydding Neath 57 B8
Rhydfudr Ceredig 111 D11
Rhydgaled Conwy 165 C7
Rhydgaled = Chancery Ceredig 111 B11
Rhydlewis Ceredig 92 B6
Rhydlios Gwyn 144 C3
Rhydlydan Conwy 164 E5
Rhydlydan Powys 129 E11
Rhydmoelddu Powys 113 B11
Rhydness Powys 96 C2
Rhydowen Carms 92 F3
Rhydowen Ceredig 93 B8
Rhydspence Hereford 96 B4
Rhydtalog Flint 166 D2
Rhydwen Gwyn 146 F4
Rhydwyn Anglesey 178 D4
Rhydycroesau Powys 148 C4
Rhydyfelin Carms 92 D6
Rhydyfelin Ceredig 111 B11
Rhydyfelin Powys 129 E11
Rhydyfelin Rhondda 58 B5
Rhydygele Pembs 91 G7
Rhydymain Gwyn 146 E6
Rhydymwyn Flint 166 B2
Rhydywrach Carms 73 B11
Rhyl Denb 181 E8
Rhymney Caerph 77 D10
Rhyn Wrex 148 B6
Rhynd Fife 287 E8
Rhynd Perth 286 E5
Rhynie Aberds 302 G4
Rhynie Highld 301 B8
Ribbesford Worcs 116 C5
Ribble Head N Yorks 212 D5
Ribblehead N Yorks 212 D5
Ribbleton Lancs 203 G7
Ribby Lancs 202 G4
Ribchester Lancs 203 F8
Riber Derbys 170 D4
Ribigill Highld 308 D5
Riby Lincs 201 F7
Riby Cross Roads Lincs 201 F7
Riccall N Yorks 207 F8
Riccarton E Ayrs 257 B10
Richards Castle Hereford 115 D9
Richborough Port Kent 71 G10
Richings Park Bucks 66 D4
Richmond London 67 E7
Richmond N Yorks 224 E3
Richmond S Yorks 186 D6
Richmond Hill W Yorks 206 G2
Richmond's Green Essex 106 F2
Rich's Holford Som 42 G6
Rickard's Down Devon 24 B6
Rickarton Aberds 293 E10
Rickerby Cumb 239 F10
Rickerscote Staffs 151 E8
Rickford N Som 44 B3
Rickinghall Suff 125 B10
Rickleton T & W 243 G7
Rickling Essex 105 E9
Rickling Green Essex 105 F10
Rickmansworth Herts 85 G9
Rickney E Sus 23 D10
Riddell Borders 262 E2
Riddings Derbys 170 E6
Riddlecombe Devon 25 E10
Riddlesden W Yorks 205 E7
Riddrie Glasgow 268 B2
Ridgacre W Mid 133 G10
Ridge Bath 44 B5
Ridge Dorset 18 D4
Ridge Hants 32 D4
Ridge Herts 86 E2
Ridge Lancs 211 G9
Ridge Som 28 F3
Ridge Wilts 46 G3
Ridge Common Hants 34 C2
Ridge Green Sur 51 D10
Ridge Hill Gtr Man 185 B7
Ridge Lane Warks 134 E5
Ridge Row Kent 55 E8
Ridgebourne Powys 113 E11
Ridgehill N Som 60 G4
Ridgemarsh Herts 85 G8
Ridgeway Bristol 60 D6
Ridgeway Derbys 170 E5
Ridgeway Derbys 186 E6
Ridgeway Kent 54 E5
Ridgeway Newport 59 B9
Ridgeway Pembs 73 D10
Ridgeway Som 45 D8
Ridgeway Staffs 168 E5
Ridgeway Cross Hereford 98 B4
Ridgeway Moor Derbys 186 E6
Ridgewell Essex 106 C4
Ridgewood E Sus 23 B7
Ridgmont C Beds 103 D9
Ridgway Shrops 131 F7
Ridgway Sur 50 B4
Riding Gate Som 30 B2
Riding Mill Northumb 242 E2
Ridley Kent 68 G6
Ridley Northumb 241 E7
Ridley Stokoe Northumb 250 F6
Ridleywood Wrex 166 E6
Ridlington Norf 160 C6
Ridlington Rutland 136 C6
Ridlington Street Norf 160 C6
Ridsdale Northumb 251 G10
Riechip Perth 286 C4
Riemore Perth 286 C4
Rienachait Highld 306 F5
Rievaulx N Yorks 215 B11
Riff Orkney 314 E4
Riffin Aberds 303 E7
Rifle Green Torf 78 D3
Rift House Hrtlpl 234 E5
Rigg Dumfries 239 D7
Riggend N Lnrk 278 G5
Rigsby Lincs 190 F6
Rigside S Lnrk 259 B9
Riley Green Lancs 194 B6
Rileyhill Staffs 152 F2
Rilla Mill Corn 11 G11
Rillaton Corn 11 G11
Rillington N Yorks 217 E7
Rimac Lincs 191 C7
Rimington Lancs 204 D2
Rimpton Som 29 C10
Rimswell E Yorks 201 B10
Rimswell Valley E Yorks 201 B10
Rinaston Pembs 91 F9
Rindleford Shrops 132 D4
Ring o' Bells Lancs 194 E3
Ringasta Shetland 313 M5
Ringford Dumfries 237 D8
Ringing Hill Leics 153 F9
Ringinglow S Yorks 186 E3
Ringland Newport 59 B11
Ringland Norf 160 G2
Ringles Cross E Sus 37 C7
Ringlestone Kent 53 B11
Ringlestone Kent 53 B9
Ringley Gtr Man 195 F9
Ringmer E Sus 36 E6
Ringmore Devon 8 F3
Ringmore Devon 14 G4
Ringorm Moray 302 E2
Ring's End Cambs 139 C7
Ringsfield Suff 143 F8
Ringsfield Corner Suff 143 F8
Ringshall Herts 85 C7
Ringshall Suff 125 G10
Ringshall Stocks Suff 125 G10
Ringstead Norf 176 E2
Ringstead Northants 121 B9
Ringtail Green Essex 87 B11
Ringwood Hants 31 F11
Ringwould Kent 55 D11
Rinmore Aberds 292 B6
Rinnigill Orkney 314 G3
Rinsey Corn 2 D3
Rinsey Croft Corn 2 D4
Riof W Isles 304 E3
Ripe E Sus 23 C8
Ripley Derbys 170 E5
Ripley Hants 19 B9
Ripley N Yorks 214 G5
Ripley Sur 50 B5
Riplingham E Yorks 208 G5
Ripon N Yorks 214 E6
Ripper's Cross Kent 54 E3
Rippingale Lincs 155 D11
Ripple Kent 55 D10
Ripple Worcs 99 D7
Ripponden W Yorks 196 D4
Rireavach Highld 307 K5
Risabus Argyll 254 C4
Risbury Hereford 115 G10
Risby E Yorks 208 G6
Risby Lincs 189 C10
Risby Suff 124 D5
Risca Caerph 78 G2
Rise E Yorks 209 E9
Rise Carr Darl 224 B5
Rise End Derbys 170 D3
Rise Park London 87 G8
Rise Park Nottingham 171 F9
Riseden E Sus 52 G6
Riseden Kent 53 F8
Risegate Lincs 156 D4
Riseholme Lincs 189 F7
Risehow Cumb 228 E6
Riseley Beds 121 E10
Riseley Wokingham 65 G8
Rishangles Suff 126 D3
Rishton Lancs 203 G10
Rishworth W Yorks 196 D4
Rising Bridge Lancs 195 B9
Rising Sun Corn 12 G3
Risingbrook Staffs 151 E8
Risinghurst Oxon 83 D9
Risley Derbys 153 B9
Risley Warr 183 C10
Risplith N Yorks 214 F4
Rispond Highld 308 C4
Rivar Wilts 63 G10
Rivenhall Essex 88 B4
Rivenhall End Essex 88 B4
River Kent 55 E9
River W Sus 34 C6
River Bank Cambs 123 D10
Riverhead Kent 52 B4
Rivers' Corner Dorset 30 E3
Riverside Cardiff 59 D7
Riverside Plym 7 D8
Riverside Stirl 278 C6
Riverside Worcs 117 D10
Riverside Docklands Lancs 194 B4
Riverton Devon 40 G6
Riverview Park Kent 69 E7
Rivington Lancs 194 E6
Rixon Dorset 30 E3
Rixton Warr 183 C11
Roa Island Cumb 210 G4
Roach Bridge Lancs 194 B5
Roaches Gtr Man 196 G3
Roachill Devon 26 C4
Road Green Norf 142 E5
Road Weedon Northants 120 F2
Roade Northants 120 G5
Roadhead Cumb 240 C2
Roadmeetings S Lnrk 269 F7
Roadside Highld 310 C5
Roadside of Catterline Aberds 293 F10
Roadside of Kinneff Aberds 293 F10
Roadwater Som 42 F4
Roag Highld 298 E2
Roast Green Essex 105 E9
Roath Cardiff 59 D7
Roath Park Cardiff 59 D7
Rob Roy's House Argyll 284 F5
Roberton Borders 261 G10
Roberton S Lnrk 259 D10
Robertsbridge E Sus 38 C2
Robertstown Moray 302 E2
Robertstown Rhondda 77 E8
Roberttown W Yorks 197 C7
Robeston Back Pembs 73 B9
Robeston Cross Pembs 72 D5
Robeston Wathen Pembs 73 B9
Robeston West Pembs 72 D5
Robhurst Kent 54 G2
Robin Hill Staffs 168 D6
Robin Hood Derbys 186 G3
Robin Hood Lancs 194 E4
Robin Hood W Yorks 197 B10
Robin Hood's Bay N Yorks 227 D9
Robinhood End Essex 106 D4
Robins W Sus 34 B4
Robinson's End Warks 134 E6
Roborough Devon 7 C10
Roborough Devon 25 D9
Robroyston Glasgow 268 B2
Roby Mers 182 C6
Roby Mill Lancs 194 F4
Rocester Staffs 152 B2
Roch Pembs 91 G7
Roch Gate Pembs 91 G7
Rochdale Gtr Man 195 E11
Roche Corn 5 C9
Roche Grange Staffs 169 C7
Rochester Medway 69 F8
Rochester Northumb 251 D8
Rochford Essex 88 G5
Rochford Worcs 116 D2
Rock Caerph 77 F11
Rock Corn 10 F4
Rock Devon 28 G3
Rock Neath 57 C9
Rock Northumb 264 E6
Rock Som 28 C4
Rock W Sus 35 E10
Rock Worcs 116 C4
Rock End Staffs 168 D5
Rock Ferry Mers 182 D4
Rockbeare Devon 14 C6
Rockbourne Hants 31 D10
Rockcliffe Cumb 239 E9
Rockcliffe Dumfries 237 D10
Rockcliffe Flint 182 G3
Rockcliffe Lancs 195 C11
Rockcliffe Cross Cumb 239 E8
Rockfield Highld 311 L3
Rockfield Mon 79 C7
Rockford Devon 41 D9
Rockford Hants 31 F11
Rockgreen Shrops 115 B10
Rockhampton S Glos 79 G11
Rockhead Corn 11 E7
Rockhill Shrops 114 B5
Rockingham Northants 137 E7
Rockland All Saints Norf 141 D9
Rockland St Mary Norf 142 C6
Rockland St Peter Norf 141 D9
Rockley Notts 188 G2
Rockley Wilts 63 E7
Rockley Ford Som 45 C8
Rockness Glos 80 F4
Rockrobin E Sus 52 G6
Rocks Park E Sus 37 C7
Rocksavage Halton 183 E8
Rockstowes Glos 80 F3
Rockville Argyll 276 C4
Rockwell End Bucks 65 B9
Rockwell Green Som 27 C10
Rocky Hill Scilly 1 G4
Rodbaston Staffs 151 G8
Rodborough Glos 80 E4
Rodbourne Swindon 62 C6
Rodbourne Wilts 62 C2
Rodbourne Bottom Wilts 62 C2
Rodbourne Cheney Swindon 62 B6
Rodbridge Corner Essex 107 C7
Rodd Hereford 114 E6
Rodd Hurst Hereford 114 E6
Roddam Northumb 264 E2
Rodden Dorset 17 E8
Roddymoor Durham 233 D9
Rode Som 45 C10
Rode Heath E Ches 168 D3
Rode Hill Som 45 C10
Rodeheath E Ches 168 B5
Roden Telford 149 F11
Rodford S Glos 61 C7
Rodgrove Som 30 C2
Rodhuish Som 42 F4
Rodington Telford 149 G11
Rodington Heath Telford 149 G11
Rodley Glos 80 C2
Rodley W Yorks 205 F10
Rodmarton Glos 80 F6
Rodmell E Sus 36 F6
Rodmer Clough W Yorks 196 B3
Rodmersham Kent 70 G2
Rodmersham Green Kent 70 G2
Rodney Stoke Som 44 C3
Rodsley Derbys 170 G2
Rodway Som 43 F9
Rodway Telford 150 F3
Rodwell Dorset 17 F9
Roe Cross Gtr Man 185 B7
Roe End Herts 85 B8
Roe Green Gtr Man 195 G9
Roe Green Herts 86 D2
Roe Green Herts 104 E6
Roe Lee Blkburn 203 G9
Roebuck Low Gtr Man 196 F3
Roecliffe N Yorks 215 F7
Roedean Brighton 36 G4
Roehampton London 67 E8
Roesound Shetland 312 G5
Roestock Herts 86 D2
Roffey W Sus 51 G7
Rogart Highld 309 J7
Rogart Station Highld 309 J7
Rogate W Sus 34 C4
Roger Ground Cumb 221 F7
Rogerstone Newport 59 B9
Rogerton S Lnrk 268 D2
Rogiet Mon 60 B3
Rogue's Alley Cambs 139 B7
Roke Oxon 83 G10
Rokemarsh Oxon 83 G10
Roker T & W 243 F10
Rollesby Norf 161 F8
Rolleston Leics 136 C4
Rolleston Notts 172 E2
Rolleston-on-Dove Staffs 152 D4
Rollestone S Yorks 186 E5
Rollestone Wilts 46 E5
Rollestone Camp Wilts 46 E5
Rolls Mill Dorset 30 E3
Rolston E Yorks 209 D10
Rolstone N Som 59 G11
Rolvenden Kent 53 G10
Rolvenden Layne Kent 53 G11
Romaldkirk Durham 232 G5
Roman Hill Suff 143 E10
Romanby N Yorks 225 G7
Romannobridge Borders 270 F3
Romansleigh Devon 26 C2
Rome Angus 293 G7
Romesdal Highld 298 D4
Romford Dorset 31 F9
Romford Kent 52 E6
Romford London 68 B4
Romiley Gtr Man 184 C6
Romney Street Kent 68 G4
Rompa Shetland 313 L6
Romsey Hants 32 C5
Romsey Town Cambs 123 F9
Romsley Shrops 132 G5
Romsley Worcs 117 B9
Romsley Hill Worcs 117 B9
Ronachan Ho Argyll 255 B8
Ronague I o M 192 E3
Rondlay Telford 132 B4
Ronkswood Worcs 117 G7
Rood End W Mid 133 F10
Rook End Essex 105 E11
Rook Street Wilts 45 G10
Rookby Cumb 222 C6
Rookhope Durham 232 C4
Rooking Cumb 221 B8
Rookley I o W 20 E6
Rookley Green I o W 20 E6
Rooks Bridge Som 43 C11
Rooks Hill Kent 52 C5
Rook's Nest Som 42 G5
Rooksey Green Suff 125 G8
Rooksmoor Glos 80 E4
Rookwith N Yorks 214 B4
Rookwood W Sus 21 B11
Roos E Yorks 209 G11
Roose Cumb 210 F4
Roosebeck Cumb 210 F5
Roosecote Cumb 210 F4
Roost End Essex 106 C4
Rootham's Green Beds 122 F2
Rooting Street Kent 54 D3
Rootpark S Lnrk 269 E9
Ropley Hants 48 G6
Ropley Dean Hants 48 G5
Ropley Soke Hants 49 G7
Ropsley Lincs 155 C9
Rora Aberds 303 D10
Rorandle Aberds 293 B8
Rorrington Shrops 130 C5
Rosarie Moray 302 E3
Roscroggan Corn 4 G3
Rose Corn 4 E5
Rose-an-Grouse Corn 2 B2
Rose Ash Devon 26 C3
Rose Green Essex 107 F8
Rose Green Suff 107 C9
Rose Green Suff 107 D8
Rose Green W Sus 22 D6
Rose Grove Lancs 204 G2
Rose Hill Bucks 66 C2
Rose Hill Derbys 153 B7
Rose Hill E Sus 23 B7
Rose Hill Gtr Man 195 F8
Rose Hill Lancs 204 G2
Rose Hill Oxon 83 E8
Rose Hill Suff 108 C3
Rose Hill Sur 51 D7
Rose Valley Pembs 73 E8
Roseacre Kent 53 B9
Roseacre Lancs 202 F4
Rosebank E Dunb 278 G3
Rosebank S Lnrk 268 F6
Rosebery Midloth 270 D6
Rosebrae Moray 301 C11
Rosebrough Northumb 264 D4
Rosebush Pembs 91 F11
Rosecare Corn 11 B9
Rosedale Herts 86 E4
Rosedale Abbey N Yorks 226 F4
Roseden Northumb 264 E2
Rosedinnick Corn 5 B8
Rosedown Devon 24 C3
Rosefield Highld 301 D8
Rosehall Highld 309 J4
Rosehall N Lnrk 268 C4
Rosehaugh Mains Highld 300 D6
Rosehearty Aberds 303 C9
Rosehill Blkburn 195 C8
Rosehill Corn 4 E5
Rosehill Corn 5 C10
Rosehill Gtr Man 184 D3
Rosehill London 67 F9
Rosehill Pembs 72 B5
Rosehill Shrops 150 C3
Rosehill T & W 243 D8
Roseisle Moray 301 C11
Roseland Corn 6 C5
Roselands E Sus 23 E10
Rosemarket Pembs 73 D7
Rosemarkie Highld 301 D7
Rosemary Lane Devon 27 E11
Rosemelling Corn 5 D10
Rosemergy Corn 1 B4
Rosemount Perth 286 C5
Rosenannon Corn 5 B9
Rosenithon Corn 3 E8
Roser's Cross E Sus 37 C9
Rosevean Corn 5 D10
Rosevear Corn 2 E5
Roseville W Mid 133 E8
Rosevine Corn 3 B9
Rosewarne Corn 2 B4
Rosewarne Corn 4 G2
Rosewell Midloth 270 C5
Roseworth Stockton 234 G4
Roseworthy Corn 2 B4
Roseworthy Corn 4 F5
Roseworthy Barton Corn 2 B4
Rosgill Cumb 221 B10
Rosherville Kent 68 E6
Roshven Highld 289 B9
Roskear Croft Corn 4 G3
Roskhill Highld 298 E2
Roskill House Highld 300 D6
Roskorwell Corn 3 E7
Rosley Cumb 230 B2
Roslin Midloth 270 C5
Rosliston Derbys 152 F4
Rosneath Argyll 276 E5
Ross Borders 273 C9
Ross Dumfries 237 E8
Ross Northumb 264 B4
Ross Perth 285 E11
Ross Green Worcs 116 E5
Ross-on-Wye Hereford 98 G2
Rossett Wrex 166 D5
Rossett Green N Yorks 206 C2
Rossie Ochill Perth 286 F4
Rossie Priory Perth 286 D6
Rossington S Yorks 187 B10
Rosskeen Highld 300 C6
Rossland Renfs 277 G8
Rossmore Poole 19 C7
Roster Highld 310 F6
Rostherne E Ches 184 E2
Rostholme S Yorks 198 F5
Rosthwaite Cumb 220 C5
Rosthwaite Cumb 220 G4
Roston Derbys 169 G10
Rosudgeon Corn 2 D3
Rosyth Fife 280 E2
Rotchfords Essex 107 E8
Rotcombe Bath 44 B6
Rothbury Northumb 252 C3
Rotherbridge W Sus 35 C7
Rotherby Leics 154 F3
Rotherfield E Sus 37 B9
Rotherfield Greys Oxon 65 C8
Rotherfield Peppard Oxon 65 C8
Rotherham S Yorks 186 C6
Rotherhithe London 67 D11
Rothersthorpe Northants 120 F4
Rotherwas Hereford 97 D10
Rotherwick Hants 49 B8
Rothes Moray 302 E2
Rothesay Argyll 275 G11
Rothiebrisbane Aberds 303 F7
Rothiemay Crossroads Moray 302 E5
Rothiemurchus Lodge Highld 291 C11
Rothienorman Aberds 303 F7
Rothiesholm Orkney 314 D6
Rothley Leics 153 G11
Rothley Northumb 252 F2
Rothley Plain Leics 153 G11
Rothley Shield East Northumb 252 E2
Rothmaise Aberds 302 F6
Rothwell Lincs 189 B11
Rothwell Northants 136 G6
Rothwell W Yorks 197 B10
Rothwell Haigh W Yorks 197 B10
Rotsea E Yorks 209 C7
Rottal Angus 292 G5
Rotten End Essex 106 F4
Rotten End Suff 127 D7
Rotten Green Hants 49 B9
Rotten Row W Berks 64 E5
Rotten Row W Mid 118 B3
Rottingdean Brighton 36 G5
Rottington Cumb 219 C9
Rotton Park W Mid 133 F10
Roud I o W 20 E6
Rough Bank Gtr Man 196 E2
Rough Close Staffs 151 B8
Rough Common Kent 54 B6
Rough Haugh Highld 308 E7
Rough Hay Staffs 152 E4
Rougham Norf 158 E6
Rougham Suff 125 E8
Rougham Green Suff 125 E8
Roughbirchworth S Yorks 197 G9
Roughburn Highld 290 E5
Roughcote Staffs 168 G6
Roughlee Lancs 204 E2
Roughley W Mid 134 D2
Roughmoor Som 28 B2
Roughmoor Swindon 62 B6
Roughrigg N Lnrk 278 G6
Roughsike Cumb 240 B2
Roughton Lincs 174 C2
Roughton Norf 160 B4
Roughton Shrops 132 E5
Roughton Moor Lincs 174 C2
Roughway Kent 52 C6
Round Bush Herts 85 F10
Round Green Luton 103 G11
Round Maple Suff 107 C9
Round Oak Shrops 131 G7
Round Oak W Mid 133 F8
Round Spinney Northants 120 D5
Round Street Kent 69 F7
Roundbush Essex 88 E5
Roundbush Green Essex 87 C9
Roundham Som 28 F6
Roundhay W Yorks 206 F2
Round's Green W Mid 133 F9
Roundshaw London 67 G10
Roundstonefoot Dumfries 248 B4
Roundstreet Common W Sus 35 B9
Roundswell Devon 40 G4
Roundthorn Gtr Man 184 D4
Roundthwaite Cumb 222 E2
Roundway Wilts 62 G4
Roundyhill Angus 287 B7
Rous Lench Worcs 117 G10
Rousdon Devon 15 C11
Rousham Oxon 101 G9
Routenburn N Ayrs 266 C3
Routh E Yorks 209 E7
Rout's Green Bucks 84 F3
Row Corn 11 F7
Row Cumb 211 B8
Row Cumb 231 E8
Row Ash Hants 33 E8
Row Brow Cumb 229 D7
Row Green Essex 106 G4
Row Heath Essex 89 B10
Row-of-trees E Ches 184 F4
Row Town Sur 66 G4
Rowanburn Dumfries 239 B10
Rowanfield Glos 99 G8
Rowardennan Stirl 277 B7
Rowarth Derbys 185 D8
Rowbarton Som 28 B2
Rowberrow Som 44 B3
Rowde Wilts 62 G3
Rowden Devon 13 B8
Rowden N Yorks 205 B11
Rowe Head Cumb 210 D5
Rowen Conwy 180 G3
Rowfoot Northumb 240 E5
Rowford Som 28 B2
Rowhedge Essex 107 G10
Rowhill Sur 66 G4
Rowhook W Sus 50 G6
Rowington Warks 118 D4
Rowington Green Warks 118 D4
Rowland Derbys 186 G2
Rowlands Castle Hants 34 E2
Rowlands Gill T & W 242 F5
Rowland's Green Hereford 98 D3
Rowledge Sur 49 E10
Rowlestone Hereford 97 F7
Rowley E Yorks 208 G5
Rowley Shrops 130 B6
Rowley Green London 86 F2
Rowley Hill W Yorks 197 E7
Rowley Park Staffs 151 E8
Rowley Regis W Mid 133 F9
Rowley's Green W Mid 134 G6
Rowling Kent 55 C9
Rowly Sur 50 E4
Rownall Staffs 169 F7
Rowner Hants 33 G9
Rowney Green Worcs 117 C10
Rownhams Hants 32 D5
Rowrah Cumb 219 B11
Rowsham Bucks 84 B4
Rowsley Derbys 170 B3
Rowstock Oxon 64 B3
Rowston Lincs 173 D9
Rowthorne Derbys 171 C7
Rowton Shrops 149 G7
Rowton Telford 150 F2
Rowton W Ches 166 C6
Rowton Moor W Ches 166 C6
Roxburgh Borders 262 C5
Roxburgh Mains Borders 262 D5
Roxby N Lincs 200 D2
Roxby N Yorks 226 B5
Roxeth London 66 B6
Roxton Beds 122 G3
Roxwell Essex 87 D10
Royal British Legion Village Kent 53 B8
Royal Leamington Spa Warks 118 D6
Royal Oak Darl 233 G10
Royal Oak Lancs 194 G2
Royal Oak N Yorks 218 D2
Royal Tunbridge Wells = Tunbridge Wells Kent 52 F5
Royal Wootton Bassett Wilts 62 C5
Royal's Green E Ches 167 G10
Roybridge Highld 290 E4
Royd S Yorks 197 G8
Royd Moor S Yorks 197 G8
Royd Moor W Yorks 198 E2
Roydhouse W Yorks 197 E8
Roydon Essex 86 D6
Roydon Norf 141 G11
Roydon Norf 158 E4
Roydon Hamlet Essex 86 D6
Royds Green W Yorks 197 B11
Royston Glasgow 268 B2
Royston Herts 105 C7
Royston S Yorks 197 E11
Royston Water Som 28 E2
Royton Gtr Man 196 F2
Ruabon = Rhiwabon Wrex 166 G4
Ruaig Argyll 288 E2
Ruan High Lanes Corn 3 B10
Ruan Lanihorne Corn 5 G7
Ruan Major Corn 2 F6
Ruan Minor Corn 2 F6
Ruarach Highld 295 C11
Ruardean Glos 79 B10
Ruardean Hill Glos 79 B10
Ruardean Woodside Glos 79 B10
Rubery Worcs 117 B9
Rubha Ghaisinis W Isles 297 G4
Rubha Stoer Highld 306 F5
Ruchazie Glasgow 268 B3
Ruchill Glasgow 267 B11
Ruckcroft Cumb 230 C6
Ruckhall Hereford 97 D9
Ruckinge Kent 54 G4
Ruckland Lincs 190 F4
Rucklers Lane Herts 85 E9
Ruckley Shrops 131 C10
Rudbaxton Pembs 91 G9
Rudby N Yorks 225 D9
Ruddington Notts 153 C11
Ruddle Glos 79 C11
Rudford Glos 98 G5
Rudge Shrops 132 D6
Rudge Som 45 C10
Rudge Heath Shrops 132 D5
Rudgeway S Glos 60 B6
Rudgwick W Sus 50 G5
Rudhall Hereford 98 F2
Rudheath W Ches 183 G11
Rudheath Woods W Ches 184 G2
Rudhja Garbh Argyll 289 E11
Rudley Green Essex 88 E4
Rudloe Wilts 61 E10
Rudry Caerph 59 B7
Rudston E Yorks 217 F11
Rudyard Staffs 169 D7
Ruewood Shrops 149 D9
Rufford Lancs 194 D3
Rufforth York 206 C6
Ruffs Notts 171 F8
Rugby Warks 119 B10
Rugeley Staffs 151 F10
Ruggin Som 27 D11
Ruglen S Ayrs 245 C7
Rugley Northumb 264 G5
Ruilick Highld 300 E5
Ruishton Som 28 C3
Ruisigearraidh W Isles 296 C5
Ruislip London 66 B5
Ruislip Common London 66 B5
Ruislip Gardens London 66 B5
Ruislip Manor London 66 B6
Ruiton W Mid 133 E8
Ruloe W Ches 183 G9
Rumach Highld 295 G8

Rumbling Bridge Perth 279 B10
Rumbow Cottages Worcs 117 B8
Rumburgh Suff 142 G6
Rumbush W Mid 118 B2
Rumer Hill Staffs 133 B9
Rumford Corn 10 G3
Rumford Falk 279 F8
Rumney Cardiff 59 D8
Rumsam Devon 40 G5
Rumwell Som 27 C11
Runcorn Halton 183 E8
Runcton W Sus 22 C5
Runcton Holme Norf 140 B2
Rundlestone Devon 13 G7
Runfold Sur 49 D11
Runhall Norf 141 B11
Runham Norf 143 B10
Runham Norf 161 G9
Runham Vauxhall Norf 143 B10
Running Hill Head Gtr Man 196 F4
Running Waters Durham 234 C2
Runnington Som 27 C10
Runsell Green Essex 88 D3
Runshaw Moor Lancs 194 D4
Runswick Bay N Yorks 226 B6
Runwell Essex 88 G2
Ruscombe Glos 80 D4
Ruscombe Wokingham 65 D9
Ruscote Oxon 101 C8
Rush Green Essex 89 B11
Rush Green Herts 86 C5
Rush Green Herts 104 G4
Rush Green London 68 B4
Rush Green Norf 141 B11
Rush-head Aberds 303 E8
Rush Hill Bath 61 G8
Rushall Hereford 98 E2
Rushall Norf 142 G3
Rushall W Mid 133 C10
Rushall Wilts 46 B6
Rushbrooke Suff 125 E7
Rushbury Shrops 131 E10
Rushcombe Bottom Poole 18 B5
Rushden Herts 104 E6
Rushden Northants 121 D9
Rushenden Kent 70 E2
Rusher's Cross E Sus 37 B10
Rushey Mead Leicester 136 B2
Rushford Devon 12 F4
Rushford Norf 141 G8
Rushgreen Warr 183 D11
Rushington Hants 32 E5
Rushlake Green E Sus 23 B10
Rushland Cross Cumb 210 B6
Rushley Green Essex 106 D5
Rushmere C Beds 103 F8
Rushmere Suff 143 F9
Rushmere St Andrew Suff 108 B4
Rushmere Street Suff 108 B4
Rushmoor Sur 49 E11
Rushmoor Telford 150 G2
Rushmore Hants 33 E11
Rushmore Hill London 68 G3
Rushock Hereford 114 F6
Rushock Worcs 117 C7
Rusholme Gtr Man 184 B5
Rushton Dorset 18 D3
Rushton N Yorks 217 C9
Rushton Northants 136 G6
Rushton Shrops 132 B2
Rushton W Ches 167 C9
Rushton Spencer Staffs 168 C6
Rushwick Worcs 116 G6
Rushy Green E Sus 23 C7
Rushyford Durham 233 F11
Ruskie Stirl 285 G10
Ruskington Lincs 173 E9
Rusland Cumb 210 B6
Rusling End Herts 104 G4
Rusper W Sus 51 F8
Ruspidge Glos 79 C11
Russ Hill Sur 51 E8
Russel Highld 299 E8
Russell Hill London 67 G10
Russell's Green E Sus 38 E2
Russell's Hall W Mid 133 F8
Russell's Water Oxon 65 B8
Russel's Green Suff 126 C5
Rusthall Kent 52 F5
Rustington W Sus 35 G9
Ruston N Yorks 217 C9
Ruston Parva E Yorks 217 G11
Ruswarp N Yorks 227 D7
Ruthall Shrops 131 F11
Rutherford Borders 262 C4
Rutherglen S Lnrk 268 C2
Ruthernbridge Corn 5 B10
Ruthin Denb 165 D10
Ruthin V Glam 58 D3
Ruthrieston Aberdeen 293 C11
Ruthven Aberds 302 E5
Ruthven Angus 286 C6
Ruthven Highld 291 D9
Ruthven Highld 301 F8
Ruthven House Angus 287 C7
Ruthvoes Corn 5 C8
Ruthwaite Cumb 229 D10
Ruthwell Dumfries 238 D3
Ruxley London 68 E3
Ruxton Hereford 97 F11
Ruxton Green Hereford 79 B8
Ruyton-XI-Towns Shrops 149 E7
Ryal Northumb 242 C2
Ryal Fold Blkburn 195 C7
Ryall Dorset 16 C4
Ryall Worcs 99 C7
Ryarsh Kent 53 B7
Rychraggan Highld 300 F4
Rydal Cumb 221 D7
Ryde I o W 21 C7
Rydens Sur 66 F6
Rydeshill Sur 50 C3
Rydon Devon 14 G3
Rye E Sus 38 C6
Rye Common Hants 49 C9
Rye Foreign E Sus 38 C5
Rye Harbour E Sus 38 D6
Rye Park Herts 86 C5
Rye Street Worcs 98 D5
Ryebank Shrops 149 C10
Ryecroft S Yorks 186 B6
Ryecroft W Yorks 205 F7
Ryecroft Gate Staffs 168 C6
Ryeford Glos 80 E4
Ryehill E Yorks 201 B8
Ryeish Green Wokingham 65 F8
Ryelands Hereford 115 F9
Ryeworth Glos 99 G9
Ryhall Rutland 155 G10
Ryhill W Yorks 197 E11
Ryhope T & W 243 G10
Rylah Derbys 171 B7
Rylands Notts 153 B10
Rylstone N Yorks 204 B5
Ryme Intrinseca Dorset 29 E9
Ryther N Yorks 207 F7
Ryton Glos 98 E4
Ryton N Yorks 216 D5
Ryton Shrops 132 C5
Ryton T & W 242 E5
Ryton Warks 135 F7
Ryton-on-Dunsmore Warks 119 C7
Ryton Woodside T & W 242 E4

S

Sabden Lancs 203 F11
Sabine's Green Essex 87 F8
Sackers Green Suff 107 D8
Sacombe Herts 86 B4
Sacombe Green Herts 86 B4
Sacriston Durham 233 B10
Sadberge Darl 224 B6
Saddell Argyll 255 D8
Saddell Ho Argyll 255 D8
Saddington Leics 136 E3
Saddle Bow Norf 158 F2
Saddle Street Dorset 28 G5
Saddlescombe W Sus 36 E3
Sadgill Cumb 221 D9
Saffron Walden Essex 105 D10
Saffron's Cross Hereford 115 G10
Sageston Pembs 73 E9
Saham Hills Norf 141 C8
Saham Toney Norf 141 C8
Saighdinis W Isles 296 E4
Saighton W Ches 166 C6
Sain Dunwyd = St Donats V Glam 58 F2
Sain Tathon = St Athan V Glam 58 F4
St Abbs Borders 273 B8
St Abb's Haven Borders 273 B8
St Agnes Corn 4 E4
St Agnes Scilly 1 H3
St Albans Herts 85 D10
St Allen Corn 4 E6
St Andrews Fife 287 F9
St Andrew's Major V Glam 58 E6
St Andrew's Wood Devon 27 F9
St Annes Lancs 193 B10
St Anne's Park Bristol 60 E6
St Ann's Dumfries 248 E3
St Ann's Nottingham 171 G9
St Ann's Chapel Corn 12 G4
St Ann's Chapel Devon 8 F3
St Anthony Corn 3 C9
St Anthony-in-Meneage Corn 3 D7
St Anthony's T & W 243 E7
St Anthony's Hill E Sus 23 E10
St Arvans Mon 79 F8
St Asaph = Llanelwy Denb 181 G8
St Athan = Sain Tathon V Glam 58 F4
St Augustine's Kent 54 C6
St Austell Corn 5 E10
St Austins Hants 20 B2
St Bees Cumb 219 C9
St Blazey Corn 5 E11
St Blazey Gate Corn 5 E11
St Boswells Borders 262 C3
St Breock Corn 10 G5
St Breward Corn 11 F7
St Briavels Glos 79 E9
St Briavels Common Glos 79 E8
St Bride's Pembs 72 C4
St Brides Major = Saint-y-Brid V Glam 57 G11
St Bride's Netherwent Mon 60 B2
St Brides-super-Ely V Glam 58 D5
St Brides Wentlooge Newport 59 C9
St Budeaux Plym 7 D8
St Buryan Corn 1 D4
St Catherine Bath 61 E9
St Catherine's Argyll 284 G5
St Catherine's Hill Dorset 19 B8
St Chloe Glos 80 E4
St Clears = Sanclêr Carms 74 B3
St Cleer Corn 6 B5
St Clement Corn 4 G6
St Clether Corn 11 E10
St Colmac Argyll 275 G11
St Columb Major Corn 5 C8
St Columb Minor Corn 4 C6
St Columb Road Corn 5 D8
St Combs Aberds 303 C10
St Cross Hants 33 B7
St Cross South Elmham Suff 142 G5
St Cyrus Aberds 293 G9
St David's Perth 286 E3
St David's = Tyddewi Pembs 90 F5
St Day Corn 4 G4
St Decumans Som 42 E5
St Dennis Corn 5 D9
St Denys Soton 32 E6
St Devereux Hereford 97 E8
St Dials Torf 78 G3
St Dogmaels = Llandudoch Pembs 92 B3
St Dominick Corn 7 B8
St Donat's = Sain Dunwyd V Glam 58 F2
St Edith's Wilts 62 G3
St Endellion Corn 10 F5
St Enoder Corn 5 D7
St Erme Corn 4 E6
St Erney Corn 7 D7
St Erth Corn 2 B3
St Erth Praze Corn 2 B3
St Ervan Corn 10 G3
St Eval Corn 5 B7
St Ewe Corn 5 F9
St Fagans Cardiff 58 D6
St Fergus Aberds 303 D10
St Fillans Perth 285 E10
St Florence Pembs 73 E9
St Gennys Corn 11 B8
St George Bristol 60 E6
St George Conwy 181 F7
St George in the East London 67 C10
St George's Gtr Man 184 B4
St Georges N Som 59 G11
St George's Telford 150 G4
St George's V Glam 58 D5
St George's Hill Sur 66 G5
St George's Well Devon 27 F8
St Germans Corn 7 D7
St Giles Lincs 189 G7
St Giles London 67 C10
St Giles in the Wood Devon 25 D8
St Giles on the Heath Devon 12 C3
St Giles's Hill Hants 33 B7
St Gluvias Corn 3 C7
St Godwalds Worcs 117 D9
St Harmon Powys 113 C9
St Helen Auckland Durham 233 F9
St Helena Warks 134 C5
St Helens Cumb 228 E6
St Helen's E Sus 38 E4
St Helens I o W 21 D8
St Helens Mers 183 B8
St Helen's S Yorks 197 F11
St Helen's Wood E Sus 38 E4
St Helier London 67 F9
St Hilary Corn 2 C3
St Hilary V Glam 58 E4
St Ibbs Herts 104 F3
St Illtyd Bl Gwent 78 E2
St Ippollytts Herts 104 F3
St Ishmael's Pembs 72 D4
St Issey Corn 10 G4
St Ive Corn 6 B6
St Ive Cross Corn 6 B6
St Ives Cambs 122 C6
St Ives Corn 2 A2
St Ives Dorset 31 G10
St James Dorset 30 C5
St James London 67 C9
St James Norf 160 E5
St James South Elmham Suff 142 G6
St James's End Northants 120 E4
St Jidgey Corn 5 B8
St John Corn 7 E8
St John's E Sus 52 G4
St John's I o M 192 D3
St John's Sevenoaks 52 B4
St Johns London 67 D11
St John's Sevenoaks 52 B4
St John's Southborough 52 E5
St John's Sur 50 B3
St John's W Yorks 206 F4
St Johns Warks 118 C5
St John's Worcs 116 G6
St John's Chapel Devon 25 B8
St John's Chapel Durham 232 D3
St John's Fen End Norf 157 G10
St John's Highway Norf 157 G10
St John's Park I o W 21 C8
St John's Town of Dalry Dumfries 246 G4
St John's Wells Aberds 303 F7
St John's Wood London 67 C9
St Judes I o M 192 C4
St Julians Herts 85 D10
St Julians Newport 59 B10
St Just in Roseland Corn 3 B9
St Just Corn 1 C3
St Justinian Pembs 90 F4
St Katharines Wilts 63 G9
St Katherine's Aberds 303 F7
St Keverne Corn 3 E7
St Kew Corn 10 F6
St Kew Highway Corn 10 F6
St Keyne Corn 6 C4
St Lawrence Corn 5 B10
St Lawrence Essex 89 E7
St Lawrence I o W 20 F6
St Lawrence Kent 71 F11
St Leonard's Bucks 84 D6
St Leonards Dorset 31 G10
St Leonards E Sus 38 F3
St Leonards S Lnrk 268 E2
St Leonard's Street Kent 53 B7
St Levan Corn 1 E3
St Luke's Derby 152 B6
St Luke's London 67 C10
St Lythans V Glam 58 E6
St Mabyn Corn 10 G6
St Madoes Perth 286 E5
St Margaret South Elmham Suff 142 G6
St Margaret's Hereford 97 E7
St Margarets Herts 86 C5
St Margarets London 67 E7
St Margaret's at Cliffe Kent 55 E11
St Margaret's Hope Orkney 314 G4
St Mark's Glos 99 G8
St Mark's I o M 192 E3
St Martin Corn 2 E6
St Martin Corn 6 E5
St Martins Perth 286 D5
St Martin's Shrops 148 B6
St Martin's Moor Shrops 148 B6
St Mary Bourne Hants 48 C2
St Mary Church V Glam 58 E4
St Mary Cray London 68 F3
St Mary Hill V Glam 58 D3
St Mary Hoo Medway 69 D10
St Mary in the Marsh Kent 39 B9
St Marychurch Torbay 9 B8
St Mary's Orkney 314 F4
St Mary's Bay Kent 39 B9
St Maughans Mon 79 B7
St Maughans Green Mon 79 B7
St Mawes Corn 3 C8
St Mawgan Corn 5 B7
St Mellion Corn 7 B7
St Mellons Cardiff 59 C8
St Merryn Corn 10 G3
St Mewan Corn 5 E9
St Michael Caerhays Corn 5 G9
St Michael Church Som 43 G10
St Michael Penkevil Corn 5 G7
St Michael South Elmham Suff 142 G6
St Michaels Kent 53 F11
St Michaels Torbay 9 C7
St Michaels Worcs 115 D11
St Michael's Hamlet Mers 182 D5
St Michael's on Wyre Lancs 202 E5
St Minver Corn 10 F5
St Monans Fife 287 G9
St Neot Corn 6 B3
St Neots Cambs 122 E3
St Newlyn East Corn 4 D6
St Nicholas Herts 104 F5
St Nicholas Pembs 91 D7
St Nicholas V Glam 58 E5
St Nicholas at Wade Kent 71 F9
St Nicholas South Elmham Suff 142 G6
St Nicolas Park Warks 135 E7
St Ninians Stirl 278 C5
St Olaves Norf 143 D9
St Osyth Essex 89 B10
St Osyth Heath Essex 89 B10
St Owens Cross Hereford 97 G10
St Pancras London 67 C10
St Paul's Glos 80 B4
St Paul's Cray London 68 F3
St Paul's Walden Herts 104 G3
St Peter South Elmham Suff 142 G6
St Peter The Great Worcs 117 G7
St Peter's Glos 99 G8
St Peters Kent 71 F11
St Peter's T & W 243 E7
St Petrox Pembs 73 F7
St Pinnock Corn 6 C4
St Quivox S Ayrs 257 E9
St Ruan Corn 2 F6
St Stephen Corn 5 E8
St Stephens Corn 7 D8
St Stephens Corn 12 D2
St Stephen's Herts 85 D10
St Teath Corn 11 E7
St Thomas Devon 14 C4
St Thomas Swansea 57 C7
St Tudy Corn 11 F7
St Twynnells Pembs 73 F7
St Veep Corn 6 E2
St Vigeans Angus 287 C10
St Vincent's Hamlet Essex 87 G9
St Wenn Corn 5 C9
St Weonards Hereford 97 G9
St Winnow Corn 6 D2
St y-Nyll V Glam 58 D5
Saint Hill Devon 27 F9
Saint Hill W Sus 51 F11
Saint y Brid = St Brides Major V Glam 57 G11
Saintbridge Glos 80 B5
Saintbury Glos 100 D2
Saint's Hill Kent 52 E4
Saith ffynnon Flint 181 F11
Salcombe Devon 9 G9
Salcombe Regis Devon 15 D9
Salcott-cum-Virley Essex 88 C6
Salden Bucks 102 F6
Sale Gtr Man 184 C3
Sale Green Worcs 117 F8
Saleby Lincs 191 F7
Salehurst E Sus 38 C2
Salem Carms 94 F2
Salem Ceredig 128 G3
Salem Corn 4 G4
Salen Argyll 289 E7
Salen Highld 289 C8
Salendine Nook W Yorks 196 D6
Salenside Borders 261 E11
Salesbury Lancs 203 G9
Saleway Worcs 117 F8
Salford C Beds 103 D8
Salford Gtr Man 184 B4
Salford Oxon 100 F5
Salford Ford C Beds 103 D8
Salford Priors Warks 117 G11
Salfords Sur 51 D9
Salhouse Norf 160 G6
Saligo Argyll 274 G3
Salisbury Wilts 31 B10
Salkeld Dykes Cumb 230 D6
Sallachan Highld 289 C11
Sallachy Highld 295 B11
Sallachy Highld 309 J5
Salle Norf 160 E2
Salmans Kent 52 E4
Salmonby Lincs 190 G4
Salmond's Muir Angus 287 D9
Salmonhutch Devon 14 B2
Salperton Glos 99 G11
Salperton Park Glos 81 B9
Salph End Beds 121 G11
Salsburgh N Lnrk 268 C6
Salt Staffs 151 D9
Salt Coates Cumb 238 G5
Salt End E Yorks 201 B7
Salt Hill Slough 66 C3
Salta Cumb 229 B7
Saltaire W Yorks 205 F8
Saltash Corn 7 D8
Saltburn Highld 301 C7
Saltburn-by-the-Sea Redcar 235 G9
Saltby Leics 155 D7
Saltcoats Cumb 219 F11
Saltcoats E Loth 281 E9
Saltcoats N Ayrs 266 G4
Saltcotes Lancs 193 B11
Saltdean Brighton 36 G5
Salter Lancs 212 G2
Salter Street W Mid 118 C2
Salterbeck Cumb 228 F5
Salterforth Lancs 204 D3
Salters Heath Hants 48 B6
Salters Lode Norf 139 C11
Saltershill Shrops 150 D2
Salterswall W Ches 167 B10
Salterton Wilts 46 F6
Saltfleet Lincs 191 C7
Saltfleetby All Saints Lincs 191 C7
Saltfleetby St Clement Lincs 191 C7
Saltfleetby St Peter Lincs 190 D6
Saltford Bath 61 F7
Salthouse Cumb 210 F4
Salthouse Norf 177 E9
Saltley W Mid 133 F11
Saltmarsh Newport 59 C11
Saltmarshe E Yorks 199 C9
Saltness Orkney 314 G2
Saltness Shetland 313 J4
Saltney Flint 166 B5
Salton N Yorks 216 D4
Saltrens Devon 25 C7
Saltwell T & W 243 E7
Saltwick Northumb 242 B5
Saltwood Kent 55 F7
Salum Argyll 288 E2
Salvington W Sus 35 F10
Salwarpe Worcs 117 E7
Salwayash Dorset 16 B5
Sambourne Warks 117 E11
Sambourne Wilts 45 E11
Sambrook Telford 150 E4
Samhla W Isles 296 E3
Samlesbury Lancs 203 G7
Samlesbury Bottoms Lancs 194 B6
Sampford Arundel Som 27 D10
Sampford Brett Som 42 E5
Sampford Chapple Devon 25 G10
Sampford Courtenay Devon 25 G10
Sampford Moor Som 27 D10
Sampford Peverell Devon 27 E8
Sampford Spiney Devon 12 G6
Sampool Bridge Cumb 211 B9
Samuel's Corner Essex 70 B3
Samuelston E Loth 281 G9
Sanachan Highld 299 E8
Sanaigmore Argyll 274 F3
Sanclêr = St Clears Carms 74 B3
Sancreed Corn 1 D4
Sancton E Yorks 208 F4
Sand Highld 307 K4
Sand Shetland 313 J5
Sand Som 44 D2
Sand Gate Cumb 211 D7
Sand Hole E Yorks 208 F2
Sand Hutton N Yorks 207 B9
Sand Side Cumb 210 C4
Sand Side Lancs 202 C4
Sandaig Highld 295 E9
Sandal W Yorks 197 D10
Sandal Magna W Yorks 197 D10
Sandale Cumb 229 C10
Sandavore Highld 294 G6
Sandbach E Ches 168 C3
Sandbach Heath E Ches 168 C3
Sandbank Argyll 276 E3
Sandbanks Kent 70 G4
Sandbanks Poole 18 D6
Sandborough Staffs 152 F2
Sandbraes Lincs 200 G6
Sandend Aberds 302 C5
Sanderstead London 67 G10
Sandfields Glos 99 G8
Sandfields Neath 57 C8
Sandfields Staffs 134 B2
Sandford Cumb 222 B4
Sandford Devon 26 G4
Sandford Dorset 18 D4
Sandford Hants 31 G11
Sandford I o W 20 E6
Sandford N Som 44 B2
Sandford S Lnrk 268 G4
Sandford Shrops 148 E6
Sandford Shrops 149 C11
Sandford W Yorks 205 F11
Sandford Worcs 99 B7
Sandford Batch N Som 44 B2
Sandford Hill Stoke 168 G6
Sandford on Thames Oxon 83 E8
Sandford Orcas Dorset 29 C10
Sandford St Martin Oxon 101 F8
Sandfordhill Aberds 303 E11
Sandgate Kent 55 G7
Sandgreen Dumfries 237 D7
Sandhaven Aberds 303 C9
Sandhaven Argyll 276 E3
Sandhead Dumfries 236 E2
Sandhill Bucks 102 F4
Sandhill Cambs 139 F11
Sandhill S Yorks 198 F2
Sandhills Dorset 29 E11
Sandhills Dorset 29 G9
Sandhills Mers 182 C4
Sandhills Oxon 83 D9
Sandhills Sur 50 F2
Sandhills W Yorks 206 F3
Sandhoe Northumb 241 D11
Sandhole Argyll 275 D11
Sandholme E Yorks 208 G2
Sandholme Lincs 156 B6
Sandhurst Brack 65 G10
Sandhurst Glos 98 G6
Sandhurst Kent 38 B3
Sandhurst Cross Kent 38 B3
Sandhutton N Yorks 215 C7
Sandiacre Derbys 153 B9
Sandilands Lincs 191 E8
Sandilands S Lnrk 259 B9
Sandiway W Ches 183 G10
Sandleheath Hants 31 E10
Sandling Kent 53 B9
Sandlow Green E Ches 168 B3
Sandness Shetland 313 H3
Sandon Essex 88 E2
Sandon Herts 104 E6
Sandon Staffs 151 C8
Sandonbank Staffs 151 D8
Sandown I o W 21 E7
Sandown Park Kent 52 E6
Sandpit Dorset 28 G6
Sandpits Glos 98 F6
Sandplace Corn 6 D5
Sandridge Herts 85 C11
Sandridge Wilts 62 F2
Sandringham Norf 158 D3
Sands Bucks 84 G4
Sands End London 67 D9
Sandsend N Yorks 227 C7
Sandside Cumb 210 D6
Sandside Cumb 211 C9
Sandside Orkney 314 F2
Sandside Ho Highld 310 C3
Sandsound Shetland 313 J5
Sandtoft N Lincs 199 F8
Sandvoe Shetland 312 D5
Sandway Kent 53 C11
Sandwell W Mid 133 F10
Sandwich Kent 55 B10
Sandwich Bay Estate Kent 55 B11
Sandwick Cumb 221 B8
Sandwick Orkney 314 H4
Sandwick Shetland 313 L6
Sandwith Cumb 219 C9
Sandwith Newtown Cumb 219 C9
Sandy C Beds 104 B3
Sandy Carms 75 E7
Sandy Bank Lincs 174 E3
Sandy Carrs Durham 234 C3
Sandy Cross E Sus 37 C9
Sandy Cross Sur 49 D11
Sandy Down Hants 20 B2
Sandy Gate Devon 14 C5
Sandy Haven Pembs 72 D5
Sandy Lane W Yorks 205 F8
Sandy Lane Wilts 62 F3
Sandy Lane Wrex 166 G5
Sandy Way I o W 20 E5
Sandybank Orkney 314 C5
Sandycroft Flint 166 B4
Sandyford Dumfries 248 E6
Sandyford Stoke 168 E5
Sandygate Devon 14 G3
Sandygate I o M 192 C4
Sandygate S Yorks 186 D4
Sandyhills Dumfries 237 D10
Sandylake Corn 6 C2
Sandylands Lancs 211 G8
Sandylands Som 27 C10
Sandylane Swansea 56 D5
Sandypark Devon 13 D10
Sandysike Cumb 239 D9
Sangobeg Highld 308 C4
Sangomore Highld 308 C4
Sanham Green W Berks 63 F10
Sankey Bridges Warr 183 D9
Sankyns Green Worcs 116 E5
Sanna Highld 288 C6
Sanndabhaig W Isles 297 G4
Sanndabhaig W Isles 304 E6
Sannox N Ayrs 255 C11
Sanquhar Dumfries 247 B7
Sansaw Heath Shrops 149 E10
Santon Cumb 220 E2
Santon N Lincs 200 E2
Santon Bridge Cumb 220 E2
Santon Downham Suff 140 F6
Sapcote Leics 135 E9
Sapey Bridge Worcs 116 F4
Sapey Common Hereford 116 E4
Sapiston Suff 125 B8
Sapley Cambs 122 C4
Sapperton Derbys 152 C3
Sapperton Glos 80 E6
Sapperton Lincs 155 C10
Saracen's Head Lincs 156 D6
Sarclet Highld 310 E7
Sardis Carms 75 D9
Sardis Pembs 73 D10
Sarisbury Hants 33 F8
Sarn Bridgend 58 C2
Sarn Flint 181 F10
Sarn Powys 130 E4
Sarn Bach Gwyn 144 D6
Sarn Meyllteyrn Gwyn 144 C4
Sarnau Carms 74 B4
Sarnau Ceredig 110 G6
Sarnau Gwyn 147 B9
Sarnau Powys 95 E10
Sarnau Powys 148 F4
Sarnesfield Hereford 115 G7
Saron Carms 75 C10
Saron Carms 93 D7
Saron Denb 165 C8
Saron Gwyn 163 B8
Saron Gwyn 163 D7
Sarratt Herts 85 F8
Sarratt Bottom Herts 85 F8
Sarre Kent 71 G9
Sarsden Oxon 100 G5
Sarsden Halt Oxon 100 G5
Sarsgrum Highld 308 C3
Sasaig Highld 295 E8
Sascott Shrops 149 G8
Satley Durham 233 C8
Satmar Kent 55 F9
Satran Highld 294 B6
Satron N Yorks 223 F8
Satterleigh Devon 25 C11
Satterthwaite Cumb 220 G6
Satwell Oxon 65 C8
Sauchen Aberds 293 B8
Saucher Perth 286 D5
Sauchie Clack 279 C7
Sauchieburn Aberds 293 G8
Saughall W Ches 182 G5
Saughall Massie Mers 182 D3
Saughton Edin 280 G4
Saughtree Borders 250 D3
Saul Glos 80 D2
Saundby Notts 188 D3
Saundersfoot Pembs 73 E10
Saunderton Bucks 84 E3
Saunderton Lee Bucks 84 F4
Saunton Devon 40 F3
Sausthorpe Lincs 174 B5
Saval Highld 309 J5
Savary Highld 289 E8
Saveock Corn 4 F5
Saverley Green Staffs 151 B9
Savile Park W Yorks 196 C5
Savile Town W Yorks 197 C8
Sawbridge Warks 119 D10
Sawbridgeworth Herts 87 B7
Sawdon N Yorks 217 B8
Sawley Derbys 153 C9
Sawley Lancs 203 D11
Sawley N Yorks 214 F4
Sawood W Yorks 204 G6
Sawston Cambs 105 B9
Sawtry Cambs 138 G3
Sawyer's Hill Som 27 C11
Saxby Leics 154 F6
Saxby Lincs 189 D8
Saxby W Sus 35 G7
Saxby All Saints N Lincs 200 D3
Saxelbye Leics 154 E4
Saxham Street Suff 125 E11
Saxilby Lincs 188 F5
Saxlingham Norf 159 B10
Saxlingham Green Norf 142 D4
Saxlingham Nethergate Norf 142 D4
Saxlingham Thorpe Norf 142 D4
Saxmundham Suff 127 E7
Saxon Street Cambs 124 F3
Saxondale Notts 154 B3
Saxtead Suff 126 D5
Saxtead Green Suff 126 E5
Saxtead Little Green Suff 126 D5
Saxthorpe Norf 160 C2
Saxton N Yorks 206 F5
Sayers Common W Sus 36 D3
Scackleton N Yorks 216 E2
Scadabhagh W Isles 305 J3
Scaftworth Notts 187 C11
Scagglethorpe N Yorks 216 E6
Scaitcliffe Lancs 195 B9
Scaladal W Isles 305 G3
Scalan Moray 292 B4
Scalasaig Argyll 274 D4
Scalby E Yorks 199 B10
Scalby N Yorks 227 G10
Scald End Beds 121 F10
Scaldwell Northants 120 C5
Scale Hall Lancs 211 G9
Scale Houses Cumb 231 B7
Scaleby Cumb 239 E11
Scalebyhill Cumb 239 E10
Scales Cumb 210 E5
Scales Cumb 230 F2
Scales Cumb 231 C7
Scales Lancs 202 G5
Scalford Leics 154 E5
Scaling Redcar 226 C4
Scaliscro W Isles 304 F3
Scallasaig Highld 295 D10
Scallastle Argyll 289 F8
Scalloway Shetland 313 K6
Scalpay W Isles 305 J4
Scalpay Ho Highld 295 C8
Scalpsie Argyll 255 B11
Scamadale Highld 295 F9
Scamblesby Lincs 190 F3
Scamland E Yorks 207 E11
Scammadale Argyll 289 G10
Scamodale Highld 289 B10
Scampston N Yorks 217 D7
Scampton Lincs 189 F7
Scaniport Highld 300 F6
Scapa Orkney 314 F4
Scapegoat Hill W Yorks 196 D5
Scar Orkney 314 B6
Scar Head Cumb 220 G5
Scarborough N Yorks 217 B10
Scarcewater Corn 5 E8
Scarcliffe Derbys 171 B7
Scarcroft W Yorks 206 E3
Scarcroft Hill W Yorks 206 E3
Scardroy Highld 300 D2
Scarff Shetland 312 E4
Scarfskerry Highld 310 B6
Scargill Durham 223 C11
Scarinish Argyll 288 E2
Scarisbrick Lancs 193 E11
Scarness Cumb 229 E10
Scarning Norf 159 G9
Scarrington Notts 172 G2
Scarth Hill Lancs 194 F2
Scarthingwell N Yorks 206 F5
Scartho NE Lincs 201 F9
Scarvister Shetland 313 J5
Scarwell Orkney 314 D2
Scatness Shetland 313 M5
Scatraig Highld 301 F7
Scatwell Ho Highld 300 D3
Scawby N Lincs 200 F3
Scawsby S Yorks 198 G5
Scawthorpe S Yorks 198 F5
Scawton N Yorks 215 C10
Scayne's Hill W Sus 36 C5
Scethrog Powys 96 F2
Scholar Green E Ches 168 D4
Scholemoor W Yorks 205 G8
Scholes Gtr Man 194 F5
Scholes S Yorks 186 B5
Scholes W Yorks 197 B7
Scholes W Yorks 197 F7
Scholes W Yorks 204 F6
Scholes W Yorks 206 F3
Scholey Hill W Yorks 197 B11
School Aycliffe Durham 233 G11
School Green Essex 106 E4
School Green I o W 20 D2
School Green W Ches 167 C10
School Green W Yorks 205 G8
School House Dorset 28 G5
Schoolgreen Wokingham 65 F8
Schoolhill Aberds 293 D11
Sciberscross Highld 309 H7
Scilly Bank Cumb 219 B9
Scissett W Yorks 197 E8
Scleddau Pembs 91 E8
Sco Ruston Norf 160 E5
Scofton Notts 187 E10
Scole Norf 126 B2
Scole Common Norf 142 G2
Scolpaig W Isles 296 D3
Scone Perth 286 E5
Sconser Highld 295 B7
Scoonie Fife 287 G7
Scoor Argyll 274 B5
Scopwick Lincs 173 D9
Scoraig Highld 307 K5
Scorborough E Yorks 208 D6
Scorrier Corn 4 G4
Scorriton Devon 8 B4
Scorton Lancs 202 D6
Scorton N Yorks 224 E5
Scot Hay Staffs 168 F4
Scot Lane End Gtr Man 194 F6
Scotbheinn W Isles 296 F4
Scotby Cumb 239 G10
Scotch Corner N Yorks 224 E4
Scotches Derbys 170 F4
Scotforth Lancs 202 B5
Scotgate W Yorks 196 E6
Scothern Lincs 189 F8
Scotland Leics 136 D3
Scotland Leics 153 E7
Scotland Lincs 155 C10
Scotland W Berks 64 F5
Scotland End Oxon 100 E6
Scotland Gate Northumb 253 G7
Scotland Street Suff 107 D9
Scotlands W Mid 133 C8
Scotlandwell Perth 286 G5
Scots' Gap Northumb 252 F2
Scotsburn Highld 301 B7
Scotscalder Station Highld 310 D4
Scotscraig Fife 287 E8
Scotston Aberds 293 F9
Scotston Perth 286 C3
Scotstoun Glasgow 267 B10
Scotstown Highld 289 C10
Scotswood T & W 242 E5
Scotswood Windsor 66 F2
Scott Willoughby Lincs 155 B11
Scottas Highld 295 E9
Scotter Lincs 199 G11
Scotterthorpe Lincs 199 G11
Scottlethorpe Lincs 155 E11
Scotton Lincs 188 B5
Scotton N Yorks 206 B2
Scotton N Yorks 224 F3
Scottow Norf 160 E5
Scoughall E Loth 282 E2
Scoulag Argyll 266 D2
Scoulton Norf 141 C9
Scounslow Green Staffs 151 D11
Scourie Highld 306 E6
Scourie More Highld 306 E6
Scousburgh Shetland 313 M5
Scout Dike S Yorks 197 G8
Scout Green Cumb 221 D11
Scouthead Gtr Man 196 F3
Scowles Glos 79 C9
Scrabster Highld 310 B4
Scraesburgh Borders 262 F5
Scrafield Lincs 174 B4
Scragged Oak Kent 69 G10
Scrainwood Northumb 251 B11
Scrane End Lincs 174 G5
Scrapsgate Kent 70 E2
Scraptoft Leics 136 B2
Scrapton Som 28 E3
Scratby Norf 161 F10
Scrayingham N Yorks 216 G4
Scredda Corn 5 E10
Scredington Lincs 173 G9
Screedy Som 27 B9
Scremby Lincs 174 B6
Scremerston Northumb 273 F10
Screveton Notts 172 G2
Scrivelsby Lincs 174 B3
Scriven N Yorks 206 B2
Scronkey Lancs 202 D4
Scrooby Notts 187 C11
Scropton Derbys 152 C3
Scrub Hill Lincs 174 D2
Scruton N Yorks 224 G5
Scrwgan Powys 148 E3
Scuddaborg Highld 298 C3
Scuggate Cumb 239 C10
Sculcoates Hull 209 G7
Sculthorpe Norf 159 C7
Scunthorpe N Lincs 199 E11
Scurlage Swansea 56 D3
Sea Som 28 E4
Sea Mill Cumb 210 F5
Sea Mills Bristol 60 D5
Sea Mills Corn 10 G4
Sea Palling Norf 161 D8
Seaborough Dorset 28 F6
Seabridge Staffs 168 G4
Seabrook Kent 55 G7
Seaburn T & W 243 F10
Seacombe Mers 182 C4
Seacox Heath Kent 53 G8
Seacroft Lincs 175 C9
Seacroft W Yorks 206 F3
Seadyke Lincs 156 B6
Seafar N Lnrk 278 G5
Seafield Highld 311 L3
Seafield Midloth 270 C5
Seafield S Ayrs 257 E8
Seafield W Loth 269 B10
Seaford E Sus 23 F7
Seaforth Mers 182 B4
Seagrave Leics 154 F2
Seagry Heath Wilts 62 C3
Seaham Durham 234 B4
Seahouses Northumb 264 C6
Seal Kent 52 B4
Sealand Flint 166 B5
Seale Sur 49 D11
Seamer N Yorks 217 C10
Seamer N Yorks 225 C9
Seamill N Ayrs 266 F4
Searby Lincs 200 F5
Seasalter Kent 70 F6
Seascale Cumb 219 E10
Seathorne Lincs 175 B9
Seathwaite Cumb 220 C4
Seathwaite Cumb 220 F4
Seatle Cumb 211 C7
Seatoller Cumb 220 C4
Seaton Corn 6 E6
Seaton Cumb 228 E6
Seaton Devon 15 C10
Seaton Durham 243 G9
Seaton E Yorks 209 D9
Seaton Kent 55 B8
Seaton Northumb 243 B8
Seaton Rutland 137 D8
Seaton Burn T & W 242 C6
Seaton Carew Hrtlpl 234 F6
Seaton Delaval Northumb 243 B8
Seaton Ross E Yorks 207 E11
Seaton Sluice Northumb 243 B8
Seatown Aberds 302 C5
Seatown Aberds 303 D11
Seatown Dorset 16 C4
Seaureaugh Moor Corn 2 B6
Seave Green N Yorks 225 E11
Seaview I o W 21 C8
Seaville Cumb 238 G5
Seavington St Mary Som 28 E6
Seavington St Michael Som 28 D6
Seawick Essex 89 C10
Sebastopol Torf 78 F3
Sebay Orkney 314 F5
Sebergham Cumb 230 C3
Sebiston Velzian Orkney 314 D2
Seckington Warks 134 B5
Second Coast Highld 307 K4
Second Drove Cambs 139 F10
Sedbergh Cumb 222 G3
Sedbury Glos 79 G8
Sedbusk N Yorks 223 G7
Seddington C Beds 104 B3
Sedgeberrow Worcs 99 D10
Sedgebrook Lincs 155 B7
Sedgefield Durham 234 F3
Sedgeford Norf 158 B4
Sedgehill Wilts 30 B5
Sedgemere W Mid 118 B4
Sedgley W Mid 133 E8
Sedgley Park Gtr Man 195 G10
Sedgwick Cumb 211 B10
Sedlescombe E Sus 38 D3
Sedlescombe Street E Sus 38 D3
Sedrup Bucks 84 C3
Seed Kent 54 B2
Seed Lee Lancs 194 C5
Seedley Gtr Man 184 B4
Seend Wilts 62 G2
Seend Cleeve Wilts 62 G2
Seend Head Wilts 62 G2
Seer Green Bucks 85 G7
Seething Norf 142 D6
Seething Wells London 67 F7
Sefton Mers 193 G11
Segensworth Hants 33 F8
Seggat Aberds 303 E7
Seghill Northumb 243 C7
Seifton Shrops 131 G9
Seighford Staffs 151 D7
Seilebost W Isles 305 J2
Seion Gwyn 163 B8
Seisdon Staffs 132 E6
Seisiadar W Isles 304 E7
Selattyn Shrops 148 C5
Selborne Hants 49 G8
Selby N Yorks 207 G8
Selgrove Kent 54 B4
Selham W Sus 34 C6
Selhurst London 67 F10
Selkirk Borders 261 D11
Sellack Hereford 97 F11
Sellack Boat Hereford 97 F11
Sellafirth Shetland 312 D7
Sellan Corn 1 C4
Sellibister Orkney 314 B7
Sellick's Green Som 28 D2
Sellindge Kent 54 F6
Selling Kent 54 B4
Sells Green Wilts 62 G3
Selly Hill N Yorks 227 D7
Selly Oak W Mid 133 G10
Selly Park W Mid 133 G11
Selmeston E Sus 23 D8
Selsdon London 67 G10
Selsey W Sus 22 E5
Selsfield Common W Sus 51 G10
Selside Cumb 221 F10
Selside N Yorks 212 D5
Selsley Glos 80 E4
Selsmore Hants 21 B10
Selson Kent 55 B10
Selsted Kent 55 E8
Selston Notts 171 E7
Selston Common Notts 171 E7
Selston Green Notts 171 E7
Selwick Orkney 314 F2
Selworthy Som 42 D2
Sem Hill Wilts 30 B5
Semblister Shetland 313 H5
Semer Suff 107 B9
Semington Wilts 61 G11
Semley Wilts 30 B5
Sempringham Lincs 156 C2
Send Sur 50 B4
Send Grove Sur 50 C4
Send Marsh Sur 50 B4
Senghenydd Caerph 77 G10
Sennen Corn 1 D3

ennen Cove Corn 1 D3
ennybridge =
Pont Senni Powys 95 F8
erlby Notts 187 D10
errington Wilts 46 F5
essay N Yorks 215 D9
etchey Norf 158 G2
etley Hants 32 G4
eton E Loth 281 G8
eton Mains E Loth 281 F8
etter Shetland 312 E6
etter Shetland 313 H5
etter Shetland 313 J7
etter Shetland 313 L6
etiscarth Orkney 314 E3
ettle N Yorks 212 G6
ettrington N Yorks 216 E6
even Ash Som 43 G7
even Kings London 68 B3
even Sisters =
Blaendulais Neath 76 D4
even Springs Glos 81 B7
even Star Green Essex 107 F8
evenhampton Glos 99 G10
evenhampton Swindon 82 G2
evenoaks Kent 52 C4
evenoaks Common
Kent 52 C4
evenoaks Weald Kent 52 C4
evern Beach S Glos 60 B4
evern Stoke Worcs 99 C7
evernhampton Swindon 82 G2
evick End Beds 121 G11
evington Kent 54 E4
ewards End Essex 105 D11
ewardstone Essex 86 F5
ewardstonebury Essex 86 F5
ewell C Beds 103 G9
ewerby E Yorks 218 F3
eworgan Corn 2 C6
ewstern Leics 155 E7
exhow N Yorks 225 D9
ezincote Glos 100 E3
garasta Mhor W Isles 305 J2
giogarstaigh W Isles 304 B7
giwen = Skewen Neath 57 B8
hab Hill Glos 80 B6
habbington Bucks 83 D11
hackerley Shrops 132 B6
hackerstone Leics 135 B7
hacklecross Derbys 153 C8
hackleford Sur 50 D2
hackleton W Yorks 196 B3
hacklewell London 67 B10
hacklford Sur 50 D2
hade W Yorks 196 C2
hadforth Durham 234 C2
hadingfield Suff 143 G8
hadoxhurst Kent 54 F3
hadsworth Blkburn 195 B8
hadwell Glos 80 F3
hadwell London 67 C11
hadwell Norf 141 G8
hadwell W Yorks 206 F2
haffalong Staffs 169 E7
haftenhoe End Herts 105 D8
haftesbury Dorset 30 C5
haftoe S Yorks 197 E11
hafton Two Gates
Yorks 197 E11
haggs Dorset 18 E3
hakeford Shrops 150 D3
hakerley Gtr Man 195 G7
hakesfield Glos 98 E3
halbourne Wilts 63 G10
halcombe I o W 20 D3
halden Hants 49 E7
halden Green Hants 49 E7
haldon Devon 14 G4
halfleet I o W 20 D4
halford Essex 106 F4
halford Som 45 G8
halford Sur 50 D4
halford Green Essex 106 F4
halloch Moray 302 D3
hallowford Devon 25 G11
hallowford Devon 41 E8
hallowford Staffs 151 D7
halmsford Street Kent 54 C5
halstone Bucks 102 D2
hamley Green Sur 50 E4
handon Argyll 276 D5
handwick Highld 301 B8
hangton Leics 136 D4
hankhouse Northumb 243 B7
hanklin I o W 21 E7
hannochie N Ayrs 255 E10
hannochill Stirl 277 B10
hanquhar Aberds 302 F5
hanwell Fife 287 E8
hanzie Perth 286 B6
hap Cumb 221 B11
hapridge Glos 79 B11
hapwick Dorset 30 G6
hapwick Som 44 F2
harcott Wilts 46 B6
hard End W Mid 134 F3
hardlow Derbys 153 C8
hareshill Staffs 133 B8
harlston W Yorks 197 D11
harlston Common
V Yorks 197 D11
harmans Cross W Mid 118 B2
harnal Street Medway 69 E9
harnbrook Beds 121 F9
harneyford Lancs 195 C11
harnford Leics 135 E9
harnhill Green Dorset 30 F2
haroe Green Lancs 202 G6
harow N Yorks 214 E6
harp Street Norf 161 E7
harpenhoe C Beds 103 E11
harperton Northumb 251 C11
harples Gtr Man 195 E8
harpley Heath Staffs 151 B9
harpness Glos 79 E11
harp's Corner E Sus 23 B9
harpsbridge E Sus 36 C6
harpstone Bath 45 B9
harpthorne W Sus 51 G11
harptor Corn 11 G11
harpway Gate Worcs 117 D9
harrington Norf 159 B10
harrow S Yorks 186 D4
harston Gtr Man 184 D4
hatterford Worcs 132 G5
hatterling Kent 55 B9
hatton Derbys 185 E11
haugh Prior Devon 7 C10
havington E Ches 168 E2
haw Gtr Man 196 F2
haw Swindon 62 B6
haw W Berks 64 F3
haw W Yorks 204 F6
haw Wilts 61 F11
haw Common Glos 98 F3
haw Green Herts 104 E5
haw Green Lancs 194 D4
haw Green N Yorks 205 C11
haw Heath E Ches 184 F3
haw Heath Gtr Man 184 D5
haw Lands S Yorks 197 F10
Shaw Mills N Yorks 214 G5
Shaw Side Gtr Man 196 F2
Shawbank Shrops 131 G9
Shawbirch Telford 150 G2
Shawbury Shrops 149 E11
Shawclough Gtr Man 195 E11
Shawdon Hall Northumb 264 G3
Shawell Leics 135 G10
Shawfield Gtr Man 195 E11
Shawfield Staffs 169 C9
Shawfield Head
N Yorks 205 C11
Shawford Hants 33 C7
Shawford Som 45 C9
Shawforth Lancs 195 C11
Shawhead Dumfries 237 B10
Shawhead N Lnrk 268 C4
Shawhill Dumfries 238 D6
Shawlands Glasgow 267 C11
Shawsburn S Lnrk 268 E5
Shawton S Lnrk 268 F3
Shawtonhill S Lnrk 268 F3
Shay Gate W Yorks 205 F8
Sheandow Moray 302 F2
Shear Cross Wilts 45 E11
Shearington Dumfries 238 D2
Shearsby Leics 136 E2
Shearston Som 43 G9
Shebbear Devon 24 F6
Shebdon Staffs 150 D5
Shebster Highld 310 C4
Sheddens E Renf 267 D11
Shedfield Hants 33 E9
Sheen Staffs 169 C10
Sheep Hill Durham 242 F5
Sheepbridge Derbys 186 G5
Sheepdrove W Berks 63 D10
Sheeplane C Beds 103 E8
Sheepridge Bucks 65 B11
Sheepridge W Yorks 197 D7
Sheepscar W Yorks 206 G2
Sheepscombe Glos 80 C5
Sheepstor Devon 7 B11
Sheepwash Devon 25 F7
Sheepwash Northumb 253 F7
Sheepway N Som 60 D3
Sheepy Magna Leics 134 C6
Sheepy Parva Leics 134 C6
Sheering Essex 87 C8
Sheerness Kent 70 E2
Sheerwater Sur 66 G4
Sheet Hants 34 C3
Sheet Shrops 115 C10
Sheets Heath Sur 50 B2
Sheffield Corn 1 D5
Sheffield S Yorks 186 D5
Sheffield Bottom
W Berks 65 F7
Sheffield Green E Sus 36 C6
Sheffield Park S Yorks 186 D5
Shefford C Beds 104 D2
Shefford Woodlands
W Berks 63 E11
Sheigra Highld 306 C6
Sheildmuir N Lnrk 268 D5
Sheinton Shrops 132 C2
Shelderton Shrops 115 B8
Sheldon Derbys 169 B11
Sheldon Devon 27 F10
Sheldon W Mid 134 G3
Sheldwich Kent 54 B4
Sheldwich Lees Kent 54 B4
Shelf Bridgend 58 C2
Shelf W Yorks 196 B6
Shelfanger Norf 142 G2
Shelfield W Mid 133 C10
Shelfield Warks 118 E2
Shelfield Green Warks 118 E2
Shelfleys Northants 120 F4
Shelford Notts 171 G11
Shelford Warks 135 F8
Shell Worcs 117 F9
Shell Green Halton 183 D8
Shelland Suff 125 E10
Shellbrook Leics 152 F6
Shelley Essex 87 E9
Shelley Suff 107 D10
Shelley W Yorks 197 E8
Shelley Woodhouse
W Yorks 197 E8
Shellingford Oxon 82 G4
Shellow Bowells Essex 87 D10
Shellwood Cross Sur 51 D8
Shelsley Beauchamp
Worcs 116 E4
Shelsley Walsh Worcs 116 E4
Shelthorpe Leics 153 F10
Shelton Beds 121 D10
Shelton Norf 142 E4
Shelton Notts 172 G3
Shelton Shrops 149 G9
Shelton Stoke 168 F5
Shelton Green Norf 142 E4
Shelton Lock Derby 153 C7
Shelton under Harley
Staffs 150 B6
Shelve Shrops 130 D6
Shelvin Devon 27 G11
Shelvingford Kent 71 F8
Shelwick Hereford 97 C10
Shelwick Green
Hereford 97 C10
Shenfield Essex 87 G10
Shenington Oxon 101 C7
Shenley Herts 85 E11
Shenley Brook End
M Keynes 102 D6
Shenley Church End
M Keynes 102 D6
Shenley Fields W Mid 133 G10
Shenley Lodge
M Keynes 102 D6
Shenley Wood M Keynes 102 D6
Shenleybury Herts 85 E11
Shenmore Hereford 97 D7
Shennanton Dumfries 236 C5
Shennanton Ho
Dumfries 236 C5
Shenstone Staffs 134 C2
Shenstone Worcs 117 C7
Shenstone Woodend
Staffs 134 C2
Shenton Leics 135 C7
Shenval Highld 300 G4
Shenval Moray 302 G2
Shenvault Moray 301 E10
Shepeau Stow Lincs 156 G6
Shephall Herts 104 G5
Shepherd Hill W Yorks 197 C9
Shepherd's Bush London 67 C8
Shepherd's Gate Norf 157 F11
Shepherd's Green Oxon 65 C8
Shepherd's Hill Sur 50 G2
Shepherd's Patch Glos 80 E2
Shepherd's Port Norf 158 C3
Shepherdswell or
Sibertswold Kent 55 D9
Shepley W Yorks 197 F7
Shepperdine S Glos 79 F10
Shepperton Sur 66 F5
Shepperton Green Sur 66 F5
Shepreth Cambs 105 B7
Shepshed Leics 153 F9
Shepton Beauchamp
Som 28 D6
Shepton Mallet Som 44 E6
Shepton Montague Som 45 G7
Shepway Kent 53 C9
Sheraton Durham 234 D4
Sherberton Devon 13 G8
Sherborne Bath 44 B5
Sherborne Dorset 29 D10
Sherborne Glos 81 C11
Sherborne St John
Hants 48 B6
Sherbourne Warks 118 E5
Sherbourne Street Suff 107 C9
Sherburn Durham 234 C2
Sherburn N Yorks 217 D9
Sherburn Grange
Durham 234 C2
Sherburn Hill Durham 234 C2
Sherburn in Elmet
N Yorks 206 G5
Shere Sur 50 D5
Shereford Norf 159 D7
Sherfield English Hants 32 C3
Sherfield on Loddon
Hants 49 B7
Sherfin Lancs 195 B9
Sherford Devon 8 G5
Sherford Dorset 18 C4
Sherford Som 28 C2
Sheriff Hill T & W 243 E7
Sheriff Hutton N Yorks 216 F3
Sheriffhales Shrops 150 G5
Sheriff's Lench Worcs 99 B10
Sheringham Norf 177 E11
Sherington M Keynes 103 B7
Sheringwood Norf 177 E11
Shermanbury W Sus 36 D2
Shernal Green Worcs 117 E8
Shernborne Norf 158 C4
Sherrard's Green Worcs 98 B5
Sherrardspark Herts 86 C2
Sherriffhales Shrops 150 G5
Sherrington Wilts 46 F3
Sherston Wilts 61 B11
Sherwood Nottingham 171 G9
Sherwood Green Devon 25 C9
Sherwood Park Kent 52 E6
Shettleston Glasgow 268 C2
Shevington Gtr Man 194 F4
Shevington Moor
Gtr Man 194 E4
Shevington Vale
Gtr Man 194 F4
Shevlock Corn 7 D7
Shewalton N Ayrs 257 B8
Shibden Head W Yorks 196 B5
Shide I o W 20 D5
Shiel Aberds 292 B4
Shiel Bridge Highld 295 D11
Shield Row Durham 242 G6
Shieldaig Highld 299 B8
Shieldaig Highld 299 D8
Shieldhall Glasgow 267 B10
Shieldhill Dumfries 248 F2
Shieldhill Falk 279 F7
Shieldhill S Lnrk 269 G10
Shielfoot Highld 289 C8
Shielhill Angus 287 B8
Shielhill Invclyd 276 G4
Shifford Oxon 82 E5
Shifnal Shrops 132 B4
Shilbottle Northumb 252 B5
Shilbottle Grange
Northumb 252 B6
Shildon Durham 233 F10
Shillford E Renf 267 D8
Shillingford Devon 27 C7
Shillingford Oxon 83 G9
Shillingford Abbot Devon 14 D4
Shillingford St George
Devon 14 D4
Shillingstone Dorset 30 E4
Shillington C Beds 104 E2
Shillmoor Northumb 251 B9
Shilton Oxon 82 D3
Shilton Warks 135 G8
Shilvington Northumb 252 G5
Shimpling Norf 142 G3
Shimpling Suff 125 G7
Shimpling Street Suff 125 G7
Shincliffe Durham 233 C11
Shiney Row T & W 243 G8
Shinfield Wokingham 65 F8
Shingay Cambs 104 B6
Shingham Norf 140 C5
Shingle Street Suff 109 C7
Shinner's Bridge Devon 8 C5
Shinness Highld 309 H5
Shipbourne Kent 52 C5
Shipdham Norf 141 B9
Shipham Som 44 B2
Shiphay Torbay 9 B7
Shiplake Oxon 65 D9
Shiplake Bottom Oxon 65 C8
Shiplake Row Oxon 65 D9
Shiplate N Som 43 B11
Shiplaw Borders 270 F4
Shipley Derbys 170 G6
Shipley Northumb 264 F4
Shipley Shrops 132 D6
Shipley W Sus 35 C10
Shipley W Yorks 205 F8
Shipley Bridge Sur 51 E10
Shipley Common
Derbys 171 G7
Shipley Shiels Northumb 251 E7
Shipmeadow Suff 143 F7
Shipping Pembs 73 D10
Shippon Oxon 83 F7
Shipston-on-Stour
Warks 100 C5
Shipton Bucks 102 F5
Shipton Glos 81 B8
Shipton N Yorks 207 B7
Shipton Shrops 131 E11
Shipton Bellinger Hants 47 D8
Shipton Gorge Dorset 16 C5
Shipton Green W Sus 22 C4
Shipton Lee Bucks 102 G4
Shipton Moyne Glos 61 B11
Shipton Oliffe Glos 81 B8
Shipton on Cherwell
Oxon 83 B7
Shipton Solers Glos 81 B8
Shipton-under-
Wychwood Oxon 82 B3
Shiptonthorpe E Yorks 208 E3
Shirburn Oxon 83 F11
Shirdley Hill Lancs 193 E11
Shire Oak W Mid 133 C11
Shirebrook Derbys 171 B8
Shirecliffe S Yorks 186 C4
Shiregreen S Yorks 186 C5
Shirehampton Bristol 60 D4
Shiremoor T & W 243 C8
Shirenewton Mon 79 G7
Shireoaks Derbys 185 E9
Shireoaks Notts 187 E9
Shires Mill Fife 279 D10
Shirkoak Kent 54 F2
Shirl Heath Hereford 115 F8
Shirland Derbys 170 D6
Shirlett Shrops 132 D3
Shirley Derbys 170 G2
Shirley Hants 19 B9
Shirley London 67 F11
Shirley Soton 32 E6
Shirley W Mid 118 B2
Shirley Heath W Mid 118 B2
Shirley holms Hants 19 B11
Shirley Warren Soton 32 E5
Shirrell Heath Hants 33 E9
Shirwell Devon 40 F5
Shirwell Cross Devon 40 F5
Shiskine N Ayrs 255 E10
Shitterton Dorset 18 C2
Shobdon Hereford 115 E8
Shobley Hants 31 F11
Shobnall Staffs 152 E4
Shobrooke Devon 26 G5
Shoby Leics 154 F3
Shocklach W Ches 166 F6
Shocklach Green
W Ches 166 F6
Shoeburyness Sthend 70 C2
Sholden Kent 55 C11
Sholing Soton 32 E6
Sholing Common Soton 33 E7
Sholver Gtr Man 196 F3
Shoot Hill Shrops 149 G8
Shootash Hants 32 C4
Shooters Hill London 68 D2
Shootersway Herts 85 D7
Shop Corn 10 G3
Shop Corn 24 E2
Shop Devon 24 E5
Shop Corner Suff 108 E4
Shopford Cumb 240 C3
Shopnoller Som 43 G7
Shopp Hill W Sus 34 B6
Shopwyke W Sus 22 B5
Shore Gtr Man 196 D2
Shore W Yorks 196 B2
Shore Bottom Devon 28 G2
Shore Mill Highld 301 C7
Shoreditch London 67 C10
Shoreditch Som 28 C2
Shoregill Cumb 222 E5
Shoreham Kent 68 G4
Shoreham Beach W Sus 36 G2
Shoreham-by-Sea
W Sus 36 F2
Shores Green Oxon 82 D5
Shoresdean Northumb 273 F9
Shoreside Shetland 313 J4
Shoreswood Northumb 273 F8
Shoreton Highld 300 C6
Shorley Hants 33 B9
Shorncliffe Camp Kent 55 F7
Shorncote Glos 81 F8
Shorne Kent 69 E7
Shorne Ridgeway Kent 69 E7
Shorne West Kent 69 E7
Short Cross W Mid 133 G9
Short Green Norf 141 F11
Short Heath Derbys 152 G6
Short Heath W Mid 133 C9
Short Heath W Mid 133 E11
Short Street Wilts 45 D10
Shortacombe Devon 12 D6
Shortacross Corn 6 D5
Shortbridge E Sus 37 C7
Shortfield Common Sur 49 E10
Shortgate E Sus 23 B7
Shorthampton Oxon 100 G6
Shortheath Hants 49 F9
Shortheath Sur 49 E10
Shorthill Shrops 131 B8
Shortlands London 67 F11
Shortlanesend Corn 4 F6
Shortlees E Ayrs 257 B10
Shortmoor Devon 28 G2
Shortmoor Dorset 29 G7
Shorton Torbay 9 C7
Shortroods Renfs 267 B9
Shortstanding Glos 79 C9
Shortstown Beds 103 B11
Shortwood Glos 80 F4
Shortwood S Glos 61 D7
Shorwell I o W 20 E5
Shoscombe Bath 45 B8
Shoscombe Vale Bath 45 B8
Shotatton Shrops 149 E7
Shotesham Norf 142 D5
Shotgate Essex 88 G3
Shotley Northants 137 D8
Shotley Suff 108 D4
Shotley Bridge Durham 242 G3
Shotley Gate Suff 108 E4
Shotleyfield Northumb 242 G3
Shottenden Kent 54 C4
Shottermill Sur 49 G11
Shottery Warks 118 G3
Shotteswell Warks 101 B8
Shottisham Suff 108 C6
Shottle Derbys 170 F4
Shottlegate Derbys 170 F4
Shotton Durham 234 D4
Shotton Durham 234 F3
Shotton Flint 166 B4
Shotton Northumb 242 B6
Shotton Northumb 263 C8
Shotton Colliery Durham 234 C3
Shotts N Lnrk 269 C7
Shotwick W Ches 182 G4
Shouldham Norf 140 B3
Shouldham Thorpe
Norf 140 B3
Shoulton Worcs 116 F6
Shover's Green E Sus 53 G7
Shraleybrook Staffs 168 F3
Shrawardine Shrops 149 F8
Shrawley Worcs 116 E6
Shreding Green Bucks 66 C4
Shrewley Warks 118 D4
Shrewley Common
Warks 118 D4
Shrewsbury Shrops 149 G9
Shrewton Wilts 46 E5
Shripney W Sus 22 C6
Shrivenham Oxon 63 B8
Shropham Norf 141 E9
Shroton or
Iwerne Courtney Dorset 30 E5
Shrub End Essex 107 G9
Shrubs Hill Sur 66 F3
Shrutherhill S Lnrk 268 E5
Shucknall Hereford 97 C11
Shudy Camps Cambs 106 C2
Shulishadermor Highld 298 E4
Shulista Highld 298 B4
Shuna Ho Argyll 275 C8
Shurdington Glos 80 B6
Shurlock Row Windsor 65 E10
Shurnock Worcs 117 E10
Shurrery Highld 310 D4
Shurrery Lodge Highld 310 D4
Shurton Som 43 E8
Shustoke Warks 134 E4
Shut Heath Staffs 151 E7
Shute Devon 15 B11
Shute Devon 26 G5
Shute End Wilts 31 B11
Shutford Oxon 101 C7
Shuthonger Glos 99 D7
Shutlanger Northants 120 G4
Shutt Green Staffs 133 B7
Shutta Corn 6 E5
Shuttington Warks 134 B5
Shuttlesfield Kent 55 E7
Shuttlewood Derbys 187 G7
Shuttleworth Gtr Man 195 D10
Shutton Hereford 98 F3
Shwt Bridgend 57 D11
Siabost bho Dheas
W Isles 304 D4
Siabost bho Thuath
W Isles 304 D4
Siadar W Isles 304 C5
Siadar Iarach W Isles 304 C5
Siadar Uarach W Isles 304 C5
Sibbaldbie Dumfries 248 F4
Sibbertoft Northants 136 G3
Sibdon Carwood Shrops 131 G8
Sibford Ferris Oxon 101 D7
Sibford Gower Oxon 101 D7
Sible Hedingham Essex 106 E5
Sibley's Green Essex 106 F2
Sibsey Lincs 174 E5
Sibsey Fen Side Lincs 174 E4
Sibson Cambs 137 D11
Sibson Leics 135 C7
Sibster Highld 310 D7
Sibthorpe Notts 172 F3
Sibthorpe Notts 188 G2
Sibton Suff 127 D7
Sibton Green Suff 127 C7
Sicklesmere Suff 125 E7
Sicklinghall N Yorks 206 D3
Sid Devon 15 D8
Sidbrook Som 28 B3
Sidbury Devon 15 C8
Sidbury Shrops 132 F3
Sidcot N Som 44 B2
Sidcup London 68 E3
Siddal W Yorks 196 C6
Siddick Cumb 228 E6
Siddington E Ches 184 G4
Siddington Glos 81 F8
Siddington Heath
E Ches 184 G4
Side of the Moor
Gtr Man 195 E8
Sidemoor Worcs 117 C9
Sidestrand Norf 160 B5
Sideway Stoke 168 G5
Sidford Devon 15 C8
Sidlesham W Sus 22 D5
Sidlesham Common
W Sus 22 C5
Sidley E Sus 38 F2
Sidlow Sur 51 D9
Sidmouth Devon 15 D8
Sidway Staffs 150 B5
Sigford Devon 13 G11
Sigglesthorne E Yorks 209 D9
Sighthill Edin 280 G3
Sighthill Glasgow 268 B2
Sigingstone = Tresigin
V Glam 58 E3
Signet Oxon 82 C2
Sigwells Som 29 C10
Silchester Hants 64 G6
Sildinis W Isles 305 G4
Sileby Leics 153 F11
Silecroft Cumb 210 C2
Silfield Norf 142 D2
Silford Devon 24 B6
Silian Ceredig 111 G11
Silk Willoughby Lincs 173 G9
Silkstead Hants 32 C6
Silkstone S Yorks 197 F9
Silkstone Common
S Yorks 197 G9
Silloth Cumb 238 G4
Sills Northumb 251 C8
Sillyearn Moray 302 D5
Siloh Carms 94 D4
Silpho N Yorks 227 G9
Silsden W Yorks 204 D6
Silsoe C Beds 103 D11
Silton Dorset 30 B3
Silver End Essex 88 B4
Silver End W Mid 133 F8
Silver Green Norf 142 E5
Silver Hill E Sus 38 B2
Silver Knap Som 29 C11
Silver Street Glos 80 E3
Silver Street Kent 69 G11
Silver Street Som 27 C11
Silver Street Som 44 G4
Silver Street Worcs 117 B11
Silverburn Midloth 270 C4
Silverdale Lancs 211 E9
Silverdale Staffs 168 F4
Silverdale Green Lancs 211 E9
Silvergate Norf 160 D3
Silverhill E Sus 38 E3
Silverhill Park E Sus 38 E4
Silverknowes Edin 280 F4
Silverley's Green Suff 126 B5
Silvermuir S Lnrk 269 F8
Silverstone Northants 102 C3
Silverton Devon 27 G7
Silverton W Dunb 277 F8
Silvertonhill S Lnrk 268 E4
Silvertown London 68 D2
Silverwell Corn 4 F4
Silvington Shrops 116 B2
Silwick Shetland 313 J4
Sim Hill S Yorks 197 G9
Simister Gtr Man 195 F10
Simmondley Derbys 185 C8
Simm's Cross Halton 183 D8
Simm's Lane End Mers 194 G4
Simonburn Northumb 241 C9
Simonsbath Som 41 F9
Simonsburrow Devon 27 D10
Simonside T & W 243 E8
Simonstone Lancs 203 G11
Simonstone N Yorks 223 G7
Simprim Borders 272 F6
Simpson M Keynes 103 D7
Simpson Pembs 72 B5
Simpson Cross Pembs 72 B5
Simpson Green W Yorks 205 F9
Sinclair's Hill Borders 272 E6
Sinclairston E Ayrs 257 F11
Sinclairtown Fife 280 C5
Sinderby N Yorks 214 C6
Sinderhope Northumb 241 G8
Sinderland Green
Gtr Man 184 C2
Sindlesham Wokingham 65 F9
Sinfin Derby 152 C6
Sinfin Moor Derby 153 C7
Singdean Borders 250 C3
Single Hill Bath 45 B8
Singleborough Bucks 102 E5
Singleton Lancs 202 F3
Singleton W Sus 34 E5
Singlewell Kent 69 E7
Singret Wrex 166 D4
Sinkhurst Green Kent 53 E10
Sinnahard Aberds 292 B6
Sinnington N Yorks 216 B4
Sinton Worcs 116 E6
Sinton Green Worcs 116 E6
Sion Hill Bath 61 F8
Sipson London 66 D5
Sirhowy Bl Gwent 77 C11
Sisland Norf 142 D6
Sissinghurst Kent 53 F9
Sisterpath Borders 272 F5
Siston S Glos 61 D7
Sithney Corn 2 D4
Sithney Common Corn 2 D4
Sithney Green Corn 2 D4
Sittingbourne Kent 70 G2
Six Ashes Staffs 132 F5
Six Bells Bl Gwent 78 E2
Six Hills Leics 154 E2
Six Mile Bottom Cambs 123 F11
Sixhills Lincs 189 D11
Sixmile Kent 54 E6
Sixpenny Handley
Dorset 31 D7
Sizewell Suff 127 E9
Skaigh Devon 13 C8
Skail Highld 308 E7
Skaill Orkney 314 F5
Skaill Orkney 314 C4
Skaill Orkney 314 E2
Skares E Ayrs 258 F2
Skateraw E Loth 282 F4
Skaw Shetland 312 B8
Skaw Shetland 312 G7
Skeabost Highld 298 E4
Skeabrae Orkney 314 D2
Skeeby N Yorks 224 E4
Skeete Kent 54 E6
Skeffington Leics 136 C4
Skeffling E Yorks 201 D11
Skegby Notts 171 C7
Skegby Notts 188 G3
Skegness Lincs 175 C9
Skelberry Shetland 313 G6
Skelberry Shetland 313 M5
Skelbo Highld 309 K7
Skelbo Street Highld 309 K7
Skelbrooke S Yorks 198 E4
Skeldyke Lincs 156 B6
Skelfhill Borders 249 C11
Skellingthorpe Lincs 188 G6
Skellister Shetland 313 H6
Skellorn Green E Ches 184 E6
Skellow S Yorks 198 E4
Skelmanthorpe W Yorks 197 E8
Skelmersdale Lancs 194 F3
Skelmonae Aberds 303 F8
Skelmorlie N Ayrs 266 B3
Skelmuir Aberds 303 E9
Skelpick Highld 308 D7
Skelton Cumb 230 D4
Skelton E Yorks 199 B9
Skelton N Yorks 223 E11
Skelton Redcar 226 B3
Skelton York 207 B7
Skelton-on-Ure N Yorks 215 F7
Skelwick Orkney 314 B4
Skelwith Bridge Cumb 220 E6
Skendleby Lincs 174 B6
Skendleby Psalter Lincs 190 G6
Skene Ho Aberds 293 C9
Skenfrith Mon 97 G9
Skerne E Yorks 208 B6
Skerne Park Darl 224 C5
Skeroblingarry Argyll 255 E8
Skerray Highld 308 C6
Skerricha Highld 306 D7
Skerryford Pembs 72 C6
Skerton Lancs 211 G9
Sketchley Leics 135 E8
Sketty Swansea 56 C6
Skewen = Sgiwen Neath 57 B8
Skewes Corn 5 B9
Skewsby N Yorks 216 E2
Skeyton Norf 160 D4
Skeyton Corner Norf 160 D5
Skiag Bridge Highld 307 G7
Skibo Castle Highld 309 L7
Skidbrooke Lincs 190 C6
Skidbrooke North End
Lincs 190 B6
Skidby E Yorks 208 G6
Skilgate Som 27 B7
Skillington Lincs 155 D7
Skinburness Cumb 238 F4
Skinflats Falk 279 E8
Skinidin Highld 298 E2
Skinner's Bottom Corn 4 F4
Skinners Green W Berks 64 F2
Skinnet Highld 308 C5
Skinningrove Redcar 226 B4
Skipness Argyll 255 B9
Skippool Lancs 202 E3
Skiprigg Cumb 230 B3
Skipsea E Yorks 209 B9
Skipsea Brough E Yorks 209 C9
Skipton N Yorks 204 C5
Skipton-on-Swale
N Yorks 215 D7
Skipwith N Yorks 207 F9
Skirbeck Lincs 174 G4
Skirbeck Quarter Lincs 174 G4
Skirethorns N Yorks 213 G9
Skirlaugh E Yorks 209 F8
Skirling Borders 260 B3
Skirmett Bucks 65 B9
Skirpenbeck E Yorks 207 B10
Skirwith Cumb 231 E8
Skirza Highld 310 C7
Skitby Cumb 239 D10
Skitham Lancs 202 E4
Skittle Green Bucks 84 E3
Skulamus Highld 295 C8
Skullomie Highld 308 C6
Skyborry Green Shrops 114 C5
Skye Green Essex 107 G7
Skye of Curr Highld 301 G9
Skyfog Pembs 90 F6
Skyreholme N Yorks 213 G11
Slack Derbys 170 C4
Slack W Yorks 196 B3
Slack W Yorks 196 D5
Slack Head Cumb 211 D9
Slackcote Gtr Man 196 F3
Slackhall Derbys 185 E9
Slackhead Moray 302 C4
Slackholme End Lincs 191 G8
Slacks of Cairnbanno
Aberds 303 E8
Slad Glos 80 D5
Sladbrook Glos 98 F5
Slade Devon 27 F10
Slade Devon 40 D4
Slade Kent 54 C2
Slade Pembs 72 B6
Slade End Oxon 83 G9
Slade Green London 68 D4
Slade Heath Staffs 133 B8
Slade Hooton S Yorks 187 D8
Sladen Green Hants 48 C2
Slades Green Worcs 99 E7
Sladesbridge Corn 10 G6
Slaggyford Northumb 240 G5
Slaidburn Lancs 203 C10
Slaithwaite W Yorks 196 E5
Slaley Derbys 170 D3
Slaley Northumb 241 F11
Slamannan Falk 279 G7
Slape Cross Som 43 F10
Slapewath Redcar 226 B2
Slapton Bucks 103 G8
Slapton Devon 8 G6
Slapton Northants 102 B2
Slate Haugh Moray 302 C4
Slateford Edin 280 G4
Slatepit Dale Derbys 170 B4
Slattocks Gtr Man 195 F11
Slaugham W Sus 36 B3
Slaughter Hill E Ches 168 D2
Slaughterbridge Corn 11 D8
Slaughterford Wilts 61 E10
Slawston Leics 136 E5
Slay Pits S Yorks 199 F7
Sleaford Hants 49 F10
Sleaford Lincs 173 F9
Sleagill Cumb 221 B11
Sleap Shrops 149 D9
Sleapford Telford 150 F2
Sleapshyde Herts 86 D2
Sleastary Highld 309 K6
Slebech Pembs 73 B8
Sledge Green Worcs 98 E6
Sledmere E Yorks 217 G8
Sleeches Cross E Sus 52 G5
Sleepers Hill Hants 33 B7
Sleet Moor Derbys 170 E6
Sleetbeck Cumb 240 B2
Sleight Dorset 18 B5
Sleights N Yorks 227 D7
Slepe Dorset 18 C4
Sliabhna h-Airde
W Isles 296 F3
Slickly Highld 310 C6
Sliddery N Ayrs 255 E10
Slideslow Worcs 117 C9
Sligachan Hotel Highld 294 C6
Sligneach Argyll 288 G4
Sligrachan Argyll 276 C3
Slimbridge Glos 80 E2
Slindon Staffs 150 C6
Slindon W Sus 35 F7
Slinfold W Sus 50 G6
Sling Glos 79 D9
Sling Gwyn 163 B10
Slingsby N Yorks 216 E3
Slioch Aberds 302 F5
Slip End C Beds 85 B9
Slip End Herts 104 D5
Slippery Ford W Yorks 204 E6
Slipton Northants 121 B9
Slitting Mill Staffs 151 F10
Slochd Highld 301 G8
Slockavullin Argyll 275 D9
Slogan Moray 302 E3
Sloley Norf 160 E5
Sloncombe Devon 13 D10
Sloothby Lincs 191 G7
Slough Slough 66 D3
Slough Green Som 28 C3
Slough Green W Sus 36 B3
Slough Hill Suff 125 G7
Sluggan Highld 301 G8
Sluggans Highld 298 E4
Slumbay Highld 295 B10
Sly Corner Kent 54 G3
Slyfield Sur 50 C3
Slyne Lancs 211 F9
Smailholm Borders 262 B4
Small Dole W Sus 36 E2
Small End Lincs 174 D6
Small Heath W Mid 134 F2
Small Hythe Kent 53 G11
Small Way Som 44 G6
Smallbridge Gtr Man 196 D2
Smallbrook Devon 14 B3
Smallbrook Glos 79 E9
Smallburgh Norf 160 E6
Smallburn Aberds 303 E10
Smallburn E Ayrs 258 D5
Smalldale Derbys 185 E11
Smalldale Derbys 185 F9
Smalley Derbys 170 G6
Smalley Common
Derbys 170 G6
Smalley Green Derbys 170 G6
Smallfield Sur 51 E10
Smallford Herts 85 D11
Smallholm Dumfries 238 B4
Smallmarsh Devon 25 C10
Smallrice Staffs 151 C9
Smallridge Devon 28 G4
Smallshaw Gtr Man 196 G2
Smallthorne Stoke 168 E5
Smallwood E Ches 168 C4
Smallwood Worcs 117 D10
Smallwood Green Suff 125 F8
Smallwood Hey Lancs 202 D3
Smallworth Norf 141 G10
Smannell Hants 47 D11
Smardale Cumb 222 D4
Smarden Kent 53 E11
Smarden Bell Kent 53 E11
Smart's Hill Kent 52 E4
Smaull Argyll 274 G3
Smeatharpe Devon 27 E11
Smeaton Fife 280 C5
Smeeth Kent 54 F5
Smeeton Westerby
Leics 136 E3
Smelthouses N Yorks 214 G3
Smercleit W Isles 297 K3
Smerral Highld 310 F5
Smestow Staffs 133 E7
Smethcott Shrops 131 D9
Smethwick W Mid 133 F10
Smethwick Green
E Ches 168 C4
Smirisary Highld 289 B8
Smisby Derbys 152 F6
Smite Hill Worcs 117 F7
Smith End Green Worcs 116 G5
Smith Green Lancs 202 C5
Smithaleigh Devon 7 D11
Smithbrook W Sus 34 C6
Smithfield Cumb 239 D10
Smithies S Yorks 197 F11
Smithincott Devon 27 E9
Smithley S Yorks 197 G11
Smith's End Herts 105 D8
Smith's Green E Ches 168 E3
Smiths Green E Ches 184 G4
Smith's Green Essex 105 G11
Smith's Green Essex 106 C3
Smithston Aberds 302 G5
Smithstown Highld 299 B7
Smithton Highld 301 E7
Smithwood Green Suff 125 G8
Smithy Bridge Gtr Man 196 D2
Smithy Gate Flint 181 F11
Smithy Green E Ches 184 G2
Smithy Green Gtr Man 184 D5
Smithy Houses Derbys 170 F5
Smithy Lane Ends Lancs 194 E2
Smock Alley W Sus 35 D9
Smockington Leics 135 F9
Smoky Row Bucks 84 D4
Smoogro Orkney 314 F3
Smug Oak Herts 85 E10
Smyrton S Ayrs 244 G4
Smythe's Green Essex 88 B6
Snagshall E Sus 38 C3
Snaigow House Perth 286 C4
Snailbeach Shrops 131 C7
Snails Hill Som 29 E7
Snailswell Herts 104 E3
Snailwell Cambs 124 D2
Snainton N Yorks 217 C8
Snaisgill Durham 232 F5
Snaith E Yorks 198 C6
Snape N Yorks 214 C5
Snape Suff 127 F7
Snape Green Lancs 193 E11
Snape Hill Derbys 186 F5
Snape Hill S Yorks 198 G2
Snapper Devon 40 G5
Snaresbrook London 67 B11
Snarestone Leics 134 B6
Snarford Lincs 189 E9
Snargate Kent 39 B7
Snarraness Shetland 313 H4
Snatchwood Torf 78 E3
Snave Kent 39 B8
Sneachill Worcs 117 G8
Snead Powys 130 E6
Snead Common Worcs 116 D4
Sneads Green Worcs 117 D7
Sneath Common Norf 142 F3
Sneaton N Yorks 227 D7
Sneatonthorpe N Yorks 227 D8
Snedshill Telford 132 B4
Sneinton Nottingham 153 B11
Snelland Lincs 189 E9
Snelston Derbys 169 G11
Snetterton Norf 141 E9
Snettisham Norf 158 C3
Sneyd Green Stoke 168 F5
Sneyd Park Bristol 60 D5
Snibston Leics 153 G8
Snig's End Glos 98 F5
Snipeshill Kent 70 G2
Sniseabhal W Isles 297 H3
Snitter Northumb 252 C2
Snitterby Lincs 189 C7
Snitterfield Warks 118 F4
Snitterton Derbys 170 C3
Snitton Shrops 115 B11
Snittongate Shrops 115 B11
Snodhill Hereford 96 C6
Snodland Kent 69 G7
Snods Edge Northumb 242 G3
Snow End Herts 105 E8
Snow Hill E Ches 167 E10
Snow Hill W Yorks 197 C10
Snow Lea W Yorks 196 D5
Snow Street Norf 141 G11
Snowden Hill S Yorks 197 G9
Snowdown Kent 55 C8
Snowshill Glos 99 E11
Snydale W Yorks 198 D2
Soake Hants 33 E11
Soar Anglesey 178 G5
Soar Carms 94 F2
Soar Devon 9 G9
Soar Gwyn 146 B2
Soar Powys 95 E9
Soar-y-Mynydd Ceredig 112 G5
Soberton Hants 33 D10
Soberton Heath Hants 33 E10
Sockbridge Cumb 230 F6
Sockburn Darl 224 D6
Sockety Dorset 29 F7
Sodom Denb 181 G9
Sodom Shetland 313 G7
Sodom Wilts 62 C4
Sodylt Bank Shrops 148 B6
Soham Cambs 123 C11
Soham Cotes Cambs 123 B11
Soho London 67 C9
Soho Som 45 D7
Soho W Mid 133 F10
Solas W Isles 296 D4
Soldon Cross Devon 24 E4
Soldridge Hants 49 G7
Sole Street Kent 54 D5
Sole Street Kent 69 F7
Solfach = Solva Pembs 90 G5
Solihull W Mid 118 B2
Solihull Lodge W Mid 117 B11
Sollers Dilwyn Hereford 115 F8
Sollers Hope Hereford 98 E2
Sollom Lancs 194 D3
Solva = Solfach Pembs 90 G5
Somerby Leics 154 G5
Somerby Lincs 200 F5
Somercotes Derbys 170 E6
Somerdale Bath 61 F7
Somerford Dorset 19 C9
Somerford E Ches 168 B4
Somerford Staffs 133 B7
Somerford Keynes Glos 81 G8
Somerley W Sus 22 D4
Somerleyton Suff 143 D9
Somers Town London 67 C9
Somers Town Ptsmth 21 B8
Somersal Herbert
Derbys 152 B2
Somersby Lincs 190 G4
Somersham Cambs 123 B7
Somersham Suff 107 B11
Somerton Newport 59 B10
Somerton Oxon 101 F9
Somerton Som 29 B7
Somerton Suff 124 G6
Somerton Hill Som 29 B7
Somerwood Shrops 149 G11
Sompting W Sus 35 G11
Sompting Abbotts
W Sus 35 F11
Sonning Wokingham 65 D9
Sonning Common Oxon 65 C8
Sonning Eye Oxon 65 D9
Sontley Wrex 166 F4
Sookholme Notts 171 B8
Sopley Hants 19 B9
Sopwell Herts 85 D11
Sopworth Wilts 61 B10
Sorbie Dumfries 236 E6
Sordale Highld 310 C5
Sorisdale Argyll 288 C4
Sorley Devon 8 F4
Sorn E Ayrs 258 D3
Sornhill E Ayrs 258 C2
Sortat Highld 310 C6
Sotby Lincs 190 F2
Sothall S Yorks 186 E6
Sots Hole Lincs 173 C10
Sotterley Suff 143 G9
Soudley Shrops 131 E9
Soudley Shrops 150 D4
Soughley S Yorks 197 G7
Soughton = Sychdyn
Flint 166 B2
Soulbury Bucks 103 F7

Soulby Cumb 222 C4
Soulby Cumb 230 F5
Souldern Oxon 101 E10
Souldrop Beds 121 E9
Sound E Ches 167 F10
Sound Shetland 313 H5
Sound Shetland 313 J6
Sound Heath E Ches 167 F10
Soundwell S Glos 60 D6
Sour Nook Cumb 230 C3
Sourhope Borders 263 E8
Sourin Orkney 314 C4
Sourlie N Ayrs 266 G6
Sourton Devon 12 C6
Soutergate Cumb 210 C4
South Acre Norf 158 G6
South Acton London 67 D7
South Alkham Kent 55 E8
South Allington Devon 9 G10
South Alloa Falk 279 C7
South Ambersham W Sus 34 C6
South Anston S Yorks 187 E8
South Ascot Windsor 66 F2
South Ashford Kent 54 E4
South Auchmachar Aberds 303 E9
South Baddesley Hants 20 B3
South Ballachulish Highld 284 B4
South Balloch S Ayrs 245 D8
South Bank Redcar 234 G6
South Bank York 207 C7
South Barrow Som 29 B10
South Beach Northumb 243 B8
South Beach = Marian-y-de Gwyn 145 C7
South Beddington London 67 G9
South Benfleet Essex 69 B9
South Bents T & W 243 E10
South Bersted W Sus 22 C6
South Blainslie Borders 271 G10
South Bockhampton Dorset 19 B9
South Bramwith S Yorks 198 E6
South Brent Devon 8 D3
South Brewham Som 45 F8
South Bromley London 67 C11
South Broomage Falk 279 E7
South Broomhill Northumb 252 D6
South Burlingham Norf 143 B7
South Cadbury Som 29 B10
South Cairn Dumfries 236 C1
South Carlton Lincs 189 F7
South Carlton Notts 187 E9
South Carne Corn 11 E10
South Cave E Yorks 208 G4
South Cerney Glos 81 F8
South Chailey E Sus 36 D5
South Chard Som 28 F4
South Charlton Northumb 264 E5
South Cheriton Som 29 C11
South Church Durham 233 F10
South Cliffe E Yorks 208 F3
South Clifton Notts 188 G4
South Clunes Highld 300 E5
South Cockerington Lincs 190 D5
South Common Devon 28 G4
South Cornelly Bridgend 57 E10
South Corriegills N Ayrs 256 C2
South Corrielaw Dumfries 248 G5
South Cove Suff 143 G9
South Creagan Argyll 289 E11
South Creake Norf 159 B7
South Crosland W Yorks 196 E6
South Croxton Leics 154 G3
South Croydon London 67 G10
South Cuil Highld 298 C3
South Dalton E Yorks 208 D5
South Darenth Kent 68 F5
South Denes Norf 143 C10
South Down Hants 33 C7
South Down Som 28 E2
South Duffield N Yorks 207 G9
South Dunn Highld 310 D5
South Earlswood Sur 51 D9
South Elkington Lincs 190 D3
South Elmsall W Yorks 198 E3
South Elphinstone E Loth 281 G7
South End Beds 103 B10
South End Bucks 103 F7
South End Cumb 210 G4
South End E Yorks 209 E9
South End Hants 31 D10
South-end Herts 86 B6
South End N Lincs 200 C6
South End Norf 141 E9
South Erradale Highld 299 B7
South Fambridge Essex 88 F5
South Farnborough Hants 49 C11
South Fawley W Berks 63 C11
South Ferriby N Lincs 200 C3
South Field E Yorks 200 B4
South Field Windsor 66 D3
South Flobbets Aberds 303 F7
South Garth Shetland 312 D7
South Garvan Highld 289 B11
South Glendale W Isles 297 K3
South Gluss Shetland 312 F5
South Godstone Sur 51 D11
South Gorley Hants 31 E11
South Gosforth T & W 242 D6
South Green Essex 89 B8
South Green Essex 87 G11
South Green Kent 69 G11
South Green Norf 157 F10
South Green Norf 159 G11
South Green Suff 126 B3
South Gyle Edin 280 G3
South-haa Shetland 312 E5
South Hackney London 67 C11
South Ham Hants 48 C6
South Hampstead London 67 C9
South Hanningfield Essex 88 F2
South Harefield London 66 B5
South Harrow London 66 B6
South Harting W Sus 34 D3
South Hatfield Herts 86 D2
South Hayling Hants 21 B10
South Hazelrigg Northumb 264 C3
South Heath Bucks 84 E6
South Heath Essex 89 B10
South Heighton E Sus 23 E7
South-heog Shetland 312 E5
South Hetton Durham 234 B3
South Hiendley W Yorks 197 E11
South Hill Corn 12 G2
South Hill N Som 43 B10
South Hill Pembs 72 C4
South Hinksey Oxon 83 E8
South Hole Devon 24 C2
South Holme N Yorks 216 D3
South Holmwood Sur 51 D7
South Hornchurch London 68 C4
South Huish Devon 8 G3
South Hykeham Lincs 172 C6
South Hylton T & W 243 F9
South Kelsey Lincs 189 B8
South Kensington London 67 D9
South Kessock Highld 300 E6
South Killingholme N Lincs 201 D7
South Kilvington N Yorks 215 C8
South Kilworth Leics 136 G2
South Kirkby W Yorks 198 E2
South Kirkton Aberds 293 C9
South Kiscadale N Ayrs 256 D2
South Knighton Devon 14 G2
South Knighton Leicester 136 C2
South Kyme Lincs 173 F11
South Lambeth London 67 D10
South Lancing W Sus 35 G11
South Lane S Yorks 197 F9
South Leigh Oxon 82 D5
South Leverton Notts 188 E3
South Littleton Worcs 99 B11
South Lopham Norf 141 G10
South Luffenham Rutland 137 C8
South Malling E Sus 36 E6
South Marston Swindon 63 B7
South Merstham Sur 51 C9
South Middleton Northumb 263 E11
South Milford N Yorks 206 G5
South Millbrex Aberds 303 E8
South Milton Devon 8 G4
South Mimms Herts 86 E2
South Molton Devon 26 B2
South Moor Durham 242 G5
South Moreton Oxon 64 B5
South Mundham W Sus 22 C5
South Muskham Notts 172 D3
South Newbald E Yorks 208 F4
South Newbarns Cumb 210 F4
South Newington Oxon 101 E8
South Newsham Northumb 243 B8
South Newton Wilts 46 G5
South Normanton Derbys 170 D6
South Norwood London 67 F10
South Nutfield Sur 51 D10
South Ockendon Thurrock 68 C5
South Ormsby Lincs 190 F5
South Ossett W Yorks 197 D9
South Otterington N Yorks 215 B7
South Owersby Lincs 189 C9
South Oxhey Herts 85 G10
South Park Sur 51 D8
South Pelaw Durham 243 G7
South Perrott Dorset 29 F7
South Petherton Som 28 D6
South Petherwin Corn 12 E2
South Pickenham Norf 141 C7
South Pill Corn 7 D8
South Pool Devon 8 G5
South Poorton Dorset 16 B6
South Port Argyll 284 E4
South Quilquox Aberds 303 F8
South Radworthy Devon 41 G9
South Rauceby Lincs 173 F8
South Raynham Norf 159 E7
South Reddish Gtr Man 184 C5
South Reston Lincs 190 E6
South Ruislip London 66 B6
South Runcton Norf 140 B2
South Scarle Notts 172 C4
South Shian Argyll 289 E11
South Shields T & W 243 D9
South Shore Blkpool 202 G2
South Side Durham 233 F8
South Side Orkney 314 D5
South Somercotes Lincs 190 C6
South Stainley N Yorks 214 G6
South Stainmore Cumb 222 C6
South Stanley Durham 242 G5
South Stifford Thurrock 68 D6
South Stoke Oxon 64 C6
South Stoke W Sus 35 F8
South Stour Kent 54 F4
South Street E Sus 36 D5
South Street Kent 54 B5
South Street Kent 68 G6
South Street Kent 69 G10
South Street Kent 70 F6
South Street London 52 B2
South Tawton Devon 13 C9
South Tehidy Corn 4 G3
South Thoresby Lincs 190 F6
South Tidworth Wilts 47 D8
South Tottenham London 67 B10
South Town Devon 14 E5
South Town Hants 49 F7
South Twerton Bath 61 G8
South Ulverston Cumb 210 D6
South View Hants 48 C6
South Voxter Shetland 313 G5
South Walsham Norf 161 G7
South Warnborough Hants 49 D8
South Weald Essex 87 G9
South Weirs Hants 32 G3
South Weston Oxon 84 F2
South Wheatley Corn 11 C10
South Wheatley Notts 188 D3
South Whiteness Shetland 313 J5
South Widcombe Bath 44 B5
South Wigston Leics 135 D11
South Willesborough Kent 54 E4
South Willingham Lincs 189 E11
South Wimbledon London 67 E9
South Wingate Durham 234 E4
South Wingfield Derbys 170 D5
South Witham Lincs 155 F8
South Wonford Devon 24 F5
South Wonston Hants 48 F3
South Woodford London 86 G6
South Woodham Ferrers Essex 88 F4
South Wootton Norf 158 E2
South Wraxall Wilts 61 G10
South Yardley W Mid 134 G2
South Yarrows Highld 310 E7
South Yeo Devon 25 G8
South Zeal Devon 13 C9
Southall London 66 C6
Southam Cumb 219 C9
Southam Glos 99 F9
Southam Warks 119 E8
Southampton Soton 32 E6
Southay Som 28 D6
Southborough Kent 52 E5
Southborough Bromley 68 F2
Southborough Kingston-u-Thames 67 F7
Southbourne Bmouth 19 C8
Southbourne W Sus 22 B3
Southbrook Wilts 45 G10
Southburgh Norf 141 C9
Southburn E Yorks 208 C5
Southchurch Sthend 70 B2
Southcoombe Oxon 100 F6
Southcote Reading 65 E7
Southcott Corn 11 B9
Southcott Devon 24 D6
Southcott Wilts 47 B7
Southcourt Bucks 84 C4
Southcrest Worcs 117 D10
Southdean Borders 250 B4
Southdene Mers 182 B6
Southdown Bath 61 G8
Southdown Corn 7 E8
Southease E Sus 36 F6
Southend Argyll 255 G7
Southend Bucks 65 B9
Southend Glos 80 F2
Southend London 67 E11
Southend Oxon 83 E9
Southend W Berks 64 D2
Southend W Berks 64 E5
Southend Wilts 63 E7
Southend-on-Sea Sthend 69 B11
Southerhouse Shetland 313 K5
Southerly Devon 12 D6
Southern Cross Brighton 36 F3
Southern Green Herts 104 E6
Southernby Cumb 230 D3
Southernden Kent 53 D11
Southerndown V Glam 57 G11
Southerness Dumfries 237 D11
Southery Norf 140 E2
Southey Green Essex 106 E5
Southfield Northumb 243 B7
Southfields London 67 E9
Southfields Thurrock 69 C7
Southfleet Kent 68 E6
Southford I o W 20 F6
Southgate Ceredig 111 A11
Southgate London 86 G3
Southgate Norf 159 C7
Southgate Norf 160 E2
Southgate Swansea 56 D5
Southgate W Sus 51 F9
Southill C Beds 104 C3
Southill Dorset 17 E9
Southington Hants 48 D4
Southlands Dorset 17 F9
Southleigh Devon 15 C10
Southmarsh Som 45 G8
Southmead Bristol 60 D5
Southminster Essex 89 F7
Southmoor Oxon 82 F5
Southoe Cambs 122 E3
Southolt Suff 126 D3
Southorpe P'boro 137 C11
Southover Dorset 17 C8
Southover E Sus 36 F6
Southover E Sus 37 B11
Southowram W Yorks 196 C6
Southport Mers 193 D10
Southpunds Shetland 313 L6
Southrepps Norf 160 B5
Southrey Lincs 173 B10
Southrop Glos 81 E11
Southrop Oxon 101 E7
Southrope Hants 49 E7
Southsea Ptsmth 21 B8
Southsea Wrex 166 E4
Southstoke Bath 61 G8
Southtown Norf 143 B10
Southtown Orkney 314 G4
Southtown Som 28 D4
Southtown Som 44 F5
Southville Devon 8 G4
Southville Torf 78 F3
Southwaite Cumb 230 C4
Southwark London 67 D10
Southwater W Sus 35 B11
Southwater Street W Sus 35 B11
Southway Plym 7 C9
Southway Som 44 E4
Southwell Dorset 17 G9
Southwell Notts 172 E2
Southwick Hants 33 F10
Southwick Northants 137 E10
Southwick Som 43 D11
Southwick T & W 243 F9
Southwick W Sus 36 F2
Southwick Wilts 45 B10
Southwold Suff 127 B10
Southwood Derbys 153 E7
Southwood Hants 49 B10
Southwood Norf 143 B7
Southwood Som 44 G5
Southwood Worcs 116 E4
Soval Lodge W Isles 304 F5
Sowber Gate N Yorks 215 B7
Sower Carr Lancs 202 E3
Sowerby N Yorks 215 C8
Sowerby W Yorks 196 C4
Sowerby Bridge W Yorks 196 C5
Sowerby Row Cumb 230 D3
Sowley Green Suff 124 G4
Sowood W Yorks 196 D5
Sowood Green W Yorks 196 D5
Sowton Devon 14 C5
Sowton Barton Devon 14 D2
Soyal Highld 309 K5
Soyland Town W Yorks 196 C4
Spa Common Norf 160 C5
Spacey Houses N Yorks 206 C2
Spalding Lincs 156 E4
Spaldington E Yorks 207 G11
Spaldwick Cambs 122 C2
Spalford Notts 172 B4
Spanby Lincs 155 B11
Spango Invclyd 276 G4
Spanish Green Hants 49 B7
Sparham Norf 159 F11
Sparhamhill Norf 159 F11
Spark Bridge Cumb 210 C6
Sparkbrook W Mid 133 G11
Sparkford Som 29 B10
Sparkhill W Mid 133 G11
Sparkwell Devon 7 D11
Sparl Shetland 312 G5
Sparnon Corn 1 E3
Sparnon Gate Corn 4 G3
Sparrow Green Norf 159 G9
Sparrow Hill Som 44 C2
Sparrowpit Derbys 185 E9
Sparrow's Green E Sus 52 G6
Sparsholt Hants 48 G2
Sparsholt Oxon 63 B10
Spartylea Northumb 232 B3
Spath Staffs 151 B11
Spaunton N Yorks 226 G4
Spaxton Som 43 F8
Spean Bridge Highld 290 E4
Spear Hill W Sus 35 D10
Spearywell Hants 32 B4
Speckington Som 29 C9
Speed Gate Kent 68 F5
Speedwell Bristol 60 E6
Speen Bucks 84 F4
Speen W Berks 64 F3
Speeton N Yorks 218 E2
Speke Mers 182 E6
Speldhurst Kent 52 E5
Spellbrook Herts 87 B7
Spelsbury Oxon 101 G7
Spelter Bridgend 57 C11
Spen W Yorks 197 B7
Spen Green E Ches 168 C4
Spencers Wood Wokingham 65 F8
Spennells Worcs 116 C6
Spennithorne N Yorks 214 B2
Spennymoor Durham 233 E11
Spernall Warks 117 E11
Spetchley Worcs 117 G7
Spetisbury Dorset 30 G6
Spexhall Suff 143 G7
Spey Bay Moray 302 C3
Speybank Highld 291 C10
Speybridge Highld 301 G10
Speyview Moray 302 E2
Spillardsford Aberds 303 D10
Spilsby Lincs 174 B6
Spindlestone Northumb 264 C5
Spinkhill Derbys 187 F7
Spinney Hill Northants 120 E5
Spinney Hills Leicester 136 C2
Spinningdale Highld 309 L6
Spion Kop Notts 171 B9
Spirthill Wilts 62 D3
Spital Mers 182 E4
Spital Windsor 66 D3
Spital Hill S Yorks 187 C10
Spital in the Street Lincs 189 D7
Spital Tongues T & W 242 D6
Spitalbrook Herts 86 D5
Spitalfields London 67 C10
Spitalhill Derbys 169 F11
Spithurst E Sus 36 D6
Spittal Dumfries 236 D5
Spittal E Loth 281 F9
Spittal E Yorks 207 C11
Spittal Highld 310 D5
Spittal Northumb 273 E10
Spittal Pembs 91 G9
Spittal Stirl 277 D10
Spittal Houses S Yorks 186 B5
Spittal of Glenmuick Aberds 292 E5
Spittal of Glenshee Perth 292 F3
Spittalfield Perth 286 C5
Spittlegate Lincs 155 C8
Spixworth Norf 160 F4
Splatt Corn 10 F4
Splatt Corn 11 D10
Splatt Devon 25 F10
Splatt Som 43 F8
Splayne's Green E Sus 36 C6
Splott Cardiff 59 D7
Spofforth N Yorks 206 C3
Spon End W Mid 118 B6
Spon Green Flint 166 C3
Spondon Derby 153 B8
Spooner Row Norf 141 D11
Spoonleygate Shrops 132 D6
Sporle Norf 158 G6
Spotland Bridge Gtr Man 195 E11
Spott E Loth 282 F3
Spratton Northants 120 C4
Spreakley Sur 49 E10
Spreyton Devon 13 B9
Spriddlestone Devon 7 E10
Spridlington Lincs 189 E8
Sprig's Alley Oxon 84 F3
Spring Bank Cumb 229 G10
Spring Cottage Leics 152 F6
Spring End N Yorks 223 F9
Spring Gardens Som 45 D9
Spring Green Lancs 204 E4
Spring Grove London 67 D7
Spring Hill Gtr Man 196 F2
Spring Hill Lancs 195 B8
Spring Hill W Mid 133 D7
Spring Park London 67 F11
Spring Vale S Yorks 197 G9
Spring Valley I o M 192 E4
Springbank Glos 99 G8
Springboig Glasgow 268 C3
Springbourne Bmouth 19 C8
Springburn Glasgow 268 B2
Springfield Argyll 275 F11
Springfield Caerph 77 F11
Springfield Dumfries 239 D8
Springfield Essex 88 D2
Springfield Fife 287 F7
Springfield Gtr Man 194 F5
Springfield Highld 300 C6
Springfield M Keynes 103 D7
Springfield Moray 301 D10
Springfield W Mid 133 D8
Springfield W Mid 133 F9
Springfield W Mid 133 G11
Springfields Stoke 168 G5
Springhead Gtr Man 196 G3
Springhill E Renf 267 D10
Springhill I o W 20 B6
Springhill N Lnrk 269 D7
Springhill Staffs 133 B11
Springhill Staffs 133 C9
Springholm Dumfries 237 C10
Springkell Dumfries 239 B7
Springside N Ayrs 257 B9
Springthorpe Lincs 188 D5
Springwell Essex 105 C10
Springwell T & W 243 F7
Springwell T & W 243 F9
Springwells Dumfries 248 E3
Sproatley E Yorks 209 G9
Sproston Green W Ches 168 B2
Sprotbrough S Yorks 198 G4
Sproughton Suff 108 C2
Sprouston Borders 263 B7
Sprowston Norf 160 G4
Sproxton Leics 155 E7
Sproxton N Yorks 216 C2
Sprunston Cumb 230 B3
Spunhill Shrops 149 C8
Spurlands End Bucks 84 F5
Spurstow E Ches 167 D9
Spurtree Shrops 116 D2
Spynie Moray 302 C2
Spyway Dorset 16 C6
Square and Compass Pembs 91 E7
Squires Gate Blkpool 202 G2
Sraid Ruadh Argyll 288 E1
Srannda W Isles 296 C6
Sronphadruig Lodge Perth 291 F9
Stableford Shrops 132 D5
Stableford Staffs 150 B6
Stacey Bank S Yorks 186 C3
Stackhouse N Yorks 212 F6
Stackpole Pembs 73 F7
Stackpole Quay Pembs 73 F7
Stacksford Norf 141 E11
Stacksteads Lancs 195 C10
Stackyard Green Suff 107 B9
Staddiscombe Plym 7 E10
Staddlethorpe E Yorks 199 B10
Staddon Devon 24 C3
Staddon Devon 24 G5
Staden Derbys 185 G9
Stadhampton Oxon 83 F10
Stadhlaigearraidh W Isles 297 H3
Stadmorslow Staffs 168 D5
Staffield Cumb 230 C6
Staffin Highld 298 C4
Stafford Staffs 151 E8
Stafford Park Telford 132 B4
Stafford's Corner Essex 89 B7
Stafford's Green Dorset 29 C10
Stagbatch Hereford 115 F9
Stagden Cross Essex 87 C10
Stagehall Borders 271 G9
Stag's Head Devon 25 B11
Stagsden Beds 103 B9
Stagsden West End Beds 103 B9
Stain Highld 310 C7
Stainburn Cumb 228 F6
Stainburn N Yorks 205 D10
Stainby Lincs 155 E8
Staincliffe W Yorks 197 C8
Staincross S Yorks 197 E10
Staindrop Durham 233 G8
Staines Green Herts 86 C3
Staines-upon-Thames Sur 66 E4
Stainfield Lincs 155 D11
Stainfield Lincs 189 G10
Stainforth N Yorks 212 F6
Stainforth S Yorks 198 E6
Staining Lancs 202 F3
Stainland W Yorks 196 D5
Stainsacre N Yorks 227 D8
Stainsby Derbys 170 B6
Stainsby Lincs 190 G4
Stainton Cumb 211 B10
Stainton Cumb 230 F5
Stainton Cumb 239 F9
Stainton Durham 223 B11
Stainton M'bro 225 C9
Stainton N Yorks 224 F2
Stainton S Yorks 187 C9
Stainton by Langworth Lincs 189 F9
Stainton le Vale Lincs 189 C11
Stainton with Adgarley Cumb 210 E5
Staintondale N Yorks 227 F9
Stair Cumb 229 G10
Stair E Ayrs 257 E10
Stairfoot S Yorks 197 F11
Stairhaven Dumfries 236 D4
Staithes N Yorks 226 B5
Stake Hill Gtr Man 195 F11
Stake Pool Lancs 202 D4
Stakeford Northumb 253 F7
Stakenbridge Worcs 117 B7
Stalbridge Dorset 30 D2
Stalbridge Weston Dorset 30 D2
Stalham Norf 161 D7
Stalham Green Norf 161 E7
Stalisfield Green Kent 54 C3
Stallen Dorset 29 D10
Stalling Busk N Yorks 213 B8
Stallingborough NE Lincs 201 E7
Stallington Staffs 151 B8
Stalmine Lancs 202 D3
Stalmine Moss Side Lancs 202 D3
Stalybridge Gtr Man 185 B7
Stambermill W Mid 133 G8
Stamborough Som 42 F4
Stambourne Essex 106 D4
Stambourne Green Essex 106 D4
Stamford Lincs 137 B10
Stamford Bridge E Yorks 207 B10
Stamford Bridge W Ches 167 B7
Stamford Hill London 67 B10
Stamfordham Northumb 242 C3
Stamperland E Renf 267 D11
Stamshaw Ptsmth 33 G10
Stanah Cumb 220 B6
Stanah Lancs 202 E3
Stanborough Herts 86 C2
Stanbridge C Beds 103 G9
Stanbridge Dorset 31 G8
Stanbridgeford C Beds 103 G9
Stanbrook Essex 106 F2
Stanbrook Worcs 98 B6
Stanbury W Yorks 204 F6
Stand Gtr Man 195 F9
Stand N Lnrk 268 B5
Standburn Falk 279 G8
Standeford Staffs 133 B8
Standen Kent 53 E11
Standen Hall Lancs 203 E10
Standen Street Kent 53 G10
Standerwick Som 45 C10
Standford Hants 49 G10
Standford Bridge Telford 150 E4
Standingstone Cumb 229 B11
Standingstone Cumb 229 E7
Standish Glos 80 D4
Standish Gtr Man 194 E5
Standish Lower Ground Gtr Man 194 F5
Standlake Oxon 82 E5
Standon Hants 32 B6
Standon Herts 105 G7
Standon Staffs 150 B6
Standon Green End Herts 86 B5
Stane N Lnrk 269 D7
Stanecastle N Ayrs 257 E8
Stanfield Norf 159 E8
Stanfield Stoke 168 E5
Stanford C Beds 104 C3
Stanford Kent 54 F6
Stanford Norf 141 E7
Stanford Shrops 148 G6
Stanford Bishop Hereford 116 G3
Stanford Bridge Worcs 116 D4
Stanford Dingley W Berks 64 E5
Stanford End Wokingham 65 G8
Stanford Hills Notts 153 E10
Stanford in the Vale Oxon 82 G4
Stanford-le-Hope Thurrock 69 C7
Stanford on Avon Northants 119 B11
Stanford on Soar Notts 153 E10
Stanford on Teme Worcs 116 D4
Stanford Rivers Essex 87 E8
Stanfree Derbys 187 G7
Stanground P'boro 138 D4
Stanhill Lancs 195 B8
Stanhoe Norf 158 B6
Stanhope Borders 260 D4
Stanhope Durham 232 D5
Stanhope Kent 54 E3
Stanion Northants 137 F8
Stank Cumb 210 E4
Stanklyn Worcs 117 C7
Stanks W Yorks 206 F3
Stanley Derbys 170 G6
Stanley Durham 242 G5
Stanley Lancs 194 F3
Stanley Notts 171 C7
Stanley Perth 286 D5
Stanley Shrops 132 G3
Stanley Shrops 132 G5
Stanley Staffs 168 E6
Stanley W Yorks 197 C10
Stanley Wilts 62 E3
Stanley Common Derbys 170 G6
Stanley Crook Durham 233 D9
Stanley Downton Glos 80 E4
Stanley Ferry W Yorks 197 C11
Stanley Gate Lancs 194 G2
Stanley Green E Ches 184 E5
Stanley Green Poole 18 C6
Stanley Green Shrops 149 B10
Stanley Hill Hereford 98 C3
Stanley Moor Staffs 168 E6
Stanley Pontlarge Glos 99 E9
Stanleytown Rhondda 77 G8
Stanlow Staffs 132 D5
Stanlow W Ches 182 F6
Stanmer Brighton 36 F4
Stanmore Hants 33 B7
Stanmore London 85 G11
Stanmore Shrops 132 E4
Stanmore W Berks 64 D3
Stanner Powys 114 F5
Stannergate Dundee 287 D8
Stanners Hill Sur 66 G3
Stannersburn Northumb 250 F6
Stanningfield Suff 125 F7
Stanningley W Yorks 205 G10
Stannington Northumb 242 B6
Stannington S Yorks 186 D4
Stanpit Dorset 19 C9
Stansbatch Hereford 114 E6
Stansfield Suff 124 G5
Stanshope Staffs 169 E10
Stanstead Suff 106 B6
Stanstead Abbotts Herts 86 C5
Stansted Kent 68 G6
Stansted Airport Essex 105 G11
Stansted Mountfitchet Essex 105 G10
Stanthorne W Ches 167 B11
Stanton Glos 99 E11
Stanton Mon 96 G6
Stanton Northumb 252 F4
Stanton Staffs 169 F10
Stanton Suff 125 C9
Stanton by Bridge Derbys 153 D7
Stanton-by-Dale Derbys 153 B9
Stanton Chare Suff 125 C9
Stanton Drew Bath 60 G5
Stanton Fitzwarren Swindon 81 G11
Stanton Gate Notts 153 B9
Stanton Harcourt Oxon 82 D6
Stanton Hill Notts 171 C7
Stanton in Peak Derbys 170 C2
Stanton Lacy Shrops 115 B9
Stanton Lees Derbys 170 C3
Stanton Long Shrops 131 E11
Stanton-on-the-Wolds Notts 154 C2
Stanton Prior Bath 61 G7
Stanton St Bernard Wilts 62 G5
Stanton St John Oxon 83 D9
Stanton St Quintin Wilts 62 D2
Stanton Street Suff 125 D9
Stanton under Bardon Leics 153 G9
Stanton upon Hine Heath Shrops 149 E11
Stanton Wick Bath 60 G6
Stantonbury M Keynes 102 C6
Stantway Glos 80 C2
Stanwardine in the Fields Shrops 149 E8
Stanwardine in the Wood Shrops 149 D8
Stanway Essex 107 G8
Stanway Glos 99 E11
Stanway Green Essex 107 G9
Stanway Green Suff 126 C4
Stanwell Sur 66 E5
Stanwell Moor Sur 66 E4
Stanwick Northants 121 C9
Stanwick-St-John N Yorks 224 C3
Stanwix Cumb 239 F10
Stanycliffe Gtr Man 195 F11
Stanydale Shetland 313 H4
Staoinebrig W Isles 297 H3
Stape N Yorks 226 G5
Stapehill Dorset 31 G9
Stapeley E Ches 167 F11
Stapenhill Staffs 152 E5
Staple Kent 55 B9
Staple Som 42 E6
Staple Cross Devon 27 C8
Staple Fitzpaine Som 28 D3
Staple Hill S Glos 60 D6
Staple Hill Worcs 117 C9
Staple Lawns Som 28 D3
Staplecross E Sus 38 C3
Staplefield W Sus 36 B3
Stapleford Cambs 123 G9
Stapleford Herts 86 B4
Stapleford Leics 154 F6
Stapleford Lincs 172 D5
Stapleford Notts 153 B9
Stapleford Wilts 46 F5
Stapleford Abbotts Essex 87 G8
Stapleford Tawney Essex 87 F8
Staplegrove Som 28 B2
Staplehay Som 28 C2
Staplehurst Kent 53 E9
Staplers I o W 20 D6
Staples Hill W Sus 35 B8
Staplestreet Kent 70 G5
Stapleton Bristol 60 D6
Stapleton Cumb 240 C2
Stapleton Hereford 114 D6
Stapleton Leics 135 D8
Stapleton N Yorks 198 D4
Stapleton N Yorks 224 C5
Stapleton Shrops 131 C9
Stapleton Som 29 C7
Stapley Som 27 E11
Staploe Beds 122 E2
Staplow Hereford 98 C3
Stapness Shetland 313 J4
Star Fife 287 G7
Star Pembs 92 E4
Star Som 44 B2
Star Hill Mon 79 E7
Stara Orkney 314 D2
Starbeck N Yorks 206 B2
Starbotton N Yorks 213 E9
Starcross Devon 14 E5
Stareton Warks 118 C6
Stargate T & W 242 E5
Starkholmes Derbys 170 D4
Starling Gtr Man 195 E9
Starlings Green Essex 105 E9
Starr's Green E Sus 38 D3
Starston Norf 142 G4
Start Devon 8 G6
Start Hill Essex 105 G10
Startforth Durham 223 B10
Startley Wilts 62 C2
Startop's End Bucks 84 C6
Starveall S Glos 61 B9
Starvecrow Kent 52 D5
Statenborough Kent 55 B10
Statford St Andrew Suff 127 E7
Statham Warr 183 D11
Stathe Som 28 B5
Stathern Leics 154 C5
Station Hill Cumb 229 B11
Station Town Durham 234 D4
Statland Common Norf 141 D10
Staughton Green Cambs 122 D2
Staughton Highway Cambs 122 E2
Staughton Moor Beds 122 E2
Staunton Glos 79 C8
Staunton Glos 98 F5
Staunton in the Vale Notts 172 G4
Staunton on Arrow Hereford 115 E7
Staunton on Wye Hereford 97 B7
Staupes N Yorks 205 B10
Staveley Cumb 211 B7
Staveley Cumb 221 F9
Staveley Derbys 186 G6
Staveley N Yorks 215 G7
Staveley-in-Cartmel Cumb 211 B7
Staverton Devon 8 C5
Staverton Glos 99 G7
Staverton Northants 119 E10
Staverton Wilts 61 G11
Staverton Bridge Glos 99 G7
Stawell Som 43 F11
Stawley Som 27 C9
Staxigoe Highld 310 D7
Staxton N Yorks 217 D10
Staylittle Ceredig 128 F2
Staylittle = Penffordd-Lâs Powys 129 E7
Staynall Lancs 202 E3
Staythorpe Notts 172 E3
Stead W Yorks 205 D8
Steam Mills Glos 79 B10
Stean N Yorks 213 E11
Steanbow Som 44 F5
Stearsby N Yorks 216 E2
Steart Som 29 B9
Steart Som 43 D9
Stebbing Essex 106 G3
Stebbing Green Essex 106 G3
Stechford W Mid 134 F2
Stede Quarter Kent 53 F11
Stedham W Sus 34 C5
Steel Northumb 241 F10
Steel Northumb 251 G9
Steel Bank S Yorks 186 D4
Steel Cross E Sus 52 G4
Steel Green Cumb 210 D3
Steel Heath Shrops 149 B10
Steele Road Borders 250 E2
Steelend Fife 279 C10
Steeleroad-end Borders 250 E2
Steen's Bridge Hereford 115 F10
Steep Hants 34 B2
Steep Lane W Yorks 196 C4
Steep Marsh Hants 34 B3
Steephill I o W 21 F7
Steeple Dorset 18 E4
Steeple Essex 88 E6
Steeple Ashton Wilts 46 B2
Steeple Aston Oxon 101 F9
Steeple Barton Oxon 101 G8
Steeple Bumpstead Essex 106 C3
Steeple Claydon Bucks 102 F3
Steeple Gidding Cambs 138 G2
Steeple Langford Wilts 46 F4
Steeple Morden Cambs 104 C5
Steeraway Telford 132 B3
Steeton W Yorks 204 E6
Stein Highld 298 D2
Steinmanhill Aberds 303 E7
Stella T & W 242 E5
Stelling Minnis Kent 54 D6
Stelvio Newport 59 B9
Stembridge Som 28 C6
Stembridge Swansea 56 C3
Stemster Highld 310 C5
Stemster Ho Highld 310 C5
Stenalees Corn 5 D10
Stenaquoy Orkney 314 C5
Stencoose Corn 4 F4
Stenhill Devon 27 E9
Stenhouse Dumfries 247 E8
Stenhouse Edin 280 G4
Stenhousemuir Falk 279 E7
Stenigot Lincs 190 E3
Stennack Corn 2 B5
Stenness Shetland 312 F4
Stenscholl Highld 298 C4
Stenso Orkney 314 D3
Stenson Derbys 152 D6
Stenton E Loth 282 G2
Stenton Fife 280 B5
Stentwood Devon 27 F10
Stenwith Lincs 154 B6
Stepaside Corn 5 F9
Stepaside Pembs 73 D10
Stepaside Powys 129 F11
Stepping Hill Gtr Man 184 D6
Steppingley C Beds 103 D10
Stepps N Lnrk 268 B3
Sterndale Moor Derbys 169 B10
Sternfield Suff 127 E7
Sterridge Devon 40 D
Stert Wilts 46 E
Sterte Poole 18 C
Stetchworth Cambs 124 F
Stevenage Herts 104 G
Steven's Crouch E Sus 38 D
Stevenston N Ayrs 266 G
Stevenstone Devon 25 D
Steventon Hants 48 D
Steventon Oxon 83 G
Steventon Shrops 115 C1
Steventon End Essex 105 C1
Stevington Beds 121 G
Stewards Essex 87 D
Steward's Green Essex 87 E
Stewartby Beds 103 C1
Stewarton Argyll 255 F
Stewarton E Ayrs 267 F
Stewkley Bucks 103 F
Stewkley Dean Bucks 102 F
Stewley Som 28 D
Stewton Lincs 190 D
Steyne Cross I o W 21 D
Steyning W Sus 35 E1
Steynton Pembs 72 D
Stibb Corn 24 E
Stibb Cross Devon 24 E
Stibb Green Wilts 63 G
Stibbard Norf 159 D
Stibbington Cambs 137 D1
Stichill Borders 262 B
Stick Hill Kent 52 E
Sticker Corn 5 E
Stickford Lincs 174 D
Sticklepath Devon 13 C
Sticklepath Devon 40 G
Sticklepath Som 28 E
Sticklepath Som 42 F
Sticklinch Som 44 F
Stickling Green Essex 105 E
Stickney Lincs 174 D
Stiff Street Kent 69 G1
Stiffkey Norf 177 E
Stifford's Bridge Hereford 98 B
Stileway Som 44 E
Stillingfleet N Yorks 207 E
Stillington N Yorks 215 F1
Stillington Stockton 234 G
Stilton Cambs 138 F
Stinchcombe Glos 80 F
Stinsford Dorset 17 C1
Stiperstones Shrops 131 C
Stirchley Telford 132 B
Stirchley W Mid 133 G1
Stirkoke Ho Highld 310 D
Stirling Aberds 303 E1
Stirling Stirl 278 C
Stirtloe Cambs 122 D
Stirton N Yorks 204 C
Stisted Essex 106 G
Stitchcombe Wilts 63 F
Stitchin's Hill Worcs 116 G
Stithians Corn 2 B
Stittenham Highld 300 B
Stivichall W Mid 118 B
Stixwould Lincs 173 B1
Stoak W Ches 182 G
Stobhill Northumb 252 G
Stobhillgate Northumb 252 F
Stobieside S Lnrk 258 B
Stobo Borders 260 B
Stoborough Dorset 18 D
Stoborough Green Dorset 18 D
Stobs Castle Borders 250 B
Stobshiel E Loth 271 C
Stobswood Northumb 252 E
Stock Essex 87 F1
Stock Lancs 204 D
Stock N Som 60 G
Stock Green Worcs 117 F
Stock Hill Suff 125 D
Stock Wood Worcs 117 F1
Stockbridge Hants 47 G1
Stockbridge S Yorks 198 F
Stockbridge W Sus 22 C
Stockbridge W Yorks 205 E
Stockbridge Village Mers 182 C
Stockbury Kent 69 G1
Stockcross W Berks 64 F
Stockend Glos 80 D
Stocker's Head Kent 54 C
Stockerston Leics 136 D
Stockfield W Mid 134 G
Stockheath Hants 22 B
Stockholes Turbary N Lincs 199 F
Stockiemuir Stirl 277 E1
Stocking Hereford 98 E
Stocking Green Essex 105 D1
Stocking Pelham Herts 105 F
Stockingford Warks 134 E
Stockland Devon 28 G
Stockland Bristol Som 43 E
Stockland Green Kent 52 E
Stockland Green W Mid 133 E1
Stockleigh English Devon 26 F
Stockleigh Pomeroy Devon 26 G
Stockley Wilts 62 F
Stocklinch Som 28 D
Stockport Gtr Man 184 C
Stocks Green Kent 52 D
Stocksbridge S Yorks 186 B
Stocksfield Northumb 242 E
Stockstreet Essex 106 G
Stockton Hereford 115 E1
Stockton Norf 143 E
Stockton Shrops 130 C
Stockton Shrops 132 D
Stockton Telford 150 F
Stockton Warks 119 E
Stockton Wilts 46 F
Stockton Brook Staffs 168 E
Stockton Heath Warr 183 D1
Stockton-on-Tees Stockton 225 B
Stockton on Teme Worcs 116 D
Stockton on the Forest York 207 B
Stocktonwood Shrops 130 C
Stockwell Devon 27 G
Stockwell Glos 80 C
Stockwell London 67 D1
Stockwell End W Mid 133 C
Stockwell Heath Staffs 151 E1
Stockwitch Cross Som 29 C
Stockwood Bristol 60 F
Stockwood Dorset 29 F
Stockwood Vale Bath 60 F
Stodday Lancs 202 B
Stodmarsh Kent 71 G
Stody Norf 159 C1
Stoer Highld 307 G
Stoford Som 29 E
Stoford Wilts 46 F

Stoford Water Devon 27 F9
Stogumber Som 42 F5
Stogursey Som 43 E8
Stoke Devon 24 C2
Stoke Hants 22 C2
Stoke Hants 48 C2
Stoke Medway 69 D10
Stoke Plym 7 D9
Stoke Suff 108 C3
Stoke W Mid 119 B7
Stoke Abbott Dorset 29 G7
Stoke Albany Northants 136 F6
Stoke Aldermoor W Mid 119 B7
Stoke Ash Suff 126 C2
Stoke Bardolph Notts 171 G10
Stoke Bishop Bristol 60 D5
Stoke Bliss Worcs 116 E3
Stoke Bruerne Northants 102 B4
Stoke by Clare Suff 106 C4
Stoke-by-Nayland Suff 107 D9
Stoke Canon Devon 14 B4
Stoke Charity Hants 48 F3
Stoke Climsland Corn 12 G3
Stoke Common Hants 33 C7
Stoke Cross Hereford 116 G2
Stoke D'Abernon Sur 50 B6
Stoke Doyle Northants 137 F10
Stoke Dry Rutland 137 D7
Stoke Edith Hereford 98 C2
Stoke End Warks 134 D3
Stoke Farthing Wilts 31 B9
Stoke Ferry Norf 140 D4
Stoke Fleming Devon 9 F7
Stoke Gabriel Devon 8 D6
Stoke Gifford S Glos 60 D6
Stoke Golding Leics 135 D7
Stoke Goldington M Keynes 102 B6
Stoke Green Bucks 66 C3
Stoke Hammond Bucks 103 F7
Stoke Heath Shrops 150 D3
Stoke Heath W Mid 135 G7
Stoke Heath Worcs 117 D8
Stoke Hill Devon 14 C4
Stoke Hill Hereford 98 B2
Stoke Holy Cross Norf 142 C4
Stoke Lacy Hereford 98 B2
Stoke Lane Hereford 116 G2
Stoke Lyne Oxon 101 F11
Stoke Mandeville Bucks 84 C4
Stoke Newington London 67 B10
Stoke on Tern Shrops 150 D2
Stoke-on-Trent Stoke 168 F5
Stoke Orchard Glos 99 F8
Stoke Park Suff 108 C3
Stoke Poges Bucks 66 C3
Stoke Pound Worcs 117 D9
Stoke Prior Hereford 115 F10
Stoke Prior Worcs 117 D8
Stoke Rivers Devon 40 F6
Stoke Rochford Lincs 155 D8
Stoke Row Oxon 65 C7
Stoke St Gregory Som 28 B4
Stoke St Mary Som 28 C3
Stoke St Michael Som 45 D7
Stoke St Milborough Shrops 131 G11
Stoke sub Hamdon Som 29 D7
Stoke Talmage Oxon 83 F11
Stoke Trister Som 30 B2
Stoke Wake Dorset 30 F3
Stoke Water Dorset 29 G7
Stoke Wharf Worcs 117 D9
Stokeford Dorset 18 D3
Stokegorse Shrops 131 G11
Stokeham Notts 188 F3
Stokeinteignhead Devon 14 G4
Stokenchurch Bucks 84 F3
Stokenham Devon 8 G6
Stokesay Shrops 131 G8
Stokesby Norf 161 G8
Stokesley N Yorks 225 D10
Stokoe Northumb 250 F6
Stolford Som 43 D8
Ston Easton Som 44 C6
Stondon Massey Essex 87 E9
Stone Bucks 84 C3
Stone Glos 79 F11
Stone Kent 38 B6
Stone Kent 68 E5
Stone S Yorks 187 D9
Stone Som 44 G5
Stone Staffs 151 C8
Stone Worcs 117 B7
Stone Allerton Som 44 C2
Stone Bridge Corner P'boro 138 C5
Stone Chair W Yorks 196 B6
Stone Cross E Sus 23 E10
Stone Cross E Sus 37 B8
Stone Cross E Sus 52 G6
Stone Cross Kent 52 F4
Stone Cross Kent 54 F4
Stone Cross Kent 55 B10
Stone Cross W Mid 133 E10
Stone-edge Batch N Som 60 E3
Stone Head N Yorks 204 E4
Stone Heath Staffs 151 B9
Stone Hill Kent 54 D2
Stone Hill Kent 54 F5
Stone Hill S Glos 60 E6
Stone Hill S Yorks 199 F7
Stone House Cumb 212 B5
Stone in Oxney Kent 38 B6
Stone Raise Cumb 230 B4
Stone Street Kent 52 C5
Stone Street Suff 107 D9
Stone Street Suff 143 G7
Stonea Cambs 139 E9
Stoneacton Shrops 131 E10
Stonebow Worcs 99 B8
Stonebridge Essex 70 B2
Stonebridge London 67 C8
Stonebridge N Som 43 B11
Stonebridge Norf 141 E8
Stonebridge Sur 51 D7
Stonebridge W Mid 134 G4
Stonebridge Green Kent 54 D2
Stonebroom Derbys 170 D6
Stonebyres Holdings S Lnrk 268 G6
Stoneclough Gtr Man 195 F9
Stonecombe Devon 40 E6
Stonecrouch Kent 53 G7
Stonedge Borders 250 B3
Stoneferry Hull 209 G8
Stonefield Argyll 289 F11
Stonefield S Lnrk 268 D3
Stonefield Staffs 151 C7
Stonefield Castle Hotel Argyll 275 F9
Stonegate E Sus 37 B11
Stonegate N Yorks 226 D5
Stonegrave N Yorks 216 D3
Stonegravels Derbys 186 G5
Stonehall Kent 55 D9
Stonehall Worcs 99 B7
Stonehaugh Northumb 241 B7
Stonehaven Aberds 293 E10
Stonehill Sur 66 G4
Stonehills Hants 33 G7
Stonehouse Aberds 303 F8
Stonehouse Glos 80 D4
Stonehouse Northumb 240 F5
Stonehouse Plym 7 E9
Stonehouse S Lnrk 268 F5
Stonehouses Staffs 169 G7
Stoneleigh London 67 G8
Stoneleigh Warks 118 C6
Stoneley Green E Ches 167 E10
Stonely Cambs 122 D2
Stonepits Worcs 117 F10
Stonequarry W Sus 52 F2
Stoner Hill Hants 34 B2
Stones Green Essex 108 F3
Stonesby Leics 154 E6
Stonesfield Oxon 82 B5
Stonestreet Green Kent 54 F5
Stonethwaite Cumb 220 C5
Stoneton Warks 119 G9
Stonewells Moray 302 C2
Stonewood Kent 68 E5
Stoney Cross Hants 32 E3
Stoney Hill Worcs 117 C9
Stoney Middleton Derbys 186 F2
Stoney Royd W Yorks 196 C5
Stoney Stanton Leics 135 E9
Stoney Stoke Som 45 G8
Stoney Stratton Som 45 F7
Stoney Stretton Shrops 131 B7
Stoneyard Green Hereford 98 C4
Stoneybank E Loth 280 G6
Stoneybreck Shetland 313 N2
Stoneyburn W Loth 269 C9
Stoneycombe Devon 9 B7
Stoneycroft Mers 182 C5
Stoneyfield Gtr Man 195 E11
Stoneyfield Moray 301 D11
Stoneyford Derbys 170 F6
Stoneyford Devon 27 F8
Stoneygate Aberds 303 F10
Stoneygate Leicester 136 C2
Stoneyhills Essex 88 F6
Stoneykirk Dumfries 236 D2
Stoneylane Shrops 115 B11
Stoneywood Aberdeen 293 B10
Stoneywood Falk 278 E5
Stonganess Shetland 312 C7
Stonham Aspal Suff 126 F2
Stonnall Staffs 133 C11
Stonor Oxon 65 B8
Stonton Wyville Leics 136 D4
Stony Batter Hants 32 B3
Stony Cross Devon 25 B8
Stony Cross Hereford 98 B4
Stony Cross Hereford 115 D10
Stony Dale Notts 172 G2
Stony Gate T & W 243 G9
Stony Green Bucks 84 F5
Stony Heap Durham 242 G4
Stony Heath Hants 48 B5
Stony Houghton Derbys 171 B7
Stony Knaps Dorset 28 G5
Stony Littleton Bath 45 B8
Stony Stratford M Keynes 102 C5
Stonyfield Highld 300 B6
Stonyford Hants 32 D4
Stonyland Devon 25 B8
Stonymarsh Hants 32 B4
Stoodleigh Devon 26 D6
Stop-and-Call Pembs 91 D8
Stopes S Yorks 186 D3
Stopgate Devon 28 F2
Stopham W Sus 35 D8
Stopper Lane Lancs 204 D2
Stopsley Luton 104 G2
Stoptide Corn 10 F4
Stores Corner Suff 109 B7
Storeton Mers 182 E4
Storiths N Yorks 205 C7
Stormontfield Perth 286 E5
Stormore Wilts 45 D10
Stornoway W Isles 304 E6
Storridge Hereford 98 B4
Storrington W Sus 35 E9
Storrs Cumb 221 G7
Storrs S Yorks 186 D3
Storth Cumb 211 C9
Storwood E Yorks 207 E10
Stotfield Moray 302 B2
Stotfold C Beds 104 D4
Stottesdon Shrops 132 G3
Stoughton Leics 136 C2
Stoughton Sur 50 C3
Stoughton W Sus 34 E4
Stoughton Cross Som 44 D2
Stoul Highld 295 F9
Stoulton Worcs 99 B8
Stour Provost Dorset 30 C3
Stour Row Dorset 30 C4
Stourbridge W Mid 133 G8
Stourpaine Dorset 30 F5
Stourport on Severn Worcs 116 C6
Stourton Staffs 133 F7
Stourton W Yorks 206 G2
Stourton Warks 100 D5
Stourton Wilts 45 G9
Stourton Caundle Dorset 30 D2
Stourton Hill Warks 100 D6
Stout Som 44 G2
Stove Orkney 314 C6
Stove Shetland 313 L6
Stoven Suff 143 G8
Stow Borders 271 G9
Stow Lincs 155 B11
Stow Lincs 188 E5
Stow Bardolph Norf 140 B2
Stow Bedon Norf 141 D9
Stow cum Quy Cambs 123 E10
Stow Lawn W Mid 133 D8
Stow Longa Cambs 122 C2
Stow Maries Essex 88 F4
Stow-on-the-Wold Glos 100 F3
Stow Park Newport 59 B10
Stowbridge Norf 140 B2
Stowe Glos 79 D9
Stowe Hereford 96 B5
Stowe Lincs 156 G2
Stowe Shrops 114 C6
Stowe Staffs 152 G2
Stowe-by-Chartley Staffs 151 D10
Stowe Green Glos 79 D9
Stowell Glos 81 C9
Stowell Som 29 C11
Stowey Bath 44 B5
Stowfield Hereford 79 B9
Stowford Devon 12 B4
Stowford Devon 12 D4
Stowford Devon 24 E3
Stowford Devon 25 B10
Stowford Devon 41 E7
Stowgate Lincs 156 G3
Stowlangtoft Suff 125 D9
Stowmarket Suff 125 F10
Stowting Kent 54 E6
Stowting Common Kent 54 E6
Stowting Court Kent 54 E6
Stowupland Suff 125 F11
Straad Argyll 275 G11
Strachan Aberds 293 D8
Strachurmore Argyll 284 G5
Stradbroke Suff 126 C4
Stradishall Suff 124 G4
Stradsett Norf 140 C3
Stragglethorpe Lincs 172 E6
Straid S Ayrs 244 E4
Straight Soley Wilts 63 E10
Straith Dumfries 247 F8
Straiton Edin 270 B5
Straiton S Ayrs 245 C9
Straloch Aberds 303 G8
Straloch Perth 292 G2
Stramshall Staffs 151 B11
Strand Glos 80 C2
Strand London 67 C10
Strands Cumb 210 C3
Strang I o M 192 E4
Strangeways Gtr Man 184 B4
Strangford Hereford 97 F11
Stranghow Redcar 226 B3
Strangways Wilts 46 E6
Stranog Aberds 293 D10
Stranraer Dumfries 236 C2
Strata Florida Ceredig 112 D4
Stratfield Mortimer W Berks 65 G7
Stratfield Saye Hants 65 G7
Stratfield Turgis Hants 49 B7
Stratford C Beds 104 B3
Stratford Glos 99 D7
Stratford London 67 C11
Stratford Marsh London 67 C11
Stratford New Town London 67 C11
Stratford St Andrew Suff 127 E7
Stratford St Mary Suff 107 E10
Stratford Sub Castle Wilts 46 G6
Stratford Tony Wilts 31 B9
Stratford-upon-Avon Warks 118 F3
Strath Highld 299 B7
Strath Highld 310 D6
Strathallan Castle Perth 286 F3
Strathan Highld 295 F11
Strathan Highld 307 G5
Strathan Highld 308 C5
Strathan Skerray Highld 308 C6
Strathaven S Lnrk 268 G4
Strathavon Lo Moray 301 G11
Strathblane Stirl 277 F11
Strathcanaird Highld 307 J6
Strathcarron Highld 299 E9
Strathcoil Argyll 289 F8
Strathcoul Highld 310 D5
Strathdon Aberds 292 B5
Strathellie Aberds 303 C10
Strathgarve Lodge Highld 300 C4
Strathkinness Fife 287 F8
Strathmashie House Highld 291 D7
Strathmiglo Fife 286 F6
Strathmore Lodge Highld 310 E5
Strathpeffer Highld 300 D4
Strathrannoch Highld 300 B3
Strathtay Perth 286 B3
Strathvaich Lodge Highld 300 B3
Strathwhillan N Ayrs 256 B2
Strathy Highld 300 B6
Strathy Highld 310 C2
Strathyre Stirl 285 F9
Stratton Corn 24 F2
Stratton Dorset 17 C9
Stratton Glos 81 E8
Stratton Audley Oxon 102 F2
Stratton Chase Bucks 85 G7
Stratton-on-the-Fosse Som 45 C7
Stratton St Margaret Swindon 63 B7
Stratton St Michael Norf 142 E4
Stratton Strawless Norf 160 E4
Stravithie Fife 287 F9
Strawberry Bank Cumb 211 B8
Strawberry Hill E Sus 52 F5
Strawberry Hill London 67 E7
Strawberry Hill W Yorks 198 C2
Streat E Sus 36 D5
Streatham London 67 E10
Streatham Hill London 67 E10
Streatham Park London 67 E9
Streatham Vale London 67 E9
Streatley C Beds 103 F11
Streatley W Berks 64 C5
Street Cumb 222 D2
Street Lancs 202 C6
Street N Yorks 226 E4
Street Som 28 F5
Street Som 44 F3
Street Ash Som 28 E3
Street Ashton Warks 135 G9
Street Dinas Shrops 148 B6
Street End Hants 33 D9
Street End Kent 54 C6
Street End W Sus 22 D5
Street Gate T & W 242 F6
Street Houses N Yorks 206 D6
Street Lane Derbys 170 F5
Street Lydan Wrex 149 B8
Street of Kincardine Highld 291 B11
Street on the Fosse Som 44 F6
Streethay Staffs 152 G2
Streethouse W Yorks 197 C11
Streetlam N Yorks 224 F6
Streetly W Mid 133 D11
Streetly End Cambs 106 B2
Strefford Shrops 131 F8
Strelley Notts 171 G8
Strensall York 216 G2
Strensham Worcs 99 C8
Stretch Down Devon 26 E4
Stretcholt Som 43 E9
Strete Devon 8 F6
Stretford Gtr Man 184 C4
Stretford Hereford 115 F10
Stretford Court Hereford 115 F8
Strethall Essex 105 D9
Stretham Cambs 123 C10
Strettington W Sus 22 B5
Stretton Derbys 170 C5
Stretton Rutland 155 F8
Stretton Staffs 151 G7
Stretton Staffs 152 D5
Stretton W Ches 166 E6
Stretton Warr 183 E10
Stretton en le Field Leics 152 G6
Stretton Grandison Hereford 98 C2
Stretton-on-Dunsmore Warks 119 C8
Stretton-on-Fosse Warks 100 D4
Stretton Sugwas Hereford 97 C9
Stretton under Fosse Warks 135 G8
Stretton Westwood Shrops 131 D11
Strichen Aberds 303 D9
Strines Gtr Man 185 D7
Stringston Som 43 E7
Strixton Northants 121 E8
Stroat Glos 79 F9
Strode N Som 60 G4
Strom Shetland 313 J5
Stromeferry Highld 295 B10
Stromemore Highld 295 B10
Stromness Orkney 314 F2
Stronaba Highld 290 E4
Stronachlachar Stirl 285 F8
Stronachullin Lodge Argyll 275 F9
Stronchreggan Highld 290 F2
Stronchrubie Highld 307 H7
Strone Argyll 255 F7
Strone Argyll 274 G6
Strone Argyll 276 E3
Strone Highld 290 E3
Strone Highld 291 D9
Strone Highld 300 G5
Strone Invclyd 276 G5
Stronelairg Lodge Highld 291 C7
Stroneskar Argyll 275 C9
Stronmachair Stirl 285 G8
Stronmilchan Argyll 284 E5
Stronord Dumfries 236 C6
Stronsaul Argyll 276 F2
Strontian Highld 289 C10
Stronvar Stirl 285 E9
Strood Kent 53 G11
Strood Medway 69 F8
Strood Green Sur 51 D8
Strood Green W Sus 35 C8
Strood Green W Sus 50 G6
Strothers Dale Northumb 241 F11
Stroud Glos 80 D4
Stroud Hants 34 C2
Stroud Sur 50 F2
Stroud Green Essex 88 G5
Stroud Green Glos 80 D4
Stroud Green London 67 B10
Stroude Sur 66 F4
Strouden Bmouth 19 C8
Stroul Argyll 276 E4
Stroupster Highld 310 C7
Stroxton Lincs 155 C8
Stroxworthy Devon 24 D4
Struan Highld 294 B5
Struan Perth 291 G10
Strubby Lincs 191 E7
Structon's Heath Worcs 116 D5
Strugg's Hill Lincs 156 B5
Strumpshaw Norf 142 B6
Strutherhill S Lnrk 268 F5
Struthers Fife 287 G7
Struy Highld 300 F3
Stryd Anglesey 178 E2
Stryd y Facsen Anglesey 178 E4
Stryt-issa Wrex 166 F3
Stuartfield Aberds 303 E9
Stub Place Cumb 219 G11
Stubb Norf 161 E8
Stubbermere W Sus 22 B3
Stubber's Green W Mid 133 C10
Stubbings Windsor 65 C10
Stubbing's Green Suff 125 C11
Stubbington Hants 33 G9
Stubbins Lancs 195 D9
Stubbins Lancs 202 E6
Stubble Green Cumb 219 F11
Stubbles W Berks 64 D5
Stubbs Cross Kent 54 F3
Stubb's Green Norf 142 D5
Stubbs Green Norf 143 D7
Stubhampton Dorset 30 E6
Stubshaw Cross Gtr Man 194 G5
Stubton Lincs 172 F5
Stubwood Staffs 151 B11
Stuckgowan Argyll 285 G7
Stuckton Hants 31 E11
Stud Green E Ches 168 C2
Stud Green Windsor 65 D11
Studd Hill Kent 71 F7
Studdal Kent 55 D10
Studfold N Yorks 212 E6
Studham C Beds 85 B8
Studland Dorset 18 E6
Studley Warks 117 E11
Studley Wilts 62 E3
Studley Green Bucks 84 F3
Studley Green Wilts 45 B10
Studley Roger N Yorks 214 E5
Studley Royal N Yorks 214 E5
Stump Cross Essex 105 C10
Stumps Cross Glos 99 E11
Stuntney Cambs 123 B11
Stunts Green E Sus 23 C10
Sturbridge Staffs 150 C6
Sturford Wilts 45 E10
Sturgate Lincs 188 D5
Sturmer Essex 106 C3
Sturminster Common Dorset 30 E3
Sturminster Marshall Dorset 31 G7
Sturminster Newton Dorset 30 E3
Sturry Kent 71 G7
Stursdon Corn 24 E2
Sturton N Lincs 200 G3
Sturton by Stow Lincs 188 E5
Sturton le Steeple Notts 188 E3
Stuston Suff 126 B2
Stutton N Yorks 206 E5
Stutton Suff 108 E3
Styal E Ches 184 E4
Styants Bottom Kent 52 B5
Stydd Lancs 203 F9
Styrrup Notts 187 C10
Suainebost W Isles 304 B7
Suardail W Isles 304 E6
Succoth Aberds 302 F4
Succoth Argyll 284 G6
Suckley Worcs 116 G4
Suckley Green Worcs 116 G4
Suckley Knowl Worcs 116 G4
Suckquoy Orkney 314 H4
Sucksted Green Essex 105 F11
Sudborough Northants 137 G9
Sudbourne Suff 127 G8
Sudbrook Lincs 173 G7
Sudbrook Mon 60 B4
Sudbrooke Lincs 189 F8
Sudbury Derbys 152 C3
Sudbury London 67 C7
Sudbury Suff 107 C7
Sudden Gtr Man 195 E11
Suddie Highld 300 D6
Sudgrove Glos 80 D6
Suffield N Yorks 227 G9
Suffield Norf 160 C4
Sugnall Staffs 150 C5
Sugwas Pool Hereford 97 C9
Suisnish Highld 295 D7
Suladale Highld 298 D3
Sulaisiadar W Isles 304 E7
Sulby I o M 192 C4
Sulgrave Northants 101 B11
Sulgrave T & W 243 F8
Sulham W Berks 64 E6
Sulhampstead W Berks 64 F6
Sulhampstead Abbots W Berks 64 F6
Sulhampstead Bannister Upper End W Berks 64 F6
Sulhamstead W Berks 64 F6
Sulland Orkney 314 B5
Sullington W Sus 35 E9
Sullington Warren W Sus 35 E9
Sullom Shetland 312 F5
Sullom Voe Oil Terminal Shetland 312 F5
Sully V Glam 59 F7
Sumburgh Shetland 313 N6
Summer Bridge N Yorks 214 G4
Summer Heath Bucks 84 G2
Summer Hill E Sus 23 D9
Summer Hill W Mid 133 E9
Summerbridge N Yorks 214 G4
Summercourt Corn 5 D7
Summerfield Kent 55 B9
Summerfield Norf 158 B5
Summerfield Worcs 116 C6
Summerfield Park W Mid 133 F10
Summergangs Hull 209 G8
Summerhill Newport 59 B10
Summerhill Pembs 73 D11
Summerhill Staffs 133 B11
Summerhill Telford 150 F4
Summerhill Worcs 116 B6
Summerhill Wrex 166 E4
Summerhouse Darl 224 B4
Summerlands Cumb 211 B10
Summerlands Som 29 D8
Summerleaze Mon 60 B2
Summerley Derbys 186 F5
Summerscales N Yorks 205 C8
Summersdale W Sus 22 B5
Summerseat Gtr Man 195 E9
Summerston Glasgow 277 G11
Summerstown Bucks 102 G3
Summerstown London 67 E9
Summertown Oxon 83 D8
Summit Gtr Man 195 E10
Summit Gtr Man 196 D2
Summit Gtr Man 196 F2
Sun Green Gtr Man 185 B7
Sunbrick Cumb 210 E5
Sunbury Common Sur 66 E5
Sunbury-on-Thames Sur 66 F6
Sundayshill S Glos 79 G11
Sundaywell Dumfries 247 G8
Sunderland Argyll 274 G3
Sunderland Cumb 229 D9
Sunderland Lancs 202 B4
Sunderland T & W 243 F9
Sunderland Bridge Durham 233 D11
Sundhope Borders 261 D8
Sundon Park Luton 103 F11
Sundridge Kent 52 B3
Sundridge London 68 E2
Sunhill Glos 81 E10
Sunipol Argyll 288 D5
Sunk Island E Yorks 201 D9
Sunken Marsh Essex 69 C10
Sunningdale Windsor 66 F3
Sunninghill Windsor 66 F2
Sunningwell Oxon 83 E7
Sunniside Durham 233 D8
Sunniside T & W 242 F6
Sunniside T & W 243 G8
Sunny Bank Gtr Man 195 F10
Sunny Bower Lancs 203 G10
Sunny Hill Derby 152 C6
Sunnybrow Durham 233 E9
Sunnyfields S Yorks 198 F4
Sunnyhurst Blkburn 195 C7
Sunnylaw Stirl 278 B5
Sunnymead Oxon 83 D8
Sunnymeads Windsor 66 D4
Sunnymede Essex 87 G11
Sunnyside S Yorks 187 C7
Sunnyside W Sus 51 F11
Sunset Hereford 114 F6
Sunton Wilts 47 C8
Surbiton London 67 F7
Surby I o M 192 E3
Surfleet Lincs 156 D5
Surfleet Seas End Lincs 156 D5
Surlingham Norf 142 B6
Surrex Essex 107 G7
Suspension Bridge Norf 139 E10
Sustead Norf 160 B3
Susworth Lincs 199 G10
Sutcombe Devon 24 E4
Sutcombemill Devon 24 E4
Sutherland Grove Argyll 289 E11
Suton Norf 141 D11
Sutors of Cromarty Highld 301 C8
Sutterby Lincs 190 G5
Sutterton Lincs 156 B5
Sutterton Dowdyke Lincs 156 C5
Sutton Bucks 66 D4
Sutton C Beds 104 B4
Sutton Cambs 123 B8
Sutton Devon 8 G4
Sutton E Sus 23 F7
Sutton Kent 55 D10
Sutton Lincs 172 E5
Sutton London 67 G9
Sutton Mers 183 C8
Sutton N Yorks 198 B3
Sutton Norf 161 E7
Sutton Notts 154 B5
Sutton Notts 187 E11
Sutton Oxon 82 D6
Sutton P'boro 137 D11
Sutton Pembs 72 B6
Sutton S Yorks 198 E5
Sutton Shrops 132 F4
Sutton Shrops 149 D7
Sutton Shrops 149 G10
Sutton Shrops 150 C3
Sutton Som 44 G6
Sutton Staffs 150 E5
Sutton Suff 108 B6
Sutton Sur 50 D5
Sutton W Sus 35 D7
Sutton Abinger Sur 50 D6
Sutton at Hone Kent 68 E5
Sutton Bassett Northants 136 E5
Sutton Benger Wilts 62 D2
Sutton Bingham Som 29 E8
Sutton Bonington Notts 153 E10
Sutton Bridge Lincs 157 E9
Sutton Cheney Leics 135 C8
Sutton Coldfield W Mid 134 D2
Sutton Corner Lincs 157 D8
Sutton Courtenay Oxon 83 G8
Sutton Crosses Lincs 157 E8
Sutton Cum Lound Notts 187 E11
Sutton End W Sus 35 D7
Sutton Forest Side Notts 171 D8
Sutton Gault Cambs 123 B8
Sutton Green E Ches 168 B4
Sutton Green Sur 50 C4
Sutton Green W Ches 182 F5
Sutton Green Wrex 166 F6
Sutton Hall Shrops 132 C4
Sutton Heath Mers 183 C8
Sutton Hill Telford 132 C4
Sutton Holms Dorset 31 F9
Sutton Howgrave N Yorks 214 D6
Sutton in Ashfield Notts 171 D7
Sutton-in-Craven N Yorks 204 E6
Sutton in the Elms Leics 135 E10
Sutton Ings Hull 209 G8
Sutton Lakes Hereford 97 B10
Sutton Lane Ends E Ches 184 G6
Sutton Leach Mers 183 C8
Sutton Maddock Shrops 132 C4
Sutton Mallet Som 43 F11
Sutton Mandeville Wilts 31 B7
Sutton Manor Mers 183 C8
Sutton Marsh Hereford 97 C10
Sutton Mill N Yorks 204 E6
Sutton Montis Som 29 C10
Sutton on Hull Hull 209 G8
Sutton on Sea Lincs 191 E8
Sutton-on-the-Forest N Yorks 215 G11
Sutton on the Hill Derbys 152 C4
Sutton on Trent Notts 172 B3
Sutton Poyntz Dorset 17 E10
Sutton Row Wilts 31 B7
Sutton St Edmund Lincs 157 G7
Sutton St James Lincs 157 F7
Sutton St Michael Hereford 97 B10
Sutton St Nicholas Hereford 97 B10
Sutton Scarsdale Derbys 170 B6
Sutton Scotney Hants 48 F3
Sutton Street Suff 108 C6
Sutton under Brailes Warks 100 D6
Sutton-under-Whitestonecliffe N Yorks 215 C9
Sutton upon Derwent E Yorks 207 D10
Sutton Valence Kent 53 D10
Sutton Veny Wilts 45 E11
Sutton Waldron Dorset 30 D5
Sutton Weaver W Ches 183 F8
Sutton Wick Bath 44 B5
Sutton Wick Oxon 83 G7
Swaby Lincs 190 F5
Swadlincote Derbys 152 F6
Swaffham Norf 140 B6
Swaffham Bulbeck Cambs 123 E11
Swaffham Prior Cambs 123 E11
Swafield Norf 160 C5
Swaile's Green E Sus 38 C3
Swain House W Yorks 205 F9
Swainby N Yorks 225 E9
Swainshill Hereford 97 C9
Swainsthorpe Norf 142 C4
Swainswick Bath 61 F9
Swaithe S Yorks 197 G11
Swalcliffe Oxon 101 D7
Swalecliffe Kent 70 F6
Swallow Lincs 201 G7
Swallow Beck Lincs 173 B7
Swallowcliffe Wilts 31 B7
Swallowfield Wokingham 65 G8
Swallowfields Devon 8 C5
Swallowhurst Cumb 220 G2
Swallownest S Yorks 187 E7
Swallows Cross Essex 87 F10
Swalwell T & W 242 E6
Swampton Hants 48 C2
Swan Bottom Bucks 84 D6
Swan Green Suff 126 C5
Swan Green W Ches 184 G2
Swan Street Essex 107 F7
Swan Village W Mid 133 E9
Swanage Dorset 18 F6
Swanbach E Ches 167 G11
Swanbister Orkney 314 F3
Swanborough Swindon 81 G11
Swanbourne Bucks 102 F6
Swanbridge V Glam 59 F7
Swanland E Yorks 200 B3
Swanley Glos 80 F2
Swanley Kent 68 F4
Swanley Bar Herts 86 E3
Swanley Village Kent 68 F4
Swanmore Hants 33 D9
Swanmore I o W 21 C7
Swannay Orkney 314 D2
Swannington Leics 153 F8
Swannington Norf 160 F2
Swanpool Lincs 189 G7
Swanscombe Kent 68 E6
Swansea = Abertawe Swansea 56 C6
Swanside Mers 182 C6
Swanston Edin 270 B4
Swanton Abbott Norf 160 D5
Swanton Hill Norf 160 D5
Swanton Morley Norf 159 F10
Swanton Novers Norf 159 C10
Swanton Street Kent 53 B11
Swanwick Derbys 170 E6
Swanwick Hants 33 F8
Swanwick Green E Ches 167 F9
Swarby Lincs 173 G8
Swarcliffe W Yorks 206 F3
Swardeston Norf 142 C4
Swarister Shetland 312 E7
Swarkestone Derbys 153 D7
Swarland Northumb 252 C5
Swarraton Hants 48 F5
Swartha W Yorks 205 D7
Swarthmoor Cumb 210 D5
Swartland Orkney 314 D2
Swathwick Derbys 170 B5
Swaton Lincs 156 B2
Swavesey Cambs 123 D7
Sway Hants 19 B11
Swayfield Lincs 155 E9
Swaythling Soton 32 D6
Sweet Green Worcs 116 E2
Sweetham Devon 14 B3
Sweethaws E Sus 37 B8
Sweethay Som 28 C2
Sweetholme Cumb 221 B11
Sweethouse Corn 5 C11
Sweets Corn 11 B9
Sweetshouse Corn 5 C11
Sweffling Suff 126 E6
Swell Som 28 C5
Swelling Hill Hants 49 G7
Swepstone Leics 153 G7
Swerford Oxon 101 E7
Swettenham E Ches 168 B4
Swetton N Yorks 214 E3
Swffryd Caerph 78 F2
Swift's Green Kent 53 E11
Swiftsden E Sus 38 B2
Swilland Suff 126 G3
Swillbrook Lancs 202 G5
Swillington W Yorks 206 G3
Swillington Common W Yorks 206 G3
Swimbridge Devon 25 B10
Swimbridge Newland Devon 40 G6
Swinbrook Oxon 82 C3
Swincliffe N Yorks 205 B10
Swincliffe W Yorks 197 B8
Swincombe Devon 41 E7
Swinden N Yorks 204 C3
Swinderby Lincs 172 C5
Swindon Glos 99 G8
Swindon Staffs 133 E7
Swindon Swindon 63 C7
Swine E Yorks 209 F8
Swinefleet E Yorks 199 C9
Swineford S Glos 61 F7
Swineshead Beds 121 D11
Swineshead Lincs 174 G2
Swineshead Bridge Lincs 174 G2
Swinethorpe Lincs 172 B5
Swiney Highld 310 F6
Swinford Leics 119 B11
Swinford Oxon 82 D6
Swingate Notts 171 G8
Swingbrow Cambs 139 F7
Swingfield Minnis Kent 55 E8
Swingfield Street Kent 55 E8
Swingleton Green Suff 107 B9
Swinhoe Northumb 264 D6
Swinhope Lincs 190 B2
Swining Shetland 312 G6
Swinister Shetland 312 E5
Swinister Shetland 313 L6
Swinithwaite N Yorks 213 B10
Swinmore Common Hereford 98 C3
Swinnie Borders 262 F4
Swinnow Moor W Yorks 205 G10
Swinscoe Staffs 169 F10
Swinside Cumb 229 G10
Swinside Townfoot Borders 262 F6
Swinstead Lincs 155 E10
Swinton Borders 272 F6
Swinton Glasgow 268 C3
Swinton Gtr Man 195 G9
Swinton N Yorks 214 D4
Swinton N Yorks 216 E5
Swinton S Yorks 186 B6
Swinton Bridge S Yorks 187 B7
Swinton Hill Borders 272 F6
Swinton Park Gtr Man 195 G9
Swintonmill Borders 272 F6
Swiss Valley Carms 75 E8
Swithland Leics 153 G10
Swordale Highld 300 C5
Swordale Highld 309 K6
Swordland Highld 295 F9
Swordly Highld 308 C7
Sworton Heath E Ches 183 E11
Swyddffynnon Ceredig 112 D3
Swynnerton Staffs 151 B7
Swyre Dorset 16 D6
Sycamore Devon 28 F3
Sychdyn = Soughton Flint 166 B2
Sychtyn Powys 129 B9
Sydallt Wrex 166 D4
Syde Glos 81 C7
Sydenham London 67 E11
Sydenham Oxon 84 E2
Sydenham Som 43 F10
Sydenham Damerel Devon 12 F4
Syderstone Norf 158 C6
Sydling St Nicholas Dorset 17 B8
Sydmonton Hants 48 B3
Sydney E Ches 168 D2
Syerston Notts 172 F2
Syke Gtr Man 195 D11
Sykehouse S Yorks 198 D6
Sykes Lancs 203 C8
Syleham Suff 126 B4
Sylen Carms 75 D8
Symbister Shetland 313 G7
Symington Borders 271 F8
Symington S Ayrs 257 C9
Symington S Lnrk 259 B11
Symonds Green Herts 104 F4
Symonds Yat Hereford 79 B9
Symondsbury Dorset 16 C4
Synderford Dorset 28 G5
Synod Inn = Post Mawr Ceredig 111 G8
Synton Borders 261 E11
Synton Mains Borders 261 E11
Synwell Glos 80 G3
Syre Highld 308 E6
Syreford Glos 99 G10
Syresham Northants 102 C2
Syster Highld 310 C6
Syston Leics 154 G2
Syston Lincs 172 G6
Sytch Ho Green Shrops 132 E5
Sytch Lane Telford 150 E2
Sytchampton Worcs 116 D6
Sywell Northants 120 D6

T

Taagan Highld 299 C10
Tabley Hill E Ches 184 F2
Tabor Gwyn 146 F5
Tabost W Isles 305 G5
Tàbost W Isles 304 B7
Tachbrook Mallory Warks 118 E6
Tacker Street Som 42 F4
Tackley Oxon 101 G9
Tacleit W Isles 304 E3
Tacolneston Norf 142 D2
Tadcaster N Yorks 206 E5
Tadden Dorset 31 G7
Taddington Derbys 185 G10
Taddington Glos 99 E11
Taddiport Devon 25 D7
Tadhill Som 45 D7
Tadley Hants 64 G6
Tadley Oxon 64 B4
Tadlow C Beds 104 B5
Tadlow C Beds 104 B5
Tadmarton Oxon 101 D7
Tadnoll Dorset 17 D11
Tadwick Bath 61 E8
Tadworth Sur 51 B8
Tafarn-y-bwlch Pembs 91 E11
Tafarn-y-gelyn Denb 165 C11
Tafarnau-bach Bl Gwent 77 C10
Taff Merthyr Garden Village M Tydf 77 F10
Taff's Well Rhondda 58 C6
Tafolwern Powys 129 C7
Tai Conwy 164 C3
Tai-bach Powys 148 D3
Tai-mawr Conwy 165 G7
Tai-morfa Gwyn 144 D5
Tai-nant Wrex 166 F3
Tai-Ucha Denb 165 D8
Taibach Neath 57 D9
Taigh a Ghearraidh W Isles 296 D3
Taigh Bhalaigh W Isles 296 D3
Tain Highld 309 L7
Tain Highld 310 C6
Tainlon Gwyn 162 E6
Tai'r-Bull Powys 95 F9
Tai'r-heol Caerph 77 G10
Tai'r-ysgol Swansea 57 B7
Tairbeart W Isles 305 H3
Tairgwaith Neath 76 C2
Takeley Essex 105 G11
Takeley Street Essex 105 G10
Tal-sarn Ceredig 111 F10
Tal-y-bont Ceredig 128 F3
Tal-y-Bont Conwy 164 B3
Tal-y-bont Gwyn 145 E11
Tal-y-bont Gwyn 179 G10
Tal-y-cafn Conwy 180 G3
Tal-y-coed Mon 78 B6
Tal-y-llyn Gwyn 128 B4
Tal-y-waenydd Gwyn 163 F11
Tal-y-wern Powys 128 C6
Talacharn = Laugharne Carms 74 C4
Talachddu Powys 95 E11
Talacre Flint 181 E10
Talardd Gwyn 147 D7
Talaton Devon 15 B7
Talbenny Pembs 72 C4
Talbot Green Rhondda 58 C4
Talbot Heath Poole 19 C7
Talbot Village Poole 19 C7
Talbot Woods Bmouth 19 C7
Talbot's End S Glos 80 G2
Tale Devon 27 G9
Talerddig Powys 129 C8
Talgarreg Ceredig 111 G8
Talgarth Powys 96 E3
Talgarth's Well Swansea 56 D2
Talisker Highld 294 B5
Talke Staffs 168 E4
Talke Pits Staffs 168 E4
Talkin Cumb 240 F3
Talla Linnfoots Borders 260 E4
Talladale Highld 299 B9
Tallaminnoch S Ayrs 245 D10
Talland Corn 6 E4
Tallarn Green Wrex 166 G6
Tallentire Cumb 229 D8
Talley Carms 94 E2
Tallington Lincs 137 B11
Talmine Highld 308 C5
Talog Carms 92 F6
Talsarn Carms 94 F5
Talsarnau Gwyn 146 B2
Talskiddy Corn 5 B8
Talwrn Anglesey 179 F7
Talwrn Wrex 166 F3
Talybont-on-Usk Powys 96 G2
Talygarn Rhondda 58 C4
Talyllyn Powys 96 F2
Talysarn Gwyn 163 E7
Talywain Torf 78 E3
Tamanabhagh W Isles 304 F2
Tame Bridge N Yorks 225 D10
Tame Water Gtr Man 196 F3
Tamer Lane End Gtr Man 194 G6
Tamerton Foliot Plym 7 C9
Tamfourhill Falk 279 E7
Tamworth Staffs 134 C4
Tamworth Green Lincs 174 G5
Tan Hills Durham 233 B11
Tan Hinon Powys 129 F7
Tan-lan Conwy 164 C3
Tan-lan Gwyn 163 G10
Tan Office Suff 126 E2
Tan Office Green Suff 124 F5
Tan-y-bwlch Gwyn 163 G11
Tan-y-fron Conwy 165 C7
Tan-y-graig Anglesey 179 F8
Tan-y-graig Gwyn 144 B6
Tan-y-groes Ceredig 92 B5
Tan-y-mynydd Gwyn 144 C6
Tan-y-pistyll Powys 147 D11
Tan-yr-allt Denb 181 E9
Tan-yr-allt Gwyn 163 E7
Tancred N Yorks 206 B5
Tandem W Yorks 197 D7
Tanden Kent 54 F2
Tandlehill Renfs 267 C8
Tandridge Sur 51 C11
Tanerdy Carms 93 G8
Tanfield Durham 242 F5
Tanfield Lea Durham 242 G5
Tang N Yorks 205 B10
Tang Hall York 207 C8
Tangasdal W Isles 297 M2
Tangiers Pembs 73 B7
Tangley Hants 47 C10
Tanglwst Carms 92 E6
Tangmere W Sus 22 B6
Tangwick Shetland 312 F4
Tangy Argyll 255 E7
Tanhouse Lancs 194 F3
Tanis Wilts 62 G3
Tankersley S Yorks 197 G10
Tankerton Kent 70 F6
Tanlan Flint 181 E10
Tanlan Banks Flint 181 E10
Tannach Highld 310 E7
Tannachie Aberds 293 E9
Tannadice Angus 287 B8
Tanner's Green Worcs 117 C11
Tannington Suff 126 D4
Tannington Place Suff 126 D4
Tannochside N Lnrk 268 C4
Tansley Derbys 170 D4
Tansley Hill W Mid 133 F9

Tansley Knoll Derbys 170 C4
Tansor Northants 137 E11
Tanterton Lancs 202 G6
Tantobie Durham 242 G5
Tanton N Yorks 225 C10
Tanwood Worcs 117 C8
Tanworth-in-Arden Warks 118 C2
Tanyfron Wrex 166 E3
Tanygrisiau Gwyn 163 F11
Tanyrhydiau Ceredig 112 D4
Tanysgafell Gwyn 163 B10
Taobh a Chaolais W Isles 297 K3
Taobh a' Ghlinne W Isles 305 G5
Taobh a Thuath Loch Aineort W Isles 297 J3
Taobh a Tuath Loch Baghasdail W Isles 297 J3
Taobh Siar W Isles 305 H3
Taobh Tuath W Isles 296 C5
Taplow Bucks 66 C2
Tapnage Hants 33 E9
Tapton Derbys 186 G5
Tapton Hill S Yorks 186 D4
Tarbat Ho Highld 301 B7
Tarbert Argyll 255 B7
Tarbert Argyll 275 E7
Tarbert Argyll 275 G9
Tarbet Argyll 285 G7
Tarbet Highld 295 F9
Tarbet Highld 306 E6
Tarbock Green Mers 183 D7
Tarbolton S Ayrs 257 D10
Tarbrax S Lnrk 269 D10
Tardebigge Worcs 117 D10
Tardy Gate Lancs 194 B4
Tarfside Angus 292 F6
Tarland Aberds 292 C6
Tarleton Lancs 194 C3
Tarleton Moss Lancs 194 C2
Tarlogie Highld 309 L7
Tarlscough Lancs 194 E2
Tarlton Glos 81 F7
Tarn W Yorks 205 F9
Tarnbrook Lancs 203 B7
Tarnock Som 43 C11
Tarns Cumb 229 B8
Tarnside Cumb 221 G8
Tarporley W Ches 167 C9
Tarpots Essex 69 B9
Tarr Som 42 G6
Tarraby Cumb 239 F10
Tarrant Crawford Dorset 30 G6
Tarrant Gunville Dorset 30 E6
Tarrant Hinton Dorset 30 E6
Tarrant Keyneston Dorset 30 G6
Tarrant Launceston Dorset 30 F6
Tarrant Monkton Dorset 30 F6
Tarrant Rawston Dorset 30 F6
Tarrant Rushton Dorset 30 F6
Tarrel Highld 311 L2
Tarring Neville E Sus 36 G6
Tarrington Hereford 98 C2
Tarrington Common Hereford 98 D2
Tarryblake Ho Moray 302 E5
Tarsappie Perth 286 E5
Tarskavaig Highld 295 E7
Tarts Hill Shrops 149 B8
Tarves Aberds 303 F8
Tarvie Highld 300 D4
Tarvie Perth 292 G2
Tarvin W Ches 167 B7
Tarvin Sands W Ches 167 B7
Tasburgh Norf 142 D4
Tasley Shrops 132 E3
Taston Oxon 101 G7
Tat Bank W Mid 133 F9
Tatenhill Staffs 152 E4
Tatenhill Common Staffs 152 E3
Tathall End M Keynes 102 B6
Tatham Lancs 212 F2
Tathwell Lincs 190 E4
Tatling End Bucks 66 B4
Tatsfield Sur 52 B2
Tattenhall W Ches 167 D7
Tattenhoe M Keynes 102 E6
Tatterford Norf 159 D7
Tattersett Norf 158 C6
Tattershall Lincs 174 D2
Tattershall Bridge Lincs 173 D11
Tattershall Thorpe Lincs 174 D2
Tattingstone Suff 108 D2
Tattingstone White Horse Suff 108 D2
Tattle Bank Warks 118 E3
Tatton Dale E Ches 184 E2
Tatworth Som 28 F4
Taunton Gtr Man 196 G2
Taunton Som 28 C2
Taverham Norf 160 G3
Taverners Green Essex 87 B9
Tavernspite Pembs 73 C11
Tavistock Devon 12 G5
Taw Green Devon 13 B9
Tawstock Devon 25 B9
Taxal Derbys 185 F8
Tay Bridge Dundee 287 E8
Tayinloan Argyll 255 C7
Taymouth Castle Perth 285 C11
Taynish Argyll 275 E8
Taynton Glos 98 G4
Taynton Oxon 82 C2
Taynuilt Argyll 284 D4
Tayport Fife 287 E8
Tayvallich Argyll 275 E8
Tea Green Herts 104 G2
Tealby Lincs 189 C11
Tealing Angus 287 D8
Team Valley T & W 242 E6
Teams T & W 242 E6
Teanford Staffs 169 G8
Teangue Highld 295 E8
Teanna Mhachair W Isles 296 E3
Teasley Mead E Sus 52 F4
Tebay Cumb 222 E2
Tebworth C Beds 103 F9
Tedburn St Mary Devon 14 C2
Teddington Glos 99 E9
Teddington London 67 E7
Teddington Hands Worcs 99 E9
Tedsmore Shrops 149 D7
Tedstone Delamere Hereford 116 F3
Tedstone Wafer Hereford 116 F3
Teesville Redcar 225 B10
Teeton Northants 120 C3
Teffont Evias Wilts 46 G3
Teffont Magna Wilts 46 G3
Tegryn Pembs 92 E4
Teigh Rutland 155 F7
Teign Village Devon 14 E2
Teigncombe Devon 13 D9
Teigngrace Devon 14 G2
Teignmouth Devon 14 G4
Telford Telford 132 B3
Telham E Sus 38 E3
Tellisford Som 45 B10
Telscombe E Sus 36 G6
Telscombe Cliffs E Sus 36 G5
Templand Dumfries 248 F3
Temple Corn 11 G8
Temple Glasgow 267 B10
Temple Midloth 270 D6
Temple Wilts 45 E10
Temple Windsor 65 C10
Temple Balsall W Mid 118 B4
Temple Bar Carms 75 B9
Temple Bar Ceredig 111 G10
Temple Bar W Sus 22 B5
Temple Cloud Bath 44 B6
Temple Cowley Oxon 83 E8
Temple End Essex 106 C6
Temple End Suff 124 G3
Temple Ewell Kent 55 E9
Temple Fields Essex 87 C7
Temple Grafton Warks 118 G2
Temple Guiting Glos 99 F11
Temple Herdewyke Warks 119 G7
Temple Hill Kent 68 D5
Temple Hirst N Yorks 198 C6
Temple Normanton Derbys 170 B6
Temple Sowerby Cumb 231 F8
Templeborough S Yorks 186 C6
Templecombe Som 30 C2
Templehall Fife 280 C5
Templeman's Ash Dorset 28 G6
Templeton Devon 26 E5
Templeton Pembs 73 C10
Templeton W Berks 63 F11
Templeton Bridge Devon 26 E5
Templetown Durham 242 G4
Tempsford C Beds 122 G3
Ten Acres W Mid 133 G11
Ten Mile Bank Norf 140 D2
Tenandry Perth 291 G11
Tenbury Wells Worcs 115 D11
Tenby = Dinbych-y-Pysgod Pembs 73 E10
Tencreek Corn 6 E4
Tendring Essex 108 G2
Tendring Green Essex 108 F2
Tendring Heath Essex 108 F2
Tenston Orkney 314 E2
Tenterden Kent 53 G11
Terfyn Conwy 180 F6
Terfyn Gwyn 163 C9
Terhill Som 43 G7
Terling Essex 88 B3
Ternhill Shrops 150 C2
Terpersie Castle Aberds 302 G5
Terras Corn 5 E8
Terregles Banks Dumfries 237 B11
Terrible Down E Sus 23 B7
Terrick Bucks 84 D4
Terriers Bucks 84 G5
Terrington N Yorks 216 E3
Terrington St Clement Norf 157 E10
Terrington St John Norf 157 G10
Terryhorn Aberds 302 F4
Terry's Green Warks 118 C2
Terwick Common W Sus 34 C4
Teston Kent 53 C8
Testwood Hants 32 E5
Tetbury Glos 80 G5
Tetbury Upton Glos 80 F5
Tetchill Shrops 149 C7
Tetchwick Bucks 83 B11
Tetcott Devon 12 B2
Tetford Lincs 190 G4
Tetley N Lincs 199 E9
Tetney Lincs 201 G10
Tetney Lock Lincs 201 G10
Tetsworth Oxon 83 E11
Tettenhall W Mid 133 D7
Tettenhall Wood W Mid 133 D7
Tetworth Cambs 122 G4
Teuchan Aberds 303 F10
Teversal Notts 171 C7
Teversham Cambs 123 F9
Teviothead Borders 249 B10
Tewel Aberds 293 E10
Tewin Herts 86 C3
Tewin Wood Herts 86 B3
Tewitfield Lancs 211 E10
Tewkesbury Glos 99 E7
Teynham Kent 70 G3
Teynham Street Kent 70 G3
Thackley W Yorks 205 F9
Thackley End W Yorks 205 F9
Thackthwaite Cumb 229 G8
Thainston Aberds 293 F8
Thakeham W Sus 35 D10
Thame Oxon 84 D2
Thames Ditton Sur 67 F7
Thames Haven Thurrock 69 C8
Thames Head Glos 81 F7
Thamesmead London 68 C3
Thanington Kent 54 B6
Thankerton S Lnrk 259 B11
Tharston Norf 142 E3
Thatcham W Berks 64 F4
Thatto Heath Mers 183 C8
Thaxted Essex 106 E2
The Aird Highld 298 D4
The Alders Staffs 134 C3
The Arms Norf 141 D7
The Bage Hereford 96 C5
The Balloch Perth 286 F2
The Bank E Ches 168 D4
The Banks Gtr Man 185 D7
The Banks Wilts 62 D4
The Barony E Ches 167 E11
The Barony Orkney 314 D2
The Barton Wilts 62 D5
The Batch S Glos 61 E7
The Beeches Glos 81 E8
The Bell Gtr Man 194 F4
The Bents Staffs 151 C10
The Blythe Staffs 151 D10
The Bog Shrops 131 D7
The Borough Dorset 30 E2
The Borough London 67 D10
The Bourne Sur 49 E10
The Bourne Worcs 117 F9
The Bows Stirl 285 G11
The Braes Highld 295 B7
The Brampton Staffs 168 F4
The Brand Leics 153 G10
The Bratch Staffs 133 E7
The Breck Orkney 314 F3
The Brents Kent 70 G4
The Bridge Dorset 30 E3
The Broad Hereford 115 E9
The Brook Suff 125 B11
The Brushes Derbys 186 F5
The Bryn Mon 78 D4
The Burf Worcs 116 D6
The Butts Hants 49 F8
The Butts Som 45 D9
The Camp Glos 80 D6
The Camp Herts 85 D11
The Cape Warks 118 D5
The Chart Kent 52 C3
The Chequer Wrex 167 G7
The Chuckery W Mid 133 D10
The City Bucks 84 F3
The Cleaver Hereford 97 F10
The Close W Sus 22 C5
The Colony Oxon 100 D6
The Common Bath 60 G6
The Common Bucks 102 E5
The Common Dorset 30 E3
The Common Shrops 150 D3
The Common Suff 108 B2
The Common Swansea 56 C4
The Common W Sus 51 G7
The Common Wilts 47 G8
The Common Wilts 61 G11
The Common Wilts 62 C4
The Corner Kent 53 E8
The Corner Shrops 131 F8
The Cot Mon 79 F8
The Craigs Highld 309 K4
The Crofts E Yorks 218 E4
The Cronk I o M 192 C4
The Cross Hands Leics 134 C6
The Cwm Mon 79 G7
The Dell Suff 143 D9
The Delves W Mid 133 D10
The Den N Ayrs 266 E6
The Dene Durham 242 G4
The Dene Hants 47 C11
The Down Kent 53 F7
The Down Shrops 132 E3
The Downs Sur 50 F3
The Dunks Wrex 166 E4
The Eals Northumb 251 F7
The Eaves Glos 79 D10
The Fall W Yorks 197 B10
The Fence Glos 79 D8
The Flat Glos 80 B3
The Flatt Cumb 240 B3
The Flourish Derbys 153 B8
The Folly Herts 85 C11
The Folly S Glos 61 E8
The Fording Hereford 98 F3
The Forge Hereford 114 F6
The Forstal Kent 54 F4
The Forties Derbys 152 F6
The Four Alls Shrops 150 C3
The Fox Wilts 62 B6
The Foxholes Shrops 132 G2
The Frenches Hants 32 C4
The Frythe Herts 86 C2
The Garths Shetland 312 B8
The Gibb Wilts 61 D10
The Glack Borders 260 B6
The Gore Shrops 131 G11
The Grange N Yorks 225 F11
The Grange Norf 160 E2
The Green C Beds 85 B8
The Green Cambs 122 D5
The Green Cumb 210 C3
The Green Cumb 211 D7
The Green Essex 88 B3
The Green Hants 32 B3
The Green M Keynes 103 C7
The Green Norf 141 C11
The Green Norf 159 B11
The Green Northants 102 C5
The Green Oxon 101 F9
The Green S Yorks 197 G8
The Green Shrops 130 G6
The Green Warks 118 F4
The Green Wilts 45 G11
The Grove Dumfries 237 B11
The Grove Durham 242 G3
The Grove Herts 85 F9
The Grove Shrops 131 B7
The Grove Shrops 131 G8
The Grove Worcs 99 C7
The Gutter Derbys 170 F5
The Gutter Worcs 117 B9
The Hacket S Glos 61 B7
The Hague Derbys 185 C8
The Hall Shetland 312 D8
The Hallands N Lincs 200 C5
The Ham Wilts 45 C11
The Handfords Staffs 151 E7
The Harbour Kent 53 D10
The Haven W Sus 50 G5
The Headland Hrtlpl 234 E6
The Heath Norf 159 D8
The Heath Norf 160 E3
The Heath Norf 160 E4
The Heath Staffs 151 C11
The Heath Suff 108 D2
The Hem Shrops 132 B4
The Hendre Mon 79 C7
The Herberts V Glam 58 E3
The Hermitage Cambs 123 C7
The High Essex 86 C6
The Highlands E Sus 38 F2
The Hill Cumb 210 C3
The Hobbins Shrops 132 E4
The Hollands Staffs 168 D6
The Hollies Notts 172 E4
The Holmes Derbys 153 B7
The Holt Wokingham 65 D10
The Hook Worcs 98 C6
The Hope Shrops 115 B10
The Howe Cumb 211 B9
The Howe I o M 192 F2
The Humbers Telford 150 G3
The Hundred Hereford 115 E10
The Hyde London 67 B8
The Hyde Worcs 98 E6
The Hythe Essex 107 G10
The Inch Edin 280 G5
The Knab Swansea 56 D6
The Knap V Glam 58 F5
The Knapp Hereford 116 G3
The Knapp S Glos 79 G11
The Knowle W Mid 133 F9
The Laches Staffs 133 B8
The Lake Dumfries 237 E8
The Lakes Worcs 116 B5
The Lawe T & W 243 D9
The Lawns E Yorks 208 G6
The Leacon Kent 54 G3
The Leath Shrops 131 F11
The Lee Bucks 84 E6
The Lees Kent 54 C4
The Leigh Glos 99 F7
The Leys Staffs 134 C4
The Lhen I o M 192 B4
The Ling Norf 142 D6
The Lings Norf 141 B10
The Lings S Yorks 199 F7
The Linleys Wilts 61 F11
The Lunt W Mid 133 D9
The Manor W Sus 22 C4
The Marsh E Ches 168 C4
The Marsh Hereford 115 F9
The Marsh Powys 130 D6
The Marsh Shrops 150 D3
The Marsh Staffs 150 D6
The Marsh Suff 125 B11
The Marsh Suff 126 B2
The Marsh Wilts 62 C5
The Middles Durham 242 G6
The Mint Hants 34 B3
The Moor Flint 166 B4
The Moor Kent 38 B3
The Moors Hereford 97 E10
The Mount Hants 64 G2
The Mount Reading 65 E8
The Mumbles = Y Mwmbwls Swansea 56 D6
The Murray S Lnrk 268 E2
The Mythe Glos 99 E7
The Nant Wrex 166 E3
The Narth Mon 79 D8
The Neuk Aberds 293 D9
The Node Herts 104 G4
The Nook Shrops 149 C11
The Nook Shrops 150 E3
The North Mon 79 D8
The Oval Bath 61 G8
The Park Glos 99 G8
The Parks S Yorks 198 F6
The Pitts Wilts 31 B9
The Platt Oxon 83 E9
The Pludds Glos 79 B10
The Point Devon 14 E5
The Pole of Itlaw Aberds 302 D6
The Port of Felixstowe Suff 108 E5
The Potteries Stoke 168 F5
The Pound Glos 98 E4
The Quarry Glos 80 F2
The Quarry Shrops 149 G9
The Quarter Kent 53 E11
The Quarter Kent 53 G11
The Rampings Worcs 99 E7
The Rectory Lincs 156 G2
The Reddings Glos 99 G8
The Rhos Pembs 73 C8
The Rhydd Hereford 97 E9
The Riddle Hereford 115 E9
The Ridge Wilts 61 F11
The Ridges Wokingham 65 G10
The Ridgeway Herts 86 E3
The Riding Northumb 241 D10
The Riggs Borders 261 C8
The Rink Borders 261 C11
The Rise Windsor 66 F2
The Rock Telford 132 B3
The Rocks Kent 53 B8
The Rocks S Glos 61 C8
The Roe Denb 181 G8
The Rookery Herts 85 G10
The Rookery Staffs 168 D5
The Row Lancs 211 D9
The Rowe Staffs 150 B6
The Ryde Herts 86 D2
The Sands Sur 49 D11
The Scarr Glos 98 F4
The Shoe Wilts 61 E10
The Shruggs Staffs 151 C8
The Slack Durham 233 F8
The Slade W Berks 64 F4
The Smeeth Norf 157 G10
The Smithies Shrops 132 D3
The Spa Wilts 62 G2
The Spring Warks 118 C5
The Square Torf 78 F3
The Stocks Kent 38 B6
The Stocks Wilts 62 G2
The Straits Hants 49 F9
The Straits W Mid 133 E8
The Strand Wilts 46 B2
The Swillett Herts 85 F8
The Sydnall Shrops 150 C3
The Thrift Cambs 104 D6
The Throat Wokingham 65 F10
The Toft Staffs 151 F8
The Towans Corn 2 B3
The Town Scilly 1 F3
The Twittocks Glos 99 D7
The Tynings Glos 80 B6
The Vale W Mid 133 G11
The Valley E Ches 167 D11
The Valley Kent 54 C3
The Valley Leics 154 F4
The Valley Pembs 73 D10
The Vauld Hereford 97 B10
The Village Newport 78 G4
The Village W Mid 133 F7
The Village Windsor 66 E3
The Walshes Worcs 116 C6
The Warren Kent 54 E3
The Warren Wilts 63 F8
The Waterwheel Shrops 131 C7
The Weaven Hereford 97 E10
The Wells Sur 67 G7
The Wern Wrex 166 E3
The Willows NE Lincs 201 F8
The Wood Shrops 148 E6
The Wood Shrops 149 D9
The Woodlands Leics 136 D3
The Woodlands Suff 107 C11
The Woodlands Suff 108 D3
The Woods W Mid 133 D10
The Wrangle Bath 44 B4
The Wrythe London 67 F9
The Wyke Shrops 132 B4
The Wymm Hereford 97 B10
The Yeld Shrops 131 G11
Theakston N Yorks 214 B6
Thealby N Lincs 199 D11
Theale Som 44 D3
Theale W Berks 64 E6
Thearne E Yorks 209 F7
Theberton Suff 127 D8
Theddingworth Leics 136 F3
Theddlethorpe All Saints Lincs 191 D7
Theddlethorpe St Helen Lincs 191 D7
Thelbridge Barton Devon 26 E3
Thelnetham Suff 125 B10
Thelveton Norf 142 G3
Thelwall Warr 183 D10
Themelthorpe Norf 159 E11
Thenford Northants 101 C10
Theobald's Green Wilts 62 F4
Therfield Herts 104 D6
Thetford Lincs 156 F2
Thetford Norf 141 G7
Theydon Bois Essex 86 F6
Theydon Garnon Essex 87 F7
Theydon Mount Essex 87 F7
Thick Hollins W Yorks 196 E6
Thicket Mead Bath 45 B7
Thickthorn Hall Norf 142 B3
Thickwood Wilts 61 E10
Thimble End W Mid 134 E2
Thimbleby Lincs 190 G2
Thimbleby N Yorks 225 F9
Thinford Durham 233 E11
Thingley Wilts 61 E11
Thingwall Mers 182 E3
Thirdpart N Ayrs 266 F3
Thirlby N Yorks 215 C9
Thirlestane Borders 271 F11
Thirn N Yorks 214 B4
Thirsk N Yorks 215 C8
Thirtleby E Yorks 209 G9
Thistleton Lancs 202 F4
Thistleton Rutland 155 F8
Thistley Green Essex 88 B2
Thistley Green Suff 124 B3
Thixendale N Yorks 216 G6
Thockrington Northumb 241 B11
Tholomas Drove Cambs 139 B7
Tholthorpe N Yorks 215 F9
Thomas Chapel Pembs 73 D10
Thomas Close Cumb 230 C4
Thomastown Aberds 302 F5
Thomastown Rhondda 58 B4
Thompson Norf 141 D8
Thomshill Moray 302 D2
Thong Kent 69 E7
Thongsbridge W Yorks 196 F6
Thoralby N Yorks 213 B10
Thoresby Notts 187 G10
Thoresthorpe Lincs 191 F7
Thoresway Lincs 189 B11
Thorganby Lincs 190 B2
Thorganby N Yorks 207 E9
Thorgill N Yorks 226 F4
Thorington Suff 127 C8
Thorington Street Suff 107 D10
Thorlby N Yorks 204 C5
Thorley Herts 87 B7
Thorley I o W 20 D3
Thorley Houses Herts 105 G9
Thorley Street Herts 87 B7
Thorley Street I o W 20 D3
Thormanby N Yorks 215 E9
Thorn Devon 13 D9
Thorn Powys 114 E5
Thorn Hill S Yorks 186 C6
Thornaby on Tees Stockton 225 B9
Thornage Norf 159 B11
Thornborough Bucks 102 E4
Thornborough N Yorks 214 D5
Thornbury Devon 24 F6
Thornbury Hereford 116 F2
Thornbury S Glos 79 G10
Thornbury W Yorks 205 G9
Thornby Cumb 239 G7
Thornby Northants 120 B3
Thorncliff W Yorks 197 E8
Thorncliffe Staffs 169 D8
Thorncombe Dorset 28 G5
Thorncombe Dorset 30 G5
Thorncombe Street Sur 50 E4
Thorncote Green C Beds 104 B3
Thorncross I o W 20 E4
Thorndon Suff 126 D2
Thorndon Cross Devon 12 C6
Thorne Corn 24 G2
Thorne S Yorks 199 E7
Thorne Coffin Som 29 D8
Thorne Moor Devon 12 D3
Thorne St Margaret Som 27 C9
Thornehillhead Devon 24 D6
Thornend Wilts 62 D3
Thorner W Yorks 206 E3
Thornes Staffs 133 C11
Thornes W Yorks 197 D10
Thorney Bucks 66 D4
Thorney Notts 188 G5
Thorney P'boro 138 C5
Thorney Som 28 C6
Thorney Close T & W 243 G9
Thorney Crofts E Yorks 201 C8
Thorney Green Suff 125 E11
Thorney Hill Hants 19 B9
Thorney Island W Sus 22 C3
Thorney Toll P'boro 138 C6
Thorneywood Notts 171 G9
Thornfalcon Som 28 C3
Thornford Dorset 29 E10
Thorngrafton Northumb 241 D7
Thorngrove Som 43 G11
Thorngumbald E Yorks 201 B8
Thornham Norf 176 E2
Thornham Fold Gtr Man 195 F11
Thornham Magna Suff 126 C2
Thornham Parva Suff 126 C2
Thornhaugh P'boro 137 C11
Thornhill Cardiff 59 C7
Thornhill Cumb 219 D10
Thornhill Derbys 185 E11
Thornhill Dumfries 247 D9
Thornhill Soton 33 E7
Thornhill Stirl 278 B3
Thornhill Torf 78 F3
Thornhill W Yorks 197 D9
Thornhill Wilts 62 D5
Thornhill Edge W Yorks 197 D8
Thornhill Lees W Yorks 197 D8
Thornhill Park Hants 33 E7
Thornhills W Yorks 197 C7
Thornholme E Yorks 218 G2
Thornicombe Dorset 30 G5
Thornielee Borders 261 B10
Thornley Durham 233 D8
Thornley Durham 234 D3
Thornliebank E Renf 267 D10
Thornly Park Renfs 267 C9
Thornroan Aberds 303 F8
Thorns N Yorks 223 E7
Thorns Suff 124 F4
Thorns Green Ches 184 E3
Thornseat S Yorks 186 C2
Thornsett Derbys 185 D8
Thornthwaite Cumb 229 F10
Thornthwaite N Yorks 205 B9
Thornton Angus 287 C7
Thornton Bucks 102 D5
Thornton E Yorks 207 D11
Thornton Fife 280 B5
Thornton Lancs 202 E2
Thornton Leics 135 B9
Thornton Lincs 174 B2
Thornton M'bro 225 C9
Thornton Mers 193 G10
Thornton Northumb 273 F9
Thornton Pembs 72 D6
Thornton W Yorks 205 G8
Thornton Curtis N Lincs 200 D5
Thornton Heath London 67 F10
Thornton Hough Mers 182 E4
Thornton in Craven N Yorks 204 D4
Thornton in Lonsdale N Yorks 212 E3
Thornton-le-Beans N Yorks 225 G7
Thornton-le-Clay N Yorks 216 F3
Thornton-le-Dale N Yorks 216 C6
Thornton le Moor Lincs 189 B9
Thornton-le-Moor N Yorks 215 B7
Thornton-le-Moors W Ches 182 G6
Thornton-le-Street N Yorks 215 B8
Thornton Rust N Yorks 213 B9
Thornton Steward N Yorks 214 B3
Thornton Watlass N Yorks 214 B4
Thorntonhall S Lnrk 267 D11
Thorntonloch E Loth 282 G4
Thornton Park Northumb 273 F8
Thornwood Common Essex 87 D7
Thornydykes Borders 272 F2
Thoroton Notts 172 G3
Thorp Gtr Man 196 F2
Thorp Arch W Yorks 206 D4
Thorpe Cumb 230 F5
Thorpe Derbys 169 E11
Thorpe E Yorks 208 D5
Thorpe Lincs 191 E7
Thorpe N Yorks 213 G10
Thorpe Norf 143 D8
Thorpe Notts 172 F3
Thorpe Sur 66 F4
Thorpe Abbotts Norf 126 B3
Thorpe Acre Leics 153 E10
Thorpe Arnold Leics 154 E5
Thorpe Audlin W Yorks 198 D3
Thorpe Bassett N Yorks 217 E7
Thorpe Bay Shend 70 B2
Thorpe by Water Rutland 137 D7
Thorpe Common Suff 108 D5
Thorpe Constantine Staffs 134 B5
Thorpe Culvert Lincs 175 C7
Thorpe Edge W Yorks 205 F9
Thorpe End Norf 160 G5
Thorpe Fendykes Lincs 175 C7
Thorpe Green Essex 108 G3
Thorpe Green Lancs 194 C5
Thorpe Green Suff 125 G8
Thorpe Green Sur 66 F4
Thorpe Hamlet Norf 142 B4
Thorpe Hesley S Yorks 186 B5
Thorpe in Balne S Yorks 198 E5
Thorpe in the Fallows Lincs 188 E6
Thorpe Langton Leics 136 E4
Thorpe Larches Durham 234 F3
Thorpe Latimer Lincs 156 B2
Thorpe-le-Soken Essex 108 G3
Thorpe le Street E Yorks 208 E2
Thorpe le Vale Lincs 190 C2
Thorpe Lea Sur 66 E4
Thorpe Malsor Northants 120 B6
Thorpe Mandeville Northants 101 B10
Thorpe Market Norf 160 B4
Thorpe Marriot Norf 160 F3
Thorpe Morieux Suff 125 G8
Thorpe on the Hill Lincs 172 B6
Thorpe on The Hill W Yorks 197 B10
Thorpe Row Norf 141 B9
Thorpe St Andrew Norf 142 B5
Thorpe St Peter Lincs 175 C7
Thorpe Salvin S Yorks 187 E8
Thorpe Satchville Leics 154 G4
Thorpe Street Suff 125 B10
Thorpe Thewles Stockton 234 G4
Thorpe Tilney Lincs 173 D10
Thorpe Underwood N Yorks 206 B5
Thorpe Underwood Northants 136 G5
Thorpe Waterville Northants 137 G10
Thorpe Willoughby N Yorks 207 G7
Thorpe Wood N Yorks 207 G7
Thorpeness Suff 127 F9
Thorpland Norf 140 B2
Thorrington Essex 89 B9
Thorverton Devon 26 G6
Thoulstone Wilts 45 D10
Thrandeston Suff 126 B2
Thrapston Northants 121 B9
Thrashbush N Lnrk 268 B5
Threapland Cumb 229 D9
Threapland N Yorks 213 G9
Threapwood Staffs 169 G8
Threapwood W Ches 166 F6
Three Ashes Hants 64 G6
Three Ashes Hereford 97 G10
Three Ashes Shrops 115 B7
Three Ashes Som 45 D7
Three Bridges Argyll 284 F4
Three Bridges Lincs 190 D6
Three Bridges W Sus 51 F9
Three Burrows Corn 4 F4
Three Chimneys Kent 53 F10
Three Cocked Hat Norf 143 D8
Three Cocks = Aberllynfi Powys 96 D3
Three Crosses Swansea 56 C5
Three Cups Corner E Sus 37 C10
Three Gates Dorset 29 F10
Three Hammers Corn 11 D10
Three Holes Norf 139 C10
Three Holes Cross Corn 10 G6
Three Leg Cross E Sus 53 G7
Three Legged Cross Dorset 31 F9
Three Maypoles W Mid 118 B2
Three Mile Cross Wokingham 65 F8
Three Oaks E Sus 38 E4
Three Sisters Denb 165 C9
Threehammer Common Norf 160 E6
Threekingham Lincs 155 B11
Threelows Staffs 169 F9
Threemile Cross Wokingham 65 F8
Threemilestone Corn 4 G5
Threemiletown W Loth 279 F11
Threepwood Borders 271 G10
Threewaters Corn 5 B10
Threlkeld Cumb 230 F2
Threshers Bush Essex 87 D7
Threshfield N Yorks 213 G9
Thrigby Norf 161 G9
Thringarth Durham 232 G4
Thringstone Leics 153 F8
Thrintoft N Yorks 224 G6
Thriplow Cambs 105 B8
Throapham S Yorks 187 D8
Throckenholt Lincs 139 B7
Throcking Herts 104 E6
Throckley T & W 242 D5
Throckmorton Worcs 99 B9
Throop Dorset 18 C2
Throphill Northumb 252 F4
Thropton Northumb 252 C2
Throsk Stirl 279 C7
Througham Glos 80 D6
Throughgate Dumfries 247 G9
Throwleigh Devon 13 C9
Throwley Kent 54 B3
Throwley Forstal Kent 54 C3
Throxenby N Yorks 217 B10
Thrumpton Notts 153 C10
Thrumpton Notts 188 E2
Thrumster Highld 310 E7
Thrunton Northumb 264 G3
Thrupe Som 44 D6
Thrupp Glos 80 E5
Thrupp Oxon 82 F3
Thrupp Oxon 83 B7
Thruscross N Yorks 205 B9
Thrushelton Devon 12 D4
Thrussington Leics 154 F2
Thruxton Hants 47 D9
Thruxton Hereford 97 E8
Thrybergh S Yorks 187 B7
Thulston Derbys 153 C8
Thunder Bridge W Yorks 197 E7
Thunder Hill Norf 161 F8
Thundergay N Ayrs 255 C9
Thunder's Hill E Sus 23 C9
Thundersley Essex 69 B9
Thundridge Herts 86 B5
Thurcaston Leics 153 G11
Thurcroft S Yorks 187 D7
Thurdon Corn 24 E3
Thurgarton Norf 160 C3
Thurgarton Notts 171 F11
Thurgoland S Yorks 197 G9
Thurlaston Leics 135 D10
Thurlaston Warks 119 C9
Thurlbear Som 28 C3
Thurlby Lincs 156 F2
Thurlby Lincs 172 C6
Thurlby Lincs 191 F7
Thurleigh Beds 121 F11
Thurlestone Devon 8 G3
Thurloxton Som 43 G9
Thurlstone S Yorks 197 G8
Thurlton Norf 143 D8
Thurlton Links Norf 143 D8
Thurlwood E Ches 168 D4
Thurmaston Leics 136 B2
Thurnby Leics 136 C2
Thurne Norf 161 F8
Thurnham Kent 53 B10
Thurnham Lancs 202 C5
Thurning Norf 159 D11
Thurning Northants 137 G11
Thurnscoe S Yorks 198 F3
Thurnscoe East S Yorks 198 F3
Thursby Cumb 239 G8
Thursford Norf 159 C9
Thursford Green Norf 159 C9
Thursley Sur 50 F2
Thurso Highld 310 C5
Thurso East Highld 310 C5
Thurstaston Mers 182 E2
Thurston Suff 125 D8
Thurston Clough Gtr Man 196 F3
Thurston End Suff 124 G5
Thurstonfield Cumb 239 F8
Thurstonland W Yorks 197 E7
Thurton Norf 142 C6
Thurvaston Derbys 152 B2
Thurvaston Derbys 152 B4
Thuxton Norf 141 B10
Thwaite N Yorks 223 F7
Thwaite Suff 126 D2
Thwaite Flat Cumb 210 E4
Thwaite Head Cumb 220 G6
Thwaite St Mary Norf 142 E6
Thwaites W Yorks 205 E7
Thwaites Brow W Yorks 205 E7
Thwing E Yorks 217 E11
Tibbermore Perth 286 E4
Tibberton Glos 98 G5
Tibberton Telford 150 E3
Tibberton Worcs 117 F8
Tibenham Norf 142 F2
Tibshelf Derbys 170 C6
Tibshelf Wharf Notts 170 C6
Tibthorpe E Yorks 208 B5
Ticehurst E Sus 53 G7
Tichborne Hants 48 G5
Tickencote Rutland 137 B9
Tickenham N Som 60 E3
Ticket Wood Devon 8 G4
Tickford End M Keynes 103 C7
Tickhill S Yorks 187 C9
Ticklerton Shrops 131 E9
Tickmorend Glos 80 F4
Ticknall Derbys 153 E7
Tickton E Yorks 209 E7
Tidbury Green W Mid 117 B11
Tidcombe Wilts 47 B9
Tiddington Oxon 83 E11
Tiddington Warks 118 F4
Tidebrook E Sus 37 B10
Tideford Corn 6 D6
Tideford Cross Corn 6 C6
Tidenham Glos 79 F9
Tidenham Chase Glos 79 F9
Tideswell Derbys 185 F11
Tidmarsh W Berks 64 E6
Tidmington Warks 100 D5
Tidnor Hereford 97 D11
Tidpit Hants 31 D9
Tidworth Wilts 47 D8
Tiers Cross Pembs 72 C6
Tiffield Northants 120 G3
Tifty Aberds 303 E7
Tigerton Angus 293 G7
Tigh-na-Blair Perth 285 F11
Tighnabruaich Argyll 275 F10
Tighnacachla Argyll 274 G3
Tighnafiline Highld 307 L3
Tighness Argyll 284 G6
Tigley Devon 8 C5
Tilbrook Cambs 121 D11
Tilbury Thurrock 68 D6
Tilbury Green Essex 106 C4
Tilbury Juxta Clare Essex 106 C5
Tile Cross W Mid 134 F3
Tile Hill W Mid 118 B5
Tilegate Green Essex 87 D8
Tilehouse Green W Mid 118 B3
Tilehurst Reading 65 E7
Tilekiln Green Essex 105 G10
Tiley Dorset 29 F11
Tilford Sur 49 E11
Tilford Common Sur 49 E11
Tilford Reeds Sur 49 E11
Tilgate W Sus 51 G9
Tilgate Forest Row W Sus 51 G
Tilkey Essex 106 G
Tilland Corn 6 C
Tillathrowie Aberds 302 F
Tillers' Green Glos 98 E
Tilley Shrops 149 D1
Tilley Green Shrops 149 D1
Tillicoultry Clack 279 B
Tillietudlem S Lnrk 268 F
Tillingham Essex 89 E
Tillington Hereford 97 B
Tillington Staffs 151 E
Tillington W Sus 35 C
Tillington Common Hereford 97 B
Tillislow Devon 12 C
Tillworth Devon 28 G
Tilly Down Hants 47 D1
Tilly Lo Aberds 293 C
Tillyarblet Angus 293 G
Tillybirloch Aberds 293 C
Tillycorthie Aberds 303 G
Tillydrine Aberds 293 D
Tillyfour Aberds 293 B
Tillyfourie Aberds 293 B
Tillygarmond Aberds 293 D
Tillygreig Aberds 303 G
Tillykerrie Aberds 303 G
Tillynaught Aberds 302 C
Tilmanstone Kent 55 C1
Tilney All Saints Norf 157 F1
Tilney cum Islington Norf 157 G1
Tilney Fen End Norf 157 G1
Tilney High End Norf 157 F1
Tilney St Lawrence Norf 157 G1
Tilsdown Glos 80 F
Tilshead Wilts 46 D
Tilsmore E Sus 37 C
Tilsop Shrops 116 C
Tilstock Shrops 149 B1
Tilston W Ches 167 E
Tilstone Bank W Ches 167 D
Tilstone Fearnall W Ches 167 C
Tilsworth C Beds 103 G
Tilton on the Hill Leics 136 B
Tilts S Yorks 198 F
Tiltups End Glos 80 F
Tilty Essex 105 F1
Timberden Bottom Kent 68 G
Timberhonger Worcs 117 C
Timberland Lincs 173 D1
Timbersbrook E Ches 168 C
Timberscombe Som 42 E
Timble N Yorks 205 C
Timbold Hill Kent 54 B
Timbrelham Corn 12 E
Timperley Gtr Man 184 D
Timsbury Bath 45 B
Timsbury Hants 32 C
Timsgearraidh W Isles 304 E
Timworth Suff 125 D
Timworth Green Suff 125 D
Tincleton Dorset 17 C1
Tindale Cumb 240 F
Tindale Crescent Durham 233 F
Tindon End Essex 106 E
Tingewick Bucks 102 E
Tingley W Yorks 197 B
Tingon Shetland 312 E
Tingrith C Beds 103 E1
Tingwall Orkney 314 D
Tinhay Devon 12 E
Tinkers End Bucks 102 F
Tinshill W Yorks 205 F1
Tinsley S Yorks 186 C
Tinsley Green W Sus 51 F
Tintagel Corn 11 D
Tintern Parva Mon 79 E
Tintinhull Som 29 D
Tintwistle Derbys 185 B
Tinwald Dumfries 248 G
Tinwell Rutland 137 B1
Tipner Ptsmth 33 G1
Tippacott Devon 41 D
Tipper's Hill Warks 134 F
Tipperty Aberds 302 C
Tipperty Aberds 303 G
Tipple Cross Devon 12 D
Tipps End Norf 139 D1
Tip's Cross Essex 87 E
Tiptoe Hants 19 B1
Tipton W Mid 133 E
Tipton Green W Mid 133 E
Tipton St John Devon 15 C
Tiptree Essex 88 B
Tiptree Heath Essex 88 B
Tir-y-berth Caerph 77 F1
Tir-y-dail Carms 75 C1
Tirabad Powys 95 C
Tiraghoil Argyll 288 G
Tircanol Swansea 57 B
Tirdeunaw Swansea 57 B
Tirinie Perth 291 G1
Tirley Glos 98 F
Tirley Knowle Glos 98 F
Tiroran Argyll 288 G
Tirphil Caerph 77 E1
Tirril Cumb 230 F
Tirryside Highld 309 H
Tisbury Wilts 30 B
Tisman's Common W Sus 50 G
Tissington Derbys 169 E1
Titchberry Devon 24 B
Titchfield Hants 33 F
Titchfield Common Hants 33 F
Titchfield Park Hants 33 F
Titchmarsh Northants 121 B1
Titchwell Norf 176 E
Titcomb W Berks 63 F1
Tithby Notts 154 B
Tithe Barn Hillock Mers 183 B
Tithebarn Staffs 169 G
Titley Hereford 114 E
Titlington Northumb 264 F
Titmore Green Herts 104 F
Titsey Sur 52 C
Titson Corn 24 G
Tittenhurst Windsor 66 F
Tittensor Staffs 151 B
Titterhill Shrops 131 G1
Tittle Row Windsor 65 C1
Tittleshall Norf 159 E
Titton Worcs 116 D
Titty Hill W Sus 34 B
Tiverton Devon 27 E
Tiverton W Ches 167 C
Tivetshall St Margaret Norf 142 F
Tivetshall St Mary Norf 142 F
Tividale W Mid 133 E
Tivington Som 42 D
Tivington Knowle Som 42 E
Tivoli Cumb 228 G
Tivy Dale S Yorks 197 F
Tixall Staffs 151 E

xover Rutland 137 C9
ab Orkney 314 F5
ab Shetland 313 M5
ad Row Suff 143 F10
admoor Derbys 170 E4
bermory Argyll 289 D7
beronochy Argyll 275 C8
bha Beag W Isles 296 D5
bha Mor W Isles 297 H3
bhtarol W Isles 304 E3
bson W Isles 304 E3
by's Hill Lincs 191 C7
cher Aberds 302 F6
ckenham Wilts 62 D4
ckenham Wick Wilts 62 C4
ckholes Blkburn 195 C7
ckington S Glos 60 B6
ckwith N Yorks 206 C5
dber Dorset 30 C4
dding Hereford 115 B8
ddington C Beds 103 F10
ddington Glos 99 E10
ddington W Sus 35 G8
ddlehills Aberds 303 E10
dd's Green Herts 104 F4
denham Glos 100 D4
dhill Angus 287 D8
dhills Cumb 239 E9
dhills Durham 233 E10
dlachie Aberds 293 B8
dmorden W Yorks 196 C2
dpool Corn 4 G4
drig Borders 261 F10
dwick S Yorks 187 E7
ft Cambs 123 F7
ft Lincs 155 F11
ft Shetland 312 F6
ft Warks 119 C9
ft Hill Durham 233 F9
ft Hill Lincs 174 C2
ft Monks Norf 143 E8
ft next Newton Lincs 189 D8
ftrees Norf 159 D7
fts Highld 310 C7
ftshaw W Yorks 197 B7
ftwood Norf 159 G9
gston Northumb 252 C6
kavaig Highld 295 D8
kers Green Oxon 65 D8
kyngton London 67 C7
lastadh a Chaolais
V Isles 304 E3
lastadh bho Thuath
V Isles 304 D7
lborough Corn 11 F9
lcarne Corn 2 B5
lcarne Corn 2 C5
lcarne Wartha Corn 2 B5
ldish Corn 5 D8
lgus Mount Corn 4 G3
lhurst E Sus 53 G7
ll Bar Mers 183 C7
ll Bar Rutland 137 B10
ll Bar S Yorks 198 F5
ll End W Mid 133 E9
ll of Birness Aberds 303 F10
lladine Worcs 117 F7
lland Som 42 G6
llard Farnham Dorset 30 D6
llard Royal Wilts 30 D6
llbar End W Mid 119 B7
ller Fratrum Dorset 17 B7
ller Porcorum Dorset 17 B7
ller Whelme Dorset 29 G8
llerford Dorset 17 B7
llerton N Yorks 215 G10
llerton Notts 154 C2
llesbury Essex 89 C7
llesby M'bro 225 B10
lleshunt D'Arcy Essex 88 C6
lleshunt Knights
ssex 88 C6
lleshunt Major Essex 88 C5
llie Highld 300 D5
lm W Isles 304 E6
lmers Herts 86 E4
lpuddle Dorset 17 C11
lskithy Corn 4 G3
lvaddon Downs Corn 4 G3
lvah Highld 291 D10
lworth London 67 F7
m an Fhuadain
V Isles 305 G5
maknock Perth 286 E2
matin Highld 301 G8
mbreck Highld 300 F6
mbui Perth 286 B2
mchrasky Highld 290 B4
mdoun Highld 290 C3
mich Highld 300 B6
mich Highld 300 G3
mich House Highld 300 E5
mintoul Aberds 292 D3
mintoul Moray 292 B3
mlow Warks 119 E9
mnaven Moray 302 F4
mnavoulin Moray 302 G2
mperrow Corn 4 G5
mpkin Staffs 168 E6
mpset's Bank E Sus 52 G2
mpsleibhe Argyll 289 F8
mthorn Derbys 185 F9
n Mon 78 F5
n Breigam V Glam 58 D3
n-Pentre Rhondda 77 F7
n-teg Rhondda 58 B5
n-y-pistyll Caerph 77 F11
nbridge Kent 52 D5
nderghie Dumfries 236 F6
ndu Bridgend 57 E11
ne Som 27 C11
ne Green Som 27 C11
nedale Som 27 C10
ng Kent 53 D10
ng Shrops 132 B5
ng W Yorks 205 G10
ng Forge Shrops 132 B5
ng Green Kent 54 C3
ng Norton Shrops 132 B5
ng Park W Yorks 205 F9
ng Street W Yorks 205 G9
nge Leics 153 E8
nge Corner Kent 70 F2
nge Fold Gtr Man 195 F8
nge Moor Gtr Man 195 E8
ngham Sur 49 D11
ngland Dumfries 237 D8
ngue Highld 308 D5
ngue End Lincs 156 F3
ngwell M Keynes 103 C7
ngwynlais Cardiff 58 C6
nmawr Neath 57 B10
nna = Tonnau Neath 57 B9
nnau = Tonna Neath 57 B9
ntine Lancs 194 G4
nwell Herts 86 B4
nypandy Rhondda 77 G7
nyrefail Rhondda 58 B4
ot Baldon Oxon 83 E9
ot Hill Essex 87 E8
ot Hill Staffs 169 G9
othill Hants 32 D5
Toothill Swindon 62 C6
Toothill W Yorks 196 C6
Tooting Graveney
London 67 E9
Top End Beds 121 E10
Top Green Notts 172 F3
Top Lock Gtr Man 194 F6
Top o' th' Lane Lancs 194 C5
Top o' th' Meadows
Gtr Man 196 F3
Top of Hebers Gtr Man 195 F11
Top Valley Nottingham 171 F9
Topcliffe N Yorks 215 D8
Topcliffe W Yorks 197 B9
Topcroft Norf 142 E5
Topcroft Street Norf 142 E5
Topham S Yorks 198 D6
Topleigh W Sus 34 D6
Toppesfield Essex 106 D4
Toppings Gtr Man 195 E8
Toprow Norf 142 D3
Topsham Devon 14 D5
Torbeg N Ayrs 255 E10
Torboll Farm Highld 309 K7
Torbothie N Lnrk 269 D7
Torbreck Highld 309 J7
Torbrex Stirl 278 C5
Torbryan Devon 8 B6
Torbush N Lnrk 268 D6
Torcross Devon 8 G6
Torcroy Highld 291 D9
Tore Highld 300 D6
Torfrey Corn 6 E2
Torgyle Highld 290 B5
Torinturk Argyll 275 G9
Torkington Gtr Man 184 D6
Torksey Lincs 188 F4
Torlum W Isles 296 F3
Torlundy Highld 290 F3
Tormarton S Glos 61 D9
Tormisdale Argyll 254 B2
Tormitchell S Ayrs 244 E6
Tormore Highld 295 E8
Tormore N Ayrs 255 D9
Tornagrain Highld 301 E7
Tornahaish Aberds 292 C4
Tornapress Highld 299 E8
Tornaveen Aberds 293 C8
Torness Highld 300 G5
Toronto Durham 233 E9
Torpenhow Cumb 229 D10
Torphichen W Loth 279 G9
Torphin Edin 270 B4
Torphins Aberds 293 C8
Torpoint Corn 7 E8
Torquay Torbay 9 C8
Torquhan Borders 271 F8
Torr Devon 7 E11
Torr Devon 8 C2
Torra Argyll 254 B4
Torran Argyll 275 C9
Torran Highld 298 E5
Torran Highld 301 B7
Torrance E Dunb 277 F8
Torrans Argyll 288 G6
Torranyard N Ayrs 267 G7
Torre Som 42 E4
Torre Torbay 9 C8
Torridon Highld 299 D9
Torridon Ho Highld 299 D8
Torries Aberds 293 B8
Torrin Highld 295 C7
Torrisdale Highld 308 C6
Torrisdale Castle Argyll 255 D8
Torrisdale-Square
Argyll 255 D8
Torrish Highld 311 H3
Torrisholme Lancs 211 G9
Torroble Highld 309 J5
Torroy Highld 309 K5
Torrpark Corn 11 D10
Torry Aberdeen 293 C11
Torry Aberds 302 F4
Torryburn Fife 279 D10
Torsonce Borders 271 G9
Torsonce Mains
Borders 271 G9
Torterston Aberds 303 E10
Torthorwald Dumfries 238 B2
Tortington W Sus 35 F8
Torton Worcs 116 C6
Tortworth S Glos 80 G2
Torvaig Highld 298 E4
Torver Cumb 220 G5
Torwood Falk 278 E6
Torwoodlee Mains
Borders 261 B11
Torworth Notts 187 D11
Tosberry Devon 24 C3
Toscaig Highld 295 B9
Toseland Cambs 122 E4
Tosside N Yorks 203 B11
Tostock Suff 125 E9
Tot Hill Hants 64 G3
Totaig Highld 295 C10
Totaig Highld 298 D2
Totardor Highld 294 B5
Tote Highld 298 E4
Tote Hill Hants 32 C4
Tote Hill W Sus 34 C5
Totegan Highld 310 C2
Totford Hants 48 F5
Totham Hill Essex 88 C5
Totham Plains Essex 88 C5
Tothill Lincs 190 E6
Totland I o W 20 D2
Totley S Yorks 186 F4
Totley Brook S Yorks 186 E4
Totley Rise S Yorks 186 E4
Totmonslow Staffs 151 B9
Totnell Dorset 29 F10
Totnes Devon 8 C6
Totnor Hereford 97 E11
Toton Notts 153 C10
Totronald Argyll 288 D3
Totscore Highld 298 C3
Tottenham London 86 G4
Tottenham Hale London 67 B10
Tottenhill Norf 158 G2
Tottenhill Row Norf 158 G2
Totteridge Bucks 84 G5
Totteridge London 86 G2
Totternhoe C Beds 103 G9
Totteroak S Glos 61 C8
Totterton Shrops 131 F7
Totties W Yorks 197 F7
Tottington Gtr Man 195 E9
Tottington Norf 141 D7
Tottlebank Cumb 210 C6
Tottleworth Lancs 203 G10
Totton Hants 32 E5
Touchen End Windsor 65 D11
Toulston N Yorks 206 E5
Toulton Som 43 G7
Toulvaddie Highld 311 L2
Tournaig Highld 307 L3
Toux Aberds 303 D9
Tovil Kent 53 C9
Tow House Northumb 241 E7
Tow Law Durham 233 D8
Towan Corn 10 G3
Towan Cross Corn 4 F4
Toward Argyll 266 B2
Towcester Northants 102 B3
Towednack Corn 1 B5
Tower End Norf 158 F3
Tower Hamlets Kent 55 E10
Tower Hill Devon 12 C3
Tower Hill E Ches 184 F6
Tower Hill Essex 108 E5
Tower Hill Herts 85 E8
Tower Hill Mers 194 G2
Tower Hill Sur 51 D7
Tower Hill W Mid 133 E11
Tower Hill W Sus 35 B11
Towerage Bucks 84 G4
Towerhead N Som 44 B2
Towersey Oxon 84 D2
Towie Aberds 292 B6
Towie Aberds 302 G5
Towie Aberds 303 C8
Towiemore Moray 302 E3
Town Barton Devon 14 C2
Town End Bucks 84 F3
Town End Cambs 139 D8
Town End Cumb 211 B7
Town End Cumb 211 C8
Town End Cumb 212 C2
Town End Cumb 220 D6
Town End Cumb 221 E8
Town End Cumb 221 F7
Town End Cumb 231 F8
Town End Derbys 185 F11
Town End E Yorks 207 C10
Town End Mers 183 D7
Town End W Yorks 196 D5
Town Fields W Ches 167 B10
Town Green Gtr Man 183 B9
Town Green Lancs 194 F2
Town Green Norf 161 G7
Town Head Cumb 220 D6
Town Head Cumb 221 E8
Town Head Cumb 222 C2
Town Head Cumb 222 C3
Town Head Cumb 231 F7
Town Head Cumb 231 F8
Town Head Cumb 231 G8
Town Head Cumb 231 G9
Town Head Derbys 185 F11
Town Head N Yorks 204 B2
Town Head N Yorks 212 F5
Town Head Staffs 169 F8
Town Head W Yorks 204 D6
Town Kelloe Durham 234 D3
Town Lane Gtr Man 183 B11
Town Littleworth
E Sus 36 D6
Town of Lowton
Mers 183 B10
Town Park Telford 132 B3
Town Row E Sus 52 G5
Town Street Glos 98 F6
Town Yetholm Borders 263 D8
Townend Derbys 185 E9
Townend Staffs 151 B9
Townend W Dunb 277 F8
Townfield Durham 232 B5
Towngate Cumb 230 B6
Towngate Lincs 156 G2
Townhead Argyll 275 G11
Townhead Cumb 229 D7
Townhead Cumb 230 D6
Townhead Cumb 231 E8
Townhead Dumfries 237 E8
Townhead N Lnrk 268 B4
Townhead Northumb 251 E9
Townhead S Ayrs 244 C6
Townhead S Yorks 186 E4
Townhead S Yorks 197 G7
Townhead of Greenlaw
Dumfries 237 C9
Townhill Fife 280 D2
Townhill Swansea 56 C6
Townhill Park Hants 33 E7
Townlake Devon 12 G4
Townland Green Kent 54 G2
Town's End Bucks 102 G2
Town's End Dorset 18 B3
Town's End Dorset 18 E5
Town's End Dorset 29 F9
Towns End Hants 48 B5
Towns End Som 30 D2
Town's End Som 45 D7
Townsend Bath 44 B5
Townsend Bucks 84 D2
Townsend Devon 25 B10
Townsend Herts 85 D10
Townsend Oxon 63 B11
Townsend Pembs 72 D4
Townsend Som 44 C4
Townsend Stoke 168 F6
Townsend Wilts 46 B3
Townsend Wilts 46 B4
Townsend Fold Lancs 195 C10
Townshend Corn 2 C3
Townwell S Glos 79 G11
Towthorpe E Yorks 217 G8
Towthorpe York 207 B8
Towton N Yorks 206 F5
Towyn Conwy 181 F7
Toxteth Mers 182 D5
Toynton All Saints
Lincs 174 C5
Toynton Fen Side
Lincs 174 C5
Toynton St Peter Lincs 174 C6
Toy's Hill Kent 52 C3
Trabboch E Ayrs 257 E10
Traboe Corn 2 E6
Trabrown Borders 271 F10
Tracebridge Som 27 C9
Tradespark Highld 301 D8
Tradespark Orkney 314 F4
Trafford Park Gtr Man 184 B3
Traigh Ho Highld 295 F8
Trallong Powys 95 F9
Trallwn Rhondda 77 G9
Trallwn Swansea 57 B7
Tram Inn Hereford 97 E9
Tramagenna Corn 11 E7
Tranch Torf 78 E3
Tranent E Loth 281 G8
Tranmere Mers 182 D4
Trantlebeg Highld 310 D2
Trantlemore Highld 310 D2
Tranwell Northumb 252 G5
Trapp Carms 75 B11
Traprain E Loth 281 F11
Trap's Green Warks 118 D2
Trapshill W Berks 63 G11
Traquair Borders 261 C8
Trash Green W Berks 65 F7
Travellers' Rest Carms 74 B5
Trawden Lancs 204 F4
Trawscoed Powys 95 E11
Trawsfynydd Gwyn 146 B4
Trawsnant Ceredig 111 D11
Tre-Aubrey V Glam 58 E4
Tre-Beferad V Glam 58 F3
Tre-boeth Swansea 57 B7
Tre-derwen Powys 148 F4
Tre-Forgan Neath 76 D3
Tre-gagle Mon 79 D8
Tre-Gibbon Rhondda 77 E7
Tre Gwyr = Gowerton
Swansea 56 B5
Tre-gynwr Carms 74 B6
Tre-hill V Glam 58 E5
Tre-Ifor Rhondda 77 D7
Tre-lan Flint 165 B11
Tre-Mostyn Flint 181 F10
Tre-pit V Glam 58 E2
Tre-Taliesin Ceredig 128 E3
Tre-vaughan Carms 93 G8
Tre-wyn Mon 96 G6
Treadam Mon 78 B5
Treaddow Hereford 97 G10
Treal Corn 2 F6
Trealaw Rhondda 77 G8
Treales Lancs 202 G4
Trearddur Anglesey 178 F3
Treaslane Highld 298 D3
Treath Corn 3 D7
Treator Corn 10 F4
Trebanog Rhondda 77 G8
Trebanos Neath 76 E2
Trebarber Corn 5 C7
Trebartha Corn 11 F11
Trebarwith Corn 11 D7
Trebarwith Strand Corn 10 D6
Trebeath Corn 11 D11
Trebell Green Corn 5 C11
Treberfydd Powys 96 F2
Trebetherick Corn 10 F4
Trebilcock Corn 5 C9
Treble's Holford Som 43 G7
Treborough Som 42 F4
Trebudannon Corn 5 C7
Trebullett Corn 12 F2
Treburgett Corn 11 F7
Treburgie Corn 6 C4
Treburley Corn 12 F3
Treburrick Corn 10 G3
Trebyan Corn 5 C11
Trecastle Powys 95 F7
Trecenydd Caerph 58 B6
Trecott Devon 25 G10
Trecwn Pembs 91 E9
Trecynon Rhondda 77 E7
Tredannick Corn 10 G6
Tredaule Corn 11 E10
Tredavoe Corn 1 D5
Treddiog Pembs 91 F7
Tredegar Bl Gwent 77 D10
Trederwen Powys 148 F5
Tredethy Corn 11 G7
Tredington Glos 99 F8
Tredington Warks 100 C5
Tredinnick Corn 1 C4
Tredinnick Corn 5 D10
Tredinnick Corn 6 B3
Tredinnick Corn 6 D4
Tredinnick Corn 10 G4
Tredogan V Glam 58 F5
Tredomen Caerph 77 G10
Tredomen Powys 96 E2
Tredown Devon 24 D2
Tredrizzick Corn 10 F5
Tredunnock Mon 78 G5
Tredustan Powys 96 E2
Tredworth Glos 80 B4
Treen Corn 1 B4
Treen Corn 1 E3
Treesmill Corn 5 D11
Treeton S Yorks 186 D6
Tref y Clawdd =
Knighton Powys 114 C5
Trefaes Gwyn 144 C5
Trefanny Hill Corn 6 D4
Trefasser Pembs 91 D7
Trefdraeth Anglesey 178 G6
Trefdraeth = Newport
Pembs 91 D11
Trefecca Powys 96 E2
Trefechan Ceredig 111 A11
Trefechan M Tydf 77 D8
Trefechan Wrex 166 F3
Trefeglwys Powys 129 E9
Trefeitha Powys 96 E2
Trefenter Ceredig 112 D2
Treffgarne Pembs 91 G9
Treffynnon Pembs 90 F6
Treffynnon = Holywell
Flint 181 F11
Trefgarn Owen Pembs 91 F7
Trefil Bl Gwent 77 C10
Trefilan Ceredig 111 F11
Trefin = Trevine Pembs 90 E6
Treflach Shrops 148 D5
Trefnanney Powys 148 F4
Trefnant Denb 181 G9
Trefonen Shrops 148 D5
Trefor Anglesey 178 E5
Trefor Gwyn 162 F5
Treforda Corn 11 E7
Treforest Rhondda 58 B5
Treforgan Ceredig 92 B4
Treforys = Morriston
Swansea 57 B7
Trefriw Conwy 164 C3
Trefrize Corn 12 F2
Trefynwy = Monmouth
Mon 79 C8
Tregada Corn 12 E2
Tregadgwith Corn 1 D4
Tregadillett Corn 12 E2
Tregaian Anglesey 178 F6
Tregajorran Corn 4 G3
Tregamere Corn 5 C8
Tregardock Corn 10 E6
Tregare Mon 78 C6
Tregarland Corn 6 D5
Tregarlandbridge Corn 6 D4
Tregarne Corn 3 E7
Tregaron Ceredig 112 F3
Tregarrick Mill Corn 6 D4
Tregarth Gwyn 163 B10
Tregath Gwyn 163 B10
Tregatillian Corn 5 C8
Tregatta Corn 11 D7
Tregavarah Corn 1 D4
Tregear Corn 2 E5
Tregeare Corn 11 D10
Tregeiriog Wrex 148 C3
Tregele Anglesey 178 C5
Tregellist Corn 10 F6
Tregeseal Corn 1 C3
Tregew Corn 3 C8
Tregidden Corn 2 E6
Treginnis Pembs 90 G4
Treglemais Pembs 90 F6
Tregole Corn 11 B9
Tregolls Corn 2 B6
Tregolwyn =
Colwinston V Glam 58 D2
Tregona Corn 5 B7
Tregonce Corn 10 G4
Tregonetha Corn 5 C9
Tregonna Corn 10 G4
Tregonning Corn 5 D7
Tregony Corn 5 G8
Tregoodwell Corn 11 E8
Tregorden Corn 10 G6
Tregorrick Corn 5 E10
Tregoss Corn 5 C9
Tregoyd Powys 96 D4
Tregoyd Mill Powys 96 D3
Tregreenwell Corn 11 E7
Tregrehan Mills Corn 5 E10
Tregroes Ceredig 93 C8
Tregullon Corn 5 C11
Tregunna Corn 10 G5
Tregurrian Corn 5 B7
Tregurtha Downs Corn 2 C2
Tregyddulan Pembs 91 D7
Tregynon Powys 129 D11
Trehafod Rhondda 77 G8
Trehafren Powys 129 E11
Trehan Corn 7 D8
Treharris M Tydf 77 F9
Trehemborne Corn 10 G3
Treherbert Rhondda 76 F6
Trehunist Corn 6 C6
Trekeivesteps Corn 11 G10
Trekenner Corn 12 F2
Trekenning Corn 5 C8
Treknow Corn 11 D7
Trelales = Laleston
Bridgend 57 F11
Trelan Corn 2 F6
Trelash Corn 11 C9
Trelassick Corn 5 E7
Trelawnyd Flint 181 F9
Trelech Carms 92 E5
Treleddyd-fawr Pembs 90 F5
Treleigh Corn 4 G4
Treletert = Letterston
Pembs 91 F8
Trelew Corn 3 B8
Trelewis M Tydf 77 F10
Treligga Corn 11 E7
Trelights Corn 10 F5
Trelill Corn 10 F6
Trelion Corn 5 E8
Treliske Corn 4 F6
Trelissick Corn 3 B8
Treliver Corn 5 B9
Trellech Mon 79 D8
Trelleck Grange Mon 79 E7
Trelogan Flint 181 E10
Treloquithack Corn 2 D5
Trelowia Corn 6 D5
Trelowth Corn 5 E9
Trelystan Powys 130 C5
Tremadog Gwyn 163 G9
Tremail Corn 11 D9
Tremain Ceredig 92 B4
Tremaine Corn 11 D10
Tremains Bridgend 58 D2
Tremar Corn 6 B5
Trematon Corn 7 D7
Trematon Castle Corn 7 D8
Tremayne Corn 2 B4
Trembraze Corn 6 B5
Tremedda Corn 1 B5
Tremeirchion Denb 181 G9
Tremethick Cross Corn 1 C4
Tremore Corn 5 C10
Tremorebridge Corn 5 C10
Tremorfa Cardiff 59 D8
Trenance Corn 4 C6
Trenance Corn 5 B7
Trenance Corn 5 C9
Trenance Corn 10 G4
Trenant Corn 6 B4
Trenant Corn 10 G5
Trenarren Corn 5 F10
Trenay Corn 6 B3
Trench Telford 150 G3
Trench Green Oxon 65 D7
Trench Wood Kent 52 D5
Trencreek Corn 4 C6
Trencrom Corn 2 B2
Trendeal Corn 5 E7
Trenear Corn 2 C5
Treneglos Corn 11 D10
Trenerth Corn 2 B4
Trenewan Corn 6 E3
Trengune Corn 11 C9
Trenhorne Corn 11 F11
Treninnick Corn 4 C6
Trenoon Corn 2 F6
Trenoweth Corn 3 C7
Trent Dorset 29 D9
Trent Vale Stoke 168 G5
Trentham Stoke 168 G5
Trentishoe Devon 40 D6
Trentlock Derbys 153 C9
Trenwheal Corn 2 C4
Treoes V Glam 58 D2
Treopert = Granston
Pembs 91 E7
Treorchy = Treorci
Rhondda 77 F7
Treorci = Treorchy
Rhondda 77 F7
Treowen Caerph 78 F2
Treowen Powys 130 E2
Trequite Corn 10 F6
Tre'r-ddôl Ceredig 128 E3
Trer Ilai = Leighton
Powys 130 B4
Trerhyngyll V Glam 58 D4
Trerise Corn 2 F6
Trerose Corn 3 D7
Trerulefoot Corn 6 D6
Tresaith Ceredig 110 G5
Tresamble Corn 3 B7
Tresarrett Corn 11 G7
Tresavean Corn 2 B6
Tresawle Corn 5 F7
Tresawsen Corn 4 F5
Trescoll Corn 5 C10
Trescott Staffs 132 D6
Trescowe Corn 2 C3
Tresean Corn 4 D5
Tresevern Croft Corn 2 B6
Tresham Glos 80 G3
Tresigin = Sigingstone
V Glam 58 E3
Tresillian Corn 5 F7
Tresimwn = Bonvilston
V Glam 58 E5
Tresinney Corn 11 E8
Tresinwen Pembs 91 C7
Treskerby Corn 4 G4
Treskillard Corn 2 B5
Treskilling Corn 5 D10
Treskinnick Cross Corn 11 B10
Treslothan Corn 2 B5
Tresmeer Corn 11 D10
Tresowes Green Corn 2 D3
Tresoweshill Corn 2 D4
Tresparrett Corn 11 C8
Tresparrett Posts Corn 11 C8
Tressady Highld 309 J7
Tressait Perth 291 G10
Tresta Shetland 312 D8
Tresta Shetland 313 H5
Treswell Notts 188 F3
Treswithian Corn 4 G2
Treswithian Downs Corn 4 G2
Trethellan Water Corn 2 B6
Trethevy Corn 11 D7
Trethewell Corn 3 B9
Trethewey Corn 1 E3
Trethillick Corn 10 F4
Trethomas Caerph 59 B7
Trethosa Corn 5 E8
Trethowel Corn 5 E10
Trethurgy Corn 5 D10
Tretio Pembs 90 F5
Tretire Hereford 97 G10
Tretower Powys 96 G3
Treuddyn Flint 166 D3
Trevadlock Corn 11 F11
Trevail Corn 4 D5
Trevalga Corn 11 D7
Trevalgan Corn 1 A5
Trevalyn Wrex 166 D5
Trevance Corn 10 G4
Trevanger Corn 10 F5
Trevanson Corn 10 G5
Trevarrack Corn 1 C5
Trevarren Corn 5 C8
Trevarrian Corn 4 B6
Trevarrick Corn 5 G9
Trevarth Corn 4 G4
Trevaughan Carms 73 B11
Trevaughan Carms 93 G7
Treveal Corn 1 A5
Trevegean Corn 1 D3
Treveighan Corn 11 F7
Trevellas Corn 4 E4
Trevelmond Corn 6 C4
Trevelver Corn 10 G5
Trevemper Corn 4 D6
Treven Corn 11 D7
Trevena Corn 2 D4
Trevenen Corn 2 D5
Trevenen Bal Corn 2 D5
Trevenning Corn 11 F7
Treveor Corn 5 G9
Treverbyn Corn 5 D10
Treverbyn Corn 6 B4
Treverva Corn 3 C7
Trevescan Corn 1 E3
Trevethin Torf 78 E3
Trevia Corn 11 E7
Trevigro Corn 6 B6
Trevilder Corn 10 G6
Trevilla Corn 3 B8
Trevilson Corn 4 D6
Trevine Corn 10 F5
Trevine = Trefin Pembs 90 E6
Treviscoe Corn 5 D8
Treviskey Corn 2 B6
Trevithal Corn 1 D5
Trevoll Corn 4 D6
Trevone Corn 10 F3
Trevor Wrex 166 G3
Trevor Uchaf Denb 166 G2
Trevorrick Corn 10 G4
Trevowah Corn 4 D5
Trevowhan Corn 1 B4
Trew Corn 2 D4
Trewalder Corn 11 E7
Trewarmett Corn 11 D7
Trewartha Corn 2 B2
Trewartha Corn 3 B10
Trewassa Corn 11 D8
Treween Corn 11 E10
Trewellard Corn 1 C3
Trewen Corn 11 E11
Trewen Corn 11 F7
Trewen Mon 79 G7
Trewennack Corn 2 D5
Trewennan Corn 11 E7
Trewern Powys 148 G5
Trewetha Corn 10 E6
Trewethen Corn 10 F6
Trewethern Corn 10 F6
Trewey Corn 1 B5
Trewidland Corn 6 D5
Trewindle Corn 6 C2
Trewint Corn 6 C5
Trewint Corn 11 B9
Trewint Corn 11 E10
Trewithian Corn 3 B9
Trewithick Corn 11 D11
Trewollock Corn 5 G10
Trewoodloe Corn 12 G2
Trewoofe Corn 1 D4
Trewoon Corn 2 F5
Trewoon Corn 5 E9
Treworga Corn 5 G7
Treworgan Common
Mon 78 D6
Treworlas Corn 3 B9
Treworld Corn 11 C8
Trewornan Corn 10 G5
Treworrick Corn 6 B4
Treworthal Corn 3 B9
Trewyddel = Moylgrove
Pembs 92 C2
Treyarnon Corn 10 G3
Treyford W Sus 34 D4
Trezaise Corn 5 D9
Trezelah Corn 1 C5
Triangle Glos 79 E8
Triangle Staffs 133 B11
Triangle W Yorks 196 C4
Trickett's Cross Dorset 31 G9
Triffleton Pembs 91 G9
Trillacott Corn 11 D11
Trimdon Durham 234 E3
Trimdon Colliery
Durham 234 D3
Trimdon Grange
Durham 234 D3
Trimingham Norf 160 B5
Trimley Lower Street
Suff 108 D5
Trimley St Martin Suff 108 D5
Trimley St Mary Suff 108 D5
Trimpley Worcs 116 B5
Trims Green Herts 87 B7
Trimsaran Carms 75 E7
Trimstone Devon 40 E3
Trinafour Perth 291 G9
Trinant Caerph 78 E2
Tring Herts 84 C6
Tring Wharf Herts 84 C6
Tringford Herts 84 C6
Trinity Angus 293 G8
Trinity Devon 27 F7
Trinity Edin 280 F4
Trinity Fields Staffs 151 D8
Trisant Ceredig 112 B4
Triscombe Som 43 F7
Trislaig Highld 290 F2
Trispen Corn 4 E6
Tritlington Northumb 252 E6
Troan Corn 5 C7
Trochry Perth 286 C3
Trodigal Argyll 255 E7
Troearhiwgwair
Bl Gwent 77 D11
Troedrhiwdalar Powys 113 G9
Troedrhiwffenyd
Ceredig 93 C8
Troedrhiwfuwch Caerph 77 E10
Troedyraur Ceredig 92 B6
Troedyrhiw M Tydf 77 E9
Trofarth Conwy 180 G5
Trolliloes E Sus 23 C10
Tromode I o M 192 E4
Trondavoe Shetland 312 F5
Troon Corn 2 B5
Troon S Ayrs 257 C8
Trooper's Inn Pembs 73 C7
Trosaraidh W Isles 297 K3
Trossachs Hotel Stirl 285 G9
Troston Suff 125 C7
Trostre Carms 56 B4
Trostrey Common Mon 78 E5
Troswell Corn 11 C11
Trotshill Worcs 117 F7
Trotten Marsh W Sus 34 B4
Trottiscliffe Kent 68 G6
Trotton W Sus 34 C4
Trough Gate Lancs 195 C11
Troutbeck Cumb 221 E8
Troutbeck Cumb 230 F3
Troutbeck Bridge Cumb 221 F8
Trow Green Glos 79 D9
Troway Derbys 186 F5
Trowbridge Cardiff 59 C8
Trowbridge Wilts 45 B11
Trowell Notts 153 B9
Trowle Common Wilts 45 B10
Trowley Bottom Herts 85 C9
Trows Borders 262 C5
Trowse Newton Norf 142 B4
Troy Town Kent 52 D2
Troy Town Kent 54 E5
Troy Town Medway 69 F8
Troydale W Yorks 205 G10
Truas Corn 11 D7
Trub Gtr Man 195 F11
Trudoxhill Som 45 E8
True Street Devon 8 C6
Trueman's Heath
Worcs 117 B11
Trull Som 28 C2
Trumaisgearraidh
W Isles 296 D4
Trumfleet S Yorks 198 E6
Trumpan Highld 298 C2
Trumpet Hereford 98 D3
Trumpington Cambs 123 F8
Trumpsgreen Sur 66 F3
Trunch Norf 160 C5
Trunnah Lancs 202 E2
Truro Corn 4 G6
Truscott Corn 12 D2
Trusham Devon 14 E3
Trusley Derbys 152 B5
Trussall Corn 2 D5
Trussell Corn 11 D10
Trusthorpe Lincs 191 E8
Truthan Corn 4 E6
Truthwall Corn 2 C2
Trwstllewelyn Powys 130 D3
Tryfil Anglesey 178 E6
Trysull Staffs 133 E7
Trythogga Corn 1 C5
Tubbs Mill Corn 5 G9
Tubney Oxon 82 F6
Tubslake Kent 53 G9
Tuckenhay Devon 8 D6
Tuckermarsh Devon 7 B8
Tuckerton Som 28 B3
Tuckhill Shrops 132 F5
Tucking Mill Bath 61 G9
Tuckingmill Corn 4 G3
Tuckingmill Corn 11 F7
Tuckingmill Wilts 30 B6
Tuckton Bmouth 19 C8
Tuddenham Suff 108 B3
Tuddenham Suff 124 C4
Tuddenham St Martin
Suff 108 B3
Tudeley Kent 52 D6
Tudeley Hale Kent 52 D6
Tudhay Devon 28 G4
Tudhoe Durham 233 D11
Tudhoe Grange Durham 233 E11
Tudor Hill W Mid 134 D2
Tudorville Hereford 97 G11
Tudweiliog Gwyn 144 B4
Tuebrook Mers 182 C5
Tuesley Sur 50 E3
Tuesnoad Kent 54 E2
Tuffley Glos 80 C4
Tufnell Park London 67 B9
Tufton Hants 48 D3
Tufton Pembs 91 F10
Tugby Leics 136 C5
Tugford Shrops 131 F11
Tughall Northumb 264 D6
Tulchan Lodge Angus 292 F3
Tullecombe W Sus 34 B4
Tullibardine Perth 286 F3
Tullibody Clack 279 B7
Tullich Argyll 284 F4
Tullich Highld 299 E9
Tullich Highld 300 G6
Tullich Muir Highld 301 B7
Tulliemet Perth 286 B3
Tulloch Aberds 293 F9
Tulloch Aberds 303 F8
Tulloch Highld 290 E5
Tulloch Perth 286 E4
Tulloch Castle Highld 300 C5
Tulloch-gribban
Highld 301 G9
Tullochgorm Argyll 275 D10
Tullochroisk Perth 285 B11
Tullochvenus Aberds 293 C7
Tulloes Angus 287 C9
Tullybannocher Perth 285 E11
Tullybelton Perth 286 D4
Tullycross Stirl 277 D9
Tullyfergus Perth 286 C6
Tullymurdoch Perth 286 B5
Tullynessle Aberds 293 B7
Tulse Hill London 67 E10
Tumble = Y Tymbl Carms 75 C8
Tumbler's Green Essex 106 F6
Tumby Lincs 174 D2
Tumby Woodside Lincs 174 D3
Tummel Bridge Perth 285 B11
Tumpy Green Glos 80 E2
Tumpy Lakes Hereford 97 B10
Tunbridge Hill Medway 69 E10
Tunbridge Wells =
Royal Tunbridge Wells
Kent 52 F5
Tunga W Isles 304 E6
Tungate Norf 160 D5
Tunley Bath 45 B7
Tunley Glos 80 E6
Tunnel Hill Worcs 98 C6
Tunnel Pits N Lincs 199 G8
Tunshill Gtr Man 196 E2
Tunstall E Yorks 209 G12
Tunstall Kent 69 G11
Tunstall Lancs 212 E2
Tunstall N Yorks 224 F4
Tunstall Norf 143 B8
Tunstall Staffs 150 D5
Tunstall Stoke 168 E5
Tunstall Suff 127 G7
Tunstall T & W 243 G9
Tunstead Derbys 185 G10
Tunstead Gtr Man 196 G4
Tunstead Norf 160 E5
Tunworth Hants 49 D7
Tupsley Hereford 97 C10
Tupton Derbys 170 B5
Tur Langton Leics 136 E4
Turbary Common Poole 19 C7
Turf Hill Gtr Man 196 E2
Turfdown Corn 5 B11
Turfholm S Lnrk 259 B8
Turfmoor Devon 28 G3
Turfmoor Shrops 149 F7
Turgis Green Hants 49 B7
Turin Angus 287 B9
Turkdean Glos 81 B10
Turkey Island Hants 33 E9
Turkey Island W Sus 34 D3
Turkey Tump Hereford 97 F10
Turleigh Wilts 61 G10
Turleygreen Shrops 132 F5
Turlin Moor Poole 18 C5
Turmer Hants 31 F10
Turn Lancs 195 D10
Turnalt Argyll 275 C9
Turnastone Hereford 97 D7
Turnberry S Ayrs 244 B6
Turnchapel Plym 7 E9
Turnditch Derbys 170 F3
Turner Green Lancs 203 G8
Turner's Green E Sus 23 B10
Turner's Green E Sus 52 G6
Turner's Green W Berks 64 F4
Turner's Green Warks 118 D3
Turners Hill W Sus 51 F10
Turners Puddle Dorset 18 C2
Turnerwood S Yorks 187 E8
Turnford Herts 86 E5
Turnhouse Edin 280 G3
Turnhurst Stoke 168 E5
Turnstead Milton
Derbys 185 E8
Turnworth Dorset 30 F4
Turrerich Perth 286 D2
Turriff Aberds 303 D7
Tursdale Durham 234 D2
Turton Bottoms Blkburn 195 D8
Turves Cambs 138 D6
Turves Green W Mid 117 B10
Turvey Beds 121 G8
Turville Bucks 84 G3
Turville Heath Bucks 84 G2
Turweston Bucks 102 D2
Tushielaw Borders 261 F8
Tutbury Staffs 152 D4
Tutnall Worcs 117 C9
Tutnalls Glos 79 E10
Tutshill Glos 79 G8
Tutt Hill Kent 54 D3
Tuttington Norf 160 D4
Tutts Clump W Berks 64 E5
Tutwell Corn 12 F3
Tuxford Notts 188 G2
Twatt Orkney 314 D2
Twatt Shetland 313 H5
Twechar E Dunb 278 F4
Tweedale Telford 132 C4
Tweeddaleburn
Borders 270 E5
Tweedmouth Northumb 273 E9
Tweedsmuir Borders 260 E3
Twelve Heads Corn 4 G5
Twelve Oaks E Sus 37 C11
Twelvewoods Corn 6 B4
Twemlow Green E Ches 168 B3
Twenties Kent 71 F10
Twenty Lincs 156 E3
Twerton Bath 61 G8
Twickenham London 67 E7
Twigworth Glos 98 G6
Twineham W Sus 36 D3
Twineham Green W Sus 36 C3
Twinhoe Bath 45 B8
Twinstead Essex 107 D7
Twinstead Green Essex 106 D6
Twiss Green Warr 183 B11
Twist Devon 28 G3
Twiston Lancs 204 E2
Twitchen Devon 41 G9
Twitchen Shrops 115 B7
Twitchen Mill Devon 41 G9
Twitham Kent 55 B9
Twitton Kent 52 B4
Two Bridges Devon 13 G8
Two Bridges Glos 79 D11
Two Burrows Corn 4 F4
Two Dales Derbys 170 C3
Two Gates Staffs 134 C4
Two Mile Ash M Keynes 102 D6
Two Mile Ash W Sus 35 B10
Two Mile Hill Bristol 60 E6
Two Mile Oak Cross
Devon 8 B6
Two Mills W Ches 182 G5
Two Pots Devon 40 E4
Two Waters Herts 85 D9
Twr Anglesey 178 E2
Twycross Leics 134 C6
Twydall Medway 69 F9
Twyford Bucks 102 F3
Twyford Derbys 152 D6
Twyford Dorset 30 D5
Twyford Hants 33 C7
Twyford Leics 154 G4
Twyford Lincs 155 E8
Twyford Norf 159 E10
Twyford Oxon 101 D9
Twyford Shrops 148 D6
Twyford Wokingham 65 D9
Twyford Worcs 99 B10
Twyford Common
Hereford 97 D10
Twyn-Allws Mon 78 C3
Twyn Shôn-Ifan
Caerph 77 G11
Twyn-y-Sheriff Mon 78 D6
Twyn-yr-odyn V Glam 58 E6
Twynholm Dumfries 237 D8
Twyning Glos 99 D7
Twyning Green Glos 99 D8
Twynllanan Carms 94 G5
Twynmynydd Carms 75 C11
Twynyrodyn M Tydf 77 D9
Twywell Northants 121 B9
Ty-coch Swansea 56 C6
Ty-draw Conwy 164 D5
Ty-draw Swansea 57 C7
Ty-fry Mon 78 F6
Ty-hen Carms 92 G6
Ty-hen Gwyn 144 C3
Ty-isaf Carms 56 B4
Ty Llwyn Bl Gwent 77 D11
Ty-mawr Anglesey 179 D7
Ty Mawr Carms 93 C10
Ty-mawr Conwy 181 F7
Ty Mawr Cwm Conwy 164 F6
Ty-nant Conwy 165 G7
Ty-nant Gwyn 147 D8
Ty-Newydd Ceredig 111 D10
Ty-Sign Caerph 78 G2
Ty-uchaf Powys 147 E10
Tyberton Hereford 97 D7
Tyburn W Mid 134 E2

Tyby Norf 159 D11
Tycroes Carms 75 C10
Tycrwyn Powys 148 F2
Tydd Gote Lincs 157 F9
Tydd St Giles Cambs 157 F8
Tydd St Mary Lincs 157 F8
Tyddewi = St Davids Pembs 90 F5
Tyddyn Powys 129 F9
Tyddyn Angharad Denb 165 F9
Tyddyn Dai Anglesey 178 C6
Tyddyn-mawr Gwyn 163 G9
Tye Hants 22 C2
Tye Common Essex 87 G11
Tye Green Essex 87 C10
Tye Green Essex 87 D7
Tye Green Essex 87 F11
Tye Green Essex 105 D11
Tye Green Essex 105 G10
Tye Green Essex 106 G5
Tyegate Green Norf 161 G7
Tyersal W Yorks 205 G9
Tyganol V Glam 58 E4
Tyla Mon 78 C2
Tylagwyn Bridgend 58 B2
Tyldesley Gtr Man 195 G7
Tyle Carms 94 F3
Tyle-garw Rhondda 58 C4
Tyler Hill Kent 70 G6
Tylers Causeway Herts 86 D3
Tylers Green Bucks 84 G6
Tyler's Green Essex 87 D8
Tyler's Green Sur 51 C11
Tyler's Hill Bucks 85 E7
Tylorstown Rhondda 77 F8
Tylwch Powys 129 G9
Ty-Ion Gwyn 163 D7
Ty'n-y-bryn Rhondda 58 B4
Tyn-y-celyn Wrex 148 B3
Tyn-y-coed Shrops 148 D4
Ty'n-y-coedcae Caerph 59 B7
Tyn-y-cwm Swansea 75 E10
Ty-n-y-fedwen Powys 148 C2
Ty'n-y-ffordd Denb 181 G8
Tyn-y-ffridd Powys 148 C2
Ty'n-y-garn Bridgend 57 E11
Tyn-y-graig Powys 113 G10
Ty'n-y-groes Conwy 180 G3
Ty'n-y-maes Gwyn 163 C10
Tyn-y-pwll Anglesey 178 D6
Ty'n-yr-eithin Ceredig 112 E3
Tynant Rhondda 58 B5
Tyncelyn Ceredig 112 E2
Tyndrum Stirl 285 D7
Tyne Dock T & W 243 D9
Tyne Tunnel T & W 243 D8
Tyneham Dorset 18 E3
Tynehead Midloth 271 D7
Tynemouth T & W 243 D9
Tynewydd Ceredig 92 B4
Tynewydd Neath 76 D4
Tynewydd Rhondda 76 F6
Tyning Bath 45 B7
Tyninghame E Loth 282 F2
Tynron Dumfries 247 E8
Tyntesfield N Som 60 E4
Tyntetown Rhondda 77 F9
Tynyfedw Conwy 165 B7
Tynygongl Anglesey 179 E8
Tynygraig Ceredig 112 D3
Tynyrwtra Powys 129 F7
Tŷ'r-felin-isaf Conwy 164 C5
Tyrells End C Beds 103 E9
Tyrell's Wood Sur 51 B7
Tyrie Aberds 303 C9
Tyringham M Keynes 103 B7
Tyseley W Mid 134 G2
Tythecott Devon 24 D6
Tythegston Bridgend 57 F11
Tytherington E Ches 184 F6
Tytherington S Glos 61 B7
Tytherington Som 45 D9
Tytherington Wilts 46 E2
Tytherleigh Devon 28 G4
Tytherton Lucas Wilts 62 E2
Tyttenhanger Herts 85 D11
Tywardreath Corn 5 E11
Tywardreath Highway Corn 5 D11
Tywyn Conwy 180 F3
Tywyn Gwyn 110 C2

U

Uachdar W Isles 296 F3
Uags Highld 295 B9
Ubberley Stoke 168 F6
Ubbeston Green Suff 126 C6
Ubley Bath 44 B4
Uckerby N Yorks 224 E4
Uckfield E Sus 37 C7
Uckinghall Worcs 99 D7
Uckington Glos 99 G8
Uckington Shrops 131 B11
Uddingston S Lnrk 268 C3
Uddington S Lnrk 259 C9
Udimore E Sus 38 D5
Udley N Som 60 G3
Udny Green Aberds 303 G8
Udny Station Aberds 303 G9
Udston S Lnrk 268 D3
Udstonhead S Lnrk 268 F4
Uffcott Wilts 62 D6
Uffculme Devon 27 E9
Uffington Lincs 137 B11
Uffington Oxon 63 B10
Uffington Shrops 149 G10
Ufford P'boro 137 C11
Ufford Suff 126 G5
Ufton Warks 119 E7
Ufton Green W Berks 64 F6
Ufton Nervet W Berks 64 F6
Ugadale Argyll 255 E8
Ugborough Devon 8 D3
Ugford Wilts 46 G5
Uggeshall Suff 143 G8
Ugglebarnby N Yorks 227 D7
Ughill S Yorks 186 C3
Ugley Essex 105 F10
Ugley Green Essex 105 F10
Ugthorpe N Yorks 226 C5
Uidh W Isles 297 M2
Uig Argyll 276 E2
Uig Argyll 288 D3
Uig Highld 296 F7
Uig Highld 298 C3
Uigen W Isles 304 E2
Uigshader Highld 298 E4
Uisken Argyll 274 B4
Ulaw Aberds 303 G9
Ulbster Highld 310 E7
Ulcat Row Cumb 230 G4
Ulceby Lincs 190 G6
Ulceby N Lincs 200 E6
Ulceby Skitter N Lincs 200 E6
Ulcombe Kent 53 D10
Uldale Cumb 229 D10
Uley Glos 80 F3
Ulgham Northumb 252 E6
Ullapool Highld 307 K6
Ullcombe Devon 28 F2
Ullenhall Warks 118 D2
Ullenwood Glos 80 B6
Ulleskelf N Yorks 206 E6
Ullesthorpe Leics 135 F10
Ulley S Yorks 187 D7
Ullingswick Hereford 97 B11
Ullington Worcs 100 B2
Ullinish Highld 294 B5
Ullock Cumb 229 G10
Ullock Cumb 229 G7
Ulnes Walton Lancs 194 D4
Ulpha Cumb 220 G3
Ulrome E Yorks 209 B9
Ulshaw N Yorks 214 B2
Ulsta Shetland 312 E6
Ulva House Argyll 288 F6
Ulverley Green W Mid 134 G2
Ulverston Cumb 210 D5
Ulwell Dorset 18 E6
Umberleigh Devon 25 C10
Unapool Highld 306 F7
Unasary W Isles 297 J3
Under Bank W Yorks 196 F6
Under the Wood Kent 71 F8
Under Tofts S Yorks 186 D4
Underbarrow Cumb 221 G9
Undercliffe W Yorks 205 G9
Underdale Shrops 149 G10
Underdown Devon 14 D3
Underhill London 86 F3
Underhill Wilts 45 G11
Underhoull Shetland 312 C7
Underling Green Kent 53 D9
Underriver Kent 52 C5
Underriver Ho Kent 52 C5
Underton Shrops 132 E3
Underwood Newport 59 B11
Underwood Notts 171 E7
Underwood Pembs 73 C7
Underwood Plym 7 D10
Undley Suff 140 G3
Undy Mon 60 B2
Ungisiadar W Isles 304 F3
Unifirth Shetland 313 H4
Union Cottage Aberds 293 D10
Union Mills I o M 192 E4
Union Street E Sus 53 G8
United Downs Corn 4 G4
Unstone Derbys 186 F5
Unstone Green Derbys 186 F5
Unsworth Gtr Man 195 F10
Unthank Cumb 230 B3
Unthank Cumb 230 D5
Unthank Cumb 231 C8
Unthank Derbys 186 F4
Unthank End Cumb 230 D5
Up Cerne Dorset 29 G11
Up End M Keynes 103 B8
Up Exe Devon 26 G6
Up Green Hants 65 G9
Up Hatherley Glos 99 G8
Up Holland Lancs 194 F4
Up Marden W Sus 34 E3
Up Mudford Som 29 D9
Up Nately Hants 49 C7
Up Somborne Hants 47 G11
Up Sydling Dorset 29 G10
Upavon Wilts 46 C6
Upchurch Kent 69 F10
Upcott Devon 24 D2
Upcott Devon 25 F11
Upcott Devon 25 F9
Upcott Devon 40 F3
Upcott Hereford 114 G6
Upcott Som 27 C11
Upend Cambs 124 F3
Upgate Norf 160 F2
Upgate Street Norf 141 E11
Upgate Street Norf 142 E5
Uphall Dorset 29 G9
Uphall W Loth 279 G11
Uphall Station W Loth 279 G11
Upham Devon 26 F5
Upham Hants 33 C8
Uphampton Hereford 115 E7
Uphampton Worcs 116 E6
Uphempston Devon 8 C6
Uphill N Som 43 B10
Uphill Manor N Som 43 B10
Uplands Glos 80 D5
Uplands Swansea 56 C6
Uplawmoor E Renf 267 D8
Upleadon Glos 98 F5
Upleadon Court Glos 98 F5
Upleatham Redcar 226 B2
Uplees Kent 70 G3
Uploders Dorset 16 C6
Uplowman Devon 27 D8
Uplyme Devon 16 C2
Upminster London 68 B5
Upnor Medway 69 E9
Upottery Devon 28 F2
Uppacott Devon 25 B9
Uppat Highld 311 J2
Uppend Essex 105 F9
Upper Affcot Shrops 131 F8
Upper Ardchronie Highld 309 L6
Upper Ardgrain Aberds 303 F9
Upper Ardroscadale Argyll 275 G11
Upper Arley Worcs 132 G5
Upper Armley W Yorks 205 G11
Upper Arncott Oxon 83 B10
Upper Astley Shrops 149 F10
Upper Aston Shrops 132 E6
Upper Astrop Northants 101 D10
Upper Badcall Highld 306 E6
Upper Bangor Gwyn 179 G9
Upper Basildon W Berks 64 D5
Upper Batley W Yorks 197 B8
Upper Battlefield Shrops 149 F10
Upper Beeding W Sus 35 E11
Upper Benefield Northants 137 F9
Upper Bentley Worcs 117 D9
Upper Bighouse Highld 310 D2
Upper Birchwood Derbys 170 E6
Upper Blainslie Borders 271 G10
Upper Boat Rhondda 58 B6
Upper Boddam Aberds 302 F6
Upper Boddington Northants 119 G9
Upper Bogrow Highld 309 L7
Upper Bogside Moray 302 D2
Upper Bonchurch I o W 21 F7
Upper Booth Derbys 185 D10
Upper Borth Ceredig 128 F2
Upper Boyndlie Aberds 303 C9
Upper Brailes Warks 100 D6
Upper Brandon Parva Norf 141 B10
Upper Breakish Highld 295 C8
Upper Breinton Hereford 97 C9
Upper Broadheath Worcs 116 F6
Upper Brockholes W Yorks 196 B5
Upper Broughton Notts 154 D3
Upper Broxwood Hereford 115 G7
Upper Bruntingthorpe Leics 136 F2
Upper Brynamman Carms 76 C2
Upper Buckenhill Hereford 97 E11
Upper Bucklebury W Berks 64 F4
Upper Bullington Hants 48 E3
Upper Burgate Hants 31 D11
Upper Burnhaugh Aberds 293 D10
Upper Bush Medway 69 F7
Upper Caldecote C Beds 104 B3
Upper Cam Glos 80 F3
Upper Canada N Som 43 B11
Upper Canterton Hants 32 E3
Upper Catesby Northants 119 F10
Upper Catshill Worcs 117 C9
Upper Chapel Powys 95 C10
Upper Cheddon Som 28 B2
Upper Chicksgrove Wilts 31 B7
Upper Church Village Rhondda 58 B5
Upper Chute Wilts 47 C9
Upper Clapton London 67 B10
Upper Clatford Hants 47 E11
Upper Coberley Glos 81 B7
Upper College Shrops 149 C11
Upper Colwall Hereford 98 C5
Upper Common Hants 48 D6
Upper Cotburn Aberds 303 D7
Upper Cotton Staffs 169 F9
Upper Coullie Aberds 293 B9
Upper Cound Shrops 131 C11
Upper Coxley Som 44 E4
Upper Cudworth S Yorks 197 F11
Upper Culphin Aberds 302 D6
Upper Cumberworth W Yorks 197 F8
Upper Cwm-twrch Powys 76 C3
Upper Cwmbran Torf 78 F3
Upper Dallachy Moray 302 C3
Upper Deal Kent 55 C11
Upper Dean Beds 121 D10
Upper Dean Devon 8 C4
Upper Denby W Yorks 197 D8
Upper Denby W Yorks 197 F8
Upper Denton Cumb 240 D4
Upper Derraid Highld 301 F10
Upper Diabaig Highld 299 C8
Upper Dicker E Sus 23 D9
Upper Dinchope Shrops 131 G9
Upper Dormington Hereford 97 D11
Upper Dounreay Highld 310 C4
Upper Dovercourt Essex 108 E4
Upper Dowdeswell Glos 81 B8
Upper Druimfin Argyll 289 D7
Upper Dunsforth N Yorks 215 G8
Upper Dunsley Herts 84 C6
Upper Eashing Sur 50 E3
Upper Eastern Green W Mid 134 G5
Upper Eathie Highld 301 C7
Upper Edmonton London 86 G4
Upper Egleton Hereford 98 C2
Upper Elkstone Staffs 169 D9
Upper Ellastone Staffs 169 G10
Upper Elmers End London 67 F11
Upper End Derbys 185 F9
Upper End Glos 81 C10
Upper End Glos 81 D8
Upper End Leics 154 G4
Upper Enham Hants 47 D11
Upper Farmcote Shrops 132 E5
Upper Farringdon Hants 49 F8
Upper Feorlig Highld 298 E2
Upper Fivehead Som 28 C4
Upper Forge Shrops 132 F4
Upper Framilode Glos 80 C3
Upper Froyle Hants 49 E9
Upper Gambolds Worcs 117 D9
Upper Gills Highld 310 B7
Upper Glenfintaig Highld 290 E4
Upper Godney Som 44 E3
Upper Goldstone Kent 71 G9
Upper Gornal W Mid 133 E8
Upper Gravenhurst C Beds 104 D2
Upper Green Essex 105 E8
Upper Green Mon 78 B5
Upper Green Suff 124 E4
Upper Green W Berks 63 G11
Upper Green W Yorks 197 B9
Upper Grove Common Hereford 97 F11
Upper Guist Norf 159 D10
Upper Hackney Derbys 170 C3
Upper Hale Sur 49 D10
Upper Halistra Highld 298 D2
Upper Halliford Sur 66 F5
Upper Halling Medway 69 G7
Upper Ham Worcs 99 D7
Upper Hambleton Rutland 137 B8
Upper Hamnish Hereford 115 F10
Upper Harbledown Kent 54 B6
Upper Hardres Court Kent 55 C7
Upper Hardwick Hereford 115 F8
Upper Hartfield E Sus 52 G3
Upper Hartshay Derbys 170 E5
Upper Haselor Worcs 99 C10
Upper Hatton Staffs 150 B6
Upper Haugh S Yorks 186 B6
Upper Hawkhillock Aberds 303 F10
Upper Hayesden Kent 52 E5
Upper Hayton Shrops 131 G10
Upper Heath Shrops 131 F11
Upper Heaton W Yorks 197 D7
Upper Hellesdon Norf 160 G4
Upper Helmsley N Yorks 207 B9
Upper Hengoed Shrops 148 C5
Upper Hergest Hereford 114 G5
Upper Heyford Northants 120 F3
Upper Heyford Oxon 101 F9
Upper Hill Glos 79 F11
Upper Hill Hereford 115 G9
Upper Hindhope Borders 251 B7
Upper Holloway London 67 B9
Upper Holton Suff 127 B8
Upper Hopton W Yorks 197 D7
Upper Horsebridge E Sus 23 C9
Upper Howsell Worcs 98 B5
Upper Hoyland S Yorks 197 G11
Upper Hulme Staffs 169 C8
Upper Hyde I o W 21 E7
Upper Ifold Sur 50 G4
Upper Inglesham Swindon 82 F2
Upper Inverbrough Highld 301 F8
Upper Kergord Shetland 313 H6
Upper Kidston Borders 270 G4
Upper Kilcott Glos 61 B9
Upper Killay Swansea 56 C5
Upper Killeyan Argyll 254 C3
Upper Kinsham Hereford 115 D7
Upper Knockando Moray 301 E11
Upper Lambourn W Berks 63 C10
Upper Landywood Staffs 133 B9
Upper Langford N Som 44 B3
Upper Langwith Derbys 171 B8
Upper Layham Suff 107 C10
Upper Leigh Staffs 151 B10
Upper Lenie Highld 300 G5
Upper Littleton N Som 60 G5
Upper Loads Derbys 170 B4
Upper Lochton Aberds 293 D8
Upper Lode Worcs 99 E7
Upper London Staffs 151 G11
Upper Longwood Shrops 132 B2
Upper Ludstone Shrops 132 D6
Upper Lybster Highld 310 F6
Upper Lydbrook Glos 79 B10
Upper Lyde Hereford 97 C9
Upper Lye Hereford 115 D7
Upper Maes-coed Hereford 96 D6
Upper Marsh W Yorks 204 F6
Upper Midhope S Yorks 186 B2
Upper Midway Derbys 152 E5
Upper Milovaig Highld 297 G7
Upper Milton Oxon 82 B3
Upper Milton Som 44 D4
Upper Minety Wilts 81 G8
Upper Mitton Worcs 116 C6
Upper Moor Worcs 99 B9
Upper Moor Side W Yorks 205 G10
Upper Morton S Glos 79 G11
Upper Nash Pembs 73 E8
Upper Netchwood Shrops 132 E2
Upper Newbold Derbys 186 G5
Upper Nobut Staffs 151 B10
Upper North Dean Bucks 84 F4
Upper Norwood London 67 F10
Upper Norwood W Sus 34 D6
Upper Obney Perth 286 D4
Upper Ochrwyth Caerph 59 B8
Upper Oddington Glos 100 F4
Upper Ollach Highld 295 B7
Upper Padley Derbys 186 F2
Upper Pickwick Wilts 61 E11
Upper Pollicott Bucks 84 C2
Upper Poppleton York 207 C7
Upper Port Highld 301 G10
Upper Postern Kent 52 D6
Upper Quinton Warks 100 B3
Upper Race Torf 78 F3
Upper Ratley Hants 32 C4
Upper Ridinghill Aberds 303 D10
Upper Rissington Glos 82 B2
Upper Rochford Worcs 116 D2
Upper Rodmersham Kent 70 G2
Upper Sandaig Highld 295 D9
Upper Sanday Orkney 314 F5
Upper Sapey Hereford 116 E3
Upper Saxondale Notts 154 B3
Upper Seagry Wilts 62 C3
Upper Shelton C Beds 103 C9
Upper Sheringham Norf 177 E10
Upper Shirley London 67 G11
Upper Shirley Soton 32 E6
Upper Siddington Glos 81 F8
Upper Skelmorlie N Ayrs 266 B4
Upper Slackstead Hants 32 B5
Upper Slaughter Glos 100 G3
Upper Solva Pembs 90 G5
Upper Soudley Glos 79 C11
Upper Stanton Drew Bath 60 G6
Upper Staploe Beds 122 F2
Upper Stoke Norf 142 C5
Upper Stoke W Mid 135 G7
Upper Stondon C Beds 104 D2
Upper Stowe Northants 120 F2
Upper Stratton Swindon 63 B7
Upper Street Hants 31 D11
Upper Street Norf 142 G3
Upper Street Norf 160 B5
Upper Street Norf 160 E6
Upper Street Norf 160 F6
Upper Street Norf 161 F7
Upper Street Suff 108 E2
Upper Street Suff 124 G5
Upper Street Suff 126 G2
Upper Strensham Worcs 99 D8
Upper Studley Wilts 45 B10
Upper Sundon C Beds 103 F10
Upper Swainswick Bath 61 F9
Upper Swanmore Hants 33 D9
Upper Swell Glos 100 F3
Upper Sydenham London 67 E10
Upper Tankersley S Yorks 186 B4
Upper Tean Staffs 151 B10
Upper Threapwood W Ches 166 F6
Upper Thurnham Lancs 202 C5
Upper Tillyrie Perth 286 G5
Upper Tooting London 67 E9
Upper Tote Highld 298 D5
Upper Town Derbys 170 D3
Upper Town Derbys 170 E2
Upper Town Durham 233 D7
Upper Town Hereford 97 B11
Upper Town N Som 60 F4
Upper Town Suff 125 D8
Upper Town W Yorks 204 G6
Upper Town Wilts 62 D3
Upper Treverward Shrops 114 B5
Upper Tysoe Warks 100 C6
Upper Up Glos 81 F8
Upper Upham Wilts 63 D8
Upper Upnor Medway 69 E9
Upper Vobster Som 45 D8
Upper Walthamstow London 67 B11
Upper Wardington Oxon 101 B9
Upper Wardley W Sus 34 B4
Upper Weald M Keynes 102 D5
Upper Weedon Northants 120 F2
Upper Welland Worcs 98 C5
Upper Wellingham E Sus 36 E6
Upper Welson Hereford 114 G5
Upper Westholme Som 44 E5
Upper Weston Bath 61 F8
Upper Weybread Suff 126 B4
Upper Whiston S Yorks 187 D7
Upper Wick Glos 80 F2
Upper Wick Worcs 116 G6
Upper Wield Hants 48 F6
Upper Wigginton Shrops 148 B6
Upper Winchendon Bucks 84 C2
Upper Witton W Mid 133 E11
Upper Wolvercote Oxon 83 D7
Upper Wolverton Worcs 117 G8
Upper Woodend Aberds 293 B8
Upper Woodford Wilts 46 F6
Upper Woolhampton W Berks 64 F5
Upper Wootton Hants 48 C5
Upper Wraxall Wilts 61 E10
Upper Wyche Hereford 98 C5
Upperby Cumb 239 G10
Upperdale Derbys 185 G11
Uppermill Gtr Man 196 F3
Uppersound Shetland 313 J6
Upperthong W Yorks 196 F6
Upperthorpe Derbys 187 E7
Upperthorpe N Lincs 199 G9
Upperton E Sus 23 E10
Upperton Oxon 83 G11
Upperton W Sus 35 C7
Uppertown Derbys 170 C4
Uppertown Highld 300 F4
Uppertown Highld 310 B7
Uppertown Northumb 241 C9
Uppertown Orkney 314 G4
Upperwood Derbys 170 D3
Uppincott Devon 26 G5
Uppingham Rutland 137 D7
Uppington Dorset 31 F8
Uppington Shrops 132 B2
Upsall N Yorks 215 B9
Upshire Essex 86 E6
Upsher Green Suff 107 C8
Upstreet Kent 71 G8
Upthorpe Glos 80 E3
Upthorpe Suff 125 C9
Upton Bucks 84 C3
Upton Cambs 122 B3
Upton Corn 11 G11
Upton Corn 24 G2
Upton Cumb 230 D2
Upton Devon 8 G4
Upton Devon 27 G9
Upton Dorset 17 E10
Upton Dorset 18 C5
Upton E Yorks 209 C8
Upton Hants 32 D5
Upton Hants 47 B11
Upton I o W 21 C7
Upton Kent 71 F11
Upton Leics 135 D7
Upton Lincs 188 D5
Upton London 68 C2
Upton Mers 182 D3
Upton Mers 183 D7
Upton Norf 161 G7
Upton Northants 120 E4
Upton Notts 172 E2
Upton Notts 188 F2
Upton Oxon 64 B4
Upton Oxon 82 C2
Upton P'boro 138 C2
Upton Slough 66 D3
Upton Som 27 B7
Upton Som 29 B7
Upton W Ches 166 B6
Upton W Yorks 198 E3
Upton Warks 118 F2
Upton Wilts 45 G11
Upton Bishop Hereford 98 F2
Upton Cheyney S Glos 61 F7
Upton Cressett Shrops 132 E3
Upton Crews Hereford 98 F2
Upton Cross Corn 11 G11
Upton End C Beds 104 E2
Upton Field Notts 172 E2
Upton Green Norf 161 G7
Upton Grey Hants 49 D7
Upton Heath W Ches 166 B6
Upton Hellions Devon 26 G4
Upton Lea Bucks 66 C3
Upton Lovell Wilts 46 E2
Upton Magna Shrops 149 G11
Upton Noble Som 45 F8
Upton Park London 68 C2
Upton Pyne Devon 14 B4
Upton Rocks Halton 183 D8
Upton St Leonards Glos 80 C5
Upton Scudamore Wilts 45 D11
Upton Snodsbury Worcs 117 G8
Upton upon Severn Worcs 99 C7
Upton Warren Worcs 117 D8
Upwaltham W Sus 34 E6
Upware Cambs 123 C10
Upwell Norf 139 C9
Upwey Dorset 17 E9
Upwick Green Herts 105 G9
Upwood Cambs 138 G5
Uradale Shetland 313 K6
Urafirth Shetland 312 F5
Uragaig Argyll 274 D4
Urchfont Wilts 46 B4
Urdimarsh Hereford 97 B10
Ure Shetland 312 F4
Ure Bank N Yorks 214 E6
Urgashay Som 29 C9
Urgha W Isles 305 J3
Urgha Beag W Isles 305 H3
Urishay Common Hereford 96 D6
Urlar Perth 286 C2
Urlay Nook Stockton 225 C7
Urmston Gtr Man 184 C3
Urpeth Durham 242 G6
Urquhart Highld 300 D5
Urquhart Moray 302 C2
Urra N Yorks 225 E11
Urray Highld 300 D5
Ushaw Moor Durham 233 C10
Usk Mon 78 E5
Usselby Lincs 189 C9
Usworth T & W 243 F8
Utkinton W Ches 167 B8
Utley W Yorks 204 E6
Uton Devon 14 B2
Utterby Lincs 190 C4
Uttoxeter Staffs 151 C11
Uwchmynydd Gwyn 144 D3
Uxbridge London 66 C5
Uxbridge Moor London 66 C5
Uyea Shetland 312 D5
Uyeasound Shetland 312 C7
Uzmaston Pembs 73 C7

V

Vachelich Pembs 90 F5
Vadlure Shetland 313 J4
Vagg Som 29 D8
Vaila Hall Shetland 313 J4
Vaivoe Shetland 312 G7
Vale W Yorks 196 B2
Vale Down Devon 12 D6
Vale of Health London 67 B9
Valeswood Shrops 149 E7
Valley = Y Fali Anglesey 178 F3
Valley Park Hants 32 C6
Valley Truckle Corn 11 E7
Valleyfield Dumfries 237 D8
Valsgarth Shetland 312 B8
Valtos Highld 298 C5
Van Caerph 59 B7
Van Powys 129 F9
Vange Essex 69 B8
Vanlop Shetland 313 M5
Varchoel Powys 148 G4
Varfell Corn 2 C2
Varteg Torf 78 D3
Vassa Shetland 313 H6
Vastern Wilts 62 C5
Vatsetter Shetland 312 E7
Vatsetter Shetland 313 L5
Vatten Highld 298 E2
Vaul Argyll 288 E2
Vauxhall London 67 D10
Vauxhall Mers 182 C4
Vauxhall W Mid 133 F11
Vaynol Hall Gwyn 163 B8
Vaynor M Tydf 77 C8
Veensgarth Shetland 313 J6
Velator Devon 40 F3
Veldo Hereford 97 C11
Velindre Powys 96 D3
Vellanoweth Corn 2 C2
Vellow Som 42 F5
Velly Devon 24 C3
Veness Orkney 314 D5
Venn Devon 8 F4
Venn Green Devon 24 E5
Venn Ottery Devon 15 C7
Venngreen Devon 24 E5
Vennington Shrops 130 B6
Venn's Green Hereford 97 B10
Venny Tedburn Devon 14 B2
Venterdon Corn 12 G3
Vention Devon 40 E3
Ventnor I o W 21 F7
Venton Devon 7 D11
Ventongimps Corn 4 E5
Ventonleague Corn 2 B3
Venus Hill Herts 85 E8
Veraby Devon 26 B3
Vermentry Shetland 313 H5
Vernham Bank Hants 47 B10
Vernham Dean Hants 47 B10
Vernham Row Hants 47 B10
Vernham Street Hants 47 B11
Vernolds Common Shrops 131 G9
Verwood Dorset 31 F9
Veryan Corn 3 B10
Veryan Green Corn 5 G8
Vicarage Devon 15 D10
Vicarscross W Ches 166 B6
Vickerstown Cumb 210 F3
Victoria Corn 5 C9
Victoria S Yorks 197 F7
Victoria Dock Village Hull 200 B6
Victoria Park Bucks 84 C4
Victory Gardens Renfs 267 B10
Vidlin Shetland 312 G6
Viewpark N Lnrk 268 C4
Vigo W Mid 133 C10
Vigo Village Kent 68 G6
Vinegar Hill Mon 60 B2
Vinehall Street E Sus 38 C3
Vines Cross E Sus 23 B9
Viney Hill Glos 79 D11
Vinney Green S Glos 61 D7
Virginia Water Sur 66 F3
Virginstow Devon 12 C3
Viscar Corn 2 C6
Vobster Som 45 D8
Voe Shetland 312 E5
Voe Shetland 313 G6
Vogue Corn 4 G4
Vole Som 43 D11
Vowchurch Hereford 97 D7
Vowchurch Common Hereford 97 D7
Voxmoor Som 27 D10
Voxter Shetland 312 F5
Voy Orkney 314 E2
Vron Gate Shrops 130 B6
Vulcan Village Mers 183 C9

W

Waberthwaite Cumb 220 G2
Wackerfield Durham 233 G9
Wacton Hereford 116 F2
Wacton Norf 142 E3
Wacton Common Norf 142 F3
Wadbister Shetland 313 J6
Wadborough Worcs 99 B8
Wadbrook Devon 28 G4
Waddesdon Bucks 84 B2
Waddeton Devon 9 D7
Waddicar Mers 182 B5
Waddicombe Devon 26 B5
Waddingham Lincs 189 B7
Waddington Lancs 203 E10
Waddington Lincs 173 C7
Waddingworth Lincs 189 G11
Waddon Devon 14 F3
Waddon London 67 G10
Wade Hall Lancs 194 C4
Wadebridge Corn 10 G5
Wadeford Som 28 E4
Wadenhoe Northants 137 G10
Wades Green E Ches 167 C11
Wadesmill Herts 86 B5
Wadhurst E Sus 52 G6
Wadshelf Derbys 186 G4
Wadsley S Yorks 186 C4
Wadsley Bridge S Yorks 186 C4
Wadswick Wilts 61 F10
Wadwick Hants 48 C2
Wadworth S Yorks 187 B9
Waen Denb 165 B10
Waen Denb 165 C7
Waen Flint 181 G11
Waen Powys 129 E9
Waen Aberwheeler Denb 165 B9
Waen-fâch Powys 148 F4
Waen Goleugoed Denb 181 G9
Waen-pentir Gwyn 163 B9
Waen-wen Gwyn 163 B9
Wag Highld 311 G4
Wagbeach Shrops 131 C7
Wagg Som 28 B6
Waggersley Staffs 151 B7
Waggs Plot Devon 28 G4
Wain Lee Staffs 168 D5
Wainfelin Torf 78 E3
Wainfleet All Saints Lincs 175 D7
Wainfleet Bank Lincs 175 D7
Wainfleet St Mary Lincs 175 D8
Wainfleet Tofts Lincs 175 D7
Wainford Norf 142 E6
Waingroves Derbys 170 F6
Wainhouse Corner Corn 11 B9
Wainscott Medway 69 E8
Wainstalls W Yorks 196 B4
Waitby Cumb 222 D5
Waithe Lincs 201 G9
Wake Green W Mid 133 G11
Wake Hill N Yorks 214 E3
Wake Lady Green N Yorks 226 F3
Wakefield W Yorks 197 C10
Wakeley Herts 104 F6
Wakerley Northants 137 D9
Wakes Colne Essex 107 F7
Wakes Colne Green Essex 107 E7
Walberswick Suff 127 C9
Walberton W Sus 35 F7
Walbottle T & W 242 D5
Walby Cumb 239 E10
Walcombe Som 44 D5
Walcot Bath 61 F9
Walcot Lincs 155 B11
Walcot N Lincs 199 C11
Walcot Oxon 82 B4
Walcot Shrops 130 F6
Walcot Swindon 63 C7
Walcot Telford 149 G11
Walcot Worcs 99 B8
Walcot Green Norf 142 G2
Walcote Leics 135 G11
Walcote Warks 118 F2
Walcott Lincs 173 D10
Walcott Norf 161 C7
Walden N Yorks 213 C10
Walden Head N Yorks 213 C9
Walden Stubbs N Yorks 198 D5
Waldersey Cambs 139 C8
Waldershaigh S Yorks 186 B3
Walderslade Medway 69 G9
Walderton W Sus 34 E3
Walditch Dorset 16 C5
Waldley Derbys 152 B2
Waldridge Durham 243 G7
Waldringfield Suff 108 C5
Waldringfield Heath Suff 108 B5
Waldron E Sus 23 B8
Waldron Down E Sus 37 C8
Wales S Yorks 187 E7
Wales Som 29 C9
Wales Bar S Yorks 187 E7
Wales End Suff 106 B5
Walesby Lincs 189 C10
Walesby Notts 187 G11
Walesby Grange Lincs 189 C10
Waleswood S Yorks 187 E7
Walford Hereford 97 G11
Walford Hereford 115 C7
Walford Shrops 149 E8
Walford Som 28 B3
Walford Staffs 150 C6
Walford Heath Shrops 149 F8
Walgherton E Ches 167 F11
Walgrave Northants 120 C6
Walham Glos 98 G6
Walham Green London 67 D9
Walhampton Hants 20 B2
Walk Mill Lancs 204 G3
Walkden Gtr Man 195 G8
Walker T & W 243 E7
Walker Barn E Ches 185 G7
Walker Fold Lancs 203 E9
Walkerburn Borders 261 B9
Walkeringham Notts 188 C3
Walkerith Lincs 188 C3
Walkern Herts 104 F5
Walker's Green Hereford 97 B10
Walker's Heath W Mid 117 B11
Walkerville N Yorks 224 F4
Walkford Dorset 19 C10
Walkhampton Devon 7 B10
Walkington E Yorks 208 F5
Walkley S Yorks 186 D4
Walkmill Shrops 131 E7
Walkmills Shrops 131 D9
Wall Corn 2 B4
Wall Northumb 241 D10
Wall Staffs 134 B2
Wall Bank Shrops 131 E10
Wall End Cumb 210 C4
Wall End Kent 71 G8
Wall Heath W Mid 133 F7
Wall Hill Gtr Man 196 F3
Wall Mead Bath 45 B7
Wall Nook Durham 233 B10
Wall under Heywood Shrops 131 E10
Wallacestone Falk 279 F8
Wallaceton Dumfries 247 F8
Wallacetown S Ayrs 245 C7
Wallacetown S Ayrs 257 E8
Wallacetown Shetland 313 H5
Wallands Park E Sus 36 E6
Wallasey Mers 182 C4
Wallbank Lancs 195 D11
Wallbrook W Mid 133 E8
Wallcrouch E Sus 53 G7
Wallend London 68 C2
Waller's Green Hereford 98 D3
Walley's Green E Ches 167 C11
Wallingford Oxon 64 B6
Wallington Hants 33 F9
Wallington Herts 104 E5
Wallington London 67 G9
Wallington Heath W Mid 133 C9
Wallingwells Notts 187 E9
Wallis Pembs 91 F10
Wallisdown Poole 19 C7
Walliswood Sur 50 F6
Wallow Green Glos 80 F4
Wallridge Northumb 242 B3
Walls Shetland 313 J4
Wallsend T & W 243 D7
Wallston V Glam 58 E6
Wallsuches Gtr Man 195 E7
Wallsworth Glos 98 G6
Wallyford E Loth 281 G7
Walmer Kent 55 C11
Walmer Bridge Lancs 194 C3
Walmersley Gtr Man 195 E
Walmgate Stray York 207 C
Walmley W Mid 134 E
Walmsgate Lincs 190 F
Walnut Grove Perth 286 E
Walnut Tree M Keynes 103 D
Walnuttree Green Herts 105 G
Walpole Som 43 E
Walpole Suff 127 C
Walpole Cross Keys Norf 157 F1
Walpole Highway Norf 157 G1
Walpole Marsh Norf 157 F
Walpole St Andrew Norf 157 F1
Walpole St Peter Norf 157 F
Walrow Som 43 D1
Walsal End W Mid 118 B
Walsall W Mid 133 D
Walsall Wood W Mid 133 C1
Walsden W Yorks 196 C
Walsgrave on Sowe W Mid 135 G
Walsham le Willows Suff 125 C
Walshaw Gtr Man 195 E
Walshford N Yorks 206 C
Walsoken Cambs 157 G
Walson Mon 97 G
Walston S Lnrk 269 F1
Walsworth Herts 104 E
Walters Ash Bucks 84 F
Walter's Green Kent 52 E
Walterston V Glam 58 E
Walterstone Hereford 96 F
Waltham Kent 54 D
Waltham NE Lincs 201 G
Waltham Abbey Essex 86 E
Waltham Chase Hants 33 D
Waltham Cross Herts 86 E
Waltham on the Wolds Leics 154 D
Waltham St Lawrence Windsor 65 D1
Waltham's Cross Essex 106 E
Walthamstow London 67 B1
Walton Bucks 84 C
Walton Cumb 240 E
Walton Derbys 170 B
Walton Leics 135 F1
Walton M Keynes 103 D
Walton Mers 182 C
Walton P'boro 138 C
Walton Powys 114 F
Walton Shrops 115 B
Walton Som 44 F
Walton Staffs 151 C
Walton Staffs 151 D
Walton Suff 108 D
Walton Telford 149 F1
Walton W Yorks 197 D1
Walton W Yorks 206 D
Walton Warks 118 G
Walton Cardiff Glos 99 E
Walton Court Bucks 84 C
Walton East Pembs 91 G1
Walton Elm Dorset 30 D
Walton Grounds Northants 101 E1
Walton Heath Hants 33 F1
Walton Highway Norf 157 G
Walton in Gordano N Som 60 E
Walton-le-Dale Lancs 194 B
Walton Manor Oxon 83 D
Walton-on-Thames Sur 66 F
Walton on the Hill Staffs 151 E
Walton on the Hill Sur 51 B
Walton-on-the-Naze Essex 108 G
Walton on the Wolds Leics 153 F1
Walton-on-Trent Derbys 152 F
Walton Pool Worcs 117 B
Walton St Mary N Som 60 E
Walton Summit Lancs 194 B
Walton Warren Norf 158 F
Walton West Pembs 72 C
Walwen Flint 181 F1
Walwen Flint 181 G1
Walwen Flint 182 F
Walwick Northumb 241 C1
Walworth Darl 224 B
Walworth London 67 D1
Walworth Gate Darl 233 G1
Walwyn's Castle Pembs 72 C
Wambrook Som 28 F
Wampool Cumb 238 G
Wanborough Sur 50 D
Wanborough Swindon 63 C
Wandel Dyke S Lnrk 259 D1
Wandle Park London 67 F1
Wandon End Herts 104 G
Wandsworth London 67 E
Wangford Suff 127 B
Wanlip Leics 154 G
Wanlockhead Dumfries 259 G
Wannock E Sus 23 E
Wansford E Yorks 209 B
Wansford P'boro 137 D1
Wanshurst Green Kent 53 D
Wanson Corn 24 G
Wanstead London 68 B
Wanstrow Som 45 E
Wanswell Glos 79 E1
Wantage Oxon 63 B1
Wants Green Worcs 116 F
Wapley S Glos 61 D
Wappenbury Warks 119 D
Wappenham Northants 102 B
Wapping London 67 C1
Warbleton E Sus 23 B1
Warblington Hants 22 B
Warborough Oxon 83 G
Warboys Cambs 138 G
Warbreck Blkpool 202 F
Warbstow Corn 11 C1
Warbstow Cross Corn 11 C1
Warburton Gtr Man 184 D
Warburton Green Gtr Man 184 E
Warcop Cumb 222 B
Ward End W Mid 134 F
Ward Green S Yorks 197 G1
Ward Green Suff 125 E1
Ward Green Cross Lancs 203 F
Warden Kent 70 E
Warden Northumb 241 D1
Warden Powys 114 E
Warden Hill Glos 99 G
Warden Point I o W 20 D
Warden Street C Beds 104 C
Wardhedges C Beds 103 D1
Wardhill Orkney 314 D
Wardington Oxon 101 B
Wardlaw Borders 261 F
Wardle E Ches 167 D1

ardle Gtr Man 196 D2
ardle Bank E Ches 167 D10
ardley Gtr Man 195 G9
ardley Rutland 136 C6
ardley T & W 243 E7
ardley W Sus 34 B4
ardlow Derbys 185 G11
ardour Wilts 30 B6
ardpark N Lnrk 278 F5
ardrobes Bucks 84 E4
ardsend E Ches 184 E6
ardy Hill Cambs 139 G9
are Herts 86 C5
are Kent 71 G9
are Street Kent 53 B9
areham Dorset 18 D4
arehorne Kent 54 G3
aren Mill Northumb 264 C4
arenford Northumb 264 D4
arenton Northumb 264 C4
areside Herts 86 B5
aresley Cambs 122 G4
aresley Worcs 116 C6
arfield Brack 65 E11
arfleet Devon 9 E7
argate Lincs 156 C4
argrave Mers 183 C9
argrave Wokingham 65 D9
arham Hereford 97 D9
arham Norf 176 E6
arhill Gtr Man 185 B7
aring's Green W Mid 118 C2
ark Northumb 241 B9
ark Northumb 263 B8
ark Common
orthumb 263 B8
arkleigh Devon 25 C10
arkton Northants 121 B7
arkworth Northants 101 C9
arkworth Northumb 252 B6
arlaby N Yorks 224 G6
arland W Yorks 196 C2
arleggan Corn 6 B3
arleigh Bath 61 G9
arley Essex 87 G9
arley Town W Yorks 196 B5
arley Woods W Mid 133 F10
arlingham Sur 51 B11
armbrook Derbys 170 E3
armfield W Yorks 197 C11
armingham E Ches 168 C2
arminghurst W Sus 35 D10
armington Northants 137 E11
armington Warks 101 B8
arminster Wilts 45 D11
arminster Common
ilts 45 E11
armlake Kent 53 C10
armley S Glos 61 E7
armley Hill S Glos 61 E7
armley Tower S Glos 61 E7
rmonds Hill
orthants 121 D9
rmsworth S Yorks 198 G4
rmwell Dorset 17 D11
rnborough Green
ants 49 C8
arndon Worcs 117 F7
arners End Herts 85 D8
arnford Hants 33 C10
arnham W Sus 51 G7
arningcamp W Sus 35 F8
arninglid W Sus 36 B2
arpsgrove Oxon 83 F10
arren Dorset 18 C3
arren E Ches 184 G5
arren Pembs 72 F6
arren S Yorks 186 B5
arren Corner Hants 34 B2
arren Corner Hants 49 D10
arren Heath Suff 108 C4
arren Row Windsor 65 C10
arren Street Kent 54 C2
arrenby Redcar 235 F7
arren's Green Herts 104 F5
arrington M Keynes 121 G7
arrington Warr 183 D10
arriston Edin 280 F5
arsash Hants 33 F7
arsill N Yorks 214 F4
arslow Staffs 169 D9
arsop Vale Notts 171 B8
arstock W Mid 117 B11
arstone Staffs 133 B9
arter E Yorks 208 C3
arthermarske
Yorks 214 D4
arthill N Yorks 207 B9
artle Aberds 293 C7
artling E Sus 23 D11
artnaby Leics 154 E4
arton Lancs 194 B2
arton Lancs 211 E9
arton Northumb 252 C2
arton Warks 134 C5
arton Bank Lancs 194 B2
arwick Warks 118 E5
arwick Bridge Cumb 239 F11
arwick on Eden
mb 239 F11
arwick Wold Sur 51 C10
arwicksland Cumb 239 B10
asbister Orkney 314 C3
asdale Head Cumb 220 D3
ash Derbys 185 E9
ash Common W Berks 64 G3
ash Dyke Norf 157 F10
ash Water W Berks 64 G3
ashall Green Herts 105 E8
ashaway Corn 5 B10
ashbourne Devon 8 E5
ashbrook Som 44 C2
ashbrook Suff 108 C2
ashbrook Street Suff 108 C2
asherwall Staffs 168 F6
ashfield Devon 26 D6
ashfold N Yorks 223 E11
ashford Som 42 E5
ashford Worcs 117 D11
ashford Pyne Devon 26 E4
ashingborough Lincs 189 G8
ashingley Cambs 138 F2
ashington T & W 243 F8
ashington W Sus 35 E10
ashington Village
& W 243 F8
ashmere Green Suff 107 B8
ashpit W Yorks 196 F6
ashwood Heath
Mid 134 F2
asing W Berks 64 G5
askerley Durham 233 B7
asp Green Sur 51 D10
asperton Warks 118 F5
asps Nest Lincs 173 C9
ass N Yorks 215 D11
aste Green Warks 118 D4
astor Devon 8 F2
atch House Green
ssex 106 G3
atchet Som 42 E5
atchfield Oxon 63 B8
Watchfield Som 43 D10
Watchgate Cumb 221 F10
Watchhill Cumb 229 C9
Watchill Dumfries 238 D6
Watchill Dumfries 248 G3
Watcombe Torbay 9 B8
Watendlath Cumb 220 B5
Water Devon 13 E11
Water Lancs 195 B10
Water Eaton M Keynes 103 E7
Water Eaton Oxon 83 C8
Water End Beds 104 B2
Water End C Beds 103 D11
Water End C Beds 104 B5
Water End E Yorks 207 F11
Water End Essex 105 C11
Water End Hants 49 C7
Water End Herts 85 C8
Water End Herts 86 E2
Water Fryston W Yorks 198 B3
Water Garth Nook
Cumb 210 F3
Water Houses N Yorks 213 F7
Water Newton Cambs 138 D2
Water Orton Warks 134 E3
Water Stratford Bucks 102 E3
Water Yeat Cumb 210 B5
Waterbeach Cambs 123 D9
Waterbeach W Sus 22 B5
Waterbeck Dumfries 238 B6
Waterdale Herts 85 E10
Waterden Norf 159 B7
Waterditch Hants 19 B9
Waterend Bucks 84 F3
Waterend Cumb 229 G8
Waterend Glos 80 C3
Waterend Herts 86 C2
Waterfall Staffs 169 E9
Waterfoot Argyll 255 D9
Waterfoot Cumb 230 G5
Waterfoot E Renf 267 D11
Waterfoot Lancs 195 C10
Waterford Hants 20 B2
Waterford Herts 86 C4
Watergate Corn 6 E4
Watergate Corn 11 E8
Watergore Som 28 D6
Waterhales Essex 87 F8
Waterham Kent 70 G5
Waterhay Wilts 81 G9
Waterhead Angus 292 F6
Waterhead Cumb 221 E7
Waterhead Devon 8 F3
Waterhead Dumfries 248 E5
Waterhead on
Minnoch S Ayrs 245 E9
Waterheads Borders 270 E4
Waterheath Norf 143 E8
Waterhouses Durham 233 C9
Waterhouses Staffs 169 E9
Wateringbury Kent 53 C7
Waterlane Glos 80 E6
Waterlip Som 45 E7
Waterloo Blkburn 195 B7
Waterloo Corn 11 G8
Waterloo Derbys 170 C6
Waterloo Gtr Man 196 G2
Waterloo Highld 295 C8
Waterloo Mers 182 B4
Waterloo N Lnrk 268 E6
Waterloo Norf 126 B2
Waterloo Norf 143 B9
Waterloo Norf 160 F4
Waterloo Pembs 73 E7
Waterloo Perth 286 D4
Waterloo Poole 18 C6
Waterloo Shrops 149 C9
Waterloo Park Mers 182 B4
Waterloo Port Gwyn 163 C7
Waterlooville Hants 33 F11
Waterman Quarter
Kent 53 E10
Watermead Glos 80 B5
Watermeetings S Lnrk 259 G11
Watermill E Sus 38 E2
Watermillock Cumb 230 G4
Watermoor Glos 81 E8
Waterperry Oxon 83 D10
Waterrow Som 27 B9
Water's Nook Gtr Man 195 F7
Waters Upton Telford 150 F2
Watersfield W Sus 35 D8
Watersheddings
Gtr Man 196 F2
Waterside Aberds 292 B5
Waterside Aberds 303 G10
Waterside Blkburn 195 C8
Waterside Bucks 85 E7
Waterside Cumb 229 B10
Waterside Derbys 185 E8
Waterside E Ayrs 245 B10
Waterside E Ayrs 267 G9
Waterside E Dunb 278 G3
Waterside E Renf 267 D10
Waterside S Yorks 199 E7
Waterside Sur 51 D11
Waterside Telford 150 F2
Waterslack Lancs 211 D9
Waterstein Highld 297 G7
Waterstock Oxon 83 D10
Waterston Pembs 72 D6
Waterthorpe S Yorks 186 E6
Waterton Aberds 303 F9
Waterton Bridgend 58 D2
Watford Herts 85 F10
Watford Northants 120 D2
Watford Gap Staffs 134 C2
Watford Heath Herts 85 G10
Watford Park Caerph 58 B6
Wath Cumb 222 D3
Wath N Yorks 214 D6
Wath N Yorks 214 F2
Wath N Yorks 216 D3
Wath Brow Cumb 219 C10
Wath upon Dearne
S Yorks 198 G2
Watherston Borders 271 F8
Watledge Glos 80 E4
Watley's End S Glos 61 C7
Watlington Norf 158 G2
Watlington Oxon 83 G11
Watnall Notts 171 F8
Watness Shetland 313 H3
Watten Highld 310 D6
Wattisfield Suff 125 C10
Wattisham Suff 125 G10
Wattisham Stone Suff 125 G10
Wattlefield Norf 142 D2
Wattlesborough Heath
Shrops 149 G7
Watton E Yorks 208 C6
Watton Norf 141 C8
Watton at Stone Herts 86 B4
Watton Green Norf 141 C8
Watton's Green Essex 87 F8
Wattston N Lnrk 268 B5
Wattstown Rhondda 77 G8
Wattsville Caerph 78 G2
Wauchan Highld 295 G11
Waulkmill Lodge
Orkney 314 F3
Waun Gwyn 163 C9
Waun Powys 148 F4
Waun Beddau Pembs 90 F5
Waun Fawr Ceredig 128 G2
Waun-Lwyd Bl Gwent 77 D11
Waun-y-clyn Carms 75 E7
Waun y Gilfach Bridgend 57 D10
Waunarlwydd Swansea 56 B6
Waunclunda Carms 94 E3
Waunfawr Gwyn 163 D8
Waungilwen Carms 92 D6
Waungron Swansea 75 E9
Waunlwyd Bl Gwent 77 D11
Wavendon M Keynes 103 D8
Wavendon Gate
M Keynes 103 D8
Waverbridge Cumb 229 B10
Waverton Cumb 229 B10
Waverton W Ches 167 C7
Wavertree Mers 182 D5
Wawcott W Berks 63 F11
Wawne E Yorks 209 F7
Waxham Norf 161 D8
Waxholme E Yorks 201 B10
Way Kent 71 F10
Way Village Devon 26 E5
Way Wick N Som 59 G11
Waye Devon 13 G11
Wayend Street Hereford 98 D4
Wayfield Medway 69 F9
Wayford Som 28 F6
Waymills Shrops 167 G9
Wayne Green Mon 78 B6
Way's Green W Ches 167 B10
Waytown Devon 24 C5
Waytown Devon 40 G5
Wdig = Goodwick
Pembs 91 D8
Weachyburn Aberds 302 D6
Weacombe Som 42 E6
Weald Oxon 82 E4
Wealdstone London 67 B7
Wearde Corn 7 D8
Weardley W Yorks 205 E11
Weare Som 44 C2
Weare Giffard Devon 25 C7
Wearhead Durham 232 D3
Wearne Som 28 B6
Weasdale Cumb 222 E3
Weasenham All Saints
Norf 158 E6
Weasenham St Peter
Norf 159 E7
Weaste Gtr Man 184 B4
Weatherhill Sur 51 E10
Weatheroak Hill
Worcs 117 C11
Weaverham W Ches 183 G10
Weavering Street Kent 53 B9
Weaverslake Staffs 152 F2
Weaverthorpe N Yorks 217 E9
Webbington Som 43 B11
Webheath Worcs 117 D10
Webscott Shrops 149 E9
Wecock Hants 33 E11
Wedderlairs Aberds 303 F8
Wedderlie Borders 272 E2
Weddington Kent 55 B9
Weddington Warks 135 E7
Wedhampton Wilts 46 B5
Wedmore Som 44 D2
Wednesbury W Mid 133 D9
Wednesbury Oak
W Mid 133 E9
Wednesfield W Mid 133 C8
Weecar Notts 172 B4
Weedon Bucks 84 B4
Weedon Bec Northants 120 F2
Weedon Lois Northants 102 B2
Weeford Staffs 134 C2
Week Devon 8 C5
Week Devon 12 E5
Week Devon 25 B9
Week Devon 26 D2
Week Green Corn 11 B10
Week St Mary Corn 11 B10
Weeke Devon 26 F3
Weeke Hants 48 G3
Weekley Northants 137 G7
Weekmoor Som 27 B10
Weeks I o W 21 C7
Weel E Yorks 209 F7
Weeley Essex 108 G2
Weeley Heath Essex 108 G3
Weelsby NE Lincs 201 F9
Weem Perth 286 C2
Weeping Cross Staffs 151 E8
Weethley Warks 117 F11
Weethley Bank Warks 117 G11
Weethley Gate Warks 117 G11
Weeting Norf 140 F5
Weeton E Yorks 201 C11
Weeton Lancs 202 G3
Weeton N Yorks 205 D11
Weetwood W Yorks 205 F11
Weetwood Common
W Ches 167 B8
Weetwood Hall
Northumb 264 D2
Weir Essex 69 B10
Weir Lancs 195 B11
Weir Quay Devon 7 C8
Weirbrook Shrops 148 E6
Welborne Norf 159 G11
Welborne Common
Norf 141 B11
Welbourn Lincs 173 E7
Welburn N Yorks 216 C3
Welburn N Yorks 216 F4
Welbury N Yorks 225 E7
Welby Lincs 155 B9
Welches Dam Cambs 139 F9
Welcombe Devon 24 D2
Weld Bank Lancs 194 D5
Weldon Northants 137 F8
Weldon Northumb 252 D4
Welford Northants 136 G2
Welford W Berks 64 E2
Welford-on-Avon
Warks 118 G3
Welham Leics 136 E5
Welham Notts 188 E2
Welham Som 45 G7
Welham Green Herts 86 D2
Welhambridge E Yorks 207 G11
Well Hants 49 D9
Well Lincs 190 G6
Well N Yorks 214 C5
Well Bottom Dorset 30 D6
Well End Bucks 65 B11
Well End Herts 86 F2
Well Green Gtr Man 184 D3
Well Heads W Yorks 205 G7
Well Hill Kent 68 G3
Well Place Oxon 65 B7
Well Street Kent 53 B7
Well Town Devon 26 F6
Welland Worcs 98 C5
Welland Stone Worcs 98 D6
Wellbank Angus 287 D8
Wellbrook E Sus 37 B9
Welldale Dumfries 238 D5
Weller's Town Kent 52 E4
Wellesbourne Warks 118 F5
Wellheads Aberds 302 F4
Wellhouse W Berks 64 E4
Wellhouse W Yorks 196 E5
Welling London 68 D3
Wellingborough
Northants 121 D7
Wellingham Norf 159 E7
Wellingore Lincs 173 D7
Wellington Cumb 219 E11
Wellington Hereford 97 B9
Wellington Som 27 C10
Wellington Telford 150 G3
Wellington Heath
Hereford 98 C4
Wellington Hill W Yorks 206 F2
Wellisford Som 27 C9
Wellow Bath 45 B8
Wellow I o W 20 D3
Wellow NE Lincs 201 F9
Wellow Notts 171 B11
Wellow Wood Hants 32 C3
Wellpond Green Herts 105 G8
Wellroyd W Yorks 205 F10
Wells Som 44 D5
Wells Green E Ches 167 E11
Wells-Next-The-Sea
Norf 176 E6
Wellsborough Leics 135 C7
Wellsprings Som 28 B2
Wellstye Green Essex 87 B10
Wellswood Torbay 9 C8
Welltown Corn 6 B2
Wellwood Fife 279 D11
Welney Norf 139 E10
Welsford Devon 24 C3
Welsh Bicknor Hereford 79 B9
Welsh End Shrops 149 B10
Welsh Frankton Shrops 149 C7
Welsh Harp London 67 B8
Welsh Hook Pembs 91 F8
Welsh Newton Hereford 79 B7
Welsh Newton
Common Hereford 79 B8
Welsh St Donats V Glam 58 D4
Welshampton Shrops 149 B8
Welshpool Powys 130 B4
Welshwood Park Essex 107 F10
Welstor Devon 13 G10
Welton Bath 45 C7
Welton Cumb 230 C3
Welton E Ayrs 258 D2
Welton E Yorks 200 B3
Welton Lincs 189 F8
Welton Northants 119 D11
Welton Hill Lincs 189 E8
Welton le Marsh Lincs 175 B7
Welton le Wold Lincs 190 D3
Welwick E Yorks 201 C10
Welwyn Herts 86 B2
Welwyn Garden City
Herts 86 C2
Wem Shrops 149 D10
Wembdon Som 43 F9
Wembley London 67 B7
Wembley Park London 67 B7
Wembury Devon 7 F10
Wembworthy Devon 25 F11
Wemyss Bay Invclyd 266 B3
Wenallt Ceredig 112 C3
Wenallt Gwyn 146 F4
Wenallt Gwyn 165 G7
Wendens Ambo Essex 105 D10
Wendlebury Oxon 83 B9
Wendling Norf 159 G8
Wendover Bucks 84 D5
Wendover Dean Bucks 84 E5
Wendron Corn 2 C5
Wendy Cambs 104 B6
Wenfordbridge Corn 11 F7
Wenhaston Suff 127 B8
Wenhaston Black
Heath Suff 127 C8
Wennington Cambs 122 B4
Wennington Lancs 212 E2
Wennington London 68 C4
Wensley Derbys 170 C3
Wensley N Yorks 213 B11
Wentbridge W Yorks 198 D3
Wentnor Shrops 131 E7
Wentworth Cambs 123 B9
Wentworth S Yorks 186 B5
Wenvoe V Glam 58 E6
Weobley Hereford 115 G8
Weobley Marsh
Hereford 115 G8
Weoley Castle W Mid 133 G10
Wepham W Sus 35 F8
Wepre Flint 166 B3
Wereham Norf 140 C3
Wereham Row Norf 140 C3
Wereton Staffs 168 E3
Wergs W Mid 133 C7
Wern Gwyn 145 B10
Wern Powys 77 B10
Wern Powys 147 G9
Wern Powys 148 E5
Wern Powys 148 G5
Wern Shrops 148 C5
Wern Swansea 56 C4
Wern ddu Shrops 148 D4
Wern-Gifford Mon 96 G6
Wern-olau Swansea 56 B5
Wern Tarw Bridgend 58 C3
Wern-y-cwrt Mon 78 D5
Wern-y-gaer Flint 166 B2
Werneth Gtr Man 196 G2
Werneth Low Gtr Man 185 C7
Wernffrwd Swansea 56 C4
Wernlas Shrops 148 E6
Wernrheolydd Mon 78 C5
Wernyrheolydd Mon 78 C5
Werrington Corn 12 D2
Werrington P'boro 138 C3
Werrington Staffs 168 F6
Wervin W Ches 182 G6
Wescoe Hill N Yorks 205 D11
Wesham Lancs 202 G4
Wessington Derbys 170 D5
West Aberthaw V Glam 58 F4
West Acre Norf 158 F5
West Acton London 67 C7
West Adderbury Oxon 101 D9
West Allerdean
Northumb 273 F9
West Allotment T & W 243 C8
West Alvington Devon 8 G4
West Amesbury Wilts 46 E6
West Anstey Devon 26 B5
West Appleton N Yorks 224 G4
West Ardhu Argyll 288 D6
West Ardsley W Yorks 197 B9
West Ardwell Dumfries 236 E2
West Arthurlie E Renf 267 D9
West Ashby Lincs 190 G3
West Ashford Devon 40 F4
West Ashling W Sus 22 B4
West Ashton Wilts 45 B11
West Auckland Durham 233 F9
West Ayton N Yorks 217 C9
West Bagborough Som 43 G7
West Bank Bl Gwent 78 D2
West Bank Halton 183 E8
West Barkwith Lincs 189 E11
West Barnby N Yorks 226 C6
West Barnes London 67 F8
West Barns E Loth 282 F3
West Barsham Norf 159 C8
West Bay Dorset 16 C5
West Beckham Norf 160 B2
West Bedfont Sur 66 E5
West Benhar N Lnrk 269 C7
West Bergholt Essex 107 F9
West Bexington Dorset 16 D6
West Bilney Norf 158 F4
West Blackdene
Durham 232 D3
West Blackdown Devon 12 E5
West Blatchington
Brighton 36 F3
West Bold Borders 261 B9
West Boldon T & W 243 E9
West Bourton Dorset 30 B3
West Bowling W Yorks 205 G9
West Bradford Lancs 203 E10
West Bradley Som 44 F5
West Bretton W Yorks 197 E9
West Bridgford Notts 153 B11
West Brompton London 67 D9
West Bromwich
W Mid 133 E10
West Broughton
Derbys 152 C2
West Buckland Devon 41 G7
West Buckland Som 27 C11
West Burnside Aberds 293 F8
West Burrafirth
Shetland 313 H4
West Burton N Yorks 213 B10
West Burton W Sus 35 E7
West Butsfield Durham 233 C8
West Butterwick
N Lincs 199 F10
West Byfleet Sur 66 G4
West Caister Norf 161 G10
West Calder W Loth 269 C10
West Camel Som 29 C9
West Carlton W Yorks 205 E10
West Carr Hull 209 G7
West Carr N Lincs 199 F8
West Chadsmoor Staffs 151 G9
West Challow Oxon 63 B11
West Charleton Devon 8 G5
West Chelborough
Dorset 29 F8
West Chevington
Northumb 252 D6
West Chiltington W Sus 35 D9
West Chiltington
Common W Sus 35 D9
West Chinnock Som 29 E7
West Chirton T & W 243 D8
West Chisenbury Wilts 46 C6
West Clandon Sur 50 C4
West Cliff Bmouth 19 C7
West Cliff N Yorks 227 C7
West Cliffe Kent 55 E10
West Clyne Highld 311 J2
West Clyth Highld 310 F6
West Coker Som 29 E8
West Common Hants 32 G6
West Compton Dorset 17 C7
West Compton Som 44 E5
West Cornforth
Durham 234 E2
West Cowick E Yorks 199 C7
West Cranmore Som 45 E7
West Cross Kent 53 G10
West Cross Swansea 56 D6
West Crudwell Wilts 80 G6
West Clyne Highld 311 J2
West Clyth Highld 310 F6
West Cullery Aberds 293 C9
West Curry Corn 11 C11
West Curthwaite Cumb 230 B2
West Darlochan Argyll 255 E7
West Dean W Sus 34 E5
West Dean Wilts 32 B3
West Deeping Lincs 138 B2
West Denant Pembs 72 C6
West Denton T & W 242 D5
West Derby Mers 182 C5
West Dereham Norf 140 C3
West Didsbury Gtr Man 184 C4
West Down Devon 40 E4
West Down Hants 47 F11
West Downs Corn 5 C10
West Drayton London 66 D5
West Drayton Notts 188 G2
West Dulwich London 67 E10
West Ealing London 67 C7
West Edge Derbys 170 C4
West Ella E Yorks 200 B4
West End Beds 121 E11
West End Beds 121 G9
West End Brack 65 E11
West End Bracknell 66 G2
West End Caerph 78 F2
West End Cumb 239 F8
West End Dorset 30 G6
West End Esher 66 G6
West End E Yorks 201 B9
West End E Yorks 208 G4
West End E Yorks 209 B9
West End E Yorks 209 G9
West End E Yorks 217 G11
West End Glos 80 F5
West End Hants 33 E7
West End Hants 33 F9
West End Hants 48 F6
West End Herts 86 D3
West End Kent 54 B2
West End Kent 71 F7
West End Lancs 195 B8
West End Lancs 211 G8
West End Leics 153 F8
West End Lincs 174 F5
West End Lincs 190 B5
West End Mon 78 F6
West End N Som 60 F3
West End N Yorks 205 B8
West End N Yorks 206 E6
West End N Yorks 207 F7
West End Norf 141 B8
West End Norf 161 G10
West End Oxon 64 B5
West End Oxon 82 E6
West End S Glos 61 B8
West End S Lnrk 269 F9
West End S Yorks 199 F7
West End Som 44 C5
West End Som 45 G7
West End Suff 143 G9
West End Surry Heath 49 E10
West End W Sus 36 D2
West End W Yorks 197 B8
West End W Yorks 205 F10
West End Wilts 30 C6
West End Wilts 31 C7
West End Wilts 62 D3
West End Windsor 65 D10
West End Worcs 99 D11
West End = Marian-y-
mor Gwyn 145 C7
West End Green Hants 65 G7
West-end Town V Glam 58 F3
West Ewell Sur 67 G8
West Farleigh Kent 53 C8
West Farndon
Northants 119 G10
West Felton Shrops 148 D6
West Fenton E Loth 281 E9
West Ferry Dundee 287 D8
West Field N Lincs 200 D6
West Field York 207 C7
West Fields W Berks 64 F3
West Firle E Sus 23 D7
West Fleetham
Northumb 264 D5
West Flodden
Northumb 263 C10
West Garforth W Yorks 206 G3
West Ginge Oxon 64 B2
West Gorton Gtr Man 184 B5
West Grafton Wilts 63 G8
West Green Hants 49 B8
West Green London 67 B10
West Green S Yorks 197 F11
West Green W Sus 51 F9
West Greenskares
Aberds 303 C7
West Grimstead Wilts 32 B2
West Grinstead W Sus 35 C11
West Haddlesey
N Yorks 198 B5
West Haddon Northants 120 C2
West Hagbourne Oxon 64 B4
West Hagley Worcs 133 G8
West Hall Cumb 240 D3
West Hallam Derbys 170 G6
West Halton N Lincs 200 C2
West Ham Hants 48 C6
West Ham London 68 C2
West Hampstead London 67 B9
West Handley Derbys 186 F5
West Hanney Oxon 82 G6
West Hanningfield
Essex 88 F2
West Hardwick W Yorks 198 D2
West Harling Norf 141 G9
West Harlsey N Yorks 225 F8
West Harnham Wilts 31 B10
West Harptree Bath 44 B5
West Harrow London 66 B6
West Harting W Sus 34 C3
West Harton T & W 243 E9
West Hatch Som 28 C3
West Hatch Wilts 30 B6
West Head Norf 139 B11
West Heath E Ches 168 C4
West Heath Hants 48 B5
West Heath Hants 49 B11
West Heath London 68 D3
West Heath W Mid 117 B10
West Helmsdale Highld 311 H4
West Hendon London 67 B8
West Hendred Oxon 64 B2
West Herrington
T & W 243 G8
West Heslerton N Yorks 217 D8
West Hewish N Som 59 G11
West Hill Devon 15 C7
West Hill E Sus 38 E4
West Hill E Yorks 218 F3
West Hill London 67 E8
West Hill N Som 60 D3
West Hill Som 30 B2
West Hill Staffs 151 G9
West Hill W Sus 51 G10
West Hill Wilts 61 F11
West Hoathly W Sus 51 G11
West Holme Dorset 18 D3
West Holywell T & W 243 C8
West Horndon Essex 68 B6
West Horrington Som 44 D5
West Horsley Sur 50 C5
West Horton Northumb 264 C2
West Hougham Kent 55 E9
West Houlland
Shetland 313 H4
West Houses Lincs 174 E4
West Howe Bmouth 19 B7
West Howetown Som 42 G2
West Huntington York 207 B8
West Huntspill Som 43 E10
West Hurn Dorset 19 B8
West Hyde Herts 85 G8
West Hynish Argyll 288 F1
West Hythe Kent 54 G6
West Ilkerton Devon 41 D8
West Ilsley W Berks 64 C3
West Itchenor W Sus 22 C3
West Jesmond T & W 243 D7
West Keal Lincs 174 C5
West Kennett Wilts 62 F6
West Kensington
London 67 D8
West Kilbride N Ayrs 266 F4
West Kilburn London 67 C8
West Kingsdown Kent 68 G5
West Kingston W Sus 35 G9
West Kington Wilts 61 D10
West Kington Wick
Wilts 61 D10
West Kinharrachie
Aberds 303 F9
West Kirby Mers 182 D2
West Kirkby Mers 182 D2
West Knapton N Yorks 217 D7
West Knighton Dorset 17 D10
West Knoyle Wilts 45 G11
West Kyloe Northumb 273 G11
West Kyo Durham 242 G5
West Lambrook Som 28 D6
West Langdon Kent 55 D10
West Langwell Highld 309 J6
West Lavington W Sus 34 C5
West Lavington Wilts 46 C4
West Layton N Yorks 224 D2
West Lea Durham 234 B4
West Leake Notts 153 D10
West Learmouth
Northumb 263 B9
West Leigh Devon 25 F11
West Leigh Hants 22 B2
West Leigh Som 42 G6
West Lexham Norf 158 F6
West Lilling N Yorks 216 F2
West Linton Borders 270 E2
West Liss Hants 34 B3
West Littleton S Glos 61 D9
West Lockinge Oxon 64 B2
West Looe Corn 6 E5
West Luccombe Som 41 D11
West Lulworth Dorset 18 E2
West Lutton N Yorks 217 F8
West Lydford Som 44 G5
West Lydiatt Hereford 97 C11
West Lyn Devon 41 D8
West Lyng Som 28 B4
West Lynn Norf 158 E2
West Mains Borders 271 F11
West Mains S Lnrk 268 E2
West Malling Kent 53 B7
West Malvern Worcs 98 B5
West Marden W Sus 34 E3
West Marina E Sus 38 F3
West Markham Notts 188 G2
West Marsh NE Lincs 201 E9
West Marton N Yorks 204 C3
West Mathers Aberds 293 G9
West Melbury Dorset 30 C5
West Melton S Yorks 198 G2
West Meon Hants 33 C10
West Meon
Woodlands Hants 33 B10
West Merkland Highld 308 F3
West Mersea Essex 89 C8
West Milton Dorset 16 B6
West Minster Kent 70 E2
West Molesey Sur 66 F6
West Monkseaton
T & W 243 C8
West Monkton Som 28 B3
West Moor T & W 243 C7
West Moors Dorset 31 G9
West Morden Dorset 18 B4
West Morriston
Borders 272 G2
West Morton W Yorks 205 E7
West Mudford Som 29 C9
West Muir Angus 293 G7
West Myreriggs Perth 286 C6
West Ness N Yorks 216 D3
West Newham
Northumb 242 B3
West Newton E Yorks 209 F9
West Newton Norf 158 D3
West Newton Som 28 B3
West Norwood London 67 E10
West Ogwell Devon 14 G2
West Orchard Dorset 30 D4
West Overton Wilts 62 F6
West Panson Devon 12 C2
West Park Hrtlpl 234 E5
West Park Hull 200 B5
West Park Mers 183 B7
West Park T & W 243 D9
West Park W Yorks 205 F11
West Parley Dorset 19 B7
West Pasture Durham 232 G4
West Peckham Kent 52 C6
West Pelton Durham 242 G6
West Pennard Som 44 F4
West Pentire Corn 4 C5
West Perry Cambs 122 D2
West Pontnewydd Torf 78 F3
West Poringland Norf 142 C5
West Porlock Som 41 D11
West Portholland Corn 5 G9
West Porton Renfs 277 G8
West Pulham Dorset 30 F2
West Putford Devon 24 D5
West Quantoxhead Som 42 E6
West Rainton Durham 234 B2
West Rasen Lincs 189 D9
West Ravendale
NE Lincs 190 B2
West Raynham Norf 159 D7
West Retford Notts 187 E11
West Rounton N Yorks 225 E8
West Row Suff 124 B3
West Royd W Yorks 205 F9
West Rudham Norf 158 D6
West Ruislip London 66 B5
West Runton Norf 177 E11
West Saltoun E Loth 271 B9
West Sandford Devon 26 G4
West Sandwick
Shetland 312 E6
West Scholes W Yorks 205 G7
West Scrafton N Yorks 213 C11
West Shepton Som 44 E6
West Side Bl Gwent 77 D11
West Side Orkney 314 C5
West Skelston
Dumfries 247 F8
West Sleekburn
Northumb 253 G7
West Somerton Norf 161 F9
West Southbourne
Bmouth 19 C8
West Stafford Dorset 17 D10
West Stockwith Notts 188 C3
West Stoke Devon 13 G9
West Stoke Som 29 D7
West Stoke W Sus 22 B4
West Stonesdale
N Yorks 223 E7
West Stoughton Som 44 D2
West Stour Dorset 30 C3
West Stourmouth Kent 71 G9
West Stow Suff 124 C6
West Stowell Wilts 62 G6
West Strathan Highld 308 C5
West Stratton Hants 48 E4
West Street Kent 54 C2
West Street Kent 55 C10
West Street Medway 69 D8
West Street Suff 125 C9
West Tanfield N Yorks 214 D5
West Taphouse Corn 6 C3
West Tarbert Argyll 275 G9
West Tarring W Sus 35 G10
West Third Borders 262 B4
West Thirston
Northumb 252 D5
West Thorney W Sus 22 C3
West Thurrock Thurrock 68 D5
West Tilbury Thurrock 69 D7
West Tisted Hants 33 B11
West Tofts Norf 140 E6
West Tofts Perth 286 D5
West Tolgus Corn 4 G3
West Torrington Lincs 189 E10
West Town Bath 60 G4
West Town Devon 14 B3
West Town Devon 24 C4
West Town Hants 21 B10
West Town Hereford 115 E8
West Town N Som 60 F3
West Town Som 44 F4
West Town W Sus 36 D3
West Tytherley Hants 32 B3
West Tytherton Wilts 62 E2
West Vale W Yorks 196 C5
West View Hrtlpl 234 D5
West Village V Glam 58 E3
West Walton Norf 157 G9
West Walton Highway
Norf 157 G9
West Watergate Corn 6 E4
West Watford Herts 85 F10
West Wellow Hants 32 D3
West Wemyss Fife 280 C6
West Wick N Som 59 G11
West Wickham Cambs 106 B2
West Wickham London 67 F11
West Williamston
Pembs 73 D8
West Willoughby Lincs 173 G7
West Winch Norf 158 F2
West Winterslow Wilts 47 G8
West Wittering W Sus 21 B11
West Witton N Yorks 213 B11
West Woodburn
Northumb 251 F9
West Woodhay W Berks 63 G11
West Woodlands Som 45 E9
West Worldham Hants 49 F8
West Worlington Devon 26 E3
West Worthing W Sus 35 G10
West Wratting Cambs 124 G2
West Wycombe Bucks 84 G4
West Wylam Northumb 242 E4
West Yatton Wilts 61 E11
West Yell Shetland 312 E6
West Yeo Som 43 G10
West Yoke Kent 68 F5
West Youlstone Corn 24 D3
Westacott Devon 40 G5
Westbere Kent 71 G7
Westborough Lincs 172 G5
Westbourne Bmouth 19 C7
Westbourne Suff 108 B2
Westbourne W Sus 22 B3
Westbourne Green
London 67 C9
Westbrook Hereford 96 C5
Westbrook Kent 71 E10
Westbrook Sur 50 E3
Westbrook W Berks 64 E2
Westbrook Warr 183 C9
Westbrook Wilts 62 F3
Westbrook Green Norf 142 G2
Westbrook Hay Herts 85 D8
Westburn S Lnrk 268 C3
Westbury Bucks 102 D2
Westbury Shrops 131 B7
Westbury Wilts 45 C11
Westbury Leigh Wilts 45 C11
Westbury-on-Severn
Glos 80 C2
Westbury on Trym Bristol 60 D5
Westbury Park Bristol 60 D5
Westbury-sub-Mendip
Som 44 D4
Westby Lancs 202 G3
Westby Lincs 155 D9
Westcliff-on-Sea
Sthend 69 B11
Westcombe Som 29 B7
Westcombe Som 45 F7
Westcot Oxon 63 B10
Westcote Glos 100 G4
Westcotes Leicester 135 C11
Westcott Bucks 84 B2
Westcott Devon 27 G8
Westcott Shrops 131 C8
Westcott Sur 50 D6
Westcott Barton Oxon 101 F8
Westcourt Wilts 63 G8
Westcroft M Keynes 102 E6
Westcroft W Mid 133 C8
Westdean E Sus 23 F8
Westdene Brighton 36 F3
Westdown Camp Wilts 46 D4
Westdowns Corn 11 E7
Westend Oxon 100 G6
Westend S Glos 79 G10
Westend Town
Northumb 241 D7
Westenhanger Kent 54 F6
Wester Aberchalder
Highld 300 G5
Wester Arboll Highld 311 L2
Wester Auchinloch
N Lnrk 278 G3
Wester Auchnagallin
Highld 301 F10
Wester Balgedie Perth 286 G5
Wester Brae Highld 300 C6
Wester Broomhouse
E Loth 282 F3
Wester Craiglands
Highld 301 D7
Wester Culbeuchly
Aberds 302 C6
Wester Dalvoult
Highld 291 B11
Wester Dechmont
W Loth 269 B10
Wester Deloraine
Borders 261 E8
Wester Denoon Angus 287 C7
Wester Ellister Argyll 254 B2
Wester Essendy Perth 286 C5
Wester Essenside
Borders 261 E10
Wester Feddal Perth 286 G2
Wester Fintray
Aberds 293 B10
Wester Galgantray
Highld 301 E8
Wester Gospetry Fife 286 G5
Wester Gruinards
Highld 309 K5
Wester Hailes Edin 270 B4
Wester Housebyres
Borders 262 B2
Wester Kershope
Borders 261 D9
Wester Lealty Highld 300 B6
Wester Lix Stirl 285 E9
Wester Milton Highld 301 D9
Wester Mosshead
Aberds 302 F5
Wester Newburn Fife 287 G8
Wester Ord Aberds 293 C10
Wester Parkgate
Dumfries 248 F2
Wester Quarff Shetland 313 K6
Wester Skeld Shetland 313 J4
Wester Strath Highld 300 D6
Wester Watten Highld 310 D6
Westerdale Highld 310 D5
Westerdale N Yorks 226 D3
Westerfield Shetland 313 H5
Westerfield Suff 108 B3
Westerfolds Moray 301 C11
Westergate W Sus 22 C6
Westerham Kent 52 C2
Westerhope T & W 242 D5
Westerleigh S Glos 61 D8
Westerleigh Hill S Glos 61 D8
Western Bank Cumb 229 B10
Western Downs Staffs 151 E8
Western Heights Kent 55 E10
Western Hill Durham 233 C11
Western Park
Leicester 135 C11
Westerton Aberds 293 B9
Westerton Aberds 302 E5
Westerton Angus 287 B10
Westerton Durham 233 E10
Westerton Moray 302 D3
Westerton W Sus 22 B5
Westertown Aberds 303 F7
Westerwick Shetland 313 J4
Westfield Bath 45 C7
Westfield Cumb 228 F5
Westfield E Sus 38 D4
Westfield Hants 21 B10
Westfield Hereford 98 B4
Westfield Highld 310 C4
Westfield N Lnrk 278 G4
Westfield Norf 141 B9

Westfield Redcar 235 G7
Westfield S Yorks 186 E6
Westfield Sur 50 B4
Westfield W Loth 279 G8
Westfield W Yorks 197 C8
Westfield W Yorks 205 E9
Westfield Sole Kent 69 G9
Westfields Dorset 30 F2
Westfields Hereford 97 C9
Westfields of Rattray Perth 286 C5
Westford Som 27 C10
Westgate Durham 232 D4
Westgate N Lincs 199 F9
Westgate Norf 176 E4
Westgate Norf 177 E7
Westgate Hill W Yorks 197 B8
Westgate on Sea Kent 71 E10
Westgate Street Norf 160 E3
Westhall Aberds 302 G6
Westhall Suff 143 G8
Westhall Hill Oxon 82 C3
Westham Dorset 17 F9
Westham E Sus 23 E10
Westham Som 44 D2
Westhampnett W Sus 22 B5
Westhay Som 44 E2
Westhead Lancs 194 F2
Westhide Hereford 97 C11
Westhill Aberds 293 C10
Westhill E Yorks 209 F10
Westhill Highld 301 E7
Westhope Hereford 115 G9
Westhope Shrops 131 F9
Westhorp Northants 119 G10
Westhorpe Lincs 156 C4
Westhorpe Notts 171 E11
Westhorpe Suff 125 D10
Westhoughton Gtr Man 195 F7
Westhouse N Yorks 212 E3
Westhouses Derbys 170 D6
Westhumble Sur 51 C7
Westing Shetland 312 C7
Westington Glos 100 D2
Westlake Devon 8 E2
Westland Argyll 275 G11
Westland Green Herts 105 G8
Westlands Staffs 168 G4
Westlands Worcs 117 E7
Westlea Northumb 252 G6
Westlea Swindon 62 C6
Westleigh Devon 25 B7
Westleigh Devon 27 D9
Westleigh Gtr Man 194 G6
Westleton Suff 127 D8
Westley Shrops 131 B7
Westley Suff 124 E6
Westley Heights Essex 69 B7
Westley Waterless Cambs 124 F2
Westlington Bucks 84 C3
Westlinton Cumb 239 E9
Westmancote Worcs 99 D8
Westmarsh Kent 71 G9
Westmeston E Sus 36 E4
Westmill Herts 104 E3
Westmill Herts 105 F7
Westminster London 67 D10
Westmoor End Cumb 229 D8
Westmuir Angus 287 B7
Westness Orkney 314 D3
Westnewton Cumb 229 C8
Westnewton Northumb 263 C10
Westoe T & W 243 D9
Weston Bath 61 F8
Weston Devon 15 D9
Weston Devon 27 G10
Weston Dorset 17 G9
Weston Dorset 29 F8
Weston E Ches 168 E2
Weston E Ches 184 G5
Weston Halton 183 E8
Weston Hants 34 C2
Weston Hereford 115 F7
Weston Herts 104 E5
Weston Lincs 156 D5
Weston N Yorks 205 D9
Weston Northants 101 B11
Weston Notts 172 B3
Weston Pembs 73 C8
Weston S Lnrk 269 F10
Weston Shrops 114 C6
Weston Shrops 131 E11
Weston Shrops 148 D5
Weston Shrops 149 D11
Weston Soton 32 E6
Weston Staffs 151 D9
Weston Suff 143 F8
Weston W Berks 63 E11
Weston Bampfylde Som 29 C10
Weston Beggard Hereford 97 C11
Weston by Welland Northants 136 E5
Weston Colley Hants 48 F4
Weston Colville Cambs 124 G2
Weston Common Soton 33 E7
Weston Corbett Hants 49 D7
Weston Coyney Stoke 168 G6
Weston Ditch Suff 124 B3
Weston Favell Northants 120 E5
Weston Green Cambs 124 G2
Weston Green Norf 160 G2
Weston Green Sur 67 F7
Weston Heath Shrops 150 G5
Weston Hills Lincs 156 E5
Weston in Arden Warks 135 F7
Weston-in-Gordano N Som 60 E2
Weston Jones Staffs 150 E5
Weston Longville Norf 160 F2
Weston Lullingfields Shrops 149 E8
Weston Manor I o W 20 D2
Weston Mill Plym 7 D9
Weston-on-Avon Warks 118 G3
Weston-on-the-Green Oxon 83 B8
Weston-on-Trent Derbys 153 D8
Weston Park Bath 61 F8
Weston Patrick Hants 49 D7
Weston Point Halton 183 E7
Weston Rhyn Shrops 148 B5
Weston-sub-Edge Glos 100 C2
Weston-super-Mare N Som 59 G10
Weston Town Som 45 E8
Weston Turville Bucks 84 C5
Weston under Lizard Staffs 150 G6
Weston under Penyard Hereford 98 G2
Weston under Wetherley Warks 119 D7
Weston Underwood Derbys 170 G3
Weston Underwood M Keynes 121 G7
Westonbirt Glos 61 B11
Westoncommon Shrops 149 D8
Westoning C Beds 103 E10
Westonwharf Shrops 149 D8
Westonzoyland Som 43 G11
Westow N Yorks 216 F5
Westowe Som 42 G6
Westown Devon 27 E10
Westown Perth 286 E6
Westport Argyll 255 E7
Westport Som 28 D5
Westquarter Falk 279 F8
Westra V Glam 58 E6
Westridge Green W Berks 64 D5
Westrigg W Loth 269 B8
Westrip Glos 80 D4
Westrop Wilts 61 E11
Westrop Green W Berks 64 E4
Westruther Borders 272 F2
Westry Cambs 139 D7
Westthorpe Derbys 187 F7
Westvale Mers 182 B6
Westville Devon 8 G4
Westville Notts 171 F8
Westward Cumb 229 C11
Westward Ho! Devon 24 B6
Westweekmoor Devon 12 C4
Westwell Kent 54 D3
Westwell Oxon 82 D2
Westwell Leacon Kent 54 D3
Westwells Wilts 61 F11
Westwick Cambs 123 D8
Westwick Durham 223 B11
Westwick Norf 160 D5
Westwick Row Herts 85 D9
Westwood Devon 14 B6
Westwood Devon 14 E5
Westwood Kent 55 D7
Westwood Kent 71 F11
Westwood Notts 171 E7
Westwood P'boro 138 D3
Westwood S Lnrk 268 E2
Westwood Wilts 45 B10
Westwood Wilts 46 G6
Westwood Heath W Mid 118 B5
Westwood Park Essex 107 E9
Westwood Park Gtr Man 184 B3
Westwoodside N Lincs 188 B3
Westy Warr 183 D10
Wetham Green Kent 69 F10
Wetheral Cumb 239 G11
Wetheral Plain Cumb 239 F11
Wetherby W Yorks 206 D4
Wetherden Suff 125 E10
Wetherden Upper Town Suff 125 D10
Wetheringsett Suff 126 D2
Wethersfield Essex 106 E4
Wethersta Shetland 312 G5
Wetherup Street Suff 126 E2
Wetley Rocks Staffs 169 F7
Wetmore Staffs 152 E5
Wettenhall E Ches 167 C10
Wettenhall Green E Ches 167 C10
Wettles Shrops 131 F8
Wetton Staffs 169 D10
Wetwang E Yorks 208 B4
Wetwood Staffs 150 C5
Wexcombe Wilts 47 B9
Wexham Street Bucks 66 C3
Weybourne Norf 177 E10
Weybourne Sur 49 D11
Weybread Suff 142 G4
Weybridge Sur 66 G5
Weycroft Devon 16 B2
Weydale Highld 310 C5
Weyhill Hants 47 D10
Weymouth Dorset 17 F9
Weythel Powys 114 F4
Whaddon Bucks 102 E6
Whaddon Cambs 104 B6
Whaddon Glos 80 C4
Whaddon Glos 99 G9
Whaddon Wilts 31 B11
Whaddon Wilts 61 G11
Whaddon Gap Cambs 104 B6
Whale Cumb 230 G6
Whaley Derbys 187 G8
Whaley Bridge Derbys 185 E8
Whaley Thorns Derbys 187 G8
Whaligoe Highld 310 E7
Whalley Lancs 203 F10
Whalley Banks Lancs 203 F10
Whalley Range Gtr Man 184 C4
Whalleys Lancs 194 F3
Whalton Northumb 252 G4
Wham N Yorks 212 G5
Whaplode Lincs 156 E6
Whaplode Drove Lincs 156 G6
Whaplode St Catherine Lincs 156 E6
Wharf Warks 119 G8
Wharfe N Yorks 212 F5
Wharles Lancs 202 F4
Wharley End C Beds 103 C8
Wharmley Northumb 241 D9
Wharncliffe Side S Yorks 186 C3
Wharram le Street N Yorks 217 F7
Wharram Percy N Yorks 217 G7
Wharton Hereford 115 F10
Wharton Lincs 188 C4
Wharton W Ches 167 B11
Wharton Green W Ches 167 B11
Whashton N Yorks 224 D3
Whasset Cumb 211 C10
Whatcombe Dorset 30 G4
Whatcote Warks 100 C6
Whatcroft W Ches 167 B11
Whateley Staffs 134 D4
Whatfield Suff 107 B10
Whatley Som 28 F5
Whatley Som 45 D8
Whatlington E Sus 38 D3
Whatmore Shrops 116 C2
Whatsole Street Kent 54 E6
Whatstandwell Derbys 170 E4
Whatton Notts 154 B4
Whauphill Dumfries 236 E6
Whaw N Yorks 223 E9
Wheal Alfred Corn 2 B3
Wheal Baddon Corn 4 G5
Wheal Busy Corn 4 G4
Wheal Frances Corn 4 E5
Wheal Kitty Corn 4 E4
Wheal Rose Corn 4 G4
Wheal Hold Hants 64 G5
Wheatacre Norf 143 E9
Wheatcroft Derbys 170 D5
Wheatenhurst Glos 80 D3
Wheathall Shrops 131 C9
Wheathampstead Herts 85 C11
Wheathill Shrops 132 G2
Wheathill Som 44 G5
Wheatley Devon 14 C4
Wheatley Hants 49 E9
Wheatley Oxon 83 D9
Wheatley S Yorks 198 G5
Wheatley W Yorks 196 B5
Wheatley Hill Durham 234 D3
Wheatley Hills S Yorks 198 G6
Wheatley Lane Lancs 204 F2
Wheatley Park S Yorks 198 F5
Wheaton Aston Staffs 151 G7
Wheddon Cross Som 42 F2
Wheedlemont Aberds 302 G4
Wheelbarrow Town Kent 55 D7
Wheeler End Bucks 84 G4
Wheelerstreet Sur 50 E2
Wheelock E Ches 168 D3
Wheelock Heath E Ches 168 D2
Wheelton Lancs 194 C5
Wheelton Lancs 194 C6
Wheelton Lancs 194 D5
Wheelton Lancs 194 D6
Wheen Angus 292 F5
Wheldale W Yorks 198 B3
Wheldrake York 207 D9
Whelford Glos 81 F11
Whelley Gtr Man 194 F5
Whelp Street Suff 107 B8
Whelpley Hill Herts 85 E7
Whelpo Cumb 230 D2
Whelston Flint 182 F2
Whempstead Herts 104 G6
Whenby N Yorks 216 F2
Whepstead Suff 124 F6
Wherry Town Corn 1 D5
Wherstead Suff 108 C3
Wherwell Hants 47 E11
Wheston Derbys 185 F10
Whetley Cross Dorset 29 G7
Whetsted Kent 53 D7
Whetstone Leics 135 D11
Whetstone London 86 G3
Whettleton Shrops 131 G8
Whicham Cumb 210 C2
Whichford Warks 100 E6
Whickham T & W 242 E6
Whickham Fell T & W 242 F6
Whiddon Devon 40 F5
Whiddon Down Devon 13 C9
Whifflet N Lnrk 268 C4
Whigstreet Angus 287 C8
Whilton Northants 120 E2
Whilton Locks Northants 120 E2
Whim Farm Borders 270 E4
Whimble Devon 24 G5
Whimple Devon 14 B6
Whimpwell Green Norf 161 D7
Whinburgh Norf 141 B10
Whin Lane End Lancs 202 E3
Whinfield Darl 224 B6
Whinhall N Lnrk 268 B5
Whinmoor W Yorks 206 F3
Whinney Hill S Yorks 187 C7
Whinney Hill Stockton 225 B7
Whinnieliggate Dumfries 237 D9
Whinny Heights Blkburn 195 B7
Whinnyfold Aberds 303 F10
Whins of Milton Stirl 278 C5
Whins Wood W Yorks 205 F7
Whipcott Devon 27 D9
Whippendell Botton Herts 85 E9
Whippingham I o W 20 C6
Whipsiderry Corn 4 C6
Whipsnade C Beds 85 B8
Whipton Devon 14 C5
Whirley Grove E Ches 184 F5
Whirlow S Yorks 186 E4
Whisby Lincs 172 B6
Whissendine Rutland 154 G6
Whissonsett Norf 159 E8
Whisterfield E Ches 184 G4
Whistlefield Argyll 276 C2
Whistlefield Argyll 276 C4
Whistley Green Wokingham 65 E9
Whistlow Oxon 101 F9
Whiston Mers 183 C7
Whiston Northants 120 E6
Whiston S Yorks 186 D6
Whiston Staffs 151 G7
Whiston Staffs 169 F8
Whiston Cross Mers 183 C7
Whiston Cross Shrops 132 C5
Whitacre Heath Warks 134 E4
Whitbarrow Village Cumb 230 F4
Whitbeck Cumb 210 C2
Whitbourne Hereford 116 F4
Whitbourne Moor Wilts 45 D10
Whitburn T & W 243 E10
Whitburn W Loth 269 C8
Whitburn Colliery T & W 243 E10
Whitby N Yorks 227 C7
Whitby W Ches 182 F5
Whitbyheath W Ches 182 F5
Whitchurch Bath 60 F6
Whitchurch Bucks 102 G5
Whitchurch Cardiff 59 C7
Whitchurch Devon 12 G5
Whitchurch Hants 48 D3
Whitchurch Hereford 79 B9
Whitchurch Pembs 90 F5
Whitchurch Shrops 167 G8
Whitchurch Som 30 C2
Whitchurch Canonicorum Dorset 16 B3
Whitchurch Hill Oxon 64 D6
Whitchurch-on-Thames Oxon 64 D6
Whitcombe Dorset 17 D10
Whitcombe Som 29 C10
Whitcot Shrops 131 E7
Whitcott Keysett Shrops 130 G5
White Ball Som 27 D9
White Colne Essex 107 F7
White Coppice Lancs 194 D6
White Cross Bath 44 B5
White Cross Bath 44 B6
White Cross Corn 2 E5
White Cross Corn 5 D7
White Cross Hereford 97 C9
White Cross Som 43 D10
White Cross Wilts 45 G9
White Cross Hill Cambs 123 B9
White End Worcs 98 E5
White Gate Gtr Man 195 G11
White Gate Som 28 F4
White Grit Shrops 130 D6
White Hall Herts 104 G5
White Hill Bath 45 B8
White Hill W Yorks 204 E6
White Hill Wilts 45 G10
White Hills Northants 120 E4
White House Suff 108 B2
White Houses Notts 188 F2
White Lackington Dorset 17 B10
White Ladies Aston Worcs 117 G8
White-le-Head Durham 242 G5
White Lee W Yorks 197 B8
White Lund Lancs 211 G8
White Mill Carms 93 G9
White Moor Derbys 170 F5
White Ness Shetland 313 J5
White Notley Essex 88 B3
White Oak Kent 68 F4
White Ox Mead Bath 45 B8
White Pit Lincs 190 F5
White Post Kent 52 E4
White Post Notts 171 D10
White Rocks Hereford 97 G8
White Roding or White Roothing Essex 87 C9
White Stake Lancs 194 B4
White Stone Hereford 97 C11
White Waltham Windsor 65 D10
Whiteacen Moray 302 E2
Whiteacre Kent 54 D6
Whiteacre Heath Warks 134 E4
Whiteash Green Essex 106 E5
Whitebirk Blkburn 195 B8
Whitebog Highld 301 C7
Whitebridge Highld 290 B6
Whitebrook Mon 79 D8
Whiteburn Borders 271 F11
Whitebushes Sur 51 D9
Whitecairn Dumfries 236 D4
Whitecairns Aberds 293 B11
Whitecastle S Lnrk 269 G10
Whitechapel Lancs 203 E7
Whitechapel London 67 C10
Whitechurch Maund Hereford 97 B11
Whitecleat Orkney 314 F5
Whitecliff Glos 79 C9
Whiteclosegate Cumb 239 F10
Whitecote W Yorks 205 F10
Whitecraig E Loth 281 G7
Whitecraigs E Renf 267 D11
Whitecroft Glos 79 D10
Whitecrook W Dunb 267 B10
Whitecross Corn 2 C2
Whitecross Corn 6 E2
Whitecross Corn 10 G5
Whitecross Falk 279 F9
Whitecross Som 28 C6
Whitecross Staffs 151 E7
Whiteface Highld 309 L7
Whitefarland N Ayrs 255 C9
Whitefaulds S Ayrs 245 B7
Whitefield Aberds 303 G7
Whitefield Dorset 18 C4
Whitefield Gtr Man 195 F10
Whitefield Perth 286 D5
Whitefield Som 27 B9
Whitefield Lane End Mers 183 D7
Whiteflat E Ayrs 258 D2
Whiteford Aberds 303 G7
Whitegate W Ches 167 B10
Whitehall Blkburn 195 C7
Whitehall Bristol 60 E6
Whitehall Devon 27 E10
Whitehall Devon 40 F4
Whitehall Hants 49 C8
Whitehall Herts 104 E6
Whitehall W Sus 35 C10
Whitehall Village Orkney 314 D6
Whitehaven Cumb 219 B9
Whitehaven Shrops 148 E5
Whitehawk Brighton 36 G4
Whiteheath Gate W Mid 133 F9
Whitehill E Sus 37 B8
Whitehill Hants 49 G9
Whitehill Kent 54 B4
Whitehill Midloth 271 B7
Whitehill Moray 302 D5
Whitehill S Lnrk 268 D4
Whitehill Staffs 168 E3
Whitehills Aberds 302 C6
Whitehills S Lnrk 268 E2
Whitehills T & W 243 E7
Whiteholme Blkpool 202 E2
Whitehouse Aberds 293 B8
Whitehouse Argyll 275 G9
Whitehouse Common W Mid 134 D2
Whitehouse Green W Berks 65 F7
Whiteinch Glasgow 267 B10
Whitekirk E Loth 281 E10
Whiteknights Reading 65 E8
Whiteknowes Aberds 293 C7
Whitelackington Som 28 D5
Whitelaw S Lnrk 268 G2
Whiteleaf Bucks 84 E4
Whiteleas T & W 243 E9
Whiteleaved Oak Glos 98 D5
Whitelee Borders 262 C3
Whitelee Northumb 250 B6
Whitelees S Ayrs 257 C9
Whiteley Bank I o W 21 E7
Whiteley Green E Ches 184 F6
Whiteley Village Sur 66 G5
Whitelye Mon 79 E8
Whitemans Green W Sus 36 B4
Whitemire Moray 301 D9
Whitemoor Corn 5 D9
Whitemoor Nottingham 171 G8
Whitemoor Warks 118 C5
Whitemore Staffs 168 C5
Whitenap Hants 32 C5
Whiteoak Green Oxon 82 C4
Whiteparish Wilts 32 C2
Whitepits Wilts 45 F10
Whiterashes Aberds 303 G8
Whiterigg Borders 262 C3
Whiterock Bridgend 58 D2
Whiterow Highld 310 E7
Whiterow Moray 301 D10
White's Green W Sus 34 B6
Whiteshill Glos 80 D4
Whiteshill S Glos 60 D6
Whiteside Northumb 240 D6
Whiteside W Loth 269 B9
Whitesmith E Sus 23 C8
Whitespots Dumfries 247 F10
Whitestaunton Som 28 E3
Whitestone Aberds 293 D8
Whitestone Devon 14 C3
Whitestone Devon 40 D3
Whitestone Warks 135 F7
Whitestones Aberds 303 D8
Whitestreet Green Suff 107 D9
Whitewall Common Mon 60 B2
Whitewall Corner N Yorks 216 E5
Whiteway Bath 61 G8
Whiteway Dorset 18 E3
Whiteway Glos 80 C6
Whiteway Glos 80 F4
Whitewell Aberds 303 C9
Whitewell Corn 11 E7
Whitewell Highld 291 C11
Whitewell Lancs 203 D9
Whitewell Wrex 167 G7
Whitewell Bottom Lancs 195 C10
Whiteworks Devon 13 G8
Whitfield Kent 55 D10
Whitfield Northants 102 D2
Whitfield Northumb 241 F7
Whitfield S Glos 79 G11
Whitfield Court Sur 50 B3
Whitfield Hall Northumb 241 F7
Whitford Devon 15 B11
Whitford = Chwitffordd Flint 181 F10
Whitgift E Yorks 199 C10
Whitgreave Staffs 151 D7
Whithaugh Borders 249 F11
Whithebir Orkney 314 C5
Whithorn Dumfries 236 E6
Whiting Bay N Ayrs 256 D2
Whitington Norf 140 D4
Whitkirk W Yorks 206 G3
Whitland = Hendy-Gwyn Carms 73 B11
Whitlaw Borders 271 F9
Whitleigh Plym 7 C9
Whitletts S Ayrs 257 E9
Whitley Gtr Man 194 F5
Whitley N Yorks 198 C5
Whitley Reading 65 E8
Whitley S Yorks 186 C4
Whitley W Mid 119 B7
Whitley Wilts 61 F11
Whitley Bay T & W 243 C9
Whitley Bridge N Yorks 198 C5
Whitley Chapel Northumb 241 F10
Whitley Head W Yorks 204 E6
Whitley Heath Staffs 150 D6
Whitley Lower W Yorks 197 D8
Whitley Reed W Ches 183 E10
Whitley Row Kent 52 C3
Whitley Sands T & W 243 C9
Whitley Thorpe N Yorks 198 C5
Whitley Wood Reading 65 F8
Whitlock's End W Mid 118 B2
Whitminster Glos 80 D3
Whitmoor Devon 27 E9
Whitmore Dorset 31 F9
Whitmore Staffs 168 G4
Whitmore Park W Mid 134 G6
Whitnage Devon 27 D8
Whitnash Warks 118 E6
Whitnell Som 43 F8
Whitney Bottom Som 28 E4
Whitney-on-Wye Hereford 96 B5
Whitrigg Cumb 229 D10
Whitrigg Cumb 238 F6
Whitriggs Borders 262 F3
Whitsbury Hants 31 D10
Whitslaid Borders 271 G11
Whitsome Borders 273 E7
Whitsomehill Borders 273 F7
Whitson Newport 59 C11
Whitstable Kent 70 F6
Whitstone Corn 11 B11
Whittingham Northumb 264 G3
Whittingslow Shrops 131 F8
Whittington Glos 99 G10
Whittington Lancs 212 D2
Whittington Norf 140 D4
Whittington Shrops 148 C6
Whittington Staffs 133 G7
Whittington Staffs 134 B3
Whittington Staffs 150 C5
Whittington Warks 134 D5
Whittington Worcs 117 G7
Whittington Moor Derbys 186 G5
Whittleford Warks 134 E6
Whittle-le-Woods Lancs 194 C5
Whittlebury Northants 102 C3
Whittlesey Cambs 138 D5
Whittlesford Cambs 105 B9
Whittlestone Head Blkburn 195 D8
Whitton Borders 263 E7
Whitton Hereford 115 C8
Whitton London 66 E6
Whitton N Lincs 200 C2
Whitton Northumb 252 C3
Whitton Powys 114 D5
Whitton Shrops 115 C11
Whitton Stockton 234 G3
Whitton Suff 108 B2
Whittonditch Wilts 63 E9
Whittonstall Northumb 242 F3
Whittytree Shrops 115 B8
Whitway Hants 48 B3
Whitwell Derbys 187 F8
Whitwell Herts 104 G3
Whitwell I o W 20 F6
Whitwell N Yorks 224 F5
Whitwell Rutland 137 B8
Whitwell-on-the-Hill N Yorks 216 F4
Whitwell Street Norf 160 E2
Whitwick Leics 153 F8
Whitwood W Yorks 198 C2
Whitworth Lancs 195 D11
Whixall Shrops 149 C10
Whixley N Yorks 206 B4
Whoberley W Mid 118 B6
Wholeflats Falk 279 E8
Whome Orkney 314 G3
Whorlton Durham 224 C2
Whorlton N Yorks 225 E9
Whydown E Sus 38 F2
Whygate Northumb 241 B7
Whyke W Sus 22 C5
Whyle Hereford 115 E11
Whyteleafe Sur 51 B10
Wibdon Glos 79 F9
Wibsey W Yorks 205 G8
Wibtoft Leics 135 F9
Wichenford Worcs 116 E5
Wichling Kent 54 B2
Wick Bmouth 19 C8
Wick Devon 27 G11
Wick Highld 310 D7
Wick S Glos 61 E8
Wick Shetland 313 K6
Wick Som 28 B6
Wick Som 43 C10
Wick Som 43 E8
Wick V Glam 58 E2
Wick W Sus 35 G8
Wick Wilts 31 C11
Wick Worcs 99 B9
Wick Episcopi Worcs 116 G6
Wick Hill Brack 65 E11
Wick Hill Kent 53 E10
Wick Hill Wokingham 65 G9
Wick Rocks S Glos 61 E8
Wick St Lawrence N Som 59 F11
Wick Street Glos 80 D5
Wicken Cambs 123 C11
Wicken Northants 102 D4
Wicken Bonhunt Essex 105 E9
Wicken Green Village Norf 158 C6
Wickenby Lincs 189 E9
Wicker Street Green Suff 107 C9
Wickersley S Yorks 187 C7
Wickford Essex 88 G3
Wickham Hants 33 E9
Wickham W Berks 63 E11
Wickham Bishops Essex 88 C4
Wickham Green Suff 125 D11
Wickham Green W Berks 63 E11
Wickham Heath W Berks 64 F2
Wickham Market Suff 126 F6
Wickham St Paul Essex 106 D6
Wickham Skeith Suff 125 D11
Wickham Street Suff 124 G5
Wickham Street Suff 125 D11
Wickhambreaux Kent 55 B8
Wickhambrook Suff 124 G4
Wickhamford Worcs 99 C11
Wickhampton Norf 143 B8
Wickham's Cross Som 44 G4
Wickhurst Kent 52 D4
Wicklane Bath 45 B7
Wicklewood Norf 141 C11
Wickmere Norf 160 C3
Wickridge Street Glos 98 F6
Wickstreet E Sus 23 D8
Wickwar S Glos 61 B8
Widbrook Wilts 45 B10
Widcombe Bath 61 G9
Widdington Essex 105 E10
Widdrington Northumb 253 D7
Widdrington Station Northumb 252 E6
Widecombe in the Moor Devon 13 F10
Widegates Corn 6 D5
Widemarsh Hereford 97 C10
Widemouth Bay Corn 24 G2
Wideopen T & W 242 C6
Widewall Orkney 314 G4
Widewell Plym 7 C9
Widford Essex 87 D11
Widford Herts 86 B6
Widgham Green Cambs 124 F3
Widham Wilts 62 B5
Widley Hants 33 F11
Widmer End Bucks 84 F5
Widmerpool Notts 154 D2
Widmoor Bucks 66 B2
Widmore London 68 F2
Widnes Halton 183 D8
Wierton Kent 53 D9
Wig Powys 130 F2
Wig Fach Bridgend 57 F10
Wigan Gtr Man 194 F5
Wiganthorpe N Yorks 216 E3
Wigbeth Dorset 31 F8
Wigborough Som 28 D6
Wiggaton Devon 15 C8
Wiggenhall St Germans Norf 157 G11
Wiggenhall St Mary Magdalen Norf 157 G11
Wiggenhall St Mary the Virgin Norf 157 G11
Wiggenhall St Peter Norf 158 G2
Wiggens Green Essex 106 C3
Wiggington Staffs 134 B4
Wigginstall Staffs 169 C9
Wigginton Herts 84 C6
Wigginton Oxon 101 E7
Wigginton Shrops 148 B6
Wigginton Staffs 134 B4
Wigginton York 207 B7
Wigginton Bottom Herts 84 D6
Wigginton Heath Oxon 101 D7
Wigglesworth N Yorks 204 B2
Wiggonby Cumb 239 G7
Wiggonholt W Sus 35 D9
Wighill N Yorks 206 D5
Wighton Norf 159 B8
Wightwick Manor Staffs 133 D7
Wigley Derbys 186 G4
Wigley Hants 32 D4
Wigmarsh Shrops 149 D7
Wigmore Hereford 115 D8
Wigmore Medway 69 G10
Wigsley Notts 188 G5
Wigsthorpe Northants 137 G10
Wigston Leics 136 D2
Wigston Magna Leics 136 D2
Wigston Parva Leics 135 F9
Wigthorpe Notts 187 E9
Wigtoft Lincs 156 B5
Wigton Cumb 229 B11
Wigtown Dumfries 236 D6
Wigtwizzle S Yorks 186 B2
Wike W Yorks 206 E2
Wike Well End S Yorks 199 E7
Wilbarston Northants 136 F6
Wilberfoss E Yorks 207 C10
Wilberlee W Yorks 196 E5
Wilburton Cambs 123 C9
Wilby Norf 141 F10
Wilby Northants 121 D7
Wilby Suff 126 C4
Wilcot Wilts 62 G6
Wilcott Shrops 149 F7
Wilcott Marsh Shrops 149 F7
Wilcove Corn 7 D8
Wilcrick Newport 60 B2
Wild Mill Bridgend 58 C2
Wilday Green Derbys 186 G4
Wildboarclough E Ches 169 B7
Wilde Street Suff 124 B4
Wilden Beds 121 F11
Wilden Worcs 116 C6
Wildern Hants 33 E7
Wildernesse Kent 52 B4
Wilderspool Warr 183 D10
Wilderswood Gtr Man 194 E6
Wildhern Hants 47 C11
Wildhill Herts 86 D3
Wildmanbridge S Lnrk 268 E6
Wildmoor Hants 49 B7
Wildmoor Oxon 83 F7
Wildmoor Worcs 117 B9
Wildridings Brack 65 F11
Wildsworth Lincs 188 B4
Wildwood Staffs 151 E8
Wilford Nottingham 153 B11
Wilgate Green Kent 54 B3
Wilkesley E Ches 167 G10
Wilkhaven Highld 311 L3
Wilkieston W Loth 270 B2
Wilkin Throop Som 29 C11
Wilkinthroop Som 29 C11
Wilksby Lincs 174 C3
Will Row Lincs 191 D7
Willacy Lane End Lancs 202 F5
Willand Devon 27 E8
Willand Som 27 E11
Willand Moor Devon 27 E8
Willard's Hill E Sus 38 C2
Willaston E Ches 167 E11
Willaston Shrops 149 B11
Willaston W Ches 182 F4
Willen M Keynes 103 C7
Willenhall W Mid 119 B7
Willenhall W Mid 133 D9
Willerby E Yorks 208 G6
Willerby N Yorks 217 D10
Willersey Glos 100 D2
Willersley Hereford 96 B6
Willesborough Kent 54 E4
Willesborough Lees Kent 54 E4
Willesden London 67 C8
Willesden Green London 67 C8
Willesley Leics 152 G6
Willesley Wilts 61 B11
Willett Som 42 G6
Willey Shrops 132 D3
Willey Warks 135 G9
Willey Green Sur 50 C2
Willhayne Som 28 E4
Williamhope Borders 261 C10
William's Green Suff 107 C9
Williamscott Oxon 101 B9
Williamslee Borders 270 G6
Williamstown Rhondda 77 G8
Williamthorpe Derbys 170 B6
Willian Herts 104 E4
Willicote Pastures Worcs 100 B3
Willingale Essex 87 D9
Willingcott Devon 40 E3
Willingdon E Sus 23 E9
Willingham Cambs 123 C8
Willingham Suff 143 G8
Willingham by Stow Lincs 188 E5
Willingham Green Cambs 124 G2
Willington Beds 104 B2
Willington Derbys 152 D5
Willington Durham 233 D9
Willington Kent 53 C9
Willington T & W 243 D8
Willington Warks 100 D5
Willington Corner W Ches 167 B8
Willington Quay T & W 243 D8
Willisham Suff 125 G11
Willisham Tye Suff 125 G11
Willitoft E Yorks 207 F10
Williton Som 42 E5
Willoughbridge Staffs 168 G3
Willoughby Lincs 191 G7
Willoughby Warks 119 D10
Willoughby Hills Lincs 174 F4
Willoughby-on-the-Wolds Notts 154 D2
Willoughby Waterleys Leics 135 E11
Willoughton Lincs 188 C6
Willow Green W Ches 183 F10
Willow Green Worcs 116 F5
Willow Holme Cumb 239 F9
Willowbank Bucks 66 B5
Willows Gtr Man 195 F8
Willows Green Essex 88 B2
Willowtown Bl Gwent 77 C11
Willsbridge S Glos 61 E7
Willslock Staffs 151 C11
Willstone Shrops 131 D9
Willsworthy Devon 12 E6
Wilmcote Warks 118 F3
Wilmington Bath 61 G7
Wilmington Devon 15 B10
Wilmington E Sus 23 E8
Wilmington Kent 68 E4
Wilmington Green E Sus 23 D8
Wilminstone Devon 12 F5
Wilmslow E Ches 184 E4
Wilmslow Park E Ches 184 E5
Wilnecote Staffs 134 C4
Wilney Green Norf 141 G11
Wilpshire Lancs 203 G9
Wilsden W Yorks 205 F7
Wilsden Hill W Yorks 205 F7
Wilsford Lincs 173 G8
Wilsford Wilts 46 B6
Wilsford Wilts 46 F6
Wilsham Devon 41 D9
Wilshaw W Yorks 196 F6
Wilsic S Yorks 187 B9
Wilsill N Yorks 214 G3
Wilsley Green Kent 53 F9
Wilsley Pound Kent 53 F9
Wilsom Hants 49 F8
Wilson Hereford 97 G11
Wilson Leics 153 E8
Wilsontown S Lnrk 269 D9
Wilstead Beds 103 C11
Wilsthorpe Derbys 153 C9
Wilsthorpe Lincs 155 G11
Wilstone Herts 84 C6
Wilstone Green Herts 84 C6
Wilthorpe S Yorks 197 F10
Wilton Borders 261 G11
Wilton Cumb 219 C10
Wilton Hereford 97 G11
Wilton N Yorks 217 C7
Wilton Redcar 225 B11
Wilton Som 28 C2
Wilton Wilts 46 G5
Wilton Wilts 63 G9
Wilton Park Bucks 85 G7
Wiltown Devon 27 D11
Wiltown Som 28 C5
Wimbish Essex 105 D11
Wimbish Green Essex 106 D2
Wimble Hill Hants 49 D10
Wimblebury Staffs 151 G10
Wimbledon London 67 E8
Wimblington Cambs 139 E8
Wimbolds Trafford W Ches 182 G6
Wimboldsley W Ches 167 C11
Wimborne Minster Dorset 18 B6
Wimborne St Giles Dorset 31 E8
Wimbotsham Norf 140 B2
Wimpole Cambs 104 B6
Wimpson Soton 32 E5
Wimpstone Warks 100 B4
Wincanton Som 30 B2
Winceby Lincs 174 B4
Wincham W Ches 183 F11
Winchburgh W Loth 279 G11
Winchcombe Glos 99 F10
Winchelsea E Sus 38 D6
Winchelsea Beach E Sus 38
Winchester Hants 33
Winchestown Bl Gwent 77 C
Winchet Hill Kent 53
Winchfield Hants 49
Winchfield Hurst Hants 49
Winchmore Hill Bucks 84 C
Winchmore Hill London 86 G
Wincle E Ches 169 E
Wincobank S Yorks 186 C
Wind Hill Cumb 210 E
Wind Hill Pembs 73 F
Winder Cumb 219 B1
Windermere Cumb 221 F
Winderton Warks 100 C
Windhill Highld 300 E
Windhill S Yorks 198 G
Windhill W Yorks 205 F
Windhouse Shetland 312 D
Winding Wood W Berks 63 E1
Windle Hill W Ches 182 F
Windlehurst Gtr Man 185 D
Windlesham Sur 66 G
Windley Derbys 170 F
Windmill Corn 10 G
Windmill Flint 181 G1
Windmill Flint 182 G
Windmill Hill Bristol 60 E
Windmill Hill E Sus 23 C1
Windmill Hill Halton 183 E
Windmill Hill Kent 69 F1
Windmill Hill Som 28 D4
Windmill Hill W Yorks 197 D1
Windmill Hill Worcs 99 B8
Windrush Glos 81 C1
Windsor N Lincs 199 E9
Windsor Windsor 66 D3
Windsor Green Suff 125 G7
Windsoredge Glos 80 E4
Windwhistle Som 28 F5
Windy Arbor Mers 183 D7
Windy Arbour Warks 118 C5
Windy Hill Wrex 166 E4
Windy Nook T & W 243 E7
Windy-Yett E Ayrs 267 E9
Windydoors Borders 261 B10
Windygates Fife 287 G7
Windyharbour E Ches 184 G4
Windyknowe W Loth 269 B9
Windywalls Borders 263 C7
Wineham W Sus 36 C2
Winestead E Yorks 201 C9
Winewall Lancs 204 E4
Winfarthing Norf 142 F2
Winford I o W 21 E7
Winford N Som 60 F4
Winforton Hereford 96 B5
Winfrith Newburgh Dorset 18 E2
Wing Bucks 103 G7
Wing Rutland 137 C7
Wingate Durham 234 D4
Wingates Gtr Man 195 F7
Wingates Northumb 252 D4
Wingerworth Derbys 170 B5
Wingfield C Beds 103 F10
Wingfield S Yorks 186 B6
Wingfield Suff 126 B4
Wingfield Wilts 45 B10
Wingfield Green Suff 126 B4
Wingfield Park Derbys 170 E5
Wingham Kent 55 B8
Wingham Green Kent 55 B8
Wingham Well Kent 55 B8
Wingmore Kent 55 D7
Wingrave Bucks 84 B5
Winkburn Notts 172 D2
Winkfield Brack 66 E2
Winkfield Place Brack 66 E2
Winkfield Row Brack 65 E11
Winkhill Staffs 169 E9
Winkhurst Green Kent 52 D3
Winklebury Hants 48 C6
Winkleigh Devon 25 F10
Winksley N Yorks 214 E5
Winkton Dorset 19 B9
Winlaton T & W 242 E5
Winlaton Mill T & W 242 E5
Winless Highld 310 D7
Winllan Powys 148 E4
Winmarleigh Lancs 202 D5
Winmarleigh Moss Lancs 202 D4
Winnal Hereford 97 E9
Winnal Common Hereford 97 E9
Winnall Hants 33 B7
Winnall Worcs 116 D6
Winnard's Perch Corn 5 B8
Winnersh Wokingham 65 E9
Winnington Staffs 150 B4
Winnington W Ches 183 G10
Winnington Green Shrops 148 G6
Winnothdale Staffs 169 G8
Winscales Cumb 228 F6
Winscombe N Som 44 B2
Winsdon Hill Luton 103 G11
Winsford Som 42 G2
Winsford W Ches 167 B10
Winsh-wen Swansea 57 B7
Winsham Devon 40 F3
Winsham Som 28 F5
Winshill Staffs 152 E5
Winsick Derbys 170 B6
Winskill Cumb 231 D7
Winslade Devon 24 D5
Winslade Hants 49 D7
Winsley N Yorks 214 G4
Winsley Wilts 61 G10
Winslow Bucks 102 F5
Winslow Mill Hereford 98 D2
Winson Glos 81 D9
Winson Green W Mid 133 F10
Winsor Hants 32 E4
Winstanley Gtr Man 194 G5
Winstanleys Gtr Man 194 F5
Winster Cumb 221 G8
Winster Derbys 170 C2
Winston Durham 224 B2
Winston Suff 126 E3
Winston Green Suff 126 E3
Winstone Glos 81 D7
Winswell Devon 25 E7
Winter Gardens Essex 69 C9
Winter Well Som 28 C3
Winterborne Bassett Wilts 62 E6
Winterborne Came Dorset 17 D10
Winterborne Clenston Dorset 30 G4
Winterborne Herringston Dorset 17 D9
Winterborne Houghton Dorset 30 G4
Winterborne Kingston Dorset 18 B3
Winterborne Monkton Dorset 17 D9

...avigator mapping

...ain is based on Ordnance Survey mapping, and ...ational Grid, it can be used with in-car or handheld ...g identifiable waypoints such as road junctions, ...ways and farms, or assessing your position in relation to ...he features shown on the map.

...ur receiver, choose British Grid as the location format and for ...datum select Ordnance Survey (this may be described as Ord ...y GB or similar, or more specifically as OSGB36). Your receiver will automatically convert the latitude/longitude co-ordinates transmitted by GPS into compatible National Grid data.

Positional accuracy of any particular feature is limited to 50–100m, due to the limitations of the original survey and the scale of Navigator mapping.

For further information see www.gps.gov.uk

...National Grid square SE.

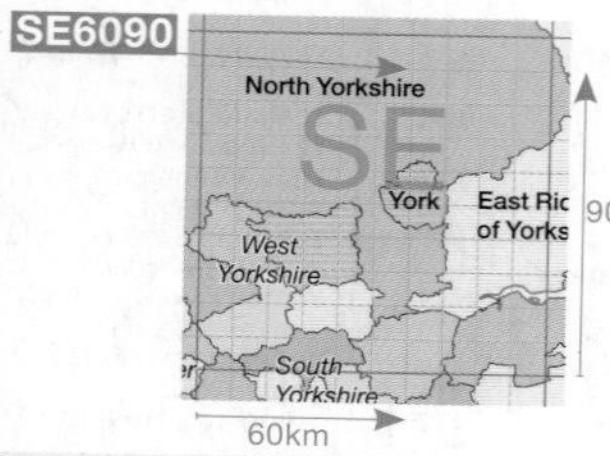

SE6090
North Yorkshire
SE
York
East Ri of Yorks
West Yorkshire
South Yorkshire
90km
60km

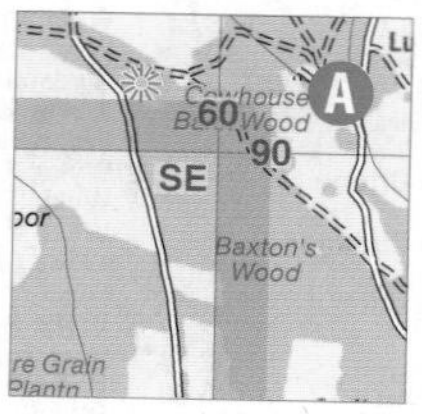

60
90
SE
A
Baxton's Wood

Greater London

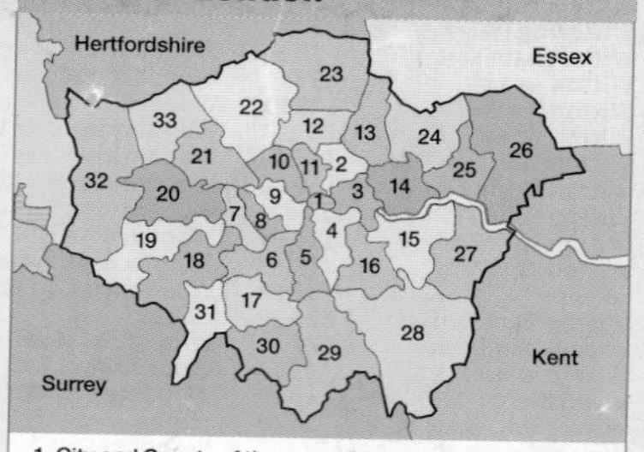

Hertfordshire
Essex
Surrey
Kent

1 City and County of the City of London
2 Hackney
3 Tower Hamlets
4 Southwark
5 Lambeth
6 Wandsworth
7 Hammersmith and Fulham
8 Royal Borough of Kensington and Chelsea
9 City of Westminster
10 Camden
11 Islington
12 Haringey
13 Waltham Forest
14 Newham
15 Greenwich
16 Lewisham
17 Merton
18 Richmond upon Thames
19 Hounslow
20 Ealing
21 Brent
22 Barnet
23 Enfield
24 Redbridge
25 Barking and Dagenham
26 Havering
27 Bexley
28 Bromley
29 Croydon
30 Sutton
31 Kingston upon Thames
32 Hillingdon
33 Harrow

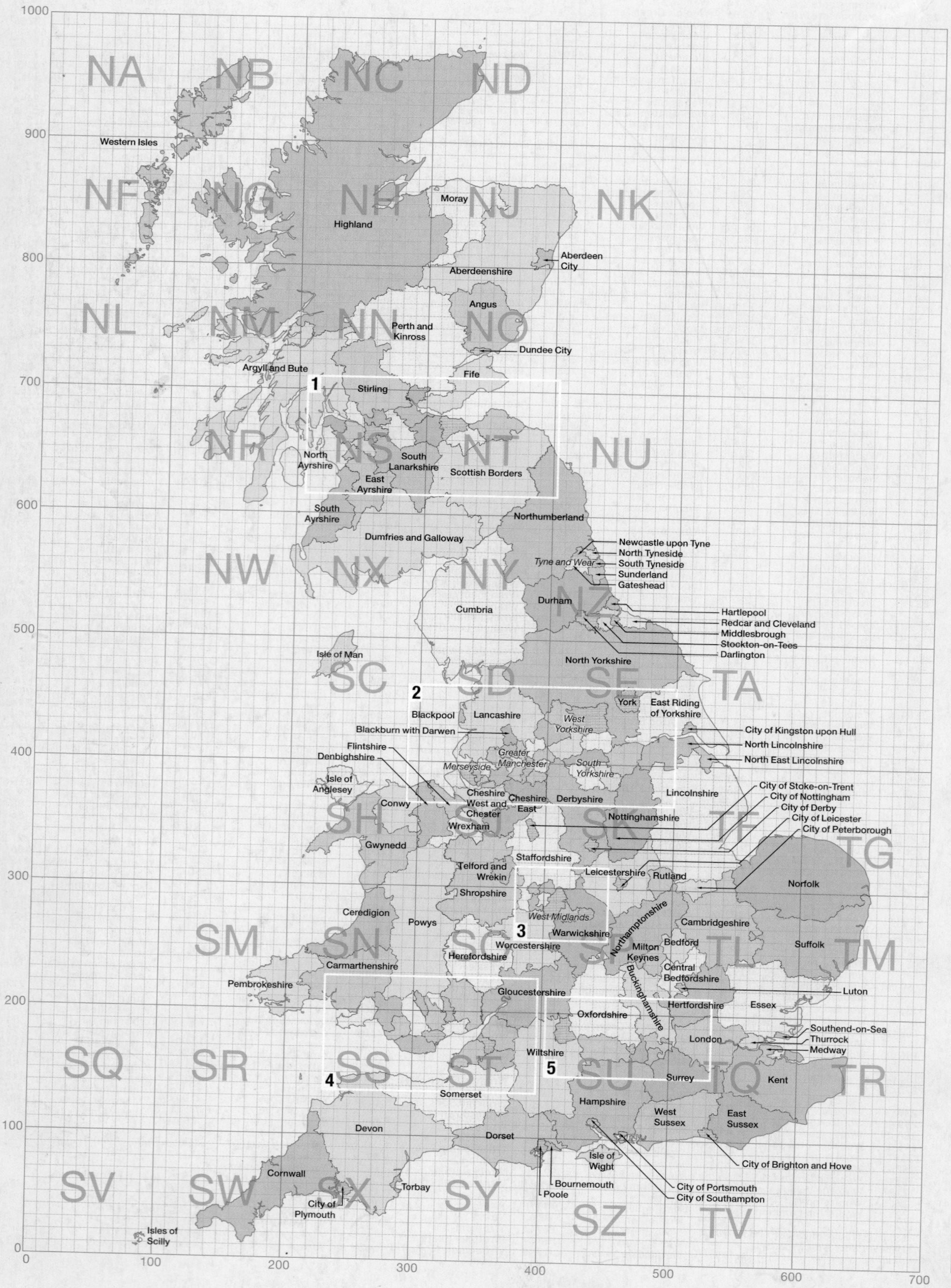

NA
NB
NC
ND
Western Isles
NF
NG
NH
NJ
NK
Moray
Highland
Aberdeen City
Aberdeenshire
NL
NM
NN
NO
Angus
Perth and Kinross
Dundee City
Argyll and Bute
Fife
Stirling
NR
NS
NT
NU
North Ayrshire
South Lanarkshire
East Ayrshire
Scottish Borders
South Ayrshire
Dumfries and Galloway
Northumberland
Newcastle upon Tyne
North Tyneside
South Tyneside
Sunderland
Gateshead
Tyne and Wear
NW
NX
NY
NZ
Cumbria
Durham
Hartlepool
Redcar and Cleveland
Middlesbrough
Stockton-on-Tees
Darlington
Isle of Man
North Yorkshire
SC
SD
SE
TA
Blackpool
Lancashire
York
East Riding of Yorkshire
Blackburn with Darwen
West Yorkshire
City of Kingston upon Hull
North Lincolnshire
North East Lincolnshire
Flintshire
Denbighshire
Greater Manchester
Merseyside
South Yorkshire
Isle of Anglesey
Conwy
Cheshire West and Chester
Cheshire East
Derbyshire
Lincolnshire
City of Stoke-on-Trent
City of Nottingham
City of Derby
City of Leicester
City of Peterborough
SH
SJ
SK
TF
TG
Wrexham
Nottinghamshire
Gwynedd
Staffordshire
Telford and Wrekin
Leicestershire
Rutland
Norfolk
Shropshire
Ceredigion
Powys
West Midlands
Warwickshire
Northamptonshire
Cambridgeshire
SM
SN
SO
SP
TL
TM
Suffolk
Worcestershire
Herefordshire
Bedford
Milton Keynes
Carmarthenshire
Central Bedfordshire
Pembrokeshire
Luton
Buckinghamshire
Gloucestershire
Hertfordshire
Essex
Oxfordshire
Southend-on-Sea
Thurrock
Medway
London
Wiltshire
SQ
SR
SS
ST
SU
TQ
TR
Surrey
Kent
Somerset
Hampshire
West Sussex
East Sussex
Devon
Dorset
Isle of Wight
City of Brighton and Hove
Cornwall
Torbay
Bournemouth
Poole
City of Portsmouth
City of Southampton
City of Plymouth
SV
SW
SX
SY
SZ
TV
Isles of Scilly
1000
900
800
700
600
500
400
300
200
100
0
100
200
300
400
500
600
700
1
2
3
4
5

1 Central Scotland

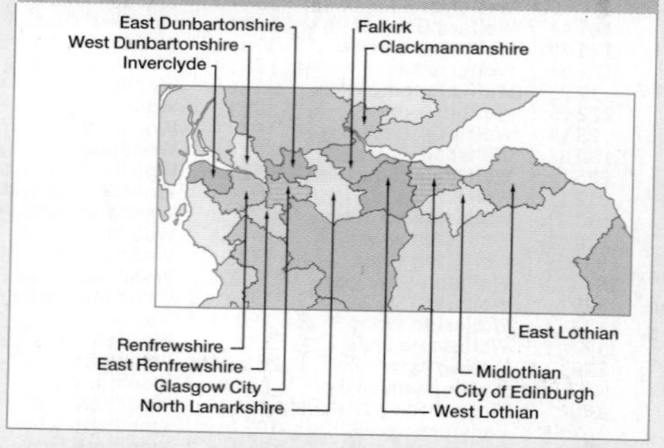

East Dunbartonshire
West Dunbartonshire
Inverclyde
Falkirk
Clackmannanshire
Renfrewshire
East Renfrewshire
Glasgow City
North Lanarkshire
East Lothian
Midlothian
City of Edinburgh
West Lothian

2 Northern England

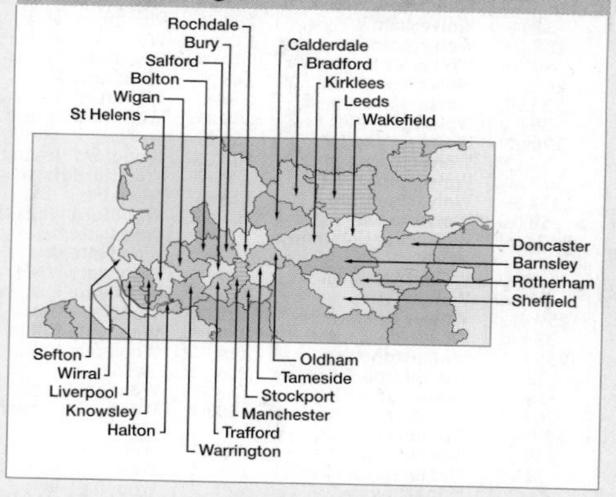

Rochdale
Bury
Salford
Bolton
Wigan
St Helens
Calderdale
Bradford
Kirklees
Leeds
Wakefield
Doncaster
Barnsley
Rotherham
Sheffield
Sefton
Wirral
Liverpool
Knowsley
Halton
Oldham
Tameside
Stockport
Manchester
Trafford
Warrington

3 West Midlands

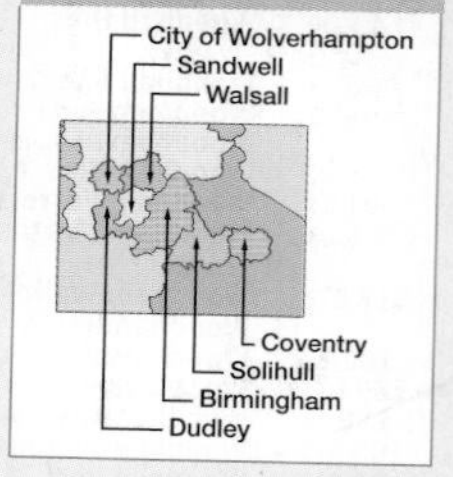

City of Wolverhampton
Sandwell
Walsall
Coventry
Solihull
Birmingham
Dudley

4 South Wales and Bristol area

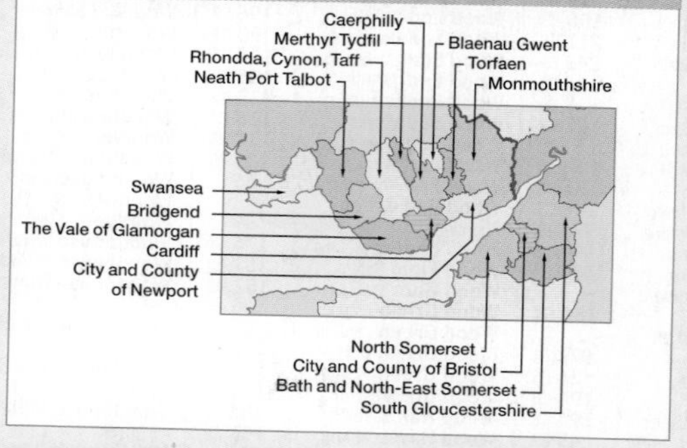

Caerphilly
Merthyr Tydfil
Rhondda, Cynon, Taff
Neath Port Talbot
Blaenau Gwent
Torfaen
Monmouthshire
Swansea
Bridgend
The Vale of Glamorgan
Cardiff
City and County of Newport
North Somerset
City and County of Bristol
Bath and North-East Somerset
South Gloucestershire

5 Thames Valley

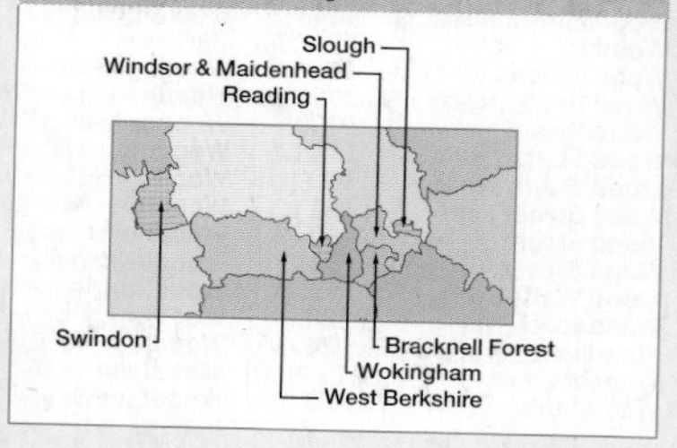

Slough
Windsor & Maidenhead
Reading
Swindon
Bracknell Forest
Wokingham
West Berkshire

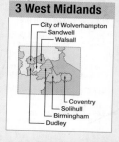

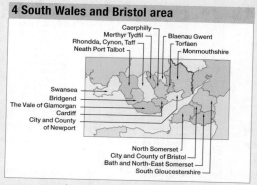

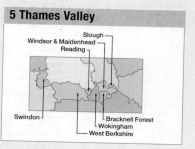